# Rayden & Jackson on Divorce and Family Matters

## Volume 2(2)    Statutory materials

**Statutory instruments**
**European material**
**Court fees**

While every care has been taken to ensure the accuracy of this work, no responsibility for loss or damage occasioned to any person acting or refraining from action as a result of any statement in it can be accepted by the authors, editors or publishers.

# Rayden & Jackson on Divorce and Family Matters

Eighteenth edition

## Volume 2(2)   Statutory materials

**Statutory instruments**
**European material**
**Court fees**

**Mark Everall** MA (OXON)
One of Her Majesty's Counsel and of the Western Circuit

**Nigel Dyer** BA (DUNELM)
Barrister

**Philip Waller** LLB (EXON)
Senior District Judge of the Family Division

**Rebecca Bailey-Harris**
Barrister, Professor of Law, University of Bristol

*Consulting Editors*

**The Rt Hon Sir Mathew Thorpe**
One of Her Majesty's Lord Justices of Appeal

**GJ Maple** LLB (LOND)
District Judge of the Principal Registry of the Family Division

LexisNexis®
Butterworths

**Members of the LexisNexis Group worldwide**

| | |
|---|---|
| United Kingdom | LexisNexis Butterworths, a Division of Reed Elsevier (UK) Ltd, Halsbury House, 35 Chancery Lane, LONDON, WC2A 1EL, and RSH, 1–3 Baxter's Place, Leith Walk EDINBURGH EH1 3AF |
| Argentina | LexisNexis Argentina, BUENOS AIRES |
| Australia | LexisNexis Butterworths, CHATSWOOD, New South Wales |
| Austria | LexisNexis Verlag ARD Orac GmbH & Co KG, VIENNA |
| Canada | LexisNexis Butterworths, MARKHAM, Ontario |
| Chile | LexisNexis Chile Ltda, SANTIAGO DE CHILE |
| Czech Republic | Nakladatelství Orac sro, PRAGUE |
| France | Editions du Juris-Classeur SA, PARIS |
| Germany | LexisNexis Deutschland GmbH, FRANKFURT and MUNSTER |
| Hong Kong | LexisNexis Butterworths, HONG KONG |
| Hungary | HVG-Orac, BUDAPEST |
| India | LexisNexis Butterworths, NEW DELHI |
| Italy | Giuffrè Editore, MILAN |
| Malaysia | Malayan Law Journal Sdn Bhd, KUALA LUMPUR |
| New Zealand | LexisNexis Butterworths, WELLINGTON |
| Poland | Wydawnictwo Prawnicze LexisNexis, WARSAW |
| Singapore | LexisNexis Butterworths, SINGAPORE |
| South Africa | LexisNexis Butterworths, DURBAN |
| Switzerland | Stämpfli Verlag AG, BERNE |
| USA | LexisNexis, DAYTON, Ohio |

© Reed Elsevier (UK) Ltd 2004

Published by LexisNexis Butterworths

A CIP Catalogue record for this book is available from the British Library.

ISBN 1-405-70528-0

QM LIBRARY
(MILE END)

ISBN 1 405 70528 0
ISBN for the complete set of volumes 0 406 94823 2

Typeset by Columns Design Ltd, Reading, England.
Printed and bound in Great Britain by CPI Bath.

Visit LexisNexis Butterworths at www.lexisnexis.co.uk

# Contents

## Volume 2(1)    Statutory materials

## Statutes

# Appendix 1   Alphabetical table of statutes

# Volume 2(2)   Statutory materials

# Statutory instruments, European material, Court fees

## Appendix 2   Chronological table of rules, regulations and orders

# Appendix 2   Alphabetical table of rules, regulations and orders

## Appendix 3    European material

## Appendix 4    Court fees

# Rules, Regulations and Orders

**ORDERS IN COUNCIL UNDER THE EVIDENCE (FOREIGN, DOMINION AND COLONIAL DOCUMENTS) ACT 1933 AND THE OATHS AND EVIDENCE (OVERSEAS AUTHORITIES AND COUNTRIES) ACT 1963**

The requirements in the various Orders, as to the authentication of copies of entries in the marriage registers, are as follows:

| Country and number of instrument | Certifying officer (if specified) | Mode of authentication (if specified) |
|---|---|---|
| ADEN SI 1965 No 1527 | Entries in Registers of Christian Marriages; | |
| | (i) The Registrar General of Births, Deaths and Marriages or | (i) The seal of the General Registry Office; |
| | (ii) The Marriage Registrar or | (ii) The signature of the certifying officer; |
| | (iii) Any other person entrusted under the Marriage (Christian) Ordinance with the custody of the relevant marriage register | (iii) The signature of the certifying officer; |
| | Entries in Register of Parsi Marriages; | |
| | (i) The Registrar General of Births, Deaths and Marriages or | (i) The seal of the General Registry Office; |
| | (ii) The Registrar of Parsi Marriages | (ii) The signature of the certifying officer; |
| | Entries in The Marriage Certificate Book under the Marriage (Special Provisions) Ordinance; | |
| | (i) The Registrar General of Births, Deaths and Marriages or | (i) The seal of the General Registry Office; |
| | (ii) The Registrar of Special Marriages | (ii) The signature of the certifying officer; |
| ANTIGUA SI 1965 No 312 | (1) The Registrar General | The seal of the General Register Office and the signature of the certifying officer: |
| | or | |
| | (2) the Assistant Registrar of a Parish or a Marriage Officer | The signature of the certifying officer. |

| Country and number of instrument | Certifying officer (if specified) | Mode of authentication (if specified) |
|---|---|---|
| AUSTRALIA SR & O 1938 No 739 NAURU ISLAND | The Administrator of Nauru. | The signature of the Administrator and the seal or stamp of the Administration of Nauru. |
| NEW GUINEA | The Registrar-General or the deputy Registrar-General or a District Registrar or deputy District Registrar of Births, Deaths and Marriages. | The signature of the certifying officer and the seal or stamp of the Registrar General or a District Registrar as the case may be. |
| NEW SOUTH WALES | The Registrar-General or Deputy Registrar-General or a District Registrar of Births, Deaths and Marriages. | The signature and seal of the certifying officer. |
| NORFOLK ISLAND | The Registrar of Births, Marriages and Deaths. | The signature of the Registrar. |
| NORTHERN TERRITORY | The Registrar-General or the deputy Registrar-General of Births, Marriages and Deaths. | The signature and seal of the certifying officer. |
| PAPUA | The Registrar-General or the deputy Registrar General or a District Registrar or Assistant District Registrar. | The signature of the certifying officer and the seal or stamp of the General Registry for Papua or a District Registry Office as the case may be. |
| QUEENSLAND | The Registrar-General or the Deputy Registrar-General. | The signature of the certifying officer. |
| SEAT OF GOVERNMENT | The Principal Registrar or the deputy Principal Registrar or a District Registrar or deputy District Registrar of Births, Deaths and Marriages. | The signature of the certifying officer and the seal or stamp of the Principal Registrar or a District Registrar as the case may be. |
| SOUTH AUSTRALIA | The Principal or Deputy Registrar of Births, Deaths and Marriages. | The signature and seal of the certifying officer. |

| Country and number of instrument | Certifying officer (if specified) | Mode of authentication (if specified) |
|---|---|---|
| AUSTRALIA—*contd* TASMANIA | The Registrar-General. | The signature and seal of the certifying officer. |
| VICTORIA | The Government Statist or the Assistant Government Statist. | The signature of the certifying officer. |
| WESTERN AUSTRALIA | The Registrar-General or the Deputy Registrar-General. | The signature of the certifying officer. |
| BAHAMAS SI 1961 No 2041 | The Registrar-General. | The Seal of the General Register Office and the signature of the Registrar General. |
| BARBADOS SI 1962 No 641 | The Registrar of the Island of Barbados. | The signature of the certifying officer. |
| BASUTOLAND (now Lesotho) SI 1965 No 1719 | The Registrar of Marriages or a Marriage Officer. | The signature of the certifying officer. |
| BECHUANALAND (now Botswana) SI 1965 No 1720 | The Registrar of Marriages or a Marriage Officer. | The signature of the certifying officer. |
| BELGIUM SR & O 1933 No 383 | Officier de l'état civil or deputy; or Greffier of a tribunal of first instance or deputy. | The printed and stamped emblem of the communal administration. |
| BERMUDA SI 1961 No 2042 | The Registrar-General or the Assistant Registrar-General. | The seal of the office of the Registrar-General and the signature of the certifying officer. |
| BRITISH ANTARCTIC TERRITORY SI 1962 No 2605 | | The signature and seal of the Registrar-General. |
| BRITISH GUIANA (now Guyana) SI 1961 No 2043 | The Registrar-General or an officer acting as his deputy. | The seal of the General Register office and the signature of the certifying officer. |
| BRITISH HONDURAS SI 1961 No 2044 | The Registrar-General or the Deputy Registrar-General. | The signature of the certifying officer. |

| Country and number of instrument | Certifying officer (if specified) | Mode of authentication (if specified) |
| --- | --- | --- |
| CANADA<br>SI 1962 No 2606<br>BRITISH COLUMBIA | The Director or Acting Director of Vital Statistics, a District Registrar or Deputy District Registrar of Births, Deaths and Marriages. | |
| MANITOBA | The Recorder of Vital Statistics. | |
| NEWFOUNDLAND | The Registrar General or any registering officer appointed by or under the relevant statute. | |
| NORTHWEST TERRITORIES | The Registrar General or a Deputy Registrar General. | |
| NOVA SCOTIA | The Registrar General, Deputy Registrar General or any person appointed to perform the functions of the Deputy Registrar General during his absence or incapacity. | |
| PRINCE EDWARD ISLAND | The Director of Vital Statistics. | |
| QUEBEC | The Prothonotary or Deputy Prothonotary of the Superior Court of the District. | |
| SASKATCHEWAN | The District or Assistant Director of Vital Statistics. | |
| YUKON TERRITORY | The Registrar General. | |
| CAYMAN ISLANDS<br>SI 1965 No 313 | The Registrar-General or a Marriage Officer. | The signature and seal of the Registrar-General or the signature of the Marriage Officer concerned. |
| DENMARK<br>SI 1969 No 144 | The Pastor of the Parish; in respect of civil mariages in Copenhagen the municipal authorities, in provisional towns and in Frederiksberg the Mayor, and in rural parishes the Executive. | The signature and seal of the certifying officer. |

| Country and number of instrument | Certifying officer (if specified) | Mode of authentication (if specified) |
|---|---|---|
| DOMINICA<br>SI 1961 No 2045 | | The signature of the Registrar-General, the Chief or the Senior Clerk to the Registrar of the Supreme Court, a Registrar or a Marriage Officer. |
| FALKLAND ISLANDS<br>SI 1962 No 2607 | | The signature and seal of the Registrar-General. |
| FIJI<br>SI 1961 No 2046 | | The signature and seal of the Registrar-General. |
| FRANCE<br>SR & O 1937<br>No 515 | Officier de l'état civil or deputy; or Greffier en chef of a tribunal or deputy. | The seal or printed or stamped emblem of the mairie (mayoralty) or of the greffe (record office). |
| GERMANY, FEDERAL REPUBLIC OF and LAND BERLIN<br>SI 1970 No 819 | The Registrar (Der Standesbeamte), Register of Births or Marriages or Deaths. | The signature and seal or stamp of the certifying officer. |
| GIBRALTAR<br>SI 1961 No 2047 | The Marriage Registrar. | The seal and signature of the certifying officer. |
| GRENADA<br>SI 1966 No 82 | Entries in the General Marriage Register Book: The Registrar General or the Deputy Registrar General.<br>Entries in Marriage Register Book:<br>A Registrar of Marriages, a Deputy Registrar of Marriages or a Marriage Officer. | The signature of the certifying officer and the seal or stamp of the General Register Office.<br><br>The signature of the certifying officer. |
| HONG KONG<br>SI 1962 No 642 | The Registrar of Marriages or a Deputy Registrar of Marriages or a Deputy Registrar General, a Legal Assistant or Assistant Registrar in the Registrar General's Department. | The seal of the Registrar of Marriages and the signature of the certifying officer. |
| IRELAND, REPUBLIC OF<br>SI 1969 No 1059 | Registrar-General (Registers of Births, Marriages and Deaths or Registers of Marriages). | The seal of the Registrar General. |

| Country and number of instrument | Certifying officer (if specified) | Mode of authentication (if specified) |
| --- | --- | --- |
| IRELAND, REPUBLIC OF— *contd* | A Superintendent Registrar, an Assistant Superintendent Registrar, a Registrar, or an Assistant Registrar (Register of Births, Marriages and Deaths). | The signature of the certifying officer. |
| | A Registrar of Marriages or a Deputy Registrar of Marriages (Registers of Marriages). | The signature of the certifying officer. |
| ITALY SI 1969 No 145 | The Registrar (Ufficiale dello stato civile) of Births, Marriages and Deaths or his deputy. | The signature of the certifying officer. |
| JAMAICA SI 1962 No 643 | The Registrar General or the Assistant Registrar General. | The seal of the General Register Office and the signature of the certifying officer. |
| KENYA SI 1965 No 1712 | | The seal of the Registrar-General or the signature of a Registrar of Marriages. |
| LUXEMBOURG SI 1972 No 116 | Registrar (Officier de l'état civil or Zivilstandesbeamte) | The signature of the Registrar and the seal of the Commune |
| | or | or |
| | Clerk to the Tribunal of first instance (Greffier du Tribunal de première instance or Gerichtssekretär). | The signature of the Clerk to the tribunal of first instance and the seal of the tribunal. |
| MAURITIUS SI 1961 No 2048 | The Registrar-General, the Deputy Registrar-General or the Assistant Registrar-General. | The seal of the Office of the Registrar-General and the signature of the certifying officer. |
| MONTSERRAT SI 1962 No 644 | The Registrar-General. | The seal of the General Registry Office and the signature of the certifying officer. |
| THE NETHERLANDS SI 1970 No 284 (B) | Civil Registrar (De ambtenaar van de burgerlijke stand) | |
| | or | |
| | Clerk to a District Court (De Griffier van de Arrondissementsrechtbank) | In each case the signature of the certifying officer. |
| | or | |

| Country and number of instrument | Certifying officer (if specified) | Mode of authentication (if specified) |
|---|---|---|
| THE NETHERLANDS–*contd* | Keeper of the National Archives (Derijksarchivaris in de provincie). | |
| NEW ZEALAND SI 1959 No 1306 | The Registrar-General or Deputy Registrar-General. | The signature or seal of the certifying officer. |
| SAINT LUCIA SI 1965 No 1721 | The Registrar of Civil Status, the Deputy Registrar, a District Registrar, a Deputy District Registrar or a Status Officer. | The signature of the certifying officer. |
| ST HELENA SI 1961 No 2049 | The Registrar-General or an officer acting as his deputy. | The signature of the certifying officer. |
| SARAWAK SI 1961 No 2050 | The Senior Marriage Registrar or a Marriage Registrar. | (1) Church marriages: the signature and seal of the certifying officer. (2) Civil marriages: the signature of the certifying officer. |
| SEYCHELLES SI 1962 No 2608 | (1) Entries in Register of Marriages: the Chief Officer of the Civil Status or a Civil Status Officer. (2) Entries in Register of Christian Marriages: The Chief Officer of the Civil Status or a Minister. | The signature of the certifying officer. |
| SIERRA LEONE SI 1962 No 2609 | (1) Entries in Register of Christian Marriages: the Registrar-General, the Deputy Registrar-General or a Minister of Religion. (2) Entries in Registers of Civil and Mohammedan Marriages: the Registrar-General or the Deputy Registrar-General. | The signature of the certifying officer. |
| SWAZILAND SI 1965 No 1865 | The Registrar of Births, Marriages and Deaths, or the Assistant Registrar of Births, Marriages and Deaths. | The signature of the certifying officer. |

| Country and number of instrument | Certifying officer (if specified) | Mode of authentication (if specified) |
|---|---|---|
| TANGANYIKA (now Tanzania) SI 1961 No 2051 | A Registrar, Deputy Registrar or Assistant Registrar of Marriages. | The signature of the certifying officer. |
| TURKS AND CAICOS ISLANDS SI 1966 No 83 | The Registrar of Deeds. | The signature of the certifying officer. |
| UGANDA SI 1961 No 2052 | (1) Entries in Marriage Register Book: a registrar. (2) Entries in Register of Mohammedan Marriages: the Registrar-General or a registrar. | The signature of the certifying officer. |
| UNITED STATES OF AMERICA SI 1969 No 146 | | In respect of all States the authentication necessary is the signature of the certifying officer or any other officer who may, from time to time, be authorised to perform the certifying functions at present performed by the officer designated. |
| ALABAMA | State Registrar or County Probate Judge. | |
| ALASKA | State Registrar of Vital Statistics or Local Registrars: Magistrates and District Judges. | |
| ARIZONA | Clerk of Superior Court. | |
| ARKANSAS | Director, Bureau of Vital Statistics, or County Clerk. | |
| CALIFORNIA | Chief, Bureau of Vital Statistics, or County Recorder. | |
| COLORADO | Court Clerk of Records or Chief, Records and Statistics Section. | |
| CONNECTICUT | Chief, Public Health Statistics Section or Local Registrar. | |
| DELAWARE | Chief, Bureau of Vital Statistics, or Local Registrar. | |
| DISTRICT OF COLUMBIA | Deputy Clerk, Marriage Bureau or Clerk, US District Court. | |
| FLORIDA | Director, Bureau of Vital Statistics, or County Judge. | |
| GEORGIA | County Ordinary. | |
| HAWAII | Registrar General. | |
| IDAHO | Director, Bureau of Vital Statistics, or County Recorder. | |
| ILLINOIS | County Clerk. | |
| INDIANA | Clerk of Circuit Court or Clerk of Superior Court. | |

| Country and number of instrument | Certifying officer (if specified) | Mode of authentication (if specified) |
|---|---|---|
| USA—*contd* | | |
| IOWA | Director, Records and Statistics Section, or County Clerk. | In respect of all States the authentication necessary is the signature of the certifying officer or any other officer who may, from time to time, be authorised to perform the certifying functions at present performed by the officer designated. |
| KANSAS | Director, Division of Vital Statistics and Records, or Probate Judge. | |
| KENTUCKY | Director, Office of Vital Statistics, or County Court Clerk. | |
| LOUISIANA | Clerk of Court, or City Registrar of New Orleans. | |
| MAINE | Director, Division of Research and Vital Records, or Town, and City Clerks. | |
| MARYLAND | Chief, Division of Vital Records, County Clerk of Circuit Court or Clerk of Court of Common Pleas of Baltimore. | |
| MASSACHUSETTS | Secretary of the Commonwealth, Town and City Clerks or Local Registrars of Vital Statistics. | |
| MICHIGAN | Chief, Vital Records Section or County Clerks. | |
| MINNESOTA | District Court Clerk. | |
| MISSISSIPPI | Director, Division of Public Health Statistics, or County Circuit Clerk. | |
| MISSOURI | Supervisor, Vital Records, or Recorder of Deeds. | |
| MONTANA | Clerk of District Court. | |
| NEBRASKA | Director, Bureau of Vital Statistics, or County Clerk. | |
| NEVADA | Recorder or Chief, Section of Vital Statistics. | |
| NEW HAMPSHIRE | Director, Bureau of Vital Statistics, Town or City Clerk. | |
| NEW JERSEY | Chief, Vital Statistics and Registration, or Local Registrar. | |
| NEW MEXICO | County Clerk. | |
| NEW YORK | | |
| (a) other than New York City | Director, Bureau of Vital Records, or County Clerk. | |
| (b) New York City | City Clerk. | |
| NORTH CAROLINA | Chief, Public Health Statistics Section or County Register of Deeds. | |

| Country and number of instrument | Certifying officer (if specified) | Mode of authentication (if specified) |
|---|---|---|
| USA—*contd* | | In respect of all States the authentication necessary is the signature of the certifying officer or any other officer who may, from time to time, be authorised to perform the certifying functions at present performed by the officer designated. |
| NORTH DAKOTA | County Judge. | |
| OHIO | Probate Judge. | |
| OKLAHOMA | Clerk of Court. | |
| OREGON | State Registrar or County Clerk. | |
| PENNSYLVANIA | County Clerk. | |
| RHODE ISLAND | Chief, Division of Vital Statistics, Local Registrar, Town or City Clerk. | |
| SOUTH CAROLINA | State Registrar or Probate Judge. | |
| SOUTH DAKOTA | Director, Division of Public Health Statistics, or County Clerk of Court. | |
| TENNESSEE | State Registrar or County Court Clerk. | |
| TEXAS | County Clerk. | |
| UTAH | County Clerk. | |
| VERMONT | Secretary of State, Town or City Clerk. | |
| VIRGINIA | State Registrar or Clerk of Court. | |
| WASHINGTON | State Registrar of Vital Statistics or County Auditor. | |
| WEST VIRGINIA | County Clerk. | |
| WISCONSIN | Director, Bureau of Vital Statistics, Register of Deeds or City Health Officer. | |
| WYOMING | Director, Division of Vital Statistics, or County Clerk. | |
| ZANZIBAR SI 1961 No 2053 | A Registrar of Marriages. | The signature of the certifying officer. |

## MAINTENANCE ORDERS ACT 1950 (SUMMARY JURISDICTION) RULES 1950

**Dated** 15 December 1950

**SI 1950 No 2035**

I, William Allen, Viscount Jowitt, Lord High Chancellor of Great Britain, in exercise of the powers conferred upon me by section 29 of the Summary Jurisdiction Act 1879, as extended by section 5, subsections (1) and (3) of section 25 and subsection (1) of section 28 of the Maintenance Orders Act 1950, as those provisions of the said Act of 1950 are adapted by subsection (2) of section 30 thereof, and of all other powers enabling me in this behalf, do hereby make the following Rules—

PART I

TRANSFER OF WIFE MAINTENANCE PROCEEDINGS

**1.** (1) Where proceedings under [section 1 of the Domestic Proceedings and Magistrates' Courts Act 1978], are begun against a defendant residing in Scotland or Northern Ireland in a court having jurisdiction by virtue of [subsection (3) of section 1 of the said Act], then, upon an application in that behalf made by the defendant in accordance with paragraph (2) of this Rule, a justice acting for the same place as that court may, if it appears that the case could be more conveniently heard in a court of summary jurisdiction having jurisdiction in the place where the parties last ordinarily resided together as man and wife, determine that the proceedings shall be removed into the last-mentioned court.

(2) An application under the foregoing paragraph may be made orally or in writing by or on behalf of the defendant and, unless the defendant applies in person, there shall be lodged with the clerk of the court in which the proceedings under the said [section 1] have been begun a statutory declaration by the defendant which shall state the grounds upon which the application is made and the address of the defendant to which notices may be sent.

(3) The justice adjudicating on an application made under paragraph (1) of this Rule shall, unless he determines that the application shall be refused forthwith, afford to the complainant an opportunity of making representations, either orally or in writing, thereon.

(4) Where a justice determines under paragraph (1) of this Rule that the proceedings under the said [section 1] shall be removed into another court of summary jurisdiction, he shall cause the clerk of the court in which the said proceedings have been begun to send to the clerk of that other court the complaint, a copy of the summons and any other relevant documents; and, on receipt thereof in that other court, the complaint shall be deemed to have been made in, and the summons to have been issued by, that other court, and any justice acting for the same place as that other court may appoint a time and place for the hearing of the proceedings which, upon notice thereof being sent by registered post to the complainant and defendant, shall be deemed to have been the time and place appointed in the summons.

PART II

PROCEDURE UNDER PART II OF THE ACT IN RELATION TO MAINTENANCE ORDERS MADE BY COURTS OF SUMMARY JURISDICTION IN ENGLAND

**2.** (1) An application for the registration in a court in Scotland or Northern Ireland under Part II of the Act of a maintenance order made by a court of summary jurisdiction in England may be made, either orally or in writing by or on behalf of the person entitled to the payments thereunder, to a justice acting for the same place as the court which made the order; and, unless the applicant appears in person, there shall be lodged with the clerk of the court which made the order a statutory declaration by the applicant which shall contain the particulars specified in paragraph (2) of this Rule.

(2)  A statutory declaration lodged under the foregoing paragraph shall state—

(a)  the address of the person liable to make the payments under the order;

(b)  the reason why it is convenient that the order should be enforced in Scotland or Northern Ireland, as the case may be;

(c)  unless a certificate of arrears is lodged under section 20 of the Act, the amount of any arrears due under the order;

(d)  that the order is not already registered under Part II of the Act.

(3)  If it appears to the justice dealing with an application made as aforesaid that the person liable to make the payments under the order resides in Scotland or Northern Ireland, and that it is convenient that the order should be enforceable there, he shall cause the clerk of the court which made the order to send to the sheriff-clerk of the sheriff court in Scotland, or, as the case may be, to the clerk of the court of summary jurisdiction in Northern Ireland, having jurisdiction in the place in which the person liable to make the payments under the order appears to be—

(a)  a certified copy of the order;

(b)  the certificate of arrears or statutory declaration (if any);

(c)  if no statutory declaration has been lodged, written notice of the address of the person liable to make the payments under the order.

(4)  A memorandum of any proceedings taken under the foregoing provisions of this Rule for the registration of a maintenance order in a court in Scotland or Northern Ireland shall be entered in the register; and on the receipt by the clerk of the court which made the order (who shall be the prescribed officer of that court for the purposes of subsection (4) of section 17 of the Act) of notice under the said subsection (4) of the registration of the order he shall cause particulars of the notice to be registered in his court by means of a memorandum entered and signed by him in the register.

**3.**  (1)  An application to a court of summary jurisdiction in England under subsection (5) of section 22 of the Act to adduce evidence in connection with a maintenance order made by that court and registered in a court in Scotland or Northern Ireland may be made orally by or on behalf of the applicant and the proceedings may be ex parte.

(2)  The court in which application is made under the last foregoing paragraph shall cause a transcript or summary of any evidence taken therein to be sent to the clerk of the court in which the order is registered.

(3)  The clerk of the court of summary jurisdiction in England by which a maintenance order registered in a court in Scotland or Northern Ireland was made shall be the prescribed officer to whom any transcript or summary of evidence adduced in the court in Scotland or Northern Ireland under the said subsection (5) shall be sent.

**4.**  (1)  Where a maintenance order made by a court of summary jurisdiction in England and registered in a court in Scotland or Northern Ireland is varied under subsection (1) of section 22 of the Act by the court in which it is registered, the clerk of the court which made the order shall be the prescribed officer to whom, under subsection (1) of section 23 of the Act, notice of the variation shall be given; and on receipt of such notice he shall cause particulars of the same to be registered in his court by means of a memorandum entered and signed by him in the register.

(2)  Where a maintenance order made by a court of summary jurisdiction in England and registered in a court in Scotland or Northern Ireland is discharged or

varied by the court which made it, the clerk of that court shall give notice of the discharge or variation to the clerk of the court in which the order is registered by sending to him a certified copy of the order discharging or varying the maintenance order.

**5.**   (1) An application under subsection (2) of section 24 of the Act for the cancellation of the registration of a maintenance order made by a court of summary jurisdiction in England and registered in a court in Scotland or Northern Ireland may be made, either orally or in writing by or on behalf of the person liable to make the payments thereunder, to a justice acting for the same place as the court which made the order; and, unless the applicant appears in person, there shall be lodged with the clerk of the court which made the order a statutory declaration by the applicant stating the facts upon which he relies in support of the application.

(2)   If it appears to the justice dealing with an application made as aforesaid that the person liable to make the payments under the order has ceased to reside in Scotland or Northern Ireland, as the case may be, he shall cause the clerk of the court which made the order to send notice to that effect to the clerk of the court in which the order is registered.

**6.**   On the cancellation under section 24 of the Act of the registration in a court in Scotland or Northern Ireland of a maintenance order made by a court of summary jurisdiction in England, the clerk of the last-mentioned court shall be the prescribed officer to whom, under subsection (3) of the said section 24, notice of the cancellation shall be given; and on receipt of such notice he shall cause particulars of the same to be registered in his court by means of a memorandum entered and signed by him in the register.

PART III

PROCEDURE IN COURTS OF SUMMARY JURISDICTION IN ENGLAND UNDER PART II OF THE ACT IN RELATION TO MAINTENANCE ORDERS MADE BY COURTS IN SCOTLAND OR NORTHERN IRELAND.

**7.**   The clerk of the court of summary jurisdiction in England specified in paragraph (b) of subsection (3) of section 17 of the Act shall be the prescribed officer for the purpose of subsection (2) of the said section 17, and on receiving, in pursuance of that section, a certified copy of a maintenance order made by a court in Scotland or Northern Ireland he shall cause the order to be registered in his court by means of a memorandum entered and signed by him in the register, and shall send written notice to the clerk of the court by which the order was made that it has been duly registered.

**8.**   An application for the variation under subsection (1) of section 22 of the Act of the rate of the payments under a maintenance order registered under Part II of the Act in a court of summary jurisdiction in England shall be made by way of complaint in accordance with the [Magistrates' Courts Act 1952], and thereupon a summons may be issued directed to any person whom the justice to whom the complaint is made may consider proper to answer the same.

**9.**   (1) An application to a court of summary jurisdiction in England under subsection (5) of section 22 of the Act to adduce evidence in connection with a maintenance order registered therein under Part II of the Act may be made orally by or on behalf of the applicant and the proceedings may be ex parte.

(2)   The court in which application is made under the last foregoing paragraph shall cause a transcript or summary of any evidence taken therein to be sent to the clerk of the court in Scotland or Northern Ireland by which the order was made.

(3) The clerk of the court of summary jurisdiction in England in which a maintenance order is registered under Part II of the Act shall be the prescribed officer to whom any transcript or summary of evidence adduced under the said subsection (5) in the court in Scotland or Northern Ireland by which the order was made shall be sent.

**9A.** (1) An application to a magistrates' court under section 21(2) of the Act to adduce evidence in connection with a maintenance order made by the Court of Session and registered in the magistrates' court under Part I of the Act of 1958 by virtue of section 1(2) of the Act of 1958 may be made orally by or on behalf of the applicant and the proceedings may be ex parte.

(2) The court in which application is made under paragraph (1) above shall cause a transcript or summary of any evidence taken therein to be sent to the Deputy Principal Clerk of Session.

**9B.** (1) Where, in the exercise of the duty imposed by section 19(2) of the Act or in the exercise of the powers conferred by virtue of section 18(2ZA) or section 22(1A) or (1E) of the Act, a court of summary jurisdiction orders that payments under a registered order are to be made by a particular means, the clerk of the court shall record on the copy of the order the means of payment which the court has ordered and notify in writing, as soon as practicable, the person liable to make payments under the order of how payments are to be made.

(2) Where, in the exercise of any of the aforesaid powers, the court orders payment to the clerk of the court, or to the clerk of any other magistrates' court, by a method of payment falling within section 59(6) of the Magistrates' Courts Act 1980 (standing order, etc), the clerk of the court to whom payments are to be made shall notify the person liable to make the payments under the order of the number and location of the account into which the payments should be made.

(3) Where, under section 60(4) of the Magistrates' Courts Act 1980, as modified by section 22(1E) of the Act, the clerk of the court receives an application from an interested party for the method of payment to be varied, the clerk shall notify in writing, as soon as practicable, that party and, where practicable, any other interested party, of the result of the application, including any decision to refer the matter to the court; where the clerk grants the application, he shall record the variation on the copy of the order.

**10.** (1) Where a maintenance order registered under Part II of the Act in a court of summary jurisdiction in England is varied under subsection (1) of section 22 of the Act by that court, the clerk of the court shall—

(a) give notice of the variation to the clerk of the court in Scotland or Northern Ireland by which the order was made; and

(b) if the order is registered in the High Court under Part I of the Act of 1958 by virtue of section 1(1) of the Act of 1958, give notice of the variation to the appropriate officer of the High Court;

by sending to the clerk of the court and, where necessary, the appropriate officer of the High Court, a certified copy of the order of variation.

(2) Where a maintenance order registered under Part II of the Act in a court of summary jurisdiction in England is discharged or varied by any other court, the clerk of the court in which it is registered shall be the prescribed officer to whom under section 23(2) of the Act notice of the discharge or variation shall be given; and on receipt of a certified copy of an order discharging or varying the registered order, he shall cause particulars of the same to be registered in his court by means of a memorandum entered and signed by him in the register.

**11.** (1) An application under subsection (1) of section 24 of the Act for the cancellation of the registration of a maintenance order registered under Part II of the Act in a court of summary jurisdiction in England shall be made to the clerk of that court by lodging with him a written application in that behalf (which shall state the date of the registration of the order) together with a copy of the order the registration of which it is sought to cancel.

(2) Where, in pursuance of an application made as aforesaid, the clerk cancels the registration of the maintenance order he shall send written notice of the cancellation to the clerk of the court by which the order was made and, where the order is registered in the High Court under Part I of the Act of 1958 by virtue of section 1(2) of the Act of 1958, to the appropriate officer of the High Court.

**12.**   Where a maintenance order is registered under Part II of the Act in a court of summary jurisdiction in England, the clerk of that court shall be the prescribed officer to whom notice shall be sent under subsection (2) of section 24 of the Act that the person liable to make the payments under the order has ceased to reside in England; and on receipt of such notice the clerk shall cancel the registration of the order and shall send written notice of the cancellation to the clerk of the court by which the order was made and, where the order is registered in the High Court under Part I of the Act of 1958 by virtue of section 1(2) of the Act of 1958, to the appropriate officer of the High Court.

**12A.**   Where the clerk of a magistrates' court in which a maintenance order is registered under Part I of the Act of 1958 receives a notice of cancellation under section 24(3) of the Act from the appropriate officer of the High Court, he shall—
  (a)  cause the particulars of such notice to be entered in the register; and
  (b)  cancel the registration under the said Part I; and
  (c)  give notice of the cancellation to the appropriate officer of the court in Scotland or Northern Ireland, as the case may be, which made the order, that is to say either—
    (i)  the Deputy Principal Clerk of Session, in the case of the Court of Session; or
    (ii)  the Chief Registrar of the Queen's Bench Division (Matrimonial), in the case of the High Court of Justice in Northern Ireland.

PART IV

FORMS

**13.**   (1)  A notice under subsection (4) of section 19 of the Act that the payments under a maintenance order made by a sheriff court in Scotland or a court of summary jurisdiction in Northern Ireland have become payable through or to any officer or person shall be in the form number 1 in the Schedule to these Rules, or any form to the like effect, and shall be sent by registered post by the clerk of that court to the person liable to make the payments under the order at his last known address.

(2)  A notice under the said subsection (4) that the payments under a maintenance order made by a court of summary jurisdiction in England have, on its registration under Part II of the Act in a court in Scotland or Northern Ireland, ceased to be payable through or to any officer or person shall be in the form number 2 in the Schedule to these Rules, or any form to the like effect, and shall be sent by registered post by the clerk of the first-mentioned court to the person liable to make the payments under the order at his last known address.

**14.**   A certificate lodged under subsection (1) of section 20 of the Act as to the amount of any arrears due under a maintenance order made by a court of summary jurisdiction in England shall be in the form number 3 in the Schedule to these Rules, or any form to the like effect.

**15.** A notice under subsection (5) or subsection (5A) of section 24 of the Act of the cancellation of the registration under Part II of the Act of a maintenance order in a court of summary jurisdiction in England shall be in the form number 4 in the Schedule to these Rules, or any form to the like effect, and shall be sent by registered post by the clerk of that court to the person liable to make the payments under the order at his last known address.

PART V

INTERPRETATION AND COMMENCEMENT

**16.** (1) In Parts II to V of these Rules, unless the context otherwise requires, the following expressions have the meanings hereby respectively assigned to them—

'maintenance order' has the same meaning as in Part II of the Act;

'the Act' means the Maintenance Orders Act 1950;

'the Act of 1958' means the Maintenance Orders Act 1958;

'appropriate officer of the High Court' means the Senior Registrar of the Principal Registry of the Family Division of the High Court or the district registrar of the relevant district registry;

'register' means the register kept in accordance with rule 54 of the Magistrates' Courts Rules 1968;

and other expressions used in these Rules have the meanings assigned to them in section 28 of the Act.

(2) References in Part III of these Rules to the clerk of the court by which the order was made shall be construed, in relation to a maintenance order made by a county court in Northern Ireland, as references to the Clerk of the Crown and Peace for the appropriate county in Northern Ireland.

(3) The Interpretation Act 1889 shall apply to the interpretation of these Rules as it applies to the interpretation of an Act of Parliament.

**17.** These Rules may be cited as the Maintenance Orders Act 1950 (Summary Jurisdiction) Rules 1950, and shall come into operation on the first day of January 1951.

Dated the fifteenth day of December 1950.

*Jowitt, C.*

SCHEDULE                                                              Rules 13 to 15

FORMS

1

*Notice to person liable to make payments that sums payable under a maintenance order registered in a court of summary jurisdiction in England have become payable through collecting officer. (Maintenance Orders Act 1950, s 19(4).)*

In the [county of                                    . Petty Sessional Division of                              ].
Court of Summary Jurisdiction sitting at
To AB, of

You are hereby given notice that the sums payable by you under (*insert particulars of maintenance order*) made on the              day of         , 19    , by (*state court in Scotland or Northern Ireland by which order was made*) and registered in this Court under Part II of the Maintenance Orders Act 1950, have, under an order of this Court dated the
day of            , 19    , become payable through [*or* to] the Collecting Officer of this Court [*or* the Court of Summary Jurisdiction sitting at                     ].

Payments under the order (including payments in respect of any sums due at the date of the receipt by you of this notice) should henceforth be sent to me [*or* to the said Collecting Office] at (state address).

Dated the           day of       19  .

> AB,
> Clerk [and Collecting Officer] of
> the Court of Summary Jurisdiction
> sitting at   .

### 2

*Notice to person liable to make payments that sums payable under a maintenance order made by a court of summary jurisdiction in England have ceased to be payable to or through any officer or person. (Maintenance Orders Act 1950, s 19(4).)*

In the [county of         . Petty Sessional Division of        ].
Court of Summary Jurisdiction sitting at
To AB, of

You are hereby given notice that the sums payable by you under (*insert particulars of maintenance order*) made on the      day of  , 19  , by this Court have, by reason of the registration of the said order in (*state court in Scotland or Northern Ireland in which order is registered*), ceased to be payable through [*or* to] (*state officer or person through or to whom payments have hitherto been required to be made*).

Payments under the order (including payments in respect of any sums due at the date of the receipt by you of this notice) should henceforth be paid to (*state name and address of the person entitled to payments under the order*) [, unless you receive, or have meanwhile received, notice from the clerk of the said court in Northern Ireland that they are to be paid to any other person].

Dated the        day of      19  .

> AB,
> Clerk [and Collecting Officer] of
> the Court of Summary Jurisdiction
> sitting at   .

### 3

*Certificate of Arrears. (Maintenance Orders Act 1950, s 20(1).)*

I hereby certify that the arrears due at the date of this certificate under (*insert particulars of maintenance order*) made on the    day of  , 19  , by the Court of Summary Jurisdiction sitting at      , the payments whereunder are at present required to be made to [*or* through] me, amount to      .

Dated the       day of     19  .

> AB,
> Collecting Officer of the Court of
> Summary Jurisdiction sitting at
>    .

### 4

*Notice of cancellation of registration of maintenance order in magistrates' court (Maintenance Orders Act 1950, s 24(5).)*

........................................................Magistrates' Court (*Code*)

Date:

To:

Address:

You are hereby given notice that the registration in this Court under Part II of the Maintenance Orders Act 1950 of [*insert particulars of maintenance order*] made on the
          day of          19   , by [*state court in Scotland or Northern Ireland by which order was made*] has been cancelled.

[Sums payable by you under the said order have, by reason of the cancellation of the registration of the said order, ceased to be payable through the clerk of [*this court*] [the magistrates' court at

                                        ] [by the following method of payment falling within section 59(6) of the Magistrates' Courts Act 1980 (standing order, etc) namely                    ], [by an attachment of earnings order].

Payments under the order [including payments in respect of any sums due at the date of receipt by you of this notice] should henceforth be paid to [*state name and address of person entitled to payments under the order*], unless you receive, or have meanwhile received, notice from the clerk of a competent court that they are to be paid to any other person.]

                                                            Justices' Clerk

## MAGISTRATES' COURTS (MAINTENANCE ORDERS ACT 1958) Rules 1959

**Dated** 1 January 1959

**SI 1959 No 3**

PART I

PROCEDURE UNDER PART I OF THE ACT

*Applications for registration under section 2(3) of the Act*

**1.**  An application for the registration in the High Court of a magistrates' court order need not be in writing or on oath.

*Manner in which magistrates' court is to be satisfied as to various matters*

**2.**  (1) An applicant wishing to show, in accordance with section 2A(1) of the Act, that the order to which the application relates, though deemed to have been made by a magistrates' court in England, was in fact made in another part of the United Kingdom or a country or territory outside the United Kingdom and that by the law of that part or of that country or territory interest is recoverable under the order may do so by producing the original court order or an authenticated copy thereof showing the date or time from which and the rate at which interest is so recoverable.

(2) For the purposes of paragraph (1) of this Rule, a copy shall be deemed to be authenticated if it purports to be certified by a judge or official of the court which made the original order to be a true copy of the original order, but it shall not be necessary to prove the signature or official position of the person appearing to have given such a certificate.

(3) Where an application for the registration in the High Court of a magistrates' court order is granted, the court shall be satisfied in the manner provided by paragraph (5) of this Rule that no process for the enforcement of the order issued before the grant of the application remains in force.

(4) Where the court receives notice given under section 5 of the Act (which relates to the cancellation of registration), the court shall be satisfied in the manner provided by paragraph (5) of this Rule that no process for the enforcement of the order issued before the giving of the notice remains in force and that no proceedings for the variation of the order are pending in a magistrates' court.

(5) For the purpose of satisfying the court as to the matters referred to in paragraphs (3) and (4) of this Rule—

(a)  if the person through or to whom payments are ordered to be made is the *clerk of* [justices' chief executive for] a magistrates' court, there shall be produced a certificate in that behalf purporting to be *signed by the clerk* [signed by the justices' chief executive] in the form numbered 1, 2 or 3, as the case may be, in the Schedule to these Rules;

(b)  in any other case, there shall be produced a document purporting to be a statutory declaration in that behalf in the form numbered 5 or 6, as the case may be, in the Schedule to these Rules.

**Note**. Words 'clerk of' substituted by words 'justices' chief executive for' in square brackets by SI 2001/615, r 2(iii), Schedule, para 17, as from 1 April 2001. Words 'signed by the clerk' substituted by words 'signed by the justices' chief executive' in square brackets by SI 2001/615, r 2(iii), Schedule, para 19, as from 1 April 2001.

*Receipt by magistrates' court of notice of registration in the High Court of order previously registered in magistrates' court*

**2A.**   Where a magistrates' court receives from the High Court notice of the registration in the High Court of an order made by a sheriff court in Scotland or a court of summary jurisdiction in Northern Ireland and previously registered in that magistrates' court in accordance with section 17(4) of the Act of 1950, the *clerk of* [justices' chief executive for] the court shall cause the particulars of such notice to be entered in the register.

**Note**. Inserted by SI 1980/1896, r 3. Words 'clerk of' substituted by words 'justices' chief executive for' in square brackets by SI 2001/615, r 2(iii), Schedule, para 17, as from 1 April 2001.

*Copy of magistrates' court order sent to the High Court for registration*

**3.**   (1) Where an application for the registration of a magistrates' court order is granted and the court is satisfied that no process issued for the enforcement of the order before the grant of the application remains in force, the court shall, in accordance with paragraph (c) of subsection (4) of section two of the Act, cause *the clerk* [the justices' chief executive] to send a copy of the order, certified to be a true copy thereof in the form numbered 7 in the Schedule to these Rules to the proper officer of the High Court.

(2) Where the court is satisfied in accordance with Rule 1A above that interest is recoverable under the order in respect of which the application has been granted the court shall, in accordance with section 2A(1) of the Act, cause *the clerk* [the justices' chief executive] to send, together with the certified copy of the order mentioned in paragraph (1) of this rule, a certificate in respect of the interest so recoverable in the form numbered 4 in the Schedule to these Rules to the appropriate officer of the High Court.

**Note**. Words 'the clerk' in both places they occur substituted by words 'the justices' chief executive' in square brackets by SI 2001/615, r 2(iii), Schedule, para 18, as from 1 April 2001.

*Registration of High Court or county court order in a magistrates' court*

**4.**   Where a *clerk of* [justices' chief executive for] a magistrates' court in accordance with paragraph (b) of subsection (2) of section two of the Act receives from an officer of the High Court or the registrar of a county court a certified copy of a High Court or county court order, he shall cause the order to be registered in his court by means of a memorandum entered and signed by him in the register and shall send written notice to that officer of the High Court or the registrar of the county court, as the case may be, that it has been duly registered.

**Note**. Words 'clerk of' substituted by words 'justices' chief executive for' in square brackets by SI 2001/615, r 2(iii), Schedule, para 17, as from 1 April 2001.

*Registration in magistrates' court of order made in Court of Session or High Court in Northern Ireland*

**4A.**   Where a *clerk of* [justices' chief executive for] a magistrates' court, in pursuance of section 2(2)(b) of the Act, receives from the appropriate officer of the original court in Scotland or Northern Ireland a certified copy of an order made by the Court of Session or the High Court in Northern Ireland, he shall cause the order to be registered in his court by means of a memorandum entered and signed by him in the register and shall send written notice to the appropriate officer of the High Court and to the appropriate officer of the original court that the order has been duly registered.

**Note**. Inserted by SI 1980/1896, r 5. Words 'clerk of' substituted by words 'justices' chief executive for' in square brackets by SI 2001/615, r 2(iii), Schedule, para 17, as from 1 April 2001.

*Notices as respects payments through a clerk of a magistrates' court*

**5.**   (1) A notice under subsection (6ZC) of section 2 of the Act, that the payments under a High Court or county court order or an order made by the Court of Session or the High Court in Northern Ireland have, on its registration in a magistrates' court, become payable through the *clerk of* [justices' chief executive for] a magistrates' court shall be given by the *clerk of* [justices' chief executive for] the court of registration in the form numbered 8 in the Schedule to these Rules.

(2) A notice under subsection (6ZC) of section 2 of the Act, that the payments under a magistrates' court order or an order made by a sheriff court in Scotland or a court of summary jurisdiction in Northern Ireland and registered in a magistrates' court under Part II of the Act of 1950 have, on its registration in the High Court, ceased to be payable to a *clerk to* [justices' chief executive for] a magistrates' court shall be given by the *clerk of* [justices' chief executive for] the administering court and shall be in the form numbered 9 in the Schedule to these Rules and, where payments have been payable *through a clerk* [through a justices' chief executive] other than the *clerk of* [justices' chief executive for] the administering court, he shall send a copy of the said notice to *that other clerk* [that other justices' chief executive].

(3) A notice under subsection (5)(b) of section five of the Act that the registration in a magistrates' court of a High Court or county court order or an order made by the Court of Session or the High Court in Northern Ireland has been cancelled and that payments thereunder have ceased to be payable through a *clerk of* [justices' chief executive for] a magistrates' court shall be given by the *clerk of* [justices' chief executive for] the court of registration and shall be in the form numbered 10 in the Schedule to these Rules and, where payments have been payable *through a clerk* [through a justices' chief executive] other than the *clerk of* [justices' chief executive for] the court of registration, he shall send a copy of the said notice to *that other clerk* [that other justices' chief executive].

(4) A notice given in accordance with the preceding provisions of this Rule shall be delivered to the person liable to make payments under the order to which the notice relates or sent by post to that person at his last known address.

**Note**. Words 'clerk of' in each place they appear substituted by words 'justices' chief executive for' in square brackets by SI 2001/615, r 2(iii), Schedule, para 17. Words 'through a clerk' in both places they occur substituted by words 'through a justices' chief executive' in square brackets by SI 2001/615, r 2(iii), Schedule, para 20, as from 1 April 2001. Words 'that other clerk' in both places they occur substituted by words 'that other justices' chief executive' in square brackets by SI 2001/615, r 2(iii), Schedule, para 20, as from 1 April 2001.

**5A.**   (1) Where, in the exercise of the duty imposed by section 2(6ZA)(b) of the Act, or in the exercise of the powers conferred by section 3(2A) or (2B) or section 4(2A), (5A) or (5B) of the Act, a magistrates' court orders that payments under a registered order are to be made by a particular means, the clerk of the court shall record on the copy of the order the means of payment which the court has ordered and [the justices' chief executive shall] notify in writing, as soon as practicable, the person liable to make payments under the order of how the payments are to be made.

(2) Where, in the exercise of any of the aforesaid powers, the court orders that payments be made by the debtor to the creditor or by the debtor to the *clerk of* [justices' chief executive for] the court or to the *clerk of* [justices' chief executive for] any other magistrates' court by a method of payment falling within section 59(6) of the Magistrates' Courts Act 1980 (standing order, etc), the *clerk of* [justices' chief executive for] the court which makes the order to whom payments are to be made shall notify the person liable to make the payments under the order of the number and location of the account into which the payments should be made.

(3) Where, under section 60(4) of the Magistrates' Courts Act 1980, as applied by section 4(5A) of the Act or as modified by section 4(5B) of the Act, the *clerk of* [justices' chief executive for] the court receives an application from an interested party for the method of payment to be varied, *the clerk* [the justices' chief executive shall] shall notify in writing, as soon as practicable, that party and, where practicable, any other interested party, of the result of the application, including any decision to refer the matter to the court; where *the clerk* [the clerk of the court grants] grants the application he shall record the variation on the copy of the order.

**Note**. Words 'the justices' chief executive shall' in square brackets inserted, words 'clerk of' in each place they occur substituted by words 'justices' chief executive for' in square brackets, and words 'the clerk' in both places substituted by words 'the justices' chief executive shall' and 'the clerk of the court grants' in square brackets, by SI 2001/615, r 2(iii), paras 17, 22, 23, as from 1 April 2001.

*Remission to the original court of application for variation of registered maintenance order*

**6.** An order under subsection (4) of section four of the Act remitting an application for the variation of a High Court or county court order registered in a magistrates' court to the original court shall be in the form numbered 11 in the Schedule to these Rules.

*Notice of variation, remission, discharge or cancellation of registration by a magistrates' court of a registered order*

**7.** (1) Where a High Court or county court order registered in a magistrates' court is, under subsection (2) of section four of the Act, varied by a magistrates' court, the *clerk of* [justices' chief executive for] the last-mentioned court shall give notice of the variation to the High Court or county court, as the case may be.

(2) Where an application for the variation of a High Court or county court order registered in a magistrates' court is, under subsection (4) of section four of the Act, remitted to the original court by a magistrates' court, the *clerk of* [justices' chief executive for] the last-mentioned court shall give notice of the remission to the High Court or county court, as the case may be.

(3) Where the registration of a High Court or county court order in a magistrates' court is, under subsection (4) of section five of the Act, cancelled by the court of registration, the *clerk of* [justices' chief executive for] the last-mentioned court shall give notice of cancellation to the High Court or county court, as the case may be, stating, if such be the case, that the cancellation is in consequence of a notice given under subsection (1) of the said section five.

(3A) Where the registration in a magistrates' court of an order made in the Court of Session or the High Court in Northern Ireland is cancelled under section 5(4) of the Act by that magistrates' court, the *clerk of* [justices' chief executive for] that magistrates' court shall give notice of the cancellation to the appropriate officer of the original court and to the appropriate officer of the High Court (where the order is registered by virtue of Part II of the Act of 1950).

(3B) Where the registration in a magistrates' court of an order under Part II of the Act of 1950 is cancelled by that magistrates' court by virtue of section 5(4) of the Act the *clerk of* [justices' chief executive for] the court shall give notice of the cancellation to the appropriate officer of the original court and to the appropriate officer of the High Court (where the order is registered under Part I of the Act).

(4) Where a magistrates' court order registered in the High Court is varied or discharged by a magistrates' court, the *clerk of* [justices' chief executive for] the last-mentioned court shall give notice of the variation or discharge, as the case may be, to the High Court.

(5) Notice under the preceding provisions of this Rule shall be given by sending to the appropriate officer of the High Court or the registrar of the county court, as the case may be, a copy of the order of variation, remission, cancellation or discharge, as the case may be, certified to be a true copy thereof by the *clerk of* [justices' chief executive for] the magistrates' court and marked, in the case of a High Court maintenance order, with the title and cause number, if any, and in the case of a county court maintenance order with the plaint or application number.

(6) For the purposes of the preceding paragraph the appropriate officer of the High Court shall be—

(a) in relation to a High Court order registered in a magistrates' court, the officer to whom notice of registration was given under Rule 4 of these Rules;

(b) in relation to a magistrates' court order registered in the High Court, the officer to whom a copy of the order was sent under Rule 3 of these Rules.

(7) Where a magistrates' court order registered in the High Court is discharged by a magistrates' court and it appears to the last-mentioned court that no arrears remain to be recovered, notice under subsection (3) of section five of the Act shall be given by an endorsement in the form numbered 12 in the Schedule to these Rules on the certified copy of the order of discharge referred to in paragraph (5) of this Rule.

**Note**. Words 'clerk of' in each place they occur substituted by words 'justices' chief executive for' in square brackets by SI 2001/615, r 2(iii), Schedule, para 17. Paras (3A), (3B) inserted by SI 1980/1896, r 7, as from 1 April 2001.

*Notices received from the High Court or a county court or from a person entitled to payments*

**8.** Subject to Rule 8A below where any notice is received—

(a) of the registration in the High Court of a magistrates' court order;

(b) of the discharge or variation by the High Court or a county court of a High Court or county court order registered in a magistrates' court;

(bb) of the discharge or variation by the Court of Session or High Court in Northern Ireland of an order made by such court and registered in a magistrates' court;

(c) under subsection (1) or (2) of section five of the Act (which relates to the cancellation of registration);

the *clerk of* [justices' chief executive for] the magistrates' court shall cause particulars of the notice to be registered in his court by means of a memorandum entered and signed by him in the register and, in the case of a notice under subsection (1) or (2) of section five of the Act, shall cause the person in possession of any warrant of commitment, issued but not executed, for the enforcement of the order to be informed of the giving of the notice.

**Note**. Words 'subject to Rule 8A below' and para (bb) inserted by SI 1980/1896, r 9. Words 'clerk of' substituted by words 'justices' chief executive for' in square brackets by SI 1980/615, r 2(iii), Schedule, para 17, as from 1 April 2001.

*Notice of cancellation of registration in High Court under Part I of the Act*

**8A.**   Where any notice is received by a court that the registration of an order in the High Court has been cancelled under section 5(4) of the Act, the *clerk of* [justices' chief executive for] the court shall cause the particulars of the notice to be entered in the register.

**Note**. Inserted by SI 1980/1896, r 9. Words 'clerk of' substituted by words 'justices' chief executive for' in square brackets by SI 2001/615, r 2(iii), Schedule, para 17, as from 1 April 2001.

*jurisdiction as respects complaints for variation of High Court maintenance orders*

**9.**   Rule 34 of the Magistrates' Courts Rules 1952 (which relates to jurisdiction to hear certain complaints), shall apply to a complaint for the variation of a High Court or county court order registered in a magistrates' court as if the order were a magistrates' court maintenance order made by the court of registration and as if in paragraph (4) of the said Rule for the words 'shall cause' there were substituted the words 'may cause'.

PART II

*Repealed.*

PART III

MISCELLANEOUS AND SUPPLEMENTAL

*Administering court to be informed of proceedings in foreign court*

**21.**   Where any decision is reached, or warrant of distress or commitment is issued, in pursuance of a complaint or application relating to a maintenance order or the enforcement of a maintenance order (including an application under section twelve of the Act, which relates to the determination whether payments are earnings), being a complaint or application heard by a magistrates' court other than the administering court—

   (a)  the *clerk of* [justices' chief executive for] the first-mentioned court shall forthwith send by post to the *clerk of* [justices' chief executive for] the administering court an extract from the register containing a minute or memorandum of the decision or of the issue of the warrant as the case may be;

   (b)  on receipt of the extract *the last-mentioned clerk* [the last-mentioned justices' chief executive] shall enter the minute or memorandum in his register.

**Note**. Words 'clerk of' (in both places) and 'the last-mentioned clerk' substituted by words 'justices' chief executive' and 'the last-mentioned justices' chief executive' in square brackets by SI 2001/615, r 2(iii), Schedule, paras 17, 24, as from 1 April 2001.

*Review of committals, etc*

**22.**   (1) Where for the purpose of enforcing a maintenance order a magistrates' court has exercised its power under subsection (2) of section sixty-five of the Magistrates' Courts Act 1952, or subsection (3) or (5) of section eighteen of the Act to postpone the issue of a warrant of commitment and under the terms of the postponement the warrant falls to be issued, the *clerk of* [justices' chief executive for] the court shall give notice to the defendant in the form numbered 15 in the Schedule to these Rules and shall attach to the said notice a copy of the form numbered 16 of the said Schedule.

(2) An application under subsection (1) of the said section eighteen requesting that the warrant shall not be issued shall be in the form numbered 16 in the Schedule to these Rules and shall be delivered to the *clerk of* [justices' chief executive for] the court or sent to him by post.

**Note**. Words 'clerk of' (in both places) substituted by words 'justices' chief executive' in square brackets by SI 2001/615, r 2(iii), Schedule, paras 17, 24, as from 1 April 2001.

(3) For the purposes of subsection (2) of the said section eighteen the period for the receipt by *the clerk* [the justices' chief executive] of an application under subsection (1) of the said section shall be the period of eight days beginning with the day on which *the clerk* [the justices' chief executive] sends to the defendant the notice referred to in paragraph (1) of this Rule.

(4) An application under subsection (4) of the said section eighteen requesting that a warrant of commitment which has been executed shall be cancelled shall be in the form numbered 17 in the Schedule to these Rules.

(5) Where an application by a defendant under subsection (1) or (4) of the said section eighteen is considered by the court the *clerk of* [justices' chief executive for] the court shall give notice of the decision of the court, if the person in question is not present—

    (a)  to the person in whose favour the maintenance order in question was made; and

    (b)  except where an application under subsection (1) of the said section eighteen is dismissed, to the defendant.

(6) Where on considering an application by a defendant under subsection (4) of the said section eighteen the court—

    (a)  makes an order under paragraph (b) of subsection (5) of the said section for the cancellation of the warrant of commitment; or

    (b)  remits under subsection (6) of the said section the whole or any part of the sum in respect of which the warrant was issued;

the *clerk of* [justices' chief executive for] the court shall forthwith give written notice of the decision to the person in charge of the prison or other place in which the defendant is detained.

**Note**. Words 'clerk of' in each place they occur substituted by words 'justices' chief executive for' in square brackets by SI 2001/615, r 2(iii), Schedule, para 17, as from 1 April 2001. Words 'the clerk' in both places they occur substituted by words 'the justices' chief executive' in square brackets by SI 2001/615, r 2(iii), Schedule, paras 18, 25, as from 1 April 2001.

*Warrants of commitment*

**23.** A warrant of commitment for the enforcement of a maintenance order, being an affiliation order or an order enforceable as an affiliation order, issued in pursuance of a complaint under section seventy-four of the Magistrates' Courts Act 1952, as amended by section sixteen of the Act, shall be in the form numbered 18 in the Schedule to these Rules:

Provided that where the issue of the warrant has been postponed under section sixty-five of the Magistrates' Courts Act 1952, or under section eighteen of the Act the warrant shall be in the form numbered 19 in the Schedule to these Rules.

*Revocations*

**24.** (1) The forms of warrants of commitment numbered 20 and 21 in the Schedule to the Bastardy (Forms) Order 1915, shall be omitted therefrom and the form numbered 88 in the Schedule to the Magistrates' Courts (Forms) Rules 1952, shall cease to apply to a warrant of commitment the issue of which has been postponed under section sixty-five of the Magistrates' Courts Act 1952, or under section eighteen of the Act, being a warrant of commitment for the enforcement of a maintenance order.

(2) The forms numbered 23, 24 and 25 in the Schedule to the Bastardy (Forms) Order 1915 (which relate to the attachment of pension or income), shall be omitted therefrom.

(3) The following provisions of the Magistrates' Courts Rules 1952, are hereby revoked, that is to say—
(a) paragraph (8) of Rule 34 (which relates to the giving of information as respects certain proceedings in a foreign court); and
(b) Rule 36 (which relates to the attachment of income or pension).

*Interpretation*

**25.** (1) Subsection (3) of section one of the Act shall apply to the interpretation of Part I of these Rules as it applies to the interpretation of Part I of the Act.

(2) Section twenty-one of the Act shall apply to the interpretation of these Rules as it applies to the interpretation of the Act.

(3) The Interpretation Act 1889, shall apply to the interpretation of these Rules as it applies to the interpretation of an Act of Parliament.

(4) In these Rules—
'the Act' means the Maintenance Orders Act 1958;
'the Act of 1950' means the Maintenance Orders Act 1950;
'appropriate officer of the High Court' means the Senior Registrar of the Principal Registry of the Family Division of the High Court or such district registrar as may be specified by the applicant;
'appropriate officer of the original court' means—
(i) the Sheriff-clerk, in the case of a sheriff court in Scotland;
(ii) the clerk of petty sessions, in the case of a magistrates' court in Northern Ireland;
(iii) the Deputy Principal Clerk of Session, in the case of the Court of Session;
(iv) the Chief Registrar of the Queen's Bench Division (Matrimonial), in the case of the High Court of Justice in Northern Ireland.

(5) Any reference in these Rules to the administering court in relation to a maintenance order or a related attachment of earnings order is a reference to the magistrates' court—
(a) which made the maintenance order;
(b) in which the maintenance order is registered under the Act, under Part II of the Maintenance Orders Act 1950, or under the Maintenance Orders (Facilities for Enforcement) Act 1920; or
(c) by which the maintenance order was confirmed under the Maintenance Orders (Facilities for Enforcement) Act 1920.

(6) Any reference in these Rules to the register is a reference to the register kept in accordance with Rule 54 of the Magistrates' Courts Rules 1968.

(7) Any reference in these Rules to a form in the Schedule to these Rules shall include a reference to a form to the like effect with such variations as the circumstances may require.

**Note**. The Interpretation Act 1889 is replaced by the Interpretation Act 1978.

*Citation and commencement*

**26.** These Rules may be cited as the Magistrates' Courts (Maintenance Orders Act 1958) Rules 1959, and shall come into operation on the sixteenth day of February 1959.

SCHEDULE

FORMS

\*　　\*　　\*　　\*　　\*

4

*Certificate in respect of interest recoverable under a maintenance order*
*(MO Act 1958, s 2A(1))*

I hereby certify that the rate of interest shown in accordance with subsection (1) of section 2A of the Maintenance Orders Act 1958 to be recoverable in respect of (insert particulars of maintenance order, or, if application relates only to a part of the order relating to a lump sum, insert particulars of that part of the order)
is ...............................................................................................................................
and that the date from which it is so recoverable is ...................................................
to ...........................................................................................................................

Dated the　　　　　day of　　　　　　　　　, 19　　.
　　　　　　　　　　　　　　　　　　　JC,
　　　　　　　　　　　　　　　　　　　CLERK OF THE MAGISTRATES' COURT
　　　　　　　　　　　　　　　　　　　SITTING AT　　　　　　　　　　　　　　.

5

*Declaration that no process for enforcement remains in force*
*(MO Act 1958, s 2(3))*

I, GH, of　　　　　　　　, do solemnly and sincerely declare that at the date of this declaration no process remains in force for the enforcement of (insert particulars of maintenance order, or if application relates only to a part of the order relating to a lump sum, insert particulars of that part of the order) made on the　　　day of　　　　, 19　　, by the Magistrates' Court sitting at　　　　　　　, whereunder I am entitled to receive payment[s].

And I make this solemn declaration, conscientiously believing the same to be true by virtue of the provisions of the Statutory Declarations Act 1835.

Declared at　　　　　　　, the　　　　　day of　　　　　　, 19　　before me,
　　　　　　　　　　　　　　　　　　　JP,
　　　　　　　　　　　　　　　　　　　Justice of the Peace for the [county] of
　　　　　　　　　　　　　　　　　　　(Or other description)

6

*Declaration that no process for enforcement remains in force and no proceedings for variation*
*are pending*
*(MO Act 1958, s 5(4)(c))*

I, GH, of　　　　　　　　, do solemnly and sincerely declare that at the date of this declaration no process remains in force for the enforcement and no proceedings are pending in a Magistrates' Court for the variation of (insert particulars of maintenance order, or if application relates only to a part of the order relating to a lump sum, insert particulars of that part of the order) made on the　　　day of　　　　, 19　　, by the [High Court] [　　　County Court] [Court of Session] [High Court in Northern Ireland] whereunder I am entitled to receive payment[s].

And I make this solemn declaration, conscientiously believing the same to be true by virtue of the provisions of the Statutory Declarations Act 1835.
　　　　　　　　　　　　　　　　　　　GH

Declared at　　　　　　　, the　　　　　day of　　　　　　, 19　　before me,
　　　　　　　　　　　　　　　　　　　JP,
　　　　　　　　　　　　　　　　　　　Justice of the Peace for the [county] of
　　　　　　　　　　　　　　　　　　　(Or other description)

\*　　\*　　\*　　\*　　\*

10
*Notice of cancellation of registration*
*(MO Act 1958, s 5(5))*

To

Magistrates' Court (*Code*)

Address:

You are hereby given notice that the registration in this Court under Part I of the Maintenance Orders Act 1958, (*insert particulars of maintenance order*) made on the day of         19     by the [High Court] [         County Court] [Court of Session] [High Court in Northern Ireland] has been cancelled.

Sums payable by you under the said order have by reason of the cancellation of the registration of the said order ceased to be payable [through the *clerk of* [justices' chief executive for] [this court] [the magistrates' court at              ]], [by the following method of payment falling within section 59(6) of the Magistrates' Courts Act 1980 (standing order, etc) namely,              ], [by an attachment of earnings order] [by direct payment to              ].

Payments under the order (including payments in respect of any sum due on the date of the receipt by you of this notice) should henceforth be paid to (*state name and address of person entitled to payments under the order*).

*Justices' Clerk* [Justices' Chief Executive]

11
*Order remitting to the original court application for variation of registered maintenance order*
*(MO Act 1958, s 4(4))*

In the [county of              . Petty Sessional Division              ].
Before the Magistrates' Court sitting at              .
Complaint has been made by CD, of              , (hereinafter called the complainant) who states that by (*insert particulars of maintenance order*) made on the         day of         19     by the [High Court] [         County Court] and registered on the         day of         19     in the Magistrates' Court sitting at              . AB (hereinafter called the defendant) [*or* he/she] was ordered (*state shortly terms of original order, and mention any subsequent order and effect thereof*):

And the complainant has applied for the said order to be varied by an order requiring         on the ground that.

[And the said complaint has been sent to the *Clerk of* [Justices' Chief Executive for] this Court in pursuance of Rule 34 of the Magistrates' Courts Rules 1952].

It appearing to this Court that it is appropriate to remit the application to the [High Court] [         County Court], it is ordered that the application be so remitted.

Dated the         day of         19

JP,
Justice of the Peace for the [county] first above mentioned
*or* By order of the Court
JC
Clerk of the Magistrates' Court sitting at

12
*Endorsement that no arrears remain to be recovered*
*(MO Act 1958, s 5(3))*

In the [county of              . Petty Sessional Division of              ].
Before the Magistrates' Court sitting at              .

Whereas it appeared to this Court this day on discharging (*insert particulars of maintenance order*) that no arrears remain to be recovered thereunder notice is hereby given under subsection (3) of section five of the Maintenance Orders Act 1958.

Dated the                    day of                          19

JC

*Clerk of* [Justices' Chief Executive for]<br>
the Magistrates' Court sitting at

*    *    *    *    *

**15**
*Notice that warrant of commitment falls to be issued*
(*MO Act 1958, s 18(1)*)

In the [county of                              . Petty Sessional Division                          ].
Before the Magistrates' Court sitting at

To AB, of

PLEASE READ THIS NOTICE CAREFULLY

On the            day of              , 19    , this Court postponed the issue of a warrant of commitment in your case for the enforcement of (*insert particulars of maintenance order*) (*insert the terms of postponement*).

You have failed to comply with these terms of postponement and the warrant committing you to prison for a term of                  now falls to be issued unless you pay under the maintenance order [the sum] [the net sum, after making deductions in respect of income tax,] of

If you consider that there are grounds for not issuing the warrant you may make an application to the Court on the attached form requesting that the warrant shall not be issued and stating those grounds.

If no such application is received by me on or before the        day of          , 19    , and you fail to pay the sum referred to above the warrant will be issued.

If such an application is received by me on or before the        day of          , 19    , it will be considered by a justice who may either refer it to the Court for further consideration or dismiss the application and issue the warrant forthwith.

Dated the            day of                  19

JC

*Clerk of* [Justices' Chief Executive for]<br>
the Magistrates' Court sitting at

**16**
*Application requesting that warrant should not be issued*
(*MO Act 1958, s 18(1)*)

To the Magistrates' Court sitting at

I, AB, of                              , have received the notice sent to me by the *clerk of* [Justices' Chief Executive for] the Court and dated the                          day of , 19    .

I hereby request that the warrant of commitment shall not be issued. The grounds of my request are as follows—

Dated the              day of          , 19    .

AB

Note. This application should be delivered or sent by post to the *Clerk of* [Justices' Chief Executive for] the Court (*insert address*).

17
*Application requesting that warrant should be cancelled*
(*MO Act 1958, s 18(4)*.)

To the Magistrates' Court sitting at
I, AB, hereby request that the warrant of commitment under which I am for the time being imprisoned [or otherwise detained] should be cancelled. The grounds of my request are as follows—

Dated the         day of      , 19  .

AB

**Note.** Words 'clerk of', 'Clerk of' and 'Justices' Clerk' in each place they occur substituted by words 'justices' chief executive for', 'Justices' Chief Executive' and 'Justices Chief Executive for' in square brackets by SI 2001/615, r 2(iii), Schedule, paras 17, 26–28, as from 1 April 2001.

## FOREIGN MARRIAGE ORDER 1970

**Dated** 19 October 1970

**SI 1970 No 1539**

Her Majesty, by virtue and in exercise of the powers conferred on Her by sections 18 and 21 of the Foreign Marriage Act 1892, as amended by sections 4(2) and (6) of the Foreign Marriage Act 1947, or otherwise in Her Majesty vested, is pleased, by and with the advice of Her Privy Council, to order, and it is hereby ordered, as follows:

**1.** This Order may be cited as the Foreign Marriage Order 1970. It shall come into operation on 1 January 1971.

**2.** (1) Unless otherwise provided in this Order, expressions used in this Order shall have the same meanings as in the Foreign Marriage Act, 1892.

(2) The Interpretation Act 1889 shall apply for the interpretation of this Order as it applies for the interpretation of an Act of Parliament.

**Note.** The Interpretation Act 1889 is replaced by Interpretation Act 1978.

**3.** (1) Before a marriage is solemnised in a foreign country under the Foreign Marriage Acts 1892 to 1947, the marriage officer must be satisfied:
   (a) that at least one of the parties is a British subject; and
   (b) that the authorities of that country will not object to the solemnisation of the marriage; and
   (c) that insufficient facilities exist for the marriage of the parties under the law of that country; and
   (d) that the parties will be regarded as validly married by the law of the country to which each party belongs.

(2) If a marriage officer, by reason of anything in this Article, refuses to solemnise or allow to be solemnised in his presence the marriage of any person requiring such marriage to be solemnised, that person shall have the same right to appeal to the Secretary of State as is given by section 5 of the Foreign Marriage Act 1892.

**4.** (1) In special cases, where the Secretary of State is satisfied that for some good reason the requirements of the Foreign Marriage Act 1892 as to residence and notice for a marriage intended to be solemnised under the Act cannot be complied with, and he is satisfied that the intended marriage is not clandestine and that adequate public notice of the intended marriage has been given in the place or places where each of the parties resided not less than fifteen days next preceding the giving of such notice, he may authorise the marriage officer to dispense with those requirements.

(2) In cases falling under paragraph (1) of this Article, the oath under section 7 of the Foreign Marriage Act 1892 shall omit the matter specified in subsection (b) of that section.

**5.** For the purpose of marriages to be solemnised by or before a consular officer who is a marriage officer, every place within the curtilage or precincts of the building which is for the time being used for the purpose of his office shall be part of the official house of such marriage officer, and every place to which the public have ordinary access in such official house shall be deemed to be part of the office of such marriage officer.

**6.** Where a certified copy of an entry in a marriage register kept under section 9 of the Foreign Marriage Act 1892, relating to a party shown to be from Scotland or Northern Ireland is received by the Registrar General, he shall send a copy of that entry to the Registrar General for Scotland or Northern Ireland, as the case may require.

**7.** (1) Where a marriage between parties, of whom one at least is a British subject, has been duly solemnised or has taken place in a foreign country in accordance with the local law of the country, either party to the marriage, being a British subject, may produce to the consul of Her Majesty's Government in the United Kingdom for the district in which the marriage has been solemnised or has taken place (or in the absence of such officer to the appropriate consul of any other Government who, by arrangement with Her Majesty's Government in the United Kingdom, have undertaken consular representation in that district on behalf of Her Majesty's Government in the United Kingdom) a certified copy of the entry in the marriage register duly authenticated by the appropriate authority in that country or a marriage certificate issued by the appropriate authority of the country, accompanied by a translation into English, and may request him to accept the certificate as a certificate of marriage issued in accordance with the local law and to certify the translation; and the consul on payment of the appropriate fee, shall, if he is satisfied that the certificate has been duly issued by the appropriate authority and that the translation is a true one, transmit the said certificate and translation, together with his own certificate regarding the accuracy of the translation, to the Registrar General or, in the case of any certificate relating to a party shown to be from Scotland or Northern Ireland, to the Registrar General for Scotland or Northern Ireland as the case may require.

(2) Any person shall be entitled to have from the appropriate Registrar General a certified copy of any document received by that Registrar General as aforesaid, on payment of fees in respect of the provision of the copy and any necessary search for the document. The fees shall be the fees which are for the time being charged by the appropriate Registrar General for the provision of a certified copy of, and any necessary search for, an entry in the records in his custody of marriages performed in England and Wales, Scotland or Northern Ireland, as the case may be.

(3) Any copy of any foreign marriage certificate issued by the appropriate Registrar General under the provisions of paragraph (2) of this Article shall, without further proof, be received in evidence to the like extent as if it were a certificate duly issued by the authorities of the foreign country in which the marriage was celebrated.

**8.** The forms in the Schedule to this Order shall be used in all cases to which they are applicable.

**9.** (1) The Foreign Marriage Order 1964 and the Foreign Marriage (Amendment) Order 1967 are hereby revoked.

(2) Section 38 of the Interpretation Act 1889 shall apply in relation to the said Orders as if the present Order were an Act of Parliament and as if the said Orders were enactments repealed by an Act of Parliament.

*W. G. Agnew*

**Note.** Interpretation Act 1889, s 38 is replaced by Interpretation Act 1978, ss 17(2)(a) and 16(2).

SCHEDULE                                                                                       Art 8

FORMS

NO. 1—NOTICE OF MARRIAGE

*(Section 2 of the Foreign Marriage Act 1892)*

To [Her Majesty's Consul-General *or* Consul *or* Vice-Consul] at

I hereby give you notice that a marriage is intended to be had within three calendar months from the date hereof between me and the other party herein named and described (that is to say):

| Name and Surname | Condition | Profession | Age | Residence | Length of Residence |
|---|---|---|---|---|---|
| AB | ........................ | | | | |
| CD | ........................ | | | | |

Witness my hand, this          day of

(Signed) AB, *or*

CD

NO. 2—FORM OF OATH

*(Section 7 of the Foreign Marriage Act 1892)*

I, AB, of ...................., make oath and say as follows:

**1.**   A marriage is proposed to be solemnised between me and CD.

**2.**   I believe that there is not any impediment in kindred or alliance, or other lawful hindrance to the above marriage.

**3.**   Both I and CD have for three weeks immediately preceding this date had our usual residence within the district of [*here insert the official title of the marriage officer, and the place where he is appointed to reside*], that is to say, I at ................, and CD at ...............

[to be omitted in cases falling under Article 4 of the Order]

**4.**   [I am not under the age of 18 years] [*or as the case may be*, I am under the age of 18 years and the widow/er of EF who died on the                 day of                 ] [*or*, I am under the age of 18 years and the consent of GH and IJ, whose consent is required by law to my marriage, is given as shown by the writing under their/his/her hand now shown to me and marked [                  ]] [*or*, I am under the age of 18 years and there is no person whose consent to my marriage is required] [*or*, I am under the age of 18 years and the necessity of obtaining the consent of the persons whose consent to my marriage is required by law has been dispensed with].

**5.**   [CD is not under the age of 18 years] [*or, as the case may be*, CD is under the age of 18 years and the widow/er of KL who died on the                 day of                 ] [*or*, CD is under the age of 18 years and the consent of MN and OP, whose consent is required by law to his/her marriage, is given as shown by the writing under their/his/her hand now shown to me and marked [             ]] [*or*, CD is under the age of 18 years and there is no person whose consent to his/her marriage is required] [*or*, CD is under the age of 18 years and the necessity of obtaining the consent of the persons whose consent to his/her marriage is required by law has been dispensed with].

**6.**   I make the foregoing statements solemnly and deliberately, conscientiously believing the same to be true, well knowing that if any person knowingly and wilfully makes a false oath or signs a false notice under the Foreign Marriage Act 1892, for the purpose of procuring a marriage, he may be guilty of an offence under section 3 of the Perjury Act 1911; and well knowing also that any person who, being married or single, shall marry any other person during the life of the husband or wife or either party as the case may be, may be guilty of an offence under section 57 of the Offences against the Person Act 1861.

Sworn at ................................................

this ................ day of .................... 19 ...                  AB

Before me, XY, HM Consul (*or as the case may be*)

at .............................................................................

XY (Official seal)

NO. 3—CERTIFICATE OF COPY OF MARRIAGE REGISTER

(*s 10( 1) of the Foreign Marriage Act 1892*)

I, ................, Her Majesty's Consul [*or as the case may be*], residing at ...............,
hereby certify that this is a true copy of the entries of marriages registered in this office, from the entry of the marriage of AB and CD number *one*, to the entry of the marriage of EF and GH, number *two*.

Witness my hand and seal this          day of          19   .
(Signature and official seal of marriage officer).

## MAGISTRATES' COURTS (ATTACHMENT OF EARNINGS) RULES 1971

**Dated** 13 May 1971

**SI 1971 No 809**

*Citation and operation*

**1.**   These Rules may be cited as the Magistrates' Courts (Attachment of Earnings) Rules 1971 and shall come into operation on 2 August 1971.

*Interpretation*

**2.**   (1) Sections 2 and 25(1) of the Act shall apply to the interpretation of these Rules as they apply to the interpretation of the Act.

(2)  The Interpretation Act 1889 shall apply to the interpretation of these Rules as it applies to the interpretation of an Act of Parliament.

(3)  Any reference in these Rules to 'the Act' is a reference to the Attachment of Earnings Act 1971.

(4)  Any reference in these Rules to any enactment or rule is a reference to that enactment or rule as amended by any enactment or rule.

(5)  *Any reference in these Rules to a form in the Schedule to these Rules shall include a reference to a form to the like effect with such variations as the circumstances may require.*

(6)  Any reference in these Rules to an attachment of earnings order shall be construed subject to the provisions of Rule 23.

**Note.** Interpretation Act 1889 is replaced by Interpretation Act 1978. Para 5 revoked by SI 2003/1236, rr 2, 3, with effect from 20 June 2003.

*Revocation*

**3.**   (1) Rules 10 to 20 and 23(2) of the Magistrates' Courts (Maintenance Orders Act 1958) Rules 1959, the Magistrates' Courts (Attachment of Earnings) Rules 1967 and paragraph 9 of the Schedule to the Justices' Clerks Rules 1970 are hereby revoked.

(2)  The forms numbered 13, 14 and 20 in the Schedule to the Magistrates' Courts (Maintenance Orders Act 1958) Rules 1959 shall be omitted therefrom.

*Jurisdiction as respects complaints for an attachment of earnings order*

**4.**   A magistrates' court shall have jurisdiction to hear a complaint for an attachment of earnings order if it would have jurisdiction to enforce payment of any arrears under the related maintenance order.

*Attachment of earnings order*

**5.**   *An attachment of earnings order shall be in the form numbered 1 in the Schedule to these Rules.*
**Note.** Revoked by SI 2003/1236, rr 2, 4.

*Service of orders and notices*

**6.**   (1) Where a magistrates' court makes an attachment of earnings order or an order varying or discharging such an order, the *clerk of* [justices' chief executive for] the court shall cause a copy of the order to be served on the employer and shall send a copy of the order to the debtor.

(2)  Where an attachment of earnings order made by a magistrates' court ceases to have effect as provided in section 8 or 11 of the Act, notice of cessation shall be given to the employer.

(3)  The notice required by the preceding paragraph shall be given by the *clerk of* [justices' chief executive for] the magistrates' court—

(a) which made or confirmed the maintenance order (in a case to which section 11(1)(c) of the Act applies);
(b) in which the maintenance order is registered under any enactment (in a case to which section 11(1)(a), (b) or (d) of the Act applies);
(c) which issued the warrant of commitment or exercised the power conferred by section 65(2) of the Magistrates' Courts Act 1952 (in a case to which section 8 of the Act applies).

**Note.** Words 'clerk of' in both places substituted by words 'justices' chief executive for' in square brackets by SI 2001/615, r 2(iii), Schedule, para 32, as from 1 April 2001.

*Particulars of debtor*

**7.** The particulars of the debtor for the purpose of enabling him to be identified, so far as they are known, are to be included in an attachment of earnings order under section 6(3) of the Act shall be—
(a) full name and address;
(b) place of work;
(c) nature of work and works number, if any.

*Notice of application for appropriate variation order*

**8.** The *clerk of* [justices' chief executive for] a magistrates' court, by which an application under section 10 of the Act for the appropriate variation of an attachment of earnings order is to be heard, shall give notice in writing of the time and place appointed for the hearing of the application to the person entitled to receive payment under the related maintenance order (whether directly or through the officer of any court).

**Note.** Words 'clerk of' substituted by words 'justices' chief executive for' in square brackets by SI 2001/615, r 2(iii), Schedule, para 32, as from 1 April 2001.

*Jurisdiction as respects complaints for the discharge and variation of attachment of earnings orders*

**9.** (1) This Rule shall apply to a complaint for the discharge or variation of an attachment of earnings order except where the related maintenance order—
(a) is an affiliation order to which section 88(2)(a) of the Children and Young Persons Act 1933 applies;
(b) is an order made under section 87 of that Act;
(c) is an order made under section 43 of the National Assistance Act 1948;
(d) is an order made under section 30 of the Children and Young Persons Act 1963.

(2) Where a complaint is made to a justice of the peace acting for the same petty sessions area as the court which made the attachment of earnings order and it appears to him that—
(a) the person in whose favour the attachment of earnings order was made, or
(b) the debtor,
is for the time being in some petty sessions area other than that for which the justice is acting, or that the complainant is the *clerk of* [justices' chief executive for] a magistrates' court acting for such other area, then, if it appears to the justice that the complaint may be more conveniently dealt with by a magistrates' court acting for that other area, he may cause the *clerk of* [justices' chief executive for] the court to send the complaint by post to the *clerk of* [justices' chief executive for] the other court and for that purpose shall write down the complaint, if this has not already been done.

(3) On receipt by the *clerk of* [justices' chief executive for] a magistrates' court of a complaint under the preceding paragraph, he shall bring the complaint before the court and the court shall issue a summons requiring the person appropriate under section 19(4) of the Act to appear before it, and shall hear and determine the complaint.

**Note.** Words 'clerk of' in each place substituted by words 'justices' chief executive for' in square brackets by SI 2001/615, r 2(iii), Schedule, para 32, as from 1 April 2001.

*Complaints for variation or discharge of attachment of earnings orders against persons outside
United Kingdom*

**10.**  (1) Where a complaint for the variation or discharge of an attachment of
earnings order is made against a person who resides outside the United Kingdom
and that person does not appear at the time and place appointed for the hearing of
the complaint, then, subject to paragraph (2) of this Rule, the court may, if it thinks it
reasonable in all the circumstances to do so, proceed to hear and determine the
complaint in accordance with section 20(3) of the Act if it is proved to the satisfaction
of the court that the complainant has taken any of the following steps to give the
person against whom the complaint is made notice of the complaint and of the time
and place appointed for the hearing thereof, that is to say—

   (a)  has caused written notice of the matters aforesaid to be delivered to the said
        person;
   (b)  has caused written notice of the matters aforesaid to be sent by post
        addressed to the said person at his last known or usual place of abode or at
        his place of business or at some other address at which there is ground for
        believing that it will reach him; or
   (c)  has caused notice of the matters aforesaid to be inserted in one or more
        newspapers on one or more occasions.

   (2)  Where it is proposed to take any such steps as are mentioned in sub-paragraph
(b) or (c) of the preceding paragraph, the complainant shall apply for directions to a
justice of the peace acting for the same petty sessions area as the court by which the
complaint is to be heard, and the taking of such steps shall be effective for the
purposes of this Rule only if they were taken in accordance with the directions given
by the said justice.

   (3)  Paragraph (1) of Rule 55 of the Magistrates' Courts Rules 1968 shall apply for
the purpose of proving the delivery of a written notice in pursuance of sub-paragraph
(a) of paragraph (1) of this Rule as it applies for the purpose of proving the service of
a summons.

   In relation to a solemn declaration made outside the United Kingdom, paragraph
(1) of the said Rule 55, as applied by this paragraph, shall have effect as if for the
reference to the authorities mentioned in the said paragraph (1) there were
substituted a reference to a consular officer of Her Majesty's Government in the
United Kingdom or any person for the time being authorised by law, in the place
where the declarant is, to administer an oath for any judicial or other legal purpose.

   (4)  Paragraph (2) of the said Rule 55 shall apply for the purpose of proving the
sending of a written notice in pursuance of sub-paragraph (b) of paragraph (1) of
this Rule, or the insertion of a notice in a newspaper in pursuance of sub-
paragraph (c) thereof, as it applies for the purpose of proving the service of any
process, provided, as respects the insertion of a notice in a newspaper, that a copy
of the newspaper containing the notice is annexed to the certificate.

*Complaints by debtors for variation or discharge of attachment of earnings orders against persons
who cannot be found*

**11.**  (1) Where a complaint by the debtor for the variation or discharge of an
attachment of earnings order is made against a person and that person does not
appear at the time and place appointed for the hearing of the complaint, then, subject
to paragraph (2) of this Rule, the court may, if it thinks it reasonable in all the circumstances to do so, proceed to hear and determine the complaint, notwithstanding
the absence of proof that that person had knowledge of the summons as required by
Rule 82(2) of the Magistrates' Courts Rules 1968, if it is proved to the satisfaction of
the court that the summons in respect of the complaint was served in accordance with
the provisions of Rule 82(1)(b) or (c) of those Rules and the complainant has caused
notice of the complaint and of the time and place appointed for the hearing thereof
to be inserted in one or more newspapers on one or more occasions.

(2)  Where it is proposed to rely upon the provisions of the preceding paragraph of this Rule, the complainant shall apply for directions to a justice of the peace acting for the same petty sessions area as the court by which the complaint is to be heard, and the giving of notice in a newspaper shall be effective for the purposes of this Rule only if the notice was given in accordance with the directions given by the said justice.

(3)  Paragraph (2) of Rule 55 of the Magistrates' Courts Rules 1968 shall apply for the purpose of proving the insertion of a notice in a newspaper in pursuance of paragraph (1) of this Rule as it applies for the purpose of proving the service of any process, providing that a copy of the newspaper containing the notice is annexed to the certificate.

*Variation of attachment of earnings order on change of employment*

**12.**    Where an attachment of earnings order has lapsed under section 9(4) of the Act on the debtor's ceasing to be in the employment of the person to whom the order was directed and it appears to a magistrates' court, acting for the same petty sessions area as the court which made the order, that the debtor has subsequently entered the employment of a person (whether the same as before or another), the court may, of its own motion, vary the order by directing it to that person and may make any consequential amendment to the order made necessary by this variation.

*Discharge of attachment of earnings order by court of its own motion*

**13.**    (1)  Where it appears to a magistrates' court acting for the same petty sessions area as the magistrates' court which made the attachment of earnings order that the debtor is not in the employment of the person to whom the order is directed and that the likelihood of the debtor's entering the employment of any person is not such as to justify preserving the order, the court may, of its own motion, discharge the order.

(2)  Where a magistrates' court has made an attachment of earnings order and, by virtue of section 7, 21 or 30 of the Matrimonial Proceedings and Property Act 1970, the related maintenance order ceases to have effect because of the remarriage of the person entitled to receive payments under it, a magistrates' court acting for the same petty sessions area as that court may, of its own motion, discharge the attachment of earnings order, if there are no arrears to be recovered.

*Temporary variation of protected earnings rate*

**14.**    (1)  A justice of the peace acting for the same petty sessions area as the magistrates' court which made the attachment of earnings order may, on a written application made by the debtor on the ground of a material change in the debtor's resources and needs since the order was made or last varied, by order (hereinafter referred to as a temporary variation order) vary the attachment of earnings order for a period of not more than four weeks by an increase of the protected earnings rate.

(2)  *A temporary variation order shall be in the form numbered 3 in the Schedule to these Rules.*

(3)  The *clerk of* [justices' chief executive for] the magistrates' court which made the attachment of earnings order shall cause a copy of any temporary variation order to be served on the employer and shall give him notice if the temporary variation order is discharged and *the clerk* [the justices' chief executive] shall also send a copy to the person entitled to receive payments under the related maintenance order (whether directly or through an officer of any court).

(4)  Where an application for the variation or discharge of an attachment of earnings order is made to a magistrates' court and there is in existence a temporary variation order in respect of the attachment of earnings order, the court may, of its own motion, discharge the temporary variation order.

**Note.**  Para (2) revoked by SI 2003/1236, rr 2, 5, with effect from 20 June 2003. Words 'clerk of' and 'the clerk' substituted by words 'justices' chief executive for' and 'the justices' chief executive' in square brackets by SI 2001/615, r 2(v), Schedule, paras 32, 33, as from 1 April 2001.

*Consolidated attachment orders*

**15.**   (1)  In this Rule references to an attachment of earnings order are references to such an order made by a magistrates' court and do not include such an order made to secure payments under a magistrates' court maintenance order.

(2)  Where a magistrates' court has power to make more than one attachment of earnings order in respect of the liabilities of a debtor, it may make a consolidated attachment order to discharge those liabilities.

(3)  Where a magistrates' court has power to make an attachment of earnings order in respect of a debtor who is already subject to such an order (whether or not it is itself a consolidated attachment order) made by any magistrates' court, the court may, subject to the provisions of this Rule, discharge the existing order and make a consolidated attachment order in respect of that debtor.

(4)  Where two or more attachment of earnings orders (whether or not they are themselves consolidated attachment orders) made by magistrates' courts are in existence in respect of one debtor, a magistrates' court acting for the same petty sessions areas as one of those courts may, subject to the provisions of this Rule, discharge the existing orders and make a consolidated attachment order in respect of that debtor.

(5)  A magistrates' court may exercise the power conferred under paragraphs (2) to (4) of this Rule either of its own motion or on the application of the debtor.

(6)  A debtor may apply to a magistrates' court for a consolidated attachment order—

(i)   in a case to which paragraph (2) or (3) of this Rule applies, during the hearing of the proceedings for the enforcement of the fine or other liability;

(ii)  in a case to which paragraph (4) of this Rule applies, by complaint.

(7)  Where an employer applies in writing to the *clerk of* [justices' chief executive for] a magistrates' court which has power to make a consolidated attachment order requesting the court to make such an order, *the clerk* [the justices' chief executive] shall bring the application before the court, and, if it appears to the court that the application is justified, the court shall proceed as if it had determined of its own motion to make such an order.

(8)  Before a magistrates' court exercises of its own motion the powers conferred under paragraph (4) of this Rule, it shall cause written notice to be given to the debtor of his right to make representations to the court.

(9)  Where a magistrates' court has power to make a consolidated attachment order under paragraph (3) or (4) of this Rule and a relevant attachment of earnings order has been made by a magistrates' court acting for another petty sessions area, the first mentioned court shall cause notice to be given to the *clerk of* [justices' chief executive for] the second mentioned court and shall not discharge that attachment of earnings order unless the enforcement of the sum to which the order relates is transferred to the first mentioned court under section 72 of the Magistrates' Courts Act 1952 (transfer of fines), paragraph 7 of Schedule 10 to the Administration of Justice Act 1970 (transfer of enforcement of legal aid contribution orders) or Rule 16 of these Rules as the case may be.

(10)  Where a magistrates' court makes a consolidated attachment order, it shall specify in the order such normal deduction rate as the court thinks reasonable and this rate may be less than the sum of the normal deduction rates specified in any attachment of earnings orders discharged by the court.

**Note.** Words 'clerk of' in both places and words 'the clerk' substituted by words 'justices' chief executive for' and 'the justices' chief executive' in square brackets by SI 2001/615, r 2(v), Schedule, paras 32, 33,as from 1 April 2001. See also SI 2004/176, reg 4A (inserted by SI 2004/107, reg 2).

*Transfer of fines etc with a view to making consolidated attachment order*

**16.**   (1)  Where a magistrates' court has made or has power to make an attachment of earnings order to secure—

(a) the payment of any sum adjudged to be paid by a conviction or treated (by any enactment relating to the collection and enforcement of fines, costs, compensation or forfeited recognisances) as so adjudged to be paid, or

(b) the payment of any sum required to be paid by a legal aid contribution order,

and a magistrates' court acting for some other petty sessions area has made an attachment of earnings order in respect of the debtor, then, if the debtor does not reside in either petty sessions area, the first mentioned court may make an order making payment of that sum enforceable in the petty sessions area for which the second mentioned court acted.

(2) As from the date on which an order is made under paragraph (1) of this Rule with respect to any sum, all functions under any enactment relating to that sum which, if no such order had been made, would have been exercisable by the court which made the order, shall be exercisable by a court acting for the petty sessions area specified in the order, or the *clerk of* [justices' chief executive for] that court, as the case may be, and not otherwise.

(3) The making of an order under paragraph (1) of this Rule with respect to any sum shall not prejudice the power to make a subsequent order with respect to that sum under that paragraph or under section 72 or 72A of the Magistrates' Courts Act 1952 or paragraph 7 of Schedule 10 to the Administration of Justice Act 1970.

**Note.** Words 'clerk of' substituted by words 'justices' chief executive for' in square brackets by SI 2001/615, r 2(v), Schedule, para 32, as from 1 April 2001.

*Disposal of sums paid under consolidated attachment orders*

**17.** (1) A *clerk of* [justices' chief executive for]a magistrates' court receiving a payment under a consolidated attachment order shall, subject to paragraph (2) below, apply the money in payment of the sums secured by the order, paying first any sums previously secured by an attachment of earnings order which was discharged in consequence of the making of the consolidated attachment order.

(2) Where two or more attachment of earnings orders were discharged in consequence of the making of the consolidated attachment order the sums due under the orders shall be paid in the chronological order of the orders.

**Note.** Words 'clerk of' substituted by words 'justices' chief executive for' in square brackets by SI 2001/615, r 2(v), Schedule, para 32, as from 1 April 2001.

*Method of making payment under attachment of earnings order*

**18.** (1) A *clerk of* [justices' chief executive for] a magistrates' court to whom any payment under an attachment of earnings order is to be made shall notify the employer and the person entitled to receive payments under the related maintenance order of the hours during which, and the place at which, payments are, subject to the provisions of this Rule, to be made and received.

(2) If an employer sends by post any payments under an attachment of earnings order to a *clerk of* [justices' chief executive for] a magistrates' court, he shall do so at his own risk and expense.

(3) A *clerk of* [justices' chief executive for] a magistrates' court may send by post any payment under an attachment of earnings order to the person entitled to receive payments under the related maintenance order at the request and at the risk of that person.

**Note.** Words 'clerk of' in each place substituted by words 'justices' chief executive for' in square brackets by SI 2001/615, r 2(v), Schedule, para 32, as from 1 April 2001.

*Payments under attachment of earnings order after imprisonment imposed*

**19.** (1) Where imprisonment or other detention has been imposed for the purpose of enforcing a maintenance order, the *clerk of* [justices' chief executive for] a magistrates' court to whom any payment under a related attachment of earnings order is to be made—

    (a)   in relation to such a payment shall be a person authorised to receive the said payment for the purposes of section 67(2) of the Magistrates' Courts Act 1952 (which relates to release from custody and reduction of detention on payment);

    (b)   on receiving such a payment shall notify the person authorised for the said purposes by Rule 45(1) of the Magistrates' Courts Rules [1981] of the sum received.

    (2)  Where a person receives notice of the receipt of a sum under the preceding paragraph of this Rule, he shall note the receipt of that sum on the warrant of commitment, if any, held by him.

**Note.** Words 'clerk of' substituted by words 'justices' chief executive for' in square brackets by SI 2001/615, r 2(v), Schedule, para 32, as from 1 April 2001.

### *Service of orders and notices*

**20.**   Where under section 14 of the Act (which relates to statements of earnings, etc) an order is directed to the debtor or to a person appearing to be an employer of the debtor or where under these Rules a copy of an order is to be served or a notice is to be given to any person—

    (a)   service may be effected on, or notice may be given to a person, other than a corporation, by delivering it to the person to whom it is directed or by sending it by post in a letter addressed to him at his last known or usual place of abode or, in the case of an employer or a person appearing to be an employer of the debtor, at his place of business;

    (b)   service may be effected on, or notice given to, a corporation by delivering the document at, or sending it to—

        (i)   such office or place as the corporation may, for the purpose of this Rule, have specified in writing to the court in relation to the debtor or to a class or description of person to which he belongs, or

        (ii)   the registered office of the corporation if that office is in England and Wales or, if there is no registered office in England and Wales, any place therein where the corporation trades or conducts its business.

### *County court records*

**21.**   (1)  Where a *clerk of* [justices' chief executive for] a magistrates' court causes a copy of an order or notice to be given to any person under Rule 6 of these Rules, he shall cause a copy of the order or notice to be given also to the *County Court Registrar* [District Judge] for the district in which the debtor resides.

    (2)  Where the *clerk of* [justices' chief executive for] a magistrates' court which has made an attachment of earnings order is informed of a debtor's change of address, he shall notify the new address to the *County Court Registrar* [District Judge] for the district in which the debtor resided before the change of address.

**Note.** Words 'clerk of' in both places substituted by words 'justices' chief executive for' in square brackets by SI 2001/615, r 2(v), Schedule, para 32, as from 1 April 2001. Words 'County Court Registrar' in both places substituted by words 'District Judge' in square brackets by the Courts and Legal Services Act 1990, s 74, as from 1 January 1991.

### *Justices' clerks*

**22.**   (1)  The things specified in paragraph (2) of this Rule, being things authorised to be done by, to or before a single justice of the peace for a petty sessions area, may be done by, to or before the justices' clerk for that area.

    (2)  The things referred to in paragraph (1) above are—

    (a)   the power to make an order under section 14(1) or (2) of the Act (power of court to obtain statements of earnings, etc) before the hearing of an application to a magistrates' court for an attachment of earnings order, or for the variation or discharge of such an order;

(b) the determination that a complaint for the discharge or variation of an attachment of earnings order be dealt with by a magistrates' court acting for another petty sessions area in accordance with Rule 9 of these Rules;

(c) the giving of directions under Rule 10 or 11 of these Rules;

(d) the discharge or variation by the court of its own motion of an attachment of earnings order in accordance with Rule 12 or 13 or these Rules;

(e) the temporary variation of an attachment of earnings order by an increase of the protected earnings rate in accordance with Rule 14 of these Rules;

(f) the making of an order under Rule 16 of these Rules (transfer of fines, etc with view to making consolidated attachment order).

*Application of these Rules to attachment of earnings orders in respect of fines etc*

**23.** (1) In the application of these Rules to attachment of earnings orders to secure—

(a) the payment of any sum adjudged to be paid by a conviction or treated (by any enactment relating to the collection of fines, costs, compensation or forfeited recognisances) as so adjudged to be paid, or

(b) the payment of any sum required to be paid by a legal aid contribution order, the exceptions and modifications specified in the following provisions of this Rule shall apply.

(2) Rules 4, 5, 8, 9, 10, 11 and 19 shall not apply.

(3) *An attachment of earnings order shall be in the form numbered 2 in the Schedule to these Rules.*

(4) Rule 14 (temporary variation of protected earnings rate) shall have effect as if in paragraph (3) the words 'and *the clerk* [justices' chief executive] shall also send a copy to the person entitled to receive payments under the related maintenance order (whether directly or through an officer of any court)' were omitted.

(5) Rule 18 (method of making payment under attachment of earnings order) shall have effect as if in paragraph (1) the words 'and the person entitled to receive payments under the related maintenance order' and paragraph (3) were omitted.

**Note.** In para (2) reference to '5' and para (3) revoked by SI 2003/1236, rr 2, 6, as from 20 June 2003. In para (4) words 'the clerk' substituted by words 'justices' chief executive' in square brackets by SI 2001/615, r 2(v), Schedule, para 33, as from 1 April 2001.

*Transitional provisions*

**24.** *The clerk of a magistrates' court which before the coming into force of these Rules made an attachment of earnings order, which has not ceased to have effect or been discharged, shall send to the employer and to the County Court Registrar for the district in which the debtor resides a copy of the order in the form numbered 4 in the Schedule.*

**Note.** Revoked by SI 2003/1236, rr 2, 7, as from 20 June 2003.

## BLOOD TESTS (EVIDENCE OF PATERNITY) REGULATIONS 1971

**Dated** 12 November 1971

**SI 1971 No 1861**

*Citation and commencement*

**1.** These Regulations may be cited as the Blood Tests (Evidence of Paternity) Regulations 1971 and shall come into operation on 1 March 1972.

*Interpretation*

**2.** (1) In these Regulations, unless the context otherwise requires—
'the Act' means the Family Law Reform Act 1969;
'court' means a court which gives a direction for the use of *blood tests* [scientific tests] in pursuance of section 20(1) of the Act;
'direction' means a direction given as aforesaid;
'direction form' means Form 1 in Schedule 1 to these Regulations;
'photograph' means a recent photograph, taken full face without a hat, of the size required for insertion in a passport;
*'sample' means blood taken for the purpose of tests;* ['sample' means bodily fluid or bodily tissue taken for the purpose of scientific tests;]
*'sampler' means a registered medical practitioner or tester nominated in a direction form to take blood samples for the purposes of the direction;* ['sampler' means a registered medical practitioner, or a person who is under the supervision of such a practitioner and is either a registered nurse or registered [biomedical scientist], or a tester;]
'subject' means a person from whom a court directs that *blood samples* [bodily samples] shall be taken;
*'tester' means a person appointed by the Lord Chancellor to carry out blood tests;* ['tester' means an individual employed to carry out tests by a body which has been accredited for the purposes of section 20 of the Act either by the Lord Chancellor or by a body appointed by him for those purposes and which has been nominated in a direction to carry out tests;]
'tests' mean *blood tests* [scientific tests] carried out under Part III of the Act and includes any test made with the object of ascertaining the inheritable *characteristics of blood* [characteristics of bodily fluids or bodily tissue].
(2) A reference in these Regulations to a person who is under a disability is a reference to a person who has not attained the age of 16 years or who is suffering from a mental disorder within the meaning of the Mental Health Act 1959 and is incapable of understanding the nature and purpose of *blood tests* [scientific tests].
(3) The Interpretation Act 1889 shall apply to the interpretation of these Regulations as it applies to the interpretation of an Act of Parliament.

**Note.** The Interpretation Act 1889 is replaced by Interpretation Act 1978. In para (1) words 'blood tests' in both places they occur substituted by words 'scientific tests' in square brackets, definitions 'sample' and 'sampler' substituted by subsequent definitions 'sample' and 'sampler' respectively, in definition 'subject' words 'blood samples' substituted by words 'bodily samples' in square brackets, definition 'tester' substituted by subsequent definition 'tester', in definition 'tests' words 'characteristics of blood' substituted by words 'characteristics of bodily fluids or bodily tissue' in square brackets, all by SI 2001/773, regs 2, 4, 5, as from 1 April 2001. In definition 'sampler' words 'biomedical scientist' in square brackets substituted by SI 2004/2033, regs 1, 3, as from 27 July 2004.

In para (2) words 'blood tests' substituted by words 'scientific tests' in square brackets by SI 2001/773, regs 2, 5, as from 1 April 2001.

*Direction form*

**3.** A sampler shall not take a sample from a subject unless Parts I and II of the direction form have been completed and the direction form purports to be signed by the proper officer of the court or some person on his behalf.

*Subjects under disability to be accompanied to sampler*

**4.** A subject who is under a disability who attends a sampler for the taking of a sample shall be accompanied by a person of full age who shall identify him to the sampler.

*Taking of samples*

**5.** (1) Without prejudice to the provisions of rules of court, a sampler may make arrangements for the taking of samples from the subjects or may change any arrangements already made and make other arrangements.

(2) Subject to the provisions of these Regulations, where a subject attends a sampler in accordance with arrangements made under a direction, the sampler shall take a sample from him on that occasion.

(3) A sampler shall not take a sample from a subject if—

    (i) [in the case of a blood sample] he has reason to believe that the subject has been transfused with blood within the three months immediately preceding the day on which the sample is to be taken; or

    (ii) in his opinion, tests on a sample taken at that time from that subject could not effectively be carried out for the purposes of and in accordance with the direction; and

    (iii) in his opinion, the taking of a sample might have an adverse effect on the health of the subject.

(4) A sampler may take a sample from a subject who has been injected with a blood product or blood plasma, if, in his opinion, the value of any tests done on that sample would not be thereby affected, but shall inform the tester that the subject was so injected.

(5) Where a sampler does not take a sample from a subject in accordance with arrangements made for the taking of that sample and no other arrangements are made, he shall return the direction form relating to that subject to the court, having stated on the form his reason for not taking the sample and any reason given by the subject (or the person having the care and control of the subject) for any failure to attend in accordance with those arrangements.

(6) A subject who attends a sampler for the taking of a sample may be accompanied by his legal representative.

**Note.** In para (3)(i) words 'in the case of a blood sample' in square brackets inserted by SI 2001/773, regs 2, 6, as from 1 April 2001.

*Sampling procedure*

**6.** (1) A sampler shall comply with the provisions of this Regulation, all of which shall be complied with in respect of one subject before any are complied with in respect of any other subject; so however that a report made in accordance with the provisions of section 20(2) of the Act or any other evidence relating to the samples or the tests made on the samples shall not be challenged solely on the grounds that a sampler has not acted in accordance with the provisions of this Regulation.

(2) Before a sample is taken from any subject who has attained the age of 12 months by the date of the direction, the sampler shall ensure that a photograph of that subject is affixed to the direction form relating to that subject *unless the direction form is accompanied by a certificate from a medical practitioner that the subject is suffering from a mental disorder and that a photograph of him cannot or should not be taken.*

(3) Before a sample is taken from a subject, he, or where he is under a disability the person of full age accompanying him, shall complete the declaration in Part V of the direction form (that that subject is the subject to whom the direction form relates and, where a photograph is affixed to the direction form, that the photograph is a photograph of that subject) which shall be signed in the presence of and witnessed by the sampler.

(4) *Where a subject is suffering from a mental disorder, the sampler shall not take a sample from him unless the sampler is in possession of a certificate from a medical practitioner that the taking of a blood sample from the subject will not be prejudicial to his proper care and treatment.*

(5) A sample shall not be taken from any subject unless—

(a) he or, where he is under a disability, the person having the care and control of him, has signed a statement on the direction form that he consents to the sample being taken; or

(b) where he is under a disability and is not accompanied by the person having the care and control of him, the sampler is in possession of a statement in writing, purporting to be signed by that person that he consents to the sample being taken[; or

(c) where he is under the age of sixteen years, and the person with care and control of him does not consent, the court has nevertheless ordered that sample be taken].

(6) The sampler shall affix to the direction form any statement referred to in sub-paragraph (b) of the preceding paragraph.

(7) If a subject or, where he is under a disability, the person having the care and control of him, does not consent to the taking of a sample, he may record on the direction form his reasons for withholding his consent.

(8) When the sampler has taken a sample he shall place it in a suitable container and shall affix to the container a label giving the full name, age and sex of the subject from whom it was taken and the label shall be signed by the sampler *and by that subject, or, if he is under a disability, the person accompanying him.*

(9) The sampler shall state in Part VII of the direction form that he has taken the sample and the date on which he did so.

**Note.** In para (2) words 'unless the direction' to the end revoked, para (4) revoked, in para (5) sub-para (c) and word 'or' immediately preceding it inserted and in para (8) words from 'and by that subject' to the end revoked by SI 2001/733, regs 2, 7, as from 1 April 2001.

*Despatch of samples to tester*

**7.** (1) When a sampler has taken samples, he shall, where he is not himself the tester, pack the containers together with the relevant direction forms and shall despatch them forthwith to the tester by post by *special delivery service* [recorded delivery] or shall deliver them or cause them to be delivered to the tester by some person other than a subject or a person who has accompanied a subject to the sampler.

(2) If at any time a sampler despatches to a tester samples from some only of the subjects and has not previously despatched samples taken from the other subjects, he shall inform the tester whether he is expecting to take any samples from those other subjects and, if so, from whom and on what date.

**Note.** In para (1) words 'special delivery service' substituted by words 'recorded delivery' in square brackets by SI 2001/773, regs 2, 8, as from 1 April 2001.

*Procedure where sampler nominated is unable to take the samples*

**8.** (1) Where a sampler is unable himself to take samples from all or any of the subjects, he may nominate another *medical practitioner or tester* [sampler] to take the samples which he is unable to take.

(2) The sampler shall record the nomination of the other sampler on the relevant direction forms and shall forward them to the sampler nominated by him.

**Note.** In para (1) words 'medical practitioner or tester' substituted by words 'sampler' in square brackets by SI 2001/773, regs 2, 9, as from 1 April 2001.

*[Accredication*

**8A.**   (1) Subject to paragraph (2), a body shall not be eligible for accreditation for the purposes of section 20 of the Act unless it is accredited to ISO/IEC/17025 by an accreditation body which complies with the requirements of ISO Guide 58.

(2) A body which employs a person who at the date of the coming into force of the Blood Tests (Evidence of Paternity) (Amendment) Regulations 2001 was a tester appointed by the Lord Chancellor shall, until three years after that date, be eligible for accreditation for the purposes of section 20 of the Act notwithstanding that it does not comply with paragraph (1).]

**Note.** Inserted by SI 2001/773, regs 2, 10, as from 1 April 2001.

*Testing of samples*

**9.**   (1) Samples taken for the purpose of giving effect to a direction shall (so far as practicable) all be tested by the same tester.

(2) A tester shall not make tests on any samples for the purpose of a direction unless he will, in his opinion, be able to show from the results of those tests (whether alone or together with the results of tests on any samples which he has received and tested or expects to receive subsequently) that a subject is or is not excluded from being *the father of a subject whose paternity is in dispute* [the father or mother of the person whose parentage falls to be determined].

**Note.** In para (2) words 'the father of a subject whose paternity is in dispute' substituted by words 'the father or mother of the person whose parentage falls to be determined' in square brackets by SI 2001/773, regs 2, 11, as from 1 April 2001.

*Report by tester*

**10.**   On completion of the tests in compliance with the direction, the tester shall forward to the court a report in Form 2 in Schedule 1 to these Regulations, together with the appropriate direction forms.

*Procedure where tests not made*

**11.**   If at any time it appears to a tester that he will be unable to make tests in accordance with the direction, he shall inform the court, giving his reasons, and shall return the direction forms in his possession to the court.

*Fees*

**12.**   *(1) The charges that may be made by samplers shall be those specified in the first two columns of Part I of Schedule 2 to these Regulations.*

*[Fees*

**12.**   (1) A sampler may charge £27.50 for making the arrangements to take a sample.

(2) The charge in paragraph (1) is payable whether or not a sample is taken.]

**Note.** Substituted by SI 2004/596, regs 3, 4, as from 1 April 2004 (in relation to samples taken on or after that date).

SCHEDULE 1                                                    Regulations 2(1) and 10

FORM 1

*Direction Form*

*Family Law Reform Act 1969*

[*Insert title of proceedings*]

..........................................

v

..........................................

Reference No of direction .......................................

Full name and date of birth of person ...................................................................
to be tested to whom this form relates.

PART I

*Notification of Direction*

The ........................................................................... [*name and address of court*]
on ............................ day of .................................................... 19 ........ directed that
*blood tests* [scientific tests] be carried out in respect of the persons whose names are
set out below for the purpose of ascertaining the *paternity* [parentage] of ..............
............................................. [*name of person whose paternity* [parentage] *is in dispute*]
and that *blood samples* [bodily samples] be taken from the person named below on
or before the ...................................... day of .................................... 19 ........
The name of the person appearing to the court to have the care and control of
the person to whom this form relates who is under 16/suffering from a mental
disorder within the meaning of the Mental Health Act 1959 [*Delete as appropriate*]
and is incapable of understanding the nature and purpose of *blood tests* [scientific
tests], is ..........................................

.................................... (Signed)
Proper Officer of the Court

| Name | Address | Age |
|------|---------|-----|
| ..................... | ........................................................... | ................... |
| ..................... | ........................................................... | ................... |
| ..................... | ........................................................... | ................... |
| ..................... | ........................................................... | ................... |
| ..................... | ........................................................... | ................... |

PART II

*Request to sampler to take sample*

To ............................................................... [*name and address of sampler*].
[*Delete if sampler is also tester*] You are hereby requested to take a *blood sample*
[bodily sample] from .......................................................................... [*name of person
to whom form relates*].
[[*The sample is to be taken notwithstanding the refusal to consent of the
person with care and control of ......................................................................... (*name
of person to whom form relates*).] Delete if not applicable.]

You are further requested to send the sample taken to ........................................
........................................ [*name and address of tester* [name and address of accredited body]] [*or the tester by whom you have arranged for tests to be made*].

[Other samples will be taken as follows: [*To be completed where all the samples from the parties named in Part I are not to be taken by the same sampler*]

*Name of person from whom sample will be taken*          *Name, address and telephone number*
                                                                                                                  *of sampler*

................................................................          ................................................................
................................................................          ................................................................
................................................................          ................................................................
                                                                                                  ....................................(Signed)

[Being unable to comply with the request set out below, I have nominated ................................ [*name and address of nominee*] to take the sample.
                                                                                                  ....................................(Signed)

PART III

*Photograph*

[*For use where sampler named above nominates another sampler*]
   Below is a photograph of the person to whom this form relates, being a person who has attained the age of twelve months.

PART IV

[*To be completed by the sampler* [where sample is of blood]]
   I have questioned ................................ [*Insert name of person to whom form relates or, in the case of person under 16 or suffering from mental disability, person accompanying that person*] and it appears that he/she/the party to whom this form relates—
   has/has not [*Delete as appropriate*] been transferred with blood in the last three months [*Delete as appropriate*];
   has not been injected with a blood product or plasma substitute [*Delete as appropriate*];
   has been injected with a blood product/blood plasma [*Delete as appropriate*] on or about ................................
and that the value of any tests will thereby be/not be affected [*Delete as appropriate*].
                                                                                                  ....................................(Signed)
                                                                                                                  (Sampler)

PART V

*Declaration*

[*To be completed where the person to whom the form relates has attained the age of sixteen and is not suffering from a mental disability.*]
   I ................................ [*insert full name and address of person to whom the form relates*] declare that the photograph affixed to Part III of this form is a photograph of me and that I am a person in respect of whom the above-named court gave a direction that *blood tests* [scientific tests] be made. I hereby consent/do not consent [*Delete as appropriate*] to the taking of a *blood sample* [bodily sample] from me for the purpose of such tests.

[I do not consent because ....................................................................................................]
[*To be deleted unless the person making the declaration withholds consent and wishes to record the reason for so doing*]

I understand that it is a serious offence punishable by imprisonment to personate another person for the purpose of providing a *blood sample* [bodily sample].

Date ..................................... .............................................. (Signed)

The above was explained to the declarant who stated that he/she understood it and signed it in my presence.

Date ..................................... .............................................. (Signed)
(Sampler)

PART VI

*Declaration*

[*To be completed where the person to whom the form relates has not attained the age of sixteen or is suffering from a mental disability.*]

I ..................................... [*full name and address of person accompanying the subject*] [being the person having the care and control of ...........................................
[*name of person to whom form relates*] [*Delete if not applicable*]] declare that the person whom I identify to .................................................................. [*insert name of sampler*] [and whose photograph is affixed to Part III of this form [*Delete as appropriate*]] is, to the best of my knowledge and belief .............................................. [who is the son/daughter of ................................... [*insert the name of mother of person identified*]].

I, being the person having the care and control of the person to whom this form relates, consent/do not consent to the taking of a sample. [I do not consent because:—]
[*To be completed if the person making the declaration withholds consent and wishes to record the reason for so doing*].

I understand that it is a serious offence punishable by imprisonment to personate another person for the purpose of providing a *blood sample* [bodily sample] or to proffer the wrong child for that purpose.

Date ..................................... .............................................. (Signed)

The above was explained to the declarant who stated that he/she understood it and signed it in my presence.

Date ..................................... .............................................. (Signed)
(Sampler)

PART VII

[*To be completed by sampler*]

I have today taken a *blood sample* [bodily sample] from ..................................... to whom this form relates, whose [apparent] age is ..................... years. [I identified him/her from the photograph affixed to this form.] [He/She was [also] identified to me by .............] [*Delete as appropriate*]

Date ..................................... .............................................. (Signed)
(Sampler)

OBSERVATIONS
[*Any observations by the sampler which may assist the tester shall be inserted here.*]

PART VIII

[*To be completed by sampler*]

The person to whom this form relates did not attend on the date originally arranged [or on a new date arranged by me ] [*Delete if inappropriate*].

His/Her reasons given to me for failing to attend were as follows:

Date ....................................... ............................................... (Signed)

(Sampler)

[PART VIIIA

Request to accredited body to carry out tests

To ................................................................. (name and address of accredited body).

You are hereby requested to carry out scientific tests on a bodily sample from ..................................................... (name of person to whom form relates).]

PART IX

[*To be completed by tester*]

I have today received at ......................................................... [*insert place of receipt*] the sample referred to in Part VII of this form.

[It was received by *special delivery service* [recorded delivery]].

[It was handed to me by .....................................] [*Delete as appropriate*].

Date ..................................... ............................................... (Signed)

(Tester)

**Note.** In Parts I, II, words 'blood tests' in both places substituted by words 'scientific tests' in square brackets, word 'paternity' in both places substituted by word 'parentage' in square brackets, words 'blood samples' substituted by words 'bodily samples' in square brackets, words 'blood tests' substituted by words 'scientific tests' in square brackets and words 'blood sample' substituted by words 'bodily sample' in square brackets, by SI 2001/773, regs 2, 12, as from 1 April 2001.

Words from '['The sample' to 'not applicable]' inserted by SI 2001/773, regs 2, 13, as from 1 April 2001. Words 'name and address of tester' substituted by words 'name and address of accredited body' in square brackets and words from 'or the tester' to 'to be made' revoked by SI 2001/773, regs 2, 13, as from 1 April 2003.

In Part IV words 'where sample is of blood' in square brackets inserted by SI 2001/773, regs 2, 14, as from 1 April 2001.

In Part V words 'blood sample' in both places substituted by words 'bodily sample' in square brackets and words 'blood tests' substituted by words 'scientific tests' in square brackets by SI 2001/773, regs 2, 12, as from 1 April 2001.

In Parts VI, VII, words 'blood sample' substituted by words 'bodily sample' in square brackets by SI 2001/773, regs 2, 12, as from 1 April 2001.

Part VIIIA inserted by SI 2001/773, regs 2, 15, as from 1 April 2001.

In Part IX words 'special delivery service' substituted by words 'recorded delivery' in square brackets by SI 2001/773, regs 2, 16, as from 1 April 2001.

FORM 2

*Report by Tester*

Ref No of Proceedings ..................

*Family Law Reform Act 1969*

To:  { *Registrar* [Court Manager], ....................  High Court of Justice, Strand, London, W.C.2.
  { *Justices' Clerk* [Justices' Chief Executive], ........  County Court
                                                            Magistrates' Court.

                          v                                                    1
                                                                               2

_____

PART I

I, ......... , *being a blood tester appointed by the Lord Chancellor for the purpose of Part III* [being employed to carry out scientific tests by a body which has been accredited for the purposes of section 20] of the Family Law Reform Act 1969, certify that I have carried out *blood tests* [scientific tests] (the details of which are given in Part II of this Report) on samples provided by the persons named in this direction, *viz*,

From the results obtained ......... is excluded/is not excluded from possible paternity [parentage] of .........

Reason for conclusion:

Comments on value, if any, of tests in determining whether any person tested is the father [or mother] of the person whose *paternity* [parentage] is in dispute:

                                                            Signed  ...............
                                                            Status  ...............
                                                            Address ...............

PART II

*Test Report* [Report of Scientific Tests]

NOTE
¹ Complete as appropriate.
² Insert title of proceedings.

**Note.** Words 'Registrar' and 'Justices' Clerk' substituted by words 'Court Manager' and 'Justices' Chief Executive' respectively in square brackets by SI 2001/773, regs 2, 17, as from 1 April 2001. Words from 'being a blood tester' to 'Part III' substituted by words from 'being employed' to 'section 20' in square brackets by SI 2001/773, regs 2, 17. Words 'blood tests' substituted by words 'scientific tests' in square brackets and word 'Mr' revoked by SI 2001/773, regs 2, 17, as from 1 April 2001.

Words 'paternity' in both places substituted by word 'parentage' in square brackets, words 'or mother' inserted and words 'Test Report' substituted by words 'Report of Scientific Tests' in square brackets by SI 2001/773, regs 2, 17, as from 1 April 2001.

Regulation 12      SCHEDULE 2

*CHARGES MADE BY SAMPLERS*

*PART I*

*Samplers*

*The charges which may be made by a sampler in respect of one direction requesting him to take samples shall be as follows:*

|  | Charge from 1 July 1992 £ | Charge before 1 July 1992 £ |
|---|---|---|
| For making all necessary arrangements (whether or not samples are taken) | 17.40 | 16.50 |
| For making further arrangements (whether or not samples are taken) to give effect to a variation by the court of a direction | 17.40 | 16.50 |
| For taking sample— | 17.40 | 16.50 |
| from first subject | 8.70 | 8.20 |
| from each subject after first |  |  |
| For taking second or subsequent samples from one or more subjects— |  |  |
| if one such sample | 17.40 | 16.50 |
| if two such samples | 26.10 | 24.70 |
| if three or more such samples | 43.50 | 41.20 |

**Note.** Revoked by SI 2004/596, regs 3, 5, as from 1 April 2004.


## MAGISTRATES' COURTS (BLOOD TESTS) RULES 1971

**Dated** 6 December 1971

**SI 1971 No 1991**

**1.** These Rules may be cited as the Magistrates' Courts (Blood Tests) Rules 1971 and shall come into operation on 1 March 1972.

**2.**    (1)  In these Rules save where the context otherwise requires—
    'the Act' means the Family Law Reform Act 1969;
    'the applicant' means an applicant for a direction;
    *'blood samples' and 'blood tests'* ['bodily samples' and 'scientific tests'] have the same meaning as in Part III of the Act;
    'complaint' means a complaint in the hearing of which the *paternity* [parentage] of any person falls to be determined;
    'court' means a magistrates' court;
    'direction' means a direction given in accordance with the provisions of section 20(1) of the Act;
    'direction form' means Form 1 in Schedule 1 to the Blood Tests (Evidence of Paternity) Regulations 1971;
    'photograph' means a recent photograph, taken full face without a hat, of the size required for insertion in a passport;
    'proceedings' means any proceedings in a magistrates' court for the hearing of a complaint;
    *'sampler' means a registered medical practitioner or tester, nominated in a direction form to take blood samples for the purpose of the direction;* ['sampler' means a registered medical practitioner, or a person who is under the supervision of such a

practitioner and is either a registered nurse or a registered [biomedical scientist], or a tester;]

'subject' means a person from whom a court directs that *blood samples* [bodily samples] shall be taken;

*'tester' means a person appointed by the Secretary of State to carry out blood tests* ['tester' means an individual employed to carry out tests by a body which has been accredited for the purposes of section 20 of the Act either by the Lord Chancellor or by a body appointed by him for those purposes and which has been nominated in a direction to carry out tests].

(2) Any reference in these Rules to a form other than a direction form is a reference to a form contained in the Schedule to these Rules.

(3) Any reference in these Rules to a person who is under a disability is a reference to a person who has not attained the age of 16 years or who is suffering from a mental disorder within the meaning of the Mental Health Act 1959 and is incapable of understanding the nature and purpose of *blood tests* [bodily tests].

(4) The Interpretation Act 1889 shall apply to the interpretation of these Rules as it applies to the interpretation of an Act of Parliament.

**Note.** The Interpretation Act 1889 is replaced by Interpretation Act 1978. In para (1) in definition 'blood samples and blood tests' words 'bodily samples and scientific tests' substituted for words 'blood samples and blood tests', in definition 'complaint' word 'paternity' substituted by word 'parentage' in square brackets, definitions 'sampler' and 'tester' substituted and in definition 'subject' words 'blood samples' substituted by words 'bodily samples' in square brackets by SI 2001/776, rr 3, 4. In definition 'sampler' words 'biomedical scientist' substituted by SI 2004/2033, art 6, as from 27 July 2004. In para (3) words 'blood tests' substituted by words 'bodily tests' in square brackets by SI 2001/776, rr 3, 5, as from 1 April 2001.

**3.** *Form 1 shall be served on any person who makes a complaint in the hearing of which it appears to the justices' clerk that the paternity of any person falls to be determined and on any person who is served with a summons to answer such a complaint.*

**Note.** Revoked by SI 2001/776, rr 3, 6, as from 1 April 2001.

**4.** A party to any proceedings may apply in writing to the court for a direction at any time after the making of the complaint, and, on receipt of the application, the *justices' clerk* [justices' chief executive] shall inform the other party to the proceedings that the application has been made and that he may consent to the court giving a direction before commencement of the hearing of the complaint.

**Note.** Words 'justices' clerk' substituted by words 'justices' chief executive' in square brackets by SI 2001/776, rr 3, 7, as from 1 April 2001.

**5.** A court may give a direction in the absence of the applicant and the other party to the proceedings if it appears to the court that that other party, or, where he is under a disability, the person having the care and control of him has consented to the giving of the direction.

**6.** The court, when giving a direction shall name the person appearing to the court to have the care and control of any subject who is under a disability.

**7.** A direction shall be in Form 2 and a copy of it shall be served on every subject or, where the subject is under a disability, on the person named in the direction as having the care and control of him.

**8.** Within 14 days, or such longer period as the court may order, of the giving of the direction, the applicant, unless he has been granted legal aid under the Legal Aid and Advice Act 1949 [now Legal Aid Act 1988] shall pay to the *justices' clerk* [justices' chief executive] such sum as appears to the *justices' clerk* [justices' chief executive] to be sufficient to pay the fees of the sampler and tester in respect of taking and testing samples for the purpose of giving effect to the direction.

**Note.** Words 'justices' clerk' in both places substituted by words 'justices' chief executive' in square brackets by SI 2001/776, rr 3, 7, as from 1 April 2001.

**9.**   Within 14 days, or such longer period as the court may order, of service of a copy of the direction, each subject who is not under a disability and the person having the care and control of a subject who is under a disability but has attained the age of 12 months by the date of the direction shall furnish to the *justices' clerk* [justices' chief executive] a photograph of the subject:

*Provided that this requirement shall not apply in the case of a subject who is suffering from a mental disorder if the medical practitioner in whose care he is certifies that a photograph cannot or should not be taken of the subject.*

**Note.** Words 'justices' clerk' substituted by words 'justices' chief executive' in square brackets, and proviso revoked by SI 2001/776, rr 3, 7, 8, as from 1 April 2001.

**10.**   (1) If any person fails to comply with the provisions of Rule 8 or 9 of these Rules, the *justices' clerk* [justices' chief executive] shall not take any further steps required of him by these Rules without first informing the court and receiving its instructions to do so.

(2) If the court is informed by the *justices' clerk* [justices' chief executive] in accordance with paragraph (1) of this Rule, it may vary or revoke the direction or may make such order as to the hearing or the continuation of the hearing of the complaint as appears to the court to be appropriate in all the circumstances and shall cause the parties to be notified.

**Note.** Words 'justices' clerk' in both places substituted by words 'justices' chief executive' in square brackets by SI 2001/776, rr 3, 7, as from 1 April 2001.

**11.**   Where a court has given a direction and the justices' clerk is satisfied that the requirements of Rule 8 of these Rules (where applicable) have been met and he is in possession of a photograph (or a certificate under the proviso to Rule 9 of these Rules) in respect of each subject who has attained the age of 12 months by the date of the direction, the *justices' clerk* [justices' chief executive] shall arrange for *blood samples to be taken and for blood tests to be made* [bodily samples to be taken and for scientific tests to be made] on those samples, or shall arrange for the parties' solicitors to make the arrangements on his behalf.

**Note.** Words 'justices' clerk' and 'blood samples to be taken and for blood tests to be made' substituted by words 'justices' chief executive' and words 'bodily samples to be taken and for scientific tests to be made' respectively by SI 2001/776, rr 3, 7, 9, as from 1 April 2001.

**12.**   When arrangements have been made for the taking of samples, the *justices' clerk* [justices' chief executive] shall—

(a) give notice in Form 3 to each subject or, where a subject is under a disability, the person having the care and control of the subject, of the arrangements made for the taking of samples from the subject and shall require him, or where he is under a disability, the person having the care and control of him, to comply with the arrangements;

(b) complete Parts I and II of a direction form in respect of each subject and send the direction form to the sampler who is to take the *blood sample* [bodily sample] from that subject.

**Note.** Words 'justices' clerk' and 'blood sample' substituted by words 'justices' chief executive' and 'bodily sample' respectively by SI 2001/776, rr 3, 7, 10, as from 1 April 2001.

**13.**   When a direction form is returned to the court by a sampler, or by a tester, unless it is accompanied by a report under section 20(2) of the Act, the court shall cause a copy of the form to be served on each party to the proceedings and shall consider any entries made on the direction form by the sampler, tester or any other person and may vary or revoke the direction or make such order as to the hearing or the continuation of the hearing of the complaint as appears to the court to be appropriate in all the circumstances.

**14.**   On receipt of the report by the tester under section 20(2) of the Act, the *justices' clerk* [justices' chief executive] shall serve a copy of the report on each of the parties to the proceedings.

**Note.** Words 'justices' clerk' substituted by words 'justices' chief executive' by SI 2001/776, rr 3, 7, as from 1 April 2001.

**15.**   The *justices' clerk* [justices' chief executive] shall use any sum paid to him under Rule 8 of these Rules in paying the fees to the sampler *and tester* and shall repay the balance, if any, to the applicant.

**Note.** Words 'justices' clerk' substituted by words 'justices' chief executive' and words 'and tester' revoked by SI 2001/776, rr 3, 7, 11, as from 1 April 2001.

**16.**   Service of any document required to be served by these Rules may be effected by delivering it to the person upon whom it is required to be served or to his solicitor or by sending it by first class post to him at his last known or usual place of abode or to his solicitor at his office.

Rule 2(2)

## SCHEDULE

FORM 1

*FAMILY LAW REFORM ACT 1969*

*An explanation of the use of blood tests in paternity disputes (MC (BT) Rules 1971, r 3)*

*Introduction*

   *In a case where there is a dispute about the paternity of a child blood tests may provide important evidence and courts now have power to order their use if a party in a case asks for them. This leaflet explains about blood tests and how to get them.*

*Evidence from the blood tests*

   *A small amount of blood is taken from the mother, her child and the man said to be the child's father. Tests upon this blood can show that the man is not the father of the child. They cannot definitely prove that a man is the father, but they can in some cases show that he is likely to be the father. Giving blood for this purpose is simple and not harmful to the health.*

*Applying for blood tests*

   *Any party in a case where the paternity of a child is disputed can apply for blood tests. If both parties agree, the court may order tests before the case is heard. If one party does not agree, the case must come before the court which will then decide whether or not to order tests.*

*Refusal to comply with an order*

   *No-one can be forced to give a blood sample. But if a person does not comply with the court's order, the court will consider his reason, and if it does not think he has good reason for not complying, it can draw its own conclusions. One of these may be that the person knew that the result of tests might not support his case.*

*Arrangements for giving blood*

   *When blood tests are ordered, the parties (and the person looking after the child, if not one of the parties) will be told to attend a named doctor at a stated time and place. Anyone who cannot keep the appointment must tell the doctor immediately so that another appointment can be made. Failure to do this may be taken as a refusal to undergo tests. It is important that the three samples of blood are taken by the same doctor at the same time. Distance may make this impossible, but if the mother, child and man said to be the father are living in the same area they will have to attend the same doctor on the same day.*

*Identification of parties*

*It is essential that the right people are tested. For this purpose a passport size photograph must be provided of all parties over 12 months old. A child under 12 months is identified by the person who is looking after it. Giving a blood sample instead of someone else or allowing the wrong child to be tested is a serious offence. The penalty is a fine of up to £400 or imprisonment for up to two years. The blood test itself can show that the wrong person has been tested.*

*Cost of blood tests*

*The cost of blood tests may be as much as £36. This must be paid by the person asking for the tests before they will be carried out. However, a party to a case where the paternity of a child is disputed may be entitled to legal aid, and if he or she is, the cost of the test may be paid by the legal aid fund. Anyone involved in this type of case should consult a solicitor about this possibility.*

*Effect of blood transfusion*

*Blood transfusion within 3 months of the tests can effect their value. If a person has had a recent transfusion, his solicitor or the clerk of the court should be informed before the court orders tests.*

*Report*

*When tests have been carried out, the tester will send a written report to the court and a copy of this will be sent to the parties to the case.*

*Further information*

*Further information about the procedure may be obtained from a solicitor or from the clerk of the court which is dealing with the case.*

**Note.** Revoked by SI 2001/776, rr 3, 12, as from 1 April 2001.


FORM 2

FAMILY LAW REFORM ACT 1969


*Blood Test* [Scientific Test] *direction (MC (BT) Rules 1971, r 7)*

In the .................................................................................................. Magistrates'
                                              Court
.................................................................................................... Complainant
                                              and
....................................................................................................Defendant

By virtue of the power conferred upon the court by section 20(1) of the Family Law Reform Act 1969 and on the application of ............................ the court hereby directs that *blood tests* [scientific tests] be used to ascertain whether such tests show that ........................................................ is or is not excluded from being the father of ........................................................ and that for that purpose *blood samples* [bodily samples] shall be taken from:

And it is further ordered that such samples shall be taken before the          day of              19  .

By order of the court,

......................................................

Justices' Clerk.

Address ...............................................

Dated ....................... 19 .

The person appearing to the court to have the care and control of ................ being a person who [has not attained the age of sixteen years] [is suffering from a mental disorder within the meaning of the Mental Health Act 1959 and is incapable of understanding the nature and purpose of *blood tests* [scientific tests]] is .....................

.............................................................

**Note.** Words 'Blood Test', 'blood samples' and words 'blood tests' in both places they occur substituted by words 'Scientific Test', 'bodily samples' and 'scientific tests' respectively by SI 2001/776, rr 3, 13, as from 1 April 2001.

FORM 3

FAMILY LAW REFORM ACT 1969

*Requirement to give blood sample* [bodily sample] (*MC* (*BT*) *Rules 1971, r 12*)

To ............................................................................. [*Name of subject/person having care and control of subject*].

Further to the direction for the carrying out of *blood tests* [scientific tests] given on ........... 19 by the ........................................ Magistrates' Court, a copy of which has been served on you, you are hereby required, for the purpose of giving effect to the direction, to attend on ..................................... [*insert title and name of sampler*] at ................................... [*insert address at which sample is to be taken*] at ................. a.m./ p.m. on ....................................... 19 for a *blood sample* [bodily sample] to be taken from you.

.............................................

*Justices' Clerk* [Justices' Chief Executive].

Address .....................................................

*Note.* Any travelling or other expenses reasonably incurred in complying with this requirement are payable in the first instance by the person who applied to the court for the direction, namely                                              whose solicitors are                of                    . The court has power to deal with these expenses when it makes an order for costs at the end of the proceedings.

**Note.** Words 'blood sample' in both places they occur, 'blood tests' and 'Justices' Clerk' substituted by words 'bodily sample', 'scientific tests' and 'Justices' Chief Executive' respectively by SI 2001/776, rr 3, 14, as from 1 April 2001.

## MATRIMONIAL CAUSES (DECREE ABSOLUTE) GENERAL ORDER 1972

**Dated** 20 July 1972

**1.** (1) This Order may be cited as the Matrimonial Causes (Decree Absolute) General Order 1972 and shall come into operation on 1 September 1972.

(2) In this Order a decree means a decree of divorce or nullity of marriage.

**2.** [(1) Subject to paragraph (2)], in relation to any decree nisi granted after the coming into operation of this Order the period of six months specified in section 5(7) of the Matrimonial Causes Act 1965 shall be reduced to six weeks and accordingly the decree shall not be made absolute until the expiration of six weeks from its grant unless the court by special order fixes a shorter period.

[(2)  Where the period of six weeks mentioned in paragraph (1) would expire on a day on which the office or registry of the court in which the cause is proceeding is closed, the period shall be extended until the end of the first day thereafter on which the office or registry is open.]

**Note.** The words in square brackets were added by the 1973 General Order with effect from 2 April 1973.

## ADOPTION (DESIGNATION OF OVERSEAS ADOPTIONS) ORDER 1973

**Dated** 1 January 1973

**SI 1973 No 19**

**1.**  This Order may be cited as the Adoption (Designation of Overseas Adoptions) Order 1973 and shall come into operation on 1 February 1973.

**2.**  The Interpretation Act 1889 shall apply to the interpretation of this Order as it applies to the interpretation of an Act of Parliament.

**Note.** The Interpretation Act 1889 is replaced by Interpretation Act 1978.

**3.**  (1)  An adoption of an infant is hereby specified as an overseas adoption if it is an adoption effected in a place in relation to which this Article applies and under the law in force in that place.

(2)  Subject to paragraph (2A) as respects any adoption effected before the date on which this Order comes into operation, this Article applies in relation to any place which, at that date, forms part of a country or territory described in Part I or II of the Schedule to this Order and as respects any adoption effected on or after that date, this Article applies in relation to any place which, at the time the adoption is effected, forms part of a country or territory which at that time is a country or territory described in Part I or II of the Schedule to this Order.

(2A)  This Article also applies, as respects any adoption effected on or after 5th April 1993, in relation to any place which, at the time the adoption is effected, forms part of the People's Republic of China.

(3)  In this Article the expression—

'infant' means a person who at the time when the application for adoption was made had not attained the age of 18 years and had not been married;

'law' does not include customary or common law.

**4.**  (1)  Evidence that an overseas adoption has been effected may be given by the production of a document purporting to be—

(a)  a certified copy of an entry made, in accordance with the law of the country or territory concerned, in a public register relating to the recording of adoptions and showing that the adoptions and showing that the adoption has been effected; or

(b)  a certificate that the adoption has been effected, signed or purporting to be signed by a person authorised by the law of the country or territory concerned to sign such a certificate, or a certified copy of such certificate.

(2)  Where a document produced by virtue of paragraph (1) of this Article is not in English, the Registrar General or the Registrar General of Births, Deaths and Marriages for Scotland, as the case may be, may require the production of an English translation of the document before satisfying himself of the matters specified in section 8 of the Adoption Act 1968.

(3)  Nothing in this Article shall be construed as precluding proof, in accordance with the Evidence (Foreign, Dominion and Colonial Documents) Act 1933, or the Oaths and Evidence (Overseas Authorities and Countries) Act 1963, or otherwise, that an overseas adoption has been effected.

SCHEDULE

PART I

COMMONWEALTH COUNTRIES AND UNITED KINGDOM DEPENDENT TERRITORIES

| | |
|---|---|
| Australia | Malaysia |
| Bahamas | Malta |
| Barbados | Mauritius |
| Bermuda | Montserrat |
| Botswana | New Zealand |
| British Honduras | Nigeria |
| British Virgin Islands | Pitcairn |
| Canada | St. Christopher, Nevis and Anguilla |
| Cayman Islands | St. Vincent |
| The Republic of Cyprus | Seychelles |
| Dominica | Singapore |
| Fiji | Southern Rhodesia |
| Ghana | Sri Lanka |
| Gibraltar | Swaziland |
| Guyana | Tanzania |
| Hong Kong | Tonga |
| Jamaica | Trinidad and Tobago |
| Kenya | Uganda |
| Lesotho | Zambia |
| Malawi | |

PART II

OTHER COUNTRIES AND TERRITORIES

Austria
Belgium
Denmark (including Greenland and the Faroes)
Finland
France (including Réunion, Martinique, Guadeloupe and French Guyana)
The Federal Republic of Germany and Land Berlin (West Berlin)
Greece
Iceland
The Republic of Ireland
Israel
Italy
Luxembourg
The Netherlands (including Suriname and the Antilles)
Norway
Portugal (including the Azores and Madeira)
South Africa and South West Africa
Spain (including the Balearics and the Canary Islands)
Sweden
Switzerland
Turkey
The United States of America
Yugoslavia

## MATRIMONIAL CAUSES (DECREE ABSOLUTE) GENERAL ORDER 1973

**Dated** 15 March 1973

**Note.** This Order extends the normal period of six weeks after which a decree nisi of dissolution or nullity of marriage can be made absolute in cases where, the court office being closed, the time for appeal is extended. See p 4076, where the amendment has been incorporated.

## RECIPROCAL ENFORCEMENT OF MAINTENANCE ORDERS (DESIGNATION OF RECIPROCATING COUNTRIES) ORDER 1974

**Dated** 26 March 1974

**SI 1974 No 556**

Whereas Her Majesty is satisfied that, in the event of the benefits conferred by Part I of the Maintenance Orders (Reciprocal Enforcement) Act 1972 being applied to, or to particular classes of, maintenance orders made by the courts of each of the countries and territories specified in column (1) of the Schedule to this Order, similar benefits will in that country or territory be applied to, or to those classes of, maintenance orders made by the courts of the United Kingdom:

And whereas Her Majesty considers the provisions contained in Article 4 of this Order expedient for the purpose of securing the matters set out in section 24 of the said Act of 1972:

Now, therefore, Her Majesty, in exercise of the powers conferred by sections 1 and 24 of the Maintenance Orders (Reciprocal Enforcement) Act 1972, is pleased, by and with the advice of Her Privy Council, to order, and it is hereby ordered, as follows—

**1.**   This Order may be cited as the Reciprocal Enforcement of Maintenance Orders (Designation of Reciprocating Countries) Order 1974 and shall come into operation on 8 May 1974.

**2.**   (1)   In this Order—

'the Act of 1972' means the Maintenance Orders (Reciprocal Enforcement) Act 1972;

'the Act of 1920' means the Maintenance Orders (Facilities for Enforcement) Act 1920;

'column (1)' and 'column (2)' mean respectively columns (1) and (2) of the Schedule to this Order.

(2)   The Interpretation Act 1889 shall apply for the interpretation of this Order as it applies for the interpretation of an Act of Parliament.

**Note.** The Interpretation Act 1889 is replaced by Interpretation Act 1978.

**3.**   Each of the countries and territories specified in column (1) is hereby designated as a reciprocating country for the purposes of Part I of the Act of 1972 as regards maintenance orders of the description specified in respect of that country or territory in column (2).

**4.**   (1)   Sections 5, 12 to 15, 17, 18 and 21 of the Act of 1972 shall apply in relation to a maintenance order transmitted under section 2 or 3 of the Act of 1920 to one of the countries and territories specified in column (1), being an order of the description specified in respect of that country or territory in column (2) to which immediately before the coming into operation of this Order the Act of 1920 applied, as they apply in relation to a maintenance order sent to that country or territory in pursuance of section 2 of the Act of 1972 or made by virtue of section 3 or 4 of the Act of 1972 and confirmed by a competent court in that country or territory.

(2)   Sections 8 to 21 of the Act of 1972 shall apply in relation to a maintenance order made in one of the countries and territories specified in column (1), being an order of the description specified in respect of that country or territory in column

(2) to which immediately before the coming into operation of this Order the Act of 1920 applied and not being an order which immediately before that date is registered in the High Court or the High Court of Justice in Northern Ireland under section 1 of the Act of 1920, as they apply in relation to a registered order.

(3) A maintenance order made by a court in one of the countries and territories specified in column (1) being an order of the description specified in respect of that country or territory in column (2) which has been confirmed by a court in England, Wales or Northern Ireland under section 4 of the Act of 1920 and is in force immediately before the coming into operation of this Order, shall be registered under section 7(5) of the Act of 1972 in like manner as if it had been confirmed by that court in England, Wales or Northern Ireland under subsection (2) of that section.

(4) Any proceedings brought under or by virtue of any provision of the Act of 1920 in a court in England, Wales or Northern Ireland which are pending immediately before the coming into operation of this Order, being proceedings affecting a person resident in one of the countries and territories specified in column (1), shall be continued as if they had been brought under or by virtue of the corresponding provision of the Act of 1972.

SCHEDULE                                                                    Article 3

COUNTRIES AND TERRITORIES DESIGNATED AS RECIPROCATING COUNTRIES

| (1)<br>Country or territory | (2)<br>Description of maintenance orders to which designation extends |
| --- | --- |
| Australian Capital Territory | Maintenance orders other than—<br>(a) *provisional affiliation orders and*<br>(b) orders obtained by or in favour of a public authority |
| British Columbia | Maintenance orders generally |
| Gibraltar | Maintenance orders generally |
| Manitoba | Maintenance orders generally |
| New South Wales | Maintenance orders other than—<br>(a) *provisional affiliation orders, and*<br>(b) orders obtained by or in favour of a public authority |
| New Zealand | Maintenance orders generally |
| Northern Territory of Australia | Maintenance orders other than—<br>(a) *provisional affiliation orders, and*<br>(b) orders obtained by or in favour of a public authority |
| Nova Scotia | Maintenance orders other than—<br>(a) maintenance orders of the description contained in paragraph (b) of the definition of 'maintenance orders' in section 21(1) of the Act of 1972 (orders for the payment of birth and funeral expenses of child) and<br>(b) orders obtained by or in favour of a public authority |
| Ontario | Maintenance orders other than—<br>(a) *provisional affiliation orders*<br>(b) maintenance orders of the description contained in the said paragraph (b), and |

| (1)<br>Country or territory | (2)<br>Description of maintenance orders to<br>which designation extends |
|---|---|
| | (c) *provisional maintenance orders made by virtue of the Matrimonial Proceedings (Polygamous Marriages) Act 1972 or any corresponding legislation in Ontario* |
| Queensland | Maintenance orders other than—<br>(a) *provisional affiliation orders, and*<br>(b) orders obtained by or in favour of a public authority |
| South Australia | Maintenance orders other than—<br>(a) *provisional affiliation orders, and*<br>(b) orders obtained by or in favour of a public authority |
| Tasmania | Maintenance orders other than—<br>(a) *provisional affiliation orders, and*<br>(b) orders obtained by or in favour of a public authority |
| Victoria | Maintenance orders other than—<br>(a) *provisional affiliation orders, and*<br>(b) orders obtained by or in favour of a public authority |

**Note.** Words printed in italics in column (2) omitted by SI 1979 No 116.

## THE MAINTENANCE ORDERS (FACILITIES FOR ENFORCEMENT) (REVOCATION) ORDER 1974

**Dated** 26 March 1974

**SI 1974 No 557**

Her Majesty, in exercise of the powers conferred by section 19 of the Maintenance Orders Act 1958, is pleased, by and with the advice of Her Privy Council, to order, and it is hereby ordered, as follows—

**1.**   This Order may be cited as the Maintenance Orders (Facilities for Enforcement) (Revocation) Order 1974 and shall come into operation on 8 May 1974.

**2.**   (1) Insofar as the Maintenance Orders (Facilities for Enforcement) Order 1959, provides that the Maintenance Orders (Facilities for Enforcement) Act 1920 shall extend to the countries and territories specified in paragraph (2) below, that Order is hereby revoked, and accordingly the names of those countries and territories shall be omitted from the First Schedule to that Order.

(2)   The countries and territories referred to in paragraph (1) above are—
(a)   Australia, Territory for the Seat of Government of the Commonwealth (Australian Capital Territory);
(b)   British Columbia;
(c)   Gibraltar;
(d)   Manitoba;
(e)   New South Wales;
(f)   New Zealand;
(g)   Northern Territory of Australia;
(h)   Nova Scotia;

(i)  Ontario;
(j)  Queensland;
(k)  South Australia;
(l)  Tasmania;
(m)  Victoria.

## MAGISTRATES' COURTS (RECIPROCAL ENFORCEMENT OF MAINTENANCE ORDERS) RULES 1974

**Dated** 4 April 1974

**SI 1974 No 668**

**1.**  These Rules may be cited as the Magistrates' Courts (Reciprocal Enforcement of Maintenance Orders) Rules 1974 and shall come into operation on 8 May 1974.

**2.**  (1)  In these Rules, unless the context otherwise requires—
      'the Act' means the Maintenance Orders (Reciprocal Enforcement) Act 1972; and
      'his register', in relation to a *justices' clerk*, means the register kept by that clerk in pursuance of rule 54 of the Magistrates' Courts Rules 1968.
  (2)  The Interpretation Act 1889 shall apply for the interpretation of these Rules as it applies for the interpretation of an Act of Parliament.
**Note.** Interpretation Act 1889 is replaced by Interpretation Act 1978.

**3.**  The officer of any court, by or in relation to whom anything is to be done in pursuance of any provision of Part I of the Act shall, where that court is a magistrates' court, be the *justices' clerk.*

**4.**  (1)  An application under section 2 of the Act (transmission of maintenance order made in the United Kingdom for enforcement in reciprocating country) may, where the court which made the maintenance order which the application relates is a magistrates' court, be made in writing by or on behalf of the payee under the order.
  (2)  Any application made in pursuance of paragraph (1) above shall—
  (a)  specify the date on which the order was made;
  (b)  contain such particulars as are known to the applicant of the whereabouts of the payer and the nature and location of his assets;
  (c)  specify any matters likely to assist in the identification of the payer;
  (d)  where possible, be accompanied by a recent photograph of the payer.
  (3)  In this rule, 'the payer' means the payer under the order to which the application relates.

**4A.**  (1)  In this rule 'an application' means—
  (a)  an application under section 3 of the Act for a provisional maintenance order against a person residing in a reciprocating country,
  (b)  an application under section 5 of the Act for the variation or revocation of a maintenance order made in the United Kingdom, or
  (c)  an application under section 9 of the Act for the variation or revocation of a maintenance order registered by a court in the United Kingdom.
  (2)  An application shall be filed in an appropriate form.
  (3)  On receipt of such an application the justices' clerk shall—
  (a)  fix the date, time and place for a hearing or a directions appointment, and
  (b)  notify the applicant of the date, time and place so fixed.

**4B.**  (1)  This rule applies to proceedings under section 5(5), 7 or 9(6) of the Act for the confirmation of a provisional order made in a reciprocating country.

(2) On receipt of the order and accompanying documents referred to in section 5(5), 7 or 9(6) of the Act, the justices' clerk shall—

(a) fix the date, time and place for a hearing or a directions appointment allowing sufficient time for service under this rule to be effected at least 21 days before the date so fixed, and

(b) serve a copy of the order and documents on the resident party together with a notice stating the date, time and place so fixed.

(3) Within 14 days of service under this rule the resident party shall file an answer to the provisional order in an appropriate form.

**4C.** (1) Schedule A1 to these Rules shall apply to proceedings pursuant to rule 4A and 4B above.

(2) In Schedule A1 as it applies to rule 4A, 'the resident party' and 'the non-resident party' shall be taken to mean—

(a) in the case of an application under sub-paragraph (a) of rule 4A(1), the applicant and the respondent respectively;

(b) in the case of an application under sub-paragraph (b) of rule 4A(1), the payee and the payer respectively under the order in question; and

(c) in the case of an application under sub-paragraph (c) of rule 4A(1), the payer and the payee respectively under the order in question.

(3) In rule 4B and in Schedule A1 as it applies to that rule, 'the resident party' and 'the non-resident party' shall be taken to mean the payer and the payee respectively under the order in question.

**5.** A document setting out or summarising any evidence, required by section 3(5)(b), 5(4) or 9(5) of the Act (provisional orders) to be authenticated shall be authenticated by a certificate, signed by one of the justices before whom that evidence was given, that the document is the original document containing or recording or, as the case may be, summarising that evidence or a true copy of that document.

**6.** (1) Subject to paragraph (2) below, any documents required by section 5(4) or 9(5) of the Act to be sent to a court in a reciprocating country shall be sent to that court by post.

(2) Where the court to which the documents are to be sent is in a country specified in Schedule 1 to these Rules, such documents shall be sent to the Secretary of State for transmission to that court.

**7.** (1) For the purposes of compliance with section 5(9) of the Act (revocation by United Kingdom court of provisional order) there shall be served on the person on whose application the maintenance order was made a notice which shall—

(a) set out the evidence received or taken, as the case may be, in pursuance of that subsection;

(b) inform that person that it appears to the court that the maintenance order ought not to have been made; and

(c) inform that person that if he wishes to make representations with respect to the evidence set out in the notice he may do so orally or in writing and that if he wishes to adduce further evidence he should notify the clerk of the magistrates' court which made the maintenance order.

(2) Where a justices' clerk receives notification that the person on whose application the maintenance order was made wishes to adduce further evidence, he shall fix a date for the hearing of such evidence and shall send that person written notice of the date fixed.

**8.** (1) Where a certified copy of an order, not being a provisional order, is received by a justices' clerk who is required under any provision of Part I of the Act to register the order, he shall cause the order to be registered in his court by means of a minute or memorandum entered and signed by him in his register.

(2) Where any magistrates' court makes or confirms an order which is required under section 7(5) or 9(10) of the Act to be registered, the justices' clerk shall enter and sign a minute or memorandum thereof in his register.

(3) Every minute or memorandum entered in pursuance of paragraph (1) or (2) above shall specify the section of the Act under which the order in question is registered.

**9.** (1) When an order is registered under section 6(3) of the Act, the court shall order that payment of sums due thereunder shall be made to the clerk of the registering court during such hours and at such places as that clerk may direct.

(1A) A justices' clerk to whom payments are ordered to be made (whether by virtue of an order under paragraph (1) above or by virtue of an order of the court under the Act) shall send those payments by post to the court which made the order or to such other person or authority as that court or the Secretary of State may from time to time direct:

Provided that if the court which made the order is in one of the countries or territories specified in Schedule 2 to these Rules the justices' clerk shall unless the Secretary of State otherwise directs send any such sums to the Crown Agents for Overseas Governments and Administrations for transmission to the person to whom they are due.

(2) Where it appears to a justices' clerk to whom payments by way of periodical payments under any maintenance order are made that any sums payable under the order are in arrear he may and, if such sums are in arrear to an amount equal to four times the sum payable weekly under the order, he shall, whether the person for whose benefit the payment should have been made requests him to do so or not, proceed in his own name for the recovery of those sums, unless it appears to him that it is unreasonable in the circumstances to do so.

**9A.** Without prejudice to Rule 9 above, the justices' clerk of the registering court shall take reasonable steps to notify the person to whom payments are due under a registered order of the means of enforcement available in respect of it, including, in an appropriate case, the possibility of registration of the whole or a part of the order in the High Court under Part I of the Maintenance Orders Act 1958.

**9B.** (1) Where, in the exercise of the duty imposed under rule 9(1) above, or in the exercise of the powers conferred by virtue of section 7(5A), section 8(4A) or section 9(1ZA) of the Act, the court orders that payments under the order are to be made by a particular means, the clerk of the court shall record on the copy of the order the means of payment which the court has ordered and notify in writing, as soon as practicable, the person liable to make payments under the order of how payments are to be made.

(2) Where, in the exercise of the aforesaid powers, the court orders payment to the clerk of the court, or to the clerk of any other magistrates' court, by a method of payment falling within section 59(6) of the Magistrates' Courts Act 1980 (standing order, etc), the clerk of the court to whom payments are to be made shall notify the person liable to make the payments under the order of the number and location of the account into which the payments are to be made.

(3) Where, under section 60(4) of the Magistrates' Courts Act 1980, as modified by section 9(1ZA) of the Act, the clerk of the court receives an application from an interested party for the method of payment to be varied, the clerk shall notify in writing, as soon as practicable, that party and, where practicable, any other interested party, of the result of the application, including any decision to refer the matter to the court; where the clerk grants the application, he shall record the variation on the copy of the order.

**10.** (1) Subject to paragraph (2) below, where a request is made by or on behalf of a court in a reciprocating country for the taking in England and Wales of the evidence of a person residing therein, the following magistrates' courts shall have power under section 14(1) of the Act (obtaining of evidence needed for purpose of certain proceedings) to take that evidence, that is to say—
    (a) where the maintenance order to which the proceedings in the court in the reciprocating country relate was made by a magistrates' court, the court which made the order;
    (b) where the maintenance order to which those proceedings relate is registered in a magistrates' court, the court in which the order is registered;
    (c) a magistrates' court which has received such a request from the Secretary of State.

(2) The power conferred by paragraph (1) above may, with the agreement of a court having that power, be exercised by any other magistrates' court which, because the person whose evidence is to be taken resides within its jurisdiction or for any other reason, the first-mentioned court considers could more conveniently take the evidence; but nothing in this paragraph shall derogate from the power of any court specified in paragraph (1) above.

(3) Subject to paragraph (4) below, where the evidence of any person is to be taken by a magistrates' court under the foregoing provisions of this rule—
    (a) the evidence shall be taken in the same manner as if that person were a witness in proceedings on a complaint;
    (b) any oral evidence so taken shall be put into writing and read to the person who gave it, who shall be required to sign the document; and
    (c) the justices by whom the evidence of any person is so taken shall certify at the foot of any document setting out the evidence of, or produced in evidence by, that person that such evidence was taken, or document received in evidence, as the case may be, by them.

(4) Where such a request as is mentioned in paragraph (1) above includes a request that the evidence be taken in a particular manner, the magistrates' court by which the evidence is taken shall, so far as circumstances permit, comply with that request.

(5) Any document such as is mentioned in paragraph (3)(c) above shall be sent—
    (a) where the request for the taking of the evidence was made by or on behalf of a court in a country specified in Schedule 1 to these Rules, to the Secretary of State for transmission to that court;
    (b) in any other case, to the court in the reciprocating country by or on behalf of which the request was made.

**11.** Any request under section 14(5) of the Act for the taking or providing of evidence by a court in a reciprocating country shall, where made by a magistrates' court, be communicated in writing to the court in question.

**12.** (1) Where a magistrates' court makes an order, not being a provisional order, varying a maintenance order to which section 5 of the Act (variation and revocation of maintenance order made in the United Kingdom) applies, the justices' clerk shall send written notice of the making of the order to the Secretary of State; and where the order is made by virtue of paragraph (a) or (b) of subsection (3) of that section, he shall send such written notice to the court in a reciprocating country which would, if the order had been a provisional order, have had power to confirm the order.

(2) Where a magistrates' court revokes a maintenance order to which section 5 of the Act applies, the justices' clerks shall send written notice of the revocation to the Secretary of State and to the court in a reciprocating country which has power to confirm that maintenance order, or by which the order has been confirmed, or in which the order is registered for enforcement, as the case may be.

(3) Where under section 9 of the Act (variation and revocation of maintenance order registered in United Kingdom court) a magistrates' court makes an order, not being a provisional order, varying or revoking a registered order, the justices' clerk shall send written notice of the making of the order to the court in a reciprocating country which made the registered order.

(4) Where under section 7(2) of the Act (confirmation by United Kingdom court of provisional maintenance order made in reciprocating country) a magistrates' court confirms an order to which section 7 of the Act applies, the justices' clerk shall send written notice of the confirmation to the court in a reciprocating country which made the order.

**13.** (1) Where a justices' clerk—
  (a) registers under section 6(3) of the Act (registration in United Kingdom court of maintenance order made in reciprocating country) an order to which section 6 of the Act applies; or
  (b) registers under section 7(5) of the Act an order which has been confirmed in pursuance of section 7(2) of the Act,
he shall send written notice to the Secretary of State that the order has been duly registered.

(3) Where a justices' clerk registers a maintenance order under section 10(4) of the Act, he shall send written notice to the Secretary of State that the order has been duly registered.

**14.** (1) Where a justices' clerk cancels the registration of a maintenance order under section 10(1) of the Act (cancellation of registration and transfer of order), he shall send written notice of the cancellation to the payer under the order.

(2) Where a justices' clerk registers a maintenance order under section 6(3), 7(5), 9(10), 10(4), 10(5) or 23(3) of the Act, he shall send to the payer under the order written notice stating—
  (a) that the order has been duly registered;
  (b) that sums due under the order should be paid to the justices' clerk; and
  (c) the hours during which and the place at which such payments should be made.

## SCHEDULE A1

RULES OF PROCEDURE

**1.** In this Schedule, and in any rule where this Schedule applies to proceedings pursuant to that rule, unless the context otherwise requires—
  'business day' means any day other than—
  (a) a Saturday, Sunday, Christmas or Good Friday; or
  (b) a bank holiday, that is to say, a day which is, or is to be observed as, a bank holiday, or a holiday, under the Banking and Financial Dealings Act 1971, in England and Wales,
  'directions appointment' means a hearing for directions under paragraph 4 below,
  'file' means deposit with the justices' clerk,
  'justices' clerk' has the meaning assigned to it by section 70 of the Justices of the Peace Act 1979 and includes any person who performs a justices' clerk's functions by virtue of paragraph 12 below,
  'leave' includes approval,
  'note' includes a record made by mechanical or electronic means, and
  'proceedings' means proceedings to which this Schedule applies.

*Transfer of proceedings*

**2.** (1) Where—
  (a) any proceedings are relevant proceedings within the meaning of section 93 of the Children Act 1989, and
  (b) the justices' clerk or the court receives a request in writing from the resident party that the proceedings be transferred to another magistrates' court,
the justices' clerk or court shall issue a certificate in the appropriate form, granting or refusing the request in accordance with any Order made by the Lord Chancellor under Part I of Schedule 11 to the Children Act 1989.

  (2) Where a request is granted under paragraph (1) the justices' clerk shall send a copy of the certificate—
  (a) to the resident party,
  (b) to the Lord Chancellor's Department, and
  (c) to the magistrates' court to which the proceedings are to be transferred.

  (3) Any consent given or refused by a justices' clerk in accordance with any Order made by the Lord Chancellor under Part I of Schedule 11 shall be recorded in writing by the justices' clerk at the time it is given or refused or as soon as practicable thereafter.

*Service*

**3.** (1) Where service of a document is required by this Schedule or by a rule where this Schedule applies to proceedings pursuant to that rule it may be effected, unless the contrary is indicated—
  (a) if the person to be served is not known by the person serving to be acting by solicitor—
      (i) by delivering it to him personally, or
      (ii) by delivering it at, or by sending it by first-class post to, his residence or last known residence, or
  (b) if the person to be served is known by the person serving to be acting by solicitor—
      (i) by delivering the document at, or sending it by first-class post to, the solicitor's address for service,
      (ii) where the solicitor's address for service includes a numbered box at a document exchange, by leaving the document at that document exchange or at a document exchange which transmits documents on every business day to that document exchange, or
      (iii) by sending a legible copy of the document by facsimile transmission to the solicitor's office.

  (2) In this paragraph, 'first-class post' means first-class post which has been pre-paid or in respect of which pre-payment is not required.

  (3) A document shall, unless the contrary is proved, be deemed to have been served—
  (a) in the case of service by first-class post, on the second business day after posting, and
  (b) in the case of service in accordance with sub-paragraph 1(b)(ii), on the second business day after the day on which it is left at the document exchange.

  (4) In any proceedings where this Schedule, or a rule where this Schedule applies, requires a document to be served, the court or the justices' clerk may, without prejudice to any power under paragraph 4 below, direct that—
  (a) the requirement shall not apply;
  (b) the time specified by the rules for complying with the requirement shall be abridged to such extent as may be specified in the direction;
  (c) service shall be effected in such manner as may be specified in the direction.

*Directions*

**4.** (1) The justices' clerk or the court may give, vary or revoke directions for the conduct of the proceedings, including—

(a)  the timetable for the proceedings,

(b)  varying the time within which or by which an act is required by this Schedule or by a rule where this Schedule applies to proceedings pursuant to that rule to be done,

(c)  the service of documents, and

(d)  the submission of evidence,

and the justices' clerk shall, on receipt of an application or of any other document by which proceedings are commenced, consider whether such directions need to be given.

(2) Where the justices' clerk or a single justice who is holding a directions appointment considers, for whatever reason, that it is inappropriate to give a direction on a particular matter, he shall refer the matter to the court which may give any appropriate direction.

(3) Directions under sub-paragraph (1) may be given, varied or revoked either—

(a)  of the justices' clerk's or the court's own motion having given the resident party an opportunity to attend and be heard or to make written representations, or

(b)  on the written request of either party specifying the direction which is sought.

(4) On receipt of a request under sub-paragraph (3)(b) the justices' clerk shall—

(a)  make the direction sought, or

(b)  fix a date for a hearing to consider the request.

*Timing of proceedings*

**5.** (1) Any period of time fixed by this Schedule or by a rule where this Schedule applies to proceedings pursuant to that rule, or by any order or direction, for doing any act shall be reckoned in accordance with this rule.

(2) Where the period, being a period of 7 days or less, would include a day which is not a business day, that day shall be excluded.

(3) Where the time fixed for filing a document with the justices' clerk expires on a day on which the justices' clerk's office is closed, and for that reason the document cannot be filed on that day, the document shall be filed in time if it is filed on the next day on which the justices' clerk's office is open.

(4) Where this Schedule or a rule where this Schedule applies to proceedings pursuant to that rule provides a period of time within which or by which a certain act is to be performed in the course of relevant proceedings, that period may not be extended otherwise than by a direction of the justices' clerk or the court under paragraph 4(1) above.

(5) At the—

(a)  transfer to a court of proceedings,

(b)  postponement or adjournment of any hearing or directions appointment in the course of relevant proceedings, or

(c)  conclusion of any such hearing or directions appointment other than one at which the proceedings are determined, or so soon thereafter as is practicable,

the justices' clerk or the court shall—

(i)  fix a date upon which the proceedings shall come before the justices' clerk or the court again for such purposes as the justices' clerk or the court directs, which date shall, where paragraph (a) applies, be as soon as possible after the transfer, and

(ii)  give notice to the resident party of the date so fixed.

*Attendance at directions appointment and hearing*

**6.** (1) The resident party shall attend a directions appointment of which he has been given notice in accordance with paragraph 4 above unless the justices' clerk or the court otherwise directs.

(2) Where at the time and place appointed for a hearing or directions appointment the resident party does not appear the justices' clerk or the court shall not proceed with the hearing or appointment unless—

(a) the proceedings relate to an application filed by the resident party, or

(b) the court is satisfied that the resident party has received reasonable notice of the hearing or appointment.

(3) Where at the time and place appointed for a hearing or directions appointment the non-resident party does not appear the court may proceed with the hearing or appointment where the proceedings relate to an order or application sent by the Lord Chancellor to the court under the Act.

(4) Nothing in this Schedule shall be taken as preventing either party from appearing at any hearing or directions appointment.

*Documentary evidence*

**7.** (1) A party shall file, at or by such time as the justices' clerk or the court directs or, in the absence of a direction, before the hearing or appointment—

(a) written statements of the substance of the oral evidence which he intends to adduce at a hearing or a directions appointment, which shall—

(i) be dated,

(ii) be signed by the person making the statement,

(iii) contain a declaration that the maker of the statement believes it to be true and understands that it may be placed before the court, and

(iv) show in the top right-hand corner of the first page—

(a) the initials and surname of the person making the statement,

(b) the number of the statement in relation to the maker,

(c) the date on which the statement was made, and

(d) the party on whose behalf it is filed, and

(b) copies of any documents upon which he intends to rely at a hearing or a directions appointment.

(2) A party may, subject to any direction of the justices' clerk or the court about the timing of statements under this rule, file a statement which is supplementary to a statement served under sub-paragraph (1).

(3) Where a non-resident party files a statement or document under this rule, he shall also file a copy of it for service on the resident party; and the justices' clerk shall on receipt of that copy serve it on the resident party.

(4) At a hearing or directions appointment a party may not without the leave of the justices' clerk, in the case of a directions appointment, or the court—

(a) adduce evidence, or

(b) seek to rely on a document,

in respect of which he has failed to comply with the requirements of sub-paragraphs (1) and, where applicable, (3).

*Amendment*

**8.** (1) A party amending a document shall file the amended document with the justices' clerk; and the amendments shall be identified.

(2) Paragraph 7(3) above applies to an amended document filed under this paragraph.

*Oral evidence*

**9.** The justices' clerk or the court shall keep a note of the substance of any oral evidence given at a hearing or directions appointment.

*Hearing*

**10.** (1) Before the hearing, the justice or justices who will be dealing with the case shall read any documents which have been filed under paragraph 7 above in respect of the hearing.

(2) The justices' clerk at a directions appointment, or the court at a hearing or directions appointment, may give directions as to the order of speeches and evidence.

(3) After the final hearing, the court shall make its decision as soon as is practicable.

(4) Before the court makes an order or refuses an application, the justices' clerk shall record in writing—

(a) the names of the justice or justices constituting the court by which the decision is made, and

(b) in consultation with the justice or justices, the reasons for the court's decision and any findings of fact.

(5) After the court announces its decision, the justices' clerk shall as soon as practicable make a record in writing of any order.

(6) Where, under subsection (4) of section 7 of the Domestic Proceedings and Magistrates' Courts Act 1978, a court decides to treat an application under section 7 as if it were an application for an order under section 2 of that Act, the court shall indicate orally which of grounds (a) and (b) in that subsection it considers applicable and a memorandum of that decision and the grounds therefor shall be entered in the court's register.

*Confidentiality of documents*

**11.** (1) No document, other than a record of an order, held by the court and relating to any proceedings shall be disclosed, other than to—

(a) a party,

(b) the legal representative of a party,

(c) the Lord Chancellor's Department, or

(d) the Legal Aid Board,

without leave of the justices' clerk or the court.

*Delegation by justices' clerk*

**12.** (1) In this paragraph, 'employed as a clerk in court' has the same meaning as in rule 2(1) of the Justices' Clerks (Qualifications of Assistants) Rules 1979.

(2) Anything authorised to be done by, to or before a justices' clerk under this Schedule or under a rule to which this Schedule applies may be done instead by, to or before a person employed as a clerk in court where that person is appointed by the magistrates' courts committee to assist him and where that person has been specifically authorised by the justices' clerk for that purpose.

(3) Any authorisation by the justices' clerk under sub-paragraph (2) shall be recorded in writing at the time the authority is given or as soon as practicable thereafter.

*Application of section 97 of the Magistrates' Courts Act 1980*

**13.** (1) Subject to sub-paragraph (2) below, section 97 of the Magistrates' Courts Act 1980 shall apply to proceedings to which this Schedule applies as it applies to a hearing of a complaint under that section.

(2) The power of a justice under section 97 of that Act to issue a witness summons may be exercised by a justices' clerk.

## SCHEDULE 1                                              Rules 6(2) and 10(5)

RECIPROCATING COUNTRIES TO WHICH DOCUMENTS ARE TRANSMITTED VIA THE SECRETARY
OF STATE

British Columbia
New Zealand
Nova Scotia
Ontario
Ghana
India
Kenya
New Brunswick
Northwest Territories of Canada
The Republic of South Africa
Alberta[1]
Saskatchewan[1]
Turks and Caicos Islands[1]
United Republic of Tanzania (except Zanzibar)[1]
Papua New Guinea[2]
Zimbabwe[2]
Nunavat[3]


## SCHEDULE 2                                                      Rule 9(1)

COUNTRIES AND TERRITORIES IN WHICH SUMS ARE PAYABLE THROUGH CROWN AGENTS FOR
OVERSEAS GOVERNMENTS AND ADMINISTRATIONS

Gibraltar
Barbados
Bermuda
Ghana
Kenya
Fiji[1]
Hong Kong[1]
Singapore[1]
Turks and Caicos Islands[1]
United Republic of Tanzania (except Zanzibar)[1]
Anguilla[2]
Falkland Islands and Dependencies[2]
St Helena[2]

**Note.** Countries and Territories marked [1] and Rule 13(3) added by SI 1979 No 170 with
effect from 1 April 1979. Countries and Territories marked [2] added by SI 1983 No 1148
with effect from 1 September 1983. There is no Rule 13(2). Country marked [3] added by
SI 2002/1724, as from 20 August 2002.


## MAGISTRATES' COURTS (GUARDIANSHIP OF MINORS) RULES 1974

**Dated** 11 April 1974

**SI 1974 No 706**

The Lord Chancellor, in exercise of the powers conferred on him by section 3 of the
Marriage Act 1949 and by section 15 of the Justices of the Peace Act 1949, as extended
by section 122 of the Magistrates' Courts Act 1952, section 16(5) of the Guardianship
of Minors Act 1971 and that section as applied by sections 1(6), 3(3) and 4(3) of the

Guardianship Act 1973, and section 3(4) of the said Act of 1973 after consultation with the Rule Committee appointed under the said section 15, hereby makes the following Rules—

*Citation and commencement*

**1.**   These Rules may be cited as the Magistrates' Courts (Guardianship of Minors) Rules 1974 and shall come into operation on 8 May 1974.

*Interpretation*

**2.**   (1) In these Rules, the following expressions have the meanings hereby respectively assigned to them, that is to say—

'the Act of 1949' means the Marriage Act 1949;

*'the Act of 1971' means the Guardianship of Minors Act 1971;*

*'the Act of 1973' means the Guardianship Act 1973;*

'court' means a magistrates' court;

'the Rules of 1968' means the Magistrates' Courts Rules 1968, as amended;

*'supervision order' means an order made by a magistrates' court under section 2(2)(a) of the Act of 1973 providing for the supervision of a minor by a probation officer or local authority.*

(2) In these Rules, unless the context otherwise requires, any reference to a rule or to the Schedule shall be construed as a reference to a rule contained in these Rules or to the Schedule thereto, and any reference in a rule to a paragraph shall be construed as a reference to a paragraph of that rule.

(3) *In these Rules, any reference to a form in the Schedule shall be construed as including a reference to a form to the like effect with such variations as the circumstances may require.*

(4) In these Rules, unless the context otherwise requires, any reference to any enactment shall be construed as a reference to that enactment as amended, extended or applied by any subsequent enactment.

(5) The Interpretation Act 1889 shall apply for the interpretation of these Rules as it applies for the interpretation of an Act of Parliament.

**Note.**   The definitions and para (3), printed in italics, omitted by SI 1991 No 1991 with effect from 14 October 1991.

*Revocation*

**3.**   The Guardianship of Infants (Summary Jurisdiction) Rules 1925 and the Guardianship of Infants (Summary Jurisdiction) Rules 1944 are hereby revoked.

*Applications under Guardianship of Minors Acts 1971 and 1973 to be by complaint*

**4.**   *Revoked.*

*Procedure for applications for consent to marriage*

**5.**   (1) An application for the consent of the court to the marriage of a minor under section 3 of the Act of 1949 (marriages of persons under 18) may be made, either orally or in writing, to a justice of the peace [for the commission area in which] the applicant or any respondent resides.

(2) Upon receiving such an application as is referred to in paragraph (1) the justice shall, where the application was in consequence of a refusal to give consent to the marriage, give to any person whose consent is required and who has refused consent a notice of the application and of the date, time and place appointed for the hearing thereof.

(3) Rule 82 of the Rules of 1968 (service of summons, etc) shall apply in relation to the service of a notice given in accordance with paragraph (2) as it applies in relation to the service of a summons issued on a person other than a corporation.

(4) The provisions of Part II of the Magistrates' Courts Act 1952 relating to the hearing of a complaint and of rule 14 of the Rules of 1968 (order of evidence and speeches) shall apply to the hearing of such an application as is referred to in paragraph (1) as if it were made by way of complaint but as if for any reference therein to the complainant, the complaint, the defendant and his defence there were substituted references, respectively, to the applicant, the application, the respondent and his case.

*Provisions for certain hearings to be in camera*

**6.**   *Revoked.*

*Notice to local authority of proposal to commit minor to its care*

**7.**   *Revoked.*

*Substitution of new supervisor for minor*

**8.**   *Revoked.*

*Defendants to application for variation or discharge of order*

**9.**   *Revoked.*

*Defendants to applications regarding access to minors by grandparents*

**9A.**   *Revoked.*

*Copy of extract from register to be sent to grandparent applying under section 14A(1)*

**9B.**   *Revoked.*

# MAGISTRATES' COURTS (RECIPROCAL ENFORCEMENT OF MAINTENANCE ORDERS) (REPUBLIC OF IRELAND) RULES 1975

**Dated** 27 February 1975

**SI 1975 No 286**

The Lord Chancellor, in exercise of the powers conferred on him by section 15 of the Justices of the Peace Act 1949, as extended by section 122 of the Magistrates' Courts Act 1952, and sections 2(3) and (4), 3(5)(b) and (c), (6A) and (6C), 5(2), 6(2), (3), (6) and (9), 8(5) and (6), 9(3), 10(1) to (5) and (7), 14(1), 16(1) and 18(1) of the Maintenance Orders (Reciprocal Enforcement) Act 1972, as extended by Article 3 of the Reciprocal Enforcement of Maintenance Orders (Republic of Ireland) Order 1974 (which sections are set out in Schedule 2 to that Order) and after consultation with the Rule Committee appointed under the said section 15, hereby makes the following Rules—

**1.**   These Rules may be cited as the Magistrates' Courts (Reciprocal Enforcement of Maintenance Orders) (Republic of Ireland) Rules 1975 and shall come into operation on 1 April 1975.

**2.**   (1) In these Rules, unless the context otherwise requires—
   'the Act' means the Maintenance Orders (Reciprocal Enforcement) Act 1972 as applied with such exceptions, adaptations and modifications as are specified in the Reciprocal Enforcement of Maintenance Orders (Republic of Ireland) Order 1974; and

'his register', in relation to a justices' clerk, means the register kept by that clerk in pursuance of rule 54 of the Magistrates' Courts Rules 1968.

(2) The Interpretation Act 1889 shall apply to the interpretation of these Rules as it applies to the interpretation of an Act of Parliament.

**Note.** Interpretation Act 1889 is replaced by Interpretation Act 1978.

**3.** The officer of any court, by or in relation to whom anything is to be done in pursuance of any provision of Part I of the Act shall, where the court is a magistrates' court, be the justices' clerk.

**4.** (1) An application under section 2 of the Act (transmission of maintenance order made in United Kingdom for enforcement in Republic of Ireland) may, where the court which made the maintenance order to which the application relates is a magistrates' court, be made in writing by or on behalf of the payee under the order.

(2) Any application made in pursuance of paragraph (1) above shall—

(a) specify the date on which the order was made;

(b) contain such particulars as are known to the applicant of the whereabouts of the payer;

(c) specify any matters likely to assist in the identification of the payer;

(d) where possible, be accompanied by a recent photograph of the payer.

(3) In this rule, 'the payer' means the payer under the order to which the application relates.

**4A.** (1) An application under section 3 of the Act for a provisional order or under section 5 of the Act for the variation or revocation of a maintenance order or a provisional order made in the United Kingdom shall be filed in an appropriate form.

(2) On receipt of such an application the justices' clerk shall—

(a) fix the date, time and place for a hearing or a directions appointment; and

(b) notify the applicant of the date, time and place so fixed.

**4B.** (1) Schedule A1 to these Rules shall apply to proceedings pursuant to rule 4A above.

(2) In Schedule A1 as it applies to rule 4A, 'the resident party' and 'the non-resident party' shall be taken to mean—

(a) in the case of an application for a provisional order, the applicant and the respondent respectively, and

(b) in the case of an application for the variation or revocation of a maintenance order or a provisional order, the payee and the payer respectively under the order in question.

**5.** A document setting out or summarising any evidence, required by section 3(5)(b) or 5(2) of the Act to be authenticated, shall be authenticated by a certificate, signed by one of the justices before whom that evidence was given, that the document is the original document setting out or, as the case may be, summarising that evidence or a true copy of that document.

**6.** Where under section 3(6A) of the Act a person is required to be notified of the date fixed for the hearing at which confirmation of a provisional order is to be considered, the clerk of the magistrates' court which made the provisional order shall send that person written notice of the date fixed.

**7.** Any documents required by section 5(4) of the Act to be sent to a court in the Republic of Ireland shall be sent to that court by post.

**8.** (1) Where a justices' clerk is required under any provision of Part I of the Act to register an order, he shall cause the order to be registered in his court by means of a minute or memorandum entered and signed by him in his register.

(2) Every minute or memorandum entered in pursuance of paragraph (1) above shall specify the section of the Act under which the order in question is registered.

**9.** (1) Any notice required under section 6(6) of the Act (notice of registration in United Kingdom court of maintenance order made in Republic of Ireland) to be served on the payer under a maintenance order shall, where the order is registered in a magistrates' court, be in the form in Part I of the Schedule to these Rules, or in a form to the like effect.

(2) Where a magistrates' court to which an appeal is made under section 6(7) of the Act sets aside the registration of a maintenance order, the justices' clerk shall send written notice of the court's decision to the payee under the order.

(3) Any notice required under section 6(10) of the Act (notice that maintenance order made in Republic of Ireland has not been registered in United Kingdom court) to be given to the payee under a maintenance order shall, where the appropriate court is a magistrates' court, be in the form in Part II of the Schedule to these Rules or in a form to the like effect.

**10.** (1) When an order is registered under section 6(3) of the Act, the court shall order that payment of sums due thereunder shall be made to the clerk of the registering court during such hours and at such place as that clerk may direct.

(1A) A justices' clerk to whom payments are ordered to be made (whether by virtue of an order under paragraph (1) above or by virtue of an order of the court under the Act) shall send those payments by post to the payee under the order, or where a public authority has been authorised by the payee to receive the payments, to that public authority.

(2) Where it appears to a justices' clerk to whom payments under any maintenance order are made that any sums payable under the order are in arrear he shall, if the person for whose benefit the payment should have been made so requests in writing, proceed in his own name for the recovery of those sums, unless it appears to him that it is unreasonable in the circumstances to do so.

(3) Where it appears to such a justices' clerk that any sums payable under the order are in arrear to an amount equal to four times the sum payable weekly under the order he shall give to the person for whose benefit the payment should have been made notice in writing stating the particulars of the arrears.

**10A.** (1) Where, in the exercise of the duty imposed under rule 10(1) above, or in the exercise of the powers conferred by virtue of section 8(4A) of the Act, the court orders that payments under the order are to be made by a particular means, the clerk of the court shall record on the copy of the order the means of payment which the court has ordered and notify in writing, as soon as practicable, the person liable to make payments under the order of how payments are to be made.

(2) Where, in the exercise of the aforesaid powers, the court orders payment to the clerk of the court, or to the clerk of any other magistrates' court, by a method of payment falling within section 59(6) of the Magistrates' Courts Act 1980 (standing order, etc), the clerk of the court to whom payments are to be made shall notify the person liable to make the payments under the order of the number and location of the account into which the payments are to be made.

**11.** (1) Subject to paragraph (2) below, where a request is made by or on behalf of a court in the Republic of Ireland for the taking in England and Wales of the evidence of a person residing therein, the following magistrates' courts shall have power under section 14(1) of the Act (obtaining of evidence needed for purpose of certain proceedings) to take that evidence, that is to say—

(a) where the maintenance order to which the proceedings in the court in the Republic of Ireland relate was made by a magistrates' court, the court which made the order;

(b) where the maintenance order to which those proceedings relate is registered in a magistrates' court which has received such a request from the Secretary of State.

(2) The power conferred by paragraph (1) above may, with the agreement of a court having that power, be exercised by any other magistrates' court which, because the person whose evidence is to be taken resides within its jurisdiction or for any other reason, the first-mentioned court considers could more conveniently take the evidence; but nothing in this paragraph shall derogate from the power of any court specified in paragraph (1) above.

(3) Subject to paragraph (4) below, where the evidence of any person is to be taken by a magistrates' court under the foregoing provisions of this rule—

(a) the evidence shall be taken in the same manner as if that person were a witness in proceedings on a complaint;

(b) any oral evidence so taken shall be put into writing and read to the person who gave it, who shall be required to sign the document; and

(c) the justices by whom the evidence of any person is so taken shall certify at the foot of any document setting out the evidence of, or produced in evidence by, that person that such evidence was taken, or document received in evidence, as the case may be, by them.

(4) Where such a request as is mentioned in paragraph (1) above includes a request that the evidence be taken in a particular manner, the magistrates' court by which the evidence is taken shall, so far as circumstances permit, comply with that request.

**12.** Where a magistrates' court makes an order varying or revoking a maintenance order to which section 5 of the Act (variation and revocation of maintenance order made in United Kingdom) applies, the justices' clerk shall send written notice of the making of the order to the Secretary of State.

**13.** (1) Where a justices' clerk registers under section 6(3) of the Act (registration in United Kingdom court of maintenance order made in Republic of Ireland an order to which section 6 of the Act applies), he shall send written notice to the Secretary of State that the order has been duly registered.

(2) Where a justices' clerk cancels the registration of a maintenance order under section 10(1) of the Act (cancellation of registration and transfer of order), he shall send written notice of the cancellation to the payer under the order.

(3) Where a justices' clerk registers a maintenance order under section 10(4) of the Act, he shall send written notice to the Secretary of State and to the payer under the order that the order has been duly registered.

**14.** (1) Where the clerk of a magistrates' court receives from the Secretary of State a notice of the issue of the summons or other originating document in proceedings in the Republic of Ireland in relation to the making, variation or revocation of a maintenance order and it appears to that justices' clerk that the person against whom those proceedings have been instituted is residing within the petty sessions area for which the court acts, the justices' clerk shall serve the notice on that person by sending it by post in a registered letter addressed to him at his last known or usual place of abode.

(2) Where it appears to a justices' clerk who has received such a notice from the Secretary of State that the person against whom the proceedings have been instituted is not so residing, the justices' clerk shall send the notice to the Secretary of State.

(3) Where a justices' clerk serves a notice in pursuance of paragraph (1) above he shall send a document which establishes that the notice was so served to the Secretary of State for transmission to the responsible authority in the Republic of Ireland.

SCHEDULE A1

RULES OF PROCEDURE

**1.** In this Schedule, and in any rule where this Schedule applies to proceedings pursuant to that rule, unless the context otherwise requires—
'business day' means any day other than—
(a) a Saturday, Sunday, Christmas or Good Friday; or
(b) a bank holiday, that is to say, a day which is, or is to be observed as, a bank holiday, or a holiday, under the Banking and Financial Dealings Act 1971, in England and Wales,
'directions appointment' means a hearing for directions under paragraph 4 below,
'file' means deposit with the justices' clerk,
'justices' clerk' has the meaning assigned to it by section 70 of the Justices of the Peace Act 1979 and includes any person who performs a justices' clerk's functions by virtue of paragraph 12 below,
'leave' includes approval,
'note' includes a record made by mechanical or electronic means, and
'proceedings' means proceedings to which this Schedule applies.

*Transfer of proceedings*

**2.** (1) Where—
(a) any proceedings are relevant proceedings within the meaning of section 93 of the Children Act 1989, and
(b) the justices' clerk or the court receives a request in writing from the resident party that the proceedings be transferred to another magistrates' court,
the justices' clerk or court shall issue a certificate in the appropriate form, granting or refusing the request in accordance with any Order made by the Lord Chancellor under Part I of Schedule 11 to the Children Act 1989.
(2) Where a request is granted under paragraph (1) the justices' clerk shall send a copy of the certificate—
(a) to the resident party,
(b) to the Lord Chancellor's Department, and
(c) to the magistrates' court to which the proceedings are to be transferred.
(3) Any consent given or refused by a justices' clerk in accordance with any Order made by the Lord Chancellor under Part I of Schedule 11 shall be recorded in writing by the justices' clerk at the time it is given or refused or as soon as practicable thereafter.

*Service*

**3.** (1) Where service of a document is required by this Schedule or by a rule where this Schedule applies to proceedings pursuant to that rule it may be effected, unless the contrary is indicated—
(a) if the person to be served is not known by the person serving to be acting by solicitor—
(i) by delivering it to him personally, or
(ii) by delivering it at, or by sending it by first-class post to, his residence or last known residence, or
(b) if the person to be served is known by the person serving to be acting by solicitor—
(i) by delivering the document at, or sending it by first-class post to, the solicitor's address for service,
(ii) where the solicitor's address for service includes a numbered box at a document exchange, by leaving the document at that document

exchange or at a document exchange which transmits documents on every business day to that document exchange, or

(iii) by sending a legible copy of the document by facsimile transmission to the solicitor's office.

(2) In this paragraph, 'first-class post' means first-class post which has been pre-paid or in respect of which pre-payment is not required.

(3) A document shall, unless the contrary is proved, be deemed to have been served—

(a) in the case of service by first-class post, on the second business day after posting, and

(b) in the case of service in accordance with sub-paragraph 1 (b) (ii), on the second business day after the day on which it is left at the document exchange.

(4) In any proceedings where this Schedule, or a rule where this Schedule applies, requires a document to be served, the court or the justices' clerk may, without prejudice to any power under paragraph 4 below, direct that—

(a) the requirement shall not apply;

(b) the time specified by the rules for complying with the requirement shall be abridged to such extent as may be specified in the direction;

(c) service shall be effected in such manner as may be specified in the direction.

*Directions*

**4.** (1) The justices' clerk or the court may give, vary or revoke directions for the conduct of the proceedings, including—

(a) the timetable for the proceedings,

(b) varying the time within which or by which an act is required by this Schedule or by a rule where this Schedule applies to proceedings pursuant to that rule to be done,

(c) the service of documents, and

(d) the submission of evidence,

and the justices' clerk shall, on receipt of an application or of any other document by which proceedings are commenced, consider whether such directions need to be given.

(2) Where the justices' clerk or a single justice who is holding a directions appointment considers, for whatever reason, that it is inappropriate to give a direction on a particular matter, he shall refer the matter to the court which may give any appropriate direction.

(3) Directions under sub-paragraph (1) may be given, varied or revoked either—

(a) of the justices' clerk's or the court's own motion having given the resident party an opportunity to attend and be heard or to make written representations, or

(b) on the written request of either party specifying the direction which is sought.

(4) On receipt of a request under sub-paragraph (3) (b) the justices' clerk shall—

(a) make the direction sought, or

(b) fix a date for a hearing to consider the request.

*Timing of proceedings*

**5.** (1) Any period of time fixed by this Schedule or by a rule where this Schedule applies to proceedings pursuant to that rule, or by any order or direction, for doing any act shall be reckoned in accordance with this rule.

(2) Where the period, being a period of 7 days or less, would include a day which is not a business day, that day shall be excluded.

(3) Where the time fixed for filing a document with the justices' clerk expires on a day on which the justices' clerk's office is closed, and for that reason the document cannot be filed on that day, the document shall be filed in time if it is filed on the next day on which the justices' clerk's office is open.

(4) Where this Schedule or a rule where this Schedule applies to proceedings pursuant to that rule provides a period of time within which or by which a certain act is to be performed in the course of relevant proceedings, that period may not be extended otherwise than by a direction of the justices' clerk or the court under paragraph 4(1) above.

(5) At the—

(a) transfer to a court of proceedings,

(b) postponement or adjournment of any hearing or directions appointment in the course of relevant proceedings, or

(c) conclusion of any such hearing or directions appointment other than one at which the proceedings are determined, or so soon thereafter as is practicable,

the justices' clerk or the court shall—

    (i) fix a date upon which the proceedings shall come before the justices' clerk or the court again for such purposes as the justices' clerk or the court directs, which date shall, where paragraph (a) applies, be as soon as possible after the transfer, and

    (ii) give notice to the resident party of the date so fixed.

*Attendance at directions appointment and hearing*

**6.** (1) The resident party shall attend a directions appointment of which he has been given notice in accordance with paragraph 4 above unless the justices' clerk or the court otherwise directs.

(2) Where at the time and place appointed for a hearing or directions appointment the resident party does not appear the justices' clerk or the court shall not proceed with the hearing or appointment unless—

(a) the proceedings relate to an application filed by the resident party, or

(b) the court is satisfied that the resident party has received reasonable notice of the hearing or appointment.

(3) Where at the time and place appointed for a hearing or directions appointment the non-resident party does not appear the court may proceed with the hearing or appointment where the proceedings relate to an order or application sent by the Lord Chancellor to the court under the Act.

(4) Nothing in this Schedule shall be taken as preventing either party from appearing at any hearing or directions appointment.

*Documentary evidence*

**7.** (1) A party shall file, at or by such time as the justices' clerk or the court directs or, in the absence of a direction, before the hearing or appointment—

(a) written statements of the substance of the oral evidence which he intends to adduce at a hearing or a directions appointment, which shall—

    (i) be dated,

    (ii) be signed by the person making the statement,

    (iii) contain a declaration that the maker of the statement believes it to be true and understands that it may be placed before the court, and

    (iv) show in the top right-hand corner of the first page—

        (a) the initials and surname of the person making the statement,

        (b) the number of the statement in relation to the maker,

        (c) the date on which the statement was made, and

        (d) the party on whose behalf it is filed, and

(b) copies of any documents upon which he intends to rely at a hearing or a directions appointment.

(2) A party may, subject to any direction of the justices' clerk or the court about the timing of statements under this rule, file a statement which is supplementary to a statement served under sub-paragraph (1).

(3) Where a non-resident party files a statement or document under this rule, he shall also file a copy of it for service on the resident party; and the justices' clerk shall on receipt of that copy serve it on the resident party.

(4) At a hearing or directions appointment a party may not without the leave of the justices' clerk, in the case of a directions appointment, or the court—

(a) adduce evidence, or

(b) seek to rely on a document,

in respect of which he has failed to comply with the requirements of sub-paragraphs (1) and, where applicable, (3).

*Amendment*

**8.** (1) A party amending a document shall file the amended document with the justices' clerk; and the amendments shall be identified.

(2) Paragraph 7(3) above applies to an amended document filed under this paragraph.

*Oral evidence*

**9.** The justices' clerk or the court shall keep a note of the substance of any oral evidence given at a hearing or directions appointment.

*Hearing*

**10.** (1) Before the hearing, the justice or justices who will be dealing with the case shall read any documents which have been filed under paragraph 7 above in respect of the hearing.

(2) The justices' clerk at a directions appointment, or the court at a hearing or directions appointment, may give directions as to the order of speeches and evidence.

(3) After the final hearing, the court shall make its decision as soon as is practicable.

(4) Before the court makes an order or refuses an application, the justices' clerk shall record in writing—

(a) the names of the justice or justices constituting the court by which the decision is made, and

(b) in consultation with the justice or justices, the reasons for the court's decision and any findings of fact.

(5) After the court announces its decision, the justices' clerk shall as soon as practicable make a record in writing of any order.

(6) Where, under subsection (4) of section 7 of the Domestic Proceedings and Magistrates' Courts Act 1978, a court decides to treat an application under section 7 as if it were an application for an order under section 2 of that Act, the court shall indicate orally which of grounds (a) and (b) in that subsection it considers applicable and a memorandum of that decision and the grounds therefor shall be entered in the court's register.

*Confidentiality of documents*

**11.** (1) No document, other than a record of an order, held by the court and relating to any proceedings shall be disclosed, other than to—

(a) a party,

(b) the legal representative of a party,

(c) the Lord Chancellor's Department, or

(d) the Legal Aid Board,

without leave of the justices' clerk or the court.

*Delegation by justices' clerk*

**12.** (1) In this paragraph, 'employed as a clerk in court' has the same meaning as in rule 2(1) of the Justices' Clerks (Qualifications of Assistants) Rules 1979.

(2) Anything authorised to be done by, to or before a justices' clerk under this Schedule or under a rule to which this Schedule applies may be done instead by, to or before a person employed as a clerk in court where that person is appointed by the magistrates' courts committee to assist him and where that person has been specifically authorised by the justices' clerk for that purpose.

(3) Any authorisation by the justices' clerk under sub-paragraph (2) shall be recorded in writing at the time the authority is given or as soon as practicable thereafter.

*Application of section 97 of the Magistrates' Courts Act 1980*

**13.** (1) Subject to sub-paragraph (2) below, section 97 of the Magistrates' Courts Act 1980 shall apply to proceedings to which this Schedule applies as it applies to a hearing of a complaint under that section.

(2) The power of a justice under section 97 of that Act to issue a witness summons may be exercised by a justices' clerk.

SCHEDULE 1

PART I                                                                          Rule 9(1)

Notice to payer of registration of maintenance order
To[1]
I hereby give notice that on          day of          19  I registered a maintenance order (copy attached) made by the                    court in the Republic of Ireland ordering you to pay[2]                    the sum of[3]
You are entitled to appeal to the                    magistrates' court within one calendar month from the date of service of this notice to set aside the registration of the order on one of the following grounds:—

(a) that the registration is contrary to public policy;
(b) if you did not appear in the proceedings in the Republic of Ireland, that you were not served with the summons or other notice of the proceedings either in sufficient time to enable you to arrange for your defence or in accordance with the law of the place where you were residing;
(c) that the order is irreconcilable with a judgment given in the United Kingdom in proceedings between you and the above-mentioned payee.

JC
*Justices' Clerk*

[1] Insert name and address of payer.
[2] Insert name and address of payee.
[3] Insert amount and period, eg monthly.

PART II                                                                         Rule 9(3)

Notice to payee that maintenance order has not been registered
To[1]
I hereby give notice that I have not registered a maintenance order made by the court in the Republic of Ireland ordering[2]

to pay you the sum of[3]                              on the ground that[4]
You are entitled to appeal against my decision to the                    magistrates' court to have the order registered.

If you wish to appeal, you may do so by completing and returning to me the notice of appeal set out below. Unless you are present in court or legally represented when the appeal is heard, the court may dismiss the case. If you wish to be legally represented, you may apply to[5]                    for legal aid and advice.

JC

Justices' Clerk

[1] Insert name and address of payee.
[2] Insert name and address of payer.
[3] Insert amount and period, eg, monthly.
[4] Insert one of the grounds specified in section 6(5) of the Maintenance Orders (Reciprocal Enforcement) Act 1972.
[5] Insert the name and address of the Secretary of the appropriate legal aid committee.

MAINTENANCE ORDERS (RECIPROCAL ENFORCEMENT) ACT 1972

Appeal by way of complaint

Magistrates' Court (Code)

Date:
Defendant:
Address:
Matter of     The                    Court at                    in the Republic of
Complaint:   Ireland having on                    made a maintenance order requiring the defendant to pay to the undersigned complainant the sum of £        [weekly or as the case may be] and the order having been sent to the Justices' Clerk for the said Magistrates' Court for registration; the Justices' Clerk has refused to register the order on the ground that

I hereby appeal to the said Magistrates' Court against the refusal to register this order.

Signed                    (Complainant)

## RECOVERY ABROAD OF MAINTENANCE (CONVENTION COUNTRIES) ORDER 1975

**Dated** 18 March 1975

**SI 1975 No 423**

**1.**   This Order may be cited as the Recovery Abroad of Maintenance (Convention Countries) Order 1975 and shall come into operation on 12 April 1975.
**2.**   The countries and territories specified in the Schedule to this Order, being countries and territories outside the United Kingdom to which the United Nations Convention on the Recovery Abroad of Maintenance done at New York on 20th June 1956 extends, are hereby declared to be convention countries for the purposes of Part II of the Maintenance Orders (Reciprocal Enforcement) Act 1972.

SCHEDULE                                                        Article 2

CONVENTION COUNTRIES

| | |
|---|---|
| Algeria | Bosnia and Herzegovina[3] |
| Australia[3] | Brazil |
| Austria | Burkino Faso[3] |
| Barbados | Cape Verde[3] |
| Belgium | Central African Republic |

Chile
Croatia[3]
Cyprus[3]
Czech Republic[3]
Denmark
Ecuador
Finland
France (including the overseas departments of Guadeloupe, Guiana, Martinique and Réunion)
  Comoro Archipelago
  French Polynesia
  New Caledonia and Dependencies
  St Pierre and Miquelon
Germany
Greece
Guatemala
Haiti
Holy See
Hungary
Ireland[4]
Israel
Italy
Luxembourg
Mexico[3]

Monaco
Morocco
Netherlands (Kingdom in Europe, Netherlands Antilles and Aruba[3])
New Zealand[3]
Niger
Norway
Pakistan
Philippines
Poland
Portugal
Romania[3]
Slovakia[3]
Slovenia[3]
Spain
Sri Lanka
Suriname[2]
Sweden
Switzerland[1]
The former Yugoslav Republic of Macedonia[3]
Tunisia
Turkey
Uruguay[3]
Yugoslavia

[1] *Switzerland was added to the schedule by SI 1978 No 279 with effect from 23 March 1978.*
[2] *Suriname was added by SI 1982 No 1530 with effect from 1 December 1982.*
[3] *Countries added or names changed by SI 1996 No 1925 with effect from 1 September 1996.*
[4] *Ireland added by SI 2002/2839, art 2(2), with effect from 15 January 2003.*

## MAGISTRATES' COURTS (RECOVERY ABROAD OF MAINTENANCE) RULES 1975

**Dated** 21 March 1975

**SI 1975 No 488**

The Lord Chancellor, in exercise of the power conferred on him by section 15 of the Justices of the Peace Act 1949, as extended by section 122 of the Magistrates' Courts Act 1952, section 5(1) of the Justices of the Peace Act 1968 and sections 27(8) to (10), 32(1) to (3), (6) and (8), 33(4) and (5), 35(4) and 38(2) of the Maintenance Orders (Reciprocal Enforcement) Act 1972, after consultation with the Rule Committee appointed under the said section 15, hereby makes the following Rules—

**1.**   These Rules may be cited as the Magistrates' Courts (Recovery Abroad of Maintenance) Rules 1975 and shall come into operation on 12 April 1975.

**2.**   (1) In these Rules, unless the context otherwise requires—
    'the Act' means the Maintenance Orders (Reciprocal Enforcement) Act 1972; and
    'his register', in relation to a justices' clerk, means the register kept by that clerk in pursuance of rule 54 of the Magistrates' Courts Rules 1968.
    (2) The Interpretation Act 1889 shall apply to the interpretation of these Rules as it applies to the interpretation of an Act of Parliament.

**Note.** Interpretation Act 1889 is replaced by Interpretation Act 1978.

**3.**   The officer of any court, by or in relation to whom anything is to be done in pursuance of any provision of Part II of the Act, shall, where that court is a magistrates' court, be the justices' clerk.

**3A.**   (1) On receipt of an application for the recovery of maintenance in England and Wales sent from the Lord Chancellor to a magistrates' court under section 27B of the Act, the justices' clerk shall—

(a)  fix the date, time and place for a hearing or a directions appointment, allowing sufficient time for service under this rule to be effected at least 21 days before the date so fixed; and

(b)  serve copies of the application and any accompanying documents, together with a notice stating the date, time and place so fixed, on the respondent.

(2) Within 14 days of service under this rule, the respondent shall file an answer to the application in the appropriate form.

**4.**   Where a magistrates' court dismisses an application under section 27A of the Act (application for recovery of maintenance), or an application by a person in a convention country for the variation of a registered order, the justices' clerk shall send written notice of the court's decision to the Secretary of State and any such notice shall include a statement of the justices' reasons for their decision.

**5.**   (1) Where a magistrates' court makes an order which is required under section 27C(7) of the Act to be registered, the justices' clerk shall enter and sign a minute or memorandum of the order in his register.

(2) Where a justices' clerk in pursuance of section 32(2) or (3) of the Act (transfer of orders), receives a certified copy of an order, he shall cause the order to be registered in his court by means of a minute or memorandum entered and signed by him in his register.

(3) Every minute or memorandum entered in pursuance of paragraph (1) or (2) above shall specify the section and subsection of the Act under which the order in question is registered.

**5A.**   Where an application under section 26(1) or (2) of the Act or a certificate under section 26(3A) of the Act is required to be registered in a magistrates' court in pursuance of the Recovery of Maintenance (United States of America) Order 1979, the justices' clerk shall enter and sign a minute or memorandum of the application or certificate in his register.

**6.**   (1) Where a justices' clerk registers an order in pursuance of section 27C(7) or 32(2) or (3) of the Act, he shall send written notice to the Secretary of State that the order has been duly registered.

(2) Where a justices' clerk is required by section 32(6) of the Act to give notice of the registration of an order he shall do so by sending written notice to the officer specified in that subsection that the order has been duly registered.

**7.**   (1) A justices' clerk to whom payments are made by virtue of section 27C, section 33(3A) or section 34A of the Act shall send those payments by post to such person or authority as the Lord Chancellor may from time to time direct.

(2) Where it appears to the justices' clerk to whom payments under a registered order are made that any sums payable under the order are in arrear he may and, if such sums are in arrear to an amount equal

(a)  in the case of payments to be made monthly or less frequently, to twice the sum payable periodically; or

(b)  in any other case, to four times the sum payable periodically,

he shall, whether the person for whose benefit the payment should have been made requests him to do so or not, proceed in his own name for the recovery of those sums, unless it appears to him that it is unreasonable in the circumstances to do so.

**7A.** (1) Where, in the exercise of the duty imposed under section 27C of the Act, or in the exercise of the powers conferred by virtue of section 33(3A) or section 34A of the Act, the court orders that payments under the order are to be made by a particular means, the clerk of the court shall record on the copy of the order the means of payment which the court has ordered and notify in writing, as soon as practicable, the person liable to make payments under the order of how the payments are to be made.

(2) Where, in the exercise of any of the aforesaid powers, the court orders payment to the clerk of the court, or to the clerk of any other magistrates' court, by a method of payment falling within section 59(6) of the Magistrates' Courts Act 1980 (standing order, etc) the clerk of the court to whom payments are to be made shall notify the person liable to make the payments under the order of the number and location of the account into which the payments are to be made.

(3) Where, under section 34A(4) of the Act, the clerk of the court receives an application from an interested party for the method of payment to be varied, the clerk shall notify in writing, as soon as practicable, that party and, where practicable, any other interested party, of the result of the application, including any decision to refer the matter to the court; where the clerk grants the application he shall record the variation on the copy of the order.

**7B.** (1) In this rule 'an application' means an application under section 34 of the Act for the variation or revocation of a registered order.

(2) An application which is made directly to the registering court shall be filed in an appropriate form.

(3) On receipt of an application, either filed in accordance with paragraph (2) or sent from the Lord Chancellor under section 34(3) of the Act, the justices' clerk shall—

(a) fix the date, time and place for a hearing or a directions appointment; and

(b) notify the applicant of the date, time and place so fixed.

**8.** (1) Notice under section 35(4) of the Act (variation of orders by magistrates' courts) of the making of an application for the variation or revocation of a registered order and of the time and place appointed for the hearing of the complaint shall be in the form specified in the Schedule to these Rules and shall be sent by post by the justices' clerk to the Secretary of State for onward transmission to the appropriate authority in the convention country in which the respondent is residing.

(2) The time appointed for the hearing of the said application shall be not less than six weeks later than the date on which the said notice is sent to the Secretary of State.

**9.** (1) Where a magistrates' court receives from the Secretary of State a request under section 38(1) of the Act (taking evidence at request of court in convention country) to take the evidence of any person, that evidence shall be taken in accordance with the provisions of this rule.

(2) Subject to paragraph (3) below—

(a) the evidence shall be taken in the same manner as if the person concerned were a witness in proceedings on a complaint;

(b) any oral evidence so taken shall be put into writing and read to the person who gave it, who shall be required to sign the document; and

(c) the justices by whom the evidence of any person is so taken shall certify at the foot of any document setting out the evidence of, or produced in evidence by, that person that such evidence was taken, or document received in evidence, as the case may be, by them.

(3) Where the request referred to in section 38(1) of the Act includes a request that the evidence be taken in a particular manner, the court by which the evidence is taken shall, so far as circumstances permit, comply with that request.

**10.** (1) Where a justices' clerk receives from the Secretary of State a request under section 38(1) of the Act to take the evidence of any person, that evidence shall be taken in accordance with the provisions of this rule.

(2) Subject to paragraph (3) below—

(a) the person whose evidence is to be taken shall be examined on oath by or before the justices' clerk;

(b) any oral evidence shall be put into writing and read to that person who shall be required to sign the document; and

(c) the justices' clerk shall certify at the foot of any document setting out the evidence of, or produced in evidence by, that person that such evidence was taken, or document received in evidence, as the case may be, by him.

(3) Where the request referred to in section 38(1) of the Act includes a request that the evidence be taken in a particular manner the justices' clerk by whom the evidence is taken shall, so far as circumstances permit, comply with that request.

(4) For the purposes of this rule a justices' clerk shall have the like power to administer oaths as has a single justice of the peace.

**11.** Any document such as is mentioned in paragraph (2)(c) of rule 9 or 10 of these Rules shall be sent to the Secretary of State for onward transmission to the appropriate authority in the convention country in which the request referred to in section 38(1) of the Act originated.

**12.** (1) Schedule 2 shall apply to proceedings pursuant to rules 3A and 7B above.

(2) In Schedule 2 as it applies to rule 3A, 'the resident party' and 'the non-resident party' shall be taken to mean the respondent and the applicant respectively.

(3) In Schedule 2 as it applies to rule 7B, 'the resident party' and 'the non-resident party' shall be taken to mean the payer and the payee under the order in question respectively.

SCHEDULE 1                                                                    Rule 8(1)

FORM OF NOTICE UNDER SECTION 35(4) OF THE MAINTENANCE ORDERS (RECIPROCAL ENFORCEMENT) ACT 1972

Magistrates' Court (*Code*)

Date                                 :

To the defendant     :

    of                          :

Complaint has been made by

The complainant       :

    of                          :

who states that by an order made on

under the                                Act by

the                                  Magistrates' Court you were

ordered as follows:

and applies for that order to be [revoked] [varied by an order requiring                                ] on the ground that

The hearing of the complaint will be on

Date of hearing          :                           at            m.

    at the                     :                 Magistrates' Court.

JC

Justices' Clerk

NOTE: If you do not appear at the time and place specified above the court may proceed in your absence. If you wish to make written representations to the court you may do so on the enclosed form.

SCHEDULE 2

RULES OF PROCEDURE

**1.** In this Schedule, and in any rule where this Schedule applies to proceedings pursuant to that rule, unless the context otherwise requires—

'business day' means any day other than—

(a)  a Saturday, Sunday, Christmas or Good Friday; or

(b)  a bank holiday, that is to say, a day which is, or is to be observed as, a bank holiday, or a holiday, under the Banking and Financial Dealings Act 1971, in England and Wales,

'directions appointment' means a hearing for directions under paragraph 4 below,

'file' means deposit with the justices' clerk,

'justices' clerk' has the meaning assigned to it by section 70 of the Justices of the Peace Act 1979 and includes any person who performs a justices' clerk's functions by virtue of paragraph 12 below,

'leave' includes approval,

'note' includes a record made by mechanical or electronic means, and

'proceedings' means proceedings to which this Schedule applies.

*Transfer of proceedings*

**2.**  (1)  Where—

(a)  any proceedings are relevant proceedings within the meaning of section 93 of the Children Act 1989, and

(b)  the justices' clerk or the court receives a request in writing from the resident party that the proceedings be transferred to another magistrates' court,

the justices' clerk or court shall issue a certificate in the appropriate form, granting or refusing the request in accordance with any Order made by the Lord Chancellor under Part I of Schedule 11 to the Children Act 1989.

(2)  Where a request is granted under paragraph (1) the justices' clerk shall send a copy of the certificate—

(a)  to the resident party,

(b)  to the Lord Chancellor's Department, and

(c)  to the magistrates' court to which the proceedings are to be transferred.

(3)  Any consent given or refused by a justices' clerk in accordance with any Order made by the Lord Chancellor under Part I of Schedule 11 shall be recorded in writing by the justices' clerk at the time it is given or refused or as soon as practicable thereafter.

*Service*

**3.**  (1)  Where service of a document is required by this Schedule or by a rule where this Schedule applies to proceedings pursuant to that rule it may be effected, unless the contrary is indicated—

(a)  if the person to be served is not known by the person serving to be acting by solicitor—

(i)  by delivering it to him personally, or

(ii)  by delivering it at, or by sending it by first-class post to, his residence or last known residence, or

(b)  if the person to be served is known by the person serving to be acting by solicitor—

(i)  by delivering the document at, or sending it by first-class post to, the solicitor's address for service,

(ii)  where the solicitor's address for service includes a numbered box at a document exchange, by leaving the document at that document

exchange or at a document exchange which transmits documents on every business day to that document exchange, or
   (iii)   by sending a legible copy of the document by facsimile transmission to the solicitor's office.
   (2) In this paragraph, 'first-class post' means first-class post which has been pre-paid or in respect of which pre-payment is not required.
   (3) A document shall, unless the contrary is proved, be deemed to have been served—
   (a)   in the case of service by first-class post, on the second business day after posting, and
   (b)   in the case of service in accordance with sub-paragraph 1(b)(ii), on the second business day after the day on which it is left at the document exchange.
   (4) In any proceedings where this Schedule, or a rule where this Schedule applies, requires a document to be served, the court or the justices' clerk may, without prejudice to any power under paragraph 4 below, direct that—
   (a)   the requirement shall not apply;
   (b)   the time specified by the rules for complying with the requirement shall be abridged to such extent as may be specified in the direction;
   (c)   service shall be effected in such manner as may be specified in the direction.

*Directions*

**4.**   (1) The justices' clerk or the court may give, vary or revoke directions for the conduct of the proceedings, including—
   (a)   the timetable for the proceedings,
   (b)   varying the time within which or by which an act is required by this Schedule or by a rule where this Schedule applies to proceedings pursuant to that rule to be done,
   (c)   the service of documents, and
   (d)   the submission of evidence,
and the justices' clerk shall, on receipt of an application or of any other document by which proceedings are commenced, consider whether such directions need to be given.
   (2) Where the justices' clerk or a single justice who is holding a directions appointment considers, for whatever reason, that it is inappropriate to give a direction on a particular matter, he shall refer the matter to the court which may give any appropriate direction.
   (3) Directions under sub-paragraph (1) may be given, varied or revoked either—
   (a)   of the justices' clerk's or the court's own motion having given the resident party an opportunity to attend and be heard or to make written representations, or
   (b)   on the written request of either party specifying the direction which is sought.
   (4) On receipt of a request under sub-paragraph (3)(b) the justices' clerk shall—
   (a)   make the direction sought, or
   (b)   fix a date for a hearing to consider the request.

*Timing of proceedings*

**5.**   (1) Any period of time fixed by this Schedule or by a rule where this Schedule applies to proceedings pursuant to that rule, or by any order or direction, for doing any act shall be reckoned in accordance with this rule.
   (2) Where the period, being a period of 7 days or less, would include a day which is not a business day, that day shall be excluded.
   (3) Where the time fixed for filing a document with the justices' clerk expires on a day on which the justices' clerk's office is closed, and for that reason the document cannot be filed on that day, the document shall be filed in time if it is filed on the next day on which the justices' clerk's office is open.

(4) Where this Schedule or a rule where this Schedule applies to proceedings pursuant to that rule provides a period of time within which or by which a certain act is to be performed in the course of relevant proceedings, that period may not be extended otherwise than by a direction of the justices' clerk or the court under paragraph 4(1) above.

(5) At the—

(a) transfer to a court of proceedings,

(b) postponement or adjournment of any hearing or directions appointment in the course of relevant proceedings, or

(c) conclusion of any such hearing or directions appointment other than one at which the proceedings are determined, or so soon thereafter as is practicable,

the justices' clerk or the court shall—

    (i) fix a date upon which the proceedings shall come before the justices' clerk or the court again for such purposes as the justices' clerk or the court directs, which date shall, where paragraph (a) applies, be as soon as possible after the transfer, and

    (ii) give notice to the resident party of the date so fixed.

*Attendance at directions appointment and hearing*

**6.** (1) The resident party shall attend a directions appointment of which he has been given notice in accordance with paragraph 4 above unless the justices' clerk or the court otherwise directs.

(2) Where at the time and place appointed for a hearing or directions appointment the resident party does not appear the justices' clerk or the court shall not proceed with the hearing or appointment unless—

(a) the proceedings relate to an application filed by the resident party, or

(b) the court is satisfied that the resident party has received reasonable notice of the hearing or appointment.

(3) Where at the time and place appointed for a hearing or directions appointment the non-resident party does not appear the court may proceed with the hearing or appointment where the proceedings relate to an order or application sent by the Lord Chancellor to the court under the Act.

(4) Nothing in this Schedule shall be taken as preventing either party from appearing at any hearing or directions appointment.

*Documentary evidence*

**7.** (1) A party shall file, at or by such time as the justices' clerk or the court directs or, in the absence of a direction, before the hearing or appointment—

(a) written statements of the substance of the oral evidence which he intends to adduce at a hearing or a directions appointment, which shall—

    (i) be dated,

    (ii) be signed by the person making the statement,

    (iii) contain a declaration that the maker of the statement believes it to be true and understands that it may be placed before the court, and

    (iv) show in the top right-hand corner of the first page—

        (a) the initials and surname of the person making the statement,

        (b) the number of the statement in relation to the maker,

        (c) the date on which the statement was made, and

        (d) the party on whose behalf it is filed, and

(b) copies of any documents upon which he intends to rely at a hearing or a directions appointment.

(2) A party may, subject to any direction of the justices' clerk or the court about the timing of statements under this rule, file a statement which is supplementary to a statement served under sub-paragraph (1).

(3) Where a non-resident party files a statement or document under this rule, he shall also file a copy of it for service on the resident party; and the justices' clerk shall on receipt of that copy serve it on the resident party.

(4) At a hearing or directions appointment a party may not without the leave of the justices' clerk, in the case of a directions appointment, or the court—

(a) adduce evidence, or

(b) seek to rely on a document,

in respect of which he has failed to comply with the requirements of sub-paragraphs (1) and, where applicable, (3).

*Amendment*

**8.** (1) A party amending a document shall file the amended document with the justices' clerk; and the amendments shall be identified.

(2) Paragraph 7(3) above applies to an amended document filed under this paragraph.

*Oral evidence*

**9.** The justices' clerk or the court shall keep a note of the substance of any oral evidence given at a hearing or directions appointment.

*Hearing*

**10.** (1) Before the hearing, the justice or justices who will be dealing with the case shall read any documents which have been filed under paragraph 7 above in respect of the hearing.

(2) The justices' clerk at a directions appointment, or the court at a hearing or directions appointment, may give directions as to the order of speeches and evidence.

(3) After the final hearing, the court shall make its decision as soon as is practicable.

(4) Before the court makes an order or refuses an application, the justices' clerk shall record in writing—

(a) the names of the justice or justices constituting the court by which the decision is made, and

(b) in consultation with the justice or justices, the reasons for the court's decision and any findings of fact.

(5) After the court announces its decision, the justices' clerk shall as soon as practicable make a record in writing of any order.

(6) Where, under subsection (4) of section 7 of the Domestic Proceedings and Magistrates' Courts Act 1978, a court decides to treat an application under section 7 as if it were an application for an order under section 2 of that Act, the court shall indicate orally which of grounds (a) and (b) in that subsection it considers applicable and a memorandum of that decision and the grounds therefor shall be entered in the court's register.

*Confidentiality of documents*

**11.** (1) No document, other than a record of an order, held by the court and relating to any proceedings shall be disclosed, other than to—

(a) a party,

(b) the legal representative of a party,

(c) the Lord Chancellor's Department, or

(d) the Legal Aid Board,

without leave of the justices' clerk or the court.

*Delegation by justices' clerk*

**12.** (1) In this paragraph, 'employed as a clerk in court' has the same meaning as in rule 2(1) of the Justices' Clerks (Qualifications of Assistants) Rules 1979.

(2) Anything authorised to be done by, to or before a justices' clerk under this Schedule or under a rule to which this Schedule applies may be done instead by, to or before a person employed as a clerk in court where that person is appointed by the magistrates' courts committee to assist him and where that person has been specifically authorised by the justices' clerk for that purpose.

(3) Any authorisation by the justices' clerk under sub-paragraph (2) shall be recorded in writing at the time the authority is given or as soon as practicable thereafter.

*Application of section 97 of the Magistrates' Courts Act 1980*

**13.** (1) Subject to sub-paragraph (2) below, section 97 of the Magistrates' Courts Act 1980 shall apply to proceedings to which this Schedule applies as it applies to a hearing of a complaint under that section.

(2) The power of a justice under section 97 of that Act to issue a witness summons may be exercised by a justices' clerk.

## RECIPROCAL ENFORCEMENT OF MAINTENANCE ORDERS (DESIGNATION OF RECIPROCATING COUNTRIES) ORDER 1975

**Dated** 19 December 1975

**SI 1975 No 2187**

At the Court at Buckingham Palace, the 19 day of December 1975
Present,
The Queen's Most Excellent Majesty in Council

Whereas Her Majesty is satisfied that, in the event of the benefits conferred by Part I of the Maintenance Orders (Reciprocal Enforcement) Act 1972, being applied to, or to particular classes of, maintenance orders made by the courts of each of the countries and territories specified in column (1) of the Schedule to this Order, similar benefits will in that country or territory be applied to, or to those classes of, maintenance orders made by the courts of the United Kingdom:

And whereas Her Majesty considers the provisions contained in Article 4 of this Order expedient for the purpose of securing the matters set out in section 24 of the said Act of 1972:

Now, therefore, Her Majesty, in exercise of the powers conferred by sections 1 and 24 of the Maintenance Orders (Reciprocal Enforcement) Act, 1972, is pleased, by and with the advice of Her Privy Council, to order, and it is hereby ordered, as follows—

**1.** This Order may be cited as the Reciprocal Enforcement of Maintenance Orders (Designation of Reciprocating Countries) Order 1975 and shall come into operation on 28 January 1976.

**2.** (1) In this Order—

'the Act of 1972' means the Maintenance Orders (Reciprocal Enforcement) Act 1972;

'the Act of 1920' means the Maintenance Orders (Facilities for Enforcement) Act 1920;

'column (1)' and 'column (2)' mean respectively columns (1) and (2) of the Schedule to this Order.

(2) The Interpretation Act 1889 shall apply for the interpretation of this Order as it applies for the interpretation of an Act of Parliament.

**Note.** Interpretation Act 1889 is replaced by Interpretation Act 1978.

**3.** Each of the countries and territories specified in column (1) is hereby designated as a reciprocating country for the purposes of Part I of the Act of 1972 as regards maintenance orders of the description specified in respect of that country or territory in column (2).

**4.** (1) Sections 5, 12 to 15, 17, 18 and 21 of the Act of 1972 shall apply in relation to a maintenance order transmitted under section 2 or 3 of the Act of 1920 to one of the countries and territories specified in column (1), being an order of the description specified in respect of that country or territory in column (2) to which immediately before the coming into operation of this Order the Act of 1920 applied, as they apply in relation to a maintenance order sent to that country or territory in pursuance of section 2 of the Act of 1972 or made by virtue of section 3 or 4 of the Act of 1972 and confirmed by a competent court in that country or territory.

(2) Sections 8 to 21 of the Act of 1972 shall apply in relation to a maintenance order made in one of the countries and territories specified in column (1), being an order of the description specified in respect of that country or territory in column (2) to which immediately before the coming into operation of this Order the Act of 1920 applied and not being an order which immediately before that date is registered in the High Court or the High Court of Justice in Northern Ireland under section 1 of the Act of 1920, as they apply in relation to a registered order.

(3) A maintenance order made by a court in one of the countries and territories specified in column (1) being an order of the description specified in respect of that country or territory in column (2) which has been confirmed by a court in England, Wales or Northern Ireland under section 4 of the Act of 1920 and is in force immediately before the coming into operation of this Order, shall be registered under section 7(5) of the Act of 1972 in like manner as if it had been confirmed by that court in England, Wales or Northern Ireland under subsection (2) of that section.

(4) Any proceedings brought under or by virtue of any provision of the Act of 1920 in a court in England, Wales or Northern Ireland which are pending immediately before the coming into operation of this Order, being proceedings affecting a person resident in one of the countries and territories specified in column (1), shall be continued as if they had been brought under or by virtue of the corresponding provision of the Act of 1972.

SCHEDULE                                                    Article 3

COUNTRIES AND TERRITORIES DESIGNATED AS RECIPROCATING COUNTRIES

| (1)<br>Country or territory | (2)<br>Description of maintenance orders to which designation extends |
| --- | --- |
| Barbados | Maintenance orders generally. |
| Bermuda | Maintenance orders generally. |
| Ghana | Maintenance orders other than—<br>(a) affiliation orders, and<br>(b) maintenance orders of the description contained in paragraph (b) of the definition of 'maintenance order' in the said section 21(1). |
| India | Maintenance orders other than—<br>(a) affiliation orders<br>(b) maintenance orders of the description contained in paragraph (b) of the definition of 'maintenance order' in the said section 21(1); and<br>(c) orders obtained by or in favour of a public authority. |
| Kenya | Maintenance orders other than—<br>(a) affiliation orders, and |

| (1) Country or territory | (2) Description of maintenance orders to which designation extends |
|---|---|
| | (b) maintenance orders of the description contained in paragraph (b) of the definition of 'maintenance order', in the said section 21(1). |
| Malta | Maintenance orders generally. |
| New Brunswick | Maintenance orders other than— |
| | (a) affiliation orders; |
| | (b) maintenance orders of the description contained in paragraph (b) of the definition of 'maintenance order' in the said section 21(1); and |
| | (c) orders obtained by or in favour of a public authority. |
| Northwest Territories of Canada | Maintenance orders other than— |
| | (a) affiliation orders; |
| | (b) maintenance order of the description contained in paragraph (b) of the definition of 'maintenance order' in the said section 21(1); and |
| | (c) orders obtained by or in favour of a public authority. |
| The Republic of South Africa | Maintenance orders other than— |
| | (a) affiliation orders, and |
| | (b) maintenance orders of the description contained in paragraph (b) of the definition of 'maintenance order' in the said section 21(1). |

## MAINTENANCE ORDERS (FACILITIES FOR ENFORCEMENT) (REVOCATION) ORDER 1975

**Dated** 19 December 1975

**SI 1975 No 2188**

Her Majesty, in exercise of the powers conferred by section 19 of the Maintenance Orders Act 1958, is pleased, by and with the advice of Her Privy Council, to order, and it is hereby ordered, as follows—

**1.**   This Order may be cited as the Maintenance Orders (Facilities for Enforcement) (Revocation) Order 1975 and shall come into operation on 28 January, 1976.

**2.**   (1) Insofar as the Maintenance Orders (Facilities for Enforcement) Order 1959 provides that the Maintenance Orders (Facilities for Enforcement) Act 1920, shall extend to the countries and territories specified in paragraph (2) below, that Order is revoked, and accordingly the names of those countries and territories shall be omitted from the First Schedule to that Order.

   (2) The countries and territories referred to in paragraph (1) above are—

   Barbados;
   Bermuda;
   Ghana;
   India;
   Kenya Colony;
   Kenya Protectorate;
   Malta;
   New Brunswick;
   Northwest Territories of Canada;
   The Republic of South Africa.

## EVIDENCE (PROCEEDINGS IN OTHER JURISDICTIONS) (CAYMAN ISLANDS) ORDER 1978

**Dated** 20 December 1978

**SI 1978 No 1890**

At the Court at Buckingham Palace, the 20th day of December 1978
Present,
The Queen's Most Excellent Majesty in Council

Her Majesty, in exercise of the powers conferred upon Her by section 10(3) of the Evidence (Proceedings in Other Jurisdictions) Act 1975 and of all other powers enabling Her in that behalf, is pleased, by and with the advice of Her Privy Council, to order, and it is hereby ordered, as follows—

**1.** (1) This Order may be cited as the Evidence (Proceedings in Other Jurisdictions) (Cayman Islands) Order 1978.
(2) This Order shall come into operation on 10 January 1979.

**2.** The Interpretation Act 1889 shall apply, with the necessary adaptations, for the purpose of interpreting this Order and otherwise in relation thereto as it applies for the purpose of interpreting, and in relation to, Acts of Parliament.
**Note.** Interpretation Act 1889 is replaced by Interpretation Act 1978.

**3.** Sections 1 to 3 and 5 to 10 of, and Schedule 2 to, the Evidence (Proceedings in Other Jurisdictions) Act 1975, with the exceptions, adaptations and modifications specified in the Schedule hereto, shall extend to the Cayman Islands.

SCHEDULE TO THE ORDER        Article 3

PROVISIONS OF THE EVIDENCE (PROCEEDINGS IN OTHER JURISDICTIONS) ACT 1975 AS EXTENDED TO THE CAYMAN ISLANDS

EVIDENCE FOR CIVIL PROCEEDINGS

*Application to Grand Court for assistance in obtaining evidence for civil proceedings in other court*

**1.** Where an application is made to the Grand Court for an order for evidence to be obtained in the Cayman Islands, and the court is satisfied—
   (a) that the application is made in pursuance of a request issued by or on behalf of a court or tribunal ('the requesting court') exercising jurisdiction in a country or territory outside the Cayman Islands; and
   (b) that the evidence to which the application relates is to be obtained for the purposes of civil proceedings which either have been instituted before the requesting court or whose institution before that court is contemplated,
the Grand Court shall have the powers conferred on it by the following provisions of this Act.

*Power of Grand Court to give effect to application for assistance*

**2.** (1) Subject to the provisions of this section, the Grand Court shall have power, on any such application as is mentioned in section 1 above, by order to make such provision for obtaining evidence in the Cayman Islands as may appear to the court to be appropriate for the purpose of giving effect to the request in pursuance of which the application is made; and any such order may require a person specified therein to take such steps as the court may consider appropriate for that purpose.

(2) Without prejudice to the generality of subsection (1) above but subject to the provisions of this section, an order under this section may, in particular, make provision—

  (a)  for the examination of witnesses, either orally or in writing;
  (b)  for the production of documents;
  (c)  for the inspection, photographing, preservation, custody or detention of any property;
  (d)  for the taking of samples of any property and the carrying out of any experiments on or with any property;
  (e)  for the medical examination of any person;
  (f)  without prejudice to paragraph (e) above, for the taking and testing of samples of blood from any person.

(3) An order under this section shall not require any particular steps to be taken unless they are steps which can be required to be taken by way of obtaining evidence for the purposes of civil proceedings in the court making the order (whether or not proceedings of the same description as those to which the application of the order relates); but this subsection shall not preclude the making of an order requiring a person to give testimony (either orally or in writing) otherwise than on oath where this is asked for by the requesting court.

(4) An order under this section shall not require a person—

  (a)  to state what documents relevant to the proceedings to which the application for the order relates are or have been in his possession, custody or power; or
  (b)  to produce any documents other than particular documents specified in the order as being documents appearing to the court making the order to be, or to be likely to be, in his possession, custody or power.

(5) A person who, by virtue of an order under this section, is required to attend at any place shall be entitled to the like conduct money and payment for expenses and loss of time as on attendance as a witness in civil proceedings before the court making the order.

*Privilege of witnesses*

**3.**  (1) A person shall not be compelled by virtue of an order under section 2 above to give any evidence which he could not be compelled to give—

  (a)  in civil proceedings in the Cayman Islands; or
  (b)  subject to subsection (2) below, in civil proceedings in the country or territory in which the requesting court exercises jurisdiction.

(2) Subsection (1)(b) above shall not apply unless the claim of the person in question to be exempt from giving the evidence is either—

  (a)  supported by a statement contained in the request (whether it is so supported unconditionally or subject to conditions that are fulfilled); or
  (b)  conceded by the applicant for the order;

and where such a claim made by any person is not supported or conceded as aforesaid he may (subject to the other provisions of this section) be required to give the evidence to which the claim relates but that evidence shall not be transmitted to the requesting court if that court, on the matter being referred to it, upholds the claim.

(3) Without prejudice to subsection (1) above, a person shall not be compelled by virtue of an order under section 2 above to give any evidence if his doing so would be prejudicial to the security of the United Kingdom, the Cayman Islands or any other territory for which the United Kingdom is responsible under international law; and a certificate signed by or on behalf of the Governor to the effect that it would be so prejudicial for that person to do so shall be conclusive evidence of that fact.

(4) In this section references to giving evidence include references to answering any question and to producing any document and reference in subsection (2) above to the transmission of evidence given by a person shall be construed accordingly.

EVIDENCE FOR CRIMINAL PROCEEDINGS

\*   \*   \*   \*   \*

EVIDENCE FOR INTERNATIONAL PROCEEDINGS

*Power of Grand Court to assist in obtaining evidence for international proceedings*

**6.** (1) The Governor may by order direct that, subject to such exceptions, adaptations or modifications as may be specified in the order, the provisions of sections 1 to 3 above shall have effect in relation to international proceedings of any description specified in the order.

(2) An order under this section may direct that sections 89 to 95 inclusive of the Penal Code shall have effect in relation to international proceedings to which the order applies as it has effect in relation to a judicial proceeding in a tribunal of a foreign state.

(3) In this section 'international proceedings' means proceedings before the International Court of Justice or any other court, tribunal, commission, body or authority (whether consisting of one or more persons) which, in pursuance of any international agreement or any resolution of the General Assembly of the United Nations, exercises any jurisdiction or performs any functions of a judicial nature or by way of arbitration, conciliation or inquiry or is appointed (whether permanently or temporarily) for the purposes of exercising any jurisdiction or performing any such functions.

SUPPLEMENTARY

*Rules of court*

**7.** The power to make rules of court conferred by section 21 of the Grand Court Law includes power to make rules of court—

(a) as to the manner in which applications may be made under section 1 above;

(b) as to the circumstances in which an order can be made under section 2 above;

(c) as to the manner of making references under subsection (2) of section 3 above.

*Consequential amendments and repeals*

**8.** (2) The enactments mentioned in Schedule 2 to this Act are hereby repealed as respects the Cayman Islands to the extent specified in the third column of that Schedule.

(3) Nothing in this section shall affect—

(a) any application to any court or judge which is pending at the commencement of this Act;

(b) any certificate given for the purposes of any such application;

(c) any power to make an order on such an application; or

(d) the operation or enforcement of any order made on such an application.

(4) Subsection (3) above is without prejudice to section 38(2) of the Interpretation Act 1889 (effect of repeals).

*Interpretation*

**9.** (1) In this Act

'civil proceedings', in relation to the requesting court, means proceedings in any civil or commercial matter;

'Governor' means the Governor of the Cayman Islands;

'Grand Court' means the Grand Court of the Cayman Islands;

'requesting court' has the meaning given in section 1 above;

'property' includes any land, chattel or other corporeal property of any description;

'request' includes any commission, order or other process issued by or on behalf of the requesting court.

(3) Any power conferred by this Act to make an order includes power to revoke or vary any such order by a subsequent order.

(4) Nothing in this Act shall be construed as enabling any court to make an order that is binding on the Crown or on any person in his capacity as an officer or servant of the Crown.

(5) Except so far as the context otherwise requires, any reference in this Act to any enactment is a reference to that enactment as amended or extended by or under any other enactment.

*Commencement*

**10.** The provisions of this Act shall come into force on such date as the Governor may by notice published in the Gazette of the Cayman Islands appoint.

SCHEDULE 2 TO THE ACT         Section 8(2)

REPEALS

| Chapter | Short Title | Extent |
|---|---|---|
| 19 & 20 Vict c 113. | The Foreign Tribunals Evidence Act 1856. | The whole Act. |
| 22 Vict c 20. | The Evidence by Commission Act 1859. | The whole Act. |
| 33 & 34 Vict c 52. | The Extradition Act 1870. | Section 24. |
| 48 & 49 Vict c 74. | The Evidence by Commission Act 1885. | The whole Act. |
| 1966 c 41. | The Arbitration (International Investment Disputes) Act 1966. | In section 3(1), paragraph (b) together with the word 'and' immediately preceding that paragraph. In section 7(e), subsection (2) of the section 3 there set out. |

**EVIDENCE (PROCEEDINGS IN OTHER JURISDICTIONS) (FALKLAND ISLANDS AND DEPENDENCIES) ORDER 1978**

**Dated** 20 December 1978

**SI 1978 No 1891**

At the Court at Buckingham Palace, the 20th day of December 1978<br>Present,<br>The Queen's Most Excellent Majesty in Council

Her Majesty, in exercise of the powers conferred upon Her by section 10(3) of the Evidence (Proceedings in Other Jurisdictions) Act 1975 and of all other powers enabling Her in that behalf, is pleased, by and with the advice of Her Privy Council, to order, and it is hereby ordered, as follows—

**1.** (1) This Order may be cited as the Evidence (Proceedings in Other Jurisdictions) (Falkland Islands and Dependencies) Order 1978.

(2) This Order shall come into operation on 10 January 1979.

**2.** The Interpretation Act 1889 shall apply, with the necessary adaptations, for the purpose of interpreting this Order and otherwise in relation thereto as it applies for the purpose of interpreting, and in relation to, Acts of Parliament.

**Note.** The Interpretation Act 1889 is replaced by Interpretation Act 1978.

**3.** Sections 1 to 3 and 5 to 10 of, and Schedules 1 and 2 to, the Evidence (Proceedings in Other Jurisdictions) Act 1975, with the exceptions, adaptations and modifications specified in the Schedule hereto, shall extend to the Falkland Islands and its Dependencies.

SCHEDULE TO THE ORDER                                         Article 3

PROVISIONS OF THE EVIDENCE (PROCEEDINGS IN OTHER JURISDICTIONS) ACT 1975 AS
EXTENDED TO THE FALKLAND ISLANDS AND DEPENDENCIES

EVIDENCE FOR CIVIL PROCEEDINGS

*Application to Supreme Court for assistance in obtaining evidence for civil proceedings in other court*

**1.** Where an application is made to the Supreme Court for an order for evidence to be obtained in the Colony, and the court is satisfied—
- (a) that the application is made in pursuance of a request issued by or on behalf of a court or tribunal ('the requesting court') exercising jurisdiction in a country or territory outside the Colony; and
- (b) that the evidence to which the application relates is to be obtained for the purposes of civil proceedings which either have been instituted before the requesting court or whose institution before that court is contemplated,

the Supreme Court shall have the powers conferred on it by the following provisions of this Act.

*Power of Supreme Court to give effect to application for assistance*

**2.** (1) Subject to the provisions of this section, the Supreme Court shall have power, on any such application as is mentioned in section 1 above, by order to make such provision for obtaining evidence in the Colony as may appear to the court to be appropriate for the purpose of giving effect to the request in pursuance of which the application is made; and any such order may require a person specified therein to take such steps as the court may consider appropriate for that purpose.

(2) Without prejudice to the generality of subsection (1) above but subject to the provisions of this section, an order under this section may, in particular, make provision—
- (a) for the examination of witnesses, either orally or in writing;
- (b) for the production of documents;
- (c) for the inspection, photographing, preservation, custody or detention of any property;
- (d) for the taking of samples of any property and the carrying out of any experiments on or with any property;
- (e) for the medical examination of any person;
- (f) without prejudice to paragraph (e) above, for the taking and testing of samples of blood from any person.

(3) An order under this section shall not require any particular steps to be taken unless they are steps which can be required to be taken by way of obtaining evidence, for the purposes of civil proceedings in the court making the order (whether or not proceedings of the same description as those to which the application for the order relates); but this subsection shall not preclude the making of an order requiring a person to give testimony (either orally or in writing) otherwise than on oath where this is asked for by the requesting court.

(4) An order under this section shall not require a person—
- (a) to state what documents relevant to the proceedings to which the application for the order relates are or have been in his possession, custody or power; or

(b) to produce any documents other than particular documents specified in the order as being documents appearing to the court making the order to be, or to be likely to be, in his possession, custody or power.

(5) A person who, by virtue of an order under this section, is required to attend at any place shall be entitled to the like conduct money and payment for expenses and loss of time as on attendance as a witness in civil proceedings before the court making the order.

*Privilege of witnesses*

**3.** (1) A person shall not be compelled by virtue of an order under section 2 above to give any evidence which he could not be compelled to give—

(a) in civil proceedings in the Colony; or

(b) subject to subsection (2) below, in civil proceedings in the country or territory in which the requesting court exercises jurisdiction.

(2) Subsection (1)(b) above shall not apply unless the claim of the person in question to be exempt from giving the evidence is either—

(a) supported by a statement contained in the request (whether it is so supported unconditionally or subject to conditions that are fulfilled); or

(b) conceded by the applicant for the order;

and where such a claim made by any person is not supported or conceded as aforesaid he may (subject to the other provisions of this section) be required to give evidence to which the claim relates but that evidence shall not be transmitted to the requesting court if that court, on the matter being referred to it, upholds the claim.

(3) Without prejudice to subsection (1) above, a person shall not be compelled by virtue of an order under section 2 above to give any evidence if his doing so would be prejudicial to the security of the United Kingdom, the Colony or any other territory for which the United Kingdom is responsible under international law; and a certificate signed by or on behalf of the Governor to the effect that it would be so prejudicial for that person to do so shall be conclusive evidence of that fact.

(4) In this section references to giving evidence include references to answering any question and to producing any document and the reference in subsection (2) above to the transmission of evidence given by a person shall be construed accordingly.

EVIDENCE FOR CRIMINAL PROCEEDINGS

\*     \*     \*     \*     \*

EVIDENCE FOR INTERNATIONAL PROCEEDINGS

*Power of Supreme Court to assist in obtaining evidence for international proceedings*

**6.** (1) The Governor may by order direct that, subject to such exceptions, adaptations or modifications as may be specified in the order, the provisions of sections 1 to 3 above shall have effect in relation to international proceedings of any description specified in the order.

(2) An order under this section may direct that section 1(4) of the Perjury Act 1911 shall have effect in relation to international proceedings to which the order applies as it has effect in relation to a judicial proceeding in a tribunal of a foreign state.

(3) In this section 'international proceedings' means proceedings before the International Court of Justice or any other court, tribunal, committee, body or authority (whether consisting of one or more persons) which, in pursuance of any international agreement or any resolution of the General Assembly of the United Nations, exercises any jurisdiction or performs any functions of a judicial nature or by way of arbitration, conciliation or inquiry or is appointed (whether permanently or temporarily) for the purpose of exercising any jurisdiction or performing any such functions.

SUPPLEMENTARY

*Rules of court*

**7.**   The power to make rules of court under section 69 of the Administration of Justice Ordinance shall include power to make rules of court—

(a) as to the manner in which any such application as is mentioned in section 1 above is to be made;

(b) subject to the provisions of this Act, as to the circumstances in which an order can be made under section 2 above; and

(c) as to the manner in which any such reference as is mentioned in section 3(2) above is to be made;

and any such rules may include such incidental supplementary and consequential provision as may be considered necessary or expedient.

*Consequential amendment and repeals*

**8.**   (1) The enactment mentioned in Schedule 1 to this Act shall have effect subject to the amendment there specified, being an amendment consequential on the provisions of this Act.

(2) The enactments mentioned in Schedule 2 to this Act are hereby repealed to the extent specified in the third column of that Schedule.

(3) Nothing in this section shall affect—

(a) any application to any court or judge which is pending at the commencement of this Act;

(b) any certificate given for the purposes of any such application;

(c) any power to make an order on such an application; or

(d) the operation or enforcement of any order made on such an application.

(4) Subsection (3) above is without prejudice to section 38(2) of the Interpretation Act 1889 (effect of repeals).

*Interpretation*

**9.**   (1) In this Act—

'civil proceedings', in relation to the requesting court, means proceedings in any civil or commercial matter;

'the Colony' means the Colony of the Falkland Islands and includes its Dependencies;

'requesting court' has the meaning given in section 1 above;

'property' includes any land, chattel or other corporeal property of any description;

'request' includes any commission, order or other process issued by or on behalf of the requesting court;

'Supreme Court' means the Supreme Court of the Colony.

(3) Any power conferred by this Act to make an order includes power to revoke or vary any such order by a subsequent order.

(4) Nothing in this Act shall be construed as enabling any court to make an order that is binding on the Crown or on any person in his capacity as an officer or servant of the Crown.

(5) Except so far as the context otherwise requires, any reference in this Act to any enactment is a reference to that enactment as amended or extended by or under any other enactment.

*Commencement*

**10.**   (2) The provisions of this Act shall come into force on such date as the Governor may by order appoint.

SCHEDULES

SCHEDULE 1 TO THE ACT                                         Section 8(1)

CONSEQUENTIAL AMENDMENT

*The Perjury Act 1911*

In the Perjury Act 1911 after section 1 there shall be inserted—

*False unsworn statement under Evidence (Proceedings in Other Jurisdictions) Act 1975.*

1A. If any person, in giving any testimony (either orally or in writing) otherwise than on oath, where required to do so by an order under section 2 of the Evidence (Proceedings in Other Jurisdictions) Act 1975, makes a statement—
  (a) which he knows to be false in a material particular, or
  (b) which is false in a material particular and which he does not believe to be true,
he shall be guilty of an offence and shall be liable on conviction on indictment to imprisonment for a term not exceeding two years or a fine or both.'


SCHEDULE 2 TO THE ACT                                         Section 8(2)

REPEALS

| Chapter | Short Title | Extent |
|---------|-------------|--------|
| 19 & 20 Vict c 113. | The Foreign Tribunals Evidence Act 1856. | The whole Act. |
| 22 Vict c 20. | The Evidence by Commission Act 1859. | The whole Act. |
| 33 & 34 Vict c 52. | The Extradition Act 1870. | Section 24. |
| 48 & 49 Vict c 74. | The Evidence by Commission Act 1885. | The whole Act. |
| 53 & 54 Vict c 37. | The Foreign Jurisdiction Act 1890. | In Schedule 1 the entries relating to the Foreign Tribunals Evidence Act 1856, the Evidence by Commission Act 1859 and the Evidence by Commission Act 1885. |
| 1963 c 27. | The Oaths and Evidence (Overseas Authorities and Countries) Act 1963. | Section 4. |
| 1966 c 41. | The Arbitration (International Investment Disputes) Act 1966. | In section 3(1), paragraph (b) together with the word 'and' immediately preceding that paragraph. In section 7 (e), subsection (2) of the section 3 there set out. |

**EVIDENCE (PROCEEDINGS IN OTHER JURISDICTIONS)
(GIBRALTAR) ORDER 1978**

**Dated** 20 December 1978

**SI 1978 No 1892**

At the Court at Buckingham Palace, the 20th day of December 1978

Present,

The Queen's Most Excellent Majesty in Council

Her Majesty, in exercise of the powers conferred upon Her by section 10(3) of the Evidence (Proceedings in Other Jurisdictions) Act 1975, or otherwise in Her Majesty vested, is pleased, by and with the advice of Her Privy Council, to order, and it is hereby ordered, as follows—

**1.** This Order may be cited as the Evidence (Proceedings in Other Jurisdictions) (Gibraltar) Order 1978 and shall come into operation on 10 January 1979.

**2.** The Interpretation Act 1889 shall apply, with the necessary adaptations, for the purpose of interpreting this Order and otherwise in relation thereto as it applies for the purpose of interpreting, and in relation to, Acts of Parliament.

**Note.** Interpretation Act 1889 is replaced by the Interpretation Act 1978.

**3.** Subsections (2), (3) and (4) of section 8 of the Evidence (Proceedings in Other Jurisdictions) Act 1975 and the provisions of Schedule 2 to that Act that relate to the Foreign Tribunals Evidence Act 1856, the Evidence by Commission Act 1859, the Extradition Act 1870, the Evidence by Commission Act 1885 and section 3(1)(b) of the Arbitration (International Investment Disputes) Act 1966, as amended in its application to Gibraltar, shall extend to Gibraltar.


**EVIDENCE (PROCEEDINGS IN OTHER JURISDICTIONS) (SOVEREIGN BASE AREAS OF AKROTIRI AND DHEKELIA) ORDER 1978**

**Dated** 20 December 1978

**SI 1978 No 1920**

At the Court at Buckingham Palace, the 20th day of December 1978

Present,

The Queen's Most Excellent Majesty in Council

Her Majesty, in exercise of the powers conferred upon Her by section 10(3) of the Evidence (Proceedings in Other Jurisdictions) Act 1975 and of all other powers enabling Her in that behalf, is pleased, by and with the advice of Her Privy Council, to order, and it is hereby ordered, as follows—

**1.** (1) This Order may be cited as the Evidence (Proceedings in Other Jurisdictions) (Sovereign Base Areas of Akrotiri and Dhekelia) Order 1978.
(2) This Order shall come into operation on 10 January 1979.

**2.** The Interpretation Act 1889 shall apply, with the necessary adaptations, for the purpose of interpreting this Order and otherwise in relation thereto as it applies for the purpose of interpreting, and in relation to, Acts of Parliament.

**3.** Sections 1 to 3 and 5 to 10 of, and Schedule 2 to, the Evidence (Proceedings in Other Jurisdictions) Act 1975, with the exceptions, adaptations and modifications specified in the Schedule hereto, shall extend to the Sovereign Base Areas of Akrotiri and Dhekelia.

SCHEDULE TO THE ORDER                                                         Article 3

PROVISIONS OF THE EVIDENCE (PROCEEDINGS IN OTHER JURISDICTIONS) ACT 1975 AS
EXTENDED TO THE SOVEREIGN BASE AREAS

EVIDENCE OF CIVIL PROCEEDINGS

*Application to Judge's Court for assistance in obtaining evidence for civil proceedings in other court*

**1.** Where an application is made to the Judge's Court for an order for evidence to be obtained in the Sovereign Base Areas, and the court is satisfied—
  (a) that the application is made in pursuance of a request issued by or on behalf of a court or tribunal ('the requesting court') exercising jurisdiction in a country or territory outside the Sovereign Base Areas; and
  (b) that the evidence to which the application relates is to be obtained for the purposes of civil proceedings which either have been instituted before the requesting court or whose institution before that court is contemplated,
the Judge's Court shall have the powers conferred on it by the following provisions of this Act.

*Power of Judge's Court to give effect to application for assistance*
**2.** (1) Subject to the provisions of this section, the Judge's Court shall have power, on any such application as is mentioned in section 1 above, by order to make such provision for obtaining evidence in the Sovereign Base Areas as may appear to the court to be appropriate for the purpose of giving effect to the request in pursuance of which the application is made; and any such order may require a person specified therein to take such steps as the court may consider appropriate for that purpose.
  (2) Without prejudice to the generality of subsection (1) above but subject to the provisions of this section, an order under this section may, in particular, make provision—
  (a) for the examination of witnesses, either orally or in writing;
  (b) for the production of documents;
  (c) for the inspection, photographing, preservation, custody or detention of any property;
  (d) for the taking of samples of any property and the carrying out of any experiments on or with any property;
  (e) for the medical examination of any person;
  (f) without prejudice to paragraph (e) above, for the taking and testing of samples of blood from any person.
  (3) An order under this section shall not require any particular steps to be taken unless they are steps which can be required to be taken by way of obtaining evidence for the purposes of civil proceedings in the court making the order (whether or not proceedings of the same description as those to which the application for the order relates); but this subsection shall not preclude the making of an order requiring a person to give testimony (either orally or in writing) otherwise than on oath where this is asked for by the requesting court.
  (4) An order under this section shall not require a person—

(a) to state what documents relevant to the proceedings to which the application for the order relates are or have been in his possession, custody or power; or

(b) to produce any documents other than particular documents specified in the order as being documents appearing to the court making the order to be, or to be likely to be, in his possession, custody or power.

(5) A person who, by virtue of an order under this section, is required to attend at any place shall be entitled to the like conduct money and payment for expenses and loss of time as on attendance as a witness in civil proceedings before the court making the order.

*Privilege of witnesses*

**3.** (1) A person shall not be compelled by virtue of an order under section 2 above to give any evidence which he could not be compelled to give—

(a) in civil proceedings in the Sovereign Base Areas; or

(b) subject to subsection (2) below, in civil proceedings in the country or territory in which the requesting court exercises jurisdiction.

(2) Subsection (1)(b) above shall not apply unless the claim of the person in question to be exempt from giving the evidence is either—

(a) supported by a statement contained in the request (whether it is so supported unconditionally or subject to conditions that are fulfilled); or

(b) conceded by the applicant for the order;

and where such a claim made by any person is not supported or conceded as aforesaid he may (subject to the other provisions of this section) be required to give the evidence to which the claim relates but that evidence shall not be transmitted to the requesting court if that court, on the matter being referred to it, upholds the claim.

(3) Without prejudice to subsection (1) above, a person shall not be compelled by virtue of an order under section 2 above to give any evidence if his doing so would be prejudicial to the security of the United Kingdom, the Sovereign Base Areas, or any other territory for which the United Kingdom is responsible under international law; and a certificate signed by or on behalf of the Administrator to the effect that it would be so prejudicial for that person to do so shall be conclusive evidence of that fact.

(4) In this section references to giving evidence include references to answering any question and to producing any document and the reference in subsection (2) above to the transmission of evidence given by a person shall be construed accordingly.

EVIDENCE FOR CRIMINAL PROCEEDINGS

\*     \*     \*     \*     \*

EVIDENCE FOR INTERNATIONAL PROCEEDINGS

*Power of Judge's Court to assist in obtaining evidence for international proceedings*

**6.** (1) The Administrator may by order direct that, subject to such exceptions, adaptations or modifications as may be specified in the order, the provisions of sections 1 to 3 above shall have effect in relation to international proceedings of any description specified in the order.

(2) An order under this section may direct that sections 110 to 112 inclusive of the Criminal Code shall have effect in relation to international proceedings to which the order applies as it has effect in relation to a judicial proceeding in a tribunal of a foreign state.

(3) In this section 'international proceedings' means proceedings before the International Court of Justice or any other court, tribunal, commission, body or authority (whether consisting of one or more persons) which, in pursuance of any international agreement or any resolution of the General Assembly of the United Nations, exercises any jurisdiction or performs any functions of a judicial nature or by way or arbitration, conciliation or inquiry or is appointed (whether permanently or temporarily) for the purpose of exercising any jurisdiction or performing any such functions.

SUPPLEMENTARY

*Rules of Court*

**7.** The power to make Rules of Court under subsection (2) of section 102 of the Civil Procedure Ordinance, section 176 of the Criminal Procedure Ordinance, and section 63 of the Courts Ordinance, shall include powers to make Rules of Court—
   (a) as to the manner in which any such application as is mentioned in section 1 above is to be made;
   (b) subject to the provisions of this Act, as to the circumstances in which an order can be made under section 2 above; and
   (c) as to the manner in which any such reference as is mentioned in section 3(2) above is to be made;
and any such rules may include such incidental, supplementary and consequential provision as the authority making the rules may consider necessary or expedient.

*Consequential amendments and repeals*

**8.** (2) The enactments mentioned in Schedule 2 to this Act are hereby repealed as respects the Sovereign Base Areas to the extent specified in the third column of that schedule.
   (3) Nothing in this section shall affect—
   (a) any application to the court or judge which is pending at the commencement of this Act;
   (b) any certificate given for the purposes of any such application;
   (c) any power to make an order on such an application; or
   (d) the operation or enforcement of any order made on such an application.
   (4) Subsection (3) above is without prejudice to section 38(2) of the Interpretation Act 1889 (effect of repeals).

*Interpretation*

**9.** (1) In this Act—
   'Administrator', in relation to the Sovereign Base Areas, means the Administrator of the Sovereign Base Areas and includes any person or persons administering the Government of the Sovereign Base areas;
   'civil proceedings', in relation to the requesting court, means proceedings in any civil or commercial matter;
   'Judge's Court' means the Judge's Court of the Sovereign Base Areas of Akrotiri and Dhekelia;
   'requesting court' has the meaning given in section 1 above;
   'property' includes any land, chattel or other corporeal property of any description;
   'request' includes any commission, order or other process issued by or on behalf of the requesting court;
   'Sovereign Base Areas' means the Sovereign Base Areas of Akrotiri and Dhekelia.
   (3) Any power conferred by this Act to make an order includes power to revoke or vary any such order by a subsequent order.
   (4) Nothing in this Act shall be construed as enabling any court to make an order that is binding on the Crown or on any person in his capacity as an officer or servant of the Crown.
   (5) Except so far as the context otherwise requires, any reference in this Act to any enactment is a reference to that enactment as amended or extended by or under any other enactment.

*Commencement*

**10.** (2) The provisions of this Act shall come into force on such date as the Administrator may by order appoint.

SCHEDULE 2 TO THE ACT                                      Section 8(2)

REPEALS

| Chapter | Short Title | Extent |
|---|---|---|
| 19 & 20 Vict c 113. | The Foreign Tribunals Evidence Act 1856. | The whole Act. |
| 22 Vict c 20. | The Evidence by Commission Act 1859. | The whole Act. |
| 33 & 34 Vict c 52. | The Extradition Act 1870. | Section 24. |
| 48 & 49 Vict c 74. | The Evidence by Commission Act 1885. | The whole Act. |
| 53 & 54 Vict c 37. | The Foreign Jurisdiction Act 1890. | In Schedule 1 the entries relating to the Foreign Tribunals Evidence Act 1856, the Evidence by Commission Act 1859 and the Evidence by Commission Act 1885 but without prejudice to any Order in Council made in respect of any of those Acts before the commencement of this Act. |
| 1966 c 41. | The Arbitration (International Investment Disputes) Act 1966. | In section 3(1), paragraph (b) together with the word 'and' immediately preceding that paragraph.<br>In section 7(e), subsection (2) of the section 3 there set out. |
| 1968 c 64. | The Civil Evidence Act 1968. | Section 17(2). |

## RECIPROCAL ENFORCEMENT OF MAINTENANCE ORDERS (DESIGNATION OF RECIPROCATING COUNTRIES) ORDER 1979

**Dated** 6 February 1979

**SI 1979 No 115**

Whereas Her Majesty is satisfied that, in the event of the benefits conferred by Part I of the Maintenance Orders (Reciprocal Enforcement) Act 1972 being applied to, or to particular classes of, maintenance orders made by the courts of each of the countries and territories specified in column (1) of the Schedule to this Order, similar benefits will in that country or territory be applied to, or to those classes of, maintenance orders made by the courts of the United Kingdom:

And whereas Her Majesty considers the provisions contained in Article 6 of this Order expedient for the purpose of securing the matters set out in section 24 of the said Act of 1972:

Now, therefore, Her Majesty, in exercise of the powers conferred by sections 1, 24 and 45(1) of the Maintenance Orders (Reciprocal Enforcement) Act 1972, is pleased, by and with the advice of Her Privy Council, to order, and it is hereby ordered, as follows—

**1.** This Order may be cited as the Reciprocal Enforcement of Maintenance Orders (Designation of Reciprocating Countries) Order 1979 and shall come into operation on 1 April 1979.

**2.** In this Order—

'the Act of 1972' means the Maintenance Orders (Reciprocal Enforcement) Act 1972;

'the Act of 1920' means the Maintenance Orders (Facilities for Enforcement) Act 1920;

'the Order of 1974' means the Reciprocal Enforcement of Maintenance Orders (Designation of Reciprocating Countries) Order 1974;

'column (1)' and 'column (2)' in Articles 3 and 6 below mean respectively columns (1) and (2) of the Schedule to this Order.

**3.** Each of the countries and territories specified in column (1) is hereby designated as a reciprocating country for the purposes of Part I of the Act of 1972 as regards maintenance orders of the description specified in respect of that country or territory in column (2).

[1] **4.** The Order of 1974 shall be varied by omitting in column (2) of the Schedule to that Order the words '(a) provisional affiliation orders, and' in respect of the following countries or territories (which are specified in column (1) of that Schedule)—

Australian Capital Territory;

New South Wales;

Northern Territory of Australia;

Queensland;

South Australia;

Tasmania;

Victoria.

[1] **5.** The Order of 1974 shall be varied by omitting in column (2) of the Schedule to that Order in respect of Ontario the words '(a) provisional affiliation orders,' and the words '(c) provisional maintenance orders made by virtue of the Matrimonial Proceedings (Polygamous Marriages) Act 1972 or any corresponding legislation in Ontario'.

**6.** (1) Sections 5, 12 to 15, 17, 18 and 21 of the Act of 1972 shall apply in relation to a maintenance order transmitted under section 2 or 3 of the Act of 1920 to one of the countries and territories specified in column (1), being an order of the description specified in respect of that country or territory in column (2) to which immediately before the coming into operation of this Order the Act of 1920 applied, as they apply in relation to a maintenance order sent to that country or territory in pursuance of section 2 of the Act of 1972 or made by virtue of section 3 or 4 of the Act of 1972 and confirmed by a competent court in that country or territory.

(2) Sections 8 to 21 of the Act of 1972 shall apply in relation to a maintenance order made in one of the countries and territories specified in column (1), being an order of the description specified in respect of that country or territory in column (2) to which immediately before the coming into operation of this Order the Act of 1920 applied and not being an order which immediately before that date is registered in the High Court or the High Court of Justice in Northern Ireland under section 1 of the Act of 1920, as they apply in relation to a registered order.

(3) A maintenance order made by a court in one of the countries and territories specified in column (1) being an order of the description in respect of that country or territory in column (2) which has been confirmed by a court in England, Wales or Northern Ireland under section 4 of the Act of 1920 and is in force immediately before the coming into operation of this Order, shall be registered under section 7(5) of the Act of 1972 in like manner as if it had been confirmed by that court in England, Wales or Northern Ireland under subsection (2) of that section.

---

[1] See p 4310, where the 1974 order, as amended, is set out.

(4) Any proceedings brought under or by virtue of any provision of the Act of 1920 in a court in England, Wales or Northern Ireland which are pending immediately before the coming into operation of this Order, being proceedings affecting a person resident in one of the countries and territories specified in column (1), shall be continued as if they had been brought under or by virtue of the corresponding provision of the Act of 1972.

SCHEDULE                                                                     Article 2

COUNTRIES AND TERRITORIES DESIGNATED AS RECIPROCATING COUNTRIES

| (1)<br>Country or territory | (2)<br>Description of maintenance orders<br>to which designations extends |
|---|---|
| Alberta . . . . | Maintenance orders other than—<br>(a) provisional affiliation orders;<br>(b) maintenance orders of the description contained in paragraph (b) of the definition of 'maintenance order' in section 21(1) of the Act of 1972;<br>(c) orders obtained by or in favour of a public authority. |
| Fiji . . . . . | Maintenance orders generally. |
| Hong Kong . . . | Maintenance orders generally. |
| Norfolk Island . . . | Maintenance orders other than orders obtained by or in favour of a public authority. |
| Saskatchewan . . . | Maintenance orders other than—<br>(a) provisional affiliation orders; and<br>(b) maintenance orders of the description contained in the said paragraph (b). |
| Singapore . . . . | Maintenance orders generally. |
| Turks and Caicos Islands | Maintenance orders other than—<br>(a) affiliation orders;<br>(b) maintenance orders of the description contained in the said paragraph (b); and<br>(c) orders obtained by or in favour of a public authority. |
| United Republic of Tanzania (except Zanzibar) | Maintenance orders other than—<br>(a) affiliation orders;<br>(b) maintenance orders of the description contained in the said paragraph (b); and<br>(c) orders obtained by or in favour of a public authority. |
| Western Australia . . | Maintenance orders other than orders obtained by or in favour of a public authority. |

## MAINTENANCE ORDERS (FACILITIES FOR ENFORCEMENT) (REVOCATION) ORDER 1979

**Dated** 6 February 1979

**SI 1979 No 116**

Her Majesty, in exercise of the powers conferred by section 19 of the Maintenance Orders Act 1958, is pleased, by and with the advice of Her Privy Council, to order, and it is hereby ordered, as follows—

**1.** This Order may be cited as the Maintenance Orders (Facilities for Enforcement) (Revocation) Order 1979 and shall come into operation on 1 April 1979.

**2.** (1) In so far as the Maintenance Orders (Facilities for Enforcement) Order 1959 provides that the Maintenance Orders (Facilities for Enforcement) Act 1920 shall extend to the countries and territories specified in paragraph (2) below, that Order is hereby revoked, and accordingly the names of those countries and territories shall be omitted from the First Schedule to that Order.

(2) The countries and territories referred to in paragraph (1) above are—
Alberta;
Fiji;
Hong Kong;
Norfolk Island;
Saskatchewan;
Singapore;
Turks and Caicos Islands;
Western Australia.

**3.** The Maintenance Orders (Facilities for Enforcement) (Tanganyika) Order 1964 is hereby revoked.

## EVIDENCE (PROCEEDINGS IN OTHER JURISDICTIONS) (ISLE OF MAN) ORDER 1979

**Dated** 19 December 1979

**SI 1979 No 1711**

At the Court at Buckingham Palace, the 19th day of December 1979

Present,

The Queen's Most Excellent Majesty in Council

Her Majesty, in exercise of the powers conferred upon Her by section 10(3) of the Evidence (Proceedings in Other Jurisdictions) Act 1975 is pleased, by and with the advice of Her Privy Council, to order, and it is hereby ordered, as follows—

**1.** This Order may be cited as the Evidence (Proceedings in Other Jurisdictions) (Isle of Man) Order 1979 and shall come into operation on 1 February 1980.

**2.** The provisions of the Evidence (Proceedings in Other Jurisdictions) Act 1975 shall extend to the Isle of Man subject to the exceptions, adaptations and modifications specified in Schedule 1 to this Order.

**3.** The provisions of the Evidence (European Court) Order 1976 shall extend to the Isle of Man subject to the modifications specified in Schedule 2 to this Order.

SCHEDULE 1                                                                 Article 2

EXCEPTIONS, ADAPTATIONS AND MODIFICATIONS IN THE EXTENSION OF THE EVIDENCE (PROCEEDINGS IN OTHER JURISDICTIONS) ACT 1975 TO THE ISLE OF MAN

**1.** (1) Any reference in the Evidence (Proceedings in Other Jurisdictions) Act 1975—
(a) to the High Court shall be construed as including a reference to Her Majesty's High Court of Justice of the Isle of Man;
(b) to an indictment shall be construed as a reference to an information;
(c) to the United Kingdom shall, except in section 5(1), be construed as including the Isle of Man.

(2) Any reference in the said Act of 1975, as extended to the Isle of Man by this Order, to an enactment of Tynwald shall be construed as a reference to that enactment as amended or replaced by or under any other enactment of Tynwald.

**2.** Section 4 (Extension of powers of High Court etc in relation to obtaining evidence for proceedings in that court) shall be omitted.

**3.** In section 5(1) (Power of United Kingdom Court to assist in obtaining evidence for criminal proceedings in overseas court), for the reference to the United Kingdom there shall be substituted a reference to the Isle of Man.

**4.** In section 6(2) (Power of United Kingdom court to assist in obtaining evidence for international proceedings), for the enactments referred to therein there shall be substituted a reference to section 1(4) of the Perjury Act 1952 (an Act of Tynwald).

**5.** In section 7 (Rules of court), for the enactments referred to therein there shall be substituted a reference to section 35 of the Isle of Man Judicature Act 1883 (an Act of Tynwald).

**6.** In section 9 (Interpretation), subsection (2) shall be omitted.

**7.** In section 10 (Short title, commencement and extent), subsections (2) and (3) shall be omitted.

**8.** For Schedule 1 (Consequential Amendments), substitute the following provision—

'SCHEDULE 1                                                                Section 8(1)

CONSEQUENTIAL AMENDMENTS

*In Perjury Act 1952 (an Act of Tynwald)*
   In the Perjury Act 1952 (an Act of Tynwald) after section 1 there shall be inserted—
   "1A. False unsworn statement under Evidence (Proceedings in Other Jurisdictions) Act 1975.

If any person, in giving any testimony (either orally or in writing) otherwise than on oath, where required to do so by an order under section 2 of the Evidence (Proceedings in Other Jurisdictions) Act 1975 (an Act of Parliament extended to the Isle of Man by the Evidence (Proceedings in Other Jurisdictions) (Isle of Man) Order 1979), makes a statement—
   (a) which he knows to be false in a material particular, or
   (b) which is false in a material particular and which he does not believe to be true,
he shall be guilty of an offence and shall be liable on conviction on information to imprisonment for a term not exceeding two years or a fine or both.".'

**9.** In Schedule 2 (Repeals), the reference to the German Conventions Act 1955, the Northern Ireland Act 1962, the Arbitration (International Investment Disputes) Act 1966, the Civil Evidence Act 1968 and the Civil Evidence Act (Northern Ireland) 1971 shall be omitted.

   (*Schedule 2, relating to evidence for proceedings before the European Court of Justice, is not reproduced.*)


## MAGISTRATES' COURTS (RECIPROCAL ENFORCEMENT OF MAINTENANCE ORDERS) (HAGUE CONVENTION COUNTRIES) RULES 1980

**Dated** 31 January 1980

**SI 1980 No 108**

The Lord Chancellor, in exercise of the powers conferred on him by the provisions specified in Schedule 1 to these Rules and after consultation with the Rule Committee appointed under section 15 of the Justices of the Peace Act 1949 hereby makes the following Rules—

**1.**   These Rules may be cited as the Magistrates' Courts (Reciprocal Enforcement of Maintenance Orders) (Hague Convention Countries) Rules 1980 and shall come into operation on 1 March 1980.

**2.**   In these Rules, unless the context otherwise requires—

'the Act' means the Maintenance Orders (Reciprocal Enforcement) Act 1972 as applied with such exceptions, adaptations and modifications as are specified in the Reciprocal Enforcement of Maintenance Orders (Hague Convention Countries) Order 1979; and

'his register', in relation to a justices' clerk means the register kept by that clerk in pursuance of Rule 54 of the Magistrates' Courts Rules 1968.

**3.**   The officer of any court, by or in relation to whom anything is to be done in pursuance of any provision of Part I of the Act shall, where that court is a magistrates' court, be the justices' clerk.

**4.**   (1) An application under section 2 of the Act (transmission of maintenance order made in the United Kingdom for recognition and enforcement in Hague Convention country) shall where the court which made the maintenance order to which the application relates is a magistrates' court, be made in writing by or on behalf of the payee under the order.

(2) Any application made in pursuance of paragraph (1) above shall—

(a) specify the date on which the order was made;

(b) contain such particulars as are known to the applicant of the whereabouts of the payer and the nature and location of his assets;

(c) specify any matters likely to assist in the identification of the payer;

(d) where possible, be accompanied by a recent photograph of the payer.

(3) In this rule 'the payer' means the payer under the order to which the application relates.

**4A.**   (1) In this rule, 'an application' means—

(a) an application under section 3 of the Act for a maintenance order against a person residing in a Hague Convention country,

(b) an application under section 5 of the Act for the variation *or revocation* of a maintenance order made in the United Kingdom, or

(c) an application under section 9 of the Act for the variation or revocation of a maintenance order registered by a court in the United Kingdom.

(2) An application shall be filed in an appropriate form.

(3) On receipt of such an application the justices' clerk shall—

(a) fix the date, time and place for a hearing or a directions appointment, and

(b) notify the applicant of the date, time and place so fixed.

**Note.** In para (1)(c) words 'or revocation' revoked by SI 1999/2002, as from 16 August 1999.

**4B.**   (1) Schedule 2A to these Rules shall apply to proceedings pursuant to rule 4A above.

(2) In Schedule 2A as it applies to rule 4A, 'the resident party' and 'the non-resident party' shall be taken to mean—

(a) in the case of an application under sub-paragraph (a) of rule 4A(1), the applicant and the respondent respectively,

(b) in the case of an application under sub-paragraph (b) of rule 4A(1), the payee and payer respectively under the order in question, and

(c) in the case of an application under sub-paragraph (c) of rule 4A(1), the payer and payee respectively under the order in question.

**5.** (1) Where a justices' clerk is required under any provision of Part I of the Act to register a maintenance order, he shall cause the order to be registered in his court by means of a minute or memorandum entered and signed by him in his register.

(2) Every minute or memorandum entered in pursuance of paragraph (1) above shall specify the section of the Act under which the order in question is registered.

(3) Where a maintenance order is under any provision of Part I of the Act registered in a magistrates' court, the justices' clerk shall send written notice of the registration to the Secretary of State.

**6.** Where under section 5(4)(b) of the Act a copy of any representations made or evidence adduced by or on behalf of the payer in an application by the payee for the variation or revocation of a maintenance order to which section 5 of the Act applies, is required to be served on the payee before the hearing, the clerk of the magistrates' court to which the application is made shall arrange for a copy of such representations or evidence to be sent to the payee by post.

**7.** (1) Any notice required under section 6(8) of the Act (notice of registration in United Kingdom court of maintenance order made in Hague Convention country) to be served on the payer under a maintenance order shall, where the order is registered in a magistrates' court, be in the form in Part I of Schedule 2 to these Rules, or in a form to the like effect.

(2) Where a magistrates' court to which an appeal is made under section 6(9) of the Act sets aside the registration of a maintenance order, the justices' clerk shall send written notice of the court's decision to the Secretary of State.

(3) Any notice required under section 6(11) of the Act (notice that maintenance order made in Hague Convention country has not been registered in United Kingdom court) to be given to the payee under a maintenance order shall, where the appropriate court is a magistrates' court, be in the form in Part I of Schedule 2 to these Rules or in a form to the like effect.

**8.** (1) When an order is registered under section 6(3) of the Act, the court shall order that payment of sums due thereunder shall be made to the clerk of the registering court during such hours and at such place as that clerk may direct.

(1A) A justices' clerk to whom payments are ordered to be made (whether by virtue of an order under paragraph (1) above or by virtue of an order of the court under the Act) shall send those payments by post to the payee under the order.

(2) Where it appears to a justices' clerk to whom payments by way of periodical payments under any maintenance order are to be made that any sums payable under the order are in arrear he may and, if such sums are in arrear to an amount equal to four times the sum payable weekly under the order, he shall, whether the person for whose benefit the payment should have been made requests him to do so or not, proceed in his own name for the recovery of those sums, unless it appears to him that it is unreasonable in the circumstances to do so.

**8A.** Without prejudice to Rule 8 above, the justices' clerk of the registering court shall take reasonable steps to notify the person to whom payments are due under a registered order of the means of enforcement available in respect of it, including, in an appropriate case, the possibility of registration of the whole or part of the order in the High Court under Part I of the Maintenance Orders Act 1958.

**8B.** (1) Where, in the exercise of the duty imposed under rule 8(1) above, or in the exercise of the powers conferred by virtue of section 8(4A) or section 9(1ZA) of the Act, the court orders that payments under the order are to be made by a particular means, the clerk of the court shall record on the copy of the order the means of payment which the court has ordered and notify in writing, as soon as practicable, the person liable to make payments under the order of how payments are to be made.

(2) Where, in the exercise of any of the aforesaid powers, the court orders payment to the clerk of the court, or to the clerk of any other magistrates' court, by a method of payment falling within section 59(6) of the Magistrates' Courts Act 1980 (standing order, etc), the clerk of the court to whom payments are to be made shall notify the person liable to make the payments under the order of the number and location of the account into which the payments are to be made.

(3) Where, under section 60(4) of the Magistrates' Courts Act 1980, as modified by section 9(1ZA) of the Act, the clerk of the court receives an application from an interested party for the method of payment to be varied, the clerk shall notify in writing, as soon as practicable, that party and, where practicable, any other interested party, of the result of the application, including any decision to refer the matter to the court; where the clerk then grants the application, he shall record the variation on the copy of the order.

**9.**   (1) Subject to paragraph (2) below, where a request is made by or on behalf of a court in a Hague Convention country for the taking in England and Wales of the evidence of a person residing therein, the following magistrates' courts shall have power under section 14(1) of the Act (obtaining of evidence needed for purpose of certain proceedings) to take that evidence, that is to say—

(a) where the maintenance order to which the proceedings in the court in the Hague Convention country relate was made by a magistrates' court, the court which made the order;

(b) where the maintenance order to which those proceedings in the court in the Hague Convention country relate was made by a court in a Hague Convention country, the court in which the order is registered;

(c) a magistrates' court which has received such a request from the Secretary of State.

(2) The power conferred by paragraph (1) above may, with the agreement of a court having that power, be exercised by any other magistrates' court which, because the person whose evidence is to be taken resides within its jurisdiction or for any other reason, the first-mentioned court considers could more conveniently take the evidence; but nothing in this paragraph shall derogate from the power of any court specified in paragraph (1) above.

(3) Subject to paragraph (4) below, where the evidence of any person is to be taken by a magistrates' court under the foregoing provisions of this Rule—

(a) the evidence shall be taken in the same manner as if that person were a witness in proceedings on a complaint;

(b) any oral evidence so taken shall be put into writing and read to the person who gave it who shall be required to sign the document; and

(c) the justices by whom the evidence of any person is so taken shall certify at the foot of any document setting out the evidence of, or produced in evidence by, that person that such evidence was taken, or document received in evidence, as the case may be, by them.

(4) Where such a request as is mentioned in paragraph (1) above includes a request that the evidence be taken in a particular manner, the magistrates' court by which the evidence is taken shall, so far as circumstances permit, comply with that request.

**10.**   (1) Where a justices' clerk cancels the registration of a maintenance order under section 10(1) of the Act (cancellation of registration and transfer of order) he shall send written notice of the cancellation to the payer under the order.

(2) Where a justices' clerk registers a maintenance order under section 10(4) of the Act, he shall send written notice to the Secretary of State and to the payer under the order that the order has been duly registered.

**11.** Where a justices' clerk serves a notice on a payer under a maintenance order who resides in a Hague Convention country under any provision of Part I of the Act, he shall send a document which establishes that the notice was so served to the Secretary of State.

**12.** (1) Where the clerk of a magistrates' court receives from the Secretary of State notice of the institution of proceedings, including notice of the substance of the claim, in a Hague Convention country in relation to the making, variation or revocation of a maintenance order and it appears to the justices' clerk that the person against whom those proceedings have been instituted is residing within the petty sessions area for which the court acts, the justices' clerk shall serve the notice on that person by sending it by post in a registered letter addressed to him at his last known or usual place of abode.

(2) Where it appears to a justices' clerk who has received such a notice from the Secretary of State that the person against whom the proceedings have been instituted is not so residing, the justices' clerk shall return the notice to the Secretary of State with an intimation to that effect.

## SCHEDULE 1

ENABLING POWERS

Section 15 of the Justices of the Peace Act 1949, as extended by section 122 of the Magistrates' Courts Act 1952;

The following provisions of the Maintenance Orders (Reciprocal Enforcement) Act 1972, as extended by Article 3 of the Reciprocal Enforcement of Maintenance Orders (Hague Convention Countries) Order 1979, namely,

section 2(3) and (4) (see Rules 3 and 4);
section 3(5)(b), (6A) and (6D) (see Rule 3);
section 5(3), (4)(c), (6), (7) and (10) (see Rules 3 and 5);
section 5(4)(b) (see Rule 6);
section 6(2), (3), (5), (6), (7), (8), (10), (11) and (12) (see Rules 3, 5, 7 and Schedule 2);
section 8(5) (see Rule 8);
section 8(6) (see Rule 3);
section 9(3), (4)(b) and (c), (6), (7) and (8) (see Rules 3 and 5);
section 10(1), (2), (3), (4), (5) and (7) (see Rules 3, 5 and 10);
section 11(1)(b) (see Rule 3);
section 14(1) (see Rule 9);
section 16(1) (see Rule 8);
section 18(1) (see Rule 9).
(Note: the references to Rules are to the Rules in this SI which give effect to the enabling powers to which the Rules relate.)

## SCHEDULE 2

PART I

Notice to payer of registration of maintenance order.

To[1]
I hereby give notice that on            day of                         19    I registered a
maintenance order (copy attached) made by the                              Court in[2]
                  ordering you to pay [3]                   the sum of [4]
You are entitled to appeal to the                     magistrates' court within *one calendar month* [two calendar months] from the date of the service of this notice to set aside the registration of the order on one of the following grounds:—

(a)   that the court making the order did not have jurisdiction to do so;[5]

(b)   that the registration is contrary to public policy;

(c)   that the order was obtained by fraud in connection with a matter of procedure;

(d)   that proceedings between you and the payee and having the same purpose are pending before a court in the United Kingdom and those proceedings were instituted before these proceedings;

(e)   that the order is incompatible with a judgment given in proceedings between you and the payee and having the same purpose, either in the United Kingdom or in a Hague Convention country;

(f)   if you did not appear in the proceedings in the Hague Convention country, that you were not given notice of the institution of the proceedings, including notice of the substance of the claim, in accordance with the law of that country and in sufficient time to enable you to defend the proceedings.

*JC* [J.C.E.]
*Clerk of the Court* [Justices' Chief Executive].

---

[1] Insert name and address of payer.

[2] Insert name of Hague Convention country.

[3] Insert name of payee.

[4] Insert amount in sterling and period, eg monthly.

[5] Jurisdiction may be based—

(a)   on the habitual residence of the payer or payee in that State;

(b)   on the payer and payee being nationals of that State;

(c)   on your submission to the jurisdiction of the court; or

(d)   in the case of an order made on divorce, etc on any ground which is recognised by United Kingdom law.

PART II

Rule 7(3)

Notice to payee that maintenance order has not been registered.

To[1]

I hereby give notice that I have not registered a maintenance order made by the court in[2]                    ordering[3]                    to pay you the sum of[4]                    on the ground that[5]

You are entitled to appeal against my decision to the                    magistrates' court within *one calendar month* [two calendar months] from the date when this notice was given to have the order registered.

If you wish to appeal, you may do so by completing and returning to me the notice of appeal set out opposite. Unless you are present in court or legally represented when the appeal is heard the court may dismiss the case. If you wish to be legally represented and need legal aid or advice you may apply to the Area Secretary, The Law Society, 14 (London West) Legal Aid Area, Area Headquarters, 29–37 Red Lion Street, London WC1R 4PP.

*JC* [J.C.E.]
*Clerk of the Court* [Justices' Chief Executive].

---

[1] Insert name and address of payee.

[2] Insert name of Hague Convention country.

[3] Insert name and address of payer.

[4] Insert amount in sterling and period, eg monthly.

[5] Insert one of the grounds specified in section 6(5), (6) or (7) of the Maintenance Orders (Reciprocal Enforcement) Act 1972 (as extended by the Reciprocal Enforcement of Maintenance (Hague Convention Countries) Order 1979).

MAINTENANCE ORDERS (RECIPROCAL ENFORCEMENT) ACT 1972

Appeal by way of *complaint* [application]

Magistrates' Court (Code)

Date:
Defendant:
Address:

Matter of Complaint.

The           Court at          in        having on
      made a maintenance order requiring the defendant to pay the undersigned complainant the sum of £    [weekly or as the case may be] and the order having been sent to the *Justices' Clerk* [Justices' Chief Executive] for the said Magistrates' Court for registration; the *Justices' Clerk* [Justices' Chief Executive] has refused to register the order on the ground that
      I hereby appeal to the said Magistrates' Court against the refusal to register this order.

Signed                      (*Complainant* [Applicant])

**Note.** In Parts I, II, references to 'JC', 'Clerk of the Court' and 'Justices' Clerk' substituted by references to 'J.C.E.' and 'Justices' Chief Executive' by SI 2001/615, r 2(ix), Schedule, para 69, as from 1 April 2001. In Part II, words 'one calendar month' substituted by words 'two calendar months' and words 'complaint' and 'Complainant' substituted by words 'application' and 'Applicant' respectively by SI 1999/2002, rr 3, 4, as from 16 August 1999.

## SCHEDULE 2A

RULES OF PROCEDURE

**1.** In this Schedule, and in any rule where this Schedule applies to proceedings pursuant to that rule, unless the context otherwise requires—
      'business day' means any day other than—
(a) a Saturday, Sunday, Christmas or Good Friday; or
(b) a bank holiday, that is to say, a day which is, or is to be observed as, a bank holiday, or a holiday, under the Banking and Financial Dealings Act 1971, in England and Wales,
      'directions appointment' means a hearing for directions under paragraph 4 below,
      'file' means deposit with the justices' clerk,
      'justices' clerk' has the meaning assigned to it by section 70 of the Justices of the Peace Act 1979 and includes any person who performs a justices' clerk's functions by virtue of paragraph 12 below,
      'leave' includes approval,
      'note' includes a record made by mechanical or electronic means, and
      'proceedings' means proceedings to which this Schedule applies.

*Transfer of proceedings*

**2.** (1) Where—
(a) any proceedings are relevant proceedings within the meaning of section 93 of the Children Act 1989, and
(b) the justices' clerk or the court receives a request in writing from the resident party that the proceedings be transferred to another magistrates' court,
the justices' clerk or court shall issue a certificate in the appropriate form, granting or refusing the request in accordance with any Order made by the Lord Chancellor under Part I of Schedule 11 to the Children Act 1989.
      (2) Where a request is granted under paragraph (1) the justices' clerk shall send a copy of the certificate—

    (a)  to the resident party,

    (b)  to the Lord Chancellor's Department, and

    (c)  to the magistrates' court to which the proceedings are to be transferred.

    (3) Any consent given or refused by a justices' clerk in accordance with any Order made by the Lord Chancellor under Part I of Schedule 11 shall be recorded in writing by the justices' clerk at the time it is given or refused or as soon as practicable thereafter.

*Service*

**3.**   (1) Where service of a document is required by this Schedule or by a rule where this Schedule applies to proceedings pursuant to that rule it may be effected, unless the contrary is indicated—

    (a)  if the person to be served is not known by the person serving to be acting by solicitor—

        (i)  by delivering it to him personally, or

       (ii)  by delivering it at, or by sending it by first-class post to, his residence or last known residence, or

    (b)  if the person to be served is known by the person serving to be acting by solicitor—

        (i)  by delivering the document at, or sending it by first-class post to, the solicitor's address for service,

       (ii)  where the solicitor's address for service includes a numbered box at a document exchange, by leaving the document at that document exchange or at a document exchange which transmits documents on every business day to that document exchange, or

      (iii)  by sending a legible copy of the document by facsimile transmission to the solicitor's office.

    (2) In this paragraph, 'first-class post' means first-class post which has been pre-paid or in respect of which pre-payment is not required.

    (3) A document shall, unless the contrary is proved, be deemed to have been served—

    (a)  in the case of service by first-class post, on the second business day after posting, and

    (b)  in the case of service in accordance with sub-paragraph 1(b)(ii), on the second business day after the day on which it is left at the document exchange.

    (4) In any proceedings where this Schedule, or a rule where this Schedule applies, requires a document to be served, the court or the justices' clerk may, without prejudice to any power under paragraph 4 below, direct that—

    (a)  the requirement shall not apply;

    (b)  the time specified by the rules for complying with the requirement shall be abridged to such extent as may be specified in the direction;

    (c)  service shall be effected in such manner as may be specified in the direction.

*Directions*

**4.**   (1) The justices' clerk or the court may give, vary or revoke directions for the conduct of the proceedings, including—

    (a)  the timetable for the proceedings,

    (b)  varying the time within which or by which an act is required by this Schedule or by a rule where this Schedule applies to proceedings pursuant to that rule to be done,

    (c)  the service of documents, and

    (d)  the submission of evidence,

and the justices' clerk shall, on receipt of an application or of any other document by which proceedings are commenced, consider whether such directions need to be given.

(2) Where the justices' clerk or a single justice who is holding a directions appointment considers, for whatever reason, that it is inappropriate to give a direction on a particular matter, he shall refer the matter to the court which may give any appropriate direction.

(3) Directions under sub-paragraph (1) may be given, varied or revoked either—

(a) of the justices' clerk's or the court's own motion having given the resident party an opportunity to attend and be heard or to make written representations, or

(b) on the written request of either party specifying the direction which is sought.

(4) On receipt of a request under sub-paragraph (3)(b) the justices' clerk shall—

(a) make the direction sought, or

(b) fix a date for a hearing to consider the request.

*Timing of proceedings*

**5.** (1) Any period of time fixed by this Schedule or by a rule where this Schedule applies to proceedings pursuant to that rule, or by any order or direction, for doing any act shall be reckoned in accordance with this rule.

(2) Where the period, being a period of 7 days or less, would include a day which is not a business day, that day shall be excluded.

(3) Where the time fixed for filing a document with the justices' clerk expires on a day on which the justices' clerk's office is closed, and for that reason the document cannot be filed on that day, the document shall be filed in time if it is filed on the next day on which the justices' clerk's office is open.

(4) Where this Schedule or a rule where this Schedule applies to proceedings pursuant to that rule provides a period of time within which or by which a certain act is to be performed in the course of relevant proceedings, that period may not be extended otherwise than by a direction of the justices' clerk or the court under paragraph 4(1) above.

(5) At the—

(a) transfer to a court of proceedings,

(b) postponement or adjournment of any hearing or directions appointment in the course of relevant proceedings, or

(c) conclusion of any such hearing or directions appointment other than one at which the proceedings are determined, or so soon thereafter as is practicable,

the justices' clerk or the court shall—

(i) fix a date upon which the proceedings shall come before the justices' clerk or the court again for such purposes as the justices' clerk or the court directs, which date shall, where paragraph (a) applies, be as soon as possible after the transfer, and

(ii) give notice to the resident party of the date so fixed.

*Attendance at directions appointment and hearing*

**6.** (1) The resident party shall attend a directions appointment of which he has been given notice in accordance with paragraph 4 above unless the justices' clerk or the court otherwise directs.

(2) Where at the time and place appointed for a hearing or directions appointment the resident party does not appear the justices' clerk or the court shall not proceed with the hearing or appointment unless—

(a) the proceedings relate to an application filed by the resident party, or

(b) the court is satisfied that the resident party has received reasonable notice of the hearing or appointment.

(3) Where at the time and place appointed for a hearing or directions appointment the non-resident party does not appear the court may proceed with the hearing or appointment where the proceedings relate to an order or application sent by the Lord Chancellor to the court under the Act.

(4) Nothing in this Schedule shall be taken as preventing either party from appearing at any hearing or directions appointment.

*Documentary evidence*

**7.**   (1) A party shall file, at or by such time as the justices' clerk or the court directs or, in the absence of a direction, before the hearing or appointment—
  (a)  written statements of the substance of the oral evidence which he intends to adduce at a hearing or a directions appointment, which shall—
      (i)  be dated,
      (ii)  be signed by the person making the statement,
      (iii)  contain a declaration that the maker of the statement believes it to be true and understands that it may be placed before the court, and
      (iv)  show in the top right-hand corner of the first page—
          (a)  the initials and surname of the person making the statement,
          (b)  the number of the statement in relation to the maker,
          (c)  the date on which the statement was made, and
          (d)  the party on whose behalf it is filed, and
  (b)  copies of any documents upon which he intends to rely at a hearing or a directions appointment.

(2) A party may, subject to any direction of the justices' clerk or the court about the timing of statements under this rule, file a statement which is supplementary to a statement served under sub-paragraph (1).

(3) Where a non-resident party files a statement or document under this rule, he shall also file a copy of it for service on the resident party; and the justices' clerk shall on receipt of that copy serve it on the resident party.

(4) At a hearing or directions appointment a party may not without the leave of the justices' clerk, in the case of a directions appointment, or the court—
  (a)  adduce evidence, or
  (b)  seek to rely on a document,
in respect of which he has failed to comply with the requirements of sub-paragraphs (1) and, where applicable, (3).

*Amendment*

**8.**   (1) A party amending a document shall file the amended document with the justices' clerk; and the amendments shall be identified.

(2) Paragraph 7(3) above applies to an amended document filed under this paragraph.

*Oral evidence*

**9.**   The justices' clerk or the court shall keep a note of the substance of any oral evidence given at a hearing or directions appointment.

*Hearing*

**10.**   (1) Before the hearing, the justice or justices who will be dealing with the case shall read any documents which have been filed under paragraph 7 above in respect of the hearing.

(2) The justices' clerk at a directions appointment, or the court at a hearing or directions appointment, may give directions as to the order of speeches and evidence.

(3) After the final hearing, the court shall make its decision as soon as is practicable.

(4) Before the court makes an order or refuses an application, the justices' clerk shall record in writing—
  (a)  the names of the justice or justices constituting the court by which the decision is made, and

(b) in consultation with the justice or justices, the reasons for the court's decision and any findings of fact.

(5) After the court announces its decision, the justices' clerk shall as soon as practicable make a record in writing of any order.

(6) Where, under subsection (4) of section 7 of the Domestic Proceedings and Magistrates' Courts Act 1978, a court decides to treat an application under section 7 as if it were an application for an order under section 2 of that Act, the court shall indicate orally which of grounds (a) and (b) in that subsection it considers applicable and a memorandum of that decision and the grounds therefor shall be entered in the court's register.

*Confidentiality of documents*

**11.** (1) No document, other than a record of an order, held by the court and relating to any proceedings shall be disclosed, other than to—
(a) a party,
(b) the legal representative of a party,
(c) the Lord Chancellor's Department, or
(d) the Legal Aid Board,
without leave of the justices' clerk or the court.

*Delegation by justices' clerk*

**12.** (1) In this paragraph, 'employed as a clerk in court' has the same meaning as in rule 2(1) of the Justices' Clerks (Qualifications of Assistants) Rules 1979.

(2) Anything authorised to be done by, to or before a justices' clerk under this Schedule or under a rule to which this Schedule applies may be done instead by, to or before a person employed as a clerk in court where that person is appointed by the magistrates' courts committee to assist him and where that person has been specifically authorised by the justices' clerk for that purpose.

(3) Any authorisation by the justices' clerk under sub-paragraph (2) shall be recorded in writing at the time the authority is given or as soon as practicable thereafter.

*Application of section 97 of the Magistrates' Courts Act 1980*

**13.** (1) Subject to sub-paragraph (2) below, section 97 of the Magistrates' Courts Act 1980 shall apply to proceedings to which this Schedule applies as it applies to a hearing of a complaint under that section.

(2) The power of a justice under section 97 of that Act to issue a witness summons may be exercised by a justices' clerk.


## ATTACHMENT OF EARNINGS (EMPLOYER'S DEDUCTION) ORDER 1980

**Dated** 14 April 1980

**SI 1980 No 558**

The Lord Chancellor, in exercise of the powers conferred on him by section 7(4)(a) and (5) of the Attachment of Earnings Act 1971, hereby makes the following Order—
**1.** This Order may be cited as the Attachment of Earnings (Employer's Deduction) Order 1980 and shall come into operation on 1 June 1980.
**2.** On any occasion when, after the coming into operation of this Order, an employer makes a deduction from a debtor's earnings in compliance with an attachment of earnings order, he shall be entitled to deduct, in addition, 50 pence towards his clerical and administrative costs, in lieu of the sum of 13 pence prescribed by the Attachment of Earnings (Employer's Deduction) Order 1975, and section 7(4)(a) of the Attachment of Earnings Act 1971 shall have effect accordingly.

**3.**  The Attachment of Earnings (Employer's Deduction) Order 1975 is hereby revoked.

## EVIDENCE (PROCEEDINGS IN OTHER JURISDICTIONS) (GUERNSEY) ORDER 1980

**Dated** 17 December 1980

**SI 1980 No 1956**

At the Court at Buckingham Palace, the 17th day of December 1980

Present,

The Queen's Most Excellent Majesty in Council

Her Majesty, in exercise of the powers conferred upon Her by section 10(3) of the Evidence (Proceedings in Other Jurisdictions) Act 1975, is pleased, by and with the advice of Her Privy Council, to order, and it is hereby ordered, as follows—

**1.**  This Order may be cited as the Evidence (Proceedings in Other Jurisdictions) (Guernsey) Order 1980 and shall come into operation on 10 January 1981.

**2.**  In this Order and in the Schedules hereto the following expressions have the meanings hereby respectively assigned to them—
'the Bailiwick' means the Bailiwick of Guernsey and the territorial waters adjacent thereto;
'the appropriate Court' means—
(a)  as respects the Island of Guernsey, the Royal Court sitting as an Ordinary Court;
(b)  as respects the Island of Alderney, the Court of Alderney;
(c)  as respects the Island of Sark, the Court of the Seneschal of Sark.

**3.**  The provisions of the Evidence (Proceedings in Other Jurisdictions) Act 1975 shall extend to the Bailiwick subject to the exceptions, adaptations and modifications specified in Schedule 1 to this Order.

**4.**  The provisions of the Evidence (European Court) Order 1976 shall extend to the Bailiwick subject to the exceptions, adaptations and modifications specified in Schedule 2 to this Order.

SCHEDULE 1                                                    Article 3

EXCEPTIONS, ADAPTATIONS AND MODIFICATIONS IN THE EXTENSION OF THE EVIDENCE (PROCEEDINGS IN OTHER JURISDICTIONS) ACT 1975 TO THE BAILIWICK

**1.**  (1)  For any reference in the Evidence (Proceedings in Other Jurisdictions) Act 1975, as extended to the Bailiwick by this Order, to the High Court, the Court of Session or the High Court of Justice in Northern Ireland, there shall be substituted a reference to the appropriate Court.
(2)  For any reference in the said Act, as extended, to the United Kingdom, except the reference in section 3(3), there shall be substituted a reference to the Bailiwick.
**2.**  In section 3(3), after the words 'the United Kingdom' there shall be inserted the words 'or the Bailiwick'.
**3.**  Section 4 shall be omitted.
**4.**  Section 6(2) shall be omitted.

**5.** In section 7, for the words from the beginning of the section to the words 'Northern Ireland Act 1962', there shall be substituted the words—

'The power of the Royal Court sitting as a Full Court to make rules of court under Article 64 of the Reform (Guernsey) Law 1948, and section 12 of the Royal Court of Guernsey (Miscellaneous Reform Provisions) Law 1950.'

**6.** Section 8(1), together with Schedule 1 to the Act, shall be omitted.

**7.** In section 10, subsections (2) and (3) shall be omitted.

SCHEDULE 2                                                                 Article 4

EXCEPTIONS, ADAPTATIONS AND MODIFICATIONS TO THE EVIDENCE (EUROPEAN COURT) ORDER 1976 IN ITS EXTENSION TO THE BAILIWICK

**1.** In Article 2, after the words 'Act 1975' there shall be inserted the words '(as extended, subject to adaptations, to the Bailiwick of Guernsey by the Evidence (Proceedings in Other Jurisdictions) (Guernsey) Order 1980)'.

**2.** Article 3 shall be omitted.

## MAGISTRATES' COURTS RULES 1981

**Dated** 20 March 1981

**SI 1981 No 552**

*'These Rules are printed excluding the modifications necessary to the procedure created by the Crime and Disorder Act 1997, ss 51, 52 and Sch 3. The modifications, made by SI 1998/3046 with effect from 4 January 1999, are not relevant to this work.'*

GENERAL

*Citation, operation and revocations*

**1.** (1) These Rules may be cited as the Magistrates' Courts Rules 1981 and shall come into operation on 6 July 1981.

(2) The Rules mentioned in the Schedule to these Rules are hereby revoked; but where proceedings were commenced before 6 July 1981 and the old enactments within the meaning of paragraphs 1 and 2(2) of Schedule 8 to the Magistrates' Courts Act 1980 continue to apply by virtue of paragraph 2(1) of the said Schedule 8, the provisions of the Rules so mentioned continue to apply and nothing in these Rules affects those provisions.

*Interpretation*

**2.** (1) In these Rules—

'the Act of 1978' means the Domestic Proceedings and Magistrates' Courts Act 1978;

'the Act of 1980' means the Magistrates' Courts Act 1980;

'the Act of 1989' means the Children Act 1989;

'the Act of 1998' means the Crime and Disorder Act 1998;

'the Act of 2000' means the Powers of Criminal Courts (Sentencing) Act 2000;

'child' means a person who has not attained the age of 18;

'court computer system' means a computer or computer system which is used to assist to discharge and record the business of the court;

'electronic signature' is as much of anything in electronic form as

(a) is incorporated into or otherwise logically associated with any electronic communication or electronic data; and

(b) purports to be so incorporated or associated for the purpose of being used in establishing the authenticity of the communication or data, the integrity of the communication, or both;

'*contribution order*' *has the meaning assigned to it in paragraph 23(2) of Schedule 2 to the Act of 1989;*

'judgment summons' has the meaning assigned to it by rule 58.

(2) *In these Rules* '*legal aid order*' *and* '*statement of means*' *have the meanings assigned to them by regulation 31(1) of the Legal Aid in Criminal Proceedings (General) Regulations 1968.*

[(2) In these Rules 'representation order' has the meaning assigned to it by section 14 of the Access to Justice Act 1999.]

(3) In these Rules a reference to the person with whom a child has his home shall be construed in accordance with the Act of 1989, except that, in the case of any child in the care of a local authority, the local authority shall be treated for the purposes of these Rules as the person with whom the child has his home.

(4) In these Rules a reference to 'the authorised persons for the police area' is a reference to the persons employed by a local authority in that area or by the chief officer of police or the police authority for that area who are authorised by the chief officer of police to execute warrants.

(5) Any requirement in these Rules that a document shall be in the prescribed form shall be construed as a requirement that the document shall be in the form prescribed in that behalf by rules made under section 144 of the Act of 1980, or a form to like effect.

(6) In these Rules any reference to a rule shall be construed as a reference to a rule contained in these Rules; and any reference in a rule to a paragraph shall be construed as a reference to a paragraph of that rule.

[(7) Subject to rules 15 and 99, where these Rules require a document to be given or sent or a notice to be communicated in writing, it may, with the consent of the addressee, be sent by electronic communication.

(8) Electronic communication means a communication transmitted (whether from one person to another, from one device to another or from a person to a device or vice versa)—

(a) by means of a telecommunication system (within the meaning of the Telecommunications Act 1984); or

(b) by other means but while in an electronic form.]

**Note.** In para (1) definition 'the Act of 1998' inserted by SI 2000/3361, r 2(1), (2), as from 15 January 2001. Definitions 'the Act of 2000', 'court computer system', 'electronic signature' inserted and definition 'contribution order' revoked by SI 2003/1236, rr 9, 11(a)–(c), as from 20 June 2003. Para (2) substituted and paras (7), (8), inserted by SI 2003/1236, rr 9, 11(d), (e), as from 20 June 2003.

*Saving for the Family Proceedings Courts (Children Act 1989) Rules 1991 and the Family Proceedings Courts (Matrimonial Proceedings etc) Rules 1991*

**3.** The provisions of these Rules shall have effect subject to the provisions of the Family Proceedings Courts (Children Act 1989) Rules 1991 and the Family Proceedings Courts (Matrimonial Proceedings etc) Rules 1991.

INFORMATION AND COMPLAINT

*Information and complaint*

**4.** (1) An information may be laid or complaint made by the prosecutor or complainant in person or by his counsel or solicitor or other person authorised in that behalf.

(2) Subject to any provision of the Act of 1980 and any other enactment, an information or complaint need not be in writing or on oath.

(3) It shall not be necessary in an information or complaint to specify or negative an exception, exemption, proviso, excuse or qualification, whether or not it accompanies the description of the offence or matter of complaint contained in the enactment creating the offence or on which the complaint is founded.

\*     \*     \*     \*     \*

*Certification of records*

**38.** For the purposes of section 84(2) of the Act of 1978 (which provides that a copy of any record made by virtue of section 84 of the reasons for a decision of a magistrates' court shall, if certified by such officer of the court as may be prescribed, be admissible as evidence of those reasons) the certifying officer shall be the *clerk of* [justices' chief executive for] the magistrates' court concerned.

**Note.** Words 'clerk of' substituted by words 'justices' chief executive for' in square brackets by SI 2001/610, rr 2, 3 as from 1 April 2001.

ORDERS FOR PERIODICAL PAYMENTS

*Method of making periodical payments*

**39.** (1) Where a magistrates' court makes a means of payment order, the clerk of the court shall record on the order for periodical payments to which the means of payment order relates, the means of payment which the court has ordered and [the justices' chief executive shall] notify in writing, as soon as practicable, the person liable to make payments under the order of how payments are to be made.

(2) Where the court orders that payments by the debtor to the creditor are to be made to the *clerk of* [justices' chief executive for] the court or to the *clerk of* [justices' chief executive for] any other magistrates' court under section 59(3)(b) of the Act of 1980, *the clerk to whom* [the justices' chief executive to whom] the payments are ordered to be made shall notify the person liable to make the payments of the hours during which, and the place at which, payments are to be made.

(3) The *clerk of* [justices' chief executive for] the court to whom any periodical payments are made shall send them by post to—
   (a) the person entitled to them; or
   (b) if the person entitled to them is a child, to the child or to the person with whom the child has his home:
Provided that *the clerk may* [the justices' chief executive may]—
   (a) at the request of the person entitled to the payments; or
   (b) if the person entitled to them is a child, at the request of the child or the person with whom the child has his home,
make other arrangements for making the payments.

(4) If a person makes any periodical payments to the *clerk of* [justices' chief executive for] a magistrates' court otherwise than in person at *the clerk's office* [the office of the justices' chief executive], he shall do so at his own risk and expense.

(5) Where the court orders that payments by the debtor to the creditor be made by a method of payment falling within section 59(6) of the Act of 1980 (standing order, etc), the *clerk of* [justices' chief executive for] the court shall notify the person liable to make payments under the order of the number and location of the account into which the payments should be made.

(6) Where the *clerk of* [justices' chief executive for] a magistrates' court receives an application from an interested party under section 20ZA(2) of the Act of 1978, section 60(4) of the Act of 1980 or paragraph 6A(2) of Schedule 1 to the Children Act 1989 for the method of payment to be varied, *the clerk shall notify* [the justices' chief executive shall notify] in writing as soon as practicable, that party and, where practicable, any other interested party, of the result of the application, including any decision to refer the matter to the court; where *the clerk grants* [the clerk of the court grants] the application, he shall record the variation on the order for periodical payments to which the variation relates.

(7) In this rule 'means of payment order' means an order of a magistrates' court under paragraphs (a) to (d) of section 59(3) of the Act of 1980.

**Note.** Words 'clerk of' in each place they occur substituted by words 'justices' chief executive for' in square brackets by SI 2001/610, rr 2, 3 as from 1 April 2001. In para (1) words 'the justices' chief executive shall' in square brackets inserted by SI 2001/610, rr 2, 8(a); in para (2) words 'the clerk to whom' substituted by words 'the justices' chief executive to whom' in square brackets by SI 2001/610, rr 2, 8(b); in para (3) words 'the clerk may' substituted by words 'the justices' chief executive may' in square brackets by SI 2001/610, rr 2, 8(c); in para (4) words 'the clerks office' substituted by words 'the office of the justices' chief executive' in square brackets by SI 2001/610, rr 2, 8(d); in para (6) words 'the clerk shall notify' and 'the clerk grants' substituted by words 'the justices' chief executive shall notify' and 'the clerk of the court grants' in square brackets by SI 2001/610, rr 2, 8(e), all as from 1 April 2001.

*Duty of clerk to notify arrears of periodical payments*

**40.**   *Where an order under section 59(1) of the Act requires periodical payments to be made to the clerk of [justices' chief executive for] a magistrates' court and the payments are at any time in arrears to an amount equal—*

  (a)   *in the case of payments to be made monthly or less frequently, to twice the sum payable periodically; or*

  (b)   *in any other case, to four times the sum payable periodically,*

*the clerk shall [the justices' chief executive shall], unless it appears to him that it is unnecessary or inexpedient to do so, give to the person entitled to the payments or, if that person is a child, to the child or the person with whom the child has his home notice in writing stating the particulars of the arrears.*

**Note.** Revoked by SI 2003/1236, rr 9, 28, as from 20 June 2003. (Words 'clerk of' and 'the clerk shall' therein substituted by words 'justices' chief executive for' and 'the justices' chief executive shall' substituted by SI 2001/610, rr 2, 3, 7 as from 1 April 2001.)

*Revocation, variation, etc, of orders for periodical payments*

**41.**   (1)   This rule shall apply to a complaint for the revocation, discharge, revival, alteration or variation of a magistrates' court maintenance order or order enforceable as a magistrates' court maintenance order, but shall not apply—

  (a)   where jurisdiction is confined by paragraph (a) of subsection (2) of section 88 of the Children and Young Persons Act 1933 to courts appointed for the commission area where the person liable is residing;

  (b)   where an order has been made under the proviso to subsection (4) of that section;

  (c)   to a contribution order;

  (d)   to a complaint for an order under section 26(4) of the Children Act 1948;

  (e)   to a complaint for an order under section 22(1) of the Maintenance Orders Act 1950.

(2)   A complaint to which this rule applies may be made to a justice of the peace acting for the same petty sessions area as the responsible court or to a justice of the peace acting for the petty sessions area where the complainant is for the time being.

(3)   A justice of the peace shall not take action on a complaint to which this rule applies unless either the complainant has furnished him with written particulars—

  (a)   of the nature of the evidence that the complainant proposes to adduce at the hearing of the complaint and the names and addresses and, if known to him, the occupations of his witnesses; and

  (b)   of the occupations of the complainant and defendant and the address of the complainant and last address of the defendant known to the complainant,

or the justice is acting for the same petty sessions area as the responsible court and it appears to him that the last address of the defendant known to the complainant is within that area.

(4)   Where a complaint to which this rule applies is made to a justice of the peace acting for the same petty sessions area as the responsible court, and it appears to him that either of the places stated in the said particulars as being the addresses

of the complainant and defendant is within another petty sessions area, then, if the justice determines that the complaint could more conveniently be dealt with by a magistrates' court acting for that other petty sessions area, he shall cause the *clerk of* [justices' chief executive for] the responsible court to send by post to the *clerk of* [justices' chief executive for] that other court the complaint, the said particulars and a copy of any relevant record of reasons for a decision kept in pursuance of rule 36.

(5) Where the places stated in the said particulars as being the addresses of the complainant and the defendant appear to the justice to be outside the petty sessions area for which the justice is acting and in other and different petty sessions areas, the reference in the last preceding paragraph to another petty sessions area shall be construed as a reference to such one of those other areas aforesaid as appears to the justice convenient.

(6) On receipt by the *clerk of* [justices' chief executive for] a magistrates' court of a complaint, the particulars and a copy of any relevant record of reasons under paragraph (4), he shall bring the complaint before the court, and the court shall issue a summons requiring the defendant to appear before it, and shall hear and determine the complaint.

(7) Where a complaint to which this rule applies is made to a justice of the peace acting for a petty sessions area other than that for which the responsible court acts, the justice shall cause the *clerk of* [justices' chief executive for] the magistrates' court acting for that other petty sessions area to send the complaint, the said particulars and the said copy of any relevant record of reasons by post to the *clerk of* [justices' chief executive for] the responsible court; and the *clerk of* [justices' chief executive for] the responsible court shall bring the complaint before the court; and thereupon paragraphs (4) to (6) shall have effect as if the complaint had been made and the particulars and the copy of any relevant record of reasons furnished to a justice of the peace acting for the same petty sessions area as the responsible court.

(8) Notwithstanding the foregoing provisions of this rule, a justice to whom a complaint is made may refer the complaint to the responsible court which may, in such case or when the complaint is brought before the court in accordance with paragraph (6), cause the complaint, the particulars and the copy of any relevant record of reasons to be sent by post to the *clerk of* [justices' chief executive for] the court which made the original order and *that clerk* [that chief executive] and that court shall proceed in accordance with the provisions of paragraph (6).

(9) Where a magistrates' court makes an order on a complaint to which this rule applies affecting an order made by another magistrates' court or affecting an order under which payments are made to the *clerk of* [justices' chief executive for] another magistrates' court, the *clerk of* [justices' chief executive for] the first-mentioned court shall cause a copy of the order to be sent to the *clerk of* [justices' chief executive for] that other court.

(10) In this rule 'responsible court' means—

(a) where payments under the order are made to the *clerk of* [justices' chief executive for] a magistrates' court, that court;

(b) where payments are not so made, the court which made the order.

**Note.** Words 'clerk of' in each place they occur substituted by words 'justices' chief executive for' in square brackets, and words 'that clerk' substituted by words 'that chief executive' in square brackets by SI 2001/610, rr 2, 3, 6 as from 1 April 2001.

*Application for sums under affiliation order to be paid to person having custody of child*

**42.** *Revoked.*

*Service of copy of order*

**43.** Where a magistrates' court makes, revokes, discharges, suspends, revives, alters or varies a magistrates' courts maintenance order or order enforceable as a magistrates' courts maintenance order or allows time or further time for payment of a lump sum under any such order or orders payment of a lump sum under any such order to be paid by instalments or varies any such order for payment by instalments the court shall cause a copy of its order to be served on the defendant by delivering it to him or by sending it by post in a letter addressed to him at his last known or usual place of abode.

*Remission of sums due under order*

**44.**   (1)  Before remitting the whole or any part of a sum due under a magistrates' courts maintenance order or an order enforceable as a magistrates' courts maintenance order under section 95 of the Act of 1980, the court shall, except save where it appears to it to be unnecessary or impracticable to do so, cause the person in whose favour the order is made or, if that person is a child, the child or the person with whom the child has his home to be notified of its intention and shall afford to such person a reasonable opportunity to make representations to the court, either orally at an adjourned hearing of the complaint for enforcement or in writing and such representations shall be considered by the court.

(2)  Any written representations may be considered by the court if they purport to be signed by or on behalf of the person in whose favour the order is made or, if that person is a child, by or on behalf of the child or the person with whom the child has his home.

*Duty of clerk* [justices' chief executive] *to notify remarriage of person entitled to payments under a maintenance order*

**45.**   (1)  Where the *clerk of* [justices' chief executive for] a magistrates' court to whom any payments under an order to which this rule applies are required to be made is notified in writing by or on behalf of the person entitled to payments under such an order, the person liable to make payments under such an order or the personal representatives of either of those persons that the person so entitled has remarried, *the clerk shall* [the justices' chief executive shall] forthwith in writing so notify *the clerk or other appropriate officer of* [the justices' chief executive for or other appropriate officer of] each of the courts mentioned in paragraph (2) *of which he is not the clerk* [for which he is not the justices' chief executive]

(2)  The courts referred to in paragraph (1) are—

(a)  any court which has made a relevant order or, in the case of a provisional order made under section 3 of the Maintenance Orders (Facilities for Enforcement) Act 1920 or section 3 of the Maintenance Orders (Reciprocal Enforcement) Act 1972, the court which confirmed the order;

(b)  if a relevant order has been transmitted abroad for registration under section 2 of the said Act of 1920 or section 2 of the said Act of 1972 the court in which the order is registered, and

(c)  if a complaint for the enforcement of a relevant order has been sent to a court under rule 59(2), that court.

(3)  This rule applies to an order in relation to which section 4(2) of the Act of 1978 applies, an order to which section 38 of the Matrimonial Causes Act 1973 applies and an attachment of earnings order made to secure payments under either of the above-mentioned orders and in paragraph (2) 'relevant order' means any such order to which the payments referred to in paragraph (1) relate.

**Note.** Words 'clerk of' substituted by words 'justices' chief executive for' in square brackets, words 'the clerk shall' substituted by words 'the justices' chief executive shall' in square brackets, words 'the clerk or other appropriate officer' substituted by words 'the justices' chief executive for or other appropriate officer' in square brackets and words 'of which he is not the clerk' substituted for words 'for which he is not the justices' chief executive' in square brackets, by SI 2001/610, rr 2, 3, 7, 9 as from 1 April 2001.

SATISFACTION, ENFORCEMENT AND APPLICATION OF PAYMENTS

\* \* \* \* \*

*To whom payments are to be made*

**48.** (1) A person adjudged by the conviction of a magistrates' court to pay any sum shall, unless the court otherwise directs, pay that sum, or any instalment of that sum, to the *clerk of* [justices' chief executive for] the court.

(2) Where payment of any sum or instalment of any sum adjudged to be paid by the conviction or order of a magistrates' court is made to any person other than the *clerk of* [justices' chief executive for] the court, that person, unless he is the person to whom the court has directed payment to be made or, in the case of a child, is the person with whom the child has his home, shall, as soon as may be, account for and, *if the clerk* [if the justices' chief executive] so requires, pay over the sum or instalment to the *clerk of* [justices' chief executive for] the court.

(3) Where payment of any sum adjudged to be paid by the conviction or order of a magistrates' court, or any instalment of such a sum, is directed to be made to the *clerk of* [justices' chief executive for] some other magistrates' court, the *clerk of* [justices' chief executive for] the court that adjudged the sum to be paid shall pay over any sums received by him on account of the said sum or instalment to the *clerk of* [justices' chief executive for] that other court.

**Note.** Words 'clerk of' in each place they occur substituted by words 'justices' chief executive for' in square brackets and words 'if the clerk' substituted by words 'if the justices' chief executive' in square brackets, by SI 2001/610, rr 2, 3, 10 as from 1 April 2001.

*Duty of clerk* [justices' chief executive] *to give receipt*

**49.** The *clerk of* [justices' chief executive for] a magistrates' court shall give or send a receipt to any person who makes a payment to him in pursuance of a conviction or order of a magistrates' court and who asks for a receipt.

**Note.** Words 'clerk of' in both places they occur substituted by words 'justices' chief executive for' in square brackets by SI 2001/610, rr 2, 3 as from 1 April 2001.

*Relief of collecting officer*

**50.** *Revoked.*

*Application for further time*

**51.** An application under section 75(2) of the Act of 1980 or section 22 of the Act of 1978, unless the court requires the applicant to attend, be made in writing.

*Notice of date of hearing of means inquiry etc*

**52.** Where a magistrates' court, under subsection (1) of section 86 of the Act of 1980 (power of magistrates' court to fix day for appearance of offender at means inquiry etc), has fixed a day on which an offender must appear in person before the court and, under subsection (3) of that section, fixes a later day in substitution for the day previously fixed, service of the notice of the substituted day may be effected in any manner in which service of a summons may be effected under rule 99(1).

\* \* \* \* \*

*Notice to defendant before enforcing order*

**53.** (1) A warrant of distress shall not be issued for failure to pay a sum enforceable as a civil debt unless the defendant has been previously served with a copy of the minute of the order, or the order was made in his presence and the warrant is issued on that occasion.

(2) A warrant of commitment shall not be issued for disobedience to an order of a magistrates' court unless the defendant has been previously served with a copy of the minute of the order, or the order was made in his presence and the warrant is issued on that occasion:

Provided that this paragraph shall not apply to—

(a) an order to pay money; or

(b) an expedited order under section 16(2) and (6) of the Act of 1978.

(3) A copy of the minute of the order shall be served under this rule by delivering it to the defendant or by sending it to him by post in a letter addressed to him at his last known or usual place of abode.

(4) In relation to an order under section 16 of the Act of 1978 (other than an expedited order under subsections (2) and (6) of that section) paragraphs (2) and (3) shall have effect as if for the references to a copy of a minute of the order there were substituted references to a copy of the order.

*Execution of distress warrant*

**54.**   (1) A warrant of distress issued for the purpose of levying a sum adjudged to be paid by a summary conviction or order—

(a) shall name or otherwise describe the person against whom the distress is to be levied;

(b) shall be directed to the constables of the police area in which the warrant is issued or to the *authorised persons* [civilian enforcement officers] for the police area specified in the warrant, or to a person named in the warrant and shall, subject to, and in accordance with, the provisions of this rule, require them to levy the said sum by distress and sale of the goods belonging to the said person;

(c) may where it is directed to the constables of a police area, instead of being executed by any of those constables, be executed by any person under the direction of a constable.

(2) The warrant shall authorise the person charged with the execution of it to take as well as any money any goods of the person against whom the distress is levied; and any money so taken shall be treated as if it were the proceeds of the sale of goods taken under the warrant.

(3) The warrant shall require the person charged with the execution to pay the sum to be levied to the *clerk of* [justices' chief executive for] the court that issued the warrant.

[(3A) A warrant to which this rule applies may be executed by the persons to whom it was directed or by any of the following persons, whether or not the warrant was directed to them—

(a) a constable for any police area in England and Wales, acting in his own police area;

(b) where the warrant is one to which section 125A of the Act of 1980 applies, a civilian enforcement officer within the meaning of section 125A of the Act of 1980;

(c) where the warrant is one to which section 125A of the Act of 1980 applies, any of the individuals described in section 125B(1) of the Act of 1980;

and in this rule any reference to the person charged with the execution of a warrant includes any of the above persons who is for the time being authorised to execute the warrant, whether or not they have the warrant in their possession at the time.

(3B) A person executing a warrant of distress shall—

(a) either—

(i) if he has the warrant with him, show it to the person against whom the distress is levied, or

(ii) otherwise, state where the warrant is and what arrangements may be made to allow the person against whom distress is levied to inspect it;

(b) explain, in ordinary language, the sum for which distress is levied and the reason for the distress;

(c) where the person executing the warrant is one of the persons referred to in paragraph (3A)(b) or (c) above, show the person against whom the distress is levied a written statement under section 125A(4) or 125B(4) as appropriate; and

(d) in any case, show documentary proof of his identity.]

(4) *There shall not be taken under the warrant the wearing apparel or bedding of any person or his family or the tools and implements of his trade.*

[(4) There shall not be taken under the warrant the clothing or bedding of any person or his family or the tools, books, vehicles or other equipment which he personally needs to use in his employment, business or vocation, provided that in this paragraph the word 'person' shall not include a corporation.]

(5) The distress levied under any such warrant as aforesaid shall be sold within such period beginning not earlier than the 6th day after the making of the distress as may be specified in the warrant, or if no period is specified in the warrant, within a period beginning on the 6th day and ending on the 14th day after the making of the distress:

Provided that with the consent in writing of the person against whom the distress is levied the distress may be sold before the beginning of the said period.

[(5A) The clerk of the court which issued the warrant may, on the application of the person charged with the execution of it, extend the period within which the distress must be sold by any number of days not exceeding 60; but following the grant of such an application there shall be no further variation or extension of that period.]

(6) The said distress shall be sold by public auction or in such other manner as the person against whom the distress is levied may in writing allow.

(7) Notwithstanding anything in the preceding provisions of this rule, the said distress shall not be sold if the sum for which the warrant was issued and the charges of taking and keeping the distress have been paid.

(8) Subject to any direction to the contrary in the warrant, where the distress is levied on household goods, the goods shall not, without the consent in writing of the person against whom the distress is levied, be removed from the house until the day of sale; and so much of the goods shall be impounded as is in the opinion of the person executing the warrant sufficient to satisfy the distress, by affixing to the articles impounded a conspicuous mark.

(9) The *constable or other* person charged with the execution of any such warrant as aforesaid shall cause the distress to be sold, and may deduct out of the amount realised by the sale all costs and charges incurred in effecting the sale; and he shall return to the owner the balance, if any, after retaining the amount of the sum for which the warrant was issued and the proper costs and charges of the execution of the warrant.

(10) The *constable or other* person charged with the execution of any such warrant as aforesaid shall as soon as practicable send to the *clerk of* [justices' chief executive for] the court that issued it a written account of the costs and charges incurred in executing it; and *the clerk shall* [the justices' chief executive shall] allow the person against whom the distress was levied to inspect the account within one month after the levy of the distress at any reasonable time to be appointed by the court.

(11) If any person pays or tenders to the *constable or other* person charged with the execution of any such warrant as aforesaid the sum mentioned in the warrant, or produces a receipt for that sum given by the *clerk of* [justices' chief executive for] the court that issued the warrant, and also pays the amount of the costs and charges of the distress up to the time of the payment or tender or the production of the receipt, the constable or other person as aforesaid shall not execute the warrant, or shall cease to execute it, as the case may be.

**Note.** In para (1)(b) words 'authorised persons' substituted by words 'civilian enforcement officers' by SI 2001/167, r 3(1) as from 19 February 2001. In para (3) words 'clerk of' substituted for words 'justices' chief executive for' in square brackets by SI 2001/610, rr 2, 3 as from 1 April 2001. Paras (3A), (3B): inserted by SI 2001/167, r 3(2) as from 1 April 2001. Para (4): substituted by SI 1999/2765, r 2 as from 1 November 1999. Para (5A): inserted by SI 2001/167, r 3(3) as from 1 February 2001. In paras (9)–(11) words 'constable or other' revoked by SI 2001/167, r 3(4). In paras (10), (11) words 'clerk of' substituted by words 'justices' chief executive for' in square brackets, and words 'the clerk shall' substituted by words 'the justices' chief executive shall' in square brackets by SI 2001/610, rr 2, 3, 7 as from 1 April 2001.

*Payment after imprisonment imposed*

**55.** (1) The persons authorised for the purposes of section 79(2) of the Act of 1980 to receive a part payment are—
  (a) unless there has been issued a warrant of distress or commitment, the *clerk of* [justices' chief executive for] the court enforcing payment of the sum, or any person appointed under section 88 of that Act to supervise the offender;
  (b) where the issue of a warrant of commitment has been suspended on conditions which provide for payment to be made to the *clerk of* [justices' chief executive for] some other magistrates' court, *that clerk* [that chief executive];
  (c) any constable holding a warrant of distress or commitment or, where the warrant is directed to some other person, that person;
  (d) the governor or keeper of the prison or place in which the defaulter is detained, or other person having lawful custody of the defaulter:
    Provided that—
    (i) the said governor or keeper shall not be required to accept any sum tendered in part payment under the said subsection (2) except on a weekday between 9 o'clock in the morning and 5 o'clock in the afternoon; and
    (ii) no person shall be required to receive in part payment under the said subsection (2) an amount which, or so much of an amount as, will not procure a reduction of the period for which the defaulter is committed or ordered to be detained.

(2) Where a person having custody of a defaulter receives payment of any sum he shall note receipt of the sum on the warrant of commitment.

(3) Where the *clerk of* [justices' chief executive for] a court other than the court enforcing payment of the sums receives payment of any sum he shall inform the *clerk of* [justices' chief executive for] the other court.

(4) Where a person appointed under section 88 of the Act of 1980 to supervise an offender receives payment of any sum, he shall send it forthwith to the *clerk of* [justices' chief executive for] the court which appointed him.

(5) If the period of imprisonment imposed on any person in default of payment of a sum adjudged to be paid by a conviction or order of a magistrates' court, or for want of sufficient distress to satisfy such a sum, is reduced through part payments to less than 5 days, he may be committed either to a prison or to a place certified by the Secretary of State under section 134 of the Act of 1980, or, if he is already in prison, the Secretary of State may transfer him to a place so certified.

**Note.** Words 'clerk of' in each place they occur substituted by words 'justices' chief executive for' in square brackets by SI 2001/610, rr 2, 3 as from 1 April 2001. In para (1)(b) words 'that clerk' substituted by words 'that chief executive' in square brackets by SI 2001/610, rr 2, 6.

*Order for supervision*

**56.** (1) Unless an order under section 88(1) of the Act of 1980 is made in the offender's presence, the *clerk of* [justices' chief executive for] the court making the order shall deliver to the offender, or serve on him by post, notice in writing of the order.

(2) It shall be the duty of any person for the time being appointed under the said section to advise and befriend the offender with a view to inducing him to pay the sum adjudged to be paid and thereby avoid committal to custody and to give any information required by a magistrates' court about the offender's conduct and means.

**Note.** Words 'clerk of' susbstituted by words 'justices' chief executive for' in square brackets by SI 2001/610, rr 2, 3 as from 1 April 2001.

*Transfer of fine order*

**57.**   (1) The *clerk of a magistrates' court* [justices' chief executive for a magistrates' court] which has made a transfer of fine order under section 89 or 90 or section 90 as applied by section 91 of the Act of 1980 shall send to the clerk of the court having jurisdiction under the order a copy of the order.

(2) Where a magistrates' court has made a transfer of fine order in respect of a sum adjudged to be paid by a court in Scotland or in Northern Ireland *the clerk of the magistrates' court* [justices' chief executive for the magistrates' court] shall send a copy of the order to the clerk of the Scottish court or to the clerk of the Northern Irish court, as the case may be.

(3) Where the *clerk of a magistrates' court* [justices' chief executive for a magistrates' court] receives a copy of a transfer of fine order (whether made in England and Wales, or in Scotland or in Northern Ireland) specifying that court as the court by which payment of the sum in question is to be enforceable, he shall thereupon, if possible, deliver or send by post to the offender notice in writing *in the prescribed form.*

(4) Where under a transfer of fine order a sum adjudged to be paid by a Scottish court or by a Northern Irish court is enforceable by a magistrates' court—

  (a) if the sum is paid, *the clerk of the magistrates' court* [justices' chief executive for the magistrates' court] shall send it to the clerk of the Scottish court or to the clerk of the Northern Irish court, as the case may be;

  (b) if the sum is not paid, *the clerk of the magistrates' court* [justices' chief executive for the magistrates' court] shall inform the clerk of the Scottish court or the clerk of the Northern Irish court, as the case may be, of the manner in which the adjudication has been satisfied or that the sum, or any balance thereof, appears to be irrecoverable.

**Note.** In paras (1), (3) words 'clerk of a magistrates' court' substituted by words 'justices' chief executive for a magistrates' court' in square brackets by SI 2001/610, rr 2, 11. In paras (2), (4) words 'the clerk of the magistrates' court' in each place they occur substituted by words 'justices' chief executive for the magistrates' court' by SI 2001/610, rr 2, 11 as from 1 April 2001. In para (3) words 'in the prescribed form' revoked by SI 2003/1236, rr 9, 30 as from 20 June 2003.

*Civil debt: judgment summons*

**58.**   (1) A summons issued on a complaint made for the purposes of section 96 of the Act of 1980 (in these rules referred to as a 'judgment summons') shall be served on the judgment debtor personally:

Provided that if a justice of the peace is satisfied by evidence on oath that prompt personal service of the summons is impracticable, he may allow the summons to be served in such a way as he may think just.

(2) Unless the judgment debtor appears and consents to an immediate hearing, the court shall not hear the complaint unless the summons was served at least 3 clear days before the hearing.

(3) Service of a judgment summons outside the commission area for which the justice issuing the summons acted may, without prejudice to any other provision of these rules enabling service of a summons to be proved, be proved by affidavit.

*Enforcement of affiliation orders, etc*

**59.** (1) Subject to the following provisions of this rule, a complaint for the enforcement of a magistrates' courts maintenance order, or an order enforceable as a magistrates' courts maintenance order, shall be heard by the court that made the order:

Provided that—

(a) where—

    (i) the complainant is the person in whose favour the order was made or, if that person is a child, is the child or the person with whom the child has his home; and

    (ii) the complainant resides in a petty sessions area other than that for which the court acts; and

    (iii) payment is directed to be made either to the complainant or the *clerk of* [justices' chief executive for] a magistrates' court acting for that petty sessions area,

the complaint may be heard by the last-mentioned court;

(b) where the complainant is the *clerk of* [justices' chief executive for] a magistrates' court, the complaint may be heard by that court.

(2) Where a complaint is made to a justice of the peace for the enforcement of such an order as aforesaid and it appears to him that the defendant is for the time being in some petty sessions area other than that for which the justice is acting and that the order may be more conveniently enforced by a magistrates' court acting for that area, the justice shall cause the *clerk of* [justices' chief executive for] the court to send the complaint by post to the *clerk of* [justices' chief executive for] a magistrates' court acting for that other petty sessions area, and for that purpose shall write down the complaint if this has not already been done.

(3) On receipt by the *clerk of* [justices' chief executive for] a magistrates' court of a complaint sent under the last preceding paragraph, he shall bring it before the court; and the court shall issue a summons or warrant for procuring the appearance of the defendant before it, and shall hear and determine the complaint.

(4) If, after a complaint has been sent to the *clerk of* [justices' chief executive for] a magistrates' court under this rule, the *clerk of* [justices' chief executive for] the court to which the complaint was made receives any payment under the order, he shall forthwith send by post to *the clerk to whom* [the justices' chief executive to whom] the complaint was sent a certificate of the amount of the payment and of the date when it was made.

(5) If, after a complaint has been sent as aforesaid, payment under the order is made, not to the *clerk of* [justices' chief executive for] the court to which the complaint was originally made, but to the person specified in the order or, in the case of a child, to the person with whom the child has his home, that person shall forthwith *inform the clerk* [inform the justices' chief executive] of the amount and date as aforesaid and *the clerk shall forthwith send* [the justices' chief executive shall forthwith send] a certificate of the amount and date as required by the last preceding paragraph.

(6) A certificate under this rule purporting to be signed by the *clerk of* [justices' chief executive for] the court to which the complaint was originally made shall be admissible as evidence on the hearing of the complaint that the amount specified in the certificate was paid on the date so specified.

(7) This rule shall not apply—

(a) where jurisdiction is confined by section 88(2)(a) of the Children and Young Persons Act 1933, to courts having jurisdiction in the place where the person liable is residing;

(b) to a contribution order.

**Note.** Words 'clerk of' in each place they occur substituted by words 'justices' chief executive for' in square brackets by SI 2001/610, rr 2, 3 as from 1 April 2001. In para (4) words 'the clerk to whom' substituted by words 'the justices' chief executive to whom' by SI 2001/610, rr 2, 12(a). In para (5) words 'inform the clerk' and 'the clerk shall forthwith send' substituted by words 'inform the justices' chief executive' and 'the justices' chief executive shall forthwith send' respectively by SI 2001/610, r 2, 12(b).

*Enforcement where periodical payments made under more than one order*

**60.** (1) Where periodical payments are required to be made to any person by another person under more than one periodical payments order, proceedings for the recovery of the payments may be brought by way of one complaint. Any such complaint shall indicate the payments due under each order referred to in the complaint.

(2) Any sum paid to the *clerk of* [justices' chief executive for] a magistrates' court on any date by a person liable to make payments under 2 or more periodical payments orders which is less than the total sum required to be paid on that date to *that clerk* [that chief executive] by that person in respect of those orders (being orders one of which requires payments to be made for the benefit of a child to the person with whom the child has his home and one or more of which requires payments to be made to that person either for his own benefit or for the benefit of another child who has his home with him) shall be apportioned between the orders in proportion to the amounts respectively due under each order over a period of one year and if, as a result of the apportionment, the payments under any such order are no longer in arrears the residue shall be applied to the amount due under the other order or (if there is more than one other order) shall be apportioned as aforesaid between the other orders.

(3) For the purposes of calculating the apportionment of any sum under paragraph (2)—

(a) a month shall be treated as consisting of 4 weeks; and

(b) a year shall be treated as consisting of 52 weeks.

**Note.** Words 'clerk of' and 'that clerk' substituted by words 'justices' chief executive for' and 'that chief executive' in square brackets by SI 2001/610, rr 2, 3, 6 as from 1 April 2001.

*Notice of adjudication on complaint for enforcement of a magistrates' court maintenance order, etc*

**61.** A magistrates' court shall give notice in writing to the complainant of its adjudication on a complaint for the enforcement of a magistrates' courts maintenance order, or order enforceable as a magistrates' courts maintenance order, unless the complainant is present or is the *clerk of* [justices' chief executive for] the court.

**Note.** Words 'clerk of' substituted by words 'justices' chief executive for' in square brackets by SI 2001/610, rr 2, 3 as from 1 April 2001.

*Particulars relating to payment of lump sum under a magistrates' court maintenance order, etc to be entered in register*

**62.** Where a magistrates' court allows time for payment of a lump sum required to be paid under a magistrates' courts maintenance order, or order enforceable as a magistrates' courts maintenance order, or orders that any such lump sum shall be paid by instalments or varies the number of instalments payable, the amount of any instalment payable or the date on which any instalment becomes payable, particulars thereof shall be entered in the register or in any separate record kept for the purpose of recording particulars of lump sum payments.

*Notice of date of reception in custody and discharge*

**63.** (1) Where in proceedings to enforce a magistrates' courts maintenance order, or an order enforceable as a magistrates' courts maintenance order, the defendant is committed to custody, then on his discharge the governor or keeper of the prison or place of detention shall send to the *clerk of* [justices' chief executive for] the court that committed the defendant a certificate showing the dates of the defendant's reception and discharge; and *that clerk* [that chief executive] shall, if the payments under the order are required to be made to the clerk of any other court, send the certificate to the *last-mentioned clerk* [last-mentioned justices' chief executive].

(2) Where a magistrates' court issues a warrant of commitment for a default in paying a sum adjudged to be paid by a summary conviction then on the discharge of the defaulter the governor or keeper of the prison or place of detention shall send to the *clerk of* [justices' chief executive for] the court a certificate showing the dates of the defaulter's reception and discharge.

**Note.** Words 'clerk of' in each place they occur substituted by words 'justices' chief executive for' in square brackets by SI 2001/610, rr 2, 3 as from 1 April 2001. In para (1) words 'that clerk' and 'last-mentioned clerk' substituted by words 'that chief executive' and 'last-mentioned justices' chief executive' in square brackets by SI 2001/610, rr 2, 6, 13.

*Direction that money found on defaulter shall not be applied in satisfaction of debt*

**64.** Where the defaulter is committed to, or ordered to be detained in, a prison or other place of detention, any direction given under section 80(2) of the Act of 1980 shall be endorsed on the warrant of commitment.

*Particulars of fine enforcement to be entered in register*

**65.** (1) Where the court on the occasion of convicting an offender of an offence issues a warrant of commitment for a default in paying a sum adjudged to be paid by the conviction or, having power to issue such a warrant, fixes a term of imprisonment under section 77(2) of the Act of 1980, the reasons for the court's action shall be entered in the register, or any separate record kept for the purpose of recording particulars of fine enforcement.

(2) There shall be entered in the register, or any such record, particulars of any—

  (a)  means inquiry under section 82 of the Act of 1980;

  (b)  hearing under subsection (5) of the said section 82;

  (c)  allowance of further time for the payment of a sum adjudged to be paid by a conviction;

  (d)  direction that such a sum shall be paid by instalments including any direction varying the number of instalments payable, the amount of any instalments payable and the date on which any instalment becomes payable;

  (e)  distress for the enforcement of such a sum;

  (f)  attachment of earnings order for the enforcement of such a sum;

  (g)  order under that Act placing a person under supervision pending payment of such a sum;

  (h)  order under section 85(1) of that Act remitting the whole or any part of a fine;

  (i)  order under section 120(4) of that Act remitting the whole or any part of any sum enforceable under that section (forfeiture of recognizance);

  (j)  authority granted under section 87(3) of that Act authorising the taking of proceedings in the High Court or county court for the recovery of any sum adjudged to be paid by a conviction;

  (k)  transfer of fine order made by the court;

  (l)  order transferring a fine to the court;

  (m)  order under *section 32(1) of the Powers of Criminal Courts Act 1973* [section 140(1) of the Act of 2000] specifying the court for the purpose of enforcing a fine imposed or a recognizance forfeited by the Crown Court; and

  (n)  any fine imposed or recognizance forfeited by a coroner which has to be treated as imposed or forfeited by the court.

**Note.** In para (2)(m) words 'section 32(1) of the Powers of Criminal Courts Act 1977' substituted by words 'section 140(1) of the Act of 2000' in square brackets by SI 2003/1236, rr 9, 31, as from 20 June 2003.

REGISTER

*Register of convictions, etc*

**66.**　(1)　The *clerk of* [justices' chief executive for] every magistrates' court shall keep a register in which there shall be entered—

(a)　a minute or memorandum of every adjudication of the court;

(b)　a minute or memorandum of every other proceeding or thing required by these rules or any other enactment to be so entered.

(2)　*The register shall be in the prescribed form, and entries in the register shall include, where relevant, such particulars as are provided for in the said form.*

[(2)　The register may be stored in electronic form on the court computer system and entries in the register shall include, where relevant, the following particulars—

(a)　the name of the informant, complainant or applicant;

(b)　the name and date of birth (if known) of the defendant or respondent;

(c)　the nature of offence, matter of complaint or details of the application;

(d)　the date of offence or matter of complaint;

(e)　the plea or consent to order; and

(f)　the minute of adjudication.]

(3)　Particulars of any entry relating to a decision about bail or the reasons for any such decisions or the particulars of any certificate granted under section 5(6A) of the Bail Act 1976 may be made in a book separate from that in which the entry recording the decision itself is made, but any such separate book shall be regarded as forming part of the register.

(3A)　Where, by virtue of subsection (3A) of section 128 of the Act of 1980, an accused gives his consent to the hearing and determination in his absence of any application for his remand on an adjournment of the case under sections 5, 10(1) or 18(4) of that Act, the court shall cause the consent of the accused, and the date on which it was notified to the court, to be entered in the register.

(3B)　Where any consent mentioned in paragraph (3A) is withdrawn, the court shall cause the withdrawal of the consent and the date on which it was notified to the court to be entered in the register.

(4)　On the summary trial of an information the accused's plea shall be entered in the register.

(5)　Where a court tries any person summarily in any case in which he may be tried summarily only with his consent, the court shall cause his consent to be entered in the register and, if the consent is signified by a person representing him in his absence, the court shall cause that fact also to be entered in the register.

(6)　Where a person is charged before a magistrates' court with an offence triable either way the court shall cause the entry in the register to show whether he was present when the proceedings for determining the mode of trial were conducted and, if they were conducted in his absence, whether they were so conducted by virtue of section 18(3) of the Act of 1980 (disorderly conduct on his part) or by virtue of section 23(1) of that Act (consent signified by person representing him).

(7)　In any case to which section 22 of the Act of 1980 (certain offences triable either way to be tried summarily if value involved is small) applies, the court shall cause its decision as to the value involved or, as the case may be, the fact that it is unable to reach such a decision to be entered in the register.

(8)　Where a court has power under section 53(3) of the Act of 1980 to make an order with the consent of the defendant without hearing evidence, the court shall cause any consent of the defendant to the making of the order to be entered in the register.

*(9) The entry in the column of the register headed 'Nature of Offence' shall show clearly, in case of conviction or dismissal, what is the offence of which the accused is convicted or, as the case may be, what is the offence charged in the information that is dismissed.*

[(9) In the case of conviction or dismissal, the register shall clearly show the nature of the offence of which the accused is convicted or, as the case may be, the nature of the offence charged in the information that is dismissed.]

(10) An entry of a conviction in the register shall state the date of the offence.

[(10A) Where a court is required under [section 130(3) of the Act of 2000] to give reasons for not making a compensation order the court shall cause the reasons given to be entered in the register.]

[(10B) Where a court passes a custodial sentence, the court shall cause a statement of whether it obtained and considered a pre-sentence report before passing sentence to be entered in the register.]

*(11) The entries shall be signed or their accuracy certified by one of the justices, or the justice, before whom the proceedings to which they relate took place, or by the clerk who was present when those proceedings took place or, in the case of an entry required by paragraphs (3A) and (3B), where the consent or withdrawal of consent was not given or made (as the case may be) when the accused was present before the court, by the clerk or justice who received the notification:*

*Provided that, where the proceedings took place before a justice or justices sitting elsewhere than in a petty sessional court-house, the justice or, as the case may be, one of the justices may instead of signing an entry in the register, send to the clerk whose duty it is to keep the register a signed return of the proceedings containing the particulars required to be entered in the register; and the clerk shall enter the return in the register.*

*(11A) Any certificate made by virtue of paragraph (11) shall be kept with and as part of the register.*

(12) Every register shall be open to inspection during reasonable hours by any justice of the peace, or any person authorised in that behalf by a justice of the peace or the Secretary of State.

**Note.** In Para (1) words 'clerk of' substituted by words 'justices' chief executive for' in square brackets by SI 2001/610, rr 2, 3 as from 1 April 2001. Para (2) substituted by SI 2003/1236, rr 9, 32(1) and para (9) substituted by SI 2003/1236, rr 9, 32(2) both as from 20 June 2003. Para (10A); inserted by SI 1988/2132, r 2(d), and para (10B) inserted by SI 1992/2072, r 2(1). In para (10A) words 'section 130(3) of the Act of 2000' substituted by SI 2003/1236, rr 9, 32(3), as from 20 June 2003. Paras (11), (11A) revoked by SI 2003/1236, rr 9, 32(4) as from 20 June 2003.

EVIDENCE—GENERAL

*Proof of service, handwriting, etc*

**67.** (1) The service on any person of a summons, process, notice or document required or authorised to be served in any proceedings before a magistrates' court, and the handwriting or seal of a justice of the peace or other person on any warrant, summons, notice, process or documents issued or made in any such proceedings, may be proved in any legal proceedings by a document purporting to be a solemn declaration in the prescribed form made before a justice of the peace, commissioner for oaths, clerk of a magistrates' court or registrar of a county court or a sheriff or sheriff clerk (in Scotland) or a clerk of petty sessions (in Northern Ireland).

*(2) The service of any process or other document required or authorised to be served, the proper addressing, pre-paying and posting or registration for the purposes of service of a letter containing such a document, and the place, date and time of posting or registration of any such letter, may be proved in any proceedings before a magistrates' court by a document purporting to be a certificate signed by the person by whom the service was effected or the letter posted or registered.*

[(2) The service of any process or other document required or authorised to be served may be proved in any proceedings before a magistrates' court by a document purporting to be a certificate signed by the person by whom the service was effected.]

(3) References in paragraph (2) to the service of any process shall, in their application to a witness summons, be construed as including references to the payment or tender to the witness of his costs and expenses.

[(4) Any process or other document produced by the court computer system on a given day shall be sufficient evidence that the process or other document was sent to the person to whom it is addressed within 2 days of it being produced, unless the contrary is proved.]

**Note.** Para (2) substituted and para (4) inserted by SI 2003/1236, rr 9, 33 as from 20 June 2003.

### Proof of proceedings

**68.** The register of a magistrates' court, or *any document purporting to be* an extract from the register *and to be* certified by *the clerk* [the justices' chief executive] as a true extract, shall be admissible in any legal proceedings as evidence of the proceedings of the court entered in the register.

**Note.** Words 'any document purporting to be' and 'and to be' revoked by SI 2003/1236, rr 9, 34 as from 20 June 2003. Words 'the clerk' substituted by words 'the justices' chief executive' in square brackets by SI 2001/610, rr 2, 5 as from 1 April 2001.

### Proof that magistrates' court maintenance orders, etc, have not been revoked, etc

**69.** A certificate purporting to be signed by the c*lerk of* [the justices' chief executive for] a magistrates' court, and stating that no minute or memorandum of an order revoking, discharging, suspending, reviving, altering or varying a magistrates' court maintenance order, or order enforceable as a magistrates' court maintenance order or an order made under Part I of the Act of 1978 enforceable otherwise than as a magistrates' court maintenance order made by the court is entered in the register of the court shall, in any proceedings relating to the enforcement of the order or the revocation, discharge, suspension, revival, alteration or variation of the order, be evidence that the order has not been revoked, discharged, suspended, revived, altered or varied.

**Note.** Words 'clerk of' substituted by words 'justices' chief executive for' in square brackets by SI 2001/610, rr 2, 3 as from 1 April 2001.

\*   \*   \*   \*   \*

APPEAL TO CROWN COURT

### Documents to be sent to Crown Court

**74.** (1) A *clerk of* [justices' chief executive for] a magistrates' court shall as soon as practicable send to the appropriate officer of the Crown Court any notice of appeal to the Crown Court given to the *clerk of* [justices' chief executive for] the court.

(2) The *clerk of* [justices' chief executive for] a magistrates' court shall send to the appropriate officer of the Crown Court, with the notice of appeal, a copy of the extract of the magistrates' court register relating to that decision and of the last known or usual place of abode of the parties to the appeal.

(3) Where any person, having given notice of appeal to the Crown Court, has been granted bail for the purposes of the appeal the *clerk of* [justices' chief executive for] the court from whose decision the appeal is brought shall before the day fixed for the hearing of the appeal send to the appropriate officer of the Crown Court—

(a) in the case of bail in criminal proceedings, a copy of the record made in pursuance of section 5 of the Bail Act 1976 relating to such bail;

(b) in the case of bail otherwise than in criminal proceedings, the recognizance entered into by the appellant relating to such bail.

(4) Where, in any such case as is referred to in paragraph 3(b), the recognizance in question has been entered into otherwise than before the magistrates' court from whose decision the appeal is brought, or the *clerk of* [justices' chief executive for] that court, the person who took the recognizance shall send it forthwith to *that clerk* [that chief executive]

(5) Where a notice of appeal is given in respect of a hospital order or guardianship order made under section 60 of the Mental Health Act 1959, the *clerk of* [justices' chief executive for] the magistrates' court from which the appeal is brought shall send with the notice to the appropriate officer of the Crown Court any written evidence considered by the court under subsection (1)(a) of the said section 60.

(6) Where a notice of appeal is given in respect of an appeal against conviction by a magistrates' court the *clerk of* [justices' chief executive for] the court shall send with the notice to the appropriate officer of the Crown Court any admission of facts made for the purposes of the summary trial under section 10 of the Criminal Justice Act 1967.

[(7) Where a notice of appeal is given in respect of an appeal against sentence by a magistrates' court, and where that sentence was a custodial sentence, the [justices' chief executive for] the court shall send with the notice to the appropriate office of the Crown Court a statement of whether the magistrates' court obtained and considered a pre-sentence report before passing such sentence.]

**Note.** Words 'clerk of' in each place they occur substituted by words 'justices' chief executive for' in square brackets and in para (4) words 'that clerk' substituted by words 'that chief executive' in square brackets, by SI 2001/610, rr 2, 3, 6 as from 1 April 2001. Para (7): inserted by SI 1992/2072, r 2(m).

*Abandonment of appeal*

**75.**   Where notice to abandon an appeal has been given by the appellant, any recognizance conditioned for the appearance of the appellant at the hearing of the appeal shall have effect as if conditioned for the appearance of the appellant before the court from whose decision the appeal was brought at a time and place to be notified to the appellant by the *clerk of* [justices' chief executive for] that court.

**Note.** Words 'clerk of' substituted by words 'justices' chief executive for' in square brackets by SI 2001/610, rr 2, 3 as from 1 April 2001.

CASE STATED

*Application to state case*

**76.**   (1) An application under section 111(1) of the Act of 1980 shall be made in writing and signed by or on behalf of the applicant and shall identify the question or questions of law or jurisdiction on which the opinion of the High Court is sought.

(2) Where one of the questions on which the opinion of the High Court is sought is whether there was evidence on which the magistrates' court could come to its decision, the particular finding of fact made by the magistrates' court which it is claimed cannot be supported by the evidence before the magistrates' court shall be specified in such application.

(3) Any such application shall be sent to the *clerk of* [justices' chief executive for] the magistrates' court whose decision is questioned.

**Note.** Words 'clerk of' substituted by words 'justices' chief executive for' in square brackets by SI 2001/610, rr 2, 3 as from 1 April 2001.

*Consideration of draft case*

**77.** (1) Within 21 days after receipt of an application made in accordance with rule 76, the *clerk of* [justices' chief executive for] the magistrates' court whose decision is questioned shall, unless the justices refuse to state a case under section 111(5) of the Act of 1980, send a draft case in which are stated the matters required under rule 81 to the applicant or his solicitor and shall send a copy thereof to the respondent or his solicitor.

(2) Within 21 days after receipt of the draft case under paragraph (1), each party may make representations thereon. Any such representations shall be in writing and signed by or on behalf of the party making them and shall be sent to the clerk [the justices' chief executive].

(3) Where the justices refuse to state a case under section 111(5) of the Act and they are required by the High Court by order of mandamus under section 111(6) to do so, this rule shall apply as if in paragraph (1)—

(a) for the words 'receipt of an application made in accordance with rule 76' there were substituted the words 'the date on which an order of mandamus under section 111(6) of the Act of 1980 is made'; and

(b) the words 'unless the justices refuse to state a case under section 111(5) of the Act of 1980' were omitted.

**Note.** In para (1) words 'clerk of' substituted by words 'justices' chief executive for' in square brackets, and in para (2) words 'the clerk' substituted by words 'the justices' chief executive' in square brackets by SI 2001/610, rr 2, 3, 5 as from 1 April 2001.

*Preparation and submission of final case*

**78.** (1) Within 21 days after the latest day on which representations may be made under rule 77, the justices whose decision is questioned shall make such adjustments, if any, to the draft case prepared for the purposes of that rule as they think fit, after considering any such representations, and shall state and sign the case.

(2) A case may be stated on behalf of the justices whose decision is questioned by any 2 or more of them and may, if the justices so direct, be signed on their behalf by their clerk.

(3) Forthwith after the case has been stated and signed the *clerk of* [justices' chief executive for] the court shall send it to the applicant or his solicitor, together with any statement required by rule 79.

**Note.** Words 'clerk of' substituted by words 'justices' chief executive for' in square brackets by SI 2001/610, rr 2, 3 as from 1 April 2001.

*Extension of time limits*

**79.** (1) If the *clerk of* [justices' chief executive for] a magistrates' court is unable to send to the applicant a draft case under paragraph (1) of rule 77 within the time required by that paragraph, he shall do so as soon as practicable thereafter and the provisions of that rule shall apply accordingly; but in that event the *clerk shall* [the justices' chief executive shall] attach to the draft case, and to the final case when it is sent to the applicant or his solicitor under rule 78(3), a statement of the delay and the reasons therefor.

(2) If the *clerk of* [justices' chief executive for] a magistrates' court receives an application in writing from or on behalf of the applicant or the respondent for an extension of the time within which representations on the draft case may be made under paragraph (2) of rule 77, together with reasons in writing therefor, *he may by notice in writing* [the clerk of the magistrates' court may by notice in writing] sent to the applicant or respondent as the case may be [by the justices' chief executive] extend the time and the provisions of that paragraph and of rule 78 shall apply accordingly; but in that event *the clerk shall* [the justices' chief executive shall] attach to the final case, when it is sent to the applicant or his solicitor under rule 78(3), a statement of the extension and the reasons therefor.

(3) If the justices are unable to state a case within the time required by paragraph (1) of rule 78, they shall do so as soon as practicable thereafter and the provisions of that rule shall apply accordingly; but in that event *the clerk* [the justices' chief executive] shall attach to the final case, when it is sent to the applicant or his solicitor under rule 78(3), a statement of the delay and the reasons therefor.

**Note.** Words 'clerk of' and 'the clerk shall' in both places, words 'he may by notice in writing' and words 'the clerk' substituted by words 'justices' chief executive for', 'the justices' chief executive shall', 'the clerk of the magistrates' court may by notice in writing' and 'the justices' chief executive' respectively, by SI 2001/610, rr 2, 3, 5, 7, 17, as from 1 April 2001.

*Service of documents*

**80.**   Any document required by rules 76 to 79 to be sent to any person shall either be delivered to him or be sent by post in a registered letter or by recorded delivery service and, if sent by post to an applicant or respondent, shall be addressed to him at his last known or usual place of abode.

*Content of case*

**81.**   (1) A case stated by the magistrates' court shall state the facts found by the court and the question or questions of law or jurisdiction on which the opinion of the High Court is sought.

(2) Where one of the questions on which the opinion of the High Court is sought is whether there was evidence on which the magistrates' court could come to its decision, the particular finding of fact which it is claimed cannot be supported by the evidence before the magistrates' court shall be specified in the case.

(3) Unless one of the questions on which the opinion of the High Court is sought is whether there was evidence on which the magistrates' court could come to its decision, the case shall not contain a statement of evidence.

$$* \quad * \quad * \quad * \quad *$$

SUMMONS

*Form of summons*

**98.**   (1) A summons shall be signed by the justice issuing it or state his name and be authenticated by the signature of the clerk of a magistrates' court.

(2) A summons requiring a person to appear before a magistrates' court to answer to an information or complaint shall state shortly the matter of the information or complaint and shall state the time and place at which the defendant is required by the summons to appear.

(3) A single summons may be issued against a person in respect of several informations or complaints; but the summons shall state the matter of each information or complaint separately and shall have effect as several summonses, each issued in respect of one information or complaint.

[(4) In this rule where a signature is required, an electronic signature incorporated into the document shall satisfy this requirement.]

**Note.** Para (4) inserted by SI 2003/1236, rr 9, 42 as from 20 June 2003.

*Service of summons, etc*

**99.**   (1) Service of a summons issued by a justice of the peace on a person other than a corporation may be effected—

(a) by delivering it to the person to whom it is directed; or
(b) by leaving it for him with some person at his last known or usual place of abode; or
(c) by sending it by post in a letter addressed to him at his last known or usual place of abode.

(2) *Omitted.*

(3) Service for the purposes of the Act of 1980 of a summons issued by a justice of the peace on a corporation may be effected by delivering it at, or sending it by post to, the registered office of the corporation, if that office is in the United Kingdom, or, if there is no registered office in the United Kingdom, any place in the United Kingdom where the corporation trades or conducts its business.

(4) Paragraph (3) shall have effect in relation to a document (other than a summons) issued by a justice of the peace as it has effect in relation to a summons so issued, but with the substitution of references to England and Wales for the references to the United Kingdom.

(5) Any summons or other document served in manner authorised by the preceding provisions of this rule shall, for the purposes of any enactment other than the Act of 1980 or these Rules requiring a summons or other document to be served in any particular manner, be deemed to have been as effectively served as if it had been served in that manner; and nothing in this rule shall render invalid the service of a summons or other document in that manner.

(6) Sub-paragraph (c) of paragraph (1) shall not authorise the service by post of—

(a) a summons requiring the attendance of any person to give evidence or produce a document or thing; or

(b) a summons issued under any enactment relating to the liability of members of the naval, military or air forces of the Crown for the maintenance of their wives and children, whether legitimate or illegitimate.

(7) In the case of a summons issued on an application for an order under section 16 or 17(1) of the Act of 1978 (powers of court to make orders for the protection of a party to a marriage or a child of the family) service of the summons shall not be effected in manner authorised by sub-paragraph (b) or (c) of paragraph (1) unless a justice of the peace is satisfied by evidence on oath that prompt personal service of the summons is impracticable and allows service to be effected in such manner.

(8) Where this rule or any other of these Rules provides that a summons or other document may be sent by post to a person's last known or usual place of abode that rule shall have effect as if it provided also for the summons or other document to be sent in the manner specified in the rule to an address given by that person for that purpose.

(9) This rule shall not apply to a judgment summons.

\*       \*       \*       \*       \*

*Application for alteration of maintenance agreement under s 35 of Matrimonial Causes Act 1973 or under s 15 of the Family Law Reform Act 1987*

**105.** An application to a magistrates' court under section 35 of the Matrimonial Causes Act 1973 or under section 15 of the Family Law Reform Act 1987 for the alteration of a maintenance agreement shall be by complaint.

*Proceedings against person outside the United Kingdom on application for variation, etc of certain maintenance orders*

**106.** (1) The period referred to in section 41(2A) of the Maintenance Orders (Reciprocal Enforcement) Act 1972 (which provides that, subject to certain conditions, a magistrates' court may, if it is satisfied that the respondent has been outside the United Kingdom during such period as may be prescribed by rules, proceed on an application made under sections 11B or 11C of the Guardianship of Minors Act 1971 notwithstanding that the respondent has not been served with the summons) shall be the whole of the period beginning one month before the making of the application and ending with the date of the hearing.

(2) Before proceeding in any such case as is referred to in the said section 41(2A), the court shall be satisfied that, in addition to the matter referred to in those subsections, the applicant has taken steps to notify the respondent of the making of the application and of the time and place appointed for the hearing by—

(a) causing a notice in writing to that effect to be delivered to the respondent; or

(b) causing a notice in writing to that effect to be sent by post addressed to the respondent at his last known or usual place of abode or at his place of business or at such other address at which there is ground for believing that it will reach the respondent, in accordance with directions given for the purpose by a justice of the peace acting for the same petty sessions area as that of the court; or

(c) causing a notice to that effect to be inserted in one or more newspapers, in accordance with directions given as aforesaid;

and that it is reasonable in all the circumstances to proceed in the absence of the respondent.

(3) In any such case as is referred to in the said section 41(2A), the court shall not make the order for which the application is made unless it is satisfied that during the period of 6 months immediately preceding the making of the application the respondent was continuously outside the United Kingdom or was not in the United Kingdom on more than 30 days and that, having regard to any communication to the court in writing purporting to be from the respondent, it is reasonable in all the circumstances so to do.

(4) Paragraph (1) of rule 67 of these Rules shall apply for the purpose of proving the delivery of a written notice in pursuance of paragraph (2)(a) as it applies for the purpose of proving the service of a summons.

In relation to a solemn declaration made outside the United Kingdom, paragraph (1) of the said rule 67 as applied by this paragraph, shall have effect as if for the reference to the authorities mentioned in the said paragraph (1) there were substituted a reference to a consular officer of Her Majesty's Government in the United Kingdom or any person for the time being authorised by law, in the place where the declarant is, to administer an oath for any judicial or other legal purpose.

(5) Paragraph (2) of the said rule 67 shall apply for the purpose of proving the sending of a written notice in pursuance of paragraph (2)(b) or the insertion of a notice in a newspaper in pursuance of paragraph (2)(c) as it applies for the purpose of proving the service of any process, provided, as respects the insertion of a notice in a newspaper, that a copy of the newspaper containing the notice is annexed to the certificate.

\*   \*   \*   \*   \*

*Signature of forms prescribed by rules made under the Act of 1980*

**109.** (1) Subject to paragraph (2), where any form prescribed by Rules made or having effect as if made under section 144 of the Act of 1980 contains provision for signature by a justice of the peace only, the form shall have effect as if it contained provision in the alternative for signature by the clerk of a magistrates' court.

(2) This rule shall not apply to any form of warrant, other than a warrant of commitment or of distress, or to any form prescribed in the Magistrates' Courts (Forms) Rules 1981.

[(3) In this rule where a signature is required on a form of warrant other than an arrest, remand or commitment warrant, an electronic signature incorporated into the document will satisfy this requirement.]

**Note.** Para (3) inserted by SI 2003/1236, rr 9, 45 as from 20 June 2003.

\*   \*   \*   \*   \*

*[Applications for variation or discharge of orders under the Crime and Disorder Act 1998]*

[**114.** An application for variation or discharge of any of the following orders shall be by complaint:
  (a) a parenting order, under section 9(5) of the Crime and Disorder Act 1998;
  (b) a child safety order, under section 12(4) of that Act;
  (c) a reparation order, under paragraph 2 of Schedule 5 to that Act;
  (d) an action plan order, under that paragraph.]

**Note.** Inserted by SI 1998/2167, r 4(4) as from 30 September 1998.

SCHEDULE                                                                    Rule 1(2)

REVOCATIONS

| Rules revoked | References |
|---|---|
| The Magistrates' Courts Rules 1968 | SI 1968/1920. |
| The Magistrates' Courts (Amendment) Rules 1969 | SI 1969/1711. |
| The Magistrates' Courts (Amendment) Rules 1970 | SI 1970/1004. |
| The Magistrates' Courts (Amendment) (No 2) Rules 1970 | SI 1970/1791. |
| The Magistrates' Courts (Amendment) Rules 1973 | SI 1973/790. |
| The Magistrates' Courts (Amendment) Rules 1975 | SI 1975/126. |
| The Magistrates' Courts (Amendment) (No 2 ) Rules 1975 | SI 1975/518. |
| The Magistrates' Courts (Amendment) Rules 1977 | SI 1977/1174. |
| The Magistrates' Courts (Amendment) Rules 1978 | SI 1978/147. |
| The Magistrates' Courts (Amendment) (No 2) Rules 1978 | SI 1978/758. |
| The Magistrates' Courts (Amendment) Rules 1979 | SI 1979/1221. |
| The Magistrates' Courts (Amendment) Rules 1980 | SI 1980/510. |
| The Magistrates' Courts (Amendment) (No 2) Rules 1980 | SI 1980/1583. |

## RECIPROCAL ENFORCEMENT OF FOREIGN JUDGMENTS (SURINAME) ORDER 1981

**Dated** 31 May 1981

**SI 1981 No 735**

Whereas an Exchange of Notes, a copy whereof is set out in Schedule 1 to this Order, took place on 2 September 1970 between the Government of the United Kingdom of Great Britain and Northern Ireland and the Government of the Kingdom of the Netherlands extending the Convention providing for the Reciprocal Recognition and Enforcement of Judgments in Civil Matters signed at The Hague on 17 November 1967 to the territory of Suriname, then part of the Kingdom of the Netherlands:

And whereas on 25 November 1975 the territory of Suriname became the sovereign State of the Republic of Suriname and the Government of the Republic of Suriname declared in its communication of 29 November 1975 to the Secretary-General of the United Nations, a copy whereof is set out in Part I of Schedule 2 to this Order, that it be presumed that the Republic of Suriname has succeeded to the rights and obligations of the Kingdom of the Netherlands in respect of the said Convention:

And whereas by Note of 17 May 1980, a copy whereof is set out in Part II of Schedule 2 to this Order, the Government of the Republic of Suriname informed the Government of the United Kingdom that, in the event of a decision by the Government of the Republic of Suriname to make a declaration of non-succession in respect of the said Convention, it will take into account a six months' period of notice:

And whereas Her Majesty is satisfied that, in the event of Part I of the Foreign Judgments (Reciprocal Enforcement) Act 1933 being extended to judgments given in the superior courts of the Republic of Suriname, substantial reciprocity of treatment will, under the terms of the said Convention, be assured as respects the enforcement in the Republic of Suriname of judgments given in the superior courts of the United Kingdom; and is accordingly minded to direct that Part I of the said Act shall extend to the Republic of Suriname:

And whereas it is expedient to specify the courts in the Republic of Suriname which are, for the purposes of that Act, to be deemed to be superior courts, and necessary, in order to give effect to the said Convention, to make certain provisions in relation to matters with respect to which there is power to make rules of court for the purpose of Part I of the said Act:

Now, therefore, Her Majesty, by virtue and in exercise of the powers conferred on Her by sections 1 and 3 of the said Act, and of all other powers enabling Her in that behalf, is pleased, by and with the advice of Her Privy Council, to order, and it is hereby ordered, as follows—

**1.** This Order may be cited as the Reciprocal Enforcement of Foreign Judgments (Suriname) Order 1981 and shall come into operation on 13 May 1981.

**2.** Part I of the Foreign Judgments (Reciprocal Enforcement) Act 1933 shall extend to the Republic of Suriname.

**3.** The following courts of the Republic of Suriname shall be deemed superior courts of the Republic of Suriname for the purposes of Part I of the Foreign Judgments (Reciprocal Enforcement) Act 1933, that is to say—

The Hof van Justitie van Suriname;
The Kantongerecht in het Eerste Kanton;
The Kantongerecht in het Derde Kanton.

**4.** No security for costs shall be required to be given by any person making application for the registration of a judgment of a superior court of the Republic of Suriname.

**5.** A judgment of a superior court of the Republic of Suriname shall, in the absence of proof to the contrary, be deemed to be capable of execution in the Republic of Suriname if a certified copy of the judgment is produced bearing the seal of the court and the executory formula 'In naam van de Republiek'.

**6.** The rate of interest due under the law of the Republic of Suriname upon the sum in respect of which a judgment of a superior court of the Republic of Suriname is given shall be deemed to be that specified in the judgment or any certificate of the original court accompanying the judgment and, if no rate is so specified, no interest shall be deemed to be due thereon under the law of the Republic of Suriname.

**7.** A translation of the judgment of a superior court of the Republic of Suriname or of any other document accompanying an application for registration of such a judgment shall, if certified by a sworn translator or by a diplomatic or consular officer of either the United Kingdom or the Republic of Suriname, be accepted without further authentication.

SCHEDULE 1

EXCHANGE OF NOTES

\* \* \* \* \*

SCHEDULE 2

PART I

Declaration

\*   \*   \*   \*   \*

PART II

Note

\*   \*   \*   \*   \*

## CIVIL COURTS ORDER 1983

**Dated** 11 May 1983

**SI 1983 No 713**

The Lord Chancellor, in exercise of the powers conferred on him by section 99(1) of the Supreme Court Act 1981; by section 29(1) of the Administration of Justice Act 1982; by section 1(1) of the Matrimonial Causes Act 1967; by section 55 of the County Courts Act 1959; by section 96 of the Bankruptcy Act 1914 and section 218(5) of the Companies Act 1948; and by section 67(1) and (2) of the Race Relations Act 1976, hereby makes the following Order—

**1.** This Order may be cited as the Civil Courts Order 1983 and shall come into operation on 1 August 1983.

*District Registries of the High Court*

\*   \*   \*   \*   \*

**4.** (1) There shall be a district registry of the High Court at each of the places specified in the first column of Schedule 1 to this Order.

(2) The name of every place so specified shall be the name of the district registry at that place, except that the name of the district registry at Brecon shall be the Brecknock District Registry, the name of the district registry at Chatham shall be the Medway District Registry, the name of the district registry at Margate shall be the Thanet District Registry and the name of the district registry at Torquay shall be the Torquay and Newton Abbot District Registry.

(3) A district registry which is appointed a Chancery district registry by the Rules of the Supreme Court 1965 is denoted by the words '(Chancery)' beneath the name of the place at which the district registry is situated.

(4) The district of each district registry shall be the area comprising the districts for the time being of the county courts named in the second column of Schedule 1 to this Order opposite the name of the place at which the district registry is situated.

*County Courts*

\*   \*   \*   \*   \*

**6.** (1) There shall be a county court at each of the places mentioned in the first column of Schedule 3 to this Order.

(2) The name of every place so specified shall be the name of the county court at that place except where the contrary is specified in Schedule 4 to this Order.

(3) The entries in respect of the City of London in Schedules 3 and 4 to this Order stem from section 42 of the Courts Act 1971 and are not made by virtue of section 29 of the Administration of Justice Act 1982.

(4) The letters 'D.R.' in the first column of Schedule 3 to this Order denote a district registry of the High Court.

**7.** For the purpose of section 1(1) of the Matrimonial Causes Act 1967, where the word 'Divorce' appears in the second column of Schedule 3 to this Order opposite a place name in the first column, the county court at that place is hereby designated as a divorce county court and that county court is also designated as a court of trial.

\*     \*     \*     \*     \*

**11.** The Orders specified in Schedule 5 to this Order are hereby revoked.

## SCHEDULE 1

Article 4(1)

| First Column | Second Column |
|---|---|
| NAME OF PLACE | DISTRICTS DEFINED BY REFERENCE TO COUNTY COURT DISTRICTS |
| Aberystwyth | Aberystwyth |
| Barnsley | Barnsley |
| Barnstaple | Barnstaple |
| Barrow-in-Furness | Barrow-in-Furness |
| Basingstoke | Basingstoke |
| Bath | Bath<br>Trowbridge |
| Bedford | Bedford |
| Birkenhead | Birkenhead |
| Birmingham (Chancery) | Birmingham<br>Redditch |
| Blackburn | Blackburn |
| Blackpool | Blackpool |
| Blackwood | Blackwood |
| Bolton | Bolton |
| Boston | Boston<br>Skegness |
| Bournemouth | Bournemouth<br>Poole |
| Bradford | Bradford |
| Brecon | Brecknock |

| First Column | Second Column |
|---|---|
| NAME OF PLACE | DISTRICTS DEFINED BY REFERENCE TO COUNTY COURT DISTRICTS |
| Bridgend | Bridgend<br>Neath and Port Talbot |
| . . .[1] | . . .[1] |
| Brighton | Brighton<br>Haywards Heath<br>Lewes |
| Bristol<br>(Chancery) | Bristol<br>Weston Super Mare |
| Burnley | Accrington<br>Burnley<br>Nelson<br>Rawtenstall |
| Bury | Bury |
| Bury St. Edmunds | Bury St. Edmunds |
| Caernarfon | Caernarfon<br>Conwy and Colwyn<br>Porthmadog |
| Cambridge | Cambridge |
| Canterbury | Ashford<br>Canterbury |
| Cardiff<br>(Chancery) | Cardiff |
| Carlisle | Carlisle<br>Penrith |
| Carmarthen | Carmarthen<br>Llanelli |
| Chatham | Dartford<br>Gravesend |
| Chelmsford | Chelmsford |
| Cheltenham | Cheltenham |
| Chester | Chester<br>Runcorn |
| Chesterfield | Chesterfield<br>Worksop |

| First Column | Second Column |
| --- | --- |
| NAME OF PLACE | DISTRICTS DEFINED BY REFERENCE TO COUNTY COURT DISTRICTS |
| Chichester | Chichester |
| Colchester | . . .[2] Colchester and Clacton |
| Coventry | Banbury Coventry Nuneaton Stratford on Avon Warwick |
| Crewe | Crewe Northwich |
| Croydon | Bromley Croydon |
| Darlington | Darlington |
| Derby | Burton upon Trent Buxton Derby |
| Dewsbury | Dewsbury |
| Doncaster | Doncaster Goole Rotherham |
| Dudley | Dudley Kidderminster Stourbridge |
| Durham | Bishop Auckland Durham |
| Eastbourne | Eastbourne |
| Exeter | Exeter |
| Gloucester | Gloucester |
| Great Grimsby | Great Grimsby |
| . . .[1] | . . .[1] |
| Guildford | Aldershot and Farnham Epsom Guildford Reigate |
| Halifax | Halifax |

| First Column | Second Column |
|---|---|
| NAME OF PLACE | DISTRICTS DEFINED BY REFERENCE TO COUNTY COURT DISTRICTS |
| Harlow | . . .[2] <br> Harlow <br> Hertford |
| Harrogate | Harrogate |
| Hartlepool | Hartlepool |
| Hastings | Hastings |
| Haverfordwest | Haverfordwest |
| Hereford | Hereford <br> Ludlow |
| Huddersfield | Huddersfield |
| Ipswich | Ipswich |
| Keighley | Keighley <br> Skipton |
| Kendal | Kendal |
| King's Lynn | King's Lynn |
| Kingston upon Hull | Kingston upon Hull |
| Lancaster | Lancaster |
| Leeds (Chancery) | Leeds |
| Leicester | Leicester <br> Loughborough <br> Melton Mowbray |
| Lincoln | Grantham <br> Lincoln <br> Newark |
| Liverpool (Chancery) | Liverpool |
| Llangefni | Llangefni |
| Lowestoft | Lowestoft |
| Luton | Hitchin <br> Luton |
| Macclesfield | Macclesfield |

| First Column | Second Column |
|---|---|
| NAME OF PLACE | DISTRICTS DEFINED BY REFERENCE TO COUNTY COURT DISTRICTS |
| Maidstone | Maidstone |
| Manchester (Chancery) | Altrincham Manchester |
| Mansfield | Mansfield |
| Margate | Thanet |
| Merthyr Tydfil | Merthyr Tydfil |
| Middlesbrough | Middlesbrough |
| Milton Keynes | Aylesbury Milton Keynes |
| Newcastle upon Tyne (Chancery) | . . .[3] . . .[3] . . .[3] [Morpeth and Berwick][3] Newcastle upon Tyne |
| Newport (Gwent) | . . .[4] . . .[4] Newport (Gwent) Pontypool |
| Newport (Isle of Wight) | Newport (Isle of Wight) |
| Northampton | . . .[5] Kettering Northampton Rugby Wellingborough |
| Norwich | Norwich |
| Nottingham | Nottingham |
| Oldham | Oldham Tameside |
| Oxford | Oxford |
| Peterborough | Huntingdon Peterborough |
| Plymouth | Plymouth |
| Pontefract | Pontefract |
| Pontypridd | Aberdare . . .[6] Pontypridd |

| First Column | Second Column |
|---|---|
| **NAME OF PLACE** | **DISTRICTS DEFINED BY REFERENCE TO COUNTY COURT DISTRICTS** |
| Portsmouth | Portsmouth |
| Preston (Chancery) | Chorley<br>Preston |
| Reading | Newbury<br>Reading<br>Slough |
| Rhyl | . . .[7]<br>Rhyl |
| . . .[7] | . . .[7] |
| Romford | Basildon<br>. . .[1]<br>Ilford<br>Romford |
| St Helens | St Helens |
| Salford | Salford |
| Salisbury | Salisbury |
| Scarborough | . . .[3]<br>Scarborough |
| Scunthorpe | Scunthorpe |
| Sheffield | Sheffield |
| Shrewsbury | Shrewsbury<br>Telford |
| Southampton | Southampton |
| Southend-on-Sea | Southend-on-Sea |
| Southport | Southport |
| South Shields | North Shields<br>South Shields |
| Stafford | Stafford |
| Stockport | Stockport |
| Stoke on Trent | Stoke on Trent |
| Sunderland | Consett<br>Gateshead<br>Sunderland |

| First Column | Second Column |
|---|---|
| **NAME OF PLACE** | **DISTRICTS DEFINED BY REFERENCE TO COUNTY COURT DISTRICTS** |
| Swansea | Swansea |
| Swindon | Swindon |
| Taunton | Taunton |
| Torquay | Torquay and Newton Abbot |
| Truro | Bodmin<br>. . .[8]<br>Penzance<br>Truro |
| Tunbridge Wells | Tunbridge Wells |
| Wakefield | Wakefield |
| Walsall | . . .[9]<br>Tamworth<br>Walsall |
| Warrington | Warrington |
| Welshpool | Welshpool<br>Newtown |
| . . .[8] | . . .[8] |
| Weymouth | Weymouth |
| Whitehaven | Whitehaven<br>. . .[9] |
| Wigan | Leigh<br>Wigan |
| Winchester | Winchester |
| Wolverhampton | Wolverhampton |
| Worcester | Evesham<br>Worcester |
| . . .[9] | . . .[9]<br>Whitehaven |
| Worthing | Horsham<br>Worthing |
| Wrexham | Mold<br>Oswestry<br>Wrexham |

| First Column | Second Column |
|---|---|
| NAME OF PLACE | DISTRICTS DEFINED BY REFERENCE TO COUNTY COURT DISTRICTS |
| Yeovil | Yeovil |
| York | York |

**Note.** Entries numbered 1 omitted by SI 1997/3187, art 2, as from 20 December 1999. Entries numbered 2 omitted by SI 1997/2310, art 3, as from 1 December 1997. Entries numbered 3 omitted by SI 1997/2762, art 3, as from 15 December 1997. Entries numbered 4 omitted by SI 2001/4025, art 2, as from 1 April 2002. Entries numbered 5 omitted by SI 1999/216, art 3, as from 1 March 1999. Entries numbered 6 omitted by SI 2000/2738, art 2, as from 1 December 2000. Entries numbered 7 omitted by SI 1998/1880, art 3, as from 7 September 1998. Entries numbered 8 omitted by SI 1998/2910, art 3, as from 24 December 1998. Entries numbered 9 omitted by SI 2000/1482, art 2, as from 3 July 2000.

\*     \*     \*     \*     \*

## SCHEDULE 3

Article 6(1)

| Column 1 NAME OF PLACE | Column 2 ADDITIONAL JURISDICTION |
|---|---|
| Aberdare | Bankruptcy |
| Aberystwyth (D.R.) | . . . Bankruptcy Divorce |
| Accrington | Divorce |
| Aldershot | Divorce |
| . . .¹ | |
| Altrincham | Divorce |
| Ashford | |
| Aylesbury | Bankruptcy |
| Banbury | Bankruptcy |
| Barnet | Divorce |
| Barnsley (D.R.) | Bankruptcy Divorce |
| Barnstaple (D.R.) | . . . Bankruptcy Divorce |
| Barrow-in-Furness (D.R.) | . . . Bankruptcy Divorce |

| Column 1 NAME OF PLACE | Column 2 ADDITIONAL JURISDICTION |
|---|---|
| Basildon | |
| Basingstoke (D.R.) | Divorce |
| Bath (D.R.) | Bankruptcy Divorce |
| Bedford (D.R.) | Bankruptcy Divorce |
| . . .¹ | |
| Birkenhead (D.R.) | Bankruptcy Divorce |
| Birmingham (D.R.) | . . . Bankruptcy Divorce Race Relations |
| Bishop Auckland | Divorce |
| . . .² | |
| Blackburn (D.R.) | Bankruptcy Divorce |
| Blackpool (D.R.) | . . . Bankruptcy Divorce |

| Column 1 NAME OF PLACE | Column 2 ADDITIONAL JURISDICTION | Column 1 NAME OF PLACE | Column 2 ADDITIONAL JURISDICTION |
|---|---|---|---|
| Blackwood (D.R.) | Bankruptcy Divorce | Bury St Edmunds (D.R.) | Bankruptcy Divorce |
| . . .[1] | | Buxton | |
| Bodmin | Divorce | Caernarfon (D.R.) | . . . Bankruptcy Divorce |
| Bolton (D.R.) | Bankruptcy Divorce | Caerphilly | |
| Boston (D.R.) | . . . Bankruptcy Divorce | . . .[5] | . . .[5] |
| Bournemouth (D.R.) | Bankruptcy Divorce | Cambridge (D.R.) | Bankruptcy Divorce Race Relations |
| Bow | Divorce | Canterbury (D.R.) | . . . Bankruptcy Divorce Race Relations |
| Bradford (D.R.) | Bankruptcy Divorce | Cardiff (D.R.) | . . . Bankruptcy Divorce Race Relations |
| . . .[2] | | | |
| . . .[3] | Divorce | Carlisle (D.R.) | Bankruptcy Divorce Race Relations |
| Brentford | Divorce | Carmarthen (D.R.) | . . . Bankruptcy Divorce |
| Bridgend (D.R.) | Bankruptcy Divorce | | |
| . . .[4] | . . .[4] | Chatham (D.R.) | . . . Bankruptcy Divorce |
| . . .[1] | | | |
| Brighton (D.R.) | . . . Bankruptcy Divorce | Chelmsford (D.R.) | Bankruptcy Divorce |
| Bristol (D.R.) | . . . Bankruptcy Divorce Race Relations | Cheltenham (D.R.) | Bankruptcy |
| | | . . .[6] | |
| Bromley | Divorce | Chester (D.R.) | . . . Bankruptcy |
| Burnley (D.R.) | Bankruptcy Divorce | | |
| Burton-on-Trent | Bankruptcy Divorce | Chesterfield (D.R.) | Bankruptcy Divorce |
| Bury (D.R.) | Divorce | Chichester (D.R.) | Divorce |

| Column 1 NAME OF PLACE | Column 2 ADDITIONAL JURISDICTION | Column 1 NAME OF PLACE | Column 2 ADDITIONAL JURISDICTION |
|---|---|---|---|
| Chorley | Divorce | Exeter (D.R.) | . . . Bankruptcy Divorce Race Relations |
| City of London | . . . | | |
| Clerkenwell | | Gateshead | Divorce |
| Colchester (D.R.) | . . . Bankruptcy Divorce | Gloucester (D.R.) | . . . Bankruptcy Divorce |
| Colwyn Bay | | Goole | |
| Consett | Divorce | Grantham | |
| . . . 7 | | Gravesend | |
| Coventry (D.R. | Bankruptcy Divorce | . . . 4 | |
| Crewe (D.R.) | Bankruptcy Divorce | . . . | . . . 4 Bankruptcy |
| Croydon (D.R.) | Bankruptcy Divorce | Grimsby (D.R.) | . . . Bankruptcy Divorce |
| Darlington (D.R.) | Bankruptcy Divorce | Guildford (D.R.) | Bankruptcy Divorce |
| Dartford | | Halifax (D.R.) | Bankruptcy Divorce |
| Derby (D.R.) | Bankruptcy Divorce | Harlow (D.R.) | Divorce |
| Dewsbury (D.R.) | Bankruptcy Divorce | Harrogate (D.R.) | Bankruptcy Divorce |
| Dolgellau | | Hartlepool (D.R.) | . . . Divorce |
| Doncaster (D.R.) | Bankruptcy Divorce | Hastings (D.R.) | Bankruptcy Divorce |
| Dudley (D.R.) | Bankruptcy Divorce | Haverfordwest (D.R.) | . . . Bankruptcy Divorce |
| Durham (D.R.) | Bankruptcy Divorce | | |
| Eastbourne (D.R.) | Bankruptcy Divorce | Haywards Heath | |
| Edmonton | Divorce | . . . 5 | |
| Epsom | Divorce | Hereford (D.R.) | Bankruptcy Divorce |
| Evesham | | | |

| Column 1 NAME OF PLACE | Column 2 ADDITIONAL JURISDICTION | Column 1 NAME OF PLACE | Column 2 ADDITIONAL JURISDICTION |
|---|---|---|---|
| Hertford | Bankruptcy Divorce | Leigh | Divorce |
| High Wycombe | | Lewes | |
| Hitchin | Divorce | . . .[9] | |
| . . .[8] | | Lincoln (D.R.) | Bankruptcy Divorce |
| Horsham | Divorce | Liverpool (D.R.) | . . . Bankruptcy Divorce |
| Huddersfield (D.R.) | Bankruptcy Divorce | Llanelli | Divorce |
| Huntingdon | | Llangefni (D.R.) | Bankruptcy Divorce |
| Ilford | Divorce | . . .[5] | |
| Ipswich (D.R.) | . . . Bankruptcy Divorce | Lowestoft (D.R.) | . . . Divorce |
| Keighley (D.R.) | Divorce | Ludlow | |
| Kendal (D.R.) | Bankruptcy Divorce | Luton (D.R.) | Bankruptcy Divorce |
| Kettering | | Macclesfield (D.R.) | Bankruptcy Divorce |
| Kidderminster | Bankruptcy | Maidstone (D.R.) | Bankruptcy Divorce |
| King's Lynn (D.R.) | . . . Bankruptcy Divorce | Manchester (D.R.) | . . . Bankruptcy Divorce Race Relations |
| Kingston-upon- Hull (D.R.) | . . . Bankruptcy Divorce | Mansfield (D.R.) | Divorce |
| Kingston-upon- Thames | Bankruptcy Divorce | Margate (D.R.) | . . . Divorce |
| Lambeth | | Marylebone | Race Relations |
| Lancaster (D.R.) | Bankruptcy Divorce | Melton Mowbray | |
| Leeds (D.R.) | . . . Bankruptcy Divorce Race Relations | Merthyr Tydfil (D.R.) | Bankruptcy Divorce |
| Leicester (D.R.) | Bankruptcy Divorce | Middlesbrough (D.R.) | . . . Bankruptcy Divorce |

| Column 1 NAME OF PLACE | Column 2 ADDITIONAL JURISDICTION | Column 1 NAME OF PLACE | Column 2 ADDITIONAL JURISDICTION |
|---|---|---|---|
| Milton Keynes (D.R.) | Bankruptcy Divorce | Penrith | Divorce |
| Mold | | Penzance | [Divorce][5] |
| . . .[6] | | Peterborough (D.R.) | Bankruptcy Divorce |
| Morpeth | Divorce | Plymouth (D.R.) | . . . Bankruptcy Divorce Race Relations |
| Neath | Bankruptcy Divorce | | |
| Nelson | Divorce | Pontefract (D.R.) | Divorce |
| Newark | | Pontypool | |
| Newbury | Bankruptcy | Pontypridd (D.R.) | Bankruptcy Divorce |
| Newcastle upon Tyne (D.R.) | . . . Bankruptcy Divorce Race Relations | Poole | . . . |
| Newport (Gwent) (D.R.) | . . . Bankruptcy Divorce | Portsmouth (D.R.) | . . . Bankruptcy Divorce |
| Newport (Isle of Wight) (D.R.) | . . . Bankruptcy Divorce | Preston (D.R.) | . . . Bankruptcy Divorce |
| Northampton (D.R.) | Bankruptcy Divorce | Rawtenstall | Divorce |
| North Shields | Divorce | Reading (D.R.) | Bankruptcy Divorce |
| Northwich | | Redditch | |
| Norwich (D.R.) | Bankruptcy Divorce | Redhill | Divorce |
| Nottingham (D.R.) | Bankruptcy Divorce Race Relations | Rhyl (D.R.) | Bankruptcy Divorce |
| | | . . .[8] | . . .[8] |
| Nuneaton | | Romford (D.R.) | Bankruptcy Divorce |
| Oldham (D.R.) | Bankruptcy Divorce | Rotherham | Divorce |
| Oswestry | | Rugby | |
| Oxford (D.R.) | Bankruptcy Divorce Race Relations | Runcorn | Divorce |
| | | St. Albans | Bankruptcy |

| Column 1 NAME OF PLACE | Column 2 ADDITIONAL JURISDICTION | Column 1 NAME OF PLACE | Column 2 ADDITIONAL JURISDICTION |
|---|---|---|---|
| St. Helens (D.R.) | Divorce | Stourbridge | Bankruptcy |
| Salford (D.R.) | Bankruptcy Divorce | Stratford upon Avon | |
| Salisbury (D.R.) | Bankruptcy Divorce | Sunderland (D.R.) | . . . Bankruptcy Divorce |
| Scarborough (D.R.) | Bankruptcy Divorce | Swansea (D.R.) | . . . Bankruptcy Divorce |
| Scunthorpe (D.R.) | Bankruptcy Divorce | Swindon (D.R.) | Bankruptcy Divorce |
| Sheffield (D.R.) | Bankruptcy Divorce | Tameside | Bankruptcy Divorce |
| Shoreditch | | Tamworth | |
| Shrewsbury (D.R.) | Bankruptcy Divorce | Taunton (D.R.) | Bankruptcy Divorce |
| Skegness | | Telford | Divorce |
| Skipton | Divorce | Torquay (D.R.) | . . . Bankruptcy Divorce |
| Slough | Bankruptcy Divorce | Trowbridge | Divorce |
| Southampton (D.R.) | . . . Bankruptcy Divorce Race Relations | Truro (D.R.) | . . . Bankruptcy Divorce |
| Southend-on-Sea (D.R.) | Bankruptcy Divorce | Tunbridge Wells (D.R.) | Bankruptcy Divorce |
| Southport (D.R.) | Divorce | Uxbridge | Divorce |
| South Shields (D.R.) | Divorce | Wakefield (D.R.) | Bankruptcy Divorce |
| Stafford (D.R.) | Bankruptcy Divorce | Walsall (D.R.) | Bankruptcy Divorce |
| Staines | Divorce | Wandsworth | Divorce |
| Stockport (D.R.) | Bankruptcy Divorce | Warrington (D.R.) | Bankruptcy Divorce |
| Stoke-on-Trent (D.R.) | Bankruptcy Divorce | Warwick | Bankruptcy |
| | | Watford | Divorce |

| Column 1 | Column 2 | Column 1 | Column 2 |
| NAME OF PLACE | ADDITIONAL JURISDICTION | NAME OF PLACE | ADDITIONAL JURISDICTION |
| --- | --- | --- | --- |
| Wellingborough | | Wolverhampton (D.R.) | Bankrupcty Divorce |
| Welshpool (D.R.) | Bankruptcy Divorce | Woolwich | |
| . . .[5] | . . .[5] | Worcester (D.R.) | Bankrupcty Divorce |
| West Kensington | | Workington | . . . |
| Weston Super Mare | Divorce | | Bankruptcy Divorce |
| Weymouth (D.R.) | . . . Bankruptcy Divorce | Worksop | |
| | | Worthing (D.R.) | Divorce |
| Whitehaven (D.R.) | Bankruptcy[10] Divorce | Wrexham (D.R.) | Bankruptcy Divorce Race Relations |
| Wigan (D.R.) | Bankruptcy Divorce | Yeovil (D.R.) | Bankruptcy Divorce |
| Willesden | Divorce | York (D.R.) | Bankruptcy Divorce |
| Winchester (D.R.) | Bankrupcty Divorce | | |

**Note.** References to 'Admiralty' in column 2 in each place revoked by SI 1999/1011, art 4(a) as from 26 April 1999. Entries numbered 1 revoked by SI 1997/2762, art 4, as from 15 December 1997. Entries numbered 2, 3, revoked or amended by SI 1997/2310, art 4, as from 1 December 1997. Entries numbered 4 revoked or amended by SI 1999/3187, art 2, as from 20 December 1999. Entries numbered 5 revoked or amended by SI 1998/2910, art 4, as from 24 December 1998. Entries numbered 6 revoked by SI 2001/4025, art 2, as from 1 April 2002. Entries numbered 7 revoked by SI 1999/216, art 4, as from 1 March 1999. Entries numbered 8 revoked by SI 1998/1880, art 4, as from 7 September 1998. Entries numbered 9 revoked by SI 2000/1482, art 2, as from 2 July 2000. Entries numbered 10 amended by SI 2000/1317, as from 1 January 2001.

## SCHEDULE 4

Article 6(2)

1. The name of the county court at Aldershot shall be the Aldershot and Farnham County Court.

2. The name of the county court at Brecon shall be the Brecknock County Court.

3. ...

4. The name of the county court at Chatham shall be the Medway County Court.

5. The name of the county court for the City of London shall be the Mayor's and City of London Court.

6. The name of the county court at Colwyn Bay shall be the Conwy and Colwyn Bay County Court.

7. The name of the county court at Grimsby shall be the Great Grimsby County Court.

8. The name of the county court at Margate shall be the Thanet County Court.

9. The name of the county court at Neath shall be the Neath and Port Talbot County Court.

10. The name of the county court at Marylebone shall be the Central London County Court.

10A. The name of the court at Morpeth shall be the Morpeth and Berwick County Court.

11. The name of the county court at Redhill shall be the Reigate County Court.

12. The name of the county court at Welshpool shall be the Welshpool and Newtown County Court.

13. The name of the county court at West Kensington shall be the West London County Court.

**Note.** Para 3 revoked by SI 1998/2910, art 5, as from 24 December 1998. Para 10A added by SI 1997/2762, art 5, as from 15 December 1997.

\*    \*    \*    \*    \*

## MAINTENANCE ORDERS (FACILITIES FOR ENFORCEMENT) (REVOCATION) ORDER 1983

**Dated** 27 July 1983

### SI 1983 No 1124

Her Majesty, in exercise of the powers conferred by section 19 of the Maintenance Orders Act 1958, is pleased, by and with the advice of Her Privy Council, to order, and it is hereby ordered, as follows—

**1.** This Order may be cited as the Maintenance Orders (Facilities for Enforcement) (Revocation) Order 1983 and shall come into operation in September 1983.

**2.** In this Order—

(a) 'the Order of 1959' means the Maintenance Orders (Facilities for Enforcement) Order 1959;

(b) 'the Act of 1920' means the Maintenance Orders (Facilities for Enforcement) Act 1920.

**3.** (1) In so far as the Order of 1959 provides that the Act of 1920 shall extend to the countries and territories specified in paragraph (2) below, that Order is hereby revoked, and accordingly the names of those countries and territories shall be omitted from the First Schedule to that Order.

(2) The countries and territories referred to in paragraph (1) above are—

Anguilla

Falkland Islands and Dependencies

Isle of Man

Papua

St. Helena.

**4.** In so far as the Order of 1959, as it has effect by virtue of paragraph 3 of Schedule 2 to the Zimbabwe Act 1979, provides that the Act of 1920 shall extend to Zimbabwe, that Order is hereby revoked and, accordingly, the name of Southern Rhodesia shall be omitted from the First Schedule to that Order.

**RECIPROCAL ENFORCEMENT OF MAINTENANCE ORDERS
(DESIGNATION OF RECIPROCATING COUNTRIES) ORDER 1983**

**Dated** 27 July 1983

**SI 1983 No 1125**

Whereas Her Majesty is satisfied that, in the event of the benefits conferred by Part I of the Maintenance Orders (Reciprocal Enforcement) Act 1972 being applied to, or to particular classes of, maintenance orders made by the courts of each of the countries and territories specified in column (1) of the Schedule to this Order, similar benefits will in that country or territory be applied to, or to those classes of, maintenance orders made by the courts of the United Kingdom:

And whereas Her Majesty considers the provisions contained in Article 5 of this Order expedient for the purpose of securing the matters set out in section 24 of the said Act of 1972:

Now, therefore, Her Majesty, in exercise of the powers conferred by sections 1, 24 and 45(1) of the Maintenance Orders (Reciprocal Enforcement) Act 1972, is pleased, by and with the advice of Her Privy Council, to order, and it is hereby ordered, as follows—

**1.** This Order may be cited as the Reciprocal Enforcement of Maintenance Orders (Designation of Reciprocating Countries) Order 1983 and shall come into operation on 1st September 1983.

**2.** In this Order—

'the Act of 1972' means the Maintenance Orders (Reciprocal Enforcement) Act 1972;

'the Act of 1920' means the Maintenance Orders (Facilities for Enforcement) Act 1920;

'the Order of 1974' means the Reciprocal Enforcement of Maintenance Orders (Designation of Reciprocating Countries) Order 1974;

'column (1)' and 'column (2)' in Articles 3 and 5 below mean respectively columns (1) and (2) of the Schedule to this Order.

**3.** Each of the countries and territories specified in column (1) is hereby designated as a reciprocating country for the purposes of Part I of the Act of 1972 as regards maintenance orders of the description specified in respect of that country or territory in column (2).

**4.** Column (2) of the Schedule to the 1974 Order shall be varied as follows—

(a) in the entry in respect of Manitoba for the words 'other than provisional affiliation orders' there shall be substituted the words 'generally';

(b) for the entry in respect of New Zealand there shall be substituted the following entry—

'Maintenance orders generally'; and

(c) in the entry relating to Nova Scotia for the words 'the said paragraph (b), and' in paragraph (a) there shall be substituted the words 'paragraph (b) of the definition of "maintenance order" in section 21(1) of the Act of 1972 (orders for the payment of birth and funeral expenses of child), and'.

**5.** (1) Sections 5, 12 to 15, 17, 18 and 21 of the Act of 1972 shall apply in relation to a maintenance order transmitted under section 2 or 3 of the Act of 1920 to one of the countries and territories specified in column (1), being an order of the description specified in respect of that country or territory in column (2) to which immediately before the coming into operation of this Order the Act of 1920 applied, as they apply in relation to a maintenance order sent to that country or territory in pursuance of section 2 of the Act of 1972 or made by virtue of section 3 or 4 of the Act of 1972 and confirmed by a competent court in that country or territory.

**Note.** The Order of 1974 (as amended) is printed at p 4310.

(2) Sections 8 to 21 of the Act shall apply in relation to a maintenance order made in one of the countries and territories specified in column (1), by an order of the description specified in respect of that country or territory in column (2) to which immediately before the coming into operation of this Order the Act of 1920 applied and not being an order which immediately before that date is registered in the High Court or the High Court of Justice in Northern Ireland under section 1 of the Act of 1920, as they apply in relation to a registered order.

(3) A maintenance order made by a court in one of the countries and territories specified in column (1) being an order of the description specified in respect of that country or territory in column (2) which has been confirmed by a court in England, Wales or Northern Ireland under section 4 of the Act of 1920 and is in force immediately before the coming into operation of this Order, shall be registered under section 7(5) of the Act of 1972 in like manner as if it had been confirmed by that court in England, Wales or Northern Ireland under subsection (2) of that section.

(4) Any proceedings brought under or by virtue of any provision of the Act of 1920 in a court in England, Wales or Northern Ireland which are pending immediately before the coming into operation of this Order, being proceedings affecting a person resident in one of the countries or territories specified in column (1), shall be continued as if they had been brought under or by virtue of the corresponding provision of the Act of 1972.

## SCHEDULE

Article 3

COUNTRIES AND TERRITORIES DESIGNATED AS RECIPROCATING COUNTRIES

| (1)<br>Country or territory | (2)<br>Description of maintenance orders to which designation extends |
|---|---|
| Anguilla | Maintenance orders generally |
| Falkland Islands and Dependencies | Maintenance orders generally |
| Isle of Man | Maintenance orders generally |
| Nauru | Maintenance orders generally |
| Papua New Guinea | Maintenance orders other than provisional affiliation orders |
| St Helena | Maintenance orders generally |
| Zimbabwe | Maintenance orders other than—<br>(a) affiliation orders; and<br>(b) maintenance orders of the description contained in paragraph (b) of the definition of 'maintenance order' in section 21(1) of the Act of 1972 (orders for the payment of birth and funeral expenses of child) |

## ADOPTION AGENCIES REGULATIONS 1983

**Dated** 30 December 1983

**SI 1983 No 1964**

The Secretary of State for Social Services in relation to England and the Secretary of State for Wales in relation to Wales, in exercise of their powers under section 32 of the Adoption Act 1958 and section 4(1) of the Children Act 1975, and of all other powers enabling them in that behalf, hereby make the following regulations—

*Citation, commencement, extent and interpretation*

**1.** (1) These regulations may be cited as the Adoption Agencies Regulations 1983 and shall come into operation on 27 May 1984.

(2) These regulations shall not apply to Scotland.

(3) In these regulations, unless the context otherwise requires—

'the Act' means the Adoption Act 1976;

'the Children Act' means the Children Act 1989;

['the 2000 Act' means the Care Standards Act 2000;]

'adoption agency' means *an approved adoption society* [an appropriate voluntary organisation] or local authority;

'adoption panel' means a panel established in accordance with regulation 5;

['independent review panel' means a panel constituted under section 9A of the Act;]

'prospective adopter' means a person who proposes to adopt a child;

['registration authority' means in relation to an agency, the registration authority which may exercise in relation to that agency, functions to which section 36A of the [2000] Act applies;]

['specified offence' means an offence specified in Schedule 2.]

(4) Any reference in these regulations to any provision made by or contained in any enactment or instrument shall, except insofar as the context otherwise requires, be construed as including a reference to any provision which may re-enact or replace it, with or without modification.

(5) Any reference in these regulations to a numbered regulation or the Schedule is to the regulation bearing that number in or the Schedule to these regulations and any reference in a regulation or the Schedule to a numbered paragraph is a reference to that paragraph bearing that number in that regulation or the Schedule.

**Note.** In para (3) definitions 'the 2000 Act' and 'registration authority' inserted by SI 2003/367, reg 25(1), (2)(a), (c) as from 30 April 2003. In the definition 'adoption agency' words 'an approved adoption society' substituted by words 'an appropriate voluntary organisation' in square brackets by SI 2003/367, reg 25(1), (2)(b) as from 30 April 2003. Definition 'independent review panel' inserted, in relation to England, by SI 2004/190, reg 13(1), (2)(a), as from 30 April 2004 (as amended by SI 2004/1868, reg 3(1), (2)(a)). In definition 'registration authority' reference to '2000' in square brackets inserted, in relation to England, by SI 2004/190, reg 13(1), (2)(b), as from 30 April 2004 (as amended by SI 2004/1868, reg 3(1), (2)(a)), Definition 'specified offence' inserted by SI 1997/2308, reg 2(1), (2) as from 17 October 1997.

*Approval of adoption societies*

**2.** *(1) An application to the Secretary of State under section 3 of the Act (approval of adoption societies) shall be made in writing on a form supplied by the Secretary of State.*

*(2) An unincorporated body of persons shall not apply for approval under section 3 of the Act.*

**Note.** Revoked by SI 2003/367, reg 25(1), (3), as from 30 April 2003.

*Annual reports and information to be provided by approved adoption societies*

**3.** *Every approved adoption society shall—*
  (a) *furnish the Secretary of State with two copies of the society's annual report as soon as is reasonably practicable after the issue thereof and with such other information as and when the Secretary of State may from time to time require;*
  (b) *notify the Secretary of State in writing of any change in the society's name or in the address of its registered or head office within one month after such change;*
  (c) *where the society proposes to cease, or expects to cease, to act as an adoption society, so notify the Secretary of State in writing not less than one month, or as soon as is reasonably practicable, before the date when the society will cease, or expects to cease, so to act; and*
  (d) *where the society has ceased to act as an adoption society, notify the Secretary of State in writing that it has ceased so to act as soon thereafter as is reasonably practicable.*

**Note.** Revoked by SI 2003/367, reg 25(1), (3), as from 30 April 2003.

*Application of regulations to certain adoption agencies*

**4.** Where an adoption agency operates only for the purpose of putting persons into contact with other adoption agencies and for the purpose of putting such agencies into contact with each other or for either of such purposes, regulation 5 and, to the extent that it requires consultation with the adoption panel and the making of arrangements for the exercise of the panel's functions, regulation 6, shall not apply to such an agency.

*Establishment of adoption panel and appointment of members*

**5.** (1) Subject to paragraphs (2), (3) and (6), an adoption agency shall establish at least one adoption panel and shall appoint no more than 10 persons, including at least one man and one woman, to be members of such a panel.

(2) The adoption agency shall appoint as chairman of an adoption panel a person who has such experience in adoption work as the agency considers appropriate and the other members of the panel shall include—
  (a) subject to paragraph (6), two social workers in the employment of the adoption agency,
  (b) subject to paragraph (6), at least one member of the adoption agency's management committee where the agency is an approved adoption society or, where the adoption agency is a local authority, at least one member of that authority's social services committee,
  (c) the person nominated as the medical adviser to the adoption agency under regulation 6(4) (or one of them if more than one are nominated), for so long as that person is so nominated, and
  (d) at least three other persons ('independent persons'), not being members or employees of the adoption agency, or elected members, where the agency is a local authority who shall where reasonably practicable include an adoptive parent and an adopted person who must be at least 18 years of age.

(3) The adoption agency shall appoint one of the members of the adoption panel as vice-chairman, who, where the chairman of the panel has died or ceased to hold office, or is unable to perform his duties by reason of illness, absence from England and Wales or any other cause, shall act as the chairman for so long as there is no chairman able to do so.

(4) An adoption panel shall make the recommendations specified in regulation 10 only when, subject to paragraph (6), at least six of its members meet as a panel and those members include the chairman or vice-chairman and a social worker in the employment of the adoption agency.

(5) An adoption panel shall keep a written record of any of the recommendations specified in regulation 10 which it makes and the reasons for them.

(6) Any two but no more than three local authorities may establish a joint adoption panel, and where a joint adoption panel is established—

(a) the maximum number of members who may be appointed to that panel shall be increased to eleven,

(b) the chairman shall be appointed by agreement between the local authorities,

(c) one social worker in the employment of each local authority and one member of each local authority's social services committee shall be appointed to the panel,

(d) three independent persons shall be appointed to the panel by agreement between the local authorities,

(e) the vice-chairman shall be appointed from the members of the panel by agreement between the local authorities, and

(f) the quorum set out in paragraph (4) shall be increased to seven.

[(7) Where a local authority are operating executive arrangements, paragraphs (2)(b) and (6)(c) shall have effect as if the references in those paragraphs to a local authority's social services committee were references to—

(a) the authority's executive; or

(b) an overview and scrutiny committee of the authority where the committee's functions under section 21 of the Local Government Act 2000 (overview and scrutiny committees) relate wholly or partly to any social services functions of the authority.

(8) In paragraph (7)—

(a) 'executive', 'executive arrangements' and 'overview and scrutiny committee' have the same meaning as in Part II of the Local Government Act 2000; and

(b) 'social services functions' has the same meaning as in section 1A of the Local Authority Social Services Act 1970 (meaning of 'social services functions').]

**Note.** Paras (7), (8) inserted in relation to England by SI 2001/2237, arts 1, 2, 39 as from 11 July 2001 and in relation to Wales by SI 2002/808, arts 2, 35 as from 1 April 2002.

*Tenure of office of members*

**5A.** (1) Subject to the provisions of this regulation and regulation 5B a member of the adoption panel shall hold office for a term not exceeding three years, and may not hold office as a member of that panel for more than two consecutive terms without an intervening period of at least three years.

[(1A) Where—

(a) a member of an adoption panel holds office and is in his second consecutive term as a member of that panel; and

(b) his term of office is due to expire on or after 31st October 2003.

the adoption agency may extend the term of office of that member for a further period not exceeding two years.]

(2) An adoption agency shall so arrange the tenure of office of the members of the panel so that so far as possible the term of office of at least one third of its members shall expire each year.

(3) The medical adviser member of the adoption panel shall hold office only for so long as he is the medical adviser nominated under regulation 6(4).

(4) A member may resign his office at any time after appointment by giving notice in writing to that effect to the adoption agency, or if he is a member of a joint adoption panel, by giving notice to one of the local authorities whose panel it is.

(5) Subject to paragraph (6), if an adoption agency is of the opinion that a member is unfit or unable to hold office, the agency may terminate his office by giving him notice in writing with reasons.

(6) If the member whose appointment is to be terminated under paragraph (5) is a member of a joint adoption panel, his appointment may only be terminated with the agreement of all the local authorities whose panel it is.

(7) Where a member is appointed to replace a person whose appointment has been terminated for any reason before the expiry of the term for which he has been appointed, that member shall hold office as a member of that panel for the unexpired part of the term of the person whom he replaces, and may not hold office for more than one consecutive term after the expiry of that term without an intervening period of three years.

**Note.** Para (1A) inserted in relation to England by SI 2003/2555, reg 2 as from 27 October 2003 (and in relation to Wales by SI 2003/3223, reg 2 as from 11 December 2003).

*Establishment of new panels on 1 November 1997*

**5B.** (1) All members of an adoption panel established before 1st November 1997, shall cease to hold office on that date.

(2) With effect from the 1 November 1997, an adoption agency shall establish a new adoption panel in accordance with regulations 5 and 5A.

*Adoption agency arrangements for adoption work*

**6.** (1) An adoption agency shall, in consultation with the adoption panel and to the extent specified in paragraph (5) with the adoption agency's medical adviser, make arrangements which shall be set out in writing to govern the exercise of the agency's and the panel's functions and such arrangements shall be *reviewed by the agency not less than once every three years* [kept under review and, where appropriate, revised by the agency].

(2) Subject to regulations 14 and 15, the arrangements referred to in paragraph (1) shall include provision—

(a)  for maintaining the confidentiality and safekeeping of adoption information, case records and the indexes to them,

(b)  for authorising access to such records and indexes or disclosure of information by virtue of regulation 15, and

(c)  for ensuring that those for whom access ir provided or to whom disclosure is made by virtue of regulation 15(2)(a) agree in writing before such authorisation is given that such records, indexes and information will remain confidential, so however that a child who is placed for adoption or who has been adopted and his prospective adopter or adoptive parent shall not be required to give such agreement in respect of that child's adoption.

(3) *The adoption agency shall satisfy itself that social work staff employed on the agency's work have had such experience and hold such qualifications as the adoption agency considers appropriate to that work.*

(4) The adoption agency shall nominate at least one registered medical practitioner to be the agency's medical adviser.

(5) The adoption agency's medical adviser shall be consulted in relation to the arrangements for access to and disclosure of health information which is required or permitted by virtue of regulation 15.

**Note.** In para (1) words 'reviewed by the agency not less than once every three years' substituted by words 'kept under review and, where appropriate, revised by the agency' and para (3) revoked by SI 2003/367, reg 25, as from 30 April 2003.

*Adoption agency's duties in respect of a child and his parents or guardian*

**7.** (1) When an adoption agency is considering adoption for a child it shall either—

(a)  in respect of the child, having regard to his age and understanding, and as the case may be his parents or guardian, so far as is reasonably practicable—

> (i) provide a counselling service for them,
> (ii) explain to them the legal implications of and procedures in relation to adoption and freeing for adoption, and
> (iii) provide them with written information about the matters referred to in head (ii), or

(b) satisfy itself that the requirements of sub-paragraph (a) have been carried out by another adoption agency.

(2) Where, following the procedure referred to in paragraph (1), an adoption agency is considering adoption for a child, the agency shall—

(a) set up a case record in respect of the child and place on it any information obtained by virtue of this regulation,

(b) obtain, so far as is reasonably practicable, such particulars of the parents or guardian and having regard to his age and understanding the child as are referred to in Parts I and II to V of the Schedule together with any other relevant information which may be requested by the adoption panel,

(c) arrange and obtain a written report by a registered medical practitioner on the child's health which shall deal with the matters specified in Part II of the Schedule, unless such a report has been made within six months before the setting up of the case record under sub-paragraph (a) and is available to the agency,

(d) arrange such other examinations and screening procedures of and tests on the child and, so far as is reasonably practicable, his parents, as are recommended by the adoption agency's medical adviser, and obtain a copy of the written report of such examinations, screening procedures and tests, and

(e) prepare a written report containing the agency's observations on the matters referred to in this regulation, which shall be passed together with all information obtained by it by virtue of this regulation to the adoption panel or to another adoption agency.

(3) Where the father of a child does not have parental responsibility for the child and his identity is known to the adoption agency, it shall so far as it considers reasonably practicable and in the interests of the child—

(a) carry out in respect of the father the requirements of paragraph (1)(a) as if they applied to him unless the agency is satisfied that another adoption agency has so complied with those requirements,

(b) obtain the particulars of him referred to in Parts III and IV of the Schedule together with any other relevant information which may be requested by the adoption panel, and arrange and obtain a copy of the written report of such examinations, screening procedures and tests on him as are recommended by the adoption agency's medical adviser, and

(c) ascertain so far as possible whether he intends to apply for custody of the child.

*Adoption agency's duties in respect of a prospective adopter*

**8.** (1) When an adoption agency is considering whether a person may be suitable to be an adoptive parent, either—

(a) it shall—
> (i) provide a counselling service for him,
> (ii) explain to him the legal implications of and procedures in relation to adoption, and
> (iii) provide him with written information about the matters referred to in head (ii), or

(b) it shall satisfy itself that the requirements of sub-paragraph (a) have been carried out in respect of him by another adoption agency.

(2) Where, following the procedure referred to in paragraph (1) [and subject to regulation 8A], an adoption agency considers that a person may be suitable to be an adoptive parent, it shall—

(a) set up a case record in respect of him and place on it any information obtained by virtue of this regulation [and regulation 8A],

(b) obtain such particulars as are referred to in Part VI of the Schedule together with, so far as is reasonably practicable, any other relevant information which may be requested by the adoption panel,

(c) obtain a written report by a registered medical practitioner on the prospective adopter's health which shall deal with the matters specified in Part VII of the Schedule, unless such a report has been made within six months before the setting up of the case record under sub-paragraph (a) and is available to the agency,

(d) obtain a written report in respect of any premises which that person intends to use as his home if he adopts a child,

(e) obtain written reports of the interviews with two persons nominated by the prospective adopter to provide personal references for him,

(f) obtain a written report from the prospective adopter's local authority in relation to him,

(g) prepare a written report which shall include the agency's assessment of the prospective adopter's suitability to be an adoptive parent and any other observations of the agency on the matters referred to in this regulation.

(h) notify the prospective adopter that his application is to be referred to the adoption panel and at the same time send a copy of the agency's assessment referred to in paragraph (g) to the prospective adopter inviting him to send any observations in writing on that assessment to the agency within 28 days [beginning with the date on which the notification was sent,], and

(i) at the end of the period of 28 days referred to in sub-paragraph (h), (or earlier if any observations made by the prospective adopter on the assessment are received before the 28 days has expired), pass the written report referred to in sub-paragraph (g) and any written observations made by the prospective adopter together with all information obtained by the agency by virtue of this regulation, to the adoption panel or to another adoption agency.

**Note.** In para (2) words 'and subject to regulation 8A', in sub-para (a) words 'and regulation 8A' and in sub-para (h) words from 'beginning with' to 'was sent', in square brackets inserted by SI 1997/2308, reg 2(3) as from 17 October 1997.

[*Criminal convictions of a prospective adopter*

**8A.** (1) An adoption agency shall, so far as practicable, take steps to obtain information about any previous criminal convictions and any cautions given by a constable in respect of criminal offences which relate to a prospective adopter and the members of his household *over the age of 18* [aged 18 or over] when considering under regulation 8(1) whether a person may be suitable to be an adoptive parent.

(2) An adoption agency shall not consider a person to be suitable to be an adoptive parent or, as the case may be, shall consider a person no longer to be suitable, if he or any member of his household *over the age of 18* [aged 18 or over]—

(a) has been convicted of a specified offence [committed at the age of 18 or over]; or

(b) has been cautioned by a constable in respect of a specified offence which, at the time the caution was given, he admitted.

(3) The adoption agency shall notify a prospective adopter in writing as soon as possible after becoming aware that, by virtue of paragraph (2), he is not (or, as the case may be, is no longer) considered suitable to be an adoptive parent and the notification shall specify the conviction or, as the case may be, the caution in question.]

**Note.** Inserted by SI 1997/2308, reg 2(4) as from 17 October 1997. Words 'over the age of 18' in both places substituted by words 'aged 18 or over' in square brackets and words 'committed at the age of 18 or over' in square brackets inserted by SI 2001/2992, reg 3 (in relation to England) and by SI 2003/710, reg 21 (in relation to Wales) as from 1 October 2001 and 30 April 2003 respectively.

*Adoption agency's duties in respect of proposed placement*

**9.**   (1) Subject to paragraph (2), an adoption agency shall refer its proposal to place a particular child for adoption with a prospective adopter, which it considers may be appropriate, together with a written report containing its observations on the proposal and any information relevant to the proposed placement, to its adoption panel.

(2) An adoption agency shall refer its proposal to place a child for adoption to the adoption panel only if—

(a) any other adoption agency which has made a decision in accordance with regulation 11(1) that adoption is in the best interests of the child or that the prospective adopter is suitable to be an adoptive parent, has been consulted concerning the proposal, and

(b) any local authority or voluntary organisation which has parental respons- ibility for the child by virtue of section 18 or 21 of the Act (freeing for adoption and variation of order to substitute one adoption agency for another) or in whose care the child is, has been consulted and agrees with the proposal.

(3) An adoption agency which has a proposal to place a particular child for adoption with a prospective adopter shall set up case records in respect of them to the extent that it has not already set up such records and place on the appropriate record any information, reports and decisions referred to it by another adoption agency together with any information to be passed to the adoption panel by virtue of this regulation in respect of them.

(4) An adoption agency shall obtain, so far as is reasonably practicable, any other relevant information which may be requested by the adoption panel in connection with the proposed placement.

*Adoption panel functions*

**10.**   (1) Subject to paragraphs (2) and (3), an adoption panel shall consider the case of every child, prospective adopter and proposed placement referred to it by the adoption agency and shall make one or more of the recommendations to the agency, as the case may be, as to—

(a) whether adoption is in the best interests of a child and, if the panel recommends that it is, whether an application under section 18 of the Act (freeing child for adoption) should be made to free the child for adoption,

(b) whether a prospective adopter is suitable to be an adoptive parent, and

(c) whether a prospective adopter would be a suitable adoptive parent for a particular child.

(2) An adoption panel may make the recommendations specified in paragraph (1) at the same time or at different times, so however that it shall make the recommendation specified in paragraph (1)(c) in respect of a particular child and prospective adopter only if—

(a) that recommendation is to be made at the same meeting of the panel at which a recommendation has been made that adoption is in the best interests of the child, or

(b) an adoption agency decision has been made in accordance with regulation 11(1) that adoption is in the best interests of the child, and

(c)   in either case—

   (i)   the recommendation specified in paragraph (1)(c) is to be made at the same meeting of the panel at which a recommendation has been made that the prospective adopter is suitable to be an adoptive parent, or

   (ii)   an adoption agency decision has been made in accordance with regulation 11(1) that the prospective adopter is suitable to be an adoptive parent.

(3)   In considering what recommendations to make the panel shall have regard to the duties imposed upon the adoption agency by sections 6 and 7 of the Act (duty to promote welfare of child and religious upbringing of adopted child) and shall, as the case may be—

(a)   consider and take into account all the information and reports passed to it by virtue of regulations 7(2)(c), 8(2)(g) and 9(1),

(b)   request the adoption agency to obtain any other relevant information which the panel considers necessary,

(c)   obtain legal advice in relation to each case together with advice on an application for an adoption order or, as the case may be, an application to free a child for adoption.

*Adoption agency decisions and notifications*

**11.**   (1) An adoption agency shall make a decision on a matter referred to in regulation 10(1)(a) or (c) only after taking into account the recommendation of the adoption panel made by virtue of that regulation on such matter.

(1A)   No member of an adoption panel shall take part in any decision made by the adoption agency under paragraph (1).

(2)   As soon as possible after making such a decision the adoption agency shall, as the case may be, notify in writing—

(a)   the parents of the child, including his father if he does not have parental responsibility for the child but only where the agency considers this to be in the child's interests, or the guardian of the child, if their whereabouts are known to the agency, of its decision as to whether it considers adoption to be in the best interests of the child,

(b)   the person to be notified under sub-paragraph (a), if it considers adoption to be in the best interests of the child, of its decision as to whether an application under section 18 of the Act (freeing child for adoption) should be made to free the child for adoption, and

(c)   *omitted*

(d)   the prospective adopter of its decision that he would be suitable as such for a particular child.

*Adoption agency decisions and notifications—prospective adopters*

**11A.**   (1) In relation to a matter referred to in regulation 10(1)(b) (panel recommendations—prospective adopters) the adoption agency shall take into account the recommendation of the adoption panel made by virtue of that regulation on that matter before making its decision.

(2)   No member of an adoption panel [or an independent review panel] shall take part in any decision made by the agency under paragraph (1).

(3)   If the agency decide to approve the prospective adopter as suitable to be an adoptive parent, the agency shall notify the prospective adopter in writing of its decision.

(4)   [Except in a case where paragraph (2) of regulation 8A applies,] if the agency consider that the prospective adopter is not suitable to be an adoptive parent, the agency shall—

(a) notify the prospective adopter in writing that it proposes not to approve him as suitable to be an adoptive parent;

(b) send with that notification their reasons together with a copy of the recommendation of the adoption panel, if different; and

(c) *invite the prospective adopter to submit any representations he wishes to make within 28 days.*

[(c) notify the prospective adopter in writing that within 28 days—

    (i) he may submit any representations he wishes to make in writing to the agency; or

    (ii) he may apply to the Secretary of State for a review by an independent review panel of the agency's proposal not to approve him as suitable to be [an adoptive parent] (referred to in this regulation as a 'qualifying determination')]

(5) If within the period of 28 days referred to in paragraph (4), *the prospective adopter has not made any representations* [the prospective adopter has not applied to the Secretary of State for a review by an independent review panel of the qualifying determination or made any representations to the agency], the agency may proceed to make its decision and shall notify the prospective adopter in writing of its decision together with the reasons for that decision.

[(5A) If the agency receives notification from the Secretary of State that a prospective adopter has applied to the Secretary of State for a review by an independent review panel of the qualifying determination, it shall within 7 days after the date of that notification submit to the Secretary of State—

[(a) all of the documents and information which were passed to the adoption panel in accordance with regulation 8(2)(i);

(b) any relevant information in relation to the prospective adopter which was obtained by the agency after the date on which the documents and information referred to in sub-paragraph (a) were passed to the adoption panel; and

(c) the documents referred to in paragraph (4)(a) and (b)].]

(6) If within the period of 28 days referred to in paragraph (4) the agency receive further representations from the prospective adopter, it may refer the case together with all the relevant information to its adoption panel for further consideration.

(7) The adoption panel shall reconsider any case referred to it under paragraph (6) and make a fresh recommendation to the agency as to whether the prospective adopter is suitable to be an adoptive parent.

(8) *The agency shall make a decision on the case but if the case has been referred to the adoption panel under paragraph (6) it shall make the decision only after taking into account any recommendation of the adoption panel made by virtue of paragraph (7).*

[(8) The agency shall make a decision on the case and, in addition to the requirements of paragraph (1),—

(a) if the prospective adopter has applied to the Secretary of State for a review by an independent review panel of the qualifying determination, it shall make the decision only after taking into account any recommendation of that panel made in accordance with the Independent Review of Determinations (Adoption) Regulations 2004; or

(b) if the case has been referred to an adoption panel under paragraph (6), it shall make the decision only after taking into account any recommendation of the adoption panel made by virtue of paragraph (7).]

(9) As soon as possible after making the decision under paragraph (8), the agency shall notify the prospective adopter in writing of its decision, stating its reasons for that decision if they do not consider the prospective adopter to be suitable to be an adoptive parent, and [, if the case has been referred to an adoption panel under paragraph (6),] of the adoption panel's recommendation, if this is different from the agency's decision.

[(9A)  In a case where an independent review panel has made a recommendation, the agency shall send to the independent review panel a copy of the notification referred to in paragraph (9).]

**Note.** Inserted by SI 1997/649, reg 2(10).

In Para (2) words 'or an independent review panel' in square brackets inserted, in relation to England, by SI 2004/190, reg 13(1), (3)(a) as from 30 April 2004: (for effect see reg 1(3) thereof (as amended by SI 2004/1868, reg 3(1), (2)(a)). In para (4): words from 'Except in' to 'regulation (8A) applies,' in square brackets inserted by SI 1997/2308, reg 2(5) as from 17 October 1997. Para (4)(c) substituted, in relation to England, by SI 2004/190, reg 13(1), (3)(b) as from 30 April 2004 (for effect see reg 1(3) thereof (as amended by SI 2004/1868, reg 3(1), (2)(a)), and in sub-para (c)(ii) words 'a prospective adopter' substituted by words 'an adoptive parent' in square brackets by SI 2004/1868, reg 4 as from 20 August 2004. In para (5) words 'the prospective adopter has not made any representations' revoked and subsequent words 'the prospective adopter has not applied to the Secretary of State for a review by an independent review panel of the qualifying determination or made any representations to the agency' in square brackets substituted, in relation to England, by SI 2004/190, reg 13(1), (3)(c) as from 30 April 2004 (for effect see reg 1(3) thereof (as amended by SI 2004/1868, reg 3(1), (2)(a)). Para (5A) inserted, in relation to England, by SI 2004/190, reg 13(1), (3)(d) as from 30 April 2004 (for effect see reg 1(3) thereof (as amended by SI 2004/1868, reg 3(1), (2)(a)) and sub-paras (a)–(c) substituted, for sub-paras (a)–(d), by SI 2004/1081, reg 2 as from 30 April 2004. Para (8) substituted, in relation to England, by SI 2004/190, reg 13(1), (3)(e) as from 30 April 2004 (for effect see reg 1(3) thereof (as amended by SI 2004/1868, reg 3(1), (2)(a)), In para (9) words from ', if the case' to 'under paragraph (6)' in square brackets inserted and para (9A) inserted, in relation to England, by SI 2004/190, reg 13(1), (3)(f), (g), as from 30 April 2004 (for effect see reg 1(3) thereof (as amended by SI 2004/1868, reg 3(1), (2)(a)).

*Placement for adoption*

**12.**  (1)  Where an adoption agency has decided in accordance with regulation 11(1) that a prospective adopter would be a suitable adoptive parent for a particular child it shall provide the prospective adopter with written information about the child, his personal history and background, including his religious and cultural background, his health history and current state of health, together with the adoption agency's written proposals in respect of the adoption, including proposals as to the date of placement for adoption with the prospective adopter.

(2)  If the prospective adopter accepts the adoption agency's proposals the agency shall—

(a)    inform the child of the proposed placement for adoption with the prospective adopter where the child is capable of understanding the proposal,

(aa)   notify in writing the parent or guardian of the child, if their whereabouts are known to the agency, of the proposed placement for adoption, unless the parent or guardian has made a declaration under section 18(6) or 19(4) of the Act (declaration as to no further involvement with child),

(aaa)  where the father of the child does not have parental responsibility for him and his identity is known to the agency, notify the father of the proposed placement provided the agency considers this to be in the best interests of the child,

(b)    send a written report of the child's health history and current state of health to the prospective adopter's registered medical practitioner, if any, before the proposed placement, together with particulars of the proposed placement,

(c)    notify the local authority and the *district health authority* [Health Authority or Primary Care Trust] in whose area the prospective adopter resides in writing before the placement with particulars of the proposed placement,

(d)    notify the local education authority in whose area the prospective adopter resides in writing before the placement with particulars of the proposed placement if the child is of compulsory school age within the meaning of section 35 of the Education Act 1944 or the adoption agency's medical adviser considers the child to be handicapped,

(e)   [subject to regulation 8A] place the child with the prospective adopter, so however that where the child already has his home with the prospective adopter the agency shall notify the prospective adopter in writing of the date the child is placed with him by the agency for adoption,

(f)   *omitted*

(g)   ensure that the child is visited within one week of the placement and on such other occasions as the adoption agency considers necessary in order to supervise the child's well-being,

(h)   ensure that written reports are obtained of such visits,

(i)   provide such advice and assistance to the prospective adopter as the agency considers necessary,

(j)   make appointments for the child to be examined by a registered medical practitioner and for a written assessment on the state of his health and his need for health care to be made—

(i)   at least once in every period of six months before the child's second birthday, and

(ii)   at least once in every period of twelve months after the child's second birthday, unless the child is of sufficient understanding to make an informed decision and refuses to submit to the examination, and

(k)   review the placement of the child within four weeks of placement, not more than three months after that review unless an application for an adoption order has been made, and at least every six months thereafter until an application for an adoption order is made.

(3)   The agency who carry out the review referred to in paragraph (2)(k) shall—

(a)   set out in writing the arrangements governing the manner in which the case of each child shall be reviewed and shall draw the written arrangements to the attention of the child, where reasonably practicable having regard to his age and understanding, to the prospective adopters, and to any other person the agency considers relevant,

(b)   have regard so far as reasonably practicable to the considerations specified in Part VIII of the Schedule, and

(c)   ensure that—

(i)   the information obtained in respect of a child's case,

(ii)   details of the proceedings at any meeting arranged by the agency to consider any aspect of the review of the case, and

(iii)   details of any decision made in the course of or as a result of the review,

are recorded in writing.

(4)   The agency who carry out the review shall, so far as reasonably practicable, notify details of the result of the review and of any dcision taken by them in consequence of the review to—

(a)   the child where he is of sufficient age and understanding;

(b)   his parents, except where a freeing order has been made under section 18 of the Act and that order has not been revoked,

(c)   his father, if he does not have parental responsibility for him and his identity is known, provided that the agency considers this to be in the child's interests;

(d)   the prospective adopters; and

(e)   any other person whom they consider ought to be notified.

**Note.** In para (2)(c) words 'district health authority' substituted by words 'Health Authority or Primary Care Trust' in square brackets by SI 2002/2469, reg 14, Sch 11, as from 10 October 2002. In para (2)(e) words 'subject to regulation 8A' in square brackets inserted by SI 1997/2308, reg 2(6) as from 17 October 1997.

*Review of case where no placement made within six months of freeing for adoption*

**13.**   (1)  Where a child has been freed for adoption by virtue of an order under section 18 of the Act (freeing child for adoption) and six months have elapsed since the making of that order and the child does not have his home with a prospective adopter, the adoption agency which has parental responsibility for the child by virtue of section 18 or 21 of the Act (freeing for adoption and variation of order to substitute one agency for another) shall review that child's case to determine why no placement has been made and what action if any should be taken to safeguard and promote his welfare.

(2)  A case to which paragraph (1) applies shall be subject to such a review at intervals of not more than six months.

*Information on adoption*

**13A.**   As soon as practicable after the making of an adoption order in respect of a child, the adoption agency shall—

(a)  provide the adopters with such information about the child as they consider appropriate; and

(b)  at the same time advise the adopters that this information should be made available to the child at a time when they consider it is appropriate but no later than the child's eighteenth birthday.

*Confidentiality and preservation of case records*

**14.**   (1)  Subject to regulation 15, any information obtained or recommendations or decisions made by virtue of these regulations shall be treated by the adoption agency as confidential.

(2)  Where a case record has been set up by an adoption agency under regulations 7(2)(a), 8(2)(a) or 9(3) in respect of a child or a prospective adopter, any report, recommendation or decision made by that agency by virtue of these regulations in respect of that child or that prospective adopter shall be placed on the case record relating to that child or, as the case may be, that prospective adopter, and any case records set up by the agency together with the indexes to them shall be kept in a place of special security.

(3)  Subject to regulation 16(2), an adoption agency shall preserve the indexes to all its case records and the case records in respect of those cases in which an adoption order is made in a place of special security for at least 75 years and shall preserve other case records in a place of special security for so long as it considers appropriate, so however that any case records and indexes may be so preserved on microfilm or such other system as reproduces the total contents of any such record or index.

(4)  The adoption agency shall ensure that the place of special security referred to in paragraphs (2) and (3) [is suitable to] preserve the records *etc* [(together with any indices not part of the records)], so far as is possible, and in particular minimise the risk of damage from fire or water.

**Note.** In para (4) words 'is suitable to' in square brackets inserted and words 'etc' substituted by words '(together with any indices not part of the records)' by SI 1997/2308, reg 2(7), as from 17 October 1997.

*Access to case records and disclosure of information*

**15.**   (1)  Subject to paragraph (3), an adoption agency shall provide such access to its case records and the indexes to them and disclose such information in its possession, as may be required—

(a)  to those holding an inquiry under section 81 of the Children Act (inquiries), for the purposes of such an inquiry,

(b) to the Secretary of State,

[(bb) the registration authority]

(c) subject to the provisions of sections 29(7) and 32(3) of the Local Government Act 1974 (investigations and disclosure), to a Local Commissioner, appointed under section 23 of that Act (Commissioners for Local Administration), for the purposes of any investigation conducted in accordance with Part III of that Act,

(cc) to any person appointed by the adoption agency for the purposes of the consideration by the agency of any representations (including complaints),

(d) to the persons and authorities referred to in regulations 11 and 12 to the extent specified in those regulations,

(e) to a *guardian ad litem* [children's guardian] or reporting officer appointed under rules made pursuant to section 65 of the Act (*guardian ad litem* [children's guardian] and reporting officer) for the purposes of the discharge of his duties in that behalf, and

(f) to a court having power to make an order under the Act.

(2) Subject to paragraph (3), an adoption agency may provide such access to its case records and the indexes to them and disclose such information in its possession, as it thinks fit—

(a) for the purposes of carrying out its functions as an adoption agency, and

(b) to a person who is authorised in writing by the Secretary of State to obtain information for the purposes of research.

(3) A written record shall be kept by an adoption agency of any access provided or disclosure made by virtue of this regulation.

**Note.** Para (1)(bb) inserted by SI 2003/367, reg 25, as from 30 April 2003. In Para (1)(ee) words 'guardian ad litem' in both places substituted by words 'children's guardian' in square brackets by SI 2002/3220, art 2 as from 31 January 2003.

*Transfer of case records*

**16.** (1) Subject to paragraphs (2) and (3), an adoption agency may transfer a copy of a case record (or part thereof) to another adoption agency when it considers this to be in the interests of a child or prospective adopter to whom the record relates, and a written record shall be kept of any such transfer.

(2) *An approved adoption society which intends to cease to act or exist as such shall forthwith either transfer its case records to another adoption agency having first obtained the Secretary of State's approval for such transfer, or transfer its case records—*

(a) *to the local authority in whose area the society's head office is situated; or*

(b) *in the case of a society which amalgamates with another approved adoption society to form a new approved adoption society, to the new society.*

[(2) An appropriate voluntary organisation which intends to cease to act or exist as such shall forthwith either transfer its case records to another adoption agency having first obtained the registration authority's approval for such transfer, or transfer its case records—

(a) to the local auithority in whose area the organisation's principal office is situated; or

(b) in the case of an organisation that amalgamates with another approved voluntary organisation to form a new approved voluntary organisation, to the new organisation.]

(3) An adoption agency to which case records are transferred by virtue of paragraph (2)(a) or (b) shall notify the *Secretary of State* [registration authority] in writing of such transfer.

**Note.** Para (2) substituted by SI 2003/367, reg 25(6)(a) as from 30 April 2003 (see also SI 2003/365, art 2, Schedule, paras 1, 3). In para (3) words 'Secretary of State' substituted by words 'registration authority' in square brackets by SI 2003/367, reg 25(6)(b) as from 30 April 2003.

*Progress reports under section 19 of the Act*

**17.**   Where parental responsibility for a child who is in Great Britain has been transferred from one adoption agency ('the existing agency') to another ('the substitute agency') by virtue of an order under section 21 of the Act (variation of section 18 order), the substitute agency shall provide such information to the existing agency as that agency considers necessary for it to comply with its duty under section 19(2) and (3) of the Act.

*[Local authority reports in non agency cases*

**17A.**   [A local authority which is required by section 22(2) of the Act to investigate an application for an adoption order in respect of a child who was not placed with the applicant by an adopion agency shall, so far as practicable, take steps to obtain information about any previous criminal convictions and any cautions given by a constable in respect of criminal offences which relate to the applicant and other members of his household over the age of 18.]

**Note.** Inserted by SI 1997/2308, reg 2(8) as from 17 October 1997.

*Revocations*

**18.**   The Adoption Agencies Regulations 1976 and the Adoption Agencies (Amendment) Regulations 1981 are hereby revoked.

Signed by authority of the Secretary of State for Social Services.

SCHEDULE                                   Regulations 7(2)(b) and (c)
                                            and (3)(b), and 8(2)(b) and (c)

PART I

PARTICULARS RELATING TO THE CHILD

   1. Name, sex, date and place of birth and address.
   2. Whether legitimate or illegitimate at birth and, if illegitimate whether subsequently legitimated.
   3. Nationality.
   4. Physical description.
   5. Personality and social development.
   6. Religion, including details of baptism, confirmation or equivalent ceremonies.
   7. Details of any wardship proceedings and of any court orders, or agreement under section 4 of the Children Act, relating to parental responsibility for the child, or to his custody and maintenance.
   8. Details of any brothers and sisters, including dates of birth, arrangements in respect of care and custody and whether any brother or sister is also being considered for adoption.
   9. Extent of access to members of the child's natural family and, if the child is illegitimate, his father, and in each case the nature of the relationship enjoyed.
   10. If the child has been in the case of a local authority or voluntary organisation, details (including dates) of any placements with foster parents, or other arrangements in respect of the care of the child, including particulars of the persons with whom the child has had his home and observations on the care provided.
   11. Names, addresses and types of schools attended, with dates and educational attainments.
   12. Any special needs in relation to the child's health (whether physical or mental) and his emotional and behavioural development, and how those are to be met.

12A. Any educational needs which the child has and how these needs are to be met, the result of any assessment carried out in respect of any special educational needs under the Education Act 1996, and how any needs identified in the statement of special educational needs made under section 324 of that Act are to be met.

13. What, if any, rights to or interest in property or any claims to damages, under the Fatal Accidents Act 1976 or otherwise, the child stands to retain or lose if adopted.

14. Wishes and feelings in relation to adoption and, as the case may be, an application under section 18 of the Act (freeing child for adoption), including any wishes in respect of religious and cultural upbringing.

15. Any other relevant information which the agency considers may assist the panel.

PART II

MATTERS TO BE COVERED IN REPORT ON THE CHILD'S HEALTH

1. Name, date of birth, sex, weight and height.
2. A neo-natal report on the child, including—
(a)   details of the birth, and any complications,
(b)   results of a physical examination and screening tests,
(c)   details of any treatment given,
(d)   details of any problem in management and feeding,
(dd) how his health and medical history has affected his physical, intellectual, emotional, social or behavioural development,
(e)   any other relevant information which may assist the panel,
(f)   the name and address of any doctor who may be able to provide further information about any of the above matters.
3 A full health history and examination of the child, including—
(a)   details of any serious illness, disability, accident, hospital admission or attendance at an out-patient department, and in each case any treatment given,
(b)   details and dates of immunisations,
(c)   a physical and developmental assessment according to age, including an assessment of vision and hearing and of neurological, speech and language development and any evidence of emotional disorder,
(d)   for a child over five years of age, the school health history (if available),
(e)   any other relevant information which may assist the panel.
4. The signature, name, address and qualifications of the registered medical practitioner who prepared the report, the date of the report and of the examinations carried out together with the name and address of any doctor (if different) who may be able to provide further information about any of the above matters.

PART III

PARTICULARS RELATING TO EACH NATURAL PARENT, INCLUDING WHERE APPROPRIATE THE FATHER OF AN ILLEGITIMATE CHILD

1. Name, date and place of birth and address.
2. Marital status and date and place of marriage (if any).
3. Past and present relationship (if any) with the other natural parent, including comments on its stability.
4. Physical description.
5. Personality.
6. Religion.
7. Educational attainments.
8. Past and present occupations and interests.

9. Names and brief details of the personal circumstances of the parents and any brothers and sisters of the natural parent, with their ages or ages at death.

10. Wishes and feelings in relation to adoption and, as the case may be, an application under section 18 of the Act (freeing child for adoption), including any wishes in respect of the child's religious and cultural upbringing.

11. Any other relevant information which the agency considers may assist the panel.

PART IV

PARTICULARS RELATING TO THE HEALTH OF EACH NATURAL PARENT INCLUDING WHERE APPROPRIATE THE FATHER OF AN ILLEGITIMATE CHILD

1. Name, date of birth, sex, weight and height.

2. A family health history, covering the parents, the brothers and sisters (if any) and the other children (if any) of the natural parent with details of any serious physical or mental illness and inherited and congenital disease.

3. Past health history, including details of any serious physical or mental illness, disability, accident, hospital admission or attendance at an out-patient department, and in each case any treatment given.

4. A full obstetric history of the mother, including any problems in the ante-natal, labour and post-natal periods, with the results of any tests carried out during or immediately after pregnancy.

5. Details of any present illness, including treatment and prognosis.

6. Any other relevant information which the agency considers may assist the panel.

7. The signature, name, address and qualifications of any registered medical practitioner who supplied any of the information in this Part together with the name and address of any doctor (if different) who may be able to provide further information about any of the above matters.

PART V

PARTICULARS RELATING TO A GUARDIAN

1. Particulars referred to in paragraphs 1, 6, 10 and 11 of Part III.

PART VI

PARTICULARS RELATING TO THE PROSPECTIVE ADOPTER

1. Name, date and place of birth and address.

2. Domicile.

3. Marital status, date and place of marriage (if any) and comments on stability of relationship.

4. Details of any previous marriage.

5. If a married person proposes to adopt a child alone, the reasons for this.

6. Physical description.

7. Personality.

8. Religion, and whether willing to follow any wishes of a child or his natural parents or guardian in respect of the child's religious and cultural upbringing.

9. Educational attainments.

10. Past and present occupations and interests.

11. Details of income and comments on the living standards of the household.

12. Details of other members of the prospective adopter's household (including any children of the prospective adopter even if not resident in the household).

13. Details of the parents and any brothers or sisters of the prospective adopter, with their ages or ages at death.

14. Attitudes to adoption of such other members of the prospective adopter's household and family as the agency considers appropriate.

15. Previous experience of caring for children as step-parent, foster parent, child-minder or prospective adopter and assessment of ability in this respect, together where appropriate with assessment of ability in bringing up the prospective adopter's own children.

16. Reasons for wishing to adopt a child and extent of understanding of the nature and effect of adoption.

17. Assessment of ability to bring up an adopted child throughout his childhood.

18. Details of any adoption allowance payable.

19. Names and address of two referees who will give personal references on the prospective adopter.

20. Name and address of the prospective adopter's registered medical practitioner, if any.

21. Any other relevant information which the agency considers may assist the panel.

PART VII

MATTERS TO BE COVERED IN REPORT ON HEALTH OF THE PROSPECTIVE ADOPTER

1. Name, date of birth, sex, weight and height.

2. A family health history, covering the parents, the brothers and sisters (if any) and the children (if any) of the prospective adopter, with details of any serious physical or mental illness and inherited and congenital disease.

3. Marital history, including (if applicable) reasons for inability to have children.

4. Past health history, including details of any serious physical or mental illness, disability, accident, hospital admission or attendance at an out-patient department, and in each case any treatment given.

5. Obstetric history (if applicable).

6. Details of any present illness, including treatment and prognosis.

7. A full medical examination.

8. Details of any daily consumption of alcohol, tobacco and habit-forming drugs.

9. Any other relevant information which the agency considers may assist the panel.

10. The signature, name, address and qualifications of the registered medical practitioner who prepared the report, the date of the report and of the examinations carried out together with the name and address of any doctor (if different) who may be able to provide further information about any of the above matters.

PART VIII

CONSIDERATIONS TO BE INCLUDED IN REVIEW

1. The child's needs (including his educational needs), progress and development, and whether any changes are needed to help meet those needs or to assist his progress or development.

2. Any arrangements for contact, and whether there is need for any change in such arrangements.

3. Existing arrangements for the child's medical and dental care and treatment, and health and dental surveillance.

4. The possible need for an appropriate course of action to assist any necessary change of such care, treatment or surveillance.

5. The possible need for preventive measures, such as vaccination and immunisation, and screening for vision and hearing.

[SCHEDULE 2

OFFENCES IN ENGLAND AND WALES

**1.** An offence under section 1 of the Sexual Offences Act 1956 (rape).
**2.** An offence specified in Schedule 1 to the Children and Young Persons Act 1933 except for—
  (a)   the offence of common assault or battery; or
  [(aa)  in a case where the offender was under 18 at the time the offence was committed, an offence contrary to section 47 of the Offences Against the Person Act 1861 (assault occasioning actual bodily harm); or]
  (b)   in a case where the offender was under 20 at the time the offence was committed, an offence contrary to sections 6, 2 or 13 of the Sexual Offences Act 1956 (sexual intercourse with a girl between 13 and 16, buggery or indecency between men).
**3.** An offence under section 1(1) of the Indecency with Children Act 1960 (indecent conduct towards young child).
**4.** An offence under section 54 of the Criminal Law Act 1977 (inciting a girl under 16 to have incestuous sexual intercourse).
**5.** An offence contrary to section 1 of the Protection of the Children Act 1978 (indecent photographs of children).
**6.** An offence contrary to section 160 of the Criminal Justice Act 1988 (the possession of indecent photographs of children).
**7.** An offence contrary to section 170 of the Customs and Excise Management Act 1979 in relation to goods prohibited to be imported under section 42 of the Customs Consolidation Act 1876 (prohibitions and restrictions relating to pornography) where the prohibited goods include indecent photographs of children under the age of 16.

OFFENCES IN SCOTLAND

\*      \*      \*      \*      \*

OFFENCES IN NORTHERN IRELAND

\*      \*      \*      \*      \*

**Note.** Inserted by SI 1997/2308, reg 2(9), Schedule. Para (2)(aa) inserted in relation to England by SI 1999/2768, reg 2 as from 31 October 1999, and in relation to Wales by SI 2001/3443, reg 2, as from 1 November 2001.

**RECIPROCAL ENFORCEMENT OF JUDGMENTS (ADMINISTRATION OF JUSTICE ACT 1920, PART II) (CONSOLIDATION) ORDER 1984**

**Dated** 8 February 1984

**SI 1984 No 129**

At the Court at Buckingham Palace, the 8th day of February 1984

Present,

The Queen's Most Excellent Majesty in Council

Her Majesty, by virtue and in exercise of the powers conferred on Her by section 14 of the Administration of Justice Act 1920 or otherwise in Her Majesty vested, is pleased, by and with the advice of Her Privy Council, to order, and it is hereby ordered, as follows—

1. This Order may be cited as the Reciprocal Enforcement of Judgments (Administration of Justice Act 1920, Part II) (Consolidation) Order 1984 and shall come into operation on 8 February 1984.

2. Part II of the Administration of Justice Act 1920 shall extend to the countries and territories specified in Schedule 1 to this Order.

3. The Orders specified in Schedule 2 to this Order are hereby revoked.

## SCHEDULE 1

Article 2

Anguilla
Antigua and Barbuda
Bahamas
Barbados
Belize
Bermuda
Botswana
British Indian Ocean Territory*
British Virgin Islands*
Cayman Islands*
Christmas Island
Cocos (Keeling) Islands
Republic of Cyprus
Dominica
Falkland Islands
Fiji
The Gambia
Ghana
<. . .>
Grenada
Guyana
Hong Kong
Jamaica
Kenya
Kiribati
Lesotho
Malawi
Malaysia
Malta
Mauritius

Montserrat*
Newfoundland
Territory of Norfolk Island
Northern Territory of Australia
Papua New Guinea
Queensland
St Christopher and Nevis
St Helena
St Lucia
St Vincent and the Grenadines
Saskatchewan
Seychelles
Sierra Leone
Singapore
Solomon Islands
South Australia
Sovereign Base Areas of Akrotiri and
   Dhekelia in Cyprus*
Sri Lanka
Swaziland
Tanzania
Tasmania
Trinidad and Tobago
Turks and Caicos Islands*
Tuvalu
Uganda
Victoria
Western Australia
Zambia
Zimbabwe

**Note.** Countries and territories marked * added by SI 1985 No 1994 with effect from 1 February 1986 and entry 'Gibraltar' revoked by SI 1997/2601, art 2 with effect from 1 February 1998.

## SCHEDULE 2

Article 3

ORDERS REVOKED

| Date on which Order made | Countries or territories to which Order applied | References |
| --- | --- | --- |
| 10 August 1921 | Cyprus and Gibraltar. | SR & O 1921/1394 |
| 31 October 1921 | Colony of Sierra Leone and Island of St Vincent. | SR & O 1921/1692 |
| 31 October 1921 | Sierra Leone, Somaliland and Zanzibar Protectorates. | SR & O 1921/1693 |
| 21 November 1921 | South Australia. | SR & O 1921/1806 |
| 6 February 1922 | Ceylon, Grenada and Trinidad and Tobago. | SR & O 1922/125 |
| 6 February 1922 | Western Australia. | SR & O 1922/126 |
| 15 March 1922 | Nigeria Protectorate and Tanganyika Territory. | SR & O 1922/291 |
| 15 March 1922 | Colony of Nigeria and the Straits Settlements. | SR & O 1922/292 |
| 1 April 1922 | Hong Kong and Basutoland. | SR & O 1922/353 |
| 1 April 1922 | Bechuanaland Protectorate, Swaziland and Wei-hai-wei. | SR & O 1922/354 |
| 25 May 1922 | British Guiana, St Lucia, Seychelles and Gold Coast Colony. | SR & O 1922/573 |
| 20 June 1922 | Northern Rhodesia and Uganda Protectorate. | SR & O 1922/719 |
| 14 July 1922 | British Solomon Islands and Nyasaland Protectorates. | SR & O 1922/810 |
| 14 July 1922 | Leeward Islands, Dominica and Gilbert and Ellice Islands. | SR & O 1922/811 |
| 13 October 1922 | British Honduras and Barbados. | SR & O 1922/1206 |
| 4 May 1923 | Newfoundland. | SR & O 1923/562 |
| 4 May 1923 | New Zealand. | SR & O 1923/563 |
| 4 May 1923 | Kenya Protectorate and Southern Rhodesia. | SR & O 1923/564 |
| 4 May 1923 | Falkland Islands, Fiji and the Colonies of The Gambia and Kenya. | SR & O 1923/565 |
| 20 February 1924 | Federated Malay States, Johore and Northern Territories of the Gold Coast. | SR & O 1924/253 |
| 20 February 1924 | Ashanti, Bermuda, Jamaica and Mauritius. | SR & O 1924/254 |
| 9 October 1924 | Bahamas. | SR & O 1924/1220 |
| 7 November 1924 | Kedah. | SR & O 1924/1270 |
| 7 November 1924 | Victoria. | SR & O 1924/1271 |

| Date on which Order made | Countries or territories to which Order applied | References |
|---|---|---|
| 2 May 1925 | Territory of New Guinea. | SR & O 1925/449 |
| 2 May 1925 | Northern Territory of Australia and Territory of Norfolk Island. | SR & O 1925/450 |
| 1 February 1926 | Territory of Papua. | SR & O 1926/91 |
| 25 February 1926 | New South Wales. | SR & O 1926/217 |
| 7 February 1927 | St Helena. | SR & O 1927/60 |
| 6 February 1928 | Saskatchewan. | SR & O 1928/86 |
| 22 March 1928 | Queensland. | SR & O 1928/252 |
| 27 November 1930 | Malta. | SR & O 1930/987 |
| 17 March 1932 | Tasmania. | SR & O 1932/127 |

## ADOPTION RULES 1984

**Dated** 17 February 1984

**SI 1984 No 265**

The Lord Chancellor, in exercise of the powers conferred on him by section 9(3) of the Adoption Act 1958, as amended by paragraph 22 of Schedule 3 to the Children Act 1975, and section 12(1) of the Adoption Act 1968, as amended by Part III of Schedule 4 to the Children Act 1975, and all other powers enabling him in that behalf, hereby makes the following rules—

PART I

INTRODUCTORY

*Citation and commencement*

**1.** These rules may be cited as the Adoption Rules 1984 and shall come into operation on 27 May 1984.

*Interpretation*

**2.** (1) In these rules, unless the context otherwise requires—
['the Act' means the Adoption Act 1976;]
'adoption agency' means a local authority or approved adoption society;
['CA of the receiving State' means, in relation to a Convention country other than the United Kingdom, the Central Authority of the Receiving State;
'CA of the State of origin' means, in relation to a Convention country other than the United Kingdom, the Central Authority of the State of origin;
'Central Authority' means, in relation to England, the Secretary of State for Health, and in relation to Wales, the National Assembly for Wales;]
'the child' means the person whom the applicant for an adoption order or an order authorising a proposed foreign adoption proposes to adopt, or, as the case may be, the person the adoption agency proposes should be freed for adoption;
['children's guardian' means an officer of the service appointed to act on behalf of the child in accordance with section 65(1)(a) of the Act;]
['Convention' means the Convention on Protection of Children and Co-operation in respect of Intercountry Adoption, concluded at the Hague on 29th May 1993;]
*'Convention proceedings' means proceedings in the High Court on an application for a Convention adoption order and proceedings in the High Court under the Act;*

['Convention proceedings' means proceedings in the High Court or a county court for a Convention adoption order or in connection with a Convention adoption order or a Convention adoption;]

'the court' means the High Court and any county court [falling within the class specified for the commencement of proceedings under the Act by an Order under Part I of Schedule 11 to the Children Act 1989];

['Hague Convention Regulations' means the Intercountry Adoption (Hague Convention) Regulations 2003;]

'interim order' means an order under [section 25 of the Act];

'order authorising a proposed foreign adoption' means an order under [section 55 of the Act];

'process' means, in the High Court, a summons and, in a county court, an application;

'proper officer' means, in the High Court, [a district judge] of the Principal Registry of the Family Division and, in a county court, the person defined as 'proper officer' by Order 1(3) of the County Court Rules 1981; *and*

['receiving State' means the state in which it is proposed that the child will bcome habitually resident;]

'regular armed forces of the Crown' means the Royal Navy, the Regular Armed Forces as defined by section 225 of the Army Act 1955, the Regular Air Force as defined by section 223 of the Air Force Act 1955, the Queen Alexandra's Royal Naval Nursing Service and the Women's Royal Naval Service.

['reporting officer' means an officer of the service appointed in accordance with section 65(1)(b) of the [Act; and]]

['State of origin' means the state in which the child is habitually resident].

[(2) Except where a contrary intention appears, a word or phrase used in these rules shall have the same meaning as in the Children Act 1989 or, where the word or phrase does not appear in that Act, as in the Act.]

(3) In these rules a form referred to by number means the form so numbered in Schedule 1 to these rules, or a form substantially to the like effect, with such variations, as the circumstances may require.

**Note.** In para (1) definition 'the Act' substituted by SI 1991/1880, r 3(1), definitions 'CA of the receiving State', 'CA of the State of origin' and 'Central Authority' inserted by SI 2003/183, r 3(a) as from 1 June 2003, definition 'children's guardian' inserted by SI 2001/819, rr 2, 4 as from 1 April 2001, definition 'Convention' inserted by SI 2003/183, r 3(b) as from 1 June 2003, definition 'Convention proceedings' substituted by SI 2003/183, r 3(c) as from 1 June 2003, in definition 'the court' words from 'falling within the class' to 'Children Act 1989' in square brackets substituted by SI 1991/1880, r 3(1), definition 'Hague Convention Regulations' inserted by SI 2003/183, r 3(d) as from 1 June 2003, in definition 'interim order' words 'section 25 of the Act' in square brackets substituted by SI 1991/1880, r 3(1), in definition 'order authorising a proposed foreign adoption' words 'section 55 of the Act' in square brackets substituted by SI 1991/1880, r 3(1), in definition 'proper officer' words 'a district judge' in square brackets substituted by SI 1991/1880, r 3(1), in definition 'proper officer' word 'and' revoked by SI 2003/183, r 3(e) as from 1 June 2003, definition 'receiving State' inserted by SI 2003/183, r 3(f) as from 1 June 2003, definition 'reporting officer' inserted by SI 2001/819, rr 2, 4 as from 1 April 2001, in definition 'reporting officer' word 'Act' substituted by words 'Act; and' in square brackets by SI 2003/183, r 3(g) as from 1 June 2003 and definition 'State of origin' inserted by SI 2003/183, r 3(h) as from 1 June 2003.

Para (2): substituted by SI 1991/1880, rule 3(2).

*Extent and application of other rules*

**3.** (1) These rules shall apply to proceedings in the High Court and in a county court under the Act and Part IV of these rules shall apply to Convention proceedings, commenced on or after *27 May 1984* [1 June 2003].

(2) *Subject to the provisions of these rules and any enactment, the Rules of the Supreme Court 1965 and the County Court Rules 1981 shall apply with the necessary modifications to*

*proceedings in the High Court or a county court under the Act.*

[(2) Subject to the provisions of these rules and to any enactment, the Rules of the Supreme Court 1965 and the County Court Rules 1981 in force immediately before 26 April 1999 shall continue to apply, with any necessary modifications, to proceedings in the High Court or a county court under the Act, and any reference in these rules to those rules shall be construed accordingly.]

(3) For the purposes of paragraph (2) any provision of these rules authorising or requiring anything to be done shall be treated as if it were a provision of the Rules of the Supreme Court 1965 or the County Court Rules 1981 as the case may be.

[(3A) In any proceedings concerning an adoption in accordance with the Convention relating to Adoption concluded at the Hague on 15th November 1965, the Adoption Rules 1984 in force immediately before 1st June 2003 shall continue to apply, with any necessary modifications, to proceedings in the High Court.]

(4) Unless the contrary intention appears, any power which by these rules may be exercised by the court may be exercised by the proper officer.

**Note.** In para (1) words '27 May 2003' substituted by words '1 June 2003' by SI 2003/183, r 4(a) as from 1 June 2003. Para (2) substituted by SI 1999/1477, r 2 as from 16 June 1999. Para (3A) inserted by SI 2003/183, r 4(b) as from 1 June 2003.

PART II

FREEING FOR ADOPTION

*Commencement of proceedings*

**4.** (1) Proceedings to free a child for adoption shall be commenced—
   (a) by originating summons in Form 1 issued out of the Principal Registry of the Family Division; or
   (b) by filing in the office of a county court an originating application in Form 1.
(2) The applicant shall be the adoption agency and the respondents shall be—
   (a) each parent or guardian of the child;
   (b) any local authority or voluntary organisation which has parental responsibility for, is looking after, or is caring for the child;
   (c) *omitted*;
   (d) *omitted*;
   (e) *omitted*;
   (f) any person liable by virtue of any order or agreement to contribute to the maintenance of the child; and
   (g) in the High Court, the child.
(3) The court may at any time direct that any other person or body, *save in a county court the child,* be made a respondent to the process.
(4) On filing the originating process the applicant shall pay the appropriate fee and supply three copies of—
   (a) Form 1, together with any other documents required to be supplied, and
   (b) a report in writing covering all the relevant matters specified in Schedule 2 to these rules.

**Note.** In para (3) words, 'save in a county court the child,' in italics revoked by SI 2001/819, rr 2, 5, as from 1 April 2001.

*Appointment and duties of reporting officer*

**5.** (1) As soon as practicable after the originating process has been filed or at any stage thereafter, if it appears that a parent or guardian of the child is willing to agree to the making of an adoption order and is in England or Wales, the proper officer shall appoint a reporting officer in respect of that parent or guardian, and shall send to him a copy of the originating process and any documents attached thereto and of the report supplied by the applicant.

(2)  The same person may be appointed as reporting officer in respect of two or more parents or guardians of the child.

(3)  *The reporting officer shall be appointed from a panel established by regulations under section 41(7) of the Children Act 1989, if any, but shall not be a member or employee of the applicant or any respondent body nor have been involved in the making of any arrangements for the adoption of the child.*

[(3)  The reporting officer shall not be a member or employee of the applicant or any respondent body nor have been involved in the making of any arrangements for the adoption of the child.]

(4)  The reporting officer shall—

(a)  ensure so far as is reasonably practicable that any agreement to the making of an adoption order is given freely and unconditionally and with full understanding of what is involved;

(b)  confirm that the parent or guardian has been given an opportunity of making a declaration under section 18(6) of the Act that he prefers not to be involved in future questions concerning the adoption of the child;

(c)  witness the signature by the parent or guardian of the written agreement to the making of an adoption order;

(d)  investigate all the circumstances relevant to that agreement and any such declaration;

(e)  where it is proposed to free for adoption a child whose parents were not married to each other at the time of his birth and whose father is not his guardian, interview any person claiming to be the father in order to be able to advise the court on the matters listed in section 18(7) of the Act; but if more than one reporting officer has been appointed, the proper officer shall nominate one of them to conduct the interview; and

(f)  on completing his investigations make a report in writing to the court, drawing attention to any matters which, in his opinion, may be of assistance to the court in considering the application.

(5)  With a view to obtaining the directions of the court on any matter, the reporting officer may at any time make such interim report to the court as appears to him to be necessary and, in particular, the reporting officer shall make a report if a parent or guardian of the child is unwilling to agree to the making of an adoption order, and in such a case the proper officer shall notify the applicant.

(6)  The court may, at any time before the final determination of the application, require the reporting officer to perform such further duties as the court considers necessary.

(7)  The reporting officer shall attend any hearing of the application if so required by the court.

(8)  Any report made to the court under this rule shall be confidential.

**Note.**  Para (3) substituted by SI 2001/819, rr 2, 6, as from 1 April 2001.

*Appointment and duties of guardian ad litem* [children's guardian]

**6.**   (1)  As soon as practicable after the originating process has been filed, or after receipt of the statement of facts supplied under rule 7, if it appears that a parent or guardian of the child is unwilling to agree to the making of an adoption order, the proper officer shall appoint a *guardian ad litem* [children's guardian] of the child and shall send to him a copy of the originating process, together with any documents attached thereto, the statement of facts and the report supplied by the applicant.

(2)  Where there are special circumstances and it appears to the court that the welfare of the child requires it, the court may at any time appoint a *guardian ad litem* [children's guardian] of the child, and where such an appointment is made the court shall indicate any particular matters which it requires the *guardian ad litem* [children's guardian] to investigate, and the proper officer shall send the

*guardian ad litem* [children's guardian] a copy of the originating process together with any documents attached thereto and the report supplied by the applicant.

(3) The same person may be appointed as reporting officer under rule 5(1) in respect of a parent or guardian who appears to be willing to agree to the making of an adoption order, and as *guardian ad litem* [children's guardian] of the child under this rule, and, whether or not so appointed as reporting officer, the guardian ad litem may be appointed as reporting officer in respect of a parent or guardian of the child who originally was unwilling to agree to the making of an adoption order but who later signifies his or her agreement.

*(4) In the High Court, unless the applicant desires some other person to act as guardian ad litem, the Official Solicitor shall, if he consents, be appointed as the guardian ad litem of the child.*

*(5) In a county court and where, in the High Court, the Official Solicitor does not consent to act as guardian ad litem, or the applicant desires some other person so to act, the guardian ad litem shall be appointed from a panel established by regulations under section 41(7) of the Children Act 1989, if any, but shall not be a member or employee of the applicant or any respondent body nor have been involved in the making of any arrangements for the adoption of the child.*

[(5) The children's guardian shall not be a member or employee of the applicant or any respondent body nor have been involved in the making of any arrangements for the adoption of the child.]

(6) With a view to safeguarding the interests of the child before the court, the *guardian ad litem* [children's guardian] shall, so far as is reasonably practicable—
   (a) investigate—
      (i) so far as he considers necessary, the matters alleged in the originating process, the report supplied by the applicant and, where appropriate, the statement of facts supplied under rule 7, and
      (ii) any other matters which appear to him to be relevant to the making of an order freeing the child for adoption;
   (b) advise whether, in his opinion, the child should be present at the hearing of the process; and
   (c) perform such other duties as appear to him to be necessary or as the court may direct.

(7) On completing his investigations the *guardian ad litem* [children's guardian] shall make a report in writing to the court, drawing attention to any matters which, in his opinion, may be of assistance to the court in considering the application.

(8) With a view to obtaining the directions of the court on any matter, the *guardian ad litem* [children's guardian] may at any time make such interim report to the court as appears to him to be necessary.

(9) The court may, at any time before the final determination of the application, require the *guardian ad litem* [children's guardian] to perform such further duties as the court considers necessary.

(10) The *guardian ad litem* [children's guardian] shall attend any hearing of the application unless the court otherwise orders.

(11) Any report made to the court under this rule shall be confidential.

**Note.** Words 'guardian ad litem' in each place they occur substituted by words 'children's guardian' in square brackets, para (4) revoked and para (5) substituted by SI 2001/819, rr 2, 3, 7, all from 1 April 2001.

*Statement of facts in dispensation cases*

**7.** (1) Where the adoption agency applying for an order freeing a child for adoption intends to request the court to dispense with the agreement of a parent or guardian of the child on any of the grounds specified in section 16(2) of the Act, the request shall, unless otherwise directed, be made in the originating process, or, if made subsequently, by notice to the proper officer and there shall be attached to the originating process or notice three copies of the statement of facts on which the applicant intends to rely.

(2) Where the applicant has been informed by a person with whom the child has been placed for adoption that he wishes his identity to remain confidential, the statement of facts supplied under paragraph (1) shall be framed in such a way as not to disclose the identity of that person.

(3) Where a statement of facts has been supplied under paragraph (1), the proper officer shall, where and as soon as practicable, inform the parent or guardian of the request to dispense with his agreement and shall send to him a copy of the statement supplied under paragraph (1).

(4) The proper officer shall also send a copy of the statement supplied under paragraph (1) to the *guardian ad litem* [children's guardian] and to the reporting officer if a different person.

**Note.** Words 'guardian ad litem' substituted by words 'children's guardian' in square brackets by SI 2001/819, rr 2, 3(a) as from 1 April 2001.

*Agreement*

**8.** (1) Any document signifying the agreement of a person to the making of an adoption order may be in Form 2, and, if executed by a person outside England and Wales before the commencement of the proceedings, shall be filed with the originating process.

(2) If the document is executed in Scotland it shall be witnessed by a Justice of the Peace or a Sheriff.

(3) If the document is executed in Northern Ireland it shall be witnessed by a Justice of the Peace.

(4) If the document is executed outside the United Kingdom it shall be witnessed by one of the following persons—

(a) any person for the time being authorised by law in the place where the document is executed to administer an oath for any judicial or other legal purpose;

(b) a British consular officer;

(c) a notary public; or

(d) if the person executing the document is serving in any of the regular armed forces of the Crown, an officer holding a commission in any of those forces.

*Notice of hearing*

**9.** (1) As soon as practicable after receipt of the originating process, the proper officer shall list the case for hearing by a judge, and shall serve notice of the hearing on all the parties, the reporting officer and the *guardian ad litem* [children's guardian] (if appointed) in Form 3.

(2) The reporting officer and the *guardian ad litem* [children's guardian] (if appointed), but no other person, shall be served with a copy of the originating process and the report supplied by the applicant, and that report shall be confidential.

(3) If, at any stage before the hearing of the process, it appears to the court that directions for the hearing are required, the court may give such directions as it considers necessary and, in any event, the court shall, not less than four weeks before the date fixed for the hearing under paragraph (1), consider the documents relating to the process with a view to giving such further directions for the hearing as appear to the court to be necessary.

**Note.** Words 'guardian ad litem' substituted by words 'children's guardian' in square brackets by SI 2001/819, rr 2, 3(a) as from 1 April 2001.

*The hearing*

**10.**   (1) On the hearing of the process, any person upon whom notice is required to be served under rule 9 may attend and be heard on the question whether an order freeing the child for adoption should be made.

(2) Any member or employee of a party which is a local authority, adoption agency or other body may address the court if he is duly authorised in that behalf.

(3) Where the court has been informed by the applicant that the child has been placed with a person (whether alone or jointly with another) for adoption and that person wishes his identity to remain confidential, the proceedings shall be conducted with a view to securing that any such person is not seen by or made known to any respondent who is not already aware of his identity except with his consent.

(4) Subject to paragraph (5) the judge shall not make an order freeing the child for adoption except after the personal attendance before him of a representative of the applicant duly authorised in that behalf and of the child.

(5) If there are special circumstances which, having regard to the report of the *guardian ad litem* [children's guardian] (if any), appear to the court to make the attendance of the child unnecessary, the court may direct that the child need not attend.

(6) If there are special circumstances which appear to the court to make the attendance of any other party necessary, the court may direct that that party shall attend.

**Note.** Words 'guardian ad litem' substituted by words 'children's guardian' in square brackets by SI 2001/819, rr 2, 3(a) as from 1 April 2001.

*Proof of identity of child, etc*

**11.**   (1) Where the child who is the subject of the proceedings is identified in the originating process by reference to a birth certificate which is the same, or relates to the same entry in the Registers of Births, as a birth certificate exhibited to a form of agreement, the child so identified shall be deemed, unless the contrary appears, to be the child to whom the form of agreement refers.

(2) Where the child has previously been adopted, paragraph (1) shall have effect as if for the references to a birth certificate and to the Registers of Births there were substituted respectively references to a certified copy of an entry in the Adopted Children Register and to that Register.

(3) Where the precise date of the child's birth is not proved to the satisfaction of the court, the court shall determine the probable date of his birth and the date so determined may be specified in the order freeing the child for adoption as the date of his birth.

(4) Where the place of birth of the child cannot be proved to the satisfaction of the court but it appears probable that the child was born in the United Kingdom, the Channel Islands or the Isle of Man, he may be treated as having been born in the registration district and sub-district in which the court sits, and in any other case (where the country of birth is not proved) the particulars of the country of birth may be omitted from the order freeing the child for adoption.

*Application for revocation of order freeing a child for adoption*

**12.**   (1) An application by a former parent for an order revoking an order freeing the child for adoption shall be made in Form 4 in the proceedings commenced under rule 4.

(2) Notice of the proceedings shall be served on all parties and on any adoption agency which has parental responsibility for the child by virtue of section 21 of the Act, save that notice shall not be served on a party to the proceedings who was joined as a party by virtue of rule 4(2)(b).

(3) As soon as practicable after receipt of the application, the proper officer shall list the case for hearing by a judge and shall appoint a *guardian ad litem* [children's guardian] of the child in accordance with rule 6(4) or (5) and shall send to him a copy of the application and any documents attached thereto.

(4) The *guardian ad litem* [children's guardian] shall have the same duties as if he had been appointed under rule 6 but as if in that rule—

(a) the reference to an order freeing the child for adoption was a reference to the revocation of an order freeing the child for adoption; and

(b) each reference to the report supplied by the applicant was omitted.

**Note.** Words 'guardian ad litem' in both places substituted by words 'children's guardian' in square brackets by SI 2001/819, rr 2, 3(a) as from 1 April 2001.

*Substitution of one adoption agency for another*

**13.** (1) An application under section 21(1) of the Act shall be made in Form 5 in the proceedings commenced under rule 4.

(2) Notice of any order made under section 21 of the Act shall be sent by the court to the court which made the order under section 18 of the Act (if a different court) and to any former parent (as defined in section 19(1) of the Act) of the child.

PART III

ADOPTION ORDERS

*Application for a serial number*

**14.** If any person proposing to apply to the court for an adoption order wishes his identity to be kept confidential, he may, before commencing proceedings, apply to the proper officer for a serial number to be assigned to him for the purposes of identifying him in the proposed process and a number shall be assigned to him accordingly.

*Commencement of proceedings*

**15.** (1) Proceedings for an adoption order shall be commenced—

(a) by originating summons in Form 6 issued out of the Principal Registry of the Family Division; or

(b) by filing in the office of a county court an originating application in Form 6.

(2) The applicant shall be the proposed adopter and the respondents shall be—

(a) each parent or guardian (not being an applicant) of the child, unless the child is free for adoption;

(b) any adoption agency having parental responsibility for the child by virtue of section 18 or 21 of the Act;

(c) any adoption agency named in the application or in any form of agreement to the making of the adoption order as having taken part in the arrangements for the adoption of the child;

(d) any local authority to whom the applicant has given notice under section 22 of the Act of his intention to apply for an adoption order;

(e) any local authority or voluntary organisation which has parental responsibility for, is looking after or, is caring for the child;

(f) *omitted*;

(g) *omitted*;

(h) any person liable by virtue of any order or agreement to contribute to the maintenance of the child;

(i) *revoked*;

(j) where the applicant proposes to rely on section 15(1)(b)(ii) of the Act, the spouse of the applicant; and

(k) in the High Court, the child.

(3) The court may at any time direct that any other person or body, *save in a county court the child,* be made a respondent to the process.

(4) On filing the originating process the applicant shall pay the appropriate fee and supply three copies of—

(a) Form 6, together with any other documents required to be supplied, and

(b) where the child was not placed for adoption with the applicant by an adoption agency, save where the applicant or one of the applicants is a parent of the child, reports by a registered medical practitioner made not more than three months earlier on the health of the child and of each applicant, covering the matters specified in Schedule 3 to these rules.

**Note.** In para (3) words ', save in a county court the child,' revoked by SI 2001/819, rr 2, 8, as from 1 April 2001.

*Preliminary examination of application*

**16.** If it appears to the proper officer on receipt of the originating process for an adoption order that the court—

(a) may be precluded, by virtue of section 24(1) of the Act, from proceeding to hear the application, or

(b) may for any other reason appearing in the process have no jurisdiction to make an adoption order,

he shall refer the process to the judge or district judge for directions.

*Appointment and duties of reporting officer*

**17.** (1) As soon as practicable after the originating process has been filed or at any stage thereafter, if the child is not free for adoption and if it appears that a parent or guardian of the child is willing to agree to the making of an adoption order and is in England and Wales, the proper officer shall appoint a reporting officer in respect of that parent or guardian, and shall send to him a copy of the originating process and any documents attached thereto.

(2) The same person may be appointed as reporting officer in respect of two or more parents or guardians of the child.

*(3) The reporting officer shall be appointed from a panel established by regulations under section 41(7) of the Children Act 1989, if any, but shall not be a member or employee of any respondent body (except where a local authority is made a respondent only under rule 15(2)(d)) nor have been involved in the making of any arrangements for the adoption of the child.*

[(3) The reporting officer shall not be a member or employee of the applicant or any respondent body (except where a local authority is made a respondent only under rule 15(2)(d)) nor have been involved in the making of any arrangement for the adoption of the child.]

(4) The reporting officer shall—

(a) ensure so far as is reasonably practicable that any agreement to the making of the adoption order is given freely and unconditionally and with full understanding of what is involved;

(b) witness the signature by the parent or guardian of the written agreement to the making of the adoption order;

(c) investigate all the circumstances relevant to that agreement; and

(d) on completing his investigations make a report in writing to the court, drawing attention to any matters which, in his opinion, may be of assistance to the court in considering the application.

(5) Paragraphs (5) to (8) of rule 5 shall apply to a reporting officer appointed under this rule as they apply to a reporting officer appointed under that rule.

**Note.** Para (3) substituted by SI 2001/819, rr 2, 9, as from 1 April 2001.

*Appointment and duties of guardian ad litem* [children's guardian]

**18.** (1) As soon as practicable after the originating process has been filed, or after receipt of the statement of facts supplied under rule 19, if the child is not free for adoption and if it appears that a parent or guardian of the child is unwilling to agree to the making of the adoption order, the proper officer shall appoint a *guardian ad litem* [children's guardian] of the child and shall send him a copy of the originating process together with any documents attached thereto.

(2) Where there are special circumstances and it appears to the court that the welfare of the child requires it, the court may at any time appoint a *guardian ad litem* [children's guardian] of the child and where such an appointment is made the court shall indicate any particular matters which it requires the *guardian ad litem* [children's guardian] to investigate, and the proper officer shall send the *guardian ad litem* [children's guardian] a copy of the originating process together with any documents attached thereto.

[(2A) Where an application is made for a Convention adoption order under rule 28, the proper officer shall as soon as possible appoint a children's guardian of the child and shall send him a copy of the originating process together with any documents attached thereto.]

(3) The same person may be appointed as reporting officer under rule 17(1) in respect of a parent or guardian who appears to be willing to agree to the making of the adoption order, and as *guardian ad litem* [children's guardian] of the child under this rule, and, whether or not so appointed as reporting officer, the *guardian ad litem* [children's guardian] may be appointed as reporting officer in respect of a parent or guardian of the child who originally was unwilling to agree to the making of an adoption order but who later signifies his or her agreement.

*(4) In the High Court, unless the applicant desires some other person to act as guardian ad litem, the Official Solicitor shall, if he consents, be appointed as the guardian ad litem of the child.*

*(5) In a county court and where, in the High Court, the Official Solicitor does not consent to act as guardian ad litem, or the applicant desires some other person so to act, the guardian ad litem shall be appointed from a panel established by regulations under section 41(7) of the Children Act 1989, if any, but shall not be a member or employee of any respondent body (except where a local authority is made a respondent only under rule 15(2)(d)) nor have been involved in the making of any arrangements for the adoption of the child.*

[(5) The children's guardian shall not be a member or employee of the applicant or any respondent body (except where a local authority is made a respondent only under rule 15(2)(d)) nor have been involved in the making of any arrangements for the adoption of the child.]

(6) With a view to safeguarding the interests of the child before the court the *guardian ad litem* [children's guardian] shall, so far as is reasonably practicable—

(a) investigate—
  (i) so far as he considers necessary, the matters alleged in the originating process, any report supplied under rule 22(1) or (2) [, any reports filed under the Convention or Hague Convention Regulations] and, where appropriate, the statement of facts supplied under rule 19;
  (ii) any other matters which appear to him to be relevant to the making of an adoption order [/Convention adoption order];
(b) advise whether, in his opinion, the child should be present at the hearing of the process; and
(c) perform such other duties as appear to him to be necessary or as the court may direct.

(7) Paragraphs (7) to (11) of rule 6 shall apply to a *guardian ad litem* [children's guardian] appointed under this rule as they apply to a *guardian ad litem* [children's guardian] appointed under that rule.

**Note.** Words 'guardian ad litem' in each place they occur substituted by words 'children's guardian' in square brackets by SI 2001/819, rr 2, 3(a) as from 1 April 2001. Para (4) revoked and para (5) substituted by SI 2001/819, rr 2, 10 as from 1 April 2001. In para (6)(a) words ', any reports filed under the Convention or Hague Convention Regulations' and '/Convention adoption order' in square brackets inserted by SI 2003/183, r 5(c), (d), as from 1 June 2003.

### Statement of facts in dispensation cases

**19.** (1) Where the child is not free for adoption and the applicant for the adoption order intends to request the court to dispense with the agreement of a parent or guardian of the child on any of the grounds specified in section 16(2) of the Act, the request shall, unless otherwise directed, be made in the originating process or, if made subsequently, by notice to the proper officer and there shall be attached to the originating process or notice three copies of the statement of facts on which the applicant intends to rely.

(2) Where a serial number has been assigned to the applicant under rule 14, the statement of facts supplied under paragraph (1) shall be framed in such a way as not to disclose the identity of the applicant.

(3) Where a statement of facts has been supplied under paragraph (1), the proper officer shall, where and as soon as practicable, inform the parent or guardian of the request to dispense with his agreement and shall send to him a copy of the statement supplied under paragraph (1).

(4) The proper officer shall also send a copy of the statement supplied under paragraph (1) to the *guardian ad litem* [children's guardian] and to the reporting officer if a different person.

**Note.** Words 'guardian ad litem' substituted by words 'children's guardian' in square brackets by SI 2001/819, rr 2, 3(a), as from 1 April 2001.

### Agreement

**20.** (1) Any document signifying the agreement of a person to the making of the adoption order may be in Form 7, and, if executed by a person outside England and Wales before the commencement of the proceedings, shall be filed with the originating process.

(2) If the document is executed outside England and Wales it shall be witnessed by one of the persons specified in rule 8(2), (3) or (4), according to the country in which it is executed.

### Notice of hearing

**21.** (1) Subject to paragraph (4), the proper officer shall list the case for hearing by a judge as soon as practicable after the originating process has been filed, and shall serve notice of the hearing on all the parties, the reporting officer and the *guardian ad litem* [children's guardian] (if appointed) in Form 8.

(2) In a case where section 22 of the Act applies, the proper officer shall send a copy of the originating process and, where appropriate, of the report supplied under rule 15(4), to the local authority to whom notice under that section was given.

(3) No person other than the reporting officer, the *guardian ad litem* [children's guardian] (if appointed) and, in cases where section 22 of the Act applies, the local authority to whom notice under that section was given, shall be served with a copy of the originating process.

(4) Where section 22 of the Act applies, the proper officer shall list the case for hearing on a date not less than three months from the date of the notice given to the local authority under that section.

(5) If, at any stage before the hearing of the process, it appears to the court that directions for the hearing are required, the court may give such directions as it considers necessary and, in any event, the court shall, not less than four weeks before the date fixed for the hearing under paragraph (1), consider the documents relating to the process with a view to giving such further directions for the hearing as appear to the court to be necessary.

**Note.** Words 'guardian ad litem' substituted by words 'children's guardian' in square brackets by SI 2001/819, rr 2, 3(a), as from 1 April 2001.

*Reports by adoption agency or local authority*

**22.**   (1) Where the child was placed for adoption with the applicant by an adoption agency, that agency shall supply, within six weeks of receipt of the notice of hearing under rule 21, three copies of a report in writing covering the matters specified in Schedule 2 to these rules.

(2) Where the child was not placed for adoption with the applicant by an adoption agency, the local authority to whom the notice under section 22 of the Act was given shall supply, within six weeks of receipt of the notice of hearing under rule 21, three copies of a report in writing covering the matters specified in Schedule 2 to these rules.

(3) The court may request a further report under paragraph (1) or (2) and may indicate any particular matters it requires such a further report to cover.

(4) The proper officer shall send a copy of any report supplied under paragraph (1) or (2) to the reporting officer and to the *guardian ad litem* [children's guardian] (if appointed).

(5) No other person shall be supplied with a copy of any report supplied under paragraph (1) or (2) and any such report shall be confidential.

**Note.** Words 'guardian ad litem' substituted by words 'children's guardian' in square brackets by SI 2001/819, rr 2, 3(a), as from 1 April 2001.

*The hearing*

**23.**   (1) On the hearing of the process, any person upon whom notice is required to be served under rule 21 may attend and be heard on the question whether an adoption order should be made.

(2) Any member or employee of a party which is a local authority, adoption agency or other body may address the court if he is duly authorised in that behalf.

(3) If a serial number has been assigned to the applicant under rule 14, the proceedings shall be conducted with a view to securing that he is not seen by or made known to any respondent who is not already aware of the applicant's identity except with his consent.

(4) Subject to paragraphs (5) and (7), the judge shall not make an adoption order or an interim order except after the personal attendance before him of the applicant and the child.

(5) If there are special circumstances which, having regard to the report of the *guardian ad litem* [children's guardian] (if any), appear to the court to make the attendance of the child unnecessary, the court may direct that the child need not attend.

(6) If there are special circumstances which appear to the court to make the attendance of any other party necessary, the court may direct that that party shall attend.

(7) In the case of an application under section 14(1A) or (1B) of the Act, the judge may in special circumstances make an adoption order or an interim order after the personal attendance of one only of the applicants, if the originating process is verified by an affidavit sworn by the other applicant or, if he is outside

the United Kingdom, by a declaration made by him and witnessed by any of the persons specified in rule 8(4).

**Note.** Words 'guardian ad litem' substituted by words 'children's guardian' in square brackets by SI 2001/819, rr 2, 3(a), as from 1 April 2001.

*Proof of identity of child, etc*

**24.** (1) Where the child who is the subject of the proceedings is identified in the originating process by reference to a birth certificate which is the same, or relates to the same entry in the Registers of Births, as a birth certificate exhibited to a form of agreement, the child so identified shall be deemed, unless the contrary appears, to be the child to whom the form of agreement refers.

(2) Where the child has previously been adopted, paragraph (1) shall have effect as if for the references to a birth certificate and to the Registers of Births there were substituted respectively references to a certified copy of an entry in the Adopted Children Register and to that Register.

(3) Subject to paragraph (5), where the precise date of the child's birth is not proved to the satisfaction of the court, the court shall determine the probable date of his birth and the date so determined may be specified in the adoption order as the date of his birth.

(4) Subject to paragraph (5), where the place of birth of the child cannot be proved to the satisfaction of the court but it appears probable that the child was born in the United Kingdom, the Channel Islands or the Isle of Man, he may be treated as having been born in the registration district and sub-district in which the court sits, and in any other case (where the country of birth is not proved) the particulars of the country of birth may be omitted from the adoption order.

(5) Where the child is free for adoption, any order made identifying the probable date and place of birth of the child in the proceedings under section 18 of the Act shall be sufficient proof of the date and place of birth of the child in proceedings to which this rule applies.

*Further proceedings after interim order*

**25.** Where the court has made an interim order, the proper officer shall list the case for further hearing by a judge on a date before the order expires and shall send notice in Form 8 of the date of the hearing to all the parties and to the *guardian ad litem* [children's guardian] (if appointed) not less than one month before that date.

**Note.** Words 'guardian ad litem' substituted by words 'children's guardian' in square brackets by SI 2001/819, rr 2, 3(a), as from 1 April 2001.

*Committal of child to care on refusal of adoption order*

**26.** *Revoked.*

PART IV

CONVENTION PROCEEDINGS

*Introductory*

**27.** (1) This Part of these rules shall apply to Convention proceedings and, subject to the provisions of this Part of these rules, Parts I, III and V of these rules shall apply, with the necessary modifications, to Convention proceedings as they apply to proceedings in the High Court [or a county court] under the Act.

(2) *Any reference in this Part of these rules to the nationality of a person who is not solely a United Kingdom national means that person's nationality as determined in accordance with section 70 of the Act.*

**Note.** In para (1) words 'or a county court' in square brackets inserted and para (2) revoked by SI 2003/183, r 6, as from 1 June 2003.

*Originating process*

**28.**   (1)  An applicant for a Convention adoption order shall state in his originating process that he is applying for a Convention adoption order.
   (2)  The originating process—
   (a)  need not contain paragraphs corresponding to paragraphs 2, 24 or 25 of Form 6 but
   (b)  shall contain the additional information required by Schedule 4 to these rules.

*Evidence as to nationality*

**29.**   *(1)  Any document (or copy of a document) which is to be used for the purposes of satisfying the court as to the nationality of the applicant or of the child shall be attached to the originating process.*
   *(2)  Where the applicant claims that for the purposes of section 17(2)(a), (4)(a) or (5)(a) of the Act he or the child is a national of a Convention country, he shall attach to the originating process a statement by an expert as to the law of that country relating to nationality applicable to that person.*
**Note.** Revoked by SI 2901/183, r 7, as from 1 June 2003.

*Statement at hearing*

**30.**   *The requirement that the conditions in section 17(2), (3) and (4) or (5) of the Act are satisfied immediately before the order is made may be established by—*
   *(a)  oral evidence at the hearing of an application for a Convention adoption order, or*
   *(b)  a document executed by the applicant containing a statement to that effect attested in accordance with rule 44 and such a statement shall be admissible in evidence without further proof of the signature of the applicant.*

[*Statement at hearing*

**30.**   The requirements prescribed by regulations 21 and 32 of the Hague Convention Regulations may be established by a document executed by the applicant containing a statement to that effect attested in accordance with rule 44 and such a statement shall be admissible in evidence without further proof of the signature of the applicant.]
**Note.** Substituted by SI 2003/183, r 8, as from 1 June 2003.

*Orders*

**31.**   *Within 7 days after a Convention adoption order has been drawn up, the proper officer shall by notice to the Registrar General request him to send the information to the designated authorities of any Convention country—*
   *(a)  of which the child is a national;*
   *(b)  in which the child was born;*
   *(c)  in which the applicant habitually resides; or*
   *(d)  of which the applicant is a national.*
**Note.** Revoked by SI 2003/183, r 9, as from 1 June 2003.

ADDITIONAL PROVISIONS FOR CASES WHERE CHILD IS NOT A UNITED KINGDOM NATIONAL

*Scope of rules 33 to 36*

**32.**   *Rules 33 to 36 shall apply to any case where the child is not a United Kingdom national, and in such a case—*

(a)  the provisions in Part III of these rules, other than rules 17 and 20 (agreement to adoption), and

(b)  paragraphs 9 to 14 of Form 6,

*shall apply with the necessary modifications to take account of section 17(6)(a) of the Act.*

**Note.** Revoked by SI 2003/183, r 9, as from 1 June 2003.

*Evidence as to foreign law relating to consents and consultations*

**33.**   *The applicant shall file, with his originating process, a statement by an expert as to the provisions relating to consents and consultations of the internal law relating to adoption of the Convention country of which the child is a national.*

**Note.** Revoked by SI 2003/183, r 9, as from 1 June 2003.

*Form of consent etc*

**34.**   (1) Any document signifying the consent of a person to, or otherwise containing the opinion of a person on the making of, the Convention adoption order shall be in a form which complies with the internal law relating to adoption of the Convention country of which the child is *a national* [habitually resident]: provided that where the court is not satisfied that a person consents with full understanding of what is involved, it may call for further evidence.

(2) A document referred to in paragraph (1) shall, if sufficiently witnessed, be admissible as evidence of the consent or opinion contained therein without further proof of the signature of the person by whom it is executed.

(3) A document referred to in paragraph (1) shall, if executed before the date of the applicant's originating process referred to in rule 28(2), be attached to that process.

**Note.** Words 'a national' substituted by words 'habitually resident' in square brackets by SI 2003/183, r 10, as from 1 June 2003.

*Notice of hearing*

**35.**   (1)  When serving notice of the hearing on the persons specified in rule 21, the proper officer shall also serve notice on any person—

(a)  whose consent to the making of the order is required, not being an applicant, or

(b)  who, in accordance with the internal law relating to adoption of the Convention country of which the child is a national [habitually resident], has to be consulted about, but does not have to consent to, the adoption.

(2)  Any person served or required to be served with notice under this rule shall be treated as if he had been served or was required to be served with notice under rule 21.

**Note.** Words 'a national' substituted by words 'habitually resident' in square brackets by SI 2003/183, r 10, as from 1 June 2003.

*Proper officer to receive opinions on adoption*

**36.**   *For the purposes of this rule and of section 17(7)(a) of the Act, the Senior District Judge of the Principal Registry of the Family Division is the proper officer of the court to whom any person whose consent is required under or who is consulted in pursuance of the internal law relating to adoption of the Convention country of which the child is a national may communicate his consent or other opinion on the adoption.*

**Note.** Revoked by SI 2003/183, r 11, as from 1 June 2003.

PROCEEDINGS UNDER SECTION 52 OR 53 OF THE ACT

*Application to annul or revoke adoption*

**37.**   (1)  An application for an order under section 52(1) or 53(1) of the Act shall be made by originating process issued out of the Principal Registry of the Family Division in Form 9; and the person filing the process shall be described as the applicant and the adopted person and any adopter, not being the applicant, shall be described as a respondent.

(2)  An application under section 53(1) of the Act shall not, except with the leave of the court, be made later than 2 years after the date of the adoption to which it relates.

*[Application to annul Convention adoption or Convention adoption order*

**37A.**   (1)  An application for the annulment of a Convention adoption or a Convention adoption order under section 53(1) of the Act shall be made by originating process issued out of the Principal Registry of the Family Division in Form 9, and may be made by—

(a)  the adopter or adopters, or

(b)  the adopted person, or

(c)  the relevant Central Authority, or

(d)  the adoption agency, or

(e)  the local authority to whom notice under section 22 of the Act was given (if different), or

(f)  the Secretary of State for the Home Department.

(2)  The adopted person and any adopter, not being the applicant, shall be respondents and the court may require notice of the application to be served on such other persons as it thinks fit.]

**Note.** Inserted by SI 2003/183, r 12, as from 1 June 2003.

*[Application for directions where a full adoption has not been made*

**37B.**   (1)  An application for a direction under section 39(3A) of the Act—

(a)  may be made by the adopted child, the adopter or adopters or the birth parents of the child; and

(b)  shall be made by originating process issued out of the Principal Registry of the Family Division in Form 15A.

(2)  The person filing the process shall be described as the applicant.

(3)  The respondents shall be—

(a)  the adopter or adopters (if not the applicant),

(b)  the birth parents (if not the applicant),

(c)  the adoption agency,

(d)  the local authority to whom notice under section 22 of the Act was given (if different),

(e)  the Attorney-General

and the court may require notice of the application to be served on such other persons as it thinks fit including the child, having regard to the child's age and degree of maturity.

(4)  Any direction given in accordance with section 39(3A) of the Act shall be in Form 15B.]

**Note.** Inserted by SI 2003/183, r 12, as from 1 June 2003.

*Application to declare adoption invalid or determination invalid or affected*

**38.**   An application for an order or decision under section 52 or 53 of the Act shall be made by originating process issued out of the Principal Registry of the

Family Division in Form 10; and the person filing the process shall be described as the applicant and the adopted person and any adopter, not being the applicant, shall be described as a respondent.

*Evidence in support of application*

**39.** (1) Evidence in support of an application under section 52 or 53 of the Act shall be given by means of an affidavit in Form 11 which shall be filed within 14 days after the issue of the originating process.

(2) Where the application is made under section 53 of the Act there shall be exhibited to the affidavit a statement of the facts and, *subject to rule 42*, there shall be filed with the affidavit expert evidence of any provision of foreign law relating to adoption on which the applicant intends to rely.

(3) The court may order any deponent to give oral evidence concerning the facts stated in, or exhibited to, his affidavit.

**Note.** Words ', subject to rule 42,' revoked by SI 2003/183, r 13, as from 1 June 2003.

*Guardian ad litem* [children's guardian]

**40.** Where the adopted person is under the age of 18 on the date on which an application under section 52 or 53 of the Act is made, rule 18(2) [, (2A)] and (4) to (7) shall apply to the application as it applies to an application for an adoption order [/Convention adoption order] as if the references in rule 18 to the making of an adoption order [/Convention adoption order] were references to the granting of an application under section 52 or 53 of the Act.

**Note.** Words 'Guardian ad litem' substituted by words 'children's guardian' in square brackets by SI 2001/819, rr 2, 3(a), as from 1 April 2001. Reference to ', (2A)' and words '/Convention adoption order' in both places in square brackets inserted by SI 2003/183, r 14, as from 1 June 2003.

*Notice of order made under section 52 or 53 etc*

**41.** (1) Where under section 52 or 53 of the Act the court has ordered that an adoption be annulled or revoked or that an adoption or a determination shall cease to be valid in Great Britain, the proper officer shall serve notice of the order on the Registrar General [and, where it relates to a Convention adoption order or a Convention adoption, the relevant Central Authority], and shall state in the notice—

  (a) the date of the adoption;

  (b) the name and address of the authority which granted the adoption; and

  (c) the names of the adopter or adopters and of the adopted person as given in the affidavit referred to in rule 39.

(2) *A notice under paragraph (1) in respect of the annulment or revocation of an adoption shall request the Registrar General to send the information to the designated authorities of any Convention country—*

  *(a) in which the adoption was granted;*

  *(b) of which the adopted person is a national; or*

  *(c) in which the adopted person was born.*

(3) *Revoked.*

**Note.** In para (1) words 'and, where it relates to a Convention adoption order or a Convention adoption, the relevant Central Authority' in square brackets inserted and para (2) revoked by SI 2003/183, r 15, as from 1 June 2003. (Para (3) revoked by SI 1991/1880, r 28(3)).

SUPPLEMENTARY

*Evidence as to specified or notified provisions*

**42.** *(1) Where the applicant seeks to satisfy the court as to any question which has arisen or is likely to arise concerning a provision—*

    (a)  *of the internal law of the Convention country of which the applicant or any other person is or was a national,*

    (b)  *which has been specified in an order—*

        (i)  *under section 17(8) of the Act (a 'specified provision'), or*

        (ii)  *under section 54(4) of the Act (a 'notified provision'),*

*expert evidence of the specified or notified provision shall, where practicable, be attached to the originating process.*

    *(2) Paragraph (1) shall apply, in the case of a person who is or was a United Kingdom national, for the purposes of a notified provision in respect of a specified country as it applies for the purposes of a notified provision in respect of a Convention country of which a person is or was a national.*

**Note.** Revoked by SI 2003/183, r 16, as from 1 June 2003.

*Interim order*

**43.**  *Where the applicant is a national or both applicants are nationals of a Convention country, the court shall take account of any specified provision (as defined in section 17(8) of the Act) of the internal law of that country before any decision is made to postpone the determination of the application and to make an interim order.*

**Note.** Revoked by SI 2003/183, r 16, as from 1 June 2003.

*Witnessing of documents*

**44.**  A document shall be sufficiently attested for the purposes of this Part of these rules if it is witnessed by one of the following persons—

    (a)  if it is executed in England and Wales, the reporting officer, a Justice of the Peace, an officer of a county court appointed for the purposes of section 58(1)(c) of the County Courts Act 1984 or a justices' clerk within the meaning of section 70 of the Justices of the Peace Act 1979; or

    (b)  if it is executed elsewhere, any person specified in rule 8(2), (3) or (4), according to the country in which it is executed.

*Service of documents*

**45.**  (1) Any document to be served for the purposes of this Part of these rules may be served out of the jurisdiction without the leave of the court.

    (2) Any document served out of the jurisdiction in a country in which English is not an official language shall be accompanied by a translation of the document in the official language of the country in which service is to be effected or, if there is more than one official language of the country, in any one of those languages which is appropriate to the place in that country where service is to be effected.

*Translation of documents*

**46.**  Where a translation of any document is required for the purposes of Convention proceedings, the translation shall, unless otherwise directed, be provided by the applicant.

PART V

MISCELLANEOUS

*Application for removal, return etc, of child*

**47.**  (1) An application—

    (a)  for leave under section 27 or 28 of the Act to remove a child from the home of a person with whom the child lives,

(b) under section 29(2) of the Act for an order directing a person not to remove a child from the home of a person with whom the child lives,

(c) under section 29(1) of the Act for an order for the return of a child who has been removed from the home of a person with whom the child lives,

(d) under section 30(2) of the Act for leave to give notice of an intention not to give a home to a child or not to allow a child to remain in a person's home, or

(e) under section 20(2) of the Act for leave to place a child for adoption,

shall be made in accordance with paragraph (2).

(2) The application under paragraph (1) shall be made—

(a) if an application for an adoption order or an order under section 18 or 20 of the Act is pending, by process on notice in those proceedings; or

(b) if no such application is pending, by filing an originating process in the court.

(3) *Revoked.*

(4) Any respondent to the originating process made under paragraph (2)(b) who wishes to claim relief shall do so by means of an answer to the process which shall be made within 7 days of the service of the copy of the process on the respondent.

(5) Subject to paragraph (6), the proper officer shall serve a copy of the process, and of any answer thereto, and a notice of the date of the hearing—

(a) in a case where proceedings for an adoption order or an order under section 18 or 20 of the Act are pending (or where such proceedings have subsequently been commenced), on all the parties to those proceedings and on the reporting officer and *guardian ad litem* [children's guardian], if any;

(b) in any other case, on any person against whom an order is sought on the applicant and on the local authority to whom the prospective adopter has given notice under section 22 of the Act; and

(c) in any case, on such other person or body, not being the child, as the court thinks fit.

(6) If in any application under this rule a serial number has been assigned to a person who has applied or who proposes to apply for an adoption order, or such a person applies to the proper officer in that behalf before filing the originating process and a serial number is assigned accordingly—

(a) the proper officer shall ensure that the documents served under paragraph (5) do not disclose the identity of that person to any other party to the application under this rule who is not already aware of that person's identity, and

(b) the proceedings on the application under this rule shall be conducted with a view to securing that he is not seen by or made known to any party who is not already aware of his identity except with his consent.

(7) Unless otherwise directed, any prospective adopter who is served with a copy of an application under this rule and who wishes to oppose the application shall file his process for an adoption order within 14 days or before or at the time of the hearing of the application under this rule, whichever is the sooner.

(8) The court may at any time give directions, and if giving directions under paragraph (7) shall give further directions, as to the conduct of any application under this rule and in particular as to the appointment of a *guardian ad litem* [children's guardian] of the child.

(9) Where an application under paragraph (1)(a) or (d) is granted or an application under paragraph (1)(b) or (c) is refused, the judge may thereupon, if process for an adoption order has been filed, treat the hearing of the application as the hearing of the process for an adoption order and refuse an adoption order accordingly.

(10) Where an application under this rule is determined the proper officer shall serve notice of the effect of the determination on all the parties.

(11) Paragraphs (6) to (10) shall apply to an answer made under this rule as they apply to an originating process made under this rule as if the answer were the originating process.

**Note.** Words 'guardian ad litem' substituted by words 'children's guardian' in square brackets by SI 2001/819, rr 2, 3(a), as from 1 April 2001.

[*Application for removal, return etc, of child in Convention proceedings*

**47A.** (1) Paragraph (2) shall apply where—
  (a) a notice under regulation 18(1) of the Hague Convention Regulations has been given but has not been complied with; or
  (b) before such a notice was given an application for a Convention adoption order has been made and not disposed of.

(2) Where this paragraph applies an application for the return of the child shall be made by the local authority to whom notice under section 22 of the Act was given by filing an originating process in the court or, where paragraph (1)(b) applies, by process on notice in the existing proceedings.

(3) The respondents shall be—
  (a) the prospective adopter or adopters,
  (b) the children's guardian,
  (c) the adoption agency

and the court may require notice of the application to be served on such other persons as it thinks fit, including the child, having regard to the child's age and degree of maturity.

(4) Any respondent who wishes to contest the notice shall, within 7 days of service of the notice upon him, file and serve an answer.

(5) The proper officer shall list the case for hearing on a date not more than 21 days from the date the application under paragraph (2) was submitted to the court.]

**Note.** Inserted by SI 2003/183, r 17, as from 1 June 2003.

[*Specific applications in Convention proceedings*

**47B.** (1) Where a Convention adoption order is to be or has been sought and has not been disposed of the applicant or proposed applicant may apply to the court for an order—
  (a) permitting the child to be known by a new surname, or
  (b) permitting the child to be removed from the United Kingdom for a period of one month or more.

(2) The application under paragraph (1) shall be made—
  (a) if an application for a Convention adoption order under section 17 of the Act is pending, by process on notice in those proceedings; or
  (b) if no such application is pending, by filing an originating process in the court.

(3) The proper officer shall serve a copy of the process and a notice of the date of the hearing—
  (a) in a case where proceedings for an adoption order are pending on all the parties to those proceedings and on the children's guardian; and
  (b) in any other case, on the adoption agency and the local authority to whom notice under section 22 of the Act was given (if different).]

**Note.** Inserted by SI 2003/183, r 17, as from 1 June 2003.

*Proposed foreign adoption proceedings*

**48.** (1) Proceedings for an order authorising a proposed foreign adoption shall be commenced—

   (a)  by originating summons in Form 6 issued out of the Principal Registry of the Family Division; or

   (b)  by filing in the office of the county court within whose district the child is an originating application in Form 6.

(2) Subject to paragraph (3), Part III of these rules except rule 15(i) and Part V except rule 52(1)(d) shall apply to an application for an order authorising a proposed foreign adoption as if such an order were an adoption order.

(3) An applicant for an order authorising a proposed foreign adoption shall provide expert evidence of the law of adoption in the country in which he is domiciled and an affidavit as to that law sworn by such a person as is mentioned in section 4(1) of the Civil Evidence Act 1972 (that is to say a person who is suitably qualified on account of his knowledge or experience to give evidence as to that law) shall be admissible in evidence without notice.

*Amendment and revocation of orders*

**49.** (1) An application under paragraph 4 of Schedule 1 to the Act for the amendment of an adoption order or the revocation of a direction to the Registrar General, or under section 52 of the Act for the revocation of an adoption order, may be made ex parte in the first instance, but the court may require notice of the application to be served on such persons as it thinks fit.

(2) Where the application is granted, the proper officer shall send to the Registrar General a notice specifying the amendments or informing him of the revocation and shall give sufficient particulars of the order to enable the Registrar General to identify the case.

*[Power to court to limit cross examination*

**49A.** The court may limit the issues on which a children's guardian or a reporting officer may be cross-examined.]

**Note.** Inserted by SI 2001/819, rr 2, 11, as from 1 April 2001.

*Service of documents*

**50.** (1) Subject to rule 45 and unless otherwise directed, any document under these rules may be served—

   (a)  on a corporation or body of persons, by delivering it at, or sending it by post to, the registered or principal office of the corporation or body;

   (b)  on any other person, by delivering it to him, or by sending it by post to him at his usual or last known address.

(2) The person effecting service of any document under these rules shall make, sign and file a certificate showing the date, place and mode of service. If he has failed to effect service of any document, he shall make, sign and file a certificate of non-service showing the reason why service has not been effected.

*Costs*

**51.** (1) On the determination of proceedings to which these rules apply or on the making of an interim order, the judge may make such order as to the costs as he thinks just and, in particular, may order the applicant to pay—

   (a)  the expenses incurred by the reporting officer and the *guardian ad litem* [children's guardian] (if appointed),

   (b)  the expenses incurred by any respondent in attending the hearing, or such part of those expenses as the judge thinks proper.

(2) Order 62 of the Rules of the Supreme Court 1965 and Order 38 of the County Court Rules 1981 shall not apply to costs in proceedings under the Act and

Parts 43, 44 (except rules 44.9 to 44.12), 47 and 48 of the Civil Procedures Rules 1998 shall apply to costs in those proceedings with the following modifications—

(a) in rule 43.2(1)(c)(ii) of the Civil Procedure Rules, 'district judge' includes a district judge of the Principal Registry of the Family Division; and

(b) rule 44.3(2) of *the 1998 Rules* [the Civil Procedure Rules] (costs follow the event) shall not apply.]

[(3) Except in the case of an appeal against a decision of an authorised court officer (to which rules 47.20 to 47.23 of the Civil Procedure Rules apply), an appeal against a decision in assessment proceedings relating to costs in proceedings under the Act shall be dealt with in accordance with the following paragraphs of this rule.

(4) An appeal within paragraph (3) shall lie as follows—

(a) where the decision appealed against was made by a district judge of the High Court or a costs judge (as defined by rule 43.2(1)(b) of the Civil Procedure Rules), to a judge of the High Court; or

(b) where the decision appealed against was made by a district judge of a county court, to a judge of that court.

(5) Part 52 of the Civil Procedure Rules applies to every appeal within paragraph (3), and any reference in Part 52 to a judge or a district judge shall be taken to include a district judge of the Principal Registry of the Family Division.

(6) The Civil Procedure Rules apply to an appeal to which part 52 or rules 47.20 to 47.23 of those Rules apply in accordance with paragraph (3) in the same way as they apply to any other appeal within Part 52 or rules 47.20 to 47.23 as the case may be; accordingly the Rules of the Supreme Court 1965 and the County Court Rules 1981 shall not apply to any such appeal.]

**Note.** Para (1) numbered as such and para (2) inserted by SI 1999/1477, r 4, as from 16 June 1999 (para (1) applying to any assessment of costs made on or after that date but so that, as a general rule, no costs for work done before that date shall be disallowed if they would have been allowed on taxation before that date). In para (1)(a) words 'guardian ad litem' substituted by words 'children's guardian' in square brackets by SI 2001/819, rr 2, 3(a) as from 1 April 2001. In para (2)(b) words 'the 1998 Rules' substituted by words 'the Civil Procedure Rules' in square brackets and paras (3)–(6) inserted by SI 2003/183, r 18, as from 24 February 2003.

*Notice and copies of orders etc*

**52.** (1) In proceedings to which these rules apply orders shall be made in the form indicated in this paragraph—

| Description of order | Form |
| --- | --- |
| (a) Order under section 18 of the Act | 12 |
| (b) Order under section 20 of the Act | 13 |
| (c) Interim order | 14 |
| (d) Adoption order | 15 |
| (e) Convention adoption order | 15 (with the word 'Convention' inserted where appropriate) |
| (f) Order authorising a proposed foreign adoption | 15 (with the words 'order authorising a proposed foreign adoption' substituted for the words 'adoption order' wherever they appear). |

(2) Where an adoption order is made by a court sitting in Wales in respect of a child who was born in Wales (or is treated under rule 24(4) as having been born in the registration district and sub-district in which that court sits) and the adopter so requests before the order is drawn up, the proper officer shall obtain a translation into Welsh of the particulars set out in the order.

(3) Within 7 days of the making of an order in proceedings to which these rules

apply, the proper officer shall send a copy of the order (and of any translation into Welsh obtained under paragraph (2)) to the applicant.

(4) Within 7 days of the making of an order to which paragraph (1)(d), (e) or (f) applies, the proper officer shall send a copy of the order (and of any translation into Welsh obtained under paragraph (2)) to the Registrar General and, [where paragraph (e) applies, to the Central Authority;] *in the case of a Convention adoption order, shall comply with rule 31*; where a translation into Welsh under paragraph (2) has been obtained, the English text shall prevail.

(5) Where an order to which paragraph (1)(a), (b), (d), (e) or (f) applies is made or refused or an order to which paragraph (1)(c) applies is made, the proper officer shall serve notice to that effect on every respondent.

(6) *Revoked.*

(7) The proper officer shall serve notice of the making of an order to which paragraph (1)(a), (b), (d), (e) or (f) applies on any court in Great Britain which appears to him to have made any such order as is referred to in section 12(8) of the Act (orders relating to parental responsibility for, and the maintenance of the child).

(8) A copy of any order may be supplied to the Registrar General at his request.

(9) A copy of any order may be supplied to the applicant.

(10) A copy of any order may be supplied to any other person with the leave of the court.

[(11) Within 7 days of the making of an order to annul a Convention adoption order or a Convention adoption, the proper officer shall send a copy of the order to the applicant, every respondent, the relevant Central Authority and the Registrar General.]

**Note.** In para (4) words 'where paragraph (e) applies, to the Central Authority;' in square brackets inserted and words 'in the case of a Convention adoption order, shall comply with rule 31;' revoked, and para 11 inserted by SI 2003/183, r 19, as from 1 June 2003.

*Custody, inspection and disclosure of documents and information*

**53.** (1) All documents relating to proceedings under the Act (or under any previous enactment relating to adoption) shall, while they are in the custody of the court, be kept in a place of special security.

(2) A party who is an individual and is referred to in a confidential report supplied to the court by an adoption agency, a local authority, a reporting officer or a *guardian ad litem* [children's guardian] may inspect, for the purposes of the hearing, that part of any such report which refers to him, subject to any direction given by the court that—

(a) no part of one or any of the reports shall be revealed to that party, or

(b) the part of one or any of the reports referring to that party shall be revealed only to that party's legal advisers, or

(c) the whole or any other part of one or any of the reports shall be revealed to that party.

(3) Any person who obtains any information in the course of, or relating to, any proceedings mentioned in paragraph (1) shall treat that information as confidential and shall only disclose it if—

(a) the disclosure is necessary for the proper exercise of his duties, or

(b) the information is requested—

    (i) by a court or public authority (whether in Great Britain or not) having power to determine adoptions and related matters, for the purpose of the discharge of its duties in that behalf, or

    (ii) by the Registrar General, or a person authorised in writing by him, where the information requested relates only to the identity of any adoption agency which made the arrangements for placing the child for adoption in the actual custody of the applicants, and of any local authority which was notified of the applicant's intention to apply for an adoption order in respect of the child, or

(iii) by a person who is authorised in writing by the Secretary of State to obtain the information for the purposes of research.

[(3A) Nothing in this rule shall prevent the disclosure of a document prepared by an officer of the service for the purpose of—

(a) enabling a person to perform functions required under section 62(3A) of the Justices of the Peace Act 1997; and

(b) assisting an officer of the service who is appointed by the court under any enactment to perform his functions.

(3B) Nothing in this rule shall prevent the disclosure of any document relating to proceedings by an officer of the service to any other officer of the service unless that other officer is involved in the same proceedings but on behalf of a different party.]

(4) Save as required or authorised by a provision of any enactment or of these rules or with the leave of the court, no document or order held by or lodged with the court in proceedings under the Act (or under any previous enactment relating to adoption) shall be open to inspection by any person, and no copy of any such document or order, or of an extract from any such document or order, shall be taken by or issued to any person.

**Note.** In para (2) words 'guardian ad litem' substituted by words 'children's guardian' in square brackets and paras (3A), (3B) inserted by SI 2001/819, rr 2, 3(a), 12, as from 1 April 2001.

*Revocations*

**54.** Except to the extent that they continue to apply for the purposes of the determination of an application for an adoption order, a Convention adoption order or a provisional adoption order made before the commencement date of these rules in the High Court or a county court, as the case may be, the following rules are hereby revoked—

(i) The Adoption (High Court) Rules 1976,

(ii) The Adoption (County Court) Rules 1976,

(iii) The Convention Adoption Rules 1978,

(iv) The Adoption (County Court) (Amendment) Rules 1978,

(v) The Adoption (High Court) (Amendment) Rules 1978,

(vi) The Adoption (County Court) (Amendment) Rules 1979,

(vii) The Adoption (High Court) (Amendment) Rules 1982 and

(viii) The Adoption (County Court) (Amendment) Rules 1982.

SCHEDULE 1                                                                        Rule 2(2)

GENERAL FORMS

Form 1

Originating Process for an Order Freeing a Child for Adoption
(Heading—High Court)
In the High Court of Justice
Family Division

                                                                    No          of 19

In the matter of the Adoption Act 1958 and
In the matter of the Children Act 1975 and
In the matter of                      a child
Let         of                      attend at the Royal Courts of Justice, Strand, London WC2, on a date to be fixed for the hearing of the application of                      of

for an order—

1.  That the said child be freed for adoption;
2.  That the costs of this application be provided for;
And take notice that the grounds of the application are as follows—
(Continue as in body of the county court originating process below, from the words 'I, an authorised officer ...')
(Heading—County Court)

In the                       County Court
Number of matter

In the matter of the Adoption Act 1976
In the matter of              a child
I, an authorised officer of the          of          being an adoption agency
wishing to free for adoption          , a child, hereby give the following further
particulars in support of the application.
1.  This application is/is not made with the consent of                     (and
          ), the parent(s)/guardian(s) of the child.

*Particulars of the child*

2.  Identity etc. The child is of the      sex and is not and has not been married.
He/she was born on the      day of          19  and is the person to whom
the attached birth/adoption certificate relates (*or*, was born on or about the      day
of          19  , in          ). He/she is a          national.
3.  Parentage, etc. The child is the child of          whose last known address
was          (*or* deceased) and          whose last known address was
          (*or* deceased).
(4.  The guardian(s) of the child (other than the mother or father of the child
is/are          of          (and          of          ).)
(5.  Parental agreement. I understand that the said          (and
          ) is/are willing to agree to the making of an adoption
order.)
(6.  I request the judge to dispense with the agreement of          on the
ground(s) that          (and          ) and there are attached hereto three
copies of a statement of the facts on which I intend to rely.)
7.  Home, etc. The child is currently living with          of          and
has been living there since the      day of          19  . (The child has been
placed with them for adoption (and they wish their identity to remain confidential).)
(8.  The child is being looked after by          (who have parental
responsibility for the child).)
(9.  Maintenance.          of          is liable by virtue of an order
made by the          court at          on the      day of
19  , (*or* by an agreement dated the          day of          19  ) to contribute
to the maintenance of the child.)
(10.  I attach hereto signed by the mother/father/guardian of the child a
declaration that he/she prefers not to be involved in future questions concerning
the adoption of the child.)r
(11.  The child's parents were not married to each other at the time of his birth
and          of          who is/claims to be the father does/does not
intend to apply for an order under section 4(1)(a) of the Children Act 1989 or for
a residence order in respect of the child.)
(12.  No proceedings relating in whole or in part to the child have been
completed or commenced in any court in England and Wales or elsewhere
(except).)
I accordingly apply on behalf of          for an order freeing the child for
adoption.
Dated this          day of          19

*Notes*

(Heading.) Enter the first name(s) and surname as shown in the certificate referred to in paragraph 2; otherwise enter the first name(s) and surname by which the child is known.

If the application is made to a county court, it may be made to any county court which has been designated as a divorce county court under section 33 of the Matrimonial and Family Proceedings Act 1984.

Paragraph 2. If the child has previously been adopted, a certified copy of the entry in the Adopted Children Register should be attached and not a certified copy of the original entry in the Registers of Births. Where a certificate is not attached, enter the place, including the country, of birth if known.

Paragraph 3. If the child has previously been adopted, give the names of his adoptive parents and not those of his natural parents. If the child's parents were not married to each other at the time of his birth and the father has parental responsibility for the child, give details under paragraph 12 of the court order or the agreement which provides for parental responsibility.

Paragraph 4. Enter particulars of any person appointed by deed or will in accordance with the provisions of the Guardianship of Infants Acts 1886 and 1925, or the Guardianship of Minors Act 1971, or by a court of competent jurisdiction or under section 5 of the Children Act 1989, to be a guardian. Do not include any person who has the custody of the child only. Delete this paragraph if the child has no guardian.

Paragraphs 5 and 6. Enter either in paragraph 5 or 6 the names of the persons mentioned in paragraphs 3 and 4, except that in the case of a child whose parents were not married to each other at the time of his birth the father of the child should be entered only if he has parental responsibility for the child by virtue of a court order or by agreement or he has a residence order in respect of the child. Where it is sought to dispense with parental agreement, enter in paragraph 6 one or more of the grounds set out in section 16(2) of the Act.

Paragraph 7. Enter the name and address of the person with whom the child has his home.

Paragraph 8. This paragraph should be completed where the child is being looked after by a local authority or a voluntary organisation.

Paragraph 9. This paragraph should be completed where some person or body is liable to contribute to the maintenance of the child under a court order or agreement.

Paragraph 12. State the nature of the proceedings and the date and effect of any orders made.

Form 2

Agreement to an Adoption Order (Freeing Cases)

(*Heading as in Form 1*)

IF YOU ARE IN ANY DOUBT ABOUT YOUR LEGAL RIGHTS YOU SHOULD OBTAIN LEGAL ADVICE *BEFORE* SIGNING THIS FORM.

Whereas an application is to be/has been made by        for an order freeing      , a child, for adoption:

And whereas the child is the person to whom the birth certificate attached marked 'A' relates:

(And whereas the child is at least six weeks old:)

I, the undersigned      of      being a parent/guardian of the child hereby state as follows—

(1) I consent to the application of                    an adoption agency, for an order freeing the child for adoption.

(2) I understand that the effect of an adoption order would be to deprive me permanently of parental responsibility for the child and to vest it in the adopters; and in particular I understand that, if and when an adoption order is made, I shall have no right to see or get in touch with the child or to have him/her returned to me.

(3) I further understand that the court cannot make an order freeing a child for adoption without the agreement of each parent or guardian of the child to the making of an adoption order, unless the court dispenses with that agreement on the ground that the person concerned—

(a) cannot be found or is incapable of giving agreement, or

(b) is withholding his agreement unreasonably, or

(c) has persistently failed without reasonable cause to discharge his parental responsibility in relation to the child, or

(d) has abandoned or neglected the child, or

(e) has persistently ill-treated the child, or

(f) has seriously ill-treated the child and the rehabilitation of the child within the household of the parent or guardian is unlikely.

(4) I further understand that, when the application for an order freeing the child for adoption is heard, this document may be used as evidence of my agreement to the making of an adoption order unless I inform the court that I no longer agree.

(5) I hereby freely, and with full understanding of what is involved, agree unconditionally to the making of an adoption order.

(6) (I have been given an opportunity of making a declaration that I prefer not to be involved in future questions concerning the adoption of the child. I understand that if I make such a declaration I will not be told when the child has been adopted or whether he had been placed for adoption. I further understand that I will not be able to apply for a revocation of the order freeing the child for adoption if I make such a declaration. I hereby freely declare, with full understanding of what is involved, that I do not wish to be involved in future questions concerning the adoption of the child.)

(7) (I have been given an opportunity of making a declaration that I prefer not to be involved in future questions concerning the adoption of the child, and the effect of making such a declaration has been explained to me. I do not wish to make such a declaration.)

(8) (I have not received or given any payment or reward for, or in consideration of, the adoption of the child, for any agreement to the making of an adoption order or consent to the making of an application for an order freeing the child for adoption, for placing the child for adoption with any person or making any arrangements for the adoption of the child (other than a payment to an adoption agency for their expenses incurred in connection with the adoption).)

Signature:

This form, duly completed, was signed by the said                    before me at
                    on the          day of                    19   .

Signature:

Address

Description

*NOTES*
(*Heading*)

(a) Insert the name of the adoption agency applying for the order.

(b) Insert the first name(s) and surname of the child as known to the person giving agreement.

(c) If the child has previously been adopted a certified copy of the entry in the Adopted Children Register should be attached and not a certified copy of the original entry in the Registers of Births.

(d) Where two or more forms of agreement are supplied to the court at the same time they may both or all refer to a certificate attached to one of the forms of agreement.

*Paragraphs 6 and 7*

If the parent or guardian does not make the declaration the adoption agency must, after twelve months have passed from the making of the order freeing the child for adoption, inform the parent or guardian whether an adoption order has been made in respect of the child, and, if not, whether the child has his home with a person with whom he has been placed for adoption. Further, if no adoption order has been made in respect of the child or the child does not have his home with a person with whom he has been placed for adoption, then the parent or guardian may apply to the court for revocation of the order freeing the child for adoption.

*Witness Statement*

In England and Wales, the document should be witnessed by the reporting officer. In Scotland, it should be witnessed by a Justice of the Peace or a Sheriff, and in Northern Ireland, by a Justice of the Peace. Outside the United Kingdom it should be witnessed by a person authorised by law in the place where the document is signed to administer an oath for any judicial or legal purpose, a British consular officer, a notary public, or, if the person executing the document is serving in the regular armed forces of the Crown, an officer holding a commission in any of those forces.

Form 3

Notice of Hearing of an Application for an Order Freeing a Child for Adoption

(*Heading as in Form 1*)

To
of
 Whereas an application for an order freeing for adoption   , a child of
the   sex born on the   day of   19 , has been made by
   of
 And whereas   (and   ) was/were appointed reporting
officer(s) (and   was appointed *guardian ad litem* [children's guardian]
of the child);
Take notice—

1. That the said application will be heard before the judge at   on the
day of   19 , at   o'clock and that you may then appear and be heard on the question whether an order freeing the child for adoption should be made.

2. That you are not obliged to attend the hearing unless you wish to do so or the court notifies you that your attendance is necessary.

3. That while the said application is pending, if the child is being looked after by the applicant, then a parent or guardian of the child who has not consented to the making of the application must not, except with the leave of the court, remove the child from the home of the person with whom the child has his home against the will of that person.

(4. That the court has been requested to dispense with your agreement to the making of an adoption order on the ground(s) that   and the statement of the facts on which the applicant intends to rely is attached.)

It would assist the court if you would complete the attached form and return it to me.

Dated the                    day of                    19   .

—District Judge

.......................................................................................................................................................

To the Senior District Judge of the Family Division/District Judge of the County Court.
Number              of 19  .
I received notice of the hearing of the application on the              day of
19  .
I wish/do not wish to oppose the application.
I wish/do not wish to appear and be heard on the question whether an order should be made.

(signature)
(address)
(date)

*Notes*

*Preamble*

Enter the first name(s) and the surname of the child as shown in the originating process. Enter the name of the applicant agency and the name(s) of the reporting officer(s) (and of the *guardian ad litem* [children's guardian, if appointed).

**Note.** Words 'guardian ad litem' in both places, substituted by words 'children's guardian' in square brackets by SI 2001/819, rr 2, 3(b), as from 1 April 2001.

Form 4

Application for Revocation of an Order Freeing a Child for Adoption

(*Heading as in Form 1*)

On the              day of                    19   this court made an order freeing
, a child, for adoption.
I/We              (and              ) of (address), the former parent(s) of the child, apply for revocation of that order on the grounds that—
  1. No adoption order has been made in respect of the child, and
  2. The child does not have his home with a person with whom he has been placed for adoption, and
  3. I/We wish to resume parental responsibility because
signed
dated

*Notes*

  (a)  The application must be made to the court which made the original order, and not earlier than 12 months from the date of that order.
  (b)  A parent or guardian of the child who has made a declaration (referred to in section 18(6) of the Act) that he prefers not to be involved in future questions concerning the adoption of the child may not make application for revocation of the order.
  (c)  State the reasons relied upon for the revocation of the order.

Form 5

Application for Substitution of One Adoption Agency for Another

(*Heading as in Form 1*)

I, an authorised officer of the                    of                    , and I, an authorised officer of the            of            , both being adoption agencies, wishing to transfer the parental responsibility for            , a child, from            to                    hereby give the following further particulars in support of our application.

1. On the            day of                    19  , the court made an order freeing the child for adoption under section 18 of the Adoption Act. A copy of that order is attached.

2. The transfer would be in the best interests of the child because

3. The administrative reasons why the transfer is desirable are

(4. The former parent(s),                    of                    (and                    of                    ), has/have been informed of the making of this application.)

Dated etc

(signatures)
(addresses)

*Notes*

*Preamble*

Enter the names of the two agencies concerned and enter the name of the child as shown in the order referred to in paragraph 1.

*Paragraphs 2 and 3*

State concisely the reasons it is desired to transfer the child between the agencies.

*Paragraph 4*

A former parent is a person as defined in section 19(1) of the Adoption Act. This paragraph should be deleted only if there are no former parents.

Form 6

Originating Process for an Adoption Order [/Convention Adoption Order]/ Order Authorising a Proposed Foreign Adoption

(*Heading as in Form 1*)

I/We, the undersigned,                    (and                    ,) wishing to adopt            , a child, hereby give the following further particulars in support of my/our application.

PART 1

Particulars of the applicant(s)

1. *Name and address etc*

*Name of (first) applicant in full*
Address
Occupation
Date of Birth
Relationship (if any) to the child
(Name of (second) applicant in full
Address
Occupation
Date of Birth
Relationship (if any) to the child                                    )

2. *Domicile*

I am/we are/one of us (namely            ) is domiciled in England and Wales/
Scotland/Northern Ireland/the Channel Islands/the Isle of Man.

3. *Status*

We are married to each other and our marriage certificate (or other evidence of
marriage) is attached (*or* I am unmarried/a widow/a widower/a divorcee) (*or* I am
applying alone as a married person and can satisfy the court that            ).

(4. I am applying alone for an adoption order in respect of my own child and
can satisfy the court that the other natural parent                .)

(5. *Health*

A report on my/our health, made by a registered medical practitioner on the
day of            19   , is attached.)

*Notes*

*Heading*

Enter the first name(s) and surname of the child as shown in any certificate
referred to in paragraph 6 below; otherwise enter the first name(s) and surname
by which the child was known before being placed for adoption.

If the application is made to a county court, it may be made to any county court
which has been designated as a divorce county court under section 33 of the
Matrimonial and Family Proceedings Act 1984.

Paragraph 1—Insert the address where the applicant has his home and the place
(if different) where documents may be served upon him.

Paragraph 2—May be deleted if the application is for an order authorising a
proposed foreign adoption [/Convention adoption order].

Paragraph 3—Documentary evidence of marital status should be supplied. A
married applicant can apply alone if he or she can satisfy the court that his or her
spouse cannot be found, or that they have separated and are living apart and that the
separation is likely to be permanent, or that by reason of physical or mental ill health
the spouse is incapable of making an application for an adoption order. Any
documentary evidence on which the applicant proposes to rely should be attached to
the application. The name and address (if known) of the spouse should be supplied,
and the marriage certificate (or other evidence of marriage) should be attached.

Paragraph 4—State the reason to be relied upon eg that the other natural
parent is dead, or cannot be found, or that there is some other reason, which
should be specified, justifying his or her exclusion. Documentary evidence, eg a
death certificate, should be supplied where appropriate.

Paragraph 5—A separate health report is required in respect of each applicant,
and the report must have been made during the period of three months before
the date of the application. No report is required, however, if the child was placed
for adoption with applicant by an adoption agency, or if he is the child of the

applicant or either of them [, or if the application is for a Convention adoption order].

PART 2

Particulars of the child.

### 6. *Identity etc*

The child is of the      sex and is not and has not been married. He/she was born on the          day of                    19    and is the person to whom the attached birth/adoption certificate relates (*or* was born on or about the        day of 19  , in                  ). He/she is a              national.

### (7. *Health*

A report on the health of the child, made by a registered medical practitioner on the          day of                  19    , is attached.)

(8.  The child is free for adoption pursuant to section 18 of the Adoption Act, and I/we attach hereto the order of the                  court, dated                  , to that effect. Parental responsibility for the child was thereby vested in                    (and was transferred to            by order of the                  court under section 21 of the Adoption Act on                    19    ).)

### (9. *Parentage, etc*

The child is the child of                    whose last known address was (*or* deceased) and                  whose last known address was                    (*or* deceased).)

(10.  The guardian(s) of the child (other than the mother or the father of the child) is/are              of                  (and                  of                  ).)

### (11. *Parental agreement*

I/We understand that the said                  (and                  ) is/are willing to agree to the making of an adoption order in pursuance of my/our application.)

(12.  I/we request the judge to dispense with the agreement of              (and              ) on the ground(s) that                  (and                  ) and there are attached hereto three copies of a statement of the facts upon which I/we intend to rely.)

### (13. *Care etc*

The child is being looked after by                  (who have parental responsibility for the child).)

### (14. *Maintenance*

              of                                is liable by virtue of an order made by the                court at                  on the              day of                    19    , (*or* by an agreement dated the                  day of                  19    ) to contribute to the maintenance of the child.)

### 15. *Proposed names*

If an adoption order is made in pursuance of this application, the child is to be known by the following names:
Surname
Other names

*Notes*

Paragraph 6—If the child has previously been adopted a certified copy of the entry in the Adopted Children Register should be attached and not a certified copy of the original entry in the Registers of Births. Where a certificate is not attached, enter the place (including the country) of birth if known.

Paragraph 7—The report must have been made during the period of three months before the date of the application. No report is required, however, if the child was placed for adoption with the applicant by an adoption agency, or if he is the child of the applicant or either of them [or, if the application is for a Convention adoption order].

Paragraph 8—[Where the application being made is for a Convention adoption order and the order freeing the child for adoption was made in Scotland or Northern Ireland replace the words 'section 18 of the Adoption Act' with either 'section 18 of the Adoption (Scotland) Act 1978' or 'Article 17(1) or 18(1) of the Adoption (Northern Ireland) Order 1987' as appropriate,] The order made by the court freeing the child for adoption and any order made under section 21 [or corresponding Scotland or Northern Ireland legislation] should be attached.

Paragraph 9—This paragraph and paragraphs 10 to 14 only apply if the child is not free for adoption. If the child has previously been adopted, give the names of his adoptive parents and not those of his natural parents. If the parents of the child were not married to each other at the time of his birth and the father has parental responsibility for the child, give details under paragraph 19 of the court order or the agreement which provides for parental responsibility.

Paragraph 10—Enter particulars of any person appointed by deed or will in accordance with the provisions of the Guardianship of Infants Acts 1886 and 1925, or the Guardianship of Minors Act 1971 or by a court of competent jurisdiction or under section 5 of the Children Act 1989, to be a guardian. Do not include any person who has the custody of the child only. Delete this paragraph if the child has no guardian.

Paragraphs 11 and 12—Enter either in paragraph 11 or 12 the names of the persons mentioned in paragraphs 9 and 10, except that in the case of a child whose parents were not married to each other at the time of his birth the father of the child should be entered only if he has parental responsibility for the child by virtue of a court order or by agreement he has a residence order in respect of the child. Where it is sought to dispense with parental agreement, enter in paragraph 12 one or more of the grounds set out in section 16(2) of the Act.

Paragraph 13—This paragraph should be completed where the child is being looked after by a local authority or a voluntary organisation.

Paragraph 14—This paragraph should be completed where some person or body is liable to contribute to the maintenance of the child under a court order or agreement.

PART 3

*General*

16. The child has lived with me/us continuously since the                             day of                19   (and has accordingly had his home with me/us for the five years preceding the date of this application).

17. The child was (placed with me/us for adoption on the                             day of                19   by                          , an adoption agency) (*or* received into my/our home in the following circumstances:

                                                                                                ).

(18. I/we notified the                          Council on the                          day of 19   , of my/our intention to apply for an adoption order in respect of the child.)

19. No proceedings relating in whole or in part to the child other than as stated in paragraph 8 have been completed or commenced in any court in England and Wales or elsewhere (except                          ).

20. I/we have not received or given any payment or reward for, or in consideration of, the adoption of the child, for any agreement to the making of an adoption order, the transfer of the home of the child with a view to adoption or the making of any arrangements for adoption (except as follows:

).

21. As far as I/we know, the only person(s) or bod(y)(ies) who have taken part in the arrangements for the child's adoption are

(22. For the purpose of this application reference may be made to                of
.)

(23. I/we desire that my/our identity should be kept confidential, and the serial number of this application is                .)

(24. I/we intend to adopt the child under the law of or within                which is the country of my/our domicile, and evidence as to the law of adoption in that country is filed with this process.)

(25. I/we desire to remove the child from the British Isles for the purpose of adoption.

I/we accordingly apply for an adoption order [/a Convention adoption order]/an order authorising a proposed foreign adoption in respect of the child.

Dated this                day of                19   .

Signature(s)

*Notes*

Paragraphs 16 and 17—Under section 13 of the Act, an adoption order cannot be made unless the child has had his home with the applicants or one of them—

(a) for at least 13 weeks if the applicant or one of them is a parent, step-parent or relative of the child or if the child was placed with the applicant by an adoption agency or in pursuance of an order of the High Court;

[(aa) for at least 6 months if the proposed adoption is be effected by a Convention adoption order;]

(b) for at least 12 months in any other case.

Paragraph 18—Notice does not have to be given if the child was placed with the applicant by an adoption agency. Where notice does have to be given, no order can be made until the expiration of three months from the date of the notice.

Paragraph 19—The nature of the proceedings and the date and effect of any orders made should be stated. The court cannot proceed with the application if a previous application made by the same applicant in relation to the child was refused, unless one of the conditions in section 24(1) of the Act is satisfied. The court must dismiss the application if it considers that, where the application is made by a married couple of whom one is a parent and the other a step-parent of the child, or by a step-parent of the child alone, the matter would be better dealt with under Part I of the Children Act 1989.

Paragraph 21—Enter the name and address of the adoption agency or individual who took part in the arrangements for placing the child for adoption in the home of the applicant. [In Convention proceedings it is only necessary to specify those that took part in the arrangements in the country where the order is made.]

Paragraph 22—Where the applicant or one of the applicants is a parent of the child, or a relative as defined by section 72(1) of the Act or the child was placed with the applicant by an adoption agency [or if the application is for a Convention adoption order], no referee need be named.

Paragraph 23—If the applicant wishes his identity to be kept confidential, the serial number obtained under rule 14 should be given.

**Note.** In Part 1: in Form heading words '/Convention adoption order' inserted, and in Notes: in para 2 words '/Convention adoption order' and in para 5 words ', or if the application is for a Convention adoption order' in square brackets inserted by SI 2003/183, r 20(b), (c) as from 1 June 2003.

In Part 2: Notes: in para 7 words ', or if the application is for a Convention adoption order', in para 8 words from 'Where the application' to 'as appropriate.' and words 'or corresponding Scotland or Northern Ireland legislation,' in square brackets inserted by SI 2003/183, r 20(c), (d)(i) as from 1 June 2003.

In Part 3: words '/a Convention adoption order' in square brackets inserted by SI 2003/183, r 20(h) as from 1 June 2003.

In Part 3: Notes: in paras 16, 17 sub-para (aa) inserted, in para 21 words from 'In Convention proceedings' to 'where the order is to be made.' in square brackets inserted and in para 22 words 'or if the application is for a Convention adoption order' in square brackets inserted by SI 2003/183, r 20(e)–(g) as from 1 June 2003.


Form 7

Agreement to an Adoption Order [/Convention Adoption Order]/Proposed Foreign Adoption

(*Heading as in Form 1*)

IF YOU ARE IN ANY DOUBT ABOUT YOUR LEGAL RIGHTS YOU SHOULD OBTAIN LEGAL ADVICE *BEFORE* SIGNING THIS FORM.

Whereas an application is to be/has been made by            and
(*or* under serial No       ) for an adoption order [, a Convention adoption order] or order authorising a proposed foreign adoption in respect of                          a child;

And whereas the child is the person to whom the birth certificate attached marked 'A' relates:

(And whereas the child is at least six weeks old:)

I, the undersigned             of           being a parent/guardian of the child hereby state as follows:

(1) I understand that the effect of an adoption order [/a Convention adoption order]/an order authorising a proposed foreign adoption will be to deprive me permanently of the parental responsibility for the child and to vest them in the applicant(s); and in particular I understand that, if an order is made, I shall have no right to see or get in touch with the child or to have him/her returned to me.

(2) I further understand that the court cannot make an adoption order [/a Convention adoption order]/an order authorising the proposed foreign adoption of the child without the agreement of each parent or guardian of the child unless the court dispenses with an agreement on the ground that the person concerned—

(a)  cannot be found or is incapable of giving agreement, or

(b)  is withholding his agreement unreasonably, or

(c)  has persistently failed without reasonable cause to discharge the parental responsibility for the child, or

(d)  has abandoned or neglected the child, or

(e)  has persistently ill-treated the child, or

(f)  has seriously ill-treated the child and the rehabilitation of the child within the household of the parent or guardian is unlikely.

(3) I further understand that when the application for an adoption order [/a Convention adoption order]/order authorising the proposed foreign adoption of the child is heard, this document may be used as evidence of my agreement to the making of the order unless I inform the court that I no longer agree.

(4) I hereby freely, and with full understanding of what is involved, agree unconditionally to the making of an adoption order [/a Convention adoption order]/an order authorising the proposed foreign adoption of the child in pursuance of the application.

(5)  As far as I know, the only person(s) or body(ies) who has/have taken part in the arrangements for the child's adoption is/are                (and                ).

(6)  I have not received or given any payment or reward for, or in consideration of, the adoption of the child, for any agreement to the making of an adoption order or placing the child for adoption with any person or making arrangements for the adoption of the child (other than payment to an adoption agency for their expenses incurred in connection with the adoption).

Signature:

This form, duly completed, was signed by the said                before me at                on the                day of                19   .

Signature:
Address:
Description:

*Notes*

*Preamble.* Insert either the name(s) of the applicant(s) or the serial No assigned to the applicant(s) for the purposes of the application.

Insert the first name(s) and surname of the child as known to the person giving agreement.

If the child has previously been adopted a certified copy of the entry in the Adopted Children Register should be attached and not a certified copy of the original entry in the Registers of Births.

Where two or more forms of agreement are supplied to the court at the same time they may both or all refer to a certificate attached to one of the forms of agreement.

The father of a child who was not married to the child's mother when the child was born is not a parent for this purpose unless he has parental responsibility by virtue of a court order or an agreement or he has a residence order in respect of the child; 'guardian' also means a person appointed by deed or will in accordance with the provisions of the Guardianship of Infants Acts 1886 and 1925 or the Guardianship of Minors Act 1971, or by a court of competent jurisdiction, or under section 5 of the Children Act 1989, to be the guardian of the child.

*Paragraph 3.* Notice will be given of the hearing of the application and of the court by which it is to be heard. After the making of the application a parent or guardian who has agreed cannot remove the child from the home of the applicant(s) except with the leave of the court.

*Paragraph 5.* Enter the name and address of the adoption agency or individual who took part in the arrangements for placing the child in the home of the applicant(s).

*Witness statement.* In England and Wales the document should be witnessed by the reporting officer. In Scotland, it should be witnessed by a Justice of the Peace or a Sheriff, and in Northern Ireland by a Justice of the Peace. Outside the United Kingdom it should be witnessed by a person authorised by law in the place where the document is signed to administer an oath for any judicial or legal purpose, a British consular officer, a notary public, or, if the person executing the document is serving in the regular armed forces of the Crown, an officer holding a commission in any of those forces.

**Note.** Words '/Convention Adoption Order', ', a Convention adoption order' and words '/a Convention adoption order' in each place, inserted by SI 2003/183, r 21(b), (c) as from 1 June 2003.

Form 8

Notice of Hearing of an Application for an Adoption Order/an Order Authorising a Proposed Foreign Adoption [/a Convention Adoption Order]

(*Heading as in Form 1*)

To                 of
Whereas an application for an adoption order/an order authorising a proposed foreign adoption [/a Convention adoption order] in respect of                 , a child of the           sex born on the           day of                 19 , has been made (by           (and           ) of                 ) (*or* under the serial number                 ) *and whereas(and                 ) was/were appointed reporting officer(s) (and                 was appointed guardian ad litem [children's guardian] of the child);* [and whereas                 who is an officer of CAFCASS appointed to act on behalf of the child/and whereas                 who is an officer of CAFCASS appointed to prepare a report]

*TAKE NOTICE—*

(1. That the said application will be heard before the judge at                 on the           day of           19 , at           o'clock and that you may then appear and be heard on the question whether an adoption order/an order authorising a proposed foreign adoption [/a Convention adoption order] should be made.)

(2. That if you wish to appear and be heard on the question whether an adoption order/an order authorising a proposed foreign adoption [/a Convention adoption order] should be made, you should give notice to the court on or before the day of           19 , in order that a time may be fixed for your appearance.)

3. That you are not obliged to attend the hearing unless you wish to do so or the court notifies you that your attendance is necessary.

4. That while the application is pending, a parent or guardian of the child who has agreed to the making of an order must not, except with the leave of the court, remove the child from the home of the applicant.

(5. That the application states that the child has had his home with the applicant for the five years preceding the application and accordingly, if that is correct, no person is entitled, against the will of the applicant, to remove the child from the applicant's home except with the leave of the court or under authority conferred by an enactment or on the arrest of the child.)

(6. That the court has been requested to dispense with your agreement to the making of an order on the ground(s) that                 and a statement of the facts on which the applicant intends to rely is attached.)

It would assist the court if you would complete the attached form and return it to me.
Dated the                 day of                 19 .

District Judge
...........................................................................................................................
To the Senior District Judge of the Family Division/District Judge of the County Court.

No
I received the notice of the hearing of the application on the                 day of
                19 .
I wish/do not wish to oppose the application.
I wish/do not wish to appear and be heard on the question whether an order should be made.

(signature)
(address)
(date)

*Notes* Paragraph numbers in these notes refer to the appropriate paragraph in the form.

When this form is used under rule 25(2) to give notice of a further hearing of an application it is to be amended so as to refer to a further hearing and so as to give particulars of the interim order.

*Preamble.* Enter the name(s) and surname of the child as shown in the originating process. Enter the name of the applicant(s) unless the applicant has obtained a serial number, in which case the second part in brackets should be completed. [In every Convention case an officer of CAFCASS is appointed to act on behalf of the child. Where a foreign adoption is proposed an officer of CAFCASS is appointed to report.]

*Paragraphs 1 and 2.* Paragraph 1 should be completed and paragraph 2 struck out where the notice is addressed to any respondent where the applicant does not wish his identity to be kept confidential. When a serial number has been assigned to the applicant and the notice is addressed to an individual respondent other than the spouse of the applicant, paragraph 1 should be struck out and paragraph 2 completed.

*Paragraph 5.* This paragraph should be deleted except where it appears from the originating process that the child has had his home with the applicant for five years.

*Paragraph 6.* Unless deleted, this paragraph should contain the grounds specified in the originating application.

**Note.** Words '/a Convention adoption order' in square brackets in each place they occur inserted, words from 'and whereas' to 'of the child' substituted by words 'and whereas' to 'prepare a report' in square brackets, and in the Notes to the Preamble words from 'In every Convention case' to 'appointed to report.' in square brackets inserted, by SI 2003/183, r 22(a)–(c) as from 1 June 2003.

Form 9

Originating Process for the Annulment or Revocation of an Adoption

In the High Court
Family Division                                                  No        of 19
    In the Matter of        and
    In the Matter of the Adoption Act 1976
Let        of        attend at the Royal Courts of Justice, Strand, London WC2A 2LL on a date to be fixed for the hearing of the application of
    of        for an order—
    1. That the adoption which was authorised on the        day of
19    at        , by which        (and        ) was (*or* were) authorised to adopt the said        be annulled (*or* revoked).
    (2. That the leave of the court be granted for the purpose of making this application out of time.)
    3. That the costs of this application be provided for.
Dated this        day of        19  .
This summons was taken out by        of        , solicitor for the above named        .

*Notes*

    This form is for use when the adoption is to be *annulled or revoked under section 52(1) or 53(1)* [revoked under 52(1) or annulled under section 53(1)] of the Adoption Act 1976. An application may not be made unless either the adopter or both adopters, as the case may be, or the adopted person habitually resides in Great Britain immediately before the application is made.

    *Preamble.* Enter the full names by which the adopted person has been known since the adoption.

    *Paragraph 1.* Enter the description and address of the authority by which adoption was authorised.

    *Paragraph 2.* Except with the leave of the court, an application to annul an adoption may not be made later than two years after the date of the adoption to which it relates.

**Note.** Words 'annulled or revoked under section 52(1) or 53(1)' substituted by words 'revoked under section 52(1) or annulled under section 53(1)' in square brackets by SI 2003/183, r 23, as from 1 June 2003.

Form 10

Originating Process for an Order that an Overseas Adoption or a
Determination Cease to be Valid or that a Determination has been Affected
by a Subsequent Determination

(*Heading as in Form 9*)

Let                      of                      attend at the Royal Courts of Justice, Strand, London WC2A 2LL on a date to be fixed for the hearing of the application of                      of                      for—

(1. An order that an overseas adoption which was authorised on the          day of          19    at          , by which                      (and                      ) was (*or* were) authorised to adopt the said          do cease to be valid in Great Britain;)

(2. *An order that a determination made by an authority of a Convention country (or a specified country) to authorise (or review the authorisation of) a Convention adoption (or an adoption order made under any enactment in force in a specified country and corresponding to sections 12(1) and 17 of the Adoption Act 1976) do cease to be valid in Great Britain;)*

(3. *An order that a determination made by an authority of a Convention country (or a specified country) to give (or review) a decision revoking (or annulling) a Convention adoption (or an adoption order made under any enactment in force in a specified country and corresponding to sections 12(1) and 17 of the Adoption Act 1976) (or an order made under section 12(1) of the Adoption Act 1976 as a Convention adoption order) do cease to be valid in Great Britain;)*

[(2. An order that a determination made by an authority of a specified country to authorise or review the authorisation of an adoption order made under any enactment in force in a specified country and corresponding to sections 12(1) and 17 of the Adoption Act 1976 do cease to be valid in Great Britain;)

(3. An order that a determination made by an authority of a specified country to give or review a decision revoking or annulling an order made under any enactment in force in a specified country and corresponding to sections 12(1) and 17 of the Adoption Act 1976 do cease to be valid in Great Britain;)]

(4. A decision as to the extent, if any, to which a determination mentioned in paragraph 2 (*or* 3) above has been affected by a subsequent determination;)

(5. An order that the costs of this application be provided for.)

Dated this                      day of                      19   .

This summons was taken out by                      of                      , solicitor for the above named

*Notes*

This form is principally for use if the applicant claims that the adoption or determination is contrary to public policy or that the authority which purported to authorise the adoption or make the determination was not competent to entertain the case. The applicant should delete the paragraphs which are not relevant.

*Paragraph 1.* An overseas adoption is one occurring in a place, under the law of that place, listed in the Schedule to the Adoption (Designation of Overseas Adoptions) Order 1973; *a Convention adoption is an overseas adoption of a description designated in such an order as that of an adoption regulated by the Hague Convention on the Adoption of Children 1965.*

*Paragraphs 2 and 3. A Convention country means a country designated by an order of the Secretary of State as a country in which the Hague Convention on the Adoption of Children 1965 is in force (section 72(1) of the 1976 Act).* A specified country means those countries listed in the Schedule to the Adoption (Designation of Overseas Adoptions) Order 1973.

**Note.** Paras 2, 3 substituted, and in the Notes relating to para 1 words from '; a Convention' to the end' revoked and in the note to paras 2, 3 words from 'A Convention' to '1976 Act).' revoked by SI 2003/183, r 24, as from 1 June 2003.

Form 11

Affidavit in Support of Application under Sections 52 and 53 of the Adoption Act 1976

(*Heading as in Form 9*)

I/we                              of                              hereby make oath and say that the particulars set out in this affidavit are true.
   1. Name of (first) adopter in full
      Address
   2. Name of second adopter in full
      Address
   3. Name of adopted person in full
   (4. The said                         (and the said                        ) habitually reside(s) in Great Britain.)
   5. The adopted person is of the                     sex, is a national of                     and was born at                     on the                     day of                     19   .
   6. On the                     day of                     19    the said                          (and                     ) was (*or* were) authorised to adopt the said                          by                     at                     and those persons are the persons to whom the certified copy of an entry in a public register (or other evidence of adoption) which is exhibited to this affidavit relates.
   (7. At the time at which the adoption was authorised the said                          was a national of                     and resided in                     (the said                     was a national of                     and resided in                     ) and the adopted person was a national of                     and resided in                     .)
*or*
   (7. *For other applications details of the marriage or, as appropriate, of the determination or determinations should be given and any necessary documentary evidence relating thereto supplied.*)
   (8. A statement of the facts is exhibited to this affidavit.)

*Sworn, etc*
   This affidavit is filed on behalf of the applicant(s).

*Notes*

*Paragraph 3.* Enter the name(s) by which the adopted person has been known since the adoption.

*Paragraph 4.* This paragraph is not required for applications made under section 53(2) of the Adoption Act 1976. Where this paragraph is required, no application may be made to the court unless the adopter or, as the case may be, both adopters or the adopted person habitually reside in Great Britain immediately before the application is made. Therefore, the name(s) of either the adopter(s) or the adopted person should be entered.

*Paragraph 6.* Enter the description and the full address of the authority which authorised the adoption. Evidence of the adoption may be given either by a certified copy of an entry in a public register relating to adoptions or by a certificate that the adoption has been effected signed by a person who is authorised by the law of the country concerned to do so.

*Paragraph 7.* This paragraph should be completed where the application is made under section 53(2) of the Adoption Act 1976. Enter the name of the first adopter and of the second adopter, if applicable.

*Paragraph 8.* A statement of facts is not required for an application to revoke a convention adoption under section 52(1) of the Adoption Act 1976. Expert evidence as to notified provisions may be necessary. In that or any other case where the applicant intends to rely on any provision of foreign law relating to adoption, any accompanying affidavit thereon must be sworn by a person who is suitably qualified on account of his knowledge or experience to give evidence as to the law concerned.

Form 12

Order Freeing a Child for Adoption

(*Heading as in Form 1*)

Whereas an application has been made by                         of                 , being an adoption agency, for an order freeing for adoption             , a child of the           sex, the child of                     (and                 );
It is ordered that the child be freed for adoption and that parental responsibility for the child be vested in the applicant;
(and as regards costs it is ordered that                             ;)
(and whereas the precise date of the child's birth has not been proved to the satisfaction of the court but the court has determined the probable date of his/her birth to be the                 day of                         19  ;)
(and whereas it has been proved to the satisfaction of the court that the child was born in                         (country);)
(and whereas the place of birth of the child has not been proved to the satisfaction of the court (but it appears probable that the child was born in the United Kingdom, the Channel Islands or the Isle of Man, the child is treated as having been born in the registration district of                 and sub-district of                     in the county of                 );)
(and whereas it has been proved to the satisfaction of the court that the child is identical with                 to whom the entry numbered         made on the     day of           19   , in the Register of Births for the registration district of                 and sub-district of                     in the county of                     relates
(*or* with             to whom the entry numbered             and dated the             day of                 19   , in the Adopted Children Register relates);)
It is directed that this order is sufficient proof of the above particulars for the purposes of any future adoption application in respect of the child.
And it is further recorded that                         (and                 ) being a parent or guardian of the child made a declaration that he/she prefers not to be involved in future questions concerning the adoption of the child.

Dated this                 day of                     19  .

Form 13

Order Revoking an Order Freeing a Child for Adoption/Dismissing an Application to Revoke an Order Freeing a Child for Adoption

(*Heading as in Form 1*)

Whereas an application has been made by                 of                 (and         of                 ) for an order revoking an order freeing for adoption

, a child of the                    sex, the child of                          (and
          ), such order having been made by the                    court on the
     day of                    19   ;
   It is ordered that the said order be revoked and that parental responsibility for
the child be vested in                    (and                    );
(and it is ordered that                    of                    do make periodical payments
to the child in the sum of £          payable                    ;)
   (It is ordered that the application be dismissed (and that the applicant(s) shall
not make further application under section 20 of the Adoption Act 1976);)
(and it is ordered that                    , the adoption agency which obtained the
order under section 18 of the Adoption Act 1976, is released from the duty of
complying further with section 19(3) of that Act as respects the applicant(s).)
   (And as regards costs it is ordered that                    .)
Dated this                    day of                    19  .

## Form 14

### Interim Order

(*Heading as in Form 1*)

   Whereas an application has been made by                    of                    (and
               ) for an adoption order in respect of                    , a child of the
sex, the child/adopted child of                    (and                    );
   It is ordered that the determination of the application be postponed and that
the applicant(s) do have the parental responsibility of the child until the     day of
          19   , by way of a probationary period (*or* that the determination of the
application be postponed to the                    day of                    19   , and that the
applicant(s) do have the parental responsibility of the child until that day by way of
a probationary period) (upon the following terms, namely                    );
(and as regards costs it is ordered that                    ;)
(and it is ordered that the application be further heard before the judge at
on the          day of                    19 , at                    o'clock.)
Dated this                    day of                    19  .

## Form 15

### (Convention) Adoption Order/Order Authorising a Proposed Foreign Adoption

(*Heading as in Form 1*)

   Whereas an application has been made by                    of                    whose
occupation is                    (and                    whose occupation is                    )
for an adoption order/an order authorising a proposed foreign adoption/a
Convention adoption order in respect of                    , a child of the                    sex, the
child/adopted child of                    (and                    );
   It is ordered that (the applicant(s) do adopt the child) (*or* the applicant(s) be
authorised to remove the child from Great Britain for the purpose of adopting
him/her under the law of or within the country in which the applicant is/applicants
are domiciled, and that the parental responsibility for the child (including the legal
custody of the child) be vested in the applicant(s).
   (And as regards costs, it is ordered that                    ;)
   (And it is recorded that the                    , being an adoption agency, placed the
child for adoption with the applicant(s)/the                    Council was notified of the
applicant(s) intention to adopt the child;)
   (And whereas the child was freed for adoption by the                    court on the
          day of                    19   ;)

(And whereas the precise date of the child's birth has not been proved to the satisfaction of the court but the court has determined the probable date of his/her birth to be the                    day of                              19   ;)

(And whereas it has been proved to the satisfaction of the court that the child was born in                              (country);)

(And whereas the place of birth of the child has not been proved to the satisfaction of the court (but it appears probable that the child was born in the United Kingdom, the Channel Islands or the Isle of Man, the child is treated as having been born in the registration district of                    and sub-district of                    in the county of                    );)

(And whereas it has been proved to the satisfaction of the court that the child was born on the            day of                    19   (and is identical with                    to whom the entry numbered            made on the                    day of 19   , in the Register of Births for the registration district of                    and sub-district of                    in the county of                    relates) (*or* with to whom the entry numbered            and dated the                    day of            19   , in the Adopted Children Register relates);)

(And whereas the name or names and surname stated in the application as those by which the child is to be known are                    ;)

It is directed that the Registrar General shall make in the Adopted Children Register an entry in the form specified by regulations made by him recording the particulars set out in this order (and that the entry shall be marked with the words 'Convention order');

(And it is further directed that the aforesaid entry in the Register of Births/ Adopted Children Register be marked with the words 'adopted'/'readopted'/ 'proposed foreign adoption'/'proposed foreign readoption'.)

Dated this                    day of                    19   .

[Form 15A

Application to the High Court for a Direction under s 39(3A) of the Adoption Act 1976]

# IN THE HIGH COURT OF JUSTICE

### PRINCIPAL REGISTRY OF THE FAMILY DIVISION

|  |  |
|---|---|
| NO. AA | of 20 |
| CS | of 20 |

### IN THE MATTER OF THE ADOPTION ACT 1976

### IN THE MATTER OF

**A CHILD**

Note: Enter the full name by which the adopted person has been known since the adoption.

Let

of

attend at the Royal Courts of Justice, Strand, London WC2A 2LL on a date to be fixed for the hearing of the application

of

of

for:-

Note: Enter the description and authority by which the Convention adoption was authorised.

1. A direction that a Convention adoption which was authorised

on the            day of                          [19    ] [20    ]

at                                                                              ,

by which

(and                                                                          )

was (or were) authorised to adopt the said

Note: The Convention means the Convention on Protection of Children and Co-operation in respect of Intercountry Adoption, concluded at the Hague on 29th May 1993.

was not, under the law of the country in which the adoption was effected, a full adoption; (that the consents referred to in Articles 4(c) and (d) of the Convention have not been given for a full adoption) (that the United Kingdom is not the receiving State (within the meaning of Article 2 of the Convention)); and that it would be more favourable for the said

if a direction under section 39(3A) of the Adoption Act 1976 was given.

**A15A**   Application to the High Court for a direction under s.39(3A) of the Adoption Act 1976 (6.03)

2.  A direction that section 39(2) of the Adoption Act 1976 shall not apply to
the said

(to the extent that

Note: Please insert
details of the extent
to which s.39 (2)
of the Adoption Act
1976 should not
apply.

).

3.  An order that the costs of this application be provided for.

Dated this                          day of                                      20

This summons was taken out by

of                                                                                         ,

solicitor for the                                                                        .

This form is for use if the applicant claims that the Convention adoption is not, under the law of the
country that made the adoption, a full adoption; that the consents required under Articles 4(c) and (d)
of the Convention have not been given for a full adoption (or the UK is not the receiving State within
the meaning of Article 2 of the Convention); and that it would be more favourable to the child if a
direction was given under s.39 (3A) of the Adoption Act 1976.

**Form 15B**
Direction of the High Court that s.39(2) of the Adoption Act 1976 should not apply, or should apply to such extent as is directed by the court

IN THE HIGH COURT OF JUSTICE

**PRINCIPAL REGISTRY OF THE FAMILY DIVISION**

**NO. AA of 20**

**CS of 20**

**IN THE MATTER OF THE ADOPTION ACT 1976**

**IN THE MATTER OF**

**A CHILD**

Note: Enter the full name by which the adopted person has been known since the adoption.

Upon the application of and upon hearing and upon hearing (and upon reading ).
The High Court is satisfied that: -
**1.** The adoption of the said

was effected as a Convention adoption

Note: Enter the date and the country within which the Convention adoption was made.

on the day of                    [19    ] [20    ]

in

; and

**2.** Under the law of that country the adoption was not effected as a full adoption;

and

**3.** *(The consents referred to in Articles 4(c) and (d) of the Convention have not been given for a full adoption) *(The United Kingdom is not the receiving State (within the meaning of Article 2 of the Convention)); and

Note: *Delete as appropriate.

**4.** In all the circumstances it would be more favourable for the said ,

for a direction to be given under section 39(3A) of the Adoption Act 1976.

**It is hereby directed that: -**

*(Section 39(2) of the Adoption Act 1976 shall not apply to the said ).

*(Section 39(2) of the Adoption Act 1976 shall apply to the said ,

Note: *Delete as appropriate.

with the following modifications: ).

(and as regards costs it is ordered that ).

Dated this day of                    20

SCHEDULE 2                                                         Rule 4(4)

MATTERS TO BE COVERED IN REPORTS SUPPLIED UNDER RULES 4(4), 22(1) OR 22(2)

So far as is practicable, the report supplied by the adoption agency or, in the case of a report supplied under rule 22(2), the local authority shall include all the following particulars—

1.   *The Child*

   (a)  Name, sex, date and place of birth and address;
   (b)  whether the child's parents were married to each other at the time of his birth and, if not, whether he was subsequently legitimated;
   (c)  nationality;
   (d)  physical description;
   (e)  personality and social development;
   (f)  religion, including details of baptism, confirmation or equivalent ceremonies;
   (g)  details of any wardship proceedings and of any court orders relating to parental responsibility for the child or to maintenance and residence;
   (h)  details of any brothers and sisters, including dates of birth, arrangements concerning with whom they are to live and whether any brother or sister is the subject of a parallel application;
   (i)  extent of contact with members of the child's natural family and, if the child's parents were not married to each other at the time of his birth, his father, and in each case the nature of the relationship enjoyed;
   (j)  if the child has been in the care of a local authority or is in such care, or is being, or has been, looked after by such authority or organisation, details (including dates) of any placements with foster parents, or other arrangements in respect of the care of the child, including particulars of the persons with whom the child has had his home and observations on the care provided;
   (k)  date and circumstances of placement with prospective adopter [and where a Convention adoption is proposed, details of the arrangements which were made for the transfer of the child to the UK and that they were in accordance with regulation 12(8) of the Hague Convention Regulations;];
   (l)  names, addresses and types of schools attended, with dates, and educational attainments;
   (m) any special needs in relation to the child's health (whether physical or mental) and his emotional and behavioural development and whether he is subject to a statement under the Education Act 1981;
   (n)  what, if any, rights to or interest in property or any claim to damages, under the Fatal Accidents Act 1976 or otherwise, the child stands to retain or lose if adopted;
   (o)  wishes and feelings in relation to adoption and the application, including any wishes in respect of religious and cultural upbringing; and
   (p)  any other relevant information which might assist the court.

2.   *Each natural parent*

   (a)  Name, date and place of birth and address;
   (b)  marital status and date and place of marriage (if any);
   (c)  past and present relationship (if any) with the other natural parent, including comments on its stability;
   (d)  physical description;
   (e)  personality;
   (f)  religion;
   (g)  educational attainments;

(h) past and present occupations and interests;
(i) so far as available, names and brief details of the personal circumstances of the parents and any brothers and sisters of the natural parent, with their ages or ages at death;
(j) wishes and feelings in relation to adoption and the application, including any wishes in respect of the child's religious and cultural upbringing;
(k) reasons why any of the above information is unavailable; and
(l) any other relevant information which might assist the court.

3. *Guardian(s)*

Give the details required under paragraph 2(a), (f), (j) and (l).

4. *Prospective adopter(s)*

(a) Name, date and place of birth and address;
(b) relationship (if any) to the child;
(c) marital status, date and place of marriage (if any) and comments on stability of relationship;
(d) details of any previous marriage;
(e) if a parent and step-parent are applying, the reasons why they prefer adoption to a residence order;
(f) if a natural parent is applying alone, the reasons for the exclusion of the other parent;
(g) if a married person is applying alone, the reasons for this;
(h) physical description;
(i) personality;
(j) religion, and whether willing to follow any wishes of the child or his parents or guardian in respect of the child's religious and cultural upbringing;
(k) educational attainments;
(l) past and present occupations and interests;
(m) particulars of the home and living conditions (and particulars of any home where the prospective adopter proposes to live with the child, if different);
(n) details of income and comments on the living standards of the household;
(o) details of other members of the household (including any children of the prospective adopter even if not resident in the household);
(p) details of the parents and any brothers or sisters of the prospective adopter, with their ages or ages at death;
(q) attitudes to the proposed adoption of such other members of the prospective adopter's household and family as the adoption agency or, as the case may be, the local authority considers appropriate;
(r) previous experience of caring for children as step-parent, foster parent, child-minder or prospective adopter and assessment of ability in this respect, together where appropriate with assessment of ability in bringing up the prospective adopter's own children;
(s) reasons for wishing to adopt the child and extent of understanding of the nature and effect of adoption;
(t) any hopes and expectations for the child's future;
(u) assessment of ability to bring up the child throughout his childhood;
(v) details of any adoption allowance payable;
(w) confirmation that any referees have been interviewed, with a report of their views and opinion of the weight to be placed thereon; and
(x) any other relevant information which might assist the court.

5.   *Actions at the adoption agency or local authority supplying the report*

(a)  Reports under rule 4(4) or 22(1)—
   (i)   brief account of the agency's actions in the case, with particulars and dates of all written information and notices given to the child, his natural parents and the prospective adopter;
   (ii)  details of alternatives to adoption considered;
   (iii) reasons for considering that adoption would be in the child's best interests (with date of relevant decision); and
   (iv)  reasons for considering that the prospective adopter would be suitable to be an adoptive parent and that he would be suitable for this child (with dates of relevant decisions) or, if the child has not yet been placed for adoption, reasons for considering that he is likely to be so placed.

   *or*

(b)  Reports under rule 22(2)—
   (i)   confirmation that notice was given under section 22 of the Act, with the date of that notice;
   (ii)  brief account of the local authority's actions in the case; and
   (iii) account of investigations whether child was placed in contravention of section 11 of the Act.

6.   *Generally*

(a)  Whether any respondent appears to be under the age of majority or under a mental disability; and
(b)  whether, in the opinion of the body supplying the report, any other person should be made a respondent (for example, a person claiming to be the father of a child whose parents were not married to each other at the time of his birth, a spouse or ex-spouse of a natural parent, a relative of a deceased parent, or a person with parental responsibility).

[6A.

Further information to be provided in proceedings relating to a Convention adoption/foreign adoption
(a)  where the UK is the State of origin confirmation that an order has been made under section 18(1) of the Act, section 18 of the Adoption (Scotland) Act 1978 or Article 17(1) or 18(1) of the Adoption Northern Ireland Order 1987;
(b)  where the UK is the State of origin confirmation that, after possibilities for placement of the child within the UK have been given due consideration, an intercountry adoption is in the child's best interests;
(c)  confirmation that, in the case of a foreign adoption, the requirements of regulations made under section 56A of the Adoption Act 1976 have been complied with and, in the case of a Convention adoption, that the requirements of the Intercountry Adoption (Hague Convention) Regulations 2003 have been complied with; and
(d)  for the Convention adoption where the United Kingdom is either the State of origin or the receiving State confirmation that the Central Authorities of both States have agreed that the adoption may proceed. The documents supplied by the CA of the State of origin should be attached to the report together with a translation if necessary.]

*7.   Conclusions*

(This part of the report should contain more than a simple synopsis of the information above. As far as possible, the court should be given a fuller picture of the child, his natural parents and, where appropriate, the prospective adopter.)

(a) Except where the applicant or one of them is a parent of the child, a summary by the medical adviser to the body supplying the report, of the health history and state of health of the child, his natural parents and, if appropriate, the prospective adopter, with comments on the implications for the order sought and on how any special health needs of the child might be met;

(b) opinion on whether making the order sought would be in the child's best long-term interests, and on how any special emotional, behavioural and educational needs of the child might be met;

(c) opinion on the effect on the child's natural parents of making the order sought;

(d) if the child has been placed for adoption, opinion on the likelihood of full integration of the child into the household, family and community of the prospective adopter, and on whether the proposed adoption would be in the best long-term interests of the prospective adopter;

(e) opinion, if appropriate, on the relative merits of adoption and a residence order; and

(f) final conclusions and recommendations whether the order sought should be made (and, if not, alternative proposals).

**Note.** In para 1(k) words from 'and where a Convention adoption' to 'Hague Convention Regulations' in square brackets and para 6A, inserted by SI 2003/183, r 27, as from 1 June 2003.

SCHEDULE 3                                                     Rule 15(4)

REPORTS ON THE HEALTH OF THE CHILD AND OF THE APPLICANT(S)

This information is required for reports on the health of a child and of his prospective adopter(s). Its purpose is to build up a full picture of their health history and current state of health, including strengths and weaknesses. This will enable the local authority's medical adviser to base his advice to the court on the fullest possible information, when commenting on the health implications of the proposed adoption. The reports made by the examining doctor should cover, as far as practicable, the following matters.

*1.   The child*

Name, date of birth, sex, weight and height.

A.   A health history of each natural parent, so far as is possible, including—

(i) name, date of birth, sex, weight and height;

(ii) a family health history, covering the parents, the brothers and sisters and the other children of the natural parent, with details of any serious physical or mental illness and inherited and congenital disease;

(iii) past health history, including details of any serious physical or mental illness, disability, accident, hospital admission or attendance at an out-patient department, and in each case any treatment given;

(iv) a full obstetric history of the mother, including any problems in the ante-natal, labour and post-natal periods, with the results of any tests carried out during or immediately after pregnancy;

(v) details of any present illness including treatment and prognosis;

(vi)   any other relevant information which might assist the medical adviser; and

(vii)   the name and address of any doctor(s) who might be able to provide further information about any of the above matters.

B.   A neo-natal report on the child, including—

(i)   details of the birth, and any complications;

(ii)   results of a physical examination and screening tests;

(iii)   details of any treatment given;

(iv)   details of any problem in management and feeding;

(v)   any other relevant information which might assist the medical adviser; and

(vi)   the name and address of any doctor(s) who might be able to provide further information about any of the above matters.

C.   A full health history and examination of the child, including—

(i)   details of any serious illness, disability, accident, hospital admission or attendance at an out-patient department, and in each case any treatment given;

(ii)   details and dates of immunisations;

(iii)   a physical and developmental assessment according to age, including an assessment of vision and hearing and of neurological, speech and language development and any evidence of emotional disorder;

(iv)   for a child over five years of age, the school health history (if available);

(v)   any other relevant information which might assist the medical adviser; and

(vi)   the name and address of any doctor(s) who might be able to provide further information about any of the above matters.

D.   The signature, name, address and qualifications of the registered medical practitioner who prepared the report, and the date of the report and of the examinations carried out.

2.   *The Applicant*

(If there is more than one applicant, a report on each applicant should be supplied covering all the matters listed below.)

A.   (i)   name, date of birth, sex, weight and height;

(ii)   a family health history, covering the parents, the brothers and sisters and the children of the applicant, with details of any serious physical or mental illness and inherited and congenital disease:

(iii)   marital history, including (if applicable) reasons for inability to have children;

(iv)   past health history, including details of any serious physical or mental illness, disability, accident, hospital admission or attendance at an out-patient department, and in each case any treatment given;

(v)   obstetric history (if applicable);

(vi)   details of any present illness, including treatment and prognosis;

(vii)   a full medical examination.

(viii)   details of any daily consumption of alcohol, tobacco and habit-forming drugs;

(ix)   any other relevant information which might assist the medical adviser; and

(x)   the name and address of any doctor(s) who might be able to provide further information about any of the above matters.

B.   The signature, name, address and qualifications of the registered medical practitioner who prepared the report, and the date of the report and of the examinations carried out.

SCHEDULE 4                                                    Rule 28(2)(b)

MODIFICATION TO FORM 6 FOR THE PURPOSES OF CONVENTION PROCEEDINGS

Form 6 shall contain the following additional paragraphs after paragraph 25—

PART 3

*Additional Information Required for a Convention Adoption Application*

26.   *The Child*

The child—

(a)   is a United Kingdom national (or a national of                which is a
Convention country) and

(b)   habitually resides at               which is in British territory (or a Convention
country).

27.   *The Applicants*

We are applying together, in reliance on section 17(4)(a) of the Act, and the first applicant
is a United Kingdom national (or a national of                which is a
Convention country) and the second applicant is a United Kingdom national (or a
national of               which is a Convention country) and we habitually reside at
which is in Great Britain.

( *or*

27.   *The Applicants*

We are applying together in reliance on section 17(4)(b) of the Act, and are both United
Kingdom nationals, and we are habitually resident at               which is in British territory
(or a Convention country).)

( *or*

27.   *The Applicant*

I am applying alone in reliance on section 17(5)(a) of the Act, and am a United
Kingdom national (or a national of               which is a Convention country) and
habitually reside at               which is in Great Britain.)

( *or*

27.   *The Applicant*

I am applying alone in reliance on section 17(5)(b) of the Act, and am a United Kingdom
national and habitually reside at               which is in British territory (or a
Convention country).)

28.   *Specified Provisions*

We are both (or I am), accordingly, nationals of the same (or a national of a) Convention
country, namely               and there are no specified provisions in respect of that country (or
there are no relevant specified provisions in respect of that country because               ).

*Notes*

Paragraphs 26 and 27. Documentary evidence of nationality should be exhibited. Where a
child or an applicant is a national of a Convention country, evidence as to the law of the
country relating to nationality applicable to that person should be supplied. Where the child is
not a United Kingdom national, evidence as to the provisions relating to consents and
consultations of the internal law relating to adoption of the Convention country of which the
child is a national should be supplied. Any affidavit on foreign law must be sworn by a
person who is suitably qualified on account of his knowledge or experience to give evidence as
to the law concerned. British territory is defined in section 72(1) of the Act.

Paragraph 28. 'Specified provision' is defined in section 17(8) of the Act. Expert evidence
as to specified provisions may be necessary; if so any affidavit on foreign law must be sworn

*by a person who is suitably qualified on account of his knowledge or experience to give evidence as to the law concerned.*

...

[**26** Where the United Kingdom is the receiving State and—

The Child

    (i)   to be adopted has not attained the age of 18 years at the date of the application; and

    (ii)  was habitually resident in        which is a Convention country outside the British Islands on the date on which the Article 17(c) agreement was made.

The Applicants

    (iii)  Both spouses (in the case of an application by a married couple) or the applicant (in the case of an application by one person) have attained the age of 21 years and have been habitually resident In the British Islands for a period of not less than one year ending with the date of the application; and

    (iv)  [Both spouses (in the case of an application by a married couple) or the applicant (in the case of an application by one person) are British citizens by virtue of the British Nationality Act 1981.] [Whereas,
(insert name of applicant(s) is/are not a British citizen by virtue of the British Nationality Act 1981, the Home Office has confirmed that the child is authorised to enter and reside permanently in the United Kingdom.]

**27** Where the United Kingdom is the State of origin—

The Child

    (i)   to be adopted has not attained the age of 18 years at the date of the application;

    (ii)  is free for adoption by virtue of an order made under section 18 of the 1976 Act, section 18 of the Adoption (Scotland) Act 1978, or Article 17(1) or 18(1) of the Adoption (Northern Ireland) Order 1987; and

    (iii)  is habitually resident in which is part of the British Islands on the date of the application.

The Applicants

Both spouses (in the case of an application by a married couple) or the applicant (in the case of an application by one person) have attained the age of 21 years and are habitually resident in     which is a Convention country outside the British Islands on the date of the application.

**Notes**

Paragraph 26. The report on the child prepared by the CA of the State of origin should be exhibited where the United Kingdom is the receiving State. In sub-paragraph (iv) insert the words in square brackets which apply. Where the applicant or one or more of the applicants is not a British citizen by virtue of the British Nationality Act 1981, notice of confirmation from the Home Office that the child is authorised to enter and reside permanently in the United Kingdom should be exhibited.]

**Note.** Paras 26–28, substituted by paras 26, 27, by SI 2003/183, r 28, as from 1 June 2003.

## MAGISTRATES' COURTS (ADOPTION) RULES 1984

**Dated** 24 April 1984

### SI 1984 No 611

The Lord Chancellor, in exercise of the power conferred on him by section 144 of the Magistrates' Courts Act 1980 after consultation with the Rule Committee appointed under that section, hereby makes the following Rules—

PART I

INTRODUCTORY

*Citation, operation and revocations*

**1.** (1) These Rules may be cited as the Magistrates' Courts (Adoption) Rules 1984 and shall come into operation on 27 May 1984.

(2) The Magistrates' Courts (Adoption) Rules 1976, the Magistrates' Courts (Adoption) (Amendment) Rules 1979 and the Magistrates' Courts (Adoption) (Amendment) Rules 1981 are hereby revoked; but where an application for an adoption order has been made before 27 May 1984 and has not been determined by that date, the provisions of the said Rules continue to apply in connection with that application and nothing in these Rules affects those provisions.

*Interpretation*

**2.** (1) In these Rules, the following expressions shall, unless the context otherwise requires, have the meaning hereby respectively assigned to them, that is to say—

'the 1976 Act' means the Adoption Act 1976;

'the 1989 Act' means the Children Act 1989;

'adoption agency' means a local authority or approved adoption society;

'the child' means the person whom the applicant for an adoption order proposes to adopt or, as the case may be, the person the adoption agency proposes should be freed for adoption;

['children's guardian' means an officer of the service appointed to act on behalf of the child in accordance with section 65(1)(a) of the 1976 Act;]

'interim order' means an order under section 25 of the 1976 Act;

'regular armed forces of the Crown' means the Royal Navy, the Regular Armed Forces as defined by section 225 of the Army Act 1955, the Regular Air Force as defined by section 223 of the Air Force Act 1955, the Queen Alexandra's Royal Naval Nursing Service and the Women's Royal Naval Service;

['reporting officer' means an officer of the service appointed in accordance with section 65(1)(b) of the 1976 Act;].

(2) Expressions which are used in these Rules which are used in the 1976 Act and the 1989 Act have the same meaning as in those Acts.

(3) In these Rules, unless the context otherwise requires, any reference to a rule or to a Schedule shall be construed as a reference to a rule contained in these Rules or to a Schedule hereto, and any reference in a rule to a paragraph shall be construed as a reference to a paragraph of that rule.

(4) In these Rules, any reference to a form shall be construed as a reference to the form so numbered in Schedule 1 to these Rules or to a form substantially to the like effect, with such variations as the circumstances may require.

**Note.** Definitions 'children's guardian' and 'reporting officer' inserted by SI 2001/820, rr 2, 4, as from 1 April 2001.

*Extent*

**3.** These Rules shall apply only to proceedings under the 1976 Act.

PART II

FREEING FOR ADOPTION

*The application*

**4.** (1) An application to free a child for adoption shall be in Form 1 and shall be made to a family proceedings court acting for the area within which either the child or a parent or guardian of the child is at the date of the application by delivering it, or sending it by post to that court, together with all documents referred to in the application.

(2) The applicant shall be the adoption agency and the respondents shall be—

(a) each parent or guardian of the child;

(b) any local authority or voluntary organisation which has parental responsibility for, is looking after, or which is caring for, the child;

(c) [*omitted*]

(d) [*omitted*]

(e) [*omitted*]

(f) any person liable by virtue of any order or agreement to contribute to the maintenance of the child.

(3) The court may at any time direct that any other person or body, except the child, be made a respondent to the application.

(4) The applicant shall supply to the *justices' clerk* [justice's chief executive] three copies of—

(a) Form 1, together with any other documents required to be supplied, and

(b) a report in writing covering all the relevant matters specified in Schedule 2.

**Note.** Words 'justice's clerk' substituted by words 'justice's chief executive' by SI 2001/615, r 2(xi) Schedule, para 71, as from 1 April 2001.

*Appointment and duties of reporting officer*

**5.** (1) As soon as practicable after the application has been made or at any stage thereafter, if it appears that a parent or guardian of the child is willing to agree to the making of an adoption order and is in England or Wales, the court shall appoint a reporting officer in respect of that parent or guardian, and shall send to him a copy of the application and any documents attached thereto and of the report supplied by the applicant.

(2) The same person may be appointed as reporting officer in respect of two or more parents or guardians of the child.

(3) *The reporting officer shall be appointed from a panel established in accordance with any regulations made by the Secretary of State under section 41(7) of the Children Act 1989 but shall not be a member or employee of the applicant or any respondent body nor have been involved in the making of any arrangements for the adoption of the child.*

[(3) The reporting officer shall not be a member or employee of the applicant or any respondent body nor have been involved in the making of any arrangements for the adoption of the child.]

(4) The reporting officer shall—

(a) ensure so far as is reasonably practicable that any agreement to the making of an adoption order is given freely and unconditionally and with full understanding of what is involved;

(b) confirm that the parent or guardian has been given an opportunity of making a declaration under section 18(6) of the 1976 Act that he prefers not to be involved in future questions concerning the adoption of the child;

(c) witness the signature by the parent or guardian of the written agreement to the making of an adoption order;

(d) investigate all the circumstances relevant to that agreement and any such declaration;

(e) where it is proposed to free a child whose mother and father were not married at the time of his birth for adoption and his father is not his guardian, interview any person claiming to be the father in order to be able to advise the court on the matters listed in section 18(7) of the 1976 Act; but if more than one reporting officer has been appointed, the court shall nominate one of them to conduct the interview; and

(f) on completing his investigations make a report in writing to the court, drawing attention to any matters which, in his opinion, may be of assistance to the court in considering the application.

(5) With a view to obtaining the directions of the court on any matter, the reporting officer may at any time make such interim report to the court as appears to him to be necessary; and in particular, the reporting officer shall make a report if a parent or guardian of the child is unwilling to agree to the making of an adoption order, and in such a case the *justices' clerk* [justice's chief executive] shall notify the applicant.

(6) The court may, at any time before the final determination of the application, require the reporting officer to perform such further duties as the court considers necessary.

(7) The reporting officer shall attend any hearing of the application if so required by the court.

(8) Any report made to the court under this rule shall be confidential.

(9) The powers of the court to appoint a reporting officer under paragraph (1), to nominate one reporting officer to conduct an interview under paragraph (4)(e), to give directions following the making of an interim report in accordance with paragraph (5) and to require the reporting officer to perform further duties under paragraph (6) shall also be exercisable, before the hearing of the application, by a single justice or by the justices' clerk.

**Note.** Para (3) substituted by SI 2001/820, rr 2, 5, as from 1 April 2001. In para (5) words 'justice's clerk' substituted by words 'justice's chief executive' in square brackets by SI 2001/615, r 2(xi), Schedule, para 71.


*Appointment and duties of guardian ad litem* [children's guardian]

**6.** (1) As soon as practicable after the application has been made, or after receipt of the statement of facts supplied under rule 7, if it appears that a parent or guardian of the child is unwilling to agree to the making of an adoption order, the court shall appoint a *guardian ad litem* [children's guardian] of the child and shall send to him a copy of the application, together with any documents attached thereto, the statement of facts and the report supplied by the applicant.

(2) Where there are special circumstances and it appears to the court that the welfare of the child requires it, the court may at any time appoint a *guardian ad litem* [children's guardian] of the child, and where such an appointment is made the court shall indicate any particular matters which it requires the *guardian ad litem* [children's guardian] to investigate, and the court shall send the *guardian ad litem* [children's guardian] a copy of the application, together with any documents attached thereto, and the report supplied by the applicant.

(3) The same person may be appointed as reporting officer under rule 5(1) in respect of a parent or guardian who appears to be willing to agree to the making of an adoption order, and as *guardian ad litem* [children's guardian] of the child under this rule; and, whether or not so appointed as reporting officer, the *guardian ad litem* [children's guardian] may be appointed as reporting officer in respect of a parent or guardian of the child who originally was unwilling to agree to the making of an adoption order but who later signifies his or her agreement.

*(4) The guardian ad litem shall be appointed from a panel established in accordance with any regulations made by the Secretary of State under section 41(7) of the Children Act 1989*

*but shall not be a member or employee of the applicant or any respondent body nor have been involved in the making of any arrangements for the adoption of the child.*

[(4) The children's guardian shall not be a member or employee of the applicant or any respondent body nor have been involved in the making of any arrangements for the adoption of the child.]

(5) With a view to safeguarding the interests of the child before the court, the *guardian ad litem* [children's guardian] shall, so far as is reasonably practicable—

    (a) investigate—

        (i) so far as he considers necessary, the matters alleged in the application, the report supplied by the applicant and, where appropriate, the statement of facts supplied under rule 7, and

        (ii) any other matters which appear to him to be relevant to the making of an order freeing the child for adoption;

    (b) advise whether, in his opinion, the child should be present at the hearing of the application; and

    (c) perform such other duties as appear to him to be necessary or as the court may direct.

(6) On completing his investigations the *guardian ad litem* [children's guardian] shall make a report in writing to the court, drawing attention to any matters which, in his opinion, may be of assistance to the court in considering the application.

(7) With a view to obtaining the directions of the court on any matter, the *guardian ad litem* [children's guardian] may at any time make such interim report to the court as appears to him to be necessary.

(8) The court may, at any time before the final determination of the application, require the *guardian ad litem* [children's guardian] to perform such further duties as the court considers necessary.

(9) The *guardian ad litem* [children's guardian] shall attend any hearing of the application unless the court otherwise orders.

(10) Any report made to the court under this rule shall be confidential.

(11) The powers of the court to appoint a *guardian ad litem* [children's guardian] under paragraph (1) or (2), to require the performance by the *guardian ad litem* [children's guardian] of particular duties in accordance with paragraph (2), (5)(c) or (8), and to give directions following the making of an interim report in accordance with paragraph (7) shall also be exercisable, before the hearing of the application, by a single justice or by the justices' clerk.

**Note.** Words 'guardian ad litem' in each place they occur substituted by words 'children's guardian' in square brackets and para (4) substituted by SI 2001/820, rr 2, 3, 6, as from 1 April 2001.

*Statement of facts in dispensation cases*

**7.** (1) Where the adoption agency applying for an order freeing a child for adoption intends to request the court to dispense with the agreement of a parent or guardian of the child on any of the grounds specified in section 16(2) of the 1976 Act, the request shall, unless otherwise directed, be made in the application, or, if made subsequently, by notice to the *justices' clerk* [justices' chief executive], and there shall be attached to the application or notice three copies of the statement of facts on which the applicant intends to rely.

(2) Where the applicant has been informed by a person with whom the child has been placed for adoption that he wishes his identity to remain confidential, the statement of facts supplied under paragraph (1) shall be framed in such a way as not to disclose the identity of that person.

(3) Where a statement of facts has been supplied under paragraph (1), the *justices' clerk* [justices' chief executive] shall, where and as soon as practicable, inform the parent or guardian of the request to dispense with his agreement and shall send to him a copy of the statement supplied under paragraph (1).

*Joint application for parental responsibility by adoption agencies*

**13.** (1) An application by two adoption agencies under section 21(1) of the 1976 Act shall be made in the appropriate form prescribed in Schedule 1 to these Rules to a court acting for the area within which the child is at the date of the application by delivering it, or sending it by post to that court, together with all documents referred to in the application.

(2) Notice of any order made under section 21 of the 1976 Act shall be sent by the court to the court which made the order under section 18 of the 1976 Act (if a different court) and to any former parent (as defined in section 19(1) of the 1976 Act) of the child.

PART III

ADOPTION ORDERS

*Application for a serial number*

**14.** If any person proposing to apply to a domestic court for an adoption order wishes his identity to be kept confidential, he may, before making his application, apply to the *justices' clerk* [justices' chief executive] for a serial number to be assigned to him for the purposes of identifying him in connection with the proposed application, and a number shall be assigned to him accordingly.

**Note.** Words 'justices' clerk' substituted by words 'justices' chief executive' in square brackets by SI 2001/615, r 2(xi), Schedule, para 71, as from 1 April 2001.

*The application*

**15.** (1) An application for an adoption order shall be in Form 6 and shall be made to a family proceedings court acting for the area within which the child is at the date of the application by delivering it, or sending it by post to that court, together with all documents referred to in the application.

(2) The applicant shall be the proposed adopter and the respondents shall be—

(a) each parent or guardian (not being an applicant) of the child, unless the child is free for adoption;

(b) any adoption agency having parental responsibility for the child by virtue of section 18 or 21 of the 1976 Act;

(c) any adoption agency named in the application or in any form of agreement to the making of the adoption order as having taken part in the arrangements for the adoption of the child;

(d) any local authority to whom the applicant has given notice under section 18 of the 1975 Act of his intention to apply for an adoption order;

(e) any local authority or voluntary organisation which has parental responsibility for, is looking after, or is caring for, the child;

(f) [*omitted*]

(g) [*omitted*]

(h) [*omitted*]

(i) [*omitted*]

(j) where the applicant proposes to rely on section 15(1)(b)(ii) of the 1976 Act, the spouse of the applicant.

(3) The court may at any time direct that any other person or body, except the child, be made a respondent to the application.

(4) The applicant shall supply to the *justices' clerk* [justices' chief executive] three copies of—

(a) Form 6, together with any other documents required to be supplied, and

(b) where the child was not placed for adoption with the applicant by an adoption agency, save where the applicant or one of the applicants is a parent of the child, reports by a registered medical practitioner made not more than three months earlier on the health of the child and of each applicant, covering the matters specified in Schedule 3.

**Note.** Words 'justices' clerk' substituted by words 'justices' chief executive' in square brackets by SI 2001/615, r 2(xi), Schedule, para 71, as from 1 April 2001.

*Preliminary examination of application*

**16.** If it appears to the *justices' clerk* [justices' chief executive] on receipt of the application for an adoption order that the court—

(a) may be precluded, by virtue of section 24(1) of the 1976 Act, from proceeding to hear the application, or

(b) may, for any other reason appearing in the application, have no jurisdiction to make an adoption order,

he shall bring the relevant matter to the attention of the court and the application shall not be proceeded with unless the court gives directions as to the further conduct of the application.

**Note.** Words 'justices' clerk' substituted by words 'justices' chief executive' in square brackets by SI 2001/615, r 2(xi), Schedule, para 71, as from 1 April 2001.

*Appointment and duties of reporting officer*

**17.** (1) As soon as practicable after the application has been made or at any stage thereafter, if the child is not free for adoption and if it appears that a parent or guardian of the child is willing to agree to the making of an adoption order and is in England and Wales, the court shall appoint a reporting officer in respect of that parent or guardian, and shall send to him a copy of the application and any documents attached thereto.

(2) The same person may be appointed as reporting officer in respect of two or more parents or guardians of the child.

(*3*) *The reporting officer shall be appointed from a panel established in accordance with any regulations made by the Secretary of State under section 41(7) of the Children Act 1989, but shall not be a member or employee of any respondent body (except where a local authority is made a respondent only under rule 15(2)(d)) nor have been involved in the making of any arrangements for the adoption of the child.*

[(3) The reporting officer shall not be a member or employee of the applicant or any respondent body (except where a local authority is made a respondent only under rule 15(2)(d)) nor have been involved in the making of any arrangements for the adoption of the child.]

(4) The reporting officer shall—

(a) ensure so far as is reasonably practicable that any agreement to the making of the adoption order is given freely and unconditionally and with full understanding of what is involved;

(b) witness the signature by the parent or guardian of the written agreement to the making of the adoption order;

(c) investigate all the circumstances relevant to that agreement; and

(d) on completing his investigations make a report in writing to the court, drawing attention to any matters which, in his opinion, may be of assistance to the court in considering the application.

(5) Paragraphs (5) to (8) of rule 5 shall apply to a reporting officer appointed under this rule as they apply to a reporting officer appointed under that rule; and paragraph (9) of rule 5 shall apply in relation to the appointment of a reporting officer under this rule as it applies in relation to such an appointment made under that rule.

**Note.** Para (3) substituted by SI 2001/820, rr 2, 7, as from 1 April 2001.

*Appointment and duties of guardian ad litem* [children's guardian]

**18.**   (1) As soon as practicable after the application has been made, or after receipt of the statement of facts supplied under rule 19, if the child is not free for adoption and if it appears that a parent or guardian of the child is unwilling to agree to the making of the adoption order, the court shall appoint a *guardian ad litem* [children's guardian] of the child and shall send him a copy of the application together with any documents attached thereto.

(2) Where there are special circumstances and it appears to the court that the welfare of the child requires it, the court may at any time appoint a *guardian ad litem* [children's guardian] of the child and where such an appointment is made the court shall indicate any particular matters which it requires the *guardian ad litem* [children's guardian] to investigate and the court shall send the *guardian ad litem* [children's guardian] a copy of the application together with any documents attached thereto.

(3) The same person may be appointed as reporting officer under rule 17(1) in respect of a parent or guardian who appears to be willing to agree to the making of the adoption order, and as *guardian ad litem* [children's guardian] of the child under this rule; and, whether or not so appointed as reporting officer, the *guardian ad litem* [children's guardian] may be appointed as reporting officer in respect of a parent or guardian of the child who originally was unwilling to agree to the making of an adoption order but who later signifies his or her agreement.

*(4) The guardian ad litem [children's guardian] shall be appointed from a panel established in accordance with any regulations made by the Secretary of State under section 41(7) of the Children Act 1989 but shall not be a member or employee of any respondent body (except where a local authority is made a respondent only under rule 15(2)(d)) nor have been involved in the making of any arrangements for the adoption of the child.*

[(4) The children's guardian shall not be a member or employee of the applicant or any respondent body (except where a local authority is made a respondent only under rule 15(2)(d)) nor have been involved in the making of any arrangements for the adoption of the child.]

(5) With a view to safeguarding the interests of the child before the court the *guardian ad litem* [children's guardian] shall so far as is reasonably practicable—
   (a) investigate—
      (i)   so far as he considers necessary, the matters alleged in the application, any report supplied under rule 22(1) or (2) and, where appropriate, the statement of facts supplied under rule 19;
      (ii)  any other matters which appear to him to be relevant to the making of an adoption order;
   (b) advise whether, in his opinion, the child should be present at the hearing of the application; and
   (c) perform such other duties as appear to him to be necessary or as the court may direct.

(6) Paragraphs (6) to (10) of rule 6 shall apply to a *guardian ad litem* [children's guardian] appointed under this rule as they apply to a *guardian ad litem* [children's guardian] appointed under that rule; and paragraph (11) of rule 6 shall apply in relation to the appointment of a *guardian ad litem* [children's guardian] under this rule as it applies in relation to such an appointment made under that rule.

**Note.** Words 'guardian ad litem' in each place they occur substituted by words 'children's guardian' in square brackets and para (4) substituted by SI 2001/820, rr 2, 3, 8, as from 1 April 2001.

*Statement of facts in dispensation cases*

**19.**   (1) Where the child is not free for adoption and the applicant for the adoption order intends to request the court to dispense with the agreement of a parent or guardian of the child on any of the grounds specified in section 16(2) of the 1976

Act, the request shall, unless otherwise directed, be made in the application or, if made subsequently, by notice to the *justices' clerk* [justices' chief executive] and there shall be attached to the application or notice three copies of the statement of facts on which the applicant intends to rely.

(2) Where a serial number has been assigned to the applicant under rule 14, the statement of facts supplied under paragraph (1) shall be framed in such a way as not to disclose the identity of the applicant.

(3) Where a statement of facts has been supplied under paragraph (1), the *justices' clerk* [justices' chief executive] shall, where and as soon as practicable, inform the parent or guardian of the request to dispense with his agreement and shall send to him a copy of the statement supplied under paragraph (1).

(4) The *justices' clerk* [justices' chief executive] shall also send a copy of the statement supplied under paragraph (1) to the *guardian ad litem* [children's guardian] and to the reporting officer if a different person.

**Note.** Words 'justices' clerk' in each place substituted by words 'justices' chief executive' in square brackets by SI 2001/615, r 2(xi), Schedule, para 71, as from 1 April 2001. Words 'guardian ad litem' substituted by words 'children's guardian' in square brackets by SI 2001/820, rr 2, 3, as from 1 April 2001.

*Agreement*

**20.** (1) Any document signifying the agreement of a person to the making of the adoption order may be in Form 7, and, if executed by a person outside England and Wales before the commencement of the proceedings, shall be filed with the application.

(2) If the document is executed outside England and Wales it shall be witnessed by one of the persons specified in rule 8(2), (3) or (4), according to the country in which it is executed.

*Notice of hearing*

**21.** (1) Subject to paragraph (4), as soon as practicable after the application has been made the *justices' clerk* [justices' chief executive] shall fix a time for the hearing of the application and shall serve notice of the hearing on all the parties, the reporting officer and the guardian ad litem (if appointed) in Form 8.

(2) In a case where section 22 of the 1976 Act applies, the *justices' clerk* [justices' chief executive] shall send a copy of the application and, where appropriate, of the report supplied under rule 15(4), to the local authority to whom notice under that section was given.

(3) No person other than the reporting officer, the *guardian ad litem* [children's guardian] (if appointed) and, in cases where section 22 of the 1976 Act applies, the local authority to whom notice under that section was given, shall be served with a copy of the application.

(4) Where section 22 of the 1976 Act applies, the *justices' clerk* [justices' chief executive] shall fix a time for the hearing so that the hearing takes place on a date not less than three months from the date of the notice given to the local authority under that section.

**Note.** Words 'justices' clerk' in each place substituted by words 'justices' chief executive' in square brackets by SI 2001/615, r 2(xi), Schedule, para 71, as from 1 April 2001. Words 'guardian ad litem' substituted by words 'children's guardian' in square brackets by SI 2001/820, rr 2, 3, as from 1 April 2001.

*Reports by adoption agency or local authority*

**22.** (1) Where the child was placed for adoption with the applicant by an adoption agency, that agency shall supply, within six weeks of receipt of the notice of hearing under rule 21, three copies of a report in writing covering the matters specified in Schedule 2.

(2) Where the child was not placed for adoption with the applicant by an adoption agency, the local authority to whom the notice under section 22 of the 1976 Act was given shall supply, within six weeks of receipt of the notice of hearing under rule 21, three copies of a report in writing covering the matters specified in Schedule 2.

(3) The court may request a further report under paragraph (1) or (2) and may indicate any particular matters it requires such a further report to cover.

(4) The *justices' clerk* [justices' chief executive] shall send a copy of any report supplied under paragraph (1) or (2) to the reporting officer and to the *guardian ad litem* [children's guardian] (if appointed).

(5) No other person shall be supplied with a copy of any report supplied under paragraph (1) or (2) and any such report shall be confidential.

**Note.** Words 'justices' clerk' substituted by words 'justices' chief executive' in square brackets by SI 2001/615, r 2(xi), Schedule, para 71, as from 1 April 2001. Words 'guardian ad litem' substituted by words 'children's guardian' in square brackets by SI 2001/820, rr 2, 3, as from 1 April 2001.

*The hearing*

**23.**   (1) On the hearing of the application any person upon whom notice is required to be served under rule 21 may attend and be heard on the question whether an adoption order should be made.

(2) Any member or employee of a party which is a local authority, adoption agency or other body may address the court if he is duly authorised in that behalf.

(3) If a serial number has been assigned to the applicant under rule 14, the proceedings shall be conducted with a view to securing that he is not seen by or made known to any respondent who is not already aware of the applicant's identity except with his consent.

(4) Subject to paragraphs (5) and (7), the court shall not make an adoption order or an interim order except after the personal attendance before the court of the applicant and the child.

(5) If there are special circumstances which, having regard to the report of the *guardian ad litem* [children's guardian] (if any), appear to the court to make the attendance of the child unnecessary, the court may direct that the child need not attend.

(6) If there are special circumstances which appear to the court to make the attendance of any other party necessary, the court may direct that that party shall attend.

(7) In the case of an application under section 14(1A) or (1B) of the 1976 Act, the court may in special circumstances make an adoption order or an interim order after the personal attendance of one only of the applicants, if the application is verified by a declaration made by the applicant who does not attend and witnessed by a justice of the peace, a justices' clerk within the meaning of section 70 of the Justices of the Peace Act 1979, or, if made outside the United Kingdom, by any of the persons specified in rule 8(4).

**Note.** Words 'guardian ad litem' substituted by words 'children's guardian' in square brackets by SI 2001/820, rr 2, 3, as from 1 April 2001.

*Proof of identity of child, etc*

**24.**   (1) Where proof of the identity of the child is required for any purpose, any fact tending to establish his identity with a child to whom a document relates may be proved by affidavit.

(2) Where any such fact is proved by affidavit, the attendance of a witness at the hearing to prove that fact shall not be compelled unless the fact is disputed or for some special reason his attendance is required by the court.

(3) Subject to paragraph (5), where the precise date of the child's birth is not proved to the satisfaction of the court, the court shall determine the probable date of his birth and the date so determined may be specified in the adoption order as the date of his birth.

(4) Subject to paragraph (5), where the place of birth of the child cannot be proved to the satisfaction of the court but it appears probable that the child was born in the United Kingdom, the Channel Islands or the Isle of Man, he may be treated as having been born in the registration district and sub-district in which the court sits, and in any other case (where the country of birth is not proved) the particulars of the country of birth may be omitted from the adoption order.

(5) Where the child is free for adoption, any order made identifying the probable date and place of birth of the child in the proceedings under section 14 of the 1975 Act shall be sufficient proof of the date and place of birth of the child in proceedings to which this rule applies.

*Further proceedings after interim order*

**25.** Where the court has made an interim order, the justices' clerk shall fix a time for the further hearing of the application, such hearing to be on a date before the order expires, and shall send notice in Form 8 of the date of the hearing to all the parties and to the *guardian ad litem* [children's guardian] (if appointed) not less than one month before that date.

**Note.** Words 'guardian ad litem' substituted by words 'children's guardian' in square brackets by SI 2001/820, rr 2, 3, as from 1 April 2001.

*Committal of child to care on refusal of adoption order*

**26.** *Revoked.*

PART **IV**

MISCELLANEOUS

*Application for removal, return etc, of child*

**27.** (1) An application—
  (a) for leave under section 27 or 28 of the 1976 Act to remove a child from the home of a person with whom the child lives,
  (b) under section 29(1) of the 1976 Act for an order for the return of a child who has been removed from the home of a person with whom the child lives,
  (c) under section 29(2) of the 1976 Act for an order directing a person not to remove a child from the home of a person with whom the child lives,
  (d) under section 30(2) of the 1976 Act, for leave to give notice of an intention not to allow a child to remain in a person's home, or
  (e) under section 20(2) of the 1976 Act, for leave to place a child for adoption,
shall be made in accordance with paragraph (2).
  (2) The application under paragraph (1) shall be made by complaint—
  (a) if an application for an adoption order or an order under section 18 or 20 of the 1976 Act is pending, to the family proceedings court in which the application is pending; or
  (b) if no such application is pending, to the family proceedings court in whose area the applicant lives or, in the case of an application made under section 28 of the 1976 Act, the court in whose area the child is:

Provided that if an application is pending under paragraph (1) above, any further application concerning the home of the child shall be made to the family proceedings court in which that original application is pending.

(3) The respondents shall be—

(a) in a case where proceedings for an adoption order or an order under section 18 or 20 of the 1976 Act are pending (or where such proceedings have subsequently been commenced), all the parties to those proceedings;

(b) in any other case, any person against whom an order is sought in the application and the local authority to whom the prospective adopter has given notice under section 22 of the 1976 Act; and

(c) in any case, such other person or body, not being the child, as the court thinks fit.

(4) If in any application under this rule a serial number has been assigned to a person who has applied or who proposes to apply for an adoption order, or such a person applies to the *justices' clerk* [justices' chief executive] in that behalf before making that application and a serial number is assigned accordingly—

(a) the *justices' clerk* [justices' chief executive] shall ensure that a summons directed to any of the respondents does not disclose the identity of that person to any respondent to the application under this rule who is not already aware of that person's identity, and

(b) the proceedings on the application under this rule shall be conducted with a view to securing that he is not seen by or made known to any party who is not already aware of his identity except with his consent.

(5) The *justices' clerk* [justices' chief executive] shall serve notice of the time fixed for the hearing on the reporting officer and *guardian ad litem* [children's guardian] (if any), together with a copy of the complaint: and on the hearing of the application the reporting officer and *guardian ad litem* [children's guardian] may attend and be heard on the question of whether the application made should be granted.

(6) Unless otherwise directed, any prospective adopter who is a respondent under this rule and who wishes to oppose the application shall make his application for an adoption order within 14 days of the service upon him of the summons or before or at the time of the hearing of the application under this rule, whichever is the sooner.

(7) The court may at any time give directions, and if giving directions under paragraph (6) shall give directions, as to the conduct of any application under this rule and in particular as to the appointment of a *guardian ad litem* [children's guardian] of the child.

(8) Any member or employee of a party which is a local authority, adoption agency or other body may address the court at the hearing of an application under this rule if he is duly authorised in that behalf.

(9) Where an application under paragraph (1)(a) or (d) is granted or an application under paragraph (1)(b) or (c) is refused, the court may thereupon, if application for an adoption order has been made, treat the hearing of the application as the hearing of the application for an adoption order and refuse an adoption order accordingly.

(10) Where an application under this rule is determined the *justices' clerk* [justices' chief executive] shall serve notice of the effect of the determination on all the parties.

(11) A search warrant issued by a justice of the peace under section 29(4) of the 1976 Act (which relates to premises specified in an information to which an order made under the said section 29(1) relates, authorising a constable to search the said premises and if he finds the child to return the child to the person on whose application the said order was made) shall be in a warrant form as per section 102 of the 1989 Act (warrant to search for or remove a child) or a form to the like effect.

**Note.** Words 'justices' clerk' in both places substituted by words 'justices' chief executive' in square brackets by SI 2001/615, r 2(xi), Schedule, para 71, as from 1 April 2001. Words 'guardian ad litem' in each place substituted by words 'children's guardian' in square brackets by SI 2001/820, rr 2, 3, as from 1 April 2001.

*Amendment and revocation of orders*

**28.** (1) Any application made under paragraph 4 of Schedule 1 to the 1976 Act for the amendment of an adoption order or the revocation of a direction to the Registrar General, or under section 52 of, and Schedule 2 to, the 1976 Act (or section 1(1) of the Adoption Act 1960), for the revocation of an adoption order, shall be in Form 9, and shall be made to a family proceedings court acting for the same petty sessions area as the family proceedings court which made the adoption order, by delivering it or sending it by post to the *clerk to the justices* [justices' chief executive].

(2) Notice of the application shall be given by the *justices' clerk* [justices' chief executive] to such persons (if any) as the court thinks fit.

(3) Where the application is granted, the *justices' clerk* [justices' chief executive] shall send to the Registrar General a notice specifying the amendments or informing him of the revocation and shall give sufficient particulars of the order to enable the Registrar General to identify the case.

**Note.** Words 'justices' clerk' in both places and 'clerk to the justices' substituted by words 'justices' chief executive' in square brackets by SI 2001/615, r 2(xi), Schedule, paras 71, 73.

[*Power to court to limit cross-examination*

**28A.** the court may limit the issues on which a children's guardian or a reporting officer may be cross-examined.]

**Note.** Inserted by SI 2001/820, rr 2, 9, as from 1 April 2001.

*Service of documents*

**29.** (1) Unless otherwise directed, any document under these rules may be served—

(a) on a corporation or body of persons, by delivering it at, or sending it by post to, the registered or principal office of the corporation or body;

(b) on any other person, by delivering it to him, or by sending it by post to him at his usual or last known address.

(2) A note of service or non-service shall be endorsed on a copy of Form 3 or Form 8.

(3) In the case of a document sent by post to a person's usual or last known address in accordance with paragraph (1)(b), the court may treat service as having been effected notwithstanding that the document has been returned undelivered.

*Costs*

**30.** (1) On the determination of an application or on the making of an interim order, the court may make such order as to the costs as it thinks just and, in particular, may order the applicant to pay—

(a) the expenses incurred by the reporting officer and the *guardian ad litem* [children's guardian] (if appointed), and

(b) the expenses incurred by any respondent in attending the hearing,

or such part of those expenses as the court thinks proper.

(2) Determination of an application in this rule includes a refusal to proceed with the application or withdrawal of the application.

**Note.** Words 'guardian ad litem' substituted by words 'children's guardian' in square brackets by SI 2001/820, rr 2, 3, as from 1 April 2001.

*Notice and copies of orders, etc*

**31.** (1) In applications to which these rules apply orders shall be made in the form indicated in this paragraph—

| *Description of order* | *Form* |
| --- | --- |
| (a) Order under section 18 of the 1976 Act | 10 |
| (b) Order under section 20 of the 1976 Act | 11 |
| (c) Interim order | 12 |
| (d) Adoption order | 13 |

(2) Where an adoption order is made by a court sitting in Wales in respect of a child who was born in Wales (or is treated under rule 24(4) as having been born in the registration district and sub-district in which that court sits) and the adopter so requests before the order is drawn up, the *justices' clerk* [justices' chief executive] shall supply a translation into Welsh of the particulars set out in the order.

(3) Within 7 days of the making of an order in an application to which these rules apply, the *justices' clerk* [justices' chief executive] shall send a copy of the order (and of any translation into Welsh required to be supplied under paragraph (2)) to the applicant.

(4) Within 7 days of the making of an adoption order, the *justices' clerk* [justices' chief executive] shall send a copy of the order (and of any translation into Welsh supplied under paragraph (2)) to the Registrar General; where a translation into Welsh under paragraph (2) has been supplied, the English text shall prevail.

(5) Where an order to which paragraph 1(a), (b) or (d) applies is made or refused or an order to which paragraph 1(c) applies is made, the *justices' clerk* [justices' chief executive] shall serve notice to that effect on every respondent.

(6) [*omitted*]

(7) The *justices' clerk* [justices' chief executive] shall serve notice of the making of an order to which paragraph 1(a), (b) or (d) applies on any court in Great Britain which appears to him to have made any such order as is referred to in section 12(3) of the 1976 Act (orders relating to parental responsibility for, and the maintenance of, the child).

(8) A copy of any order may be supplied to the Registrar General at his request.

(9) A copy of any order may be supplied to the applicant.

(10) A copy of any order may be supplied to any other person with the leave of the court.

**Note.** Words 'justices' clerk' in each place substituted by words 'justices' chief executive' in square brackets by SI 2001/615, r 2(xi), Schedule, para 71.

*Keeping of registers, custody, inspection and disclosure of documents and information*

**32.** (1) Such part of the register kept in pursuance of rules made under the Magistrates' Courts Act 1980, as relates to proceedings under Part II of the 1976 Act shall be kept in a separate book and shall contain the particulars shown in Form 14 and the book shall not contain particulars of any other proceedings except proceedings under the 1976 Act (or under any previous enactment relating to adoption).

(2) Any declaration by a parent or guardian or a former parent of a child that he prefers not to be involved in future questions concerning the adoption of the child which is required to be recorded by the court in accordance with section 18(6) or 19(4) of the 1976 Act shall be recorded in the book kept in pursuance of paragraph (1).

(3) The book kept in pursuance of paragraph (1) and all other documents relating to proceedings mentioned in that paragraph shall, while they are in the custody of the court, be kept in a place of special security.

(4) A party who is an individual and is referred to in a confidential report supplied to the court by an adoption agency, a local authority, a reporting officer or a *guardian ad litem* [children's guardian] may, for the purposes of the hearing, be supplied with a copy of that part of any such report which refers to him, subject to any direction given by the court that—

(a)  no part of one or any of the reports shall be revealed to that party, or

(b)  the part of one or any of the reports referring to that party shall be revealed only to that party's legal advisers, or

(c)  the whole or any other part of one or any of the reports be revealed to that party.

(5) Any person who obtains any information in the course of, or relating to, any proceedings mentioned in paragraph (1), shall treat that information as confidential and shall only disclose it if—

(a)  the disclosure is necessary for the proper exercise of his duties, or

(b)  the information is requested—

(i)  by a court or public authority (whether in Great Britain or not) having power to determine adoptions and related matters, for the purpose of the discharge of its duties in that behalf, or

(ii)  by the Registrar General, or a person authorised in writing by him, where the information requested relates only to the identity of any adoption agency which made the arrangements for placing the child for adoption in the actual custody of the applicants, and of any local authority which was notified of the applicant's intention to apply for an adoption order in respect of the child, or

(iii)  by a person who is authorised in writing by the Secretary of State to obtain the information for the purposes of research.

[(5A) Nothing in this rule shall prevent the disclosure of a document prepared by an officer of the service for the purpose of—

(a)  enabling a person to perform functions required under section 62(3A) of the Justices of the Peace Act 1997; and

(b)  assisting an officer of the service who is appointed by the court under any enactment to perform his functions.

(5B) Nothing in this rule shall prevent the disclosure of any document relating to proceedings by an officer of the service to any other officer of the service unless that other officer is involved in the same proceedings but on behalf of a different party.]

(6) Save as required or authorised by a provision of any enactment or of these Rules or with the leave of the court, no document or order held by or lodged with the court in proceedings under the 1976 Act (or under any previous enactment relating to adoption) shall be open to inspection by any person, and no copy of any such document or order, or of an extract from any such document or order, shall be taken by or issued to any person.

**Note.** In para (4) words 'guardian ad litem' substituted by 'children's guardian' in square brackets and paras (5A), (5B) inserted by SI 2001/820, rr 2, 3, 10, as from 1 April 2001.

*Proceedings to be by way of complaints etc*

**33.**   Save in so far as special provision is made by these Rules, proceedings on an application shall be regulated in the same manner as proceedings on complaint, and accordingly for the purposes of this rule the application shall be deemed to be a complaint, the applicant to be a complainant, the respondents to be defendants and any notice served under these rules to be a summons; but nothing in this rule shall be construed as enabling a warrant of arrest to be issued for failure to appear in answer to any such notice.

SCHEDULE 1                                                    Rule 2(4)

FORMS

FORM 1                                                        Rule 4(1)

APPLICATION FOR AN ORDER FREEING A CHILD FOR ADOPTION

To the                                    .............Family Proceedings Court

I, an authorised officer of the            of            being an adoption agency
wishing to free for adoption        , a child, hereby give the following further
particulars in support of the application.

1. This application is/is not made with the consent of            (and
         ), the parent(s)/guardian(s) of the child.

*Particulars of the child*

2. Identity etc. The child is of the      sex and is not and has not been married.
He/she was born on the      day of            19   and is the person to whom the
attached birth/adoption certificate relates (*or* was born on or about the      day of
         19   , in         ). He/she is a            national.
3. Parentage etc. The child is the child of            whose last known address
was            (*or* deceased) and            whose last known address was
         (*or* deceased).
(4. The guardian(s) of the child (other than the mother or father of the child)
is/are         of         (and         of         ).)
(5. Parental agreement. I understand that the said         (and            )
is/are willing to agree to the making of an adoption order.)
(6. I request the court to dispense with the agreement of            on the
ground(s) that            (and            ) and there are attached hereto three
copies of a statement of the facts on which I intend to rely.)
7. Care, etc. The child is currently living with            of            and has
been living there since the      day of            19   . (The child has been placed
with them for adoption (and they wish their identity to remain confidential).)
(8. The child is looked after by            (who have the powers and duties of the
parent or guardian of the child) (*or* the parental responsibility for the child).)
(9. Maintenance.         of            is liable, by virtue of an order made
by the            court at         on the      day of            19   (*or* by an
agreement dated the      day of            19   ), to contribute to the maintenance
of the child.)
(10. I attach hereto signed by the mother/father/guardian of the child a
declaration that he/she prefers not to be involved in future questions concerning
the adoption of the child.)
(11. The father and mother of the child were not married to each other at the
time of his birth and         of            who is/claims to be the father—
    (i)  does/does not intend to apply for an order under section 4(1)(a) of the
         1989 Act,
    (ii) does/does not intend to apply for a residence order.)
(12. No proceedings relating in whole or in part to the child have been completed
or commenced in England and Wales or elsewhere (except         ).)

I accordingly apply on behalf of            for an order freeing the child for
adoption.

Dated this      day of            19   .

*Notes*

An application to a domestic court must be made to a court within the area in which either the child or his parent or guardian is.

Introduction: Enter the first name(s) and surname as shown in the certificate referred to in paragraph 2; otherwise enter the first name(s) and surname by which the child is known.

Paragraph 2: If the child has previously been adopted, a certified copy of the entry in the Adopted Children Register should be attached and not a certified copy of the original entry in the Registers of Births. Where a certificate is not attached, enter the place, including the country, of birth if known.

Paragraph 3: If the child has previously been adopted, give the names of his adoptive parents and not those of his natural parents. If the father and mother were not married to each other at the time of the birth and a court has made an order giving the father parental responsibility for the child, or if the father has legal custody of the child by virtue of a court order, give details of that order under paragraph 12.

Paragraph 4: Enter particulars of any person appointed under section 5 of the 1989 Act to be a guardian. Do not include any person who has the custody of the child only. Delete this paragraph if the child has no guardian.

Paragraphs 5 and 6: Enter either in paragraph 5 or 6 the names of the persons mentioned in paragraphs 3 and 4, except that if the father and mother of the child were not married at the time of his birth the father of the child should be entered only if a court has made an order giving him parental responsibility for the child. Where it is sought to dispense with parental agreement, enter in paragraph 6 one or more of the grounds set out in section 16(2) of the 1976 Act.

Paragraph 7: Enter the name and address of the person with whom the child has his home.

Paragraph 8: This paragraph should be completed where the child is being looked after by a local authority or a voluntary organisation.

Paragraph 9: This paragraph should be completed where some person or body is liable to contribute to the maintenance of the child under a court order or agreement.

Paragraph 12: State the nature of the proceedings and the date and effect of any orders made.

FORM 2                                                                          Rule 8

AGREEMENT TO AN ADOPTION ORDER (FREEING CASES)

IF YOU ARE IN ANY DOUBT ABOUT YOUR LEGAL RIGHTS YOU SHOULD OBTAIN LEGAL ADVICE
BEFORE SIGNING THIS FORM

Whereas an application is to be/has been made by               for an order freeing
            , a child, for adoption:

And whereas the child is the person to whom the birth certificate attached marked 'A' relates:

(And whereas the child is at least six weeks old:)

I, the undersigned               of               being a parent/guardian of the child hereby state as follows—

(1) I consent to the application of               an adoption agency, for an order freeing the child for adoption.

(2) I understand that the effect of an adoption order would be to deprive me permanently of parental responsibility for the child and to vest that in the adopters: and in particular I understand that, if and when an adoption order is made, I shall have no right to see or get in touch with the child or to have him/her returned to me.

(3) I further understand that the court cannot make an order freeing a child for adoption without the agreement of each parent or guardian of the child to the making of an adoption order, unless the court dispenses with that agreement on the ground that the person concerned—

(a) cannot be found or is incapable of giving agreement, or

(b) is withholding his agreement unreasonably, or

(c) has persistently failed without reasonable cause to discharge his parental responsibility in relation to the child, or

(d) has abandoned or neglected the child, or

(e) has persistently ill-treated the child, or

(f) has seriously ill-treated the child and the rehabilitation of the child within the household of the parent or guardian is unlikely.

(4) I further understand that, when the application for an order freeing the child for adoption is heard, this document may be used as evidence of my agreement to the making of an adoption order unless I inform the court that I no longer agree.

(5) I hereby freely, and with full understanding of what is involved, agree unconditionally to the making of an adoption order.

(6) (I have been given an opportunity of making a declaration that I prefer not to be involved in future questions concerning the adoption of the child. I understand that if I make such a declaration I will not be told when the child has been adopted or whether he has been placed for adoption. I further understand that I will not be able to apply for a revocation of the order freeing the child for adoption if I make such a declaration. I hereby freely declare, with full understanding of what is involved, that I do not wish to be involved in future questions concerning the adoption of the child.)

(7) (I have been given an opportunity of making a declaration that I prefer not to be involved in future questions concerning the adoption of the child, and the effect of making such a declaration has been explained to me. I do not wish to make such a declaration.)

(8) I have not received or given any payment or reward for, or in consideration of, the adoption of the child, for any agreement to the making of an adoption order or consent to the making of an application for an order freeing the child for adoption, for placing the child for adoption with any person or making any arrangements for the adoption of the child (other than a payment to an adoption agency for their expenses incurred in connection with the adoption).

Signature:

This form, duly completed, was signed by the said                before me at             on the      day of               19   .

Signature:
Address
Description

*Notes*

Heading: (a) Insert the name of the adoption agency applying for the order.

(b) Insert the first name(s) and surname of the child as known to the person giving agreement.

(c) If the child has previously been adopted a certified copy of the entry in the Adopted Children Register should be attached and not a certified copy of the original entry in the Registers of Births.

(d) Where two or more forms of agreement are supplied to the court at the same time they may both or all refer to a certificate attached to one of the forms of agreement.

Paragraphs 6 and 7: If the parent or guardian does not make the declaration the adoption agency must, after twelve months have passed from the making of the order freeing the child for adoption, inform the parent or guardian whether an adoption order has been made in respect of the child, and, if not, whether the child has his home with a person with whom he has been placed for adoption. Further, if no adoption order has been made in respect of the child or the child does not have his home with a person with whom he has been placed for adoption, then the parent or guardian may apply to the court for revocation of the order freeing the child for adoption.

Paragraph 8: Any such payment or reward is illegal, except payment to an adoption agency in respect of their expenses incurred in connection with the adoption.

Witness statement: In England and Wales, the document should be witnessed by the reporting officer. In Scotland, it should be witnessed by a Justice of the Peace or a Sheriff, and in Northern Ireland, by a Justice of the Peace. Outside the United Kingdom it should be witnessed by a person authorised by law in the place where the document is signed to administer an oath for any judicial or legal purpose, a British consular officer, a notary public, or, if the person executing the document is serving in the regular armed forces of the Crown, an officer holding a commission in any of those forces.

FORM 3                                                                                           Rule 9(1)

NOTICE OF HEARING OF AN APPLICATION FOR AN ORDER FREEING A CHILD FOR ADOPTION

...................Family Proceedings Court

To
of

Whereas an application for an order freeing for adoption             , a child of the          sex born on the     day of             19    has been made by
of
And whereas             (and          ) was/were appointed reporting officer(s) (and          was appointed *guardian ad litem* [children's guardian] of the child);

TAKE NOTICE—

1. That the said application will be heard before the court at                 on the
          day of             19   , at     o'clock and that you may then appear and be heard on the question whether an order freeing the child for adoption should be made.

2. That you are not obliged to attend the hearing unless you wish to do so or the court notifies you that your attendance is necessary.

3. That while the said application is pending, if the child is being looked after by the applicant, then a parent or guardian of the child who has not consented to the making of the application must not, except with the leave of the court, remove the child from the home of the person with whom the child lives against the will of that person.

(4. That the court has been requested to dispense with your agreement to the making of an adoption order on the ground(s) that             and the statement of the facts on which the applicant intends to rely is attached.)

It would assist the court if you would complete the attached form and return it to me by        .

Dated the     day of          19   .

*Justices' Clerk* [Justices' Chief Executive]

To the *Clerk to the Justices* [Chief Executive to the Justices].

Freeing for adoption: (*state name of child*)
I received notice of the hearing of the application on the          day of
19   .
I wish/do not wish to oppose the application.
I wish/do not wish to appear and be heard on the question whether an order should be made.

(signature)<br>
(address)<br>
(date)

*Notes*

   Preamble: Enter the first name(s) and the surname of the child as shown in the application. Enter the name of the applicant agency and the name(s) of the reporting officer(s) (and of the *guardian ad litem* [children's guardian], if appointed).

**Note.** Words 'guardian ad litem' in both places substituted by words 'children's guardian' in square brackets by SI 2001/820, rr 2, 3, as from 1 April 2001. Words 'Justices' Clerk' and 'Clerk to the Justices' in square brackets substituted by SI 2001/615, r 2(xi), Schedule, para 75, as from 1 April 2001.

FORM 4                                                            Rule 12(1)

APPLICATION FOR REVOCATION OF AN ORDER FREEING A CHILD FOR ADOPTION

To the                                        .................Family Proceedings Court

   On the     day of          19    this court made an order freeing          ,
a child, for adoption.

   I/We          (and          ) of (*address*), the former parent(s) of the child, apply for revocation of that order on the grounds that:

   1.  No adoption order has been made in respect of the child, and
   2.  The child does not have his home with a person with whom he has been placed for adoption, and
   3.  I/We wish to resume parental responsibility for the child because (*state the reasons relied upon for the revocation of the order*)

signed
dated

*Notes*

   (a)  The application must be made to the court which made the original order, and not earlier than 12 months from the date of that order.
   (b)  A parent or guardian of the child who has made a declaration (referred to in section 18(6) of the 1976 Act) that he prefers not to be involved in future questions concerning the adoption of the child may not make application for revocation of the order.

FORM 5                                                            Rule 13(1)

APPLICATION FOR TRANSFER OF PARENTAL RESPONSIBILITY BETWEEN ADOPTION AGENCIES

To the                                        .................Family Proceedings Court

   I, an authorised officer of the          of          , and I, an authorised officer of the          of          , both being adoption agencies, wishing to

transfer the parental responsibility for                    , a child, from                    to
     hereby give the following further particulars in support of our application.

     1.  On the      day of           19    the court made an order freeing the child for
adoption under section 18 of the Children Act 1976. A copy of that order is attached.
     2.  The transfer would be in the best interests of the child because
     3.  The administrative reasons why the transfer is desirable are
     (4. The    former    parent(s)            of            (and            of
            ), has/have been informed of the making of this application.)

Dated etc

                                                                (signatures)
                                                                (addresses)

*Notes*

     Preamble: Enter the names of the two agencies concerned and enter the name
of the child as shown in the order referred to in paragraph 1.
     Paragraphs 2 and 3: State concisely the reasons it is desired to transfer the child
between the agencies.
     Paragraph 4: A former parent is a person as defined in section 19(1) of the 1976
Act. This paragraph should be deleted only if there are no former parents.

FORM 6                                                          Rule 15(1)

APPLICATION FOR AN ADOPTION ORDER

To the                                        ......... Family Proceedings Court

I/We, the undersigned,            (and            ,) wishing to adopt            ,
a child, hereby give the following particulars in support of my/our application.

PART 1

Particulars of the applicant(s)

     *1.  Name and address, etc*

Name of (first) applicant in full
Address
Occupation
Date of Birth
Relationship (if any) to the child
Name of (second) applicant in full
Address
Occupation
Date of Birth
Relationship (if any) to the child

     *2.  Domicile*

     I am/we are/one of us (namely            ) is domiciled in England and
Wales/Scotland/Northern Ireland/the Channel Islands/the Isle of Man.

     *3.   Status*

     We are married to each other and our marriage certificate (or other evidence of
marriage) is attached (*or* I am unmarried/a widow/a widower/a divorcee) (*or* I am
applying alone as a married person and can satisfy the court that            ).

     (4.  I am applying alone for an adoption order in respect of my own child and
can satisfy the court that the other natural parent            .)

(*5. Health*

A report on my/our health, made by a registered medical practitioner on the day of          19  , is attached.)

*Notes*

The application must be made to a family proceedings court within whose area the child is.

Introduction: Enter the first name(s) and surname of the child as shown in any certificate referred to in paragraph 6 below; otherwise enter the first name(s) and surname by which the child was known before being placed for adoption.

Paragraph 1: Insert the address where the applicant has his home and the place (if different) where documents may be served upon him.

Paragraph 3: Documentary evidence of marital status should be supplied. A married applicant can apply alone if he or she can satisfy the court that his or her spouse cannot be found, or that they have separated and are living apart and that the separation is likely to be permanent, or that by reason of physical or mental ill health the spouse is incapable of making an application for an adoption order. Any documentary evidence on which the applicant proposes to rely should be attached to the application. The name and address (if known) of the spouse should be supplied, and the marriage certificate (or other evidence of marriage) should be attached.

Paragraph 4: State the reason to be relied upon eg that the other natural parent is dead, or cannot be found, or that there is some other reason, which should be specified, justifying his or her exclusion. Documentary evidence, eg a death certificate, should be supplied where appropriate.

Paragraph 5: A separate health report is required in respect of each applicant, and the report must have been made during the period of three months before the date of the application. No report is required, however, if the child was placed for adoption with the applicant by an adoption agency, or if he is the child of the applicant or either of them.

PART 2

Particulars of the child.

6. *Identity, etc*

The child is of the        sex and is not and has not been married. He/she was born on the       day of          19   and is the person to whom the attached birth/adoption certificate relates (or was born on or about the      day of 19  , in           ). He/she is a        national.

(7. *Health*

A report on the health of the child, made by a registered medical practitioner on the       day of          19  , is attached.)

(8. The child is free for adoption pursuant to section 18 of the Children Act 1976, and I/we attach hereto the order of the            court, dated           , to that effect. The parental responsibility for the child was thereby vested in           (and was transferred to          by order of the           court under section 21 of the 1976 Act on         19  ).)

(9. *Parentage, etc*

The child is the child of          whose last known address was (*or* deceased) and          whose last known address was         (*or* deceased).)

(10. The guardian(s) of the child (other than the mother or the father of the child) is/are        of          (and          of          ).)

(*11. Parental agreement*

I/We understand that the said            (and            ) is/are willing to agree to the making of an adoption order in pursuance of my/our application.)

(12. I/we request the court to dispense with the agreement of            (and            ) on the ground(s) that            (and            ) and there are attached hereto three copies of a statement of the facts upon which I/we intend to rely.)

(*13. Persons by whom child looked after*

The child is being looked after by            (who have parental responsibility for him).)

(*14. Maintenance*

            of            is liable by virtue of an order made by the            court at            on the            day of            19  , (*or* by an agreement dated the    day of            19  ) to contribute to the maintenance of the child.)

*15. Proposed names*

If an adoption order is made in pursuance of this application, the child is to be known by the following names:

Surname
Other names

*Notes*

Paragraph 6: If the child has previously been adopted a certified copy of the entry in the Adopted Children Register should be attached and not a certified copy of the original entry in the Registers of Births. Where a certificate is not attached, enter the place (including the country) of birth if known.

Paragraph 7: The report must have been made during the period of three months before the date of the application. No report is required, however, if the child was placed for adoption with the applicant by an adoption agency, or if he is the child of the applicant or either of them.

Paragraph 8: The order made by the court freeing the child for adoption and any order made under section 21 of the 1976 Act should be attached.

Paragraph 9: This paragraph and paragraphs 10 to 14 only apply if the child is not free for adoption. If the father and mother of the child were not married to each other at the time of his birth, and a court has made an order giving the father parental responsibility for the child, give details of the order under paragraph 19.

Paragraph 10: Enter particulars of any person appointed under section 5 of the 1989 Act to be a guardian. Do not include any person who has the custody of the child only. Delete this paragraph if the child has no guardian.

Paragraphs 11 and 12: Enter either in paragraph 11 or 12 the names of the persons mentioned in paragraphs 9 and 10, except that if the father and mother of the child were not married at the time of his birth the father of the child should be entered only if a court has made an order giving the father parental responsibility for the child. Where it is sought to dispense with parental agreement, enter in paragraph 12 one or more of the grounds set out in section 16(2) of the 1976 Act.

Paragraph 13: This paragraph should be completed where the child is being looked after by a local authority or a voluntary organisation.

Paragraph 14: This paragraph should be completed where some person or body is liable to contribute to the maintenance of the child under a court order or agreement.

PART 3

*General*

16. The child has lived with me/us continuously since the        day of 19    (and has accordingly had his home with me/us for the five years preceding the date of this application).

17. The child was (placed with me/us for adoption on the        day of 19   by         , an adoption agency) (*or* received into my/our home in the following circumstances:

(18. I/we/one of us (namely      ) notified the        Council on the      day of       19  , of my/our intention to apply for an adoption order in respect of the child.)

19. No proceedings relating in whole or in part to the child other than as stated in paragraph 8 have been completed or commenced in any court in England and Wales or elsewhere (except        ).

20. I/we have not received or given any payment or reward for, or in consideration of, the adoption of the child, for any agreement to the making of an adoption order, the transfer of the home of the child with a view to adoption or the making of any arrangements for adoption (except as follows:       ).

21. As far as I/we know, the only person(s) or bod(y)(ies) who have taken part in the arrangements for the child's adoption are

(22. For the purpose of this application reference may be made to        of      .)

(23. I/we desire that my/our identity should be kept confidential, and the serial number of this application is      .)

I/we accordingly apply for an adoption order in respect of the child.

Dated this      day of          19  .

                                        Signature(s)

*Notes*

Paragraphs 16 and 17: Under section 13 of the 1976 Act, an adoption order cannot be made unless the child has had his home with the applicants or one of them:

(a) for at least 13 weeks if the applicant or one of them is a parent, step-parent or relative of the child or if the child was placed with the applicant by an adoption agency or in pursuance of an order of the High Court;

(b) for at least 12 months in any other case.

Paragraph 18: Notice does not have to be given if the child was placed with the applicant by an adoption agency. Where notice does have to be given, no order can be made until the expiration of three months from the date of the notice.

Paragraph 19: The nature of the proceedings and the date and effect of any orders made should be stated. The court cannot proceed with the application if a previous application made by the same applicant in relation to the child was refused, unless one of the conditions of section 24(1) of the 1976 Act is satisfied. The court must dismiss the application if it considers that, where the application is made by a married couple of whom one is a parent and the other a step-parent of the child, or by a step-parent of the child alone, the matter would be better dealt with under Part I of the Children Act 1989.

Paragraph 21: Enter the name and address of the adoption agency or individual who took part in the arrangements for placing the child for adoption in the home of the applicant.

Paragraph 22: Where the applicant or one of the applicants is a parent of the child, or a relative as defined by section 72 of the 1976 Act or the child was placed with the applicant by an adoption agency, no referee need be named.

Paragraph 23: If the applicant wishes his identity to be kept confidential, the serial number obtained under rule 14 should be given.

FORM 7                                                                                        Rule 20

AGREEMENT TO AN ADOPTION ORDER

IF YOU ARE IN ANY DOUBT ABOUT YOUR LEGAL RIGHTS YOU SHOULD OBTAIN LEGAL ADVICE
**BEFORE** SIGNING THIS FORM

Whereas an application is to be/has been made by               and               (*or* under serial No     ) for an adoption order in respect of               , a child;

And whereas the child is the person to whom the birth certificate attached marked 'A' relates:

(And whereas the child is at least six weeks old:)

I, the undersigned               of               being a parent/guardian of the child hereby state as follows:

(1) I understand that the effect of an adoption order will be to deprive me permanently of parental responsibility for the child and to vest that in the applicant(s); and in particular I understand that, if an order is made, I shall have no right to see or get in touch with the child or to have him/her returned to me.

(2) I further understand that the court cannot make an adoption order without the agreement of each parent or guardian of the child unless the court dispenses with an agreement on the ground that the person concerned—

(a)  cannot be found or is incapable of giving agreement, or

(b)  is withholding his agreement unreasonably, or

(c)  has persistently failed without reasonable cause to discharge parental responsibility for the child, or

(d)  has abandoned or neglected the child, or

(e)  has persistently ill-treated the child, or

(f)  has seriously ill-treated the child and the rehabilitation of the child within the household of the parent or guardian is unlikely.

(3) I further understand that when the application for an adoption order is heard this agreement may be used as evidence of my agreement to the making of the order unless I inform the court that I no longer agree.

(4) I hereby freely, and with full understanding of what is involved, agree unconditionally to the making of an adoption order in pursuance of the application.

(5) As far as I know, the only person(s) or bod(y)(ies) who has/have taken part in the arrangements for the child's adoption is/are               (and               ).

(6) I have not received or given any payment or reward for, or in consideration of, the adoption of the child, for any agreement to the making of an adoption order or placing the child for adoption with any person or making arrangements for the adoption of the child (other than payment to an adoption agency for their expenses incurred in connection with the adoption).

Signature:

This form, duly completed, was signed by the said               before me at
on the        day of               19  .

Signature:
Address:
Description:

*Notes*

Preamble: Insert either the name(s) of the applicant(s) or the serial No assigned to the applicant(s) for the purposes of the application.

Insert the first name(s) and surname of the child as known to the person giving agreement.

If the child has previously been adopted a certified copy of the entry in the Adopted Children Register should be attached and not a certified copy of the original entry in the Registers of Births.

Where two or more forms of agreement are supplied to the court at the same time they may both or all refer to a certificate attached to one of the forms of agreement.

A father who was not married to the mother of a child at the time of his birth is not a parent for this purpose, but is a guardian if a court has made an order giving him parental responsibility for the child; 'guardian' also means a person appointed under section 5 of the 1989 Act to be the guardian of the child.

Paragraph 3: Notice will be given of the hearing of the application and of the court by which it is to be heard. After the making of the application a parent or guardian who has agreed to the making of an adoption order cannot remove the child from the applicant's home without leave of the court.

Paragraph 5: Enter the name and address of the adoption agency or individual who took part in the arrangements for placing the child in the home of the applicant(s).

Witness statement: In England and Wales the document should be witnessed by the reporting officer. In Scotland, it should be witnessed by a Justice of the Peace or a Sheriff, and in Northern Ireland by a Justice of the Peace. Outside the United Kingdom it should be witnessed by a person authorised by law in the place where the document is signed to administer an oath for any judicial or legal purpose, a British consular officer, a notary public, or, if the person executing the document is serving in the regular armed forces of the Crown, an officer holding a commission in any of those forces.

FORM 8                                                                     Rule 21(1)

NOTICE OF HEARING OF AN APPLICATION FOR AN ADOPTION ORDER

................Family Proceedings Court

To                    of

Whereas an application for an adoption order in respect of            , a child of the
        sex born on the          day of            19  , has been made (by
(and              ) of                    ) (*or* under the serial number      ) and whereas
            (and              ) was/were appointed reporting officer(s) (and
            was appointed *guardian ad litem* [children's guardian] of the child);


TAKE NOTICE:

(1. That the said application will be heard before the court at            on the
day of                19  , at      o'clock and that you may then appear and be heard
on the question whether an adoption order should be made.)

(2. That if you wish to appear and be heard on the question whether an adoption
order should be made, you should give notice to the court on or before the    day of
            19  , in order that a time may be fixed for your appearance.)

3. That you are not obliged to attend the hearing unless you wish to do so or the
court notifies you that your attendance is necessary.

4. That while the application is pending, a parent or guardian of the child who
has agreed to the making of an order must not, except with the leave of the court,
remove the child from the home of the applicant.

(5. That the application states that the child has had his home with the applicant for the five years preceding the application and accordingly, if that is correct, no person is entitled, against the will of the applicant, to remove the child from the applicant's home except with the leave of the court or under authority conferred by an enactment or on the arrest of the child.)

(6. That the court has been requested to dispense with your agreement to the making of an order on the ground(s) that            and a statement of the facts on which the applicant intends to rely is attached.)

It would assist the court if you would complete the attached form and return it to me by

Dated the        day of                  19    .

Justices' Clerk

To the Clerk to the Justices.

Application for an adoption order: (*state name of child*)
I received the notice of the hearing of the application on the      day of           19    .
I wish/do not wish to oppose the application.
I wish/do not wish to appear and be heard on the question whether an order should be made.

(signature)<br>(address)<br>(date)

*Notes*

When this form is used under rule 25 to give notice of a further hearing of an application it is to be amended so as to refer to a further hearing and so as to give particulars of the interim order.

Preamble: Enter the name(s) and surname of the child as shown in the application. Enter the name of the applicant(s) unless the applicant has obtained a serial number, in which case the second part in brackets should be completed.

Paragraphs 1 and 2: Paragraph 1 should be completed and paragraph 2 struck out where the notice is addressed to any respondent where the applicant does not wish his identity to be kept confidential. When a serial number has been assigned to the applicant and the notice is addressed to an individual respondent other than the spouse of the applicant, paragraph 1 should be struck out and paragraph 2 completed.

Paragraph 5: This paragraph should be deleted except where it appears from the application that the child has had his home with the applicant for five years.

Paragraph 6: Unless deleted, this paragraph should contain the grounds specified in the application.

**Note.** Words 'guardian ad litem' substituted by words 'children's guardian' in square brackets by SI 2001/820, r 2, 3, as from 1 April 2001.

FORM 9                                                      Rule 28(1)

APPLICATION TO AMEND OR REVOKE ADOPTION ORDER

To the                          ....................Family Proceedings Court

1. Identification of the adoption order to be amended or revoked

Name of adopters:
Date of adoption order:

2. Particulars of the applicant

Name:

Address:

Relationship (if any) to the child (*or* if no such relationship, state reason for application):

If application is made under section 50 of the 1976 Act, state the amendments desired and the facts relied on in support of the application:

If application is made under section 50 of the 1976 Act, state the facts relied on in support of the application:

I apply for the adoption order to be amended or revoked in accordance with this application.

Dated this     day of          19   .

Signature

FORM 10                                                            Rule 31(1)

ORDER FREEING A CHILD FOR ADOPTION

....................Family Proceedings Court

    Whereas an application has been made by          of          , being an adoption agency, for an order freeing for adoption          , a child of the sex, the child of          (and          );

    It is ordered that the child be freed for adoption and that parental responsibility for the child be vested in the applicant;

(and as regards costs it is ordered that          ;)

(and whereas the precise date of the child's birth has not been proved to the satisfaction of the court but the court has determined the probable date of his/her birth to be the     day of          19   ;)

(and whereas it has been proved to the satisfaction of the court that the child was born in          (*country*);)

(and whereas the place of birth of the child has not been proved to the satisfaction of the court (but it appears probable that the child was born in the United Kingdom, the Channel Islands or the Isle of Man, the child is treated as having been born in the registration district of          and sub-district of          in the county of          );)

(and whereas it has been proved to the satisfaction of the court that the child is identical with          to whom the entry numbered          made on the     day of          19   , in the Register of Births for the registration district of          and sub-district of          in the county of          relates (*or* with          to whom the entry numbered          and dated the     day of          19   , in the Adopted Children Register relates);)

    It is directed that this order is sufficient proof of the above particulars for the purposes of any future adoption application in respect of the child.

    And it is further recorded that          (and          ) being a parent or guardian of the child made a declaration under section 18(6) of the 1976 Act that he/she prefers not to be involved in future questions concerning the adoption of the child.

Dated this     day of          19   .

Justice of the Peace<br>
[*or* By order of the Court<br>
Clerk of the Court]

FORM 11                                                                     Rule 31(1)

ORDER REVOKING AN ORDER FREEING A CHILD FOR ADOPTION/DISMISSING AN APPLICATION
TO REVOKE AN ORDER FREEING A CHILD FOR ADOPTION

......................Family Proceedings Court

Whereas an application has been made by              of              (and
              ) for an order revoking an order freeing for adoption              , a child
of the        sex, the child of              (and              ), such order having been
made by the                    court on the      day of              19   :

It is ordered that the said order be revoked and that parental responsibility for
the child be vested in                    (and              );
(and it is ordered that              of              do make periodical payments
to the child in the sum of £        payable                    ;)

It is ordered that the application be dismissed (and that the applicant(s) shall
not make further application under section 20 of the 1976 Act);
(and it is ordered that              , the adoption agency which obtained the
order under section 18 of the 1976 Act, is released from the duty of complying
further with section 19(3) of that Act as respects the applicant(s).)

(And as regards costs is ordered that                    .)

Dated this      day of                    19   .

Justice of the Peace
[*or* By order of the Court
Clerk of the Court]

FORM 12                                                                     Rule 31(1)

INTERIM ORDER

......................Family Proceedings Court

Whereas an application has been made by              of              (and
              ) for an adoption order in respect of              a child of the        sex,
the child/adopted child of              (and              );

It is ordered that the determination of the application be postponed and that the
applicant(s) do have parental responsibility for the child until the      day of
19   , by way of a probationary period (*or* that the determination of the application
be postponed to the      day of              19   , and that the applicant(s) do have
parental responsibility for the child until that day by way of a probationary period)
(upon the following terms, namely              );
(and as regards costs it is ordered that              ;)
(and it is ordered that the application be further heard before the court at
on the      day of              19   , at      o'clock.)

Dated this      day of                    19   .

Justice of the Peace
[*or* By order of the Court
Clerk of the Court]

FORM 13                                                                     Rule 31(1)

ADOPTION ORDER

......................Family Proceedings Court

Whereas an application has been made by              of              whose
occupation is              (and              whose occupation is              ) for an
adoption order in respect of              , a child of the        sex, the child/adopted
child of              (and              );

It is ordered that the applicant(s) do adopt the child and that parental responsibility be vested in the applicant(s).

(And as regards costs, it is ordered that                ;)

(And it is recorded that the                , being an adoption agency, placed the child for adoption with the applicant(s)/the                Council was notified of the applicant(s) intention to adopt the child;)

(And whereas the child was freed for adoption by the                court on the day of                19   ;)

(And whereas the precise date of the child's birth has not been proved to the satisfaction of the court but the court has determined the probable date of his/her birth to be the                day of                19   ;)

(And whereas it has been proved to the satisfaction of the court that the child was born in                (*country*);)

(And whereas the place of birth of the child has not been proved to the satisfaction of the court (but it appears probable that the child was born in the United Kingdom, the Channel Islands or the Isle of Man, the child is treated as having been born in the registration district of                and sub-district of                in the county of                );)

(And whereas it has been proved to the satisfaction of the court that the child was born on the   day of                19   (and is identical (with                to whom the entry numbered                made on the   day of                19   , in the Register of Births for the registration district of                and sub-district of                in the county of                relates) (*or* with                to whom the entry numbered                and dated the   day of                19   , in the Adopted Children Register relates);)

(And whereas the name or names and surname stated in the application as those by which the child is to be known are                ;)

It is directed that the Registrar General shall make in the Adopted Children Register an entry in the form specified by regulations made by him recording the particulars set out in this order;

(And it is further directed that the aforesaid entry in the Register of Births/ Adopted Children Register be marked with the words 'adopted'/'readopted').

Dated this       day of                19   .

Justice of the Peace
[*or* By order of the Court
Clerk of the Court]

FORM 14

REGISTER OF ADOPTIONS

In the [county of      ] [Petty Sessional Division of      ].

Rule 32(1)

| No | Date of decision | Name and address of applicant | Name of child | Sex of child prior to adoption | Age of child | Name of child after adoption | Minute of decision | Signature of justice adjudicating |
|----|------------------|-------------------------------|---------------|--------------------------------|--------------|------------------------------|--------------------|-----------------------------------|
| | | | | | | | | |

SCHEDULE 2                                                                      Rule 4(4)

MATTERS TO BE COVERED IN REPORTS SUPPLIED UNDER RULES 4(4), 22(1) or 22(2)

So far as is practicable, the report supplied by the adoption agency or, in the case of a report supplied under rule 22(2), the local authority shall include all the following particulars:

1. *The Child*

   (a) Name, sex, date and place of birth and address;
   (b) whether the child's father and mother were married to each other at the time of his birth;
   (c) nationality;
   (d) physical description;
   (e) personality and social development;
   (f) religion, including details of baptism, confirmation or equivalent ceremonies;
   (g) details of any wardship proceedings and of any court orders relating to parental responsibility for the child or to maintenance and residence;
   (h) details of any brothers and sisters, including dates of birth, arrangements concerning with whom they are to live and whether any brother or sister is the subject of a parallel application;
   (i) extent of contact with members of the child's natural family and, if the father and mother of the child were not married to each other at the time of his birth, his father, and in each case the nature of the relationship enjoyed;
   (j) if the child has been looked after by, or is in the care of a local authority, or has been cared for by a voluntary organisation, details (including dates) of any placements with foster parents, or other arrangements in respect of the care of the child, including particulars of the persons with whom the child has had his home and observations on the care provided;
   (k) date and circumstances of placement with prospective adopter;
   (l) names, addresses and types of schools attended, with dates, and educational attainments;
   (m) any special needs in relation to the child's health (whether physical or mental) and his emotional and behavioural development and whether he is subject to a statement under the Education Act 1981;
   (n) what, if any, rights to or interests in property or any claim to damages, under the Fatal Accidents Act 1976 or otherwise, the child stands to retain or lose if adopted;
   (o) wishes and feelings in relation to adoption and the application, including any wishes in respect of religious and cultural upbringing; and
   (p) any other relevant information which might assist the court.

2. *Each Natural Parent, including where appropriate the father who was not married to the child's mother at the time of his birth*

   (a) Name, date and place of birth and address;
   (b) marital status and date and place of marriage (if any);
   (c) past and present relationship (if any) with the other natural parent, including comments on its stability;
   (d) physical description;
   (e) personality;
   (f) religion;
   (g) educational attainments;
   (h) past and present occupations and interests;
   (i) so far as available, names and brief details of the personal circumstances of the parents and any brothers and sisters of the natural parent, with their ages or ages at death;

(j)  wishes and feelings in relation to adoption and the application, including any wishes in respect of the child's religious and cultural upbringing;
(k)  reasons why any of the above information is unavailable; and
(l)  any other relevant information which might assist the court.

### 3. Guardian

Give the details required under paragraph 2(a), (f), (j), and (l).

### 4. Prospective Adopter

(a)  Name, date and place of birth and address;
(b)  relationship (if any) to the child;
(c)  marital status, date and place of marriage (if any) and comments on stability of relationship;
(d)  details of any previous marriage;
(e)  if a parent and step-parent are applying, the reason why they prefer adoption to a residence order;
(f)  if a natural parent is applying alone, the reasons for the exclusion of the other parent;
(g)  if a married person is applying alone, the reasons for this;
(h)  physical description;
(i)  personality;
(j)  religion, and whether willing to follow any wishes of the child or his parents or guardian in respect of the child's religious and cultural upbringing;
(k)  educational attainments;
(l)  past and present occupations and interests;
(m) particulars of the home and living conditions (and particulars of any home where the prospective adopter proposes to live with the child, if different);
(n)  details of income and comments on the living standards of the household;
(o)  details of other members of the household (including any children of the prospective adopter even if not resident in the household);
(p)  details of the parents and any brothers or sisters of the prospective adopter, with their ages or ages at death;
(q)  attitudes to the proposed adoption of such other members of the prospective adopter's household and family as the adoption agency or, as the case may be, the local authority considers appropriate;
(r)  previous experience of caring for children as step-parent, foster parent, child-minder or prospective adopter and assessment of ability in this respect, together where appropriate with assessment of ability in bringing up the prospective adopter's own children;
(s)  reasons for wishing to adopt the child and extent of understanding of the nature and effect of adoption;
(t)  any hopes and expectations for the child's future;
(u)  assessment of ability to bring up the child throughout his childhood;
(v)  details of any adoption allowance payable;
(w) confirmation that any referees have been interviewed, with a report of their views and opinion of the weight to be placed thereon; and
(x)  any other relevant information which might assist the court.

### 5. Actions of the adoption agency or local authority supplying the report

(a)  Reports under rules 4(4) or 22(1)—
    (i)  brief account of the agency's actions in the case, with particulars and dates of all written information and notices given to the child, his natural parents and the prospective adopter;

      (ii)  details of alternatives to adoption considered;

      (iii)  reasons for considering that adoption would be in the child's best interests (with date of relevant decision); and

      (iv)  reasons for considering that the prospective adopter would be suitable to be an adoptive parent and that he would be suitable for this child (with dates of relevant decisions) or, if the child has not yet been placed for adoption, reasons for considering that he is likely to be so placed;

OR

  (b)  Reports under rule 22(2)—

      (i)  confirmation that notice was given under section 22 of the 1976 Act, with the date of that notice;

      (ii)  brief account of the local authority's actions in the case; and

      (iii)  account of investigations whether child was placed in contravention of section 11 of the 1976 Act.

## 6. *Generally*

  (a)  Whether any respondent appears to be under the age of majority or under a mental disability; and

  (b)  whether, in the opinion of the body supplying the report, any other person should be made a respondent (for example, a person who was not married to the mother of the child at the time of his birth and who claims to be the father of the child, a spouse or ex-spouse of a natural parent, a relative of a deceased parent, or a person with parental responsibility).

## 7. *Conclusions*

(This part of the report should contain more than a simple synopsis of the information above. As far as possible, the court should be given a fuller picture of the child, his natural parents and, where appropriate, the prospective adopter.)

  (a)  Except where the applicant or one of them is a parent of the child, a summary by the medical adviser to the body supplying the report, of the health history and state of health of the child, his natural parents and, if appropriate, the prospective adopter, with comments on the implications for the order sought and on how any special health needs of the child might be met;

  (b)  opinion on whether making the order sought would be in the child's best long-term interests, and on how any special emotional, behavioural and educational needs of the child might be met;

  (c)  opinion on the effect on the child's natural parents of making the order sought;

  (d)  if the child has been placed for adoption, opinion on the likelihood of full integration of the child into the household, family and community of the prospective adopter, and on whether the proposed adoption would be in the best long-term interests of the prospective adopter;

  (e)  opinion, if appropriate, on the relative merits of adoption and a residence order; and

  (f)  final conclusions and recommendations whether the order sought should be made (and, if not, alternative proposals).

SCHEDULE 3                                            Rule 15(4)

REPORTS ON THE HEALTH OF THE CHILD AND OF THE APPLICANT(S)

This information is required for reports on the health of a child and of his prospective adopter(s). Its purpose is to build up a full picture of their health history and current state of health, including strengths and weaknesses. This will enable the local authority's medical adviser to base his advice to the court on the fullest possible information, when commenting on the health implications of the proposed adoption. The reports made by the examining doctor should cover, as far as practicable, the following matters.

## 1. The Child

Name, date of birth, sex, weight and height.
- A.  A health history of each natural parent, so far as is possible, including:
  - (i)   name, date of birth, sex, weight and height;
  - (ii)  a family health history, covering the parents, the brothers and sisters and the other children of the natural parent, with details of any serious physical or mental illness and inherited and congenital disease;
  - (iii) past health history, including details of any serious physical or mental illness, disability, accident, hospital admission or attendance at an out-patient department, and in each case any treatment given;
  - (iv)  a full obstetric history of the mother, including any problems in the ante-natal, labour and post-natal periods, with the results of any tests carried out during or immediately after pregnancy;
  - (v)   details of any present illness including treatment and prognosis;
  - (vi)  any other relevant information which might assist the medical adviser; and
  - (vii) the name and address of any doctor(s) who might be able to provide further information about any of the above matters.
- B.  A neo-natal report on the child, including—
  - (i)   details of the birth, and any complications;
  - (ii)  results of a physical examination and screening tests;
  - (iii) details of any treatment given;
  - (iv)  details of any problem in management and feeding;
  - (v)   any other relevant information which might assist the medical adviser; and
  - (vi)  the name and address of any doctor(s) who might be able to provide further information about any of the above matters.
- C.  A full health history and examination of the child, including—
  - (i)   details of any serious illness, disability, accident, hospital admission or attendance at an out-patient department, and in each case any treatment given;
  - (ii)  details and dates of immunisations;
  - (iii) a physical and developmental assessment according to age, including an assessment of vision and hearing and of neurological, speech and language development and any evidence of emotional disorder;
  - (iv)  for a child over five years of age, the school health history (if available);
  - (v)   any other relevant information which might assist the medical adviser; and
  - (vi)  the name and address of any doctor(s) who might be able to provide further information about any of the above matters.
- D.  The signature, name, address and qualifications of the registered medical practitioner who prepared the report, and the date of the report and of the examinations carried out.

## 2. The Applicant

(If there is more than one applicant, a report on each applicant should be supplied covering all the matters listed below.)

A.    (i)   name, date of birth, sex, weight and height;

      (ii)  a family health history, covering the parents, the brothers and sisters and the children of the applicant, with details of any serious physical or mental illness and inherited and congenital disease;

    (iii)  marital history, including (if applicable) reasons for inability to have children;

    (iv)  past health history, including details of any serious physical or mental illness, disability, accident, hospital admission or attendance at an out-patient department, and in each case any treatment given;

     (v)  obstetric history (if applicable);

    (vi)  details of any present illness, including treatment and prognosis;

   (vii)  a full medical examination;

  (viii)  details of any daily consumption of alcohol, tobacco and habit-forming drugs;

    (ix)  any other relevant information which might assist the medical adviser; and

     (x)  the name and address of any doctor(s) who might be able to provide further information about any of the above matters.

B. The signature, name, address and qualifications of the registered medical practitioner who prepared the report, and the date of the report and of the examinations carried out.

## EVIDENCE (PROCEEDINGS IN OTHER JURISDICTIONS) (ANGUILLA) ORDER 1986

**Dated** 12 February 1986

**SI 1986 No 218**

At the Court at Buckingham Palace, the 12th day of February 1986

Present,

The Queen's Most Excellent Majesty in Council

Her Majesty, in exercise of the powers conferred upon Her by section 10(3) of the Evidence (Proceedings in Other Jurisdictions) Act 1975, is pleased, by and with the advice of Her Privy Council, to order, and it is hereby ordered, as follows—

**1.** This Order may be cited as the Evidence (Proceedings in Other Jurisdictions) (Anguilla) Order 1986 and shall come into operation on 1 April 1986.

**2.** Sections 1 to 3, 5, 6 and 8 to 10 of, and Schedule 2 to, the Evidence (Proceedings in Other Jurisdictions) Act 1975, with the exceptions, adaptations and modifications specified in the Schedule hereto, shall extend to Anguilla.

SCHEDULE TO THE ORDER                           Article 2

PROVISIONS OF THE EVIDENCE (PROCEEDINGS IN OTHER JURISDICTIONS) ACT 1975 AS EXTENDED TO ANGUILLA

*Evidence for civil proceedings*

**1.** Where an application is made to the Eastern Caribbean Supreme Court for an order for evidence to be obtained in Anguilla, and the court is satisfied—

  (a) that the application is made in pursuance of a request issued by or on behalf of a court or tribunal ('the requesting court') exercising jurisdiction in a country or territory outside Anguilla; and

(b) that the evidence to which the application relates is to be obtained for the purposes of civil proceedings which either have been instituted before the requesting court or whose institution before that court is contemplated,

the Eastern Caribbean Supreme Court shall have the powers conferred on it by the following provisions of this Act.

**2.** (1) Subject to the provisions of this section, the Eastern Caribbean Supreme Court shall have power, on any such application as is mentioned in section 1 above, by order to make such provision for obtaining evidence in Anguilla as may appear to the court to be appropriate for the purpose of giving effect to the request in pursuance of which the application is made; and any such order may require a person specified therein to take such steps as the court may consider appropriate for that purpose.

(2) With prejudice to the generality of subsection (1) above but subject to the provisions of this section, an order under this section may, in particular, make provision—

(a) for the examination of witnesses, either orally or in writing;

(b) for the production of documents;

(c) for the inspection, photographing, preservation, custody or detention of any property;

(d) for the taking of samples of any property and the carrying out of any experiments on or with any property;

(e) for the medical examination of any person;

(f) without prejudice to paragraph (e) above, for the taking and testing of samples of blood from any person.

(3) An order under this section shall not require any particular steps to be taken unless they are steps which can be required to be taken by way of obtaining evidence for the purposes of civil proceedings in the court making the order (whether or not proceedings of the same description as those to which the application for the order relates); but this subsection shall not preclude the making of an order requiring a person to give testimony (either orally or in writing) otherwise than on oath where this is asked for by the requesting court.

(4) An order under this section shall not require a person—

(a) to state what documents relevant to the proceedings to which the application for the order relates are or have been in his possession, custody or power, or

(b) to produce any documents other than particular documents specified in the order as being documents appearing to the court making the order to be, or to be likely to be, in his possession, custody or power.

(5) A person who, by virtue of an order under this section, is required to attend at any place shall be entitled to the like conduct money and payment for expenses and loss of time as on attendance as a witness in civil proceedings before the court making the order.

**3.** (1) A person shall not be compelled by virtue of an order under section 2 above to give any evidence which he could not be compelled to give—

(a) in civil proceedings in Anguilla; or

(b) subject to subsection (2) below, in civil proceedings in the country or territory in which the requesting court exercises jurisdiction.

(2) Subsection (1)(b) above shall not apply unless the claim of the person in question to be exempt from giving the evidence is either—

(a) supported by a statement contained in the request (whether it is so supported unconditionally or subject to conditions that are fulfilled); or

(b) conceded by the applicant for the order;

and where such a claim made by any person is not supported or conceded as aforesaid he may (subject to the other provisions of this section) be required to give the evidence to which the claim relates but that evidence shall not be transmitted to the requesting court if that court, on the matter being referred to it, upholds the claim.

(3) Without prejudice to subsection (1) above, a person shall not be compelled by virtue of an order under section 2 above to give any evidence if his doing so would be prejudicial to the security of the United Kingdom, Anguilla or any other territory for which the United Kingdom is responsible under international law; and a certificate signed by or on behalf of the Governor to the effect that it would be so prejudicial for that person to do so shall be conclusive evidence of that fact.

(4) In this section references to giving evidence include references to answering any question and to producing any document and the reference in subsection (2) above to the transmission of evidence given by a person shall be construed accordingly.

EVIDENCE FOR CRIMINAL PROCEEDINGS

\*     \*     \*     \*     \*

EVIDENCE FOR INTERNATIONAL PROCEEDINGS

**6.** (1) The Governor may by order direct that, subject to such exceptions, adaptations or modifications as may be specified in the order, the provisions of sections 1 to 3 above shall have effect in relation to international proceedings of any description specified in the order.

(2) An order under this section may direct that the provisions of the Perjury Act 1873 shall have effect in relation to international proceedings to which the order applies as it has effect in relation to a judicial proceeding in a tribunal of a foreign state.

(3) In this section 'international proceedings' means proceedings before the International Court of Justice or any other court, tribunal, commission, body or authority (whether consisting of one or more persons) which, in pursuance of any international agreement or any resolution of the General Assembly of the United Nations, exercises any jurisdiction or performs any functions of a judicial nature or by way of arbitration, conciliation or inquiry or is appointed (whether permanently or temporarily) for the purpose of exercising any jurisdiction or performing any such functions.

*Supplementary*

**8.** (2) The enactments mentioned in Schedule 2 to this Act are hereby repealed as respects Anguilla to the extent specified in the third column of that Schedule.

(3) Nothing in this section shall affect—

(a) any application to any court or judge which is pending at the commencement of this Act;

(b) any certificate given for the purposes of any such application;

(c) any power to make an order on such an application; or

(d) the operation or enforcement of any order made on such an application.

(4) Subsection (3) above is without prejudice to section 18(2) of the Interpretation and General Clauses Act (effect of repeals).

**9.** (1) In this Act—

'civil proceedings', in relation to the requesting court, means proceedings in any civil or commercial matter;

'Eastern Caribbean Supreme Court' means the Eastern Caribbean Supreme Court established by the Anguilla, Montserrat and Virgin Islands (Supreme Court) Order 1983;

'Governor' means the Governor of Anguilla;

'property' includes any land, chattel or other corporeal property of any description;

'request' includes any commission, order or other process issued by or on behalf of the requesting court;

'requesting court' has the meaning given in section 1 above.

(3) Any power conferred by this Act to make an order includes power to revoke or vary any such order by a subsequent order.

(4) Nothing in this Act shall be construed as enabling any court to make an order that is binding on the Crown or on any person in his capacity as an officer or servant of the Crown.

(5) Except so far as the context otherwise requires, any reference in this Act to any enactment is a reference to that enactment as amended or extended by or under any other enactment.

**10.** The provisions of this Act shall come into force on such date as the Governor may by order appoint.

SCHEDULE 2 TO THE ACT                                                    Section 8(2)

REPEALS

| Chapter | Short Title | Extent |
|---|---|---|
| 19 & 20 Vict c 113. | The Foreign Tribunals Evidence Act 1856. | The whole Act. |
| 22 Vict c 20. | The Evidence by Commission Act 1859. | The whole Act. |
| 33 & 34 Vict c 52. | The Extradition Act 1870. | Section 24. |
| 48 & 49 Vict c 74. | The Evidence by Commission Act 1885. | The whole Act. |
| 1966 c 41. | The Arbitration (International Investment Disputes) Act 1966. | In section 3(1), paragraph (b). |

**Note.** This Order is printed as published: there is no Ord 7, Ord 8(1) or Ord 9(2).

## THE MAGISTRATES' COURTS (CHILD ABDUCTION AND CUSTODY) RULES 1986

**Dated** 1 July 1986

**SI 1986 No 1141**

### ARRANGEMENT OF RULES

RULE
1. Citation and commencement
2. Interpretation
3. Stay of proceedings pending in a magistrates' court
4. Dismissal of complaint
5. Resumption of proceedings after stay
6. Further stay of proceedings or dismissal of complaint
7. Notice of registration of order in respect of a child
8. Authenticated copy of magistrates' court order
9. Application for declaration of unlawful removal of a child

The Lord Chancellor, in exercise of the power conferred upon him by section 144 of the Magistrates' Courts Act 1980, as extended by sections 10 and 24 of the Child Abduction and Custody Act 1985, after consultation with the Rule Committee appointed under the said section 144, hereby makes the following Rules—

*Citation and commencement*

**1.**   These Rules may be cited as the Magistrates' Courts (Child Abduction and Custody) Rules 1986 and shall come into operation on 1 August 1986.

*Interpretation*

**2.**   In these Rules—
'complaint' includes an application under Rule 14 of the Magistrates' Courts (Children and Young Persons) Rules 1970;
'Contracting State' means a Contracting State defined in section 2 of the 1985 Act;
'the 1985 Act' means the Child Abduction and Custody Act 1985;
'the Hague Convention' means the Convention defined in section 1(1) of the 1985 Act;
'the High Court' means the High Court in England and Wales, the High Court in Northern Ireland or the High Court of Justice of the Isle of Man.

*Stay of proceedings pending in a magistrates' court*

**3.**   Where any proceedings in which a decision falls to be made on the merits of rights of custody (as construed under section 9 of the 1985 Act) are pending in a magistrates' court and that court receives notice from the High Court or the Court of Session that an application in respect of the child concerned has been made under the Hague Convention, the magistrates' court shall order that all further proceedings in the proceedings pending before it shall be stayed, and shall cause notice to be given to the parties to the proceedings accordingly.

*Dismissal of complaint*

**4.**   Where a magistrates' court which has stayed any proceedings under Rule 3 above receives notice from the High Court or the Court of Session that an order has been made under Article 12 of the Hague Convention for the return of the child concerned, the court shall dismiss the complaint and cause notice to be given to the parties to the proceedings accordingly.

*Resumption of proceedings after stay*

**5.**   Where a magistrates' court which has stayed any proceedings under Rule 3 above receives notice from the High Court or Court of Session that an order for the return of the child concerned has been refused (other than in the circumstances set out in the third paragraph of Article 12 of the Hague Convention), the court shall order that the stay be lifted, shall so notify the parties to the proceedings, and shall proceed to deal with the complaint accordingly.

*Further stay of proceedings or dismissal of complaint*

**6.**   Where a magistrates' court which has stayed any proceedings under Rule 3 above receives notice from the High Court or Court of Session that an order has been made under the third paragraph of Article 12 of the Hague Convention staying or dismissing the application thereunder, the court shall continue the stay on the proceedings pending before it or, in a case where the High Court or Court of Session has dismissed the application, dismiss the complaint, and shall cause notice to be given to the parties accordingly.

*Notice of registration of order in respect of a child*

**7.**   Where any proceedings such as are mentioned in section 20(2)(a), (b) or (c) of the 1985 Act are pending in a magistrates' court and that court receives notice from the High Court or the Court of Session that an application has been made under section 16 of that Act for the registration of a decision made in respect of the child in proceedings commenced before the proceedings which are pending (other than a decision mentioned in section 20(3) of the 1985 Act) or that such a decision has been registered under the said section 16, the court shall cause notice to be given to the parties to those proceedings that it has received notice of the application or of the registration, as the case may be.

*Authenticated copy of magistrates' court order*

**8.**   (1) A person who wishes to make an application under the Hague Convention in a Contracting State other than the United Kingdom and who wishes to obtain from a magistrates' court an authenticated copy of a decision of that court relating to the child in respect of whom the application is to be made shall apply in writing to the justices' clerk for that court.
  (2)  An application under paragraph (1) above shall specify—
  (a)  the name and date or approximate date of birth of the child concerned;
  (b)  the date or approximate date of the proceedings in which the decision of the court was given, and the nature of those proceedings;
  (c)  the Contracting State in which the application in respect of the child is to be made;
  (d)  the relationship of the applicant to the child concerned;
  (e)  the postal address of the applicant.
  (3)  A justices' clerk who receives an application for an authenticated copy of a decision under this rule shall send by post to the applicant at the address indicated in the application for the purposes an authenticated copy of the decision concerned.
  (4)  For the purposes of paragraph (3) of this rule a copy of a decision shall be deemed to be authenticated if it is accompanied by a statement signed by the justices' clerk that it is a true copy of the decision concerned.

*Application for declaration of unlawful removal of a child*

**9.**   An application to a magistrates' court under section 23(2) of the 1985 Act (declaration that the removal of a child from the United Kingdom has been unlawful) may be made orally or in writing in the course of the custody proceedings (as defined in section 27 of that Act).

## CHILD ABDUCTION AND CUSTODY (PARTIES TO CONVENTIONS) ORDER 1986

**Dated** 8 July 1986

**SI 1986 No 1159**

Her Majesty, in exercise of the powers conferred on Her by sections 2 and 13 of the Child Abduction and Custody Act 1985, is pleased, by and with the advice of Her Privy Council, to order, and it is hereby ordered, as follows—
**1.**   This Order may be cited as the Child Abduction and Custody (Parties to Conventions) Order 1986, and shall come into operation on 1 August 1986.

**2.** (1) In this Article of, and in Schedule 1 to, this Order, 'the Convention' means the Convention on the Civil Aspects of International Child Abduction which was signed at The Hague on 25 October 1980.

    (2) (a) The Contracting States to the Convention shall be as specified in the first column of Schedule 1 to this Order.

        (b) Where the Convention applies, or applies only, to a particular territory or particular territories specified in a declaration made by a Contracting State under Article 39 or 40 of the Convention, the territory or territories in question shall be as specified in the second column of Schedule 1 to this Order.

        (c) The date of the coming into force of the Convention as between the United Kingdom and any State or territory so specified shall be as specified in the third column of Schedule 1 to this Order.

**3.** (1) In this Article of, and in Schedule 2 to, this Order, 'the Convention' means the European Convention on Recognition and Enforcement of Decisions concerning Custody of Children and on the Restoration of Custody of Children which was signed in Luxembourg on 20 May 1980.

    (2) (a) The Contracting States to the Convention shall be as specified in the first column of Schedule 2 to this Order.

        (b) Where the Convention applies, or applies only, to a particular territory or particular territories specified by a Contracting State under Article 24 or 25 of the Convention, the territory or territories in question shall be as specified in the second column of Schedule 2 to this Order.

        (c) The date of the coming into force of the Convention as between the United Kingdom and any State or territory so specified shall be as specified in the third column of Schedule 2 to this Order.

[SCHEDULE 1

Article 2

CONVENTION ON THE CIVIL ASPECTS OF INTERNATIONAL CHILD ABDUCTION, THE HAGUE, 25TH OCTOBER 1980

| *Contracting States to the Convention* | *Territories specified in Declarations under Article 39 or 40 of the Convention* | *Date of Coming into Force as between the United Kingdom and the State or Territory* |
| --- | --- | --- |
| Argentina | — | 1st June 1991 |
| Australia | Australian States and mainland Territories | 1st January 1987 |
| Austria | — | 1st October 1988 |
| The Bahamas | — | 1st January 1994 |
| Belarus | — | 1st September 2003 |
| Belgium | — | 1st May 1999 |
| Belize | — | 1st October 1989 |
| Bosnia and Herzegovina | — | 7th April 1992 |
| Burkina Faso | — | 1st August 1992 |
| Canada | Ontario | 1st August 1986 |
| | New Brunswick | 1st August 1986 |
| | British Columbia | 1st August 1986 |
| | Manitoba | 1st August 1986 |
| | Nova Scotia | 1st August 1986 |
| | Newfoundland | 1st August 1986 |

| Contracting States to the Convention | Territories specified in Declarations under Article 39 or 40 of the Convention | Date of Coming into Force as between the United Kingdom and the State or Territory |
| --- | --- | --- |
| | Prince Edward Island | 1st August 1986 |
| | Quebec | 1st August 1986 |
| | Yukon Territory | 1st August 1986 |
| | Saskatchewan | 1st November 1986 |
| | Alberta | 1st February 1987 |
| | Northwest Territories | 1st April 1988 |
| Chile | — | 1st May 1994 |
| China | Hong Kong Special Administrative Region | 1st September 1997 |
| | Macau Special Administrative Region | 1st March 1999 |
| Colombia | — | 1st March 1996 |
| Croatia | — | 1st December 1991 |
| Cyprus | — | 1st February 1995 |
| Czech Republic | — | 1st March 1998 |
| Denmark | — | 1st July 1991 |
| Ecuador | — | 1st April 1992 |
| Estonia | — | 1st September 2003 |
| Fiji | — | 1st September 2003 |
| Finland | — | 1st August 1994 |
| France | — | 1st August 1986 |
| Germany | — | 1st December 1990 |
| Georgia | — | 1st October 1997 |
| Germany | — | 1st December 1990 |
| Greece | — | 1st June 1993 |
| Honduras | — | 1st March 1994 |
| Hungary | — | 1st September 1986 |
| Iceland | — | 1st November 1996 |
| Ireland | — | 1st October 1991 |
| Israel | — | 1st December 1991 |
| Italy | — | 1st May 1995 |
| Latvia | — | 1st September 2003 |
| Luxembourg | — | 1st January 1987 |
| Macedonia | — | 1st December 1991 |
| Malta | — | 1st March 2002 |
| Mauritius | — | 1st June 1993 |
| Mexico | — | 1st September 1991 |
| Monaco | — | 1st February 1993 |
| Netherlands | — | 1st September 1990 |
| New Zealand | — | 1st August 1991 |
| Norway | — | 1st April 1989 |
| Panama | — | 1st May 1994 |
| Peru | — | 1st September 2003 |
| Poland | — | 1st November 1992 |
| Portugal | — | 1st August 1986 |
| Romania | — | 1st February 1993 |
| St Kitts and Nevis | — | 1st August 1994 |
| Serbia and Montenegro | — | 27th April 1992 |
| Slovakia | — | 1st February 2001 |
| Slovenia | — | 1st June 1994 |

| Contracting States to the Convention | Territories specified in Declarations under Article 39 or 40 of the Convention | Date of Coming into Force as between the United Kingdom and the State or Territory |
|---|---|---|
| South Africa | — | 1st October 1997 |
| Spain | — | 1st September 1987 |
| Sweden | — | 1st June 1989 |
| Switzerland | — | 1st August 1986 |
| Turkey | — | 1st August 2001 |
| Turkmenistan | — | 1st March 1998 |
| United States of America | — | 1st July 1988 |
| Uruguay | — | 1st September 2003 |
| Uzbekistan | — | 1st September 2003 |
| Venezuela | — | 1st January 1997 |
| Zimbabwe | — | 1st July 1995] |

**Note:** Substituted by SI 2003/1518, art 3, Schedule, as from 12 June 2003.

[SCHEDULE 2                                                                                          Article 3

EUROPEAN CONVENTION ON RECOGNITION AND ENFORCEMENT OF DECISIONS CONCERNING CUSTODY OF CHILDREN AND ON THE RESTORATION OF CUSTODY OF CHILDREN, LUXEMBOURG, 20TH MAY 1980

| Contracting States to the Convention | Territories specified in Declarations under Article 24 or 25 of the Convention | Date of Coming into Force of Convention as between the United Kingdom and the State or Territory |
|---|---|---|
| Austria | — | 1st August 1986 |
| Belgium | — | 1st August 1986 |
| Cyprus | — | 1st October 1986 |
| Czech Republic | — | 1st July 2000 |
| Denmark | — | 1st August 1991 |
| Finland | — | 1st August 1994 |
| France | — | 1st August 1986 |
| Germany | — | 1st February 1991 |
| Greece | — | 1st July 1993 |
| Iceland | — | 1st November 1996 |
| Ireland | — | 1st October 1991 |
| Italy | — | 1st June 1995 |
| Latvia | — | 1st August 2002 |
| Liechtenstein | — | 1st August 1997 |
| Luxembourg | — | 1st August 1986 |
| Malta | — | 1st February 2000 |
| Netherlands | — | 1st September 1990 |
| Norway | — | 1st May 1989 |
| Poland | — | 1st March 1996 |
| Portugal | — | 1st August 1986 |
| Spain | — | 1st August 1986 |
| Sweden | — | 1st July 1989 |
| Switzerland | — | 1st August 1986 |
| Turkey | — | 1st June 2000] |

**Note:** Substituted by SI 2003/1518, art 3, Schedule as from 12 June 2003.

## THE MAGISTRATES' COURTS (CIVIL JURISDICTION AND JUDGMENTS ACT 1982) RULES 1986

**Dated** 17 November 1986

**SI 1986 No 1962**

ARRANGEMENT OF RULES

The Lord Chancellor, in exercise of the powers conferred on him by section 144 of the Magistrates' Courts Act 1980, as extended by section 145 of that Act, section 2A(1) of the Maintenance Orders Act 1958, sections 2(3), 8(5) and 33(4) of the Maintenance Orders (Reciprocal Enforcement) Act 1972 and sections 12 and 48 of the Civil Jurisdiction and Judgments Act 1982, after consultation with the Rule Committee under the said section 144, hereby makes the following Rules—

PART I

CITATION, COMMENCEMENT AND INTERPRETATION

*Citation and commencement*

**1.** These Rules may be cited as the Magistrates' Courts (Civil Jurisdiction and Judgments Act 1982) Rules 1986 and shall come into operation on 1 January 1987.

*Interpretation*

**2.** In these Rules—
'the 1982 Act' means the Civil Jurisdiction and Judgments Act 1982;
'[the court's register]', in relation to a [justices' chief executive], means the register kept by [the justices' chief executive] in pursuance of Rule 66 of the Magistrates' Courts Rules 1981.

**Note.** In definition 'the courts register' (definition 'his register' as originally enacted) words 'the Court's register' substituted by SI2001/615, r 2(xiv), Schedule, para 80(a) as from 1 April 2001. Words 'justices' chief executive' and 'the justices' chief executive' substituted for words 'justices' clerk' by SI 2001/615, r 2(xiv), Schedule, para 80(b), (c) as from 1 April 2001.

PART II

REGISTRATION OF MAINTENANCE ORDERS

*The prescribed officer*

**3.**   The prescribed officer of a magistrates' court for the purposes of the 1982 Act [and the Civil Jurisdiction and Judgements order 2001] shall be the justices' clerk.

**Note.** Words 'and the Civil Jurisdiction and Judgements Order 2001' in square brackets inserted by SI 2002/194, r 4 as from 1 March 2002.

*Registration of maintenance orders*

**4.**   (1) Where a *justices' clerk* [justices' chief executive] receives an application under Article 31 of the 1968 Convention for enforcement of a maintenance order made in a Contracting State other than the United Kingdom he shall, subject to Articles 27 and 28 of that Convention and to paragraphs (3) and (4) of this Rule, cause the order to be registered in his court by means of a minute or memorandum entered and signed by him in *his register* [the court's register].

[(1A Where a justices' chief executive receives an application under Article 38 of the Regulation for enforcement of a maintenance order made in a Regulation State other than the United Kingdom he shall, subject to Articles 34 and 35 of the Regulation and to paragraphs (3) and (4) of this Rule, cause the order to be registered in his court by means of a minute or memorandum entered and signed by him in the court's register.]

(2) Before registering an order under paragraph (1) [or (1A)] of this Rule the *justices' clerk* [justices' chief executive] shall take such steps as he thinks fit for the purpose of ascertaining whether the payer under the order to which the application relates is residing within the jurisdiction of the court, and shall consider any information he possesses (whether provided by the applicant or otherwise) as to the nature and location of the payer's assets.

(3) If, after taking such steps and considering such information as are mentioned in paragraph (2) above, the *justices' clerk* [justices' chief executive] is satisfied that the payer under the order is not residing within the jurisdiction of the court he shall, subject to paragraph (4) of this Rule, refuse the application and return the documents relating thereto to the *Secretary of State* [Lord Chancellor] with a statement giving such information as he possesses as to the whereabouts of the payer and the nature and location of his assets.

(4) If, after taking such steps and considering such information as are mentioned in paragraph (2) above, the *justices' clerk* [justices' chief executive] is satisfied that the payer is not residing within the jurisdiction of the court but that there are assets against which, after registration in the High Court under Part I of the Maintenance Orders Act 1958, the order could be enforced, he shall cause the order to be registered in accordance with paragraph (1) [or (1A)] of this Rule.

Provided that where the *justices' clerk* [justices' chief executive] is of the opinion that the payer is residing within the jurisdiction of another magistrates' court in England and Wales he may, if he thinks fit, and notwithstanding the provisions of this paragraph, refuse the application and return the documents relating thereto to the *Secretary of State* [Lord Chancellor] in accordance with paragraph (3) above.

(5) If the *justices' clerk* [justices' chief executive] refuses an application made under Article 31 of the 1968 Convention [or under Article 38 of the Regulation], he shall cause notice of his decision to be sent to the applicant, at the address provided by the applicant.

(6) Where an order has been registered under paragraph (1) [or (1A)] of this Rule the *justices' clerk* [justices' chief executive] who was responsible for its registration shall cause a written notice stating that it has been duly registered in his court to be sent to—

(a)  the *Secretary of State* [Lord Chancellor];

(b)  the payer under the order to which the registration relates;

(c)  the applicant, at the address provided by the applicant.

(7) Where an order has been registered under paragraph (1) [or (1A)] of this Rule and the *justices' clerk* [justices' chief executive] who was responsible for its registration is of the opinion that the order, or a part thereof, is one which would be appropriate for enforcement in the High Court he shall notify the applicant accordingly and shall notify the applicant also of the possibility of an application by the applicant for registration of the whole or part of the order in the High Court under Part I of the Maintenance Orders Act 1958.

**Note.** Words 'justices' clerk' in each place they occur substituted by words 'justices' chief executive' in square brackets by SI 2001/615, r 2(xiv), Schedule, para 78 as from 1 April 2001. In para (1) words 'the register' substituted by words 'the court's register' in square brackets by SI 2001/615, r 2(xiv), Schedule, para 81 as from 1 April 2001. Para (1A) inserted by SI 2002/194, r 5(a) as from 1 March 2002. In paras (2), (4), (6), (7) words 'or (1A)' in square brackets inserted by SI 2002/194, r 5(b) as from 1 March 2002. In paras (3), (4), (6) words 'Secretary of State' substituted by words 'Lord Chancellor' in square brackets by SI 2002/194, r 3 as from 1 March 2002. In para (5) words 'or under Article 38 of the Regulation' in square brackets inserted by SI 2002/194, r 5(c) as from 1 March 2002.

*Appeals from decision as to registration*

**5.**  An appeal under Article 36 or under Article 40 of the 1968 Convention [or under Article 43 of the Regulation] shall be by way of complaint to the magistrates' court in which the order is registered, or in which the application for its registration has been refused, as the case may be.

**Note.** Words 'or under Article 43 of the Regulation' in square brackets inserted by SI 2002/194, r 6 as from 1 March 2002.

*Payment of sums due under a registered order*

**6.**  (1) When an order is registered under section 5(3) of the 1982 Act [or under Article 38 of the Regulation], the court shall order that payment of sums due thereunder shall be made to the *clerk of* [justices' chief executive for] the registering court during such hours and at such place as *that clerk* [that justices' chief executive] may direct.

(1A) The *justices' clerk* [justices' chief executive] to whom payments are ordered to be made (whether by virtue of an order under paragraph (1) above or by virtue of an order of the court under the 1982 Act) shall send those payments by post to the court which made the order or to such other person or authority as that court or the *Secretary of State* [Lord Chancellor] may from time to time direct.

(2) Where it appears to a *justices' clerk* [justices' chief executive] to whom payments by way of periodical payments under any maintenance order are made ... that any sums payable under the order are in arrear he may and, if such sums are in arrear to an amount equal to four times the sum payable weekly, he shall, whether the person for whose benefit the payment should have been made requests him to do so or not, proceed in his own name for the recovery of those sums, unless it appears to him that it is unreasonable in the circumstances to do so.

(3) Without prejudice to the foregoing provisions of this Rule, the *justices' clerk* [justices' chief executive] of the registering court shall take reasonable steps to notify the person to whom payments are due under a registered order of the means of enforcement available in respect of it, including, in an appropriate case,

the possibility of registration of the whole or part of the order in the High Court under Part I of the Maintenance Orders Act 1958.

**Note.** Paras (1), (1A) substituted, for para (1) as originally enacted, by SI 1992/457, r 2, Schedule, para 19. In para (1) words 'or under Article 38 of the Regulation' in square brackets inserted by SI 2002/194, r 7 as from 1 March 2002, words 'clerk of' substituted by words 'justices' chief executive for' in square brackets and words 'that clerk' substituted by words 'that justices' chief executive' in square brackets by SI 2001/615, r 2(xiv), Schedule, paras 79, 82 as from 1 April 2001. In para (1A) words 'justices' clerk' substituted by words 'justices' chief executive' in square brackets by SI 2001/615, r 2(xiv), Schedule, para 78 as from 1 April 2001, and words 'Secretary of State' substituted by words 'Lord Chancellor' in square brackets by SI 2002/194, r 3 as from 1 March 2002. In para (2) words 'justices' clerk' substituted by words 'justices' chief executive' in square brackets by SI 2001/615, r 2(xiv), Schedule, para 78 as from 1 April 2001 and words omitted revoked by SI 1992/457, r 2, Schedule, para 19. In para (3) words 'justices' clerk' substituted by words 'justices' chief executive' in square brackets by SI 2001/615, r 2(xiv), Schedule, para 78 as from 1 April 2001.

**6A.**    (1)  Where, in the exercise of the duty imposed under Rule 6(1) above, or in the exercise of the powers conferred by virtue of section 5(6B) of the Act of 1982, the court orders that payments under the order are to be made by a particular means, the clerk of the court shall record on the order the means of payment which the court has ordered and [the justices' chief executive shall] notify in writing, as soon as practicable, the person liable to make payments under the order of how payments are to be made.

(2)  Where, in the exercise of the aforesaid powers, the court orders payment to the *clerk of* [justices' chief executive for] the court, or to the *clerk of* [justices' chief executive for] any other magistrates' court, by a method of payment falling within section 59(6) of the Magistrates' Courts Act 1980 (standing order, etc), the *clerk of* [justices' chief executive for] the court to whom payments are to be made shall notify the person liable to make the payments under the order of the number and location of the account into which the payments are to be made.

**Note.** Words 'the justices' chief executive' in square brackets inserted and words 'clerk of' in each place substituted by words 'justices' chief executive for' in square brackets by SI 2001/615, r 2(xiv), Schedule, paras 79, 83, as from 1 April 2001.

*Variation and revocation of registered orders*

**7.**  Where a maintenance order which has been registered for enforcement in a magistrates' court has been varied or revoked by an order made by a competent court in a Contracting State [or a Regulation State] the *justices' clerk* [justices' chief executive] for the court in which the order is registered shall, on receiving notice of the variation or revocation, register the order of variation or revocation by means of a minute or memorandum entered and signed by him in his register, and shall cause notice of the same to be given in writing by post to the payee and to the payer under the order to which the variation or revocation relates.

**Note.** Words 'or a Regulation State' in square brackets inserted by SI 2002/194, r 9 as from 1 March 2002. Words 'justices' clerk' substituted by words 'justices' chief executive' in square brackets by SI 2001/615, r 2(xiv), schedule, para 78 as from 1 April 2002.

*Transfer of registered orders*

**8.**    (1)  Where the *justices' clerk* [justices' chief executive] for the court where an order is registered is of the opinion that the payer under the registered order is residing within the jurisdiction of another magistrates' court in England and Wales he shall transfer the order to that other court by sending the information and documents relating to the registration of the order (that is, the information and documents required under Articles 46 and 47 of the Convention [or under Article 53 of the Regulation, as appropriate]) to the *justices' clerk* [justices' chief executive] for that other court, and shall cause notice of the same to be given to the payee under the order to which the transfer relates, and to the *Secretary of State* [Lord Chancellor].

Provided that where an application is pending in the registering court for the registration of the whole or part of the order in the High Court under Part I of the Maintenance Orders Act 1958, the *justices' clerk* [justices' chief executive] shall not transfer the order, or such part of it to which the application relates, under this paragraph.

(2) On the transfer of an order under paragraph (1) above the *justices' clerk* [justices' chief executive] for the court to which it is transferred shall register the order in the like manner as if an application for registration had been received under Rule 4 of these Rules.

(3) The *justices' clerk* [justices' chief executive] who is required by the foregoing provisions of this Rule to send to the *justices' clerk* [justices' chief executive] for another court information and documents relating to the registration of an order shall send with that information and those documents—

(a) a certificate of arrears, if applicable, signed by him;

(b) a statement giving such information as he possesses as to the whereabouts of the payer and the nature and location of his assets; and

(c) any other relevant documents in his possession relating to the case.

**Note.** Words 'justice's clerk' in each place substituted by words 'justices' chief executive' in square brackets by SI 2001/615, r 2(xiv), Schedule, para 78 as from 1 April 2002. Words 'or under Article 53 of the Regulation, as appropriate' in square brackets inserted and words 'Secretary of State' substituted by words 'Lord Chancellor' in square brackets by SI 2002/194, rr 3, 10 as from 1 March 2002.

### Cancellation of registered orders

**9.** Subject to Rule 8 of these Rules, where the *justices' clerk* [justices' chief executive] for the court where an order is registered is of the opinion that the payer under the registered order is not residing within the jurisdiction of that court and has no assets against which, after registration in the High Court under Part I of the Maintenance Orders Act 1958, the order could be enforced he shall cancel the registration of the order and shall cause notice of the same to be given to the payee under the order to which the cancellation relates and shall send the information and documents relating to the registration of the order (that is, the information and documents required under Articles 46 and 47 of the Convention [or under Article 53 of the Regulation, as appropriate]) to the *Secretary of State* [Lord Chancellor], together with such information and documents as are referred to in Rule 8(3)(a), (b) and (c) of these Rules.

**Note.** Words 'justices' clerk' substituted by words 'justices' chief executive' in square brackets by SI 2001/615, r 2(xiv), Schedule, para 78 as from 1 April 2001. Words 'or under Article 53 of the Regulation, as appropriate' in square brackets inserted and words 'Secretary of State' substituted by words 'Lord Chancellor' in square brackets by SI 2002/194, rr 3, 10 as from 1 March 2002.

PART III

APPLICATIONS FOR MAINTENANCE UNDER ARTICLE 5(2) OF THE 1968 CONVENTION

### Complaint against a person residing outside the United Kingdom

**10.** (1) This Rule applies where a complaint is made to a magistrates' court by a person who is domiciled or habitually resident in England and Wales against a person residing in a Contracting State [or a Regulation State] other than the United Kingdom, and the complaint is one in respect of which the court has jurisdiction to make a maintenance order by virtue of Article 5(2) of the 1968 Convention [or Article 5(2) of the Regulation].

(2) On the making of a complaint to which paragraph (1) of this Rule applies, the following documents, that is to say—

(a) notice of the institution of the proceedings, including a statement of the grounds of the complaint;

(b) a statement signed by the *justices' clerk* [justices' chief executive], giving such information as he possesses as to the whereabouts of the defendant;

(c) a statement giving such information as *the clerk* [the justices' chief executive] possesses for facilitating the identification of the defendant; and

(d) where available, a photograph of the defendant;

shall be sent by that clerk to the *Secretary of State* [Lord Chancellor].

(3) The *justices' clerk* [justices' chief executive] shall give the defendant notice in writing of the date fixed for the hearing by sending the notice by post addressed to his last known or usual place of abode.

(4) Where the defendant makes any written representations or adduces any documentary evidence in advance of the hearing, a copy of the representations or evidence shall be served on the complainant by the *justices' clerk* [justices' chief executive] before the hearing.

(5) In considering whether or not to make a maintenance order pursuant to a complaint to which paragraph (1) of this Rule applies, where the defendant does not appear and is not represented at the hearing the court shall take into account any representations made and any evidence adduced by him or on his behalf under paragraph (4) above and, where the defendant does appear or is represented at the hearing, the court may take any such representations or evidence into account in addition to any oral representations made or evidence adduced at the hearing.

(6) Where a maintenance order has been made under this Rule [in respect of a complaint in relation to which the court has jurisdiction by virtue of Article 5(2) of the 1968 Convention], the *justices' clerk* [justices' chief executive] shall cause notice thereof to be given to the defendant by sending a copy of the order by post addressed to his last known or usual place of abode and, on application by the complainant, shall give to the complainant the following documents, that is to say—

(a) a certified copy of the order;

(b) a written statement signed by the justices' clerk as to whether or not the defendant appeared in the proceedings in which the order was made, and, if he did not appear, the original or a certified copy of a document which establishes that the document mentioned in paragraph (2)(a) of this Rule had been served on the defendant;

(c) a document which establishes that notice of the order was sent to the defendant; and

(d) a written statement signed by the justices' clerk as to whether or not the complainant received legal aid in the proceedings;

with a view to an application being made by the complainant for registration and enforcement under Articles 31 and 32 of the 1968 Convention.

[(7) Where a maintenance order has been made under this Rule in respect of a complaint in relation to which the court has jurisdiction by virtue of Article 5(2) of the Regulation, the justices' chief executive shall cause notice thereof to be given to the defendant by sending a copy of the order by post addressed to his last known or usual place of abode and, on application by the complainant, shall give to the complainant the following documents-

(a) a certified copy of the order; and

(b) a completed certificate in the form of Annex V to the Regulation;

with a view to an application being made by the complainant for registration and enforcement under Articles 38 and 39 of the Regulation.]

**Note.** In para (1) words 'or a Regulation State' and 'or Article 5(2) of the Regulation' in square brackets inserted by SI 2002/194, r 12(a) as from 1 March 2002. In para (2) words 'justice's clerk' and 'the clerk' substituted by words 'justices' chief executive' and 'the justices' chief executive' in square brackets by SI 2001/615, r 2(xiv), Schedule, paras 78, 82 as from1 April 2001, and words 'Secretary of State' substituted by words 'Lord Chancellor' by SI 2002/194, r 3 as from1 March 2002. In paras (3), (4), (6) words 'justices' clerk' substituted by words 'justices' chief executive' in square brackets by SI 2001/615, r 2(xiv), Schedule, para 78 as from 1 April 2001. In para (6) words from 'in respect of' to 'the 1968 Convention' in square brackets and para (7) inserted by SI 2002/194, r12(b), (c) as from 1 March 2002.

*Application for variation and revocation of a maintenance order*

**11.**   (1) This Rule applies where an application is made to a magistrates' court for the variation or revocation of a maintenance order where the payer under the order is residing in a Contracting State [or a Regulation State] other than the United Kingdom.

(2) Where an application to which this Rule applies is made by the payee, the following documents, that is to say—

(a) notice of the institution of the proceedings, including a statement of the grounds of the application;

(b) a statement signed by the *justices' clerk* [justices' chief executive], giving such information as he possesses as to the whereabouts of the respondent;

(c) a statement giving such information as the clerk possesses for facilitating the identification of the respondent; and

(d) where available, a photograph of the respondent;

shall be sent by *that clerk* [that justices' chief executive] to the *Secretary of State* [Lord Chancellor].

(3) Where an application to which this Rule applies is made by the payee—

(a) the *justices' clerk* [justices' chief executive] shall give the respondent notice in writing of the date fixed for the hearing by sending the notice by post addressed to his last known or usual place of abode;

(b) where the respondent makes any written representations or adduces any documentary evidence in advance of the hearing, a copy of the representations or evidence shall be served on the applicant by the *justices' clerk* [justices' chief executive] before the hearing;

(c) the court, in considering whether to vary or revoke the order, shall, where the payer does not appear and is not represented at the hearing, take into account any representations made and any evidence adduced by or on his behalf under sub-paragraph (b) above and, where the payer does appear or is represented at the hearing, the court may take any such representations or evidence into account, in addition to any oral representations or evidence adduced at the hearing.

(4) Where an application to which this Rule applies is made by the payer, the *justices' clerk* [justices' chief executive] shall arrange for the service of the document mentioned in paragraph (2)(a) of this Rule on the payee.

(5) Where upon an application *to which this Rule applies* [to vary or revoke a maintenance order where the payer under the order is residing in a contracting state] the court varies or revokes the order, the *justices' clerk* [justices' chief executive] shall cause notice thereof to be given to the respondent by sending a copy of the order of variation or revocation by post addressed to his last known or usual place of abode and, on application by the applicant, shall give to the applicant the following documents, that is to say—

(a) a certified copy of the order of variation or revocation;

(b) a written statement, signed by the justices' clerk as to whether or not the respondent appeared in the proceedings for the variation or revocation of the order and if he did not appear the original or a certified copy of a document which establishes that the notice of the institution of the proceedings had been served on the respondent;

(c) a document which establishes that notice of the order of variation or revocation was sent to the respondent; and

(d) a written statement signed by the justices' clerk as to whether or not the applicant or the respondent received legal aid in the proceedings;

with a view to an application being made by the applicant for registration and enforcement of the order of variation or revocation under Articles 31 and 32 of the 1968 Convention.

[(6) Where upon an application to vary or revoke a maintenance order where the payer under the order is residing in a Regulation State the court varies or revokes the order, the justices' chief executive shall cause notice thereof to be given to the respondent by sending a copy of the order of variation or revocation by post addressed to his last known or usual place of abode and, on application by the applicant, shall give to the applicant the following documents—

(a) a certified copy of the order of variation or revocation; and

(b) a completed certificate in the form of Annex V to the Regulation;

with a view to an application being made by the applicant for registration and enforcement of the order of variation or revocation under Articles 38 and 39 of the Regulation.]

**Note.** Words 'justices' clerk' in each place they occur substituted by words 'justices' chief executive' in square brackets and words 'that clerk' substituted by words 'that justices' chief executive' in square brackets, by SI 2001/615, r 2(xiv), Schedule, paras 78, 82 as from 1 April 2004.

In para (1) words 'or a Regulation State' in square brackets inserted and in para (2) words 'Secretary of State' substituted by words 'Lord Chancellor' in square brackets, by SI 2002/194, rr 3, 13(a) as from 1 March 2002.

In para (5) words 'to which this Rule applies' substituted by words from 'to vary' to 'contracting state' in square brackets and para (6) inserted, by SI 2002/194, r 13(b), (c) as from 1 March 2002.

*Copies of, and certificates in connection with, maintenance orders*

**12.** (1) Without prejudice to the provisions of *Rule 10(6) and Rule 11(5)* [Rules 10(6), 10(7), 11(5) and 11(6)] of these Rules, a person wishing to obtain for the purposes of an application for recognition or enforcement in a Contracting State [or a Regulation State] a copy of a maintenance order made by a magistrates' court in England and Wales, and a certificate giving particulars relating to the order and the proceedings in which it was made may apply in writing to the *justices' clerk* [justices' chief executive] for that court.

(2) An application under paragraph (1) above shall specify—

(a) the names of the parties to the proceedings in the magistrates' court;

(b) the date or approximate date of the proceedings in which the maintenance order was made, and the nature of those proceedings;

(c) the Contracting State [or the Regulation State] in which the application for recognition or enforcement has been made or is to be made;

(d) the postal address of the applicant.

(3) A *justices' clerk* [justices' chief executive] who receives an application under paragraph (1) of this Rule shall send by post to the applicant at the address indicated in the application for the purposes an authenticated copy of the order concerned.

(4) For the purposes of paragraph (3) of this Rule a copy of an order shall be deemed to be authenticated if it is accompanied by a statement signed by the *justices' clerk* [justices' chief executive] that it is a true copy of the order concerned and giving particulars of the proceedings in which it was made.

(5) A person wishing to obtain for the purposes of an application made or to be made in another Contracting State [or in another Regulation State] or in another part of the United Kingdom in connection with a maintenance order which is

registered in a magistrates' court in England and Wales a certificate giving particulars of any payments made and any arrears which have accrued under the order while so registered may apply in writing to the *justices' clerk* [justices' chief executive] for the registering court, and a *justices' clerk* [justices' chief executive] who receives such an application shall send by post to the applicant at the address indicated in the application for the purposes a certificate giving the information so requested.

**Note.** Words justices' clerk' in each place they occur substituted by words 'justices' chief executive' in square brackets by SI 2001/615, r 2(xiv), Schedule, para 78 as from 1 April 2001. In para (1) words 'Rule 10(6) and Rule 11(5)' substituted by words 'Rules 10(6), 10(7), 11(5) and 11(6)' in square brackets and words 'or a Regulation State' in square brackets inserted by SI 2002/194, r 14(a) as from 1 March 2002. in para (2)(c) words 'or the Regulation State' and in para (5) words 'or in another Regulation State' in square brackets inserted by SI 2002/194, r 14(b), (c) as from 1 March 2002.

PART IV

EVIDENCE IN MAINTENANCE PROCEEDINGS

*Admissibility of documents*

**13.**   (1) Subject to paragraph (2) of this Rule, a statement contained in—

(a) a document which purports to set out or summarise evidence given in proceedings in a court in another part of the United Kingdom or another Contracting State [or another Regulation State];

(b) a document which purports to have been received in evidence in proceedings in a court in another part of the United Kingdom or another Contracting State [or another Regulation State];

(c) a document which purports to set out or summarise evidence taken in another part of the United Kingdom or in another Contracting State [or another Regulation State] for the purpose of proceedings in a court in England and Wales under the 1982 Act [or the Regulation], whether in response to a request made by such a court or otherwise; or

(d) a document which purports to record information relating to the payments made under an order of a court in another part of the United Kingdom or another Contracting State [or another Regulation State]

shall, in any proceedings in a magistrates' court in England and Wales relating to a maintenance order to which the 1982 Act [or the Regulation] applies, be admissible as evidence of any fact stated therein to the same extent as oral evidence of that fact is admissible in those proceedings.

(2) Paragraph (1) of this Rule shall not apply unless the document concerned has been made or authenticated by the court in the other part of the United Kingdom or the other Contracting State [or another Regulation State], as the case may be, or by a judge or official of that court, in accordance with paragraph (3), (4) or (5) of this Rule.

(3) A document purporting to set out or summarise evidence given as mentioned in paragraph (1)(a) above, or taken as mentioned in paragraph (1)(c) above, shall be deemed to be authenticated for the purposes of that paragraph if the document purports to be certified by the judge or official before whom the evidence was given or by whom it was taken, or to be the original document containing or recording or, as the case may be, summarising, the evidence or a true copy of that document.

(4) A document purporting to have been received in evidence as mentioned in paragraph (1)(b) above, or to be a copy of a document so received, shall be deemed to be authenticated for the purposes of that paragraph if the document purports to be certified by a judge or official of the court in question to be, or to be a true copy of, a document which has been so received.

(5) A document purporting to record information as mentioned in paragraph (1)(d) above shall be deemed to be authenticated for the purposes of that

paragraph if the document purports to be certified by a judge or official of the court in question to be a true record of the payments made under the order concerned.

(6) It shall not be necessary in any proceedings in which evidence is to be received under this Rule to prove the signature or official position of the person appearing to have given such a certificate.

(7) Nothing in this Rule shall prejudice the admission in evidence of any document which is admissible in evidence apart from this Rule.

(8) Any request by a magistrates' court in England and Wales for the taking or providing of evidence by a court in another part of the United Kingdom or another Contracting State [or another Regulation State] for the purpose of proceedings under the 1982 Act [or the Regulation] shall be communicated in writing to the court in question.

**Note.** Words 'or another Regulation State', 'or the Regulation' and 'or the other Regulation State' in square brackets in each place they occur inserted by SI 2002/194, r 15 as from 1 March 2002.

*Evidence for the purposes of proceedings outside England and Wales*

**14.** (1) Subject to paragraph (2) below, where for the purposes of any proceedings in a court in another part of the United Kingdom or in a Contracting State [or in a Regulation State] other than the United Kingdom relating to a maintenance order a request is made by or on behalf of that court for the taking in England and Wales of evidence of a person residing therein relating to matters specified in the request, the following magistrates' courts shall have power to take that evidence, that is to say—
  (a) where the maintenance order to which the proceedings in the court in the other part of the United Kingdom or Contracting State [or Regulation State] relate was made by a magistrates' court, the court which made the order;
  (b) where the maintenance order to which those proceedings relate is registered in a magistrates' court, the court in which the order is registered;
  (c) a magistrates' court which has received such a request from the *Secretary of State* [Lord Chancellor].

(2) The power conferred by paragraph (1) above may, with the agreement of a court having that power, be exercised by any other magistrates' court which, because the person whose evidence is to be taken resides within its jurisdiction or for any other reason, the first mentioned court considers could more conveniently take the evidence; but nothing in this paragraph shall derogate from the power of any court specified in paragraph (1) above.

(3) Before taking the evidence of a person under paragraph (1) or (2) above, a magistrates' court shall give notice of the time and place at which the evidence is to be taken to such persons and in such manner as it thinks fit.

(4) Subject to paragraph (5) below, where the evidence of a person is to be taken by a magistrates' court under the foregoing provisions of this Rule—
  (a) the evidence shall be taken in the same manner as if that person were a witness in proceedings on a complaint;
  (b) any oral evidence so taken shall be put into writing and read to the person who gave it, who shall be required to sign the document; and
  (c) the justices by whom the evidence of any person is so taken shall certify at the foot of any document setting out the evidence of, or produced in evidence by, that person that such evidence was taken, or a document received in evidence, as the case may be, by them.

(5) Where such a request as is mentioned in paragraph (1) above includes a request that the evidence be taken in a particular manner, the magistrates' court by which the evidence was taken shall, so far as circumstances permit, comply with that request.

(6) Any document such as is mentioned in paragraph (4)(c) above shall be sent to the court in the Contracting State [or the Regulation State] by or on behalf of which the request was made.

**Note.** Words 'or in a Regulation State', 'or Regulation State 'or the Regulation State' in square brackets inserted by SI 2002/194, r 16 as from 1 March 2002. Words 'Secretary of State' substituted by words 'Lord Chancellor' in square brackets by SI 2002/14, r 3 as from 1 March 2002.

PART V

*Amendments*

**15.**   The enactments and instruments mentioned in the Schedule to this Order shall have effect with the amendments there specified.

SCHEDULE                                                                      Rule 15

AMENDMENTS

PART I

RULES

THE MAGISTRATES' COURTS (MAINTENANCE ORDERS ACT 1958) RULES 1959

\*       \*       \*       \*       \*

EVIDENCE (PROCEEDINGS IN OTHER JURISDICTIONS) (TURKS AND CAICOS ISLANDS) ORDER 1987

**Dated** 21 July 1987

**SI 1987 No 1266**

At the Court at Buckingham Palace, the 21st day of July 1987

Present,

The Queen's Most Excellent Majesty in Council

Her Majesty, in exercise of the powers conferred upon Her by section 10(3) of the Evidence (Proceedings in Other Jurisdictions) Act 1975, is pleased, by and with the advice of Her Privy Council, to order, and it is hereby ordered, as follows:

**1.**   This Order may be cited as the Evidence (Proceedings in Other Jurisdictions) (Turks and Caicos Islands) Order 1987 and shall come into force on 19th August 1987.

**2.**   Sections 1 to 10 of, and Schedule 2 to, the Evidence (Proceedings in Other Jurisdictions) Act 1975, with the exceptions, adaptations and modifications specified in the Schedule hereto, shall extend to the Turks and Caicos Islands.

SCHEDULE TO THE ORDER                                                        Article 2

PROVISIONS OF THE EVIDENCE (PROCEEDINGS IN OTHER JURISDICTIONS) ACT 1975 AS EXTENDED TO THE TURKS AND CAICOS ISLANDS

EVIDENCE FOR CIVIL PROCEEDINGS

*Application to Supreme Court for assistance in obtaining evidence for civil proceedings in other court*

**1.**   Where an application is made to the Supreme Court for an order for evidence to be obtained in the Turks and Caicos Islands, and the court is satisfied—

(a) that the application is made in pursuance of a request issued by or on behalf of a court or tribunal ('the requesting court') exercising jurisdiction in a country or territory outside the Turks and Caicos Islands; and

(b) that the evidence to which the application relates is to be obtained for the purposes of civil proceedings which either have been instituted before the requesting court or whose institution before that court is contemplated,

the Supreme Court shall have the powers conferred on it by the following provisions of this Act.

*Power of Supreme Court to give effect to application for assistance*

**2.** (1) Subject to the provisions of this section, the Supreme Court shall have power, on any such application as is mentioned in section 1 above, by order to make such provision for obtaining evidence in the Turks and Caicos Islands as may appear to the court to be appropriate for the purpose of giving effect to the request in pursuance of which the application is made; and any such order may require a person specified therein to take such steps as the court may consider appropriate for that purpose.

(2) Without prejudice to the generality of subsection (1) above but subject to the provisions of this section, an order under this section may, in particular, make provision—

(a) for the examination of witnesses, either orally or in writing;

(b) for the production of documents;

(c) for the inspection, photographing, preservation, custody or detention of any property;

(d) for the taking of samples of any property and the carrying out of any experiments on or with any property;

(e) for the medical examination of any person;

(f) without prejudice to paragraph (e) above, for the taking and testing of samples of blood from any person.

(3) An order under this section shall not require any particular steps to be taken unless they are steps which can be required to be taken by way of obtaining evidence for the purposes of civil proceedings in the court making the order (whether or not proceedings of the same description as those to which the application for the order relates); but this subsection shall not preclude the making of an order requiring a person to give testimony (either orally or in writing) otherwise than on oath where this is asked for by the requesting court.

(4) An order under this section shall not require a person—

(a) to state what documents relevant to the proceedings to which the application for the order relates are or have been in his possession, custody or power; or

(b) to produce any documents other than particular documents specified in the order as being documents appearing to the court making the order to be, or to be likely to be, in his possession, custody or power.

(5) A person who, by virtue of an order under this section, is required to attend at any place shall be entitled to the like conduct money and payment for expenses and loss of time as on attendance as a witness in civil proceedings before the court making the order.

*Privilege of witnesses*

**3.** (1) A person shall not be compelled by virtue of an order under section 2 above to give any evidence which he could not be compelled to give—

(a) in civil proceedings in the Turks and Caicos Islands; or

(b) subject to subsection (2) below, in civil proceedings in the country or territory in which the requesting court exercises jurisdiction.

(2) Subsection (1)(b) above shall not apply unless the claim of the person in question to be exempt from giving the evidence is either—

(a) supported by a statement contained in the request (whether it is so supported unconditionally or subject to conditions that are fulfilled); or

(b) conceded by the applicant for the order;

and where such a claim made by any person is not supported or conceded as aforesaid he may (subject to the other provisions of this section) be required to give the evidence to which the claim relates but that evidence shall not be transmitted to the requesting court if that court, on the matter being referred to it, upholds the claim.

(3) Without prejudice to subsection (1) above, a person shall not be compelled by virtue of an order under section 2 above to give any evidence if his doing so would be prejudicial to the security of the United Kingdom, the Turks and Caicos Islands or any other territory for which the United Kingdom is responsible under international law; and a certificate signed by or on behalf of the Governor to the effect that it would be so prejudicial for that person to do so shall be conclusive evidence of that fact.

(4) In this section references to giving evidence include references to answering any question and to producing any document and the reference in subsection (2) above to the transmission of evidence given by a person shall be construed accordingly.

*Extensions of powers of Supreme Court in relation to obtaining evidence for proceedings in that court*

**4.** Sections 93 to 96 of the Civil Procedure Ordinance shall apply to any hearing under this Act before an examiner or commissioner appointed by the Supreme Court or a judge thereof, including a hearing conducted by an examiner or commissioner appointed to take evidence outside the jurisdiction of the Supreme Court, as if the hearing were a trial of any cause or matter before the Supreme Court.

EVIDENCE FOR CRIMINAL PROCEEDINGS

\*    \*    \*    \*    \*

EVIDENCE FOR INTERNATIONAL PROCEEDINGS

\*    \*    \*    \*    \*

SUPPLEMENTARY

*Rules of court*

**7.** The power to make rules of court under section 16 of the Supreme Court Ordinance shall include power to make rules of court—

(a) as to the manner in which any such application as is mentioned in section 1 above is to be made;

(b) subject to the provisions of this Act, as to the circumstances in which an order can be made under section 2 above; and

(c) as to the manner in which any such reference as is mentioned in section 3(2) above is to be made;

and any such rules may include such incidental, supplementary and consequential provisions as the authority making the rules may consider necessary or expedient.

*Consequential amendment and repeals*

**8.** (1) The enactments mentioned in Schedule 2 to this Act are hereby repealed as respects the Turks and Caicos Islands to the extent specified in the third column of that Schedule.

(2) Nothing in this section shall affect—

(a) any application to any court or judge which is pending at the commencement of this Act;

(b) any certificate given for the purposes of any such application;

(c) any power to make an order on such an application; or

(d) the operation or enforcement of any order made on such an application.

(3) Subsection (2) above is without prejudice to sections 21 to 24 of the Interpretation Ordinance.

*Interpretation*

**9.** (1) In this Act—
'civil proceedings', in relation to the requesting court, means proceedings in any civil or commercial matter;
'Governor' means the Governor of the Turks and Caicos Islands;
'property' includes any land, chattel or other corporeal property of any description;
'request' includes any commission, order or other process issued by or on behalf of the requesting court;
'requesting court' has the meaning given in section 1 above;
'Supreme Court' means the Supreme Court of the Turks and Caicos Islands.

(2) Any power conferred by this Act to make an order includes power to revoke or vary any such order by a subsequent order.

(3) Nothing in this Act shall be construed as enabling any court to make an order that is binding on the Crown or on any person in his capacity as an officer or servant of the Crown.

(4) Except so far as the context otherwise requires, any reference in this Act to any enactment is a reference to that enactment as amended or extended by or under any other enactment.

(5) Nothing in this Act shall be construed as affecting the provisions of the Confidential Relationships Ordinance 1979, the Banking Ordinance 1979 or the Companies Ordinance 1981.

*Commencement*

**10.** The provisions of the Act shall come into force on such date as the Governor may by order appoint.

SCHEDULE 2 TO THE ACT                                          Section 8(1)

REPEALS

| Chapter | Short Title | Extent |
|---|---|---|
| 19 & 20 Vict c 113 | The Foreign Tribunals Evidence Act 1856. | The whole Act. |
| 22 Vict c 20 | The Evidence by Commission Act 1859. | The whole Act. |
| 33 & 34 Vict c 52 | The Extradition Act 1870. | Section 24. |
| 48 & 49 Vict c 74 | The Evidence by Commission Act 1885. | The whole Act. |
| 1966 c 41 | The Arbitration (International Investment Disputes) Act 1966. | In section 3(1), paragraph (b). |

## INCOME SUPPORT (GENERAL) REGULATIONS 1987

**Dated** 20 November 1987

**SI 1987 No 1967**

\*      \*      \*      \*      \*

*Liable relative payments*

**25.**    Regulations 29 to *44* [42], 46 to 52 and Chapter VIII of this Part shall not apply to any payment which is to be calculated in accordance with Chapter VII thereof (liable relatives).

**Note.** Reference to '44' substituted by subsequent reference '42' in square brackets by SI 2003/455, reg 2, Sch 1, para 7 as from 6 April 2004; for transitional arrangements in connection with the introduction of child tax credit see reg 7 thereof.

*Child support*

**25A.**    Regulations 29, 31, 32, 40 and 42 and Chapter VII of this Part shall not apply to any payment which is to be calculated in accordance with Chapter VIIA of this Part (child support).

\*      \*      \*      \*      \*

*Interpretation*

**54.**    In this Chapter, unless the context otherwise requires—
'claimant' includes a young claimant;
'liable relative' means—

(a) a spouse or former spouse of a claimant or of a member of the claimant's family;

(b) a parent of a child or young person who is a member of the claimant's family or of a young claimant;

(c) a person who has not been adjudged to be the father of a child or young person who is a member of the claimant's family or of a young claimant where that person is contributing towards the maintenance of that child, young person or young claimant and by reason of that contribution he may reasonably be treated as the father of that child, young person or young claimant;

(d) a person liable to maintain another person by virtue of section 26(3)(c) of the Act (liability to maintain) where the latter is the claimant or a member of the claimant's family,

and, in this definition, a reference to a child's, young person's or young claimant's parent includes any person in relation to whom the child, young person or young claimant was treated as a child or a member of the family;

'payment' means a periodical payment or any other payment made by or derived from a liable relative including, except in the case of a discretionary trust, any payment which would be so made or derived upon application being made by the claimant but which has not been acquired by him but only from the date on which it could be expected to be acquired were an application made; but it does not include any payment—

(a) arising from a disposition of property made in contemplation of, or as a consequence of—

    (i) an agreement to separate; or

    (ii) any proceedings for judicial separation, divorce or nullity of marriage;

(b) made after the death of the liable relative;

(c) made by way of a gift but not in aggregate or otherwise exceeding £250 in the period of 52 weeks beginning with the date on which the payment, or if there is more than one such payment the first payment, is made; and, in the case of a claimant who continues to be in receipt of income support at the end of the period of 52 weeks, this provision shall continue to apply thereafter with the modification that any subsequent period of 52 weeks shall begin with the first day of the benefit week in which the first payment is made after the end of the previous period of 52 weeks;

(d) *to which regulation 44(2) applies (modifications in respect of children and young persons);*

(e) made—

    (i) to a third party in respect of the claimant or a member of the claimant's family; or

    (ii) to the claimant or to a member of the claimant's family in respect of a third party.

where having regard to the purpose of the payment, the terms under which it is made and its amount it is unreasonable to take it into account;

(f) in kind;

(g) to, or in respect of, a child or young person who is to be treated as not being a member of the claimant's household under regulation 16 (circumstances in which a person is to be treated as being or not being a member of the same household);

(h) which is not a periodical payment, to the extent that any amount of that payment—

    (i) has already been taken into account under this Part by virtue of a previous claim or determination; or

    (ii) has been recovered under section 27(1) of the Act (prevention of duplication of payments) or is currently being recovered; or

    (iii) at the time the determination is made, has been used by the claimant except where he has deprived himself of that amount for the purpose of securing entitlement to income support or increasing the amount of that benefit;

'periodical payment' means—

(a) a payment which is made or is due to be made at regular intervals in pursuance of a court order or agreement for maintenance;

(b) in a case where the liable relative has established a pattern of making payments at regular intervals, any such payment;

(c) any payment not exceeding the amount of income support payable had that payment not been made;

(d) any payment representing a commutation of payments to which sub-paragraphs (a) or (b) of this definition applies whether made in arrears or in advance,

but does not include a payment to be made before the first benefit week pursuant to the claim which is not so made;

'young claimant' means a person aged 16 or over but under 19 who makes a claim for income support.

**Note.** In definition 'payment' para (d) revoked by SI 2003/455, reg 2, Sch 1, para 14 as from 6 April 2004; for transitional arrangements in connection with the introduction of child tax credit see reg 7 thereof.

*Treatment of liable relative payments*

**55.** Subject to regulation 55A and except where regulation 60(1) (liable relative payments to be treated as capital) applies a payment shall—

(a) to the extent that it is not a payment of income, be treated as income;

(b) be taken into account in accordance with the following provisions of this Chapter.

*Disregard of payments treated as not relevant income*

**55A.**   Where the Secretary of State treats any payment as not being relevant income for the purposes of section 74A of the Social Security Administration Act 1992 (payment of benefit where maintenance payments collected by Secretary of State), that payment shall be disregarded in calculating a claimant's income.

*Period over which periodical payments are to be taken into account*

**56.**   (1)  The period over which a periodical payment is to be taken into account shall be—

(a)  in a case where the payment is made at regular intervals, a period equal to the length of that interval;

(b)  in a case where the payment is due to be made at regular intervals but is not so made, such number of weeks as is equal to the number (and any fraction shall be treated as a corresponding fraction of a week) obtained by dividing the amount of that payment by the weekly amount of that periodical payment as calculated in accordance with regulation 58(4) (calculation of the weekly amount of a liable relative payment);

(c)  in any other case, a period equal to a week.

(2)  The period under paragraph (1) shall begin on the date on which the payment is treated as paid under regulation 59 (date on which a liable relative payment is to be treated as paid).

*Period over which payments other than periodical payments are to be taken into account*

**57.**   (1)  Subject to paragraph (2), the number of weeks over which a payment other than a periodical payment is to be taken into account shall be equal to the number (and any fraction shall be treated as a corresponding fraction of a week) obtained by dividing that payment *by*—

(a)  *where the payment is in respect of the claimant or the claimant and any child or young person who is a member of the family, the aggregate* [by the aggregate] of £2 and the amount of income support which would be payable had the payment not been made;

(b)  *where the payment is in respect of one, or more than one, child or young person who is a member of the family, the lesser of the amount (or the aggregate of the amounts) prescribed under Schedule 2, in respect of—*

(i)  *the personal allowance of the claimant and each such child or young person;*

(ii)  *any family and lone parent premium;*

[(iia)  *any enhanced disability premium in respect of such a child or young person]*

(iii)  *any disabled child premium in respect of such a child; and*

(iv)  *any carer premium if, but only if, that premium is payable because the claimant is in receipt, or is treated as being in receipt, of invalid care allowance [carer's allowance] by reason of the fact that he is caring for such a child or young person who is severely disabled;*

*and the aggregate of £2 and the amount of income support which would be payable had the payment not been made.*

(2)  Where a liable relative makes a periodical payment and any other payment concurrently and the weekly amount of that periodical payment, as calculated in accordance with regulation 58 (calculation of the weekly amount of a liable relative payment), is less than—

(a)  *in a case where the periodical payment is in respect of the claimant or the claimant and any child or young person who is a member of the family, the aggregate of £2 and the amount of income support which would be payable had the payments not been made; or*

(b)  in a case where the periodical payment is in respect of one or more than one child or young person who is a member of the family, the aggregate of the amount prescribed in Schedule 2 in respect of each such child or young person and any family and lone parent premium,

that other payment shall, subject to paragraph (3), be taken into account over a period of such number of weeks as is equal to the number obtained (and any fraction shall be treated as a corresponding fraction of a week) by dividing that payment by an amount equal to the extent of the difference between the amount *referred to in sub-paragraph (a) or (b), as the case may be* [as calculated under this paragraph], and the weekly amount of the periodical payment.

(3)  If—

(a)  the liable relative ceases to make periodical payments, the balance (if any) of the other payment shall be taken into account over the number of weeks equal to the number (and any fraction shall be treated as a corresponding fraction of a week) obtained by dividing that balance by the amount referred to in *sub-paragraph (a) or (b) of* paragraph (1), *as the case may be;*

(b)  the amount of any subsequent periodical payment varies, the balance (if any) of the other payment shall be taken into account over a period of such number of weeks as is equal to the number obtained (and any fraction shall be treated as a corresponding fraction of a week) by dividing that balance by an amount equal to the extent of the difference between the amount referred to in sub-paragraph (a) or (b) of paragraph (2) and the weekly amount of the subsequent periodical payment.

(4)  The period under paragraph (1) or (2) shall begin on the date on which the payment is treated as paid under regulation 59 (date on which a liable relative payment is treated as paid) and under paragraph (3) shall begin on the first day of the benefit week in which the cessation or variation of the periodical payment occurred.

**Note.** In para (1) words from 'by M to 'family, the aggregate substituted by words 'by the aggregate' in square brackets by SI 2003/455, r 2, Sch 1, para 15(a) as from 6 April 2004. Para (1)(b), in para (2)(a) words from '(a) in a case' to 'of the family' and para (2)(b) and word 'or' immediately preceding it, revoked by SI 2003/455, reg 2, Sch 1, para 15(b), (c) as from 6 April 2004. Para (1)(b)(iia) inserted by SI 2000/2629, reg 2(b) as from 9 April 2001 (as amended by SI 2001/859, reg 5). In para (1)(b)(iv) words 'invalid case allowance' substituted by words 'carer's allowance' by SI 2002/2497, reg 3, Sch 2, paras 1, 2 as from 1 April 2003. In para (2) words 'referred to in sub-paragraph (a) or (b), as he case may be' substituted by words 'as calculated under this paragraph' in square brackets by SI 2003/455, reg 2, sch 1, para 15(b). In para (3) words 'sub-paragraph (a) or (b) of', 'as the case may be' and 'sub-paragraph (a) or (b) of' revoked by SI 2003/455, reg 2, Sch 1, para 15(d). For further information in relation to transitional arrangements in connection with the introduction of child tax credit see SI 2003/455, reg 7.

*Calculation of the weekly amount of a liable relative payment*

**58.**  (1) Where a periodical payment is made or is due to be made at intervals of one week, the weekly amount shall be the amount of that payment.

(2) Where a periodical payment is made or is due to be made at intervals greater than one week and those intervals are monthly, the weekly amount shall be determined by multiplying the amount of the payment by 12 and dividing the product by 52.

(3) Where a periodical payment is made or is due to be made at intervals and those intervals are neither weekly nor monthly, the weekly amount shall be determined by dividing that payment by the number equal to the number of weeks (including any part of a week) in that interval.

(4) Where a payment is made and that payment represents a commutation of periodical payments whether in arrears or in advance, the weekly amount shall be

the weekly amount of the individual periodical payments so commutated as calculated under paragraphs (1) to (3) as is appropriate.

(5) The weekly amount of a payment to which regulation 57 applies (period over which payments other than periodical payments are to be taken into account) shall be equal to the amount of the divisor used in calculating the period over which the payment or, as the case may be, the balance is to be taken into account.

*Date on which a liable relative payment is to be treated as paid*

**59.** (1) A periodical payment is to be treated as paid—
   (a) in the case of a payment which is due to be made before the first benefit week pursuant to the claim, on the day in the week in which it is due to be paid which corresponds to the first day of the benefit week;
   (b) in any other case, on the first day of the benefit week in which it is due to be paid unless, having regard to the manner in which income support is due to be paid in the particular case, it would be more practicable to treat it as paid on the first day of a subsequent benefit week.

(2) Subject to paragraph (3), any other payment shall be treated as paid—
   (a) in the case of a payment which is made before the first benefit week pursuant to the claim, on the day in the week in which it is paid which corresponds to the first day of the benefit week;
   (b) in any other case, on the first day of the benefit week in which it is paid unless, having regard to the manner in which income support is due to be paid in the particular case, it would be more practicable to treat it as paid on the first day of a subsequent benefit week.

(3) Any other payment paid on a date which falls within the period in respect of which a previous payment is taken into account, not being a periodical payment, is to be treated as paid on the first day following the end of that period.

*Liable relative payments to be treated as capital*

**60.** (1) Subject to paragraph (2), where a liable relative makes a periodical payment concurrently with any other payment, and the weekly amount of the periodical payment as calculated in accordance with regulation 58(1) to (4) (calculation of the weekly amount of a liable relative payment), is equal to or greater than the amount referred to in sub-paragraph (a) of regulation 57(2) (period over which payments other than periodical payments are to be taken into account) less the £2 referred to therein, or sub-paragraph (b) of that regulation, as the case may be, the other payment shall be treated as capital.

(2) If, in any case, the liable relative ceases to make periodical payments, the other payment to which paragraph (1) applies shall be taken into account under paragraph (1) of regulation 57 but, notwithstanding paragraph (4) thereof, the period over which the payment is to be taken into account shall begin on the first day of the benefit week following the last one in which a periodical payment was taken into account.

CHAPTER VIIA.   CHILD SUPPORT

*Interpretation*

**60A.** In this Chapter—
   'child support maintenance' means such periodical payments as are referred to in section 3(6) of the Child Support Act 1991 [and shall include any payments made by the Secretary of State in lieu of such payments];
   'maintenance *assessment* [calculation]' has the same meaning as in the Child Support Act 1991 by virtue of section 54 of that Act.

**Note.** In definition 'child support maintenance' words 'and shall include any payments made by the Secretary of State in lieu of such payments' in square brackets inserted by SI 2000/3176, reg 2(1)(a), in relation to certain cases as from 3 March 2003. For further effect see SI 2000/3176, art 1 and SI 2003/192, art 6 (as amended by SI 2003/346, art 2). In definition 'maintenance assessment' words 'assessment' substituted by words 'calculation' in square brackets by SI 2001/158, reg 6, in relation to certain cases as from 3 March 2003; for savings see reg 10 thereof (as amended by SI 2003/347, regs 2, 4 and SI 2000/3186 (as amended by SI 2004/2415, reg 8)).

*Treatment of child support maintenance*

**60B.**   Subject to regulation 60E, all payments of child support maintenance shall to the extent that they are not payments of income be treated as income and shall be taken into account on a weekly basis in accordance with the following provisions of this Chapter.

*Calculation of the weekly amount of payments of child support maintenance*

**60C.**   (1) The weekly amount of child support maintenance shall be determined in accordance with the following provisions of this regulation.

(2) Where payments of child support maintenance are made weekly, the weekly amount shall be the amount of that payment.

(3) Where payments of child support maintenance are made monthly, the weekly amount shall be determined by multiplying the amount of the payment by 12 and dividing the product by 52.

(4) Where payments of child support are made at intervals and those intervals are not a week or a month, the weekly amount shall be determined by dividing that payment by the number equal to the number of weeks (including any part of a week) in that interval.

(5) Where a payment is made and that payment represents a commutation of child support maintenance the weekly amount shall be the weekly amount of the individual child support maintenance payments so commuted as calculated in accordance with paragraphs (2) to (4) as appropriate.

(6) Paragraph (2), (3) or, as the case may be, (4) shall apply to any payments made at the intervals specified in that paragraph whether or not—

(a) the amount paid is in accordance with the maintenance *assessment* [calculation], and

(b) the intervals at which the payments are made are in accordance with the intervals specified by the Secretary of State under regulation 4 of the Child Support (Collection and Enforcement) Regulations 1992.

**Note.** In para (6)(a) word 'assessment' substituted by word 'calculation' in square brackets by SI 2001/158, reg 6(1), (2) in relation to certain cases as from 3 March 2003 (see reg 1(3) thereof and SI 2003/192, arts 3, 8, Schedule); for savings see reg 10 thereof (as amended by SI 2004/2415, reg 8).

*Date on which child support maintenance is to be treated as paid*

**60D.**   (1) Subject to paragraph (2), a payment of child support maintenance is to be treated as paid—

(a) subject to sub-paragraph (aa), in the case of a payment which is due to be paid before the first benefit week pursuant to the claim, on the day in the week in which it is due to be paid which corresponds to the first day of the benefit week;

(aa) in the case of any amount of a payment which represents arrears of maintenance for a week prior to the first benefit week pursuant to a claim, on the day of the week in which it became due which corresponds to the first day of the benefit week;

(b) in any other case, on the first day of the benefit week in which it is due to be paid or the first day of the first succeeding benefit week in which it is practicable to take it into account.

(2) Where a payment to which paragraph (1)(b) refers is made to the Secretary of State and then transmitted to the person entitled to receive it, the payment shall be treated as paid on the first day of the benefit week in which it is transmitted or, where it is not practicable to take it into account in that week, the first day of the first succeeding benefit week in which it is practicable to take the payment into account.

*Disregard of payments treated as not relevant income*

**60E.** Where the Secretary of State treats any payment of child support maintenance as not being relevant income for the purposes of section 74A of the Social Security Administration Act 1992 (payment of benefit where maintenance payments collected by Secretary of State), that payment shall be disregarded in calculating a claimant's income.

## MAGISTRATES' COURTS (FAMILY LAW ACT 1986) RULES 1988

**Dated** 26 February 1988

**SI 1988 No 329**

ARRANGEMENT OF RULES

1. Citation and commencement.
2. Interpretation.
3. Registration of Part I orders.
4. Notice of revocation or variation of a registered order, and of cancellation of registration.
5. *Revoked.*
6. Duty to give statement of other proceedings.
7. Stay of proceedings.

The Lord Chancellor, in exercise of the powers conferred upon him by section 144 of the Magistrates' Courts Act 1980, as extended by section 145 of that Act and by sections 27, 39 and 42(1) of the Family Law Act 1986, section 15 of the Guardianship of Minors Act 1971 and section 100(7) of the Children Act 1975, after consultation with the Rule Committee appointed under the said section 144, hereby makes the following Rules:

*Citation and commencement*

**1.** These Rules may be cited as the Magistrates' Courts (Family Law Act 1986) Rules 1988 and shall come into force on 4th April 1988.

*Interpretation*

**2.** (1) In these Rules the following expressions have the meaning hereby respectively assigned to them—
　　'the Act' means the Family Law Act 1986;
　　'commission area' has the same meaning as in the Justices of the Peace Act 1979;
　　'Part I order' means a Part I order within the meaning of any of sections 1, 32, 40 and 42(5) and (6) of the Act;
　　'specified dependent territory' means a dependent territory specified in column 1 of Schedule 1 to the Family Law Act 1986 (Dependent Territories) Order 1991;

'the appropriate court' means, in relation to Scotland, the Court of Session and, in relation to Northern Ireland, the High Court and, in relation to a specified dependent territory, means the corresponding court in that territory;
'the Deputy Principal Clerk' means the Deputy Principal Clerk of Session;
'the Master' means the Master (Care and Protection) of the High Court in Northern Ireland.

(2) Any requirement in these Rules for any matter to be entered in the register of a magistrates' court is a requirement that it be entered in the register kept by the clerk of that court in accordance with Rule 66 of the Magistrates' Courts Rules 1981.

*Registration of Part I orders*

**3.** (1) An application under section 27 of the Act for the registration in the appropriate court of a Part I order made by a magistrates' court in England and Wales shall be made in writing in Form 1 in the Schedule to these Rules or in a similar form containing the information specified in the said Form 1, to the court which made the order.

(2) An application to which paragraph (1) above relates shall be accompanied by the following documents, namely—
(a) a certified copy of the order;
(b) where the order has been varied, a certified copy of any variation order which is in force;
(c) any other document relevant to the application.

(3) Subject to paragraph (4) below, if it appears to the court to which an application is made in accordance with paragraphs (1) and (2) above that the order to which the application relates is in force it shall cause the clerk of the court to send a copy of the application, together with copies of the documents set out in paragraph (2) above, to the Deputy Principal Clerk or the Master of the appropriate court, or the corresponding officer of the appropriate court in a specified dependent territory, or to more than one of those persons, as the case may be.

(4) If it appears to the court to which an application is made in accordance with paragraphs (1) and (2) above that the order to which the application relates is no longer in force in respect of a child in respect of whom the order was made or that any such child has attained the age of 16, it shall refuse to send the documents referred to in paragraph (2) above to the appropriate court, or shall indicate thereon with respect to which child or children the order is not to be registered, and the clerk of the court shall notify the applicant of its refusal or indication accordingly.

(5) A memorandum of the granting of an application made in accordance with paragraphs (1) and (2) above shall be entered in the register of the court to which the application was made.

(6) Where the clerk of the court which granted an application made in accordance with paragraphs (1) and (2) above receives notice of the registration in the appropriate court of the order he shall cause particulars of the notice to be entered in the register of his court.

*Notice of revocation or variation of a registered order, and of cancellation of registration*

**4.** (1) Where a Part I order made by a magistrates' court in England and Wales and registered in the appropriate court in Scotland, Northern Ireland or a specified dependent territory is revoked or varied, the clerk of the court making the order of revocation or variation shall cause a certified copy of that order to be sent to the Deputy Principal Clerk or the Master of the appropriate court, or the corresponding officer of the appropriate court in a specified dependent territory, or to more than one of those persons, as the case may be, and to the court which made the Part I order, if that court is different from the court making the order of revocation or variation.

(2) Where the clerk of the court which made an order revoking or varying a registered order receives notice of the registration in the appropriate court of the order of revocation or variation he shall cause particulars of the notice to be entered in the register of his court.

(3) Where the clerk of the court which made a Part I order receives, in accordance with paragraph (1) above, a certified copy of an order of revocation or variation of that order by another court, he shall cause notice thereof to be entered in the register of his court.

(4) Where the clerk of a court which made a Part I order receives notice of the registration in the appropriate court of an order revoking or varying the Part I order he shall cause particulars of the notice to be entered in the register of his court.

(5) Where the clerk of a court which made a Part I order receives notice of the cancellation of the registration of that order in the appropriate court, he shall cause particulars of the notice to be entered in the register of his court.

*Courts authorised to hear applications under the Guardianship of Minors Act 1971 and Part II of the Children Act 1975*

**5.**   *Revoked.*

*Duty to give statement of other proceedings*

**6.**   (1) A party to proceedings for or relating to a Part I order in a magistrates' court in England and Wales who knows of other proceedings (including proceedings out of the jurisdiction and concluded proceedings) which relate to the child concerned shall provide to the court a statement giving the information set out in Form 2 in the Schedule to these Rules, and, for this purpose, the clerk of a magistrates' court in which proceedings for or relating to a Part I order are pending shall, as soon in those proceedings as may be practicable, notify the parties of the provisions of this rule by sending to each party a notice in the said Form 2 or in a similar form.

(2) Paragraph (1) above shall not apply in relation to proceedings commenced in a magistrates' court before 4th April 1988.

*Stay of proceedings*

**7.**   (1) Where under section 5(2) of the Act a magistrates' court stays proceedings on an application for a Part I order it shall cause notice of the stay to be given to the parties to the proceedings.

(2) Where under section 5(3) of the Act a magistrates' court removes a stay granted in accordance with section 5(2) it shall cause notice of the removal of the stay to be given to the parties to the proceedings and shall proceed to deal with the application accordingly.

SCHEDULE                                                                Rule 3(1) and 6

FORM 1                                                                        Rule 3(1)

APPLICATION FOR REGISTRATION IN SCOTLAND, NORTHERN IRELAND OR A SPECIFIED DEPENDENT TERRITORY OF A PART I ORDER (SECTION 27 OF FAMILY LAW ACT 1986)

....................................................................................Magistrates' Court (Code)

Date:

To the Justices' Clerk,....................................................Magistrates' Court (address)

Name of applicant:

Address:

Order made on:          (date)

To be registered in: (Scotland, Northern Ireland, specified dependent territory or more than one of these)

Name of child:

Date of birth:

Address (or suspected whereabouts) of child:

Name of person with whom child is presently residing (or suspected to be residing):

The applicant's interest under the order is

.......................................................................................................................................

(State whether the order has been served on each person named)

[The order is not registered in any other court]

[The order is already registered in .............................................................................]
To the best of the applicant's information and belief the order is in force and [no other order affecting the child is in force in the place where the order is to be registered] [the following other orders are in force in the place where the order is to be registered]

Signed by the applicant

.............................................

**Note.** This application must be accompanied by a certified copy of the order to which it relates, a certified copy of any variation order which is in force, and any other document which is relevant to the application.

FORM 2                                                                              Rule 6

NOTICE OF REQUIREMENT TO GIVE PARTICULARS OF OTHER PROCEEDINGS (S 39 FAMILY LAW ACT 1986)

...................................................................................Magistrates' Court (Code)

Date:

To:

Address:

Concerning the application of:                                        (*name of applicant*)

under:        (*statute*)

As a party to these proceedings you are required to inform the court if you know of any other proceedings (including proceedings out of the jurisdiction and concluded proceedings) relating to: (name of child).

The information you should provide, if known, is:
   (a)   the place in which and the court in which the other proceedings were instituted;
   (b)   the names of the parties to the proceedings and their relationship to the child;
   (c)   the nature and current state of the proceedings and the relief claimed;
   (d)   if the relief claimed in the proceedings before this court was not claimed in the other proceedings, the reasons why it was not claimed in the other proceedings.

The information should be provided in writing addressed to the Justices' Clerk, at the address below.

Justices' Clerk
...................................Magistrates' court

Address..................................................................................................................
......................................................................................................................................

## MAGISTRATES' COURTS (CHILDREN AND YOUNG PERSONS) RULES 1988

**Dated** 23 May 1988

**SI 1988 No 913**

ARRANGEMENT OF RULES

\*      \*      \*      \*      \*

PART I

GENERAL

*Citation and commencement*

**1.**   These Rules may be cited as the Magistrates' Courts (Children and Young Persons) Rules 1988 and shall come into force on 1st August 1988.

*Interpretation*

**2.**   (1) In these Rules the following expressions have the meanings hereby respectively assigned to them, that is to say—
'the Act of 1933' means the Children and Young Persons Act 1933;
'the Act of 1969' means the Children and Young Persons Act 1969;
'the Act of 1989' means the Children Act 1989;
'child' means a person under the age of fourteen;
'court' means a juvenile court except that in Part VII it means a magistrates' court, whether a juvenile court or not;
'parent', in the case of a child or young person whose father and mother were not married to each other at the time of his birth, has the same meaning as it has in section 70(1A) and (1B) of the Children and Young Persons Act 1969;
'register' means the separate register kept for the juvenile court pursuant to rule 37 of these Rules;
'young person' means a person who has attained the age of fourteen and is under the age of seventeen.
(2) In these Rules, unless the context otherwise requires, any reference to a rule, Part or Schedule shall be construed as a reference to a rule contained in these Rules, a Part thereof or a Schedule thereto, and any reference in a rule to a paragraph shall be construed as a reference to a paragraph of that rule.

*Revocations and savings etc*

**3.**   (1) Subject to paragraph (3), the Rules specified in Schedule 1 are hereby revoked.
(2) Subject to paragraph (3), the provisions of the Magistrates' Courts Rules 1981 shall have effect subject to these Rules.
(3) Nothing in these Rules shall apply in connection with any proceedings begun before the coming into force thereof.

\*    \*    \*    \*    \*

PART III

PROCEEDINGS RELATING TO SUPERVISION ORDERS

*Application and interpretation of Part III*

**13.**   (1) This Part shall apply in connection with proceedings in a court in the case of any person in relation to whom proceedings are brought or proposed to be brought under—
(a)  any of the following provisions of the Act of 1969, namely—
  (i)  *omitted,*
  (ii)  section 15 (variation and discharge of supervision orders),
  (iii)  *omitted;*
(b)  section 72 or 73 of the Social Work (Scotland) Act 1968 (persons subject to supervision requirements or orders moving from or to Scotland);

(c)   section 189 or 390 of the Criminal Procedure (Scotland) Act 1975 (young person subject to Scottish probation order resident in England or Wales); or

(d)   regulations made under section 25 of the Act of 1989 (authority to retain child in secure accommodation),

except that rules 14, 20(2), 24 and 25 shall not apply in connection with proceedings under the enactments mentioned in sub-paragraphs (b) and (c) above, rules 14(3)(c) and (d) and 25 shall not apply in connection with proceedings of the kind mentioned in paragraph (d), and rule 26 shall apply only in connection with proceedings of that kind.

(2)   In this Part of the Rules the following expressions have the meanings hereby respectively assigned to them, that is to say—

'the applicant' means the person by whom proceedings are brought or proposed to be brought;

'the appropriate local authority' means—

(a)   *omitted,*

(b)   in relation to proceedings under section 15 of the Act of 1969, the local authority whose area is named in the supervision order in pursuance of section 18(2) of that Act, and

(c)   *omitted;*

'guardian' has the same meaning as in section 70(1) and (2) of the Act of 1969;

'the relevant infant' means a person in relation to whom proceedings are brought or proposed to be brought as mentioned in paragraph (1);

'reside' has the meaning assigned to it by section 70(1) of the Act of 1969;

'the respondent' means the relevant infant except that—

(a)   in relation to proceedings under section 15 of the Act of 1969 in which the relevant infant is the applicant it means the supervisor of the relevant infant, and

(b)   *omitted.*

*Notice by persons proposing to bring care etc proceedings*

**14.**   (1)   An applicant proposing to bring proceedings shall send a notice to the clerk of the court specifying the grounds for the proceedings and the names and addresses of the persons to whom a copy of the notice is sent in pursuance of paragraph (2).

(2)   Without prejudice to section 34(2) of the Act of 1969 and regulations made under section 25 of the Act of 1989, the applicant shall—

(a)   send to each of the persons mentioned in paragraph (3) a copy of the said notice, and

(b)   notify each of those persons of the date, time and place, appointed for the hearing unless a summons is issued for the purpose of securing his attendance thereat.

(3)   The persons referred to in paragraph (2) are the following persons other than the person who is the applicant—

(a)   the relevant infant, unless it appears to the applicant inappropriate to notify him in pursuance of paragraph (2), having regard to his age and understanding;

(b)   the parent or guardian of the relevant infant if the whereabouts of such parent or guardian is known to the applicant or can readily be ascertained by him;

(c)   any grandparent of the relevant infant if the whereabouts of such grandparent is known to the applicant or can readily be ascertained by him;

(d)   any foster parent or other person with whom the relevant infant has had his home for a period of, or periods amounting in total to, not less than 42 days, ending not more than six months before the date of the application, if the whereabouts of such a person is known to the applicant or can readily be ascertained by him;

(dd) where the father and mother of the relevant infant were not married to each other at the time of his birth, any person who is known to the applicant to have made an application for an order under section 4 of the Family Law Reform Act 1987 (parental rights and duties of father) which has not yet been determined;

(e)  the appropriate local authority;

(f)  *omitted;*

(g)  where the proceedings are for the variation or discharge of a supervision order which names a person other than the appropriate authority as the supervisor, that supervisor.

(4)  *Omitted.*

*Notice to parent or guardian of party status*

**15.**  *Revoked.*

*Appointment and duties of guardian ad litem*

**16.**  *Revoked.*

*Applications by grandparents to be parties to proceedings*

**17.**  *Revoked.*

*Rights of parents and guardians*

**18.**  Without prejudice to any provision of these Rules which provides for a parent or guardian to take part in proceedings, the relevant infant's parent or guardian shall be entitled—

(a)  to meet any allegations made against him in the course of the proceedings by cross-examining any witness and calling or giving evidence (and shall call or give evidence at the conclusion of the evidence for the respondent and the evidence, if any, for the applicant in rebuttal but before either the respondent or the applicant addresses the court under rule 14(4) or (5) of the Magistrates' Courts Rules 1981 (as applied by rule 20(3) of these Rules); and

(b)  to make representations to the court, and shall do so at any such stage after the conclusion of the evidence in the hearing as the court considers appropriate.

*Rights of other persons*

**19.**  (1) Without prejudice to any other provision of these Rules which provides for a parent, guardian or grandparent to take part in proceedings, any person to whom this paragraph applies shall be entitled to make representations to the court, and shall do so at any such stage after the conclusion of the evidence in the hearing as the court considers appropriate.

(2)  The preceding paragraph applies to—

(a)  any person who is required to be given notice of the proceedings by virtue of rule 14(3)(d) of these Rules; and

(b)  any other person who is not a party to the proceedings and who satisfies the court that both of the criteria specified in the next following paragraph are met.

(3)  The criteria mentioned in the preceding paragraph are—

(a)  that the person in question has demonstrated an interest in the infant's welfare which has been maintained until the commencement of the proceedings;

(b)  that the representations of that person are likely to be of relevance to the proceedings and to the welfare of the relevant infant.

*Adjournment of proceedings and procedure at hearing*

**20.**   (1)  The court may, at any time, whether before or after the beginning of the hearing, adjourn the hearing, and, when so doing, may either fix the date, time and place at which the hearing is to be resumed or, leave the date, time and place to be determined later by the court; but the hearing shall not be resumed at that date, time and place unless the court is satisfied that the applicant, the respondent, any other party to the proceedings and any person to whom rule 19(1) applies have had adequate notice thereof.

(2)  Subject to the provisions of the Act of 1969, sections 56, 57 and 123 of the Magistrates' Courts Act 1980 (non-appearance of parties and defects in process) shall apply to the proceedings as if they were by way of complaint and as if any references therein to the complainant, to the defendant and to the defence were, respectively, references to the applicant, to the respondent or any other party to the proceedings and to his case.

(3)  Subject to the provisions of the next following paragraph, rules 14 and 16(1) of the Magistrates' Courts Rules 1981 (order of evidence and speeches and form of order) shall apply to the proceedings as if they were by way of complaint and as if any references therein to the complainant, to the defendant and to the defence were, respectively, references to the applicant, to the respondent and to his case.

(4)  *Omitted.*

(5)  *Omitted.*

*Duty of court to explain nature of proceedings; evidence and order of speeches*

**21.**   (1)  Except where the relevant infant is the applicant or where, by virtue of any enactment, the court may proceed in his absence, before proceeding with the hearing the court shall inform him of the general nature both of the proceedings and of the grounds on which they are brought, in terms suitable to his age and understanding, or if by reason of his age and understanding or his absence it is impracticable so to do, shall so inform any parent or guardian of his present at the hearing.

(2)  *Omitted.*

(3)  *Omitted.*

*Conduct of case on behalf of relevant infant*

**22.**   (1)  Except where—

(a)  the relevant infant or his parent or guardian is legally represented,

(b)  *omitted,*

(c)  *omitted,*

the court shall, unless the relevant infant otherwise requests, allow his parent or guardian to conduct the case on his behalf, subject however to the provisions of rule 23(2).

(2)  If the court thinks it appropriate to do so it may, unless the relevant infant otherwise requests, allow a relative of his or some other responsible person to conduct the case on his behalf.

*Power of court to hear evidence in absence of relevant infant and to require parent or guardian to withdraw*

**23.**   (1)  Where the evidence likely to be given, is such that in the opinion of the court it is in the interests of the relevant infant that the whole, or any part, of the evidence should not be given in his presence, then, unless the relevant infant is conducting his own case, the court may hear the whole or part of the evidence, as it thinks appropriate, in his absence:

Provided that evidence relating to the character or conduct of the relevant infant shall be heard in his presence.

(2) If the court is satisfied that in the special circumstances it is appropriate so to do, it may require a parent, guardian or grandparent of the relevant infant or any other person entitled to make representations by virtue of rule 19 to withdraw from the court while the relevant infant gives evidence or makes a statement:

Provided that the court shall inform the person so excluded of the substance of any allegations made against him by the relevant infant.

*Duty of court to explain procedure to relevant infant at end of applicant's case*

**24.**   If it appears to the court after hearing the evidence in support of the applicant's case that he has made out a *prima facie* case it shall tell the relevant infant or the person conducting the case on his behalf under rule 22 that he may give evidence or make a statement and call witnesses.

*Consideration of reports*

**25.**   (1) The court shall arrange for copies of any written report of a probation officer, local authority, local education authority, educational establishment or registered medical practitioner before the court to be made available, so far as practicable before the hearing, to—

(a)  the applicant;

(b)  the appropriate local authority, where it is not the applicant;

(c)  the legal representative, if any, of the relevant infant;

(d)  the parent or guardian of the relevant infant;

(e)  *omitted*;

(f)  the relevant infant, except where the court otherwise directs on the ground that it appears to it impracticable to disclose the report having regard to the age and understanding of the infant or undesirable to do so having regard to serious harm which thereby be suffered by him; and

(g)  any other person who is a party to the proceedings.

(2) Copies of any such report may, if the court considers it desirable to do so, be shown to any person who is required to be given notice of the proceedings in pursuance of rule 14(3)(d) of these Rules and to any other person who is entitled to make representations to the court by virtue of rule 19(1) of these Rules.

(3) Where the court is satisfied that the applicant's case has been proved—

(a)  *omitted*;

(b)  the court shall take into consideration such information as to the relevant infant's general conduct, home surroundings, school record and medical history as may be necessary to enable it to deal with the case in his best interests and, in particular, shall take into consideration such information as aforesaid which is provided in pursuance of section 9 of the Act of 1969;

(c)  if such information as aforesaid is not fully available, the court shall consider the desirability of adjourning the case for such inquiry as may be necessary;

(d)  any written report of a probation officer, local authority, local education authority, educational establishment or registered medical practitioner may be received and considered by the court without being read aloud; and

(e)  if the court considers it necessary in the interests of the relevant infant, it may require him or his parent or guardian, if present, to withdraw from the court.

(4) In any case in which the relevant infant is not legally represented and where a report which has not been made available to him in accordance with a direction under paragraph (1)(f) has been considered without being read aloud in pursuance of paragraph (3)(d) or where the relevant infant, his parent or guardian has been required to withdraw from the court in pursuance of paragraph (3)(e), then—

(a)  the relevant infant shall be told the substance of any part of the information given to the court bearing on his character or conduct which the court considers to be material to the manner in which the case should be dealt with unless it appears to it impracticable so to do having regard to his age and understanding, and

(b) the relevant infant's parent or guardian, if present, shall be told the substance of any part of such information which the court considers to be material as aforesaid and which has reference to his character or conduct or to the character, conduct, home surroundings or health of the relevant infant;

and, if such a person, having been told the substance of any part of such information desires to produce further evidence with reference thereto, the court, if it thinks the further evidence would be material, shall adjourn the proceedings for the production thereof and shall, if necessary in the case of a report, require the attendance at the adjourned hearing of the person who made the report.

*Consideration of reports: secure accommodation proceedings*

**26.**    (1) This rule applies only in connection with proceedings brought under regulations made under section 25 of the Act of 1989.

(2) The court shall arrange for copies of any written report before the court to be made available, so far as practicable before the hearing, to—

(a) the applicant;

(b) the legal representative, if any, of the relevant infant;

(c) the parent or guardian of the relevant infant;

(d) the relevant infant, except where the court otherwise directs on the ground that it appears to it impracticable to disclose the report having regard to the age and understanding of the infant or undesirable to do so having regard to serious harm which might thereby be suffered by him;

and copies of such a report may, if the court considers it desirable to do so, be shown to any person who is required to be given notice of the proceedings in pursuance of rule 14(3)(d) of these Rules.

(3) In any case in which the court has determined that the relevant criteria are satisfied, the court shall, for the purpose of determining the maximum period of authorisation to be specified in the order, take into consideration such information as it considers necessary for that purpose, including such information which is provided in pursuance of section 9 of the Act of 1969.

(4) Any written report may be received and considered by the court without being read aloud.

*Duty of court to explain manner in which it proposes to deal with case and effect of order*

**27.**    (1) Before finally disposing of the case the court shall in simple language inform the relevant infant, any person conducting the case on his behalf, and his parent or guardian, if present, of the manner in which it proposes to deal with the case and allow any of those persons so informed to make representations:

Provided that the relevant infant shall not be informed as aforesaid if the court considers it undesirable or, having regard to his age and understanding, impracticable so to inform him.

(2) On making any order, the court shall in simple language suitable to his age and understanding explain to the relevant infant the general nature and effect of the order unless it appears to it impracticable so to do having regard to his age and understanding or, in the case of an order requiring his parent or guardian to enter into a recognizance, it appears to it undesirable so to do; and shall in any case give such an explanation to the relevant infant's parent or guardian, if present.

*Leave of court for withdrawal of discharge applications*

**28.**    *Revoked.*

PART IV

PROCEEDINGS IN RELATION TO ACCESS TO CHILDREN IN CARE AND RESOLUTIONS
CONCERNING PARENTAL RIGHTS AND DUTIES

*Application and interpretation of Part IV*

**29.** *Revoked.*

*Notice of complaint*

**30.** *Revoked.*

*Appointment and duties of guardian ad litem*

**31.** *Revoked.*

*Evidence of guardian ad litem*

**32.** *Revoked.*

*Rights of persons other than parties*

**33.** *Revoked.*

*Evidence and procedure generally*

**34.** *Revoked.*

*Power of the court to hear evidence in absence of child, etc*

**35.** *Revoked.*

\*      \*      \*      \*      \*

## MAGISTRATES' COURTS (INCREASE OF LUMP SUMS) ORDER 1988

**Dated** 20 June 1988

**SI 1988 No 1069**

In exercise of the powers conferred upon me by section 4(5) of the Affiliation
Proceedings Act 1957, section 12B(2) of the Guardianship of Minors Act 1971,
section 35A(2) of the Children Act 1975 and section 2(3) of the Domestic
Proceedings and Magistrates' Courts Act 1978, I hereby make the following Order:
**1.** This Order may be cited as the Magistrates' Courts (Increase of Lump Sums)
Order 1988 and shall come into force on 25th July 1988.
**2.** For the purposes *of section 4(5) of the Affiliation Proceedings Act 1957, section
12B(2) of the Guardianship of Minors Act 1971, section 35A(2) of the Children Act 1975
and* section 2(3) of the Domestic Proceedings and Magistrates' Courts Act 1978 the
maximum amount of any lump sum required to be paid by an order referred to in
any of those provisions is hereby fixed at £1,000.
**Note.** Words from 'of section' to 'Children Act 1975 and' in italics spent.

## MATRIMONIAL CAUSES (COSTS) RULES 1988

**Dated** 26 July 1988

### SI 1988 No 1328

**Note.** Following the repeal of the original enabling powers, these Rules (with the exception or r 10 and Sch 2) were continued in force as from 14 October 1991 by SI 1991/1832, as if they were part of those Rules and were applied to the taxation of costs in matrimonial causes and in proceedings under the Children Act 1989. Following the revocation of SI 1991/1832 by SI 1999/1012, these Rules have lapsed as from 26 April 1999.

## REIMBURSEMENT OF COSTS (MONETARY LIMIT) ORDER 1988

**Dated** 27 July 1988

### SI 1988 No 1342

The Lord Chancellor, in exercise of the powers conferred on him by section 53(1) of the Administration of Justice Act 1985 and with the concurrence of the Treasury, hereby makes the following Order—

**1.** This Order may be cited as the Reimbursement of Costs (Monetary Limit) Order 1988 and shall come into force on 1st October 1988.

**2.** The amount prescribed for the purposes of section 53 of the Administration of Justice Act 1985 (reimbursement of additional costs resulting from death or incapacity of presiding judge etc) is £8000.

## ADOPTION ALLOWANCE SCHEMES ORDER 1989

**Dated** 8 February 1989

### SI 1989 No 166

*Citation and commencement*

**1.** This Order may be cited as the Adoption Allowance Schemes Order 1989 and shall come into force on i4th February 1989.

*Repeals*

**2.** Section 57(7) of the Adoption Act 1976 (expiry after seven years of section 57(4) of the 1976 Act which provides for adoption allowance schemes) is hereby repealed.

## ACCESS TO PERSONAL FILES (SOCIAL SERVICES) REGULATIONS 1989

**Dated** 17 February 1989

### SI 1989 No 206

**Note.** These Regulations lapsed on the repeal of the enabling powers by the Data Protection Act 1998, s 74(2), Sch 16, Pt I as from 1 March 2000.

## CIVIL LEGAL AID (ASSESSMENT OF RESOURCES) REGULATIONS 1989

**Dated** 3 March 1989

### SI 1989 No 338

*Note. Following the repeal of the enabling provisions by the Access to Justice Act 1999, s 106, Sch 15, Pt I, these Regulations have lapsed except insofar as they may continue to have effect by virtue of SI 2000/774, art 5, as from 1 April 2000.*

ARRANGEMENT OF REGULATIONS

The Lord Chancellor, in exercise of the powers conferred on him by sections 15(1), 16, 34 and 43 of the Legal Aid Act 1988 and with the consent of the Treasury, hereby makes the following Regulations—

*Citation and commencement*

**1.**   These Regulations may be cited as the Civil Legal Aid (Assessment of Resources) Regulations 1989 and shall come into force on 1st April 1989.

*Revocations*

**2.**   The Regulations specified in Schedule 1 are hereby revoked.

*Interpretation*

**3.**   (1)  In these Regulations, unless the context otherwise requires—
'the Act' means the Legal Aid Act 1988;
'area committee', 'Area Director' and 'assessment officer' have the meanings assigned to them by the Civil Legal Aid (General) Regulations 1989;
'certificate' means a legal aid certificate issued in accordance with the Civil Legal Aid (General) Regulations 1989;
'child' means a person—
(a) under the age that is for the time being the upper limit of compulsory school age within the meaning of the Education Act 1944; or
(b) over the limit of compulsory school age and either receiving full-time instruction at an educational establishment or undergoing training for a trade, profession or vocation;

'contribution' has the meaning assigned to it by the Civil Legal Aid (General) Regulations 1989;

'disposable capital' and 'disposable income' have the meanings assigned to them by regulation 4;

'income' includes—

(a) benefits,

(b) privileges, and

(c) any sum payable (whether voluntarily or under a court order, the terms of any instrument or otherwise) for the purpose of the maintenance of a child;

'income based jobseeker's allowance' has the meaning given by section 1(4) of the Jobseekers Act 1995, but excludes any sum treated as payable by way of a jobseeker's allowance by virtue of section 26 of that Act;

'legal aid' means representation under Part IV of the Act;

'make an assessment', in relation to the assessment officer, means to assess the disposable income, disposable capital and contribution of the person concerned;

'period of computation' means the period of 12 months next ensuing from the date of the application for a certificate, or such other period of 12 months as in the particular circumstances of any case the assessment officer may consider to be appropriate;

'person concerned' means the person—

(a) whose disposable income and disposable capital are to be assessed or reassessed; or

(b) whose resources are to be treated as the resources of any other person under these Regulations.

(2) Any reference in these Regulations to a regulation or Schedule by number means the regulation or Schedule so numbered in these Regulations.

*Computation of disposable income, disposable capital and contribution*

**4.**   (1) Subject to the provisions of these Regulations, the assessment officer shall—

(a) take into account the financial resources of the person concerned; and

(b) compute his income and capital in accordance with Schedules 2 and 3;

and, in these Regulations, 'disposable income' and 'disposable capital' mean the amounts of income and capital available for the making of a contribution after the person concerned's income and capital have been computed in accordance with those Schedules.

(2) Subject to paragraph (3) below, legal aid shall be available to a person whose disposable income does not exceed £7,595 [£7,777] [£7,940] a year but a person may be refused legal aid where—

(a) his disposable capital exceeds £6,750; and

(b) it appears to the Area Director that he could afford to proceed without legal aid.

(3) Where the subject matter of the dispute in respect of which the legal aid application has been made includes a claim in respect of personal injuries legal aid shall be available to a person whose disposable income does not exceed £8,370 [£8,571] [£8,751] a year but a person may be refused legal aid where—

(a) his disposable capital exceeds £8,560; and

(b) it appears to the Area Director that he could afford to proceed without legal aid.

(4) A person who desires to receive legal aid shall be liable to make the following contributions—

(a) where his disposable income in the period of computation exceeds £2,563 [£2,625] [£2,680], a monthly contribution in respect of disposable income payable throughout the period while the certificate is in force of one thirty-sixth of the excess;

(b) where his disposable capital exceeds £3,000, a contribution in respect of disposable capital not greater than the excess.

(5) In this regulation 'personal injuries' includes any death and any disease or other impairment of a person's physical or mental condition.

**Note.** Sums '£7,595'. And '£8,370' and '£2,563' substituted by sums '£7,777', '£8,571' and '£2,625' in square brackets by SI 1998/664, reg 2 as from 6 April 1998 and further substituted by sums '£7,940', and '£8,751' and '£2,680' in square brackets by SI 1999/813, reg 2, subject to savings, as from 12 April 1999.

*Subject matter of dispute*

**5.**   (1) In computing the income or capital of the person concerned, there shall be excluded the value of the subject matter of the dispute in respect of which the legal aid application has been made.

(2) Periodical payments of maintenance (whether made voluntarily or otherwise) shall not be treated as the subject matter of the dispute for the purposes of paragraph (1).

*Application in representative, fiduciary or official capacity*

**6.**   Where an application for legal aid is made by a person who is concerned in the proceedings only in a representative, fiduciary or official capacity, the assessment officer shall, in computing the income and capital of that person and the amount of any contribution to be made—

(a) where so requested by the Area Director, assess the value of any property or estate or the amount of any fund out of which that person is entitled to be indemnified and the disposable income, disposable capital and contribution of any persons (including that person if appropriate), who might benefit from the outcome of the proceedings; and

(b) except in so far as they are assessed under paragraph (a), disregard the personal resources of that person.

*Resources of spouses etc*

**7.**   (1) Subject to paragraph (2), in computing the income and capital of the person concerned the resources of his or her spouse shall be treated as his or her resources.

(2) The resources of the spouse of the person concerned shall not be treated as his or her resources if—

(a) the spouse has a contrary interest in the dispute in respect of which the legal aid application is made; or

(b) the person concerned and the spouse are living separate and apart.

(3) Paragraphs (1) and (2) above and Schedules 2 and 3 shall apply to a man and a woman who are living with each other in the same household as husband and wife as it applies to the parties to a marriage.

**7A.**   (1) Where it appears to the assessment officer that—

(a) the person concerned has transferred any resources to another person;

(b) another person is or has been maintaining the person concerned in the proceedings to which the application relates or any other proceedings, or

(c) any of the resources of another person are or have been made available to the person concerned,

the assessment officer shall have power to treat all or any part of the resources of that other person as the resources of the person concerned.

(2) Where paragraph (1) applies:

(a) the question of what is or is not a resource of that other person shall be determined, as nearly as the circumstances permit, in accordance with the provisions of these Regulations excluding this regulation, and

(b)  the assessment officer shall assess or estimate the value of those resources to the best of his judgment.

(3)  In this regulation 'person' (except in the phrase 'person concerned') includes a company, partnership, body of trustees and any body of persons whether corporate or not corporate.

*Resources of an applicant who is a child*

**8.**  *Omitted.*

*Deprivation or conversion of resources*

**9.**  Where it appears to the assessment officer that the person concerned has with intent to reduce the amount of his disposable income or disposable capital whether for the purpose of making himself eligible for legal aid, reducing his liability to pay a contribution towards legal aid or otherwise—

(a)  directly or indirectly deprived himself of any resources; or

(b)  converted any part of his resources into resources which under these Regulations are to be wholly or partly disregarded, or in respect of which nothing is to be included in determining the resources of that person;

the resources of which he has so deprived himself or which he has so converted shall be treated as part of his resources or as not so converted as the case may be and, for this purpose, resources which are to be wholly or partly disregarded shall include the repayment of money borrowed on the security of a dwelling.

*Notification of the assessment officer's decision*

**10.**  (1) The assessment officer shall make an assessment of the disposable income, disposable capital and contribution of the person concerned.

(2)  The assessment made under paragraph (1) shall be communicated in writing to the Area Director and the assessment officer may draw attention to any special circumstances affecting the manner in which any contribution is to be made.

*Duty of the person concerned to report change in financial circumstances*

**11.**  The person concerned shall [forthwith] inform the Area Director of any change in his financial circumstances which has occurred since the original assessment was made and which he has reason to believe might affect the terms on which the certificate was granted or its continuation.

**Note.** Word 'forthwith' in square brackets inserted by SI 1998/664, reg 3, as from 6 April 1998.

*Further assessments*

**12.**  (1) Where—

(a)  it appears that the circumstances upon which the assessment officer has assessed the disposable income or disposable capital of the person concerned have altered so that—

(i)  his disposable income may have increased by an amount greater than £750 or decreased by an amount greater than £300; or

(ii)  his disposable capital may have increased by an amount greater than £750; or

(b)  the Area Director considers that the current financial circumstances of the person concerned are such that he could afford to proceed without legal aid,

the assessment officer shall make a further assessment of the person's disposable income or disposable capital or contribution as the case may be in accordance with the provisions of Schedules 2 and 3, unless (in relation to sub-paragraph (a)) it appears to him unlikely that any significant change in that person's liability to make a contribution will result from any such further assessment

(2) For the purposes of the further assessment, the period of computation shall be the period of 12 months following from the date of the request for a reassessment or such other period of twelve months as in the particular circumstances of the case the assessment officer may consider to be appropriate.

(3) Where a further assessment is made the amount and value of every resource of a capital nature acquired since the date of the legal aid application shall be ascertained as at the date of receipt of that resource.

*Further assessment of resources outside the original period of computation*

**13.** *Revoked.*

*Amendment of assessment due to error or receipt of new information*

**14.** Where—
- (a) it appears to the assessment officer that there has been some error or mistake in the assessment of a person's disposable income, disposable capital or contribution or in any computation or estimate upon which such assessment was based, and that it would be just and equitable to correct the error or mistake; or
- (b) new information which is relevant to the assessment has come to light,

the assessment officer shall make an amended assessment and give written notice to the Area Director of the amended assessment and of any of the circumstances giving rise to it which he considers to merit special attention.

*Power of assessment officer to estimate the resources of the person concerned*

**15.** (1) Where the Area Director informs the assessment officer that the person concerned requires a certificate as a matter of urgency and the officer is not satisfied that he can make an assessment and communicate it to the Area Director by the time that he is requested so to do, the officer may, on the basis of the information then available to him, make an estimate of the disposable income and disposable capital of the person concerned and of his *maximum* contribution.

(2) The assessment officer shall communicate any estimate made under paragraph (1) to the Area Director in writing and, until the making of a full assessment, the estimate shall be treated as if it were an assessment and section 17(1) of the Act and regulation 4(2) and (4) above shall have effect as if the disposable income, disposable capital and contribution of the person concerned were of the amounts specified in the estimate.

(3) In any case in which the assessment officer makes an estimate under paragraph (1) he shall, upon receiving such additional information as he may require, make an assessment and shall communicate it to the Area Director in writing and the assessment shall for all purposes take the place of the estimate.

**Note.** In para (1) word 'maximum' revoked by SI 1993/788, reg 6(2).

SCHEDULE 1                                                                                                    Regulation 2

REGULATIONS REVOKED

\*      \*      \*      \*      \*

SCHEDULE 2                                                                                                    Regulation 4

COMPUTATION OF INCOME

**1.** The income of the person concerned from any source shall be taken to be the income which that person may reasonably expect to receive (in cash or in kind) during the period of computation and, in the absence of other means of ascertaining it, shall be taken to be the income received during the preceding year.

**2.**   The income in respect of any emolument, benefit or privilege which is received otherwise than in cash shall be estimated at such sum as in all the circumstances is just and equitable.

**3.**   (1) The income from a trade, business or gainful occupation other than an employment at a wage or salary shall be deemed to be the profits therefrom which have accrued or will accrue to the person concerned in respect of the period of computation, and, in computing such profits, the assessment officer may have regard to the profits of the last accounting period of such trade, business or gainful occupation for which accounts have been prepared.

(2) In ascertaining the profits under paragraph (1), there shall be deducted all sums necessarily expended to earn those profits, but no deduction shall be made in respect of the living expenses of that person or of any member of his family or household, except in so far as such member of his family or household is wholly or mainly employed in such trade or business and such living expenses form part of his remuneration.

**4.**   (1) In computing the income of the person concerned, there shall be deducted the total amount of tax which it is estimated would be payable by the person concerned if his income (as computed in accordance with paragraphs 1 to 3 above but not taking into account the provisions of regulation 5) were his income for a fiscal year and his liability for tax in that year were to be ascertained by reference to that income and not by reference to his income in any other year or period.

(2) For the purposes of this paragraph, tax shall be estimated at the rate provided by and after making all appropriate allowances, deductions or reliefs in accordance with the statutory provisions relating to income tax in force for the fiscal year in which the legal aid application is made.

**4A.**   In computing the income of the person concerned, there shall be deducted any sums payable (net of council tax benefit) by the person concerned in respect of the council tax to which he is liable by virtue of section 6 of the Local Government Finance Act 1992.

**5.**   Where the person concerned or his spouse is in receipt of income based jobseeker's allowance or of income support paid under the Social Security Contributions and Benefits Act 1992, the person concerned shall, for the period during which income based jobseeker's allowance or income support is received, be deemed to have a disposable income which does not exceed the figure for the time being specified in regulation 4(4)(a).

**6.**   (1) In computing disposable income the following payments under the Social Security Contributions and Benefits Act 1992 shall be disregarded—

   (a)   disability living allowance;
   (b)   attendance allowance paid under section 64 or Schedule 8 paragraphs 4 or 7(2);
   (c)   constant attendance allowance paid under section 104 as an increase to a disablement pension;
   (d)   any payment made out of the social fund.

(2) In computing disposable income, a payment made under the Community Care (Direct Payments) Act 1996 [or under regulations made under section 57 of the Health and Social Care Act 2001 (direct payments)] shall be disregarded.

**6A.**   In computing disposable income there shall be disregarded—

   (a)   so much of any back to work bonus received under section 26 of the Jobseekers Act 1995 as is by virtue of that section to be treated as payable by way of a jobseeker's allowance;
   (b)   any payment made by the Secretary of State under the Earnings Top-up Scheme 1996.

**7.**   Where the income of the person concerned consists, wholly or in part, of a wage or salary from employment, there shall be deducted—

    (a)  the reasonable expenses of travelling to and from his place of employment;

    (b)  the amount of any payments reasonably made for membership of a trade union or professional organisation; and

    (c)  where it would be reasonable so to do, an amount to provide for the care of any dependent child living with the person concerned during the time that person is absent from home by reason of his employment; and

    (d)  the amount of any contribution paid, whether under a legal obligation or not, to an occupational pension scheme within the meaning of the Social Security Pensions Act 1975 or to a personal pension scheme within the meaning of the Social Security Act 1986.

**8.**   There shall be a deduction in respect of contributions payable by the person concerned (whether by deduction or otherwise) under the Social Security Contributions and Benefits Act 1992 of the amount estimated to be so payable in the 12 months following the application for a certificate.

**9.**   (1) In the case of a householder, there shall be a deduction in respect of rent of the main or only dwelling of the amount of the net rent payable, or such part thereof as is reasonable in the circumstances, and the assessment officer shall decide which is the main dwelling where the person concerned resides in more than one dwelling in which he has an interest.

    (2) For the purposes of this paragraph, 'rent' includes—

    (a)  the annual rent payable; and

    (b)  a sum in respect of yearly outgoings borne by the householder including, in particular, a reasonable allowance towards any necessary expenditure on repairs and insurance and any annual instalment (whether of interest or of capital) payable in respect of a mortgage debt or heritable security charged on the house in which the householder resides or has an interest;

and, in calculating the amount of rent payable, any housing benefit paid under the Social Security Contributions and Benefits Act 1992 shall be deducted from the amount of rent payable.

    (3) In this paragraph, the expression 'net rent' means the rent less any proceeds of sub-letting any part of the premises in respect of which the said rent is paid or the outgoings are incurred except that, where any person or persons other than the person concerned, his or her spouse or any dependant of his or hers is accommodated, otherwise than as a sub-tenant, in the premises for which the rent is paid, the rent may be deemed to be reduced by an amount reasonably attributable to such other person or persons.

    (4) In sub-paragraph (2)(b) above, the amount to be included as 'rent' in respect of any annual instalment payable in respect of a mortgage debt or heritable security shall not exceed an amount bearing the same proportion to the amount of the annual instalment as £100,000 bears to the debt secured.

**10.**   If the person concerned is not a householder, there shall be a deduction in respect of the cost of his living accommodation of such amount as is reasonable in the circumstances.

**11.**   (1) Subject to paragraph (2), in computing the income of the person concerned there shall be a deduction—

    (a)  in respect of the maintenance of the spouse of the person concerned, where the spouses are living together;

    (b)  in respect of the maintenance of any dependent child and of any dependent relative of the person concerned, where such persons are members of his household;

at the following rates—

        (i)  in the case of a spouse at a rate equivalent to the difference between the income support allowance for a couple where both members are aged not less than 18 (which is specified in column 2 of paragraph 1(3)(c) of Schedule 2 Part I of the Income Support (General) Regulations 1987), and the allowance for a single person aged not less than 25 (which is specified in column 2 of paragraph 1(1)(e) of Schedule 2 Part I of those Regulations);

(ii) in the case of a dependent child or a dependent relative [aged 18 or under], at a rate equivalent to the amount specified for the time being in paragraph 2 of Part I of Schedule 2 to the Income Support (General) Regulations 1987 appropriate to the age of the child or relative; then

[(iii) in the case of a dependent child or a dependent relative aged 19 or over, at a rate equivalent to the amount which would have been specified in accordance with paragraph 11(1)(b)(ii) immediately before he attained the age of 19].

(2) The assessment officer may reduce any rate provided by virtue of sub-paragraph (1) by taking into account the income and other resources of the dependent child or other dependant to such extent as appears to the officer to be just and equitable.

(3) In ascertaining whether a child is a dependent child or whether a person is a dependent relative for the purposes of this paragraph, regard shall be had to their income and other resources.

**12.** Where the person concerned is making and, throughout such period as the assessment officer may consider to be adequate, has regularly made bona fide payments for the maintenance of—

(a) a spouse who is living apart;

(b) a former spouse;

(c) a child; or

(d) a relative;

who is not a member of the household of the person concerned, there shall be a deduction at the rate of such payments or at such rate (not exceeding the rate of such payments) as in all the circumstances is reasonable.

**13.** Where the person concerned is required to, or may reasonably provide for any other matter, the assessment officer may make an allowance of such amount as he considers to be reasonable in the circumstances of the case.

**14.** In computing the income from any source, there shall be disregarded such amount, if any, as the assessment officer considers to be reasonable having regard to the nature of the income or to any other circumstances of the case.

**Note.** In para 6(2) words from 'or under' to '(direct payments)' in square brackets inserted in relation to England by SI 2003/762, reg 11(1), Sch 1 as from 8 April 2003 and in relation to Wales by SI 2004/1748, reg 12, Sch 2, para 1 as from 8 July 2004. In para 11(1)(b)(ii) words 'aged 18 or under' in square brackets and para 11(1)(b)(iii), inserted by SI 1998/664, reg 4 as from 6 April 1998.

SCHEDULE 3                                                                    Regulation 4

COMPUTATION OF CAPITAL

**1.** (1) Subject to paragraph (2) and to the provisions of these Regulations, in computing the capital of the person concerned, there shall be included the amount or value of every resource of a capital nature belonging to him on the date the legal aid application is made.

(2) Where it comes to the attention of the assessment officer that, between the date the legal aid application is made and the assessment, there has been a substantial fluctuation in the value of a resource or there has been a substantial variation in the nature of a resource affecting the basis of computation of its value,

or any resource has ceased to exist or a new resource has come into the possession of the person concerned, the officer shall compute the capital resources of that person in the light of such facts and the resources as so computed shall be taken into account in the assessment.

**2.** In so far as any resource of a capital nature does not consist of money, its amount or value shall be taken to be—

   (a) the amount which that resource would realise if sold in the open market or, if there is only a restricted market for that resource, the amount which it would realise in that market, or

   (b) the amount or value assessed in such manner as appears to the assessment officer to be just and equitable.

**3.** Where money is due to the person concerned, whether it is payable immediately or otherwise and whether payment is secured or not, its value shall be taken to be its present value.

**4.** Where the person concerned stands in relation to a company in a position analogous to that of a sole owner or partner in the business of that company, the assessment officer may, in lieu of ascertaining the value of his stocks, shares, bonds or debentures in that company, treat that person as if he were the sole owner or partner and compute the amount of his capital in respect of that resource in accordance with paragraph 5 below.

**5.** Where the person concerned is or is to be treated as the sole owner of, or a partner in, any business, the value of such business to him or his share shall be taken to be either—

   (a) such sum, or his share of such sum, as the case may be, as could be withdrawn from the assets of such business without substantially impairing the profits of such business or its normal development; or

   (b) such sum as that person could borrow on the security of his interest in such business without [substantially ]injuring the commercial credit of that business;

whichever is the greater.

**6.** The value of any interest in reversion or remainder on the termination of a prior estate, whether legal or equitable, in any real or personal property or in a trust or other fund, whether the person concerned has the sole interest or an interest jointly or in common with other persons or whether his interest is vested or contingent, shall be computed in such manner as is both equitable and practicable.

**7.** Where the person concerned or his spouse is in receipt of income based jobseeker's allowance or of income support paid under the Social Security Contributions and Benefits Act 1992, the person concerned shall, for the period during which income based jobseeker's allowance or income support is received, be deemed to have disposable capital not exceeding the figure for the time being specified in regulation 4(4)(b).

**8.** In computing the amount of capital of the person concerned, there shall be disregarded—

   (a) so much of any back to work bonus received under section 26 of the Jobseekers Act 1995 as is by virtue of that section to be treated as payable by way of a jobseeker's allowance; and

   (b) the whole of any payment made out of the social fund under the Social Security Contributions and Benefits Act 1992,

or any arrears of payments made under the Community Care (Direct Payments) Act 1996 [or under regulations made under section 57 of the Health and Social Care Act 2001 (direct payments)].

**9.** Save in exceptional circumstances, no sum shall be included in the amount of the capital of the person concerned in respect of—

   (a) the household furniture and effects of the dwelling house occupied by him;

   (b) articles of personal clothing; and

(c) the tools and equipment of his trade, unless they form part of the plant or equipment of a business to which the provisions of paragraph 5 of this Schedule apply.

**10.** (1) In computing the amount of capital of the person concerned, the value of any interest in the main or only dwelling in which he resides shall be taken to be the amount for which that interest could be sold in the open market, subject to the following rules—

(a) the amount to be allowed in respect of any mortgage debt or heritable security shall not exceed £100,000;

(b) the first £100,000 of the value of that interest, after the application of the rule in paragraph (a), shall be disregarded.

(2) Where the person concerned resides in more than one dwelling in which he has an interest, the assessment officer shall decide which is the main dwelling and shall take into account the amount for which any interest in a dwelling which is not the main dwelling could be sold in the open market; provided that the total amount to be allowed in respect of any mortgage debts or heritable securities over all such dwellings, together with any amount allowed under sub-paragraph (1)(a) in respect of the main dwelling, shall not exceed £100,000.

**11.** Where the person concerned has received or is entitled to receive from a body of which he is a member a sum of money by way of financial assistance towards the cost of the proceedings in respect of which the legal aid application is made, such sum shall be disregarded.

**12.** The value to the person concerned of any life assurance or endowment policy shall be taken to be the amount which the person concerned could readily borrow on the security thereof.

**13.** Where under any statute, bond, covenant, guarantee or other instrument, the person concerned is under a contingent liability to pay any sum or is liable to pay a sum not yet ascertained, an allowance shall be made of such an amount as is reasonably likely to become payable within the 12 months immediately following the date of the application for a certificate.

**14.** Where the person concerned produces evidence which satisfies the assessment officer that the debt or part of the debt will be discharged within the twelve months immediately following the date of the legal aid application, an allowance may be made in respect of any debt owing by the person concerned (other than a debt secured on the dwelling or dwellings in which he resides) to the extent to which the assessment officer considers reasonable.

**14A.** (1) Where the person concerned is of pensionable age and his annual disposable income (excluding any net income derived from capital) is less than the figure for the time being prescribed in regulation 4(4)(a) there shall be disregarded the amount of capital as specified in the following table—

| annual disposable income (excluding net income derived from capital) | amount of capital disregard |
| --- | --- |
| up to £370 | £35,000 |
| £371–670 | £30,000 |
| £671–970 | £25,000 |
| £971–1,270 | £20,000 |
| £1,271–1,570 | £15,000 |
| £1,571–1,870 | £10,000 |
| £1,871 and above | £5,000 |

(2) In this Schedule 'pensionable age' means—

(a) in the case of a man, the age of 65 [60]; and

(b) in the case of a woman, the age of 60,

**14B.** *Omitted.*

**15.** In computing the capital of the person concerned, there may also be disregarded such an amount of capital (if any) as the assessment officer may, in his discretion, decide having regard to all the circumstances of the case.

**Note.** In para 5(b) word 'substantially' in square brackets inserted and in para 14A(2)(a) number '65' substituted by number '60' in square brackets by SI 1998/664, regs 5, 6, with effect from 6 April 1998. In para 8(b) words from 'or under' to '(direct payments)' in square brackets inserted in relation to England by SI 2003/762, reg 11(1), Sch 1 as from 8 April 2003 and in relation to Wales by SI 2004/1748, reg 12, Sch 2, para 1 as from 1 November 2004.

## CIVIL LEGAL AID (GENERAL) REGULATIONS 1989

**Dated** 3 March 1989

### SI 1989 No 339

Following the repeal of the enabling provisions by the Access to Justice Act 1999, s 106, Sch 15, para 1, these Regulations have lapsed except insofar as they may continue to have effect by virtue of SI 2000/774, art 5 and SI 2001/916, art 4, Sch 2, as from 1 April 2000.

## ARRANGEMENT OF REGULATIONS

**Note:** Regulations 148–152 not herein printed.

The Lord Chancellor, in exercise of the powers conferred on him by sections 2(7), 6(2), (3), 15(3), 16(6), 17, 31, 34 and 43 of and paragraph 11 of Schedule 1 to the Legal Aid Act 1988 and all other powers enabling him in that behalf, after consulting the General Council of the Bar, the Law Society, the Supreme Court Rule Committee, the County Court Rule Committee, the Matrimonial Causes Rule Committee and the Magistrates' Courts Rule Committee and with the consent of the Treasury hereby makes the following Regulations—

PART I

GENERAL

*Citation, commencement, revocations and transitional provisions*

**1.** (1) These Regulations may be cited as the Civil Legal Aid (General) Regulations 1989 and shall come into force on 1st April 1989.

(2) The Regulations specified in Schedule 1 are hereby revoked.

(3) Where a review by an area committee under regulation 104, 105 or 106 relates to an assessment made before 1st June 1989, paragraphs (5) and (6) of regulation 105 shall not apply and the assisted person's solicitor or counsel may, within 21 days of the area committee's decision, appeal in writing to a committee appointed by the Board.

*Scope*

**2.**   (1) Subject to section 15(7)(a) of the Act and paragraph (2) below, these Regulations apply for the purposes of the provision of civil legal aid under Part IV of the Act.

(2) Where the Board has entered into a franchising contract, regulations relevant to the remuneration and payment of expenses of legal representatives and the manner in which any determination which may be required for those purposes may be made, reviewed or appealed against shall apply except to the extent that the franchising contract makes different express provision.

*Interpretation*

**3.**   (1) In these Regulations, unless the context otherwise requires—

'the Act' means the Legal Aid Act 1988;

'affidavit of costs and resources' means an affidavit which includes the matters specified in Schedule 2 and which is sworn by a person in support of his application for an order under section 18 of the Act;

'appropriate area committee' means the area committee in whose area an application for a certificate has been granted or refused and includes an area committee to whose area an application has been transferred under these Regulations;

'area committee' means an area committee appointed by the Board in accordance with regulation 4;

'Area Director' means an Area Director appointed by the Board in accordance with regulation 4 and includes any person duly authorised to act on his behalf;

'assessment officer' means a person authorised by the Secretary of State or the Board to assess the disposable income, disposable capital and contribution of the person concerned;

'assisted person' means a person in respect of whom a certificate issued under these Regulations is in force and, for the purposes of Part XI only, includes a person in respect of whom a certificate has been, but is no longer, in force;

'authorised summary proceedings' means proceedings in a magistrates' court for which legal aid is available by virtue of Part I of Schedule 2 to the Act;

['CPR' means the Civil Procedure Rules 1998, and a reference to a rule or Part prefixed by 'CPR', means the rule, or (as the case may be) Part so numbered in the CPR;]

'certificate' means a legal aid certificate issued in accordance with these Regulations (or any regulations revoked by these Regulations) and includes an amendment to a certificate issued under Part VII and, unless the context otherwise requires, an emergency certificate;

'contract' means a contract entered into by the Board with other persons or bodies pursuant to its powers under section 4 of the Act;

'contribution' means the contribution payable under section 16(1) of the Act in respect of the costs of representation;

['costs judge' has the meaning given in CPR rule 43.2(1)(b); 'costs officer' has the meaning given in CPR rule 43.2(1)(c);]

'court' includes—

(a) in relation to proceedings tried or heard at first instance by a master or *taxing master* [costs judge] of the Supreme Court, a registrar of the Family Division of the High Court, a district registrar or the registrar of a county court, that master or registrar;

(b) in relation to proceedings on appeal to the Court of Appeal, the registrar of civil appeals;

['detailed assessment' has the meaning given in CPR rule 43.4;]

'disposable capital' and 'disposable income' mean the amounts of capital and income available for the making of a contribution after capital and income have been computed in accordance with the Civil Legal Aid (Assessment of Resources) Regulations 1989;

'EEC lawyer' has the same meaning as in the European Communities (Services of Lawyers) Order 1978;

'emergency certificate' means a certificate issued under Part III of these Regulations;

'family proceedings' has the meaning assigned by section 32 of the Matrimonial and Family Proceedings Act 1984;

'franchisee' means a person or body (other than the Board) acting under the terms of a franchising contract;

'fund' means the legal aid fund;

'legal aid' means representation under Part IV of the Act;

'legal aid area' has the meaning assigned by regulation 4(1);

'legal aid only costs' means those costs which would not be allowed as inter partes costs, but which are payable from the fund subject to determination under regulation 107A(2);

'legal executive' means a fellow of the Institute of Legal Executives;

*'master' in relation to an application for an order under section 18 of the Act in respect of proceedings in or on appeal from the Chancery or Queen's Bench Division of the High Court, means a taxing master of the Supreme Court or a district registrar of the High Court; and in relation to such an application made in respect of proceedings in or on appeal from the Family Division of the High Court, means a registrar of the said Division or a district registrar of the High Court;*

'patient' means a person who, by reason of mental disorder within the meaning of the Mental Health Act 1983, is incapable of managing and administering his property and affairs;

'recognised mediator' means a mediator who is recognised by the Board for the purposes of conducting a meeting described in section 15(3F) of the Act;

'relevant authority' means the Area Director in the case of an assessment and the *taxing officer* [costs officer] in the case of a *taxation* [detailed assessment];

'special Children Act proceedings' means proceedings under the Children Act 1989 for which representation must be granted to the applicant regardless of sections 15(1) to (3) of the Act;

'standard basis' and 'indemnity basis', in relation to the *taxation* [detailed assessment] of costs, have the meanings assigned by *Order 62, rule 12 of the Rules of the Supreme Court 1965* [CPR rule 44.4];

'substantive certificate' means a certificate issued to replace an emergency certificate which is still in force.

*'taxing officer' has the same meanings in relation to proceedings governed by Order 38 of the County Court Rules 1981, Order 62 of the Rules of the Supreme Court and the Matrimonial Causes (Costs) Rules 1988 respectively, as it has in those rules.*

(2) Any reference in these Regulations to a regulation or Schedule by number means the regulation or Schedule so numbered in these Regulations.

(3) References in these Regulations to costs shall, unless the context otherwise requires, be construed as including references to fees, charges, disbursements, expenses and remuneration.

**Note.** In para (1) definitions 'CPR', 'costs judge' and 'costs officer' and 'detailed assessment' inserted, in definition 'court' in para (a) words 'taxing master' substituted by words 'costs judge' in square brackets, definitions 'master' and 'taxing officer' revoked, in definition 'relevant authority' words 'taxing officer' and ' taxation' substituted by words 'costs officer' and 'detailed assessment' in square brackets, in definition 'standard basis' and 'indemnity basis' words 'taxation' substituted by words 'detailed assessment' in square brackets and words 'Order 62, rule 12 of the Rules of the Supreme Court 1965' substituted by words 'CPR rule 44.4' in square brackets by regs 3, 4 as from 20 March 2000.

*Exclusion from civil legal aid of prescribed bodies*

**3A.**   Representation under Part IV of the Act shall not be available to any body acting in a representative, fiduciary or official capacity for the purposes of proceedings under the Children Act 1989.

*Area committees, Area Directors and legal aid areas*

**4.**   (1)  The Board shall, for the purposes of administering the Act, appoint—
(a)  area committees, and
(b)  Area Directors,
in respect of areas (in these Regulations referred to as 'legal aid areas') to be specified by the Board.

(2)  Area committees and Area Directors so appointed shall exercise functions respectively delegated to them by the Board or conferred on them by these Regulations.

(3)  Where and to the extent that a franchising contract permits the franchisee to exercise any of the functions of an Area Director, the functions may be exercised by the franchisee on the Area Director's behalf.

*Powers exercisable by courts*

**5.**   Where the power to do any act or exercise any jurisdiction or discretion is conferred by any provision of these Regulations on a court, it may, unless it is exercisable only during the trial or hearing of the action, cause or matter, be exercised—
(a)  in respect of proceedings in a county court or the Family Division of the High Court, by the registrar;
(b)  in respect of proceedings in the Chancery or Queen's Bench Division of the High Court, by a judge, master or district registrar;
(c)  in respect of proceedings in the Court of Appeal, by a single judge of that Court or by the registrar of civil appeals;
(d)  in respect of proceedings in the House of Lords, by the Clerk of the Parliaments;
(e)  by any person who, under any enactment or rules of court, is capable of exercising the jurisdiction of the court in relation to the proceedings in question.

*Powers exercisable by Area Directors*

**6.**   (1)  Where an area committee is required or entitled to perform any function under these Regulations, that function may, subject to paragraph (2), be performed on behalf of that committee by the Area Director.

(2)  Paragraph (1) shall not empower an Area Director to determine an appeal under regulation 39.

*Computation of time*

**7.**   (1)  Where, under these Regulations, an act is required to be done within a specified period after or from a specified date, the period of time so fixed starts immediately after that date.

(2)  The period within which an act is required or authorised to be done under these Regulations may, if the Area Director thinks fit, be extended and any such period may be extended although the application for extension is not made until after the expiration of the period.

*Service of notices*

**8.**   (1)  Where by virtue of these Regulations any document is required to be served (whether the expression 'serve' or the expression 'send' or 'send by post' or any other expression is used) the document may be served—

(a) if the person to be served is acting in person, by delivering it to him personally or by delivering it at, or sending it by post to, his address for service or, if he has no address for service—

    (i) by delivering the document at his residence or by sending it by post to his last known residence, or

    (ii) in the case of a proprietor of a business, by delivering the document at his place of business or by sending it by post to his last known place of business;

(b) if the person to be served is acting by a solicitor—

    (i) by delivering the document at, or by sending it by post to, the solicitor's address for service, or

    (ii) where the solicitor's address for service includes a numbered box at a document exchange, by leaving the document at that document exchange or at a document exchange which transmits documents daily to that document exchange.

(2) Any document which is left at a document exchange in accordance with paragraph (1)(b)(ii), shall, unless the contrary is proved, be deemed to have been served on the second day after the day on which it is left.

*Availability of documents to the court*

**9.** Any document sent to a court office or registry or filed or exhibited under the provisions of these Regulations may, on request, be made available for the use of the court at any stage of the proceedings.

PART II

APPLICATIONS FOR CERTIFICATES

*Applications to be made to Area Directors*

**10.** Any person who wishes to be granted legal aid for the purposes of proceedings may apply for a certificate—

(a) if resident in the United Kingdom, to any Area Director, or

(b) if resident elsewhere, to the Area Director of one of the legal aid areas nominated by the Board for this purpose.

*Form and lodgment of application*

**11.** Every application—

(a) shall be made in writing on a form approved by the Board or in such other written form as the Area Director may accept; and

(b) shall be lodged with the Area Director.

*Contents of application*

**12.** (1) Subject to regulation 12A every application shall—

(a) state the name of the solicitor selected by the applicant to act for him;

(b) contain such information and be accompanied by such supporting documents (including any welfare report) as may be necessary to enable—

    (i) the Area Director to determine the nature of the proceedings in respect of which legal aid is sought and whether it is reasonable that representation should be granted; and

    (ii) the assessment officer to assess the disposable income, disposable capital and contribution of the applicant.

(2) *Omitted.*

(3) An applicant shall, if required to do so for the purpose of providing additional material, supply such further information or documents as may be required or attend for an interview.

*Certificate relating to special Children Act proceedings*

**12A.** (1) Where a person is entitled to legal aid for special Children Act proceedings, his solicitor shall lodge with the Area Director an application on a form approved by the Board at the first available opportunity and in any event within three working days of receiving instructions to act for that person in such proceedings.

(2) The application shall—

(a) state the name of the solicitor selected by the applicant to act for him; and

(b) contain a statement signed by the solicitor to the effect that legal aid is sought in respect of proceedings to which section 15(1) to (3) of the Act do not apply.

(3) Work done by a solicitor in relation to special Children Act proceedings prior to the issue of a certificate shall be deemed to be work done while such a certificate is in force provided that the application was lodged at the first available opportunity and in any event within the time specified in paragraph (1).

*Applications by persons resident outside United Kingdom*

**13.** (1) Subject to paragraph (2), where the applicant resides outside the United Kingdom and cannot be present in England or Wales while his application is considered, his application shall be—

(a) written in English or in French; and

(b) except where the applicant is a member of Her Majesty's armed forces, sworn—

    (i) if the applicant resides within the Commonwealth or the Republic of Ireland, before any justice of the peace or magistrate or any person for the time being authorised by law in the place where he resides to administer an oath for any judicial or other legal purpose, or

    (ii) if the applicant resides elsewhere, before a British consular officer or any other person for the time being authorised to exercise the functions of such an officer or having authority to administer an oath in that place; and

(c) accompanied by a statement in writing, signed by some responsible person who has knowledge of the facts, certifying that part of the application which relates to the applicant's disposable income and disposable capital.

(2) The requirements of paragraph (1) may be waived by the Area Director where compliance with them would cause serious difficulty, inconvenience or delay and the application otherwise satisfies the requirements of regulations 11 and 12.

*Child Abduction and Custody Act 1985*

**14.** (1) A person whose application under the Hague Convention or the European Convention has been submitted to the Central Authority in England and Wales pursuant to section 3(2) or section 14(2) of the Child Abduction and Custody Act 1985 and on whose behalf a solicitor in England and Wales has been instructed in connection with the application—

(a) shall be eligible to receive legal aid whether or not his financial resources are such as to make him eligible to receive it under regulations made under the Legal Aid Act 1988;

(b) shall not be refused legal aid by virtue of subsections (2) and (3) of section 15 of the said Act of 1988; and

(c) shall not be required to pay a contribution to the legal aid fund;

and these Regulations (with the exception of those provisions relating to assessment of disposable income and capital, eligibility on the merits and payment of contribution) shall apply accordingly.

(2) In this regulation the 'Hague Convention' means the convention defined in section 1(1) of the Child Abduction and Custody Act 1985 and the 'European Convention' means the convention defined in section 12(1) of that Act.

*Registration of certain foreign orders and judgments*

**15.** (1) This regulation applies to any person who—

(a) appeals to a magistrates' court against the registration of or the refusal to register a maintenance order made in a Hague Convention country pursuant to the Maintenance Orders (Reciprocal Enforcement) Act 1972; or

(b) applies for the registration of a judgment under section 4 of the Civil Jurisdiction and Judgments Act 1982.

(2) Subject to paragraph (3), a person to whom this regulation applies—

(a) shall be eligible to receive legal aid whether or not his financial resources are such as to make him eligible to receive it under regulations made under the Legal Aid Act 1988;

(b) shall not be refused legal aid by virtue of subsections (2) and (3) of section 15 of the said Act of 1988;

(c) shall not be required to pay a contribution to the legal aid fund;

and these Regulations (with the exception of those provisions relating to assessment of disposable income and capital, eligibility on the merits and payment of contribution) shall apply accordingly.

(3) A person shall not be given legal aid under this regulation in respect of any appeal or application as is mentioned in paragraph (1) unless he benefited from complete or partial legal aid or exemption from costs or expenses in the country in which the maintenance order was made or the judgment was given.

(4) In this regulation, 'Hague Convention country' has the same meaning as in the Reciprocal Enforcement of Maintenance Orders (Hague Convention Countries) Order 1979 and 'the Maintenance Orders (Reciprocal Enforcement) Act 1972' means that Act as applied with such exceptions, adaptations and modifications as are specified in the said 1979 Order.

*Application on behalf of minors and patients*

**16.** (1) Subject to paragraph (5), an application for legal aid for a minor or patient shall be made on his behalf by a person of full age and capacity and—

(a) where the application relates to proceedings which are required by rules of court to be brought or defended by a next friend or guardian ad litem, the person making the application shall be the next friend or guardian ad litem; or,

(b) where the application relates to proceedings which have not actually begun, the person who, subject to any order of the court, intends to act in either of those capacities when the proceedings begin, shall make the application; or,

(c) where the application is made by a minor who is entitled to begin, prosecute or defend any proceedings without a next friend or guardian ad litem, the person making the application shall be that minor's solicitor.

(2) *Omitted.*

(3) Any certificate issued to a minor or patient shall be in his name, stating the name of the person who has applied for it on his behalf.

(4) In any matter relating to the issue, amendment, revocation or discharge of a certificate issued to a minor or patient, and in any other matter which may arise between an assisted person who is a minor or patient and the Area Director, the person who is named in the certificate as the next friend, guardian ad litem or (where there is no next friend or guardian ad litem) solicitor of the minor or patient shall be treated for all purposes (including the receipt of notices) as the agent of the minor or patient.

(5) An Area Director may, where the circumstances appear to make it desirable, waive all or any of the requirements of the preceding paragraphs of this regulation.

*Power to transfer application to another area office*

**17.**   *If it appears to an Area Director that an application could, without prejudice to the applicant, be more conveniently or appropriately dealt with in another area office, the papers relating to the application shall be transferred to that other office.*

[(1) If it appears to an Area Director that an application or certificate could be more conveniently or appropriately dealt with in another area office, he may transfer the application or certificate to that other office.]

[(2) Where a certificate is transferred under this regulation to another area office, the certificate shall, for all purposes, including any obligation by the assisted person to continue to pay a contribution, continue as if it were a certificate issued by that area office.]

**Note.** Sub-s (1) substituted and numbered as such and para (2) inserted by SI 1999/1113, reg 3, as from 6 May 1999.

*Reference to the assessment officer for assessment of resources*

**18.**   (1) Subject to section 15(3B) to (3D) of the Act and except where he has previously refused the application, the Area Director shall refer to the assessment officer so much of it as is relevant to the assessment of the applicant's disposable income and disposable capital; and (subject to paragraph (2) and regulation 21) no application shall be approved until the assessment officer has assessed the applicant's disposable income, disposable capital and contribution in accordance with the Civil Legal Aid (Assessment of Resources) Regulations 1989.

(2) Where an Area Director approves an application relating to proceedings—
- (a) in the House of Lords or on appeal from a magistrates' court in any action, cause or matter in which the applicant was an assisted person in the court below; or
- (b) by way of a new trial ordered by a court in any action, cause or matter in which the applicant was an assisted person;

he shall not require the assessment officer to re-assess the assisted person's disposable income and disposable capital.

PART III

EMERGENCY CERTIFICATES

*Application for emergency certificate*

**19.**   (1) Any person who desires legal aid as a matter of urgency may apply to an Area Director for an emergency certificate on a form approved by the Board or in such other manner as the Area Director may accept as sufficient in the circumstances of the case.

(2) Subject to paragraph (3), an application for an emergency certificate shall contain such information and be accompanied by such documents as may be necessary to enable the Area Director to determine the nature of the proceedings for which legal aid is sought and the circumstances in which it is required and whether—
- (a) the applicant is likely to fulfil the conditions under which legal aid may be granted under the Act and these Regulations; and
- (b) it is in the interests of justice that the applicant should, as a matter of urgency, be granted legal aid;

and the applicant shall furnish such additional information and documents (if any) as may be sufficient to constitute an application for a certificate under Part II of these Regulations.

(3) If it appears to the Area Director that the applicant cannot at the time of making the application reasonably furnish the information required under paragraph (2), or any part of it, that Area Director shall nevertheless have the power to issue an

emergency certificate subject to such conditions as to the furnishing of additional information as he thinks fit.

*Refusal of emergency certificate*

**20.** An application for an emergency certificate may be refused—
  (a) on one of the grounds on which a substantive certificate may be refused under regulation 34; or
  (b) on the ground that the applicant is unlikely to fulfil the conditions under which legal aid may be granted; or
  (c) on the ground that it is not in the interests of justice that legal aid be granted as a matter of urgency.

*Issue and effect of emergency certificate*

**21.** (1) An Area Director shall have power to approve an application made under regulation 19 and to issue an emergency certificate without reference to the assessment officer.
  (2) *Omitted.*
  (3) Where an Area Director issues an emergency certificate, he shall send the emergency certificate (together with a copy) to the solicitor selected by the applicant, and a copy of the certificate to the applicant.
  (4) An emergency certificate shall have the same effect in all respects as a substantive certificate and any person holding an emergency certificate shall, while it is in force, be deemed for the purposes of the proceedings to which the emergency certificate relates to be an assisted person.

*Duration of emergency certificate*

**22.** An emergency certificate shall remain in force until—
  (a) it is discharged or revoked in accordance with Part X of these Regulations; or
  (b) it is merged in a substantive certificate under regulation 23; or
  (c) the expiry of any period (including any extension of that period granted under regulation 24(1)) allowed for the duration of the emergency certificate.

*Merger in substantive certificate*

**23.** (1) Where a substantive certificate is issued, the emergency certificate shall merge in the substantive certificate and the substantive certificate shall take effect from the date upon which the emergency certificate was issued in respect of the proceedings specified in the emergency certificate.
  (2) Where an emergency certificate is merged in a substantive certificate, the substantive certificate shall state—
  (a) the date of issue of the emergency certificate, and
  (b) that the emergency certificate has been continuously in force from that date until the date of the substantive certificate.

*Extension and expiry of emergency certificate*

**24.** (1) The Area Director (whose decision shall be final) may extend the period allowed for the duration of an emergency certificate where—
  (a) the applicant is offered a substantive certificate in respect of the proceedings to which the emergency certificate relates and either fails to signify his acceptance or appeals against the terms of the offer; or
  (b) the application for a substantive certificate in respect of the proceedings to which the emergency certificate relates has been refused and either notice of appeal has been given to the appropriate area committee within the time limits laid down by regulation 36 or the time limit for doing so has not expired; or
  (c) there are exceptional circumstances.

(2)  Where an emergency certificate is extended under paragraph (1)(a) or (b), no further work may be done or steps taken under the certificate.

*Notification of extension of emergency certificate*

**25.**   (1)  Where an emergency certificate is extended, the Area Director shall—
- (a)  forthwith issue a notice to that effect;
- (b)  send the notice (together with a copy) to the solicitor acting for the person to whom the emergency certificate was issued; and
- (c)  send a copy of the notice to the person to whom the emergency certificate was issued.

(2)  It shall be the duty of the solicitor to notify forthwith any counsel whom he may have instructed that the certificate has been extended.

(3)  A solicitor who receives notice that an emergency certificate has been extended under regulation 24 shall, if proceedings have begun or otherwise upon their commencement—
- (a)  send a copy of the notice by post to the appropriate court office or registry, and
- (b)  serve notice of the fact upon any other persons who are parties to the proceedings,

and, if any other person becomes a party to the proceedings, serve a similar notice upon that person.

PART IV
DETERMINATION OF APPLICATIONS

*Power to notify other parties of application*

**26.**   (1)  On receiving an application for a certificate, the Area Director may, if he thinks fit—
- (a)  notify any party to the proceedings in respect of which the application is made; and
- (b)  ask that party whether he is willing to delay taking any further step in, or in relation to, the proceedings until the application has been determined.

(2)  When the Area Director has determined the application, he shall so inform any party notified under this regulation.

*Meeting with a mediator in family matters*

**26A.**   Subsection (3F) of section 15 of the Act shall not apply—
- (a)  where there is no recognised mediator available to the applicant or any other party to the proceedings to hold a meeting under that subsection; or
- (b)  where—
    - (i)  the applicant is likely to fulfil the conditions under which legal aid may be granted under the Act and these Regulations;
    - (ii)  it is in the interests of justice that the applicant should, as a matter of urgency, be granted legal aid; and
    - (iii)  an application for an emergency certificate under regulation 19 has been made.

*Financial eligibility*

**27.**   (1)  Where the assessment officer assesses that an applicant has disposable income of an amount which makes him ineligible for legal aid, the Area Director shall refuse the application.

(2)  Where the assessment officer assesses that an applicant, having disposable income of an amount which makes him eligible for legal aid, has disposable capital of an amount which renders him liable to be refused legal aid, the Area Director shall refuse the application if it appears to him that the probable costs of the

applicant in the proceedings in respect of which the application was made would not exceed the contribution payable by the applicant.

*Eligibility on the merits*

**28.**   (1)  Without prejudice to the generality of section 15(2) to (3C) and (3E) of the Act and subject to paragraph (2), an application for a certificate shall only be approved after the Area Director has considered all the questions of fact or law arising in the action, cause or matter to which the application relates and the circumstances in which the application was made.

(2)  Where the application relates to proceedings to which section 15(3B), (3C) or (3E) of the Act apply, provided that the Area Director is satisfied that it does so relate and subject to regulation 27 (where applicable) he shall grant the application and Parts IV and V of these Regulations shall apply with any necessary modifications.

*Refusal where advantage trivial or on account of nature of proceedings*

**29.**   Without prejudice to regulations 28 and 32, an application may be refused where it appears to the Area Director that—
- (a)  only a trivial advantage would be gained by the applicant from the proceedings to which the application relates, or
- (b)  on account of the nature of the proceedings a solicitor would not ordinarily be employed.

*Refusal where other rights or facilities available*

**30.**   (1)  Without prejudice to regulation 28, an application may be refused where it appears to the Area Director that—
- (a)  the applicant has available to him rights or facilities which make it unnecessary for him to obtain legal aid; or
- (b)  the applicant has a reasonable expectation of obtaining financial or other help from a body of which he is a member,

and that he has failed to take all reasonable steps to enforce or obtain such rights, facilities or help (including permitting the Area Director to take those steps on his behalf).

(2)  Where it appears that the applicant has a right to be indemnified against expenses incurred in connection with any proceedings, it shall not, for the purposes of paragraph (1), be deemed to be a failure to take reasonable steps if he has not taken proceedings to enforce that right, whether for a declaration as to that right or otherwise.

*Determination of contribution*

**31.**   (1)  The Area Director shall, when determining an application, also determine the sums for the time being payable on account of the applicant's contribution.

(2)  *Omitted.*

(3)  *Omitted.*

*Proceedings in which others have an interest*

**32.**   (1)  When determining an application, the Area Director shall consider whether it is reasonable and proper for persons concerned jointly with or having the same interest as the applicant to defray so much of the costs as would be payable from the fund in respect of the proceedings if a certificate were issued.

(2)  In determining an application made by, or on behalf of, a person in connection with an action, cause or matter in which—
- (a)  numerous persons have the same interest, and
- (b)  in accordance with rules of court, one or more persons may sue or be sued, or may be authorised by a court to defend any such action, cause or matter on behalf of or for the benefit of all persons so interested,

the Area Director shall consider whether the rights of the applicant would be substantially prejudiced by the refusal of his application.

(3) Where an application has been approved and the Area Director considers that it is reasonable that persons concerned jointly with or having the same interest as the applicant should contribute to the cost of the proceedings, he shall add the amount which would be payable by such persons to the sums (if any) payable by the applicant under regulation 31 and shall so notify him under regulation 43(2).

(4) The Area Director may subsequently redetermine the amount of any additional sums payable under paragraph (3) where he is satisfied that the applicant has, without success, taken all reasonable steps (including permitting the Area Director to take those steps on his behalf) to obtain such payment.

*Application in representative, fiduciary or official capacity*

**33.**   Where an application is made in a representative, fiduciary or official capacity, the Area Director—
- (a)   shall take into account the value of any property or estate or the amount of any fund out of which the applicant is entitled to be indemnified and the financial resources of any persons (including the applicant if appropriate) who might benefit from the proceedings; and
- (b)   may (without prejudice to regulation 28) either—
  - (i)   approve the application, subject to the payment from the property or resources specified in sub-paragraph (a) of any sums which he may in his discretion determine, or
  - (ii)   refuse the application, if he concludes that to do so would not cause hardship.

*Refusal where assignment made to obtain legal aid*

**33A.**   Without prejudice to regulation 28, an application may be refused where it appears to the Area Director that—
- (a)   any cause of action in respect of which the application was made has been transferred to the applicant by assignment or otherwise from a body of persons corporate, or unincorporate, or by another person who would not be entitled to receive legal aid; and
- (b)   the assignment or transfer was entered into with a view to allowing the action to be commenced or continued with the benefit of a legal aid certificate.

PART V

REFUSAL OF APPLICATIONS

*Notification of refusal*

**34.**   (1) Where an application for a certificate is refused on one or more of the following grounds, namely, that—
- (a)   the assessment officer has assessed that the applicant has disposable income which makes him ineligible for legal aid; or
- (b)   the assessment officer has assessed that the applicant, having disposable income of an amount which makes him eligible for legal aid, has disposable capital of an amount which renders him liable to be refused legal aid and it appears to the Area Director that, without legal aid, the probable costs to the applicant of the proceedings in respect of which the application was made would not exceed the sums payable by the applicant on account of his contribution; or
- (c)   the proceedings to which the application relates are not proceedings for which legal aid may be given; or
- (d)   the applicant has not shown that he has reasonable grounds for taking, defending or being a party to the proceedings; or

(e) it appears unreasonable that the applicant should receive legal aid in the particular circumstances of the case,

the Area Director shall notify the applicant of the grounds on which the application has been refused and inform him of the circumstances in which he may appeal to the appropriate area committee for the decision to be reviewed.

(2) Where an application is refused on either of the grounds specified in sub-paragraphs (d) and (e) of paragraph (1), the notification given under that paragraph shall include a brief statement of the reasons why that ground applies to the applicant's case.

### Right of appeal against refusal

**35.** (1) Where an Area Director refuses an application for a certificate or an applicant is dissatisfied with the terms upon which the Area Director would be prepared to issue it, the applicant may, subject to paragraph (2), appeal to the appropriate area committee.

(2) No appeal shall lie to an area committee from—

(a) an assessment of the assessment officer, or

(b) any decision by an Area Director as to the sums payable on account of the applicant's contribution or the method by which they shall be paid except a decision as to sums payable under regulation 32(3), or

(c) the refusal of an application for an emergency certificate.

### Time and form of appeal

**36.** Every appeal shall be brought by giving to the appropriate area committee, within 14 days of the date of notice of refusal of a certificate or of the terms upon which a certificate would be issued (or such longer period as the appropriate area committee may allow), notice of appeal in writing either on a form approved by the Board or in such other written form as the Area Director may accept as sufficient in the circumstances of the case.

### Nature of appeal

**37.** Every appeal shall be by way of reconsideration of the application.

### Representation at appeal or other final application

**38.** (1) Upon an appeal the appellant may—

(a) furnish further statements, whether oral or in writing, in support of his application; and

(b) conduct the appeal himself, with or without the assistance of any person whom he may appoint for the purpose, or be represented by counsel or a solicitor or legal executive.

(2) With any necessary modifications, paragraph (1)(a) shall apply to any appeal to an area committee and, subject to regulation 58(3), paragraph (1)(b) shall apply to any appeal to an area committee on which the committee finally determines the applicant's right to receive legal aid.

### Determination of appeal

**39.** (1) The area committee shall determine the appeal in such manner as seems to it to be just and, without prejudice to the generality of the foregoing, may—

(a) dismiss the appeal; or

(b) direct the Area Director to offer a certificate subject to such terms and conditions as the area committee thinks fit;

(c) direct the Area Director to settle terms and conditions on which a certificate may be offered; or

(d) refer the matter, or any part of it, back to the Area Director for his determination or report.

(2) Any decision of an area committee with regard to an appeal shall be final, and it shall give notice of its decision, and the reasons for it, to the appellant and to any solicitor acting for him on a form approved by the Board.

*Repeated refusals of certificates*

**40.**   (1) Where a person has applied for and been refused a certificate on three separate occasions and it appears to the Area Director to whom such person applies that his conduct may amount to an abuse of the facilities provided by the Act, then the Area Director may report the matter to the appropriate area committee.

(2) If a report under paragraph (1) has been made, the area committee may—

(a) enquire whether any other area office has received an application from the person named in the report;

(b) call for a report as to the circumstances of any other such application; and

(c) if it considers that the person named in the report has abused the facilities provided by the Act, report thereon to the Board, making such recommendations as seem to the area committee to be just.

*Power to make prohibitory directions*

**41.**   (1) The Board, on receipt of a report made under regulation 40(2)(c), shall give the person named in it an opportunity of making (either by himself or by some other person acting on his behalf) representations in writing on the matter, and shall make such other enquiries as seem to be necessary; and, if they are satisfied that his conduct has amounted to an abuse of the facilities provided by the Act, may make a direction (in this regulation referred to as a 'prohibitory direction') that no consideration shall, for a period not exceeding five years, be given by an Area Director or area committee either—

(a) to any future or pending application by that person for a certificate with regard to any particular matter; or

(b) in exceptional circumstances, to any future or pending application by him whatsoever.

(2) The Board may in its discretion—

(a) include within the terms of any prohibitory direction any receiver, next friend or guardian ad litem who applies for a certificate on behalf of the person referred to in the prohibitory direction; and

(b) at any time vary or revoke any prohibitory direction in whole or in part.

(3) Where the Board makes a prohibitory direction, it shall inform the Lord Chancellor and shall, if so requested, give him its reasons for making it.

PART VI

ISSUE AND EFFECT OF CERTIFICATES

*Issue of certificate where no contribution may be payable*

**42.**   Where an application is approved relating to special Children Act proceedings or where no contribution is (for the time being) payable, the Area Director shall—

(a) issue a certificate;

(b) send the certificate (together with a copy) to the solicitor selected by the applicant; and

(c) send a copy of the certificate to the applicant together with a notice drawing the applicant's attention to the provisions of sections 16(6) and 17(1) of the Act.

*Offer of certificate where contribution payable*

**43.**   (1)  Where an application is approved for any proceedings where a contribution will be payable, the Area Director shall require—

(a)  any sums payable out of capital to be paid forthwith if the sum is readily available or, if it is not, by such time as seems to him reasonable in all the circumstances; and

(b)  the first contribution to be paid out of income to be paid forthwith with further contributions payable at monthly intervals thereafter.

(2)  The Area Director shall notify the applicant—

(a)  of the sums payable under regulation 31; and

(b)  of the terms upon which a certificate will be issued to him;

and draw to his attention the provisions of sections 16(1) and (6) and 17(1) of the Act.

*Undertaking to account for sums received from third parties*

**44.**   Where the applicant—

(a)  appears to be a member of an organisation or body which might reasonably be expected to give him financial assistance in meeting the cost of the proceedings for which the applicant has applied for legal aid; and

(b)  does not appear to have any right to be indemnified by that organisation or body against expenses incurred in connection with those proceedings,

the Area Director shall require the applicant, as a term upon which the certificate will be issued, to sign an undertaking to pay to the Board (in addition to any sums payable under regulations 31 and 32) any sum which he receives from that organisation or body on account of the cost of those proceedings.

*Acceptance and issue of certificate where contribution payable*

**45.**   (1)  An applicant who desires that a certificate should be issued to him on the terms notified to him by an Area Director shall, within 28 days of being so notified—

(a)  signify his acceptance of those terms on a form approved by the Board and lodge it with the Area Director; and

(b)  if those terms require the payment of any sums of money, give an undertaking, on a form approved by the Board, to pay those sums by the method stated in the terms and, if any sum is required to be paid before the certificate is issued, make that payment accordingly.

(2)  When an applicant has complied with so many of the requirements of paragraph (1) as are relevant to his case, the Area Director shall issue a certificate and send it to the solicitor selected by the applicant.

(3)  *Omitted.*

*Scope of certificates*

**46.**   (1)  A certificate may be issued in respect of the whole or part of proceedings and may be extended to cover appellate proceedings other than those mentioned in paragraph (2).

(2)  Except in the case of special Children Act proceedings a certificate shall not be extended to cover proceedings in the House of Lords or on appeal from a magistrates' court.

(3)  A certificate shall not relate to more than one action, cause or matter except in the case of—

(a)  family proceedings; or

(b), (c)  *omitted;*

(d)  an application for a grant of representation which is necessary to enable the action, which is the subject matter of the certificate, to be brought;

(e) an application under section 33 of the Supreme Court Act 1981 or section 52 of the County Courts Act 1984 and subsequent court proceedings; or

(f) proceedings which, under the Act, may be taken to enforce or give effect to any order or agreement made in the proceedings to which the certificate relates; and, for the purposes of this sub-paragraph, proceedings to enforce or give effect to an agreement or order shall include proceedings in bankruptcy or to wind-up a company.

*Certificates to specify parties to proceedings*

**47.**   A certificate other than one relating to family proceedings shall specify the parties to the proceedings in respect of which it is issued.

*Power to restrict costs allowable to distant solicitor*

**48.**   (1) Where the solicitor selected by the applicant to whom a certificate is issued carries on his practice at a place which is so far away from where his services will be required in acting under the certificate that his selection will result in significantly greater expense to the fund than would have been incurred if the applicant had selected another solicitor, the certificate may provide that the solicitor shall not be entitled to payment in respect of any additional costs or disbursements incurred by reason of the fact that he does not carry on his practice at or near the place where his services are required in acting under the certificate.

(2) Where a certificate includes a provision under paragraph (1), payment of such additional costs or disbursements shall not be allowed on determination of the costs.

*Effect of certificates*

**49.**   Any document purporting to be a certificate issued in accordance with these Regulations shall, until the contrary is proved, be deemed to be a valid certificate issued to the person named in it and for the purposes there set out and shall be received in evidence without further proof.

*Notification of issue of certificates*

**50.**   (1) Whenever an assisted person becomes a party to proceedings, or a party to proceedings becomes an assisted person, his solicitor shall forthwith—

(a) serve all other parties to the proceedings with notice of the issue of a certificate in a form approved by the Board; and

(b) if at any time thereafter any other person becomes a party to the proceedings, forthwith serve a similar notice on that party.

(2) Copies of the notices referred to in paragraph (1) shall form part of the papers for the use of the court in the proceedings.

(3) Where an assisted person's solicitor—

(a) commences any proceedings for the assisted person in a county court; or

(b) commences proceedings in accordance with *Order 112, rule 3 or 4 of the Rules of the Supreme Court 1965 or rule 101 or 103 of the Matrimonial Causes Rules 1977* [RSC Order 112 rules 3 or 4 in Schedule 1 to the CPR, or any of rules 3.2 to 3.5 of the Family Proceedings Rules 1991];

and at the same time files a copy of the notice to be served in accordance with paragraph (1), a copy of that notice shall be annexed to the originating process for service.

(4) A solicitor who receives a certificate from an Area Director shall, if proceedings have begun, or otherwise upon their commencement, send a copy of it by post to the appropriate court office or registry.

(5) *Omitted.*

**Note.** In para (3)(b) words from 'Order 112' to 'Matrimonial Causes Rules 1977' substituted by words from 'RSC Order' to 'Family Proceedings Rules 1991' in square brackets by SI 2000/451, reg 5, as from 20 March 2000.

PART VII

AMENDMENT OF CERTIFICATE AND ADJUSTMENT OF CONTRIBUTION

*Power to amend certificates*

**51.** The Area Director may amend a certificate where in his opinion—
- (a) there is some mistake in the certificate; or
- (b) it has become desirable for the certificate to extend to—
  - (i) proceedings; or
  - (ii) other steps; or
  - (iii) subject to regulation 46(3), other proceedings; or
  - (iv) proceedings which under the Act may be taken to enforce or give effect to any order or agreement made in the proceedings in respect of which the certificate was issued; or
  - (v) the bringing of an interlocutory appeal; or
  - (vi) proceedings in the Court of Justice of the European Communities on a reference to that Court for a preliminary ruling; or
  - (vii) representation by an EEC lawyer; or
- (c) it has become desirable to add or substitute parties to the proceedings in respect of which the certificate was issued; or
- (d) it has become desirable for the certificate to extend to any steps having the same effect as a cross-action or as a reply thereto, or a cross-appeal; or
- (e) it has become desirable for the certificate not to extend to certain of the proceedings in respect of which it was issued; or
- (f) a change of solicitor should be authorised; [or
- (g) it has become desirable to amend, impose or remove a limitation or condition on the certificate.

**Note.** Para (g) and word 'or' immediately preceding it inserted by SI 2002/711, reg 3, as from 1 April 2001.

*Power to alter contribution and amend certificate*

**52.** (1) Without prejudice to the provisions of the Civil Legal Aid (Assessment of Resources) Regulations 1989, where the assisted person's disposable income and disposable capital have been assessed the Area Director may, if he considers it to be desirable, request the assessment officer to re-assess the assisted person's financial resources and contribution.

(2) Where at any time during which a certificate is in force the Area Director is of opinion that the costs incurred or likely to be incurred under the certificate will not be more than the contribution which the assisted person has already paid he may waive (and, where necessary subsequently revive) the requirement for further payments on account of the assisted person's contribution.

(3) Without prejudice to regulation 51, the Area Director shall amend the certificate from such date as he considers appropriate—
- (a) where he re-determines the amount payable on account of the assisted person's contribution whether as a result of a re-assessment pursuant to paragraph (1) or otherwise; or
- (b) where he waives or revives (following a period of waiver) the requirement for further payments on account of the assisted person's contribution under paragraph (2).

*Making and determination of applications for amendment*

**53.** Parts II and V of these Regulations shall apply, with any necessary modifications, to applications for the amendment of certificates as they apply to applications for certificates.

*Procedure on issue of amendment*

**54.** (1) Where an Area Director amends a certificate, he shall send two copies of the amendment to the assisted person's solicitor and one copy to the assisted person.

(2) A solicitor who receives an amendment sent to him under paragraph (1) shall forthwith—

(a) if proceedings have begun or otherwise upon their commencement, send a copy of the amendment by post to the appropriate court office or registry, and

(b) except in the case of an amendment made under regulation 42, serve notice of the fact of the amendment in a form approved by the Board upon all other parties to the proceedings, and, if any other person becomes a party to the proceedings, serve similar notice upon that person.

(3) The copy of the amendment sent to the appropriate court office or registry shall form part of the papers for the court in the proceedings.

(4) Paragraphs (2) and (3) shall not apply to authorised summary proceedings, and, where an assisted person is a party to such proceedings, his solicitor shall, before or at the first hearing that takes place after the amendment has been issued, file the amendment with the *clerk to the justices* [justices' chief executive].

**Note.** Words 'clerk to the justices' substituted by words 'justices' chief executive' in square brackets by SI 2001/617, reg 2, as from 1 April 2001.

*Right to show cause on application to remove limitation*

**55.** An Area Director shall not refuse an application to amend a certificate (other than an emergency certificate) by removing a limitation imposed upon it until—

(a) notice has been served on the assisted person that the application may be refused and his certificate discharged and that he may show cause why the application should be granted; and

(b) the assisted person has been given an opportunity to show cause why his application should be granted.

*Procedure on refusal of amendment*

**56.** Where an Area Director refuses an application for the amendment of a certificate, he shall notify the assisted person's solicitor in writing, stating his reasons for so doing.

*Right of appeal against refusal of amendment*

**57.** (1) Where an Area Director refuses an application for the amendment of a certificate, the assisted person may appeal to the appropriate area committee.

(2) An appeal shall be brought by giving notice on a form approved by the Board within 14 days of the Area Director's decision to refuse the application.

*Determination of appeal against refusal of amendment*

**58.** (1) Subject to paragraph (3), the area committee shall, on an appeal under regulation 57, reconsider the application and determine the appeal in such manner as seems to it to be just and, without prejudice to the generality of the foregoing, may—

(a) dismiss the appeal; or

(b) direct the Area Director to amend the certificate in such manner as the area committee thinks fit.

(2) Any decision of an area committee with regard to an appeal shall be final, and it shall give notice of its decision, and the reasons for it, to the assisted person and to his solicitor in a form approved by the Board.

(3) Nothing in this regulation or regulation 53 shall require the area committee to allow the assisted person to conduct an appeal under this regulation himself or

to be represented on any such appeal if the area committee considers that such steps are unnecessary.

PART VIII

AUTHORITY TO INCUR COSTS

*Instructing counsel*

**59.** (1) Where it appears to an assisted person's solicitor that the proper conduct of the proceedings so requires, he may instruct counsel; but, unless authority has been given in the certificate or by the Area Director—

(a) counsel shall not be instructed in authorised summary proceedings; and

(b) a Queen's Counsel or more than one counsel shall not be instructed.

(2) Any instructions delivered to counsel under paragraph (1) shall—

(a) include a copy of the certificate (and any amendments to it) and any authority to incur costs under this Part of these Regulations;

(b) be endorsed with the legal aid reference number; and

(c) in the case of authorised summary proceedings, show the authority for counsel to be instructed;

but no fees shall be marked on any set of papers so delivered.

*Power of Board to give general authority*

**60.** The Board may give general authority to solicitors acting for assisted persons in any particular class of case to incur costs by—

(a) obtaining a report or opinion from one or more experts or tendering expert evidence:

(b) employing a person to provide a report or opinion (other than as an expert); or

(c) requesting transcripts of shorthand notes or tape recordings of any proceedings;

and, if such authority is given, the Board shall specify the maximum fee payable for any such report, opinion, expert evidence or transcript.

*Other cases where authority may be sought*

**61.** (1) Where it appears to an assisted person's solicitor to be necessary for the proper conduct of the proceedings to incur costs by taking any of the steps specified in paragraph (2), he may, unless authority has been given in the certificate, apply to the Area Director for prior authority.

(2) The steps referred to in paragraph (1) are—

(a) obtaining a report or opinion of an expert or tendering expert evidence in a case of a class not included in any general authority given under regulation 60; or

(b) paying a person, not being an expert witness, a fee to prepare a report and, if required, to give evidence in a case of a class not included in any general authority given under regulation 60; or

(c) in a case of a class included in a general authority given under regulation 60, paying a higher fee than that specified by the Board or obtaining more reports or opinions or tendering more evidence (expert or otherwise) than has been specified; or

(d) performing an act which is either unusual in its nature or involves unusually large expenditure; or

(e) bespeaking any transcripts of shorthand notes or tape recordings of any proceedings not included in any general authority given under regulation 60.

(3) Where the Area Director gives prior authority for the taking of any step referred to in paragraph (2)(a), (b), (c) or (e), he shall specify—

(a) the number of reports or opinions that may be obtained or the number of persons who may be authorised to give expert evidence, and

(b) the maximum fee to be paid for each report, opinion, transcript or to each person for tendering evidence, as the case may be.

*Reasons to be given for refusing authority*

**62.**   If an Area Director refuses an application for authority made under regulation 59 or 61, he shall give written reasons for his decision.

*Effect of obtaining and failing to obtain authority*

**63.**   (1) Subject to paragraph (2), no question as to the propriety of any step or act in relation to which prior authority has been obtained under regulation 59, 60 or 61 shall be raised on any *taxation* [detailed assessment] of costs.

(2) Where costs are incurred in accordance with and subject to the limit imposed by a prior authority given under regulation 59, 60 or 61, no question shall be raised on any *taxation* [detailed assessment] as to the amount of the payment to be allowed for the step or act in relation to which the authority was given unless the solicitor or the assisted person knew or ought reasonably to have known that the purpose for which the authority was given had failed or become irrelevant or unnecessary before the costs were incurred.

(3) Without prejudice to regulation 59, where costs are incurred in instructing a Queen's Counsel or more than one counsel, without authority to do so having been given in the certificate or under regulation 59(1), no payment in respect of those costs shall be allowed on any *taxation* [detailed assessment] unless it is also allowed on an inter partes *taxation* [detailed assessment].

(4) Where costs are incurred in instructing counsel or in taking any step or doing any act for which authority may be given under regulation 60 or 61, without authority to do so having been given in the certificate or under regulation 59, 60 or 61, payment in respect of those costs may still be allowed on *taxation* [detailed assessment].

**Note.** Words 'taxation' in each place it occurs substituted by words 'detailed assessment' in square brackets by SI 2000/451, reg 3(a) as from 20 March 2000.

*Restriction on payment otherwise than from the fund*

**64.**   Where a certificate has been issued in connection with any proceedings, the assisted person's solicitor or counsel shall not receive or be party to the making of any payment for work done in those proceedings during the currency of that certificate (whether within the scope of the certificate or otherwise) except such payments as may be made out of the fund.

PART IX

CONDUCT OF PROCEEDINGS

*Restrictions on entrusting case to others*

**65.**   (1) No solicitor or counsel acting for an assisted person shall entrust the conduct of any part of the case to any other person except another solicitor or counsel selected under section 32(1) of the Act.

(2) Nothing in paragraph (1) shall prevent a solicitor from entrusting the conduct of any part of the case to a partner of his or to a competent and responsible representative of his employed in his office or otherwise under his immediate supervision.

*Duty to report changes of circumstances*

**66.** The assisted person shall forthwith inform his solicitor of any change in his circumstances or in the circumstances of his case, which he has reason to believe might affect the terms or the continuation of his certificate.

*Provision of information*

**66A.** The Area Director or the assessment officer may at any time after the grant of a certificate require the assisted person to—
(a) provide further evidence of any information given in relation to his application for a certificate;
(b) attend for an interview for the purpose of providing such information;
(c) provide such additional information as the Area Director or the assessment officer may require.

*Duty to report abuse of legal aid*

**67.** (1) Where an assisted person's solicitor or counsel has reason to believe that the assisted person has—
(a) required his case to be conducted unreasonably so as to incur an unjustifiable expense to the fund or has required unreasonably that the case be continued; or
(b) intentionally failed to comply with any provision of regulations made under the Act concerning the information to be furnished by him or in furnishing such information has knowingly made a false statement or false representation,
the solicitor or counsel shall forthwith report the fact to the Area Director.
(2) Where the solicitor or counsel is uncertain whether it would be reasonable for him to continue acting for the assisted person, he shall report the circumstances to the Area Director.

*Power of court to refer abuse to Area Director*

**68.** (1) Subject to paragraph (2), at any time during the hearing of any proceedings to which an assisted person is a party, the court may, on the application of the Board or of its own motion, make an order referring to the Area Director the question whether the assisted person's certificate should continue where the court considers that the assisted person has—
(a) in relation to any application for a certificate, made an untrue statement as to his financial resources or has failed to disclose any material fact concerning them, whether the statement was made or the failure occurred before or after the issue of the certificate and notwithstanding that it was made or occurred in relation to an application to another area office in connection with the same proceedings; or
(b) intentionally failed to comply with these Regulations by not furnishing to his solicitor or the Area Director any material information concerning anything other than his financial resources; or
(c) knowingly made an untrue statement in furnishing such information;
and the court shall notify the Area Director of the terms of any order so made.
(2) No order shall be made under paragraph (1) by reason of any such mis-statement or failure as is referred to in paragraph (1)(a) if the assisted person satisfies the court that he used due care or diligence to avoid such mis-statement or failure but the assisted person's solicitor shall nevertheless report the circumstances to the Area Director.

*Duty to report on refusing or giving up case*

**69.**   (1) A solicitor shall inform the Area Director of his reasons for refusing to act or for giving up a case after being selected.

(2) Counsel, where he has been selected to act or is acting for an assisted person, shall inform the Area Director of his reasons for refusing to accept instructions or for giving up the case or shall, if required so to do, inform the Area Director of his reasons for entrusting it to another.

(3) Without prejudice to any other right of a solicitor or counsel to give up a case, any solicitor or counsel may give up an assisted person's case in the circumstances specified in regulation 67.

(4) Where any solicitor or counsel exercises his right to give up an assisted person's case in the circumstances specified in regulation 67, the solicitor shall make a report to the Area Director of the circumstances in which that right was exercised.

(5) Where the Area Director to whom a report is made under paragraph (4) does not discharge or revoke the assisted person's certificate, he shall require the assisted person to select another solicitor to act for him.

*Duty to report progress of proceedings*

**70.**   (1) An assisted person's solicitor and his counsel (if any) shall give the Area Director such information regarding the progress and disposal of the proceedings to which the certificate relates as the Area Director may from time to time require for the purpose of performing his functions under these Regulations [, whether in relation to the assisted person's case or any other application, certificate or contract,] and, without being required so to do, the assisted person's solicitor shall—

(a) make a report where the assisted person declines to accept a reasonable offer of settlement or a sum which is paid into court;

(b) notify the Area Director where a legal aid certificate is issued to another party to the proceedings;

[(c) notify the Area Director of any information which comes to his knowledge and which he considers may be relevant to the determination of any application or the continuance of any certificate or contract].

(2) Without prejudice to the generality of paragraph (1), an assisted person's solicitor shall, when required so to do by the Board, make a report to the Area Director, on a form approved by the Board, specifying the grounds on which he certifies that it is reasonable for the assisted person to continue to receive legal aid in respect of the proceedings to which the certificate relates.

(3) Where an assisted person's solicitor fails to make a report under paragraph (2) within 21 days of the Board's request, the Area Director shall—

(a) give notice to him and to the assisted person that the legal aid certificate may be discharged; and

(b) invite the assisted person to show cause why the certificate should not be discharged,

and the provisions of Part X of these Regulations shall apply, with any necessary modifications, where notice is given under sub-paragraph (a) above.

**Note.** In para (1) words from', whether in' to 'or contract' in square brackets and sub-para (c) inserted by SI 1999/1113, reg 4 as from 6 May 1999.

*Duty to report death, etc, of assisted person*

**71.**   A solicitor who has acted or is acting for an assisted person shall, on becoming aware that the assisted person—

(a) has died; or

(b) has had a bankruptcy order made against him, report that fact to the Area Director.

*Duty to report completion of case*

**72.**   A solicitor shall report forthwith to the Area Director either—
   (a) upon the completion of the case if he has completed the work authorised by the certificate, or
   (b) if, for any reason, he is unable to complete the work.

*Privilege, etc, not to prevent disclosure*

**73.**   (1) No solicitor or counsel shall be precluded, by reason of any privilege arising out of the relationship between counsel, solicitor and client, from disclosing to an Area Director or an area committee any information, or from giving any opinion, which he is required to disclose or give to the Area Director or that committee under the Act or these Regulations, or which may enable them to perform their functions under the Act or these Regulations [in relation to any application, certificate or contract].

   (2) For the purpose of providing information under the Act or these Regulations or to enable an Area Director or an area committee to perform its functions under the Act or these Regulations [in relation to any application, certificate or contract], any party may disclose to an Area Director or an area committee communications in relation to the proceedings concerned sent to or by the assisted person's solicitor, whether or not they are expressed to be 'without prejudice'.

**Note.** Words 'in relation to any application, certificate or contract' in both places they occur in square brackets inserted by SI 1999/1113, reg 5, as from 6 May 1999.

PART X

REVOCATION AND DISCHARGE OF CERTIFICATES

*Effect of revocation or discharge*

**74.**   (1) An Area Director may terminate a certificate by revoking or discharging it under this Part of these Regulations.

   (2) Subject to this Part of these Regulations, a person whose certificate is revoked shall be deemed never to have been an assisted person in relation to those proceedings except for the purposes of section 18 of the Act; and a person whose certificate is discharged shall, from the date of the discharge, cease to be an assisted person in the proceedings to which the certificate related.

*Revocation or discharge of emergency certificate*

**75.**   (1) The Area Director shall revoke an emergency certificate where the assessment officer assesses that the person to whom it was issued has disposable income of an amount which makes him ineligible for legal aid.

   (2) The Area Director shall revoke an emergency certificate where the assessment officer assesses that the person to whom it was issued, having disposable income of an amount which makes him eligible for legal aid, has disposable capital of an amount which renders him liable to be refused legal aid, and it appears to the Area Director that, without legal aid, the probable cost to him of the proceedings in respect of which the emergency certificate was issued would not exceed the contribution which would be payable by him.

   (3) The Area Director may revoke or discharge an emergency certificate if he is satisfied that the assisted person has failed to attend for an interview or to provide information or documents when required to do so under these Regulations, or has failed to accept an offer of a substantive certificate.

   (4) The Area Director may revoke or discharge an emergency certificate upon the expiry of such period (including any extension of that period granted under regulation 24(1)) as he may have allowed for the duration of the certificate.

   (5) No emergency certificate shall be revoked under paragraph (3) until—

(a) notice has been served on the assisted person and his solicitor that the Area Director may do so and that the assisted person may show cause why the certificate should not be revoked, and

(b) the assisted person has been given an opportunity to show cause why his certificate should not be revoked.

(6) Where notice is served under paragraph (5), no further work may be done or steps taken under the certificate unless authorised by the Area Director.

*Discharge of certificate on financial grounds*

**76.** (1) The Area Director shall discharge a certificate (other than an emergency certificate) from such date as he considers appropriate where the assessment officer assesses that the person to whom it was issued has disposable income of an amount which makes him ineligible for legal aid.

(2) The Area Director shall discharge a certificate (other than an emergency certificate) from such date as he considers appropriate where the assessment officer assesses that the person to whom it was issued, having disposable income of an amount which makes him eligible for legal aid, has disposable capital of an amount which renders him liable to be refused legal aid, and it appears to the Area Director that, without legal aid, the probable cost to him of continuing the proceedings in respect of which the certificate was issued would not exceed the contribution which would be payable.

(3) Subject to section 15(3B) to (3D) of the Act, where the Area Director considers that the current financial circumstances of the assisted person are such that he could afford to proceed without legal aid, he may, with a view to discharging the certificate, require the assessment officer to assess the assisted person's current financial resources in accordance with the Civil Legal Aid (Assessment of Resources) Regulations 1989 and may discharge the certificate from such date as he considers appropriate.

*Discharge on the merits*

**77.** The Area Director shall discharge a certificate from such date as he considers appropriate where, as a result of information which has come to his knowledge, he considers that—

(a) the assisted person no longer has reasonable grounds for taking, defending or being a party to the proceedings, or for continuing to do so; or

(b) the assisted person has required the proceedings to be conducted unreasonably so as to incur an unjustifiable expense to the fund; or

(c) it is unreasonable in the particular circumstances that the assisted person should continue to receive legal aid.

*Power to revoke or discharge for abuse of legal aid*

**78.** (1) Subject to paragraph (2), the Area Director may revoke or discharge a certificate where, as a result of information which has come to his knowledge, whether by a reference from the court under regulation 68 or otherwise, it appears to the Area Director that the assisted person has—

(a) in relation to any application for a certificate (whether for the same or different proceedings), made an untrue statement as to his financial resources or has failed to disclose any material fact concerning them, whether the statement was made or the failure occurred before or after the issue of the certificate and notwithstanding that it was made or occurred in relation to an application to another area office; or

(b) intentionally failed to comply with these Regulations by not furnishing to the Area Director or the solicitor any material information concerning any matter other than his financial resources; or

(c) knowingly made an untrue statement in furnishing such information.

(2) No certificate shall be revoked or discharged under paragraph (1) by reason of any such mis-statement or failure as is referred to in paragraph (1)(a) if the assisted person satisfies the Area Director that he used due care or diligence to avoid such mis-statement or failure.

*Power to revoke or discharge for failure to provide information etc*

**79.** The Area Director may revoke or discharge a certificate if he is satisfied that the assisted person has failed to attend for an interview or to provide information or documents when required to do so under these Regulations whether in respect of the same or different proceedings.

*Further power to discharge*

**80.** The Area Director may discharge a certificate from such date as he considers appropriate—
   (a) with the consent of the assisted person; or
   (b) where the assisted person has been required to make a contribution and any payment in respect of it is more than 21 days in arrears; or
   (c) on being satisfied, by the report of the assisted person's solicitor or otherwise, that—
      (i) the assisted person has died; or
      (ii) the assisted person has had a bankruptcy order made against him; or
      (iii) the proceedings to which the certificate relates have been disposed of; or
      (iv) the work authorised by the certificate has been completed.

*Opportunity to show cause against revocation or discharge*

**81.** (1) Except where a certificate is discharged or revoked under regulation 75 or discharged under regulation 76 or 80(a), (b), (c)(i), (iii) or (iv), no certificate shall be revoked or discharged until—
   (a) notice has been served on the assisted person that the Area Director may revoke or discharge his certificate (as the case may be) and that he may show cause why it should not be revoked or discharged; and
   (b) the assisted person has been given an opportunity to show cause why his certificate should not be revoked or discharged.

(2) Where an Area Director revokes or discharges a certificate after notice has been given under paragraph (1), the assisted person may appeal to the appropriate area committee against such revocation or discharge and the provisions of regulations 36 to 39 shall, with the necessary modifications, apply to the conduct of such appeals.

(3) Any decision with regard to an appeal under paragraph (2) shall be final, and the area committee shall give notice of its decision and the reasons for it to the appellant and to any solicitor acting for him on a form approved by the Board.

[(4) Where noticed is secured under paragraph (1)(a), no further work may be done or steps taken under the certificate rules authorised by the Area Director.]

**Note.** Para 4 inserted by SI 2002/711, reg 4 as from 8 April 2002.

*Notification of revocation or discharge*

**82.** (1) Where an Area Director revokes or discharges an assisted person's certificate, he shall, unless the costs have already been determined, forthwith issue a notice of revocation or a notice of discharge (as the case may be), and shall send the notice (together with a copy) to his solicitor, and shall (except where the certificate has been discharged because the assisted person has died) send a further copy of the notice to the assisted person.

(2) A solicitor who receives a notice of revocation or a notice of discharge sent to him under paragraph (1) shall either forthwith, or if an appeal has been brought under regulation 81(2) which has been dismissed, forthwith upon receipt by him of a notice of dismissal—

(a)  serve notice of such revocation or discharge in a form approved by the Board upon any other persons who are parties to the proceedings, and

(b)  inform any counsel, and if proceedings have been commenced send a copy of the notice by post to the appropriate court office or registry.

(3)  The copy of the notice sent to the appropriate court office or registry shall form part of the papers for the use of the court in the proceedings.

(4)  *Omitted.*

(5)  Where the Area Director has considered revoking or discharging a certificate in consequence of information brought to his knowledge by any person, he may, if he thinks fit, inform that person whether or not the certificate has been revoked or discharged.

*Effect of revocation or discharge on retainer*

**83.**  (1)  Upon receipt by him of a notice of revocation or discharge of a certificate, the retainer of any solicitor and counsel selected by or acting on behalf of the assisted person shall, subject to paragraph (2), either forthwith determine or, if an appeal has been brought under regulation 81(2) which has been dismissed, forthwith determine after receipt by him of a notice of such dismissal.

(2)  If an Area Director revokes or discharges a certificate and proceedings have commenced, the retainer of the solicitor shall not determine until he has sent to the appropriate court office or registry, and has served, any notice required by regulation 82.

*Costs to be taxed [determined by way of detailed assessment] or assessed [under regulation 105] on revocation or discharge*

**84.**  Upon the determination of a retainer under regulation 83—

(a)  the costs of the proceedings to which the certificate related, incurred by or on behalf of the person to whom it was issued, shall, as soon as is practicable after the determination of the retainer, be submitted for *taxation* [detailed assessment] or assessment [under regulation 105]; and

(b)  the fund shall remain liable for the payment of any costs so *taxed or* assessed.

**Note.** Words 'determined by way of detailed assessment' substituted for words 'taxed', words 'under regulation 105' in square brackets in both places inserted, words 'detailed assessment' substituted for word 'taxation' in square brackets and words 'taxed or' revoked by SI 2000/451, regs 3, 6, 7 as from 20 March 2000.

*Operation of statutory charge*

**85.**  (1)  Where a certificate has been revoked or discharged, section 16(6) of the Act (which provides for a charge upon property recovered or preserved for an assisted person) shall apply to any property recovered or preserved as a result of the person whose certificate has been revoked or discharged continuing to take, defend or be a party to the proceedings to which the certificate related.

(2)  For the purpose of paragraph (1), the reference to a person whose certificate has been discharged shall, where the certificate has been discharged under regulation 80(c)(i) or (ii), include his personal representatives, his trustee in bankruptcy or the Official Receiver, as the case may be.

*Right to recover costs and contribution*

**86.**  (1)  Where a certificate has been revoked—

(a)  the Board shall have the right to recover from the person to whom the certificate was issued the costs paid or payable under regulation 84(b) less any amount received from him by way of contribution; and

(b)  the solicitor who has acted under the certificate shall have the right to recover from that person the difference between the amount paid or payable out of the fund and the full amount of his solicitor and own client costs.

(2) Where a certificate has been discharged, the person to whom the certificate was issued shall remain liable for the payment of his contribution (if any) as determined or redetermined, up to the amount paid or payable by the Board under regulation 84(b) and, where he continues to take, defend or be a party to the proceedings to which the certificate related, section 17(1) of the Act shall apply in so far as the costs were incurred while he was an assisted person.

PART XI

PROPERTY AND COSTS RECOVERED FOR ASSISTED PERSONS

*Money recovered to be paid to solicitor or the Board*

**87.** (1) Subject to regulations 89 and 94, all moneys payable to an assisted person—
(a) by virtue of any agreement or order made in connection with the action, cause or matter to which his certificate relates, whether such agreement was made before or after the proceedings were taken; or
(b) being moneys payable in respect of the action, cause or matter to which his certificate relates upon the distribution of property of a person who had been adjudicated bankrupt or has entered into a deed of arrangement, or of a company in liquidation; or
(c) being moneys which were paid into court by him or on his behalf in any proceedings to which his certificate relates and which have been ordered to be repaid to him; or
(d) being moneys standing in court to the credit of any proceedings to which his certificate relates,
shall be paid or repaid, as the case may be, to the solicitor of the assisted person or, if he is no longer represented by a solicitor, to the Board, and only the solicitor, or, as the case may be, the Board, shall be capable of giving a good discharge for moneys so payable.
(2) Where the assisted person's solicitor has reason to believe that an attempt may be made to circumvent the provisions of paragraph (1), he shall inform the Board.

*Notice to trustee in bankruptcy, etc*

**88.** (1) Where moneys become payable under regulation 87(1)(b), the solicitor or the Board, as the case may be, shall send to the trustee in bankruptcy, the trustee or assignee of the deed of arrangement or the liquidator of the company in liquidation, as the case may be, notice that a certificate has been issued to the assisted person.
(2) A notice sent under paragraph (1) shall operate as a request by the assisted person for payment of the moneys payable under regulation 87(1)(b) to the assisted person's solicitor or the Board, as the case may be, and shall be a sufficient authority for that purpose.

*Exceptions to regulation 87*

**89.** Notwithstanding the requirements of regulation 87—
(a) payment of any sum under an order for costs in favour of an assisted person in authorised summary proceedings shall be made to the *clerk to the justices* [justices' chief executive], who shall pay it to the Board or as the Board shall direct, and only the *clerk to the justices* [justices' chief executive] shall be able to give a good discharge therefor; and
(b) where any moneys recovered or preserved for an assisted person in any proceedings have been paid into or remain in court and invested for the benefit of the assisted person, such part of those moneys as is not subject to

the charge created by section 16(6) of the Act in accordance with regulation 93 may be paid to the assisted person.

**Note.** Words 'clerk to the justices' in both places substituted by words 'justices' chief executive' in square brackets by SI 2001/617, reg 2 as from 1 April 2001.

*Solicitor to pay moneys recovered to the Board*

**90.** (1) An assisted person's solicitor shall forthwith—

(a) inform the Area Director of any property recovered or preserved for the assisted person and send to him a copy of the order or agreement by virtue of which the property was recovered or preserved; and

(b) subject to paragraphs (2) and (4), pay all moneys received by him under the terms of the order or agreement made in the assisted person's favour to the Board.

(2) Where the Area Director considers that the rights of the fund will thereby be safeguarded, he may direct the assisted person's solicitor to—

(a) pay to the Board under paragraph (1)(b) only such sums as, in the opinion of the Area Director, should be retained by the Board in order to safeguard the rights of the fund under any provisions of the Act and these Regulations; and

(b) pay any other moneys to the assisted person.

(3) Where—

(a) in proceedings under any of the enactments referred to in regulation 96(1) the property recovered or preserved for the assisted person includes money which by order of the court or under the terms of any agreement reached is to be used for the purpose of purchasing a home for himself or his dependants; or

(b) in any proceedings the property recovered or preserved for the assisted person includes property which, by order of the court or under the terms of any agreement reached, is to be used as a home for the assisted person or his dependants,

the assisted person's solicitor shall immediately so inform the Area Director.

(4) If the Area Director considers and directs that the provisions of regulation 96 apply to any sum of money, paragraph (1)(b) above shall not apply to it and the assisted person's solicitor shall release the money only in accordance with the provisions of regulation 96.

(5) Where the assisted person's solicitor pays moneys to the Board in accordance with this regulation, he shall identify what sums relate to costs and what to damages.

*Enforcement of orders, etc, in favour of assisted person*

**91.** (1) Where in any proceedings to which an assisted person is a party—

(a) an order or agreement is made providing for the recovery or preservation of property for the benefit of the assisted person and, by virtue of the Act, there is a first charge on the property for the benefit of the Board; or

(b) an order or agreement is made for the payment of costs to the assisted person,

the Board may take such proceedings in its own name as may be necessary to enforce or give effect to such an order or agreement.

(2) An assisted person may, with the consent of the appropriate Area Director, take proceedings (being proceedings for which representation may be granted under the Act) to give effect to an order or agreement referred to in regulation 87(1)(a).

(2A) The assisted person's solicitor may take proceedings for the recovery of costs in the circumstances to which regulation 107B applies.

(2B) Where the Board has paid costs to which regulation 92(1)(b) refers, but those costs have not been reimbursed by payment from any other party in favour of the assisted person, the solicitor shall require the consent of the Area Director before taking proceedings to which paragraph (2A) refers.

(3) Where the Board takes proceedings, it may authorise any person to swear an affidavit, file a proof, receive a dividend or take any other step in the proceedings in its name and the costs incurred by the Board in any such proceedings shall be a first charge on any property or sum so recovered.

*Retention and payment out of moneys by the Board*

**92.** (1) The costs payable by the Board in respect of any work done under a certificate, after deduction of any sums paid under regulation 100 or 101 (payments on account), shall be—

(a) the legal aid only costs;

(b) any other costs determined under regulation 107A(2);

(c) where inter partes costs paid in favour of the assisted person are received by the Board, a sum equal to the amount by which the costs received exceed the costs referred to in sub-paragraph (b) above;

(d) where all the inter partes costs as agreed or determined in accordance with any direction or order given or made in the proceedings in favour of the assisted person are received by the Board together with interest, a sum equal to the balance of interest after deduction of interest on the costs to which sub-paragraph (b) refers.

(2) Upon receipt of moneys paid to it under this Part of the Regulations the Board shall retain—

(a) subject to regulation 103 and to paragraph (1)(c) and (d) above, any sum paid under an order or agreement for costs made in favour of the assisted person in respect of the period covered by his certificate;

(b) a sum equal to the amount (if any) by which any property recovered or preserved is charged for the benefit of the Board by virtue of section 16(6) of the Act;

(c) any costs of proceedings taken by the Board under regulation 91(1),

and shall pay the balance to the assisted person.

*Interest on damages*

**92A.** (1) Where the Board receives damages paid in favour of an assisted person it shall, subject to the provisions of this regulation, pay to the assisted person a sum representing gross interest earned while the damages are being held by the Board.

(2) Without prejudice to its other powers to invest money, the Board shall maintain and may deposit in one general account at a bank or building society damages to which this regulation refers.

(3) The rate of interest payable to the assisted person by virtue of this regulation shall be $\frac{1}{2}$ per cent per annum less than the rate payable on damages deposited in the general account.

(4) The Board shall not be required to pay interest where the damages received do not exceed £500 or where the period during which they are held by the Board is less than 28 days.

(5) Interest shall be payable for the period beginning on the third business day after the date on which the damages are received by the Board down to (and including) the date on which the Board determines the amount to be retained under regulation 92(2).

(6) In this regulation—

'bank' means the Bank of England, or the branch, situated in England or Wales, or any institution authorised under the Banking Act 1987;

'building society' means the branch, situated in England or Wales, of a building society within the meaning of the Building Societies Act 1986;

'business day' means a day other than a Saturday, a Sunday, Christmas Day, Good Friday or a bank holiday under the Banking and Financial Dealings Act 1971;

'general account' means an interest bearing account opened in the name of the Board, the title of which account does not identify any assisted person.

*Operation of statutory charge on moneys in court*

**93.** Where any moneys recovered or preserved for an assisted person in any proceedings are ordered to be paid into or remain in court and invested for the benefit of the assisted person, the charge created by section 16(6) of the Act, shall attach only to such parts of those moneys as, in the opinion of the Area Director, will be sufficient to safeguard the rights of the Board under any provisions of the Act or these Regulations and the Area Director shall notify the court in writing of the amount so attached.

*Exemptions from the statutory charge*

**94.**   [(1)] The charge created by section 16(6) of the Act shall not apply to—

(a)   any interim payment made in accordance with an order made under Order 29, rule 11 or 12 of the Rules of the Supreme Court 1965, or Order 13, rule 12 of the County Court Rules 1981, or in accordance with an agreement having the same effect as such an order;

(b)   any sum or sums ordered to be paid under section 5 of the Inheritance (Provision for Family and Dependants) Act 1975;

(c)   any periodical payment of maintenance which, for this purpose, means money or money's worth paid towards the support of a spouse, former spouse, child or any other person for whose support the payer has previously been responsible or has made payments;

(d)   the first £2,500 of any money, or of the value of any property, recovered or preserved by virtue of—

    (i)   an order made, or deemed to be made, under the provisions of section 23(1)(c) or (f), 23(2), 24, 27(6)(c) or (f), or 35 of the Matrimonial Causes Act 1973; or

    (ii)   an order made, or deemed to be made, under the provisions of section 2 or 6 of the Inheritance (Provision for Family and Dependants) Act 1975 or any provision repealed by that Act; or

    (iii)   an order made, or deemed to be made, after 30th September 1977, under section 17 of the Married Women's Property Act 1882; or

    (iv)   *omitted*;

    (v)   an order for the payment of a lump sum made, or deemed to be made, under the provisions of section 60 of the Magistrates' Courts Act 1980; or

    (vi)   an order made, or deemed to be made, under the provision of section 2(1)(b) or (d), 6(1) or (5) or 20(2) of the Domestic Proceedings and Magistrates' Courts Act 1978; or

    (vii)   *omitted*;

    (viii)   an order made, or deemed to be made, under the provisions of Schedule 1 to the Children Act 1989; or

    (ix)   an agreement made after 1st March 1981 which has the same effect as an order made, or deemed to be made under any of the provisions specified in sub-paragraph (d)(i) to (viii);

(dd)   any tools of the assisted person's trade;

(e)   where the certificate was issued before 3rd May 1976, any money or property, of whatever amount or value, recovered or preserved by the virtue of an order made, or deemed to be made, under any of the provisions specified in sub-paragraph (d)(i) or (ii) before 1st August 1976 or which, if made on or after that date, give effect to a settlement entered into before that date;

(f)   any payment made in accordance with an order made by the Employment Appeal Tribunal, or in accordance with a settlement entered into after 1st November 1983 which has the same effect as such an order;

(ff)   any payment made by the Secretary of State under the Earnings Top-up Scheme 1996; or

(g)   any sum, payment or benefit which, by virtue of any provision of, or made under, an Act of Parliament, cannot be assigned or charged.

[(2) The charge created by section 16(6) of the Act shall not apply in relation to any increase in the net liability of the fund arising out of the cost of giving advice or assistance under Part III of the Act which is mediation-related advice or assistance, as defined in regulation 32(2) of the Legal Advice and Assistance Regulations 1989.]

**Note.** Para (1) numbered as such and para (2) inserted by SI 1999/2565, reg 3, as from 5 October 1999.

*Vesting and enforcement of charges*

**95.** (1) Any charge on property recovered or preserved for an assisted person arising under section 16(6) of the Act or created by virtue of regulation 96, 97 or 98 shall vest in the Board.

(2) The Board may enforce any such charge in any manner which would be available to a chargee in respect of a charge given inter partes, but the Board shall not agree to the release or postponement of the enforcement of any such charge except where regulation 96, 97 or 98 applies and then only in accordance with the provisions of those regulations.

(3) Any such charge shall according to its nature—

(a) in the case of unregistered land, be a Class B land charge within the meaning of section 2 of the Land Charges Act 1972;

(b) in the case of registered land, be a registrable substantive charge; or

(c) in a case in which the conditions specified in section 53(1) or 54(1) of the Land Registration Act 1925 are met, be protected by lodging a caution in accordance with the provisions of the relevant section,

and references to registration in regulations 96 to 98 shall be construed as references to registration or protection in accordance with paragraph (a), (b) or (c) of this regulation.

(3A) Where, in any of the circumstances described in regulation 96, 97 or 98, the property charged or to be charged is land to which the Conveyancing and Feudal Reform (Scotland) Act 1970 applies:

(a) references in those regulations to a charge executed in favour of the Board shall be construed as references to a standard security in favour of the Board within the meaning of Part II of that Act; and

(b) references in those regulations to registration shall be construed as references to the recording of a standard security in the Register of Sasines.

(4) Without prejudice to the provisions of the Land Registration Act 1925 and the Land Charges Act 1972, all conveyances and acts done to defeat, or operating to defeat, any such charge shall, except in the case of a bona fide purchaser for value without notice, be void as against the Board.

*Postponement of enforcement of charges over money*

**96.** (1) This regulation applies where in proceedings under—

(a) the Married Women's Property Act 1882;

(b) the Matrimonial Causes Act 1973;

(c) the Inheritance (Provision for Family and Dependants) Act 1975;

(d) Schedule 1 to the Children Act 1989;

(e) Part III of the Matrimonial and Family Proceedings Act 1984; or

(f) section 30 of the Law of Property Act 1925,

there is recovered or preserved for the assisted person a sum of money which by order of the court or under the terms of any agreement reached is to be used for the purpose of purchasing a home for himself or his dependants.

(2) Where the assisted person—

(a) wishes to purchase a home in accordance with the order or agreement; and

(b) agrees in writing on a form approved by the Board to comply with the conditions set out in paragraph (3), the Board may, if the Area Director is satisfied that the property to be purchased will provide adequate security for the amount of the charge created by section 16(6) of the Act, agree to defer enforcing any charge over that sum.

(3) The conditions referred to in paragraph (2) are that—

(a) the property to be purchased shall be subject to a charge executed in favour of the Board and registered in accordance with regulation 95; and

(b) interest shall accrue for the benefit of the Board in accordance with regulation 99(4).

(4) Where the Board has agreed to defer enforcement under paragraph (2), the assisted person's solicitor may release any money received by him under regulation 87 and which is the subject of the order or agreement, to the vendor or the vendor's representative on completion of the purchase of the property purchased in accordance with the order or agreement.

(5) Where—

(a) the Area Director has directed (under regulation 90(4)) that this regulation applies; and

(b) an agreement to defer enforcement under paragraph (2) above has been made, the assisted person's solicitor may release any money received by him under regulation 87 and which is the subject of the order or agreement to another solicitor or to a person providing conveyancing services to whom section 22(1) of the Solicitors Act 1974 does not apply, who has given an undertaking to, and on a form approved by, the Board that he will fulfil the obligations imposed by this regulation on the assisted person's solicitor.

(6) Where the assisted person's solicitor releases any money under paragraph (4) or (5), he shall so inform the Area Director as soon as practicable and either—

(a) provide the Area Director with sufficient information to enable him to register a charge on the property purchased in accordance with the order or agreement; or

(b) send to the Area Director a copy of any undertaking given under paragraph (5).

(7) Where any sum of money retained by the assisted person's solicitor by virtue of this regulation has not been used for the purchase of a home after a period of one year from the date of the order or agreement under which it was recovered or preserved for the assisted person, the assisted person's solicitor shall pay that sum to the Board.

*Postponement of enforcement of charges over land*

**97.**   (1) This regulation applies where, in any proceedings, there is recovered or preserved for the assisted person property which, by order of the court or under the terms of any agreement reached, is to be used as a home for the assisted person or his dependants.

(2) Where the Area Director considers that the provisions of this regulation apply to any property, he shall so direct.

(3) Where the Area Director has directed that this regulation applies to property and the assisted person—

(a) wishes to use the property as a home for himself or his dependants; and

(b) agrees in writing on a form approved by the Board to comply with the condition set out in paragraph (4),

the Board may, if the Area Director is satisfied that the property will provide adequate security for the sum referred to in paragraph (4), agree to defer enforcing any charge over that property.

(4) The condition referred to in paragraph (3) is that interest shall accrue for the benefit of the Board in accordance with regulation 99(4).

(5) Where, in a case to which this regulation applies, the charge in favour of the Board has not yet been registered in accordance with regulation 95(3) and the assisted person—

(a) wishes to purchase a different property in substitution for the property which is the subject of the order or agreement referred to in paragraph (1); and

(b) agrees in writing on a form approved by the Board to comply with the conditions set out in paragraph (6),

the Board may, if the Area Director is satisfied that the property to be purchased will provide adequate security for the amount of the charge created by section 16(6) of the Act, agree to defer enforcing any charge over that property.

(6) The conditions referred to in paragraph (5) are that—

(a) the property to be purchased shall be subject to a charge executed in favour of the Board and registered in accordance with regulation 95; and

(b) interest shall accrue for the benefit of the Board in accordance with regulation 99(4).

*Substitution of charged property*

**98.** (1) This regulation applies where the Board has agreed under regulation 96 or 97 to defer enforcing a charge created by section 16(6) of the Act and a charge over any property (whether created by the said section 16(6) or in pursuance of regulation 96 or 97 or this regulation) has been registered in favour of the Board in accordance with regulation 95.

(2) Where, in a case to which this regulation applies—

(a) the assisted person wishes to purchase a different property in substitution for that over which a charge already exists;

(b) the assisted person agrees in writing on a form approved by the Board to comply with the conditions set out in paragraph (3); and

(c) the Area Director is satisfied that the property to be purchased will provide adequate security for the amount of the charge created by section 16(6) of the Act,

the Board may agree to release that charge.

(3) The conditions referred to in paragraph (2) are that—

(a) the property to be purchased shall be subject to a charge executed in favour of the Board and registered in accordance with regulation 95; and

(b) simple interest shall accrue or continue to accrue for the benefit of the Board from the same date, on the same amounts and at the same rate as would apply if the assisted person were to retain the property over which the charge exists and the charge were not to be released.

(4) *Omitted.*

*Payment and recovery of interest*

**99.** (1) Where interest is payable by the assisted person pursuant to the provisions of regulations 96, 97 or 98, such interest shall continue to accrue until the amount of the charge created by section 16(6) of the Act is paid and the Board shall not seek to recover interest until such payment is made.

(2) The Board may take such steps as may be necessary to enforce, give effect to or terminate any agreement made under regulation 96, 97 or 98.

(3) Nothing in regulations 96 to 99 shall prevent the assisted person from making interim payments of interest or capital in respect of the amount outstanding on the charge, whether such payments are made at regular intervals or not, and any such payment of capital shall reduce that amount accordingly except that no interim payment shall be used to reduce any such sum while interest on that sum remains outstanding.

(4) *Where interest is payable by the assisted person pursuant to the provisions of regulation 96 or 97—*

(a) it shall run from the date on which the charge is first registered;

(b) it shall accrue at the rate of 8 per cent per annum (or such other rate as may from time to time be prescribed); and

(c) the capital on which it is calculated shall be the amount outstanding on the charge from time to time.

[(4) Where interest is payable by the assisted person pursuant to the provisions of regulation 96 or 97—

(a) it shall run from the date when the charge is first registered;

(b) the applicable rate shall be—

    (i) 8% per annum until 31st March 2002;

    (ii) thereafter, 1 percentage point above the Bank of England base rate current on 1st April 2002;

(c) subject to sub-paragraph (d); the applicable rate shall be varied on 1st April of each subsequent year so that it remains at the rate of 1 percentage point above the Bank of England base rate then current; and

(d) the variation set out in sub-paragraph (c) shall take place only if the application of the new base rate has the effect of varying the base rate previously applicable by 1 percentage point or more.]

(5) In paragraphs (3) and (4), the amount outstanding on the charge at any given time means the amount of the charge created by section 16(6) of the Act, calculated so as to take into account only those sums which up to that time have been either—

(a) paid by the Board in accordance with an assessment [under regulation 105] or *taxation* [detailed assessment] of costs, or

(b) recouped by the Board in the circumstances described in section 16(9) of the Act or in accordance with paragraph (3) of this regulation.

(6) In regulations 96 to 99 references to the amount of any charge created by section 16(6) of the Act shall be construed as references to the amount determined in accordance with section 16(6) and (9) of the Act or to the value of the property to which it applies at the time when it was recovered or preserved whichever is the less.

**Note.** Para (4) substituted by SI 2001/735, reg 3 as from 3 December 2001. In para (5) words 'under regulation 105' inserted and word 'taxation' substituted by words 'detailed assessment' in square brackets by SI 2000/451, regs 3(a), 6 as from 20 March 2000.

PART XII

COSTS OF ASSISTED PERSONS

*Payment on account*

**100.** (1) A solicitor acting for an assisted person under a certificate to which this regulation applies may submit a claim to the Board on a form approved by the Board for the payment of sums on account of profit costs incurred in connection with the proceedings to which the certificate relates.

(2) Counsel instructed on behalf of an assisted person under a certificate to which this regulation applies may submit a claim to the Board on a form approved by the Board for the payment of sums on account of his fees for work done in connection with the proceedings to which the certificate relates.

(3) A payment may only be made under paragraph (1) or (2) when—

(a) a period of 12 months has elapsed since the date on which the certificate was issued, or

(b) further periods of 12 months and 24 months have elapsed since that date.

(4) A claim may only be made under paragraph (1) or (2) within the period of 2 months before to 4 months after any period specified in paragraph (3)

(5) The maximum payment to be made for each claim under paragraph (1) or (2) in any one financial year shall be—

(a)  in the case of a claim under paragraph (1):
for the financial year 1993/94                                                   62%
for the financial year 1994/95                                                   70%
for the financial year 1995/96 and thereafter                                    75%

(6)  Where a solicitor's retainer has been determined and another solicitor (who is not a member of the same firm) is acting on behalf of the assisted person, the appropriate area committee may authorise payment of a sum on account of the original solicitor's costs where it appears unlikely that the costs will be *taxed* [determined by way of detailed assessment] within 6 months of the date on which the retainer was determined.

(7)  The making of a payment under this regulation shall not release a solicitor from any obligation under these Regulations to submit his costs and counsel's fees for *taxation* [detailed assessment] or assessment [under regulation 105] on conclusion of the case.

(8)  Where, after *taxation* [detailed assessment] or assessment [under regulation 105], payments made under this regulation are found to exceed the final costs of the case, the solicitor or counsel (if any) shall, on demand, repay the balance due to the fund and, where the total costs exceed any payments made under this regulation, the balance shall be paid from the fund.

(9)  Claims for payments on account made under regulation 100(1), (2) or (6) or regulation 101(1)(b) shall be made at prescribed rates where such rates are prescribed for solicitors or counsel, as the case may be, in—
(a)  the Legal Aid in Civil Proceedings (Remuneration) Regulations 1994; or
(b)  the Legal Aid in Family Proceedings (Remuneration) Regulations 1991.

**Note.** In para (6) word 'taxed' substituted by words 'determined by way of detailed assessment' in square brackets, in paras (7), (8) words 'taxation' substituted by words 'detailed assessment' and words 'under regulation 105' in square brackets inserted, by SI 2000/451, regs 3, 6, as from 20 March 2000.

*Payment on account of disbursements, in cases of hardship, etc*

**101.**   (1) Without prejudice to regulation 100, a solicitor acting for an assisted person may apply to the appropriate area committee for the payment of a sum on account of—
(a)  disbursements incurred or about to be incurred in connection with the proceedings to which the certificate relates;
(b)  profit costs or counsel's fees where the proceedings to which the certificate relates have continued for more than 12 months and it appears unlikely that an order for taxation will be made within the next 12 months and delay in the taxation of those costs or fees will cause hardship to the solicitor or counsel.

(1A)  A solicitor who has acted for an assisted person may make an application under paragraph (1)(k) notwithstanding that the proceedings to which the certificate related have concluded and that the certificate has been revoked or discharged.

(2)  Without prejudice to regulation 100, where—
(a)  the proceedings to which the certificate related have concluded or the solicitor is otherwise entitled to have his costs taxed; and
(b)  counsel acting for the assisted person has not received payment in respect of his fees for at least 6 months since the event which gave rise to the right to taxation,
counsel may apply to the appropriate area committee for payment of 75 per cent of the amount claimed on account of his fees for work done in connection with the proceedings to which the certificate related.

(3)  Without prejudice to regulation 100, where—
(a)  the proceedings to which the certificate related have concluded or the solicitor acting for the assisted person is otherwise entitled to have his bill of costs taxed;

    (b)  the solicitor commenced proceedings for taxation in accordance with the time limits laid down by rules of court; and

    (c)  the solicitor has not received payment in respect of his costs for at least six months since he submitted his bill for taxation,

he may apply to the appropriate area committee for payment of 75 per cent of the amount claimed on account of his profit costs for work done in connection with the proceedings to which the certificate related.

### Deferment of solicitor's profit costs

**102.**  Where an assisted person's solicitor has failed to comply with any provision of these Regulations and, as a result of his default or omission, the fund incurs loss—

    (a)  the appropriate area committee may defer payment of all or part of the solicitor's profit costs in connection with *the proceedings to which the certificate relates* [any proceedings] until he has complied with such provisions; and

    (b)  if the Board refers the conduct of the solicitor to the Solicitor's Disciplinary Tribunal and the solicitor is disciplined, the Board may retain any sum, payment of which has been deferred under sub-paragraph (a), in accordance with the finding of the Tribunal.

**Note.** In para (a) words 'the precedings to which the certificate relates' substituted by words 'any proceedings' in square brackets by SI 2002/3033, reg 3 as from 31 December 2002.

### [Production of documentation and disclosure of information

**102A.**  A solicitor shall promptly produce to the Commission any documentation in his possession or control, and disclose any information, which the Commission may request from time to time in connection with any proceedings in respect of which it has made payment to the solicitor.]

**Note.** Inserted by SI 2002/3033, reg 4 as from 31 December 2002.

### [Recoupment of losses and excesses

**102B.**  (1) Where the fund incurs loss in the circumstances mentioned in regulation 102, the solicitor shall pay to the Commission a sum equivalent to the amount of such loss or such proportion of that amount as the Commission considers appropriate.

    (2) Where for whatever reason a solicitor has been paid an amount greater than that to which he is entitled, the Commission may recover the excess either by way of repayment by the solicitor or by way of deduction from any other sum which may be due to him.]

**Note.** Inserted by SI 2002/3033, reg 4 as from 31 December 2002.

### Legal aid granted after costs incurred

**103.**  (1) Where, after proceedings have been instituted in any court, a party becomes an assisted person in relation to those proceedings, the provisions of section 17(1) of the Act shall apply only to so much of the costs of the proceedings as are incurred while a certificate is in force.

    (2) Any solicitor who has acted on behalf of the assisted person in the proceedings to which a certificate relates before the date of the certificate, and any solicitor who has a lien on any documents necessary for the proceedings and who has delivered them up subject to his lien, may give notice of that fact to the appropriate area committee.

    (3) Subject to paragraph (4), if moneys are recovered for the assisted person, the Board shall pay to any solicitor who has given notice under paragraph (2) out of the sum so recovered the costs to which he would have been entitled following a *solicitor and own client taxation* [a detailed assessment of solicitor and client costs under CPR rule 48.8].

(4) In any case where the sums so recovered are insufficient to pay the solicitor's costs in full in accordance with paragraph (3) and also to meet the sums paid out or payable out of the fund on the assisted person's account, the sums recovered in the proceedings shall be divided between the fund and the solicitor in the same proportions as the solicitor's costs and the cost to the fund bear to the aggregate of the two, and the first charge for the benefit of the Board imposed by virtue of section 16(6) of the Act on property recovered or preserved in the proceedings shall take effect accordingly.

(5) In any case in which the amount of—

(a) the costs payable to a solicitor under this regulation; or

(b) the inter partes costs incurred during the period in which the certificate was in force,

have not been ascertained on *taxation* [detailed assessment], they shall, for the purpose of this regulation, be assessed by the appropriate area committee and, where the committee makes an assessment under this regulation, it shall do so with a view to allowing, for the costs referred to in sub-paragraph (a) above, such costs as the solicitor would have been entitled to on a *solicitor and own client taxation* [detailed assessment of solicitor and client costs under CPR rule 48.8] and, for the costs referred to in sub-paragraph (b) above, such costs as would have been allowed on a *taxation* [detailed assessment] under regulation 107A(2).

(6) For the purposes of this regulation, work done by a solicitor—

(a) immediately prior to the issue of an emergency certificate, and

(b) at a time when no application for an emergency certificate could be made because the appropriate area office was closed,

shall be deemed to be work done while such a certificate is in force if the solicitor applies for an emergency certificate at the first available opportunity and the application is granted.

**Note.** In paras (3), (5) words 'solicitor and own client taxation' substituted by words 'detailed assessment of solicitor and client costs under CPR rule 48.8' in square brackets and in para (5) word 'taxation' in both places substituted by words 'detailed assessment' in square brackets substituted, by SI 2000/451, regs 3, 8, as from 20 March 2000.

*Remuneration of legal representatives in magistrates' courts and family proceedings*

**104.** (1) The sums to be allowed to legal representatives in connection with *authorised summary proceedings* [proceedings in a magistrates' court] shall be assessed by the Area Director.

(2) *Omitted.*

(3) In the case of *authorised summary proceedings* [proceedings in a magistrates' court] which are not family proceedings any assessment, review or appeal under these regulations shall be made in accordance with the provisions of *regulation 6 of and Schedule 1 Part I paragraph 1(1)(a) to the Legal Aid in Criminal and Care Proceedings (Costs) Regulations 1989* [the Legal Aid in Family Proceedings (Remuneration) Regulations 1991] as if the work done was work to which these provisions apply, save that *paragraphs 2 and 3 of Schedule 1, Part I* [regulation 3(4)(c)] shall not apply.

*(4) Paragraphs (4) to (8) of regulation 105 and regulation 105A shall apply where costs are assessed by an Area Director under paragraph (1) as they apply to an assessment under that regulation.*

*(5) Subject to paragraph (4), regulations 105 to 110 shall not apply to costs in respect of authorised summary proceedings.*

[(4) Paragraphs (3A) to (11) of regulation 105 shall apply and regulation 105A shall apply where costs are assessed by an Area Director under paragraph (1) as they apply to an assessment under that regulation; provided that the references to the time limit in regulation 105(3A) shall be construed as references to—

(a)   the date three months after the termination of the solicitor's retainer, where the retainer is determined before proceedings are begun, or where the assisted person's certificate is revoked or discharged; or

(b)   otherwise, the date three months after the determination of the proceedings, whether in a magistrates' court or another court.

(5) Subject to paragraph (4), regulations 105 to 110 shall not apply to costs in respect of proceedings in a magistrates' court to which this regulation applies.]

**Note.** In paras (1), (3) words 'authorised summary proceedings' substituted by words 'proceedings in a magistrates' court' in square brackets, in para (3) words from 'regulation 6' to '1989' substituted by words 'the Legal Aid in Family Proceedings (Remuneration) Regulations 1991' in square brackets and words 'paragraphs 2 and 3 of Schedule 1, Part 1' substituted by words 'regulation 3(4)(c)' in square brackets, and paras (4), (5) revoked by SI 2000/451, reg 9, as from 20 March 2000. New paras (4), (5) inserted by SI 2002/3033, reg 5, as from 31 December 2002.

*Assessment of costs*

**105.**   *(1) In this regulation and in regulation 106A, 'assessment' means an assessment of costs with a view to ensuring that [, subject to paragraph (10),] the amounts of costs to be allowed are those which would be allowed on a taxation [detailed assessment] under regulation 107A(2).*

[(1) In this regulation and regulation 106A, 'assessment' means an assessment of costs by the Area Director and payable under a certificate in accordance with this regulation and regulation 107A.]

(2) Subject to regulation 106A, where the retainer of an assisted person's solicitor or counsel is determined before proceedings are actually begun and there has been no subsequent change of solicitor or counsel under the certificate, the amount of the solicitor's costs and counsel's fees (if any) shall be assessed by the Area Director.

*(2A)   Where proceedings have begun and the solicitor is of the opinion that the total amount which he and counsel (if any) would receive after taxation under regulation 107A(2) would not be more than £500 he must apply to the Area Director for an assessment of the amount of his costs and counsel's fees (if any) in respect of the work done.*

[(2A) Subject to paragraph (12), where proceedings have begun and the total claim for costs does not exceed £2,500, the solicitor shall apply to the Area Director for an assessment of those costs.]

*(3)   Subject to paragraph (2A) and regulation 106A, where proceedings have begun and—*

(a)   *the solicitor is of the opinion that the total amount which he and counsel (if any) would receive after taxation [detailed assessment] under regulation 107A(2) would not be more than £1,000; or*

(b)   *...*

(c)   *there are special circumstances where a taxation [detailed assessment] would be against the interest of the assisted person or would increase the amount payable from the fund; or*

(d)   *after a direction or order that the assisted person's costs shall be taxed [determined by way of detailed assessment] under regulation 107A(2), the solicitor incurs costs for the purpose of recovering moneys payable to the fund,*

*the solicitor may apply to the Area Director for an assessment of the amount of his costs and counsel's fees (if any) in respect of the work done.*

[(3) Subject to paragraph (12) where proceedings have begun and the total claim for costs exceeds £2,500, the solicitor may apply to the Area Director for an assessment of those costs if—

(a)   there are special circumstances where a detailed assessment would be against the interest of the assisted person or would increase the amount payable from the fund; or

(b)   after a direction or order that the assisted person's costs shall be determined by way of detailed assessment under regulations 107(2), the solicitor incurs costs for the purpose of recovering moneys payable to the fund.]

[(3A) [Subject to paragraph (10),] an application for an assessment under this regulation shall be made—

(a) where paragraph (2) applies, within three months of the termination of the solicitor's retainer;

(b) where paragraph (2A) or (3) applies—

  (i) if the assisted person's certificate is revoked or discharged [but there has been no order for assessment or determination of costs by the court], within three months of the termination of the solicitor's retainer;

  (ii) otherwise, within the period which would have been the period specified by CPR rule 47.7 for the commencement of detailed assessment proceedings if the costs fell to be determined by way of detailed assessment.]

(4) If any solicitor or counsel is dissatisfied with any decision on an assessment in accordance with paragraph *(2) or (3)* [(2), (2A) or (3)], he may, within 21 days of that decision, make written representations to the appropriate area committee; and that committee shall review the assessment of the Area Director whether by confirming, increasing or decreasing the amount assessed by the Area Director.

(5) A solicitor or counsel who is dissatisfied with the decision of an area committee on a review under paragraph (4) may, within 21 days of the decision, apply to that committee [in writing] to certify a point of principle of general importance.

(6) Where an area committee certifies a point of principle of general importance, the solicitor or counsel may, within 21 days of the certification, appeal in writing to a committee appointed by the Board against the decision of the area committee under paragraph (4).

(7) On an appeal under paragraph (6) the committee appointed by the Board may reverse, affirm or amend the decision of the area committee under paragraph (4).

(8) The assisted person's solicitor shall within 7 days after an assessment or review under this regulation notify counsel in writing where the fees claimed on his behalf have been reduced or disallowed on assessment or review.

*[(9) Subject to paragraph (10), the time limit in paragraph (3A) may, for good reason, be extended by the Area Director.*

*(10) Where a solicitor or counsel without good reason has failed (or, if an extension were not granted, would fail) to comply with the time limit in paragraph (3A), the Area Director may, in exceptional circumstances, extend the time limit and shall consider whether it is reasonable in the circumstances to reduce the costs; provided that costs shall not be reduced unless the solicitor or counsel has been allowed a reasonable opportunity to show cause in writing why the costs should not be reduced.]*

[(10) Where a solicitor or counsel has failed to comply with the time limit in paragraph (3A), the costs shall be assessed and the Area Director shall consider what, if any, reduction is reasonable and proportionate in all the circumstances; provided that costs shall not be reduced unless the solicitor or counsel has been allowed a reasonable opportunity to show cause in writing why the costs should not be reduced.]

(11) A solicitor or counsel may appeal to the area committee against a decision made by the Area Director under paragraph (9) or (10) and such an appeal shall be commenced within 21 days of the decision by giving notice in writing to the area committee specifying the grounds of appeal.]

[(12) In any proceedings where it is or may be necessary for the court to carry out a detailed assessment of costs payable to the assisted person by another party to the proceedings, the solicitor shall not apply to the Area Director for an assessment and the total claim for costs shall be subject to that detailed assessment by the court.

(13) In this regulation, 'total claim for costs' means the claim consisting of the solicitor's profit costs (including those of any other solicitor who has acted under the certificate), counsel's fees and disbursements (if any), but excluding any element of Value Added Tax.

(14) Any costs incurred in connection with an appeal against the decision of the Area Director under this regulation shall not be deemed to be costs to which the assisted person's certificate relates.]

**Note.** Para (1) substituted by SI 2003/1312, reg 2(a) as from 1 July 2003. Para (2A) inserted by SI 1991/524, reg 3(2); substituted by SI 2003/1312, reg 2(b) as from 1 July 2003. Para (3) substituted by SI 2003/1312, reg 2(c) as from 1 July 2003. Para (3A) inserted by SI 2000/451, reg 10(2) as from 20 March 2000 and words 'Subject to paragraph (10),' in square brackets inserted by SI 2002/3033, reg 6(1) as from 31 December 2002. In para (3A)(b)(i) words from 'but there has' to 'by the court' in square brackets inserted by SI 2003/1312, reg 2(d) as from 1 July 2003. In para (4) words '(2) or (3)' substituted by words '(2), (2A) or (3)' in square brackets by SI 2003/1312, reg 2(e) as from 1 July 2003. In para (5) words 'in writing' in square brackets inserted by SI 2003/1312, reg 2(f) as from 1 July 2003. Paras (9)–(11) inserted by SI 2000/451, reg 10(3) as from 20 March 2000. Para (9) revoked and para (10) substituted by SI 2002/3033, reg 6(2), (3) as from 31 December 2002. In para (11) words '(9) or' revoked by SI 2002/3033, reg 6(4) as from 31 December 2002. Paras (12)–(14) inserted by SI 2003/1312, reg 2(g) as from 1 July 2003.

*Assisted person having financial interest in assessment*

**105A.** (1) Where an assisted person has a financial interest in any assessment, review or appeal under regulation 105 he shall have a right to make written representations to the Area Director, appropriate area committee or committee appointed by the Board as the case may be within 21 days of being notified of the right to make such representations.

(2) On an assessment to which paragraph (1) applies it shall be the duty of an assisted person's solicitor—

  (a) to supply him with a copy of his bill;

  (b) to inform him of the extent of his financial interest and his right to make written representations; and

  (c) to endorse on the bill that the assisted person has a financial interest in the assessment and that he has complied with sub-paragraphs (a) and (b) above.

(3) Where a legal representative wishes to apply for a review of the assessment of the Area Director or appeal against a decision of the area committee under regulation 105 and the assisted person has exercised his right to make representations prior to the assessment, the legal representative shall notify the assisted person of the decision to be reviewed or appealed, the grounds of appeal and his right to make further written representations.

*Agreement in respect of costs*

**106.** Omitted.

*Assessment [under regulation 105] and taxation [detailed assessment] where agreed costs have been paid*

**106A.** (1) In the circumstances described in paragraph (2) below, there shall be no *taxation* [detailed assessment] or assessment [under regulation 105] except in accordance with this regulation.

(2) The circumstances are—

  (a) where proceedings to which an assisted person has been a party are, as regards an assisted person (other than a person referred to in *Order 62, rule 16 of the Rules of the Supreme Court 1965* [CPR rule 48.5]), settled without any direction of the court as to costs on terms including a provision for the payment of agreed costs in favour of the assisted person;

(b) where proceedings to which an assisted person has been a party are brought to an end by a judgment, decree or final order and there has been agreement as to the costs to be paid in favour of the assisted person; or

(c) where the retainer of an assisted person's solicitor or counsel is determined in circumstances to which regulation 105(2) refers and there is an agreement for the payment of agreed costs in favour of the assisted person,

and the agreed costs have been paid.

*(3) The assisted person's solicitor may apply to the Area Director for an assessment limited to legal aid only costs if the solicitor is of the opinion that the amount of those costs, when determined, including counsel's fees (if any) would not be more than £1,000.*

[(3) The assisted party's solicitor shall apply to the Area Director for an assessment limited to 'legal aid only costs, if the amount of those costs including counsel's fees (if any) does not exceed £2,500.]

*(4) The assisted person's solicitor may apply for a taxation under regulation 107A(2) limited to legal aid only costs if the solicitor is of the opinion that the amount of those costs, when determined, including counsel's fees (if any), would be more than £500.*

[(4) The assisted party's solicitor shall apply for a detailed assessment under regulation 107A(2) limited to legal aid only costs, if the amount of those costs including counsel's fees (if any) exceeds £2,500.]

(5) Before any assessment or *taxation* [detailed assessment] under paragraph (3) or (4), the assisted person's solicitor shall confirm in writing to the relevant authority that the agreed costs have been paid.

(6) The relevant authority may require the production of any information which it considers relevant for the purposes of discharging its functions with respect to a determination under this regulation.

(7) Paragraphs (4) to (8) of regulation 105 shall apply where costs are assessed by an Area Director under paragraph (3) above as they apply under that regulation.

**Note.** Words 'under regulation 105' in square brackets in both places they occur inserted by SI 2000/451, reg 6 as from 20 March 2000. Word 'taxation' in both places it occurs substituted by words 'detailed assessment' in square brackets by SI 2000/451, reg 3(a) as from 20 March 2000. In para (2)(a) words 'Order 62, rule 16 of the Rules of the Supreme Court 1965' substituted by words 'CPR rule 48.5' in square brackets by SI 2000/451, reg 11 as from 20 March 2000. Paras (3), (4) substituted by SI 2003/1312, reg 3 as from 1 July 2003: see SI 2003/1312.

*Taxation [Detailed assessment] of costs*

**107.** (1) The costs of proceedings to which an assisted person is a party shall be *taxed* [determined by way of detailed assessment] in accordance with any direction or order given or made in the proceedings irrespective of the interest (if any) of the assisted person in the *taxation* [detailed assessment]; *and, for the purpose of these Regulations, an order for the taxation of the costs of a review of taxation or of the costs of an appeal from a decision of a judge on such a review shall be deemed to be a final order.*

(2) Any certificate or notice of revocation or discharge, or a copy of any such certificate or notice, shall be made available on the *taxation* [detailed assessment].

(3) Where in any proceedings to which an assisted person is a party—

(a) judgment is signed in default, the judgment shall include a direction that the costs of any assisted person shall be *taxed* [determined by way of detailed assessment] under regulation 107A(2);

(b) the court gives judgment or makes a final decree or order in the proceedings, the judgment, decree or order shall include a direction (in addition to any other direction as to *taxation* [detailed assessment]) that the costs of any assisted person shall be *taxed* [determined by way of detailed assessment] under regulation 107A(2);

(c) the plaintiff accepts money paid into court, the costs of any assisted person shall be *taxed* [determined by way of detailed assessment] on the standard basis.

(4) Where in any proceedings to which an assisted person or a former assisted person is a party and—

(a) the proceedings are, or have been, brought to an end without a direction having been given, whether under paragraph (3) or otherwise, as to the assisted person's costs being *taxed* [determined by way of detailed assessment] under regulation 107A(2); or

(b) a judgment or order in favour of an opposing party, which includes a direction that the assisted person's costs be so *taxed* [determined by way of detailed assessment], has not been drawn up or, as the case may be, entered by him; or

(c) a retainer is determined under regulation 83 in such circumstances as to require a *taxation* [detailed assessment] in accordance with the provisions of these Regulations;

the costs of that person shall be *taxed* [determined by way of detailed assessment] under regulation 107A(2) on production of a copy of the notice of discharge or revocation of the certificate at the appropriate *taxing office* [court office].

**Note.** Word 'Taxation', and 'taxation' wherever it occurs substituted by words 'Detailed assessment' and 'detailed assessment' in square brackets by SI 2000/451, reg 3(a) as from 20 March 2000. Word 'taxed' in each place it occurs substituted by words 'determined by way of detailed assessment' in square brackets by SI 2000/451, reg 3(b) as from 20 March 2000. In para (1) words from '; and, for' to the end revoked by SI 2000/451, reg 12(1) as from 20 March 2000. In para (4) words 'taxing office' substituted by words 'court office' in square brackets by SI 2000/451, reg 12(2) as from 20 March 2000.

*Basis of taxation [Detailed assessment]*

**107A.** (1) This regulation applies on any *assessment, review or taxation* [assessment under regulation 105 or detailed assessment] of the costs of an assisted person in proceedings where the costs are, or may be, paid out of the fund.

(2) Costs to which this regulation applies shall be determined on the standard basis subject to—

(a) the Legal Aid in Civil Proceedings (Remuneration) Regulations 1994 in proceedings to which those Regulations apply;

(b) the Legal Aid in Family Proceedings (Remuneration) Regulations 1991 in proceedings to which those Regulations apply.

(3) Any *assessment, review or taxation* [assessment under regulation 105 or detailed assessment] under this regulation shall—

(a) subject to the provisions of sub-paragraphs (a) and (b) of paragraph (2), be in accordance with Part XII of these Regulations;

(b) be conducted together with any determination of the costs of the proceedings required in accordance with any direction or order given or made in the proceedings;

[(c) be conducted in accordance with any conditions or limitations on the relevant certificate, whether as to the work authorised under the certificate, the maximum costs payable or otherwise;

(d) ensure that any limitation as to costs on the relevant certificate will not reduce any sums payable in respect of counsel's fees except where counsel's fees alone exceed such limitation, when paragraph (4) below will apply].

[(4) Where counsel's fees alone exceed any limitation as to costs on the relevant certificate, the excess shall be borne by the assisted person's solicitor except where he has sent counsel a copy of the certificate and any amendments in accordance with regulation 59(2)(a).]

**Note.** Word 'Taxation' substituted by words 'Detailed assessment' in square brackets by SI 2000/451, reg 3(a) as from 20 March 2000. Words 'assessment, review or taxation' in both places they occur substituted by words 'assessment under regulation 105 or detailed assessment' in square brackets by SI 2000/451, reg 13 as from 20 March 2000. Paras 1(3)(c), (d) and (4) inserted by SI 1999/1113, reg 6 as from 6 May 1999.

*Recovery of costs*

**107B.** (1) Where an agreement or order provides for costs to be paid by any other party (in this regulation referred to as 'the paying party') in favour of the assisted person, the assisted person's solicitor may recover a sum in respect of costs from the paying party subject to the provisions of this regulation and regulation 91(2B).

(2) The costs which the assisted person's solicitor may recover by virtue of this regulation shall not exceed the total of the sums referred to in sub-paragraphs (c) and (d) of regulation 92(1).

(3) The assisted person's legal representatives shall not be prevented from recovering from the paying party the sums in respect of costs to which this regulation refers by—

   *(a)   any rule of law which limits the costs recoverable by a party to proceedings to the amount which he is liable to pay his legal representatives; or*

   (a)   any rule of law which limits the costs recoverable by a party to proceedings to the amount which he is liable to pay his legal representatives [, including, without limitation, with respect to the rates for the basis of *taxation* [detailed assessment] set out in regulation 107A or any limitation as to costs on the relevant certificate or contract]; or

   (b)   regulation 64 (restriction on payment otherwise than from the fund).

(4) Subject to reimbursement of the Board in respect of costs to which regulation 92(1)(b) refers and any interest thereon, any costs recovered from the paying party by virtue of this regulation shall belong to the solicitor.

**Note.** In para (3) words from ', including, without limitation' to 'or contract' in square brackets inserted by SI 1999/1113, reg 7, as from 6 May 1999. In para (3)(a) word 'taxation' substituted by words 'detailed assessment' in square brackets by SI 2000/451, reg 3(a), as from 20 March 2000.

*Failure to apply for taxation [detailed assessment]*

**108.** Where, in any proceedings to which a former assisted person was a party, an order or agreement was made for the payment to him of costs and he has failed to ask for the costs to be *taxed* [determined by way of detailed assessment] or his certificate is discharged before *taxation* [detailed assessment], the Board may authorise the making of the application for *taxation* [detailed assessment] on his behalf and the costs of the application and of *taxation* [detailed assessment] shall be deemed to be costs in the proceedings to which the certificate related.

**Note.** Word 'taxation' in each place it occurs substituted by words 'detailed assessment' in square brackets and word 'taxed' substituted by words 'determined by way of detailed assessment' in square brackets by SI 2000/451, reg 3(a), (b), as from 20 March 2000.

*Disallowance or reduction of costs*

**109.** (1) Without prejudice to section 51(6) of the Supreme Court Act 1981, *Order 62, rules 10 and 11 of the Rule of the Supreme Court 1965 or to Order 38, rule 1(3) of the County Court Rules 1981* [or CPR rules 44.14 and 48.7], on any *taxation* [detailed assessment] of an assisted person's costs in connection with proceedings (which are not authorised summary proceedings) any wasted costs shall be disallowed or reduced, and where the solicitor has without good reason delayed putting in his bill for *taxation* [detailed assessment] the whole of the costs may be disallowed or reduced.

(2)  No costs shall be disallowed or reduced under paragraph (1) until notice has been served by the *taxing officer* [costs officer] on the solicitor whose name appears on the assisted person's certificate and, in a case where those costs relate to counsel's fees, on the assisted person's counsel, requiring the solicitor or, as the case may be, counsel to show cause orally or in writing why those costs should not be disallowed or reduced.

(3)  In this regulation 'wasted costs' has the same meaning as in section 51(7) of the Supreme Court Act 1981.

**Note.** In para (1) words from ', Order 62' to 'County Court Rules 1981' substituted by words 'or CPR rules 44.14 and 48.7' in square brackets and words 'taxation' substituted by words 'detailed assessment' in square brackets by SI 2000/451, reg 3(a), 14, as from 20 March 2000. In para (2) words 'taxing officer' substituted by words 'costs officer' in square brackets by SI 2000/451, reg 3(d) as from 20 March 2000.

*Solicitor's duty to safeguard the interests of the fund*

**110.**   It shall be the duty of an assisted person's solicitor to safeguard the interests of the fund on any inter partes *taxation* [detailed assessment] pursuant to an order for costs made in favour of the assisted person where that person may himself have no interest in the result of the *taxation* [detailed assessment], and for this purpose to take such steps as may appear to the solicitor to be necessary to *obtain a review of taxation under regulation 113 or 114* [appeal against the detailed assessment].

**Note.** Word 'taxation' in both places substituted by words 'detailed assessment' in square brackets and words 'obtain a review of taxation under regulation 113 or 114' substituted by words 'appeal against the detailed assessment' in square brackets substituted by SI 2000/451, regs 3(a), 15, as from 20 March 2000.

*Costs of applications, reports, etc, under these Regulations*

**111.**   Costs incurred by reason of any application made under Part VIII, and of any report made by an assisted person's solicitor under Part IX, of these Regulations shall be *taxed* [determined by way of detailed assessment] under regulation 107A(2) and costs incurred by reason of regulation 25, 50, 54, 82 or 124 shall be costs in the cause.

**Note.** Word 'taxed' substituted by words 'determined by way of detailed assessment' in square brackets by SI 2000/451, reg 3(b) as from 20 March 2000.

*Duty to inform counsel*

**112.**   (1)  The assisted person's solicitor shall within 7 days after the *taxation* [detailed assessment] (or provisional *taxation* [detailed assessment]) notify counsel in writing where the fees claimed on his behalf have been reduced or disallowed on *taxation* [detailed assessment], and shall endorse the bill of costs with the date on which such notice was given or that no such notice is necessary.

(2)  Where the bill of costs is endorsed that no notice under paragraph (1) is necessary, the *taxing officer* [costs officer] may issue the certificate or allocatur but, where such a notice has been given, the *taxing officer* [costs officer] shall not issue the certificate or allocatur until 14 days have elapsed from the date so endorsed.

**Note.** Word 'taxation' in each place substituted by words 'detailed assessment' in square brackets and words 'taxing officer' in each place substituted by words 'costs officer' in square brackets by SI 2000/451, reg 3(a), (d) as from 20 March 2000.

*Application to carry in objections to the taxation*

**113.**   *(1)  In this regulation, in regulation 114 and in regulation 116, 'legal aid taxation' means the taxation under regulation 107A(2) of a solicitor's bill to his own client where that bill is to be paid out of the fund.*

*(2) Where—*

*(a)   an assisted person is dissatisfied with any decision of a taxing officer as to the amount which he is entitled to recover by virtue of an order or agreement for costs made in his favour or for which he is liable by virtue of an order for costs made against him; or*

*(b)   the assisted person's solicitor is dissatisfied with any decision of the taxing officer—*

*(i)   on an inter partes taxation pursuant to an order for costs made in favour of the assisted person, or*

*(ii)   on a legal aid taxation,*

*the solicitor shall apply to the appropriate area committee for authority to carry in objections to the taxation; and if the area committee gives authority (but not otherwise) the solicitor may carry in objections in accordance with rules of court.*

**[113.**   (1) Subject to paragraph (2), detailed assessment proceedings shall be deemed to be proceedings to which the assisted person's certificate relates, whether or not it has been discharged or revoked, and the costs of such proceedings shall be paid out of the fund unless the court otherwise orders.

(2) Subject to the following paragraphs of this regulation, an assisted person's solicitor may appeal against a decision in detailed assessment proceedings in accordance with rules of court, and, if counsel acting for the assisted person notifies the solicitor that he is dissatisfied with the decision, shall do so, but the costs of any such appeal shall be deemed to be costs to which the assisted person's certificate relates only to the extent that the court hearing the appeal so orders.

(3) The assisted person shall not be required to make any contribution to the fund on account of the costs of any appeal against a decision in detailed assessment proceedings and the charge created by section 16(6) of the Act shall not apply in relation to any resulting increase in the net liability of the fund in consequence of any order made in such an appeal.

*(4) Where permission to appeal is obtained under CPR rule 47.24(2) [52.3], the assisted person's solicitor shall give written notice to that effect to the Lord Chancellor.*

*(5) The assisted person's solicitor shall send to the Lord Chancellor, together with the notice given under paragraph (4), copies of-*

*(a)   the bill of costs; and ;*

*(b)   the request for permission to appeal.*

*(6) When filing a notice of appeal [an appeal notice], the assisted person's solicitor shall file with the court a copy of the notice given under paragraph (4).*

*(7) After filing notice of appeal [an appeal notice] the assisted person's solicitor shall without delay send a copy of it to the Lord Chancellor.]*

**Note.** New regulation 13, substituted, for regs 113–118 as originally enacted, by SI 2000/451, reg 16 as from 20 March 2000.

Paras (4)–(7) revoked by SI 2003/1312, reg 4 as from 1 July 2003. In para (4) reference to '47.24(2)' substituted by reference to '52.3' in square brackets and in paras (6), (7) words 'notice of appeal' substituted by words 'an appeal notice' in square brackets by SI 2001/3735, reg 4 as from 3 December 2001.

*Application to judge to review taxation*

**114.**   *Where the assisted person or his solicitor, as the case may be, is dissatisfied with the decision of the taxing officer on any matter to which objection has been taken under regulation 113, the solicitor shall apply to the Board for authority to have the taxation reviewed; and, if the Board gives authority (but not otherwise), the solicitor may apply (or instruct counsel to apply) to a judge to review the taxation in accordance with rules of court.*

See the note to s 113 ibid.

*Appeal from review of taxation*

**115.** (1) Subject to paragraph (2) and notwithstanding that the assisted person may have no interest in the appeal or would, but for regulation 118, have an interest adverse to that of his solicitor, an assisted person's solicitor—

(a) may, with the authority of the Board, appeal from the decision of the judge on a review of taxation under regulation 114, or

(b) shall be entitled to be heard on an appeal brought by any other party,

and, on any such appeal, the solicitor may appear by counsel.

(2) Nothing in this regulation shall be deemed to confer a right of appeal in proceedings to which an assisted person is not a party where no such right exists.

(3) Where an assisted person's solicitor applies for authority under paragraph (1), he shall do so before the expiration of the time allowed by rules of court for an appeal from the decision of a judge and, for this purpose, the time so allowed shall be extended by two months.

See the note to s 113 ibid.

*Counsel dissatisfied with taxation*

**116.** (1) Where counsel acting for an assisted person is dissatisfied with any decision on a legal aid taxation, it shall be the duty of the assisted person's solicitor to report the matter to the appropriate area committee or to the Board, as the case may be, and, if the committee or the Board give authority to do so—

(a) to carry in objections to the taxation,

(b) to apply to a judge to review the taxation, or

(c) to appeal from the decision of the judge,

as the case may be, and regulations 113 to 115 and 120 shall apply as if the solicitor were the person dissatisfied.

(2) Paragraph (1) shall apply to a provisional taxation with the necessary modifications and in particular with the insertion of the words 'to inform the taxing officer that he wishes to be heard on the taxation and to attend on the taxation,' after the words 'the assisted person's solicitor'.

See the note to s 113 ibid.

*Objection by other party*

**117.** If, in proceedings to which an assisted person is a party, any other party carries in objections to the inter partes taxation or applies to a judge to review the taxation, the assisted person's solicitor may be heard on the objections or review notwithstanding that the assisted person himself may have no interest in the taxation.

See the note to s 113 ibid.

*Assisted person having no interest or adverse interest in taxation*

**118.** Where the assisted person has no interest in the taxation or would, but for the provisions of this regulation, have an interest adverse to that of his solicitor—

(a) it shall be the duty of the solicitor carrying in objections under regulation 113 or applying for a review under regulation 114 to ensure that all matters which are proper to be taken into account in consideration of the objections or on the review are placed before the taxing officer or the judge, as the case may be;

(b) the assisted person shall not be required to make any contribution to the fund on account of the costs of any proceedings arising under regulations 113 to 117 or in consequence of any order made in such proceedings; and

(c) the charge created by section 16(6) of the Act shall not apply in relation to any resulting increase in the net liability of the fund arising out of the costs of any proceedings under regulations 113 to 117 or in consequence of any order made in such proceedings.

See the note to s 113 ibid.

*Assisted person having financial interest in taxation [detailed assessment]*

**119.** (1) Where the assisted person has a financial interest in the *taxation* [detailed assessment] it shall be the duty of his solicitor—

(a)  to supply him with a copy of his bill;

(b)  to inform him of the extent of his financial interest and the steps which can be taken to safeguard that interest and, if the assisted person so requests, to give notice in accordance with rules of court to the *taxing officer* [costs officer] that the assisted person has such an interest; and

(c)  to endorse on the bill that the assisted person has a financial interest in the *taxation* [detailed assessment] and that he has complied with sub-paragraphs (a) and (b) above.

(2)  Where the assisted person has a financial interest in the *taxation* [detailed assessment] he shall not be required to make any contribution to the fund on account of the costs of the *taxation* [detailed assessment] proceedings and the charge created by section 16(6) of the Act shall not apply in relation to any resulting increase in the net liability of the fund arising out of the costs of the *taxation* [detailed assessment] proceedings.

[(3) For the purposes of paragraph (2), the cost of drawing up a bill of costs shall not be included as part of the costs of the detailed assessment proceedings.]

**Note.** Word 'taxation' in each place it occurs substituted by words 'detailed assessment' in square brackets by SI 2000/451, reg 3(a) as from 20 March 2000. In para (1)(b) words 'taxing officer' substituted by words 'costs officer' in square brackets and para (3) inserted by SI 2000/451, regs 3(d), 17 as from 20 March 2000.

*Costs to be paid out of the fund*

**120.**  ...

**Note.** Revoked by SI 2000/451, reg 18, as from 20 March 2000.

*Time limits, etc*

**121.**  ...

**Note.** Revoked by SI 2000/451, reg 18, as from 20 March 2000.

*Appointment of solicitor to intervene*

**122.** (1) The Lord Chancellor may appoint a solicitor to intervene in any *review by a judge of a taxation* [appeal against a detailed assessment under CPR rule 47.22(2) or (3)] of the costs of proceedings to which an assisted person is a party, and any such appointment may be made in respect of a *particular review* [particular such appeal] or may extend to any *review of taxation* [such appeal] during the period for which the solicitor is appointed.

(2)  ...

(3)  If, in proceedings to which an assisted person is a party, any other party *applies to a judge to review the inter partes taxation* [appeals against a detailed assessment of costs payable by one party to another] or the assisted person's solicitor *applies to a judge to review any such taxation as is referred to in* [appeals against a detailed assessment in accordance with] regulation 113, the assisted person's solicitor shall so *inform the Board and the Board shall notify the Lord Chancellor* [inform the Lord Chancellor] and inform him of the name and address of the assisted person's solicitor and, where the *subject of the review is an inter partes taxation* [subject of the appeal is a detailed assessment of costs payable by one party to another], the name and address of the solicitor acting for the other party.

(4)  The solicitor appointed by the Lord Chancellor to *intervene in a review of taxation* [intervene in an appeal against a detailed assessment] shall be entitled to production of all documents relevant to the matters in issue before the *judge* [costs officer] and to delivery of copies thereof and to appear by counsel and be heard *on*

*the review* [on the appeal], with a view to ensuring that all considerations which are proper to be taken into account are placed before the court, whether they relate to the interests of the fund or of the assisted person or to the remuneration of solicitors and counsel acting for assisted persons.

(5) On any *review* [appeal] in which a solicitor appointed by the Lord Chancellor has intervened, the judge may make such order as may be just for the payment to or by that solicitor of the costs incurred by him or any other party, and any sum due to the solicitor by virtue of any such order shall be paid by him to the Board and any sum so payable by the solicitor shall be paid out of the fund, and the solicitor shall be entitled to receive from the fund the costs he has incurred on the intervention.

*(6) A solicitor appointed by the Lord Chancellor under paragraph (1) may appeal from the decision of the judge on a review of taxation under regulation 115 and paragraphs (2) to (5) above shall apply to such an appeal as it applies to a review.*

[(6) Where rules of court provide for a further appeal from a decision on appeal from a detailed assessment ('the original appeal'), a solicitor appointed by the Lord Chancellor under paragraph (1) may appeal from the original appeal and paragraphs (2) to (5) shall apply to such a further appeal as it applies to the original appeal.]

**Note.** In para (1) words 'review by a judge of a taxation', 'particular review' and 'review of taxation' substituted by words 'appeal against a detailed assessment under CPR rule 47.22(2) or (3)', 'particular such appeal' and 'such appeal' in square brackets by SI 2000/451, reg 19(1 )(a)–(c). Para (2) revoked by SI 2000/451, reg 19(2). In para (3) words 'applies to a judge to review the inter partes taxation' substituted by words from 'appeals against a' to 'one party to another' in square brackets by SI 2000/451, reg 19(3)(a). In para (3) words 'applies to a judge to review any such taxation as is referred to in' substituted by words 'appeals against a detailed assessment in accordance with' in square brackets by SI 2000/451, reg 19(3)(b). In para (3) words 'inform the Board and the Board shall notify the Lord Chancellor' substituted by words 'inform the Lord Chancellor' in square brackets by SI 2000/451, reg 19(3)(c). In para (3) words 'subject of the review is an inter partes taxation' substituted by words from 'subject of the appeal' to 'one party to another' in square brackets by SI 2000/451, reg 19(3)(d). In para (4) words 'intervene in a review of taxation', 'judge' and 'on the review' substituted by words 'intervene in an appeal against a detailed assessment', 'costs officer' and 'on the appeal' in square brackets by SI 2000/451, reg 19(4)(a)–(c). In para (5) word 'review' substituted by word 'appeal' in square brackets by SI 2000/451, reg 19(5). Para (6) substituted by SI 2000/451, reg 19(6). All of the amendments noted above came into force on 20 March 2000.

PART XIII

COSTS AWARDED AGAINST AN ASSISTED PERSON

*Security for costs given by assisted person*

**123.**   Where in any proceedings an assisted person is required to give security for costs, the amount of such security shall not exceed the amount which could be ordered under section 17(1) of the Act.

*Assisted person's liability for costs*

**124.**   (1) Where proceedings have been concluded in which an assisted person (including, for the purpose of this regulation, a person who was an assisted person in respect of those proceedings) is liable or would have been liable for costs if he had not been an assisted person, no costs attributable to the period during which his certificate was in force shall be recoverable from him until the court has determined the amount of his liability in accordance with section 17(1) of the Act.

(2) Where the assisted person's certificate does not relate to, or has been amended so that it no longer relates to the whole of the proceedings, the court shall nevertheless make a determination under section 17(1) of the Act in respect

of that part of the proceedings to which the certificate relates.

(3) The amount of an assisted person's liability for costs shall be determined by the court which tried or heard the proceedings.

*Affidavit of means by unassisted party*

**125.** (1) Any person, not being himself an assisted person, who is a party to proceedings (other than authorised summary proceedings) to which an assisted person is a party, may file in the appropriate court office or registry an affidavit exhibiting a statement setting out the rate of his own income and amount of his own capital and any other facts relevant to the determination of his means in accordance with section 17(1) of the Act.

(2) Any person filing an affidavit under paragraph (1) shall serve a copy of it, together with the exhibit, upon the assisted person's solicitor, who shall forthwith serve him with a copy of the certificate and shall send a copy of the affidavit to the Area Director.

*Determination of liability for costs*

**126.** In determining the amount of the assisted person's liability for costs—

(a) his dwelling-house, clothes, household furniture and the tools and implements of his trade shall be left out of account to the like extent as they are left out of account by the assessment officer in determining his disposable income and disposable capital; and

(b) any document which may have been sent to the court office or registry or filed or exhibited under these Regulations shall, subject to regulation 128, be evidence of the facts stated therein.

*Postponement, adjournment or referral of determination*

**127.** The court may, if it thinks fit—

(a) postpone or adjourn the determination for such time and to such place (including chambers) as the court thinks fit; or

(b) refer to a master, registrar or the Clerk of the Parliaments or (in the case of an appeal from a decision of the Crown Court or a court of summary jurisdiction) to the chief clerk or clerk to the justices of the court from which the appeal is brought, for investigation (in chambers or elsewhere) any question of fact relevant to the determination, and require him to report his findings on that question to the court.

*Oral examination of parties*

**128.** (1) The court may, if it thinks fit, order the assisted person and any party who has filed an affidavit pursuant to regulation 125 to attend for oral examination as to his means and as to any other facts (whether stated in any document before the court or otherwise) which may be relevant to the determination of the amount of the assisted person's liability for costs and may permit any party to give evidence and call witnesses.

(2) Where the court has made an order under regulation 127(b), the person to whom the matter has been referred for investigation may exercise the power conferred on the court by this regulation.

*Order for costs*

**129.** The court may direct—

(a) that payment under the order for costs shall be limited to such amount, payable in instalments or otherwise (including an amount to be determined on *taxation* [detailed assessment]), as the court thinks reasonable having regard to all the circumstances; or

(b) where the court thinks it reasonable that no payment should be made immediately or that the assisted person should have no liability for payment, that payment under the order for costs be suspended either until such date as the court may determine or indefinitely.

**Note.** In para (a) word 'taxation' substituted by words 'detailed assessment' in square brackets by SI 2000/451, reg 3(a) as from 20 March 2000.

*Variation of order for costs*

**130.** The party in whose favour an order for costs is made may, within six years from the date on which it was made, apply to the court for the order to be varied on the ground that—
(a) material additional information as to the assisted person's means, being information which could not have been obtained by that party with reasonable diligence at the time the order was made, is available; or
(b) there has been a change in the assisted person's circumstances since the date of the order;
and on any such application the order may be varied as the court thinks fit; but save as aforesaid the determination of the court shall be final.

*Assisted person acting in representative, fiduciary or official capacity*

**131.** Where an order for costs is made against an assisted person who is concerned in the proceedings in a representative, fiduciary or official capacity, he shall have the benefit of section 17(1) of the Act and his personal resources shall not (unless there is reason to the contrary) be taken into account for that purpose, but regard shall be had to the value of the property or estate, or the amount of the fund out of which he is entitled to be indemnified.

*Assisted person a minor*

**132.** Where a minor is an assisted person, his means for the purpose of determining his liability for costs under section 17(1) of the Act shall be taken as including the means of any person whose resources have been taken into account under the Civil Legal Aid (Assessment of Resources) Regulations 1989 by the assessment officer in assessing the disposable income and disposable capital of the minor.

*Order against next friend or guardian ad litem*

**133.** Where an order for costs is made against a next friend or guardian ad litem of an assisted person who is a minor or patient, he shall have the benefit of section 17(1) of the Act as it applies to an assisted person and the means of the next friend or guardian ad litem shall, for the purposes of regulation 132, be taken as being the means of the minor or, as the case may be, of the patient.

PART XIV

COSTS OF UNASSISTED PARTIES OUT OF THE FUND

*Time and form of application*

**134.** (1) An application for an order under section 18 of the Act may be made at any time and in any manner in which an application for an order for costs might be made in respect of the same proceedings if none of the parties were receiving legal aid.

(2) Any proceedings in respect of which a separate certificate could properly be issued shall be treated as separate proceedings for the purposes of section 18 of the Act.

*Unassisted party acting in representative, fiduciary or official capacity*

**135.** Where an unassisted party is concerned in proceedings only in a representative, fiduciary or official capacity, then for the purposes of section 18(4)(b) of the Act the court shall not take into account his personal resources, but shall have regard to the value of the property, estate or fund out of which the unassisted party is entitled to be indemnified and may in its discretion also have regard to the resources of the persons, if any, including the unassisted party where appropriate, who are beneficially interested in that property, estate or fund.

*Appearance by unassisted party and Area Director*

**136.** (1) The unassisted party and the Area Director may appear at any hearing or inquiry under Parts XIII and XIV of these Regulations.

(2) The Area Director may, instead of appearing, submit written representations concerning the application and such representations shall be—

(a) supported by an affidavit sworn by the Area Director; and

(b) sent to the proper officer of the court, with a copy to the unassisted party, not less than 7 days before the hearing or inquiry to which they relate.

*Applications in respect of magistrates' court proceedings*

**137.** (1) Where an application for an order under section 18 of the Act is made in respect of authorised summary proceedings, the court, instead of making an order forthwith, may in its discretion either—

(a) adjourn the hearing of the application; or

(b) dismiss the application.

(2) If the court adjourns the hearing of the application, the unassisted party shall swear an affidavit of costs and resources containing the matters specified in Schedule 2, which he shall produce at the adjourned hearing and, not less than 21 days before the adjourned hearing, the unassisted party shall serve notice of the date and time of the hearing on the Area Director, with a copy of his affidavit of costs and resources together with any exhibits and supporting documents.

*Applications in respect of county court proceedings*

**138.** On application for an order under section 18 of the Act made in respect of proceedings in or on appeal from a county court, the court shall not make an order under that section forthwith, but may in its discretion—

(a) refer the application to the registrar for hearing and determination; or

(b) adjourn the application; or

(c) dismiss the application,

and, in this regulation and regulations 139 to 142, 'registrar' means the registrar of the county court in which the proceedings were tried or determined or from which the appeal was brought.

*Procedure where application referred to registrar for determination*

**139.** Where a court in accordance with regulation 138(a) refers an application to the registrar for hearing and determination—

(a) the provisions of regulation 142 shall apply as if the registrar were the court and the court had adjourned the hearing of the application to a date to be fixed; and

(b) the unassisted party or the Area Director may appeal to the judge on a point of law from the registrar's determination within 14 days of the date on which it was given.

*Reference to registrar for inquiry and report*

**140.** The court may, if it adjourns the hearing of an application in accordance with regulation 138(b), make an order referring it to the registrar for inquiry and report; and, if such an order is made—

(a) the court shall serve a copy of its order on the unassisted party;

(b) within 21 days of the court making its order (or such longer time as the court may allow), the unassisted party shall file an affidavit of costs and resources (with any exhibits and supporting documents) together with a copy; and

(c) the court shall serve a copy of its order and of the unassisted party's affidavit of costs and resources filed under sub-paragraph (b) on the Area Director.

*Procedure on inquiry and report*

**141.** (1) As soon as a copy of the order of the court and the affidavit of costs and resources have been served on the Area Director in accordance with regulation 140(1)(c), the registrar shall give the unassisted party and the Area Director not less than 21 days' notice of the date and time when he proposes to conduct his inquiry.

(2) In exercising his functions under this regulation, the registrar shall have the same powers as a *taxing officer* [costs officer] has in the exercise of his functions under the *County Court Rules 1981* [CPR Parts 43–48].

(3) On completing his inquiry, the registrar shall report to the court in writing, and shall at the same time send a copy of his report to the unassisted party and the Area Director.

(4) When the court has received the registrar's report, it shall give the unassisted party and the Area Director 21 days' notice of the day appointed for the hearing and determination of the application in chambers.

**Note.** In para (2) words 'taxing officer' and 'County Court Rules 1981' substituted by words 'costs officer' and 'CPR Parts 43–48' in square brackets by SI 2000/451, regs 3(d), 20 as from 20 March 2000.

*Procedure where application adjourned*

**142.** If the court adjourns the hearing of an application in accordance with regulation 138(b) but does not refer it to the registrar for inquiry and report—

(a) within 21 days of the adjournment, the unassisted party shall file an affidavit of costs and resources (with any exhibits and supporting documents) together with a copy; and

(b) not less than 21 days before the adjourned hearing, the court shall serve on the Area Director notice of the date fixed together with a copy of the affidavit of costs and resources filed under sub-paragraph (a).

*Applications in respect of proceedings in the Supreme Court and House of Lords*

**143.** (1) On an application for an order under section 18 of the Act made in respect of proceedings in the Supreme Court (except proceedings on appeal from a county court) or in the House of Lords, the court shall not make an order forthwith, but may in its discretion—

(a) refer the application to a *master* [costs judge or district judge] or registrar for hearing and determination; or

(b) adjourn the hearing of the application; or

(c) dismiss the application,

and, in relation to proceedings in the Court of Appeal, 'registrar' means the registrar of civil appeals or, in respect of appeals from the Employment Appeal Tribunal or from the Restrictive Practices Court, the registrar of that Tribunal or Court, as the case may be.

(2) Where the application is referred to a registrar under paragraph (1)(a), the provisions of regulations 139 and 142 shall apply with any necessary modifications.

[(3) In regulations 143 to 146 the expression 'district judge' means a district judge of the High Court, including a district judge of the Principal Registry of the Family Division.]

**Note.** In para (1)(a) word 'master' substituted by words 'costs judge or district judge' in square brackets and para (3) inserted by SI 2000/451, reg 21 as from 20 March 2000.

*Procedure where application referred to master for determination*

**144.** Where the court in accordance with regulation 143(1)(a) refers the application to a *master* [costs judge or district judge] for hearing and determination—

(a) the provisions of regulation 147 shall apply as if the *master* [costs judge or district judge] were the court and the court had adjourned the hearing of the application to a date to be fixed; and

(b) the *master* [costs judge or district judge] shall have the same powers as a *taxing officer* [costs officer] has in the exercise of his functions under *Order 62 of the Rules of the Supreme Court 1965* [CPR Parts 43 to 48]; and

(c) the unassisted party or the Area Director may appeal to a judge in chambers on a point of law within 14 days from the determination of the *master* [costs judge or district judge].

**Note.** Words 'master' in each place it occurs, 'taxing officer' and 'Order 62 of the Rules of the Supreme Court 1965' substituted by words 'costs judge or district judge' in each place, 'costs officer' and 'CPR Parts 43 to 48' in square brackets by SI 2000/451, regs 3(d), 21(1), 22.

*Reference to master [costs judge or district judge] for inquiry and report*

**145.** The court may, if it adjourns the hearing of an application in accordance with regulation 143(1)(b), make an order referring it to the *master* [costs judge or district judge] for inquiry and report; and if such an order is made, then within 21 days of the court making the order (or such longer time as the *master* [costs judge or district judge] may allow) the unassisted party shall—

(a) file an affidavit of costs and resources;

(b) lodge a copy of the order of the court and of his affidavit of costs and resources, together with original exhibits and any other documents necessary to support the affidavit, with the *master* [costs judge or district judge]; and at the same time

(c) serve a copy of the order of the court and of his affidavit of costs and resources (and of any exhibits and supporting documents) on the Area Director.

**Note.** Word 'master' in each place it occurs substituted by words 'costs judge or district judge' in square brackets by SI 2000/451, reg 21(2).

*Procedure on inquiry and report*

**146.** (1) Where the unassisted party has complied with the requirements of regulation 145, the *master* [costs judge or district judge] shall give the unassisted party and the Area Director not less than 21 days' notice of the date and time when he proposes to conduct his inquiry.

(2) In exercising his functions under this regulation, the *master* [costs judge or district judge] shall have the same powers as a *taxing officer* [costs officer] has in the exercise of his functions under *Order 62 of the Rules of the Supreme Court 1965* [CPR Parts 43 to 48].

(3) On completing his inquiry, the *master* [costs judge or district judge] shall report to the court in writing, and shall at the same time send a copy of his report to the unassisted party and to the Area Director.

(4) When the court has received the report of the *master* [costs judge or district judge], the unassisted party shall seek an appointment for the hearing and determination of the application in chambers, and shall give the Area Director not less than 21 days' notice of the date and time so fixed.

**Note.** Words 'master' in each place, 'taxing officer' and 'Order 62 of the Rules of the Supreme Court 1965' substituted by words 'costs judge or district judge' in each place, 'costs officer' and 'CPR Parts 43 to 48' in square brackets by SI 2000/451, regs 3(d), 21(1), 22 as from 20 March 2000.

*Procedure where application adjourned*

**147.** If the court adjourns the hearing of an application in accordance with regulation 143 but does not refer it for inquiry and report, then—
(a) within 21 days of the adjournment, the unassisted party shall file an affidavit of costs and resources together with original exhibits and any other documents necessary to support the affidavit; and
(b) not less than 21 days before the adjourned hearing, the unassisted party shall serve notice on the Area Director of the date and time of the adjourned hearing together with a copy of his affidavit of costs and resources (and of any exhibits and supporting documents).

PART XV

PARTICULAR COURTS AND TRIBUNALS

*The Lands Tribunal*

**148.**

\* \* \* \* \*

*The Employment Appeal Tribunal*

**149.**

\* \* \* \* \*

*The Commons Commissioners*

**150.**

\* \* \* \* \*

*The Restrictive Practices Court*

**151.**

\* \* \* \* \*

PART XVI

REPRESENTATION BY MEANS ON CONTRACTS

\* \* \* \* \*

SCHEDULE 1                                                          Regulation 1

REGULATIONS REVOKED

\* \* \* \* \*

SCHEDULE 2                                                         Regulation 137

MATTERS TO BE INCLUDED IN AN AFFIDAVIT OF COSTS AND RESOURCES

**1.** An estimate of the unassisted party's inter partes costs of the proceedings in respect of which his application is made, supported by—
(a) particulars of the estimated costs in the form of a summary bill of costs; and
(b) all necessary documentary evidence to substantiate each item in the bill.

**2.**   A statement, supported by evidence, of the unassisted party's financial resources of every kind during the period beginning three years before his application is made, and of his estimated future financial resources and expectations.

**3.**   A declaration that to the best of his knowledge and belief the unassisted party has not, and at any relevant time has not had and will not have any financial resources or expectations not specified in the statement described in paragraph 2 above.

**4.**   A declaration that the unassisted party has not at any time deliberately forgone or deprived himself of any financial resources or expectations with a view to furthering his application.

**5.**   A statement supported by evidence of the unassisted party's reasonable financial commitments during the period covered by his statement described in paragraph 2 above, including, if desired, his estimated solicitor and own client costs of the proceedings in respect of which his application is made.

**6.**   (1) If the unassisted party has, or at any relevant time has had, a spouse, his statements and declarations described in paragraphs 2 to 5 above shall also take account of and (to the best of his knowledge and belief) specify that spouse's financial resources, expectations and commitments, unless he or she had a contrary interest to the unassisted party in the proceedings in respect of which his application is made, or the unassisted party and his spouse are or at the relevant time were living separate and apart, or for some other reason it would be either inequitable or impracticable for the unassisted party to comply with the requirements of this paragraph.

(2)   Paragraph (1) shall apply to a man and woman who are living with each other in the same household as husband and wife as it applies to the parties to a marriage.

**7.**   Full particulars of any application for legal aid made by the unassisted party in connection with the proceedings in respect of which his application is made, including the date and reference number of any such application and the Area Director to whom it was made.

## LEGAL ADVICE AND ASSISTANCE REGULATIONS 1989

**Dated** 3 March 1989

**SI 1989 No 340**

*Note. Following the repeal of the enabling provisions by the Access to Justice Act 1999, s 106, Sch 15, Pt 1, these Regulations have lapsed in so far as they may continue to have effect by virtue of SI 2000/774, art 5, and SI 2001/916, art 4, Sch 2 as from 1 April 2000 (for certain purposes) and 2 April 2001 (for remaining purposes).*

## ARRANGEMENT OF REGULATIONS

The Lord Chancellor, in exercise of the powers conferred on him by sections 2, 9, 10, 11, 34, and 43 of the Legal Aid Act 1988, having consulted the General Council of the Bar, the Law Society, the County Court Rule Committee and the Magistrates' Courts Rule Committee, and with the consent of the Treasury, hereby makes the following Regulations—

*Citation, commencement, and transitional provisions*

**1.**   (1) These Regulations may be cited as the Legal Advice and Assistance Regulations 1989 and shall come into force on 1st April 1989.

(2) Where a review under paragraph (7) of regulation 29 relates to a claim made before 1st June 1989, paragraphs (8) and (9) of that regulation shall not apply and the solicitor may appeal in writing within 21 days of receipt of notification of the decision on the review to a committee appointed by the Board.

*Revocations*

**2.**   The Regulations specified in Schedule 1 are hereby revoked.

*Interpretation*

**3.**   (1) In these Regulations, unless the context otherwise requires—
      'ABWOR' means assistance by way of representation;
      'the Act' means the Legal Aid Act 1988;

'appropriate area committee' means the area committee in whose area an application for advice and assistance, or a claim for costs has been dealt with by an Area Director;

'area committee' has the meaning assigned to it in the Civil Legal Aid (General) Regulations 1989;

'Area Director' has the meaning assigned to it in the Civil Legal Aid (General) Regulations 1989;

'assessed deficiency' means the amount by which the sum allowed to the solicitor by the Area Director in assessing his claim under regulation 29 exceeds any contribution payable by the client to the solicitor under section 9 of the Act together with the value of any charge arising under section 11 of the Act;

'board of visitors' means a board of visitors appointed by the Secretary of State under section 6(2) of the Prison Act 1952;

'child' means a person under the age that is for the time being the upper limit of compulsory school age by virtue of section 35 of the Education Act 1944 together with any Order in Council made under that section;

'client' means a person seeking or receiving advice and assistance or on whose behalf advice and assistance is sought;

'contract' means a contract entered into by the Board with other persons or bodies pursuant to its powers under section 4 of the Act;

'costs' means the cost of giving advice or assistance, including disbursements, charges and fees;

'Costs Regulations' means the Legal Aid in Criminal and Care Proceedings (Costs) Regulations 1989;

['customs office' has the meaning assigned to it by article 2(1) of the Police and Criminal Evidence Act 1984 (Application to Customs and Excise) Order 1985;

'customs officer' means officer as defined in article 2(1) of the Police and Criminal Evidence Act 1984 (Application to Customs and Excise) Order 1985;]

'disability working allowance' means a disability working allowance under section 20(6A) of the Social Security Contributions and Benefits Act 1992;

'extension' means the grant of prior authority to exceed the limit prescribed under section 10(1) of the Act and, where appropriate, the grant of prior authority to exceed any further limit imposed under regulation 21(3) or 22(8);

'family credit' means family credit under the Social Security Contributions and Benefits Act 1992;

'franchisee' means a person or body (other than the Board) acting under the terms of a franchising contract;

'fund' means the legal aid fund;

'income based jobseeker's allowance' has the meaning given by section 1(4) of the Jobseekers Act 1995, but excludes any sum treated as payable by way of a jobseeker's allowance by virtue of section 26 of that Act;

'income support' means income support under the Social Security Contributions and Benefits Act 1992;

'patient' means a person who by reason of mental disorder within the meaning of the Mental Health Act 1983 is incapable of managing and administering his property and affairs;

'Scope Regulations' means the Legal Advice and Assistance (Scope) Regulations 1989;

'serious service offence' means an offence under any of the Army Act 1955, the Air Force Act 1955, or the Naval Discipline Act 1957 which cannot be dealt with summarily or which appears to an interviewing service policeman to be serious;

'volunteer' means a person who, for the purpose of assisting with an investigation, attends voluntarily at a police station [or a customs office] or at any other place where a constable [or customs officer] is present or accompanies a constable [or a customs officer] to a police station [or a customs office] or any such other place without having been arrested.

(2) Any reference in these Regulations to a regulation or Schedule by number means the regulation or Schedule so numbered in these Regulations.

**Note.** In para (1) definitions 'customs office' and 'customs officer' inserted and in definition 'volunteer' words 'or a customs office' and 'or customs officer' in square brackets in each place they occur inserted by SI 1999/2089, reg 3 as from 1 September 1999.

*Exercise of Area Director's functions by franchisee*

**3A.**   Where and to the extent that a franchising contract so provides, any functions of an Area Director are conferred on a franchisee, the functions may be exercised by the franchisee on the Area Director's behalf.

*Limit on cost of advice and assistance*

**4.**   (1) Subject to paragraph (2), the limit applicable under section 10(1) of the Act is—

(a) in respect of advice and assistance given in accordance with regulation 6(1), £90;

(b) in respect of advice and assistance provided to a petitioner for divorce or judicial separation which includes advice or assistance in the preparation of the petition, three times the relevant sum specified for preparation in the table in paragraph 1 (or paragraph 2 in the case of a franchisee) of Schedule 6;

(c) in respect of all other advice and assistance, twice the relevant sum referred to in sub-paragraph (b);

(2) Section 10(1) of the Act shall not apply to—

(a) advice or assistance specified in regulation 5(1)(b) of the Legal Advice and Assistance at Police Stations (Remuneration) Regulations 1989 where the interests of justice require such advice or assistance to be given as a matter of urgency; or

(b) ABWOR provided under arrangements made by the Board under regulation 7; or

(c) advice or assistance given under arrangements made by the Board under regulation 8.

*ABWOR relating to applications for further detention*

**5.**

\*      \*      \*      \*      \*

*ABWOR in proceedings before a Mental Health Review Tribunal*

**5A.**

\*      \*      \*      \*      \*

*Provision of advice and assistance at police stations etc*

**6.**

\*      \*      \*      \*      \*

*ABWOR in proceedings in magistrates' courts*

**7.**

\*      \*      \*      \*      \*

*Advice and assistance in criminal proceedings in magistrates' courts*

**8.**

\*      \*      \*      \*      \*

*Applications for advice and assistance*

**9.**   (1) An application for advice and assistance to which this regulation applies shall be made in accordance with its provisions to the solicitor from whom the advice and assistance is sought.

(2)   This regulation applies to all advice and assistance except—

(a)   advice or assistance given under regulation 6 or 8; and

(b)   ABWOR given under regulation 7, or to which Part III of the Act applies by virtue of regulation 7(1)(c) [or 9(e)] of the Scope Regulations (warrants of further detention).

(3)   Subject to paragraph (3A) and regulations 10 and 15, the application under paragraph (1) shall be made by the client in person.

(3A)   Where a franchising contract so provides and subject to compliance with any provisions specified in the contract, an application for advice and assistance may be made by telephone or by post.

(4)   Where a client makes an application under paragraph (1) he shall provide the solicitor with the information necessary to enable the solicitor to determine—

(a)   his disposable capital;

(b)   where appropriate, whether he is in receipt of income support, income based jobseeker's allowance, family credit or disability working allowance; and

(c)   where he is not in receipt of income support, income based jobseeker's allowance, family credit or disability working allowance, his disposable income.

(5)   Where an application under paragraph (1) is for advice or assistance relating to the making of a will, the client shall provide the solicitor with the information necessary to enable the solicitor to determine whether the advice or assistance would fall within regulation 4(2) of the Scope Regulations.

(6)   The information required by this regulation shall be furnished on a form approved by the Board.

**Note.** In para (2)(b) words 'or 9(e)' in square brackets inserted by SI 2001/191, reg 2 as from 19 February 2001.

*Attendance on behalf of a client*

**10.**   (1) *Where* [subject to paragraph (5), where] a client cannot for good reason attend on the solicitor in order to apply for advice and assistance in accordance with paragraph (3) of regulation 9, he may authorise another person to attend on his behalf.

(2)   Where a person authorised in accordance with paragraph (1) attends on a solicitor, he shall furnish the solicitor with the information necessary to enable the solicitor to determine—

(a)   the client's disposable capital,

(b)   where appropriate, whether the client is in receipt of income support, income based jobseeker's allowance, family credit or disability working allowance, and

(c)   where the client is not in receipt of income support, income based jobseeker's allowance, family credit or disability working allowance, the client's disposable income.

(3)   Where the application is for advice or assistance relating to the making of a will, the person authorised in accordance with paragraph (1) shall provide the solicitor with the information necessary to enable the solicitor to determine whether the advice or assistance would fall within regulation 4(2) of the Scope Regulations.

(4)   The information required by this regulation shall be furnished on a form approved by the Board.

[(5) A client may authorise another person to attend on the solicitor on his behalf in accordance with paragraph (1) only if, at the time when the authorisation is given, the client is either present in, or resides in, England and Wales.]

**Note.** In para (1) word 'where' substituted by words 'subject to paragraph (5), where' in square brackets and para (5) inserted by SI 1999/2575, reg 4, as from 5 October 1999.

*Eligibility for advice and assistance to which regulation 9 applies*

**11.** (1) A client is eligible for advice and assistance (excluding ABWOR) to which regulation 9 applies if his weekly disposable income does not exceed £77 [£80] [£83] and his disposable capital does not exceed £1,000.

(2) A client is eligible for ABWOR to which regulation 9 applies if his weekly disposable income does not exceed £166 [£172] [£178] and his disposable capital does not exceed £3,000.

**Note.** Sums '£77', '£166' substituted by sums '£80' and '£172' by SI 1998/663, reg 3 as from 1 April 1988, and further substituted by sums '£83' and '£178' by SI 1999/1814, reg 2(1) as from 12 April 1999.

*Contributions*

**12.** (1) A client shall be liable to pay weekly contributions towards the cost of ABWOR if his weekly disposable income exceeds £69 [£72] [£75] but does not exceed £166 [£172] [£178].

(2) The amount of any contribution under paragraph (1) shall be one third of the amount by which his weekly disposable income exceeds £69 [£72] [£75].

(3) The period during which contributions shall be payable shall start on the date of approval of ABWOR and shall continue until the conclusion of the proceedings to which ABWOR related or until ABWOR is withdrawn.

(4) For ABWOR to which Part III of the Act applies by virtue of regulation 7(1)(b) or 8 of the Scope Regulations, a client shall be liable (subject to paragraphs (1), (2) and (5) of this regulation) to pay one week's contribution towards the cost of ABWOR.

(5) A client whose weekly disposable income does not exceed £69 [£72] [£75] is not liable to pay any contribution towards the cost of ABWOR under section 9(6) of the Act.

(6) A client shall in no case be liable to pay any contribution towards the cost of advice and assistance other than ABWOR.

**Note.** Sums '£69' in each place and sum '£166' substituted by sums '£72' and '£172' by SI 1998/663, reg 3 as from 1 April 1998, and further substituted by sums '£75' and '£178' by SI 1999/1814, reg 2(1) as from 12 April 1999.

*Assessment of disposable income, disposable capital and contribution*

**13.** (1) Subject to paragraphs (2) and (3), a solicitor to whom an application under regulation 9 is made shall assess the disposable income and disposable capital of the client and, where appropriate, of any person whose financial resources may be treated as those of the client in accordance with Schedule 2.

(2) Where the solicitor is satisfied that any of the persons whose disposable incomes are to be assessed under paragraph (1) is directly or indirectly in receipt of *income support, income based jobseeker's allowance, family credit or disability working allowance* [any qualifying benefit], he shall take that person's disposable income as not exceeding the sum for the time being specified in the regulation 11(1).

[(2A) The following are qualifying benefits for the purposes of paragraph (2) above—

(a) income support;

(b) working families' tax credit, provided that the amount (if any) to be deducted under section 128(2)(b) of the Social Security Contributions and Benefits Act 1992 has been determined at not more than £70 a week;

   (c) disabled person's tax credit, provided that the amount (if any) to be deducted under section 129(5)(b) of the Social Security Contributions and Benefits Act 1992 has been determined at not more than £70 a week; and

   (d) income based jobseeker's allowance.]

(3) Where, in the case of an application for ABWOR to which regulation 9 applies, the solicitor is satisfied that any of the persons whose disposable capital is to be assessed under paragraph (1) is directly or indirectly in receipt of income support or income based jobseeker's allowance, he shall take that person's disposable capital as not exceeding the capital sum specified in regulation 11(2).

(4) The solicitor shall also determine in accordance with the provisions of regulation 12 the weekly contribution, if any, payable to him by the client under section 9(6) of the Act.

(5) The solicitor shall not provide advice and assistance to any person until either the form referred to in regulation 9(6) has been signed by the client or, where appropriate, the form referred to in regulation 10(4) has been signed on behalf of the client, and in any case, until the solicitor has assessed disposable income and disposable capital in accordance with paragraph (1).

**Note.** In para (2) words from 'income support,' to 'disability working allowance' subsituted by words 'any qualifying benefit' in square brackets and para (2A) inserted by SI 1999/2575, regs 5, 6, as from 5 October 1999.

*Children and patients*

**14.** (1) A solicitor shall not, except where paragraph (2) or (2A) applies, accept an application for advice and assistance from a child unless he has been authorised to do so by the Area Director and the Area Director shall withhold such authority unless he is satisfied that it is reasonable in the circumstances that the child should receive advice and assistance.

(2) A solicitor may accept an application for advice and assistance from a child who—

   (a) is arrested and held in custody at a police station or other premises;

   (b) is being interviewed in connection with a serious service offence; or

   (c) is a volunteer;

where the solicitor is satisfied that the application cannot reasonably be made by any of the persons specified in paragraph (3)(a), (c) or (d).

(2A) A solicitor may accept an application for advice and assistance from a child in relation to proceedings in which that child is entitled to begin, prosecute or defend without a next friend or guardian ad litem.

(3) A solicitor may accept an application for advice and assistance on behalf of a child or patient from—

   (a) in the case of a child, his parent or guardian or other person in whose care he is; or

   (b) in the case of a patient, a receiver appointed under Part VII of the Mental Health Act 1983 or the patient's nearest relative or guardian within the meaning of Part II of the Mental Health Act 1983; or

   (c) in the case of a child or patient, a person acting for the purposes of any proceedings as his next friend or guardian ad litem; or

   (d) in the case of a child or a patient, any other person where the Area Director is satisfied that it is reasonable in the circumstances and has given prior authority for the advice and assistance to be given to such other person on behalf of the child or patient.

*Clients resident outside England and Wales*

**15.** Where the client resides outside England and Wales, the Area Director may give the solicitor prior authority to accept a postal application for advice and assistance if the Area Director is satisfied that it is reasonable in the circumstances to do so.

*Advice and assistance from more than one solicitor*

**16.**   (1) A person shall not, except where regulation 6, 7 or 8 applies, be given advice and assistance for the same matter by more than one solicitor without the prior authority of the Area Director, and such authority may be given on such terms and conditions as the Area Director may in his discretion see fit to impose.

(2) Where regulation 6 applies, a person may be given advice and assistance for the same matter by more than one solicitor without the prior authority of the Area Director, provided that the cost of that advice and assistance shall not exceed the cost that would have been incurred had it been given by one solicitor.

*Separate matters*

**17.**   [(1)] Where two or more separate matters are involved, each matter shall be the subject of a separate application for advice and assistance provided that [(subject to paragraph (2))] matters connected with or arising from proceedings for divorce or judicial separation, whether actual or prospective between the client and his spouse, shall not be treated as separate matters for the purpose of advice and assistance.

[(2) Matters in relation to which the advice or assistance or mediation-related advice or assistance (as defined in regulation 32(1)) shall be treated as separate matters from those in relation to which the advice or assistance is not mediation-related advice or assistance.]

**Note.** Para (1) numbered as such and words '(subject to paragraph (2))' in square brackets inserted and para (2) inserted by SI 1999/2575, reg 7, as from 5 October 1999.

*Refusal of advice and assistance*

**18.**   A solicitor may for good cause either refuse to accept an application for advice and assistance or (having accepted an application) decline to give, or to continue to give advice and assistance and may, if he thinks fit, refuse to disclose his reasons for doing so to the client or person seeking advice and assistance on his behalf; but he shall give the Area Director such information about such a refusal as the Area Director may require.

*Power to require information*

**19.**   The Area Director may require a solicitor who has given advice and assistance to furnish such information as he may from time to time require for the purposes of his functions under these Regulations; and the solicitor shall not be precluded, by reason of any privilege arising out of the relationship between solicitor and client, from disclosing such information to him.

*Entrusting functions to others*

**20.**   Subject to any arrangements made by the Board under regulation 6, 7 or 8, nothing in these Regulations shall prevent a solicitor from entrusting any function under these Regulations to a partner of his or to a competent and responsible representative of his who is employed in his office or is otherwise under his immediate supervision.

*Extensions*

**21.**   (1) Subject to regulation 22(8), and except where regulation 6, 7 or 8 applies, where it appears to the solicitor that the cost of giving advice or assistance is likely to exceed the limit applicable under section 10(1) of the Act, he shall apply to the Area Director for an extension and shall furnish such information as may enable him to consider and determine that application.

(2) Where an Area Director receives an application in accordance with paragraph (1) he shall consider—

(a) whether it is reasonable for the advice and assistance to be given; and

(b) whether the estimate of the costs to be incurred in giving advice and assistance is reasonable.

(3) If the Area Director is satisfied that it is reasonable for the advice or assistance to be given and that the estimate of the costs to be incurred in giving it is reasonable, he shall grant an extension and shall prescribe such higher limit as he thinks fit and may limit the advice and assistance to such subject matter as he thinks fit.

*Applications for approval of ABWOR*

**22.**

\* \* \* \* \*

*Counsel*

**23.**

\* \* \* \* \*

*Notification of approval of assistance by way of representation*

**24.**

\* \* \* \* \*

*Withdrawal of approval of assistance by way of representation*

**25.**

\* \* \* \* \*

*Appeals against refusal of ABWOR etc*

**26.**

\* \* \* \* \*

*Determination of appeals*

**27.**

\* \* \* \* \*

*Collection and refund of contributions*

**28.** (1) Where a client is required to pay contributions the solicitor may collect them in weekly instalments or by such other periodic instalments as may be agreed between him and the client.

(1A) Where the total contribution is likely to exceed the cost of giving ABWOR, the solicitor shall not require the client to pay a sum higher than would be expected to defray his reasonable costs.

(2) Where the reasonable costs of the ABWOR are less than any contribution made by the client, the solicitor shall refund the balance.

*Costs payable out of the fund*

**29.** (1) Where the reasonable costs of the advice or assistance, including charges for disbursements, exceed any contribution payable by the client to the solicitor under section 9 of the Act together with the value of any charge arising under section 11 of the Act, the solicitor shall, except where paragraph (2) applies, submit a claim to the Area Director requesting payment of the deficiency.

\* \* \* \* \*

(7) If any solicitor or counsel is dissatisfied with any decision of the Area Director as to the payment of an assessed deficiency in the costs of advice and assistance, he may within 21 days of receipt of notification of that decision make written representations to the appropriate area committee; and that committee shall review the assessment of the Area Director whether by confirming, increasing or decreasing the amount assessed by the Area Director.

(8) A solicitor or counsel who is dissatisfied with the decision of an area committee on a review under paragraph (7) may within 21 days of receipt of notification of the decision apply to that committee to certify a point of principle of general importance.

(9) Where an area committee certifies a point of principle of general importance the solicitor or counsel may, within 21 days of receipt of notification of that certification, appeal in writing to a committee appointed by the Board against the decision of the area committee under paragraph (7).

(10) On an appeal under this regulation the committee appointed by the Board may reverse, affirm or amend the decision of the area committee under paragraph (7).

*Basis of assessments*
**30.**

\*   \*   \*   \*   \*

*Payment on account*
**30A.**

\*   \*   \*   \*   \*

*Recovery of costs*
**31.**

\*   \*   \*   \*   \*

*Exceptions to charge on property recovered or preserved*

**32.**   [(1)] The provisions of section 11 (2)(b) of the Act shall not apply to the matters specified in Schedule 4 [or in relation to the cost of giving mediation-related advice or assistance].

[(2) In this regulation—
'mediation-related advice or assistance' means advice or assistance where—
  (a)  the advice or assistance is given to a person who is a party to mediation in a dispute relating to family matters;
  (b)  the subject matter of the advice or assistance forms all or part of the subject matter of the mediation; and
  (c)  at the time when the advice or assistance was given, the mediation has not come to an end as regards the subject matter of the advice or assistance, provided that for the purposes of this sub-paragraph mediation, as regards any matter, shall not be taken to have come to an end by reason of the parties having reached agreement, unless and until the terms of that agreement are made binding on the parties, by way of a binding agreement, a consent order, or otherwise;
'family matters' has the meaning given in section 13A(2) of the Act;
'mediation' has the meaning given in section 2(3A) of the Act.]

**Note.** Para (1) numbered as such, and words 'or in relation to the cost of giving mediation-related advice or assistance' in square brackets and para (2), inserted by SI 1999/2575, reg 8, as from 5 October 1999.

*Authority not to enforce the charge*

**33.** Where in the opinion of the solicitor—

(a) it would cause grave hardship or distress to the client to enforce the charge on any money or property recovered or preserved for him, or

(b) the charge on any property recovered or preserved could be enforced only with unreasonable difficulty because of the nature of the property,

the solicitor may apply to the appropriate area committee for authority not to enforce, either wholly or in part, the charge and, if the committee gives authority, any deficiency in the solicitor's costs shall be computed as if section 11(2)(b) of the Act did not apply to that money or property or to such part of it as the committee may have authorised.

*Costs awarded against a client*

**34.**

\* \* \* \* \*

*Costs of successful unassisted parties out of the fund*

**35.** Before making any order under section 13 of the Act, the Court shall afford the Area Director who dealt with the application under regulation 22 an opportunity to make representations.

*False statements etc*

**36.** Where a client has wilfully failed to comply with the provisions of these Regulations as to the information to be furnished by him or, in furnishing such information, has knowingly made a false statement or false representation, and after the failure occurred or the false statement or false representation was made the client received advice or assistance, the appropriate area committee may declare that the advice or assistance so given was not given under the Act and these Regulations and, if it does, shall so inform the client and the solicitor; and thereafter the Board shall be entitled to recover from the client any sums paid out of the fund in respect of the advice and assistance so given.

*Computation of time*

**37.** (1) Where, under these Regulations, an act is required to be done within a specified period after or from a specified date, the period of time so fixed starts immediately after that date.

(2) The period within which an act is required or authorised to be done under these Regulations may, if the Area Director thinks fit, be extended and any such period may be extended although the application for extension is not made until after the expiration of the period.

SCHEDULE 1                                                                 Regulation 2

\* \* \* \* \*

SCHEDULE 2                                                              Regulation 13(1)

ASSESSMENT OF RESOURCES

**1.** In this Schedule, unless the context otherwise requires—

'capital' means the amount or value of every resource of a capital nature;

'income' means the total income from all sources which the person concerned has received or may reasonably expect to receive in respect of the seven days up to and including the date of his application;

'the person concerned' means the person whose disposable capital and disposable income are to be assessed.

**2.** The provisions of this Schedule apply to a man and a woman who are living with each other in the same household as husband and wife as they apply to the parties to a marriage.

**3.** Any question arising under this Schedule shall be decided by the solicitor to whom the client has applied and that solicitor, in deciding any such question, shall have regard to any guidance which may from time to time be given by the Board as to the application of this Schedule.

**4.** The disposable capital and disposable income of the person concerned shall be the capital and income as assessed by the solicitor after deducting any sums which are to be left out of account or for which allowance is to be made under the provisions of this Schedule.

**5.** The resources of any person who, under section 26(3) and (4) of the Social Security Act 1986 is liable to maintain a child or who usually contributes substantially to a child's maintenance, or who has care and control of the child, not being a person who has such care and control by reason of any contract or for some temporary purpose, may be treated as the resources of the child, if, having regard to all the circumstances, including the age and resources of the child and to any conflict of interest it appears just and equitable to do so.

**6.** If it appears to the solicitor that the person concerned has, with intent to reduce the disposable capital or disposable income whether for the purpose of making himself eligible for advice and assistance, reducing his liability to pay a contribution in respect of the costs of advice and assistance or otherwise,

(a)  directly or indirectly deprived himself of any resource or

(b)  converted any part of his resources into resources which are to be left out of account wholly or partly,

the resources of which he has so deprived himself or which he has so converted shall be treated as part of his resources or as not so converted, as the case may be.

**7.**  (1)  In computing the capital and income of the person concerned, there shall be left out of account the value of the subject matter of any claim in respect of which he is seeking advice or assistance.

(2)  In computing the capital and income of the person concerned, the resources of any spouse of his shall be treated as his resources unless—

(i)   the spouse has a contrary interest in the matter in respect of which he is seeking advice and assistance, or

(ii)  the person concerned and his spouse are living separate and apart, or

(iii) in all the circumstances of the case it would be inequitable or impractical to do so.

(3)  In computing the capital and income of the person concerned, there shall be left out of account so much of any back to work bonus received under section 26 of the Jobseekers Act 1995 as is by virtue of that section to be treated as payable by way of a jobseeker's allowance.

**8.**  In computing the capital of the person concerned—

(a)   there shall be left out of account the value of his household furniture and effects, of his clothes and of tools and implements of his trade;

(aa)  the value of the main or only dwelling in which he resides shall be taken to be the amount for which that interest could be sold in the open market, subject to the following rules—

(i)   the amount to be allowed in respect of any mortgage debt or heritable security shall not exceed £100,000;

(ii)  the first £100,000 of the value of that interest, after the application of the rule in paragraph (i), shall be disregarded;

(b)   where the person concerned resides in more than one dwelling in which he has an interest there shall be taken into account the amount for which any interest in a dwelling which is not the main dwelling could be sold in the open market; provided that the total amount to be allowed in respect of any mortgage debts or heritable securities over all such dwellings, together with any amount allowed under paragraph (aa)(i) in respect of the main dwelling, shall not exceed £100,000;

(c) where the person concerned has living with him one or more of the following persons, namely, a spouse whose resources are required to be aggregated with his, a dependent child or a dependent relative wholly or substantially maintained by him, a deduction shall be made of £335 in respect of the first person £200 in respect of the second and £100 in respect of each further person.

**9.** In computing the income of the person concerned—

  (a) there shall be left out of account—

    (i) any income tax paid or payable on income treated under the provisions of this Schedule as his income;

    (ii) contributions estimated to have been paid under the Social Security Acts 1975–1988 or any scheme made under those Acts during or in respect of the seven days up to and including the date of the application for advice and assistance;

  (b) there shall be a deduction in respect of the spouse of the person concerned, if the spouses are living together, in respect of the maintenance of any dependent child and in respect of the maintenance of any dependent relative of the person concerned, being (in either of such cases) a member of his or her household, at the following rates—

    (i) in the case of a spouse at a rate equivalent to the difference between the income support allowance for a couple where both members are aged not less than 18 (which is specified in column 2 of paragraph 1(3)(c) of Schedule 2 Part I of the Income Support (General) Regulations 1987 and the allowance for a single person aged not less than 25 (which is specified in column 2 of paragraph 1(1)(e) of Schedule 2, Part I to those Regulations;

    (ii) in the case of a dependent child [aged 18 or under] or a dependent relative at a rate equivalent to the amount specified for the time being in paragraph 2 of Part I of Schedule 2 to the Income Support (General) Regulations 1987 appropriate to the age of the child or relative;

    [(iii) in the case of a dependent child or a dependent relative aged 19 or over, at a rate equivalent to the amount which would have been specified for the time being in accordance with paragraph 9(b)(ii) immediately before he attained the age of 19].

**9A.** (1) In computing disposable income the following payments made under the Social Security Contributions and Benefits Act 1992 shall be disregarded—

  (a) disability living allowance;

  (b) attendance allowance paid under section 64 or Schedule 8 paragraph 4 or 7(2);

  (c) constant attendance allowance paid under section 104 as an increase to a disablement pension; or

  (d) any payment made out of the social fund.

(2) In computing disposable income, a payment made under the Community Care (Direct Payments) Act 1996 [or under regulations made under section 57 of the Health and Social Care Act 2001 (direct payments)] shall be disregarded.

**9B.** In computing the disposable income of any person there shall be disregarded any payment made by the Secretary of State under the Earnings Top-up Scheme 1996.

**10.** If the person concerned is making bona fide payments for the maintenance of a spouse who is living apart, of a former spouse, of a child or relative who is not (in any such case) a member of the household of the person concerned, there shall be a deduction of such payment as was or will be made in respect of the seven days up to and including the date of the application for advice and assistance.

**11.** Where it appears to the solicitor that there has been some error or mistake in the assessment of the disposable income, disposable capital or contribution of the person concerned, he may reassess the disposable income or disposable capital or contribution or, as the case may be, amend the assessment and in the latter case the amended assessment shall for all purposes be substituted for the original assessment.

**Note.** In para 9(b)(ii) words 'aged 18 or under' in square brackets and 9(b)(iii) inserted by SI 1998/663, reg 4 as from 6 April 1998. In para 9A(2) words 'or under regulations made under section 57 of the Health and Social Care Act 2001 (direct payments)' in square brackets inserted by SI 2003/762, reg 11(1), Sch 1 in relation to England as from 8 April 2003 and by SI 2004/1748, reg 12, Sch 2, para 1 in relation to Wales as from 1 November 2004.

SCHEDULE 3                                                                Regulation 13(4)

*Revoked.*

SCHEDULE 4                                                                Regulation 32

EXCEPTIONS TO CHARGE ON PROPERTY RECOVERED OR PRESERVED

The provisions of section 11(2)(b) of the Act shall not apply to—
  (a)  any periodical payment of maintenance, which for this purpose means money or money's worth paid towards the support of a spouse, former spouse, child or any other person for whose support the payer has previously been responsible or has made payments;
  (b)  any property recovered or preserved for the client as a result of advice and assistance given to him by the solicitor which comprises the client's main or only dwelling, or any household furniture or tools of trade;
  (c)  (without prejudice to (b) above) the first £2,500 of any money or of the value of any property recovered or preserved by virtue of—
     (i)  an order made, or deemed to be made, under the provisions of section 23(1)(c) or (f), 23(2), 24, 27(6)(c) or (f), or 35 of the Matrimonial Causes Act 1973;
     (ii)  an order made, or deemed to be made, under the provisions of section 2 or 6 of the Inheritance (Provision for Family and Dependants) Act 1975;
     (iii)  an order made, or deemed to be made, under section 17 of the Married Women's Property Act 1882; or
     (iv)  an order made, or deemed to be made, under the provisions of section 4(2)(b) of the Affiliation Proceedings Act 1957; or
     (v)  an order for the payment of a lump sum made, or deemed to be made, under the provisions of section 60 of the Magistrates' Courts Act 1980; or
     (vi)  an order made, or deemed to be made, under the provisions of section 2(1)(b) or (d), 6(1) or (5), 11(2)(b) or (3)(b) or 20(2) of the Domestic Proceedings and Magistrates' Courts Act 1978; or
     (vii)  an order made, or deemed to be made, under section 9(2)(b), 10(1)(b)(ii), 11(b)(ii) of the Guardianship of Minors Act 1971 or under section 11B, 11C or 11D of that Act; or
     (viii)  an order made, or deemed to be made, under section 34(1)(c) or 35 of the Children Act 1975; or
     (ix)  an agreement which has the same effect as an order made, or deemed to be made, under any of the provisions specified in this sub-paragraph;
  (d)  one-half of any redundancy payment within the meaning of Part VI of the Employment Protection (Consolidation) Act 1978 recovered or preserved for the client;
  (e)  any payment of money in accordance with an order made under section 136 of the Employment Protection (Consolidation) Act 1978 by the Employment Appeal Tribunal;

(f) any sum, payment or benefit which, by virtue of any provision of or made under an Act of Parliament, cannot be assigned or charged.

SCHEDULE 5                                                                   Regulation 34

COSTS AWARDED AGAINST A CLIENT

**1.**   No costs attributable to the period during which a client was in receipt of ABWOR shall be recoverable from him until the court has determined the amount of his liability in accordance with section 12 of the Act:
Provided that where the ABWOR does not relate to or has been withdrawn so that it no longer relates to the whole of the proceedings the court shall nevertheless make a determination in respect of that part of the proceedings to which the approval of ABWOR relates.
**2.**   The court may, if it thinks fit, refer to the *clerk to the justices* [justices' chief executive] for investigation any question of fact relevant to the determination, requiring him to report his findings on that question to the court.
**3.**   In determining the amount of the client's liability his dwelling-house, clothes, household furniture and the tools and implements of his trade shall be left out of account to the like extent as they are left out of account by the solicitor in determining the client's disposable capital.
**4.**   Any person, not being himself a client, who is a party to proceedings to which the client is a party may, at any time before the judgment, lodge with the *clerk to the justices* [justices' chief executive] an affidavit exhibiting thereto a statement setting out the rate of his own income and amount of his own capital and any other facts relevant to the determination of his means in accordance with section 12 of the Act and shall serve a copy thereof together with the exhibit upon the client's solicitor and such affidavit and exhibit shall be evidence of the facts stated therein.
**5.**   The court may, if it thinks fit, order the client and any party who has filed an affidavit in accordance with paragraph (4) of this Schedule to attend for oral examination as to his means and as to any other facts relevant to the determination of the amount of the client's liability and may permit any party to give evidence and call witnesses thereon.
**6.**   The court may direct—
   (a) that payment under the order for costs shall be limited to such amount payable in instalments or otherwise as the court thinks reasonable having regard to all the circumstances; or
   (b) where the court thinks it reasonable for payment under sub-paragraph (a) not to be made immediately, that payment under the order for costs be suspended either until such date as the court may determine or sine die.
**7.**   The party in whose favour an order is made may within 6 years from the date thereof apply to the court for the order to be varied on the grounds that—
   (a) material additional information as to the client's means, being information which could not have been obtained by that party with reasonable diligence at the time the order was made, is available; or
   (b) there has been a change in the client's circumstances since the date of the order, and
on any such application the order may be varied as the court thinks fit but save as aforesaid the determination of the court shall be final.
**8.**   Where an order for costs is made against a client who is concerned in the proceedings solely in a representative, fiduciary or official capacity, he shall have the benefit of section 12(1) of the Act and his personal resources shall not (unless there is reason to the contrary) be taken into account for that purpose, but regard shall be had to the value of the property or estate, or the amount of the fund out of which he is entitled to be indemnified.
**9.**   Where a client is a child, his means for the purpose of determining his liability for costs under section 12(1) of the Act shall be taken as including the means of

any person whose disposable income and disposable capital has, by virtue of Schedule 2, been included in assessing the child's resources.

**10.** Where an order for costs is made against a next friend or guardian ad litem of a client who is a child or patient, he shall have the benefit of section 12(1) of the Act in like manner as it applies to a client, and the means of the next friend or guardian ad litem shall be taken as being the means of the child as defined in paragraph 9 or, as the case may be, of the patient.

**Note.** In paras 2, 4 words 'clerk to the justices' substituted by words 'justices' chief executive' in square brackets by SI 2001/829, reg 3, as from 1 April 2001.

## LEGAL ADVICE AND ASSISTANCE (SCOPE) REGULATIONS 1989

**Dated** 23 March 1989

**SI 1989 No 550**

*Following the repeal of the enabling provisions by the Access to Justice Act 1999, s 106, Sch 15, Pt 1, these Regulations have lapsed except insofar as they may continue to have effect by virtue of SI 2000/774, art 5, and SI 2001/916, art 4, Sch 2 as from 1 April 2000 (for certain purposes) and 2 April 2001 (for remaining purposes).*

ARRANGEMENT OF REGULATIONS

1. Citation and commencement.
2. Interpretation.
3. Excluded services.
4A. Services under contracts and grants.
5. Transition.
6. Application of Part III of the Act to ABWOR.
7. Proceedings in magistrates' courts.
8. Proceedings in county courts.
8A. Proceedings in the Crown Court.
9. Other proceedings.
Schedule: Proceedings in magistrates' courts in which ABWOR is available.

The Lord Chancellor, in exercise of the powers conferred on him by sections 8 and 43 of the Legal Aid Act 1988, hereby makes the following Regulations of which a draft has, in accordance with section 36(3)(b) of that Act, been laid before and approved by resolution of each House of Parliament—

PART I

GENERAL

*Citation and commencement*

**1.** These Regulations may be cited as the Legal Advice and Assistance (Scope) Regulations 1989 and shall come into force on 1st April 1989.

*Interpretation*

**2.** In these Regulations, unless the context otherwise requires—
   'ABWOR' means assistance by way of representation;
   'the Act' means the Legal Aid Act 1988;
   'client' means a person seeking or receiving advice or assistance or on whose behalf advice or assistance is sought;

\*      \*      \*      \*      \*

'mental disorder' has the meaning assigned to it in section 1 of the Mental Health Act 1983;

\* \* \* \* \*

EXCLUSIONS FROM PART II OF THE ACT

*Excluded services*

**3.**

**Note.** This regulation was substituted for regs 3, 4 as originally enacted, by SI 1999/3377, regs 4, 6, as from 1 January 2000.

The services excluded relate to crime, clinical negligence and personal injury and are not set out in full.

\* \* \* \* \*

*Proceedings in Magistrates' Courts*

**7.**

\* \* \* \* \*

[(5) Part III of the Act applies to ABWOR given to—
(a) a respondent in proceedings in a magistrates' court under the following sections of the Crime and Disorder Act 1998:
   (i)  section 2 (sex offender orders);
   (ii)  section 11 (child safety orders); or
   (iii)  section 8 (parenting orders), where the application is for a parenting order by virtue of section 8(1 ) (a), (b) or (c); or
(b) an applicant in proceedings in a magistrates' court to vary or discharge an order made against that applicant, or a respondent in proceedings in a magistrates' court to vary or discharge an order made against that respondent, under any of the provisions referred to in sub-paragraph (a) above.]

\* \* \* \* \*

**Note.** Para (5) inserted by SI 1998/2831, reg 4 as from 1 December 1998.

*Proceedings in county courts*

**8.** Part III of the Act applies to ABWOR given by a solicitor at a hearing in any proceedings in a county court to a party who is not receiving and has not been refused representation in connection with those proceedings, where the court—
   (i)  is satisfied that the hearing should proceed on the same day;
   (ii)  is satisfied that that party would not otherwise be represented; and
   (iii)  requests a solicitor who is within the precincts of the court for purposes other than the provision of ABWOR in accordance with this regulation, or approves a proposal from such a solicitor, that he provide that party with ABWOR.

\* \* \* \* \*

*[Proceedings in the Crown Court*

**8A.**   Part III of the Act applies to ABWOR given to—
  (a)   an appellant in an appeal to the Crown Court under section 4 or section 10 of the Crime and Disorder Act 1998;
  (b)   a respondent in proceedings in the Crown Court under section 8 of the Crime and Disorder Act 1998, where the application is for a parenting order made against him by virtue of section 8(1)(c) of that Act; or
  (c)   an applicant in proceedings in the Crown Court to vary or discharge an order made against that applicant, or a respondent in proceedings in the Crown Court to vary or discharge an order made against that respondent, under the provision referred to in sub-paragraph (b) above.]

**Note.** Inserted by SI 1998/2831, regs 3, 6 as from 1 December 1998: see SI 1998/2831, reg 1(b).

## THE MAGISTRATES' COURTS (SOCIAL SECURITY ACT 1986) (TRANSFER OF ORDERS TO MAINTAIN AND ENFORCEMENT OF MAINTENANCE ORDERS) RULES 1990

**Dated** 17 September 1990

**SI 1990 No 1909**

The Lord Chancellor, in exercise of the powers conferred on him by section 144 of the Magistrates' Courts Act 1980 as extended by section 145 of that Act, after consultation with the Rule Committee appointed under the said section 144, hereby makes the following Rules—

**1.**   (1) These Rules may be cited as the Magistrates' Courts (Social Security Act 1986) (Transfers of Orders to Maintain and Enforcement of Maintenance Orders) Rules 1990 and shall come into force on 15th October 1990.
  (2) In these Rules, 'personal allowance element', 'the dependent parent' and 'the liable parent' have the same meaning as in section 24A of the Social Security Act 1986 ('the 1986 Act').

**2.**   Where under section 24A of the 1986 Act the Secretary of State gives notice in writing to a magistrates' court which has made an order under section 24(4) of that Act, transferring to a dependent parent (by virtue of subsection (3)) or transferring back from the dependent parent to himself (by virtue of subsection (7)) the right to receive the payments under the order (exclusive of any personal allowance element), the clerk of that court shall amend the order by substituting the name of the dependent parent for that of the Secretary of State or the name of the Secretary of State for that of the dependent parent, as appropriate.

**3.**   *Where a clerk amends an order made under section 24(4) in accordance with rule 2 of these Rules, he shall—*
  *(a)   make a written record of the fact that, the circumstances in which and the date on which, he has done so, and shall keep it with the register kept under rule 66 of the Magistrates' Courts Rules 1981; and*
  *(b)   send a copy of the amended order, as soon as practicable, to the Secretary of State, the liable parent and the dependent parent.*

**[3.**   Where a clerk amends an order made under section 24(4) in accordance with rule 2 of these Rules—
  (a)   he shall make a written record of the fact that, the circumstances in which and the date on which, he has done so, and shall keep it with the register kept under rule 66 of the Magistrates' Courts Rules 1981; and
  (b)   the justices' chief executive shall send a copy of the amended order, as soon as practicable, to the Secretary of State, the liable parent and the dependent parent.]

**Note.** Substituted by SI 2001/615, r 2(xviii), Schedule, para 89 as from 1 April 2001.

**4.** Where an application within paragraph (a) or (b) of section 24B(5) of the 1986 Act is made to a magistrates' court, the *clerk of* [justices' chief executive for] the court shall, after giving notice to the Secretary of State of any such application, notify the parties to the application that he has done so and that the Secretary of State is entitled to appear and be heard on the application.

**Note.** Words 'clerk of' substituted by words 'justices' chief executive for' in square brackets by SI 2001/615, r 2(xviii), Schedule, para 90, as from 1 April 2001.

## HIGH COURT AND COUNTY COURTS JURISDICTION ORDER 1991

**Dated** 19 March 1991

**SI 1991 No 724**

The Lord Chancellor, in exercise of the powers conferred upon him by sections 1 and 120 of the Courts and Legal Services Act 1990, having consulted as required by section 1(9) of that Act, hereby makes the following Order a draft of which has, in accordance with section 120(4) of that Act, been laid before and approved by resolution of each House of Parliament—

*Title and commencement*

**1.** This Order may be cited as the High Court and County Courts Jurisdiction Order 1991 and shall come into force on 1st July 1991.

*Jurisdiction*

**2.** (1) A county court shall have jurisdiction under—
  (a) sections 146 and 147 of the Law of Property Act 1925,

*   *   *   *   *

  (g) section 41 of the Administration of Justice Act 1970,

*   *   *   *   *

  (j) section 87 of the Magistrates' Courts Act 1980,

*   *   *   *   *

  (l) sections 15, 16, 21, 25 and 139 of the County Courts Act 1984,
  (m) section 39(4) of, and paragraph 3(1) of Schedule 3 to, the Legal Aid Act 1988,

*   *   *   *   *

  (p) sections 13 and 14 of the Trusts of Land and Appointment of Trustees Act 1996,
whatever the amount involved in the proceedings and whatever the value of any fund or asset connected with the proceedings.
  (2) A county court shall have jurisdiction under—
  (a) section 10 of the Local Land Charges Act 1975, and
  (b) section 10(4) of the Rentcharges Act 1977,
where the sum concerned or amount claimed does not exceed £5,000.
  (3) A county court shall have jurisdiction under the following provisions of the Law of Property Act 1925 where the capital value of the land or interest in land which is to be dealt with does not exceed £30,000—
  (a) sections 3, 49, 66, 181 and 188;
  (b) proviso (iii) to paragraph 3 of Part III of Schedule 1;
  (c) proviso (v) to paragraph 1(3) of Part IV of Schedule 1;
  (d) provisos (iii) and (iv) to paragraph 1(4) of Part IV of Schedule 1.

(4) A county court shall have jurisdiction under sections 89, 90, 91 and 92 of the Law of Property Act 1925 where the amount owing in respect of the mortgage or charge at the commencement of the proceedings does not exceed £30,000.

(5) A county court shall have jurisdiction under the proviso to section 136(1) of the Law of Property Act 1925 where the amount or value of the debt or thing in action does not exceed £30,000.

(6) A county court shall have jurisdiction under section 1(6) of the Land Charges Act 1972—

(a) in the case of a land charge of Class C(i), C(ii) or D(i), if the amount does not exceed £30,000;

(b) in the case of a land charge of Class C(iii), if it is for a specified capital sum of money not exceeding £30,000 or, where it is not for a specified capital sum, if the capital value of the land affected does not exceed £30,000;

(c) in the case of a land charge of Class A, Class B, Class C(iv), Class D(ii), Class D(iii) or Class E, if the capital value of the land affected does not exceed £30,000;

(d) in the case of a land charge of Class F, if the land affected by it is the subject of an order made by the court under section 1 of the Matrimonial Homes Act 1983 or an application for an order under that section relating to that land has been made to the court;

(e) in a case where an application under section 23 of the Deeds of Arrangement Act 1914 could be entertained by the court.

(7) A county court shall have jurisdiction under sections 69, 70 and 71 of the Solicitors Act 1974 where a bill of costs relates wholly or partly to contentious business done in a county court and the amount of the bill does not exceed £5,000.

(8) The enactments and statutory instruments listed in the Schedule to this Order are amended as specified therein, being amendments which are consequential on the provisions of this article.

*Injunctions*

**3.** The High Court shall have jurisdiction to hear an application for an injunction made in the course of or in anticipation of proceedings in a county court where a county court may not, by virtue of regulations under section 38(3)(b) of the County Courts Act 1984 or otherwise, grant such an injunction.

*Allocation—Commencement of proceedings*

**4.** Subject to articles [4A] 5 and 6, proceedings in which both the county courts and the High Court have jurisdiction may be commenced either in a county court or in the High Court.

**Note.** Reference to '4A' inserted by SI 1999/1014, art 4, as from 26 April 1999.

**[4A.** Except for proceedings to which article 5 applies, a claim for money in which county courts have jurisdiction may only be commenced in the High Court if the financial value of the claim is more than £15,000.]

**Note.** Inserted by SI 1999/1014, art 5 as from 26 April 1999.

**5.** *(1) Proceedings in which county courts have jurisdiction and which include a claim for damages in respect of personal injuries shall be commenced in a county court, unless the value of the action is £50,000 or more.*

[(1) Proceedings which include a claim for damages in respect of personal injuries may only be commenced in the High Court if the financial value of the claim is £50,000 or more].

(2) In this article 'personal injuries' means personal injuries to the *plaintiff* [claimant] or any other person, and includes disease, impairment of physical or mental condition, and death.

[(3) This article does not apply to proceedings which include a claim for damages in respect of an alleged breach of duty of care committed in the course of the provision of clinical or medical services (including dental or nursing services).]

**Note.** Para (1) substituted, in para (2) word 'plaintiff' substituted by word 'claimant' and para (3) inserted by SI 1999/1014, arts 3, 6, as from 26 April 1999.

**6.** Applications and appeals under *section 19 of the Local Government Finance Act 1982* [section 17 of the Audit Commission Act 1998] and appeals under *section 20* [section 18] of that Act shall be commenced in the High Court.

**Note.** Words 'section 19 of the Local Government Finance Act 1982' and 'section 20' substituted by words 'section 17 of the Audit Commission Act 1998' and 'section 18' by virtue of the Audit Commission Act 1998, s 54(2), Sch 4, para 4(1) as from 11 September 1998.

**7.**

**Note.** Revoked by SI 1999/1014, art 7, as from 26 April 1999.

*Enforcement*

**8.** (1) Subject to paragraph (1A) a judgment or order of a county court for the payment of a sum of money which it is sought to enforce wholly or partially by execution against goods—

   (a) shall be enforced only in the High Court where the sum which it is sought to enforce is £5,000 or more;

   (b) shall be enforced only in a county court where the sum which it is sought to enforce is less than *£1,000* [£600];

   (c) in any other case may be enforced in either the High Court or a county court.

*   *   *   *   *

(2) Section 85(1) of the County Courts Act 1984 is amended by the insertion, at the beginning of the subsection, of the words 'Subject to article 8 of the High Court and County Courts Jurisdiction Order 1991'.

**Note.** In para (1)(6) sum '£1,000' substituted by sum '£600' in square brackets by SI 1999/1014, art 8, as from 26 April 1999.

*   *   *   *   *

*Definition of value of action*

**9.** *(1) For the purposes of articles 5 and 7—*

   *(a) the value of an action for a sum of money, whether specified or not, is the amount which the plaintiff or applicant reasonably expects to recover;*

   *(b) an action for specified relief other than a sum of money—*

      *(i) has a value equal to the amount of money which the plaintiff or applicant could reasonably state to be the financial worth of the claim to him, or*

      *(ii) where there is no such amount, has no quantifiable value;*

   *(c) an action which includes more than one claim—*

      *(i) if one or more of the claims is of a kind specified in paragraph (b)(ii), has no quantifiable value;*

      *(ii) in any other case, has a value which is the aggregate of the values of the claims as determined in accordance with paragraphs (a) and (b)(i).*

*(2) In determining the value of an action under paragraph (1), claims for—*

   *(a) unspecified further or other relief,*

   *(b) interest, other than interest pursuant to a contract, and*

   *(c) costs,*

*shall be disregarded.*

*(3) In determining the value, under paragraph (1), of an action which is brought by more than one plaintiff or applicant regard shall be had to the aggregate of the expectations or interests of all the plaintiffs or applicants.*

*(4) In determining the value of an action under paragraph (1)(a)—*

(a) the sum which the plaintiff or applicant reasonably expects to recover shall be reduced by the amount of any debt which he admits that he owes to a defendant in that action and which arises from the circumstances which give rise to the action;

(b) no account shall be taken of a possible finding of contributory negligence, except to the extent, if any, that such negligence is admitted;

(c) where the plaintiff seeks an award of provisional damages as described in section 32A(2)(a) of the Supreme Court Act 1981, no account shall be taken of the possibility of a future application for further damages;

(d) the value shall be taken to include sums which, by virtue of section 22 of the Social Security Act 1989, are required to be paid to the Secretary of State.

[**9.** For the purposes of Articles 4A and 5, the financial value of the claim shall be calculated in accordance with rule 16.3(6) of the Civil Procedure Rules 1998.]

**Note.** Substituted by SI 1999/1014, art 9 as from 26 April 1999.

**10.** ...

**Note.** Revoked by SI 1999/1014, art 10, as from 26 April 1999.

*Crown proceedings—transitional provisions*

          *    *    *    *    *

*Savings*

**12.** This Order shall not apply to—

(a) family proceedings within the meaning of Part V of the Matrimonial and Family Proceedings Act 1984;

(b) ...

**Note.** Para (b) revoked by SI 1999/1014, art 11, as from 26 April 1999.

## SCHEDULE

PART I—ACTS

| Chapter | Short Title | Amendment |
|---|---|---|
| | * * * * * | |
| 15 & 16 Geo 5 c 20 | Law of Property Act 1925 | (1) In sections 3(7), 49(4), 66(4), paragraph 3A of Part III of Schedule 1 and paragraph 1(3A) and (4A) of Part IV of Schedule 1, for the words 'the county court limit' is substituted '£30,000', and the words 'or net annual value for rating' are omitted. (2) In sections 30(2) and 147(5) the words from 'where the' onwards are omitted. (3) In sections 89(7), 90(3), 91(8), 92(2), 136(3), 181(2) and 188(2), for the words 'the county court limit' is substituted '£30,000'; (4) In section 146(13), paragraphs (a) and (b) are omitted. (5) In section 205(1), paragraph (iiiA) is omitted. |
| | * * * * * | |

| Chapter | Short Title | Amendment |
|---------|-------------|-----------|
| 1970 c 31 | Administration of Justice Act 1970 | In section 41, subsections (4) and (4A) are omitted. |
| 1972 c 61 | Land Charges Act 1972 | (1) The following is substituted for section 1(6A):<br>'(6A) The county courts have jurisdiction under subsection (6) above—<br>(a) in the case of a land charge of Class C(i), C(ii) or D(i), if the amount does not exceed £30,000;<br>(b) in the case of a land charge of Class C(iii), if it is for a specified capital sum of money not exceeding £30,000 or, where it is not for a specified capital sum, if the capital value of the land affected does not exceed £30,000;<br>(c) in the case of a land charge of Class A, Class B, Class C(iv), Class D(ii), Class D(iii) or Class E if the capital value of the land affected does not exceed £30,000;<br>(d) in the case of a land charge of Class F, if the land affected by it is the subject of an order made by the court under section 1 of the Matrimonial Homes Act 1983 or an application for an order under that section relating to that land has been made to the court;<br>(e) in a case where an application under section 23 of the Deeds of Arrangement Act 1914 could be entertained by the court.'<br>(2) Section 1(6B) is omitted. |

\*　　\*　　\*　　\*　　\*

| Chapter | Short Title | Amendment |
|---------|-------------|-----------|
| 1974 c 47 | Solicitors Act 1974 | In section 69—<br>(a) in subsection (3), for the words 'the county court limit' is substituted '£5,000'; and<br>(b) subsection (4) is omitted. |
| 1975 c 76 | Local Land Charges Act 1975 | The following is substituted for section 10(8) and (8A):<br>'(8) Where the amount claimed by way of compensation under this section does not exceed £5,000, proceedings for the recovery of such compensation may be begun in a county court.' |

| Chapter | Short Title | Amendment |
|---------|-------------|-----------|
| | * * * * * | |
| 1980 c 43 | Magistrates' Courts Act 1980 | In section 87, subsections (2) and 2(A) are omitted. |
| | * * * * * | |
| 1982 c 53 | Administration of Justice Act 1982 | In paragraph 8 of Schedule 3 the words from 'if the limit' to the end are omitted. |
| 1984 c 28 | County Courts Act 1984 | (1) In section 15(1) the words from 'where the debt' to the end are omitted. |
| | | (2) In section 15(2), paragraph (a) and the words 'any hereditament or to' in paragraph (b) are omitted. |
| | | (3) Section 15(3) is omitted. |
| | | (4) In section 16, paragraph (b) and the word 'and' immediately before it are omitted. |
| | | (5) In section 21(1) the words from 'where the net annual value' to the end are omitted. |
| | | (6) In section 21(2) the words from 'being an action' to the end are omitted. |
| | | (7) In section 21, subsections (5) and (6) are omitted. |
| | | (8) In section 24(2)(c), the references to sections 30(2), 146(13) and 147(5) are omitted. |
| | | (9) In section 25, the words from 'where it is shown' to the end are omitted. |
| | | (10) In section 139(2) the words ', if the net annual value for rating of the land does not exceed the county court limit,' are omitted. |
| | | (11) In section 147(1), paragraph (b) of the definition of 'the county court limit' and, in paragraph (c) of that definition, the words 'or (b)' are omitted. |
| | * * * * * | |
| 1988 c 34 | Legal Aid Act 1988 | (1) In section 39(4) the words from 'notwithstanding' onwards are omitted. |
| | | (2) Paragraph 3(3)(b) of Schedule 3, and the word 'or' immediately preceding it, are omitted. |

* * * * *

PART II—STATUTORY INSTRUMENTS

| *Year and number* | *Title* | *Amendment* |
|---|---|---|
| SI 1981/1123 | County Courts Jurisdiction Order 1981 | In the table in article 2, the entries relating to the following provisions are omitted: <br> (1) sections 39, 40, 41, 45, 47, 68 and 146 of the County Courts Act 1959 and, in so far as it relates to the Law of Property Act 1925 and the Land Charges Act 1925, the First Schedule to that Act; <br> (2) section 69(3) of the Solicitors Act 1974; <br> (3) section 139(5) of the Consumer Credit Act 1974. |
| SI 1981/1749 | County Courts Appeals Order 1981 | The following is substituted for article 2: <br> '2. There shall be no right of appeal under section 77 of the County Courts Act 1984 without the leave either of the judge of the county court or of the Court of Appeal where: <br> (a) the claim (or counter-claim, if larger) is for an amount not exceeding— <br> (i) in the case of proceedings in which the county courts have jurisdiction by virtue of section 15 or 16 of the County Courts Act 1984, £2,500 and <br> (ii) in the case of proceedings in which the county courts have jurisdiction by virtue of section 23 or 32 of the County Courts Act 1984, £15,000; or <br> (b) the determination sought to be appealed from was made by the judge acting in an appellate capacity.' |

\*     \*     \*     \*     \*

# ARRANGEMENTS FOR PLACEMENT OF CHILDREN (GENERAL) REGULATIONS 1991

**Dated** 2 April 1991

**SI 1991 No 890**

ARRANGEMENT OF REGULATIONS

1. Citation, commencement and interpretation.
2. Application of Regulations.
3. Making of arrangements.
4. Considerations on making and contents of arrangements.

The Secretary of State for Health, in exercise of the powers conferred by sections 23(2)(a) and (f)(ii) and (5), 59(2) and (3) and 104(4) of, and paragraphs 12, 13 and 14 of Schedule 2, 4(1) and (2)(d) of Schedule 4, 7(1) and (2)(g) of Schedule 5 and paragraph 10(1) and (2)(f) of Schedule 6 to the Children Act 1989 and of all other powers enabling him in that behalf hereby makes the following Regulations—

*Citation, commencement and interpretation*

**1.** (1) These Regulations may be cited as the Arrangements for Placement of Children (General) Regulations 1991 and shall come into force on 14th October 1991.

(2) In these Regulations, unless the context otherwise requires—

'the Act' means the Children Act 1989;

'area authority' means, in relation to a child who is or is to be placed, the local authority in whose area the child is or is to be placed, where the child is looked after by a different authority;

'care case' means a case in which the child is in the care of a local authority;

'placement' subject to regulation 13 means—

(a) the provision of accommodation and maintenance by a local authority for any child whom they are looking after by any of the means specified in section 23(2)(a), *(b), (c), (d)* [(aa)] or *(f)* of the Act (accommodation and maintenance of child looked after by a local authority);

(b) the provision of accommodation for a child by a voluntary organisation by any of the means specified in section 59(1)(a), *(b), (c), (d)* [(aa)] or *(f)* of the Act (provision of accommodation by voluntary organisations), and

(c) the provision of accommodation for a child in a *registered children's home* [private children's home], and the expressions 'place' and 'placed' shall be construed accordingly;

'responsible authority' means—

(a) in relation to a placement by a local authority (including one in which the child is accommodated and maintained in a voluntary home or a *registered children's home* [private children's home]), the local authority which place the child,

(b) in relation to a placement by a voluntary organisation of a child who is not looked after by a local authority, the voluntary organisation which place the child, and

(c) in relation to a placement in a *registered children's home* [private children's home] of a child who is neither looked after by a local authority nor accommodated in such a home by a voluntary organisation, the person carrying on the home.

(3) Any notice required under these Regulations is to be given in writing and may be sent by post.

(4) In these Regulations, unless the context otherwise requires—

(a) any reference to a numbered regulation is to the regulation in these Regulations bearing that number and any reference in a regulation to a numbered paragraph is to the paragraph of that regulation bearing that number;

(b) any reference to a numbered Schedule is to the Schedule to those Regulations bearing that number.

**Note.** In para (2) definition 'placement' references to '(b), (c), (d)' in both places substituted by reference '(aa)' in square brackets and in para (c) words 'registered children's home' substituted by words 'private children's home' in square brackets, and in definition 'responsible authority' words 'registered children's home' in both places substituted by words 'private children's home' in square brackets, by SI 2002/546, reg 2 in relation to England as from 1 April 2002 and by SI 2002/2935, regs 5, 13 in relation to Wales as from 31 December 2002.

*Application of Regulations*

**2.** (1) Subject to paragraph (2) and (3), these Regulations apply to placements—

(a) by a local authority of any child;

(b) by a voluntary organisation of a child who is not looked after by a local authority;

(c) in a *registered children's home* [private children's home] of a child who is neither looked after by a local authority nor accommodated in such a home by a voluntary organisation, by a person carrying on the home.

(2) These Regulations shall not apply to placements of a child, otherwise than by a local authority or voluntary organisation—

*(a) in an independent school which is a children's home within the meaning of section 63(6) of the Act; or*

*(b) in a special school (as defined in section 182 of the Education Act 1993) which is not maintained by a local education authority, or otherwise out of public funds* [, in a school which is a children's home within the meaning of section 1(6) of the Care Standards Act 2000].

(3) These regulations shall not apply to any placement of a child for adoption under the Adoption Act 1976.

**Note.** In para (1)(c) words 'registered children's home' substituted by words 'private children's home' in square brackets and in para (2) words from '—(a) in an independent' to the end substituted by words ', in a school which is a children's home within the meaning of section (6) of the Care Standards Act 2000' in square brackets, by SI 2002/546, reg 2(1), (2) in relation to England as from 1 April 2002, and SI 2002/2935, regs 5(1), (2), 13 in relation to Wales as from 31 December 2002.

*Making of arrangements*

**3.** (1) Before they place a child the responsible authority shall, so far as is reasonably practicable, make immediate and long-term arrangements for that placement, and for promoting the welfare of the child who is to be placed.

(2) Where it is not practicable to make those arrangements before the placement, the responsible authority shall make them as soon as reasonably practicable thereafter.

(3) In the case of a child to whom section 20(11) of the Act applies (child aged 16 or over agreeing to be provided with accommodation) the arrangements shall so far as reasonably practicable be agreed by the responsible authority with the child before a placement is made and if that is not practicable as soon as reasonably practicable thereafter.

(4) In any other case in which a child is looked after or accommodated but is

not in care the arrangements shall so far as reasonably practicable be agreed by the responsible authority with—

(a)  a person with parental responsibility for the child, or

(b)  if there is no such person the person who is caring for the child,

before a placement is made and if that is not practicable as soon as reasonably practicable thereafter.

(5)  Any arrangements made by the responsible authority under this regulation shall be recorded in writing.

*Considerations on making and contents of arrangements*

**4.**   (1)  The considerations to which the responsible authority are to have regard so far as reasonably practicable in making the arrangements referred to in regulation 3 in each case are the general considerations specified in Schedule 1, the considerations concerning the health of a child specified in Schedule 2 and the considerations concerning the education of a child specified in Schedule 3.

(2)  Except in a care case, the arrangements referred to in regulation 3 shall include, where practicable, arrangements concerning the matters specified in Schedule 4.

*Notification of arrangements*

**5.**   (1)  The responsible authority shall, so far as is reasonably practicable, notify the following persons in writing of the arrangements to place a child, before the placement is made—

(a)  any person an indication of whose wishes and feelings have been sought under section 22(4), section 61(2) or section 64(2) of the Act (consultation prior to decision making in respect of children looked after by a local authority, provided with accommodation by a voluntary organisation or in a *registered children's home* [private children's home]);

(b)   *the district health authority for the district in which the child is living;*

[(b)the Primary Care Trust, or *if there is no Primary Care Trust,* the Health Authority, for the area in which the child is living and, if it is different, for the area in which the child is to be placed;]

(c)  the local education authority for the area in which the child is living [and, if it is different, for the area in which the child is to be placed];

(d)  the child's registered medical practitioner [and, where applicable, any registered medical practitioner with whom the child is to be registered following the placement];

(e)  *omitted;*

(f)  the area authority;

(g)  any person who is caring for the child immediately before the arrangements are made;

(h)  except in a care case, any person in whose favour a contact order is in force with respect to the child, and

(i)  in a care case, any person who has contact with the child pursuant to section 34 of the Act (contact with a child in care by parents etc) or to an order under that section.

(2)  Where it is not practicable to give the notification before the placement, it shall be given as soon as reasonably practicable thereafter.

(3)  The responsible authority shall send a copy of the arrangements referred to in regulation 3 or such part of the arrangements as they consider will not prejudice the welfare of the child with the notification referred to in paragraph (1) but in the case of notification to those specified in paragraph (1)(b) to (i) they shall send details of only such part of the arrangements as they consider those persons need to know.

**Note.** In para (1)(a) words 'registered children's home' substituted by words 'private children's home' in square brackets by SI 2002/546, reg 2(1), (2) in relation to England as from 1 April 2002 and by SI 2002/2935, reg 5(1), (2), 13 in relation to Wales as from 31 December 2002. Para (1)(b) substituted by SI 2002/546, reg 2(1), (5)(a) in relation to England as from 1 April 2002 and a corresponding amendment is made by SI 2002/3013, reg 2(1), (2)(a) in relation to Wales as from 1 January 2003. In para (1)(b) words 'if there is no Primary Care Trust' revoked by SI 2002/2469, reg 4, Sch 1, Pt 2, para 52 as from 1 October 2002. In para (1)(c) words from 'and, if it' to 'to be placed' in square brackets and in para (1)(d) words from 'and, where applicable' to 'following the placement' in square brackets inserted by SI 2002/546, reg 2(1), (5)(b), (c) in relation to England as from 1 April 2002 and by SI 2002/3013, reg 2(1), (2)(b), (c) in relation to Wales as from 1 January 2003.

## *Arrangements for contact*

**6.** In operating the arrangements referred to in paragraph 6 of Schedule 4, a voluntary organisation or a person carrying on a *registered children's home* [private children's home] shall, unless it is not reasonably practicable or consistent with the child's welfare, endeavour to promote contact between the child and the persons mentioned in that paragraph.

**Note.** Words 'registered children's home' substituted by words 'private children's home' in square brackets by SI 2002/546, reg 2(1), (2) in relation to England as from 1 April 2002 and by SI 2002/2935, regs 5, 13 as from 31 December 2002.

## *Health requirements* [Health Assessments]

**7.** *(1) A responsible authority shall, so far as reasonably practicable before a placement is made and if that is not reasonably practicable as soon as practicable after the placement is made—*
  *(a) ensure that arrangements are made for the child to be examined by a registered medical practitioner and*
  *(b) require the practitioner who has carried out the examination to make a written assessment of the state of health of the child and his need for health care*
*unless the child has been so examined and such assessment has been made within a period of three months immediately preceding the placement or the child is of sufficient understanding and he refuses to submit to the examination.*

*(2) During the placement of the child the responsible authority shall ensure that arrangements are made for a child to be provided with health care services, including medical and dental care and treatment.*

[**7.** (1) Subject to paragraphs (3) and (4), a responsible authority shall—
  (a) before making a placement, or if that is not reasonably practicable, as soon as reasonably practicable after a placement is made, make arrangements for a registered medical practitioner to conduct an assessment, which may include a physical examination, of the child's state of health;
  (b) require the registered medical practitioner who conducts the assessment to prepare a written report of the assessment which addresses the matters listed in Schedule 2; and
  (c) having regard to the matters listed in Schedule 2 and, unless paragraph (4) applies, to the assessment report, prepare a plan for the future health care of the child if one is not already in existence.

(2) A responsible authority shall ensure that each child is provided during the placement with—
  (a) health care services, including medical and dental care and treatment; and
  (b) advice and guidance on health, personal care and health promotion issues appropriate to his needs.

(3) Paragraph (1) does not apply if within a period of three months immediately preceding the placement the child's health has been assessed, and a report of the assessment prepared in accordance with that paragraph.

(4) Sub-paragraphs (a) and (b) of paragraph (1) do not apply if the child, being of sufficient understanding to do so, refuses to consent to the assessment.]

**Note.** Substituted by SI 2002/546, reg 2(1), (6) in relation to England as from 1 April 2002 and by SI 2002/3013, reg 2(1), (3) in relation to Wales as from 1 January 2003.

*Establishment of records*

**8.**   (1) A responsible authority shall establish, if one is not already in existence, a written case record in respect of each child whom it places.

(2) The record shall include—

(a)   a copy of the arrangements referred to in regulation 3;

(b)   a copy of any written report in its possession concerning the welfare of the child;

(c)   a copy of any document considered or record established in the course of or as a result of a review of the child's case;

(d)   details of arrangements for contact, of contact orders and of other court orders relating to the child; and

(e)   details of any arrangements whereby another person acts on behalf of the local authority or organisation which placed the child.

*Retention and confidentiality of records*

**9.**   (1) A case record relating to a child who is placed shall be retained by the responsible authority until the seventy-fifth anniversary of the date of birth of the child to whom it relates or, if the child dies before attaining the age of 18, for a period of 15 years beginning with the date of his death.

(2) The requirement of paragraph (1) may be complied with either by retaining the original written record, or a copy of it, or by keeping all of the information from such record in some other accessible form (such as by means of a computer).

(3) A responsible authority shall secure the safe keeping of case records and shall take all necessary steps to ensure that information contained in them is treated as confidential, subject only to—

(a)   any provision of or made under or by virtue of, a statute under which access to such records or information may be obtained or given;

(b)   any court order under which access to such records or information may be obtained or given.

*Register*

**10.**   (1) A local authority shall, in respect of every child placed in their area (by them and any other responsible authority) and every child placed by them outside their area, enter into a register to be kept for the purpose—

(a)   the particulars specified in paragraph (3), and

(b)   such of the particulars specified in paragraph (4) as may be appropriate.

(2) A voluntary organisation and a person carrying on a *registered children's home* [private children's home] shall, in respect of every child placed by them, enter into a register to be kept for the purpose—

(a)   the particulars specified in paragraph (3), and

(b)   such of the particulars specified in paragraph (4) as may be appropriate.

(3) The particulars to be entered into the register in accordance with paragraph (1) or (2) are—

(a)   the name, sex and date of birth of the child;

(b)   the name and address of the person with whom the child is placed and, if different, of those of the child's parent or other person not being a parent of his who has parental responsibility for him;

(c)   in the case of a child placed on behalf of a local authority by a voluntary organisation or in a *registered children's home* [private children's home], the name of the authority;

(d) whether the child's name is entered on any local authority register indicating that the child is at risk of being abused;

(e) whether the child's name is entered on the register maintained under paragraph 2 of Schedule 2 to the Act (register of disabled children);

(f) the date on which each placement of the child began and terminated and the reason for each termination;

(g) in a care case the name of the local authority in whose care the child is;

(h) the legal provisions under which the child is being looked after or cared for.

(4) The additional particulars to be entered in the register, where appropriate in accordance with paragraph (1) or (2) are—

(a) in the case of a child placed by a local authority in respect of whom arrangements have been made for the area authority to carry out functions pursuant to regulation 12 a note that the arrangements were made and the name of the other local authority with whom they were made; and

(b) in the case of a child who has been placed, in respect of whom arrangements have been made for supervision of the placement to be carried out on behalf of a responsible authority (otherwise than pursuant to regulation 12), a note that the arrangements were made and the name of person with whom the arrangements were made.

(5) Entries in registers kept in accordance with this regulation shall be retained until the child to whom the entry relates attains the age of 23 or, if the child has died before attaining 23, the period of 5 years beginning with the date of his death.

(6) The requirements of paragraph (1) may be complied with either by retaining the original register, or a copy of it, or by keeping all of the information from such a register in some other accessible form (such as by means of a computer).

(7) A responsible authority shall secure the safe keeping of registers kept in accordance with this regulation and shall take all necessary steps to ensure that information contained in them is treated as confidential, subject only to—

(a) any provision of or made under or by virtue of a statute under which access to such registers or information may be obtained or given;

(b) any court order under which access to such registers or information may be obtained or given.

**Note.** Words 'registered children's home' in both places substituted by words 'private children's home' in square brackets by SI 2002/546, reg 2(1), (2) in relation to England as from 1 April 2002 and by SI 2002/2935, regs 5, 13 in relation to Wales as from 31 December 2002.

*Access by* guardians ad litem *[officers of the service] to records and register*

**11.** Each voluntary organisation, where they are not acting as an authorised person, and every person carrying on a *registered children's home* [private children's home] shall provide a *guardian ad litem* [officer of the service] of a child—

(a) such access as may be required to—

(i) case records and registers maintained in accordance with these Regulations; and

(ii) the information from such records or registers held in whatever form (such as by means of computer);

(b) such copies of the records or entries in the registers as he may require.

**Note.** Words 'guardians ad litem' and 'guardian ad litem' substituted by words 'officers of the service' and 'officer of the service' in square brackets and words 'registered children's home' substituted by words 'private children's home' in square brackets by SI 2002/546, reg 2(1), (2), (7) in relation to England as from 1 April 2002 and by SI 2002/2935, regs 5, 13 in relation to Wales as from 31 December 2002.

*Arrangements between local authorities and area authorities*

**12.** Where arrangements are made by a local authority which is looking after a child with an area authority for the area authority to carry out functions in relation to a placement on behalf of the local authority—

(a) the local authority shall supply the area authority with all such information as is necessary to enable the area authority to carry out those functions on behalf of the local authority;

(b) the area authority shall keep the local authority informed of the progress of the child and, in particular, shall furnish reports to the local authority following each visit to the home in which the child is placed and following each review of the case of the child carried out by the area authority on behalf of the local authority;

(c) the local authority and the area authority shall consult each other from time to time as necessary, and as soon as reasonably practicable after each such review of the case of the child, with regard to what action is required in relation to him.

*Application of Regulations to short-term placements*

**13.** (1) This regulation applies where a responsible authority has arranged to place a child in a series of short-term placements at the same place and the arrangement is such that no single placement is to last for more than four weeks and the total duration of the placements is not to exceed 120 days in any period of 12 months.

(2) Any series of short-term placements to which this regulation applies may be treated as a single placement for the purposes of these Regulations.

---

SCHEDULE 1 Regulation 4(1)

CONSIDERATIONS TO WHICH RESPONSIBLE AUTHORITIES ARE TO HAVE REGARD

**1.** In the case of a child who is in care, whether an application should be made to discharge the care order.

**2.** Where the responsible authority is a local authority whether the authority should seek a change in the child's legal status.

**3.** Arrangements for contact, and whether there is any need for changes in the arrangements in order to promote contact with the child's family and others so far as is consistent with his welfare.

**4.** The responsible authority's immediate and long term arrangements for the child, previous arrangements in respect of the child, and whether a change in those arrangements is needed and consideration of alternative courses of action.

**5.** Where the responsible authority is a local authority, whether an independent visitor should be appointed if one has not already been appointed.

**6.** Whether arrangements need to be made for the time when the child will no longer be looked after by the responsible authority.

**7.** Whether plans need to be made to find a permanent substitute family for the child.

SCHEDULE 2 Regulation 4(1)

HEALTH CONSIDERATIONS TO WHICH RESPONSIBLE AUTHORITIES ARE TO HAVE REGARD

**1.** The child's state of health [including his physical, emotional and mental health].

**2.** The child's health history [including, as far as practicable, his family health history].

**3.** The effect of the child's health and health history on his development.

**4.** Existing arrangements for the child's medical and dental care and treatment and health and dental surveillance.

**5.** The possible need for an appropriate course of action which should be identified to assist necessary change of such care, treatment or surveillance.

**6.** The possible need for preventive measures, such as vaccination and immunisation, and screening for vision and hearing [and for advice and guidance on health, personal care and health promotion issues appropriate to the child's needs].

**Note.** In para 1 words 'including his physical, emotional and mental health' in square brackets, in para 2 words 'including, as far as practicable, his family health history' in square brackets and in para 6 words from 'and for advice' to 'child's needs' in square brackets, inserted by SI 2002/546, reg 2(1), (8) in relation to England as from 1 April 2002 and by SI 2002/3013, reg 2(1), (4) in relation to Wales as from 1 January 2003.

SCHEDULE 3                                                    Regulation 4(1)

EDUCATIONAL CONSIDERATIONS TO WHICH RESPONSIBLE AUTHORITIES ARE TO HAVE REGARD

**1.** The child's educational history.
**2.** The need to achieve continuity in the child's education.
**3.** The need to identify any educational need which the child may have and to take action to meet that need.
**4.** The need to carry out any assessment in respect of any special educational need under the *Education Act 1981* [Education Act 1996] and meet any such needs identified in a statement of special educational needs made under *section 7* [section 324] of that Act.

**Note.** In para 4 words 'Education Act 1981' and 'section 7' substituted by words 'Education Act 1996' and 'section 324' in square brackets by SI 2002/546, reg 2(1), (9) in relation to England from 1 April 2002 and by SI 2002/2935, regs 5(1), (6), 13 in relation to Wales as from 31 December 2002.

SCHEDULE 4                                                    Regulation 4(2)

MATTERS TO BE INCLUDED IN ARRANGEMENTS TO ACCOMMODATE CHILDREN WHO ARE NOT IN CARE

**1.** The type of accommodation to be provided and its address together with the name of any person who will be responsible for the child at that accommodation on behalf of the responsible authority.
**2.** The details of any services to be provided for the child.
**3.** The respective responsibilities of the responsible authority and—
  (a) the child;
  (b) any parent of his; and
  (c) any person who is not a parent of his but who has parental responsibility for him.
**4.** What delegation there has been by the persons referred to in paragraph 3(b) and (c) of this Schedule to the responsible authority of parental responsibility for the child's day to day care.
**5.** The arrangements for involving those persons and the child in decision making with respect to the child having regard—
  (a) to the local authority's duty under sections 20(6) (involvement of children before provision of accommodation) and 22(3) to (5) of the Act (general duties of the local authority in relation to children looked after by them);
  (b) the duty of the voluntary organisation under section 61(1) and (2) of the Act (duties of voluntary organisations); and
  (c) the duty of the person carrying on a *registered children's home* [private children's home] under section 64(1) and (2) of the Act (welfare of children in *registered children's homes* [private children's homes]).
**6.** The arrangements for contact between the child and—
  (a) his parents;
  (b) any person who is not a parent of his but who has parental responsibility for him; and
  (c) any relative, friend or other person connected with him,

and if appropriate, the reasons why contact with any such person would not be reasonably practicable or would be inconsistent with the child's welfare.

**7.** The arrangements for notifying changes in arrangements for contact to any of the persons referred to in paragraph 6.

**8.** In the case of a child aged 16 or over whether section 20(11) (accommodation of a child of 16 or over despite parental opposition) applies.

**9.** The expected duration of arrangements and the steps which should apply to bring the arrangements to an end, including arrangements for rehabilitation of the child with the person with whom he was living before the voluntary arrangements were made or some other suitable person, having regard in particular, in the case of a local authority looking after a child, to section 23(6) of the Act (duty to place children where practicable with parents etc) and paragraph 15 of Schedule 2 to the Act (maintenance of contact between child and family).

**Note.** In para 5(c) words 'registered children's home' and 'registered children's homes' substituted by words 'private children's home' and 'private children's homes' in square brackets by SI 2002/546, reg 2(1), (2) in relation to England as from 1 April 2002 and by SI 2002/2935, regs 5(1), (2), 13 in relation to Wales as from 31 December 2002.

## CONTACT WITH CHILDREN REGULATIONS 1991

**Dated** 2 April 1991

**SI 1991 No 891**

The Secretary of State for Health, in exercise of the powers conferred by section 34(8) of the Children Act 1989 and all other powers enabling him in that behalf, hereby makes the following Regulations—

*Citation, commencement and interpretation*

**1.** (1) These Regulations may be cited as the Contact with Children Regulations 1991 and shall come into force on 14th October 1991.

(2) Any notice required under these Regulations is to be given in writing and may be sent by post.

(3) In these Regulations unless the context requires otherwise—

(a) any reference to a numbered section is to the section in the Children Act 1989 bearing that number;

(b) any reference to a numbered regulation is to the regulation in these Regulations bearing that number; and

(c) any reference to a Schedule is to the Schedule to these Regulations.

*Local authority refusal of contact with child*

**2.** Where a local authority has decided under section 34(6) to refuse contact with a child that would otherwise be required by virtue of section 34(1) or a court order, the authority shall, as soon as the decision has been made, notify the following persons in writing of those parts of the information specified in the Schedule as the authority considers those persons need to know—

(a) the child, if he is of sufficient understanding;

(b) the child's parents;

(c) any guardian of his;

(d) where there was a residence order in force with respect to the child immediately before the care order was made, the person in whose favour the order was made;

(e) where immediately before the care order was made, a person had care of the child by virtue of an order made in the exercise of the High Court's inherent jurisdiction with respect to children, that person; and

(f) any other person whose wishes and feelings the authority consider to be relevant.

*Departure from terms of court order on contact under section 34*

**3.** The local authority may depart from the terms of any order under section 34 (parental contact etc with children in care) by agreement between the local authority and the person in relation to whom the order is made and in the following circumstance and subject to the following condition—

    (a) where the child is of sufficient understanding, subject to agreement also with him; and

    (b) a written notification shall be sent to the persons specified in regulation 2 containing those parts of the information specified in the Schedule as the authority considers those persons need to know, within seven days of the agreement to depart from the terms of the order.

*Notification of variation or suspension of contact arrangements*

**4.** Where a local authority varies or suspends any arrangements made (otherwise than under an order made under section 34) with a view to affording any person contact with a child in the care of that local authority, written notification shall be sent to those persons specified in regulation 2 containing those parts of the information specified in the Schedule as the authority considers those persons need to know, as soon as the decision is made to vary or suspend the arrangements.

---

SCHEDULE                                           Regulations 2, 3, and 4

INFORMATION TO BE CONTAINED IN WRITTEN NOTIFICATION

**1.** Local authority's decision.
**2.** Date of the decision.
**3.** Reasons for the decision.
**4.** Duration (if applicable).
**5.** Remedies available in case of dissatisfaction.

---

## DEFINITION OF INDEPENDENT VISITORS (CHILDREN) REGULATIONS 1991

**Dated** 2 April 1991

**SI 1991 No 892**

The Secretary of State for Health, in exercise of the powers conferred by paragraph 17(7) of Schedule 2 to the Children Act 1989 and of all other powers enabling him in that behalf hereby makes the following Regulations:

*Citation and commencement*

**1.** These Regulations may be cited as the Definition of Independent Visitors (Children) Regulations 1991 and shall come into force on 14th October 1991.

*Independent visitors*

**2.** A person appointed by a local authority as an independent visitor under paragraph 17(1) of Schedule 2 to the Children Act 1989 shall be regarded as independent of the local authority appointing him in the following circumstances:

    (a) where the person appointed is not connected with the local authority by virtue of being—

> (i) a member of the local authority or any of their committees or sub-committees, whether elected or co-opted [, or a council manager of the Local Authority (within the meaning of section 11(4)(b) of the Local Government Act 2000 (local authority executives))]; or
> (ii) an officer of the local authority employed in the Social Services Department of that authority; or
> (iii) a spouse of any such person;
> (b) where the child who is to receive visits from the person appointed is accommodated by an organisation other than the local authority, and the person appointed is not—
> > (i) a member of that organisation; or
> > (ii) a patron or trustee of that organisation; or
> > (iii) an employee of that organisation, whether paid or not; or
> > (iv) a spouse of any such person.

**Note.** In para 2(a)(i) words from ', or a council' to 'executives))' in square brackets inserted by SI 2001/2237, arts 1(2), 2(x), 40 in relation to England as from 11 July 2001 and by SI 2002/808, arts 2(v), 36 in relation to Wales as from 1 April 2002.

## PLACEMENT OF CHILDREN WITH PARENTS ETC REGULATIONS 1991

**Dated** 2 April 1991

**SI 1991 No 893**

ARRANGEMENT OF REGULATIONS

SCHEDULES

The Secretary of State for Health, in exercise of the powers conferred by sections 23(5) and (9) and 104(4) of, and paragraph 14 of Schedule 2 to, the Children Act 1989 and of all other powers enabling him in that behalf hereby makes the following Regulations—

*Citation, commencement and interpretation*

**1.** (1) These Regulations may be cited as the Placement of Children with Parents etc Regulations 1991 and shall come into force on 14th October 1991.

(2) In these Regulations, unless the context otherwise requires—

'the Act' means the Children Act 1989;

'area authority' means, in relation to a child who is or is to be placed, the local authority in whose area the child is or is to be placed where the child is in the care of a different authority;

*'guardian ad litem' means a guardian ad litem appointed pursuant to section 41 of the Act (representation of child and his interests in certain proceedings) or under rules made under section 65 of the Adoption Act 1976 (panels for selection of guardians ad litem and reporting officers);*

'placement' means allowing a child who is in the care of a local authority to live pursuant to section 23(5) of the Act (placement of a child in care with parents etc) with—

(a)  a parent of the child,

(b)  a person who is not a parent of the child but who has parental responsibility for him, or

(c)  where there was a residence order in force with respect to him immediately before the care order was made a person in whose favour the residence order was made,

and the expressions 'place' and 'placed' shall be construed accordingly and 'placed with' a person means being allowed to live with that person pursuant to that section;

'placement decision' means a decision to place a child which is made in accordance with regulation 5(2) (placement decisions by director of social services or nominated person);

'supervisory duties' means the duties imposed by regulation 9 (support and supervision of placements).

(3)  Any notice required under these Regulations is to be in writing and any such notice may be sent by post.

(4)  In these Regulations, unless the context otherwise requires—

(a)  any reference to a numbered regulation is to the regulation in these Regulations bearing that number and any reference in a regulation to a numbered paragraph is to the paragraph of that regulation bearing that number;

(b)  any reference to a numbered Schedule is to the Schedule to these Regulations bearing that number.

**Note.** In para (2) definition 'guardian ad litem' revoked by SI 2002/546, reg 3(1), (2) in relation to England as from 1 April 2002 and by SI 2002/2935, regs (1), (2), 13 in relation to Wales as from 31 December 2002.

*Scope of Regulations*

**2.**   (1)  These Regulations shall apply to every child who is in the care of a local authority and who is or is proposed to be placed.

(2)  Where a child who is to be placed is aged 16 or over regulations 3, 6, 7, 8, 9 and 12 shall not apply.

(3)  These Regulations shall not apply to the placement of a child for adoption pursuant to the Adoption Act 1976.

(4)  Nothing in these Regulations shall require the temporary removal of a child from the person with whom he is already living and with whom he may be placed, before a placement decision is made concerning him.

(5)  These Regulations shall not apply in a case to the extent that they are incompatible with any order made by a court under section 34 of the Act (parental contact with children in care etc), or any direction of a court which has effect under paragraph 16(5) of Schedule 14 to the Act (transitional provision as to directions) in that case.

*Enquiries and assessment*

**3.**   (1) Before a placement decision is made, a local authority shall make all necessary enquiries in respect of—

(a)  the health of the child;

(b)  the suitability of the person with whom it is proposed that the child should be placed;

(c)  the suitability of the proposed accommodation, including the proposed sleeping arrangements;

(d)  the educational and social needs of the child; and

(e)  the suitability of all other members of the household, aged 16 and over, in which it is proposed a child will live.

(2)  In considering the suitability of a person as required by paragraph (1)(b) or (e), the local authority shall, so far as practicable, take into account the particulars specified in paragraphs 1 and 2 respectively of Schedule 1.

*Duties of local authorities in relation to placements*

**4.**   A local authority shall satisfy themselves that the placement of a child is the most suitable way of performing their duty under section 22(3) of the Act (general duty of local authority in respect of children looked after by them) and that the placement is the most suitable having regard to all the circumstances.

*Placement decisions by director of social services or nominated person*

**5.**   (1) A placement shall be made only after a placement decision has been made.

(2)  The decision to place a child shall be made on behalf of the local authority by the director of social services appointed by the authority under section 6 of the Local Authority Social Services Act 1970 (director of social services) or by an officer of the local authority nominated in writing for that purpose by the director.

*Immediate placements*

**6.**   (1) Subject to paragraph (2), nothing in regulation 3 shall prevent the immediate placement of a child pursuant to a placement decision in circumstances in which the local authority consider that to be necessary and in accordance with their duty under section 22(3) of the Act and in such a case the authority shall take steps to ensure that the provisions of these Regulations that would otherwise have to be complied with before the placement decision is made are complied with as soon as practicable thereafter.

(2)  Before an immediate placement is made pursuant to this regulation a local authority shall—

(a)  arrange for the person with whom the child is to be placed to be interviewed in order to obtain as much of the information specified in paragraph 1 of Schedule 1 as can be readily ascertained at the interview, and

(b)  arrange to obtain as much of the information specified in paragraph 2 of Schedule 1 in relation to other members of the household aged 16 and over, in which it is proposed the child will live, as can be readily ascertained at the time of that interview.

*Provisions of agreements*

**7.**   Following a placement decision the local authority shall seek to reach agreement with the person with whom the child is to be placed on all the particulars, so far as is practicable, specified in Schedule 2 and the placement shall not be put into effect unless and until such an agreement on all such particulars has been reached and recorded in writing and a copy of it has been given or sent to that person.

*Notification of placements*

**8.** (1) Subject to paragraph (3) the local authority shall, so far as practicable, give notice to all the persons whose wishes and feelings have been sought in relation to the decision to place the child pursuant to section 22(4) of the Act (persons to be consulted concerning local authority decisions) and to those persons specified in paragraph (4) of—
  (a) the placement decision, and
  (b) details of where the child is to be placed.
(2) Where the child is placed with a person other than a parent the local authority's notice under paragraph (1) to the persons referred to in the paragraph shall contain—
  (a) the name and address of the person with whom the child is placed;
  (b) particulars of arrangements for contact with the child;
  (c) any other particulars relating to the care and welfare of the child which it appears to the local authority ought to be supplied.
(3) A local authority shall not be required to give notice under paragraph (1) in the case of a person whose whereabouts are unknown to the authority, or cannot be readily ascertained, or in any case where the authority determine that to give such notice would not be in accordance with their duty under section 22(3) of the Act.
(4) For the purposes of paragraph (1) the persons specified are—
  *(a) the district health authority for the district in which the child is living;*
  [(a) the Primary Care Trust, or ..., the Health Authority, for the area in which the child is living and, if it is different, for the area in which the child is to be placed;]
  (b) the local education authority for the area in which the child is living [and, if it is different, for the area in which the child is to be placed];
  (c) the child's registered medical practitioner [and, where applicable, any registered medical practitioner with whom the child is to be registered following the placement];
  (d) the area authority;
  (e) any person, not being an officer of a local authority, who has been caring for the child immediately before the placement; and
  (f) where there was a residence order in force with respect to the child immediately before the care order was made, the person in whose favour the residence order was made.

**Note.** Para (4)(a) substituted in relation to England by SI 2002/546, reg 3(1), (3)(a) as from 1 April 2002 and words (omitted) therein revoked by SI 2002/2469, reg 4, Sch 1, Pt 2, para 53 as from 1 October 2002. In para (4)(b) words from 'and, if it is' to 'to be placed' in square brackets and in sub-para (c) words from 'and, where applicable' to 'following the placement' in square brackets inserted in relation to England by SI 2002/546, ref 3(1), (3)(b), (c) as from 1 April 2002.

*Support and supervision of placements*

**9.** (1) A local authority shall satisfy themselves that the welfare of each child who has been placed by them continues to be appropriately provided for by his placement and for that purpose the authority shall—
  (a) give such advice and assistance to the person with whom the child is placed as appears to the local authority to be necessary;
  (b) make arrangements for a person authorised by the local authority to visit the child from time to time as necessary but in any event—
    (i) within one week of the beginning of the placement,
    (ii) at intervals of not more than 6 weeks during the first year of the placement,
    (iii) thereafter at intervals of not more than three months and also whenever reasonably requested by the child or the person with whom the child is placed,

and for the person so authorised to make arrangements, so far as practicable, on each visit to see the child alone.

(2)  On each occasion on which a child is visited in pursuance of this regulation by any person authorised by the local authority which placed the child the local authority shall cause a written report on the child to be prepared by that person.

*Placements outside England and Wales*

**10.**   A local authority which make arrangements to place a child outside England and Wales in accordance with the provisions of paragraph 19 of Schedule 2 to the Act (placement of child in care outside England and Wales) shall take steps to ensure that, so far as is reasonably practicable, requirements corresponding with the requirements of these Regulations are complied with in relation to that child as would be required to be complied with under these Regulations if the child were placed in England and Wales.

*Termination of placements*

**11.**   (1) If it appears to a local authority that the placement is no longer in accordance with their duty in respect of the child under section 22(3) of the Act or would prejudice the safety of the child, they shall terminate the placement and shall remove the child forthwith from the person with whom he is placed.

(2)  Where, in the case of a child who has been placed in the area of an area authority by another local authority, it appears to the area authority that it would be detrimental to the welfare of the child if he continued to be so placed, the area authority may remove the child forthwith from the person with whom he is placed.

(3)  Where a child is removed under paragraph (2) the area authority shall forthwith notify the other authority of that fact and that authority shall make other arrangements for the care of the child as soon as is practicable.

*Notification of termination of placements*

**12.**   In relation to a decision to terminate a placement a local authority shall, so far as is reasonably practicable—

(a)  give notice in writing of any decision to terminate the placement before it is terminated to—
  (i)   the child, having regard to his age and understanding,
  (ii)  the other persons whose wishes and feelings have been sought in relation to the decision to terminate the placement pursuant to section 22(4) of the Act,
  (iii) the person with whom the child is placed,
  (iv)  the other persons to whom regulation 8(1) refers; and
(b)  give notice in writing of the termination of the placement to all those persons, other than the child and the person with whom the child is placed.

*Application of Regulations to short-term placements*

**13.**   (1) This regulation applies where a local authority has arranged to place a child in a series of short-term placements with the same person and the arrangement is such that no single placement is to last for more than four weeks and the total duration of the placements is not to exceed 120 days in any period of 12 months.

(2)  Any series of short-term placements to which this regulation applies may be treated as a single placement for the purpose of these Regulations.

(3)  Regulation 9(1)(b) shall apply in relation to short-term placements to which this regulation applies as if for paragraphs (1)(b)(i) to (iii) of that regulation there were substituted—

'(i)  on a day when the child is in fact placed ('a placement day') within the first seven placement days of a series of short-term placements, and

(ii)  thereafter, if the series of short-term placements continues, on placement days falling at intervals of not more than six months or, if the interval between placements exceeds six months, during the next placement.'

SCHEDULE 1                                                    Regulation 3(2)

PARTICULARS TO BE TAKEN INTO ACCOUNT IN CONSIDERING SUITABILITY OF PERSONS AND HOUSEHOLDS

**1.**  In respect of a person with whom it is proposed the child should be placed—
  (a)  age;
  (b)  health;
  (c)  personality;
  (d)  marital status and particulars of any previous marriage;
  (e)  previous experience of looking after and capacity to look after children and capacity to care for the child;
  (f)  the result of any applications to have a child placed with him or to adopt a child or of any application for registration *under section 71 (registration as child-minder) of the Act* [for child minding or day care] and details of any prohibition on his acting as a child-minder, providing day care, or caring for foster children privately or children in a voluntary or registered children's home;
  (g)  details of children in his household, whether living there or not;
  (h)  religious persuasion and degree of observance, racial origin and cultural and linguistic background;
  (i)  past and present employment and leisure activities and interests;
  (j)  details of the living standards and particulars of accommodation of his household;
  (k)  *subject to the provisions of the Rehabilitation of Offenders Act 1974, any criminal conviction.*
  [(k)  details of criminal offences of which he has been convicted, or in respect of which he has been cautioned by a constable and which, at the time the caution was given, he admitted.]

**Note.**  In para 1(f) words 'under section 71 (registration as child-minder) of the Act' substituted by words 'for child minding or day care' in square brackets and para (k) substituted by SI 2002/546, reg 3(1), (4) in relation to England as from 1 April 2002.

**2.**  In respect of members of the household aged 16 and over of a person with whom a child is to be placed, so far as is practicable, all the particulars specified in paragraph (1)(a), (b), (c), (d), (f), (i), and (k) of this Schedule.

SCHEDULE 2                                                      Regulation 7

PARTICULARS ON WHICH THERE SHOULD BE AGREEMENT WITH THE PERSON WITH WHOM A CHILD IS TO BE PLACED

**1.**  The authority's plans for the child and the objectives of the placement.
**2.**  The arrangements for support of the placement.
**3.**  Arrangements for visiting the child in connection with the supervision of the placement by the person authorised by or on behalf of the local authority or area authority, and frequency of visits and reviews of the child's case under regulations made under section 26 of the Act (review of cases).
**4.**  Arrangements for contact, if any (including prohibition of contact) in pursuance of section 34 of the Act (parental contact etc for children in care).

**5.** Removal of the child from the placement in the circumstances specified in regulation 11.

**6.** The need to notify the local authority of relevant changes in circumstances of the person with whom the child is placed, including any intention to change his address, changes in the household in which the child will live and any serious occurrence involving the child such as injury or death.

**7.** The provision of a statement concerning the health of the child, the child's need for health care and surveillance, and the child's educational needs and the local authority's arrangements to provide for all such needs.

**8.** Any arrangements for any delegation and exercise of responsibility for consent to medical examination or treatment.

**9.** The need to ensure that any information relating to any child or his family or any other person given in confidence to the person with whom the child is placed in connection with the placement is kept confidential and that such information is not disclosed to any person without the consent of the local authority.

**10.** The circumstances in which it is necessary to obtain in advance the approval of the local authority for the child living, even temporarily, in a household other than the household of the person with whom the child has been placed.

**11.** The arrangements for requesting a change in the agreement.

## REPRESENTATIONS PROCEDURE (CHILDREN) REGULATIONS 1991

**Dated** 2 April 1991

**SI 1991 No 894**

ARRANGEMENT OF REGULATIONS

PART I

*Introductory*

1. Citation and commencement.
2. Interpretation.

PART II

*Representations and their consideration*

3. Local authority action.
3A. Local resolution.
4. Preliminaries.
5. Appointment of independent person.
6. Consideration by local authority with independent person.
7. Withdrawal of representations.
8. Notification to complainant and reference to panel.
9. Recommendations.

PART III

*Review of procedure*

10. Monitoring of operation of procedure.

PART IV

*Application of Regulations to voluntary organisations and registered children's homes*

11. Application to voluntary organisations and registered children's homes.
11A. Exceptions to application of Regulations.

12.    Special cases.

The Secretary of State for Health, in exercise of the powers conferred by sections 24(15) and 26(5) and (6), 59(4) and (5) and 104(4) of, and paragraph 10(2)(1) of Schedule 6 and paragraph 6 of Schedule 7 to, the Children Act 1989, and all other powers enabling him in that behalf, hereby makes the following Regulations—

PART I

INTRODUCTORY

*Citation and commencement*

**1.**    These Regulations may be cited as the Representations Procedure (Children) Regulations 1991, and shall come into force on 14th October 1991.

*Interpretation*

**2.**    (1)  In these Regulations, unless the context otherwise requires—
'the Act' means the Children Act 1989;
'complainant' means a person *qualifying for advice and assistance* [falling within section 23A, 23C, 24 or 24B(3) of the Act making any representations] about the discharge of their functions by a local authority under Part III of the Act in relation to him, or a person specified in section 26(3)(a) to (e) of the Act making any representations;
'independent person' means in relation to representations made to, or treated as being made to, a local authority, a person who is neither a member nor an officer of that authority;
'panel' means a panel of 3 persons;
'representations' means representations referred to in sections *24(14)* [24D(1)] or 26(3) of the Act;
['section 26A advocate' means a person who is appointed to provide assistance to the complainant under arrangements made by a local authority under section 26A(1) of theAct].
(2)  Any notice required under these Regulations is to be given in writing and may be sent by post.
(3)  In these Regulations unless the context requires otherwise—
(a)  any reference to a numbered section is to the section in the Act bearing that number;
(b)  any reference to a numbered regulation is to the regulation in these Regulations bearing that number, and any reference in a regulation to a numbered paragraph is to the paragraph of that regulation bearing that number.

**Note.** In para (1) definition 'complainant' words 'qualifying for advice and assistance' substituted by words from 'falling within' to 'any representations' and in definition 'representations' reference to '24(14)' substituted by reference to '24D(1)' in square brackets by SI 2001/2189, reg 13(1), (2) in relation to Wales and by SI 2001/2874, reg 13(1), (2) in relation to England, both from 1 October 2001. In para (1) definition 'section 26A advocate' inserted by SI 2004/719, regs 6, 7 in relation to England as from 1 April 2004.

PART II

REPRESENTATIONS AND THEIR CONSIDERATION

*Local authority action*

**3.**    (1)  The local authority shall appoint one of their officers to assist the authority in the co-ordination of all aspects of their consideration of the representations.
(2)  The local authority shall take all reasonable steps to ensure that everyone involved in the handling of the representations, including independent persons, is familiar with the procedure set out in these Regulations.

*[Local resolution*

**3A.** (1) Where a local authority receive any representation from a person specified in section 24D(1) they shall—

(a) provide the person appointed under regulation 3(1) with a written summary of the representation;

(b) endeavour by informal means to reach a settlement to the satisfaction of the complainant within 14 days; and

(c) if at the end of 14 days no resolution has been achieved, notify the person appointed under regulation 3(1).]

**Note.** Inserted by SI 2001/2874, regs 13(1), (3), 14 in relation to England as from 1 October 2001.

*Preliminaries*

**4.** (1) Where *a local authority receive representations from any complainant, except from a person to whom section 26(3)(e) may apply, they*—

[(a) a person to whom it applies is dissatisfied with the outcome of the procedure set out in regulation 3A; or

(b) a local authority receive representations from any other complainant, except from a person to whom section 26(3)(e) may apply,

the local authority] shall send to the complainant an explanation of the procedure set out in these Regulations, and offer assistance and guidance on the use of the procedure, or give advice on where he may obtain it.

(2) Where oral representations are made, the authority shall forthwith cause them to be recorded in writing, and sent to the complainant [and any section 26A advocate], who shall be given the opportunity to comment on the accuracy of the record.

(2A) The authority shall consider any comments made by the complainant [and any section 26A advocate] under paragraph (2) and shall make any amendments to the record which they consider to be necessary.

(3) For the purposes of the following provisions of these Regulations the written record referred to in paragraph (2), as amended where appropriate in accordance with paragraph (2A), shall be deemed to be the representations.

(4) Where a local authority receive representations from a person to whom they consider section 26(3)(e) may apply they shall—

(a) forthwith consider whether the person has a sufficient interest in the child's welfare to warrant his representations being considered by them;

(b) if they consider that he has a sufficient interest, cause the representations to be dealt with in accordance with the provisions of these Regulations, and send to the complainant an explanation of the procedure set out in the Regulations, and offer assistance and guidance on the use of the procedure, or give advice on where he may obtain it;

(c) if they consider that he has not got a sufficient interest they shall notify him accordingly in writing, and inform him that no further action will be taken;

(d) if they consider it appropriate to do so having regard to his understanding, they shall notify the child of the result of their consideration.

(5) Where paragraph (4)(b) applies, the date at which the authority conclude that the person has a sufficient interest shall be treated for the purpose of these Regulations as the date of receipt of the representations.

**Note.** In para (1) words from 'a local authority' to 'may apply, they' substituted by paras (a), (b) and words 'the local authority' in square brackets by SI 2001/2874, reg 13 in relation to England as from 1 October 2001. In paras (2), (2A) words 'and any section 26A advocate' in square brackets inserted by SI 2004/719, reg 6(1), (3) in relation to England as from 1 April 2004 and by SI 2004/1448, reg 6 in relation to Wales as from 1 June 2004.

*Appointment of independent person*

**5.**   Where the local authority receive representations under regulation 4 they shall appoint an independent person to take part in the consideration of them, unless regulation 4(4)(c) applies.

*Consideration by local authority with independent person*

**6.**   (1)  The local authority shall consider the representations with the independent person and formulate a response within 28 days of their receipt.

(2)  The independent person shall take part in any discussions which are held by the local authority about the action (if any) to be taken in relation to the child in the light of the consideration of the representations.

*Withdrawal of representations*

**7.**   The representations may be withdrawn at any stage by the person making them [or any section 26A advocate acting on his behalf].

**Note.** Words 'or any section 26A advocate acting on his behalf' in square brackets inserted by SI 2004/719, reg 6(1), (4) in relation to England as from 1 April 2004 and by SI 2004/1448, reg 6, as from 1 June 2004 in relation to Wales.

*Notification to complainant and reference to panel*

**8.**   (1)  The local authority shall give notice within the period specified in regulation 6 to—

(a)  the complainant [and any section 26A advocate];

(b)  if different, the person on whose behalf the representations were made, unless the local authority consider that he is not of sufficient understanding or it would be likely to cause serious harm to his health or emotional condition;

(c)  the independent person;

(d)  any other person whom the local authority consider has sufficient interest in the case,

of the proposed result of their consideration of the representations and the complainant's right to have the matter referred to a panel under paragraph (2).

(2)  If the complainant [, or any section 26A advocate on his behalf] informs the authority in writing within 28 days of the date on which notice is given under paragraph (1) that he is dissatisfied with the proposed result and wishes the matter to be referred to a panel for consideration of the representations, a panel shall be appointed by the local authority for that purpose.

(3)  The panel shall include at least one independent person.

(4)  The panel shall meet within 28 days of the receipt by the local authority of the complainant's request that the matter be referred to a panel.

(5)  At that meeting the panel shall consider—

(a)  any oral or written submissions that the complainant [(or any section 26A advocate on his behalf)] or the local authority wish to make; and

(b)  if the independent person appointed under regulation 5 is different from the independent person on the panel, any oral or written submissions which the independent person appointed under regulation 5 wishes to make.

(6)  If the complainant wishes to attend the meeting of the panel he may be accompanied throughout the meeting [by any section 26A advocate or] by another person of his choice, and may nominate [the section 26A advocate or] that other person to speak on his behalf.

**Note.** In para (1)(a) words 'and any section 26A advocate', in para (2) words ', or any section 26A advocate on his behalf', in para (5)(a) words '(or any section 26A advocate on his behalf)', in para (6) words 'by any section 26A advocate or' and 'the section 26A advocate or' in square brackets inserted by SI 2004/719, regs 6(1), (5), 7 in relation to England as from 1 April 2004 and by SI 2004/1448, regs 6(1), (5), 7 in relation to Wales as from 1 June 2004.

*Recommendations*

**9.**   (1) When a panel meets under regulation 8, they shall decide on their recommendations and record them with their reasons in writing within 24 hours of the end of the meeting referred to in regulation 8.

(2) The panel shall give notice of their recommendations to—

(a)   the local authority;

(b)   the complainant [and any section 26A advocate];

(c)   the independent person appointed under regulation 5 if different from the independent person on the panel;

(d)   any other person whom the local authority considers has sufficient interest in the case.

(3) The local authority shall, together with the independent person appointed to the panel under regulation 8(3) consider what action if any should be taken in relation to the child in the light of the representation, and that independent person shall take part in any discussions about any such action.

**Note.** In para (2)(a) words 'and any section 26A advocate' in square brackets inserted by SI 2004/719, reg 6, in relation to England, as from 1 April 2004 and by SI 2004/1448, reg 6, in relation to Wales, as from 1 June 2004.

PART III

REVIEW OF PROCEDURE

*Monitoring of operation of procedure*

**10.**   (1) Each local authority shall monitor the arrangements that they have made with a view to ensuring that they comply with the Regulations by keeping a record of each representation received, the outcome of each representation, and whether there was compliance with the time limits specified in regulations 6(1), 8(4) and 9(1).

(2) For the purposes of such monitoring, each local authority shall, at least once in every period of twelve months, compile a report on the operation in that period of the procedure set out in these Regulations.

(3) The first report referred to in paragraph (2) shall be compiled within twelve months of the date of coming into force of these Regulations.

PART IV

APPLICATION OF REGULATIONS TO VOLUNTARY ORGANISATIONS AND REGISTERED CHILDREN'S HOMES AND IN SPECIAL CASES

*Application to voluntary organisations and registered children's homes*

**11.**   (1) The provisions of Parts I to III of these Regulations shall apply where accommodation is provided for a child by a voluntary organisation, and he is not looked after by a local authority, as if—

(a)   for references to 'local authority' there were substituted references to 'voluntary organisation';

(b)   for the definition in regulation 2(1) of 'complainant' there were substituted—
'   "complainant" means

(a)   any child who is being provided with accommodation by a voluntary organisation;

(b)   any parent of his;

(c)   any person who is not a parent of his but who has parental responsibility for him;

(d)   such other person as the voluntary organisation consider has a sufficient interest in the child's welfare to warrant his representations being considered by them';

(c) for the definition in regulation 2(1) of 'independent person' there were substituted—
' "independent person" means in relation to representations made to, or treated as being made to a voluntary organisation, a person who is not an officer of that voluntary organisation nor a person engaged in any way in furthering its objects, nor the spouse of any such person;' and

(d) for the definition in regulation 2(1) of 'representations' there were substituted—
' "representations" means representations referred to in section 59(4) about the discharge by the voluntary organisation of any of their functions relating to section 61 and any regulations made under it in relation to the child.';

(e) for the reference in regulation 4(1) and (4) to a person to whom section 26(3)(e) may apply or to whom the local authority consider section 26(3)(e) may apply there was substituted a reference to a person who may fall within sub-paragraph (d) in the definition of 'complainant' in these Regulations.

(2) The provisions of Parts I to III of these Regulations shall apply where accommodation is provided for a child in a *registered children's home* [private children's home], but where a child is neither looked after by a local authority nor accommodated on behalf of a voluntary organisation, as if—

(a) for references to 'local authority' there were substituted references to 'the person carrying on the home';

(b) for the definition in regulation 2(1) of 'complainant' there were substituted—
' "complainant" means—
  (i) any child who is being provided with accommodation in a *registered children's home* [private children's home];
  (ii) a parent of his;
  (iii) any person who is not a parent of his but who has parental responsibility for him;
  (iv) such other person as the person carrying on the home considers has a sufficient interest in the child's welfare to warrant his representations being considered by them;';

(c) for the definition in regulation 2(1) of 'independent person' there were substituted—
' "independent person" means in relation to representations made to a person carrying on a *registered children's home* [private children's home], a person who is neither involved in the management or operation of that home nor financially interested in its operation, nor the spouse of any such person;';

(d) for the definition in regulation 2(1) of 'representations' there were substituted—
' "representations" means any representations (including any complaint) made in relation to the person carrying on the *registered children's home* [private children's home] by a complainant about the discharge of his functions relating to section 64.';

(e) for the reference in regulation 4(1) and (4) to a person to whom section 26(3)(e) may apply or to whom the local authority consider section 26(3)(e) may apply there was substituted a reference to a person who may fall within sub-paragraph (d) in the definition of 'complainant' in these Regulations.

**Note.** Words 'registered children's home' in each place substituted by words 'private children's home' in square brackets by SI 2002/546, reg 5(a) in relation to England as from 1 April 2002 and by SI 2002/2935, reg 8(a) in relation to Wales as from 31 December 2002.

*Exceptions to application of Regulations*

**11A.**   These Regulations shall not apply to representations made by a child or a person in respect of a child who is being provided with accommodation, otherwise than by a local authority or voluntary organisation—

(a)   *in an independent school which is a children's home within the meaning of section 63(6) of the Act; or*

(b)   *in a special school (as defined in section 182 of the Education Act 1993) which is not maintained by a local education authority, or otherwise out of public funds* [, in a school which is a children's home within the meaning of section 1 (6) of the Care Standards Act 2000].

**Note.** Paras (a), (b) revoked and subsequent words from ', in a school' to 'Care Standards Act 2000' in square brackets substituted by SI 2002/546, reg 5(b) in relation to England as from 1 April 2002.

*Special cases including application to representations by foster parents*

**12.**   (1) Where representations would fall to be considered by more than one local authority, they shall be considered by the authority which is looking after the child or by the authority within whose area the child is ordinarily resident where no authority has that responsibility.

(2) The provisions of Parts I to III of, and of regulation 12(1) of, these Regulations, shall apply to the consideration by a local authority of any representations (including any complaint) made to them by any person exempted or seeking to be exempted under paragraph 4 of Schedule 7 to the Act (foster parents: limits on numbers of foster children) about the discharge of their functions under that paragraph as if—

(a)   for the definition in regulation 2(1) of 'complainant' there were substituted: 'a person exempted or seeking to be exempted under paragraph 4 of Schedule 7 to the Act making any representations;';

(b)   for the definition in regulation 2(1) of 'representations' there were substituted: 'representations referred to in paragraph 6 of Schedule 7 to the Act';

(c)   in regulation 4(1) the words 'except from a person to whom section 26(3)(e) may apply' were omitted;

(d)   regulation 4(4) and (5) were omitted.

## REVIEW OF CHILDREN'S CASES REGULATIONS 1991

**Dated** 2 April 1991

**SI 1991 No 895**

ARRANGEMENT OF REGULATIONS

SCHEDULES

1. Elements to be included in review.
2. Considerations to which responsible authorities are to have regard.
3. Health considerations to which responsible authorities are to have regard.

The Secretary of State for Health, in exercise of the powers conferred by sections 26(1) and (2), 59(4)(a) and (5) and 104(4) of and paragraph 10(1) and (2)(1) of Schedule 6 to the Children Act 1989 and of all other powers enabling him in that behalf hereby makes the following Regulations—

*Citation, commencement and interpretation*

**1.**  (1)  These Regulations may be cited as the Review of Children's Cases Regulations 1991 and shall come into force on 14th October 1991.

(2)  In these Regulations, unless the context otherwise requires—
'the Act' means the Children Act 1989;
...
'independent visitor' means an independent visitor appointed under paragraph 17 of Schedule 2 to the Act;
'responsible authority' means in relation to—
(a) a child who is being looked after by a local authority, that authority;
(b) a child who is being provided with accommodation by a voluntary organisation otherwise than on behalf of a local authority, that voluntary organisation;
(c) a child who is being provided with accommodation in a *registered children's home* [private children's home] otherwise than on behalf of a local authority or voluntary organisation, the person carrying on that home.

(3)  Any notice required under these Regulations is to be given in writing and may be sent by post.

(4)  In these Regulations, unless the context otherwise requires—
(a) any reference to a numbered regulation is to the regulation in these Regulations bearing that number and any reference in any regulation to a numbered paragraph is to the paragraph of that regulation bearing that number;
(b) any reference to a numbered Schedule is to the Schedule to these Regulations bearing that number.

**Note.** In para (1) definition 'guardian ad litem' revoked and in definition 'responsible authority' in para (c) words 'registered children's home' substituted by words 'private children's home' in square brackets by SI 2002/546, reg 4 in relation to England as from 1 April 2002 and by SI 2002/2935, regs 7, 13 in relation to Wales as from 31 December 2002.

*Review of children's cases*

**2.**  Each responsible authority shall review in accordance with these Regulations the case of each child while he is being looked after or provided with accommodation by them.

*[Independent reviewing officers*

**2A.**  (1)  Each responsible authority must appoint a person ('the independent reviewing officer') in respect of each case to carry out the functions mentioned in section 26(2A) of the Act, which are—
(a) participating in the review of the case in question;
(b) monitoring the performance of the authority's functions in respect of the review;
(c) referring the case to an officer of the Children and Family Court Advisory and Support Service, if the independent reviewing officer considers it appropriate to do so.

(2) The independent reviewing officer must be registered as a social worker in a register maintained by the General Social Care Council [or by the Care Council for Wales] under section 56 of the Care Standards Act 2000 or in a corresponding register maintained under the law of Scotland or Northern Ireland.

(3) The independent reviewing officer must, in the opinion of the responsible authority, have sufficient relevant social work experience to undertake the functions mentioned in paragraph (1) in relation to the case.

(4) A person who is an employee of the responsible authority may not be appointed as an independent reviewing officer in a case if he is involved in the management of the case or is under the direct management of—

(a)  a person involved in the management of the case;

(b)  a person with management responsibilities in relation to a person mentioned in sub-paragraph (a); or

(c)  a person with control over the resources allocated to the case.

(5) The independent reviewing officer must—

(a)  as far as reasonably practicable attend any meeting held in connection with the review of the child's case; and

(b)  chair any such meeting that he attends.

(6) The independent reviewing officer must, as far as reasonably practicable, take steps to ensure that the review is conducted in accordance with these Regulations and in particular to ensure—

(a)  that the child's views are understood and taken into account;

(b)  that the persons responsible for implementing any decision taken in consequence of the review are identified; and

(c)  that any failure to review the case in accordance with these Regulations or to take proper steps to make arrangements in accordance with regulation 8 is brought to the attention of persons at an appropriate level of seniority within the responsible authority.

(7) If the child whose case is reviewed wishes to take proceedings under the Act on his own account, for example to apply to the court for contact or for discharge of a care order, it is the function of the independent reviewing officer—

(a)  to assist the child to obtain legal advice; or

(b)  to establish whether an appropriate adult is able and willing to provide such assistance or bring the proceedings on the child's behalf.]

**Note.** Inserted by SI 2004/1419, reg 2(1), (2) in relation to England as from 27 September 2004; a corresponding amendment has been made by SI 2004/1449, reg 2(1), (2) in relation to Wales as from 1 September 2004. In para (2) words 'or by the Care Council for Wales' in square brackets inserted by SI 2004/2253, reg 2 as from 27 September 2004. See also the disapplication of para (2) above, in relation to an independent reviewing officer appointed during the period from 27 September 2004 to 31 March 2005, by the Review of Children's Cases (Amendment No 2 and Transitional Arrangements) (England) Regulations 2004, SI 2004/2253, reg 3.

*Time when case is to be reviewed*

**3.**   *(1)  Each case is first to be reviewed within four weeks of the date upon which the child begins to be looked after or provided with accommodation by a responsible authority.*

*(2)  The second review shall be carried out not more than three months after the first and thereafter subsequent reviews shall be carried out not more than six months after the date of the previous review.*

[(1) Each case must first be reviewed within four weeks of the date on which the child begins to be looked after or provided with accommodation by the responsible authority.

(2) The second review must be carried out no more than three months after the first and thereafter subsequent reviews must be carried out no more than six months after the date of the previous review.

(3) A review must be carried out before the time specified in paragraph (1) or (2) if the independent reviewing officer so directs.

(4) This regulation is subject to regulation 11 (application of regulations to short periods).]

**Note.** Substituted by SI 2004/1419, reg 2(1), (3) in relation to England as from 27 September 2004; a corresponding amendment has been made by SI 2004/1449, reg 2(1), (3) in relation to Wales as from 1 September 2004.

*Manner in which cases are to be reviewed*

**4.** (1) Each responsible authority shall set out in writing their arrangements governing the manner in which the case of each child shall be reviewed and shall draw the written arrangements to the attention of those specified in regulation 7(1).

(2) The responsible authority which are looking after or providing accommodation for a child shall make arrangements to coordinate the carrying out of all aspects of the review of that child's case.

(3) The responsible authority shall appoint one of their officers to assist the authority in the coordination of all the aspects of the review.

(4) The manner in which each case is reviewed shall, so far as practicable, include the elements specified in Schedule 1.

(5) Nothing in these Regulations shall prevent the carrying out of any review under these Regulations and any other review, assessment or consideration under any other provision at the same time.

*Considerations to which responsible authorities are to have regard*

**5.** The considerations to which the responsible authority are to have regard so far as is reasonably practicable in reviewing each case are the general considerations specified in Schedule 2 and the considerations concerning the health of the child specified in Schedule 3.

*Health reviews*

**6.** *The responsible authority shall make arrangements for a child who continues to be looked after or provided with accommodation by them to be examined by a registered medical practitioner and for a written assessment on the state of health of the child and his need for health care to be made—*

*(a)   at least once in every period of six months before the child's second birthday, and*

*(b)   at least once in every period of twelve months after the child's second birthday,*

*unless the child is of sufficient understanding and he refuses to submit to the examination.*

[(1) Subject to paragraph (2), the responsible authority shall, in respect of each child who continues to be looked after or provided with accommodation by them—

(a) arrange for an assessment, which may include a physical examination, of the child's state of health, to be conducted by a registered medical practitioner, or a registered nurse or registered midwife acting under the supervision of a registered medical practitioner—

   (i) at least once in every period of six months before the child's fifth birthday; and

   (ii) at least once in every period of twelve months after the child's fifth birthday;

(b) require the person who carried out the assessment to prepare a written report which addresses the matters listed in Schedule 2; and

(c) review the plan for the future health of the child prepared under regulation 7(1)(c) of the Arrangements for Placement of Children (General) Regulations 1991 at the intervals set out in sub-paragraphs (i) and (ii) of paragraph (a).

(2) Sub-paragraphs (a) and (b) of paragraph (1) do not apply if the child, being of sufficient understanding to do so, refuses to consent to the assessment.]

**Note.** Substituted by SI 2002/546, reg 4(1), (4) in relation to England as from 1 April 2002 and (subject to minor variation) by SI 2002/3013, reg 3(1), (2) in relation to Wales as from 1 January 2003.

*Consultation, participation and notification*

**7.**    (1) Before conducting any review the responsible authority shall, unless it is not reasonably practicable to do so, seek and take into account the views of—

(a)  the child;

(b)  his parents;

(c)  any person who is not a parent of his but who has parental responsibility for him; and

(d)  any other person whose views the authority consider to be relevant;

including, in particular, the views of those persons in relation to any particular matter which is to be considered in the course of the review.

(2)  The responsible authority shall so far as is reasonably practicable involve the persons whose views are sought under paragraph (1) in the review including, where the authority consider appropriate, the attendance of those persons at part or all of any meeting which is to consider the child's case in connection with any aspect of the review of that case.

(3)  The responsible authority shall, so far as is reasonably practicable, notify details of the result of the review and of any decision taken by them in consequence of the review to—

(a)  the child;

(b)  his parents;

(c)  any person who is not a parent of his but who has parental responsibility for him; and

(d)  any other person whom they consider ought to be notified.

*Arrangements for implementation of decisions arising out of reviews*

**8.**    The responsible authority shall make arrangements themselves or with other persons to implement any decision which the authority propose to make in the course, or as a result, of the review of a child's case.

*[Independent reviewing officer to be notified of failure to implement etc*

**8A.**    The responsible authority must inform the independent reviewing officer of—

(a)  any significant failure to make arrangements in accordance with regulation 8; or

(b)  any significant change of circumstances occurring after the review that affects those arrangements.]

**Note.** Inserted by SI 2004/1419, reg 2(1), (4) in relation to England as from 27 September 2004 and (subject to minor variation) by SI 2004/1449, reg 2(1), (4) in relation to Wales as from 1 September 2004.

*Monitoring arrangements for reviews*

**9.**    Each responsible authority shall monitor the arrangements which they have made with a view to ensuring that they comply with these Regulations.

*Recording review information*

**10.**   Each responsible authority shall ensure that—

(a)   information obtained in respect of the review of a child's case,

(b)   details of the proceedings at any meeting arranged by the authority at which the child's case is considered in connection with any aspect of the review of that case, and

(c)   details of any decisions made in the course of or as a result of the review,

are recorded in writing.

*Application of Regulations to short periods*

**11.**   (1) This regulation applies to cases in which a responsible authority has arranged that a child should be looked after or provided with accommodation for a series of short periods at the same place and the arrangement is such that no single period is to last for more than four weeks and the total duration of the periods is not to exceed 120 days in any period of 12 months.

(2) Regulation 3 shall not apply to a case to which this regulation applies, but instead—

(a)   each such case is first to be reviewed within three months of the beginning of the first of the short periods;

(b)   if the case continues, the second review shall be carried out not more than six months after the first; and

(c)   thereafter, if the case continues, subsequent reviews shall be carried out not more than six months after the date of the previous review.

(3) For the purposes of regulation 6, a child shall be treated as continuing to be looked after or provided with accommodation throughout the period that this regulation applies to his case.

*Transitional provisions*

**Note:** Regulation 12 (Transitional provisions) applying to placements before 14 October 1991 not printed here. See 16th Edition, Vol 2, p 4537.

*Exception to application of Regulations*

**13.**   These Regulations shall not apply in the case of a child who is being provided with accommodation, otherwise than *on behalf of a local authority or voluntary organisation*—

(a)   *in an independent school which is a children's home within the meaning of section 63(6) of the Act; or*

(b)   *in a special school (as defined in section 182 of the Education Act 1993) which is not maintained by a local education authority, or otherwise out of public funds* [by a local authority or a voluntary organisation, in a school which is in a children's home within the meaning of section 1(6) of the Care Standards Act 2000].

**Note.** Words from 'on behalf of' to the end revoked and subsequent words from 'by a local' to 'Care Standards Act 2000' in square brackets substituted by SI 2002/546, reg 4 in relation to England as from 1 April 2002 and by SI 2002/2935, regs 7, 13 in relation to Wales as from 31 December 2002.

**13A.**   These Regulations shall not apply in the case of a child who is placed for adoption under the Adoption Act 1976.

SCHEDULE 1                                                        Regulation 4(4)

ELEMENTS TO BE INCLUDED IN REVIEW

**1.** Keeping informed of the arrangements for looking after the child and of any relevant change in the child's circumstances.

**2.** Keeping informed of the name and address of any person whose views should be taken into account in the course of the review.

**3.** Making necessary preparations and providing any relevant information to the participants in any meeting of the responsible authority which considers the child's case in connection with any aspect of the review.

**4.** Initiating meetings of relevant personnel of the responsible authority and other relevant persons to consider the review of the child's case.

**5.** Explaining to the child any steps which he may take under the Act including, where appropriate—

(a) his right to apply, with leave, for a section 8 order (residence, contact and other orders with respect to children),

(b) where he is in care, his right to apply for the discharge of the care order, and

(c) the availability of the procedure established under the Act for considering representations.

**6.** Making decisions or taking steps following review decisions arising out of or resulting from the review.

SCHEDULE 2                                                          Regulation 5

CONSIDERATIONS TO WHICH RESPONSIBLE AUTHORITIES ARE TO HAVE REGARD

**1.** In the case of a child who is in care, whether an application should be made to discharge the care order.

**2.** Where the responsible authority are a local authority whether they should seek a change in the child's legal status.

**3.** Arrangements for contact, and whether there is any need for changes in the arrangements in order to promote contact with the child's family and others so far as is consistent with his welfare.

**4.** Any special arrangements that have been made or need to be made for the child, including the carrying out of assessments either by a local authority or other persons, such as those in respect of special educational need under the *Education Act 1981* [Education Act 1996].

**5.** The responsible authority's immediate and long term arrangements for looking after the child or providing the child with accommodation (made pursuant to the provisions of the Arrangements for Placement of Children (General) Regulations 1991), whether a change in those arrangements is needed and consideration of alternative courses of action.

**6.** Where the responsible authority are a local authority, whether an independent visitor should be appointed if one has not already been appointed.

**7.** The child's educational needs, progress and development.

**8.** Whether arrangements need to be made for the time when the child will no longer be looked after or provided with accommodation by the responsible authority.

**9.** Whether plans need to be made to find a permanent substitute family for the child.

**Note.** In para 4 words 'Education Act 1981' substituted by words 'Education Act 1996' in square brackets by SI 2002/546, reg 4 in relation to England as from 1 April 2002 and by SI 2002/2935, regs 7, 13 in relation to Wales as from 31 December 2002.

SCHEDULE 3                                                    Regulation 5

HEALTH CONSIDERATIONS TO WHICH RESPONSIBLE AUTHORITIES ARE TO HAVE REGARD

**1.** The child's state of health [including his physical, emotional and mental health].
**2.** The child's health history [including, as far as practicable, his family health and history].
**3.** The effect of the child's health and health history on his development.
**4.** Existing arrangements for the child's medical and dental care and treatment and health and dental surveillance.
**5.** The possible need for an appropriate course of action which should be identified to assist necessary change of such care, treatment or surveillance.
**6.** The possible need for preventive measures, such as vaccination and immunisation, and screening for vision and hearing [, and for advice and guidance on health, personal care and health promotion issues appropriate to the child's needs].
**Note.** In para 1 words 'including his physical, emotional and mental health', in para 2 words 'including, as far as practicable, his family health and history' and in para 6 words from ', and for advice' to 'child's needs' in square brackets inserted by SI 2002/546, reg 41), (7) in relation to England as from 1 April 2002 and by SI 2002/3013, reg 3(1), (3) in relation to Wales as from 1 January 2003.

## FOSTER PLACEMENT (CHILDREN) REGULATIONS 1991

**Dated** 3 April 1991

**SI 1991 No 910**
**Note.** These Regulations are revoked by SI 2002/57, reg 51 in relation to England as from 1 April 2002 and by SI 2003/237, reg 53(a) in relation to Wales as from 1 April 2003.

## ADOPTED PERSONS (CONTACT REGISTER) (FEES) RULES 1991

**Dated** 8 April 1991

**SI 1991 No 952**
The Secretary of State for Health, in exercise of the powers conferred on him by section 51A(3) and (5) of the Adoption Act 1976 and of all other powers enabling him in that behalf, hereby makes the following Rules—

*Citation, commencement and interpretation*
**1.** (1) These Rules may be cited as the Adopted Persons (Contact Register) (Fees) Rules 1991 and shall come into force on 1st May 1991.
  (2) In these Rules—
    'the Act' means the Adoption Act 1976;
    'the register' means the Adoption Contact Register maintained by the Registrar General under section 51A(1) of the Act.

*Fees payable for entries in the register*
**2.** (1) The fee payable for the entry of the name and address of an adopted person in the register under section 51A(3) of the Act is *£9.50* [£15.00].
  (2) The fee payable for the entry of the name and address of a relative of an adopted person in the register under section 51A(5) of the Act is *£27.50* [£30.00].
**Note.** Sums '£9.50' and '£27.50' substituted by sums '£15.00' and '£30.00' in square brackets by SI 1998/615, reg 2 as from 1 April 1998.

## THE COUNTY COURTS (INTEREST ON JUDGMENT DEBTS) ORDER 1991

**Dated** 20 May 1991

**SI 1991 No 1184**

The Lord Chancellor, in exercise of the powers conferred on him by section 74 of the County Courts Act 1984 and with the concurrence of the Treasury, hereby makes the following Order—

*Citation, commencement, interpretation and savings*

**1.**   (1) This Order may be cited as the County Courts (Interest on Judgment Debts) Order 1991 and shall come into force on 1st July 1991.

(2)  In this Order, unless the context otherwise requires—

'administration order' means an order under section 112 of the 1984 Act;

'given', in relation to a relevant judgment, means 'given or made';

'judgment creditor' means the person who has obtained or is entitled to enforce the relevant judgment and 'debtor' means the person against whom it was given;

'judgment debt' means a debt under a relevant judgment;

*'relevant judgment' means a judgment or order of a county court for the payment of a sum of money of not less than £5,000 and, in relation to a judgment debt, means the judgment or order which gives rise to the judgment debt;*

['relevant judgment' means a judgment or order of a county court for the payment of a sum of money (a) of not less than £5,000 or (b) in respect of a debt which is a qualifying debt for the purposes of the Late Payment of Commercial Debts (Interest) Act 1998 and, in relation to a judgment debt, means the judgment or order which gives rise to the judgment debt;]

'the 1984 Act' means the County Courts Act 1984.

(3)  Where in accordance with the provisions of this Order interest ceases to accrue on a specified day, interest shall cease to accrue at the end of that day.

(4)  Nothing in this Order shall apply where the relevant judgment is given before 1st July 1991.

**Note.** Definition 'relevant judgment' substituted by SI 1998/2400, art 2 as from 1 November 1998.

*The general rule*

**2.**   (1) Subject to the following provisions of this Order, every judgment debt under a relevant judgment shall, to the extent that it remains unsatisfied, carry interest under this Order from the date on which the relevant judgment was given.

(2)  In the case of a judgment or order for the payment of a judgment debt, other than costs, the amount of which has to be determined at a later date, the judgment debt shall carry interest from that later date.

(3)  Interest shall not be payable under this Order where the relevant judgment—

(a)  is given in proceedings to recover money due under an agreement regulated by the Consumer Credit Act 1974;

(b)  grants—

    (i)  the landlord of a dwelling house, or

    (ii)  the mortgagee under a mortgage of land which consists of or includes a dwelling house,

a suspended order for possession.

(4)  Where the relevant judgment makes financial provision for a spouse or a child, interest shall only be payable on an order for the payment of not less than £5,000 as a lump sum (whether or not the sum is payable by instalments).

For the purposes of this paragraph, no regard shall be had to any interest payable under section 23(6) of the Matrimonial Causes Act 1973.

*Interest where payment deferred*

**3.**   Where under the terms of the relevant judgment payment of a judgment debt—

    (a)  is not required to be made until a specified date, or

    (b)  is to be made by instalments,

interest shall not accrue under this Order—

        (i)   until that date, or

        (ii)  on the amount of any instalment, until it falls due,

as the case may be.

*Interest and enforcement or other proceedings*

**4.**   (1)  Where a judgment creditor takes proceedings in a county court to enforce payment under a relevant judgment, the judgment debt shall cease to carry interest thereafter, except where those proceedings fail to produce any payment from the debtor in which case interest shall accrue as if those proceedings had never been taken.

(2)  For the purposes of this article 'proceedings to enforce payment under a relevant judgment' include any proceeding for examining or summoning a judgment debtor or attaching a debt owed to him, but do not include proceedings under the Charging Orders Act 1979.

(3)  Where an administration order or an attachment of earnings order is made, interest shall not accrue during the time the order is in force.

*Rate of interest*

**5.**   (1)  Subject to paragraph (2), where a judgment debt carries interest the rate of interest shall be the rate for the time being specified in section 17 of the Judgments Act 1838.[1]

(2)  Where a judgment debt carries interest and has been given for a sum expressed in a currency other than sterling, a county court may order that the rate of interest shall be such rate as the court thinks fit (instead of the rate otherwise applicable under paragraph (1)) and, where the court makes such an order, section 17 of the Judgments Act 1838 shall have effect in relation to the judgment debt as if the rate specified in the order were substituted for the rate specified in that section.

*Appropriation of interest*

**6.**   (1)  Where the debtor is indebted to the same judgment creditor under two or more judgments or orders, money paid by him shall be applied to satisfy such of the judgments as the debtor may stipulate or, where no such stipulation is made, according to their priority in time.

(2)  Money paid by the debtor in respect of any judgment debt shall be appropriated first to discharge or reduce the principal debt and then towards the interest.

(1)  See Judgment Debts (Rate of Interest) Order 1993, p 5060.

## HIGH COURT (DISTRIBUTION OF BUSINESS) ORDER 1991

**Dated** 30 April 1991

**SI 1991 No 1210**

The Lord Chancellor, in exercise of the powers conferred upon him by section 61(3)(a) and (c) of the Supreme Court Act 1981, hereby makes the following Order—

**1.**   This Order may be cited as the High Court (Distribution of Business) Order 1991.

**2.**   There shall be assigned to the Family Division all business in the High Court of any of the following descriptions—

(a) all proceedings under—
　　(i) the Domestic Violence and Matrimonial Proceedings Act 1976;
　　(ii) the Child Abduction and Custody Act 1985;
　　(iii) the Family Law Act 1986;
　　(iv) section 30 of the Human Fertilisation and Embryology Act 1990; and
(b) all proceedings for the purpose of enforcing an order made in any proceedings of a type described in paragraph 3 of Schedule 1 to the Supreme Court Act 1981.

**3.** Paragraph 3 of Schedule 1 to the Supreme Court Act 1981 shall be amended in accordance with the Schedule to this Order, being an amendment which is consequential on the provisions of article 2 above.

**4.** This Order shall come into force on 14th October 1991.

SCHEDULE

The following shall be added after paragraph 3(e) of Schedule 1 to the Supreme Court Act 1981—

'(f) all proceedings under—
　　(i) the Domestic Violence and Matrimonial Proceedings Act 1976;
　　(ii) the Child Abduction and Custody Act 1985;
　　(iii) the Family Law Act 1986;
　　(iv) section 30 of the Human Fertilisation and Embryology Act 1990; and
(g) all proceedings for the purpose of enforcing an order made in any proceedings of a type described in this paragraph.'

## COUNTY COURT REMEDIES REGULATIONS 1991

**Dated** 21 May 1991

**SI 1991 No 1222**

The Lord Chancellor, in exercise of the powers conferred on him by section 38 of the County Courts Act 1984, hereby makes the following Regulations a draft of which has, in accordance with section 38(7) of that Act, been laid before and approved by resolution of each House of Parliament—

**1.** These Regulations may be cited as the County Court Remedies Regulations 1991 and shall come into force on 1st July 1991.

**2.** In these Regulations, 'prescribed relief' means relief of any of the following kinds—
(a) an order requiring a party to admit any other party to premises for the purpose of inspecting or removing documents or articles which may provide evidence in any proceedings, whether or not the proceedings have been commenced;
(b) an interlocutory injunction—
　　(i) restraining a party from removing from the jurisdiction of the High Court assets located within that jurisdiction; or
　　(ii) restraining a party from dealing with assets whether located within the jurisdiction of the High Court or not.

**3.** (1) Subject to the following provisions of this regulation, a county court shall not grant prescribed relief or vary or revoke an order made by the High Court granting such relief.

(2) Paragraph (1) shall not apply to—
(a) any county court held by a judge of the Court of Appeal or judge of the High Court sitting as a judge for any county court district;

\*　　\*　　\*　　\*　　\*

(3)  A county court may grant relief of a kind referred to in regulation 2(b)—

(a)  when exercising jurisdiction in family proceedings within the meaning of Part V of the Matrimonial and Family Proceedings Act 1984;

(b)  for the purpose of making an order for the preservation, custody or detention of property which forms or may form the subject matter of proceedings;

(c)  in aid of execution of a judgment or order made in proceedings in a county court to preserve assets until execution can be levied upon them, or

*    *    *    *    *

(4)  Paragraph (1) shall not—

(a)  affect or modify powers expressly conferred on a county court by or under any enactment other than section 38 of the County Courts Act 1984; or

(b)  prevent a county court from varying an order granting prescribed relief where all the parties are agreed on the terms of the variation.

**4.**   An application to the High Court for relief of a kind referred to in regulation 2(a) in county court proceedings shall be deemed to include an application for transfer of the proceedings to the High Court.

**5.**   (1) After an application for prescribed relief has been disposed of by the High Court, the proceedings shall, unless the High Court orders otherwise, be transferred to a county court if—

(a)  they were transferred to the High Court; or

(b)  apart from these Regulations, they should have been commenced in a county court.

(2)  Where an order is made on an ex parte application, the application shall not be treated as disposed of for the purposes of paragraph (1) until any application to set aside or vary the order has been heard, or until the expiry of 28 days (or such other period as the Court may specify) during which no such application has been made.


## FAMILY PROCEEDINGS RULES 1991

**Dated** 1 May 1991

**SI 1991 No 1247**

These Rules and the Appendices containing prescribed forms are printed as currently in force in Division C of the Service to this Edition.


## FAMILY PROCEEDINGS COURTS (CHILDREN ACT 1989) RULES 1991

**Dated** 25 May 1991

**SI 1991 No 1395**

ARRANGEMENT OF RULES

PART I

*Introductory*

PART II

*General*

## PART IIA

*Proceedings under section 30 of the Human Fertilisation and Embryology Act 1990*

## PART III

*Miscellaneous*

## SCHEDULES

PART I   INTRODUCTORY

*Citation, commencement and interpretation*

**1.**   (1)   These Rules may be cited as the Family Proceedings Courts (Children Act 1989) Rules 1991 and shall come into force on 14th October 1991.

(2)   Unless a contrary intention appears—

a section or schedule referred to means the section or schedule in the Act of 1989,

'application' means an application made under or by virtue of the Act of 1989 or under these Rules, and 'applicant' shall be construed accordingly,

'business day' means any day other than—

(a)   a Saturday, Sunday, Christmas Day or Good Friday; or

(b)   a bank holiday, that is to say, a day which is, or is to be observed as, a bank holiday, or a holiday, under the Banking and Financial Dealings Act 1971, in England and Wales,

'child'—

(a)   means, in relation to any relevant proceedings, subject to sub-paragraph (b), a person under the age of 18 with respect to whom the proceedings are brought, and

(b)   where paragraph 16(1) of Schedule 1 applies, also includes a person who has reached the age of 18,

['children and family reporter' means an officer of the service who has been asked to prepare a welfare report under section 7(1)(a),]

['children's guardian'—

(a)   means an officer of the service appointed under section 41 for the child with respect to whom the proceedings are brought; but

(b)   does not include such an officer appointed in relation to proceedings specified by rule 21A,]

'contribution order' has the meaning assigned to it by paragraph 23(2) of Schedule 2,

'court' means a family proceedings court constituted in accordance with sections 66 and 67 of the Magistrates' Courts Act 1980 or, in respect of those proceedings prescribed in rule 2(5), a single justice who is a member of a family panel,

'directions appointment' means a hearing for directions under rule 14(2),

'emergency protection order' means an order under section 44,

'file' means deposit with the *justices' clerk* [justices' chief executive],

'form' means a form in Schedule 1 to these Rules with such variation as the circumstances of the particular case may require,

*'guardian ad litem' means a guardian ad litem, appointed under section 41, of the child with respect to whom the proceedings are brought,*

['justices' chief executive' means a justices' chief executive appointed under section 40 of the Justices of the Peace Act 1997;]

'justices' clerk' has the meaning assigned to it by section 70 of the Justices of the Peace Act 1979 and includes any person who performs a justices' clerk's functions by virtue of rule 32,

'leave' includes approval,

'note' includes a record made by mechanical means,

['officer of the service' has the same meaning as in the Criminal Justice and Court Services Act 2000,]

'parental responsibility' has the meaning assigned to it by section 3,

'parties' in relation to any relevant proceedings means the respondents specified for those proceedings in the third column of Schedule 2 to these Rules, and the applicant,

'recovery order' means an order under section 50,

'relevant proceedings' has the meaning assigned to it by section 93(3),

'section 8 order' has the meaning assigned to it by section 8(2),

'specified proceedings' has the meaning assigned to it by section 41(6) and rule 2(2),

'the 1981 rules' means the Magistrates' Courts Rules 1981,
'the Act of 1989' means the Children Act 1989,
'welfare officer' means a person who has been asked to prepare a welfare report
under *section 7* [section 7(1)(b)].

**Note.** In para (2) definitions 'children and family reporter', 'children's guardian' and 'officer of the service' inserted, definition 'guardian ad litem' revoked and in definition 'welfare officer' words 'section 7' substituted by words 'section 7(1)(b)' in square brackets, by SI 2001/818, rr 2, 3(a)–(c) as from 1 April 2001. In para (2) definition 'file' words 'justices' chief executive' in square brackets substituted for words 'justice's clerk' and definition 'justices' chief executive' inserted by SI 2001/615, r 2(xx), Schedule, paras 93, 94 as from 1 April 2001.

*Matters prescribed for the purposes of the Act of 1989*

**2.**    (1) The parties to proceedings in which directions are given under section 38(6), and any person named in such a direction, form the prescribed class for the purposes of section 38(8)(b) (application to vary directions made with interim care or interim supervision order).

(2) The following proceedings [(in a family proceedings court)] are specified for the purposes of section 41 in accordance with subsection (6)(i) thereof—
(a) proceedings (in a family proceedings court) under section 25;
(b) applications under section 33(7);
(c) proceedings under paragraph 19(1) of Schedule 2;
(d) applications under paragraph 6(3) of Schedule 3.

(3) The applicant for an order that has been made under section 43(1) and the persons referred to in section 43(11) may, in any circumstances, apply under section 43(12) for a child assessment order to be varied or discharged.

(4) The following persons form the prescribed class for the purposes of section 44(9)(b) (application to vary directions)—
(a) the parties to the application for the order in respect of which it is sought to vary the directions;
(b) the *guardian ad litem* [children's guardian];
(c) the local authority in whose area the child concerned is ordinarily resident;
(d) any person who is named in the directions.

(5) The following proceedings are prescribed for the purposes of section 93(2)(i) as being proceedings with respect to which a single justice may discharge the functions of a family proceedings court, that is to say, proceedings—
(a) where an ex parte application is made, under section 10, 44(1), 48(9), 50(1), 75(1) or 102(1),
(b) subject to rule 28, under section 11(3) or 38(1),
(c) under sections 4(3)(b), 7, 14, 34(3)(b), 37, 41, 44(9)(b) and (11)(b)(iii), 48(4), 91(15) or (17), or paragraph 11(4) of Schedule 14,
(d) in accordance with any Order made by the Lord Chancellor under Part I of Schedule 11, and
(e) in accordance with rule 3 to 8, 10 to 19, 21, 22, or 27.

**Note.** In para (2) words '(in a family proceedings court)' in square brackets inserted by SI 1991/1991, r 26, Sch 2, para 8(1). In para (4)(b) words 'guardian ad litem' substituted by words 'children's guardian' in square brackets by SI 2001/818, rr 2 4(a) as from 1 April 2001.

## PART II   GENERAL

*Application for leave to commence proceedings*

**3.**    (1) Where the leave of the court is required to bring any relevant proceedings, the person seeking leave shall file—
(a) a written request for leave in Form C2 setting out the reasons for the application; and

(b) a draft of the application (being the documents referred to in rule 4(1A)) for the making of which leave is sought together with sufficient copies for one to be served on each respondent.

(2) On considering a request for leave filed under paragraph (1), the court shall—

(a) grant the request, whereupon the *justices' clerk* [justices' chief executive] shall inform the person making the request of the decision, or

(b) direct that a date be fixed for a hearing of the request, whereupon the justices' clerk shall fix such a date and [the justices' chief executive shall] give such notice as the court directs to the person making the request and to such other persons as the court requires to be notified, of the date so fixed.

(3) Where leave is granted to bring any relevant proceedings, the application shall proceed in accordance with rule 4; but paragraph (1)(a) of that rule shall not apply.

**Note.** In para (2) words 'justices' clerk' substituted by words 'justices chief executive' in square brackets and words 'the justices' chief executive' in square brackets inserted by SI 2001/615, r 2(xx), Schedule, paras 93, 97.

*Application*

**4.** (1) Subject to paragraph (4), an applicant shall—

(a) file the documents referred to in paragraph (1A) below (which documents shall together be called 'the application') together with sufficient copies for one to be served on each respondent, and

(b) serve a copy of the application, together with Form C6 and such (if any) of Forms C7 and C10A as are given to him by the *justices' clerk* [justices' chief executive] under paragraph (2)(b), on each respondent such minimum number of days prior to the date fixed under paragraph (2)(a) as is specified in relation to that application in column (ii) of Schedule 2 to these Rules.

(1A) The documents to be filed under paragraph (1)(a) above are:

(a) (i) whichever is appropriate of Forms C1 to C5 or C51, and

(ii) such of the supplemental Forms C10 or C11 to C20 as may be appropriate, or

(b) where there is no appropriate form a statement in writing of the order sought, and where the application is made in respect of more than one child, all the children shall be included in one application.

(2) *On receipt of the documents filed under paragraph (1)(a), the justices' clerk shall—*

(a) *fix the date, time and place for a hearing or a directions appointment, allowing sufficient time for the applicant to comply with paragraph (1)(b),*

(b) *endorse the date, time and place so fixed upon Form C6, and where appropriate, Form C6A, and*

(c) *return forthwith to the applicant the copies of the application and Form C10A if filed with it, together with Form C6 and such of Forms C6A and C7 as are appropriate.*

[(2) On receipt by the justices' chief executive of the documents filed under paragraph (1)(a)—

(a) the justices' clerk shall fix the date, time and place for a hearing or a directions appointment, allowing sufficient time for the applicant to comply with paragraph (1)(b), and

(b) the justices' chief executive shall—

(i) endorse the date, time and place so fixed upon Form C6, and where appropriate, Form C6A, and

(ii) return forthwith to the applicant the copies of the application and Form C10A if filed with it, together with Form C6, and such of Forms C6A and C7 as are appropriate.]

(3) The applicant shall, at the same time as complying with paragraph (1)(b), serve Form 6A on the persons set out in relation to the relevant class of proceedings in column (iv) of Schedule 2 to these Rules.

(4) An application for—

(a) a section 8 order,

(b) an emergency protection order,

(c) a warrant under section 48(9),

(d) a recovery order, or

(e) a warrant under section 102(1),

may, with leave of the justices' clerk, be made ex parte in which case the applicant shall—

(i) file with the *justices' clerk* [justices' chief executive] or the court the application in the appropriate form in Schedule 1 to these Rules at the time when the application is made or as directed by the justices' clerk, and

(ii) in the case of an application for a prohibited steps order, or a specific issue order, under section 8 or an emergency protection order, and also in the case of an application for an order under section 75(1) where the application is ex parte, serve a copy of the application on each respondent within 48 hours after the making of the order.

(5) Where the court refuses to make an order on an ex parte application it may direct that the application be made inter partes.

(6) In the case of proceedings under Schedule 1, the application under paragraph (1) shall be accompanied by a statement in Form C10A setting out the financial details which the applicant believes to be relevant to the application together with sufficient copies for one to be served on each respondent.

**Note.** In para (1)(b), (4)(i) words 'justices clerk' substituted by words 'justices' chief executive' in square brackets and para (2) substituted by SI 2001/615, r 2(xx), Schedule, paras 93, 100, as from 1 April 2001.

*Withdrawal of application*

**5.** (1) An application may be withdrawn only with leave of the court.

(2) Subject to paragraph (3), a person seeking leave to withdraw an application shall file and serve on the parties a written request for leave setting out the reasons for the request.

(3) The request under paragraph (2) may be made orally to the court if the parties and, if appointed, the *guardian ad litem* [children's guardian] or the *welfare officer* [welfare officer or children and family reporter] are present.

(4) Upon receipt of a written request under paragraph (2), the court shall—

(a) if—

(i) the parties consent in writing,

(ii) any *guardian ad litem* [children's guardian] has had an opportunity to make representations, and

(iii) the court thinks fit,

grant the request; in which case the *justices' clerk* [justices' chief executive] shall notify the parties, the *guardian ad litem* [children's guardian] and the *welfare officer* [welfare officer or children and family reporter] of the granting of the request; or

(b) the justices' clerk shall fix a date for the hearing of the request and [the justices' chief executive shall] give at least 7 days' notice to the parties, the *guardian ad litem* [children's guardian] and the *welfare officer* [welfare officer or children and family reporter] of the date fixed.

**Note.** Words 'guardian ad litem' in each place substituted by words 'children's guardian' in square brackets and words 'welfare officer' in each place substituted by words 'welfare officer or children and family reporter' in square brackets, by SI 2001/818, rr 2, 4(a), (b) as from 1 April 2001. Words 'justices' clerk' substituted by words 'justices' chief executive' in square brackets and words 'the justices' chief executive shall' in square brackets inserted by SI 2001/615, r 2(xx), Schedule, paras 93, 97 as from 1 April 2001.

*Transfer of proceedings*

**6.**   (1) Where, in any relevant proceedings, the *justices' clerk* [justices' chief executive] or the court receives a request in writing from a party that the proceedings be transferred to another family proceedings court or to a county court, the *justices' clerk* [justices' chief executive] or court shall issue an order or certificate in the appropriate form in Schedule 1 to these Rules, granting or refusing the request in accordance with any Order made by the Lord Chancellor under Part I of Schedule 11.

(2) Where a request is granted under paragraph (1), the *justices' clerk* [justices' chief executive] shall send a copy of the order—

(a)  to the parties,

(b)  to any *guardian ad litem* [children's guardian], and

(c)  to the family proceedings court or to the county court to which the proceedings are to be transferred.

(3) Any consent given or refused by a justices' clerk in accordance with any Order made by the Lord Chancellor under Part I of Schedule 11 shall be recorded in writing by the justices' clerk at the time it is given or refused or as soon as practicable thereafter.

(4) Where a request to transfer proceedings to a county court is refused under paragraph (1), the person who made the request may apply in accordance with rule 4.6 of the Family Proceedings Rules 1991 for an order under any Order made by the Lord Chancellor under Part I of Schedule 11.

**Note.** In paras (1), (2) words 'justices' clerk in each place substituted by words 'justices' chief executive' in square brackets by SI 2001/615, r 2(xx), Schedule, para 83 as from 1 April 2001. In para (2)(b) words 'guardian ad litem' by words 'children's guardian' in square brackets by SI 2001/818, rr 2, 4(a) as from 1 April 2001.

*Parties*

**7.**   (1)  The respondents to relevant proceedings shall be those persons set out in the relevant entry in column (iii) of Schedule 2 to these Rules.

(2)  In any relevant proceedings a person may file a request in Form C2 that he or another person—

(a)  be joined as a party, or

(b)  cease to be a party.

(3)  On considering a request under paragraph (2) the court shall, subject to paragraph (4)—

(a)  grant it without a hearing or representations, save that this shall be done only in the case of a request under paragraph (2)(a), whereupon the *justices' clerk* [justices' chief executive] shall inform the parties and the person making the request of that decision, or

(b)  order that a date be fixed for the consideration of the request, whereupon the *justices' clerk* [justices' chief executive] shall give notice of the date so fixed, together with a copy of the request—

(i)  in the case of a request under paragraph (2)(a), to the applicant, and

(ii)  in the case of a request under paragraph (2)(b), to the parties, or

(c)  invite the parties or any of them to make written representations, within a specified period, as to whether the request should be granted; and upon the expiry of the period the court shall act in accordance with sub-paragraph (a) or (b).

(4)  Where a person with parental responsibility requests that he be joined under paragraph (2)(a), the court shall grant his request.

(5)  In any relevant proceedings the court may direct—

(a)  that a person who would not otherwise be a respondent under these Rules be joined as a party to the proceedings, or

(b)  that a party to the proceedings cease to be a party.

**Note.** In para (3) words 'justices' clerk' in both places substituted by words 'justices' chief executive' in square brackets by SI 2001/615m r 2(xx), Schedule, para 93 as from 1 April 2001.

*Service*

**8.**   (1) Where service of a document is required by these Rules (and not by a provision to which section 105(8) (service of notice or other document under the Act) applies) it may be effected—

    (a)  if the person to be served is not known by the person serving to be acting by solicitor—

        (i)  by delivering it to him personally, or

        (ii)  by delivering it at or by sending it by first-class post to, his residence or his last known residence, or

    (b)  if the person to be served is known by the person serving to be acting by solicitor—

        (i)  by delivering the document at, or sending it by first-class post to, the solicitor's address for service,

        (ii)  where the solicitor's address for service includes a numbered box at a document exchange, by leaving the document at that document exchange or at a document exchange which transmits documents on every business day to that document exchange, or

        (iii)  by sending a legible copy of the document by facsimile transmission to the solicitor's office.

    (2) In this rule, 'first-class post' means first-class post which has been pre-paid or in respect of which pre-payment is not required.

    (3) Where a child who is a party to any relevant proceedings is required by these Rules to serve a document, service shall be effected by—

    (a)  the solicitor acting for the child,

    (b)  where there is no such solicitor, the *guardian ad litem* [children's guardian], or

    (c)  where there is neither such a solicitor nor a *guardian ad litem* [children's guardian], the *justices' clerk* [justices' chief executive].

    (4) Service of any document on a child shall, subject to any direction of the justices' clerk or the court, be effected by service on—

    (a)  the solicitor acting for the child,

    (b)  where there is no such solicitor, the *guardian ad litem* [children's guardian], or

    (c)  where there is neither such a solicitor nor a *guardian ad litem* [children's guardian], with leave of the justices' clerk or the court, the child.

    (5) Where the justices' clerk or the court refuses leave under paragraph (4)(c), a direction shall be given under paragraph (8).

    (6) A document shall, unless the contrary is proved, be deemed to have been served—

    (a)  in the case of service by first-class post, on the second business day after posting, and

    (b)  in the case of service in accordance with paragraph (1)(b)(ii), on the second business day after the day on which it is left at the document exchange.

    (7) At or before the first directions appointment in, or hearing of, relevant proceedings, whichever occurs first, the applicant shall file a statement in Form C9 that service of—

    (a)  a copy of the application and other documents referred to in rule 4(1)(b) has been effected on each respondent, and

    (b)  notice of the proceedings has been effected under rule 4(3);

and the statement shall indicate—

        (i)  the manner, date, time and place of service, or

        (ii)  where service was effected by post, the date, time and place of posting.

    (8) In any relevant proceedings, where these rules require a document to be served, the court or the justices' clerk may, without prejudice to any power under rule 14, direct that—

(a) the requirement shall not apply;

(b) the time specified by the rules for complying with the requirement shall be abridged to such extent as may be specified in the direction;

(c) service shall be effected in such manner as may be specified in the direction.

**Note.** In paras (3), (4), words 'guardian ad litem' in each place substituted by words 'children's guardian' in square brackets by SI 2001/818, rr 2, 4(a) as from 1 April 2001. In para (3)(c) words 'justices' clerk' substituted by words 'justices' chief executive in square brackets by SI 2001/615, r 2(xx), Schedule, para 93, as from 1 April 2001.

### *Acknowledgement of application*

**9.** Within 14 days of service of an application for a section 8 order or an application under Schedule 1, each respondent shall file and serve on the parties an acknowledgement of the application in Form C7.

### *Appointment of guardian ad litem [children's guardian]*

**10.** (1) As soon as practicable after the commencement of specified proceedings or the transfer of such proceedings to the court, the justices' clerk or the court shall appoint a *guardian ad litem* [children's guardian] unless—

(a) such an appointment has already been made by the court which made the transfer and is subsisting, or

(b) the justices' clerk or the court considers that such an appointment is not necessary to safeguard the interests of the child.

(2) At any stage in specified proceedings a party may apply, without notice to the other parties unless the justices' clerk or the court otherwise directs, for the appointment of a *guardian ad litem* [children's guardian].

(3) The justices' clerk or the court shall grant an application under paragraph (2) unless it is considered that such an appointment is not necessary to safeguard the interests of the child, in which case reasons shall be given; and a note of such reasons shall be taken by the justices' clerk.

(4) At any stage in specified proceedings the justices' clerk or the court may appoint a *guardian ad litem* [children's guardian] even though no application is made for such an appointment.

[(4A) The justices' chief executive or the court may, in specified proceedings, appoint more than one children's guardian in respect of the same child.]

(5) The *justices' clerk* [justices' chief executive] shall, as soon as practicable, notify the parties and any *welfare officer* [welfare officer or children and family reporter] of an appointment under this rule or, as the case may be, of a decision not to make such an appointment.

(6) Upon the appointment of a *guardian ad litem* [children's guardian] the *justices' clerk* [justices' chief executive] shall, as soon as practicable, notify him of the appointment and serve on him copies of the application and of documents filed under rule 17(1).

(7) *A guardian ad litem appointed from a panel established by regulations made under section 41(7) shall not—*

(a) *be a member, officer or servant of a local authority which, or an authorised person (within the meaning of section 31(9)) who, is a party to the proceedings unless he is employed by such an authority solely as a member of a panel of guardians ad litem and reporting officers;*

(b) *be, or have been, a member, officer or servant of a local authority or voluntary organisation (within the meaning of section 105(1)) who has been directly concerned in that capacity in arrangements relating to the care, accommodation or welfare of the child during the five years prior to the commencement of the proceedings;*

(c) *be a serving probation officer (except that a probation officer who has not in that capacity been previously concerned with the child or his family and who is employed part-time may, when not engaged in his duties as a probation officer, act as a guardian ad litem).*

[(7) A children's guardian appointed by the justices' chief executive or by the court under this rule shall not—

(a) be a member, officer or servant of a local authority which, or an authorised person (within the meaning of section 31(9)) who, is a party to the proceedings;

(b) be, or have been, a member, officer or servant of a local authority or voluntary organisation (within the meaning of section 105(1)) who has been directly concerned in that capacity in arrangements relating to the care, accommodation or welfare of the child during the five years prior to the commencement of the proceedings; or

(c) be a serving probation officer who has, in that capacity, been previously concerned with the child or his family.]

(8) When appointing a *guardian ad litem* [children's guardian], the justices' clerk or the court shall consider the appointment of anyone who has previously acted as *guardian ad litem* [children's guardian] of the same child.

(9) The appointment of a *guardian ad litem* [children's guardian] under this rule shall continue for such time as is specified in the appointment or until terminated by the court.

(10) When terminating an appointment in accordance with paragraph (9), the court shall give reasons in writing for so doing, a note of which shall be taken by the justices' clerk.

(11) Where the justices' clerk or the court appoints a *guardian ad litem* [children's guardian] in accordance with this rule or refuses to make such an appointment, the justices' clerk shall record the appointment or refusal in the appropriate form in Schedule 1 to these Rules.

**Note.** Words 'guardian ad litem' in each place they occur substituted by words 'children's guardian' in square brackets by SI 2001/818, rr 2, 4(a) as from 1 April 2001. Para (4A) inserted and para (7) substituted by SI 2001/818, rr 2, 5 as from 1 April 2001. In paras (5), (6) words 'justices' clerk' substituted by words 'justices' chief executive' in square brackets by SI 2001/615, r 2(xx), Schedule, para 93 as from 1 April 2001. In para (5) words 'welfare officer' substituted by words 'welfare officer or children and family reporter' in square brackets by SI 2001/818, rr 2, 4(b).

*[Powers and duties of officers of the service]*

**11.** *(1) In carrying out his duty under section 41(2), the guardian ad litem shall have regard to the principle set out in section 1(2) and the matters set out in section 1(3)(a) to (f) as if for the word 'court' in that section there were substituted the words 'guardian ad litem'.*

*(2) The guardian ad litem shall—*

*(a) appoint a solicitor to represent the child, unless such a solicitor has already been appointed, and*

*(b) give such advice to the child as is appropriate having regard to his understanding and, subject to rule 12(1)(a), instruct the solicitor representing the child on all matters relevant to the interests of the child, including possibilities for appeal, arising in the course of the proceedings.*

*(3) Where it appears to the guardian ad litem that the child—*

*(a) is instructing his solicitor direct, or*

*(b) intends to, and is capable of, conducting the proceedings on his own behalf, he shall so inform the court through the justices' clerk and thereafter—*

> *(i) shall perform all of his duties set out in this rule, other than duties under paragraph (2)(a) and such other duties as the justices' clerk or the court may direct,*

> *(ii) shall take such part in the proceedings as the justices' clerk or the court may direct, and*

> *(iii) may, with leave of the justices' clerk or the court, have legal representation in his conduct of those duties.*

*(4) The guardian ad litem shall, unless excused by the justices' clerk or the court, attend all directions appointments in, and hearings of, the proceedings and shall advise the justices' clerk or the court on the following matters—*

(a) *whether the child is of sufficient understanding for any purpose including the child's refusal to submit to a medical or psychiatric examination or other assessment that the court has power to require, direct or order;*

(b) *the wishes of the child in respect of any matter relevant to the proceedings, including his attendance at court;*

(c) *the appropriate forum for the proceedings;*

(d) *the appropriate timing of the proceedings or any part of them;*

(e) *the options available to it in respect of the child and the suitability of each such option including what order should be made in determining the application;*

(f) *any other matter concerning which the justices' clerk or the court seeks his advice or concerning which he considers that the justices' clerk or the court should be informed.*

*(5) The advice given under paragraph (4) may, subject to any order of the court, be given orally or in writing; and if the advice be given orally, a note of it shall be taken by the justices' clerk or the court.*

*(6) The guardian ad litem shall, where practicable, notify any person whose joinder as a party to those proceedings would be likely, in the guardian ad litem's opinion, to safeguard the interests of the child, of that person's right to apply to be joined under rule 7(2) and shall inform the justices' clerk or the court—*

(a) *of any such notification given,*

(b) *of anyone whom he attempted to notify under this paragraph but was unable to contact, and*

(c) *of anyone whom he believes may wish to be joined to the proceedings.*

*(7) The guardian ad litem shall, unless the justices' clerk or the court otherwise directs, not less than 7 days before the date fixed for the final hearing of the proceedings, file a written report advising on the interests of the child; and the justices' clerk shall, as soon as practicable, serve a copy of the report on the parties.*

*(8) The guardian ad litem shall serve and accept service of documents on behalf of the child in accordance with rule 8(3)(b) and (4)(b) and, where the child has not himself been served, and has sufficient understanding, advise the child of the contents of any documents so served.*

*(9) The guardian ad litem shall make such investigations as may be necessary for him to carry out his duties and shall, in particular—*

(a) *contact or seek to interview such persons as he thinks appropriate or as the court directs,*

(b) *if he inspects records of the kinds referred to in section 42, bring to the attention of the court, through the justices' clerk, and such other persons as the justices' clerk or the court may direct, all such records and documents which may, in his opinion, assist in the proper determination of the proceedings, and*

(c) *obtain such professional assistance as is available to him which he thinks appropriate or which the justices' clerk or the court directs him to obtain.*

*(10) In addition to his duties under other paragraphs of this rule, the guardian ad litem shall provide to the justices' clerk and the court such other assistance as may be required.*

*(11) A party may question the guardian ad litem about oral or written advice tendered by him to the justices' clerk or the court under this rule.*

[(1) In carrying out his duty under section 7(1)(a) or section 41(2), the officer of the service shall have regard to the principle set out in section 1(2) and the matters set out in section 1(3)(a) to (f) as if for the word 'court' in that section there were substituted the words 'officer of the service'.

(2) The officer of the service shall make such investigations as may be necessary for him to carry out his duties and shall, in particular—

(a) contact or seek to interview such persons as he thinks appropriate or as the court directs;

(b) obtain such professional assistance as is available to him which he thinks appropriate or which the justices' clerk or the court directs him to obtain.

(3) In addition to his duties, under other paragraphs of this rule, or rules 11A or 11B, the officer of the service shall provide to the justices' chief executive, the justices' clerk and the court such other assistance as he or it may require.

(4) A party may question the officer of the service about oral or written advice tendered by him to the justices' chief executive, the justices' clerk or the court.]

**Note.** Substituted by SI 2001/818, rr 2, 6 as from 1 April 2001.

*[Additional powers and duties of children's guardian*

**11A.** (1) The children's guardian shall—
  (a) appoint a solicitor to represent the child unless such a solicitor has already been appointed; and
  (b) give such advice to the child as is appropriate having regard to his understanding and, subject to rule 12(1)(a), instruct the solicitor representing the child on all matters relevant to the interests of the child including possibilities for appeal, arising in the course of proceedings.

(2) Where it appears to the children's guardian that the child—
  (a) is instructing his solicitor direct; or
  (b) intends to conduct and is capable of conducting the proceedings on his own behalf,
he shall inform the court through the justices' chief executive and from then he—
       (i) shall perform all of his duties set out in rule 11 and this rule, other than those duties under paragraph (1)(a) of this rule, and such other duties as the justices' clerk or the court may direct;
      (ii) shall take such part in the proceedings as the justices' clerk or the court may direct; and
     (iii) may, with the leave of the justices' clerk or the court, have legal representation in the conduct of those duties.

(3) Unless excused by the justices' clerk or the court, the children's guardian shall attend all directions appointments in and hearings of the proceedings and shall advise the court on the following matters—
  (a) whether the child is of sufficient understanding for any purpose including the child's refusal to submit to a medical or psychiatric examination or other assessment that the court has the power to require, direct or order;
  (b) the wishes of the child in respect of any matter relevant to the proceedings including his attendance at court;
  (c) the appropriate forum for the proceedings;
  (d) the appropriate timing of the proceedings or any part of them;
  (e) the options available to it in respect of the child and the suitability of each such option including what order should be made in determining the application; and
  (f) any other matter concerning which the justices' chief executive, the justices' clerk or the court seeks his advice or concerning which he considers that the justices' chief executive, the justices' clerk or the court should be informed,

(4) The advice given under paragraph (3) may, subject to any order of the court, be given orally or in writing; and if the advice be given orally, a note of it shall be taken by the justices' clerk or the court.

(5) The children's guardian shall, where practicable, notify any person whose joinder as a party to those proceedings would be likely, in the opinion of the officer of the service, to safeguard the interests of the child of that person's right to apply to be joined under rule 7(2) and shall inform the justices' chief executive or the court—
  (a) of any such notification given;
  (b) of anyone whom he attempted to notify under this paragraph but was unable to contact; and
  (c) of anyone whom he believes may wish to be joined to the proceedings.

*Solicitor for child*

**12.** (1) A solicitor appointed under section 41(3) or in accordance with *rule 11(2)(a)* [rule 11A(1)(a)] shall represent the child—

(a) in accordance with instructions received from the *guardian ad litem* [children's guardian] (unless the solicitor considers, having taken into account the views of the *guardian ad litem* [children's guardian] and any direction of the court under *rule 11(3)* [rule 11A(2)], that the child wishes to give instructions which conflict with those of the *guardian ad litem* [children's guardian] and that he is able, having regard to his understanding, to give such instructions on his own behalf in which case he shall conduct the proceedings in accordance with instructions received from the child), or

(b) where no *guardian ad litem* [children's guardian] has been appointed for the child and the condition in section 41(4)(b) is satisfied, in accordance with instructions received from the child, or

(c) in default of instructions under (a) or (b), in furtherance of the best interests of the child.

(2) A solicitor appointed under section 41(3) or in accordance with *rule 11(2)(a)* [rule 11A(1)(a)] shall serve and accept service of documents on behalf of the child in accordance with rule 8(3)(a) and (4)(a) and, where the child has not himself been served and has sufficient understanding, advise the child of the contents of any document so served.

(3) Where the child wishes an appointment of a solicitor under section 41(3) or in accordance with *rule 11(2)(a)* [rule 11A(1)(a)] to be terminated, he may apply to the court for an order terminating the appointment; and the solicitor and the *guardian ad litem* [children's guardian] shall be given an opportunity to make representations.

(4) Where the *guardian ad litem* [children's guardian] wishes an appointment of a solicitor under section 41(3) to be terminated, he may apply to the court for an order terminating the appointment; and the solicitor and, if he is of sufficient understanding, the child, shall be given an opportunity to make representations.

(5) When terminating an appointment in accordance with paragraph (3) or (4), the court shall give reasons for so doing, a note of which shall be taken by the justices' clerk.

(6) Where the justices' clerk or the court appoints a solicitor under section 41(3) or refuses to make such an appointment, the justices' clerk shall record the appointment or refusal in the appropriate form in Schedule 1 to these Rules and [the justices' chief executive shall] serve a copy on the parties and, where he is appointed, on the solicitor.

**Note.** Words 'rule 11(2)(a)' in each place it occurs substituted by words 'rule 11A(1)(a)' in square brackets and 'rule 11(3)' substituted by words 'rule 11A(2)' in square brackets by SI 2001/818, rr 2, 8(a), (b) as from 1 April 2001. Words 'guardian ad litem' in each place they occur substituted by words 'children's guardian' in square brackets by SI 2001/818, rr 2, 4(a) as from 1 April 2001. In para (6) words 'the justices' chief executive shall' in square brackets inserted by SI 2001/615, r 2(xx), Schedule, para 97.

*Welfare officer*

**13.** (1) Where the court or a justices' clerk has directed that a written report be made by a welfare officer [in accordance with section 7(1)(b)], the report shall be filed at or by such time as the court or justices' clerk directs or, in the absence of such a direction, at least 14 days before a relevant hearing; and the *justices' clerk* [justices' chief executive] shall, as soon as practicable, serve a copy of the report on the parties and any *guardian ad litem* [children's guardian].

(2) In paragraph (1), a hearing is relevant if the *justices' clerk* [justices' chief executive] has given the welfare officer notice that his report is to be considered at it.

(3) After the filing of a written report by a welfare officer, the court or the justices' clerk may direct that the welfare officer attend any hearing at which the report is to be considered; and—

(6) The children's guardian shall, unless the justices' clerk or the court otherwise directs, not less than 14 days before the date fixed for the final hearing of the proceedings—

   (a)  file a written report advising on the interests of the child; .

   (b)  serve a copy of the filed report on the other parties.

(7) The children's guardian shall serve and accept service of documents on behalf of the child in accordance with rule 8(3)(b) and (4)(b) and, where the child has not himself been served, and has sufficient understanding, advise the child of the contents of any document so served.

(8) If the children's guardian inspects records of the kinds referred to in section 42, he shall bring to the attention of—

   (a)  the court, through the justices' chief executive; and

   (b)  unless the court or the justices' clerk otherwise directs, the other parties to the proceedings,

all records and documents which may, in his opinion, assist in the proper determination of the proceedings.

(9) The children's guardian shall ensure that, in relation to a decision made by the justices' clerk or the court in the proceedings—

   (a)  if he considers it appropriate to the age and understanding of the child, the child is notified of that decision; and

   (b)  if the child is notified of the decision, it is explained to the child in a manner appropriate to his age and understanding.]

**Note.** Inserted by SI 2001/818, rr 2, 7 as from 1 April 2001: see SI 2001/818, r 1.

*[Additional powers and duties of a children and family reporter*

**11B.**   (1) In addition to his duties under rule 11, the children and family reporter shall—

   (a)  notify the child of such contents of his report (if any) as he considers appropriate to the age and understanding of the child, including any reference to the child's own views on the application and the recommendation of the children and family reporter; and

   (b)  if he does notify the child of any contents of his report, explain them to the child in a manner appropriate to his age and understanding.

   (2) Where the court has—

   (a)  directed that a written report be made by a children and family reporter; and

   (b  notified the children and family reporter that his report is to be considered at a hearing,

the children and family reporter shall-

       (i)  file his report; and

      (ii)  serve a copy on the other parties and on the children's guardian (if any),

by such time as the court may direct and if no direction is given, not less than 14 days before that hearing.

(3) The court may direct that the children and family reporter attend any hearing at which his report is to be considered.

(4) The children and family reporter shall advise the court if he considers that the joinder of a person as a party to the proceedings would be likely to safeguard the interests of the child.

(5) The children and family reporter shall consider whether it is in the best interests of the child for the child to be made a party to the proceedings.

(6) If the children and family reporter considers the child should be made a party to the proceedings he shall notify the court of his opinion together with the reasons for that opinion.]

**Note.** Inserted by SI 2001/818, rr 2, 7 as from 1 April 2001.

(a)   except where such a direction is given at a hearing attended by the welfare officer, the *justices' clerk* [justices' chief executive] shall inform the welfare officer of the direction; and

(b)   at the hearing at which the report is considered any party may question the welfare officer about his report.

[(3A)  The welfare officer shall consider whether it is in the best interests of the child for the child to be made a party to the proceedings.

(3B)  If the welfare officer considers that the child should be made a party to the proceedings he shall notify the court of his opinion together with the reasons for that opinion.]

(4)  This rule is without prejudice to the court's power to give directions under rule 14.

**Note.** In para (1) words 'in accordance with section 7(1)(b)' in square brackets and paras (3A), (3B) inserted by SI 2001/818, rr 2, 9, as from 1 April 2001. In paras (1)-(3) words 'justices clerk' substituted by words 'justices' chief executive' in square brackets by SI 2001/615, r 2(xx), Schedule, para 93 as from 1 April 2001. In para (1) words 'guardian ad litem' substituted by words 'children's guardian' in square brackets by SI 2011/818, rr 2, 4(a) as from 1 April 2001.

*Directions*

**14.**   (1)  In this rule, 'party' includes the *guardian ad litem* [children's guardian] and, where a request or direction concerns a report under section 7, the *welfare officer* [welfare officer or children and family reporter].

(2)  In any relevant proceedings the justices' clerk or the court may, subject to paragraph (5), give, vary or revoke directions for the conduct of the proceedings, including—

(a)   the timetable for the proceedings;

(b)   varying the time within which or by which an act is required, by these Rules, to be done;

(c)   the attendance of the child;

(d)   the appointment of a *guardian ad litem* [children's guardian] *whether under section 41 or otherwise,* or of a solicitor under section 41(3);

(e)   the service of documents;

(f)   the submission of evidence including experts' reports;

(g)   the preparation of welfare reports under section 7;

(h)   the transfer of the proceedings to another court in accordance with any Order made by the Lord Chancellor under Part I of Schedule 11;

(i)   consolidation with other proceedings;

and the justices' clerk shall, on receipt of an application [by the justices' chief executive], or where proceedings have been transferred to his court, consider whether such directions need to be given.

(3)  Where the justices' clerk or a single justice who is holding a directions appointment considers, for whatever reason, that it is inappropriate to give a direction on a particular matter, he shall refer the matter to the court which may give any appropriate direction.

(4)  Where a direction is given under paragraph (2)(h), an order shall be issued in the appropriate form in Schedule 1 to these Rules and the *justices' clerk* [justices' chief executive] shall follow the procedure set out in rule 6(2).

(5)  Directions under paragraph (2) may be given, varied or revoked either—

(a)   of the justices' clerk or the court's own motion [the justices' chief executive] having given the parties notice of the intention to do so and an opportunity to attend and be heard or to make written representations,

(b)   on the written request in Form C2 of a party specifying the direction which is sought, filed and served on the other parties, or

(c)   on the written request in Form C2 of a party specifying the direction which is sought, to which the other parties consent and which they or their representatives have signed.

(6) In an urgent case, the request under paragraph (5)(b) may, with the leave of the justices' clerk or the court, be made—

(a) orally,

(b) without notice to the parties, or

(c) both as in sub-paragraph (a) and as in sub-paragraph (b).

(7) On receipt of a request [by the justices' chief executive] under paragraph (5)(b) the justices' clerk shall fix a date for the hearing of the request and [the justices' chief executive shall] give not less than 2 days' notice in Form C6 to the parties of the date so fixed.

(8) On considering a request under paragraph (5)(c) the justices' clerk or the court shall either—

(a) grant the request, whereupon the *justices' clerk* [justices' chief executive] shall inform the parties of the decision, or

(b) direct that a date be fixed for the hearing of the request, whereupon the justices' clerk shall fix such a date and [the justices' chief executive shall] give not less than 2 days' notice to the parties of the date so fixed.

(9) Subject to rule 28, a party may request, in accordance with paragraph 5(b) or (c), that an order be made under section 11(3) or, if he is entitled to apply for such an order, under section 38(1), and paragraphs (6), (7) and (8) shall apply accordingly.

(10) Where, in any relevant proceedings, the court has power to make an order of its own motion, the power to give directions under paragraph (2) shall apply.

(11) Directions of the justices' clerk or a court which are still in force immediately prior to the transfer of relevant proceedings to another court shall continue to apply following the transfer, subject to any changes of terminology which are required to apply those directions to the court to which the proceedings are transferred, unless varied or discharged by directions under paragraph (2).

(12) The justices' clerk or the court shall record the giving, variation or revocation of a direction under this rule in the appropriate form in Schedule 1 to these Rules and [the justices' chief executive shall] serve, as soon as practicable, a copy of the form on any party who was not present at the giving, variation or revocation.

**Note.** In paras (1), (2) words 'guardian ad litem' substituted by words 'children's guardian' in square brackets by SI 2001/818, rr 2, 4(a) as from 1 April 2001 and in para (1) words 'welfare officer' substituted by words 'welfare officer or children and family reporter' in square brackets by SI 2001/818, rr 2, 4(b) as from 1 April 2001. In para (2)(d) words 'whether under section 41 or otherwise' revoked by SI 2001/818, rr 2, 10 as from 1 April 2001 and words 'by the justices' chief executive' in square brackets inserted by SI 2001/615, r 2(xx), Schedule, para 99 as from 1 April 2001. In paras (4), (8)(a) words 'justices' clerk' substituted by words 'justices' chief executive' in square brackets by SI 2001/615, r 2(xx), Schedule, para 93 as from 1 April 2001. In para (5)(a) words 'the justices' chief executive' in square brackets inserted by SI 2001/615, r 2(xx), Schedule, para 98 as from 1 April 2001. In paras (7), (8), (12) words 'by the justices' chief executive' and 'the justices' chief executive shall' in square brackets inserted by SI 2001/615, r 2(xx), Schedule, paras 97, 99 as from 1 April 2001.

*Timing of proceedings*

**15.** (1) Any period of time fixed by these Rules, or by any order or direction, for doing any act shall be reckoned in accordance with this rule.

(2) Where the period, being a period of 7 days or less, would include a day which is not a business day, that day shall be excluded.

(3) Where the time fixed for filing a document with the *justices' clerk* [justices' chief executive] expires on a day on which the *justices' clerk's office* [office of the justices' chief executive] is closed, and for that reason the document cannot be

filed on that day, the document shall be filed in time if it is filed on the next day on which the *justices' clerk's office* [office of the justices' chief executive] is open.

(4) Where these Rules provide a period of time within which or by which a certain act is to be performed in the course of relevant proceedings, that period may not be extended otherwise than by a direction of the justices' clerk or the court under rule 14.

(5) At the—

(a) transfer to a court of relevant proceedings,

(b) postponement or adjournment of any hearing or directions appointment in the course of relevant proceedings, or

(c) conclusion of any such hearing or directions appointment other than one at which the proceedings are determined, or so soon thereafter as is practicable,

*the justices' clerk or the court shall—*

(i) *fix a date upon which the proceedings shall come before the justices' clerk or the court again for such purposes as the justices' clerk or the court directs, which date shall, where paragraph (a) applies, be as soon as possible after the transfer, and*

(ii) *give notice to the parties and to the guardian ad litem or the welfare officer of the date so fixed.*

[(i) the justices' clerk shall fix a date upon which the proceedings shall come before him or the court again for such purposes as he or the court directs, which date shall, where paragraph (a) applies, be as soon as possible after the transfer, and

(ii) the justices' chief executive shall give notice to the parties and to the *guardian ad litem* [children's guardian] or the *welfare officer* [welfare officer or children and family reporter] of the date so fixed].

**Note.** In para (3) words 'justices' clerk' and 'justices' clerk's office' in both places substituted by words 'justices' chief executive' and 'office of the justices' chief executive' in square brackets by SI 2001/615, r 2(xx), Schedule, paras 93, 95 as from 1 April 2001. In para (5) words from 'the justices' clerk or the court shall' to the end substituted by subsequent sub-paras (i), (ii) by SI 2001/615, r 2(xx), Schedule, para 96 as from 1 April 2001; in new sub-para (ii) words 'guardian ad litem' and words 'welfare officer' substituted by words 'children's guardian' and 'welfare officer or children and family reporter' in square brackets by SI 2001/818. rr 2, 4(a), (b) as from 1 April 2001.

*Attendances at directions appointment and hearing*

**16.** (1) Subject to paragraph (2), a party shall attend a directions appointment of which he has been given notice in accordance with rule 14(5) unless the justices' clerk or the court otherwise directs.

(2) Relevant proceedings shall take place in the absence of any party including the child if—

(a) the court considers it in the interests of the child, having regard to the matters to be discussed or the evidence likely to be given, and

(b) the party is represented by a *guardian ad litem* [children's guardian] or solicitor;

and when considering the interests of the child under sub-paragraph (a) the court shall give the *guardian ad litem* [children's guardian], solicitor for the child and, if he is of sufficient understanding, the child, an opportunity to make representations.

(3) Subject to paragraph (4) below, where at the time and place appointed for a hearing or directions appointment the applicant appears but one or more of the respondents do not, the justices' clerk or the court may proceed with the hearing or appointment.

(4) The court shall not begin to hear an application in the absence of a respondent unless—

(a) it is proved to the satisfaction of the court that he received reasonable notice of the date of the hearing; or

(b) the court is satisfied that the circumstances of the case justify proceeding with the hearing.

(5) Where at the time and place appointed for a hearing or directions appointment, one or more respondents appear but the applicant does not, the court may refuse the application, or, if sufficient evidence has previously been received, proceed in the absence of the applicant.

(6) Where at the time and place appointed for a hearing or directions appointment neither the applicant nor any respondent appears, the court may refuse the application.

(7) If the court considers it expedient in the interests of the child, it shall hear any relevant proceedings in private when only the officers of the court, the parties, their legal representatives and such other persons as specified by the court may attend.

**Note.** In para (2) words 'guardian ad litem' in both places substituted by words 'children's guardian' in square brackets by SI 2001/818, rr 2, 4(a) as from 1 April 2001.

*Documentary evidence*

**17.**   (1) Subject to paragraphs (4) and (5), in any relevant proceedings a party shall file and serve on the parties, any *welfare officer* [welfare officer or children and family reporter] and any *guardian ad litem* [children's guardian] of whose appointment he has been given notice under rule 10(5)—

  (a) written statements of the substance of the oral evidence which the party intends to adduce at a hearing of, or a directions appointment in, those proceedings, which shall—

    (i) be dated,

    (ii) be signed by the person making the statement,

    (iii) contain a declaration that the maker of the statement believes it to be true and understands that it may be placed before the court, and

    (iv) show in the top right hand corner of the first page—

        (a) the initials and surname of the person making the statement,

        (b) the number of the statement in relation to the maker,

        (c) the date on which the statement was made, and

        (d) the party on whose behalf it is filed; and

  (b) copies of any documents, including, subject to rule 18(3), experts' reports, upon which the party intends to rely, at a hearing of, or a directions appointment in, those proceedings,

at or by such time as the justices' clerk or the court directs or, in the absence of a direction, before the hearing or appointment.

(2) A party may, subject to any direction of the justices' clerk or the court about the timing of statements under this rule, file and serve on the parties a statement which is supplementary to a statement served under paragraph (1).

(3) At a hearing or directions appointment a party may not, without the leave of the justices' clerk, in the case of a directions appointment, or the court—

  (a) adduce evidence, or

  (b) seek to rely on a document,

in respect of which he has failed to comply with the requirements of paragraph (1).

(4) In proceedings for a section 8 order a party shall—

  (a) neither file nor serve any document other than as required or authorised by these Rules, and

  (b) in completing a form prescribed by these Rules, neither give information, nor make a statement, which is not required or authorised by that form,

without the leave of the justices' clerk or the court.

(5) In proceedings for a section 8 order, no statement or copy may be filed under paragraph (1) until such time as the justices' clerk or the court directs.

**Note.** In para (1) words 'welfare officer' and 'guardian ad litem' substituted by words 'welfare officer or children and family reporter' and 'children's guardian' in square brackets by SI 2001/818, rr 2, 4(a), (b) as from 1 April 2001.

*Expert evidence—examination of child*

**18.** (1) No person may, without the leave of the justices' clerk or the court, cause the child to be medically or psychiatrically examined, or otherwise assessed, for the purpose of the preparation of expert evidence for use in the proceedings.

(2) An application for leave under paragraph (1) shall, unless the justices' clerk or the court otherwise directs, be served on all the parties to the proceedings and on the *guardian ad litem* [children's guardian].

(3) Where the leave of the justices' clerk or the court has not been given under paragraph (1), no evidence arising out of an examination or assessment to which that paragraph applies may be adduced without the leave of the court.

**Note.** Words 'guardian ad litem' substituted by words 'children's guardian' in square brackets by SI 2001/818, r 2, 4(a) as from 1 April 2001.

*Amendment*

**19.** (1) Subject to rule 17(2), a document which has been filed or served in any relevant proceedings may not be amended without the leave of the justices' clerk or the court which shall, unless the justices' clerk or the court otherwise directs, be requested in writing.

(2) On considering a request for leave to amend a document the justices' clerk or the court shall either—

(a) grant the request, whereupon the *justices' clerk* [justices' chief executive] shall inform the person making the request of that decision, or

(b) invite the parties or any of them to make representations, within a specified period, as to whether such an order should be made.

(3) A person amending a document shall file it with the *justices' clerk* [justices' chief executive] and serve it on those persons on whom it was served prior to amendment; and the amendments shall be identified.

**Note.** Words 'justices' clerk in both places substituted by words 'justices' chief executive' in square brackets by SI 2001/615, r 2(xx), Schedule, para 93 as from 1 April 2001.

*Oral evidence*

**20.** The justices' clerk or the court shall keep a note of the substance of the oral evidence given at a hearing of, or directions appointment in, relevant proceedings.

*Hearing*

**21.** (1) Before the hearing, the justice or justices who will be dealing with the case shall read any documents which have been filed under rule 17 in respect of the hearing.

(2) The justices' clerk at a directions appointment, or the court at a hearing or directions appointment, may give directions as to the order of speeches and evidence.

(3) Subject to directions under paragraph (2), at a hearing of, or directions appointment in, relevant proceedings, the parties and the *guardian ad litem* [children's guardian] shall adduce their evidence in the following order—

(a) the applicant,

(b) any party with parental responsibility for the child,

(c) other respondents,

(d) the *guardian ad litem* [children's guardian],

(e) the child if he is a party to the proceedings and there is no *guardian ad litem* [children's guardian].

(4) After the final hearing of relevant proceedings, the court shall make its decision as soon as is practicable.

(5) Before the court makes an order or refuses an application or request, the justices' clerk shall record in writing—

(a) the names of the justice or justices constituting the court by which the decision is made, and

(b) in consultation with the justice or justices, the reasons for the court's decision and any findings of fact.

(6) When making an order or when refusing an application, the court, or one of the justices constituting the court by which the decision is made, shall—

(a) where it makes a finding of fact state such finding and complete Form C22; and

(b) state the reasons for the court's decision.

*(7) After the court announces its decision, the justices' clerk shall as soon as practicable—*

*(a) make a record of any order made in the appropriate form in Schedule 1 to these Rules or, where there is no such form, in writing; and*

*(b) subject to paragraph (8), serve a copy of any order made on the parties to the proceedings and on any person with whom the child is living.*

[(7) As soon as practicable after the court announces its decision—

(a) the justices' clerk shall make a record of any order made in the appropriate form in Schedule 1 to these Rules or, where there is no such form, in writing; and

(b) subject to paragraph (8), the justices' chief executive shall serve a copy of any order made on the parties to the proceedings and on any person with whom the child is living.]

(8) Within 48 hours after the making of an order under section 48(4), or the making, ex parte, of—

(a) a section 8 order,

(b) an order under section 44, 48(9), 50 or 75(1),

the applicant shall serve a copy of the order in the appropriate form in Schedule 1 to these Rules on—

    (i) each party,

    (ii) any person who has actual care of the child, or who had such care immediately prior to the making of the order, and

    (iii) in the case of an order referred to in sub-paragraph (b), the local authority in whose area the child lives or is found.

**Note.** In para (3) words 'guardian ad litem' in each place substituted by words 'children's guardian' in square brackets by SI 2001/818, rr 2, 4(a) as from 1 April 2001. Para (7) substituted by SI 2001/615, r 2(xx), Schedule, para 101.

## PART IIA   PROCEEDINGS UNDER SECTION 30 OF THE HUMAN FERTILISATION AND EMBRYOLOGY ACT 1990

*Interpretation*

**21A.** (1) In this Part of these Rules—

'the 1990 Act' means the Human Fertilisation and Embryology Act 1990;

'the birth father' means the father of the child, including a person who is treated as being the father of the child by section 28 of the 1990 Act where he is not the husband within the meaning of section 30 of the 1990 Act;

'the birth mother' means the woman who carried the child;

'the birth parents' means the birth mother and the birth father;

*'the guardian ad litem' means the guardian appointed in accordance with rule 21E;*

'the husband and wife' means the persons who may apply for a parental order where the conditions set out in section 30(1) of the 1990 Act are met;

'parental order' means an order under section 30 of the 1990 Act (parental orders in favour of gamete donors) providing for a child to be treated in law as a child of the parties to a marriage;

['parental order reporter' means an officer of the service appointed under s 41 of the Children Act 1989 in relation to proceedings specified by paragraph (2)].

(2) Applications under section 30 of the 1990 Act are specified proceedings for the purposes of section 41 of the Children Act 1989 in accordance with section 41(6)(i) of that Act.

**Note.** Definition 'the guardian ad litem' revoked and definition 'parental order reporter' inserted by SI 2001/818, rr 2, 11 as from 1 April 2001.

### *Application of the remaining provisions of these Rules*

**21B.** Subject to the provisions of this Part, the remaining provisions of these Rules shall apply as appropriate with any necessary modifications to proceedings under this Part except that rules 7(1), 9, 10(1)(b), 10(11), *11(2)* [11A(1)], *11(3)* [11A(2)] and 12 shall not apply.

**Note.** References to '11(2)' and '11(3)' substituted by references '11A(1)' and '11A(2)' in square brackets by SI 2001/818, rr 2, 12 as from 1 April 2001.

### *Parties*

**21C.** The applicants shall be the husband and wife and the respondents shall be the persons set out in the relevant entry in column (iii) of Schedule 2.

### *Acknowledgement*

**21D.** Within 14 days of the service of an application for a parental order, each respondent shall file and serve on all the other parties an acknowledgement in Form C52.

### *Appointment and duties of the guardian ad litem [parental order reporter]*

**21E.** (1) As soon as practicable after the application has been filed, the justices' clerk shall consider the appointment of a *guardian ad litem* [parental order reporter] in accordance with section 41(1) of the Children Act 1989.

(2) ...

(3) In addition to such of the matters set out in *rule 11* [rules 11 and 11A] as are appropriate, the *guardian ad litem* [parental order reporter] shall—

(i) investigate the matters set out in section 30(1) to (7) of the 1990 Act;

(ii) so far as he considers necessary, investigate any matter contained in the application form or other matter which appears relevant to the making of a parental order;

(iii) advise the court on whether there is any reason under section 6 of the Adoption Act 1976, as applied with modifications by the Parental Orders (Human Fertilisation and Embryology) Regulations 1994 to refuse the parental order.

**Note.** Words 'guardian ad litem' in each place substituted by words 'parental order reporter' in square brackets, para (2) revoked and in para (3) words 'rule 11' substituted by words 'rules 11 and 11A' in square brackets by SI 2001/818, rr 2, 13 as from 1 April 2004.

### *Personal attendance of applicants*

**21F.** The court shall not make a parental order except upon the personal attendance before it of the applicants.

### *Copies of orders*

**21G.** (1) Where a parental order is made by a court sitting in Wales in respect of a child who was born in Wales and the applicants so request before the order is drawn up, the *justices' clerk* [justices' chief executive] shall obtain a translation into Welsh of the particulars set out in the order.

(2) Within 7 days after the making of a parental order, the *justices' clerk* [justices' chief executive] shall send a copy of the order to the Registrar General.

(3) A copy of any parental order may be supplied to the Registrar General at his request.

**Note.** Words 'justices' clerk' in both places substituted by words 'justices' chief executive' in square brackets by SI 2001/615, r 2(xx), Schedule, para 93 as from 1 April 2001.

*Amendment and revocation of orders*

**21H.**   (1) Any application made under paragraph 4 of Schedule 1 to the Adoption Act 1976 as modified by the Parental Orders (Human Fertilisation and Embryology) Regulations 1994 for the amendment of a parental order or for the revocation of a direction to the Registrar General shall be made to a family proceedings court for the same petty sessions area as the family proceedings court which made the parental order, by delivering it to or sending it by post to the *clerk to the justices* [justices' chief executive].

(2) Notice of the application shall be given by the *justices' clerk* [justices' chief executive] to such persons (if any) as the court thinks fit.

(3) Where the application is granted, the *justices' clerk* [justices' chief executive] shall send to the Registrar General a notice specifying the amendments or informing him of the revocation and shall given sufficient particulars of the order to enable the Registrar General to identify the case.

**Note.** Words 'clerk to the justices' and 'justices' clerk' in both places substituted by words 'justices' chief executive' in square brackets by SI 2001/615, r 2(xx), Schedule, para 93, 102 as from 1 April 2001.

*Keeping of registers, custody, inspection and disclosure of documents and information*

**21I.**   (1) Such part of the register kept in pursuance of rules made under the Magistrates' Courts Act 1980 as relates to proceedings for parental orders shall be kept in a separate book and the book shall not contain particulars of any other proceedings.

(2) The book kept in pursuance of paragraph (1) and all other documents relating to the proceedings for a parental order shall, while they are in the custody of the court, be kept in a place of special security.

(3) Any person who obtains information in the course of, or relating to proceedings for a parental order, shall treat the information as confidential and shall only disclose it if—

(a) the disclosure is necessary for the proper exercise of his duties, or

(b) the information is requested—

   (i) by a court or public authority (whether in Great Britain or not) having the power to determine proceedings for a parental order and related matters, for the purpose of the discharge of its duties in that behalf, or

   (ii) by a person who is authorised in writing by the Secretary of State to obtain the information for the purposes of research.

*Application for removal, return etc of child*

**21J.**   (1) An application under sections 27(1), 29(1) or 29(2) of the Adoption Act 1976 as applied with modifications by the Parental Orders (Human Fertilisation and Embryology) Regulations 1994 shall be made by complaint to the family proceedings court in which the application under section 30 of the 1990 Act is pending.

(2) The respondents shall be all the parties to the proceedings under section 30 and such other person or body, not being the child, as the court thinks fit.

(3) The *justices' clerk* [justices' chief executive] shall serve notice of the time fixed for the hearing, together with a copy of the complaint on the guardian ad litem who

may attend on the hearing of the application and be heard on the question of whether the application should be granted.

(4) The court may at any time give directions as to the conduct of the application under this rule.

(5) Where an application under this rule is determined, the *justices' clerk* [justices' chief executive] shall serve notice of the determination on all the parties.

(6) A search warrant issued by a justice of the peace under section 29(4) of the Adoption Act 1976 (applied as above) (which relates to premises specified in an information to which an order made under the said section 29(1) relates, authorising a constable to search the said premises and if he finds the child to return the child to the person on whose application the said order was made) shall be in a warrant form as if issued under section 102 of the Children Act 1989 (warrant to search for or remove a child) or a form to the like effect.

**Note.** Words 'justices' clerk' in both places substituted by words 'justices' chief executive' in square brackets by SI 2001/615, r 2(xx), Schedule para 93 as from 1 April 2001.


## PART III   MISCELLANEOUS

*Costs*

**22.**   (1) In any relevant proceedings, the court may, at any time during the proceedings in that court, make an order that a party pay the whole or any part of the costs of any other party.

(2) A party against whom the court is considering making a costs order shall have an opportunity to make representations as to why the order should not be made.

*[Power of court to limit cross-examination*

**22A.**   The court may limit the issues on which an officer of the service may be cross-examined.]

**Note.** Inserted by SI 2001/818, rr 2, 14 as from 1 April 2001.

*Confidentiality of documents*

**23.**   (1) No document, other than a record of an order, held by the court and relating to relevant proceedings shall be disclosed, other than to—

(a) a party,

(b) the legal representative of a party,

(c) the *guardian ad litem* [children's guardian].

(d) the *Legal Aid Board* [Legal Services Commission], or

(e) a *welfare officer* [welfare officer or children and family reporter],

[(f) an expert whose instruction by a party has been authorised by a court,] without leave of the justices' clerk or the court.

(2) Nothing in this rule shall prevent the notification by the court or the *justices' clerk* [justices' chief executive] of a direction under section 37(1) to the authority concerned.

*(3) Nothing in this rule shall prevent the disclosure of a document prepared by a guardian ad litem for the purpose of—*

*(a) enabling a person to perform functions required by regulations made under section 41(7);*

*(b) assisting a guardian ad litem or a reporting officer (within the meaning of section 65(1)(b) of the Adoption Act 1976) who is appointed under any enactment to perform his functions.*

[(3) Nothing in this rule shall prevent the disclosure of a document prepared by an officer of the service for the purpose of—

(a) enabling a person to perform functions required under section 62(3A) of the Justices of the Peace Act 1997;

(b) assisting an officer of the service who is appointed by the court under any enactment to perform his functions.]

   [(4) Nothing in this rule shall prevent the disclosure of any document relating to proceedings by an officer of the service to any other officer of the service unless that other officer is involved in the same proceedings but on behalf of a different party.]

**Note.** In para (1)(c) words 'guardian ad litem' substituted by words 'children's guardian' in square brackets by SI 2001/818, rr 2, 4(a) as from 1 April 2001. In para (1)(d) words 'Legal Aid Board' substituted by words 'Legal Services Commission' in square brackets by virtue of the Access to Justice Act 1999, s 105, Sch 14, Pt II, para 3(3) as from 1 April 2000 (subject to transitional provisions and savings, by SI 2000/774, arts 2, 5). In para (1)(e) words 'welfare officer' substituted by words 'welfare officer or children and family reporter' in square brackets by SI 2001/818, rr 2, 4(b) as from 1 April 2001. Para (1)(f) and word 'or' immediately preceding it inserted by SI 2001/818, rr 2, 15(a) as from 1 April 2001. In para (2) words 'justices' clerk' substituted by words 'justices' chief executive' in square brackets by SI 2001/615, r 2(xx), Schedule, para 93 as from 1 April 2001. Para (3) inserted by SI 1997/1895, r 2; substituted by SI 2001/818, rr 2, 15(b) as from 1 April 2001. Para (4) inserted by SI 2001/818, rr 2, 15(c) as from 1 April 2001.

*Enforcement of residence order*

**24.**   Where a person in whose favour a residence order is in force wishes to enforce it he shall file a written statement describing the alleged breach of the arrangements settled by the order, whereupon the *justices' clerk shall* [justices' chief executive shall] fix a date, time and place for a hearing of the proceedings and give notice as soon as practicable, to the person wishing to enforce the residence order and to any person whom it is alleged is in breach of the arrangements settled by that order, of the date fixed.

**Note.** Words 'justices' clerk shall' substituted by words 'justices' chief executive shall' in square brackets by SI 2001/615, r 2(xx), Schedule, para 97 as from 1 April 2001.

*Notification of consent*

**25.**   (1) Consent for the purposes of—
   (a) section 16(3), or
   (b) section 38A(2)(b)(ii) or 44A(2)(b)(ii), or
   (c) paragraph 19(1) of Schedule 2,
shall be given either—
         (i) orally in court, or
        (ii) in writing to the *justices' clerk* [justices' chief executive] or the court and signed by the person giving his consent.
   (2) Any written consent given for the purposes of subsection (2) of section 38A or section 44A, shall include a statement that the person giving consent—
   (a) is able and willing to give to the child the care which it would be reasonable to expect a parent to give him; and
   (b) understands that the giving of consent could lead to the exclusion of the relevant person from the dwelling-house in which the child lives.

**Note.** Words 'justices' clerk' substituted by words 'justices' chief executive' in square brackets by SI 2001/615, r 2(xx) Schedule, para 93 as from 1 April 2001.

*Exclusion requirements: interim care orders and emergency protection orders*

**25A.**   (1) This rule applies where the court includes an exclusion requirement in an interim care order or an emergency protection order.
   (2) The applicant for an interim care order or emergency protection order shall
   (a) prepare a separate statement of the evidence in support of the application for an exclusion requirement;

(b) serve the statement personally on the relevant person with a copy of the order containing the exclusion requirement (and of any power of arrest which is attached to it);

(c) inform the relevant person of his right to apply to vary or discharge the exclusion requirement.

(3) Where a power of arrest is attached to an exclusion requirement in an interim care order or an emergency protection order, a copy of the order shall be delivered to the officer for the time being in charge of the police station for the area in which the dwelling-house in which the child lives is situated (or of such other station as the court may specify) together with a statement that the relevant person has been served with the order or informed of its terms (whether by being present when the order was made or by telephone or otherwise).

(4) Rules 12A(3), 20 (except paragraphs (1) and (3)) and 21 of the Family Proceedings Courts (Matrimonial Proceedings etc) Rules 1991 shall apply, with the necessary modifications, for the service, variation, discharge and enforcement of any exclusion requirement to which a power of arrest is attached as they apply to an order made on an application under Part IV of the Family Law Act 1996.

(5) The relevant person shall serve the parties to the proceedings with any application which he makes for the variation or discharge of the exclusion requirement.

(6) Where an exclusion requirement ceases to have effect whether—

(a) as a result of the removal of a child under section 38A(10) or 44A(10),

(b) because of the discharge of the interim care order or emergency protection order, or

(c) otherwise,

the applicant shall inform—

(i) the relevant person,

(ii) the parties to the proceedings,

(iii) any officer to whom a copy of the order was delivered under paragraph (3), and

(iv) (where necessary) the court.

(7) Where the court includes an exclusion requirement in an interim care order or an emergency protection order of its own motion, paragraph (2) shall apply with the omission of any reference to the statement of the evidence.

*Secure accommodation*

**26.** In proceedings under section 25, the *justices' clerk* [justices' chief executive] shall, if practicable, arrange for copies of all written reports before the court to be made available before the hearing to—

(a) the applicant,

(b) the parent or guardian of the child,

(c) any legal representative of the child,

(d) the *guardian ad litem* [children's guardian], and

(e) the child, unless the *justices' clerk* [justices' chief executive] or the court otherwise directs;

and copies of such reports may, if the court considers it desirable, be shown to any person who is entitled to notice of the proceedings in accordance with these Rules.

**Note.** Words 'justices' clerk' in both places substituted by words 'justices' chief executive' in square brackets by SI 2001/615, r 2(xx), Schedule, para 93 as from 1 April 2001. Words 'guardian ad litem' substituted by words 'children's guardian' in square brackets by SI 2001/818, rr 2, 4(a) as from 1 April 2001.

*Investigation under section 37*

**27.** (1) This rule applies where a direction is given to an appropriate authority by a family proceedings court under section 37(1).

(2) On giving a direction the court shall adjourn the proceedings and the justices' clerk or the court shall record the direction in the appropriate form in Schedule 1 to these Rules.

(3) A copy of the direction recorded under paragraph (2) shall, as soon as practicable after the direction is given, be served by the *justices' clerk* [justices' chief executive] on the parties to the proceedings in which the direction is given and, where the appropriate authority is not a party, on that authority.

(4) When serving the copy of the direction on the appropriate authority the *justices' clerk* [justices' chief executive] shall also serve copies of such of the documentary evidence which has been, or is to be, adduced in the proceedings as the court may direct.

(5) Where a local authority informs the court of any of the matters set out in section 37(3)(a) to (c) it shall do so in writing.

**Note.** Words 'justices' clerk' in both places substituted by words 'justices' chief executive' in square brackets by SI 2001/615, r 2(xx), Schedule, para 93 as from 1 April 2001.

*Limits on the power of a justices' clerk or a single justice to make an order under section 11(3) or section 38(1)*

**28.** A justices' clerk or single justice shall not make an order under section 11(3) or section 38(1) unless—

(a) a written request for such an order has been made to which the other parties and any *guardian ad litem* [children's guardian] consent and which they or their representatives have signed,

(b) a previous such order has been made in the same proceedings, and

(c) the terms of the order sought are the same as those of the last such order made.

**Note.** Words 'guardian ad litem' substituted by words 'children's guardian' in square brackets by SI 2001/818, rr 2, 4(a) as from 1 April 2001.

*Appeals to a family proceedings court under section 77(6) and paragraph 8(1) of Schedule 8*

**29.** (1) An appeal under section 77(6) or paragraph 8(1) of Schedule 8 shall be by application in accordance with rule 4.

(2) An appeal under section 77(6) shall be brought within 21 days from the date of the step to which the appeal relates.

*Contribution orders*

**30.** (1) An application for a contribution order under paragraph 23(1) of Schedule 2 shall be accompanied by a copy of the contribution notice served in accordance with paragraph 22(1) of that Schedule and a copy of any notice served by the contributor under paragraph 22(8) of that Schedule.

(2) Where a local authority notifies the court of an agreement reached under paragraph 23(6) of Schedule 2, it shall do so in writing through the *justices' clerk* [justices' chief executive].

(3) An application for the variation or revocation of a contribution order under paragraph 23(8) of Schedule 2 shall be accompanied by a copy of the contribution order which it is sought to vary or revoke.

**Note.** Words 'justices' clerk' substituted by words 'justices' chief executive' in square brackets by SI 2001/615, r 2(xx), Schedule, para 93 as from 1 April 2001.

*Direction to local education authority to apply for education supervision order*

**31.** (1) For the purposes of section 40(3) and (4) of the Education Act 1944, a direction by a magistrates' court to a local education authority to apply for an education supervision order shall be given in writing.

(2) Where, following such a direction, a local education authority informs the court that they have decided not to apply for an education supervision order, they shall do so in writing.

*Applications and orders under sections 33 and 34 of the Family Law Act 1986*

**31A.**   (1) In this rule 'the 1986 Act' means the Family Law Act 1986.

(2) An application under section 33 of the 1986 Act shall be in Form C4 and an order made under that section shall be in Form C30.

(3) An application under section 34 of the 1986 Act shall be in Form C3 and an order made under that section shall be in Form C31.

(4) An application under section 33 or section 34 of the 1986 Act may be made ex parte in which case the applicant shall file the application—

(a) where the application is made by telephone, within 24 hours after the making of the application, or

(b) in any other case at the time when the application is made,

and shall serve a copy of the application on each respondent 48 hours after the making of the order.

(5) Where the court refuses to make an order on an ex parte application it may direct that the application be made inter partes.

*Delegation by justices' clerk*

**32.**   (1) In this rule, 'employed as a clerk in court' has the same meaning as in rule (1) of the Justices' Clerks (Qualifications of Assistants) Rules 1979.

(2) Anything authorised to be done by, to or before a justices' clerk under these Rules, or under paragraphs 13 to 15C of the Schedule to the Justices' Clerks Rules 1970 as amended by Schedule 3 to these Rules, may be done instead by, to or before a person employed as a clerk in court where that person is appointed by the magistrates' courts committee to assist him and where that person has been specifically authorised by the justices' clerk for that purpose.

(3) Any authorisation by the justices' clerk under paragraph (2) shall be recorded in writing at the time the authority is given or as soon as practicable thereafter.

*Application of section 97 of the Magistrates' Courts Act 1980*

**33.**   Section 97 of the Magistrates' Courts Act 1980 shall apply to relevant proceedings in a family proceedings court as it applies to a hearing of a complaint under that section.

*Disclosure of addresses*

**33A.**   (1) Nothing in these Rules shall be construed as requiring any party to reveal the address of their private residence (or that of any child) except by order of the court.

(2) Where a party declines to reveal an address in reliance upon paragraph (1) he shall give notice of that address to the court in Form C8 and that address shall not be revealed to any person except by order of the court.

*Setting aside on failure of service*

**33B.**   Where an application has been sent to a respondent in accordance with rule 8(1) and, after an order has been made on the application, it appears to the court that the application did not come to the knowledge of the respondent in due time, the court may of its own motion set aside the order and may give such directions as it thinks fit for the rehearing of the application.

*Consequential and minor amendments, savings and transitionals*

**34.**   (1) Subject to paragraph (3) the consequential and minor amendments in Schedule 3 to these Rules shall have effect.

(2) Subject to paragraph (3), the provisions of the 1981 Rules shall have effect subject to these Rules.

(3) Nothing in these Rules shall affect any proceedings which are pending (within the meaning of paragraph 1 of Schedule 14 to the Act of 1989) immediately before these Rules come into force.

## SCHEDULE 1

### FORMS

**Note:** The forms prescribed by Schedule 1 are identical to those prescribed by Schedule 1 to the Family Proceedings Rules 1991. The forms are printed after those rules in Division C of the Service to this Edition.

## SCHEDULE 2 (Rules 4 and 7)
### RESPONDENTS AND NOTICE

| (i) Provision under which proceedings brought | (ii) Minimum number of days prior to hearing or directions appointment for service under rule 4(1)(b) | (iii) Respondents | (iv) Persons to whom notice is to be given |
|---|---|---|---|
| All applications. | See separate entries below. | Subject to separate entries below, | Subject to separate entries below, |
| | | every person whom the applicant believes to have parental responsibility for the child; | the local authority providing accommodation for the child; |
| | | where the child is the subject of a care order, every person whom the applicant believes to have had parental responsibility immediately prior to the making of the care order; | persons who are caring for the child at the time when the proceedings are commenced; in the case of proceedings brought in respect of a child who is alleged to be staying in a refuge which is certificated under section 51(1) or (2), the person who is providing the refuge. |
| | | in the case of an application to extend, vary or discharge an order, the parties to the proceedings leading to the order which it is sought to have extended, varied or discharged; | |

| (*i*) Provision under which proceedings brought | (*ii*) Minimum number of days prior to hearing or directions appointment for service under rule 4(1)(b) | (*iii*) Respondents | (*iv*) Persons to whom notice is to be given |
|---|---|---|---|
| | | in the case of specified proceedings, the child. | |
| Section *4(1)(a)* [4(1)(c)], 4(3), 5(1), 6(7), 8, 13(1), 16(6), 33(7), 77(6), Schedule 1, paragraph 19(1), 23(1) or 23(8) of Schedule 2, paragraph 8(1) of Schedule 8, or paragraph 11(3) or 16(5) of Schedule 14. | 14 days | Except for proceedings under section 77(6), Schedule 2, or paragraph 8(1) of Schedule 8, as for 'all applications' above, and in the case of proceedings under Schedule 1, those persons whom the applicant believes to be interested in or affected by the proceedings:

in the case of an application under paragraph 11(3)(b) or 16(5) of Schedule 14, any person, other than the child, named in the order or directions which it is sought to discharge or vary;

in the case of proceedings under section 77(6), the local authority against whose decision the appeal is made;

in the case of an application under paragraph 23(1) of Schedule 2, the contributor; in the case of an application under paragraph 23(8) of Schedule 2— | As for 'all applications' above, and:

in the case of an application under paragraph 19(1) of Schedule 2, the parties to the proceedings leading to the care order;

in the case of an application under section 5(1), the father of the child if he does not have parental responsibility. |

| (*i*) Provision under which proceedings brought | (*ii*) Minimum number of days prior to hearing or directions appointment for service under rule 4(*1*)(*b*) | (*iii*) Respondents | (*iv*) Persons to whom notice is to be given |
|---|---|---|---|
| | | (i) if the applicant is the local authority, the contributor, and (ii) if the applicant is the contributor, the local authority.<br><br>In the case of an application under paragraph 8(1) of Schedule 8, the local authority against whose decision the appeal is made.<br><br>In the case of an application for a section 8 order, every person whom the applicant believes—<br>(i) to be named in a court order with respect to the same child, which has not ceased to have effect,<br>(ii) to be a party to pending proceedings in respect of the same child, or<br>(iii) to be a person with whom the child has lived for at least three years prior to the application, unless, in a case to which (i) or (ii) applies, the applicant believes | |

| (*i*) Provision under which proceedings brought | (*ii*) Minimum number of days prior to hearing or directions appointment for service under rule 4(1)(b) | (*iii*) Respondents | (*iv*) Persons to whom notice is to be given |
|---|---|---|---|
| | | that the court order or pending proceedings are not relevant to the application. | |
| Section 36(1), 39(1), 39(2), 39(3), 39(4), 43(1), or paragraph 6(3), 15(2) or 17(1) of Schedule 3. | 7 days | As for 'all applications' above, and: | As for 'all applications' above, and: |
| | | in the case of an application under section 39(2) or (3), the supervisor; | in the case of an application for an order under section 43(1)— |
| | | in the case of proceedings under paragraph 17(1) of Schedule 3, the local education authority concerned; | (i) every person whom the applicant believes to be a parent of the child, (ii) every person whom the applicant believes to be caring for the child, |
| | | in the case of proceedings under section 36 or paragraph 15(2) or 17(1) of Schedule 3, the child. | (iii) every person in whose favour a contact order is in force with respect to the child, and (iv) every person who is allowed to have contact with the child by virtue of an order under section 34. |
| Section 31, 34(2), 34(3), 34(4), 34(9) or 38(8)(b). | 3 days | As for 'all applications' above, and: | As for 'all applications' above, and: |
| | | in the case of an application under section 34, the person whose contact with the | in the case of an application under section 31— (i) every person whom the |

| (i) Provision under which proceedings brought | (ii) Minimum number of days prior to hearing or directions appointment for service under rule 4(1)(b) | (iii) Respondents | (iv) Persons to whom notice is to be given |
|---|---|---|---|
| | | child is the subject of the application. | applicant believes to be a party to pending relevant proceedings in respect of the same child, and (ii) every person whom the applicant believes to be a parent without parental responsibility for the child. |
| Section 43(12). | 2 days | As for 'all applications' above. | Those of the persons referred to in section 43(11)(a) to (e) who were not party to the application for the order which it is sought to have varied or discharged. |
| Section 25, 44(1), 44(9)(b), 45(4), 45(8), 46(7), 48(9), 50(1), 75(1) or 102(1). | 1 day | Except for applications under section 75(1) or 102(1), as for 'all applications' above, and: in the case of an application under section 44(9)(b)— (i) the parties to the application for the order in respect of which it is sought to vary the directions; (ii) any person who was caring for the child prior to the making of the order; and | As for 'all applications' above, and: in the case of an application under section 44(1), every person whom the applicant believes to be a parent of the child; in the case of an application under section 44(9)(b)— (i) the local authority in whose area the child is living, and (ii) any person |

| (*i*) Provision under which proceedings brought | (*ii*) Minimum number of days prior to hearing or directions appointment for service under rule 4(1)(*b*) | (*iii*) Respondents | (*iv*) Persons to whom notice is to be given |
|---|---|---|---|
| | | (iii) any person whose contact with the child is affected by the direction which it is sought to have varied; | whom the applicant believes to be affected by the direction which it is sought to have varied. |
| | | in the case of an application under section 50, the person whom the applicant alleges to have effected or to have been or to be responsible for the taking or keeping of the child; | |
| | | in the case of an application under section 75(1), the registered person; | |
| | | in the case of an application under section 102(1), the person referred to in section 102(1) and any person preventing or likely to prevent such a person from exercising powers under enactments mentioned in subsection (6) of that section. | |
| Section 30 of the Human Fertilisation and Embryology Act 1990. | 14 days | The birth parents (except where the applicants seek to dispense with their agreement under section 30(6) of the Human Fertilisation and Embryology Act 1990) and any | Any local authority or voluntary organisation that has at any time provided accommodation for the child. |

| (*i*) | (*ii*) | (*iii*) | (*iv*) |
|---|---|---|---|
| Provision under which proceedings brought | Minimum number of days prior to hearing or directions appointment for service under rule 4(1)(b) | Respondents | Persons to whom notice is to be given |
| | | | other persons or body with parental responsibility for the child at the date of the application. |

**Note.** In entry beginning 'Section 4(1)(a), 4(3)' reference to '4(1)(a)' substituted by reference '4(1)(c)' by SI 2003/2840, r 3. This amendment came into force on 1 December 2003 (being the date on which the Adoption and Children Act 2002, s 111 came into force): see SI 2003/3079, art 2 and SI 2003/2840, r 1.

SCHEDULE 3

\*   \*   \*   \*   \*

## FAMILY PROCEEDINGS COURTS (CONSTITUTION) RULES 1991

**Dated** 11 June 1991

**SI 1991 No 1405**

The Lord Chancellor, in exercise of the powers conferred on him by section 144 of the Magistrates' Courts Act 1980, after consultation with the Rule Committee appointed under the said section 144, hereby makes the following Rules—

*Citation, commencement, revocations and savings*

**1.**   (1) These Rules may be cited as the Family Proceedings Courts (Constitution) Rules 1991 and shall come into force on 14th October 1991, except that for the purposes of rules 4(1), 8, 11(2) and 12(1), these Rules shall come into force on 12th August 1991.

(2) Subject to paragraph (3), the Rules mentioned in the Schedule to these Rules are hereby revoked.

(3) Nothing in these Rules shall affect any proceedings which are pending (within the meaning of paragraph 1 of Schedule 14 to the Act of 1989) immediately before these Rules come into force.

*Interpretation*

**2.**   (1) In these Rules, unless a contrary intention appears—
any reference to a rule shall be construed as a reference to a rule contained in these Rules and any reference in a rule to a paragraph shall be construed as a reference to a paragraph of that rule;
'commission area' has the meaning assigned to it by section 1 of the Act of 1979 but does not include *the inner London area or the City of London* [any petty sessions area within the Greater London Commission Area];
… ;
'panel' means 'family panel', within the meaning of section 92 of the Act of 1989;

'petty sessions area' has the meaning assigned to it by section 4 of the Act of 1979 but does not include *the inner London area or any petty sessional division thereof, or the City of London* [any petty sessions area within the Greater London Commission Area];

*'stipendiary magistrate' means a magistrate appointed under section 13 of the Act of 1979;*

['District Judge (Magistrates' Court) means a District Judge (Magistrates' Courts) appointed under section 10A(1) of the Justices of the Peace Act 1997 or a Deputy District Judge (Magistrates' Courts) appointed under section 10B(1) of that Act;]

'the Act of 1979' means the Justices of the Peace Act 1979;

'the Act of 1989' means the Children Act 1989.

(2) Any reference in these Rules to a justice for a petty sessions area shall be construed as a reference to a justice who ordinarily acts in and for that area.

**Note.** In para (1) definition 'commission area' words 'the inner London area or the City of London' substituted by words 'the Greater London Commission Area' in square brackets by SI 2003/3367, rr 2, 3(a) as from 1 January 2004. In para (1) definition 'inner London area' (omitted) revoked by SI 2003/3367, rr 2, 3(b) as from 1 January 2004. In para (1) definition 'petty sessions area' words 'the inner London area or any petty sessional division thereof, or the City of London' substituted by words 'any petty sessions area within the Greater London Commission Area' in square brackets by SI 2003/3367, rr 2, 3(c) as from 1 January 2004. In para (1) definition 'District Judge (Magistrates' Courts)' substituted, for definition 'stipendiary magistrate' as originally enacted, by SI 2000/1873, r 2 as from 31 August 2000 (see SI 2000/1873, r 1 and SI 2000/1920, art 3(a)).

*Extent*

**3.** *These Rules do not apply in the inner London area or in the City of London.* [These Rules do not apply in the Greater London Commission Area.]

**Note.** Substituted by SI 2003/3367, rr 2, 4 as from 1 January 2004.

*Appointments and formation of panel*

**4.** (1) The justices for each petty sessions area shall, at a meeting held in October 1991, and before 14th October 1991, of which seven days' notice shall be given to each justice for that area, appoint, in accordance with the provisions of these Rules, justices to form a panel for that area who shall, subject to rule 5(4), serve thereon for a term commencing on 14th October 1991 and expiring on 31st December 1993.

(2) The justices for each petty sessions area shall, at the meeting held in October 1993 in accordance with rules made under section 18 of the Act of 1979 for the purpose of electing a chairman of the justices, and thereafter at the said meeting in every third year, appoint, in accordance with the provisions of these Rules, justices to form a panel for that area who shall, subject to rule 5(4), serve thereon for a term of three years commencing on 1st January in the following year.

(3) The number of justices appointed to the panel for a petty sessions area shall be such as the justices for that area at the time of appointment think sufficient for family proceedings courts in the area.

(4) Nominations shall be permitted but where voting is necessary it shall be by secret ballot.

(5) The justices for a petty sessions area may at any time, subject to rule 5(1), appoint one or more additional members of the panel who shall serve thereon until the end of the period for which the other members of the panel were appointed.

*Eligibility and removal*

**5.** (1) A justice shall not be appointed to a panel unless—

(a) he is a justice of the petty sessions area for which the panel is being formed;

(b) he has acted as a justice for a minimum period of one year;

(c) he has indicated that he is willing to serve as a member of the panel; and

(d) where he is appointed under rule 4(1), he will not attain the age of 70 years during the term of his appointment and has undertaken that he intends to serve as a member of the panel for the full term of the appointment.

(2) A justice shall be eligible for appointment to a panel whether or not he—

(a) has been a member of that panel before, or

(b) is, or has been, a member of any other panel.

(3) A *stipendiary magistrate* [District Judge (Magistrates' Courts)] who has been nominated by the Lord Chancellor to hear family proceedings shall be a member of any panel for a petty sessions area or areas which is situated in the commission area or areas to which he is appointed and every such nomination shall be for a specified period and shall be revocable by the Lord Chancellor.

(4) The Lord Chancellor may remove from a panel any justice who, in the Lord Chancellor's opinion, is unsuitable to serve on a family proceedings court.

**Note.** In para (3) words 'stipendiary magistrate' substituted by words 'District Judge (Magistrates' Courts)' in square brackets by SI 2000/1873, r 4(a) as from 31 August 2000 (see SI 2000/1873, r 1 and SI 2000/1920, art 3).

*Vacancies in membership of panel*

**6.** If a vacancy occurs in the membership of a panel for a petty sessions area, the justices for that area shall, as soon as practicable, unless they consider that it is not necessary, and subject to rule 5, appoint a justice to fill the vacancy who shall serve on the panel until the end of the period for which the other members were appointed.

*Temporary transfer of justices between panels*

**7.** (1) Subject to paragraph (4), the justices' clerk for one petty sessions area ('the *first area*') may make a request to the justices' clerk for another petty sessions area ('the *second area*') for the temporary transfer of one or more justices from the panel for the second area to the panel for the first area for the purpose of hearing family proceedings specified in the request.

(2) The justices' clerk for the second area shall grant a request under paragraph (1) where he considers that the better administration of justice will be served by such a transfer, and the justice or justices who are to be nominated by him for the transfer agree to be transferred.

(3) A justices' clerk who grants a request under paragraph (1) shall do so in writing.

(4) Where the first area falls within a different commission area to the second area, a justice or justices shall only be transferred under this rule where the Lord Chancellor appoints the justice or justices who are nominated for the transfer to the commission area within which the first area falls for the purpose of the proceedings specified in the request.

(5) The transfer of a justice or justices under this rule shall not prevent the justice or justices transferred from sitting in a family proceedings court in the second area.

[*Temporary transfer of justices between panels*

**7.** (1) A justices' chief executive for a petty sessions area may nominate a justice or justices from the panel for that area for temporary transfer to the panel for another petty sessions area within his commission area for the purpose of hearing family proceedings specified in his nomination if he is satisfied that the better administration of justice will be served by such transfer, and the justice or justices so nominated agree to be transferred.

(2) A justices' chief executive for one commission area ('the first commission area') may make a request to the justices' chief executive for another commission area ('the second commission area') for the temporary transfer of one or more justices from the panel for a petty sessions area within the second commission area to the panel for a petty sessions area within the first commission area for the purpose of hearing family proceedings specified in the request.

(3) The justices' chief executive for the second commission area shall grant a request under paragraph (2) where he considers that the better administration of justice will be served by such transfer, and the justice or justices nominated by him for the transfer agree to be transferred.

(4) A justices' chief executive who grants a request under paragraph (2) shall do so in writing.

(5) The transfer of a justice or justices under this rule shall not prevent the justice or justices transferred from sitting in a family proceedings court in the petty sessions area from which he or they are transferred.

(6) A justice who is not a District Judge (Magistrates' Courts) shall only be transferred under this rule to a petty sessions area in a different commission area if the Lord Chancellor appoints the justice nominated for the transfer to the commission area within which the petty sessions area falls for the purpose of the proceedings specified in the request.]

**Note.** Substituted by SI 2001/615, r 2(xxi), Schedule, para 104 as from 1 April 2001.

*Chairman and deputy chairmen of panel*

**8.** (1) The members of each panel shall, in accordance with the provisions of this rule and rule 9, on the occasion of their appointment or as soon as practicable thereafter, meet and elect from amongst their number a chairman and as many deputy chairmen as will ensure, subject to rule 10(3), that each family proceedings court sits under the chairmanship of a person so elected.

(2) Nominations for chairman and one or more deputy chairmen may be made by the members of the panel to the *justices' clerk* [justices' chief executive] but, where voting is necessary, it shall be by secret ballot.

(3) If a vacancy occurs in the chairmanship or deputy chairmanship, the members of the panel shall, as soon as practicable, elect by secret ballot a chairman or, as the case may be, deputy chairman, to hold office for the remainder of the period for which the members serve.

**Note.** Words 'justices' clerk' substituted by words 'justices' chief executive' in square brackets by SI 2001/615, r 2(xxi), Schedule, para 103 as from 1 April 2001.

*Conduct of ballots generally*

**9.** (1) Where, under a ballot conducted under any provision of these Rules, there is an equality of votes between any candidates, and the addition of a vote would entitle one of them to be elected, the *justices' clerk* [justices' chief executive] shall forthwith decide between those candidates by lot.

(2) Where, under a ballot conducted under any provision of these Rules, a ballot paper is returned unmarked or it is marked in such a manner that there is a doubt as to the identity of the justice or justices for whom the vote is cast, the ballot paper or the vote, as the case may be, shall be rejected when the votes are counted.

**Note.** Words 'justices' clerk' substituted by words 'justices' chief executive' in square brackets by SI 2001/615, r 2(xxi), Schedule, para 103 as from 1 April 2001.

*Composition of family proceedings courts*

**10.** (1) The members of a panel shall meet as often as may be necessary but not less than twice a year to make arrangements connected with the sitting of family proceedings courts and to discuss questions connected with the work of those courts.

(2) The justices to sit in each family proceedings court shall be chosen from the panel in such manner as the panel may determine so as to ensure that section 66(1) of the Magistrates' Courts Act 1980 (which requires a family proceedings court to be composed of not more than three justices of the peace, including, so far as practicable, both a man and a woman), is complied with.

(3) Except as is provided by paragraph (4), where a *stipendiary magistrate* [District Judge (Magistrates' Courts)] is chosen to sit in a family proceedings court under paragraph (2) he shall preside, but where a *stipendiary magistrate* [District Judge (Magistrates' Courts)] is not so chosen, the court shall sit under the chairmanship of the chairman or a deputy chairman elected under rule 8.

(4) If, at any sitting of a family proceedings court, a *stipendiary magistrate* [District Judge (Magistrates' Courts)], the chairman or a deputy chairman who was chosen to sit as a member of the court cannot do so owing to circumstances unforeseen when the justices to sit were chosen under paragraph (2), the members of that court shall choose one of their number to preside.

**Note.** Words 'stipendiary magistrate' in each place substituted by words 'District Judge (Magistrates' Courts)' in square brackets by SI 2000/1873, r 4(a), as from 1 August 2000.

*Combined panels*

**11.** (1) Where, immediately before 14th October 1991, there exists a combined domestic court panel ('the first panel') in respect of two or more petty sessions areas there shall, with effect from 14th October 1991, be a combined family panel ('the second panel') for those areas and in relation to the second panel these Rules shall have effect as if—

(a)  a direction for its formation had, before 14th October 1991, been made under paragraph (2) by the magistrates' courts committee for the areas in question, save that paragraphs (4) and (5) shall not apply, and

(b)  the direction stated under paragraph (6) that the number of justices to serve as members, and the number of members to be provided by each area, were to be the same as for the first panel.

(2) Subject to the provisions of this rule, a magistrates' courts committee may make a direction for the formation or dissolution of a combined panel in respect of two or more petty sessions areas in the same commission area, of which at least one is a petty sessions area for which the committee acts.

(3) A direction under paragraph (2) shall not be made unless the magistrates' courts committee has consulted the justices for each petty sessions area specified in the direction for which it acts.

(4) A direction under paragraph (2) shall be notified forthwith to the justices for each petty sessions area specified in the direction.

(5) If a magistrates' courts committee makes a direction under paragraph (2) which specifies a petty sessions area or petty sessions areas for which it does not act, the direction shall have no effect unless, before the date on which it is to come into effect, a corresponding direction has been made by the magistrates' courts committee or committees for the area or areas in question.

(6) A direction for the formation of a combined panel shall state—

(a)  the number of justices who are to serve as members of the combined panel, which shall be such as the magistrates' courts committee thinks sufficient for family proceedings courts in the petty sessions areas specified in the direction; and

(b)  the number of members thereof to be provided by each area, which shall, as nearly as may be, be the proportion which the number of justices for that area bears to the total number of justices for the petty sessions areas specified in the direction.

(7) A direction for the formation or dissolution of a combined panel under paragraph (2) shall have effect—

(a)  where it is a direction for the formation of a combined panel and is made before 14th October 1991, on that date,

(b)  where sub-paragraph (a) does not apply and the direction is consequential upon the making of an order under section 23 of the Act of 1979, on the date on which that order comes into force, and

(c) in any other case, on 1st January in the year following the next October meeting of the justices for each of the areas concerned held in accordance with rules made under section 18 of the Act of 1979 for the purpose of electing a chairman of the justices.

(8) For the purposes of paragraph (7)(b), a direction is consequential upon the making of an order under the said section 23 if it is made after that order is made (but before it comes into force) and specifies a petty sessions area which is the subject of such an order.

(9) A magistrates' courts committee which has made a direction for the formation of a combined panel may at any time make a further direction to increase the number of justices specified under paragraph (6)(a) and any such further direction shall state the petty sessions area or petty sessions areas by which the additional member or members is or are to be provided.

(10) A further direction in relation to a combined panel under paragraph (9) shall have effect forthwith or, in the case of a direction which specifies a petty sessions area or petty sessions areas for which the magistrates' courts committee does not act, as soon as corresponding further directions have been made under that paragraph by the magistrates' courts committee or committees for the area or areas in question.

(11) A combined panel formed by a direction made under paragraph (2), shall be the panel for the petty sessions areas specified in the direction and, in relation to any such combined panel, subject to rule 12(4), these Rules shall have effect accordingly.

(12) On the coming into effect of a direction made under this rule (other than a further direction under paragraph (9)), any existing panel in respect of any of the petty sessions areas specified in the direction shall dissolve and any appointments thereto shall cease.

*Appointment of justices to combined panel*

**12.** (1) Where a magistrates' courts committee has made a direction for the formation of a combined panel under rule 11(2), the justices for each petty sessions area specified in the direction shall, at a meeting of the justices held in accordance with paragraph (2), appoint, subject to paragraph (3), such number of justices from the petty sessions areas in question as is stated in the direction, to serve as members of the combined panel, for a term commencing at the same time as the direction will have effect and expiring at the same time as will end the term of appointment of any justices for the time being appointed under rule 4(1) or, where that term has expired, rule 4(2), to form a panel which is not specified in the direction.

(2) The meeting referred to in paragraph (1) shall be—

(a) where the direction is made before 14th October 1991, the meeting referred to in rule 4(1);

(b) where sub-paragraph (a) does not apply and the direction is consequential upon the making of an order under section 23 of the Act of 1979, within the meaning of rule 11(8), a meeting held as soon as practicable after the direction has been made; and

(c) in any other case, the meeting referred to in rule 11(7)(c).

(3) In relation to the appointment of justices under paragraph (1), rules 4(4), 5(1)(b)–(d), (2) and (3), and 9 of these Rules shall apply as they apply in relation to appointments under rule 4.

(4) Subject to rule 13, after the first appointments to a combined panel have been made in accordance with paragraph (1), these Rules shall have effect in relation to the combined panel as if—

(a) in rule 4—

(i) references to appointments to a panel in paragraph (2) of that rule were references to appointments to the combined panel of such number of justices from the petty sessions area as is stated in the direction; and

    (ii)  paragraphs (3) and (5) thereof were omitted;
  (b)  for paragraph (1)(a) of rule 5 there were substituted the following paragraph—

    '(1)(a)  The members of a combined panel provided by each petty sessions area for which the panel is formed shall be appointed from amongst the justices for that area.';

  (c)  for rule 6 there were substituted the following rule—

    **'6.**  If a vacancy occurs in the number of justices forming a combined panel or if a further direction is made under rule 11(9), the justices for the appropriate petty sessions area shall as soon as practicable appoint such a justice or justices as might have been appointed to the panel under rule 5.';

  (d)  in rule 7, where the first area or the second area is one of the petty sessions areas for which the combined panel has been formed, the references to those areas included the other petty sessions areas in respect of which the combined panel has been formed.

*Appointments of justices to a panel as a consequence of a dissolution of a combined panel*

**13.**  (1) Where a magistrates' courts committee makes a direction under rule 11(2), for the dissolution of a combined panel, the justices for each petty sessions area specified in the direction shall (unless the petty sessions area is also specified in a direction for the formation of a combined panel), at a meeting of the justices held in accordance with paragraph (2), appoint, subject to paragraph (3), justices to form a panel for that area for a term commencing at the same time as the direction will have effect and expiring at the same time as will end the term of appointment of any justices for the time being appointed under rule 4(1) or, where that term has expired, rule 4(2), to form a panel which is not specified in the direction.

  (2)  The meeting referred to in paragraph (1) shall be—
  (a)  where the direction is consequential upon the making of an order under section 23 of the 1979 Act, within the meaning of rule 11(8), a meeting held as soon as practicable after the direction has been made; and
  (b)  in any other case, the meeting of the justices referred to in rule 11(7)(c).

  (3)  In relation to the appointment of justices under paragraph (1), rules 4(3), (4) and (5), 5(1), (2) and (3) and 9 shall apply as they apply in relation to appointments under rule 4.

SCHEDULE                                         Rule 1(2)

REVOCATIONS

\*    \*    \*    \*    \*

## EMERGENCY PROTECTION ORDER (TRANSFER OF RESPONSIBILITIES) REGULATIONS 1991

**Dated** 19 June 1991

**SI 1991 No 1414**

The Secretary of State for Health, in exercise of the powers conferred by section 52(3) and (4) and section 104(4) of the Children Act 1989 and of all other powers enabling him in that behalf, hereby makes the following Regulations—

*Citation and commencement*

**1.**  These Regulations may be cited as the Emergency Protection Order (Transfer of Responsibilities) Regulations 1991 and shall come into force on 14th October 1991.

*Transfer of responsibilities under emergency protection orders*

**2.**   Subject to regulation 5 of these Regulations, where—
   (a)   an emergency protection order has been made with respect to a child;
   (b)   the applicant for the order was not the local authority within whose area the child is ordinarily resident; and
   (c)   that local authority are of the opinion that it would be in the child's best interests for the applicant's responsibilities under the order to be transferred to them,

that authority shall (subject to their having complied with the requirements imposed by regulation 3(1) of these Regulations) be treated, for the purposes of the Children Act 1989, as though they and not the original applicant had applied for, and been granted, the order.

*Requirements to be complied with by local authorities*

**3.**   (1) In forming their opinion under regulation 2(c) of these Regulations the local authority shall consult the applicant for the emergency protection order and have regard to the following considerations—
   (a)   the ascertainable wishes and feelings of the child having regard to his age and understanding;
   (b)   the child's physical, emotional and educational needs for the duration of the emergency protection order;
   (c)   the likely effect on him of any change in his circumstances which may be caused by a transfer of responsibilities under the order;
   (d)   his age, sex, family background;
   (e)   the circumstances which gave rise to the application for the emergency protection order;
   (f)   any directions of a court and other orders made in respect of the child;
   (g)   the relationship (if any) of the applicant for the emergency protection order to the child, and
   (h)   any plans which the applicant may have in respect of the child.
   (2)   The local authority shall give notice, as soon as possible after they form the opinion referred to in regulation 2(c), of the date and time of the transfer to—
   (a)   the court which made the emergency protection order,
   (b)   the applicant for the order, and
   (c)   those (other than the local authority) to whom the applicant for the order gave notice of it.

   (3)   A notice required under this regulation shall be given in writing and may be sent by post.

*When responsibility under emergency protection order transfers*

**4.**   The time at which responsibility under any emergency protection order is to be treated as having been transferred to a local authority shall be the time stated as the time of transfer in the notice given in accordance with regulation 3 of these Regulations by the local authority to the applicant for the emergency protection order or the time at which notice is given to him under that regulation, whichever is the later.

*Exception for children in refuges*

**5.**   These Regulations shall not apply where the child to whom the emergency protection order applies is in a refuge in respect of which there is in force a Secretary of State's certificate issued under section 51 of the Children Act 1989 (refuges for children at risk) and the person carrying on the home or, the foster parent providing the refuge, having taken account of the wishes and feelings of the child, has decided that the child should continue to be provided with the refuge for the duration of the order.

## FAMILY PROCEEDINGS COURTS (CONSTITUTION) (METROPOLITAN AREA) RULES 1991

**Dated** 11 June 1991

**SI 1991 No 1426**

**Note.** The Rules are revoked by SI 2003/2960, r 3(1), except in relation to any proceedings pending (within the meaning of the Children Act 1989, Sch 14, para 1) before 1 January 2004 (see rr 1(1)(b) and 3(2) thereof).

## PARENTAL RESPONSIBILITY AGREEMENT REGULATIONS 1991

**Dated** 27 June 1991

**SI 1991 No 1478**

The Lord Chancellor, in exercise of the powers conferred on him by section 4(2) and 104 of the Children Act 1989, and of all other powers enabling him in that behalf, hereby makes the following Regulations—

*Citation, commencement and interpretation*

**1.**    (1)  These Regulations may be cited as the Parental Responsibility Agreement Regulations 1991 and shall come into force on 14th October 1991.

(2)  In these Regulations, 'the Principal Registry' means the principal registry of the Family Division of the High Court.

*Form of parental responsibility agreement*

**2.**    A parental responsibility agreement shall be made in the form set out in the Schedule to these Regulations.

*Recording of parental responsibility agreement*

**3.**    (1)  A parental responsibility agreement shall be recorded by the filing of the agreement, together with two copies, in the Principal Registry.

(2)  Upon the filing of documents under paragraph (1), an officer of the Principal Registry shall seal the copies and send one to the child's mother and one to the child's father.

(3)  The record of an agreement under paragraph (1) shall be made available, during office hours, for inspection by any person upon—

(a)  written request to an officer of the Principal Registry, and

(b)  payment of such fee as may be prescribed in an Order under section 41 of the Matrimonial and Family Proceedings Act 1984 (Fees in family proceedings).

SCHEDULE                                                        Regulation 2

*FORM OF AGREEMENT*

*Parental Responsibility Agreement*              **Keep this form in a safe**
*Section 4(1)(b) Children Act 1989*              **place**
                                                 *Date recorded at the Principal Registry*
**Read the notes on the other side before**      *of the Family Division*
**you make this agreement.**

**This is a Parental Responsibility Agreement regarding**

   *the Child*      *Name*

               *Boy or Girl*   *Date of Birth*   *Date of 18th birthday*

**Between**

   *the Mother*    *Name*

               *Address*

**and**   *the Father*   *Name*

               *Address*

*We declare that*     *we are the mother and father of the above child and we agree that the*
*child's father shall have parental responsibility for the child (in*
*addition to the mother having parental responsibility).*

               *Signed* (**Mother**)        *Signed* (**Father**)

               *Date*                *Date*

**Certificate of**   *The following evidence of*   *The following evidence of*
**Witness**       *identity was produced by the*  *identity was produced by the*
               *person signing above:*     *person signing above:*

               *Signed in the presence of:*   *Signed in the presence of:*
               *Name of Witness*       *Name of Witness*

               *Address*               *Address*

               *Signature of Witness*     *Signature of Witness*

               *[A Justice of the Peace]*    *{A Justice of the Peace]*
               *[Justices' Clerk]*          *[Justices' Clerk]*
               *[An Officer of the Court*    *[An Officer of the Court*
               *authorised by the judge to*   *authorised by the judge to*
               *administer oaths]*         *administer oaths]*

*C(PRA)*

*Notes about the Parental Responsibility Agreement*
*Read these notes before you make the agreement*

## About the Parental Responsibility Agreement

*The making of this agreement will affect the legal position of the mother and the father. You should both seek legal advice before you make the Agreement. You can obtain the name and address of a solicitor from the Children Panel (0171–242 1222) or from*
   *—your local family proceedings court, or county court*
   *—a Citizen's Advice Bureau*
   *—a Law Centre*
   *—a local library.*
   *You may be eligible for legal aid.*

## When you fill in the Agreement

*Please use black ink (the Agreement will be copied). Put the name of one child only. If the father is to have parental responsibility for more than one child, fill in a separate form for each child.* **Do not sign the Agreement.**

## When you have filled in the Agreement

*Take it to a local family proceedings court, or county court, or the Principal Registry of the Family Division (the address is below).*

*A justice of the peace, a justices' clerk, or a court official who is authorised by the judge to administer oaths, will witness your signature and he or she will sign the certificate of the witness.*

**To the mother:**   *When you make the declaration you will have to prove that you are the child's mother so take to the court the child's full birth certificate. You will also need evidence of your identity showing a photograph and signature (for example, a photocard, official pass or passport).*

**To the father:**   *You will need evidence of your identity showing a photograph and signature (for example, a photocard, official pass or passport).*

## When the Certificate has been signed and witnessed

*Make 2 copies of the other side of this form. You do not need to copy these notes.*

*Take, or send, this form and the copies to The Principal Registry of the Family Division, Somerset House, Strand, London WC2R 1LP.*

*The Registry will record the Agreement and keep this form. The copies will be stamped and sent back to each parent at the address on the Agreement. The Agreement will not take effect until it has been received and recorded at the Principal Registry of the Family Division.*

## Ending the Agreement

*Once a parental responsibility agreement has been made it can only end*
   *—by an order of the court made on the application of any person who has parental responsibility for the child*
   *—by an order of the court made on the application of the child with leave of the court*
   *—when the child reaches the age of 18.*

---

C(PRA) (Notes)

[Parental Responsibility Agreement
Section 4(1)(b) Children Act 1989

**Keep this form in a safe place**
*Date recorded at the Principal Registry
of the Family Division*

**Read the notes on the other side
before you make this agreement.**

[**This is a Parental Responsibility Agreement regarding**

the Child            *Name*

                        *Boy or Girl        Date of Birth        Date of 18th birthday*

**Between**

the Mother        *Name*

                        *Address*

**and**    the Father    *Name*

                        *Address*

We declare that    we are the mother and father of the above child and we
                        agree that the father shall have parental responsibility for
                        the child (in addition to the mother having parental
                        responsibility).

Signed (**Mother**)                    Signed (**Father**)


Date                                        Date


**Certificate of**        The following evidence of        The following evidence of
**Witness**            identity was produced by the    identity was produced by the
                        person signing above:            person signing above:


Signed in the presence of:        Signed in the presence of:
*Name of Witness*                    *Name of Witness*


*Address*                                *Address*


*Signature of Witness*                *Signature of Witness*


[A Justice of the Peace]            {A Justice of the Peace]
[Justices' Clerk]                        [Justices' Clerk]
[An Officer of the Court            [An Officer of the Court
authorised by the judge            authorised by the judge
to administer oaths]                    to administer oaths]

C(PRA)

*Notes about the Parental Responsibility Agreement*

**Read these notes before you make the agreement**

**About the Parental Responsibility Agreement**

The making of this agreement will affect the legal position of the mother and the father. You should both seek legal advice before you make the Agreement. You can obtain the name and address of a solicitor from the Children Panel (020 7242 1222) or from
  —your local family proceeding court, or county court
  —a Citizen's Advice Bureau
  —a Law centre
  —a local library.
You may be eligible for public funding.

**When you fill in the Agreement**

Please use black ink (the Agreement will be copied). Put the name of one child only. If the father is to have parental responsibility for more than one child, fill in a separate form for each child. **Do not sign the Agreement.**

**When you have filled in the Agreement**

Take it to a local family proceedings court, or county court, or the Principal Registry of the Family Division (the address is below).

A justice of the Peace, a Justices' Clerk, or a court official who is authorised by the judge to administer oaths, will witness your signature and he or she will sign the certificate of the witness.

**To the mother:**   When you make the declaration you will have to prove that you are the child's mother so take to the court the child's full birth certificate.
          You will also need evidence of your identity showing a photograph and signature (for example, a photocard, official pass or passport).

**To the father:**   You will need evidence of your identity showing a photograph and signature (for example, a photocard, official pass or passport).

**When the Certificate has been signed and witnessed**

Make 2 copies of the other side of this form. You do not need to copy these notes. Take, or send, this form and the copies to **The Principal Registry of the Family Division, First Avenue 42–49 High Holborn, London WC1V 6NP**.

The Registry will record the Agreement and keep this form. The copies will be stamped and sent back to each parent at the address on the Agreement. The Agreement will not take effect until it has been received and recorded at the Principal Registry of the Family Division.

**Ending the Agreement**

Once a parental responsibility agreement has been made it can only end
  —by an order of the court made on the application of any person who has parental responsibility for the child
  —by an order of the court made on the application of the child with leave of the court
  —when the child reaches the age of 18.]

**C(PRA) (Notes)**

**Note.** Substituted by SI 1994/3157, reg 2, Sch; Form further substituted by SI 2001/2262, reg 2, Schedule as from 1 September 2001.

## CHILDREN (SECURE ACCOMMODATION) REGULATIONS 1991

**Dated** 30 June 1991

**SI 1991 No 1505**

ARRANGEMENT OF REGULATIONS

The Secretary of State for Health, in exercise of the powers conferred by sections 25(2) and (7) and 104(4) of and paragraphs 4(1) and (2)(d) and (i) of Schedule 4, 7(1) and (2)(f) and (3) of Schedule 5 and 10(1) and (2)(j) and (3) of Schedule 6 to the Children Act 1989 and of all other powers enabling him in that behalf hereby makes the following Regulations—

*Citation and commencement*

**1.** These Regulations may be cited as the Children (Secure Accommodation) Regulations 1991 and shall come into force on 14th October 1991.

*Interpretation*

**2.** (1) In these Regulations, unless the context otherwise requires—
'the Act' means the Children Act 1989;
'children's home' means a *registered* [private] children's home, a community home or a voluntary home;
'independent visitor' means a person appointed under paragraph 17 of Schedule 2 to the Act;
'secure accommodation' means accommodation which is provided for the purpose of restricting the liberty of children to whom section 25 of the Act (use of accommodation for restricting liberty) applies.

(2) Any reference in these regulations to a numbered regulation shall be construed as a reference to the regulation bearing that number in these Regulations, and any reference in a regulation to a numbered paragraph is a reference to the paragraph bearing that number in that regulation.

**Note.** In definition 'children's home' word 'registered' substituted by word 'private' in square brackets by SI 2002/546, r 7(a) in relation to England as from 1 April 2002 and by SI 2002/2935, regs 10(a), 13 in relation to Wales as from 31 December 2002.

*Approval by Secretary of State of secure accommodation in a children's home*

**3.**  Accommodation in a children's home shall not be used as secure accommodation unless it has been approved by the Secretary of State for such use and approval shall be subject to such terms and conditions as he sees fit.

*Placement of a child aged under 13 in secure accommodation in a children's home*

**4.**  A child under the age of 13 years shall not be placed in secure accommodation in a children's home without the prior approval of the Secretary of State to the placement of that child and such approval shall be subject to such terms and conditions as he sees fit.

*Children to whom section 25 of the Act shall not apply*

**5.**  (1) Section 25 of the Act shall not apply to a child who is detained under any provision of the Mental Health Act 1983 or in respect of whom an order has been made under *section 53 of the Children and Young Persons Act 1933 (punishment of certain grave crimes)* [section 90 or 91 of the Powers of the Criminal Courts (Sentencing) Act 2000 (detention at Her Majesty's pleasure or for specified period)].

(2) Section 25 of the Act shall not apply to a child—

(a) to whom section 20(5) of the Act (accommodation of persons over 16 but under 21) applies and who is being accommodated under that section,

(b) in respect of whom an order has been made under section 43 of the Act (child assessment order) and who is kept away from home pursuant to that order.

**Note.** In para (1) words from 'section 53' to 'crimes)' substituted by words from 'section 90' to specified period)' in square brackets by SI 2002/546, reg 7(b) in relation to England as from 1 April 2002 and by SI 2002/2935, regs 10(b), 13 in relation to Wales as from 31 December 2002.

*Detained and remanded children to whom section 25 of the Act shall have effect subject to modifications*

**6.**  (1) Subject to regulation 5, section 25 of the Act shall have effect subject to the modification specified in paragraph (2) in relation to children who are being looked after by a local authority and are of the following descriptions—

(a) children detained under section 38(6) of the Police and Criminal Evidence Act 1984 (detained children), and

(b) children remanded to local authority accommodation under section 23 of the Children and Young Persons Act 1969 (remand to local authority accommodation) but only if—

(i) the child is charged with or has been convicted of a violent or sexual offence, or of an offence punishable in the case of an adult with imprisonment for a term of 14 years or more, or

(ii) the child has a recent history of absconding while remanded to local authority accommodation, and is charged with or has been convicted of an imprisonable offence alleged or found to have been committed while he was so remanded.

(2) The modification referred to in paragraph (1) is that, for the words 'unless it appears' to the end of subsection (1), there shall be substituted the following words—
'unless it appears that any accommodation other than that provided for the purpose of restricting liberty is inappropriate because—
(a) the child is likely to abscond from such other accommodation, or
(b) the child is likely to injure himself or other people if he is kept in any such other accommodation'.

*Children to whom section 25 of the Act shall apply and have effect subject to modifications*

**7.** (1) Subject to regulation 5 and paragraphs (2) and (3) of this regulation section 25 of the Act shall apply (in addition to children looked after by a local authority)—
(a) to children, other than those looked after by a local authority, who are accommodated by health authorities, [Primary Care Trusts,] National Health Service trusts established under section 5 of the National Health Service and Community Care Act 1990 [, NHS foundation trusts] or local education authorities, and
(b) to children, other than those looked after by a local authority, who are accommodated in *residential care homes, nursing homes or mental nursing homes* [care homes or independent hospitals].
(2) In relation to the children of a description specified in paragraph (1)(a) section 25 of the Act shall have effect subject to the following modifications—
(a) for the words 'who is being looked after by a local authority' in subsection (1) there shall be substituted the words 'who is being provided with accommodation by a health authority, [a Primary Care Trust,] a National Health Service trust established under section 5 of the National Health Service and Community Care Act 1990 [, NHS foundation trusts] or a local education authority'; and
(b) for the words 'local authorities' in subsection (2)(c) there shall be substituted the words 'health authorities, [Primary Care Trusts,] National Health Service trusts [, NHS foundation trusts] or local education authorities'.
(3) In relation to the children of a description specified in paragraph (1)(b), section 25 of the Act shall have effect subject to the following modifications—
(a) for the words 'who is being looked after by a local authority' in subsection (1) there shall be substituted the words 'who is being provided with accommodation in a *residential care home, a nursing home or a mental nursing home* [care home or an independent hospital]'; and
(b) for the words 'local authorities' in subsection (2)(c) there shall be substituted the words 'persons carrying on *residential care homes, nursing homes or mental nursing homes* [care homes or independent hospitals]'.

**Note.** In para (1)(a) words ', Primary Care Trusts' in square brackets inserted, in relation to England and Wales, by SI 2000/694, art 3, Schedule, Pt II, para 4(a) as from 1 April 2000 and ', NHS foundation trusts' in square brackets inserted by SI 2004/696, art 3(1), Sch 1, para 9(a) as from 1 April 2004. In para (1)(b) words 'residential care homes, nursing homes or mental nursing homes' substituted by words 'care homes or independent hospitals' in square brackets in relation to England by SI 2002/546, reg 7(c)(i) as from 1 April 2002 and in relation to Wales by SI 2002/2935, regs 10(c)(i), 13 as from 31 December 2002. In para (2)(a) words ', a Primary Care Trust' in square brackets inserted, in relation to England and Wales, by SI 2000/694, art 3, Schedule, Pt II, para 4(b)(i) as from 1 April 2000, and words ', an NHS foundation trust' in square brackets inserted by SI 2004/696, art 3(1), Sch 1, para 9(b) as from 1 April 2004. In para (2)(b) words ', Primary Care Trusts' in square brackets inserted, in relation to England and Wales, by SI 2000/694, art 3, Schedule, Pt II, para 4(b)(ii) as from 1 April 2000, and words ', NHS foundation trusts' in square brackets inserted by SI 2004/696, art 3(1), Sch 1, para 9(c) as from 1 April 2004. In para (3)(a) words 'residential care home, a nursing home or a mental nursing home' substituted by words 'care home or an independent hospital' in square brackets in relation to England by SI 2002/546, reg 7(c)(ii) as from 1 April 2002 and in relation to Wales by SI 2002/2935, regs 10(c)(ii), 13 as from 31 December 2002. In para (3)(b) words 'residential care homes, nursing homes or mental nursing homes' substituted by words 'care homes or independent hospitals' in square brackets in relation to England by SI 2002/546, reg 7(c)(i) as from 1 April 2002 and in relation to Wales by SI 2002/2935, regs 10(c)(i), 13 as from 31 December 2002.

*Applications to court*

**8.**   Subject to section 101 of the Local Government Act 1972 [or to provisions in or under sections 14 to 20 of the Local Government Act 2000], applications to a court under section 25 of the Act in respect of a child shall be made only by the local authority which are looking after that child.

**Note.** Words '[or to provisions in or under sections 14 to 20 of the Local Government Act 2000]' in square brackets inserted by SI 2001/2237, arts 1(2), 2(y), 41 as from 11 July 2001 in relation to England and by SI 2002/808, arts 2(w), 37, as from 1 April 2002 in relation to Wales.

*Duty to give information of placement in children's homes*

**9.**   Where a child is placed in secure accommodation in a children's home which is managed by a person, organisation or authority other than the local authority which is looking after him, the person who, or the organisation or the authority which manages that accommodation shall inform the authority which are looking after him that he has been placed there, within 12 hours of his being placed there, with a view to obtaining their authority to continue to keep him there if necessary.

*Maximum period in secure accommodation without court authority*

**10.**   (1)  Subject to paragraphs (2) and (3), the maximum period beyond which a child to whom section 25 of the Act applies may not be kept in secure accommodation without the authority of a court is an aggregate of 72 hours (whether or not consecutive) in any period of 28 consecutive days.

(2)  Where authority of a court to keep a child in secure accommodation has been given, any period during which the child has been kept in such accommodation before the giving of that authority shall be disregarded for the purposes of calculating the maximum period in relation to any subsequent occasion on which the child is placed in such accommodation after the period authorised by court has expired.

(3)  Where a child is in secure accommodation at any time between 12 midday on the day before and 12 midday on the day after a public holiday or a Sunday, and—

  (a)  during that period the maximum period specified in paragraph (1) expires, and

  (b)  the child had, in the 27 days before the day on which he was placed in secure accommodation, been placed and kept in such accommodation for an aggregate of more than 48 hours,

the maximum period does not expire until 12 midday on the first day, which is not itself a public holiday or a Sunday, after the public holiday or Sunday.

*Maximum initial period of authorisation by a court*

**11.**   Subject to regulations 12 and 13 the maximum period for which a court may authorise a child to whom section 25 of the Act applies to be kept in secure accommodation is three months.

*Further period of authorisation by a court*

**12.**   Subject to regulation 13 a court may from time to time authorise a child to whom section 25 of the Act applies to be kept in secure accommodation for a further period not exceeding 6 months at any one time.

*Maximum periods of authorisation by court for remanded children*

**13.**   (1) The maximum period for which a court may from time to time authorise a child who has been remanded to local authority accommodation under section 23 of the Children and Young Persons Act 1969 to be kept in secure accommodation (whether the period is an initial period or a further period) is the period of the remand.

(2) Any period of authorisation in respect of such a child shall not exceed 28 days on any one occasion without further court authorisation.

*Duty to inform parents and others in relation to children in secure accommodation in a children's home*

**14.**   Where a child to whom section 25 of the Act applies is kept in secure accommodation in a children's home and it is intended that an application will be made to a court to keep the child in that accommodation, the local authority which are looking after the child shall if practicable inform of that intention as soon as possible—

(a)  his parent,

(b)  any person who is not a parent of his but who has parental responsibility for him,

(c)  the child's independent visitor, if one has been appointed, and

(d)  any other person who that local authority consider should be informed.

*Appointment of persons to review placement in secure accommodation in a children's home*

**15.**   Each local authority looking after a child in secure accommodation in a children's home shall appoint at least three persons, at least one of whom is neither a member nor an officer of a local authority by or on behalf of which the child is being looked after, who shall review the keeping of the child in such accommodation for the purposes of securing his welfare within one month of the inception of the placement and then at intervals not exceeding three months where the child continues to be kept in such accommodation.

*Review of placement in secure accommodation in a children's home*

**16.**   (1) The persons appointed under regulation 15 to review the keeping of a child in secure accommodation shall satisfy themselves as to whether or not—

(a)  the criteria for keeping the child in secure accommodation continue to apply;

(b)  the placement in such accommodation in a children's home continues to be necessary; and

(c)  any other description of accommodation would be appropriate for him,

and in doing so shall have regard to the welfare of the child whose case is being reviewed.

(2) In undertaking the review referred to in regulation 15 the persons appointed shall, if practicable, ascertain and take into account the wishes and feelings of—

(a)  the child,

(b)  any parent of his,

(c)  any person not being a parent of his but who has parental responsibility for him,

(d)  any other person who has had the care of the child, whose views the persons appointed consider should be taken into account,

(e)  the child's independent visitor if one has been appointed, and

(f)  the person, organisation or local authority managing the secure accommodation in which the child is placed if that accommodation is not managed by the authority which is looking after that child.

(3) The local authority shall, if practicable, inform all those whose views are required to be taken into account under paragraph (2) of the outcome of the review, what action, if any, the local authority propose to take in relation to the child in the light of the review, and their reasons for taking or not taking such action.

*Records to be kept in respect of a child in secure accommodation in a children's home*

**17.**   Whenever a child is placed in secure accommodation in a children's home the person, organisation or local authority which manages that accommodation shall ensure that a record is kept of—

(a)  the name, date of birth and sex of that child,

(b)  the care order or other statutory provision by virtue of which the child is in the children's home and in either case particulars of any other local authority involved with the placement of the child in that home,

(c)  the date and time of his placement in secure accommodation, the reason for his placement, the name of the officer authorising the placement and where the child was living before the placement,

(d)  all those informed by virtue of regulation 9, 14 or 16(3) in their application to the child,

(e)  court orders made in respect of the child by virtue of section 25 of the Act,

(f)  reviews undertaken in respect of the child by virtue of regulation 15,

(g)  the date and time of any occasion on which the child is locked on his own in any room in the secure accommodation other than his bedroom during usual bedtime hours, the name of the person authorising this action, the reason for it and the date on which and time at which the child ceases to be locked in that room, and

(h)  the date and time of his discharge and his address following discharge from secure accommodation

and the Secretary of State may require copies of these records to be send to him at any time.

*Voluntary homes and registered children's homes not to be used for restricting liberty*

**18.**   *Revoked.*

*Revocation of Secure Accommodation (No 2) Regulations 1983 and the Amendment Regulations*

**19.**   The Secure Accommodation (No 2) Regulations 1983 and the Secure Accommodation (No 2) (Amendment) Regulations 1986 are hereby revoked.

## REFUGES (CHILDREN'S HOMES AND FOSTER PLACEMENTS) REGULATIONS 1991

**Dated** 30 June 1991

**SI 1991 No 1507**

*Citation and commencement*

**1.**   These Regulations may be cited as the Refuges (Children's Homes and Foster Placements) Regulations 1991 and shall come into force on 14th October 1991.

*Interpretation*

**2.** (1) In these Regulations unless the context otherwise requires—

'certificate' means a certificate issued under section 51 (refuges for children at risk);

'designated officer' means a police officer for the time being designated for the purpose of these Regulations by the chief officer for the police area within which—

(a) a home which is provided as a refuge in pursuance of section 51(1) is situated, or

(b) a foster parent who provides a refuge in pursuance of section 51(2) lives;

'home' means a *registered children's home* [private children's home] or voluntary home;

'responsible person' in relation to a child means—

(a) except where a person has care of the child as mentioned in paragraph (b) below—

    (i) a parent of his,

    (ii) a person who is not a parent of his, but who has parental responsibility for him, and

    (iii) any person who for the time being has care of him not being a person providing a refuge;

(b) any person who for the time being has care of the child by virtue of a care order, emergency protection order or section 46 (removal and accommodation of children by police in cases of emergency) as the case may be.

(2) Any reference in these Regulations to a numbered section is a reference to the section in the Children Act 1989 bearing that number.

**Note.** In para (1) definition 'home' words 'registered children's home' substituted by words 'private children's home' in square brackets by SI 2002/546, reg 6(a) in relation to England and as from 1 April 2002 and by SI 2002/2935, regs 9(a), 13 in relation to Wales as from 31 December 2001.

*Requirements*

**3.** (1) The provisions of this regulation shall apply while a certificate is in force with respect to a home or a foster parent.

(2) A child may not be provided with a refuge unless it appears to the person providing the refuge that the child is at risk of harm unless the child is or continues to be provided with a refuge.

(3) As soon as is reasonably practicable after admitting a child to a home for the purpose of providing a refuge or after a foster parent provides a refuge for a child, and in any event within 24 hours of such provision, the person providing the refuge for the child shall—

(a) notify the designated officer that a child has been admitted to the home, or provided with refuge by a foster parent, together with the telephone number by which the person providing the refuge for the child may be contacted,

(b) if he knows the child's name, notify the designated officer of that name, and

(c) if he knows the child's last permanent address, notify the designated officer of that address.

(4) Where subsequently the person providing the refuge discovers the child's name or last permanent address he shall immediately notify the designated officer accordingly.

(5) As soon as is reasonably practicable after providing the refuge for the child, and in any event within 24 hours of becoming aware of the identity of the responsible person for the child, the person providing the refuge shall give to the designated officer the name and address of the responsible person.

(6)  The requirements of paragraph (7) of this regulation shall apply where the designated officer has been notified or is otherwise aware—
(a)  that a child is being provided with a refuge, and
(b)  of the name and address of a responsible person.
(7)  The designated officer shall—
(a)  inform the responsible person—
  (i)  that the child is being provided with a refuge,
  (ii)  by whom the refuge is being provided,
(b)  notify the responsible person of a telephone number by which the person providing the refuge for the child may be contacted,
(c)  not disclose to any person the address of the place at which the refuge is provided.
(8)  Where a child ceases to be provided with a refuge, the person who provided him with the refuge shall notify the designated officer.
(9)  No child shall be provided with a refuge in any one place for a continuous period of more than 14 days or for more than 21 days in any period of 3 months.

\*     \*     \*     \*     \*

## CHILDREN (ALLOCATION OF PROCEEDINGS) ORDER 1991

**Dated** 20 June 1991

**SI 1991 No 1677**

The Lord Chancellor, in exercise of the powers conferred on him by section 92(9) and (10) of, and Part I of Schedule 11 to, the Children Act 1989, and of all other powers enabling him in that behalf, hereby makes the following Order—

*Citation, commencement and interpretation*

**1.**   (1) This Order may be cited as the Children (Allocation of Proceedings) Order 1991 and shall come into force on 14th October 1991.
(2)  In this Order, unless the context otherwise requires—
'child'—
(a)  means, subject to sub-paragraph (b), a person under the age of 18 with respect to whom proceedings are brought, and
(b)  where the proceedings are under Schedule 1, also includes a person who has reached the age of 18;
'London commission area' has the meaning assigned to it by section 2(1) of the Justices of the Peace Act 1979;
'petty sessions area' has the meaning assigned to it by section 4 of the Justices of the Peace Act 1979; and
'the Act' means the Children Act 1989, and a section, Part or Schedule referred to by number alone means the section, Part or Schedule so numbered in that Act.

*Classes of county court*

**2.**   For the purposes of this Order there shall be the following classes of county court:
(a)  divorce county courts, being those courts designated for the time being as divorce county courts by an order under section 33 of the Matrimonial and Family Proceedings Act 1984;
(b)  family hearing centres, being those courts set out in Schedule 1 to this Order;
(c)  care centres, being those courts set out in column (ii) of Schedule 2 to this Order.

COMMENCEMENT OF PROCEEDINGS

*Proceedings to be commenced in magistrates' court*

**3.** (1) Subject to paragraphs (2) and (3) and to article 4, proceedings under any of the following provisions shall be commenced in a magistrates' court:

(a) section 25 (use of accommodation for restricting liberty);

(b) section 31 (care and supervision orders);

(c) section 33(7) (leave to change name of or remove from United Kingdom child in care);

(d) section 34 (parental contact);

(e) section 36 (education supervision orders);

(f) section 43 (child assessment orders);

(g) section 44 (emergency protection orders);

(h) section 45 (duration of emergency protection orders etc);

(i) section 46(7) (application for emergency protection order by police officer);

(j) section 48 (powers to assist discovery of children etc);

(k) section 50 (recovery orders);

(l) section 75 (protection of children in an emergency);

(m) section 77(6) (appeal against steps taken under section 77(1));

(n) section 102 (powers of constable to assist etc);

(o) paragraph 19 of Schedule 2 (approval of arrangements to assist child to live abroad);

(p) paragraph 23 of Schedule 2 (contribution orders);

(q) paragraph 8 of Schedule 8 (certain appeals);

(r) section 21 of the Adoption Act 1976;

(s) ... ;

(t) section 20 of the Child Support Act 1991 (appeals) where the proceedings are to be dealt with in accordance with the Child Support Appeals (Jurisdiction of Courts) Order 1993;

(u) section 30 of the Human Fertilisation and Embryology Act 1990 (parental orders in favour of gamete donors).

(2) Notwithstanding paragraph (1) and subject to paragraph (3), proceedings of a kind set out in sub-paragraph (b), (e), (f), (g), (i) or (j) of paragraph (1), and which arise out of an investigation directed, by the High Court or a county court, under section 37(1), shall be commenced—

(a) in the court which directs the investigation, where that court is the High Court or a care centre, or

(b) in such care centre as the court which directs the investigation may order.

(3) Notwithstanding paragraphs (1) and (2), proceedings of a kind set out in sub-paragraph (a) to (k), (n) or (o) of paragraph (1) shall be commenced in a court in which are pending other proceedings, in respect of the same child, which are also of a kind set out in those sub-paragraphs.

**Note.** Para (1)(s) revoked by SI 2001/775, arts 3, 4 as from 1 April 2001.

*Application to extend, vary or discharge order*

**4.** (1) Subject to paragraphs (2) and (3), proceedings under the Act, or under the Adoption Act 1976—

(a) to extend, vary or discharge an order, or

(b) the determination of which may have the effect of varying or discharging an order,

shall be commenced in the court which made the order.

(2) Notwithstanding paragraph (1), an application for an order under section 8 which would have the effect of varying or discharging an order made, by a county court, in accordance with section 10(1)(b) shall be made to a divorce county court.

(3) Notwithstanding paragraph (1), an application to extend, vary or discharge an order made, by a county court, under section 38, or for an order which would have the effect of extending, varying or discharging such an order, shall be made to a care centre.

(4) A court may transfer proceedings commenced in accordance with paragraph (1) to any other court in accordance with the provisions of articles 5 to 13.

TRANSFER OF PROCEEDINGS

*Disapplication of enactments about transfer*

**5.** Sections 38 and 39 of the Matrimonial and Family Proceedings Act 1984 shall not apply to proceedings under the Act or under the Adoption Act 1976.

*Transfer from one magistrates' court to another*

**6.** (1) A magistrates' court (the 'transferring court') shall transfer proceedings under the Act or to which this article applies to another magistrates' court (the 'receiving court') where—

- (a) having regard to the principle set out in section 1(2), the transferring court considers that the transfer is in the interests of the child—
  - (i) because it is likely significantly to accelerate the determination of the proceedings,
  - (ii) because it would be appropriate for those proceedings to be heard together with other family proceedings which are pending in the receiving court, or
  - (iii) for some other reason, and
- (b) the receiving court, by its justices' clerk (as defined by rule 1(2) of the Family Proceedings Courts (Children Act 1989) Rules 1991, consents to the transfer.

(2) This article applies to proceedings—

- (a) under the Act;
- (b) under the Adoption Act 1976;
- (c) of the kind mentioned in sub-paragraph *(s)*, (t) or (u) of article 3(1) [and under section 55A of the Family Law Act 1986];
- [(d) under section 11 of the Crime and Disorder Act 1998 (child safety orders)].

**Note.** In para (2)(c) reference to '(s),' revoked and words 'and under section 55A of the Family Law Act 1986' in square brackets inserted by SI 2001/775, arts 3, 5 as from 1 April 2001. Para (2)(d) inserted by SI 1998/2166, art 2 as from 30 September 1998.

*Transfer from magistrates' court to county court by magistrates' court*

**7.** (1) Subject to paragraphs (2), (3) and (4) and to articles 15 to 18, a magistrates' court may, upon application by a party or of its own motion, transfer to a county court proceedings of any of the kinds mentioned in article 3(1) [or proceedings under section 55A of the Family Law Act 1986] where it considers it in the interests of the child to do so having regard, first, to the principle set out in section 1(2) and, secondly, to the following questions:

- (a) whether the proceedings are exceptionally grave, important or complex, in particular—
  - (i) because of complicated or conflicting evidence about the risks involved to the child's physical or moral well-being or about other matters relating to the welfare of the child;
  - (ii) because of the number of parties;
  - (iii) because of a conflict with the law of another jurisdiction;
  - (iv) because of some novel and difficult point of law; or
  - (v) because of some question of general public interest;

(b) whether it would be appropriate for those proceedings to be heard together with other family proceedings which are pending in another court; and

(c) whether transfer is likely significantly to accelerate the determination of the proceedings, where—

(i) no other method of doing so, including transfer to another magistrates' court, is appropriate, and

(ii) delay would seriously prejudice the interests of the child who is the subject of the proceedings.

(2) Notwithstanding paragraph (1), proceedings of the kind mentioned in sub-paragraph (g) to (j), (l), (m), (p) or (q) of article 3(1) shall not be transferred from a magistrates' court.

(3) Notwithstanding paragraph (1), proceedings of the kind mentioned in sub-paragraph (a) or (n) of article 3(1) shall only be transferred from a magistrates' court to a county court in order to be heard together with other family proceedings which arise out of the same circumstances as gave rise to the proceedings to be transferred and which are pending in another court.

(4) Notwithstanding paragraphs (1) and (3), proceedings of the kind mentioned in article 3(1)(a) shall not be transferred from a magistrates' court which is not a family proceedings court within the meaning of section 92(1).

**Note.** In para (1) words 'or proceedings under section 55A of the Family Law Act 1986' in square brackets inserted by SI 2001/775, arts 3, 6 as from 1 April 2001.

**8.** Subject to articles 15 to 18, a magistrates' court may transfer to a county court proceedings under the Act or under the Adoption Act 1976, being proceedings to which article 7 does not apply, where, having regard to the principle set out in section 1(2), it considers that in the interests of the child the proceedings can be dealt with more appropriately in that county court.

*Transfer from magistrates' court following refusal of magistrates' court to transfer*

**9.** (1) Where a magistrates' court refuses to transfer proceedings under article 7, a party to those proceedings may apply to the care centre listed in column (ii) of Schedule 2 to this Order against the entry in column (1) for the petty sessions area or London commission area in which the magistrates' court is situated for an order under paragraph (2).

(2) Upon hearing an application under paragraph (1) the court may transfer the proceedings to itself where, having regard to the principle set out in section 1(2) and the questions set out in article 7(1)(a) to (c), it considers it in the interests of the child to do so.

(3) Upon hearing an application under paragraph (1) the court may transfer the proceedings to the High Court where, having regard to the principle set out in section 1(2), it considers—

(a) that the proceedings are appropriate for determination in the High Court, and

(b) that such determination would be in the interests of the child.

(4) This article shall apply (with the necessary modifications) to proceedings brought under Parts I and II as it applies where a magistrates' court refuses to transfer proceedings under article 7.

*Transfer from one county court to another*

**10.** (1) Subject to articles 15 to 17, a county court (the 'transferring court') shall transfer proceedings to which this article applies to another county court (the 'receiving court') where—

(a) the transferring court, having regard to the principle set out in section 1(2), considers the transfer to be in the interests of the child, and

(b) the receiving court is—

    (i) of the same class or classes, within the meaning of article 2, as the transferring court, or

    (ii) to be presided over by a judge or district judge who is specified by directions under section 9 of the Courts and Legal Services Act 1990 for the same purposes as the judge or district judge presiding over the transferring court.

(2) This article applies to proceedings—

(a) under the act;

(b) under the Adoption Act 1976;

(c) of the kind mentioned in sub-paragraph *(s)*, (t) or (u) of article 3(1) [and under section 55A of the Family Law Act 1986];

[(d) under section 11 of the Crime and Disorder Act 1998 (child safety orders)].

**Note.** In para (2)(c) reference to '(s),' revoked and words 'and under section 55A of the Family Law Act 1986' in square brackets inserted by SI 2001/775, arts 3, 5 as from 1 April 2001. Para (2)(d) inserted by SI 1998/2166, art 2 as from 30 September 1998.

*Transfer from county court to magistrates' court by county court*

**11.** (1) A county court may transfer to a magistrates' court before trial proceedings which were transferred under article 7(1) where the county court, having regard to the principle set out in section 1(2) and the interests of the child, considers that the criterion cited by the magistrates' court as the reason for transfer—

(a) in the case of the criterion in article 7(1)(a), does not apply,

(b) in the case of the criterion in article 7(1)(b), no longer applies, because the proceedings with which the transferred proceedings were to be heard have been determined,

(c) in the case of the criterion in article 7(1)(c), no longer applies.

(2) Paragraph (1) shall apply (with the necessary modifications) to proceedings under Parts I and II brought in, or transferred to, a county court as it applies to proceedings transferred to a county court under article 7(1).

*Transfer from county court to High Court by county court*

**12.** (1) A county court may transfer proceedings under the Act or the Adoption Act 1976 to the High Court where, having regard to the principle set out in section 1(2), it considers—

(a) that the proceedings are appropriate for determination in the High Court, and

(b) that such determination would be in the interests of the child.

(2) This article applies to proceedings—

(a) under the act;

(b) under the Adoption Act 1976;

(c) of the kind mentioned in sub-paragraph (s), (t) or (u) of article 3(1).

*Transfer from High Court to county court*

**13.** (1) Subject to articles 15, 16 and 18, the High Court may transfer to a county court proceedings under the Act or the Adoption Act 1976 where, having regard to the principle set out in section 1(2), it considers that the proceedings are appropriate for determination in such a court and that such determination would be in the interests of the child.

(2) This article applies to proceedings—

(a) under the act;

(b) under the Adoption Act 1976;

(c) of the kind mentioned in sub-paragraph (s), (t) or (u) of article 3(1).

ALLOCATION OF PROCEEDINGS TO PARTICULAR COUNTY COURTS

*Commencement*

**14.** Subject to articles 18, 19 and 20 and to rule 2.40 of the Family Proceedings Rules 1991 (Application under Part I or II of the Children Act 1989 where matrimonial cause is pending), an application under the Act or under the Adoption Act 1976 which is to be made to a county court shall be made to a divorce county court.

*Proceedings under Part I or II or Schedule 1*

**15.** (1) Subject to paragraph (3), where an application under Part I or II or Schedule 1 is to be transferred from a magistrates' court to a county court, it shall be transferred to a divorce county court.

(2) Subject to paragraph (3), where an application under Part I or II or Schedule 1, other than an application for an order under section 8, is to be transferred from the High Court to a county court, it shall be transferred to a divorce county court.

(3) Where an application under Part I or II or Schedule 1, other than an application for an order under section 8, is to be transferred to a county court for the purpose of consolidation with other proceedings, it shall be transferred to the court in which those other proceedings are pending.

*Orders under section 8 of the Children Act 1989*

**16.** (1) An application for an order under section 8 in a divorce county court, which is not also a family hearing centre, shall, if the court is notified that the application will be opposed, be transferred for trial to a family hearing centre.

(2) Subject to paragraph (3), where an application for an order under section 8 is to be transferred from the High Court to a county court it shall be transferred to a family hearing centre.

(3) Where an application for an order under section 8 is to be transferred to a county court for the purpose of consolidation with other proceedings, it may be transferred to the court in which those other proceedings are pending whether or not it is a family hearing centre; but paragraph (1) shall apply to the application following the transfer.

*Application for adoption or freeing for adoption*

**17.** (1) Subject to article 22, proceedings in a divorce county court, which is not also a family hearing centre, under section 12 or 18 of the Adoption Act 1976 shall, if the court is notified that the proceedings will be opposed, be transferred for trial to a family hearing centre.

(2) Where proceedings under the Adoption Act 1976 are to be transferred from a magistrates' court to a county court, they shall be transferred to a divorce county court.

*Applications under Part III, IV or V*

**18.** (1) An application under Part III, IV or V, if it is to be commenced in a county court, shall be commenced in a care centre.

(2) An application under Part III, IV or V which is to be transferred from the High Court to a county court shall be transferred to a care centre.

(3) An application under Part III, IV or V which is to be transferred from a magistrates' court to a county court shall be transferred to the care centre listed against the entry in column(1) of Schedule 2 to this Order for the petty sessions area or London commission area in which the relevant magistrates' court is situated.

*Principal Registry of the Family Division*

**19.** The principal registry of the Family Division of the High Court shall be treated, for the purposes of this Order, as if it were a divorce county court, a family hearing centre and a care centre listed against every entry in column (i) of Schedule 2 to this Order (in addition to the entries against which it is actually listed).

*Lambeth, Shoreditch and Woolwich County Courts*

**20.** Notwithstanding articles 14, 16 and 17, an application for an order under section 8 or under the Adoption Act 1976 may be made to and tried in Lambeth, Shoreditch or Woolwich County Court.

MISCELLANEOUS

*Contravention of provision of this Order*

**21.** Where proceedings are commenced or transferred in contravention of a provision of this Order, the contravention shall not have the effect of making the proceedings invalid; and no appeal shall lie against the determination of proceedings on the basis of such contravention alone.

*Transitional provision—proceedings under Adoption Act 1976*

**22.** Proceedings under the Adoption Act 1976 which are commenced in a county court prior to the coming into force of this Order may, notwithstanding article 17(1), remain in that court for trial.

SCHEDULE 1                                                                    Article 2

FAMILY HEARING CENTRES

**Midland . . . Circuit**

Birmingham County Court
Coventry County Court
Derby County Court
[Dudley County Court]
[. . .]
Leicester County Court
Lincoln County Court
Mansfield County Court
Northampton County Court
Nottingham County Court
. . .
. . .
Stafford County Court
Stoke-on-Trent County Court
Telford County Court
Walsall County Court
Wolverhampton County Court

**Northern Circuit**

Worcester County Court
Blackburn County Court
Bolton County Court

Carlisle County Court
Lancaster County Court
Liverpool County Court
Manchester County Court
[Oldham County Court]

**North Eastern Circuit**

Stockport County Court
Barnsley County Court
Bradford County Court
Darlington County Court
Dewsbury County Court
Doncaster County Court
Durham County Court
[Grimsby County Court]
Halifax County Court
Harrogate County Court
Huddersfield County Court
Keighley County Court
Kingston-upon-Hull County Court
Leeds County Court
Newcastle-upon-Tyne County Court
Pontefract County Court
Rotherham County Court

Scarborough County Court
Sheffield County Court
Skipton County Court
Sunderland County Court
Teesside County Court
Wakefield County Court
York County Court

**South Eastern Circuit**

[Barnet County Court]
[Bedford County Court]
Brighton County Court
Bow County Court
Brentford County Court
Bromley County Court
Cambridge County Court
Canterbury County Court
Chelmsford County Court
Chichester County Court
Colchester and Clacton County Court
Croydon County Court
[Dartford County Court]
Edmonton County Court
Guildford County Court
Hitchin County Court
Ilford County Court
Ipswich County Court
[King's Lynn County Court]
Kingston-upon-Thames County Court
Luton County Court
Maidstone County Court
Medway County Court
Milton Keynes County Court
Norwich County Court
[Oxford County Court
Peterborough County Court]
Reading County Court
Romford County Court
Slough County Court
Southend County Court

Wandsworth County Court
Watford County Court

**Wales and Chester Circuit**

Willesden County Court
Aberystwyth County Court
Caernarfon County Court
Cardiff County Court
Carmarthen County Court
Chester County Court
Crewe County Court
Haverfordwest County Court
Llangefni County Court
Macclesfield County Court
Merthyr Tydfil County Court
Newport (Gwent) County Court
[Pontypridd County Court]
Rhyl County Court
Swansea County Court
Warrington County Court
Welshpool and Newtown County Court

**Western Circuit**

[Barnstaple County Court]
Wrexham County Court
Basingstoke County Court
[Bath County Court]
Bournemouth County Court
Bristol County Court
Exeter County Court
Gloucester County Court
Plymouth County Court
Portsmouth County Court
[Salisbury County Court]
Southampton County Court
Swindon County Court
Taunton County Court
Truro County Court
[Weymouth County Court]
[Yeovil County Court]

**Note.** In Heading 'Midland Circuit': words omitted revoked by SI 2001/775, arts 3, 7(1), (2)(a) as from 1 April 2001.

Under heading 'Midland Circuit': entry 'Dudley County Court' inserted by SI 1994/3138, art 3, entry 'Grimsby County Court' (omitted) inserted by SI 1994/3138, art 3 and revoked by SI 2001/775, arts 3, 7(1), (2)(b) as from 1 April 2001, entries 'Oxford County Court' and 'Peterborough County Court' (omitted) revoked by SI 2001/775, arts 3, 7(1), (2)(b) as from 1 April 2001.

Under heading 'Northern Circuit': entry 'Oldham County Court' inserted by SI 1999/524, art 2(a) as from 1 April 1999 and entry 'Grimsby County Court' inserted by SI 2001/775, arts 3, 7(1), (3) as from 1 April 2001.

Under heading 'South Eastern Circuit': entry 'Barnet County Court' inserted by SI 2000/2670, art 2 as from 23 October 2000, entries 'Bedford County Court', 'Dartford County Court' and 'King's Lynn County Court' inserted by SI 1994/3138, art 3 and entries 'Oxford County Court' and 'Peterborough County Court' inserted by SI 2001/775, arts 3, 7(1), (4) as from 1 April 2001.

Under heading 'Wales and Chester Circuit': entry 'Pontypridd County Court' inserted by SI 1995/1649, art 2.

Under heading 'Western Circuit': entry 'Barnstaple County Court' inserted by SI 1999/524, art 2(b) as from 1 April 1999, entries 'Bath County Court' and 'Weymouth County Court' inserted by SI 1994/3138, art 3, entry 'Salisbury County Court' inserted by SI 1997/1897, art 5 as from 1 September 1997 and entry 'Yeovil County Court' inserted by SI 2001/1656, art 2 as from 4 June 2001.

## SCHEDULE 2                                                                 Article 2

CARE CENTRES

| (i)<br>*Petty Sessions Area* | (ii)<br>*Care Centres* |
|---|---|
| | **Midland ... Circuit** |
| ... | ... |
| Aldridge and Brownhills | Wolverhampton County Court |
| Alfreton and Belper | Derby County Court |
| Ashby-De-La-Zouch | Leicester County Court |
| Atherstone and Coleshill | Coventry County Court |
| ... | ... |
| Bewdley and Stourport | Worcester County Court |
| ... | ... |
| Birmingham | Birmingham County Court |
| Boston | Lincoln County Court |
| Bourne and Stamford | Lincoln County Court |
| Bridgnorth | Telford County Court |
| ... | ... |
| Bromsgrove | Worcester County Court |
| Burton-upon-Trent | [Derby County Court] |
| Caistor | Lincoln County Court |
| Cannock | Wolverhampton County Court |
| ... | ... |
| Cheadle | Stoke-on-Trent County Court |
| Chesterfield | Derby County Court |
| City of Hereford | Worcester County Court |
| Congleton | Stoke-on-Trent County Court |
| Corby | Northampton County Court |
| Coventry | Coventry County Court |
| Crewe and Nantwich | Stoke-on-Trent County Court |
| Daventry | Northampton County Court |
| Derby and South Derbyshire | Derby County Court |
| ... | ... |
| Drayton | Telford County Court |
| Dudley | Wolverhampton County Court |
| East Retford | Nottingham County Court |
| ... | ... |
| Eccleshall | Stoke-on-Trent County Court |
| Elloes | Lincoln County Court |
| ... | ... |
| Gainsborough | Lincoln County Court |
| Glossop | Derby County Court |
| Grantham | Lincoln County Court |
| ... | ... |
| Halesowen | Wolverhampton County Court |

| *(i)* Petty Sessions Area | *(ii)* Care Centres |
| --- | --- |
| . . . | . . . |
| High Peak | Derby County Court |
| . . . | . . . |
| Ilkeston | Derby County Court |
| Kettering | Northampton County Court |
| Kidderminster | Worcester County Court |
| Leek | Stoke-on-Trent County Court |
| Leicester (City) | Leicester County Court |
| Leicester (County) | Leicester County Court |
| Lichfield | Stoke-on-Trent County Court |
| Lincoln District | Lincoln County Court |
| Loughborough | Leicester County Court |
| Louth | Lincoln County Court |
| Ludlow | Telford County Court |
| Lutterworth | Leicester County Court |
| Malvern Hills | Worcester County Court |
| Mansfield | Nottingham County Court |
| Market Bosworth | Leicester County Court |
| Market Harborough | Leicester County Court |
| Market Rasen | Lincoln County Court |
| Melton and Belvoir | Leicester County Court |
| Mid-Warwickshire | Coventry County Court |
| Mid-Worcestershire | Worcester County Court |
| Newark and Southwell | Nottingham County Court |
| Newcastle-under-Lyme | Stoke-on-Trent County Court |
| . . . | . . . |
| . . . | . . . |
| Northampton | Northampton County Court |
| North Herefordshire | Worcester County Court |
| . . . | . . . |
| . . . | . . . |
| Nottingham | Nottingham County Court |
| Nuneaton | Coventry County Court |
| Oswestry | Telford County Court |
| . . . | . . . |
| . . . | . . . |
| Pirehill North | Stoke-on-Trent County Court |
| Redditch | Worcester County Court |
| Rugby | Coventry County Court |
| Rugeley | Wolverhampton County Court |
| Rutland | Leicester County Court |
| . . . | . . . |
| Seisdon | Wolverhampton County Court |
| Sleaford | Lincoln County Court |
| Shrewsbury | Telford County Court |
| Solihull | Birmingham County Court |
| South Herefordshire | Worcester County Court |
| South Warwickshire | Coventry County Court |
| Spilsby and Skegness | Lincoln County Court |
| Stoke-on-Trent | Stoke-on-Trent County Court |
| Stone | Stoke-on-Trent County Court |
| Stourbridge | Wolverhampton County Court |

| *(i)*<br>*Petty Sessions Area* | *(ii)*<br>*Care Centres* |
| --- | --- |
| Sutton Coldfield | Birmingham County Court |
| Tamworth | Stoke-on-Trent County Court |
| Telford | Telford County Court |
| . . . | . . . |
| Towcester | Northampton County Court |
| Uttoxeter | Stoke-on-Trent County Court |
| Vale of Evesham | Worcester County Court |
| Warley | Wolverhampton County Court |
| Walsall | Wolverhampton County Court |
| Wellingborough | Northampton County Court |
| West Bromwich | Wolverhampton County Court |
| West Derbyshire | Derby County Court |
| . . . | . . . |
| . . . | . . . |
| Wolds | Lincoln County Court |
| Wolverhampton | Wolverhampton County Court |
| . . . | . . . |
| Worcester City | Worcester County Court |
| Worksop | Nottingham County Court |

**Northern Circuit**

| | |
| --- | --- |
| Appleby | Carlisle County Court |
| Ashton-under-Lyne | Manchester County Court |
| Barrow with Bootle | Lancaster County Court |
| Blackburn | Blackburn County Court |
| Blackpool | Lancaster County Court |
| Bolton | Manchester County Court |
| Burnley | Blackburn County Court |
| Bury | Manchester County Court |
| Carlisle | Carlisle County Court |
| Chorley | Blackburn County Court |
| Darwen | Blackburn County Court |
| Eccles | Manchester County Court |
| Fylde | Lancaster County Court |
| Hyndburn | Blackburn County Court |
| Kendal and Lonsdale | Lancaster County Court |
| Keswick | Carlisle County Court |
| Knowsley | Liverpool County Court |
| Lancaster | Lancaster County Court |
| Leigh | Manchester County Court |
| Liverpool | Liverpool County Court |
| Manchester | Manchester County Court |
| Middleton and Heywood | Manchester County Court |
| North Lonsdale | Lancaster County Court |
| North Sefton | Liverpool County Court |
| Oldham | Manchester County Court |
| Ormskirk | Liverpool County Court |
| Pendle | Blackburn County Court |
| Penrith and Alston | Carlisle County Court |
| Preston | Blackburn County Court |
| Ribble Valley | Blackburn County Court |
| Rochdale | Manchester County Court |

| *(i)* Petty Sessions Area | *(ii)* Care Centres |
| --- | --- |
| Rossendale | Blackburn County Court |
| St Helens | Liverpool County Court |
| Salford | Manchester County Court |
| South Lakes | Lancaster County Court |
| South Ribble | Blackburn County Court |
| South Sefton | Liverpool County Court |
| South Tameside | Manchester County Court |
| Stockport | Manchester County Court |
| Trafford | Manchester County Court |
| West Allerdale | Carlisle County Court |
| Whitehaven | Carlisle County Court |
| Wigan | Liverpool County Court |
| Wigton | Carlisle County Court |
| Wirral | Liverpool County Court |
| Wyre | Lancaster County Court |

**North Eastern Circuit**

| | |
| --- | --- |
| Bainton Beacon | Kingston-upon-Hull County Court |
| Barnsley | Sheffield County Court |
| Batley and Dewsbury | Leeds County Court |
| Berwick-upon-Tweed | Newcastle-upon-Tyne County Court |
| Beverley | Kingston-upon-Hull County Court |
| Blyth Valley | Newcastle-upon-Tyne County Court |
| Bradford | Leeds County Court |
| Brighouse | Leeds County Court |
| Calder | Leeds County Court |
| Chester-le-Street | Newcastle-upon-Tyne County Court |
| Claro | York County Court |
| Coquetdale | Newcastle-upon-Tyne County Court |
| Darlington | Teesside County Court |
| Derwentside | Newcastle-upon-Tyne County Court |
| Dickering | Kingston-upon-Hull County Court |
| Doncaster | Sheffield County Court |
| Durham | Newcastle-upon-Tyne County Court |
| Easington | Sunderland County Court |
| Easingwold | York County Court |
| Gateshead | Newcastle-upon-Tyne County Court |
| [Grimsby and Cleethorpes | Kingston-upon-Hull County Court |
| Goole and Howdenshire | Kingston-upon-Hull County Court] |
| Hartlepool | Teesside County Court |
| Holme Beacon | Kingston-upon-Hull County Court |
| Houghton-le-Spring | Sunderland County Court |
| . . . | . . . |
| Huddersfield | Leeds County Court |
| Keighley | Leeds County Court |
| Kingston-upon-Hull | Kingston-upon-Hull County Court |
| Langbaurgh East | Teesside County Court |
| Leeds | Leeds County Court |
| Middle Holderness | Kingston-upon-Hull County Court |
| Morley | Leeds County Court |
| Morpeth Ward | Newcastle-upon-Tyne County Court |
| Newcastle-upon-Tyne | Newcastle-upon-Tyne County Court |

| (i)<br>Petty Sessions Area | (ii)<br>Care Centres |
| --- | --- |
| Northallerton | Teesside County Court |
| North Holderness | Kingston-upon-Hull County Court |
| [North Lincolnshire | Kingston-upon-Hull County Court] |
| North Tyneside | Newcastle-upon-Tyne County Court |
| Pontefract | Leeds County Court |
| Pudsey and Otley | Leeds County Court |
| Richmond | Teesside County Court |
| Ripon Liberty | York County Court |
| Rotherham | Sheffield County Court |
| Ryedale | York County Court |
| Scarborough | York County Court |
| Sedgefield | Newcastle-upon-Tyne County Court |
| Selby | York County Court |
| Sheffield | Sheffield County Court |
| Skyrack and Wetherby | Leeds County Court |
| South Holderness | Kingston-upon-Hull County Court |
| South Hunsley Beacon | Kingston-upon-Hull County Court |
| South Tyneside | Sunderland County Court |
| Staincliffe | Leeds County Court |
| Sunderland | Sunderland County Court |
| Teesdale and Wear Valley | Newcastle-upon-Tyne County Court |
| Teesside | Teesside County Court |
| Todmorden | Leeds County Court |
| Tynedale | Newcastle-upon-Tyne County Court |
| Wakefield | Leeds County Court |
| Wansbeck | Newcastle-upon-Tyne County Court |
| Whitby Strand | Teesside County Court |
| Wilton Beacon | Kingston-upon-Hull County Court |
| York | York County Court |

**South Eastern Circuit**

| | |
| --- | --- |
| [Abingdon | Oxford County Court] |
| Ampthill | Luton County Court |
| Arundel | Brighton County Court |
| Ashford and Tenterden | [Canterbury County Court] |
| Aylesbury | Milton Keynes County Court |
| Barnet | Principal Registry of the Family Division |
| Barking and Dagenham | Principal Registry of the Family Division |
| Basildon | Chelmsford County Court |
| Battle and Rye | Brighton County Court |
| . . . | . . . |
| Bedford | Luton County Court |
| Bexhill | Brighton County Court |
| Bexley | Principal Registry of the Family Division |
| [Bicester | Oxford County Court] |
| Biggleswade | Luton County Court |
| Bishop's Stortford | Watford County Court |
| Brent | Principal Registry of the Family Division |
| Brentwood | Chelmsford County Court |
| Brighton | Brighton County Court |
| Bromley | Principal Registry of the Family Division |
| Buckingham | Milton Keynes County Court |

| (i)<br>Petty Sessions Area | (ii)<br>Care Centres |
| --- | --- |
| Burnham | Milton Keynes County Court |
| Cambridge | [Cambridge County Court] |
| Canterbury and St Augustine | [Canterbury County Court] |
| Chelmsford | Chelmsford County Court |
| Chertsey | Guildford County Court |
| Cheshunt | Watford County Court |
| Chichester and District | Brighton County Court |
| Chiltern | Milton Keynes County Court |
| Colchester | Chelmsford County Court |
| Crawley | Brighton County Court |
| Cromer | Norwich County Court |
| Crowborough | Brighton County Court |
| Croydon | Principal Registry of the Family Division |
| Dacorum | Watford County Court |
| Dartford | Medway County Court |
| [Didcot and Wantage | Oxford County Court] |
| Diss | Norwich County Court |
| Dorking | Guildford County Court |
| Dover and East Kent | [Canterbury County Court] |
| Downham Market | Norwich County Court |
| Dunmow | Chelmsford County Court |
| Dunstable | Luton County Court |
| Ealing | Principal Registry of the Family Division |
| Eastbourne | Brighton County Court |
| [East Cambridgeshire | Cambridge County Court] |
| East Dereham | Norwich County Court |
| [East Oxfordshire | Oxford County Court] |
| . . . | . . . |
| Enfield | Principal Registry of the Family Division |
| Epping and Ongar | Chelmsford County Court |
| Epsom | Guildford County Court |
| Esher and Walton | Guildford County Court |
| Fakenham | Norwich County Court |
| Farnham | Guildford County Court |
| Faversham and Sittingbourne | Medway County Court |
| [Fenland | Peterborough County Court] |
| Folkestone and Hythe | [Canterbury County Court] |
| The Forest | Reading County Court |
| Freshwell and South Hinckford | Chelmsford County Court |
| Godstone | Guildford County Court |
| Guildford | Guildford County Court |
| Gravesham | Medway County Court |
| Great Yarmouth | Norwich County Court |
| Hailsham | Brighton County Court |
| Halstead and Hedingham | Chelmsford County Court |
| Harlow | Chelmsford County Court |
| Harrow Gore | Principal Registry of the Family Division |
| Haringey | Principal Registry of the Family Division |
| Harwich | Chelmsford County Court |
| Hastings | Brighton County Court |
| [Haverhill and Sudbury | Ipswich County Court] |
| Havering | Principal Registry of the Family Division |

| (i)<br>Petty Sessions Area | (ii)<br>Care Centres |
| --- | --- |
| [Henley | Oxford County Court] |
| Hertford and Ware | Watford County Court |
| Hillingdon | Principal Registry of the Family Division |
| Horsham | Brighton County Court |
| Hounslow | Principal Registry of the Family Division |
| Hove | Brighton County Court |
| Hunstanton | Norwich County Court |
| [Huntingdonshire | Peterborough County Court] |
| . . . | . . . |
| King's Lynn | Norwich County Court |
| Kingston-upon-Thames | Principal Registry of the Family Division |
| Leighton Buzzard | Luton County Court |
| Lewes | Brighton County Court |
| . . . | . . . |
| Luton | Luton County Court |
| Maidenhead | Reading County Court |
| Maidstone | Medway County Court |
| Maldon and Witham | Chelmsford County Court |
| . . . | . . . |
| Medway | Medway County Court |
| Merton | Principal Registry of the Family Division |
| Mid-Hertfordshire | Watford County Court |
| Mid-Sussex | Brighton County Court |
| . . . | . . . |
| Milton Keynes | Milton Keynes County Court |
| Newham | Principal Registry of the Family Division |
| [North East Suffolk | Ipswich County Court] |
| North Hertfordshire | Watford County Court |
| [North Oxfordshire and Chipping Norton | Oxford County Council] |
| North Walsham | Norwich County Court |
| [North West Suffolk | Ipswich County Court] |
| Norwich | Norwich County Court |
| [Oxford | Oxford County Council] |
| Peterborough | Peterborough County Court |
| . . . | . . . |
| Reading and Sonning | Reading County Court |
| Redbridge | Principal Registry of the Family Division |
| Reigate | Guildford County Court |
| Richmond-upon-Thames | Principal Registry of the Family Division |
| . . . | . . . |
| Rochford and Southend-on-Sea | Chelmsford County Court |
| Saffron Walden | Chelmsford County Court |
| St Albans | Watford County Court |
| [St Edmundsbury and Stowmarket | Ipswich County Court] |
| . . . | . . . |
| Sevenoaks | Medway County Court |
| Slough | Reading County Court |
| [South East Suffolk | Ipswich County Court] |
| South Mimms | Watford County Court |
| Staines and Sunbury | Guildford County Court |
| Stevenage | Watford County Court |
| Steyning | Brighton County Court |

| (i)<br>Petty Sessions Area | (ii)<br>Care Centres |
| --- | --- |
| . . . | . . . |
| . . . | . . . |
| Sutton | Principal Registry of the Family Division |
| Swaffham | Norwich County Court |
| Tendring | Chelmsford County Court |
| [Thanet | Canterbury County Court] |
| Thetford | Norwich County Court |
| Thurrock | Chelmsford County Court |
| Tonbridge and Malling | Medway County Court |
| . . . | . . . |
| Tunbridge Wells and Cranbrook | Medway County Court |
| Waltham Forest | Principal Registry of the Family Division |
| Watford | Watford County Court |
| West Berkshire | Reading County Court |
| Windsor | Reading County Court |
| . . . | . . . |
| [Witney | Oxford County Court] |
| Woking | Guildford County Court |
| . . . | . . . |
| [Woodstock | Oxford County Council] |
| Worthing | Brighton County Court |
| Wycombe | Milton Keynes County Court |
| Wymondham | Norwich County Court |

**Wales and Chester Circuit**

| | |
| --- | --- |
| Ardudwy-is-Artro | [Caernarfon County Court] |
| Ardudwy-uwch-Artro | [Caernarfon County Court] |
| Bangor | [Caernarfon County Court] |
| Bedwellty | Newport (Gwent) County Court |
| Berwyn | Rhyl County Court |
| Brecon | [Pontypridd County Court] |
| Caernarfon and Gwyrfai | [Caernarfon County Court] |
| Cardiff | Cardiff County Court |
| Carmarthen North | Swansea County Court |
| Carmarthen South | Swansea County Court |
| Ceredigion Ganol | Swansea County Court |
| Chester | Chester County Court |
| Cleddau | Swansea County Court |
| Colwyn | Rhyl County Court |
| Congleton | Stoke-on-Trent County Court |
| Conwy and Llandudno | [Caernarfon County Court] |
| Crewe and Nantwich | Stoke-on-Trent County Court |
| Cynon Valley | [Pontypridd County Court] |
| De Ceredigion | Swansea County Court |
| Dinefwr | Swansea County Court |
| Dyffryn Clwyd | Rhyl County Court |
| East Gwent | Newport (Gwent) County Court |
| Eifionydd | [Caernarfon County Court] |
| Ellesmere Port and Neston | Chester County Court |
| Estimaner | [Caernarfon County Court] |

| (i) | (ii) |
|---|---|
| *Petty Sessions Area* | *Care Centres* |
| Flint | Rhyl County Court |
| Gogledd Ceredigion | Swansea County Court |
| Gogledd Preseli | Swansea County Court |
| Halton | Warrington County Court |
| Hawarden | Rhyl County Court |
| Llandrindod Wells | [Pontypridd County Court] |
| Llanelli | Swansea County Court |
| Lliw Valley | Swansea County Court |
| Lower Rhymney Valley | Cardiff County Court |
| Macclesfield | Warrington County Court |
| Machynlleth | [Chester County Court] |
| Merthyr Tydfil | [Pontypridd County Court] |
| Miskin | [Pontypridd County Court] |
| Mold | Rhyl County Court |
| Nant Conwy | [Caernarfon County Court] |
| Neath | Swansea County Court |
| Newcastle and Ogmore | Cardiff County Court |
| Newport | Newport (Gwent) County Court |
| Newton | [Chester County Court] |
| North Anglesey | [Caernarfon County Court] |
| Penllyn | [Caernarfon County Court] |
| Port Talbot | Swansea County Court |
| Pwllheli | [Caernarfon County Court] |
| Rhuddlan | Rhyl County Court |
| South Anglesey | [Caernarfon County Court] |
| South Pembrokeshire | Swansea County Court |
| Swansea | Swansea County Court |
| Talybont | [Caernarfon County Court] |
| Upper Rhymney Valley | [Pontypridd County Court] |
| Vale of Glamorgan | Cardiff County Court |
| Vale Royal | Chester County Court |
| Warrington | Warrington County Court |
| Welshpool | [Chester County Court] |
| Wrexham Maelor | Rhyl County Court |
| Ystradgynlais | Swansea County Court |
| | |
| | **Western Circuit** |
| Alton | Portsmouth County Court |
| Andover | Portsmouth County Court |
| Axminster | Taunton County Court |
| Barnstaple | Taunton County Court |
| Basingstoke | Portsmouth County Court |
| Bath and Wansdyke | Bristol County Court |
| Bideford and Great Torrington | Taunton County Court |
| Blandford and Sturminster | Bournemouth County Court |
| Bodmin | Truro County Court |
| Bournemouth | Bournemouth County Court |
| Bristol | Bristol County Court |
| Bridport | Bournemouth County Court |
| Cheltenham | Bristol County Court |

| *(i)*<br>*Petty Sessions Area* | *(ii)*<br>*Care Centres* |
| --- | --- |
| Christchurch | Bournemouth County Court |
| Cirencester, Fairford and Tetbury | [Swindon County Court] |
| Cullompton | Taunton County Court |
| Dorchester | Bournemouth County Court |
| Droxford | Portsmouth County Court |
| Dunheved and Stratton | Truro County Court |
| Eastleigh | Portsmouth County Court |
| East Penwith | Truro County Court |
| East Powder | Truro County Court |
| Exeter | Plymouth County Court |
| Exmouth | Plymouth County Court |
| Falmouth and Kerrier | Truro County Court |
| Fareham | Portsmouth County Court |
| Forest of Dean | Bristol County Court |
| Gloucester | Bristol County Court |
| Gosport | Portsmouth County Court |
| Havant | Portsmouth County Court |
| Honiton | Taunton County Court |
| Hythe | Bournemouth County Court |
| Isle of Wight | Portsmouth County Court |
| Isles of Scilly | Truro County Court |
| Kennet | [Swindon County Court] |
| Kingsbridge | Plymouth County Court |
| Long Ashton | Bristol County Court |
| Lymington | Bournemouth County Court |
| Mendip | Taunton County Court |
| North Avon | Bristol County Court |
| North Cotswold | Bristol County Court |
| North Wiltshire | [Swindon County Court] |
| Odiham | Portsmouth County Court |
| Okehampton | Plymouth County Court |
| Penwith | Truro County Court |
| Petersfield | Portsmouth County Court |
| Plymouth | Plymouth County Court |
| Plympton | Plymouth County Court |
| Portsmouth | Portsmouth County Court |
| Poole | Bournemouth County Court |
| Pydar | Truro County Court |
| Ringwood | Bournemouth County Court |
| Romsey | Bournemouth County Court |
| Salisbury | [Swindon County Court] |
| Sedgemoor | Taunton County Court |
| Shaftesbury | Bournemouth County Court |
| Sherborne | Bournemouth County Court |
| Southampton | Portsmouth County Court |
| South East Cornwall | Plymouth County Court |
| South Gloucestershire | Bristol County Court |
| South Molton | Taunton County Court |
| South Somerset | Taunton County Court |
| Swindon | [Swindon County Court] |
| Taunton Deane | Taunton County Court |
| Tavistock | Plymouth County Court |

| (i)<br>*Petty Sessions Area* | (ii)<br>*Care Centres* |
| --- | --- |
| Teignbridge | Plymouth County Court |
| Tewkesbury | Bristol County Court |
| Tiverton | Taunton County Court |
| Torbay | Plymouth County Court |
| Totnes | Plymouth County Court |
| Totton and New Forest | Bournemouth County Court |
| Truro and South Powder | Truro County Court |
| Wareham and Swanage | Bournemouth County Court |
| West Somerset | Taunton County Court |
| Weston-Super-Mare | Bristol County Court |
| West Wiltshire | [Swindon County Court] |
| Weymouth and Portland | Bournemouth County Court |
| Wimborne | Bournemouth County Court |
| Winchester | Portsmouth County Court |
| Wonford | Plymouth County Court |

| (i)<br>*London Commission Area* | (ii)<br>*Care Centres* |
| --- | --- |
| Inner London Area and<br>   City of London | Principal Registry of the<br>   Family Division |

**Note.** Heading '**Midland Circuit**': words omitted revoked by SI 2001/775, arts 3, 8(1), (2)(a) as from 1 April 2001. Under heading '**Midland Circuit**': entries 'Abingdon', 'Barton-on-Humber', 'Bicester', 'Brigg', 'Cambridge', 'Didcot and Wantage', 'East Oxfordshire', 'Ely', 'Epworth and Goole', 'Grimsby and Cleethorpes', 'Henley', 'Huntingdon', 'Newmarket', 'North Oxfordshire and Chipping Norton', 'North Witchford', 'Oxford', 'Peterborough', 'Scunthorpe', 'Toseland', 'Wisbech', 'Witney' and 'Woodstock' (omitted) revoked by SI 2001/775, arts 3, 8(1), (2)(b) as from 1 April 2001.

   Under heading '**North Eastern Circuit**': entries 'Grimsby and Cleethorpes', 'Goole and Howdenshire' and 'North Lincolnshire' inserted and entry 'Howdenshire' (omitted) revoked by SI 2001/775, arts 3, 8(1), (3)(a)–(c) all from 1 April 2001.

   Under heading '**South Eastern Circuit**': entries 'Abingdon', 'Bicester', 'Didcot and Wantage', 'East Oxfordshire', 'Henley', 'North Oxfordshire and Chipping Norton', 'Oxford', 'Witney' and 'Woodstock' inserted by SI 2001/775, arts 3, 8(1), (4)(a)–(e), (h), (i) as from 1 April 2001; in entries 'Ashford and Tenterden', 'Canterbury and St Augustine', 'Dover and East Kent' and 'Folkstone and Hythe' words 'Canterbury County Court' in square brackets substituted by SI 1994/3138, arts 2, 5(a); entries 'Beccles', 'Ely', 'Ipswich', 'Lowestoft', 'Mildenhall', 'Risbridge', 'Saxmundham', 'Stow', 'Sudbury and Cosford', 'Toseland', 'Wisbech' and 'Woodbridge' (omitted) revoked by SI 2003/331, art 2(a), (d), (h), (m), (o) as from 1 April 2003; in entry 'Cambridge' in column (ii) words 'Cambridge County Court' in square brackets substituted by SI 2003/331, art 2(b) as from 1 April 2003; entries 'East Cambridgeshire', 'Haverhill and Sudbury' and 'South East Suffolk' inserted by SI 2003/331, art 2(c), (f), (n) as from 1 April 2003; entry 'Fenland' substituted for entry 'Felixstowe', entry 'Huntingdonshire' substituted for entry 'Huntingdon', entry 'North East Suffolk' substituted for entry 'Newmarket', entry 'North West Suffolk' substituted for entry 'North Witchford', entry 'St Edmundsbury and Stowmarket' substituted for entry 'St Edmundsbury', all as originally enacted, by SI 2003/331, art 2(e), (g), (j), (l) as from 1 April 2003; entries 'Margate' and 'Ramsgate' (omitted) revoked by SI 1994/3138, arts 2, 4(a) and entry 'Thanet' inserted by SI 1994/3138, arts 2, 4(b).

   Under heading '**Wales and Chester Circuit**': in entries 'Ardudwy-is-Artro', 'Ardudwy-uwch-Artro', 'Bangor', 'Caernarfon and Gwyrfai', 'Conwy and Llandudno', 'Eifionydd', 'Estimaner', 'Nant Conwy', 'North Anglesey', 'Penllyn', 'Pwllheli', 'South Anglesey' and

'Talybont' words 'Caernarfon County Court' in square brackets substituted by SI 1994/3138, arts 2, 5(d); in entries 'Brecon', 'Cynon Valley', 'Llandrindod Wells' and 'Upper Rhymney Valley' words 'Pontypridd County Court' in square brackets substituted by SI 1995/1649, art 3; in entries 'Machynlleth', 'Newton' and 'Welshpool' words 'Chester County Court' in square brackets substituted by SI 1994/3138, arts 2, 5(b).

Under heading '**Western Circuit**': in entries 'Cirencester, Fairford and Tetbury', 'Kennet', 'North Wiltshire', 'Swindon' and 'West Wiltshire' words 'Swindon County Court' in square brackets substituted by SI 1994/3138, arts 2, 5(c); in entry 'Salisbury' words 'Swindon County Court' in square brackets substituted by SI 1997/1897, art 6 as from 1 September 1997.

## CHILDREN (ALLOCATION OF PROCEEDINGS) (APPEALS) ORDER 1991

**Dated** 25 July 1991

**SI 1991 No 1801**

The Lord Chancellor, in exercise of the powers conferred on him by section 94(10) of the Children Act 1989, and of all other powers enabling him in that behalf, hereby makes the following Order—

*Citation, commencement and interpretation*

**1.** (1) This Order may be cited as the Children (Allocation of Proceedings) (Appeals) Order 1991 and shall come into force on 14th October 1991.

(2) In this Order—

'district judge' includes an assistant district judge and a deputy district judge; and

'circuit judge' means any person who is capable of sitting as a judge for a county court district and who is allocated to hear appeals permitted by this Order in accordance with directions given under section 9 of the Courts and Legal Services Act 1990.

*Appeals*

**2.** Where a district judge orders the transfer of proceedings to a magistrates' court in accordance with article 11 of the Children (Allocation of Proceedings) Order 1991 an appeal may be made against that decision—

(a) to a judge of the Family Division of the High Court, or

(b) except where the order was made by a district judge or deputy district judge of the principal registry of the Family Division, to a circuit judge.

**FAMILY LAW ACT 1986 (DEPENDENT TERRITORIES) ORDER 1991**

**Dated** 24 July 1991

**SI 1991 No 1723**

Her Majesty, in exercise of the powers conferred upon Her by section 43 of the Family Law Act 1986 is pleased, by and with the advice of Her Privy Council, to order, and it is hereby ordered, as follows—

**1.**   This Order may be cited as the Family Law Act 1986 (Dependent Territories) Order 1991 and shall come into force on 14th October 1991.

**2.**   In this Order—
  'the Act' means the Family Law Act 1986;
  'specified dependent territory' means a dependent territory specified in column 1 of Schedule 1 to this Order;
  'Part I order' has the meaning given by section 1(1) of the Act;
  'part of the United Kingdom' has the meaning given by section 42(1) of the Act.

**3.**   (1)  This Order applies in relation to a specified dependent territory from the date specified opposite the name of that territory in column 2 of Schedule 1 to this Order.

  (2)  Part I of the Act shall apply, for the purpose of regulating, as between any specified dependent territory and any part of the United Kingdom, the jurisdiction of courts to make Part I orders, and the recognition and enforcement of orders corresponding to such orders, with the modifications specified in Schedule 2 of this Order.

  (3)  Each Part of Schedule 3 to this Order shall have effect for the construction of Part I of the Act as modified by this Order in relation to the specified dependent territory named in the heading to that Part of that Schedule.

**4.**   This Order does not extend to any territory outside the United Kingdom.

*G. I. de Deney*
Clerk of the Privy Council

SCHEDULE 1                                                                   Article 2

SPECIFIED DEPENDENT TERRITORIES

| *Dependent Territory* | *Date from which this Order applies* |
| --- | --- |
| The Isle of Man | 14th October 1991 |

SCHEDULE 2                                                                 Article 3(2)

MODIFICATIONS OF PART I OF THE FAMILY LAW ACT 1986

*Chapter I—Preliminary*

**1.**   (1)  In section 1(1) after paragraph (e) insert—
  '(f) an order made by a court in a specified dependent territory corresponding to an order within paragraphs (a) to (e) above.'
  (2)  In section 1(2)—
  (a)  in paragraph (a), after 'subsection (1)(c)' insert 'or (f)';
  (b)  in paragraph (c), after 'paragraph (e)' insert 'or (f)'.
  (3)  In section 1(3) after paragraph (b) insert—
  'and

(c) excludes any order falling within subsection (1)(f) above made before the date specified opposite the name of the territory concerned in Column 2 of Schedule 1 to the Family Law Act 1986 (Dependent Territories) Order 1991, as from time to time in force.'

*Chapter II—Jurisdiction of courts in England and Wales*

**2.** (1) In section 2A(2), for 'Scotland or Northern Ireland' substitute 'Scotland, Northern Ireland or a specified dependent territory'.

(2) In section 2A(3)—

(a) in paragraph (a), after 'section 13(6)(a)(i)), or' insert 'a corresponding dependent territory order, or';

(b) in paragraph (b), after 'this Act' insert ', or a corresponding dependent territory order,'.

**3.** (1) In section 3(1)(b), after 'United Kingdom' insert 'or a specified dependent territory'.

(2) In section 3(2), for 'Scotland or Northern Ireland' substitute 'Scotland, Northern Ireland or a specified dependent territory'.

(3) In section 3(3)—

(a) in paragraph (a), after 'section 13(6)(a)(i)), or' insert 'a corresponding dependent territory order, or';

(b) in paragraph (b), after 'this Act' insert ', or a corresponding dependent territory order,'.

**4.** (1) In section 6(1), for 'Scotland or Northern Ireland'—

(a) (in the first place) substitute 'Scotland, Northern Ireland or a specified dependent territory'; and

(b) (in the second place) substitute 'Scotland, Northern Ireland or the territory'.

(2) In section 6(3), for 'Scotland or Northern Ireland' substitute 'Scotland, Northern Ireland or a specified dependent territory'.

(3) In section 6(4)—

(a) in paragraph (a), after 'section 13(6)(a)(i)), or' insert 'a corresponding dependent territory order, or';

(b) in paragraph (b), after 'this Act' insert ', or a corresponding dependent territory order,'.

*Chapter III—Jurisdiction of courts in Scotland*

**5.** In section 10(a)(ii) and (b)(ii), after 'United Kingdom' insert 'or a specified dependent territory'.

**6.** (1) In section 11(1), after 'United Kingdom' insert 'or a specified dependent territory'.

(2) In section 11(2)—

(a) in paragraph (a), after the words 'section 13(6)(a)(ii))' insert 'or a corresponding dependent territory order';

(b) in paragraph (b), after 'this Act' insert ', or a corresponding dependent territory order,'.

**7.** (1) In section 13(3) and (4), after 'United Kingdom' insert 'or a specified dependent territory'.

(2) In section 13(5)—

(a) in paragraph (a), after 'paragraph (a)(ii) of that subsection), or' insert 'a corresponding dependent territory order, or';

(b) in paragraph (b), after 'this Act' insert ', or a corresponding dependent territory order,'.

(3) In section 13(6)(a)(ii)—

(a) after 'this Act' insert 'or a corresponding dependent territory provision';

(b) after 'United Kingdom' insert 'or a specified dependent territory'.

**8.** In section 15(1)—
(a) in paragraph (a), after 'United Kingdom' insert 'or in a specified dependent territory';
(b) in paragraph (b), after 'United Kingdom' insert 'and any specified dependent territory';
(c) after 'the other court in the United Kingdom' insert 'or in the specified dependent territory'.

*Chapter IV—Jurisdiction of courts in Northern Ireland*

**9.** (1) In section 20(1)(b), after 'United Kingdom' insert 'or in a specified dependent territory'.
(2) In section 20(2), for 'England and Wales or Scotland' substitute 'England and Wales, Scotland or a specified dependent territory'.
(3) In section 20(3)—
(a) in paragraph (a), after 'section 13(6)(a)(i)), or' insert 'a corresponding dependent territory order, or';
(b) in paragraph (b), after 'this Act' insert ', or a corresponding dependent territory order,'.
**10.** (1) In section 21(3), for 'England and Wales or Scotland' substitute 'England and Wales, Scotland or a specified dependent territory'.
(2) In section 21(4)—
(a) in paragraph (a), for 'section 13(6)(a)(i), or' substitute 'section 13(6)(a)(i)), or a corresponding dependent territory order, or';
(b) in paragraph (b), after 'this Act' insert ', or a corresponding dependent territory order,'.
**11.** (1) In section 23(1), for 'England and Wales or Scotland'—
(a) (in the first place) substitute 'England and Wales, Scotland or a specified dependent territory'; and
(b) (in the second place) substitute 'England and Wales, Scotland or the territory'.
(2) In section 23(3), for 'England and Wales or Scotland' substitute 'England and Wales, Scotland or a specified dependent territory'.
(3) In section 23(4)—
(a) in paragraph (a), after 'section 13(6)(a)(i)), or' insert 'a corresponding dependent territory order, or';
(b) in paragraph (b), after 'this Act' insert ', or a corresponding dependent territory order,'.

*Chapter V—Recognition and Enforcement*

**12.** In section 25(1)—
(a) after the words 'a court in any part of the United Kingdom' insert 'or in a specified dependent territory';
(b) after the words 'shall be recognised in any other part' insert 'or, in the case of a dependent territory order, any part';
(c) for the words 'in that other part', in both places where they occur, substitute 'in that part'.
**13.** In section 26, after 'United Kingdom' insert 'and a specified dependent territory'.
**14.** (1) In section 27(1), after 'under this section' insert ', or in a specified dependent territory under a corresponding provision'.
(2) In section 27(3), after 'part of the United Kingdom' insert 'or dependent territory'.
(3) In section 27(4)—
(a) after 'the appropriate court' insert 'in any part of the United Kingdom'; and

(b) after 'subsection (3) above' insert 'or under a corresponding dependent territory provision,'.

**15.** In section 28(2)—

(a) in paragraph (a), after 'United Kingdom' insert 'or in a specified dependent territory'; and

(b) in paragraph (b), after 'United Kingdom' insert 'and any specified dependent territory'.

**16.** (1) In section 31(1), after 'United Kingdom' insert 'or specified dependent territory'.

(2) In section 31(2), after 'outside the United Kingdom' insert 'and any specified dependent territory'.

**17.** (1) In section 32(1)—

(a) in the definition of 'the appropriate court', after 'the Court of Session' insert 'and, in relation to a specified dependent territory, means the corresponding court in that territory';

(b) in the definition of 'Part I order', in paragraph (a), after 'this Part' insert 'or the corresponding dependent territory provisions'.

(2) In section 32(3)(a), after 'this Part' insert 'or the corresponding dependent territory provisions, as the case may be,'.

*Chapter VI—Miscellaneous and supplemental*

**18.** In section 33(3), after 'United Kingdom' insert 'and any specified dependent territory'.

**19.** (1) In section 35(2), after 'specified in the order,' insert 'or out of any specified dependent territory (within the meaning of the Family Law Act 1986 (Dependent Territories) Order 1991) specified in the order,'.

(2) In section 35(3), after 'any part of the United Kingdom' insert 'or any specified dependent territory'.

**20.** (1) In section 36(1)—

(a) after 'in the United Kingdom' insert 'or any specified dependent territory'; and

(b) after 'specified part of it' insert 'or from any such territory'.

(2) In section 36(2)—

(a) after 'this section applies' insert ', made by a court in one part of the United Kingdom or in a specified dependent territory,';

(b) after 'shall have effect in each' insert 'other part, or, in the case of an order made in a dependent territory, each';

(c) the words 'other than the part in which it was made' shall be omitted;

(d) in paragraphs (a) and (b), the word 'other' shall be omitted.

**21.** In section 37(1), after 'part of it' insert 'or from a specified dependent territory'.

**22.** (1) In section 38(2)—

(a) in paragraph (a), after 'of which he is a ward), or' insert 'in a specified dependent territory, or'; and

(b) in paragraph (b), after 'United Kingdom' insert 'or in a specified dependent territory'.

(2) In section 38(3)(a) and (b), after 'United Kingdom' insert 'or the specified dependent territory'.

**23.** (1) In section 41(1)—

(a) in paragraph (b) after 'United Kingdom' insert 'or in a specified dependent territory';

(b) after 'that part of the United Kingdom', in both places, insert 'or that territory'.

(2) In section 41(2)—

(a) after 'the part of the United Kingdom' insert 'or the territory';

(b) in paragraph (a), after 'that part of the United Kingdom' insert 'or that territory';

(c) in paragraph (b), after 'the United Kingdom' insert 'or in a specified dependent territory'.

(3) In section 41(3)—

(a) after 'a Part of the United Kingdom' insert 'or a specified dependent territory';

(b) in paragraph (b)—

    (i) after 'outside that part of the United Kingdom' insert 'or that territory';

    (ii) after 'a court in any part of the United Kingdom' insert 'or in any specified dependent territory'.

**24.** (1) In section 42(1)—

(a) after the definition of 'certified copy' insert—

'' 'corresponding dependent territory order', 'corresponding dependent territory provision' and similar expressions, in relation to a specified dependent territory, shall be construed in accordance with Schedule 3 to the Family Law Act 1986 (Dependent Territories) Order 1991 as from time to time in force;

'dependent territory' has the meaning given by section 43(2) of this Act;';

(b) after the definition of 'prescribed' insert—

'' 'specified dependent territory' means a dependent territory for the time being specified in Schedule 1 to the said Order of 1991.'.

(2) In section 42(2), for 'England and Wales or in Northern Ireland' substitute 'England and Wales, Northern Ireland or a specified dependent territory'.

(3) In section 42(4), after paragraph (c) insert—

'(d) if the proceedings are in a specified dependent territory, means any child who has been treated by both parties as a child of their family, except a child who has been placed with those parties as foster parents by a public authority in that territory.'.

(4) In section 42(6), after paragraph (d) insert—

'(e) an order under a corresponding dependent territory provision.'

(5) In section 42(7)(a), after 'United Kingdom' insert 'and any specified dependent territory'.

SCHEDULE 3                                                    Article 3(3)

INTERPRETATION OF CERTAIN EXPRESSIONS IN PART I OF THE FAMILY LAW ACT 1986 AS
MODIFIED BY SCHEDULE 2 TO THIS ORDER

PART I

*The Isle of Man*

**1.** In section 1(1)(f) 'an order made by the court in a specified dependent territory corresponding to an order within paragraphs (a) to (e) above' means—

(a) an order under section 9 of the Family Law Act 1991 (an Act of Tynwald), or any of the following enactments (being enactments repealed by that Act)—

    (i) section 3(5) of the Guardianship of Infants Act 1953 (an Act of Tynwald), so far as it relates to the custody of infants;

    (ii) section 4(1) of that Act, except so far as it relates to costs, but including that section as applied by section 3(1) of the Legitimacy Act 1962 (an Act of Tynwald);

    (iii) section 42(1) or (2) of the Judicature (Matrimonial Causes) Act 1976 (an Act of Tynwald);

    (iv) section 8(2) or 18(1)(ii) of the Domestic Proceedings Act 1983 (an Act of Tynwald);

    (v) section 34(1) of that Act;

  (vi) section 49(1) of that Act, so far as it relates to the custody of or access to a child;

 (b) an order made by the High Court of Justice of the Isle of Man in the exercise of its jurisdiction relating to wardship or its inherent jurisdiction with respect to children—

  (i) so far as it gives care of a child to any person or provides for contact with or access to, or the education of, a child but

  (ii) excluding an order varying or revoking such an order, or an order relating to a child of whom care or control is (immediately after the making of the order) vested in a public authority in the Isle of Man.

**2.** In each of sections 2A(3), 3(3), 6(4), 11(2), 13(5), 20(3), 21(4) and 23(4)—

 (a) in paragraph (a) 'corresponding dependent territory order' means an order under section 3(3) of the Child Custody Act 1987 (an Act of Tynwald);

 (b) in paragraph (b) 'corresponding dependent territory order' means an order under section 4(2) of that Act.

**3.** In section 13(6)(a)(ii), 'corresponding dependent territory provision' means section 2(2) or 5(3) of the Child Custody Act 1987 (an Act of Tynwald).

**4.** (1) In section 27(1) 'corresponding provision' means section 7 of the Child Custody Act 1987 (an Act of Tynwald).

 (2) In section 27(4) 'corresponding dependent territory provision' means section 12(3) of that Act.

**5.** (1) In section 32(1) 'the corresponding court' means the High Court of Justice of the Isle of Man.

 (2) In section 32(1) and (3)(a) 'the corresponding dependent territory provisions' means Part I of the Child Custody Act 1987 (an Act of Tynwald).

**6.** In section 42(6)(e) 'corresponding dependent territory provision' means—

 (a) section 42(6) or (7) of the Judicature (Matrimonial Causes) Act 1976 (an Act of Tynwald);

 (b) section 18(6) of the Domestic Proceedings Act 1983 (an Act of Tynwald).

## LEGAL AID (DISCLOSURE OF INFORMATION) REGULATIONS 1991

**Dated** 25 July 1991

**SI 1991 No 1753**

*The Lord Chancellor, in exercise of the powers conferred on him by sections 31, 34 and 43 of the Legal Aid Act 1988, hereby makes the following Regulations—*

**1.** *These Regulations may be cited as the Legal Aid (Disclosure of Information) Regulations 1991 and shall come into force on 19 August 1991.*

**2.** *Notwithstanding the relationship between or rights of a legal representative and client or any privilege arising out of such relationship, the legal representative shall not be precluded from disclosing to any person authorised by the Board to request it, any information which relates to advice, assistance and representation provided to a client or former client of his where that client is or was a legally assisted person which is requested for the purpose of enabling the Board to discharge its functions under the Legal Aid Act 1988.*

**Note.** Following the repeal of the enabling provisions by the Access to Justice Act 1999, s 106, Sch 15, Pt 1,these Regulations have lapsed except insofar as they may continue to have effect by virtue of SI 2000/774, art 5, and SI 2001/916, art 4, Sch 2 as from 1 April 2000 for certain purposes, and 2 April 2001 for remaining purposes.

 (A registered European lawyer may provide professional activities by way of legal advice and assistance or legal aid, and this provision shall be interpreted accordingly: see European Communities (Lawyer's Practice) Regulations 2000, SI 2000/1119, reg 14.)

## CHILDREN AND YOUNG PERSONS (DESIGNATION OF ISLE OF MAN ORDERS) ORDER 1991

**Dated** 9 September 1991

**SI 1991 No 2031**

The Secretary of State for Health, in exercise of powers conferred by sections 26(1) and 69(3) of the Children and Young Persons Act 1969 and of all other powers enabling him in that behalf hereby makes the following Order—

*Citation and commencement*

**1.** This Order may be cited as the Children and Young Persons (Designation of Isle of Man Orders) Order 1991 and shall come into force on 14 October 1991.

*Designation*

**2.** A care order made under section 50 of the Children and Young Persons Act 1966 (an Act of Tynwald) being an order which satisfies the conditions set out in section 26(1) of the Children and Young Persons Act 1969 (transfers between England and Wales and the Channel Islands or Isle of Man) is hereby designated for the purposes of section 26 of that Act.

*Revocation*

**3.** The Children and Young Persons (Designation of Isle of Man Order) Order 1971 is hereby revoked.

## CHILDREN (PRESCRIBED ORDERS—NORTHERN IRELAND, GUERNSEY AND ISLE OF MAN) REGULATIONS 1991

**Dated** 9 September 1991

**SI 1991 No 2032**

The Secretary of State for Health, in exercise of the powers conferred by section 101 of the Children Act 1989, and of all other powers enabling him in that behalf, hereby makes the following Regulations—

*Citation, commencement, interpretation and extent*

**1.** (1) These Regulations may be cited as the Children (Prescribed Orders— Northern Ireland, Guernsey and Isle of Man) Regulations 1991 and shall come into force on 14 October 1991.

(2) In these Regulations unless the context requires otherwise—
'the Act' means the Children Act 1989;
'the authority' means the local authority in whose care the child is by virtue of a care order under the Act;
'the Board' means a Health and Social Services Board in Northern Ireland established under article 16 of the Health and Personal Social Services (Northern Ireland) Order 1972;
'the Children Board' means the States Children Board in Guernsey;
'the Department' means the Department of Health and Social Security of the Isle of Man;
'the Northern Ireland Act' means the Children and Young Persons Act (Northern Ireland) 1968;
'the Act of Tynwald' means the Children and Young Persons Act 1966 (an Act of Tynwald).

(3) In these Regulations, unless the context requires otherwise, any reference to a numbered regulation is to the regulation in these Regulations bearing that number and any reference in any regulation to a numbered paragraph is to the paragraph of that regulation bearing that number.

(4) This regulation and regulations 2, 6 and 8 shall extend to Northern Ireland.

*Transfer of care orders from England and Wales to Northern Ireland*

**2.** (1) A care order being an order made by a court in England and Wales, which appears to the Secretary of State to correspond in its effect to an order which may be made under a provision in force in Northern Ireland, shall in the circumstances prescribed in paragraph (2) have effect for all the purposes of the Northern Ireland Act as if it were an order under section 95(1)(b) of that Act committing the child to the care of the Board for the area in which it is proposed that he will live.

(2) The circumstances referred to in paragraph (1) are that the court has given its approval under paragraph 19(1) of Schedule 2 to the Act to the authority arranging or assisting in arranging for the child to live in Northern Ireland.

(3) The care order shall cease to have effect for the purposes of the law of England and Wales if the following conditions are satisfied—

(a) the Board for the area in which the child will live in Northern Ireland has notified the court referred to in paragraph (2) in writing that it agrees to take over the care of the child; and

(b) the authority has notified the court referred to in paragraph (2) that it agrees to the Board taking over the care of the child.

*Transfer of care orders to England and Wales from the Isle of Man*

**3.** (1) A relevant order within the meaning of section 56(6) of the Act of Tynwald (being an order made by a court in the Isle of Man which appears to the Secretary of State to correspond in its effect to an order which may be made under the Act) shall in the circumstances prescribed in paragraph (2) have effect for all the purposes of the Act in England and Wales as if it were a care order under section 31 of the Act placing the child in question in the care of the local authority in whose area he is to live.

(2) The circumstances prescribed are—

(a) that the relevant order was made otherwise than on a finding of guilt;

(b) that either—

(i) the court has given leave under sub-section (2) of section 56 of the Act of Tynwald for the Department to make arrangements for the child to be received into the care of that authority; or

(ii) the court has directed under sub-section (5) of that section that the said sub-section (2) shall not apply in relation to the order in question; and

(c) that the authority has agreed in writing to receive the child into its care.

*Transfer of care orders from England and Wales to the Isle of Man*

**4.** The conditions prescribed for the purposes of section 101(4) of the Act (child in care taken to live in the Isle of Man) in the case of a child who is taken to live in the Isle of Man are that—

(a) the court has given its approval under paragraph 19(1) of Schedule 2 to the Act to the authority arranging or assisting in arranging for the child to live in the Isle of Man;

(b) the Department has notified the court referred to in paragraph (a) in writing that it agrees to receive the child into its care; and

(c) the authority has notified the court referred to in paragraph (a) that it agrees to the Department receiving the child into care.

*Transfer of care orders from England and Wales to Guernsey*

**5.**   The conditions prescribed for the purposes of section 101(4) of the Act in the case of a child who is taken to live in Guernsey are that—

(a)   the court has given its approval under paragraph 19(1) of Schedule 2 to the Act to the authority arranging or assisting in arranging for the child to live in care in Guernsey;

(b)   the Children Board has notified the Guernsey Juvenile Court in writing that it agrees to receive the child into its care; and

(c)   the authority has notified the Guernsey Juvenile Court that it agrees to the Children Board receiving the child into care; and

(d)   the Guernsey Juvenile Court has made a fit person order in respect of the child.

*Transfer of recovery orders from England and Wales to Northern Ireland*

**6.**   (1)   Where an authority has reason to believe that a child has been unlawfully taken to, or is being unlawfully kept in Northern Ireland, or has run away to Northern Ireland, or is missing and believed to be in Northern Ireland, a recovery order made by a court in England and Wales under section 50 of the Act (being an order which appears to the Secretary of State to correspond in its effect to an order which may be made under any provision in force in Northern Ireland) shall have effect for all purposes of the law of Northern Ireland as if it were an order made under section 50 of the Act by a magistrates' court within the meaning of the Magistrates' Courts (Northern Ireland) Order 1981.

(2)   Where a child is subject to a recovery order which is to have effect in Northern Ireland as mentioned in paragraph (1), any reasonable expenses incurred by an authorised person within the meaning of section 50(7) of the Act shall be recoverable from the authority in whose care the child was.

*Transfer of recovery orders to England and Wales from the Isle of Man*

**7.**   (1)   For all purposes of the Act in England and Wales a recovery order under section 98B of the Act of Tynwald (being an order made by a court in the Isle of Man which appears to the Secretary of State to correspond in its effect to an order which may be made under the Act) shall in the circumstances prescribed in paragraph (2) have effect as if it were a recovery order made under section 50 of the Act.

(2)   The circumstances referred to in paragraph (1) are that section 98A of the Act of Tynwald applies to the child in question otherwise than by virtue of an order committing him to the care of the Department on a finding of guilt.

*Amendments to Children and Young Persons Act 1969*

**8.**   (1)   The following consequential amendments shall be made to section 25 of the Children and Young Persons Act 1969 (transfers between England or Wales and Northern Ireland)—

(a)   in subsection (1)—

(i)   after the words 'training school order' there shall be inserted the words 'or by any order which has effect as if it were a fit person order';

(ii)   for the words 'as if it were a care order' to the end of that subsection there shall be substituted the words 'in a case in which there was a fit person order (or an order having effect as if it were a fit person order), as if it were a care order under section 31 of the Children Act 1989 and in a case in which there was a training school order as if it were a supervision order imposing a residence requirement as mentioned in section 12AA of this Act.';

(b) in subsection (2)—
  (i) after the words 'committed by a care order' there shall be inserted the words 'to which paragraph 36 of Schedule 14 to the Children Act (criminal care order transitional provisions) applies';
  (ii) after the words 'interim order' there shall be inserted the words 'or who is to accommodate a person pursuant to a supervision order imposing a residence requirement as mentioned in section 12AA of this Act';
  (iii) the words 'or to the care of the Secretary of State' shall be omitted;
  (iv) for '83(3)(a), 88(3), 90 and 91(3)' there shall be substituted '88(3) and 90';
  (v) for the words 'a fit person order' there shall be substituted the words 'the supervision order';
(c) in subsection (3)—
  (i) the words 'or the Ministry of Home Affairs' shall be omitted;
  (ii) for the words 'or care order' there shall be substituted the words ', care order or supervision order';
  (iii) in paragraph (b) after the words 'care order' there shall be inserted the words 'or supervision order';
  (iv) sub-paragraph (1) of paragraph (b) shall be omitted;
(d) in subsection (4) the words 'or the Ministry of Home Affairs' and the word 'Ministry' shall be omitted.

(2) The following consequential amendments shall be made to section 26 of the Children and Young Persons Act 1969 (transfers between England or Wales and the Channel Islands or the Isle of Man)—
(a) in subsection (1) after the words 'interim order' there shall be inserted 'or as a supervision order imposing a residence requirement as mentioned in section 12AA of this Act' and at the end of the subsection there shall be inserted the words 'and 'care order' means an order made under section 31 of the Children Act 1989.';
(b) for the words in subsection (2) from ', subject to the following subsection' to the end of the subsection (3) there shall be substituted 'be deemed to be the subject of a care order placing the child in the care of a named local authority or, where the relevant order was made as a criminal disposal in criminal proceedings, a supervision order imposing a residence requirement as mentioned in section 12AA of this Act with a requirement that the child be accommodated by a designated local authority.'

## CHILDREN (SECURE ACCOMMODATION) (NO 2) REGULATIONS 1991

**Dated** 6 September 1991

**SI 1991 No 2034**

The Secretary of State for Health, in exercise of the powers conferred by section 25(2)(c) of the Children Act 1989 and of all other powers enabling him in that behalf hereby makes the following Regulations—

*Citation and commencement*

**1.** (1) These Regulations may be cited as the Children (Secure Accommodation) (No 2) Regulations 1991 and shall come into force on 14th October 1991 immediately after the Children (Secure Accommodation) Regulations 1991.

*Applications to court—special cases*

**2.** (1) Applications to a court under section 25 of the Children Act 1989 in respect of a child provided with accommodation by a health authority [, a Primary Care Trust], a National Health Service trust established under section 5 of the National Health Service and Community Care Act 1990 [, an NHS foundation trust] or a local education authority shall, unless the child is looked after by a local authority, be made only by the health authority, [Primary Care Trust,] National Health Service trust [, an NHS foundation trust] or local education authority providing accommodation for the child.

(2) Applications to a court under section 25 of the Children Act 1989 in respect of a child provided with accommodation in a *residential care home, nursing home or mental nursing home* [care home or independent hospital] shall, unless the child is looked after by a local authority, be made only by the person carrying on the home in which accommodation is provided for the child.

**Note.** In para (1) words ', a Primary Care Trust' in square brackets inserted in relation to England and Wales by SI 2000/694, art 3, Schedule, Pt II, para 5 as from 1 April 2000. In para (1) words ', an NHS Foundation Trust' and ', NHS foundation trust' in square brackets inserted by SI 2004/696, art 3, Sch 1, para 10, Sch 3 as from 1 April 2004. In para (1) words 'Primary Care Trust' in square brackets inserted, in relation to England, by SI 2002/546, reg 8(a) as from 1 April 2002. In para (2) words 'residential care home, nursing home or mental nursing home' substituted by words 'care home or independent hospital' in square brackets by SI 2002/546, reg 8(b) in relation to England as from 1 April 2002 and by SI 2002/2935, regs 11, 13 in relation to Wales as from 31 December 2002.

## MAGISTRATES' COURTS (COSTS AGAINST LEGAL REPRESENTATIVES IN CIVIL PROCEEDINGS) RULES 1991

**Dated** 16 September 1991

**SI 1991 No 2096**

The Lord Chancellor, in exercise of the powers conferred upon him by section 144 of the Magistrates' Courts Act 1980, after consultation with the Rule Committee appointed under that section, hereby makes the following Rules—

*Citation, commencement and interpretation*

**1.** (1) These Rules may be cited as the Magistrates' Courts (Costs Against Legal Representatives in Civil Proceedings) Rules 1991 and shall come into force on 14 October 1991.

(2) In these Rules—

'interested party' means the party benefiting from the wasted costs order and, where he is a legally assisted person, within the meaning of section 2(11) of the 1988 Act, the Legal Aid Board;

'the 1988 Act' means the Legal Aid Act 1988;

'wasted costs order' means any action taken by a court under section 145A of the Magistrates' Courts Act 1980.

*General*

**2.** (1) A wasted costs order may provide that the whole or any part of the wasted costs incurred by a party shall be disallowed or (as the case may be) met by the legal or other representative concerned and the court shall specify the amount of such costs.

(2) Subject to paragraph (7) below, a court may make a wasted costs order either on the application of a party to the proceedings or on its own motion and when doing so the justices' clerk shall make a record of the order in writing, and the reasons for the decision of the court.

(3) Before making a wasted costs order, the court shall allow the legal or other representative a reasonable opportunity to appear before it and show cause why the order should not be made.

(4) Subject to paragraphs (5) and (6) below, any payments which are required to be made by a legal or other representative under a wasted costs order shall be made to the party who has incurred the wasted costs.

(5) Where the party who has incurred wasted costs is receiving assistance by way of representation under Part III of the 1988 Act and which has been approved under regulation 22 of the Legal Advice and Assistance Regulations 1989, any payments which are required to be made by a legal or other representative under a wasted costs order shall be paid to the *justices' clerk* [justices' chief executive] in accordance with regulation 31 of those Regulations.

(6) Where the party who has incurred wasted costs is being granted representation under Part IV of the 1988 Act, any payments which are required to be made by a legal or other representative under a wasted costs order shall be paid to the *justices' clerk* [justices' chief executive] in accordance with regulation 89(a) of the Civil Legal Aid (General) Regulations 1989.

(7) A court shall not make a wasted costs order after the end of the period of six months beginning with the date on which the proceedings are disposed of by the court.

(8) Where a wasted costs order has been made, the *justices' clerk* [justices' chief executive] shall, as soon as practicable, serve a copy of the order on any interested party and on the legal or other representative concerned.

**Note.** Words 'justices' clerk' in each place substituted by words 'justices' chief executive' in square brackets by SI 2001/615, r 2(xxiv), Schedule, para 120 as from 1 April 2001.

*Appeals*

**3.** (1) A legal or other representative against whom a wasted costs order is made may appeal to the Crown Court.

(2) Subject to paragraph (4) below, an appeal shall be instituted within 21 days of the wasted costs order being made by the appellant giving notice in writing to the *justices' clerk of* [justices' chief executive for] the court which made the order, stating the grounds of appeal.

(3) The appellant shall, as soon as practicable after instituting the appeal, serve a copy of the notice and grounds of appeal, including any application for an extension of the time in which to appeal granted under paragraph (4) below, on any interested party.

(4) The time limit within which an appeal may be instituted may, for good reason, be extended before or after it expires by a judge of the Crown Court and, where it is so extended, the court to which the appeal is made shall give notice of the extension to the appellant, the *justices' clerk of* [justices' chief executive for] the court which made the wasted costs order and any interested party.

(5) The court to which the appeal is made shall give notice of the hearing date to the appellant, the *justices' clerk of* [justices' chief executive for] the court which made the wasted costs order and any interested party and shall allow the interested party to make representations either orally or in writing.

(6) The court hearing the appeal may affirm, vary or revoke the order as it thinks fit and shall notify its decision to the appellant, any interested party and the *justices' clerk of* [justices' chief executive for] the court which made the order.

**Note.** Words 'justices' clerk of' in each place substituted by words 'justices' chief executive for' in square brackets by SI 2001/615, r 2(xxiv) Schedule, para 121 as from 1 April 2001.

## ADOPTION ALLOWANCE REGULATIONS 1991

**Dated** 9 September 1991

**SI 1991 No 2030**

*Citation, commencement and interpretation*

**1.** (1) These Regulations may be cited as the Adoption Allowance Regulations 1991 and shall come into force on 14 October 1991.

(2) In these Regulations unless the context otherwise requires—
'the Act' means the Adoption Act 1976;
'adopters' means the persons who have adopted or intend to adopt a child or, where there is only one such person, that person;
'adoption agency' means an approved adoption society *or a local authority*;
'adoption panel' means a panel established in accordance with regulation 5 of the Adoption Agencies Regulations 1983;
<. . .>
'child benefit' means a benefit under section 1 of the Child Benefit Act 1975;
'fostering allowance' means the amount of money paid by way of maintenance for a child placed with a foster parent pursuant to section 23(2)(a) or section 59(1)(a) of the Children Act 1989 (placement with foster parents and others by local authorities and voluntary organisations);
['disability living allowance' means a disability living allowance under section 37ZA of the Social Security Act 1975;]
'income support' means income support under section 20 of the Social Security Act 1986;
<. . .>
'unemployment benefit' means unemployment benefit under section 14 of the Social Security Act 1975.

(3) In these Regulations unless the context otherwise requires, a reference to a numbered regulation is to the regulation in these Regulations bearing that number, and a reference to a numbered paragraph is to the paragraph of that regulation bearing that number.

**Note.** Para (2): in definition 'adoption agency' words 'or a local authority' revoked by SI 2003/1348, reg 15(1) in relation to England as from 31 October 2003 and by SI 2004/1011, reg 16(1) in relation to Wales as from 1 October 2004, and definitions 'attendance allowance' and 'mobility allowance' revoked and definition 'disability living allowance' inserted by SI 1991/2742, reg 18(1), (2).

*Circumstances in which an allowance may be paid*

**2.** (1) Without prejudice to paragraph (3), an allowance may be paid where one or more of the circumstances specified in paragraph (2) exists and the adoption agency—
(a) is making the arrangements for the child's adoption; and
(b) has decided—
    (i) in accordance with regulation 11(1) of the Adoption Agencies Regulations 1983 that the adoption by the adopters would be in the child's best interests, and
    (ii) after considering the recommendation of the adoption panel, that such adoption is not practicable without payment of an allowance.

(2) The circumstances referred to in paragraph (1) are—
(a) where the adoption agency is satisfied that the child has established a strong and important relationship with the adopters before the adoption order is made;
(b) where it is desirable that the child be placed with the same adopters as his brothers or sisters, or with a child with whom he has previously shared a home;

(c) where at the time of the placement for adoption the child—
  (i) is mentally or physically disabled or suffering from the effects of emotional or behavioural difficulties, and
  (ii) needs special care which requires a greater expenditure of resources than would be required if the child were not so disabled, or suffering from the effects of emotional or behavioural difficulties;
(d) where at the time of the placement for the adoption the child was mentally or physically disabled, or suffering from the effects of emotional or behavioural difficulties and as a result at a later date he requires more care and a greater expenditure of resources than were required at the time he was placed for adoption because there is—
  (i) a deterioration in the child's health or condition, or
  (ii) an increase in his age; or
(e) where at the time of the placement for adoption it was known that there was a high risk that the child would develop an illness or disability and as a result at a later date he requires more care and a greater expenditure of resources than were required at the time he was placed for adoption because such illness or disability occurs.

(3) An allowance may be paid by the agency where before these Regulations come into force—
(a) an allowance was being paid by the agency to the adopters in respect of a child in accordance with a scheme which is revoked by section 57A(4) of the Act (revocation of schemes approved under section 57(4) of the Act) or under section 57(5)(b) of the Act (revocation of scheme by the Secretary of State) and the adopters have agreed to receive (instead of such allowance) an allowance complying with these Regulations, or
(b) the agency decided that the adopters are eligible to receive an allowance in accordance with a scheme which is revoked by section 57A(4) of the Act or under section 57(5)(b) of the Act and—
  (i) no payment has been made pursuant to that decision, and
  (ii) any conditions to which the agency's decision to pay such an allowance is subject are satisfied.

(4) In each case before an allowance is payable the adoption agency shall require the adopters to have agreed to—
(a) inform the adoption agency immediately if—
  (i) the child no longer has his home with them (or either of them), if they have changed their address, or if the child dies, or
  (ii) there is any change in their financial circumstances or the financial needs or resources of the child; and
(b) complete and supply the adoption agency with an annual statement of their financial circumstances and the financial circumstances of the child.

(5) An allowance may not be paid from a date before the date of placement for adoption and may be paid from such later date as may be determined by the adoption agency and notified to the adopters.

*Amount of the allowance*

**3.** (1) The allowance shall be of such amount as the adoption agency determines in accordance with paragraphs (2) to (4).

(2) In determining the amount of allowance the adoption agency shall take into account—
(a) the financial resources available to the adopters including any financial benefit which would be available in respect of the child when adopted;
(b) the amount required by the adopters in respect of their reasonable outgoings and commitments (excluding outgoings in respect of the child); and
(c) the financial needs and resources of the child.

(3) In assessing the income available to the adopters the adoption agency shall disregard mobility and attendance allowance payable in respect of the child and, where the adopters are in receipt of income support, child benefit.

(4) The allowance paid by the adoption agency shall not—

(a) include any element of remuneration for the care of the child by the adopters;

(b) exceed the amount of the fostering allowance excluding any element of remuneration in that allowance which would be payable if the child were fostered by the adopters.

*Procedure in determining whether an allowance should be paid*

**4.** (1) Subject to paragraphs (2) and (3), an adoption agency shall, before an adoption order is made in respect of a child whose adoption they are arranging or have arranged—

(a) consider whether an allowance may be paid in accordance with paragraphs (1) and (2) of regulation 2 (circumstances in which an allowance may be paid);

(b) supply information to the adopters about allowances including the basis upon which amounts of allowances are determined;

(c) give notice in writing in accordance with paragraph (4) to the adopters of their proposed decision as to whether an allowance should be paid and the proposed amount, if any, which would be payable;

(d) consider any representations received from the adopters within the period specified in the notice;

(e) make a decision as to whether an allowance should be paid, determine the amount, if any, which would be payable and notify the adopters of that decision and determination.

(2) The adoption agency shall not be required—

(a) in a case where the adopters may agree in accordance with regulation 2(3)(a) to receive payments complying with these Regulations instead of payments which are made to them in accordance with a scheme revoked by section 57A(4) of the Act (revocation of schemes approved under section 57(4) of the Act) or under section 57(5)(b) of the Act (revocation of scheme by the Secretary of State)—

    (i) to comply with sub-paragraph (a) of paragraph (1),

    (ii) to comply with sub-paragraph (b) of that paragraph before the adoption order is made provided that they do so as soon as is reasonably practicable after 14 October 1991, or

    (iii) to comply with sub-paragraphs (c) to (e) of that paragraph unless and until an application is received by the agency for an allowance to be made under these Regulations instead of under a scheme which has been revoked; or

(b) in a case where regulation 2(3)(b) applies, to comply with either of the following—

    (i) sub-paragraph (a) of paragraph (1), or

    (ii) sub-paragraphs (b) to (e) of that paragraph before an adoption order is made provided that they do so as soon as is reasonably practicable after 14 October 1991;

(c) in a case to which regulation 2(2)(d) or (e) of these Regulations applies, to determine the amount of an allowance unless or until—

    (i) there is a deterioration in the child's health or condition, or an increase in his age (in a case to which regulation 2(2)(d) applies), or

    (ii) the onset of the illness or disability (in a case to which regulation 2(2)(e) applies,

and as a result the child requires more care and a greater expenditure of resources than were required at the time at which he was placed for adoption.

(3) An approved adoption society which holds itself out as not being an adoption agency which normally pays allowances shall not be required to comply with sub-paragraphs (a) and (b) of paragraph (1) and need comply with sub-paragraphs (c), (d) and (e) of that paragraph as respects any adopters only if they have considered whether or not to pay an allowance to those adopters.

(4) A notice under paragraph (1)(c) shall state the period of time within which the adopters may make representations to the adoption agency concerning the proposed decision or determination and the adoption agency shall not make a decision or determination under paragraph (1)(e) until after the expiry of that period.

*Information about allowances*

**5.** After a decision has been made to pay an allowance, the adoption agency shall notify the adopters in writing of the following—
  (a) the method of the determination of the amount of the allowance;
  (b) the amount of the allowance as initially determined;
  (c) the date of the first payment of the allowance;
  (d) the method of payment of the allowance and frequency with which and the period for which payment will be made;
  (e) the arrangements and procedure for review, variation and termination of the allowance;
  (f) the responsibilities of—
      (i) the agency under regulation 6, and
      (ii) the adopters pursuant to their agreement under paragraph (4) of regulation 2,
    in respect of the allowance in the event of a change in circumstances of the adopters or the child.

*Renew, variation and termination of allowances*

**6.** (1) The adoption agency shall review an allowance—
  (a) annually, on receipt of a statement from the adopters as to—
      (i) their financial circumstances;
      (ii) the financial needs and resources of the child;
      (iii) their address and whether the child still has a home with them (or either of them); and
  (b) if any change in the circumstances of the adopters or the child, including any change of address, comes to their notice.

(2) The adoption agency may vary or suspend payment of the allowance if, as a result of a review, they consider that the adopters' need for it has changed or ceased since the amount of the allowance was last determined.

(3) Where the adopters fail to supply the adoption agency with an annual statement in accordance with their agreement under regulation 2(4)(b), the adoption agency may deem the adopters' need for an allowance to have ceased until such time as a statement is supplied.

(4) Where payment of an allowance is suspended the agency may recommence payment if as a result of a review the adoption agency considers that the financial circumstances of the adopters have become such that an allowance should be paid.

(5) The adoption agency shall terminate payment of an allowance when—
  (a) the child ceases to have a home with the adopters (or either of them);
  (b) the child ceases full-time education and commences employment or qualifies for a placement on a Government training scheme;
  (c) the child qualifies for income support or unemployment benefit in his own right:
  (d) the child attains the age of eighteen, unless he continues in full-time education, when it may continue until he attains the age of twenty-one so long as he continues in full-time education; or

(e) any period agreed between the adoption agency and the adopters for the payment of the allowance expires.

*Confidentiality, preservation and access to records*

**7.** (1) Subject to regulation 15 of the Adoption Agencies Regulations 1983, any information obtained or recommendations received or decisions made by virtue of these Regulations shall be treated by the adoption agency as confidential.

(2) The adoption agency shall place a record of the details of each allowance in respect of a child including details of any determination under regulation 3 and review under regulation 6 on the case records that they are required to set up under the Adoption Agencies Regulations 1983.

## LEGAL AID IN FAMILY PROCEEDINGS (REMUNERATION) REGULATIONS 1991

**Dated** 9 September 1991

**SI 1991 No 2038**

Following the repeal of the enabling provisions by the Access to Justice Act 1999, s 106, Sch 15, Pt I, these Regulations have lapsed except in so far as they may continue to have effect by virtue of SI 2000/774, art 5 as from 1 April 2000.

The Lord Chancellor, in exercise of the powers conferred on him by sections 2(5), (7), 34 and 43 of the Legal Aid Act 1988 and all other powers enabling him in that behalf, having had regard to the matters specified in section 34(9) and consulted the General Council of the Bar and the Law Society, and with the consent of the Treasury, hereby makes the following Regulations—

*Citation, commencement and transitional provisions*

**1.** (1) These Regulations may be cited as the Legal Aid in Family Proceedings (Remuneration) Regulations 1991 and shall come into force on 14 October 1991.

(2) Subject to paragraph (3), these Regulations shall apply to remuneration payable in respect of work done on or after 14 October 1991 and remuneration payable in respect of work done in proceedings commenced before that date shall be determined as if these Regulations and the Legal Aid in Criminal and Care Proceedings (Costs) (Amendment) (No 3) Regulations 1991 had not been made.

Provided that regulation 3 of, and Schedule 1 to, these Regulations shall apply to remuneration payable in respect of work done on or after 14 October 1991 in relation to care proceedings (within the meaning of section 27 of the Legal Aid Act 1988) as if those proceedings were care proceedings within the meaning of these Regulations.

(3) For the purposes of determining remuneration payable in respect of work done before 14 October 1991 in relation to proceedings of a kind described in paragraph (a) of the definition of 'prescribed family proceedings', Schedule 2 to the Rules shall have effect as if that Schedule were substituted for Schedule 2(a) to these Regulations and Schedule 2 (as so substituted) shall have effect as it had effect during the year in which the work in question was done.

*Interpretation*

**2.** (1) In these Regulations, unless the context otherwise requires—
'the relevant authority' means the Area Director in the case of an assessment and the *taxing officer* [costs officer] in the case of a *taxation* [detailed assessment], and 'determination' shall mean an assessment or *taxation* [detailed assessment] as the case may be;

'care proceedings' means proceedings for an order under Parts IV or V of the
    Children Act 1989 and includes proceedings under section 25 of that Act
    (secure accommodation orders);
'fee-earner' means a solicitor, a legal executive or any clerk who regularly does
    work for which it is appropriate to make a direct charge to a client;
'the General Regulations' means the Civil Legal Aid (General) Regulations
    1989;
'prescribed family proceedings' means—
(a)  proceedings commenced before 14 October 1991 with respect to which
    rules made under section 50 of the Matrimonial Causes Act 1973 applied
    immediately before the date of the coming into force of these Regulations;
(b)  proceedings commenced on or after 14 October 1991 to which those rules
    would have applied if they had continued in force on and after that date
    [, other than proceedings under Part IV of the Family Law Act 1996];
(c)  proceedings under the Children Act 1989, excluding care proceedings;
(d)  proceedings under section 20 or 27 of the Child Support Act 1991 in the
    High Court, a county court or a magistrates' court;
(e)  proceedings under section 30 of the Human Fertilisation and Embryology
    Act 1990 in the High Court, a county court or a magistrates' court.
'the Rules' means the Matrimonial Causes (Costs) Rules 1988.
(2)  Unless the context otherwise requires—
(a)  expressions used in the Rules, the Family Proceedings Rules 1991 and in the
    General Regulations shall have the same meanings as in those Rules or
    Regulations; *and*
[(aa) the expressions 'detailed assessment', 'costs judge' and 'costs officer' shall
    have the meanings given to them in Part 43 of the Civil Procedure Rules
    1998; and]
(b)  any reference in these Regulations to a regulation, Part or Schedule by
    number means the regulation, Part or Schedule so numbered in these
    Regulations.

**Note.** In para (1) definition 'the relevant authority' words 'taxing officer' and word 'taxation'
in both places substituted by words 'costs officer' and 'detailed assessment' by SI 2001/830,
reg 3(1) as from 2 April 2001. In para (1) definition 'prescribed family proceedings' words
'[, other than proceedings under part IV of the Family Law Act 1996]' in square brackets
inserted by SI 1997/2394, reg 2 as from 1 November 1997. In para (2) sub-para (aa) inserted
(and word immediately preceding it revoked) by SI 2001/830, reg 3(2) as from 2 April 2001.

*Remuneration*

**3.**  (1)  The sums to be allowed to legal representatives in connection with family
proceedings shall be determined in accordance with these Regulations, Part XII of
the General Regulations, the Family Proceedings (Costs) Rules 1991 and
paragraphs 1(3), (4)(a) and (5) and paragraph 2(2)(a) of Part I of Schedule 1 to
the Rules.

[(1A) The following paragraphs of this regulation shall apply solely on a
determination under regulation 107A of the General Regulations.]

(2)  Subject to the following paragraphs, the amounts to be allowed on determination under this regulation shall be—
(a)  in accordance with Schedule 1 where the certificate was issued in relation to
    care proceedings;
(b)  in accordance with Schedule 2 where the certificate was issued in relation to
    prescribed family proceedings, or, in relation to proceedings in a
    magistrates' court, any family proceedings other than care proceedings [or
    proceedings under Part IV of the Family Law Act 1996];
[(bb) in accordance with the county court rate in column 3 of Schedule 2(a)
    where the certificate was issued in relation to proceedings in the High

Court, a county court or a magistrates' court under Part IV of the Family Law Act 1996;]

(c)  in accordance with [the Legal Aid in Civil Proceedings (Remuneration) Regulations 1994] where the certificate was issued in relation to family proceedings not falling within *sub-paragraphs (a) and (b)* [sub-paragraph (a), (b) or (bb);]

(d)  in accordance with paragraph (2) of rule 8 of the Rules where the costs incurred relate to the kind of work to which that paragraph applies;

(e)  in accordance with paragraph 1(1) of Part I of Schedule 1 to the Rules where no provision is made in the Schedules to these Regulations for the kind of work to which the costs relate.

(3) Where a certificate relating to proceedings under paragraph 2(c) is extended to cover proceedings falling within sub-paragraphs (a) or (b), the amounts to be allowed on determination shall be in accordance with Schedule 1 or 2 as the case may be, or, if it is extended to cover proceedings falling within both sub-paragraphs, in accordance with Schedule 2.

[(3A) Where a certificate relating to proceedings under paragraph (2)(c) is extended to cover proceedings falling within sub-paragraph (bb), the amounts to be allowed on determination shall be in accordance with that sub-paragraph.]

(4)  On determination the relevant authority—

(a)  in allowing costs under item 4 of Part I of Schedule 1, shall allow costs at the higher rate where the work was done by a fee-earner whose office is situated within legal aid area 1;

(b)  in allowing costs under item 4 of Part I of Schedule 2(a), shall allow costs at the higher rate where at the time when the relevant work was done the proceedings were conducted in the principal registry or in another court on the South-Eastern Circuit;

[(bb) in allowing costs under Parts I to III and V of Schedule 1 and Part I to III and V of Schedule 2, shall [, subject to paragraph (4A),] allow the rates specified *for franchisees* in Schedules 1A and 2A where the work done was done by a person or body *(other than the Board) action under the terms of a franchising contract which was entered into by the Board pursuant to its powers under section 4 of the Legal Aid Act 1988* [who is authorised to carry out work in family proceedings by a contract with the Legal Services Commission] and references in these Regulations to Schedule 1 or 2 shall, in relation to *work done by franchisees* [such work], be construed as references to Schedule 1A or, as the case may be, 2A;]

(c)  may allow a larger amount than that specified in column 2 or column 3, as the case may be, of Parts I, II, III and V of Schedules 1 and 2(a) where it appears to him reasonable to do so having regard to—

(i)  the exceptional competence with which the work was done, or

(ii)  the exceptional expedition with which the work was done, or

(iii)  any other exceptional circumstances of the case *including, in the case of care proceedings, the fact that the solicitor was a member of the Law Society's Children Act panel*

but, without prejudice to regulation 109 of the General Regulations or rules 15 or 16 of the Rules, the relevant authority may in respect of any item in Part I, II, III or V of Schedule 1 or 2(a) allow a lower amount than that specified in column 2 or column 3 of that Part, as the case may be, where it appears to him reasonable to do so having regard to any failure on the part of the solicitor to provide timely preparation or advice, or for any similar reason.

[(4A) Except in relation to prescribed family proceedings in a magistrates' court, where paragraph (4)(bb) applies and the relevant work is done by a member of a relevant panel the relevant authority shall, subject to paragraph (4B), allow whichever is the higher of—

(a) an amount 15% higher than the amount in Schedule 1A or (as the case may be) 2A(a) which he would have allowed but for this paragraph and paragraph (4)(c); and

(b) if he decides to award such an amount, a larger amount than that specified in column 2 or column 3, as the case may be, of Parts I, II, III and V of Schedule 1A or (as the case may be) 2A(a), awarded in accordance with paragraph (4)(c).

(4B) Paragraph (4A) shall not apply in relation to any item if, but for that paragraph, the relevant authority would, in accordance with regulation 3(4)(c), have allowed a lower amount for that item than the one in Part I, II, III or V of Schedule 1A or 2A(a).]

(5) Without prejudice to regulation 109 of the Legal Aid General Regulations or rules 14 or 15 of the Rules, where a standard fee is specified in Part IV of Schedules 1 or 2(a) for work done by junior counsel that fee shall be allowed unless the relevant authority considers that it would be unreasonable to do so, in which case he shall allow such lesser or greater fee as may be reasonable—

Provided that the fee allowed shall not exceed any maximum fee which is specified unless the relevant authority considers that, owing to the time and labour expended by counsel or to any other special circumstance of the case, the maximum fee specified would not provide reasonable remuneration for some or all of the work done, in which case the fee to be allowed shall be in the discretion of the relevant authority.

(6) For the purpose of determining which of the brief fees provided by item 12 of Schedule 1 and item 13 of Schedule 2(a) should be allowed—

(a) a one hour fee shall be allowed where the hearing lasts for one hour or less than one hour;

(b) a half day fee shall be allowed where the hearing lasts for more than one hour and

   (i) begins and ends before the luncheon adjournment; or

   (ii) begins after the luncheon adjournment and ends before 5.30 pm;

(c) a full day fee shall be allowed where the hearing lasts for more than one hour and

   (i) begins before and ends after the luncheon adjournment but before 5.30 pm; or

   (ii) begins after the luncheon adjournment and ends after 5.30 pm; and

(d) a more than a full day fee shall be allowed where the hearing

   (i) begins before the luncheon adjournment and ends after 5.30 pm on the same day; or

   (ii) begins on one day and continues into a subsequent day.

(7) In exercising his discretion under this regulation or in relation to any provision of the Schedules where the amount of costs to be allowed is in his discretion, the relevant authority shall exercise his discretion in accordance with paragraph 1(2) of Part I of Schedule 1 to the Rules.

(8) Disbursements (other than counsel's fees) for which no allowance is made in Schedules 1 or 2(a) shall be determined and allowed, or disallowed, according to the general principles applicable to the taxation of costs in *RSC Order 62* [Parts 43 to 48 of the Civil Procedure Rules 1998].

[(9) In this regulation—

(a) 'relevant panel' means—

   (i) the Solicitors' Family Law Association Accredited Specialist Panel; or

   (ii) in relation to work done under a certificate which includes proceedings relating to children, the Law Society's Children Act Panel; and

  [(iii) The Law Society Family Law Panel Advanced; and]

(b) 'proceedings relating to children' means proceedings in which the welfare of children is determined, including, without limitation, proceedings under the Children Act 1989 or under the inherent jurisdiction of the High Court in relation to children.]

**Note.** Para (1A) inserted by SI 1994/230, reg 5.

In para (2)(b) words 'or proceedings under Part IV of the Family Law Act 1996' in square brackets and sub-para (bb) inserted by SI 1997/2394, reg 3(a), (b) as from 1 November 1997. In para (2)(c) words 'the Legal Aid in Civil Proceedings (Remuneration) Regulations 1994' in square brackets substituted by SI 1994/230, reg 6, and words 'sub-paragraphs (a) and (b)' substituted by words 'sub-paragraph (a), (b) or (bb)' in square brackets by SI 1997/2394, reg 3(c) as from 1 November 1997.

Para (3A) inserted by SI 1997/2394, reg 4 as from 1 November 1997.

Para (4): sub-para (bb) inserted by SI 1996/650, reg 2; in sub-para (bb) words ', subject to paragraph (4A),' in square brackets inserted, words 'for franchisees' revoked words from '(other than the Board)' to 'Legal Aid Act 1988' substituted by words from 'who is authorised' to 'Legal Services Commission' in square brackets and words 'work done by franchisees' substituted by words 'such work' in square brackets by SI 2001/830, reg 4(1) (a)–(d) as from 2 April 2001; in sub-para (c)(iii) words 'including, in the case of care proceedings, the fact that the solicitor was a member of the Law Society's Children Act panel' revoked by SI 2001/830, reg 4(2) as from 2 April 2001.

Paras (4A), (4B) inserted by SI 2001/830, reg 4(3) as from 2 April 2001.

In para (8) words 'RSC Order 62' substituted by words 'Parts 43 to 48 of the Civil Procedure Rules 1998' in square brackets by SI 2001/830, reg 4(4) as from 2 April 2001.

Para (9) inserted by SI 2001/830, reg 4(5) as from 2 April 2001 and (9)(a)(iii) inserted by SI 2002/710, reg 3 as from 8 April 2002.

**Note:** The figures set out in Schedule 1 below apply to work done on or after 14 October 1991 but before 1 April 1992.

## SCHEDULE 1

## CARE PROCEEDINGS

## PART I

PREPARATION

| Column 1 | Column 2<br>High Court | Column 3<br>County Court or<br>Magistrates' Court |
|---|---|---|
| ITEM | | |
| 1.  Writing routine letters | £4.00 per item | £3.50 per item |
| 2.  Receiving routine letters | £2.00 per item | £1.75 per item |
| 3.  Routine telephone calls | £4.00 per item | £3.50 per item |
| 4.  All other preparation work | £62.50 per hour | £55.50 per hour |
| including any work which was | (£66.75 per hour | £58.50 per hour |
| reasonably done arising out of or | for a fee-earner whose office is situated within | |
| incidental to the proceedings, | legal aid area 1) | |
| interviews with client, witnesses, and | | |
| other parties; obtaining evidence; | | |
| preparation and consideration of, and | | |
| dealing with, documents, | | |
| negotiations and notices; dealing with | | |
| letters written and received and | | |
| telephone calls which are not routine | | |
| 5.  Travelling and waiting time in | | |
| connection with the above matters | £30.50 per hour | £28.00 per hour |

PREPARATION

| Column 1 | Column 2<br>High Court | Column 3<br>County Court or<br>Magistrates' Court |
| --- | --- | --- |

## PART II

CONFERENCES WITH COUNSEL

| | | |
| --- | --- | --- |
| 6. Attending counsel in conference | £35.50 per hour | £31.00 per hour |
| 7. Travelling and waiting | £30.50 per hour | £28.00 per hour |

## PART III

ATTENDANCES

| | | |
| --- | --- | --- |
| 8. Attending with counsel at the trial or hearing of any cause or the hearing of any summons or other application at court, or other appointment | £35.50 per hour | £31.00 per hour |
| 9. Attending without counsel at the trial or hearing of any cause or the hearing of any summons or other application at court, or other appointment | £61.00 per hour | £61.00 per hour |
| 10. Travelling and waiting | £30.50 per hour | £28.00 per hour |

## PART IV

FEES FOR JUNIOR COUNSEL

| | | |
| --- | --- | --- |
| 11. With a brief on an unopposed application for an injunction, or procedural issue | Standard £84.50<br>Maximum £140.00 | £73.00<br>£121.00 |
| 12. With a brief on the trial of a cause or matter or on the hearing of an application where the hearing lasts for | | |
| (a) one hour | Standard £127.50<br>Maximum £256.00 | £109.00<br>£218.50 |
| (b) a half day | Standard £176.50<br>Maximum £291.00 | £152.00<br>£256.00 |
| (c) a full day | Standard £352.00<br>Maximum £559.00 | £304.00<br>£486.00 |
| (d) more than a full day | Discretionary | Discretionary |
| 13. For each day or part of a day on which the trial of a cause or matter, or the hearing of an ancillary application, or a children appointment, is continued after the first day | Discretionary | Discretionary |
| 14. Conference (including time reasonably spent in preparation and conference, but not otherwise remunerated) | Standard £19.50<br>per half hour | Standard £17.00<br>per half hour |
| 15. (a) Complex items of written work (such as advices on evidence, opinions and affidavits of a substantial nature, requests for particulars or answers) | Standard £92.00<br>per item | Standard £79.00<br>per item |

FEES FOR JUNIOR COUNSEL

| Column 1 | Column 2<br>High Court | Column 3<br>County Court or<br>Magistrates' Court |
|---|---|---|
|    (b) All other written work | Standard £54.50<br>per item | Standard £48.00<br>per item |
| 16.  Except where the court is within 40<br>      kilometres of Charing Cross or where<br>      there is no local Bar in the court town,<br>      or within 40 kilometres thereof, for<br>      travelling time | Standard £17.70<br>per hour<br>plus expenses | Standard £15.20<br>per hour<br>plus expenses |

## SCHEDULE 1

## CARE PROCEEDINGS

## PART I

PREPARATION

| Column 1 | Column 2<br>High Court | Column 3<br>County Court or<br>Magistrates' Court |
|---|---|---|
| **ITEM** | | |
| 1.  Writing routine letters | £4.15 per item | £3.60 per item |
| 2.  Receiving routine letters | £2.05 per item | £1.80 per item |
| 3.  Routine telephone calls | £4.15 per item | £3.60 per item |
| 4.  All other preparation work<br>    including any work which was<br>    reasonably done arising out of or<br>    incidental to the proceedings,<br>    interviews with client, witnesses, and<br>    other parties, obtaining evidence;<br>    preparation and consideration of, and<br>    dealing with, documents,<br>    negotiations and notices; dealing with<br>    letters written and received and<br>    telephone calls which are not routine | £64.50 per hour<br>(£68.75 per hour<br>for a fee-earner whose office is situated within<br>legal aid area 1) | £57.25 per hour<br>£60.25 per hour |
| 5.  Travelling and waiting time in<br>    connection with the above matters | £31.50 per hour | £28.75 per hour |

## PART II

CONFERENCES WITH COUNSEL

| | | |
|---|---|---|
| 6.  Attending counsel in conference | £36.50 per hour | £32.00 per hour |
| 7.  Travelling and waiting | £31.50 per hour | £28.75 per hour |

## PART III

ATTENDANCES

| | | |
|---|---|---|
| 8.  Attending with counsel at the trial or<br>    hearing of any cause or the hearing<br>    of any summons or other application<br>    at court, or other appointment | £36.50 per hour | £32.00 per hour |

ATTENDANCES

| Column 1 | Column 2<br>High Court | Column 3<br>County Court or<br>Magistrates' Court |
|---|---|---|
| 9.  Attending without counsel at the trial or hearing of any cause or the hearing of any summons or other application at court, or other appointment | £63.00 per hour | £63.00 per hour |
| 10. Travelling and waiting | £31.50 per hour | £28.75 per hour |

## PART IV

FEES FOR JUNIOR COUNSEL

| Column 1 | Column 2<br>High Court | Column 3<br>County Court or<br>Magistrates' Court |
|---|---|---|
| 11. With a brief on an unopposed application for an injunction, or procedural issue | Standard £87.00<br>Maximum £144.00 | £75.00<br>£125.00 |
| 12. With a brief on the trial of a cause or matter or on the hearing of an application where the hearing lasts for | | |
| (a) one hour | Standard £131.50<br>Maximum £264.00 | £112.50<br>£225.00 |
| (b) a half day | Standard £182.00<br>Maximum £300.00 | £157.00<br>£264.00 |
| (c) a full day | Standard £363.00<br>Maximum £576.00 | £313.00<br>£501.00 |
| (d) more than a full day | Discretionary | Discretionary |
| 13. For each day or part of a day on which the trial of a cause or matter, or the hearing of an ancillary application, or a children appointment, is continued after the first day | Discretionary | Discretionary |
| 14. Conference (including time reasonably spent in preparation and conference, but not otherwise remunerated) | Standard £20.00<br>per ½ hour | Standard £17.50<br>per ½ hour |
| 15. (a) Complex items of written work (such as advices on evidence, opinions and affidavits of a substantial nature, requests for particulars or answers) | Standard £94.75<br>per item | Standard £81.50<br>per item |
| (b) All other written work | Standard £56.25<br>per item | Standard £49.50<br>per item |
| 16. Except where the court is within 40 kilometres of Charing Cross or where there is no local Bar in the court town, or within 40 kilometres thereof, for travelling time | Standard £18.25<br>per hour<br>+ expenses | Standard £15.65<br>per hour<br>+ expenses |

## PART V

TAXATION AND REVIEW OF TAXATION (HIGH COURT AND COUNTY COURT ONLY)

| Column 1 | Column 2 | Column 3 |
|---|---|---|
| 17. Preparing the bill (where allowable) and completing the taxation (excluding preparing for and attending the taxation) | £31.50–£88.00 | £31.50–£50.25 |

TAXATION AND REVIEW OF TAXATION (HIGH COURT AND COUNTY COURT ONLY)

| Column 1 | Column 2<br>High Court | Column 3<br>County Court or<br>Magistrates' Court |
|---|---|---|
| 18. Preparing for and attending the taxation (including travelling and waiting) | Discretionary | Discretionary |
| 19. Review by district judge or judge (including preparation) | Discretionary | Discretionary |

**Note:** Schedules 1 and 1A set out below apply to costs incurred on and after 1 April 1996. The figures in italics apply to work done on or after 8 July 1996.

## SCHEDULE 1

## CARE PROCEEDINGS

## PART I

PREPARATION

| Column 1 | Column 2<br>High Court | Column 3<br>County Court or<br>Magistrates' Court |
|---|---|---|
| ITEM | | |
| 1. Writing routine letters | £4.25 per item | £3.65 per item |
| 2. Receiving routine letters | £2.05 per item | £1.80 per item |
| | *£2.10 per item* | *£1.85 per item* |
| 3. Routine telephone calls | £4.25 per item | £3.65 per item |
| 4. All other preparation work including any work which was reasonably done arising out of or incidental to the proceedings, interviews with client, witnesses, and other parties; obtaining evidence; preparation and consideration of, and dealing with, documents, negotiations and notices; dealing with letters written and received and telephone calls which are not routine | £65.50 per hour<br>(£69.75 per hour<br>for a fee-earner whose office is situated within legal aid area 1) | £58.00 per hour<br>£61.25 per hour |
| 5. Travelling and waiting time in connection with the above matters | £32.00 per hour | £29.25 per hour |

## PART II

CONFERENCES WITH COUNSEL

| | | |
|---|---|---|
| 6. Attending counsel in conference | £37.00 per hour | £32.50 per hour |
| 7. Travelling and waiting | £32.00 per hour | £29.25 per hour |

## PART III

ATTENDANCES

| | | |
|---|---|---|
| 8. Attending with counsel at the trial or hearing of any cause or the hearing of any summons or other application at court, or other appointment | £37.00 per hour | £32.50 per hour |

ATTENDANCES

| Column 1 | Column 2<br>High Court | Column 3<br>County Court or<br>Magistrates' Court |
|---|---|---|
| 9. Attending without counsel at the trial or hearing of any cause or the hearing of any summons or other application at court, or other appointment | £64.00 per hour | £64.00 per hour |
| 10. Travelling and waiting | £32.00 per hour | £29.25 per hour |

## PART IV

FEES FOR JUNIOR COUNSEL

| | Column 2<br>High Court | Column 3<br>County Court or<br>Magistrates' Court |
|---|---|---|
| 11. With a brief on an unopposed application for an injunction, or procedural issue | Standard £88.25<br>Maximum £146.25 | £76.25<br>£127.00 |
| 12. With a brief on the trial of a cause or matter or on the hearing of an application where the hearing lasts for | | |
| (a) one hour | Standard £133.50<br>Maximum £268.00 | £114.25<br>£228.50 |
| (b) a half day | Standard £184.75<br>Maximum £304.50 | £159.25<br>£268.00 |
| (c) a full day | Standard £368.50<br>Maximum £584.75 | £317.75<br>£508.50 |
| (d) more than a full day | Discretionary | Discretionary |
| 13. For each day or part of a day on which the trial of a cause or matter, or the hearing of an ancillary application, or a children appointment, is continued after the first day | Discretionary | Discretionary |
| 14. Conference (including time reasonably spent in preparation and conference, but not otherwise remunerated) | Standard £20.25<br>per ½ hour | Standard £17.75<br>per ½ hour |
| 15. (a) Complex items of written work (such as advices on evidence, opinions and affidavits of a substantial nature, requests for particulars or answers) | Standard £96.25<br>per item | Standard £82.75<br>per item |
| (b) All other written work | Standard £57.00<br>per item | Standard £50.25<br>per item |
| 16. Except where the court is within 40 kilometres of Charing Cross or where there is no local Bar in the court town, or within 40 kilometres thereof, for travelling time | Standard £18.50<br>per hour<br>+ expenses | Standard £15.85<br>per hour<br>+ expenses |

## PART V

TAXATION AND REVIEW OF TAXATION (HIGH COURT AND COUNTY COURT ONLY)

| | Column 2<br>High Court | Column 3<br>County Court or<br>Magistrates' Court |
|---|---|---|
| 17. Preparing the bill (where allowable) and completing the taxation (excluding preparing for and attending the taxation) | £32.00–£89.25 | £32.00–£51.00 |

TAXATION AND REVIEW OF TAXATION (HIGH COURT AND COUNTY COURT ONLY)

| Column 1 | Column 2<br>High Court | Column 3<br>County Court or<br>Magistrates' Court |
|---|---|---|
| 18. Preparing for and attending the taxation (including travelling and waiting) | Discretionary | Discretionary |
| 19. Review by district judge or judge (including preparation) | Discretionary | Discretionary |

## SCHEDULE 1A
## CARE PROCEEDINGS
## PART I

PREPARATION

| Column 1 | Column 2<br>High Court | Column 3<br>County Court or<br>Magistrates' Court |
|---|---|---|
| **ITEM** | | |
| 1. Writing routine letters | £4.25 per item | £3.70 per item |
| 2. Receiving routine letters | £2.10 per item | £1.85 per item |
| 3. Routine telephone calls | £4.20 per item<br>*£4.25 per item* | £3.70 per item |
| 4. All other preparation work including any work which was reasonably done arising out of or incidental to the proceedings, interviews with client, witnesses, and other parties; obtaining evidence; preparation and consideration of, and dealing with, documents, negotiations and notices; dealing with letters written and received and telephone calls which are not routine | £66.50 per hour<br>(£70.75 per hour<br>for a fee-earner whose office is situated within<br>legal aid area 1) | £59.00 per hour<br>£62.00 per hour |
| 5. Travelling and waiting time in connection with the above matters | £32.50 per hour | £29.50 per hour |

## PART II

CONFERENCES WITH COUNSEL

| | Column 2 High Court | Column 3 County Court or Magistrates' Court |
|---|---|---|
| 6. Attending counsel in conference | £37.50 per hour | £33.00 per hour |
| 7. Travelling and waiting | £32.50 per hour | £29.50 per hour |

## PART III

ATTENDANCES

| | Column 2 High Court | Column 3 County Court or Magistrates' Court |
|---|---|---|
| 8. Attending with counsel at the trial or hearing of any cause or the hearing of any summons or other application at court, or other appointment | £37.50 per hour | £33.00 per hour |
| 9. Attending without counsel at the trial or hearing of any cause or the hearing of any summons or other application at court, or other appointment | £65.00 per hour | £65.00 per hour |
| 10. Travelling and waiting | £32.50 per hour | £29.50 per hour |

TAXATION AND REVIEW OF TAXATION (HIGH COURT AND COUNTY COURT ONLY)

| Column 1 | Column 2<br>High Court | Column 3<br>County Court |
|---|---|---|

## PART V

TAXATION AND REVIEW OF TAXATION (HIGH COURT AND COUNTY COURT ONLY)

| | | Column 2<br>High Court | Column 3<br>County Court |
|---|---|---|---|
| 17. | Preparing the bill (where allowable) and completing the taxation (excluding preparing for and attending the taxation) | £32.50–£90.75 | £32.70–£51.75 |
| 18. | Preparing for and attending the taxation (including travelling and waiting) | Discretionary | Discretionary |
| 19. | Review by district judge or judge (including preparation) | Discretionary | Discretionary |

**Note:** The figures set out in Schedule 2 below apply to work done on or after 14 October 1991 but before 1 April 1992.

## SCHEDULE 2

PRESCRIBED FAMILY PROCEEDINGS

### (a) **High Court and county court proceedings**

### PART I

PREPARATION

| Column 1 | Column 2<br>High Court | Column 3<br>County Court |
|---|---|---|

ITEM

| | | Column 2<br>High Court | Column 3<br>County Court |
|---|---|---|---|
| 1. | Writing routine letters | £4.00 per item | £3.50 per item |
| 2. | Receiving routine letters | £2.00 per item | £1.75 per item |
| 3. | Routine telephone calls | £4.00 per item | £3.50 per item |
| 4. | All other preparation work including any work which was reasonably done arising out of or incidental to the proceedings, interviews with client, witnesses, and other parties; obtaining evidence; preparation and consideration of, and dealing with, documents, negotiations and notices; dealing with letters written and received and telephone calls which are not routine | Where the proceedings were conducted in the principal registry or in another court on the South-Eastern Circuit at the time when the relevant work was done:<br>£44.50 per hour<br>All other circuits:<br>£41.75 per hour | £39.00 per hour<br><br>£37.00 per hour |
| 5. | In addition to items 1–4 above, to cover the general care and conduct of the proceedings | plus 50% | plus 50% |
| 6. | Travelling and waiting time in connection with the above matters | £35.50 per hour | £28.00 per hour |

### PART II

CONFERENCES WITH COUNSEL

| | | | |
|---|---|---|---|
| 7. | Attending counsel in conference | £35.50 per hour | £31.00 per hour |
| 8. | Travelling and waiting | £30.50 per hour | £28.00 per hour |

ATTENDANCES

| Column 1 | Column 2<br>High Court | Column 3<br>County Court |
|---|---|---|

## PART III

ATTENDANCES

| | | |
|---|---|---|
| 9. Attending with counsel at the trial or hearing of any cause or the hearing of any summons or other application at court, or other appointment | £35.50 per hour | £31.00 per hour |
| 10. Attending without counsel at the trial or hearing of any cause or the hearing of any summons or other application at court, or other appointment | £53.50 per hour | £50.50 per hour |
| 11. Travelling and waiting | £30.50 per hour | £28.00 per hour |

## PART IV

FEES FOR JUNIOR COUNSEL

| | | |
|---|---|---|
| 12. With a brief on an unopposed application for an injunction, or procedural issue | Standard £84.50<br>Maximum £140.00 | £73.00<br>£121.00 |
| 13. With a brief on the trial of a cause or matter or on the hearing of an ancillary application or on a children appointment where the hearing lasts for | | |
| (a) one hour | Standard £127.50<br>Maximum £256.00 | £109.00<br>£218.50 |
| (b) a half day | Standard £176.50<br>Maximum £291.00 | £152.00<br>£256.00 |
| (c) a full day | Standard £352.00<br>Maximum £559.00 | £304.00<br>£486.00 |
| (d) more than a full day | Discretionary | Discretionary |
| 14. For each day or part of a day on which the trial of a cause or matter, or the hearing of an ancillary application, or a children appointment, is continued after the first day | Discretionary | Discretionary |
| 15. Conference (including time reasonably spent in preparation and conference, but not otherwise remunerated), | Standard £19.50<br>per half hour | Standard £17.00<br>per half hour |
| 16. (a) Complex items of written work (such as advices on evidence, opinions and affidavits of a substantial nature, requests for particulars or answers) | Standard £92.00<br>per item | Standard £79.00<br>per item |
| (b) All other written work | Standard £54.50<br>per item | Standard £48.00<br>per item |
| 17. Except where the court is within 40 kilometres of Charing Cross or where there is no local Bar in the court town, or within 40 kilometres thereof, for travelling time | Standard £17.70<br>per hour<br>plus expenses | Standard £15.20<br>per hour<br>plus expenses |

FEES FOR JUNIOR COUNSEL

| Column 1 | Column 2<br>High Court | Column 3<br>County Court |
|---|---|---|

## PART V

TAXATION AND REVIEW OF TAXATION

| | | |
|---|---|---|
| 18. Preparing the bill (where allowable) and completing the taxation (excluding preparing for and attending the taxation) | £30.50–£85.50 | £30.50–£48.75 |
| 19. Preparing for and attending the taxation (including travelling and waiting) | Discretionary | Discretionary |
| 20. Review by district judge or judge (including preparation) | Discretionary | Discretionary |

### (b) Magistrates' court proceedings

| Class of work | Rate |
|---|---|
| Preparation | £42 per hour (£44.50 per hour for a fee-earner whose office is situated within legal aid area 1) |
| Advocacy | £53 per hour |
| Attendance at court where counsel assigned | £28.50 per hour |
| Travelling and waiting | £23.50 per hour |
| Routine letters written and routine telephone calls | £3.25 per item (£3.40 per item for a fee-earner whose office is situated within legal aid area 1) |

**Note:** The figures set out in Schedule 2 below apply to work done on and after 1 April 1992 but before 1 April 1996.

## SCHEDULE 2

PRESCRIBED FAMILY PROCEEDINGS

### (a) High Court and county court proceedings

## PART I

PREPARATION

| Column 1 | Column 2<br>High Court | Column 3<br>County Court |
|---|---|---|
| ITEM | | |
| 1. Writing routine letters | £4.15 per item | £3.60 per item |
| 2. Receiving routine letters | £2.05 per item | £1.80 per item |
| 3. Routine telephone calls | £4.15 per item | £3.60 per item |
| 4. All other preparation work including any work which was reasonably done | | |

PREPARATION

| Column 1 | Column 2<br>High Court | Column 3<br>County Court |
|---|---|---|
| arising out of or incidental to the proceedings, interviews with client, witnesses, and other parties; obtaining evidence; preparation and consideration of, and dealing with, documents, negotiations and notices; dealing with letters written and received and telephone calls which are not routine | Where the proceedings were conducted in the principal registry or in another court on the South-Eastern Circuit at the time when the relevant work was done:<br>£46.00 per hour<br>All other circuits:<br>£43.00 per hour | £40.25 per hour<br><br>£38.20 per hour |
| 5.  In addition to items 1–4 above, to cover the general care and conduct of the proceedings | + 50% | + 50% |
| 6.  Travelling and waiting time in connection with the above matters | £31.50 per hour | £28.75 per hour |

## PART II

CONFERENCES WITH COUNSEL

| | Column 2<br>High Court | Column 3<br>County Court |
|---|---|---|
| 7.  Attending counsel in conference | £36.50 per hour | £32.00 per hour |
| 8.  Travelling and waiting | £31.50 per hour | £28.75 per hour |

## PART III

ATTENDANCES

| | Column 2<br>High Court | Column 3<br>County Court |
|---|---|---|
| 9.  Attending with counsel at the trial or hearing of any cause or the hearing of any summons or other application at court, or other appointment | £36.50 per hour | £32.00 per hour |
| 10.  Attending without counsel at the trial or hearing of any cause or the hearing of any summons or other application at court, or other appointment | £55.00 per hour | £52.00 per hour |
| 11.  Travelling and waiting | £31.50 per hour | £28.75 per hour |

## PART IV

FEES FOR JUNIOR COUNSEL

| Column 1 | Column 2<br>High Court | Column 3<br>County Court |
|---|---|---|
| 12.  With a brief on an unopposed application for an injunction, or procedural issue | Standard £87.00<br>Maximum £144.00 | £75.00<br>£125.00 |
| 13.  With a brief on the trial of a cause or matter or on the hearing of an ancillary application or on a children appointment where the hearing lasts for | | |
| (a) one hour | Standard £131.50<br>Maximum £264.00 | £112.50<br>£225.00 |
| (b) a half day | Standard £182.00<br>Maximum £300.00 | £157.00<br>£264.00 |

FEES FOR JUNIOR COUNSEL

| Column 1 | Column 2<br>High Court | Column 3<br>County Court |
|---|---|---|
|    (c) a full day | Standard £363.00<br>Maximum £576.00 | £313.00<br>£501.00 |
|    (d) more than a full day | Discretionary | Discretionary |
| 14.  For each day or part of a day on which the trial of a cause or matter, or the hearing of an ancillary application, or a children appointment, is continued after the first day | Discretionary | Discretionary |
| 15.  Conference (including time reasonably spent in preparation and conference, but not otherwise remunerated) | Standard £20.00<br>per ½ hour | Standard £17.50<br>per ½ hour |
| 16.  (a) Complex items of written work (such as advices on evidence, opinions and affidavits of a substantial nature, requests for particulars or answers) | Standard £94.75<br>per item | Standard £81.50<br>per item |
|    (b) All other written work | Standard £56.25<br>per item | Standard £49.50<br>per item |
| 17.  Except where the court is within 40 kilometres of Charing Cross or where there is no local Bar in the court town, or within 40 kilometres thereof, for travelling time | Standard £18.25<br>per hour<br>+ expenses | Standard £15.65<br>per hour<br>+ expenses |

## PART V

TAXATION AND REVIEW OF TAXATION

| | | |
|---|---|---|
| 18.  Preparing the bill (where allowable) and completing the taxation (excluding preparing for and attending the taxation) | £31.50–£88.0 | £31.50–£50.25 |
| 19.  Preparing for and attending the taxation (including travelling and waiting) | Discretionary | Discretionary |
| 20.  Review by district judge or judge (including preparation) | Discretionary | Discretionary |

## (b) Magistrates' court proceedings

| Class of work | Rate |
|---|---|
| Preparation | £43.25 per hour<br>(£46.00 per hour for a fee-earner whose office is situated within legal aid area 1) |
| Advocacy | £54.50 per hour |
| Attendance at court where counsel assigned | £29.50 per hour |
| Travelling and waiting | £24.25 per hour |

| Class of work | Rate |
|---|---|
| Routine letters written and routine telephone calls | £3.35 per item (£3.50 per item for a fee-earner whose office is situated within legal aid area 1) |

**Note:** Schedules 2 and 2A set out below apply to costs incurred on or after 1 April 1996. The figures in italics apply to work done on or after 8 July 1996.

## SCHEDULE 2

PRESCRIBED FAMILY PROCEEDINGS

### (a) High Court and county court proceedings

## PART I

PREPARATION

| Column 1 | Column 2 High Court | Column 3 County Court |
|---|---|---|
| ITEM | | |
| 1.   Writing routine letters | £4.25 per item | £3.65 per item |
| 2.   Receiving routine letters | £2.05 per item | £1.80 per item |
| | *£2.10 per item* | *£1.85 per item* |
| 3.   Routine telephone calls | £4.25 per item | £3.65 per item |
| 4.   All other preparation work including any work which was reasonably done arising out of or incidental to the proceedings, interviews with client, witnesses, and other parties; obtaining evidence; preparation and consideration of, and dealing with, documents, negotiations and notices; dealing with letters written and received and telephone calls which are not routine | Where the proceedings were conducted in the principal registry or in another court on the South-Eastern Circuit at the time when the relevant work was done: £46.75 per hour All other circuits: £43.75 per hour | £41.00 per hour £38.75 per hour |
| 5.   In addition to items 1–4 above, to cover the general care and conduct of the proceedings | + 50% | + 50% |
| 6.   Travelling and waiting time in connection with the above matters | £32.00 per hour | £29.25 per hour |

## PART II

CONFERENCES WITH COUNSEL

| Column 1 | Column 2 High Court | Column 3 County Court |
|---|---|---|
| 7.   Attending counsel in conference | £37.00 per hour | £32.50 per hour |
| 8.   Travelling and waiting | £32.00 per hour | £29.25 per hour |

## PART III

ATTENDANCES

| Column 1 | Column 2<br>High Court | Column 3<br>County Court |
|---|---|---|
| 9. Attending with counsel at the trial or hearing of any cause or the hearing of any summons or other application at court, or other appointment | £37.00 per hour | £32.50 per hour |
| 10. Attending without counsel at the trial or hearing of any cause or the hearing of any summons or other application at court, or other appointment | £55.75 per hour | £52.75 per hour |
| 11. Travelling and waiting | £32.00 per hour | £29.25 per hour |

## PART IV

FEES FOR JUNIOR COUNSEL

| | | |
|---|---|---|
| 12. With a brief on an unopposed application for an injunction, or procedural issue | Standard £88.25<br>Maximum £146.25 | £76.25<br>£127.00 |
| 13. With a brief on the trial of a cause or matter or on the hearing of an ancillary application or on a children appointment where the hearing lasts for | | |
| (a) one hour | Standard £133.50<br>Maximum £268.00 | £114.25<br>£228.50 |
| (b) a half day | Standard £184.75<br>Maximum £304.50 | £159.25<br>£268.00 |
| (c) a full day | Standard £368.50<br>Maximum £584.75 | £317.75<br>£508.50 |
| (d) more than a full day | Discretionary | Discretionary |
| 14. For each day or part of a day on which the trial of a cause or matter, or the hearing of an ancillary application, or a children appointment, is continued after the first day | Discretionary | Discretionary |
| 15. Conference (including time reasonably spent in preparation and conference, but not otherwise remunerated), | Standard £20.25<br>per ½ hour | Standard £17.75<br>per ½ hour |
| 16. (a) Complex items of written work (such as advices on evidence, opinions and affidavits of a substantial nature, requests for particulars or answers) | Standard £96.25<br>per item | Standard £82.75<br>per item |
| (b) All other written work | Standard £57.00<br>per item | Standard £50.25<br>per item |
| 17. Except where the court is within 40 kilometres of Charing Cross or where there is no local Bar in the court town, or within 40 kilometres thereof, for travelling time | Standard £18.50<br>per hour<br>+ expenses | Standard £15.85<br>per hour<br>+ expenses |

## PART V

TAXATION AND REVIEW OF TAXATION

| Column 1 | Column 2<br>High Court | Column 3<br>County Court |
|---|---|---|
| 18. Preparing the bill (where allowable) and completing the taxation (excluding preparing for and attending the taxation) | £32.00–£89.25 | £32.00–£51.75 |
| 19. Preparing for and attending the taxation (including travelling and waiting) | Discretionary | Discretionary |
| 20. Review by district judge or judge (including preparation) | Discretionary | Discretionary |

### (b) Magistrates' court proceedings

| Class of work | Rate |
|---|---|
| Preparation | £44.00 per hour (£46.75 per hour for a fee-earner whose office is situated within legal aid area 1) |
| Advocacy | £55.25 per hour |
| Attendance at court where counsel assigned | £30.00 per hour |
| Travelling and waiting | £24.60 per hour |
| Routine letters written and routine telephone calls | £3.40 per item (£3.55 per item for a fee-earner whose office is situated within legal aid area 1) |

## SCHEDULE 2A

PRESCRIBED FAMILY PROCEEDINGS

### (a) High Court and county court proceedings

## PART I

PREPARATION

| Column 1 | Column 2<br>High Court | Column 3<br>County Court |
|---|---|---|
| ITEM | | |
| 1. Writing routine letters | £4.25 per item | £3.70 per item |
| 2. Receiving routine letters | £2.10 per item | £1.85 per item |
| 3. Routine telephone calls | £4.20 per item<br>£4.25 *per item* | £3.70 per item |
| 4. All other preparation work including any work which was reasonably done arising out of or incidental to the proceedings, interviews with client, witnesses, and other parties; obtaining evidence; preparation and consideration of, and dealing with, documents, negotiations and notices; | Where the proceedings were conducted in the principal registry or in another court on the South-Eastern Circuit at the time when the relevant work was done: | |

PREPARATION

| Column 1 | Column 2<br>High Court | Column 3<br>County Court |
|---|---|---|
| dealing with letters written and received and telephone calls which are not routine | £47.50 per hour<br>All other circuits:<br>£44.25 per hour | £41.50 per hour<br><br>£39.25 per hour |
| 5. In addition to items 1–4 above, to cover the general care and conduct of the proceedings | + 50% | + 50% |
| 6. Travelling and waiting time in connection with the above matters | £32.50 per hour | £29.50 per hour |

## PART II

CONFERENCES WITH COUNSEL

| | | |
|---|---|---|
| 7. Attending counsel in conference | £37.50 per hour | £33.00 per hour |
| 8. Travelling and waiting | £32.50 per hour | £29.50 per hour |

## PART III

ATTENDANCES

| | | |
|---|---|---|
| 9. Attending with counsel at the trial or hearing of any cause or the hearing of any summons or other application at court, or other appointment | £37.50 per hour | £33.00 per hour |
| 10. Attending without counsel at the trial or hearing of any cause or the hearing of any summons or other application at court, or other appointment | £56.75 per hour | £53.50 per hour |
| 11. Travelling and waiting | £32.50 per hour | £29.50 per hour |

## PART V

TAXATION AND REVIEW OF TAXATION

| | | |
|---|---|---|
| 18. Preparing the bill (where allowable) and completing the taxation (excluding preparing for and attending the taxation) | £32.50–£90.75 | £32.50–£51.00<br>*£51.75* |
| 19. Preparing for and attending the taxation (including travelling and waiting) | Discretionary | Discretionary |
| 20. Review by district judge or judge (including preparation) | Discretionary | Discretionary |

### (b) Magistrates' court proceedings

| Class of work | Rate |
|---|---|
| Preparation | £44.50 per hour (£47.50 per hour for a fee-earner whose office is situated within legal aid area 1) |
| Advocacy | £56.25 per hour |
| Attendance at court where counsel assigned | £30.25 per hour |

| Class of work | Rate |
|---|---|
| Travelling and waiting | £25.00 per hour |
| Routine letters written and routine telephone calls | £3.45 per item (£3.60 per item for a fee-earner whose office is situated within legal aid area 1) |

## FAMILY PROCEEDINGS COURTS (MATRIMONIAL PROCEEDINGS ETC) RULES 1991

**Dated** 31 August 1991

**SI 1991 No 1991**

ARRANGEMENT OF RULES

PART III

*Consequential and Minor Amendments*

26.  Consequential and minor amendments

PART IV

*Revocations*

27.  Revocations

SCHEDULES

Schedule 1—Forms
Schedule 2—Consequential and minor amendments
Schedule 3—Revocations

The Lord Chancellor, in exercise of the powers conferred on him by section 144 of the Magistrates' Courts Act 1980 after consultation with the Rule Committee appointed under that section, hereby makes the following Rules—

PART I

INTRODUCTORY

*Citation, commencement and transitional*

**1.**  (1) These Rules may be cited as the Family Proceedings Courts (Matrimonial Proceedings etc) Rules 1991 and shall come into force on 14 October 1991 except that paragraph 3(7) of Schedule 2 to these Rules shall come into force on 7 October 1991.

(2) Nothing in these Rules shall affect any proceedings which are pending (within the meaning of paragraph 1 of Schedule 14 to the Children Act 1989) immediately before these Rules come into force.

PART II

MATRIMONIAL PROCEEDINGS UNDER THE DOMESTIC PROCEEDINGS AND MAGISTRATES' COURTS ACT 1978

*Interpretation, application and savings*

**2.**  (1) In this Part of these Rules, unless a contrary intention appears—
any reference to a rule shall be construed as a reference to a rule contained in these Rules; and any reference in a rule to a paragraph shall be construed as a reference to a paragraph of that rule,
'application' means an application for an order made under or by virtue of *the Act or, as the case may be, the Family Law Act 1996* [the Act, the Family Law Act 1986 or the Family Law Act 1996, as the case may be] and 'applicant' shall be construed accordingly,
'business day' means any day other than—
(a)  a Saturday, Sunday, Christmas Day or Good Friday; or
(b)  a bank holiday, that is to say, a day which is, or is to be observed as, a bank holiday or a holiday under the Banking and Financial Dealings Act 1971, in England and Wales,
'court' means a family proceedings court constituted in accordance with sections 66 and 67 of the Magistrates' Courts Act 1980 or, in respect of those proceedings prescribed in rule 25, a single justice who is a member of a family panel,
'directions appointment' means a hearing for directions under rule 6(1),
'file' means deposit with the justices' clerk,
'form' means a form in Schedule 1 to these Rules and, where a form is referred to by number, means the form so numbered in that schedule with such variation as the circumstances of the particular case may require,

'note' includes a record made by mechanical means,

'respondent' includes, as the case may be, more than one respondent,

'the Act' means the Domestic Proceedings and Magistrates' Courts Act 1978.

(2) Expressions used in this Part of these Rules have the meaning which they bear *in the Act or, as the case may be, in the Family Law Act 1996* [in the Act, the Family Law Act 1986 or the Family Law Act 1996, as the case may be].

(3) This part of these Rules shall not apply in relation to any such application or order as is referred to in paragraph 1 or 2 of Schedule 1 to the Domestic Proceedings and Magistrates' Courts Act 1978 (transitional provisions); and, accordingly, the Magistrates' Courts (Matrimonial Proceedings) Rules 1960 shall continue to apply in relation to any such application or order but with the following modification, that is to say, on any complaint made by virtue of paragraph 2(d) of the said Schedule 1 for the variation or revocation of a provision requiring access to a child to be given to a grandparent, rule 7 of the said Rules of 1960 shall be construed as applying to the complaint as it applies to a complaint made by virtue of section 8 of the Matrimonial Proceedings (Magistrates' Courts) Act 1960 and as if paragraph (5) of that rule included a reference to that grandparent.

(4) Subject to rule 1(2), the provisions of the Magistrates' Courts Rules 1981 shall have effect subject to this Part of these Rules.

**Note.** Words 'the Act or, as the case may be, the Family Law Act 1996' and 'in the Act or, as the case may be, in the Family Law Act 1996' substituted by words 'the Act, the Family Law Act 1986 or the Family Law Act 1996, as the case may be' and 'in the Act, the Family Law Act 1996, as the case may be' in square brackets by SI 2001/778, rr 4, 6 as from 1 April 2001.

*Applications*

**3.**   (1) Subject to paragraph (3) and rule 3A, an applicant shall—
- (a)  file the application in the appropriate form in Schedule 1 to these Rules or, where there is no such form, in writing, together with sufficient copies for one to be served on the respondent, and
- (b)  serve a copy of the application, endorsed in accordance with paragraph (2)(b), together with any notice attached under paragraph (2)(c), on the respondent at least 21 days prior to the date fixed under paragraph (2)(a).

*(2) On receipt of the documents filed under paragraph (1)(a), the justices' clerk shall—*
- *(a)  fix the date, time and place for a hearing or a directions appointment, allowing sufficient time for the applicant to comply with paragraph (1)(b),*
- *(b)  endorse the date, time and place so fixed upon the copies of the application filed by the applicant, and,*
- *(c)  omitted*
- *(d)  return the copies to the applicant forthwith.*

[(2) On receipt by the justices' chief executive of the documents filed under paragraph (1)(a)—
- (a)  the justices' clerk shall fix the date, time and place for a hearing or a directions appointment, allowing sufficient time for the applicant to comply with paragraph (1)(b), and
- (b)  the justices' chief executive shall—
    - (i)  endorse the date, time and place so fixed upon the copies of the application filed by the applicant, and
    - (ii)  return the copies to the applicant forthwith.]

**Note.** Para (2) substituted by SI 2001/615, r 2(xxiii), Schedule, para 112.

(3) A court may proceed on an application made orally where it is made by virtue of section 6(4) of the Act and where an application is so made paragraph (1) shall not apply.
- (4)  *omitted*

*Applications under Part IV of the Family Law Act 1996*

**3A.**   (1) An application for an occupation order or a non-molestation order under Part IV of the Family Law Act 1996 (Family Homes and Domestic Violence) shall be made in Form FL401.

(2) An application for an occupation order or a non-molestation order which is made in other proceedings which are pending shall be made in Form FL401.

(3) An application in Form FL401 shall be supported—

(a) by a statement which is signed and is declared to be true; or

(b) with the leave of the court, by oral evidence.

(4) An application in form FL401 may, with the leave of the justices' clerk or of the court, be made ex parte, in which case

(a) the applicant shall file with the *justices' clerk* [justices' chief executive] or the court the application at the time when the application is made or as directed by the justices' clerk; and

(b) the evidence in support of the application shall state the reasons why the application is made ex parte.

(5) An application made on notice (together with any statement supporting it and a notice in Form FL402) shall be served by the applicant on the respondent personally not less than 2 business days prior to the date on which the application will be heard.

(6) The court or the justices' clerk may abridge the period specified in paragraph (5).

(7) Where the applicant is acting in person, service of the application may, with the leave of the justices' clerk, be effected in accordance with rule 4.

(8) Where an application for an occupation order or a non-molestation order is pending, the court shall consider (on the application of either party or of its own motion) whether to exercise its powers to transfer the hearing of that application to another court and the justices' clerk or the court shall make an order for transfer in Form FL417 if it seems necessary or expedient to do so.

(9) Where an order for transfer is made, the *justices' clerk* [justices' chief executive] shall send a copy of the order—

(a) to the parties, and

(b) to the family proceedings court or to the county court to which the proceedings are to be transferred.

(10) A copy of an application for an occupation order under section 33, 35 or 36 of the Family Law Act 1996 shall be served by the applicant by first-class post on the mortgagee or, as the case may be, the landlord of the dwelling-house in question, with a notice in Form FL416 informing him of his right to make representations in writing or at any hearing.

(11) The applicant shall file a statement in Form FL415 after he has served the application.

(12) Rule 33A of the Family Proceedings Courts (Children Act 1989) Rules 1991 (disclosure of addresses) shall apply for the purpose of preventing the disclosure of addresses where an application is made in Form FL401 as it applies for that purpose in proceedings under the Children Act 1989.

**Note.** Words 'justices clerk' substituted by words 'justices' chief executive' in both places by SI 2001/615, r 2(xxiii), Schedule, para 111 as from 1 April 2001.

*[Applications under section 55A of the Family Law Act 1986*

**3B.**   (1) An application for a declaration of parentage under section 55A of the Family Law Act 1986 shall be made in Form FL 423.

(2) An application in Form FL 423 shall be supported by a statement which is signed and is declared to be true. Provided that if the applicant is under the age of 18, the statement shall, unless otherwise directed, be made by his next friend.

(3) A statement under paragraph (2) may contain statements of information or belief with the sources and grounds thereof.

(4) Within 14 days of service of the application the respondent shall file and serve on the parties an answer to the application in Form FL 423.

(5) Where the respondent or one of the respondents is a child, the justices' clerk or the court may at any stage in the proceedings appoint a guardian ad litem, but only if it considers that such an appointment is necessary to safeguard the interests of the child.

(6) The justices' chief executive shall send a copy of the application and every document accompanying it and of any answer to the Attorney General if he has notified the court that he wishes to intervene in the proceedings.

(7) When all answers to the application have been filed the applicant shall issue and serve on all respondents to the application a request for directions for the conduct of the proceedings, including directions as to any other persons who should be made respondents to the application or given notice of the proceedings.

(8) When giving directions in accordance with paragraph (7) the court shall consider whether it is desirable that the Attorney General should argue before it any question relating to the proceedings, and if it does so consider and the Attorney General agrees to argue that question—
  (i) the justices' chief executive shall send a copy of the application and every document accompanying it and of any answer to the Attorney General;
  (ii) the Attorney General need not file an answer; and
  (iii) the court shall give him directions requiring him to serve on all parties to the proceedings a summary of his argument.

(9) Persons given notice of proceedings pursuant to directions given in accordance with paragraph (7) shall within 21 days after service of the notice upon them be entitled to apply to the court to be joined as parties.

(10) The Attorney General may file an answer to the application within 21 days after directions have been given in accordance with paragraph (7) and no directions for the hearing shall be given until that period and the period referred to in paragraph (9) have expired.

(11) The Attorney General, in deciding whether it is necessary or expedient to intervene in the proceedings, may have a search made for, and may inspect and obtain a copy of, any document filed in the court offices which relates to any other family proceedings referred to in the proceedings.

(12) Where the justices' clerk or the court is considering whether or not to transfer proceedings under section 55A of the Family Law Act 1986 to another court, rules 6, 14(2)(h), (4) and (11) and 32 of the Family Proceedings Courts (Children Act 1989) Rules 1991 shall apply as appropriate.

(13) A declaration made in accordance with section 55A of the Family Law Act 1986 shall be in form FL 424.

(14) The prescribed officer for the purposes of section 55A(7) of the Family Law Act 1986 shall be the justices' chief executive, who shall, within 21 days after a declaration of parentage has been made, send to the Registrar General a copy of the declaration and of the application.]

**Note.** Inserted by SI 2001/778, rr 4, 7 as from 1 April 2001.

*Service*

**4.**   (1) Where service of a document is required by these Rules it may be effected, unless the contrary is indicated—
  (a) if the person to be served is not known by the person serving to be acting by solicitor—
    (i) by delivering it to him personally, or
    (ii) by delivering at, or by sending it by first-class post to, his residence or his last known residence, or

(b) if the person to be served is known by the person serving to be acting by solicitor—
  (i) by delivering the document at, or sending it by first-class post to, the solicitor's address for service,
  (ii) where the solicitor's address for service includes a numbered box at a document exchange, by leaving the document at that document exchange or at a document exchange which transmits documents on every business day to that document exchange, or
  (iii) by sending a legible copy of the document by facsimile transmission to the solicitor's office.

(2) In this rule, 'first-class post' means first-class post which has been pre-paid or in respect of which pre-payment is not required.

(3) A document shall, unless the contrary is proved, be deemed to have been served—
  (a) in the case of service by first-class post, on the second business day after posting, and
  (b) in the case of service in accordance with paragraph (1)(b)(ii), on the second business day after the day on which it is left at the document exchange.

(4) At or before the first directions appointment in, or hearing of, the proceedings, whichever occurs first, the applicant shall file a statement that service of a copy of the application has been effected on the respondent and the statement shall indicate—
  (a) the manner, date, time and place of service, or
  (b) where service was effected by post, the date, time and place of posting.

(5) In any proceedings under the Act, the justices' clerk or the court may direct that a requirement in this Part of these Rules to serve a document shall not apply or shall be effected in such manner as the justices' clerk or the court directs.

*Answer to application*

**5.** Within 14 days of service of an application for an order under section 2, 6, 7 or 20 of the Act, the respondent shall file and serve on the parties an answer to the application in the appropriate form in Schedule 1 to these Rules.

*Directions*

**6.** (1) In any proceedings under the Act, the justices' clerk or the court may, subject to paragraph (3), give, vary or revoke directions for the conduct of the proceedings, including—
  (a) the timetable for the proceedings;
  (b) varying the time within which or by which an act is required, by this Part of these Rules, to be done;
  (c) the service of documents; and
  (d) the submission of evidence;
and the justices' clerk shall, on receipt of an application [by the justices' chief executive], consider whether such directions need to be given.

(2) Where the justices' clerk or a single justice who is holding a directions appointment considers, for whatever reason, that it is inappropriate to give a direction on a particular matter, he shall refer the matter to the court which may give any appropriate direction.

(3) Directions under paragraph (1) may be given, varied or revoked either—
  (a) of the justices' clerk's or the court's own motion [the justices' chief executive] having given the parties notice of the intention to do so and an opportunity to attend and be heard or to make written representations,
  (b) on the written request of a party specifying the direction which is sought, which request has been filed and served on the other parties, or

   (c)   on the written request of a party specifying the direction which is sought, to which the other parties consent and which they or their representatives have signed.

(4)   In an urgent case, the request under paragraph (3)(b) may, with the leave of the justices' clerk or the court, be made—

   (a)   orally,

   (b)   without notice to the other parties, or

   (c)   both as in sub-paragraph (a) and as in sub-paragraph (b).

(5)   On receipt of a request [by the justices' chief executive] under paragraph (3)(b) the justices' clerk shall fix a date for the hearing of the request and [the justices' chief executive shall] give not less than 2 days' notice to the parties of the date so fixed.

(6)   On considering a request under paragraph (3)(c) the justices' clerk or the court shall either—

   (a)   grant the request, whereupon the *justices' clerk* [justices' chief executive] shall inform the parties of the decision, or

   (b)   direct that a date be fixed for the hearing of the request, whereupon the *justices' clerk* [justices' chief executive] shall fix such a date and [the justices' chief executive shall] give not less than 2 days' notice to the parties of the date so fixed.

(7)   The justices' clerk or the court shall take a note of the giving, variation or revocation of a direction under this rule and [the justices' chief executive shall] serve, as soon as practicable, a copy of the note on any party who was not present at the giving, variation or revocation.

**Note.** Amended by SI 2001/615, r 2(xxiii), Schedule, paras 111, 113–115 as from 1 April 2001.

*Timing of proceedings*

**7.**   (1)   Any period of time fixed by this Part of these Rules, or by any order or direction, for the doing of any act shall be reckoned in accordance with this rule.

(2)   Where the period, being a period of 7 days or less, would include a day which is not a business day, that day shall be excluded.

(3)   Where the time fixed for filing a document with the *justices' clerk* [justices' chief executive] expires on a day on which the *justices' clerk's office* [office of the justices' chief executive] is closed, and for that reason the document cannot be filed on that day, the document shall be filed in time if it is filed on the next day on which the *justices' clerk's office* [office of the justices' chief executive] is open.

(4)   Where these Rules provide a period of time within which or by which a certain act is to be performed in the course of proceedings, that period may not be extended otherwise than by a direction of the justices' clerk or the court under rule 6(1).

(5)   At the—

   (a)   postponement or adjournment of any hearing or directions appointment in the course of proceedings, or

   (b)   conclusion of any such hearing or directions appointment other than one at which the proceedings are determined, or as soon thereafter as is practicable,

the justices' clerk or the court shall—

     (i)   *fix a date upon which the proceedings shall come before the justices' clerk or the court again for such purposes as the justices' clerk or the court directs, and*

     (ii)   *give notice to the parties of the date so fixed.*

    [(i)   the justices' clerk shall fix a date upon which the proceedings shall come before him or the court again for such purposes as he or the court directs, and

     (ii)   the justices' chief executive shall serve, in accordance with these Rules, a copy of the order made on the parties to the proceedings.]

**Note.** Amended by SI 2001/615, r 2(xxiii), Schedule, para 111 as from 1 April 2001.

*Attendance at directions appointment and hearing*

**8.** (1) Subject to paragraph (2), a party shall attend a directions appointment of which he has been given notice in accordance with rule 6(3) unless the justices' clerk of the court otherwise directs.

(2) Subject to rules 18(2) and 22(2), the court shall not begin to hear an application in the absence of the respondent unless—

(a) it is proved to the satisfaction of the court that he received reasonable notice of the date of the hearing; or

(b) the court is satisfied that the circumstances of the case justify proceeding with the hearing.

(3) Where, at the time and place appointed for a hearing, the respondent appears but the applicant does not, the court may refuse the application or, if sufficient evidence has previously been received, proceed in the absence of the applicant.

(4) Where at the time and place appointed for a hearing neither the applicant nor the respondent appears, the court may refuse the application.

*Documentary evidence*

**9.** (1) In any proceedings the parties shall file and serve on the other parties—

(a) written statements of the substance of the oral evidence which the party intends to adduce at a hearing of, or a directions appointment in, those proceedings, which shall—

  (i) be dated,

  (ii) be signed by the person making the statement, and

  (iii) contain a declaration that the maker of the statement believes it to be true and understands that it may be placed before the court, and

(b) copies of any documents upon which the party intends to rely at a hearing of, or a directions appointment in, those proceedings,

at or by such time as the justices' clerk or the court directs or, in the absence of a direction, before the hearing or appointment.

(2) A party may, subject to any direction of the justices' clerk or the court about the timing of statements under this rule, file and serve on the parties a statement which is supplementary to a statement served under paragraph (1).

(3) At a hearing or directions appointment a party may not, without the leave of the justices' clerk in the case of a directions appointment, or the court—

(a) adduce evidence, or

(b) seek to rely on a document,

in respect of which he has failed to comply with the requirements of paragraph (1).

*Amendment*

**10.** (1) Subject to rule 9(2), a copy of a document which has been filed or served in any proceedings may not be amended without the leave of the justices' clerk or the court which shall, unless the justices' clerk or the court otherwise directs, be requested in writing.

(2) On considering a request for leave to amend a document the justices' clerk or the court shall either—

(a) grant the request, whereupon the *justices' clerk* [justices' chief executive] shall inform the person making the request of that decision, or

(b) invite the parties or any of them to make representations, within a specified period, as to whether such an order should be made.

(3) A person amending a document shall file it with the *justices' clerk* [justices' chief executive] and serve it on those persons on whom it was served prior to amendment, and the amendments shall be identified.

**Note.** Amended by SI 2001/615, r 2(xxii), Schedule, para 111 as from 1 April 2001.

*Oral evidence*

**11.** The justices' clerk or the court shall keep a note of the substance of the oral evidence given at a hearing of, or directions appointment in, any proceedings.

*Hearing*

**12.** (1) Before the hearing, the justice or justices who will be dealing with the case shall read any documents which have been filed under rule 9 in respect of the hearing.

(2) The justices' clerk at a directions appointment or the court at a hearing or directions appointment, may give directions as to the order of speeches and evidence.

(3) Subject to directions under paragraph (2), at a hearing of, or directions appointment in, proceedings, the parties shall adduce their evidence in the following order—

(a) the applicant,

(b) the respondent other than the child, and

(c) the child if he is a respondent.

(4) After the final hearing of proceedings, the court shall make its decision as soon as is practicable.

(5) Before the court makes an order or refuses an application, the justices' clerk shall record in writing—

(a) the names of the justice or justices constituting the court by which the decision is made, and

(b) in consultation with the justice or justices, the reasons for the court's decision and any findings of fact.

(6) When making an order or when refusing an application, the court, or one of the justices constituting the court by which the decision is made, shall state any findings of fact and the reasons for the court's decision.

(7) *After the court announces its decision, the justices' clerk shall as soon as practicable—*

(a) *make a record of any order made in the appropriate form in Schedule 1 to these Rules, or, where there is no such form, in writing; and*

(b) *serve, in accordance with these Rules, a copy of any order made on the parties to the proceedings.*

[(7) After the court announces its decision—

(a) the justices' clerk shall, as soon as practicable, make a record of the order made in the appropriate form, in writing, and

(b) the justices' chief executive shall serve, in accordance with these Rules, a copy of the order made on the parties to the proceedings.]

(8) The *justices' clerk* [justices' chief executive] shall supply a copy of the record of the reasons for a decision made in pursuance of paragraph (5)(b) to any person on request, if satisfied that it is required in connection with an appeal or possible appeal.

**Note.** Amended by SI 2001/615, r 2(xxii), Schedule, paras 111, 117 as from 1 April 2001.

*Hearing of applications under Part IV of the Family Law Act 1996*

**12A.** (1) This rule applies to the hearing of applications under the Part IV of the Family Law Act 1996 and the following forms shall be used in connection with such hearings—

(a) a record of the hearing shall be made on Form FL405, and

(b) any order made on the hearing shall be issued in Form FL404.

(2) Where an order is made on an application made ex parte, a copy of the order together with a copy of the application and of any statement supporting it shall be served by the applicant on the respondent personally.

(3) Where the applicant is acting in person, service of a copy of an order made on an application made ex parte shall be effected by the *justices' clerk* [justices' chief executive] if the applicant so requests.

(4) Where the application is for an occupation order under section 33, 35 or 36 of the Family Law Act 1996, a copy of any order made on the application shall be served by the applicant by first-class post on the mortgagee or, as the case may be, the landlord of the dwelling-house in question.

(5) A copy of an order made on an application heard inter partes shall be served by the applicant on the respondent personally.

(6) Where the applicant is acting in person, service of a copy of the order made on an application heard inter partes may, with the leave of the justices' clerk, be effected in accordance with rule 4.

(7) The court may direct that a further hearing be held in order to consider any representations made by a mortgagee or a landlord.

**Note.** Amended by SI 2001/615, r 2(xxii), Schedule, para 111 as from 1 April 2001.

*Applications to vary etc orders made under Part IV of the Family Law Act 1996*

**12B.** An application to vary, extend or discharge an order made under Part IV of the Family Law Act 1996 shall be made in Form FL403 and rules 12 and 12A shall apply to the hearing of such an application.

*Costs*

**13.** (1) In any proceedings, the court may, at any time during the proceedings, make an order that a party pay the whole or any part of the costs of any other party.

(2) A party against whom the court is considering making a costs order shall have an opportunity to make representations as to why the order should not be made.

*Confidentiality of documents*

**14.** No document, other than a record of an order, held by the court and relating to proceedings shall be disclosed other than to—
  (a) a party,
  (b) the legal representative of a party, or
  (c) the *Legal Aid Board* [Legal Services Commission],
without leave of the justices' clerk or the court.

**Note.** Words 'Legal Aid Board' substituted by words '[Legal Services Commission]' in square brackets by virtue of the Access to Justice Act 1999, s 105, Sch 14, Pt II, para 3(3) as from 1 April (SI 2000/744, arts 2, 5).

*Delegation by justices' clerk*

**15.** (1) In this rule, 'employed as a clerk in court' has the same meaning as in rule 2(1) of the Justices' Clerks (Qualifications of Assistants) Rules 1979.

(2) Anything authorised to be done by, to or before a justices' clerk under this Part of these Rules, or under paragraph 15 or 15D of the Schedule to the Justices' Clerks Rules 1970 as amended by Schedule 2 to these Rules, may be done instead by, to or before a person employed as a clerk in court where that person is appointed by the Magistrates' Courts Committee to assist him and where that person has been specifically authorised by the justices' clerk for that purpose.

(3) Any authorisation by the justices' clerk under paragraph (2) shall be recorded in writing [by the justices' chief executive] at the time the authority is given or as soon as practicable thereafter.

**Note.** Amended by SI 2001/615, r 2(xxii), Schedule, para 114, as from 1 April 2001.

*Application of enactments governing procedure in proceedings brought on complaint*

**16.**   (1)  Section 53(3) of the Magistrates' Courts Act 1980 (orders with the consent of the defendant without hearing evidence) shall apply to applications under section 20 of the Act for the variation of orders for periodical payments as it applies to complaints for the variation of the rate of any periodical payments ordered by magistrates' court to be made.

(2)  Section 97 of the Magistrates' Courts Act 1980 (issue of a witness summons) shall apply to proceedings as it applies to a hearing of a complaint under that section.

*Orders made under section 6 in the absence of the respondent*

**17.**   For the purposes of subsection (9)(a), (b) and (c) of section 6 of the Act, evidence of the consent of the respondent to the making of the order, of the financial resources of the respondent and of the financial resources of the child shall be by way of a written statement in the appropriate form in Schedule 1 to these Rules signed by the respondent or, where the application is in respect of financial provision for a child and the child has completed the appropriate form, the child.

*Application under section 7*

**18.**   (1)  Where, under subsection (4) of section 7 of the Act, a court decides to treat an application under section 7 as if it were an application for an order under section 2 of the Act, the court shall indicate orally which of grounds (a) and (b) in that subsection it considers applicable and a memorandum of the decision and the grounds therefore shall be entered in the court's register.

(2)  Where a court decides as aforesaid and the respondent is not then present or represented in court, or the respondent or his representative does not then agree to the continuance of the hearing, the court shall adjourn the hearing and the *justices' clerk* [justices' chief executive] shall serve notice of the decision and the grounds therefor on the respondent in the appropriate form in Schedule 1 to these Rules.

**Note.** Amended by SI 2001/615, r 2(xxiii), Schedule, para 114 as from 1 April 2001.

*Respondents on applications under section 20 or section 20A*

**19.**   (1)  The respondent on an application for the variation or revocation of an order under section 20 of the Act shall be the party to the marriage in question other than the applicant and, where the order requires payments to be made to or in respect of a child who is 16 years of age or over, that child.

(2)  The respondents on an application for the revival of an order under section 20A of the Act shall be the parties to the proceedings leading to the order which it is sought to have revived.

*Enforcement of orders made on applications under Part IV of the Family Law Act 1996*

**20.**   (1)  Where a power of arrest is attached to one or more of the provisions ('the relevant provisions') of an order made under Part IV of the Family Law Act 1996—

(a)  the relevant provisions shall be set out in Form FL406 and the form shall not include any provisions of the order to which the power of arrest was not attached; and

(b)  a copy of the form shall be delivered to the officer for the time being in charge of any police station for the applicant's address or of such other police station as the court may specify.

The copy of the form delivered under sub-paragraph (b) shall be accompanied by a statement showing that the respondent has been served with the order or informed of its terms (whether by being present when the order was made or by telephone or otherwise).

(2) Where an order is made varying or discharging the relevant provisions, the *justices* [justices' chief executive] shall—

(a) immediately inform the officer who received a copy of the form under paragraph (1) and, if the applicant's address has changed, the officer for the time being in charge of the police station for the new address; and

(b) deliver a copy of the order to any officer so informed.

(3) An application for the issue of a warrant for the arrest of the respondent shall be made in Form FL407 and the warrant shall be issued in Form FL408 and delivered by the *justices clerk* [justices' chief executive] to the officer for the time being in charge of any police station for the respondent's address or of such other police station as the court may specify.

(4) The court before whom a person is brought following his arrest may—

(a) determine whether the facts, and the circumstances which led to the arrest, amounted to disobedience of the order, or

(b) adjourn the proceedings and, where such an order is made, the arrested person may be released and

  (i) be dealt with within 14 days of the day on which he was arrested; and

  (ii) be given not less than 2 business days' notice of the adjourned hearing.

Nothing in this paragraph shall prevent the issue of a notice under paragraph (8) if the arrested person is not dealt with within the period mentioned in sub-paragraph (b)(i) above.

(5) Paragraphs (6) to (13) shall apply for the enforcement of orders made on applications under Part IV of the Family Law Act 1996 by committal order.

(6) Subject to paragraphs (11) and (12), an order shall not be enforced by committal order unless—

(a) a copy of the order in Form FL404 has been served personally on the respondent; and

(b) where the order requires the respondent to do an act, the copy has been so served before the expiration of the time within which he was required to do the act and was accompanied by a copy of any order, made between the date of the order and the date of service, fixing that time.

(7) At the time when the order is drawn up, the *justices clerk* [justices' chief executive] shall—

(a) where the order made is (or includes) a non-molestation order, and

(b) where the order made is an occupation order and the court so directs,

issue a copy of the order, indorsed with or incorporating a notice as to the consequences of disobedience, for service in accordance with paragraph (6).

(8) If the respondent fails to obey the order, the *justices clerk* [justices' chief executive] shall, at the request of the applicant, issue a notice in Form FL418 warning the respondent that an application will be made for him to be committed and, subject to paragraph (12), the notice shall be served on him personally.

(9) The request for issue of the notice under paragraph (8) shall be treated as a complaint and shall—

(a) identify the provisions of the order or undertaking which it is alleged have been disobeyed or broken;

(b) list the ways in which it is alleged that the order or undertaking has been disobeyed or broken;

(c) be supported by a statement which is signed and is declared to be true and which states the grounds on which the application is made,

and, unless service is dispensed with under paragraph (12), a copy of the statement shall be served with the notice.

(10)  If an order in Form FL419 (a committal order) is made, it shall include provision for the issue of a warrant of committal in Form FL420 and, unless the court otherwise orders—

(a)  a copy of the order shall be served personally on the person to be committed either before or at the time of the execution of the warrant; or

(b)  the order for the issue of the warrant may be served on the person to be committed at any time within 36 hours after the execution of the warrant.

(11)  An order requiring a person to abstain from doing an act may be enforced by committal order notwithstanding that a copy of the order has not been served personally if the court is satisfied that, pending such service, the respondent had notice thereof either—

(a)  by being present when the order was made;

(b)  by being notified of the terms of the order whether by telephone or otherwise.

(12)  The court may dispense with service of a copy of the order under paragraph (6) or a notice under paragraph (8) if the court thinks it just to do so.

(13)  Where service of a notice to show cause is dispensed with under paragraph (12) and a committal order is made, the court may of its own motion fix a date and time when the person to be committed is to be brought before the court.

(14)  Paragraphs (6) to (10), (12) and (13) shall apply to the enforcement of undertakings with the necessary modifications and as if—

(a)  for paragraph (6) there were substituted the following—

'(6)  A copy of Form FL422 recording the undertaking shall be delivered by the *justices clerk* [justices' chief executive] to the party giving the undertaking

(a)  by handing a copy of the document to him before he leaves the court building; or

(b)  where his place of residence is known, by posting a copy to him at his place of residence; or

(c)  through his solicitor,

and, where delivery cannot be effected in this way, the *justices clerk* [justices' chief executive] shall deliver a copy of the document to the party for whose benefit the undertaking is given and that party shall cause it to be served personally as soon as is practicable.';

(b)  in paragraph (12), the words from 'a copy' to 'paragraph (6) or' were omitted.

(15)  Where a person in custody under a warrant or order, desires to apply to the court for his discharge, he shall make his application in writing attested by the governor of the prison showing that he has purged or is desirous of purging his contempt and the *justices clerk* [justices' chief executive] shall, not less than one day before the application is heard, serve notice of it on the party (if any) at whose instance the warrant or order was issued.

(16)  The court by whom an order of committal is made may by order direct that the execution of the order of committal shall be suspended for such period or on such terms or conditions as it may specify.

(17)  Where execution of an order of committal is suspended by an order under paragraph (16), the applicant for the order of committal must, unless the court otherwise directs, serve on the person against whom it was made a notice informing him of the making and terms of the order under that paragraph.

(18)  The court may adjourn consideration of the penalty to be imposed for contempts found proved and such consideration may be restored if the respondent does not comply with any conditions specified by the court.

(19)  Where the court makes a hospital order in Form FL413 or a guardianship order in Form FL414 under the Mental Health Act 1983, the *justices clerk* [justices' chief executive] shall—

(a) send to the hospital any information which will be of assistance in dealing with the patient;

(b) inform the applicant when the respondent is being transferred to hospital.

(20) Where a transfer direction given by the Secretary of State under section 48 of the Mental Health Act 1983 is in force in respect of a person remanded in custody by the court, the *justices clerk* [justices' chief executive] shall notify—

(a) the governor of the prison to which that person was remanded; and

(b) the hospital where he is detained,

of any committal hearing which that person is required to attend and the justices' clerk shall give notice in writing to the hospital where that person is detained of any further remand.

(21) An order for the remand of the respondent shall be in Form FL409 and an order discharging the respondent from custody shall be in form FL421.

(22) In paragraph (4) 'arrest' means arrest under a power of arrest attached to an order or under a warrant of arrest.

**Note.** Amended by SI 2001/615, r 2(xxiii), Schedule, para 111 as from 1 April 2001.

*Applications under Part IV of the Family Law Act 1996: bail*

**21.** (1) An application for bail made by a person arrested under a power of arrest or a warrant of arrest may be made either orally or in writing.

(2) Where an application is made in writing, it shall contain the following particulars—

(a) the full name of the person making the application;

(b) the address of the place where the person making the application is detained at the time when the application is made;

(c) the address where the person making the application would reside if he were to be granted bail;

(d) the amount of the recognizance in which he would agree to be bound; and

(e) the grounds on which the application is made and, where a previous application has been refused, full particulars of any change in circumstances which has occurred since that refusal.

(3) An application made in writing shall be signed by the person making the application or by a person duly authorised by him in that behalf or, where the person making the application is a minor or is for any reason incapable of acting, by a guardian ad litem acting on his behalf and a copy shall be served by the person making the application on the applicant for the Part IV order.

(4) The following forms shall be used:

(a) the recognizance of the person making the application shall be in Form FL410 and that of a surety in Form FL411;

(b) a bail notice in Form FL412 shall be given to the respondent where he is remanded on bail.

*Proceedings by or against a person outside England and Wales for variation or revocation of orders under section 20*

**22.** (1) The jurisdiction conferred on a court by virtue of section 20 of the Act shall, subject to the provisions of this rule, be exercisable even though the proceedings are brought by or against a person residing outside England and Wales.

(2) Subject to paragraph (3), where a court is satisfied that the respondent has been outside England and Wales for the whole of the period beginning one month before the making of the application and ending with the date of the hearing, it may proceed with an application made under section 20 of the Act provided that—

(a) the applicant has taken steps to notify the respondent of the making of the application and of the time and place appointed for the hearing by—

(i)   causing a notice in writing to that effect to be delivered to the respondent;

(ii)   causing a notice in writing to that effect to be sent by post addressed to the respondent at his last known or usual place of abode or at his place of business or at such other address at which there is ground for believing that it will reach the respondent, in accordance with directions given for the purpose by a justice acting for the same petty sessions area as that of the court; or

(iii)   causing a notice to that effect to be inserted in one or more newspapers, in accordance with directions given as aforesaid; and

(b)   it is reasonable in all the circumstances to proceed in the absence of the respondent.

(3)   The court shall not make the order for which the application is made unless it is satisfied that during the period of 6 months immediately preceding the making of the application the respondent was continuously outside England and Wales or was not in England and Wales on more than 30 days and that, having regard to any communication to the court in writing purporting to be from the respondent, it is reasonable in all the circumstances to do so.

(4)   A court shall not exercise its powers under section 20 of the Act so as to increase the amount of any periodical payments required to be made by any person under the Act unless the order under that section is made at a hearing at which that person appears or a statement has been filed under rule 4(4) that service of a copy of the application has been effected on the respondent.

(5)   Paragraph (1) of rule 67 of the Magistrates' Courts Rules 1981 shall apply for the purpose of proving the delivery of a written notice in pursuance of paragraph (2)(a)(i) as it applies for the purpose of proving the service of a summons. In relation to a solemn declaration made outside the United Kingdom, paragraph (1) of the said rule 67, as applied by this paragraph, shall have effect as if for the reference to the authorities mentioned in the said paragraph (1) there were substituted a reference to a consular officer of Her Majesty's Government in the United Kingdom or any person for the time being authorised by law, in the place where the declarant is, to administer an oath for any judicial or other legal purpose.

(6)   Paragraph (2) of the said rule 67 shall apply for the purpose of proving the sending of a written notice in pursuance of paragraph (2)(a)(ii) or the insertion of a notice in a newspaper in pursuance of paragraph (2)(a)(iii) as it applies for the purpose of proving the service of any process, provided, as respects the insertion of a notice in a newspaper, that a copy of the newspaper containing the notice is annexed to the certificate.

*Entries in court's registers*

**23.**   (1)   Where the *justices' clerk* [justices chief executive] receives notice of any direction made by the High Court or a county court under section 28 of the Act by virtue of which an order made by the court under the Act ceases to have effect, particulars thereof shall be entered in the court's register.

(2)   Where the hearing of an application under section 2 of the Act is adjourned after the court has decided that it is satisfied of any ground mentioned in section 1 and the parties to the proceedings agree to the resumption of the hearing in accordance with section 31 by a court which includes justices who were not sitting when the hearing began, particulars of the agreement shall be entered in the court's register.

**Note.** Amended by SI 2001/615, r 2(xxiii), Schedule, para 111 as from 1 April 2001.

*Setting aside on failure of service*

**24.**   Where an application has been sent to a respondent in accordance with rule 4(1) and, after an order has been made on the application, it appears to the court that the application did not come to the knowledge of the respondent in due time, the court may of its own motion set aside the order and may give such directions as it thinks fit for the rehearing of the application.

*Proceedings with respect to which a single justice may discharge the functions of a court*

**25.**   The following proceedings are prescribed as proceedings with respect to which a single justice may discharge the functions of a court, that is to say, proceedings—

(a)   in which an application is made ex parte for an occupation order or a non-molestation order under Part IV of the Family Law Act 1996;

(b)   in accordance with rules 3, 3A(2), (6) and (8), 4, 6 (except paragraph (2)), 7 to 14 and 20(4).

PART III

CONSEQUENTIAL AND MINOR AMENDMENTS

**26.**   The consequential and minor amendments set out in Schedule 2 to these Rules shall have effect.

PART IV

REVOCATION

**27.**   The revocation set out in Schedule 3 to these Rules shall have effect.

SCHEDULE 1                                                          Rule 2(1)

FORMS                                                           Rule 3(1)(a)

FORM 1

APPLICATION FOR ORDER UNDER SECTION 2 (DPMC ACT 1978)

In the .................................................................. Magistrates' Court

at ...........................................................................................................

Date

Respondent

Address

The application of

Tel. No

Address

*Note: If you are concerned about giving your address you may give an alternative address where papers can be served. However, you must notify the court of your actual address.*

who applies for an order under section 2 of the Domestic Proceedings and Magistrates' Courts Act 1978 on the ground(s) that the respondent—

[(a)  has failed to provide reasonable maintenance for the applicant]

[(b)  has failed to provide, or to make a proper contribution towards, reasonable maintenance for any child of the family]

[(c)  has behaved in such a way that the applicant cannot reasonably be expected to live with the respondent]

[(d)  has deserted the applicant]

If ground (c) is alleged indicate briefly below the circumstances alleged to support that ground

MAT. 1

My solicitor's address for service
(if applicable) is

Tel.

Fax No.

I wish the payments to be made

☐ direct to a bank/building
society account

The name of the bank/building society is

_____

_____

Bank/building
society sort
code

Account number

☐ by the attachment of earnings order

☐ in the following way

If you would like another
method of payment to be used
please give details in the box

☐ No preference

I declare that the information I have given is correct and complete to the best of my knowledge.

Signed                                          Date

**What you (the applicant) must do next**

- fill in the attached Statement of Means of Applicant

- fill in your name in the appropriate box on the Notice of [Hearing] [Directions Appointment]

- take or send this form to the court with an extra copy for the respondent to be served. The top copy will be kept by the court and the other copy given or sent back to you for service

- you must then serve that copy of the form on the respondent according to the rules

STATEMENT OF MEANS OF APPLICANT

- Please complete all parts of the form which apply to you

- Continue on a separate sheet if necessary

**1** Personal details

Surname

Forename(s)

☐ Mr ☐ Mrs ☐ Miss ☐ Ms ☐ Other

☐ Married ☐ Single ☐ Other (specify)

Age

Address

Postcode

**2** Dependants *(people you support financially)*

Children living with you

| Name(s) | Age |
|---------|-----|
|         |     |

Children not living with you

| Name(s) | Age |
|---------|-----|
|         |     |

Amount of any maintenance being paid

Other dependants
*(give details—including whether you have these responsibilities on a part-time basis)*

**3** Employment

I am ☐ employed as a

☐ self-employed as a

☐ unemployed

☐ a pensioner

My employer is
*(State name and address)*

Jobs other than main job

Self-employment annual turnover £

☐ I am not in arrears with my national insurance contributions, income tax and VAT

☐ I am in arrears and I owe £

Give details of contracts and other work in hand

Give details of any sums due in respect of work done

**4**   Bank accounts and savings

(a)  I have ☐ bank or building society account(s)

| Name of account | Average balance in a/c over last 6 months |
|---|---|
|  |  |

(b)  I have ☐ savings account(s)

| Name of account | Amount in account |
|---|---|
|  |  |

When filling in sections 6, 7, and 9. Please give amounts on a weekly OR monthly basis. DO NOT put some weekly and some monthly figures

**5**   Property

I live in
☐ my own property
☐ lodgings
☐ jointly owned property
☐ council property
☐ privately rented property
☐ other. Please state

|  |
|---|

Value of (jointly) owned property  £ _____

**6**   Income  Amounts are per week/month*
*Delete as appropriate

| | |
|---|---|
| My usual take home pay *(including overtime, commission, bonuses etc)* | £ |
| Income support | £ |
| Child benefit(s) | £ |
| Other state benefit(s) | £ |
| My pension(s) | £ |
| Others living in my home give me | £ |
| Other income *(give details below)* | |
|  | £ |
|  | £ |
|  | £ |
| Total income | £ |

**7**   **Expenses** *(do not include any payments made by other members of the household out of their own income)*

I have regular expenses as follows: *(do not include payments on any arrears)*

Amounts are per week/month.*   *Delete as appropriate.*

| | |
|---|---|
| Mortgage *(including second mortgage)* | £ |
| Rent | £ |
| Community charge | |
| Gas | £ |
| Electricity | £ |
| Water charges | £ |
| TV rental and licence | £ |
| HP repayments | £ |
| Mail order | £ |
| Housekeeping, food, school meals | £ |
| Travelling expenses | £ |
| Children's clothing & pocket money | £ |
| Maintenance payments | £ |
| Others (but not credit debt payments or court orders) | £ |
| | £ |
| | £ |
| | £ |
| Total expenses | £ |

**8**   **Court orders**

| Court | Case No | Amount outstanding | Payment per month |
|---|---|---|---|
| | | | |

**9**   **Money you owe on essential bills**

Please state the amount of any arrears owing and the amount of any payments you make towards these arrears.

Payments are per week/month.*   *Delete as appropriate.*

| | Total amount outstanding | Amount of payment |
|---|---|---|
| Rent | £ | |
| Mortgage | £ | |
| Community charge | £ | |
| Water rates | £ | |
| Fuel debts:   Gas | £ | |
| Electricity | £ | |
| Other | £ | |
| Maintenance arrears | £ | |
| Total priority debts | £ | |

**10**   **Other commitments**

Give details of payments on any credit cards, other loans, storecards, loans from family etc.

| | Total amount outstanding | Amount of payment |
|---|---|---|
| | £ | |
| | £ | |
| | £ | |
| | £ | |
| | £ | |
| | £ | |
| Total | £ | |

**11**   **Declaration**

I declare that the details I have given above are true to the best of my knowledge

Signed

Dated

## NOTICE OF A [HEARING] [DIRECTIONS APPOINTMENT]

The respondent must read this Notice as soon as this form is served on him/her

About the [Hearing] [Directions Appointment]

name of applicant (to be completed by applicant)

has made an application to the Court.

*To be completed by the court*        Case No

The Court will hear this at

on

at       o'clock

the time allowed is

Both the applicant and the respondent are hereby informed that, if there is a child of the family who is under the age of 18, the court shall not dismiss or make a final order on the application until it has been decided whether to exercise any of its powers under the Children Act 1989 with respect to the child.

What you (the respondent) must do

• There is a copy of the application and the applicant's statement of means with this Notice. Read the application and statement of means now. You do not have to fill in any part. You must complete the form of Answer including the Statement of Means of Respondent enclosed and follow the instructions on the first page of the Answer regarding service.

Rule 5                          RESPONDENT'S ANSWER

In the .............................................................................................................................. Magistrates' Court

at .........................................................................................................................................................

Case No

(See the Notice of [Hearing]
[Directions Appointment] for
this number.)

Respondent's name and address

*These boxes to be completed by the respondent*

To the respondent:

You will get with this form a copy of

- a Notice of Hearing or Directions Appointment
- an application that has been made to the court
- the applicant's statement of means

Please

- read the Notice first
- then read the application and the applicant's statement of means
- answer the questions on this form and complete the attached Statement of Means of Respondent
  (which forms part of this Answer)

You must return this Answer including the Statement of Means of Respondent to the court and serve a copy
on the applicant within 14 days from the date of service on you of this form.

(Respondent's Answer continued)

1. About the application

Please    • read the application form before you answer the question
            • continue on another sheet if there is not enough room, putting the number of the question on the sheet.

My full name is
Put the surname last

My full address for
service is

Do you have legal
representation?

No ☐
Yes ☐

Please say who your solicitor is

Name

Address

Tel. No                          Fax

Do you accept that you should be a
respondent in this application?

If no, you do not need to complete
the rest of this form.

Yes ☐
No ☐

Please give reason and sign below

Do you intend to contest this
application?

No ☐
Yes ☐

Give reason

(Respondent's Answer continued)

2.   a.  Is everything in the           Yes ☐
        application true to the best of
        your knowledge?          No ☐

Please explain

    b.  Is there anything else the      No ☐
       Court should know about
       this application?       Yes ☐

Please give details

    c.  Do you intend to make an     No ☐
       application?             Yes ☐

Please give details

      Do you agree with        Yes ☐
      the proposed method
      of payment?           No ☐

Please give details

I wish the payments to be made

☐  direct to a bank/building
    society account
The name of the bank/building society is

_____

_____

Bank/building   _____
society sort
code         _____
Account number  _____

☐  by the attachment of earnings order

☐  in the following way

If you would like another
method of payment to be used
please give details in the box

☐  No preference

3.  I declare that the information I have given is true and correct to the best of my knowledge.

Signed

Date

## STATEMENT OF MEANS OF RESPONDENT

- Please complete all parts of the form which apply to you

- Continue on a separate sheet if necessary

**1** Personal details

Surname

Forename(s)

☐ Mr   ☐ Mrs   ☐ Miss   ☐ Ms   ☐ Other

☐ Married   ☐ Single   ☐ Other (specify)

Age

Address

Postcode

**2** Dependants *(people you support financially)*

Children living with you

| Name(s) | Age |
|---------|-----|
|         |     |

Children not living with you

| Name(s) | Age |
|---------|-----|
|         |     |

Amount of any maintenance being paid

Other dependants
*(give details—including whether you have these responsibilities on a part-time basis)*

**3** Employment

I am   ☐ employed as a

☐ self-employed as a

☐ unemployed

☐ a pensioner

My employer is
*(State name and address)*

Jobs other than main job

Self-employment annual turnover   £

☐ I am not in arrears with my national insurance contributions, income tax and VAT

☐ I am in arrears and I owe   £

Give details of contracts and other work in hand

Give details of any sums due in respect of work done

**4** Bank accounts and savings

(a) I have ☐ bank or building society account(s)

| Name of account | Average balance in a/c over last 6 months |
|---|---|
| | |
| | |
| | |

(b) I have ☐ savings account(s)

| Name of account | Amount in account |
|---|---|
| | |
| | |
| | |

When filling in sections 6, 7, and 9, please give amounts on a weekly OR monthly basis. DO NOT put some weekly and some monthly figures

**5** Property

I live in
☐ my own property
☐ lodgings
☐ jointly owned property
☐ council property
☐ privately rented property
☐ other. Please state

Value of (jointly) owned property £

**6** Income  Amounts are per week/month*
*Delete as appropriate

| | |
|---|---|
| My usual take home pay *(including overtime, commission, bonuses etc)* | £ |
| Income support | £ |
| Child benefit(s) | £ |
| Other state benefit(s) | £ |
| My pension(s) | £ |
| Others living in my home give me | £ |
| Other income *(give details below)* | |
| | £ |
| | £ |
| | £ |
| Total income | £ |

**7** Expenses *(do not include any payments made by other members of the household out of their own income)*

I have regular expenses as follows: *(do not include payments on any arrears)*
Amounts are per week/month.* *\* Delete as appropriate.*

| | |
|---|---|
| Mortgage *(including second mortgage)* | £ |
| Rent | £ |
| Community charge | |
| Gas | £ |
| Electricity | £ |
| Water charges | £ |
| TV rental and licence | £ |
| HP repayments | £ |
| Mail order | £ |
| Housekeeping, food, school meals | £ |
| Travelling expenses | £ |
| Children's clothing & pocket money | £ |
| Maintenance payments | £ |
| Others (but not credit debt payments or court orders) | £ |
| | £ |
| | £ |
| | £ |
| Total expenses | £ |

**8** Court orders

| Court | Case No | Amount outstanding | Payment per month |
|---|---|---|---|
| | | | |

**9** Money you owe on essential bills

Please state the amount of any arrears owing and the amount of any payments you make towards these arrears.

Payments are per week/month.* *\* Delete as appropriate.*

| | | Total amount outstanding | Amount of payment |
|---|---|---|---|
| Rent | | £ | |
| Mortgage | | £ | |
| Community charge | | £ | |
| Water rates | | £ | |
| Fuel debts: | Gas | £ | |
| | Electricity | £ | |
| | Other | £ | |
| Maintenance arrears | | £ | |
| Total priority debts | | £ | |

**10** Other commitments

Give details of payments on any credit cards, other loans, storecards, loans from family etc.

| | Total amount outstanding | Amount of payment |
|---|---|---|
| | £ | |
| | £ | |
| | £ | |
| | £ | |
| | £ | |
| | £ | |
| Total | £ | |

**11** Declaration

I wish the payments to be made ☐ direct to a bank/building society account

The name of the bank/building society is
_____

**Bank/building** _____
**society sort** 
**code** _____

**Account number** _____

☐ by the attachment of earnings order

☐ in the following way
If you would like another method of payment to be used please give details in the box

☐ No preference

I declare that the details I have given above are true to the best of my knowledge

Signed 

Dated _____

Rule 3(1)(a)

## FORM 2

### APPLICATION FOR ORDER UNDER SECTION 6 (DPMC ACT 1978)

In the ................................................................................................. Magistrates' Court

at ......................................................................................................................................

Date

Respondent

Address

The application of

Tel. No

Address

*Note: If you are concerned about giving your address you may give an alternative address where papers can be served. However, you must notify the court of your actual address.*

who applies for an order for financial provision under section 6 of the Domestic Proceedings and Magistrates' Courts Act 1978 on the ground that s/he/the respondent has agreed to—

[the making of periodical payments to the applicant/respondent to the amount of £          per          for a term of          beginning on          ]

[the payment of a lump sum to the applicant/respondent to the amount of £          ]

[the making of periodical payments to
(being a child of the family)/the applicant/the respondent for the benefit of          (being a child of the family to the amount of £          per          for a term of          beginning on          ]

[the payment of a lump sum to          (being a child of the family)/the applicant/the respondent for the benefit of          (being a child of the family) to the amount of £          ]

MAT. 2

Is the agreement relating to periodical payments to a child of the family in writing?

☐ Yes    ☐ No

If yes, please state the date on which it was made.

My solicitor's address for service
(if applicable) is

Tel.

Fax No.

I wish the payments to be made

☐ direct to a bank/building
society account
The name of the bank/building society is

_____

_____

Bank/building    _____
society sort      _____
code
Account number   _____

☐ by the attachment of earnings order

☐ in the following way

If you would like another
method of payment to be used
please give details in the box

☐ No preference

I declare that the information I have given is correct and complete to the best of my knowledge.

Signed                                    Date

**What you (the applicant) must do next**

- fill in the attached Statement of Means of Applicant

- fill in your name in the appropriate box on the Notice of [Hearing] [Directions Appointment]

- take or send this form to the court with an extra copy for the respondent to be served. The top copy will be kept by the court and the other copy given or sent back to you for service

- you must then serve that copy of the form on the respondent according to the rules

## STATEMENT OF MEANS OF APPLICANT

- Please complete all parts of the form which apply to you

- Continue on a separate sheet if necessary

### 1 Personal details

Surname

Forename(s)

☐ Mr ☐ Mrs ☐ Miss ☐ Ms ☐ Other

☐ Married ☐ Single ☐ Other (specify)

Age

Address

Postcode

### 2 Dependants *(people you support financially)*

Children living with you

| Name(s) | Age |
|---|---|
| | |
| | |

Children not living with you

| Name(s) | Age |
|---|---|
| | |
| | |

Amount of any maintenance being paid

Other dependants
*(give details—including whether you have these responsibilities on a part-time basis)*

### 3 Employment

I am ☐ employed as a

☐ self-employed as a

☐ unemployed

☐ a pensioner

My employer is
*(State name and address)*

Jobs other than
main job

Self-employment annual turnover £

☐ I am not in arrears with my national insurance contributions, income tax and VAT

☐ I am in arrears and I owe £

Give details of contracts and other work in hand

Give details of any sums due in respect of work done

**4** Bank accounts and savings

(a) I have ☐ bank or building society account(s)

| Name of account | Average balance in a/c over last 6 months |
|---|---|
| | |

(b) I have ☐ savings account(s)

| Name of account | Amount in account |
|---|---|
| | |

When filling in sections 6, 7, and 9, please give amounts on a weekly OR monthly basis. DO NOT put some weekly and some monthly figures

**5** Property

I live in
☐ my own property
☐ lodgings
☐ jointly owned property
☐ council property
☐ privately rented property
☐ other. Please state

Value of (jointly) owned property  £

**6** Income Amounts are per week/month*
*Delete as appropriate

| | |
|---|---|
| My usual take home pay *(including overtime, commission, bonuses etc)* | £ |
| Income support | £ |
| Child benefit(s) | £ |
| Other state benefit(s) | £ |
| My pension(s) | £ |
| Others living in my home give me | £ |
| Other income *(give details below)* | |
| | £ |
| | £ |
| | £ |
| Total income | £ |

**7** **Expenses** *(do not include any payments made by other members of the household out of their own income)*

I have regular expenses as follows: *(do not include payments on any arrears)*
Amounts are per week/month.* *\* Delete as appropriate.*

| | |
|---|---|
| Mortgage *(including second mortgage)* | £ |
| Rent | £ |
| Community charge | |
| Gas | £ |
| Electricity | £ |
| Water charges | £ |
| TV rental and licence | £ |
| HP repayments | £ |
| Mail order | £ |
| Housekeeping, food, school meals | £ |
| Travelling expenses | £ |
| Children's clothing & pocket money | £ |
| Maintenance payments | £ |
| Others (but not credit debt payments or court orders) | £ |
| | £ |
| | £ |
| | £ |
| Total expenses | £ |

**8** **Court orders**

| Court | Case No | Amount outstanding | Payment per month |
|---|---|---|---|
| | | | |

**9** **Money you owe on essential bills**

Please state the amount of any arrears owing and the amount of any payments you make towards these arrears.

Payments are per week/month.* *\* Delete as appropriate.*

| | | Total amount outstanding | Amount of payment |
|---|---|---|---|
| Rent | | £ | |
| Mortgage | | £ | |
| Community charge | | £ | |
| Water rates | | £ | |
| Fuel debts: | Gas | £ | |
| | Electricity | £ | |
| | Other | £ | |
| Maintenance arrears | | £ | |
| Total priority debts | | £ | |

**10** **Other commitments**

Give details of payments on any credit cards, other loans, storecards, loans from family etc.

| | Total amount outstanding | Amount of payment |
|---|---|---|
| | £ | |
| | £ | |
| | £ | |
| | £ | |
| | £ | |
| | £ | |
| Total | £ | |

**11** **Declaration**

I wish the payments to be made ☐ direct to a bank/building society account

The name of the bank/building society is

_____

_____

Bank/building society sort code _____

Account number _____

☐ by the attachment of earnings order

☐ in the following way

If you would like another method of payment to be used please give details in the box

☐ No preference

I declare that the details I have given above are true to the best of my knowledge

Signed

Dated _____

## NOTICE OF A [HEARING] [DIRECTIONS APPOINTMENT]

The respondent must read this Notice as soon as this form is served on him/her

About the [Hearing] [Directions Appointment]

name of applicant (to be completed by applicant)

has made an application to the Court.

*To be completed by the court*   Case No

The Court will hear this at

on

at                    o'clock

the time allowed is

Both the applicant and the respondent are hereby informed that, if there is a child of the family who is under the age of 18, the court shall not dismiss or make a final order on the application until it has been decided whether to exercise any of its powers under the Children Act 1989 with respect to the child.

What you (the respondent) must do

• There is a copy of the application and the applicant's statement of means with this Notice. Read the application and statement of means now. You do not have to fill in any part. You must complete the form of Answer including the Statement of Means of Respondent enclosed and follow the instructions on the first page of the Answer regarding service.

Rule 5                          **RESPONDENT'S ANSWER**

In the ......................................................................................................................................... Magistrates' Court

at ..............................................................................................................................................................................

Case No

(See the Notice of [Hearing]
[Directions Appointment] for
this number.)

Respondent's name and address

*These boxes to be completed by the respondent*

To the respondent:

You will get with this form a copy of

- a Notice of Hearing or Directions Appointment
- an application that has been made to the court
- the applicant's statement of means

Please

- read the Notice first
- then read the application and the applicant's statement of means
- answer the questions on this form and complete the attached Statement of Means of Respondent
  (which forms part of this Answer)

You must return this Answer including the Statement of Means of Respondent to the court and serve a copy
on the applicant within 14 days from the date of service on you of this form.

(Respondent's Answer continued)

1. About the application

Please • read the application form before you answer the question
• continue on another sheet if there is not enough room, putting the number of the question on the sheet.

My full name is
Put the surname last

My full address for
service is

No ☐
Do you have legal
representation?                    Yes ☐

Please say who your solicitor is

Name

Address

Tel. No                          Fax

Yes ☐
Do you accept that you should be a
respondent in this application?     No ☐

If no, you do not need to complete
the rest of this form.

Please give reason and sign below

No ☐
Do you intend to contest this
application?                        Yes ☐

Give reason

(Respondent's Answer continued)

2.  a.  Is everything in the
        application true to the best of
        your knowledge?

    Yes ☐

    No ☐

    | Please explain |
    | --- |
    | |

    b.  Is there anything else the
        Court should know about
        this application?

    No ☐

    Yes ☐

    | Please give details |
    | --- |
    | |

    c.  Do you intend to make an
        application?

    No ☐

    Yes ☐

    | Please give details |
    | --- |
    | |

    I wish the payments to be made

    ☐ direct to a bank/building
       society account

    The name of the bank/building society is

    _____

    _____

    Bank/building   _____
    society sort    _____
    code
    Account number  _____

    ☐ by the attachment of earnings order

    ☐ in the following way

    If you would like another
    method of payment to be used
    please give details in the box

    | |
    | --- |

    ☐ No preference

3.  I declare that the information I have given is true and correct to the best of my knowledge.

Date [                    ]

Signed [                    ]

STATEMENT OF MEANS OF RESPONDENT

- Please complete all parts of the form which apply to you

- Continue on a separate sheet if necessary

**1** Personal details

Surname

Forename(s)

☐ Mr   ☐ Mrs   ☐ Miss   ☐ Ms   ☐ Other

☐ Married   ☐ Single   ☐ Other (specify)

Age

Address

Postcode

**2** Dependants *(people you support financially)*

Children living with you

| Name(s) | Age |
|---------|-----|
|         |     |

Children not living with you

| Name(s) | Age |
|---------|-----|
|         |     |

Amount of any maintenance being paid

Other dependants
*(give details—including whether you have these responsibilities on a part-time basis)*

**3** Employment

I am   ☐ employed as a

☐ self-employed as a

☐ unemployed

☐ a pensioner

My employer is
*(State name and address)*

Jobs other than
main job

Self-employment annual turnover   £

☐   I am not in arrears with my national insurance
contributions, income tax and VAT

☐   I am in arrears and I owe   £

Give details of contracts and other work in hand

Give details of any sums due in respect of work done

**4**   Bank accounts and savings

(a)  I have  ☐  bank or building society account(s)

| Name of account | Average balance in a/c over last 6 months |
|---|---|
| | |
| | |
| | |
| | |

(b)  I have  ☐  savings account(s)

| Name of account | Amount in account |
|---|---|
| | |
| | |
| | |
| | |

When filling in sections 6, 7, and 9, please give amounts on a weekly OR monthly basis. DO NOT put some weekly and some monthly figures

**5**   Property

I live in  ☐  my own property
      ☐  lodgings
      ☐  jointly owned property
      ☐  council property
      ☐  privately rented property
      ☐  other. Please state

Value of (jointly) owned property  £

**6**   Income  Amounts are per week/month*
      *Delete as appropriate

| | |
|---|---|
| My usual take home pay *(including overtime, commission, bonuses etc)* | £ |
| Income support | £ |
| Child benefit(s) | £ |
| Other state benefit(s) | £ |
| My pension(s) | £ |
| Others living in my home give me | £ |
| Other income *(give details below)* | |
| | £ |
| | £ |
| | £ |
| Total income | £ |

**7** Expenses *(do not include any payments made by other members of the household out of their own income)*

I have regular expenses as follows: *(do not include payments on any arrears)*

Amounts are per week/month.*   * *Delete as appropriate.*

| | |
|---|---|
| Mortgage *(including second mortgage)* | £ |
| Rent | £ |
| Community charge | |
| Gas | £ |
| Electricity | £ |
| Water charges | £ |
| TV rental and licence | £ |
| HP repayments | £ |
| Mail order | £ |
| Housekeeping, food, school meals | £ |
| Travelling expenses | £ |
| Children's clothing & pocket money | £ |
| Maintenance payments | £ |
| Others (but not credit debt payments or court orders) | £ |
| | £ |
| | £ |
| | £ |
| Total expenses | £ |

**8** Court orders

| Court | Case No | Amount outstanding | Payment per month |
|---|---|---|---|
| | | | |

**9** Money you owe on essential bills

Please state the amount of any arrears owing and the amount of any payments you make towards these arrears.

Payments are per week/month.*   * *Delete as appropriate.*

| | | Total amount outstanding | Amount of payment |
|---|---|---|---|
| Rent | | £ | |
| Mortgage | | £ | |
| Community charge | | £ | |
| Water rates | | £ | |
| Fuel debts: | Gas | £ | |
| | Electricity | £ | |
| | Other | £ | |
| Maintenance arrears | | £ | |
| Total priority debts | | £ | |

**10** Other commitments

Give details of payments on any credit cards, other loans, storecards, loans from family etc.

| | Total amount outstanding | Amount of payment |
|---|---|---|
| | £ | |
| | £ | |
| | £ | |
| | £ | |
| | £ | |
| | £ | |
| Total | £ | |

**11** Declaration

I wish the payments to be made   ☐ **direct to a bank/building society account**

The name of the bank/building society is

_____

_____

**Bank/building society sort code**   _____

_____

**Account number** _____

☐ **by the attachment of earnings order**

☐ **in the following way**

If you would like another method of payment to be used please give details in the box

☐ **No preference**

I declare that the details I have given above are true to the best of my knowledge

Signed

Dated

Rule 3(1)(a)

**FORM 3**

**APPLICATION FOR ORDER UNDER SECTION 7** (DPMC ACT 1978)

In the ........................................................................................... Magistrates' Court

at ...........................................................................................................................

Date

Respondent

Address

The application of

Address

Tel. No

*Note: If you are concerned about giving your address you may give an alternative address where papers can be served. However, you must notify the court of your actual address.*

who applies for an order for financial provision under section 7 of the Domestic Proceedings and Magistrates' Courts Act 1978, not exceeding the aggregate of the payments made to the applicant during the last three months; and states that he/she has been living apart from h.............. husband/wife for a continuous period exceeding three months, neither of them have deserted the other, and that h.............. husband/wife has been making periodical payments for [h.............. benefit] [and] [the benefit of (name(s))] being a child/children of the family].

The aggregate amount of the payments made during the last three months is £................

MAT. 2

My solicitor's address for service
(if applicable) is

Tel.

Fax No

I wish the payments to be made   ☐ direct to a bank/building
society account
The name of the bank/building society is

Bank/building
society sort
code
Account number

☐ by the attachment of earnings order

☐ in the following way

If you would like another
method of payment to be used
please give details in the box

☐ No preference

I declare that the information I have given is correct and complete to the best of my knowledge.

Signed

Date

**What you (the applicant) must do next**

- fill in the attached Statement of Means of Applicant

- fill in your name in the appropriate box on the Notice of [Hearing] [Directions Appointment]

- take or send this form to the court with an extra copy for the respondent to be served. The top copy will be kept by the court and the other copy given or sent back to you for service

- you must then serve that copy of the form on the respondent according to the rules

## STATEMENT OF MEANS OF APPLICANT

- • Please complete all parts of the form which apply to you

- • Continue on a separate sheet if necessary

### 1   Personal details

Surname

Forename(s)

☐ Mr   ☐ Mrs   ☐ Miss   ☐ Ms   ☐ Other

☐ Married   ☐ Single   ☐ Other (specify)

Age

Address

Postcode

### 2   Dependants *(people you support financially)*

Children living with you

| Name(s) | Age |
|---|---|
| | |

Children not living with you

| Name(s) | Age |
|---|---|
| | |

Amount of any maintenance being paid

**Other dependants**
*(give details—including whether you have these responsibilities on a part-time basis)*

### 3   Employment

I am ☐ employed as a

☐ self-employed as a

☐ unemployed

☐ a pensioner

My employer is
*(State name and address)*

Jobs other than
main job

Self-employment annual turnover   £

☐ I am not in arrears with my national insurance contributions, income tax and VAT

☐ I am in arrears and I owe   £

Give details of contracts and other work in hand

Give details of any sums due in respect of work done

**4**  Bank accounts and savings

(a)  I have ☐  bank or building society account(s)

| Name of account | Average balance in a/c over last 6 months |
|---|---|
|  |  |

(b)  I have ☐  savings account(s)

| Name of account | Amount in account |
|---|---|
|  |  |

When filling in sections 6, 7, and 9, please give amounts on a weekly OR monthly basis. DO NOT put some weekly and some monthly figures

**5**  Property

I live in  ☐  my own property

☐  lodgings

☐  jointly owned property

☐  council property

☐  privately rented property

☐  other. Please state

|  |
|---|

| Value of (jointly) owned property | £ |
|---|---|

**6**  Income  Amounts are per week/month*

*Delete as appropriate

| | |
|---|---|
| My usual take home pay *(including overtime, commission, bonuses etc)* | £ |
| Income support | £ |
| Child benefit(s) | £ |
| Other state benefit(s) | £ |
| My pension(s) | £ |
| Others living in my home give me | £ |
| Other income *(give details below)* | |
|  | £ |
|  | £ |
|  | £ |
| Total income | £ |

**7** Expenses *(do not include any payments made by other members of the household out of their own income)*

I have regular expenses as follows: *(do not include payments on any arrears)*
Amounts are per week/month.* *Delete as appropriate.*

| | |
|---|---|
| Mortgage *(including second mortgage)* | £ |
| Rent | £ |
| Community charge | |
| Gas | £ |
| Electricity | £ |
| Water charges | £ |
| TV rental and licence | £ |
| HP repayments | £ |
| Mail order | £ |
| Housekeeping, food, school meals | £ |
| Travelling expenses | £ |
| Children's clothing & pocket money | £ |
| Maintenance payments | £ |
| Others (but not credit debt payments or court orders) | £ |
| | £ |
| | £ |
| | £ |
| Total expenses | £ |

**8** Court orders

| Court | Case No | Amount outstanding | Payment per month |
|---|---|---|---|
| | | | |

**9** Money you owe on essential bills

Please state the amount of any arrears owing and the amount of any payments you make towards these arrears.

Payments are per week/month.* *Delete as appropriate.*

| | | Total amount outstanding | Amount of payment |
|---|---|---|---|
| Rent | | £ | |
| Mortgage | | £ | |
| Community charge | | £ | |
| Water rates | | £ | |
| Fuel debts: | Gas | £ | |
| | Electricity | £ | |
| | Other | £ | |
| Maintenance arrears | | £ | |
| Total priority debts | | £ | |

**10** Other commitments

Give details of payments on any credit cards, other loans, storecards, loans from family etc.

| | Total amount outstanding | Amount of payment |
|---|---|---|
| | £ | |
| | £ | |
| | £ | |
| | £ | |
| | £ | |
| | £ | |
| Total | £ | |

**11** Declaration

I wish the payments to be made ☐ **direct to a bank/building society account**
The name of the bank/building society is

_____

_____

Bank/building
society sort
code _____

Account number _____

☐ **by the attachment of earnings order**

☐ **in the following way**
If you would like another
method of payment to be used
please give details in the box

☐ **No preference**

I declare that the details I have given above are true to the best of my knowledge

Signed

Dated _____

## NOTICE OF A [HEARING] [DIRECTIONS APPOINTMENT]

The respondent must read this Notice as soon as this form is served on him/her

About the [Hearing] [Directions Appointment]

name of applicant (to be completed by applicant)

has made an application to the Court.

*To be completed by the court*   Case No

The Court will hear this at

on

at                                                    o'clock

the time allowed is

Both the applicant and the respondent are hereby informed that, if there is a child of the family who is under the age of 18, the court shall not dismiss or make a final order on the application until it has been decided whether to exercise any of its powers under the Children Act 1989 with respect to the child.

What you (the respondent) must do

• There is a copy of the application and the applicant's statement of means with this Notice. Read the application and statement of means now. You do not have to fill in any part. You must complete the form of Answer including the Statement of Means of Respondent enclosed and follow the instructions on the first page of the Answer regarding service.

Rule 5                                **RESPONDENT'S ANSWER**

In the .................................................................................................................. Magistrates' Court

at .........................................................................................................................................

Case No

(See the Notice of [Hearing]
[Directions Appointment] for
this number.)

Respondent's name and address

*These boxes to be completed by the respondent*

To the respondent:

You will get with this form a copy of

- a Notice of Hearing or Directions Appointment
- an application that has been made to the court
- the applicant's statement of means

Please

- read the Notice first
- then read the application and the applicant's statement of means
- answer the questions on this form and complete the attached Statement of Means of Respondent
  (which forms part of this Answer)

You must return this Answer including the Statement of Means of Respondent to the court and serve a copy
on the applicant within 14 days from the date of service on you of this form.

(Respondent's Answer continued)

1. About the application

Please
- read the application form before you answer the question
- continue on another sheet if there is not enough room, putting the number of the question on the sheet.

**My full name is**
Put the surname last

**My full address for service is**

**Do you have legal representation?**

No ☐
Yes ☐

Please say who your solicitor is

Name

Address

Tel. No                    Fax

**Do you accept that you should be a respondent in this application?**

If no, you do not need to complete the rest of this form.

Yes ☐
No ☐

Please give reason and sign below

**Do you intend to contest this application?**

No ☐
Yes ☐

Give reason

(Respondent's Answer continued)

2.  a.  Is everything in the
        application true to the best of
        your knowledge?

        Yes ☐

        No ☐

        Please explain

    b.  Is there anything else the
        Court should know about
        this application?

        No ☐

        Yes ☐

        Please give details

    c.  Do you intend to make an
        application?

        No ☐

        Yes ☐

        Please give details

        I wish the payments to be made

        ☐ direct to a bank/building
           society account
           The name of the bank/building society is

           _____

           _____

           Bank/building    _____
           society sort     _____
           code             _____
           Account number   _____

        ☐ by the attachment of earnings order

        ☐ in the following way

        If you would like another
        method of payment to be used
        please give details in the box

        ☐ No preference

3.  I declare that the information I have given is true and correct to the best of my knowledge.

    Date _____        Signed _____

## STATEMENT OF MEANS OF RESPONDENT

- • Please complete all parts of the form which apply to you

- • Continue on a separate sheet if necessary

### 1 Personal details

Surname

Forename(s)

☐ Mr ☐ Mrs ☐ Miss ☐ Ms ☐ Other

☐ Married ☐ Single ☐ Other (specify)

Age

Address

Postcode

### 2 Dependants *(people you support financially)*

Children living with you

| Name(s) | Age |
|---------|-----|
|         |     |

Children not living with you

| Name(s) | Age |
|---------|-----|
|         |     |

Amount of any maintenance being paid

Other dependants
*(give details—including whether you have these responsibilities on a part-time basis)*

### 3 Employment

I am ☐ employed as a

☐ self-employed as a

☐ unemployed

☐ a pensioner

My employer is
*(State name and address)*

Jobs other than
main job

Self-employment annual turnover £

☐ I am not in arrears with my national insurance contributions, income tax and VAT

☐ I am in arrears and I owe £

Give details of contracts and other work in hand

Give details of any sums due in respect of work done

**4** Bank accounts and savings

(a) I have ☐ bank or building society account(s)

| Name of account | Average balance in a/c over last 6 months |
|---|---|
|  |  |
|  |  |
|  |  |

(b) I have ☐ savings account(s)

| Name of account | Amount in account |
|---|---|
|  |  |
|  |  |
|  |  |

When filling in sections 6, 7, and 9, please give amounts on a weekly OR monthly basis. DO NOT put some weekly and some monthly figures

**5** Property

I live in
☐ my own property
☐ lodgings
☐ jointly owned property
☐ council property
☐ privately rented property
☐ other. Please state

Value of (jointly) owned property £

**6** Income  Amounts are per week/month*
*Delete as appropriate

| | |
|---|---|
| My usual take home pay *(including overtime, commission, bonuses etc)* | £ |
| Income support | £ |
| Child benefit(s) | £ |
| Other state benefit(s) | £ |
| My pension(s) | £ |
| Others living in my home give me | £ |
| Other income *(give details below)* | £ |
| | £ |
| | £ |
| Total income | £ |

**7** Expenses *(do not include any payments made by other members of the household out of their own income)*

I have regular expenses as follows: *(do not include payments on any arrears)*
Amounts are per week/month.* *Delete as appropriate.*

| | |
|---|---|
| Mortgage *(including second mortgage)* | £ |
| Rent | £ |
| Community charge | |
| Gas | £ |
| Electricity | £ |
| Water charges | £ |
| TV rental and licence | £ |
| HP repayments | £ |
| Mail order | £ |
| Housekeeping, food, school meals | £ |
| Travelling expenses | £ |
| Children's clothing & pocket money | £ |
| Maintenance payments | £ |
| Others (but not credit debt payments or court orders) | £ |
| | £ |
| | £ |
| | £ |
| Total expenses | £ |

**8** Court orders

| Court | Case No | Amount outstanding | Payment per month |
|---|---|---|---|
| | | | |

**9** Money you owe on essential bills

Please state the amount of any arrears owing and the amount of any payments you make towards these arrears.

Payments are per week/month.* *Delete as appropriate.*

| | | Total amount outstanding | Amount of payment |
|---|---|---|---|
| Rent | | £ | |
| Mortgage | | £ | |
| Community charge | | £ | |
| Water rates | | £ | |
| Fuel debts: | Gas | £ | |
| | Electricity | £ | |
| | Other | £ | |
| Maintenance arrears | | £ | |
| Total priority debts | | £ | |

**10** Other commitments

Give details of payments on any credit cards, other loans, storecards, loans from family etc.

| | Total amount outstanding | Amount of payment |
|---|---|---|
| | £ | |
| | £ | |
| | £ | |
| | £ | |
| | £ | |
| | £ | |
| Total | £ | |

**11** Declaration

I wish the payments to be made  ☐ **direct to a bank/building society account**
**The name of the bank/building society is**

_____

_____

**Bank/building society sort code** _____

**Account number** _____

☐ **by the attachment of earnings order**

☐ **in the following way**
If you would like another method of payment to be used please give details in the box

☐ **No preference**

I declare that the details I have given above are true to the best of my knowledge

Signed

Dated

Rule 3(1)(a)                                 FORM 4

## APPLICATION FOR ORDER UNDER SECTION 20 (DPMC ACT 1978)

In the ................................................................................................ Magistrates' Court

at ............................................................................................................

Date

Respondent

Address

The application of

Tel. No

Address

*Note: If you are concerned about giving your address you may give an alternative address where papers can be served. However, you must notify the court of your actual address.*

who applies under section 20 of the Domestic Proceedings and Magistrates' Courts Act 1978 for an order

[to [vary] [revoke] an order made under [section 2(1)(a)] [section 2(1)(b)] [section 2(1)(c)] [section 2(1)(d)]]

[to [vary] [revoke] an order made under section 6]

[for the payment of a lump sum [to the other party to the marriage] [to a child of the family] [to the other party to the marriage for the benefit of a child of the family]]

[to [vary] [revoke] an order made under section 7]

[to [vary] [revoke] an order made under section 19]

Please give details of any relevant court proceedings involving yourself and the respondent.

Proceedings are not pending or in progress            ☐

Proceedings are pending or in progress.              ☐
Details are given below. (*Please include the
name of the court and the case number of the
proceedings if known.*)

The effect of the order

Please give details of the financial provision you wish the
court to make, including the amount and any method of payment
requested.

(Note: you do need to fill this in if you are applying to
revoke an order.)

MAT. 4

My solicitor's address for service
(if applicable) is

Tel.

Fax No

I wish the payments to be made

☐ direct to a bank/building
society account
The name of the bank/building society is

_____

_____

Bank/building
society sort
code

Account number

☐ by the attachment of earnings order

☐ in the following way

If you would like another
method of payment to be used
please give details in the box

☐ No preference

I declare that the information I have given is correct and complete to the best of my knowledge.

Signed

Date

**What you (the applicant) must do next**

- fill in the attached Statement of Means of Applicant

- fill in your name in the appropriate box on the Notice of [Hearing] [Directions Appointment]

- take or send this form to the court with an extra copy for the respondent to be served. The top copy will be kept by the court and the other copy given or sent back to you for service

- you must then serve that copy of the form on the respondent according to the rules

## STATEMENT OF MEANS OF APPLICANT

- Please complete all parts of the form which apply to you

- Continue on a separate sheet if necessary

### 1  Personal details

Surname

Forename(s)

☐ Mr   ☐ Mrs   ☐ Miss   ☐ Ms   ☐ Other

☐ Married   ☐ Single   ☐ Other (specify)

Age

Address

Postcode

### 2  Dependants *(people you support financially)*

Children living with you

| Name(s) | Age |
|---------|-----|
|         |     |

Children not living with you

| Name(s) | Age |
|---------|-----|
|         |     |

Amount of any maintenance being paid

Other dependants
*(give details—including whether you have these responsibilities on a part-time basis)*

### 3  Employment

I am   ☐ employed as a

☐ self-employed as a

☐ unemployed

☐ a pensioner

My employer is
*(State name and address)*

Jobs other than main job

Self-employment annual turnover   £

☐ I am not in arrears with my national insurance contributions, income tax and VAT

☐ I am in arrears and I owe   £

Give details of contracts and other work in hand

Give details of any sums due in respect of work done

| 4 | Bank accounts and savings |

(a) I have ☐ bank or building society account(s)

| Name of account | Average balance in a/c over last 6 months |
|---|---|
|  |  |
|  |  |
|  |  |

(b) I have ☐ savings account(s)

| Name of account | Amount in account |
|---|---|
|  |  |
|  |  |
|  |  |

When filling in sections 6, 7, and 9, please give amounts on a weekly OR monthly basis. DO NOT put some weekly and some monthly figures

| 5 | Property |

I live in
☐ my own property
☐ lodgings
☐ jointly owned property
☐ council property
☐ privately rented property
☐ other. Please state

Value of (jointly) owned property  £

| 6 | Income  Amounts are per week/month* |

*Delete as appropriate

| My usual take home pay *(including overtime, commission, bonuses etc)* | £ |
| Income support | £ |
| Child benefit(s) | £ |
| Other state benefit(s) | £ |
| My pension(s) | £ |
| Others living in my home give me | £ |
| Other income *(give details below)* | |
|  | £ |
|  | £ |
|  | £ |
| Total income | £ |

**7**    **Expenses** *(do not include any payments made by other members of the household out of their own income)*

I have regular expenses as follows: *(do not include payments on any arrears)*
Amounts are per week/month.*   * *Delete as appropriate.*

| | |
|---|---|
| Mortgage *(including second mortgage)* | £ |
| Rent | £ |
| Community charge | |
| Gas | £ |
| Electricity | £ |
| Water charges | £ |
| TV rental and licence | £ |
| HP repayments | £ |
| Mail order | £ |
| Housekeeping, food, school meals | £ |
| Travelling expenses | £ |
| Children's clothing & pocket money | £ |
| Maintenance payments | £ |
| Others (but not credit debt payments or court orders) | £ |
| | £ |
| | £ |
| | £ |
| Total expenses | £ |

**8**    Court orders

| Court | Case No | Amount outstanding | Payment per month |
|---|---|---|---|
| | | | |

**9**    Money you owe on essential bills

Please state the amount of any arrears owing and the amount of any payments you make towards these arrears.

Payments are per week/month.*   * *Delete as appropriate.*

| | | Total amount outstanding | Amount of payment |
|---|---|---|---|
| Rent | | £ | |
| Mortgage | | £ | |
| Community charge | | £ | |
| Water rates | | £ | |
| Fuel debts: | Gas | £ | |
| | Electricity | £ | |
| | Other | £ | |
| Maintenance arrears | | £ | |
| Total priority debts | | £ | |

**10**    Other commitments

Give details of payments on any credit cards, other loans, storecards, loans from family etc.

| | Total amount outstanding | Amount of payment |
|---|---|---|
| | £ | |
| | £ | |
| | £ | |
| | £ | |
| | £ | |
| | £ | |
| Total | £ | |

**11**    Declaration

I wish the payments to be made   ☐ **direct to a bank/building society account**
The name of the bank/building society is
_____

**Bank/building society sort code** _____

**Account number** _____

☐ **by the attachment of earnings order**

☐ **in the following way**
If you would like another method of payment to be used please give details in the box

☐ **No preference**

I declare that the details I have given above are true to the best of my knowledge

Signed

Dated

## NOTICE OF A [HEARING] [DIRECTIONS APPOINTMENT]

The respondent must read this Notice as soon as this form is served on him/her

About the [Hearing] [Directions Appointment]

name of applicant (to be completed by applicant)

has made an application to the Court.

*To be completed by the court*        Case No

The Court will hear this at

on

at                                                           o'clock

the time allowed is

What you (the respondent) must do

• There is a copy of the application and the applicant's statement of means with this Notice. Read the application and statement of means now. You do not have to fill in any part. You must complete the form of Answer including the Statement of Means of Respondent enclosed and follow the instructions on the first page of the Answer regarding service.

Rule 5                                   **RESPONDENT'S ANSWER**

In the ..................................................................................................................... Magistrates' Court

at ...............................................................................................................................................

|  | Case No |  |
|---|---|---|

(See the Notice of [Hearing] [Directions Appointment] for this number.)

Respondent's name and address

*These boxes to be completed by the respondent*

To the respondent:

You will get with this form a copy of

- a Notice of Hearing or Directions Appointment
- an application that has been made to the court
- the applicant's statement of means

Please

- read the Notice first
- then read the application and the applicant's statement of means
- answer the questions on this form and complete the attached Statement of Means of Respondent (which forms part of this Answer)

You must return this Answer including the Statement of Means of Respondent to the court and serve a copy on the applicant within 14 days from the date of service on you of this form.

(Respondent's Answer continued)

1. About the application

Please   • read the application form before you answer the question
              • continue on another sheet if there is not enough room, putting the number of the question on the sheet.

**My full name is**
Put the surname last

**My full address for service is**

No ☐

**Do you have legal representation?**      Yes ☐

Please say who your solicitor is

Name

Address

Tel. No             Fax

Yes ☐

**Do you accept that you should be a respondent in this application?**      No ☐

If no, you do not need to complete the rest of this form.

Please give reason and sign below

No ☐

**Do you intend to contest this application?**      Yes ☐

Give reason

(Respondent's Answer continued)

2.  a. Is everything in the
       application true to the best of
       your knowledge?

Yes ☐

No ☐

Please explain

b. Is there anything else the
   Court should know about
   this application?

No ☐

Yes ☐

Please give details

c. Do you intend to make an
   application?

No ☐

Yes ☐

Please give details

I wish the payments to be made

☐ direct to a bank/building
   society account
The name of the bank/building society is

_____

_____

Bank/building          _____
society sort           _____
code
Account number         _____

☐ by the attachment of earnings order

☐ in the following way

If you would like another
method of payment to be used
please give details in the box

☐ No preference

3. I declare that the information I have given is true and correct to the best of my knowledge.

Signed

Date

## STATEMENT OF MEANS OF RESPONDENT

- Please complete all parts of the form which apply to you

- Continue on a separate sheet if necessary

### **1** Personal details

Surname

Forename(s)

☐ Mr    ☐ Mrs    ☐ Miss    ☐ Ms    ☐ Other

☐ Married    ☐ Single    ☐ Other (specify)

Age

Address

Postcode

### **2** Dependants *(people you support financially)*

Children living with you

| Name(s) | Age |
|---------|-----|
|         |     |
|         |     |

Children not living with you

| Name(s) | Age |
|---------|-----|
|         |     |
|         |     |

Amount of any maintenance being paid

Other dependants
*(give details—including whether you have these responsibilities on a part-time basis)*

### **3** Employment

I am    ☐ employed as a

☐ self-employed as a

☐ unemployed

☐ a pensioner

My employer is
*(State name and address)*

Jobs other than
main job

Self-employment annual turnover    £

☐ I am not in arrears with my national insurance contributions, income tax and VAT

☐ I am in arrears and I owe    £

Give details of contracts and other work in hand

Give details of any sums due in respect of work done

**4** Bank accounts and savings

(a) I have ☐ bank or building society account(s)

| Name of account | Average balance in a/c over last 6 months |
|---|---|
| | |
| | |
| | |

(b) I have ☐ savings account(s)

| Name of account | Amount in account |
|---|---|
| | |
| | |
| | |

When filling in sections 6, 7, and 9, please give amounts on a weekly OR monthly basis. DO NOT put some weekly and some monthly figures

**5** Property

I live in
☐ my own property
☐ lodgings
☐ jointly owned property
☐ council property
☐ privately rented property
☐ other. Please state

Value of (jointly) owned property £ _____

**6** Income  Amounts are per week/month*
*Delete as appropriate

| | |
|---|---|
| My usual take home pay *(including overtime, commission, bonuses etc)* | £ |
| Income support | £ |
| Child benefit(s) | £ |
| Other state benefit(s) | £ |
| My pension(s) | £ |
| Others living in my home give me | £ |
| Other income *(give details below)* | |
| | £ |
| | £ |
| | £ |
| Total income | £ |

**7** **Expenses** *(do not include any payments made by other members of the household out of their own income)*

I have regular expenses as follows: *(do not include payments on any arrears)*
Amounts are per week/month.* *\* Delete as appropriate.*

| | |
|---|---|
| Mortgage *(including second mortgage)* | £ |
| Rent | £ |
| Community charge | |
| Gas | £ |
| Electricity | £ |
| Water charges | £ |
| TV rental and licence | £ |
| HP repayments | £ |
| Mail order | £ |
| Housekeeping, food, school meals | £ |
| Travelling expenses | £ |
| Children's clothing & pocket money | £ |
| Maintenance payments | £ |
| Others (but not credit debt payments or court orders) | £ |
| | £ |
| | £ |
| | £ |
| Total expenses | £ |

**8** **Court orders**

| Court | Case No | Amount outstanding | Payment per month |
|---|---|---|---|
| | | | |

**9** **Money you owe on essential bills**

Please state the amount of any arrears owing and the amount of any payments you make towards these arrears.

Payments are per week/month.* *\* Delete as appropriate.*

| | | Total amount outstanding | Amount of payment |
|---|---|---|---|
| Rent | | £ | |
| Mortgage | | £ | |
| Community charge | | £ | |
| Water rates | | £ | |
| Fuel debts: | Gas | £ | |
| | Electricity | £ | |
| | Other | £ | |
| Maintenance arrears | | £ | |
| Total priority debts | | £ | |

**10** **Other commitments**
Give details of payments on any credit cards, other loans, storecards, loans from family etc.

| | Total amount outstanding | Amount of payment |
|---|---|---|
| | £ | |
| | £ | |
| | £ | |
| | £ | |
| | £ | |
| | £ | |
| Total | £ | |

**11** **Declaration**

I wish the payments to be made ☐ direct to a bank/building society account
The name of the bank/building society is
_____
_____

Bank/building
society sort     _____
code
Account number  _____

☐ by the attachment of earnings order

☐ in the following way

If you would like another
method of payment to be used
please give details in the box

☐ No preference

I declare that the details I have given above are true to the best of my knowledge

Signed

Dated _____

Rule 17                                        FORM 5

**WRITTEN STATEMENT TO EVIDENCE THE CONSENT AND FINANCIAL RESOURCES OF THE RESPONDENT TO THE MAKING OF AN ORDER UNDER SECTION 6** (DPMC ACT 1978, s.6(9)(a) and (b))

---

Concerning the application made by (applicant's name)                    to be heard on (date)

\* I, (full name)                         , hereby consent to the making of an order for financial provision under section 6 of the Domestic Proceedings and Magistrates' Courts Act 1978 in the terms set out in the application dated                    which I have received.

OR (if you are completing this form before an application is served)

\* I, (full name)                         , hereby consent to the making of an order for financial provision under section 6 of the Domestic Proceedings and Magistrates' Courts Act 1978 in the following terms—

    [the making of periodical payments to me/the applicant to the amount of £              per                    for a term of                    beginning on                    ]

    [the payment of a lump sum to me/the applicant to the amount £                    (specify condition of payment)]

    [the making of periodical payments to                    (being
    a child of the family)/me/the applicant for the benefit of
    (being a child of the family) to the amount of £                    per                    for a term
    of                    beginning on                    ]

    [the payment of a lump sum to                    (being
    a child of the family)/me/the applicant for the benefit of
    (being a child of the family) to the amount of £                    (specify condition of payment)]

\* Delete whichever is inappropriate

I (full name),                                        declare that my financial resources are as indicated in the following statement of means:

    MAT. 5

## STATEMENT OF MEANS OF RESPONDENT

- Please complete all parts of the form which apply to you

- Continue on a separate sheet if necessary

### 1 Personal details

Surname

Forename(s)

☐ Mr ☐ Mrs ☐ Miss ☐ Ms ☐ Other

☐ Married ☐ Single ☐ Other (specify)

Age

Address

Postcode

### 2 Dependants *(people you support financially)*

Children living with you

| Name(s) | Age |
|---------|-----|
|         |     |

Children not living with you

| Name(s) | Age |
|---------|-----|
|         |     |

Amount of any maintenance being paid

**Other dependants**
*(give details—including whether you have these responsibilities on a part-time basis)*

### 3 Employment

I am ☐ employed as a

☐ self-employed as a

☐ unemployed

☐ a pensioner

My employer is
*(State name and address)*

Jobs other than
main job

Self-employment annual turnover £

☐ I am not in arrears with my national insurance
contributions, income tax and VAT

☐ I am in arrears and I owe £

Give details of contracts and other work in hand

Give details of any sums due in respect of work done

### 4  Bank accounts and savings

(a)  I have ☐ bank or building society account(s)

| Name of account | Average balance in a/c over last 6 months |
|---|---|
| | |
| | |
| | |

(b)  I have ☐ savings account(s)

| Name of account | Amount in account |
|---|---|
| | |
| | |
| | |

When filling in sections 6, 7, and 9, please give amounts on a weekly OR monthly basis. DO NOT put some weekly and some monthly figures

### 5  Property

I live in
☐ my own property
☐ lodgings
☐ jointly owned property
☐ council property
☐ privately rented property
☐ other. Please state

Value of (jointly) owned property   £

### 6  Income  Amounts are per week/month*
*Delete as appropriate*

| | |
|---|---|
| My usual take home pay *(including overtime, commission, bonuses etc)* | £ |
| Income support | £ |
| Child benefit(s) | £ |
| Other state benefit(s) | £ |
| My pension(s) | £ |
| Others living in my home give me | £ |
| Other income *(give details below)* | |
| | £ |
| | £ |
| | £ |
| Total income | £ |

**7** Expenses *(do not include any payments made by other members of the household out of their own income)*

I have regular expenses as follows: *(do not include payments on any arrears)*
Amounts are per week/month.* *\* Delete as appropriate.*

| | |
|---|---|
| Mortgage *(including second mortgage)* | £ |
| Rent | £ |
| Community charge | |
| Gas | £ |
| Electricity | £ |
| Water charges | £ |
| TV rental and licence | £ |
| HP repayments | £ |
| Mail order | £ |
| Housekeeping, food, school meals | £ |
| Travelling expenses | £ |
| Children's clothing & pocket money | £ |
| Maintenance payments | £ |
| Others (but not credit debt payments or court orders) | £ |
| | £ |
| | £ |
| | £ |
| Total expenses | £ |

**8** Court orders

| Court | Case No | Amount outstanding | Payment per month |
|---|---|---|---|
| | | | |

**9** Money you owe on essential bills

Please state the amount of any arrears owing and the amount of any payments you make towards these arrears.

Payments are per week/month.* *\* Delete as appropriate.*

| | | Total amount outstanding | Amount of payment |
|---|---|---|---|
| Rent | | £ | |
| Mortgage | | £ | |
| Community charge | | £ | |
| Water rates | | £ | |
| Fuel debts: | Gas | £ | |
| | Electricity | £ | |
| | Other | £ | |
| Maintenance arrears | | £ | |
| Total priority debts | | £ | |

**10** Other commitments

Give details of payments on any credit cards, other loans, storecards, loans from family etc.

| | Total amount outstanding | Amount of payment |
|---|---|---|
| | £ | |
| | £ | |
| | £ | |
| | £ | |
| | £ | |
| | £ | |
| Total | £ | |

**11** Declaration

I declare that the details I have given above are true to the best of my knowledge

Signed

Dated

Rule 17                                   FORM 6


### WRITTEN STATEMENT TO EVIDENCE THE FINANCIAL RESOURCES OF A CHILD
(DPMC ACT 1978, s.6(9)(c))

---

\* I, (full name)                         , declare that to the best of my knowledge and belief

[(full name of child)                     has no financial resources] [the financial resources of

(full name of child)                      are as follows—]


OR (if the child is completing this form)

\* I, (*full name*)                       , declare that [I have no financial resources] [my financial resources are as follows—]


MAT. 6

STATEMENT OF MEANS OF CHILD

- Please complete all parts of the form which apply to you

- Continue on a separate sheet if necessary

**1** Personal details

Surname

Forename(s)

☐ Mr   ☐ Mrs   ☐ Miss   ☐ Ms   ☐ Other

☐ Married   ☐ Single   ☐ Other (specify)

Age

Address

Postcode

**2** Dependants *(people you support financially)*

Children living with you

| Name(s) | Age |
|---|---|
|  |  |
|  |  |

Children not living with you

| Name(s) | Age |
|---|---|
|  |  |
|  |  |

Amount of any maintenance being paid

Other dependants
*(give details—including whether you have these responsibilities on a part-time basis)*

**3** Employment

I am  ☐ employed as a

☐ self-employed as a

☐ unemployed

☐ a pensioner

My employer is
*(State name and address)*

Jobs other than
main job

Self-employment annual turnover   £

☐ I am not in arrears with my national insurance
contributions, income tax and VAT

☐ I am in arrears and I owe   £

Give details of contracts and other work in hand

Give details of any sums due in respect of work done

## 4  Bank accounts and savings

(a) I have ☐ bank or building society account(s)

| Name of account | Average balance in a/c over last 6 months |
|---|---|
|  |  |

(b) I have ☐ savings account(s)

| Name of account | Amount in account |
|---|---|
|  |  |

When filling in sections 6, 7, and 9, please give amounts on a weekly OR monthly basis. DO NOT put some weekly and some monthly figures

## 5  Property

I live in

☐ my own property

☐ lodgings

☐ jointly owned property

☐ council property

☐ privately rented property

☐ other. Please state

|  |
|---|

Value of (jointly) owned property

£ _____

## 6  Income  Amounts are per week/month*
*Delete as appropriate

| | |
|---|---|
| My usual take home pay *(including overtime, commission, bonuses etc)* | £ |
| Income support | £ |
| Child benefit(s) | £ |
| Other state benefit(s) | £ |
| My pension(s) | £ |
| Others living in my home give me | £ |
| Other income *(give details below)* | |
|  | £ |
|  | £ |
|  | £ |
| Total income | £ |

**7** **Expenses** *(do not include any payments made by other members of the household out of their own income)*

I have regular expenses as follows: *(do not include payments on any arrears)*
Amounts are per week/month.* *\* Delete as appropriate.*

| | |
|---|---|
| Mortgage *(including second mortgage)* | £ |
| Rent | £ |
| Community charge | |
| Gas | £ |
| Electricity | £ |
| Water charges | £ |
| TV rental and licence | £ |
| HP repayments | £ |
| Mail order | £ |
| Housekeeping, food, school meals | £ |
| Travelling expenses | £ |
| Children's clothing & pocket money | £ |
| Maintenance payments | £ |
| Others (but not credit debt payments or court orders) | £ |
| | £ |
| | £ |
| | £ |
| Total expenses | £ |

**8** Court orders

| Court | Case No | Amount outstanding | Payment per month |
|---|---|---|---|
| | | | |

**9** Money you owe on essential bills

Please state the amount of any arrears owing and the amount of any payments you make towards these arrears.

Payments are per week/month.* *\* Delete as appropriate.*

| | | Total amount outstanding | Amount of payment |
|---|---|---|---|
| Rent | | £ | |
| Mortgage | | £ | |
| Community charge | | £ | |
| Water rates | | £ | |
| Fuel debts: | Gas | £ | |
| | Electricity | £ | |
| | Other | £ | |
| Maintenance arrears | | £ | |
| Total priority debts | | £ | |

**10** Other commitments

Give details of payments on any credit cards, other loans, storecards, loans from family etc.

| | Total amount outstanding | Amount of payment |
|---|---|---|
| | £ | |
| | £ | |
| | £ | |
| | £ | |
| | £ | |
| | £ | |
| Total | £ | |

**11** Declaration

I declare that the details I have given above are true to the best of my knowledge

Signed

Dated

Rule 18(2)                                    FORM 7

### NOTICE OF DECISION TO TREAT APPLICATION FOR ORDER UNDER SECTION 7
### AS APPLICATION FOR ORDER UNDER SECTION 2 (DPMC Act 1978, s.7(4))

.................................................................................................................. Magistrates' Court

Date                                                          Case No

To the
Respondent

Address

You are hereby notified that the above-named Magistrates' Court at the hearing of the application made on (date)            by
your husband/wife for an order under section 7 of the Domestic Proceedings and Magistrates' Courts Act 1978 (being an order for
financial provision not exceeding the aggregate of the payments made to the applicant during the preceding three months) has
decided, under subsection (4) of section 7, to treat the application as if it were an application under section 2 (for an order for such
payments as the court may specify) because the court considers that the orders which it has the power to make under section 7

[would not  provide reasonable maintenance for the applicant]

[would not  provide, or make a proper contribution towards, reasonable maintenance for the child(ren) of the family]

* The hearing has been adjourned until            (time) on            (date)

Justices' Clerk

You should complete the tear-off slip below and return it as soon as possible. If you are represented by a solicitor show this form to him
before returning it.

MAT. 7

\* At this hearing the court will have power to make any order for financial provision which it thinks fit on the evidence disclosed. You may feel therefore that it is in your interests to appear at the adjourned hearing.

----------------------------------------------------------------------------------------------------

*Tear off along here*

The *Clerk to the Justices* [Justices' Chief Executive]

.......................................................................................................Magistrates' Court

Address...........................................................................................

.......................................................................................................

Name...............................................................................................

Hearing date...................................................................................

\* I will not contest the application

\* I will contest the application on the following grounds: †

\* Delete whichever is inappropriate

† State briefly your reasons for contesting the application. If your reasons include an allegation about the behaviour of your wife/husband set out the main facts which you will rely on in support of your allegation.

Signed.........................................................................................

Date............................................................................................

**Note.** Words 'Clerk to the Justices' substituted by words 'Justices' Chief Executive' in square brackets by SI 2001/615, r 2(xxiii), Schedule, para 119, as from 1 April 2001.

Rule 3(2)(c)                                    FORM 8

*Omitted*

Rule 12(7)(a)                                FORM 9

### ORDERS UNDER SECTION 2, 6 OR 7 (DPMC Act 1978)

.......................................................................................... Magistrates' Court

Date            [                    ]        Case No      [                    ]

Respondent      [                                    ]

Address         [                                    ]

Child(ren) of the Family      [ Name                          Date of Birth ]

On the application of          [                          ]

Address         [                          ]

Application     [ Particulars                              ]

(section [1] [6] [7] of the Domestic Proceedings and Magistrates' Courts Act 1978)
[The application is granted and] it is ordered that:

MAT. 9

ORDERS FOR FINANCIAL PROVISION

s.2(1)(a)/      [The respondent pay to the applicant £            per
s.6/s.7         from                              until                                    ]


s.2(1)(b)/      [The respondent pay to the applicant a lump sum of £
s.6             (specify conditions of payment)]


s.2(1)(c)/      [The [respondent/applicant] pay [to the applicant/respondent/]
s.6/            for the benefit of (name of child)]
s.7


                [to (name of child)

                £               per              from
                until                                    ]


s.2(1)(d)/      [The [respondent/applicant] pay [to the applicant/respondent]
s.6/s.7         for the benefit of (name of child)]


                [to (name of child)


                a lump sum of £                          (specify conditions of payment)]


                [Payments under the above orders are to be made in the following way:]



                                SUPPLEMENTARY


                [(Any appropriate direction under section 25(2)]


                [The respondent pay costs of £                    to the applicant
                (specify conditions of payment)]



                                                        Justice of the Peace
                                                    [By Order of the Court
                                                        Justices' Clerk]

| Rule 12(7)(a) | FORM 10 |
|---|---|
| | *omitted* |

| Rule 21 | FORM 11 |
|---|---|
| | *omitted* |

| Rule 21 | FORM 12 |
|---|---|
| | *omitted* |

| Rule 20(5) | FORM 13 |
|---|---|
| | *omitted* |

**Note.** The Forms relating to proceedings under Part IV of the Family Law Act 1996 (the FL series) referred to in these rules are published with the full series of these forms with the Family Proceedings Rules 1991, Appendix 1 in Division C of the Service to this Edition.

## SCHEDULE 2

## CONSEQUENTIAL AND MINOR AMENDMENTS

\* \* \* \* \*

**Note.** The amendments are included in the rules as printed.

\* \* \* \* \*

## SCHEDULE 3

## REVOCATIONS

\* \* \* \* \*

## TRANSFER OF FUNCTIONS (MAGISTRATES' COURTS AND FAMILY LAW) ORDER 1992

**Dated** 12 March 1992

**SI 1992 No 709**

*Citation and commencement*

**1.** (1) This Order may be cited as the Transfer of Functions (Magistrates' Courts and Family Law) Order 1992.

(2) This Order shall come into force on 1st April 1992.

*Transfer of functions relating to magistrates' courts and related matters*

**2.** (1) The functions of the Secretary of State under—

(a) the Justices of the Peace Act 1979,

(b) any rules or regulations made under the Act of 1979, and

(c) the provisions specified in Schedule 1 to this Order (which confer functions in respect of magistrates' courts committees, the committee of magistrates, juvenile courts, the powers of magistrates' courts, justices' clerks, proceedings in magistrates' courts and connected matters),

are hereby transferred to the Lord Chancellor.

(2) In paragraph (1) above the reference to rules and regulations made under the Act of 1979 includes a reference to any rules or regulations having effect as if made under the Act or which continue to have effect by virtue of any provision of that Act.

(3) In—

(a) the provisions mentioned in paragraph (1) above, except the provisions mentioned in paragraph (4) below, and

(b) section 20(5) of the Prosecution of Offences Act 1985 (application of section 61(4) of the Act of 1979 to the recovery, under regulations made under section 20, of sums paid by the Legal Aid Board or out of central funds),

for the words 'Secretary of State', wherever they occur, there shall be substituted 'Lord Chancellor'.

(4) The provisions referred to in paragraph (3) above are—

(a) section 38(4) of and Schedule 1 to the Act of 1979; and

(b) in the Justices of the Peace Act 1949 (Compensation) Regulations 1978, in regulation 2(1) (interpretation), the definition of local authority.

(5) In section 38(4) of the Act of 1979 (power of either the Lord Chancellor or the Secretary of State to require committee of magistrates to consider the report on certain matters) the words 'or the Secretary of State' shall be omitted.

(6) In the Petty Sessions Areas (Divisions and Names) Regulations 1988, in regulation 6, for the words 'Home Office, Queen Anne's Gate, London SW1H 9AT by a date' there shall be substituted 'at an address and by a date'.

*Transfer of certain functions relating to family law*

**3.** (1) The functions of the Secretary of State under the provisions specified in Schedule 2 to this Order (which confer miscellaneous functions with respect to family law) are hereby transferred to the Lord Chancellor.

(2) In the provisions specified in that Schedule for the words 'Secretary of State', wherever they occur, there shall be substituted 'Lord Chancellor'.

*Transfer of functions relating to reciprocal enforcement of maintenance orders*

**4.** (1) The functions of the Secretary of State—

(a)  under the Maintenance Orders (Facilities for Enforcement) Act 1920,
(b)  arising by virtue of—
    (i)  paragraph 2 of Schedule 2 to the South Africa Act 1962, or
    (ii)  paragraph 3 of Schedule 2 to the Zimbabwe Act 1979
    (which continue the operation of the Act of 1920 in relation to the Republic of South Africa and Zimbabwe respectively), or
(c)  under any rules made under the Act of 1920,
are hereby transferred to the Lord Chancellor.

(2) In the provisions mentioned in paragraph (1) above (including the provisions of the Act of 1920 continued as mentioned in that paragraph) any reference to the Secretary of State shall be construed as a reference to the Lord Chancellor.

(3) The functions of the Secretary of State—
(a)  under the Maintenance Orders (Reciprocal Enforcement) Act 1972,
(b)  arising by virtue of—
    (i)  the Reciprocal Enforcement of Maintenance Orders (Republic of Ireland) Order 1974 (which applies Part I of the Act of 1972, with modifications, in relation to the Republic of Ireland),
    (ii)  the Reciprocal Enforcement of Maintenance Orders (Hague Convention Countries) Order 1979 (which applies Part I of the Act of 1972, with modifications, in relation to the Hague Convention countries), or
    (iii)  the Recovery of Maintenance (United States of America) Order 1979 (which applies Part II of the Act of 1972, with modifications, in relation to specified States of the United States of America), or
(c)  under any rules or regulations made under or by virtue of the Act of 1972 or by virtue of any Order mentioned in sub-paragraph (b) above,
apart from the functions mentioned in paragraph (4) below, are hereby transferred to the Lord Chancellor.

(4) The functions referred to in paragraph (3) above are the functions of the Secretary of State in so far as they relate to any matter concerning—
(a)  a court in Scotland; or
(b)  a person residing in Scotland or having assets there or believed to reside or have assets there.

(5) In the provisions referred to in paragraph (3) above (including the provisions of the Act of 1972 as applied or modified as mentioned in that paragraph) references to the Secretary of State shall be construed, so far as necessary, as references to the Lord Chancellor.

(6) The functions of the Secretary of State under—
(a)  section 5(1) of the Civil Jurisdiction and Judgments Act 1982 (recognition and enforcement of maintenance orders), and
(b)  any provision of rules 3 to 14 of the Magistrates' Courts (Civil Jurisdiction and Judgements Act 1982) Rules 1986
as respects England and Wales are hereby transferred to the Lord Chancellor.

(7) In section 5(1) of the Act of 1982 for paragraphs (a) and (b) there shall be substituted—
'(a)  as respects England and Wales and Northern Ireland, by the Lord Chancellor; and
(b)  as respects Scotland, by the Secretary of State.'

*Supplementary*

**5.** (1) Any instrument made before the coming into force of this Order shall have effect, so far as may be necessary for the purpose or in consequence of the transfers effected by this Order, as if references to the Secretary of State were references to the Lord Chancellor.

(2) This Order does not affect the validity of anything done by or in relation to the Secretary of State before the coming into force of this Order, and anything which at the time of the coming into force of this Order is in process of being done by or in relation to the Secretary of State may, if it relates to a function transferred by this Order, be continued by or in relation to the Lord Chancellor.

(3) Anything done by the Secretary of State for the purpose of a function transferred by this Order, if in force at the coming into force of this Order, shall have effect, so far as required for continuing its effect after the coming into force of this Order, as if done by the Lord Chancellor.

(4) Documents or forms produced for use in connection with any function transferred by this Order may be used even though they contain references to the Secretary of State and those references shall be construed so far as necessary as references to the Lord Chancellor.

## SCHEDULE 1

FUNCTIONS RELATING TO MAGISTRATES' COURTS ETC TRANSFERRED BY ARTICLE 2

| Title and chapter or number | Provision confirming function |
| --- | --- |
| The Children and Young Persons Act 1933 (c 12). | Schedule 2 (powers with respect to juvenile courts). |
| The Clerks of the Peace and Justices' Clerks (Compensation) Regulations 1965 (SI 1965/517). | Any provision of the Regulations. |
| The Magistrates' Courts Act 1980 (c 43). | Section 68 (powers with respect to combined family panels). |
| | Section 137(4) (power to vary provision made by Part I of Schedule 6 to the act with respect to fees taken by clerks to justices). |
| The Magistrates' Courts Rules 1981 (SI 1981/552). | Rule 66(12) (power to authorise inspection of registers kept by clerks of magistrates' courts). |

\*    \*    \*    \*    \*

## SCHEDULE 2

FUNCTIONS RELATING TO FAMILY LAW TRANSFERRED BY ARTICLE 3

| Title and chapter or number | Provision confirming function |
| --- | --- |
| The Family Law Reform Act 1969 (c 46). | Section 22(1) (power to make regulations as to the manner of giving effect to directions as to scientific tests and the taking of samples for the purposes of establishing paternity). |
| Blood Tests (Evidence of Paternity) Regulations 1971 (SI 1971/1861). | Regulation 2(1) (so far as it confers the function of appointing testers). |
| The Domestic Proceedings and Magistrates' Courts Act 1978 (c 22). | Section 2(3) (power to determine, by order, the maximum amount of lump sum required to be paid under an order of a magistrates' court made in matrimonial proceedings). |

| Title and chapter or number | Provision confirming function |
|---|---|
| The Magistrates' Courts Act 1980 (c 43). | In section 59 (orders for periodical payments: means of payment), subsection (8) (power by regulations to confer on magistrates' courts the power to order that periodical payments be made by a method of payment other than those specified in subsection (3) of the section), subsection (10) (power to apply other enactments to such methods of payment) and subsection (11) (power to be exercised by statutory instrument). In section 94A (interest on arrears), subsection (1) (power by order to provide that a magistrates' court may order that interest shall be paid on arrears under certain maintenance orders), subsection (2) (power to prescribe rate of interest) and subsection (6) (power exercisable by statutory instrument). |
| The Magistrates' Courts (Adoption) Rules 1984 (SI 1984/611). | Rule 32(5)(b)(iii) (authorisation of person to obtain information relating to adoption proceedings for the purposes of research). |
| The Children Act 1989 (c 41). | Section 97(4) (power by order to dispense with ban on publication of material intended or likely to identify children involved in proceedings before magistrates' courts etc). In Schedule 1 (financial provision for children), paragraph 5(2) (power by order to fix maximum amount of lump sum payment). |

## CHILD SUPPORT (INFORMATION, EVIDENCE AND DISCLOSURE) REGULATIONS 1992

**Dated** 20 July 1992

**SI 1992 No 1812**

ARRANGEMENT OF REGULATIONS

Whereas a draft of this instrument was laid before Parliament in accordance with section 52(2) of the Child Support Act 1991 and approved by a resolution of each House of Parliament:

Now, therefore, the Secretary of State for Social Security, in exercise of the powers conferred by section 4(4), 6(9), 7(5), 14(1) and (3), 50(5), 51, 54 and 57 of, and paragraphs 16(10) of Schedule 1 to and 2(4) of Schedule 2 to, the Child Support Act 1991 and of all other powers enabling him in that behalf, hereby makes the following Regulations—

PART I

GENERAL

*Citation, commencement and interpretation*

**1.**   (1) These Regulations may be cited as the Child Support (Information, Evidence and Disclosure) Regulations 1992 and shall come into force on 5th April 1993.

(2) In these Regulations, unless the context otherwise requires—

"the Act" means the Child Support Act 1991;

"appropriate authority" means—

   (a) in relation to housing benefit, the housing or local authority concerned; and

   (b) in relation to council tax benefit, the billing authority or, in Scotland, the levying authority;

*"local authority" means, in relation to England and Wales, the council of a county, a metropolitan district, a London Borough or the Common Council of the City of London and, in relation to Scotland, a regional council or an islands council;*

["local authority" means, in relation to England, a county council, a district council, a London borough council, the Common Council of the City of London or the Council of the Isles of Scilly and, in relation to Wales, a county council or a county borough council and, in relation to Scotland, a council constituted under section 2 of the Local Government etc (Scotland) Act 1994;]

*"Maintenance Assessments and Special Cases Regulations" means the Child Support (Maintenance Assessments and Special Cases) Regulations 1992;*

["Maintenance Calculations and Special Cases Regulations" means the Child Support (Maintenance Calculations and Special Cases) Regulations 2000;]

*"Maintenance Assessment Procedure Regulations" means the Child Support (Maintenance Assessment Procedure) Regulations 1992;*

["Maintenance Calculation Procedure Regulations" means the Child Support (Maintenance Calculation Procedure) Regulations 2000;]

"parent with care" means a person who, in respect of the same child or children, is both a parent and a person with care;

"related proceedings" means proceedings in which a relevant court order was or is being sought;

"relevant court order" means—

    (a) an order as to periodical or capital provision or as to variation of property rights made under an enactment specified in paragraphs (a) to (e) of section 8(11) of the Act or prescribed under section 8(11)(f) of the Act in relation to a qualifying child or a relevant person; or

    (b) an order under Part II of the Children Act 1989 (Orders With Respect To Children In Family Proceedings) in relation to a qualifying child or, in Scotland, an order under section 3 of the Law Reform (Parent and Child) (Scotland) Act 1986 or a decree of declarator under section 7 of that Act in relation to a qualifying child;

"relevant person" means—

    (a) a person with care;

    (b) an *absent parent* [a non-resident parent];

    (c) a parent who is treated as *an absent parent* [a non-resident parent] under *regulation 20 of the Maintenance Assessments and Special Cases Regulations* [regulation 8 of the Maintenance Calculations and Special Cases Regulations];

    (d) where the application for an *assessment* [a calculation] is made by a child under section 7 of the Act, that child,

in respect of whom *a maintenance assessment has been applied for or is or has been in force* [a maintenance calculation has been applied for, or has been treated as applied for under section 6(3) of the Act, or is or has been in force].

(3) In these Regulations, unless the context otherwise requires, a reference—

    (a) to a numbered regulation is to the regulation in these Regulations bearing that number;

    (b) in a regulation to a numbered paragraph is to the paragraph in that regulation bearing that number;

    (c) in a paragraph to a lettered or numbered sub-paragraph is to the sub-paragraph in that paragraph bearing that letter or number.

**Note.** In para (2): definition "local authority" substituted, definition "Maintenance Assessments and Special Cases Regulations" substituted by subsequent definition "Maintenance Calculations and Special Cases Regulations", definition "Maintenance Assessment Procedure Regulations" substituted by subsequent definition "Maintenance Calculation Procedure Regulations", in definition "relevant person" in paras (b), (c) words "an absent parent" substituted by words "a non-resident parent" in square brackets, in para (c) words "regulation 20 of the Maintenance Assessments and Special Cases Regulations" substituted by words "regulation 8 of the Maintenance Calculations and Special Cases Regulations" in square brackets, in para (d) words "an assessment" substituted by words "a calculation" in square brackets and words "a maintenance assessment has been applied for or is or has been in force" substituted by words from "a maintenance calculation" to "has been in force" in square brackets, by SI 2001/161, regs 2(1), (2), 3(1)(a), (b), (2), 5(1)(a), (b) as from 3 March 2003 in relation to certain cases: for effect see SI 2001/161, reg 1(3)(d) (and SI 2003/192, arts 3, 8, Schedule) and for transitional provisions see reg 10(Z1), (1), (3) thereof.

PART II

FURNISHING OF INFORMATION OR EVIDENCE

*Persons under a duty to furnish information or evidence*

**2.** *(1) Where an application for a maintenance assessment [or for a review of a maintenance assessment] has been made under the Act, [or a child support officer is conducting or proposing to conduct a review under section 19 of the Act,] a person falling* *within a category listed in paragraph (2) shall, subject to the restrictions specified in that paragraph, furnish such information or evidence as is required by the Secretary of State [or a child support officer] and which is needed to enable a determination to be made in relation to one or more of the matters listed in regulation 3(1), and the person concerned has that information or evidence in his possession or can reasonably be expected to acquire that information or evidence.*

[(1) A person falling within a category listed in paragraph (2) shall furnish such information or evidence—

    (a)  with respect to the matter or matters specified in that paragraph in relation to that category; and

    (b)  which is in his possession or which he can reasonably be expected to acquire,

as is required by the Secretary of State *to enable a decision to be made under section 11, 12, 16 or 17 of the Act* [and is needed for any of the purposes specified in regulation 3(1)].]

[*(1A) A person falling within paragraph (2)(a) or (e) shall furnish such information or evidence as is required by the Secretary of State and is needed by him to enable a decision to be made in relation to the matters listed in regulation 3(1)(h) and (hh) where the person concerned has that information or evidence in his possession or can reasonably be expected to acquire it.*]

[(1A) In such cases as the Secretary of State may determine, a person falling within a category listed in paragraph (2) shall furnish such information or evidence as the Secretary of State may determine which is information or evidence—

    (a)  with respect to the matter or matters specified in that paragraph in relation to that category;

    (b)  needed by the Secretary of State for the purpose specified in regulation 3(1A); and

    (c)  in that person's possession or which that person can reasonably be expected to acquire.]

(2) The persons who may be required to furnish information or evidence, and the matter or matters with respect to which such information or evidence may be required, are as follows—

    (a)  the relevant persons, with respect to the matters listed in regulation 3(1);

[(aa) where regulation 8(1) of the Maintenance Calculations and Special Cases Regulations applies (persons treated as non-resident parents), a parent of or a person who provides day to day care for the child in respect of whom a maintenance calculation has been applied for or has been treated as applied for or is or has been in force, with respect to the matter listed in sub-paragraph (1) of regulation 3(1);]

    (b)  a person who is alleged to be a parent of a child with respect to whom an application for a maintenance *assessment has been made* [calculation has been made, or has been treated as made], or in relation to whom a maintenance *assessment has been made* [calculation has been made, or has been treated as made] *in respect of which a child support officer is conducting or proposing to conduct a review and that person*] denies that he is one of that child's parents, with respect to the matters listed in sub-paragraphs (b) and (d) of regulation 3(1);

[(ba) the current or recent employer of a person falling within sub-paragraph (b), with respect to the matters listed in sub-paragraphs (d) and (e) of regulation 3(1);]

    (c)  the current or recent employer of the *absent parent* [non-resident parent] *or the parent with care* in relation to whom an application for a maintenance *assessment has been made* [calculation has been made, or has been treated as made,] [or in relation to whom a maintenance *assessment has been made* [calculation has been made, or has been treated as made,] *and a child support officer is conducting or proposing to conduct a review of that assessment]*, with respect to the matters listed in sub-paragraphs (d), (e), (f), (h)[, (hh)] and (j) of regulation 3(1);

[(cc) persons employed in the service of the Crown or otherwise in the discharge of Crown functions, where they are the current or recent employer of the *absent parent* [non-resident parent] *or the parent with care* in relation to whom an application for a maintenance *assessment has been made* [calculation has been made, or has been treated as made,] [or in relation to whom a maintenance *assessment has been made* [calculation has been made, or has been treated as made,] *and a child support officer is conducting or proposing to conduct a review of that assessment]*, with respect to the matters listed in sub-paragraphs (d), (e), (f), (h)[, (hh)] and (j) of regulation 3(1);

(cd) persons employed in the service of the Crown or otherwise in the discharge of Crown functions, where they are the current or recent employer of a person falling within sub-paragraph (b), with respect to the matters listed in sub-paragraphs (d) and (e) of regulation 3(1);]

(d) the local authority in whose area a person falling within a category listed in sub-paragraphs (a) and (b) above resides or has resided, with respect to the *matter* [matters] listed in sub-paragraph (a)[, (d), (e), (f), (h) and (hh)] of regulation 3(1);

(e) a person specified in paragraph (3) below, in any case where, in relation to the qualifying child or qualifying children or the *absent parent* [non-resident parent]—
  (i)  there is or has been a relevant court order; or
  (ii) there have been, or are pending, related proceedings before a court,
with respect to the matters listed in sub-paragraphs [(aa), (ab),] (g), (h) and (k) of regulation 3(1);

[(f) a person who acts or has acted as an accountant for the absent parent, including where that person is self-employed, in relation to any business accounts of that parent with respect to the matters listed in sub-paragraphs (e), (f), (h) and (hh) of regulation 3(1);

(g) a company or partnership for whom the absent parent is providing or has provided services under a contract for services with respect to the matters listed in sub-paragraphs (e) and (f) of regulation 3(1); and

(h) persons employed in the service of the Crown or otherwise in the discharge of Crown functions—
  (i)  under [the Road Traffic (Northern Ireland) Order 1981,] sections 97 to 99A of the Road Traffic Act 1988 or Part II of the Vehicle Excise and Registration Act 1994 with respect to the matter listed in sub-paragraph (e) of regulation 3(1); or
  (ii) under the Prison Act 1952[, the Prison Act (Northern Ireland) 1953 or the Prisons (Scotland) Act 1989] with respect to the matter listed in sub-paragraph (e) of regulation 3(1)].

(3) The persons who may be required to furnish information or evidence in relation to a relevant court order or related proceedings under the provisions of paragraph (2)(e) are—
  (a) in England and Wales—
    (i)   in relation to the High Court, the senior district judge of the principal registry of the Family Division or, where proceedings were instituted in a district registry, the district judge;
    (ii)  in relation to a county court, the proper officer of that court within the meaning of Order 1, Rule 3 of the County Court Rules 1981;
    (iii) in relation to a magistrates' court, the *clerk to the justices of* [justices' chief executive for] that court;

(b) in Scotland—
    (i) in relation to the Court of Session, the Deputy Principal Clerk of Session;
    (ii) in relation to a sheriff court, the sheriff clerk.

**Note.** Original para (1) substituted by SI 1999/1510, art 6(a) as from 1 June 1999. Words in square brackets therein inserted by SI 1995/3261, reg 7(2). In new para (1) words "to enable a decision to be made under section 11, 12, 16 or 17 of the Act" substituted by words "and is needed for any of the purposes specified in regulation 3(1)" in square brackets by SI 2003/3206, reg 2(1), (2)(a) as from 7 January 2004 (only for the purposes of any case in respect of which the Child Support, Pensions and Social Security Act 2000, s 12 has not come into force and for so long as that section is not in force for the purposes of such a case): see SI 2003/3206, reg 1(2), (3).

Para (1A): inserted by SI 1996/1945, reg 7(2); substituted by SI 2003/3206, reg 2(1), (2)(b) as from 7 January 2004 (only for the purposes of any case in respect of which the Child Support, Pensions and Social Security Act 2000, s 12 has not come into force and for so long as that section is not in force for the purposes of such a case): see SI 2003/3206, reg 1(2), (3).

Para (2)(aa) inserted by SI 2002/1204, reg 4(a) as from 3 March 2003 in relation to certain cases: for effect see SI 2002/1204, reg 1(3)(b) and SI 2003/192, arts 3, 8, Schedule.

In para (2)(b) words from "assessment has been made" to "and that person" in square brackets substituted by SI 1995/3261, reg 7(3), (4).

In para (2)(b), (c), (cc) words "assessment has been made" substituted by words "calculation has been made, or has been treated as made" in square brackets by SI 2001/161, reg 5(2)(c) as from 3 March 2003 in relation to certain cases: for transitional provisions see reg 10(Z1), (1), (3) thereof. In para (2)(b) words "in respect of which a child support officer is conducting or proposing to conduct a review" revoked by SI 1999/1510, art 6(b)(i) as from 1 June 1999.

Para (2)(ba) inserted by SI 1995/123, reg 2.

In para (2)(c) words "absent parent" substituted by words "non-resident parent" in square brackets by SI 2001/161, reg 2(1) as from 3 March 2003 in relation to certain cases: for effect see SI 2001/161, reg 1(3)(d) and SI 2003/192, arts 3, 8, Schedule. In para (2)(c), (cc) words "or the parent with care" revoked by SI 2001/161, reg 5(2)(a) as from 3 March 2003 in relation to certain cases: for effect see SI 2001/161, reg 1(3)(d) and SI 2003/192, arts 3, 8, Schedule. In para (2)(c) words beginning with the words "or in relation to" in square brackets inserted by SI 1995/3261, reg 7(1), (4).

In para (2)(c), (cc) words "and a child support officer is conducting or proposing to conduct a review of that assessment" revoked by SI 1999/1510, art 6(b)(ii) as from 1 June 1999 and references to ", (hh)" in square brackets inserted by SI 2001/161, reg 5(2)(b) as from 31 January 2001 (for effect see reg 1(3)(a)). Para (2)(cc), (cd) inserted by SI 1995/1045, reg 22. In para (2)(cc) words "absent parent" substituted by words "non-resident parent" in square brackets by SI 2001/161, reg 2(1) as from 3 March 2003 in relation to certain cases: for effect see SI 2001/161, reg 1(3)(d) and SI 2003/192, arts 3, 8, Schedule. In para (2)(cc) words beginning with the words "or in relation to" in square brackets inserted by SI 1995/3261, reg 7(1), (4).

In para (2)(d) word "matter" substituted by word "matters" in square brackets by SI 2001/161, reg 5(2)(d)(i) as from 31 January 2001 (for effect see reg 1(3)(a)). In para (2)(d) words ", (d), (e), (f), (h) and (hh)" in square brackets inserted by SI 2001/161, reg 5(2)(d)(ii) as from 31 January 2001 (for effect see reg 1(3)(a)).

In para (2)(e) words "absent parent" substituted by words "non-resident parent" in square brackets by SI 2001/161, reg 2(1) as from 3 March 2003 in relation to certain cases: for effect see SI 2001/161, reg 1(3)(d) and SI 2003/192, arts 3, 8, Schedule. In para (2)(e) words "(aa), (ab)," in square brackets inserted by SI 1996/1945, reg 7(3).

Para (2)(f)–(h) inserted by SI 2001/161, reg 5(2)(e) as from 30 January 2001 (for effect see SI 2001/161, reg 1(3)(a)). In para (2)(h)(i) words "the Road Traffic (Northern Ireland) Order 1981," in square brackets inserted by SI 2002/1204, reg 4(b)(i) as from 30 April 2002. In para (2)(h)(ii) words ", the Prison Act (Northern Ireland) 1953 or the Prisons (Scotland) Act 1989" in square brackets inserted by SI 2002/1204, reg 4(b)(ii) as from 30 April 2002.

In para (3)(a)(iii) words "clerk to the justices of" substituted by words "justices' chief executive for" in square brackets by SI 2001/161, reg 4 as from 1 April 2001.

*Purposes for which information or evidence may be required*

**3.** (1) The Secretary of State [*or a child support officer*] may require information or evidence under the provisions of regulation 2 only if that information or evidence is needed to enable—

(a) a decision to be made as to whether, in relation to an application for a maintenance *assessment* [calculation], there exists a qualifying child, *an absent parent* [a non-resident parent] and a person with care;

[(aa) a decision to be made as to whether there is in force a written maintenance agreement made before 5th April 1993, or a maintenance order [made on or after the date prescribed for the purposes of section 4(10)(a) of the Act which has been in force for at least a year from the date it was made], in relation to a qualifying child and the person who is at that time the *absent parent* [non-resident parent] of that child;

(ab) a decision to be made as to whether a person with care has parental responsibility for a qualifying child for the purposes of section 5(1) of the Act;]

(b) a decision to be made as to whether *a child support officer* [the Secretary of State] has jurisdiction to make a maintenance *assessment* [calculation] under section 44 of the Act;

(c) a decision to be made, where more than one application has been made, as to which application is to be proceeded with;

(d) *an absent parent* [a non-resident parent] to be identified;

(e) *an absent parent* [a non-resident parent] to be traced;

(f) the amount of child support maintenance payable by an absent parent [a non-resident parent] to be *assessed* [calculated];

(g) the amount payable under a relevant court order to be ascertained;

(h) the amounts specified in sub-paragraphs (f) and (g) to be recovered from *an absent parent* [a non-resident parent];

[(hh) a decision to be made as to whether to take action under section 35(1) or 38(1) of the Act or to apply under section 36(1) of the Act for an order for recovery by means of garnishee proceedings or a charging order;]

(i) the amount of interest payable with respect to arrears of child support maintenance to be determined;

(j) the amount specified in sub-paragraph (i) to be recovered from an *absent parent* [a non-resident parent];

(k) any related proceedings to be identified;

[(l) a determination as to who is in receipt of child benefit, payable under Part IX of the Social Security Contributions and Benefits Act 1992, either for a child who may be a relevant other child for the purposes of Schedule 1 to the Act, or for the qualifying child where a parent may fall to be treated as a non-resident parent under the Maintenance Calculations and Special Cases Regulations].

[(1A) The Secretary of State may require information or evidence to be provided under the provisions of regulation 2(1A) only for the purpose of verifying whether information or evidence which he holds, or has held, is correct.]

(2) The information or evidence to be furnished in accordance with regulation 2 may in particular include information and evidence as to—

(a) the habitual residence of the person with care, the *absent parent* [non-resident parent] and any child in respect of whom *an application for a maintenance assessment has been made* [the maintenance calculation has been applied for, or has been treated as applied for];

(b) the name and address of the person with care and of the *absent parent* [non-resident parent], their marital status, and the relationship of the person with care to any child in respect of whom *the application for a maintenance* assessment has been made [the maintenance calculation has been applied for, or has been treated as applied for];

(c) the name, address and date of birth of any such child, that child's marital status, and any education that child is undergoing;

(d) the persons who have parental responsibility for (*or* [and], in Scotland, parental rights over) any qualifying child where there is more than one person with care;

(e) the time spent by a qualifying child in respect of whom *an application for a maintenance assessment has been made* [the maintenance calculation has been applied for, or has been treated as applied for] with each person with care, where there is more than one such person;

(f) the matters relevant for determining, in a case falling within section 26 of the Act (disputes about parentage), whether that case falls within one of the Cases set out in subsection (2) of that section, and if it does not, the matters relevant for determining the parentage of a child whose parentage is in dispute;

(g) the name and address of any current or recent employer of *an absent parent* [a non-resident parent] *or a parent with care*, and the gross earnings and the deductions from those earnings deriving from each employment;

(h) the address from which *an absent parent* [a non-resident parent] *or parent with care* who is self-employed carries on his trade or business, the trading name, [the total taxable profits derived from his employment as a self-employed earner, as submitted to, or as issued to him by, the Inland Revenue,] and the gross receipts and expenses and other outgoings of the trade or business;

(i) any other income of *an absent parent* [a non-resident parent] *and a parent with care*;

(j) *any income, other than earnings, of a qualifying child;*

(k) amounts payable and paid under a relevant court order or a maintenance agreement;

(l) the persons living in the same household as the *absent parent* [non-resident parent] *or living in the same household as the parent with care*, their relationship to the *absent parent* [non-resident parent] *or the parent with care, as the case may be*, and to each other, and, in the case of the children of any such party, the dates of birth of those children;

(m) *the matters set out in sub-paragraphs (g) and (h) in relation to the persons specified in sub-paragraph (l) other than any children living in the same household as the absent parent or the parent with care, as the case may be;*

(n) *income other than earnings of the persons living in the same household as the absent parent or the parent with care;*

(o) *benefits related to disability that the absent parent, parent with care and other persons living in the same household as the absent parent or the parent with care are entitled to or would be entitled to if certain conditions were satisfied;*

(p) *the housing costs to be taken into account for the purposes of determining assessable or disposable income [any application made under the Act or any question arising in connection with such an application];*

(q) the identifying details of any bank, building society or similar account held in the name of the *absent parent* [non-resident parent] *or the person with care*, and statements relating to any such account;

(r) the matters relevant for determining whether—

    (i) a maintenance *assessment* [calculation] has ceased to have effect *or should be cancelled* under the provisions of paragraph 16 of Schedule 1 to the Act;

    (ii) a person is a child within the meaning of section 55 of the Act;

[(s)  the making of, and the amount of, any qualifying transfer or compensating transfer
     within the meaning of Schedule 3A to the Maintenance Assessments and Special
     Cases Regulations.]

**Note.** In para (1) words "or a child support officer" in square brackets inserted by
SI 1995/3261, reg 8, revoked by SI 1999/1510, art 7(a) as from 1 June 1999: see
SI 1999/1510, art 3(1). In paras (1)(a), (b), 2(r)(i) word "assessment" substituted by
words "calculation" in square brackets by SI 2001/161, reg 2(2) as from 3 March 2003 in
relation to certain cases: for effect see SI 2001/161, reg 1(3)(d) and SI 2003/192, arts 3,
8, Schedule. In paras (1)(a), (d)–(f), (h), (j), (2)(g)–(i) words "an absent parent"
substituted by words "a non-resident parent" in square brackets by SI 2001/161, reg 2(1)as
from 3 March 2003 in relation to certain cases: for effect see SI 2001/161, reg 1(3)(d) and
SI 2003/192, arts 3, 8, Schedule. Para (1)(aa), (ab), (hh) inserted by SI 1996/1945,
reg 8(2), (3). In para (1)(aa) words from "made on or after" to "it was made" in square
brackets inserted by SI 2001/161, reg 6(1)(a) as from 3 March 2003 in relation to certain
cases: for effect see SI 2001/161, reg 1(3)(d) and SI 2003/192, arts 3, 8, Schedule. In
paras (1)(aa), (2)(a), (b), (l), (q) words "absent parent" in each place substituted by
words "non-resident parent" in square brackets by SI 2001/161, reg 2(1) as from 3 March
2003 in relation to certain cases: for effect see SI 2001/161, reg 1(3)(d) and SI 2003/192,
arts 3, 8, Schedule. In para (1)(b) words "a child support officer" substituted by words
"the Secretary of State" in square brackets by SI 1999/1510, art 7(b) as from 1 June 1999.
In para (1)(f) word "assessed" substituted by word "calculated" in square brackets by
SI 2001/161, reg 2(3) as from 3 March 2003 in relation to certain cases: for effect
see SI 2001/161, reg 1(3)(d) and SI 2003/192, arts 3, 8, Schedule. Para (1)(l) inserted
by SI 2001/161, reg 6(1)(b) as from 3 March 2003 in relation to certain cases: for effect
see SI 2001/161, reg 1(3)(d) and SI 2003/192, arts 3, 8, Schedule.

   Para (1A) inserted by SI 2003/3206, reg 2(1), (3) as from 7 January 2004 (only for the
purposes of any case in respect of which the Child Support, Pensions and Social Security
Act 2000, s 12 has not come into force and for so long as that section is not in force for the
purposes of such a case): see SI 2003/3206, reg 1(2), (3).

   In para (2)(a), (e) words "an application for a maintenance assessment has been made"
substituted by words "the maintenance calculation has been applied for, or has been
treated as applied for" in square brackets by SI 2001/161, reg 6(2)(a) as from 3 March
2003 in relation to certain cases: for effect see SI 2001/161, reg 1(3)(d) and SI 2003/192,
arts 3, 8, Schedule. In para (2)(b) words "the application for a maintenance assessment
has been made" substituted by words "the maintenance calculation has been applied for,
or has been treated as applied for" in square brackets by SI 2001/161, reg 6(2)(a) as from
3 March 2003 in relation to certain cases: for effect see SI 2001/161, reg 1(3)(d) and
SI 2003/192, arts 3, 8, Schedule. In para (2)(d) word "or" substituted by word "and" in
square brackets by SI 1998/58, reg 32(a) as from 19 January 1998. In para (2)(g) words
"or a parent with care", in para (2)(h) words "or parent with care" and in para (2)(j)
words "and a parent with care" revoked by SI 2001/161, reg 6(2)(b)(i)–(iii) as from
3 March 2003 in relation to certain cases: for effect see SI 2001/161, reg 1(3)(d) and
SI 2003/192, arts 3, 8, Schedule. In para (2)(h) words from "the total taxable" to "the
Inland Revenue," in square brackets inserted by SI 1999/977, reg 4(1), (2) as from
4 October 1999. In para (2)(j), (m)–(p) revoked by SI 2001/161, reg 6(2)(c) as from
3 March 2003 in relation to certain cases: for effect see SI 2001/161, reg 1(3)(d) and
SI 2003/192, arts 3, 8, Schedule. In para (2)(l) words "or living in the same household as
the parent with care" and words "or the parent with care, as the case may be" revoked by
SI 2001/161, reg 6(2)(b)(iv) as from 3 March 2003 in relation to certain cases: for effect
see SI 2001/161, reg 1(3)(d) and SI 2003/192, arts 3, 8, Schedule. In para (2)(p) words
"assessable or disposable income" substituted by words "any application made under the
Act or any question arising in connection with such an application" in square brackets by
SI 1998/58, reg 32(b) as from 19 January 1998. In para (2)(q) words "or the person with
care" revoked by SI 2001/161, reg 6(2)(b)(v) as from 3 March 2003 in relation to certain
cases: for effect see SI 2001/161, reg 1(3)(d) and SI 2003/192, arts 3, 8, Schedule. In para
(2)(r)(i) words "or should be cancelled" revoked by SI 2001/161, reg 6(2)(b)(vi) as from
3 March 2003 in relation to certain cases: for effect see SI 2001/161, reg 1(3)(d) and
SI 2003/192, arts 3, 8, Schedule. Para (2)(s) inserted by SI 1995/1045, reg 23; revoked
by SI 2001/161, reg 6(2)(c) as from 3 March 2003 in relation to certain cases: for effect
see SI 2001/161, reg 1(3)(d) and SI 2003/192, arts 3, 8, Schedule.

*Contents of request for information or evidence*

**3A.**    [Any request by the Secretary of State in accordance with regulations 2 and 3 for the provision of information or evidence shall set out the possible consequences of failure to provide such information or evidence [including details of the offences provided for in section 14A of the Act for failure to provide, or providing false, information].]

**Note.** Inserted by SI 1995/326, reg 9; substituted by SI 1999/1510, art 8 as from 1 June 1999. Words from 'including details of' to 'providing false, information' in square brackets by SI 2001/161, reg 6(3) as from 1 January 2001.

**4.**    <. . .>

**Note.** Revoked by SI 2001/161, reg 7(1) as from 31 January 2001.

*Time within which information or evidence is to be furnished*

**5.**    (1) Subject to *paragraph (2) and* the provisions of *regulations 2(5), 6(1) and 17(5) of the Maintenance Assessment Procedure Regulations* [regulation 3(4) of the Maintenance Calculation Procedure Regulations], information or evidence furnished in accordance with regulations 2 and 3 shall be furnished as soon as is reasonably practicable in the particular circumstances of the case.

(2) <. . .>

**Note.** Amended by SI 1999/1510, art 9(a) as from 1 June 1999 and by SI 2001/161, reg 3 as from a day to be appointed.

*Continuing duty of persons with care*

**6.**    Where a person with care with respect to whom a maintenance *assessment* [calculation] has been made believes that, by virtue of section 44 or 55 of, or paragraph 16 of Schedule 1 to, the Act, the *assessment* [calculation] has ceased to have effect *or should be cancelled*, she shall, as soon as is reasonably practicable, inform the Secretary of State of that belief, and of the reasons for it, and shall provide such other information as the Secretary of State may reasonably require, with a view to assisting the Secretary of State *or a child support officer* in determining whether the *assessment* [calculation] has ceased to have effect, *or should be cancelled*.

**Note.** Word 'assessment' in each place substituted by word 'calculation' by SI 2001/161, reg 2 as from 3 March 2003 in relation to certain cases and words 'or should be cancelled' revoked by SI 2001/161, reg 7 as from 3 March in relation to certain cases: for further effect see reg 10 thereof. Words 'or a child support officer' revoked by SI 1999/1510, art 10 as from 1 June 1999.

*Powers of inspectors in relation to Crown residences*

**7.**    Subject to Her Majesty not being in residence, an inspector appointed under section 15 of the Act may enter any Crown premises for the purpose of exercising any powers conferred on him by that section.

PART III

DISCLOSURE OF INFORMATION

*Disclosure of information to a court or tribunal*

**8.**    [(1)] The Secretary of State or *a child support officer* may disclose any information held by *them* [him] for the purposes of the Act to—
(a)  a court;
(b)  any tribunal or other body or person mentioned in the Act;
(c)  *any tribunal or other body or person mentioned in the Act;*

[(cc) a person with a right of appeal under the Act to an appeal tribunal,]
where such disclosure is made for the purposes of any proceedings before any of
those bodies relating to this Act *or to the benefit Acts* [, to the benefit Acts or to the
Jobseekers Act 1995].

[(2) For the purposes of this regulation 'proceedings' includes the determination of an application referred to *a child support* [an] appeal tribunal under
section 28D(1)(b) of the Act.]

[(3) The Secretary of State *or a child support officer* may disclose information held
by *them* [him] for the purposes of the Act to a court in any case where—

(a) that court has exercised any power it has to make, vary or revive a
maintenance order or to vary a maintenance agreement; and

(b) such disclosure is made for the purposes of any proceedings before that
court in relation to that maintenance order or that maintenance agreement
or for the purposes of any matters arising out of those proceedings.]

**Notes.** Para (1) numbered as such by SI 1996/2907, reg 63. In para (1) words 'or a child
support officer' revoked, and word 'them' substituted by word 'him' in square brackets by
SI 1999/1510, art 11(a)(i), (ii) as from 1 June 1999: see SI 1999/1510, art 3(1). Para (1)(c)
revoked by SI 1999/1510, art 11(a)(iii) as from 29 November 1999. Para (1)(cc) inserted by
SI 2004/2415, reg 3 as from 16 September 2004 for certain purposes (see SI 2004/2415, reg
1(2)(b)(i)) and in respect of remaining purposes this amendment shall come into force on
the day on which the Child Support, Pensions and Social Security Act 2000, ss 1(2), 8, 9,
Sch 3, para 11(2), (7) come into force for remaining purposes: see SI 2004/2415,
reg 1(2)(b)(ii). In para (1) words 'or to the benefit Acts' substituted by words ', to the benefit
Acts or to the Jobseekers Act 1995' in square brackets by SI 1998/58, reg 33(2) as from 19
January 1998.

Para (2) inserted by SI 1996/2907, reg 63. In para (2) words 'a child support' substituted
by word "an" in square brackets by SI 1999/1510, art 11(b) as from 1 June 1999.

Para (3) inserted by SI 1998/58, reg 33(3) as from 19 January 1998. In para (3) words 'or a
child support officer' revoked by SI 1999/1510, art 11(c)(i) as from 1 June 1999. In para (3)
word "them" substituted by word "him" in square brackets by SI 1999/1510, art 11(c)(ii) as
from 1 June 1999.

**9.** <. . .>

**Note.** Revoked by SI 1999/977, reg 4(1), (3) as from 6 April 1999.

[*Disclosure of information to other persons*

**9A.** (1) The Secretary of State or *a child support officer* may disclose information
*given to him by* [held by him for the purposes of the Act relating to] one party to a
maintenance *assessment* [calculation] to another party to that *assessment* [calculation]
where, in the opinion of the Secretary of State or *a child support officer*,
such information is essential to inform the party to whom it would be given
as to—

(a) *why an application for a maintenance assessment under section 4, 6 or 7 of the Act*
[why he has decided not to make a maintenance calculation in response to
an application made under section 4 or 7 of the Act or treated as made
under section 6 of the Act], or an application for *a review under section 17 or
18 of the Act* [revision under section 16 of the Act or a decision under section
17 of the Act superseding an earlier decision] has been rejected;

(b) why, although an application for a maintenance *assessment* [calculation]
referred to in sub-paragraph (a) has been accepted, that *assessment* [calcula-
tion] cannot, at the time in question, be proceeded with or why a maintenance
*assessment* [calculation] will not be made following that application;

(c) *why a mainenance assessment* [calculation] has ceased to have effect *or has
been cancelled;*

(d) how a maintenance *assessment* [calculation] has been calculated, in so far as
the matter has been dealt with by the notification given under *regulation 10*

*of the Maintenance Assessment Procedure Regulations* [regulation 23 of the Maintenance Calculation Procedure Regulations];

[(e)  why a decision has been made not to arrange for, or to cease, collection of any child support maintenance under section 29 of the Act;

(f)  why a particular method of enforcement, under section 31, 33, 35, 36, 38 or 40 of the Act of an amount due under a maintenance *assessment* [calculation] has been adopted in a particular case; or

(g)  why a decision has been made not to enforce, or to cease to enforce, under section 31 or 33 of the Act the amount due under a maintenance *assessment* [calculation].]

(2)  For the purposes of this regulation, 'party to a maintenance *assessment* [calculation]' means—

(a)  a relevant person;

(b)  a person appointed by the Secretary of State under regulation *regulation 3A of the Child Support Appeal Tribunals (Procedure) Regulations 1992* [34 of the Social Security and Child Support (Decisions and Appeals) Regulations 1999];

[(c)  the personal representative of a relevant person where—

(i)  a *review* [revision, supersession] or appeal was pending at the date of death of that person and the personal representative is dealing with that *review* [revision, supersession] or appeal on behalf of that person; or

(ii)  an application for a *departure direction* [variation] has been made but not determined at the date of death of that person and the personal representative is dealing *with that application on behalf of that person* [on behalf of that person with any matters arising in connection with the determination of that application].]

(3)  Any application for informaton under this regulation shall be made to the Secretary of State or *a child support officer* in writing setting out the reasons for the application.

(4)  Except where a person gives written permission to the Secretary of State or *a child support officer* that the information in relation to him mentioned in sub-paragraphs (a) and (b) below may be conveyed to other persons, any information given under the provisions of paragraph (1) shall not contain—

(a)  the address of any person other than the recipient of the information in question (other than the address of the office of *the child support officer concerned* [the officer concerned who is exercising functions of the Secretary of State under the Act]) or any other information the use of which could reasonably be expected to lead to any such person being located;

(b)  any other information the use of which could reasonably be expected to lead to any person, other than a qualifying child or a relevant person, being identified.]

**Note.** Inserted by SI 1995/1045, reg 24.

In para (1) words 'or a child support officer' revoked by SI 1999/1510, art 12(a) as from 1 June 1999. In para (1) words 'given to him' substituted by words 'held by him for the purposes of the Act relating to' in square brackets by SI 1999/977, reg 4(1), (4) as from 6 April 1999. In paras (1), (2) word 'assessment' in each place it occurs substituted by word 'calculation' in square brackets by SI 2001/161, reg 2(2) as from 3 March 2003 in relation to certain cases: for effect see SI 2001/161, reg 1(3)(d) and SI 2003/192, arts 3, 8, Schedule. In para (1)(a) words 'why an application for a maintenance assessment under section 4, 6 or 7 of the Act' substituted by words from 'why he has' to 'section 6 of the Act' in square brackets by SI 2001/161, reg 7(3)(a) as from 3 March 2003 in relation to certain cases: for effect see SI 2001/161, reg 1(3)(d) and SI 2003/192, arts 3, 8, Schedule. In para (1)(a) words 'review under section 17 or 18 of the Act' substituted by words from 'revision under section 16' to 'an earlier decision' in square brackets by SI 1999/1510, art 12(b) as from 1 June 1999. In para (1)(c) words 'or has been cancelled' revoked by SI 2001/161, reg 7(3)(b) as from 3 March

2003 in relation to certain cases: for effect see SI 2001/161, reg 1(3)(d) and SI 2003/192, arts 3, 8, Schedue. In para (1)(d) words 'regulation 10 of the Maintenance Assessment Procedure Regulations' substituted by words 'regulation 23 of the Maintenance Calculation Procedure Regulations' in square brackets by SI 2001/161, reg 3(3)(b) as from 3 March 2003 in relation to certain cases: for effect see SI 2001/161, reg 1(3)(d) and SI 2003/192, arts 3, 8, Schedue. Para (1)(e)–(g) inserted by SI 1995/3261, reg 11.

In para (2)(b) words 'regulation 3A of the Child Support Appeal Tribunals (Procedure) Regulations 1992' substituted by words '34 of the Social Security and Child Support (Decisions and Appeals) Regulations 1999' in square brackets by SI 1999/1510, art 12(c)(i) as from 1 June 1999. Para (2)(c) substituted by SI 1996/2907, reg 64.

In para (2)(c)(i) word 'review' in both places substituted by words 'revision, supesession' in square brackets by SI 1999/1510, art 12(c)(ii) as from 1 June 1999. In para (2)(c)(ii) words 'departure direction' substituted by word 'variation' in square brackets by SI 2002/161 as from 3 March 2003 in relation to certain cases: for effect see SI 2001/161, reg 1(3)(d) and SI 2003/192, arts 3, 8, Schedule. In para (2)(c)(ii) words 'dealing with that application on behalf of that person' substituted by words from 'on behalf of that person' to 'that application' in square brackets by SI 1998/58, reg 34 as from 19 January 1998. In paras (3), (4) words 'or a child support officer' revoked by SI 1999/1510, art 12(a) as from 1 June 1999.

In para (4)(a) words 'the child support officer concerned' substituted by words from 'the officer concerned' to 'under that Act' in square brackets by SI 1999/1510, art 12(d) as from 1 June 1999.

**10.**  <. . .>

**Note.** Substituted, together with 10A for s 10 as originally enacted by SI 1995/3261, reg 12. Revoked by SI 1999/1510, art 13 as from 1 June 1999.

**10A.**  <. . .>

**Note.** Substituted, together with 10 for s 10 as originally enacted by SI 1995/3261, reg 12. Revoked by SI 1999/1510, art 13 as from 1 June 1999.

*Employment to which section 50 of the Act applies*

**11.** For the purposes of section 50 of the Act (unauthorised disclosure of information) the following kinds of employment are prescribed in addition to those specified in paragraphs (a) to (e) of section 50(5)—

(a)  the Comptroller and Auditor General;

(b)  the Parliamentary Commissioner for Administration;

(c)  the Health Service Commissioner for England;

(d)  the Health Service Commissioner for Wales;

(e)  *the Health Service Commissioner for Scotland* [the Scottish Public Services Ombudsman;];

(f )  any member of the staff of the National Audit Office;

(g)  any other person who carries out the administrative work of that Office, or who provides, or is employed in the provision of, services to it;

(h)  any officer of any of the Commissioners [or of the Ombudsman] referred to in paragraphs (b) to (e) above; and

(i)  any person who provides, or is employed in the provision of, services to the Department of Social Security.

## CHILD SUPPORT (MAINTENANCE ASSESSMENT [MAINTENANCE CALCULATION] PROCEDURE) REGULATIONS 1992

**Note.** Words "Maintenance Assessment" in italics revoked and subsequent words in square brackets substituted by virtue of the Child Support, Pensions and Social Security Act 2000, s 1(2)(a): to be appointed: see the Child Support, Pensions and Social Security Act 2000, s 86(2).

**Dated** 20 July 1992

**SI 1992 No 1813**

**Note.** *These Regulations are revoked with savings by SI 2001/157, reg 30 (as amended by SI 2003/347, reg 2(1), (2)(b) and SI 2003/328, reg 7(1), (6)); for further savings see reg 31, Sch 3 thereto (as amended by SI 2004/2415, reg 6(1), (3)) and SI 2000/3186 (as amended by SI 2004/2415, reg 8) as from 3 March 2003 in relation to certain cases: for effect see SI 2001/157, reg 1(5) and SI 2003/192, arts 3, 4, 8, Schedule.*

## ARRANGEMENT OF REGULATIONS

Whereas a draft of this instrument was laid before Parliament in accordance with section 52(2) of the Child Support Act 1991 and approved by a resolution of each House of Parliament:

Now, therefore, the Secretary of State for Social Security, in exercise of the powers conferred by sections 3(3), 5(3), 6(1), 12, 16, 17, 18, 42(3), 46(11), 51, 52(4), 54 and 55 of, and paragraphs 11, 14 and 16 of Schedule 1 to, the Child Support Act 1991 and of all other powers enabling him in that behalf, hereby makes the following Regulations—

PART I

GENERAL

*Citation, commencement and interpretation*

**1.** (1) These Regulations may be cited as the Child Support (Maintenance Assessment Procedure) Regulations 1992 and shall come into force on 5th April 1993.

(2) In these Regulations, unless the context otherwise requires—
"the Act" means the Child Support Act 1991;
"applicable amount"[, except in regulation 40ZA,] is to be construed in accordance with Part IV of the Income Support Regulations;
"applicable amounts Schedule" means Schedule 2 to the Income Support Regulations;

"award period" means a period in respect of which an award of family credit or disability working allowance is made;

"balance of the reduction period" means, in relation to a direction that is or has been in force, the portion of the period specified in a direction in respect of which no reduction of relevant benefit has been made;

"benefit week", in relation to income support, has the same meaning as in the Income Support Regulations, [in relation to jobseeker's allowance has the same meaning as in the Jobseeker's Allowance Regulations,] and, in relation to family credit and disability working allowance, is to be construed in accordance with the Social Security (Claims and Payments) Regulations 1987;

[ *"designated authority" has the meaning it has in regulation 2(1) of the Social Security (Work-focused Interviews) Regulations 2000;*]

["designated authority" means—
   (a) the Secretary of State;
   (b) a person providing services to the Secretary of State;
   (c) a local authority;
   (d) a person providing services to, or authorised to exercise any functions of, any such authority;]

"direction" means reduced benefit direction;

*"disability working allowance" has the same meaning as in the Social Security Contributions and Benefits Act 1992;*

["disability working allowance" means an award of disability working allowance under section 129 of the Social Security Contributions and Benefits Act 1992 which was awarded with effect from a date falling before 5th October 1999;]

"day to day care" has the same meaning as in the Maintenance Assessments and Special Cases Regulations;

"effective application" means any application that complies with the provisions of regulation 2;

"effective date" means the date on which a maintenance assessment takes effect for the purposes of the Act;

["family credit" means an award of family credit under section 128 of the Social Security Contributions and Benefits Act 1992 which was awarded with effect from a date falling before 5th October 1999;]

"Income Support Regulations" means the Income Support (General) Regulations 1987;

"Information, Evidence and Disclosure Regulations" means the Child Support (Information, Evidence and Disclosure) Regulations 1992;

["the Jobseeker's Allowance Regulations" means the Jobseeker's Allowance Regulations 1996;]

["Maintenance Arrangements and Jurisdiction Regulations" means the Child Support (Maintenance Arrangements and Jurisdiction) Regulations 1992;]

"Maintenance Assessments and Special Cases Regulations" means the Child Support (Maintenance Assessments and Special Cases) Regulations 1992;

"maintenance period" has the meaning prescribed in regulation 33;

"obligation imposed by section 6 of the Act" is to be construed in accordance with section 46(1) of the Act;

[ *"official error" means an error made by an officer of the Department of Social Security acting as such which no person outside that Department caused or to which no person outside that Department materially contributed;*]

["official error" means an error made by—
   (a) an officer of the Department of Social Security, the Board or the Department for Education and Employment acting as such which no person outside any of those Departments caused or to which no person outside any of those Departments materially contributed;

(*b*)  *a person employed by a designated authority acting on behalf of the authority,*
       *which no person outside that authority caused or to which no person outside that*
       *authority materially contributed*
[(b) a person employed by a designated authority acting on behalf of the
     authority, which no person outside that authority caused or to which no
     person outside that authority materially contributed,

but excludes any error of law which is only shown to have been an error by
virtue of a subsequent decision of a Child Support Commissioner or the
court];]
"parent with care" means a person who, in respect of the same child or children,
is both a parent and a person with care;
"the parent concerned" means the parent with respect to whom a direction is
given;
"protected income level" has the same meaning as in paragraph 6(6) of
Schedule 1 to the Act;
"relevant benefit" means income support, [income-based jobseeker's allowance,]
*family credit or disability working allowance* [or an award of family credit or
disability working allowance which was awarded with effect from a date falling
before 5th October 1999];
"relevant person" means—
    (a) a person with care;
    (b) an absent parent;
    (c) a parent who is treated as an absent parent under regulation 20 of the
        Maintenance Assessments and Special Cases Regulations;
    (d) where the application for an assessment is made by a child under
        section 7 of the Act, that child,
in respect of whom a maintenance assessment has been applied for or is or
has been in force.
(3) In these Regulations, references to a direction as being "in operation",
suspended", or "in force" shall be construed as follows—
a direction is "in operation" if, by virtue of that direction, relevant benefit is
    currently being reduced;
a direction is "suspended" if ... —
    (a) after that direction has been given, relevant benefit ceases to be
        payable, or *becomes payable at one of the rates indicated in regulation 40(3)*
        [the circumstances in regulation 40(3) or regulation 40ZA(4), as the
        case may be, apply]; ...
    (b) at the time that the direction is given, *relevant benefit is payable at one of*
        *the rates indicated in regulation 40(3)* [the circumstances in regulation
        40(3) or regulation 40ZA(4), as the case may be, apply; or]
    [(c) at the time that the direction is given one or more of the deductions
        set out in regulation 40A is being made from the income support [or
        income-based jobseeker's allowance] payable to or in respect of the
        parent concerned,]
and these Regulations provide for relevant benefit payable from a later date
to be reduced by virtue of the same direction;
a direction is "in force" if it is either in operation or is suspended,
and cognate terms shall be construed accordingly.
(4) The provisions of Schedule 1 shall have effect to supplement the meaning
of "child" in section 55 of the Act.
(5) The provisions of these Regulations shall have general application to cases
prescribed in regulations 19 to 26 of the Maintenance Assessments and Special
Cases Regulations as cases to be treated as special cases for the purposes of the Act,
and the terms "absent parent" and "person with care" shall be construed
accordingly.

(6) Except where express provision is made to the contrary, where, by any provision of the Act or of these Regulations—

(a) any document is given or sent to the Secretary of State, that document shall, subject to paragraph (7), be treated as having been so given or sent on the day it is received by the Secretary of State; and

(b) any document is given or sent to any [other] person, that document shall, if sent by post to that person's last known or notified address, and subject to paragraph (8), be treated as having been given or sent on the second day after the day of posting, excluding any Sunday or any day which is a bank holiday in England, Wales, Scotland or Northern Ireland under the Banking and Financial Dealings Act 1971.

(7) Except where the provisions of regulation *8(6), 24(2), 29(3) or 31(6)(a)* [*9(1)* or 18(4)] apply, the Secretary of State may treat a document given or sent to him as given or sent on such day, earlier than the day it was received by him, as he may determine, if he is satisfied that there was unavoidable delay in his receiving the document in question.

(8) Where, by any provision of the Act or of these Regulations, and in relation to a particular application, notice or notification—

(a) more than one document is required to be given or sent to a person, and more than one such document is sent by post to that person but not all the documents are posted on the same day; or

(b) documents are required to be given or sent to more than one person, and not all such documents are posted on the same day,

all those documents shall be treated as having been posted on the later or, as the case may be, the latest day of posting.

(9) In these Regulations, unless the context otherwise requires, a reference—

(a) to a numbered Part is to the Part of these Regulations bearing that number;

(b) to a numbered Schedule is to the Schedule to these Regulations bearing that number;

(c) to a numbered regulation is to the regulation in these Regulations bearing that number;

(d) in a regulation or Schedule to a numbered paragraph is to the paragraph in that regulation or Schedule bearing that number;

(e) in a paragraph to a lettered or numbered sub-paragraph is to the sub-paragraph in that paragraph bearing that letter or number.

**Note.** Para (2): in definition "applicable amount" words "except in regulation 40ZA" in square brackets inserted by SI 1996/1345, reg 5(2)(a); in definition "benefit week" words from "in relation to" to "Jobseeker's Allowance Regulations," in square brackets inserted by SI 1996/1345, reg 5(2)(a); definition "designated authority" (as inserted by SI 2000/897, reg 16(5), Sch 6, para 8(a)) substituted by SI 2002/1703, reg 17, Sch 2, para 3 as from 30 September 2002; definition "disability working allowance" substituted by SI 1999/2566, reg 5(1), (2) as from 5 October; definition "family credit" inserted by SI 1999/2566, reg 5(1), (3) as from 5 October 1999; definition "the Jobseeker's Allowance Regulations" inserted by SI 1996/1345, reg 5(2)(a); definition "Maintenance Arrangements and Jurisdiction Regulations" inserted by SI 1995/123, reg 4; definition "official error" (as inserted by SI 1999/1047, reg 2(a)) substituted by SI 2000/897, reg 16(5), Sch 6, para 8(b) as from 3 April 2000; in definition "official error" sub-para (b) and subsequent words in square brackets substituted by SI 2000/1596, reg 6 as from 19 June 2000; in definition "relevant benefit" words "income-based jobseeker's allowance," in square brackets inserted by SI 1996/1345, reg 5(2)(a); in definition "relevant benefit" words "family credit or disability working allowance" substituted by words "or an award of family credit or disability working allowance which was awarded with effect from a date falling before 5th October 1999" in square brackets by SI 1999/2566, reg 5(1), (4) as from 5 October 1999.

In para (3) words omitted revoked by SI 1995/3261, reg 15 and words "or, as the case may be, regulation 40ZA(4)" in square brackets inserted by SI 1996/1345, reg 5(2)(b); in sub-para (a) words "becomes payable at one of the rates indicated in regulation 40(3)" substituted by words "the circumstances in regulation 40(3) or regulation 40ZA(4), as the case may be, apply" in square brackets by SI 2003/2779, reg 3(1), (2)(a) as from 5 November 2003; in sub-para (b) words "relevant benefit is payable at one of the rates indicated in regulation 40(3)" substituted by words ", the circumstances in regulation 40(3) or regulation 40ZA(4), as the case may be, apply; or" in square brackets by SI 2003/2779, reg 3(1), (2)(b) as from 5 November 2003; sub-para (c) inserted by SI 1995/3261, reg 15 and words "or income-based jobseeker's allowance" in square brackets inserted by SI 1996/1345, reg 5(2)(b). In para (6)(b) word "other" in square brackets inserted by SI 1996/3196, reg 5. In para (7) words "8(6), 24(2), 29(3) or 31(6)(a)" substituted by words "9(1) or 18(4)" in square brackets by SI 1999/1047, reg 2(b) as from 1 June 1999.

PART II

APPLICATIONS FOR A MAINTENANCE ASSESSMENT

*Applications under section 4, 6 or 7 of the Act*

**2.**   (1) Any person who applies for a maintenance assessment under section 4 or 7 of the Act shall do so on a form (a 'maintenance application form') provided by the Secretary of State.

(2) Maintenance application forms provided by the Secretary of State under section 6 of the Act or under paragraph (1) shall be supplied without charge by such persons as the Secretary of State appoints or authorises for that purpose.

(3) A completed maintenance application form shall be given or sent to the Secretary of State.

(4) Subject to paragraph (5), an application for a maintenance assessment under the Act shall be an effective application if it is made on a maintenance application form and that form has been completed in accordance with the Secretary of State's instructions.

(5) Where an application is not effective under the provisions of paragraph (4), the Secretary of State may—

(a) give or send the maintenance application form to the person who made the application, together, if he thinks appropriate, with a fresh maintenance application form, and request that the application be resubmitted so as to comply with the provisions of that paragraph; or

(b) request the person who made the application to provide such additional information or evidence as the Secretary of State specifies,

and if a completed application form or, as the case may be, the additional information or evidence requested is received by the Secretary of State within 14 days of the date of his request, he shall treat the application as made on the date on which the earlier or earliest application would have been treated as made had it been effective under the provisions of paragraph (4).

(6) Subject to paragraph (7), a person who has made an effective application may amend his application by notice in writing to the Secretary of State at any time before a maintenance assessment is made.

(7) No amendment under paragraph (6) shall relate to any change of circumstances arising after the effective date of a maintenance assessment resulting from an effective application.

*Applications on the termination of a maintenance assessment*

**3.**   (1) Where a maintenance assessment has been in force with respect to a person with care and a qualifying child and that person is replaced by another person with care, an application for a maintenance assessment with respect to that person with care and that qualifying child may for the purposes of regulation 30(2)(b)(ii) and subject to paragraph (3) be treated as having been received on a date earlier than that on which it was received.

(2) Where a maintenance assessment has been made in response to an application by a child under section 7 of the Act and either—

    (a) *a child support officer* [the Secretary of State] cancels that assessment following a request from that child; or

    (b) that child ceases to be a child for the purposes of the Act,

any application for a maintenance assessment with respect to any other children who were qualifying children with respect to the earlier maintenance assessment may for the purposes of regulation 30(2)(b)(ii) and subject to paragraph (3) be treated as having been received on a date earlier than that on which it was received.

(3) No application for a maintenance assessment shall be treated as having been received under paragraph (1) or (2) on a date—

    (a) more than 8 weeks earlier than the date on which the application was received; or

    (b) on or before the first day of the maintenance period in which the earlier maintenance assessment ceased to have effect.

**Note.** In para (2)(a) words "a child support officer" substituted for words "the Secretary of State" in square brackets by SI 1999/1047, reg 3 as from 1 June 1999.

*Multiple applications*

**4.** (1) The provisions of Schedule 2 shall apply in cases where there is more than one application for a maintenance assessment.

(2) The provisions of paragraphs 1, 2 and 3 of Schedule 2 relating to the treatment of two or more applications as a single application shall apply where no request is received for the Secretary of State to cease acting in relation to all but one of the applications.

(3) Where, under the provisions of paragraph 1, 2 or 3 of Schedule 2, two or more applications are to be treated as a single application, that application shall be treated as an application for a maintenance assessment to be made with respect to all of the qualifying children mentioned in the applications, and the effective date of that assessment shall be determined by reference to the earlier or earliest application.

*Notice to other persons of an application for a maintenance assessment*

**5.** (1) Subject to paragraph (2A), where an effective application for a maintenance assessment has been made the Secretary of State shall as soon as is reasonably practicable give notice in writing of that application to the relevant persons other than the applicant.

(2) The Secretary of State shall, subject to paragraph (2A), give or send to any person to whom notice has been given under paragraph (1) a form (a 'maintenance enquiry form') and a written request that the form be completed and returned to him for the purpose of enabling the application for the maintenance assessment to be proceeded with.

(2A) The provisions of paragraphs (1) and (2) shall not apply where the Secretary of State is satisfied that an application for a maintenance assessment can be dealt with in the absence of a completed and returned maintenance enquiry form.

(3) Where the person to whom notice is being given under paragraph (1) is an absent parent, that notice shall specify the effective date of the maintenance assessment if one is to be made, and set out in general terms the provisions relating to interim maintenance assessments.

*Response to notification of an application for a maintenance assessment*

**6.** (1) Any person who has received a maintenance enquiry form given or sent under regulation 5(2) shall complete that form in accordance with the Secretary of State's instructions and return it to the Secretary of State within 14 days of its having been given or sent.

(2) Subject to paragraph (3), a person who has returned a completed maintenance enquiry form may amend the information he has provided on that form at any time before a maintenance assessment is made by notifying the Secretary of State in writing of the amendments.

(3) No amendment under paragraph (2) shall relate to any change of circumstances arising after the effective date of any maintenance assessment made in response to the application in relation to which the maintenance enquiry form was given or sent.

**7.** (1) Where *the child support officer concerned* [the Secretary of State] is informed of the death of a qualifying child with respect to whom an application for a maintenance assessment has been made, he shall—

(a) proceed with the application as if it had not been made with respect to that child if he has not yet made an assessment;

(b) treat any assessment already made by him as not having been made if the relevant persons have not been notified of it and proceed with the application as if it had not been made with respect to that child.

(2) Where all of the qualifying children with respect to whom an application for a maintenance assessment has been made have died, and either the assessment has not been made or the relevant persons have not been notified of it, *the child support officer* [the Secretary of State] shall treat the application as not having been made.

**Note.** Words "the child support officer concerned" and "the child support officer" substituted by words "the Secretary of State" in square brackets by SI 1999/1047, reg 4(a), (b) as from 1 June 1999.

## PART III

### INTERIM MAINTENANCE ASSESSMENTS

*[Categories of interim maintenance assessment]*

**8.** [(1) Where [the Secretary of State] serves notice under section 12(4) of the Act of his intention to make an interim maintenance assessment, he shall not make that interim assessment before the end of a period of 14 days, commencing with the date that notice was given or sent.

(2) There shall be four categories of interim maintenance assessment, Category A, Category B, Category C, and Category D interim maintenance assessments.

(3) An interim maintenance assessment made by *a child support officer* [the Secretary of State] shall be—

(a) a Category A interim maintenance assessment, where any information, other than information referred to in sub-paragraph (b), that is required by him to enable him to make an assessment in accordance with the provisions of Part I of Schedule 1 to the Act has not been provided by that absent parent, and that parent has that information in his possession or can reasonably be expected to acquire it;

(b) a Category B interim maintenance assessment, where the information that is required by him as to the income of the partner or other member of the family of the absent parent or parent with care for the purposes of the calculation of the income of that partner or other member of the family under regulation 9(2), 10, 11(2) or 12(1) of the Maintenance Assessments and Special Cases Regulations—

(i) has not been provided by that partner or other member of the family, and that partner or other member of the family has that information in his possession or can reasonably be expected to acquire it; or

      (ii)  has been provided by that partner or other member of the family to the absent parent or parent with care, but the absent parent or parent with care has not provided it to the Secretary of State *or the child support officer;*

  (c)  a Category C interim maintenance assessment where—

      (i)  the absent parent is a self-employed earner as defined in regulation 1(2) of the Maintenance Assessments and Special Cases Regulations; and

      (ii)  the absent parent is currently unable to provide, but has indicated that he expects within a reasonable time to be able to provide, information to enable *a child support officer* [the Secretary of State] to determine the earnings of that absent parent in accordance with paragraphs 3 to 5 of Schedule 1 to the Maintenance Assessments and Special Cases Regulations; and

      (iii)  no maintenance order as defined in section 8(11) of the Act or written maintenance agreement as defined in section 9(1) of the Act is in force with respect to children in respect of whom the Category C interim maintenance assessment would be made; or

  (d)  a Category D interim maintenance assessment where it appears to *a child support officer* [the Secretary of State], on the basis of information available to him as to the income of the absent parent, that the amount of any maintenance assessment made in accordance with Part I of Schedule 1 to the Act applicable to that absent parent may be higher than the amount of a Category A interim maintenance assessment in force in respect of him;

  (e)  in this regulation and in regulation 8A, "family" and "partner" have the same meanings as in the Maintenance Assessments and Special Cases Regulations.]

**Note.** Substituted, together with regs 8A–8D for reg 8 as originally enacted, by SI 1995/3261, reg 16. In para (1) words "a child support officer" substituted by words "the Secretary of State" in square brackets by SI 1999/1047, reg 5(a) as from 1 June 1999. In para (3) words "or the child support officer" in each place substituted by words "the Secretary of State" in square brackets, and words "or the child support officer" revoked by by SI 1999/1047, reg 5(b)(i), (ii) as from 1 June 1999.

*[Amount of an interim maintenance assessment]*

**[8A.**  (1) The amount of child support maintenance fixed by a Category A interim maintenance assessment shall be 1.5 multiplied by the amount of the maintenance requirement in respect of the qualifying child or qualifying children concerned calculated in accordance with the provisions of paragraph 1 of Schedule 1 to the Act, and paragraphs 2 to 9 of that Schedule shall not apply to Category A interim maintenance assessments.

    (2) Subject to paragraph (5), the amount of child support maintenance fixed by a Category B interim maintenance assessment shall be determined in accordance with paragraphs (3) and (4).

    (3) Where *a child support officer* [the Secretary of State] is unable to determine the exempt income—

  (a)  of an absent parent under regulation 9 of the Maintenance Assessments and Special Cases Regulations because he is unable to determine whether regulation 9(2) of those Regulations applies;

  (b)  of a parent with care under regulation 10 of those Regulations because he is unable to determine whether regulation 9(2) of those Regulations, as modified by and applied by regulation 10 of those Regulations applies,

the amount of the Category B interim maintenance assessment shall be the maintenance assessment calculated in accordance with Part I of Schedule 1 to the Act on the assumption that—

(i) in a case falling within sub-paragraph (a), regulation 9(2) of those Regulations does apply;

(ii) in a case falling within sub-paragraph (b), regulation 9(2) of those Regulations as modified by and applied by regulation 10 of those Regulations does apply.

*(4) Where the disposable income of an absent parent, calculated in accordance with regulation 12(1)(a) of the Maintenance Assessments and Special Cases Regulations, would, without taking account of the income of any member of his family, bring him within the provisions of paragraph 6 of Schedule 1 to the Act (protected income), and a child support officer is unable to ascertain the disposable income of the other members of his family, the amount of the Category B interim maintenance assessment shall be the maintenance assessment calculated in accordance with Part I of Schedule 1 to the Act on the assumption that the provisions of paragraph 6 of Schedule 1 to the Act do not apply to the absent parent.*

[(4) Where *a child support officer* [the Secretary of State] is unable to ascertain the income of other members of the family of an absent parent so that the disposable income of that absent parent can be calculated in accordance with regulation 12(1)(a) of the Maintenance Assessments and Special Cases Regulations, the amount of the Category B interim maintenance assessment shall be the maintenance assessment calculated in accordance with Part I of Schedule 1 to the Act on the assumption that the provisions of paragraph 6 of that Schedule do not apply to the absent parent.]

(5) Where the application of the provisions of paragraph (3) or (4) would result in the amount of a Category B interim maintenance assessment being more than 30 per centum of the net income of the absent parent as calculated in accordance with regulation 7 of the Maintenance Assessments and Special Cases Regulations, those provisions shall not apply to that absent parent and instead, the amount of that Category B interim maintenance assessment shall be 30 per centum of his net income as so calculated and where that calculation results in a fraction of a penny, that fraction shall be disregarded.

(6) The amount of child support maintenance fixed by a Category C interim maintenance assessment shall be £30.00 but *a child support officer* [the Secretary of State] may set a lower amount, including a nil amount, if he thinks it reasonable to do so in all the circumstances of the case.

(7) Paragraph 6 of Schedule 1 to the Act shall not apply to Category C interim maintenance assessments.

(8) *A child support officer* [The Secretary of State] shall notify the person with care where he is considering setting a lower amount for a Category C interim maintenance assessment in accordance with paragraph (6) and shall take into account any relevant representations made by that person with care in deciding the amount of that Category C interim maintenance assessment.

(9) The amount of child support maintenance fixed by a Category D interim maintenance assessment shall be calculated or estimated by applying to the absent parent's income, in so far as *the child support officer* [the Secretary of State] is able to determine it at the time of the making of that Category D interim maintenance assessment, the provisions of Part I of Schedule 1 to the Act and regulations made under it, subject to the modification that—

(a) paragraphs 6 and 8 of that Schedule shall not apply;

(b) only paragraphs (1)(a) and (5) of regulation 9 of the Maintenance Assessments and Special Cases Regulations shall apply; and

(c) heads (b) and (c) of sub-paragraph (3) of paragraph 1 of Schedule 1 to the Maintenance Assessments and Special Cases Regulations shall not apply.

(10) Where the absent parent referred to in paragraph (9) is an employed earner as defined in regulation 1 of the Maintenance Assessments and Special Cases Regulations and *the child support officer* [the Secretary of State] is unable to calculate the net income of that absent parent, his net income shall be estimated under the provisions of paragraph (2A)(a) and (b) of that regulation.]

**Note.** Substituted, together with regs 8, 8B–8D for reg 8 as originally enacted, by SI 1995/3261, reg 16. In paras (3), (4) words "a child support officer" substituted by words "the Secretary of State" in square brackets by SI 1999/1047, reg 6(a) as from 1 June 1999. Para (4) substituted by SI 1998/58, reg 35 as from 19 January 1998. In para (6) words "a child support officer" substituted by words "the Secretary of State" in square brackets by SI 1999/1047, reg 6(a) as from 1 June 1999. In para (8) words "A child support officer" substituted by words "The Secretary of State" in square brackets by SI 1999/1047, reg 6(a) as from 1 June 1999. In paras (9), (10) words "the child support officer" substituted by words "the Secretary of State" in square brackets by SI 1999/1047, reg 6(b) as from 1 June 1999.

**8B.**

[< . . .>]

**Note.** Substituted, together with regs 8, 8A, 8C, 8D for reg 8 as originally enacted, by SI 1995/3261, reg 16. Revoked by SI 1999/1047, reg 7 as from 1 June 1999.

[*Effective date of an interim maintenance assessment*

[**8C.** [(1) Except where regulation 3(5) of the Maintenance Arrangements and Jurisdiction Regulations (effective date of maintenance assessment where court order in force), regulation *9(9) or* 33(7) or paragraph (2) applies, the effective date of an interim maintenance assessment shall be—

(a) in respect of a Category A interim maintenance assessment, subject to *regulations 8B, 9(2) and (3) and* sub-paragraph (d), such date, being not earlier than the first and not later than the seventh day following the date upon which that interim maintenance assessment was made, as falls on the same day of the week as the date determined in accordance with regulation 30(2)(a)(ii) or (b)(ii) as the case may be;

(b) in respect of a Category B interim maintenance assessment made after 22nd January 1996, subject to sub-paragraph (d) *and to regulations 31 to 31C,* the date specified in regulation 30(2)(a)(ii) or (b)(ii) as the case may be;

(c) in respect of a Category C interim maintenance assessment, subject to sub-paragraph (d) *and regulations 31 to 31C,* the date set out in sub-paragraph (a);

(d) in respect of a Category A, Category B or Category C interim maintenance assessment, where the application of the provisions of sub-paragraph (a), (b) or (c) would otherwise set an effective date for an interim maintenance assessment earlier than the end of a period of eight weeks from the date upon which—

(i) the maintenance enquiry form referred to in regulation 30(2)(a)(i) was given or sent to an absent parent; or

(ii) the application made by an absent parent referred to in regulation 30(2)(b)(i) was received by the Secretary of State,

in circumstances where that absent parent has complied with the provisions of regulation 30(2)(a)(i) or (b)(i) or paragraph (2A) of that regulation applies, the date determined in accordance with regulation 30(2)(a)(i) or (b)(i).

(2) *The effective date of an interim maintenance assessment made under section 12(1)(b) or (c) of the Act shall, subject to regulations 8B, 9(2), (3) and (9), or 33(7), and, as regards Category B and Category C interim maintenance assessments to regulations 31 to 31C* [The effective date of an interim maintenance assessment made under section 12(1)(b) of the Act shall, subject to regulation 33(7)], be such date, not earlier than the first and not later than the seventh day following the date upon which that interim maintenance assessment was made, as falls on the same day of the week as the effective date of the maintenance assessment calculated in accordance with Part I of Schedule 1 to the Act which *is being reviewed* [the Secretary of State is proposing to supersede with a decision under section 17 of the Act].

(3) In cases where the effective date of an interim maintenance assessment is determined under paragraph (1), *regulation 8B or 9(2), (3) or (9)*, where a maintenance assessment, except a maintenance assessment falling within regulation 8D(7), is made after an interim maintenance assessment has been in force, child support maintenance calculated in accordance with Part I of Schedule 1 to the Act shall be payable in respect of the period preceding that during which the interim maintenance assessment was in force.

(4) The child support maintenance payable under the provisions of paragraph (3) shall be payable in respect of the period between the effective date of the assessment (or, where separate assessments are made for different periods under paragraph 15 of Schedule 1 to the Act, the effective date of the assessment in respect of the earliest such period) and the effective date of the interim maintenance assessment.]

**Note.** Substituted, together with regs 8–8B, 8D for reg 8 as originally enacted, by SI 1995/3261, reg 16. In para (1) words "9(9) or", "to regulations 8B, 9(2) and (3) and", "and regulations 31 to 31C" and "and to regulations 31 to 3" revoked by SI 1999/1047, reg 8(a)–(d) as from 1 June 1999. In para (2) words from "The effective date" to "regulations 31 to 31C" substituted by words from "The effective date" to "regulation 33(7)" in square brackets by SI 1999/1047, reg 8(e)(i) as from 1 June 1999 and words "is being reviewed" substituted by words from "the Secretary of State" to "the Act" in square brackets, by SI 1999/1047, reg 8(e) as from 1 June 1999. In para (3) words "regulation 8B or 9(2), (3) or (9)," revoked by SI 1999/1047, reg 8(f) as from 1 June 1999.

[*Miscellaneous provisions in relation to interim maintenance assessments*

[**8D.**   (1) Subject to paragraph (2), where a maintenance assessment calculated in accordance with Part I of Schedule 1 to the Act is made following an interim maintenance assessment, the amount of child support maintenance payable in respect of the period after 18th April 1995, during which that interim maintenance assessment was in force shall be that fixed by the maintenance assessment.

[(1A) The reference in paragraph (1) to a maintenance assessment calculated in accordance with Part I of Schedule 1 to the Act shall include a maintenance assessment falling within regulation 30A(2).]

(2) Paragraph (1) shall not apply where a maintenance assessment calculated in accordance with Part I of Schedule 1 to the Act falls within paragraph (7).

(3) < . . . >

(4) The provisions of regulations *29, 31 to 31C, 32, 33(5) and 55* [32 and 33(5)] shall not apply to a Category A or Category D interim maintenance assessment.

(5) Subject to paragraph (6) *and regulation 9(15)*, an interim maintenance assessment shall cease to have effect on the first day of the maintenance period during which the Secretary of State receives the information which enables *a child support officer* [him] to make the maintenance assessment or assessments in relation to the same absent parent, person with care, and qualifying child or qualifying children, calculated in accordance with Part I of Schedule 1 to the Act.

(6) *Subject to regulation 9(15)*, where *a child support officer* [the Secretary of State] has insufficient information or evidence to enable him to make a maintenance assessment calculated in accordance with Part I of Schedule 1 to the Act for the whole of the period beginning with the effective date applicable to a particular case, an interim maintenance assessment made in that case shall cease to have effect—

(a) on 18th April 1995 where by that date the Secretary of State has received the information or evidence set out in paragraph (7); or

(b) on the first day of the maintenance period after 18th April 1995 in which the Secretary of State has received that information or evidence.

(7) The information or evidence referred to in paragraph (6) is information or evidence enabling *a child support officer* [the Secretary of State] to make a

maintenance assessment calculated in accordance with Part I of Schedule 1 to the Act, for a period beginning after the effective date applicable to that case, in respect of the absent parent, parent with care and qualifying child or qualifying children in respect of whom the interim maintenance assessment referred to in paragraph (6) was made.

[(8) Where the information or evidence referred to in paragraph (6)(a) or (b) is that there has been an award of income support[, state pension credit] or an income-based jobseeker's allowance, the Secretary of State shall be treated as having received that information or evidence on the first day in respect of which income support [, state pension credit] or an income-based jobseeker's allowance was payable under that award.]

**Note.** Substituted, together with regs 8–8C for reg 8 as originally enacted, by SI 1995/3261, reg 16. Para (1A) inserted by SI 1998/58, reg 36 as from 19 January 1998. Para (3) revoked by SI 1999/1047, reg 9(a) as from 1 June 1999. In para (4) words "29, 31 to 31C, 32, 33(5) and 55" substituted by words "32 and 33(5)" in square brackets by SI 1999/1047, reg 9(b) as from 1 June 1999. In para (5) words "and regulation 9(15)" revoked and words "a child support officer" substituted by word "him" in square brackets by SI 1999/1047, reg 9(c) as from 1 June 1999. In para (6) words "Subject to regulation 9(15)," revoked, and words "a child support officer" substituted by words "the Secretary of State" in square brackets by SI 1999/1047, reg 9(d) as from 1 June 1999. In para (7) words "a child support officer" substituted by words "the Secretary of State" in square brackets by SI 1999/1047, reg 9(e) as from 1 June 1999. In para (8) substituted by SI 1996/3196, reg 6 and words ", state pension credit" in square brackets in both places they occur inserted by SI 2003/2779, reg 3(1), (3) as from 5 November 2003.

*Cancellation of an interim maintenance assessment*

**9.** (1) Where a child support officer is satisfied that there was unavoidable delay by the absent parent in—

    (i) completing and returning a maintenance enquiry form under the provisions of regulation 6(1);

    (ii) providing information or evidence that is required by the Secretary of State for the determination of an application for a maintenance assessment; or

    (iii) providing information or evidence that is required by a child support officer to enable him to conduct or complete a review under section 16, 17, 18 or 19 of the Act,

he may cancel an interim maintenance assessment which is in force.

(2) Where a child support officer cancels a Category A, Category B or Category D interim maintenance assessment in accordance with the provisions of paragraph (1), and he is satisfied that there was unavoidable delay for only part of the period during which that assessment was in force, and that another Category A, Category B or Category D interim maintenance assessment should be made, the effective date of that other Category A, or Category D interim maintenance assessment shall, subject to paragraph (3), be the first day of the maintenance period following the date upon which, in the opinion of the child support officer, the delay became avoidable and the effective date of that other Category B interim maintenance assessment made after 22nd January 1996 shall be the date set out in regulation 8C(1)(b).

(3) Where the Category A or Category B interim maintenance assessment cancelled in accordance with the provisions of paragraph (1) was made prior to 18th April 1995 and the effective date of any new Category A or Category B interim maintenance assessment would, by virtue of paragraph (2), be prior to 18th April 1995, the effective date of that new Category A or Category B interim maintenance assessment shall be the first day of the maintenance period which begins on or after 18th April 1995.

(4) Where in respect of any Category A or Category B interim maintenance assessment in force before 18th April 1995 the delay referred to in paragraph (1)

became avoidable before 18th April 1995, that Category A or Category B interim maintenance assessment may not be cancelled with effect from a date earlier than the date the delay became avoidable.

(5) Subject to paragraph (1), where a child support officer is satisfied that it would be appropriate to make an interim maintenance assessment the Category of which is different from that of the interim maintenance assessment in force, he may cancel the interim maintenance assessment which is in force with effect from—

    (i) subject to sub-paragraph (ii), whichever is the later of the first day of the maintenance period in which he becomes so satisfied or the first day of the maintenance period which begins on or after 18th April 1995; or

    (ii) where he is satisfied that the interim maintenance assessment in force should be replaced by a Category B interim maintenance assessment, whichever is the later of the effective date of the interim maintenance assessment in force or 22nd January 1996.

(6) Where an interim maintenance assessment is cancelled under the provisions of paragraph (5)(ii) and that interim maintenance assessment was made immediately following a previous interim maintenance assessment, a child support officer shall also cancel that previous interim maintenance assessment with effect from the effective date of that previous interim maintenance assessment or 22nd January 1996 whichever is the later.

(7) Where an interim maintenance assessment has been cancelled in the circumstances set out in paragraph (5)(ii) or (6), payments made under that interim maintenance assessment shall be treated as payments made under the Category B interim maintenance assessment which replaces it.

(8) In paragraph (5), 'Category' in relation to an interim maintenance assessment means Category A, Category B, Category C or Category D, as the case may be.

(9) Where a child support officer makes an interim maintenance assessment following the cancellation of an interim maintenance assessment in accordance with paragraph (5), the effective date of the fresh interim maintenance assessment shall be—

    (i) subject to sub-paragraph (ii), the date upon which that cancellation took effect;

    (ii) where the fresh interim maintenance assessment is a Category B interim maintenance assessment, subject to paragraphs (10) and (11), the date determined in accordance with regulation 8C(1)(b) or 22nd January 1996, whichever is later.

(10) Where paragraph (9)(ii) applies and the interim maintenance assessment cancelled in accordance with paragraph (5) caused a court order to cease to have effect in accordance with regulation 3(6) of the Maintenance Arrangements and Jurisdiction Regulations, the effective date of the Category B interim maintenance assessment referred to in paragraph (9)(ii) shall be the date upon which that cancellation took effect.

(11) Where paragraphs (6) and (9)(ii) apply and the interim maintenance assessment cancelled in accordance with paragraph (6) caused a court order to cease to have effect in accordance with regulation 3(6) of the Maintenance Arrangements and Jurisdiction Regulations, the effective date of the Category B interim maintenance assessment referred to in paragraph 9(ii) shall be the date upon which the cancellation in accordance with paragraph (6) took effect.

(12) A child support officer may cancel an interim maintenance assessment which is in force with effect from such date as he considers appropriate in all the circumstances on the grounds that—

    (a) there was a material procedural error in connection with the making of the assessment; or

    (b) he is satisfied that he did not, or has subsequently ceased to have jurisdiction to make that interim maintenance assessment.

(13) Where a child support officer has cancelled an interim maintenance assessment under paragraph (12), a relevant person may apply to the Secretary of State for a review of that cancellation under section 18(3) of the Act and the provisions of section 18(5) to (8) shall apply to that review.

(14) Where, following a review under section 18(3) of the Act, a child support officer sets aside the cancellation of the interim maintenance assessment which has been cancelled under paragraph (12), the effective date of the reinstated interim maintenance assessment shall be the date on which the cancelled interim maintenance assessment ceased to have effect or 22nd January 1996 whichever is the later.

(15) An interim maintenance assessment in force which is made under section 12(1)(b) or (c) of the Act shall be cancelled by a child support officer with effect from the effective date of that interim maintenance assessment as soon as is reasonably practicable after he has received the information or evidence which enables him to carry out or to complete a review under section 16, 17, 18 or 19 of the Act.

(16) Where an interim maintenance assessment has been cancelled under paragraph (15), payments made under it shall be treated as payments made under the maintenance assessment being reviewed under section 16, 17, 18 or 19 of the Act or under any maintenance assessment made following the review which replaces for the relevant period the maintenance assessment being reviewed.

*[Interim maintenance assessments which follow other interim maintenance assessments*

**[9.** (1) Where an interim maintenance assessment is being revised on the ground specified in regulation 17(1)(b) and the Secretary of State is satisfied—

(a) that another Category A, Category B or Category D maintenance assessment should be made, and

(b) that there has been unavoidable delay for part of the period during which the assessment which is being revised was in force,

the effective date of that other—

(i) Category A or Category D interim maintenance assessment shall be the first day of the maintenance period following the date upon which, in the opinion of the Secretary of State, the delay became avoidable;

(ii) Category B interim maintenance assessment shall be the date set out in regulation 8C(1)(b).

(2) Where an interim maintenance assessment is revised on either of the grounds set out in regulation 17(4) or (5), payments made under that interim maintenance assessment before the revision shall be treated as payments made under the Category B interim maintenance assessment which replaces it.

(3) Subject to paragraphs (5) and (6), where the Secretary of State makes a Category B interim maintenance assessment following the revision of an interim maintenance assessment in accordance with regulation 17(4), the effective date of that Category B interim maintenance assessment shall be the date determined in accordance with regulation 8C(1)(b).

(4) Where the Secretary of State makes a fresh interim maintenance assessment following the supersession of an interim maintenance assessment in accordance with regulation 20(7), the effective date of that fresh interim maintenance assessment shall be the date from which that supersession took effect.

(5) Where the Secretary of State cancels upon a revision an interim maintenance assessment in accordance with regulation 17(4) which caused a court order to cease to have effect in accordance with regulation 3(6) of the Maintenance Arrangements and Jurisdiction Regulations, the effective date of the Category B interim maintenance assessment referred to in regulation 17(4) shall be the date on which that revision took effect.

(6) Where the revision of an interim maintenance assessment in accordance with regulation 17(5) caused a court order to cease to have effect in accordance with regulation 3(6) of the Maintenance Arrangements and Jurisdiction Regulations, the effective date of the Category B interim maintenance assessment referred to in regulation 17(4) shall be the date on which that revision took effect.]

**Note.** Substituted, together with reg 9A for reg 9 as originally enacted, by SI 1995/3261, reg 17. Regs 9, 9A substituted by new reg 9, by SI 1999/1047, reg 10 as from 1 June 1999: see SI 1999/1047, reg 1(1).

**[9A. . . .]**

[. . .]

**Note.** Substituted, together with reg 9A for reg 9 as originally enacted, by SI 1995/3261, reg 17. Regs 9, 9A substituted, by new reg 9, by SI 1999/1047, reg 10 as from 1 June 1999.

PART IV

NOTIFICATIONS FOLLOWING CERTAIN DECISIONS BY CHILD SUPPORT OFFICERS

*Notification of a new or a fresh maintenance assessment*

**10.** [(1) Where a child support officer—

[(a) makes a new or fresh maintenance assessment following an application under section 4, 6 or 7 of the Act, a review under section 16 [of the Act of a

*[continued on next right-hand page]*

maintenance assessment the effective date of which is on or before 8th December 1996 or a review under section] 17, 18 or 19 of the Act, or the giving or cancellation of a departure direction;

(b) makes a new interim maintenance assessment under section 12 of the Act, substitutes an interim maintenance assessment for one which is in force in accordance with regulation 8 or 9, or gives or cancels a departure direction; or]

(c) makes a maintenance assessment calculated in accordance with Part I of Schedule 1 to the Act where an interim maintenance assessment is or has been in force,

he shall immediately notify the relevant person, so far as that is reasonably practicable, of the amount of the child support maintenance under that assessment.]

[(1) A person with a right of appeal to an appeal tribunal under—

(a) section 20 of the Act; and

(b) section 20 of the Act as extended by paragraph 3(1)(b) of Schedule 4C to the Act,

shall be given notice of that right and of the decision to which that right relates.]

[(1A) ...

(1B) ...

(1C) ...]

(2) [Subject to [paragraphs (2A) and (2B)], a notification under paragraph (1)] [of a new or fresh maintenance assessment made under section 11, 16 or 17] shall set out, in relation to the maintenance assessment in question—

(a) the maintenance requirement;

(b) the effective date of the assessment;

[(c) the net and assessable income of the absent parent and, where relevant, the amount determined under regulation 9(1)(b) of the Maintenance Assessments and Special Cases Regulations (housing costs);]

[(cc) where relevant, the absent parent's protected income level and the amount of the maintenance assessment before the adjustment in respect of protected income specified in paragraph 6(2) of Schedule 1 to the Act was carried out;]

[(d) the net and assessable income of the parent with care, and, where relevant, an amount in relation to housing costs determined in the manner specified in regulation 10 of the Maintenance Assessments and Special Cases Regulations (calculation of exempt income of parent with care);]

(e) details as to the minimum amount of child support maintenance payable by virtue of regulations made under paragraph 7 of Schedule 1 to the Act; and

(f) details as to apportionment where a case is to be treated as a special case for the purposes of the Act under section 42 of the Act;

[(h) any amount determined in accordance with Schedule 3A or 3B to the Maintenance Assessments and Special Cases Regulations (qualifying transfer of property and travel costs);]

[(i) where the notification under paragraph (1)(a) ... follows the giving, or cancellation of a departure direction, the amounts calculated in accordance with Part I of Schedule 1 to the Act, or in accordance with regulation 8A, which have been changed as a result of the giving or cancellation of that departure direction].

[(2A) Where a new Category A [Category C or Category D] interim maintenance assessment is made, or a fresh Category A [Category C or Category D] interim maintenance assessment is made following *a review under section 16 of the Act of a maintenance assessment the effective date of which is on or before 8th December 1996 or a review under section 19(1)* [a revision of a maintenance assessment under section 16 of the Act or a supersession of a maintenance assessment under section 17 of the Act], a notification under paragraph (1) shall set out, in relation to that interim maintenance assessment, the maintenance requirement and the effective date.]

[(2AA) Where a fresh Category D interim maintenance assessment is made following the giving or cancellation of a departure direction, a notification under paragraph (1) shall set out in relation to that interim maintenance assessment the amounts calculated in accordance with regulation 8A which have changed as a result of the giving or cancellation of that departure direction.]

[(2B) A notification under paragraph (1) in relation to a Category B interim maintenance assessment shall set out in relation to it—

[(a) the matters listed in sub-paragraphs (a), (b) and (d) to (f) of paragraph (2);

(b) where known, the absent parent's assessable income; and

(c) where the Category B interim maintenance assessment is made following the giving or cancellation of a departure direction, the amounts calculated in accordance with regulation 8A which have changed as a result of the giving or cancellation of that departure direction].]

(3) Except where a person gives written permission to the Secretary of State that the information, in relation to him, mentioned in sub-paragraphs (a) and (b) below may be conveyed to other persons, any document given or sent under the provisions of paragraph (1) or (2) shall not contain—

(a) the address of any person other than the recipient of the document in question (other than the address of the office *of the child support officer concerned* [of the officer concerned who is exercising functions of the Secretary of State under the Act]) or any other information the use of which could reasonably be expected to lead to any such person being located;

(b) any other information the use of which could reasonably be expected to lead to any person, other than a qualifying child or a relevant person, being identified.

*(4) Subject to paragraph (5), a notification under paragraph (1) shall include information as to the following provisions—*

*(a) where a new maintenance assessment is made following an application under the Act or a fresh maintenance assessment is made following a review under section 16 of the Act, sections 16, 17 and 18 of the Act;*

*(b) where a fresh maintenance assessment is made following a review under section 17 of the Act, or following a review under section 19 of the Act where the child support officer conducting such a review is satisfied that if an application were to be made under section 17 of the Act it would be appropriate to make a fresh maintenance assessment, sections 16 and 18 of the Act;*

*(c) where a fresh maintenance assessment is made following a review under section 18 of the Act, sections 16, 17 and 20 of the Act;*

*(d) where a fresh maintenance assessment is made following a review under section 19 of the Act, sections 16, 17 and 18 of the Act;*

*(e) where a fresh maintenance assessment is made following the giving of a departure direction, sections 16, 17 and 18 of the Act.*

*(5) Where a new Category A Category C or Category D interim maintenance assessment is made or a fresh Category A Category C or Category D interim maintenance assessment is made following a review under section 16 or 19(1) of the Act, a notification under paragraph (1) shall include information as to sections 16 and 19(1) of the Act.]*

*(6) Where a fresh Category D interim maintenance assessment is made following the giving or cancellation of a departure direction, a notification under paragraph (1) shall include information as to sections 16 and 19(1) of the Act.*

[(4) Where a decision as to a maintenance assessment is made under section 11, 12, 16 or 17 of the Act, a notification under paragraph (1) shall include information as to the provisions of sections 16 and 17 of the Act.]

**Note.** Para (1) substituted by SI 1999/1047, reg 11(a) as from 1 June 1999. Paras (1A)–(1C) inserted by SI 1998/2799, reg 2(2)(d)(ii) as from 7 December 1998; revoked by SI 1999/1047, reg 11(b) as from 1 June 1999. In para (2) words from "Subject to" to "under paragraph (1)" in square brackets substituted by SI 1995/123, reg 6(2) and words "paragraphs (2A) and (2B)" in square brackets substituted by SI 1995/1045, reg 30(3).

In para (2) words "of a new or fresh maintenance assessment made under section 11, 16 or 17" in square brackets inserted by SI 1999/1047, reg 11(c)(i) as from 1 June 1999.

Para (2)(c) substituted by SI 1995/3261, reg 18(3), sub-para (cc) inserted by SI 1995/3261, reg 18(4), sub-para (d) substituted by SI 1995/3261, reg 18(5), sub-para (h) inserted by SI 1995/3261, reg 18(6) and sub-para (i) inserted by SI 1996/2907, reg 67(3). In para (2) in sub-para (i) words omitted revoked by SI 1999/1047, reg 11(c)(ii) as from 1 June 1999: see SI 1999/1047, reg 1(1). In para (2A) inserted by SI 1995/123, reg 6(3), (5) and words "Category C or Category D" in square brackets in both places they occur inserted by SI 1995/1045, reg 30(4), (6). In para (2A) words from "a review" to "19(1)" substituted by words from "a revision" to "of the Act" in square brackets by SI 1999/1047, reg 11(d) as from 1 June 1999. Para (2AA) inserted by SI 1996/2907, reg 67(4), (7). Para (2B) inserted by SI 1995/1045, reg 30(5); sub-paras (a)–(c) substituted, for sub-paras (a), (b) as originally enacted, by SI 1996/2907, reg 67(5). In para (3)(a) words "of the child support officer concerned" substituted by words from "of the officer concerned" to "under the Act" in square brackets by SI 1999/1047, reg 11(e) as from 1 June 1999. Paras (4)–(6) substituted, by para (4), by SI 1999/1047, reg 11(f) as from 1 June 1999.

*[Notification of increase or reduction in the amount of a maintenance assessment*

**[10A.** (1) Where, in a case falling within paragraph (2B) of regulation 22 of the Maintenance Assessments and Special Cases Regulations (multiple applications relating to an absent parent), *a child support officer* [the Secretary of State] has increased or reduced one or more of the other maintenance assessments referred to in that paragraph following the making of the fresh assessment referred to in sub-paragraph (c) of that paragraph, he shall, so far as that is reasonably practicable, immediately notify the relevant persons in respect of whom each maintenance assessment so increased or reduced was made of—

   (a)  the making of that fresh assessment;

   (b)  the amount of the increase or reduction in that maintenance assessment; and

   (c)  the date on which that increase or reduction shall take effect,

and the notification shall include information as to the provisions of *section 18* [sections 16 and 17] of the Act.

(2) Except where a person gives written permission to the Secretary of State that the information in relation to him mentioned in sub-paragraphs (a) and (b) below may be conveyed to other persons, any document given or sent under the provisions of paragraph (1) shall not contain—

   (a)  the address of any person other than the recipient of the document in question (other than the address of the office of *the child support officer concerned* [of the officer concerned who is exercising functions of the Secretary of State under the Act]) or any other information the use of which could reasonably be expected to lead to any such person being located;

   (b)  any other information the use of which could reasonably be expected to lead to any person, other than a qualifying child or a relevant person, being identified.]

**Note.** Inserted by SI 1998/58, reg 38 as from 19 January 1998. In para (1) words "a child support officer" substituted by words "the Secretary of State" in square brackets and words "section 18" substituted by words "sections 16 and 17" in square brackets by SI 1999/1047, reg 12(a) as from 1 June 1999. In para (2)(a) words "of the child support officer concerned" substituted by words from "of the officer" to "under the Act" in square brackets by SI 1999/1047, reg 12(b) as from 1 June 1999.

*Notification of a refusal to conduct a review*

**11.** <. . .>
**Note.** Revoked by SI 1999/1047, reg 13 as from 1 June 1999.

**12.** <. . .>
**Note.** Revoked by SI 1999/1047, reg 13 as from 1 June 1999.

**13.** <. . .>
**Note.** Revoked by SI 1999/1047, reg 13 as from 1 June 1999.

**14.** <. . .>
**Note.** Revoked by SI 1999/1047, reg 13 as from 1 June 1999.

**15.** <. . .>
**Note.** Revoked by SI 1999/1047, reg 13 as from 1 June 1999.

**[15A.** <. . .>
**Note.** Inserted by SI 1995/3261, reg 22 and revoked by SI 1999/1047, reg 13 as from 1 June 1999.

*Notification when an applicant under section 7 of the Act ceases to be a child*

**16.** Where a maintenance assessment has been made in response to an application by a child under section 7 of the Act and that child ceases to be a child for the purposes of the Act, *a child support officer* [the Secretary of State] shall immediately notify, so far as that is reasonably practicable—

  (a)  the other qualifying children who have attained the age of 12 years and the absent parent with respect to whom that maintenance assessment was made; and

  (b)  the person with care.

**Note.** Words "a child support officer" substituted by words "the Secretary of State" in square brackets by SI 1999/1047, reg 14 as from 1 June 1999.

*Notification that an appeal has lapsed*

**[16A.** *Where a case falls within section 20A(1) of the Act and the appeal that has been brought under section 20 of the Act lapses under the provisions of section 20A(2) of the Act a child support officer shall, so far as that is reasonably practicable, notify the relevant persons that that appeal has lapsed.*]

Where an appeal lapses in accordance with section 16(6) of the Act, the Secretary of State shall, so far as is reasonably practicable, notify the relevant persons that that appeal has lapsed.]

**Note.** Inserted by SI 1995/3261, reg 23; substituted by SI 1999/1047, reg 15 as from 1 June 1999.

PART V

PERIODICAL REVIEWS [*PART V REVISIONS AND SUPERSESSIONS*]
**Note.** Substituted by SI 1999/1047, reg 16 as from 1 June 1999.

PART V

PERIODICAL REVIEWS

*Intervals between periodical reviews and notice of a periodical review*

**17.** (1) Subject to regulation 18, where a maintenance assessment in force is—

  (a)  an assessment that has not been previously reviewed;

  (b)  a fresh assessment following an earlier review under section 16 of the Act; or

(c) a fresh assessment following a review under section 17 of the Act, where before 22 January 1996 a child support officer decided, in accordance with section 17(3) of the Act, to proceed with a review,

that assessment shall be reviewed by a child support officer under section 16 of the Act after it has been in force for a period of—

    (i) in the case of an assessment the effective date of which is on or before 18th April 1994, 52 weeks;

    (ii) in the case of an assessment the effective date of which is after 18th April 1994, 104 weeks.

(2) Where a maintenance assessment in force is a fresh assessment, following—

(a) a review under section 17 of the Act where, after 22nd January 1996, a child support officer decided, in accordance with section 17(3) of the Act, to proceed with that review; or

(b) a review under section 18 or 19 of the Act,

that assessment shall be reviewed by a child support officer under section 16 of the Act after it has been in force for a period of—

    (i) in a case where the effective date of the assessment that has been reviewed was on or before 18th April 1994, 52 weeks;

    (ii) in a case where the effective date of the assessment that has been reviewed was after 18th April 1994, 104 weeks,

less, in either case, *the period between the effective date of the assessment that has been reviewed and the effective date of the fresh assessment following that review* [the period between the effective date of the fresh assessment following the latest review carried out under sub-paragraph (a) or (b) and whichever is the later of—

  (aa) the effective date of the assessment falling within sub-paragrah (a) of paragraph (1); or

  (bb) the effective date of the assessment made following the review referred to in sub-paragraph (b) or (c) of paragraph (1)]

. . .

(3) A child support officer may decide not to conduct a review under paragraph (1) if a fresh maintenance assessment following such a review would cease to have effect within 28 days of the effective date of that fresh assessment.

(4) Before a child support officer conducts a review under section 16 of the Act, he shall give 14 days' notice of the proposed review to the relevant persons.

(5) Subject to paragraphs (6) and (7), a child support officer shall request every person to whom he is giving notice under paragraph (4) to provide, within 14 days, and in accordance with the provisions of regulations 2 and 3 of the Information, Evidence and Disclosure Regulations such information or evidence as to his current circumstances as may be specified and shall set out the possible consequences of failure to provide that information or evidence.

(6) *The provisions of paragraph (5) shall not apply in relation to any person to whom or in respect of whom income support or income-based jobseeker's allowance is payable or to a person with care where income support or income-based jobseeker's allowance is payable to or in respect of the absent parent.*

. . .

[(6) The provisions of paragraph (5) shall not apply in relation to—

(a) any person or in respect of whom income support or income-based jobseeker's allowance is payable;

(b) a person with care where income support or income-based jobseeker's allowance is payable to or in respect of the absent parent;

(c) an absent parent or parent with care to whom regulation 10A of the Maintenance Assessments and Special Cases Regulations applies; or

(d) a parent with care where that regulation applies to the absent parent.]

(7) The provisions of paragraph (5) shall not apply in relation to a relevant person where—

(a) the case is one prescribed in regulation 22 or 23 of the Maintenance Assessments and Special Cases Regulations as a case to be treated as a special case for the purposes of the Act;

(b) there has been a review under section 16 of the Act in relation to another maintenance assessment in force relating to that person;

(c) the child support officer concerned has notified that person of the assessments following that review not earlier than 13 weeks prior to the date a review under section 16 of the Act is due under paragraph (1); and

(d) the child support officer has no reason to believe that there has been a change in that person's circumstances.

[(8) Nothing in this Part requires a review of a maintenance assessment which has not been in force for 104 weeks before 7th December 1998.]

**Note.** In para (2) words from 'the period' to 'been reviewed' substituted by words from 'the period' to 'paragraph (1)' and para (6) substituted by SI 1998/58 as from 19 January 1998. Para (8) inserted by SI 1998/2799 as from 7 December 1998.

[*Revision of decision*

**17.** (1) Subject to paragraphs (6) and (8), any decision may be revised by the Secretary of State—

(a) if the Secretary of State receives an application for the revision of a decision under section 16 of the Act within one month of the date of notification of the decision or within such longer time as may be allowed by regulation 18;

(b) if—

(i) the Secretary of State notifies a person, who applied for a decision to be revised within the period specified in sub-paragraph (a), that the application is unsuccessful because the Secretary of State is not in possession of all of the information or evidence needed to make a decision; and

(ii) that person reapplies for a decision to be revised within one month of the notification described in head (i) above, or such longer period as the Secretary of State is satisfied is reasonable in the circumstances of the case, and provides in that application sufficient evidence or information to enable a decision to be made;

(c) if the decision arose from an official error;

(d) if the Secretary of State is satisfied that the original decision was erroneous due to a misrepresentation of, or failure to disclose, a material fact and that the decision was more advantageous to the person who misrepresented or failed to disclose that fact than it would otherwise have been but for that error;. . .

(e) if the Secretary of State commences action leading to the revision of a decision within one month of the date of notification of the decision [; or

(f) if an appeal is made under section 20 of the Act against a decision within the time prescribed in regulation 31 of the Social Security and Child Support (Decisions and Appeals) Regulations 1999, or in a case to which regulation 32 of those Regulations applies within the time prescribed in that regulation, but the appeal has not been determined].

(2) A decision may be revised by the Secretary of State in consequence of a departure direction where that departure direction takes effect on the effective date.

(3) Subject to regulation 20(6) a decision of the Secretary of State under section 12 of the Act may be revised where—

(a) the Secretary of State receives information which enables him to make a maintenance assessment calculated in accordance with Part I of Schedule 1 to the Act for the whole of the period beginning with the effective date applicable to a particular case; or

(b) the Secretary of State is satisfied that there was unavoidable delay by the absent parent in—
  (i) completing and returning a maintenance enquiry form under the provisions of regulation 6(1);
  (ii) providing information or evidence that is required by him for the determination of an application for a maintenance assessment; or
  (iii) providing information or evidence that is required by him to enable him to revise a decision under section 16 of the Act or supersede a decision under section 17 of the Act.

(4) Where an interim maintenance assessment is in force which is not a Category B interim maintenance assessment and the Secretary of State is satisfied that it would be appropriate to make a Category B interim maintenance assessment, he may revise the interim maintenance assessment which is in force.

(5) Where the Secretary of State revises an interim maintenance assessment in accordance with paragraph (4) and that interim maintenance assessment was made immediately following a previous interim maintenance assessment, he may also revise that previous interim maintenance assessment.

(6) Paragraph (1) shall apply neither—
(a) in respect of a material change of circumstances which—
  (i) occurred since *the date as from which the decision had effect* [the date on which the decision was made]; or
  (ii) is expected, according to information or evidence which the Secretary of State has, to occur; nor
(b) where—
  (i) an appeal against a decision has been brought but not determined; and
  (ii) from the point of view of the appellant, a revision of that decision, if made, would be less to his advantage than the original decision.

(7) In paragraphs (1), (2) and (6) and regulation 18(3) "decision" means a decision of the Secretary of State under section 11 or 12 of the Act and any supersession of such a decision.

(8) Paragraph (1) shall apply in relation to—
(a) any decision of the Secretary of State with respect to a reduced benefit direction or a person's liability under section 43 of the Act; and
(b) the supersession of any such decision under section 17 as extended by paragraph 2 of Schedule 4C to the Act,
as it applies in relation to any decision of the Secretary of State under sections 11, 12 or 17 of the Act.]

**Note.** Substituted, together with regs 18–24, for regs 17, 18, 18A–18D, 19–26, 26A, 27–29 as previously enacted, by SI 1999/1047, reg 16 as from 1 June 1999. In new para (1)(d) word omitted revoked by SI 2004/2415, reg 4(a) as from 16 September 2004. New para (1)(f) and word "; or" immediately preceding it inserted by SI 2004/2415, reg 4(b) as from 16 September 2004. In new para (6)(a)(i) words "the date as from which the decision had effect" substituted by words "the date on which the decision was made" in square brackets by SI 2000/1596, reg 7 as from 19 June 2000.

*Review under section 16 of the Act to be substituted for review under section 17 of the Act*

**18.**   Where after 22nd January 1996 a child support officer considers that he is likely to be required under section 17(3) of the Act to make one or more fresh maintenance assessments if he conducts a review under that section and the application for that review was received by the Secretary of State not earlier than 8 weeks prior to the date upon which the next review of the maintenance assessment in force is due under the provisions of section 16 of the Act, the child support officer shall carry out a review under section 16 of the Act instead of the review under section 17 of the Act for which application has been made.

[*Late applications for a revision*

**18.** (1) The period of one month specified in regulation 17(1)(a) may be extended where the requirements specified in the following provisions of this regulation are met.

(2) An application for an extension of time shall be made by a relevant person or a person acting on his behalf.

(3) An application for an extension of time under this regulation shall—

(a) be made within 13 months of the date on which notification of the decision which it is sought to have revised was given or sent; and

(b) contain particulars of the grounds on which the extension of time is sought and shall contain sufficient details of the decision which it is sought to have revised to enable that decision to be identified.

(4) The application for an extension of time shall not be granted unless the person making the application or any person acting for him satisfies the Secretary of State that—

(a) it is reasonable to grant that application;

(b) the application for a decision to be revised has merit; and

(c) special circumstances are relevant to the application for an extension of time, and as a result of those special circumstances, it was not practicable for the application for a decision to be revised to be made within one month of the date of notification of the decision which it is sought to have revised.

(5) In determining whether it is reasonable to grant an application for an extension of time, the Secretary of State shall have regard to the principle that the greater the time that has elapsed between the expiration of the period of one month described in regulation 17(1)(a) from the date of notification of the decision which it is sought to have revised and the making of the application for an extension of time, the more compelling should be the special circumstances on which the application is based.

(6) In determining whether it is reasonable to grant the application for an extension of time, no account shall be taken of the following—

(a) that the person making the application for an extension of time or any person acting for him was unaware of or misunderstood the law applicable to his case (including ignorance or misunderstanding of the time limits imposed by these Regulations); or

(b) that a Child Support Commissioner or a court has taken a different view of the law from that previously understood and applied.

(7) An application under this regulation for an extension of time which has been refused may not be renewed.]

**Note.** Substituted, together with regs 17, 19–24, for regs 17, 18, 18A–18D, 19–26, 26A, 27–29 as previously enacted, by SI 1999/1047, reg 16 as from 1 June 1999.

[PART VA

. . .]

**Note.** Inserted by SI 1998/2799, reg 2(3) as from 7 December 1998; substituted, together with Pts V, VI, VII, by new Pt V, by SI 1999/1047, reg 16 as from 1 June 1999.

[**18A.** . . .]

[. . .]

**Note.** Inserted by SI 1998/2799, reg 2(3) as from 7 December 1998; substituted, together with Pts V, VI, VII, by new Pt V, by SI 1999/1047, reg 16 as from 1 June 1999.

[**18B.** . . .]

[. . .]

**Note.** Inserted by SI 1998/2799, reg 2(3) as from 7 December 1998; substituted, together with Pts V, VI, VII, by new Pt V, by SI 1999/1047, reg 16 as from 1 June 1999.

**[18C. . . .]**

**[. . .]**

**Note.** Inserted by SI 1998/2799, reg 2(3) as from 7 December 1998; substituted, together with Pts V, VI, VII, by new Pt V, by SI 1999/1047, reg 16 as from 1 June 1999.

**[18D. . . .]**

**[. . .]**

**Note.** Inserted by SI 1998/2799, reg 2(3) as from 7 December 1998; substituted, together with Pts V, VI, VII, by new Pt V, by SI 1999/1047, reg 16 as from 1 June 1999.

**[PART VI**

**. . .]**

**Note.**

Note. Substituted, together with Pts V, VA, VII, by new Pt V, by SI 1999/1047, reg 16 as from 1 June 1999: see SI 1999/1047, reg 1(1).

PART VI

REVIEWS ON A CHANGE OF CIRCUMSTANCES

*Conduct of a review on a change of circumstances*

**19.** (1) Where a child support officer proposes to conduct a review under section 17 of the Act, he shall give 14 days' notice of the proposed review to the relevant persons.

(2) Any application made under section 17 of the Act after 22nd January 1996 shall be in writing and shall give details of the change of circumstances in respect of which a review is sought.

(3) Where a child support officer conducts the review in respect of which notification has been given in accordance with paragraph (1), he shall take into account any information in relation to a change of circumstances notified to him in writing by a relevant person.

(4) *Omitted.*

(5) Where a maintenance assessment is in force with respect to a parent with care and an absent parent in response to an application by the parent with care under section 6 of the Act, and the parent with care authorises the Secretary of State to take action under the Act to recover child support maintenance from that absent parent in relation to an additional child of whom she is a parent with care and he is an absent parent, that authorisation shall be treated by the Secretary of State as an application for a review under section 17 of the Act.

*[Date from which revised decision takes effect*

**19.** Where the date from which a decision took effect is found to be erroneous on a revision under section 16 of the Act, the revision shall take effect from the date on which the revised decision would have taken effect had the error not been made.]

**Notes.** Substituted, together with regs 17, 18, 20–24, for regs 17, 18, 18A–18D, 19–26, 26A, 27–29 as previously enacted, by SI 1999/1047, reg 16 as from 1 June 1999.

*Fresh assessments following a review on a change of circumstances*

**20.** (1) Subject to paragraphs (2) to (5) and regulations 21 and 22, a child support officer who has completed a review of an original assessment under section 17 of the Act shall not make a fresh assessment if the difference between the amount of child support maintenance fixed by that assessment and the amount that would be fixed if a fresh assessment were to be made as a result of the review of that assessment is less than £10.00 per week.

(2) Where a child support officer who has completed a review of an original assessment under section 17 of the Act determines that, were a fresh assessment to be made as a result of the review of that assessment, the circumstances of the absent parent are such that the provisions of paragraph 6 of Schedule 1 to the Act would apply to that fresh assessment, he shall not make a fresh assessment if—

    (a) where the amount fixed by the original assessment is less than the amount that would be fixed by the fresh assessment, the difference between the two amounts is less than £5.00 a week; and

    (b) where the amount fixed by the original assessment is more than the amount that would be fixed by the fresh assessment, the difference between the two amounts is less than £1.00 a week.

(3) Where a child support officer who has completed a review of an original assessment under section 17 of the Act determines that were a fresh assessment to be made as a result of the review of that assessment, the children in respect of whom that fresh assessment would be made are not identical with the children in respect of whom the original assessment was made, he shall not make a fresh assessment if the difference between the amount of child support maintenance fixed by the original assessment and the amount that would be fixed if a fresh assessment were to be made as a result of the review of an original assessment is less than £1.00 per week.

(4) Where a child support officer on completing a review under section 17 of the Act determines that—

    (a) the absent parent is, by virtue of paragraph 5(4) of Schedule 1 to the Act, to be taken for the purposes of that Schedule to have no assessable income; or

    (b) the case falls within paragraph 7(2) of Schedule 1 to the Act,

he shall make a fresh maintenance assessment.

(5) Where a child support officer, on completing a review under section 17 of the Act of a case falling within sub-paragraph (4) of paragraph 5 of Schedule 1 to the Act, determines that the case no longer falls within that sub-paragraph, he shall make a fresh assessment.

[*Supersession of decisions*

**20.** (1) Subject to paragraphs (9) and (10), for the purposes of section 17 of the Act, the cases and circumstances in which a decision ("a superseding decision") may be made under that section are set out in paragraphs (2) to (7).

(2) A decision may be superseded by a decision made by the Secretary of State acting on his own initiative—

    (a) where he is satisfied that the decision is one in respect of which there has been a material change of circumstances since the decision was made;

    (b) where he is satisfied that the decision was made in ignorance of, or was based upon a mistake as to, some material fact; or

    (c) in consequence of a departure direction or of a revision or supersession of a decision with respect to a departure direction.

(3) Except where paragraph (8) applies, a decision may be superseded by a decision made by the Secretary of State where—

(a) an application is made on the basis that—

    (i) there has been a change of circumstances *since the decision was made* [since the date from which the decision had effect]; or

    (ii) it is expected that a change of circumstances will occur; and

(b) the Secretary of State is satisfied that the change of circumstances is or would be material.

(4) A decision may be superseded by a decision made by the Secretary of State where—

(a) an application is made on the basis that the decision was made in ignorance of, or was based upon a mistake as to, a fact; and

(b) the Secretary of State is satisfied that the fact is or would be material.

[(4A) A decision may be superseded by a decision made by the Secretary of State—

(a) where an application is made on the basis that; or

(b) acting on his own initiative where,

the decision to be superseded is a decision of an appeal tribunal or of a Child Support Commissioner that was made in accordance with section 28ZB(4)(b) of the Act, in a case where section 28ZB(5) of the Act applies.]

(5) A decision, other than a decision given on appeal, may be superseded by a decision made by the Secretary of State—

(a) acting on his own initiative where he is satisfied that the decision was erroneous in point of law; or

(b) where an application is made on the basis that the decision was erroneous in point of law.

(6) An interim maintenance assessment may be superseded by a decision made by the Secretary of State where he receives information which enables him to make a maintenance assessment calculated in accordance with Part I of Schedule 1 to the Act for a period beginning after the effective date of that interim maintenance assessment.

(7) Subject to paragraphs (4) and (5) of regulation 17, where the Secretary of State is satisfied that it would be appropriate to make an interim maintenance assessment the category of which is different from that of the interim maintenance assessment which is in force, he may make a decision which supersedes the interim maintenance assessment which is in force.

(8) This paragraph applies—

(a) where any paragraph of regulation 21 applies; and

(b) in the case of a Category A or Category D interim maintenance assessment.

(9) The cases and circumstances in which a decision may be superseded shall not include any case or circumstance in which a decision may be revised.

(10) Paragraphs (2) to (6) shall apply neither in respect of—

(a) a decision to refuse an application for a maintenance assessment; nor

(b) a decision to cancel a maintenance assessment.

(11) For the purposes of section 17 of the Act as extended by paragraph 2 of Schedule 4C to the Act, paragraphs (2) to (5) shall apply in relation to—

(a) a decision with respect to a reduced benefit direction or a person's liability under section 43 of the Act; and

(b) any decision of the Secretary of State under section 17 of the Act as extended by paragraph 2 of Schedule 4C to the Act,

whether as originally made or as revised under section 16 of the Act as extended by paragraph 1 of Schedule 4C to the Act, as they apply in relation to any decision as to a maintenance assessment save that paragraph (8) shall not apply in respect of such a decision.]

**Note.** Substituted, together with regs 17–19, 21–24, for regs 17, 18, 18A–18D, 19–26, 26A, 27–29 as previously enacted, by SI 1999/1047, reg 16 as from 1 June 1999.

In new para (3)(a)(i) words "since the decision was made" substituted by words "since the date from which the decision had effect" in square brackets by SI 2000/1596, reg 8 as from 19 June 2000. New para (4A) inserted by SI 2003/1050, reg 5(1) as from 5 May 2003.

*Fresh assessments following a review on a change of circumstances: special case prescribed by regulation 22 of the Maintenance Assessments and Special Cases Regulations*

**21.** (1) The provisions of paragraphs (2) and (3) shall apply on a review under section 17 of the Act where a case is to be treated as a special case for the purposes of the Act by virtue of regulation 22 of the Maintenance Assessments and Special Cases Regulations.

(2) Where there is a change in the circumstances of the absent parent (whether or not there is also a change in the circumstances of one or more of the persons with care), a child support officer shall not make fresh assessments if the difference between the aggregate amount of child support maintenance fixed by the original assessments and the aggregate amount that would be fixed if fresh assessments were to be made as a result of the review of these original assessments is less than £10.00 per week or, where the circumstances of the absent parent are such that the provisions of paragraph 6 of Schedule 1 to the Act would apply to those fresh assessments, that difference is less than—

(a) where the aggregate amount fixed by the original assessments is less than the aggregate amount that would be fixed by the fresh assessments, £5.00 a week; and

(b) where the aggregate amount fixed by the original assessments is more than the aggregate amount that would be fixed by the fresh assessments, £1.00 a week.

(3) Where there is a change in the circumstances of one or more of the persons with care but not in that of the absent parent, the provisions of regulation 20 shall apply in relation to a review of each original assessment.

[*Circumstances in which a decision may not be superseded*

[**21.** (1) A decision of the Secretary of State shall not be superseded in any of the circumstances specified in the following paragraphs of this regulation.

(2) Except where paragraph (3) or (4) applies and subject to paragraph (5) and regulation 22, this paragraph applies where the difference between—

(a) the amount of child support maintenance ("the amount") fixed in accordance with the original decision; and

(b) the amount which would be fixed in accordance with a superseding decision,

is less than £10.00 per week.

(3) Subject to paragraph (5), this paragraph applies where the circumstances of the absent parent are such that the provisions of paragraph 6 of Schedule 1 to the Act would apply and either—

(a) the amount fixed in accordance with the original decision is less than the amount that would be fixed in accordance with a superseding decision and the difference between the two amounts is less than £5.00 per week; or

(b) the amount fixed in accordance with the original decision is more than the amount that would be fixed in accordance with the superseding decision and the difference between the two amounts is less than £1.00 per week.

(4) Subject to paragraph (5), this paragraph applies where—

(a) the children, in respect of whom child support maintenance would be fixed in accordance with a superseding decision, are not the same children for whom child support maintenance was fixed in accordance with the original decision; and

    (b)  the difference between—
         (i)  the amount of child support maintenance ("the amount") fixed in accordance with the original decision; and
        (ii)  the amount which would be fixed in accordance with a superseding decision,
is less than £1.00 per week.

    (5)  This regulation shall not apply where—
    (a)  the absent parent is, by virtue of paragraph 5(4) of Schedule 1 to the Act, to be taken for the purposes of that Schedule to have no assessable income;
    (b)  the case falls within paragraph 7(2) of Schedule 1 to the Act; or
    (c)  it appears to the Secretary of State that the case no longer falls within paragraph 5(4) of Schedule 1 to the Act.
    (6)  In this regulation—
"original decision" means the decision which would be superseded but for the application of this regulation; and
"superseding decision" means a decision which would supersede the original decision but for the application of this regulation.]

**Note.** Substituted, together with regs 17–20, 22–24, for regs 17, 18, 18A–18D, 19–26, 26A, 27–29 as previously enacted, by SI 1999/1047, reg 16 as from 1 June 1999.

*Fresh assessments following a review on a change of circumstances: special case prescribed by regulation 23 of the Maintenance Assessments and Special Cases Regulations*

**22.**  (1)  The provisions of paragraph (2) shall apply on a review under section 17 of the Act where a case is to be treated as a special case for the purposes of the Act by virtue of regulation 23 of the Maintenance Assessments and Special Cases Regulations.

    (2)  Where there is a change in the circumstances of the person with care or in the circumstances of one or more of the absent parents, the provisions of regulation 20 shall apply to a review of each original assessment.

*[Special cases and circumstances for which regulation 21 is modified*

**[22.**  Where an application is made for a supersession on the basis of a change of circumstances which is relevant to more than one maintenance assessment, regulation 21 shall apply with the following modifications—
    (a)  before the word "amount" in each place it occurs there shall be inserted the word "aggregate"; and
    (b)  for the word "decision" in each place it occurs there shall be substituted the word "decisions".]

**Note.** Substituted, together with regs 17–21, 23, 24, for regs 17, 18, 18A–18D, 19–26, 26A, 27–29 as previously enacted, by SI 1999/1047, reg 16 as from 1 June 1999.

*Reviews conducted under section 19 of the Act as if a review under section 17 of the Act had been applied for*

**23.**  The provisions of regulations 20, 21 and 22 shall apply to a review under section 19 of the Act which has been conducted as if an application for a review under section 17 of the Act had been made.

*[Date from which a decision is superseded*

**[23.**  (1)  Except in a case to which paragraph (2) applies, where notice is given under regulation 24 in the period which begins 28 days before an application for a supersession is made and ends 28 days after that application is made, the superseding decision of which notice was given under regulation 24 shall take effect as from the first day of the maintenance period in which that application was made.

(2) *Where a decision is superseded* [Subject to paragraph (19), where a decision is superseded] by a decision made by the Secretary of State in a case to which regulation 20(2)(a) applies on the basis of evidence or information which was also the basis of a decision made under section 9 or 10 of the Social Security Act 1998 the superseding decision under section 17 shall take effect as from the first day of the maintenance period in which that evidence or information was first brought to the attention of an officer exercising the functions of the Secretary of State under the Act.

(3) Where a superseding decision is made in a case to which either paragraph (2)(b) or (5)(a) of regulation 20 applies, the decision shall take effect as from the first day of the maintenance period in which the decision was made.

(4) *Where a superseding decision is made* [Subject to paragraph (19), where a superseding decision is made] in a case to which regulation 20(3)(a)(i), (4) or (5)(b) applies, the decision shall take effect as from the first day of the maintenance period in which the application for a supersession was made.

(5) Where a superseding decision is made in a case to which regulation 20(3)(a)(ii) applies, the decision shall take effect as from the first day of the maintenance period in which the change of circumstances is due to occur.

(6) Subject to paragraphs (1), (3) and (14), in a case to which regulation 24 applies, a superseding decision shall take effect as from the first day of the maintenance period in which falls the date which is 28 days after the date on which the Secretary of State gave notice to the relevant persons under that regulation.

(7) For the purposes of paragraph (6), where the relevant persons are notified on different dates, the period of 28 days shall be counted from the date of the latest notification.

(8) For the purposes of paragraphs (6) and (7)—
(a) notification includes oral and written notification;
(b) where a person is notified in more than one way, the date on which he is notified is the date on which he was first given notification; and
(c) the date of written notification is the date on which it was handed or sent to the person.

(9) Regulation 1(6) shall not apply in a case to which paragraph (8)(c) applies.

(10) Where—
(a) a decision made by an appeal tribunal under section 20 of the Act or by a Child Support Commissioner is superseded on the ground that it was erroneous due to a misrepresentation of, or that there was a failure to disclose, a material fact; and
(b) the Secretary of State is satisfied that the decision was more advantageous to the person who misrepresented or failed to disclose that fact than it would otherwise have been but for that error,
the superseding decision shall take effect as from the date the decision of the appeal tribunal or, as the case may be, the Child Support Commissioner took, or was to take effect.

(11) Any decision given under section 17 of the Act in consequence of a determination which is a relevant determination for the purposes of section 28ZC of the Act (restrictions on liability in certain cases of error) shall take effect as from the date of the relevant determination.

(12) Where the Secretary of State supersedes a decision in accordance with regulation 20(6), the superseding decision shall take effect as from the first day of the maintenance period in which the Secretary of State has received the information referred to in that paragraph.

(13) Where the Secretary of State supersedes a decision in accordance with regulation 20(7), the superseding decision shall take effect as from the first day of the maintenance period in which the Secretary of State became satisfied that it would be appropriate to make an interim maintenance assessment the category of which is different from that of the maintenance assessment which is in force.

(14) Where a decision is superseded in consequence of a departure direction or a revision or supersession of a decision with respect to a departure direction—

(a) paragraph (6) above shall not apply; and

(b) the superseding decision shall take effect as from the date on which the departure direction or, as the case may be, the revision or supersession, took effect.

(15) Where a decision with respect to a reduced benefit direction is superseded because the direction ceases to be in force in accordance with regulation 41(a), the superseding decision shall have effect as from—

(a) where the direction is in operation immediately before it ceases to be in force, the last day of the benefit week during the course of which the parent concerned complied with the obligations imposed by section 6 of the Act; or

(b) where the direction is suspended immediately before it ceases to be in force, the date on which the parent concerned complied with the obligations imposed by section 6 of the Act.

(16) Where a decision with respect to a reduced benefit direction is superseded because the direction ceases to be in force in accordance with regulation 41(b), the superseding decision shall have effect as from—

(a) where the direction is in operation immediately before it ceases to be in force, the last day of the benefit week during the course of which the application under regulation 41(b) was made; or

(b) where the direction is suspended immediately before it ceases to be in force, the date on which the application under regulation 41(b) was made.

(17) Where a decision with respect to a reduced benefit direction is superseded because the direction ceases to be in force in accordance with regulation 41(c) or (d), the superseding decision shall have effect as from—

(a) where the direction is in operation immediately before it ceases to be in force, the last day of the benefit week during the course of which the Secretary of State is supplied with information that enables him to make the assessment;

(b) where the direction is suspended immediately before it ceases to be in force, the date on which the Secretary of State is supplied with information that enables him to make the assessment.

(18) Where a decision with respect to a reduced benefit direction is superseded because the direction ceases to be in force in accordance with regulation 47(1), the superseding decision shall have effect as from the last day of the benefit week preceding the benefit week on the first day of which, in accordance with the provisions of regulation 36(4), the further direction comes into operation, or would come into operation but for the provisions of regulation 40 or 40ZA.

[(19) Where a superseding decision is made in a case to which regulation 20(2)(a) or (3) applies and the material circumstance is the death of a qualifying child or a qualifying child ceasing to be a qualifying child, the decision shall take effect as from the first day of the maintenance period in which the change occurred.]

[(20) Where a superseding decision is made in a case to which regulation 20(4A) applies that decision shall take effect from the first day of the maintenance period following the date on which the appeal tribunal or the Child Support Commissioner's decision would have taken effect had it been decided in accordance with the determination of the Child Support Commissioner or the court in the appeal referred to in section 28ZB(1)(b) of the Act.]]

**Note.** Substituted, together with regs 17–22, 24, for regs 17, 18, 18A–18D, 19–26, 26A, 27–29 as previously enacted, by SI 1999/1047, reg 16 as from 1 June 1999. In para (2) words "Where a decision is superseded " substituted by words "Subject to paragraph (19), where a decision is superseded" in square brackets by SI 2000/1596, reg 9(a) as from 19 June 2000. In para (4) words "Where a superseding decision is made" substituted by words "Subject to paragraph (19), where a superseding decision is made" in square brackets by SI 2000/1596, reg 9(b) as from 19 June 2000. Para (19) inserted by SI 2000/1596, reg 9(c) as from 19 June 2000. Para (20): inserted by SI 2003/1050, reg 5(2) as from 5 May 2003.

*    *    *    *    *

**Note.** Substituted, together with Pts V, VA, VI, by new Pt V, by SI 1999/1047, reg 16 as from 1 June 1999.

PART VII

REVIEWS OF A DECISION BY A CHILD SUPPORT OFFICER

*Time limits for an application for a review of a decision by a child support officer*

**24.** (1) Subject to paragraph (2), the Secretary of State shall not refer any application for a review under section 18(1), (3) or (4) of the Act or under section 18 of the Act as extended by regulation 9(6) to a child support officer unless that application is received by the Secretary of State within 28 days of the date of notification to the applicant of the decision whose review he seeks.

(2) Where the Secretary of State receives an application for a review under section 18(1), (3) or (4) of the Act or under section 18 of the Act as extended by regulation 9(6) more than 28 days after the date of notification to the applicant of the decision whose review he seeks, the Secretary of State may refer that application to a child support officer if he is satisfied that there was unavoidable delay in making the application.

(3) Where—

(a) a child support officer refuses an application for a maintenance assessment on the grounds of lack of jurisdiction;

(b) the applicant makes no application at that stage for that refusal to be reviewed under section 18(1)(a) of the Act but applies to a court for a maintenance order in relation to the children concerned;

(c) the court refuses to make a maintenance order on the grounds of lack of jurisdiction; and

(d) the applicant then makes an application for the refusal mentioned in subparagraph (a) to be reviewed under section 18(1)(a) of the Act,

the date the applicant is notified of the court's decision shall, for the purposes of paragraphs (1) and (2), be treated as the date of notification to the applicant of the decision whose review he seeks.

[*Procedure where the Secretary of State proposes to supersede a decision on his own initiative*

**24.** *Where the Secretary of State on his own initiative proposes to make a decision superseding a decision other than in consequence of a decision with respect to a departure direction or a revision or supersession of such a decision he shall notify the relevant persons who could be materially affected by the decision of that intention.*]

**Note.** Substituted, together with regs 17–23, for regs 17, 18, 18A–18D, 19–26, 26A, 27–29 as previously enacted, by SI 1999/1047, reg 16 as from 1 June 1999.

*Notice of a review of a decision by a child support officer*

**25.** . . .

. . .

**Note.** Substituted, together with regs 17, 18, 18A–18D, 19–24, 26, 26A, 27–29, by new regs 17–24, by SI 1999/1047, reg 16 as from 1 June 1999.

**26.** . . .

. . .

**Note.** Substituted, together with regs 17, 18, 18A–18D, 19–25, 26A, 27–29, by new regs 17–24, by SI 1999/1047, reg 16 as from 1 June 1999.

[**26A.** . . .]

[. . .]

**Note.** Inserted by SI 1993/913, reg 11; substituted, together with regs 17, 18, 18A–18D, 19–26, 27–29, by new regs 17–24, by SI 1999/1047, reg 16 as from 1 June 1999.

**27.** . . .

. . .

**Note.** Substituted, together with regs 17, 18, 18A–18D, 19–26, 26A, 28, 29, by new regs 17–24, by SI 1999/1047, reg 16 as from 1 June 1999.

**28.** . . .

. . .

**Note.** Substituted, together with regs 17, 18, 18A–18D, 19–26, 26A, 27, 29, by new regs 17–24, by SI 1999/1047, reg 16 as from 1 June 1999.

**29.** . . .

. . .

**Note.** Substituted, together with regs 17, 18, 18A–18D, 19–26, 26A, 27, 28, by new regs 17–24, by SI 1999/1047, reg 16 as from 1 June 1999.

PART VIII

COMMENCEMENT AND TERMINATION OF MAINTENANCE ASSESSMENTS AND MAINTENANCE
PERIODS

*Effective dates of new maintenance assessments*

**30.** (1) Subject to [[regulations 8C (effective dates of interim maintenance assessments), 30A (effective dates in particular cases), 33(7) (maintenance periods)] and to regulation 3(5)[, (7) or (8)] of the Maintenance Arrangements and Jurisdiction Regulations (maintenance assessments where court order in force),] the effective date of a new maintenance assessment following an application under section 4, 6 or 7 of the Act shall be the date determined in accordance with paragraphs (2) to (4).

[(2) Where no maintenance assessment made in accordance with Part I of Schedule 1 to the Act is in force with respect to the person with care and absent parent, the effective date of a new assessment shall be—

(a) in a case where the application for a maintenance assessment is made by a person with care or by a child under section 7 of the Act—

   (i) eight weeks from the date on which a maintenance enquiry form has been given or sent to an absent parent, where such date is on or after 18th April 1995 and where within four weeks of the date that form was given or sent, it has been returned by the absent parent to the Secretary of State and it contains his name, address and written confirmation that he is the parent of the child or children in respect of whom the application for a maintenance assessment was made;

   (ii) in all other circumstances, the date a maintenance enquiry form is given or sent to an absent parent;

(b) in a case where the application for a maintenance assessment is made by an absent parent—

    (i)  eight weeks from the date on which an application made by an absent parent was received by the Secretary of State, where such date is on or after 18th April 1995 and where, on, or within four weeks of, the date of receipt of that maintenance application, the absent parent has provided his name, address and written confirmation that he is the parent of the child or children in respect of whom the application was made;

    (ii)  in all other circumstances, the date an effective maintenance application form is received by the Secretary of State;

[(c)  in a case where the application for a maintenance assessment is an application in relation to which the provisions of regulation 3 have been applied, the date an effective maintenance application form is received by the Secretary of State.]]

[(2A)  Where *a child support officer* [the Secretary of State] is satisfied that there was unavoidable delay by the absent parent in providing the information listed in sub-paragraphs (a)(i) or (b)(i) of paragraph (2) within the time specified in those sub-paragraphs, he may apply the provisions of those sub-paragraphs for the purpose of setting the effective date of a maintenance assessment even though that information was not provided within the time specified in those sub-paragraphs.]

    (3)  The provisions of regulation 1(6)(b) shall not apply to paragraph (2)(a).

    (4)  Where *a child support officer* [the Secretary of State] is satisfied that an absent parent has deliberately avoided receipt of a maintenance enquiry form, he may determine the date on which the form would have been given or sent but for such avoidance, and that date shall be the relevant date for the purposes of paragraph (2)(a).

**Note.** In para (1) words ending with the words "court order in force)," in square brackets inserted by SI 1995/123, reg 7 and words "regulations 8C (effective dates of interim maintenance assessments" and ",(7) or (8)" in square brackets substituted by SI 1995/3261, regs 32(2), 36(2). Para (2) substituted by SI 1995/1045, reg 36(3); sub-para (c) inserted by SI 1995/3261, reg 32(3). Para (2A) inserted by SI 1995/1045, reg 36(4); words "a child support officer" substituted by words "the Secretary of State" in square brackets by SI 1999/1047, reg 17 as from 1 June 1999.

In para (4) words "a child support officer" substituted by words "the Secretary of State" in square brackets by SI 1999/1047, reg 17 as from 1 June 1999.

[*Effective dates of new maintenance assessments in particular cases*

**30A.**  (1)  Subject to regulation 33(7), where a new maintenance assessment is made in accordance with Part I of Schedule 1 to the Act following an interim maintenance assessment which has ceased to have effect in the circumstances set out in regulation 8D(6), the effective date of that maintenance assessment shall be the date upon which that interim maintenance assessment ceased to have effect in accordance with that regulation.

[(2)  Where *a child support officer* [the Secretary of State] receives the information or evidence to enable him to make a maintenance assessment, calculated in accordance with the provisions of Part I of Schedule 1 to the Act, for the period from the date set by regulation 3(7) of the Maintenance Arrangements and Jurisdiction Regulations or regulation 30(2)(a) or (b), as the case may be, to the effective date of the maintenance assessment referred to in paragraph (1), the maintenance assessment first referred to in this paragraph shall, subject to regulation 33(7), have effect for that period.]

[(3)  The effective date of a new maintenance assessment made in respect of a person with care and an absent parent shall, where the circumstances set out in paragraph (4) apply, be the first day of the first maintenance period after the *child support officer* [Secretary of State] has received the information or evidence referred to in paragraph (4)(c) or 13th January 1997, whichever is the later.

(4) The circumstances referred to in paragraph (3) are where—

(a) paragraphs (1) and (2) do not apply to that person with care and that absent parent;

(b) no maintenance assessment made in accordance with the provisions of Part I of Schedule 1 to the Act is in force in relation to that person with care and that absent parent; and

(c) on or after 13th January 1997, *a child support officer* [the Secretary of State] has sufficient information or evidence to enable him to make a new maintenance assessment, calculated in accordance with the provisions of Part I of Schedule 1 to the Act, in relation to that person with care and that absent parent but in respect only of a period beginning after the effective date applicable in their case by virtue of regulation 30(2).

(5) Where the information or evidence referred to in paragraph (3) is that there has been an award of income support[, state pension credit] or an income-based job seeker's allowance, the Secretary of State shall be treated as having received the information or evidence which enables *a child support officer* [him] to make the assessment referred to in that paragraph on the first day in respect of which income support[, state pension credit] or an income-based jobseeker's allowance was payable under that award.

(6) Where, in a case falling within paragraph (3), *a child support officer* [the Secretary of State] receives the information or evidence to enable him to make a maintenance assessment calculated in accordance with the provisions of Part I of Schedule 1 to the Act, for the period from the effective date applicable to that case under regulation 30(2)(a) or (b), as the case may be, to the effective date of the assessment referred to in paragraph (3), the maintenance assessment first referred to in this paragraph shall have effect for that period.

(7) Paragraphs (3) to (6) shall not apply where a case falls within regulation 33(7), or regulation 3 of the Maintenance Agreements and Jurisdiction Regulations (relationship between maintenance assessments and certain court orders).]]

**Note.** Inserted by SI 1995/3261, reg 33. Para (2) substituted by SI 1996/3196, reg 8(2), and words a child support officer "substituted by words "the Secretary of State" in square brackets by SI 1999/1047, reg 18(a) as from 1 June 1999. Para (3) inserted by SI 1996/3196, reg 8(3), and words "child support officer" substituted by words "Secretary of State" in square brackets by SI 1998/58, reg 40 as from 19 January 1998. Para (4) inserted by SI 1996/3196, reg 8(3), and words "a child support officer" substituted by words "the Secretary of State" in square brackets by SI 1999/1047, reg 18(a) as from 1 June 1999. Para (5) inserted by SI 1996/3196, reg 8(3), and words ", state pension credit" in square brackets in both places they occur inserted by SI 2003/2779, reg 3(1), (3) as from 5 November 2003, and words "a child support officer" substituted by word "him" in square brackets by SI 1999/1047, reg 18(b) as from 1 June 1999. Para (6) inserted by SI 1996/3196, reg 8(3), and words "a child support officer" substituted by words "the Secretary of State" in square brackets by SI 1999/1047, reg 18(a) as from 1 June 1999. Para (7): inserted by SI 1996/3196, reg 8(3).

**31.**   . . .

. . .

**Note.** Revoked by SI 1999/1047, reg 19 as from 1 June 1999.

[**31A.**   . . .]

[. . .]

**Note.** Substituted, together with regs 31, 31B, 31C for reg 31 as originally enacted, by SI 1995/3261, reg 34; Revoked by SI 1999/1047, reg 19 as from 1 June 1999.

[**31B.**   . . .]

[. . .]

**Note.** Substituted, together with regs 31, 31A, 31C for reg 31 as originally enacted, by SI 1995/3261, reg 34; revoked by SI 1999/1047, reg 19 as from 1 June 1999.

**[31C.  . . . .]**

[. . .]

**Note.** Substituted, together with regs 31–31B for reg 31 as originally enacted, by SI 1995/3261, reg 34. Revoked by SI 1999/1047, reg 19 as from 1 June 1999.

*Cancellation of a maintenance assessment*

**32.**    Where *a child support officer* [the Secretary of State] cancels a maintenance assessment under paragraph 16(2) or (3) of Schedule 1 to the Act, the assessment shall cease to have effect from the date of receipt of the request for the cancellation of the assessment or from such later date as *the child support officer* [he] may determine.

**Note.** Words "a child support officer" substituted by words "the Secretary of State" in square brackets and words "the child support officer" substituted for word "he" in square brackets by SI 1999/1047, reg 20 as from 1 June 1999.

[*Cancellation of maintenance assessments made under section 7 of the Act where the child is no longer habitually resident in Scotland*

**32A.**    (1) Where a maintenance assessment made in response to an application by a child under section 7 of the Act is in force and that child ceases to be habitually resident in Scotland, *a child support officer* [the Secretary of State] shall cancel that assessment.

(2) In any case where paragraph (1) applies, the assessment shall cease to have effect from the date that *the child support officer* [the Secretary of State] determines is the date on which the child concerned ceased to be habitually resident in Scotland.]

**Note.** Words "a child support officer" and words "the child support officer" substituted by words "the Secretary of State" in both places in square by SI 1999/1047, reg 21 as from 1 June 1999.

[*Notification of intention to cancel a maintenance assessment under paragraph 16(4A) of Schedule 1 to the Act*

**32B.**    (1) *A child support officer* [The Secretary of State] shall, if it is reasonably practicable to do so, give written notice to the relevant persons of his intention to cancel a maintenance assessment under paragraph 16(4A) of Schedule 1 to the Act.

(2) Where a notice under paragraph (1) has been given, *a child support officer* [the Secretary of State] shall not cancel that maintenance assessment before the end of a period of 14 days commencing with the date that notice was given or sent.]

**Note.** Inserted by SI 1995/3261, reg 35, and SI 1995/3265, reg 2. Words "A child support officer" and "a child support officer" substituted by words "The Secretary of State" and "the Secretary of State" in square brackets by SI 1999/1047, reg 22 as from 1 June 1999.

*Maintenance periods*

**33.**    (1) The child support maintenance payable under a maintenance assessment shall be calculated at a weekly rate and be in respect of successive maintenance periods, each such period being a period of 7 days.

(2) Subject to paragraph (6), the first maintenance period shall commence on the effective date of the first maintenance assessment, and each succeeding maintenance period shall commence on the day immediately following the last day of the preceding maintenance period.

(3) The maintenance periods in relation to a fresh maintenance assessment *following a review under section 16, 17, 18 or 19 of the Act* [made upon the supersession of a decision under section 17 of the Act] shall coincide with the maintenance periods in relation to the earlier assessment, had it continued in force, and the first maintenance period in relation to a fresh assessment shall commence on the day following the last day of the last maintenance period in relation to the earlier assessment.

(4) The amount of child support maintenance payable in respect of a maintenance period which includes the effective date of a fresh maintenance assessment shall be the amount of maintenance payable under that fresh assessment.

(5) The amount of child support maintenance payable in respect of a maintenance period during the course of which a cancelled maintenance assessment ceases to have effect shall be the amount of maintenance payable under that assessment.

(6) Where a case is to be treated as a special case for the purposes of the Act by virtue of regulation 22 of the Maintenance Assessments and Special Cases Regulations (multiple applications relating to an absent parent) and an application is made by a person with care in relation to an absent parent where—

(a) there is already a maintenance assessment in force in relation to that absent parent and a different person with care; or

(b) sub-paragraph (a) does not apply, but before a maintenance assessment is made in relation to that application, a maintenance assessment is made in relation to that absent parent and a different person with care,

the maintenance periods in relation to an assessment made in response to that application shall coincide with the maintenance periods in relation to the earlier maintenance assessment, except where regulation 3(7) of the Maintenance Arrangements and Jurisdiction Regulations or paragraph (8) applies, and the first such period shall, subject to paragraph (9), commence not later than 7 days after the date of notification to the relevant persons of the later maintenance assessment.

(7) Subject to regulation 3(7) of the Maintenance Arrangements and Jurisdiction Regulations and to paragraph (8), the effective date of a maintenance assessment made in response to an application falling within paragraph (6) shall be the date upon which the first maintenance period in relation to that application commences in accordance with that paragraph.

(8) The first maintenance period in relation to a maintenance assessment which is made in response to an application falling within paragraph (6) and which immediately follows an interim maintenance assessment shall commence on the effective date of the interim maintenance assessment or 22nd January 1996 whichever is the later, and the effective date of that maintenance assessment shall be the date upon which that first maintenance period commences.

(9) Where the case is one to which, if paragraphs (6) and (7) did not apply, regulation 30(2)(a)(i) or (b)(i) would apply, and the first maintenance period would, under the provisions of paragraph (6), commence during the 8-week period referred to in sub-paragraph (a) or (b) of that regulation, the first maintenance period shall commence not later than 7 days after the expiry of that period of 8 weeks.

**Note.** In para (3) words 'following a review under section 16, 17, 18 or 19 of the Act' substituted by words 'made upon the supersession of a decisionm under section 17 of the Act' in square brackets by SI 1999/1047, reg 23 as from 1 June 1999.

PART IX

REDUCED BENEFIT DIRECTIONS

*Prescription of disability working allowance for the purposes of section 6 of the Act*

**34.**    Disability working allowance shall be a benefit of a prescribed kind for the purposes of section 6 of the Act.

*Periods for compliance with obligations imposed by section 6 of the Act*

**35.**    (1)  Where the Secretary of State considers that a parent has failed to comply with an obligation imposed by section 6 of the Act he shall serve written notice on that parent that, unless she complies with that obligation, he intends to refer the case to a child support officer for the child support officer to take action under section 46 of the Act if the child support officer considers such action to be appropriate.

(2)  The Secretary of State shall not refer a case to a child support officer prior to the expiry of a period of—

(a)  2 weeks from the date he serves notice under paragraph (1) on the parent in question; or

(b)  6 weeks from that date, where, before the expiry of 2 weeks from service of that notice, he has received from the parent in question in writing her reasons why she believes that if she were to be required to comply with an obligation imposed by section 6 of the Act, there would be a risk, as a result of that compliance, of her or any child or children living with her suffering harm or undue distress,

and the notice shall contain a statement setting out the provisions of sub-paragraphs (a) and (b).

(3)  Where a child support officer serves written notice on a parent under section 46(2) of the Act, the period to be specified in that notice shall be 14 days.

[*Circumstances in which a reduced benefit direction shall not be given*

**35A.**    *A child support officer* [The Secretary of State] shall not after 22nd January 1996 give a reduced benefit direction where—

(a)  income support is paid to or in respect of the parent in question and the applicable amount of the claimant for income support includes one or more of the amounts set out in paragraph 15(3), (4) or (6) of Part IV of Schedule 2 to the Income Support (General) Regulations 1987; or

[(aa)  income-based jobseeker's allowance is paid to or in respect of the parent in question and the applicable amount of the claimant for income-based jobseeker' s allowance includes one or more of the amounts set out in paragraph 20(4), (5) or (7) of Schedule 1 to the Jobseeker's Allowance Regulations; or]

(b)  an amount equal to one or more of the amounts specified in sub-paragraph (a) is included, by virtue of regulation 9 of the Maintenance Assessments and Special Cases Regulations, in the exempt income of the parent in question and family credit or disability working allowance is paid to or in respect of that parent [;or

(c)  an amount prescribed under section 9(5)(c) of the Tax Credits Act 2002 (increased elements of child tax credit for children or young persons with a disability) is included in an award of child tax credit payable to the parent in question or a member of that parent's family living with him].]

**Note.** Inserted by SI 1995/3261, reg 37. Words "A child support officer" substituted by words "The Secretary of State" in square brackets by SI 1999/1047, reg 25 as from 1 June 1999, para (aa) inserted by SI 1996/1345, reg 5(5), and para (c) and word "; or" immediately preceding it inserted by SI 2003/328, reg 5 as from 6 April 2003.

*Amount of and period of reduction of relevant benefit under a reduced benefit direction*

**36.**   (1) The reduction in the amount payable by way of a relevant benefit to, or in respect of, the parent concerned and the period of such reduction by virtue of a direction shall be determined in accordance with paragraphs (2) to (9).

(2) Subject to paragraph (6) and regulations 37, 38(7) [, 40 and 40ZA], there shall be a reduction for a period of [156 weeks] from the day specified in the direction under the provisions of section 46(9) of the Act in respect of each such week equal to

$$[0.4 \times B]$$

where B is an amount equal to the weekly amount, in relation to the week in question, specified in column (2) of paragraph 1(1)(e) of the applicable amounts Schedule.

(3)   . . .

(4) [Subject to paragraphs [(4A),] (5), (5A) and (5B)], a direction shall come into operation on the first day of the second benefit week following the review, carried out by *the adjudication officer* [the Secretary of State] in consequence of the direction, of the relevant benefit that is payable.

[(4A) Subject to paragraphs (5), (5A) and (5B), where a reduced benefit direction ("the subsequent direction") is made on a day when a reduced benefit direction ("the earlier direction") is in force in respect of the same parent, the subsequent direction shall come into operation on the day immediately following the day on which the earlier direction ceased to be in force.]

(5) Where the relevant benefit is income support and the provisions of regulation 26(2) of the Social Security (Claims and Payments) Regulations 1987 (deferment of payment of different amount of income support) apply, a direction shall come into operation on such later date as may be determined by the Secretary of State in accordance with those provisions.

[(5A) Where the relevant benefit is family credit or disability working allowance and, at the time a direction is given, a lump sum payment has already been made under the provisions of regulation 27(1A) of the Social Security (Claims and Payments) Regulations 1987 (payment of family credit or disability working allowance by lump sum) the direction shall, subject to paragraph (5B), come into operation on the first day of any benefit week which immediately follows the period in respect of which the lump sum payment was made, or the first day of any benefit week which immediately follows 18th April 1995 if later.

(5B) Where the period in respect of which the lump sum payment was made is not immediately followed by a benefit week, but family credit or disability working allowance again becomes payable, or income support [or income-based job-seeker's allowance] becomes payable, during a period of 52 weeks from the date the direction was given, the direction shall come into operation on the first day of the second benefit week which immediately follows the expiry of a period of 14 days from service of the notice specified in paragraph (5C).

(5C) Where paragraph (5B) applies, the parent to or in respect of whom family credit or disability working allowance has again become payable, or income support [or income-based jobseeker's allowance] has become payable, shall be notified in writing by [the Secretary of State] that the amount of family credit, disability working allowance [, income support or income-based jobseeker's allowance] paid to or in respect of her will be reduced in accordance with the provisions of paragraph (5B) if she continues to fail to comply with the obligations imposed by section 6 of the Act.

(5D) Where—

(a) family credit or disability working allowance has been paid by lump sum under the provisions of regulation 27(1A) of the Social Security (Claims and Payments) Regulations 1987 (whether or not a benefit week immediately follows the period in respect of which the lump sum payment was made); and

(b) where income support [or income-based jobseeker's allowance] becomes payable to or in respect of a parent to or in respect of whom family credit or disability working allowance was payable at the time the direction referred to in paragraph (5A) was made, income support [or, as the case may be, income-based jobseeker' s allowance] shall become a relevant benefit for the purposes of that direction and the amount payable by way of income support [or, as the case may be, income-based jobseeker' s allowance] shall be reduced in accordance with that direction.

(5E) In circumstances to which paragraph (5A) or (5B) applies, where no relevant benefit has become payable during a period of 52 weeks from the date on which a direction was given, it shall lapse.]

[(6) Where the benefit payable is income support or income-based jobseekers allowance and there is a change in the benefit week whilst a direction is in operation, the period of the reduction specified in paragraph (2) shall be a period greater than 155 weeks but less than 156 weeks and ending on the last day of the last benefit week falling entirely within the period of 156 weeks specified in that paragraph.]

(7) Where the weekly amount specified in column (2) of paragraph 1(1)(e) of the applicable amounts Schedule changes on a day when a direction is in operation, the amount of the reduction of the relevant benefit shall be changed—

(a) where the benefit is income support [or income-based jobseeker's allowance], from the first day of the first benefit week to commence for the parent concerned on or after the day that weekly amount changes;

(b) where the benefit is family credit or disability working allowance, from the first day of the next award period of that benefit for the parent concerned commencing on or after the day that weekly amount changes.

(8) Only one direction in relation to a parent shall be in force at any one time.

(9) . . .

**Note.** In para (2) first words in square brackets substituted by SI 1996/1345, reg 5(6)(a) and words and formula in square brackets substituted by SI 1996/1945, reg 14(2). In para (3) words in square brackets substituted by SI 1996/1345, reg 5(6)(a), revoked by SI 1996/1945, reg 14(3). In para (4) words from "Subject to" to "(5A) and (5B)" in square brackets substituted by SI 1995/1045, reg 38(2) and number "(4A)," in square brackets inserted by SI 1996/1945, reg 14(4), and words "the adjudication officer" substituted by words "the Secretary of State" in square brackets by SI 1999/1047, reg 26(a) as from 29 November 1999. Para (4A) inserted by SI 1996/1945, reg 14(5). Paras (5A)–(5E) inserted by SI 1995/1045, reg 38(3). In para (5B) words "or income-based jobseeker's allowance" in square brackets inserted by SI 1996/1345, reg 5(6)(b). In para (5C) words "or income-based jobseeker's allowance" in square brackets inserted by SI 1996/1345, reg 5(6)(c), and words "a child support officer" substituted by words "the Secretary of State" in square brackets by SI 1999/1047, reg 26(b) as from 1 June 1999, and words ", income support or income-based jobseeker's allowance" in square brackets substituted by SI 1996/1345, reg 5(6)(c). In para (5D)(b) words "or income-based jobseeker's allowance" in square brackets inserted by SI 1996/1345, reg 5(6)(d) and words "or, as the case may be, income-based jobseeker's allowance" in square brackets in both places they occur inserted by SI 1996/1345, reg 5(6)(d). In para (6) words in square brackets inserted by SI 1996/1345, reg 5(6)(b); substituted by SI 1996/1945, reg 14(6). Para (7) words in square brackets inserted by SI 1996/1345, reg 5(6)(b). Para (9): revoked by SI 1996/1945, reg 14(3).

*Modification of reduction under a reduced benefit direction to preserve minimum entitlement to relevant benefit*

**37.** Where in respect of any benefit week the amount of the relevant benefit that would be payable after it has been reduced following a direction would, but for this regulation, be nil or less than the minimum amount of that benefit that is payable as determined—

(a) in the case of income support, by regulation 26(4) of the Social Security (Claims and Payments) Regulations 1987;

(aa) in the case of income-based jobseeker's allowance, by regulation 87A of the Jobseeker's Allowance Regulations 1996;

(b) in the case of family credit and disability working allowance, by regulation 27(2) of the Social Security (Claims and Payments) Regulations 1987,

the amount of that reduction shall be decreased to such extent as to raise the amount of that benefit to the minimum amount that is payable.

*Suspension of a reduced benefit direction when relevant benefit ceases to be payable*

**38.** (1) Where relevant benefit ceases to be payable to, or in respect of, the parent concerned at a time when a direction is in operation, that direction shall, subject to paragraph (2), be suspended for a period of 52 weeks from the date the relevant benefit has ceased to be payable.

(2) Where a direction has been suspended for a period of 52 weeks and no relevant benefit is payable at the end of that period, it shall cease to be in force.

(3) Where a direction is suspended and relevant benefit again becomes payable to or in respect of the parent concerned, the amount payable by way of that benefit shall, subject to regulations 40, [40ZA,] 41 and 42, be reduced in accordance with that direction for the balance of the reduction period.

(4) The amount or, as the case may be, amounts of the reduction to be made during the balance of the reduction period shall be determined in accordance with regulation 36(2) ...

(5) No reduction in the amount of benefit under paragraph (3) shall be made before the expiry of a period of 14 days from service of the notice specified in paragraph (6), and the provisions of regulation 36(4) shall apply as to the date when the direction again comes into operation.

(6) Where relevant benefit again becomes payable to or in respect of a parent with respect to whom a direction is suspended she shall be notified in writing by *a child support officer* [the Secretary of State] that the amount of relevant benefit paid to or in respect of her will again be reduced, in accordance with the provisions of paragraph (3), if she continues to fail to comply with the obligations imposed by section 6 of the Act.

(7) Where a direction has ceased to be in force by virtue of the provisions of paragraph (2), a further direction in respect of the same parent given on account of that parent's failure to comply with the obligations imposed by section 6 of the Act in relation to one or more of the same qualifying children shall, unless it also ceases to be in force by virtue of the provisions of paragraph (2), be in operation for the balance of the reduction period relating to the direction that has ceased to be in force, and the provisions of paragraph (4) shall apply to it.

**Note.** In para (3) words in square brackets inserted by SI 1996/1345, reg 5(8) and in para (4) words omitted revoked by SI 1996/1945, reg 15. In para (6) words "a child support officer" substituted by words "the Secretary of State" in square brackets by SI 1999/1047, reg 27 as from 1 June 1999.

*Reduced benefit direction where family credit or disability working allowance is payable and income support becomes payable*

**39.** (1) Where a direction is in operation in respect of a parent to whom or in respect of whom family credit or disability working allowance is payable, and income support or income-based jobseeker's allowance becomes payable to or in respect of that parent, income support or, as the case may be, income-based jobseeker's allowance shall become a relevant benefit for the purposes of that direction, and the amount payable by way of income support or, as the case may be, income-based jobseeker's allowance shall be reduced in accordance with that direction for the balance of the reduction period.

(2) The amount or, as the case may be, the amounts of the reduction to be made during the balance of the reduction period shall be determined in accordance with regulation 36(2).

*Suspension of a reduced benefit direction when a modified applicable amount is payable [(income support)]*

**40.** (1) Where a direction is given or is in operation at a time when income support is payable to or in respect of the parent concerned *but her applicable amount falls to be calculated under the provisions mentioned in paragraph (3)* [but the circumstances in paragraph (3) apply to her], that direction shall be suspended for so long as *the applicable amount falls to be calculated under the provisions mentioned in that paragraph* [those circumstances apply], or 52 weeks, whichever period is the shorter.
   [(1A) . . .]
   (2) Where a case falls within paragraph (1) [. . .] and a direction has been suspended for a period of 52 weeks, it shall cease to be in force.
   (3) *The provisions of paragraph (1) shall apply where the applicable amount in relation to the parent concerned falls to be calculated under—*
   (a) *regulation 19 of and Schedule 4 to the Income Support Regulations (applicable amounts for persons in residential care and nursing homes);*
   (b) *regulation 21 of and paragraphs 1 to 3 of Schedule 7 to the Income Support Regulations (patients);*
   (c) *regulation 21 of and paragraphs 10B, 10C <. . .> and 13 of Schedule 7 to the Income Support Regulations (persons in residential accommodation).*
   [(3) The circumstances referred to in paragraph (1) are that—
   (a) she is resident in a care home or an independent hospital;
   (b) she is being provided with a care home service or an independent health care service; or
   (c) her applicable amount falls to be calculated under regulation 21 of and any of paragraphs 1 to 3 of Schedule 7 to the Income Support Regulations (patients).
   (4) In paragraph (3)—
   "care home" has the meaning assigned to it by section 3 of the Care Standards Act 2000;
   "care home service" has the meaning assigned to it by section 2(3) of the Regulation of Care (Scotland) Act 2001;
   "independent health care service" has the meaning assigned to it by section 2(5)(a) and (b) of the Regulation of Care (Scotland) Act 2001; and
   "independent hospital" has the meaning assigned to it by section 2 of the Care Standards Act 2000.]

**Note.** Provision heading words "when a modified applicable amount is payable" substituted by words "(income support)" in square brackets by SI 2003/2779, reg 3(1), (4)(a) as from 5 November 2003. In para (1) words "but her applicable amount falls to be calculated under the provisions mentioned in paragraph (3)" and "as the applicable amount falls to be calculated under the provisions mentioned in that paragraph" substituted by words "but the circumstances in paragraph (3) apply to her" and "those circumstances apply" in square brackets by SI 2003/2779, reg 3(1), (4)(b) as from 5 November 2003. Para (1A) inserted by SI 1995/1045, reg 39(2); revoked by SI 2003/2779, reg 3(1), (4)(c) as from 5 November 2003. In para (2) words omitted inserted by SI 1995/1045, reg 39(3); revoked by SI 2003/2779, reg 3(1), (4)(d) as from 5 November 2003. Para (3) substituted by new paras (3), (4) by SI 2003/2779, reg 3(1), (4)(e) as from 5 November 2003.

[*Suspension of a reduced benefit direction in the case of modifed applicable amounts in jobseeker's allowance [(income-based jobseeker's allowance)]*

**40ZA.** (1) Where a direction is given or is in operation at a time when income-based jobseeker's allowance is payable to or in respect of the parent concerned *but* *her applicable amount falls to be calculated under the provisions mentioned in paragraph (4)* [but the circumstances in paragraph (4) apply to her], that direction shall be suspended for so long as *the applicable amount falls to be calculated under those provisions* [those circumstances apply], or 52 weeks, whichever period is the shorter.

(2) . . .

(3) Where a case falls within paragraph (1) . . . and a direction has been suspended for a period of 52 weeks, it shall cease to be in force.

*(4) The provisions of paragraph (1) shall apply where the applicable amount in relation to the parent concerned falls to be calculated under—*

(a) *regulation 85 of and paragraph 1 or 2 of Schedule 5 to the Jobseeker's Allowance Regulations (patients);*

(b) *regulation 85 of and paragraph 8, 9 or 15 of Schedule 5 to the Jobseeker's Allowance Regulations (persons in residential accommodation); or*

(c) *regulation 86 of and Schedule 4 to the Jobseeker's Allowance Regulations (applicable amounts for persons in residential care and nursing homes).*

[(4) The circumstances referred to in paragraph (1) are that—

(a) she is resident in a care home or an independent hospital;

(b) she is being provided with a care home service or an independent health care service; or

(c) her applicable amount falls to be calculated under regulation 85 of and paragraph 1 or 2 of Schedule 5 to the Jobseeker's Allowance Regulations (patients).

(5) In paragraph (4)—

"care home" has the meaning assigned to it by section 3 of the Care Standards Act 2000;

"care home service" has the meaning assigned to it by section 2(3) of the Regulation of Care (Scotland) Act 2001;

"independent health care service" has the meaning assigned to it by section 2(5)(a) and (b) of the Regulation of Care (Scotland) Act 2001; and

"independent hospital" has the meaning assigned to it by section 2 of the Care Standards Act 2000.]]

**Note.** Inserted by SI 1996/1345, reg 5(10). Provision heading words "in the case of modifed applicable amounts in jobseeker's allowance" substituted by words "(income-based jobseeker's allowance)" in square brackets by SI 2003/2779, reg 3(1), (5)(a) as from 5 November 2003. In para (1) words "but her applicable amount falls to be calculated under the provisions mentioned in paragraph (4)" and "the applicable amount falls to be calculated under those provisions" substituted by words "but the circumstances in paragraph (4) apply to her" and "those circumstances apply" in square brackets by SI 2003/2779, reg 3(1), (5)(b) as from 5 November 2003. Para (2) revoked, in para (3) words omitted and para (4) substituted by new paras (4), (5) by SI 2003/2779, reg 3(1), (5)(c)–(e) as from 5 November 2003.

*Suspension of a reduced benefit direction where certain deductions are being made from income support*

**40A.** *Revoked.*

**Note.** Inserted by SI 1995/3261, reg 38. Revoked with savings by SI 1996/3196, reg 9; for savings see reg 16(3) thereof.

*Termination of a reduced benefit direction following compliance with obligations imposed by section 6 of the Act*

**41.** (1) Where a parent with care with respect to whom a direction is in force complies with the obligations imposed by section 6 of the Act, that direction shall cease to be in force on the date determined in accordance with paragraph (2) or (3), as the case may be.

(2) Where the direction is in operation, it shall cease to be in force on the last day of the benefit week during the course of which the parent concerned complied with the obligations imposed by section 6 of the Act.

(3) Where the direction is suspended, it shall cease to be in force on the date on which the parent concerned complied with the obligations imposed by section 6 of the Act.

[*Termination of reduced benefit direction*

**41.** A reduced benefit direction shall cease to be in force—

(a) where a parent with care, with respect to whom such a direction is in force, complies with the obligations imposed by section 6 of the Act;

(b) upon an application made for the purpose where the Secretary of State is satisfied that a parent with care, with respect to whom such a direction is in force, should not be required to comply with the obligations imposed by section 6 of the Act;

(c) where a qualifying child of a parent with respect to whom a direction is in force applies for a maintenance assessment to be made with respect to him under section 7 of the Act and an assessment is made in response to that application in respect of all of the qualifying children in relation to whom the parent concerned failed to comply with the obligations imposed by section 6 of the Act; or

(d) where—

  (i) an absent parent applies for a maintenance assessment to be made under section 4 of the Act with respect to all of his qualifying children in relation to whom the other parent of those children is a person with care;

  (ii) a direction is in force with respect to that other parent following her failure to comply with the obligations imposed by section 6 of the Act in relation to those qualifying children; and

  (iii) an assessment is made in response to that application by the absent parent for a maintenance assessment.]

**Note.** Substituted, for regs 41–46 as originally enacted, by SI 1999/1047, reg 28 as from 1 June 1999.

**42.** . . .

. . .

**Note.** Substituted, together with regs 41, 43–46, by new reg 41, by SI 1999/1047, reg 28 as from 1 June 1999.

**43.** . . .

. . .

**Note.** Substituted, together with regs 41, 42, 44–46, by new reg 41, by SI 1999/1047, reg 28 as from 1 June 1999.

**44.** . . .

. . .

**Note.** Substituted, together with regs 41–43, 45, 46, by new reg 41, by SI 1999/1047, reg 28 as from 1 June 1999.

**45.** . . .

. . .

**Note.** Substituted, together with regs 41–44, 46, by new reg 41, by SI 1999/1047, reg 28 as from 1 June 1999.

**46.** . . .

. . .

**Note.** Note. Substituted, together with regs 41–45, by new reg 41, by SI 1999/1047, reg 28 as from 1 June 1999.

*Reduced benefit directions where there is an additional qualifying child*

**47.** (1) Where a direction is in operation or would be in operation but for the provisions of regulation 40 [or 40ZA] and *a child support officer* [the Secretary of State] gives a further direction with respect to the same parent on account of that parent failing to comply with the obligations imposed by section 6 of the Act in relation to an additional qualifying child of whom she is a person with care, the earlier direction shall cease to be in force . . . .

(2) Where a further direction comes into operation in a case falling within paragraph (1), the provisions of regulation 36 shall apply to it.

[(3) Where—

(a) a direction ("the earlier direction") has ceased to be in force by virtue of regulation 38(2); and

(b) [the Secretary of State] gives a direction ("the further direction") with respect to the same parent on account of that parent's failure to comply with the obligations imposed by section 6 of the Act in relation to an additional qualifying child,

as long as that further direction remains in force, no additional direction shall be brought into force with respect to that parent on account of her failure to comply with the obligations imposed by section 6 of the Act in relation to one or more children in relation to whom the earlier direction was given.]

(4) Where a case falls within paragraph (1) or (3) and the further direction, but for the provisions of this paragraph would cease to be in force by virtue of the provisions of regulation 41 or 42, but the earlier direction would not have ceased to be in force by virtue of the provisions of those regulations, the later direction shall continue in force for a period ("the extended period") calculated in accordance with the provisions of paragraph (5) and the reduction of relevant benefit [for the extended period shall be determined in accordance with regulation 36(2)].

(5) The extended period for the purposes of paragraph (4) shall be

$$[(156 - F - S) \text{ weeks}]$$

where—

F is the number of weeks for which the earlier direction was in operation; and

S is the number of weeks for which the later direction has been in operation.

(6) . . .

(7) . . .

(8) In this regulation "an additional qualifying child" means a qualifying child of whom the parent concerned is a person with care and who was either not such a qualifying child at the time the earlier direction was given or had not been born at the time the earlier direction was given.

**Note.** In para (1) words "or 40ZA" in square brackets inserted by SI 1996/1345, reg 5(11) and words "a child support officer" substituted by words "the Secretary of State" in square brackets and words omitted revoked by SI 1999/1047, reg 29(a)(i), (ii) as from 1 June 1999. Para (3) substituted by SI 1996/1945, reg 17(2), and in sub-para (b) words "a child support officer" substituted by words "the Secretary of State" in square brackets by SI 1999/1047, reg 29(b) as from 1 June 1999. In para (4) words in square brackets substituted by SI 1996/1945, reg 17(3). In para (5) formula in square brackets substituted by SI 1996/1945, reg 17(4). Paras (6), (7): revoked by SI 1996/1945, reg 17(5).

*Suspension and termination of a reduced benefit direction where the sole qualifying child ceases to be a child or where the parent concerned ceases to be a person with care*

**48.**   (1)  Where, whilst a direction is in operation—

(a)  there is, in relation to that direction, only one qualifying child, and that child ceases to be a child within the meaning of the Act; or

(b)  the parent concerned ceases to be a person with care,

the direction shall be suspended from the last day of the benefit week during the course of which the child ceases to be a child within the meaning of the Act, or the parent concerned ceases to be a person with care, as the case may be.

(2)  Where, under the provisions of paragraph (1), a direction has been suspended for a period of 52 weeks and no relevant benefit is payable at that time, it shall cease to be in force.

(3)  If during the period specified in paragraph (1) the former child again becomes a child within the meaning of the Act or the parent concerned again becomes a person with care and relevant benefit is payable to or in respect of that parent, a reduction in the amount of that benefit shall be made in accordance with the provisions of paragraphs (3) to (7) of regulation 38.

*Notice of termination of a reduced benefit direction*

**49.**   (1)  Where a direction ceases to be in force under the provisions of regulations 41 to 44 or 46 to 48, or is suspended under the provisions of regulation 48, a child support officer shall serve notice of such termination or suspension, as the case may be, on the adjudication officer and shall specify the date on which the direction ceases to be in force or is suspended, as the case may be.

(2)  Any notice served under paragraph (1) shall set out the reasons why the direction has ceased to be in force or has been suspended.

(3)  The parent concerned shall be served with a copy of any notice served under paragraph (1).

*[Notice of termination of a reduced benefit direction*

**49.**   Where a direction ceases to be in force under the provisions of regulations 41, 47 or 48, or is suspended under the provisions of regulation 48, the Secretary of State shall serve notice of such a termination or suspension, as the case may be, on the parent concerned and shall specify the date on which the direction ceases to be in force or is suspended, as the case may be.]

**Note.** Substituted by SI 1999/1047, reg 30 as from 1 June 1999.

*Notice of termination of suspension of a reduced benefit direction*

**[49A.**   . . .]

[. . .]

**Note.** Inserted by SI 1995/3261, reg 39; revoked by SI 1996/3196, reg 9.

*Rounding provisions*

**50.**   Where any calculation made under this Part of these Regulations results in a fraction of a penny, that fraction shall be treated as a penny if it exceeds one half, and shall otherwise be disregarded.

PART X

MISCELLANEOUS PROVISIONS

*Persons who are not persons with care*

**51.**   (1) For the purposes of the Act the following categories of person shall not be persons with care—

(a) a local authority;

(b) a person with whom a child who is looked after by a local authority is placed by that authority under the provisions of the Children Act 1989 except where that person is a parent of such a child and the local authority allow the child to live with that parent under section 23(5) of that Act;

(c) in Scotland, a person with whom a child is boarded out by a local authority under the provisions of section 21 of the Social Work (Scotland) Act 1968.

(2) In paragraph (1) above—

'local authority' means, in relation to England and Wales, the council of a county, a metropolitan district, a London Borough or the Common Council of the City of London and, in relation to Scotland, a regional council or an islands council;

'a child who is looked after by a local authority' has the same meaning as in section 22 of the Children Act 1989.

**52.**  . . .

**Note.** Revoked by SI 1999/1047, reg 31 as from 1 June 1999.

*Authorisation of representative*

**53.**   (1) A person may authorise a representative, whether or not legally qualified, to receive notices and other documents on his behalf and to act on his behalf in relation to the making of applications and the supply of information under any provision of the Act or these Regulations.

(2) Where a person has authorised a representative for the purposes of paragraph (1) who is not legally qualified, he shall confirm that authorisation in writing to the Secretary of State.

**54.**  . . .

**Note.** Revoked by SI 1999/1047, reg 31 as from 1 June 1999.

**55.**  . . .

**Note.** Revoked by SI 1999/1047, reg 31 as from 1 June 1999.

**56.**  . . .

**Note.** Revoked by SI 1999/1047, reg 31 as from 1 June 1999.

**57.**  . . .

**Note.** Inserted by SI 1993/913, reg 16; revoked by SI 1999/1047, reg 31 as from 1 June 1999.

SCHEDULE 1

MEANING OF 'CHILD' FOR THE PURPOSES OF THE ACT                                Regulation 1(4)

*Persons of 16 or 17 years of age who are not in full-time non-advanced education*

**1.**   (1) Subject to sub-paragraph (3), the conditions which must be satisfied for a person to be a child within section 55(1)(c) of the Act are—

(a) the person is registered for work or for training under *youth training* [work-based training for young people or, in Scotland, Skillseekers training] with—

      (i)  the Department of Employment;

     (ii)  the Ministry of Defence;

   (iii)  in England and Wales, a local education authority within the meaning of the Education Acts 1944 to 1992;

   (iv)  in Scotland, an education authority within the meaning of section 135(1) of the Education (Scotland) Act 1980 (interpretation); or

    (v)  for the purposes of applying Council Regulation (EEC) No. 1408/71, any corresponding body in another member State;

(b)  the person is not engaged in remunerative work, other than work of a temporary nature that is due to cease before the end of the extension period which applies in the case of that person;

(c)  the extension period which applies in the case of that person has not expired; and

(d)  immediately before the extension period begins, the person is a child for the purposes of the Act without regard to this paragraph.

(2)  For the purposes of paragraphs (b), (c) and (d) of sub-paragraph (1), the extension period—

(a)  begins on the first day of the week in which the person would no longer be a child for the purposes of the Act but for this paragraph; and

(b)  where a person ceases to fall within section 55(1)(a) of the Act or within paragraph 5—

      (i)  on or after the first Monday in September, but before the first Monday in January of the following year, ends on the last day of the week which falls immediately before the week which includes the first Monday in January in that year;

     (ii)  on or after the first Monday in January but before the Monday following Easter Monday in that year, ends on the last day of the week which falls 12 weeks after the week which includes the first Monday in January in that year;

   (iii)  at any other time of the year, ends on the last day of the week which falls 12 weeks after the week which includes the Monday following Easter Monday in that year.

(3)  A person shall not be a child for the purposes of the Act under this paragraph if—

(a)  he is engaged in training under *youth training* [work-based training for young people or, in Scotland, Skillseekers training]; or

(b)  he is entitled to income support [or income-based jobseeker's allowance].

*Meaning of "advanced education" for the purposes of section 55 of the Act*

**2.**  For the purposes of section 55 of the Act "advanced education" means education of the following description—

(a)  a course in preparation for a degree, a Diploma of Higher Education, a higher national diploma, a higher national diploma or higher national certificate of the Business and [Technology] Education Council or the Scottish Vocational Education Council or a teaching qualification; or

(b)  any other course which is of a standard above that of an ordinary national diploma a national diploma or national certificate of the Business and [Technology] Education Council or the Scottish Vocational Education Council, the advanced level of the General Certificate of Education, a Scottish certificate of education (higher level) or a Scottish certificate of sixth year studies.

*Circumstances in which education is to be treated as full-time education*

**3.**  For the purposes of section 55 of the Act education shall be treated as being full-time if it is received by a person attending a course of education at a recognised educational establishment and the time spent receiving instruction or tuition, undertaking supervised study, examination or practical work or taking part in any exercise, experiment or project for which provision is made in the curriculum of the course, exceeds 12 hours per week, so however that in calculating the time spent in pursuit of the course, no account shall be taken of time occupied by meal breaks or spent on unsupervised study, whether undertaken on or off the premises of the educational establishment.

*Interruption of full-time education*

**4.** (1) Subject to sub-paragraph (2), in determining whether a person falls within section 55(1)(b) of the Act no account shall be taken of a period (whether beginning before or after the person concerned attains age 16) of up to 6 months of any interruption to the extent to which it is accepted that the interruption is attributable to a cause which is reasonable in the particular circumstances of the case; and where the interruption or its continuance is attributable to the illness or disability of mind or body of the person concerned, the period of 6 months may be extended for such further period as *a child support officer* [the Secretary of State] considers reasonable in the particular circumstances of the case.

(2) The provisions of sub-paragraph (1) shall not apply to any period of interruption of a person' s full-time education which is likely to be followed immediately or which is followed immediately by a period during which—

(a) provision is made for the training of that person, and for an allowance to be payable to that person, under *youth training* [work-based training for young people or, in Scotland, Skillseekers training]; or

(b) he is receiving education by virtue of his employment or of any office held by him.

*Circumstances in which a person who has ceased to receive full-time education is to be treated as continuing to fall within section 55(1) of the Act*

**5.** (1) Subject to sub-paragraphs (2) and (5), a person who has ceased to receive full-time education (which is not advanced education) shall, if—

(a) he is under the age of 16 when he so ceases, from the date on which he attains that age; or

(b) he is 16 or over when he so ceases, from the date on which he so ceases,

be treated as continuing to fall within section 55(1) of the Act up to and including the week including the terminal date or if he attains the age of 19 on or before that date up to and including the week including the last Monday before he attains that age.

(2) In the case of a person specified in sub-paragraph (1)(a) or (b) who had not attained the upper limit of compulsory school age when he ceased to receive full-time education, the terminal date in his case shall be that specified in paragraph (a), (b) or (c) of sub-paragraph (3), whichever next follows the date on which he would have attained that age.

(3) In this paragraph the "terminal date" means—

(a) the first Monday in January; or

(b) the Monday following Easter Monday; or

(c) the first Monday in September,

whichever first occurs after the date on which the person's said education ceased.

(4) In this paragraph "compulsory school age" means—

(a) in England and Wales, compulsory school age as determined in accordance with section 9 of the Education Act 1962;

(b) in Scotland, school age as determined in accordance with sections 31 and 33 of the Education (Scotland) Act 1980.

(5) A person shall not be treated as continuing to fall within section 55(1) of the Act under this paragraph if he is engaged in remunerative work, other than work of a temporary nature that is due to cease before the terminal date.

(6) Subject to sub-paragraphs (5) and (8), a person whose name was entered as a candidate for any external examination in connection with full-time education (which is not advanced education), which he was receiving at that time, shall so long as his name continued to be so entered before ceasing to receive such education be treated as continuing to fall within section 55(1) of the Act for any week in the period specified in sub-paragraph (7).

(7) Subject to sub-paragraph (8), the period specified for the purposes of sub-paragraph (6) is the period beginning with the date when that person ceased to receive such education ending with—

(a) whichever of the dates in sub-paragraph (3) first occurs after the conclusion of the examination (or the last of them, if there are more than one); or

(b) the expiry of the week which includes the last Monday before his 19th birthday,

whichever is the earlier.

(8) The period specified in sub-paragraph (7) shall, in the case of a person who has not attained the age of 16 when he so ceased, begin with the date on which he attained that age.

*Interpretation*

**6.**

In this Schedule—

"Education Acts 1944 to 1992" has the meaning prescribed in section 94(2) of the Further and Higher Education Act 1992;

"remunerative work" means work of not less than 24 hours a week—

(a) in respect of which payment is made; or

(b) which is done in expectation of payment;

"week" means a period of 7 days beginning with a Monday;

"*youth training* [work-based training for young people or, in Scotland, Skillseekers training]" means—

(a) arrangements made under section 2 of the Employment and Training Act 1973 (functions of the Secretary of State) or section 2 of the Enterprise and New Towns (Scotland) Act 1990;

(b) arrangements made by the Secretary of State for persons enlisted in Her Majesty's forces for any special term of service specified in regulations made under section 2 of the Armed Forces Act 1966 (power of Defence Council to make regulations as to engagement of persons in regular forces); or

(c) for the purposes of the application of Council Regulation (EEC) No 1408/71, any corresponding provisions operated in another member State,

for purposes which include the training of persons who, at the beginning of their training, are under the age of 18.

**Note.** In paras 1(1)(a), (3)(a), 4(2)(a) words "youth training" substituted by words from "work-based training" to "Skillseekers training" in square brackets by SI 1999/977, reg 5 as from 6 April 1999. In para 1(3)(b) words in square brackets inserted by SI 1996/1345, reg 5(12). In para 2 words in square brackets substituted by SI 1993/913, reg 17. In para 4(1) words "a child support officer" substituted by words "the Secretary of State" in square brackets by SI 1999/1047, reg 32 as from 1 June 1999. In para 6 definition "youth training" words "work-based training for young people or, in Scotland, Skillseekers training" substituted for words "youth training" in square brackets by SI 1999/977, reg 5 as from 6 April 1999.

SCHEDULE 2

MULTIPLE APPLICATIONS                                                    Regulation 4

*No maintenance assessment in force: more than one application for a maintenance assessment by the same person under section 4 or 6 or under sections 4 and 6 of the Act*

**1.** (1) Where a person makes an effective application for a maintenance assessment under section 4 or 6 of the Act and, before that assessment is made, makes a subsequent effective application under that section with respect to the same absent parent or person with care, as the case may be, those applications shall be treated as a single application.

(2) Where a parent with care makes an effective application for a maintenance assessment—

(a) under section 4 of the Act; or

(b) under section 6 of the Act,

and, before that assessment is made, makes a subsequent effective application—

(c) in a case falling within paragraph (a), under section 6 of the Act; or

(d) in a case falling within paragraph (b), under section 4 of the Act,

with respect to the same absent parent, those applications shall, if the parent with care does not cease to fall within section 6(1) of the Act, be treated as a single application under section 6 of the Act, and shall otherwise be treated as a single application under section 4 of the Act.

*No maintenance assessment in force: more than one application by a child under section 7 of the Act*

**2.** Where a child makes an effective application for a maintenance assessment under section 7 of the Act and, before that assessment is made, makes a subsequent effective application under that section with respect to the same person with care and absent parent, both applications shall be treated as a single application for a maintenance assessment.

*No maintenance assessment in force: applications by different persons for a maintenance assessment*

**3.** (1) Where the Secretary of State receives more than one effective application for a maintenance assessment with respect to the same person with care and absent parent, he shall *refer each such application to a child support officer and, if no maintenance assessment has been made in relation to any of the applications, the child support officer shall* [, if no maintenance assessment has been made in relation to any of the applications,] determine which application he shall proceed with in accordance with sub-paragraphs (2) to (11).

(2) Where there is an application by a person with care under section 4 or 6 of the Act and an application by an absent parent under section 4 of the Act, *the child support officer* [the Secretary of State] shall proceed with the application of the person with care.

(3) Where there is an application for a maintenance assessment by a qualifying child under section 7 of the Act and a subsequent application is made with respect to that child by a person who is, with respect to that child, a person with care or an absent parent, *the child support officer* [the Secretary of State] shall proceed with the application of that person with care or absent parent, as the case may be.

(4) Where, in a case falling within sub-paragraph (3), there is more than one subsequent application, *the child support officer* [the Secretary of State] shall apply the provisions of sub-paragraph (2), (8), (9) or (11), as is appropriate in the circumstances of the case, to determine which application he shall proceed with.

(5) Where there is an application for a maintenance assessment by more than one qualifying child under section 7 of the Act in relation to the same person with care and absent parent, *the child support officer* [the Secretary of State] shall proceed with the application of the elder or, as the case may be, eldest of the qualifying children.

(6) Where a case is to be treated as a special case for the purposes of the Act under regulation 19 of the Maintenance Assessments and Special Cases Regulations (both parents are absent) and an effective application is received from each absent parent, *the child support officer* [the Secretary of State] shall proceed with both applications, treating them as a single application for a maintenance assessment.

(7) Where, under the provisions of regulation 20 of the Maintenance Assessments and Special Cases Regulations (persons treated as absent parents), two persons are to be treated as absent parents and an effective application is received from each such person, *the child support officer* [the Secretary of State] shall proceed with both applications, treating them as a single application for a maintenance assessment.

(8) Where there is an application under section 6 of the Act by a parent with care and an application under section 4 of the Act by another person with care who has parental responsibility for (or, in Scotland, parental rights over) the qualifying child or qualifying children with respect to whom the application under section 6 of the Act was made, *the child support officer* [the Secretary of State] shall proceed with the application under section 6 of the Act by the parent with care.

(9) Where—

(a) more than one person with care makes an application for a maintenance assessment under section 4 of the Act in respect of the same qualifying child or qualifying children (whether or not any of those applications is also in respect of other qualifying children);

(b) each such person has parental responsibility for (or, in Scotland, parental rights over) that child or children; and

(c) under the provisions of regulation 20 of the Maintenance Assessments and Special Cases Regulations one of those persons is to be treated as an absent parent,

*the child support officer* [the Secretary of State] shall proceed with the application of the person who does not fall to be treated as an absent parent under the provisions of regulation 20 of those Regulations.

(10) Where, in a case falling within sub-paragraph (9), there is more than one person who does not fall to be treated as an absent parent under the provisions of regulation 20 of those Regulations, *the child support officer* [the Secretary of State] shall apply the provisions of paragraph (11) to determine which application he shall proceed with.

(11) Where—

(a) more than one person with care makes an application for a maintenance assessment under section 4 of the Act in respect of the same qualifying child or qualifying children (whether or not any of those applications is also in respect of other qualifying children); and

(b) either—

(i) none of those persons has parental responsibility for (or, in Scotland, parental rights over) that child or children; or

(ii) the case falls within sub-paragraph (9)(b) but *the child support officer* [the Secretary of State] has not been able to determine which application he is to proceed with under the provisions of sub-paragraph (9),

*the child support officer* [the Secretary of State] shall proceed with the application of the principal provider of day to day care, as determined in accordance with sub-paragraph (12).

(12) Where—

(a) the applications are in respect of one qualifying child, the application of that person with care with whom the child spends the greater or, as the case may be, the greatest proportion of his time;

(b) the applications are in respect of more than one qualifying child, the application of that person with care with whom the children spend the greater or, as the case may be, the greatest proportion of their time, taking account of the time each qualifying child spends with each of the persons with care in question;

(c) *the child support officer* [the Secretary of State] cannot determine which application he is to proceed with under paragraph (a) or (b), and child benefit is paid in respect of the qualifying child or qualifying children to one but not any other of the applicants, the application of the applicant to whom child benefit is paid;

(d) *the child support officer* [the Secretary of State] cannot determine which application he is to proceed with under paragraph (a), (b) or (c), the application of that applicant who in the opinion of *the child support officer* [the Secretary of State] is the principal provider of day to day care for the child or children in question.

(13) Subject to sub-paragraph (14), where, in any case falling within sub-paragraphs (2) to (11), the applications are not in respect of identical qualifying children, the application that *the child support officer* [the Secretary of State] is to proceed with as determined by those paragraphs shall be treated as an application with respect to all of the qualifying children with respect to whom the applications were made.

(14) Where *the child support officer* [the Secretary of State] is satisfied that the same person with care does not provide the principal day to day care for all of the qualifying children with respect to whom an assessment would but for the provisions of this paragraph be made under sub-paragraph (13), he shall make separate assessments in relation to each person with care providing such principal day to day care.

*Maintenance assessment in force: subsequent application for a maintenance assessment with respect to the same persons*

**4.** Where a maintenance assessment is in force and a subsequent application is made under the same section of the Act for an assessment with respect to the same person with care, absent parent, and qualifying child or qualifying children as those with respect to whom the assessment in force has been made, that application shall not be proceeded with ...

*Maintenance assessment in force: subsequent application for a maintenance assessment under section 6 of the Act*

**5.** Where a maintenance assessment is in force following an application under section 4 or 7 of the Act and the person with care makes an application under section 6 of the Act, any maintenance assessment made in response to that application shall replace the assessment currently in force.

*Maintenance assessment in force: subsequent application for a maintenance assessment in respect of additional children*

**6.** *(1) Where a maintenance assessment made in response to an application by an absent parent under section 4 of the Act is in force and that assessment is not in respect of all of hi children who are in the care of the person with care with respect to whom that assessment has been made, an assessment made in response to an application by that person with care under section 4 of the Act with respect to—*

(a)   *the children in respect of whom the assessment currently in force was made; and*

(b)   *the additional child or, as the case may be, one or more of the additional children in that person's care who are children of that absent parent,*

*shall replace the assessment currently in force.*

(2)   *Where—*

(a)   *a maintenance assessment made in response to an application by an absent parent or a person with care under section 4 of the Act is in force;*

(b)   *that assessment is not in respect of all of the children of the absent parent who are in the care of the person with respect to whom that assessment has been made; and*

(c)   *the absent parent makes a subsequent application in respect of an additional qualifying child or additional qualifying children of his in the care of the same person,*

*that application shall be treated as an application for a maintenance assessment in respect of all of the qualifying children concerned, and the assessment made shall replace the assessment currently in force.*

[(1)   Where there is in force a maintenance assessment made in response to an application under section 4 of the Act by an absent parent or person with care and that assessment is not in respect of all of the absent parent's children who are in the care of the person with care with respect to whom that assessment was made—

(a)   if that absent parent or that person with care makes an application under section 4 of the Act with respect to the children in respect of whom the assessment currently in force was made and the additional child or one or more of the additional children in the care of that person with care who are children of that absent parent, an assessment made in response to that application shall replace the assessment currently in force;

(b)   if that absent parent or that person with care makes an application under section 4 of the Act in respect of an additional qualifying child or additional qualifying children of that absent parent in the care of that person with care, that application shall be treated as an application for a maintenance assessment in respect of all the qualifying children concerned and the assessment made shall replace the assessment currently in force.]

(3)   Where a maintenance assessment made in response to an application by a child under section 7 of the Act is in force and the person with care [or the absent parent] of that child makes an application for a maintenance assessment under section 4 of the Act in respect of [one or more *children of the absent parent who are in her care* [children of that absent parent who are in the care of that person with care], that application shall be treated as an application for a maintenance assessment with respect to all the *children of the absent parent who are in her care* [children of that absent parent who are in the care of that person with care], and], that assessment shall replace the assessment currently in force.

**Note.** In para 3(1) words "refer each such application to a child support officer and, if no maintenance assessment has been made in relation to any of the applications, the child support officer shall" substituted by words from ", if no maintenance" to "the applications," in square brackets by SI 1999/1047, reg 33(a)(i) as from 1 June 1999. In para 3(2)–(14) words "the child support officer" in each place substituted by words "the Secretary of State" in square brackets by SI 1999/1047, reg 33(a)(ii) as from 1 June 1999. In para 4 words omitted revoked by SI 1999/1047, reg 33(b) as from 1 June 1999. Para 6(1), (2) substituted by new sub-para (1) by SI 1998/58, reg 41(2) as from 19 January 1998. In para 6(3) words "or the absent parent" in square brackets inserted by SI 1998/58, reg 41(3)(a) as from 19 January 1998, words from "one or" to ", and" in square brackets substituted by SI 1993/913, reg 18, and words "children of the absent parent who are in her care" in both places substituted by words "children of that absent parent who are in the care of that person with care" in square brackets by SI 1998/58, reg 41(3)(b) as from 19 January 1998.

# CHILD SUPPORT (MAINTENANCE ASSESSMENTS AND SPECIAL CASES) REGULATIONS 1992

**Dated** 20 July 1992

**SI 1992 No 1815**

*These Regulations are revoked by SI 2001/155, reg 15(1) (as amended by SI 2003/347, reg 2(1), (2)(c)) as from 3 March 2003 in relation to certain cases. For further effect see SI 2001/155, reg 1(4) and SI 2003/192, arts 3, 8, Schedule. For savings SI 2001/155, reg 15(2)–(6) and SI 2000/3186 (as amended by SI 2004/2415, reg 8).*

## ARRANGEMENT OF REGULATIONS

SCHEDULES

Schedule 1—Calculation of N and M.
Schedule 2—Amounts to be disregarded when calculating or estimating N and M.
Schedule 3—Eligible housing costs.
Schedule 3A—Amount to be allowed in respect of transfers of property.
Schedule 3B—Amount to be allowed in respect of travelling costs.
Schedule 4—Cases where child support maintenance is not to be payable.
Schedule 5—Provisions applying to cases to which section 43 of the Act and regulation 28 apply.

Whereas a draft of this instrument was laid before Parliament in accordance with section 52(2) of the Child Support Act 1991 and approved by a resolution of each House of Parliament:

Now, therefore, the Secretary of State for Social Security, in exercise of the powers conferred by sections 42, 43, 51, 52(4) and 54 of, and paragraphs 1, 2 and 4 to 9 of Schedule 1 to, the Child Support Act 1991 and of all other powers enabling him in that behalf, hereby makes the following Regulations—

PART I

GENERAL

*Citation, commencement and interpretation*

**1.** (1)  These Regulations may be cited as the Child Support (Maintenance Assessments and Special Cases) Regulations 1992 and shall come into force on 5th April 1993.

(2) In these Regulations unless the context otherwise requires—

"the Act" means the Child Support Act 1991;

["care home" has the meaning assigned to it by section 3 of the Care Standards Act 2000;

"care home service" has the meaning assigned to it by section 2(3) of the Regulation of Care (Scotland) Act 2001;]

["Child Benefit Rates Regulations" means the Child Benefit and Social Security (Fixing and Adjustment of Rates) Regulations 1976;]

["child tax credit" means a child tax credit under section 8 of the Tax Credits Act 2002;]

"claimant" means a claimant for income support;

"Contributions and Benefits Act" means the Social Security Contributions and Benefits Act 1992;

["Contributions and Benefits (Northern Ireland) Act" means the Social Security Contributions and Benefits (Northern Ireland) Act 1992;]

"council tax benefit" has the same meaning as in the Local Government Finance Act 1992;

["couple" means a married or unmarried couple;]

"course of advanced education" means

(a) a full-time course leading to a postgraduate degree or comparable qualification, a first degree or comparable qualification, a Diploma of Higher Education, a higher national diploma, a higher national diploma or higher national certificate of the Business and [Technology] Education Council or the Scottish Vocational Education Council or a teaching qualification; or

(b) any other full-time course which is a course of a standard above that of an ordinary national diploma, a national diploma or national certificate of the Business and [Technology] Education Council or the Scottish Vocational Education Council, the advanced level of the General Certificate of Education, a Scottish certificate of education (higher level) or a Scottish certificate of sixth year studies;

"covenant income" means the gross income payable to a student under a Deed of Covenant by a parent;

"day" includes any part of a day;

["day to day care" means—

(a) care of not less than 104 nights in total during the 12 month period ending with the relevant week; or

(b) where, in the opinion of the *child support officer, a period other than 12 months but ending with the relevant week* [Secretary of State, a period other than 12 months] is more representative of the current arrangements for the care of the child in question, care during that period of not less in total than the number of nights which bears the same ratio to 104 nights as that period bears to 12 months,

and for the purpose of this definition—

(i) where a child is a boarder at a boarding school, or is an in-patient in a hospital, the person who, but for those circumstances, would otherwise provide day to day care of the child shall be treated as providing day to day care during the periods in question;

[(ii) in relation to an application for child support maintenance, "relevant week" shall have the meaning ascribed to it in head (ii) of sub-paragraph (a) of the definition of "relevant week" in this paragraph;

*(iii) in relation to a review of a maintenance assessment under section 16 of the Act "relevant week" means the period of 7 days immediately preceding whichever is the later of the date on which a request is made to an absent parent or to a person with care for information or evidence under regulation 17(5) of the Maintenance Assessment Procedure Regulations; or*

*(iv) in relation to a review under section 17, 18(1)(a), (1)(b), (2) or (6A) or 19(1)(a) to (c) or (6) of the Act, "relevant week" shall have the meaning ascribed to it in sub-paragraph (a), (c), (d), (e) or (f), as the case may be, of the definition of "relevant week" in this paragraph*

[(iii) in a case where notification is given under regulation 24 of the Maintenance Assessment Procedure Regulations to the relevant persons on different dates, "relevant week" means the period of seven days immediately preceding the date of the latest notification].]]

["Departure Direction and Consequential Amendments Regulations" means the Child Support Departure Direction and Consequential Amendments Regulations 1996;]

. . .

"earnings" has the meaning assigned to it by paragraph *1 or 3* [1, 2A or 3], as the case may be, of Schedule 1;

["earnings top-up" means the allowance paid by the Secretary of State under the rules specified in the Earnings Top-up Scheme;

"The Earnings Top-up Scheme" has the Earnings Top-up Scheme 1996;]

"effective date" means the date on which a maintenance assessment takes effect for the purposes of the Act;

"eligible housing costs" shall be construed in accordance with Schedule 3;

"employed earner" has the same meaning as in section 2(1)(a) of the Contributions and Benefits Act [except that it shall include a person gainfully employed in Northern Ireland];

["family" means—

(a) a married or unmarried couple (including the members of a polygamous marriage);

(b) a married or unmarried couple (including the members of a polygamous marriage) and any child or children living with them for whom at least one member of that couple has day to day care;

(c) where a person who is not a member of a married or unmarried couple has day to day care of a child or children, that person and any such child or children;

and for the purposes of this definition a person shall not be treated as having day to day care of a child who is a member of that person's household where the child in question is being looked after by a local authority within the meaning of section 22 of the Children Act 1989 or, in Scotland, where the child is boarded out with that person by a local authority under the provisions of section 21 of the Social Work (Scotland) Act 1968;]

[. . .]

"grant" means any kind of educational grant or award and includes any scholarship, exhibition, allowance or bursary but does not include a payment made under section 100 of the Education Act 1944 or section 73 of the Education (Scotland) Act 1980;

"grant contribution" means any amount which a Minister of the Crown or an education authority treats as properly payable by another person when assessing the amount of a student's grant and by which that amount is, as a consequence, reduced;

"home" means—

(a)   the dwelling in which a person and any family of his normally live; or

(b)   if he or they normally live in more than one home, the principal home of that person and any family of his,

and for the purpose of determining the principal home in which a person normally lives no regard shall be had to residence in *a residential care home or a nursing home* [a care home or an independent hospital or to the provision of a care home service or an independent health care service] during a period which does not exceed 52 weeks or, where it appears to the *child support officer* [Secretary of State] that the person will return to his principal home after that period has expired, such longer period as *that officer* [the Secretary of State] considers reasonable to allow for the return of that person to that home;

"housing benefit" has the same meaning as in section 130 of the Contributions and Benefits Act;

"Housing Benefit Regulations" means the Housing Benefit (General) Regulations 1987;

"Income Support Regulations" means the Income Support (General) Regulations 1987;

["independent health care service" has the meaning assigned to it by section 2(5)(a) and (b) of the Regulation of Care (Scotland) Act 2001;

"independent hospital" has the meaning assigned to it by section 2 of the Care Standards Act 2000;]

["Independent Living (1993) Fund" means the charitable trust of that name established by a deed made between the Secretary of State for Social Security of the one part and Robin Glover Wendt and John Fletcher Shepherd of the other part;]

["Independent Living (Extension) Fund" means the charitable trust of that name established by a deed made between the Secretary of State for Social Security of the one part and Robin Glover Wendt and John Fletcher Shepherd of the other part;]

["the Jobseekers Act" means the Jobseekers Act 1995;]

"Maintenance Assessment Procedure Regulations" means the Child Support (Maintenance Assessment Procedure) Regulations 1992;

"married couple" means a man and a woman who are married to each other and are members of the same household;

"non-dependant" means a person who is a non-dependant for the purposes of either—

   (a)  regulation 3 of the Income Support Regulations; or

   (b)  regulation 3 of the Housing Benefit Regulations,

      or who would be a non-dependant for those purposes if another member of the household in which he is living were entitled to income support or housing benefit as the case may be;

. . .

"occupational pension scheme " has the same meaning as in *section 66(1) of the Social Security Pensions Act 1975* [section 1 of the Pension Schemes Act 1993];

"ordinary clothing or footwear" means clothing or footwear for normal daily use, but does not include school uniforms, or clothing or footwear used solely for sporting activities;

"parent with care" means a person who, in respect of the same child or children, is both a parent and a person with care;

"partner" means—

   (a)  in relation to a member of a married or unmarried couple who are living together, the other member of that couple;

   (b)  in relation to a member of a polygamous marriage, any other member of that marriage with whom he lives;

"patient" means a person (other than a person who is serving a sentence of imprisonment or detention in a young offender institution within the meaning of the Criminal Justice Act 1982 as amended by the Criminal Justice Act 1988) who is regarded as receiving free in-patient treatment within the meaning of the Social Security (Hospital In-Patients) Regulations 1975;

"person" does not include a local authority;

"personal pension scheme" has the same meaning as in [section 1 of the Pensions Schemes Act 1993] and, in the case of a self-employed earner, includes a scheme approved by the Inland Revenue under Chapter IV of Part XIV of the Income and Corporation Taxes Act 1988;

"polygamous marriage" means any marriage during the subsistence of which a party to it is married to more than one person and in respect of which any ceremony of marriage took place under the law of a country which at the time of that ceremony permitted polygamy;

["Primary Care Trust" means a Primary Care Trust established under section 16A of the National Health Service Act 1977;]

"prisoner" means a person who is detained in custody pending trial or sentence upon conviction or under a sentence imposed by a court other than a person whose detention is under the Mental Health Act 1983 or the Mental Health (Scotland) Act 1984;

["profit-related pay" means any payment by an employer calculated by reference to actual or anticipated profits;]

["qualifying transfer" has the meaning assigned to it in Schedule 3A;]

"relevant child" means a child of an absent parent or a parent with care who is a member of the same family as that parent;

"relevant Schedule" means Schedule 2 to the Income Support Regulations (income support applicable amounts);

["relevant week" means—

   (a)  in relation to an application for child support maintenance—

      (i)  in the case of the applicant, the period of seven days immediately preceding the date on which the appropriate maintenance assessment application form (being an effective application within the meaning of regulation 2(4) of the Maintenance Assessment Procedure Regulations) is submitted to the Secretary of State;

     (ii)  in the case of a person to whom a maintenance assessment enquiry form is given or sent as the result of such an application, the period of

seven days immediately preceding the date on which that form is given or sent to him or, as the case may be, the date on which it is treated as having been given or sent to him under regulation 1(6)(b) of the Maintenance Assessment Procedure Regulations;
(b) where a decision ("the original decision") is to be—
    (i) revised under section 16 of the Act; or
    (ii) superseded by a decision under section 17 of the Act on the basis that the original decision was made in ignorance of, or was based upon a mistake as to some material fact or was erroneous in point of law,
    the period of seven days which was the relevant week for the purposes of the original decision;
(c) where a decision ("the original decision") is to be superseded by a decision under section 17 of the Act—
    (i) on an application made for the purpose on the basis that a material change of circumstances has occurred since the original decision was made, the period of seven days immediately preceding the date on which that application was made;
    (ii) subject to paragraph (b), in a case where a relevant person is given notice under regulation 24 of the Maintenance Assessment Procedure Regulations, the period of seven days immediately preceding the date of that notification;
    except that where, under paragraph 15 of Schedule 1 to the Act, the Secretary of State makes separate maintenance assessments in respect of different periods in a particular case, because he is aware of one or more changes of circumstances which occurred after the date which is applicable to that case under paragraph (a), (b) or (c) the relevant week for the purposes of each separate assessment made to take account of each such change of circumstances, shall be the period of seven days immediately preceding the date on which notification was given to the Secretary of State of the change of circumstances relevant to that separate maintenance assessment;]

. . .

"retirement annuity contract" means an annuity contract for the time being approved by the Board of Inland Revenue as having for its main object the provision of a life annuity in old age or the provision of an annuity for a partner or dependant and in respect of which relief from income tax may be given on any premium;
"self-employed earner" has the same meaning as in section 2(1)(b) of the Contributions and Benefits Act [except that it shall include a person gainfully employed in Northern Ireland otherwise than in employed earner's employment (whether or not he is also employed in such employment)];
["state pension credit" means the social security benefit of that name payable under the State Pension Credit Act 2002;]
"student" means a person, other than a person in receipt of a training allowance, who is aged less than 19 and attending a full-time course of advanced education or who is aged 19 or over and attending a full-time course of study at an educational establishment; and for the purposes of this definition—
(a) a person who has started on such a course shall be treated as attending it throughout any period of term or vacation within it, until the last day of the course or such earlier date as he abandons it or is dismissed from it;
(b) a person on a sandwich course (within the meaning of paragraph 1(1) of Schedule 5 to the [Education (Mandatory Awards) (No 2) Regulations 1993]) shall be treated as attending a full-time course of advanced education or, as the case may be, of study;

"student loan" means a loan which is made to a student pursuant to arrangements made under section 1 of the Education (Student Loans) Act 1990;

. . .

"training allowance" has the same meaning as in regulation 2 of the Income Support Regulations;

"unmarried couple" means a man and a woman who are not married to each other but are living together as husband and wife;

"weekly council tax" means the annual amount of the council tax in question payable in respect of the year in which the effective date falls, divided by 52;

"[work-based training for young people or, in Scotland, Skillseekers training]" means—

    (a) arrangements made under section 2 of the Employment and Training Act 1973 or section 2 of the Enterprise and New Towns (Scotland) Act 1990; or

    (b) arrangements made by the Secretary of State for persons enlisted in Her Majesty's forces for any special term of service specified in regulations made under section 2 of the Armed Forces Act 1966 (power of Defence Council to make regulations as to engagement of persons in regular forces);

    for purposes which include the training of persons who, at the beginning of their training, are under the age of 18;

[ *"working families' tax credit" means a working families' tax credit under section 128 of the Contributions and Benefits Act;*]

["working tax credit" means a working tax credit under section 10 of the Tax Credits Act 2002;]

"year" means a period of 52 weeks.

[(2A) Where any provision of these Regulations requires the income of a person to be estimated and that or any other provision of these Regulations requires that the amount of such estimated income is to be taken into account for any purpose after deducting from it a sum in respect of income tax or of primary Class 1 contributions under the Contributions and Benefits Act [or, as the case may be, the Contributions and Benefits (Northern Ireland) Act] or of contributions paid by that person towards an occupational or personal pension scheme, then [subject to sub-paragraph (e)]—

    (a) the amount to be deducted in respect of income tax shall be calculated by applying to that income the rates of income tax applicable at the [relevant week] less only the personal relief to which that person is entitled under Chapter 1 of Part VII of the Income and Corporation Taxes Act 1988 (personal relief); but if the period in respect of which that income is to be estimated is less than a year, the amount of the personal relief deductible under this sub-paragraph shall be calculated on a pro rata basis [and the amount of income to which each tax rate applies shall be determined on the basis that the ratio of that amount to the full amount of the income to which each tax rate applies is the same as the ratio of the proportionate part of that personal relief to the full personal relief];

    (b) the amount to be deducted in respect of Class 1 contributions under the Contributions and Benefits Act [or, as the case may be, the Contributions and Benefits (Northern Ireland) Act] shall be calculated by applying to that income the appropriate primary percentage applicable in the relevant week; and

    (c) the amount to be deducted in respect of contributions paid by that person towards an occupational . . . pension scheme shall be one-half of the sums so [paid, and]

    [(d) the amount to be deducted in respect of contributions towards a personal pension scheme shall be one half of the contributions paid by that person or, where that scheme is intended partly to provide a capital sum to discharge a mortgage secured on that person's home, 37.5 per centum of those contributions;

(e) in relation to any bonus or commission which may be included in that person's income—
   (i) the amount to be deducted in respect of income tax shall be calculated by applying to the gross amount of that bonus or commission the rate or rates of income tax applicable in the relevant week;
   (ii) the amount to be deducted in respect of primary Class 1 contributions under the Contributions and Benefits Act [or, as the case may be, the Contributions and Benefits (Northern Ireland) Act] . . . shall be calculated by applying to the gross amount of that bonus or commission the appropriate main primary percentage applicable in the relevant week [but no deduction shall be made in respect of the portion (if any) of the bonus or commission which, if inserted to estimated income, would cause such income to exceed the upper earnings limit for Class 1 contributions as provided for in section 5(1)(b) of the Contributions and Benefits Act [or, as the case may be, the Contributions and Benefits (Northern Ireland) Act]]; and
   (iii) the amount to be deducted in respect of contributions paid by that person in respect of the gross amount of that bonus or commission towards an occupational pension scheme shall be one half of any sum so paid.]]

(3) In these Regulations, unless the context otherwise requires, a reference—
(a) to a numbered Part is to the Part of these Regulations bearing that number;
(b) to a numbered Schedule is to the Schedule to these Regulations bearing that number;
(c) to a numbered regulation is to the regulation in these Regulations bearing that number;
(d) in a regulation or Schedule to a numbered paragraph is to the paragraph in that regulation or Schedule bearing that number;
(e) in a paragraph to a lettered or numbered sub-paragraph is to the sub-paragraph in that paragraph bearing that letter or number.

(4) [These Regulations are subject to the provisions of Parts VIII and IX of the Departure Direction and Consequential Amendments Regulations and] the regulations in Part II and the provisions of the Schedules to these Regulations are subject to the regulations relating to special cases in Part III.

**Note.** Para (2): definitions "care home" and "care home service" inserted by SI 2003/2779, reg 4(1), (2)(c) as from 5 November 2003; definition "Child Benefit Rates Regulations" inserted by SI 1996/1803, reg 7; definition "child tax credit" inserted by SI 2003/328, reg 6(1), (2)(a) as from 6 April 2003; definition "Contributions and Benefits (Northern Ireland) Act" inserted by SI 1996/3196, reg 10(2); definition "couple" inserted by SI 1993/913, reg 19(2); in definition "course of advanced education", in sub-paras (a), (b) word "Technology" substituted by SI 1993/913, reg 19(2); "day to day care" substituted by SI 1995/1045, reg 41(2); in definition "day to day care" words "child support officer, a period other than 12 months but ending with the relevant week" substituted by words from "Secretary of State" to "12 months" in square brackets by SI 1999/1510, art 14(1)(a)(i) as from 1 June 1999; in definition "day to day care" sub-paras (ii)–(iv) substituted, for sub-para (ii) as originally enacted, by SI 1995/3261, reg 40(2)(a) and sub-para (iii) further substituted for sub-paras (iii), (iv) by SI 1999/1510, art 14(1)(a)(ii) as from 1 June 1999; definition "Departure Direction and Consequential Amendments Regulations" inserted by SI 1996/2907, reg 68(2) and SI 1998/58, reg 42(2)(a); definition "disabled person's tax credit" (omitted) revoked by SI 2003/328, reg 6(1), (2)(b) as from 6 April 2003; in definition "earnings" words "1 or 3" substituted by words "1, 2A or 3" in square brackets by SI 1999/977, reg 6(1), (2)(a) as from 4 October 1999; definition "earnings top-up" inserted by SI 1996/1945, reg 18(2); definition "The Earnings Top-up Scheme" inserted by SI 1996/1945, reg 18(2); in definition "employed earner" words "except that it shall include a person gainfully employed in Northern Ireland" in square brackets inserted by SI 1998/58, reg 42(2)(b) as from 19 January 1998; definition "family" substituted by SI 1996/1945, reg 18(3); definition "family credit" (now omitted) inserted by SI 1996/3196, reg 10(2), revoked by SI 2003/328, reg 6(1), (2)(b) as from 6 April 2003; in definition "home" words "a residential care home or a nursing home" substituted by words from "a care home" to "health care service" in square brackets by SI 2003/2779, reg 4(1), (2)(a) as from 5 November 2003; in definition "home" words "child support officer" and "that officer" substituted by words "Secretary of State" and "the Secretary of State" in square brackets by SI 1999/1510, art 14(b) as from 1 June 1999; definitions "independent health care service" and "independent hospital" inserted by SI 2003/2779, reg 4(1), (2)(d) as from 5 November 2003; definition "Independent Living (1993) Fund" inserted by SI 1993/913, reg 19(2); definition "Independent Living (Extension) Fund" inserted by SI 1993/913, reg 19(2); definition "the Jobseekers Act" inserted by SI 1996/1345, reg 6(2); definition "nursing home" (omitted) revoked by SI 2003/2779, reg 4(1), (2)(b) as from 5 November 2003; in definition "occupational pension scheme" words "section 66(1) of the Social Security Pensions Act 1975" substituted by words "section 1 of the Pension Schemes Act 1993" in square brackets by SI 1998/58, reg 42(2)(c) as from 19 January 1998; in definition "personal pension scheme" words "section 1 of the Pensions Schemes Act 1993" in square brackets substituted by SI 1996/3196, reg 10(2); definition "Primary Care Trust" inserted by SI 2002/2469, reg 11, Sch 8 as from 1 October 2002; definition "profit-related pay" inserted by SI 1996/3196, reg 10(2); definition "qualifying transfer" inserted by SI 1995/1045, reg 41(2); definition "relevant week" substituted by SI 1999/1510, art 14(1)(c) as from 1 June 1999; definition "residential care home" (omitted) revoked by SI 2003/2779, reg 4(1), (2)(b) as from 5 November 2003; in definition "self-employed earner" words from "except that" to "such employment)" in square brackets inserted by SI 1998/58, reg 42(2)(e) as from 19 January 1998; definition "state pension credit" inserted by SI 2003/2779, reg 4(1), (2)(e) as from 5 November 2003; in definition "student" words "Education (Mandatory Awards) (No 2) Regulations 1993" in square brackets substituted by SI 1995/1045, reg 41(2); definition omitted revoked by SI 1993/913, reg 19(2); in definition "youth training" words "youth training" substituted by words "work-based training for young people or, in Scotland, Skillseekers training" by SI 1999/977, reg 6(1), (2)(b) as from 6 April 1999: see SI 1999/977, reg 1(2); definition "working families' tax credit" inserted by SI 1999/2566, reg 2(3), Sch 2, Pt III; substituted by definition "working tax credit" SI 2003/328, reg 6(1), (2)(c) as from" 6 April 2003.

Para (2A): inserted by SI 1993/913, reg 19(3); words "or, as the case may be, the Contributions and Benefits (Northern Ireland Act" in square brackets in each place they occur inserted by SI 1996/3196, reg 10(3); words "subject to sub-paragraph (e)" in square brackets inserted by SI 1995/1045, reg 41(3)(a); in sub-para (a) words "relevant week" in square brackets substituted by SI 1995/1045, reg 41(3)(b); in sub-para (a) words from "and the amount" to "personal relief" in square brackets inserted by SI 1998/58, reg 42(3) as from 19 January 1998; in sub-para (c) words omitted revoked by SI 1995/1045, reg 41(3); in sub-para (c) words "paid, and" in square brackets substituted by SI 1995/1045, reg 41(3)(c); sub-para (d) inserted by SI 1995/1045, reg 41(3); sub-para (e) inserted by SI 1995/1045, reg 41(3); in sub-para (e)(ii) words omitted revoked by SI 1996/3196, reg 10(3); in sub-para (e) words in square brackets beginning with the words "but no deduction" inserted by SI 1995/3261, reg 40(3).

Para (4): words from "These Regulations" to "Regulations and" in square brackets inserted by SI 1996/2907, reg 68(3).

PART II

CALCULATION OR ESTIMATION OF CHILD SUPPORT MAINTENANCE

*Calculation or estimation of amounts*

**2.** (1) Where any amount *falls to be taken into account for the purposes of these Regulations* [is to be considered in connection with any calculation made under these Regulations], it shall be calculated or estimated as a weekly amount and, except where the context otherwise requires, any reference to such an amount shall be construed accordingly.

(2) Subject to [regulations 11(6) and (7) and 13(2) and [regulation 8A(5)] of the Maintenance Assessment Procedure Regulations], where any calculation made under [the Act or] these Regulations results in a fraction of a penny that fraction shall be treated as a penny if it is either one half or exceeds one half, otherwise it shall be disregarded.

(3) *A child support officer* [The Secretary of State] shall calculate the amounts to be taken into account for the purposes of these Regulations by reference, as the case may be, to the dates, weeks, months or other periods specified herein provided that if he becomes aware of a material change of circumstances occurring after such date, week, month or other period but before the effective date, he shall take that change of circumstances into account.

**Note.** In para (1): words "falls to be taken into account for the purposes of these Regulations" substituted by words "is to be considered in connection with any calculation made under these Regulations" in square brackets by SI 1998/58, reg 43 as from 19 January 1998. In para (2) words from "regulations 11(6) and (7)" to "Maintenance Assessment Procedure Regulations" in square brackets substituted by SI 1995/1045, reg 42 and words "regulation 8A(5)" in square brackets substituted by SI 1995/3262, reg 3 and words "the Act or" in square brackets inserted by SI 1995/1045, reg 42. Para (3): words "A child support officer" substituted by words "The Secretary of State" in square brackets by SI 1999/1510, art 15 as from 1 June 1999.

*Calculation of AG*

**3.**   (1)  The amounts to be taken into account for the purposes of calculating AG in the formula set out in paragraph 1(2) of Schedule 1 to the Act are—

(a)  with respect to each qualifying child, an amount equal to the amount specified in column (2) of paragraph 2 of the relevant Schedule for a person of the same age (income support personal allowance for child or young person);

[(b) with respect to a person with care of one or more qualifying children—

(i)   where one or more of those children is aged less than 11, an amount equal to the amount specified in column (2) of paragraph 1(1)(e) of the relevant Schedule (income support personal allowance for a single claimant aged not less than 25);

(ii)  where none of those children are aged less than 11 but one or more of them is aged less than 14, an amount equal to 75 per centum of the amount specified in head (i) above; and

(iii)  where none of those children are aged less than 14 but one or more of them is aged less than 16, an amount equal to 50 per centum of the amount specified in head (i) above;]

(c)  *an amount equal to—*

(i)   *the amount specified in paragraph 3(b) of the relevant Schedule; or*

(ii)  *where the person with care is a lone parent as defined in regulation 2(1) of the Income Support Regulations, the amount specified in paragraph 3(a) of the relevant Schedule*

[(c) an amount equal to the amount specified in paragraph 3(1)(b) of the relevant Schedule.]

(d)   . . .

(2) The amounts referred to in paragraph (1) shall be the amounts applicable at the effective date.

**Note.** Para (1)(b) substituted by SI 1994/227, reg 4(2).

Para (1)(c) substituted by SI 1998/58, reg 44 as from 6 April 1998.

Para (1)(d) revoked by SI 1996/1803, reg 8.

*Basic rate of child benefit*

**4.**   For the purposes of paragraph 1(4) of Schedule 1 to the Act 'basic rate' means the rate of child benefit which is specified in regulation 2(1)(a)(i) or 2(1)(b) of the Child Benefit Rates Regulations (weekly rate for only, elder or eldest child and for other children) applicable to the child in question at the effective date.

*support officer* [Secretary of State] shall estimate their respective entitlements having regard to such information as is available but where sufficient information on which to base an estimate is not available the parent and that other person shall be treated as entitled to that income in equal shares.

(5) Where any income normally received at regular intervals has not been received it shall, if it is due to be paid and there are reasonable grounds for believing it will be received, be treated as if it had been received.

**Note.** In para (1)(b) words in square brackets inserted by SI 1996/1345, reg 6(6), (7)(a). In para (3)(a) words "youth training" substituted by words from "work-based training" to "Skillseekers training" in square brackets by SI 1999/977, reg 6(1), (3) as from 6 April 1999. In para (4) words "child support officer" substituted by words "Secretary of State" in square brackets by SI 1999/1510, art 16 as from 1 June 1999.

*Net income: calculation or estimation of M*

**8.**    For the purposes of paragraph 5(2) of Schedule 1 to the Act, the amount of M (net income of the parent with care) shall be calculated in the same way as N is calculated under regulation 7 but as if references to the absent parent were references to the parent with care.

*Exempt income: calculation or estimation of E*

**9.**    (1)    For the purposes of paragraph 5(1) of Schedule 1 to the Act, the amount of E (exempt income of absent parent) shall, subject to paragraphs (3) and (4), be the aggregate of the following amounts—

(a)    an amount equal to the amount specified in column (2) of paragraph 1(1)(e) of the relevant Schedule (income support personal allowance for a single claimant aged not less than 25);

(b)    an amount in respect of housing costs determined in accordance with regulations 14 to [16 and 18];

[(bb)    where applicable, an amount in respect of a qualifying transfer of property determined in accordance with Schedule 3A;]

(c)    . . .

(d)    where, if the parent were a claimant aged less than 60, the conditions in paragraph 11 of the relevant Schedule (income support disability premium) would be satisfied in respect of him, an amount equal to the amount specified in column (2) of paragraph 15(4)(a) of that Schedule (income support disability premium);

(e)    where—

(i)    if the parent were a claimant, the conditions in paragraph 13 of the relevant Schedule (income support severe disability premium) would be satisfied, an amount equal to the amount specified in column (2) of paragraph 15(5)(a) of that Schedule (except that no such amount shall be taken into account in the case of an absent parent in respect of whom *an invalid care allowance* [a carer's allowance] under section 70 of the Contributions and Benefits Act is payable to some other person);

(ii)    if the parent were a claimant, the conditions in paragraph 14ZA of the relevant Schedule (income support carer premium) would be satisfied in respect of him, an amount equal to the amount specified in column (2) of paragraph 15(7) of that Schedule;

[(iii)    if the parent were a claimant, the conditions in paragraph 13A of the relevant Schedule (income support enhanced disability premium) would be satisfied in respect of him, an amount equal to the amount specified in paragraph 15(8)(b) of that Schedule;]

*The general rule*

**5.**   For the purposes of paragraph 2(1) of Schedule 1 to the Act—
   (a)  the value of C, otherwise than in a case where the other parent is the person with care, is nil; and
   (b)  the value of P is 0.5.

*The additional element*

**6.**   [(1)  For the purposes of the formula in paragraph 4(1) of Schedule 1 to the Act, the value of R is—
   (a)  where the maintenance assessment in question relates to one qualifying child, 0.15;
   (b)  where the maintenance assessment in question relates to two qualifying children, 0.20; and
   (c)  where the maintenance assessment in question relates to three or more qualifying children, 0.25.]
   (2) For the purposes of the alternative formula in paragraph 4(3) of Schedule 1 to the Act—
   (a)  the value of Z is [1.5];
   (b)  the amount for the purposes of paragraph (b) of the definition of Q is the same as the amount specified in [regulation *3(1)(c)(i)* [3(1)(c)]] (income support family premium) in respect of each qualifying child.

**Note.** Para (1) substituted by SI 1994/227, reg 4(3). Para (2): in sub-para (a) figure "1.5" in square brackets substituted by SI 1995/1045, reg 43, and in sub-para (b) words in square brackets beginning with the word "regulation" substituted by SI 1996/1803, reg 10 and number "3(1)(c)(i)" substituted by "3(1)(c)" in square brackets by SI 1998/58, reg 45 as from 6 April 1998.

*Net income: calculation or estimation of N*

**7.**   (1)  Subject to the following provisions of this regulation, for the purposes of the formula in paragraph 5(1) of Schedule 1 to the Act, the amount of N (net income of absent parent) shall be the aggregate of the following amounts—
   (a)  the amount, determined in accordance with Part I of Schedule 1, of any earnings of the absent parent;
   (b)  the amount, determined in accordance with Part II of Schedule 1, of any benefit payments under the Contributions and Benefits Act [or the Jobseekers Act] paid to or in respect of the absent parent;
   (c)  the amount, determined in accordance with Part III of Schedule 1, of any other income of the absent parent;
   (d)  the amount, determined in accordance with Part IV of Schedule 1, of any income of a relevant child which is treated as the income of the absent parent;
   (e)  any amount, determined in accordance with Part V of Schedule 1, which is treated as the income of the absent parent.
   (2) Any amounts referred to in Schedule 2 shall be disregarded.
   (3) Where an absent parent's income consists—
   (a)  only of a *youth training* [work-based training for young people or, in Scotland, Skillseekers training] allowance; or
   (b)  in the case of a student, only of grant, an amount paid in respect of grant contribution or student loan or any combination thereof; or
   (c)  only of prisoner's pay,

then for the purposes of determining N such income shall be disregarded.
   (4) Where a parent and any other person are beneficially entitled to any income but the shares of their respective entitlements are not ascertainable the *child*

(f)    where, if the parent were a claimant, the conditions in paragraph 3 of the relevant Schedule (income support family premium) would be satisfied in respect of a relevant child of that parent [. . .], the amount specified in [sub-paragraph (b) of] that paragraph or, where those conditions would be satisfied only by virtue of the case being one to which paragraph (2) applies, half that amount;

(g)    in respect of each relevant child—

    (i)   an amount equal to the amount of the personal allowance for that child, specified in column (2) of paragraph 2 of the relevant Schedule (income support personal allowance) or, where paragraph (2) applies, half that amount;

    (ii)  if the conditions set out in paragraph 14(b) and (c) of the relevant Schedule (income support disabled child premium) are satisfied in respect of that child, an amount equal to the amount specified in column (2) of paragraph 15(6) of the relevant Schedule or, where paragraph (2) applies, half that amount;

    [(iii)  if the conditions set out in paragraph 13A of the relevant Schedule (income support enhanced disability premium) are satisfied in respect of that child, an amount equal to the amount specified in paragraph 15(8)(a) of that Schedule or, where paragraph (2) applies, half that amount;]

*(h)    where the absent parent in question or his partner is living in—*

    *(i)   accommodation provided under Part III of the National Assistance Act 1948;*

    *(ii)  accommodation provided under paragraphs 1 and 2 of Schedule 8 to the National Health Service Act 1977; or*

    *(iii)  a nursing home or residential care home,*

    *the amount of the fees paid in respect of the occupation of that accommodation or, as the case may be, that home but where a local authority has determined that the absent parent in question or his partner is entitled to housing benefit in respect of fees for that accommodation or that home, the net amount of such fees after deduction of housing benefit;*

[(h)    where the absent parent or his partner is resident in a care home or an independent hospital or is being provided with a care home service or an independent health care service, the amount of fees paid in respect of that home, hospital or service, as the case may be, but where it has been determined that the absent parent in question or his partner is entitled to housing benefit in respect of fees for that home, hospital or service, as the case may be, the net amount of such fees after deduction of housing benefit;]

[(i)    where applicable, an amount in respect of travelling costs determined in accordance with Schedule 3B.]

(2) This paragraph applies where—

(a)  the absent parent has a partner;

(b)  the absent parent and the partner are parents of the same relevant child; and

(c)  the income of the partner, calculated under regulation 7(1) [(but excluding the amount mentioned in sub-paragraph (d) of that regulation)] as if that partner were an absent parent to whom that regulation applied, exceeds the aggregate of—

    (i)   the amount specified in column 2 of paragraph 1(1)(e) of the relevant Schedule (income support personal allowance for a single claimant aged not less than 25);

    (ii)  half the amount of the personal allowance for that child specified in column (2) of paragraph 2 of the relevant Schedule (income support personal allowance);

(iii) half the amount of any income support disabled child premium specified in column (2) of paragraph 15(6) of that Schedule in respect of that child; [and]

(iv) half the amount of any income support family premium specified in paragraph [3 [(1)](b) of the relevant Schedule] except where such premium is payable irrespective of that child; ...

[(v) where a departure direction has been given on the grounds that a case falls within regulation 27 of the Departure Direction and Consequential Amendments Regulations (partner's contribution to housing costs), the amount of the housing costs which corresponds to the percentage of the housing costs mentioned in regulation 40(7) of those Regulations].

(3) Where an absent parent does not have day to day care of any relevant child for 7 nights each week but does have day to day care of one or more such children for fewer than 7 nights each week, [any amount] to be taken into account under sub-paragraphs (1)(c) [or (f)] shall be reduced so that they bear the same proportion to the amounts referred to in those sub-paragraphs as the average number of nights each week in respect of which such care is provided has to 7.

(4) Where an absent parent has day to day care of a relevant child for fewer than 7 nights each week, any amounts to be taken into account under sub-paragraph (1)(g) in respect of such a child shall be reduced so that they bear the same proportion to the amounts referred to in that sub-paragraph as the average number of nights each week in respect of which such care is provided has to 7.

(5) The amounts referred to in paragraph (1) are the amounts applicable at the effective date.

**Note.** In para (1)(b) words "16 and 18" in square brackets substituted by SI 1996/1945, reg 19. Para (1)(bb) inserted by SI 1995/1045, reg 44(2). Para (1)(c) revoked by SI 1998/58, reg 47(2)(a) as from 6 April 1998. In para (1)(e)(i) words "an invalid care allowance" substituted by words "a carer's allowance" in square brackets by SI 2003/328, reg 6(1), (3) as from 1 April 2003. Para (1)(e)(iii) inserted by SI 2002/1204, reg 5(a) as from 30 April 2002. In para (1)(f) words "but he is not a lone parent as defined in regulation 2(1) of the Income Support Regulations" substituted by words "but he is not a parent to whom sub-paragraph (c) applies" in square brackets by SI 1998/58, reg 46(3) as from 19 January 1998. In para (1)(f) words omitted revoked by SI 1998/58, reg 47(2)(b) as from 6 April 1998 and words "sub-paragraph (b) of" in square brackets inserted by SI 1996/1803, reg 11(2)(b). Para (1)(g)(iii) inserted by SI 2002/1204, reg 5(b) as from 30 April 2002. Para (1)(h) substituted by SI 2003/2779, reg 4(1), (3) as from 5 November 2003. Para (1)(i) inserted by SI 1995/1045, reg 44(2).

In para (2), sub-para (c) words "(but excluding the amount mentioned in sub-paragraph (d) of that regulation)" in square brackets inserted by SI 1993/913, reg 20, in (2)(c)(iii) word "and" in square brackets inserted by SI 1995/1045, reg 44(3), in (2)(c)(iv) words in square brackets ending with the words "the relevant Schedule" substituted by SI 1996/1803, reg 11(3), in (2)(c)(iv) number "(1)" inserted by SI 1998/58, reg 47(3) as from 6 April 1998, in (2)(c)(iv) words omitted revoked by SI 1995/1045, reg 43(3) and (2)(c)(v) inserted by SI 1996/2907, reg 68(4).

In para (3) words "any amount" in square brackets substituted by SI 1996/1803, reg 11(1), (4)(a) and words "or (f)" in square brackets substituted by SI 1996/1803, reg 11(1), (4)(b).

*Exempt income: calculation or estimation of F*

**10.** (1) For the purposes of paragraph 5(2) of Schedule 1 to the Act, the amount of F (exempt income of parent with care) shall be calculated in the same way as E is calculated under regulation 9 but as if references to the absent parent were references to the parent with care except that—

(a) sub-paragraph (bb) of paragraph (1) of that regulation shall not apply unless at the time of the making of the qualifying transfer the parent with care would have been the absent parent had the Child Support Act 1991 been in force at the date of the making of the transfer; and

(b) paragraphs (3) and (4) of that regulation shall apply only where the parent with care shares day to day care of the child mentioned in those paragraphs with one or more other persons.

*Assessable income: family credit or disability working allowance paid to or in respect of a parent with care or an absent parent*

**10A.** (1) Subject to paragraph (2), where *working families' tax credit or disabled person's tax credit* [working tax credit] is paid to or in respect of a parent with care or an absent parent, that parent shall, for the purposes of Schedule 1 to the Act, be taken to have no assessable income.

(2) Paragraph (1) shall apply to an absent parent only if—
(a) he is also a parent with care; and
(b) either—
  (i) a maintenance assessment in respect of a child in relation to whom he is a parent with care is in force; or
  (ii) the *child support officer* [Secretary of State] is considering an application for such an assessment to be made.]

**Note.** Inserted by SI 1996/3196, reg 11. In para (1) words "working families' tax credit or disabled person's tax credit" in both places substituted by words "working tax credit" in square brackets by SI 2003/328, reg 6(1), (4) as from 6 April 2003. In para (2)(b)(ii) words "child support officer " substituted by words "Secretary of State" in square brackets by SI 1999/1510, art 16 as from 1 June 1999.

[*Assessable income: state pension credit paid to or in respect of a parent with care or an absent parent*

**10B.** Where state pension credit is paid to or in respect of a parent with care or an absent parent, that parent shall, for the purposes of Schedule 1 to the Act, be taken to have no assessable income.]

**Note.** Inserted by SI 2003/2779, reg 4(1), (4) as from 5 November 2003.

*Protected income*

**11.** (1) For the purposes of paragraph 6 of Schedule 1 to the Act the protected income level of an absent parent shall, [subject to paragraphs (3), (4)[, (6) and (6A)]], be the aggregate of the following amounts—
(a) where—
  (i) the absent parent does not have a partner, an amount equal to the amount specified in column (2) of paragraph 1(1)(e) of the relevant Schedule (income support personal allowance for a single claimant aged not less than 25 years);
  (ii) the absent parent has a partner, an amount equal to the amount specified in column (2) of paragraph 1(3)(c) of the relevant Schedule (income support personal allowance for a couple where both members are aged not less than 18 years);
  (iii) the absent parent is a member of a polygamous marriage, an amount in respect of himself and one of his partners, equal to the amount specified in sub-paragraph (ii) and, in respect of each of his other partners, an amount equal to the difference between the amounts specified in sub-paragraph (ii) and sub-paragraph (i);
(b) an amount in respect of housing costs determined in accordance with regulations 14, 15, 16 and 18, or, in a case where the absent parent is a non-dependant member of a household who is treated as having no housing costs by [regulation 15(4)], the non-dependant amount which would be calculated in respect of him under [paragraphs (1), (2) and (9) of regulation 63 of the Housing Benefit Regulations (non-dependant

deductions) if he were a non-dependant in respect of whom a calculation were to be made under those paragraphs (disregarding any other provision of that regulation)];

[(c) . . .]

(d) where, if the parent were a claimant, the conditions in paragraph 11 of the relevant Schedule (income support disability premium) would be satisfied, an amount equal to the amount specified in column (2) of paragraph 15(4) of that Schedule (income support disability premium);

(e) where, if the parent were a claimant, the conditions in paragraph 13 or 14ZA of the relevant Schedule (income support severe disability and carer premiums) would be satisfied in respect of either or both premiums, an amount equal to the amount or amounts specified in column (2) of paragraph 15(5) or, as the case may be, (7) of that Schedule in respect of that or those premiums (income support premiums);

(f) where, if the parent were a claimant, the conditions in paragraph 3 of the relevant Schedule (income support family premium) would be satisfied . . ., the amount specified in [sub-paragraph (b) of] that paragraph;

(g) in respect of each child who is a member of the family of the absent parent—

    (i) an amount equal to the amount of the personal allowance for that child, specified in column (2) of paragraph 2 of the relevant Schedule (income support personal allowance);

    (ii) if the conditions set out in paragraphs 14(b) and (c) of the relevant Schedule (income support disabled child premium) are satisfied in respect of that child, an amount equal to the amount specified in column (2) of paragraph 15(6) of the relevant Schedule;

(h) where, if the parent were a claimant, the conditions specified in Part III of the relevant Schedule would be satisfied by the absent parent in question or any member of his family in relation to any premium not otherwise included in this regulation, an amount equal to the amount specified in Part IV of that Schedule (income support premiums) in respect of that premium;

[(i) where the absent parent or his partner is resident in a care home or an independent hospital or is being provided with a care home service or an independent health care service, the amount of fees paid in respect of that home, hospital or service, as the case may be, but where it has been determined that the absent parent in question or his partner is entitled to housing benefit in respect of fees for that home, hospital or service, as the case may be, the net amount of such fees after deduction of housing benefit;]

(i) *where the absent parent in question or his partner is living in—*

    (i) *accommodation provided under Part III of the National Assistance Act 1948;*

    (ii) *accommodation provided under paragraphs 1 and 2 of Schedule 8 to the National Health Service Act 1977; or*

    (iii) *a nursing home or residential care home,*

*the amount of the fees paid in respect of the occupation of that accommodation or, as the case may be, that home but where housing benefit is paid to the absent parent in question or his partner in respect of fees for that accommodation or that home the net amount of such fees after deduction of housing benefit*

[(j) where—

    (i) the absent parent is, or that absent parent and any partner of his are, the only person or persons resident in, and liable to pay council tax in respect of, the home for which housing costs are included under sub-paragraph (b), the amount of weekly council tax for which he is liable in respect of that home, less any applicable council tax benefit;

    (ii)  where other persons are resident with the absent parent in, and liable to pay council tax in respect of, the home for which housing costs are included under sub-paragraph (b), an amount representing the share of the weekly council tax in respect of that home applicable to the absent parent, determined by dividing the total amount of council tax due in that week by the number of persons liable to pay it, less any council tax benefit applicable to that share, provided that, if the absent parent is required to pay and pays more than that share because of default by one or more of those other persons, the amount for the purposes of this regulation shall be the amount of weekly council tax the absent parent pays, less any council tax benefit applicable to such amount;]

(k)  an amount of [£30.00];

[(kk) an amount in respect of travelling costs determined in accordance with Schedule 3B];

(l)  where the income of—

    (i)  the absent parent in question;

    (ii)  any partner of his; and

    (iii)  any child or children for whom an amount is included under sub-paragraph (g)(i);

exceeds the sum of the amounts to which reference is made in sub-paragraphs [(a) to (kk)], [15 per centum] of the excess.

(2) For the purposes of sub-paragraph (l) of paragraph (1) "income" shall be calculated—

(a)  in respect of the absent parent in question or any partner of his, in the same manner as N (net income of absent parent) is calculated under regulation 7 except—

    (i)  there shall be taken into account the basic rate of any child benefit and any maintenance which in either case is in payment in respect of any member of the family of the absent parent;

    (ii)  there shall be deducted the amount of any maintenance under a maintenance order which the absent parent or his partner is paying in respect of a child in circumstances where an application for a maintenance assessment could not be made in accordance with the Act in respect of that child; < . . . >

    [(iii)  to the extent that it falls under sub-paragraph (b), the income of any child in that family shall not be treated as the income of the parent or his partner and Part IV of Schedule 1 shall not apply; < . . . >]

    [(iv)  paragraph 27 of Schedule 2 shall apply as though the reference to paragraph 3(2) and (4) of Schedule 3 were omitted;

    (v)  there shall be deducted the amount of any maintenance which is being paid in respect of a child by the absent parent or his partner under an order requiring such payment made by a court outside Great Britain; and]

    [(vi)  there shall be taken into account any child tax credit which is payable to the absent parent or his partner; and]

(b)  in respect of any child in that family, as being the total of [that child's relevant income (within the meaning of paragraph 23 of Schedule 1), there being disregarded any maintenance in payment to or in respect of him,] but only to the extent that such income does not exceed the amount included under sub-paragraph (g) of paragraph (1) (income support personal allowance for a child and income support disabled child premium) reduced, as the case may be, under paragraph (4).

(3) Where an absent parent does not have day to day care of any child (whether or not a relevant child) for 7 nights each week but does have day to day care of one

or more such children for fewer than 7 nights each week, [any amount] to be taken into account under [sub-paragraph (f)] of paragraph (1) ( . . . income support family premium) shall be reduced so that they bear the same proportion to the amounts referred to in those sub-paragraphs as the average number of nights each week in respect of which such care is provided has to 7.

(4) Where an absent parent has day to day care of a child (whether or not a relevant child) for fewer than 7 nights each week any amounts in relation to that child to be taken into account under sub-paragraph (g) of paragraph (1) (income support personal allowance for child and income support disabled child premium) shall be reduced so that they bear the same proportion to the amounts referred to in that sub-paragraph as the average number of nights in respect of which such care is provided has to 7.

(5) The amounts referred to in paragraph (1) shall be the amounts applicable at the effective date.

[(6) If the application of the above provisions of this regulation would result in the protected income level of an absent parent being less than 70 per centum of his net income, as calculated in accordance with regulation 7, those provisions shall not apply in his case and instead his protected income level shall be 70 per centum of his net income as so calculated.]

[(6A)    In a case to which paragraph (6) does not apply, if the application of paragraphs (1) to (5) and of regulation 12(1)(a) would result in the amount of child support maintenance payable being greater than 30 per centum of the absent parent's net income calculated in accordance with regulation 7, paragraphs (1) to (5) shall not apply in his case and instead his protected income level shall be 70 per centum of his net income as so calculated.]

[(7)      Where any calculation under paragraph (6) [or (6A)] results in a fraction of a penny, that fraction shall be treated as a penny.]

**Note.** In para (1)(i) words from "but where" to "housing benefit" in square brackets inserted by SI 1995/3261, reg 43(3), words in square brackets beginning with the words "subject to paragraphs (3), (4)" substituted by SI 1995/1045, reg 46(2), words ", (6) and (6A)" in square brackets substituted by SI 1996/1945, reg 20(2). In para (1)(b) words "regulation 15(4)" in square brackets substituted by SI 1995/3261, reg 43(2) and words from "paragraphs (1), (2) and (9)" to "that regulation)" in square brackets substituted by SI 1995/1045, reg 46(2). Para (1)(c) substituted by SI 1998/58, reg 48(a) as from 19 January 1998, revoked by SI 1998/58, reg 49(2)(a) as from 6 April 1998. In para (1)(f) words omitted revoked by SI 1998/58, reg 49(2)(b) as from 6 April 1998 and words "sub-paragraph (b) of" in square brackets inserted by SI 1996/1803, reg 12(2)(b)(ii). Para (1)(i) substituted by SI 2003/2779, reg 4(1), (5) as from 5 November 2003. Para (1)(j) substituted by SI 1995/1045, reg 46(2) and in para (k) sum "£30.00" in square brackets substituted by SI 1994/227, reg 4(4). Para (1)(kk) inserted by SI 1995/1045, reg 46(2). In para (1)(l) words "(a) to (kk)" in square brackets substituted by SI 1995/1045, reg 46(2) and words "15 per centum" in square brackets substituted by SI 1994/227, reg 4(5).

In para (2)(a)(ii) word omitted revoked by SI 1995/1045, reg 46(3). Para (2)(a)(iii) inserted by SI 1995/1045, reg 46(4) and word omitted revoked by SI 1995/3261, reg 43(4). Para (2)(a)(iv), (v) inserted by SI 1995/3261, reg 43(5). Para (2)(a)(vi) inserted by SI 2003/328, reg 6(1), (5) as from 6 April 2003. In para (2)(b) words from "that child's relevant income" to "in respect of him," in square brackets substituted by SI 1995/1045, reg 46(5).

In para (3) words "any amount" in square brackets substituted by SI 1996/1803, reg 12(3) and words "sub-paragraph (f)" in square brackets substituted by SI 1998/58, reg 49(3) as from 6 April 1998: see SI 1998/58, reg 1(3). In para (3) words omitted revoked by SI 1996/1803, reg 12(3).

Para (6) inserted by SI 1995/1045, reg 46(6). Para (6A) inserted by SI 1996/1945 reg 20(3).

Para (7) inserted by SI 1995/1045, reg 46(6); words in square brackets inserted by SI 1996/1945, reg 20(4).

*Disposable income*

**12.** (1) For the purposes of paragraph 6(4) of Schedule 1 to the Act (protected income), the disposable income of an absent parent shall be—

  (a)  except in a case to which regulation 11(6) or (6A) applies, the aggregate of his income and any income of any member of his family calculated in like manner as under regulation 11(2);

  (b)  subject to sub-paragraph (c), in a case to which regulation 11(6) or (6A) applies, his net income as calculated in accordance with regulation 7; and

  (c)  in a case to which regulation 11(6) applies and the absent parent is paying maintenance under an order of a kind mentioned in regulation 11(2)(a)(ii) or (v), his net income as calculated in accordance with regulation 7 less the amount of maintenance he is paying under that order.

  (2)  Subject to paragraph (3), where a maintenance assessment has been made with respect to the absent parent and payment of the amount of that assessment would reduce his disposable income below his protected income level the amount of the assessment shall be reduced by the minimum amount necessary to prevent his disposable income being reduced below his protected income level.

  (3)  Where the prescribed minimum amount fixed by regulations under paragraph 7 of Schedule 1 to the Act is applicable (such amount being specified in regulation 13) the amount payable under the assessment shall not be reduced to less than the prescribed minimum amount.

*The minimum amount*

**13.** (1) Subject to regulation 26, for the purposes of paragraph 7(1) of Schedule 1 to the Act the minimum amount shall be 5 per centum of the amount specified in paragraph 1(1)(e) of the relevant Schedule (income support personal allowance for single claimant aged not less than 25).

  (2)  Where an amount calculated under paragraph (1) results in a sum other than a multiple of 5 pence, it shall be treated as the sum which is the next higher multiple of 5 pence.

*Eligible housing costs*

**14.** Schedule 3 shall have effect for the purpose of determining the costs which are eligible to be taken into account as housing costs for the purposes of these Regulations.

*Amount of housing costs*

**15.** (1) Subject to the provisions of this regulation and [regulations 16 and 18], a parent's housing costs shall be the aggregate of the eligible housing costs payable in respect of his home.

  (2)  Where a local authority has determined that a parent is entitled to housing benefit, the amount of his housing costs shall, subject to paragraphs (4) to (9), be the weekly amount treated as rent under regulations 10 and 69 of the Housing Benefit Regulations (rent and calculation of weekly amounts) less the amount of housing benefit.

  (3)  Where a parent has eligible housing costs and another person who is not a member of his family is also liable to make payments in respect of the home, the amount of the parent's housing costs shall be his share of those costs [but, where that other person does not make those payments in circumstances where head (a) of paragraph 4(2) of Schedule 3 applies, the eligible housing costs of that parent shall include the housing costs for which, because of that failure to pay, that parent is treated as responsible under that head].

  (4)–(9)  . . .

[[(4)] A parent shall be treated as having no housing costs where he is a non-dependant member of a household and is not responsible for meeting housing costs except to another member, or other members, of that household.]

**Note.** Para (1): words in square brackets substituted by SI 1995/1045, reg 48(2). In Para (3) words from "but," to "that head." in square brackets inserted by SI 1998/58, reg 50 as from 19 January 1998: see SI 1998/58, reg 1(2). Paras (4)–(9): revoked by SI 1995/1045, reg 48(3). Second para (4), originally para (10), renumbered as para (4) by SI 1995/3261, reg 44; substituted by SI 1995/1045, reg 48(4). *Weekly amount of housing costs*

**16.**  (1) *Where a parent pays housing costs* [Where housing costs are payable by a parent]—

- (a) on a weekly basis, the amount of such housing costs shall subject to paragraph (2), be the weekly rate payable at the effective date;
- (b) on a monthly basis, the amount of such housing costs shall subject to paragraph (2), be the monthly rate payable at the effective date, multiplied by 12 and divided by 52;
- (c) by way of rent payable to a housing association, as defined in section 1(1) of the Housing Associations Act 1985 which is registered in accordance with section 5 of that Act, or to a local authority, on a free week basis, that is to say the basis that he pays an amount by way of rent for a given number of weeks in a 52 week period, with a lesser number of weeks in which there is no liability to pay ("free weeks"), the amount of such housing costs shall be *the amount which he pays* [the amount payable]—
  - (i) in the relevant week if it is not a free week; or
  - (ii) in the last week before the relevant week which is not a free week, if the relevant week is a free week;
- (d) on any other basis, the amount of such housing costs shall, subject to paragraph (2), be the rate payable at the effective date, multiplied by the number of payment periods, or the nearest whole number of payment periods (any fraction of one half being rounded up), falling within a period of 365 days and divided by 52.

(2) Where housing costs consist of payments on a repayment mortgage and the absent parent or parent with care has not provided information or evidence as to the rate of repayment of the capital secured and the interest payable on that mortgage at the effective date and that absent parent or parent with care has provided a statement from the lender, in respect of a period ending not more than 12 months prior to the first day of the relevant week, for the purposes of the calculation of exempt income under regulation 9 and protected income under regulation 11—

- (a) if the amount of capital repaid for the period covered by that statement is shown on it, the rate of repayment of capital owing under that mortgage shall be calculated by reference to that amount; and
- (b) if the amount of capital owing and the interest rate applicable at the end of the period covered by that statement are shown on it, the interest payable on that mortgage shall be calculated by reference to that amount and that interest rate.]

**Note.** Substituted by SI 1996/1945, reg 22. In para (1) words "Where a parent pays housing costs" substituted by words "Where housing costs are payable by a parent" in square brackets by SI 1998/58, reg 51(a). In para (1)(c) words "the amount which he pays" substituted by words "the amount payable" in square brackets by SI 1998/58, reg 51(b) as from 19 January 1998.

the other parent is an absent parent, as if the value of C was the assessable income of the other parent;

Y   is—

(i)   the amount of child support maintenance assessed under Schedule 1 to the Act payable by the other parent if he is an absent parent or which would be payable if he were an absent parent, and for the purposes of such calculation the value of C shall be the assessable income of the parent treated as an absent parent under paragraph (2); or,

(ii)   if there is no such other parent, shall be nil;

J   is the total of the weekly average number of nights for which day to day care is provided by the person who is treated as the absent parent in respect of each child included in the maintenance assessment and shall be calculated to 2 decimal places;

L   is the number of children who are included in the maintenance assessment in question.

(5)   Where the value of T calculated under the provisions of paragraph (4) is less than zero, no child support maintenance shall be payable.

(6)   The liability to pay any amount calculated under paragraph (4) shall be subject to the provision made for protected income and minimum payments under paragraphs 6 and 7 of Schedule 1 to the Act.

**Note.** Amended by SI 1999/1510, art 16 as from 1 June 1999.

*One parent is absent and the other is treated as absent*

**21.**   (1)   Where the circumstances of a case are that one parent is an absent parent and the other parent is treated as an absent parent by regulation 20(2), that case shall be treated as a special case for the purposes of the Act.

(2)   For the purpose of assessing the child support maintenance payable by an absent parent where this case applies, each reference in Schedule 1 to the Act to a parent who is a person with care shall be treated as a reference to a person who is treated as an absent parent by regulation 20(2).

*Multiple applications relating to an absent parent*

**22.**   [(1)   Where an application for a maintenance assessment has been made in respect of an absent parent and—

(a)   at least one other application for a maintenance assessment has been made in relation to the same absent parent (or a person who is treated as an absent parent by regulation 20(2)) but to different children; or

(b)   at least one maintenance assessment is in force in relation to the same absent parent or a person who is treated as an absent parent by regulation 20(2) but to different children,

that case shall be treated as a special case for the purposes of the Act.]

[(2)   For the purposes of assessing the amount of child support maintenance payable in respect of each application where [paragraph (1)(a)] applies [or in respect of the application made in circumstances where paragraph (1)(b) applies], for references to the assessable income of an absent parent in the Act and in these Regulations[, and subject to paragraph (2ZA),] there shall be substituted references to the amount calculated by the formula—

$$\left( (A + T) \times \frac{B}{D} \right) - CS$$

where—

A is the absent parent's assessable income;

T is the sum of the amounts allowable in the calculation or estimation of his exempt income by virtue of Schedule 3A;

B is the maintenance requirement calculated in respect of the application in question;

D is the sum of the maintenance requirements as calculated for the purposes of each assessment relating to the absent parent in question; and

CS is the amount (if any) allowable by virtue of Schedule 3A in calculating or estimating the absent parent's exempt income in respect of a relevant qualifying transfer of property in respect of the assessment in question.]

[(2ZA) Where a case falls within regulation 39(1)(a) of the Departure Direction and Consequential Amendment Regulations, for the purposes of assessing the amount of child support maintenance payable in respect of an application for child support maintenance before a departure direction in respect of the maintenance assessment in question is given, for references to the assessable income of an absent parent in the Act and in these Regulations there shall be substituted references to the amount calculated by the formula—

$$(A + T) \times \frac{B}{D}$$

where A, T, B and D have the same meanings as in paragraph (2).]

[(2A) Where paragraph (1)(b) applies, and a maintenance assessment has been made in respect of the application referred to in paragraph (1), each maintenance assessment in force at the time of that assessment shall be reduced using the formula for calculation of assessable income set out in paragraph (2) and each reduction shall take effect on the date specified in regulation 33(7) of the Maintenance Assessment Procedure Regulations.]

[(2B) Where—

(a) a case is treated as a special case for the purposes of the Act by virtue of paragraph (1);

(b) more than one maintenance assessment is in force in respect of the absent parent; and

(c) *any of those assessments is reviewed under section 16, 17, 18 or 19 of the Act and a fresh assessment is to be made,*

[(c) any of those assessments falls to be replaced by a fresh assessment to be made by virtue of a revision under section 16 of the Act or a decision under section 17 of the Act superseding an earlier decision,]

the formula set out in paragraph (2) or, as the case may be, paragraph (2ZA) shall be applied to calculate or estimate the amount of child support maintenance payable under that fresh assessment.

(2C) Where a maintenance assessment falls within sub-paragraph (b) of paragraph (2B) but *it is not reviewed under any of the provisions set out in* [not within] sub-paragraph (c) of that paragraph, the formula set out in paragraph (2) or, as the case may be, paragraph (2ZA) shall be applied to determine whether that maintenance assessment should be increased or reduced as a result of the making of a fresh assessment under sub-paragraph (c) and any increase or reduction shall take effect from the effective date of that fresh assessment.]

(3) Where more than one maintenance assessment has been made with respect to the absent parent and payment by him of the aggregate of the amounts of those assessments would reduce his disposable income below his protected income level, the aggregate amount of those assessments shall be reduced (each being reduced by reference to the same proportion as those assessments bear to each other) by the minimum amount necessary to prevent his disposable income being reduced below his protected income level provided that the aggregate amount payable under those assessments shall not be reduced to less than the minimum amount prescribed in regulation 13(1).

[(4) Where the aggregate of the child support maintenance payable by the absent parent is less than the minimum amount prescribed in regulation 13(1), the child support maintenance payable shall be—

(a) that prescribed minimum amount apportioned between the two or more applications in the same ratio as the maintenance requirements in question bear to each other; or

(b) where, because of the application of regulation 2(2), such an apportionment produces an aggregate amount which is different from that prescribed minimum amount, that different amount.]

(5) Payment of each of the maintenance assessments calculated under this regulation shall satisfy the liability of the absent parent (or a person treated as such) to pay child support maintenance.

**Note.** Para (1) substituted by SI 1995/3261, reg 45(2). Para (2) substituted by SI 1995/1045, reg 51, for circumstances in which a child support officer shall not make a fresh assessment see regs 63(1)–(3), 64(1), (3), words "paragraph (1)(a)" in square brackets substituted by SI 1995/3261, reg 45(3), words "or in respect of the application made in circumstances where paragraph (1)(b) applies" in square brackets inserted by SI 1995/3261, reg 45(3) and words ", and subject to paragraph (2ZA)," in square brackets substituted by SI 1996/2907, reg 68(5)(a). Para (2ZA): inserted by SI 1996/2907, reg 68(5)(b). Para (2A): inserted by SI 1995/3261, reg 45(4). Paras (2B), (2C) inserted by SI 1998/58, reg 53 as from 19 January 1998. Para (2B)(c) substituted by SI 1999/1510, art 18(a) as from 1 June 1999. In para (2C) words "it is not reviewed under any of the provisions set out in" substituted by words "not within" in square brackets by SI 1999/1510, art 18(b) as from 1 June 1999: see SI 1999/1510, art 3(1). Para (4) substituted by SI 1993/913, reg 23.

*Person caring for children of more than one absent parent*

**23.** (1) Where the circumstances of a case are that—

(a) a person is a person with care in relation to two or more qualifying children; and

(b) in relation to at least two of those children there are different persons who are absent parents or persons treated as absent parents by regulation 20(2); that case shall be treated as a special case for the purposes of the Act.

(2) Subject to paragraph (2A) in calculating the maintenance requirements for the purposes of this case, for any amount which (but for this paragraph) would have been included under regulation 3(1)(b) or (c) (amounts included in the calculation of AG) there shall be substituted an amount calculated by dividing the amount which would have been so included by the relevant number.

(2A) In applying the provisions of paragraph (2) to the amount which is to be included in the maintenance requirements under regulation 3(1)(b)—

(a) first take the amount specified in head (i) of regulation 3(1)(b) and divide it by the relevant number;

(b) then apply the provisions of regulation 3(1)(b) as if the references to the amount specified in column (2) of paragraph 1(1)(e) of the relevant Schedule were references to the amount which is the product of the calculation required by head (a) above, and as if, in relation to an absent parent, the only qualifying children to be included in the assessment were those qualifying children in relation to whom he is the absent parent.

(3) In paragraphs (2) and (2A) 'the relevant number' means the number equal to the total number of persons who, in relation to those children, are either absent parents or persons treated as absent parents by regulation 20(2) except that where in respect of the same child both parents are persons who are either absent parents or persons who are treated as absent parents under that regulation, they shall count as one person.

(4) Where the circumstances of a case fall within this regulation and the person with care is the parent of any of the children, for C in paragraph 2(1) of Schedule 1 to the Act (the assessable income of that person) there shall be substituted the amount which would be calculated under regulation 22(2) if the references therein to an absent parent were references to a parent with care.

*Persons with part-time care—not including a person treated as an absent parent*

**24.** (1) Where the circumstances of a case are that—
  (a) two or more persons who do not live in the same household each provide day to day care for the same qualifying child; and
  (b) those persons do not include any parent who is treated as an absent parent of that child by regulation 20(2),
that case shall be treated as a special case for the purposes of the Act.
  (2) For the purposes of this case—
  (a) the person whose application for a maintenance assessment is being proceeded with shall, subject to paragraph (b), be entitled to receive all of the child support maintenance payable under the Act in respect of the child in question;
  (b) on request being made to the Secretary of State by—
    (i) that person; or
    (ii) any other person who is providing day to day care for that child and who intends to continue to provide that care,
    the Secretary of State may make arrangements for the payment of any child support maintenance payable under the Act to the persons who provide such care in the same ratio as that in which it appears to the Secretary of State, that each is to provide such care for the child in question;
  (c) before making an arrangement under sub-paragraph (b), the Secretary of State shall consider all of the circumstances of the case and in particular the interests of the child, the present arrangements for the day to day care of the child in question and any representations or proposals made by the persons who provide such care for that child.

*Care provided in part by a local authority*

**25.** (1) Where the circumstances of a case are that a local authority and a person each provide day to day care for the same qualifying child, that case shall be treated as a special case for the purposes of the Act.
  (2) Subject to paragraph (3), in a case where this regulation applies—
  (a) child support maintenance shall be calculated in respect of that child as if this regulation did not apply;
  (b) the amount so calculated shall be divided by 7 so as to produce a daily amount;
  (c) in respect of each night for which day to day care for that child is provided by a person other than the local authority, the daily amount relating to that period shall be payable by the absent parent (or, as the case may be, by the person treated as an absent parent under regulation 20(2));
  (d) child support maintenance shall not be payable in respect of any night for which the local authority provides day to day care for that qualifying child.
  (3) In a case where more than one qualifying child is included in a child support maintenance assessment application and where this regulation applies to at least one of those children, child support maintenance shall be calculated by applying the formula—

$$S \times \left( \frac{A}{7 \times B} \right)$$

where—
  S   is the total amount of child support maintenance in respect of all qualifying children included in that maintenance assessment application, calculated as if this regulation did not apply;
  A   is the aggregate of the number of nights of day to day care for all qualifying children included in that maintenance assessment application provided in each week by a person other than the local authority;

B   is the number of qualifying children in respect of whom the maintenance assessment application has been made.

*Cases where child support maintenance is not to be payable*

**26.**   (1)  Where the circumstances of a case are that—
(a)  but for this regulation the minimum amount prescribed in regulation 13(1) would apply; and
(b)  any of the following conditions are satisfied—
  (i)   the income of the absent parent includes one or more of the payments or awards specified in Schedule 4 or would include such a payment but for a provision preventing the receipt of that payment by reason of it overlapping with some other benefit payment or would, in the case of the payments referred to in paragraph (a)(i) or (iv) of that Schedule, include such a payment if the relevant contribution conditions for entitlement had been satisfied;
  (ii)  an amount to which regulation *11(1)(c) or (f)* [11(1)(f)] applies (protected income: income support family premium) is taken into account in calculating or estimating under paragraphs (1) to (5) of regulation 11 the protected income of the absent parent;
  (iii) the absent parent is a child within the meaning of section 55 of the Act;
  (iv)  the absent parent is a prisoner; or
  (v)   the absent parent is a person in respect of whom N (as calculated or estimated under regulation 7(1)) is less than the minimum amount prescribed by regulation 13(1),
the case shall be treated as a special case for the purposes of the Act.
(2)  For the purposes of this case—
(a)  the requirement in paragraph 7(2) of Schedule 1 to the Act (minimum amount of child support maintenance fixed by an assessment to be the prescribed minimum amount) shall not apply;
(b)  the amount of the child support maintenance to be fixed by the assessment shall be nil.

**Note.** Amended by SI 1998/58, reg 54 as from 6 April 1998.

*Child who is a boarder or an in-patient*

**27.**   (1)  Where the circumstances of a case are that—
(a)  a qualifying child is a boarder at a boarding school or is an in-patient in a hospital; and
(b)  by reason of those circumstances, the person who would otherwise provide day to day care is not doing so,
that case shall be treated as a special case for the purposes of the Act.
(2)  For the purposes of this case, section 3(3)(b) of the Act shall be modified so that for the reference to the person who usually provides day to day care for the child there shall be substituted a reference to the person who would usually be providing such care for that child but for the circumstances specified in paragraph (1).

*Child who is allowed to live with his parent under section 23(5) of the Children Act 1989*

**27A.**   (1)  Where the circumstances of a case are that a qualifying child who is in the care of a local authority in England and Wales is allowed by the authority to live with a parent of his under section 23(5) of the Children Act 1989, that case shall be treated as a special case for the purposes of the Act.
(2)  For the purposes of this case, section 3(3)(b) of the Act shall be modified so that for the reference to the person who usually provides day to day care for the

child there shall be substituted a reference to the parent of a child whom the local authority allow the child to live with under section 23(5) of the Children Act 1989.

*Amount payable where absent parent is in receipt of income support or other prescribed benefit*

**28.** (1) Where the condition specified in section 43(1)(a) of the Act is satisfied in relation to an absent parent (assessable income to be nil where income support, income-based jobseeker's allowance or other prescribed benefit is paid), the prescribed conditions for the purposes of section 43(1)(b) of the Act are that—
  (a) the absent parent is aged 18 or over;
  (b) he does not satisfy the conditions in paragraph *(3)(a) or (b)* [3(1)(a) or (b) of the relevant Schedule (income support family premium) and does not have day to day care of any child (whether or not a relevant child); and
  (c) his income does not include one or more of the payments or awards specified in Schedule 4 (other than by reason of a provision preventing receipt of overlapping benefits or by reason of a failure to satisfy the relevant contribution conditions).
  (2) For the purposes of section 43(2)(a) of the Act, the prescribed amount shall be equal to the minimum amount prescribed in regulation 13(1) for the purposes of paragraph 7(1) of Schedule 1 to the Act.
  (3) Subject to paragraph (4), where—
  (a) an absent parent is liable under section 43 of the Act and this regulation to make payments in place of payments of child support maintenance with respect to two or more qualifying children in relation to whom there is more than one parent with care; or
  (b) that absent parent and his partner (within the meaning of regulation 2(1) of the Social Security (Claims and Payments) Regulations 1987) are both liable to make such payments,
the prescribed amount mentioned in paragraph (2) shall be apportioned between the persons with care in the same ratio as the maintenance requirements of the qualifying child or children in relation to each of those persons with care bear to each other.
  (4) If, in making the apportionment required by paragraph (3), the effect of the application of regulation 2(2) would be such that the aggregate amount payable would be different from the amount prescribed in paragraph (2) the Secretary of State shall adjust that apportionment so as to eliminate that difference; and that adjustment shall be varied from time to time so as to secure that, taking one week with another and so far as is practicable, each person with care receives the amount which she would have received if no adjustment had been made under this paragraph.
  (5) The provisions of Schedule 5 shall have effect in relation to cases to which section 43 of the Act and this regulation apply.]

**Note.** Amended by SI 1998/58, reg 55 as from 6 April 1998.

SCHEDULE 1

CALCULATION OF N AND M

PART I  EARNINGS

*Chapter 1*

*Earnings of an employed earner*

**1.** (1) Subject to sub-paragraphs (2) and (3), "earnings" means in the case of employment as an employed earner, any remuneration or profit derived from that employment and includes—
  (a) any bonus, commission, [payment in respect of overtime,] royalty or fee;

[(aa)  any profit-related pay, whether paid in anticipation of, or following, the calculation of profits;]

(b)  any holiday pay except any payable more than 4 weeks after termination of the employment;

(c)  any payment by way of a retainer;

[(d)  any payments made by the parent's employer in respect of any expenses not wholly, exclusively and necessarily incurred in the performance of the duties of the employment, including any payment made by the parent's employer in respect of—

    (i)  travelling expenses incurred by that parent between his home and place of employment; and

    (ii)  expenses incurred by that parent under arrangements made for the care of a member of his family owing to that parent's absence from home;]

(e)  any award of compensation made under section 68(2) or 71(2)(a) of the Employment Protection (Consolidation) Act 1978 (remedies and compensation for unfair dismissal);

(f)  any such sum as is referred to in section 112 of the Contributions and Benefits Act (certain sums to be earnings for social security purposes);

(g)  any statutory sick pay under Part I of the Social Security and Housing Benefits Act 1982 or statutory maternity pay under Part V of the Social Security Act 1986;

[(gg)  any statutory paternity pay under Part 12ZA of the Contributions and Benefits Act or any statutory adoption pay under Part 12ZB of that Act;]

(h)  any payment in lieu of notice and any compensation in respect of the absence or inadequacy of any such notice but only insofar as such payment or compensation represents loss of income;

(i)  any payment relating to a period of less than a year which is made in respect of the performance of duties as—

    (i)  an auxiliary coastguard in respect of coast rescue activities;

    (ii)  a part-time fireman in a fire brigade maintained in pursuance of the Fire Services Acts 1947 to 1959;

    (iii)  a person engaged part-time in the manning or launching of a lifeboat;

    (iv)  a member of any territorial or reserve force prescribed in Part I of Schedule 3 to the Social Security (Contributions) Regulations 1979;

(j)  any payment made by a local authority to a member of that authority in respect of the performance of his duties as a member, other than any expenses wholly, exclusively and necessarily incurred in the performance of those duties.

(2)  Earnings shall not include—

(a)  any payment in respect of expenses wholly, exclusively and necessarily incurred in the performance of the duties of the employment [except any such payment which is made in respect of housing costs and those housing costs are included in the calculation of the exempt or protected income of the absent parent under regulation 9(1)(b) or, as the case may be, regulation 11(1)(b)];

(b)  any occupational pension;

(c)  any payment where—

    (i)  the employment in respect of which it was made has ceased; and

    (ii)  a period of the same length as the period by reference to which it was calculated has expired since that cessation but prior to the effective date;

(d)  any advance of earnings or any loan made by an employer to an employee;

(e)  any amount received from an employer during a period when the employee has withdrawn his services by reason of a trade dispute;

(f)  any payment in kind;

(g)  where, in any week or other period which falls within the period by reference to which earnings are calculated, earnings are received both in respect of a previous employment and in respect of a subsequent employment, the earnings in respect of the previous employment;

[(h) any tax-exempt allowance made by an employer to an employee [except any such allowance which is made in respect of housing costs and those housing costs are included in the calculation of the exempt or protected income of the absent parent under regulation 9(1)(b) or, as the case may be, regulation 11(1)(b)].]

(3)  The earnings to be taken into account for the purposes of calculating N and M shall be gross earnings less—

(a)  any amount deducted from those earnings by way of—

(i)   income tax;

(ii)  primary Class 1 contributions under the Contributions and Benefits Act [or under the Social Security Contributions and Benefits (Northern Ireland) Act 1992]; and

(b)  one half of any sums paid by the parent towards an [occupational pension scheme];

[(c) one half of any sums paid by the parent towards a personal pension scheme, or, where that scheme is intended partly to provide a capital sum to discharge a mortgage secured upon the parent's home, 37.5 per centum of any such sums.]

**2.**   [(1)  Subject to sub-paragraphs [(1A)] to (4), the amount of the earnings to be taken into account for the purpose of calculating N and M shall be calculated or estimated by reference to the average earnings at the relevant week having regard to such evidence as is available in relation to that person's earnings during such period as appears appropriate to the *child support officer* [Secretary of State] beginning not earlier than eight weeks before the relevant week and ending not later than the date of the assessment and for the purpose of that calculation or estimate he may consider evidence of that person's cumulative earnings during the period beginning with the start of the year of assessment (within the meaning of section 832 of the Income and Corporation Taxes Act 1988) in which the relevant week falls and ending with a date no later than the date of the assessment.]

[(1A)  Subject to sub-paragraph (4), where a person has claimed, or has been paid, *working families' tax credit or disabled person's tax credit* [working tax credit or child tax credit] on any day during the period beginning not earlier than eight weeks before the relevant week and ending not later than the date on which the assessment is made, the *child support officer* [Secretary of State] may have regard to the amount of earnings taken into account in determining entitlement to those benefits in order to calculate or estimate the amount of earnings to be taken into account for the purposes of calculating N and M, notwithstanding the fact that entitlement to those benefits may have been determined by reference to earnings attributable to a period other than that specified in sub-paragraph (1).]

[(2)      Where a person's earnings during the period of 52 weeks ending with the relevant week include—

(a)  a bonus, commission, or payment of profit-related pay made in anticipation of the calculation of profits which is paid separately from or in relation to a longer period than, the other earnings with which it is paid; or

(b)  a payment in respect of profit-related pay made following the calculation of the employer's profits,

the amount of that bonus, commission or profit-related payment shall be determined for the purposes of the calculation of earnings by aggregating any such payments received in that period and dividing by 52.]

(3) Subject to sub-paragraph (4), the amount of any earnings of a student shall be determined by aggregating the amount received in the year ending with the relevant week and dividing by 52 or, where the person in question has been a student for less than a year, by aggregating the amount received in the period starting with his becoming a student and ending with the relevant week and dividing by the number of complete weeks in that period.

[(3A) Where a case is one to which regulation 30A(1) or (3) of the Maintenance Assessment Procedure Regulations applies (effective dates of new maintenance assessments in particular cases), the term "relevant week" shall, for the purpose of this paragraph, mean the period of 7 days immediately preceding the date on which the information or evidence is received which enables [the Secretary of State] to make a new maintenance assessment calculated in accordance with the provisions of Part I of Schedule 1 to the Act in respect of that case for a period beginning after the effective date applicable to that case.]

(4) Where a calculation would, but for this sub-paragraph, produce an amount which, in the opinion of the *child support officer* [Secretary of State], does not accurately reflect the normal amount of the earnings of the person in question, such earnings, or any part of them, shall be calculated by reference to such other period as may, in the particular case, enable the normal weekly earnings of that person to be determined more accurately and for this purpose the [Secretary of State] shall have regard to—

(a) the earnings received, or due to be received, from any employment in which the person in question is engaged, has been engaged or is due to be engaged;

(b) the duration and pattern, or the expected duration and pattern, of any employment of that person.

*Chapter 2*

*Earnings of a self-employed earner*

**[2A.** (1) Subject to paragraphs 2B, 2C, 4 and 5A, "earnings" in the case of employment as a self-employed earner shall have the meaning given by the following provisions of this paragraph.

(2) "Earnings" means the total taxable profits from self-employment of that earner as submitted to the Inland Revenue, less the following amounts—

(a) any income tax relating to the taxable profits from the self-employment determined in accordance with sub-paragraph (3);

(b) any National Insurance Contributions relating to the taxable profits from the self-employment determined in accordance with sub-paragraph (4);

(c) one half of any premium paid in respect of a retirement annuity contract or a personal pension scheme or, where that scheme is intended partly to provide a capital sum to discharge a mortgage or charge secured upon the self-employed earner's home, 37.5 per centum of the contributions payable.

(3) For the purposes of sub-paragraph (2)(a) the income tax to be deducted from the total taxable profits shall be determined in accordance with the following provisions—

(a) subject to head (d), an amount of earnings equivalent to any personal allowance applicable to the earner by virtue of the provisions of Chapter 1 of Part VII of the Income and Corporation Taxes Act 1988 (personal reliefs) shall be disregarded;

(b) subject to head (c), an amount equivalent to income tax shall be calculated in relation to the earnings remaining following the application of head (a) (the "remaining earnings");

(c) the tax rate applicable at the effective date shall be applied to all the remaining earnings, where necessary increasing or reducing the amount payable to take account of the fact that the earnings relate to a period greater or less than one year;

(d) the amount to be disregarded by virtue of head (a) shall be calculated by reference to the yearly rate applicable at the effective date, that amount being reduced or increased in the same proportion to that which the period represented by the taxable profits bears to the period of one year.

(4) For the purposes of sub-paragraph (2)(b) above, the amount to be deducted in respect of National Insurance Contributions shall be the total of—

(a) the amount of Class 2 contributions (if any) payable under section 11(1) or, as the case may be, (3), of the Contributions and Benefits Act; and

(b) the amount of Class 4 contributions (if any) payable under section 15(2) of that Act,

at the rates applicable at the effective date.

**2B.** (1) Where—

(a) a self-employed earner cannot provide the *child support officer* [Secretary of State] with the total taxable profit figure from self-employment for the period concerned as submitted to the Inland Revenue, but can provide a copy of his tax calculation notice; or

(b) the *child support officer* [Secretary of State] becomes aware that the total taxable profit figure from the self-employment submitted by the self-employed earner has been revised by the Inland Revenue,

the earnings of that earner shall be calculated by reference to the income from employment as a self-employed earner as set out in the tax calculation notice issued in relation to his case, and if a revision of the figures included in that notice has occurred, by reference to the revised notice.

(2) In this paragraph and elsewhere in this Schedule—

"submitted to" means submitted to the Inland Revenue in accordance with their requirements by or on behalf of the self-employed earner; and

a "tax calculation notice" means a document issued by the Inland Revenue containing information as to the income of a self-employed earner;

a "revision of the figures" means the revision of the figures relating to the total taxable profit of a self-employed earner following an enquiry under section 9A of the Taxes Management Act 1970 or otherwise by the Inland Revenue.

**2C.** Where the *child support officer* [Secretary of State] accepts that it is not reasonably practicable for the self-employed earner to provide information relating to his total taxable profits from self-employment in the form submitted to, or (where paragraph 2B applies) as issued or revised by, the Inland Revenue, "earnings" in relation to that earner shall have the meaning given by paragraph 3 of this Schedule.]

**3.** (1) *Subject* [Where paragraph 2C applies, and subject] to sub-paragraphs (2) and (3) and to paragraph 4, "earnings" in the case of employment as a self-employed earner means the gross receipts of the employment including, where an allowance in the form of periodic payments is paid under section 2 of the Employment and Training Act 1973 or section 2 of the Enterprise and New Towns (Scotland) Act 1990 in respect of the relevant week for the purpose of assisting him in carrying on his business, the total of those payments made during the period by reference to which his earnings are determined under paragraph 5.

(2) Earnings shall not include—

(a) any allowance paid under either of those sections in respect of any part of the period by reference to which his earnings are determined under paragraph 5 if no part of that allowance is paid in respect of the relevant week;

(b) any income consisting of payments received for the provision of board and lodging accommodation unless such payments form the largest element of the recipient's income.

(3) [Subject to sub-paragraph (7),] There shall be deducted from the gross receipts referred to in sub-paragraph (1)—

(a) [except in a case to which paragraph 4 applies,] any expenses which are reasonably incurred and are wholly and exclusively defrayed for the purposes of the earner's business in the period by reference to which his earnings are determined under paragraph 5(1) or, where paragraph 5(2) applies, any such expenses relevant to the period there mentioned (whether or not defrayed in that period);

(b) [except in a case to which paragraph 4 [or 5(2)] applies,] any value inserted tax paid in the period by reference to which earnings are determined in excess of value inserted tax received in that period;

(c) any amount in respect of income tax determined in accordance with sub-paragraph (5);

(d) any amount in respect of National Insurance contributions determined in accordance with sub-paragraph (6);

(e) one half of any premium paid in respect of a retirement annuity contract or a personal pension scheme[, or, where that scheme is intended partly to provide a capital sum to discharge a mortgage or charge secured upon the parent's home, 37.5 per centum of the contributions payable].

(4) For the purposes of sub-paragraph (3)(a)—

(a) such expenses include—

   (i) repayment of capital on any loan used for the replacement, in the course of business, of equipment or machinery, or the repair of an existing business asset except to the extent that any sum is payable under an insurance policy for its repair;

  (ii) any income expended in the repair of an existing business asset except to the extent that any sum is payable under an insurance policy for its repair;

 (iii) any payment of interest on a loan taken out for the purposes of the business;

(b) such expenses do not include—

   (i) repayment of capital on any other loan taken out for the purposes of the business;

  (ii) any capital expenditure;

 (iii) the depreciation of any capital asset;

 (iv) any sum employed, or intended to be employed, in the setting up or expansion of the business;

  (v) any loss incurred before the beginning of the period by reference to which earnings are determined;

 (vi) any expenses incurred in providing business entertainment;

(vii) any loss incurred in any other employment in which he is engaged as a self-employed earner.

[(5) For the purposes of sub-paragraph (3)(c), the amount in respect of income tax shall be determined in accordance with the following provisions—

(a) subject to head (c), an amount of chargeable earnings equivalent to any personal allowance applicable to the earner by virtue of the provisions of Chapter 1 of Part VII of the Income and Corporation Taxes Act 1988 (personal reliefs) shall be disregarded;

(b) [subject to head (bb),] an amount equivalent to income tax shall be calculated with respect to taxable earnings at the rates applicable at the effective date;

[(bb) where taxable earnings are determined over a period of less or more than one year, the amount of earnings to which each tax rate applies shall be reduced or increased in the same proportion to that which the period represented by the chargeable earnings bears to the period of one year;]

(c) the amount to be disregarded by virtue of head (a) shall be calculated by reference to the yearly rate applicable at the effective date, that amount being reduced or increased in the same proportion to that which the period represented by the chargeable earnings bears to the period of one year;

(d) in this sub-paragraph, "taxable earnings" means the chargeable earnings of the earner following the disregard of any applicable personal allowances.]

(6) For the purposes of sub-paragraph (3)(d), the amount to be deducted in respect of National Insurance contributions shall be the total of—

(a) the amount of Class 2 contributions (if any) payable under section 11(1) or, as the case may be, [(3)] of the Contributions and Benefits Act; and

(b) the amount of Class 4 contributions (if any) payable under section 15(2) of that Act,

at the rates applicable [to the chargeable earnings] at the effective date.

[(7) In the case of a self-employed earner whose employment is carried on in partnership or is that of a share fisherman within the meaning of the Social Security (Mariners' Benefits) Regulations 1975, sub-paragraph (3) shall have effect as though it requires—

(a) a deduction from the earner's estimated or, where appropriate, actual share of the gross receipts of the partnership or fishing boat, of his share of the sums likely to be deducted or, where appropriate, deducted from those gross receipts under heads (a) and (b) of that sub-paragraph; and

(b) a deduction from the amount so calculated of the sums mentioned in heads (c) to (e) of that sub-paragraph.]

[(8) In sub-paragraphs (5) and (6) "chargeable earnings" means the gross receipts of the employment less any deductions mentioned in sub-paragraph (3)(a) and (b).]

**4.** In a case where a person is self-employed as a childminder the amount of earnings referable to that employment shall be one-third of the gross receipts.

**5.** (1) Subject to sub-paragraphs [(2) to (3)]—

(a) where a person has been a self-employed earner for 52 weeks or more including the relevant week, the amount of his earnings shall be determined by reference to the average of the earnings which he has received in the 52 weeks ending with the relevant week;

(b) where the person has been a self-employed earner for a period of less than 52 weeks including the relevant week, the amount of his earnings shall be determined by reference to the average of the earnings which he has received during that period.

(2) [Subject to sub-paragraph (2A), where] a person who is a self-employed earner provides in respect of the employment a profit and loss account and, where appropriate, a trading account or a balance sheet or both, and the profit and loss account is in respect of a period at least 6 months but not exceeding 15 months and that period terminates within the [24 months] immediately preceding the effective date, the amount of his earnings shall be determined by reference to the average of the earnings over the period to which the profit and loss account relates and such earnings shall include receipts relevant to that period (whether or not received in that period).

[(2A) Where the *child support officer* [Secretary of State] is satisfied that, in relation to the person referred to in sub-paragraph (2) there is more than one profit and loss account, each in respect of different periods, both or all of which satisfy the conditions mentioned in that sub-paragraph, the provisions of that sub-paragraph shall apply only to the account which relates to the latest such period, unless *the officer* [the Secretary of State] is satisfied that the latest such account is not available for reasons beyond the control of that person, in which case he may have regard to any such other account which satisfies the requirements of that sub-paragraph.]

(3) Where a calculation would, but for this sub-paragraph, produce an amount which, in the opinion of the *child support officer* [Secretary of State], does not accurately reflect the normal amount of the earnings of the person in question, such earnings, or any part of them, shall be calculated by reference to such other period as may, in the particular case, enable the normal weekly earnings of that person to be determined more accurately and for this purpose the child support officer shall have regard to—

(a) the earnings received, or due to be received, from any employment in which the person in question is engaged, or has been engaged or is due to be engaged;

(b) the duration and pattern, or the expected duration and pattern, of any employment of that person.

(4) In sub-paragraph (2)—

(a) "balance sheet" means a statement of the financial position of the employment disclosing its assets, liabilities and capital at the end of the period in question;

(b) "profit and loss account" means a financial statement showing net profit or loss of the employment for the period in question; and

(c) "trading account" means a financial statement showing the revenue from sales, the cost of those sales and the gross profit arising during the period in question.

[(5) Subject to sub-paragraph (3), where a person has claimed, or has been paid, *working families' tax credit or disabled person's tax credit* [working tax credit or child tax credit] on any day during the period beginning not earlier than eight weeks before the relevant week and ending not later than the date on which the assessment is made, the *child support officer* [Secretary of State] may have regard to the amount of earnings taken into account in determining entitlement to those benefits in order to calculate or estimate the amount of earnings to be taken into account for the purposes of calculating N and M, notwithstanding the fact that entitlement to those benefits may have been determined by reference to earnings attributable to a period other than that specified in sub-paragraph (1).]

[(6) This paragraph applies only where the earnings of a self-employed earner have the meaning given by paragraph 3 of this Schedule.]

**[5A.** (1) Subject to sub-paragraph (2) of this paragraph, the earnings of a self-employed earner may be determined in accordance with the provisions of paragraph 2A only where the total taxable profits concerned relate to a period of not less than 6, and not more than 15 months, which terminated not more than 24 months prior to the relevant week.

(2) Where there is more than one total taxable profit figure which would satisfy the conditions set out in sub-paragraph (1), the earnings calculation shall be based upon the figure pertaining to the latest such period.

(3) Where, in the opinion of the *child support officer* [Secretary of State], information as to the total taxable profits of the self-employed earner which would satisfy the criteria set out in sub-paragraphs (1) and (2) of this paragraph does not accurately reflect the normal weekly earnings of the self-employed earner, the earnings of that earner can be calculated by reference to the provisions of paragraphs 3 and 5 of this Schedule.]

**Note.** Para 1: in sub-para (1)(a) words "payment in respect of overtime," in square brackets inserted by SI 1995/1045, reg 54(2), sub-para (1)(aa) inserted by SI 1996/3196, reg 13(2), sub-para (1)(d) substituted by SI 1996/1945, reg 24(2), sub-para (1)(gg) inserted by SI 2004/2415, reg 5(1), (2) as from 16 September 2004, in sub-para (2)(a) words from "except any such payment" to "regulation 11(1)(b)" in square brackets inserted by SI 1998/58, reg 56(2)(a) as from 19 January 1998, sub-para (2)(h) inserted by SI 1996/3196, reg 13(2) and in sub-para (2)(h) words from "except any such allowance" to "regulation 11(1)(b)" in square brackets inserted by SI 1998/58, reg 56(2)(b) as from 19 January 1998, in sub-para

(3)(a)(ii) words "or under the Social Security Contributions and Benefits (Northern Ireland) Act 1992" in square brackets inserted by SI 1995/1045, reg 54(2), in sub-para (3)(b) words "occupational pension scheme" in square brackets substituted by SI 1995/1045, reg 54(3) and sub-para (3)(c) inserted by SI 1995/1045, reg 54(2).

Para 2: sub-para (1) substituted by SI 1995/1045, reg 54(4) and in sub-para (1) number "(1A)" in square brackets substituted by SI 1996/3196, reg 13(3)(a), in sub-paras (1), (1A), (4) words "child support officer" substituted by words "Secretary of State" in square brackets in each place they occur by SI 1999/1510, art 19(a)(i) as from 1 June 1999, sub-paras (1A), (3A) inserted by SI 1996/3196, reg 13(3)(b), (d) and in sub-para (1A) words "working families' tax credit or disabled person's tax credit" substituted by words "working tax credit or child tax credit" in square brackets by SI 2003/328, reg 6(1), (6)(a) as from 6 April 2003, sub-para (2) substituted by SI 1996/3196, reg 13(3)(c) and in sub-para (3A) words "a child support officer" substituted by words "the Secretary of State" in square brackets by SI 1999/1510, art 19(a)(ii) as from 1 June 1999.

Paras 2A–2C inserted by SI 1999/977, reg 6(1), (5)(a) as from 4 October 1999. In paras 2B, 2C words "child support officer" in each place they occur substituted by words "Secretary of State" in square brackets by SI 1999/977, reg 6(5), as amended by SI 1999/1510, art 46 as from 4 October 1999.

In para 3(1) word "Subject" substituted by words "Where paragraph 2C applies, and subject" in square brackets by SI 1999/977, reg 6(1), (5)(b) as from 4 October 1999. In para 3(3) words "Subject to sub-paragraph (7)," in square brackets inserted by SI 1993/913, reg 27. In para 3(3)(a) words "except in a case to which paragraph 4 applies," in square brackets inserted by SI 1993/913, reg 27. In para 3(3)(b) words from "except in a case" to "applies," in square brackets inserted by SI 1993/913, reg 27 and words "or 5(2)" in square brackets inserted by SI 1995/1045, reg 54(5). In para 3(3)(e) words from ", or, where" to "contributions payable" in square brackets inserted by SI 1995/1045, reg 54(5). Para 3(5) substituted by SI 1996/3196, reg 13(4). In para 3(5)(b) words "subject to head (bb)," in square brackets inserted by SI 1998/58, reg 56(3)(a) as from 19 January 1998: see SI 1998/58, reg 1(2). Para 3(5)(bb) inserted by SI 1998/58, reg 56(3)(b) as from 19 January 1998. In para 3(6)(a) number "(3)" in square brackets substituted by SI 1995/1045, reg 54(7) and words "to the chargeable earnings" in square brackets inserted by SI 1993/913, reg 27. Para 3(7) inserted by SI 1993/913, reg 27; substituted by SI 1995/1045, reg 54(8). Para 3(8) inserted by SI 1993/913, reg 27.

In para 5(1) words "(2) to (3)" in square brackets substituted by SI 1995/1045, reg 54(9). In para 5(2) words "Subject to sub-paragraph (2A), where" and words "24 months" in square brackets substituted by SI 1995/1045, reg 54(9). Para 5(2A) inserted by SI 1995/1045, reg 54(9). In para 5(2A), (3), (5) words "child support officer" substituted by words "Secretary of State" in square brackets by SI 1999/1510, art 19(b)(ii) as from 1 June 1999 and in sub-para (2A) words "the officer" substituted by words "the Secretary of State" in square brackets by SI 1999/1510, art 19(b)(i) as from 1 June 1999. Para 5(5) inserted by SI 1996/3196, reg 13(5). In para 5(5) words "working families' tax credit or disabled person's tax credit" substituted by words "working tax credit or child tax credit" in square brackets by SI 2003/328, reg 6(1), (6)(a) as from 6 April 2003. Para 5(6) inserted by SI 1999/977, reg 6(1), (5)(c) as from 4 October 1999.

Para 5A inserted by SI 1999/977, reg 6(1), (5)(d) as from 4 October 1999 and in sub-para (3) words "child support officer" substituted by words "Secretary of State" in square brackets by SI 1999/977, reg 6(5), as amended by SI 1999/1510, art 46 as from 4 October 1999.

PART II   BENEFIT PAYMENTS

**6.**   (1) The benefit payments to be taken into account in calculating or estimating N and M shall be determined in accordance with this Part.

(2) 'Benefit payments' means any benefit payments under the Contributions and Benefits Act or the Jobseekers Act except amounts to be disregarded by virtue of Schedule 2.

(3) The amount of any benefit payment to be taken into account shall be determined by reference to the rate of that benefit applicable at the effective date.

**7.**   (1) Where a benefit payment under the Contributions and Benefits Act includes an adult or child dependency increase—

(a) if that benefit is payable to a parent, the income of that parent shall be calculated or estimated as if it did not include that amount;

(b) if that benefit is payable to some other person but includes an amount in respect of the parent, the income of the parent shall be calculated or estimated as if it included that amount.

(1A) For the purposes of sub-paragraph (1), an addition to a contribution-based jobseeker's allowance under regulation 9(4) [regulations 10(4)] of the Jobseeker's Allowance (Transitional Provisions) Regulations 1995 [1996] shall be treated as a dependency increase included with a benefit under the Contributions and Benefits Act.

(2)–revoked.

(6) Where child benefit in respect of a relevant child is in payment at the rate specified in regulation 2(1)(a)(ii) of the Child Benefit Rates Regulations, the difference between that rate and the basic rate applicable to that child, as defined in regulation 4.

**Note.** para 7(1A) amended by SI 1999/977, reg 6(1), (5) as from 6 April 1999 and para 7(2)–(5) revoked by SI 2003/328, reg 6 (1), (6)(b) as from 6 April 2003.

PART III  OTHER INCOME

**8.** The amount of the other income to be taken into account in calculating or estimating N and M shall be the aggregate of the following amounts determined in accordance with this Part.

**9.** Any periodic payment of pension or other benefit under an occupational or personal pension scheme or a retirement annuity contract or other such scheme for the provision of income in retirement.

**[9A.** (1) Where a war disablement pension includes an adult or child dependency increase—
(a) if that pension, including the dependency increase, is payable to a parent, the income of that parent shall be calculated or estimated as if it did not include that amount;
(b) if that pension, including the dependency increase, is payable to some other person but includes an amount in respect of the parent, the income of the parent shall be calculated or estimated as if it included that amount.

(2)  For the purposes of this paragraph, a "war disablement pension" includes a war widow's pension [and a war widower's pension], a payment made to compensate for non-payment of such a pension, and a pension or payment analogous to such a pension or payment paid by the government of a country outside Great Britain.]

**10.** Any payment received on account of the provision of board and lodging which does not come within Part I of this Schedule.

**11.** Subject to regulation 7(3)(b) and paragraph 12, any payment to a student of—
(a) grant;
(b) an amount in respect of grant contribution;
(c) covenant income except to the extent that it has been taken into account under sub- paragraph (b);
(d) a student loan.

**12.** The income of a student shall not include any payment—
(a) intended to meet tuition fees or examination fees;
(b) intended to meet additional expenditure incurred by a disabled student in respect of his attendance on a course;
(c) intended to meet additional expenditure connected with term time residential study away from the student's educational establishment;
(d) on account of the student maintaining a home at a place other than that at which he resides during his course;

   (e)  intended to meet the cost of books, and equipment (other than special equipment) or, if not so intended, an amount equal to the amount allowed under *regulation 38(2)(f) of the Family Credit (General) Regulations 1987 towards such costs* [regulation 62(2A)(b) of the Income Support (General) Regulations 1987 towards such costs];

   (f)  intended to meet travel expenses incurred as a result of his attendance on the course.

**13.**   Any interest, dividend or other income derived from capital.

**14.**   Any maintenance payments in respect of a parent.

**[14A.**   (1) Subject to sub-paragraph (2), the amount of any earnings top-up paid to or in respect of the absent parent or the parent with care.

(2) Subject to sub-paragraphs (3) and (4), where earnings top-up is payable and the amount which is payable has been calculated by reference to the weekly earnings of either the absent parent and another person or the parent with care and another person—

   (a)  if during the period which is used to calculate his earnings under paragraph 2 or, as the case may be, paragraph 5, the normal weekly earnings of that parent exceed those of the other person, the amount payable by way of earnings top-up shall be treated as the income of that parent;

   (b)  if during that period, the normal weekly earnings of that parent equal those of the other person, half of the amount payable by way of earnings top-up shall be treated as the income of that parent;

   (c)  if during that period, the normal weekly earnings of that parent are less than those of that other person, the amount payable by way of earnings top-up shall not be treated as the income of that parent.

(3) Where any earnings top-up is in payment and, not later than the effective date, the person, or, if more than one, each of the persons by reference to whose engagement and normal engagement in remunerative work that payment has been calculated is no longer the partner of the person to whom that payment is made, the payment in question shall be treated as the income of the parent in question only where that parent is in receipt of it.

(4) Where earnings top-up is in payment and, not later than the effective date, either or both of the persons by reference to whose engagement and normal engagement in remunerative work that payment has been calculated has ceased to be employed, half of the amount payable by way of earnings top-up shall be treated as the income of the parent in question.]

**[14B.**   (1) Subject to sub-paragraph (2), payments to a person of working tax credit shall be treated as the income of the parent who has qualified for them by his normal engagement in remunerative work at the rate payable at the effective date.

(2) Where working tax credit is payable and the amount which is payable has been calculated by reference to the earnings of the absent parent and another person—

   (a)  if during the period which is used to calculate his earnings under paragraph 2 or, as the case may be, paragraph 5, the normal weekly earnings of that parent exceed those of the other person, the amount payable by way of working tax credit shall be treated as the income of that parent;

   (b)  if during that period the normal weekly earnings of that parent equal those of the other person, half of the amount payable by way of working tax credit shall be treated as the income of that parent; and

   (c)  if during that period the normal weekly earnings of that parent are less than those of that other person, the amount payable by way of working tax credit shall not be treated as the income of that parent.]

**15.**   Any other payments or other amounts received on a periodical basis which are not otherwise taken into account under Part I, II, IV or V of this Schedule [except payments or other amounts which—

(a)  are excluded from the definition of "earnings" by virtue of paragraph 1(2);

(b)  are excluded from the definition of "the relevant income of a child" by virtue of paragraph 23; or

(c)  are the share of housing costs attributed by virtue of paragraph (3) of regulation 15 to any former partner of the parent of the qualifying child in respect of whom the maintenance assessment is made and are paid to that parent.].

**16.**  (1) Subject to sub-paragraphs (2) to [(7)] the amount of any income to which this Part applies shall be calculated or estimated—

(a)  where it has been received in respect of the whole of the period of 26 weeks which ends at the end of the relevant week, by dividing such income received in that period by 26;

(b)  where it has been received in respect of part of the period of 26 weeks which ends at the end of the relevant week, by dividing such income received in that period by the number of complete weeks in respect of which such income is received and for this purpose income shall be treated as received in respect of a week if it is received in respect of any day in the week in question.

(2) The amount of maintenance payments made in respect of a parent—

(a)  where they are payable weekly and have been paid at the same amount in respect of each week in the period of 13 weeks which ends at the end of the relevant week, shall be the amount equal to one of those payments;

(b)  in any other case, shall be the amount calculated by aggregating the total amount of those payments received in the period of 13 weeks which ends at the end of the relevant week and dividing by the number of weeks in that period in respect of which maintenance was due.

(3) In the case of a student—

(a)  the amount of any grant and any amount paid in respect of grant contribution shall be calculated by apportioning it equally between the weeks in respect of which it is payable;

(b)  the amount of any covenant income shall be calculated by dividing the amount payable in respect of a year by 52 (or, where such amount is payable in respect of a lesser period, by the number of complete weeks in that period) and, subject to sub-paragraph (4), deducting £5.00;

(c)  the amount of any student loan shall be calculated by apportioning the loan equally between the weeks in respect of which it is payable and, subject to sub-paragraph (4), deducting £10.00.

(4) For the purposes of sub-paragraph (3)—

(a)  not more than £5.00 shall be deducted under sub-paragraph (3)(b);

(b)  not more than £10.00 in total shall be deducted under sub-paragraphs (3)(b) and (c).

(5) Where in respect of the period of 52 weeks which ends at the end of the relevant week a person is in receipt of interest, dividend or other income which has been produced by his capital, the amount of that income shall be calculated by dividing the aggregate of the income so received by 52.

(6) Where a calculation would, but for this sub-paragraph, produce an amount which, in the opinion of the *child support officer* [Secretary of State], does not accurately reflect the normal amount of the other income of the person in question, such income, or any part of it, shall be calculated by reference to such other period as may, in the particular case, enable the other income of that person to be determined more accurately and for this purpose the *child support officer* [Secretary of State] shall have regard to the nature and pattern of receipt of such income.

[(7) This paragraph shall not apply to payments of working tax credit referred to in paragraph 14B.]

**Note.** Para 9A: inserted by SI 1999/977, reg 6(1), (5)(f) as from 6 April 1999. In para 9A(2) words "and a war widower's pension" in square brackets inserted by SI 2003/2779, reg 4(1), (6)(a) as from 5 November 2003.

In para 12(e) words "regulation 38(2)(f) of the Family Credit (General) Regulations 1987 towards such costs" substituted by words from "regulation 62(2A)(b)" to "towards such costs" in square brackets by SI 2003/328, reg 6(1), (6)(c) as from 6 April 2003.

Para 14A: inserted by SI 1996/1945, reg 24(4).

Para 14B: inserted by SI 2003/328, reg 6(1), (6)(d) as from 6 April 2003.

In para 15 words "except payments or other amounts which are excluded from the definition of "earnings" by virtue of paragraph 1(2)" (inserted by SI 1996/1945, reg 24(5)) substituted by words from "except payments" to "that parent." in square brackets by SI 1998/58, reg 56(4) as from 19 January 1998.

In para 16(1) reference to "(6)" substituted by reference to "(7)" in square brackets by SI 2003/328, reg 6(1), (6)(e)(i) as from 6 April 2003. In para 16(6) in both places words "child support officer" substituted by words "Secretary of State" in square brackets by SI 1999/1510, art 19(c) as from 1 June 1999. Para 16(7) inserted by SI 2003/328, reg 6(1), (6)(e)(ii) as from 6 April 2003.

PART IV   INCOME OF CHILD TREATED AS INCOME OF PARENT

**17.** The amount of any income of a child which is to be treated as the income of the parent in calculating or estimating N and M shall be the aggregate of the amounts determined in accordance with this Part.

**18.** Where a child has income which falls within the following paragraphs of this Part and that child is a member of the family of his parent (whether that child is a qualifying child in relation to that parent or not), the relevant income of that child shall be treated as that of his parent.

**19.** Where child support maintenance is being assessed for the support of only one qualifying child, the relevant income of that child shall be treated as that of the parent with care.

**20.** Where child support maintenance is being assessed to support more than one qualifying child, the relevant income of each of those children shall be treated as that of the parent with care to the extent that it does not exceed the aggregate of—

  (a)  the amount determined under—
    (i)  regulation 3(1)(a) (calculation of AG) in relation to the child in question; and
    (ii) the total of any other amounts determined under regulation 3(1)(b) [and (c)] which are applicable in the case in question divided by the number of children for whom child support maintenance is being calculated,

  less the basic rate of child benefit (within the meaning of regulation 4) for the child in question; and

  (b)  [one-and-a-half times] the total of the amounts calculated under regulation 3(1)(a) (income support personal allowance for child or young person) in respect of that child and regulation *3(1)(c)(i)* [3(1)(c)] (income support family premium).

**21.** Where child support maintenance is not being assessed for the support of the child whose income is being calculated or estimated, the relevant income of that child shall be treated as that of his parent to the extent that it does not exceed the amount determined under regulation 9(1)(g).

**22.** [(1)] Where a benefit under the Contributions and Benefits Act includes an adult or child dependency increase in respect of a relevant child, the relevant income of that child shall be calculated or estimated as if it included that amount.

[(1A) For the purposes of sub-paragraph (1), an addition to a contribution-based jobseeker's allowance under [regulation 10(4)] of the Jobseeker's Allowance (Transitional Provisions) Regulations [1996] shall be treated as a dependency increase included with a benefit under the Contributions and Benefits Act.]

[(1B) (1) Where a war disablement pension includes a dependency allowance paid in respect of a relevant child, the relevant income of that child shall be calculated or estimated as if it included that amount.

(2) For the purposes of this paragraph, a "war disablement pension" includes a war widow's pension [and a war widower's pension], a payment made to compensate for non-payment of such a pension, and a pension or payment analogous to such a pension or payment paid by the government of a country outside Great Britain.]

**23.** For the purposes of this Part, "the relevant income of a child" does not include—

    (a) any earnings of the child in question;

    (b) payments by an absent parent *in respect of* [to] the child for whom maintenance is being assessed;

    (c) where the class of persons who are capable of benefiting from a discretionary trust include the child in question, payments from that trust except in so far as they are made to provide for food, ordinary clothing and footwear, gas, electricity or fuel charges or housing costs; or

    (d) any interest payable on arrears of child support maintenance for that child;

    [(e) the first £10 of any other income of that child.]

**24.** The amount of the income of a child which is treated as the income of the parent shall be determined in the same way as if such income were the income of the parent.

**Note.** In para 20(a)(ii) words "and (c)" in square brackets substituted by SI 1996/1803, reg 17(3)(a). In para 20(b) words "one-and-a-half times" in square brackets substituted by SI 1995/1045, reg 54(10), and number "3(1)(c)(i)" substituted by number "3(1)(c)" in square brackets by SI 1998/58, reg 56(5) as from 6 April 1998.

Para 22(1) numbered as such, and sub-para (1A) inserted, by SI 1996/1345, reg 6(4)(b). In para 22(1A) words "regulation 9(4)" substituted by words "regulation 10(4)" in square brackets by SI 1999/977, reg 6(1), (g)(i) as from 6 April 1999 and year "1995" substituted by year "1996" in square brackets by SI 1999/977, reg 6(1), (5)(g)(ii) as from 6 April 1999. Para 22(1B) inserted by SI 1999/977, reg 6(1), (5)(h) as from 6 April 1999. In para 22(1B)(2) words "and a war widower's pension" in square brackets inserted by SI 2003/2779, reg 4(1), (6)(b) as from 5 November 2003.

In para 23(b) words "in respect of" substituted by word "to" in square brackets substituted by SI 1998/58, reg 56(6) as from 19 January 1998 and sub-para (e) inserted by SI 1995/1045, reg 54(11).

PART V    AMOUNTS TREATED AS THE INCOME OF A PARENT

**25.** The amounts which fall to be treated as income of the parent in calculating or estimating N and M shall include amounts to be determined in accordance with this Part.

**26.** Where *a child support officer* [the Secretary of State] is satisfied—

    (a) that a person has performed a service either—

        (i) without receiving any remuneration in respect of it; or

        (ii) for remuneration which is less than that normally paid for that service;

    (b) that the service in question was for the benefit of—

        (i) another person who is not a member of the same family as the person in question; or

        (ii) a body which is neither a charity nor a voluntary organisation;

    (c) that the service in question was performed for a person who, or as the case may be, a body which was able to pay remuneration at the normal rate for the service in question;

    (d) that the principal purpose of the person undertaking the service without receiving any or adequate remuneration is to reduce his assessable income for the purposes of the Act; and

    (e) that any remuneration foregone would have fallen to be taken into account as earnings, the value of the remuneration forgone shall be estimated by *a child support officer* [the Secretary of State] and an amount equal to the value so estimated shall be treated as income of the person who performed those services.

**27.**   Subject to paragraphs 28 to 30, where *the child support officer* [the Secretary of State] is satisfied that, otherwise than in the circumstances set out in paragraph 26, a person has intentionally deprived himself of—

> (a)  any income or capital which would otherwise be a source of income;
>
> (b)  any income or capital which it would be reasonable to expect would be secured by him,

with a view to reducing the amount of his assessable income, his net income shall include the amount estimated by *a child support officer* [the Secretary of State] as representing the income which that person would have had if he had not deprived himself of or failed to secure that income or, as the case may be, that capital.

**28.**   No amount shall be treated as income by virtue of paragraph 27 in relation to—

> (a)  if the parent satisfies the conditions for payment of the rate of child benefit specified in regulation 2(1)(a)(ii) of the Child Benefit Rates Regulations, an amount representing the difference between that rate and the basic rate, as defined in regulation 4;
>
> (b)  if the parent is a person to, or in respect of, whom income support is payable, a contribution-based jobseeker's allowance;
>
> (c)  a payment from a discretionary trust or a trust derived from a payment made in consequence of a personal injury.

**29.**   Where an amount is included in the income of a person under paragraph 27 in respect of income which would become available to him on application, the amount included under that paragraph shall be included from the date on which it could be expected to be acquired.

**30.**   Where *a child support officer* [the Secretary of State] determines under paragraph 27 that a person has deprived himself of capital which would otherwise be a source of income, the amount of that capital shall be reduced at intervals of 52 weeks, starting with the week which falls 52 weeks after the first week in respect of which income from it is included in the calculation of the assessment in question, by an amount equal to the amount which *the child support officer* [the Secretary of State] estimates would represent the income from that source in the immediately preceding period of 52 weeks.

**31.**   Where a payment is made on behalf of a parent or a relevant child in respect of food, ordinary clothing or footwear, gas, electricity or fuel charges, housing costs or council tax, an amount equal to the amount which *the child support officer* [the Secretary of State] estimates represents the value of that payment shall be treated as the income of the parent in question except to the extent that such amount is—

> (a)  disregarded under paragraph 38 of Schedule 2;
>
> (b)  a payment of school fees paid by or on behalf of someone other than the absent parent.

**32.**   Where paragraph 26 applies the amount to be treated as the income of the parent shall be determined as if it were earnings from employment as an employed earner and in a case to which paragraph 27 or 31 applies the amount shall be determined as if it were other income to which Part III of this Schedule applies.

**Note.** Amended by SI 1999/1510, art 19 as from 1 June 1999.

SCHEDULE 2

AMOUNTS TO BE DISREGARDED WHEN CALCULATING OR ESTIMATING N AND M

**1.**   The amounts referred to in this Schedule are to be disregarded when calculating or estimating N and M (parent's net income).

**2.** An amount in respect of income tax applicable to the income in question where not otherwise allowed for under these Regulations.

**3.** Where a payment is made in a currency other than sterling, an amount equal to any banking charge or commission payable in converting that payment to sterling.

**4.** Any amount payable in a country outside the United Kingdom where there is a prohibition against the transfer to the United Kingdom of that amount.

**5.** Any compensation for personal injury and any payments from a trust fund set up for that purpose.

**6.** Any advance of earnings or any loan made by an employer to an employee.

**7.** Any payment by way of, or any reduction or discharge of liability resulting from entitlement to, housing benefit or council tax benefit.

**8.** Any disability living allowance, mobility supplement or any payment intended to compensate for the non-payment of any such allowance or supplement.

**9.** Any payment which is—
   (a) an attendance allowance under section 64 of the Contributions and Benefits Act;
   (b) an increase of disablement pension under section 104 or 105 of that Act (increases where constant attendance needed or for exceptionally severe disablement);
   (c) a payment made under regulations made in exercise of the power conferred by Schedule 8 to that Act (payments for pre-1948 cases);
   (d) an increase of an allowance payable in respect of constant attendance under that Schedule;
   (e) payable by virtue of articles 14, 15, 16, 43 or 44 of the Personal Injuries (Civilians) Scheme 1983 (allowances for constant attendance and exceptionally severe disablement and severe disablement occupational allowance) or any analogous payment; or
   (f) a payment based on the need for attendance which is paid as part of a war disablement pension.

**10.** Any payment under section 148 of the Contributions and Benefits Act (pensioners' Christmas bonus).

**11.** Any social fund payment within the meaning of Part VIII of the Contributions and Benefits Act.

**12.** Any payment made by the Secretary of State to compensate for the loss (in whole or in part) of entitlement to housing benefit.

**13.** Any payment made by the Secretary of State to compensate for loss of housing benefit supplement under regulation 19 of the Supplementary Benefit (Requirements) Regulations 1983.

**14.** Any payment made by the Secretary of State to compensate a person who was entitled to supplementary benefit in respect of a period ending immediately before 11th April 1988 but who did not become entitled to income support in respect of a period beginning with that day.

**15.** Any concessionary payment made to compensate for the non-payment of income support [, state pension credit], [income-based jobseeker's allowance,] disability living allowance, or any payment to which paragraph 9 applies.

**16.** Any payments of child benefit to the extent that they do not exceed the basic rate of that benefit as defined in regulation 4.

**17.** Any payment made under regulations 9 to 11 or 13 of the Welfare Food Regulations 1988 (payments made in place of milk tokens or the supply of vitamins).

**18.** Subject to paragraph 20 and to the extent that it does not exceed £10.00—
   (a) war disablement pension or war widows pension [or war widower's pension] or a payment made to compensate for non-payment of such a pension;

(b) a pension paid by the government of a country outside Great Britain and which either—

   (i) is analogous to a war disablement pension; or

   (ii) is analogous to a war widow's pension [or war widower's pension].

**19.** (1) Except where sub-paragraph (2) applies and subject to sub-paragraph (3) and paragraphs 20, 38 and 47, [up to £20.00] of any charitable or voluntary payment made, or due to be made, at regular intervals.

(2) Subject to sub-paragraph (3) and paragraphs 38 and 47, any charitable or voluntary payment made or due to be made at regular intervals which is intended and used for an item other than food, ordinary clothing or footwear, gas, electricity or fuel charges, housing costs of any member of the family or the payment of council tax.

(3) Sub-paragraphs (1) and (2) shall not apply to a payment which is made by a person for the maintenance of any member of his family or of his former partner or of his children.

(4) For the purposes of sub-paragraph (1) where a number of charitable or voluntary payments fall to be taken into account they shall be treated as though they were one such payment.

**20.** (1) Where, but for this paragraph, more than [£20.00] would be disregarded under paragraphs 18 and 19(1) in respect of the same week, only [£20.00] in aggregate shall be disregarded and where an amount falls to be deducted from the income of a student under paragraph 16(3)(b) or (c) of Schedule 1, that amount shall count as part of the [£20.00] disregard allowed under this paragraph.

(2) Where any payment which is due to be paid in one week is paid in another week, sub-paragraph (1) and paragraphs 18 and 19(1) shall have effect as if that payment were received in the week in which it was due.

**21.** In the case of a person participating in arrangements for training made under section 2 of the Employment and Training Act 1973 or section 2 of the Enterprise and New Towns (Scotland) Act 1990 (functions in relation to training for employment etc.) or attending a course at an employment rehabilitation centre established under section 2 of the 1973 Act—

   (a) any travelling expenses reimbursed to the person;

   (b) any living away from home allowance under section 2(2)(d) of the 1973 Act or section 2(4)(c) of the 1990 Act;

   (c) any training premium,

but this paragraph, except in so far as it relates to a payment mentioned in sub-paragraph (a), (b) or (c), does not apply to any part of any allowance under section 2(2)(d) of the 1973 Act or section 2(4)(c) of the 1990 Act.

**22.** Where a parent occupies a dwelling as his home and that dwelling is also occupied by a person, other than a non-dependant or a person who is provided with board and lodging accommodation, and that person is contractually liable to make payments in respect of his occupation of the dwelling to the parent, the amount or, as the case may be, the amounts specified in [paragraph 19 of Schedule 9 to the Income Support (General) Regulations 1987 which would have applied if he had been in receipt of income support].

**23.** Where a parent, who is not a self-employed earner, is in receipt of rent or any other money in respect of the use and occupation of property other than his home, that rent or other payment to the extent of any sums which that parent is liable to pay by way of—

   [(a) payments which are to be taken into account as eligible housing costs under sub- paragraphs (b), (c), (d) and (t) of paragraph 1 of Schedule 3 (eligible housing costs for the purposes of determining exempt income and protected income) and paragraph 3 of that Schedule (exempt income: additional provisions relating to eligible housing costs);]

(b) council tax payable in respect of that property;

(c) water and sewerage charges payable in respect of that property.

**24.** [For each week in which a parent provides] board and lodging accommodation in his home otherwise than as a self-employed earner—

(a) £20.00 of any payment for that accommodation made by[, on behalf or in respect of] the person to whom that accommodation is provided; and

(b) where any such payment exceeds £20.00, 50 per centum of the excess.

**25.** Any payment made to a person in respect of an adopted child who is a member of his family that is made in accordance with any regulations made under section 57A or pursuant to section 57A(6) of the Adoption Act 1976 (permitted allowances) or, as the case may be, [section 51A] of the Adoption (Scotland) Act 1978 (schemes for the payment of allowances to adopters)—

(a) where the child is not a child in respect of whom child support maintenance is being assessed, to the extent that it exceeds [the aggregate of the amounts to be taken into account in the calculation of E under regulation 9(1)(g)], reduced, as the case may be, under regulation 9(4);

(b) in any other case, to the extent that it does not exceed the amount of the income of a child which is treated as that of his parent by virtue of Part IV [of Schedule 1.].

**26.** Where a local authority makes a payment in respect of the accommodation and maintenance of a child in pursuance of paragraph 15 of Schedule 1 to the Children Act 1989 (local authority contribution to child's maintenance) to the extent that it exceeds the amount referred to in [regulation 9(1)(g)] (reduced, as the case may be, under regulation 9(4)).

**27.** Any payment received under a policy of insurance taken out to insure against the risk of being unable to maintain repayments on a loan taken out to acquire an interest in, or to meet the cost of repairs or improvements to, the parent's home and used to meet such repayments, to the extent that the payment received under that policy [exceeds] [the total of the amount of the payments set out in paragraphs 1(b), 3(2) and (4) of Schedule 3 as modified, where applicable, by regulation 18.]

**28.** In the calculation of the income of the parent with care, any maintenance payments made by the absent parent in respect of his qualifying child.

**29.** Any payment made by a local authority to a person who is caring for a child under section 23(2)(a) of the Children Act 1989 (provision of accommodation and maintenance by a local authority for children whom the authority is looking after) or, as the case may be, section 21 of the Social Work (Scotland) Act 1968 or by a voluntary organisation under section 59(1)(a) of the Children Act 1989 (provision of accommodation by voluntary organisations) or by a care authority under regulation 9 of the Boarding Out and Fostering of Children (Scotland) Regulations 1985 (provision of accommodation and maintenance for children in care).

**30.** Any payment made by a health authority [, or Primary Care Trust], local authority or voluntary organisation in respect of a person who is not normally a member of the household but is temporarily in the care of a member of it.

**31.** Any payment made by a local authority under section 17 or 24 of the Children Act 1989 or, as the case may be, section 12, 24 or 26 of the Social Work (Scotland) Act 1968 (local authorities' duty to promote welfare of children and powers to grant financial assistance to persons looked after, or in, or formerly in, their care).

**32.** Any resettlement benefit which is paid to the parent by virtue of regulation 3 of the Social Security (Hospital In-Patients) Amendment (No. 2) Regulations 1987 (transitional provisions).

**33.** (1) Any payment or repayment made—

(a) as respects England and Wales, under regulation 3, 5 or 8 of the National Health Service (Travelling Expenses and Remission of Charges) Regulations 1988 (travelling expenses and health service supplies);

(b) as respects Scotland, under regulation 3, 5 or 8 of the National Health Service (Travelling Expenses and Remission of Charges) (Scotland) Regulations 1988 (travelling expenses and health service supplies).

(2) Any payment or repayment made by the Secretary of State for Health, the Secretary of State for Scotland or the Secretary of State for Wales which is analogous to a payment or repayment mentioned in sub-paragraph (1).

**34.** Any payment made (other than a training allowance), whether by the Secretary of State or any other person, under the Disabled Persons Employment Act 1944 or in accordance with arrangements made under section 2 of the Employment and Training Act 1973 to assist disabled persons to obtain or retain employment despite their disability.

**35.** Any contribution to the expenses of maintaining a household which is made by a non-dependant member of that household.

**36.** Any sum in respect of a course of study attended by a child payable by virtue of regulations made under section 81 of the Education Act 1944 (assistance by means of scholarship or otherwise), or by virtue of section 2(1) of the Education Act 1962 (awards for courses of further education) or section 49 of the Education (Scotland) Act 1980 (power to assist persons to take advantage of educational facilities).

[**36A** Any sum in respect of financial assistance given, or given under arrangements made, by the Secretary of State (in relation to England) or the National Assembly for Wales (in relation to Wales) under section 14 of the Education Act 2002 (power of Secretary of State and National Assembly for Wales to give financial assistance for purposes related to education), to a child.]

**37.** Where a person receives income under an annuity purchased with a loan which satisfies the following conditions—

(a) that loan was made as part of a scheme under which not less than 90 per centum of the proceeds of the loan were applied to the purchase by the person to whom it was made of an annuity ending with his life or with the life of the survivor of two or more persons (in this paragraph referred to as "the annuitants") who include the person to whom the loan was made;

(b) that the interest on the loan is payable by the person to whom it was made or by one of the annuitants;

(c) that at the time the loan was made the person to whom it was made or each of the annuitants had attained the age of 65;

(d) that the loan was secured on a dwelling in Great Britain and the person to whom the loan was made or one of the annuitants owns an estate or interest in that dwelling; and

(e) that the person to whom the loan was made or one of the annuitants occupies the dwelling on which it was secured as his home at the time the interest is paid,

the amount, calculated on a weekly basis equal to—

(i) where, or insofar as, section 26 of the Finance Act 1982 (deduction of tax from certain loan interest) applies to the payments of interest on the loan, the interest which is payable after the deduction of a sum equal to income tax on such payments at the basic rate for the year of assessment in which the payment of interest becomes due;

(ii) in any other case the interest which is payable on the loan without deduction of such a sum.

**38.** Any payment of the description specified in paragraph 39 of Schedule 9 to the Income Support Regulations (disregard of payments made under certain trusts and disregard of certain other payments) and any income derived from the investment of such payments.

**39.** Any payment made to a juror or witness in respect of attendance at court other than compensation for loss of earnings or for loss of a benefit payable under the Contributions and Benefits Act [or the Jobseekers Act].

**40.**   Any special war widows' payment made under—
   (a)  the Naval and Marine Pay and Pensions (Special War Widows Payment) Order 1990 made under section 3 of the Naval and Marine Pay and Pensions Act 1865;
   (b)  the Royal Warrant dated 19th February 1990 amending the Schedule to the Army Pensions Warrant 1977;
   (c)  the Queen's Order dated 26th February 1990 made under section 2 of the Air Force (Constitution) Act 1917;
   (d)  the Home Guard War Widows Special Payments Regulations 1990 made under section 151 of the Reserve Forces Act 1980;
   (e)  the Orders dated 19th February 1990 amending Orders made on 12th December 1980 concerning the Ulster Defence Regiment made in each case under section 140 of the Reserve Forces Act 1980,
and any analogous payment by the Secretary of State for Defence to any person who is not a person entitled under the provisions mentioned in sub-paragraphs (a) to (e).

**41.**   Any payment to a person as holder of the Victoria Cross or the George Cross or any analogous payment.

**42.**   Any payment made either by the Secretary of State for the Home Department or by the Secretary of State for Scotland under a scheme established to assist relatives and other persons to visit persons in custody.

**43.**   Any amount by way of a refund of income tax deducted from profits or emoluments chargeable to income tax under Schedule D or Schedule E.

**44.**   Maintenance payments (whether paid under the Act or otherwise) insofar as they are not treated as income under Part III or IV [of Schedule 1.].

**45.**   Where following a divorce or separation—
   (a)  capital is divided between the parent and the person who was his partner before the divorce or separation; and
   (b)  that capital is intended to be used to acquire a new home for that parent or to acquire furnishings for a home of his,
income derived from the investment of that capital for one year following the date on which that capital became available to the parent.

**[46.**   Except in the case of a self-employed earner, payments in kind.]

**47.**   Any payment made by the Joseph Rowntree Memorial Trust from money provided to it by the Secretary of State for Health for the purpose of maintaining a family fund for the benefit of severely handicapped children.

**48.**   Any payment of expenses to a person who is—
   (a)  engaged by a charitable or voluntary body; or
   (b)  a volunteer,
if he otherwise derives no remuneration or profit from the body or person paying those expenses.

**[48A.**   Any guardian's allowance under Part III of the Contributions and Benefits Act.

**48B.**   Any payment in respect of duties mentioned in paragraph 1(1)(i) of Chapter 1 of Part I of Schedule 1 relating to a period of one year or more.]

**[48C.**   Any payment to a person under section 1 of the Community Care (Direct Payments) Act 1996 or section 12B of the Social Work (Scotland) Act 1968 [or under regulations made under section 57 of the Health and Social Care Act 2001 (direct payments)] in respect of his securing community care services, as defined in section 46 of the National Health Services and Community Care Act 1990.]

**[48D.**   Any payment of child tax credit.]

**[48E.**
Any payment made by a local authority, or by the National Assembly for Wales, to a person relating to a service which is provided to develop or sustain the capacity of that person to live independently in his accommodation.]

**[48F.**    Any supplementary pension under article 29(1A) of the Naval, Military and Air Forces etc (Disablement and Death) Service Pensions Order 1983 (pensions to widows and widowers) or under article 27(3) of the Personal Injuries (Civilians) Scheme 1983 (pensions to widows and widowers).]

**49.**    In this Schedule—

"concessionary payment" means a payment made under arrangements made by the Secretary of State with the consent of the Treasury which is charged either to the National Insurance Fund or to a Departmental Expenditure Vote to which payments of benefit under the Contributions and Benefits Act [or the Jobseekers Act] are charged;

"health authority" means a health authority established under the National Health Service Act 1977 or the National Health Service (Scotland) Act 1978;

"mobility supplement" has the same meaning as in regulation 2(1) of the Income Support Regulations;

"war disablement pension" and "war widow" have the same meanings as in section 150(2) of the Contributions and Benefits Act [or the Jobseekers Act].

**Note.** In para 15 words ", state pension credit" in square brackets inserted by SI 2003/2779, reg 4(1), (7)(a) as from 5 November 2003 and words "income-based jobseeker's allowance," in square brackets inserted by SI 1996/1345, reg 6(5). In para 18 words "or war widower's pension" in square brackets in both places they occur inserted by SI 2003/2779, reg 4(1), (7)(b) as from 5 November 2003. In para 19(1) words in square brackets substituted by SI 1996/481, reg 3(2). In para 20(1) sums in square brackets substituted by SI 1996/481, reg 3(3). In para 22 words from "paragraph 19 of" to "of income support" in square brackets substituted by SI 2003/328, reg 6(1), (7)(a) as from 6 April 2003. Para 23(a) substituted by SI 1993/913, reg 28. In para 24 first words in square brackets substituted, and words in square brackets in sub-para (a) inserted, by SI 1995/1045, reg 55(2), (3). In para 25 words "section 51" substituted by words "section 51A" in square brackets by SI 1999/977, reg 6(1), (6) as from 6 April 1999, words from "the aggregate" to "regulation 9(1)(g)" in square brackets substituted by SI 1993/913, reg 29, words "of Schedule 1." in square brackets inserted by SI 1998/58, reg 57 as from 19 January 1998. In para 26 words "regulation 9(1)(g)" in square brackets substituted by SI 1993/913, reg 30. In para 27 first word in square brackets substituted by SI 1995/1045, reg 55(4); words in square brackets substituted by SI 1995/3261, reg 46. In para 30 words ", or Primary Care Trust" in square brackets inserted by SI 2002/2469, reg 9, Sch 6 as from 1 October 2002. Para 36A inserted by SI 2004/2415, reg 5(1), (3) as from 16 September 2004. In para 39 words "or the Jobseekers Act" in square brackets inserted by SI 1996/1345, reg 6(6). In para 44 words "of Schedule 1." in square brackets inserted by SI 1998/58, reg 57 as from 19 January 1998. Para 46 substituted by SI 1993/913, reg 31. Paras 48A, 48B inserted by SI 1993/913, reg 32. Para 48C inserted by SI 1996/3196, reg 14 and words "or under regulations made under section 57 of the Health and Social Care Act 2001 (direct payments)" in square brackets inserted in relation to England as from 8 April 2003 by SI 2003/762, reg 11(2), Sch 2 and in relation to Wales as from 1 November 2004 by SI 2004/1748, reg 12, Sch 2, para 2. Para 48D inserted by SI 2003/328, reg 6(1), (7)(b) as from 6 April 2003. Para 48E (as originally inserted by SI 2003/328, reg 6(1), (7)(c)) substituted by SI 2003/2779, reg 4(1), (7)(c) as from 5 November 2003. Para 48F inserted by SI 2003/2779, reg 4(1), (7)(d) as from 5 November 2003. In para 49 words "or the Jobseekers Act" in square brackets in both places they occur inserted by SI 1996/1345, reg 6(7)(c).

## SCHEDULE 3

ELIGIBLE HOUSING COSTS

*Eligible housing costs for the purposes of determining exempt income and protected income*

**1.**    Subject to the following provisions of this Schedule, *the following payments* [the following amounts payable] in respect of the provision of a home shall be eligible to be taken into account as housing costs for the purposes of these Regulations—

(a)    *payments of, or by way of,* [amounts payable by way of] rent;

(b)    *mortgage interest payments;*

[(b) amounts payable by way of mortgage interest;]

(c) *interest payments* [amounts payable by way of interest] under a hire purchase agreement to buy a home;

(d) *interest payments* [amounts payable by way of interest] on loans for repairs and improvements to the home[, including interest on a loan for any service charge imposed to meet the cost of such repairs and improvements;]

(e) *payments* [amounts payable] by way of ground rent or in Scotland, payments by way of feu duty;

(f) *payments* [amounts payable] under a co-ownership scheme;

(g) *payments* [amounts payable] in respect of, or in consequence of, the use and occupation of the home;

(h) where the home is a tent, *payments* [amounts payable] in respect of the tent and the site on which it stands;

(i) *payments* [amounts payable] in respect of a licence or permission to occupy the home (whether or not board is provided);

(j) *payments* [amounts payable] by way of mesne profits or, in Scotland, violent profits;

(k) *payments of, or by way of,* [amounts payable by way of] service charges, the payment of which is a condition on which the right to occupy the home depends;

(l) *payments* [amounts payable] under or relating to a tenancy or licence of a Crown tenant;

(m) mooring charges payable for a houseboat;

(n) where the home is a caravan or a mobile home, *payments* [amounts payable] in respect of the site on which it stands;

(o) any contribution payable by a parent resident in an almshouse provided by a housing association which is either a charity of which particulars are entered in the register of charities established under section 4 of the Charities Act 1960 (register of charities) or an exempt charity within the meaning of that Act, which is a contribution towards the cost of maintaining that association's almshouses and essential services in them;

(p) *payments* [amounts payable] under a rental purchase agreement, that is to say an agreement for the purchase of a home under which the whole or part of the purchase price is to be paid in more than one instalment and the completion of the purchase is deferred until the whole or a specified part of the purchase price has been paid;

(q) where, in Scotland, the home is situated on or pertains to a croft within the meaning of section 3(1) of the Crofters (Scotland) Act 1955, the *payment* [amount payable] in respect of the croft land;

(r) where the home is provided by an employer (whether under a condition or term in a contract of service or otherwise), *payments* [amounts payable] to that employer in respect of the home, including *payments made by the employer deducting the payment in question* [any amounts deductible by the employer] from the remuneration of the parent in question;

(s) < . . . >

(t) *payments in respect of a loan taken out to pay off another loan but only to the extent that it was incurred [in respect of payments eligible to be taken into account as housing costs by virtue of the other provisions of this Schedule*

[(t) amounts payable in respect of a loan taken out to pay off another loan but only to the extent that it was incurred in respect of amounts eligible to be taken into account as housing costs by virtue of other provisions of this Schedule.]

*Loans for repairs and improvements to the home*

2   [Subject to paragraph 2A (loans for repairs and improvements in transitional cases), for the purposes of] of paragraph 1(d) "repairs and improvements" means major repairs necessary to maintain the fabric of the home and any of the following measures undertaken with a view to improving its fitness for occupation—
  (a)  installation of a fixed bath, shower, wash basin or lavatory, and necessary associated plumbing;
  (b)  damp proofing measures;
  (c)  provision or improvement of ventilation and natural lighting;
  (d)  provision of electric lighting and sockets;
  (e)  provision or improvement of drainage facilities;
  (f)  improvement of the structural condition of the home;
  (g)  improvements to the facilities for the storing, preparation and cooking of food;
  (h)  provision of heating, including central heating;
  (i)  provision of storage facilities for fuel and refuse;
  (j)  improvements to the insulation of the home;
  (k)  other improvements which the *child support officer* [Secretary of State] considers reasonable in the circumstances.

*[Loans for repairs and improvements in transitional cases*

**2A.**   In the case of a loan entered into before the first date upon which a maintenance application or enquiry form is given or sent or treated as given or sent to the relevant person, for the purposes of paragraph 1(d) "repairs and improvements" means repairs and improvements of any description whatsoever.]

*Exempt income: additional provisions relating to eligible housing costs*

**3.**   (1) The additional provisions made by this paragraph shall have effect only for the purpose of calculating or estimating exempt income.
  (2)  Subject to sub-paragraph (6), where the home of an absent parent or, as the case may be, a parent with care, is subject to a mortgage or charge and that parent *makes periodical payments* [is liable to make periodical payments] to reduce the capital secured by that mortgage or charge of an amount provided for in accordance with the terms thereof, *the amount of those payments* [those amounts payable] shall be eligible to be taken into account as the housing costs of that parent.
  [(2A)  Where an absent parent or as the case may be a parent with care has entered into a loan for repairs or improvements of a kind referred to in paragraph 1(d) and that parent *makes periodical payments* [is liable to make periodical payments] of an amount provided for in accordance with the terms of that loan to reduce the amount of that loan, *the amount of those payments* [those amounts payable] shall be eligible to be taken into account as housing costs of that parent.]
  (3)  Subject to sub-paragraph (6), where the home of an absent parent or, as the case may be, a parent with care, is held under an agreement and *certain payments made* [certain amounts payable] under that agreement are included as housing costs by virtue of paragraph 1 of this Schedule, *the weekly amount of any other payments which are made* [any other amounts payable] in accordance with that agreement by the parent in order either—
  (a)  to reduce his liability under that agreement; or
  (b)  to acquire the home to which it relates,
shall also be eligible to be taken into account as housing costs.
  (4)   Where a policy of insurance has been obtained and retained for the purpose of discharging a mortgage or charge on the home of the parent in

question, the amount of the *premiums paid* [premiums payable] under that policy shall be eligible to be taken into account as a housing cost [including for the avoidance of doubt such a policy of insurance whose purpose is to secure the payment of monies due under the mortgage or charge in the event of the unemployment, sickness or disability of the insured.]

[(4A) Where–
  (a) an absent parent or parent with care has obtained a loan which constitutes an eligible housing cost falling within sub-paragraph (d) or (t) of paragraph 1; and
  (b) a policy of insurance has been obtained and retained, the purpose of which is solely to secure the payment of monies due under that loan in the event of the unemployment, sickness or disability of the insured person,
the amount of the premiums payable under that policy shall be eligible to be taken into account as a housing cost.]

[(5) Where a policy of insurance has been obtained and retained for the purpose of discharging a mortgage or charge on the home of the parent in question and also for the purpose of accruing profits on the maturity of the policy, there shall be eligible to be taken into account as a housing cost—
  (a) where the sum secured by the mortgage or charge does not exceed £60,000, the whole of the *premiums paid* [premiums payable] under that policy; and
  (b) where the sum secured by the mortgage or charge exceeds £60,000, the part of the *premiums paid* [premiums payable] under that policy which are necessarily incurred for the purpose of discharging the mortgage or charge or, where that part cannot be ascertained, 0.0277 per centum of the amount secured by the mortgage or charge.]

[(5A) Where a plan within the meaning of regulation 4 of the Personal Equity Plans Regulations 1989 has been obtained and retained for the purpose of discharging a mortgage or charge on the home of the parent in question and also for the purpose of accruing profits upon the realisation of the plan, there shall be eligible to be taken into account as a housing cost—
  (a) where the sum secured by the mortgage or charge does not exceed £60,000, the whole of the premiums payable in respect of the plan; and
  (b) where the sum secured by the mortgage or charge exceeds £60,000, that part of the premiums payable in respect of the plan which is necessarily incurred for the purpose of discharging the mortgage or charge or, where that part cannot be ascertained, 0.0277 per centum of the amount secured by the mortgage or charge.

(5B) Where a personal pension plan has been obtained and retained for the purpose of discharging a mortgage or charge on the home of the parent in question and also for the purpose of securing the payment of a pension to him, there shall be eligible to be taken into account as a housing cost 25 per centum of the contributions payable in respect of that personal pension plan [derived from a personal pension scheme].]

(6) For the purposes of sub-paragraphs (2) and (3), housing costs shall not include—
  (a) [any payments in excess of those required] to be made under or in respect of a mortgage, charge or agreement to which either of those sub-paragraphs relate;
  (b) *payments* [amounts payable] under any second or subsequent mortgage on the home to the extent that [they would not be eligible] to be taken into account as housing costs;
  (c) premiums payable in respect of any policy of insurance against loss caused by the destruction of or damage to any building or land.

*Conditions relating to eligible housing costs*

**4.**   (1)   Subject to the following provisions of this paragraph the housing costs referred to in this Schedule shall be included as housing costs only where—
   [(a) they are necessarily incurred for the purpose of purchasing, renting or otherwise securing possession of the home for the parent and his family, or for the purpose of carrying out repairs and improvements to that home;]
   (b) the parent or, if he is one of a family, he or a member of his family, is responsible for those costs; and
   (c) the liability to meet those costs is to a person other than a member of the same household.

[(1A) For the purposes of sub-paragraph (1)(a) "repairs and improvements" shall have the meaning given in paragraph 2 of this Schedule.]

(2) For the purposes of sub-paragraph (1)(b) a parent shall be treated as responsible for housing costs where—
   (a)   because the person liable to meet those costs is not doing so, he has to meet those costs in order to continue to live in the home and either he was formerly the partner of the person liable, or he is some other person whom it is reasonable to treat as liable to meet those costs; or
   (b)   he pays a share of those costs in a case where—
       (i)   he is living in a household with other persons;
      (ii)   those other persons include persons who are not close relatives of his or his partner;
     (iii)   a person who is not such a close relative is responsible for those costs under the preceding provisions of this paragraph or has an equivalent responsibility for housing expenditure; and
      (iv)   it is reasonable in the circumstances to treat him as sharing that responsibility.

[(3)       Subject to sub-paragraph (4), payments on a loan shall constitute an eligible housing cost only if that loan has been obtained for the purposes specified in sub-paragraph (1)(a).

(4) Where a loan has been obtained only partly for the purposes specified in sub-paragraph (1)(a), the eligible housing cost shall be limited to that part of the payment attributable to those purposes.]

*Accommodation also used for other purposes*

**5.**   Where amounts are payable in respect of accommodation which consists partly of residential accommodation and partly of other accommodation, only such proportion thereof as is attributable to residential accommodation shall be eligible to be taken into account as housing costs.

*Ineligible service and fuel charges*

**6.**   Housing costs shall not include—
   [(a) where the costs are inclusive of ineligible service charges within the meaning of paragraph 1(a)(i) of Schedule 1 to the Housing Benefit (General) Regulations 1987 (ineligible service charges), the amounts specified as ineligible in paragraph 1A of that Schedule;]
   [(aa)  . . .
   (b) where the costs are inclusive of any of the items mentioned in paragraph 5(2) of Schedule 1 to the Housing Benefit (General) Regulations 1987 (payment in respect of fuel charges), the deductions prescribed in that paragraph unless the parent provides evidence on which the actual or approximate amount of the service charge for fuel may be estimated, in which case the estimated amount; . . .
   (c) charges for water, sewerage or allied environmental services and where the amount of such charges is not separately identified, such part of the charges in question as is attributable to those services [and

(d) where the costs are inclusive of charges, other than those which are not to be included by virtue of sub-paragraphs (a) to (c), that part of those charges which exceeds the greater of the following amounts—
  (i) the total of the charges other than those which are ineligible service charges within the meaning of paragraph 1 of Schedule 1 to the Housing Benefit Regulations (housing costs);
  (ii) 25 per centum of the total amount of eligible housing costs,
  and for the purposes of this sub-paragraph, where the amount of those charges is not separately identifiable, that amount shall be such amount as is reasonably attributable to those charges.]

*Interpretation*

**7.** In this Schedule except where the context otherwise requires—
  "close relative" means a parent, parent-in-law, son, son-in-law, daughter, daughter-in-law, step-parent, step-son, step-daughter, brother, sister, or the spouse of any of the preceding persons or, if that person is one of an unmarried couple, the other member of that couple;
  "co-ownership scheme" means a scheme under which the dwelling is let by a housing association and the tenant, or his personal representative, will, under the terms of the tenancy agreement or of the agreement under which he became a member of the association, be entitled, on his ceasing to be a member and subject to any conditions stated in either agreement, to a sum calculated by reference directly or indirectly to the value of the dwelling;
  "housing association" has the meaning assigned to it by section 1(1) of the Housing Association Act 1985.

**Note.** In para 1 words "the following payments" substituted by words "the following amounts payable" in square brackets by SI 1998/58, reg 58(2)(a) as from 19 January 1998. In para 1(a) words "payments of, or by way of," substituted by words "amounts payable by way of" in square brackets, para 1(b) substituted, in sub-paras (c), (d) words "interest payments" substituted by words "amounts payable by way of interest" in square brackets by SI 1998/58, reg 58(2)(b), (c), (d) as from 19 January 1998. In para 1(d) words from ", including interest" to "repairs and improvements;" in square brackets inserted by SI 1993/913, reg 33. In para 1(e)–(j), (l), (n), (p), (r) word "payments" substituted by words "amounts payable" in square brackets by SI 1998/58, reg 58(2)(e) as from 19 January 1998. In para 1(k) words "payments of, or by way of," substituted by words "amounts payable by way of" in square brackets by SI 1998/58, reg 58(2)(b) as from 19 January 1998: see SI 1998/58, reg 1(2). In para 1(q) word "payment" substituted by words "amount payable" in square brackets by SI 1998/58, reg 58(2)(f) as from 19 January 1998. In para 1(r) words "payments made by the employer deducting the payment in question" substituted by words "any amounts deductible by the employer" in square brackets by SI 1998/58, reg 58(2)(g)(ii) as from 19 January 1998. Para 1(s) revoked by SI 1993/913, reg 33. Para 1(t) substituted by SI 1998/58, reg 58(2)(h) as from 19 January 1998.
  In para 2 words from "Subject to paragraph" to "purposes of" in square brackets substituted by SI 1995/1045, reg 56(3). In para 2(k) words "child support officer" substituted by words "Secretary of State" in square brackets by SI 1999/1510, art 20 as from 1 June 1999.
  Para 2A inserted by SI 1995/1045, reg 56(4).
  In para 3(2), (2A) words "makes periodical payments" substituted by words "is liable to make periodical payments" and words "the amount of those payments" substituted by words "those amounts payable" in square brackets by SI 1998/58, reg 58(3)(a) as from 19 January 1998. Para 3(2A) inserted by SI 1995/3261, reg 47(2). In para 3(3) words "certain payments made" substituted by words "certain amounts payable" in square brackets and words "the weekly amount of any other payments which are made" substituted by words "any other amounts payable" in square brackets by SI 1998/58, reg 58(3)(b)(i), (ii) as from 19 January 1998. In para 3(4) words "premiums paid" substituted by words "premiums payable" in square brackets by SI 1998/58, reg 58(3)(c) as from 19 January 1998. In para 3(4) words from "including for" to "of the insured." in square brackets inserted by SI 1995/1045, reg 56(5). Para 3(4A) inserted by SI 1996/3196, reg 15(3)(a). Para 3(5) substituted by SI 1994/227, reg 4(8). In para 3(5)(a), (b) words "premiums paid" substituted by words "premiums payable"

in square brackets by SI 1998/58, reg 58(3)(c) as from 19 January 1998. Para 3(5A) inserted by SI 1995/1045, reg 56(5). Para 3(5B) inserted by SI 1995/1045, reg 56(5). In para 3(5B) words "derived from a personal pension scheme" in square brackets inserted by SI 1996/3196, reg 15(3)(b). In para 3(6)(a) words "any payments in excess of those required" in square brackets substituted by SI 1995/1045, reg 56(5) and in sub-para (6)(b) word "payments" substituted by words "amounts payable" in square brackets by SI 1998/58, reg 58(3)(d) as from 19 January 1998. In para 3(6)(b) words "they would not be eligible" in square brackets substituted by SI 1995/1045, reg 56(5).

Para 4(1)(a) substituted, and sub-paras (1A), (3), (4) inserted, by SI 1996/3196, reg 15(4).

Para 6: sub-para (a) substituted by SI 1995/3261, reg 47(3)(i); sub-para (aa) inserted by SI 1995/1045, reg 56(6), revoked by SI 1995/3261, reg 47(3)(ii); in sub-para (b) word omitted revoked, and sub-para (d) and preceding "and" inserted, by SI 1995/3261, reg 47(3)(iii), (iv).

## SCHEDULE 3A

### AMOUNT TO BE ALLOWED IN RESPECT OF TRANSFERS OF PROPERTY

*Interpretation*

**1.** (1) In this Schedule—
"property" means—
  (a) a legal estate or an equitable interest in land; or
  (b) a sum of money which is derived from or represents capital, whether in cash or in the form of a deposit with—
    (i) the Bank of England;
    (ii) an authorised institution or an exempted person within the meaning of the Banking Act 1987;
    (iii) a building society incorporated or deemed to be incorporated under the Building Societies Act 1986;
  (c) any business asset as defined in sub-paragraph (2) (whether in the form of money or an interest in land or otherwise);
  (d) any policy of insurance which has been obtained and retained for the purpose of providing a capital sum to discharge a mortgage or charge secured upon an estate or interest in land which is also the subject of the transfer (in this Schedule referred to as an endowment policy);
"qualifying transfer" means a transfer of property—
  (a) which was made in pursuance of a court order made, or a written maintenance agreement executed, before 5th April 1993;
  (b) which was made between the absent parent and either the parent with care or a relevant child [, or both whether jointly or otherwise including, in Scotland, in common property];
  (c) which was made at a time when the absent parent and the parent with care were living separate and apart;
  *(d) the effect of which is that the parent with care or a relevant child is beneficially entitled (subject to any mortgage or charge) to the whole of the asset transferred;*
  [(d) the effect of which is that (subject to any mortgage or charge) the parent with care or a relevant child is solely beneficially entitled to the property of which the property transferred forms the whole or part, or the business asset, or the parent with care is beneficially entitled to that property or that asset together with the relevant child or absent parent or both, jointly or otherwise or, in Scotland, in common property, or the relevant child is so entitled together with the absent parent;] and
  *(e) which was not made expressly for the purpose only of compensating the parent with care for the loss of any right to apply for or receive periodical payments or a capital sum in respect of herself;*
  [(e) which was not made for the purpose only of compensating the parent with care either for the loss of a right to apply for, or receive, periodical

payments or a capital sum in respect of herself, or for any reduction in the amount of such payments or sum;]

"compensating transfer" means a transfer of property which would be a qualifying transfer (disregarding the requirement of paragraph (e) of the definition of "qualifying transfer") if it were made by the absent parent, but which is made by the parent with care in favour of the absent parent *or a* [, or] relevant child [or both jointly or otherwise, or, in Scotland, in common property];

"relevant date" means the date of the making of the court order or the execution of the written maintenance agreement in pursuance of which the qualifying transfer was made.

(2) For the purposes of sub-paragraph (1) "business asset" means an asset, whether in the form of money or an interest in land or otherwise which, prior to the date of transfer was used in the course of a trade or business carried on—

(a) by the absent parent as a sole trader;

(b) by the absent parent in partnership, whether with the parent with care or not;

(c) by a close company within the meaning of sections 414 and 415 of the Income and Corporation Taxes Act 1988 in which the absent parent was a participator at the date of the transfer.

(3) Where the condition specified in regulation 10(a) is satisfied this Schedule shall apply as if references—

(a) to the parent with care were references to the absent parent; and

(b) to the absent parent were references to the parent with care.

*Evidence to be produced in connection with the allowance for transfers of property*

**2.** (1) Where the absent parent produces to the Secretary of State—

(a) contemporaneous evidence in writing of the making of a court order or of the execution of a written maintenance agreement, which requires the relevant person to make a qualifying transfer of property;

(b) evidence in writing and whether contemporaneous or not as to—

(i) the fact of the transfer;

(ii) the value of the property transferred at the relevant date;

(iii) the amount of any mortgage or charge outstanding at the relevant date,

an amount in respect of the relevant value of the transfer determined in accordance with the following provisions of this Schedule shall be allowed in calculating or estimating the exempt income of the absent parent.

(2) Where the evidence specified in sub-paragraph (1) is not produced within a reasonable time after the Secretary of State has been notified of the wish of the absent parent that *a child support officer* [the Secretary of State] consider the question, *the officer* [he] shall determine the question on the basis that the relevant value of the transfer is nil.

*Consideration of evidence produced by other parent*

**[3.** (1) Where an absent parent has notified the Secretary of State that he wishes him to consider whether an amount should be allowed in respect of the relevant value of a qualifying transfer, the Secretary of State shall—

(a) give notice to the other parent of that application; and

(b) have regard in determining the application to any representations made by the other parent which are received within the period specified in sub-paragraph (2).

(2) The period specified in this sub-paragraph is one month from the date on which the notice referred to in sub-paragraph (1)(a) above was sent or such longer period as the Secretary of State is satisfied is reasonable in the circumstances of the case.]

*Computation of qualifying value—business assets and land*

**4.**    (1)  Subject to paragraph 6, where the property *which is the subject of the transfer* [transferred] by the absent parent is, or includes, an estate or interest in land, or a business asset, the qualifying value of that estate, interest or asset shall be determined in accordance with the formula—

$$QV = \frac{VT - MC}{2}$$

*where*—

(i)    *QV is the qualifying value,*

(ii)   *VT is the value of the estate or interest in land or the value of the asset (as the case may be) calculated at the relevant date, and*

(iii)  *MC is the amount of the principal outstanding at the relevant date under any mortgage or charge on the estate, interest or asset*

$$[QV = (VP - MCP)/2 - (VAP - MCR) - VCR$$

where—

QV is the qualifying value,

VP is the value at the relevant date of the business asset or the property of which the estate or interest forms the whole or part,

and

for the purposes of this calculation it is assumed that the estate, interest or asset held on the relevant date by the absent parent or by the absent parent and the parent with care is held by them jointly in equal shares or, in Scotland, in common property;

MCP is the amount of any mortgage or charge outstanding immediately prior to the relevant date on the business asset or on the property of which the estate or interest forms the whole or part;

VAP is the value calculated at the relevant date of the business asset or of the property of which the estate or interest forms the whole or part beneficially owned by the absent parent immediately following the transfer (if any);

MCR is, where immediately after the transfer the absent parent is responsible for discharging a mortgage or charge on the business asset or on the property of which the estate or interest forms the whole or part, the amount calculated at the relevant date which is a proportion of any such mortgage or charge outstanding immediately following the transfer, being the same percentage as VAP bears to that property as a whole; and

VCR is the value of any charge in favour of the absent parent on the business asset or on the property of which the estate or interest forms the whole or part, being the amount specified in the court order or written maintenance agreement in relation to the charge, or the amount of a proportion of the value of the business asset or the property on the relevant date specified in the court order or written maintenance agreement].

(2)  For the purposes of sub-paragraph (1) the value of an estate or interest in land is to be determined upon the basis that the parent with care and any relevant child, if in occupation of the land, would quit on completion of the sale.

*Computation of qualifying value—cash, deposits and endowment policies*

**5.**    Subject to paragraph 6, where the property which is the subject of the qualifying transfer is, or includes—

(i) a sum of money whether in cash or in the form of a deposit with the Bank of England, an authorised institution or exempted person within the meaning of the Banking Act 1987, or a building society incorporated or deemed to be incorporated under the Building Societies Act 1986, derived from or representing capital; or

(ii) an endowment policy,

the amount of the qualifying value shall be determined by applying the formula—

$$QV = \frac{VT}{2}$$

where—

(a) QV is the qualifying value; and

(b) VT is the amount of cash, the balance of the account or the surrender value of the endowment policy on the relevant date [and for the purposes of this calculation it is assumed that the cash, balance or policy held on the relevant date by the absent parent and the parent with care is held by them jointly in equal shares or, in Scotland, in common property].

*Transfers wholly in lieu of periodical payments for relevant child*

**6.** Where the evidence produced in relation to a transfer to, or in respect of, a relevant child, shows expressly that the whole of that transfer was made exclusively in lieu of periodical payments in respect of that child—

(a) in a case to which paragraph 4 applies, *for the formula given in that paragraph there shall be substituted the following—QV = VT − MC* [the qualifying value shall be treated as being twice the qualifying value calculated in accordance with that paragraph]; and

(b) in a case to which paragraph 5 applies, the qualifying value shall be *the value of the transfer* [treated as being twice the qualifying value calculated in accordance with that paragraph].

*Multiple transfers to related persons*

**7.** (1) Where there has been more than one qualifying transfer from the absent parent—

(a) to the same parent with care;

(b) to or for the benefit of the same relevant child;

(c) to or for the benefit of two or more relevant children with respect to all of whom the same persons are respectively the parent with care and the absent parent;

or any combination thereof, the relevant value by reference to which the allowance is to be calculated in accordance with paragraph 10 shall be the aggregate of the qualifying transfers calculated individually in accordance with the preceding paragraphs of this Schedule, less the value of any compensating transfer or where there has been more than one, the aggregate of the values of the compensating transfers so calculated.

(2) Except as provided by sub-paragraph (1), the values of transfers shall not be aggregated for the purposes of this Schedule.

*Computation of the value of compensating transfers*

**8.** [Subject to paragraph 8A, the value of] a compensating transfer shall be determined in accordance with paragraph 4 to 7 above, but as if any reference in those paragraphs—

(a) to the absent parent were a reference to the parent with care;

(b) to the parent with care were a reference to the absent parent; and

(c) to a qualifying transfer were a reference to a compensating transfer.

**[8A.** (1) This paragraph applies where—
(a) the property which is the subject of a compensating transfer is or includes cash or deposits as defined in paragraph 5(i);
(b) that property was acquired by the parent with care after the relevant date;
(c) the absent parent has no legal interest in that property;
(d) if that property is or includes cash obtained by a mortgage or charge, that mortgage or charge was executed by the parent with care after the relevant date and was of property to the whole of which she is legally entitled; and
(e) the effect of the compensating transfer is that the parent with care or a relevant child is beneficially entitled (subject to any mortgage or charge) to the whole of the absent parent's legal estate in the land which is the subject of the qualifying transfer.

(2) Where sub-paragraph (1) applies, the qualifying value of the compensating transfer shall be the amount of the cash or deposits transferred pursuant to the court order or written maintenance agreement referred to in head (a) of the definition of "qualifying transfer" in paragraph 1(1).]

*Computation of relevant value of a qualifying transfer*

**9.** The relevant value of a qualifying transfer shall be calculated by deducting from the qualifying value of the qualifying transfer the qualifying value of any compensating transfer between the same persons as are parties to the qualifying transfer.

*Amount to be allowed in respect of a qualifying transfer*

**10.** For the purposes of regulation 9(1)(bb), the amount to be allowed in the computation of E, or in case where regulation 10(a) applies, F, shall be—
(a) where the relevant value calculated in accordance with paragraph 9 is less than £5,000, nil;
(b) where the relevant value calculated in accordance with paragraph 9 is at least £5,000, but less than £10,000, £20.00 per week;
(c) where the relevant value calculated in accordance with paragraph 9 is at least £10,000, but less than £25,000, £40.00 per week;
(d) where the relevant value calculated in accordance with paragraph 9 is not less than £25,000, £60.00 per week.

**11.** This Schedule in its application to Scotland shall have effect as if—
(a) in paragraph 1 for the words "legal estate or equitable interest in land" [and in head (e) of paragraph 8A(1), for the words "legal estate in the land"] there were substituted the words "an interest in land within the meaning of section 2(6) of the Conveyancing and Feudal Reform (Scotland) Act 1970";
(b) in paragraph 4 the word "estate," and the words "estate or" in each place where they respectively occur were omitted [;
(c) in paragraphs 1, 2, 4 and 8A for the word "mortgage" there were substituted the words "heritable security].]

**Note.** Inserted by SI 1995/1045, reg 57, Sch 1.
In para 1(1) definition "qualifying transfer" in para (b) words from ", or both whether" to "in common property" in square brackets inserted by SI 1999/977, reg 6(1), (7)(a)(i) as from 6 April 1999. In para 1(1) in definition "qualifying transfer" paras (d), (e) substituted by SI 1999/977, reg 6(1), (7)(a)(ii), (iii) as from 6 April 1999. In para 1(1) definition "compensating transfer" words "or a" substituted by word ", or" in square brackets, and words from "or both jointly" to "in common property" in square brackets inserted by SI 1999/977, reg 6(1), (7)(b)(i), (ii) as from 6 April 1999.
In para 2(2) words "a child support officer" and "the officer" substituted by words "the Secretary of State" and "he" in square brackets by SI 1999/1510, art 21(a)(i), (ii) as from 1 June 1999.

Para 3: substituted by SI 1999/1510, art 21(b) as from 1 June 1999.

In para 4(1) words "which is the subject of the transfer" substituted by word "transferred" in square brackets by SI 1999/977, reg 6(1), (7)(c)(i) as from 6 April 1999.

In para 4(1) words from "QV = " to "interest or asset" substituted by words from "QV = (VP" to "written maintenance agreement" in square brackets by SI 1999/977, reg 6(1), (7)(c)(ii) as from 6 April 1999.

In para 5(b) words from "and for the" to "in common property" in square brackets inserted by SI 1999/977, reg 6(1), (7)(d) as from 6 April 1999.

In para 6(a) words "for the formula given in that paragraph there shall be substituted the following—QV = VT – MC" substituted by words from "the qualifying value" to "with that paragraph" in square brackets by SI 1999/977, reg 6(1), (7)(e)(i) as from 6 April 1999.

In para 6(b) words "the value of the transfer" substituted by words from "treated as being" to "with that paragraph" in square brackets by SI 1999/977, reg 6(1), (7)(e)(ii) as from 6 April 1999.

In para 8 words "Subject to paragraph 8A, the value of" in square brackets substituted by SI 1995/3261, reg 48(1). Para 8A: inserted by SI 1995/3261, reg 48(2).

In para 11(a) words from "and in head" to "in the land"" in square brackets and para (c) inserted by SI 1999/977, reg 6(1), (7)(f)(i), (ii) as from 6 April 1999: see SI 1999/977, reg 1(2).

## SCHEDULE 3B

AMOUNT TO BE ALLOWED IN RESPECT OF TRAVELLING COSTS

*Interpretation*

**1.** In this Schedule—

"day" means, in relation to a person who attends at a work place for one period of work which commences before midnight of one day and concludes the following day, the first of those days;

"journey" means a single journey, and "pair of journeys" means two journeys in opposing directions, between the same two places;

"relevant employment" means an employed earner's employment in which the relevant person is employed and in the course of which he is required to attend at a work place, and "relevant employer" means the employer of the relevant person in that employment;

"relevant person" means—

(a) in the application of the provisions of this Schedule to regulation 9, the absent parent or the parent with care; and

(b) in the application of the provisions of this Schedule to regulation 11, the absent parent;

*"straight-line distance" means the straight-line distance measured in miles and calculated to 2 decimal places, and, where that distance is not a whole number of miles, rounded to the nearest whole number of miles, a distance which exceeds a whole number of miles by 0.50 of a mile being rounded up;*

["straight-line distance" means the straight-line distance measured in kilometres and calculated to 2 decimal places, and, where that distance is not a whole number of kilometres, rounded to the nearest whole number of kilometres, a distance which exceeds a whole number of kilometres by 0.50 of a kilometre being rounded up;]

"travelling costs" means the costs of—

(a) purchasing either fuel or a ticket for the purpose of travel;

(b) contributing to the costs borne by a person other than a relevant employer in providing transport; or

(c) paying another to provide transport,

which are incurred by the relevant person in travelling between the relevant person's home and his work place, and where he has more than one relevant employment between any of his work places in those employments;

"work place" means the relevant person's normal place of employment in a relevant employment, and "deemed work place" means a place which has been selected by the *child support officer* [Secretary of State] pursuant either to paragraph 8(2) or 15(2) for the purpose of calculating the amount to be allowed in respect of the relevant person's travelling costs.

*Computation of amount allowable in respect of travelling costs*

**2.**   For the purpose of regulation 9 and regulation 11 an amount in respect of the travelling costs of the relevant person shall be determined in accordance with the following provisions of this Schedule if the relevant person—

(a)   has travelling costs; and

(b)   provides the information required to enable the amount of the allowance to be determined.

*Computation in cases where there is one relevant employment and one work place in that employment*

**3.**   Subject to paragraphs 21 to 23, where the relevant person has one relevant employment and is normally required to attend at only one work place in the course of that employment the amount to be allowed in respect of travelling costs shall be determined in accordance with paragraphs 4 to 7 below.

**4.**   There shall be calculated or, if that is impracticable, estimated—

(a)   the straight-line distance between the relevant person's home and his work place;

(b)   the number of journeys between the relevant person's home and his work place which he makes during a period comprising a whole number of weeks which appears to the *child support officer* [Secretary of State] to be representative of his normal pattern of work, there being disregarded any pair of journeys between his work place and his home and where the first journey is from his work place to his home and where the time which elapses between the start of the first journey and the conclusion of the second is not more than two hours.

**5.**   The results of the calculation or estimate produced by sub-paragraph (a) of paragraph 4 shall be multiplied by the result of the calculation or estimate required by sub-paragraph (b) of that paragraph.

**6.**   The product of the multiplication required by paragraph 5 shall be divided by the number of weeks in the period.

**7.**   Where the result of the division required by paragraph 6 is less than or equal to *150* [240], the amount to be allowed in respect of the relevant person's travelling costs shall be nil, and where it is greater than *150* [240] the weekly allowance to be made in respect of the relevant person's travelling costs shall be *10 pence* [6 pence] multiplied by the number by which that number exceeds *150* [240].

*Computation in cases where there is more than one work place but only one relevant employment*

**8.**   (1) Subject to sub-paragraph (2) and paragraphs 21 to 23 below, where the relevant person has one relevant employment but attends at more than one work place the amount to be allowed in respect of travelling costs for the purposes of regulations 9 and 11 shall be determined in accordance with paragraphs 9 to *13* [14].

(2) Where it appears that the relevant person works at more than one work place but his pattern of work is not sufficiently regular to enable the calculation of the amount to be allowed in respect of his travelling costs to be made readily, the *child support officer* [Secretary of State] may—

(a)   select a place which is either one of the relevant person's work places or some other place which is connected with the relevant employment; and

(b) apply the provisions of paragraphs 4 to 7 above to calculate the amount of the allowance to be made in respect of travelling costs upon the basis that the relevant person makes one journey from his home to the deemed work place and one journey from the deemed work place to his home on each day on which he attends at a work place in connection with relevant employment,

and the provisions of paragraphs 9 to *13* [14] shall not apply.

(3) For the purposes of sub-paragraph (2)(b) there shall be disregarded any day upon which the relevant person attends at a work place and in order to travel to or from that work place he undertakes a journey in respect of which—

(a) the travelling costs are borne wholly or in part by the relevant employer; or

(b) the relevant employer provides transport for any part of the journey for the use of the relevant person,

and where he attends at more than one work place on the same day that day shall be disregarded only if the condition specified in this sub-paragraph is satisfied in respect of all the work places at which he attends on that day.

**9.**   There shall be calculated, or if that is impracticable, estimated—

(a) the straight-line distances between the relevant person's home and each work place; and

(b) the straight-line distances between each of the relevant person's work places, other than those between which he does not ordinarily travel.

**10.**   Subject to paragraph 11, there shall be calculated for each pair of places referred to in paragraph 9 the number of journeys which the relevant person makes between them during a period comprising a whole number of weeks which appears to the *child support officer* [Secretary of State] to be representative of the normal working pattern of the relevant person.

**11.**   For the purposes of the calculation required by paragraph 10 there shall be disregarded—

(a) any pair of journeys between the same work place and the relevant person's home where the first journey is from his work place to his home and the time which elapses between the start of the first journey and the conclusion of the second is not more than two hours; and

(b) any journey in respect of which—

(i) the travelling costs are borne wholly or in part by the relevant employer; or

(ii) the relevant employer provides transport for any part of the journey for the use of the relevant person.

**12.**   The result of the calculation of the number of journeys made between each pair of places required by paragraph 10 shall be multiplied by the result of the calculation or estimate of the straight-line distance between them required by paragraph 9.

**13.**   All the products of the multiplications required by paragraph 12 shall be inserted together and the resulting sum divided by the number of weeks in the period.

**14.**   Where the result of the division required by paragraph 13 is less than or equal to *150* [240], the amount to be allowed in respect of travelling costs shall be nil, and where it is greater than *150* [240], the weekly allowance to be made in respect of the relevant person's travelling costs shall be *10 pence* [6 pence] multiplied by the number by which that number exceeds *150* [240].

*Computation in cases where there is more than one relevant employment*

**15.**   (1)   Subject to sub-paragraph (2) and paragraphs 21 to 23, where the relevant person has more than one relevant employment the amount to be allowed in respect of travelling costs for the purposes of regulations 9 and 11 shall be determined in accordance with paragraphs 16 to 20.

(2) Where it appears that in respect of any of his relevant employments, whilst the relevant person works at more than one work place, his pattern or work is not sufficiently regular to enable the calculation of the amount to be allowed in respect of his travelling costs to be made readily, the *child support officer* [Secretary of State]—

(a) may select a place which is either one of the relevant person's work places in that relevant employment or some other place which is connected with that relevant employment;

(b) may calculate the weekly average distance travelled in the course of his journeys made in connection with the relevant employment upon the basis that—

(i) the relevant person makes one journey from his home, or from another work place or deemed work place in another relevant employment, to the deemed work place and one journey from the deemed work place to his home, or to another work place or deemed work place in another relevant employment, on each day on which he attends at a work place in connection with the relevant employment in relation to which the deemed work place has been selected, and

(ii) the distance he travels between those places is the straight-line distance between them; and

(c) shall disregard any journeys made between work places in the relevant employment in respect of which a deemed work place has been selected.

(3) For the purposes of sub-paragraph (2)(b) there shall be disregarded any day upon which the relevant person attends at a work place and in order to travel to or from that work place he undertakes a journey in respect of which—

(a) the travelling costs are borne wholly or in part by the relevant employer; or

(b) the relevant employer provides transport for any part of the journey for the use of the relevant person,

and where in the course of the particular relevant employment he attends at more than one work place on the same day, that day shall be disregarded only if the condition specified in this paragraph is satisfied in respect of all the work places at which he attends on that day in the course of that employment.

**16.** There shall be calculated, or if that is impracticable, estimated—

(a) the straight-line distances between the relevant person's home and each work place; and

(b) the straight-line distances between each of the relevant person's work places, except—

(i) those between which he does not ordinarily travel, and

(ii) those for which a calculation of the distance from the relevant person's home is not required by virtue of paragraph 15(c).

**[17.** Subject to paragraph 17A, there shall be calculated, or if that is impracticable estimated, for each pair of places referred to in paragraph 16 between which straight-line distances are required to be calculated or estimated, the number of journeys which the relevant person makes between them during a period comprising a whole number of weeks which appears to the *child support officer* [Secretary of State] to be representative of the normal working pattern of the relevant person.

**17A.** For the purposes of the calculation required by paragraph 17, there shall be disregarded—

(a) any pair of journeys between the same work place and his home where the first journey is from his work place to his home and the time which elapses between the start of the first journey and the conclusion of the second is not more than two hours; and

(b) any journey in respect of which—

(i) the travelling costs are borne wholly or in part by the relevant employer; or

(ii) the relevant employer provides transport for any part of the journey for the use of the relevant person.]

**18.** The result of the calculation or estimate of the number of journeys made between each pair of places required by paragraph 17 shall be multiplied by the result of the calculation or estimate of the straight-line distance between them required by paragraph 16.

**19.** All the products of the multiplications required by paragraph 18, shall be inserted together and the resulting sum divided by the number of weeks in the period.

**20.** Where the result of the division required by paragraph 19, plus where appropriate the result of the calculation required by paragraph 15 in respect of a relevant employment in which a deemed work place has been selected, is less than or equal to *150* [240] the amount to be allowed in respect of travelling costs shall be nil, and where it is greater than *150* [240], the weekly allowance to be made in respect of the relevant person's travelling costs shall be *10 pence* [6 pence] multiplied by the number by which that number exceeds *150* [240].

*Relevant employments in respect of which no amount is to be allowed*

**21.** (1) No allowance shall be made in respect of travelling costs in respect of journeys between the relevant person's home and his work place or between his work place and his home in a particular relevant employment if the condition set out in paragraph 22 or 23 is satisfied in respect of that employment.

(2) The condition mentioned in paragraph 22, or as the case may be 23, is satisfied in relation to a case where the relevant person has more than one work place in a relevant employment only where the employer provides assistance of the kind mentioned in that paragraph in respect of all of the work places to or from which the relevant person travels in the course of that employment, but those journeys in respect of which that assistance is provided shall be disregarded in computing the total distance travelled by the relevant person in the course of the relevant employment.

**22.** The condition is that relevant employer provides transport of any description in connection with the employment which is available to the relevant person for any part of the journey between his home and his work place or between his work place and his home.

**23.** The condition is that the relevant employer bears any part of the travelling costs arising from the relevant person travelling between his home and his work place or between his work place and his home in connection with that employment, and for the purposes of this paragraph he does not bear any part of that cost where he does no more than—

(a) make a payment to the relevant person which would fall to be taken into account in determining the amount of the relevant person's net income;

(b) make a loan to the relevant person;

(c) pay to the relevant person an increased amount of remuneration,

to enable the relevant person to meet those costs himself.]

**Note.** Inserted by SI 1995/1045, reg 57, Sch 2.

Para 1: definition "straight-line distance" substituted by SI 2004/2415, reg 5(1), (4)(a) as from 16 September 2004; in definition "work place" words "child support officer" substituted by words "Secretary of State" in square brackets by SI 1999/1510, art 22 as from 1 June 1999.

In paras 4(b), 8(2), 10, 15(2), 17 words "child support officer" substituted by words "Secretary of State" in square brackets by SI 1999/1510, art 22 as from 1 June 1999.

In paras 7, 14, 20 references to "150" in each place it occurs substituted by references "240" in square brackets by SI 2004/2415, reg 5(1), (4)(b)(i) as from 16 September 2004.

In paras 7, 14, 20 words "10 pence" substituted by words "6 pence" in square brackets substituted by SI 2004/2415, reg 5(1), (4)(b)(ii) as from 16 September 2004.

In para 8(1), (2) references to "13" substituted by references to "14" in square brackets substituted by SI 2004/2415, reg 5(1), (4)(c) as from 16 September 2004.

Paras 17, 17A: substituted, for para 17 as originally enacted, by SI 1995/3261, reg 49.

## SCHEDULE 4

CASES WHERE CHILD SUPPORT MAINTENANCE IS NOT TO BE PAYABLE

The payments and awards specified for the purposes of regulation 26(1)(b)(i) are—

(a) the following payments under the Contributions and Benefits Act—
   [(i)   incapacity benefit under section 30A;
   (ii)   long-term incapacity benefit for widows under section 40;
   (iii)  long-term incapacity benefit for widowers under section 41;]
   (iv)   maternity allowance under section 35;
   (v)   . . .
   (vi)   attendance allowance under section 64;
   (vii)  severe disablement allowance under section 68;
   (viii) *invalid care allowance* [carer's allowance] under section 70;
   (ix)   disability living allowance under section 71;
   (x)   disablement benefit under section 103;
   (xi)   . . .
   (xii)  statutory sick pay within the meaning of section 151;
   (xiii) statutory maternity pay within the meaning of section 164;
(b) awards in respect of disablement made under (or under provisions analogous to)—
   (i)   the War Pensions (Coastguards) Scheme 1944;
   (ii)   the War Pensions (Naval Auxiliary Personnel) Scheme 1964;
   (iii)  the Pensions (Polish Forces) Scheme 1964;
   (iv)   the War Pensions (Mercantile Marine) Scheme 1964;
   (v)   the Royal Warrant of 21st December 1964 (service in the Home Guard before 1945);
   (vi)   the Order by Her Majesty of 22nd December 1964 concerning pensions and other grants in respect of disablement or death due to service in the Home Guard after 27th April 1952;
   (vii)  the Order by Her Majesty (Ulster Defence Regiment) of 4th January 1971;
   (viii) the Personal Injuries (Civilians) Scheme 1983;
   (ix)   the Naval Military and Air Forces Etc. (Disablement and Death) Service Pensions Order 1983; and
(c) payments from [the Independent Living (1993) Fund or the Independent Living (Extension) Fund].

**Note.** Para (a)(i)–(iii) substituted by SI 1995/1045, reg 58. Para (a)(v) revoked by SI 1995/1045, reg 58. In para (a)(viii) words "invalid care allowance" substituted by words "carer's allowance" in square brackets and para (a)(xi) revoked by SI 2003/328, reg 6(1), (8) as from 1 April 2003. In para (c) words in square brackets substituted by SI 1993/913, reg 34.

## SCHEDULE 5

PROVISIONS APPLYING TO CASES TO WHICH SECTION 43 OF THE ACT AND REGULATION 28 APPLY

[1   . . .
2   . . .
3   . . .
[3A   . . .]
4   . . .
5   . . .
6   . . .
7   . . .
[7A   . . .]

**8** . . .

**9** The provisions of paragraphs (1) and (2) of regulation 5 of the Child Support (Collection and Enforcement) Regulations 1992 shall apply to the transmission of payments in place of payments of child support maintenance under section 43 of the Act and regulation 28 as they apply to the transmission of payments of child support maintenance.]

**Note.** Inserted by SI 1993/913, reg 26(3), Schedule. Paras 1–3, para 3A (as originally inserted by SI 1995/1045, reg 59(4)), paras 4–7, para 7A (as originally inserted by SI 1993/925, reg 2(3)(iv)) and para 8 revoked by SI 1999/1510, art 23 as from 1 June 1999.

## CHILD SUPPORT (ARREARS, INTEREST AND ADJUSTMENT OF MAINTENANCE ASSESSMENTS) REGULATIONS 1992

**Dated** 20 July 1992

**SI 1992 No 1816**

ARRANGEMENT OF REGULATIONS

Whereas a draft of this instrument was laid before Parliament in accordance with section 52(2) of the Child Support Act 1991 and approved by a resolution of each House of Parliament:

Now, therefore, the Secretary of State for Social Security, in exercise of the powers conferred by sections 41, 51, 52(4) and 54 of the Child Support Act 1991 and of all other powers enabling him in that behalf, hereby makes the following Regulations—

PART I

GENERAL

*Citation, commencement and interpretation*

**1.** (1)  These Regulations may be cited as the Child Support (Arrears, Interest and Adjustment of Maintenance Assessments) Regulations 1992 and shall come into force on 5th April 1993.

(2)  In these Regulations, unless the context otherwise requires—

*"absent parent" includes a person treated as an absent parent by virtue of regulation 20 of the Maintenance Assessments and Special Cases Regulations;*

"the Act" means the Child Support Act 1991;

"arrears" means arrears of child support maintenance;

"arrears of child support maintenance" is to be construed in accordance with section 41(1) and (2) of the Act;

"arrears notice" has the meaning prescribed in regulation 2;

["Maintenance Calculation Procedure Regulations" means the Child Support (Maintenance Calculation Procedure) Regulations 2000;]

*"due date" has the meaning prescribed in regulation 3;*

*"Maintenance Assessments and Special Cases Regulations" means the Child Support (Maintenance Assessments and Special Cases) Regulations 1992;*

*"Maintenance Assessment Procedure Regulations" means the Child Support (Maintenance Assessment Procedure) Regulations 1992;*

["non-resident parent" includes a person treated as such under regulation 8 of the Child Support (Maintenance Calculations and Special Cases) Regulations 2000;]

"parent with care" means a person who, in respect of the same child or children, is both a parent and a person with care;

"relevant person" has the same meaning as in the *Maintenance Assessment Procedure Regulations* [Maintenance Calculation Procedure Regulations]

["state pension credit" means the social security benefit of that name payable under the State Pension Credit Act 2002].

(3) In these Regulations, unless the context otherwise requires, a reference—

(a)  to a numbered regulation is to the regulation in these Regulations bearing that number;

(b)  in a regulation to a numbered paragraph is to the paragraph in that regulation bearing that number;

(c)  in a paragraph to a lettered or numbered sub-paragraph is to the sub-paragraph in that paragraph bearing that letter or number.

**Note.** Para (2): definitions "absent parent", "due date", "Maintenance Assessments and Special Cases Regulations" and "Maintenance Assessment Procedure Regulations" revoked by SI 2001/162, reg 5(1), (2)(a) as from 3 March 2003 in relation to certain cases; for savings see reg 6(Z1) thereof (as inserted by SI 2003/347, reg 2(3), (4)(a)), (1), (2) and SI 2000/3186 (as amended by SI 2004/2415, reg 8). For further effect see SI 2001/162, reg 1(3) and SI 2003/192, arts 3, 5, 8, Schedule.

Para (2): definitions "Maintenance Calculation Procedure Regulations" and "non-resident parent" inserted by SI 2001/162, reg 5(1), (2)(b), (c) as from 3 March 2003 in relation to certain cases; for savings see reg 6(Z1) thereof (as inserted by SI 2003/347, reg 2(3), (4)(a)),

(1), (2) and SI 2000/3186 (as amended by SI 2004/2415, reg 8). For further effect see SI 2001/162, reg 1(3) and SI 2003/192, arts 3, 5, 8, Schedule.

Para (2): in definition "relevant person" words "Maintenance Assessment Procedure Regulations" substituted by words "Maintenance Calculation Procedure Regulations" in square brackets by SI 2001/162, reg 5(1), (2)(d); as from 3 March 2003 in relation to certain cases; for savings see reg 6(Z1) thereof (as inserted by SI 2003/347, reg 2(3), (4)(a)), (1), (2) and SI 2000/3186 (as amended by SI 2004/2415, reg 8). For further effect see SI 2001/162, reg 1(3) and SI 2003/192, arts 3, 5, 8, Schedule.

Para (2): definition "state pension credit" inserted by SI 2002/3019, reg 26(1), (2) as from 6 October 2003.

PART II

AREARS OF CHILD SUPPORT MAINTENANCE AND INTEREST ON ARREARS

**Note.** Words "and Interest on Arrears" revoked by SI 2001/162, reg 5(1), (3) as from 3 March 2003 in relation to certain cases; for savings see reg 6(Z1) thereof (as inserted by SI 2003/347, reg 2(3), (4)(a)), (1), (2) and SI 2000/3186 (as amended by SI 2004/2415, reg 8). For further effect see SI 2001/162, reg 1(3) and SI 2003/192, arts 3, 5, 8, Schedule

*Applicability of provisions as to arrears and interest and arrears notices*

**2.** (1) The provisions of paragraphs (2) to (4) and *regulations 3 to 9* [regulations 5 and 8] shall apply where—

(a) a case falls within section 41(1) of the Act; and

(b) the Secretary of State is arranging for the collection of child support maintenance under section 29 of the Act.

(2) Where the Secretary of State is considering taking action with regard to a case falling within paragraph (1), he shall serve a notice (an "arrears notice") on the *absent parent* [non-resident parent].

(3) An arrears notice shall—

(a) itemise the payments of child support maintenance due and not paid;

(b) set out in general terms the provisions as to arrears *and interest* contained in this regulation and *regulations 3 to 9* [regulations 5 and 8]; and

(c) request the *absent parent* [non-resident parent] to make payment of all outstanding arrears.

(4) Where an arrears notice has been served under paragraph (2), no duty to serve a further notice under that paragraph shall arise in relation to further arrears unless those further arrears have arisen after an intervening continuous period of not less than 12 weeks during the course of which all payments of child support maintenance due from the *absent parent* [non-resident parent] have been paid on time in accordance with regulations made under section 29 of the Act.

**Note.** Provision heading: words "and interest" in revoked by SI 2001/162, reg 5(1), (3)(b)(i) as from 3 March 2003 in relation to certain cases; for savings see reg 6(Z1) thereof (as inserted by SI 2003/347, reg 2(3), (4)(a)), (1), (2) and SI 2000/3186 (as amended by SI 2004/2415, reg 8). For further effect see SI 2001/162, reg 1(3) and SI 2003/192, arts 3, 5, 8, Schedule.

In para (1) words "regulations 3 to 9" substituted by words "regulations 5 and 8" in square brackets by SI 2001/162, reg 5(1), (3)(b)(ii) as from 3 March 2003 in relation to certain cases; for savings see reg 6(Z1) thereof (as inserted by SI 2003/347, reg 2(3), (4)(a)), (1), (2) and SI 2000/3186 (as amended by SI 2004/2415, reg 8). For further effect see SI 2001/162, reg 1(3) and SI 2003/192, arts 3, 5, 8, Schedule.

In paras (2), (3)(c), (4) words "absent parent" substituted by words "non-resident parent" in square brackets by SI 2001/162, reg 5(1), (3)(b)(iv) as from 3 March 2003 in relation to certain cases; for savings see reg 6(Z1) thereof (as inserted by SI 2003/347, reg 2(3), (4)(a)), (1), (2) and SI 2000/3186 (as amended by SI 2004/2415, reg 8). For further effect see SI 2001/162, reg 1(3) and SI 2003/192, arts 3, 5, 8, Schedule.

In para (3)(b) words "and interest" revoked and words "regulations 3 to 9" substituted by words "regulations 5 and 8" in square brackets by SI 2001/162, reg 5(1), (3)(b)(ii), (iii) as from 3 March 2003 in relation to certain cases; for savings see reg 6(Z1) thereof (as inserted by SI 2003/347, reg 2(3), (4)(a)), (1), (2) and SI 2000/3186 (as amended by SI 2004/2415, reg 8). For further effect see SI 2001/162, reg 1(3) and SI 2003/192, arts 3, 5, 8, Schedule.

*Liability to make payments of interest with respect to arrears*
**3.** (1) Subject to paragraph (2) and regulations 4 and 5, interest shall be payable with respect to any amount of child support maintenance due in accordance with a maintenance assessment and not paid by the date specified by the Secretary of State in accordance with regulations made under section 29 of the Act (the "due date"), and shall be payable in respect of the period commencing on that day and terminating on the date that amount is paid.

(2) Subject to paragraph (3), interest with respect to arrears shall only be payable if the Secretary of State has served an arrears notice in relation to those arrears, and shall not be payable in respect of any period terminating on a date earlier than 14 days prior to the date the arrears notice is served on the absent parent.

(3) Where the Secretary of State has served an arrears notice, the provisions of paragraph (2) shall not apply in relation to further arrears unless the conditions mentioned in regulation 2(4) are satisfied.

(4) Subject to paragraph (6), where, *following a review under section 16, 17, 18 or 19 of the Act or* [by virtue of a revision under section 16 of the Act, a decision under section 17 of the Act superseding an earlier decision or of] an appeal under section 20 of the Act, a fresh maintenance assessment is made with retrospective effect, interest in respect of the relevant retrospective period shall be payable with respect to the arrears calculated by reference to that fresh assessment.

(5) The provisions of paragraph (4) shall apply to a fresh assessment *following a review under section 16, 17, 18 or 19 of the Act or* [made by virtue of a revision under section 16 of the Act, a decision under section 17 of the Act superseding an earlier decision or of] an appeal under section 20 of the Act prior to any adjustment of that assessment under the provisions of regulation 10.

(6) For the purposes of paragraph (4), where *the review under section 16, 17, 18 or 19 of the Act or an appeal under section 20 of the Act results in* [by virtue of a revision under section 16 of the Act, a decision under section 17 of the Act superseding an earlier decision or of an appeal under section 20 of the Act there is] an increased assessment, and arrears in relation to that assessment arise, no interest shall be payable with respect to the arrears relating to the additional maintenance payable under that assessment in respect of any period prior to the date the absent parent is notified of the increased assessment.

**Note.** In paras (4), (5) words "following a review under section 16, 17, 18 or 19 of the Act or" substituted by words from "by virtue of a revision" to "decision or of" and "made by virtue" to "decision or of" in square brackets, and in para (6) words "the review under section 16, 17, 18 or 19 of the Act or an appeal under section 20 of the Act results in" substituted by words from "by virtue of a revision" to "the Act there is" in square brackets, by SI 1999/1510, art 24 as from 1 June 1999.

*Circumstances in which no liability to pay interest arises*
**4.** (1)     An absent parent shall not be liable to make payments of interest [with respect to arrears—
  (a) in respect of any day which falls after 17th April 1995; or
  (b) in respect of any period if either of the conditions set out in paragraph (2) is satisfied in relation to that period.]
(2) The conditions referred to in paragraph (1) are—
  (a) the absent parent did not know, and could not reasonably have been expected to know, of the existence of the arrears; or
  (b) the arrears have arisen solely in consequence of an operational or administrative error on the part of the Secretary of State . . ..

[(3) An absent parent who pays all outstanding arrears . . . within 28 days of the due date shall not be liable to make payments of interest with respect to those arrears.]

**Note.** In para (1) words from "with respect to arrears—" to "to that period." in square brackets substituted by SI 1995/1045, reg 7(1), (2). In para (2)(b) words omitted revoked by SI 1999/1510, art 25 as from 1 June 1999. Para (3): inserted by SI 1993/913, reg 36 and words omitted revoked by SI 1995/1045, reg 7(1), (3).

*Payment of arrears by agreement*

**5.** [(1) The Secretary of State may at any time enter into an agreement with an absent parent (an "arrears agreement") for the *absent parent* [non-resident parent] to pay all outstanding arrears by making payments on agreed dates of agreed amounts.

(2) Where an arrears agreement has been entered into, the Secretary of State shall prepare a schedule of the dates on which payments of arrears shall be made and the amount to be paid on each such date, and shall send a copy of the schedule to such persons as he thinks fit.]

(3) *If an arrears agreement is entered into within 28 days of the due date, and the terms of that agreement are adhered to by the absent parent, there shall be no liability to make payments of interest under the provisions of regulation 3 with respect to the arrears in relation to which the arrears agreement was entered into.*

(4) *If an arrears agreement is entered into later than 28 days after the due date and the terms of that agreement are adhered to by the absent parent, there shall, with respect to the arrears in relation to which that agreement was entered into, be no liability to make payments of interest in respect of any period commencing on the date that agreement was entered into.*

(5) The Secretary of State may at any time enter into a further arrears agreement with the *absent parent* [non-resident parent] in relation to all arrears then outstanding.

(6) Where the terms of any arrears agreement are not adhered to by an absent parent, interest shall be payable with respect to arrears in accordance with the provisions of regulation 3.

(7) It shall be an implied term of any arrears agreement that any payment of child support maintenance that becomes due whilst that agreement is in force shall be made by the due date.

**Note.** Paras (1), (2) substituted by SI 1993/913, reg 37. In paras (1), (5) words "absent parent" substituted by words "non-resident parent" in square brackets by SI 2001/162, reg 5(1), (3)(c)(i) as from 3 March 2003 in relation to certain cases; for savings see reg 6(Z1) thereof (as inserted by SI 2003/347, reg 2(3), (4)(a)), (1), (2) and SI 2000/3186 (as amended by SI 2004/2415, reg 8). For further effect see SI 2001/162, reg 1(3) and SI 2003/192, arts 3, 5, 8, Schedule.

Paras (3), (4), (6) revoked by SI 2001/162, reg 5(1), (3)(c)(ii) as from 3 March 2003 in relation to certain cases; for savings see reg 6(Z1) thereof (as inserted by SI 2003/347, reg 2(3), (4)(a)), (1), (2) and SI 2000/3186 (as amended by SI 2004/2415, reg 8). For further effect see SI 2001/162, reg 1(3) and SI 2003/192, arts 3, 5, 8, Schedule.

*Rate of interest and calculation of interest*

**6.** (1) The rate of interest payable where liability to pay interest under regulation 3 arises shall be one per centum per annum above the median base rate prevailing from time to time calculated on a daily basis.

(2) Interest shall be payable only with respect to arrears of child support maintenance and shall not be payable with respect to any interest that has already become due.

(3) For the purposes of paragraph (1)—

(a) the median base rate, in relation to a year or part of a year, is the base rate quoted by the reference banks; or, if different base rates are quoted, the rate which, when the base rate quoted by each bank is ranked in a descending sequence of seven, is fourth in the sequence;

(b)   *the reference banks are the seven largest institutions—*

    (i)   *authorised < . . . > under the Banking Act 1987, and*

    (ii)   *incorporated in and carrying on a deposit-taking business within the United Kingdom,*

which quote a base rate in sterling; and

[(b)   the reference banks are the seven largest persons for the time being who—

    (i)   have permission under Part 4 of the Financial Services and Markets Act 2000 to accept deposits,

    (ii)   are incorporated in the United Kingdom and carrying on there a regulated activity of accepting deposits, and

    (iii)   quote a base rate in sterling; and]

(c)   the size of *an institution* [a person] is to be determined by reference to *its* [his] total consolidated gross assets in sterling, as shown in *its* [his] audited end-year accounts last published.

(4) In paragraph (3)(c), the reference to the consolidated gross assets of *an institution* [a person] is a reference to the consolidated gross assets of *that institution* [that person] together with any subsidiary (within the meaning of section 736 of the Companies Act 1985).

[(5) Where any calculation of interest payable under this Part of these Regulations results in a fraction of a penny, that fraction shall be disregarded.]

[(6)        Paragraph (3)(b) must be read with—

(a)   section 22 of the Financial Services and Markets Act 2000;

(b)   any relevant order under that section; and

(c)   Schedule 22 to that Act.]

**Note.** Para (3)(b) substituted by SI 2001/3649, art 424(1) as from 1 December 2001. In para (3)(c) words "an institution" and "its" in both places substituted by words "a person" and "his" in square brackets by SI 2001/3649, art 424(2) as from 1 December 2001. In para (4) words "an institution" and "that institution" substituted by words "a person" and "that person" in square brackets by SI 2001/3649, art 424(3) as from 1 December 2001. Para (5) inserted by SI 1993/913, reg 38 and Para (6): inserted by SI 2001/3649, art 424(4) as from 1 December 2001.

*Receipt and retention of interest paid*

**7.**   (1) Payments of interest with respect to arrears shall be made in accordance with regulations under section 29 of the Act as though they were payments of child support maintenance payable in accordance with a maintenance assessment, and shall be made within 14 days of being demanded by the Secretary of State.

(2) Subject to paragraph (3), where the Secretary of State has been authorised to recover child support maintenance under section 6 of the Act and income support [or income-based jobseeker's allowance] is paid to or in respect of the parent with care, interest with respect to arrears relating to the period during which income support [or income-based jobseeker's allowance] is paid shall be payable to the Secretary of State and may be retained by him.

(3) Where a case falls within paragraph (2), but the Secretary of State considers that, if the absent parent had made payments of child support maintenance due from him in accordance with that assessment, the parent with care would not have been entitled to income support [or income-based jobseeker's allowance], any interest shall be payable to the parent with care.

(4) Where the child support maintenance payable under a maintenance assessment is payable to more than one person, any interest in respect of arrears under that assessment shall be apportioned in the same ratio as the child support maintenance that is payable, and the provisions of paragraphs (1) to (3) shall apply to each amount of interest so apportioned.

**Note.** In para (2) words "or income-based jobseeker's allowance" in square brackets in both places they occur inserted by SI 1996/1345, reg 3(1), (2)(a). In para (3) words "or income-based jobseeker's allowance" in square brackets inserted by SI 1996/1345, reg 3(1), (2)(a).

*[Retention of recovered arrears of child support maintenance by the Secretary of State*

**8.** (1) This regulation applies where—

(i) the Secretary of State recovers arrears from an *absent parent* [a non-resident parent] under section 41 of the Act; and

(ii) income support [or income-based jobseeker's allowance] is paid to or in respect of the person with care or was paid to or in respect of that person at the date or dates upon which the payment or payments of child support maintenance referred to in paragraph (2) should have been made.

(2) Where paragraph (1) applies, the Secretary of State may retain such amount of those arrears as is equal to the difference between the amount of income support [or income-based jobseeker's allowance] that was paid to or in respect of the person with care and the amount of income support [or income-based jobseeker's allowance] that he is satisfied would have been paid had the *absent parent* [non-resident parent] paid, by the due dates, the amounts due under the child support *maintenance assessment* [maintenance calculation] in force or to be taken to have been in force by virtue of the provisions of section 41(2A) of the Act.]

**Note.** Substituted by SI 1995/3261, reg 2. In paras (1)(i), (2) words "an absent parent" substituted by words "non-resident parent" in square brackets by SI 2001/162, reg 5(1), (3)(d)(i) as from 3 March 2003 in relation to certain cases; for savings see reg 6(Z1) thereof (as inserted by SI 2003/347, reg 2(3), (4)(a)), (1), (2) and SI 2000/3186 (as amended by SI 2004/2415, reg 8). For further effect see SI 2001/162, reg 1(3) and SI 2003/192, arts 3, 5, 8, Schedule. In para (1)(ii) words "or income-based jobseeker's allowance" in square brackets inserted by SI 1996/1345, reg 3. In para (2) words "or income-based jobseeker's allowance" in square brackets in both places they occur inserted by SI 1996/1345, reg 3. In para (2) words "maintenance assessment" substituted by words "maintenance calculation" in square brackets by SI 2001/162, reg 5(1), (3)(d)(ii) as from 3 March 2003 in relation to certain cases; for savings see reg 6(Z1) thereof (as inserted by SI 2003/347, reg 2(3), (4)(a)), (1), (2) and SI 2000/3186 (as amended by SI 2004/2415, reg 8). For further effect see SI 2001/162, reg 1(3) and SI 2003/192, arts 3, 5, 8, Schedule.

PART III

ATTRIBUTION OF PAYMENTS AND ADJUSTMENT OF THE AMOUNT PAYABLE UNDER A MAINTENANCE ASSESSMENT

**Note.** Word "Assessment" substituted by word "Calculation" in square brackets by SI 2001/162, reg 5(1), (4)(a) as from 3 March 2003 in relation to certain cases; for savings see reg 6(Z1) thereof (as inserted by SI 2003/347, reg 2(3), (4)(a)), (1), (2) and SI 2000/3186 (as amended by SI 2004/2415, reg 8). For further effect see SI 2001/162, reg 1(3) and SI 2003/192, arts 3, 5, 8, Schedule.

*Attribution of payments*

**9.** Where a maintenance *assessment* [calculation] is or has been in force and there are arrears of child support maintenance, the Secretary of State may attribute any payment of child support maintenance made by an *absent parent* [non-resident parent] to child support maintenance due as he thinks fit.

**Note.** Words "assessment" and "absent parent" substituted by words "calculation" and "non-resident parent" in square brackets by SI 2001/162, reg 5(1), (4)(b), (c) as from 3 March 2003 in relation to certain cases; for savings see reg 6(Z1) thereof (as inserted by SI 2003/347, reg 2(3), (4)(a)), (1), (2) and SI 2000/3186 (as amended by SI 2004/2415, reg 8). For further effect see SI 2001/162, reg 1(3) and SI 2003/192, arts 3, 5, 8, Schedule.

*[Adjustment of the amount payable under a maintenance assessment [calculation]*

**10.**   [(1)  Where for any reason, including the retrospective effect of a *new or fresh* maintenance *assessment* [calculation], there has been an overpayment of child support maintenance, *a child support officer* [the Secretary of State] may, for the purpose of taking account of that overpayment—

(a)  apply the amount overpaid to reduce any arrears of child support maintenance due under any previous maintenance *assessment* [calculation] made in respect of the same relevant persons; or

(b)  where there is no previous relevant maintenance *assessment* [calculation] or an overpayment remains after the application of sub-paragraph (a), and subject to paragraph (4), adjust the amount payable under a current maintenance *assessment* [calculation] by such amount as he considers appropriate in all the circumstances of the case having regard in particular to—

   (i)  the circumstances of the *absent parent* [non-resident parent] and the person with care;

   (ii)  the amount of the overpayment in relation to the amount due under the current maintenance *assessment* [calculation]; and

   (iii)  the period over which it would be reasonable for the overpayment to be rectified.

(2) *Where a child support officer [the Secretary of State] has adjusted the amount payable under a maintenance assessment under the provisions of paragraph (1) and that maintenance assessment is subsequently [replaced by a fresh maintenance assessment made by virtue of a revision under section 16 of the Act or of a decision under section 17 of the Act superseding an earlier decision], that adjustment shall, subject to paragraph (3), continue to apply to the amount payable under that fresh maintenance assessment unless a child support officer [the Secretary of State] is satisfied that such adjustment would not be appropriate in all the circumstances of the case.*

(3) *Where a child support officer [the Secretary of State] is satisfied that the adjustment referred to in paragraph (2) would not be appropriate, he may cancel that adjustment or he may adjust the amount payable under that fresh maintenance assessment as he sees fit, having regard to the matters specified in heads (i) to (iii) of sub-paragraph (b) of paragraph (1).*

[(3A)    Where there has been a voluntary payment, the Secretary of State may—

(a)  apply the amount of the voluntary payment to reduce any arrears of child support maintenance due under any previous maintenance calculation made in respect of the same relevant persons; or

(b)  where there is no previous relevant maintenance calculation or an amount of the voluntary payment remains after the application of sub-paragraph (a), and subject to paragraph (4), adjust the amount payable under a current maintenance calculation by such amount as he considers appropriate in all the circumstances of the case having regard in particular to—

   (i)  the circumstances of the non-resident parent and the person with care;

   (ii)  the amount of the voluntary payment in relation to the amount due under the current maintenance calculation; and

   (iii)  the period over which it would be reasonable for the voluntary payment to be taken into account.]

(4) Any adjustment under the provisions of paragraph (1), (2) *or (3)* [(3A) or regulation 15D of the Social Security and Child Support (Decisions and Appeals) Regulations 1999] shall not reduce the amount payable under a maintenance *assessment* [calculation] to less than *the minimum amount prescribed under paragraph 7* [an amount equivalent to a flat rate fixed by paragraph 4(1)] of Schedule 1 to the Act.]

**Note.** Provision heading: word "assessment" substituted by word "calculation" in square brackets by SI 2001/162, reg 5(1), (4)(a) as from 3 March 2003 in relation to certain cases; for savings see reg 6(Z1) thereof (as inserted by SI 2003/347, reg 2(3), (4)(a)), (1), (2) and SI 2000/3186 (as amended by SI 2004/2415, reg 8). For further effect see SI 2001/162, reg 1(3) and SI 2003/192, arts 3, 5, 8, Schedule.

Substituted by SI 1995/1045, reg 8. In para (1) words "new or fresh" revoked by SI 2001/162, reg 5(1), (4)(d)(i) as from 3 March 2003 in relation to certain cases; for savings see reg 6(Z1) thereof (as inserted by SI 2003/347, reg 2(3), (4)(a)), (1), (2) and SI 2000/3186 (as amended by SI 2004/2415, reg 8). For further effect see SI 2001/162, reg 1(3) and SI 2003/192, arts 3, 5, 8, Schedule.

In para (1) word "assessment" in each place it occurs substituted by word "calculation" in square brackets by SI 2001/162, reg 5(1), (4)(b) as from 3 March 2003 in relation to certain cases; for savings see reg 6(Z1) thereof (as inserted by SI 2003/347, reg 2(3), (4)(a)), (1), (2) and SI 2000/3186 (as amended by SI 2004/2415, reg 8). For further effect see SI 2001/162, reg 1(3) and SI 2003/192, arts 3, 5, 8, Schedule.

In paras (1)–(3) words "a child support officer" in each place they occur substituted by words "the Secretary of State" in square brackets by SI 1999/1510, art 26(a) as from 1 June 1999.

In para (1)(b)(i) words "absent parent" substituted by words "non-resident parent" in square brackets by SI 2001/162, reg 5(1), (4) as from 3 March 2003 in relation to certain cases; for savings see reg 6(Z1) thereof (as inserted by SI 2003/347, reg 2(3), (4)(a)), (1), (2) and SI 2000/3186 (as amended by SI 2004/2415, reg 8). For further effect see SI 2001/162, reg 1(3) and SI 2003/192, arts 3, 5, 8, Schedule.

Paras (2), (3) revoked by SI 2000/3185, reg 14(1) in relation to certain cases and for the purposes of any revision, supersession or appeal in relation to a decision which is made as provided in the Child Support (Transitional Provisions) Regulations 2000, reg 3 as from 3 March 2003 (as amended by SI 2003/347, reg 2(1), (2)(a)); for savings see reg 14(2)–(4) thereof and SI 2000/3186 (as amended by SI 2004/2415, reg 8). For further effect see SI 2000/3185, reg 1(1), (2) and SI 2003/192, arts 3, 7(a), 8, Schedule. In para (2) words from "revised as a result" to "maintenance assessment made substituted by words from "replaced by a fresh" to "earlier decision" in square brackets by SI 1999/1510, art 26(b) as from 1 June 1999.

Para (3A) inserted by SI 2001/162, reg 5(1), (4)(d)(ii) as from 3 March 2003 in relation to certain cases; for savings see reg 6(Z1) thereof (as inserted by SI 2003/347, reg 2(3), (4)(a)), (1), (2) and SI 2000/3186 (as amended by SI 2004/2415, reg 8). For further effect see SI 2001/162, reg 1(3) and SI 2003/192, arts 3, 5, 8, Schedule.

In para (4) words "(2) or (3)" substituted by words "(3A) or regulation 15D of the Social Security and Child Support (Decisions and Appeals) Regulations 1999" in square brackets, word "assessment" substituted by word "calculation" in square brackets and words "the minimum amount prescribed under paragraph 7" substituted by words "an amount equivalent to a flat rate fixed by paragraph 4(1)" in square brackets by SI 2001/162, reg 5(1), (4)(b), (d)(iii)(aa), (bb) as from 3 March 2003 in relation to certain cases; for savings see reg 6(Z1) thereof (as inserted by SI 2003/347, reg 2(3), (4)(a)), (1), (2) and SI 2000/3186 (as amended by SI 2004/2415, reg 8). For further effect see SI 2001/162, reg 1(3) and SI 2003/192, arts 3, 5, 8, Schedule.

*[Reimbursement of a repayment of overpaid child maintenance*

**10A.** (1) The Secretary of State may require a relevant person to repay the whole or a part of any payment by way of reimbursement made to an *absent parent* [non-resident parent] under section 41B(2) of the Act where the overpayment referred to in section 41B(1) of the Act arose—

(a) in respect of the amount payable under a maintenance *assessment* [calculation] calculated in accordance with Part I of Schedule 1 to the Act and where income support[, state pension credit] [or income-based jobseeker's allowance], family credit or disability working allowance was not in payment to that person at any time during the period in which that overpayment occurred or at the date or dates on which the payment by way of reimbursement was made; or

(b) in respect of the amount payable under an interim maintenance assessment and that amount has not been varied under regulation 8D(1) of the

Maintenance Assessment Procedure Regulations following the making of a maintenance assessment calculated in accordance with Part I of Schedule 1 to the Act.

(2) In a case falling within section 4 or 7 of the Act, where the circumstances set out in section 41B(6) apply, the Secretary of State may retain out of the child support maintenance collected by him in accordance with section 29 of the Act such sums as cover the amount of any payment by way of reimbursement required by him from the relevant person under section 41B(3) of the Act.]

**Notes.**
**Amendment:** Inserted by SI 1995/3261, reg 3. In para (1) words "absent parent" substituted by words "non-resident parent" in square brackets and word "assessment" substituted by word "calculation" in square brackets by SI 2001/162, reg 5(1), (4)(b), (c) as from 3 March 2003 in relation to certain cases; for savings see reg 6(Z1) (as inserted by SI2003/347, reg 2(3), (4)(a)), (1), (2) thereof and SI 2000/3186 (as amended by SI 2004/2415, reg 8). For further effect see SI 2001/162, reg 1(3) and SI 2003/192, arts 3, 5, 8, Schedule.

In para (1)(a) words ", state pension credit" in square brackets inserted by SI 2002/3019, reg 26(1), (3) as from 6 October 2003 and words "or income-based jobseeker's allowance" in square brackets inserted by SI 1996/1345, reg 3.

In para (1), in sub-para (a) words ", family credit or disability working allowance" and sub-para (b) revoked by SI 2001/162, reg 5(1), (4)(e) as from 3 March 2003 in relation to certain cases; for savings see reg 6(Z1) (as inserted by SI2003/347, reg 2(3), (4)(a)), (1), (2) thereof and SI 2000/3186 (as amended by SI 2004/2415, reg 8). For further effect see SI 2001/162, reg 1(3) and SI 2003/192, arts 3, 5, 8, Schedule.

*[Repayment of a reimbursement of a voluntary payment*

**10B.**   The Secretary of State may require a relevant person to repay the whole or any part of any payment by way of reimbursement made to a non-resident parent under section 41B(2) of the Act where—

(a) a voluntary payment was made;
(b) section 41B(1A) applies; and

income support [, state pension credit] or income-based jobseeker's allowance was not in payment to that person at any time during the period in which the voluntary payment was made or at the date or dates on which the payment by way of reimbursement was made.]

**Note.** Inserted by SI 2001/162, reg 5(1), (4)(f) as from 3 March 2003 in relation to certain cases; for savings see reg 6(Z1) (as inserted by SI2003/347, reg 2(3), (4)(a)), (1), (2) thereof and SI 2000/3186 (as amended by SI 2004/2415, reg 8). For further effect see SI 2001/162, reg 1(3) and SI 2003/192, arts 3, 5, 8, Schedule. Words ", state pension credit" in square brackets inserted by SI 2002/3019, reg 26(1), (3) as from 6 October 2003.

PART IV

MISCELLANEOUS

*Notifications following a cancellation or adjustment under the provisions of regulation 10*

**11.**   [(1) Where *a child support officer* [the Secretary of State] has, under the provisions of regulation 10, cancelled an adjustment in accordance with the provisions of paragraph (3) of that regulation or adjusted the amount payable under a maintenance assessment, he shall immediately notify the relevant persons, so far as is reasonably practicable, of the cancellation or, of the amount and period of the adjustment, and the amount payable during the period of the adjustment.]

(2) A notification under paragraph (1) shall include information as to the provisions of *regulation 12(1) and regulation 13(1) in so far as it relates to time limits for an application for a review under regulation 12(1)* [regulations 12 to 15].

**Note.** Provision heading: substituted by SI 1995/1045, reg 9(2).
Para (1) substituted by SI 1995/1045, reg 9(3), words "a child support officer" substituted

by words "the Secretary of State" in square brackets substituted by SI 1999/1510, art 27(a) as from 1 June 1999. In para (2) words "regulation 12(1) and regulation 13(1) in so far as it relates to time limits for an application for a review under regulation 12(1)" substituted by words "regulations 12 to 15" in square brackets by SI 1999/1510, art 27(b) as from 1 June 1999.

*Review of cancellations or adjustments under regulation 10 [Extension of the application of Schedule 4C to the Act]*

**12.** *(1) Where an adjustment made under regulation 10 has been cancelled under paragraph (3) of that regulation or where the amount payable under a maintenance assessment has been adjusted under the provisions of that regulation, a relevant person may apply to the Secretary of State for a review of that cancellation or adjustment as if it were a case falling within section 18 of the Act and—*

*(a)  section 18(5), (7), (8) and regulations made under section 18(11); and*

*(b)  subject to the modifications set out in paragraph (2), section 18(6) and (9),*

*shall apply to such a review.*

*(2) The modifications referred to in paragraph (1) are—*

*(a)  section 18(6) of the Act shall have effect as if for the words "the refusal, assessment or cancellation in question" there are substituted the words "the adjustment of the amount payable, or the cancellation of the adjustment of the amount payable, under regulation 10 of the Child Support (Arrears, Interest and Adjustment of Maintenance Assessments) Regulations 1992";*

*(b)  section 18(9) of the Act shall have effect as if for the words "a maintenance assessment or (as the case may be) a fresh maintenance assessment should be made" there are substituted the words "a cancelled adjustment should be reinstated or a revised adjustment of the amount payable under regulation 10 of the Child Support (Arrears, Interest and Adjustment of Maintenance Assessments) Regulations 1992 should be made.".*

*(3)  Where an adjustment has been cancelled or the amount payable under a maintenance assessment has been adjusted under the provisions of regulation 10, a child support officer may reinstate that cancelled adjustment or revise that adjustment if he is satisfied that one or more of the circumstances set out in paragraphs (a) to (c) of section [19(2)] of the Act apply to that cancellation or that adjustment.*

[Schedule 4C to the Act is hereby extended so that it applies to any decision with respect to the adjustment of amounts payable under maintenance assessments for the purpose of taking account of overpayments of child support maintenance.]

**Note.** Substituted, together with regs 13–17, for regs 12–15 as originally enacted, by SI 1999/1510, art 28 as from 1 June 1999.

*Procedure and notifications on applications and reviews under regulation 12 [Revision of decisions]*

**13.** *(1) The provisions of regulations 24 to 26 of the Maintenance Assessment Procedure Regulations shall apply to an application for a review under regulation 12(1).*

*(2) Where a child support officer refuses an application for a review under regulation 12(1) on the grounds set out in section 18(6) of the Act (as applied by regulation 12), he shall immediately notify the applicant, so far as that is reasonably practicable, and shall give the reasons for his refusal in writing.*

*(3) Where a child support officer adjusts the amount payable under a maintenance assessment following a review under regulation 12(1) or (3), he shall immediately notify the relevant persons, so far as that is reasonably practicable, of the amount and period of the adjustment, and the amount payable during the period of adjustment.*

*(4) Where a child support officer refuses to adjust the amount payable under a maintenance assessment following a review under regulation 12(1) he shall immediately notify the relevant persons, so far as that is reasonably practicable, of the refusal, and shall give the reasons for his refusal in writing.*

*(5) Where a child support officer refuses to reinstate, or reinstates, a cancelled adjustment following a review under regulation 12(1), he shall immediately notify the relevant persons, so far as that is reasonably practicable, of the refusal or reinstatement, as the case may be, and shall give reasons for his refusal in writing.*

*(6) A notification under paragraphs (2), (4) and (5), and under paragraph (3) following a review under regulation 12(1), shall include information as to the provisions of section 20 of the Act.*

*(7) A notification under paragraph (3) following a review under regulation 12(3) shall include information as to the provisions of section 18 of the Act.*

[(1)  A decision may be revised by the Secretary of State—

(a)  if the Secretary of State receives an application for the revision of a decision under section 16 of the Act as extended by regulation 12 above within one month of the date of notification of the decision or within such longer time as may be allowed by regulation 14;

(b)  if the decision arose from an official error;

(c)  if the Secretary of State commences action leading to the revision of a decision within one month of the date of notification of the decision; or

(d)  if the Secretary of State is satisfied that the original decision was erroneous due to a misrepresentation of, or failure to disclose, a material fact and that the decision was more advantageous to the person who misrepresented or failed to disclose that fact than it would otherwise have been but for that error.

(2) In paragraph (1)—

"decision" means a decision of the Secretary of State—

(a)  adjusting the amount payable under a maintenance assessment; or

(b)  cancelling an adjustment of an amount payable under a maintenance assessment,

under regulation 10 and a decision superseding such a decision;

"official error" means an error made by an officer of the Department of Social Security acting as such which no person outside that Department caused or to which no person outside that Department materially contributed.

(3) Paragraph (1) shall not apply in respect of a change of circumstances which occurred since the date as from which the decision had effect.]

**Note.** Substituted, together with regs 12, 14–17, for regs 12–15 as originally enacted, by SI 1999/1510, art 28 as from 1 June 1999.

*Non-disclosure of information to third parties [Late application for revision]*

**14.**   *The provisions of regulation 10(3) of the Maintenance Assessment Procedure Regulations shall apply to any document given or sent under the provisions of regulation 11 or 13.*

[(1)  The period of one month specified in regulation 13(1)(a) may be extended where the conditions specified in the following provisions of this regulation are satisfied.

(2)  An application for an extension of time shall be made by a relevant person or a person acting on his behalf.

(3)  An application for an extension of time under this regulation shall—

(a)  be made within 13 months of the date on which notification of the decision which it is sought to have revised was given or sent; and

(b)  contain particulars of the grounds on which the extension of time is sought and shall contain sufficient details of the decision which it is sought to have revised to enable that decision to be identified.

(4)  An application for an extension of time shall not be granted unless the person making the application or any person acting for him satisfies the Secretary of State that—

(a)  it is reasonable to grant the application;

(b) the application for a revision has merit; and

(c) special circumstances are relevant to the application for an extension of time and as a result of those special circumstances, it was not practicable for the application for a decision to be revised to be made within one month of the date of notification of the decision which it is sought to have revised.

(5) In determining whether it is reasonable to grant an application for an extension of time, the Secretary of State shall have regard to the principle that the greater the time that has elapsed between the expiration of one month described in regulation 13(1)(a) from the date of notification of the decision which it is sought to have revised and the making of the application for an extension of time, the more compelling should be the special circumstances on which the application is based.

(6) In determining whether it is reasonable to grant the application for an extension of time, no account shall be taken of the following—

(a) that the person making the application for an extension of time or any person acting for him was unaware of or misunderstood the law applicable to his case (including ignorance or misunderstanding of the time limits imposed by these Regulations); or

(b) that a Child Support Commissioner or a court has taken a different view of the law from that previously understood and applied.

(7) An application under this regulation for an extension of time which has been refused may not be renewed.]

**Note.** Substituted, together with regs 12, 13, 15–17, for regs 12–15 as originally enacted, by SI 1999/1510, art 28 as from 1 June 1999.

*Applicability of regulations 1(6) and 53 to 56 of the Maintenance Assessment Procedure Regulations [Date from which revised decision takes effect]*

**15.** *Regulations 1(6) and 53 to 56 of the Maintenance Assessment Procedure Regulations shall apply to the provisions of these Regulations.*

[Where the date as from which a decision took effect is found to be erroneous on a revision under section 16 of the Act as extended by regulation 12 above, the revision shall take effect as from the date on which the revised decision would have taken effect had the error not been made.]

**Note.** Substituted, together with regs 12–14, 16, 17, for regs 12–15 as originally enacted, by SI 1999/1510, art 28 as from 1 June 1999.

*[Supersession of decisions*

**16.** [(1) For the purposes of section 17 of the Act as extended by regulation 12 above, the cases and circumstances in which a decision adjusting the amount payable under a maintenance assessment may be superseded by a decision under that section as extended are set out in paragraphs (2) to (4).

(2) A decision may be superseded by a decision made by the Secretary of State acting on his own initiative where he is satisfied that the decision—

(a) is one in respect of which there has been a material change of circumstances since the decision was made; or

(b) was made in ignorance of, or was based upon a mistake as to, some material fact.

(3) A decision may be superseded by a decision made by the Secretary of State where an application is made on the basis that—

(a) there has been a change of circumstances since the decision was made and the Secretary of State is satisfied that the change of circumstances is or would be material; or

(b) the decision was made in ignorance of, or was based upon a mistake as to, a fact and the Secretary of State is satisfied that the fact is or would be material.

(4) A decision, other than a decision given on appeal, may be superseded by a decision made by the Secretary of State—

(a) acting on his own initiative where he is satisfied that the decision was erroneous in point of law; or

(b) where an application is made on the basis that the decision was erroneous in point of law.

(5) The cases and circumstances in which a decision may be superseded under section 17 of the Act as extended by regulation 12 above shall not include any case or circumstance in which a decision may be revised.]

**Note.** Substituted, together with regs 12–15, 17, for regs 12–15 as originally enacted, by SI 1999/1510, art 28 as from 1 June 1999.

*[Application of regulations 1(6), 10(3) and 53 of the Maintenance Assessment Procedure Regulations*

**17.** [(1) The provisions of regulation 10(3) of the Maintenance Assessment Procedure Regulations shall apply to any notification—

(a) under regulation 11; and

(b) of a decision under the provisions of regulation 13, 14 or 16.

(2) Regulations 1(6) and 53 of the Maintenance Assessment Procedure Regulations shall apply to the provisions of these Regulations.]

**Note.** Substituted, together with regs 12–16, for regs 12–15 as originally enacted, by SI 1999/1510, art 28 as from 1 June 1999.

## CHILD SUPPORT (COLLECTION AND ENFORCEMENT) REGULATIONS 1992

**Dated** 17 August 1992

**SI 1992 No 1989**

ARRANGEMENT OF REGULATIONS

PART IV

*Liability orders*

SCHEDULES

The Secretary of State for Social Security, in exercise of the powers conferred by sections 29(2) and (3), 31(8), 32(1) to (5) and (7) to (9), 34(1), 35(2), (7) and (8), 39(1), (3) and (4), 40(4), (8) and (11), 51, 52 and 54 of the Child Support Act 1991 and of all other powers enabling him in that behalf, hereby makes the following Regulations—

PART I

GENERAL

*Citation, commencement and interpretation*

**1.**   (1) These Regulations may be cited as the Child Support (Collection and Enforcement) Regulations 1992 and shall come into force on 5th April 1993.

*(2)  In these Regulations "the Act" means the Child Support Act 1991.*

[(2)  In these Regulations—

"the Act" means the Child Support Act 1991;

"the 2000 Act" means the Child Support, Pensions and Social Security Act 2000;

"interest" means interest which has become payable under section 41 of the Act before its amendment by the 2000 Act; and

"voluntary payment" means a payment as defined in section 28J of the Act and Regulations made under that section.]

[(2A) Except in relation to regulation 8(3)(a) and Schedule 2, in these Regulations "fee" means an assessment fee or a collection fee, which for these purposes have the same meaning as in the Child Support Fees Regulations 1992 prior to their revocation by the Child Support (Collection and Enforcement and Miscellaneous Amendments) Regulations 2000.]

(3) Where under any provision of the Act or of these Regulations—

(a) any document or notice is given or sent to the Secretary of State, it shall be treated as having been given or sent on the day it is received by the Secretary of State; and

(b) any document or notice is given or sent to any other person, it shall, if sent by post to that person's last known or notified address, be treated as having been given or sent on *the second day after the day of posting, excluding any Sunday or any day which is a bank holiday under the Banking and Financial Dealings Act 1971* [the day that it is posted].

(4) In these Regulations, unless the context otherwise requires, a reference—

(a) to a numbered Part is to the Part of these Regulations bearing that number;

(b) to a numbered regulation is to the regulation in these Regulations bearing that number;

(c) in a regulation to a numbered or lettered paragraph or sub-paragraph is to the paragraph or sub-paragraph in that regulation bearing that number or letter;

(d) in a paragraph to a lettered or numbered sub-paragraph is to the sub-paragraph in that paragraph bearing that letter or number;

(e) to a numbered Schedule is to the Schedule to these Regulations bearing that number.

**Note.** Para (2) substituted and para (2A) inserted by SI 2001/162, reg 2(1), (2)(a), (b) as from 3 March 2003 in relation to certain cases; for savings see reg 6(Z1) (as inserted by SI 2003/347, reg 2(3), (4)(a)), (1), (2) thereof and SI 2000/3186 (as amended by SI 2004/2415, reg 8). For further effect see SI 2001/62, reg 1(3) and SI 2003/192, arts 3, 5, 8, Schedule. In para (3)(b) words from "the second day" to "Banking and Financial Dealings Act 1971" substituted by words "the day that it is posted" in square brackets by SI 2001/162, reg 2(1), (2)(c) as from 3 March 2003 in relation to certain cases; for savings see reg 6(Z1) (as inserted by SI 2003/347, reg 2(3), (4)(a)), (1), (2) thereof and SI 2000/3186 (as amended by SI 2004/2415, reg 8). For further effect see SI 2001/62, reg 1(3) and SI 2003/192, arts 3, 5, 8, Schedule.

PART II

COLLECTION OF CHILD SUPPORT MAINTENANCE

*Payment of child support maintenance*

**2.** (1) Where a maintenance *assessment* [calculation] has been made under the Act and the case is one to which section 29 of the Act applies, the Secretary of State may specify that payments of child support maintenance shall be made by the liable person—

(a) to the person caring for the child or children in question or, where an application has been made under section 7 of the Act, to the child who made the application;

(b) to, or through, the Secretary of State; or

(c) to, or through, such other person as the Secretary of State may, from time to time, specify.

(2) In paragraph (1) and in the rest of this Part, "liable person" means a person liable to make payments of child support maintenance.

**Note.** In para (1) word "assessment" substituted by word "calculation" in square brackets by SI 2001/162, reg 2(1), (3)(a) as from 3 March 2003 in relation to certain cases; for savings see reg 6(Z1) (as inserted by SI 2003/347, reg 2(3), (4)(a)), (1), (2) thereof and SI 2000/3186 (as amended by SI 2004/2415, reg 8). For further effect see SI 2001/62, reg 1(3) and SI 2003/192, arts 3, 5, 8, Schedule.

*Method of payment*

**3.** (1) Payments of child support maintenance[, penalty payments, interest and fees] shall be made by the liable person by whichever of the following methods the Secretary of State specifies as being appropriate in the circumstances—

    (a)  by standing order;
    (b)  by any other method which requires one person to give his authority for payments to be made from an account of his to an account of another's on specific dates during the period for which the authority is in force and without the need for any further authority from him;
    (c)  by an arrangement whereby one person gives his authority for payments to be made from an account of his, or on his behalf, to another person or to an account of that other person;
    (d)  by cheque or postal order;
    (e)  in cash;
    [(f)  by debit card].

    [(1A)  In paragraph (1), "debit card" means a card, operating as a substitute for a cheque, that can be used to obtain cash or to make a payment at a point of sale whereby the card holder's bank or building society account is debited without deferment of payment.]

    (2)  The Secretary of State may direct a liable person to take all reasonable steps to open an account from which payments under the maintenance *assessment* [calculation] may be made in accordance with the method of payment specified under paragraph (1).

**Note.** In para (1) words ", penalty payments, interest and fees" in square brackets and sub-para (f) inserted, para (1A) inserted and in para (2) word "assessment" substituted by word "calculation" in square brackets by SI 2001/162, reg 2(1), (3)(a)–(c) as from 3 March 2003 in relation to certain cases; for savings see reg 6(Z1) (as inserted by SI 2003/347, reg 2(3), (4)(a)), (1), (2) thereof and SI 2000/3186 (as amended by SI 2004/2415, reg 8). For further effect see SI 2001/62, reg 1(3) and SI 2003/192, arts 3, 5, 8, Schedule.

*Interval of payment*

**4.**  (1)  The Secretary of State shall specify the day and interval by reference to which payments of child support maintenance are to be made by the liable person and may from time to time vary such day or interval.

    [(2)  In specifying the day and interval of payment the Secretary of State shall have regard to the following factors—
    (a)  the circumstances of the person liable to make the payments and in particular the day upon which and the interval at which any income is payable to that person;
    (b)  any preference indicated by that person;
    (c)  any period necessary to enable the clearance of cheques or otherwise necessary to enable the transmission of payments to the person entitled to receive them,
and, subject to those factors, to any other matter which appears to him to be relevant in the particular circumstances of the case.]

**Note.** Para (2) substituted by SI 1995/1045, reg 12.

*Transmission of payments*

**5.**  (1)  Payments of child support maintenance made through the Secretary of State or other specified person shall be transmitted to the person entitled to receive them in whichever of the following ways the Secretary of State specifies as being appropriate in the circumstances—
    (a)  by a transfer of credit to an account nominated by the person entitled to receive the payments;
    (b)  by cheque, girocheque or other payable order;
    (c)  in cash.

    (2)  [Subject to paragraph (3), the Secretary of State] shall specify the interval by reference to which the payments referred to in paragraph (1) are to be transmitted to the person entitled to receive them.

[(3) Except where the Secretary of State is satisfied in the circumstances of the case that it would cause undue hardship to either the person liable to make the payments or the person entitled to receive them, the interval referred to in paragraph (2) shall not differ from the interval referred to in regulation 4.

(4) Subject to paragraph (3) and regulation 4(2), the interval referred to in paragraph (2) and that referred to in regulation 4 may be varied from time to time by the Secretary of State.]

**Note.** In para (2) words in square brackets substituted by SI 1995/1045, reg 13(2) and paras (3), (4) substituted by SI 1995/1045, reg 13(3).

*[Voluntary payments*

**5A.** (1) Regulation 5(1) shall apply in relation to voluntary payments as if—
  (a) for the words "Payment of child support maintenance" there were substituted the words "Voluntary payments"; and
  (b) the words "or other specified person" were omitted.

(2) In determining when the Secretary of State shall transmit a voluntary payment to the person entitled to it, the Secretary of State shall have regard to the factor in regulation 4(2)(c).]

**Note.** Inserted by SI 2001/162, reg 2(1), (3)(d) as from 3 March 2003 in relation to certain cases; for savings see reg 6(Z1) (as inserted by SI 2003/347, reg 2(3), (4)(a)), (1), (2) thereof and SI 2000/3186 (as amended by SI 2004/2415, reg 8). For further effect see SI 2001/62, reg 1(3) and SI 2003/192, arts 3, 5, 8, Schedule.

*Representations about payment arrangements*

**6.** The Secretary of State shall, insofar as is reasonably practicable, provide the liable person and the person entitled to receive the payments of child support maintenance with an opportunity to make representations with regard to the matters referred to in regulations 2 to 5 and the Secretary of State shall have regard to those representations in exercising his powers under those regulations.

*Notice to liable person as to requirements about payment*

**7.** (1) [In the case of child support maintenance,] the Secretary of State shall send the liable person a notice stating—
  (a) the amount of child support maintenance payable;
  (b) to whom it is to be paid;
  (c) the method of payment; and
  (d) the day and interval by reference to which payments are to be made;
  [(e) the amount of any payment of child support maintenance which is overdue and which remains outstanding].

[(1A) In the case of penalty payments, interest or fees, the Secretary of State shall send the liable person a notice stating—
  (a) the amount of child support maintenance payable;
  (b) the amount of arrears;
  (c) the amount of the penalty payment, interest or fees to be paid, as the case may be;
  (d) the method of payment;
  (e) the day by which payment is to be made; and
  (f) information as to the provisions of sections 16 and 20 of the Act.]

(2) A notice under paragraph (1) shall be sent to the liable person as soon as is reasonably practicable after—
  (a) the making of a maintenance *assessment* [calculation], and
  (b) after any change in the requirements referred to in any previous such notice.

[(3) A notice under paragraph (1A) shall be sent to the liable person as soon as reasonably practicable after the decision to require a payment of the penalty payment, interest or fees has been made.]

**Note.** In para (1) words "In the case of child support maintenance," in square brackets and sub-para (e) inserted, para (1A) inserted and in para (2)(a) word "assessment" substituted by word "calculation" in square brackets, and para (3) inserted, by SI 2001/162, reg 2(1), (3)(a), (e)(i)–(iii) as from 3 March 2003 in relation to certain cases; for savings see reg 6(Z1) (as inserted by SI 2003/347, reg 2(3), (4)(a)), (1), (2) thereof and SI 2000/3186 (as amended by SI 2004/2415, reg 8). For further effect see SI 2001/62, reg 1(3) and SI 2003/192, arts 3, 5, 8, Schedule.

[PART IIA

COLLECTION OF PENALTY PAYMENTS]

[*Payment of a financial penalty*

**7A.** (1) This regulation applies where a maintenance calculation is, or has been, in force, the liable person is in arrears with payments of child support maintenance, and the Secretary of State requires the liable person to pay penalty payments to him.

(2) For the purposes of regulation 7(1)(e) a payment will be overdue if it is not received by the time that the next payment of child support maintenance is due.

(3) The Secretary of State may require a penalty payment to be made if the outstanding amount is not received within 7 days of the notification in regulation 7(1)(e) or if the liable person fails to pay all outstanding amounts due on dates and of amounts as agreed between the liable person and the Secretary of State.

(4) Payments of a penalty payment shall be made within 14 days of the notification referred to in regulation 7(1A).

(5) In this Part a "liable person" means a person liable to make a penalty payment and in Part II and in this Part "penalty payment" is to be construed in accordance with section 41A of the Act.]

**Note.** Inserted by SI 2001/162, reg 2(1), (4) as from 3 March 2003 in relation to certain cases; for savings see reg 6(Z1) (as inserted by SI 2003/347, reg 2(3), (4)(a)), (1), (2) thereof and SI 2000/3186 (as amended by SI 2004/2415, reg 8). For further effect see SI 2001/62, reg 1(3) and SI 2003/192, arts 3, 5, 8, Schedule.

PART III

DEDUCTION FROM EARNINGS ORDERS

*Interpretation of this Part*

**8.** (1) For the purposes of this Part—
["defective" means in relation to a deduction from earnings order that it does not comply with the requirements of regulations 9 to 11 and such failure to comply has made it impracticable for the employer to comply with his obligations under the Act and these Regulations;]
*"disposable income" means the amount determined under [regulation 12(1)(a)] of the Child Support (Maintenance Assessments and Special Cases) Regulations 1992;*
"earnings" shall be construed in accordance with paragraphs (3) and (4);
*"exempt income" means the amount determined under regulation 9 of the Child Support (Maintenance Assessments and Special Cases) Regulations 1992;*
[*"interim maintenance assessment" means a Category A, Category B, Category C or Category D interim maintenance assessment within the meaning of [regulation 8(3)] of the Child Support (Maintenance Assessment Procedure) Regulations 1992;*]
"net earnings" shall be construed in accordance with paragraph (5);

"normal deduction rate" means the rate specified in a deduction from earnings order (expressed as a sum of money per week, month or other period) at which deductions are to be made from the liable person's net earnings;

"pay-day" in relation to a liable person means an occasion on which earnings are paid to him or the day on which such earnings would normally fall to be paid;

["protected earnings proportion" means the proportion referred to in regulation 11(2);]

*"prescribed minimum amount" means the minimum amount prescribed in regulation 13 of the Child Support (Maintenance Assessments and Special Cases) Regulations 1992;*

*"protected earnings rate" means the level of earnings specified in a deduction from earnings order (expressed as a sum of money per week, month or other period) below which deductions of child support maintenance shall not be made for the purposes of this Part;*

*"protected income level" means the level of protected income determined in accordance with [paragraphs (1) to (5) of] regulation 11 of the Child Support (Maintenance Assessments and Special Cases) Regulations 1992.*

(2) For the purposes of this Part the relationship of employer and employee shall be treated as subsisting between two persons if one of them as a principal and not as a servant or agent, pays to the other any sum defined as earnings under paragraph (1) and "employment", "employer" and "employee" shall be construed accordingly.

(3) Subject to paragraph (4), "earnings" are any sums payable to a person—

(a) by way of wages or salary (including any fees, bonus, commission, overtime pay or other emoluments payable in addition to wages or salary or payable under a contract of service);

(b) by way of pension (including an annuity in respect of past service, whether or not rendered to the person paying the annuity, and including periodical payments by way of compensation for the loss, abolition or relinquishment, or diminution in the emoluments, of any office or employment);

(c) by way of statutory sick pay.

(4) "Earnings" shall not include—

(a) sums payable by any public department of the Government of Northern Ireland or of a territory outside the United Kingdom;

(b) pay or allowances payable to the liable person as a member of Her Majesty's forces [other than pay or allowances payable by his employer to him as a special member of a reserve force (within the meaning of the Reserve Forces Act 1996)];

(c) pension, allowances or benefit payable under any enactment relating to social security;

(d) pension or allowances payable in respect of disablement or disability;

(e) guaranteed minimum pension within the meaning of the Social Security Pensions Act 1975;

[(f) working tax credit payable under section 10 of the Tax Credits Act 2002].

(5) "Net earnings" means the residue of earnings after deduction of—

(a) income tax;

(b) primary class I contributions under Part I of the Contributions and Benefits Act 1992;

(c) amounts deductible by way of contributions to a superannuation scheme which provides for the payment of annuities or [lump] sums—

   (i) to the employee on his retirement at a specified age or on becoming incapacitated at some earlier age; or

   (ii) on his death or otherwise, to his personal representative, widow, relatives or dependants.

**Note.** Para (1): definition "defective" inserted by SI 1995/1045, reg 14; definitions "disposable income", "exempt income", "interim maintenance assessment", "prescribed minimum amount", "protected earnings rate" and "protected income level" revoked by SI 2001/162, reg 2(1), (5)(a)(i) as from 3 March 2003 in relation to certain cases; for savings see reg 6(Z1) (as inserted by SI 2003/347, reg 2(3), (4)(a)), (1), (2) thereof and SI 2000/3186 (as amended by SI 2004/2415, reg 8), for further effect see SI 2001/62, reg 1(3) and SI 2003/192, arts 3, 5, 8, Schedule; in definition "disposable income" words "regulation 12(1)(a)" in square brackets substituted by SI 1995/1045, reg 14; definition "interim maintenance assessment" inserted by SI 1995/1045, reg 14; in definition "interim maintenance assessment" words "regulation 8(3)" in square brackets substituted by SI 1996/1945, reg 3; definition "protected earnings proportion" inserted by SI 2001/162, reg 2(1), (5)(a)(ii) as from 3 March 2003 in relation to certain cases; for savings see reg 6(Z1) (as inserted by SI 2003/347, reg 2(3), (4)(a)), (1), (2) thereof and SI 2000/3186 (as amended by SI 2004/2415, reg 8), for further effect see SI 2001/62, reg 1(3) and SI 2003/192, arts 3, 5, 8, Schedule; in definition "protected income level" words "paragraphs (1) to (5) of" in square brackets inserted by SI 1995/1045, reg 14.

In para (4)(b) words from "other than pay" to "Reserve Forces Act 1996)" in square brackets inserted by SI 1999/977, reg 2(1), (2) as from 6 April 1999: see SI 1999/977, reg 1(2). Para (4)(f) inserted by SI 2003/328, reg 2 as from 6 April 2003. In para (5) word in square brackets substituted by SI 1993/913, reg 41.

*Deduction from earnings orders*

**9.** A deduction from earnings order shall specify—
   (a) the name and address of the liable person;
   (b) the name of the employer at whom it is directed;
   (c) where known, the liable person's place of work, the nature of his work and any works or pay number;
   [(cc)    where known, the liable person's national insurance number;]
   [(d) the normal deduction rate or rates and the date upon which each is to take effect;
   (e) the *protected earnings rate* [protected earnings proportion];]
   (f) the address to which amounts deducted from earnings are to be sent.

**Note.** Para (cc) inserted by SI 1995/3261, reg 6 and paras (d), (e) substituted by SI 1995/1045, reg 15. In para (e) words "protected earnings rate" substituted by words "protected earnings proportion" in square brackets by SI 2001/162, reg 2(1), (5)(b) as from 3 March 2003 in relation to certain cases; for savings see reg 6(Z1) (as inserted by SI 2003/347, reg 2(3), (4)(a)), (1), (2) thereof and SI 2000/3186 (as amended by SI 2004/2415, reg 8). For further effect see SI 2001/62, reg 1(3) and SI 2003/192, arts 3, 5, 8, Schedule.

*Normal deduction rate*

**10.** (1) The period by reference to which [a normal deduction rate] rate is set shall be the period by reference to which the liable person's earnings are normally paid or, if none, such other period as the Secretary of State may specify.

(2) *The Secretary of State, in specifying the normal deduction rate, shall not include any amount in respect of arrears or interest[, in a case where there is a current assessment,] if, [at the date of making of any current maintenance assessment other than an interim maintenance assessment]—*
   (a) *the liable person's disposable income was below the level specified in paragraph (3); or*
   (b) *the deduction of such an amount from the liable person's disposable income would have reduced his disposable income below the level specified in paragraph (3).*

(3) *The level referred to in paragraph (2) is the liable person's protected income level less the prescribed minimum amount.*

In para (1) words "a normal deduction rate" in square brackets substituted by SI 1995/1045, reg 16(2).

Paras (2), (3) revoked by SI 2001/162, reg 2(1), (5)(c) as from 3 March 2003 in relation to certain cases; for savings see reg 6(Z1) (as inserted by SI 2003/347, reg 2(3), (4)(a)), (1), (2) thereof and SI 2000/3186 (as amended by SI 2004/2415, reg 8). For further effect see SI

2001/62, reg 1(3) and SI 2003/192, arts 3, 5, 8, Schedule. In para (2) words ", in a case where there is a current assessment," in square brackets inserted by SI 1995/1045, reg 16(3) and words from "at the date of making" to "interim maintenance assessment" in square brackets substituted by SI 1995/1045, reg 16(3).

*Protected earnings rate [Protected earnings proportion]*

**11.** (1) The period by reference to which the *protected earnings rate* [protected earnings proportion] is set shall be the same as the period by reference to which the normal deduction rate is set under regulation 10(1).

(2) The amount to be specified as the *protected earnings rate* [protected earnings proportion] in respect of any period shall *[except where paragraph (3) or paragraph (4) applies,]* be an amount equal to *the liable person's exempt income* [60% of the liable person's net earnings] in respect of that period as calculated at the date of the current *assessment* [maintenance calculation].

[(3) *Where an interim maintenance assessment [, except a Category B interim maintenance assessment,] is in force the protected earnings rate shall be—*
  (a) *where there is some knowledge of the liable person's circumstances, the aggregate of the following amounts at the date of the making of the assessment—*
    (i) *the personal allowance applicable by virtue of paragraph 1(1)(e) of Schedule 2 to the Income Support (General) Regulations 1987 (in this paragraph referred to as "the relevant Schedule") or if he is known to have a partner, that applicable for a couple under paragraph 1(3)(c) of that Schedule;*
    (ii) *the personal allowance applicable by virtue of the relevant Schedule in respect of any child or young person who is known to be living with the relevant person (and where the age of the child or young person is not known it shall be assumed to be less than 11);*
    (iii) *the amount of any premium applicable by virtue of the relevant Schedule which is known to be applicable in the circumstances of the case; and*
    (iv) *£30;*
  (b) *in any other case the personal allowance specified in paragraph 1(1)(e) of the relevant Schedule at the date mentioned in sub-paragraph (a), plus £30.*

[(4) *Where there is a liability to make payments of child support maintenance but no maintenance assessment is in force—*
  (a) *in a case where the last maintenance assessment was a Category A or Category C interim maintenance assessment, the protected earnings rate shall be the amount which would be produced by the application of the provisions of paragraph (3) if a Category A or Category C interim maintenance assessment were in force;*
  (b) *subject to sub-paragraph (a), in a case where the absent parent provides sufficient evidence to satisfy the Secretary of State that his circumstances have changed since the last occasion on which his exempt income was calculated for the purposes of a decision under the Act, the protected earnings rate shall be the exempt amount as it would be calculated in consequence of that change of circumstances if regulation 9 of the Child Support (Maintenance Assessments and Special Cases) Regulations 1992 applied in his case; and*
  (c) *in any other case, the protected earnings rate shall be the amount of the liable person's exempt income as it was on the last occasion that amount was calculated for the purposes of a decision under the Act.]]*

**Note.** Provision heading substituted by SI 2001/162, reg 2(1), (5)(d)(i) as from 3 March 2003 in relation to certain cases; for savings see reg 6(Z1) (as inserted by SI 2003/347, reg 2(3), (4)(a)), (1), (2) thereof and SI 2000/3186 (as amended by SI 2004/2415, reg 8). For further effect see SI 2001/62, reg 1(3) and SI 2003/192, arts 3, 5, 8, Schedule.

In para (1) words "protected earnings rate" substituted by words "protected earnings proportion" in square brackets by SI 2001/162, reg 2(1), (5)(d)(ii) as from 3 March 2003 in relation to certain cases; for savings see reg 6(Z1) (as inserted by SI 2003/347, reg 2(3), (4)(a)), (1), (2) thereof and SI 2000/3186 (as amended by SI 2004/2415, reg 8). For further effect see SI 2001/62, reg 1(3) and SI 2003/192, arts 3, 5, 8, Schedule.

In para (2) words "protected earnings rate", "the liable person's exempt income" and "assessment" substituted by words "protected earnings proportion", "60% of the liable person's net earnings" and "calculation" in square brackets by SI 2001/162, reg 2(1), (5)(d)(ii), (iii)(bb), (cc) as from 3 March 2003 in relation to certain cases; for savings see reg 6(Z1) (as inserted by SI 2003/347, reg 2(3), (4)(a)), (1), (2) thereof and SI 2000/3186 (as amended by SI 2004/2415, reg 8). For further effect see SI 2001/62, reg 1(3) and SI 2003/192, arts 3, 5, 8, Schedule. In para (2) words "except where paragraph (3) or paragraph (4) applies," in square brackets inserted by SI 1995/1045, reg 17(1), (2), revoked by SI 2001/162, reg 2(1), (5)(d)(iii)(aa) as from 3 March 2003 in relation to certain cases; for savings see reg 6(Z1) (as inserted by SI 2003/347, reg 2(3), (4)(a)), (1), (2) thereof and SI 2000/3186 (as amended by SI 2004/2415, reg 8). For further effect see SI 2001/62, reg 1(3) and SI 2003/192, arts 3, 5, 8, Schedule.

Paras (3), (4) inserted by SI 1995/1045, reg 17(1), (3); revoked by SI 2001/162, reg 2(1), (5)(d)(iv) as from 3 March 2003 in relation to certain cases; for savings see reg 6(Z1) (as inserted by SI 2003/347, reg 2(3), (4)(a)), (1), (2) thereof and SI 2000/3186 (as amended by SI 2004/2415, reg 8). For further effect see SI 2001/62, reg 1(3) and SI 2003/192, arts 3, 5, 8, Schedule.

In para (3) words ", except a Category B interim maintenance assessment," in square brackets inserted by SI 1996/1945, reg 4. Para (4) substituted by SI 1999/1510, art 29 as from 1 June 1999.

*Amount to be deducted by employer*

**12.**   (1) Subject to the provisions of this regulation, an employer who has been served with a copy of a deduction from earnings order in respect of a liable person in his employment shall, each pay-day, make a deduction from the net earnings of that liable person of an amount equal to the normal deduction rate.

(2) Where the deduction of the normal deduction rate would reduce the liable person's net earnings below the *protected earnings rate* [protected earnings proportion] the employer shall deduct only such amount as will leave the liable person with net earnings equal to the *protected earnings rate* [protected earnings proportion].

(3) Where the liable person receives a payment of earnings at an interval greater or lesser than the interval specified in relation to the normal deduction rate and the *protected earnings rate* [protected earnings proportion] ("the specified interval") the employer shall. for the purpose of such payments, take as the normal deduction rate and the *protected earnings rate* [protected earnings proportion] such amounts (to the nearest whole penny) as are in the same proportion to the interval since the last pay-day as the normal deduction rate and the *protected earnings rate* [protected earnings proportion] bear to the specified interval.

[(3A) Where on any pay-day the liable person receives a payment of earnings covering a period longer than the period by reference to which the normal deduction rate is set, the employer shall, subject to paragraph (2), make a deduction from the net earnings paid to that liable person on that pay-day of an amount which is in the same proportion to the normal deduction rate as that longer period is to the period by reference to which that normal deduction rate is set.]

(4) Where, on any pay-day, the employer fails to deduct an amount due under the deduction from earnings order or deducts an amount less than the amount of the normal deduction rate the shortfall shall, subject to the operation of paragraph (2), be deducted in addition to the normal deduction rate at the next available pay-day or days.

(5) *Where, on any pay-day, the liable person's net earnings are less than his protected earnings rate the amount of the difference shall be carried forward to his next pay-day and treated as part of his protected earnings in respect of that pay-day.*

(6) Where, on any pay-day, an employer makes a deduction from the earnings of a liable person in accordance with the deduction from earnings order he may also

deduct an amount not exceeding £1 in respect of his administrative costs and such deduction for administrative costs may be made notwithstanding that it may reduce the liable person's net earnings below the *protected earnings rate* [protected earnings proportion].

**Note.** In paras (2), (3), (6) words "protected earnings rate" in both places substituted by words "protected earnings proportion" in square brackets by SI 2001/162, reg 2(1), (5)(e)(i) as from 3 March 2003 in relation to certain cases; for savings see reg 6(Z1) (as inserted by SI 2003/347, reg 2(3), (4)(a)), (1), (2) thereof and SI 2000/3186 (as amended by SI 2004/2415, reg 8). For further effect see SI 2001/62, reg 1(3) and SI 2003/192, arts 3, 5, 8, Schedule. Para (3A) inserted by SI 1998/58, reg 6 as from 19 January 1998. Para (5) revoked by SI 2001/162, reg 2(1), (5)(e)(ii) as from 3 March 2003 in relation to certain cases; for savings see reg 6(Z1) (as inserted by SI 2003/347, reg 2(3), (4)(a)), (1), (2) thereof and SI 2000/3186 (as amended by SI 2004/2415, reg 8). For further effect see SI 2001/62, reg 1(3) and SI 2003/192, arts 3, 5, 8, Schedule.

*Employer to notify liable person of deduction*

**13.** (1) An employer making a deduction from earnings for the purposes of this Part shall notify the liable person in writing of the amount of the deduction, including any amount deducted for administrative costs under regulation 12(6).

(2) Such notification shall be given not later than the pay-day on which the deduction is made or, where that is impracticable, not later than the following pay-day.

*Payment by employer to Secretary of State*

**14.** (1) Amounts deducted by an employer under a deduction from earnings order (other than any administrative costs deducted under regulation 12(6)) shall be paid to the Secretary of State by the 19th day of the month following the month in which the deduction is made.

(2) Such payment may be made—
   (a) by cheque;
   (b) by automated credit transfer; or
   (c) by such other method as the Secretary of State may specify.

*Information to be provided by liable person*

**15.** (1) The Secretary of State may, in relation to the making or operation of a deduction from earnings order, require the liable person to provide the following details—
   (a) the name and address of his employer;
   (b) the amount of his earnings and anticipated earnings;
   (c) his place of work, the nature of his work and any works or pay number;
and it shall be the duty of the liable person to comply with any such requirement within 7 days of being given written notice to that effect.

(2) A liable person in respect of whom a deduction from earnings order is in force shall notify the Secretary of State in writing within 7 days of every occasion on which he leaves employment or becomes employed or re-employed.

*Duty of employers and others to notify Secretary of State*

**16.** (1) Where a deduction from earnings order is served on a person on the assumption that he is the employer of a liable person but the liable person to whom the order relates is not in his employment, the person on whom the order was served shall notify the Secretary of State of that fact in writing, at the address specified in the order, within 10 days of the date of service on him of the order.

(2) Where an employer is required to operate a deduction from earnings order and the liable person to whom the order relates ceases to be in his employment the employer shall notify the Secretary of State of that fact in writing, at the address specified in the order, within 10 days of the liable person ceasing to be in his employment.

(3) Where an employer becomes aware that a deduction from earnings order is in force in relation to a person who is an employee of his he shall, within 7 days of the date on which he becomes aware, notify the Secretary of State of that fact in writing at the address specified in the order.

*Requirement to review deduction from earnings orders*

**17.** [(1) Subject to paragraph (2), the Secretary of State shall review a deduction from earnings order in the following circumstances—
  (a) where there is a change in the amount of the maintenance *assessment* [calculation];
  (b) where any arrears *and interest on arrears* [, penalty payment, interest or fees] payable under the order are paid off.
(2) There shall be no obligation to review a deduction from earnings order under paragraph (1) where the normal deduction rates specified in the order take account of the changes which will arise as a result of the circumstances specified in sub-paragraph (a) or (b) of that paragraph.]

**Note.** Substituted by SI 1995/1045, reg 18. In para (1)(a) word "assessment" substituted by word "calculation" in square brackets and in para (1)(b) words "and interest on arrears" substituted by words ", penalty payment, interest or fees" in square brackets by SI 2001/162, reg 2(1), (5)(f) as from 3 March 2003 in relation to certain cases; for savings see reg 6(Z1) (as inserted by SI 2003/347, reg 2(3), (4)(a)), (1), (2) thereof and SI 2000/3186 (as amended by SI 2004/2415, reg 8). For further effect see SI 2001/62, reg 1(3) and SI 2003/192, arts 3, 5, 8, Schedule.

*Power to vary deduction from earnings orders*

**18.** (1) The Secretary of State may (whether on a review under regulation 17 or otherwise) vary a deduction from earnings order so as to—
  (a) include any amount which may be included in such an order or exclude or decrease any such amount;
  (b) substitute a subsequent employer for the employer at whom the order was previously directed.
(2) The Secretary of State shall serve a copy of any deduction from earnings order, as varied, on the liable person's employer and on the liable person.

*Compliance with deduction from earnings orders as varied*

**19.** (1) Where a deduction from earnings order has been varied and a copy of the order as varied has been served on the liable person's employer it shall, subject to paragraph (2), be the duty of the employer to comply with the order as varied.
(2) The employer shall not be under any liability for non-compliance with the order, as varied, before the end of the period of 7 days beginning with the date on which a copy of the order, as varied, was served on him.

*Discharge of deduction from earnings orders*

**20.** [(1) The Secretary of State may discharge a deduction from earnings order where it appears to him that—
(a)   no further payments are due under it;
(b)   the order is ineffective or some other way of securing that payments are made would be more effective;

   (c)  the order is defective;

   (d)  the order fails to comply in a material respect with any procedural provision of the Act or regulations made under it other than provision made in regulation 9, 10 or 11;

   (e)  at the time of the making of the order he did not have, or subsequently ceased to have, jurisdiction to make a deduction from earnings order; or

   (f)  in the case of an order made at a time when there is in force *an interim maintenance assessment* [a default or interim maintenance decision], it is inappropriate to continue deductions under the order having regard to the compliance or the attempted compliance with the *maintenance assessment* [maintenance calculation] by the liable person.]

(2) The Secretary of State shall give written notice of the discharge of the deduction from earnings order to the liable person and to the liable person's employer.

**Note.** Para (1) substituted by SI 1995/1045, reg 19. In para (1)(f) words "an interim maintenance assessment" and "maintenance assessment" substituted by words "a default or interim maintenance decision" and "maintenance calculation" in square brackets by SI 2001/162, reg 2(1), (5)(g) as from 3 March 2003 in relation to certain cases; for savings see reg 6(Z1) (as inserted by SI 2003/347, reg 2(3), (4)(a)), (1), (2) thereof and SI 2000/3186 (as amended by SI 2004/2415, reg 8). For further effect see SI 2001/62, reg 1(3) and SI 2003/192, arts 3, 5, 8, Schedule.

*Lapse of deduction from earnings orders*

**21.**   (1) A deduction from earnings order shall lapse (except in relation to any deductions made or to be made in respect of the employment not yet paid to the Secretary of State) where the employer at whom it is directed ceases to have the liable person in his employment.

(2) The order shall lapse from the pay-day coinciding with, or, if none, the pay-day following, the termination of the employment.

(3) A deduction from earnings order which has lapsed under this regulation shall nonetheless be treated as remaining in force for the purposes of regulations 15 and 24.

(4) Where a deduction from earnings order has lapsed under paragraph (1) and the liable person recommences employment (whether with the same or another employer), the order may be revived from such date as may be specified by the Secretary of State.

(5) Where a deduction from earnings order is revived under paragraph (4), the Secretary of State shall give written notice of that fact to, and serve a copy of the notice on, the liable person and the liable person's employer.

(6) Where an order is revived under paragraph (4), no amount shall be carried forward under regulation 12(4) *or (5)* from a time prior to the revival of the order.

**Note.** In para (6) words "or (5)" revoked by SI 2001/162, reg 2(1), (5)(h) as from 3 March 2003 in relation to certain cases; for savings see reg 6(Z1) (as inserted by SI 2003/347, reg 2(3), (4)(a)), (1), (2) thereof and SI 2000/3186 (as amended by SI 2004/2415, reg 8). For further effect see SI 2001/62, reg 1(3) and SI 2003/192, arts 3, 5, 8, Schedule.

*Appeals against deduction from earnings orders*

**22.**   (1)  A liable person in respect of whom a deduction from earnings order has been made may appeal to the magistrates' court, or in Scotland the sheriff, having jurisdiction in the area in which he resides.

   (2)  Any appeal shall—

   (a)  be by way of complaint for an order or, in Scotland, by way of application;

   (b)  be made within 28 days of the date on which the matter appealed against arose.

(3) An appeal may be made only on one or both of the following grounds—
(a) that the deduction from earnings order is defective;
(b) that the payments in question do not constitute earnings.
(4) Where the court or, as the case may be, the sheriff is satisfied that the appeal should be allowed the court, or sheriff, may—
(a) quash the deduction from earnings order; or
(b) specify which, if any, of the payments in question do not constitute earnings.

*Crown employment*

**23.** Where a liable person is in the employment of the Crown and a deduction from earnings order is made in respect of him then for the purposes of this Part—
(a) the chief officer for the time being of the Department, office or other body in which the liable person is employed shall be treated as having the liable person in his employment (any transfer of the liable person from one Department, office or body to another being treated as a change of employment); and
(b) any earnings paid by the Crown or a minister of the Crown, or out of the public revenue of the United Kingdom, shall be treated as paid by that chief officer.

*Priority as between orders*

**24.** (1) *Where an employer would, but for this paragraph, be obliged, on any payday, to make deductions under two or more deduction from earnings orders he shall—*
(a) *deal with the orders according to the respective dates on which they were made, disregarding any later order until an earlier one has been dealt with;*
(b) *deal with any later order as if the earnings to which it relates were the residue of the liable person's earnings after the making of any deduction to comply with any earlier order.*

(2) Where an employer would, but for this paragraph, be obliged to comply with *one or more deduction from earnings orders* [a deduction from earnings order] and one or more attachment of earnings orders he shall—
(a) in the case of an attachment of earnings order which was made either wholly or in part in respect of the payment of a judgment debt or payments under an administration order, deal first with the deduction from earnings order *or orders* and thereafter with the attachment of earnings order as if the earnings to which it relates were the residue of the liable person's earnings after the making of deductions to comply with the deduction from earnings order *or orders*;
(b) in the case of any other attachment of earnings order, *deal with the orders according to the respective dates on which they were made in like manner as under paragraph (1)* [he shall—
   (i) deal with the orders according to the respective dates on which they were made, disregarding any later order until an earlier one has been dealt with;
   (ii) deal with any later order as if the earnings to which it relates were the residue of the liable person's earnings after the making of any deduction to comply with any earlier order].
"Attachment of earnings order" in this paragraph means an order made under the Attachment of Earnings Act 1971 or under regulation 32 of the Community Charge (Administration and Enforcement) Regulations 1989 [or under regulation 37 of the Council Tax (Administration and Enforcement) Regulations 1992].
(3) Paragraph (2) does not apply to Scotland.
(4) In Scotland, where an employer would, but for this paragraph be obliged to comply with *one or more deduction from earnings orders* [a deduction from earnings order] and one or more diligences against earnings he shall deal first with the

deduction from earnings order *or orders* and thereafter with the diligence against earnings as if the earnings to which the diligence relates were the residue of the liable person's earnings after the making of deductions to comply with the deduction from earnings order *or orders.*

**Note.** Para (1) revoked by SI 2001/162, reg 2(1), (5)(i)(i) as from 3 March 2003 in relation to certain cases; for savings see reg 6(Z1) (as inserted by SI 2003/347, reg 2(3), (4)(a)), (1), (2) thereof and SI 2000/3186 (as amended by SI 2004/2415, reg 8). For further effect see SI 2001/62, reg 1(3) and SI 2003/192, arts 3, 5, 8, Schedule.

In para (2) words "one or more deduction from earnings orders" substituted by words "a deduction from earnings order" in square brackets, in sub-para (a) words "or orders" in both places revoked, in sub-para (b) words from ", deal with the orders" to "as under paragraph (1)" substituted by words from "he shall" to "earlier order" in square brackets, by SI 2001/162, reg 2(1), (5)(i)(iii)(aa), (bb), (ii) as from 3 March 2003 in relation to certain cases; for savings see reg 6(Z1) (as inserted by SI 2003/347, reg 2(3), (4)(a)), (1), (2) thereof and SI 2000/3186 (as amended by SI 2004/2415, reg 8). For further effect see SI 2001/62, reg 1(3) and SI 2003/192, arts 3, 5, 8, Schedule. In para (2) words "or under regulation 37 of the Council Tax (Administration and Enforcement) Regulations 1992" in square brackets inserted by SI 1993/913, reg 42.

In para (4) words "one or more deduction from earnings orders" substituted by words "a deduction from earnings order" in square brackets and words "or orders" revoked by SI 2001/162, reg 2(1), (5)(i)(iii) as from 3 March 2003 in relation to certain cases; for savings see reg 6(Z1) (as inserted by SI 2003/347, reg 2(3), (4)(a)), (1), (2) thereof and SI 2000/3186 (as amended by SI 2004/2415, reg 8). For further effect see SI 2001/62, reg 1(3) and SI 2003/192, arts 3, 5, 8, Schedule.

*Offences*

**25.** The following regulations are designated for the purposes of section 32(8) of the Act (offences relating to deduction from earnings orders)—

[(aa)     regulation 14(1);]
[(ab)]     regulation 15(1) and (2);
(b)  regulation 16(1), (2) and (3);
(c)  regulation 19(1).

**Note.** Para (aa) inserted and para (ab) numbered as such by SI 1999/977, reg 2(1)–(3) as from 6 April 1999.

PART IV

LIABILITY ORDERS

*Extent of this Part*

**26.**   This Part, except regulation 29(2), does not apply to Scotland.

*Notice of intention to apply for a liability order*

**27.**   (1)  The Secretary of State shall give the liable person at least 7 days notice of his intention to apply for a liability order under section 33(2) of the Act.

(2)  Such notice shall set out the amount of child support maintenance which it is claimed has become payable by the liable person and has not been paid and the amount of any interest *in respect of arrears payable under section 41(3) of the Act* [, penalty payments or fees which have become payable and have not been paid].

(3)  Payment by the liable person of any part of the amounts referred to in paragraph (2) shall not require the giving of a further notice under paragraph (1) prior to the making of the application.

**Note.** In para (2) words "in respect of arrears payable under section 41(3) of the Act" substituted by words ", penalty payments or fees which have become payable and have not been paid " in square brackets by SI 2001/162, reg 2(1), (6)(a) as from 3 March 2003 in relation to certain cases; for savings see reg 6(Z1) (as inserted by SI 2003/347, reg 2(3),

(4)(a)), (1), (2) thereof and SI 2000/3186 (as amended by SI 2004/2415, reg 8). For further effect see SI 2001/62, reg 1(3) and SI 2003/192, arts 3, 5, 8, Schedule.

*Application for a liability order*

**28.** (1) An application for a liability order shall be by way of complaint for an order to the magistrates' court having jurisdiction in the area in which the liable person resides.

(2) An application under paragraph (1) may not be instituted more than 6 years after the day on which payment of the amount in question became due.

(3) A warrant shall not be issued under section 55(2) of the Magistrates' Courts Act 1980 in any proceedings under this regulation.

*Liability orders*

**29.** (1) A liability order shall be made in the form prescribed in Schedule 1.

(2) A liability order made by a court in England or Wales or any corresponding order made by a court in Northern Ireland may be enforced in Scotland as if it had been made by the sheriff.

(3) A liability order made by the sheriff in Scotland or any corresponding order made by a court in Northern Ireland may, subject to paragraph (4), be enforced in England and Wales as if it had been made by a magistrates' court in England and Wales.

(4) A liability order made by the sheriff in Scotland or a corresponding order made by a court in Northern Ireland shall not be enforced in England or Wales unless registered in accordance with the provisions of Part II of the Maintenance Orders Act 1950 and for this purpose—

(a) a liability order made by the sheriff in Scotland shall be treated as if it were a decree to which section 16(2)(b) of that Act applies (decree for payment of aliment);

(b) a corresponding order made by a court in Northern Ireland shall be treated as if it were an order to which section 16(2)(c) of that Act applies (order for alimony, maintenance or other payments).

*Enforcement of liability orders by distress*

**30.** (1) A distress made pursuant to section 35(1) of the Act may be made anywhere in England and Wales.

(2) The person levying distress on behalf of the Secretary of State shall carry with him the written authorisation of the Secretary of State, which he shall show to the liable person if so requested, and he shall hand to the liable person or leave at the premises where the distress is levied—

(a) copies of this regulation, regulation 31 and Schedule 2;

(b) a memorandum setting out the amount which is the appropriate amount for the purposes of section 35(2) of the Act;

(c) a memorandum setting out details of any arrangement entered into regarding the taking of possession of the goods distrained; and

(d) a notice setting out the liable person's rights of appeal under regulation 31 giving the Secretary of State's address for the purposes of any appeal.

(3) A distress shall not be deemed unlawful on account of any defect or want of form in the liability order.

(4) If, before any goods are seized, the appropriate amount (including charges arising up to the time of the payment or tender) is paid or tendered to the Secretary of State, the Secretary of State shall accept the amount and the levy shall not be proceeded with.

(5) Where the Secretary of State has seized goods of the liable person in pursuance of the distress, but before sale of those goods the appropriate amount

(including charges arising up to the time of the payment or tender) is paid or tendered to the Secretary of State, the Secretary of State shall accept the amount, the sale shall not be proceeded with and the goods shall be made available for collection by the liable person.

*Appeals in connection with distress*

**31.** (1) A person aggrieved by the levy of, or an attempt to levy, a distress may appeal to the magistrates' court having jurisdiction in the area in which he resides.

(2) The appeal shall be by way of complaint for an order.

(3) If the court is satisfied that the levy was irregular, it may—

(a) order the goods distrained to be discharged if they are in the possession of the Secretary of State;

(b) order an award of compensation in respect of any goods distrained and sold of an amount equal to the amount which, in the opinion of the court, would be awarded by way of special damages in respect of the goods if proceedings under section 35(6) of the Act were brought in trespass or otherwise in connection with the irregularity.

(4) If the court is satisfied that an attempted levy was irregular, it may by order require the Secretary of State to desist from levying in the manner giving rise to the irregularity.

*Charges connected with distress*

**32.** Schedule 2 shall have effect for the purpose of determining the amounts in respect of charges in connection with the distress for the purposes of section 35(2)(b) of the Act.

*Application for warrant of commitment*

**33.** (1) For the purposes of enabling an inquiry to be made under section *40* [39A] of the Act as to the liable person's conduct and means, a justice of the peace having jurisdiction for the area in which the liable person resides may—

(a) issue a summons to him to appear before a magistrates' court and (if he does not obey the summons) issue a warrant for his arrest; or

(b) issue a warrant for his arrest without issuing a summons.

(2) In any proceedings under [sections 39A and 40] of the Act, a statement in writing to the effect that wages of any amount have been paid to the liable person during any period, purporting to be signed by or on behalf of his employer, shall be evidence of the facts there stated.

(3) Where an application under section [39A] of the Act has been made but no warrant of commitment is issued or term of imprisonment fixed, the application may be renewed on the ground that the circumstances of the liable person have changed.

**Note.** In paras (1), (3) reference to "40" substituted by reference to "39A" in square brackets and in para (2) words "section 40" substituted by words "section 39A and 40" in square brackets by SI 2001/162, reg 2(1), (6)(b) as from 31 May 2001 (see SI 2001/162, reg 1(2A) (as inserted by SI 2001/1775, reg 2)).

*Warrant of commitment*

**34.** (1) A warrant of commitment shall be in the form specified in Schedule 3, or in a form to the like effect.

(2) The amount to be included in the warrant under section 40(4)(a)(ii) of the Act in respect of costs shall be such amount as in the view of the court is equal to the costs reasonably incurred by the Secretary of State in respect of the costs of commitment.

(3) A warrant issued under section 40 of the Act may be executed anywhere in England and Wales by any person to whom it is directed or by any constable acting within his police area.

(4) A warrant may be executed by a constable notwithstanding that it is not in his possession at the time but such warrant shall, on the demand of the person arrested, be shown to him as soon as possible.

(5) Where, after the issue of a warrant, part-payment of the amount stated in it is made, the period of imprisonment shall be reduced proportionately so that for the period of imprisonment specified in the warrant there shall be substituted a period of imprisonment of such number of days as bears the same proportion to the number of days specified in the warrant as the amount remaining unpaid under the warrant bears to the amount specified in the warrant.

(6) Where the part-payment is of such an amount as would, under paragraph (5), reduce the period of imprisonment to such number of days as have already been served (or would be so served in the course of the day of payment), the period of imprisonment shall be reduced to the period already served plus one day.

*[Disqualification from driving order*

**35.** (1) For the purposes of enabling an enquiry to be made under section 39A of the Act as to the liable person's livelihood, means and conduct, a justice of the peace having jurisdiction for the area in which the liable person resides may issue a summons to him to appear before a magistrates' court and to produce any driving licence held by him, and, where applicable, its counterpart, and, if he does not appear, may issue a warrant for his arrest.

(2)   In any proceedings under sections 39A and 40B of the Act, a statement in writing to the effect that wages of any amount have been paid to the liable person during any period, purporting to be signed for or on behalf of his employer, shall be evidence of the facts there stated.

(3) Where an application under section 39A of the Act has been made but no disqualification order is made, the application may be renewed on the ground that the circumstances of the liable person have changed.

(4) A disqualification order shall be in the form prescribed in Schedule 4.

(5) The amount to be included in the disqualification order under section 40B(3)(b) of the Act in respect of the costs shall be such amount as in the view of the court is equal to the costs reasonably incurred by the Secretary of State in respect of the costs of the application for the disqualification order.

(6) An order made under section 40B(4) of the Act may be executed anywhere in England and Wales by any person to whom it is directed or by any constable acting within his police area, if the liable person fails to appear or produce or surrender his driving licence or its counterpart to the court.

(7) An order may be executed by a constable notwithstanding that it is not in his possession at the time but such order shall, if demanded, be shown to the liable person as soon as reasonably practicable.

(8) In this regulation "driving licence" means a licence to drive a motor vehicle granted under Part III of the Road Traffic Act 1988.]

**Note.** Inserted by SI 2001/162, reg 2(1), (6)(c) as from 2 April 2001.

SCHEDULE 1                                                      Regulation 29(1)

LIABILITY ORDER PRESCRIBED FORM

Section 33 of the Child Support Act 1991 and regulation 29(1) of the Child Support (Collection and Enforcement) Regulations 1992

........................................Magistrates' Court

Date:

Defendant:

Address:

On the complaint of the Secretary of State for Social Security that the sums specified below are due from the defendant under the Child Support Act 1991 and Part IV of the Child Support (Collection and Enforcement) Regulations 1992 and are outstanding, it is adjudged that the defendant is liable to pay the aggregate amount specified below.

Sum payable and outstanding                — child support maintenance
                                           — interest
                                           [— penalty payments
                                           — fees]
                                           — other periodical payments collected
                                           by virtue of section 30 of the Child
                                           Support Act 1991    Aggregate
                                           amount in respect of which the
                                           liability order is made:

Justice of the Peace

(*or* by order of the Court
Clerk of the Court)

**Note.** In table, entries "—penalty payments" and "—fees" inserted by SI 2001/162, reg 2(1), (7) as from 3 March 2003 in relation to certain cases; for savings see reg 6(Z1) (as inserted by SI 2003/347, reg 2(3), (4)(a)), (1), (2) thereof and SI 2000/3186 (as amended by SI 2004/2415, reg 8). For further effect see SI 2001/62, reg 1(3) and SI 2003/192, arts 3, 5, 8, Schedule.

SCHEDULE 2                                                     Regulation 32

CHARGES CONNECTED WITH DISTRESS

**1.** The sum in respect of charges connected with the distress which may be aggregated under section 35(2)(b) of the Act shall be set out in the following Table—

| (1) Matter connected with distress | (2) Charge |
|---|---|
| A  For making a visit to premises with a view to levying distress (whether the levy is made or not): | Reasonable costs and fees incurred, but not exceeding an amount which, when aggregated with charges under this head for any previous visits made with a view to levying distress in relation to an amount in respect of which the liability order concerned was made, is not greater than the relevant amount calculated under paragraph 2(1) with respect to the visit. |
| B  For levying distress | An amount (if any) which, when aggregated with charges under head A for any visits made with a view to levying distress in relation to an amount in respect of which the liability order concerned was made, is equal to the relevant amount calculated under paragraph 2(1) with respect to the levy. |
| BB For preparing and sending a letter advising the liable person that the written authorisation of the Secretary of State is with the person levying the distress and requesting the total sum due | £10 |
| C  For the removal and storage of goods for the purposes of sale: | Reasonable costs and fees incurred. |
| D  For the possession of goods as described in paragraph 2(3)— (i) for close possession (the person in possession on behalf of the Secretary of State to provide his own board): (ii) for walking possession: | £4.50 per day.  10p per day. |
| E  For appraisement of an item distrained, at the request in writing of the liable person: | Reasonable fees and expenses of the broker appraising. |
| F  For other expenses of, and commission on, a sale by auction— | |

| (1) Matter connected with distress | (2) Charge |
|---|---|
| (i) where the sale is held on the auctioneer's premises: | The auctioneer's commission fee and out-of-pocket expenses (but not exceeding in aggregate 15 per cent of the sum realised), together with reasonable costs and fees incurred in respect of advertising. |
| (ii) where the sale is held on the liable person's premises: | The auctioneer's commission fee (but not exceeding 7½ per cent of the sum realised), together with the auctioneer's out-of-pocket expenses and reasonable costs and fees incurred in respect of advertising. |
| G  For other expenses incurred in connection with a proposed sale where there is no buyer in relation to it: | Reasonable costs and fees incurred. |

**2.**   (1) In heads A and B of the table to paragraph 1, 'the relevant amount' with respect to a visit or a levy means—

(a)  where the sum due at the time of the visit or of the levy (as the case may be) does not exceed £100, £12.50;

(b)  where the sum due at the time of the visit or of the levy (as the case may be) exceeds £100, 12½ per cent on the first £100 of the sum due, 4 per cent on the next £400, 2½ per cent on the next £1,500, 1 per cent on the next £8,000 and ¼ per cent on any additional sum;

and the sum due at any time for these purposes means so much of the amount in respect of which the liability order concerned was made as is outstanding at the time.

(2)  Where a charge has arisen under head B with respect to an amount, no further charge may be aggregated under head A or B in respect of that amount.

(3)  The Secretary of State takes close or walking possession of goods for the purposes of head D of the Table to paragraph 1 if he takes such possession in pursuance of an agreement which is made at the time that the distress is levied and which (without prejudice to such other terms as may be agreed) is expressed to the effect that, in consideration of the Secretary of State not immediately removing the goods distrained upon from the premises occupied by the liable person and delaying the sale of the goods, the Secretary of State may remove and sell the goods after a later specified date if the liable person has not by then paid the amount distrained for (including charges under this Schedule); and the Secretary of State is in close possession of goods on any day for these purposes if during the greater part of the day a person is left on the premises in physical possession of the goods on behalf of the Secretary of State under such an agreement.

**3.**   (1) Where the calculation under this Schedule of a percentage of a sum results in an amount containing a fraction of a pound, that fraction shall be reckoned as a whole pound.

(2)  In the case of dispute as to any charge under this Schedule, the amount of the charge shall be taxed.

(3)  Such a taxation shall be carried out by the district judge of the county court for the district in which the distress is or is intended to be levied, and he may give such directions as to the costs of the taxation as he thinks fit; and any such costs directed to be paid by the liable person to the Secretary of State shall be added to the sum which may be aggregated under section 35(2) of the Act.

(4) References in the Table in paragraph 1 to costs, fees and expenses include references to amounts payable by way of value added tax with respect to the supply of goods or services to which the costs, fees and expenses relate.

SCHEDULE 3                                                          Regulation 34(1)

FORM OF WARRANT OF COMMITMENT

Section 40 of the Child Support Act 1991 and regulation 34(1) of the Child Support (Collection and Enforcement) Regulations 1992

.............................Magistrates Court

Date:

Liable Person:

Address:

A liability order ("the order") was made against the liable person by the (.............) Magistrates' Court on (...................) under section 33 of the Child Support Act 1991 ("the Act") in respect of an amount of (...............).

The court is satisfied—
      (i) that the Secretary of State sought under section 35 of the Act to levy by distress the amount then outstanding in respect of which the order was made;

(and/or)
      that the Secretary of State sought under section 36 of the Act to recover through the (..........................) County Court, by means of (garnishee proceedings) *or* (a charging order), the amount then outstanding in respect of which the order was made;
      (ii) that such amount, or any portion of it, remains unpaid; and
      (iii) having inquired in the liable person's presence as to his means and as to whether there has been (wilful refusal) *or* (culpable neglect) on his part, the court is of the opinion that there has been (wilful refusal) *or* (culpable neglect) on his part.

The decision of the court is that the liable person be (committed to prison) (detained) for (.............) unless the aggregate amount mentioned below in respect of which this warrant is made is sooner paid. (*Note:* The period of imprisonment will be reduced as provided by regulation 34(5) and (6) of the Child Support (Collection and Enforcement) Regulations 1992 if part-payment is made of the aggregate amount.)

This warrant is made in respect of—
Amount outstanding (including any interest, [penalty payments, fees,] costs and charges).............................
Costs of commitment of the Secretary of State:...........................

Aggregate amount:..........................

And you *(name of person or persons to whom warrant is directed)* are hereby required to take the liable person and convey him to *(name of prison or place of detention)* and there deliver him to the (governor) (officer in charge) thereof; and you, the (governor) (officer in charge), to receive the liable person into your custody and keep him for *(period of imprisonment)* from the date of his arrest under this warrant or until he be sooner discharged in due course of law.

Justice of the Peace

(or by order of the Court<br>Clerk of the Court).

**Note.** In paras (i), (iii) word "or" in each place revoked, and words "penalty payments, fees," in square brackets inserted by SI 2001/162, reg 2(1), (8)(a)–(c) as from 3 March 2003 in relation to certain cases; for savings see reg 6(Z1) (as inserted by SI 2003/347, reg 2(3), (4)(a)), (1), (2) thereof and SI 2000/3186 (as amended by SI 2004/2415, reg 8). For further effect see SI 2001/62, reg 1(3) and SI 2003/192, arts 3, 5, 8, Schedule.


SCHEDULE 4                                                      Regulation 35(4)

FORM OF ORDER OF DISQUALIFICATION FROM HOLDING OR OBTAINING A DRIVING LICENCE

Sections 39A and 40B of the Child Support Act 1991 and regulation 35 of the Child Support (Collection and Enforcement) Regulations 1992.

.............................Magistrates' Court

Date:

Liable Person:

Address:

A liability order ("the order") was made against the liable person by the [                ] Magistrates' Court on [                ] under section 33 of the Child Support Act 1991 ("the Act") in respect of an amount of [          ].

The court is satisfied—

> (i)   that the Secretary of State sought under section 35 of the Act to levy by distress the amount then outstanding in respect of which the order was made;

[and/or]

that the Secretary of State sought under section 36 of the Act to recover through [                ] County Court by means of [garnishee proceedings] [a charging order], the amount then outstanding in respect of which the order was made;

> (ii)   that such amount, or any proportion of it, remains unpaid; and
> (iii)  having inquired in the liable person's presence as to his means and whether there has been [wilful refusal] [culpable neglect] on his part.

The decision of the court is that the liable person be disqualified from [holding or obtaining] a driving licence from [date] for [period] unless the aggregate amount in respect of which this order is made is sooner paid*

This order is made in respect of—

Amount outstanding (including any interest, fees, penalty payments, costs and charges):

Aggregate amount:

And you [the liable person] shall surrender to the court any driving licence and counterpart held.

Justice of the Peace

[*or* by order of the Court
Clerk of the Court]

**\*Note:** The period of disqualification may be reduced as provided by section 40B(5)(a) of the Act if part payment is made of the aggregate amount. The order will be revoked by section 40B(5)(b) of the Act if full payment is made of the aggregate amount.]

**Note.** Inserted by SI 2001/162, reg 2(1), (9), Schedule as from 2 April 2001, being the date the Child Support, Pensions and Social Security Act 2000, s 16 came into force (see SI 2000/3354, art 2(3) and SI 2001/162, reg 1(2)).

## CHILD SUPPORT (COLLECTION AND ENFORCEMENT OF OTHER FORMS OF MAINTENANCE) REGULATIONS 1992

**Dated** 26 October 1992

**SI 1992 No 2643**

*Citation, commencement and interpretation*

**1.** (1) These Regulations may be cited as the Child Support (Collection and Enforcement of Other Forms of Maintenance) Regulations 1992 and shall come into force on 5th April 1993.

(2) In these Regulations—

'the Act' means the Child Support Act 1991;

'child of the family' has the same meaning as in the Matrimonial Causes Act 1973 or, in Scotland, the Family Law (Scotland) Act 1985; and

'periodical payments' includes secured periodical payments.

*Periodical payments and categories of person prescribed for the purposes of section 30 of the Act*

**2.** The following periodical payments and categories of persons are prescribed for the purposes of section 30(1) of the Act—

(a) payments under a maintenance order made in relation to a child in accordance with the provisions of section 8(6) (periodical payments in addition to child support maintenance), 8(7) (periodical payments to meet expenses incurred in connection with the provision of instruction or training) or 8(8) of the Act (periodical payments to meet expenses attributable to disability);

(b) any periodical payments under a maintenance order or, in Scotland, registered minutes of agreement, which are payable to or for the benefit of a spouse or former spouse who is the person with care of a child who is a qualifying child in respect of whom a child support maintenance assessment [maintenance calculation] is in force in accordance with which the Secretary of State has arranged for the collection of child support maintenance under section 29 of the Act; and

(c) any periodical payments under a maintenance order payable to or for the benefit of a former child of the family of the person against whom the order is made, that child having his home with the person with care.

**Note.** In para (b) words 'maintenance assessment' substituted by words' maintenence calculation' in square brackets by SI 2001/162, reg 3 as from 3 March 2003 in relation to certain cases; for effect see SI 2001/162, reg 1(3), SI 2003/192, arts 3, 5, 8, Schedule, and SI 2003/347, reg 2.

*Collection and enforcement—England and Wales*

**3.**  In relation to England and Wales, sections 29(2) and (3) and 31 to *40* [40B] of the Act, and any regulations made under those sections, shall apply for the purpose of enabling the Secretary of State to enforce any obligation to pay any amount which he is authorised to collect under section 30 of the Act, with the modification that any reference in those sections or regulations to child support maintenance shall be read as a reference to any of the periodical payments mentioned in regulation 2 above, and any reference to a maintenance assessment [maintenance calculation] shall be read as a reference to any of the maintenance orders mentioned in that regulation.

**Note.** Reference to '40' substituted by reference to '40B' and words 'maintenance assessment' substituted by words' maintenence calculation' in square brackets by SI 2001/162, reg 3 as from 3 March 2003 in relation to certain cases; for effect see SI 2001/162, reg 1(3), SI 2003/192, arts 3, 5, 8, Schedule, and SI 2003/347, reg 2.

*Collection and enforcement—Scotland*

**4.**  In relation to Scotland, for the purpose of enforcing any obligation to pay any amount which the Secretary of State is authorised to collect under section 30 of the Act—

(a) the Secretary of State may bring any proceedings and take any other steps (other than diligence against earnings) which could have been brought or taken by or on behalf of the person to whom the periodical payments are payable; and

(b) sections 29(2) and (3), 31 and 32 of the Act, and any regulations made under those sections, shall apply, with the modification that any reference in those sections or regulations to child support maintenance shall be read as a reference to any of the periodical payments mentioned in regulation 2 above, and any reference to a *maintenance assessment* [maintenance assessment] shall be read as a reference to any of the maintenance orders mentioned in that regulation.

**Note.** In para (b) words 'maintenance assessment' substituted by words' maintenence calculation' in square brackets by SI 2001/162, reg 3 as from 3 March 2003 in relation to certain cases; for effect see SI 2001/162, reg 1(3), SI 2003/192, arts 3, 5, 8, Schedule, and SI 2003/347, reg 2.

*Collection and enforcement—supplementary*

**5.**  Nothing in regulation 3 or 4 applies to any periodical payment which falls due before the date specified by the Secretary of State by a notice in writing to the absent parent [non-resident parent] that he is arranging for those payments to be collected, and that date shall be not earlier than the date the notice is given.

**Note.** Words 'absent parent' substituted by words 'non-resident parent' in square brackets by SI 2001/162, reg 3 as from 3 March 2003 in relation to certain cases; for effect see SI 2001/162, reg 1(3), SI 2003/192, arts 3, 5, 8, Schedule, and SI 2003/347, reg 2.

## CHILD SUPPORT (MAINTENANCE ARRANGEMENTS AND JURISDICTION) REGULATIONS 1992

**Dated** 26 October 1992

**SI 1992 No 2645**

*Citation, commencement and interpretation*

**1.** (1) These Regulations may be cited as the Child Support (Maintenance Arrangements and Jurisdiction) Regulations 1992 and shall come into force on 5th April 1993.

(2) In these Regulations—
"the Act" means the Child Support Act 1991;
*["Maintenance Assessment Procedure Regulations" means the Child Support (Maintenance Assessment Procedure) Regulations 1992;]*
["Maintenance Calculation Procedure Regulations" means the Child Support (Maintenance Calculation Procedure) Regulations 2000;]
*"Maintenance Assessments and Special Cases Regulations" means the Child Support (Maintenance Assessments and Special Cases) Regulations 1992;*
["Maintenance Calculations and Special Cases Regulations" means the Child Support (Maintenance Calculations and Special Cases) Regulations 2000;]
"effective date" means the date on which a maintenance *assessment* [calculation] takes effect for the purposes of the Act;
"maintenance order" has the meaning given in section 8(11) of the Act.

(3) In these Regulations, unless the context otherwise requires, a reference—
(a) to a numbered regulation is to the regulation in these Regulations bearing that number;
(b) in a regulation to a numbered paragraph is to the paragraph in that regulation bearing that number;
(c) in a paragraph to a lettered or numbered sub-paragraph is to the sub-paragraph in that paragraph bearing that letter or number.

**Note.** In para (2): definition "Maintenance Assessment Procedure Regulations" inserted by SI 1995/1045, reg 25, substituted by definition "Maintenance Calculation Procedure Regulations" by SI 2001/161, reg 3(1)(b) as from 3 March 2003 in relation to certain cases, for effect and transitional provisions see SI 2001/161, reg 1(3)(d), 10(Z1), (1), (3) and SI 2003/192, arts 3, 8, Schedule; definition "Maintenance Calculations and Special Cases Regulations" substituted by definition "Maintenance Calculations and Special Cases Regulations" by SI 2001/161, reg 3(1)(a) as from 3 March 2003 in relation to certain cases, for effect and transitional provisions see SI 2001/161, reg 1(3)(d), 10(Z1), (1), (3) and SI 2003/192, arts 3, 8, Schedule, and in definition "effective date" word "assessment" substituted by word "calculation" in square brackets by SI 2001/161, reg 2(2) as from 3 March 2003 in relation to certain cases, for effect and transitional provisions see SI 2001/161, reg 1(3)(d), 10(Z1), (1), (3) and SI 2003/192, arts 3, 8, Schedule.Prescription of enactments for the purposes of section 8(11) of the Act

**2.** The following enactments are prescribed for the purposes of section 8(11)(f) of the Act—
(a) the Conjugal Rights (Scotland) Amendment Act 1861;
(b) the Court of Session Act 1868;
(c) the Sheriff Courts (Scotland) Act 1907;
(d) the Guardianship of Infants Act 1925;
(e) the Illegitimate Children (Scotland) Act 1930;
(f) the Children and Young Persons (Scotland) Act 1932;
(g) the Children and Young Persons (Scotland) Act 1937;
(h) the Custody of Children (Scotland) Act 1939;
(i) the National Assistance Act 1948;
(j) the Affiliation Orders Act 1952;

(k)  the Affiliation Proceedings Act 1957;
(l)  the Matrimonial Proceedings (Children) Act 1958;
(m) the Guardianship of Minors Act 1971;
(n)  the Guardianship Act 1973;
(o)  the Children Act 1975;
(p)  the Supplementary Benefits Act 1976;
(q)  the Social Security Act 1986;
(r)  the Social Security Administration Act 1992.

*Relationship between maintenance assessments and certain court orders*

**3.**  [(1)     Orders made under the following enactments are of a kind prescribed
for the purposes of section 10(1) of the Act—
(a)  the Conjugal Rights (Scotland) Amendment Act 1861;
(b)  the Court of Session Act 1868;
(c)  the Sheriff Courts (Scotland) Act 1907;
(d)  the Guardianship of Infants Act 1925;
(e)  the Illegitimate Children (Scotland) Act 1930;
(f)  the Children and Young Persons (Scotland) Act 1932;
(g)  the Children and Young Persons (Scotland) Act 1937;
(h)  the Custody of Children (Scotland) Act 1939;
(i)  the National Assistance Act 1948;
(j)  the Affiliation Orders Act 1952;
(k)  the Affiliation Proceedings Act 1957;
(l)  the Matrimonial Proceedings (Children) Act 1958;
(m) the Guardianship of Minors Act 1971;
(n)  the Guardianship Act 1973;
(o)  Part II of the Matrimonial Causes Act 1973;
(p)  the Children Act 1975;
(q)  the Supplementary Benefits Act 1976;
(r)  the Domestic Proceedings and Magistrates Courts Act 1978;
(s)  Part III of the Matrimonial and Family Proceedings Act 1984;
(t)  the Family Law (Scotland) Act 1985;
(u)  the Social Security Act 1986;
(v)  Schedule 1 to the Children Act 1989;
(w)  the Social Security Administration Act 1992.]
(2) Subject to paragraphs (3) and (4), where a maintenance *assessment*
[calculation] is made with respect to—
(a)  all of the children with respect to whom an order falling within paragraph
      (1) is in force; or
(b)  one or more but not all of the children with respect to whom an order
      falling within paragraph (1) is in force and where the amount payable
      under the order to or for the benefit of each child is separately specified,
that order shall, so far as it relates to the making or securing of periodical
payments to or for the benefit of the children with respect to whom the
maintenance *assessment* [calculation] has been made, cease to have effect [on the
effective date of the maintenance calculation].
(3) The provisions of paragraph (2) shall not apply where a maintenance order
has been made in accordance with section 8(7) or (8) of the Act.
(4) In Scotland, where—
(a)  an order has ceased to have effect by virtue of the provisions of paragraph
      (2) to the extent specified in that paragraph; and
(b)  *a child support officer* [the Secretary of State] no longer has jurisdiction to
      make a maintenance *assessment* [calculation] with respect to a child with
      respect to whom the order ceased to have effect,

that order shall, so far as it relates to that child, again have effect from the date *a child support officer* [the Secretary of State] no longer has jurisdiction to make a maintenance *assessment* [calculation] with respect to that child.

(5) *[Subject to regulation 33(7) of the Maintenance Assessment Procedure Regulations,] where a maintenance assessment is made with respect to children with respect to whom an order falling within paragraph (1) is in force, the effective date of that assessment shall be two days after the assessment is made.*

(6) *Where the provisions of paragraph (2) apply to an order, that part of the order to which those provisions apply shall cease to have effect from the effective date of the maintenance assessment.*

[(7) *Where at the time an interim maintenance assessment was made there was in force with respect to children in respect of whom that interim maintenance assessment was made an order falling within paragraph (1), the effective date of a maintenance assessment subsequently made in accordance with Part I of Schedule 1 to the Act in respect of those children shall be the effective date of that interim maintenance assessment as determined under paragraph (5).]*

[(8) *[Subject to regulation 33(7) of the Maintenance Assessment Procedure Regulations,] where—*

   (a) *a maintenance assessment is made in accordance with Part I of Schedule 1 to the Act in respect of children with respect to whom an order falling within paragraph (1) was in force; and*

   (b) *that order ceases to have effect on or after 18th April 1995, for reasons other than the making of an interim maintenance assessment, but prior to the date on which the maintenance assessment is made and after—*

      (i) *the date on which a maintenance enquiry form referred to in regulation 5(2) of the Maintenance Assessment Procedure Regulations was given or sent to the absent parent, where the application for a maintenance assessment was made by a person with care or a child under section 7 of the Act; or*

      (ii) *the date on which a maintenance application which complies with the provisions of regulation 2 of the Maintenance Assessment Procedure Regulations was received by the Secretary of State from an absent parent,*

*the effective date of that maintenance assessment shall be the day following that on which the court order ceased to have effect.]*

**Note.** Para (1) substituted by SI 1995/1045, reg 27(2). In para (2) word "assessment" in both places it occurs substituted by words "calculation" in square brackets and in para (a) words "on the effective date of the maintenance calculation" in square brackets inserted by SI 2001/161, regs 2(2), 8(1)(a) as from 3 March 2003 in relation to certain cases; for effect and transitional provisions see SI 2001/161, reg 1(3)(d), 10(Z1), (1), (3) and SI 2003/192, arts 3, 8, Schedule.

In para (4) words "a child support officer" in both places substituted by words "the Secretary of State" in square brackets by SI 1999/1510, art 31(1) as from 1 June 1999. In para (4) word "assessment" in both places it occurs substituted by words "calculation" in square brackets by SI 2001/161, reg 2(2) as from 3 March 2003 in relation to certain cases; for effect and transitional provisions see SI 2001/161, reg 1(3)(d), 10(Z1), (1), (3) and SI 2003/192, arts 3, 8, Schedule.

Paras (5)–(8) revoked by SI 2001/161, reg 8(1)(b) ) as from 3 March 2003 in relation to certain cases; for effect and transitional provisions see SI 2001/161, reg 1(3)(d), 10(Z1), (1), (3) and SI 2003/192, arts 3, 8, Schedule. In para (5) words "Subject to regulation 33(7) of the Maintenance Assessment Procedure Regulations," in square brackets inserted by SI 1995/3261, reg 13. Para (7) inserted by SI 1995/123, reg 3. Para (8) inserted by SI 1995/1045, reg 27(3) and words in square brackets inserted by SI 1995/3261, reg 13.

*Relationship between maintenance assessments and certain agreements*

**4.** (1) Maintenance agreements within the meaning of section 9(1) of the Act are agreements of a kind prescribed for the purposes of section 10(2) of the Act.

(2) Where a maintenance assessment [calculation] is made with respect to—

(a) all of the children with respect to whom an agreement falling within paragraph (1) is in force; or

(b) one or more but not all of the children with respect to whom an agreement falling within paragraph (1) is in force and where the amount payable under the agreement to or for the benefit of each child is separately specified,

that agreement shall, so far as it relates to the making or securing of periodical payments to or for the benefit of the children with respect to whom the maintenance *assessment* [calculation] has been made, become unenforceable from the effective date of the *assessment* [calculation].

(3) Where an agreement becomes unenforceable under the provisions of paragraph (2) to the extent specified in that paragraph, it shall remain unenforceable in relation to a particular child until such date as *a child support officer* [the Secretary of State] no longer has jurisdiction to make a maintenance *assessment* [calculation] with respect to that child.

**Note.** In paras (2), (3) word "assessment" in each place it occurs substituted by words "calculation" in square brackets by SI 2001/161, reg 2(2) as from 3 March 2003 in relation to certain cases; for effect and transitional provisions see SI 2001/161, reg 1(3)(d), 10(Z1), (1), (3) and SI 2003/192, arts 3, 8, Schedule. In para (3) words "a child support officer" substituted by words "the Secretary of State" in square brackets by SI 1999/1510, art 31(1) as from 1 June 1999.

*Notifications by child support officers [the Secretary of State]*

**5.** (1) Where *a child support officer* [the Secretary of State] is aware that an order of a kind prescribed in paragraph (2) is in force and considers that the making of a maintenance *assessment* [calculation] has affected, or is likely to affect, that order, he shall notify the persons prescribed in paragraph (3) in respect of whom that maintenance *assessment* [calculation] is in force, and the persons prescribed in paragraph (4) holding office in the court where the order in question was made or subsequently registered, of the *assessment* [calculation] and its effective date.

(2) The prescribed orders are those made under an enactment mentioned in regulation 3(1).

(3) The prescribed persons in respect of whom the maintenance *assessment* [calculation] is in force are—

(a) a person with care;

(b) *an absent parent* [a non-resident parent];

(c) a person who is treated as *an absent parent* [a non-resident parent] under *regulation 20 of the Maintenance Assessments and Special Cases Regulations* [regulation 8 of the Maintenance Calculations and Special Cases Regulations];

(d) a child who has made an application for a maintenance *assessment* [calculation] under section 7 of the Act.

(4) The prescribed person holding office in the court where the order in question was made or subsequently registered is—

(a) in England and Wales—

  (i) in relation to the High Court, the senior district judge of the principal registry of the Family Division or, where proceedings were instituted in a district registry, the district judge;

  (ii) in relation to a county court, the proper officer of that court within the meaning of Order 1, Rule 3 of the County Court Rules 1981;

  (iii) in relation to a magistrates' court, the *clerk to the justices of* [justices' chief executive for] that court;

(b) in Scotland—

  (i) in relation to the Court of Session, the Deputy Principal Clerk of Session;

  (ii) in relation to a sheriff court, the sheriff clerk.

**Note.** Provision heading: words "child support officers" substituted by words "the Secretary of State" in square brackets by SI 1999/1510, art 31(2) as from 1 June 1999: see SI 1999/1510, art 3(1). In para (1) words "a child support officer" substituted by words "the Secretary of State" in square brackets substituted by SI 1999/1510, art 31(1) as from 1 June 1999: see SI 1999/1510, art 3(1). In paras (1), (3) word "assessment" in each place it occurs substituted by words "calculation" in square brackets by SI 2001/161, reg 2(2) as from 3 March 2003 in relation to certain cases; for effect and transitional provisions see SI 2001/161, reg 1(3)(d), 10(Z1), (1), (3) and SI 2003/192, arts 3, 8, Schedule. In para (3)(b), (c) words "an absent parent" substituted by words "a non-resident parent" in square brackets and in para (3)(c) words "regulation 20 of the Maintenance Assessments and Special Cases Regulations" substituted by words "regulation 8 of the Maintenance Calculations and Special Cases Regulations" in square brackets by SI 2001/161, regs 2(1), 3(2) as from 3 March 2003 in relation to certain cases; for effect and transitional provisions see SI 2001/161, reg 1(3)(d), 10(Z1), (1), (3) and SI 2003/192, arts 3, 8, Schedule. In para (4)(a)(iii) words "clerk to the justices of" substituted by words "justices' chief executive for" in square brackets by SI 2001/161, reg 4 as from 1 April 2001.

*Notification by the court*

**6.** (1) Where a court is aware that a maintenance *assessment* [calculation] is in force and makes an order mentioned in regulation 3(1) which it considers has affected, or is likely to affect, that *assessment* [calculation], the person prescribed in paragraph (2) shall notify the Secretary of State to that effect.

(2) The prescribed person is the person holding the office specified below in the court where the order in question was made or subsequently registered—

(a) in England and Wales—
    (i) in relation to the High Court, the senior district judge of the principal registry of the Family Division or, where proceedings were instituted in a district registry, the district judge;
    (ii) in relation to a county court, the proper officer of that court within the meaning of Order 1, Rule 3 of the County Court Rules 1981;
    (iii) in relation to a magistrates' court, the *clerk to the justices of* [justices' chief executive for] that court;

(b) in Scotland—
    (i) in relation to the Court of Session, the Deputy Principal Clerk of Session;
    (ii) in relation to a sheriff court, the sheriff clerk.

**Note.** In para (1) word "assessment" in both places it occurs substituted by words "calculation" in square brackets by SI 2001/161, reg 2(2) as from 3 March 2003 in relation to certain cases; for effect and transitional provisions see SI 2001/161, reg 1(3)(d), 10(Z1), (1), (3) and SI 2003/192, arts 3, 8, Schedule. In para (2)(a)(iii) words "clerk to the justices of" substituted by words "justices' chief executive for" in square brackets by SI 2001/161, reg 4 as from 1 April 2001.

*Cancellation of a maintenance assessment on grounds of lack of jurisdiction*

**7.** (1) Where—
(a) a person with care;
(b) an absent parent; or
(c) a qualifying child

with respect to whom a maintenance assessment is in force ceases to be habitually resident in the United Kingdom, *a child support officer* [the Secretary of State] shall cancel that assessment.

(2) Where the person with care is not an individual, paragraph (1) shall apply as if sub-paragraph (a) were omitted.

(3) Where *a child support officer* [the Secretary of State] cancels a maintenance assessment under paragraph (1) or by virtue of paragraph (2), the assessment shall cease to have effect from the date that *the child support officer* [the Secretary of State] determines is the date on which—

(a) where paragraph (1) applies, the person with care, absent parent or qualifying child; or

(b) where paragraph (2) applies, the absent parent or qualifying child

with respect to whom the assessment was made ceases to be habitually resident in the United Kingdom.

[(4) Where a parent is treated as an absent parent for the purposes of the Act and of the Maintenance Assessments and Special Cases Regulations by virtue of regulation 20 of those Regulations, he shall be treated as an absent parent for the purposes of paragraphs (1) to (3).]

**Note.** Revoked by SI 2001/161, reg 8(2) as from 3 March 2003 in relation to certain cases; for effect and transitional provisions see SI 2001/161, reg 1(3)(d), 10(Z1), (1), (3) and SI 2003/192, arts 3, 8, Schedule. Words "a child support officer" in each place and words "the child support officer" substituted by words "the Secretary of State" in square brackets by SI 1999/1510, art 31(1), (3) as from 1 June 1999. Para (4) inserted by SI 1993/913, reg 45.

[*Prescription for the purposes of jurisdiction*

**7A.**   (1) The companies prescribed for the purposes of section 44(2A)(c) of the Act (non-resident parents not habitually resident in the United Kingdom but employed by prescribed companies) are companies which employ employees to work outside the United Kingdom but make calculations and payment arrangements in relation to the earnings of those employees in the United Kingdom so that a deduction from earnings order may be made under section 31 of the Act in respect of the earnings of any such employee who is a liable person for the purposes of that section.

(2) The following bodies are prescribed for the purposes of section 44(2A)(d) of the Act (non-resident parents not habitually resident in the United Kingdom but employed by a prescribed body)—

(a) a National Health Service Trust established by order made under section 5 of the National Health Service and Community Care Act 1990 ("the 1990 Act") or under section 12A of the National Health Service (Scotland) Act 1978 ("the 1978 Act");

[(aa) an NHS foundation trust within the meaning of section 1(1) of the Health and Social Care (Community Health and Standards) Act 2003;]

(b) a Primary Care Trust established by order made under section 16A of the National Health Service Act 1977;

(c) a Health Authority established under section 8 of the National Health Service Act 1977 ("the 1977 Act");

(d) a Special Health Authority established under section 11 of the 1977 Act;

[(da) a Strategic Health Authority established under section 8 of the 1977 Act;]

(e) a local authority, and for this purpose "local authority" means, in relation to England, a county council, a district council, a London borough council, the Common Council of the City of London or the Council of the Isles of Scilly and, in relation to Wales, a county council or a county borough council and, in relation to Scotland, a council constituted under section 2 of the Local Government etc (Scotland) Act 1994;

(f) a Health and Social Service Trust established by order made under Article 10 of the Health and Personal Social Services (Northern Ireland) Order 1991;

(g) a Health and Social Services Board established by order made under Article 16 of the Health and Personal Social Services (Northern Ireland) Order 1972 ("the 1972 Order");

(h) the Central Services Agency established by order made under Article 26 of the 1972 Order;

(i) a Special Agency established by order made under Article 3 of the Health and Personal Social Services (Special Agencies) (Northern Ireland) Order 1990;

(j)   a Health Board constituted under section 2 of the 1978 Act; and
(k)   a Special Health Board constituted under section 2 of the 1978 Act.]

**Note.** Inserted by SI 2001/161, reg 8(3) as from 31 January 2001. Para (2)(aa) inserted by SI 2004/696, art 3(1), Sch 1, para 13 as from 1 April 2004. and para (2)(da) inserted by SI 2002/2469, reg 4, Sch 1, Pt 2, para 60 as from 1 October 2002.

*Maintenance assessments and maintenance orders made in error*

**8.**   (1)      Where—
(a)   at the time that a maintenance *assessment* [calculation] with respect to a qualifying child was made a maintenance order was in force with respect to that child;
[(aa)   the maintenance order has ceased to have effect by virtue of the provisions of regulation 3;]
(b)   the *absent parent* [non-resident parent] has made payments of child support maintenance due under that *assessment* [calculation]; and
(c)   *the child support officer [the Secretary of State] cancels that assessment on the grounds that it was made in error,* [the Secretary of State revises the decision as to the maintenance calculation under section 16 of the Act and decides that no child support maintenance was payable on the ground that the previous decision was made in error,]
the payments of child support maintenance shall be treated as payments under the maintenance order and that order shall be treated as having continued in force.
   (2) Where—
(a)   at the time that a maintenance order with respect to a qualifying child was made a maintenance *assessment* [calculation] was in force with respect to that child;
[(aa)      the maintenance *assessment* [calculation] *is cancelled or* ceases to have effect;]
(b)   the *absent parent* [non-resident parent] has made payments of maintenance due under that order; and
(c)   the maintenance order is revoked by the court on the grounds that it was made in error,
the payments under the maintenance order shall be treated as payments of child support maintenance and the maintenance *assessment* [calculation] shall be treated *as not having been cancelled [or, as the case may be,* as not having ceased to have effect].

**Note.** In paras (1), (2) word "assessment" in each place substituted by words "calculation" in square brackets by SI 2001/161, reg 2(2) as from 3 March 2003 in relation to certain cases; for effect and transitional provisions see SI 2001/161, reg 1(3)(d), 10(Z1), (1), (3) and SI 2003/192, arts 3, 8, Schedule. Para (1)(aa) inserted by SI 1993/913, reg 46.
   In paras (1)(b), (2)(b) words "absent parent" substituted by words "non-resident parent" in square brackets by SI 2001/161, reg 2(1) as from 3 March 2003 in relation to certain cases; for effect and transitional provisions see SI 2001/161, reg 1(3)(d), 10(Z1), (1), (3) and SI 2003/192, arts 3, 8, Schedule. In para (1)(c) words "the child support officer" substituted by words "the Secretary of State" in square brackets by SI 1999/1510, art 31(3) as from 1 June 1999.
   In para (1)(c) words from "[the Secretary of State]" to "made in error," substituted by words from "the Secretary of State revises" to "was made in error," in square brackets substituted by SI 2001/161, reg 9(a) as from 3 March 2003 in relation to certain cases; for effect and transitional provisions see SI 2001/161, reg 1(3)(d), 10(Z1), (1), (3) and SI 2003/192, arts 3, 8, Schedule.
   Para (2)(aa) inserted by SI 1993/913, reg 46. In para (2)(aa) words "is cancelled or" revoked by SI 2001/161, reg 9(b) as from 3 March 2003 in relation to certain cases; for effect and transitional provisions see SI 2001/161, reg 1(3)(d), 10(Z1), (1), (3) and SI 2003/192, arts 3, 8, Schedule
   In para (2) words "as not having been cancelled or, as the case may be," revoked by SI 2001/161, reg 9(c) as from 3 March 2003 in relation to certain cases; for effect and

transitional provisions see SI 2001/161, reg 1(3)(d), 10(Z1), (1), (3) and SI 2003/192, arts 3, 8, Schedule.

In para (2) words "or, as the case may be, as not having ceased to have effect" in square brackets inserted by SI 1993/913, reg 46.

*Cases in which application may be made under section 4 or 7 of the Act*

**9.**   The provisions of section 4(10) or 7(10) of the Act shall not apply to prevent an application being made under those sections after 22nd January 1996 where a decision has been made by the relevant court either that it has no power to vary or that it has no power to enforce a maintenance order in a particular case.

## JUDGMENT DEBTS (RATE OF INTEREST) ORDER 1993

**Dated** 9 March 1993

**SI 1993 No 564**

The Lord Chancellor, in exercise of the powers conferred on him by section 44 of the Administration of Justice Act 1970 and with the concurrence of the Treasury, hereby makes the following Order:

**1.**   This Order may be cited as the Judgments Debts (Rate of Interest) Order 1993 and shall come into force on 1 April 1993.

**2.**   In relation to any judgment entered up after the coming into force of this Order, section 17 of the Judgments Act 1838 shall be amended so as to substitute for the rate specified in that section, as the rate at which judgment debts shall carry interest, the rate of 8 per cent per annum.

## RECOVERY OF MAINTENANCE (UNITED STATES OF AMERICA) ORDER 1993

**Dated** 10 March 1993

**SI 1993 No 591**

Whereas Her Majesty is satisfied that arrangements have been made in the States of the United States of America specified in the Schedule to this Order to ensure that applications by persons in the United Kingdom for the recovery of maintenance from persons in those States can be entertained by courts in those States:

And whereas Her Majesty is satisfied that in the interest of reciprocity it is desirable to ensure that applications by persons in those States for the recovery of maintenance from persons in the United Kingdom can be entertained by courts in the United Kingdom:

Now, therefore, Her Majesty, in exercise of the powers conferred upon Her by sections 40 and 45(1) of the Maintenance Orders (Reciprocal Enforcement) Act 1972, is pleased, by and with the advice of Her Privy Council, to order, and it is hereby ordered, as follows—

**1.**   (1) This Order may be cited as the Recovery of Maintenance (United States of America) Order 1993.

(2) This Order shall come into force on 5 April 1993.

**2.**   In this Order, unless the context otherwise requires—

'the Act' means the Maintenance Orders (Reciprocal Enforcement) Act 1972;

'specified State' means a State specified in the Schedule to this Order.

**3.** (1) The provisions of Part II of the Act shall apply in relation to a specified State as they apply in relation to a convention country, subject to the modification set out in paragraph (2) below.

(2) After section 26(3) of the Act there shall be inserted—

'(3A) An application under subsection (1) or (2) above, for the purpose of recovering maintenance from a person in a specified State within the meaning of the Recovery of Maintenance (United States of America) Order 1993, and a certificate signed by a justice of the peace or, where the applicant is residing in Scotland, the sheriff, to the effect that the application sets forth facts from which it may be determined that the respondent owes a duty to maintain the applicant and any other person named in the application and that a court in the specified State may obtain jurisdiction of the respondent or his property, shall be registered in the court in the prescribed manner by the appropriate officer or, in Scotland, by the sheriff clerk in the Maintenance Orders (Reciprocal Enforcement) Act 1972 register.'.

**4.** The following orders are hereby revoked:

(a) the Recovery of Maintenance (United States of America) 1979;

(b) the Recovery Abroad of Maintenance (United States of America) Order 1981; and

(c) the Recovery of Maintenance (United States of America) (Variation) Order 1984.

SCHEDULE                                                                                          Article 2

|  | *Specified States* |  |
| --- | --- | --- |
| Alaska | | Colorado |
| Arizona | | Connecticut |
| Arkansas | | Delaware |
| California | | Florida |
| Georgia | | New Jersey |
| Hawaii | | New Mexico |
| Idaho | | New York |
| Illinois | | North Carolina |
| Indiana | | North Dakota |
| Iowa | | Ohio |
| Kansas | | Oklahoma |
| Kentucky | | Oregon |
| Louisiana | | Pennsylvania |
| Maine | | Rhode Island |
| Maryland | | South Dakota |
| Massachusetts | | Tennessee |
| Michigan | | Texas |
| Minnesota | | Utah |
| Missouri | | Vermont |
| Montana | | Virginia |
| Nebraska | | Washington |
| Nevada | | Wisconsin |
| New Hampshire | | Wyoming |

**RECIPROCAL ENFORCEMENT OF MAINTENANCE ORDERS (HAGUE CONVENTION COUNTRIES) ORDER 1993**

**Dated** 10 March 1993

**SI 1993 No 593**

Whereas Her Majesty is satisfied that arrangements have been made in the countries and territories specified in Schedule 1 to this Order to ensure that maintenance orders made by courts in the United Kingdom against persons in those countries and territories can be enforced there:

And whereas Her Majesty is satisfied that in the interest of reciprocity it is desirable to ensure that maintenance orders made by courts in the countries and territories specified in Schedule 1 to this Order against persons in the United Kingdom can be enforced in the United Kingdom:

Now, therefore, Her Majesty, in exercise of the powers conferred by sections 40 and 45(1) of the Maintenance Orders (Reciprocal Enforcement) Act 1972 is pleased, by and with the advice of Her Privy Council, to order, and it is hereby ordered, as follows—

**1.**   This Order may be cited as the Reciprocal Enforcement of Maintenance Orders (Hague Convention Countries) Order 1993 and shall come into force on 5th April 1993.

**2.**   In this Order, unless the context otherwise requires—

'Act' means the Maintenance Orders (Reciprocal Enforcement) Act 1972;

'court in a Hague Convention country' includes any judicial or administrative authority in a Hague Convention country;

'Hague Convention' means the Convention on the Recognition and Enforcement of Decisions Relating to Maintenance Obligations concluded at The Hague on 2nd October 1973; and

'Hague Convention country' means a country or territory specified in Schedule 1 to this Order, being a country or territory (other than the United Kingdom) in which the Hague Convention is in force.

**3.**   (1) The provisions of Part I of the Act shall apply in relation to a Hague Convention country as they apply in relation to a reciprocating country, subject to the exceptions, adaptations and modifications set out in Schedule 2 to this Order.

(2) Accordingly, Part I of the Act shall, in relation to—

(a)  maintenance orders made by courts in the United Kingdom against persons in a Hague Convention country, and

(b)  maintenance orders made by courts in a Hague Convention country against persons in the United Kingdom,

have effect as set out in Schedule 3 to this Order.

**4.**   The Orders specified in Schedule 4 to this Order are hereby revoked.

SCHEDULE 1

Article 2

HAGUE CONVENTION COUNTRIES

Australia
Denmark
Federal Republic of Germany
Finland
France
Italy
Luxembourg
Netherlands (Kingdom in Europe and Netherlands Antilles)
Norway

Portugal
Republic of Estonia
Republic of Poland
Slovakia
Spain
Sweden
Switzerland
The Czech Republic
Turkey

**Note.** Entry 'Australia' inserted by SI 2002/2838, art 2 as from 15 January 2003. Entries 'Republic of Estonia', 'Republic of Poland' inserted by SI 1999/1318, art 2 as from 28 June 1999. Entry 'Spain' inserted by SI 2001/2567, art 2 as from 31 August 2001.

SCHEDULE 2         Article 3(1)

MODIFICATIONS TO PART I OF THE ACT

**1.** Section 1 shall not apply.
**2.** (1) Section 2 shall be amended as follows.
(2) In subsection (1)—
(a) for the words "before or after the commencement of this Part of this Act" there shall be substituted the words "before, on or after 5th April 1993";
(b) the words "or has assets" shall be omitted;
(c) for the word "reciprocating" there shall be substituted the words "Hague Convention"; and
(d) before the word "enforcement" there shall be inserted the words "recognition and".
(3) In subsection (2), for the words "provisional order" there shall be substituted the words "maintenance order made under section 3 of this Act".
(4) In subsection (4)—
(a) the words "or has assets" shall be omitted;
(b) for the word "reciprocating" where it first occurs there shall be substituted the words "Hague Convention";
(c) for paragraph (b), there shall be substituted—
"(b) a certificate signed by that officer certifying that the order is enforceable and that it is no longer subject to the ordinary forms of review;";
(d) the words "and the nature and location of his assets in that country", in both places where they occur, shall be omitted;
(e) in paragraph (e), the word "and" shall be omitted;
(f) after paragraph (f), there shall be inserted;
"(g) a written statement signed by that officer as to whether or not the payer appeared in the proceedings in which the maintenance order was made and, if he did not appear, the original or a certified copy of a document which establishes that notice of the institution of the proceedings, including notice of the substance of the claim, was served on the payer;";
(h) a document which establishes that notice of the order was sent to the payer; and
(i) a written statement signed by that officer as to whether or not the payee received legal aid either in the said proceedings or in connection with the said application,";
(g) after the words "that officer" where they last occur there shall be inserted the words ", in the case of a court in England and Wales or Northern Ireland, to the Lord Chancellor, or in the case of a court in Scotland,";
(h) after the words "transmitted by" there shall be inserted the words "the Lord Chancellor, or, as the case may be,"; and

(i) for the words "responsible authority in the reciprocating country" there shall be substituted the words "appropriate authority in the Hague Convention country".

(5) In subsection (5), after the words "applies, and" there shall be inserted the words "subject to section 5".

**3.** (1) Section 3 shall be amended as follows.

(2) For subsection (1) there shall be substituted—

"(1) Where an application is made to a magistrates' court for a maintenance order by a person who is habitually resident in England and Wales against a person residing in a Hague Convention country and the court would have jurisdiction to determine the application under the Domestic Proceedings and Magistrates' Courts Act 1978 or the Children Act 1989 if at any time when the proceedings were instituted that person—

(a) were residing in England and Wales, and

(b) received reasonable notice of the date of the hearing of the application,

the court shall subject to the following provisions of this subsection have jurisdiction to determine the application."

(3) Subsection (2) shall be omitted.

(4) For subsection (5) there shall be substituted—

"(5) On the making of an application to which subsection (1) above applies, the following documents, that is to say—

(a) notice of the institution of the proceedings, including notice of the substance of the application;

(b) a statement signed by the prescribed officer of the court giving such information as he possesses as to the whereabouts of the respondent;

(c) a statement giving such information as the officer possesses for facilitating the identification of the respondent; and

(d) where available, a photograph of the respondent,

shall be sent by that officer to the Lord Chancellor with a view to their being transmitted by the Lord Chancellor to the appropriate authority in the Hague Convention country in which the respondent is residing for service on him of the document mentioned in paragraph (a) above if the Lord Chancellor is satisfied that the statement relating to the whereabouts of the respondent gives sufficient information to justify that being done.".

(5) For subsection (6) there shall be substituted—

"(6) In considering whether or not to make a maintenance order pursuant to an application to which subsection (1) above applies the court shall take into account any representations made and any evidence adduced by or on behalf of the respondent.

(6A) Where the respondent makes any representations or adduces any evidence, a copy of the representations or evidence shall be served on the applicant by the prescribed officer of the court before the hearing.

(6B) The prescribed officer of the court shall give the respondent notice in writing of the date fixed for the hearing by sending the notice by post addressed to his last known or usual place of abode.

(6C) A maintenance order pursuant to an application to which subsection (1) above applies shall not be made unless the document mentioned in paragraph (a) of subsection (5) above has been served on the respondent in accordance with the law for the service of such documents in the Hague Convention country in which he is residing or in such other manner as may be authorised by the Lord Chancellor not less than six weeks previously.

(6D) Where a maintenance order has been made under this section, the prescribed officer of the court shall send the following documents, that is to say—

(a) a certified copy of the order;

(b) a certificate signed by that officer certifying that the order is enforceable and that it is no longer subject to the ordinary forms of review;

(c) a written statement, signed by that officer as to whether or not the respondent appeared in the proceedings in which the order was made, and, if he did not appear, the original or a certified copy of a document which establishes that the document mentioned in paragraph (a) of subsection (5) above has been served on the payer in accordance with subsection (6C) above;

(d) a document which establishes that notice of the order was sent to the respondent; and

(e) a written statement signed by that officer as to whether or not the applicant received legal aid in the proceedings,

to the Lord Chancellor with a view to their being transmitted by him to the appropriate authority in the Hague Convention country in which the respondent resides for recognition and enforcement of the order.

(6E) A maintenance order made under this section may, subject to section 5 of this Act, be enforced, varied or revoked in like manner as any other maintenance order made by a magistrates' court.".

(6) In subsection (7)—

(a) after the words "a magistrates' court" there shall be inserted the words "by a person who is habitually resident in Northern Ireland"; and

(b) for the word "reciprocating" there shall be substituted the words "Hague Convention".

**4.** (1) Section 4 shall be amended as follows.

(2) For subsection (1) there shall be substituted the following subsections—

"(1) The sheriff shall have jurisdiction in any action to which this section applies if at the time when the proceedings were instituted—

(a) the pursuer is habitually resident in Scotland and resides within the jurisdiction of the sheriff; and

(b) the sheriff is satisfied that, to the best of the information or belief of the pursuer, the defender is residing in a Hague Convention country; and

(c) the sheriff would not, apart from this subsection, have jurisdiction in that action.

(2) This section applies to any action for the payment, variation or revocation of aliment which is competent in the sheriff court, and includes an action of affiliation and aliment, but does not include an action of separation and aliment or adherence and aliment, or any action containing a crave for the custody of a child.".

(3) In subsection (3), for the words "referred to in" there shall be substituted "in which the sheriff has jurisdiction by virtue of".

(4) For subsection (4) there shall be substituted—

"(4) In any action in which the sheriff has jurisdiction by virtue of subsection (1) above, no decree shall be granted in favour of the pursuer unless a copy of the initial writ or summons has been served on the defender in the prescribed manner and in sufficient time to enable him to arrange for his defence.".

(5) Subsections (5) and (6) shall be omitted.

**5.** For section 5 there shall be substituted—

**"5.** (1) This section applies to a maintenance order a certified copy of which has been sent to a Hague Convention country for recognition and enforcement of the order.

(2) The jurisdiction of a magistrates' court to revoke or vary a maintenance order shall be exercisable notwithstanding that the proceedings for the revocation or variation, as the case may be, of the order are brought by or against a person residing in a Hague Convention country.

(3) Where subsection (1) of section 60 of the Magistrates' Courts Act 1980 (revocation, variation etc of orders for periodical payment) applies in relation to a maintenance order to which this section applies, that subsection shall have effect as if for the words "by order on complaint," there were substituted "on an application being made, by order".

(4) Where an application is made by the payee to a court in England and Wales or Northern Ireland for the variation or revocation of an order to which this section applies, and the payer is residing in a Hague Convention country, the prescribed officer of the court shall send to the Lord Chancellor notice of the institution of the proceedings, including notice of the substance of the application, with a view to its being transmitted by him to the appropriate authority in the Hague Convention country for service on the payer.

(5) Where an application is made by the payee to a court in England and Wales or Northern Ireland for the variation or revocation of an order to which this section applies, and the payer is residing in a Hague Convention country—

(a)  the court, in considering whether or not to vary or revoke the order, shall take into account any representations made and any evidence adduced by or on behalf of the payer;

(b)  a copy of any such representations or evidence shall be served on the payee in the prescribed manner before the hearing;

(c)  the prescribed officer of the court shall give the payer notice in writing of the date fixed for the hearing by sending the notice by post addressed to his last known or usual place of abode.

(6) Where an application is made by the payee to a court in England and Wales or Northern Ireland for the variation or revocation of an order to which this section applies, and the payer is residing in a Hague Convention country, the order shall not be varied or revoked unless the document mentioned in subsection (4) above has been served on the payer in accordance with the law for the service of such a document in the Hague Convention country not less than six weeks previously.

(7) Where an application is made by the payer to a court in England and Wales or Northern Ireland for the variation or revocation of an order to which this section applies, the prescribed officer of the court shall arrange for the service of the document mentioned in subsection (4) above on the payee.

(8) Where an order to which this section applies has been varied or revoked by a court in the United Kingdom the prescribed officer of the court shall send the following documents, that is to say—

(a)  a certified copy of the order of variation or revocation;

(b)  a certificate signed by that officer certifying that the order of variation or revocation is enforceable and that it is no longer subject to the ordinary forms of review;

(c)  a written statement, signed by that officer as to whether or not the respondent or, in Scotland the defender, appeared in the proceedings for the variation or revocation of the order, and, if he did not appear, the original or a certified copy of a document which establishes that notice of the institution of the proceedings has been served on the respondent, or, as the case may be, the defender; and

(d)  a document which establishes that notice of the order of variation or revocation was sent to the respondent; and

(e)  a written statement signed by that officer as to whether or not the payer or the payee received legal aid in the proceedings,

in the case of a court in England and Wales or Northern Ireland, to the Lord Chancellor, or, in the case of a court in Scotland, to the Secretary of State, with a view to their being transmitted by him to the appropriate authority in the Hague Convention country for recognition and enforcement of the order of variation or revocation.

(9) Where a maintenance order to which this section applies has been varied by an order made by a court in the United Kingdom . . . the maintenance order shall, as from the date on which the order of variation took effect, have effect as varied by that order.

(10) Where a maintenance order to which this section applies has been revoked by an order made by a court in the United Kingdom . . . the maintenance order shall, as from the date on which the order of revocation took effect, be deemed to have ceased to have effect except as respects any arrears due under the maintenance order at that date.

(11) . . .

(12) In the application of this section to Northern Ireland, in subsection (8), for the word "respondent", in each place where it occurs, there shall be substituted "defendant".".

**6.**   For section 6 there shall be substituted—

**"6.** (1) This section applies to a maintenance order made whether before, on or after 5th April 1993 by a competent court in a Hague Convention country.

(2) Where a certified copy of an order to which this section applies is received by the Lord Chancellor or the Secretary of State from a Hague Convention country, and it appears to him that the payer under the order is residing in the United Kingdom, he shall send the copy of the order and the accompanying documents to the prescribed officer of the appropriate court.

(3) Where the prescribed officer of the appropriate court receives from the Lord Chancellor or the Secretary of State a certified copy of an order to which this section applies, he shall, subject to the following subsections, register the order in the prescribed manner in that court.

(4) Before registering an order under this section an officer of a court shall take such steps as he thinks fit for the purpose of ascertaining whether the payer under the order is residing within the jurisdiction of the court, and if after taking those steps he is satisfied that the payer is not so residing he shall return the certified copy of the order and the accompanying documents to the Lord Chancellor or the Secretary of State, as the case may be, with a statement giving such information as he possesses as to the whereabouts of the payer.

(5)

(a) The prescribed officer of the appropriate court may refuse to authorise the registration of the order if the court in the Hague Convention country by or before which the order was made did not have jurisdiction to make the order; and for these purposes a court in a Hague Convention country shall be considered to have jurisdiction if—

   (i) either the payer or the payee had his habitual residence in the Hague Convention country at the time when the proceedings were instituted; or

   (ii) the payer and the payee were nationals of that country at that time; or

   (iii) the respondent in those proceedings had submitted to the jurisdiction of the court, either expressly or by defending on the merits of the case without objecting to the jurisdiction; or

   (iv) in the case of an order made by reason of a divorce or a legal separation or a declaration that a marriage is void or annulled, the court is recognised by the law of the part of the United Kingdom in which enforcement is sought as having jurisdiction to make the order.

(b) In deciding whether a court in a Hague Convention country had jurisdiction to make an order the prescribed officer shall be bound by any finding of fact on which the court based its jurisdiction.

(6) The prescribed officer of the appropriate court may refuse to authorise the registration of the order—

    (a)  if such registration is manifestly contrary to public policy;

    (b)  if the order was obtained by fraud in connection with a matter of procedure;

    (c)  if proceedings between the same parties and having the same purpose are pending before a court in the same part of the United Kingdom and those proceedings were the first to be instituted; or

    (d)  if the order is incompatible with an order made in proceedings between the same parties and having the same purpose, either in the United Kingdom or in another country, provided that the latter order itself fulfils the conditions necessary for its registration and enforcement under this Part of this Act.

(7) Without prejudice to subsection (6) above, if the payer did not appear in the proceedings in the Hague Convention country in which the order was made, the prescribed officer of the appropriate court shall refuse to authorise the registration of the order unless notice of the institution of the proceedings, including notice of the substance of the claim, was served on the payer in accordance with the law of that Hague Convention country and if, having regard to the circumstances, the payer had sufficient time to enable him to defend the proceedings.

(8) If the order is registered under subsection (3) above, the prescribed officer of the appropriate court shall serve notice in a prescribed form on the payer and give notice to the payee that the order has been registered.

(9) The payer may, before the end of the period of one calendar month beginning with the date of service of the said notice, appeal to the court in which the order is registered to set aside the registration of the order on one of the grounds set out in paragraphs (5), (6) and (7) above.

(10) If the payer appeals to the court in which the order is registered to set aside the registration of the order, the prescribed officer of the court shall give notice to the payee of the appeal and of the date of the hearing of the appeal.

(11) If the prescribed officer refuses to register the order, he shall give notice to the payee in a prescribed form that registration has been refused.

(12) A payee to whom notice has been given by the prescribed officer of any court under subsection (11) above may, before the end of the period of *one calendar month* [two calendar months] beginning with the date when notice was given, appeal to that court against the refusal to register the order.

(13) If the payee appeals to the court against the refusal to register the order, the prescribed officer of the court shall give notice to the payer of the appeal and of the date of the hearing of the appeal.

(14)  In the application of this section to Scotland—

    (a)  in subsection (8), for the words "serve notice in a prescribed form on" there shall be substituted the words "intimate to in the prescribed manner";

    (b)  in subsection (9), for the words "service of the said notice" there shall be substituted the words "the said intimation";

    (c)  in subsections (9), (10), (12) and (13), for any reference to an appeal there shall be substituted a reference to an application and cognate expressions shall be construed accordingly; and

    (d)  in subsection (11), for the words "in a prescribed form" there shall be substituted the words "in the prescribed manner".

(15)  In the application of this section to Northern Ireland, in subsection (5), for the word "respondent" there shall be substituted "defendant"."

**7.**   Section 7 shall not apply.

**8.** (1) Section 8 shall be amended as follows.

(2) In subsection (1), for the words "subsection (2)" there shall be substituted the words "subsections (2), (2A) and (2B)".

(3) After subsection (2), there shall be inserted—

"(2A) Where in a maintenance order made in a Hague Convention country there are provisions which are not enforceable under this Part of this Act, this section shall apply only to the remaining provisions of the order.

(2B) The payee under a registered order may request the partial enforcement of that order.".

(4) In subsection (4), after the words "magistrates' court" where they first occur, there shall be inserted the words "in England and Wales".

(5) In subsection (5), the words "or facilitating the enforcement of" shall be omitted.

(6) For subsections (7), (8) and (9) there shall be substituted—

"(7) Subject to subsection (8) below, a sum of money payable under a registered order shall be payable in accordance with the order, or such part thereof as the payee may have requested should be enforced, as from the date on which the order took effect.

(8) Where a registered order was made by a court in a Hague Convention country before the date of the entry into force of the Hague Convention between the United Kingdom and that country, no sum of money falling due before that date shall be payable in accordance with the order.

(9) In the application of this section to Scotland—

(a) subsections (2) to (5) shall be omitted; and

(b) in subsection (6), for the word "evidence" there shall be substituted the words "sufficient evidence".".

**9.** (1) Section 9 shall be amended as follows.

(2) For subsection (1) there shall be substituted—

"(1) Subject to the provisions of this section—

(a) the registering court shall have the like power, on an application made by the payer or payee under a registered order, to vary [the method of payment of] the order as if it had been made by the registering court and as if that court had had jurisdiction to make it;

(b) the jurisdiction of a magistrates' court to vary [the method of payment of] a registered order shall be exercisable notwithstanding that the proceedings for the variation of the order are brought by or against a person residing in a Hague Convention country.".

[(2A) Subsection (1ZA) shall be amended as follows—

(a) at the end of paragraph (za), there shall be inserted the words

"and for the words "revoke, revive or vary the order", there were substituted "vary the order in accordance with subsection (3)"";

(b) after paragraph (za), there shall be inserted the following paragraph—

"(zab) as if subsection (2) were omitted;";

(c) in paragraph (a), for the words from "as if in subsection (3)" to "there were inserted—", there shall be substituted

"as if in subsection (3)—

(i) for the words "shall include", there were substituted "means the,";

(ii) for the words "paragraphs (a) to (d) of section 59(3) above" there were substituted "subsection (3A) below"; and

(iii) after that subsection there were inserted—".

(2B) Subsection (1ZB) shall be amended as follows—

(a) at the end of paragraph (za), there shall be inserted the words—

"and for the words "revoke, revive or vary the order", there were substituted "vary the order in accordance with paragraph (3)"";

(b) after paragraph (za), there shall be inserted the following paragraph—
"(zab) as if paragraph (2) were omitted;";
(c) in paragraph (a), for the words from "as if in paragraph (3)" to "there were inserted—", there shall be substituted
"as if in paragraph (3)—
    (i) for the words "shall include", there were substituted "means the";
    (ii) for the words "sub-paragraphs (a) to (d) of Article 85(3)" there were substituted "paragraph (3A)"; and
    (iii) after that paragraph there were inserted—".]
(3) Subsections (1A) and (1B) shall be omitted.
(4) For subsections (2) to (11) there shall be substituted—
"(2) The registering court shall not vary a registered order unless—
(a) the payer under the order had his habitual residence in the United Kingdom at the time when the proceedings to vary the order were instituted; or
(b) the respondent in those proceedings had submitted to the jurisdiction of the registering court, either expressly or by defending on the merits of the case without objecting to the jurisdiction.
(3) . . .
(4) . . .
(5) . . .
(6) . . .
(7) . . .
(8) Where a registered order has been varied by the registering court or by a court in a Hague Convention country, the prescribed officer of the registering court shall register the variation order in the prescribed manner.
(9) Where a registered order has been varied by the registering court or by a court in a Hague Convention country, the registered order shall, as from the date on which the variation order took effect, have effect as so varied.
(10) In the application of this section to Northern Ireland, in subsections (2) and (7), for the word "respondent" in each place where it occurs, there shall be substituted "defendant".
[(11) This section shall not apply to a court in Scotland.]".

**10.** (1) Section 10 shall be amended as follows.
(2) For subsection (1) there shall be substituted—
"(1) Where a registered order is revoked by an order made by a court in a Hague Convention country and notice of the revocation is received by the registering court, the prescribed officer of the registering court shall cancel the registration; but any arrears due under the registered order at the date on which the order of revocation took effect, other than, in the case of a registered order made by a court in a Hague Convention country before the date of the entry into force of the Hague Convention between the United Kingdom and that country, arrears due before that date, shall continue to be recoverable as if the registration had not been cancelled.".
(3) In subsection (2)—
(a) in relation to England and Wales and Northern Ireland, for the words "is not residing within the jurisdiction of that court and has no assets within that jurisdiction against which the order can be effectively enforced" there shall be substituted the words "has ceased to reside within the jurisdiction of that court"; and
(b) in relation to Scotland, for those words there shall be substituted the words "is not residing in Scotland".
(4) In subsection (3), the words "or has assets" shall be omitted.
(5) In subsection (5)—
(a) for the words "Secretary of State" there shall be substituted the words "Lord Chancellor"; and

(b) for the words "residing or has assets" there shall be substituted the words "still residing".

(6) In subsection (6)—

(a) the words "or has assets" shall be omitted;

(b) for the words "residing and has no assets within the jurisdiction of the court" there shall be substituted the words "so residing"; and

(c) for the words "Secretary of State" there shall be substituted the words "Lord Chancellor".

(7) In subsection (7)—

(a) for the words "Secretary of State" there shall be substituted the words "Lord Chancellor"; and

(b) the words "and the nature and location of his assets" shall be omitted.

(8) In subsection (8), in paragraph (a), the word "and" shall be omitted and after paragraph (b) there shall be inserted—

"; and"

(c) for the words "Lord Chancellor", in each place where they occur, there shall be substituted the words "Secretary of State".

**11.**   (1) Section 11 shall be amended as follows.

(2) In subsection (1)—

(a) the words "at any time" shall be omitted;

(b) after the words "appears to" there shall be inserted the words "the Lord Chancellor or";

(c) the words "and has no assets" shall be omitted;

(d) for the word "responsible" where it first occurs there shall be substituted the word "appropriate";

(e) the words "or, if having regard to all the circumstances he thinks it proper to do so, to the responsible authority in another reciprocating country" and the words "and a certified copy of any order varying that order" shall be omitted;

(f) after the words "information as" there shall be inserted the words "the Lord Chancellor or"; and

(g) the words "and the nature and location of his assets" shall be omitted.

(3) Subsection (2) shall be omitted.

**12.**   For section 12 there shall be substituted—

"**12.**   Where in pursuance of section 9 above a registering court makes or refuses to make an order varying a registered order, the payer or the payee under the registered order shall have the like right of appeal (if any) from the order of variation or from the refusal to make it as he would have if the registered order had been made by the registering court.".

**13.**   (1) Section 13 shall be amended as follows.

(2) In subsection (1)—

(a) in paragraph (a), for the word "reciprocating" there shall be substituted the words "Hague Convention";

(b) after paragraph (c) there shall be added—

"or

(d) a document purporting to be signed by a judicial officer, official or other competent person in a Hague Convention country which establishes that certain documents were served on a person,".

(3) In subsection (2), for the words "judge, magistrate" there shall be substituted the words "judicial officer".

(4) In subsection (3), the word "magistrate" shall be omitted.

**14.**   (1)  Section 14 shall be amended as follows.

(2) In subsection (1)—

(a)  for the word "reciprocating" there shall be substituted the words "Hague Convention";

(b)  for the words from "in the prescribed manner" to the end there shall be substituted the following words—

"by the prescribed officer of the court—

(a)  in England and Wales or Northern Ireland, to the Lord Chancellor, or

(b)  in Scotland, to the Secretary of State,

for transmission to the appropriate authority in the Hague Convention country".

(3) In subsection (2), for paragraphs (a) and (b) there shall be substituted the words "out of moneys provided by Parliament".

(4) In subsections (3) and (4) respectively, for the word "reciprocating" there shall be substituted the words "Hague Convention".

(5) For subsection (5) there shall be substituted—

"(5)   A court in—

(a)  England and Wales or Northern Ireland may for the purpose of any proceedings in that court under this Part of this Act relating to a maintenance order to which this Part of this Act applies send to the Lord Chancellor, or

(b)  Scotland may for the purpose of such proceedings in that court relating to such an action, send to the Secretary of State,

for transmission to the appropriate authority in a Hague Convention country a request for a court in a Hague Convention country to take or provide evidence relating to such matters as may be specified in the request.".

**15.**   (1)  Section 15 shall be amended as follows.

(2) In paragraphs (a) and (c) respectively, for the word "reciprocating" there shall be substituted the words "Hague Convention".

(3) The word "magistrate" in each place where it occurs shall be omitted.

**16.**   (1)  Section 16 shall be amended as follows.

(2) In subsections (3) and (5)(a), for the word "reciprocating" there shall be substituted the words "Hague Convention".

(3) In subsection (5)(a), the words "or (if earlier) the date on which it is confirmed by a court in the United Kingdom" shall be omitted.

(4) In subsection (5)(b), for the words "a court in the United Kingdom or (if earlier) the date on which the last order varying that order is confirmed by such a court" there shall be substituted the words "the registering court".

**17.**   (1)  Section 17 shall be amended as follows.

(2) In subsection (5A), for the word "reciprocating" there shall be substituted the words "Hague Convention".

(3) For subsections (6) and (7) there shall be substituted—

"(6) A magistrates' court in Northern Ireland shall have jurisdiction to hear a complaint for the variation or revocation—

(a)  of a maintenance order made by such a court, and to which section 5 of this Act applies; or

(b)  to hear a complaint for the variation of a registered order which is registered in that court,

if the defendant to the complaint is residing in a Hague Convention country and if the court would have had jurisdiction to hear the complaint had the defendant been residing in Northern Ireland and been served with a summons to appear before the court to answer the complaint.

(7) Where the respondent to an application—

(a)  for the variation or revocation of a maintenance order made by a magistrates' court, and to which section 5 of this Act applies; or

(b) for the variation of a registered order registered in a magistrates' court, does not appear at the time and place appointed for the hearing of the application, but the court is satisfied that the respondent is residing in a Hague Convention country and that the requirements of section 5(4), (6) or (7) or section 9(3), as the case may be, have been complied with, the court may proceed to hear and determine the application at the time and place appointed for the hearing or for any adjourned hearing as if the respondent had appeared at that time and place.".

**18.** (1) Section 18 shall be amended as follows.

(2) In subsection (1)(b), (c), (d) and (f) respectively, for the word "reciprocating" there shall be substituted the words "Hague Convention".

(3) Subsection (1)(e) shall be omitted.

**19.** (1) Section 19 shall be amended as follows.

(2) In paragraphs (a), (b), (c) and (e) respectively, for the word "reciprocating" there shall be substituted the words "Hague Convention".

(3) Paragraph (d) shall be omitted.

**20.** Section 20 shall not apply.

**21.** (1) Section 21(1) shall be amended as follows.

(2) In subsection (1)—

(a) after the word "Act" where it first occurs there shall be inserted the words "unless the context otherwise requires";

(b) in the definition of "the appropriate court" the words "or having assets", in both places where they occur, and the words "or has assets" shall be omitted and for the words "a sheriff court" there shall be substituted the words "the sheriff court";

(c) in the definition of "certificate of arrears" for the words "or, as the case may be" to the end there shall be substituted the words "except any arrears the accrued before the date of the entry into force of the Hague Convention between the United Kingdom and the Hague Convention country in which the payer is residing or, as the case may be, that to the best of his information or belief there are no arrears due thereunder at the date of the certificate;";

(d) in the definition of "court" at the end there shall be inserted the words "and 'competent court in a Hague Convention country' means a court having jurisdiction on one of the grounds specified in section 6(5)(a) above;";

(e) for the definition of "maintenance order" there shall be substituted the following definition—

"'maintenance order' means an order (however described), including any settlement made by or before a competent court in a Hague Convention country, of any of the following descriptions, and, in the case of an order which is not limited to the following descriptions, the part of the order which is so limited, that is to say—

    (a) an order (including an affiliation order or order consequent upon an affiliation order) which provides for the periodical payment of sums of money towards the maintenance of any person, being a person whom the person liable to make payments under the order is, according to the law applied in the place where the order was made, liable to maintain;

    (AA) an order which has been made in Scotland, on or after the granting of a decree of divorce, for the payment of a periodical allowance by one party to the marriage to the other party;

    (b) an affiliation order or order consequent upon an affiliation order, being an order which provides for the payment by a person adjudged, found or declared to be a child's father of expenses incidental to the child's birth or, where the child has died, of his funeral expenses; and

(c) an order within the foregoing provisions of this definition made against a payer on the application of a public body which claims reimbursement of sums of money payable under the order with respect to the payee if the reimbursement can be obtained by the public body under the law to which it is subject,

and in the case of a maintenance order which has been varied (including a maintenance order which has been varied either by a court in the United Kingdom or by a competent court in a Hague Convention country whether or not the original order was made by such a court), means that order as varied:

Provided that the expression 'maintenance order' shall not include an order made in a Hague Convention country of a description which that country or the United Kingdom has reserved the right under Article 26 of the Hague Convention not to recognise or enforce;";

(f) in the definition of "order" before the words "as respects Scotland" there shall be inserted the words "means an order however described giving effect to a decision rendered by a court and";

(g) in the definition of "payee" at the end there shall be inserted the words "and includes a public body which has provided benefits for the payee and which is entitled *ipso jure* under the law to which it is subject to claim enforcement of the said order to the extent of the benefits so provided in place of the said person;";

(h) the definitions of "provisional order" and "reciprocating country" shall be omitted;

(i) in the definition of "registered order" there shall be inserted at the end the words "and 'registered' and 'registration' shall be construed accordingly;"; and

(j) the definition of "the responsible authority" shall be omitted.

(3) Subsection (2) shall be omitted.

**22.** Sections 22, 23 and 24 shall not apply.

**Note.** Para 5: in sub-ss (9), (10) words omitted, and sub-s (11) revoked by SI 1999/1318, art 3(1)(a), (b) as from 28 June 1999. In para 6 in sub-s (12) words "one calendar month" substituted by words "two calendar months" in square brackets by SI 1999/1318, art 3(2)(a) as from 28 June 1999. In para 9(2) in sub-s (1) words "the method of payment of" in square brackets in both places they occur inserted by SI 1999/1318, art 3(2)(b) as from 28 June 1999. Para 9(2A), (2B): inserted by SI 1999/1318, art 3(2)(c) as from 28 June 1999. In para 9(4) sub-ss (3)–(7) revoked and sub-s (11) inserted by SI 1999/1318, art 3(3)(a), (b) as from 28 June 1999.

SCHEDULE 3          Article 3(2)

PART I OF THE ACT AS MODIFIED BY SCHEDULE 2

ORDERS MADE BY COURTS IN THE UNITED KINGDOM

*Transmission of maintenance orders made in United Kingdom for the recognition and enforcement in Hague Convention country*

**2.** (1) Subject to subsection (2) below, where the payer under a maintenance order made, whether before, on or after 5th April 1993, by a court in the United Kingdom is residing in a Hague Convention country, the payee under the order may apply for the order to be sent to that country for recognition and enforcement.

(2) Subsection (1) above shall not have effect in relation to a maintenance order made under section 3 of this Act or to an order by virtue of a provision of Part II of this Act.

(3) Every application under this section shall be made in the prescribed manner to the prescribed officer of the court which made the maintenance order to which the application relates.

(4) If, on an application duly made under this section to the prescribed officer of a court in the United Kingdom, that officer is satisfied that the payer under the maintenance order to which the application relates is residing in a Hague Convention country, the following documents, that is to say—

(a) a certified copy of the maintenance order;

(b) a certificate signed by that officer certifying that the order is enforceable and that it is no longer subject to the ordinary forms of review;

(c) a certificate of arrears so signed;

(d) a statement giving such information as the officer possesses as to the whereabouts of the payer;

(e) a statement giving such information as the officer possesses for facilitating the identification of the payer;

(f) where available, a photograph of the payer;

(g) a written statement signed by that officer as to whether or not the payer appeared in the proceedings in which the maintenance order was made and, if he did not appear, the original or a certified copy of a document which establishes that notice of the institution of the proceedings, including notice of the substance of the claim, was served on the payer;

(h) a document which establishes that notice of the order was sent to the payer; and

(i) a written statement signed by that officer as to whether or not the payee received legal aid either in the said proceedings or in connection with the said application,

shall be sent by that officer, in the case of a court in England and Wales or Northern Ireland, to the Lord Chancellor, or, in the case of a court in Scotland, to the Secretary of State, with a view to their being transmitted by the Lord Chancellor, or, as the case may be, the Secretary of State, to the appropriate authority in the Hague Convention country if he is satisfied that the statement relating to the whereabouts of the payer gives sufficient information to justify that being done.

(5) Nothing in this section shall be taken as affecting any jurisdiction of a court in the United Kingdom with respect to a maintenance order to which this section applies, and subject to section 5 any such order may be enforced, varied or revoked accordingly.

*Power of magistrates' court to make maintenance order against person residing in Hague Convention country*

**3.**   (1) Where an application is made to a magistrates' court for a maintenance order by a person who is habitually resident in England and Wales against a person residing in a Hague Convention country and the court would have jurisdiction to determine the application under the Domestic Proceedings and Magistrates' Courts Act 1978 or the Children Act 1989 if at any time when the proceedings were instituted that person—

(a) were residing in England and Wales, and

(b) received reasonable notice of the date of the hearing of the application,

the court shall subject to the following provisions of this section have jurisdiction to determine the application.

(4) No enactment (or provision made under an enactment) requiring or enabling—

(a) a court to transfer proceedings from a magistrates' court to a county court or the High Court, or

(b) a magistrates' court to refuse to make an order on an application on the ground that any matter in question is one that would be more conveniently dealt with by the High Court,

shall apply in relation to an application to which subsection (1) above applies.

(5) On the making of an application to which subsection (1) above applies, the following documents, that is to say—

(a) notice of the institution of the proceedings, including notice of the substance of the application;

(b) a statement signed by the prescribed officer of the court giving such information as he possesses as to the whereabouts of the respondent;

(c) a statement giving such information as the officer possesses for facilitating the identification of the respondent; and

(d) where available, a photograph of the respondent,

shall be sent by that officer to the Lord Chancellor with a view to their being transmitted by the Lord Chancellor to the appropriate authority in the Hague Convention country in which the respondent is residing for service on him of the document mentioned in paragraph (a) above if the Lord Chancellor is satisfied that the statement relating to the whereabouts of the respondent gives sufficient information to justify that being done.

(6) In considering whether or not to make a maintenance order pursuant to an application to which subsection (1) above applies the court shall take into account any representations made and any evidence adduced by or on behalf of the respondent.

(6A) Where the respondent makes any representations or adduces any evidence, a copy of the representations or evidence shall be served on the applicant by the prescribed officer of the court before the hearing.

(6B) The prescribed officer of the court shall give the respondent notice in writing of the date fixed for the hearing by sending the notice by post addressed to his last known or usual place of abode.

(6C) A maintenance order pursuant to an application to which subsection (1) above applies shall not be made unless the document mentioned in paragraph (a) of subsection (5) above has been served on the respondent in accordance with the law for the service of such documents in the Hague Convention country in which he is residing or in such other manner as may be authorised by the Lord Chancellor not less than six weeks previously.

(6D) Where a maintenance order has been made under this section, the prescribed officer of the court shall send the following documents, that is to say—

(a) a certified copy of the order;

(b) a certificate signed by that officer certifying that the order is enforceable and that it is no longer subject to the ordinary forms of review;

(c) a written statement, signed by that officer as to whether or not the respondent appeared in the proceedings in which the order was made, and, if he did not appear, the original or a certified copy of a document which establishes that the document mentioned in paragraph (a) of subsection (5) above has been served on the payer in accordance with subsection (6C) above;

(d) a document which establishes that notice of the order was sent to the respondent; and

(e) a written statement signed by that officer as to whether or not the applicant received legal aid in the proceedings,

to the Lord Chancellor with a view to their being transmitted by him to the appropriate authority in the Hague Convention country in which the respondent resides for recognition and enforcement of the order.

(6E) A maintenance order made under this section may, subject to section 5 of this Act, be enforced, varied or revoked in like manner as any other maintenance order made by a magistrates' court.

(7) In the application of this section to Northern Ireland—
(a) for subsection (1) there shall be substituted—
"(1) Where a complaint is made to a magistrates' court by a person who is habitually resident in Northern Ireland against a person residing in a Hague Convention country and the complaint is one on which the court would have jurisdiction by virtue of any enactment to make a maintenance order if—
(a) that person were residing in Northern Ireland, and
(b) a summons to appear before the court to answer the complaint had been duly served on him,
the court shall have jurisdiction to hear the complaint and may make a maintenance order on the complaint.", and
(b) for subsection (4) there shall be substituted—
"(4) No enactment empowering a magistrates' court to refuse to make an order on a complaint on the ground that any matter in question is one which would be more conveniently dealt with by the High Court of Justice in Northern Ireland shall apply in relation to a complaint to which subsection (1) above applies.".

*Power of sheriff to make maintenance order against person residing in Hague Convention country*

**4.**   (1) The sheriff shall have jurisdiction in any action to which this section applies if at the time when the proceedings were instituted—
(a) the pursuer is habitually resident in Scotland and resides within the jurisdiction of the sheriff; and
(b) the sheriff is satisfied that, to the best of the information or belief of the pursuer, the defender is residing in a Hague Convention country; and
(c) the sheriff would not, apart from this subsection, have jurisdiction in that action.
(2) This section applies to any action for the payment, variation or revocation of aliment which is competent in the sheriff court, and includes an action of affiliation and aliment, but does not include an action of separation and aliment or adherence and aliment, or any action containing a crave for the custody of a child.
(3) Where in any action in which the payment of aliment in respect of a child is claimed, being an action in which the sheriff has jurisdiction by virtue of subsection (1) above, the sheriff is satisfied—
(a) that there are grounds on which a maintenance order containing a provision requiring the payment of aliment in respect of that child may be made in that action, but
(b) that he has no power to make that order unless he also makes an order providing for the custody of the child,
then, for the purpose of enabling the sheriff to make the maintenance order, the pursuer shall be deemed to be a person to whom the custody of the child has been committed by a decree of the sheriff which is for the time being in force.
(4) In any action in which the sheriff has jurisdiction by virtue of subsection (1) above, no decree shall be granted in favour of the pursuer unless a copy of the initial writ or summons has been served on the defender in the prescribed manner and in sufficient time to enable him to arrange for his defence.

*Variation and revocation of maintenance order made in United Kingdom*

**5.**   (1) This section applies to a maintenance order a certified copy of which has been sent to a Hague Convention country for recognition and enforcement of the order.
(2) The jurisdiction of a magistrates' court to revoke or vary a maintenance order shall be exercisable notwithstanding that the proceedings for the revocation

or variation, as the case may be, of the order are brought by or against a person residing in a Hague Convention country.

(3) Where subsection (1) of section 60 of the Magistrates' Courts Act 1980 (revocation, variation etc of orders for periodical payment) applies in relation to a maintenance order to which this section applies, that subsection shall have effect as if for the words "by order on complaint," there were substituted "on an application being made, by order".

(4) Where an application is made by the payee to a court in England and Wales or Northern Ireland for the variation or revocation of an order to which this section applies, and the payer is residing in a Hague Convention country, the prescribed officer of the court shall send to the Lord Chancellor notice of the institution of the proceedings, including notice of the substance of the application, with a view to its being transmitted by him to the appropriate authority in the Hague Convention country for service on the payer.

(5) Where an application is made by the payee to a court in England and Wales or Northern Ireland for the variation or revocation of an order to which this section applies, and the payer is residing in a Hague Convention country—

(a)  the court, in considering whether or not to vary or revoke the order, shall take into account any representations made and any evidence adduced by or on behalf of the payer;

(b)  a copy of any such representations or evidence shall be served on the payee in the prescribed manner before the hearing;

(c)  the prescribed officer of the court shall give the payer notice in writing of the date fixed for the hearing by sending the notice by post addressed to his last known or usual place of abode.

(6) Where an application is made by the payee to a court in England and Wales or Northern Ireland for the variation or revocation of an order to which this section applies, and the payer is residing in a Hague Convention country, the order shall not be varied or revoked unless the document mentioned in subsection (4) above has been served on the payer in accordance with the law for the service of such a document in the Hague Convention country not less than six weeks previously.

(7) Where an application is made by the payer to a court in England and Wales or Northern Ireland for the variation or revocation of an order to which this section applies, the prescribed officer of the court shall arrange for the service of the document mentioned in subsection (4) above on the payee.

(8) Where an order to which this section applies has been varied or revoked by a court in the United Kingdom the prescribed officer of the court shall send the following documents, that is to say—

(a)  a certified copy of the order of variation or revocation;

(b)  a certificate signed by that officer certifying that the order of variation or revocation is enforceable and that it is no longer subject to the ordinary forms of review;

(c)  a written statement, signed by that officer as to whether or not the respondent or, in Scotland the defender, appeared in the proceedings for the variation or revocation of the order, and, if he did not appear, the original or a certified copy of a document which establishes that notice of the institution of the proceedings has been served on the respondent, or, as the case may be, the defender; and

(d)  a document which establishes that notice of the order of variation or revocation was sent to the respondent; and

(e)  a written statement signed by that officer as to whether or not the payer or the payee received legal aid in the proceedings,

in the case of a court in England and Wales or Northern Ireland, to the Lord Chancellor, or, in the case of a court in Scotland, to the Secretary of State, with a view to their being transmitted by him to the appropriate authority in the Hague Convention country for recognition and enforcement of the order of variation or revocation.

(9) Where a maintenance order to which this section applies has been varied by an order made by a court in the United Kingdom . . . the maintenance order shall, as from the date on which the order of variation took effect, have effect as varied by that order.

(10) Where a maintenance order to which this section applies has been revoked by an order made by a court in the United Kingdom . . . the maintenance order shall, as from the date on which the order of revocation took effect, be deemed to have ceased to have effect except as respects any arrears due under the maintenance order at that date.

(11) . . .

(12) In the application of this section to Northern Ireland, in subsection (8), for the word "respondent" in each place where it occurs, there shall be substituted "defendant".

ORDERS MADE BY COURTS IN HAGUE CONVENTION COUNTRIES

*Registration in United Kingdom court of maintenance order made in Hague Convention country*

**6.** (1) This section applies to a maintenance order made whether before, on or after 5th April 1993 by a competent court in a Hague Convention country.

(2) Where a certified copy of an order to which this section applies is received by the Lord Chancellor or the Secretary of State from a Hague Convention country, and it appears to him that the payer under the order is residing in the United Kingdom, he shall send the copy of the order and the accompanying documents to the prescribed officer of the appropriate court.

(3) Where the prescribed officer of the appropriate court receives from the Lord Chancellor or the Secretary of State a certified copy of an order to which this section applies, he shall, subject to the following subsections, register the order in the prescribed manner in that court.

(4) Before registering an order under this section an officer of a court shall take such steps as he thinks fit for the purpose of ascertaining whether the payer under the order is residing within the jurisdiction of the court, and if after taking those steps he is satisfied that the payer is not so residing he shall return the certified copy of the order and the accompanying documents to the Lord Chancellor or the Secretary of State, as the case may be, with a statement giving such information as he possesses as to the whereabouts of the payer.

(5)

(a) The prescribed officer of the appropriate court may refuse to authorise the registration of the order if the court in the Hague Convention country by or before which the order was made did not have jurisdiction to make the order; and for these purposes a court in a Hague Convention country shall be considered to have jurisdiction if—

  (i) either the payer or the payee had his habitual residence in the Hague Convention country at the time when the proceedings were instituted; or

  (ii) the payer and the payee were nationals of that country at that time; or

  (iii) the respondent in those proceedings had submitted to the jurisdiction of the court, either expressly or by defending on the merits of the case without objecting to the jurisdiction; or

  (iv) in the case of an order made by reason of a divorce or a legal separation or a declaration that a marriage is void or annulled, the court is recognised by the law of the part of the United Kingdom in which enforcement is sought as having jurisdiction to make the order.

(b) In deciding whether a court in a Hague Convention country had jurisdiction to make an order the prescribed officer shall be bound by any finding of fact on which the court based its jurisdiction.

(6) The prescribed officer of the appropriate court may refuse to authorise the registration of the order—

(a) if such registration is manifestly contrary to public policy;

(b) if the order was obtained by fraud in connection with a matter of procedure;

(c) if proceedings between the same parties and having the same purpose are pending before a court in the same part of the United Kingdom and those proceedings were the first to be instituted; or

(d) if the order is incompatible with an order made in proceedings between the same parties and having the same purpose, either in the United Kingdom or in another country, provided that the latter order itself fulfils the conditions necessary for its registration and enforcement under this Part of this Act.

(7) Without prejudice to subsection (6) above, if the payer did not appear in the proceedings in the Hague Convention country in which the order was made, the prescribed officer of the appropriate court shall refuse to authorise the registration of the order unless notice of the institution of the proceedings, including notice of the substance of the claim, was served on the payer in accordance with the law of that Hague Convention country and if, having regard to the circumstances, the payer had sufficient time to enable him to defend the proceedings.

(8) If the order is registered under subsection (3) above, the prescribed officer of the appropriate court shall serve notice in a prescribed form on the payer and give notice to the payee that the order has been registered.

(9) The payer may, before the end of the period of one calendar month beginning with the date of service of the said notice, appeal to the court in which the order is registered to set aside the registration of the order on one of the grounds set out in paragraphs (5), (6) and (7) above.

(10) If the payer appeals to the court in which the order is registered to set aside the registration of the order, the prescribed officer of the court shall give notice to the payee of the appeal and of the date of the hearing of the appeal.

(11) If the prescribed officer refuses to register the order, he shall give notice to the payee in a prescribed form that registration has been refused.

(12) A payee to whom notice has been given by the prescribed officer of any court under subsection (11) above may, before the end of the period of *one calendar month* [two calendar months] beginning with the date when notice was given, appeal to that court against the refusal to register the order.

(13) If the payee appeals to the court against the refusal to register the order, the prescribed officer of the court shall give notice to the payer of the appeal and of the date of the hearing of the appeal.

(14) In the application of this section to Scotland—

(a) in subsection (8), for the words "serve notice in a prescribed form on" there shall be substituted the words "intimate to in the prescribed manner";

(b) in subsection (9), for the words "service of the said notice" there shall be substituted the words "the said intimation";

(c) in subsections (9), (10), (12) and (13) for any reference to an appeal there shall be substituted a reference to an application and cognate expressions shall be construed accordingly; and

(d) in subsection (11), for the words "in a prescribed form" there shall be substituted the words "in the prescribed manner".

(15) In the application of this section to Northern Ireland, in subsection (5), for the word "respondent" there shall be substituted "defendant".

*Enforcement of maintenance order registered in United Kingdom court*

**8.** (1) Subject to subsections (2), (2A) and (2B) below, a registered order may be enforced in the United Kingdom as if it had been made by the registering court and as if that court had had jurisdiction to make it; and proceedings for or with respect to the enforcement of any such order may be taken accordingly.

(2) Subsection (1) above does not apply to an order which is for the time being registered in the High Court under Part I of the Maintenance Orders Act 1958 or to an order which is for time being registered in the High Court of Justice in Northern Ireland under Part II of the Maintenance and Affiliation Orders Act (Northern Ireland) 1966.

(2A) Where in a maintenance order made in a Hague Convention country there are provisions which are not enforceable under this Part of this Act, this section shall apply only to the remaining provisions of the order.

(2B) The payee under a registered order may request the partial enforcement of that order.

(3) Any person for the time being under an obligation to make payments in pursuance of a registered order shall give notice of any change of address to the *clerk* [appropriate officer] of the registering court, and any person failing without reasonable excuse to give such a notice shall be liable on summary conviction to a fine not exceeding level 2 on the standard scale.

[(3A) In subsection (3) above "appropriate officer" means—

(a) in relation to a magistrates' court in England and Wales, the justices' chief executive for the court; and

(b) in relation to a court elsewhere, the clerk of the court.]

(4) An order which by virtue of this section is enforceable by a magistrates' court in England and Wales shall, subject to the modifications of sections 76 and 93 of the Magistrates' Courts Act 1980 specified in subsections (4A) and (4B) below, be enforceable as if it were a magistrates' court maintenance order made by that court.

In this subsection, "magistrates' court maintenance order" has the same meaning as in section 150(1) of the Magistrates' Courts Act 1980.

(4A) Section 76 (enforcement of sums adjudged to be paid) shall have effect as if for subsections (4) to (6) there were substituted the following subsections—

"(4) Where proceedings are brought for the enforcement of a magistrates' court maintenance order under this section, the court may vary the order by exercising one of its powers under subsection (5) below.

(5) The powers of the court are—

(a) the power to order that payments under the order be made directly to *the clerk of the court or the clerk of any other magistrates' court* [a justices' chief executive];

(b) the power to order that payments under the order be made to *the clerk of the court, or to the clerk of any other magistrates' court,* [a justices' chief executive] by such method of payment falling within section 59(6) above (standing order, etc) as may be specified;

(c) the power to make an attachment of earnings order under the Attachment of Earnings Act 1971 to secure payments under the order.

(6) In deciding which of the powers under subsection (5) above it is to exercise, the court shall have regard to any representations made by the debtor (within the meaning of section 59 above).

(7) Subsection (4) of section 59 above (power of court to require debtor to open account) shall apply for the purposes of subsection (5) above as it applies for the purposes of that section but as if for paragraph (a) there were substituted—

"(a) the court proposes to exercise its power under paragraph (b) of section 76(5) below, and"."

(4B)  In section 93 (complaint for arrears), subsection (6) (court not to impose imprisonment in certain circumstances) shall have effect as if for paragraph (b) there were substituted—

"(b) if the court is of the opinion that it is appropriate—
    (i)  to make an attachment of earnings order; or
    (ii)  to exercise its power under paragraph (b) of section 76(5) above.".

(5) The magistrates' court by which an order is enforceable by virtue of this section, and the officers thereof, shall take all such steps for enforcing the order as may be prescribed.

(6) In any proceedings for or with respect to the enforcement of an order which is for the time being registered in any court under this Part of this Act a certificate of arrears sent to the prescribed officer of the court shall be evidence of the facts stated therein.

(7) Subject to subsection (8) below, a sum of money payable under a registered order shall be payable in accordance with the order, or such part thereof as the payee may have requested should be enforced, as from the date on which the order took effect.

(8) Where a registered order was made by a court in a Hague Convention country before the date of the entry into force of the Hague Convention between the United Kingdom and that country, no sum of money falling due before that date shall be payable in accordance with the order.

(9) In the application of this section to Scotland—
(a)  subsections (2) to (5) shall be omitted; and
(b)  in subsection (6), for the word "evidence" there shall be substituted the words "sufficient evidence".

*Variation of maintenance order registered in United Kingdom court*

**9.**  (1)  Subject to the provisions of this section—
(a)  the registering court shall have the like power, on an application made by the payer or payee under a registered order, to vary [the method of payment of] the order as if it had been made by the registering court and as if that court had had jurisdiction to make it;
(b)  the jurisdiction of a magistrates' court to vary [the method of payment of] a registered order shall be exercisable notwithstanding that the proceedings for the variation of the order are brought by or against a person residing in a Hague Convention country.

(1ZA)  Where the registering court is a magistrates' court in England and Wales, section 60 of the Magistrates' Courts Act 1980 (revocation, variation etc of orders for periodical payment) shall have effect in relation to the registered order—
(za) as if in subsection (1) for the words "by order on complaint" there were substituted "on an application being made, by order [and for the words "revoke, revive or vary the order", there were substituted "vary the order in accordance with subsection (3)"]";
[(zab)  as if subsection (2) were omitted;]
(a)  *as if in subsection (3) for the words "paragraphs (a) to (d) of section 59(3) above" there were substituted "subsection (3A) below" and after that subsection there were inserted—* [as if in subsection (3)—
    (i)  for the words "shall include", there were substituted "means the";
    (ii)  for the words "paragraphs (a) to (d) of section 59(3) above" there were substituted "subsection (3A) below"; and
    (iii)  after that subsection there were inserted—]
"(3A)  The powers of the court are—
(a)  the power to order that payments under the order be made directly to *the clerk of the court or the clerk of any other magistrates' court* [a justices' chief executive];

(b) the power to order that payments under the order be made to *the clerk of the court, or to the clerk of any other magistrates' court,* [a justices' chief executive] by such method of payment falling within section 59(6) above (standing order, etc) as may be specified;

(c) the power to make an attachment of earnings order under the Attachment of Earnings Act 1971 to secure payments under the order.";

(b) as if in subsection (4) for paragraph (b) there were substituted—

"(b) payments under the order are required to be made to *the clerk of the court, or to the clerk of any other magistrates' court* [a justices' chief executive], by any method of payment falling within section 59(6) above (standing order, etc)",

and as if after the words "the court" there were inserted "which made the order";

(c) as if in subsection (5) for the words "to the clerk" there were substituted "in accordance with paragraph (a) of subsection (3A) above";

(d) as if in subsection (7), paragraph (c) and the word "and" immediately preceding it were omitted;

(e) as if in subsection (8) for the words "paragraphs (a) to (d) of section 59(3) above" there were substituted "subsection (3A) above";

(f) as if for subsections (9) and (10) there were substituted the following subsections—

"(9) In deciding, for the purposes of subsections (3) and (8) above, which of the powers under subsection (3A) above it is to exercise, the court shall have regard to any representations made by the debtor.

(10) Subsection (4) of section 59 above (power of court to require debtor to open account) shall apply for the purposes of subsection (3A) above as it applies for the purposes of that section but as if for paragraph (a) there were substituted—

"(a) the court proposes to exercise its power under paragraph (b) of section 60(3A) below, and".".

[(1ZB) Where the registering court is a court of summary jurisdiction in Northern Ireland, Article 86 of the Magistrates' Court (Northern Ireland) Order 1981 (revocation, variation etc, of orders for periodical payment) shall have effect in relation to the registered order—

(za) as if in paragraph (1) for the words "by order on complaint" there were substituted "on an application being made, by order" and for the words "revoke, revive or vary the order", there were substituted "vary the order in accordance with paragraph (3)";

(zab) as if paragraph (2) were omitted;

(a) as if in paragraph (3)—
    (i) for the words "shall include", there were substituted "means the",
    (ii) for the words "sub-paragraphs (a) to (d) of Article 85(3)" there were substituted "paragraph (3A)", and
    (iii) after that paragraph there were inserted—

"(3A) The powers of the court are—

(a) the power to order that payments under the order be made directly to the collecting officer;

(b) the power to order that payments under the order be made to the collecting officer by such method of payment falling within Article 85(7) (standing order, etc) as may be specified;

(c) the power to make an attachment of earnings order under Part IX to secure payments under the order;"

(b) as if in paragraph (4) for sub-paragraph (b) there were substituted—

"(b) payments under the order are required to be made to the collecting officer by any method of payment falling within Article 85(7) (standing order, etc)";

and as if after the words "petty sessions" there were inserted "for the petty
sessions district for which the court which made the order acts";

(c)  as if in paragraph (5) for the words "to the collecting officer" there were
substituted "in accordance with sub-paragraph (a) of paragraph (3A)";

(d)  as if in paragraph (7), sub-paragraph (c) and the word "and" immediately
preceding it were omitted;

(e)  as if in paragraph (8) for the words "sub-paragraphs (a) to (d) of Article
85(3)" there were substituted "paragraph (3A)";

(f)  as if for paragraphs (9) and (10) there were substituted the following
paragraphs—

"(9)  In deciding, for the purposes of paragraphs (3) and (8), which of the
powers under paragraph (3A) it is to exercise, the court shall have regard to any
representations made by the debtor.

(10)  Paragraph (5) of Article 85 (power of court to require debtor to open
account) shall apply for the purposes of paragraph (3A) as it applies for the
purpose of that Article but as if for sub-paragraph (a) there were substituted—

"(a)  the court proposes to exercise its power under sub-paragraph (b) of Article
86(3A), and".".]

(2) The registering court shall not vary a registered order unless—

(a)    the payer under the order had his habitual residence in the United
Kingdom at the time when the proceedings to vary the order were instituted; or

(b)    the respondent in those proceedings had submitted to the jurisdiction of the
registering court, either expressly or by defending on the merits of the case
without objecting to the jurisdiction.

(3) ...

(4) ...

(5) ...

(6) ...

(7) ...

(8) Where a registered order has been varied by the registering court or by a
court in a Hague Convention country, the prescribed officer of the registering
court shall register the variation order in the prescribed manner.

(9) Where a registered order has been varied by the registering court or by a
court in a Hague Convention country, the registered order shall, as from the date
on which the variation order took effect, have effect as so varied.

(10)    In the application of this section to Northern Ireland, in subsections
(2) and (7), for the word "respondent" in each place where it occurs, there shall
be substituted "defendant".

[(11)    This section shall not apply to a court in Scotland.]

*Cancellation of registration and transfer of order*

**10.**    (1)  Where a registered order is revoked by an order made by a court in a
Hague Convention country and notice of the revocation is received by the
registering court, the prescribed officer of the registering court shall cancel the
registration; but any arrears due under the registered order at the date on which
the order of revocation took effect, other than, in the case of a registered order
made by a court in a Hague Convention country before the date of the entry into
force of the Hague Convention between the United Kingdom and that country,
arrears due before that date, shall continue to be recoverable as if the registration
had not been cancelled.

(2) Where the prescribed officer of the registering court is of opinion that the
payer under a registered order has ceased to reside within the jurisdiction of that
court, he shall cancel the registration of the order and, subject to subsection (3)
below, shall send the certified copy of the order to the Lord Chancellor.

(3) Where the prescribed officer of the registering court, being a magistrates' court, is of opinion that the payer is residing within the jurisdiction of another magistrates' court in that part of the United Kingdom in which the registering court is, he shall transfer the order to that other court by sending the certified copy of the order to the prescribed officer of that other court.

(4) On the transfer of an order under subsection (3) above the prescribed officer of the court to which it is transferred shall, subject to subsection (6) below, register the order in the prescribed manner in that court.

(5) Where the certified copy of an order is received by the Lord Chancellor under this section and it appears to him that the payer under the order is still residing in the United Kingdom, he shall transfer the order to the appropriate court by sending the certified copy of the order together with the related documents to the prescribed officer of the appropriate court and, subject to subsection (6) below, that officer shall register the order in the prescribed manner in that court.

(6) Before registering an order in pursuance of subsection (4) or (5) above an officer of a court shall take such steps as he thinks fit for the purpose of ascertaining whether the payer is so residing, and if after taking those steps he is satisfied that the payer is not residing within the jurisdiction of the court he shall send the certified copy of the order to the Lord Chancellor.

(7) The officer of a court who is required by any of the foregoing provisions of this section to send to the Lord Chancellor or to the prescribed officer of another court the certified copy of an order shall send with that copy—

(a) a certificate of arrears signed by him;

(b) a statement giving such information as he possesses as to the whereabouts of the payer; and

(c) any relevant documents in his possession relating to the case.

(8) In the application of this section to Scotland—

(a) in subsection (2), for the words "within the jurisdiction of that court" there shall be substituted the words "in Scotland";

(b) subsections (3) and (4) shall be omitted; and

(c) for the words "Lord Chancellor", in each place where they occur, there shall be substituted the words "Secretary of State".

*Steps to be taken by Lord Chancellor or Secretary of State where payer under certain orders is not residing in the United Kingdom*

11.   (1) If it appears to the Lord Chancellor or the Secretary of State that the payer under a maintenance order, a certified copy of which has been received by him from a Hague Convention country, is not residing in the United Kingdom or, in the case of an order which subsequently became a registered order, has ceased to reside therein, he shall send to the appropriate authority in that country—

(a) the certified copy of the order in question and a certified copy of any order varying that order;

(b) if the order has at any time been a registered order, a certificate of arrears signed by the prescribed officer;

(c) a statement giving such information as the Lord Chancellor or the Secretary of State possesses as to the whereabouts of the payer; and

(d) any other relevant documents in his possession relating to the case.

**APPEALS**

*Appeals*

**12.**   Where in pursuance of section 9 above a registering court makes or refuses to make an order varying a registered order, the payer or the payee under the registered order shall have the like right of appeal (if any) from the order of variation or from the refusal to make it as he would have if the registered order had been made by the registering court.

EVIDENCE

*Admissibility of evidence given in Hague Convention country*

**13.**    (1) A statement contained in—

(a) a document, duly authenticated, which purports to set out or summarise evidence given in proceedings in a court in a Hague Convention country; or

(b) a document, duly authenticated, which purports to set out or summarise evidence taken in that country for the purpose of proceedings in a court in the United Kingdom under this Part of this Act, whether in response to a request made by such a court or otherwise; or

(c) a document, duly authenticated, which purports to have been received in evidence in proceedings in a court in that country or to be a copy of a document so received; or

(d) a document purporting to be signed by a judicial officer, official or other competent person in a Hague Convention country which establishes that certain documents were served on a person,

shall in any proceedings in a court in the United Kingdom relating to a maintenance order to which this Part of this Act applies be admissible as evidence of any fact stated therein to the same extent as oral evidence of that fact is admissible in those proceedings.

(2) A document purporting to set out or summarise evidence given as mentioned in subsection (1)(a) above, or taken as mentioned in subsection (1)(b) above, shall be deemed to be duly authenticated for the purposes of that subsection if the document purports to be certified by the judicial officer or other person before whom the evidence was given, or, as the case may be, by whom it was taken, to be the original document containing or recording, or, as the case may be, summarising, that evidence or a true copy of that document.

(3) A document purporting to have been received in evidence as mentioned in subsection (1)(c) above, or to be a copy of a document so received, shall be deemed to be duly authenticated for the purposes of that subsection if the document purports to be certified by a judge or officer of the court in question to have been, or to be a true copy of a document which has been, so received.

(4) It shall not be necessary in any such proceedings to prove the signature or official position of the person appearing to have given such a certificate.

(5) Nothing in this section shall prejudice the admission in evidence of any document which is admissible in evidence apart from this section.

*Obtaining of evidence needed for purpose of certain proceedings*

**14.**    (1) Where for the purpose of any proceedings in a court in a Hague Convention country relating to a maintenance order to which this Part of this Act applies a request is made by or on behalf of that court for the taking in the United Kingdom of the evidence of a person residing therein relating to matters specified in the request, such court in the United Kingdom as may be prescribed shall have power to take that evidence and, after giving notice of the time and place at which the evidence is to be taken to such persons and in such manner as it thinks fit, shall take the evidence in such manner as may be prescribed.

Evidence taken in compliance with such a request shall be sent by the prescribed officer of the court—

(a) in England and Wales or Northern Ireland, to the Lord Chancellor, or

(b)  in Scotland, to the Secretary of State,

for transmission to the appropriate authority in the Hague Convention country.

(2) Where any person, not being the payer or the payee under the maintenance order to which the proceedings in question relate, is required by virtue of this section to give evidence before a court in the United Kingdom, the court may order that there shall be paid out of moneys provided by Parliament such sums as appear to the court reasonably sufficient to compensate that person for the expense, trouble or loss of time properly incurred in or incidental to his attendance.

(3) Section 97(1), (3) and (4) of the Magistrates' Courts Act 1980 (which provide for compelling the attendance of witnesses, etc) shall apply in relation to a magistrates' court having power under subsection (1) above to take the evidence of any person as if the proceedings in the court in a Hague Convention country for the purpose of which a request for the taking of the evidence has been made were proceedings in the magistrates' court and had been begun by complaint.

(4) Paragraphs 71 and 73 of Schedule 1 to the Sheriff Courts (Scotland) Act 1907 (which provide for the citation of witnesses, etc) shall apply in relation to a sheriff having power under subsection (1) above to take the evidence of any person as if the proceedings in the court in a Hague Convention country for the purpose of which a request for the taking of the evidence has been made were proceedings in the sheriff court.

(5) A court in—

(a)  England and Wales or Northern Ireland may for the purpose of any proceedings in that court under this Part of this Act relating to a maintenance order to which this Part of this Act applies send to the Lord Chancellor, or

(b)  Scotland may for the purpose of such proceedings in that court relating to such an action, send to the Secretary of State,

for transmission to the appropriate authority in a Hague Convention country a request for a court in a Hague Convention country to take or provide evidence relating to such matters as may be specified in the request.

(6) In the application of this section to Northern Ireland, in subsection (3), for the reference to section 97(1), (3) and (4) of the Magistrates' Courts Act 1980 there shall be substituted a reference to Articles 118(1), (3) and (4), 119 and 120 of the Magistrates' Courts (Northern Ireland) Order 1981.

*Order, etc made in Hague Convention country need not be proved*

**15.**   For the purposes of this Part of this Act, unless the contrary is shown—

(a)  any order made by a court in a Hague Convention country purporting to bear the seal of that court or to be signed by any person in his capacity as a judge or officer of the court, shall be deemed without further proof to have been duly sealed or, as the case may be, to have been signed by that person;

(b)  the person by whom the order was signed shall be deemed without further proof to have been a judge or officer, as the case may be, of that court when he signed it and, in the case of an officer, to have been authorised to sign it; and

(c)  a document purporting to be a certified copy of an order made by a court in a Hague Convention country shall be deemed without further proof to be such a copy.

SUPPLEMENTAL

*Payment of sums under orders made in Hague Convention countries: conversion of currency*

**16.**   (1) Payment of sums due under a registered order shall, while the order is registered in a court in England, Wales or Northern Ireland, be made in such manner and to such person as may be prescribed.

(2) Where the sums required to be paid under a registered order are expressed in a currency other than the currency of the United Kingdom, then, as from the relevant date, the order shall be treated as if it were an order requiring the payment of such sums in the currency of the United Kingdom as, on the basis of the rate of exchange prevailing at that date, are equivalent to the sums so required to be paid.

(3) Where the sum specified in any statement, being a statement of the amount of any arrears due under a maintenance order made by a court in a Hague Convention country, is expressed in a currency other than the currency of the United Kingdom, that sum shall be deemed to be such sum in the currency of the United Kingdom as, on the basis of the rate of exchange prevailing at the relevant date, is equivalent to the sum so specified.

(4) For the purposes of this section a written certificate purporting to be signed by an officer of any bank in the United Kingdom certifying that a specified rate of exchange prevailed between currencies at a specified date and that at such a rate a specified sum in the currency of the United Kingdom is equivalent to a specified sum in another specified currency shall be evidence of the rate of exchange so prevailing on that date and of the equivalent sums in terms of the respective currencies.

(5) In this section "the relevant date" means—

(a)  in relation to a registered order or to a statement of arrears due under a maintenance order made by a court in a Hague Convention country, the date on which the order first becomes a registered order;

(b)  in relation to a registered order which has been varied, the date on which the last order varying that order is registered in the registering court.

(6) In the application of this section to Scotland—

(a)  subsection (1) shall not apply;

(b)  in subsection (4), for the word "evidence" there shall be substituted the words "sufficient evidence".

### Proceedings in magistrates' courts

**17.**    (4)    Anything authorised or required by this Part of this Act to be done by, to or before the magistrates' court by, to or before which any other thing was done may be done by, to or before any magistrates' court acting for the same petty sessions area (or, in Northern Ireland, petty sessions district) as that court.

(5) Any application which by virtue of a provision of this Part of this Act is made to a magistrates' court in Northern Ireland shall be made by complaint.

(5A)  Where the respondent to an application for the variation or revocation of—

(a)  a maintenance order made by a magistrates' court in England and Wales, being an order to which section 5 of this Act applies; or

(b)  a registered order which is registered in such a court,

is residing in a Hague Convention country, a magistrates' court in England and Wales shall have jurisdiction to hear the application (where it would not have such jurisdiction apart from this subsection) if it would have had jurisdiction to hear it had the respondent been residing in England and Wales.

(6) A magistrates' court in Northern Ireland shall have jurisdiction to hear a complaint for the variation or revocation—

(a)  of a maintenance order made by such a court, and to which section 5 of this Act applies; or

(b)  to hear a complaint for the variation of a registered order which is registered in that court,

if the defendant to the complaint is residing in a Hague Convention country and if the court would have had jurisdiction to hear the complaint had the defendant been residing in Northern Ireland and been served with a summons to appear before the court to answer the complaint.

(7) Where the respondent to an application—

(a) for the variation or revocation of a maintenance order made by a magistrates' court, and to which section 5 of this Act applies; or

(b) for the variation of a registered order registered in a magistrates' court,

does not appear at the time and place appointed for the hearing of the application, but the court is satisfied that the respondent is residing in a Hague Convention country, and that the requirements of section 5(4), (6) or (7) or section 9(3), as the case may be, have been complied with, the court may proceed to hear and determine the application at the time and place appointed for the hearing or for any adjourned hearing as if the respondent had appeared at that time and place.

(7A) In the application of this section to Northern Ireland, in subsection (7)—

(a) for the word "respondent", in each place where it occurs, there shall be substituted "defendant"; and

(b) for the words "an application" and "the application", in each place where they occur, there shall be substituted "a complaint" and "the complaint" respectively.

*Magistrates' courts rules*

**18.** (1) Without prejudice to the generality of the power to make rules under section 144 of the Magistrates' Courts Act 1980 (magistrates' courts rules) provision may be made by such rules with respect to any of the following matters, namely—

(a) the circumstances in which anything authorised or required by this Part of this Act to be done by, to or before a magistrates' court acting for a particular petty sessions area or by, to or before an officer of that court may be done by, to or before a magistrates' court acting for such other petty sessions area as the rules may provide or by, to or before an officer of that court;

(b) the orders made, or other things done, by a magistrates' court, or an officer of such a court, under this Part of this Act, or by a court in a Hague Convention country, notice of which is to be given to such persons as the rules may provide and the manner in which such notice shall be given;

(c) the cases and manner in which courts in Hague Convention countries are to be informed of orders made, or other things done, by a magistrates' court under this Part of this Act;

(d) the cases and manner in which a justices' clerk may take evidence needed for the purpose of proceedings in court in a Hague Convention country relating to a maintenance order to which this Part of this Act applies;

(f) the circumstances and manner in which magistrates' courts may for the purposes of this Part of this Act communicate with courts in Hague Convention countries.

(1A) For the purpose of giving effect to this Part of this Act, rules made under section 144 of the Magistrates' Courts Act 1980 may make, in relation to any proceedings brought under or by virtue of this Part of this Act, any provision not covered by subsection (1) above which—

(a) falls within subsection (2) of section 93 of the Children Act 1989, and

(b) may be made in relation to relevant proceedings under that section.

(2) Rules with respect to the matters mentioned in subsection (1) above may be made in accordance with Article 13 of the Magistrates' Courts (Northern Ireland) Order 1981 in relation to proceedings or matters in magistrates' courts in Northern Ireland under this Part of this Act.

*Rules for sheriff court*

**19.**   Without prejudice to the generality of the powers conferred on the Court of Session by section 32 of the Sheriff Courts (Scotland) Act 1971 to regulate by act of sederunt the procedure of the sheriff court, the said powers shall include power—

(a)   to prescribe the decrees granted, or other things done, by the sheriff, or an officer of the sheriff court, under this Part of this Act, or by a court in a Hague Convention country, notice of which is to be given to such persons as the act of sederunt may provide and the manner in which such notice shall be given;

(b)   to provide that evidence needed for the purpose of proceedings in a court in a Hague Convention country relating to a maintenance order to which this Part of this Act applies may, in such cases and manner as the act of sederunt may provide, be taken by a sheriff clerk or sheriff clerk depute;

(c)   to prescribe the cases and manner in which courts in a Hague Convention country are to be informed of decrees granted, or other things done, by the sheriff under this Part of this Act;

(e)   to prescribe the circumstances and manner in which the sheriff may for the purposes of this Part of this Act communicate with courts in a Hague Convention country.

*Interpretation of Part I*

**21.**   (1)   In this Part of this Act unless the context otherwise requires—

"affiliation order" means an order (however described) adjudging, finding or declaring a person to be the father of a child, whether or not it also provides for the maintenance of the child;

"the appropriate court", in relation to a person residing in England and Wales or in Northern Ireland means a magistrates' court, and in relation to a person residing in Scotland means the sheriff court, within the jurisdiction of which that person is residing;

"certificate of arrears", in relation to a maintenance order, means a certificate certifying that the sum specified in the certificate is to the best of the information or belief of the officer giving the certificate the amount of the arrears due under the order at the date of the certificate except any arrears that accrued before the date of the entry into force of the Hague Convention between the United Kingdom and the Hague Convention country in which the payer is residing, or, as the case may be, that to the best of his information or belief there are no arrears due thereunder at the date of the certificate;

"certified copy", in relation to an order of a court, means a copy of the order certified by the proper officer of the court to be a true copy;

"court" includes any tribunal or person having power to make, confirm, enforce, vary or revoke a maintenance order and "competent court in a Hague Convention country" means a court having jurisdiction on one of the grounds specified in section 6(5)(a) above;

"maintenance order" means an order (however described), including any settlement made by or before a competent court in a Hague Convention country, of any of the following descriptions, and in the case of an order which is not limited to the following descriptions, the part of the order which is so limited, that is to say—

(a)   an order (including an affiliation order or order consequent upon an affiliation order) which provides for the periodical payment of sums of money towards the maintenance of any person, being a person whom the person liable to make payments under the order is, according to the law applied in the place where the order was made, liable to maintain;

(AA) an order which has been made in Scotland, on or after the granting of a decree of divorce, for the payment of a periodical allowance by one party to the marriage to the other party;

(b) an affiliation order or order consequent upon an affiliation order, being an order which provides for the payment by a person adjudged, found or declared to be a child's father of expenses incidental to the child's birth or, where the child has died, of his funeral expenses; and

(c) an order within the foregoing provisions of this definition made against a payer on the application of a public body which claims reimbursement of sums of money payable under the order with respect to the payee if the reimbursement can be obtained by the public body under the law to which it is subject,

and in the case of a maintenance order which has been varied (including a maintenance order which has been varied either by a court in the United Kingdom or by a competent court in a Hague Convention country whether or not the original order was made by such a court), means that order as varied:

Provided that the expression "maintenance order" shall not include an order made in a Hague Convention country of a description which that country or the United Kingdom has reserved the right under Article 26 of the Hague Convention not to recognise or enforce;

"order" means an order however described giving effect to a decision rendered by a court and, as respects Scotland, includes any interlocutor, and any decree or provision contained in an interlocutor;

"payee", in relation to a maintenance order, means the person entitled to the payments for which the order provides and includes a public body which has provided benefits for the payee and which is entitled *ipso jure* under the law to which it is subject to claim enforcement of the said order to the extent of the benefits so provided in place of the said person;

"payer", in relation to a maintenance order, means the person liable to make payments under the order;

"prescribed", in relation to a magistrates' court in England and Wales or in Northern Ireland, means prescribed by rules made under section 144 of the Magistrates' Court Act 1980 or by rules made in accordance with Article 13 of the Magistrates' Courts (Northern Ireland) Order 1981, as the case may be, and in relation to any other court means prescribed by rules of court;

"registered order" means a maintenance order which is for the time being registered in a court in the United Kingdom under this Part of this Act and "registered" and "registration" shall be construed accordingly;

"registering court", in relation to a registered order, means the court in which that order is for the time being registered under this Part of this Act;

"revoke" and "revocation" include discharge.

(3) Any reference in this Part of this Act to the payment of money for the maintenance of a child shall be construed as including a reference to the payment of money for the child's education.

**Note.** Section 5: in sub-ss (9), (10) words omitted and sub-s (11) revoked by SI 1999/1318, art 4(a), (b) as from 28 June 1999. Section 6: in sub-s (12) words "one calendar month" substituted by words "two calendar months" in square brackets by SI 1999/1318, art 5 as from 28 June 1999. Section 8: in sub-s (3) word "clerk" substituted by words "appropriate officer" in square brackets by SI 2001/410, art 2, Schedule as from 1 April 2001, sub-s (3A) inserted by SI 2001/410, art 2, Schedule as from 1 April 2001, in sub-s (4A) in substituted sub-s (5)(a) words "the clerk of the court or the clerk of any other magistrates' court" substituted by words "a justices' chief executive" in square brackets by SI 2001/410, art 2, Schedule as from 1 April 2001, and in substituted sub-s (5)(b) words "the clerk of the court, or to the clerk of any other magistrates' court," substituted by words "a justices' chief executive" in square brackets by SI 2001/410, art 2, Schedule as from 1 April 2001.

Section 9: in sub-s (1)(a), (b) words "the method of payment of" in square brackets inserted, in sub-s (1ZA)(za) words from "and for the words" to "subsection (3)''" in square brackets inserted, sub-s (1ZA)(zab) inserted, in sub-s (1ZA)(a) words "as if in subsection (3) for the words "paragraphs (a) to (d) of section 59(3) above" there were substituted "subsection (3A) below" and after that subsection there were inserted—" substituted by words from "as if in subsection (3)" to "there were inserted—" in square brackets by SI 1999/1318, art 6(a), (c)(i)–(iii) as from 28 June 1999; in sub-s (1ZA) in inserted sub-s (3A)(a), words "the clerk of the court or the clerk of any other magistrates' court" substituted by words "a justices' chief executive" in square brackets by SI 2001/410, art 2, Schedule as from 1 April 2001, in sub-s (1ZA) in substituted sub-s (3A)(b) words "the clerk of the court, or to the clerk of any other magistrates' court," substituted by words "a justices' chief executive" in square brackets by SI 2001/410, art 2, Schedule as from 1 April 2001, in sub-s (1ZA)(b) in substituted sub-s (4)(b) words "the clerk of the court, or to the clerk of any other magistrates' court" substituted by words "a justices' chief executive" in square brackets by SI 2001/410, art 2, Schedule as from 1 April 2001; sub-s (1ZB) inserted by SI 1999/1318, art 6(d) as from 28 June 1999; sub-ss (3)–(7) revoked by SI 1999/1318, art 7(a) as from 28 June 1999; sub-s (11) inserted by SI 1999/1318, art 7(b) as from 28 June 1999.

**SCHEDULE 4**

Article 4

REVOCATIONS

| Title | Reference |
|---|---|
| The Reciprocal Enforcement of Maintenance Orders (Hague Convention Countries) Order 1979 | SI No 1979/1317 |
| The Reciprocal Enforcement of Maintenance Orders (Hague Convention Countries) (Variation) Order 1981 | SI No 1981/837 |
| The Reciprocal Enforcement of Maintenance Orders (Hague Convention Countries) (Variation) (No 2) Order 1981 | SI No 1981/1545 |
| The Reciprocal Enforcement of Maintenance Orders (Hague Convention Countries) (Variation) (No 3) Order 1981 | SI No 1981/1674 |
| The Reciprocal Enforcement of Maintenance Orders (Hague Convention Countries) (Variation) Order 1983 | SI No 1983/885 |
| The Reciprocal Enforcement of Maintenance Orders (Hague Convention Countries) (Variation) (No 2) Order 1983 | SI No 1983/1523 |
| The Reciprocal Enforcement of Maintenance Orders (Hague Convention Countries) (Variation) Order 1987 | SI No 1987/1282 |

**RECIPROCAL ENFORCEMENT OF MAINTENANCE ORDERS (REPUBLIC OF IRELAND) ORDER 1993**

**Dated** 10 March 1993

**SI 1993 No 594**

Whereas Her Majesty is satisfied that arrangements have been made in the Republic of Ireland to ensure that maintenance orders made by courts in the United Kingdom against persons in the Republic of Ireland can be enforced there:

And whereas Her Majesty is satisfied that in the interest of reciprocity it is desirable to ensure that maintenance orders made by courts in the Republic of Ireland against persons in the United Kingdom can be enforced in the United Kingdom:

Now, therefore, Her Majesty, in exercise of the powers conferred by sections 40 and 45(1) of the Maintenance Orders (Reciprocal Enforcement) Act 1972, is pleased, by and with the advice of Her Privy Council, to order, and it is hereby ordered, as follows—

**1.** This Order may be cited as the Reciprocal Enforcement of Maintenance Orders (Republic of Ireland) Order 1993 and shall come into force on 5th April 1993.

**2.** (1) The provisions of Part I of the Maintenance Orders (Reciprocal Enforcement) Act 1972 (in this Order referred to as 'the Act') shall apply in relation to the Republic of Ireland as they apply in relation to a reciprocating country, subject to the exceptions, adaptations and modifications set out in Schedule 1 to this Order.

(2) Accordingly, Part I of the Act shall, in relation to—

(a) maintenance orders made by courts in the United Kingdom against persons in the Republic of Ireland, and

(b) maintenance orders made by courts in the Republic of Ireland against persons in the United Kingdom,

have effect as set out in Schedule 2 to this Order.

**3.** The Reciprocal Enforcement of Maintenance Orders (Republic of Ireland) Order 1974 is hereby revoked.

SCHEDULE 1            Article 2(1)

MODIFICATIONS TO PART I OF THE ACT

**1.** Section 1 shall not apply.

**2.** (1) Section 2 shall be amended as follows.

(2) In subsection (1)—

(a) for the words 'before or after the commencement of this Part of this Act' there shall be substituted the words 'before, on or after 5th April 1993'; and

(b) the words 'or has assets' shall be omitted.

(3) In subsection (4)—

(a) the words 'or has assets' shall be omitted;

(b) the words 'and the nature and location of his assets in that country', in both places where they occur, shall be omitted;

(c) in paragraph (e), the word 'and' shall be omitted and after paragraph (f) there shall be inserted the following paragraphs:

'(g) if the payer did not appear in the proceedings in which the maintenance order was made, the original or a certified copy of a document which establishes that notice of the institution of the proceedings was served on the payer;

(h) a document which establishes that notice of the order was sent to the payer; and

     (i)   if the payee received legal aid in the proceedings, a written statement to that effect signed by that officer';

  (d) after the words 'that officer', where they last occur, there shall be inserted the words ', in the case of a court in England and Wales or Northern Ireland, to the Lord Chancellor, or in the case of a court in Scotland,'; and

  (e) after the words 'transmitted by' there shall be inserted the words 'the Lord Chancellor, or, as the case may be,'.

**3.**   (1) Section 3 shall be amended as follows.

  (2) In subsection (5)—

  (a) after paragraph (c) there shall be inserted—

    '(ca) a notice addressed to the payer stating that a provisional order has been made, that it has no effect unless and until confirmed with or without alteration by the court making the order, and that in considering whether or not to confirm the provisional order the court will take into account any representations made or any evidence adduced by or on behalf of the payer within three weeks from the date of service of the notice;'; and

  (b) for the words 'Secretary of State' in both places where they occur, there shall be substituted the words 'Lord Chancellor'.

  (3) For subsection (6) there shall be substituted—

'(6) The court which made a provisional order by virtue of this section shall not earlier than three weeks after the date of service of the notice referred to in paragraph (ca) of subsection (5) above consider whether or not to confirm the order and with or without alteration and shall take into account any representations made and any evidence adduced by or on behalf of the payer.

(6A) Where the payer makes any representations or adduces any evidence a copy of the representations or evidence shall be served on the person on whose application the provisional order was made before the date of the hearing at which confirmation of the provisional order will be considered and that person shall be notified in the prescribed manner of the date fixed for the hearing.

(6B) The court shall not confirm such an order unless the documents mentioned in paragraphs (a), (b), (c) and (ca) of subsection (5) above have been served on the payer in accordance with the law for the service of such documents in the Republic of Ireland and in sufficient time to enable him to arrange for his defence.

(6C) Where an order has been confirmed under this section, the prescribed officer of the court shall—

  (a) send to the payer by registered post notice of the confirmation of the order; and

  (b) send the following documents, that is to say—

    (i) a certified copy of the maintenance order as confirmed;

    (ii) a certificate signed by that officer certifying that the order is enforceable in the United Kingdom;

    (iii) if the payer did not appear in the proceedings in which the order was confirmed, the original or a certified copy of a document which establishes that the documents mentioned in paragraphs (a), (b), (c) and (ca) of subsection (5) above have been served on the payer;

    (iv) a document which establishes that notice of the confirmation of the order has been sent to the payer by registered post;

    (v) if the payee received legal aid in the proceedings, a written statement to that effect signed by that officer,

    to the Lord Chancellor with a view to their being transmitted by him to the responsible authority in the Republic of Ireland.

(6D) Where the court decides not to confirm a provisional order, it shall revoke the order.'.

**4.** (1) Section 4 shall be amended as follows.

(2) For subsection (1) there shall be substituted the following subsections—

'(1) The sheriff shall have jurisdiction in any action to which this section applies if—

(a) the pursuer resides within the jurisdiction of the sheriff;

(b) the sheriff is satisfied that, to the best of the information or belief of the pursuer, the defender is residing in the Republic of Ireland; and

(c) the sheriff would not, apart from this subsection, have jurisdiction in that action.

(2) This section applies to any action for the payment, variation or revocation of aliment which is competent in the sheriff court, and includes an action of affiliation and aliment, but does not include an action of separation and aliment or adherence and aliment, or any action containing a crave for the custody of a child.'.

(3) In subsection (3), for the words 'referred to in' there shall be substituted 'in which the sheriff has jurisdiction by virtue of'.

(4) For subsection (4) there shall be substituted—

'(4) In any action referred to in subsection (1) above, no decree shall be granted in favour of the pursuer unless—

(a) a copy of the initial writ or summons together with a copy of the warrant for citation has been sent to the responsible authority in the Republic of Ireland for service on the defender; and

(b) a copy of the initial writ or summons has been served on the defender in accordance with the law for the service of such documents in the Republic of Ireland and in sufficient time to enable him to arrange for his defence; and

(c) the grounds of action have been substantiated by sufficient evidence, and section 36(3) of the Sheriff Courts (Scotland) Act 1971 shall not apply in relation to any such action which is a summary cause.'.

(5) Subsections (5) and (6) shall be omitted.

**5.** For section 5 there shall be substituted—

'**5.** (1) This section applies to a maintenance order a certified copy of which has been sent to the Republic of Ireland in pursuance of section 2 of this Act and to a provisional order made in pursuance of section 3 of this Act which has been confirmed by a court in England and Wales or Northern Ireland under that section.

(2) Where subsection (1) of section 60 of the Magistrates' Courts Act 1980 (revocation, variation etc of orders for periodical payment) applies in relation to a maintenance order to which this section applies, that subsection shall have effect as if for the words "by order on complaint," there were substituted "on an application being made, by order".

(3) Where an application is made to a court in England and Wales or Northern Ireland by the payee for the variation or revocation of an order to which this section applies, and the payer is residing in the Republic of Ireland, the prescribed officer of the court shall send to the Lord Chancellor a certified copy of the application together with a document, authenticated in the prescribed manner, setting out or summarising the evidence in support of the application, with a view to their being transmitted by him to the responsible authority in the Republic of Ireland for service on the payer.

(4) A court in England and Wales or Northern Ireland shall not vary or revoke such an order before the expiry of three weeks from the date of service of the documents mentioned in subsection (3) above and before varying or revoking the order shall take into account any representations made and any evidence adduced by or on behalf of the payer.

(5) Where such an order is varied or revoked by a court in England and Wales or Northern Ireland, a certified copy of the order of the court and a

statement as to the service of the documents mentioned in subsection (3) above on the payer shall be sent to the court in the Republic of Ireland by which the order is being enforced.

(6) Where a maintenance order to which this section applies has been varied by an order made by a court in the United Kingdom, the maintenance order shall, as from the date on which the order of variation was made, have effect as varied by that order.

(7) Where a maintenance order to which this section applies has been revoked by an order made by a court in the United Kingdom, the maintenance order shall, as from the date on which the order of revocation was made, be deemed to have ceased to have effect except as respects any arrears due under the maintenance order at that date.'.

**6.** (1) Section 6 shall be amended as follows.

(2) For subsection (1) there shall be substituted—

'(1) This section applies to a maintenance order made whether before, on or after 5th April 1993 by a court in the Republic of Ireland.'.

(3) In subsection (2)—

(a) after the words 'received by' there shall be inserted the words 'the Lord Chancellor or';

(b) for the words 'the Secretary of State' in the second place where they occur, there shall be substituted the word 'him';

(c) the words 'or has assets' shall be omitted; and

(d) after the words 'copy of the order' there shall be inserted the words 'and the accompanying documents'.

(4) In subsection (3)—

(a) after the words 'receives from' there shall be inserted the words 'the Lord Chancellor or'; and

(b) for the words 'subsection (4)' there shall be substituted the words 'the following subsections'.

(5) In subsection (4)—

(a) the words 'has no assets' shall be omitted;

(b) for the words 'residing and has no assets within the jurisdiction of the court' there shall be substituted the words 'so residing';

(c) the words 'and the nature and location of his assets' shall be omitted; and

(d) after the words 'copy of the order' there shall be inserted the words 'and the accompanying documents to the Lord Chancellor or, as the case may be,'.

(6) After subsection (4) there shall be added—

'(5) The order shall not be registered—

(a) if such registration is contrary to public policy;

(b) if the payer did not appear in the proceedings in the Republic of Ireland and he was not served in accordance with the law of the place where he was residing with the summons or other notice of the institution of the proceedings in sufficient time to enable him to arrange for his defence;

(c) if the order is irreconcilable with a judgment given in the United Kingdom in proceedings between the same parties.

(6) If the order is registered under this section, the prescribed officer of the appropriate court shall serve notice in a prescribed form on the payer and give notice to the payee that the order has been registered.

(7) The payer may within one calendar month from the date of service of the said notice appeal to the court in which the order is registered to set aside the registration of the order on one of the grounds set out in subsection (5) above.

(8) If the payer appeals to the appropriate court to set aside the registration of the order, the prescribed officer of the court shall give notice to the payee of the appeal and of the date of the hearing of the appeal.

(9) If the payer appeals to the appropriate court to set aside the registration of the order, the court may, on the application of the payer, stay, or in Scotland sist, the proceedings if either—

(a) enforcement of the maintenance order has been suspended in the Republic of Ireland pending the determination of any form of appeal; or

(b) the time for an appeal has not yet expired and enforcement has been suspended pending the making of an appeal,

and in the latter case the court may lay down the time within which the proceedings will be stayed or sisted.

(10) If the order is not registered by virtue of subsection (5) above, the prescribed officer shall give notice to the payee in a prescribed form that the order has not been registered.

(11) A payee to whom notice has been given by the officer of any court under subsection (10) above may within one calendar month of the date of the notice appeal to that court to set aside the decision not to register the order.

(12) In the application of this section to Scotland—

(a) in subsection (6), for the words "serve notice on" there shall be substituted the words "intimate to";

(b) in subsection (7), for the words "service of the said notice" there shall be substituted the words "the said intimation"; and

(c) in subsections (7) to (11), for any reference to an appeal there shall be substituted a reference to an application and cognate expressions shall be construed accordingly.'.

**7.** Section 7 shall not apply.

**8.** (1) Section 8 shall be amended as follows.

(2) In subsection (1), for the words 'subsection (2)' there shall be substituted the words 'subsections (1A), (2), (2A) and (2B)'.

(3) After subsection (1) there shall be inserted—

'(1A) During the period within which an appeal to set aside the registration of a registered order may be made under section 6(7), and until any such appeal has been determined, no measures of enforcement may be taken against the property of the payer other than those designed to protect the interests of the payee:

Provided that nothing in this subsection shall be construed as preventing a registered order from being registered as mentioned in subsection (2) below.'.

(4) After subsection (2) there shall be inserted—

'(2A) Where in a maintenance order made in the Republic of Ireland there are provisions which are not enforceable, this section shall apply only to the remaining provisions of the order.

(2B) The payee under a registered order may request the partial enforcement of that order.'

(5) In subsection (4), after the words 'magistrates' court' where they first occur, there shall be inserted the words 'in England and Wales'.

(6) In subsection (5), the words 'or facilitating the enforcement of' shall be omitted.

(7) For subsections (7), (8) and (9) there shall be substituted—

'(7) Subject to subsection (8) below, sums of money payable under a registered order shall be payable in accordance with the order, or such part thereof as the payee may have requested should be enforced, as from the date on which the order took effect.

(8) No sums of money accruing before 1st April 1975 under a registered order shall be payable in accordance with the order.

(9) In the application of this section to Scotland—

(a) in subsection (1A), for any reference to an appeal there shall be substituted a reference to an application;

(b) subsections (2) to (5) shall be omitted; and

(c) in subsection (6), for the word "evidence" there shall be substituted the words "sufficient evidence".'.

**9.**   For section 9 there shall be substituted—

'**9.**   (1) Where a registered order has been varied by a court in the Republic of Ireland, the registered order shall, as from the date on which the order of variation took effect or 1st April 1975, whichever is the later, have effect as varied by that order.

(2) Where a registered order has been revoked by a court in the Republic of Ireland, the registered order shall, as from the date on which the order of revocation took effect or 1st April 1975, whichever is the later, be deemed to have ceased to have effect except as respects any arrears due under the registered order at that date.

(3) The prescribed officer of the registering court shall register in the prescribed manner any order varying a registered order.'

**10.**   (1) Section 10 shall be amended as follows.

(2) For subsection (1) there shall be substituted—

'(1) Where a registered order is revoked by an order made by a court in the Republic of Ireland and notice of the revocation is received by the registering court, the prescribed officer of the registering court shall cancel the registration; but any arrears due under the registered order at the date on which the order of revocation took effect or 1st April 1975, whichever is the later, shall continue to be recoverable as if the registration had not been cancelled.'.

(3) In subsection (2)—

(a) in relation to England and Wales and Northern Ireland, for the words 'is not residing within the jurisdiction of that court and has no assets within that jurisdiction against which the order can be effectively enforced' there shall be substituted the words 'has ceased to reside within the jurisdiction of that court'; and

(b) in relation to Scotland, for those words there shall be substituted the words 'is not residing in Scotland'.

(4) In subsection (3), the words 'or has assets' shall be omitted.

(5) In subsection (5)—

(a) for the words 'Secretary of State' there shall be substituted the words 'Lord Chancellor'; and

(b) for the words 'residing or has assets' there shall be substituted the words 'still residing'.

(6) In subsection (6)—

(a) the words 'or has assets' shall be omitted;

(b) for the words 'residing and has no assets within the jurisdiction of the court' there shall be substituted the words 'so residing'; and

(c) for the words 'Secretary of State' there shall be substituted the words 'Lord Chancellor'.

(7) In subsection (7)—

(a) for the words 'Secretary of State' there shall be substituted the words 'Lord Chancellor'; and

(b) the words 'and the nature and location of his assets' shall be omitted.

(8) In subsection (8), in paragraph (a), the word 'and' shall be omitted and after paragraph (b) there shall be inserted—

'; and

(c) for the words "Lord Chancellor", in each place where they occur, there shall be substituted the words "Secretary of State".'.

**11.**   (1) Section 11 shall be amended as follows.

(2) In subsection (1)—

(a) the words 'at any time' shall be omitted;

(b) after the words 'appears to' there shall be inserted the words 'the Lord Chancellor or';

(c) the words 'and has no assets', the words 'or, if having regard to all the circumstances he thinks it proper to do so, to the responsible authority in another reciprocating country', the words 'and a certified copy of any order varying that order' and the words 'and the nature and location of his assets' shall be omitted; and

(d) in paragraph (c), after the words 'information as' there shall be inserted the words 'the Lord Chancellor or'.

(3) Subsection (2) shall be omitted.

**12.** For section 12 there shall be substituted—

'**12.** (1) No appeal shall lie from a provisional order made in pursuance of section 3 of this Act by a court in England and Wales or Northern Ireland.

(2) Where in pursuance of that section any such court confirms or refuses to confirm such a provisional order, the payer or payee under the order shall have the like right of appeal (if any) from the confirmation of, or refusal to confirm, the provisional order as he would have if that order were not a provisional order and the court had made or, as the case may be, refused to make the order on the occasion on which it confirmed or, as the case may be, refused to confirm the order.

(3) Nothing in subsection (2) shall be construed as affecting any right of appeal conferred by any other enactment.'.

**13.** (1) Section 13 shall be amended as follows.

(2) In subsection (1), after paragraph (c) there shall be added—

'(d) a document purporting to be signed by a judge or officer of a court in the Republic of Ireland which establishes that certain documents were served on a person,'.

(3) In subsections (2) and (3), the word 'magistrate' in each place where it occurs shall be omitted.

**14.** (1) Section 14 shall be amended as follows.

(2) In subsection (1), for the words from 'in the prescribed manner' to the end there shall be substituted the following words—

'by the prescribed officer of the court—

(a) in England and Wales or Northern Ireland, to the Lord Chancellor, or

(b) in Scotland, to the Secretary of State,

for transmission to the responsible authority in the Republic of Ireland.'.

(3) For subsection (5) there shall be substituted—

'(5) A court in—

(a) England and Wales or Northern Ireland may for the purpose of any proceedings in that court under this Part of this Act relating to a maintenance order to which this Part of this Act applies, send to the Lord Chancellor, or

(b) Scotland may for the purpose of such proceedings in that court relating to such an action, send to the Secretary of State,

for transmission to the responsible authority in the Republic of Ireland a request for a court in the Republic of Ireland to take or provide evidence relating to such matters as may be specified in the request.'.

**15.** In section 15, the word 'magistrate' in each place where it occurs shall be omitted.

**16.** In section 16, subsections (2) to (6) shall be omitted.

**17.** (1) Section 17 shall be amended as follows.

(2) In subsection (6), in paragraph (a) the word 'or' and paragraph (b), shall be omitted.

(3) In subsection (7), paragraph (b) shall be omitted.

**18.** Section 20 shall not apply.

**19.** (1) Section 21(1) shall be amended as follows.

(2) In subsection (1)—

(a) in the definition of 'the appropriate court' the words 'or having assets', in both places where they occur, and the words 'or has assets' shall be omitted and for the words 'a sheriff court' there shall be substituted the words 'the sheriff court';

(b) in the definition of 'certificate of arrears' after the words 'date of the certificate' there shall be inserted the words 'except any arrears due under the order in respect of a period ending before 1st April 1975' and for the words 'that date' there shall be substituted the words 'the date of the certificate';

(c) in the definition of 'maintenance order' for the words 'payment of a lump sum or the making of periodical payments' there shall be substituted the words 'periodical payment of sums of money';

(d) for the definition of 'provisional order' there shall be substituted the following definition—

' "provisional order" means an order made by a court in England and Wales or Northern Ireland which is provisional only and has no effect unless and until confirmed, with or without alteration, by that court;';

(e) the definition of 'reciprocating country' shall be omitted; and

(f) in the definition of 'responsible authority', after the words 'similar to those of' there shall be inserted the words 'the Lord Chancellor or'.

(3) In subsection (2), for the words 'payment of a lump sum or the making of periodical payments' there shall be substituted the words 'periodical payment of sums of money'.

**20.** Sections 22, 23 and 24 shall not apply.

SCHEDULE 2        Article 2(2)

PART I OF THE ACT AS MODIFIED BY SCHEDULE 1

ORDERS MADE BY COURTS IN THE UNITED KINGDOM

*Transmission of maintenance order made in United Kingdom for enforcement in the Republic of Ireland*

**2.** (1) Subject to subsection (2) below, where the payer under a maintenance order made, whether before, on or after 5th April 1993, by a court in the United Kingdom is residing in the Republic of Ireland, the payee under the order may apply for the order to be sent to that country for enforcement.

(2) Subsection (1) above shall not have effect in relation to a provisional order or to an order made by virtue of a provision of Part II of this Act.

(3) Every application under this section shall be made in the prescribed manner to the prescribed officer of the court which made the maintenance order to which the application relates.

(4) If, on an application duly made under this section to the prescribed officer of a court in the United Kingdom, that officer is satisfied that the payer under the maintenance order to which the application relates is residing in the Republic of Ireland, the following documents, that is to say—

(a) a certified copy of the maintenance order;

(b) a certificate signed by that officer certifying that the order is enforceable in the United Kingdom;

(c) a certificate of arrears so signed;

(d) a statement giving such information as the officer possesses as to the whereabouts of the payer;

(e) a statement giving such information as the officer possesses for facilitating the identification of the payer;

(f)   where available, a photograph of the payer;

(g)   if the payer did not appear in the proceedings in which the maintenance order was made, the original or a certified copy of a document which establishes that notice of the institution of the proceedings was served on the payer;

(h)   a document which establishes that notice of the order was sent to the payer; and

(i)   if the payee received legal aid in the proceedings, a written statement to that effect signed by that officer,

shall be sent by that officer, in the case of a court in England and Wales or Northern Ireland, to the Lord Chancellor, or, in the case of a court in Scotland, to the Secretary of State, with a view to their being transmitted by the Lord Chancellor, or, as the case may be, the Secretary of State, to the responsible authority in the Republic of Ireland if he is satisfied that the statement relating to the whereabouts of the payer gives sufficient information to justify that being done.

(5)   Nothing in this section shall be taken as affecting any jurisdiction of a court in the United Kingdom with respect to a maintenance order to which this section applies, and any such order may be enforced, varied or revoked accordingly.

*Power of magistrates' court to make and confirm provisional maintenance order against person residing in the Republic of Ireland*

**3.**   (1)   Where an application is made to a magistrates' court for a maintenance order against a person residing in the Republic of Ireland and the court would have jurisdiction to determine the application under the Domestic Proceedings and Magistrates' Courts Act 1978 or the Children Act 1989 if that person—

(a)   were residing in England and Wales, and

(b)   received reasonable notice of the date of the hearing of the application, the court shall (subject to subsection (2) below) have jurisdiction to determine the application.

(2)   A maintenance order made by virtue of this section shall be a provisional order.

(4)   No enactment (or provision made under an enactment) requiring or enabling—

(a)   a court to transfer proceedings from a magistrates' court to a county court or the High Court, or

(b)   a magistrates' court to refuse to make an order on an application on the ground that any matter in question is one that would be more conveniently dealt with by the High Court,

shall apply in relation to an application to which subsection (1) above applies.

(5)   Where a court makes a maintenance order which is by virtue of this section a provisional order, the following documents, that is to say—

(a)   a certified copy of the maintenance order;

(b)   a document, authenticated in the prescribed manner, setting out or summarising the evidence given in the proceedings;

(c)   a certificate signed by the prescribed officer of the court certifying that the grounds stated in the certificate are the grounds on which the making of the order might have been opposed by the payer under the order;

(ca) a notice addressed to the payer stating that a provisional order has been made, that it has no effect unless and until confirmed with or without alteration by the court making the order, and that in considering whether or not to confirm the provisional order the court will take into account any representations made or any evidence adduced by or on behalf of the payer within three weeks from the date of service of the notice;

(d) a statement giving such information as was available to the court as to the whereabouts of the payer;

(e) a statement giving such information as the officer possesses for facilitating the identification of the payer; and

(f) where available, a photograph of the payer,

shall be sent by that officer to the Lord Chancellor with a view to their being transmitted by the Lord Chancellor to the responsible authority in the Republic of Ireland if he is satisfied that the statement relating to the whereabouts of the payer gives sufficient information to justify that being done.

(6) The court which made a provisional order by virtue of this section shall not earlier than three weeks after the date of service of the notice referred to in paragraph (ca) of subsection (5) above consider whether or not to confirm the order and with or without alteration and shall take into account any representations made and any evidence adduced by or on behalf of the payer.

(6A) Where the payer makes any representations or adduces any evidence, a copy of the representations or evidence shall be served on the person on whose application the provisional order was made before the date of the hearing at which confirmation of the provisional order will be considered and that person shall be notified in the prescribed manner of the date fixed for the hearing.

(6B) The court shall not confirm such an order unless the documents mentioned in paragraphs (a), (b), (c) and (ca) of subsection (5) above have been served on the payer in accordance with the law for the service of such documents in the Republic of Ireland and in sufficient time to enable him to arrange for his defence.

(6C) Where an order has been confirmed under this section, the prescribed officer of the court shall—

(a) send to the payer by registered post notice of the confirmation of the order; and

(b) send the following documents, that is to say—

   (i) a certified copy of the maintenance order as confirmed;

   (ii) a certificate signed by that officer certifying that the order is enforceable in the United Kingdom;

   (iii) if the payer did not appear in the proceedings in which the order was confirmed, the original or a certified copy of a document which establishes that the documents mentioned in paragraphs (a), (b), (c) and (ca) of subsection (5) above have been served on the payer;

   (iv) a document which establishes that notice of the confirmation of the order has been sent to the payer by registered post;

   (v) if the payee received legal aid in the proceedings, a written statement to that effect signed by that officer,

to the Lord Chancellor with a view to their being transmitted by him to the responsible authority in the Republic of Ireland.

(6D) Where the court decides not to confirm a provisional order, it shall revoke the order.

(7) In the application of this section to Northern Ireland—

(a) for subsection (1) there shall be substituted—

'(1) Where a complaint is made to a magistrates' court against a person residing in the Republic of Ireland and the complaint is one on which the court would have jurisdiction by virtue of any enactment to make a maintenance order if—

(a) that person were residing in Northern Ireland, and

(b) a summons to appear before the court to answer the complaint had been duly served on him,

the court shall have jurisdiction to hear the complaint and may (subject to subsection (2) below) make a maintenance order on the complaint.', and

(b) for subsection (4) there shall be substituted—

'(4) No enactment empowering a magistrates' court to refuse to make an order on a complaint on the ground that any matter in question is one which would be more conveniently dealt with by the High Court of Justice in Northern Ireland shall apply in relation to a complaint to which subsection (1) above applies.'.

**Note:** There is no sub-para (3) to para 3.

*Power of sheriff to make maintenance order against person residing in the Republic of Ireland*

**4.** (1) The sheriff shall have jurisdiction in any action to which this section applies if—

(a) the pursuer resides within the jurisdiction of the sheriff;

(b) the sheriff is satisfied that, to the best of the information or belief of the pursuer, the defender is residing in the Republic of Ireland; and

(c) the sheriff would not, apart from this subsection, have jurisdiction in that action.

(2) This section applies to any action for the payment, variation or revocation of aliment which is competent in the sheriff court, and includes an action of affiliation and aliment, but does not include an action of separation and aliment or adherence and aliment, or any action containing a crave for the custody of a child.

(3) Where in any action in which the payment of aliment in respect of a child is claimed, being an action in which the sheriff has jurisdiction by virtue of subsection (1) above, the sheriff is satisfied—

(a) that there are grounds on which a maintenance order containing a provision requiring the payment of aliment in respect of that child may be made in that action, but

(b) that he has no power to make that order unless he also makes an order providing for the custody of the child,

then, for the purpose of enabling the sheriff to make the maintenance order, the pursuer shall be deemed to be a person to whom the custody of the child has been committed by a decree of the sheriff which is for the time being in force.

(4) In any action in which the sheriff has jurisdiction by virtue of subsection (1) above, no decree shall be granted in favour of the pursuer unless—

(a) a copy of the initial writ or summons together with a copy of the warrant for citation has been sent to the responsible authority in the Republic of Ireland for service on the defender; and

(b) a copy of the initial writ or summons has been served on the defender in accordance with the law for the service of such documents in the Republic of Ireland and in sufficient time to enable him to arrange for his defence; and

(c) the grounds of action have been substantiated by sufficient evidence, and section 36(3) of the Sheriff Courts (Scotland) Act 1971 shall not apply in relation to any such action which is a summary cause.

*Variation and revocation of maintenance order made in United Kingdom*

**5.** (1) This section applies to a maintenance order a certified copy of which has been sent to the Republic of Ireland in pursuance of section 2 of this Act and to a provisional order made in pursuance of section 3 of this Act which has been confirmed by a court in England and Wales or Northern Ireland under that section.

(2) Where subsection (1) of section 60 of the Magistrates' Courts Act 1980 (revocation, variation etc of orders for periodical payment) applies in relation to a maintenance order to which this section applies, that subsection shall have effect as if for the words 'by order on complaint,' there were substituted 'on an application being made, by order'.

(3) Where an application is made to a court in England and Wales or Northern Ireland by the payee for the variation or revocation of an order to which this section applies, and the payer is residing in the Republic of Ireland, the prescribed officer of the court shall send to the Lord Chancellor a certified copy of the application, together with a document, authenticated in the prescribed manner, setting out or summarising the evidence in support of the application, with a view to their being transmitted by him to the responsible authority in the Republic of Ireland for service on the payer.

(4) A court in England and Wales or Northern Ireland shall not vary or revoke such an order before the expiry of three weeks from the date of service of the documents mentioned in subsection (3) above and before varying or revoking the order shall take into account any representations made and any evidence adduced by or on behalf of the payer.

(5) Where such an order is varied or revoked by a court in England and Wales or Northern Ireland a certified copy of the order of the court and a statement as to the service of the documents mentioned in subsection (3) above on the payer shall be sent to the court in the Republic of Ireland by which the order is being enforced.

(6) Where a maintenance order to which this section applies has been varied by an order made by a court in the United Kingdom, the maintenance order shall, as from the date on which the order of variation was made, have effect as varied by that order.

(7) Where a maintenance order to which this section applies has been revoked by an order made by a court in the United Kingdom, the maintenance order shall, as from the date on which the order of revocation was made, be deemed to have ceased to have effect except as respects any arrears due under the maintenance order at that date.

### ORDERS MADE BY COURTS IN THE REPUBLIC OF IRELAND

*Registration in United Kingdom court of maintenance order made in the Republic of Ireland*

**6.** (1) This section applies to a maintenance order made whether before, on or after 5th April 1993 by a court in the Republic of Ireland.

(2) Where a certified copy of an order to which this section applies is received by the Lord Chancellor or the Secretary of State from the responsible authority in the Republic of Ireland, and it appears to him that the payer under the order is residing in the United Kingdom, he shall send the copy of the order and the accompanying documents to the prescribed officer of the appropriate court.

(3) Where the prescribed officer of the appropriate court receives from the Lord Chancellor or the Secretary of State a certified copy of an order to which this section applies, he shall, subject to the following subsections, register the order in the prescribed manner in that court.

(4) Before registering an order under this section an officer of a court shall take such steps as he thinks fit for the purpose of ascertaining whether the payer under the order is residing within the jurisdiction of the court, and if after taking those steps he is satisfied that the payer is not so residing he shall return the certified copy of the order and the accompanying documents to the Lord Chancellor or, as the case may be, the Secretary of State with a statement giving such information as he possesses as to the whereabouts of the payer.

(5) The order shall not be registered—

(a) if such registration is contrary to public policy;

(b) if the payer did not appear in the proceedings in the Republic of Ireland and he was not served in accordance with the law of the place where he was residing with the summons or other notice of the institution of the proceedings in sufficient time to enable him to arrange for his defence;

(c)  if the order is irreconcilable with a judgment given in the United Kingdom in proceedings between the same parties.

(6)  If the order is registered under this section, the prescribed officer of the appropriate court shall serve notice in a prescribed form on the payer and give notice to the payee that the order has been registered.

(7)  The payer may within one calendar month from the date of service of the said notice appeal to the court in which the order is registered to set aside the registration of the order on one of the grounds set out in subsection (5) above.

(8)  If the payer appeals to the appropriate court to set aside the registration of the order, the prescribed officer of the court shall give notice to the payee of the appeal and of the date of the hearing of the appeal.

(9)  If the payer appeals to the appropriate court to set aside the registration of the order, the court may, on the application of the payer, stay, or in Scotland sist, the proceedings if either—

(a)  enforcement of the maintenance order has been suspended in the Republic of Ireland pending the determination of any form of appeal; or

(b)  the time for an appeal has not yet expired and enforcement has been suspended pending the making of an appeal,

and in the latter case the court may lay down the time within which the proceedings will be stayed or sisted.

(10)  If the order is not registered by virtue of subsection (5) above, the prescribed officer shall give notice to the payee in a prescribed form that the order has not been registered.

(11)  A payee to whom notice has been given by the officer of any court under subsection (10) above may within one calendar month of the date of the notice appeal to that court to set aside the decision not to register the order.

(12)  In the application of this section to Scotland—

(a)  in subsection (6), for the words 'serve notice on' there shall be substituted the words 'intimate to';

(b)  in subsection (7), for the words 'service of the said notice' there shall be substituted the words 'the said intimation'; and

(c)  in subsections (7) to (11), for any reference to an appeal there shall be substituted a reference to an application and cognate expressions shall be construed accordingly.

*Enforcement of maintenance order registered in United Kingdom*

**8.**  (1)  Subject to subsections (1A), (2), (2A) and (2B) below, a registered order may be enforced in the United Kingdom as if it had been made by the registering court and as if that court had had jurisdiction to make it; and proceedings for or with respect to the enforcement of any such order may be taken accordingly.

(1A)  During the period within which an appeal to set aside the registration of a registered order may be made under section 6(7) and until any such appeal has been determined, no measures of enforcement may be taken against the property of the payer other than those designed to protect the interests of the payee:

Provided that nothing in this subsection shall be construed as preventing a registered order from being registered as mentioned in subsection (2) below.

(2)  Subsection (1) above does not apply to an order which is for the time being registered in the High Court under Part I of the Maintenance Orders Act 1958 or to an order which is for the time being registered in the High Court of Justice in Northern Ireland under Part II of the Maintenance and Affiliation Orders Act (Northern Ireland) 1966.

(2A)  Where in a maintenance order made in the Republic of Ireland there are provisions which are not enforceable, this section shall apply only to the remaining provisions of the order.

(2B) The payee under a registered order may request the partial enforcement of that order.

(3) Any person for the time being under an obligation to make payments in pursuance of a registered order shall give notice of any change of address to the *clerk of* [appropriate officer] the registering court, and any person failing without reasonable excuse to give such a notice shall be liable on summary conviction to a fine not exceeding level 2 on the standard scale.

[(3A) In subsection (3) above 'appropriate officer' means—

(a) in relation to a magistrates' court in England and Wales, the justices' chief executive for the court; and

(b) in relation to a magistrates' court elsewhere, the clerk of the court.]

(4) An order which by virtue of this section is enforceable by a magistrates' court in England and Wales shall subject to the modifications of sections 76 and 93 of the Magistrates' Courts Act 1980 specified in subsections (4A) and (4B) below be enforceable as if it were a magistrates' court maintenance order made by that court.

In this subsection, 'magistrates' court maintenance order' has the same meaning as in section 150(1) of the Magistrates' Courts Act 1980.

(4A) Section 76 (enforcement of sums adjudged to be paid) shall have effect as if for subsections (4) to (6) there were substituted the following subsections—

'(4) Where proceedings are brought for the enforcement of a magistrates' court maintenance order under this section, the court may vary the order by exercising one of its powers under subsection (5) below.

(5) The powers of the court are—

(a) the power to order that payments under the order be made directly to *the clerk of the court or the clerk of any other magistrates' court* [a justices' chief executive];

(b) the power to order that payments under the order be made to *the clerk of the court or the clerk of any other magistrates' court* [a justices' chief executive], by such method of payment falling within section 59(6) above (standing order, etc) as may be specified;

(c) the power to make an attachment of earnings order under the Attachment of Earnings Act 1971 to secure payments under the order.

(6) In deciding which of the powers under subsection (5) above it is to exercise, the court shall have regard to any representations made by the debtor (within the meaning of section 59 above).

(7) Subsection (4) of section 59 above (power of court to require debtor to open account) shall apply for the purposes of subsection (5) above as it applies for the purposes of that section but as if for paragraph (a) there were substituted—

"(a) the court proposes to exercise its power under paragraph (b) of section 76(5) below, and" '.

(4B) In section 93 (complaint for arrears), subsection (6) (court not to impose imprisonment in certain circumstances) shall have effect as if for paragraph (b) there were substituted—

'(b) if the court is of the opinion that it is appropriate—

(i) to make an attachment of earnings order; or

(ii) to exercise its power under paragraph (b) of section 76(5) above.'

(5) The magistrates' court by which an order is enforceable by virtue of this section, and the officers thereof, shall take all such steps for enforcing the order as may be prescribed.

(6) In any proceedings for or with respect to the enforcement of an order which is for the time being registered in any court under this Part of this Act a certificate of arrears sent to the prescribed officer of the court shall be evidence of the facts stated therein.

(7) Subject to subsection (8) below, sums of money payable under a registered order shall be payable in accordance with the order, or such part thereof as the

payee may have requested should be enforced, as from the date on which the order took effect.

(8) No sums of money accruing before 1st April 1975 under a registered order shall be payable in accordance with the order.

(9) In the application of this section to Scotland—

(a) in subsection (1A), for any reference to an appeal there shall be substituted a reference to an application;

(b) subsections (2) to (5) shall be omitted; and

(c) in subsection (6), for the word 'evidence' there shall be substituted the words 'sufficient evidence'.

**Note.** In sub-para (3) words 'clerk of' substituted by words 'appropriate officer' in square brackets, sub-s (3A) inserted, and in sub-s (4A) words 'the clerk of the court or the clerk of any other magistrates' court' in both places substituted by words 'a justices' chief executive' in square brackets, by SI 2001/410, art 2, Schedule, as from 1 April 2001.

*Variation and revocation of maintenance order registered in United Kingdom court*

**9.** (1) Where a registered order has been varied by a court in the Republic of Ireland, the registered order shall, as from the date on which the order of variation took effect or 1st April 1975, whichever is the later, have effect as varied by that order.

(2) Where a registered order has been revoked by a court in the Republic of Ireland, the registered order shall, as from the date on which the order of revocation took effect or 1st April 1975, whichever is the later, be deemed to have ceased to have effect except as respects any arrears due under the registered order at that date.

(3) The prescribed officer of the registering court shall register in the prescribed manner any order varying a registered order.

*Cancellation of registration and transfer of order*

**10.** (1) Where a registered order is revoked by an order made by a court in the Republic of Ireland and notice of the revocation is received by the registering court, the prescribed officer of the registering court shall cancel the registration; but any arrears due under the registered order at the date on which the order of revocation took effect or 1st April 1975, whichever is the later, shall continue to be recoverable as if the registration had not been cancelled.

(2) Where the prescribed officer of the registering court is of opinion that the payer under a registered order has ceased to reside within the jurisdiction of that court, he shall cancel the registration of the order and, subject to subsection (3) below, shall send the certified copy of the order to the Lord Chancellor.

(3) Where the prescribed officer of the registering court, being a magistrates' court, is of opinion that the payer is residing within the jurisdiction of another magistrates' court in that part of the United Kingdom in which the registering court is, he shall transfer the order to that other court by sending the certified copy of the order to the prescribed officer of that other court.

(4) On the transfer of an order under subsection (3) above the prescribed officer of the court to which it is transferred shall, subject to subsection (6) below, register the order in the prescribed manner in that court.

(5) Where the certified copy of an order is received by the Lord Chancellor under this section and it appears to him that the payer under the order is still residing in the United Kingdom, he shall transfer the order to the appropriate court by sending the certified copy of the order together with the related documents to the prescribed officer of the appropriate court and, subject to subsection (6) below, that officer shall register the order in the prescribed manner in that court.

(6) Before registering an order in pursuance of subsection (4) or (5) above an officer of a court shall take such steps as he thinks fit for the purpose of ascertaining whether the payer is so residing, and if after taking those steps he is satisfied that the payer is not residing within the jurisdiction of the court he shall send the certified copy of the order to the Lord Chancellor.

(7) The officer of a court who is required by any of the foregoing provisions of this section to send to the Lord Chancellor or to the prescribed officer of another court the certified copy of an order shall send with that copy—

(a) a certificate of arrears signed by him;

(b) a statement giving such information as he possesses as to the whereabouts of the payer; and

(c) any relevant documents in his possession relating to the case.

(8) In the application of this section to Scotland—

(a) in subsection (2), for the words 'within the jurisdiction of that court' there shall be substituted the words 'in Scotland';

(b) subsections (3) and (4) shall be omitted; and

(c) for the words 'Lord Chancellor' in each place where they occur, there shall be substituted the words 'Secretary of State'.

*Steps to be taken by Lord Chancellor or Secretary of State where payer under certain orders is not residing in the United Kingdom*

**11.** (1) If it appears to the Lord Chancellor or the Secretary of State that the payer under a maintenance order, a certified copy of which has been received by him from the Republic of Ireland, is not residing in the United Kingdom, he shall send to the responsible authority in that country—

(a) the certified copy of the order in question;

(b) if the order has at any time been a registered order, a certificate of arrears signed by the prescribed officer;

(c) a statement giving such information as the Lord Chancellor or the Secretary of State possesses as to the whereabouts of the payer; and

(d) any other relevant documents in his possession relating to the case.

APPEALS

*Appeals*

**12.** (1) No appeal shall lie from a provisional order made in pursuance of section 3 of this Act by a court in England and Wales or Northern Ireland.

(2) Where in pursuance of that section any such court confirms or refuses to confirm such a provisional order, the payer or payee under the order shall have the like right of appeal (if any) from the confirmation of, or refusal to confirm, the provisional order as he would have if that order were not a provisional order and the court had made or, as the case may be, refused to make the order on the occasion on which it confirmed or, as the case may be, refused to confirm the order.

(3) Nothing in subsection (2) shall be construed as affecting any right of appeal conferred by any other enactment.

EVIDENCE

*Admissibility of evidence given in the Republic of Ireland*

**13.** (1) A statement contained in—

(a) a document, duly authenticated, which purports to set out or summarise evidence given in proceedings in a court in the Republic of Ireland; or

(b) a document, duly authenticated, which purports to set out or summarise evidence taken in that country for the purpose of proceedings in a court in the United Kingdom under this Part of this Act, whether in response to a request made by such a court or otherwise; or

(c) a document, duly authenticated, which purports to have been received in evidence in proceedings in a court in that country or to be a copy of a document so received; or

(d) a document purporting to be signed by a judge or officer of a court in the Republic of Ireland which establishes that certain documents were served on a person,

shall in any proceedings in a court in the United Kingdom relating to a maintenance order to which this Part of this Act applies be admissible as evidence of any facts stated therein to the same extent as oral evidence of that fact is admissible in those proceedings.

(2) A document purporting to set out or summarise evidence given as mentioned in subsection (1)(a) above, or taken as mentioned in subsection (1)(b) above, shall be deemed to be duly authenticated for the purposes of that subsection if the document purports to be certified by the judge or other person before whom the evidence was given or, as the case may be, by whom it was taken, to be the original document containing or recording, or, as the case may be, summarising, that evidence or a true copy of that document.

(3) A document purporting to have been received in evidence as mentioned in subsection (1)(c) above, or to be a copy of a document so received, shall be deemed to be duly authenticated for the purposes of that subsection if the document purports to be certified by a judge or officer of the court in question to have been, or to be a true copy of a document which has been, so received.

(4) It shall not be necessary in any such proceedings to prove the signature or official position of the person appearing to have given such a certificate.

(5) Nothing in this section shall prejudice the admission in evidence of any document which is admissible in evidence apart from this section.

*Obtaining of evidence needed for purpose of certain proceedings*

**14.** (1) Where for the purpose of any proceedings in a court in the Republic of Ireland relating to a maintenance order to which this Part of this Act applies a request is made by or on behalf of that court for the taking in the United Kingdom of the evidence of a person residing therein relating to matters specified in the request, such court in the United Kingdom as may be prescribed shall have power to take that evidence and, after giving notice of the time and place at which the evidence is to be taken to such persons and in such manner as it thinks fit, shall take the evidence in such manner as may be prescribed.

Evidence taken in compliance with such a request shall be sent by the prescribed officer of the court—

(a) in England and Wales or Northern Ireland, to the Lord Chancellor, or

(b) in Scotland, to the Secretary of State,

for transmission to the responsible authority in the Republic of Ireland.

(2) Where any person, not being the payer or the payee under the maintenance order to which the proceedings in question relate, is required by virtue of this section to give evidence before a court in the United Kingdom, the court may order that there shall be paid—

(a) if the court is a court in England, Wales or Scotland, out of moneys provided by Parliament; and

(b) if the court is a court in Northern Ireland, out of moneys provided by Parliament,

such sums as appear to the court reasonably sufficient to compensate that person for the expense, trouble or loss of time properly incurred in or incidental to his attendance.

(3) Section 97(1), (3) and (4) of the Magistrates' Courts Act 1980 (which provide for compelling the attendance of witnesses, etc) shall apply in relation to a magistrates' court having power under subsection (1) above to take the evidence of any person as if the proceedings in the court in the Republic of Ireland for the purpose of which a request for the taking of the evidence has been made were proceedings in the magistrates' court and had been begun by complaint.

(4) Paragraphs 71 and 73 of Schedule 1 to the Sheriff Courts (Scotland) Act 1907 (which provide for the citation of witnesses, etc) shall apply in relation to a sheriff having power under subsection (1) above to take the evidence of any person as if the proceedings in the court in the Republic of Ireland for the purpose of which a request for the taking of the evidence has been made were proceedings in the sheriff court.

(5) A court in—

(a) England and Wales or Northern Ireland may for the purpose of any proceedings in that court under this Part of this Act relating to a maintenance order to which this Part of this Act applies, send to the Lord Chancellor, or

(b) Scotland may for the purpose of such proceedings in that court relating to such an action, send to the Secretary of State,

for transmission to the responsible authority in the Republic of Ireland a request for a court in the Republic of Ireland to take or provide evidence relating to such matters as may be specified in the request.

(6) In the application of this section to Northern Ireland, in subsection (3), for the reference to section 97(1), (3) and (4) of the Magistrates' Courts Act 1980 there shall be substituted a reference to Articles 118(1), (3) and (4), 119 and 120 of the Magistrates' Courts (Northern Ireland) Order 1981.

*Order, etc made in the Republic of Ireland need not be proved*

**15.** For the purposes of this Part of this Act, unless the contrary is shown—

(a) any order made by a court in the Republic of Ireland purporting to bear the seal of that court or to be signed by any person in his capacity as a judge or officer of the court, shall be deemed without further proof to have been duly sealed or, as the case may be, to have been signed by that person;

(b) the person by whom the order was signed shall be deemed without further proof to have been a judge or officer, as the case may be, of that court when he signed it and, in the case of an officer, to have been authorised to sign it; and

(c) a document purporting to be a certified copy of an order made by a court in the Republic of Ireland shall be deemed without further proof to be such a copy.

SUPPLEMENTAL

*Payment of sums under orders made in the Republic of Ireland*

**16.** Payment of sums due under a registered order shall, while the order is registered in a court in England, Wales or Northern Ireland, be made in such manner and to such person as may be prescribed.

*Proceedings in magistrates' courts*

**17.** (4) Anything authorised or required by this Part of this Act to be done by, to or before the magistrates' court by, to or before which any other thing was done may be done by, to or before any magistrates' court acting for the same petty sessions area (or, in Northern Ireland, petty sessions district) as that court.

(5) Any application which by virtue of a provision of this Part of this Act is made to a magistrates' court in Northern Ireland shall be made by complaint.

(5A) Where the respondent to an application for the variation or revocation of—

(a) a maintenance order made by a magistrates' court in England and Wales, being an order to which section 5 of this Act applies; or

(b) a registered order which is registered in such a court,

is residing in the Republic of Ireland, a magistrates' court in England and Wales shall have jurisdiction to hear the application (where it would not have such jurisdiction apart from this subsection) if it would have had jurisdiction to hear it had the respondent been residing in England and Wales.

(6) A magistrates' court in Northern Ireland shall have jurisdiction to hear a complaint for the variation or revocation of a maintenance order made by such a court, being an order to which section 5 of this Act applies, if the defendant to the complaint is residing in the Republic of Ireland and the court would have jurisdiction to hear the complaint had the defendant been residing in Northern Ireland.

(7) Where the respondent to an application for the variation or revocation of a maintenance order made by a magistrates' court, being an order to which section 5 of this Act applies, does not appear at the time and place appointed for the hearing of the application, but the court is satisfied that the respondent is residing in the Republic of Ireland, the court may proceed to hear and determine the application at the time and place appointed for the hearing or for any adjourned hearing in like manner as if the respondent had appeared at that time and place.

(7A) In the application of this section to Northern Ireland, in subsection (7)—

(a) for the word 'respondent', in each place where it occurs, there shall be substituted 'defendant'; and

(b) for the words 'an application' and 'the application', in each place where they occur, there shall be substituted 'a complaint' and 'the complaint' respectively.

**Note:** There are no sub-paras (1)–(3) to para 17.

*Magistrates' courts rules*

**18.** (1) Without prejudice to the generality of the power to make rules under section 144 of the Magistrates' Courts Act 1980 (magistrates' courts rules), provision may be made by such rules with respect to any of the following matters, namely—

(a) the circumstances in which anything authorised or required by this Part of this Act to be done by, to or before a magistrates' court acting for a particular petty sessions area or by, to or before an officer of that court may be done by, to or before a magistrates' court acting for such other petty sessions area as the rules may provide or by, to or before an officer of that court;

(b) the orders made, or other things done, by a magistrates' court, or an officer of such a court, under this Part of this Act, or by a court in the Republic of Ireland, notice of which is to be given to such persons as the rules may provide and the manner in which such notice shall be given;

(c) the cases and manner in which courts in the Republic of Ireland are to be informed of orders made, or other things done, by a magistrates' court under this Part of this Act;

(d) the cases and manner in which a justices' clerk may take evidence needed for the purpose of proceedings in a court in the Republic of Ireland relating to a maintenance order to which this Part of this Act applies;

(e) the circumstances and manner in which cases may be remitted by magistrates' courts to courts in the Republic of Ireland;

(f) the circumstances and manner in which magistrates' courts may for the purposes of this Part of this Act communicate with courts in the Republic of Ireland.

(1A) For the purpose of giving effect to this Part of this Act, rules made under section 144 of the Magistrates' Courts Act 1980 may make, in relation to any proceedings brought under or by virtue of this Part of this Act, any provision not covered by subsection (1) above which—

(a) falls within subsection (2) of section 93 of the Children Act 1989, and

(b) may be made in relation to relevant proceedings under that section.

(2) Rules with respect to the matters mentioned in subsection (1) above may be made in accordance with Article 13 of the Magistrates' Courts (Northern Ireland) Order 1981 in relation to proceedings or matters in magistrates' courts in Northern Ireland under this Part of this Act.

*Rules for sheriff court*

**19.** Without prejudice to the generality of the powers conferred on the Court of Session by section 32 of the Sheriff Courts (Scotland) Act 1971 to regulate by act of sederunt the procedure of the sheriff court, the said powers shall include power—

(a) to prescribe the decrees granted, or other things done, by the sheriff, or an officer of the sheriff court, under this Part of this Act, or by a court in the Republic of Ireland, notice of which is to be given to such persons as the act of sederunt may provide and the manner in which such notice shall be given;

(b) to provide that evidence needed for the purpose of proceedings in a court in the Republic of Ireland relating to a maintenance order to which this Part of this Act applies may, in such cases and manner as the act of sederunt may provide, be taken by a sheriff clerk or sheriff clerk depute;

(c) to prescribe the cases and manner in which courts in the Republic of Ireland are to be informed of decrees granted, or other things done, by the sheriff under this Part of this Act;

(d) to prescribe the circumstances and manner in which cases may be remitted by the sheriff to courts in the Republic of Ireland;

(e) to prescribe the circumstances and manner in which the sheriff may for the purposes of this Part of this Act communicate with courts in the Republic of Ireland.

*Interpretation of Part I*

**21.** (1) In this Part of this Act—

'affiliation order' means an order (however described) adjudging, finding or declaring a person to be the father of a child, whether or not it also provides for the maintenance of the child;

'the appropriate court', in relation to a person residing in England and Wales or in Northern Ireland means a magistrates' court, and in relation to a person residing in Scotland means the sheriff court, within the jurisdiction of which that person is residing;

'certificate of arrears', in relation to a maintenance order, means a certificate certifying that the sum specified in the certificate is to the best of the information or belief of the officer giving the certificate the amount of the arrears due under the order at the date of the certificate except any arrears due under the order in respect of a period ending before 1st April 1975 or, as the case may be, that to the best of his information or belief there are no arrears due thereunder at the date of the certificate;

'certified copy', in relation to an order of a court, means a copy of the order certified by the proper officer of the court to be a true copy;

'court' includes any tribunal or person having power to make, confirm, enforce, vary or revoke a maintenance order;

'maintenance order' means an order (however described) of any of the following descriptions, that is to say—

(a) an order (including an affiliation order or order consequent upon an affiliation order) which provides for the periodical payment of sums of money towards the maintenance of any person, being a person whom the person liable to make payments under the order is, according to the law applied in the place where the order was made, liable to maintain;

(aa) an order which has been made in Scotland, on or after the granting of a decree of divorce, for the payment of a periodical allowance by one party to the marriage to the other party; and

(b) an affiliation order or order consequent upon an affiliation order, being an order which provides for the payment by a person adjudged, found or declared to be a child's father of expenses incidental to the child's birth or, where the child has died, of his funeral expenses,

and, in the case of a maintenance order which has been varied, means that order as varied;

'order', as respects Scotland, includes any interlocutor, and any decree or provision contained in an interlocutor;

'payee', in relation to a maintenance order, means the person entitled to the payments for which the order provides;

'payer', in relation to a maintenance order, means the person liable to make payments under the order;

'prescribed', in relation to a magistrates' court in England and Wales or in Northern Ireland, means prescribed by rules made under section 144 of the Magistrates' Courts Act 1980 or by rules made in accordance with Article 13 of the Magistrates' Courts (Northern Ireland) Order 1981, as the case may be, and in relation to any other court means prescribed by rules of court;

'provisional order' means an order made by a court in England and Wales or Northern Ireland which is provisional only and has no effect unless and until confirmed, with or without alteration, by that court;

'registered order' means a maintenance order which is for the time being registered in a court in the United Kingdom under this Part of this Act;

'registering court', in relation to a registered order, means the court in which that order is for the time being registered under this Part of this Act;

'the responsible authority', in relation to the Republic of Ireland, means any person who in that country has functions similar to those of the Lord Chancellor or the Secretary of State under this Part of this Act; and

'revoke' and 'revocation' include discharge.

(2) For the purposes of this Part of this Act an order shall be taken to be a maintenance order so far (but only so far) as it relates to the periodical payment of sums of money as mentioned in paragraph (a) of the definition of 'maintenance order' in subsection (1) above, to the payment of a periodical allowance as mentioned in paragraph (aa) of that definition, or to the payment by a person adjudged, found or declared to be a child's father of any such expenses as are mentioned in paragraph (b) of that definition.

(3) Any reference in this Part of this Act to the payment of money for the maintenance of a child shall be construed as including a reference to the payment of money for the child's education.

## CHILD MAINTENANCE (WRITTEN AGREEMENTS) ORDER 1993

**Dated** 3 March 1993

**SI 1993 No 620**

The Lord Chancellor, in exercise of the powers conferred on him by section 8(5) of the Child Support Act 1991, hereby makes the following Order—

**1.** This Order may be cited as the Child Maintenance (Written Agreements) Order 1993 and shall come into force on 5th April 1993.

**2.** Section 8 shall not prevent a court from exercising any power which it has to make a maintenance order in relation to a child in any circumstances in which paragraphs (a) and (b) of section 8(5) apply.

## CHILDREN (ADMISSIBILITY OF HEARSAY EVIDENCE) ORDER 1993

**Dated** 3 March 1993

**SI 1993 No 621**

The Lord Chancellor, in exercise of the powers conferred on him by section 96(3) of the Children Act 1989, hereby makes the following Order—

*Citation and commencement*

**1.** This Order may be cited as the Children (Admissibility of Hearsay Evidence) Order 1993 and shall come into force on 5th April 1993.

*Admissibility of hearsay evidence*

**2.** In—
    (a)  civil proceedings before the High Court or a county court; and
    (b)   (i)  family proceedings, and
          (ii)  civil proceedings under the Child Support Act 1991 in a magistrates' court,
evidence given in connection with the upbringing, maintenance or welfare of a child shall be admissible notwithstanding any rule of law relating to hearsay.

*Revocation*

**3.** The Children (Admissibility of Hearsay Evidence) Order 1991 is hereby revoked.

## HIGH COURT (DISTRIBUTION OF BUSINESS) ORDER 1993

**Dated** 3 March 1993

**SI 1993 No 622**

The Lord Chancellor, in exercise of the powers conferred on him by section 61(3)(a) and (c) of the Supreme Court Act 1981, hereby makes the following Order—

**1.** This Order may be cited as the High Court (Distribution of Business) Order 1993 and shall come into force on 5th April 1993.

**2.** There shall be assigned to the Family Division all proceedings in the High Court under the Child Support Act 1991.

**3.** In consequence of the provision made by article 2, paragraph 3 of Schedule 1 to the Supreme Court Act 1981 shall be amended by the insertion, after subparagraph (g), of the following—
'(h) all proceedings under the Child Support Act 1991.'.

## FAMILY PROCEEDINGS COURTS (CHILD SUPPORT ACT 1991) RULES 1993

**Dated** 11 March 1993

**SI 1993 No 627**

The Lord Chancellor, in exercise of the powers conferred on him by section 144 of the Magistrates' Courts Act 1980, after consultation with the Rule Committee appointed under that section, hereby makes the following Rules—

*Citation, commencement, interpretation and transitional provision*

**1.** These Rules may be cited as the Family Proceedings Courts (Child Support Act 1991) Rules 1993 and shall come into force on 5th April 1993.

**2.** In these rules—
'the Act of 1991' means the Child Support Act 1991,
'court' means a family proceedings court constituted in accordance with sections 66 and 67 of the Magistrates' Courts Act 1980 or a single justice who is a member of a family panel.

**3.** Rules 6 to 8 shall apply only to applications filed on or after 5th April 1993.

**4.** (1) Rules 2 to 16 of the Family Proceedings Courts (Matrimonial Proceedings etc) Rules 1991 shall apply as appropriate to an appeal under section 20 (appeal against decision of child support officer), where the proceedings are to be dealt with in accordance with the Child Support Appeals (Jurisdiction of Courts) Order 1993 <. . .>).

(2) The respondent to an appeal under section 20 of the Act of 1991 shall be the Secretary of State.

(3) <. . .>

(4) Where the justices' clerk or the court is considering whether or not to transfer proceedings under *section 20 or 27* [section 20] of the Act of 1991 to another court, rules 6, 14(2)(h), (4) and (11) and rule 32 of the Family Proceedings Courts (Children Act 1989) Rules 1991 shall also apply as appropriate.

**Note.** In para (1) words omitted revoked, para (3) revoked and in para (4) words 'section 20 or 27' substituted by words 'section 20' in square brackets by SI 2001/778, r 3 as from 1 April 2001.

*Disclosure of information under the Act of 1991*

**5.** Where the Secretary of State requires a person mentioned in regulation 2(2) or (3)(a) of the Child Support (Information, Evidence and Disclosure) Regulations 1992 to furnish information or evidence for a purpose mentioned in regulation 3(1) of those Regulations, nothing in rule 23 of the Family Proceedings Courts (Children Act 1989) Rules 1991 or rule 14 of the Family Proceedings Courts (Matrimonial Proceedings etc) Rules 1991 (confidentiality of documents) shall prevent that person from furnishing the information or evidence sought or shall require him to seek leave of the court before doing so.

*Applications for relief which is precluded by the Act of 1991*

**6.** (1) Where an application is made for an order which, in the opinion of the justices' clerk, the court would be prevented from making by section 8 or 9 of the

Act of 1991, *he* [the justices' chief executive] may send a notice in the appropriate form to the applicant and the provisions of rule 4(1) to (3) of the Family Proceedings Courts (Matrimonial Proceedings etc) Rules 1991 (service) shall apply as appropriate.

(2) Where a notice is sent under paragraph (1), no requirement of any rules, except for those of this rule, as to the service of the application or as to any other procedural step applicable to the making of an application of the type in question, shall apply unless and until the court directs that such rules shall apply or that they shall apply to such extent and subject to such modifications as may be specified in the direction.

(3) Where an applicant who has been sent a notice under paragraph (1) informs the *justices' clerk* [justices' chief executive] in writing, within 14 days of the date of service of the notice, that he wishes to persist with his application, the justices' clerk shall give such directions as he considers appropriate for the matter to be heard and determined by the court and, without prejudice to the generality of the foregoing, such directions may provide for the hearing to be ex parte.

(4) Where directions are given under paragraph (3), the *justices' clerk* [justices' chief executive]shall inform the applicant of the directions and, in relation to the other parties—

    (a) where the hearing is to be ex parte, inform them briefly—
        (i) of the nature and effect of the notice under this rule,
        (ii) that the matter is being resolved ex parte, and
        (iii) that they will be informed of the result in due course; and
    (b) where the hearing is to be inter partes, inform them of—
        (i) the circumstances which led to the directions being given, and
        (ii) the directions.

(5) Where a notice has been sent under paragraph (1) and the *justices' clerk* [justices' chief executive] is not informed under paragraph (3) the application shall be treated as having been withdrawn.

(6) Where the matter is heard pursuant to directions under paragraph (3) and the court determines that it would be prevented by section 8 or 9 of the Act of 1991 from making the order sought by the application, it shall dismiss the application.

(7) Where the court dismisses an application under this rule it shall give its reasons in writing, copies of which shall be sent to the parties by the *justices' clerk* [justices' chief executive].

(8) In this rule, 'the matter' means the question whether the making of an order in the terms sought by the application would be prevented by section 8 or 9 of the Act of 1991.

(9) Rule 15 of the Family Proceedings Courts (Matrimonial Proceedings etc) Rules 1991 (delegation by justices' clerk) shall apply as appropriate to anything authorised to be done by or to a justices' clerk under this rule or rule 7.

**Note.** Amended by SI 2001/615, r 2(xxix), Schedule, paras 131, 132 as from 1 April 2001.

*Modification of rule 6 in relation to non-free standing applications*

**7.** Where a notice is sent under rule 6(1) in respect of an application which is contained in an application, answer or other document ('the document') which contains material extrinsic to the application—

    (a) the document shall, until the contrary is directed under sub-paragraph (c) of this rule, be treated as if it did not contain the application in respect of which the notice was served;
    (b) the *justices' clerk* [justices' chief executive] shall send to the respondents a copy of the notice under rule 6(1) and a notice informing the respondents of the effect of sub-paragraph (a) of this paragraph; and

(c) if it is determined, under rule 6, that the court would not be prevented by section 8 or 9 of the Act of 1991 from making the order sought by the application, the court shall direct that the document shall be treated as if it contained the application, and it may give such directions as it considers appropriate for the conduct of the proceedings in consequence of that direction.

**Note.** Amended by SI 2001/615, r 2(xxix), Schedule, para 132 as from 1 April 2001.

*Forms*

**8.** Appendix 1 to these Rules (new form CSA1) shall have effect.

**9.** In rules 10 to 12 of these Rules, references to a form—
   (a) by number with the prefix 'CHA' are references to the forms so numbered in Schedule 1 to the Family Proceedings Courts (Children Act 1989) Rules 1991; and
   (b) by number alone are references to the forms so numbered in Schedule 1 to the Family Proceedings Courts (Matrimonial Proceedings etc) Rules 1991.

**10.** For Form CHA13 there shall be substituted the form contained in Appendix 2 to these Rules.

**11.** (1) The amendments in paragraph (2) shall be made to—
   (a) Form CHA14 (Statement of Means);
   (b) Form 1 (Application for Order Under Section 2), Form 2 (Application for Order Under Section 6), Form 3 (Application for Order Under Section 7) and Form 4 (Application for Order Under Section 20), in the Statement of Means of the Applicant and the Statement of Means of the Respondent respectively.
   (2) The forms mentioned in paragraph (1) are amended as follows—
   (a) in section 6, after 'Other state benefit(s)' there shall be inserted 'Child Support Agency maintenance';
   (b) in section 7, after 'pocket money' there shall be inserted 'Child Support Agency payments';
   (c) in section 9, after 'Other' there shall be inserted 'Child Support Agency arrears';
   (d) in sections 7 and 9, for 'Community charge' there shall be substituted 'Council tax'.

**12.** In form CHA15 (Application for Variation/Discharge of an Order for Financial Provision), there shall be substituted for section 4 the provision contained in Appendix 3 to these Rules.

**Note:** Forms CHA13, 14 and 15 referred to above were replaced in the 'C' Series of Forms in Appendix 1 to the Family Proceedings Rules 1991. The forms are printed in Division C of the Service to this Edition.

APPENDIX 1

Rule 8

In the<br>
at

Magistrates' Court

**Notice under Rule 7(1)**
**The Family Proceedings Courts (Child Support Act 1991) Rules 1993**

**Case No**

To                                    of

I have considered your                          dated the
and the other relevant papers in these proceedings. I have formed the opinion
that the court would be prevented from making the order mentioned in the notice
sent to you on                                    [in respect of the following
children:

] because

If you wish to dispute this and argue that the court should continue to deal with your application, you must say so in writing and send it to the court office by                              . If you do this a hearing will be fixed at which you will be able to say why you think the court would be able to make the order in question.

The address of the court office is:

Dated this                 day of                              19

Clerk to the Justices

## APPENDIX 2

\*   \*   \*   \*   \*

## APPENDIX 3

\*   \*   \*   \*   \*

## CHILD SUPPORT APPEALS (JURISDICTION OF COURTS) ORDER 1993

**Dated** 31 March 1993

**SI 1993 No 961**

*These Regulations are revoked in relation to England and Wales by SI 2002/1915 art 2 and in relation to Scotland by SSI 2003/96, art 6 as from 3 March 2003 for certain purposes (the remaining purposes shall be commenced in relation to particular types of cases on the date on which the Child Support, Pensions and Social Security Act 2000, s 10 comes into force for the purposes of that type of case).*

Whereas a draft of the above Order has been laid before and approved by resolution of each House of Parliament:

Now, therefore, the Lord Chancellor in relation to England and Wales and the Lord Advocate in relation to Scotland, in exercise of the power conferred on them by section 45(1) and (7) of the Child Support Act 1991 and the Lord Advocate in exercise of the power conferred on him by section 58(7) of that Act, hereby make the following Order—

*Title, commencement and interpretation*

**1.**   This Order may be cited as the Child Support Appeals (Jurisdiction of Courts) Order 1993 and shall come into force on 5th April 1993.
**2.**   In this Order, 'the Act' means the Child Support Act 1991.

*Parentage appeals to be made to courts*

**3.**   An appeal under section 20 of the Act shall be made to a court instead of to a child support appeal tribunal in the circumstances mentioned in article 4.
**4.**   The circumstances are that—
  (a) the decision against which the appeal is brought was made on the basis that a particular person (whether the applicant or some other person) either was, or was not, a parent of a child in question, and

(b) the ground of the appeal will be that the decision should not have been made on that basis.

**5.** (1) For the purposes of article 3 above, an appeal may be made to a court in Scotland if—

(a) the child in question was born in Scotland; or

(b) the child, the absent parent or the person with care of the child is domiciled in Scotland on the date when the appeal is made or is habitually resident in Scotland on that date.

(2) Where an appeal to a court in Scotland is to be made to the sheriff, it shall be to the sheriff of the sheriffdom where—

(a) the child in question was born; or

(b) the child, the absent parent or the person with care of the child is habitually resident on the date when the appeal is made.

*Modification of section 20(2) to (4) of the Act in relation to appeals to courts*

**6.** In relation to an appeal which is to be made to a court in accordance with this Order, the reference to the chairman of a child support appeal tribunal in section 20(2) of the Act shall be construed as a reference to the court.

**7.** In relation to an appeal which has been made to a court in accordance with this Order, the references to the tribunal in section 20(3) and (4) of the Act shall be construed as a reference to the court.

*Amendment of the Law Reform (Parent and Child) (Scotland) Act 1986*

**8.** In section 8 (Interpretation) of the Law Reform (Parent and Child) (Scotland) Act 1986 at the end of the definition of 'action for declarator' there shall be inserted the words 'but does not include an appeal under section 20 (Appeals) of the Child Support Act 1991 made to the court by virtue of an order made under section 45 (jurisdiction of courts in certain proceedings) of that Act;'.

## CHILD SUPPORT (MISCELLANEOUS AMENDMENTS AND TRANSITIONAL PROVISIONS) REGULATIONS 1994

**Dated** 3 February 1994

**SI 1994 No 227**

PART I

GENERAL

*Citation and commencement*

**1.** These regulations may be cited as the Child Support (Miscellaneous Amendments and Transitional Provisions) Regulations 1994 and shall come into force on the 7 February 1994.

PART II

AMENDMENT OF REGULATIONS

\* \* \* \* \*

PART III

TRANSITIONAL PROVISIONS

**6.** (1) In this Part and Part IV of these Regulations—

'the Act' means the Child Support Act 1991;

'excess' means the amount by which the formula amount exceeds the old amount;

'existing case' means a case in which before the date when these Regulations come into force, a maintenance assessment has been made which has an effective date which also falls before that date;

'formula amount' means the amount of child support maintenance that would, but for the provisions of this Part of these Regulations, be payable under the maintenance assessment in force on the date these Regulations come into force or, if there is no such assessment, under the first assessment to come into force on or after that date;

'new case' means a case in which the effective date of the maintenance assessment falls on or after the date when these Regulations come into force;

'old amount' means, subject to paragraph (2) below, the aggregate weekly amount which was payable under the orders, agreements or arrangements mentioned in regulation 7(1)(a) below;

'pending case' means a case in which an application for a maintenance assessment has been made before the date when these Regulations come into force but no maintenance assessment has been made before that date;

'Procedure Regulations' means the Child Support (Maintenance Assessment Procedure) Regulations 1992;

'transitional amount' means an amount determined in accordance with regulation 8 below; and

'transitional period' means a period of, where the formula amount does not exceed £60, 52 weeks, and in any other case 78 weeks, beginning—

(a) in relation to an existing case, with the day that the maintenance assessment in that case *is reviewed* [was reviewed or, as the case may be, a decision is made superseding an earlier decision] following an application under regulation 10(1) to (3) below;

(b) in relation to a new case, the effective date of the maintenance assessment in that case;

(c) in relation to a pending case, the effective date of the maintenance assessment in that case or the date when these Regulations come into force, whichever is the later.

(2) In determining the old amount the *child support officer* [Secretary of State] shall disregard any payments in kind and any payments made to a third party on behalf of or for the benefit of the qualifying child or qualifying children or the person with care.

**Note.** In para (1) definition 'transitional period' words 'is reviewed' substituted by words from 'was reviewed' to 'earlier decision' and in para (2) words 'child support officer' substituted by words 'Secretary of State' by SI 1999/1510, art 32 as from 1 June 1999.

*Scope of this Part*

**7.** (1) Subject to paragraph (2) below, this Part of these Regulations applies to cases where—

(a) on 4th April 1993, and at all times thereafter until the date when a maintenance assessment was or is made under the Act, there was in force, in respect of one or more of the qualifying children in respect of whom an application for a maintenance assessment was or is made under the Act and the absent parent concerned, one or more—

(i) maintenance orders;

(ii) orders under section 151 of the Army Act 1955 (deductions from pay for maintenance of wife or child) or section 151 of the Air Force Act 1955 (deduction from pay for maintenance of wife or child) or arrangements corresponding to such an order and made under Article

       1(b) or 3 of the Naval and Marine Pay and Pensions (Deductions for Maintenance) Order 1959; or

   (iii) maintenance agreements (being agreements which are made or evidenced in writing); and

(b) the absent parent was on the relevant date and continues to be a member of a family, as defined in regulation 1(2) of the Child Support (Maintenance Assessments and Special Cases) Regulations 1992, which includes one or more children;

(c) the formula amount exceeds the old amount.

(2) Nothing in this Part of these Regulations applies to—

(a) a Category A or Category D interim maintenance assessment within the meaning of regulation 8(3) of the Procedure Regulations and made under section 12 of the Act;

(b) a case falling within the provisions of Part II of the Schedule to the Child Support Act 1991 (Commencement No 3 and Transitional Provisions) Order 1992 (modification of maintenance assessment in certain cases); or

(c) a maintenance assessment calculated in accordance with Part I of Schedule 1 to the Act which is made following a Category A or Category D interim maintenance assessment within the meaning of regulation 8 of the Procedure Regulations where that Category A or Category D interim maintenance assessment is made after 22nd January 1996.

(3) In sub-paragraph (1)(b) above 'the relevant date' means—

(a) in an existing case, the date these Regulations come into force;

(b) in a new case, the effective date of the maintenance assessment in that case; and

(c) in a pending case, the effective date of the maintenance assessment in that case or the date on which these Regulations come into force, whichever is the later.

*Transitional amount of child support maintenance*

**8.** (1) In a case to which this Part of these Regulations applies the amount of child support maintenance payable under a maintenance assessment during the transitional period shall, instead of being the formula amount, be the transitional amount.

(2) The transitional amount is—

(a) where the formula amount is not more than £60, an amount which is £20 greater than the old amount;

(b) where the formula amount is more than £60—

   (i) during the first 26 weeks of the transitional period, the old amount plus either 25 per centum of the excess or £20.00, whichever is the greater;

   (ii) during the next 26 weeks of the transitional period, the old amount plus either 50 per centum of the excess or £40.00, whichever is the greater; and

   (iii) during the last 26 weeks of the transitional period, the old amount plus either 75 per centum of the excess or £60.00, whichever is the greater.

(3) If in any case the application of the provisions of this Part of these Regulations would result in an amount of child support maintenance becoming payable which is greater than the formula amount, then those provisions shall not apply or, as the case may be, shall cease to apply to that case and the amount of child support maintenance payable in that case shall be the formula amount.

PART **IV**

PROCEDURE ETC

*Interpretation*

**9.**   In this Part of these Regulations 'the Procedure Regulations' means the Child Support (Maintenance Assessment Procedure) Regulations 1992.

*Procedure*

**10.**   (1)  The provisions of Part III of these Regulations shall not apply to a case in which there is a maintenance assessment in force on the date they come into force unless the absent parent in relation to whom that assessment was made makes an application for a review of that assessment under section 17 of the Act [before 1st June 1999 or an application on or after that date for a decision under section 17 of the Act superseding an earlier decision].

(2)  Such an application must be made not later than 3 months after the date when these Regulations come into force, but if an application is made after that period it may be accepted if the Secretary of State is satisfied that there is good reason for its being made late.

*(3)  Where a maintenance assessment is reviewed solely because of the coming into force of Part III of these Regulations the provisions of regulations 10(2) and 19 of the Procedure Regulations shall not apply in relation to that review but instead the child support officer shall notify to the relevant persons (as defined in regulation 1(2) of those Regulations) details of how the provisions of Part III of these Regulations have been applied in that case.*

[(3)  Regulation 10(2) of the Procedure Regulations shall not apply in respect of a decision made solely for the purpose of applying Part III of these Regulations but instead the Secretary of State shall notify the relevant persons (as defined in regulation 1(2) of the Procedure Regulations) of the detail of how the provisions of Part III of these Regulations have been applied in that case.]

**Note.** Amended by SI 1999/1510, art 33 as from 1 June 1999.

*Reviews*

**11.**   *(1)  The provisions of the following paragraphs shall apply where there is a review of a previous assessment under section 17, 18 or 19 of the Act (reviews) at any time when the amount payable under that assessment is or was the transitional amount.*

*(2)  Where the child support officer determines that, were a fresh assessment to be made as a result of the review, the amount payable under it (disregarding the provisions of Part III of these Regulations) (in this regulation called 'the reviewed formula amount') would be—*

*(a)  more than the formula amount, the amount of child support maintenance payable shall be the transitional amount plus the difference between the formula amount and the reviewed formula amount;*

*(b)  less than the formula amount but more than the transitional amount, the amount of child support maintenance payable shall be the transitional amount;*

*(c)  less than the transitional amount, the amount of child support maintenance payable shall be the reviewed formula amount.*

*(3)  The child support officer shall, in determining the reviewed formula amount on a review under section 17 of the Act, apply the provisions of regulations 20 to 22 of the Procedure Regulations.*

*(4)  Where a child support officer makes a fresh maintenance assessment following a review under section 18 or 19 of the Act, the effective date of that fresh maintenance assessment shall be the date prescribed under regulations 31 to 31C of the Maintenance Assessment Procedure Regulations or the first day of the maintenance period following 18th April 1995, whichever is the later.*

[*Revision and supersession*

**11.** (1) The provisions of the following paragraphs shall apply where the Secretary of State proposes to make a decision under section 16 (revision of decisions) or 17 (decisions superseding earlier decisions) of the Act with respect to a maintenance assessment under which the amount payable was the transitional amount.

(2) Where a fresh maintenance assessment would be made by virtue of a decision under section 16 or 17 of the Act and the amount payable under that assessment (disregarding the provisions of Part III of these Regulations) (in this regulation called 'the new formula amount') would be—

(a) more than the formula amount, the amount of child support maintenance payable shall be the transitional amount plus the difference between the formula amount and the new formula amount;

(b) less than the formula amount but more than the transitional amount, the amount of the child support maintenance payable shall be the transitional amount;

(c) less than the transitional amount, the amount of child support maintenance payable shall be the new formula amount.

(3) Regulations 21 and 22 of the Procedure Regulations shall apply as if the new formula amount were the amount which would be fixed in accordance with a decision superseding an earlier decision.

(4) Where the effective date of a fresh maintenance assessment made by virtue of a revision under section 16 of the Act or of a decision under section 17 of the Act superseding an earlier decision would, apart from this regulation, be before 18th April 1995—

(a) the fresh maintenance assessment; and

(b) the decision under section 16 or, as the case may be, section 17,

shall have effect as from 18th April 1995.]

**Note.** Substituted by SI 1999/1510, art 34 as from 1 June 1999.

*Reviews consequent on the amendments made by Part II*

**12.** *(1) Where a child support officer reviews a maintenance assessment in consequence only of the amendments made by Part II of these Regulations he shall not make a fresh assessment if the difference between the amount of child support maintenance fixed by the assessment currently in force and the amount that would be fixed if a fresh assessment were to be made as a result of the review is less than £1.00 a week.*

*(2) For the purposes of regulations 17(2) (intervals between periodical reviews and notice of a periodical review) and 31 (effective date of maintenance assessments following a review under sections 16 to 19 of the Act) of the Procedure Regulations, a review such as is mentioned in paragraph (1) above shall be disregarded.*

*(3) Except in relation to the amendment made by regulation 4(8) above, notwithstanding anything in regulation 31 of the Procedure Regulations the effective date of a maintenance assessment such as is mentioned in paragraph (1) above shall be the date when these Regulations come into force.*

[*Decisions consequent on the amendments made by Part II*

**12.** (1) A fresh maintenance assessment shall not be made by virtue of a decision under section 17 of the Act superseding an earlier decision in consequence only of the amendments made by Part II of these Regulations where the amount of child support maintenance fixed by the assessment currently in force and the amount that would be fixed if a fresh assessment were to be made under that section is less than £1.00 a week.

(2) Except in relation to the amendment made by regulation 4(8) above, where a fresh maintenance assessment is made by virtue of a decision under section 17 of

the Act superseding an earlier decision in consequence only of the amendments made by Part II of these Regulations, the date as from which—

(a) the fresh maintenance assessment; and

(b) the decision under section 16 or, as the case may be, section 17,

shall have effect shall be 7th February 1994.]

**Note.** Substituted by SI 1999/1510, art 35 as from 1 June 1999.

**13.** . . .

**Note.** Revoked by SI 1999/1510, art 36 as from 1 June 1999.

**14.** . . .

**Note.** Revoked by SI 1999/1510, art 36 as from 1 June 1999.

## LEGAL AID IN CIVIL PROCEEDINGS (REMUNERATION) REGULATIONS 1994

**Dated** 2 February 1994

**SI 1994 No 228**

*These Regulations, following the repeal of the enabling provisions by the Access to Justice Act 1999, s 106, Sch 15, Pt I, have lapsed, except in so far as they may continue to have effect by virtue of SI 2000/774, art 5 and SI 2001/916, art 4, Sch 2, effective from 1 April 2000.*

*Citation, commencement and transitional provisions*

**1.** (1) These Regulations may be cited as the Legal Aid in Civil Proceedings (Remuneration) Regulations 1994 and shall come into force on 25th February 1994.

(2) Subject to paragraph (3) below, these Regulations apply to proceedings in respect of which a certificate is granted on or after 25th February 1994.

(3) Where a certificate was granted before 25th February 1994 to an assisted person whose solicitor represents any other assisted person in the same proceedings under a certificate granted on or after 25th February 1994, the provisions of these Regulations shall not apply as regards the costs payable under the later certificate.

(4) Proceedings in respect of which a certificate was granted before 25th February 1994 shall be treated as if these Regulations had not been made notwithstanding any amendment issued under Part VII of the General Regulations on or after that date.

*Interpretation*

**2.** (1) In these Regulations—

'CCR Order 38' means Order 38 of the County Court Rules 1981;

['CPR' means the Civil Procedure Rules 1998, and a reference to a rule or Part, prefixed by 'CPR', means the rule (or as the case may be) Part so numbered in the CPR;]

'General Regulations' means the Civil Legal Aid (General) Regulations 1989;

'legal aid area' means an area specified by the Board under regulation 4(1) of the General Regulations and 'legal aid area 1' means the area so numbered by the Board;

'prescribed rate' means the fee or hourly rate specified in the Schedules to these Regulations corresponding to the relevant item or class of work, the level of court and the location of the solicitor's office;

'relevant authority' means the Area Director in the case of an assessment and the taxing officer in the case of a taxation;

<. . .>

(2) Unless the context otherwise requires, expressions used in *RSC Order 62, CCR Order 38* [CPR Parts 43 to 48] or in the General Regulations shall have the same meanings as in those Rules or Regulations.

**Note.** In para (1) definition 'CCR Order 38' substituted by definition 'CPR' and definition 'RSC Order 62' (omitted) revoked and in para (2) words 'RSC Order 62, CCR Order 38' substituted by words 'CPR Parts 43 to 48' in square brackets, by SI 1999/3098, reg 3(1), (2) as from 31 December 1999.

*Scope*

**3.** These regulations apply to proceedings to which Part IV of the Legal Aid Act 1988 applies except—
   (a) proceedings in the House of Lords;
   (b) proceedings in the Court of Appeal;
   (c) proceedings in magistrates' courts;
   (d) proceedings to which regulation 3(2)(a) or 3(2)(b) of the Legal Aid in Family Proceedings (Remuneration) Regulations 1991 applies;
   (e) proceedings to which section 29 of the Legal Aid Act 1988 applies;
   (f) proceedings to which Part XV of the General Regulations (Particular Courts and Tribunals) applies.

*Remuneration*

**4.** (1) *The amounts* [Subject to paragraphs (3A) to (3D), the amounts] to be allowed to solicitors on a determination of the costs of an assisted person under regulation 107A of the General Regulations shall be:—
   [(a) in accordance with Schedule 1 to these Regulations or, where the work done was done by a person or body (other than the Board) acting under the terms of a franchising contract which was entered into by the Board pursuant to its powers under section 4 of the Legal Aid Act 1988, in accordance with Schedule 2;]
   (b) in accordance with *paragraph (2) of RSC Order 62, rule 17* [CPR rule 44.4(6)] where the costs incurred relate to the kind of work to which that paragraph applies;
   (c) in accordance with *paragraph 1(1) of Appendix 2, Part I to RSC Order 62, or CCR Order 38 rule 3(3A) or (3B), whichever is applicable* [CPR rules 44.3 to 44.5], where no provision is made in the [Schedules] to these Regulations for the kind of work to which the costs relate.
   (2) The relevant authority, in determining costs referred to at 3 in the [Schedules] to these Regulations, shall allow costs at the higher rate specified where the office of the solicitor for the assisted person where the work was done is situated within legal aid area 1.
   (3) *The relevant authority* [Subject to paragraphs (3A) to (3D), the relevant authority] shall determine disbursements (including counsel's fees) in accordance with *RSC Order 62 or CCR Order 38, whichever is applicable* [CPR Parts 43 to 48].
   [(3A) Paragraphs (3B) to (3D) apply where proceedings are allocated to the fast track, and in those paragraphs 'advocate's costs' means the costs of an advocate for preparing for the trial and, if the claim proceeds to trial, for appearing at the trial, and 'fixed fast track trial costs' means the amount of fast track trial costs which could be awarded under CPR rule 46.2(1) in respect of a claim.
   (3B) Where, but for this paragraph, the amount to be allowed in respect of advocate's costs would have exceeded the fixed fast track trial costs, the amount to be allowed in respect of advocate's costs shall be equal to the fixed fast track trial costs.

(3C) Where, but for this paragraph, the amount to be allowed in respect of the costs of a legal representative's attendance at the trial to assist the advocate would have exceeded the amount prescribed by CPR rule 46.3(2), the amount to be allowed in respect of those costs shall be equal to the amount prescribed by CPR rule 46.3(2).

(3D) Paragraphs (3B) and (3C) shall have effect regardless of the awards actually made by the court under CPR Part 46.]

(4) Subject to these Regulations, the sums to be allowed to legal representatives in connection with the representation of an assisted person in proceedings to which these Regulations apply, shall be determined in accordance with Part XII of the General Regulations, RSC Order 62 and CCR Order 38 [Part XII of the General Regulations and CPR Parts 43 to 48].

**Note.** In para (1) words 'The amounts' substituted by words 'Subject to paragraphs (3A) to (3D), the amounts' in square brackets by SI 1999/3098, reg 5(1) as from 31 December 1999. Para (1)(a) substituted by SI 1996/645, reg 2. In para (1)(b) words 'paragraph (2) of RSC Order 62, rule 17' substituted by words 'CPR rule 44.4(6)' in square brackets by SI 1999/3098, reg 4(1) as from 31 December 1999. In para (1)(c) words 'paragraph 1(1) of Appendix 2, Part I to RSC Order 62, or CCR Order 38 rule 3(3A) or (3B), whichever is applicable' substituted by words 'CPR rules 44.3 to 44.5' in square brackets by SI 1999/3098, reg 4(2) as from 31 December 1999. In para (2) word 'Schedules' in square brackets substituted by SI 1996/645, reg 2. In para (3) words 'The relevant authority' and 'RSC Order 62 or CCR Order 38, whichever is applicable' substituted by words 'Subject to paragraphs (3A) to (3D), the relevant authority' and 'CPR Parts 43 to 48' in square brackets by SI 1999/3098, reg 5(2) as from 31 December 1999. Paras (3A)–(3D) inserted by SI 1999/3098, reg 5(3) as from 31 December 1999. In para (4) words 'Part XII of the General Regulations, RSC Order 62 and CCR Order 38' substituted by words 'Part XII of the General Regulations and CPR Parts 43 to 48' in square brackets by SI 1999/3098, reg 4(4) as from 31 December 1999.

*Enhancement*

**5.** (1) Upon a determination the relevant authority may allow fees at more than the prescribed rate subject to the provisions of this regulation where it appears to the relevant authority, taking into account all the relevant circumstances, that—

(a) the work was done with exceptional competence, skill or expertise;

(b) the work was done with exceptional dispatch; or

(c) the case involved exceptional circumstances or complexity.

(2) Where the relevant authority considers that any item or class of work should be allowed at more than the prescribed rate, it shall apply to that item or class of work a percentage enhancement in accordance with the following provisions of this regulation.

(3) In determining the percentage by which fees should be enhanced above the prescribed rate the relevant authority shall have regard to—

(a) the degree of responsibility accepted by the solicitor;

(b) the care, speed and economy with which the case was prepared;

(c) the novelty, weight and complexity of the case.

(4) Except in proceedings to which paragraph (5) applies, the percentage above the prescribed rate by which fees for work may be enhanced shall not exceed 100%.

(5) In proceedings in the High Court, the relevant authority may allow an enhancement exceeding 100% where it considers that, in comparison with work in other High Court proceedings which would merit 100% enhancement, the item or class of work relates to exceptionally complex matters which have been handled with exceptional competence or dispatch.

(6) In proceedings to which paragraph (5) applies, the percentage above the prescribed rate by which fees for work may be enhanced may exceed 100% but shall not exceed 200%.

(7) The relevant authority may have regard to the generality of proceedings to which these Regulations apply in determining what is exceptional within the meaning of this regulation.

*Reduction of costs*

**6.** (1) Upon a determination the relevant authority may allow costs in respect of any item or class of work at less than the prescribed rate where it appears reasonable to do so having regard to the competence or dispatch with which the item or class of work was done.

(2) Paragraph (1) is without prejudice to regulation 109 of the General Regulations.

SCHEDULE

| Column 1 | Column 2 High Court | Column 3 County Court |
| --- | --- | --- |
| **WORK** | | |
| 1. Routine letters out | £7.40 per item | £6.50 per item |
| 2. Routine telephone calls | £4.10 per item | £3.60 per item |
| 3. All other preparation work including any work which was reasonably done arising out of or incidental to the proceedings, interviews with client, witnesses, and other parties; obtaining | £74.00 per hour (£78.50 per hour where solicitor's office situated within legal aid area 1) | £65.00 per hour £69.00 per hour |

| Column 1 | Column 2 High Court | Column 3 County Court |
| --- | --- | --- |
| evidence; preparation and consideration of, and dealing with, documents, negotiations and notices; dealing with letters written and received and telephone calls which are not routine. | | |
| 4. Attending counsel in conference or at the trial or hearing of any summons or application at court, or other appointment. | £36.40 per hour | £32.00 per hour |
| 5. Attending without counsel at the trial or hearing of any cause or the hearing of any summons or other application at court, or other appointment. | £74.00 per hour | £65.00 per hour |
| 6. Travelling and waiting in connection with the above matters. | £32.70 per hour | £28.75 per hour |

**Note:** The above Schedule applies to work done between 25 February 1994 and 1 April 1996.

## SCHEDULE 1

| Column 1 | Column 2<br>High Court | Column 3<br>County Court or<br>Magistrates' Court |
|---|---|---|

**WORK**

| | | |
|---|---|---|
| 1.  Routine letters out | £7.40 per item | £6.50 per item |
| 2.  Routine telephone calls | £4.10 per item | £3.60 per item |
| 3.  All other preparation work including any work which was reasonably done arising out of or incidental to the proceedings, interviews with client, witnesses, and other parties; obtaining evidence; preparation and consideration of, and dealing with, documents, negotiations and notices; dealing with letters written and received and telephone calls which are not routine. | £74.00 per hour (£78.50 per hour where solicitor's office situated within legal aid area 1) | £65.00 per hour £69.00 per hour |
| 4.  Attending counsel in conference or at the trial or hearing of any summons or application at court, or other appointment. | £36.40 per hour | £32.00 per hour |
| 5.  Attending without counsel at the trial or hearing of any cause or the hearing of any summons or other application at court, or other appointment. | £74.00 per hour | £65.00 per hour |
| 6.  Travelling and waiting in connection with the above matters. | £32.70 per hour | £28.75 per hour |

## SCHEDULE 2

| Column 1 | Column 2<br>High Court | Column 3<br>County Court or<br>Magistrates' Court |
|---|---|---|

**WORK**

| | | |
|---|---|---|
| 1.  Routine letters out | £7.50 per item | £6.60 per item |
| 2.  Routine telephone calls | £4.15 per item | £3.65 per item |
| 3.  All other preparation work including any work which was reasonably done arising out of or incidental to the proceedings, interviews with client, witnesses, and other parties; obtaining evidence; preparation and consideration of, and dealing with, documents, negotiations and notices; dealing with letters written and received and telephone calls which are not routine. | £75.00 per hour (£79.50 per hour where solicitor's office situated within legal aid area 1) | £66.00 per hour £70.00 per hour |

| Column 1 | Column 2<br>High Court | Column 3<br>County Court or<br>Magistrates' Court |
|---|---|---|
| 4.  Attending counsel in conference or at the trial or hearing of any summons or application at court, or other appointment. | £37.00 per hour | £32.50 per hour |
| 5.  Attending without counsel at the trial or hearing of any cause or the hearing of any summons or other application at court, or other appointment. | £75.00 per hour | £66.00 per hour |
| 6.  Travelling and waiting in connection with the above matters. | £33.25 per hour | £29.20 per hour |

**Note:** Schedule 1 above applies to work done by franchisees and Schedule 2 to non-franchisees. Both Schedules apply to work done on and after 1 April 1996.

## PARENTAL ORDERS (HUMAN FERTILISATION AND EMBRYOLOGY) REGULATIONS 1994

**Dated** 28 October 1994

**SI 1994 No 2767**

*Citation, commencement, interpretation and extent*

**1.**   (1) These Regulations may be cited as the Parental Orders (Human Fertilisation and Embryology) Regulations 1994 and shall come into force on 1st November 1994.
   (2)  In these Regulations unless the context otherwise requires—
'the 1990 Act' means the Human Fertilisation and Embryology Act 1990;
'the 1976 Act' means the Adoption Act 1976 and references to sections are to sections of the 1976 Act;
'the Order' means the Adoption (Northern Ireland) Order 1987 and references to articles are to articles of the Order;
'parental order' means an order under section 30 of the 1990 Act (parental orders in favour of gamete donors) providing for a child to be treated in law as a child of the parties to a marriage.
   (3)  These Regulations extend to England and Wales and Northern Ireland.

*Application of Adoption Act 1976 provisions with modifications to parental orders and application for such orders*

**2.**   The provisions of the 1976 Act set out in column 1 of Schedule 1 to these Regulations shall have effect with the modifications (if any) set out in column 2 of that Schedule in relation to parental orders made in England and Wales and applications for such orders, as they have effect in relation to adoption and applications for adoption orders.

*Application of Adoption (Northern Ireland) Order 1987 provisions with modifications to parental orders and applications for such orders*

**3.**   The provisions of the Order set out in column 1 of Schedule 2 to these Regulations shall have effect with the modifications (if any) set out in column 2 of that Schedule in relation to parental orders made in Northern Ireland and applications for such orders as they have effect in relation to adoption and applications for adoption orders.

*References in enactments to be read as references to parental orders etc*

**4.**   Schedule 3 shall have effect so that the references mentioned in column 2, where they appear in the enactments mentioned in relation to them in column 1, shall be read in relation to parental orders and applications for such orders as provided for in column 2.

SCHEDULE 1                   Regulation 2

APPLICATION OF ADOPTION ACT 1976 PROVISIONS WITH MODIFICATIONS TO PARENTAL
ORDERS AND APPLICATIONS FOR SUCH ORDERS

| Column 1<br>provisions of the 1976 Act | Column 2<br>modifications |
|---|---|

**Applications by gamete donors for a parental order**

1. (a) Section 6 (duty to promote the welfare of the child)
   (i) As if for the words 'the adoption of a child' there were substituted the words 'an application for a parental order'; and
   (ii) as if the words 'or adoption agency' were omitted.

   (b) Section 12(1) to (3) (adoption orders)
   (i) As if for the words 'an adoption order' on each occasion they appear there were substituted the words 'a parental order';
   (ii) as if in subsection (1) for the word 'adopters' there were substituted the words 'husband and wife' and as if for the words 'an authorised' there were substituted the word 'the'.

   (c) Section 24(1) (restrictions on making adoption orders)
   (i) As if for the words 'an adoption order' there were substituted the words 'a parental order'; and
   (ii) as if for the words 'a British adoption order' there were substituted the words 'such an order'.

   (d) Section 27(1) (restrictions on removal while application is pending)
   As if for the words 'an adoption order is pending in a case where a parent or guardian of the child has agreed to the making of the adoption order (whether or not he knows the identity of the applicant)' there were substituted the words 'a parental order is pending'.

   (e) Section 29 (return of a child taken away in breach of section 27 or 28 of the 1976 Act)
   (i) As if for paragraphs (a) to (c) of subsections (1) and (2) there were substituted the words
   '(a) section 27 as applied with modifications by regulation 2

| Column 1 provisions of the 1976 Act | Column 2 modifications |
|---|---|
| | of and paragraph 1(d) of Schedule 1 to the Parental Orders (Human Fertilisation and Embryology) Regulations 1994, |
| | (b) section 27 of the Adoption (Scotland) Act 1978 as applied with modifications by regulation 2 of and Schedule 1 to the Parental Orders (Human Fertilisation and Embryology) (Scotland) Regulations 1994, |
| | (c) Article 28 of the Adoption (Northern Ireland) Order 1987 as applied with modifications by regulation 3 of and paragraph 2(d) of Schedule 2 to the Parental Orders (Human Fertilisation and Embryology) Regulations 1994.'; and |
| | (ii) as if for the words 'an authorised' there were substituted on each occasion they appear the word 'the'. |
| **Effect of a parental order** 2. Section 39(1)(a), (2), (4) and (6) (status conferred by adoption) | (i) As if for the words 'an adopted child' there were substituted, on each occasion they appear, the words 'a child who is the subject of a parental order'; |
| | (ii) as if in section 39(1)(a) the words 'where the adopters are a married couple,' were omitted and for the words 'child of the marriage' there were substituted the words 'child of the marriage of the husband and wife'; |
| | (iii) as if in section 39(2) for the word 'adopters' there were substituted the words 'persons who obtain the parental order' and the words 'or adopter' and the words 'subject to subsection (3),' were omitted; |
| | (iv) as if in section 39(6) for the word 'adoption' there were substituted the words 'the making of the parental order' and the words 'Subject to the provisions of this |

| Column 1 | Column 2 |
|---|---|
| *provisions of the 1976 Act* | *modifications* |

Part,' and ', or after 31st December 1975, whichever is the later' were omitted.

### Interpretation of certain events consequent upon the making of a parental order

3. (a) Section 42 (rules of construction for instruments concerning property)

(i) As if in section 42(2) for the words 'section 39(1)' there were substituted the words 'section 39(1)(a) as applied with modifications by regulation 2 of and paragraph 2 of Schedule 1 to the Parental Orders (Human Fertilisation and Embryology) Regulations 1994';

(ii) as if in section 42(2), for the words 'of the adoptive parent or parents' there were substituted the words 'in respect of whom the husband and wife have obtained a parental order';

(iii) as if in section 42(2)(a) for the words 'adopted child' there were substituted the words 'child the subject of the parental order' and for the word 'adoption' there were substituted the words 'the parental order';

(iv) as if in section 42(2)(b) for the word 'adopted' there were substituted the words 'in respect of whom parental orders were made';

(v) as if in section 42(4) for the word 'adoption' there were substituted the words 'making of the parental order' and for the words 'adopted child' there were substituted the words 'child the subject of the parental order';

(vi) as if in section 42(5) for the word 'adopt' there were substituted the words 'obtain a parental order in respect of' and as if after the words in section 42(4) 'section 39(2)' and, in section 42(5) 'section 39', there were inserted the words 'as applied with modifications by regulation 2 of and paragraph 2 of Schedule 1 to the Parental Orders (Human Fertilisation and Embryology) Regulations 1994'.

| Column 1<br>*provisions of the 1976 Act* | Column 2<br>*modifications* |
|---|---|
| (b) Section 44 (property devolving with peerages etc) | As if for the words 'an adoption' on each occasion they appear there were substituted the words 'the making of a parental order'. |
| (c) Section 45 (protection of trustees and personal representatives) | As if in section 45(1) for the words 'adoption has been effected' there were substituted the words 'parental order has been made'. |
| (d) Section 46 (meaning of 'disposition') | (i) As if for the words 'this Part' on each occasion they appear and in section 46(5) the words 'the Part', there were substituted the words 'sections 39, 42, 44, 45 and 47 as applied with modifications by regulation 2 of and paragraphs 2 and 3(a), (b), (c) and (e) respectively of Schedule 1 to the Parental Orders (Human Fertilisation and Embryology) Regulations 1994'; and<br>(ii) as if in section 46(2) for the word 'applies' there were substituted the word 'apply'. |
| (e) Section 47 (miscellaneous enactments) | (i) As if for subsection (1) there were substituted the words '(1) Section 39(2) as applied with modifications by regulation 2 of and paragraph 2 of Schedule 1 to the Parental Orders (Human Fertilisation and Embryology) Regulations 1994 does not apply so as to prevent a child who is the subject of a parental order from continuing to be treated as the child of a person who was in law the child's mother or father before the order was made, for the purposes of the table of kindred and affinity in Schedule 1 to the Marriage Act 1949 and of sections 10 and 11 (incest) of the Sexual Offences Act 1956' and<br>(ii) as if in subsection (2) for the words 'Section 39' there were substituted the words 'Section 39 as applied with modifications by regulation 2 of and paragraph 2 of Schedule 1 to the Parental Orders (Human Fertilisation and Embryology) Regulations 1994'. |

| Column 1<br>*provisions of the 1976 Act* | Column 2<br>*modifications* |
|---|---|

**Registration**

4. (a) Section 50 (Adopted Children Register)

(i) As if for the words 'Adopted Children Register' on each occasion they appear, except on the second occasion in section 50(3), there were substituted the words 'Parental Order Register';

(ii) as if in section 50(1) for the words 'adoption orders' there were substituted the words 'parental orders';

(iii) as if in section 50(2) for the word 'adoption' there were substituted the words 'parental order';

(iv) as if in section 50(2) for the words 'adopted person' there were substituted the words 'person who is the subject of the parental order';

(v) as if in section 50(3) for the words 'every person shall be entitled to search that index and to have a certified copy of any entry in the Adopted Children Register in all respects upon and subject to the same terms' there were substituted the following words: 'the Registrar General shall—

(a) cause a search to be made of that index on behalf of any person or permit that person to search that index himself, and

(b) issue to any person a certified copy of any entry in the Parental Order Register,

in all respects, except as to the entitlement of any person to search that index, upon and subject to the same terms';

(vi) as if in section 50(4) for the words 'marked "Adopted" ' there were substituted the words 'marked "Re-registered by the Registrar General" pursuant to paragraph 1(3) of Schedule 1 as applied with modifications by regulation 2 of and paragraph 8(a) of Schedule 1 to the Parental Orders (Human Fertilisation and Embryology) Regulations 1994';

| Column 1 provisions of the 1976 Act | Column 2 modifications |
|---|---|
| | (vii) as if in section 50(5) after the words 'section 51' there were inserted the words 'as applied with modifications by regulation 2 of and paragraph 4(b) of Schedule 1 to the Parental Orders (Human Fertilisation and Embryology) Regulations 1994'; |
| | (viii) as if in section 50(5)(c) and (6) for the words 'an adoption order' on each occasion they appear there were substituted the words 'a parental order'; and |
| | (ix) as if in section 50(7) for the words 'adoptions and the amendment of adoption orders' there were substituted the words 'parental orders and the amendment of such orders'. |
| (b) Section 51(1) to (6) and (9) (disclosure of birth records of adopted children) | (i) As if in section 51(1) for the words 'an adopted person' there were substituted the words 'a person who is the subject of a parental order'; |
| | (ii) as if in section 51(2) for the words 'an adopted person under the age of 18 years' there were substituted the words 'a person who is the subject of a parental order and who is under the age of 18 years'; |
| | (iii) as if section 51(3)(a)(i) and (d) were omitted; |
| | (iv) as if in section 51(3)(a)(iii), (b)(ii) and (c)(ii) for the words 'adoption order' there were substituted the words 'parental order'; |
| | (v) as if in section 51(4) for the words from 'Where' to '1978' there were substituted the words 'Where a person who is the subject of a parental order and who is in England and Wales applies for information under subsection (1),'; and |
| | (vi) as if section 51(5)(a) and (c) were omitted. |
| **Procedure** 5. (a) Section 61(1) (evidence of agreement and consent) | (i) As if for the words 'this Act' there were substituted the words 'section 30 of the Human Fertilisation and Embryology Act 1990'; |

| Column 1<br>*provisions of the 1976 Act* | Column 2<br>*modifications* |
|---|---|
| | (ii) as if the words '(other than an order to which section 17(6) applies)' were omitted; and |
| | (iii) as if for the words 'and, if the document signifying the agreement or consent is witnessed in accordance with rules, it' there were substituted 'and any such written consent'. |
| (b) Section 63(2) (appeals etc) | (i) As if the words 'Subject to subsection (3)' were omitted; and |
| | (ii) as if for the words 'this Act' there were substituted the words 'section 30 of the Human Fertilisation and Embryology Act 1990'. |
| (c) Section 64 (proceedings to be in private) | As if for the words 'under this Act' there were substituted the words 'pursuant to section 30 of the Human Fertilisation and Embryology Act 1990'. |

**Orders, rules and regulations**

| | |
|---|---|
| 6. Section 67(1), (2), (5) and (6) (orders, rules and regulations) | (i) As if after the words 'this Act' on each occasion they appear, there were inserted the words 'as applied with modifications by regulation 2 of and Schedule 1 to the Parental Orders (Human Fertilisation and Embryology) Regulations 1994'; |
| | (ii) as if in section 67(2) the words ', except section 3(1),' were omitted; and |
| | (iii) as if in section 67(6) after the words 'paragraph 1(1) of Schedule 1' there were inserted the words 'as applied with modifications by regulation 2 of and paragraphs 4(b) and 8(a) respectively of Schedule 1 to the Parental Orders (Human Fertilisation and Embryology) Regulations 1994'. |

**Interpretation**

| | |
|---|---|
| 7. Section 72(1) (interpretation) | (i) As if after the definition of 'guardian' there were inserted the words ' "husband and wife" means, in relation to the provisions of this Act as they have effect in relation to parental orders and applications |

| Column 1 | Column 2 |
|---|---|
| provisions of the 1976 Act | modifications |

|  | for such orders, the husband and wife as defined in section 30 of the Human Fertilisation and Embryology Act 1990;'; and |
|---|---|
|  | (ii) as if after the definition of 'parent' there were inserted the words ' "parental order" means an order under section 30 of the Human Fertilisation and Embryology Act 1990;'. |

### Schedule 1 to the 1976 Act (registration of adoptions)

| 8. (a) Schedule 1, paragraph 1 | (i) As if in paragraph 1(1) for the words 'adoption order' there were substituted the words 'parental order'; |
|---|---|
|  | (ii) as if in paragraph 1(1) for the words 'Adopted Children Register' there were substituted the words 'Parental Order Register'; |
|  | (iii) as if paragraph 1(2) were omitted; |
|  | (iv) as if in paragraph 1(3) for the words from 'application to a court' to 'time in force)' there were substituted the words 'application to a court for a parental order'; |
|  | (v) as if in paragraph 1(3) for the words 'any adoption order' there were substituted the words 'any parental order'; |
|  | (vi) as if in paragraph 1(3) for the words 'marked with the word "Adopted" ' there were substituted the words 'marked with the words "Re-registered by the Registrar General" '; |
|  | (vii) as if paragraph 1(4) were omitted; and |
|  | (viii) as if in paragraph 1(5) for the words 'an adoption order' there were substituted the words 'a parental order'. |
| (b) Schedule 1, paragraph 2 | (i) As if in paragraph 2(1) for the words 'an adoption order' there were substituted the words 'a parental order'; |
|  | (ii) as if in paragraph 2(1) the words 'or the Adopted Children Register' were omitted; |

| Column 1<br>*provisions of the 1976 Act* | Column 2<br>*modifications* |
|---|---|
| | (iii) as if in paragraph 2(1) for the words ' "Adopted (Scotland)" or, as the case may be, "Re-adopted (Scotland)" ' there were substituted the words ' "Re registered (Scotland)" '; |
| | (iv) as if in paragraph 2(1) the words from 'and where, after an entry has been so marked' to the end of the sub-paragraph were omitted; |
| | (v) as if in paragraph 2(2) for the words 'register of adoptions' there were substituted the words 'register of parental orders'; |
| | (vi) as if in paragraph 2(2) for the words 'an order has been made in that country authorising the adoption of a child' there were substituted the words 'a parental order has been made in that country in respect of a child'; |
| | (vii) as if in paragraph 2(2) the words 'or the Adopted Children Register' were omitted; |
| | (viii) as if in paragraph 2(2) for the words 'marked with the word "Adopted" or "Re-adopted", as the case may require' there were substituted the words 'marked with the word '"Re-registered" '; and |
| | (ix) as if in paragraph 2(3) for the words 'so marked' there were substituted the words 'marked in accordance with the provisions of sub-paragraph (1) or (2)'; and |
| | (x) as if paragraph 2(4) and (5) were omitted. |
| (c) Schedule 1, paragraph 4 | (i) As if for the words 'an adoption order' on each occasion they appear there were substituted the words 'a parental order'; |
| | (ii) as if for the words 'Adopted Children Register' on each occasion they appear there were substituted the words 'Parental Order Register'; |
| | (iii) as if in paragraph 4(1) for the words 'adopter or of the adopted person' there were substituted the words 'husband or wife or of the person who is |

| Column 1<br>provisions of the 1976 Act | Column 2<br>modifications |
|---|---|
| | the subject of the parental order'; |
| | (iv) as if in paragraph 4(1)(a) for the words 'adopter or the adopted person' there were substituted the words 'husband or wife or the child who is the subject of the parental order'; |
| | (v) as if in paragraph 4(1)(a) for the words 'given to the adopted person' there were substituted the words 'given to that child' and the words ', or taken by him,' were omitted; |
| | (vi) as if in paragraph 4(1)(b) the words 'or (4)' were omitted; |
| | (vii) as if in paragraph 4(4) after the words 'section 50' there were inserted the words 'as applied with modifications by regulation 2 of and paragraph 4(a) of Schedule 1 to the Parental Orders (Human Fertilisation and Embryology) Regulations 1994'; and |
| | (viii) as if paragraph 4(5) were omitted. |

SCHEDULE 2                                        Regulation 3

APPLICATION OF ADOPTION (NORTHERN IRELAND) ORDER 1987 PROVISIONS WITH
MODIFICATIONS TO PARENTAL ORDERS AND APPLICATIONS FOR SUCH ORDERS

\*     \*     \*     \*     \*

SCHEDULE 3                                        Regulation 4

REFERENCES IN ENACTMENTS TO BE READ AS REFERENCES TO PARENTAL ORDERS ETC

| Column 1 | Column 2 |
|---|---|
| 1. Article 37 of the Births and Deaths Registration (Northern Ireland) Order 1976 | In article 37(1) the words 'article 52(1)(a)' and 'article 50' shall be read as though they were followed by the words 'as applied with modifications by regulation 3 of and paragraph 5(c) of Schedule 2 to the Parental Orders (Human Fertilisation and Embryology) Regulations 1994.' and the reference to 'Adopted Children Register' shall be read as a reference to 'Parental Order Register'. |
| 2. Paragraph 5(a) of Schedule 8 to the Children Act 1989 | The reference in sub-paragraph (a) to a person who proposes to adopt a child under arrangements made by an adop- |

| Column 1 | Column 2 |
| --- | --- |
| | tion agency within the meaning of the Acts or Order mentioned in that sub-paragraph shall be read as including a reference to a person who proposes to be treated as the parent of a child by virtue of a parental order and the enactments about adoption as applied by these Regulations. |
| 3. Sections 27(2) and 28(5)(c) of the 1990 Act | The references to a child who is treated by virtue of adoption as not being the child of any person other than the adopter or adopters shall be read as references to a child who is treated by virtue of the making of a parental order as not being the child of any person other than the husband and wife as defined by section 30 of the 1990 Act. |

## CHILD ABDUCTION AND CUSTODY ACT 1985 (ISLE OF MAN) ORDER 1994

**Dated** 2 November 1994

**SI 1994 No 2799**

**1.**   This Order may be cited as the Child Abduction and Custody Act 1985 (Isle of Man) Order 1994 and shall come into force on 6 December 1994.

**2.**   In this Order 'the Act' means the Child Abduction and Custody Act 1985.

**3.**   The Act shall have effect in the United Kingdom as if any reference in the Act to any order which may be made, or any proceedings which may be brought or any other thing which may be done in, or in any part of, the United Kingdom, included a reference to any corresponding order which may be made, or as the case may be, proceedings which may be brought or other thing which may be done in the Isle of Man.

## FORMS OF ENTRY FOR PARENTAL ORDERS REGULATIONS 1994

**Dated** 23 November 1994

**SI 1994 No 2981**

The Registrar General in exercise of the powers conferred on him by section 67(5) of, and paragraph 1(1) of Schedule 1 to the Adoption Act 1976 as applied, with modifications, by regulation 2 of and paragraphs 6 and (8)(a) of Schedule 1 to the Parental Orders (Human Fertilisation and Embryology) Regulations 1994, with the approval of the Secretary of State in accordance with section 67(6) of that Act as applied with modifications by paragraph 6 of Schedule 1 to those Regulations, of powers conferred by section 26(3) of the Welsh Language Act 1993, and of all other powers enabling him in that behalf, hereby makes the following Regulations—

*Citation and commencement*

**1.** These Regulations may be cited as the Forms of Entry for Parental Orders Regulations 1994 and shall come into force on 15 December 1994.

*Forms of entry in the Parental Order Register*

**2.** The entry to be made in the Parental Order Register pursuant to a direction made by—

(a) a court sitting in England, shall be in the form set out in Schedule 1 to these Regulations,

(b) a court sitting in Wales, shall be in the form set out in Schedule 2 to these Regulations.

SCHEDULE 1                                                              Regulation 2(a)

FORM OF ENTRY IN THE PARENTAL ORDER REGISTER (ENGLAND)

| | |
|---|---|
| **BIRTH** | Entry No |
| Registration district          Administrative area <br><br> Sub-district | |
| 1.  Date and place of birth        **CHILD** | |
| 2.  Name and surname | 3.  Sex |
| 4.  Name and surname        **FATHER** | |
| 5.  Place of birth | 6.  Occupation |
| 7.  Name and surname        **MOTHER** | |
| 8(a)  Place of birth | 8(b)  Occupation |
| 9(a)  Maiden surname | 9(b)  Surname at marriage if different from maiden surname |
| 10.  Usual address (if different from place of child's birth) | |
| 11.  Date of registration | 12.  Signature of registering officer |
| 13.  Name given after registration, and surname | |

SCHEDULE 2                                                    Regulation 2(b)

FORM OF ENTRY IN THE PARENTAL ORDER REGISTER (WALES)

| **BIRTH—GENEDIGAETH** | Entry no<br>Colnod Rhif |
|---|---|

| | |
|---|---|
| Registration district<br>Dosbarth cofrestru | Administrative area |
| Sub-district<br>Is-ddosbarth | Rhanbarth gweinyddol |

| | | |
|---|---|---|
| 1. Date and place<br>   of birth | **CHILD—Y PLENTYN** | |
| Dyddiad a lle y ganwyd | | |
| 2. Name and Surname<br>   Enw a chyfenw | | 3. Sex<br><br>Rhyw |
| 4. Name and surname<br>   Enw a chyfenw | **FATHER—TAD** | |
| 5. Place of birth<br>   Lle y ganwyd | 6. Occupation<br>   Gwaith | |
| 7. Name and Surname<br>   Enw a chyfenw | **MOTHER—MAM** | |
| 8(a) Place of birth<br>     Lle y ganwyd | 8(b) Occupation<br>     Gwaith | |
| 9(a) Maiden surname<br>     Cyfenw morwynol | 9(b) Surname at marriage if different from<br>     maiden surname<br>     Cyfenw adeg priodi os yn wahanol i'r<br>     cyfenw morwynol | |
| 10. Usual address (if different from place<br>    of child's birth) | Cyfeiriad arferol (os yn wahanol i le geni'r<br>plentyn) | |
| 11. Date of registration<br><br>Dyddiad cofrestru | 12. Signature of registering officer<br>    Llofnod y swyddog cofrestru | |
| 13. Name given after registration and surname<br>    Enw a roddwyd wedi cofrestru, a chyfenw | | |

## LEGAL AID IN CONTEMPT PROCEEDINGS (REMUNERATION) REGULATIONS 1995

**Dated** 30 March 1995

**SI 1995 No 948**

**Note.** Following the repeal of the enabling provisions by the Access to Justice Act 1999, s 106, Sch 15, Pt I, these Regulations have lapsed except in so far as they may continue to have effect for the purposes specified by SI 2000/774, art 5 and SI 2001/916, art 4, Sch 2, as from 2 April 2001.

*Citation, commencement and revocations*

**1.** (1) These Regulations may be cited as the Legal Aid in Contempt Proceedings (Remuneration) Regulations 1995 and shall come into force on 24th April 1995.

(2) The Legal Aid in Contempt Proceedings (Remuneration) Regulations 1991 and the Legal Aid in Contempt Proceedings (Remuneration) (Amendment) Regulations 1992 are hereby revoked.

*Scope and transitional provisions*

**2.** These Regulations shall apply to the determination of remuneration for any work done by a legal representative pursuant to an order for representation under section 29 of the Act made on or after 24th April 1995, and where an order under that section was made before that date the remuneration payable shall be determined as if these Regulations had not come into force.

*Interpretation*

**3.** In these Regulations—
'the Act' means the Legal Aid Act 1988;
'area committee' has the meaning assigned to it by regulation 4 of the Civil Legal Aid (General) Regulations 1989;
'the Costs Regulations' means the Legal Aid in Criminal and Care Proceedings (Costs) Regulations 1989 as in force on any day of appearance in respect of which a legal representative claims remuneration under these Regulations;
'day of appearance', in relation to a legal representative, means a day or any part of a day on which he represents any person pursuant to an order for representation made under section 29 of the Act;
'fee-earner' means an authorised litigator within the meaning of section 119(1) of the Courts and Legal Services Act 1990 or any person who regularly does work in respect of which it is appropriate for an authorised litigator to make a direct charge to a client, and any reference to grades of fee-earner shall be construed in accordance with regulation 6(4) of the Costs Regulations as nearly as the circumstances permit;
'franchisee' means a person or body (other than the Board) acting under the terms of a franchising contract.

*The appropriate authority*

**4.** (1) Subject to paragraph (2), the appropriate authority for the purposes of these Regulations shall be—
(a) in the case of proceedings in the Court of Appeal, Criminal Division, the registrar of criminal appeals;
(b) in the case of proceedings in the Crown Court, an officer appointed by the Lord Chancellor for the purposes of regulation 3(1)(b) of the Costs Regulations;

(c) in any other case, the Board.

(2) The appropriate authority shall appoint or authorise the appointment of determining officers to act on its behalf under these Regulations in accordance with directions given by it or on its behalf.

*Claims for remuneration*

**5.** (1) Any claim for remuneration shall be submitted to the appropriate authority in such form and manner as it may direct and shall be submitted within 3 months of the completion of the work in respect of which the claim is made.

(2) The legal representative shall supply such further information and documents as the appropriate authority may require.

(3) The time limit within which the claim for remuneration must be submitted may, for good reason, be extended by the appropriate authority.

*Standard fee*

**6.** (1) Subject to regulation 7, the total remuneration payable under these Regulations shall be a standard fee of £72.75 for each day of appearance.

(2) Where the assisted person is represented by two legal representatives, that standard fee shall be divided into £46.50 for each day of appearance for the legal representative appearing as an advocate and £26.25 for each day of appearance for the other legal representative.

*Exceptional remuneration*

**7.** (1) A legal representative may, when he claims remuneration for work done pursuant to an order under section 29 of the Act, claim that there are exceptional circumstances which justify remuneration greater than the standard fee specified in regulation 6.

(2) The appropriate authority shall consider the claim, any further particulars, information or documents submitted by the legal representative under regulation 5(2) and any other relevant information and shall decide whether there are such exceptional circumstances.

(3) If the appropriate authority decides that there are such exceptional circumstances, it may allow any legal representative such fee as appears to it to be reasonable (having regard to the amount of the standard fee specified in regulation 6) for such work as appears to it to have been reasonably done. If it decides that there are not such exceptional circumstances, no fee shall be payable under this regulation and the standard fee specified in regulation 6 shall apply.

(4) The fee allowed to a legal representative (other than counsel) under this regulation for any work shall not exceed the rates set out in paragraphs 1(1)(a) and (b) and 1A of Part I of Schedule 1 to the Costs Regulations as appropriate to the type of work, the court in which the proceedings took place, the grade and the situation of the office of the fee-earner who did the work and whether the work was done by a franchisee.

(5) In the application of paragraph (4) the rates appropriate to the Crown Court shall apply to proceedings in all courts other than magistrates' courts.

(6) Where the fee-earner who did the work was not assigned by the court under section 32(5) of the Act, the fee allowed for his work shall not exceed the rate set out in paragraphs 1(1)(a) and (b) and 1A of Part I of Schedule 1 to the Costs Regulations as appropriate to the lowest grade of fee-earner which the appropriate authority considers would have been competent to do the work.

(7) The total of the fees allowed to counsel under this regulation in respect of proceedings covered by any one order for representation under section 29 of the Act shall not exceed the amounts set out in the Table in Part II of Schedule 2 to the Costs Regulations as appropriate to a single junior counsel instructed in an appeal to the Crown Court against conviction.

*Review and appeal*

**8.**   A legal representative who is dissatisfied with a decision made under regulation 5(3) or regulation 7(2) or with the remuneration allowed under regulation 7(3) may proceed—

(a)   where the Board is the appropriate authority, in accordance with regulations 12, 13 and 17 of the Costs Regulations, except that any application for review shall be made to, and any review shall be carried out by, an area committee nominated by the Board;

(b)   in any other case, in accordance with regulations 14 to 17 of the Costs Regulations;

as if those regulations referred to remuneration allowed under these Regulations.

*Payment of costs and recovery of overpayments*

**9.**   Regulations 10 and 10A of the Costs Regulations shall apply with the necessary modifications to the remuneration payable to any legal representative under these Regulations.

## RECIPROCAL ENFORCEMENT OF MAINTENANCE ORDERS (UNITED STATES OF AMERICA) ORDER 1995

**Dated** 18 October 1995

**SI 1995 No 2709**

Whereas Her Majesty is satisfied that arrangements have been made in the States of the United States of America specified in Schedule 1 to this Order to ensure that maintenance orders made by courts in the United Kingdom can be enforced there:

And whereas Her Majesty is satisfied that in the interest of reciprocity it is desirable to ensure that maintenance orders made by courts in those States can be enforced in the United Kingdom:

Now, therefore, Her Majesty, in exercise of the powers conferred by section 40 of the Maintenance Orders (Reciprocal Enforcement) Act 1972, is pleased, by and with the advice of Her Privy Council, to order, and it is hereby ordered, as follows—

**1.**   This Order may be cited as the Reciprocal Enforcement of Maintenance Orders (United States of America) Order 1995 and shall come into force on 1st December 1995.

**2.**   In this Order, unless the context otherwise requires—

'the Act' means the Maintenance Orders (Reciprocal Enforcement) Act 1972; and

'specified State' means a State specified in Schedule 1 to this Order.

**3.**   The provisions of Part I of the Act shall apply, with the exceptions, adaptations, and modifications specified in Schedule 2 to this Order, to maintenance orders made by courts in the United Kingdom and to maintenance orders made by courts in a specified State, and accordingly Part I of the Act shall, in relation to such orders, have effect as set out in Schedule 3 to this Order.

SCHEDULE 1                                                     Article 2

SPECIFIED STATES

| | |
|---|---|
| Alaska | Nebraska |
| Arizona | Nevada |
| Arkansas | New Jersey |
| California | [New Mexico] |
| [Colorado] | New York |
| Connecticut | North Caroline |
| Delaware | North Dakota |
| Florida | [Ohio] |
| [Georgia, Idaho and Illinois] | Oklahoma |
| Indiana | Oregon |
| Iowa | Pennsylvania |
| Kansas | South Dakota |
| Kentucky | [Tennessee] |
| Louisiana | Texas |
| Maine | Utah |
| Maryland | Vermont |
| Massachusetts | Virginia |
| [Michigan] | Washington |
| Minnesota | West Virginia |
| Missouri | Wisconsin |
| Montana | Wyoming |

**Note.** Amended by SI 2003/776, art 2, as from 15 May 2003.

SCHEDULE 2                                                     Article 3

MODIFICATIONS TO PART I OF THE ACT

**1.**   Section 1 shall not apply.

**2.**   (1)  Section 2 shall be amended as follows.

(2)  In subsection (1)—

(a)  for the words 'before or after the commencement of this Part of this Act' there shall be substituted the words 'before, on or after 1st December 1995';

(b)  for the words 'reciprocating country' there shall be substituted the words 'specified State'; and

(c)  for the word 'country' there shall be substituted the word 'State'.

(3)  In subsection (2)—

(a)  the words 'a provisional order or to' shall be omitted; and

(b)  after the word 'Act' there shall be added the words 'as applied to a specified State by the Recovery of Maintenance (United States of America) Order 1993'.

(4)  In subsection (4)—

(a)  for the words 'reciprocating country' where they first occur there shall be substituted the words 'specified State';

(b)  in paragraph (a), for the words 'a certified copy' there shall be substituted the words 'three certified copies';

(c)  in paragraph (c), at the end there shall be inserted the words 'or, in Scotland, signed by the applicant or his solicitor';

(d)  for paragraph (d) there shall be substituted—

'(d)  a sworn statement signed by the payee giving the following information—

(i)   the address of the payee;

(ii)  such information as is known as to the whereabouts of the payer; and

    (iii) a description, so far as is known, of the nature and location of
          any assets of the payer available for execution;';

(e) after the words 'that officer' where they last occur there shall be inserted
    the words ', in the case of a court in England and Wales or Northern
    Ireland, to the Lord Chancellor, or, in the case of a court in Scotland,';

(f) for the words 'Secretary of State' in the second place where they occur,
    there shall be substituted the word 'him'; and

(g) for the words 'responsible authority in the reciprocating country' there
    shall be substituted the words 'appropriate authority in the specified
    State'.

(5) In subsection (5), after the word 'and' there shall be inserted the words
', subject to section 5 below,'.

**3.**   Sections 3 and 4 shall not apply.

**4.**   For section 5 there shall be substituted—

'**5.**   (1) This section applies to a maintenance order certified copies of which
have been sent in pursuance of section 2 to a specified State for enforcement.

    (2) The jurisdiction of a court in the United Kingdom to revoke, revive or
vary a maintenance order shall be exercisable notwithstanding that the
proceedings for the revocation, revival or variation, as the case may be, of the
order are brought by or against a person residing in a specified State.

    (3) Where subsection (1) of section 60 of the Magistrates' Courts Act 1980
(revocation, variation, etc of orders for periodical payment) applies in relation
to a maintenance order to which this section applies, that subsection shall have
effect as if for the words 'by order on complaint' there were substituted 'on an
application being made, by order'.

    (4) Where an application is made by the payee to a court in the United
Kingdom for the variation or revocation of an order to which this section
applies, and the payer is residing in a specified State, the prescribed officer of
the court shall—

(a) in the case of a court in England and Wales or Northern Ireland, send to
    the Lord Chancellor, or, in the case of a court in Scotland, send to the
    Secretary of State, notice of the institution of the proceedings, including
    notice of the substance of the application, with a view to its being
    transmitted to the appropriate authority in the specified State for service
    on the payer; and

(b) give the payer notice in writing of the date fixed for the hearing by
    sending the notice by post addressed to his last known or usual place of
    abode.

    (5) Where such an application is made—

(a) the order shall not be varied or revoked unless the document mentioned
    in subsection (4)(a) above has been served on the payer in accordance
    with the law for the service of such a document in the specified State;

(b) the court, in considering whether or not to vary or revoke the order, shall
    take into account any representations made and any evidence adduced
    by or on behalf of the payer; and

(c) a copy of any such representations or evidence shall be served on the
    payee in the prescribed manner before the hearing.

    (6) Where an application is made by the payer to a court in the United
Kingdom for the variation or revocation of an order to which this section
applies, the prescribed officer of the court shall arrange for the service of notice
of institution of the proceedings, including notice of the substance of the
application, on the payee.

    (7) Where an order to which this section applies is varied or revoked by a
court in the United Kingdom the prescribed officer of the court shall send the
following documents, that is to say—

    (a) three certified copies of the order of variation or revocation; and

    (b) a written statement, signed by that officer as to whether both the payer and the payee under the order appeared in the proceedings, and, if only the applicant appeared, the original or a certified copy of a document which establishes that notice of the institution of the proceedings had been served on the other party,

in the case of a court in England and Wales or Northern Ireland, to the Lord Chancellor, or, in the case of a court in Scotland, to the Secretary of State, with a view to their being transmitted by him to the appropriate authority in the specified State for registration and enforcement of the order of variation or revocation.

    (8) Where a maintenance order to which this section applies has been varied by an order made by a court in the United Kingdom or by a court in a specified State, the maintenance order shall, as from the date on which the order of variation took effect, have effect as varied by that order.

    (9) Where a maintenance order to which this section applies has been revoked by an order made by a court in the United Kingdom or by a court in a specified State, the maintenance order shall, as from the date on which the order of revocation took effect, be deemed to have ceased to have effect except in respect of any arrears due under the maintenance order at that date.

    (10) Where a maintenance order to which this section applies has been varied or revoked by an order made by a court in a specified State, the prescribed officer of the court shall register the order of variation or revocation in the prescribed manner.'.

**5.**   (1) Section 6 shall be amended as follows.

    (2) For subsection (1) there shall be substituted—

    '(1) This section applies to a maintenance order made, whether before, on or after 1st December 1995, by a court in a specified State.'.

    (3) In subsection (2)—

    (a) after the words 'received by' there shall be inserted the words 'the Lord Chancellor or';

    (b) for the words 'responsible authority in a reciprocating country' there shall be substituted the words 'appropriate authority in a specified State'; and

    (c) for the words 'Secretary of State' in the second place where they occur, there shall be substituted the word 'him'.

    (4) In subsection (3), after the words 'receives from' there shall be inserted the words 'the Lord Chancellor or'.

    (5) In subsection (4), after the words 'copy of the order to' there shall be inserted the words 'the Lord Chancellor or' and after the words 'Secretary of State' there shall be inserted ', as the case may be,'.

**6.**   Section 7 shall not apply.

**7.**   (1) Section 8 shall be amended as follows.

    (2) For subsection (7) there shall be substituted—

    '(7) Sums of money payable under a registered order shall be payable in accordance with the order as from the date on which the order was made.'.

    (3) Subsection (8) shall be omitted.

**8.**   (1) Section 9 shall be amended as follows.

    (2) For subsection (1) there shall be substituted—

    '(1) Subject to the provisions of this section—

    (a) the registering court shall have the like power, on an application made by the payer or payee under a registered order, to vary the order as if it had been made by the registering court and as if that court had had jurisdiction to make it;

    (b) the jurisdiction of a magistrates' court to vary a registered order shall be exercisable notwithstanding that proceedings for the variation of the order are brought by or against a person residing in a specified State.'.

(3) In subsection (1B), the words 'or revoke' shall be omitted.

(4) For subsections (2) to (11) there shall be substituted—

'(2) Where an application is made by the payer to a registering court in the United Kingdom for the variation of a registered order, and the payee is residing in a specified State, the prescribed officer of the court shall—

(a) in the case of a court in England and Wales or Northern Ireland, send to the Lord Chancellor, or, in the case of a court in Scotland, send to the Secretary of State, notice of the institution of the proceedings with a view to its being transmitted by him to the appropriate authority in the specified State for service on the payee; and

(b) give the payee notice in writing of the date fixed for the hearing by sending the notice by post addressed to his last known or usual place of abode.

(3) Where such an application is made—

(a) the order shall not be varied unless the document mentioned in paragraph (a) of subsection (2) above has been served on the payee in accordance with the law for the service of such a document in the specified State;

(b) the court, in considering whether or not to make or vary the order, shall take into account any representations made and any evidence adduced by or on behalf of the payee; and

(c) a copy of any such representations and evidence shall be served on the payer by the prescribed officer of the court before the hearing.

(4) Where an application is made by the payee to a registering court in the United Kingdom for the variation of a registered order, and the payer is residing in the United Kingdom, the prescribed officer of the court shall serve the document mentioned in paragraph (a) of subsection (2) above on the payer.

(5) Where a registered order is varied by a registering court in the United Kingdom the prescribed officer of the court shall send the following documents, that is to say—

(a) three certified copies of the order of variation; and

(b) a written statement signed by that officer as to whether both the payer and the payee under the order appeared in the proceedings for the variation of the order and, if only the applicant appeared, the original or a certified copy of a document which establishes that notice of the institution of the proceedings had been served on the other party,

in the case of a court in England and Wales or Northern Ireland, to the Lord Chancellor, or, in the case of a court in Scotland, to the Secretary of State, with a view to their being transmitted by him to the appropriate authority in the specified State.

(6) Where a registered order has been varied by the registering court or by a court in a specified State, the prescribed officer of the registering court shall register the variation order in the prescribed manner.

(7) Where a registered order has been varied by the registering court or by a court in a specified State, the registered order shall, as from the date on which the variation order took effect, have effect as so varied.'.

**9.** (1) Section 10 shall be amended as follows.

(2) For subsection (1) there shall be substituted—

'(1) Where a registered order is revoked by an order made by a court in a specified State and notice of the revocation is received by the registering court, the prescribed officer of the registering court shall cancel the registration; but any arrears due under the registered order at the date on which the order of revocation took effect, shall continue to be recoverable as if the registration had not been cancelled.'.

(3) In subsections (2), (5), (6) and (7), for the words 'Secretary of State' in each place where they occur, there shall be substituted the words 'Lord Chancellor'.

(4) In paragraph (a) of subsection (7), there shall be added the words 'or, in Scotland, by the applicant or his solicitor'.

(5) In subsection (8), in paragraph (a), the word 'and' shall be omitted and after paragraph (b) there shall be inserted—

'; and
> (c) for the words "Lord Chancellor", in each place where they occur, there shall be substituted the words "Secretary of State".'

**10.** (1) Section 11 shall be amended as follows.

(2) In subsection (1)—

(a) after the words 'appears to' there shall be inserted the words 'the Lord Chancellor or';

(b) for the words 'reciprocating country' where they first occur there shall be substituted the words 'specified State';

(c) for the words 'responsible authority in that country' there shall be substituted the words 'appropriate authority in that State';

(d) for the words 'responsible authority in another reciprocating country' there shall be substituted the words 'appropriate authority in another specified State';

(e) in paragraph (b), at the end there shall be added the words 'or, in Scotland, by the applicant or his solicitor'; and

(f) after the words 'information as' there shall be inserted the words 'the Lord Chancellor or'.

(3) For subsection (2) there shall be substituted—

'(2) Where the documents mentioned in subsection (1) are sent to the appropriate authority in a specified State other than that in which the order in question was made, the Lord Chancellor or the Secretary of State shall inform the appropriate authority in the specified State in which that order was made of what he has done.'.

**11.** For section 12 there shall be substituted the following section—

'**12.** Where in pursuance of section 9 a registering court makes, or refuses to make, an order varying a registered order, the payer or the payee under the registered order shall have the like right of appeal (if any) from the order of variation or from the refusal to make it as he would have if the registered order had been made by the registering court.'.

**12.** (1) Section 13 shall be amended as follows.

(2) In subsection (1)—

(a) for the words 'reciprocating country' there shall be substituted the words 'specified State'; and

(b) in paragraphs (b) and (c), for the word 'country' there shall be substituted the word 'State'.

(3) In subsection (3), for the words 'officer of the court in question' there shall be substituted the words 'other person before whom the evidence was given'.

**13.** (1) Section 14 shall be amended as follows.

(2) In subsection (1)—

(a) for the words 'reciprocating country' where they first occur there shall be substituted the words 'specified State'; and

(b) for the words from 'in the prescribed manner' to the end there shall be substituted the following words—

'by the prescribed officer of the court—

(a) in England and Wales or Northern Ireland, to the Lord Chancellor; or

(b) in Scotland, to the Secretary of State,

for transmission to the appropriate authority in the specified State'.

(3) In subsection (2), for paragraphs (a) and (b) there shall be substituted the words 'out of moneys provided by Parliament'.

(4) In subsections (3) and (4), for the words 'reciprocating country' there shall be substituted the words 'specified State'.

(5) For subsection (5) there shall be substituted—

'(5) A court in—

  (a) England and Wales or Northern Ireland may, for the purpose of any proceedings in that court under this Part of this Act relating to a maintenance order to which this Part of this Act applies, send to the Lord Chancellor; or

  (b) Scotland may, for the purpose of such proceedings in that court relating to such an order, send to the Secretary of State,

for transmission to the appropriate authority in a specified State a request for a court in that State to take or provide evidence relating to such matters as may be specified in the request.'.

**14.** In section 15, in paragraph (a) and (c), for the words 'reciprocating country' there shall be substituted the words 'specified State'.

**15.** (1) Section 16 shall be amended as follows.

(2) In subsections (3) and (5)(a), for the words 'reciprocating country' there shall be substituted the words 'specified State'.

(3) In subsection (5), the words 'or (if earlier) the date on which it is confirmed by a court in the United Kingdom' shall be omitted.

(4) In subsection (5)(b), for the words 'a court in the United Kingdom or (if earlier) the date on which the last order varying that order is confirmed by such a court' there shall be substituted the words 'the registering court'.

**16.** (1) Section 17 shall be amended as follows.

(2) In subsection (5A), for the word 'reciprocating' there shall be substituted the words 'specified State'.

(3) For subsections (6) and (7) there shall be substituted—

'(6) A magistrates' court in Northern Ireland shall have jurisdiction—

  (a) to hear a complaint for the variation or revocation of a maintenance order made by such a court, and to which section 5 of this Act applies; or

  (b) to hear a complaint for the variation of a registered order which is registered in that court,

if the defendant to the complaint is residing in a specified State and if the court would have had jurisdiction to hear the complaint had the defendant been residing in Northern Ireland and been served with a summons to appear before the court to answer the complaint.

(7) Where the respondent to an application—

  (a) for the variation or revocation of a maintenance order made by a magistrates' court, and to which section 5 of this Act applies; or

  (b) for the variation of a registered order registered in a magistrates' court,

does not appear at the time and place appointed for the hearing of the application, but the court is satisfied that the respondent is residing in a specified State, and that the requirements of section 5(4) or (6) or section 9(2) and (4), as the case may be, have been complied with, the court may proceed to hear and determine the application at the time and place appointed for the hearing or for any adjourned hearing as if the respondent had appeared at that time and place.'.

**17.** (1) Section 18 shall be amended as follows.

(2) In subsection (1)—

  (a) in paragraphs (b) and (d), for the words 'reciprocating country' there shall be substituted the words 'specified State' and, in paragraphs (c) and (f), for the words 'reciprocating countries' there shall be substituted the words 'specified States'; and

  (b) paragraph (e) shall be omitted.

**18.** (1) Section 19 shall be amended as follows.

(2) In paragraphs (a) and (b), for the words 'reciprocating country' there shall be substituted the words 'specified State' and, in paragraphs (c) and (e), for the words 'reciprocating countries' there shall be substituted the words 'specified States'.

(3) Paragraph (d) shall be omitted.

**19.** Section 20 shall not apply.

**20.** (1) Section 21 shall be amended as follows.

(2) In subsection (1)—

(a) after the word 'Act' where it first occurs there shall be inserted the words 'unless the context otherwise requires';

(b) in the definition of 'certificate of arrears', after the word 'officer' there shall be inserted the words 'or, in Scotland, the applicant or his solicitor';

(c) in the definition of 'maintenance order'—

   (i) the word 'and' in the first place where it occurs shall be omitted; and

   (ii) after paragraph (b) there shall be inserted the following paragraph—

   '(c) an order within the foregoing provisions of this definition made against a payer on the application of a public body which claims reimbursement of sums of money payable under the order with respect to the payee if reimbursement can be obtained by the public body under the law to which it is subject,';

(d) the definition of 'provisional order' shall be omitted;

(e) the definition of 'reciprocating country' shall be omitted;

(f) in the definition of 'registered order' there shall be inserted at the end the words 'and "registered" and "registration" shall be construed accordingly';

(g) the definition of 'the responsible authority' shall be omitted; and

(h) after the definition of 'revoke' and 'revocation' there shall be inserted the following definition—

' "specified State" means a State specified in Schedule 1 to the Reciprocal Enforcement of Maintenance Orders (United States of America) Order 1995'.

**21.** Sections 22, 23 and 24 shall not apply.

SCHEDULE 3                                              Article 3

PART I OF THE ACT AS MODIFIED BY SCHEDULE 2

ORDERS MADE BY COURTS IN THE UNITED KINGDOM

*Transmission of maintenance order made in United Kingdom for enforcement in specified State*

**2.** (1) Subject to subsection (2) below, where the payer under a maintenance order made, whether before, on or after 1st December 1995, by a court in the United Kingdom is residing or has assets in a specified State, the payee under the order may apply for the order to be sent to that State for enforcement.

(2) Subsection (1) above shall not have effect in relation to an order made by virtue of a provision of Part II of this Act as applied to a specified State by the Recovery of Maintenance (United States of America) Order 1993.

(3) Every application under this section shall be made in the prescribed manner to the prescribed officer of the court which made the maintenance order to which the application relates.

(4) If, on an application duly made under this section to the prescribed officer of a court in the United Kingdom, that officer is satisfied that the payer under the maintenance order to which the application relates is residing or has assets in a specified State, the following documents, that is to say—

(a) three certified copies of the maintenance order;

(b) a certificate signed by that officer certifying that the order is enforceable in the United Kingdom;

(c)   a certificate of arrears so signed or, in Scotland, signed by the applicant or
his solicitor;

(d)   a sworn statement signed by the payee giving the following information—

(i)   the address of the payee;

(ii)   such information as is known as to the whereabouts of the payer; and

(iii)   a description, so far as is known, of the nature and location of any
assets of the payer available for execution;

(e)   a statement giving such information as the officer possesses for facilitating
the identification of the payer; and

(f)   where available, a photographer of the payer;

shall be sent by that officer, in the case of a court in England and Wales or
Northern Ireland, to the Lord Chancellor, or, in the case of a court in Scotland, to
the Secretary of State, with a view to their being transmitted by him to the
appropriate authority in the specified State if he is satisfied that the statement
relating to the whereabouts of the payer and the nature and location of his assets
gives sufficient information to justify that being done.

(5)   Nothing in this section shall be taken as affecting any jurisdiction of a court
in the United Kingdom with respect to a maintenance order to which this section
applies, and, subject to section 5 below, any such order may be enforced, varied or
revoked accordingly.

*Variation and revocation of maintenance order made in United Kingdom*

**5.**   (1)   This section applies to a maintenance order certified copies of which have
been sent in pursuance of section 2 to a specified State for enforcement.

(2)   The jurisdiction of a court in the United Kingdom to revoke, revive or vary
a maintenance order shall be exercisable notwithstanding that the proceedings for
the revocation, revival or variation, as the case may be, of the order are brought by
or against a person residing in a specified State.

(3)   Where subsection (1) of section 60 of the Magistrates' Courts Act 1980
(revocation, variation, etc of orders for periodical payment) applies in relation to a
maintenance order to which this section applies, that subsection shall have effect as
if for the words 'by order on complaint' there were substituted 'on an application
being made, by order'.

(4)   Where an application is made by the payee to a court in the United Kingdom
for the variation or revocation of an order to which this section applies, and
the payer is residing in a specified State, the prescribed officer of the court
shall—

(a)   in the case of a court in England and Wales or Northern Ireland, send to
the Lord Chancellor, or, in the case of a court in Scotland, send to the
Secretary of State, notice of the institution of the proceedings, including
notice of the substance of the application, with a view to its being transmitted to the appropriate authority in the specified State for service on the
payer; and

(b)   give the payer notice in writing of the date fixed for the hearing by sending
the notice by post addressed to his last known or usual place of abode.

(5)   Where such an application is made—

(a)   the order shall not be varied or revoked unless the document mentioned in
subsection (4)(a) above has been served on the payer in accordance with
the law for the service of such a document in the specified State;

(b)   the court, in considering whether or not to vary or revoke the order, shall
take into account any representations made and any evidence adduced by
or on behalf of the payer; and

(c)   a copy of any such representations or evidence shall be served on the payee
in the prescribed manner before the hearing.

(6) Where an application is made by the payer to a court in the United Kingdom for the variation or revocation of an order to which this section applies, the prescribed officer of the court shall arrange for the service of notice of institution of the proceedings, including notice of the substance of the application, on the payee.

(7) Where an order to which this section applies is varied or revoked by a court in the United Kingdom the prescribed officer of the court shall send the following documents, that is to say—

(a) three certified copies of the order of variation or revocation; and

(b) a written statement, signed by that officer as to whether both the payer and the payee under the order appeared in the proceedings, and, if only the applicant appeared, the original or a certified copy of a document which establishes that notice of the institution of the proceedings had been served on the other party;

in the case of a court in England and Wales or Northern Ireland, to the Lord Chancellor, or, in the case of a court in Scotland, to the Secretary of State, with a view to their being transmitted by him to the appropriate authority in the specified State for registration and enforcement of the order of variation or revocation.

(8) Where a maintenance order to which this section applies has been varied by an order made by a court in the United Kingdom or by a court in a specified State, the maintenance order shall, as from the date on which the order of variation took effect, have effect as varied by that order.

(9) Where a maintenance order to which this section applies has been revoked by an order made by a court in the United Kingdom or by a court in a specified State, the maintenance order shall, as from the date on which the order of revocation took effect, be deemed to have ceased to have effect except in respect of any arrears due under the maintenance order at that date.

(10) Where a maintenance order to which this section applies has been varied or revoked by an order made by a court in a specified State, the prescribed officer of the court shall register the order of variation or revocation in the prescribed manner.

ORDERS MADE BY COURTS IN SPECIFIED STATES

*Registration in United Kingdom court of maintenance order made in a specified State*

**6.**   (1) This section applies to a maintenance order made, whether before, on or after 1st December 1995, by a court in a specified State.

(2) Where a certified copy of an order to which this section applies is received by the Lord Chancellor or the Secretary of State from the appropriate authority in a specified State, and it appears to him that the payer under the order is residing or has assets in the United Kingdom, he shall send the copy of the order to the prescribed officer of the appropriate court.

(3) Where the prescribed officer of the appropriate court receives from the Lord Chancellor or the Secretary of State a certified copy of an order to which this section applies, he shall, subject to subsection (4) below, register the order in the prescribed manner in that court.

(4) Before registering an order under this section an officer of a court shall take such steps as he thinks fit for the purpose of ascertaining whether the payer under the order is residing or has assets within the jurisdiction of the court, and if after taking those steps he is satisfied that the payer is not residing and has no assets within the jurisdiction of the court he shall return the certified copy of the order to the Lord Chancellor or the Secretary of State, as the case may be, with a statement giving such information as he possesses as to the whereabouts of the payer and the nature and location of his assets.

*Enforcement of maintenance order registered in United Kingdom court*

**8.**   (1) Subject to subsection (2) below, a registered order may be enforced in the United Kingdom as if it had been made by the registering court and as if that court had had jurisdiction to make it; and proceedings for or with respect to the enforcement of any such order may be taken accordingly.

(2) Subsection (1) above does not apply to an order which is for the time being registered in the High Court under Part I of the Maintenance Orders Act 1958 or to an order which is for the time being registered in the High Court of Justice in Northern Ireland under Part II of the Maintenance and Affiliation Orders Act (Northern Ireland) 1966.

(3) Any person for the time being under an obligation to make payments in pursuance of a registered order shall give notice of any change of address to the clerk of the registering court, and any person failing without reasonable excuse to give such a notice shall be liable on summary conviction to a fine not exceeding level 2 on the standard scale.

(4) An order which by virtue of this section is enforceable by a magistrates' court shall, subject to the modifications of sections 76 and 93 of the Magistrates' Courts Act 1980 specified in subsections (4A) and (4B) below, and subject to the modifications of Article 98 of the Magistrates' Courts (Northern Ireland) Order 1981 specified in subsection (4C) below, be enforceable as if it were a magistrates' courts maintenance order made by that court.

In this subsection 'magistrates' court maintenance order' has the same meaning as in section 150(1) of the Magistrates' Courts Act 1980.

(4A) Section 76 (enforcement of sums adjudged to be paid) shall have effect as if for subsections (4) to (6) there were substituted the following subsections—

'(4) Where proceedings are brought for the enforcement of a magistrates' court maintenance order under this section, the court may vary the order by exercising one of its powers under subsection (5) below.

(5) The powers of the court are—
   (a) the power to order that payments under the order be made directly to the clerk of the court or the clerk of any other magistrates' court;
   (b) the power to order that payments under the order be made to the clerk of the court, or to the clerk of any other magistrates' court, by such method of payment falling within section 59(6) above (standing order, etc) as may be specified;
   (c) the power to make an attachment of earnings order under the Attachment of Earnings Act 1971 to secure payments under the order.

(6) In deciding which of the powers under subsection (5) above it is to exercise, the court shall have regard to any representations made by the debtor (within the meaning of section 59 above).

(7) Subsection (4) of section 59 above (power of court to require debtor to open account) shall apply for the purposes of subsection (5) above as it applies for the purposes of that section but as if for paragraph (a) there were substituted—

"(a) the court proposes to exercise its power under paragraph (b) of section 76(5) below, and".'

(4B) In section 93 (complaint for arrears), subsection (6) (court not to impose imprisonment in certain circumstances) shall have effect as if for paragraph (b) there were substituted—

'(b) if the court is of the opinion that it is appropriate—
      (i) to make an attachment of earnings order; or
      (ii) to exercise its power under paragraph (b) of section 76(5) above.'

(4C) Article 98 of the Magistrates' Courts (Northern Ireland) Order 1981 (enforcement of sums adjudged to be paid) shall have effect—

    (a)  as if for paragraph (7)(a) there were substituted the following paragraph—
        '(a)  if the court is of the opinion that it is appropriate—
           (i)  to make an attachment of earnings order; or
           (ii)  to exercise its power under paragraph (8C)(b)';
    (b)  as if for paragraphs (8B) to (8D) there were substituted the following paragraphs—
        '(8B)  Upon the appearance of a person or proof of service of the summons on him as mentioned in paragraph (4) for the enforcement of an order to which this Article applies, the court or resident magistrate may vary the order, by exercising one of the powers under paragraph (8C).
        (8C)  The powers mentioned in paragraph (8B) are—
        (a)  the power to order that payments under the order be made directly to the collecting officer;
        (b)  the power to order that payments under the order be made to the collecting officer, by such method of payment falling within Article 85(7) (standing order, etc) as may be specified;
        (c)  the power to make an attachment of earnings order under Part IX to secure payments under the order.
    (8D)  In deciding which of the powers under paragraph (8C) is to be exercised, the court or, as the case may be, a resident magistrate shall have regard to any representations made by the debtor (within the meaning of Article 85).
    (8E)  Paragraph (5) of Article 85 (power of court to require debtor to open account) shall apply for the purposes of paragraph (8C) as it applies for the purposes of that Article but as if for sub-paragraph (a) there were substituted—
        '(a)  the court proposes to exercise its power under sub-paragraph (b) of Article 98(8C), and'.'
    (5)  The magistrates' court by which an order is enforceable by virtue of this section, and the officers thereof, shall take all such steps for enforcing or facilitating the enforcement of the order as may be prescribed.
    (6)  In any proceedings for or with respect to the enforcement of an order which is for the time being registered in any court under this Part of this Act a certificate of arrears sent to the prescribed officer of the court shall be evidence of the facts stated therein.
    (7)  Sums of money payable under a registered order shall be payable in accordance with the order as from the date on which the order was made.
    (9)  In the application of this section to Scotland—
    (a)  subsections (2) to (5) shall be omitted; and
    (b)  in subsection (6), for the word 'evidence' there shall be substituted the words 'sufficient evidence'.

*Variation of maintenance order registered in United Kingdom court*

**9.**    (1)  Subject to the provisions of this section—
    (a)  the registering court shall have the like power, on an application made by the payer or payee under a registered order, to vary the order as if it had been made by the registering court and as if that court had had jurisdiction to make it;
    (b)  the jurisdiction of a magistrates' court to vary a registered order shall be exercisable notwithstanding that proceedings for the variation of the order are brought by or against a person residing in a specified State.
    (1ZA)  Where the registering court is a magistrates' court in England and Wales, section 60 of the Magistrates' Courts Act 1980 (revocation, variation, etc of orders for periodical payment) shall have effect in relation to the registered order—
    (za)  as if in subsection (1) for the words 'by order on complaint' there were substituted 'on an application being made, by order';

(a) as if in subsection (3) for the words 'paragraphs (a) to (d) of section 59(3) above' there were substituted 'subsection (3A) below' and after that subsection there were inserted—

'(3A) The powers of the court are—

  (a) the power to order that payments under the order be made directly to the clerk of the court or the clerk of any other magistrates' court;

  (b) the power to order that payments under the order be made to the clerk of the court, or to the clerk of any other magistrates' court, by such method of payment falling within section 59(6) above (standing order, etc) as may be specified;

  (c) the power to make an attachment of earnings order under the Attachment of Earnings Act 1971 to secure payments under the order.';

(b) as if in subsection (4) for paragraph (b) there were substituted—

'(b) payments under the order are required to be made to the clerk of the court, or to the clerk of any other magistrates' court, by any method of payment falling within section 59(6) above (standing order, etc)',

and as if after the words 'the court' there were inserted 'which made the order';

(c) as if in subsection (5) for the words 'to the clerk' there were substituted 'in accordance with paragraph (a) of subsection (3A) above';

(d) as if in subsection (7), paragraph (c) and the word 'and' immediately preceding it were omitted;

(e) as if in subsection (8) for the words 'paragraphs (a) to (d) of section 59(3) above' there were substituted 'subsection (3A) above';

(f) as if for subsections (9) and (10) there were substituted the following subsections—

'(9) In deciding, for the purposes of subsections (3) and (8) above, which of the powers under subsection (3A) above it is to exercise, the court shall have regard to any representations made by the debtor.

(10) Subsection (4) of section 59 above (power of court to require debtor to open account) shall apply for the purposes of subsection (3A) above as it applies for the purposes of that section but as if for paragraph (a) there were substituted—

"(a) the court proposes to exercise its power under paragraph (b) of section 60(3A) below, and".'

(1ZB) Where the registering court is a court of summary jurisdiction in Northern Ireland, Article 86 of the Magistrates' Courts (Northern Ireland) Order 1981 (revocation, variation, etc of orders for periodical payment) shall have effect in relation to the registered order—

(a) as if in paragraph (3) for the words 'sub-paragraphs (a) to (d) of Article 85(3)' there were substituted 'paragraph (3A)' and after that paragraph there were inserted—

'(3A) The powers of the court are—

  (a) the power to order that payments under the order be made directly to the collecting officer;

  (b) the power to order that payments under the order be made to the collecting officer by such method of payment falling within Article 85(7) (standing order, etc) as may be specified;

  (c) the power to make an attachment of earnings order under Part IX to secure payments under the order.';

(b) as if in paragraph (4) for sub-paragraph (b) there were substituted—

'(b) payments under the order are required to be made to the collecting officer by any method of payment falling within Article 85(7) (standing order, etc)',

and as if the after words 'petty sessions' there were inserted 'for the petty sessions district for which the court which made the order acts';
(c) as if in paragraph (5) for the words 'to the collecting officer' there were substituted 'in accordance with sub-paragraph (a) of paragraph (3A)';
(d) as if in paragraph (7), sub-paragraph (c) and the word 'and' immediately preceding it were omitted;
(e) as if in paragraph (8) for the words 'sub-paragraphs (a) to (d) of Article 85(3)' there were substituted 'paragraph (3A)';
(f) as if for paragraphs (9) and (10) there were substituted the following paragraphs—

'(9) In deciding, for the purposes of paragraphs (3) and (8) above, which of the powers under paragraph (3A) it is to exercise, the court shall have regard to any representations made by the debtor.

(10) Paragraph (5) of Article 85 (power of court to require debtor to open account) shall apply for the purposes of paragraph (3A) as it applies for the purposes of that Article but as if for sub-paragraph (a) there were substituted—

"(a) the court proposes to exercise its power under sub-paragraph (b) of Article 86(3A), and".'

(1A) The powers conferred by subsection (1) above are not exercisable in relation to so much of a registered order as provides for the payment of a lump sum.

(1B) The registering court shall not vary a registered order if neither the payer nor the payee under the order is resident in the United Kingdom.

(2) Where an application is made by the payer to a registering court in the United Kingdom for the variation of a registered order, and the payee is residing in a specified State, the prescribed officer of the court shall—

(a) in the case of a court in England and Wales or Northern Ireland, send to the Lord Chancellor, or, in the case of a court in Scotland, send to the Secretary of State, notice of the institution of the proceedings with a view to its being transmitted by him to the appropriate authority in the specified State for service on the payee; and

(b) give the payee notice in writing of the date fixed for the hearing by sending the notice by post addressed to his last known or usual place of abode.

(3) Where such an application is made—

(a) the order shall not be varied unless the document mentioned in paragraph (a) of subsection (2) above has been served on the payee in accordance with the law for the service of such a document in the specified State;

(b) the court, in considering whether or not to make or vary the order, shall take into account any representations made and any evidence adduced by or on behalf of the payee; and

(c) a copy of any such representations and evidence shall be served on the payer by the prescribed officer of the court before the hearing.

(4) Where an application is made by the payee to a registering court in the United Kingdom for the variation of a registered order, and the payer is residing in the United Kingdom, the prescribed officer of the court shall serve the document mentioned in paragraph (a) of subsection (2) above on the payer.

(5) Where a registered order is varied by a registering court in the United Kingdom the prescribed officer of the court shall send the following documents, that is to say—

(a) three certified copies of the order of variation;

(b) a written statement signed by that officer as to whether both the payer and the payee under the order appeared in the proceedings for the variation of the order, and, if only the applicant appeared, the original or a certified copy of a document which establishes that notice of the institution of the proceedings had been served on the other party, in the case of a court in England and Wales or Northern Ireland, to the Lord Chancellor, or, in the case of a court in Scotland, to the Secretary of State, with a view to their being transmitted by him to the appropriate authority in the specified State.

(6) Where a registered order has been varied by the registering court or by a court in a specified State, the prescribed officer of the registering court shall register the variation order in the prescribed manner.

(7) Where a registered order has been varied by the registering court or by a court in a specified State, the registered order shall, as from the date on which the variation order took effect, have effect as so varied.

*Cancellation of registration and transfer of order*

**10.** (1) Where a registered order is revoked by an order made by a court in a specified State and notice of the revocation is received by the registering court, the prescribed officer of the registering court shall cancel the registration; but any arrears due under the registered order at the date on which the order of revocation took effect, shall continue to be recoverable as if the registration had not been cancelled.

(2) Where the prescribed officer of the registering court is of opinion that the payer under a registered order is not residing within the jurisdiction of that court and has no assets within that jurisdiction against which the order can be effectively enforced, he shall cancel the registration of the order and, subject to subsection (3) below, shall send the certified copy of the order to the Lord Chancellor.

(3) Where the prescribed officer of the registering court, being a magistrates' court, is of opinion that the payer is residing or has assets within the jurisdiction of another magistrates' court in that part of the United Kingdom in which the registering court is, he shall transfer the order to that other court by sending the certified copy of the order to the prescribed officer of that other court.

(4) On the transfer of an order under subsection (3) above the prescribed officer of the court to which it is transferred shall, subject to subsection (6) below, register the order in the prescribed manner in that court.

(5) Where the certified copy of an order is received by the Lord Chancellor under this section and it appears to him that the payer under the order is residing or has assets in the United Kingdom, he shall transfer the order to the appropriate court by sending the certified copy of the order together with the related documents to the prescribed officer of the appropriate court and, subject to subsection (6) below, that officer shall register the order in the prescribed manner in that court.

(6) Before registering an order in pursuance of subsection (4) or (5) above an officer of a court shall take such steps as he thinks fit for the purpose of ascertaining whether the payer is residing or has assets within the jurisdiction of the court, and if after taking those steps he is satisfied that the payer is not residing and has no assets within the jurisdiction of the court he shall send the certified copy of the order to the Lord Chancellor.

(7) The officer of a court who is required by any of the foregoing provisions of this section to send to the Lord Chancellor or to the prescribed officer of another court the certified copy of an order shall send with that copy—

(a) a certificate of arrears signed by him or, in Scotland, by the applicant or his solicitor;

(b) a statement giving such information as he possesses as to the whereabouts of the payer and the nature and location of his assets; and

(c) any relevant documents in his possession relating to the case.

(8) In the application of this section to Scotland—

(a) in subsection (2), for the words 'within the jurisdiction of that court' there shall be substituted the words 'in Scotland';

(b) subsections (3) and (4) shall be omitted; and

(c) for the words 'Lord Chancellor', in each place where they occur, there shall be substituted the words 'Secretary of State'.

*Steps to be taken by Lord Chancellor or Secretary of State where payer under certain orders is not residing in United Kingdom*

**11.**   (1) If at any time it appears to the Lord Chancellor or the Secretary of State that the payer under a maintenance order, a certified copy of which has been received by him from a specified State, is not residing and has no assets in the United Kingdom, he shall send to the appropriate authority in that State or, if having regard to all the circumstances he thinks it proper to do so, to the appropriate authority in another specified State—

(a) the certified copy of the order in question and a certified copy of any order varying that order;

(b) if the order has at any time been a registered order, a certificate of arrears signed by the prescribed officer or, in Scotland, by the applicant or his solicitor;

(c) a statement giving such information as the Lord Chancellor or the Secretary of State possesses as to the whereabouts of the payer and the nature and location of his assets; and

(d) any other relevant documents in his possession relating to the case.

(2) Where the documents mentioned in subsection (1) are sent to the appropriate authority in a specified State other than that in which the order in question was made, the Lord Chancellor or the Secretary of State shall inform the appropriate authority in the specified State in which that order was made of what he has done.

APPEALS

*Appeals*

**12.**   Where in pursuance of section 9 a registering court makes, or refuses to make, an order varying a registered order, the payer or the payee under the registered order shall have the like right of appeal (if any) from the order of variation or from the refusal to make it as he would have if the registered order had been made by the registering court.

EVIDENCE

*Admissibility of evidence given in specified State*

**13.**   (1) A statement contained in—

(a) a document, duly authenticated, which purports to set out or summarise evidence given in proceedings in a court in a specified State; or

(b) a document, duly authenticated, which purports to set out or summarise evidence taken in such a State for the purpose of proceedings in a court in the United Kingdom under this Part of this Act, whether in response to a request made by such a court or otherwise; or

(c) a document, duly authenticated, which purports to have been received in evidence in proceedings in a court in such a State or to be a copy of a document so received,

shall in any proceedings in a court in the United Kingdom relating to a maintenance order to which this Part of this Act applies be admissible as evidence of any fact stated therein to the same extent as oral evidence of that fact is admissible in those proceedings.

(2) A document purporting to set out or summarise evidence given as mentioned in subsection (1)(a) above, or taken as mentioned in subsection (1)(b) above, shall be deemed to be duly authenticated for the purposes of that subsection if the document purports to be certified by the judge, magistrate or other person before whom the evidence was given, or, as the case may be, by whom it was taken, to be the original document containing or recording, or, as the case may be, summarising, that evidence or a true copy of that document.

(3) A document purporting to have been received in evidence as mentioned in subsection (1)(c) above, or to be a copy of a document so received, shall be deemed to be duly authenticated for the purposes of that subsection if the document purports to be certified by a judge, magistrate or other person before whom the evidence was given to have been, or to be a true copy of a document which has been, so received.

(4) It shall not be necessary in any such proceedings to prove the signature or official position of the person appearing to have given such a certificate.

(5) Nothing in this section shall prejudice the admission in evidence of any document which is admissible in evidence apart from this section.

*Obtaining of evidence needed for purpose of certain proceedings*

**14.** (1) Where for the purpose of any proceedings in a court in a specified State relating to a maintenance order to which this Part of this Act applies a request is made by or on behalf of that court for the taking in the United Kingdom of the evidence of a person residing therein relating to matters specified in the request, such court in the United Kingdom as may be prescribed shall have power to take that evidence and, after giving notice of the time and place at which the evidence is to be taken to such persons and in such manner as it thinks fit, shall take the evidence in such manner as may be prescribed.

Evidence taken in compliance with such a request shall be sent by the prescribed officer of the court—

(a) in England and Wales or Northern Ireland, to the Lord Chancellor; or

(b) in Scotland, to the Secretary of State,

for transmission to the appropriate authority in the specified State.

(2) Where any person, not being the payer or the payee under the maintenance order to which the proceedings in question relate, is required by virtue of this section to give evidence before a court in the United Kingdom, the court may order that there shall be paid out of moneys provided by Parliament such sums as appear to the court reasonably sufficient to compensate that person for the expense, trouble or loss of time properly incurred in or incidental to his attendance.

(3) Section 97(1), (3) and (4) of the Magistrates' Courts Act 1980 (which provide for compelling the attendance of witnesses, etc) shall apply in relation to a magistrates' court having power under subsection (1) above to take the evidence of any person as if the proceedings in the court in a specified State for the purpose of which a request for the taking of the evidence has been made were proceedings in the magistrates' court and had been begun by complaint.

(4) Paragraphs 71 and 73 of Schedule 1 to the Sheriff Courts (Scotland) Act 1907 (which provide for the citation of witnesses, etc) shall apply in relation to a sheriff having power under subsection (1) above to take the evidence of any person as if the proceedings in the court in a specified State for the purpose of which a request for the taking of the evidence has been made were proceedings in the sheriff court.

(5) A court in—

(a) England and Wales or Northern Ireland may, for the purpose of any proceedings in that court under this Part of this Act relating to a maintenance order to which this Part of this Act applies send to the Lord Chancellor; or

(b) Scotland may, for the purpose of such proceedings in that court relating to such an order, send to the Secretary of State,

for transmission to the appropriate authority in a specified State a request for a court in that State to take or provide evidence relating to such matters as may be specified in the request.

(6) In the application of this section to Northern Ireland, in subsection (3), for the reference to section 97(1), (3) and (4) of the Magistrates' Courts Act 1980 there shall be substituted a reference to Articles 118(1), (3) and (4), 119 and 120 of the Magistrates' Courts (Northern Ireland) Order 1981.

*Order etc made in specified State need not be proved*

**15.** For the purposes of this Part of this Act, unless the contrary is shown—
(a) any order made by a court in a specified State purporting to bear the seal of that order or to be signed by any person in his capacity as a judge, magistrate or officer of the court, shall be deemed without further proof to have been duly sealed or, as the case may be, to have been signed by that person;
(b) the person by whom the order was signed shall be deemed without further proof to have been a judge, magistrate or officer, as the case may be, of that court when he signed it and, in the case of an officer, to have been authorised to sign it; and
(c) a document purporting to be a certified copy of an order made by a court in a specified State shall be deemed without further proof to be such a copy.

SUPPLEMENTAL

*Payment of sums due under orders made in specified State; conversion of currency*

**16.** (1) Payment of sums due under a registered order shall, while the order is registered in a court in England, Wales or Northern Ireland, be made in such manner and to such person as may be prescribed.

(2) Where the sums required to be paid under a registered order are expressed in a currency other than the currency of the United Kingdom, then, as from the relevant date, the order shall be treated as if it were an order requiring the payment of such sums in the currency of the United Kingdom as, on the basis of the rate of exchange prevailing at that date, are equivalent to the sums so required to be paid.

(3) Where the sum specified in any statement, being a statement of the amount of any arrears due under a maintenance order made by a court in a specified State, is expressed in a currency other than the currency of the United Kingdom, that sum shall be deemed to be such sum in the currency of the United Kingdom as, on the basis of the rate of exchange prevailing at the relevant date, is equivalent to the sum so specified.

(4) For the purposes of this section a written certificate purporting to be signed by an officer of any bank in the United Kingdom certifying that a specified rate of exchange prevailed between currencies at a specified date and that at such rate a specified sum in the currency of the United Kingdom is equivalent to a specified sum in another specified currency shall be evidence of the rate of exchange so prevailing on that date and of the equivalent sums in terms of the respective currencies.

(5) In this section 'the relevant date' means—
(a) in relation to a registered order or to a statement of arrears due under a maintenance order made by a court in a specified State, the date on which the order first becomes a registered order;
(b) in relation to a registered order which has been varied, the date on which the last order varying that order is registered in the registering court.

(6) In the application of this section to Scotland—
(a) subsection (1) shall not apply; and
(b) in subsection (4), for the word 'evidence' there shall be substituted the words 'sufficient evidence'.

*Proceedings in magistrates' courts*

**17.** (4) Anything authorised or required by this Part of this Act to be done by, to or before the magistrates' court by, to or before which any other thing was done may be done by, to or before any magistrates' court acting for the same petty sessions area (or, in Northern Ireland, petty sessions district) as that court.

(5) Any application which by virtue of a provision of this Part of this Act is made to a magistrates' court in Northern Ireland shall be made by complaint.

(5A) Where the respondent to an application for the variation or revocation of—

(a) a maintenance order made by a magistrates' court in England and Wales, being an order to which section 5 of this Act applies; or

(b) a registered order which is registered in such a court,

is residing in a specified State, a magistrates' court in England and Wales shall have jurisdiction to hear the application (where it would not have such jurisdiction apart from this subsection) if it would have had jurisdiction to hear it had the respondent been residing in England and Wales.

(6) A magistrates' court in Northern Ireland shall have jurisdiction—

(a) to hear a complaint for the variation or revocation of a maintenance order made by such a court, and to which section 5 of this Act applies; or

(b) to hear a complaint for the variation of a registered order which is registered in that court,

if the defendant to the complaint is residing in a specified State and if the court would have had jurisdiction to hear the complaint had the defendant been residing in Northern Ireland and been served with a summons to appear before the court to answer the complaint.

(7) Where the respondent to an application—

(a) for the variation or revocation of a maintenance order made by a magistrates' court, and to which section 5 of this Act applies; or

(b) for the variation of a registered order registered in a magistrates' court,

does not appear at the time and place appointed for the hearing of the application, but the court is satisfied that the respondent is residing in a specified State, and that the requirements of section 5(4) or (6) or section 9(2) and (4), as the case may be, have been complied with, the court may proceed to hear and determine the application at the time and place appointed for the hearing or for any adjourned hearing as if the respondent had appeared at that time and place.

(7A) In the application of this section to Northern Ireland, in subsection (7)—

(a) for the word 'respondent', in each place where it occurs, there shall be substituted 'defendant'; and

(b) for the words 'an application' and 'the application', in each place where they occur, there shall be substituted 'a complaint' and 'the complaint' respectively.

**Note:** There are no sub-paras (1)–(3) to para 17.

*Magistrates' courts rules*

**18.** (1) Without prejudice to the generality of the power to make rules under section 144 of the Magistrates' Courts Act 1980 (magistrates' courts rules), provision may be made by such rules with respect to any of the following matters, namely—

(a) the circumstances in which anything authorised or required by this Part of this Act to be done by, to or before a magistrates' court acting for a particular petty sessions area or by, to or before an officer of that court may be done by, to or before a magistrates' court acting for such other petty sessions area as the rules may provide or by, to or before an officer of that court;

(b) the orders made, or other things done, by a magistrates' court, or an officer of such a court, under this Part of this Act, or by a court in a specified State, notice of which is to be given to such persons as the rules may provide and the manner in which such notice shall be given;

(c) the cases and manner in which courts in specified States are to be informed of orders made, or other things done, by a magistrates' court under this Part of this Act;

(d) the cases and manner in which a justices' clerk may take evidence needed for the purpose of proceedings in a court in a specified State relating to a maintenance order to which this Part of this Act applies;

(f) the circumstances and manner in which magistrates' courts may for the purposes of this Part of this Act communicate with courts in specified States.

(1A) For the purpose of giving effect to this Part of this Act, rules made under section 144 of the Magistrates' Courts Act 1980 may make, in relation to any proceedings brought under or by virtue of this Part of this Act, any provision not covered by subsection (1) above which—

(a) falls within subsection (2) of section 93 of the Children Act 1989, and

(b) may be made in relation to relevant proceedings under that section.

(2) Rules with respect to the matters mentioned in subsection (1) above may be made in accordance with Article 13 of the Magistrates' Courts (Northern Ireland) Order 1981 in relation to proceedings or matters in magistrates' courts in Northern Ireland under this Part of this Act.

**Note:** There is no para (1)(e).

*Rules for sheriff court*

**19.** Without prejudice to the generality of the powers conferred on the Court of Session by section 32 of the Sheriff Courts (Scotland) Act 1971 to regulate by act of sederunt the procedure of the sheriff court, the said powers shall include power—

(a) to prescribe the decrees granted, or other things done, by the sheriff, or an officer of the sheriff court, under this Part of this Act, or by a court in a specified State, notice of which is to be given to such persons as the act of sederunt may provide and the manner in which such notice shall be given;

(b) to provide that evidence needed for the purpose of proceedings in a court in a specified State relating to a maintenance order to which this Part of this Act applies may, in such cases and manner as the act of sederunt may provide, be taken by a sheriff clerk or sheriff clerk depute;

(c) to prescribe the cases and manner in which courts in specified States are to be informed of decrees granted, or other things done, by the sheriff under this Part of this Act;

(e) to prescribe the circumstances and manner in which the sheriff may for the purposes of this Part of this Act communicate with courts in specified States.

*Interpretation of Part I*

**21.** (1) In this part of this Act unless the context otherwise requires—

'affiliation order' means an order (however described) adjudging, finding or declaring a person to be the father of a child, whether or not it also provides for the maintenance of the child;

'the appropriate court', in relation to a person residing or having assets in England and Wales or in Northern Ireland means a magistrates' court, and in relation to a person residing or having assets in Scotland means a sheriff court, within the jurisdiction of which that person is residing or has assets;

'certificate of arrears', in relation to a maintenance order, means a certificate certifying that the sum specified in the certificate is to the best of the information or belief of the officer or, in Scotland, the applicant or his solicitor giving the certificate the amount of the arrears due under the order at the date of the certificate or, as the case may be, that to the best of his information or belief there are no arrears due thereunder at that date;

'certified copy', in relation to an order of a court, means a copy of the order certified by the proper officer of the court to be a true copy;

'court' includes any tribunal or person having power to make, confirm, enforce, vary or revoke a maintenance order;

'maintenance order' means an order (however described) of any of the following descriptions, that is to say—

(a) an order (including an affiliation order or order consequent upon an affiliation order) which provides for the payment of a lump sum or the making of periodical payments towards the maintenance of any person, being a person whom the person liable to make payments under the order is, according to the law applied in the place where the order was made, liable to maintain;

(aa) an order which has been made in Scotland, on or after the granting of a decree of divorce, for the payment of a periodical allowance by one party to the marriage to the other party;

(b) an affiliation order or order consequent upon an affiliation order, being an order which provides for the payment by a person adjudged, found or declared to be a child's father of expenses incidental to the child's birth or, where the child has died, of his funeral expenses.

(c) an order within the foregoing provisions of this definition made against a payer on the application of a public body which claims reimbursement of sums of money payable under the order with respect to the payee if reimbursement can be obtained by the public body under the law to which it is subject,

and, in the case of a maintenance order which has been varied, means that order as varied;

'order', as respects Scotland, includes any interlocutor, and any decree or provision contained in an interlocutor;

'payee', in relation to a maintenance order, means the person entitled to the payments for which the order provides;

'payer', in relation to a maintenance order, means the person liable to make payments under the order;

'prescribed', in relation to a magistrates' court in England and Wales or in Northern Ireland, means prescribed by rules made under section 144 of the Magistrates' Courts Act 1980 or by rules made in accordance with Article 13 of the Magistrates' Courts (Northern Ireland) Order 1981, as the case may be, and in relation to any other court means prescribed by rules of court;

'registered order' means a maintenance order which is for the time being registered in a court in the United Kingdom under this Part of this Act and 'registered' and 'registration' shall be construed accordingly;

'registering court', in relation to a registered order, means the court in which that order is for the time being registered under this Part of this Act;

'revoke' and 'revocation' include discharge;

'specified State' means a State specified in Schedule 1 to the Reciprocal Enforcement of Maintenance Orders (United States of America) Order 1995.

(3) Any reference in this Part of this Act to the payment of money for the maintenance of a child shall be construed as including a reference to the payment of money for the child's education.

**MAGISTRATES' COURTS (RECIPROCAL ENFORCEMENT OF MAINTENANCE ORDERS) (UNITED STATES OF AMERICA) RULES 1995**

**Dated** 27 October 1995

**SI 1995 No 2802**

The Lord Chancellor, in exercise of the powers conferred on him by section 144 of the Magistrates' Courts Act 1980, after consultation with the Rule Committee appointed under that section, hereby makes the following Rules—

*Citation and commencement*

**1.** These Rules may be cited as the Magistrates' Courts (Reciprocal Enforcement of Maintenance Orders) (United States of America) Rules 1995 and shall come into force on 1st December 1995.

*Interpretation*

**2.** In these Rules 'the 1980 Rules' means the Magistrates' Courts (Reciprocal Enforcement of Maintenance Orders) (Hague Convention Countries) Rules 1980 and any reference to a rule by number alone shall be construed as a reference to the rule so numbered in the 1980 Rules.

*Application of the 1980 Rules*

**3.** Rules 2 to 12 of and Schedule 1A to the 1980 Rules shall apply in respect of the matters which are to be prescribed under Part I of the Maintenance Orders (Reciprocal Enforcement) Act 1972 as set out in Schedule 3 to the Reciprocal Enforcement of Maintenance Orders (United States of America) Order 1995 as if—

(a) for the reference in rule 2 of the Magistrates' Courts (Reciprocal Enforcement of Maintenance Orders) (Hague Convention Countries) Order 1979 there were substituted a reference to the Magistrates' Courts (Reciprocal Enforcement of Maintenance Orders) (United States of America) Order 1995;

(b) for rule 4(2)(b) there were substituted the following—
'(b) contain a sworn statement signed by the payee giving the following information—
(i) the address of the payee;
(ii) such information as is known as to the whereabouts of the payer; and
(iii) a description, so far as is known, of the nature and location of any assets of the payer available for execution;';

(c) rules 4A(1)(a) and 4B(2)(a) were omitted;

(d) for the reference to section 5(4)(b) of the Act in rule 6 there were substituted a reference to rule 5(5)(c);

(e) rule 7 were omitted;

(f) for references in rules 4, 9, 11 and 12 to 'Hague Convention country', wherever they appear, there were substituted references to 'specified State'.

## HUMAN FERTILISATION AND EMBRYOLOGY (STATUTORY STORAGE PERIOD FOR EMBRYOS) REGULATIONS 1996

**Dated** 22 February 1996

**SI 1996 No 375**

*Citation, commencement and interpretation*

**1.** (1) These Regulations may be cited as the Human Fertilisation and Embryology (Statutory Storage Period for Embryos) Regulations 1996 and shall come into force on 1st May 1996.

(2) In these Regulations—

'the Act' means the Human Fertilisation and Embryology Act 1990;

'the relevant date' is either 1st August 1991 or the date on which the embryo in question is first placed in storage, whichever is the later;

'the relevant persons' means the two persons whose gametes are used to bring about the creation of an embryo; and

'the woman being treated' means the woman in whom, at the relevant date it is intended that such an embryo may be placed, whether or not she is one of the relevant persons.

*Extension of statutory storage period in respect of embryos*

**2.** (1) In the circumstances specified in paragraph (2) below, section 14(4) of the Act (statutory storage period in respect of embryos) shall have effect as if for five years there were substituted the appropriate period specified in the Schedule to these Regulations.

(2) Those circumstances are that—

(a) each of the relevant persons has confirmed in writing that that person has no objection to any embryo which is created using gametes provided by that person being stored for a period in excess of five years for use in the provision of treatment services;

(b) the woman being treated is aged under 50 on the relevant date and the treatment in question would not result in her being a surrogate mother within the meaning of section 1(2) of the Surrogacy Arrangements Act 1985; and

(c) in the written opinion of two registered medical practitioners, one of the relevant persons, or, where she is not one of those persons, the woman being treated, has or is likely to become prematurely and completely infertile.

(3) In the circumstances mentioned in paragraph (4) below, section 14(4) of the Act shall have effect as if for five years there were substituted—

(a) if the woman being treated is aged 45 or under on the relevant date, ten years; or

(b) if she is aged 46 or over, the appropriate period specified in the Schedule to these Regulations.

(4) Those circumstances are—

(a) the circumstances specified in paragraph (2)(a) and (b) above; and

(b) that in the written opinion of a registered medical practitioner one of the relevant persons or, where she is not one of those persons, the woman being treated—

(i) has, or is likely to develop significantly impaired fertility, or

(ii) has a gene or genes such that a child born with that gene or those genes may suffer from such physical or mental abnormalities as to be seriously disabled.

SCHEDULE  Regulation 2(1) and (3)

The appropriate period mentioned in regulation 2(1) and (3) in respect of any embryo is the period of years specified in the second column of this Schedule corresponding to the age on the relevant date of the woman being treated and which is specified in the first column of this Schedule.

| Column 1<br>Age on relevant date of the woman being treated | Column 2<br>Appropriate period (in years) |
|---|---|
| 16 | 39 |
| 17 | 38 |
| 18 | 37 |
| 19 | 36 |
| 20 | 35 |
| 21 | 34 |
| 22 | 33 |
| 23 | 32 |
| 24 | 31 |
| 25 | 30 |
| 26 | 29 |
| 27 | 28 |
| 28 | 27 |
| 29 | 26 |
| 30 | 25 |
| 31 | 24 |
| 32 | 23 |
| 33 | 22 |
| 34 | 21 |
| 35 | 20 |
| 36 | 19 |
| 37 | 18 |
| 38 | 17 |
| 39 | 16 |
| 40 | 15 |
| 41 | 14 |
| 42 | 13 |
| 43 | 12 |
| 44 | 11 |
| 45 | 10 |
| 46 | 9 |
| 47 | 8 |
| 48 | 7 |
| 49 | 6 |

## CHILD SUPPORT DEPARTURE DIRECTION AND CONSEQUENTIAL AMENDMENTS REGULATIONS 1996

**Dated** 20 November 1996

**SI 1996 No 2907**

*These Regulations are revoked with savings by SI 2001/156, reg 33 in relation to certain cases as from 3 March 2003 (as amended by SI 2003/347, reg 2(5)); for further savings and effect see SI 2000/3186 (as amended by SI 2004/2415, reg 8) and SI 2001/156, reg 1(1) and SI 2003/192, arts 3, 8, Schedule.*

## ARRANGEMENT OF REGULATIONS

PART XI

*Transitional provisions*

47. Transitional provisions—application before 2nd December 1996.
48. Effective date of departure direction for a case falling within regulation 47.
49. Transitional provisions—no application before 2nd December 1996.
50. Transitional provisions—new maintenance assessment made before 2nd December 1996 whose effective date is on or after 2nd December 1996.

PART XII

*Revocation*

51. Revocation of the Departure Direction Anticipatory Application Regulations.

PART XIII

*Consequential amendments*

52–68. Regulations containing consequential amendments.

Whereas a draft of this instrument was laid before Parliament in accordance with section 52(2) of the Child Support Act 1991 and approved by a resolution of each House of Parliament:

Now, therefore, the Secretary of State for Social Security, in exercise of the powers conferred by sections 14(3), 21, 28A(3), 28B(2)(b), 28C, 28E(5), 28F, 28G, 28I(4)(c), 42, 51, 52(4) and 54 of, and paragraph 5 of Schedule 1, paragraphs 2, 4, 6, 7 and 9 of Schedule 4A and Schedule 4B to, the Child Support Act 1991 and of all other powers enabling him in that behalf, after consultation with the Council on Tribunals in accordance with section 8 of the Tribunals and Inquiries Act 1992, hereby makes the following Regulations:

PART I

GENERAL

*Citation, commencement and interpretation*

**1.** (1) These Regulations may be cited as the Child Support Departure Direction and Consequential Amendments Regulations 1996 and shall come into force on 2nd December 1996.

(2) In these Regulations, unless the context otherwise requires—

'the Act' means the Child Support Act 1991;

'the Appeal Regulations' means the Child Support Appeal Tribunals (Procedure) Regulations 1992;

'applicant' has the same meaning as in Schedule 4B to the Act;

'application' means [, except in regulations 32A to 32G,] an application for a departure direction;

'Arrears Regulations' means the Child Support (Arrears, Interest and Adjustment of Maintenance Assessments) Regulations 1992;

'Contributions and Benefits Act' means the Social Security Contributions and Benefits Act 1992;

'Departure Direction Anticipatory Application Regulations' means the Child Support Departure Direction (Anticipatory Application) Regulations 1996;

'departure direction application form' means the form provided by the Secretary of State in accordance with regulation 4(1);

[*'designated authority' has the meaning it has in regulation 2(1) of the Social Security (Work-focused Interviews) Regulations 2000*]

['designated authority' means—

(a) the Secretary of State;

(b) a person providing services to the Secretary of State;

(c) a local authority; or

(d) a person providing services to, or authorised to exercise any functions of, any such authority;]

'effective date' in relation to a departure direction means the date on which that direction takes effect;

'Information, Evidence and Disclosure Regulations' means the Child Support (Information, Evidence and Disclosure) Regulations 1992;

'Maintenance Arrangements and Jurisdiction Regulations' means the Child Support (Maintenance Arrangements and Jurisdiction) Regulations 1992;

'Maintenance Assessment Procedure Regulations' means the Child Support (Maintenance Assessment Procedure) Regulations 1992;

'Maintenance Assessments and Special Cases Regulations' means the Child Support (Maintenance Assessments and Special Cases) Regulations 1992;

'maintenance period' has the same meaning as in regulation 33 of the Maintenance Assessment Procedure Regulations;

'non-applicant' means—

(a) where the application has been made by a person with care, the absent parent;

(b) where the application has been made by an absent parent, the person with care;

['*official error' means an error made by an officer of the Department of Social Security acting as such which no person outside the Department caused or to which no person outside the Department materially contributed;*]

['official error' means an error made by—

(a) an officer of the Department of Social Security acting as such which no person outside that Department caused or to which no person outside that Department materially contributed;

*(b) a person employed by a designated authority acting on behalf of the authority, which no person outside that authority caused or to which no person outside that authority materially contributed*

[(b) a person employed by a designated authority acting on behalf of the authority, which no person outside that authority caused or to which no person outside that authority materially contributed,

but excludes any error of law which is only shown to have been an error by virtue of a subsequent decision of a Child Support Commissioner or the court];]

'partner' has the same meaning as in paragraph (2) of regulation 1 of the Maintenance Assessments and Special Cases Regulations;

'relevant person' means—

(a) an absent parent, or a person who is treated as an absent parent under regulation 20 of the Maintenance Assessments and Special Cases Regulations (persons treated as absent parents), whose liability under a maintenance assessment may be affected by any departure direction given following an application;

(b) a person with care, or a child to whom section 7 of the Act applies, where the amount of child support maintenance payable under a maintenance assessment relevant to that person with care or that child may be affected by any departure direction given following an application.

(3) In these Regulations, unless the context otherwise requires, a reference—

(a) to the Schedule, is to the Schedule to these Regulations;

(b) to a numbered regulation is to the regulation in these Regulations bearing that number;

(c) in a regulation or the Schedule to a numbered paragraph is to the paragraph in that regulation or the Schedule bearing that number;

(d) in a paragraph to a lettered or numbered sub-paragraph is to the sub-paragraph in that paragraph bearing that letter or number.

**Note.** Para (2): in definition 'application' words ', except in regulations 32A to 32G,' in square brackets inserted by SI 1999/1047, reg 34(a) as from 1 June 1999; definition 'designated authority' (inserted by SI 2000/897, reg 16(5), Sch 6, para 9(a)) substituted by SI 2002/1703, reg 17, Sch 2, para 5 as from 30 September 2002; definition 'official error' (inserted by SI 1999/1047, reg 34(b)) substituted by SI 2000/897, reg 16(5), Sch 6, para 9(b) as from 3 April 2000; in definition 'official error' sub-para (b) and subsequent words in square brackets substituted by SI 2000/1596, reg 10 as from 19 June 2000.

*Documents*

**2.** (1) Except where express provision is made to the contrary, where, under any provision of these Regulations—

(a) any document is given or sent to the Secretary of State, that document shall, subject to paragraph (2), be treated as having been so given or sent on the date it is received by the Secretary of State; and

(b) any document is given or sent to any other person, that document shall, if sent by post to that person's last known or notified address, and subject to paragraph (3), be treated as having been given or sent on the second day after the day of posting, excluding any Sunday or any day which is a Bank Holiday in England, Wales, Scotland or Northern Ireland under the Banking and Financial Dealings Act 1971.

(2) The Secretary of State may treat any document given or sent to him as given or sent on such day, earlier than the day it was received by him, as he may determine, if he is satisfied that there was unavoidable delay in his receiving the document in question.

(3) Where, by any provision of these Regulations, and in relation to a particular application, notice or notification—

(a) more than one document is required to be given or sent to a person, and more than one such document is sent by post to that person but not all the documents are posted on the same day; or

(b) documents are required to be given or sent to more than one person, and not all such documents are posted on the same day,

all those documents shall be treated as having been posted on the later or, as the case may be, the latest day of posting.

*Determination of amounts*

**3.** (1) Where any amount is required to be determined for the purposes of these Regulations, it shall be determined as a weekly amount and, except where the context otherwise requires, any reference to such an amount shall be construed accordingly.

(2) Where any calculation made under these Regulations results in a fraction of a penny that fraction shall be treated as a penny if it is either one half or exceeds one half and shall be otherwise disregarded.

PART II

PROCEDURE ON AN APPLICATION FOR A DEPARTURE DIRECTION AND PRELIMINARY CONSIDERATION

*Application for a departure direction*

**4.** (1) Every application shall be made in writing on a form (a 'departure direction application form') provided by the Secretary of State, or in such other manner, being in writing, as the Secretary of State may accept as sufficient in the circumstances of any particular case.

(2) Departure direction application forms shall be supplied without charge by such persons as the Secretary of State authorises for that purpose.

(3) Every application shall be given or sent to the Secretary of State or to such persons as he may authorise for that purpose.

(4) Where an application is defective at the date when it is received, or has been made in writing but not on the departure direction application form provided by the Secretary of State, the Secretary of State may refer that application to the person who made it or, as the case may be, supply him with a departure direction application form.

(5) In a case to which paragraph (4) applies, if the departure direction application form is received by the Secretary of State properly completed—

(a) within the specified period, he shall treat the application as if it had been duly made in the first instance;

(b) outside the specified period, unless he is satisfied that the delay has been unavoidable, he shall treat the application as a fresh application made on the date upon which the properly completed departure direction application form was received.

(6) An application which is made on a departure direction application form is, for the purposes of paragraph (5), properly completed if completed in accordance with the instructions on the form and defective if not so completed.

(7) In a case to which paragraph (4) applies, the specified period for the purposes of paragraph (5) shall be the period of 14 days commencing with the date upon which, in accordance with paragraph (4), the application is referred to the person who made the defective application or a departure direction application form is given or sent to the person who made a written application but not on a departure direction application form.

(8) For the purposes of paragraph (7), the provisions of regulation 2 shall apply to an application referred to in paragraph (4).

(9) A person applying for a departure direction may authorise a representative, whether or not legally qualified, to receive notices and other documents on his behalf, and to act on his behalf in relation to an application.

(10) Where a person has, under paragraph (9), authorised a representative who is not legally qualified, he shall confirm that authorisation in writing, or as otherwise required, to the Secretary of State, unless such authorisation has already been approved by the Secretary of State under regulation 53 of the Maintenance Assessment Procedure Regulations (authorisation of representative).

(11) <. . .>

(12) <. . .>

(13) <. . .>

(14) <. . .>

**Note.** Paras (11)–(14) revoked by SI 1999/1047, reg 35, as from 1 June 1999.

*Amendment or withdrawal of application*

**5.** A person who has made an application may amend or withdraw his application by notice in writing to the Secretary of State at any time prior to a determination being made in relation to that application.

*Provision of information*

**6.** (1) Where an application has been made, the Secretary of State may request further information or evidence from the applicant to enable that application to be determined.

(2) Any information or evidence requested by the Secretary of State in accordance with paragraph (1) shall be given within *14 days* [one month, or such longer period as the Secretary of State is satisfied is reasonable in the circumstances of the case,] of the request for such information or evidence having been given or sent.

(3) Where the time limit specified in paragraph (2) is not complied with, the Secretary of State may determine that application, in the absence of that information or evidence.

**Note.** In para (2) words ' days' substituted by words from 'one month' to 'circumstances of the case,' in square brackets substituted by SI 1999/1047, reg 36 as from 1 June 1999.

*Rejection of application on completion of a preliminary consideration*

**7.** (1) The Secretary of State may, on completing a preliminary consideration of an application, reject that application on the ground set out in section 28B(2)(b) of the Act if it appears to him that the difference between the current amount and the revised amount is less than £1.00.

(2) Where an application has been rejected in accordance with paragraph (1), the Secretary of State shall, as soon as reasonably practicable, give notice of that rejection to the relevant persons.

*Procedure in relation to the determination of an application*

**8.** (1) Subject to paragraph (4), where an application has not failed within the meaning of section 28D of the Act, the Secretary of State shall[, unless he is satisfied on the information or evidence available to him that a departure direction is unlikely to be given]—

(a) give notice of that application to the relevant persons other than the applicant;

(b) send to them details of the grounds on which the application has been made and any relevant information or evidence the applicant has given, except details, information or evidence falling within paragraph (2);

(c) invite representations in writing from the relevant persons other than the applicant on any matter relating to that application; and

(d) set out the provisions of paragraphs (2), (5) and (6) in relation to such representations.

(2) The details, information or evidence referred to in paragraphs (1)(b), (6) and (7) are—

(a) medical evidence or medical advice that has not been disclosed to the applicant or a relevant person and which the Secretary of State considers would be harmful to the health of the applicant or that relevant person if disclosed to him;

(b) the address of a relevant person, or of any child in relation to whom the assessment was made in respect of which the application has been made, or any other information which could reasonably be expected to lead to that person or that child being located, where that person has not agreed to disclosure of that address or that information, it is not known to the other party to that assessment and—

(i) the Secretary of State is satisfied that that address or that information is not necessary for the determination of that application; or

(ii) the Secretary of State is satisfied that that address or that information is necessary for the determination of that application and that there would be a risk of harm or undue distress to that person or that child if disclosure were made.

(3) Subject to paragraph (4), the notice referred to in paragraph (1)(a) shall be given as soon as reasonably practicable after—

(a) completion of the preliminary consideration of that application under section 28B of the Act; or

(b) where the Secretary of State has requested information or evidence under regulation 6, receipt of that information or evidence or the expiry of the period . . . referred to in regulation 6(2).

(4) The provisions of paragraphs (1) and (3) shall not apply where information or evidence requested in accordance with regulation 6 has not been received by the Secretary of State within the period specified in paragraph (2) of that regulation and the Secretary of State is satisfied on the information or evidence available to him that a departure direction should not be given.

[(4A) Where the provisions of paragraph (1) have not been complied with because the Secretary of State was satisfied on the information or evidence available to him that a departure direction was unlikely to be given, but on further consideration of the application he is minded to give a departure direction in that case, he shall, before doing so, comply with the provisions of this regulation.]

(5) Where the Secretary of State does not receive written representations from a relevant person within 14 days of the date on which representations were invited under paragraph (1), (6) or (7) he may, in the absence of written representations from that person, proceed to determine the application.

(6) The Secretary of State may, if he considers it reasonable to do so, send to the applicant a copy of any written representations made following an invitation under paragraph (1)(c), whether or not they were received within the time specified in paragraph (5), except to the extent that the representations contain information or evidence which falls within paragraph (2), and invite him to submit representations in writing on any matters contained in those representations.

(7) Where any information or evidence requested by the Secretary of State under regulation 6 is received after notification has been given under paragraph (1), the Secretary of State may, if he considers it reasonable to do so and except where that information or evidence falls within paragraph (2), send a copy of such information or evidence to the relevant persons and invite them to submit representations in writing on that information or evidence.

(8) . . .

(9) Where the Secretary of State has determined an application he shall, as soon as is reasonably practicable—

(a) notify the relevant persons of that determination;

(b) where a departure direction has been given, *refer the case to a child support officer* [make a decision in accordance with regulation 17(2) or 20(2)(c) of the Maintenance Assessment Procedure Regulations].

(10) A notification under paragraph (9)(a) shall set out—

(a) the reasons for that determination;

(b) where a departure direction has been given, the basis on which the amount of child support maintenance is to be fixed by any assessment made in consequence of that direction.

(11) . . .

**Note.** In para (1) words from ', unless' to 'given' in square brackets inserted by SI 1998/58, reg 7(2) as from 19 January 1998. In para (3)(b) words omitted revoked by SI 1999/1047, reg 37(a) as from 1 June 1999. Para (4A) inserted by SI 1998/58, reg 7(3) as from 19 January 1998. Para (8) revoked by SI 2000/1596, reg 11 as from 19 June 2000. In para (9)(b) words 'refer the case to a child support officer' substituted by words from 'make a decision' to 'Maintenance Assessment Procedure Regulations' in square brackets by SI 1999/1047, reg 37(c) as from 1 June 1999. Para (11) revoked by SI 1999/1047, reg 37(d) as from 1 June 1999.

[*Procedure in relation to determination of an application for a revision or a supersession of a decision with respect to a departure direction*

**8A.**   (1) Subject to the modifications described in paragraph (2), regulation 8 shall apply to any application for a revision or a supersession of a decision with respect to a departure direction as it applies to an application for a departure direction.

(2) The modifications described in this paragraph are—

(a) for paragraph (1) there shall be substituted the following paragraphs—

'(1) Except where paragraph (1A) applies, the Secretary of State shall—

(a) give notice of an application for a revision or a supersession of a decision with respect to a departure direction to the relevant persons other than the applicant;

(b) inform them of the grounds on which the application has been made and any relevant information or evidence the applicant has given, except details, information or evidence falling within paragraph (2);

(c) invite representations from the relevant persons other than the applicant on any matter relating to that application; and

(d) explain the provisions of paragraphs (2), (5) and (6) in relation to such representations.

(1A) This paragraph applies where an application for a revision or a supersession has been made and the Secretary of State is satisfied on the information or evidence available to him that either—

(a) a revision or supersession of a departure direction is unlikely to be made; or

(b) in a case where the applicant was the applicant for the decision which is to be revised or superseded, a ground on which the decision to be revised or superseded was made no longer applies.';

(b) paragraphs (3), (4) and (7) shall be omitted;

(c) in paragraph (4A) for the words from 'that a departure direction' to the words 'in that case' there shall be substituted the words 'that a decision revising or superseding a decision with respect to a departure direction was unlikely to be made, but on further consideration of the application he is minded to make such a decision';

(d) in paragraph (5)—

  (i) for the words '(1), (6) or (7)' there shall be substituted the words '(1) or (6)';

  (ii) after the word 'application' there shall be added the words 'for a decision revising or superseding a decision';

(e) in paragraph (8)—

  (i) for the words 'In deciding whether to give a departure direction' there shall be substituted the words 'Before deciding whether or not to make a decision revising or, as the case may be, superseding a decision as to a departure direction in consequence of an application for such a decision'; and

  (ii) in sub-paragraph (a), for the words 'by the applicant for that direction' there shall be substituted the words 'in connection with the application';

(f) for paragraphs (9) and (10) there shall be substituted the following paragraph—

'(9) Where the Secretary of State has determined an application made for the purpose of revising or superseding a decision he shall, as soon as is reasonably practicable, notify the relevant persons of—

(a) that determination;

(b) the reasons for it; and

(c) where appropriate, the basis on which the amount of child support maintenance is to be fixed by any fresh assessment made in consequence of that determination.'.]

**Note.** Inserted by SI 1999/1047, reg 38 as from 1 June 1999.

*[Departure directions and persons in receipt of income support[, state pension credit], income-based jobseeker's allowance, working families' tax credit or disabled person's tax credit [or working tax credit]*

**9.** (1) The costs referred to in regulations 13 to 18 shall not constitute special expenses where they are or were incurred—

(a) by an absent parent to or in respect of whom income support[, state pension credit] or income-based jobseeker's allowance is or was in payment at the date on which any departure direction given in response to that application would take effect;

(b) by a person with care to or in respect of whom income support[, state pension credit], income-based jobseeker's allowance [or working tax credit] is or was in payment at the date on which any departure direction given in response to that application would take effect; or

(c) by a person with care where, at the date on which any departure direction given in response to that application would take effect, income support[, state pension credit] or income-based jobseeker's allowance is or was in payment to or in respect of the absent parent of the child or children in relation to whom the maintenance assessment in question is made.

(2) A transfer shall not constitute a transfer of property for the purposes of paragraph 3(1)(b) or 4(1)(b) of Schedule 4B to the Act, or of regulations 21 and 22, where the application is made—

(a) by an absent parent to or in respect of whom income support[, state pension credit] or income-based jobseeker's allowance is or was in payment at the date on which any departure direction given in response to that application would take effect;

(b) by a person with care and, at the date on which any departure direction given in response to that application would take effect, income support[, state pension credit] or income-based jobseeker's allowance is or was in payment to or in respect of the absent parent of the child or children in relation to whom the maintenance assessment in question is made.

(3) A case shall not constitute a case under regulations 23 to 29 where the application is made—

(a) by an absent parent to or in respect of whom income support[, state pension credit] or income-based jobseeker's allowance is or was in payment at the date on which any departure direction given in response to that application would take effect;

(b) by an absent parent where, at the date on which any departure direction given in response to that application would take effect, income support[, state pension credit], income-based jobseeker's allowance [or working tax credit] is or was in payment to or in respect of the person with care of the child or children in relation to whom the maintenance assessment in question is made;

(c) by a person with care where, at the date on which any departure direction given in response to that application would take effect, income support[, state pension credit] or income-based jobseeker's allowance is or was in payment to or in respect of the absent parent of the child or children in relation to whom the maintenance assessment is made.]

**Note.** Substituted by SI 1998/58, reg 8 as from 19 January 1998. Provision heading: words ', state pension credit' in square brackets inserted by SI 2003/2779, reg 2 as from 5 November 2003 and words ', working families' tax credit or disabled person's tax credit' substituted by words 'or working tax credit' in square brackets by SI 2003/328, reg 4(1), (2) as from 6 April 2003. Words ', state pension credit' in each place they occur in square brackets inserted by SI 2003/2779, reg 2(a) as from 5 November 2003. Words ', working families' tax credit or disabled person's tax credit' in both places substituted by words 'or working tax credit' in square brackets by SI 2003/328, reg 4(1), (2) as from 6 April 2003.

*Departure directions and interim maintenance assessments*

**10.**   (1) For the purposes of section 28A(1) of the Act, the term 'maintenance assessment' does not include—

   (a)  a Category A or Category C interim maintenance assessment;
   (b)  a Category B interim maintenance assessment where the application is made under paragraph 2 of Schedule 4B to the Act in respect of expenses prescribed by regulation 18 and that Category B interim maintenance assessment was made because the applicant fell within paragraph (3)(b) of regulation 8 of the Maintenance Assessment Procedure Regulations;
   (c)  a Category D interim maintenance assessment, where the application is made under paragraph 3 or 4 of Schedule 4B to the Act or by an absent parent under paragraph 2 or 5 of that Schedule.

   (2) For the purposes of this regulation, Category A, Category B, Category C and Category D interim maintenance assessments are defined in regulation 8(3) of the Maintenance Assessment Procedure Regulations (categories of interim maintenance assessment).

**11.**   <. . .>
**Note.** Revoked by SI 1999/1047, reg 39, as from 1 June 1999.

*Meaning of 'current assessment' for the purposes of the Act [Meaning of 'current assessment' for the purposes of the Act]*

**11A.**   *[Where—*
   *(a)   an application under section 28A of the Act has been made in respect of a current assessment;*
   *(b)   after the making of that application that current assessment has been in the case of a maintenance assessment the effective date of which is on or before 8th December 1996, reviewed by a child support officer under section 16 of the Act, or, in the case of any assessment, revised by the Secretary of State under section 16 of the Act after 6th December 1998, or reviewed under section 17, 18 or 19 of the Act, whether or not that review was initiated by a reference under section 28B(4) of the Act; and*
   *(c)   following that review, a fresh maintenance assessment has been made—*
      *(i)   the effective date of which is the same as the effective date of that current assessment; or*
      *(ii)  which takes effect on the correct date applicable to that current assessment in circumstances where that current assessment has been reviewed on grounds which include the ground that its effective date was incorrect,*
   *references to the current assessment in sections 28B(3), 28C(2)(a) and 28F(5) of, and in paragraph 8 of Schedule 4A and paragraphs 2, 3 and 4 of Schedule 4B to, the Act shall have effect as if they were references to that fresh maintenance assessment.]*
[Where—
   (a)  an application under section 28A of the Act has been made in respect of a current assessment; and
   (b)  after the making of that application, a fresh maintenance assessment has been made upon a revision of a decision as to a maintenance assessment under section 16 of the Act,
references to the current assessment in sections 28B(3), 28C(2)(a) and 28F(5) of, and in paragraph 8 of Schedule 4A and paragraphs 2, 3 and 4 of Schedule 4B to, the Act shall have effect as if they were references to the fresh maintenance assessment.]

**Note.** Substituted by SI 1999/1047, reg 40 (originally inserted by SI 1998/58, reg 10) as from 1 June 1999.

*Meaning of 'benefit' for the purposes of section 28E of the Act*

**12.** For the purposes of section 28E of the Act, 'benefit' means income support [, state pension credit], income-based jobseeker's allowance, *working families' tax credit, disabled person's tax credit* [working tax credit], housing benefit, and council tax benefit.

**Note.** Words ', state pension credit' in square brackets inserted by SI 2003/2779, reg 2(a) as from 5 November 2003 and words 'working families' tax credit, disabled person's tax credit' substituted by words 'working tax credit' in square brackets by SI 2003/328, reg 4(1), (3) as from 6 April 2003.

PART III

SPECIAL EXPENSES

*Costs incurred in travelling to work*

**13.** (1) Subject to paragraphs (2) and (3), the following costs shall constitute expenses for the purposes of paragraph 2(2) of Schedule 4B to the Act where they are incurred by the applicant for the purposes of travel between his home and his normal place of work—

   (a) the cost of purchasing a ticket for such travel;

   (b) the cost of purchasing fuel, where such travel is by a vehicle which is not carrying fare-paying passengers; or

   (c) in exceptional circumstances, the taxi fare for a journey which must unavoidably be undertaken during hours when no other reasonable mode of travel is available,

and any minor incidental costs, such as tolls or fees for the use of a particular road or bridge, incurred in connection with such travel.

   (2) Where the Secretary of State considers any costs referred to in paragraph (1) to be unreasonably high or to have been unreasonably incurred he may substitute such lower amount as he considers reasonable, including a nil amount.

   (3) Costs which can be set off against the income of the applicant under the Income and Corporation Taxes Act 1988 shall not constitute expenses for the purposes of paragraph (1).

*Contact costs*

**14.** (1) Where at the time a departure direction is applied for a set pattern has been established as to frequency of contact between the absent parent and a child in respect of whom the current assessment was made, the following costs, based upon that pattern and incurred by that absent parent for the purpose of maintaining contact with that child, shall, subject to paragraphs (2) to (6), constitute expenses for the purposes of paragraph 2(2) of Schedule 4B to the Act—

   (a) the cost of purchasing a ticket for travel for the purpose of maintaining that contact;

   (b) the cost of purchasing fuel, where travel is for the purpose of maintaining that contact and is by a vehicle which is not carrying fare-paying passengers; or

   (c) the taxi fare for a journey or part of a journey to maintain that contact where the Secretary of State is satisfied that the disability of the absent parent makes it impracticable to use any other form of transport which might otherwise have been available to him,

and any minor incidental costs, such as tolls or fees for the use of a particular road or bridge, incurred in connection with such travel.

(2) Subject to paragraph (3), where the Secretary of State considers any costs referred to in paragraph (1) to be unreasonably high or to have been unreasonably incurred he may substitute such lower amount as he considers reasonable, including a nil amount.

(3) Any lower amount substituted by the Secretary of State under paragraph (2) shall not be so low as to make it impossible, in the Secretary of State's opinion, for contact to be maintained at the frequency specified in any court order made in respect of the absent parent and the child mentioned in paragraph (1) where the absent parent is maintaining contact at that frequency.

(4) Paragraph (1) shall not apply where regulation 20 of the Maintenance Assessments and Special Cases Regulations (persons treated as absent parents) applies to the applicant.

(5) Where sub-paragraph (c) of paragraph (1) applies and the applicant has, at the date an application is made, received, or at that date is in receipt of, financial assistance from any source to meet, wholly or in part, costs of maintaining contact with the child who is referred to in paragraph (1), which arise wholly from his disability and which are in excess of the costs which would be incurred if that disability did not exist, only the net amount of the costs referred to in that sub-paragraph, after the deduction of that financial assistance, shall constitute special expenses for the purposes of paragraph 2(2) of Schedule 4B to the Act.

(6) For the purposes of this regulation, a person is disabled if he is blind, deaf or dumb or is substantially or permanently handicapped by illness, injury, mental disorder or congenital deformity.

(7) Where, at the time a departure direction is applied for, no set pattern has been established as to frequency of contact between the absent parent and a child in respect of whom the current assessment was made, but the Secretary of State is satisfied that that absent parent and the person with care of that child have agreed upon a pattern of contact for the future, the costs mentioned in paragraph (1) and which are based upon that intended pattern of contact shall constitute expenses for the purposes of paragraph 2(2) of Schedule 4B to the Act, and paragraphs (2) to (6) shall apply to that application.

[(8) This regulation shall apply in relation to an application made for the purpose of superseding a decision with respect to a departure direction as though—

(a) for the words 'at the time a departure direction is applied for' in paragraphs (1) and (7) there were substituted the words 'at the time an application is made for a decision superseding a decision with respect to a departure direction';

(b) in paragraph (5), after the words 'an application' there were inserted the words 'for the supersession of a decision with respect to a departure direction'.]

**Note.** Para (8) inserted by SI 1999/1047, reg 41 as from 1 June 1999.

*Illness or disability*

**15.** (1) Subject to paragraphs (2) to (4), the costs being met by the applicant in respect of the items listed in sub-paragraphs (a) to (m), which arise from long-term illness or disability of that applicant or a dependant of that applicant and which are in excess of the costs which would be incurred if that illness or disability did not exist, shall constitute special expenses for the purposes of paragraph 2(2) of Schedule 4B to the Act—

(a) personal care and attendance;
(b) personal communication needs;
(c) mobility;
(d) domestic help;
(e) medical aids where these cannot be provided under the health service;
(f) heating;
(g) clothing;

(h) laundry requirements;
(i) payments for food essential to comply with a diet recommended by a medical practitioner;
(j) adaptations required to the applicant's home;
(k) day care;
(l) rehabilitation; or
(m) respite care.

(2) Where the Secretary of State considers any costs referred to in paragraph (1) to be unreasonably high or to have been unreasonably incurred he may substitute such lower amount as he considers reasonable, including a nil amount.

(3) [Subject to paragraph (4A),] Where—

(a) an applicant or his dependant has, at the date an application is made, received, or at that date is in receipt of, financial assistance from any source in respect of his long-term illness or disability or that of his dependant; or
(b) that applicant or his dependant is adjudged eligible for either of the allowances referred to in paragraph (4),

only the net amount of the costs incurred in respect of the items listed in paragraph (1), after the deduction of the financial assistance referred to in sub-paragraph (a) and, where applicable, the allowance referred to in sub-paragraph (b) shall constitute special expenses for the purposes of paragraph 2(2) of Schedule 4B to the Act.

(4) [Subject to paragraph (4A),] Where the Secretary of State considers that a person who has made an application in respect of special expenses falling within paragraph (1) or his dependant may be entitled to disability living allowance under section 71 of the Contributions and Benefits Act or attendance allowance under section 64 of that Act—

(a) if that applicant or his dependant has at the date of that application, or within a period of six weeks beginning with the giving or sending to him of notification of the possibility of entitlement to either of those allowances, applied for either of those allowances, the application made by that applicant shall not be determined until a decision has been made by the adjudicating authority [Secretary of State] on the eligibility for that allowance of that applicant or that dependant;
(b) if that applicant or his dependant has failed to apply for either of those allowances within the six week period specified in sub-paragraph (a), the Secretary of State shall determine the application for a departure direction made by that applicant on the basis that that applicant has income equivalent to the highest rate prescribed in respect of that allowance by or under those sections.

[(4A) Paragraphs (3) and (4) shall not apply where the dependant of an applicant is adjudged eligible for either of the allowances referred to in paragraph (4) and in all the circumstances of the case the Secretary of State considers that the costs being met by the applicant in respect of the items listed in paragraph (1) shall constitute special expenses for the purposes of paragraph 2(2) of Schedule 4B to the Act without the deductions in paragraph (3) being made.]

(5) For the purposes of this regulation, a dependant of an applicant shall be—

(a) where the applicant is an absent parent—
   (i) the partner of that absent parent;
   (ii) any child of whom that absent parent or his partner is a parent and who lives with them; or
(b) where the applicant is a parent with care—
   (i) the partner of that parent with care;
   (ii) any child of whom that parent with care or her partner is a parent and who lives with them, except any child in respect of whom the absent parent against whom the current assessment is made is the parent.

(6) For the purposes of this regulation—

(a) a person is disabled if he is blind, deaf or dumb or is substantially or permanently handicapped by illness, injury, mental disorder or congenital deformity;

(b) 'long-term illness' means an illness from which the applicant or his dependant is suffering at the date of the application and which is likely to last for at least 52 weeks from that date or if likely to be shorter than 52 weeks, for the rest of the life of that applicant or his dependant;

(c) 'the health service' has the same meaning as in section 128 of the National Health Service Act 1977 or in section 108(1) of the National Health Service (Scotland) Act 1978.

**Note.** In paras (3), (4) words 'Subject to paragraph (4A),' in square brackets inserted by SI 1998/58, reg 11(2) as from 19 January 1998. In para (4)(a) words 'adjudicating authority' substituted by words 'Secretary of State' in square brackets by SI 1999/1047, reg 42 as from 1 June 1999. Para (4A): inserted by SI 1998/58, reg 11(3) as from 19 January 1998.

*Debts incurred before the absent parent became an absent parent*

**16.** (1) Subject to paragraphs (2) to (4), repayment of debts incurred—

(a) for the joint benefit of the applicant and the non-applicant parent;

(b) for the benefit of the non-applicant parent where the applicant remains legally liable to repay the whole or part of that debt;

(c) for the benefit of any person who at the time the debt was incurred—

(i) was a child;

(ii) lived with the applicant and non-applicant parent; and

(iii) of whom the applicant or the non-applicant parent is the parent, or both are the parents; or

(d) for the benefit of any child with respect to whom the current assessment was made,

shall constitute expenses for the purposes of paragraph 2(2) of Schedule 4B to the Act where those debts were incurred before the absent parent became an absent parent in relation to a child with respect to whom the current assessment was made and at a time when the applicant and the non-applicant parent were a married or unmarried couple who were living together.

(2) Paragraph (1) shall not apply to repayment of—

(a) a debt which would otherwise fall within paragraph (1) where the applicant has retained for his own use and benefit the asset the purchase of which incurred the debt;

(b) a debt incurred for the purposes of any trade or business;

(c) a gambling debt;

(d) a fine imposed on the applicant;

(e) unpaid legal costs in respect of separation or divorce from the non-applicant parent;

(f) amounts due after use of a credit card;

(g) a debt incurred by the applicant to pay any of the items listed in sub-paragraphs (c) to (f) and (j);

(h) amounts payable by the applicant under a mortgage or loan taken out on the security of any property except where that mortgage or loan was taken out to facilitate the purchase of, or to pay for repairs or improvements to, any property which is the home of the parent with care and any child in respect of whom the current assessment was made;

(i) amounts payable by the applicant in respect of a policy of insurance of a kind referred to in paragraph 3(4) or (5) of Schedule 3 to the Maintenance Assessments and Special Cases Regulations (eligible housing costs) except where that policy of insurance was obtained or retained to discharge a mortgage or charge taken out to facilitate the purchase of, or to pay for repairs or improvements to, any property which is the home of the parent with care and any child in respect of whom the current assessment was made;

(j) a bank overdraft except where the overdraft was, at the time it was taken out, agreed to be for a specified amount repayable over a specified period;

(k) a loan obtained by the applicant, other than a loan obtained from a qualifying lender or the applicant's current or former employer;

(l) a debt in respect of which a departure direction has already been given and which has not been repaid during the period for which that direction was in force except where the maintenance assessment in respect of which that direction was given was cancelled or ceased to have effect and, during the period for which that direction was in force, a further maintenance assessment was made in respect of the same applicant, non-applicant and qualifying child with respect to whom the earlier assessment was made; or

(m) any other debt which the Secretary of State is satisfied it is reasonable to exclude.

(3) Except where the repayment is of an amount which is payable under a mortgage or loan, or in respect of a policy of insurance, which falls within the exception set out in sub-paragraph (h) or (i) of paragraph (2), repayment of a debt shall not constitute expenses for the purposes of paragraph (1) where the Secretary of State is satisfied that the applicant has taken responsibility for repayment of that debt, as, or as part of, a financial settlement with the non-applicant parent or by virtue of a court order.

(4) Where an applicant has incurred a debt partly to repay a debt or debts repayment of which would have fallen within paragraph (1), the repayment of that part of the debt incurred which is referable to the debts repayment of which would have fallen within that paragraph shall constitute expenses for the purposes of paragraph 2(2) of Schedule 4B to the Act.

(5) For the purposes of this regulation—

(a) 'married or unmarried couple' has the meaning set out in regulation 1 of the Maintenance Assessments and Special Cases Regulations;

(b) 'non-applicant parent' means—

  (i) where the applicant is the person with care, the absent parent;

  (ii) where the applicant is the absent parent, the partner of that absent parent at the time the debt in respect of which the application is made was entered into;

(c) 'qualifying lender' has the meaning given to it in section 376(4) of the Income and Corporation Taxes Act 1988;

(d) 'repairs and improvements' means major repairs necessary to maintain the fabric of the home and any of the measures set out in sub-paragraphs (a) to (j) of paragraph 2 of Schedule 3 to the Maintenance Assessments and Special Cases Regulations (eligible housing costs) and other improvements which the Secretary of State considers reasonable in the circumstances where those measures or other improvements are undertaken with a view to improving the fitness for occupation of the home.

*Pre-1993 financial commitments*

**17.** (1) A financial commitment entered into by an absent parent before 5th April 1993, except any commitment of a kind listed in paragraph (2)(b) to (g) and (j) of regulation 16 or which has been wholly or partly taken into account in the calculation of a maintenance assessment shall constitute expenses for the purposes of paragraph 2(2) of Schedule 4B to the Act where—

(a) there was in force on 5th April 1993 and at the date that commitment was entered into, *a court order or* [a maintenance order or a written] maintenance agreement made before 5th April 1993 in respect of that absent parent and every child in respect of whom, before that date, he was, or was found, or adjudged to be, the parent; ...

[(aa) at least one of the children referred to in sub-paragraph (a) is a child in respect of whom the current assessment was made; and]

(b) the Secretary of State is satisfied that it is impossible for the absent parent to withdraw from that commitment or unreasonable to expect him to do so.

(2) ...

**Note.** In para (1)(a) words 'a court order or' substituted by words 'a maintenance order or a written' in square brackets, in para (1)(a) word omitted revoked, para (1)(aa) inserted and para (2) revoked by SI 1998/58, reg 12(2), (3) as from 19 January 1998.

*Costs incurred in supporting certain children*

**18.**    (1) The costs incurred by a parent in supporting a child who is not his child but who is part of his family [and who was, at the date on which any departure direction given in response to an application under this regulation would take effect, living in the same household as that parent] (a 'relevant child') shall constitute special expenses for the purposes of paragraph 2(2) of Schedule 4B to the Act if the conditions set out in paragraph (2) are satisfied and shall, if those conditions are satisfied, equal the amount specified in paragraph (3).

(2) The conditions referred to in paragraph (1) are—

(a) *the child became a relevant child prior to 5th April 1993;*

[(a) the child became a relevant child prior to 5th April 1993 and has remained a relevant child for the whole of the period from that date to the date on which any departure direction given in response to an application under this regulation would take effect;]

(b) *subject to paragraph (7), the liability of the absent parent of a relevant child to pay maintenance to or for the benefit of that child under a court order, a written maintenance agreement or a maintenance assessment is less than the amount specified in paragraph (4), or there is no such liability; and*

[(b) subject to paragraph (7)—

(i) the liability of the absent parent of a relevant child to pay maintenance to or for the benefit of that child under a maintenance order, a written maintenance agreement or a maintenance assessment; or

(ii) any deduction from benefit under section 43 of the Act in place of payment of child support maintenance to or for the benefit of that child,

is less than the amount specified in paragraph (4), or there is no such liability or deduction; and]

(c) the net income of the parent's current partner where the relevant child is the child of that partner, calculated in accordance with paragraph (5), is less than the amount calculated in accordance with paragraph (6) ('the partner's outgoings').

(3) [Subject to paragraph (7A),] The amount referred to in paragraph (1) constituting special expenses for a case falling within this regulation is the difference between the amount specified in paragraph (4) and, subject to paragraph (7), the liability of the absent parent of a relevant child to pay maintenance of a kind mentioned in paragraph (2)(b) [(i) or any deduction from benefit mentioned in paragraph (2)(b)(ii)], and if there is no such liability [or deduction] is the amount specified in paragraph (4).

(4) [Subject to paragraphs (4A) and (4B),] The amount referred to in paragraphs (2)(b) and (3) is the aggregate of—

(a) an amount in respect of each relevant child equal to the personal allowance for that child specified in column (2) of paragraph 2 of the relevant Schedule (income support personal allowance);

(b) if the conditions set out in paragraph 14(b) and (c) [of] that Schedule (income support disabled child premium) are satisfied in respect of a relevant child, an amount equal to the amount specified in column (2) of paragraph 15(6) of that Schedule in respect of each such child; [and]

(c) *an amount equal to the income support family premium specified in paragraph 3 of that Schedule that would be payable if the parent were a claimant, except where the family includes other children of the parent; and*

[(c) *except where the family includes other children of the parent, an amount equal to the income support family premium—*

    (i) *specified in sub-paragraph (a) of paragraph 3 of that Schedule where, if the applicant were a claimant, the rate of income support family premium specified in that sub-paragraph would be applicable to him; or*

    (ii) *specified in paragraph 3(b) in all other cases*]

[(c) except where the family includes other children of the parent, an amount equal to the income support family premium specified in paragraph 3(1)(b) of that Schedule that would be payable if the parent were a claimant.]

(d) ...

[(4A) Where day to day care of the relevant child is shared between the current partner of the person making an application under this regulation and the other parent of that child, the amounts referred to in paragraph (4) shall be reduced by the proportion of those amounts which is the same as the proportion of the week in respect of which the child is not living in the same household as the applicant.]

[(4B) Where an application under paragraph (1) is made in respect of more than one relevant child and the family does not include any other children of the parent, the amount applicable under sub-paragraph (c) of paragraph (4) in respect of each relevant child shall be calculated by dividing the amount referred to in that sub-paragraph by the number of relevant children in respect of whom that application is made.]

(5) For the purposes of paragraph (2)(c), the net income of the parent's partner shall be the aggregate of—

(a) the income of that partner, calculated in accordance with regulation 7(1) of the Maintenance Assessments and Special Cases Regulations (but excluding the amount mentioned in sub-paragraph (d) of that regulation) as if that partner were an absent parent to whom that regulation applied;

(b) the child benefit payable in respect of each relevant child; and

(c) any income, other than earnings, in excess of £10.00 per week in respect of each relevant child.

(6) For the purposes of paragraph (2)(c), a current partner's outgoings shall be the aggregate of—

(a) an amount equal to the amount specified in column (2) of paragraph 1(1)(e) of the relevant Schedule (income support personal allowance for a single claimant aged not less than 25);

(b) where a departure direction has already been given in a case falling within regulation 27 in respect of the housing costs attributable to the partner, the amount determined in accordance with regulation 40(7) as the housing costs the partner is able to contribute;

(c) the amount of any reduction in the parent's exempt income, calculated under paragraph (1) of regulation 9 of the Maintenance Assessments and Special Cases Regulations, in consequence of the application of paragraph (2) of that regulation; and

(d) the amount specified in paragraph (3) [or the aggregate of those amounts where paragraph (7A) applies to that partner].

(7) The Secretary of State may, if he is satisfied that it is appropriate in the particular circumstances of the case, treat a liability of a kind mentioned in

paragraph (2)(b) [(i)] as not constituting a liability for the purposes of that paragraph and of paragraph (3).

[(7A) Where an application is made in respect of relevant children of different parents, a separate calculation shall be made in accordance with paragraphs (3) and (4) in respect of each relevant child or group of relevant children who have the same parents and the amount constituting special expenses referred to in paragraph (1) shall be the aggregate of the amounts calculated in accordance with paragraph (3) in respect of each such relevant child or group of relevant children.]

(8) For the purposes of this regulation—

(a) *a child who is not the child of a particular person is a part of that person's family where that child is the child of a current or former partner of that person;*

[(a) a child who is not the child of a particular person is a part of that person's family where—

    (i) that child is the child of a current partner of that person; or

    (ii) that child is the child of a former partner of that person and lives in the same household as the applicant for every night of each week;]

(b) 'relevant Schedule' means Schedule 2 to the Income Support (General) Regulations 1987.

**Note.** In para (1) words from 'and who' to 'parent' in square brackets inserted, para (2)(a), (b) substituted, in para (3) words 'Subject to paragraph (7A),' in square brackets, '(i) or any deduction from benefit mentioned in paragraph (2)(b)(ii)' in square brackets and 'or deduction' in square brackets inserted, in para (4) words 'Subject to paragraphs (4A) and (4B),' and word 'of' in square brackets inserted, in para (4)(b) word 'and' in square brackets inserted, para 4(c) substituted, para (4)(d) revoked, paras (4A), (4B) inserted, in para (6)(d) words 'or the aggregate of those amounts where paragraph (7A) applies to that partner' in square brackets inserted, in para (7) figure '(i)' in square brackets inserted, para (7A) inserted and para (8)(a) substituted, by SI 1998/58, reg 13(2)–(10) as from 19 January 1998. Para (4)(c) further substituted by SI 1998/58, reg 14 as from 6 April 1998.

*Special expenses for a case falling within regulation 13, 14, 16 or 17*

**19.** (1) This regulation applies where the expenses of an applicant fall within one or more of the descriptions of expenses falling within regulation 13 (travel to work costs), 14 (contact costs), 16 (debts incurred before the absent parent became an absent parent) or 17 (pre-1993 financial commitments).

(2) Special expenses for the purposes of paragraph 2(2) of Schedule 4B to the Act in respect of the expenses mentioned in paragraph (1) shall be—

(a) where the expenses fall within only one description of expenses, those expenses in excess of £15.00;

(b) where the expenses fall within more than one description of expenses, the aggregate of those expenses in excess of £15.00.

*Application for a departure direction in respect of special expenses other than those with respect to which a direction has already been given*

**20.** Where a departure direction with respect to special expenses falling within one or more of the descriptions of expenses falling within regulation 13, 14, 16 or 17 has already been given and an application with respect to special expenses falling within one or more of those descriptions of expenses is made where none of those expenses are ones with respect to which the earlier direction has been given, the special expenses with respect to which any later direction is given shall be the expenses, determined in accordance with regulation 13, 14, 16 or 17, as the case may be, with respect to which the later application is made, and the provisions of regulation 19 shall not apply.

PART IV

PROPERTY OR CAPITAL TRANSFERS

*Prescription of certain terms for the purposes of paragraphs 3 and 4 of Schedule 4B to the Act*

**21.** (1) For the purposes of paragraphs 3(1)(a) and 4(1)(a) of Schedule 4B to the Act—

(a) a court order means an order made—
  (i) under one or more of the enactments listed in or prescribed under section 8(11) of the Act; and
  (ii) in connection with the transfer of property of a kind defined in paragraph (2);

(b) an agreement means a written agreement made in connection with the transfer of property of a kind defined in paragraph (2).

(2) Subject to paragraphs (3) to (5), for the purposes of paragraph 3(1)(b) and 4(1)(b) of Schedule 4B to the Act, a transfer of property is a transfer by the absent parent of his beneficial interest in any asset to the person with care, to a child in respect of whom the current assessment was made, or to trustees where the object or one of the objects of the trust is the provision of maintenance.

(3) Where a transfer of property would not originally have fallen within paragraph (2) but the Secretary of State is satisfied that some or all of the amount of that property transferred was subsequently transferred to the person currently with care of a child in respect of whom the current assessment was made, the transfer of that property to the person currently with care shall count as a transfer of property for the purposes of paragraphs 3(1)(b) and 4(1)(b) of Schedule 4B to the Act.

(4) Where, if the Act had been in force at the time a transfer of property falling within paragraph (2) was made, the person who, at the time the application is made is the person with care would have been the absent parent and the person who, at the time the application is made is the absent parent would have been the person with care, that transfer shall not count as a transfer of property for the purposes of this regulation.

(5) For the purposes of paragraph 3(3) of Schedule 4B to the Act, the effect of a transfer of property is properly reflected in the current assessment if—

(a) the amount of child support maintenance payable under any fresh maintenance assessment which would be made in consequence of a departure direction differs from the amount of child support maintenance payable under that current assessment by less than £1.00; or

(b) the transfer referred to in paragraph (2) was for a specified period only and that period ended before the effective date of any departure direction which would otherwise have been given.

*Value of a transfer of property and its equivalent weekly value for a case falling within paragraph 3 of Schedule 4B to the Act*

**22.** (1) Where the conditions specified in paragraph 3(1) of Schedule 4B to the Act are satisfied, the value of a transfer of property for the purposes of that paragraph shall be that part of the transfer made by the absent parent (making allowance for any transfer by the person with care to the absent parent) which the Secretary of State is satisfied is in lieu of [periodical payments of] maintenance.

(2) The Secretary of State shall, in determining the value of a transfer of property in accordance with paragraph (1), assume that, unless evidence to the contrary is provided to him—

(a) the person with care and the absent parent had equal beneficial interests in the assets in relation to which the court order or agreement was made;

(b) where the person with care was married to the absent parent, one half of the value of the transfer was a transfer for the benefit of the person with care; and

(c) where the person with care has never been married to the absent parent, none of the value of the transfer was a transfer for the benefit of the person with care.

(3) The equivalent weekly value of a transfer of property shall be determined in accordance with the provisions of the Schedule.

(4) For the purposes of regulation 21 and this regulation, the term 'maintenance', means the normal day-to-day living expenses of the child with respect to whom the current assessment was made.

**Note.** In para (1) words 'periodical payments of' in square brackets inserted by SI 1998/58, reg 15, as from 19 January 1998.

PART V

ADDITIONAL CASES

*Assets capable of producing income or higher income*

**23.** (1) Subject to paragraphs (2) and (3), a case shall constitute a case for the purposes of paragraph 5(1) of Schedule 4B to the Act where—

(a) the Secretary of State is satisfied that any asset in which the non-applicant has a beneficial interest, or which he has the ability to control—

   (i) is capable of being utilised to produce income but has not been so utilised;

   (ii) has been invested in such a way that the income obtained from it is less than might reasonably be expected;

   (iii) is a chose in action which has not been enforced where the Secretary of State is satisfied that such enforcement would be reasonable;

   (iv) in Scotland, is monies due or an obligation owed, whether immediately payable or otherwise and whether the payment or obligation is secured or not and the Secretary of State is satisfied that requiring payment of the monies or the implementation of the obligation would be reasonable; or

   (v) has not been sold where the Secretary of State is satisfied that the sale of the asset would be reasonable;

(b) any asset has been transferred by the non-applicant to trustees and the non-applicant is a beneficiary of the trust so created; or

(c) any asset has become subject to a trust created by legal implication of which the non-applicant is a beneficiary.

(2) Paragraph (1) shall not apply where—

(a) the total value of the asset or assets referred to in that paragraph does not exceed £10,000.00 after deduction of the amount owing under any mortgage or charge on that asset; or

(b) the Secretary of State is satisfied that any asset referred to in that paragraph is being retained by the non-applicant to be used for a purpose which the Secretary of State considers reasonable in all the circumstances of the case [; or

(c) if the non-applicant were a claimant, paragraph 64 of Schedule 10 to the Income Support (General) Regulations 1987 (treatment of relevant trust payments) would apply to the asset referred to in that paragraph].

(3) ...

(4) For the purposes of this regulation the term 'asset' means—

(a) money, whether in cash or on deposit;

(b) a beneficial interest in land and rights in or over land;

(c) shares as defined in section 744 of the Companies Act 1985, stock and unit trusts as defined in section 6 of the Charging Orders Act 1979, gilt edged securities as defined in paragraph 1 of Schedule 2 to the Capital Gains Tax Act 1979, and other similar financial instruments.

(5) For the purposes of paragraph (4) the term 'asset' includes any asset falling within that paragraph which is located outside Great Britain.

**Note.** Para (2)(c) and word '; or' immediately preceding it inserted by SI 2002/1204, reg 3 as from 30 April 2002. Para (3) revoked by SI 1998/58, reg 16 as from 19 January 1998.

*Diversion of income*

**24.** A case shall constitute a case for the purposes of paragraph 5(1) of Schedule 4B to the Act where—

(a) the non-applicant has the ability to control the amount of income he receives, including earnings from employment or self-employment and dividends from shares, whether or not the whole of that income is derived from the company or business from which his earnings are derived; and

(b) the Secretary of State is satisfied that the non-applicant has unreasonably reduced the amount of his income which would otherwise fall to be taken into account under regulation 7 or 8 of the Maintenance Assessments and Special Cases Regulations by diverting it to other persons or for purposes other than the provision of such income for himself.

*Life-style inconsistent with declared income*

**25.** (1) Subject to paragraph (2), a case shall constitute a case for the purposes of paragraph 5(1) of Schedule 4B to the Act where the Secretary of State is satisfied that the current . . . assessment is based upon a level of income of the non-applicant which is substantially lower than the level of income required to support the overall life-style of that non-applicant.

*(2) Paragraph (1) shall not apply where—*

*(a) income support or income-based jobseeker's allowance is paid to or in respect of the non-applicant;*

*(b) the Secretary of State is satisfied that the life-style of the non-applicant is paid for—*

*(i) out of capital belonging to him; or*

*(ii) by his partner unless the non-applicant is able to influence or control the amount of income received by that partner.*

[(2) Paragraph (1) shall not apply where the Secretary of State is satisfied that the life-style of the non-applicant is paid for—

(a) out of capital belonging to him; or

(b) by his partner, unless the non-applicant is able to influence or control the amount of income received by that partner.]

(3) Where the Secretary of State is satisfied in a particular case that the provisions of paragraph (1) would apply but for the provisions of paragraph *(2)(b)(ii)* [(2)(b)], he may, whether or not any application on that ground has been made, consider whether the case falls within regulation 27.

**Note.** In para (1) word omitted revoked by SI 1998/58, reg 17(2) as from 19 January 1998. Para (2) substituted by SI 1998/58, reg 17(3) as from 19 January 1998. In para (3) number '(2)(b)(ii)' substituted by number '(2)(b)' in square brackets by SI 1998/58, reg 17(4) as from 19 January 1998.

*Unreasonably high housing costs*

**26.** A case shall constitute a case for the purposes of paragraph 5(1) of Schedule 4B to the Act where—

(a) the housing costs of the non-applicant exceed the limits set out in paragraph (1) of regulation 18 of the Maintenance Assessments and Special Cases Regulations (excessive housing costs);

(b) the non-applicant falls within paragraph (2) of that regulation or would fall within that paragraph if it applied to parents with care; and

(c) the Secretary of State is satisfied that the housing costs of the non-applicant are substantially higher than is necessary taking into account any special circumstances applicable to that non-applicant.

*Partner's contribution to housing costs*

**27.** A case shall constitute a case for the purposes of paragraph 5(1) of Schedule 4B to the Act where a partner of the non-applicant occupies the home with him and the Secretary of State considers that it is reasonable for that partner to contribute to the payment of the housing costs of the non-applicant.

*Unreasonably high travel costs*

**28.** A case shall constitute a case for the purposes of paragraph 5(1) of Schedule 4B to the Act where an amount in respect of travel to work costs has been included in the calculation of exempt income of the non-applicant under regulation 9(1)(i) of the Maintenance Assessments and Special Cases Regulations (exempt income: calculation or estimation of E) or, as the case may be, under regulation 10 of those Regulations (exempt income: calculation or estimation of F) applying regulation 9(1)(i), and the Secretary of State is satisfied that, in all the circumstances of the case, that amount is unreasonably high.

*Travel costs to be disregarded*

**29.** A case shall constitute a case for the purposes of paragraph 5(1) of Schedule 4B to the Act where—

(a) an amount in respect of travel to work costs has, in the calculation of a maintenance assessment, been included in the calculation of the exempt income of the non-applicant under regulation 9(1)(i) of the Maintenance Assessments and Special Cases Regulations or, as the case may be, under regulation 10 of those Regulations applying regulation 9(1)(i); and

(b) the Secretary of State is satisfied that the non-applicant has sufficient income remaining after the deduction of the amount that would be payable under that assessment, had the amount referred to in sub-paragraph (a) not been included in its calculation, for it to be inappropriate for all or part of that amount to be included in the exempt income of the non-applicant.

PART VI

FACTORS TO BE TAKEN INTO ACCOUNT FOR THE PURPOSES OF SECTION 28F OF THE ACT

*Factors to be taken into account and not to be taken into account in determining whether it would be just and equitable to give a departure direction*

**30.** (1) The factors to be taken into account in determining whether it would be just and equitable to give a departure direction in any case shall include—

(a) where the application is made on any ground—

    (i) whether, in the opinion of the Secretary of State, the giving of a departure direction would be likely to result in a relevant person ceasing paid employment;

    (ii) if the applicant is the absent parent, the extent, if any, of his liability to pay child maintenance under a court order or other agreement in the period prior to the effective date of the maintenance assessment;

(b) where an application is made on the ground that the case falls within regulations 13 to 20 (special expenses), whether, in the opinion of the Secretary of State—

(i) the financial arrangements made by the applicant could have been such as to enable the whole or part of the expenses cited to be paid without a departure direction being given;

(ii) the applicant has at his disposal financial resources which are currently utilised for the payment of expenses other than those arising from essential everyday requirements and which could be used to pay the whole or part of the expenses cited.

(2) The following factors are not to be taken into account in determining whether it would be just and equitable to give a departure direction in any case—

(a) the fact that the conception of a child in respect of whom the current assessment was made was not planned by one or both of the parents;

(b) whether the parent with care or the absent parent was responsible for the breakdown of the relationship between them;

(c) the fact that the parent with care or the absent parent has formed a new relationship with a person who is not a parent of the child in respect of whom the current assessment was made;

(d) the existence of particular arrangements for contact with the child in respect of whom the current assessment was made, including whether any arrangements made are being adhered to by the parents;

(e) the failure by an absent parent to make payments under a maintenance order, a written maintenance agreement, or a maintenance assessment;

(f) representations made by persons other than the relevant persons.

PART VII

EFFECTIVE DATE AND DURATION OF A DEPARTURE DIRECTION

*Refusal to give a departure direction under section 28F(4) of the Act*

**31.**   The Secretary of State shall not give a departure direction in accordance with section 28F of the Act if he is satisfied that the difference between the current amount and the revised amount is less than £1.00.

*Effective date of a departure direction*

**32.**   (1) Where an application is made on the grounds set out in section 28A(2)(a) of the Act (the effect of the current assessment) and that application is given or sent within 28 days [one month] of the date of notification of the current assessment (whether or not that assessment has been made following an interim maintenance assessment), a departure direction given in response to that application shall take effect—

(a) where it is given on grounds that relate to the whole of the period between the effective date of the current assessment and the date on which that assessment is made, on the effective date of that assessment;

(b) in a case not falling within sub-paragraph (a), on the first day of the maintenance period following the date upon which the circumstances giving rise to that application first arose.

(2) Where an application is made on the grounds set out in section 28A(2)(a) of the Act (the effect of the current assessment) and that application is given or sent later than 28 days [one month] after the date of notification of the current assessment (whether or not that assessment has been made following an interim maintenance assessment)—

(a) subject to sub-paragraph (b), a departure direction given in response to that application shall take effect on the first day of the maintenance period during which that application is received;

(b) where the Secretary of State is satisfied that there was unavoidable delay, he may, for the purposes of determining the date on which a departure direction takes effect, treat the application as if it were given or sent within 28 days [one month] of the date of notification of the current assessment.

(3) The provisions of paragraphs (1) and (2) are subject to the provisions of paragraph (6) [paragraphs (3A) and (6)] and of regulations 47 to 50.

[(3A) Where [Subject to paragraph (3B), where] an application is determined in accordance with regulation 14 and is one to which paragraph (7) of that regulation applies, a departure direction given in response to that application shall take effect—

(a) from the first day of the maintenance period immediately following the date on which the absent parent and the parent with care have agreed the pattern of contact for the future is to commence; or

(b) where no such date has been so agreed, from the first day of the maintenance period immediately following the date upon which the departure direction is given.]

[(3B) For the purposes of paragraph (3A), paragraph (8) of regulation 14 shall not apply.]

(4) Subject to paragraph (6), where an application for a departure direction is made on the grounds set out in section 28A(2)(b) of the Act (a material change in the circumstances of the case since the current assessment was made), any departure direction given shall take effect on the first day of the maintenance period during which the application was received.

(5) An application may be made on the grounds set out in section 28A(2)(b) of the Act only if the material change in the circumstances on which it is based has already occurred.

(6) Where—

(a) an application has been determined in accordance with regulation 15(4)(b);

(b) a subsequent application is made with respect to special expenses falling within regulation 15(1) each of which is an expense in respect of which the earlier application was made; and

(c) the Secretary of State is satisfied that there was good cause for the applicant or his dependant not applying for disability living allowance or, as the case may be, attendance allowance within the six week period specified in regulation 15(4)(a),

any departure direction given in response to the later application shall take effect from the date that the earlier direction had effect, or would have had effect if an earlier direction had been given.

(7) . . .

(8) . . .

**Note.** In paras (1), (2) words '28 days' substituted by words 'one month' in square brackets by SI 1999/1047, reg 43(a) as from 1 June 1999. In para (3) words 'paragraph (6)' substituted by words 'paragraphs (3A) and (6)' in square brackets by SI 1998/58, reg 18(2) as from 19 January 1998. Para (3A) inserted by SI 1998/58, reg 18(3) as from 19 January 1998 and word 'Where' substituted by words 'Subject to paragraph (3B), where' in square brackets by SI 1999/1047, reg 43(b) as from 1 June 1999. Para (3B) inserted by SI 1999/1047, reg 43(c) as from 1 June 1999. Paras (7), (8) revoked by SI 1999/1047, reg 43(d) as from 1 June 1999.

[*Revision of decisions*

**32A.** (1) Subject to paragraphs (2) and (3), a decision of the Secretary of State or any decision upon referral under section 28D(1)(b) of an appeal tribunal with respect to a departure direction may be revised by the Secretary of State under section 16 of the Act as extended by paragraph 1 of Schedule 4C to the Act—

(a) if the Secretary of State receives an application for the revision of a decision under section 16 of the Act as extended within one month of the date of notification of the decision or within such longer time as may be allowed by regulation 32B;

(b) if—

    (i) the Secretary of State notifies a person, who applied for a decision to be revised within the period specified in sub-paragraph (a), that the application is unsuccessful because the Secretary of State is not in possession of all of the information or evidence needed to make a decision; and

    (ii) that person reapplies for a decision to be revised within one month of the notification described in head (i) above or such longer period as the Secretary of State is satisfied is reasonable in the circumstances of the case, and provides in that application sufficient information or evidence to enable a decision to be made;

(c) if the decision arose from an official error;

(d) if the Secretary of State is satisfied that the original decision was erroneous due to a misrepresentation of, or failure to disclose, a material fact and that the decision was more advantageous to the person who misrepresented or failed to disclose that fact than it would otherwise have been but for that error;

(e) where a departure direction takes effect in the circumstances described in regulation 35(3); or

(f) if the Secretary of State commences action leading to the revision of a decision within one month of the date of notification of the decision.

(2) Paragraph (1) shall apply neither—

(a) in respect of a material change of circumstances which—

    (i) occurred since *the date from which the decision had effect* [the date on which the decision was made]; or

    (ii) is expected, according to information or evidence which the Secretary of State has, to occur; nor

(b) where—

    (i) an appeal against the original decision has been brought but not determined; and

    (ii) from the point of view of the appellant, a revision, if made, would be less to his advantage than the original decision.]

**Note.** Inserted by SI 1999/1047, reg 44 as from 1 June 1999. In para (2)(a)(i) words 'the date from which the decision had effect' substituted by words 'the date on which the decision was made' in square brackets by SI 2000/1596, reg 12 as from 19 June 2000.

[*Late applications for a revision*

**32B.** (1) The period of one month specified in regulation 32A(1)(a) may be extended where the requirements specified in the following provisions of this regulation are met.

(2) An application for an extension of time shall be made by a relevant person or a person acting on his behalf.

(3) An application for an extension of time under this regulation shall—

(a) be made within 13 months of the date on which notification of the decision which it is sought to have revised was given or sent; and

(b) contain particulars of the grounds on which the extension of time is sought and shall contain sufficient details of the decision which it is sought to have revised to enable that decision to be identified.

(4) The application for an extension of time shall not be granted unless the person making the application, or any person acting for him, satisfies the Secretary of State that—

(a) it is reasonable to grant that application;

(b) the application for the decision to be revised has merit; and

(c) special circumstances are relevant to the application for an extension of time,

and as a result of those special circumstances, it was not practicable for the application for a decision to be revised to be made within one month of the date of notification of the decision which it is sought to have revised.

(5) In determining whether it is reasonable to grant an application for an extension of time, the Secretary of State shall have regard to the principle that the greater the time that has elapsed between the expiration of the period of one month described in regulation 32A(1)(a) from the date of notification of the decision which it is sought to have revised and the making of the application for an extension of time, the more compelling should be the special circumstances on which the application is based.

(6) In determining whether it is reasonable to grant an application for an extension of time, no account shall be taken of the following—

(a) that the person making the application for an extension of time or any person acting for him was unaware of or misunderstood the law applicable to his case (including ignorance or misunderstanding of the time limits imposed by these Regulations);

(b) that a Child Support Commissioner or a court has taken a different view of the law from that previously understood and applied.

(7) An application under this regulation for an extension of time which has been refused may not be renewed.]

**Note.** Inserted by SI 1999/1047, reg 44 as from 1 June 1999.

*[Date from which a revision of a decision takes effect*

**32C.** Where the date from which a decision took effect is found to be erroneous on a revision, the revision shall take effect from the date on which the revised decision would have taken effect had the error not been made.]

**Note.** Inserted by SI 1999/1047, reg 44 as from 1 June 1999.

*[Supersession of decisions*

**32D.** (1) For the purposes of section 17 of the Act as it applies in relation to decisions with respect to departure directions by virtue of paragraph 2 of Schedule 4C to the Act and subject to paragraphs (6), (9) and (10), the cases and circumstances in which a decision with respect to a departure direction may be made under that section are set out in paragraphs (2) to (5).

(2) A decision may be superseded by a decision made by the Secretary of State acting on his own initiative where he is satisfied that—

(a) there has been a material change of circumstances since the decision was made; or

(b) the decision was made in ignorance of, or was based upon a mistake as to, some material fact.

(3) A decision may be superseded by a decision made by the Secretary of State where—

(a) an application is made on the basis that—

　(i) there has been a change of circumstances since the decision was made; or

　(ii) it is expected that a change of circumstances will occur; and

(b) the Secretary of State is satisfied that the change of circumstances is or would be material.

(4) A decision may be superseded by a decision made by the Secretary of State where—

(a) an application is made on the basis that the decision was made in ignorance of, or was based upon a mistake as to, a fact; and

(b) the Secretary of State is satisfied that the fact is or would be material.

(5) A decision, other than a decision given on appeal, may be superseded by a decision made by the Secretary of State—

(a) where an application is made on the basis that the decision was erroneous in point of law; or

(b) acting on his own initiative where he is satisfied that the decision was erroneous in point of law.

(6) Subject to paragraph (7), paragraphs (2)(a) and (3) shall not apply where, if a decision were to be superseded in accordance with section 17 of the Act, the difference between the current amount and the revised amount would be less than £1.00 per week.

(7) Paragraph (6) shall not apply where the Secretary of State is satisfied on the information or evidence available to him that a ground on which the decision to be superseded was made no longer applies.

(8) In paragraph (6) 'revised amount' means the amount of child support maintenance which would be fixed if a decision with respect to a maintenance assessment were to be superseded by a decision made by the Secretary of State in accordance with paragraphs (2)(a) and (3) but for the operation of paragraph (6).

(9) The cases and circumstances in which a decision may be superseded by a decision made by the Secretary of State shall not include any case or circumstance in which a decision may be revised.

(10) Subject to paragraph (11), paragraphs (2) to (5) shall apply in respect of neither—

(a) a decision to reject or refuse an application for a departure direction; nor

(b) a decision to cancel a departure direction.

(11) Paragraph (10) above shall not apply in a case to which either paragraph (2) or (3) of regulation 35 applies.]

**Note.** Inserted by SI 1999/1047, reg 44 as from 1 June 1999.

[*Date from which a superseding decision takes effect*

**32E.** (1) This regulation contains exceptions to the provisions of section 17(4) of the Act, as it applies in relation to decisions with respect to departure directions by virtue of paragraph 2 of Schedule 4C to the Act, as to the date from which decisions which supersede earlier decisions are to take effect.

(2) Subject to paragraphs (3) and (5) [(3), (5) and (12)], where—

(a) a decision is made by the Secretary of State which supersedes an earlier decision in consequence of an application having been made under section 17 of the Act as it applies in relation to decisions with respect to departure directions by virtue of paragraph 2 of Schedule 4C to the Act; and

(b) the date on which the application is made is not the first day in a maintenance period,

the decision shall take effect as from the first day of the maintenance period in which the application is made.

(3) *Where a decision* [Subject to paragraph (12), where a decision] is superseded by a decision made by the Secretary of State in a case to which regulation 32D(2)(a) applies on the basis of evidence or information which was also the basis of a decision made under section 9 or 10 of the Social Security Act 1998 the superseding decision under section 17 of the Act as extended by paragraph 2 of Schedule 7 to the Act shall take effect as from the first day of the maintenance period in which that evidence or information was first brought to the attention of an officer exercising the functions of the Secretary of State under the Act.

(4) Where a decision is superseded by a decision made by the Secretary of State under regulation 32D(3) in consequence of an application made on the basis that a material change of circumstances is expected to occur, the superseding decision shall take effect as from the first day of the maintenance period which immediately succeeds the maintenance period in which the material change of circumstances is expected to occur.

(5) Where the Secretary of State makes, on his own initiative, a decision superseding a decision in consequence of evidence or information contained in an unsuccessful application for a revision of that decision, the superseding decision shall take effect as from the first day of the maintenance period in which that application was made.

(6) Where—

(a) a decision made by an appeal tribunal under section 20 of the Act as extended by paragraph 3 of Schedule 4C to the Act is superseded on the ground that it was erroneous due to a misrepresentation of, or that there was a failure to disclose, a material fact; and

(b) the Secretary of State is satisfied that the decision was more advantageous to the person who misrepresented or failed to disclose that fact than it would otherwise have been but for that error,

the superseding decision shall take effect as from the date the decision it superseded took, or was to take, effect.

(7) Any decision given under section 17 of the Act as extended by paragraph 2 of Schedule 4C to the Act in consequence of a decision which is a relevant determination for the purposes of section 28ZC of the Act (restrictions on liability in certain cases of error) shall take effect as from the date of the relevant determination.

(8) Where a decision with respect to a departure direction is superseded by a decision under section 17 of the Act as extended by paragraph 2 of Schedule 4C to the Act because the departure direction ceases to have effect in accordance with regulation 35(1), the superseding decision shall have effect as from the date on which the decision that the maintenance assessment is cancelled or ceases to have effect, takes or took effect.

(9) Where the superseding decision referred to in paragraph (8) above is itself superseded by a further decision made under section 17 of the Act as extended by paragraph 2 of Schedule 4C to the Act in the circumstances described in regulation 35(2), that further decision shall have effect as from the effective date of the fresh maintenance assessment.

(10) Where a decision with respect to a departure direction is superseded by a decision under section 17 of the Act as extended by paragraph 2 of Schedule 4C to the Act because the departure direction is suspended in accordance with regulation 35(4), the superseding decision shall have effect as from the effective date of the later interim maintenance assessment or, as the case may be, the interim maintenance assessment which replaces a maintenance assessment.

(11) Where the superseding decision referred to in paragraph (10) above is itself superseded by a further decision under section 17 as extended because the interim maintenance assessment referred to in regulation 35(4)(c) is followed by a maintenance assessment made in accordance with the provisions of Part I of Schedule 1 to the Act or by an interim maintenance assessment to which regulation 10 does not apply, that further decision shall have effect as from the effective date of the fresh maintenance assessment or, as the case may be, interim maintenance assessment.

[(12) Where a superseding decision is made in a case to which regulation 32D(2)(a) or (3) applies and the material circumstance is the death of a qualifying child or a qualifying child ceasing to be a qualifying child, the decision shall take effect as from the first day of the maintenance period in which the change occurred.]]

**Note.** Inserted by SI 1999/1047, reg 44 as from 1 June 1999. In para (2) words '(3) and (5)' substituted by words '(3), (5) and (12)' in square brackets by SI 2000/1596, reg 13(a) as from 19 June 2000. In para (3) words 'Where a decision' substituted by words 'Subject to paragraph (12), where a decision' in square brackets by SI 2000/1596, reg 13(b) as from 19 June 2000. Para (12) inserted by SI 2000/1596, reg 13(c) as from 19 June 2000.

[*Cancellation of departure directions*

**32F.** The Secretary of State may cancel a departure direction where—
- (a) regulation 32A(1) applies and he is satisfied that it was not appropriate to have given it; or
- (b) regulation 32D applies and he is satisfied that it is no longer appropriate for it to continue to have effect.]

**Note.** Inserted by SI 1999/1047, reg 44 as from 1 June 1999.

[*Notification of right of appeal, decision and reasons for decision*

**32G.** (1) The Secretary of State shall notify a person with a right of appeal under the Act against the decision under section 16 or 17 of the Act as those sections apply in relation to decisions with respect to departure directions by virtue of paragraphs 1 and 2 of Schedule 4C to the Act with respect to a departure direction of—
- (a) that right;
- (b) that decision; and
- (c) the reasons for that decision.
- (2) A written notice provided under paragraph (1)—
- (a) shall also contain sufficient information to enable a relevant person to exercise a right of appeal; and
- (b) shall not contain any information which it is not necessary for a person to have in order to understand how the decision was reached.]

**Note.** Inserted by SI 1999/1047, reg 44 as from 1 June 1999.

**33.**

. . .

**Note.** Inserted by SI 1999/1047, reg 44 as from 1 June 1999; revoked by SI 1999/1047, reg 45 as from 1 June 1999.

**34.**

. . .

**Note.** Inserted by SI 1999/1047, reg 44 as from 1 June 1999; revoked by SI 1999/1047, reg 45 as from 1 June 1999.

[*Correction of accidental errors in departure directions*

**34A.** (1) Subject to paragraphs (3) and (4), accidental errors in any departure direction made by the Secretary of State or record of such a departure direction may, at any time, be corrected by the Secretary of State and a correction made to, or to the record of, that departure direction shall be deemed to be part of that direction or of that record.

(2) Where the Secretary of State has made a correction under the provisions of paragraph (1), he shall immediately notify the persons who were notified of the departure direction that has been corrected, so far as that is reasonably practicable.

(3) In determining whether the time limit specified in *section 28H(3) of the Act* [regulation 31(1) (time within which an appeal is to be brought) or, as the case

may be, regulation 32(1) (late appeals) of the Social Security and Child Support (Decisions and Appeals) Regulations 1999] has been complied with, there shall be disregarded any day falling before the day on which notification was given or sent under paragraph (2).

(4) The power to correct errors under this regulation shall not be taken to limit any other powers to correct errors that are exercisable apart from these Regulations.]

**Note.** Inserted by SI 1998/58, reg 19 as from 19 January 1998. In para (3) words 'section 28H(3) of the Act' substituted by words from 'regulation 31(1)' to'(Decisions and Appeals) Regulations 1999' in square brackets by SI 1999/1047, reg 46 as from 1 June 1999.

*Termination and suspension of departure directions*

**35.** (1) Subject to paragraphs (2), (3) and (4), where a departure direction has effect in relation to the amount of child support maintenance fixed by a maintenance assessment which is cancelled or ceases to have effect, that departure direction shall cease to have effect and shall not subsequently take effect.

(2) Where *a child support officer* [the Secretary of State] ceases to have jurisdiction to make a maintenance assessment and subsequently acquires jurisdiction to make a maintenance assessment in respect of the same absent parent, person with care and any child with respect to whom the earlier assessment was made, a departure direction for a case falling within paragraph 3 or 4 of Schedule 4B to the Act shall again take effect . . ..

(3) Where a departure direction had effect in relation to the amount of child support maintenance fixed by a maintenance assessment which is, under regulation 8(2) of the Maintenance Arrangements and Jurisdiction Regulations (maintenance assessments and maintenance orders made in error), treated as not having been cancelled or not having ceased to have effect, that departure direction shall again take effect . . ., except where there has, since that maintenance assessment was cancelled or ceased to have effect, been a material change of circumstances relevant to that departure direction.

(4) Where—

(a) a departure direction is in force in respect of an interim maintenance assessment or a maintenance assessment made in accordance with the provisions of Part I of Schedule 1 to the Act;

(b) that interim maintenance assessment is replaced by another ("the later interim maintenance assessment") or, as the case may be, that maintenance assessment is replaced by an interim maintenance assessment; and

(c) by virtue of regulation 10 a departure direction would not be given if that interim maintenance assessment or that later interim maintenance assessment had been in force at the time that departure direction was given,

that departure direction shall be suspended until that interim maintenance assessment or that later interim maintenance assessment has been cancelled or has ceased to have effect and shall again take effect *from the effective date of an interim maintenance assessment to which regulation 10 does not apply, or of a maintenance assessment made in accordance with the provisions of Part I of Schedule 1 to the Act, which follows the interim maintenance assessment referred to in sub-paragraph (c)* [where the interim maintenance assessment referred to in sub-paragraph (c) is followed by a maintenance assessment made in accordance with the provisions of Part I of Schedule 1 to the Act or by an interim maintenance assessment to which regulation 10 does not apply].

(5) For the purposes of paragraph (4), a departure direction which is in force shall include a departure direction which is suspended.

**Note.** In para (2) words 'a child support officer' substituted by words 'the Secretary of State' in square brackets by SI 1999/1047, reg 47(a)(i) as from 1 June 1999 and words omitted revoked by SI 1999/1047, reg 47(a)(ii) as from 1 June 1999. In para (3) words omitted revoked by SI 1999/1047, reg 47(b) as from 1 June 1999. In para (4) words from 'from the effective date' to 'sub-paragraph (c)' substituted by words from 'where the interim maintenance assessment' to 'does not apply' in square brackets by SI 1999/1047, reg 47(c) as from 1 June 1999.

PART VIII

MAINTENANCE ASSESSMENT FOLLOWING A DEPARTURE DIRECTION

*Effect of a departure direction—general*

**36.** (1) Except where a case falls within regulation 22, 41, 42 or 43, a departure direction shall specify, as the basis on which the amount of child support maintenance is to be fixed by any fresh assessment made in consequence of the direction, that the amount of net income or exempt income of the parent with care or absent parent or the amount of protected income of the absent parent be increased or, as the case may be, decreased in accordance with those provisions of regulations 37, 38 and 40 which are applicable to the particular case.

(2) Where the provisions of paragraph (1) apply to a departure direction, the amount of child support maintenance fixed by a fresh maintenance assessment shall be determined in accordance with the provisions of Part I of Schedule 1 to the Act, but with the substitution of the amounts changed in consequence of the direction for the amounts determined in accordance with those provisions.

*Effect of a departure direction in respect of special expenses—exempt income*

**37.** (1) Subject to paragraph (2), where a departure direction is given in respect of special expenses, the exempt income of the absent parent or, as the case may be, the parent with care shall be increased by [the amount specified in that departure direction being the whole or part of] the amount constituting the special expenses or the aggregate of the special expenses determined in accordance with regulations 13 to 20.

(2) Where a departure direction is given with respect to costs incurred in travelling to work or expenses which include such costs, and a component of exempt income has been determined in accordance with regulation 9(1)(i) of the Maintenance Assessments and Special Cases Regulations or regulation 10 of those Regulations applying regulation 9(1)(i), the increase in exempt income determined in accordance with paragraph (1) shall be reduced by that component of exempt income.

(3) A departure direction with respect to special expenses for a case falling within regulation 16 shall be given only for the repayment period remaining applicable to that debt at the date on which that direction takes effect except—

(a) where in consequence of the applicant's unemployment or incapacity for work, the repayment period of that debt has been extended by agreement with the creditor, a departure direction may be given to cover the additional weeks allowed for repayment; or

(b) where the Secretary of State is satisfied that, as a consequence of the income of the applicant having been substantially reduced the repayment period of that debt has been extended by agreement with the creditor, a departure direction may be given for such repayment period as the Secretary of State considers is reasonable.

(4) Where paragraph (4) of regulation 16 applies, a departure direction may be given in respect only of *repayment of* [the whole or part of the amount required to repay] that part of the debt incurred which is referable to the debt, repayment of which would have fallen within paragraph (1) of that regulation, based upon the amount, rate of repayment and repayment period agreed in respect of that part at the time it was taken out.

**Note.** In para (1) words 'the amount specified in that departure direction being the whole or part of' in square brackets inserted by SI 1998/58, reg 20(2) as from 19 January 1998. In para (4) words 'repayment of' substituted by words 'the whole or part of the amount required to repay' in square brackets by SI 1998/58, reg 20(3) as from 19 January 1998.

*Effect of a departure direction in respect of special expenses—protected income*

**38.** (1) Subject to paragraphs (2) and (3), where a departure direction is given with respect to special expenses in response to an absent parent's application, his protected income shall be determined in accordance with paragraph (1) of regulation 11 of the Maintenance Assessments and Special Cases Regulations with the modification that the increase of exempt income as determined in accordance with regulation 37 shall be added to the aggregate of the amounts mentioned in sub-paragraphs (a) to (kk) of paragraph (1) of regulation 11 of the Maintenance Assessments and Special Cases Regulations.

(2) Protected income shall not be increased in accordance with paragraph (1) on account of special expenses constituted by costs falling within regulation 18 (costs incurred in supporting certain children).

(3) Where a departure direction is given with respect to costs which include costs incurred in travelling to work, the absent parent's protected income shall be determined in accordance with paragraph (1), but without inclusion of the amount determined in accordance with sub-paragraph (kk) of regulation 11(1) of the Maintenance Assessments and Special Cases Regulations within the aggregate of the amounts mentioned in that regulation.

*Effect of a departure direction in respect of a transfer of property*

**39.** (1) Where a departure direction is given in respect of a transfer of property for a case falling within paragraph 3 of Schedule 4B to the Act—

(a) where the exempt income of an absent parent includes a component of exempt income determined in accordance with regulation 9(1)(bb) of the Maintenance Assessments and Special Cases Regulations, the exempt income of the absent parent shall be reduced by that component of exempt income;

*(b) subject to sub-paragraph (c) and paragraphs (2) and (3), the fresh maintenance assessment made in consequence of the direction shall be the maintenance assessment calculated in accordance with the provisions of paragraphs 1 to 5 and 7 to 10 of Part I of Schedule 1 to the Act, as modified by sub-paragraph (a) where that sub-paragraph is applicable to the case in question, reduced by the equivalent weekly value of the property transferred as determined in accordance with regulation 22;*

[(b) subject to sub-paragraph (c) and paragraphs (2) and (3), the fresh maintenance assessment made in consequence of the direction shall be the lower of—

(i) the amount, calculated in accordance with the provisions of paragraphs 1 to 5 and 7 to 10 of Part I of Schedule 1 to the Act, as modified in a case to which it applies by sub-paragraph (a) where that sub-paragraph is applicable to the case in question, reduced by the amount specified in that departure direction being the whole or part of the equivalent weekly value of the property transferred as determined in accordance with regulation 22; or

(ii) where the provisions of paragraph 6 of Schedule 1 to the Act (protected income) apply, the amount, calculated in accordance with the provisions of Part I of Schedule 1 to the Act, as modified in a case to which it applies by sub-paragraph (a) where that sub-paragraph is applicable to the case in question;]

(c) where the equivalent weekly value is nil, the fresh maintenance assessment made in consequence of the direction shall be the maintenance assessment calculated in accordance with the provisions of Part I of Schedule 1 to the Act, as modified by sub-paragraph (a), where that sub-paragraph is applicable to the case in question.

(2) The amount of child support maintenance fixed by an assessment made in consequence of a direction falling within paragraph (1) shall not be less than the amount prescribed by regulation 13 of the Maintenance Assessments and Special Cases Regulations.

(3) Where there has been a transfer by the applicant of property to trustees as set out in regulation 21(2) and the equivalent weekly value is greater than nil, any monies paid to the parent with care out of that trust fund for maintenance of a child with respect to whom the current assessment was made shall be disregarded in calculating the assessable income of that parent with care in accordance with the provisions of Part I of Schedule 1 to the Act.

(4) A departure direction falling within paragraph (1) shall cease to have effect at the end of the number of years of liability, as defined in paragraph 1 of the Schedule, for the case in question.

(5) Where a departure direction has ceased to have effect under the provisions of paragraph (4), the exempt income of an absent parent shall be determined as if regulation 9(1)(bb) of the Maintenance Assessments and Special Cases Regulations were omitted.

(6) Where a departure direction is given in respect of a transfer of property for a case falling within paragraph 4 of Schedule 4B to the Act, the exempt income of the absent parent shall be reduced by the component of exempt income determined in accordance with regulation 9(1)(bb) of the Maintenance Assessments and Special Cases Regulations.

(7) This regulation is subject to regulation 42.

**Note.** Para (1)(b) substituted by SI 1998/58, reg 21 as from 19 January 1998.

*Effect of a departure direction in respect of additional cases*

**40.** (1) This regulation applies where a departure direction is given for an additional case falling within paragraph 5 of Schedule 4B to the Act.

(2) In a case falling within paragraph (1)(a) of regulation 23 (assets capable of producing income or higher income), subject to paragraph (4), the net income of the non-applicant shall be increased by [the amount specified in that departure direction, being the whole or part of] an amount calculated by applying interest at the statutory rate prescribed for a judgment debt or, in Scotland, at the statutory rate in respect of interest included in or payable under a decree in the Court of Session at the date on which the departure direction is given to—

(a) any monies falling within that paragraph;

(b) the net value of any asset, other than monies, falling within that paragraph, after deduction of the amount owing on any mortgage or charge on that asset,

less any income received in respect of that asset which has been taken into account in the calculation of the current assessment.

(3) In a case falling within paragraph (1)(b) or (c) of regulation 23, subject to paragraph (4), the net income of the non-applicant shall be increased by [the amount specified in that departure direction, being the whole or part of] an amount calculated by applying interest at the statutory rate prescribed for a judgment debt, or, in Scotland, at the statutory rate in respect of interest included in or payable under a decree in the Court of Session at the date of the application to the value of the asset subject to the trust less any income received from the trust which has been taken into account in the calculation of the current assessment.

(4) In a case to which regulation 24 (diversion of income) applies, the net income of the non-applicant who is a parent of a child in respect of whom the current assessment is made shall be increased by [the amount specified in that departure direction, being the whole or part of] the amount by which the Secretary of State is satisfied that that parent has reduced his income.

(5) In a case to which regulation 25 (life-style inconsistent with declared income) applies, the net income of the non-applicant who is a parent of a child in respect of whom the current assessment is made shall be increased by [the amount specified in that departure direction, being the whole or part of] the difference between the two levels of income referred to in paragraph (1) of that regulation.

(6) In a case to which regulation 26 applies (unreasonably high housing costs) the amount of housing costs included in exempt income and the amount referred to in regulation 11(1)(b) of the Maintenance Assessments and Special Cases Regulations shall not exceed the amounts set out in regulation 18(1)(a) or (b), as the case may be, of the Maintenance Assessments and Special Cases Regulations (excessive housing costs) and the provisions of regulation 18(2) of those Regulations shall not apply.

(7) In a case to which regulation 27 applies (partner's contribution to housing costs) that part of the exempt income constituted by the eligible housing costs determined in accordance with regulation 14 of the Maintenance Assessments and Special Cases Regulations (eligible housing costs) shall, subject to paragraphs (8) and (9), be reduced by the percentage of the housing costs which the Secretary of State considers appropriate, taking into account the income of that parent and the income or estimated income of that partner.

(8) Where paragraph (7) applies, the housing costs determined in accordance with regulation 11(1)(b) of the Maintenance Assessments and Special Cases Regulations (protected income) shall remain unchanged.

(9) Where a Category B interim maintenance assessment is in force in respect of a non-applicant, the whole of the eligible housing costs may be deducted from the exempt income of that non-applicant.

(10) In a case to which regulation 28 (unreasonably high travel costs) or regulation 29 (travel costs to be disregarded) applies, for the component of exempt income determined in accordance with regulation 9(1)(i) of the Maintenance Assessments and Special Cases Regulations or in accordance with that regulation as applied by regulation 10 of those Regulations and, in the case of an absent parent, for the amount determined in accordance with regulation 11(1)(kk) of those Regulations, there shall be substituted such amount, including a nil amount, as the Secretary of State considers to be appropriate in all the circumstances of the case.

**Note.** In paras (2)–(5) words 'the amount specified in that departure direction, being the whole or part of' in square brackets inserted by SI 1998/58, reg 22 as from 19 January 1998.

*Child support maintenance payable where effect of a departure direction would be to decrease an absent parent's assessable income but case still fell within paragraph 2(3) of Schedule 1 to the Act*

**41.** (1) Subject to regulation 42 and paragraph (8), where the effect of a departure direction would, but for the following provisions of this regulation, be to reduce an absent parent's assessable income and his assessable income following that direction would be such that the case fell within paragraph 2(3) of Schedule 1 to the Act (additional element of maintenance payable), the amount of child support maintenance payable shall be determined in accordance with paragraphs (2) to (5).

(2) There shall be calculated the amount equal to A x P, where A is equal to the amount that would be the absent parent's assessable income if the departure

direction referred to in paragraph (1) had been given and P has the value prescribed in regulation 5 of the Maintenance Assessments and Special Cases Regulations.

*(3) There shall be determined the amount that would be payable under a maintenance assessment calculated by reference to the circumstances at the time the application is made, in accordance with the provisions of Part I of Schedule 1 to the Act.*

[(3) There shall be determined the amount that would be payable under a maintenance assessment made in accordance with the provisions of Part I of Schedule 1 to the Act which would be in force at the date any departure direction referred to in paragraph (1) would take effect if it were to be given.]

*(4) The lower of the amounts calculated in accordance with paragraph (2) and determined in accordance with paragraph (3) shall constitute the revised amount for the purposes of regulation 7 (rejection of application on completion of a preliminary consideration) and regulation 31 (refusal to give a departure direction under section 28F(4) of the Act), and the Secretary of State may apply regulation 7 and shall apply regulation 31 in relation to the current amount and the revised amount as so construed.*

[(4) The revised amount for the purposes of regulation 7 (rejection of application on completion of a preliminary consideration) and regulation 31 (refusal to give a departure direction under section 28F(4) of the Act) shall be the lowest of the following amounts—

(a) the amount calculated in accordance with paragraph (2);

(b) the amount determined in accordance with paragraph (3);

(c) where the provisions of paragraph 6 of Schedule 1 to the Act (protected income) as modified in a case to which they apply by the provisions of regulation 38 (effect of a departure direction in respect of special expenses—protected income) would apply if a departure direction were given, the amount payable under those provisions,

and the Secretary of State may apply regulation 7 and shall apply regulation 31 in relation to the current amount and the revised amount as so construed.]

(5) ... Where the application of the provisions of paragraph (4) results in a departure direction being given, the amount of child support maintenance payable following that direction shall be determined by *the child support officer* [the Secretary of State] as being the revised amount as defined in paragraph (4).

(6) Where the assessable income of an absent parent changes following *a review under section 16* [*by a child support officer of a maintenance assessment the effective date of which is on or before 8th December 1996 or a revision by the Secretary of State under that section after 6th December 1998, or a review under section*], 17, 18 or 19 of the Act [a decision under section 16 of the Act revising a decision as to a maintenance assessment or a decision under section 17 of the Act superseding a decision as to a maintenance assessment], the provisions of paragraphs (2) to (5) shall be applied to—

(a) the amount calculated under paragraph (2) which takes account of the change in assessable income; and

(b) the amount that would be payable under the maintenance assessment calculated in accordance with the provisions of Part I of Schedule 1 to the Act which takes account of that change in assessable income.

(7) ...

(8) Where a departure direction given in accordance with the provisions of *paragraphs (1) to (7)* [paragraphs (1) to (6)] has effect, those provisions shall apply, subject to the modifications set out in paragraph (9), where—

(a) the effect of a later direction would, but for the provisions of paragraphs (2) to (5), be to change the absent parent's assessable income and his assessable income following the direction would be such that the case fell within paragraph 2(3) of Schedule 1 to the Act (additional element of maintenance payable); and

(b) that assessable income following the later direction would be less than the assessable income would be if it were calculated in accordance with the provisions of Part I of Schedule 1 to the Act by reference to the circumstances at the time the application for the later direction is made.

(9) The modifications referred to in paragraph (8) are—

(a) in paragraph (2), A would be the absent parent's assessable income following the later direction but for the provisions of paragraphs (3) to (5);

(b) the references to regulation 7 in paragraph (4) are omitted.

**Note.** Paras (3), (4) substituted and in para (5) words omitted revoked by SI 1998/58, reg 23(2), (3) (4) as from 19 January 1998. In para (5) words 'the child support officer' substituted by words 'the Secretary of State' in square brackets by SI 1999/1047, reg 48(a) as from 1 June 1999. In para (6) words from 'a review under' to 'of the act' substituted by words from 'a decision under' to 'maintenance assessment' in square brackets by SI 1999/1047, reg 48(b) as from 1 June 1999. Para (7) revoked by SI 1998/58, reg 23(5) as from 19 January 1998. In para (8) words 'paragraphs (1) to (7)' substituted by words 'paragraphs (1) to (6)' in square brackets by SI 1998/58, reg 23(6) as from 19 January 1998.

*Application of regulation 41 where there is a transfer of property falling within paragraph 3 of Schedule 4B to the Act*

**42.** *(1) Where the application of regulation 41 to a case would result in a change in the amount of child support maintenance payable and a direction is given in respect of a transfer of property falling within paragraph 3 of Schedule 4B to the Act, regulation 41 shall be applied subject to the modifications set out in paragraphs (2) and (3).*

[(1) Where an absent parent applies for a departure direction on the grounds that the case falls within both paragraph 2 of Schedule 4B to the Act (special expenses) and paragraph 3 of that Schedule (property or capital transfers), regulation 41 shall be applied subject to the modifications set out in paragraphs (1A) to (3).

(1A) In paragraph (1) of regulation 41, the reference to a departure direction shall be construed as a reference to any departure direction that would be given if the application had been made solely on the grounds that the case falls within paragraph 2 of Schedule 4B to the Act, and the reference to the absent parent's assessable income shall be construed as a reference to the assessable income calculated in consequence of such a direction.]

(2) Where the exempt income of an absent parent includes a component of exempt income determined in accordance with regulation 9(1)(bb) of the Maintenance Assessments and Special Cases Regulations, that amount shall be excluded—

(a) in calculating the amount A defined in paragraph (2) of regulation 41;

(b) in calculating the maintenance assessment specified in paragraph (3) of regulation 41.

*(3) For the purposes of this regulation, the revised amount for the purposes of regulations 7 and 31 shall be the amount as defined in paragraph (4) of regulation 41, subject to paragraph (2) of this regulation, less the amount determined in accordance with regulation 22 (the value of a transfer of property and its equivalent weekly value for a case falling within paragraph 3 of Schedule 4B to the Act).*

[(3) For the purposes of this regulation, the revised amount for the purposes of regulations 7 and 31 shall be—

(a) subject to sub-paragraph (b), the lower of the amounts specified in sub-paragraphs (a) and (b) of paragraph (4) of regulation 41, subject to paragraph (2) of this regulation, less the amount determined in accordance with regulation 22 (value of a transfer of property and its equivalent weekly value for a case falling within paragraph 3 of Schedule 4B to the Act);

(b) where the amount specified in sub-paragraph (c) of paragraph (4) of regulation 41 is lower than the amount determined in accordance with sub-paragraph (a), that amount.]

(4) Where the application of the provisions of paragraph (3) results in a departure direction being given, the amount of child support maintenance payable following that direction shall be [determined by *the child support officer* [the Secretary of State] as being] the revised amount as defined in paragraph (3).

**Note.** Para (1) substituted by paras (1), (1A) by SI 1998/58, reg 24(2) as from 19 January 1998. Para (3) substituted by SI 1998/58, reg 24(3) as from 19 January 1998. In para (4) words from 'determined by' to 'as being' in square brackets inserted by SI 1998/58, reg 24(4) as from 19 January 1998. In para (4) words 'the child support officer' substituted by words 'the Secretary of State' in square brackets by SI 1999/1047, reg 49 as from 1 June 1999.

[*Application of regulation 41 where the case falls within paragraph 2 and paragraph 5 of Schedule 4B to the Act*

**42A.** (1) Where an absent parent applies for a departure direction on the grounds that the case falls within both paragraph 5 of Schedule 4B to the Act (additional cases) and paragraph 2 of that Schedule (special expenses), and the conditions set out in paragraph (1) of regulation 41 are satisfied, the amount of child support maintenance payable shall be determined in accordance with paragraphs (2) to (6).

(2) The application shall in the first instance be treated as an application (an 'additional cases application') made solely on the grounds that the case falls within paragraph 5 of Schedule 4B to the Act, and a determination shall be made as to whether a departure direction would be given in response to that application.

(3) Following the determination mentioned in paragraph (2), the application shall be treated as an application (a 'special expenses application') made solely on the grounds that the case falls within paragraph 2 of Schedule 4B to the Act, and the provisions of regulation 41 shall be applied to the special expenses application, subject to the provisions of paragraphs (4) to (6).

(4) Where no departure direction would be given in response to the additional cases application, the provisions of regulation 41 shall be applied to determine the amount of child support maintenance payable.

(5) Where a departure direction would be given in response to the additional cases application, the provisions of regulation 41 shall be applied to determine the amount of child support maintenance payable, subject to the modification set out in paragraph (6).

(6) For paragraph (3) of regulation 41 there shall be substituted the following paragraph—

'(3) There shall be determined the amount that would be payable under the maintenance assessment made in consequence of the direction that would be given in response to the additional cases application mentioned in paragraph (2) of regulation 42A which would be in force at the date any departure direction referred to in paragraph (1) would take effect if it were to be given.'.

(7) Where—

(a) a departure direction has been given in a case where regulation 41 has been applied and an application is then made on the grounds that the case falls within paragraph 5 of Schedule 4B to the Act; or

(b) a departure direction has been given on the grounds that the case falls within paragraph 5 of Schedule 4B to the Act, an application is then made on the grounds that the case falls within paragraph 2 of that Schedule, and the conditions set out in paragraph (1) of regulation 41 are satisfied,

the case shall be treated as a case which falls within paragraph (1), and the date of the later application treated as the date on which both applications were made.

(8) Where a departure direction is given in accordance with the provisions of paragraph (7), the earlier direction shall cease to have effect from the date the later direction has effect.]

**Note.** Inserted by SI 1998/58, reg 25 as from 19 January 1998.

*Maintenance assessment following a departure direction for certain cases falling within regulation 22 of the Maintenance Assessments and Special Cases Regulations*

**43.** (1) Where the provisions of regulation 41 or 42 are applicable to a case falling within regulation 22 of the Maintenance Assessments and Special Cases Regulations (multiple applications relating to an absent parent), those provisions shall apply for the purposes of determining the total maintenance payable in consequence of a departure direction.

(2) In a case falling within paragraph (1), the amount of child support maintenance payable in respect of each application for child support maintenance following the direction shall be the lower [lowest] of—

    (a)  the amount as determined in accordance with paragraph (3) of regulation 41, subject to the modification that regulation 22 of the Maintenance Assessments and Special Cases Regulations is applied in determining the amount that would be payable ('Y');

    (b)  the amount calculated by the formula—

$$(A \times P) \times \frac{Y}{Q}$$

where A and P have the same meanings as in regulation 41(2) and Q is the sum of the amounts calculated in accordance with sub-paragraph (a) for each assessment.

  [(c)  where the provisions of paragraph 6 of Schedule 1 to the Act (protected income) apply, as modified in a case to which they apply by the provisions of regulation 38 (effect of a departure direction in respect of special expenses—protected income) or, as the case may be, regulation 40(6), (8) or (10) (effect of a departure direction in respect of additional cases), the amount calculated as payable under those provisions].

(3) Where, in a case falling within regulation 22 of the Maintenance Assessments and Special Cases Regulations, a departure direction has been given in respect of an absent parent in a case falling within paragraph 3 of Schedule 4B to the Act (property or capital transfers), the equivalent weekly value of the transfer of property as calculated in accordance with regulation 22 of these Regulations shall be deducted from the amount of the maintenance assessment in respect of the person with care or child to or in respect of whom the property transfer was made.

**Note.** In para (2) word 'lowest' in square brackets substituted and para (c) inserted by SI 1998/58, reg 26(a), (b) as from 19 January 1998

*Maintenance assessment following a departure direction where there is a phased maintenance assessment*

**44.** Maintenance assessment following a departure direction where there is a phased maintenance assessment

(1) Where a departure direction is given in a case falling within a relevant enactment, the assessment made in consequence of that direction shall be the assessment that fixes the amount of child support maintenance that would be payable but for the provisions of that enactment ('the unadjusted departure amount').

(2) Where a departure direction takes effect on the effective date of a maintenance assessment to which the provisions of a relevant enactment become applicable, those provisions shall remain applicable to that case following the departure direction.

(3) Where a departure direction takes effect on a date later than the date on which the provisions of a relevant enactment become applicable to a maintenance assessment, the amount of child support maintenance payable in consequence of that direction shall be—

(a) where the unadjusted departure amount is more than the formula amount, the phased amount plus the difference between the unadjusted departure amount and the formula amount;

(b) where the unadjusted departure amount is more than the phased amount but less than the formula amount, the phased amount;

(c) where the unadjusted departure amount is less than the phased amount, the unadjusted departure amount.

(4) Regulation 31 shall have effect for cases falling within paragraphs (1) to (3) as if 'current amount' referred to the amount payable under the maintenance assessment that would be in force when the departure direction is given but for the provisions of the relevant enactment and 'revised amount' referred to the unadjusted departure amount.

(5) [Where the Secretary of State is satisfied that, were a decision as to a fresh maintenance assessment to be made under section 16 or, as the case may be, section 17 of the Act] in relation to a case to which the provisions of *paragraphs (1) to (3)* [paragraphs (1) and (3)] have been applied, and the amount payable under it (*'the reviewed unadjusted departure amount* [the fresh unadjusted departure amount]') would be—

(a) more than the unadjusted departure amount, the amount of child support maintenance payable shall be the amount determined in accordance with paragraph (3), plus the difference between the unadjusted departure amount and *the reviewed unadjusted departure amount* [the fresh unadjusted departure amount];

(b) less than the unadjusted departure amount but more than the phased amount, the amount of child support maintenance payable shall be the phased amount;

(c) less than the phased amount, the amount of child support maintenance payable shall be *the reviewed unadjusted departure amount* [the fresh unadjusted departure amount].

(6) In this regulation—

'the 1992 enactment' means Part II of the Schedule to the Child Support Act 1991 (Commencement No 3 and Transitional Provisions) Order 1992 (modification of maintenance assessment in certain cases);

'the 1994 enactment' means Part III of the Child Support (Miscellaneous Amendments and Transitional Provisions) Regulations 1994 (transitional provisions);

'formula amount' has the same meaning as in the relevant enactment;

'phased amount' means—

(a) where the 1992 enactment is applicable to the particular case, the modified amount as defined in paragraph 6 of that enactment;

(b) where the 1994 enactment is applicable to the particular case, the transitional amount as defined in regulation 6(1) of that enactment;

'relevant enactment' means—

(a) the 1992 enactment where that enactment is applicable to the particular case;

(b) the 1994 enactment where that enactment is applicable to the particular case.

**Note.** In para (5) words from 'Where a child support officer' to 'or 19 of the Act' substituted by words from 'Where the Secretary of State' to 'of the Act' in square brackets by SI 1999/1047, reg 50(a) as from 1 June 1999. In para (5) words 'paragraphs (1) to (3)' substituted by words 'paragraphs (1) and (3)' in square brackets by SI 1998/58, reg 27 as from 19 January 1998. In para (5) words 'the reviewed unadjusted departure amount' in each place substituted by words 'the fresh unadjusted departure amount' in square brackets by SI 1999/1047, reg 50(b) as from 1 June 1999.

PART X

MISCELLANEOUS

*Regular payments condition*

**45.** (1) For the purposes of section 28C(2)(b) of the Act (regular payments condition—reduced payments), reduced payments shall, subject to paragraph (3), be such payments as would be equal to the payments of child support maintenance fixed by the fresh maintenance assessment that would be made if the circumstances of the case were those set out in paragraph (2).

(2) The circumstances referred to in paragraph (1) are—

(a) the Secretary of State is satisfied that the case is one which falls within paragraph 2 of Schedule 4B to the Act (special expenses);

(b) the Secretary of State is satisfied that the expenses claimed by the absent parent are both being incurred and, for a case falling within regulation 13 (costs incurred in travelling to work), 14 (contact costs) or 15 (illness or disability), are neither unreasonably high nor being unreasonably incurred, and that it is just and equitable to give a departure direction in respect of the whole of those expenses; and

(c) a departure direction is given in response to the application.

(3) Where the Secretary of State considers it likely that the expenses incurred by the absent parent are lower than those claimed by him or are not reasonably incurred, he may fix such amount as he considers to be reasonable in all the circumstances of the case.

(4) Where the absent parent, following written notice under section 28C(8) of the Act, fails within 28 days of that notice to comply with the regular payments condition that was imposed on him, the application shall lapse.

*Special case—departure direction having effect from date earlier than effective date of current assessment*

**46.** (1) A case shall be treated as a special case for the purposes of the Act if the conditions specified in paragraph (2) are satisfied.

(2) The conditions are—

(a) liability to pay child support maintenance commenced earlier than the effective date of the maintenance assessment in force ('the current assessment');

(b) an application is made or treated as made in relation to the current assessment which results in a departure direction being given in respect of that assessment [or, where regulation 11A (meaning of 'current assessment' for the purposes of the Act) applies, in respect of the fresh maintenance assessment referred to in that regulation];

(c) the applicant was unable to make an application on a date falling within a period in respect of which an earlier assessment had effect because he had not been notified of that earlier assessment during that period; and

(d) if the applicant had been able to make such an application and had done so, the Secretary of State is satisfied that a departure direction would have been given in response to that application.

(3) Where a case falls within paragraph (2), references to 'the current assessment' and 'the current amount' in these Regulations shall be construed as including references to an earlier assessment falling within paragraph (2)(c) and to the amount of child support maintenance fixed by it, and these Regulations shall be applied to such an earlier assessment accordingly.

**Note.** In para (2)(b) words from 'or,' to 'regulation' in square brackets inserted by SI 1998/58, reg 28 as from 19 January 1998.

[*Cases to which regulation 11A applies*

**46A.** (1) A case where the conditions set out in paragraphs (a) to (c) [and (b)] of regulation 11A (meaning of 'current assessment' for the purposes of the Act) are satisfied shall be treated as a special case for the purposes of the Act.

(2) Where a case falls within paragraph (1), references to 'the current assessment' and 'the current amount' in these Regulations shall, subject to paragraph (3), be construed as including reference to the fresh maintenance assessment referred to in regulation 11A.

(3) Paragraph (2) shall not apply to references to 'the current assessment' in regulation 32, with the exception of the reference in paragraph (1)(a) of that regulation, and in regulations 46, 49 and 50.]

**Note.** Inserted by SI 1998/58, reg 29 as from 19 January 1998. In para (1) words 'to (c)' substituted by words 'and (b)' in square brackets by SI 1999/1047, reg 51 as from 1 June 1999.

PART XI

TRANSITIONAL PROVISIONS

*Transitional provisions—application before 2nd December 1996*

**47.** (1) This paragraph applies in any case where an application for a departure direction has been made before 2nd December 1996.

(2) Where paragraph (1) applies, the Secretary of State shall request the applicant to inform him in writing before 2nd December 1997—

(a) whether he wishes the application to be treated as an application under these Regulations in respect of the maintenance assessment in force on 2nd December 1996; and

(b) whether there have been any changes in the circumstances which are relevant for the determination or, as the case may be, redetermination of the application which have occurred since his application and, if so, what those changes are.

(3) Where the applicant fully complies with the request set out in paragraph (2), and states that he wishes the application to be treated as described in paragraph (2)(a), the Secretary of State shall treat the application as an application under these Regulations which contains the statement mentioned in section 28A(2)(a) of the Act, and paragraphs (4) to (10) and regulation 48 shall apply.

(4) Where the applicant informs the Secretary of State that there have not been any changes of the kind mentioned in paragraph (2)(b), the Secretary of State shall nevertheless invite representations in writing from the relevant persons other than the applicant.

(5) Where the applicant informs the Secretary of State that there have been changes in the circumstances of the kind mentioned in paragraph (2)(b), the Secretary of State shall—

(a) give notice that he has been informed of such changes to the relevant persons other than the applicant;

(b) send to them the information as to such changes which the applicant has given except where the Secretary of State considers that information to be information of the kind falling within paragraph (2) of regulation 8;

(c) invite representations in writing from the relevant persons other than the applicant as to such changes; and

(d) set out the provisions of paragraph (6) in relation to such representations.

(6) The following provisions shall apply to information provided under paragraph (2)(b) or representations made following an invitation made in accordance with paragraph (4) or (5)(c)—

(a) paragraphs (2) *to (11)* [to 10] of regulation 8, subject to the modification set out in paragraph (7);

(b) in relation to an applicant, regulations 6 and 7.

(7) The modification of regulation 8 mentioned in paragraph (6)(a) is that for the references to paragraph (1) or, as the case may be, paragraph (1)(c) of that regulation, there were substituted references to paragraph (5) or, as the case may be, paragraph (5)(c) of this regulation.

(8) Where the Secretary of State has not determined the application in accordance with the Departure Direction Anticipatory Application Regulations, a determination shall be made in accordance with these Regulations.

(9) Where the Secretary of State has determined the application in accordance with the Departure Direction Anticipatory Application Regulations, he shall determine whether there have been any changes in—

(a) the circumstances referred to in paragraph (2)(b);

(b) the relevant provisions of these Regulations compared with the corresponding provisions of the Departure Direction Anticipatory Application Regulations.

(10) Where the Secretary of State determines that there have been no changes of the kind referred to in paragraph (9)(a) or (b), and the relevant persons other than the applicant have not made any representations in accordance with paragraph (4), his determination of the application in accordance with the Departure Direction Anticipatory Application Regulations shall take effect.

(11) Where the Secretary of State determines that there have been changes of the kind referred to in paragraph (9)(a) or (b), or where the relevant persons other than the applicant have made representations, he shall make a determination of the application, taking those changes and representations into account, in accordance with these Regulations.

**Note.** In para (6)(a) words 'to (11)' substituted by words 'to (10)' in square brackets by SI 1999/1047, reg 52 as from 1 June 1999.

*Effective date of departure direction for a case falling within regulation 47*

**48.** (1) Where the determination made by the Secretary of State by application of the provisions of paragraphs (1) to (10) of regulation 47 is to give a departure direction, that direction shall take effect on the first day of the first maintenance period commencing on or after 2nd December 1996.

(2) Where a case falls within paragraph (1) of regulation 47, and the applicant complies with the request for information mentioned in paragraph (2) of that regulation but not by the date mentioned in that paragraph, his response shall be treated as an application for a departure direction.

*Transitional provisions—no application before 2nd December 1996*

**49.** (1) Where—

(a) a maintenance assessment was in force on 2nd December 1996;

(b) no application has been made before that date by any of the persons with respect to whom that assessment was made; and

(c) an application is made by one of those persons on the grounds set out in section 28A(2)(a) of the Act (the effect of the current assessment) on or after that date and before 2nd December 1997,

any departure direction given in response to that application shall take effect on the first day of the first maintenance period commencing on or after 2nd December 1996.

*Transitional provisions—new maintenance assessment made before 2nd December 1996 whose effective date is on or after 2nd December 1996*

**50.**   Where a new maintenance assessment is made before 2nd December 1996 but the effective date of that assessment is a date on or after 2nd December 1996—

(a) the provisions of paragraph (1) of regulation 32 shall apply as if for the reference to an application being given or sent within *28 days* [one month] of the date of notification of the current assessment there were substituted a reference to an application being given or sent before 30th December 1996;

(b) the provisions of paragraph (2) of regulation 32 shall apply as if for the reference to an application being given or sent later than *28 days* [one month] after the date of notification of the current assessment there were substituted a reference to an application being given or sent after 29th December 1996.

**Note.** Words '28 days' in both places substituted by words 'one month' in square brackets by SI 1999/1047, reg 53 as from 1 June 1999.

PART XII

REVOCATION

*Revocation of the Departure Direction Anticipatory Application Regulations*

**51.**   The Departure Direction Anticipatory Application Regulations are hereby revoked.

PART XIII

CONSEQUENTIAL AMENDMENTS

[*The consequential amendments have been incorporated into the relevant regulations as they appear in this Volume.*]

## ATTACHMENT OF DEBTS (EXPENSES) ORDER 1996

**Dated** 10 December 1996

**SI 1996 No 3098**

The Lord Chancellor, in exercise of the powers conferred on him by section 40A of the Supreme Court Act 1981 and section 109 of the County Courts Act 1984, hereby makes the following Order—

**1.**   (1) This Order may be cited as the Attachment of Debts (Expenses) Order 1996 and shall come into force on 1st January 1997.

(2)  The Attachment of Debts (Expenses) Order 1983 is hereby revoked.

**2.**   The sum which any deposit-taking institution may deduct, in accordance with section 40A(1) of the Supreme Court Act 1981 or section 109(1) of the County Courts Act 1984, shall be £55.

## CHILD ABDUCTION AND CUSTODY (FALKLAND ISLANDS) ORDER 1996

**Dated** 19 December 1996

**SI 1996 No 3156**

Her Majesty, in exercise of the powers conferred on Her by section 28 of the Child Abduction and Custody Act 1985, is pleased, by and with the advice of Her Privy Council, to order, and it is hereby ordered, as follows:

**1.**   This Order may be cited as the Child Abduction and Custody (Falkland Islands) Order 1996, and shall come into force on 1 March 1997.

**2.** Sections 1 to 24A, inclusive, section 25(1) and (2), sections 26 and 27 of, and Schedules 1 to 3, inclusive, to the Child Abduction and Custody Act 1986, modified as in the Schedule hereto, shall extend to the Falkland Islands.

**3.** For the purpose of the Schedule hereto, the term 'Governor' means the officer for the time being administering the Government of the Falkland Islands.

SCHEDULE                                                              Section 28

PROVISIONS OF THE CHILD ABDUCTION AND CUSTODY ACT 1985 AS EXTENDED TO THE FALKLAND ISLANDS

PART I    INTERNATIONAL CHILD ABDUCTION

*The Hague Convention*

**1.** (1) In this Part of this Order 'the Convention' means the Convention on the Civil Aspects of International Child Abduction which was signed at The Hague on 25th October 1980.

(2) Subject to the provisions of this Part of this Order, the provisions of that Convention set out in Schedule 1 to this Order shall have the force of law in the Falkland Islands.

*Contracting States*

**2.** (1) For the purposes of the Convention as it has effect under this Part of this Order the Contracting States shall be the United Kingdom and those for the time being specified by an Order in Council under section 2(2) of the United Kingdom Child Abduction and Custody Act 1985.

(2) An Order in Council under that section shall specify the date of the coming into force of the Convention as between the United Kingdom and any State specified in the Order. On the same date the Convention shall come into force as between the Falkland Islands and that State; and, except where the Order otherwise provides, the Convention shall apply as between the Falkland Islands and that State only in relation to wrongful removals or retentions occurring on or after that date.

(3) Where the Convention applies, or applies only, to a particular territory or particular territories specified in a declaration made by a Contracting State under Article 39 or 40 of the Convention references to that State in sub-sections (1) and (2) above shall be construed as references to that territory or those territories.

*Central Authority*

**3.** The functions under the Convention of a Central Authority shall be discharged by the Governor.

*Judicial authority*

**4.** The court having jurisdiction to entertain applications under the Convention shall be the Supreme Court of the Falkland Islands.

*Interim powers*

**5.** Where an application has been made to the Supreme Court under the Convention, the court may, at any time before the application is determined, give such interim directions as it thinks fit for the purpose of securing the welfare of the child concerned or of preventing changes in the circumstances relevant to the determination of the application.

*Reports*

**6.** Where the Governor is requested to provide information relating to a child under Article 7(d) of the Convention he may—

(a) request any public officer he believes to be appropriate to make a report to him in writing with respect to any matter which appears to him to be relevant;

(b) request any court to which a written report relating to the child has been made to send him a copy of the report;

and such a request shall be duly complied with.

*Proof of documents and evidence*

**7.** (1) For the purposes of Article 14 of the Convention a decision or determination of a judicial or administrative authority outside the Falkland Islands may be proved by a duly authenticated copy of the decision or determination; and any document purporting to be such a copy shall be deemed to be a true copy unless the contrary is shown.

(2) For the purposes of sub-paragraph (1) above a copy is duly authenticated if it bears the seal, or is signed by a judge or officer, of the authority in question.

(3) For the purposes of Articles 14 and 30 of the Convention any such document as is mentioned in Article 8 of the Convention, or a certified copy of any such document, shall be sufficient evidence of anything stated in it.

*Declaration by the Supreme Court*

**8.** The Supreme Court may, on an application made for the purposes of Article 15 of the Convention by any person appearing to the court to have an interest in the matter, make a declaration that the removal of any child from, or his retention outside the Falkland Islands was wrongful within the meaning of Article 15 of the Convention.

*Suspension of court's powers in cases of wrongful removal*

**9.** The reference in Article 16 of the Convention to deciding on the merits of rights of custody shall be construed as a reference to—

(a) making, varying or revoking a custody order, or a supervision order under section 17 of the Children Ordinance 1994; or

(b) registering or enforcing a decision under Part II of this Order.

**10.** (1) An authority having power to make rules of court may make such provision for giving effect to this Part of this Order as appears to that authority to be necessary or expedient.

(2) Without prejudice to the generality of subsection (1) above, rules of court may make provision—

(a) with respect to the procedure on applications for the return of a child and with respect to the documents and information to be furnished and the notices to be given in connection with any such application;

(b) for the giving of notices by or to a court for the purposes of the provisions of Article 16 of the Convention and paragraph 9 above and generally as respects proceedings to which those provisions apply;

(c) for enabling a person who wishes to make an application under the Convention in a Contracting State other than the Falkland Islands to obtain from any court in the Falkland Islands an authenticated copy of any decision of that court relating to the child to whom the application is to relate.

*Cost of applications*

**11.** The United Kingdom having made such a reservation as is mentioned in the third paragraph of Article 26 of the Convention, the costs mentioned in that paragraph shall not be borne by the Governor or any other authority in the Falkland Islands except so far as they fall to be so borne by virtue of the grant of legal aid or legal advice and assistance provided by funds appropriated from the Consolidated Fund of the Falkland Islands.

PART II RECOGNITION AND ENFORCEMENT OF CUSTODY DECISIONS

**12.** (1) In this Part of this Order 'the Convention' means the European Convention on Recognition and Enforcement of Decisions concerning Custody of Children and on the Restoration of Custody of Children which was signed in Luxembourg on 20th May 1980.

(2) Subject to the provisions of this Part of this Order, the provisions of that Convention set out in Schedule 2 to this order (which include Articles 9 and 10 as they have effect in consequence of a reservation made by the United Kingdom under Article 17) shall have the force of law in the Falkland Islands.

*Contracting States*

**13.** (1) For the purposes of the Convention as it has effect under this Part of this Order the Contracting States shall be the United Kingdom and those for the time being specified by an Order in Council under section 13(1) of the United Kingdom Child Abduction and Custody Act 1985.

(2) An Order in Council under that section shall specify the date of the coming into force of the Convention as between the United Kingdom and any State specified in the Order. On the same date the Convention shall come into force as between the Falkland Islands and that State.

(3) Where the Convention applies, or applies only, to a particular territory or particular territories specified by a Contracting State under Article 24 or 25 of the Convention references to that State in sub-paragraphs (1) and (2) above shall be construed as references to that territory or those territories.

*Central Authority*

**14.** The functions under the Convention of a Central Authority shall be discharged by the Governor.

*Recognition of decisions*

**15.** (1) Articles 7 and 12 of the Convention shall have effect in accordance with this paragraph.

(2) A decision to which either of those Articles applies which was made in a Contracting State other than the Falkland Islands shall be recognised in the Falkland Islands as if made by a court having jurisdiction to make it there but—

(a) the Supreme Court may, on the application of any person appearing to it to have an interest in the matter, declare on any of the grounds specified in Article 9 or 10 of the Convention that the decision is not to be recognised in the Falkland Islands; and

(b) the decision shall not be enforceable in the Falkland Islands unless registered in the appropriate court under paragraph 16 below.

(3) The references in Article 9(1)(c) of the Convention to the removal of the child are to his improper removal within the meaning of the Convention.

*Registration of decisions*

**16.** (1) A person on whom any rights are conferred by a decision relating to custody made by an authority in a Contracting State other than the Falkland Islands may make an application for the registration of the decision in an appropriate court in the Falkland Islands.

(2) The Central Authority in the Falkland Islands shall assist such a person in making such an application if a request for such assistance is made by him or on his behalf by the Central Authority of the Contracting State in question.

(3) An application under sub-paragraph (1) above or a request under sub-paragraph (2) above shall be treated as a request for enforcement for the purposes of Articles 10 and 13 of the Convention.

(4) The Supreme Court shall refuse to register a decision if—

(a) the court is of the opinion that on any of the grounds specified in Article 9 or 10 of the Convention the decision should not be recognised in any part of the Falkland Islands;

(b) the court is of the opinion that the decision is not enforceable in the Contracting State where it was made and is not a decision to which Article 12 of the Convention applies; or

(c) an application in respect of the child under Part I of this Order is pending.

(5) In this paragraph 'decision relating to custody' has the same meaning as in the Convention.

*Variation and revocation of registered decisions*

**17.** (1) Where a decision which has been registered under paragraph 16 above is varied or revoked by an authority in the Contracting State in which it was made, the person on whose behalf the application for registration of the decision was made shall notify the court in which the decision is registered of the variation or revocation.

(2) Where a court is notified under sub-paragraph (1) above of the revocation of a decision, it shall—

(a) cancel the registration, and

(b) notify such persons as may be prescribed by rules of court of the cancellation.

(3) Where a court is notified under sub-paragraph (1) above of the variation of a decision, it shall—

(a) notify such persons as may be prescribed by rules of court of the variation; and

(b) subject to any conditions which may be so prescribed, vary the registration.

(4) The court in which a decision is registered under paragraph 16 above may also, on the application of any person appearing to the court to have an interest in the matter, cancel or vary the registration if it is satisfied that the decision has been revoked or, as the case may be, varied by an authority in the Contracting State in which it was made.

*Enforcement of decisions*

**18.** Where a decision relating to custody has been registered under paragraph 16 above, the court in which it is registered shall have the same powers for the purpose of enforcing the decision as if it has been made by that court; and proceedings for or with respect to enforcement may be taken accordingly.

*Interim powers*

**19.** Where an application has been made to a court for the registration of a decision under paragraph 16 above or for the enforcement of such a decision, the court may, at any time before the application is determined, give such interim directions as it thinks fit for the purpose of securing the welfare of the child concerned or of preventing changes in the circumstances relevant to the determination of the application or, in the case of an application for registration, to the determination of any subsequent application for the enforcement of the decision.

*Suspension of court's powers*

**20.** (1) Where it appears to any court in which such proceedings as are mentioned in sub-paragraph (2) below are pending in respect of a child that—

(a) an application has been made for the registration of a decision in respect of the child under paragraph 16 above (other than a decision mentioned in sub-paragraph (3) below) or that such a decision is registered; and

(b) the decision was made in proceedings commenced before the proceedings which are pending,

the powers of the court with respect to the child in those proceedings shall be restricted as mentioned in sub-paragraph (2) below unless, in the case of an applicant for registration, the application is refused.

(2) Where sub-paragraph (1) above applies the court shall not in the case of custody proceedings make, vary, or revoke any custody order, or a supervision order under section 17 of the Children Ordinance 1994.

(3) The decision referred to in sub-paragraph (1) above is a decision which is only a decision relating to custody within the meaning of paragraph 16 of this Order by virtue of being a decision relating to rights of access.

(4) Paragraph (b) of Article 10(2) of the Convention shall be construed as referring to custody proceedings within the meaning of this Order.

*Reports*

**21.** Where the Governor is requested to make enquiries about a child under Article 15(1)(b) of the Convention he may—

(a) request a probation officer to make a report to him in writing with respect to any matter relating to the child concerned which appears to him to be relevant;

(b) request any court to which a written report relating to the child has been made to send him a copy of the report,

and any such request shall be duly complied with.

*Proof of documents and evidence*

**22.** (1) In any proceedings under this Part of this Order a decision of an authority outside the Falkland Islands may be proved by a duly authenticated copy of the decision, and any document purporting to be such a copy shall be deemed to be a true copy unless the contrary is shown.

(2) For the purposes of sub-paragraph (1) above a copy is duly authenticated if it bears the seal, or is signed by a judge or officer, of the authority in question.

(3) In any proceedings under this Part of this Order any such document as is mentioned in Article 13 of the Convention, or a certified copy of any such document, shall be sufficient evidence of anything stated in it.

*Decisions of Falkland Islands courts*

**23.** (1) Where a person on whom any rights are conferred by a decision relating to custody made by a court in the Falkland Islands makes an application to the Governor under Article 4 of the Convention with a view to securing its recognition or enforcement in another Contracting State, the Governor may require the court which made the decision to furnish him with all or any of the documents referred to in Article 13(1)(b), (c) and (d) of the Convention.

(2) Where in any custody proceedings a court in the Falkland Islands makes a decision relating to a child who has been removed from the Falklands Islands, the court may also, on an application made by any person for the purposes of Article 12 of the Convention, declare the removal to have been unlawful if it is satisfied that the applicant has an interest in the matter and that the child has been taken from or sent or kept out of the Falkland Islands without the consent of the person (or, if more than one, all the persons) having the right to determine the child's place of residence under the law of the part of the Falkland Islands in which the child was habitually resident.

(3) In this section 'decision relating to custody' has the same meaning as in the Convention.

*Rules of court*

**24.** (1) An authority having power to make rules of court may make such provision for giving effect to this Part of this Order as appears to that authority to be necessary or expedient.

(2) Without prejudice to the generality of subsection (1) above, rules of court may make provision—

(a) with respect to the procedure on applications to a court under any provision of this Part of this Order and with respect to the documents and information to be furnished and the notices to be given in connection with any such application;

(b) for the giving of directions requiring the disclosure of information about any child who is the subject of proceedings under this Part of this Order and for safeguarding its welfare.

PART III    SUPPLEMENTARY

*Power to order disclosure of child's whereabouts*

**24A.** (1) Where—

(a) in proceedings for the return of a child under Part I of this Order, or

(b) on an application for the recognition, registration or enforcement of a decision in respect of a child under Part II of this Order,

there is not available to the court adequate information as to where the child is, the court may order any person who it has reason to believe may have relevant information to disclose it to the court.

(2) A person shall not be excused from complying with an order under subsection (1) above by reason that to do so may incriminate him or his spouse of an offence; but a statement or admission made in compliance with such an order shall not be admissible in evidence against either of them in proceedings for any offence other than perjury.

*Termination of existing custody orders etc*

**25.** (1) Where—

(a) an order is made for the return of a child under Part I of this Order, or

(b) a decision with respect to a child (other than a decision mentioned in sub-paragraph (2) below) is registered under paragraph 16 of this Order,

any custody order relating to him shall cease to have effect.

(2) The decision referred to in sub-paragraph 1(b) above is a decision which is only a decision relating to custody within the meaning of paragraph 16 of this Order by virtue of being a decision relating to rights of access.

*Expenses*

**26.** There shall be paid out of money provided by Parliament—

(a) any expenses incurred by the Governor by virtue of this Order; and

(b) any increase attributable to this Order in the sums so payable under any other Act or Order.

*Interpretation*

**27.** (1) In this Order 'custody order' means (unless the contrary intention appears) any such order as is mentioned in Schedule 3 to this Order and 'custody proceedings' means proceedings in which an order within that Schedule may be made, varied or revoked.

(2) In this Order a decision relating to rights access means a decision as to the contact which a child may, or may not, have with any person.

## SCHEDULES

### SCHEDULE 1   CONVENTION ON THE CIVIL ASPECTS OF INTERNATIONAL CHILD ABDUCTION

Paragraph 1(2)

CHAPTER I—SCOPE OF THE CONVENTION

*Article 3*

The removal or the retention of a child is to be considered wrongful where—
- (a) it is in breach of rights of custody attributed to a person, an institution or any other body, either jointly or alone, under the law of the State in which the child was habitually resident immediately before the removal or retention; and
- (b) at the time of removal or retention those rights were actually exercised, either jointly or alone, or would have been so exercised but for the removal or retention.

The rights of custody mentioned in sub-paragraph (a) above may arise in particular by operation of law or by reason of a judicial or administrative decision, or by reason of an agreement having legal effect under the law of that State.

*Article 4*

The Convention shall apply to any child who was habitually resident in a Contracting State immediately before any breach of custody or access rights. The Convention shall cease to apply when the child attains the age of sixteen years.

*Article 5*

For the purposes of this Convention—
- (a) 'rights of custody' shall include rights relating to the care of the person of the child and, in particular, the right to determine the child's place of residence;
- (b) 'rights of access' shall include the right to take a child for a limited period of time to a place other than the child's habitual residence.

CHAPTER II—CENTRAL AUTHORITIES

*Article 7*

Central Authorities shall co-operate with each other and promote co-operation amongst the competent authorities in their respective States to secure the prompt return of children and to achieve the other objects of this Convention.

In particular, either directly or through any intermediary, they shall take all appropriate measures—
- (a) to discover the whereabouts of a child who has been wrongfully removed or retained;
- (b) to prevent further harm to the child or prejudice to interested parties by taking or causing to be taken provisional measures;
- (c) to secure the voluntary return of the child or to bring about an amicable resolution of the issues;
- (d) to exchange, where desirable, information relating to the social background of the child;
- (e) to provide information of a general character as to the law of their State in connection with the application of the Convention;

(f) to initiate or facilitate the institution of judicial or administrative proceedings with a view to obtaining the return of the child and, in a proper case, to make arrangements for organising or securing the effective exercise of rights of access;

(g) where the circumstances so require, to provide or facilitate the provision of legal aid and advice, including the participation of legal counsel and advisers;

(h) to provide such administrative arrangements as may be necessary and appropriate to secure the safe return of the child;

(i) to keep each other informed with respect to the operation of this Convention and, as far as possible, to eliminate any obstacles to its application.

CHAPTER III—RETURN OF CHILDREN

*Article 8*

Any person, institution or other body claiming that a child has been removed or retained in breach of custody rights may apply either to the Central Authority of the child's habitual residence or to the Central Authority of any other Contracting State for assistance in securing the return of the child.

The application shall contain—

(a) information concerning the identity of the applicant, of the child and of the person alleged to have removed or retained the child;

(b) where available, the date of birth of the child;

(c) the grounds on which the applicant's claim for return of the child is based;

(d) all available information relating to the whereabouts of the child and the identity of the person with whom the child is presumed to be.

The application may be accompanied or supplemented by—

(e) an authenticated copy of any relevant decision or agreement;

(f) a certificate or an affidavit emanating from a Central Authority, or other competent authority of the State of the child's habitual residence, or from a qualified person, concerning the relevant law of that State;

(g) any other relevant document.

*Article 9*

If the Central Authority which receives an application referred to in Article 8 has reason to believe that the child is in another Contracting State, it shall directly and without delay transmit the application to the Central Authority of that Contracting State and inform the requesting Central Authority, or the applicant, as the case may be.

*Article 10*

The Central Authority of the State where the child is shall take or cause to be taken all appropriate measures in order to obtain the voluntary return of the child.

*Article 11*

The judicial or administrative authorities of Contracting States shall act expeditiously in proceedings for the return of children.

If the judicial or administrative authority concerned has not reached a decision within six weeks from the date of commencement of the proceedings, the applicant or the Central Authority of the requested State, on its own initiative or if asked by the Central Authority of the requesting State, shall have the right to request a statement of the reasons for the delay. If a reply is received by the Central Authority of the requested State, that Authority shall transmit the reply to the Central Authority of the requesting State, or to the applicant, as the case may be.

*Article 12*

Where a child has been wrongfully removed or retained in terms of Article 3 and, at the date of the commencement of the proceedings before the judicial or administrative authority of the Contracting State where the child is, a period of less than one year has elapsed from the date of the wrongful removal or retention, the authority concerned shall order the return of the child forthwith.

The judicial or administrative authority, even where the proceedings have been commenced after the expiration of the period of one year referred to in the preceding paragraph, shall also order the return of the child, unless it is demonstrated that the child is now settled in its new environment.

Where the judicial or administrative authority in the requested State has reason to believe that the child has been taken to another State, it may stay the proceedings or dismiss the application for the return of the child.

*Article 13*

Notwithstanding the provisions of the preceding Article, the judicial or administrative authority of the requested State is not bound to order the return of the child if the person, institution or other body which opposes its return establishes that—

  (a)  the person, institution or other body having the care of the person of the child was not actually exercising the custody rights at the time of removal or retention, or had consented to or subsequently acquiesced in the removal or retention; or
  (b)  there is a grave risk that his or her return would expose the child to physical or psychological harm or otherwise place the child in an intolerable situation.

The judicial or administrative authority may also refuse to order the return of the child if it finds that the child objects to being returned and has attained an age and degree of maturity at which it is appropriate to take account of its views.

In considering the circumstances referred to in this Article, the judicial and administrative authorities shall take into account the information relating to the social background of the child provided by the Central Authority or other competent authority of the child's habitual residence.

*Article 14*

In ascertaining whether there has been a wrongful removal or retention within the meaning of Article 3, the judicial or administrative authorities of the requested State may take notice directly of the law of, and of judicial or administrative decisions, formally recognised or not in the State of the habitual residence of the child, without recourse to the specific procedures for the proof of that law or for the recognition of foreign decisions which would otherwise be applicable.

*Article 15*

The judicial or administrative authorities of a Contracting State may, prior to the making of an order for the return of the child, request that the applicant obtain from the authorities of the State of the habitual residence of the child a decision or other determination that the removal or retention was wrongful within the meaning of Article 3 of the Convention, where such a decision or determination may be obtained in that State. The Central Authorities of the Contracting States shall so far as practicable assist applicants to obtain such a decision or determination.

*Article 16*

After receiving notice of a wrongful removal or retention of a child in the sense of Article 3, the judicial or administrative authorities of the Contracting State to which the child has been removed or in which it has been retained shall not decide on the merits on rights of custody until it has been determined that the child is not to be returned under this Convention or unless an application under this Convention is not lodged within a reasonable time following receipt of the notice.

### Article 17

The sole fact that a decision relating to custody has been given in or is entitled to recognition in the requested State shall not be a ground for refusing to return a child under this Convention, but the judicial or administrative authorities of the requested State may take account of the reasons for that decision in applying this Convention.

### Article 18

The provisions of this Chapter do not limit the power of a judicial or administrative authority to order the return of the child at any time.

### Article 19

A decision under this Convention concerning the return of the child shall not be taken to be a determination on the merits of any custody issue.

### CHAPTER IV—RIGHTS OF ACCESS

### Article 21

An application to make arrangements for organising or securing the effective exercise of rights of access may be presented to the Central Authorities of the Contracting States in the same way as an application for the return of a child.

The Central Authorities are bound by the obligations of co-operation which are set forth in Article 7 to promote the peaceful enjoyment of access rights and the fulfilment of any conditions to which the exercise of those rights may be subject. The Central Authorities shall take steps to remove, as far as possible, all obstacles to the exercise of such rights. The Central Authorities, either directly or through intermediaries, may initiate or assist in the institution of proceedings with a view to organising or protecting these rights and securing respect for the conditions to which the exercise of these rights may be subject.

### CHAPTER V—GENERAL PROVISIONS

### Article 22

No security, bond or deposit, however described, shall be required to guarantee the payment of costs and expenses in the judicial or administrative proceedings falling within the scope of this Convention.

### Article 24

Any application, communication or other document sent to the Central Authority of the requested State shall be in the original language, and shall be accompanied by a translation into the official language or one of the official languages of the requested State or, where that is not feasible, a translation into French or English.

### Article 26

Each Central Authority shall bear its own costs in applying this Convention.

Central Authorities and other public services of Contracting States shall not impose any charges in relation to applications submitted under this Convention. In particular, they may not require any payment from the applicant towards the costs and expenses of the proceedings or, where applicable, those arising from the participation of legal counsel or advisers. However, they may require the payment of the expenses incurred or to be incurred in implementing the return of the child.

However, a Contracting State may, by making a reservation in accordance with Article 42, declare that it shall not be bound to assume any costs referred to in the preceding paragraph resulting from the participation of legal counsel or advisers or from court proceedings, except insofar as those costs may be covered by its system of legal aid and advice.

Upon ordering the return of a child or issuing an order concerning rights of access under this Convention, the judicial or administrative authorities may, where appropriate, direct the person who removed or retained the child, or who prevented the exercise of rights of access, to pay necessary expenses incurred by or on behalf of the applicant, including travel expenses, any costs incurred or payments made for locating the child, the costs of legal representation of the applicant, and those of returning the child.

*Article 27*

When it is manifest that the requirements of this Convention are not fulfilled or that the application is otherwise not well founded, a Central Authority is not bound to accept the application. In that case, the Central Authority shall forthwith inform the applicant or the Central Authority through which the application was submitted, as the case may be, of its reasons.

*Article 28*

A Central Authority may require that the application be accompanied by a written authorisation empowering it to act on behalf of the applicant, or to designate a representative so to act.

*Article 29*

This Convention shall not preclude any person, institution or body who claims that there has been a breach of custody or access rights within the meaning of Article 3 or 21 from applying directly to the judicial or administrative authorities of a Contracting State, whether or not under the provisions of this Convention.

*Article 30*

Any application submitted to the Central Authorities or directly to the judicial or administrative authorities of a Contracting State in accordance with the terms of this Convention, together with documents and any other information appended thereto or provided by a Central Authority, shall be admissible in the courts or administrative authorities of the Contracting States.

*Article 31*

In relation to a State which in matters of custody of children has two or more systems of law applicable in different territorial units—
  (a) any reference to habitual residence in that State shall be construed as referring to habitual residence in a territorial unit of that State;
  (b) any reference to the law of the State of habitual residence shall be construed as referring to the law of the territorial unit in that State where the child habitually resides.

*Article 32*

In relation to a State which in matters of custody of children has two or more systems of law applicable to different categories of persons, any reference to the law of that State shall be construed as referring to the legal system specified by the law of that State.

SCHEDULE 2   EUROPEAN CONVENTION ON RECOGNITION
AND ENFORCEMENT OF DECISIONS CONCERNING CUSTODY
OF CHILDREN                                               Paragraph 12(2)

*Article 1*

For the purposes of this Convention—
  (a)  'child' means a person of any nationality, so long as he is under 16 years of age and has not the right to decide on his own place of residence under the law of his habitual residence, the law of his nationality or the internal law of the State addressed;
  (b)  'authority' means a judicial or administrative authority;
  (c)  'decision relating to custody' means a decision of an authority in so far as it relates to the care of the person of the child, including the right to decide on the place of his residence, or to the right of access to him;
  (d)  'improper removal' means the removal of a child across an international frontier in breach of a decision relating to his custody which has been given in a Contracting State and which is enforceable in such a State; 'improper removal' also includes—
    (i)  the failure to return a child across an international frontier at the end of a period of the exercise of the right of access to this child or at the end of any other temporary stay in a territory other than that where the custody is exercised;
    (ii)  a removal which is subsequently declared unlawful within the meaning of Article 12.

*Article 4*

(1)  Any person who has obtained in a Contracting State a decision relating to the custody of a child and who wishes to have that decision recognised or enforced in another Contracting State may submit an application for this purpose to the central authority in any Contracting State.

(2)  The application shall be accompanied by the documents mentioned in Article 13.

(3)  The central authority receiving the application, if it is not the central authority in the State addressed, shall send the documents directly and without delay to that central authority.

(4)  The central authority receiving the application may refuse to intervene where it is manifestly clear that the conditions laid down by this Convention are not satisfied.

(5)  The central authority receiving the application shall keep the applicant informed without delay of the progress of his application.

*Article 5*

(1)  The central authority in the State addressed shall take or cause to be taken without delay all steps which it considers to be appropriate, if necessary by instituting proceedings before its competent authorities, in order—
  (a)  to discover the whereabouts of the child;
  (b)  to avoid, in particular by any necessary provisional measures, prejudice to the interests of the child or of the applicant;

   (c)  to secure the recognition or enforcement of the decision;

   (d)  to secure the delivery of the child to the applicant where enforcement is granted;

   (e)  to inform the requesting authority of the measures taken and their results.

(2) Where the central authority in the State addressed has reason to believe that the child is in the territory of another Contracting State it shall send the documents directly and without delay to the central authority of that State.

(3) With the exception of the cost of repatriation, each Contracting State undertakes not to claim any payment from an applicant in respect of any measures taken under paragraph (1) of this Article by the central authority of that State on the applicant's behalf, including the costs of proceedings and, where applicable, the costs incurred by the assistance of a lawyer.

(4) If recognition or enforcement is refused, and if the central authority of the State addressed considers that it should comply with a request by the applicant to bring in that State proceedings concerning the substance of the case, that authority shall use its best endeavours to secure the representation of the applicant in the proceedings under conditions no less favourable than those available to a person who is resident in and a national of that State and for this purpose it may, in particular, institute proceedings before its competent authorities.

*Article 7*

A decision relating to custody given in a Contracting State shall be recognised and, where it is enforceable in the State of origin, made enforceable in every other Contracting State.

*Article 9*

(1) [*Recognition and enforcement may be refused*] if—

   (a)  in the case of a decision given in the absence of the defendant or his legal representative, the defendant was not duly served with the document which instituted the proceedings or an equivalent document in sufficient time to enable him to arrange his defence; but such a failure to effect service cannot constitute a ground for refusing recognition or enforcement where service was not effected because the defendant had concealed his whereabouts from the person who instituted the proceedings in the State of origin;

   (b)  in the case of a decision given in the absence of the defendant or his legal representative, the competence of the authority giving the decisions was not founded—

      (i)  on the habitual residence of the defendant; or

     (ii)  on the last common habitual residence of the child's parents, at least one parent being still habitually resident there; or

    (iii)  on the habitual residence of the child;

   (c)  the decision is incompatible with a decision relating to custody which became enforceable in the State addressed before the removal of the child, unless the child has had his habitual residence in the territory of the requesting State for one year before his removal.

(3) In no circumstances may the foreign decision be reviewed as to its substance.

*Article 10*

(1) [*Recognition and enforcement may also be refused*] on any of the following grounds—

   (a)  if it is found that the effects of the decision are manifestly incompatible with the fundamental principles of the law relating to the family and children in the State addressed;

   (b) if it is found that by reason of a change in the circumstances including the passage of time but not including a mere change in the residence of the child after an improper removal, the effects of the original decision and manifestly no longer in accordance with the welfare of the child;

   (c) if at the time when the proceedings were instituted in the State of origin—

      (i) the child was a national of the State addressed or was habitually resident there and no such connection existed with the State of origin;

      (ii) the child was a national both of the State of origin and of the State addressed and was habitually resident in the State addressed;

   (d) if the decision is incompatible with a decision given in the State addressed or enforceable in that State after being given in a third State, pursuant to proceedings begun before the submission of the request for recognition or enforcement, and if the refusal is in accordance with the welfare of the child.

(2) Proceedings for recognition or enforcement may be adjourned on any of the following grounds—

   (a) if an ordinary form of review of the original decision has been commenced;

   (b) if proceedings relating to the custody of the child, commenced before the proceedings in the State of origin were instituted, are pending in the State addressed;

   (c) if another decision concerning the custody of the child is the subject of proceedings for enforcement or of any other proceedings concerning the recognition of the decision.

*Article 11*

(1) Decisions on rights of access and provisions of decisions relating to custody which deal with the rights of access shall be recognised and enforced subject to the same conditions as other decisions relating to custody.

(2) However, the competent authority of the State addressed may fix the conditions for the implementation and exercise of the right of access taking into account, in particular, undertakings given by the parties on this matter.

(3) Where no decision on the right of access has been taken or where recognition or enforcement of the decision relating to custody is refused, the cental authority of the State addressed may apply to its competent authorities for a decision on the right of access if the person claiming a right of access so requests.

*Article 12*

Where, at the time of the removal of a child across an international frontier, there is no enforceable decision given in a Contracting State relating to his custody, the provisions of this Convention shall apply to any subsequent decision, relating to the custody of that child and declaring the removal to be unlawful, given in a Contracting State at the request of any interested person.

*Article 13*

(1) A request for recognition or enforcement in another Contracting State of a decision relating to custody shall be accompanied by—

   (a) a document authorising the central authority of the State addressed to act on behalf of the applicant or to designate another representative for that purpose;

   (b) a copy of the decision which satisfies the necessary conditions of authenticity;

  (c)  in the case of a decision given in the absence of the defendant or his legal representative, a document which establishes that the defendant was duly served with the document which instituted the proceedings or an equivalent document;

  (d)  if applicable, any document which establishes that, in accordance with the law of the State of origin, the decision is enforceable;

  (e)  if possible, a statement indicating the whereabouts or likely whereabouts of the child in the State addressed;

  (f)  proposals as to how the custody of the child should be restored.

*Article 15*

(1)  Before reaching a decision under paragraph (1)(b) of Article 10, the authority concerned in the State addressed—

  (a)  shall ascertain the child's views unless this is impracticable having regard in particular to his age and understanding; and

  (b)  may request that any appropriate enquiries be carried out.

(2)  The cost of enquiries in any Contracting State shall be met by the authorities of the State where they are carried out.

Requests for enquiries and the results of enquiries may be sent to the authority concerned through the central authorities.

*Article 26*

(1)  In relation to a State which has in matters of custody two or more systems of law of territorial application—

  (a)  reference to the law of a person's habitual residence or to the law of a person's nationality shall be construed as referring to the system of law determined by the rules in force in that State or, if there are no such rules, to the system of law with which the person concerned is most closely connected;

  (b)  reference to the State of origin or to the State addressed shall be construed as referring, as the case may be, to the territorial unit where the decision was given or to the territorial unit where recognition or enforcement of the decision or restoration of custody is requested.

(2)  Paragraph (1)(a) of this Article also applies mutatis mutandis to States which have in matters of custody two or more systems of law of personal application.

SCHEDULE 3   CUSTODY ORDERS                      Paragraph 27(1)

**1.**  The following are the orders referred to in paragraph 27(1) of this Order—

  (a)  a care order under the Children Ordinance 1994 (as defined by section 2(1) of that Ordinance);

  (b)  a residence order within the meaning it has for the purposes of section 9 of the Children Ordinance 1994; and

  (c)  any order under—

      (i)  the Matrimonial Proceedings (Courts of Summary Jurisdiction) Ordinance 1967;

     (ii)  the Matrimonial Causes Ordinance 1979; or

    (iii)  the Guardianship of Minors Ordinance 1979,

    which is an existing order for the purposes of paragraphs 4 to 9 of Schedule 4 to the Children Ordinance 1994.

**2.**  An order made by the Supreme Court in the exercise of its jurisdiction relating to wardship so far as it gives the care and control of a child to any person.

# FAMILY LAW ACT 1996 (PART IV) (ALLOCATION OF PROCEEDINGS) ORDER 1997

**Dated** 28 July 1997

## SI 1997 No 1896

The Lord Chancellor, in exercise of the powers conferred on him by section 57 of the Family Law Act 1996, hereby makes the following Order:

**1.** (1) This Order may be cited as the Family Law Act 1996 (Part IV) (Allocation of Proceedings) Order 1997 and shall come into force on 1 October 1997.

(2) In this Order, unless the context otherwise requires—

'county court' means a county court of one of the classes specified in article 2;

'family proceedings' has the meaning assigned by section 63 and includes proceedings which are family business within the meaning of section 32 of the Matrimonial and Family Proceedings Act 1984;

'family proceedings court' has the meaning assigned by article 3;

'the Act' means the Family Law Act 1996 and a section, Part or Schedule referred to by number alone means the section, Part or Schedule so numbered in that Act.

*Classes of county court*

**2.** The classes of county court specified for the purposes of this Order are—

(a) divorce county courts, being those courts designated for the time being as divorce county courts by an order under section 33 of the Matrimonial and Family Proceedings Act 1984;

(b) family hearing centres, being those courts set out in Schedule 1 to the Children (Allocation of Proceedings) Order 1991; and

(c) care centres, being those courts set out in column (ii) of Schedule 2 to that Order.

*Classes of magistrates' court*

**3.** The classes of magistrates' court specified for the purposes of this Order are family proceedings courts, being those courts constituted in accordance with section 67 of the Magistrates' Courts Act 1980.

COMMENCEMENT OF PROCEEDINGS

*Commencement of proceedings*

**4.** (1) Subject to section 59, paragraph 1 of Schedule 7 and the provisions of this article, proceedings under Part IV may be commenced in a county court or in a family proceedings court.

(2) An application—

(a) under Part IV brought by an applicant who is under the age of eighteen; and

(b) for the grant of leave under section 43 (Leave of court required for applications by children under sixteen),

shall be commenced in the High Court.

(3) Where family proceedings are pending in a county court or a family proceedings court, an application under Part IV may be made in those proceedings.

*Application to extend, vary or discharge order*

**5.**   (1)  Proceedings under Part IV
(a)  to extend, vary or discharge an order, or
(b)  the determination of which may have the effect of varying or discharging an order,
shall be made to the court which made the order.

(2)  A court may transfer proceedings made in accordance with paragraph (1) to any other court in accordance with the provisions of articles 6 to 14.

TRANSFER OF PROCEEDINGS

*Disapplication of enactments about transfer*

**6.**   Sections 38 and 39 of the Matrimonial and Family Proceedings Act 1984 shall not apply to proceedings under Part IV.

*Transfer from one family proceedings court to another*

**7.**   A family proceedings court ('the transferring court') shall (on application or of its own motion) transfer proceedings under Part IV to another family proceedings court ('the receiving court') where—
(a)  the transferring court considers that it would be appropriate for those proceedings to be heard together with other family proceedings which are pending in the receiving court; and
(b)  the receiving court, by its justices' clerk (as defined by rule 1(2) of the Family Proceedings Courts (Children Act 1989) Rules 1991), consents to the transfer.

*Transfer from family proceedings court to county court*

**8.**   (1)  A family proceedings court may, on application or of its own motion, transfer proceedings under Part IV to a county court where it considers that—
(a)  it would be appropriate for those proceedings to be heard together with other family proceedings which are pending in that court; or
(b)  the proceedings involve
(i)  a conflict with the law of another jurisdiction;
(ii)  some novel and difficult point of law;
(iii)  some question of general public interest; or
(c)  the proceedings are exceptionally complex.

(2)  A family proceedings court must transfer proceedings under Part IV to a county court where—
(a)  a child under the age of eighteen is the respondent to the application or wishes to become a party to the proceedings; or
(b)  a party to the proceedings is a person who, by reason of mental disorder within the meaning of the Mental Health Act 1983, is incapable of managing and administering his property and affairs.

(3)  Except where transfer is ordered under paragraph (1)(a), the proceedings shall be transferred to the nearest county court.

*Transfer from family proceedings court to High Court*

**9.**   A family proceedings court may, on application or of its own motion, transfer proceedings under Part IV to the High Court where it considers that it would be appropriate for those proceedings to be heard together with other family proceedings which are pending in that Court.

*Transfer from one county court to another*

**10.**   A county court may, on application or of its own motion, transfer proceedings under Part IV to another county court where—
(a)   it considers that it would be appropriate for those proceedings to be heard together with other family proceedings which are pending in that court;
(b)   the proceedings involve the determination of a question of a kind mentioned in section 59(1) and the property in question is situated in the district of another county court; or
(c)   it seems necessary or expedient so to do.

*Transfer from county court to family proceedings court*

**11.**   A county court may, on application or of its own motion, transfer proceedings under Part IV to a family proceedings court where—
(a)   it considers that it would be appropriate for those proceedings to be heard together with other family proceedings which are pending in that court; or
(b)   it considers that the criterion
    (i)   in article 8(1)(a) no longer applies because the proceedings with which the transferred proceedings were to be heard have been determined;
    (ii)   in article 8(1)(b) or (c) does not apply.

*Transfer from county court to High Court*

**12.**   A county court may, on application or of its own motion, transfer proceedings under Part IV to the High Court where it considers that the proceedings are appropriate for determination in the High Court.

*Transfer from High Court to family proceedings court*

**13.**   The High Court may, on application or of its own motion, transfer proceedings under Part IV to a family proceedings court where it considers that it would be appropriate for those proceedings to be heard together with other family proceedings which are pending in that court.

*Transfer from High Court to county court*

**14.**   The High Court may, on application or of its own motion, transfer proceedings under Part IV to a county court where it considers that—
(a)   it would be appropriate for those proceedings to be heard together with other family proceedings which are pending in that court;
(b)   the proceedings are appropriate for determination in a county court; or
(c)   it is appropriate for an application made by a child under the age of eighteen to be heard in a county court.

*Disposal following arrest*

**15.**   Where a person is brought before—
(a)   a relevant judicial authority in accordance with section 47(7)(a), or
(b)   a court by virtue of a warrant issued under section 47(9),
and the matter is not disposed of forthwith, the matter may be transferred to be disposed of by the relevant judicial authority or court which issued the warrant or, as the case may be, which attached the power of arrest under section 47(2) or (3) if different.

MISCELLANEOUS

*Principal Registry of the Family Division*

**16.** (1) The principal registry of the Family Division of the High Court shall be treated, for the purposes of this Order, as if it were a divorce county court, a family hearing centre and a care centre.

(2) Without prejudice to article 10, the principal registry may transfer an order made in proceedings which are pending in the principal registry to the High Court for enforcement.

*Lambeth, Shoreditch and Woolwich County Courts*

**17.** Proceedings under Part IV may be commenced in, transferred to and tried in Lambeth, Shoreditch or Woolwich County Court.

*Contravention of provisions of this Order*

**18.** Where proceedings are commenced or transferred in contravention of a provision of this Order, the contravention shall not have the effect of making the proceedings invalid.

## FAMILY LAW ACT 1996 (MODIFICATIONS OF ENACTMENTS) ORDER 1997

**Dated** 28 July 1997

**SI 1997 No 1898**

The Lord Chancellor, in exercise of the powers conferred on him by paragraph 3 of Schedule 9 to the Family Law Act 1996, hereby makes the following Order:

**1.** This Order may be cited as the Family Law Act 1996 (Modifications of Enactments) Order 1997 and shall come into force on 1 October 1997.

**2.** In section 65(2)(a) of the Magistrates' Courts Act 1980 (Meaning of family proceedings) for '(m) and (n)', there shall be substituted '(m), (n) and (p)'.

**3.** < . . >

**Note.** Revoked by the Access to Justice Act 1999, s 106, Sch 15, Pt V, Table (8) as from 19 February 2001.

**CIVIL JURISDICTION AND JUDGMENTS ACT 1982 (INTERIM RELIEF) ORDER 1997**

**Dated**
12 February 1997

**SI 1997 No 302**

**1** This Order may be cited as the Civil Jurisdiction and Judgments Act 1982 (Interim Relief) Order 1997 and shall come into force on 1st April 1997.
**2** The High Court in England and Wales or Northern Ireland shall have power to grant interim relief under section 25(1) of the Civil Jurisdiction and Judgments Act 1982 in relation to proceedings of the following descriptions, namely—
  (a)  proceedings commenced or to be commenced otherwise than in a Brussels or Lugano Contracting State [or Regulation State];
  [(b) proceedings whose subject-matter is not within the scope of the Regulation as determined by Article 1 of the Regulation].
**Note.** In para (a) words "or Regulation State" inserted by SI 2001 No 3929, art 5, Sch 3, para 26(a) as from 1 March 2002.

**CHILD ABDUCTION AND CUSTODY (CAYMAN ISLANDS) ORDER 1997**

**Dated**
30 October 1997

**SI 1997 No 2574**

**1** This Order may be cited as the Child Abduction and Custody (Cayman Islands) Order 1997, and shall come into force on 2nd December 1997.
**2** Sections 1 to 24A, inclusive, section 25(1) and (2) and section 27 of and Schedules 1 to 3, inclusive, to the Child Abduction and Custody Act 1985, modified as in the Schedule hereto, shall extend to the Cayman Islands.
**3** For the purpose of the Schedule hereto, the term 'Attorney-General' means the officer so appointed for the time being by the Governor and the term 'Governor' means the officer for the time being administering the Government of the Cayman Islands.

SCHEDULE                                                                    Section 2

PROVISIONS OF THE CHILD ABDUCTION AND CUSTODY ACT 1985 AS EXTENDED TO THE CAYMAN ISLANDS

PART I

INTERNATIONAL CHILD ABDUCTION

*The Hague Convention*

**1** (1) In this Part of this Schedule 'the Convention' means the Convention on the Civil Aspects of International Child Abduction which was signed at The Hague on 25th October 1980.
  (2) Subject to the provisions of this Part of this Schedule, the provisions of that Convention set out in Appendix A to this Schedule shall have the force of law in the Cayman Islands.

*Contracting States*

**2** (1)   For the purposes of the Convention as it has effect under this Part of this Schedule the Contracting States shall be the United Kingdom and those for the time being specified by an Order in Council under section 2(2) of the United Kingdom Child Abduction and Custody Act 1985.

(2) An Order in Council under that section shall specify the date of the coming into force of the Convention as between the United Kingdom and any State specified in the Order. On the same date the Convention shall come into force as between the Cayman Islands and that State; and except where the Order otherwise provides, the Convention shall apply as between the Cayman Islands and that State only in relation to wrongful removals or retentions occurring on or after that date.

(3) Where the Convention applies, or applies only, to a particular territory or particular territories specified in a declaration made by a Contracting State under Article 39 or 40 of the Convention references to that State in sub-paragraphs (1) and (2) above shall be construed as references to that territory or those territories.

*Central Authority*

**3** The functions under the Convention of a Central Authority shall be discharged in the Cayman Islands by the Attorney-General.

*Judicial Authority*

**4** The court having jurisdiction to entertain applications under the Convention shall be the Grand Court.

*Interim powers*

**5** Where an application has been made to the Grand Court under the Convention, the court may, at any time before the application is determined, give such interim directions as it thinks fit for the purpose of securing the welfare of the child concerned or of preventing changes in the circumstances relevant to the determination of the application.

*Reports*

**6** Where the Attorney-General is requested to provide information relating to a child under Article 7(d) of the Convention he may—

  (a) request the minister for the time being responsible for social services either to make a report to him in writing with respect to any matter which appears to him to be relevant or to arrange for a suitably qualified person to make such a report to him; and

  (b) request any court to which a written report relating to the child has been made to send him a copy of the report;

and such a request shall be duly complied with.

*Proof of documents and evidence*

**7**—(1) For the purposes of Article 14 of the Convention a decision or determination of a judicial or administrative authority outside the Cayman Islands may be proved by a duly authenticated copy of the decision or determination; and any document purporting to be such a copy shall be deemed to be a true copy unless the contrary is shown.

(2) For the purposes of sub-paragraph (1) above a copy is duly authenticated if it bears the seal, or is signed by a judge or officer, of the authority in question.

(3) For the purposes of Articles 14 and 30 of the Convention any such

document as is mentioned in Article 8 of the Convention, or a certified copy of any such document, shall be sufficient evidence of anything stated in it.

*Declaration by the Grand Court*

**8** The Grand Court may, on an application made for the purposes of Article 15 of the Convention by any person appearing to the court to have an interest in the matter, make a declaration that the removal of any child from, or his retention outside the Cayman Islands was wrongful within the meaning of Article 3 of the Convention.

*Suspension of Court's powers in cases of wrongful removal*

**9** The reference in Article 16 of the Convention to deciding on the merits of rights of custody shall be construed as a reference to—
  (a)  making, varying or revoking a custody order under section 31 of the Children Law, 1995; and
  (b)  registering or enforcing a decision under Part II of this Schedule.

**10**—(1) An authority having power to make rules of court may make such provision for giving effect to this Part of this Schedule as appears to that authority to be necessary or expedient.
  (2) Without prejudice to the generality of sub-paragraph (1) above, rules of court may make provision—
  (a)  with respect to the procedure on applications for the return of a child and with respect to the documents and information to be furnished and the notices to be given in connection with any such application;
  (b)  for the giving of notices by or to a court for the purposes of the provisions of Article 16 of the Convention and paragraph 9 above and generally as respects proceedings to which those provisions apply;
  (c)  for enabling a person who wishes to make an application under the Convention in a Contracting State other than the Cayman Islands to obtain from any court in the Cayman Islands an authenticated copy of any decision of that court relating to the child to whom the application is to relate.

*Cost of applications*

**11** The United Kingdom having made such a reservation as is mentioned in the third paragraph of Article 26 of the Convention, the costs mentioned in that paragraph shall not be borne by the Governor or any other authority in the Cayman Islands except so far as they fall to be so borne by virtue of the grant of legal aid or legal advice and assistance under the Poor Persons (Legal Aid) Law 1975.

PART II

RECOGNITION AND ENFORCEMENT OF CUSTODY DECISIONS

**12**—(1) In this Part of this Schedule 'the Convention' means the European Convention on Recognition and Enforcement of Decisions concerning Custody of Children and on the Restoration of Custody of Children which was signed in Luxembourg on 20th May 1980.
  (2) Subject to the provisions of this Part of this Schedule, the provisions of that Convention set out in Appendix B to this Schedule (which include Articles 9 and 10 as they have effect in consequence of a reservation made by the United Kingdom under Article 17) shall have the force of law in the Cayman Islands.

*Contracting States*

**13**—(1) For the purposes of the Convention as it has effect under this Part of this Schedule the Contracting States shall be the United Kingdom and those for the time being specified by an Order in Council under section 13(1) of the United Kingdom Child Abduction and Custody Act 1985.

(2) An Order in Council under that section shall specify the date of the coming into force of the Convention as between the United Kingdom and any State specified in the Order. On the same date the Convention shall come into force as between the Cayman Islands and that State.

(3) Where the Convention applies, or applies only, to a particular territory or particular territories specified by a Contracting State under Articles 24 or 25 of the Convention references to that State in sub-paragraphs (1) and (2) above shall be construed as references to that territory or those territories.

*Central Authority*

**14** The functions under the Convention of a Central Authority shall be discharged in the Cayman Islands by the Attorney-General.

*Recognition of decisions*

**15**—(1) Articles 7 and 12 of the Convention shall have effect in accordance with this paragraph.

(2) A decision to which either of those Articles applies which was made in a Contracting State other than the Cayman Islands shall be recognised in the Cayman Islands as if made by a court having jurisdiction to make it there but—
  (a) the Grand Court may, on the application of any person appearing to it to have an interest in the matter, declare on any of the grounds specified in Article 9 or 10 of the Convention that the decision is not to be recognised in the Cayman Islands; and
  (b) the decision shall not be enforceable in the Cayman Islands unless registered in the Grand Court under paragraph 16 below.

(3) The references in Article 9(1)(c) of the Convention to the removal of the child are to his improper removal within the meaning of the Convention.

*Registration of decisions*

**16**—(1) A person on whom any rights are conferred by a decision relating to custody made by an authority in a Contracting State other than the Cayman Islands may make an application for the registration of the decision in the Grand Court.

(2) The Central Authority in the Cayman Islands shall assist such a person in making such an application if a request for such assistance is made by him or on his behalf by the Central Authority of the Contracting State in question.

(3) An application under sub-paragraph (1) above or a request under sub-paragraph (2) above shall be treated as a request for enforcement for the purposes of Articles 10 and 13 of the Convention.

(4) The court shall refuse to register a decision if—
  (a) it is of the opinion that on any of the grounds specified in Article 9 or 10 of the Convention the decision should not be recognised in the Cayman Islands;
  (b) it is of the opinion that the decision is not enforceable in the Contracting State where it was made and is not a decision to which Article 12 of the Convention applies; or
  (c) an application in respect of the child under Part I of this Schedule is pending.

(5) In this paragraph 'decision relating to custody' has the same meaning as in the Convention.

*Variation and revocation of registered decisions*

**17**—(1) Where a decision which has been registered under paragraph 16 above is varied or revoked by an authority in the Contracting State in which it was made, the person on whose behalf the application for registration of the decision was made shall notify the Grand Court of the variation or revocation.

(2) Where the court is notified under sub-paragraph (1) above of the revocation of a decision, it shall—

(a) cancel the registration, and

(b) notify such persons as may be prescribed by rules of court of the cancellation.

(3) Where the court is notified under sub-paragraph (1) above of the variation of a decision, it shall—

(a) notify such persons as may be prescribed by rules of court of the variation; and

(b) subject to any conditions which may be so prescribed, vary the registration.

(4) The court may also, on the application of any person appearing to the court to have an interest in the matter, cancel or vary the registration if it is satisfied that the decision has been revoked or, as the case may be, varied by an authority in the Contracting State in which it was made.

*Enforcement of decisions*

**18** Where a decision relating to custody has been registered under paragraph 16 above, the Grand Court shall have the same powers for the purpose of enforcing the decision as if it had been made by that court; and proceedings for or with respect to enforcement may be taken accordingly.

*Interim powers*

**19** Where an application has been made to the Grand Court for the registration of a decision under paragraph 16 above or for the enforcement of such a decision, the court may, at any time before the application is determined, give such interim directions as it thinks fit for the purpose of securing the welfare of the child concerned or of preventing changes in the circumstances relevant to the determination of the application or, in the case of an application for registration, to the determination of any subsequent application for the enforcement of the decision.

*Suspension of court's powers*

**20**—(1) Where it appears to any court in which such proceedings as are mentioned in sub-paragraph (2) below are pending in respect of a child that—

(a) an application has been made for the registration of a decision in respect of the child under paragraph 16 above other than a decision mentioned in sub-paragraph (3) below) or that such a decision is registered; and

(b) the decision was made in proceedings commenced before the proceedings which are pending,

the powers of the court with respect to the child in those proceedings shall be restricted as mentioned in sub-paragraph (2) below unless, in the case of an applicant for the registration, the application is refused.

(2) Where sub-paragraph (1) above applies the court shall not in the case of custody proceedings make, vary, or revoke any custody order, or any other order under section 31 of the Children Law, 1995.

(3) The decision referred to in sub-paragraph (1) above is a decision which is only a decision relating to custody within the meaning of paragraph 16 of this Schedule by virtue of being a decision relating to rights of access.

(4) Paragraph (b) of Article 10(2) of the Convention shall be construed as referring to custody proceedings within the meaning of this Schedule.

*Reports*

**21** Where the Attorney-General is requested to make enquiries about a child under Article 15(1)(b) of the Convention he may—

(a) request the Minister for the time being responsible for Social Services to make a report to him in writing with respect to any matter relating to the child concerned which appears to him to be relevant or to arrange for a suitably qualified person to make such a report to him;

(b) request any court to which a written report relating to the child has been made to send him a copy of the report;

and any such request shall be duly complied with.

*Proof of documents and evidence*

**22**—(1) In any proceedings under this Part of this Schedule a decision of an authority outside the Cayman Islands may be proved by a duly authenticated copy of the decision; and any document purporting to be such a copy shall be deemed to be a true copy unless the contrary is shown.

(2) For the purposes of sub-paragraph (1) above a copy is duly authenticated if it bears the seal, or is signed by a judge or officer, of the authority in question.

(3) In any proceedings under this Part of this Schedule any such document as is mentioned in Article 13 of the Convention, or a certified copy of any such document, shall be sufficient evidence of anything stated in it.

*Decisions of Cayman Islands courts*

**23**—(1) Where a person on whom any rights are conferred by a decision relating to custody made by a court in the Cayman Islands makes an application to the Attorney-General under Article 4 of the Convention with a view to securing its recognition or enforcement in another Contracting State, the Attorney-General may require the court which made the decision to furnish him with all or any of the documents referred to in Article 13(1)(b), (c) and (d) of the Convention.

(2) Where in any custody proceedings a court in the Cayman Islands makes a decision relating to a child who has been removed from the Cayman Islands, the court may also, on an application made by any person for the purposes of Article 12 of the Convention, declare the removal to have been unlawful if it is satisfied that the applicant has an interest in the matter and that the child has been taken from or sent or kept out of the Cayman Islands without the consent of the person (or, if more than one, all the persons) having the right to determine the child's place of residence under the law of the Cayman Islands.

(3) In this section 'decision relating to custody' has the same meaning as in the Convention.

*Rules of court*

**24**—(1) An authority having power to make rules of court may make such provision for giving effect to this Part of this Schedule as appears to that authority to be necessary or expedient.

(2) Without prejudice to the generality of subsection (1) above, rules of court may make provision—

(a) with respect to the procedure on applications to the Grand Court under any provision of this Part of this Schedule and with respect to the documents and information to be furnished and the notices to be given in connection with any such application;

   (b)  for the giving of directions requiring the disclosure of information about any child who is the subject of proceedings under this Part of this Schedule and for safeguarding its welfare.

PART III

SUPPLEMENTARY

*Power to order disclosure of child's whereabouts*

**24A**—(1)  Where—
   (a)  in proceedings for the return of a child under Part I of this Schedule; or
   (b)  on an application for the recognition, registration or enforcement of a decision in respect of a child under Part II of this Schedule,
there is not available to the court adequate information as to where the child is, the court may order any person who it has reason to believe may have relevant information to disclose it to the court.

   (2)  A person shall not be excused from complying with an order under subsection (1) above by reason that to do so may incriminate him or his spouse of an offence; but a statement or admission made in compliance with such an order shall not be admissible in evidence against either of them in proceedings for any offence other than perjury.

*Termination of existing custody orders etc*

**25**—(1)  Where—
   (a)  an order is made for the return of a child under Part I of this Schedule; or
   (b)  a decision with respect to a child (other than a decision mentioned in sub-paragraph (2) below) is registered under paragraph 16 of this Schedule;
any custody order relating to him shall cease to have effect.

   (2)  The decision referred to in sub-paragraph 1(b) above is a decision which is only a decision relating to custody within the meaning of paragraph 16 of this Schedule by virtue of being a decision relating to rights of access.

*Expenses*

**26**  There shall be paid out of money provided by the Legislative Assembly of the Islands—
   (a)  any expenses incurred by the Attorney-General by virtue of this Schedule; and
   (b)  any increase attributable to this Schedule in the sums so payable under any other Law.

*Interpretation*

**27**  In this Schedule 'custody order' means (unless the contrary intention appears) any such order as is mentioned in Appendix C to this Schedule and 'custody proceedings' means proceedings in which an order within that Appendix may be made, varied or revoked.

APPENDICES

Paragraph 1(2)

APPENDIX A

CONVENTION ON THE CIVIL ASPECTS OF INTERNATIONAL CHILD ABDUCTION

CHAPTER I

SCOPE OF THE CONVENTION

*Article 3*

The removal or the retention of a child is to be considered wrongful where—
  (a) it is in breach of rights of custody attributed to a person, an institution or any other body, either jointly or alone, under the law of the State in which the child was habitually resident immediately before the removal or retention; and
  (b) at the time of removal or retention those rights were actually exercised, either jointly or alone, or would have been so exercised but for the removal or retention.

The rights of custody mentioned in sub-paragraph (a) above may arise in particular by operation of law or by reason of a judicial or administrative decision, or by reason of an agreement having legal effect under the law of that State.

*Article 4*

The Convention shall apply to any child who was habitually resident in a Contracting State immediately before any breach of custody or access rights. The Convention shall cease to apply when the child attains the age of sixteen years.

*Article 5*

For the purposes of this Convention—
  (a) 'rights of custody' shall include rights relating to the care of the person of the child and, in particular, the right to determine the child's place of residence;
  (b) 'rights of access' shall include the right to take a child for a limited period of time to a place other than the child's habitual residence.

CHAPTER II

CENTRAL AUTHORITIES

*Article 7*

Central Authorities shall co-operate with each other and promote co-operation amongst the competent authorities in their respective States to secure the prompt return of children and to achieve the other objects of this Convention.

In particular, either directly or through any intermediary, they shall take all appropriate measures—
  (a) to discover the whereabouts of a child who has been wrongfully removed or retained;
  (b) to prevent further harm to the child or prejudice to interested parties by taking or causing to be taken provisional measures;
  (c) to secure the voluntary return of the child or to bring about an amicable resolution of the issues;
  (d) to exchange, where desirable, information relating to the social background of the child;

 (e) to provide information of a general character as to the law of their State in connection with the application of the Convention;

 (f) to initiate or facilitate the institution of judicial or administrative proceedings with a view to obtaining the return of the child and, in a proper case, to make arrangements for organising or securing the effective exercise of rights of access;

 (g) where the circumstances so require, to provide or facilitate the provision of legal aid and advice, including the participation of legal counsel and advisers;

 (h) to provide such administrative arrangements as may be necessary and appropriate to secure the safe return of the child;

 (i) to keep each other informed with respect to the operation of this Convention and, as far as possible, to eliminate any obstacles to its application.

CHAPTER III

RETURN OF CHILDREN

*Article 8*

Any person, institution or other body claiming that a child has been removed or retained in breach of custody rights may apply either to the Central Authority of the child's habitual residence or to the Central Authority of any other Contracting State for assistance in securing the return of the child.

The application shall contain—

 (a) information concerning the identity of the applicant, of the child and of the person alleged to have removed or retained the child;

 (b) where available, the date of birth of the child;

 (c) the grounds on which the applicant's claim for return of the child is based;

 (d) all available information relating to the whereabouts of the child and the identity of the person with whom the child is presumed to be.

The application may be accompanied or supplemented by—

 (e) an authenticated copy of any relevant decision or agreement;

 (f) a certificate, or an affidavit emanating from a Central Authority, or other competent authority of the State of the child's habitual residence, or from a qualified person, concerning the relevant law of that State;

 (g) any other relevant document.

*Article 9*

If the Central Authority which receives an application referred to in Article 8 has reason to believe that the child is in another Contracting State, it shall directly and without delay transmit the application to the Central Authority of that Contracting State and inform the requesting Central Authority, or the applicant, as the case may be.

*Article 10*

The Central Authority of the State where the child is shall take or cause to be taken all appropriate measures in order to obtain the voluntary return of the child.

*Article 11*

The judicial or administrative authorities of Contracting States shall act expeditiously in proceedings for the return of children.

 If the judicial or administrative authority concerned has not reached a decision within six weeks from the date of commencement of the proceedings, the applicant or the Central Authority of the requested State, on its own initiative or if asked by the Central Authority of the requesting State, shall have the right to request a statement of the reasons for the delay. If a reply is received by the Central Authority of the requested State, that Authority shall transmit the reply to the Central Authority of the requesting State, or to the applicant, as the case may be.

### Article 12

Where a child has been wrongfully removed or retained in terms of Article 3 and, at the date of the commencement of the proceedings before the judicial or administrative authority of the Contracting State where the child is, a period of less than one year has elapsed from the date of the wrongful removal or retention, the authority concerned shall order the return of the child forthwith.

The judicial or administrative authority, even where the proceedings have been commenced after the expiration of the period of one year referred to in the preceding paragraph, shall also order the return of the child, unless it is demonstrated that the child is now settled in its new environment.

Where the judicial or administrative authority in the requested state has reason to believe that the child has been taken to another State, it may stay the proceedings or dismiss the application for the return of the child.

### Article 13

Notwithstanding the provisions of the preceding Article, the judicial or administrative authority of the requested State is not bound to order the return of the child if the person, institution or other body which opposes its return establishes that—

(a) the person, institution or other body having the care of the person of the child was not actually exercising the custody rights at the time of removal or retention, or had consented to or subsequently acquiesced in the removal or retention; or

(b) there is a grave risk that his or her return would expose the child to physical or psychological harm or otherwise place the child in an intolerable situation.

The judicial or administrative authority may also refuse to order the return of the child if it finds that the child objects to being returned and has attained an age and degree of maturity at which it is appropriate to take account of its views.

In considering the circumstances referred to in this Article, the judicial and administrative authorities shall take into account the information relating to the social background of the child provided by the Central Authority or other competent authority of the child's habitual residence.

### Article 14

In ascertaining whether there has been a wrongful removal or retention within the meaning of Article 3, the judicial or administrative authorities of the requested State may take notice directly of the law of, and of judicial or administrative decisions, formally recognised or not in the State of the habitual residence of the child, without recourse to the specific procedures for the proof of that law or for the recognition of foreign decisions which would otherwise be applicable.

### Article 15

The judicial or administrative authorities of a Contracting State may, prior to the making of an order for the return of the child, request that the applicant obtain from the authorities of the State of the habitual residence of the child a decision or other determination that the removal or retention was wrongful within the meaning of Article 3 of the Convention, where such a decision or determination may be obtained in that State. The Central Authorities of the Contracting States shall so far as practicable assist applicants to obtain such a decision or determination.

*Article 16*

After receiving notice of a wrongful removal or retention of a child in the sense of Article 3, the judicial or administrative authorities of the Contracting State to which the child has been removed or in which it has been retained shall not decide on the merits of rights of custody until it has been determined that the child is not to be returned under this Convention or unless an application under this Convention is not lodged within a reasonable time following receipt of the notice.

*Article 17*

The sole fact that a decision relating to custody has been given in or is entitled to recognition in the requested State shall not be a ground for refusing to return a child under this Convention, but the judicial or administrative authorities of the requested State may take account of the reasons for that decision in applying this Convention.

*Article 18*

The provisions of this Chapter do not limit the power of a judicial or administrative authority to order the return of the child at any time.

*Article 19*

A decision under this Convention concerning the return of the child shall not be taken to be a determination on the merits of any custody issue.

CHAPTER IV

RIGHTS OF ACCESS

*Article 21*

An application to make arrangements for organising or securing the effective exercise of rights of access may be presented to the Central Authorities of the Contracting States in the same way as an application for the return of a child.

The Central Authorities are bound by the obligations of co-operation which are set forth in Article 7 to promote the peaceful enjoyment of access rights and the fulfilment of any conditions to which the exercise of those rights may be subject. The Central Authorities shall take steps to remove, as far as possible, all obstacles to the exercise of such rights. The Central Authorities, either directly or through intermediaries, may initiate or assist in the institution of proceedings with a view to organising or protecting these rights and securing respect for the conditions to which the exercise of these rights may be subject.

CHAPTER V

GENERAL PROVISIONS

*Article 22*

No security, bond or deposit, however described, shall be required to guarantee the payment of costs and expenses in the judicial or administrative proceedings falling within the scope of this Convention.

*Article 24*

Any application, communication or other document sent to the Central Authority of the requested State shall be in the original language, and shall be accompanied by a translation into the official language or one of the official languages of the requested State or, where that is not feasible, a translation into French or English.

*Article 26*

Each Central Authority shall bear its own costs in applying this Convention.

Central Authorities and other public services of Contracting States shall not impose any charges in relation to applications submitted under this Convention. In particular, they may not require any payment from the applicant towards the costs and expenses of the proceedings or, where applicable, those arising from the participation of legal counsel or advisers. However, they may require the payment of the expenses incurred or to be incurred in implementing the return of the child.

However, a Contracting State may, by making a reservation in accordance with Article 42, declare that it shall not be bound to assume any costs referred to in the preceding paragraph resulting from the participation of legal counsel or advisers or from court proceedings, except insofar as those costs may be covered by its system of legal aid and advice.

Upon ordering the return of a child or issuing an order concerning rights of access under this Convention, the judicial or administrative authorities may, where appropriate, direct the person who removed or retained the child, or who prevented the exercise of rights of access, to pay necessary expenses incurred by or on behalf of the applicant, including travel expenses, any costs incurred or payments made for locating the child, the costs of legal representation of the applicant, and those of returning the child.

*Article 27*

When it is manifest that the requirements of this Convention are not fulfilled or that the application is otherwise not well founded, a Central Authority is not bound to accept the application. In that case, the Central Authority shall forthwith inform the applicant or the Central Authority through which the application was submitted, as the case may be, of its reasons.

*Article 28*

A Central Authority may require that the application be accompanied by a written authorisation empowering it to act on behalf of the applicant, or to designate a representative so to act.

*Article 29*

This Convention shall not preclude any person, institution or body who claims that there has been a breach of custody or access rights within the meaning of Article 3 or 21 from applying directly to the judicial or administrative authorities of a Contracting State, whether or not under the provisions of this Convention.

*Article 30*

Any application submitted to the Central Authorities or directly to the judicial or administrative authorities of a Contracting State in accordance with the terms of this Convention, together with documents and any other information appended thereto or provided by a Central Authority, shall be admissible in the courts or administrative authorities of the Contracting States.

*Article 31*

In relation to a State which in matters of custody of children has two or more systems of law applicable in different territorial units—

(a) any reference to habitual residence in that State shall be construed as referring to habitual residence in a territorial unit of that State;

(b) any reference to the law of the State of habitual residence shall be construed as referring to the law of the territorial unit in that State where the child habitually resides.

*Article 32*

In relation to a State which in matters of custody of children has two or more systems of law applicable to different categories of persons, any reference to the law of that State shall be construed as referring to the legal system specified by the law of that State.

APPENDIX B

EUROPEAN CONVENTION ON RECOGNITION AND ENFORCEMENT OF DECISIONS CONCERNING CUSTODY OF CHILDREN

Paragraph 12(2)

*Article 1*

For the purposes of this Convention—

(a) 'child' means a person of any nationality, so long as he is under 16 years of age and has not the right to decide on his own place of residence under the law of his habitual residence, the law of his nationality or the internal law of the State addressed;

(b) 'authority' means a judicial or administrative authority;

(c) 'decision relating to custody' means a decision of an authority in so far as it relates to the care of the person of the child, including the right to decide on the place of his residence, or to the right of access to him;

(d) 'improper removal' means the removal of a child across an international frontier in breach of a decision relating to his custody which has been given in a Contracting State and which is enforceable in such a State; 'improper removal' also includes—

(i) the failure to return a child across an international frontier at the end of a period of the exercise of the right of access to this child or at the end of any other temporary stay in a territory other than that where the custody is exercised;

(ii) a removal which is subsequently declared unlawful within the meaning of Article 12.

*Article 4*

(1) Any person who has obtained in a Contracting State a decision relating to the custody of a child and who wishes to have that decision recognised or enforced in another Contracting State may submit an application for this purpose to the central authority in any Contracting State.

(2) The application shall be accompanied by the documents mentioned in Article 13.

(3) The central authority receiving the application, if it is not the central authority in the State addressed, shall send the documents directly and without delay to that central authority.

(4) The central authority receiving the application may refuse to intervene

where it is manifestly clear that the conditions laid down by this Convention are not satisfied.

(5) The central authority receiving the application shall keep the applicant informed without delay of the progress of his application.

*Article 5*

(1) The central authority in the State addressed shall take or cause to be taken without delay all steps which it considers to be appropriate, if necessary by instituting proceedings before its competent authorities, in order—

(a) to discover the whereabouts of the child;

(b) to avoid, in particular by any necessary provisional measures, prejudice to the interests of the child or of the applicant;

(c) to secure the recognition or enforcement of the decision;

(d) to secure the delivery of the child to the applicant where enforcement is granted;

(e) to inform the requesting authority of the measures taken and their results.

(2) Where the central authority in the State addressed has reason to believe that the child is in the territory of another Contracting State it shall send the documents directly and without delay to the central authority of that State.

(3) With the exception of the cost of repatriation, each Contracting State undertakes not to claim any payment from an applicant in respect of any measures taken under paragraph (1) of this Article by the central authority of that State on the applicant's behalf, including the costs of proceedings and, where applicable, the costs incurred by the assistance of a lawyer.

(4) If recognition or enforcement is refused, and if the central authority of the State addressed considers that it should comply with a request by the applicant to bring in that State proceedings concerning the substance of the case, that authority shall use its best endeavours to secure the representation of the applicant in the proceedings under conditions no less favourable than those available to a person who is resident in and a national of that State and for this purpose it may, in particular, institute proceedings before its competent authorities.

*Article 7*

A decision relating to custody given in a Contracting State shall be recognised and, where it is enforceable in the State of origin, made enforceable in every other Contracting State.

*Article 9*

(1) [*Recognition and enforcement may be refused*] if—

(a) in the case of a decision given in the absence of the defendant or his legal representative, the defendant was not duly served with the document which instituted the proceedings or an equivalent document in sufficient time to enable him to arrange his defence; but such a failure to effect service cannot constitute a ground for refusing recognition or enforcement where service was not effected because the defendant had concealed his whereabouts from the person who instituted the proceedings in the State of origin;

(b) in the case of a decision given in the absence of the defendant or his legal representative, the competence of the authority giving the decision was not founded—

(i) on the habitual residence of the defendant; or

(ii) on the last common habitual residence of the child's parents, at least one parent being still habitually resident there, or

(iii) on the habitual residence of the child;

(c) the decision is incompatible with a decision relating to custody which became enforceable in the State addressed before the removal of the child, unless the child has had his habitual residence in the territory of the requesting State for one year before his removal.

(3) In no circumstances may the foreign decision be reviewed as to its substance.

*Article 10*

(1) [*Recognition and enforcement may also be refused*] on any of the following grounds—
   (a) if it is found that the effects of the decision are manifestly incompatible with the fundamental principles of the law relating to the family and children in the State addressed;
   (b) if it is found that by reason of a change in the circumstances including the passage of time but not including a mere change in the residence of the child after an improper removal, the effects of the original decision and manifestly no longer in accordance with the welfare of the child;
   (c) if at the time when the proceedings were instituted in the State of origin—
      (i) the child was a national of the State addressed or was habitually resident there and no such connection existed with the State of origin;
      (ii) the child was a national both of the State of origin and of the State addressed and was habitually resident in the State addressed;
   (d) if the decision is incompatible with a decision given in the State addressed or enforceable in that State after being given in a third State, pursuant to proceedings begun before the submission of the request for recognition or enforcement, and if the refusal is in accordance with the welfare of the child.

(2) Proceedings for recognition or enforcement may be adjourned on any of the following grounds—
   (a) if an ordinary form of review of the original decision has been commenced;
   (b) if proceedings relating to the custody of the child, commenced before the proceedings in the State of origin were instituted, are pending in the State addressed;
   (c) if another decision concerning the custody of the child is the subject of proceedings for enforcement or of any other proceedings concerning the recognition of the decision.

*Article 11*

(1) Decisions on rights of access and provisions of decisions relating to custody which deal with the rights of access shall be recognised and enforced subject to the same conditions as other decisions relating to custody.

(2) However, the competent authority of the State addressed may fix the conditions for the implementation and exercise of the right of access taking into account, in particular, undertakings given by the parties on this matter.

(3) Where no decision on the right of access has been taken or where recognition or enforcement of the decision relating to custody is refused, the central authority of the State addressed may apply to its competent authorities for a decision on the right of access if the person claiming a right of access so requests.

*Article 12*

Where, at the time of the removal of a child across an international frontier, there is no enforceable decision given in a Contracting State relating to his custody, the provisions of this Convention shall apply to any subsequent decision, relating to the custody of that child and declaring the removal to be unlawful, given in a Contracting State at the request of any interested person.

*Article 13*

(1) A request for recognition or enforcement in another Contracting State of a decision relating to custody shall be accompanied by—

(a) a document authorising the central authority of the State addressed to act on behalf of the applicant or to designate another representative for that purpose;

(b) a copy of the decision which satisfies the necessary conditions of authenticity;

(c) in the case of a decision given in the absence of the defendant or his legal representative, a document which establishes that the defendant was duly served with the document which instituted the proceedings or an equivalent document;

(d) if applicable, any document which establishes that, in accordance with the law of the State of origin, the decision is enforceable;

(e) if possible, a statement indicating the whereabouts or likely whereabouts of the child in the State addressed;

(f) proposals as to how the custody of the child should be restored.

*Article 15*

(1) Before reaching a decision under paragraph (1)(b) of Article 10, the authority concerned in the State addressed—

(a) shall ascertain the child's views unless this is impracticable having regard in particular to his age and understanding; and

(b) may request that any appropriate enquiries be carried out.

(2) The cost of enquiries in any Contracting State shall be met by the authorities of the State where they are carried out.

Requests for enquiries and the results of enquiries may be sent to the authority concerned through the central authorities.

*Article 26*

(1) In relation to a State which has in matters of custody two or more systems of law of territorial application—

(a) reference to the law of a person's habitual residence or to the law of a person's nationality shall be construed as referring to the system of law determined by the rules in force in that State or, if there are no such rules, to the system of law with which the person concerned is most closely connected;

(b) reference to the State of origin or to the State addressed shall be construed as referring, as the case may be, to the territorial unit where the decision was given or to the territorial unit where recognition or enforcement of the decision or restoration of custody is requested.

(2) Paragraph (1)(a) of this Article also applies *mutatis mutandis* to States which have in matters of custody two or more systems of law of personal application.

APPENDIX C

CUSTODY ORDERS

Paragraph 27(1)

1   The following are the orders referred to in paragraph 27(1) of this Schedule—

(a) a care order as defined by section 2(1) of the Children Law, 1995;

(b) a residence order as defined by section 8(1) of the Children Law, 1995; and
(c) any order made by a court in the Cayman Islands under section 4 or section 6 of the Children Law, 1995.

**2** An order made by the Grand Court in the exercise of its jurisdiction relating to wardship so far as it gives the care and control of a child to any person.

## CIVIL JURISDICTION AND JUDGMENTS ACT 1982 (GIBRALTAR) ORDER 1997

**Dated** 30 October 1997

**SI 1997 No 2602**

**1** This Order may be cited as the Civil Jurisdiction and Judgments Act 1982 (Gibraltar) Order 1997 and shall come into force on 1st February 1998.
**2** (a) Provision corresponding to that made by the provisions of the 1968 Convention specified in paragraph (b) shall apply, so far as relevant, for the purpose of regulating, as between the United Kingdom and Gibraltar, the jurisdiction of courts and the recognition and enforcement of judgments.
    (b) Those provisions are—
        (i) Titles I–V;
        (ii) Articles 54 and 57; and
        (iii) Article 65 and the Protocol referred to therein.
**3** For the purpose stated in Article 2 above the United Kingdom and Gibraltar shall be treated as if each were a separate Contracting State and the relevant provisions of the 1968 Convention and the 1982 Act shall be construed accordingly.
**4** In determining any question as to the meaning or effect of the provision (or any part of the provision) made by Article 2 above—
    (a) regard shall be had to any relevant principles laid down by the European Court in connection with Title II of the 1968 Convention and to any relevant decision of that court as to the meaning or effect of any provision of that Title; and
    (b) without prejudice to the generality of paragraph (a), the reports mentioned in section 3(3) of the 1982 Act may be considered and shall, so far as relevant, be given such weight as is appropriate in the circumstances.
A judgment shall not be recognised under this Order if, had it been given in another Contracting State, recognition would be refused by virtue of an agreement to which Article 59 of the 1968 Convention applies.
**6** This Order extends to Northern Ireland.

## CIVIL PROCEDURE (MODIFICATION OF ENACTMENTS) ORDER 1998

**Dated** 27 November 1998

**SI 1998 No 2940**
**1** This Order may be cited as the Civil Procedure (Modification of Enactments) Order 1998 and shall come into force at the same time as the first Civil Procedure Rules made under section 2 of the Civil Procedure Act 1997.
**2** The amendments set out in this Order shall have effect.

**3**   The Judgments Act 1838 is amended as follows—
  (a)  section 17 (judgment debts to carry interest) stands as subsection (1) of that section;
  (b)  in subsection (1), for 'the time of entering up the judgment' substitute 'such time as shall be prescribed by rules of court'; and
  (c)  insert a new subsection as follows—
    '(2)  Rules of court may provide for the court to disallow all or part of any interest otherwise payable under subsection (1).'.

**4**   In section 1 of the Law Reform (Husband and Wife) Act 1962 (actions in tort between husband and wife), omit subsection (3).

**5**   The Supreme Court Act 1981 is amended as follows—
  (a)  in section 33 (powers of High Court exercisable before commencement of action), in subsection (2), omit 'in which a claim in respect of personal injuries to a person, or in respect of a person's death, is likely to be made,'; and
  (b)  in section 34 (power of High Court to order disclosure of documents, inspection of property etc)—
    (i)  omit subsection (1); and
    (ii)  in each of subsections (2) and (3), omit 'to which this subsection applies'.

**6**   The County Courts Act 1984 is amended as follows—
  (a)  omit section 47 (minors);
  (b)  in section 52 (powers of court exercisable before commencement of action), in subsection (2), omit 'in which a claim in respect of personal injuries to a person, or in respect of a person's death, is likely to be made,';
  (c)  in section 53 (power of court to order disclosure of documents, inspection of property etc)—
    (i)  omit subsection (1); and
    (ii)  in each of subsections (2) and (3), omit 'to which this section applies';
  (d)  in section 63 (assessors)—
    (i)  in subsection (1), omit 'on the application of any party';
    (ii)  omit subsection (2);
    (iii)  in subsection (3), for 'at such rate as may be prescribed' substitute 'determined by the judge'; and
    (iv)  in subsection (4), for 'subsection (2) (otherwise than on the application of a party to the proceedings)' substitute 'assisting the judge in reviewing the taxation by the district judge of the costs of any proceedings';
  (e)  in section 133 (proof of service of summonses etc), in subsection (1), omit 'under the hand of that officer'; and
  (f)  omit section 134 (summons and other process to be under seal).

# LEGAL AID (PRESCRIBED PANELS) REGULATIONS 1999

**Dated** 28 January 1999

## SI 1999 No 166

*Citation and commencement*

**1** These Regulations may be cited as the Legal Aid (Prescribed Panels) Regulations 1999 and shall come into force on 1st February 1999.

*Interpretation*

**2** *In these Regulations:*
*'the Act' means the Legal Aid Act 1988;*
*'authorised litigator' has the meaning given in section 119(1) of the Courts and Legal Services Act 1990;*
*'clinical negligence claim' means a claim for damages in respect of an alleged breach of duty of care committed in the course of the provision of clinical or medical services (including dental or nursing services);*
*'Clinical Negligence Franchise Panel' has the meaning given in regulation 3.*
*['the Commission' means the Legal Services Commission established under section 1 of the Access to Justice Act 1999.*
*'Crime Franchise Panel' has the meaning given in regulation 9.*
*'criminal proceedings' has the meaning given in regulation 10.]*
*['Family Franchise Panel' has the meaning given in regulation 5.*
*'family proceedings' has the meaning given in regulation 6.*
*'Immigration Franchise Panel' has the meaning given in regulation 7.*
*'immigration proceedings' has the meaning given in regulation 8.]*

**Note.** Following the repeal of the enabling provisions by the Access to Justice Act 1999, s 106, Sch 15, Pt I, these regulations have lapsed except insofar as they may continue to have effect by virtue of SI 2000 No 774, art 5, and SI 2001 No 916, art 4, Sch 2 as from 1 April 2000.

A registered European lawyer may provide professional activities by way of legal advice and assistance or legal aid, and these Regulations shall be interpreted accordingly: see the European Communities (Lawyer's Practice) Regulations 2000, SI 2000 No 1119, reg 4.

Defintions added by SI 1999 No 3378 with effect from 1 January 2000; further definitions added by SI 2000 No 1930 as from 2 October 2000.

\* \* \* \* \*

*Right to select legal representative in family proceedings*

**5** There shall be a panel of authorised litigators, called the Family Franchise Panel, which shall comprise those authorised litigators who from time to time are authorised under a contract with the Board to provide representation and assistance by way of representation in claims to which regulation 6 applies.

**Note.** Inserted by SI 1999 No 3378 as from 1 January 2000.

**6**—(1) This regulation applies to any family proceedings.
(2) 'Family proceedings' means proceedings which arise out of family relationships.
(3) Proceedings which arise out of family relationships include:
(a) proceedings in which the welfare of children is determined; and

(b)  all proceedings to which Parts III or IV of the Act apply under the following:
  (i)   the Matrimonial Causes Act 1973;
  (ii)  the Inheritance (Provision for Family and Dependants) Act 1975;
  (iii) the Adoption Act 1976;
  (iv)  the Domestic Proceedings and Magistrates' Courts Act 1978;
  (v)   the Matrimonial and Family Proceedings Act 1984;
  (vi)  the Child Abduction and Custody Act 1985;
  (vii) the Family Law Act 1986;
  (viii) the Children Act 1989;
  (ix)  section 30 of the Human Fertilisation and Embryology Act 1990;
  (x)   sections 20 and 27 of the Child Support Act 1991;
  (xi)  Part IV of the Family Law Act 1996;
  (xii) the inherent jurisdiction of the High Court in relation to children; and
  (xiii) in magistrates' courts, under section 43 of the National Assistance Act 1948, section 22 of the Maintenance Orders Act 1950, section 4 of the Maintenance Orders Act 1958, Part I of the Maintenance Orders (Reciprocal Enforcement) Act 1972 or section 106 of the Social Security Administration Act 1992.

(4)  'Family proceedings' does not include proceedings for judicial review.

(5)  The right conferred by section 32(1) of the Act, as regards representation and assistance by way of representation by an authorised litigator in respect of any proceedings to which this regulation applies, shall be exercisable only in relation to authorised litigators who are for the time being members of the Family Franchise Panel.

(6)  Paragraph (5) shall not affect the Board's powers under section 32(2) of the Act (assignment, or limitation on selection, of legal representative).

**Note.** Inserted by SI 1999 No 3378 as from 1 January 2000.

\* \* \* \* \*

## FAMILY PROCEEDINGS FEES ORDER 1999

**Dated** 8 March 1999

**SI 1999 No 690**

The Lord Chancellor, in exercise of the powers conferred on him by s 41 of the Matrimonial and Family Proceedings Act 1984 and s 415 of the Insolvency Act 1986 with the concurrence of the Treasury under s 41 of the Matrimonial and Family Proceedings Act 1984, and with the sanction of the Treasury under s 415(1) of the Insolvency Act 1986, makes the following Order:

**Note:** The order is printed as amended by SI 2000 No 640, SI 2000 No 938, SI 2000 No 1545, SI 2003 No 645 and SI 2003 No 719 with effect from 1 April 2000, 25 April 2000, 3 July 2000, 1 April 2003 and 6 April 2003 respectively.

*Citation and commencement*

**1**  This Order may be cited as the Family Proceedings Fees Order 1999 and shall come into force on 26th April 1999.

*Interpretation*

**2** In this Order, unless the context otherwise requires—
  (a)  a fee referred to by number means the fee so numbered in Schedule 1 to this Order;
  (b)  a rule or form referred to by number alone means the rule or form so numbered in the Family Proceedings Rules 1991; and
  (c)  expressions also used in the Family Proceedings Rules 1991 have the same meaning as in those Rules.
  [(d) 'LSC' means the Legal Services Commission established under section 1 of the Access to Justice Act 1999;
  (e)  'Funding Code' means the code approved under section 9 of the Access to Justice Act 1999.]

**Note.** Paras (d) and (e) in square brackets added by SI 2000 No 640 as from 1 April 2000.

*Fees to be taken*

**3** The fees set out in column 2 of Schedule 1 to this Order shall be taken in family proceedings in the High Court or in a county court in respect of the items described in column 1 in accordance with and subject to the directions specified in column 1.

*Exemptions, reductions and remissions*

**4**—(1) No fee shall be payable under this Order by a party who, at the time when a fee would otherwise become payable—
  *(a)  is in receipt of legal advice and assistance under Part III of the Legal Aid Act 1988 in connection with the matter to which the proceedings relate, or*
  *(b)  is in receipt of any qualifying benefit and is not in receipt of representation under Part IV of the Legal Aid Act 1988 for the purposes of the proceedings, or*
  [(a) is in receipt of—
      (i)   legal advice and assistance under Part II or Part III of the Legal Aid Act 1988 in connection with the matter to which the proceedings relate; or
      (ii)  Legal Help as defined in, and provided in accordance with, the Funding Code in connection with the matter to which the proceedings relate, or
  (b)  is in receipt of any qualifying benefit and is not in receipt of either—
      (i)   representation under Part IV of the Legal Aid Act 1988 for the purposes of the proceedings; or
      (ii)  funding provided by the LSC for the purposes of the proceedings and for which a certificate has been issued under the Funding Code certifying a decision to fund services for that party, or]
  (c)  is not a beneficiary of a trust fund in court of a value of more than £50,000 and is—
      (i)   under the age of eighteen, or
      (ii)  a person for whose financial relief an order under paragraph 2 of Schedule 1, to the Children Act 1989 is in force or is being applied for.
  (2)  The following are qualifying benefits for the purposes of paragraph (1)(b) above—
  (a)  income support;
  [(b)  *working families' tax credit, provided that the amount (if any) to be deducted under section 128(2)(b) of the Social Security Contributions and Benefits Act 1992 has been determined at not more than £70 a week;*

[(b) working tax credit provided that:
    (i)   *the party is also in receipt of child tax credit; or*
   [(i)  child tax credit is being paid to the party, or otherwise following a claim for child tax credit made jointly by the members of a married couple or an unmarried couple (as defined respectively in section 3(5) and (6) of the Tax Credits Act 2002) which includes the party; or]
   (ii)  there is a disability element or severe disability element (or both) to the tax credit received by the party; and that the gross annual income taken into account for the calculations of working tax credit is *£14,213* [£14,600] or less.]
 *(bb)  disabled persons' tax credit, provided that the amount (if any) to be deducted under section 129(5)(b) of the Social Security Contributions and Benefits Act 1992 has been determined at not more than £70 a week; and]*
 (c)  income-based jobseeker's allowance under the Jobseekers Act [1995; and]
 (d)  guarantee credit under the State Pensions Credit Act 2002.]

**Note**  Paras (1)(a) and (b) in italics omitted and paras (1)(a) and (b) in square brackets added by SI 2000 No 640 as from 1 April 2000. Para (2): sub-para (b)(I) substituted by SI 2004 No 2103 as from 31 August 2004. Para (2): in sub-para (b) sum '£14,600' substituted by SI 2004 No 2103 as from 31 August 2004. Paras (2)(b) and (bb) substituted as from 5 October 1999. Para (2)(b) in italics omitted and para (2)(b) in square brackets substituted, and sub-para (bb) omitted as from 6 April 2003. Para (2)(c): words in square brackets substituted by SI 2003 No 719 as from 6 October 2003. Sub-para (d) added by SI 2003 No 719 as from 6 October 2003.

**5**  Where it appears to the Lord Chancellor that the payment of any fee prescribed by this Order would, owing to the exceptional circumstances of the particular case, involve undue hardship, he may reduce or remit the fee in that case.

**[5A**—(1)  Subject to paragraph (2), where a fee has been paid at a time—
 (a)  when, under article 4, it was not payable, the fee shall be refunded;
 (b)  where the Lord Chancellor, if he had been aware of all the circumstances, would have reduced the fee under article 5, the amount by which the fee would have been reduced shall be refunded; and
 (c)  where the Lord Chancellor, if he had been aware of all the circumstances, would have remitted the fee under article 5, the fee shall be refunded.

   (2)  No refund shall be made under paragraph (1) unless the party who paid the fee applies within 6 months of paying the fee.

   (3)  The Lord Chancellor may extend the period of 6 months referred to in paragraph (2) if he considers that there is good reason for an application being made after the end of the period of 6 months.]

**Note.**  Article 5A added by SI 2000 No 640 as from 25 April 2000.

**6**  Where by any convention entered into by Her Majesty with any foreign power it is provided that no fee shall be required to be paid in respect of any proceedings, the fees specified in this Order shall not be taken in respect of those proceedings.

*Revocations*

**7**  The Orders specified in Schedule 2 shall be revoked, except as to any fee or other sum due or payable under those Orders before the commencement of this Order.

SCHEDULE 1

*Fees to be taken*

| Column 1<br>Number and description of fee | Column 2<br>Amount of fee |
|---|---|
| *Section 1. Fees to be taken in the High Court and in the county courts* | |
| **1 Commencement of proceedings** | |
| 1.1 On filing originating proceedings where no other fee is specified | £130 |
| 1.2 On presenting any petition, other than a second petition with leave granted under rule 2.6(4) | £180 |
| 1.3 On applying for either a non-molestation order or an occupation order under Part IV of the Family Law Act 1996, or on applying simultaneously for both a non-molestation order and an occupation order | £60 |
| 1.4 On amending a petition or presenting a second or subsequent petition with leave granted under rule 2.6(4) | £50 |
| 1.5 On filing an answer to a petition or a cross-petition | £100 |
| 1.6 On an application for an order under Part III of the Solicitors Act 1974 for the assessment of costs payable to a solicitor by his client [; or on the commencement of costs-only proceedings] | £30 |
| **Note:** Words in square brackets in fee No 1.6 added by SI 2000 No 1545 with effect from 3 July 2000. | |
| **2 Proceedings under the Children Act 1989** | |
| On filing an application or requesting leave under the following provisions of the Children Act 1989— | |
| *2.1 Parental responsibility, guardians, section 8 orders etc.* | |
| (a) section 4(1)(a), or (3), 5(1), 10(1) or (2) | £90 |
| (b) section 6(7), or 13(1) | £90 |
| *2.2 Financial provision for children* | |
| (a) paragraph 1(1), 2(1), 6(5) or 14(1) of Schedule 1 | £90 |
| (b) paragraph 1(4), 2(5), 5(6), 6(7), 6(8), 8(2), 10(2), or 11 of Schedule 1 | £90 |
| *2.3 Secure accommodation* | |
| (a) Section 25 | £90 |
| *2.4 Care, supervision, etc.* | |
| (a) section 31 | £90 |
| For the purposes of fee 2.4(a) a care order does not include an interim care order, and a supervision order does not include an interim supervision order. | |
| (b) section 33(7), 38(8)(b), 39(1), (2), (3) or (4), paragraph 6 of Schedule 3 or paragraph 11(3) of Schedule 14 | £90 |
| *2.5 Contact with child in care*　　(a) section 34(2), (3), (4) or (9) | £90 |
| *2.6 Placement abroad* | |
| (a) paragraph 19(1) of Schedule 2 | £90 |
| *2.7 Education supervision* | |
| (a) section 36(1) | £90 |
| (b) paragraph 15(2) or 17(1) of Schedule 3 | £90 |
| *2.8 Child assessment order* | |
| (a) section 43(1) | £90 |
| *2.9 Emergency protection* | |
| (a) section 43(12) | £90 |
| (b) section 44, 45, 46 or 48 | £90 |

| Column 1<br>Number and description of fee | Column 2<br>Amount of fee |
|---|---|
| **2.10 Recovery of children**<br>(a) section 50 | £90 |
| **2.11 Miscellaneous**<br>(a) section 102 | £90 |
| **2.12 Appeals**<br>(a) On commencing an appeal under section 94 of, or<br>paragraph 23(11) of Schedule 2 to, the Children Act 1989 | £90 |
| **2.13 Interim care/supervision orders**<br>(a) On an application for an interim care order or an interim<br>supervision order to be made under section 38(1) of the<br>Children Act 1989 where an application for a care order or<br>an application for a supervision order has already been made,<br>and at least one interim care order or at least one interim<br>supervision order has been made in the proceedings | £30 |

*Fee 2*
In the notes to fee 2 'numbered fee' means each of the following
fees: 2.1(a); 2.1(b); 2.2(a); 2.2(b); 2.3(a); 2.4(a); 2.4(b); 2.5(a);
2.6(a); 2.7(a); 2.7(b); 2.8(a); 2.9(a); 2.9(b); 2.10(a); 2.11(a);
2.12(a) and 2.13(a).
Where an application is made or filed, or (as the case may be)
leave is sought or an appeal commenced, under or relating to
provisions of the Children Act 1989 which are listed in two or
more different numbered fees, each of those fees shall be payable.
Where an application is made or filed, or (as the case may be)
leave is sought or an appeal commenced under or relating to
two or more provisions of the Children Act 1989 which are listed
in the same numbered fee, that fee shall be payable only once.
Where the same application is made or filed, or (as the case may
be) leave is sought or an appeal commenced, in respect of two
or more children at the same time, only one fee shall be payable
in respect of each numbered fee.

**3 Adoption and wardship applications**

| | |
|---|---|
| 3.1 On commencing proceedings under the Adoption Act 1976<br>other than under section 21 of that Act | £120 |
| 3.2 On commencing proceedings under section 21 of the<br>Adoption Act 1976 | £120 |
| 3.3 On applying for the exercise by the High Court of its<br>inherent jurisdiction with respect to children | £120 |

**4 Applications in proceedings**

| | |
|---|---|
| 4.1 On an application for an order without notice or by consent<br>(including an application to make a decree nisi absolute) except<br>where separately listed in this schedule | £30 |
| 4.2 On a request for directions for trial (other than in<br>uncontested divorce proceedings, in which no fee is chargeable)<br>except where separately listed in this schedule | £30 |
| 4.3 On an application on notice except where separately listed<br>in this schedule | £60 |
| [4.4 On an application on notice for ancillary relief, or on filing<br>a notice of intention to proceed with an application for ancillary<br>relief other than an application for an order by consent | £120] |

**Note:** Fee No 4.4 added by SI 2000 No 938 as from 25 April 2000.

**5 Appeal from a district judge**

| | |
|---|---|
| 5.1 On filing a notice of appeal from a district judge to a judge | £80 |

| Column 1<br>Number and description of fee | Column 2<br>Amount of fee |
|---|---|
| **6 Searches** | |
| 6.1 On making a search in the central index of decrees absolute kept at the Principal Registry of the Family Division for any specified period of ten calendar years or, if no such period is specified, for the ten most recent years, and, if appropriate, providing a certificate of decree absolute | £20 |
| 6.2 On making a search in the central index of parental responsibility agreements kept at the Principal Registry of the Family Division in accordance with regulations made under section 4(2) of the Children Act 1989 and, if appropriate, providing a copy of an agreement | £20 |
| 6.3 On making a search in the index of decrees absolute kept at any divorce county court or district registry for any specified period of ten calendar years or, if no period is specified, for the ten most recent years, and if appropriate, providing a certificate of decree absolute | £5 |
| **7 Copy documents** | |
| *7.1 On a request for a copy of any document (including a faxed copy where requested) or for examining a plain copy and marking it as an office copy:* | |
| *(a) per page for the first five pages of each document* | *£1* |
| *(b) per page for subsequent pages* | *25p* |
| *7.2 Where copies of any document are made available on a* | *£3* |
| [7.1 On a request for a copy of a document (other than where fee 7.2 applies): | |
| (a) for the first page (except the first page of a subsequent copy of the same document supplied at the same time) | £1 |
| (b) per page in any other case | 20p |
| Fee 7.1 shall be payable for a faxed copy or for examining a plain copy and marking it as an examined copy. | |
| Fee 7.1 shall be payable whether or not the copy is issued as an office copy. | |
| 7.2 On a request for a copy of a document required in connection with proceedings and supplied by the party making the request at the time of copying, for each page | 20p |
| 7.3 On a request for a copy of a document on a computer disk or in other electronic form, for each such copy of this Order. | £3] |
| **Note:** Fee No 7 in italics omitted and new Fee No 7 in square brackets substituted by SI 2000 No 938 with effect from 25 April 2000. | |
| *8.1 On the filing of a bill of costs for taxation (or a request for detailed assessment or a request for a detailed assessment hearing as the case may be); or on the filing of a request for a hearing date for the assessment of costs payable to a solicitor by his client pursuant to an order under Part III of the Solicitors Act 1974* | *£80* |
| *Where there is a combined party and party and legal aid determination of costs,* | |
| *fee 8.1 shall be attributed proportionately to the party and party and legal aid portions of the bill on the basis of the amount allowed.* | |
| *[Where there is a combined party and party and legal aid, or a combined party and party and LSC, or a combined party and party, legal aid and* | |

| Column 1<br>Number and description of fee | Column 2<br>Amount of fee |
|---|---|
| **7 Copy documents**—*contd* | |
| *LSC determination of costs, fee 8.1 shall be attributed proportionately to the party and party, legal aid, or LSC (as the case may be) portions of the bill on the basis of the amount allowed]  8.2 On a request for a review of taxation or an appeal against  taxation (or an appeal against a decision made in detailed   assessment proceedings as the case may be)* | *£50* |
| *8.3 On applying for the court's approval of a Legal Aid Taxation Certificate or (as the case may be) of a Legal Aid Assessment Certificate [certificate of costs payable from the Community Legal Service Fund]* | *£20* |
| [8.1 On the filing of a request for detailed assessment where the party filing the request is legally aided or is funded by the LSC and no other party is ordered to pay the costs of the proceedings | £100 |
| 8.2 On the filing of a request for a detailed assessment hearing in any case where fee 8.1 does not apply; or on the filing of a request for a hearing date for the assessment of costs payable to a solicitor by his client pursuant to an order under Part III of the Solicitors Act 1974 | £160 |
| Where there is a combined party and party and legal aid, or a combined party and party and LSC, or a combined party and party, legal aid and LSC determination of costs, fee 8.2 shall be attributed proportionately to the party and party, legal aid, or LSC (as the case may be) portions of the bill on the basis of the amount allowed. | |
| 8.3 On a request for the issue of a default costs certificate | £40 |
| 8.4 On an appeal against a decision made in detailed assessement proceedings or on a request *or an application to set aside a default costs certificate* | £100 |
| 8.5 On applying for the court's approval of a certificate of costs payable from the Community Legal Service Fund | £30 |
| 8.5 is payable at the time of applying for approval and is recoverable only against the Community Legal Service Fund.] | |
| [8.6 Application to be set aside a default costs certificate | £60] |
| **Note:** Fee No 8 in italics omitted and new Fee No 8 in square brackets substituted by SI 2000 No 938 with effect from 25 April 2000. Words in italics in fee 8.4 omitted and fee 8.6 added by SI 2003 No 645 with effect from 1 April 2003. | |
| **9 Registration of maintenance orders** | |
| On an application for a maintenance order to be– | |
| 9.1 registered under the Maintenance Orders Act 1950 or the Maintenance Orders Act 1958 | £30 |
| 9.2 sent abroad for enforcement under the Maintenance Orders (Reciprocal Enforcement)Act 1972 | £30 |
| *10 Insolvency Act 1986* | |
| *On entering a bankruptcy petition:* | |
| *(a) if presented by a debtor or the personal representative of a deceased debtor* | *£120* |
| *(b) if presented by a creditor or other person* | *£150* |
| *10.2 On entering any other petition* | *£150* |
| *One fee only is payable where more than one petition is presented in relation to a partnership.* | |

| Column 1<br>Number and description of fee | Column 2<br>Amount of fee |
|---|---|
| **10 Insolvency Act 1986—*contd*** | |
| *10.3 (a) On a request for a certificate for discharge from bankruptcy* | *£50* |
| *(b) and after the first certificate for each copy* | *£1* |
| *Requests and applications with no fee* | |
| *No fee is payable on a request or on an application to the Court by the Official Receiver when applying only in the capacity of Official Receiver to the case (and not as trustee or liquidator), or on an application to set aside a statutory demand.* | |
| Note: The editors are unsure of the relevance of bankruptcy etc fees in this Fees Order. Fee No 10 omitted by SI 2000 No 640 as from 1 April 2000. | |
| *Section 2. Fees to be taken in the county courts only* | |
| **11 Service** | |
| 11.1 On a request for service by bailiff, of any document except: | £20 |
| (a) an order for a debtor to attend the adjourned hearing of a judgment summons; | |
| (b) an interpleader summons under an execution; | |
| (c) an order made under section 23 of the Attachment of Earnings Act 1971 (enforcement provisions); or | |
| (d) an order for a debtor to attend an adjourned oral examination of his means | |
| **12 Enforcement in the county courts** | (a) Where the amount for which the warrant issues does not exceed £125 ........ £30 |
| 12.1 On an application for or in relation to enforcement of a judgment or order of a county court or through a county court, by the issue of a warrant of execution against goods except a warrant to enforce payment of a fine | |
| | (b) Where the amount for which the warrant issues exceeds £125 ........ £50 |
| 12.2 On a request for a further attempt at execution of a warrant at a new address following a notice of the reason for non-execution (except a further attempt following suspension) | £20 |
| 12.3 On an application to question a judgment debtor or other person on oath in connection with enforcement of a judgment | £40 |
| 12.4 On an application for a garnishee order nisi or a charging order nisi, or the appointment of a receiver by way of equitable execution | £50 |
| Fee 12.4 shall be payable in respect of each party against whom the order is sought. | |
| 12.5 On an application for a judgment summons | £90 |
| 12.6 On the issue of a warrant of possession or a warrant of delivery | |
| Where the recovery of a sum of money is sought in addition, no further fee is payable. | |
| 12.7 On an application for an attachment of earnings order (other than a consolidated attachment of earnings order) to | |

| Column 1<br>Number and description of fee | Column 2<br>Amount of fee |
| --- | --- |
| **12 Enforcement in the county courts** —*contd* | |
| secure money due under an order made in family proceedings<br>Fee 12.7 is payable for each defendant against whom an order<br>is sought.<br>Fee 12.7 is not payable where the attachment of earnings order<br>is made on the hearing of a judgment summons. | £60 |
| **13 Sale** | |
| 13.1 For removing or taking steps to remove goods to a place<br>of deposit | The reasonable expenses incurred |
| Fee 13.1 is to include the reasonable expenses of feeding and<br>caring for animals. | |
| 13.2 For advertising a sale by public auction pursuant to section<br>97 of the County Courts Act 1984. | The reasonable expenses incurred |
| 13.3 For the appraisement of goods | 5p in the £1 or part of a £1 of the appraised value |
| 13.4 For the sale of goods (including advertisements,<br>catalogues, sale and commission and delivery of goods) | 15p in the £1 or part of a £1 on the amount realised by the sale or such other sum as the district judge may consider to be justified in the circumstances |
| 13.5 Where no sale takes place by reason of an execution<br>being withdrawn, satisfied or stopped | (a) 10p in the £1 or part of a £1 on the value of the goods seized, the value to be the appraised value where the goods have been appraised or such other sum as the district judge may consider to be justified in the circumstances; |

| Column 1<br>Number and description of fee | Column 2<br>Amount of fee |
|---|---|
| **13 Sale** —*contd* | |
| | and in addition (b) any sum payable under fee 13.1, 13.2 or 13.3. |

*Section 3. Fees to be taken in the High Court only*

**14 Enforcement in the High Court**

| | |
|---|---|
| 14.1 On sealing a writ of execution/possession/delivery | £30 |
| Where the recovery of a sum of money is sought in addition to a writ of possession and delivery, no further fee is payable. | |
| 14.2 On an application to question a judgment debtor or other person on oath in connection with enforcement of a judgment | £40 |
| 14.3 On an application for a garnishee order nisi or a charging order nisi, or the appointment of a receiver by way of equitable execution | £50 |
| Fee 14.3 shall be payable in respect of each party against whom the order is sought. | |
| 14.4 On an application for a judgment summons | £90 |
| 14.5 On a request or application to register a judgment or order; or for leave to enforce an arbitration award; or for a certified copy of a judgment or order for use abroad | £30 |
| **15 Affidavits** | |
| On taking an affidavit or an affirmation or attestation upon honour in lieu of an affidavit or a declaration; and | £5 |
| 15.2 for each exhibit referred to and required to be marked | £2 |

## SCHEDULE 2

*Orders Revoked*

| Title | Reference |
|---|---|
| The Family Proceedings Fees Order 1991 | SI 1991/2114 |
| The Family Proceedings Fees (Amendment) Order 1995 | SI 1995/2628 |
| The Family Proceedings Fees (Amendment) Order 1996 | SI 1996/3190 |
| The Family Proceedings Fees (Amendment) Order 1997 | SI 1997/788 |
| The Family Proceedings Fees (Amendment) (No. 2) Order 1997 | SI 1997/1080 |
| The Family Proceedings Fees (Amendment) (No. 3) Order 1997 | SI 1997/1899 |
| The Family Proceedings Fees (Amendment) (No. 4) Order 1997 | SI 1997/2671 |

**FAMILY PROCEEDINGS (MISCELLANEOUS AMENDMENTS) RULES 1999**

**Dated** 25 March 1999

**SI 1999 No 1012**

**1** These Rules may be cited as the Family Proceedings (Miscellaneous Amendments) Rules 1999 and shall come into force on 26th April 1999.

*Amendments to the Family Proceedings Rules 1991*

**2** The Family Proceedings Rules 1991 shall be amended in accordance with these rules and a reference to a rule by number alone is a reference to the rule so numbered in the Family Proceedings Rules.
**3**—(1) In rules 1.2(5), 1.3 and 1.4, references to 'the County Court Rules 1981' and 'the Rules of the Supreme Court 1965' are references to the County Court Rules and the Rules of the Supreme Court in force immediately before 26th April 1999 and references to provisions of those Rules in the Family Proceedings Rules 1991 shall be read accordingly.
(2) In rule 1.3(1), after 'shall' insert 'continue to'.

*Costs in Family Proceedings*

**4**—(1) Order 38 of the County Court Rules 1981 and Order 62 of the Rules of the Supreme Court 1965 shall not apply to the assessment of costs in family proceedings and proceedings in the Family Division, and Parts 43, 44 (except rules 44.9 to 44.12), 47 and 48 of the Civil Procedure Rules 1998 ('the 1998 Rules') shall apply to the assessment of costs in those proceedings, with the following modifications:—
(a) in rule 43.2(1)(c)(ii) of the 1998 Rules, 'district judge' includes a district judge of the Principal Registry of the Family Division;
(b) rule 44.3(2) of the 1998 Rules (costs follow the event) shall not apply.
(2) The Family Proceedings (Costs) Rules 1991 are revoked.
(3) This rule applies to any assessment of costs that takes place on or after 26th April 1999, but so that, as a general rule, no costs for work done before that date shall be disallowed if they would have been allowed on taxation before that date.


**CHILD SUPPORT COMMISSIONERS (PROCEDURE) REGULATIONS 1999**

**Dated** 4 May 1999

**SI 1999 No 1305**

ARRANGEMENT OF REGULATIONS

The Lord Chancellor, in exercise of the powers conferred by sections 22(3), 24(6) and (7) and 25(2), (3) and (5) of, and paragraph 4A of Schedule 4 to, the Child Support Act 1991 and of all other powers enabling him in that behalf, after consultation with the Lord Advocate and, in accordance with section 8 of the Tribunals and Inquiries Act 1992, with the Council on Tribunals, makes the following Regulations-

PART I

GENERAL PROVISIONS

*Citation and commencement*

**1.** These Regulations may be cited as the Child Support Commissioners (Procedure) Regulations 1999 and shall come into force on 1st June 1999.

*Revocation*

**2.** The following Regulations are revoked to the extent that they relate to proceedings before the Child Support Commissioners-
  (a) the Child Support Commissioners (Procedure) Regulations 1992;
  (b) the Child Support Commissioners (Procedure) (Amendment) Regulations 1996;
  (c) the Social Security (Adjudication) and Commissioners Procedure and Child Support Commissioners (Procedure) Amendment Regulations 1997; and
  (d) the Child Support Commissioners (Procedure) (Amendment) Regulations 1997.

*Transitional provisions*

**3.**—(1) Subject to paragraphs (2) and (3), these Regulations shall apply to all proceedings before the Commissioners on or after 1st June 1999.

(2) In relation to any appeal or application for leave to appeal from any child support appeal tribunal constituted under the Act, these Regulations shall have effect with the modifications that-

(a) 'appeal tribunal' includes a reference to any such tribunal;

(b) 'Secretary of State' includes a reference to a child support officer;

(c) 'three months' shall be substituted for 'one month' in regulation 10(1) and '42 days' shall be substituted for 'one month' in regulations 11(2) and 15(1); and

(d) under regulation 11 a Commissioner may for special reasons accept an application for leave to appeal even though the applicant has not sought to obtain leave to appeal from the chairman.

(3) Any transitional question arising under any application or appeal in consequence of the coming into force of these Regulations shall be determined by a Commissioner who may for this purpose give such directions as he may think just, including modifying the normal requirements of these Regulations in relation to the application or appeal.

*Interpretation*

**4.** In these Regulations, unless the context otherwise requires-
'the Act' means the Child Support Act 1991;
'appeal tribunal' means an appeal tribunal constituted under Chapter 1 of Part I of the Social Security Act 1998;
'authorised officer' means an officer authorised by the Lord Chancellor, or in Scotland by the Secretary of State, in accordance with paragraph 4A of Schedule 4 of the Act;
'the chairman' for the purposes of regulations 10, 11 and 12 means-
  (i) the person who was the chairman or sole member of the appeal tribunal which gave the decision against which leave to appeal is being sought; or
  (ii) any other person authorised to deal with applications for leave to appeal to a Commissioner against that decision under the Act;
'Commissioner' means a Child Support Commissioner;
'legally qualified' means being a solicitor or barrister, or in Scotland, a solicitor or advocate;
'month' means a calendar month;
'office' means an Office of the Child Support Commissioners;
'party' means a party to the proceedings;
'proceedings' means any proceedings before a Commissioner, whether by way of an application for leave to appeal to, or from, a Commissioner, by way of an appeal or otherwise;
'respondent' means any person other than the applicant or appellant who was a party to the proceedings before the appeal tribunal and any other person who, pursuant to a direction given under regulation 18 is served with notice of the appeal; and
'summons', in relation to Scotland, corresponds to 'citation' and regulation 23 shall be construed accordingly.

*General powers of a Commissioner*

**5.**—(1) Subject to the provisions of these Regulations, a Commissioner may adopt any procedure in relation to proceedings before him.

(2) A Commissioner may-

(a)  extend or abridge any time limit under these Regulations (including, subject to regulations 11(3) and 15(2), granting an extension where the time limit has expired);

(b)  expedite, postpone or adjourn any proceedings.

(3) Subject to paragraph (4), a Commissioner may, on or without the application of a party, strike out any proceedings for want of prosecution or abuse of process.

(4) Before making an order under paragraph (3), the Commissioner shall send notice to the party against whom it is proposed that it should be made giving him an opportunity to make representations why it should not be made.

(5) A Commissioner may, on application by the party concerned, give leave to reinstate any proceedings which have been struck out in accordance with paragraph (3) and, on giving leave, he may give directions as to the conduct of the proceedings.

(6) Nothing in these Regulations shall affect any power which is exercisable apart from these Regulations.

*Transfer of proceedings between Commissioners*

**6.**  If it becomes impractical or inexpedient for a Commissioner to continue to deal with proceedings who are or have been before him, any other Commissioner may rehear or deal with those proceedings and any related matters.

*Delegation of functions to authorised officers*

**7.**—(1) The following functions of Commissioners may be exercised by legally qualified authorised officers, to be known as legal officers to the Commissioners-

(a)  giving directions under regulations 8, 18 and 19;

(b)  determining requests for or directing hearings under regulation 21;

(c)  summoning witnesses, and setting aside a summons made by a legal officer, under regulation 23;

(d)  postponing a hearing under regulation 5;

(e)  giving leave to withdraw or reinstate applications or appeals under regulation 24;

(f)  waiving irregularities under regulation 25 in connection with any matter being dealt with by a legal officer;

(g)  extending or abridging time, directing expedition, giving notices, striking out and reinstating proceedings under regulation 5.

(2) Any party may, within 14 days of being sent notice of the direction or order of a legal officer, make a written request to a Commissioner asking him to reconsider the matter and confirm or replace the direction or order with his own, but, unless ordered by a Commissioner, a request shall not stop proceedings under the direction or order.

*Manner of and time for service of notices, etc*

**8.**—(1) A notice to or other document for any party shall be deemed duly served if it is-

(a)  delivered to him personally; or

(b)  properly addressed and sent to him by prepaid post at the address last notified by him for this purpose, or to his ordinary address; or

(c)  served in any other manner a Commissioner may direct.

(2) A notice to or other document for a Commissioner shall be delivered or sent to the office.

(3) For the purposes of any time limit, a properly addressed notice or other document sent by prepaid post, fax or e-mail is effective from the date it is sent.

*Confidentiality*

**9.**—(1) Subject to paragraphs (3) and (4), the office shall not disclose information such as is mentioned in paragraph (2) except with the written consent of the person to whom the information relates or, in the case of a child, with the written consent of the person with care of him.

(2) The information referred to in paragraph (1) is any information provided under the Act which-

(a) relates to any person whose circumstances are relevant to the proceedings; and

(b) consists of that person's address or other information which could reasonably be expected to lead to him being located.

(3) Where-

(a) the office sends a notice to a person to whom information relates stating that the information may be disclosed in the court or proceedings unless he objects within one month of the date of the notice; and

(b) written notice of that person's objection is not received at the office within one month of the date of the notice,

then the information may be disclosed in the course of the proceedings.

(4) Where the person to whom information relates is a child, the office shall send the notice referred to in paragraph (3)(a) to the person with care of the child and where written notice of that person's objection is not received at the office within one month of the date of the notice, then the information may be disclosed in the course of the proceedings.

(5) This regulation does not apply to proceedings which relate solely to a reduced benefits direction within the meaning of section 46(11) of the Act.

PART II

APPLICATIONS FOR LEAVE TO APPEAL AND APPEALS

*Application to a Chairman for leave to appeal*

**10.**—(1) An application to a chairman for leave to appeal to a Commissioner from a decision of an appeal tribunal shall be made within one month of the date the written statement of the reasons for the decision was sent to the applicant.

(2) Where an application for leave to appeal to a Commissioner is made by the Secretary of State, the clerk to an appeal tribunal shall, as soon as may be practicable, send a copy of the application to every other party.

(3) Any party who is sent a copy of an application for leave to appeal in accordance with paragraph (2) may make representations in writing within one month of the date the application if sent.

(4) A person determining an application for leave to appeal to a Commissioner shall take into account any further representations received in accordance with paragraph (3) and shall record his decision in writing and send a copy to each party.

(5) Where an applicant has not applied for leave to appeal within one month in accordance with paragraph (1), but makes an application within one year beginning on the day the one month ends, the chairman may for special reasons accept the late application.

(6) Where in any case it is impractical, or would be likely to cause undue delay for an application for leave to appeal against a decision of an appeal tribunal to be determined by the person who was the chairman of that tribunal, that application shall be determined by any other chairman.

*Application to a Commissioner for leave to appeal*

**11.**—(1) An application to a Commissioner for leave to appeal against the decision of an appeal tribunal may be made only where the applicant has sought to obtain leave from the chairman and leave has been refused or the application has been rejected.

(2) Subject to paragraph (3) an application to a Commissioner shall be made within one month of the date that notice of the refusal or rejection was sent to the applicant by the appeal tribunal.

(3) A Commissioner may for special reasons accept a late application where the applicant failed to seek leave from the chairman within the specified time, but did so on or before the final date.

(4) In paragraph (3) the final date means the end of a period of 13 months from the date on which the decision of the appeal tribunal or, any separate statement of the reasons for it, was sent to the applicant by the appeal tribunal.

*Notice of application for leave to appeal*

**12.**—(1) An application to a chairman or a Commissioner for leave to appeal shall be made by notice in writing, and shall contain-
   (a) the name and address of the applicant;
   (b) the grounds on which the applicant intends to rely;
   (c) if the application is made late, the grounds for seeking late acceptance; and
   (d) an address for sending notices and other documents to the applicant.
(2) The notice in paragraph (1) shall have with it copies of-
   (a) the decision against which leave to appeal is sought;
   (b) if separate, the written statement of the appeal tribunal's reasons for it; and
   (c) if it is an application to a Commissioner, the notice of refusal or rejection sent to the applicant by the appeal tribunal.

(3) Where an application for leave to appeal is made to a Commissioner by the Secretary of State he shall send each respondent a copy of the notice of application and any documents sent with it when they are sent to the Commissioner.

*Determination of application*

**13.**—(1) The office shall send written notice to the applicant and each respondent of any determination of a Commissioner of an application for leave to appeal to a Commissioner.

(2) Subject to a direction by a Commissioner, where a Commissioner grants leave to appeal under regulation 11-
   (a) notice of appeal shall be deemed to have been sent on the date when notice of the determination is sent to the applicant; and
   (b) the notice of application shall be deemed to be a notice of appeal sent under regulation 14.

(3) If a Commissioner grants an application for leave to appeal he may, with the consent of the applicant and each respondent, treat and determine the application as an appeal.

*Notice of appeal*

**14.**—(1) Subject to regulation 13(2), an appeal shall be made by notice in writing and shall contain-
   (a) the name and address of the appellant;
   (b) the date on which the appellant was notified that leave to appeal had been granted;
   (c) the grounds on which the appellant intends to rely;

    (d)  if the appeal is made late, the grounds for seeking late acceptance; and

    (e)  an address for sending notices and other documents to the appellant.

    (2)  The notice in paragraph (1) shall have with it copies of-

    (a)  the notice informing the appellant that leave to appeal has been granted;

    (b)  the decision against which leave to appeal has been granted; and

    (c)  if separate, the written statement of the appeal tribunal's reasons for it.

*Time limit for appealing after leave obtained*

**15.**—(1) Subject to paragraph (2), a notice of appeal shall be valid unless it is sent to a Commissioner within one month of the date on which the appellant was sent written notice that leave to appeal had been granted.

    (2)  A Commissioner may for special reasons accept a late notice of appeal.

*Acknowledgement of a notice of appeal and notification to each respondent*

**16.** The office shall send-

    (a)  to the appellant, an acknowledgement of the receipt of the notice of appeal;

    (b)  to each respondent, a copy of the notice of appeal.

PART III

PROCEDURE

*Representation*

**17.** A party may conduct his case himself (with assistance from any person is he wishes) or be represented by any person whom he may appoint for the purpose.

*Directions on Notice of Appeal*

**18.**—(1) As soon as practicable after the receipt of a notice of appeal a Commissioner shall give any directions that appear to him to be necessary, specifying-

    (a)  the parties who are to be respondents to the appeal; and

    (b)  the order in which and the time within which any party is to be allowed to make written observations on the appeal or on the observations made by any other party.

    (2)  If in any case two or more persons who were parties to the proceedings before the appeal tribunal give notice of appeal to a Commissioner, a Commissioner shall direct which one of them is to be treated as the appellant and thereafter, but without prejudice to any rights or powers conferred on appellants by these Regulations, any other person who has given notice of appeal shall be treated as a respondent.

    (3)  Subject to an abridgement of time under regulation 5(2)(a), the time specified in directions given under paragraph (1)(b) shall be not less than one month beginning with the day on which the notice of the appeal or, as the case may be, the observations were sent to the party concerned.

**General Directions**

**19.**—(1) Where a Commissioner considers that an application or appeal made to him gives insufficient particulars to enable to question at issue to be determined, he may direct the party making the application or appeal, or any respondent, to furnish any further particulars which may be reasonably required.

    (2)  In the case of an application for leave to appeal, or an appeal from an appeal tribunal, a Commissioner may, before determining the application or

appeal, direct the tribunal to submit a statement of such facts or other matters as he considers necessary for the proper determination of that application or appeal.

(3) At any stage of the proceedings, a Commissioner may, on or without an application, give any directions as he may consider necessary or desirable for the efficient despatch of the proceedings.

(4) A Commissioner may direct any party before him to make any written observations as may seem to him necessary to enable the question at issue to be determined.

(5) An application under paragraph (3) shall be made in writing to a Commissioner and shall set out the direction which the applicant seeks.

(6) Unless a Commissioner shall otherwise determine, the office shall send a copy of an application under paragraph (3) to every other party.

*Procedure on linked case notice from the Secretary of State*

**20.** Any notice from the Secretary of State to a Commissioner under section 28ZB of the Act (Appeal involving issues that arise on appeal in other cases) shall be sent by notice in writing signed by or on behalf of the Secretary of State and shall identify, by its file reference or the names of the parties involved, each appeal or application to which it relates.

*Requests for hearings*

**21.**—(1) Subject to paragraph (2), (3) and (4), a Commissioner may determine any proceedings without a hearing.

(2) Where a request for a hearing is made by any party, a Commissioner shall grant the request unless he is satisfied that the proceedings can properly be determined without a hearing.

(3) Where a Commissioner refuses a request for a hearing, he shall send written notice to the person making the request, either before or at the same time as making his determination or decision.

(4) A Commissioner may, without an application and at any stage, direct a hearing.

*Hearings*

**22.**—(1) This regulation applies to any hearing of an application or appeal to which these Regulations apply.

(2) Subject to paragraph (3), the office shall give reasonable notice of the time and place of any hearing before a Commissioner.

(3) Unless all the parties concerned agree to a hearing at shorter notice, the period of notice specified under paragraph (2) shall be at least 14 days before the date of the hearing.

(4) If any party to whom notice of a hearing has been sent fails to appear at the hearing, the Commissioner may proceed with the case in that party's absence, or may give directions with a view to the determination of the case.

(5) Any hearing before a Commissioner shall be in public, unless the Commissioner for special reasons directs otherwise.

(6) Where a Commissioner holds a hearing the applicant or appellant, every respondent and, with the leave of a Commissioner, any other persons, shall be entitled to be present and be heard.

(7) Any person entitled to be heard at a hearing may-

(a) address the Commissioner;

(b) with the leave of the Commissioner, give evidence, call witnesses and put questions directly to any other person called as a witness.

(8) Nothing in these Regulations shall prevent a member of the Council on

Tribunals or of the Scottish Committee of the Council in his capacity as such from being present at a hearing before a Commissioner which is not held in public.

*Summoning of witnesses*

**23.**—(1) Subject to paragraph (2), a Commissioner may summon any person to attend a hearing as a witness, at such time and place as may be specified in the summons, to answer any questions or produce any documents in his custody or under his control which relate to any matter in question in the proceedings.

(2) A person shall not be required to attend in obedience to a summons under paragraph (1) unless he has been given at least 14 days' notice before the date of the hearing or, if less than 14 days, has informed the Commissioner that he accepts such notice as he has been given.

(3) Upon the application of a person summoned under this regulation, a Commissioner may set the summons aside.

(4) A Commissioner may require any witness to give evidence on oath and for this purpose an oath may be administered in due form.

*Withdrawal of applications for leave to appeal and appeals*

**24.**—(1) At any time it is determined, an applicant may withdraw an application to a Commissioner for leave to appeal against a decision of an appeal tribunal by giving written notice to a Commissioner.

(2) At any time before the decision is made, the appellant may withdraw his appeal with the leave of a Commissioner.

(3) A Commissioner may, on application by the party concerned, give leave to reinstate any application or appeal which has been withdrawn in accordance with paragraphs (1) and (2) and, on giving leave, he may make directions as to the conduct of the proceedings.

*Irregularities*

**25.** Any irregularity resulting from failure to comply with the requirements of these Regulations shall not by itself invalidate any proceedings, and the Commissioner, before reaching his decision, may waive the irregularity or take steps to remedy it.

PART IV

DECISIONS

*Determinations and decisions of a Commissioner*

**26.**—(1) The determination of a Commissioner on an application for leave to appeal shall be in writing and signed by him.

(2) The decision of a Commissioner on an appeal shall be in writing and signed by him and, unless it was a decision made with the consent of the parties he shall include the reasons.

(3) The office shall send a copy of the determination or decision and any reasons to each party.

(4) Without prejudice to paragraphs (2) and (3), a Commissioner may announce his determination or decision at the end of a hearing.

(5) When giving his decision on an application or appeal, whether in writing or orally, a Commissioner shall omit any reference to the surname of any child to whom the application or appeal relates and any other information which would be likely, whether directly or indirectly, to identify that child.

*Correction of accidental errors in decisions*

**27.**—(1) Subject to regulations 6 and 29, the Commissioner who gave the decision may at any time correct accidental errors in any decision or record of a decision.

(2) A correction made to, or to the record of, a decision shall become part of the decision or record, and the office shall send written notice of the correction to any party to whom notice of the decision has been sent.

*Setting aside decisions on certain grounds*

**28.**—(1) Subject to regulations 6 and 29, on an application made by any party, the Commissioner who gave the decision in proceedings may set it aside where it appears just to do so on the ground that-

(a) a document relating to the proceedings was not sent to, or was not at an appropriate time by, a party or his representative or was not received at an appropriate time by the Commissioner; or

(b) a party or his representative was not present at a hearing before the Commissioner; or

(c) there has been some other procedural irregularity or mishap.

(2) An application under this regulation shall be made in writing to a Commissioner within one month from the date on which the office gave written notice of the decision to the party making the application.

(3) Unless the Commissioner considers that it is unnecessary for the proper determination of an application made under paragraph (1), the office shall send a copy of it to each respondent, who shall be given a reasonable opportunity to make representations on it.

(4) The office shall send each party written notice of a determination of an application to set aside a decision and the reasons for it.

*Provisions common to regulations 27 and 28*

**29.**—(1) In regulations 27 and 28, the word 'decision' shall include determinations of applications for leave to appeal and decisions on appeals.

(2) There shall be no appeal against a correction or a refusal to correct under regulation 27 or a determination given under regulation 28.

PART IV

APPLICATIONS FOR LEAVE TO APPEAL TO THE APPELLATE COURT

*Application to a Commissioner for leave to appeal to the Appellate Court*

**30.**—(1) Subject to paragraph (2), an application to a Commissioner under section 25 of the Act for leave to appeal against a decision of a Commissioner shall be made in writing, stating the grounds of the application, within three months from the date on which the applicant was sent written notice of the decision.

(2) Subject to a direction by a Commissioner, in calculating any time for applying for leave to appeal under paragraph (1), there shall be disregarded any day before the day-

(a) on which notice was sent of a correction of a decision or the record of it under regulation 27; or

(b) on which notice was sent of a determination that a decision shall not be set aside under regulation 28.

(3) Regulations 24(1) and 24(3) shall apply to an application to a Commissioner for leave to appeal from a Commissioner's decision as they apply to the proceedings in that regulation.

## COMMUNITY LEGAL SERVICE (COSTS) REGULATIONS 2000

**Dated**  18 February 2000

**SI 2000 No 441**

PART I

GENERAL

*Citation and commencement*

**1** These Regulations may be cited as the Community Legal Service (Costs) Regulations 2000 and shall come into force on 1st April 2000.

*Interpretation*

**2**  In these Regulations:
'the Act' means the Access to Justice Act 1999;
'certificate' means a certificate issued under the Funding Code certifying a decision to fund services for the client;
['child' means a child under 18';]
'client' means an individual who receives funded services;
'Commission' means the Legal Services Commission established under section 1 of the Act;
'costs judge' has the same meaning as in the CPR;
'costs order' means an order that a party pay all or part of the costs of proceedings;
'costs order against the Commission' means an order, made under regulation 5 of the Community Legal Service (Cost Protection) Regulations 2000 (but not one under regulation 6 of those Regulations), that the Commission pay all or part of the costs of a party to proceedings who has not received funded services in relation to those proceedings under a certificate, other than a certificate which has been revoked;
'cost protection' means the limit on costs awarded against a client set out in section 11(1) of the Act;
'court' includes any tribunal having the power to award costs in favour of, or against, a party;
'CPR' means the Civil Procedure Rules 1998, and a reference to a Part or rule, prefixed by 'CPR', means the Part or rule so numbered in the CPR;
'Financial Regulations' means the Community Legal Service (Financial) Regulations 2000;
'Funding Code' means the code approved under section 9 of the Act;
'full costs' means, where a section 11(1) costs order is made against a client, the amount of costs which that client would, but for section 11(1) of the Act, have been ordered to pay;
'funded services' means services which are provided directly for a client and funded for that client by the Commission as part of the Community Legal Service under sections 4 to 11 of the Act;
['litigation friend' has the meaning given by CPR Part 21;]
'partner', in relation to a party to proceedings, means a person with whom that party lives as a couple, and includes a person with whom the party is not currently living but from whom he is not living separate and apart;
['patient' means a person who by reason of mental disorder within the meaning of the Mental Health Act 1983 is incapable of managing and administering his own affairs;]

'proceedings' include proceedings in any tribunal which is a court, as defined, in this paragraph;

'receiving party' means a party in favour of whom a costs order is made;

'Regional Director' means any Regional Director appointed by the Commission in accordance with the Funding Code and any other person authorised to act on his behalf, except a supplier;

'rules of court', in relation to a tribunal, means rules or regulations made by the authority having power to make rules or regulations regulating the practice and procedure of that tribunal and, in relation to any court, includes practice directions;

'section 11(1) costs order' means a costs order against a client where cost protection applies;

'solicitor' means solicitor or other person who is an authorised litigator within the meaning of section 119(1) of the Courts and Legal Services Act 1990;

'statement of resources' means:

(a) a statement, verified by a statement of truth, made by a party to proceedings setting out:

    (i) his income and capital and financial commitments during the previous year and, if applicable, those of his partner;

    (ii) his estimated future financial resources and expectations and, if applicable, those of his partner; and

    *(iii) a declaration that he and, if applicable, his partner, has not deliberately foregone or deprived himself of any resources or expectations, particulars of any application for funding made by him in connection with the proceedings, and any other facts relevant to the determination of his resources; or*

    [(iii) a declaration stating whether he, and if applicable his partner, has deliberately foregone or deprived himself of any resources or expectations, together (if applicable and as far as practical) with details of those resources or expectations and the manner in which they have been foregone or deprived;

    (iv) particulars of any application for funding made by him in connection with the proceedings; and

    (v) any other facts relevant to the determination of his resources; or]

(b) a statement, verified by a statement of truth, made by a client receiving funded services, setting out the information provided by the client under regulation 6 of the Financial Regulations, and stating that there has been no significant change in the client's financial circumstances since the date on which the information was provided or, as the case may be, details of any such change;

'statement of truth' has the same meaning as in CPR Part 22;

'supplier' means any person or body providing funded services to the client, including any authorised advocate (within the meaning of section 119(1) of the Courts and Legal Services Act 1990) engaged by the client's solicitor to act in proceedings.

**Note.** Words in italics omitted and words in square brackets substituted by SI 2003 No 649 as from 7 April 2003.

*Effect of these Regulations*

**3** Nothing in these Regulations shall be construed, in relation to proceedings where one or more parties are receiving, or have received, funded services, as:

(a) requiring a court to make a costs order where it would not otherwise have made a costs order; or

(b) affecting the court's power to make a wasted costs order against a legal representative.

*Termination of retainer where funding is withdrawn*

**4**—(1) The following paragraphs of this regulation apply where funding is withdrawn by revoking or discharging the client's certificate.

(2) Subject to paragraphs (3) and (4), on the revocation or discharge of the client's certificate, the retainer of any supplier acting under that certificate shall terminate immediately.

(3) Termination of retainers under paragraph (2) shall not take effect unless and until any procedures under the Funding Code for review of the decision to withdraw the client's funding are concluded, and confirm the decision to withdraw funding.

(4) The solicitor's retainer shall not terminate until he has complied with any procedures under the Funding Code that require him to send or serve notices.

Part II
Costs Orders Against Client and Against Commission

*Application of regulations 6 to 13*

**5** Regulations 6 to 13 apply only where cost protection applies.

*Security for costs*

**6** Where in any proceedings a client is required to give security for costs, the amount of that security shall not exceed the amount (if any) which is a reasonable one having regard to all the circumstances, including the client's financial resources and his conduct in relation to the dispute to which the proceedings relate.

*Assessment of resources*

**7**—(1) The first £100,000 of the value of the client's interest in the main or only dwelling in which he resides shall not be taken into account in having regard to the client's resources for the purposes of section 11(1) of the Act.

(2) Where, but only to the extent that, the court considers that the circumstances are exceptional, having regard in particular to the quantity or value of the items concerned, the court may take into account the value of the client's clothes and household furniture, or the tools and implements of his trade, in having regard to the client's resources for the purposes of section 11(1) of the Act.

(3) Subject to paragraph (4), in having regard to the resources of a party for the purposes of section 11(1) of the Act, the resources of his partner shall be treated as his resources.

(4) The resources of a party's partner shall not be treated as that party's resources if the partner has a contrary interest in the dispute in respect of which the funded services are provided.

(5) Where a party is acting in a representative, fiduciary or official capacity, the court shall not take the personal resources of the party into account for the purposes of section 11(1) of the Act, but shall have regard to the value of any property or estate, or the amount of any fund out of which he is entitled to be indemnified, and may also have regard to the resources of the persons, if any, including that party where appropriate, who are beneficially interested in that property, estate or fund.

[(6) For the purposes of section 11(1) of the Act, where a party is acting as a litigation friend to a client who is a child or a patient, the court shall not take the personal resources of the litigation friend into account in assessing the resources of the client.]

**Note.** Para (6) added by SI 2003 No 649 as from 7 April 2003.

*Statements of resources*

**8**—(1)  Any person who is a party to proceedings in which another party is a client may make a statement of resources, and file it with the court.

(2)  A person making and filing a statement of resources under paragraph (1) shall serve a copy of it on the client.

(3)  Where a copy of a statement of resources has been served under paragraph (2) not less than seven days before the date fixed for a hearing at which the amount to be paid under a section 11(1) costs order falls, or may fall, to be decided, the client shall also make a statement of resources, and shall produce it at that hearing.

*Procedures for ordering costs against client and Commission*

**9**—(1)  *Where the court makes* [Where the court is considering whether to make] a section 11(1) costs order, it shall consider whether, but for cost protection, it would have made a costs order against the client and, if so, whether it would, on making the costs order, have specified the amount to be paid under that order.

(2)  If the court considers that it would have made a costs order against the client, but that it would not have specified the amount to be paid under it, the court shall, when making the section 11(1) costs order:

(a)  specify the amount (if any) that the client is to pay under that order if, but only if:

    (i)   it considers that it has sufficient information before it to decide what amount is, in that case, a reasonable amount for the client to pay, in accordance with section 11(1) of the Act; and

    (ii)  it is satisfied that, if it were to determine the full costs at that time, they would exceed the amount referred to in sub-paragraph (i);

(b)  otherwise, it shall not specify the amount the client is to pay under the *section 11(1)* costs order.

(3)  If the court considers that it would have made a costs order against the client, and that it would have specified the amount to be paid under it, the court shall, when making the *section 11(1)* costs order:

(a)  specify the amount (if any) that the client is to pay under that order if, but only if, it considers that it has sufficient information before it to decide what amount is, in that case, a reasonable amount for the client to pay, in accordance with section 11(1) of the Act;

(b)  otherwise, it shall not specify the amount the client is to pay under the section 11(1) costs order.

(4)  Any order made under paragraph (3) shall state the amount of the full costs.

(5)  The amount (if any) to be paid by the client under an order made under paragraph (2)(b) or paragraph (3)(b), and any application for a costs order against the Commission, shall be determined in accordance with regulation 10, and at any such determination following an order made under paragraph (2)(b), the amount of the full costs shall also be assessed.

(6)  Where the court makes a section 11(1) costs order that does not specify the amount which the client is to pay under it, it may also make findings of fact, as to the parties' conduct in the proceedings or otherwise, relevant to the determination of that amount, and those findings shall be taken into consideration in that determination.

**Note.**  Words in italics in paras 1, (2)(b) and (3)(b) omitted and words in square brackets substituted by SI 2001 No 822 as from 2 April 2001.

**10**—(1)  The following paragraphs of this regulation apply where the amount to be paid under a section 11(1) costs order, or an application for a costs order against the Commission, is to be determined under this regulation, by virtue of regulation 9(5).

(2) The receiving party may, within three months after a section 11(1) costs order is made, request a hearing to determine the costs payable to him.

(3) A request under paragraph (2) shall be accompanied by:

(a)   if the section 11(1) costs order does not state the full costs, the receiving party's bill of costs, which shall comply with any requirements of relevant rules of court relating to the form and content of a bill of costs where the court is assessing a party's costs;

*(b)   a statement of resources; and*

[(b)   unless the conditions set out in paragraph (3A) are satisfied a statement of resources; and]

(c)   if the receiving party is seeking, or, subject to the determination of the amount to be paid under the section 11(1) costs order, may seek, a costs order against the Commission, written notice to that effect.

[(3A)   The conditions referred to in paragraph (3)(b) above are that—

(a)   the court is determining an application for a costs order against the Commission;

(b)   the costs were not incurred in a court of first instance.]

(4) The receiving party shall file the documents referred to in paragraph (3) with the court and at the same time serve copies of them:

(a)   on the client, if a determination of costs payable under section 11(1) of the Act is sought; and

(b)   on the Regional Director, if notice has been given under paragraph (3)(c).

(5) Where documents are served on the client under paragraph (4)(a), the client shall make a statement of resources.

(6) The client shall file the statement of resources made under paragraph (5) with the court, and serve copies of it on the receiving party and, if notice has been given under paragraph (3)(c), on the Regional Director, not more than 21 days after the client receives a copy of the receiving party's statement of resources.

(7) The client may, at the same time as filing and serving a statement of resources under paragraph (6), file, and serve on the same persons, a statement setting out any points of dispute in relation to the bill of costs referred to in paragraph (3)(a).

(8) If the client, without good reason, fails to file a statement of resources in accordance with paragraph (6), the court shall determine the amount which the client shall be required to pay under the section 11(1) costs order (and, if relevant, the full costs), having regard to the statement made by the receiving party, and the court need not hold an oral hearing for such determination.

(9) If the client files a statement of resources in accordance with paragraph (6), or the period for filing such notice expires, or if the costs payable by the client have already been determined, the court shall set a date for the hearing and, at least 14 days before that date, serve notice of it on:

(a)   the receiving party;

(b)   the client (unless the costs payable by the client have already been determined); and

(c)   if a costs order against the Commission is or may be sought, the Regional Director.

(10) The court's functions under this regulation may be exercised:

(a)   in relation to proceedings in the House of Lords, by the Clerk to the Parliaments;

(b)   in relation to proceedings in the Court of Appeal, High Court or a county court, a costs judge or a district judge;

(c)   in relation to proceedings in a magistrates' court, by a single justice or by the justices' clerk;

(d) in relation to proceedings in the Employment Appeal Tribunal, by the Registrar of that Tribunal.

(11) The amount of costs to be determined under this regulation may include the costs incurred in relation to a request made under this regulation.

**Note.** Para (3)(b) in italics omitted and sub-para (3)(b) substituted, para (3A) added by SI 2003 No 649 as from 7 April 2003.

**[10A—**(1) Subject to paragraph (2), where the court makes a section 11(1) costs order but does not specify the amount which the client is to pay under it, the court may order the client to pay an amount on account of the costs which are the subject of the order.

(2) The court may order a client to make a payment on account of costs under this regulation only if it has sufficient information before it to decide the minimum amount which the client is likely to be ordered to pay on a determination under regulation 10.

(3) The amount of the payment on account of costs shall not exceed the minimum amount which the court decides that the client is likely to be ordered to pay on such a determination.

(4) Where the court orders a client to make a payment on account of costs—
  (a) it shall order the client to make the payment into court; and
  (b) the payment shall remain in court unless and until the court—
    (i) makes a determination under regulation 10 of the amount which the client should pay to the receiving party under the section 11(1) costs order, and orders the payment on account or part of it to be paid to the receiving party in satisfaction or part satisfaction of the client's liability under that order; or
    (ii) makes an order under paragraph (5)(b) or (5)(c) of this regulation that the payment on account or part of it be repaid to the client.

(5) Where a client has made a payment on account of costs pursuant to an order under paragraph (1) of this regulation—
  (a) the receiving party shall request a hearing under regulation 10 to determine the amount of costs payable to him;
  (b) if the receiving party fails to request such a hearing within the time permitted by regulation 10(2), the payment on account shall be repaid to the client;
  (c) if upon the hearing under regulation 10 the amount of costs which it is determined that the client should pay is less than the amount of the payment on account, the difference shall be repaid to the client.**]**

**Note.** Inserted by SI 2001 No 822 as from 2 April 2001.

*Appeals, etc*

**11—**(1) Subject to the following paragraphs of this regulation, and to regulation 12, any determination made under regulation 9 or regulation 10 shall be final.

(2) Any party with a financial interest in an assessment of the full costs may appeal against that assessment, if and to the extent that that party would, but for these Regulations, be entitled to appeal against an assessment of costs by the court in which the relevant proceedings are taking place.

(3) Where, under regulation 9(2)(a), the court has specified the amount which a client is required to pay under a section 11(1) costs order, the client may apply to the court for a determination of the full costs and if, on that determination, the amount of the full costs is less than the amount which the court previously specified under regulation 9(2)(a), the client shall instead be required to pay the amount of the full costs.

(4) The receiving party or the Commission may appeal, on a point of law, against the making of a costs order against the Commission (including the amount of costs which the Commission is required to pay under the order), or against the court's refusal to make such an order.

*Variation and late determination of amount of costs*

**12**—(1) The following paragraphs of this regulation apply where the court makes a section 11(1) costs order.

(2) Where the amount (if any) which the client is required to pay under the section 11(1) costs order, together with the amount which the Commission is required to pay under any costs order against the Commission, is less than the full costs, the receiving party may, on the ground set out in paragraph (4)(a), apply to the court for an order varying the amount which the client is required to pay under the section 11(1) costs order.

(3) Where the court has not specified the amount to be paid under the section 11(1) costs order, and the receiving party has not, within the time limit in regulation 10(2), applied to have that amount determined in accordance with regulation 10, the receiving party may, on any of the grounds set out in paragraph (4), apply for a determination of the amount that the client is required to pay.

(4) The grounds referred to in paragraphs (2) and (3) are the grounds that:
(a) there has been a significant change in the client's circumstances since the date of the order;
(b) material additional information as to the client's financial resources is available, and that information could not with reasonable diligence have been obtained by the receiving party in time to make an application in accordance with regulation 10; or
(c) there were other good reasons justifying the receiving party's failure to make an application within the time limit in regulation 10(2).

(5) Any application under paragraph (2) or (3) shall be made by the receiving party within six years from the date on which the section 11(1) costs order is first made.

(6) On any application under paragraph (2), the order may be varied as the court thinks fit, but the amount of costs ordered (excluding any costs ordered to be paid under paragraph (9)) shall not exceed the amount of the full costs as stated in any previous order of the court.

(7) When the amount which the client is required to pay under the section 11(1) costs order has been determined under regulation 9(2)(a), and the receiving party applies under paragraph (2) for an order varying that amount:
(a) the receiving party shall file with the application under paragraph (2) his bill of costs, which shall comply with any requirements of relevant rules of court relating to the form and content of a bill of costs where the court is assessing a party's costs; and
(b) the court shall, when determining the application, assess the full costs.

(8) Where the receiving party has received funded services in relation to the proceedings, the Commission may make an application under paragraph (2) or paragraph (3), and:
(a) when making the application the Commission shall file with the court a statement of the receiving party's costs or, if those costs have not been assessed, the receiving party's bill of costs; and
(b) paragraphs (4) to (6) shall apply to that application as if 'the Commission' were substituted for 'the receiving party' in those paragraphs.

(9) The amount of costs to be determined under this regulation may include the costs incurred in relation to an application made under this regulation.

*Rights to appear*

**13**—(1) The Regional Director may appear at:
  (a) any hearing in relation to which notice has been given under regulation 10(3)(c);
  (b) the hearing of any appeal under regulation 11(4); or
  (c) the hearing of any application under regulation 12(8).

(2) The Regional Director may, instead of appearing under paragraph (1), give evidence in the form of a written statement to the court, verified by a statement of truth.

(3) The Regional Director shall file with the court any statement under paragraph (2), and serve a copy on the receiving party, not less than seven days before the hearing to which it relates.

PART III

PROPERTY AND COSTS RECOVERED FOR A FUNDED CLIENT

*Application of this Part*

**14**—(1) In this Part:
  'the awarded sum' means the amount of costs to be paid in accordance with a client's costs order or a client's costs agreement;
  'client's costs order' and 'client's costs agreement' mean, respectively, an order and an agreement that another party to proceedings or prospective proceedings pay all or part of the costs of a client;
  'Fund' means the Community Legal Service Fund established under section 5 of the Act;
  'the funded sum' means the amount of remuneration payable by the Commission to a supplier for the relevant work under a contract or any other arrangements that determine that supplier's remuneration, including those that apply by virtue of article 4 of the Community Legal Service (Funding) Order 2000; and, where funding is provided by the Commission under a contract which does not differentiate between the remuneration for the client's case and remuneration for other cases, means such part of the remuneration payable under the contract as may be specified in writing by the Commission as being the funded sum;
  'relevant work' means the funded services provided in relation to the dispute or proceedings to which the client's costs order or client's costs agreement relates;
  'remuneration' includes fees and disbursements and value added tax on fees and disbursements;
  'statutory charge' means the charge created by section 10(7) of the Act.

*Amount of costs under client's costs order or client's costs agreement*

**15**—(1) Subject to the following paragraphs of this regulation, the amount of the costs to be paid under a client's costs order or client's costs agreement shall, subject to regulation 16, be determined on the same basis as it would be if the costs were to be paid to a person who had not received funded services.

(2) Subject to paragraph (3), the amount of the awarded sum shall not be limited to the amount of the funded sum by any rule of law which limits the costs recoverable by a party to proceedings to the amount he is liable to pay to his legal representatives.

(3) Paragraph (2) applies only to the extent that the Commission has authorised the supplier under section 22(2)(b) of the Act to take payment for the relevant work other than that funded by the Commission.

*Costs of serving notices and other documents*

**16** The amount of costs to be paid under a client's costs order or client's costs agreement may include costs incurred in filing with the court, or serving on any other party to proceedings, notices or any other documents in accordance with these Regulations, the Financial Regulations or the Funding Code.

*Application of regulations 18 to 24*

**17**—(1)  Regulations 18 to 24 apply only where funded services have been provided under a certificate.

(2)  If the client is no longer being represented by a solicitor, all money to which regulation 18(1) applies shall be paid (or repaid) to the Commission, and all references in regulations 18(1) and 19 to the client's solicitor shall be construed as references to the Commission.

*Money recovered to be paid to solicitor*

**18**—(1)  Subject to the following paragraphs of this regulation, and to regulation 17(2), all money payable to or recovered by a client in connection with a dispute by way of damages, costs or otherwise, whether or not proceedings were begun, and whether under an order of the court or an agreement or otherwise, shall be paid to the client's solicitor, and only the client's solicitor shall be capable of giving a good discharge for that money.

(2)  Paragraph (1) shall not apply to:

(a)  any periodical payment of maintenance; or

(b)  any money recovered or preserved by a client in any proceedings which:

　　(i)  has been paid into, or remains in, court, and is invested for the client's benefit; and

　　(ii)  under regulation 50 of the Financial Regulations, is not subject to the statutory charge.

(3)  Where the client's solicitor has reason to believe that an attempt may be made to circumvent the provisions of paragraph (1), he shall inform the Commission immediately.

*Notice to third parties*

**19**—(1)  Where money is payable under regulation 18, and that money is payable by a trustee in bankruptcy, a trustee or assignee of a deed of arrangement, a liquidator of a company in liquidation, a trustee of a pension fund or any other third party ('the third party') the client's solicitor shall send to the third party notice that funded services have been funded for the client by the Commission.

(2)  Notice under paragraph (1) shall operate as a request by the client that money payable under regulation 18 be paid to his solicitor, and shall be a sufficient authority for that purpose.

*Solicitor to pay money recovered to Commission*

**20**—(1)  The client's solicitor shall forthwith:

(a)  inform the Regional Director of any money or other property recovered or preserved, and send him a copy of the order or agreement by virtue of which the property was recovered or preserved;

(b)  subject to the following paragraphs of this regulation, pay to the Commission all money or other property received by him under regulation 18.

(2)  Paragraph (1)(b) shall not apply to any money or other property to which the statutory charge does not apply, by virtue of the Financial Regulations.

(3) Where he considers it essential to protect the client's interests or welfare, the Regional Director shall pay, or direct the client's solicitor to pay, to the client any money received by way of any interim payment made in accordance with an order made under CPR rule 25.6, or in accordance with an agreement having the same effect as such an order.

(4) The Regional Director may direct the client's solicitor to:

(a) pay to the Commission under paragraph (1)(b) only such sums as, in the Regional Director's opinion, should be retained by the Commission in order to safeguard its interests; and

(b) pay any other money to the client.

(5) Where the solicitor pays money to the Commission in accordance with this regulation, he shall identify what sums relate respectively to:

(a) costs;

(b) damages;

(c) interest on costs; and

(d) interest on damages.

*Postponement of statutory charge*

**21—**(1) In this regulation:

'conveyancer' means a solicitor or any other person who lawfully provides conveyancing services;

'family proceedings' means proceedings which arise out of family relationships, including proceedings in which the welfare of children is determined. Family proceedings also include all proceedings under any one or more of the following:

(a) the Matrimonial Causes Act 1973;

(b) the Inheritance (Provision for Family and Dependants) Act 1975;vvvvv vvv vv

(c) the Adoption Act 1976;

(d) the Domestic Proceedings and Magistrates' Courts Act 1978;

(e) Part III of the Matrimonial and Family Proceedings Act 1984;

(f) Parts I, II and IV of the Children Act 1989;

(g) Part IV of the Family Law Act 1996; and

(h) the inherent jurisdiction of the High Court in relation to children;

'purchase money' means money recovered or preserved by the client in family proceedings which, by virtue of an order of the court or an agreement, is to be used to purchase a home to be used by the client or the client's dependants, and 'the purchased property' means the property purchased or to be purchased with that money.

(2) The following paragraphs of this regulation apply, and (subject to paragraph (6)) regulation 20(1)(b) does not apply, where the Commission decides to postpone enforcement of the statutory charge under regulation 52 of the Financial Regulations.

(3) The solicitor may release the purchase money to the seller or the seller's representative on completion of the purchase of the purchased property; and shall as soon as practicable provide the Commission with sufficient information to enable it to protect its interest in accordance with regulation 52(1)(c) of the Financial Regulations.

(4) The client's solicitor may release the purchase money to a conveyancer acting for the client in the purchase of the purchased property, if he is satisfied that adequate steps have been, or will be, taken to protect the interests of the Commission.

(5) The steps referred to in paragraph (4) shall include, but are not limited to, the securing of an undertaking from the conveyancer referred to in that paragraph to:

(a)  provide the information referred to in paragraph (3); and

(b)  repay the purchase money under paragraph (6).

(6) Where the purchase of the purchased property has not been completed within 12 months after the date of the Commission's decision referred to in paragraph (2), or such longer period as the Commission considers reasonable, regulation 20(1)(b) shall apply and the purchase money shall accordingly be repaid to the Commission.

*Retention and payment out of money by the Commission*

**22**—(1) The Commission shall deal with the money paid to it under this Part in accordance with this regulation.

(2) The Commission shall retain:

(a)  an amount equal to the costs incurred in taking steps under regulation 23;

(b)  an amount equal to that part of the funded sum already paid to the supplier in respect of the relevant work; and

(c)  where costs are paid to the Commission together with interest, an amount equal to that interest, less the amount of any interest payable to the supplier under paragraph (3)(b)(ii).

(3) The Commission shall pay to the supplier:

(a)  any outstanding amount of the funded sum payable to him in respect of the relevant work;

(b)  where costs are ordered or agreed to be paid to the client, and those costs are received by the Commission, and those costs (less any amount retained under paragraph (2)(a) or payable under paragraph (5)) exceed the funded sum:

    (i)  an amount equal to the amount of the excess; and

    (ii)  where those costs are paid to the Commission together with interest, an amount equal to the interest attributable to the excess referred to in sub-paragraph (i).

(4) Paragraph (5) applies where a solicitor has acted on behalf of the client in proceedings before that client receives funded services in respect of the same proceedings, or has a lien on any documents necessary to proceedings to which a client is a party, and has handed them over subject to the lien, but applies only so far as is consistent with the express terms of any contract between the Commission and the solicitor.

(5) Where the solicitor referred to in paragraph (4) gives the Commission written notice that this paragraph applies, the Commission shall pay to that solicitor the costs to which that solicitor would have been entitled if those costs had been assessed on an indemnity basis.

(6) Where the amount of costs payable under paragraph (5) have not been assessed by the court, they may instead be assessed by the Commission.

(7) Where the amount received by the Commission, less any amount retained under paragraph (2)(a), is insufficient to meet the funded sum and any sum payable under paragraph (5), the Commission shall apportion the amount received proportionately between the two.

(8) The Commission shall pay all the money paid to it under this Part, which is not paid or retained under paragraphs (2) to (5), to the client.

*Enforcement of orders etc in favour of client*

**23**—(1) Where, in relation to any dispute to which a client is a party, whether or not proceedings are begun:

(a)  an order or agreement is made providing for the recovery or preservation of property by the client (whether for himself or any other person); or

(b)  there is a client's costs order or client's costs agreement the Commission may take any steps, including proceedings in its own name, as may be necessary to enforce or give effect to that order or agreement.

(2) A client may, with the consent of the Regional Director, take proceedings to give effect to an order or agreement under which he is entitled to recover or preserve money or other property.

(3) Subject to paragraph (4), the client's solicitor may take proceedings for the recovery of costs where a client's costs order or a client's costs agreement has been made.

(4) Where the client's costs order or client's costs agreement relates wholly or partly to costs incurred in carrying out work which is remunerated, or to be remunerated, in the funded sum, but those costs have not been reimbursed by payment from any other party in favour of the client, the solicitor shall require the consent of the Regional Director before taking proceedings to which paragraph (3) refers.

(5) Where the Commission takes proceedings, it may authorise any person to make a statement, file a proof or take any other step in the proceedings in its name.

(6) The costs incurred by the Commission in taking any step to enforce an order or agreement where paragraph (1) applies shall be a first charge on any property or sum so recovered.

\*   \*   \*   \*   \*

## LEGAL SERVICES COMMISSION (DISCLOSURE OF INFORMATION) REGULATIONS 2000

**Dated** 18 February 2000

**SI 2000 No 442**

**1   Citation and commencement** These Regulations may be cited as the Legal Services Commission (Disclosure of Information) Regulations 2000 and shall come into force on 1st April 2000.

**2   Interpretation** In these Regulations:
'the Act' means the Access to Justice Act 1999;
'Commission' means the Legal Services Commission established under section 1 of the Act; and
'supplier' means any person or body who provides services funded by the Commission to a client.

**3**   The Commission may require a supplier to provide to any person authorised by the Commission to request it such information or documentation as it may from time to time require for the purpose of discharging its functions under the Act or the Legal Aid Act 1988.

**4**   Where:
(a) information or documentation is required in accordance with regulation 3; and
(b) such information or documentation relates to any service provided to a client or former client of the supplier who is or was in receipt of services funded by the Commission
the relationship between or rights of the supplier and client, or any privilege arising out of such relationship, does not preclude the supplier from disclosing such information or documentation.

**5**    For the purpose of providing information in order to enable the Commission to discharge its functions under the Act or under the Legal Aid Act 1988, any party may disclose to any person authorised by the Commission to receive them communications in relation to the proceedings concerned sent to or by the supplier, whether or not they are expressed to be 'without prejudice'.

**[6**    The Commission shall not disclose to the prosecuting authority any information which:

(a)  is in connection with the defence of the individual concerned; and

(b)  may be used for the purposes of the prosecution of that case.]

**Note.**  Para 6 inserted by SI 2001 No 857 as from 2 April 2001.

## COMMUNITY LEGAL SERVICE (FINANCIAL) REGULATIONS 2000

**Dated**  18 February 2000

**SI 2000 No 516**

PART I

GENERAL

*Citation and commencement*

**1**    These Regulations may be cited as the Community Legal Service (Financial) Regulations 2000 and shall come into force on 1st April 2000.

*Interpretation*

**2—**(1)  In these Regulations, unless the context requires otherwise:

'the Act' means the Access to Justice Act 1999;

'application' means an application to receive funded services, made by or on behalf of a client in accordance with the Funding Code;

'assessing authority' means:

(a)  the Commission, where the client's eligibility under regulation 5(6) is being assessed;

(b)  otherwise, the supplier;

'certificate' means a certificate issued under the Funding Code certifying a decision to fund services for the client;

'client' means an individual who applies for or receives funded services and, in the case of actual or contemplated proceedings, is a party or prospective party to the proceedings;

\*    \*    \*    \*    \*

'Commission' means the Legal Services Commission established under section 1 of the Act;

'CPR' means the Civil Procedure Rules 1998, and a reference to a Part or a rule, prefixed by 'CPR', means the Part or rule so numbered in the CPR;

'disposable income' and 'disposable capital' mean, respectively, the income and capital of the person concerned, calculated in accordance with regulations 16 to 37;

'family proceedings' means proceedings which arise out of family relationships, including proceedings in which the welfare of children is determined. Family proceedings also include all proceedings under any one or more of the following:

(a)  the Matrimonial Causes Act 1973;

   (b) the Inheritance (Provision for Family and Dependants) Act 1975;
   (c) the Adoption Act 1976;
   (d) the Domestic Proceedings and Magistrates' Courts Act 1978;
   (e) Part III of the Matrimonial and Family Proceedings Act 1984;
   (f) Parts I, II and IV of the Children Act 1989;
   (g) Part IV of the Family Law Act 1996; and
   (h) the inherent jurisdiction of the High Court in relation to children;
'Funding Code' means the code approved under section 9 of the Act;
'funded services' means services which are provided directly for a client and
   funded for that client by the Commission as part of the Community Legal
   Service under sections 4 to 11 of the Act;
['Multi-Party Action' means any action or actions, in which a number of clients
   have causes of action, which involve common issues of fact or law arising out
   of the same cause or event;]
'partner' except in the expression 'partner in a business' means a person with
   whom the person concerned lives as a couple, and includes a person with
   whom the person concerned is not currently living but from whom he is not
   living separate and apart;

* * * * *

'person concerned' means the person:
   (a) whose eligibility is to be assessed; or
   (b) whose resources are to be treated as the resources of the client under
      these Regulations;
'solicitor' means solicitor or other person who is an authorised litigator within the
   meaning of section 119(1) of the Courts and Legal Services Act 1990; and
'supplier' means the solicitor, mediator or agency being requested to provide or
   providing funded services to the client;
['wider public interest' means the potential of proceedings to produce real
   benefits for individuals other than the client (other than any general
   benefits which normally flow from proceedings of the type in question).]
   (2) References to the levels of service listed in paragraph (3) shall be construed
as references to the application for, or receipt or provision of, those levels of
service in accordance with the Funding Code.
   (3) The levels of service referred to in paragraph (2) are:
   (a) Legal Help;
   (b) Help at Court;
   (c) Legal Representation;
   (d) Family Mediation;
   (e) Help with Mediation;
   (f) General Family Help;
   (g) Support Funding;
   (h) Litigation Support.
**Note.** Definition of 'wider public interest' added by SI 2001 No 3663 as from 3 December
2001. Definition of 'Multi-Party Action' added by SI 2003 No 650 as from 7 April 2003.

PART II

ELIGIBILITY, ASSESSMENT AND CONTRIBUTIONS

*Financial eligibility*

**3**—(1) The following services shall be available without reference to the client's
financial resources:
   (a) services consisting exclusively of the provision of general information about
      the law and legal system and the availability of legal services;

(b) *initial* legal advice consisting of such amount of Legal Help [, and Help at Court] as is authorised under a contract to be provided without reference to the client's financial resources;

(c) Legal Representation in proceedings under the Children Act 1989 applied for by or on behalf of:

    (i) a child in respect of whom an application is made for an order under:

        (a) section 31 (care or supervision order);

        (b) section 43 (child assessment order);

        (c) section 44 (emergency protection order); or

        (d) section 45 (extension or discharge of emergency protection order);

    (ii) a parent of such a child, or a person with parental responsibility for such a child within the meaning of the Children Act 1989; or

    (iii) a child who is brought before a court under section 25 (use of accommodation for restricting liberty) who is not, but wishes to be, legally represented before the court;

(d) Legal Representation in proceedings related to any proceedings in sub-paragraph (c) which are being heard together with those proceedings or in which an order is being sought as an alternative to an order in those proceedings;

(e) Legal Representation in proceedings before a Mental Health Review Tribunal under the Mental Health Act 1983, where the client's case or application to the Tribunal is, or is to be, the subject of the proceedings;

(f) Legal Representation by a solicitor in England and Wales of a person whose application under the Hague Convention or the European Convention has been submitted to the Central Authority in England and Wales under section 3(2) or 14(2) of the Child Abduction and Custody Act 1985; and

(g) Legal Representation of a person who:

    (i) appeals to a magistrates' court against the registration of, or the refusal to register, a maintenance order made in a Hague Convention country under the Maintenance Orders (Reciprocal Enforcement) Act 1972; or

    (ii) applies for the registration of a judgment under section 4 of the Civil Jurisdiction and Judgments Act 1982 [;or]

    (iii) applies for the registration of a judgment under Council Regulation (EC) No 44/2001 of 22nd December 2000 on jurisdiction and the recognition and enforcement of judgments in civil and commercial matters]; [or

    (iv) applies for the registration of a judgment under Council Regulation (EC) No 1347/2000 of 29th May 2000 on jurisdiction and the recognition and enforcement of judgments in matrimonial matters and in matters of parental responsibility for children of both spouses.]

and who benefited from complete or partial assistance with, or exemption from, costs or expenses in the country in which the maintenance order was made or the judgment was given; [or

[(h) such services as are funded through grants under section 6(3)(c) of the Act except where the terms of the grant provide otherwise.]

(2) In this regulation:

'Central Authority' has the same meaning as in sections 3 and 14 of the Child Abduction and Custody Act 1985;

'European Convention' means the convention defined in section 12(1) of the Child Abduction and Custody Act 1985;

'Hague Convention' means the convention defined in section 1(1) of the Child Abduction and Custody Act 1985;

'Hague Convention country' has the same meaning as in the Reciprocal
Enforcement of Maintenance Orders (Hague Convention Countries) Order
1993; and

'the Maintenance Orders (Reciprocal Enforcement) Act 1972' means that Act as
applied with such exceptions, adaptations and modifications as are specified
in the Reciprocal Enforcement of Maintenance Orders (Hague Convention
Countries) Order 1993.

**Note.** Word in italics in para (1)(b), words in square brackets inserted and para (h) added
by SI 2001 No 2997 as from 1 October 2001. Para (g)(iii) added by SI 2001 No 3929 as from 1
March 2002. Para (g)(iv) added by SI 2001 No 709 as from 8 April 2002.

**4**—*(1) Subject to regulation 3, the assessing authority to which an application is made shall
determine the financial eligibility of the client in accordance with these Regulations.*

*(2) Where the assessing authority is satisfied that the client is directly or indirectly in
receipt of a qualifying benefit mentioned in paragraph (3), it shall take his disposable income
and disposable capital as not exceeding the relevant sums specified in paragraph (4).*

*(3) The following are qualifying benefits for the purposes of paragraph (2):*

*(a) income support;*

*(b) income-based jobseeker's allowance;*

*(c) working families' tax credit, provided that the amount (if any) to be deducted under
section 128(2)(b) of the Social Security Contributions and Benefits Act 1992 has been
determined at not more than £70 per week; and*

*(d) disabled person's tax credit, provided that the amount (if any) to be deducted under
section 129(5)(b) of the Social Security Contributions and Benefits Act 1992 has been
determined at not more than £70 per week.*

*(4) The relevant sums mentioned in paragraph (2) are as follows:*

*(a) where eligibility is being assessed under regulation 5(2) and the client is in receipt of
any qualifying benefit, the disposable income figure in that regulation;*

*(b) where eligibility is being assessed under paragraphs (3) or (5) of regulation 5 and the
client is in receipt of any qualifying benefit, the disposable income figure in those
paragraphs;*

*(c) where eligibility is being assessed under paragraphs (3) or (5) of regulation 5 and the
client is in receipt of a qualifying benefit in paragraph 3(a) or (b), the disposable
capital figure in those paragraphs;*

*(d) where eligibility is being assessed under regulation 5(6) and the client is in receipt of a
qualifying benefit in paragraph 3(a) or (b), the disposable income figure in regulation
38(2)(a) and the disposable capital figure in regulation 38(2)(b).*

[**4**—(1) Subject to regulation 3, the assessing authority to which an application is
made shall determine the financial eligibility of the client in accordance with these
Regulations.

(2) Where the assessing authority is satisfied that the client is in receipt, directly
or indirectly, of income support or *income-based jobseeker's allowance* [income-based
jobseeker's allowance or guarantee state pension credit (under section 1(3)(a) of
the State Pension Credit Act 2002),] it shall take his disposable income and, in
relation to paragraphs (3)(b) and (c), disposable capital, as not exceeding the
relevant sums specified in paragraph (3).

(3) The relevant sums mentioned in paragraph (2) are as follows:

(a) where eligibility is being assessed under regulation 5(2), the disposable
income figure in that paragraph;

(b) where eligibility is being assessed under regulation 5(3), the disposable
income and capital figures in that paragraph;

(c) where eligibility is being assessed under regulation 5(5) or 5(6), the
disposable income figure in regulation 38(2)(a), that is, £259 [£263], and
the disposable capital figure in regulation 38(2)(b).]

**Note.** Regulation 4 in italics omitted and reg 4 in square brackets substituted by SI 2001 No 3663 as from 3 December 2001. Amount in italics in sub-para (c) omitted and amount in square brackets substituted by SI 2002 No 709 as from 8 April 2002. Words in italics in para (2) omitted and words in square brackets inserted by SI 2003 No 650 as from 6 October 2003.

**5**—*(1)   This regulation has effect subject to regulations 3 and 4.*

*(2)   A client is eligible for Legal Help, Help at Court, and Legal Representation before the Immigration Appeal Tribunal and an adjudicator if his weekly disposable income does not exceed £84 [£87], and his disposable capital does not exceed £1,000.*

*(3)   A client is eligible for Family Mediation if his weekly disposable income does not exceed £180 [£186] and his disposable capital does not exceed £3,000.*

*(4)   A client who is eligible for Family Mediation under paragraph (3) shall also be eligible for Help with Mediation in relation to family mediation.*

*(5)   A client is eligible for Legal Representation in respect of family proceedings before a magistrates' court, other than proceedings under the Children Act 1989 or Part IV of the Family Law Act 1996, if his weekly disposable income does not exceed £180 [£186], and his disposable capital does not exceed £3,000.*

*(6)   A client is eligible for Legal Representation (other than as provided for in paragraphs (2) and (5)), General Family Help and Support Funding [, and for such other services as are required or authorised by the Lord Chancellor to be funded under section 6(8) of the Act,] if his disposable income does not exceed £8,067 [£8196] per year, but a person may be refused such services where:*

   (i)   *his disposable capital exceeds £6,750; and*

   (ii)   *it appears to the assessing authority that the probable cost of the funded services to which the application relates would not exceed the contribution payable by him under regulation 38.*

**Note.** Figures in repealed reg 5 in square brackets in paras (2)-(6) substituted by SI 2001 No 950 as from 9 April 2001. Words in square brackets in para (6) added by SI 2001 No 2997 as from 1 October 2001.

**[5**—(1)   This regulation has effect subject to regulations 3, 4 and 5A.

(2)   A client is eligible for Legal Help, Help at Court, and Legal Representation before the Immigration Appeal Tribunal and an adjudicator if his monthly disposable income does not exceed *£601* [*£611*] [£621], and his disposable capital does not exceed £3,000.

(3)   A client is eligible for Family Mediation if his monthly disposable income does not exceed *£683* [*£695*] [£707]and his disposable capital does not exceed £8,000.

(4)   A client who is eligible for Family Mediation under paragraph (3) shall also be eligible for Help with Mediation in relation to family mediation.

(5)   A client is eligible for Legal Representation in respect of family proceedings before a magistrates' court, other than proceedings under the Children Act 1989 or Part IV of the Family Law Act 1996, if his disposable income does not exceed *£683* [*£695*] [£707] per month, but a person may be refused such services where:

   (a)   his disposable capital exceeds £8,000; and

   (b)   it appears to the assessing authority that the probable cost of the funded services to which the application relates would not exceed the contribution payable by him under regulation 38.

(6)   A client is eligible for Legal Representation (other than as provided for in paragraphs (2) and (5)), General Family Help and Support Funding, and for such other services as are required or authorised by the Lord Chancellor to be funded under section 6(8) of the Act, if his disposable income does not exceed *£683* [*£695*] [£707] per month, but a person may be refused such services where:

   (a)   his disposable capital exceeds £8,000; and

   (b)   it appears to the assessing authority that the probable cost of the funded services to which the application relates would not exceed the contribution payable to him under regulation 38.]

**Note.** Figures in paras (2), (3), (5) and (6) further increased to those in square brackets by SI 2003 No 651 as from 7 April 2003.

**[5A—**(1) For the purposes of this regulation, 'gross income' means total income from all sources, before any deductions are made.

(2) This regulation does not apply to any applications to which regulation 4(2) applies.

(3) In relation to the calculation of gross income:

(a) regulations 6, 10, 11, 12 and 15 shall apply as if 'gross income' were substituted for 'disposable income' each time it appears; and

(b) regulations 21 and 23 shall not apply.

(4) Subject to regulation 3, where the gross monthly income of the person concerned exceeds £2,000 [*£2,034*] [*£2,250*] [£2,288], the assessing authority shall refuse any application for funded services.]

[(5) Where the person concerned has more than four dependant children in respect of whom he receives child benefit, the sum referred to in paragraph (4) shall be increased by £145 in respect of the fifth and each subsequent child.]

**Note.** Regulation 5 in italics omitted and regs 5, 5A and 5B substituted by SI 2001 No 3663 as from 3 December 2001. Figures in italics in regs 5 and 5A replaced by figures in square brackets by SI 2002 No 709 as from 8 April 2002. Figures in reg 5A(4) further amended and para (5) added by SI 2002 No 1766 as from 5 August 2002. Figure in reg 5A(4) further increased by SI 2003 No 650 as from 7 April 2003.

*[Waiver of eligibility limit in multi-party actions of wider public interest*

**5B—***(1) For the purposes of this regulation, a Multi-Party Action means any action or actions in which a number of clients have causes of action which involve common issues of fact or law arising out of the same cause or event.*

(2) Paragraph (3) applies where:

(a) the Commission funds Legal Representation or Support Funding in a Multi-Party Action which it considers has a significant wider public interest; and

(b) *the Commission considers it cost-effective to fund those services for a specified claimant or claimants, but not for other claimants or potential claimants who might benefit from the litigation.*

[(b) the Commission considers it cost-effective to fund those services only in relation to specific issues within the Multi-Party Action.]

(3) Where this paragraph applies, the Commission may, if it considers it equitable to do so, disapply the eligibility limits in regulations 5(6) and 5A.]

**Note.** Regulation 5 in italics omitted and regs 5, 5A and 5B substituted by SI 2001 No 3663 as from 3 December 2001. Words in italics in reg 5B omitted and words in square brackets substituted by SI 2003 No 650 as from 7 April 2003.

**[5C]—**[(1) This regulation applies to an application for the funding of legal representation to provide advocacy at an inquest into the death of a member of the immediate family of the client.

(2) Where this regulation applies, the Commission may, if it considers it equitable to do so, request the Secretary of State to disapply the eligibility limits in regulations 5(6) and 5A.

3) In considering whether to make such a request, the Commission shall have regard in particular to any applicable Convention rights under Article 2 of Schedule 1 to the Human Rights Act 1998.

(4) On receipt of a request under paragraph (2) the Secretary of State may, if he thinks fit, disapply the eligibility limits.]

**Note.** Inserted by SI 2003 No 2838, reg 3 as from 1 December 1003.

**[5D]—**[(1) This regulation applies to an application to the Commission by a client domiciled or habitually resident in another Member State for the funding of services in relation to a cross-border dispute.

(2) Where this regulation applies, the Commission must—

(a) disapply the relevant eligibility limits in regulations 5 and 5A if the client proves that he is unable to pay the cost of proceedings in England and Wales in relation to the dispute as a result of differences in the cost of living between the client's Member State of domicile or habitual residence and England and Wales; and

(b) waive part or all of any contributions payable under regulation 38, if and to such extent as the client proves that he is unable to pay them as a result of such differences in the cost of living.

(3) In this regulation—

'cross-border dispute' means a dispute where a client is domiciled or habitually resident in a Member State other than the Member State where the court is sitting or where the decision is to be enforced;

'Member State' means a member state of the European Union except Denmark.

(4) For the purposes of this regulation the Member State in which a client is domiciled shall be determined in accordance with Article 59 of Council Regulation (EC) No 44/2001 of 22 December 2000 on jurisdiction and the recognition and enforcement of judgments in civil and commercial matters.]

**Note.** Inserted as from 30 November 2004 (except in relation to applications for services made to the Commission before that date) by SI 2004 No 2899, reg 2.

*Assessment of resources*

**6** Where an application is made, the client shall provide the assessing authority with the information necessary to enable it to:

(a) determine whether he satisfies the conditions set out in regulation 4; and

(b) calculate, where relevant, his disposable income and disposable capital and those of any other person concerned.

**7—***(1) The assessing authority shall:*

*(a) subject to regulation 4(2), calculate the disposable income and disposable capital of the person concerned in accordance with regulations 16 to 37; and*

*(b) calculate any contribution payable in accordance with regulations 38 and 39.*

*(2) When calculating disposable income for the purposes of regulation 5(2), (3) or (5), the period of calculation shall be the seven days ending on the date of the application.*

*(3) When calculating disposable income for the purposes of regulation 5(6), the period of calculation shall be the 12 months starting on the date of the application or such other 12 month period as the assessing authority considers appropriate, but if there is no other practicable means of ascertaining it, the income may be taken to be the income received during the previous year.*

*(4) Where the assessing authority calculates that a client has disposable income or disposable capital of an amount which makes him ineligible to receive funded services, it shall refuse the application.*

**[7—**(1) The assessing authority shall:

(a) subject to regulation 4(2), calculate the disposable income and disposable capital of the person concerned in accordance with regulations 16 to 37;

(b) calculate the gross income of the person concerned in accordance with regulation 5A; and

(c) calculate any contribution payable in accordance with regulations 38 and 39.

(2) When calculating:

(a) disposable income for the purposes of regulation 5(2), (3), (5) or (6); or

(b) gross income for the purposes of regulation 5A
the period of calculation shall be one month.

(3) For the purposes of this regulation and regulation 15, one month means the period of one calendar month which ends on the date on which the application is made, or such other equivalent period as the Commission considers appropriate.

(4) Where the assessing authority calculates that a client has disposable income or disposable capital of an amount which makes him ineligible to receive funded services, it shall refuse the application.]

**Note.** Regulation 7 in italics omitted and reg 7 in square brackets substituted by SI 2001 No 3663 as from 3 December 2001.

**8** The supplier shall not provide any funded services to the client prior to the assessment of resources in accordance with regulation 7 other than:
(a) in accordance with Funding Code procedures; or
(b) where authorisation to do so is given by the Commission in a contract.

**9** Where the assessing authority is the supplier, any question arising under regulations 10 to 41 shall be decided by the supplier and the supplier, in deciding any such question, shall have regard to any guidance which may from time to time be given by the Commission as to the application of these Regulations.

*Application in representative, fiduciary or official capacity*

**10** Where the client is acting only in a representative, fiduciary or official capacity, the assessing authority shall, in calculating his disposable income and disposable capital, and the amount of any contribution to be made:
(a) assess the value of any property or estate or the amount of any fund out of which he is entitled to be indemnified; and
(b) unless it considers that he might benefit from the proceedings, disregard his personal resources.

*Resources of other persons*

**11**—(1) Subject to paragraph (2), in calculating the disposable income and disposable capital of the client, the resources of his partner shall be treated as his resources.

(2) The resources of the client's partner shall not be treated as his resources if he has a contrary interest in the dispute in respect of which the application is made.

(3) Except where eligibility is being assessed under regulation 5(6), where the client is a child the resources of a parent, guardian or any other person who is responsible for maintaining him, or who usually contributes substantially to his maintenance, shall be treated as his resources, unless, having regard to all the circumstances, including the age and resources of the child and any conflict of interest, it appears inequitable to do so.

(4) Where it appears to the assessing authority that:
(a) another person is or has been [or is likely to be,] substantially maintaining the person concerned, or
(b) any of the resources of another person have been [or are likely to be] made available to the person concerned,
the assessing authority may treat all or any part of the resources of that other person as the resources of the person concerned [, and may assess or estimate the value of those resources as well as it is able].

(5) In this regulation and regulation 12, 'person' includes a company, partnership, body of trustees and any body of persons, whether corporate or not corporate.

**Note** Words in square brackets in para (4) added by SI 2001 No 2997 as from 1 October 2001.

*Deprivation or conversion of resources*

**12** If it appears to the assessing authority that the person concerned has, with intent to reduce the amount of his disposable income or disposable capital, whether for the purpose of making himself eligible to receive funded services, reducing his liability to pay a contribution, or otherwise:

    (a)  directly or indirectly deprived himself of any resources,

    (b)  transferred any resources to another person, or

    (c)  converted any part of his resources into resources which under these Regulations are to be wholly or partly disregarded,

the resources which he has so deprived himself of, transferred or converted shall be treated as part of his resources or as not so converted as the case may be.

*Duty to report change in financial circumstances*

**13** The client shall forthwith inform the assessing authority of any change in his financial circumstances (or those of any other person concerned) [of which he is, or should reasonably be, aware,] which has occurred since any assessment of his resources, and which might affect the terms on which the client was assessed as eligible to receive funded services.

**Note.** Words in square brackets inserted by SI 2001 No 2997 as from 1 October 2001.

*Amendment of assessment due to error or receipt of new information*

**14** Where:

    (a)  it appears to the assessing authority that there has been an error in the assessment of a person's resources or contribution, or in any calculation or estimate upon which such assessment was based, or

    (b)  new information which is relevant to the assessment has come to light,

the assessing authority may make an amended assessment, and may take such steps as appear equitable to give effect to it in relation to any period during which funded services have already been provided.

*Further assessments*

**15** (1) Where the eligibility of the person concerned was assessed under regulation 5(6) and it appears that his circumstances may have altered so that:

    (a)  his [normal] disposable income may have increased by an amount greater than *£750* [£60] or decreased by an amount greater than *£300* [£25]; or

    (b)  his disposable capital may have increased by an amount greater than £750,

the assessing authority shall, subject to paragraph (6), make a further assessment of the person's resources and contribution (if any) in accordance with these Regulations.

(2) For the purposes of the further assessment, the period of calculation shall be the period of *12 months* [one month] following the date of the change of circumstances or such other period of 12 months as the assessing authority considers to be appropriate.

(3) Where a further assessment is made, the amount or value of every resource of a capital nature acquired since the date of the original application shall be ascertained as at the date of receipt of that resource.

(4) Any capital contribution which becomes payable as a result of a further assessment shall be payable in respect of the cost of the funded services, including costs already incurred.

(5) Where a certificate is discharged as a result of a further assessment of

capital, the assessing authority may require a contribution to be paid in respect of costs already incurred.

(6) The assessing authority may decide not to make a further assessment under paragraph (1) if it considers such a further assessment inappropriate, having regard in particular to the period during which funded services are likely to continue to be provided to the client.

**Note.** Words and figures in paras (1) and (2) omitted and words and figures in square brackets substituted by SI 2001 No 3663 as from 3 December 2001.

*Calculation of income*

**16** The income of the person concerned from any source shall be taken to be the income which that person may reasonably expect to receive (in cash or in kind) during the period of calculation [, but where the eligibility of the person concerned is being assessed under regulation 5(6), in calculating such income the Commission may have regard to his average income during such other period as it considers appropriate].

**Note.** Words in square brackets added by SI 2001 No 3663 as from 3 December 2001.

**17—**(1) The income from a trade, business or gainful occupation other than an occupation at a wage or salary shall be deemed to be whichever of the following the assessing authority considers more appropriate and practicable:

   (a) the profits which have accrued or will accrue to the person concerned in respect of the period of calculation; or
   (b) the drawings of the person concerned.

   (2) In calculating the profits under paragraph (1)(a):

   (a) the assessing authority may have regard to the profits of the last accounting period of such trade, business or gainful occupation for which accounts have been prepared; and
   (b) there shall be deducted all sums necessarily expended to earn those profits, but no deduction shall be made in respect of the living expenses of the person concerned or any member of his family or household, except in so far as that person is wholly or mainly employed in that trade or business and such living expenses form part of his remuneration.

**18—**(1) For the purposes of this regulation, 'national insurance contributions' means contributions under Part 1 of the Social Security Contributions and Benefits Act 1992.

   (2) In calculating the disposable income of the person concerned, any income tax and national insurance contributions paid or, in the case of an assessment under regulation 5(6), payable on that income in respect of the period of calculation shall be deducted.

   *(3) For the purposes of regulation 5(6), income tax and national insurance contributions payable shall be calculated in accordance with the statutory provisions in force for the fiscal year in which the application or reassessment is made.*

**Note.** Para (3) omitted by SI 2001 No 3663 as from 3 December 2001.

**19** In calculating the disposable income [or the gross income] of the person concerned, the following payments shall be disregarded:

   (a) under the Social Security Contributions and Benefits Act 1992:
       (i) disability living allowance;
       (ii) attendance allowance paid under section 64 or Schedule 8 paragraphs 4 or 7(2);
       (iii) constant attendance allowance paid under section 104 as an increase to a disablement pension;

       (iv)   any payment made out of the social fund;

     [(v)   invalid care allowance;

      (vi)   council tax benefit;]

(b)  any payment made under the Community Care (Direct Payments) Act 1996 [or under regulations made under section 57 of the Health and Social Care Act 2001 (direct payments)]; and

(c)  so much of any back to work bonus received under section 26 of the Jobseekers Act 1995 as is by virtue of that section to be treated as payable by way of jobseeker's allowance;

[(d) severe disablement allowance paid under the Social Security (Severe Disablement Allowance) Regulations 1984;

(e)  exceptionally severe disablement allowance paid under the Personal Injuries (Civilians) Scheme 1983;

(f)  *widow's and widower's* [all] pensions paid under the Naval, Military and Air Forces etc (Disability and Death) Service Pensions Order 1983; and

(g)  to the extent that it exceeds the relevant figure referred to in regulation 20(2)(b), any financial support paid under an agreement for the care of a foster child entered into in accordance with regulation 5(6) of the Foster Placement (Children) Regulations 1991.]

**Note.** Sub-paras (a)(v) and (vi) and sub-paras (d)–(g) added by SI 2001 No 3663 as from 3 December 2001. Words in italics in sub-para (f) omitted and word in square brackets substituted by SI 2002 No 709 as from 8 April 2002. Words in square brackets in line 1 inserted by SI 2002 No 1766 as from 5 August 2002. In para (b) words in square brackets inserted, in relation to England, by SI 2003 No 762, reg 11(1), Sch 1 as from 8 April 2003. In para (b) words 'or under regulations made under section 57 of the Health and Social Care Act 2001 (direct payments)' in square brackets inserted in relation to England by SI 2003 No 762, reg 11(1), Sch 1 and in relation to Wales by SI 2004 No 1748, reg 12, Sch 2, para 1 as from (in relation to England): 8 April 2003: see SI 2003 No 762, reg 1(1) and as from (in relation to Wales): 1 November 2004: see SI 2004 No 1748, reg 1(b).

**20—**(1) For the purposes of this regulation, 'the Schedule' means Schedule 2 to the Income Support (General) Regulations 1987.

(2) Subject to paragraph (3), in calculating the disposable income of the person concerned there shall be a deduction at or equivalent to the following rates (as they applied at the beginning of the period of calculation):

(a)  in respect of the maintenance of his partner, the difference between the income support allowance for a couple both aged not less than 18 (which is specified in column 2 of paragraph 1(3)(c) of the Schedule), and the allowance for a single person aged not less than 25 (which is specified in column 2 of paragraph 1(1)(e) of the Schedule); and

(b)  in respect of the maintenance of any dependant child or dependant relative of his, where such persons are members of his household:

    (i)  in the case of a dependant child or a dependant relative aged 15 or under at the beginning of the period of calculation, the amount specified at (a) in column 2 in paragraph 2(1) of the Schedule; and

    (ii)  in the case of a dependant child or a dependant relative aged 16 or over at the beginning of the period of calculation, the amount specified at (b) in column 2 in paragraph 2(1) of the Schedule.

(3) The assessing authority may reduce any rate provided by virtue of paragraph (1) by taking into account the income and other resources of the dependent child or dependant relative to such extent as appears to the assessing authority to be equitable.

(4) In ascertaining whether a child is a dependent child or whether a person is a dependant relative for the purposes of this regulation, regard shall be had to their income and other resources.

**21**  Where the person concerned is making and, throughout such period as the

assessing authority considers adequate, has regularly made payments for the maintenance of:
- (a)   a former partner;
- (b)   a child; or
- (c)   a relative

who is not a member of his household, a reasonable amount shall be deducted in respect of such payments.

**22**   *Where eligibility is being assessed under regulation 5(6), in calculating the disposable income of the person concerned from any source, such amount (if any) as the assessing authority considers reasonable, having regard to the nature of the income or to any other circumstances, shall be disregarded.*

**Note.**   Regulation 22 omitted by SI 2001 No 3663 as from 3 December 2001.

**23**—*(1)   This regulation applies only where eligibility is being assessed under regulation 5(6).*

*(2)   In calculating the disposable income of the person concerned, any sums (net of council tax benefit) payable by him in respect of the council tax to which he is liable by virtue of section 6 of the Local Government Finance Act 1992 shall be deducted.*

*(3)   Where the income of the person concerned consists, wholly or partly, of a wage or salary from employment, there shall be deducted:*
- *(a)   the reasonable expenses of travelling to and from his place of employment;*
- *(b)   the amount of any payments reasonably made for membership of a trade union or professional organisation;*
- *(c)   where it would be reasonable to do so, an amount to provide for the care of any dependant child living with the person concerned during the time that person is absent from home by reason of his employment; and*
- *(d)   the amount of any contribution paid, whether under a legal obligation or not, to an occupational pension scheme within the meaning of the Social Security Pensions Act 1975 or to a personal pension scheme within the meaning of the Social Security Act 1986.*

**[23**   Where the income of the person concerned consists, wholly or partly, of a wage or salary from employment, there shall be deducted:
- (a)   the sum of £45 per month; and
- (b)   where it would be reasonable to do so, an amount to provide for the care of any dependant child living with the person concerned during the time that person is absent from home by reason of his employment.]

**Note.**   Regulation 23 in italics omitted and reg 23 in square brackets substituted by SI 2001 No 3663 as from 3 December 2001.

**24**—*(1)   This regulation applies only where eligibility is being assessed under regulation 5(6).*

(2)   Paragraphs (3) to (5) apply only if the person concerned is a householder.

(3)   In calculating the disposable income of the person concerned, the net rent payable by him in respect of his main or only dwelling, or such part of it as is reasonable in the circumstances, shall be deducted; and the assessing authority shall decide which is the main dwelling where the person concerned resides in more than one dwelling.

(4)   For the purpose of this regulation, 'net rent' includes:
- (a)   any *annual* [monthly] rent payable;
- (b)   any *annual* [monthly] instalment (whether of interest or capital) in respect of a mortgage debt or *hereditable security up to a maximum of an amount bearing the same proportion to the amount of the annual instalment as £100,000 bears to the debt secured; and*
- (c)   *a sum in respect of yearly outgoings borne by the householder including, in particular, any water and sewerage charges, and a reasonable allowance towards any necessary expenditure on repairs and insurance.*

(5) In calculating the amount of net rent payable, there shall be deducted:

(a) any housing benefit paid under the Social Security Contributions and Benefits Act 1992;

(b) any proceeds of sub-letting any part of the premises; and

(c) an amount reasonably attributable to any person other than the person concerned, his partner or any dependent, who is accommodated in the premises otherwise than as a sub-tenant.

(6) If the person concerned is not a householder, a reasonable amount in respect of the cost of his living accommodation shall be deducted.

[(7) If no deduction has been made under regulation 20(2), the maximum amount to be deducted under paragraph (3) or, as the case may be, (6) shall be £545.]

**Note.** Para (1) omitted, words in italics in para (4) omitted and words in square brackets substituted and para (7) added by SI 2001 No 3663 as from 3 December 2001.

*Calculation of capital*

**25**   In calculating the disposable capital of the client, the amount or value of the subject matter of the dispute to which the application relates shall be excluded.

**26**   Subject to the provisions of these Regulations, in calculating the disposable capital of the person concerned, the amount or value of every resource of a capital nature belonging to him on the date on which the application is made shall be included.

**27**   In so far as any resource of a capital nature does not consist of money, its value shall be taken to be:

(a) the amount which that resource would realise if sold; or

(b) the value assessed in such other manner as appears to the assessing authority to be equitable.

**28**   Where money is due to the person concerned, whether it is payable immediately or otherwise and whether payment is secured or not, its value shall be taken to be its present value.

**29**   The value to the person concerned of any life insurance or endowment policy shall be taken to be the amount which he could readily borrow on the security of that policy.

**30**   Other than in circumstances which are exceptional having regard in particular to the quantity or value of the items concerned, nothing shall be included in the disposable capital of the person concerned in respect of:

(a) the household furniture and effects of the main or only dwelling house occupied by him;

(b) articles of personal clothing; and

(c) the tools and equipment of his trade, unless they form part of the plant or equipment of a business to which the provisions of regulation 31 apply.

**31**—(1) Where eligibility is being assessed under regulation 5(6), paragraphs (2) to (4) apply.

(2) Where the person concerned is the sole owner of or partner in a business, the value of the business to him shall be taken to be the greater of:

(a) such sum, or his share of such sum, as could be withdrawn from the assets of his business without substantially impairing its profits or normal development; and

(b) such sum as that person could borrow on the security of his interest in the business without substantially injuring its commercial credit.

(3) Where the person concerned stands in relation to a company in a position analogous to that of a sole owner or partner in a business, the assessing authority

may, instead of ascertaining the value of his stocks, shares, bonds or debentures in that company, treat that person as if he were a sole owner or partner in a business and calculate the amount of his capital in respect of that resource in accordance with paragraph (2).

(4) Where the person concerned owns solely, jointly or in common with other persons, any interest on the termination of a prior estate, whether
  (a) legal or equitable;
  (b) vested or contingent;
  (c) in reversion or remainder; and
  (d) whether in real or personal property or in a trust or other fund
the value of such interest shall be calculated in such manner as is both equitable and practicable.

(5) Where eligibility is being assessed other than under regulation 5(6), the sums mentioned in this regulation shall be disregarded.

**32**—(1) In calculating the disposable capital of the person concerned, the value of any interest in land shall be taken to be the amount for which that interest could be sold less the amount of any mortgage debt or hereditable security, subject to the following:
  (a) in calculating the value of his interests, the total amount to be deducted in respect of all mortgage debts or hereditable securities shall not exceed £100,000;
  (b) in making the deductions in sub-paragraph (a), any mortgage debt or hereditable security in respect of the main or only dwelling shall be deducted last; and
  (c) the first £100,000 of the value of his interest (if any) in the main or only dwelling in which he resides, after the application of sub-paragraphs (a) and (b), shall be disregarded.

(2) Where the person concerned resides in more than one dwelling, the assessing authority shall decide which is the main dwelling.

**33**   In calculating the disposable capital of the person concerned, there shall be disregarded:
  (a) so much of any back to work bonus received under section 26 of the Jobseekers Act 1995 as is by virtue of that section to be treated as payable by way of jobseeker's allowance; and
  (b) the whole of any payment made out of the social fund under the Social Security Contributions and Benefits Act 1992 or any arrears of payments made under the Community Care (Direct Payments) Act 1996 [or under regulations made under section 57 of the Health and Social Care Act 2001 (direct payments)].

**Note.** In para (b) words in square brackets inserted, in relation to England, by SI 2003 No 762, reg 11(1), Sch 1 as from 8 April 2003; inserted, in relation to Wales, by SI 2004 No 1748, reg 1(b) as from 1 November 2004.

**34**   *Where eligibility is being assessed under regulation 5(2), (3), or (5), and the person concerned has living with him a partner whose resources are required to be aggregated with his, or one or more dependant children or dependant relatives, a deduction shall be made of £335 in respect of the first, £200 in respect of the second and £100 in respect of each further such person.*

**Note.** Regulation 34 omitted by SI 2001 No 3663 as from 3 December 2001.

**35**—(1) Where eligibility is being assessed under regulation 5(6), the person concerned is *of pensionable age* [aged 60 or over] and his annual disposable income (excluding any net income derived from capital) is less than the *figure prescribed in* *regulation 38(2)(a)* [first figure prescribed in regulation 38(2)(a), that is, *259* [£263]], the amount of capital shown in the following table shall be disregarded:

| annual disposable income (excluding net income derived from capital) | amount of capital disregard |
|---|---|
| up to £370 | £35,000 |
| £371–670 | £30,000 |
| £671–970 | £25,000 |
| £971–1,270 | £20,000 |
| £1,271–1,570 | £15,000 |
| £1,571–1,870 | £10,000 |
| £1,871 and above | £5,000 |

| [monthly disposable income (excluding net income derived from capital | amount of capital disregard |
|---|---|
| up to £25 | £100,000 |
| £26–50 | £90,000 |
| £51–75 | £80,000 |
| £76–100 | £70,000 |
| £101–125 | £60,000 |
| £126–150 | £50,000 |
| £151–175 | £40,000 |
| £176–200 | £30,000 |
| £201–225 | £20,000 |
| £226–250 | £10,000] |

(2)  In paragraph (1) 'pensionable age' means the age of 60.

**Note.** Words in italics omitted and words in square brackets substituted by SI 2001 No 3663 as from 3 December 2001. Figure in para (1) in italics replaced by figure in square brackets by SI 2002 No 709 as from 8 April 2002.

**36**  *Where eligibility is being assessed under regulation 5(6), and under any statute, bond, covenant, guarantee or other instrument the person concerned is under a contingent liability to pay any sum or is liable to pay a sum not yet ascertained, such amount as is reasonably likely to become payable within the period of calculation shall be disregarded.*

**[36**  Where eligibility is being assessed under regulation 5(5) or 5(6), in calculating the disposable capital of the person concerned, any interim payment made to him in any court proceedings may be disregarded.]

**Note.** Regulation 36 in italics omitted and reg 36 in square brackets substituted by SI 2001 No 3663 as from 3 December 2001.

**37**  *Where eligibility is being assessed under regulation 5(6), in calculating the disposable capital of the person concerned, such amount of capital (if any) as the assessing authority considers reasonable, having regard to the nature of the capital or to any other circumstances, may be disregarded.*

**[37**  Where eligibility is being assessed under regulation 5(5) or 5(6), in calculating the disposable capital of the person concerned, any capital resource may be disregarded where:

  (a)  he is restrained from dealing with that resource by order of the court;
  (b)  he has requested the court which made the order to release part or all of that resource for use in connection with the proceedings to which the application for funding relates; and
  (c)  that request has been refused.]

**Note.** Regulation 37 in italics omitted and reg 37 in square brackets substituted by SI 2001 No 3663 as from 3 December 2001.

*Contributions*

**38**—*(1) A person whose eligibility is assessed under regulation 5(5) shall make a weekly contribution of one third of the amount by which his weekly disposable income exceeds £76 [£79].*

*(2) A person whose eligibility is assessed under regulation 5(6) shall make the following contributions:*
- *(a) where his disposable income in the period of calculation exceeds £2,723 [£2,767], monthly contributions throughout the period the certificate is in force of one thirty-sixth of the excess; and*
- *(b) where his disposable capital exceeds £3,000, a contribution of the lesser of the excess and the sum which the assessing authority considers to be the likely maximum cost of the funded services.*

*(3) If, in making an assessment under regulation 5(6), the Commission considers that there are other persons or bodies, including those who have the same or a similar interest to the client or who might benefit from any proceedings, who can reasonably be expected to contribute to the cost of the funded services, or that some other source of funding exists which could be used to contribute to that cost, a reasonable additional amount may be added to the contribution (if any) due from the client.*

*(4) The Commission may subsequently vary the amount of any additional contribution payable under paragraph (3).*

*(5) All contributions shall be payable to the assessing authority.*

**Note.** Figures in square brackets in paras (1)-(2) substituted by SI 2001 No 950 as from 9 April 2001.

*[Contributions*

**38**—(1) Subject to regulation 15, all contributions shall be:
- (a) assessed at the beginning of the case; and
- (b) payable to the assessing authority.

(2) A person whose eligibility is assessed under regulation 5(5) or 5(6) shall make the following contributions:
- (a) where his monthly disposable income exceeds £259 [£263] [£267]:
    - (i) one quarter of any such income between £255 *and* £380 [£259 *and* £386] [£263 and £393] inclusive;
    - (ii) one third of any such income between £381 *and* £505 [£387 *and* £513] [£394 and £522] inclusive; and
    - (iii) one half of his remaining disposable income; and
- (b) where his disposable capital exceeds £3,000, a contribution of the lesser of the excess and the sum which the assessing authority considers to be the likely maximum cost of the funded services.

(3) All contributions under paragraph (2)(a) shall be payable monthly throughout the period the certificate is in force.

(4) All contributions under paragraph (2)(b) shall be payable upon assessment.

(5) Paragraph (6) applies where:
- (a) eligibility is being assessed under regulation 5(5) or 5(6); and
- (b) the Commission considers that:
    - (i) there are other persons or bodies, including those who have the same or a similar interest to the client or who might benefit from any proceedings, who can reasonably be expected to contribute to the cost of the funded services; or
    - (ii) some other source of funding exists which could be used to contribute to that cost.

(6) Where this paragraph applies, the Commission may add a reasonable additional amount to the contribution (if any) due from the client.

(7) The Commission may subsequently vary the amount of any additional contribution payable under paragraph (6).

*(8) Paragraph (9) applies where:*

*(a) the Commission funds Legal Representation or Support Funding in proceedings which it considers to have a significant wider public interest; and*

*(b) the Commission considers it cost-effective to fund those services for a specified claimant or claimants, but not for other claimants or potential claimants who might benefit from the litigation.*

[(8) Paragraph (9) applies where the Commission funds Legal Representation or Support Funding in proceedings which it considers to have a significant wider public interest and either:

(a) the Commission considers it cost-effective to fund those services for a specified claimant or claimants, but not for other claimants or potential claimants who might benefit from the litigation; or

(b) the Commission is funding those services in a Multi-Party Action and it considers it cost-effective to fund those services only in relation to specific issues within that action.]

[(8) Paragraph (9) also applies where the eligibility limits have been disapplied under regulation 5C.]

(9) Where this paragraph applies, the Commission may, if it considers it equitable to do so, waive part or all of the contributions payable under this regulation.]

**Note.** Regulation 38 in italics omitted and reg 38 in square brackets substituted by SI 2001 No 3663 as from 3 December 2001. Figures in para (2)(a) in italics replaced by figures in square brackets by SI 2002 No 709 as from 8 April 2002. Figures in para (2)(a) further amended, para (8) omitted and para (8) in square brackets substituted by SI 2003 No 650 as from 7 April 2003. Para (8A) inserted by SI 2003 No 2838, reg 4 as from 1 December 2003.

**39**   Where more than one certificate is in force in respect of the client at any one time, contributions from income under only one certificate shall be payable, and the Commission may decide under which certificate contributions shall be paid.

**40**—(1) Where a certificate has been discharged or revoked and the contribution made by the client exceeds the net cost of the funded services, the excess shall be refunded to the client.

(2) The net cost of the funded services means the cost paid by the Commission less any costs recovered by the Commission from another party.

(3) Where funding is provided by the Commission under a contract which does not differentiate between the remuneration for the client's case and remuneration for other cases, or require the cost of individual cases to be assessed, the reference in paragraph (2) to the cost paid by the Commission shall be construed as a reference to such part of the remuneration payable under the contract as may be specified in writing by the Commission.

(4) For the purposes of this regulation and regulation 43, where a certificate is discharged the cost of any assessment proceedings under CPR Part 47 or of taxation in the House of Lords shall not be included as part of the cost of the funded services, and the cost of drawing up a bill is not part of the cost of assessment proceedings.

**41**   Where the Commission has revoked a certificate in accordance with Part 15 of the Funding Code:

(a) the client shall pay to the Commission all costs paid or payable by it under the certificate, less any amount already paid by way of contribution; and

(b) the solicitor shall have the right to recover from the client the difference between the amount paid or payable to him by the Commission and the full amount of his costs assessed on the indemnity basis under CPR rule 44.4.

PART III

THE STATUTORY CHARGE

*Calculation of the statutory charge*

**42**   In regulations 43 to 53:

'relevant dispute' means the dispute in connection with which funded services are provided;

'relevant proceedings' means proceedings in connection with which funded services are provided;

'recovered', in relation to property or money, means property or money recovered or preserved by a client, whether for himself or for any other person;

'statutory charge' means the charge created by section 10(7) of the Act in respect of the amount defined in regulation 43; and

'success fee' is defined in accordance with section 58 of the Courts and Legal Services Act 1990.

**43**—(1)  Subject to paragraphs *(3) and (4)* [(3), (4) and (5)], where any money or property is recovered for a client in a relevant dispute or proceedings, the amount of the statutory charge shall be the aggregate of the sums referred to in section 10(7)(a) and (b) of the Act.

(2)  For the purposes of this regulation:

(a)  the sum referred to in section 10(7)(a) shall be defined in accordance with regulation 40(2) to (4), less any contribution paid by the client;

(b)  the sum referred to in section 10(7)(b) shall include:

   (i)   any interest payable under regulation 52; and

   (ii)  any sum which the client has agreed to pay only in specific circumstances under section 10(2)(c) of the Act, including that proportion of any success fee payable by a client in receipt of Litigation Support which he has agreed should be payable to the Commission under the terms of a conditional fee agreement.

(3)  Subject to paragraph (4), the amount of the charge created by section 10(7) of the Act shall not include sums expended by the Commission in funding any of the following services:

(a)  Legal Help;

(b)  Help at Court;

(c)  Family Mediation; or

(d)  Help with Mediation.

(4)  Paragraph (3)(a) and (b) does not apply where the funded services are given in relation to family, clinical negligence or personal injury proceedings or a dispute which may give rise to such proceedings.

[(5)  Where Legal Help is provided as part of the family advice and information networks pilot, the amount of the statutory charge shall not exceed the sum which would have been expended by the Commission, had the Legal Help been provided otherwise than as a part of that pilot.]

**Note.** Para references in para (1) in italics omitted and references in square brackets inserted and para (5) added by SI 2003 No 650 as from 7 April 2003.

*Exemptions from the statutory charge*

**44**—(1)  The charge created by section 10(7) of the Act shall not apply to any of the following:

(a)  any periodical payment of maintenance;

(b)  other than in circumstances which are exceptional having regard in particular to the quantity or value of the items concerned, the client's clothes or household furniture or the tools or implements of his trade;

(c) any sum or sums ordered to be paid under section 5 of the Inheritance (Provision for Family and Dependants) Act 1975 or Part IV of the Family Law Act 1996;

(d) *the first £2,500 of any money or the value of any property recovered by virtue of an order made or deemed to be made under any of the enactments specified in paragraph (2), or an agreement which has the same effect as such an order;*

[(d) other than for the purposes of registration under regulation 52(1)(c), the first £3,000 of any money or the value of any property recovered by virtue of an order made or deemed to be made under any of the enactments specified in paragraph (2), or an agreement which has the same effect as such an order, but where the enforcement of the charge is postponed under regulation 52 this exemption will apply when the amount of the charge is paid;]

(e) one-half of any redundancy payment within the meaning of Part XI of the Employment Rights Act 1996 recovered by the client;

(f) any payment of money made in accordance with an order made by the Employment Appeal Tribunal (excluding an order for costs);

(g) where the statutory charge is in favour of the supplier, the client's main or only dwelling; or

(h) any sum, payment or benefit which, by virtue of any provision of or made under an Act of Parliament, cannot be assigned or charged.

(2) The enactments referred to in paragraph (1)(d) are:

(a) section 23(1)(c) or (f), 23(2), 24, 27(6)(c) or (f), 31(7A) or (7B), or 35 of the Matrimonial Causes Act 1973;

(b) section 2 or 6 of the Inheritance (Provision for Family and Dependants) Act 1975;

(c) section 17 of the Married Women's Property Act 1882;

(d) section 2(1)(b) or (d), 6(1) or (5), or 20(2) of the Domestic Proceedings and Magistrates' Courts Act 1978; and

(e) Schedule 1 to the Children Act 1989.

(4) In paragraph (1)(a), 'maintenance' means money or money's worth paid towards the support of a former partner, child or any other person for whose support the payer has previously been responsible or has made payments.

**Note.** Para (1)(d) in italics omitted and para (1)(d) in square brackets substituted by SI 2001 No 3663 as from 3 December 2001.

**45**—(1) Subject to paragraph (2), the statutory charge shall be in favour of the Commission.

(2) Subject to paragraph (3), where it relates to the cost of Legal Help or Help at Court, the statutory charge shall be in favour of the supplier.

(3) Where Legal Help or Help at Court has been provided, the statutory charge shall be in favour of the Commission if it attaches to money or property recovered after a certificate has been granted in relation to the same matter.

*Supplier's authority to waive statutory charge*

**46**—(1) This regulation applies only where the statutory charge is in favour of the supplier.

(2) The Commission may grant a supplier authority, either in respect of individual cases or generally, to waive either all or part of the amount of the statutory charge where its enforcement would cause grave hardship or distress to the client or would be unreasonably difficult because of the nature of the property.

*Waiver of charge in case of wider public interest*

**47**—(1) *For the purposes of this regulation, 'wider public interest' means the potential of proceedings to produce real benefits for individuals other than the client (other than any general benefits which normally flow from proceedings of the type in question).*

(2) Paragraph (3) applies where:
(a) the Commission funds Legal Representation or Support Funding in proceedings which it considers have a significant wider public interest; and
(b) the Commission considers it cost-effective to fund those services for a specified claimant or claimants, but not for other claimants or potential claimants who might benefit from the litigation.
(3) Where this paragraph applies, the Commission may, if it considers it equitable to do so, waive some or all of the amount of the statutory charge.
**Note.** Para (1) in italics omitted by SI 2001 No 3663 as from 3 December 2001.

*Application of regulations 49 to 53*

**48** Regulations 49 to 53 apply only in relation to a statutory charge in favour of the Commission.

*Operation of statutory charge where certificate revoked or discharged*

**49**—(1) Where a certificate has been revoked or discharged, section 10(7) of the Act shall apply to any money or property recovered as a result of the client continuing to pursue the relevant dispute or take, defend or be a party to the relevant proceedings.
(2) In paragraph (1), 'client' means the person whose certificate has been revoked or discharged, or, as the case may be, his personal representatives, trustee in bankruptcy or the Official Receiver.

*Operation of statutory charge on money in court*

**50**—(1) Paragraph (2) applies where any money recovered by a client in any proceedings is ordered to be paid into or remain in court and invested for the benefit of the client.
(2) Where this paragraph applies, the statutory charge shall attach only to such part of the money as, in the opinion of the Commission, will be sufficient to safeguard the interests of the Commission, and the Commission shall notify the court in writing of the amount so attached.

*Enforcement of statutory charge*

**51** Subject to regulation 52, the Commission may enforce the statutory charge in any manner which would be available to a chargee in respect of a charge given between parties.

**52**—(1) The Commission may postpone the enforcement of the statutory charge where (but only where):
(a) by order of the court or agreement it relates to property to be used as a home by the client or his dependents, or, where the relevant proceedings were family proceedings, to money to pay for such a home;
(b) the Commission is satisfied that the property in question will provide such security for the statutory charge as it considers appropriate; and
(c) as soon as it is possible to do so, the Commission registers a charge under the Land Registration Act 1925 to secure the amount in regulation 43 or, as appropriate, takes equivalent steps (whether in England and Wales or in any other jurisdiction) to protect its interest in the property.
(2) Where the client wishes to purchase a property in substitution for the property over which a charge is registered under paragraph (1)(c), the Commission may release the charge if the conditions in paragraph (1)(b) and (c) are satisfied.
(3) Where the enforcement of the statutory charge is postponed, interest shall accrue for the benefit of the Commission in accordance with regulation 53.

(4) Without prejudice to the provisions of the Land Registration Act 1925 and the Land Charges Act 1972, all conveyances and acts done to defeat, or operating to defeat, any charge shall, except in the case of a bona fide purchaser for value without notice, be void as against the Commission.

*Payment and recovery of interest*

**53**—(1) Where interest is payable by the client under regulation 52, that interest shall continue to accrue until the amount of the statutory charge is paid.

(2) The client may make interim payments of interest or capital in respect of the outstanding amount of the statutory charge, but no interim payment shall be used to reduce the capital outstanding while any interest remains outstanding.

*(3) Where interest is payable by the client under regulation 52:*
*(a) it shall run from the date when the charge is first registered;*
*(b) it shall accrue at the rate of 8% per annum; and*
*(c) the capital on which it is calculated shall be either:*
*(i) the amount of the statutory charge outstanding from time to time, less any interest accrued by virtue of regulation 52(3), or*
*(ii) where the value of the client's interest in the property at the time it was recovered was less than the amount of the statutory charge, such lower sum as the Commission considers equitable in the circumstances.*

[(3) Where interest is payable by the client under regulation 52:
(a) it shall run from the date when the charge is first registered;
(b) the applicable rate shall be:
(i) 8% per annum until 31st March 2002;
(ii) thereafter, 1 percentage point above the Bank of England base rate current on 1st April 2002;
(c) subject to sub-paragraph (d), the applicable rate shall be varied on 1st April of each subsequent year so that it remains at the rate of 1 percentage point above the Bank of England base rate then current;
(d) the variation set out in sub-paragraph (c) shall take place only if the application of the new base rate has the effect of varying the base rate previously applicable by 1 percentage point or more; and
(e) the capital on which it is calculated shall be the lesser of:
(i) the amount of the statutory charge outstanding from time to time, less any interest accrued by virtue of regulation 52(3), or
(ii) the value of the property recovered at the time of such recovery, less the amount of any exemption under regulation 44(1)(d) which would apply were the amount of the charge to be paid.]

**Note.** Para (3) in italics omitted and para (3) in square brackets substituted by SI 2001 No 3663 as from 3 December 2001.

## COMMUNITY LEGAL SERVICE (FUNDING) ORDER 2000

**Dated** 2 March 2000

**SI 2000 No 627**

*Citation and commencement*

**1** This Order may be cited as the Community Legal Service (Funding) Order 2000 and shall come into force on 1st April 2000.

*Interpretation*

**2**—(1) In this Order:
'the Act' means the Access to Justice Act 1999;
['assessing authority' means, where remuneration is payable by the Commission under a contract, the authority to which it falls at any time to assess that remuneration (including assessing by way of appeal), and shall include a Regional Director of the Commission, or the Commission's Costs Committee or Cost Appeals Committee, or the court;]
'certificate' means a certificate issued under the Funding Code certifying a decision to fund services for the client;
'client' means an individual who receives funded services;

\* \* \* \* \*

'Commission' means the Legal Services Commission established under section 1 of the Act;
'family proceedings' means proceedings, other than proceedings for judicial review, which arise out of family relationships, including proceedings in which the welfare of children is determined, and including all proceedings under one or more of the following:
  (a) the Matrimonial Causes Act 1973;
  (b) the Inheritance (Provision for Family and Dependants) Act 1975;
  (c) the Adoption Act 1976;
  (d) the Domestic Proceedings and Magistrates' Courts Act 1978;
  (e) Part III of the Matrimonial and Family Proceedings Act 1984;
  (f) Parts I, II and IV of the Children Act 1989;
  (g) Part IV of the Family Law Act 1996; and
  (h) the inherent jurisdiction of the High Court in relation to children;
'fund' means the Community Legal Service Fund established under section 5 of the Act;
'funded services' means services which are provided directly for a client and funded for that client by the Commission as part of the Community Legal Service under sections 4 to 11 of the Act;
'Funding Code' means the code approved under section 9 of the Act;

\* \* \* \* \*

(2) References to the levels of service listed in paragraph (3) shall be construed as references to the receipt or provision of those levels of service granted in accordance with the Funding Code.
(3) The levels of service referred to in paragraph (2) are:
  (a) Legal Help;
  (b) Help at Court;
  (c) Legal Representation;
  (d) Help with Mediation; and
  (e) General Family Help.
(4) In this Order, any reference to the provisions of the Civil Legal Aid (General) Regulations 1989 shall be construed as though they were amended as follows:
  (a) any reference to 'assisted person' shall be replaced by a reference to 'client';
  (b) any reference to 'authorised summary proceedings' shall be replaced by a reference to 'proceedings in a magistrates' court';
  (c) in regulation 59, the words 'legal aid' shall be replaced by 'Legal Services Commission';
  (d) in regulations 84 and 107, any reference to 'regulation 83' shall be replaced by a reference to 'regulation 4 of the Community Legal Service (Costs) Regulations 2000';
  (e) in regulation 102, the words 'or the Funding Code' shall be inserted after 'these Regulations';

(f) in regulation 104, the words 'or the Crown Court' shall be inserted after 'magistrates' court';

(g) in regulation 106A, the words 'legal aid only costs' shall be replaced by 'costs payable from the Community Legal Service Fund only'; and

(h) in regulation 113(3), the words 'section 16(6) of the Act' shall be replaced by 'section 10(7) of the Access to Justice Act 1999'.

**Note.** Definition of 'assessing authority' inserted by SI 2001 No 831 as from 2 April 2001.

*Funding of services—Direct payments*

**3**—(1) The Commission may only fund services as part of the Community Legal Service under section 6(3)(b) of the Act as follows:

(a) where a certificate was granted before 1st April 2001, to make payments in respect of the provision of Legal Representation in actual or contemplated proceedings other than the following:

    (i) personal injury;

    (ii) clinical negligence;

    (iii) family;

    (iv) immigration; or

    (v) before a Mental Health Review Tribunal;

(b) where authorisation has been given in an individual case under section 6(8)(b) of the Act.

(2) The Commission may only fund services as part of the Community Legal Service under section 6(3)(e) of the Act where authorisation for such funding has been given in an individual case under section 6(8)(b) of the Act.

**4** Where the Commission funds services under article 3(1)(a), the provisions of regulations 48, 59 to 63, 84, 100 to 102, 104 to 107A, 108 to 110, 112, 113(1), (2) and (4), 119(1), 122 and 149(7) of the Civil Legal Aid (General) Regulations 1989 shall apply.

*Remuneration under contracts*

**5**—(1) Paragraph (2) applies to contracts which have not been awarded:

(a) after competitive tendering as to price has taken place; or

(b) in relation to a particular case (including group litigation or potential group litigation); [or

(c) as part of the housing possession court duty scheme pilot; *or*

(d) as part of the alternative methods of delivery pilot][; or

(e) as part of the family advice and information networks pilot] [; or

(f) as part of the fast track asylum decision and appeals process pilot.]

(2) Subject to paragraph (1), any contract for the provision of funded services under section 6(3)(a) of the Act which provides for the levels of service in this article shall provide for payment by the Commission to be at rates no higher than the rates in the following paragraphs.

(3) [Subject to paragraphs (3A) *and (3B)* [to (3C)] in relation to:

(a) Legal Help; and

(b) Help at Court

payment shall be at rates no higher than those provided in Schedule 6, paragraphs 1 and 2 of the Legal Advice and Assistance Regulations 1989.

[(3A) In relation to Legal Help and Help at Court within any category of work mentioned in paragraph *(3B)* [(3B)(a)] which is authorised as a specific category in the schedule to the contract with the Commission under which it is provided, *payment shall be* [payment shall, subject to paragraph (7B), be] at *rates no higher than* [rates no higher than those set out in Part I of the Schedule]:

(i) 8% above those provided in Schedule 6, paragraphs 1 and 2 of the Legal Advice and Assistance Regulations 1989 in respect of fee-earners whose office is situated within the London Region of the Commission; and

(ii) 5% above those so provided in respect of all other fee-earners.

[(3AA) In relation to Legal Help and Help at Court within any category of work mentioned in paragraph (3B)(b) which is authorised as a specific category in the schedule to the contract with the Commission under which it is provided, payment shall be at rates no higher than those set out in Part II of the Schedule.]

*(3B) the categories of work mentioned in paragraph (3A) are: immigration/nationality, mental health, education, public law, community care and actions against the police.]*

[(3B) The categories of work mentioned—

(a) in paragraph (3A) are: immigration, mental health, education, public law, actions against the police etc and community care; and

(b) in paragraph (3AA) are: family, housing and employment.

(3C) In relation to any Legal Help and Help at Court provided in accordance with a contract with the Commission to which neither paragraph (3A) nor (3AA) applies, payment shall be at rates no higher than those set out in Part III of the Schedule.]

*(4) In relation to:*

*(a) Help with Mediation;*

*(b) Legal Representation before a Mental Health Review Tribunal; and*

*(c) Legal Representation before the Immigration Appeal Tribunal or an adjudicator payment shall be at rates no higher than those provided in Schedule 6, paragraphs 3 and 4 of the Legal Advice and Assistance Regulations 1989.*

[(4) In relation to Help with Mediation payment shall be at rates no higher than those set out in Part IV of the Schedule.]

\* \* \* \* \*

(5) In relation to General Family Help, payment shall be at rates no higher than the relevant rates provided in the Legal Aid in Family Proceedings (Remuneration) Regulations 1991.

(6) In relation to Legal Representation (other than as provided for in *paragraph (4)*) [paragraph (4A), or where paragraph (4A) does not apply by virtue of paragraph (4B) or the [Legal Representation referred to in *paragraph (7)*, [paragraphs (7) or (7A)]]], payment shall be at rates no higher than whichever of those provided by the Legal Aid in Civil Proceedings (Remuneration) Regulations 1994 or the Legal Aid in Family Proceedings (Remuneration) Regulations 1991 would have been applicable if the representation had been provided under Part IV of the Legal Aid Act 1988.

[(7) Paragraph (6) shall not apply to Legal Representation before—

(a) Special Commissioners of Income Tax or General Commissioners of Income Tax;

(b) a VAT and duties tribunal constituted by Schedule 12 to the Value Added Tax Act 1994; or

(c) the tribunal constituted by section 9 of the Protection of Children Act 1999.]

[(7A) In relation to Legal Representation for any proceedings under the Proceeds of Crime Act 2002 in the Crown Court or a magistrates' court, payment shall be at rates no higher than those set out for magistrates' court proceedings in Schedule 2A to the Legal Aid in Family Proceedings (Remuneration) Regulations 1991.]

[(7B) The maximum rate applicable in relation to any specialist immigration work shall be 5% greater than the maximum rate which would be applicable to that work but for this paragraph.

(7C) In paragraph (7B)—

'maximum rate' means a rate specified by this article as the rate that may not be
exceeded in relation to payment by the Commission under a contract for
the provision of funded services;

'specialist immigration work' means work carried out by a member of the Legal
Services Commission's Immigration and Asylum Accreditation Scheme who
is accredited to level 3 of that Scheme where—

    (a) immigration is authorised as a specific category of work in the schedule
to the contract with the Commission under which it is provided; and

    (b) that work is within the category of immigration.]

[(8) Where any item in the Schedule is applicable to a fee-earner, the figure to
be applied shall be—

    (a) the figure in the column headed 'London Region' if that fee-earner's office
is situated in the Commission's London Region;

    (b) otherwise, the figure in the column headed 'Outside Region.]

**Note.** Words in square brackets in article 5(3) and paras (3A) and (3B) added by SI 2000
No 1541 as from 1 July 2000. Words in italic and words in square brackets and paras
(3AA), (3B), (3C), (4) and (7A) inserted by SI 2001 No 831 as from 2 April 2001. Paras
(1)(c) and (d) added by SI 2001 No 2996 as from 1 October 2001. Sub-para (1)(e) added,
second set of para references in para (6) substituted and para (7A) added by SI 2003 No
651 as from 1 April 2003. Words in square brackets in article 5(1)(f) added by SI 2003 No
851 as from 15 April 2003. Para (3A): words 'payment shall, subject to paragraph (7B) be'
in square brackets substituted by SI 2004 No 597, art 3(1) as from 1 April 2004 (except in
relation to work carried out before that date). Paras (7B), (7C) inserted by SI 2004 No
597, art 3(3) as from 1 April 2004 (except in relation to work carried out before that
date).

**6** Where a contract entered into by the Commission in accordance with section
6(3)(a) of the Act *before 1st April 2003* provides that the procedures for assessing
the remuneration payable by the Commission shall be the same as those set out in
the Civil Legal Aid (General) Regulations 1989, the Legal Aid in Civil Proceedings
(Remuneration) Regulations 1994, or the Legal Aid in Family Proceedings
(Remuneration) Regulations 1991, the court shall assess the remuneration
accordingly.

**Note.** Words in italics omitted by SI 2003 No 651 as from 1 April 2003.

*Foreign law*

**7** The Commission may fund as part of the Community Legal Service Legal Help
relating to the preparation of applications for transmission under the provisions of
the European Agreement on the Transmission of Applications for Legal Aid.

SCHEDULE

PART I
LEGAL HELP AND HELP AT COURT—IMMIGRATION, MENTAL HEALTH, ACTIONS AGAINST
THE POLICE ETC, PUBLIC LAW, EDUCATION AND COMMUNITY CARE

| | London Region | Outside London |
|---|---|---|
| Preparation | £57.35 per hour | £52.55 per hour |
| Travel and waiting | £30.30 per hour | £29.45 per hour |
| Letters written and telephone calls | £4.40 per item | £4.10 per item |

PART II

LEGAL HELP AND HELP AT COURT—FAMILY, HOUSING AND EMPLOYMENT

|  | *London Region* | *Outside London* |
| --- | --- | --- |
| Preparation | £53.10 per hour | £50.05 per hour |
| Travel and waiting | £28.05 per hour | £28.05 per hour |
| Letters written and telephone calls | £4.10 per item | £3.95 per item |

PART III

LEGAL HELP AND HELP AT COURT—OTHER WORK CARRIED OUT UNDER CONTRACT

| *London Region* | *Outside London* |
| --- | --- |
| Preparation | £50.70 per hour | £47.80 per hour |
| Travel and waiting | £26.80 per hour | £26.80 per hour |
| Letters written and telephone calls | £3.90 per item | £3.75 per item |

PART IV

HELP WITH MEDIATION

|  | *London Region* | *Outside London* |
| --- | --- | --- |
| Preparation | £64.10 per hour | £59.95 per hour |
| Travel and waiting | £28.05 per hour | £28.05 per hour |
| Letters written and telephone calls | £4.30 per item | £4.30 per item |

PART V

LEGAL REPRESENTATION—IMMIGRATION AND MENTAL HEALTH

|  | *London Region* | *Outside London* |
| --- | --- | --- |
| Preparation | £61.20 per hour | £57.25 per hour |
| Travel and waiting | £30.30 per hour | £29.45 per hour |
| Letters written and telephone calls | £4.40 per item | £4.10 per item |
| Advocacy | £69.60 per hour | £69.60 per hour |
| Attending tribunal with counsel (Mental Health Review Tribunal only) | £32.55 per hour | £32.55 per hour] |

**Note.** Inserted by SI 2000 No 831 with effect from 831 with effect from 2 April 2001.


**COMMUNITY LEGAL SERVICE (COST PROTECTION) REGULATIONS 2000**

**Dated** 20 March 2000

**SI 2000 No 824**

**1 Citation and commencement** These Regulations may be cited as the Community Legal Service (Cost Protection) Regulations 2000 and shall come into force on 1st April 2000.

**2    Interpretation—**(1)  In these Regulations:

'the Act' means the Access to Justice Act 1999;

'certificate' means a certificate issued under the Funding Code certifying a decision to fund services for the client and 'emergency certificate' means a certificate certifying a decision to fund Legal Representation for the client in a case of emergency;

'client' means an individual who receives funded services;

'Commission' means the Legal Services Commission established under section 1 of the Act;

['costs judge' has the same meaning as in the Civil Procedure Rules 1998;]

'costs order' means an order that a party pay all or part of the costs of proceedings;

'cost protection' means the limit on costs awarded against a client set out in section 11(1) of the Act;

'court' includes any tribunal having the power to award costs in favour of, or against, a party;

'full costs' means, where a section 11(1) costs order is made against a client, the amount of costs which that client would, but for section 11(1) of the Act, have been ordered to pay;

'funded proceedings' means proceedings (including prospective proceedings) in relation to which the client receives funded services or, as the case may be, that part of proceedings during which the client receives funded services;

'funded services' means services which are provided directly for a client and funded for that client by the Commission as part of the Community Legal Service under sections 4 to 11 of the Act;

'Funding Code' means the code approved under section 9 of the Act;

'non-funded party' means a party to proceedings who has not received funded services in relation to those proceedings under a certificate, other than a certificate which has been revoked;

'partner' means a person with whom the person concerned lives as a couple, and includes a person with whom the person concerned is not currently living but from whom he is not living separate and apart;

'proceedings' include proceedings in any tribunal which is a court, as defined in this paragraph;

'receiving party' means a party in favour of whom a costs order is made;

'section 11(1) costs order' means a costs order against a client where cost protection applies;

'solicitor' means a solicitor or another person who is an authorised litigator within the meaning of section 119(1) of the Courts and Legal Services Act 1990.

(2)  References to the levels of service listed in paragraph (3) shall be construed as references to the receipt or provision of those levels of service granted in accordance with the Funding Code.

(3)  The levels of service referred to in paragraph (2) are:

(a)  Legal Help;

(b)  Help at Court;

(c)  Legal Representation;

(d)  Approved Family Help;

(e)  Investigative Support;

(f)  Litigation Support.

**Note.**  Definition of 'costs judge' inserted by SI 2001 No 823 as from 2 April 2001.

**3    Cost protection—**(1)  Cost protection shall not apply in relation to such parts of proceedings, or prospective proceedings, as are funded for the client by way of:

(a)  Help at Court or Litigation Support;
(b)  Investigative Support, except where any proceedings in respect of which the Investigative Support was given are not pursued (whether or not as funded proceedings) after the certificate for Investigative Support is discharged;
(c)  subject to paragraph (2), Legal Help.

(2) Subject to paragraph (4), where the client receives Legal Help, but later receives Legal Representation or Approved Family Help in respect of the same dispute, cost protection shall apply, both in respect of:

(a)  the costs incurred by the receiving party before the commencement of proceedings which, as regards the client, are funded proceedings by virtue of the client's receipt of Legal Help, and
(b)  the costs incurred by the receiving party in the course of proceedings which, as regards the client, are funded proceedings by virtue of the client's receipt of Legal Representation or Approved Family Help.

(3) Subject to paragraph (4), cost protection shall apply only to costs incurred by the receiving party in relation to proceedings which, as regards the client, are funded proceedings, and:

(a)  where work is done before the issue of a certificate, cost protection shall (subject to paragraphs (2) and (5)) apply only to costs incurred after the issue of the certificate;
(b)  where funding is withdrawn by discharging the client's certificate, cost protection shall apply only to costs incurred before the date when funded services under the certificate ceased to be provided.

(4) Where funding is withdrawn by revoking the client's certificate, cost protection shall not apply, either in respect of work done before or after the revocation.

(5) Cost protection shall apply to work done immediately before the grant of an emergency certificate if:

(a)  no application for such a certificate could be made because the Commission's office was closed; and
(b)  the client's solicitor applies for an emergency certificate at the first available opportunity, and the certificate is granted.

**4   Enforcement of costs order against client** Where, for the purpose of enforcing a costs order against a client (alone or together with any other judgment or order), a charging order under section 1 of the Charging Orders Act 1979 is made in respect of the client's interest in the main or only dwelling in which he resides:

(a)  that charging order shall operate to secure the amount payable under the costs order (including, without limitation, any interest) only to the extent of the amount (if any) by which the proceeds of sale of the client's interest in the dwelling (having deducted any mortgage debts) exceed £100,000; and
(b)  an order for the sale of the dwelling shall not be made in favour of the person in whose favour the charging order is made.

**5   Costs order against Commission**
(1) The following paragraphs of this regulation apply where:
(a)  funded services are provided to a client in relation to proceedings;
(b)  those proceedings are finally decided in favour of a non-funded party; and
(c)  cost protection applies.

(2) The court may, subject to the following paragraphs of this regulation, make an order for the payment by the Commission to the non-funded party of the whole or any part of the costs incurred by him in the proceedings (other than any costs that the client is required to pay under a section 11(1) costs order).

(3) An order under paragraph (2) may only be made if all the conditions set out in sub-paragraphs (a), (b), (c) and (d) are satisfied:

(a) a section 11(1) costs order is made against the client in the proceedings, and the amount (if any) which the client is required to pay under that costs order is less than the amount of the full costs;

(b) [unless there is a good reason for the delay,] the non-funded party makes a request under regulation 10(2) of the Community Legal Service (Costs) Regulations 2000 within three months of the making of the section 11(1) costs order;

(c) as regards costs incurred in a court of first instance, the proceedings were instituted by the client [, the non-funded party is an individual,] and the court is satisfied that the non-funded party will suffer *severe* financial hardship unless the order is made; and

(d) in any case, the court is satisfied that it is just and equitable in the circumstances that provision for the costs should be made out of public funds.

[(3A) An order under paragraph (2) may be made—

(a) in relation to proceedings in the House of Lords, by the Clerk to the Parliaments;

(b) in relation to proceedings in the Court of Appeal, High Court or a county court, by a costs judge or a district judge;

(c) in relation to proceedings in a magistrates' court, by a single justice or by the justices' clerk;

(d) in relation to proceedings in the Employment Appeal Tribunal, by the Registrar of that tribunal.]

(4) Where the client receives funded services in connection with part only of the proceedings, the reference in paragraph (2) to the costs incurred by the non-funded party in the relevant proceedings shall be construed as a reference to so much of those costs as is attributable to the part of the proceedings which are funded proceedings.

(5) Where a court decides any proceedings in favour of the non-funded party and an appeal lies (with or without permission) against that decision, any order made under this regulation shall not take effect:

(a) where permission to appeal is required, unless the time limit for applications for permission to appeal expires without permission being granted;

(b) where permission to appeal is granted or is not required, unless the time limit for appeal expires without an appeal being brought.

(6) Subject to paragraph (7), in determining whether the conditions in paragraph (3)(c) and (d) are satisfied, the court shall have regard to the resources of the non-funded party and of his partner.

(7) The court shall not have regard to the resources of the partner of the non-funded party if the partner has a contrary interest in the funded proceedings.

(8) Where the non-funded party is acting in a representative, fiduciary or official capacity and is entitled to be indemnified in respect of his costs from any property, estate or fund, the court shall, for the purposes of paragraph (3), have regard to the value of the property, estate or fund and the resources of the persons, if any, including that party where appropriate, who are beneficially interested in that property, estate or fund.

**Note.** Paragraph (3A) inserted by SI 2001 No 823 as from 2 April 2001. Word in italics in para (3)(c) omitted and words in square brackets in paras (3)(b) and (c) inserted by SI 2001 No 3812 as from 3 December 2001.

**6 Orders for costs against Commission—Litigation Support—**(1) Paragraph (2) applies where:

(a) the client receives Litigation Support and the certificate is not revoked;

(b) the client has effected insurance against liability in respect of costs in the proceedings, or has made other arrangements, approved by the Commission as being equivalent to such insurance;

(c) the amount of liability insured under that insurance (or covered by those other arrangements) is subject to a maximum which has been approved by the Commission; and

(d) a costs order has been made against the client in favour of a non-funded party and the actual amount of the client's liability in respect of costs under that costs order exceeds the maximum referred to in sub-paragraph (c).

(2) Where this paragraph applies, the amount of the excess referred to in paragraph (1)(d) shall, subject to paragraph (3), be paid by the Commission, not by the client, and the court shall order accordingly.

(3) The amount of the Commission's liability under this regulation shall not exceed the reasonable costs of the non-funded party incurred during the period in which Litigation Support was provided.

**7   Effect of these Regulations—**(1) No order to pay costs in favour of a non-funded party shall be made against the Commission in respect of funded proceedings except in accordance with these Regulations, and any costs to be paid under such an order shall be paid out of the Community Legal Service Fund.

(2) Nothing in these Regulations shall be construed, in relation to proceedings where one or more parties are receiving, or have received, funded services, as:

(a) requiring a court to make a costs order where it would not otherwise have made a costs order; or

(b) affecting the court's power to make a wasted costs order against a legal representative.

## PENSIONS ON DIVORCE ETC (PROVISION OF INFORMATION) REGULATIONS 2000

**Dated** 13 April 2000

**SI 2000 No 1048**

**1   Citation, commencement and interpretation—**(1) These Regulations may be cited as the Pensions on Divorce etc (Provision of Information) Regulations 2000 and shall come into force on 1st December 2000.

(2) In these Regulations—

'the 1993 Act' means the Pension Schemes Act 1993;

'the 1995 Act' means the Pensions Act 1995;

'the 1999 Act' means the Welfare Reform and Pensions Act 1999;

'the Charging Regulations' means the Pensions on Divorce etc (Charging) Regulations 2000;

'the Implementation and Discharge of Liability Regulations' means the Pension Sharing (Implementation and Discharge of Liability) Regulations 2000;

'the Valuation Regulations' means the Pension Sharing (Valuation) Regulations 2000;

'active member' has the meaning given by section 124(1) of the 1995 Act;

'day' means any day other than—

(a) Christmas Day or Good Friday; or

(b) a bank holiday, that is to say, a day which is, or is to be observed as, a bank holiday or a holiday under Schedule 1 to the Banking and Financial Dealings Act 1971;

'deferred member' has the meaning given by section 124(1) of the 1995 Act;

'implementation period' has the meaning given by section 34(1) of the 1999 Act;

'member' means a person who has rights to future benefits, or has rights to benefits payable, under a pension arrangement;

'money purchase benefits' has the meaning given by section 181(1) of the 1993 Act;

'normal benefit age' has the meaning given by section 101B of the 1993 Act;

'notice of discharge of liability' means a notice issued to the member and his former spouse by the person responsible for a pension arrangement when that person has discharged his liability in respect of a pension credit in accordance with Schedule 5 to the 1999 Act;

'notice of implementation' means a notice issued by the person responsible for a pension arrangement to the member and his former spouse at the beginning of the implementation period notifying them of the day on which the implementation period for the pension credit begins;

'occupational pension scheme' has the meaning given by section 1 of the 1993 Act;

'the party with pension rights' and 'the other party' have the meanings given by section 25D(3) of the Matrimonial Causes Act 1973;

'pension arrangement' has the meaning given in section 46(1) of the 1999 Act;

'pension credit' means a credit under section 29(1)(b) of the 1999 Act;

'pension credit benefit' means the benefits payable under a pension arrangement or a qualifying arrangement to or in respect of a person by virtue of rights under the arrangement in question which are attributable (directly or indirectly) to a pension credit;

'pension credit rights' means rights to future benefits under a pension arrangement or a qualifying arrangement which are attributable (directly or indirectly) to a pension credit;

'pension sharing order or provision' means an order or provision which is mentioned in section 28(1) of the 1999 Act;

'pensionable service' has the meaning given by section 124(1) of the 1995 Act;

'person responsible for a pension arrangement' has the meaning given by section 46(2) of the 1999 Act;

'personal pension scheme' has the meaning given by section 1 of the 1993 Act;

'qualifying arrangement' has the meaning given by paragraph 6 of Schedule 5 to the 1999 Act;

*'relevant date' has the meaning given by section 10(3) of the Family Law (Scotland) Act 1985;*

'retirement annuity contract' means a contract or scheme approved under Chapter III of Part XIV of the Income and Corporation Taxes Act 1988;

'salary related occupational pension scheme' has the meaning given by regulation 1A of the Occupational Pension Schemes (Transfer Values) Regulations 1996;

'the Regulatory Authority' means the Occupational Pensions Regulatory Authority;

'transfer day' has the meaning given by section 29(8) of the 1999 Act;

'transferee' has the meaning given by section 29(8) of the 1999 Act;

'transferor' has the meaning given by section 29(8) of the 1999 Act;

'trustees or managers' has the meaning given by section 46(1) of the 1999 Act.

**Note.** Definition of 'Relevant date' omitted by SI 2000 No 2691 as from 1 December 2000.

**2 Basic information about pensions and divorce—**(1) The requirements imposed on a person responsible for a pension arrangement for the purposes of section 23(1)(a) of the 1999 Act (supply of pension information in connection with divorce etc) are that he shall furnish—

    (a)  on request from a member, the information referred to in paragraphs (2) and (3)(b) to (f);

(b) on request from the spouse of a member, the information referred to in paragraph (3); or

(c) pursuant to an order of the court, the information referred to in paragraph (2), (3) or (4),

to the member, the spouse of the member, or, as the case may be, to the court.

(2) The information in this paragraph is a valuation of pension rights or benefits accrued under that member's pension arrangement.

(3) The information in this paragraph is—

(a) a statement that on request from the member, or pursuant to an order of the court, a valuation of pension rights or benefits accrued under that member's pension arrangement, will be provided to the member, or, as the case may be, to the court;

(b) a statement summarising the way in which the valuation referred to in paragraph (2) and sub-paragraph (a) is calculated;

(c) the pension benefits which are included in a valuation referred to in paragraph (2) and sub-paragraph (a);

(d) whether the person responsible for the pension arrangement offers membership to a person entitled to a pension credit, and if so, the types of benefits available to pension credit members under that arrangement;

(e) whether the person responsible for the pension arrangements intends to discharge his liability for a pension credit other than by offering membership to a person entitled to a pension credit; and

(f) the schedule of charges which the person responsible for the pension arrangement will levy in accordance with regulation 2(2) of the Charging Regulations (general requirements as to charges).

(4) The information in this paragraph is any other information relevant to any power with respect to the matters specified in section 23(1)(a) of the 1999 Act and which is not specified in Schedule 1 or 2 to the Occupational Pension Schemes (Disclosure of Information) Regulations 1996 (basic information about the scheme and information to be made available to individuals), or in Schedule 1 or 2 to the Personal Pension Schemes (Disclosure of Information) Regulations 1987 (basic information about the scheme and information to be made available to individuals), in a case where either of those Regulations applies.

(5) Where the member's request for, or the court order for the provision of, information includes a request for, or an order for the provision of, a valuation under paragraph (2), the person responsible for the pension arrangement shall furnish all the information requested, or ordered, to the member—

(a) within 3 months beginning with the date the person responsible for the pension arrangement receives that request or order for the provision of the information;

(b) within 6 weeks beginning with the date the person responsible for the pension arrangement receives the request, or order, for the provision of the information, if the member has notified that person on the date of the request or order that the information is needed in connection with proceedings commenced under any of the provisions referred to in section 23(1)(a) of the 1999 Act; or

(c) within such shorter period specified by the court in an order requiring the person responsible for the pension arrangement to provide a valuation in accordance with paragraph (2).

(6) Where—

(a) the member's request for, or the court order for the provision of, information does not include a request or an order for a valuation under paragraph (2); or

(b) the member's spouse requests the information specified in paragraph (3),

the person responsible for the pension arrangement shall furnish that information to the member, his spouse, or the court, as the case may be, within one month beginning with the date that person responsible for the pension arrangement receives the request for, or the court order for the provision of, the information.

(7) At the same time as furnishing the information referred to in paragraph (1), the person responsible for a pension arrangement may furnish the information specified in regulation 4(2) (provision of information in response to a notification that a pension sharing order or provision may be made).

### 3 Information about pensions and divorce: valuation of pension benefits—

(1) Where an application for financial relief under any of the provisions referred to in section 23(1)(a)(i) or (iii) of the 1999 Act (supply of pension information in connection with domestic and overseas divorce etc in England and Wales and corresponding Northern Ireland powers) has been made or is in contemplation, the valuation of benefits under a pension arrangement shall be calculated and verified for the purposes of regulation 2 of these Regulations in accordance with—

(a) paragraph (3), if the person with pension rights is a deferred member of an occupational pension scheme;

(b) paragraph (4), if the person with pension rights is an active member of an occupational pension scheme;

(c) paragraphs (5) and (6), if—
   (i) the person with pension rights is a member of a personal pension scheme; or
   (ii) those pension rights are contained in a retirement annuity contract; or

(d) paragraphs (7) to (9), if—
   (i) the pension of the person with pension rights is in payment;
   (ii) the rights of the person with pension rights are contained in an annuity contract other than a retirement annuity contract; or
   (iii) the rights of the person with pension rights are contained in a deferred annuity contract other than a retirement annuity contract.

(2) Where an application for financial provision under any of the provisions referred to in section 23(1)(a)(ii) of the 1999 Act (corresponding Scottish powers) has been made, or is in contemplation, the valuation of benefits under a pension arrangement shall be calculated and verified for the purposes of regulation 2 of these Regulations in accordance with regulation 3 of the Divorce etc (Pensions) (Scotland) Regulations 2000 (valuation).

(3) Where the person with pension rights is a deferred member of an occupational pension scheme, the value of the benefits which he has under that scheme shall be taken to be—

(a) in the case of an occupational pension scheme other than a salary related scheme, the cash equivalent to which he acquired a right under section 94(1)(a) of the 1993 Act (right to cash equivalent) on the termination of his pensionable service, calculated on the assumption that he has made an application under section 95 of that Act (ways of taking right to cash equivalent) on the date on which the request for the valuation was received; or

(b) in the case of a salary related occupational pension scheme, the guaranteed cash equivalent to which he would have acquired a right under section 94(1)(aa) of the 1993 Act if he had made an application under section 95(1) of that Act, calculated on the assumption that he has made such an application on the date on which the request for the valuation was received.

(4) Where the person with pension rights is an active member of an occupational pension scheme, the valuation of the benefits which he has accrued under that scheme shall be calculated and verified—

(a) on the assumption that the member had made a request for an estimate of the cash equivalent that would be available to him were his pensionable service to terminate on the date on which the request for the valuation was received; and

(b) in accordance with regulation 11 of and Schedule 1 to the Occupational Pension Schemes (Transfer Values) Regulations 1996 (disclosure).

(5) Where the person with pension rights is a member of a personal pension scheme, or those rights are contained in a retirement annuity contract, the value of the benefits which he has under that scheme or contract shall be taken to be the cash equivalent to which he would have acquired a right under section 94(1)(b) of the 1993 Act, if he had made an application under section 95(1) of that Act on the date on which the request for the valuation was received.

(6) In relation to a personal pension scheme which is comprised in a retirement annuity contract made before 4th January 1988, paragraph (5) shall apply as if such a scheme were not excluded from the scope of Chapter IV of Part IV of the 1993 Act by section 93(1)(b) of that Act (scope of Chapter IV).

(7) Except in a case to which, or to the extent to which, paragraph (9) applies, the cash equivalent of benefits in respect of a person referred to in paragraph (1)(d) shall be calculated and verified in such manner as may be approved in a particular case by—

(a) a Fellow of the Institute of Actuaries;

(b) a Fellow of the Faculty of Actuaries; or

(c) a person with other actuarial qualifications who is approved by the Secretary of State, at the request of the person responsible for the pension arrangement in question, as being a proper person to act for the purposes of this regulation in connection with that arrangement.

(8) Except in a case to which paragraph (9) applies, cash equivalents are to be calculated and verified by adopting methods and making assumptions which—

(a) if not determined by the person responsible for the pension arrangement in question, are notified to him by an actuary referred to in paragraph (7); and

(b) are certified by the actuary to the person responsible for the pension arrangement in question as being consistent with 'Retirement Benefit Schemes—Transfer Values (GN 11)' published by the Institute of Actuaries and the Faculty of Actuaries and current at the date on which the request for the valuation is received.

(9) Where the cash equivalent, or any portion of it represents rights to money purchase benefits under the pension arrangement in question of the person with pension rights, and those rights do not fall, either wholly or in part, to be valued in a manner which involves making estimates of the value of benefits, then that cash equivalent, or that portion of it, shall be calculated and verified in such manner as may be approved in a particular case by the person responsible for the pension arrangement in question, and by adopting methods consistent with the requirements of Chapter IV of Part IV of the 1993 Act (protection for early leavers—transfer values).

(10) Where paragraph (3), (4) or (9) has effect by reference to provisions of Chapter IV of Part IV of the 1993 Act, section 93(1)(a)(i) of that Act (scope of Chapter IV) shall apply to those provisions as if the words 'at least one year' had been omitted from section 93(1)(a)(i).

**4 Provision of information in response to a notification that a pension sharing order or provision may be made**—(1) A person responsible for a pension arrangement shall furnish the information specified in paragraph (2) to the member or to the court, as the case may be—

(a) within 21 days beginning with the date that the person responsible for the pension arrangement received the notification that a pension sharing order or provision may be made; or

(b) if the court has specified a date which is outside the 21 days referred to in sub-paragraph (a), by that date.

(2) The information referred to in paragraph (1) is—

(a) the full name of the pension arrangement and address to which any order or provision referred to in section 28(1) of the 1999 Act (activation of pension sharing) should be sent;

(b) in the case of an occupational pension scheme, whether the scheme is winding up, and, if so,—

    (i) the date on which the winding up commenced; and

    (ii) the name and address of the trustees who are dealing with the winding up;

(c) in the case of an occupational pension scheme, whether a cash equivalent of the member's pension rights, if calculated on the date the notification referred to in paragraph (1)(a) was received by the trustees or managers of that scheme, would be reduced in accordance with the provisions of *regulation 8(4), (6) or (12)* [regulation 8(4), (4A), (6) or (12)] of the Occupational Pension Schemes (Transfer Values) Regulations 1996 (further provisions as to reductions of cash equivalents);

(d) whether the person responsible for the pension arrangement is aware that the member's rights under the pension arrangement are subject to any, and if so, to specify which, of the following—

    (i) any order or provision specified in section 28(1) of the 1999 Act;

    (ii) an order under section 23 of the Matrimonial Causes Act 1973 (financial provision orders in connection with divorce etc), so far as it includes provision made by virtue of section 25B or 25C of that Act (powers to include provisions about pensions);

    (iii) an order under section 12A(2) or (3) of the Family Law (Scotland) Act 1985 (powers in relation to pensions lump sums when making a capital sum order) which relates to benefits or future benefits to which the member is entitled under the pension arrangement;

    (iv) an order under Article 25 of the Matrimonial Causes (Northern Ireland) Order 1978, so far as it includes provision made by virtue of Article 27B or 27C of that Order (Northern Ireland powers corresponding to those mentioned in paragraph (2)(d)(ii));

    (v) a forfeiture order;

    (vi) a bankruptcy order;

    (vii) an award of sequestration on a member's estate or the making of the appointment on his estate of a judicial factor under section 41 of the Solicitors (Scotland) Act 1980 (appointment of judicial factor);

(e) whether the member's rights under the pension arrangement include rights specified in regulation 2 of the Valuation Regulations (rights under a pension arrangement which are not shareable);

(f) if the person responsible for the pension arrangement has not at an earlier stage provided the following information, whether that person requires the charges specified in regulation 3 (charges recoverable in respect of the provision of basic information), 5 (charges in respect of pension sharing activity), or 6 (additional amounts recoverable in respect of pension sharing activity) of the Charging Regulations to be paid before the commencement of the implementation period, and if so,—

    (i) whether that person requires those charges to be paid in full; or

    (ii) the proportion of those charges which he requires to be paid;

(g) whether the person responsible for the pension arrangement may levy additional charges specified in regulation 6 of the Charging Regulations, and if so, the scale of the additional charges which are likely to be made;

(h) whether the member is a trustee of the pension arrangement;

(i)   whether the person responsible for the pension arrangement may request information about the member's state of health from the member if a pension sharing order or provision were to be made;

(j)   *whether the person responsible for the pension arrangement will enable the transferee to nominate a person to receive the pension credit benefit, including any lump sum which may be payable if the transferee should die before liability in respect of the pension credit has been discharged; and*

(k)   whether the person responsible for the pension arrangement requires information additional to that specified in regulation 5 (information required by the person responsible for the pension arrangement before the implementation period may begin) in order to implement the pension sharing order or provision.

**Note.** Para (2)(c) words in square brackets substituted by SI 2003 No 1727, reg 3 as from 4 August 2003. Para (2)(j) deleted by SI 2000 No 2691 as from 2 October 2000.

**5 Information required by the person responsible for the pension arrangement before the implementation period may begin** The information prescribed for the purposes of section 34(1)(b) of the 1999 Act (information relating to the transferor and the transferee which the person responsible for the pension arrangement must receive) is—

(a)   in relation to the transferor—
    (i)   all names by which the transferor has been known;
    (ii)   date of birth;
    (iii)   address;
    (iv)   National Insurance number;
    (v)   the name of the pension arrangement to which the pension sharing order or provision relates; and
    (vi)   the transferor's membership or policy number in that pension arrangement;

(b)   in relation to the transferee—
    (i)   all names by which the transferee has been known;
    (ii)   date of birth;
    (iii)   address;
    (iv)   National Insurance number; and
    (v)   if the transferee is a member of the pension arrangement from which the pension credit is derived, his membership or policy number in that pension arrangement;

(c)   where the transferee has given his consent in accordance with paragraph 1(3)(c), 3(3)(c) or 4(2)(c) of Schedule 5 to the 1999 Act (mode of discharge of liability for a pension credit) to the payment of the pension credit to the person responsible for a qualifying arrangement—
    (i)   the full name of that qualifying arrangement;
    (ii)   its address;
    (iii)   if known, the transferee's membership number or policy number in that arrangement; and
    (iv)   the name or title, business address, business telephone number, and, where available, the business facsimile number and electronic mail address of a person who may be contacted in respect of the discharge of liability for the pension credit;

(d)   where the rights from which the pension credit is derived are held in an occupational pension scheme which is being wound up, whether the transferee has given an indication whether he wishes to transfer his pension credit rights which may have been reduced in accordance with the provisions of regulation 16(1) of the Implementation and Discharge of Liability Regulations (adjustments to the amount of the pension credit—

occupational pension schemes which are underfunded on the valuation day) to a qualifying arrangement; and

(e) any information requested by the person responsible for the pension arrangement in accordance with regulation 4(2)(i) or (k).

**6 Provision of information after the death of the person entitled to the pension credit before liability in respect of the pension credit has been discharged—***(1)*
*Where the person entitled to the pension credit dies before the person responsible for the pension arrangement has discharged his liability in respect of the pension credit, the person responsible for the pension arrangement shall, within 21 days of the date of receipt of the notification of the death of the person entitled to the pension credit, notify in writing—*

*(a) the person whom the person entitled to the pension credit nominated pursuant to regulation 4(2)(j) to receive pension credit benefit; and*

*(b) any other person whom the person responsible for the pension arrangement considers should be notified, of the matters specified in paragraph (2).*

[(1) Where the person entitled to the pension credit dies before the person responsible for the pension arrangement has discharged his liability in respect of the pension credit, the person responsible for the pension arrangement shall, within 21 days of the date of receipt of the notification of the death of the person entitled to the pension credit, notify in writing any person whom the person responsible for the pension arrangement considers should be notified of the matters specified in paragraph (2).]

(2) The matters specified in this paragraph are—

(a) how the person responsible for the pension arrangement intends to discharge his liability in respect of the pension credit;

(b) whether the person responsible for the pension arrangement intends to recover charges from the person nominated to receive pension credit benefits, in accordance with regulations 2 to 9 of the Charging Regulations, and if so, a copy of the schedule of charges issued to the parties to pension sharing in accordance with regulation 2(2)(b) of the Charging Regulations (general requirements as to charges); and

(c) a list of any further information which the person responsible for the pension arrangement requires in order to discharge his liability in respect of the pension credit.

**Note.** Para (1) in italics omitted and para (5) in square brackets substituted by SI 2000 No 2691 as from 1 December 2000.

**7 Provision of information after receiving a pension sharing order or provision—**(1) A person responsible for a pension arrangement who is in receipt of a pension sharing order or provision relating to that arrangement shall provide in writing to the transferor and transferee, or, where regulation 6(1) applies, to the person other than the person entitled to the pension credit referred to in regulation 6 of the Implementation and Discharge of Liability Regulations (discharge of liability in respect of a pension credit following the death of the person entitled to the pension credit), as the case may be,—

(a) a notice in accordance with the provisions of regulation 7(1) of the Charging Regulations (charges in respect of pension sharing activity—postponement of implementation period);

(b) a list of information relating to the transferor or the transferee, or, where regulation 6(1) applies, the person other than the person entitled to the pension credit referred to in regulation 6 of the Implementation and Discharge of Liability Regulations, as the case may be, which—

(i) has been requested in accordance with regulation 4(2)(i) and (k), or, where appropriate, 6(2)(c), or should have been provided in accordance with regulation 5;

      (ii)   the person responsible for the pension arrangement considers he needs in order to begin to implement the pension sharing order or provision; and

      (iii)   remains outstanding;

  (c)  a notice of implementation; or

  (d)  a statement by the person responsible for the pension arrangement explaining why he is unable to implement the pension sharing order or agreement.

(2) The information specified in paragraph (1) shall be furnished in accordance with that paragraph within 21 days beginning with—

  (a)  in the case of sub-paragraph (a), (b) or (d) of that paragraph, the day on which the person responsible for the pension arrangement receives the pension sharing order or provision; or

  (b)  in the case of sub-paragraph (c) of that paragraph, the later of the days specified in section 34(1)(a) and (b) of the 1999 Act (implementation period).

**8 Provision of information after the implementation of a pension sharing order or provision—**(1) The person responsible for the pension arrangement shall issue a notice of discharge of liability to the transferor and the transferee, or, as the case may be, the person entitled to the pension credit by virtue of regulation 6 of the Implementation and Discharge of Liability Regulations no later than the end of the period of 21 days beginning with the day on which the discharge of liability in respect of the pension credit is completed.

(2) In the case of a transferor whose pension is not in payment, the notice of discharge of liability shall include the following details—

  (a)  the value of the transferor's accrued rights as determined by reference to the cash equivalent value of those rights calculated and verified in accordance with regulation 3 of the Valuation Regulations (calculation and verification of cash equivalents for the purposes of the creation of pension debits and credits);

  (b)  the value of the pension debit;

  (c)  any amount deducted from the value of the pension rights in accordance with regulation 9(2)(c) of the Charging Regulations (charges in respect of pension sharing activity—method of recovery);

  (d)  the value of the transferor's rights after the amounts referred to in sub-paragraphs (b) and (c) have been deducted; and

  (e)  the transfer day.

(3) In the case of a transferor whose pension is in payment, the notice of discharge of liability shall include the following details—

  (a)  the value of the transferor's benefits under the pension arrangement as determined by reference to the cash equivalent value of those rights calculated and verified in accordance with regulation 3 of the Valuation Regulations;

  (b)  the value of the pension debit;

  (c)  the amount of the pension which was in payment before liability in respect of the pension credit was discharged;

  (d)  the amount of pension which is payable following the deduction of the pension debit from the transferor's pension benefits;

  (e)  the transfer day;

  (f)  if the person responsible for the pension arrangement intends to recover charges, the amount of any unpaid charges—

      (i)   not prohibited by regulation 2 of the Charging Regulations (general requirements as to charges); and

      (ii)   specified in regulations 3 and 6 of those Regulations;

(g) How the person responsible for the pension arrangement will recover the charges referred to in sub-paragraph (f), including—

    (i)   whether the method of recovery specified in regulation 9(2)(d) of the Charging Regulations will be used;

    (ii)  the date when payment of those charges in whole or in part is required; and

    (iii) the sum which will be payable by the transferor, or which will be deducted from his pension benefits, on that date.

(4) In the case of a transferee—

(a) whose pension is not in payment; and

(b) who will become a member of the pension arrangement from which the pension credit rights were derived,

the notice of discharge of liability to the transferee shall include the following details—

    (i)   the value of the pension credit;

    (ii)  any amount deducted from the value of the pension credit in accordance with regulation 9(2)(b) of the Charging Regulations;

    (iii) the value of the pension credit after the amount referred to in sub-paragraph (b)(ii) has been deducted;

    (iv) the transfer day;

    (v)  any periodical charges the person responsible for the pension arrangement intends to make, including how and when those charges will be recovered from the transferee; and

    (vi) information concerning membership of the pension arrangement which is relevant to the transferee as a pension credit member.

(5) In the case of a transferee who is transferring his pension credit rights out of the pension arrangement from which those rights were derived, the notice of discharge of liability to the transferee shall include the following details—

(a) the value of the pension credit;

(b) any amount deducted from the value of the pension credit in accordance with regulation 9(2)(b) of the Charging Regulations;

(c) the value of the pension credit after the amount referred to in sub-paragraph (b) has been deducted;

(d) the transfer day; and

(e) details of the pension arrangement, including its name, address, reference number, telephone number, and, where available, the business facsimile number and electronic mail address, to which the pension credit has been transferred.

(6) In the case of a transferee, who has reached normal benefit age on the transfer day, and in respect of whose pension credit liability has been discharged in accordance with paragraph 1(2), 2(2), 3(2) or 4(4) of Schedule 5 to the 1999 Act (pension credits: mode of discharge— funded pension schemes, unfunded public service pension schemes, other unfunded pension schemes, or other pension arrangements), the notice of discharge of liability to the transferee shall include the following details—

(a) the amount of pension credit benefit which is to be paid to the transferee;

(b) the date when the pension credit benefit is to be paid to the transferee;

(c) the transfer day;

(d) if the person responsible for the pension arrangement intends to recover charges, the amount of any unpaid charges—

    (i)   not prohibited by regulation 2 of the Charging Regulations; and

    (ii)  specified in regulations 3 and 6 of those Regulations; and

(e) how the person responsible for the pension arrangement will recover the charges referred to in sub-paragraph (d), including—

(i) whether the method of recovery specified in regulation 9(2)(e) of the Charging Regulations will be used;

(ii) the date when payment of those charges in whole or in part is required; and

(iii) the sum which will be payable by the transferee, or which will be deducted from his pension credit benefits, on that date.

(7) In the case of a person entitled to the pension credit by virtue of regulation 6 of the Implementation and Discharge of Liability Regulations, the notice of discharge of liability shall include the following details—

(a) the value of the pension credit rights as determined in accordance with regulation 10 of the Implementation and Discharge of Liability Regulations (calculation of the value of appropriate rights);

(b) any amount deducted from the value of the pension credit in accordance with regulation 9(2)(b) of the Charging Regulations;

(c) the value of the pension credit;

(d) the transfer day; and

(e) any periodical charges the person responsible for the pension arrangement intends to make, including how and when those charges will be recovered from the payments made to the person entitled to the pension credit by virtue of regulation 6 of the Implementation and Discharge of Liability Regulations.

**9 Penalties** Where any trustee or manager of an occupational pension scheme fails, without reasonable excuse, to comply with any requirement imposed under regulation 6, 7 or 8, the Regulatory Authority may require that trustee or manager to pay within 28 days from the date of its imposition, a penalty which shall not exceed—

(a) £200 in the case of an individual, and

(b) £1,000 in any other case.

**10 Provision of information after receipt of an earmarking order—**(1) The person responsible for the pension arrangement shall, within 21 days beginning with the day that he receives—

(a) an order under section 23 of the Matrimonial Causes Act 1973, so far as it includes provision made by virtue of section 25B or 25C of that Act (powers to include provision about pensions);

(b) an order under section 12A(2) or (3) of the Family Law (Scotland) Act 1985; or

(c) an order under Article 25 of the Matrimonial Causes (Northern Ireland) Order 1978, so far as it includes provision made by virtue of Article 27B or 27C of that Order (Northern Ireland powers corresponding to those mentioned in sub-paragraph (a)),

issue to the party with pension rights and the other party a notice which includes the information specified in paragraphs (2) and (5), or (3), (4) and (5), as the case may be.

(2) Where an order referred to in paragraph (1)(a), (b) or (c) is made in respect of the pension rights or benefits of a party with pension rights whose pension is not in payment, the notice issued by the person responsible for a pension arrangement to the party with pension rights and the other party shall include a list of the circumstances in respect of any changes of which the party with pension rights or the other party must notify the person responsible for the pension arrangement.

(3) Where an order referred to in paragraph (1)(a) or (c) is made in respect of the pension rights or benefits of a party with pension rights whose pension is in payment, the notice issued by the person responsible for a pension arrangement to the party with pension rights and the other party shall include—

(a) the value of the pension rights or benefits of the party with pension rights;

(b) the amount of the pension of the party with pension rights after the order has been implemented;

(c) the first date when a payment pursuant to the order is to be made; and

(d) a list of the circumstances, in respect of any changes of which the party with pension rights or the other party must notify the person responsible for the pension arrangement.

(4) Where an order referred to in paragraph (1)(a) or (c) is made in respect of the pension rights of a party with pension rights whose pension is in payment, the notice issued by the person responsible for a pension arrangement to the party with pension rights shall, in addition to the items specified in paragraph (3), include—

(a) the amount of the pension of the party with pension rights which is currently in payment; and

(b) the amount of pension which will be payable to the party with pension rights after the order has been implemented.

(5) Where an order referred to in paragraph (1)(a), (b) or (c) is made the notice issued by the person responsible for a pension arrangement to the party with pension rights and the other party shall include—

(a) the amount of any charges which remain unpaid by—

    (i) the party with pension rights; or

    (ii) the other party,

in respect of the provision by the person responsible for the pension arrangement of information about pensions and divorce pursuant to regulation 3 of the Charging Regulations, and in respect of complying with an order referred to in paragraph (1)(a), (b) or (c); and

(b) information as to the manner in which the person responsible for the pension arrangement will recover the charges referred to in sub-paragraph (a), including—

    (i) the date when payment of those charges in whole or in part is required;

    (ii) the sum which will be payable by the party with pension rights or the other party, as the case may be; and

    (iii) whether the sum will be deducted from payments of pension to the party with pension rights, or, as the case may be, from payments to be made to the other party pursuant to an order referred to in paragraph (1)(a), (b) or (c).

## PENSIONS ON DIVORCE ETC (CHARGING) REGULATIONS 2000

**Dated** 13 April 2000

**SI 2000 No 1049**

**1 Citation, commencement and interpretation**—(1) These Regulations may be cited as the Pensions on Divorce etc (Charging) Regulations 2000 and shall come into force on 1st December 2000.

(2) In these Regulations, unless the context otherwise requires—

'the 1999 Act' means the Welfare Reform and Pensions Act 1999;

'the Provision of Information Regulations' means the Pensions on Divorce etc (Provision of Information) Regulations 2000;

'day' means any day other than—

    (a) Christmas Day or Good Friday; or

(b) a bank holiday, that is to say, a day which is, or is to be observed as, a bank holiday or a holiday under Schedule 1 to the Banking and Financial Dealings Act 1971;

'implementation period' has the meaning given by section 34(1) of the 1999 Act;

'notice of implementation' has the meaning given by regulation 1(2) of the Provision of Information Regulations;

'pension arrangement' has the meaning given to that expression in section 46(1) of the 1999 Act;

'pension credit' means a credit under section 29(1)(b) of the 1999 Act;

'pension credit benefit' has the meaning given by section 101B of the Pensions Schemes Act 1993;

'pension credit rights' has the meaning given by section 101B of the Pension Schemes Act 1993;

'pension sharing activity' has the meaning given by section 41(5) of the 1999 Act;

'pension sharing order or provision' means an order or provision which is mentioned in section 28(1) of the 1999 Act;

'person responsible for a pension arrangement' has the meaning given to that expression in section 46(2) of the 1999 Act;

'the Regulatory Authority' means the Occupational Pensions Regulatory Authority;

'the relevant date' has the meaning given by section 10(3) of the Family Law (Scotland) Act 1985;

'trustees or managers' has the meaning given by section 46(1) of the 1999 Act.

**2  General requirements as to charges**—(1) Subject to paragraph (8), a person responsible for a pension arrangement shall not recover any charges incurred in connection with—

(a) the provision of information under—

    (i) regulation 2 of the Provision of Information Regulations (basic information about pensions and divorce);

    (ii) regulation 4 of those Regulations (provision of information in response to a notification that a pension sharing order or provision may be made); or

    (iii) regulation 10 of those Regulations (provision of information after receipt of an earmarking order);

(b) complying with any order specified in section 24 of the 1999 Act (charges by pension arrangements in relation to earmarking orders); or

(c) any description of pension sharing activity specified in regulation 5 of these Regulations,

unless he has complied with the requirements of paragraphs (2) to (5).

(2) The requirements mentioned in paragraph (1) are that the person responsible for a pension arrangement shall, before a pension sharing order or provision is made—

(a) inform the member or his spouse, as the case may be, in writing of his intention to recover costs incurred in connection with any of the matters specified in sub-paragraph (a), (b) or (c) of paragraph (1); and

(b) provide the member or his spouse, as the case may be, with a written schedule of charges in accordance with paragraphs (3) and (4) in respect of those matters specified in sub-paragraph (a) or (c) of paragraph (1) for which a charge may be recoverable.

(3) No charge shall be recoverable in respect of any of the items mentioned in paragraph (4) unless the person responsible for a pension arrangement has specified in the written schedule of charges mentioned in paragraph (2)(b) that a charge may be recoverable in respect of that item.

(4) The items referred to in paragraph (3) are—
(a) the provision of a cash equivalent other than one which is provided in accordance with the provisions of—
   (i) section 93A or 94 of the 1993 Act (salary related schemes: right to statement of entitlement, and right to cash equivalent);
   (ii) regulation 11(1) of the Occupational Pension Schemes (Transfer Values) Regulations 1996 (disclosure); or
   (iii) regulation 5 (information to be made available to individuals) of, and paragraph 2(b) of Schedule 2 (provision of cash equivalent) to the Personal Pension Schemes (Disclosure of Information) Regulations 1987;
(b) subject to regulation 3(2)(b) or (c), as the case may be, the provision of a valuation in accordance with regulation 2(2) of the Provision of Information Regulations;
(c) whether a person responsible for a pension arrangement intends to recover the cost of providing membership of the pension arrangement to the person entitled to a pension credit, before or after the pension sharing order is implemented;
(d) whether the person responsible for a pension arrangement intends to recover additional charges in the circumstances prescribed in regulation 6 of these Regulations in respect of pension sharing activity described in regulation 5 of these Regulations;
(e) whether the charges are inclusive or exclusive of value added tax, where the person responsible for a pension arrangement is required to charge value added tax in accordance with the provisions of the Value Added Tax Act 1994;
(f) periodical charges in respect of pension sharing activity which the person responsible for a pension arrangement may make when a person entitled to a pension credit becomes a member of the pension arrangement from which the pension credit is derived;
(g) whether the person responsible for a pension arrangement intends to recover charges specified in regulation 10 of these Regulations.

(5) In the case of the cost referred to in paragraph (4)(c) or the charges to be imposed in respect of pension sharing activity described in regulation 5 of these Regulations, the person responsible for a pension arrangement shall provide—
(a) a single estimate of the overall cost of the pension sharing activity;
(b) a range of estimates of the overall cost of the pension sharing activity which is dependent upon the complexity of an individual case; or
(c) a breakdown of the cost of each element of pension sharing activity for which a charge shall be made.

(6) Subject to regulation 9(3) and (4), a person responsible for a pension arrangement shall recover only those sums which represent the reasonable administrative expenses which he has incurred or is likely to incur in connection with any of the activities mentioned in paragraph (1), or in relation to a pension sharing order having been made the subject of an application for leave to appeal out of time.

(7) The requirements of paragraph (2) do not apply in connection with the recovery by a person responsible for a pension arrangement of costs incurred in relation to a pension sharing order having been made the subject of an application for leave to appeal out of time.

(8) Unless the person responsible for the pension arrangement has furnished the information specified in regulation 2(2) and (3) of the Provision of Information Regulations to the member or his spouse, on request, or the court, within a period of 12 months immediately prior to the date of the request for, or the court order for the provision of, that information, the information shall be provided to the member or, where appropriate, his spouse, without charge.

**3 Charges recoverable in respect of the provision of basic information—**(1) Subject to paragraph (2), the charges prescribed for the purposes of section 23(1)(d) of the 1999 Act (charges which a person responsible for a pension arrangement may recover in respect of supplying pension information in connection with divorce etc) are any charges incurred by the person responsible for the pension arrangement in connection with the provision of any of the information set out in—

(a) regulation 2 of the Provision of Information Regulations which may be recovered in accordance with regulation 2(8) of these Regulations;

(b) regulation 4 of those Regulations; or

(c) regulation 10 of those Regulations.

(2) The charges mentioned in paragraph (1) shall not include any costs incurred by a person responsible for a pension arrangement in respect of the matters specified in sub-paragraphs (a) to (f)—

(a) any costs incurred by the person responsible for a pension arrangement which are directly related to the fulfilment of his obligations under regulation 2(3) of the Provision of Information Regulations, other than charges which may be recovered in the circumstances described in regulation 2(8) of these Regulations;

(b) any costs incurred by the person responsible for the pension arrangement as a result of complying with a request for, or an order of the court requiring, a valuation under regulation 2(2) of the Provision of Information Regulations, unless—

   (i) he is required by a member or a court to provide that valuation in less than 3 months beginning with the date the person responsible for the pension arrangement receives that request or order for the valuation;

   (ii) the valuation is requested by a member who is not entitled to a cash equivalent under any of the provisions referred to in regulation 2(4)(a);

   (iii) a member has requested a cash equivalent in accordance with any of those provisions within 12 months immediately prior to the date of the request for a valuation under regulation 2(2) of the Provision of Information Regulations;

(c) any costs incurred by the person responsible for the pension arrangement as a result of providing a valuation of benefits calculated and verified in accordance with regulation 3 of the Divorce etc (Pensions) (Scotland) Regulations 2000 (valuation), unless—

   (i) he is required by the court to provide that valuation in less than 3 months beginning with the date the person responsible for the pension arrangement receives that order;

   (ii) the valuation is requested by a member who is not entitled to a cash equivalent under any of the provisions referred to in regulation 2(4)(a);

   (iii) a member has requested a cash equivalent in accordance with any of those provisions within 12 months immediately prior to the date of the request for a valuation under regulation 2(2) of the Provision of Information Regulations; or

   (iv) the relevant date is more than 12 months immediately prior to the date the person responsible for the pension arrangement receives the request for the valuation;

(d) any costs incurred by the trustees or managers of—

   (i) an occupational pension scheme in connection with the provision of information under regulation 4 of the Occupational Pension Schemes (Disclosure of Information) Regulations 1996 (basic information about the scheme); or

      (ii)  a personal pension scheme in connection with the provision of information under regulation 4 of the Personal Pension Schemes (Disclosure of Information) Regulations 1987 (basic information about the scheme),

which the trustees or managers shall provide to the member free of charge under those Regulations;

(e)  any costs incurred by the trustees or managers of an occupational pension scheme, or a personal pension scheme, as the case may be, in connection with the provision of a transfer value in accordance with the provisions of—

    (i)  section 93A or 94 of the 1993 Act;

    (ii)  regulation 11(1) of the Occupational Pension Schemes (Transfer Values) Regulations 1996; or

    (iii)  regulation 5 of, and paragraph 2(b) of Schedule 2 to, the Personal Pension Schemes (Disclosure of Information) Regulations 1987; or

(f)  any costs not specified by the person responsible for a pension arrangement in the information on charges provided to the member pursuant to regulation 2 of the Provision of Information Regulations with the exception of any additional amounts under regulation 6(1)(a) of these Regulations.

**4  Charges in respect of the provision of information — method of recovery—**
(1) A person responsible for a pension arrangement may recover the charges specified in regulation 3(1) by using either of the methods described in sub-paragraph (a) or (b)—

(a)  requiring payment of charges at any specified time between the request for basic information and the completion of the implementation of a pension sharing order or provision, or the compliance with an order specified in section 24 of the 1999 Act, as the case may be; or

(b)  subject to paragraph (2), requiring as a condition of providing information in accordance with—

    (i)  regulation 2 of the Provision of Information Regulations; or

    (ii)  regulation 10 of those Regulations,

that payment of the charges to which regulation 3(1) refers shall be made in full by the member before the person responsible for the pension arrangement becomes obliged to provide the information.

(2) Paragraph (1)(b) shall not apply—

(a)  where a court has ordered a member to obtain the information specified in regulation 2 of the Provision of Information Regulations;

(b)  where, in accordance with regulation 2(8) of these Regulations, the person responsible for the pension arrangement shall provide that information without charge; or

(c)  where the person responsible for the pension arrangement is required to supply that information by virtue of regulation 4 of the Provision of Information Regulations.

**5  Charges in respect of pension sharing activity—**(1) The charges prescribed in respect of prescribed descriptions of pension sharing activity for the purposes of section 41(1) of the 1999 Act (charges in respect of pension sharing costs) are any costs reasonably incurred by the person responsible for the pension arrangement in connection with pension sharing activity other than those costs specified in paragraph (3).

(2) The descriptions of pension sharing activity prescribed for the purposes of section 41(1) of the 1999 Act are any type of activity which fulfils the requirements of section 41(5) of the 1999 Act.

(3) The costs specified in this paragraph are any costs which are not directly related to the costs which arise in relation to an individual case.

**6 Additional amounts recoverable in respect of pension sharing activity**—(1)
The circumstances in which a person responsible for a pension arrangement may
recover additional amounts are—

    (a) where a period of more than 12 months has elapsed between the person
responsible for the pension arrangement supplying information in
accordance with regulation 2 of the Provision of Information Regulations
and the taking effect of an order or provision specified in subsection (1) of
section 28 of the 1999 Act (activation of pension sharing); or

    (b) in the case of an occupational pension scheme, where the trustees or
managers of that scheme undertake activity from time to time associated
with pension credit rights or pension credit benefit in that scheme which
belong to a member.

(2) For the purposes of section 41(2)(d) of the 1999 Act, the additional
amounts are—

    (a) in the circumstances described in paragraph (1)(a), interest calculated at a
rate not exceeding increases in the retail prices index on the amounts of
any charges not yet due, or of any charges requested but yet to be
recovered, which are specified in the schedule of charges issued to the
member in accordance with regulation 2(2)(b) of these Regulations; and

    (b) in the circumstances described in paragraph (1)(b), an amount not
exceeding an increase calculated by reference to increases in the retail
prices index on the amounts which relate to the costs referred to in
regulation 2(4)(d) and which are specified in the schedule of charges
provided to the member and his spouse in accordance with regulation
2(2)(b).

(3) Where a person responsible for a pension arrangement intends to recover
an additional amount specified in paragraph (2)(a) in the circumstances
described in paragraph (1)(a), he shall set out this intention, the rate of interest to
be used, and the total costs recoverable in the notice of implementation and final
costs issued in accordance with regulation 7 of the Provision of Information
Regulations (provision of information after receiving a pension sharing order or
provision).

(4) Where the trustees or managers of an occupational pension scheme intend
to recover an additional amount specified in paragraph (2)(b) in the
circumstances described in paragraph (1)(b), they shall inform the parties
involved in pension sharing in writing of this intention in the schedule of charges
issued in accordance with regulation 2(2)(b) of these Regulations.

**7 Charges in respect of pension sharing activity — postponement of
implementation period**—(1) The circumstances when the start of the
implementation period may be postponed are when a person responsible for a
pension arrangement—

    (a) issues a notice to the member and the person entitled to the pension credit
no later than 21 days after the day on which the person responsible for the
pension arrangement receives the pension sharing order or provision; and

    (b) in that notice, requires the charges specified in regulation 3, 5 or 6 to be
paid before the implementation of the pension sharing order or provision is
commenced.

(2) Paragraph (1) shall apply only if the person responsible for the pension
arrangement has specified at a stage no later than in his response to the
notification that a pension sharing order or provision may be made, issued in
accordance with regulation 4 of the Provision of Information Regulations

    (a) that he requires the charges mentioned in paragraph (1) to be paid before
the implementation period is commenced; and either

    (b) whether he requires those charges to be paid in full; or

(c) the proportion of those charges which he requires to be paid as full settlement of those charges.

(3) Once payment of the charges mentioned in paragraph (1) has been made in accordance with the requirements of the person responsible for the pension arrangement—

(a) that person shall
    (i) issue the notice of implementation in accordance with regulation 7(1)(c) of the Provision of Information Regulations, and
    (ii) begin the implementation period for the pension credit,
within 21 days from the date the charges are paid, provided that the person responsible for the pension arrangement would otherwise be able to begin to implement the pension sharing order or provision, and

(b) subject to paragraph (4), that person shall not be entitled to recover any further charges in respect of the pension sharing order or provision in question.

(4) Paragraph (3)(b) shall not apply—

(a) in relation to the recovery of charges referred to in regulations 2(4)(d) and 6(2)(b); or

(b) where the pension credit depends on a pension sharing order and the order is the subject of an application for leave to appeal out of time.

**8 Charges in respect of pension sharing activity — reimbursement as between the parties to pension sharing.** A payment in respect of charges recoverable under regulation 3, 5 or 6 made by one party to pension sharing on behalf of the other party to pension sharing, shall be recoverable by the party who made the payment from that other party as a debt.

**9 Charges in respect of pension sharing activity — method of recovery—**(1) Subject to paragraphs (7) and (8), a person responsible for a pension arrangement may recover the charges specified in regulations 3, 5 and 6 by using any of the methods described in paragraph (2).

(2) The methods of recovery described in this paragraph are—

(a) subject to regulation 7 requiring the charges referred to in paragraph (1) to be paid before the implementation period for the pension sharing order or provision is commenced;

(b) deduction from a pension credit;

(c) deduction from the accrued rights of the member;

(d) where a pension sharing order or provision is made in respect of a pension which is in payment, deduction from the member's pension benefits;

(e) where liability in respect of a pension credit is discharged by the person responsible for the pension arrangement in accordance with paragraph 1(2), 2(2), or 3(2) of Schedule 5 to the 1999 Act (mode of discharge of liability for pension credits), deduction from payments of pension credit benefit; or

(f) deduction from the amount of a transfer value which is calculated in accordance with—
    (i) regulation 7 of the Occupational Pension Schemes (Transfer Values) Regulations 1996 (manner of calculation and verification of cash equivalents); or
    (ii) regulation 3 of the Personal Pension Schemes (Transfer Values) Regulations 1987 (manner of calculation and verification of cash equivalents).

(3) A person responsible for a pension arrangement shall not recover charges referred to in paragraph (1) by using any of the methods described in paragraph (2)(b), (c), (d), (e) or (f) unless—

(a) a pension sharing order or provision corresponding to any order or provision specified in subsection (1) of section 28 of the 1999 Act has been made;

(b) the implementation period has commenced;

(c) where a pension sharing order has been made, the person responsible for a pension arrangement is not aware of an appeal against the order having begun on or after the day on which the order takes effect;

(d) there are charges which are unpaid and for which the party, to whom paragraph (2)(b), (c), (d), (e) or (f) applies, is liable;

(e) the person responsible for the pension arrangement has issued a notice of implementation in accordance with regulation 7 of the Provision of Information Regulations;

(f) the person responsible for a pension arrangement specifies in the notice of implementation that recovery of the charges may be made by using any of those methods; and

(g) 21 days have elapsed since the notice of implantation was issued to the parties to pension sharing in accordance with the requirements of regulation 7 of the Provision of Information Regulations.

(4) If a pension sharing order or provision includes provision about the apportionment between the parties to pension sharing of any charge under section 41 of the 1999 Act or under corresponding Northern Ireland legislation, by virtue of section 24D of the Matrimonial Causes Act 1973 (pension sharing orders: apportionment of charges) or section 8A of the Family Law (Scotland) Act 1985 (pension sharing orders: apportionment of charges), the recovery of charges using any of the methods described in paragraph (2) by the person responsible for the pension arrangement shall comply with the terms of the order or provision.

(5) A person responsible for a pension arrangement shall not recover charges referred to in paragraph (1) by using any of the methods described in paragraph (2), from a party to pension sharing, if that party has paid in full the proportion of the charges for which he is liable.

(6) A person responsible for a pension arrangement may recover charges by using any of the methods described in paragraph (2)(b), (c) or (d)—

(a) at any time within the implementation period prescribed by section 34 of the 1999 Act ('implementation period');

(b) following an application by the trustees or managers of an occupational pension scheme, such longer period as the Regulatory Authority may allow in accordance with section 33(4) of the 1999 Act (extension of time for discharge of liability); or

(c) within 21 days after the end of the period referred to in sub-paragraph (a) or (b).

(7) Where the commencement of the implementation period is postponed, or its operation ceases in accordance with regulation 4 of the Pension Sharing (Implementation and Discharge of Liability) Regulations 2000 (postponement or cessation of implementation period where an application is made for leave to appeal out of time) a person responsible for a pension arrangement may require any outstanding charges referred to in paragraph (1) to be paid immediately, in respect of—

(a) all costs which have been incurred prior to the date of postponement or cessation; or

(b) any reasonable costs related to—

    (i) the application for leave to appeal out of time; or

    (ii) the appeal out of time itself.

(8) Paragraph (7) applies even if, prior to receiving the notification of the application for leave to appeal out of time, a person responsible for a pension arrangement has indicated to the parties to pension sharing that he will not be using the method of recovery specified in paragraph (2)(a).

**[1515]**

**10 Charges in relation to earmarking orders** The prescribed charges which a person responsible for a pension arrangement may recover in respect of complying with an order specified in section 24 of the 1999 Act are those charges which represent the reasonable administrative expenses which he has incurred or is likely to incur by reason of the order.

## PENSION SHARING (VALUATION) REGULATIONS 2000

**Dated** 13 April 2000

**SI 2000 No 1052**

**1 Citation, commencement and interpretation—**(1) These Regulations may be cited as the Pension Sharing (Valuation) Regulations 2000 and shall come into force on 1st December 2000.

(2) In these Regulations—

'the 1993 Act' means the Pension Schemes Act 1993;

'the 1995 Act' means the Pensions Act 1995;

'the 1999 Act' means the Welfare Reform and Pensions Act 1999;

['effective date' in paragraph (3) or (3A) of regulation 5 means the date as at which the assets and liabilities are valued;]

'employer' has the meaning given by section 181(1) of the 1993 Act;

'occupational pension scheme' has the meaning given by section 1 of the 1993 Act;

'pension arrangement' has the meaning given by section 46(1) of the 1999 Act;

'relevant arrangement' has the meaning given by section 29(8) of the 1999 Act;

'relevant benefits' has the meaning given by section 612 of the Income and Corporation Taxes Act 1988;

'scheme' means an occupational pension scheme;

'scheme actuary', in relation to a scheme to which section 47(1)(b) of the 1995 Act applies, means the actuary mentioned in section 47(1)(b) of that Act;

'transfer credits' has the meaning given by section 181(1) of the 1993 Act;

['transfer day' has the meaning given by section 29(8) of the 1999 Act;]

'transferor' has the meaning given by section 29(8) of the 1999 Act;

'trustees or managers' has the meaning given by section 46(1) of the 1999 Act;

'valuation day' has the meaning given by section 29(7) of the 1999 Act.

**Note.** Para (2): Definition of 'transfer day' inserted by SI 2000 No 2691, reg 10(1), (2) as from 1 December 2000. Definition of 'effective day' inserted by SI 2003 No 1727, reg 4(1), (2) as from 4 August 2003.

**2 Rights under a pension arrangement which are not shareable—**(1) Rights under a pension arrangement which are not shareable are—

(a) subject to paragraph (2), any rights accrued between 1961 and 1975 which relate to contracted-out equivalent pension benefit within the meaning of section 57 of the National Insurance Act 1965 (equivalent pension benefits, etc);

(b) any rights in respect of which a person is in receipt of—

　(i) a pension;

　(ii) an annuity;

　(iii) payments under an interim arrangement within the meaning of section 28(1A) of the 1993 Act (ways of giving effect to protected rights); or

　(iv) income withdrawal within the meaning of section 630(1) of the Income and Corporation Taxes Act 1988 (interpretation), by virtue of being the widow, widower or other dependant of a deceased person with pension rights under a pension arrangement; and

(c) any rights which do not result in the payment of relevant benefits.

(2) Paragraph (1)(a) applies only when those rights are the only rights held by a person under a pension arrangement.

**3 Calculation and verification of cash equivalents for the purposes of the creation of pension debits and credits** For the purposes of section 29 of the 1999 Act (creation of pension debits and credits), cash equivalents may be calculated and verified—

(a) where the relevant arrangement is an occupational pension scheme in accordance with regulations 4 and 5; or

(b) in any other case, in accordance with regulations 6 and 7.

**4 Occupational pension schemes: manner of calculation and verification of cash equivalents—**(1) In a case to which, or to the extent to which, paragraph (2) or (5) does not apply, cash equivalents are to be calculated and verified in such manner as may be approved in a particular case by the scheme actuary or, in relation to a scheme to which section 47(1)(b) of the 1995 Act (professional advisers) does not apply, by—

(a) a Fellow of the Institute of Actuaries;

(b) a Fellow of the Faculty of Actuaries; or

(c) a person with other actuarial qualifications who is approved by the Secretary of State, at the request of the trustees or managers of the scheme in question, as being a proper person to act for the purposes of these Regulations in connection with that scheme

and, subject to paragraph (2), in the following paragraphs of this regulation and in regulation 5 'actuary' means the scheme actuary or, in relation to a scheme to which section 47(1)(b) of the 1995 Act does not apply, the actuary referred to in sub-paragraph (a), (b) or (c) of this paragraph.

(2) Where the transferor in respect of whose rights a cash equivalent is to be calculated and verified, is a member of a scheme having particulars from time to time set out in regulations made under section 7 of the Superannuation Act 1972 (superannuation of persons employed in local government service, etc), that cash equivalent shall be calculated and verified in such manner as may be approved by the Government Actuary or by an actuary authorised by the Government Actuary to act on his behalf for that purpose and in such a case 'actuary' in this regulation and in regulation 5 means the Government Actuary or the actuary so authorised.

[(2A) Where the person with pension rights is a deferred member of an occupational pension scheme on the transfer day, the value of the benefits which he has accrued under that scheme shall be taken to be—

(a) in the case of an occupational pension scheme other than a salary related scheme, the cash equivalent to which he acquired a right under section 94(1)(a) of the 1993 Act (right to cash equivalent) on the termination of his pensionable service, calculated on the assumption that he has made an application under section 95(1) of that Act (ways of taking right to cash equivalent); or

(b) in the case of a salary related occupational pension scheme, the guaranteed cash equivalent to which he would have acquired a right under section 94(1)(aa) of the 1993 Act if he had made an application under section 95(1) of that Act.

(2B) Where the person with pension rights is an active member of an occupational pension scheme on the transfer day, the value of the benefits which he has accrued under that scheme shall be calculated and verified—

(a) on the assumption that the member had made a request for an estimate of the cash equivalent that would be available to him were his pensionable service to terminate on the transfer day; and

(b) in accordance with regulation 11 of, and Schedule 1 to, the Occupational Pension Schemes (Transfer Values) Regulations 1996 (disclosure).]

(3) Except in a case to which paragraph (5) applies, cash equivalents are to be calculated and verified by adopting methods and making assumptions which—

(a) if not determined by the trustees or managers of the scheme in question, are notified to them by the actuary; and

(b) are certified by the actuary to the trustees or managers of the scheme—

    (i) as being consistent with 'Retirement Benefit Schemes—Transfer Values (GN11)' published by the Institute of Actuaries and the Faculty of Actuaries and current on the valuation day;

    (ii) as being consistent with the methods adopted and assumptions made, at the time when the certificate is issued, in calculating the benefits to which entitlement arises under the rules of the scheme in question for a person who is acquiring transfer credits under those rules; and

    (iii) in the case of a scheme to which section 56 of the 1995 Act (minimum funding requirement) applies as providing as a minimum an amount, consistent with the methods adopted and assumptions made in calculating, for the purposes of section 57 of that Act (valuation and certification of assets and liabilities), the liabilities mentioned in section 73(3)(a), (aa), (b), (c)(i) and (d) of that Act (preferential liabilities on winding up), subject, in any case where the cash equivalent calculation is made on an individual and not a collective basis, to any adjustments which are appropriate to take account of that fact.

(4) If, by virtue of Schedule 5 to the Occupational Pension Schemes (Minimum Funding Requirement and Actuarial Valuations) Regulations 1996 (modifications), section 56 of the 1995 Act applies to a section of a scheme as if that section were a separate scheme, paragraph (3)(b)(iii) shall apply as if that section were a separate scheme and if the reference therein to a scheme were accordingly a reference to that section.

(5) Where a cash equivalent or any portion of a cash equivalent relates to money purchase benefits which do not fall to be valued in a manner which involves making estimates of the value of benefits, then that cash equivalent or that portion shall be calculated and verified in such manner as may be approved in particular cases by the trustees or managers of the scheme [, and by adopting methods consistent with the requirements of Chapter IV of Part IV of the 1993 Act (protection for early leavers—transfer values)].

**Note.** Paras (2A), (2B) inserted by SI 2000 No 2691 as from 1 December 2000. Words in square brackets in para (5) inserted by SI 2000 No 2691 as from 1 December 2000.

**5 Occupational pension schemes: further provisions as to the calculation of cash equivalents and increases and reductions of cash equivalents—**(1) Where it is the established custom for additional benefits to be awarded from the scheme at the discretion of the trustees or managers or the employer, the cash equivalent shall, unless the trustees or managers have given a direction that cash equivalents shall not take account of such benefits, take account of any such additional benefits as will accrue to the transferor if the custom continues unaltered.

(2) The trustees or managers shall not make a direction such as is mentioned in paragraph (1) unless, within 3 months before making the direction, they have consulted the actuary and have obtained the actuary's written report on the

implications for the state of funding of the scheme of making such a direction, including the actuary's advice as to whether or not in the actuary's opinion there would be any adverse implications for the funding of the scheme should the trustees or managers not make such a direction.

(3) *Subject to paragraph (6), in the case of a scheme to which section 56 of the 1995 Act applies, each respective part of the cash equivalent which relates to liabilities referred to in section 73(3)(a), (aa), (b), (c)(i) or (d) of the 1995 Act may be reduced by the percentage which is the difference between—*

    (a)  *100 per cent; and*

    (b)  *the percentage of the liabilities mentioned in the relevant paragraph of section 73(3) which the actuarial valuation shows the scheme assets as being sufficient to satisfy*

*where the actuarial valuation is the latest actuarial valuation obtained in accordance with section 57 of the 1995 Act before the valuation day.*

[(3) Subject to paragraphs (3A) and (6), where a scheme to which section 56 of the 1995 Act (minimum funding requirement) applies had, at the effective date of the actuary's last report to the trustees or managers before the valuation day in accordance with 'Retirement Benefit Schemes—Transfer Values (GN 11)' published by the Institute of Actuaries and the Faculty of Actuaries and current on the valuation day, assets that were not sufficient to pay the full amount of the cash equivalent in respect of all members, the trustees may reduce each part of the cash equivalent as shown in that report by an amount that is no greater than the percentage by which the assets are shown in that report as being insufficient to pay the full amount of the corresponding part of the cash equivalent in respect of all members of the scheme provided, in any case, that the amount of any cash equivalent after the reduction is not less than the minimum amount required under regulation 4(3)(b)(iii) to satisfy the liabilities referred to in section 73(3) of the 1995 Act (preferential liabilities on winding up) as modified by regulation 3 of the Occupational Pension Schemes (Winding Up) Regulations 1996.

[(3A) Subject to paragraph (6), in the case of a scheme to which section 56 of the 1995 Act applies which had, at the effective date of the last actuarial valuation under section 57 of the 1995 Act (valuation and certification of assets and liabilities) before the valuation day, assets that were not sufficient to pay the minimum amount of the cash equivalent in respect of the liabilities referred to in section 73(3) of the 1995 Act (preferential liabilities on winding up) as modified by regulation 3 of the Occupational Pension Schemes (Winding Up) Regulations 1996 ('the Winding Up Regulations'), the trustees or managers may reduce each part of the minimum amount of the cash equivalent, as calculated under regulation 4(3)(b)(iii), by a percentage that is no greater than the percentage which is the difference between—

    (a)  100 per cent; and

    (b)  the percentage of the liabilities mentioned in the paragraph of section 73(3) of the 1995 Act, as modified by the Winding Up Regulations, corresponding to that part which the actuarial valuation shows the scheme assets as being sufficient to satisfy.]

(4) If, by virtue of Schedule 5 to the Occupational Pension Schemes (Minimum Funding Requirement and Actuarial Valuations) Regulations 1996, section 56 of the 1995 Act applies to a section of a scheme as if that section were a separate scheme, paragraph (3) shall apply as if that section were a separate scheme, and as if the reference therein to a scheme were accordingly a reference to that section.

(5) *The reduction referred to in paragraph (3) shall not apply to a case where liability in respect of a pension credit is to be discharged in accordance with paragraph 1(2) of Schedule 5 to the 1999 Act (pension credits: mode of discharge—funded pension schemes).*

[(5) The reduction referred to in paragraph (3) shall not apply to a case where liability in respect of a pension credit is to be discharged in accordance with—

(a) paragraph 1(2) of Schedule 5 to the 1999 Act (pension credits: mode of discharge—funded pension schemes); or

(b) paragraph 1(3) of that Schedule, in a case where regulation 7(2) of the Pension Sharing (Implementation and Discharge of Liability) Regulations 2000 applies.]

(6) Where a scheme has begun to be wound up, a cash equivalent may be reduced to the extent necessary for the scheme to comply with sections 73 and 74 of the 1995 Act (discharge of liabilities by insurance, etc), and the Occupational Pension Schemes (Winding Up) Regulations 1996.

(7) If, by virtue of the Occupational Pension Schemes (Winding Up) Regulations 1996, section 73 of the 1995 Act applies to a section of a scheme as if that section were a separate scheme, paragraph (6) shall apply as if that section were a separate scheme and as if the references therein to a scheme were accordingly references to that section.

(8) Where all or any of the benefits to which a cash equivalent relates have been surrendered, commuted or forfeited before the date on which the trustees or managers discharge their liability in respect of the pension credit in accordance with the provisions of Schedule 5 to the 1999 Act, the cash equivalent of the benefits so surrendered, commuted or forfeited shall be reduced to nil.

(9) In a case where two or more of the paragraphs of this regulation fall to be applied to a calculation, they shall be applied in the order in which they occur in this regulation.

**Note.** Paras (3), (3A) substituted for para (3) by SI 2003 No 1727, reg 4(1), (3) as from 4 August 2003. Para (5) in italics omitted and para (5) in square brackets substituted by SI 2000 No 2691, reg 10(1), (4) as from 1 December 2000.

**6 Other relevant arrangements: manner of calculation and verification of cash equivalents—**(1) Except in a case to which paragraph (3) applies, cash equivalents are to be calculated and verified in such manner as may be approved in a particular case by—

(a) a Fellow of the Institute of Actuaries;

(b) a Fellow of the Faculty of Actuaries; or

(c) a person with other actuarial qualifications who is approved by the Secretary of State, at the request of the person responsible for the relevant arrangement, as being a proper person to act for the purposes of this regulation and regulation 7 in connection with that arrangement,

and in paragraph (2) 'actuary' means any person such as is referred to in sub-paragraph (a), (b) or (c) of this paragraph.

[(1A) Where the person with pension rights is a member of a personal pension scheme, or those rights are contained in a retirement annuity contract, the value of the benefits which he has accrued under that scheme or contract on the transfer day shall be taken to be the cash equivalent to which he would have acquired a right under section 94(1)(b) of the 1993 Act, if he had made an application under section 95(1) of that Act on the date on which the request for the valuation was received.

(1B) In relation to a personal pension scheme which is comprised in a retirement annuity contract made before 4th January 1988, paragraph (2) shall apply as if such a scheme were not excluded from the scope of Chapter IV of Part IV of the 1993 Act by section 93(1)(b) of that Act (scope of Chapter IV).]

(2) Except in a case to which paragraph (3) applies, cash equivalents are to be calculated and verified by adopting methods and making assumptions which—

(a) if not determined by the person responsible for the relevant arrangement, are notified to them by an actuary; and

(b) are certified by an actuary to the person responsible for the relevant arrangement as being consistent with 'Retirement Benefit Schemes—Transfer Values (GN11)', published by the Institute of Actuaries and the Faculty of Actuaries and current on the valuation day.

(3) Where a transferor's cash equivalent, or any portion of it—

(a) represents his rights to money purchase benefits under the relevant arrangement; and

(b) those rights do not fall, either wholly or in part, to be valued in a manner which involves making estimates of the value of benefits,

then that cash equivalent, or that portion of it, shall be calculated and verified in such manner as may be approved in a particular case by the person responsible for the relevant arrangement [, and by adopting methods consistent with the requirements of Chapter IV of Part IV of the 1993 Act].

(4) This regulation and regulation 7 apply to a relevant arrangement other than an occupational pension scheme.

**Note.** Paras (1A) and (1B) and words in square brackets in para (3) inserted by SI 2000 No 2691 with effect from 1 December 2000.

**7 Other relevant arrangements: reduction of cash equivalents** Where all or any of the benefits to which a cash equivalent relates have been surrendered, commuted or forfeited before the date on which the person responsible for the relevant arrangement discharges his liability for the pension credit in accordance with the provisions of Schedule 5 to the 1999 Act, the cash equivalent of the benefits so surrendered, commuted or forfeited shall be reduced in proportion to the reduction in the total value of the benefits.

## ACCESS TO JUSTICE ACT 1999 (DESTINATION OF APPEALS) ORDER 2000

**Dated**  15 April 2000

**SI 2000 No 1071**

*Citation, commencement and interpretation*

**1**—(1)  This Order may be cited as the Access to Justice Act 1999 (Destination of Appeals) Order 2000 and shall come into force on 2nd May 2000.

(2)  In this Order—

(a)  'decision' includes any judgment, order or direction of the High Court or a county court;

(b)  'family proceedings' means proceedings which are business of any description which in the High Court is for the time being assigned to the Family Division and to no other Division by or under section 61 of (and Schedule 1 to) the Supreme Court Act 1981; and

(c)  'final decision' means a decision of a court that would finally determine (subject to any possible appeal or detailed assessment of costs) the entire proceedings whichever way the court decided the issues before it.

(3)  A decision of a court shall be treated as a final decision where it—

(a)  is made at the conclusion of part of a hearing or trial which has been split into parts; and

(b)  would, if made at the conclusion of that hearing or trial, be a final decision under paragraph (2)(c).

(4)  Articles 2 to 6—

(a)  do not apply to an appeal in family proceedings; and

(b)  are subject to—

(i)  any enactment that provides a different route of appeal (other than section 16(1) of the Supreme Court Act 1981 or section 77(1) of the County Courts Act 1984); and

(ii)  any requirement to obtain permission to appeal.

*Appeals from the High Court*

**2**   Subject to articles 4 and 5, an appeal shall lie to a judge of the High Court where the decision to be appealed is made by—
  (a)  a person holding an office referred to in Part II of Schedule 2 to the Supreme Court Act 1981;
  (b)  a district judge of the High Court; or
  (c)  a person appointed to act as a deputy for any person holding such an office as is referred to in sub-paragraphs (a) and (b) or to act as a temporary additional officer in any such office.

*Appeals from a county court*

**3**—(1)  Subject to articles 4 and 5 and to paragraph (2), an appeal shall lie from a decision of a county court to the High Court.
  (2)  Subject to articles 4 and 5, where the decision to be appealed is made by a district judge or deputy district judge of a county court, an appeal shall lie to a judge of a county court.

*Appeals in a claim allocated to the multi-track or in specialist proceedings*

**4**   An appeal shall lie to the Court of Appeal where the decision to be appealed is a final decision—
  [(a) in a claim made under Part 7 of the Civil Procedure Rules 1998 and allocated to the multi-track under these Rules; or
  (b)  made in proceedings under the Companies Act 1985 or the Companies Act 1989 or to which Sections I, II or III of Part 57 or any of Parts 58 to 63 of the Civil Procedure Rules 1998 apply.].
**Note.**  Paras (a), (b) substituted by SI 2003 No 490, art 2 as from 1 April 2003.

*Appeals where decision was itself made on appeal*

**5**   Where—
  (a)  an appeal is made to a county court or the High Court (other than from the decision of an officer of the court authorised to assess costs by the Lord Chancellor); and
  (b)  on hearing the appeal the court makes a decision,
an appeal shall lie from that decision to the Court of Appeal and not to any other court.

*Transitional provisions*

**6**   Where a person has filed a notice of appeal or applied for permission to appeal before 2nd May 2000—
  (a)  this Order shall not apply to the appeal to which that notice or application relates; and
  (b)  that appeal shall lie to the court to which it would have lain before 2nd May 2000.

*Consequential amendments*

**7**   In section 16(1) of the Supreme Court Act 1981, before 'the Court of Appeal' the second time it appears, insert 'or as provided by any order made by the Lord Chancellor under section 56(1) of the Access to Justice Act 1999,'.
**8**   In section 77(1) of the County Courts Act 1984, after 'Act' insert 'and to any order made by the Lord Chancellor under section 56(1) of the Access to Justice Act 1999'.

# DIVORCE ETC (PENSIONS) REGULATIONS 2000

**Dated** 14 April 2000

**SI 2000 No 1123**

**1 Citation, commencement and transitional provisions—**(1) These Regulations may be cited as the Divorce etc (Pensions) Regulations 2000 and shall come into force on 1st December 2000.

(2) These Regulations shall apply to any proceedings for divorce, judicial separation or nullity of marriage commenced on or after 1st December 2000, and any such proceedings commenced before that date shall be treated as if these Regulations had not come into force.

**2 Interpretation** In these Regulations:
   (a) a reference to a section by number alone means the section so numbered in the Matrimonial Causes Act 1973;
   (b) 'the 1984 Act' means the Matrimonial and Family Proceedings Act 1984;
   (c) expressions defined in sections 21A and 25D(3) have the meanings assigned by those sections;
   (d) every reference to a rule by number alone means the rule so numbered in the Family Proceedings Rules 1991.

**3 Valuation—**(1) For the purposes of the court's functions in connection with the exercise of any of its powers under Part II of the Matrimonial Causes Act 1973, benefits under a pension arrangement shall be calculated and verified in the manner set out in regulation 3 of the Pensions on Divorce etc (Provision of Information) Regulations 2000, and—
   (a) the benefits shall be valued as at a date to be specified by the court (being not earlier than one year before the date of the petition and not later than the date on which the court is exercising its power);
   (b) in determining that value the court may have regard to information furnished by the person responsible for the pension arrangement pursuant to any of the provisions set out in paragraph (2); and
   (c) in specifying a date under sub-paragraph (a) above the court may have regard to the date specified in any information furnished as mentioned in sub-paragraph (b) above.

(2) The relevant provisions for the purposes of paragraph (1)(b) above are:
   (a) the Pensions on Divorce etc (Provision of Information) Regulations 2000;
   (b) regulation 5 of and Schedule 2 to the Occupational Pension Schemes (Disclosure of Information) Regulations 1996 and regulation 11 of and Schedule 1 to the Occupational Pension Schemes (Transfer Value) Regulations 1996;
   (c) section 93A or 94(1)(a) or (aa) of the Pension Schemes Act 1993;
   (d) section 94(1)(b) of the Pension Schemes Act 1993 or paragraph 2(a) (or, where applicable, 2(b)) of Schedule 2 to the Personal Pension Schemes (Disclosure of Information) Regulations 1987.

**4 Pension attachment: notices—**(1) This regulation applies in the circumstances set out in section 25D(1)(a) (transfers of pension rights).

(2) Where this regulation applies, the person responsible for the first arrangement shall give notice in accordance with the following paragraphs of this regulation to
   (a) the person responsible for the new arrangement, and
   (b) the other party.

(3) The notice to the person responsible for the new arrangement shall include copies of the following documents:

(a) every order made under section 23 imposing any requirement on the person responsible for the first arrangement in relation to the rights transferred;

(b) any order varying such an order;

(c) all information or particulars which the other party has been required to supply under any provision of rule 2.70 for the purpose of enabling the person responsible for the first arrangement:—

    (i) to provide information, documents or representations to the court to enable it to decide what if any requirement should be imposed on that person; or

    (ii) to comply with any order imposing such a requirement;

(d) any notice given by the other party to the person responsible for the first arrangement under regulation 6;

(e) where the pension rights under the first arrangement were derived wholly or partly from rights held under a previous pension arrangement, any notice given to the person responsible for the previous arrangement under paragraph (2) of this regulation on the occasion of that acquisition of rights.

(4) The notice to the other party shall contain the following particulars:

(a) the fact that the pension rights have been transferred;

(b) the date on which the transfer takes effect;

(c) the name and address of the person responsible for the new arrangement;

(d) the fact that the order made under section 23 is to have effect as if it had been made in respect of the person responsible for the new arrangement.

(5) Both notices shall be given:

(a) within the period provided by section 99 of the Pension Schemes Act 1993 for the person responsible for the first arrangement to carry out what the member requires; and

(b) before the expiry of 21 days after the person responsible for the first arrangement has made all required payments to the person responsible for the new arrangement.

**5 Pension attachment: reduction in benefits**—(1) This regulation applies where:

(a) an order under section 23 or under section 17 of the 1984 Act has been made by virtue of section 25B or 25C imposing any requirement on the person responsible for a pension arrangement;

(b) an event has occurred which is likely to result in a significant reduction in the benefits payable under the arrangement, other than:

    (i) the transfer from the arrangement of all the rights of the party with pension rights in the circumstances set out in section 25D(1)(a), or

    (ii) a reduction in the value of assets held for the purposes of the arrangement by reason of a change in interest rates or other market conditions.

(2) Where this regulation applies, the person responsible for the arrangement shall, within 14 days of the occurrence of the event mentioned in paragraph (1)(b), give notice to the other party of:

(a) that event;

(b) the likely extent of the reduction in the benefits payable under the arrangement.

(3) Where the event mentioned in paragraph (1)(b) consists of a transfer of some but not all of the rights of the party with pension rights from the arrangement, the person responsible for the first arrangement shall, within 14 days

of the transfer, give notice to the other party of the name and address of the person responsible for any pension arrangement under which the party with pension rights has acquired rights as a result of that event.

**6 Pension attachment: change of circumstances—**(1) This regulation applies where:
  (a) an order under section 23 or under section 17 of the 1984 Act has been made by virtue of section 25B or 25C imposing any requirement on the person responsible for a pension arrangement; and
  (b) any of the events set out in paragraph (2) has occurred.
  (2) Those events are:
  (a) any of the particulars supplied by the other party under rule 2.70 for any purpose mentioned in regulation 4(3)(c) has ceased to be accurate; or
  (b) by reason of the remarriage of the other party or otherwise, the order has ceased to have effect.
  (3) Where this regulation applies, the other party shall, within 14 days of the event, give notice of it to the person responsible for the pension arrangement.
  (4) Where, because of the inaccuracy of the particulars supplied by the other party under rule 2.70 or because the other party has failed to give notice of their having ceased to be accurate, it is not reasonably practicable for the person responsible for the pension arrangement to make a payment to the other party as required by the order:
  (a) it may instead make that payment to the party with pension rights, and
  (b) it shall then be discharged of liability to the other party to the extent of that payment.
  (5) Where an event set out in paragraph (2)(b) has occurred and, because the other party has failed to give notice in accordance with paragraph (3), the person responsible for the pension arrangement makes a payment to the other party as required by the order:
  (a) its liability to the party with pension rights shall be discharged to the extent of that payment, and
  (b) the other party shall, within 14 days of the payment being made, make a payment to the party with pension rights to the extent of that payment.

**7 Pension attachment: transfer of rights—**(1) This regulation applies where:
  (a) a transfer of rights has taken place in the circumstances set out in section 25D(1)(a);
  (b) notice has been given in accordance with regulation 4(2)(a) and (b);
  (c) any of the events set out in regulation 6(2) has occurred; and
  (d) the other party has not, before receiving notice under regulation 4(2)(b), given notice of that event to the person responsible for the first arrangement under regulation 6(3).
  (2) Where this regulation applies, the other party shall, within 14 days of the event, give notice of it to the person responsible for the new arrangement.
  (3) Where, because of the inaccuracy of the particulars supplied by the other party under rule 2.70 for any purpose mentioned in regulation 4(3)(c) or because the other party has failed to give notice of their having ceased to be accurate, it is not reasonably practicable for the person responsible for the new arrangement to make a payment to the other party as required by the order:
  (a) it may instead make that payment to the party with pension rights, and
  (b) it shall then be discharged of liability to the other party to the extent of that payment.
  (4) Subject to paragraph (5), where this regulation applies and the other party, within one year from the transfer, gives to the person responsible for the first arrangement notice of the event set out in regulation 6(2) in purported

compliance with regulation 7(2), the person responsible for the first arrangement shall:

(a) send that notice to the person responsible for the new arrangement, and

(b) give the other party a second notice under regulation 4(2)(b);

and the other party shall be deemed to have given notice under regulation 7(2) to the person responsible for the new arrangement.

(5) Upon complying with paragraph (4) above, the person responsible for the first arrangement shall be discharged from any further obligation under regulation 4 or 7(4), whether in relation to the event in question or any further event set out in regulation 6(2) which may be notified to it by the other party.

**8 Service**  A notice under regulation 4, 5, 6 or 7 may be sent by fax or by ordinary first class post to the last known address of the intended recipient and shall be deemed to have been received on the seventh day after the day on which it was sent.

**9 Pension sharing order not to take effect pending appeal**—(1) No pension sharing order under section 24B or variation of a pension sharing order under section 31 shall take effect earlier than 7 days after the end of the period for filing notice of appeal against the order.

(2) The filing of a notice of appeal within the time allowed for doing so prevents the order taking effect before the appeal has been dealt with.

**10 Revocation**  The Divorce etc (Pensions) Regulations 1996 and the Divorce etc (Pensions) (Amendment) Regulations 1997 are revoked.

## LEGAL AID (FUNCTIONS) ORDER 2000

**Dated**  19 July 2000

**SI 2000 No 1929**

**1 Citation and commencement**  This Order may be cited as the Legal Aid (Functions) Order 2000 and shall come into force on 1st August 2000.

**2 Interpretation**  In this Order, unless the context requires otherwise:

'the Act' means the Legal Aid Act 1988;

'the Board' means the Legal Aid Board;

'the Commission' means the Legal Services Commission established under section 1 of the Access to Justice Act 1999; and

'costs' means, in the case of a solicitor, the fees and disbursements payable under section 25 of the Act and, in the case of counsel, the fees payable under that section.

**3 Functions under Part V of the Legal Aid Act 1988**—(1) The general function conferred on the Board by section 3(2) of the Act shall include all such functions mentioned in subsection (4)(b) of that section as are required to be exercised by the Commission to enable it to determine and authorise the work to be carried out, the costs, and the method of payment of such costs, in respect of representation which is provided by means of a contract under Part II of the Act in respect of a Very High Cost Case.

(2) A Very High Cost Case is a case with regard to which, in the estimation of the Commission:

(a) if the case proceeds to trial, that trial would be likely to last for 25 days or longer; or

(b) the defence costs with regard to any one defendant (or group of defendants represented by the same firm of solicitors) are likely to amount to £150,000 or greater (such sum to include the solicitor's costs and counsel's fees and VAT).

## PROTECTION OF CHILDREN ACT 1999 (CHILD CARE ORGANISATIONS) REGULATIONS 2000

**Dated** 11 September 2000

**SI 2000 No 2432**

**1 Citation and commencement** These Regulations may be cited as the Protection of Children (Child Care Organisations) Regulations 2000, and come into force on 2nd October 2000.

**2 Prescribed enactments for the purposes of section 12(1) of the Protection of Children Act 1999** The following enactments are prescribed for the purposes of the definition of 'child care organisation' in section 12(1) of the Protection of Children Act 1999:—

(a) Local Authority Social Services Act 1970, sections 2 and 7A to 7D;

(b) Adoption Act 1976, section 9;

(c) National Health Service Act 1977, sections 8 and 15 to 18A, Schedule 5 and Schedule 5A;

(d) Registered Homes Act 1984 sections 16 and 26;

(e) Children Act 1989, sections 72 and 73, paragraph 4 of Schedule 4, paragraph 7 of Schedule 5 and paragraph 10 of Schedule 6;

(f) National Health Service and Community Care Act 1990, section 5 and Schedule 2;

(g) Criminal Justice Act 1991, sections 84 to 88A;

(h) Probation Service Act 1993, section 25; and

(i) Criminal Justice and Public Order Act 1994, sections 7 to 15.

## PROTECTION OF CHILDREN (ACCESS TO LISTS) (PRESCRIBED INDIVIDUALS) REGULATIONS 2000

**Dated** 15th September 2000

**SI 2000 No 2537**

**1 Citation, commencement and interpretation—**(1) These Regulations may be cited as the Protection of Children (Access to Lists) (Prescribed Individuals) Regulations 2000, and come into force on 9th October 2000.

(2) In these Regulations—

(a) 'the Adoption Agencies Regulations' means the Adoption Agencies Regulations 1983 [, *and*

(b) '*prospective adopter' has the same meaning as in regulation 1(3) of the Adoption Agencies Regulations.*]

['local authority' has the same meaning as in the Protection of Children Act 1999;

(c) 'prospective adopter' has the same meaning as in regulation 1(3) of the Adoption Agencies Regulations.]

Note. Words in italic omitted and words in square brackets substituted by SI 2001 No 744 as from 1 April 2001.

**2 Prescribed individuals** *For the purposes of section 103(2)(b) of the Care Standards Act 2000, a prospective adopter whose suitability to adopt a child is being considered pursuant to regulation 8(1) of the Adoption Agencies Regulations is an individual of a prescribed description.*

**2** [For the purposes of section 103(2)(b) of the Care Standards Act 2000, the following are prescribed descriptions of individual—
   (a) a prospective adopter whose suitability to adopt a child is being considered pursuant to regulation 8(1) of the Adoption Agencies Regulations; and
   (b) an individual in relation to whom a local authority is required under section 7(1A) of the Protection of Children Act 1999 (as inserted by section 98(2) of the Care Standards Act 2000) to ascertain whether he is included in any of the lists mentioned in section 7(1) of that Act.]

**Note.** Words in italic omitted and words in square brackets substituted by SI 2001 No 744 as from 1 April 2001.

**CHILD SUPPORT (TEMPORARY COMPENSATION PAYMENT SCHEME) REGULATIONS 2000**

**Dated** 30 November 2000

**SI 2000 No 3174**

**1   Citation, commencement and interpretation—**(1) These Regulations may be cited as the Child Support (Temporary Compensation Payment Scheme) Regulations 2000 and shall come into force on 31st January 2001.
   (2) In these Regulations, unless the context otherwise requires—
'the 2000 Act' means the Child Support, Pensions and Social Security Act 2000;
'the Child Support Act' means the Child Support Act 1991 before its amendment by the 2000 Act; and
'the Social Security Act' means the Social Security Act 1998.

**2   Application of the Regulations—**(1) For the purposes of section 27(2) of the 2000 Act, section 27 shall have effect as if it were modified so as to apply to cases of arrears of child support maintenance which have become due under a fresh maintenance assessment made in the following circumstances:
   (a) where the Secretary of State has given a departure direction under section 28F of the Child Support Act and—
      (i) the revised amount is higher than the current amount; and
      (ii) the effective date of the fresh maintenance assessment is a date before 1st June 1999; or
   (b) following a review under section 18 of the Child Support Act (reviews of decisions of child support officers) or a review under section 19 of that Act (reviews at instigation of child support officers) (as those provisions had effect before their substitution by section 41 of the Social Security Act),
   and the effective date of the assessment is earlier than the date on which the assessment was made; or
   (c) following an appeal to a child support appeal tribunal under section 20 of the Child Support Act (as it had effect before its substitution by section 42 of the Social Security Act) against a decision of a child support officer.

(2) In this regulation—

'current amount' means the amount of child support maintenance fixed by the current assessment; and

'revised amount' means the amount of child support maintenance fixed by the fresh maintenance assessment as a result of the departure direction given by the Secretary of State.

**3 Prescribed date** For the purposes of section 27(1)(a) of the 2000 Act, the prescribed date is 1st April [2005].

**Note.** Figure in square brackets substituted by SI 2002 No 1854, reg 3 as from 17 July 2002.

**4 Prescribed circumstances—**(1) In relation to cases of arrears which have become due under a maintenance assessment falling within section 27(1)(a) of the 2000 Act or a fresh maintenance assessment falling within section 27(1)(b) of the 2000 Act or regulation 2(1), the prescribed circumstances for the purposes of section 27(3) of the 2000 Act are that—

(a) more than 6 months of arrears of child support maintenance have become due under the maintenance assessment;

(b) at least 3 months of those arrears are due to unreasonable delay due to an act or omission by the Secretary of State or a child support officer as the case may be;

(c) the Secretary of State is authorised under section 29(1) of the Child Support Act to arrange for the collection of child support maintenance payable in accordance with the maintenance assessment;

(d) the Secretary of State is satisfied that the absent parent is, at the time the agreement is made, making such payments as are required of him in accordance with regulations made under section 29(3)(b) or (c) of the Child Support Act;

(e) where the absent parent is liable to make child support maintenance payments under a different maintenance assessment, there are no existing arrears in relation to any of them at the time the agreement is made, except for those arrears that the Secretary of State is satisfied have arisen through no fault of the absent parent; and

(f) in relation to cases under section 27(1)(b) of the 2000 Act or regulation 2(1), the absent parent has paid any arrears which he has been required to pay in relation to the maintenance assessment, or has done so except in relation to—

(i) arrears of at least 3 months which are due to unreasonable delay due to an act or omission of the Secretary of State or a child support officer as the case may be; or

(ii) any other arrears that the Secretary of State is satisfied have arisen through no fault of the absent parent.

(2) In this regulation 'agreement' means an agreement under section 27 of the 2000 Act.

**5 Terms of the agreement—**(1) For the purposes of section 27(4) of the 2000 Act, the terms which may be specified in the agreement are—

(a) the period of the agreement;

(b) payment of the child support maintenance payable in accordance with the maintenance assessment and, where relevant, the arrears, by whichever of the following methods the Secretary of State specifies as being appropriate in the circumstances—

(i) by standing order;

(ii) by any other method which requires one person to give his authority for payments to be made from an account of his to an account of another's on specific dates during the period for which the authority is in force and without the need for further authority from him;

(iii) by an arrangement whereby one person gives his authority for payments to be made from an account of his, or on his behalf, to another person or to an account of that other person;

(iv) by cheque or postal order;

(v) in cash;

(vi) by debit card;

(vii) where the Secretary of State has made a deduction from earnings order under section 31 of the Child Support Act—

(aa) by cheque;

(bb) by automated credit transfer; or

(cc) by such other method as the Secretary of State may specify;

(c) the amount of the arrears that the absent parent is required to pay (which shall include at least the last 6 months of the arrears due under the maintenance assessment);

(d) the day and interval by reference to which payments of the arrears are to be made by the absent parent; and

(e) the confirmation by the Secretary of State that he will not, while the agreement is complied with, take action to recover any of the arrears.

(2) In this regulation 'debit card' means a card, operating as a substitute for a cheque, that can be used to obtain cash or to make a payment at a point of sale whereby the card holder's bank or building society account is debited without deferment of payment.

## CHILD SUPPORT (VOLUNTARY PAYMENTS) REGULATIONS 2000

**Dated** 30 November 2000

**SI 2000 No 3177**

**1 Citation, commencement and interpretation**—(1) These Regulations may be cited as the Child Support (Voluntary Payments) Regulations 2000 and shall come into force on the day on which section 28J of the Act as inserted by the Child Support, Pensions and Social Security Act 2000 comes into force.

(2) In these Regulations—

'the Act' means the Child Support Act 1991;

'debit card' means a card, operating as a substitute for a cheque, that can be used to obtain cash or to make a payment at a point of sale whereby the card holder's bank or building society account is debited without deferment of payment;

'the Maintenance Calculations and Special Cases Regulations' means the Child Support (Maintenance Calculations and Special Cases) Regulations 2000;

'the qualifying child's home' means the home in which the qualifying child resides with the person with care and 'home' has the meaning given in regulation 1 of the Maintenance Calculations and Special Cases Regulations; and

'relevant person' means—

(a) a person with care;

(b) a non-resident parent;

(c) a parent who is treated as a non-resident parent under regulation 8 of the Maintenance Calculations and Special Cases Regulations;

(d) where the application for a maintenance calculation is made by a child under section 7 of the Act, that child, in respect of whom a maintenance calculation has been applied for, or has been treated as applied for, under section 6(3) of the Act, or is or has been in force.

**2 Voluntary payment—**(1) A payment counts as a voluntary payment if it is—
(a)  made in accordance with section 28J(2) and (4) of the Act;
(b)  of a type to which regulation 3 applies;
(c)  made on or after the effective date of the maintenance calculation made, or which would be made but for the Secretary of State's decision not to make one, and for this purpose 'effective date' means the effective date as determined in accordance with the Child Support (Maintenance Calculation Procedure) Regulations 2000; and
(d)  a payment in relation to which evidence or verification of a type to which regulation 4 applies is provided, if the Secretary of State so requires.

(2) Where the Secretary of State is considering whether a payment is a voluntary payment, he may invite representations from a relevant person.

**3 Types of payment** This regulation applies to a payment made by the non-resident parent—
(a)  by any of the following methods—
   (i)  in cash;
   (ii)  by standing order;
   (iii)  by any other method which requires one person to give his authority for payments to be made from an account of his to an account of another on specific dates during the period for which the authority is in force and without the need for any further authority from him;
   (iv)  by an arrangement whereby one person gives his authority for payments to be made from an account of his, or on his behalf, to another person or to an account of that other person;
   (v)  by cheque or postal order; or
   (vi)  by debit card, and
(b)  which is, or is in respect of,—
   (i)  a payment in lieu of child support maintenance and which is paid to the person with care;
   (ii)  a mortgage or loan taken out on the security of the property which is the qualifying child's home where that mortgage or loan was taken out to facilitate the purchase of, or to pay for essential repairs or improvements to, that property;
   (iii)  rent on the property which is the qualifying child's home;
   (iv)  mains-supplied gas, water or electricity charges at the qualifying child's home;
   (v)  council tax payable by the person with care in relation to the qualifying child's home;
   (vi)  essential repairs to the heating system in the qualifying child's home; or
   (vii)  repairs which are essential to maintain the fabric of the qualifying child's home.

**4 Evidence or verification of payment** This regulation applies to—
(a)  evidence provided by the non-resident parent in the form of—
   (i)  a bank statement;
   (ii)  a duplicate of a cashed cheque;
   (iii)  a receipt from the payee; or
   (iv)  a receipted bill or invoice; or
(b)  verification orally or in writing from the person with care.

# CHILD SUPPORT (TRANSITIONAL PROVISIONS) REGULATIONS 2000

**Dated**   4 December 2000

**SI 2000 No 3186**

PART I

GENERAL

## ARRANGEMENTS OF REGULATIONS

**1 Citation and commencement** These Regulations may be cited as the Child Support (Transitional Provisions) Regulations 2000 and shall come into force on the day on which section 29 of the 2000 Act comes fully into force.

**2 Interpretation—**(1) In Parts I to III and V except where otherwise stated—
'the Act' means the Child Support Act 1991;
['the Arrears, Interest and Adjustment Regulations' means the Child Support (Arrears, Interest and Adjustment of Maintenance Assessments) Regulations 1992;]
'the Assessment Calculation Regulations' means the Child Support (Maintenance Assessments and Special Cases) Regulations 1992;
'the Assessment Procedure Regulations' means the Child Support (Maintenance Assessment Procedure) Regulations 1992;
'the 2000 Act' means the Child Support, Pensions and Social Security Act 2000;
'calculation date' means the date the Secretary of State makes a conversion decision;
'capped amount' means the amount of income for the purposes of Part I of Schedule 1 to the Act where that income is limited by the application of paragraph 10(3) of that Schedule;
'case conversion date' means the effective date for the conversion of the non-resident parent's liability to pay child support maintenance from the rate as determined under the former Act and Regulations made under that Act, as provided for in regulation 15;
'commencement date' means the date on which section 1 of the 2000 Act, which amends section 11 of the Act, comes into force for the purposes of maintenance calculations the effective date of which, were they maintenance assessments, applying [regulation 30 or 33(7) (but not regulation 8C or 30A) of the Assessment Procedure Regulations or regulation 3(5), (7) or (8) of the Maintenance Arrangements and Jurisdiction Regulations] and subject to paragraph (2), would be the same as or later than the date prescribed for the purposes of section 4(10)(a) of the Act;
'conversion calculation' means the calculation made in accordance with regulation 16;
'conversion date' means the date on which section 1 of the 2000 Act, which amends section 11 of the Act, comes into force for all purposes;
'conversion decision' means the decision under regulation 3(1) or (4);
'Decisions and Appeals Regulations' means the Social Security and Child Support (Decisions and Appeals) Regulations 1999;
'departure direction' has the meaning given in section 54 of the former Act;
'Departure Regulations' means the Child Support Departure Direction and Consequential Amendments Regulations 1996;

'first prescribed amount' means the amount stated in or prescribed for the purposes of paragraph 4(1)(b) or (c) of Part I of Schedule 1 to the Act (flat rate for non-resident parent in receipt of benefit, pension or allowance);

'former Act' means the Act prior to its amendment by the 2000 Act;

'former assessment amount' means the amount of child support maintenance payable under a maintenance assessment on the calculation date excluding amounts payable in respect of arrears or reductions for overpayments;

'interim maintenance assessment' has the meaning given in section 54 of the former Act;

'Maintenance Arrangements and Jurisdiction Regulations' means the Child Support (Maintenance Arrangements and Jurisdiction) Regulations 1992 *prior to their amendment by the Child Support (Information, Evidence and Disclosure and Maintenance Arrangements and Jurisdiction) (Amendment) Regulations 2000*;

'maintenance assessment' has the meaning given in section 54 of the former Act other than an interim maintenance assessment;

'Maintenance Calculations and Special Cases Regulations' means the Child Support (Maintenance Calculations and Special Cases) Regulations 2000;

'maintenance period' has the meaning given in regulation 33 of the Assessment Procedure Regulations and, where in relation to a non-resident parent there is in force on the calculation date more than one maintenance assessment with more than one maintenance period, the first maintenance period to begin on or after the conversion date;

'maximum transitional amount' *means 30% of the non-resident parent's net weekly income taken into account in the conversion decision, or the subsequent decision, as the case may be* [has the meaning given in regulation 25(5), (6) or (7), whichever is applicable];

'new amount' means the amount of child support maintenance payable *in accordance with the conversion decision* [from the conversion date];

'partner' means, where there is a couple, the other member of that couple, and 'couple' for this purpose has the same meaning as in paragraph 10C(5) of Part I of Schedule 1 to the Act;

'phasing amount' means the amount determined in accordance with regulation 24;

'relevant departure direction' and 'relevant property transfer' have the meanings given in regulation 17;

'relevant other children' has the meaning given in paragraph 10C(2) of Part I of Schedule 1 to the Act and Regulations made under that paragraph;

'second prescribed amount' means the amount prescribed for the purposes of paragraph 4(2) of Part I of Schedule 1 to the Act (flat rate for non-resident parent who has a partner and who is in receipt of certain benefits);

'subsequent decision' means—

(a) any decision under section 16 or 17 of the Act to revise or supersede a conversion decision; or

(b) any such revision or supersession as decided on appeal,

whether as originally made or as revised under section 16 of the Act or decided on appeal;

'subsequent decision amount' means the amount of child support maintenance liability resulting from a subsequent decision;

'transitional amount' means the amount of child support maintenance payable during the transitional period;

'transitional period' means—

(a) the period from the case conversion date to the end of the last complete maintenance period which falls immediately prior to the—

(i) fifth anniversary of the case conversion date; or

(ii) first anniversary of the case conversion date where regulation 12(1), (2), (4) or (5) or 13 applies; or

(b) if earlier, the period from the case conversion date up to the date when the amount of child support maintenance payable by the non-resident parent is equal to the new amount or the subsequent decision amount, as the case may be; and

'the Variations Regulations' means the Child Support (Variations) Regulations 2000 .

(2) For the purposes of the definition of 'commencement date' in paragraph (1)—

(a) in the application of the Assessment Procedure Regulations, where no maintenance enquiry form, as defined in those Regulations, is given or sent to the non-resident parent, the Regulations shall be applied as if references in regulation 30 of those Regulations—

    (i) to the date when the maintenance enquiry form was given or sent to the non-resident parent were to the date on which the non-resident parent is first notified by the Secretary of State, orally or in writing, that an application for child support maintenance has been made in respect of which he is named as the non-resident parent; and

    (ii) to the return by the non-resident parent of the maintenance enquiry form containing his name, address and written confirmation that he is the parent of the child or children in respect of whom the application was made, were to the provision of this information by the non-resident parent; or

(b) in the application of the Maintenance Arrangements and Jurisdiction Regulations, where no maintenance enquiry form, as defined in the Assessment Procedure Regulations, is given or sent to the non-resident parent, regulation 3(8) shall apply as if the reference to the date when the maintenance enquiry form was given or sent were to the date on which the non-resident parent is first notified by the Secretary of State, orally or in writing, that an application for child support maintenance has been made in respect of which he is named as the non-resident parent.

(3) In these Regulations any reference to a numbered Part is to the Part of these Regulations bearing that number, any reference to a numbered regulation is to the regulation in these Regulations bearing that number and any reference in a regulation to a numbered paragraph is to the paragraph in that regulation bearing that number.

**Note.** Words in italics in para (1) omitted and words in square brackets inserted by SI 2003 No 328, reg 9(1), (2)(a)(b) as from 21 February 2003. Para (1) Para (1): definition 'the Arrears, Interest and Adjustment Regulations' inserted by SI 2004 No 2415, reg 8(1), (2)(a) as from 16 September 2004. Para (1): in definition 'maximum transitional amount' words 'has the meaning given in regulation 25(5), (6) or (7), whichever is applicable' in square brackets substituted by SI 2003 No 2779, reg 7(1), (2) as from 5 November 2003. Para (1): in definition 'new amount' words 'from the case conversion date' in square brackets substituted by SI 2004 No 2415, reg 8(1), (2)(b) as from 16 September 2004.

PART II

DECISION MAKING AND APPEALS

**3 Decision and notice of decision—**(1) Subject to paragraph (2), a decision as to the amount of child support maintenance payable under a maintenance assessment or an interim maintenance assessment made under section 11, 12, 16, 17 or 20 of the former Act may be superseded by the Secretary of State on his own initiative under section 17 of the Act, in relation to—

(a) a maintenance assessment (whenever made) which *has an effective date before the commencement date and* is in force on the calculation date;

(b) a maintenance assessment made following an application for child support maintenance which is made or treated as made as provided for in regulation 28(1);

(c) an interim maintenance assessment [whenever made] where there is sufficient information held by the Secretary of State to make a decision in accordance with this paragraph.

*(2) Where the Secretary of State acts in accordance with paragraph (1) the information used for the purposes of that supersession will be that held by the Secretary of State on the calculation date.*

[(2) Where the Secretary of State acts in accordance with paragraph (1), the information used for the purposes of that supersession will be—

(a) that held by the Secretary of State on the calculation date; or

(b) where—
    (i) regulation 5(b) applies; and
    (ii) the Secretary of State is unable to make the decision required to be made in accordance with that regulation on the basis of the information referred to in paragraph (a),

that which was used or considered to make the maintenance assessment to be superseded in accordance with regulation 3(1)(a) or (b).]

(3) Where a superseding decision referred to in paragraph (1) is made the Secretary of State shall—

(a) make a conversion calculation;

(b) calculate a new amount; and

(c) notify to the non-resident parent and the person with care and, where the maintenance assessment was made in response to an application under section 7 of the former Act, the child, in writing—
    (i) the new amount;
    (ii) where appropriate, the transitional amount;
    (iii) any phasing amount applied in the calculation of the transitional amount;
    (iv) the length of the transitional period;
    (v) the date the conversion decision was made;
    (vi) the effective date of the conversion decision;
    (vii) the non-resident parent's net weekly income;
    (viii) the number of qualifying children;
    (ix) the number of relevant other children;
    (x) where there is an adjustment for apportionment or shared care, or both, or under regulation 9 or 11 of the Maintenance Calculation and Special Cases Regulations, the amount calculated in accordance with Part I of Schedule 1 to the Act and those Regulations;
    (xi) any relevant departure direction or relevant property transfer taken into account in the conversion decision; and
    (xii) any apportionment carried out in accordance with regulation 25(3).

(4) Where at the calculation date there is an interim maintenance assessment in force and there is insufficient information held by the Secretary of State to make a maintenance assessment, or a decision in accordance with paragraph (1), the Secretary of State shall—

(a) supersede the interim maintenance assessment to make a default maintenance decision; and

(b) notify the non-resident parent, the person with care and, where the maintenance assessment was made in response to an application under section 7, the child, in writing, in accordance with regulation 15C(2) of the Decisions and Appeals Regulations.

(5) In a case to which paragraph (1)(c) or (4) applies, where after the calculation date information is made available to the Secretary of State to enable him to make a maintenance assessment he may—

(a) where the decision was made under paragraph (1)(c), revise the interim maintenance assessment in accordance with the Assessment Procedure Regulations, and supersede the conversion decision in accordance with the Decisions and Appeals Regulations;

(b) where the decision was made under paragraph (4), revise the interim maintenance assessment in accordance with the Assessment Procedure Regulations, and revise the default maintenance decision in accordance with the Decisions and Appeals Regulations.

(6) A decision referred to in paragraph (1) or (4) shall take effect from the case conversion date.

**Note.** Words in italics in para (1)(a) omitted and words in square brackets inserted by SI 2003 No 328, reg 9(1), (3)(a)(b) as from 21 February 2003. Para (2) substituted by SI 2004 No 2415, reg 8(1), (3) as from 16 September 2004.

**4 Revision, supersession and appeal of conversion decisions—**(1) Subject to this Part, where—

(a) an application is made to the Secretary of State or he acts on his own initiative to revise or supersede a conversion decision; or

(b) there is an appeal in respect of a conversion decision,

such application, action or appeal shall be decided under the Decisions and Appeals Regulations and except as otherwise provided in paragraph (2), notification shall be given in accordance with regulation 3(3).

(2) Where the Secretary of State acts in accordance with paragraph (1) he shall notify—

(a) in relation to regulation 3(3)(c)(i), the subsequent decision amount in place of the new amount; and

(b) where there has been agreement to a variation or a variation has otherwise been taken into account, the amounts calculated in accordance with the Child Support Variations Regulations.

(3) Where after the calculation date—

(a) an application is made to the Secretary of State or he acts on his own initiative to revise or supersede a maintenance assessment, an interim maintenance assessment or departure direction; or

(b) there is an appeal in respect of a maintenance assessment, an interim maintenance assessment or departure direction; and

(c) such application, action or appeal has been decided in accordance with regulations made under the former Act for the determination of such applications,

the Secretary of State may revise or supersede the conversion decision in accordance with the Decisions and Appeals Regulations.

*(4) In their application to a decision referred to in these Regulations, the Decisions and Appeals Regulations shall be modified so as to provide, on any revision or supersession of a conversion decision under section 16 or 17, respectively, of the Act, that—*

*(a) the conversion decision may include a relevant departure direction or relevant property transfer; and*

*(b) the effective date of the revision or supersession shall be as determined under the Decisions and Appeals Regulations or the case conversion date, whichever is the later.*

[(4) In their application to a decision referred to in these Regulations, the Decisions and Appeals Regulations shall be modified so as to provide—

(a) on any revision or supersession of a conversion decision under section 16 or 17 respectively of the Act, that—

(i) the conversion decision may include a relevant departure direction or relevant property transfer; and

(ii) the effective date of the revision or supersession shall be as determined under the Decisions and Appeals Regulations or the case conversion date, whichever is the later;

(b) on any appeal in respect of a conversion decision under section 16 or 17 respectively of the Act, that the time within which the appeal must be brought shall be—

    (i) within the time from the date of notification of the conversion decision against which the appeal is brought, to one month after the case conversion date of that decision; or

    (ii) as determined under the Decisions and Appeals Regulations,

whichever is the later.]

(5) In this Part, for the purposes of any revision or supersession a conversion decision shall include a subsequent decision.

**Note.** Para (4) in italics omitted and para (4) in square brackets substituted by SI 2000 No 1204 as from 30 April 2002.

**[4A Revision and supersession of an adjustment]** [Where, on or after the calculation date, an application is made to the Secretary of State or he acts on his own initiative to revise or supersede an adjustment of the amounts payable under a maintenance assessment, he may revise or supersede that adjustment in accordance with the Decisions and Appeals Regulations.]

**Note** Inserted by SI 2004 No 2415, reg 8(1), (4) as from 16 September 2004.

**5 Outstanding applications at calculation date** Where at the calculation date there is outstanding an application for a maintenance assessment or a departure direction, or under section 16 or 17 of the former Act for the revision or supersession of a maintenance assessment, an interim maintenance assessment or a departure direction, the Secretary of State may—

(a) where the application has been finally decided in accordance with Regulations made under the former Act for deciding such applications, supersede the maintenance assessment in accordance with regulation 3; or

(b) where he is unable to make a final decision on the application for—

    (i) a departure direction; or

    (ii) a revision or supersession,

supersede the maintenance assessment or the interim maintenance assessment in accordance with regulation 3.

**[5A Outstanding revisions and supersessions at calculation date]** [Regulation 5 shall apply in the same way to a decision of the Secretary of State acting on his own initiative under section 16 or 17 of the former Act to revise or supersede a maintenance assessment, an interim maintenance assessment or a departure direction as it does to an application made for the same purpose.]

**Note.** Inserted by SI 2004 No 2415, reg 8(1), (5) as from 16 September 2004.

**6 Applications for a departure direction or a variation made after calculation date**—(1) Where an application for a departure direction or a variation is made after notification of the conversion decision the Secretary of State shall—

(a) where the grounds of the application are subject only to a decision under the Departure Regulations, make a decision under the Departure Regulations;

(b) where the grounds of the application are subject to a decision or determination, as the case may be, under—

    (i) the Departure Regulations; and

    (ii) the Variations Regulations,

make a decision under the Departure Regulations; or

(c) where the grounds of the application are subject only to a determination under the Variations Regulations, treat the application as an advance application for a variation.

(2) Where the Secretary of State has made a decision or a determination in which he agrees to the departure direction or variation applied for as provided under paragraph(1) he shall—

(a) where the decision is made under paragraph (1)(a), supersede the maintenance assessment in accordance with the Assessment Procedure Regulations and the conversion decision in accordance with the Decisions and Appeals Regulations;

(b) where the decision is made under paragraph (1)(b), supersede the maintenance assessment in accordance with the Assessment Procedure Regulations and the conversion decision in accordance with the Decisions and Appeals Regulations to give effect to any relevant departure direction, and from the case conversion date any variation, in the decision; or

(c) where a determination is made under paragraph (1)(c), supersede the conversion decision in accordance with the Decisions and Appeals Regulations.

(3) Where the Secretary of State does not have the information required to make a decision under paragraph (1) he shall not revise or supersede the conversion decision.

**7 Grounds on which a conversion decision may not be revised, superseded or altered on appeal** A decision of the Secretary of State made under regulation 3 shall not be revised, superseded or altered on appeal on any of the following grounds—

(a) the use of the information held by the Secretary of State at the calculation date;

(b) that the Secretary of State took into account a relevant departure direction in the conversion decision;

(c) the application of the phasing amount in the calculation of the transitional amount;

(d) the phasing amount applied to the calculation of the transitional amount;

(e) the length of the transitional period;

(f) that an existing departure direction has not been taken into account by the Secretary of State in the transitional amount;

(g) that the Secretary of State took into account a relevant property transfer in the conversion decision, except where the application affects a relevant property transfer which has been included in the conversion decision on the grounds that—

    (i) where the person with care or, where the maintenance assessment was made in response to an application under section 7 of the former Act, the child applies for the relevant property transfer to be removed, that property transfer when awarded did not reflect the true nature, purpose or value of the property transfer; or

    (ii) *where the person with care, the non-resident parent or, where the maintenance assessment was made in response to an application under section 7 of the former Act, the child applies for the relevant property transfer to be replaced with a* variation in relation to the same transfer.

**Note.** In para (g)(ii) words omitted revoked by SI 2003 No 2779, reg 7(1), (3) as from 5 November 2003.

**8 Outstanding appeals at calculation date**—(1) Where there is an appeal outstanding at the calculation date against a maintenance assessment, an interim maintenance assessment or an application for a departure direction under the former Act, the Secretary of State shall supersede the maintenance assessment in accordance with regulation 3 using the information held at that date.

(2) When the appeal is decided—

(a) it shall be put into effect in accordance with the tribunal's decision; and

(b) the conversion decision shall be superseded in accordance with the Decisions and Appeals Regulations in consequence of the implementation of the tribunal decision.

PART III

AMOUNT PAYABLE FOLLOWING CONVERSION DECISION

**9 Amount of child support maintenance payable—**(1) *Where* [Subject to regulation 9A, where] a decision of the Secretary of State is made as provided in regulation 3(1)(a) or (b), the amount of child support maintenance payable by the non-resident parent shall, on and from the case conversion date, including but not limited to those cases referred to in regulation 14, be the new amount, *unless regulation 10 applies, in which case it shall be a transitional amount as provided for in regulations 11 to 28* [unless—

(a) regulation 10 applies, in which case it shall be a transitional amount as provided for in regulations 11 and 17 to 28; or

(b) regulation 12 or 13 applies, in which case it shall be a transitional amount as provided for in those regulations.]

(2) Where a decision under regulation 3(1)(c) relates to a Category B or C interim maintenance assessment, *regulations 10 to 28* [regulations 10 to 14 and 16 to 28] shall apply as if references to a maintenance assessment included references to such an interim maintenance assessment.

(3) In this regulation the reference to Category B or C interim maintenance assessments, and in regulation 14 the reference to Category A or D interim maintenance assessments, are to those assessments within the meaning given in regulation 8(3) of the Assessment Procedure Regulations.

**Note.** Words in italics in paras (1) and (2) omitted and words in square brackets substituted by SI 2002 No 1204, reg 8(1), (3)(a)(b) as from 30 April 2002. Para (1): words 'Subject to regulation 9A, where' in square brackets substituted by SI 2004 No 2415, reg 8(1), (6) as from 16 September 2004.

**[9A Adjustment of the amount of child support maintenance payable]—**[(1) Subject to paragraph (2), where—

(a) there has been an overpayment of child support maintenance under a maintenance assessment; and

(b) the amount payable under that maintenance assessment has been adjusted under regulation 10 of the Arrears, Interest and Adjustment Regulations as it applies to a maintenance assessment,

that adjustment shall apply to the new amount or the transitional amount in the conversion decision, as the case may be, if—

(i) the overpayment remains on the case conversion date; and

(ii) the Secretary of State considers it appropriate in all the circumstances of the case having regard to the matters set out in regulation 10(1)(b) of the Arrears, Interest and Adjustment Regulations as it applies to a conversion decision.

(2) Where the conversion decision relates to more than one parent with care, the adjustment of the amount payable under a maintenance assessment which applies to the new amount or the transitional amount, as the case may be, in accordance with paragraph (1) shall only apply in respect of the apportioned amount payable to the parent with care in relation to whom the maintenance assessment subject to the adjustment was made.

(3) In paragraph (2) the 'apportioned amount' shall have the meaning given in regulation 11(4).]

**Note.** Inserted by SI 2004 No 2415, reg 8(1), (7) as from 16 September 2004.

**[9B Attribution of payments]** [Where—
  (a) there are arrears of child support maintenance under a maintenance assessment; and
  (b) the Secretary of State has attributed any payment of child support maintenance made by an absent parent to child support maintenance due as he thinks fit, in accordance with regulation 9 of the Arrears, Interest and Adjustment Regulations as it applies to a maintenance assessment,
that attribution of payments shall apply to the new amount or the transitional amount in the conversion decision, as the case may be, if—
    (i)   the arrears remain on the case conversion date; and
    (ii)  the Secretary of State has made that attribution of payments as he thought fit, in accordance with regulation 9 of the Arrears, Interest and Adjustment Regulations as it applies to a conversion decision.]

**Note.** Inserted by SI 2004 No 2415, reg 8(1), (7) as from 16 September 2004.

**10 Circumstances in which a transitional amount is payable** This regulation applies where the new amount is a basic or reduced rate [an amount calculated under regulation 22] [, an amount calculated under regulation 26 of the Variations Regulations] or, except where regulation 12, 13 or 14 applies, a flat rate of child support maintenance; and
  (a) the former assessment amount is greater than the new amount and when the former assessment amount is decreased by the phasing amount, the resulting figure is greater than the new amount; or
  (b) the former assessment amount is less than the new amount and when the former assessment amount is increased by the phasing amount, the resulting figure is less than the new amount.

**Note.** First words in square brackets inserted by SI 2002 No 1204 as from 30 April 2002. Second words in square brackets inserted by SI 2003 No 328 as from 21 February 2003.

**11 Transitional amount—basic, reduced and most flat rate cases—**(1) Subject to *paragraph (2)* [paragraphs (2) and (3)]and regulation 25, in cases to which regulation 10 applies the transitional amount is the former assessment amount decreased, where that amount is greater than the new amount, or increased, where the latter amount is the greater, by the phasing amount.

  *(2) Where regulation 10 applies and there is at the calculation date more than one maintenance assessment in relation to the non-resident parent—*
    *(a) the amount of child support maintenance payable from the case conversion date to each person with care shall be determined by apportioning the new amount as provided in paragraph 6 of Part I of Schedule 1 to the Act and Regulations made under that Part; and*
    *(b) regulation 10 and paragraph (1) shall apply as if the references to the new amount were to the amount payable in respect of the person with care and the references to the former assessment amount were to that amount in respect of that person with care.*

  [(2) Subject to paragraph (3), where regulation 10 applies and there is at the calculation date more than one maintenance assessment in relation to the same absent parent, which has the meaning given in the former Act, the amount of child support maintenance payable from the case conversion date in respect of each person with care shall be determined by applying regulation 10 and paragraph (1) as if—
    (a) the references to the new amount were to the apportioned amount payable in respect of the person with care; and
    (b) the references to the former assessment amount were to that amount in respect of that person with care.
  (3) Where regulation 10 applies and a conversion decision is made in a circumstance to which regulation 15(3C) applies, the amount of child support maintenance payable from the case conversion date—

(a)  to a person with care in respect of whom an application for a maintenance calculation has been made or treated as made which is of a type referred to in regulation 15(3C)(b), shall be the apportioned amount payable in respect of that person with care; and

(b)  in respect of any other person with care, shall be determined by applying regulation 10 and paragraph (1) as if the references to the new amount were to the apportioned amount payable in respect of that person with care and the references to the former assessment amount were to that amount in respect of that person with care.

(4) In this regulation, 'apportioned amount' means the amount payable in respect of a person with care calculated as provided in Part I of Schedule 1 to the Act and Regulations made under that Part and, where applicable, regulations 17 to 23 and Part IV of these Regulations.]

**Note.** Words in italics in para (1) and para (2) omitted and paras (2) to (4) in square brackets inserted by SI 2003 No 328 as from 21 February 2003.

**12 Transitional amount in flat rate cases—**(1) Except where the former assessment amount is nil, where the new amount would be the first prescribed amount but is nil owing to the application of paragraph 8 of Part I of Schedule 1 to the Act the amount of child support maintenance payable for the year commencing on the case conversion date shall be a transitional amount equivalent to the second prescribed amount and thereafter shall be the new amount, *nil.*

(2) Except where the former assessment amount is nil, where the new amount would be the second prescribed amount but is nil owing to the application of paragraph 8 of Part I of Schedule 1 to the Act the amount of child support maintenance payable for the year commencing on the case conversion date shall be a transitional amount equivalent to half the second prescribed amount and thereafter shall be the new amount, *nil.*

(3) Where—

(a)  a non-resident parent has more than one qualifying child and in relation to them there is more than one person with care; and

(b)  the amount of child support maintenance payable from the case conversion date to one or some of those persons with care, but not all of them, would be nil owing to the application of paragraph 8 of Part I of Schedule 1 to the Act,

the amount of child support maintenance payable by the non-resident parent from the case conversion date shall be the new amount, *apportioned as provided in paragraph 6 of Part I of Schedule 1 to the Act and Regulations made under it, unless paragraph (4) or (5) applies* [among the persons with care, other than any in respect of whom paragraph 8 of Part I of Schedule 1 to the Act applies, in accordance with paragraph 6(2) of that Schedule, unless paragraph (4) or (5) applies].

(4) Subject to paragraph (6), where the former assessment amount is less than the new amount by an amount which is more than the second prescribed amount or, where paragraph 4(2) of Part I of Schedule 1 to the Act applies to the non-resident parent, half the second prescribed amount, the amount of child support maintenance payable by the non-resident parent shall be as provided in paragraph (1) where paragraph 4(1)(b) [or (c)] of Part I of Schedule 1 to the Act applies, and as provided in paragraph (2) where paragraph 4(2) of that Schedule applies.

(5) Subject to paragraph (6), where the former assessment amount is greater than the new amount the amount of child support maintenance payable by the non-resident parent shall be the new amount unless the new amount is less than the second prescribed amount or, where paragraph 4(2) of Part I of Schedule 1 to the Act applies to the non-resident parent, half the second prescribed amount, in which case the amount of child support maintenance payable by the non-resident parent shall be as provided in paragraph (1) where paragraph 4(1)(b) [or (c)] of

Part I of Schedule 1 to the Act applies, and as provided in paragraph (2) where paragraph 4(2) of that Schedule applies.

*(6) Where paragraph (4) or (5) applies the transitional amount shall be apportioned among the persons with care as provided in paragraph 6 of Part I of Schedule 1 to the Act and Regulations made under that Part, and the amount of child support maintenance which the non-resident parent is liable to pay to each person with care in respect of whom care of the qualifying child is shared shall be nil.*

[(6) Where paragraph (4) or (5) applies, the transitional amount shall be apportioned among the persons with care, other than any in respect of whom the former assessment amount is nil and paragraph 8 of Part I of Schedule 1 to the Act applies, in accordance with paragraph 6(2) of that Schedule.]

(7) In this regulation 'former assessment amount' means, in relation to a non-resident parent in respect of whom there is in force on the calculation date more than one maintenance assessment, the aggregate of the amounts payable under those assessments, and *in paragraph (5)* includes the amount payable where section 43 of the former Act (contribution to maintenance) applies to the non-resident parent.

**Note.** Words in italics omitted and words in square brackets substituted by SI 2002 No 1204 as from 30 April 2002.

**13 Transitional amount—certain flat rate cases—**[(1)] Where paragraph 4(2) of Part I of Schedule 1 to the Act applies and the former assessment amount is nil, the amount of child support maintenance payable for the year beginning on the case conversion date shall be a transitional amount equivalent to half the second prescribed amount and thereafter shall not be a transitional amount but shall be the new amount.

[(2) Where paragraph 4(1)(b) or (c) of Part I of Schedule 1 to the Act applies and the former assessment amount is nil, the amount of child support maintenance payable for the year beginning on the case conversion date shall be a transitional amount equivalent to half the first prescribed amount and thereafter shall not be a transitional amount but shall be the new amount.]

**Note.** Rule 13 renumbered as para (1) and para (2) added by SI 2002 No 1204 as from 30 April 2002.

**14 Certain cases where the new amount is payable** The amount of child support maintenance which the non-resident parent is liable to pay on and from the case conversion date is the new amount where—

(a) the application for the maintenance assessment referred to in regulation 3(1)(a) is determined after the case conversion date, except in a case to which regulation 28(1) applies;

(b) the former assessment amount is more than nil, including where section 43 of the former Act (contribution to maintenance) applies to the non-resident parent and the new amount is the first or second prescribed amount;

(c) the new amount is the nil rate under paragraph 5 of Part I of Schedule 1 to the Act; *or*

(d) the former assessment amount is nil and the new amount is nil owing to the application of paragraph 8 of Part I of Schedule 1 (flat rate plus shared care) to the Act; or

(e) a decision under regulation 3(1)(c) relates to a Category A or D interim maintenance assessment or a decision is made under regulation 3(4).

**Note.** Word omitted at the end of sub-para (c) by SI 2002 No 1204 as from 30 April 2002.

**15 Case conversion date—**(1) Subject to *paragraph (2)* [paragraphs (2) to (3G)], the case conversion date is the beginning of the first maintenance period on or after the conversion date.

(2) Where, on or after the commencement date, there is a maintenance assessment in force and a maintenance calculation is made to which paragraph (3) [or (3A)] applies, the case conversion date for the maintenance assessment shall be the beginning of the first maintenance period on or after the effective date of the related maintenance calculation.

(3)  *This paragraph applies where—*

(a)   *the maintenance calculation is made with respect to a relevant person who is a relevant person in relation to the maintenance assessment whether or not with respect to a different qualifying child; or*

(b)   *the maintenance calculation is made in relation to a partner ('A') of a person ('B') who is a relevant person in relation to the maintenance assessment and A or B is in receipt of a prescribed benefit.*

[(3) This paragraph applies where the maintenance calculation is made with respect to a relevant person who is a relevant person in relation to the maintenance assessment whether or not with respect to a different qualifying child.

(3A) This paragraph applies where the maintenance calculation is made in relation to a partner ('A') of a person ('B') who is a relevant person in relation to the maintenance assessment and—

(a)  A or B is in receipt of a prescribed benefit; and

(b)  either—

(i)   A is the non-resident parent in relation to the maintenance calculation and B is the absent parent in relation to the maintenance assessment; or

(ii)  A is the person with care in relation to the maintenance calculation and B is the person with care in relation to the maintenance assessment.

(3B) The case conversion date of a conversion decision made where paragraph (3C) applies is the beginning of the first maintenance period on or after the date of notification of the conversion decision.

(3C) This paragraph applies where on or after the commencement date—

(a)  there is a maintenance assessment in force;

(b)  an application is made or treated as made which, but for the maintenance assessment, would result in a maintenance calculation being made with an effective date before the conversion date;

(c)  the non-resident parent in relation to the application referred to in sub-paragraph (b) is the absent parent in relation to the maintenance assessment referred to in sub-paragraph (a); and

(d)  the person with care in relation to the application referred to in sub-paragraph (b) is a different person to the person with care in relation to the maintenance assessment referred to in sub-paragraph (a).

(3D) The case conversion date of a conversion decision made where paragraph (3E) applies is the beginning of the first maintenance period on or after the date on which the superseding decision referred to in paragraph (3E)(d) takes effect.

(3E) This paragraph applies where on or after the commencement date—

(a)  a maintenance assessment is in force in relation to a person ('C') and a maintenance calculation is in force in relation to another person ('D');

(b)  C or D is in receipt of a prescribed benefit;

(c)  either—

(i)   C is the absent parent in relation to the maintenance assessment and D is the non-resident parent in relation to the maintenance calculation; or

(ii)  C is the person with care in relation to the maintenance assessment and D is the person with care in relation to the maintenance calculation; and

(d) the decision relating to the prescribed benefit referred to in sub-paragraph (b) is superseded on the ground that C is the partner of D.

(3F) The case conversion date of a conversion decision made where paragraph (3G) applies is the beginning of the first maintenance period on or after the date from which entitlement to the prescribed benefit referred to in paragraph (3G)(c) begins.

(3G) This paragraph applies where on or after the commencement date—

(a) a person ('E') in respect of whom a maintenance assessment is in force is the partner of another person ('F') in respect of whom a maintenance calculation is in force;

(b) either—

    (i) E is the absent parent in relation to the maintenance assessment and F is the non-resident parent in relation to the maintenance calculation; or

    (ii) E is the person with care in relation to the maintenance assessment and F is the person with care in relation to the maintenance calculation; and

(c) E and F become entitled to a prescribed benefit as partners.]

(4) In *paragraph (3)* [this regulation]—

['absent parent' has the meaning given in the former Act;]

['maintenance assessment' has the meaning given in section 54 of the former Act;]

'relevant person' means, in relation to a maintenance assessment, the absent parent, *which has the meaning given in the former Act,* or person with care and, in relation to a maintenance calculation, the non-resident parent or person with care; and

'prescribed benefit' means a benefit prescribed for the purposes of paragraph 4(1)(c) of Part I of Schedule 1 to the Act.

**Note.** Words in italics in para (4) omitted and words in square brackets inserted by SI 2002 No 1204 as from 30 April 2002. Words in italics in paras (1), (3) and (4) omitted and words in square brackets substituted, paras (3) to (3G) inserted by SI 2003 No 328 as from 21 February 2003.

**16 Conversion calculation and conversion decision—**(1) A conversion calculation by the Secretary of State shall be made—

(a) in accordance with Part I of Schedule 1 to the Act;

(b) *using the information held by him at the calculation date; and*

[(b) taking into account the information used in accordance with regulation 3(2); and]

(c) taking into account any relevant departure direction or any relevant property transfer as provided in regulations 17 to *23* [23A].

(2) A conversion decision shall be treated for the purposes of any revision, supersession, appeal or application for a variation under sections 16, 17, 20 or 28G of the Act, and Regulations made in connection with such matters, as a decision under section 11 of the Act made with effect from the date of notification of that decision and, where a conversion decision has been made, the case shall for those purposes be treated as if there were a maintenance calculation in force.

[(2A) For the purposes of sections 29 to 41B of the Act and regulations made under or by virtue of those sections, a conversion decision shall be treated on or after the case conversion date as if it were a maintenance calculation.]

[(2B) For the purposes of regulation 2 of the Social Security Benefits (Maintenance Payments and Consequential Amendments) Regulations 1996 (interpretation for the purposes of section 74A of the Social Security Administration Act 1992), a conversion decision shall be treated on or after the case conversion date as it were a maintenance calculation.]

[(2C) For the purposes of regulations 9 and 10 of the Arrears, Interest and Adjustment Regulations, a conversion decision shall be treated on or after the case conversion date as if it were a maintenance calculation.]

(3) A *conversion calculation* [conversion decision] shall become a maintenance calculation when the transitional period ends or, if later, any relevant property transfer taken into account in the *calculation* [conversion calculation] ceases to have effect.

**Note.** Words in italics omitted and words in square brackets and sub-para (2A) inserted by SI 2003 No 328, reg 1(3)(a), 9(1), (7)(c)(ii) as from 21 February 2003. Para (2B) added by SI 2003 No 347, reg 3 as from 3 March 2003. Para (2C) inserted by SI 2004 No 2415, reg 8(1), (8)(b) as from 16 September 2004.

## 17 Relevant departure *decision* [direction] and relevant property transfer—

(1) A relevant departure direction means a departure direction given in relation to the maintenance assessment which is the subject of the conversion decision where that direction was given under the provisions of the former Act and Regulations made under that Act, and where it is one to which one of the following paragraphs of this regulation applies.

(2) This paragraph applies to a departure direction given on the special expenses grounds in paragraph 2(3)(b) (contact costs) or 2(3)(d) (debts) of Schedule 4B to the former Act where and to the extent that they exceed the threshold amount which is—

(a) £15 per week where the expenses fall within only one of those paragraphs and, where the expenses fall within both paragraphs, £15 per week in respect of the aggregate of those expenses, where the net weekly income is £200 or more; or

(b) £10 per week where the expenses fall within only one of those paragraphs and, where the expenses fall within both paragraphs, £10 per week in respect of the aggregate of those expenses, where the net weekly income is below £200,

and for this purpose 'net weekly income' means the income which would otherwise be taken into account for the purposes of the conversion decision including any additional income which falls to be taken into account under regulation 20.

(3) This paragraph applies to a departure direction given on the ground in paragraph 2(3)(c) (illness and disability costs) of Schedule 4B to the former Act where the illness or disability is of a relevant other child.

(4) This paragraph applies to a departure direction given on the ground in paragraph 3 (property or capital transfer) of Schedule 4B to the former Act.

(5) Subject to paragraph (6), this paragraph applies to a departure direction given on the additional cases grounds in paragraph 5(1) of Schedule 4B to the former Act and regulation 24 (diversion of income) of the Departure Regulations or paragraph 5(2)(b) of Schedule 4B to the former Act and regulation 25 (lifestyle inconsistent with declared income) of those Regulations.

*(6) Where the new amount, but for the application of a relevant departure direction referred to in paragraph (5), would be the first prescribed amount owing to the application of paragraph 4(1)(b) of Part I of Schedule 1 to the Act, or would be the nil rate under paragraph 5(a) of Part I of Schedule 1 to the Act, paragraph (5) applies where the amount of the additional net weekly income exceeds £100.*

[(6) Where, but for the application of a relevant departure direction referred to in paragraph (5), the new amount would be—

(a) the first prescribed amount owing to the application of paragraph 4(1)(b) of Part I of Schedule 1 to the Act;

(b) the amount referred to in sub-paragraph (a), but is less than that amount or is nil, owing to the application of paragraph 8 of that Part; or

(c) the nil rate under paragraph 5(a) of that Part,

paragraph (5) applies where the amount of the additional income exceeds £100.]

(7) This paragraph applies to a departure direction given on the ground in paragraph 5(2)(a) of Schedule 4B to the former Act (assets capable of producing income) where the value of the assets taken into account is greater than £65,000.

(8) A relevant property transfer is a transfer which was taken into account in the decision as to the maintenance assessment in respect of which the conversion decision is made owing to the application of Schedule 3A to the Assessment Calculation Regulations.

(9) Where—

(a) a relevant departure direction is taken into account for the purposes of a conversion calculation; or

(b) a subsequent decision is made following the application of a relevant departure direction to a maintenance assessment,

the relevant departure direction shall for the purposes of any subsequent decision, including the subsequent decision in paragraph (b), be a variation as if an application had been made under section 28G of the Act for a variation in relation to the same ground and for the same amount.

[(10) Where—

(a) a relevant property transfer is taken into account for the purposes of a conversion decision;

(b) an application is made for a variation of a type referred to in paragraph 3 of Schedule 4B to the Act and Part IV of the Variations Regulations (property or capital transfers) which relates to the same property or capital transfer as the relevant property transfer referred to in sub-paragraph (a); and

(c) the variation is agreed to,

the relevant property transfer shall cease to have effect on the effective date of the subsequent decision which resulted from the application for a variation.]

**Note.** Words in italics in heading and para (6) omitted and words in square brackets substituted by SI 2002 No 1204 with effect from 30 April 2002. Para (10): inserted by SI 2003 No 2779, reg 7(1), (4) as from 5 November 2003.

**18 Effect on conversion calculation—special expenses—**(1) Subject to paragraph (2) and regulations 22 and 23, where the relevant departure direction is one falling within paragraph (2) or (3) of regulation 17, effect shall be given to the relevant departure direction in the conversion calculation by deducting from the net weekly income of the non-resident parent the weekly amount of that departure direction and for this purpose 'net weekly income' has the meaning given in regulation 17(2).

(2) Where the income which, but for the application of this paragraph, would be taken into account in the conversion decision is the capped amount and the relevant departure direction is one falling within paragraph (2) or (3) of regulation 17 then—

(a) the weekly amount of the expenses shall first be deducted from the net weekly income of the non-resident parent which, but for the application of the capped amount, would be taken into account in the conversion decision including any additional income to be taken into account as a result of the application of paragraphs (5) or (7) of regulation 17 (additional cases);

(b) the amount by which the capped amount exceeds the figure calculated under sub-paragraph (a) shall be calculated; and

(c) effect shall be given to the relevant departure direction in the conversion calculation by deducting from the capped amount the amount calculated under sub-paragraph (b).

**19 Effect on conversion calculation—property or capital transfer** Subject to regulation 23, where the relevant departure direction is one falling within paragraph (4) of regulation 17—
  (a) the conversion calculation shall be carried out in accordance with regulation 16(1) and, where there is more than one person with care in relation to the non-resident parent, the amount of child support maintenance resulting shall be apportioned among the persons with care as provided in paragraph 6 of Part I of Schedule 1 to the Act and Regulations made under that Part; and
  (b) the equivalent weekly value of the transfer to which the relevant departure direction relates shall be deducted from the amount of child support maintenance which the non-resident parent would otherwise be liable to pay to the person with care with respect to whom the transfer was made.

**20 Effect on conversion calculation—additional cases** Subject to regulations 22 and 23, where the relevant departure direction is one falling within paragraph (5) or (7) of regulation 17 (additional cases), effect shall be given to the relevant departure direction in the conversion calculation by increasing the net weekly income of the non-resident parent which would otherwise be taken into account by the weekly amount of the additional income except that, where the amount of net weekly income calculated in this way would exceed the capped amount, the amount of net weekly income taken into account shall be the capped amount.

**21 Effect on conversion calculation—relevant property transfer—**(1) Subject to paragraph (2) and *regulation 23* [regulations 23 and 23A], a relevant property transfer shall be given effect by deducting from the net weekly income of the non-resident parent which would otherwise be taken into account the amount in relation to the relevant property transfer and for this purpose 'net weekly income' has the meaning given in regulation 17(2) but after deduction in respect of any relevant departure direction falling within paragraph (2) or (3) of regulation 17 (special expenses).
  (2) Where the net weekly income of the non-resident parent which is taken into account for the purposes of the conversion calculation is the capped amount, a relevant property transfer shall be given effect by deducting the amount in respect of the transfer from the capped amount.

**Note.** Words in italics in para (1) omitted and words in square brackets substituted by SI 2002 No 1204 as from 30 April 2002.

**22 Effect on conversion calculation—maximum amount payable where relevant departure direction is on additional cases ground—**(1) Subject to regulation 23, where this regulation applies *the amount of child support maintenance which the non-resident parent shall be liable to pay* [the new amount] shall be whichever is the lesser of—
  (a) *a weekly amount calculated by aggregating the first prescribed amount with the result of applying Part I of Schedule 1 to the Act with the additional income arising under the relevant departure direction, other than the weekly amount of any benefit, pension or allowance which the non-resident parent receives which is prescribed for the purposes of paragraph 4(1)(b) of Part I of Schedule 1 to the Act; or*
  (b) *a weekly amount calculated by applying Part I of Schedule 1 to the Act to the aggregate of the net weekly income taken into account for the purposes of the maintenance assessment which is the subject of the conversion decision and the additional income arising under the relevant departure direction.*
  [(a) a weekly amount calculated by aggregating the first prescribed amount with the result of applying Part I of Schedule 1 to the Act to the additional income arising under the relevant departure direction; or

(b) a weekly amount calculated by applying Part I of Schedule 1 to the Act to the aggregate of the additional income arising under the relevant departure direction and the weekly amount of any benefit, pension or allowance received by the non-resident parent which is prescribed for the purposes of paragraph 4(1)(b) of that Schedule.]

(2) This regulation applies where the relevant departure direction is one to which paragraph (5) or (7) of regulation 17 applies (additional cases) and the non-resident parent's liability calculated as provided in Part I of Schedule 1 to the Act, and Regulations made under that Schedule, would, but for the relevant departure direction be—

(a) the first prescribed amount;

(b) the first prescribed amount but is less than that amount or nil, owing to the application of paragraph 8 of Part I of that Schedule; or

(c) the first prescribed amount but for the application of paragraph 5(a) of that Schedule.

(3) For the purposes of paragraph (1)—

(a) 'additional income' for the purposes of sub-paragraphs (a) and (b) means such income after the application of a relevant departure direction falling within paragraph (2) or (3) of regulation 17 (special expenses) [or a relevant property transfer]; and

(b) 'weekly amount' for the purposes of sub-paragraphs (a) and (b) means the aggregate of the amounts referred to in the relevant sub-paragraph—

  (i) adjusted as provided in regulation 23(3) as if the reference in that regulation to child support maintenance were to the weekly amount; and

  (ii) after any deduction provided for in regulation 23(4) as if the reference in that regulation to child support maintenance were to the weekly amount; [and

[(c) any benefit, pension or allowance referred to in sub-paragraph (b) shall not include—

  (i) in the case of industrial injuries benefit under section 94 of the Social Security Contributions and Benefits Act 1992, any increase in that benefit under section 104 (constant attendance) or 105 (exceptionally severe disablement) of that Act;

  (ii) in the case of a war disablement pension within the meaning in section 150(2) of that Act, any award under the following articles of the Naval, Military and Air Forces etc (Disablement and Death) Service Pensions Order 1983 ('the Service Pensions Order'): article 14 (constant attendance allowance), 15 (exceptionally severe disablement allowance), 16 (severe disablement occupational allowance) or 26A (mobility supplement) or any analogous allowance payable in conjunction with any other war disablement pension; and

  (iii) any award under article 18 of the Service Pensions Order (unemployability allowances) which is an additional allowance in respect of a child of the non-resident parent where that child is not living with the non-resident parent.]

**Note.** Words in italics in para (1) omitted and words in square brackets substituted by SI 2002 No 1204 as from 30 April 2002. Paras (1)(a) and (b) in italics omitted and paras in square brackets substituted, para (3)(c) added by SI 2003 No 328 as from 21 February 2003.

**23 Effect of relevant departure direction on conversion calculation— general—**(1) Subject to paragraphs (4) and (5), where more than one relevant departure direction applies regulations 18 to 22 shall apply and the results shall be aggregated as appropriate.

(2) Paragraph 7(2) to (7) of Schedule 1 to the Act (shared care) shall apply where the rate of child support maintenance is affected by a relevant departure direction, *other than one falling within paragraph (3) of regulation 17 (illness and disability costs)*, and paragraph 7(2) of that Schedule shall be read as if after the words 'as calculated in accordance with the preceding paragraphs of this Part of this Schedule' there were inserted the words ', the Child Support (Transitional Provisions) Regulations 2000'.

(3) Subject to paragraphs (4) and (5), where the non-resident parent shares the care of a qualifying child within the meaning in Part I of Schedule 1 to the Act, or where the care of such a child is shared in part by a local authority, the amount of child support maintenance the non-resident parent is liable to pay the person with care, calculated to take account of any relevant departure direction, shall be reduced in accordance with the provisions of paragraph 7 of that Part, or regulation 9 of the Maintenance Calculations and Special Cases Regulations, as the case may be.

(4) Subject to paragraph (5), where a relevant departure direction is one falling within paragraph (4) of regulation 17 (property or capital transfer) the amount of the relevant departure direction shall be deducted from the amount of child support maintenance the non-resident parent would otherwise be liable to pay the person with care in respect of whom the transfer was made after aggregation of the effects of any relevant departure directions as provided in paragraph (1) or deduction for shared care as provided in paragraph (3).

(5) If the application of regulation 19, or paragraphs (3) or (4), would decrease the weekly amount of child support maintenance (or the aggregate of all such amounts) payable by the non-resident parent to the person with care (or all of them) to less than a figure equivalent to the first prescribed amount, the new amount shall instead be the first prescribed amount and shall be apportioned as provided in paragraph 6 of Part I of Schedule 1 to the Act, and Regulations made under that Part.

**Note.** Words in italics in para (2) omitted by SI 2002 No 1204 as from 30 April 2002.

**[23A Effect of a relevant property transfer and a relevant departure direction—general** Where—
  (a) more than one relevant property transfer applies; or
  (b) one or more relevant property transfers and one or more relevant departure directions apply,
regulation 23 shall apply as if references to a relevant departure direction were to a relevant property transfer or to the relevant property transfers and relevant departure directions, as the case may be.]

**Note.** Added by SI 2002 No 1204 as from 30 April 2002.

**24 Phasing amount—**(1) In this Part 'phasing amount' means, for the year beginning on the case conversion date, the relevant figure provided in paragraph (2), and for each subsequent year the phasing amount for the previous year aggregated with the relevant figure.

(2) The relevant figure is—
  (a) £2.50 where the relevant income is £100 or less;
  (b) £5.00 where the relevant income is more than £100 but less than £400; or
  (c) £10.00 where the relevant income is £400 or more.

(3) *For* [Subject to *paragraph (4) [paragraphs (4) and (5)]* [, (5) and (6)], for] the purposes of paragraph (2), the 'relevant income' is the net weekly income of the non-resident parent taken into account in the conversion decision.

[(4) Where the new amount is calculated under regulation 22(1), 'relevant income' for the purposes of paragraph (2) is the aggregate of the income calculated under regulation 22(1)(b).]

[(5) Where the new amount is calculated under regulation 26(1) of the Variations Regulations, the 'relevant income' for the purposes of paragraph (2) is the additional income arising under the variation.]

(6) Where a subsequent decision is made the effective date of which is the case conversion date—

(a) the reference in paragraph (3) to the conversion decision shall apply as if it were a reference to the subsequent decision; and

(b) the reference in paragraph (5) to the new amount shall apply as if it were a reference to the subsequent decision amount.]

**Note.** Words in italics in para (3) omitted and words in square brackets and para (4) added by SI 2002 No 1204, reg 8(1), (14)(a)(b) as from 30 April 2002. Para ref in para (3) added, and para (5) inserted by SI 2003 No 328, reg 9(1), (9)(a)(b) as from 21 February 2003. Para (6) inserted by SI 2003 No 2779, reg 7(1), (5)(b) as from 5 November 2003.

**25 Maximum transitional amount—**(1) Where a conversion decision is made in a circumstance *to which regulation 15(2)* [to which regulation 15(3C)] applies (maintenance assessment and related maintenance calculation), or a subsequent decision is made, the liability of the non-resident parent to pay child support maintenance during the transitional period (excluding any amount payable in respect of arrears of child support maintenance and before reduction for any amount in respect of an overpayment) shall be whichever is the lesser of—

(a) *where regulation 15(2) applies, the new amount or, where there is a subsequent decision, the subsequent decision amount; and*

[(a) the transitional amount payable under this Part added to, where applicable, the transitional amount payable under Part IV; and]

(b) the maximum transitional amount.

(2) Where—

(a) a conversion decision to which paragraph (1) applies, or a subsequent decision, results from an application made or treated as made for a maintenance calculation in respect of the same non-resident parent but a different qualifying child in relation to whom there is a different person with care (referred to in this regulation as 'the new application'); and

(b) the amount of child support maintenance payable by the non-resident parent from the case conversion date, or the effective date of the subsequent decision, as the case may be, is the maximum transitional amount,

that amount shall be apportioned as provided in paragraph (3).

(3) The apportionment referred to in paragraph (2) shall be carried out as follows—

(a) the amount of child support maintenance payable by the non-resident parent to the person with care in relation to the new application shall be calculated as provided in Part I of Schedule 1 to the Act and Regulations made under that Part and where applicable, Part IV of these Regulations, and that amount shall be the amount payable to that person with care;

[(aa) the amount of child support maintenance payable to a person with care in respect of whom there was a maintenance assessment in force immediately before the case conversion date and in respect of whom the amount payable is not calculated by reference to a phasing amount, shall be an amount calculated as provided in sub-paragraph (a) and, where applicable, regulations 17 to 23;]

(b) *the amount calculated as provided in sub-paragraph (a)* [the amounts calculated as provided in sub-paragraphs (a) and (aa)] shall be deducted from the maximum transitional amount and the remainder shall be apportioned among the other persons with care so that the proportion which each receives bears the same relation to the proportions which the others receive as those proportions would have borne in relation to each other and the new amount, or the subsequent decision amount, as the case may be, if the maximum transitional amount had not been applied.

(4) Where—

(a) apportionment under paragraph (3)(b) results in a fraction of a penny, that fraction shall be treated as a penny if it is either one half or exceeds one half, otherwise it shall be disregarded; and

(b) the application of paragraph (3)(b) would be such that the aggregate amount payable by a non-resident parent would be different from the aggregate amount payable before any such apportionment, the Secretary of State shall adjust that apportionment so as to eliminate that difference and that adjustment shall be varied from time to time so as to secure that, taking one week with another and so far as is practicable, each person with care receives the amount which she would have received if no adjustment had been made under this paragraph.

[(5) Subject to paragraphs (6) and (7), 'maximum transitional amount' means 30% of the non-resident parent's net weekly income taken into account in the conversion decision, or the subsequent decision, as the case may be.

(6) Where the new amount is calculated under regulation 22(1), 'maximum transitional amount' means 30% of the aggregate of the income calculated under regulation 22(1)(b).

(7) Where the new amount or the subsequent decision amount, as the case may be, is calculated under regulation 26(1) of the Variations Regulations 'maximum transitional amount' means 30% of the additional income arising under the variation.]

**Note.** Words in italics omitted and words in square brackets substituted by SI 2003 No 328, reg 9(1), (10)(a)(b) as from 21 February 2003. Paras (5)-(7) inserted by SI 2003 No 2779, reg 7(1), (6) as from 5 November 2003.

## 26 Subsequent decision effective on case conversion date

(1) Where there is a subsequent decision, the effective date of which is the case conversion date, the amount of child support maintenance payable shall be calculated as if the subsequent decision were a conversion decision.

(2) For the purposes of paragraph (1), regulations 9 to 25 shall apply as if references—

(a) to the calculation date, including in relation to the definition of the former assessment amount, were to—

(i) where there has been a decision under section 16, 17 or 20 in relation to the maintenance assessment, the effective date of that decision; or

(ii) where sub-paragraph (i) does not apply—

(aa) the effective date of the subsequent decision; or

(bb) if earlier, the date the subsequent decision was made;

(b) to the new amount were to the subsequent decision amount; and

(c) to the conversion decision in regulation 24(3) were to the subsequent decision.

## 27 Subsequent decision with effect in transitional period—amount payable—

(1) Subject to paragraph (6), where during the transitional period there is a subsequent decision the effective date of which is after the case conversion date, the amount of child support maintenance payable shall be the subsequent decision amount unless any of the following paragraphs applies, in which case it shall be a transitional amount as provided for in those paragraphs.

(2) Where—

(a) the new amount was greater than the former assessment amount; and

(b) the subsequent decision amount is greater than the new amount,
the amount of child support maintenance payable shall be a transitional amount calculated as the transitional amount payable immediately before the subsequent decision ('the previous transitional amount') increased by the difference between the new amount and the subsequent decision amount and the phasing amounts shall apply to that transitional amount as they would have applied to the previous transitional amount had there been no subsequent decision.

(3) Where—
(a) paragraph (2)(a) applies; and
(b) the subsequent decision amount is equal to or less than the new amount [and greater than the previous transitional amount,],
the amount of child support maintenance payable shall be the previous transitional amount and the phasing amounts shall apply as they would have applied had there been no subsequent decision.

(4) Where—
(a) the new amount was less than the former assessment amount; and
(b) the subsequent decision amount is less than the new amount,
the amount of child support maintenance payable shall be a transitional amount calculated as the previous transitional amount decreased by the difference between the new amount and the subsequent decision amount and the phasing amounts shall apply to that transitional amount as they would have applied to the previous transitional amount had there been no subsequent decision.

(5) Where—
(a) paragraph (4)(a) applies; and
(b) the subsequent decision amount is equal to or more than the new amount [and less than the previous transitional amount],
the amount of child support maintenance payable shall be the previous transitional amount and the phasing amounts shall apply as they would have applied had there been no subsequent decision.

(6) Paragraphs (2) to (5) shall not apply where the subsequent decision amount is the first or second prescribed amount *or the nil rate* [, would be the first or the second prescribed amount but is less than that amount, or is nil, owing to the application of paragraph 8 of Part I of Schedule 1 to the Act, or is the nil rate].

[(7) Where paragraph (1) applies and at the date of the subsequent decision there is more than one person with care in relation to the same non-resident parent—
(a) the amount payable to a person with care in respect of whom the amount payable is calculated by reference to a phasing amount shall be determined by applying paragraphs (1) to (5) as if references to the new amount, the subsequent decision amount and the transitional amount were to the apportioned part of the amount in question; and
(b) the amount payable in respect of any other person with care shall be the apportioned part of the subsequent decision amount.

(8) In paragraph (7), 'apportioned part' means the amount payable in respect of a person with care calculated as provided in Part I of Schedule 1 to the Act and Regulations made under that Part and, where applicable, Parts III and IV of these Regulations.

(9) *Where* [Where] a subsequent decision is made in respect of a decision which is itself a subsequent decision, paragraphs (2) to (5) shall apply as if, except in paragraphs (2)(a) and (4)(a), references to the new amount were to the subsequent decision amount which applied immediately before the most recent subsequent decision.]

[(10) [Subject to paragraph (11), where] a subsequent decision ('decision B') is made in respect of a decision which is itself a subsequent decision ('decision A') and—

(a) decision B has the same effective date as decision A; or
(b) decision B—
  (i) is a revision or alteration on appeal of decision A; and
  (ii) includes within it a determination that the effective date of decision A was incorrect,
paragraphs (2) to (5) shall apply [a]s if decision A had not been made].

[(11) In the circumstances set out in paragraph (10), paragraph (9) shall not apply where the decision in place before decision A was made was the decision which took effect from the case conversion date.]

**Note.** Words in italics omitted and words in square brackets substituted by SI 2002 No 1204, reg 8(1), (15)(a)(b)(c) as from 30 April 2002. Paras (7)-(9) added by SI 2003 No 328, reg 9(1), (11) as from 21 February 2003. Para (9) word 'Where in square brackets substituted by SI 2004 No 2415, reg 8(1)(9)(a) as from 16 September 2004. Para (10) inserted by SI 2003 No 2779, reg 7(1)(7)(b) as from 5 November 2003. Para (10): words 'Subject to paragraph (11), where' in square brackets substituted by SI 2004 No 2415, reg 8(1), (9)(b) as from 16 September 2004. Para (10): words 'as if decision A had not been made' in square brackets substituted by SI 2004 No 2415, reg 8(1), (9)(b)(ii) as from 16 September 2004. Para (11): inserted by SI 2004 No 2415, reg 8(1), (9)(c) as from 16 September 2004.

**28 Linking provisions—**(1) *Where* [Subject to paragraph (2A), where], after the commencement date but before the conversion date, an application for a maintenance calculation is made or treated as made and within the relevant period a maintenance assessment was in force in relation to the same qualifying child, non-resident parent and person with care—
  (a) the application shall be treated as an application for a maintenance assessment; and
  (b) any maintenance assessment made in response to the application shall be an assessment to which regulations 9 to 28 apply.

(2) *Where* [Subject to paragraph (2A), where], after the conversion date, an application for a maintenance calculation is made or treated as made, and within the relevant period a maintenance assessment ('the previous assessment') had been in force in relation to the same qualifying child, non-resident parent and person with care but had ceased to have effect—
  (a) the amount of child support maintenance payable by the non-resident parent from the effective date of the maintenance calculation made in response to the application shall be calculated in the same way that a conversion calculation would have been made had the previous assessment been in force on the date the calculation is made; and
  (b) the provisions of regulations 9 to 28 shall apply accordingly, including the application where appropriate of transitional amounts, phasing amounts and a transitional period, which for this purpose shall begin on the date which would have been the case conversion date in relation to the previous assessment.

[(2A) Paragraph (1) or (2) shall not apply where, before any application for a maintenance calculation of a type referred to in paragraph (1) or (2) is made or treated as made, an application for a maintenance calculation is made or treated as made in relation to either the person with care or the non-resident parent (but not both of them) to whom the maintenance assessment referred to in paragraph (1) or (2) related.]

(3) For the purposes of paragraphs (1) and (2) 'the relevant period' means 13 weeks prior to the date that the application for the maintenance calculation is made or treated as made.

(4) This paragraph applies where—
  (a) the non-resident parent is liable to pay child support maintenance of a transitional amount and there is, during the transitional period, a subsequent decision (in this regulation referred to as 'the first subsequent

decision') as a result of which the non-resident parent is liable to pay child support maintenance *at the first or second prescribed amount or the nil rate* at—
  (i) the first or second prescribed amount;
  (ii) what would be an amount referred to in head (i) but is less than that amount, or is nil, owing to the application of paragraph 8 of Part I of Schedule 1 to the Act; or
  (iii) the nil rate; and];
 (b) a second subsequent decision is made with an effective date no later than 13 weeks after the effective date of the first subsequent decision the effect of which would be that the non-resident parent would be liable to pay child support *maintenance at other than the first or second prescribed amount or the nil rate* [a rate referred to in sub-paragraph (a)].

(5) *Where* [Subject to paragraph (5A), where] paragraph (4) applies the amount of child support maintenance the non-resident parent is liable to pay from the effective date of the second subsequent decision shall be a transitional amount or, where applicable, the new amount, calculated by making a subsequent decision and, where appropriate, applying a phasing amount, as if the first subsequent decision had not occurred.

[(5A) Paragraph (5) shall not apply where, before any second subsequent decision is made, an application for a maintenance calculation is made or treated as made in relation to either the person with care or the non-resident parent (but not both of them) to whom the first subsequent decision referred to in paragraph (4) related.]

(6) This paragraph applies where during the transitional period a *conversion calculation* [conversion decision] ceases to have effect.

(7) *Where* [Subject to paragraph (7A), where] paragraph (6) applies and no later than 13 weeks after the *conversion calculation* [conversion decision] ceases to have effect *an application for child support maintenance* [an application for a maintenance calculation] is made, or treated as made, in relation to the same person with care, non-resident parent and qualifying child, the amount of child support maintenance the non-resident parent is liable to pay from the effective date of the new maintenance calculation shall be a transitional amount or, where applicable, the new amount, calculated by making a subsequent decision in relation to the *conversion calculation* [conversion decision] as if it had not ceased to have effect, and applying a phasing amount where appropriate.

[(7A) Paragraph (7) shall not apply where, before an application for a maintenance calculation of a type referred to in that paragraph is made or treated as made, an application for a maintenance calculation is made or treated as made in relation to either the person with care or the non-resident parent (but not both of them) to whom the *conversion calculation* [conversion decision] referred to in that paragraph related.]

(8) *Where* [Subject to paragraph (9)]—
 *(a)* *a conversion calculation is in force and the amount of child support maintenance payable is the new amount which is a flat rate, other than a flat rate under paragraph 4(1)(a) of Part I of Schedule 1 to the Act, or the nil rate;*
 [(a) a *conversion calculation* [conversion decision] is in force, or pursuant to regulation 16(3) a maintenance calculation is in force, ('the calculation') and the new amount—
  (i) is the first or second prescribed amount;
  (ii) would be an amount referred to in head (i), but is less than that amount, or is nil, owing to the application of paragraph 8 of Part I of Schedule 1 to the Act; or
  (iii) is the nil rate;]
 (b) after the case conversion date a subsequent decision is made;
 (c) but for the application of this regulation the subsequent decision amount would be a basic or reduced rate of child support maintenance; and

(d) within 13 weeks prior to the effective date of the subsequent decision a maintenance assessment was in force in relation to the same non-resident parent, person with care and qualifying child, under which the amount payable by the non-resident parent ('the previous assessment') was more than the amount prescribed for the purposes of paragraph 7 of Schedule 1 to the former Act;

the subsequent decision amount shall be calculated by making a subsequent decision in relation to the previous assessment as if the assessment were in force, and applying a phasing amount where appropriate.

[(9) Paragraph (8) shall not apply where, before a subsequent decision of a type referred to in paragraph (8)(b) is made, an application for a maintenance calculation is made or treated as made in relation to the person with care or the non-resident parent (but not both of them) to whom the calculation relates.]

**Note.** Words in italics omitted and words in square brackets substituted by SI 2002 No 1204 as from 30 April 2002. Words 'conversion decision' substituted for 'conversion calculation' by SI 2003 No 328 as from 21 February 2003.

PART IV

COURT ORDER PHASING

**29 Interpretation**

(1) In this Part—

'the Act' means the Child Support Act 1991;

'calculation amount' means the amount of child support maintenance that would, but for the provisions of this Part, be payable under a maintenance calculation which is in force;

'excess' means the amount by which the calculation amount exceeds the old amount;

'maintenance calculation' has the meaning given in section 54 of the Act the effective date of which is on or after the date prescribed for the purposes of section 4(10)(a) of the Act;

'old amount' means, subject to paragraph (2) below, the aggregate weekly amount which was payable under the orders, agreements or arrangements mentioned in regulation 30;

'subsequent decision' means—

(a) any decision under section 16 or 17 of the Act to revise or supersede a maintenance calculation to which regulation 31(1) applies; or

(b) any such revision or supersession as decided on appeal,

whether as originally made or as revised under section 16 of the Act or decided on appeal;

'subsequent decision amount' means the amount of child support maintenance liability resulting from a subsequent decision;

'transitional amount' means an amount determined in accordance with regulation 31; and

'transitional period' means a period beginning on the effective date of the maintenance calculation and ending 78 weeks after that date or, if earlier, on the date on which regulation 31(3) applies.

(2) In determining the old amount the Secretary of State shall disregard any payments in kind and any payments made to a third party on behalf of or for the benefit of the qualifying child or the person with care.

**30 Cases to which this Part applies** This Part applies to cases where—

(a) on 4th April 1993, and at all times thereafter until the date when a maintenance calculation is made under the Act there was in force, in respect of one or more of the qualifying children in respect of whom an application for a maintenance calculation is made or treated as made under the Act and the non-resident parent concerned, one or more—

    (i)   maintenance orders;

    (ii)  orders under section 151 of the Army Act 1955 (deductions from pay for maintenance of wife or child) or section 151 of the Air Force Act 1955 (deductions from pay for maintenance of wife or child) or arrangements corresponding to such an order and made under Article 1 or 3 of the Naval and Marine Pay and Pensions (Deductions for Maintenance) Order 1959; or

    (iii) maintenance agreements (being agreements which are made or evidenced in writing);

(b)  either—

    (i)   the non-resident parent was on the effective date of the maintenance calculation and continues to be a member of a family, as defined in regulation 1 of the Child Support (Maintenance Calculations and Special Cases) Regulations 2000 which includes one or more children; or

    (ii)  the amount of child support maintenance payable under the maintenance calculation referred to in paragraph (a) is a basic or reduced rate under paragraph 7 of Part I of Schedule 1 to the Act (shared care—basic and reduced rate); and

(c)  the calculation amount exceeds the old amount.

**31 Amount payable during the transitional period—**(1) In a case to which this Part applies, the amount of child support maintenance payable under a maintenance calculation during the transitional period shall, instead of being the calculation amount, be the transitional amount.

(2) The transitional amount is—

(a)  during the first 26 weeks of the transitional period, the old amount plus either 25 per cent of the excess or £20.00, whichever is the greater;

(b)  during the next 26 weeks of the transitional period, the old amount plus either 50 per cent of the excess or £40.00, whichever is the greater; and

(c)  during the last 26 weeks of the transitional period, the old amount plus either 75 per cent of the excess or £60.00, whichever is the greater.

(3) If in any case the application of the provisions of this Part would result in an amount of child support maintenance becoming payable which is greater than the calculation amount, then those provisions shall not apply or, as the case may be, shall cease to apply to that case and the amount of child support maintenance payable in that case shall be the calculation amount.

**32 Revision and supersession—**(1) Where the Secretary of State makes a subsequent decision in relation to a maintenance calculation to which regulation 31(1) applies, the amount of child support maintenance payable by the non-resident parent shall be—

(a)  where the subsequent decision amount is more than the calculation amount, the transitional amount plus the difference between the calculation amount and the subsequent decision amount;

(b)  where the subsequent decision amount is less than the calculation amount but more than the transitional amount, the transitional amount; or

(c)  where the subsequent decision amount is less than the calculation amount and less than or equal to the transitional amount, the subsequent decision amount.

(2) Regulation 31(2) shall apply to cases where there has been a subsequent decision as if references to the transitional amount were to the amount resulting from the application of paragraph (1).

PART V
SAVINGS

**33 Saving in relation to revision of or appeal against a conversion or subsequent decision**

(1) This regulation applies where—

(a) a conversion decision has been made under regulation 3, or a subsequent decision has been made under regulation 4, in each case where regulation *15(2)* [15(2), (3B), (3D) or (3F)] applies; and

(b) in relation to the decision referred to in paragraph (a)—

    (i)   a revised decision is made under regulation 3A(1)(e) of the Decisions and Appeals Regulations; or

    (ii)  an appeal tribunal makes a decision that the conversion decision or subsequent decision was made in error,

on the ground that regulation *15(2)* [15(2), (3B), (3D) or (3F) as the case may be] did not apply.

(2) The provisions of the former Act and Regulations made under that Act prior to any amendments or revocations made pursuant to or in consequence of the 2000 Act shall apply, until the effective date of a further conversion decision in relation to the maintenance assessment, for the purposes of that maintenance assessment as if the decision referred to in paragraph (1)(a) had not been made, subject to any revision, supersession or appeal having effect between the dates of the decisions in paragraph 1(a) and (b) which would have affected the maintenance assessment during that period but for the decision referred to paragraph 1(a).

**Note.** Regulation references in italics omitted and references in square brackets substituted by SI 2003 No 328 as from 21 February 2003.

**CHILD SUPPORT (MAINTENANCE CALCULATIONS AND SPECIAL CASES) REGULATIONS 2000**

**Dated** 18 January 2001

**SI 2001 No 155**

ARRANGEMENT OF REGULATIONS

PART I

GENERAL

PART II

CALCULATION OF CHILD SUPPORT MAINTENANCE

PART III

SPECIAL CASES

PART IV

REVOCATION AND SAVINGS

SCHEDULE:

PART I

GENERAL

**1 Citation, commencement and interpretation—**(1) These Regulations may be cited as the Child Support (Maintenance Calculations and Special Cases) Regulations 2000.

(2) In these Regulations, unless the context otherwise requires—

'the Act' means the Child Support Act 1991;

['care home' has the meaning assigned to it by section 3 of the Care Standards Act 2000;

'care home service' has the meaning assigned to it by section 2(3) of the Regulation of Care (Scotland) Act 2001;]

['child tax credit' means a child tax credit under section 8 of the Tax Credits Act 2002;]

'Contributions and Benefits Act' means the Social Security Contributions and Benefits Act 1992;

'Contributions and Benefits (Northern Ireland) Act' means the Social Security Contributions and Benefits (Northern Ireland) Act 1992;

'couple' means a man and a woman who are—

(a) married to each other and are members of the same household; or

(b) not married to each other but are living together as husband and wife;

'course of advanced education' means—

(a) a full-time course leading to a postgraduate degree or comparable qualification, a first degree or comparable qualification, a Diploma of Higher Education, a higher national diploma, a higher national diploma or higher national certificate of the Business and Technology Education Council or the Scottish Qualifications Authority or a teaching qualification; or

(b) any other full-time course which is a course of a standard above that of an ordinary national diploma, a national diploma or national certificate of the Business and Technology Education Council or the Scottish Qualifications Authority, the advanced level of the General Certificate of Education, a Scottish certificate of education (higher level), a Scottish certificate of sixth year studies or a Scottish National Qualification at Higher Level;

'day' includes any part of a day;

'day to day care' means—

    (a) care of not less than 104 nights in total during the 12 month period ending with the relevant week; or

    (b) where, in the opinion of the Secretary of State, a period other than 12 months is more representative of the current arrangements for the care of the child in question, care during that period of not less in total than the number of nights which bears the same ratio to 104 nights as that period bears to 12 months, and for the purpose of this definition—

        (i) where a child is a boarder at a boarding school or is a patient in a hospital or other circumstances apply, such as where the child stays with a person who is not a parent of the child, and which the Secretary of State regards as temporary, the person who, but for those circumstances, would otherwise provide day to day care of the child shall be treated as providing day to day care during the periods in question; and

        (ii) 'relevant week' shall have the meaning ascribed to it in the definition in this paragraph, except that in a case where notification is given under regulation 7C of the Decisions and Appeals Regulations to the relevant persons on different dates, 'relevant week' means the period of 7 days immediately preceding the date of the latest notification;

'Decisions and Appeals Regulations' means the Social Security and Child Support (Decisions and Appeals) Regulations 1999;

*'disabled person's tax credit' means a disabled person's tax credit under section 129 of the Contributions and Benefits Act;*

'effective date' means the date on which a maintenance calculation takes effect for the purposes of the Act;

'employed earner' has the same meaning as in section 2(1)(a) of the Contributions and Benefits Act except that it shall include—

    (a) a person gainfully employed in Northern Ireland; and

    (b) a person to whom section 44(2A) of the Act applies;

'family' means—

    (a) a couple (including the members of a polygamous marriage) and any member of the same household for whom one or more of them is responsible and who is a child; or

    (b) a person who is not a member of a couple and a member of the same household for whom that person is responsible and who is a child;

'home' means—

    (a) the dwelling in which a person and any family of his normally live; or

    (b) if he or they normally live in more than one home, the principal home of that person and any family of his, and for the purpose of determining the principal home in which a person normally lives no regard shall be had to residence in *a residential care home or a nursing home* [a care home or an independent hospital or the provision of a care home service or an independent health care service] during a period which does not exceed 52 weeks or, where it appears to the Secretary of State that the person will return to his principal home after that period has expired, such longer period as the Secretary of State considers reasonable to allow for the return of that person to that home;

'Income Support Regulations' means the Income Support (General) Regulations 1987;

['independent health care service' has the meaning assigned to it by section 2(5)(a) and (b) of the Regulation of Care (Scotland) Act 2001;

'independent hospital' has the meaning assigned to it by section 2 of the Care Standards Act 2000;]

'the Jobseekers Act' means the Jobseekers Act 1995;

'Maintenance Calculation Procedure Regulations' means the Child Support (Maintenance Calculation Procedure) Regulations 2000;

'net weekly income' has the meaning given in the Schedule to these Regulations;

'nursing home' has the same meaning as in regulation 19(3) of the Income Support Regulations;

'occupational pension scheme' means such a scheme within the meaning in section 1 of the Pension Schemes Act 1993 and which is approved for the purposes of Part XIV of the Income and Corporation Taxes Act 1988 [or is a statutory scheme to which section 594 of that Act applies];

'partner' means—

    (a) in relation to a member of a couple, the other member of that couple;

    (b) in relation to a member of a polygamous marriage, any other member of that marriage with whom he lives;

'patient' means a person (other than a person who is serving a sentence of imprisonment or detention in a young offender institution within the meaning of the Criminal Justice Act 1982 or the Prisons (Scotland) Act 1989 who is regarded as receiving free in-patient treatment within the meaning of the Social Security (Hospital In-Patients) Regulations 1975;

'person' does not include a local authority;

'personal pension scheme' means such a scheme within the meaning in section 1 of the Pension Schemes Act 1993 and which is approved for the purposes of Part XIV of the Income and Corporation Taxes Act 1988;

'polygamous marriage' means any marriage during the subsistence of which a party to it is married to more than one person and in respect of which any ceremony of marriage took place under the law of a country which at the time of that ceremony permitted polygamy;

'prisoner' means a person who is detained in custody pending trial or sentence upon conviction or under a sentence imposed by a court other than a person whose detention is under the Mental Health Act 1983 or the Mental Health (Scotland) Act 1984;

'relevant week' means—

    (a) in relation to an application for child support maintenance—

        (i) where the application is made by a non-resident parent, the period of 7 days immediately before the application is made; and

        (ii) in any other case, the period of 7 days immediately before the date of notification to the non-resident parent and for this purpose 'the date of notification to the non-resident parent' means the date on which the non-resident parent is first given notice by the Secretary of State under the Maintenance Calculation Procedure Regulations that an application for a maintenance calculation has been made, or treated as made, as the case may be, in relation to which the non-resident parent is named as the parent of the child to whom the application relates;

    (b) where a decision ('the original decision') is to be—

        (i) revised under section 16 of the Act; or

        (ii) superseded by a decision under section 17 of the Act on the grounds that the original decision was made in ignorance of, or was based upon a mistake as to, some material fact or was erroneous in point of law,

the period of 7 days which was the relevant week for the purposes of the original decision;

    (c) where a decision ('the original decision') is to be superseded under section 17 of the Act—

(i) on an application made for the purpose on the basis that a material change of circumstances has occurred since the original decision was made, the period of 7 days immediately preceding the date on which that application was made;

(ii) subject to sub-paragraph (b), in a case where a relevant person is given notice under regulation 7C of the Decisions and Appeals Regulations, the period of 7 days immediately preceding the date of that notification,

except that where, under paragraph 15 of Schedule 1 to the Act, the Secretary of State makes separate maintenance calculations in respect of different periods in a particular case, because he is aware of one or more changes of circumstances which occurred after the date which is applicable to that case, the relevant week for the purposes of each separate maintenance calculation made to take account of each such change of circumstances shall be the period of 7 days immediately before the date on which notification was given to the Secretary of State of the change of circumstances relevant to that separate maintenance calculation;

'residential care home' has the same meaning as in regulation 19(3) of the Income Support Regulations;

'retirement annuity contract' means an annuity contract for the time being approved by the Board of Inland Revenue as having for its main object the provision of a life annuity in old age or the provision of an annuity for a partner or dependant and in respect of which relief from income tax may be given on any premium;

'self-employed earner' has the same meaning as in section 2(1)(b) of the Contributions and Benefits Act except that it shall include a person gainfully employed in Northern Ireland otherwise than in employed earner's employment (whether or not he is also employed in such employment);

['state pension credit' means the social security benefit of that name payable under the State Pension Credit Act 2002;]

'student' means a person, other than a person in receipt of a training allowance, who is aged less than 19 and attending a full-time course of advanced education or who is aged 19 or over and attending a full-time course of study at an educational establishment; and for the purposes of this definition—

(a) a person who has started on such a course shall be treated as attending it throughout any period of term or vacation within it, until the last day of the course or such earlier date as he abandons it or is dismissed from it;

(b) a person on a sandwich course (within the meaning of paragraph 1(1) of Schedule 5 to the Education (Mandatory Awards) (No 2) Regulations 1993) shall be treated as attending a full-time course of advanced education or, as the case may be, of study;

*'training allowance' means an allowance payable under section 2 of the Employment and Training Act 1973, or section 2 of the Enterprise and New Towns (Scotland) Act 1990;*

training allowance' means a payment under section 2 of the Employment and Training Act 1973 ('the 1973 Act'), or section 2 of the Enterprise and New Towns (Scotland) Act 1990 ('the 1990 Act'), which is paid—

(a) to a person for his maintenance; and

(b) in respect of a period during which that person—

(i) is undergoing training pursuant to arrangements made under section 2 of the 1973 Act or section 2 of the 1990 Act; and

(ii) has no net weekly income of a type referred to in Part II or Part III of the Schedule;]

war widow's pension' means any pension or allowance payable for a widow which
is—

(a) granted in respect of a death due to service or war injury and payable
by virtue of the Air Force (Constitution) Act 1917, the Personal Injuries
(Emergency Provisions) Act 1939, the Pensions (Navy, Army, Air Force
and Mercantile Marine) Act 1939, the Polish Resettlement Act 1947 or
Part VII or section 151 of the Reserve Forces Act 1980;

(b) payable under so much of any Order in Council, Royal Warrant, order
or scheme as relates to death due to service in the armed forces of the
Crown, wartime service in the merchant navy or war injuries;

(c) payable in respect of death due to peacetime service in the armed
forces of the Crown before 3rd September 1939, and payable at rates,
and subject to conditions, similar to those of a pension within sub-
paragraph (b); or

(d) payable under the law of a country other than the United Kingdom
and of a character substantially similar to a pension within sub-
paragraph (a), (b) or (c),

and 'war widower's pension' shall be construed accordingly;]
'work-based training for young people or, in Scotland, Skillseekers training'
means—

(a) arrangements made under section 2 of the Employment and Training
Act 1973 or section 2 of the Enterprise and New Towns (Scotland) Act
1990; or

(b) arrangements made by the Secretary of State for persons enlisted in
Her Majesty's forces for any special term of service specified in
regulations made under section 2 of the Armed Forces Act 1966
(power of Defence Council to make regulations as to engagement of
persons in regular forces),

for purposes which include the training of persons who, at the beginning of
their training, are under the age of 18;
*'working families' tax credit' means a working families' tax credit under section 128 of the
Contributions and Benefits Act; and*
['working tax credit' means a working tax credit under section 10 of the Tax
Credits Act 2002;]
'year' means a period of 52 weeks.

(3) The following other description of children is prescribed for the purposes
of paragraph 10C(2)(b) of Schedule 1 to the Act (relevant other children)—

children other than qualifying children in respect of whom the non-resident
parent or his partner would receive child benefit under Part IX of the
Contributions and Benefits Act but who do not solely because the
conditions set out in section 146 of that Act (persons outside Great Britain)
are not met.

(4) Subject to paragraph (5), these Regulations shall come into force in
relation to a particular case on the day on which Part I of Schedule 1 to the 1991
Act as amended by the Child Support, Pensions and Social Security Act 2000
comes into force in relation to that type of case.

(5) Paragraphs (1) and (2) of regulation 4 and, for the purposes of those
provisions, this regulation shall come into force on 31st January 2001.

**Note.** Definition in italics omitted and definitions in square brackets inserted by SI 2003 No
328 as from 6 April 2003. Definitions inserted and revoked and words in square brackets by SI
2003 No 2779, regs 1, 6 as from 5 November 2003.

PART II

CALCULATION OF CHILD SUPPORT MAINTENANCE

**2 Calculation of amounts**—(1) Where any amount is to be considered in connection with any calculation made under these Regulations or under Schedule 1 to the Act, it shall be calculated as a weekly amount and, except where the context otherwise requires, any reference to such an amount shall be construed accordingly.

(2) Subject to paragraph (3), where any calculation made under these Regulations or under Schedule 1 to the Act results in a fraction of a penny that fraction shall be treated as a penny if it is either one half or exceeds one half, otherwise it shall be disregarded.

(3) Where the calculation of the basic rate of child support maintenance or the reduced rate of child support maintenance results in a fraction of a pound that fraction shall be treated as a pound if it is either one half or exceeds one half, otherwise it shall be disregarded.

(4) In taking account of any amounts or information required for the purposes of making a maintenance calculation, the Secretary of State shall apply the dates or periods specified in these Regulations as applicable to those amounts or information, provided that if he becomes aware of a material change of circumstances occurring after such date or period, but before the effective date, he shall take that change of circumstances into account.

(5) Information required for the purposes of making a maintenance calculation in relation to the following shall be the information applicable at the effective date—

(a) the number of qualifying children;

(b) the number of relevant other children;

(c) whether the non-resident parent receives a benefit, pension or allowance prescribed for the purposes of paragraph 4(1)(b) of Schedule 1 to the Act;

(d) whether the non-resident parent or his partner receives a benefit prescribed for the purposes of paragraph 4(1)(c) of Schedule 1 to the Act; and

(e) whether paragraph 5(a) of Schedule 1 to the Act applies to the non-resident parent.

**3 Reduced rate** The reduced rate is an amount calculated as follows—

$$F + (A \times T)$$

where—

F is the flat rate liability applicable to the non-resident parent under paragraph 4 of Schedule 1 to the Act;

A is the amount of the non-resident parent's net weekly income between £100 and £200; and

T is the percentage determined in accordance with the following Table—

| | 1 qualifying child of the non-resident parent | | | | 2 qualifying children of the non-resident parent | | | | 3 or more qualifying children of the non-resident parent | | | |
|---|---|---|---|---|---|---|---|---|---|---|---|---|
| Number of relevant other children of the non-resident parent | 0 | 1 | 2 | 3 or more | 0 | 1 | 2 | 3 or more | 0 | 1 | 2 | 3 or more |
| T (%) | 25 | 20.5 | 19 | 17.5 | 35 | 29 | 27 | 25 | 45 | 37.5 | 35 | 32.5 |

**4 Flat rate**—(1) The following benefits, pensions and allowances are prescribed for the purposes of paragraph 4(1)(b) of Schedule 1 to the Act—

  (a)  under the Contributions and Benefits Act—

      (i)  bereavement allowance under section 39B;

     (ii)  category A retirement pension under section 44;

    (iii)  category B retirement pension under section 48C;

    (iv)  category C and category D retirement pensions under section 78;

     (v)  incapacity benefit under section 30A;

    (vi)  *invalid care allowance* [carer's allowance] under section 70;

    (vii)  maternity allowance under section 35;

  (viii)  severe disablement allowance under section 68;

    (ix)  industrial injuries benefit under section 94;

     (x)  widowed mother's allowance under section 37;

    (xi)  widowed parent's allowance under section 39A; and

    (xii)  widow's pension under section 38;

  (b)  contribution-based jobseeker's allowance under section 1 of the Jobseekers Act;

  (c)  a social security benefit paid by a country other than the United Kingdom;

  (d)  a training allowance (other than work-based training for young people or, in Scotland, Skillseekers training); and

  (e)  a war disablement pension or war widow's pension within the meaning of section 150(2) of the Contributions and Benefits Act or a pension which is analogous to such a pension paid by the government of a country outside Great Britain; [and

  (f)  a war widow's pension or a war widower's pension]

  (2) The benefits prescribed for the purposes of paragraph 4(1)(c) of Schedule 1 to the Act are—

  (a)  income support under section 124 of the Contributions and Benefits Act; *and*

  (b)  income-based jobseeker's allowance under section 1 of the Jobseekers Act [; and

  (c)  state pension credit].

  (3) Where the non-resident parent is liable to a pay a flat rate by virtue of paragraph 4(2) of Schedule 1 to the Act—

  (a)  if he has one partner, then the amount payable by the non-resident parent shall be half the flat rate; and

  (b)  if he has more than one partner, then the amount payable by the non-resident parent shall be the result of apportioning the flat rate equally among him and his partners.

**Note.** Words in italics in para (1)(a)(vi) revoked and words in square brackets substituted by SI 2002 No 2497 as from 1 April 2003. Paa (e): words omitted revked by SI 2003 No 2779 as from 5 November 2003. Para (1)(f): sub-para (f) and word 'and' preceding inserted by SI 2003 No 2779 as from 5 November 2003. Sub-para (2)(c) inserted by SI 2002 No 3019 as from 6 October 2003.

**5 Nil rate** The rate payable is nil where the non-resident parent is—

  (a)  a student;

  (b)  a child within the meaning given in section 55(1) of the Act;

  (c)  a prisoner;

  (d)  a person who is 16 or 17 years old and—

      (i)  in receipt of income support or income-based jobseeker's allowance; or

     (ii)  a member of a couple whose partner is in receipt of income support or income-based jobseeker's allowance;

  (e)  a person receiving an allowance in respect of work-based training for young people, or in Scotland, Skillseekers training;

(f)    a person *in a residential care home or nursing home* [who is resident in a care home or an independent hospital or is being provided with a care home service or an independent health care service] who—
   (i)    is in receipt of a pension, benefit or allowance specified in regulation 4(1) or (2); or
   (ii)   has the whole or part of the cost of his accommodation met by a local authority;

(g)    a patient in hospital who is in receipt of income support whose applicable amount includes an amount under paragraph *1(a) or (b)* [(1(b) or 2] of Schedule 7 to the Income Support Regulations (patient for more than *6* [52] weeks);

[(gg) a patient in hospital who is in receipt of state pension credit and in respect of whom paragraph 2(1) of Schedule III to the State Pension Credit Regulations [2002] (patient for [more than] 52 weeks) applies;]

(h)    a person in receipt of a benefit specified in regulation 4(1) the amount of which has been reduced in accordance with the provisions of regulations *4(d)* [4] and 6 of the Social Security Hospital In-Patients Regulations 1975 (circumstances in which personal benefit is to be adjusted and adjustment of personal benefit after 52 weeks in hospital); *or*

(i)    *a person who would be liable to pay the flat rate because he satisfies the description in paragraph 4(1)(c) of Schedule 1 to the Act but his net weekly income, inclusive of—*
   (aa) *any benefit, pension or allowance that he receives which is prescribed for the purposes of paragraph 4(1)(b) of Schedule 1 to the Act; and*
   (bb) *any benefit that he or his partner receives which is prescribed for the purposes of paragraph 4(1)(c) of Schedule 1 to the Act,*
is less than £5 a week.

**Note.** Words in para (f) substituted by SI 2003 No 2779 as from 5 November 2003. Words in italics in para (g) omitted and words in square brackets substituted by SI 2003 No 1195 as from 21 May 2003. Para (gg) inserted by SI 2002 No 3019 with effect from 6 October 2003. Reference to '2002' inserted by SI 2003 No 1195 as from 21 May 2003. Words 'more than' in para (gg) substituted by SI 2003 No 1195 as from 21 May 2003. In para (h) number '4' substituted by SI 2003 No 1195 as from 21 May 2003. Word omitted in para (h) revoked by SI 2004 No 2415 as from 16 September 2004. Para (i) revoked by SI 2004 No 2415 as from 16 September 2004.

**6 Apportionment** If, in making the apportionment required by regulation 4(3) or paragraph 6 of Part I of Schedule 1 to the Act, the effect of the application of regulation 2(2) (rounding) would be such that the aggregate amount of child support maintenance payable by a non-resident parent would be different from the aggregate amount payable before any apportionment, the Secretary of State shall adjust that apportionment so as to eliminate that difference; and that adjustment shall be varied from time to time so as to secure that, taking one week with another and so far as is practicable, each person with care receives the amount which she would have received if no adjustment had been made under this paragraph.

**7 Shared care**—(1) For the purposes of paragraphs 7 and 8 of Part I of Schedule 1 to the Act a night will count for the purposes of shared care where the non-resident parent—
   (a)   has the care of a qualifying child overnight; and
   (b)   the qualifying child stays at the same address as the non-resident parent.

(2) For the purposes of paragraphs 7 and 8 of Part I of Schedule 1 to the Act, a non-resident parent has the care of a qualifying child when he is looking after the child.

(3) Subject to paragraph (4), in determining the number of nights for the purposes of shared care, the Secretary of State shall consider the 12 month period

ending with the relevant week and for this purpose 'relevant week' has the same meaning as in the definition of day to day care in regulation 1 of these Regulations.

(4) The circumstances in which the Secretary of State may have regard to a number of nights over less than a 12 month period are where there has been no pattern for the frequency with which the non-resident parent looks after the qualifying child for the 12 months preceding the relevant week, or the Secretary of State is aware that a change in that frequency is intended, and in that case he shall have regard to such lesser period as may seem to him to be appropriate, and the Table in paragraph 7(4) and the period in paragraph 8(2) of Schedule 1 to the Act shall have effect subject to the adjustment described in paragraph (5).

(5) Where paragraph (4) applies, the Secretary of State shall adjust the number of nights in that lesser period by applying to that number the ratio which the period of 12 months bears to that lesser period.

(6) Where a child is a boarder at a boarding school, or is a patient in a hospital, the person who, but for those circumstances, would otherwise have care of the child overnight shall be treated as providing that care during the periods in question.

PART III

SPECIAL CASES

**8 Persons treated as non-resident parents—**(1) Where the circumstances of a case are that—

  (a) two or more persons who do not live in the same household each provide day to day care for the same *qualifying child* [child, being a child in respect of whom an application for a maintenance calculation has been made or treated as made]; and

  (b) at least one of those persons is a parent of the child,
that case shall be treated as a special case for the purposes of the Act.

(2) For the purposes of this special case a parent who provides day to day care for a child of his is to be treated as a non-resident parent for the purposes of the Act in the following circumstances—

  (a) a parent who provides such care to a lesser extent than the other parent, person or persons who provide such care for the child in question; or

  (b) where the persons mentioned in paragraph (1)(a) include both parents and the circumstances are such that care is provided to the same extent by both but each provides care to an extent greater than or equal to any other person who provides such care for that child—

      (i) the parent who is not in receipt of child benefit for the child in question; or

      (ii) if neither parent is in receipt of child benefit for that child, the parent who, in the opinion of the Secretary of State, will not be the principal provider of day to day care for that child.

(3) For the purposes of this regulation and regulation 10 'child benefit' means child benefit payable under Part IX of the Contributions and Benefits Act.

**Note.** Words in italics in para (1)(a) omitted and words in square brackets substituted by SI 2003 No 328 as from 21 February 2003.

**9  Care provided in part by a local authority—**(1) This regulation applies where paragraph (2) applies and the rate of child support maintenance payable is the basic rate, or the reduced rate, or has been calculated following agreement to a variation where the non-resident parent's liability would otherwise have been a flat rate or the nil rate.

(2) Where the circumstances of a case are that the care of the qualifying child is shared between the person with care and a local authority and—

(a) the qualifying child is in the care of the local authority for 52 nights or more in the 12 month period ending with the relevant week; or

(b) where, in the opinion of the Secretary of State, a period other than the 12 month period mentioned in sub-paragraph (a) is more representative of the current arrangements for the care of the qualifying child, the qualifying child is in the care of the local authority during that period for no fewer than the number of nights which bears the same ratio to 52 nights as that period bears to 12 months; or

(c) it is intended that the qualifying child shall be in the care of the local authority for a number of nights in a period from the effective date,

that case shall be treated as a special case for the purposes of the Act.

(3) In a case where this regulation applies, the amount of child support maintenance which the non-resident parent is liable to pay the person with care of that qualifying child is the amount calculated in accordance with the provisions of Part I of Schedule 1 to the Act and decreased in accordance with this regulation.

(4) First, there is to be a decrease according to the number of nights spent or to be spent by the qualifying child in the care of the local authority during the period under consideration.

(5) Where paragraph (2)(b) or (c) applies, the number of nights in the period under consideration shall be adjusted by the ratio which the period of 12 months bears to the period under consideration.

(6) After any adjustment under paragraph (5), the amount of the decrease for one child is set out in the following Table—

| Number of nights in care of local authority | Fraction to subtract |
| --- | --- |
| 52–103 | One-seventh |
| 104–155 | Two-sevenths |
| 156–207 | Three-sevenths |
| 208–259 | Four-sevenths |
| 260–262 | Five-sevenths |

(7) If the non-resident parent and the person with care have more than one qualifying child, the applicable decrease is the sum of the appropriate fractions in the Table divided by the number of such qualifying children.

(8) In a case where the amount of child support maintenance which the non-resident parent is liable to pay in relation to the same person with care is to be decreased in accordance with the provisions of both this regulation and of paragraph 7 of Part I of Schedule 1 to the Act, read with regulation 7 of these Regulations, the applicable decrease is the sum of the appropriate fractions derived under those provisions.

(9) If the application of this regulation would decrease the weekly amount of child support maintenance (or the aggregate of all such amounts) payable by the non-resident parent to less than the rate stated in or prescribed for the purposes of paragraph 4(1) of Part I of Schedule 1 to the Act, he is instead liable to pay child support maintenance at a rate equivalent to that rate, apportioned (if appropriate) in accordance with paragraph 6 of Part I of Schedule 1 to the Act and regulation 6.

(10) Where a qualifying child is a boarder at a boarding school or is an in-patient at a hospital, the qualifying child shall be treated as being in the care of the local authority for any night that the local authority would otherwise have been providing such care.

(11) A child is in the care of a local authority for any night in which he is being looked after by the local authority within the meaning of section 22 of the Children Act 1989 or section 17(6) of the Children (Scotland) Act 1995.

**10 Care provided for relevant other child by a local authority** Where a child other than a qualifying child is cared for in part or in full by a local authority and the non-resident parent or his partner receives child benefit for that child, the child is a relevant other child for the purposes of Schedule 1 to the Act.

**11 Non-resident parent liable to pay maintenance under a maintenance order—**(1) Subject to paragraph (2), where the circumstances of a case are that—

  (a)  an application for child support maintenance is made or treated as made, as the case may be, with respect to a qualifying child and a non-resident parent; and
  (b)  an application for child support maintenance for a different child cannot be made under the Act but that non-resident parent is liable to pay maintenance under a maintenance order for that child,

that case shall be treated as a special case for the purposes of the Act.

  (2)  This regulation applies where the rate of child support maintenance payable is the basic rate, or the reduced rate, or has been calculated following agreement to a variation where the non-resident parent's liability would otherwise have been a flat rate or the nil rate.

  (3)  Where this regulation applies [subject to paragraph (5)], the amount of child support maintenance payable by the non-resident parent shall be ascertained by—

  (a)  calculating the amount of maintenance payable as if the number of qualifying children of that parent included any children with respect to whom he is liable to make payments under the order referred to in paragraph (1)(b); and
  (b)  apportioning the amount so calculated between the qualifying children and the children with respect to whom he is liable to make payments under the order referred to in paragraph (1)(b),

and the amount payable shall be the amount apportioned to the qualifying children, and the amount payable to each person with care shall be that amount subject to the application of apportionment under paragraph 6 of Schedule 1 to the Act and the shared care provisions in paragraph 7 of Part I of that Schedule.

  (4)  In a case where this regulation applies paragraph 7 of Part I of Schedule 1 to the Act (shared care) and regulation 10 (care provided in part by local authority) shall not apply in relation to a child in respect of whom the non-resident parent is liable to make payments under a maintenance order as provided in paragraph (1)(b).

  (5)  If the application of paragraph (3) would decrease the weekly amount of child support maintenance (or the aggregate of all such amounts) payable by the non-resident parent to the person with care (or all of them) to an amount which is less than a figure equivalent to the flat rate of child support maintenance payable under paragraph 4(1) of Schedule 1 to the Act, the non-resident parent shall instead be liable to pay child support maintenance at a rate equivalent to that flat rate apportioned (if appropriate) as provided in paragraph 6 of Schedule 1 to the Act.

**Note.** Para (3): words in square brackets inserted by SI 2004 No 2779 as from 5 November 2003. Para (5) inserted by SI 2004 No 2779 as from 5 November 2003.

**12 Child who is a boarder or an in-patient in hospital—**(1) Where the circumstances of the case are that—

  (a)  a qualifying child is a boarder at a boarding school or is an in-patient in a hospital; and
  (b)  by reason of those circumstances, the person who would otherwise provide day to day care is not doing so,

that case shall be treated as a special case for the purposes of the Act.

(2) For the purposes of this case, section 3(3)(b) of the Act shall be modified so that for the reference to the person who usually provides day to day care for the child there shall be substituted a reference to the person who would usually be providing such care for that child but for the circumstances specified in paragraph (1).

**13 Child who is allowed to live with his parent under section 23(5) of the Children Act 1989—**(1) Where the circumstances of a case are that a qualifying child who is in the care of a local authority in England and Wales is allowed by the authority to live with a parent of his under section 23(5) of the Children Act 1989, that case shall be treated as a special case for the purposes of the Act.

(2) For the purposes of this case, section 3(3)(b) of the Act shall be modified so that for the reference to the person who usually provides day to day care for the child there shall be substituted a reference to the parent of the child with whom the local authority allow the child to live with under section 23(5) of the Children Act 1989.

**14 Person with part-time care who is not a non-resident parent—**(1) Where the circumstances of a case are that—
  (a) two or more persons who do not live in the same household each provide day to day care for the same qualifying child; and
  (b) those persons do not include any parent who is treated as a non-resident parent of that child by regulation 8(2),
that case shall be treated as a special case for the purposes of the Act.
  (2) For the purposes of this case—
  (a) the person whose application for a maintenance calculation is being proceeded with shall, subject to sub-paragraph (b), be entitled to receive all of the child support maintenance payable under the Act in respect of the child in question;
  (b) on request being made to the Secretary of State by—
      (i) that person; or
      (ii) any other person who is providing day to day care for that child and who intends to continue to provide that care,
the Secretary of State may make arrangements for the payment of any child support maintenance payable under the Act to the persons who provide such care in the same ratio as that in which it appears to the Secretary of State that each is to provide such care for the child in question;
  (c) before making an arrangement under sub-paragraph (b), the Secretary of State shall consider all of the circumstances of the case and in particular the interests of the child, the present arrangements for the day to day care of the child in question and any representations or proposals made by the persons who provide such care for that child.

PART IV

REVOCATION AND SAVINGS

**15 Revocation and savings—**(1) Subject to [the Child Support (Transitional Provisions) Regulations 2000 and] paragraphs (2), (3) and (4), the Child Support (Maintenance Assessments and Special Cases) Regulations 1992 ('the 1992 Regulations') shall be revoked with respect to a particular case with effect from the date that these Regulations come into force with respect to that type of case ('the commencement date').

(2) Where before the commencement date in respect of a particular case—

(a) an application was made and not determined for—
　(i)　a maintenance assessment;
　(ii)　a departure direction; or
　(iii)　a revision or supersession of a decision;

(b) the Secretary of State had begun but not completed a revision or supersession of a decision on his own initiative;

(c) any time limit provided for in Regulations for making an application for a revision or a departure direction had not expired; or

(d) any appeal was made but not decided or any time limit for making an appeal had not expired,

the provisions of the 1992 Regulations shall continue to apply for the purposes of—

(aa) the decision on the application referred to in sub-paragraph (a);

(bb) the revision or supersession referred to in sub-paragraph (b);

(cc) the ability to apply for the revision or the departure direction referred to in sub-paragraph (c) and the decision whether to revise or to give a departure direction following any such application;

(dd) any appeal outstanding or made during the time limit referred to in sub-paragraph (d); or

(ee) any revision, supersession, appeal or application for a departure direction in relation to a decision, ability to apply or appeal referred to in sub-paragraphs (aa) to (dd) above.

(3) Where immediately before the commencement date in respect of a particular case an interim maintenance assessment was in force, the provisions of the 1992 Regulations shall continue to apply for the purposes of the decision under section 17 of the Act to make a maintenance assessment calculated in accordance with Part I of Schedule 1 to the Act before its amendment by the 2000 Act and any revision, supersession or appeal in relation to that decision.

(4) Where under regulation 28(1) of the Child Support (Transitional Provisions) Regulation 2000 an application for a maintenance calculation is treated as an application for a maintenance assessment, the provisions of the 1992 Regulations shall continue to apply for the purposes of the determination of the application and any revision, supersession or appeal in relation to any such assessment made.

(5) Where after the commencement date a maintenance assessment is revised from a date which is prior to the commencement date the 1992 Regulations shall apply for the purposes of that revision.

(6) For the purposes of this regulation—

(a) 'departure direction', 'maintenance assessment' and 'interim maintenance assessment' have the same meaning as in section 54 of the Act before its amendment by the 2000 Act;

(b) 'revision or supersession' means a revision or supersession of a decision under section 16 or 17 of the Act before their amendment by the 2000 Act; and

(c) '2000 Act' means the Child Support, Pensions and Social Security Act 2000.

**Note.** Words in square brackets in para (1) inserted by SI 2003 No 247 as from 3 March 2003.

SCHEDULE                                                    Regulation 1(2)

NET WEEKLY INCOME

PART I

GENERAL

*Net weekly income*

**1** Net weekly income means the aggregate of the net weekly income of the non-resident parent provided for in this Schedule.

*Amounts to be disregarded when calculating income*

**2** The following amounts shall be disregarded when calculating the net weekly income of the non-resident parent—

   (a)  where a payment is made in a currency other than sterling, an amount equal to any banking charge or commission payable in converting that payment to sterling;

   (b)  any amount payable in a country outside the United Kingdom where there is a prohibition against the transfer to the United Kingdom of that amount.

PART II

EMPLOYED EARNER

*Net weekly income of employed earner*

**3**—(1) The net weekly income of the non-resident parent as an employed earner shall be—

   (a)  his earnings provided for in paragraph 4 less the deductions provided for in paragraph 5 and calculated or estimated by reference to the relevant week as provided for in paragraph 6; or

   (b)  where the Secretary of State is satisfied that the person is unable to provide evidence or information relating to the deductions provided for in paragraph 5, the non-resident parent's net earnings estimated by the Secretary of State on the basis of information available to him as to the non-resident parent's net income.

(2) Where any provision of these Regulations requires the income of a person to be estimated, and that or any other provision of these Regulations requires that the amount of such estimated income is to be taken into account for any purpose, after deducting from it a sum in respect of income tax, or of primary Class 1 contributions under the Contributions and Benefits Act or, as the case may be, the Contributions and Benefits (Northern Ireland) Act, or contributions paid by that person towards an occupational pension scheme or personal pension scheme, then,

   (a)  subject to sub-paragraph (c), the amount to be deducted in respect of income tax shall be calculated by applying to that income the rates of income tax applicable at the effective date less only the personal relief to which that person is entitled under Chapter I of Part VII of the Income and Corporation Taxes Act 1988 (personal relief); but if the period in respect of which that income is to be estimated is less than a year, the amount of the personal relief deductible under this paragraph shall be calculated on a pro-rata basis and the amount of income to which each tax rate applies shall be determined on the basis that the ratio of that amount to the full amount of the income to which each tax rate applies is the same as the ratio of the proportionate part of that personal relief to the full personal relief;

   (b)  subject to sub-paragraph (c), the amount to be deducted in respect of Class 1 contributions under the Contributions and Benefits Act or, as the case may be, the Contributions and Benefits (Northern Ireland) Act, shall be calculated by applying to that income the appropriate primary percentage applicable on the effective date;

(c)  in relation to any bonus or commission which may be included in that person's income—

    (i)  the amount to be deducted in respect of income tax shall be calculated by applying to the gross amount of that bonus or commission the rate or rates of income tax applicable at the effective date;

    (ii)  the amount to be deducted in respect of primary Class 1 contributions under the Contributions and Benefits Act or, as the case may be, the Contributions and Benefits (Northern Ireland) Act, shall be calculated by applying to the gross amount of that bonus or commission the appropriate main primary percentage applicable on the effective date but no deduction shall be made in respect of the portion (if any) of the bonus or commission which, if added to the estimated income, would cause such income to exceed the upper earnings limit for Class 1 contributions as provided for in section 5(1)(b) of the Contributions and Benefits Act or, as the case may be, the Contributions and Benefits (Northern Ireland) Act;

(d)  the amount to be deducted in respect of any sums or contributions towards an occupational pension scheme or personal pension scheme shall be the full amount of any such payments made or, where that scheme is intended partly to provide a capital sum to discharge a mortgage secured upon that parent's home, 75 per centum of any such payments made.

*Earnings*

**4**—(1)  Subject to sub-paragraph (2), 'earnings' means, in the case of employment as an employed earner, any remuneration or profit derived from that employment and includes—

(a)  any bonus, commission, payment in respect of overtime, royalty or fees;

(b)  any holiday pay except any payable more than 4 weeks after termination of the employment;

(c)  any payment by way of a retainer;

(d)  any statutory sick pay under Part XI of the Contributions and Benefits Act or statutory maternity pay under Part XII of the Contributions and Benefits Act; and

[(dd) any statutory paternity pay under Part 12ZA of the Contributions and Benefits Act or any statutory adoption pay under Part 12ZB of that Act;]

(e)  any payment in lieu of notice, and any compensation in respect of the absence or inadequacy of any such notice, but only in so far as such payment or compensation represents loss of income.

(2)  Earnings for the purposes of this Part of Schedule 1 do not include—

(a)  any payment in respect of expenses wholly, exclusively and necessarily incurred in the performance of the duties of the employment;

(b)  any tax-exempt allowance made by an employer to an employee;

(c)  any gratuities paid by customers of the employer;

(d)  any payment in kind;

(e)  any advance of earnings or any loan made by an employer to an employee;

(f)  any amount received from an employer during a period when the employee has withdrawn his services by reason of a trade dispute;

(g)  any payment made in respect of the performance of duties as—

      (i)  an auxiliary coastguard in respect of coast rescue activities;

     (ii)  a part-time fireman in a fire brigade maintained in pursuance of the Fire Services Acts 1947 to 1959;

   (iii)  a person engaged part-time in the manning or launching of a lifeboat;

   (iv)  a member of any territorial or reserve force prescribed in Part I of Schedule 3 to the Social Security (Contributions) Regulations 1979;

  (h)  any payment made by a local authority to a member of that authority in respect of the performance of his duties as a member;

  (i)  any payment where—

      (i)  the employment in respect of which it was made has ceased; and

     (ii)  a period of the same length as the period by reference to which it was calculated has expired since that cessation but prior to the effective date; or

  (j)  where, in any week or other period which falls within the period by reference to which earnings are calculated, earnings are received both in respect of a previous employment and in respect of a subsequent employment, the earnings in respect of the previous employment.

*Deductions*

**5**—(1) The deductions to be taken from gross earnings to calculate net income for the purposes of this Part of the Schedule are any amount deducted from those earnings by way of—

  (a)  income tax;

  (b)  primary Class 1 contributions under the Contributions and Benefits Act or under the Contributions and Benefits (Northern Ireland) Act; or

  (c)  any sums paid by the non-resident parent towards an occupational pension scheme or personal pension scheme or, where that scheme is intended partly to provide a capital sum to discharge a mortgage secured upon that parent's home, 75 per centum of any such sums.

  (2) For the purposes of sub-paragraph (1)(a), amounts deducted by way of income tax shall be the amounts actually deducted, including in respect of payments which are not included as earnings in paragraph 4.

*Calculation or estimate*

**6**—(1) Subject to sub-paragraphs *(2) to (4)* [(3) and (4)], the amount of earnings to be taken into account for the purpose of calculating net income shall be calculated or estimated by reference to the average earnings at the relevant week having regard to such evidence as is available in relation to that person's earnings during such period as appears appropriate to the Secretary of State, beginning not earlier than 8 weeks before the relevant week and ending not later than the date of the calculation, and for the purposes of the calculation or estimate he may consider evidence of that person's cumulative earnings during the period beginning with the start of the year of assessment (within the meaning of section 832 of the Income and Corporation Taxes Act 1988) in which the relevant week falls and ending with a date no later than the date when the calculation is made.

  *(2) Subject to sub-paragraph (4), where a person has claimed, or has been paid, working families' tax credit or disabled person's tax credit on any day during the period beginning not earlier than 8 weeks before the relevant week and ending not later than the date on which the calculation is made, the Secretary of State may have regard to the amount of earnings taken into account in determining entitlement to those tax credits in order to calculate or estimate the amount of earnings to be taken into account for the purposes of calculating net earnings, notwithstanding the fact that entitlement to those tax credits may have been determined by reference to earnings attributable to a period other than that specified in sub-paragraph (1).*

(3) Where a person's earnings during the period of 52 weeks ending with the relevant week include a bonus or commission made in anticipation of the calculation of profits which is paid separately from, or in relation to a longer period than, the other earnings with which it is paid, the amount of that bonus or commission shall be determined for the purposes of the calculation of earnings by aggregating any such payments received in that period and dividing by 52.

(4) Where a calculation would, but for this sub-paragraph, produce an amount which, in the opinion of the Secretary of State, does not accurately reflect the normal amount of the earnings of the person in question, such earnings, or any part of them, shall be calculated by reference to such other period as may, in the particular case, enable the normal weekly earnings of that person to be determined more accurately, and for this purpose the Secretary of State shall have regard to—

(a) the earnings received, or due to be received from any employment in which the person in question is engaged, has been engaged or is due to be engaged; and

(b) the duration and pattern, or the expected duration and pattern, of any employment of that person.

**Note.** Para 4: sub-para (1)(dd) inserted by SI 2004 No 2415, reg 7(1), (3) as from 16 September 2004. Para (6): sub-para reference in (6)(1) substituted and sub-para (2) omitted by SI 2003 No 328 as from 6 April 2003.

## Part III

### Self-Employed Earner

*Figures submitted to the Inland Revenue*

**7**—(1) Subject to sub-paragraph (6) the net weekly income of the non-resident parent as a self-employed earner shall be his gross earnings calculated by reference to one of the following, as the Secretary of State may decide, less the deductions to which sub-paragraph (3) applies—

(a) the total taxable profits from self-employment of that earner as submitted to the Inland Revenue in accordance with their requirements by or on behalf of that earner; or

(b) the income from self-employment as a self-employed earner as set out on the tax calculation notice or, as the case may be, the revised notice.

(2) Where the information referred to in head (a) or (b) of sub-paragraph (1) is made available to the Secretary of State he may nevertheless require the information referred to in the other head from the non-resident parent and where the Secretary of State becomes aware that a revised notice has been issued he may require and use this in preference to the other information referred to in sub-paragraph (1)(a) and (b).

(3) This paragraph applies to the following deductions—

(a) any income tax relating to the gross earnings from the self-employment determined in accordance with sub-paragraph (4);

(b) any National Insurance contributions relating to the gross earnings from the self-employment determined in accordance with sub-paragraph (5); and

(c) any premiums paid by the non-resident parent in respect of a retirement annuity contract or a personal pension scheme or, where that scheme is intended partly to provide a capital sum to discharge a mortgage or a charge secured upon the parent's home, 75 per centum of the contributions payable.

(4) For the purpose of sub-paragraph (3)(a), the income tax to be deducted from the gross earnings shall be determined in accordance with the following provisions—

   (a)  subject to head (d), an amount of gross earnings equivalent to any personal allowance applicable to the earner by virtue of the provisions of Chapter I of Part VII of the Income and Corporation Taxes Act 1988 (personal relief) shall be disregarded;

   (b)  subject to head (c), an amount equivalent to income tax shall be calculated in relation to the gross earnings remaining following the application of head (a) (the 'remaining earnings');

   (c)  the tax rate applicable at the effective date shall be applied to all the remaining earnings, where necessary increasing or reducing the amount payable to take account of the fact that the earnings related to a period greater or less than one year; and

   (d)  the amount to be disregarded by virtue of head (a) shall be calculated by reference to the yearly rate applicable at the effective date, that amount being reduced or increased in the same proportion to that which the period represented by the gross earnings bears to the period of one year.

(5) For the purposes of sub-paragraph (3)(b), the amount to be deducted in respect of National Insurance contributions shall be the total of—

   (a)  the amount of Class 2 contributions (if any) payable under section 11(1) or, as the case may be, (3) of the Contributions and Benefits Act or under section 11(1) or (3) of the Contributions and Benefits (Northern Ireland) Act; and

   (b)  the amount of Class 4 contributions (if any) payable under section 15(2) of that Act, or under section 15(2) of the Contributions and Benefits (Northern Ireland) Act,

at the rates applicable at the effective date.

(6) The net weekly income of a self-employed earner may only be determined in accordance with this paragraph where the earnings concerned relate to a period which terminated not more than 24 months prior to the relevant week.

(7) In this paragraph—

'tax calculation notice' means a document issued by the Inland Revenue containing information as to the income of the self-employed earner; and

'revised notice' means a notice issued by the Inland Revenue where there has been a tax calculation notice and there is a revision of the figures relating to the income of a self-employed earner following an enquiry under section 9A of the Taxes Management Act 1970 or otherwise by the Inland Revenue.

(8) Any request by the Secretary of State in accordance with sub-paragraph (2) for the provision of information shall set out the possible consequences of failure to provide such information, including details of the offences provided for in section 14A of the Act for failing to provide, or providing false, information.

*Figures calculated using gross receipts less deductions*

**8**—(1) Where—

   (a)  the conditions of paragraph 7(6) are not satisfied; or

   (b)  the Secretary of State accepts that it is not reasonably practicable for the self-employed earner to provide information relating to his gross earnings from self-employment in the forms submitted to, or as issued or revised by, the Inland Revenue; or

   (c)  in the opinion of the Secretary of State, information as to the gross earnings of the self-employed earner which has satisfied the criteria set out in paragraph 7 does not accurately reflect the normal weekly earnings of the self-employed earner,

net income means in the case of employment as a self-employed earner his earnings calculated by reference to the gross receipts *of the employment* [in respect of employment which are of a type which would be taken into account under paragraph 7(1)] less the deductions provided for in sub-paragraph (2).

(2) The deductions to be taken from the gross receipts to calculate net earnings for the purposes of this paragraph are—

(a) any expenses which are reasonably incurred and are wholly and exclusively defrayed for the purposes of the earner's business in the period by reference to which his earnings are determined under paragraph 9(2) or (3);

(b) any value added tax paid in the period by reference to which his earnings are determined in excess of value added tax received in that period;

(c) any amount in respect of income tax determined in accordance with sub-paragraph (4);

(d) any amount of National Insurance contributions determined in accordance with sub-paragraph (4); and

(e) any premium paid by the non-resident parent in respect of a retirement annuity contract or a personal pension scheme or, where that scheme is intended partly to provide a capital sum to discharge a mortgage or a charge secured upon the parent's home, 75 per centum of contributions payable.

(3) For the purposes of sub-paragraph (2)(a)—

(a) such expenses include—

(i) repayment of capital on any loan used for the replacement, in the course of business, of equipment or machinery, or the repair of an existing business asset except to the extent that any sum is payable under an insurance policy for its repair;

(ii) any income expended in the repair of an existing business asset except to the extent that any sum is payable under an insurance policy for its repair; and

(iii) any payment of interest on a loan taken out for the purposes of the business;

(b) such expenses do not include—

(i) repayment of capital on any other loan taken out for the purposes of the business;

(ii) any capital expenditure;

(iii) the depreciation of any capital assets;

(iv) any sum employed, or intended to be employed, in the setting up or expansion of the business;

(v) any loss incurred before the beginning of the period by reference to which earnings are determined;

(vi) any expenses incurred in providing business entertainment; or

(vii) any loss incurred in any other employment in which he is engaged as a self-employed earner.

(4) For the purposes of sub-paragraph (2)(c) and (d), the amounts in respect of income tax and National Insurance contributions to be deducted from the gross receipts shall be determined in accordance with paragraph 7(4) and (5) of this Schedule as if in paragraph 7(4) references to gross earnings were references to taxable earnings and in this sub-paragraph 'taxable earnings' means the gross receipts of the earner less the deductions mentioned in sub-paragraph (2)(a) and (b).

**Note.** Words in italics in para (1) omitted and words in square brackets substituted by SI 2002 No 1204 as from 30 April 2002.

*Rules for calculation under paragraph 8*

**9**—(1) This paragraph applies only where the net income of a self-employed earner is calculated or estimated under paragraph 8 of this Schedule.

(2) Where—

(a) a non-resident parent has been a self-employed earner for 52 weeks or more, including the relevant week, the amount of his net weekly income

shall be determined by reference to the average of the earnings which he
has received in the 52 weeks ending with the relevant week; or

(b) a non-resident parent has been a self-employed earner for a period of less
than 52 weeks including the relevant week, the amount of his net weekly
income shall be determined by reference to the average of the earnings
which he has received during that period.

(3) Where a calculation would, but for this sub-paragraph, produce an amount
which, in the opinion of the Secretary of State, does not accurately reflect the
normal weekly income of the non-resident parent in question, such earnings, or
any part of them, shall be calculated by reference to such other period as may, in
the particular case, enable the normal weekly earnings of the non-resident parent
to be determined more accurately and for this purpose the Secretary of State shall
have regard to—

(a) the earnings from self-employment received, or due to be received, by him;
and

(b) the duration and pattern, or the expected duration and pattern, of any self-
employment of that non-resident parent.

*(4) Where a person has claimed, or has been paid, working families' tax credit or disabled
person's tax credit on any day during the period beginning not earlier than 8 weeks before the
relevant week and ending not later than the date on which the calculation is made, the
Secretary of State may have regard to the amount of earnings taken into account in
determining entitlement to those tax credits in order to calculate or estimate the amount of
earnings to be taken into account for the purposes of calculating net income, notwithstanding
the fact that entitlement to those tax credits may have been determined by reference to earnings
attributable to a period other than that specified in sub-paragraph (2).*

**Note.** Sub-para (4) omitted by SI 2003 No 328 as from 6 April 2003.

*Income from board or lodging*

**10** In a case where a non-resident parent is a self-employed earner who provides
board and lodging, his earnings shall include payments received for that provision
where those payments are the only or main source of income of that earner.

PART IV

TAX CREDITS

*Working families' tax credit [working tax credit]*

**11**—(1) Subject to *sub-paragraphs (2) and (3)* [sub-paragraph (2)], payments by way
of *working families' tax credit* [working tax credit] *under section 128 of the Contributions
and Benefits Act*, shall be treated as the income of the non-resident parent where he
has qualified for them by his engagement in, and normal engagement in,
remunerative work, at the rate payable at the effective date.

(2) Where working families' tax credit [working tax credit] is payable and the
amount which is payable has been calculated by reference to the *weekly earnings*
[the earnings] of the non-resident parent and another person—

(a) where during the period which is used by the Inland Revenue to calculate
his income *the normal weekly earnings* [the earnings] *(as determined in
accordance with Chapter II of Part IV of the Family Credit (General) Regulations
1987)* of that parent exceed those of the other person, the amount payable
by way of *working families' tax credit* [working tax credit] shall be treated as
the income of that parent;

(b) where during that period *the normal weekly earnings* [the earnings] of that
parent equal those of the other person, half of the amount payable by way

of *working families' tax credit* [working tax credit] shall be treated as the income of that parent; and

(c) where during that period *the normal weekly earnings* [the earnings] of that parent are less than those of that other person, the amount payable by way of *working families' tax credit* [working tax credit] shall not be treated as the income of that parent.

[(2A) For the purposes of this paragraph, 'earnings' means the employment income and the income from self-employment of the non-resident parent and the other person referred to in sub-paragraph (2), as determined for the purposes of their entitlement to working tax credit.]

(3) Where—

(a) *working families' tax credit is in payment; and*

(b) *not later than the effective date the person, or, if more than one, each of the persons by reference to whose engagement, and normal engagement, in remunerative work that payment has been calculated is no longer the partner of the person to whom that payment is made,*

the payment in question shall only be treated as the income of the non-resident parent in question where he is in receipt of it.

**Note.** Words in italics omitted and words in square brackets inserted by SI 2003 No 328 as from 26 April 2003.

*Employment Credits*

**12** Payments made by way of employment credits under section 2(1) of the Employment and Training Act 1973 to a non-resident parent who is participating in a scheme arranged under section 2(2) of the Employment and Training Act 1973 and known as the New Deal 50 plus shall be treated as the income of the non-resident parent, at the rate payable at the effective date.

*Disabled Person's Tax Credits*

**13** *Payments made by way of disabled person's tax credit under section 129 of the Contributions and Benefits Act to a non-resident parent shall be treated as the income of the non-resident parent at the rate payable at the effective date.*

**[13**—*(1) Subject to sub-paragraphs (2) and (3), payments made by way of disabled person's tax credit under section 129 of the Contributions and Benefits Act to a non-resident parent shall be treated as the income of the non-resident parent, at the rate payable at the effective date.*

(2) *Where disabled person's tax credit is payable where a non-resident parent and another person both meet the entitlement criteria for the payment and the amount which is payable has been calculated by reference to the weekly earnings of the non-resident parent and the other person—*

(a) *where during the period which is used by the Inland Revenue to calculate the non-resident parent's income the normal weekly earnings (as determined in accordance with Chapter II of Part V of the Disability Working Allowance (General) Regulations 1991) of that parent exceed those of the other person, the amount payable by way of disabled person's tax credit shall be treated as the income of that parent;*

(b) *where during that period the normal weekly earnings of that parent equal those of the other person, half of the amount payable by way of disabled person's tax credit shall be treated as the income of that parent; and*

(c) *where during that period the normal weekly earnings of that parent are less than those of that other person, the amount payable by way of disabled person's tax credit shall not be treated as the income of that parent.*

(3) *Where—*

(a) *disabled person's tax credit is in payment; and*

(b)   *not later than the effective date the person, or, if more than one, each of the persons by reference to whose entitlement that payment has been calculated is no longer the partner of the person to whom that payment is made,*

*the payment shall only be treated as the income of the non-resident parent in question where he is in receipt of it.*]

**Note.** Para 13 in italics omitted and para 13 in square brackets substituted by SI 2002 No 1204 as from 30 April 2002. Para 13 in square brackets omitted by SI 2003 No 328 as from 6 April 2003.

*[Child tax credit*

**13A** Payments made by way of child tax credit to a non-resident parent or his partner at the rate payable at the effective date.]

**Note.** Para 13A added by SI 2003 No 328 as from 6 April 2003.

PART V

OTHER INCOME

*Amount*

**14** The amount of other income to be taken into account in calculating or estimating net weekly income shall be the aggregate of the payments to which paragraph 15 applies, net of any income tax deducted and otherwise determined in accordance with this Part.

*Types*

**15** This paragraph applies to any periodic payment of pension or other benefit under an occupational or personal pension scheme or a retirement annuity contract or other such scheme for the provision of income in retirement whether or not approved by the Inland Revenue.

*Calculation or estimate and period*

**16**—(1)  The amount of any income to which this Part applies shall be calculated or estimated—

(a)   where it has been received in respect of the whole of the period of 26 weeks which ends at the end of the relevant week, by dividing such income received in that period by 26;

(b)   where it has been received in respect of part of the period of 26 weeks which ends at the end of the relevant week, by dividing such income received in that period by the number of complete weeks in respect of which such income is received and for this purpose income shall be treated as received in respect of a week if it is received in respect of any day in the week in question.

(2)  Where a calculation or estimate to which this Part applies would, but for this sub-paragraph, produce an amount which, in the opinion of the Secretary of State, does not accurately reflect the normal amount of the other income of the non-resident parent in question, such income, or any part of it, shall be calculated by reference to such other period as may, in the particular case, enable the other income of that parent to be determined more accurately and for this purpose the Secretary of State shall have regard to the nature and pattern of receipt of such income.

PART VI

BENEFITS PENSIONS AND ALLOWANCES

[**17**—(1)  Subject to paragraph (2), the net weekly income of a non-resident parent shall include payments made by way of benefits, pensions and allowances prescribed in regulation 4 for the purposes of paragraph 4(1)(b) and (c) of Schedule 1 to the Act, to a non-resident parent or his partner at the rate payable at the effective date.

(2) Paragraph (1) applies only for the purpose of establishing whether the non-resident parent is a person to whom paragraph 5(b) of Schedule 1 to the Act applies.]

**Note.** Inserted by SI 2004 No 2415, reg 7(1), (4) as from 16 September 2004.

## CHILD SUPPORT (VARIATIONS) REGULATIONS 2000

**SI 2001 No 156**

**Dated** 18th January 2001

PART I

GENERAL

**1 Citation, commencement and interpretation—**(1) These Regulations may be cited as the Child Support (Variations) Regulations 2000 and shall come into force in relation to a particular case on the day on which section 5 of the Child Support, Pensions and Social Security Act 2000 which substitutes or amends sections 28A to 28F of the Act is commenced in relation to that type of case.

(2) In these Regulations, unless the context otherwise requires—

'the Act' means the Child Support Act 1991;

'capped amount' means the amount of income for the purposes of paragraph 10(3) of Schedule 1 to the Act;

'Contributions and Benefits Act' means the Social Security Contributions and Benefits Act 1992;

'couple' has the same meaning as in paragraph 10C(5) of Schedule 1 to the Act;

'date of notification' means the date upon which notification is given in person or communicated by telephone to the recipient or, where this is not possible, the date of posting;

'date of receipt' means the day on which the information or document is actually received;

'home' has the meaning given in regulation 1(2) of the Maintenance Calculations and Special Cases Regulations;

'Maintenance Calculation Procedure Regulations' means the Child Support (Maintenance Calculation Procedure) Regulations 2000;

'Maintenance Calculations and Special Cases Regulations' means the Child Support (Maintenance Calculations and Special Cases) Regulations 2000;

'qualifying child' means the child with respect to whom the maintenance calculation falls to be made;

'relevant person' means—

(a) a non-resident parent, or a person treated as a non-resident parent under regulation 8 of the Maintenance Calculations and Special Cases Regulations, whose liability to pay child support maintenance may be affected by any variation agreed;

(b) a person with care, or a child to whom section 7 of the Act applies, where the amount of child support maintenance payable by virtue of a calculation relevant to that person with care or in respect of that child may be affected by any variation agreed; and

'Transitional Regulations' means the Child Support (Transitional Provisions) Regulations 2000.

(3) In these Regulations, unless the context otherwise requires, a reference—
(a) to a numbered Part, is to the Part of these Regulations bearing that number;
(b) to the Schedule, is to the Schedule to these Regulations;
(c) to a numbered regulation, is to the regulation in these Regulations bearing that number;
(d) in a regulation, or the Schedule, to a numbered paragraph, is to the paragraph in that regulation or the Schedule bearing that number; and
(e) in a paragraph to a lettered or numbered sub-paragraph, is to the sub-paragraph in that paragraph bearing that letter or number.

**2 Documents** Except where otherwise stated, where—
(a) any document is given or sent to the Secretary of State, that document shall be treated as having been so given or sent on the date of receipt by the Secretary of State; and
(b) any document is given or sent to any other person, that document shall, if sent by post to that person's last known or notified address, be treated as having been given or sent on the date that it is posted.

**3 Determination of amounts**—(1) Where any amount is required to be determined for the purposes of these Regulations, it shall be determined as a weekly amount and, except where the context otherwise requires, any reference to such an amount shall be construed accordingly.
(2) Where any calculation made under these Regulations results in a fraction of a penny, that fraction shall be treated as a penny if it is either one half or exceeds one half and shall be otherwise disregarded.

PART II

APPLICATION AND DETERMINATION PROCEDURE

**4 Application for a variation**—(1) Where an application for a variation is made other than in writing and the Secretary of State directs that the application be made in writing, the application shall be made either on an application form provided by the Secretary of State and completed in accordance with the Secretary of State's instructions or in such other written form as the Secretary of State may accept as sufficient in the circumstances of any particular case.
(2) An application for a variation which is made other than in writing shall be treated as made on the date of notification from the applicant to the Secretary of State that he wishes to make such an application.
(3) Where an application for a variation is made in writing other than in the circumstances to which paragraph (1) applies, the application shall be treated as made on the date of receipt by the Secretary of State.
(4) Where paragraph (1) applies and the Secretary of State receives the application within 14 days of the date of the direction, or at a later date but in circumstances where the Secretary of State is satisfied that the delay was unavoidable, the application shall be treated as made on the date of notification from the applicant to the Secretary of State that he wishes to make an application for a variation.
(5) Where paragraph (1) applies and the Secretary of State receives the application more than 14 days from the date of the direction and in circumstances where he is not satisfied that the delay was unavoidable, the application shall be treated as made on the date of receipt.
(6) An application for a variation is duly made when it has been made in accordance with this regulation and section 28A(4) of the Act.

**5 Amendment or withdrawal of application—**(1) A person who has made an application for a variation may amend or withdraw his application at any time before a decision under section 11, 16 or 17 of the Act, or a decision not to revise or supersede under section 16 or 17 of the Act, is made in response to the variation application and such amendment or withdrawal need not be in writing unless, in any particular case, the Secretary of State requires it to be.

(2) No amendment under paragraph (1) shall relate to any change of circumstances arising after what would be the effective date of a decision in response to the variation application.

**6 Rejection of an application following preliminary consideration—**(1) The Secretary of State may, on completing the preliminary consideration, reject an application for a variation (and proceed to make his decision on the application for a maintenance calculation, or to revise or supersede a decision under section 16 or 17 of the Act, without the variation, or not to revise or supersede a decision under section 16 or 17 of the Act, as the case may be) if one of the circumstances in paragraph (2) applies.

(2) The circumstances are—

(a) the application has been made in one of the circumstances to which regulation 7 applies;

(b) the application is made—

(i) on a ground in paragraph 2 of Schedule 4B to the Act (special expenses) and the amount of the special expenses, or the aggregate amount of those expenses, as the case may be, does not exceed the relevant threshold provided for in regulation 15;

(ii) on a ground in paragraph 3 of that Schedule (property or capital transfers) and the value of the property or capital transferred does not exceed the minimum value in regulation 16(4); or

(iii) on a ground referred to in regulation 18 (assets) and the value of the assets does not exceed the figure in regulation 18(3)(a), or on a ground in regulation 19(1) (income not taken into account) and the amount of the income does not exceed the figure in regulation 19(2);

(c) a request under regulation 8 has not been complied with by the applicant and the Secretary of State is not able to determine the application without the information requested; or

(d) the Secretary of State is satisfied, on the information or evidence available to him, that the application would not be agreed to, including where, although a ground is stated, the facts alleged in the application would not bring the case within the prescription of the relevant ground in these Regulations.

**7 Prescribed circumstances—**(1) This regulation applies where an application for a variation is made under *section 28G* [section 28A or 28G] of the Act and—

(a) the application is made by a relevant person and a circumstance set out in paragraph (2) applies at the relevant date;

(b) the application is made by a non-resident parent and a circumstance set out in paragraph (3) or (4) applies at the relevant date;

(c) the application is made by a person with care, or a child to whom section 7 of the Act applies, on a ground in paragraph 4 of Schedule 4B to the Act (additional cases) and a circumstance set out in paragraph (5) applies at the relevant date; or

(d) the application is made by a non-resident parent on a ground in paragraph 2 of Schedule 4B to the Act (special expenses) and a circumstance set out in paragraph (6) applies at the relevant date.

(2) The circumstances for the purposes of this paragraph are that—

(a) a default maintenance decision is in force with respect to the non-resident parent;

(b) the non-resident parent is liable to pay the flat rate of child support maintenance owing to the application of paragraph 4(1)(c) of Schedule 1 to the Act, or would be so liable but is liable to pay less than that amount, or nil, owing to the application of paragraph 8 of Schedule 1 to the Act, or the Transitional Regulations; or

(c) the non-resident parent is liable to pay child support maintenance at a flat rate of a prescribed amount owing to the application of paragraph 4(2) of Schedule 1 to the Act, or would be so liable but is liable to pay less than that amount, or nil, owing to the application of paragraph 8 of Schedule 1 to the Act, or the Transitional Regulations.

(3) The circumstances for the purposes of this paragraph are that the non-resident parent is liable to pay child support maintenance—

(a) at the nil rate owing to the application of paragraph 5 of Schedule 1 to the Act;

(b) at a flat rate owing to the application of paragraph 4(1)(a) of Schedule 1 to the Act, including where the net weekly income of the non-resident parent which is taken into account for the purposes of a maintenance calculation in force in respect of him is £100 per week or less owing to a variation being taken into account or to the application of regulation 18, 19 or 21 of the Transitional Regulations (reduction for relevant departure direction or relevant property transfer); or

(c) at a flat rate owing to the application of paragraph 4(1)(b) of Schedule 1 to the Act, or would be so liable but is liable to pay less than that amount, or nil, owing to the application of paragraph 8 of Schedule 1 to the Act, or the Transitional Regulations.

(4) The circumstances for the purposes of this paragraph are that the non-resident parent is liable to pay an amount of child support maintenance at a rate—

(a) of £5 per week or such other amount as may be prescribed owing to the application of paragraph 7(7) of Schedule 1 to the Act (shared care); or

(b) equivalent to the flat rate provided for in, or prescribed for the purposes of, paragraph 4(1)(b) of Part 1 of Schedule 1 to the Act owing to the application of—

    (i) regulation 27(5);

    (ii) regulation 9 of the Maintenance Calculations and Special Cases Regulations (care provided in part by a local authority); or

    (iii) regulation 23(5) of the Transitional Regulations.

(5) The circumstances for the purposes of this paragraph are that—

(a) the amount of the net weekly income of the non-resident parent to which the Secretary of State had regard when making the maintenance calculation was the capped amount; or

(b) the non-resident parent or a partner of his is in *receipt of working families' tax credit (as defined in section 128 of the Contributions and Benefits Act) or disabled person's tax credit (as defined in section 129 of that Act)* [working tax credit under section 10 of the Tax Credits Act 2002] and for this purpose 'partner' has the same meaning as in paragraph 10C(4) of Schedule 1 to the Act.

(6) The circumstances for the purposes of this paragraph are that the amount of the net weekly income of the non-resident parent to which the Secretary of State would have regard after deducting the amount of the special expenses would exceed the capped amount.

(7) For the purposes of paragraph (1), the 'relevant date' means the date from which, if the variation were agreed [and the application had been made under section 28G of the Act], the decision under section 16 or 17 of the Act, as the case

may be, would take effect [and if the variation were agreed, and the application had been made under section 28A of the Act, the decision under section 11 of the Act would take effect].

**Note.** Words in italics in paras (1) and (7) omitted and words in square brackets inserted by SI 2002 No 1204 as from 30 April 2002. Words in italics in sub-para (5) omitted and words in square brackets substituted by SI 2003 No 328 as from 6 April 2003.

**8 Provision of information—**(1) Where an application has been duly made, the Secretary of State may request further information or evidence from the applicant to enable that application to be determined and any such information or evidence requested shall be provided within one month of the date of notification of the request or such longer period as the Secretary of State is satisfied is reasonable in the circumstances of the case.

(2) Where any information or evidence requested in accordance with paragraph (1) is not provided in accordance with the time limit specified in that paragraph, the Secretary of State may, where he is able to do so, proceed to determine the application in the absence of the requested information or evidence.

**9 Procedure in relation to the determination of an application—**(1) Subject to paragraph (3), where the Secretary of State has given the preliminary consideration to an application and not rejected it he—

(a) shall give notice of the application to the relevant persons other than the applicant, informing them of the grounds on which the application has been made and any relevant information or evidence the applicant has given, except information or evidence falling within paragraph (2);

(b) may invite representations, which need not be in writing but shall be in writing if in any case he so directs, from the relevant persons other than the applicant on any matter relating to that application, to be submitted to the Secretary of State within 14 days of the date of notification or such longer period as the Secretary of State is satisfied is reasonable in the circumstances of the case; and

(c) shall set out the provisions of paragraphs (2)(b) and (c), (4) and (5) in relation to such representations.

(2) The information or evidence referred to in paragraphs (1)(a), (4)(a) and (7), are—

(a) details of the nature of the long-term illness or disability of the relevant other child which forms the basis of a variation application on the ground in regulation 11 where the applicant requests they should not be disclosed and the Secretary of State is satisfied that disclosure is not necessary in order to be able to determine the application;

(b) medical evidence or medical advice which has not been disclosed to the applicant or a relevant person and which the Secretary of State considers would be harmful to the health of the applicant or that relevant person if disclosed to him; or

(c) the address of a relevant person or qualifying child, or any other information which could reasonably be expected to lead to that person or child being located, where the Secretary of State considers that there would be a risk of harm or undue distress to that person or that child or any other children living with that person if the address or information were disclosed.

(3) The Secretary of State need not act in accordance with paragraph (1)—

(a) where regulation 29 applies (variation may be taken into account notwithstanding that no application has been made);

(b) where the variation agreed is one falling within paragraph 3 of Schedule 4B to the Act (property or capital transfer), the Secretary of State ceases to have jurisdiction to make a maintenance calculation and subsequently acquires jurisdiction in respect of the same non-resident parent, person with care and any child in respect of whom the earlier calculation was made;

(c) if he is satisfied on the information or evidence available to him that the application would not be agreed to, but if, on further consideration of the application, he is minded to agree to the variation he shall, before doing so, comply with the provisions of this regulation; or

(d) where—

    (i) a variation has been agreed in relation to a maintenance calculation;

    (ii) the decision as to the maintenance calculation is replaced with a default maintenance decision under section 12(1)(b) of the Act;

    (iii) the default maintenance decision is revised in accordance with section 16(1B) of the Act,

and the Secretary of State is satisfied, on the information or evidence available to him, that there has been no material change of circumstances relating to the variation since the date from which the maintenance calculation referred to in head (i) ceased to have effect.

(4) Where the Secretary of State receives representations from the relevant persons—

(a) he may, if he considers it reasonable to do so, send a copy of the representations concerned (excluding material falling within paragraph (2)) to the applicant and invite any comments he may have within 14 days or such longer period as the Secretary of State is satisfied is reasonable in the circumstances of the case; and

(b) where the Secretary of State acts under sub-paragraph (a) he shall not proceed to determine the application until he has received such comments or the period referred to in that sub-paragraph has expired.

(5) Where the Secretary of State has not received representations from the relevant persons notified in accordance with paragraph (1) within the time limit specified in sub-paragraph (b) of that paragraph, he may proceed to agree or not (as the case may be) to a variation in their absence.

(6) In considering an application for a variation, the Secretary of State shall take into account any representations received at the date upon which he agrees or not (as the case may be) to the variation from the relevant persons, including any representation received in accordance with paragraphs (1)(b), *4(a)* [(4)(a)] and (7).

(7) Where any information or evidence requested by the Secretary of State under regulation 8 is received after notification has been given under paragraph (1), the Secretary of State may, if he considers it reasonable to do so, and except where such information or evidence falls within paragraph (2), send a copy of such information or evidence to the relevant persons and may invite them to submit representations, which need not be in writing unless the Secretary of State so directs in any particular case, on that information or evidence.

(8) The Secretary of State may, if he considers it appropriate, treat an application for a variation made on one ground as if it were an application made on a different ground, and, if he does intend to do so, he shall include this information in the notice and invitation to make representations referred to in paragraphs (1), (4) and (7).

(9) Two or more applications for a variation with respect to the same maintenance calculation or application for a maintenance calculation, made or treated as made, may be considered together.

**Note.** Sub-para reference in para (6) in italics omitted and reference in square brackets inserted by SI 2002 No 1204 as from 30 April 2002.

PART III

SPECIAL EXPENSES

**10 Special expenses—contact costs—**(1) Subject to the following paragraphs of this regulation, and to regulation 15, the following costs incurred or reasonably expected to be incurred by the non-resident parent, whether in respect of himself or the qualifying child or both, for the purpose of maintaining contact with that child, shall constitute expenses for the purposes of paragraph 2(2) of Schedule 4B to the Act—

(a) the cost of purchasing a ticket for travel;

(b) the cost of purchasing fuel where travel is by a vehicle which is not carrying fare-paying passengers;

(c) the taxi fare for a journey or part of a journey where the Secretary of State is satisfied that the disability or long-term illness of the non-resident parent or the qualifying child makes it impracticable for any other form of transport to be used for that journey or part of that journey;

(d) the cost of car hire where the cost of the journey would be less in total than it would be if public transport or taxis or a combination of both were used;

(e) where the Secretary of State considers a return journey on the same day is impracticable, or the established or intended pattern of contact with the child includes contact over two or more consecutive days, the cost of the non-resident parent's, or, as the case may be, the child's, accommodation for the number of nights the Secretary of State considers appropriate in the circumstances of the case; and

(f) any minor incidental costs such as tolls or fees payable for the use of a particular road or bridge incurred in connection with such travel, including breakfast where it is included as part of the accommodation cost referred to in sub-paragraph (e).

(2) The costs to which paragraph (1) applies include the cost of a person to travel with the non-resident parent or the qualifying child, if the Secretary of State is satisfied that the presence of another person on the journey, or part of the journey, is necessary including, but not limited to, where it is necessary because of the young age of the qualifying child or the disability or long-term illness of the non-resident parent or that child.

(3) The costs referred to in paragraphs (1) and (2)—

(a) shall be expenses for the purposes of paragraph 2(2) of Schedule 4B to the Act only to the extent that they are—

(i) incurred in accordance with a set pattern as to frequency of contact between the non-resident parent and the qualifying child which has been established at or, where at the time of the variation application it has ceased, which had been established before, the time that the variation application is made; or

(ii) based on an intended set pattern for such contact which the Secretary of State is satisfied has been agreed between the non-resident parent and the person with care of the qualifying child; and

(b) shall be—

(i) where head (i) of sub-paragraph (a) applies and such contact is continuing, calculated as an average weekly amount based on the expenses actually incurred over the period of 12 months, or such lesser period as the Secretary of State may consider appropriate in the circumstances of the case, ending immediately before the first day of the maintenance period from which a variation agreed on this ground would take effect;

(ii) where head (i) of sub-paragraph (a) applies and such contact has ceased, calculated as an average weekly amount based on the expenses actually incurred during the period from the first day of the maintenance period from which a variation agreed on this ground would take effect to the last day of the maintenance period in relation to which the variation would take effect; or

(iii) where head (ii) of sub-paragraph (a) applies, calculated as an average weekly amount based on anticipated costs during such period as the Secretary of State considers appropriate.

(4) For the purposes of this regulation, costs of contact shall not include costs which relate to periods where the non-resident parent has care of a qualifying child overnight as part of a shared care arrangement for which provision is made under paragraphs 7 and 8 of Schedule 1 to the Act and regulation 7 of the Maintenance Calculations and Special Cases Regulations.

(5) Where the non-resident parent has at the date he makes the variation application received, or at that date is in receipt of, or where he will receive, any financial assistance, other than a loan, from any source to meet, wholly or in part, the costs of maintaining contact with a child as referred to in paragraph (1), only the amount of the costs referred to in that paragraph, after the deduction of the financial assistance, shall constitute special expenses for the purposes of paragraph 2(2) of Schedule 4B to the Act.

**11 Special expenses—illness or disability of relevant other child—**(1) Subject to the following paragraphs of this regulation, expenses necessarily incurred by the non-resident parent in respect of the items listed in sub-paragraphs (a) to (m) due to the long-term illness or disability of a relevant other child shall constitute special expenses for the purposes of paragraph 2(2) of Schedule 4B to the Act—

(a) personal care and attendance;

(b) personal communication needs;

(c) mobility;

(d) domestic help;

(e) medical aids where these cannot be provided under the health service;

(f) heating;

(g) clothing;

(h) laundry requirements;

(i) payments for food essential to comply with a diet recommended by a medical practitioner;

(j) adaptations required to the non-resident parent's home;

(k) day care;

(l) rehabilitation; or

(m) respite care.

(2) For the purposes of this regulation and regulation 10—

(a) a person is 'disabled' for a period in respect of which—

    (i) either an attendance allowance, disability living allowance or a mobility supplement is paid to or in respect of him;

    (ii) he would receive an attendance allowance or disability living allowance if it were not for the fact that he is a patient, though remaining part of the applicant's family; or

    (iii) he is registered blind or treated as blind within the meaning of paragraph 12(1)(a)(iii) and (2) of Schedule 2 to the Income Support (General) Regulations 1987;

and for this purpose—

    (i) 'attendance allowance' means an allowance payable under section 64 of the Contributions and Benefits Act or an increase of disablement pension under section 104 of that Act, or an award under article 14 of the Naval, Military and Air Forces Etc, (Disablement and Death) Service Pensions Order 1983 or any analogous allowance payable in conjunction with any other war disablement pension within the meaning of section 150(2) of the Contributions and Benefits Act;

(ii) 'disability living allowance' means an allowance payable under section 72 of the Contributions and Benefits Act;

(iii) 'mobility supplement' means an award under article 26A of the Naval, Military and Air Forces Etc, (Disablement and Death) Service Pensions Order 1983 or any analogous allowance payable in conjunction with any other war disablement pension within the meaning of section 150(2) of the Contributions and Benefits Act; and

(iv) 'patient' means a person (other than a person who is serving a sentence of imprisonment or detention in a young offenders institution within the meaning of the Criminal Justice Act 1982) who is regarded as receiving free in-patient treatment within the meaning of the Social Security (Hospital In-Patients) Regulations 1975;

(b) 'the health service' has the same meaning as in section 128 of the National Health Service Act 1977 or in section 108(1) of the National Health Service (Scotland) Act 1978;

(c) 'long-term illness' means an illness from which the non-resident parent or child is suffering at the date of the application or the date from which the variation, if agreed, would take effect and which is likely to last for at least 52 weeks from that date, or, if likely to be shorter than 52 weeks, for the remainder of the life of that person; and

(d) 'relevant other child' has the meaning given in paragraph 10C(2) of Schedule 1 to the Act and Regulations made under that paragraph.

(3) Where the non-resident parent has, at the date he makes the variation application, received, or at that date is in receipt of, or where he will receive any financial assistance from any source in respect of the long-term illness or disability of the relevant other child or a disability living allowance is received by the non-resident parent on behalf of the relevant other child, only the net amount of the costs incurred in respect of the items listed in paragraph (1), after the deduction of the financial assistance or the amount of the allowance, shall constitute special expenses for the purposes of paragraph 2(2) of Schedule 4B to the Act.

**12 Special expenses—prior debts**—(1) Subject to the following paragraphs of this regulation and regulation 15, the repayment of debts to which paragraph (2) applies shall constitute expenses for the purposes of paragraph 2(2) of Schedule 4B to the Act where those debts were incurred—

(a) before the non-resident parent became a non-resident parent in relation to the qualifying child; and

(b) at the time when the non-resident parent and the person with care in relation to the child referred to in sub-paragraph (a) were a couple.

(2) This paragraph applies to debts incurred—

(a) for the joint benefit of the non-resident parent and the person with care;

(b) for the benefit of the person with care where the non-resident parent remains legally liable to repay the whole or part of the debt;

(c) for the benefit of any person who is not a child but who at the time the debt was incurred—

(i) was a child;

(ii) lived with the non-resident parent and the person with care; and

(iii) of whom the non-resident parent or the person with care is the parent, or both are the parents;

(d) for the benefit of the qualifying child referred to in paragraph (1); or

(e)  for the benefit of any child, other than the qualifying child referred to in paragraph (1), who, at the time the debt was incurred—
    (i)  lived with the non-resident parent and the person with care; and
    (ii)  of whom the person with care is the parent.

(3)  Paragraph (1) shall not apply to repayment of—

(a)  a debt which would otherwise fall within paragraph (1) where the non-resident parent has retained for his own use and benefit the asset in connection with the purchase of which he incurred the debt;

(b)  a debt incurred for the purposes of any trade or business;

(c)  a gambling debt;

(d)  a fine imposed on the non-resident parent;

(e)  unpaid legal costs in respect of separation or divorce from the person with care;

(f)  amounts due after use of a credit card;

(g)  a debt incurred by the non-resident parent to pay any of the items listed in sub-paragraphs (c) to (f) and (j);

(h)  amounts payable by the non-resident parent under a mortgage or loan taken out on the security of any property except where that mortgage or loan was taken out to facilitate the purchase of, or to pay for repairs or improvements to, any property which is the home of the person with care and any qualifying child;

(i)  amounts payable by the non-resident parent in respect of a policy of insurance except where that policy of insurance was obtained or retained to discharge a mortgage or charge taken out to facilitate the purchase of, or to pay for repairs or improvements to, any property which is the home of the person with care and the qualifying child;

(j)  a bank overdraft except where the overdraft was at the time it was taken out agreed to be for a specified amount repayable over a specified period;

(k)  a loan obtained by the non-resident parent other than a loan obtained from a qualifying lender or the non-resident parent's current or former employer;

(l)  a debt in respect of which a variation has previously been agreed and which has not been repaid during the period for which the maintenance calculation which took account of the variation was in force; or

(m)  any other debt which the Secretary of State is satisfied it is reasonable to exclude.

(4)  Except where the repayment is of an amount which is payable under a mortgage or loan or in respect of a policy of insurance which falls within the exception set out in sub-paragraph (h) or (i) of paragraph (3), repayment of a debt shall not constitute expenses for the purposes of paragraph (1) where the Secretary of State is satisfied that the non-resident parent has taken responsibility for repayment of that debt as, or as part of, a financial settlement with the person with care or by virtue of a court order.

(5)  Where an applicant has incurred a debt partly to repay a debt repayment of which would have fallen within paragraph (1), the repayment of that part of the debt incurred which is referable to the debt repayment of which would have fallen within that paragraph shall constitute expenses for the purposes of paragraph 2(2) of Schedule 4B to the Act.

(6)  For the purposes of this regulation and regulation 14—

(a)  'qualifying lender' has the meaning given to it in section 376(4) of the Income and Corporation Taxes Act 1988; and

(b)  'repairs or improvements' means major repairs necessary to maintain the fabric of the home and any of the following measures—
    (i)  installation of a fixed bath, shower, wash basin or lavatory, and necessary associated plumbing;

    (ii)   damp-proofing measures;
    (iii)  provision or improvement of ventilation and natural light;
    (iv)  provision of electric lighting and sockets;
    (v)   provision or improvement of drainage facilities;
    (vi)  improvement of the structural condition of the home;
    (vii) improvements to the facilities for the storing, preparation and cooking of food;
    (viii) provision of heating, including central heating;
    (ix)  provision of storage facilities for fuel and refuse;
    (x)   improvements to the insulation of the home; or
    (xi)  other improvements which the Secretary of State considers reasonable in the circumstances.

**13 Special expenses—boarding school fees—**(1) Subject to the following paragraphs of this regulation and regulation 15, the maintenance element of the costs, incurred or reasonably expected to be incurred, by the non-resident parent for the purpose of the attendance at a boarding school of the qualifying child shall constitute expenses for the purposes of paragraph 2(2) of Schedule 4B to the Act.

    (2) Where the Secretary of State considers that the costs referred to in paragraph (1) cannot be distinguished with reasonable certainty from other costs incurred in connection with the attendance at boarding school by the qualifying child, he may instead determine the amount of those costs and any such determination shall not exceed 35% of the total costs.

    (3) Where—

    (a)  the non-resident parent has at the date the variation application is made, received, or at that date is in receipt of, financial assistance from any source in respect of the boarding school fees; or

    (b)  the boarding school fees are being paid in part by the non-resident parent and in part by another person,

a portion of the costs incurred by the non-resident parent in respect of the boarding school fees shall constitute special expenses for the purposes of paragraph 2(2) of Schedule 4B to the Act being the same proportion as the maintenance element of the costs bears to the total amount of the costs.

    (4) No variation on this ground shall reduce by more than 50% the income to which the Secretary of State would otherwise have had regard in the calculation of maintenance liability.

    (5) For the purposes of this regulation, 'boarding school fees' means the fees payable in respect of attendance at a recognised educational establishment providing full-time education which is not advanced education for children under the age of 19 and where some or all of the pupils, including the qualifying child, are resident during term time.

**14 Special expenses—payments in respect of certain mortgages, loans or insurance policies—**(1) Subject to regulation 15, the payments to which paragraph (2) applies shall constitute expenses for the purposes of paragraph 2(2) of Schedule 4B to the Act.

    (2) This paragraph applies to payments, whether made to the mortgagee, lender, insurer or the person with care—

    (a)  in respect of a mortgage or loan where—

        (i)  the mortgage or loan was taken out to facilitate the purchase of, or repairs or improvements to, a property ('the property') by a person other than the non-resident parent;

        (ii) the payments are not made under a debt incurred by the non-resident parent or do not arise out of any other legal liability of his for the period in respect of which the variation is applied for;

    (iii)  the property was the home of the applicant and the person with care when they were a couple and remains the home of the person with care and the qualifying child; and

    (iv)  the non-resident parent has no legal or equitable interest in and no charge or right to have a charge over the property; or

(b)  of amounts payable in respect of a policy of insurance taken out for the discharge of a mortgage or loan referred to in sub-paragraph (a), including an endowment policy, except where the non-resident parent is entitled to any part of the proceeds on the maturity of that policy.

**15 Thresholds for and reduction of amount of special expenses**—(1) Subject to paragraphs (2) to (4), the costs or repayments referred to in regulations 10 and 12 to 14 shall be special expenses for the purposes of paragraph 2(2) of Schedule 4B to the Act where and to the extent that they exceed the threshold amount, which is—

(a)  £15 per week where the expenses fall within only one description of expenses and, where the expenses fall within more than one description of expenses, £15 per week in respect of the aggregate of those expenses, where the relevant net weekly income of the non-resident parent is £200 or more; or

(b)  £10 per week where the expenses fall within only one description of expenses, and, where the expenses fall within more than one description of expenses, £10 per week in respect of the aggregate of those expenses, where the relevant net weekly income is below £200.

(2) Subject to paragraph (3), where the Secretary of State considers any expenses referred to in regulations 10 to 14 to be unreasonably high or to have been unreasonably incurred he may substitute such lower amount as he considers reasonable, including an amount which is below the threshold amount or a nil amount.

(3) Any lower amount substituted by the Secretary of State under paragraph (2) in relation to contact costs under regulation 10 shall not be so low as to make it impossible, in the Secretary of State's opinion, for contact between the non-resident parent and the qualifying child to be maintained at the frequency specified in any court order made in respect of the non-resident parent and that child where the non-resident parent is maintaining contact at that frequency.

(4) For the purposes of this regulation, 'relevant net weekly income' means the net weekly income taken into account for the purposes of the maintenance calculation before taking account of any variation on the grounds of special expenses.

PART IV

PROPERTY OR CAPITAL TRANSFERS

**16 Prescription of terms**—(1) For the purposes of paragraphs 3(1)(a) and (b) of Schedule 4B to the Act—

(a)  a court order means an order made—

    (i)  under one or more of the enactments listed in or prescribed under section 8(11) of the Act; and

    (ii)  in connection with the transfer of property of a kind defined in paragraph (2); and

(b)  an agreement means a written agreement made in connection with the transfer of property of a kind defined in paragraph (2).

(2) Subject to paragraphs (3) and (4), for the purposes of paragraph 3(2) of Schedule 4B to the Act, a transfer of property is a transfer by the non-resident parent of his beneficial interest in any asset to the person with care, to the

qualifying child, or to trustees where the object or one of the objects of the trust is the provision of maintenance.

(3) Where a transfer of property would not have fallen within paragraph (2) when made but the Secretary of State is satisfied that some or all of the amount of that property was subsequently transferred to the person currently with care of the qualifying child, the transfer of that property to the person currently with care shall constitute a transfer of property for the purposes of paragraph 3 of Schedule 4B to the Act.

(4) The minimum value for the purposes of paragraph 3(2) of Schedule 4B to the Act is the threshold amount which is *£5000* [£4999.99].

**Note.** Figure in para (4) in italics omitted and figure in square brackets substituted by SI 2002 No 1204 as from 30 April 2002.

**17 Value of a transfer of property—equivalent weekly value—**(1) Where the conditions specified in paragraph 3 of Schedule 4B to the Act are satisfied, the value of a transfer of property for the purposes of that paragraph shall be that part of the transfer made by the non-resident parent (making allowances for any transfer by the person with care to the non-resident parent) which the Secretary of State is satisfied is in lieu of periodical payments of maintenance.

(2) The Secretary of State shall, in determining the value of a transfer of property in accordance with paragraph (1), assume that, unless evidence to the contrary is provided to him—

(a) the person with care and the non-resident parent had equal beneficial interests in the asset in relation to which the court order or agreement was made;

(b) where the person with care was married to the non-resident parent, one half of the value of the transfer was a transfer for the benefit of the person with care; and

(c) where the person with care has never been married to the non-resident parent, none of the value of the transfer was for the benefit of the person with care.

(3) The equivalent weekly value of a transfer of property shall be determined in accordance with the provisions of the Schedule.

(4) For the purposes of regulation 16 and this regulation, the term 'maintenance' means the normal day-to-day living expenses of the qualifying child.

(5) A variation falling within paragraph (1) shall cease to have effect at the end of the number of years of liability, as defined in paragraph 1 of the Schedule, for the case in question.

PART V

ADDITIONAL CASES

**18 Assets—**(1) Subject to paragraphs (2) and (3), a case shall constitute a case for the purposes of paragraph 4(1) of Schedule 4B to the Act where the Secretary of State is satisfied there is an asset—

(a) in which the non-resident parent *has the beneficial interest* [has a beneficial interest], or which the non-resident parent has the ability to control;

(b) which has been transferred by the non-resident parent to trustees, and the non-resident parent is a beneficiary of the trust so created, in circumstances where the Secretary of State is satisfied the non-resident parent has made the transfer to reduce the amount of assets which would otherwise be taken into account for the purposes of a variation under paragraph 4(1) of Schedule 4B to the Act; or

(c) which has become subject to a trust created by legal implication of which the non-resident parent is a beneficiary.

(2) For the purposes of this regulation 'asset' means—

(a) money, whether in cash or on deposit, including any which, in Scotland, is monies due or an obligation owed, whether immediately payable or otherwise and whether the payment or obligation is secured or not and the Secretary of State is satisfied that requiring payment of the monies or implementation of the obligation would be reasonable;

(b) a legal estate or beneficial interest in land and rights in or over land;

(c) shares as defined in section 744 of the Companies Act 1985, stock and unit trusts as defined in section 6 of the Charging Orders Act 1979, gilt-edged securities as defined in Part 1 of Schedule 9 to the Taxation of Chargeable Gains Act 1992, and other similar financial instruments; or

(d) a chose in action which has not been enforced when the Secretary of State is satisfied that such enforcement would be reasonable,

and includes any such asset located outside Great Britain.

(3) Paragraph (2) shall not apply—

(a) where the total value of the assets referred to in that paragraph does not exceed £65,000 after deduction of the amount owing under any mortgage or charge on those assets;

(b) in relation to any asset which the Secretary of State is satisfied is being retained by the non-resident parent to be used for a purpose which the Secretary of State considers reasonable in all the circumstances of the case;

(c) to any asset received by the non-resident parent as compensation for personal injury suffered by him;

(d) [except where the asset is of a type specified in paragraph (2)(b) and produces income which does not form part of the net weekly income of the non-resident parent as calculated or estimated under Part III of the Schedule to the Maintenance Calculations and Special Cases Regulations,] to any asset used in the course of a trade or business; or

(e) to property which is the home of the non-resident parent or any child of his [; or

[(f) where, were the non-resident parent a claimant, paragraph 22 (treatment of payments from certain trusts) or 64 (treatment of relevant trust payments) of Schedule 10 to the Income Support (General) Regulations 1987 would apply to the asset referred to in that paragraph.]

(4) For the purposes of this regulation, where any asset is held in the joint names of the non-resident parent and another person the Secretary of State shall assume, unless evidence to the contrary is provided to him, that the asset is held by them in equal shares.

(5) Where a variation is agreed on the ground that the non-resident parent has assets for which provision is made in this regulation, the Secretary of State shall calculate the weekly value of the assets by applying the statutory rate of interest to the value of the assets and dividing by 52, and the resulting figure, aggregated with any benefit, pension or allowance [prescribed for the purposes of paragraph 4(1)(b) of Schedule 1 to the Act] which the non-resident parent receives, other than any benefits referred to in regulation 26(3), shall be taken into account as additional income under regulation 25.

(6) For the purposes of this regulation, the 'statutory rate of interest' means interest at the statutory rate prescribed for a judgment debt or, in Scotland, the statutory rate in respect of interest included in or payable under a decree in the Court of Session, which in either case applies on the date from which the maintenance calculation which takes account of the variation takes effect.

**Note.** Words in italics omitted and words in square brackets inserted by SI 2002 No 1204 as from 30 April 2002.

**19 Income not taken into account and diversion of income—**(1) Subject to paragraph (2), a case shall constitute a case for the purposes of paragraph 4(1) of Schedule 4B to the Act where—

(a) the non-resident parent's liability to pay child support maintenance under the maintenance calculation which is in force or has been applied for or treated as applied for, is, or would be, as the case may be—

    (i) the nil rate owing to the application of paragraph 5(a) of Schedule 1 to the Act; or

    (ii) a flat rate, owing to the application of paragraph 4(1)(b) of Schedule 1 to the Act, or would be a flat rate but is less than that amount, or nil, owing to the application of paragraph 8 of Schedule 1 to the Act; and

(b) the Secretary of State is satisfied that the non-resident parent is in receipt of income which would fall to be taken into account under the Maintenance Calculations and Special Cases Regulations but for the application to the non-resident parent of paragraph 4(1)(b) or 5(a) of Schedule 1 to the Act.

(2) Paragraph (1) shall apply where the income referred to in sub-paragraph (b) of that paragraph is a net weekly income of over £100.

(3) Net weekly income for the purposes of paragraph (2), in relation to earned income of a non-resident parent who is a student, shall be calculated by aggregating the income for the year ending with the relevant week (which for this purpose shall have the meaning given in the Maintenance Calculations and Special Cases Regulations) and dividing by 52, or, where the Secretary of State does not consider the result to be representative of the student's earned income, over such other period as he shall consider representative and dividing by the number of weeks in that period.

(4) A case shall constitute a case for the purposes of paragraph 4(1) of Schedule 4B to the Act where—

(a) the non-resident parent has the ability to control the amount of income he receives, including earnings from employment or self-employment, whether or not the whole of that income is derived from the company or business from which his earnings are derived, and

(b) the Secretary of State is satisfied that the non-resident parent has unreasonably reduced the amount of his income which would otherwise fall to be taken into account under the Maintenance Calculations and Special Cases Regulations by diverting it to other persons or for purposes other than the provision of such income for himself in order to reduce his liability to pay child support maintenance.

(5) Where a variation on this ground is agreed to—

(a) in a case to which paragraph (1) applies, the additional income taken into account under regulation 25 shall be the whole of the income referred to in paragraph (1)(b), aggregated with any benefit, pension or allowance [prescribed for the purposes of paragraph 4(1)(b) of Schedule 1 to the Act] which the non-resident parent receives other than any benefits referred to in regulation 26(3); and

(b) in a case to which paragraph (4) applies, the additional income taken into account under regulation 25 shall be the whole of the amount by which the Secretary of State is satisfied the non-resident parent has unreasonably reduced his income.

**Note.** Words in square brackets in para (5)(a) added by SI 2002 No 1204 as from 30 April 2002.

**20 Life-style inconsistent with declared income—**(1) Subject to paragraph (3), a case shall constitute a case for the purposes of paragraph 4(1) of Schedule 4B to the Act where—

(a) the non-resident parent's liability to pay child support maintenance under the maintenance calculation which is in force, or which has been applied for or treated as applied for, is, or would be, as the case may be—

    (i) the basic rate,

    (ii) the reduced rate,

    (iii) a flat rate owing to the application of paragraph 4(1)(a) of Schedule 1 to the Act, including where the net weekly income of the non-resident parent taken into account for the purposes of the maintenance calculation is, or would be, £100 per week or less owing to a variation being taken into account, or to the application of regulation 18, 19 or 21 of the Transitional Regulations (deduction for relevant departure direction or relevant property transfer);

    (iv) £5 per week or such other amount as may be prescribed owing to the application of paragraph 7(7) of Schedule 1 to the Act (shared care);

    (v) equivalent to the flat rate provided for in, or prescribed for the purposes of, paragraph 4(1)(b) of Schedule 1 to the Act owing to the application of—

        (aa) regulation 27(5);

        (bb) regulation 9 of the Maintenance Calculations and Special Cases Regulations (care provided in part by a local authority); or

        (cc) regulation 23(5) of the Transitional Regulations; or

    (vi) the nil rate owing to the application of paragraph 5(b) of Schedule 1 to the Act; and

(b) the Secretary of State is satisfied that the income which has been, or would be, taken into account for the purposes of the maintenance calculation is substantially lower than the level of income required to support the overall life-style of the non-resident parent.

(2) Subject to paragraph (4), a case shall constitute a case for the purposes of paragraph 4(1) of Schedule 4B to the Act where the non-resident parent's liability to pay child support maintenance under the maintenance calculation which is in force, or which has been applied for or treated as applied for, is, or would be, as the case may be—

(a) a flat rate owing to the application of paragraph 4(1)(b) of Schedule 1 to the Act, or would be a flat rate but is less than that amount, or nil, owing to the application of paragraph 8 of Schedule 1 to the Act; or

(b) the nil rate owing to the application of paragraph 5(a) of Schedule 1 to the Act,

and the Secretary of State is satisfied that the income which would otherwise be taken into account for the purposes of the maintenance calculation is substantially lower than the level of income required to support the overall life-style of the non-resident parent.

(3) Paragraph (1) shall not apply where the Secretary of State is satisfied that the life-style of the non-resident parent is paid for from—

(a) income which is or would be disregarded for the purposes of a maintenance calculation under the Maintenance Calculations and Special Cases Regulations;

(b) income which falls to be considered under regulation 19(4) (diversion of income);

(c) assets as defined for the purposes of regulation 18, or income derived from those assets;

(d) the income of any partner of the non-resident parent, except where the non-resident parent is able to influence or control the amount of income received by that partner; or

(e) assets as defined for the purposes of regulation 18 of any partner of the non-resident parent, or any income derived from such assets, except where the non-resident parent is able to influence or control the assets, their use, or income derived from them.

(4) Paragraph (2) shall not apply where the Secretary of State is satisfied that the life-style of the non-resident parent is paid for—

(a) from a source referred to in paragraph (3);

(b) from net weekly income of £100 or less; or

(c) from income which falls to be considered under regulation 19(1).

(5) Where a variation on this ground is agreed to, the additional income taken into account under regulation 25 shall be the difference between the income which the Secretary of State is satisfied the non-resident parent requires to support his overall life-style and the income which has been or, but for the application of paragraph 4(1)(b) or 5(a) of Schedule 1 to the Act, would be taken into account for the purposes of the maintenance calculation, aggregated with any benefit, pension or allowance [prescribed for the purposes of paragraph 4(1)(b) of Schedule 1 to the Act] which the non-resident parent receives other than any benefits referred to in regulation 26(3).

**Note.** Words in square brackets in para (5) added by SI 2002 No 1204 as from 30 April 2002.

PART VI
FACTORS TO BE TAKEN INTO ACCOUNT FOR THE PURPOSES OF SECTION 28F OF THE ACT

**21 Factors to be taken into account and not to be taken into account—**(1) The factors to be taken into account in determining whether it would be just and equitable to agree to a variation in any case shall include—

(a) where the application is made on any ground—

(i) whether, in the opinion of the Secretary of State, agreeing to a variation would be likely to result in a relevant person ceasing paid employment;

(ii) if the applicant is the non-resident parent, the extent, if any, of his liability to pay child maintenance under a court order or agreement in the period prior to the effective date of the maintenance calculation; and

(b) where an application is made on the ground that the case falls within regulations 10 to 14 (special expenses), whether, in the opinion of the Secretary of State—

(i) the financial arrangements made by the non-resident parent could have been such as to enable the expenses to be paid without a variation being agreed; or

(ii) the non-resident parent has at his disposal financial resources which are currently utilised for the payment of expenses other than those arising from essential everyday requirements and which could be used to pay the expenses.

(2) The following factors are not to be taken into account in determining whether it would be just and equitable to agree to a variation in any case—

(a) the fact that the conception of the qualifying child was not planned by one or both of the parents;

(b) whether the non-resident parent or the person with care of the qualifying child was responsible for the breakdown of the relationship between them;

(c) the fact that the non-resident parent or the person with care of the qualifying child has formed a new relationship with a person who is not a parent of that child;

(d) the existence of particular arrangements for contact with the qualifying child, including whether any arrangements made are being adhered to;

(e) the income or assets of any person other than the non-resident parent, other than the income or assets of a partner of the non-resident parent taken into account under regulation 20(3);

(f) the failure by a non-resident parent to make payments of child support maintenance, or to make payments under a maintenance order or a written maintenance agreement; or

(g) representations made by persons other than the relevant persons.

PART VII

EFFECT OF A VARIATION ON THE MAINTENANCE CALCULATION AND EFFECTIVE DATES

**22 Effective dates—**(1) Subject to paragraph (2), where the application for a variation is made in the circumstances referred to in section 28A(3) of the Act (before the Secretary of State has reached a decision under section 11 or 12(1) of the Act) and the application is agreed to, the effective date of the maintenance calculation which takes account of the variation shall be—

(a) where the ground giving rise to the variation existed from the effective date of the maintenance calculation as provided for in the Maintenance Calculation Procedure Regulations, that date; or

(b) where the ground giving rise to the variation arose after the effective date referred to in sub-paragraph (a), the first day of the maintenance period in which the ground arose.

(2) Where the ground for the variation applied for under section 28A(3) of the Act is a ground in regulation 12 (prior debts) or 14 (special expenses—payments in respect of certain mortgages, loans or insurance policies) and payments falling within regulation 12 or 14 which have been made by the non-resident parent constitute voluntary payments for the purposes of section 28J of the Act and Regulations made under that section, the date from which the maintenance calculation shall take account of the variation on this ground shall be the date on which the maintenance period begins which immediately follows the date on which the non-resident parent is notified under the Maintenance Calculation Procedure Regulations of the amount of his liability to pay child support maintenance.

(3) Where the ground for the variation applied for under section 28A(3) of the Act has ceased to exist by the date the maintenance calculation is made, that calculation shall take account of the variation for the period ending on the last day of the maintenance period in which the ground existed.

**23 Effect on maintenance calculation—special expenses—**(1) Subject to paragraph (2) and regulations 26 and 27, where the variation agreed to is one falling within regulation 10 to 14 (special expenses) effect shall be given to the variation in the maintenance calculation by deducting from the net weekly income of the non-resident parent the weekly amount of those expenses.

(2) Where the income which is taken into account in the maintenance calculation is the capped amount and the variation agreed to is one falling within regulation 10 to 14 then—

(a) the weekly amount of the expenses shall first be deducted from the actual net weekly income of the non-resident parent;

(b) the amount by the which the capped amount exceeds the figure calculated under sub-paragraph (a) shall be calculated; and

(c) effect shall be given to the variation in the maintenance calculation by deducting from the capped amount the amount calculated under sub-paragraph (b).

**24 Effect on maintenance calculation—property or capital transfer** Subject to regulation 27, where the variation agreed to is one falling within regulation 16 (property or capital transfers)—

(a) the maintenance calculation shall be carried out in accordance with Part 1 of Schedule 1 to the Act and Regulations made under that Part; and

(b) the equivalent weekly value of the transfer calculated as provided in regulation 17 shall be deducted from the amount of child support maintenance which he would otherwise be liable to pay to the person with care with respect to whom the transfer was made.

**25 Effect on maintenance calculation—additional cases** Subject to regulations 26 and 27, where the variation agreed to is one falling within regulations 18 to 20 (additional cases), effect shall be given to the variation in the maintenance calculation by increasing the net weekly income of the non-resident parent which would otherwise be taken into account by the weekly amount of the additional income except that, where the amount of net weekly income calculated in this way would exceed the capped amount, the amount of net weekly income taken into account shall be the capped amount.

**26 Effect on maintenance calculation—maximum amount payable where the variation is on additional cases ground—**(1) Subject to regulation 27, where this regulation applies the amount of child support maintenance which the non-resident parent shall be liable to pay shall be whichever is the lesser of—

(a) a weekly amount calculated by aggregating an amount equivalent to the flat rate stated in or prescribed for the purposes of paragraph 4(1)(b) of Schedule 1 to the Act with the amount calculated by applying that Schedule to the Act to the additional income arising under the variation, other than the weekly amount of any benefit, pension or allowance the non-resident parent receives which is prescribed for the purposes of that paragraph; or

(b) a weekly amount calculated by applying Part 1 of Schedule 1 to the Act to the additional income arising under the variation.

(2) This regulation applies where the variation agreed to is one to which regulation 25 applies and the non-resident parent's liability calculated as provided in Part 1 of Schedule 1 to the Act and Regulations made under that Schedule would, but for the variation, be—

(a) a flat rate under paragraph 4(1)(b) of that Schedule;

(b) a flat rate but is less than that amount or nil, owing to the application of paragraph 8 of that Schedule; or

(c) a flat rate under paragraph 4(1)(b) of that Schedule but for the application of paragraph 5(a) of that Schedule.

(3) For the purposes of paragraph (1)—

(a) any benefit, pension or allowance taken into account in the additional income referred to in sub-paragraph (b) shall not include—

    (i) in the case of industrial injuries benefit under section 94 of the Contributions and Benefits Act, any increase in that benefit under section 104 (constant attendance) or 105 (exceptionally severe disablement) of that Act;

    (ii) in the case of a war disablement pension within the meaning in section 150(2) of the Contributions and Benefits Act, any award under the following articles of the Naval, Military and Air Forces Etc, (Disablement and Death) Service Pensions Order 1983 ('the Service Pensions Order'): article 14 (constant attendance allowance), 15 (exceptionally severe disablement allowance), 16 (severe disablement occupational allowance) or 26A (mobility supplement) or any analogous allowances payable in conjunction with any other war disablement pension; and

> > (iii) any award under article 18 of the Service Pensions Order (unemployability allowances) which is an additional allowance in respect of a child of the non-resident parent where that child is not living with the non-resident parent;
>
> (b) 'additional income' for the purposes of sub-paragraphs (a) and (b) means such income after the application of a variation falling within regulations 10 to 14 (special expenses); and
>
> (c) 'weekly amount' for the purposes of sub-paragraphs (a) and (b) means the aggregate of the amounts referred to in the relevant sub-paragraph—
>
> > (i) adjusted as provided in regulation 27(3) as if the reference in that regulation to child support maintenance were to the weekly amount; and
> >
> > (ii) after any deduction provided for in regulation 27(4) as if the reference in that regulation to child support maintenance were to the weekly amount.

**27 Effect on maintenance calculation—general—**(1) Subject to paragraphs (4) and (5), where more than one variation is agreed to in respect of the same period regulations 23 to 26 shall apply and the results shall be aggregated as appropriate.

(2) Paragraph 7(2) to (7) of Schedule 1 to the Act (shared care) shall apply where the rate of child support maintenance is affected by a variation which is agreed to and paragraph 7(2) shall be read as if after the words 'as calculated in accordance with the preceding paragraphs of this Part of this Schedule' there were inserted the words ', Schedule 4B and Regulations made under that Schedule'.

(3) Subject to paragraphs (4) and (5), where the non-resident parent shares the care of a qualifying child within the meaning in Part 1 of Schedule 1 to the Act, or where the care of such a child is shared in part by a local authority, the amount of child support maintenance the non-resident parent is liable to pay the person with care, calculated to take account of any variation, shall be reduced in accordance with the provisions of paragraph 7 of that Part or regulation 9 of the Maintenance Calculations and Special Cases Regulations, as the case may be.

(4) Subject to paragraph (5), where the variation agreed to is one falling within regulation 16 (property or capital transfers) the equivalent weekly value of the transfer calculated as provided in regulation 17 shall be deducted from the amount of child support maintenance the non-resident parent would otherwise be liable to pay the person with care in respect of whom the transfer was made after aggregation of the effects of any other variations as provided in paragraph (1) or deduction for shared care as provided in paragraph (3).

(5) If the application of regulation 24, or paragraph (3) or (4), would decrease the weekly amount of child support maintenance (or the aggregate of all such amounts) payable by the non-resident parent to the person with care (or all of them) to less than a figure equivalent to the flat rate of child support maintenance payable under paragraph 4(1)(b) of Schedule 1 to the Act, he shall instead be liable to pay child support maintenance at a rate equivalent to that rate apportioned (if appropriate) as provided in paragraph 6 of Schedule 1 to the Act.

(6) The effect of a variation shall not be applied for any period during which a circumstance referred to in regulation 7 applies.

(7) For the purposes of regulations 23 and 25 'net weekly income' means as calculated or estimated under the Maintenance Calculations and Special Cases Regulations.

**28 Transitional provisions—conversion decisions** Where the variation is being applied for in connection with a subsequent decision within the meaning given in the Transitional Regulations, and the decision to be revised or superseded under section 16 or 17 of the Act, as the case may be, takes into account a relevant property transfer as defined and provided for in those Regulations—

(a) for the purposes of regulations 23 and 25 'capped amount' shall mean the income for the purposes of paragraph 10(3) of Schedule 1 to the Act less any deduction in respect of the relevant property transfer;

(b) for the purposes of regulation 26(3)(b) the additional income for the purposes of paragraph (1) of that regulation shall be after deduction in respect of the relevant property transfer;

(c) regulation 27(4) shall be read as if the aggregation referred to included any deduction in respect of the relevant property transfer; and

(d) regulation 27(5) shall be read as if after the reference to paragraph (3) or (4) there were a reference to any deduction in respect of the relevant property transfer.

**29 Situations in which a variation previously agreed to may be taken into account in calculating maintenance liability**—(1) This regulation applies where a variation has been agreed to in relation to a maintenance calculation.

(2) In the circumstances set out in paragraph (3), the Secretary of State may take account of the effect of such a variation upon the rate of liability for child support maintenance notwithstanding the fact that an application has not been made.

(3) The circumstances are—

(a) that the decision as to the maintenance calculation is superseded under section 17 of the Act on a change of circumstances so that the non-resident parent becomes liable to pay child support maintenance at the nil rate, or another rate which means that the variation cannot be taken into account; and

(b) that the superseding decision referred to in sub-paragraph (a) is itself superseded under section 17 of the Act on a change of circumstances so that the non-resident parent becomes liable to pay a rate of child support maintenance which can be adjusted to take account of the variation.

**30 Circumstances for the purposes of section 28F(3) of the Act** The circumstances prescribed for the purposes of section 28F(3) of the Act (Secretary of State shall not agree to a variation) are—

(a) the prescribed circumstances in regulation 6(2) or 7; and

(b) where the Secretary of State considers it would not be just and equitable to agree to the variation having regard to any of the factors referred to in regulation 21.

PART VIII

MISCELLANEOUS

**31 Regular payments condition**—(1) For the purposes of section 28C(2)(b) of the Act (payments of child support maintenance less than those specified in the interim maintenance decision) the payments shall be those fixed by the interim maintenance decision or the maintenance calculation in force, as the case may be, adjusted to take account of the variation applied for by the non-resident parent as if that variation had been agreed.

(2) The Secretary of State may refuse to consider the application for a variation where a regular payments condition has been imposed and the non-resident parent has failed to comply with it in the circumstances to which paragraph (3) applies.

(3) This paragraph applies where the non-resident parent has failed to comply with the regular payments condition and fails to make such payments which are due and unpaid within one month of being required to do so by the Secretary of State or such other period as the Secretary of State may in the particular case decide.

**32 Meaning of 'benefit' for the purposes of section 28E of the Act** For the purposes of section 28E of the Act, 'benefit' means income support, income-based jobseeker's allowance, housing benefit and council tax benefit.

PART IX

REVOCATION

**33 Revocation and savings—**(1) Subject to [the Transitional Regulations and] paragraph (2), the Child Support Departure Direction and Consequential Amendments Regulations 1996 shall be revoked with respect to a particular case with effect from the date that these Regulations come into force with respect to that type of case ('the commencement date').

(2) Where before the commencement date in respect of a particular case—
(a) an application was made and not determined for—
  (i) a maintenance assessment;
  (ii) a departure direction; or
  (iii) a revision or supersession of a decision;
(b) the Secretary of State had begun but not completed a revision or supersession of a decision on his own initiative;
(c) any time limit provided for in Regulations for making an application for a revision or a departure direction had not expired; or
(d) any appeal was made but not decided or any time limit for making an appeal had not expired,
the provisions of the Child Support Departure Direction and Consequential Amendments Regulations 1996 shall continue to apply for the purposes of—
  (aa) the decision on the application referred to in sub-paragraph (a);
  (bb) the revision or supersession referred to in sub-paragraph (b);
  (cc) the ability to apply for the revision or the departure direction referred to in sub-paragraph (c) and the decision whether to revise or to give a departure direction following any such application;
  (dd) any appeal outstanding or made during the time limit referred to in sub-paragraph (d); or
  (ee) any revision, supersession or appeal or application for a departure direction in relation to a decision, ability to apply or appeal referred to in sub-paragraphs (aa) to (dd).

(3) Where, after the commencement date, a decision with respect to a departure direction is revised from a date which is prior to the commencement date, the provisions of the Child Support Departure Direction and Consequential Amendments Regulations 1996 shall continue to apply for the purposes of that revision.

(4) Where, under regulation 28(1) of the Transitional Regulations, an application for a maintenance calculation is treated as an application for a maintenance assessment, the provisions of the Child Support Departure Direction and Consequential Amendments Regulations 1996 shall continue to apply for the purposes of an application for a departure direction in relation to any such assessment made.

(5) For the purposes of this regulation—
(a) 'departure direction' and 'maintenance assessment' means as provided in section 54 of the Act before its amendment by the 2000 Act;
(b) 'revision or supersession' means a revision or supersession of a decision under section 16 or 17 of the Act before its amendment by the 2000 Act and 'any time limit for making an application for a revision' means any time limit provided for in Regulations made under section 16 of the Act; and
(c) '2000 Act' means the Child Support, Pensions and Social Security Act 2000.

**Note.** Words in square brackets in para (1) inserted by SI 2003 No 347 as from 3 March 2003.

SCHEDULE                                                    Regulation 17(3)

EQUIVALENT WEEKLY VALUE OF A TRANSFER OF PROPERTY

**1**—(1) Subject to paragraph 3, the equivalent weekly value of a transfer of property shall be calculated by multiplying the value of a transfer of property determined in accordance with regulation 17 by the relevant factor specified in the Table set out in paragraph 2 ('the Table').

(2) For the purposes of sub-paragraph (1), the relevant factor is the number in the Table at the intersection of the column for the statutory rate and of the row for the number of years of liability.

(3) In sub-paragraph (2)—

(a) 'the statutory rate' means interest at the statutory rate prescribed for a judgment debt or, in Scotland, the statutory rate in respect of interest included in or payable under a decree in the Court of Session, which in either case applies at the date of the court order or written agreement relating to the transfer of the property;

(b) 'the number of years of liability' means the number of years, beginning on the date of the court order or written agreement relating to the transfer of property and ending on—

(i) the date specified in that order or agreement as the date on which maintenance for the youngest child in respect of whom that order or agreement was made shall cease; or

(ii) if no such date is specified, the date on which the youngest child specified in the order or agreement reaches the age of 18,

and where that period includes a fraction of a year, that fraction shall be treated as a full year if it is either one half or exceeds one half of a year, and shall otherwise be disregarded.

**2** The Table referred to in paragraph 1(1) is set out below—

THE TABLE

| Number of years of liability | Statutory Rate | | | | | | | |
|---|---|---|---|---|---|---|---|---|
| | 7.0% | 8.0% | 10.0% | 11.0% | 12.0% | 12.5% | 14.0% | 15.0% |
| 1 | .02058 | .02077 | .02115 | .02135 | .02154 | .02163 | .02192 | .02212 |
| 2 | .01064 | .01078 | .01108 | .01123 | .01138 | .01145 | .01168 | .01183 |
| 3 | .00733 | .00746 | .00773 | .00787 | .00801 | .00808 | .00828 | .00842 |
| 4 | .00568 | .00581 | .00607 | .00620 | .00633 | .00640 | .00660 | .00674 |
| 5 | .00469 | .00482 | .00507 | .00520 | .00533 | .00540 | .00560 | .00574 |
| 6 | .00403 | .00416 | .00442 | .00455 | .00468 | .00474 | .00495 | .00508 |
| 7 | .00357 | .00369 | .00395 | .00408 | .00421 | .00428 | .00448 | .00462 |
| 8 | .00322 | .00335 | .00360 | .00374 | .00387 | .00394 | .00415 | .00429 |
| 9 | .00295 | .00308 | .00334 | .00347 | .00361 | .00368 | .00389 | .00403 |
| 10 | .00274 | .00287 | .00313 | .00327 | .00340 | .00347 | .00369 | .00383 |
| 11 | .00256 | .00269 | .00296 | .00310 | .00324 | .00331 | .00353 | .00367 |
| 12 | .00242 | .00255 | .00282 | .00296 | .00310 | .00318 | .00340 | .00355 |
| 13 | .00230 | .00243 | .00271 | .00285 | .00299 | .00307 | .00329 | .00344 |
| 14 | .00220 | .00233 | .00261 | .00275 | .00290 | .00298 | .00320 | .00336 |
| 15 | .00211 | .00225 | .00253 | .00267 | .00282 | .00290 | .00313 | .00329 |
| 16 | .00204 | .00217 | .00246 | .00261 | .00276 | .00283 | .00307 | .00323 |
| 17 | .00197 | .00211 | .00240 | .00255 | .00270 | .00278 | .00302 | .00318 |
| 18 | .00191 | .00205 | .00234 | .00250 | .00265 | .00273 | .00297 | .00314 |

**3** The Secretary of State may determine a lower equivalent weekly value than that determined in accordance with paragraphs 1 and 2 where the amount of child support maintenance that would be payable in consequence of agreeing to a variation of that value is lower than the amount of the periodical payments of maintenance which were payable under the court order or written agreement referred to in regulation 16.

## CHILD SUPPORT (MAINTENANCE CALCULATION PROCEDURE) REGULATIONS 2000

**Dated** 18 January 2001

**SI 2001 No 157**

## ARRANGEMENT OF REGULATIONS

PART I

GENERAL

**1 Citation, commencement and interpretation—**(1)  These Regulations may be
cited as the Child Support (Maintenance Calculation Procedure) Regulations
2000.

(2)  In these Regulations, unless the context otherwise requires—
'the Act' means the Child Support Act 1991;
'date of notification to the non-resident parent' means the date on which the
    non-resident parent is first given notice of a maintenance application;
'effective application' means as provided for in regulation 3;
'date of receipt' means the date on which the information or document is
    actually received;
'effective date' means the date on which a maintenance calculation takes effect
    for the purposes of the Act;
'notice of a maintenance application' means notice by the Secretary of State
    under regulation 5(1) that an application for a maintenance calculation has
    been made, or treated as made, in relation to which the non-resident parent
    is named as a parent of the child to whom the application relates;

'Maintenance Calculations and Special Cases Regulations' means the Child Support (Maintenance Calculations and Special Cases) Regulations 2000;
'maintenance period' has the same meaning as in section 17(4A) of the Act;
'relevant person' means—
  (a) a person with care;
  (b) a non-resident parent;
  (c) a parent who is treated as a non-resident parent under regulation 8 of the Maintenance Calculations and Special Cases Regulations;
  (d) where the application for a maintenance calculation is made by a child under section 7 of the Act, that child,
in respect of whom a maintenance calculation has been applied for, or has been treated as applied for under section 6(3) of the Act, or is or has been in force.
  (3) The provisions in Schedule 1 shall have effect to supplement the meaning of 'child' in section 55 of the Act.
  (4) In these Regulations, unless the context otherwise requires, a reference—
  (a) to a numbered Part is to the Part of these Regulations bearing that number;
  (b) to a numbered Schedule is to the Schedule to these Regulations bearing that number;
  (c) to a numbered regulation is to the regulation in these Regulations bearing that number;
  (d) in a regulation or Schedule to a numbered paragraph is to the paragraph in that regulation or Schedule bearing that number; and
  (e) in a paragraph to a lettered or numbered sub-paragraph is to the sub-paragraph in that paragraph bearing that letter or number.
  (5) These Regulations shall come into force in relation to a particular case on the day on which the amendments to sections 5, 6, 12, 46, 51, *54 and 55* [and 54] of the Act made by the Child Support, Pensions and Social Security Act 2000 come into force in relation to that type of case.
**Note.** Numbers in italics omitted and number in square brackets inserted by SI 2002 No 1204 as from 30 April 2002.

**2 Documents** Except where otherwise stated, where—
  (a) any document is given or sent to the Secretary of State, that document shall be treated as having been so given or sent on the day that it is received by the Secretary of State; and
  (b) any document is given or sent to any other person, that document shall, if sent by post to that person's last known or notified address, be treated as having been given or sent on the day that it is posted.

PART II

APPLICATIONS FOR A MAINTENANCE CALCULATION

**3 Applications under section 4 or 7 of the Act**—(1) A person who applies for a maintenance calculation under section 4 or 7 of the Act need not normally do so in writing, but if the Secretary of State directs that the application be made in writing, the application shall be made either by completing and returning, in accordance with the Secretary of State's instructions, a form provided for that purpose, or in such other written form as the Secretary of State may accept as sufficient in the circumstances of any particular case.
  (2) An application for a maintenance calculation is effective if it complies with paragraph (1) and, subject to paragraph (4), is made on the date it is received.
  (3) Where an application for a maintenance calculation is not effective the Secretary of State may request the person making the application to provide such additional information or evidence as the Secretary of State may specify and, where the application was made on a form, the Secretary of State may request that the information or evidence be provided on a fresh form.

(4) Where the additional information or evidence requested is received by the Secretary of State within 14 days of the date of his request, or at a later date in circumstances where the Secretary of State is satisfied that the delay was unavoidable, he shall treat the application as made on the date on which the earlier or earliest application would have been treated as made had it been effective.

(5) Where the Secretary of State receives the additional information or evidence requested by him more than 14 days from the date of the request and in circumstances where he is not satisfied that the delay was unavoidable, the Secretary of State shall treat the application as made on the date of receipt of the information or evidence.

(6) Subject to paragraph (7), a person who has made an effective application may amend or withdraw the application at any time before a maintenance calculation is made and such amendment or withdrawal need not be in writing unless, in any particular case, the Secretary of State requires it to be.

(7) No amendment made under paragraph (6) shall relate to any change of circumstances arising after the effective date of a maintenance calculation resulting from an effective application.

**4 Multiple applications—**(1) The provisions of Schedule 2 shall apply in cases where there is more than one application for a maintenance calculation.

(2) The provisions of paragraphs 1, 2 and 3 of Schedule 2 relating to the treatment of two or more applications as a single application shall apply where no request is received for the Secretary of State to cease acting in relation to all but one of the applications.

(3) Where, under the provisions of paragraph 1, 2 or 3 of Schedule 2, two or more applications are to be treated as a single application, that application shall be treated as an application for a maintenance calculation to be made with respect to all of the qualifying children mentioned in the applications, and the effective date of that maintenance calculation shall be determined by reference to the earlier or earliest application.

**5 Notice of an application for a maintenance calculation—**(1) Where an effective application has been made under section 4 or 7 of the Act, or [an application] is treated as made under section 6(3) of the Act, as the case may be, the Secretary of State shall as soon as is reasonably practicable notify, orally or in writing, the non-resident parent and any other relevant persons (other than the person who has made, or is treated as having made, the application) of that application and request such information as he may require to make the maintenance calculation in such form and manner as he may specify in the particular case.

(2) Where the person to whom notice is being given under paragraph (1) is a non-resident parent, that notice shall specify the effective date of the maintenance calculation if one is to be made, and the ability to make a default maintenance decision.

(3) Subject to paragraph (4), a person who has provided information under paragraph (1) may amend the information he has provided at any time before a maintenance calculation is made and such information need not be in writing unless, in any particular case, the Secretary of State requires it to be.

(4) No amendment under paragraph (3) shall relate to any change of circumstances arising after the effective date of any maintenance calculation made in response to the application in relation to which the information was requested.

**Note.** Words in square brackets in para (1) inserted by SI 2003 No 328 as from 6 April 2003.

**6 Death of a qualifying child—**(1) Where the Secretary of State is informed of the death of a qualifying child with respect to whom an application for a maintenance calculation has been made or has been treated as made, he shall—

(a)  proceed with the application as if it had not been made with respect to that child if he has not yet made a maintenance calculation;

(b)  treat any maintenance calculation already made by him as not having been made if the relevant persons have not been notified of it and proceed with the application as if it had not been made with respect to that child.

(2)  Where all of the qualifying children with respect to whom an application for a maintenance calculation has been made have died, and either the calculation has not been made or the relevant persons have not been notified of it, the Secretary of State shall treat the application as not having been made.

PART III

DEFAULT MAINTENANCE DECISIONS

**7 Default rate—**(1) Where the Secretary of State makes a default maintenance decision under section 12(1) of the Act (insufficient information to make a maintenance calculation or to make a decision under section 16 or 17 of the Act) the default rate is as set out in paragraph (2).

(2)  The default rate for the purposes of section 12(5)(b) of the Act shall be—
£30 where there is one qualifying child of the non-resident parent;
£40 where there are two qualifying children of the non-resident parent;
£50 where there are three or more qualifying children of the non-resident parent,

apportioned, where the non-resident parent has more than one qualifying child and in relation to them there is more than one person with care, as provided in paragraph 6(2) of Part I of Schedule 1 to the Act.

(3)  Subject to paragraph (4), where any apportionment made under this regulation results in a fraction of a penny that fraction shall be treated as a penny if it is either one half or exceeds one half, otherwise it shall be disregarded.

(4)  If, in making the apportionment required by this regulation, the effect of the application of paragraph (3) would be such that the aggregate amount of child support maintenance payable by a non-resident parent would be different from the aggregate amount payable before any apportionment, the Secretary of State shall adjust that apportionment so as to eliminate that difference; and that adjustment shall be varied from time to time so as to secure that, taking one week with another and so far as is practicable, each person with care receives the amount which she would have received if no adjustment had been made under this paragraph.

PART IV

REDUCED BENEFIT DECISIONS

**8 Interpretation of Part IV—**(1) For the purposes of this Part—

'applicable amount' is to be construed in accordance with Part IV of the Income Support Regulations and regulations 83 to 86 of the Jobseeker's Allowance Regulations;

'benefit week', in relation to income support has the same meaning as in the Income Support Regulations, and in relation to jobseeker's allowance has the same meaning as in the Jobseeker's Allowance Regulations;

'Income Support Regulations' means the Income Support (General) Regulations 1987;

'Jobseeker's Allowance Regulations' means the Jobseeker's Allowance Regulations 1996;

'parent concerned' means the parent with respect to whom a reduced benefit decision is given;

'reduced benefit decision' has the same meaning as in section 46(10)(b) of the Act; and

'relevant benefit' has the same meaning as in section 46(10)(c) of the Act.

(2) In this Part references to a reduced benefit decision as being 'in operation', 'suspended' or 'in force' shall be construed as follows—

(a) a reduced benefit decision is 'in operation' if, by virtue of that decision, relevant benefit is currently being reduced;

(b) a reduced benefit decision is 'suspended' if—

(i) after that decision has been given, relevant benefit ceases to be payable, or *becomes payable at one of the rates indicated in regulation 14(4) or, as the case may be, regulation 15(4)* [the circumstances in regulation 14(4) or 15(4), as the case may be, apply;];

(ii) at the time the reduced benefit decision is given, *relevant benefit is payable at one of the rates indicated in regulation 15(4) or, as the case may be, regulation 16(4)* [the circumstances in regulation 14(4) or 15(4), as the case may be, apply,],

and these Regulations provide for relevant benefit payable from a later date to be reduced by virtue of the same reduced benefit decision; and

(c) a reduced benefit decision is 'in force' if it is either in operation or suspended

and cognate terms shall be construed accordingly.

**Note**  Para (2): words in square brackets substituted by SI 2993 No 2779, reg 5(1)(2)(a), (b) as from 5 November 2004.

**9 Period within which reasons are to be given**  The period specified for the purposes of section 46(2) of the Act (for the parent to supply her reasons) is 4 weeks from the date on which the Secretary of State serves notice under that subsection.

**[9A Period for parent to state if request still stands**  The period to be specified for the purposes of section 46(6) of the Act (period for the parent to state if her request still stands) is 4 weeks from the date on which the Secretary of State serves notice under that subsection.]

**Note.**  Added by SI 2002 No 1204 as from 30 April 2002.

**10 Circumstances in which a reduced benefit decision shall not be given**
The Secretary of State shall not give a reduced benefit decision where—

(a) income support is paid to, or in respect of, the parent in question and the applicable amount of the claimant for income support includes one or more of the amounts set out in paragraph 15(3), (4) or (6) of Part IV of Schedule 2 to the Income Support Regulations; or

(b) an income-based jobseeker's allowance is paid to, or in respect of, the parent in question and the applicable amount of the claimant for an income-based jobseeker's allowance includes one or more of the amounts set out in paragraph 20(4), (5) or (7) of Schedule 1 to the Jobseeker's Allowance Regulations [; or

(c) an amount prescribed under section 9(5)(c) of the Tax Credits Act 2002 (increased elements of child tax credit for children or young persons with a disability) is included in an award of child tax credit payable to the parent in question or a member of that parent's family living with him.]

**Note.**  Sub-para (c) added by SI 2003 No 328 as from 6 April 2003.

**11 Amount of and period of reduction of relevant benefit under a reduced benefit decision—**(1) The reduction in the amount payable by way of a relevant benefit to, or in respect of, the parent concerned and the period of such reduction by virtue of a reduced benefit decision shall be determined in accordance with paragraphs (2) to (8) below.

(2) Subject to paragraph (6) and regulations 12, 13, 14, and 15, there shall be a reduction for a period of 156 weeks from the day specified in the reduced benefit decision under the provisions of section 46(8) of the Act in respect of each such week equal to—

$$0.4 \times B$$

where B is an amount equal to the weekly amount in relation to the week in question, specified in column (2) of paragraph 1(1)(e) of Schedule 2 to the Income Support Regulations.

(3) Subject to paragraph (4), a reduced benefit decision shall come into operation on the first day of the second benefit week following the date of the reduced benefit decision.

(4) Subject to paragraph (5), where a reduced benefit decision ('the subsequent decision') is made on a day when a reduced benefit decision ('the earlier decision') is in force in respect of the same parent, the subsequent decision shall come into operation on the day immediately following the day on which the earlier decision ceased to be in force.

(5) Where the relevant benefit is income support and the provisions of regulation 26(2) of the Social Security (Claims and Payments) Regulations 1987 (deferment of payment of different amount of income support) apply, a reduced benefit decision shall come into operation on such later date as may be determined by the Secretary of State in accordance with those provisions.

(6) Where the benefit payable is income support or an income-based jobseeker's allowance and there is a change in the benefit week whilst a reduced benefit decision is in operation, the period of the reduction specified in paragraph (2) shall be a period greater than 155 weeks but less than 156 weeks and ending on the last day of the last benefit week falling entirely within the period of 156 weeks specified in that paragraph.

(7) Where the weekly amount specified in column (2) of paragraph 1(1)(e) of Schedule 2 to the Income Support Regulations changes on a day when a reduced benefit decision is in operation, the amount of the reduction of income support or income-based jobseeker's allowance shall be changed from the first day of the first benefit week to commence for the parent concerned on or after the day that weekly amount changes.

(8) Only one reduced benefit decision in relation to a parent concerned shall be in force at any one time.

**12 Modification of reduction under a reduced benefit decision to preserve minimum entitlement to relevant benefit** Where in respect of any benefit week the amount of the relevant benefit that would be payable after it has been reduced following a reduced benefit decision would, but for this regulation, be nil or less than the minimum amount of that benefit that is payable as determined—

    (a) in the case of income support, by regulation 26(4) of the Social Security (Claims and Payments) Regulations 1987;

    (b) in the case of an income-based jobseeker's allowance, by regulation 87A of the Jobseeker's Allowance Regulations,

the amount of that reduction shall be decreased to such extent as to raise the amount of that benefit to the minimum amount that is payable.

**13 Suspension of a reduced benefit decision when relevant benefit ceases to be payable**—(1) Where relevant benefit ceases to be payable to, or in respect of, the parent concerned at a time when a reduced benefit decision is in operation, that reduced benefit decision shall, subject to paragraph (2), be suspended for a period of 52 weeks from the date the relevant benefit ceases to be payable.

(2) Where a reduced benefit decision has been suspended for a period of 52 weeks and no relevant benefit is payable at the end of that period, it shall cease to be in force.

(3) Where a reduced benefit decision is suspended and relevant benefit again becomes payable to, or in respect of, the parent concerned, the amount payable by way of that benefit shall, subject to regulations 14 and 15, be reduced in accordance with that reduced benefit decision for the balance of the reduction period.

(4) The amount or, as the case may be, the amounts of that reduction to be made during the balance of the reduction period shall be determined in accordance with regulation 11(2).

(5) No reduction in the amount of benefit under paragraph (3) shall be made before the expiry of a period of 14 days from service of the notice specified in paragraph (6), and the provisions of regulation 11(3) shall apply as to the date the reduced benefit decision again comes into operation.

(6) Where relevant benefit again becomes payable to, or in respect of, a parent with respect to whom a reduced benefit decision is suspended, she shall be notified in writing by the Secretary of State that the amount of relevant benefit paid to, or in respect of, her will again be reduced, in accordance with the provisions of paragraph (3), if she falls within section 46(1) of the Act.

**14 Suspension of a reduced benefit decision *when a modified applicable amount is payable* (income support)**—(1) Where a reduced benefit decision is given or is in operation at a time when income support is payable to, or in respect of, the parent concerned *but her applicable amount falls to be calculated under the provisions mentioned in paragraph (4)* [but the circumstances in paragraph (4) apply to her], that decision shall be suspended for so long as [those circumstances apply], that decision shall be suspended for so long as *her applicable amount falls to be calculated under the provisions mentioned in that paragraph* [those circumstances apply] or 52 weeks, whichever period is the shorter.

*(2) Where a reduced benefit decision is given or is in operation at a time when income support is payable to, or in respect of, the parent concerned, but her applicable amount includes a residential allowance under regulation 17 of, and paragraph 2A of Schedule 2 to, the Income Support Regulations (applicable amounts for persons in residential care and nursing homes), that decision shall be suspended for as long as her applicable amount includes a residential allowance under that regulation and Schedule 2, or 52 weeks, whichever period is the shorter.*

(3) Where a case falls within paragraph (1) *or (2)* and a reduced benefit decision has been suspended for 52 weeks, it shall cease to be in force.

*(4) The provisions of paragraph (1) shall apply where the applicable amount in relation to the parent concerned falls to be calculated under—*

   *(a) regulation 19 of, and Schedule 4 to, the Income Support Regulations (applicable amounts for persons in residential care and nursing homes);*

   *(b) regulation 21 of, and paragraphs 1 to 3 of Schedule 7 to, the Income Support Regulations (patients);*

   *(c) regulation 21 of, and paragraphs 10B, 10C and 13 of Schedule 7 to, the Income Support Regulations (persons in local authority or residential accommodation).*

[(4) The circumstances referred to in paragraph (1) are that—

   (a) she is resident in a care home or an independent hospital;

   (b) she is being provided with a care home service or an independent health care service; or

(c)  her applicable amount falls to be calculated under regulation 21 of and any of paragraphs 1 to 3 of Schedule 7 to the Income Support Regulations (patients).

(5)  In paragraph (4)—

'care home' has the meaning assigned to it by section 3 of the Care Standards Act 2000;

'care home service' has the meaning assigned to it by section 2(3) of the Regulation of Care (Scotland) Act 2001;

'independent health care service' has the meaning assigned to it by section 2(5)(a) and (b) of the Regulation of Care (Scotland) Act 2001; and

'independent hospital' has the meaning assigned to it by section 2 of the Care Standards Act 2000.]

**Note.** Provision heading: words omitted revoked by SI 2003 No 2779, reg 5(1), (3)(a) as from 5 November 2003 (except in relation to a person to whom this provision applied before that date): see SI 2003/2779, regs 1, 9. Para (1): words 'but the circumstances in paragraph (4) apply to her' in square brackets substituted by SI 2003 No 2779, reg 5(1), (3)(b)(i) s from 5 November 2003(except in relation to a person to whom this provision applied before that date): see SI 2003/2779, regs 1, 9. Para (1): words 'those circumstances apply' in square brackets substituted by SI 2003/2779, reg 5(1), (3)(b)(ii) s from 5 November 2003(except in relation to a person to whom this provision applied before that date): see SI 2003/2779, regs 1, 9. Para (2): revoked by SI 2003 No 2779, reg 5(1), (3)(c) s from 5 November 2003(except in relation to a person to whom this provision applied before that date): see SI 2003/2779, regs 1, 9. Para (3): words omitted revoked by SI 2003 No 2779, reg 5(1), (3)(d) s from 5 November 2003(except in relation to a person to whom this provision applied before that date): see SI 2003/2779, regs 1, 9. Paras (4), (5): substituted, for para (4) as originally enacted, by SI 2003 No 2779, reg 5(1), (3)(e) s from 5 November 2003(except in relation to a person to whom this provision applied before that date): see SI 2003/2779, regs 1, 9.

**15 Suspension of a reduced benefit decision *when a modified applicable amount is payable* (income-based jobseeker's allowance)**—(1) Where a reduced benefit decision is given or is in operation at a time when an income-based jobseeker's allowance is payable to, or in respect of, the parent concerned *but her applicable amount falls to be calculated under the provisions mentioned in paragraph (4),* [but the circumstances in paragraph (4) apply to her], that reduced benefit decision shall be suspended for so long as *the applicable amount falls to be calculated under those provisions,* those circumstances apply], or 52 weeks, whichever is the shorter.

*(2)  Where a reduced benefit decision is given or is in operation at a time when an income-based jobseeker's allowance is payable to, or in respect of, the parent concerned but her applicable amount includes a residential allowance under regulation 83(c) of, and paragraph 3 of Schedule 1 to, the Jobseeker's Allowance Regulations (persons in residential care or nursing homes), that reduced benefit decision shall be suspended for so long as the applicable amount includes such a residential allowance, or 52 weeks, whichever is the shorter.*

(3)  Where a case falls within paragraph (1) *or (2)* and a reduced benefit decision has been suspended for 52 weeks, it shall cease to be in force.

*(4)  The provisions of paragraph (1) shall apply where the applicable amount in relation to the parent concerned falls to be calculated under—*

(a)  *regulation 85 of, and paragraph 1 or 2 of Schedule 5 to, the Jobseeker's Allowance Regulations (patients);*

(b)  *regulation 85 of, and paragraphs 8, 9 or 15 of Schedule 5 to, the Jobseeker's Allowance Regulations (persons in local authority or residential accommodation); or*

(c)  *regulation 86 of, and Schedule 4 to, the Jobseeker's Allowance Regulations (applicable amounts for persons in residential care and nursing homes).*

[(4)  The circumstances referred to in paragraph (1) are that—

(a)  she is resident in a care home or an independent hospital;

(b) she is being provided with a care home service or an independent health care service; or

(c) her applicable amount falls to be calculated under regulation 85 of and paragraph 1 or 2 of Schedule 5 to the Jobseeker's Allowance Regulations (patients).

(5) In paragraph (4)—

'care home' has the meaning assigned to it by section 3 of the Care Standards Act 2000;

'care home service' has the meaning assigned to it by section 2(3) of the Regulation of Care (Scotland) Act 2001;

'independent health care service' has the meaning assigned to it by section 2(5)(a) and (b) of the Regulation of Care (Scotland) Act 2001; and

'independent hospital' has the meaning assigned to it by section 2 of the Care Standards Act 2000.]

**Note.** Provision heading: words omitted revoked by SI 2003 No 2779, reg 5(1), (4)(a) as from 5 November 2003. Para (1): words 'but the circumstances in paragraph (4) apply to her' in square brackets substituted by SI 2003 N0 2779, reg 5(1), (4)(b)(i) as from 5 November 2003 (except in relation to a person to whom this provision applied before that date): see SI 2003 No 2779, regs 1, 9. Para (1): words 'those circumstances apply' in square brackets substituted by SI 2003 No 2779, reg 5(1), (4)(b)(ii) as from 5 November 2003 (except in relation to a person to whom this provision applied before that date): see SI 2003 No 2779, regs 1, 9. Para (2): revoked by SI 2003 No 2779, reg 5(1), (4)(c) as from 5 November 2003 (except in relation to a person to whom this provision applied before that date): see SI 2003 No 2779, regs 1, 9. Para (3): words omitted revoked by SI 2003 No 2779, reg 5(1), (4)(d) as from 5 November 2003 (except in relation to a person to whom this provision applied before that date): see SI 2003 No 2779, regs 1, 9. Paras (4), (5): substituted, for para (4) as originally enacted, by SI 2003 No 2779, reg 5(1), (4)(e)as from 5 November 2003 (except in relation to a person to whom this provision applied before that date): see SI 2003 No 2779, regs 1, 9.

**16 Termination of a reduced benefit decision** A reduced benefit decision shall cease to be in force—

(a) where the parent concerned—
   (i) withdraws her request under section 6(5) of the Act;
   (ii) complies with her obligation under section 6(7) of the Act; or
   (iii) consents to take a scientific test (within the meaning of section 27A of the Act);

(b) where following written notice under section 46(6)(b) of the Act, the parent concerned responds to such notice and the Secretary of State considers there are reasonable grounds;

(c) subject to regulation 13, where relevant benefit ceases to be payable to, or in respect of, the parent concerned; or

(d) where a qualifying child with respect to whom a reduced benefit decision is in force applies for a maintenance calculation to be made with respect to him under section 7 of the Act and a calculation is made in response to that application in respect of all the qualifying children in relation to whom the parent concerned falls within section 46(1) of the Act.

**17 Reduced benefit decisions where there is an additional qualifying child—**
(1) Where a reduced benefit decision is in operation, or would be in operation but for the provisions of regulations 14 and 15, and the Secretary of State gives a further reduced benefit decision with respect to the same parent concerned in relation to an additional qualifying child of whom she is a parent with care, the earlier reduced benefit decision shall cease to be in force.

(2) Where a further reduced benefit decision comes into operation in a case falling within paragraph (1), the provisions of regulation 11 shall apply to it.

(3) Where—
(a) a reduced benefit decision ('the earlier decision') has ceased to be in force by virtue of regulation 13(2); and
(b) the Secretary of State gives a further reduced benefit decision ('the further decision') with respect to the same parent concerned where that parent falls within section 46(1) of the Act,

as long as the further decision remains in force, no additional reduced benefit decision shall be brought into force with respect to that parent in relation to one or more children to whom the earlier decision was given.

(4) Where a case falls within paragraph (1) or (3) and the further decision, but for the provisions of this paragraph, would cease to be in force by virtue of the provisions of regulation 16, but the earlier decision would not have ceased to be in force by virtue of the provisions of regulation 16, the further reduced benefit decision shall remain in force for a period calculated in accordance with regulation 11.

(5) In this regulation 'additional qualifying child' means a qualifying child of whom the parent concerned is a parent with care and who was either not such a qualifying child at the time the earlier decision was given or had not been born at the time the earlier decision was given.

**18 Suspension and termination of a reduced benefit decision where the sole qualifying child ceases to be a child or where the parent concerned ceases to be a person with care**—(1) Where a reduced benefit decision is in operation and—
(a) there is, in relation to that decision, only one qualifying child, and that child ceases to be a child within the meaning of the Act; or
(b) the parent concerned ceases to be a person with care,

the decision shall be suspended from the last day of the benefit week during the course of which the child ceases to be a child within the meaning of the Act, or the parent concerned ceases to be a person with care, as the case may be.

(2) Where, under the provisions of paragraph (1), a decision has been suspended for a period of 52 weeks and no relevant benefit is payable at that time, it shall cease to be in force.

(3) If during the period specified in paragraph (2) the former child again becomes a child within the meaning of the Act or the parent concerned again becomes a person with care and relevant benefit is payable to, or in respect of, that parent, a reduction in the amount of that benefit shall be made in accordance with the provisions of paragraphs (3) to (6) of regulation 13.

**19 Notice of termination of a reduced benefit decision** Where a reduced benefit decision ceases to be in force under the provisions of regulation 16, 17 or 18 the Secretary of State shall serve notice of this on the parent concerned and shall specify the date on which the reduced benefit decision ceases to be in force.

**20 Rounding provisions** Where any calculation made under this Part results in a fraction of a penny, that fraction shall be treated as a penny if it exceeds one half and shall otherwise be disregarded.

Part V

Miscellaneous Provisions

**21 Persons who are not persons with care**—(1) For the purposes of the Act the following categories of person shall not be persons with care—
(a) a local authority;
(b) a person with whom a child who is looked after by a local authority is placed by that authority under the provisions of the Children Act 1989, except

where that person is a parent of such a child and the local authority allow
the child to live with that parent under section 23(5) of that Act;

(c) in Scotland, a family or relative with whom a child is placed by a local
authority under the provisions of section 26 of the Children (Scotland) Act
1995.

(2) In paragraph (1) above—

'family' means family other than such family defined in section 93(1) of the
Children (Scotland) Act 1995;

'local authority' means, in relation to England, a county council, a district
council, a London borough council, the Common Council of the City of
London or the Council of the Isles of Scilly and, in relation to Wales, a
county council or a county borough council, and, in relation to Scotland, a
council constituted under section 2 of the Local Government etc
(Scotland) Act 1994; and

'a child who is looked after by a local authority' has the same meaning as in
section 22 of the Children Act 1989 or section 17(6) of the Children
(Scotland) Act 1995 as the case may be.

**22 Authorisation of representative—**(1) A person may authorise a
representative, whether or not legally qualified, to receive notices and other
documents on his behalf and to act on his behalf in relation to the making of
applications and the supply of information under any provisions of the Act or
these Regulations.

(2) Where a person has authorised a representative for the purposes of
paragraph (1) who is not legally qualified, he shall confirm that authorisation in
writing to the Secretary of State.

PART VI

NOTIFICATIONS FOLLOWING CERTAIN DECISIONS

**23 Notification of a maintenance calculation—**(1) A notification of a
maintenance calculation made under section 11 or 12(2) of the Act (interim
maintenance decision) shall set out, in relation to the maintenance calculation in
question—

(a) the effective date of the maintenance calculation;

(b) where relevant, the non-resident parent's net weekly income;

(c) the number of qualifying children;

(d) the number of relevant other children;

(e) the weekly rate;

(f) the amounts calculated in accordance with Part I of Schedule 1 to the Act
and, where there has been agreement to a variation or a variation has
otherwise been taken into account, the Child Support (Variations)
Regulations 2000;

(g) where the weekly rate is adjusted by apportionment or shared care, or both,
the amount calculated in accordance with paragraph 6, 7 or 8, as the case
may be, of Part I of Schedule 1 to the Act; and

(h) where the amount of child support maintenance which the non-resident
parent is liable to pay is decreased in accordance with regulation 9 or 11 of
the Maintenance Calculations and Special Cases Regulations (care provided
in part by local authority and non-resident parent liable to pay maintenance
under a maintenance order), the adjustment calculated in accordance with
that regulation.

(2) A notification of a maintenance calculation made under section 12(1) of
the Act (default maintenance decision) shall set out the effective date of the
maintenance calculation, the default rate, the number of qualifying children on

which the rate is based, whether any apportionment has been applied under regulation 7 and shall state the nature of the information required to enable a decision under section 11 of the Act to be made by way of section 16 of the Act.

(3) Except where a person gives written permission to the Secretary of State that the information in relation to him, mentioned in sub-paragraphs (a) and (b) below, may be conveyed to other persons, any document given or sent under the provisions of paragraph (1) or (2) shall not contain—

(a) the address of any person other than the recipient of the document in question (other than the address of the office of the officer concerned who is exercising functions of the Secretary of State under the Act) or any other information the use of which could reasonably be expected to lead to any such person being located;

(b) any other information the use of which could reasonably be expected to lead to any person, other than a qualifying child or a relevant person, being identified.

(4) Where a decision as to a maintenance calculation is made under section 11 or 12 of the Act, a notification under paragraph (1) or (2) shall include information as to the provisions of sections 16, 17 and 20 of the Act.

**24 Notification when an applicant under section 7 of the Act ceases to be a child** Where a maintenance calculation has been made in response to an application by a child under section 7 of the Act and that child ceases to be a child for the purposes of the Act, the Secretary of State shall immediately notify, so far as that is reasonably practicable—

(a) the other qualifying children who have attained the age of 12 years and the non-resident parent with respect to whom that maintenance calculation was made; and

(b) the person with care.

PART VII

EFFECTIVE DATES OF MAINTENANCE CALCULATIONS

**25 Effective dates of maintenance calculations—**(1) Subject to regulations 26 to 29 [and 31], where no maintenance calculation is in force with respect to the person with care or the non-resident parent, the effective date of a maintenance calculation following an application made under section 4 or 7 of the Act, or treated as made under section 6(3) of the Act, as the case may be, shall be the date determined in accordance with paragraphs (2) to (4) below.

(2) Where the application for a maintenance calculation is made under section 4 of the Act by a non-resident parent, the effective date of the maintenance calculation shall be the date that an effective application is made or treated as made under regulation 3.

(3) Where the application for a maintenance calculation is—

(a) made under section 4 of the Act by a person with care;

(b) treated as made under section 6(3) of the Act; or

(c) made by a child under section 7 of the Act,

the effective date of the maintenance calculation shall be the date of notification to the non-resident parent.

(4) For the purposes of this regulation, where the Secretary of State is satisfied that a non-resident parent has intentionally avoided receipt of a notice of a maintenance application he may determine the date of notification to the non-resident parent as the date on which the notification would have been given to him but for such avoidance.

(5) Where in relation to a decision made under section 11 of the Act a maintenance calculation is made to which paragraph 15 of Schedule 1 to the Act

applies, the effective date of the calculation shall be the beginning of the maintenance period in which the change of circumstance to which the calculation relates occurred or is expected to occur.

**Note.** Words in square brackets inserted by SI 2003 No 328 as from 6 April 2003.

**26 Effective dates of maintenance calculations—maintenance order and application under section 4 or 7**—(1) This regulation applies, subject to regulation 28, where—

(a) no maintenance calculation is in force with respect to the person with care or the non-resident parent;

(b) an application for a maintenance calculation is made under section 4 or 7 of the Act; and

(c) *there is a maintenance order in force, made on or after the date prescribed for the purposes of section 4(10)(a) of the Act, in relation to the person with care and the non-resident parent and that order has been in force for at least one year prior to the date the application for a maintenance calculation is made.*

[(c) there is a maintenance order which—

    (i) is in force and was made on or after the date prescribed for the purposes of section 4(10)(a) of the Act;

    (ii) relates to the person with care, the non-resident parent and all the children to whom the application referred to in sub-paragraph (b) relates; and

    (iii) has been in force for at least one year prior to the date of the application referred to in sub-paragraph (b).]

(2) The effective date of the maintenance calculation shall be two months and two days after the application is made.

**Note.** Para (c) in italics omitted and para (c) in square brackets substituted by SI 2002 No 1204 as from 30 April 2002.

**27 Effective dates of maintenance calculations—maintenance order and application under section 6**—(1) This regulation applies, subject to regulation 28, where—

(a) the circumstances set out in regulation 26(1)(a) apply;

(b) an application for a maintenance calculation is treated as made under section 6(3) of the Act; and

(c) there is a maintenance order in force in relation to the person with care *and the non-resident parent* [, the non-resident parent and all the children to whom the application referred to in sub-paragraph (b) relates].

(2) The effective date of the maintenance calculation shall be 2 days after the maintenance calculation is made.

**Note.** Words in italics in sub-para (c) omitted and words in square brackets inserted by SI 2002 No 1204 as from 30 April 2002.

**28 Effective dates of maintenance calculations—maintenance order ceases** Where—

(a) a maintenance calculation is made; and

(b) there was a maintenance order in force in relation to the person with care and the non-resident parent which ceased to have effect after the date on which the application for the maintenance calculation was made but before the effective date provided for in regulation *25 or 26* [26 or 27] as the case may be,

the effective date of the maintenance calculation shall be the day following that on which the maintenance order ceased to have effect.

**Note.** Numbers in italics omitted and numbers in square brackets inserted by SI 2002 No 1204 as from 30 April 2002.

**29 Effective dates of maintenance calculations in specified cases—** [(1)]
Where an application for a maintenance calculation is made under section 4 or 7
of the Act, or treated as made under section 6(3) of the Act—

(a) except where the parent with care has made a request under section 6(5) of
the Act, where in the period of 8 weeks immediately preceding the date the
application is made, or treated as made under regulation 3, there has been
in force a maintenance calculation in respect of the same non-resident
parent and child but a different person with care, the effective date of the
maintenance calculation made in respect of the application shall be *the day
following the day* [the date] on which the previous maintenance calculation
ceased to have effect;

(b) where a maintenance calculation ('the existing calculation') is in force with
respect to the person who is the person with care in relation to the
application but who is the non-resident parent in relation to the existing
calculation, the effective date of the calculation shall be a date not later
than 7 days after the date of notification to the non-resident parent which is
the day on which a maintenance period in respect of the existing
calculation begins;

[(c) except where the parent with care has made a request under section 6(5) of
the Act, where—

   (i) in the period of 8 weeks immediately preceding the date the
application is made, or treated as made under regulation 3, a
maintenance calculation ('the previous maintenance calculation')
has been in force and has ceased to have effect;

   (ii) the parent with care in respect of the previous maintenance
calculation is the non-resident parent in respect of the application;

   (iii) the non-resident parent in respect of the previous maintenance
calculation is the parent with care in respect of the application; and

   (iv) the application relates to the same qualifying child, or all of the
same qualifying children, and no others, as the previous
maintenance calculation,

the effective date of the maintenance calculation to which the application
relates shall be the date on which the previous maintenance calculation ceased
to have effect.];

[(d) except where the parent with care has made a request under section 6(5) of
the Act, where on the date the application is made, or treated as made
under regulation 3, there is in force a maintenance calculation in relation
to the same non-resident parent and a different person with care, and the
maintenance calculation in force when the application was made has ceased
to have effect before a decision has been made in respect of that
application, the effective date of the maintenance calculation made in
response to the application shall be—

   (i) where the date of notification to the non-resident parent is before
the date on which the maintenance calculation in force has ceased
to have effect, the day following the day on which that maintenance
calculation ceases to have effect;

   (ii) where the date of notification to the non-resident parent is after the
date on which the maintenance calculation in force has ceased to
have effect, the date of notification to the non-resident parent].

[(2) Where an application is treated as made under section 6(3) of the Act,
references in sub-paragraphs (a) and (c) of paragraph (1) to 'the date the
application is made' shall mean whichever is the later of—

(a) the date of the claim for a prescribed benefit made by or in respect of the
parent with care, as determined by regulation 6 of the Social Security
(Claims and Payments) Regulations 1987; and

(b) the date on which the parent with care or her partner in the claim reports to the Secretary of State (in respect of a claim for a prescribed benefit) or to the Commissioners of Inland Revenue (in respect of a claim for a tax credit) a change of circumstances, which change—

    (i) relates to an existing claim, in respect of the parent with care, for a prescribed benefit; and

    (ii) has the effect that the parent with care is treated as applying for a maintenance calculation under section 6(1) of the Act (whether or not that section already applied to that parent with care).

(3) For the purposes of—

(a) paragraph (1), 'ceased to have effect' means ceased to have effect under paragraph 16 of Schedule 1 to the Act; and

(b) paragraph (2), 'prescribed benefit' means a benefit referred to in section 6(1) of the Act or prescribed in regulations made under that section.]

**Note.** Sub-para (c) inserted by SI 2002 No 1204 as from 30 April 2002. Regulation renumbered as para (1), words in italics omitted in para (a) and words in square brackets inserted and paras (2) and (3) added by SI 2003 No 328 as from 6 April 2003. Para (1)(d) inserted by SI 2004 No 2415, reg 6(1), (2) as from 16 September 2004.

PART VIII

REVOCATION, SAVINGS AND TRANSITIONAL PROVISIONS

**30 Revocation and savings—**(1) Subject to [the Child Support (Transitional Provisions) Regulations 2000 and] paragraph (2), the Child Support (Maintenance Assessment Procedure) Regulations 1992 shall be revoked with respect to a particular case with effect from the date that these Regulations come into force with respect to that type of case ('the commencement date').

(2) Subject to *regulation 31(2)* [regulation 31(1C)(b) and (2)], where before the commencement date in respect of a particular case—

(a) an application was made and not determined for—

    (i) a maintenance assessment;

    (ii) a departure direction; or

    (iii) a revision or supersession of a decision;

(b) the Secretary of State had begun but not completed a revision or supersession of a decision on his own initiative;

(c) any time limit provided for in Regulations for making an application for a revision or a departure direction had not expired; or

(d) any appeal was made but not decided or any time limit for making an appeal had not expired,

the provisions of the Child Support (Maintenance Assessment Procedure) Regulations 1992 shall continue to apply for the purposes of—

    (aa) the decision on the application referred to in sub-paragraph (a);

    (bb) the revision or supersession referred to in sub-paragraph (b);

    (cc) the ability to apply for the revision or the departure direction referred to in sub-paragraph (c) and the decision whether to revise or to give a departure direction following any such application;

    (dd) any appeal outstanding or made during the time limit referred to in sub-paragraph (d); or

    (ee) any revision, supersession, appeal or application for a departure direction in relation to a decision, ability to apply or appeal referred to in sub-paragraphs (aa) to (dd) above.

(3) Where immediately before the commencement date in respect of a particular case an interim maintenance assessment was in force, the provisions of the Child Support (Maintenance Assessment Procedure) Regulations 1992 shall

continue to apply for the purposes of the decision under section 17 of the Act to make a maintenance assessment calculated in accordance with Part I of Schedule 1 to the 1991 Act before its amendment by the 2000 Act and any revision, supersession or appeal in relation to that decision.

(4) Where after the commencement date a maintenance assessment is revised, cancelled or ceases to have effect from a date which is prior to the commencement date, the Child Support (Maintenance Assessment Procedure) Regulations 1992 shall apply for the purposes of that cancellation or cessation.

(5) Where under regulation 28(1) of the Child Support (Transitional Provisions) Regulations 2000 an application for a maintenance calculation is treated as an application for a maintenance assessment, the provisions of the Child Support (Maintenance Assessment Procedure) Regulations 1992 shall continue to apply for the purposes of the determination of the application and any revision, supersession or appeal in relation to any such assessment made.

(6) For the purposes of this regulation—

(a) 'departure direction', 'maintenance assessment' and 'interim maintenance assessment' have the same meaning as in section 54 of the Act before its amendment by the 2000 Act;

(b) 'revision or supersession' means a revision or supersession of a decision under section 16 or 17 of the Act before their amendment by the 2000 Act;

(c) '2000 Act' means the Child Support, Pensions and Social Security Act 2000.

**Note.** Words in square brackets in para (1) inserted by SI 2003 No 347 as from 3 March 2003. Regulation reference in para (2) substituted by SI 2003 No 328 as from 6 April 2003.

## 31 Transitional provision—effective dates and reduced benefit decisions—*(1)*
*Where a maintenance assessment is in force with respect to a non-resident parent or a parent with care and an application for a maintenance calculation is made to which regulation 29 applies, that regulation shall apply as if references to a maintenance calculation in force were to a maintenance assessment in force.*

*(2) Where—*

*(a) the application for a maintenance assessment was made before the date prescribed for the purposes of section 4(10)(a) of the Act; and*

*(b) the effective date of the maintenance assessment, if it were a maintenance assessment to which the Assessment Procedure Regulations applied ('the assessment effective date') would be later than the effective date provided for in these Regulations,*

*the application shall be treated as an application for a maintenance calculation and the effective date of that maintenance calculation shall be the assessment effective date.*

[(1) Where a maintenance assessment is, or has been, in force and an application to which regulation 29 applies is made, or is treated as made under section 6(3) of the Act, that regulation shall apply as if in paragraph (1) references to—

(a) a maintenance calculation in force were to a maintenance assessment in force;

(b) a maintenance calculation having been in force were to a maintenance assessment having been in force; and

(c) a non-resident parent in sub-paragraph (a), the first time it occurs in sub-paragraph (b) *and in sub-paragraph (c)(iii)* [, in sub-paragraph (c)(iii) and the first time it occurs in sub-paragraph (d)], were to an absent parent.

(1A) Where regulation 28(7) of the Child Support (Transitional Provisions) Regulations 2000 (linking provisions) applies, the effective date of the maintenance calculation shall be the date which would have been the beginning of the first maintenance period in respect of the conversion decision on or after what, but for this paragraph, would have been the relevant effective date provided for in regulation 25(2) to (4).

(1B) The provisions of Schedule 3 shall apply where—

(a) an effective application for a maintenance assessment has been made under the former Act ('an assessment application'); and

(b) an effective application for a maintenance calculation is made or an application for a maintenance calculation is treated as made under the Act ('a calculation application').

(1C) Where the provisions of Schedule 3 apply and, by virtue of regulation 4(3) of the Assessment Procedure Regulations, the relevant date would be—

(a) before the prescribed date, the application to be proceeded with shall be treated as an application for a maintenance assessment;

(b) on or after the prescribed date, that application shall be treated as an application for a maintenance calculation and the effective date of that maintenance calculation shall be the date which would be the assessment effective date if a maintenance assessment were to be made.

(2) Where—

(a) an application for a maintenance assessment was made before the prescribed date; and

(b) the assessment effective date of that application would be on or after the prescribed date,

the application shall be treated as an application for a maintenance calculation and the effective date of that maintenance calculation shall be the date which would be the assessment effective date if a maintenance assessment were to be made.]

(3) Paragraphs (4) to (7) shall apply where, *on or before* [immediately before] the commencement date, section 6 of the former Act applied to the parent with care.

(4) *Where a maintenance assessment was made with an effective date, applying the Assessment Procedure Regulations, or the Maintenance Arrangements and Jurisdiction Regulations, which* [Where the assessment effective date] is before the prescribed date and on or after the commencement date the parent with care notifies the Secretary of State that she is withdrawing her authorisation under subsection (1) of that section, these Regulations shall apply as if the notification were a request not to act under section 6(5) of the Act.

(5) Where a maintenance assessment was not made because section 6(2) of the former Act applied, these Regulations shall apply as if section 6(5) of the Act applied.

(6) Where a maintenance assessment was not made, section 6(2) of the former Act did not apply and a reduced benefit direction was given under section 46(5) of the former Act, these Regulations shall apply as if the reduced benefit direction were a reduced benefit decision made under section 46(5) of the Act, from the same date and with the same effect as the reduced benefit direction.

(7) Where a maintenance assessment was not made, the parent with care failed to comply with a requirement imposed on her under section 6(1) of the former Act and the Secretary of State was in the process of serving a notice or considering reasons given by the parent with care under section 46(2) or (3) of the former Act, these Regulations shall apply as if the Secretary of State was in the process of serving a notice or considering reasons under section 46(2) or (3) of the Act.

(8) For the purposes of this regulation—

(a) '2000 Act' means the Child Support, Pensions and Social Security Act 2000; ['absent parent' has the meaning given in section 3(2) of the former Act; 'assessment effective date' means the effective date of the maintenance assessment under regulation 30 or 33(7) of the Assessment Procedure Regulations or regulation 3(5), (7) or (8) of the Maintenance Arrangements and Jurisdiction Regulations, whichever applied to the maintenance assessment in question or would have applied had the effective date not been determined under regulation 8C or 30A of the Assessment Procedure Regulations;]

'Assessment Procedure Regulations' means the Child Support (Maintenance Assessment Procedure) Regulations 1992;

'commencement date' means with respect to a particular case the date these Regulations come into force with respect to that type of case;

'former Act' means the Act before its amendment by the 2000 Act;

'Maintenance Arrangements and Jurisdiction Regulations' means the Child Support (Maintenance Arrangements and Jurisdiction) Regulations 1992;

'maintenance assessment' has the meaning given in the former Act; and

'prescribed date' means the date prescribed for the purposes of section 4(10)(a) of the Act; [and

'relevant date' means the date which would be the assessment effective date of the application which is to be proceeded with in accordance with Schedule 3, if a maintenance assessment were to be made.]

(b) references in paragraphs (4) to (7) to sections 6(5), 46(5) and 46(2) and (3) of the Act mean those provisions as substituted by the 2000 Act; and

(c) in the application of the Assessment Procedure Regulations for the purposes of paragraph (4) where, on or after the prescribed date, no maintenance enquiry form, as defined in those Regulations, is given or sent to the absent parent, the Regulations shall be applied as if references in regulation 30—

  (i) to the date when the maintenance enquiry form was given or sent to the absent parent were to the date of notification to the non-resident parent;

  (ii) to the return by the absent parent of the maintenance enquiry form containing his name, address and written confirmation that he is the parent of the child or children in respect of whom the application was made were to the provision of this information by the non-resident parent; and

(d) in the application of the Maintenance Arrangements and Jurisdiction Regulations for the purposes of paragraph (4), where, on or after the prescribed date no maintenance enquiry form, as defined in the Assessment Procedure Regulations, is given or sent to the absent parent, regulation 3(8) shall be applied as if the reference to the date when the maintenance enquiry form was given or sent were a reference to the date of notification to the non-resident parent.

**Note.** Para (1): in sub-para (c) words ', in sub-paragraph (c)(iii) and the first time it occurs in sub-paragraph (d)' in square brackets substituted by SI 2004 No 2415, reg 6(1), (3) as from 16 September 2004. Words in italics in para (3) omitted and words in square brackets inserted by SI 2002 No 1204 as from 30 April 2002. Paras (1) and (2) in italics omitted and paras (1), (2) in square brackets substituted, words in italics in para (4) omitted and words in square brackets substituted and definitions in square brackets inserted by SI 2003 No 328 as from 6 April 2003.

SCHEDULE 1                                                              Regulation 1(3)

MEANING OF 'CHILD' FOR THE PURPOSES OF THE ACT

*Persons of 16 or 17 years of age who are not in full-time non-advanced education*

**1**—(1) Subject to sub-paragraph (3), the conditions which must be satisfied for a person to be a child within section 55(1)(c) of the Act are—

(a) the person is registered for work or for training under work-based training for young people or, in Scotland, Skillseekers training with—

  (i) the Department for Education and Employment;

  (ii) the Ministry of Defence;

  (iii) in England and Wales, a local education authority within the meaning of the Education Acts 1944 to 1992;

      (iv)  in Scotland, an education authority within the meaning of section 135(1) of the Education (Scotland) Act 1980 (interpretation); or

      (v)  for the purposes of applying Council Regulation (EEC) No 1408/71, any corresponding body in another member State;

(b)  the person is not engaged in remunerative work, other than work of a temporary nature that is due to cease before the end of the extension period which applies in the case of that person;

(c)  the extension period which applies in the case of that person has not expired; and

(d)  immediately before the extension period begins, the person is a child for the purposes of the Act without regard to this paragraph.

(2) For the purposes of heads (b), (c) and (d) of sub-paragraph (1), the extension period—

(a)  begins on the first day of the week in which the person would no longer be a child for the purposes of the Act but for this paragraph; and

(b)  where a person ceases to fall within section 55(1)(a) of the Act or within paragraph 5—

      (i)  on or after the first Monday in September, but before the first Monday in January of the following year, ends on the last day of the week which falls immediately before the week which includes the first Monday in January in that year;

      (ii)  on or after the first Monday in January but before the Monday following Easter Monday in that year, ends on the last day of the week which falls 12 weeks after the week which includes the first Monday in January in that year;

      (iii)  at any other time of the year, ends on the last day of the week which falls 12 weeks after the week which includes the Monday following Easter Monday in that year.

(3) A person shall not be a child for the purposes of the Act under this paragraph if—

(a)  he is engaged in training under work-based training for young people or, in Scotland, Skillseekers training; or

(b)  he is entitled to income support or an income-based jobseeker's allowance.

*Meaning of 'advanced education' for the purposes of section 55 of the Act*

**2** For the purposes of section 55 of the Act 'advanced education' means education of the following description—

(a)  a course in preparation for a degree, a Diploma of Higher Education, a higher national diploma, a higher national diploma or higher national certificate of the Business and Technology Education Council or the Scottish Qualifications Council or a teaching qualification; or

(b)  any other course which is of a standard above that of an ordinary national diploma, a national diploma or a national certificate of the Business and Technology Education Council or the Scottish Qualifications Authority, the advanced level of the General Certificate of Education, a Scottish certificate of education (higher level), a Scottish certificate of sixth year studies, or a Scottish National Qualification at Higher Level.

*Circumstances in which education is to be treated as full-time education*

**3** For the purposes of section 55 of the Act education shall be treated as being full-time if it is received by a person attending a course of education at a recognised educational establishment and the time spent receiving instruction or tuition, undertaking supervised study, examination of practical work or taking part in any exercise, experiment or project for which provision is made in the curriculum of the course, exceeds 12 hours per week, so however that in calculating the time spent in pursuit of the course, no account shall be taken of time occupied by meal breaks or spent on unsupervised study, whether undertaken on or off the premises of the educational establishment.

*Interruption of full-time education*

**4**—(1) Subject to sub-paragraph (2), in determining whether a person falls within section 55(1)(b) of the Act no account shall be taken of a period (whether beginning before or after the person concerned attains age 16) of up to 6 months of any interruption to the extent to which it is accepted that the interruption is attributable to a cause which is reasonable in the particular circumstances of the case; and where the interruption or its continuance is attributable to the illness or disability of mind or body of the person concerned, the period of 6 months may be extended for such further period as the Secretary of State considers reasonable in the particular circumstances of the case.

(2) The provisions of sub-paragraph (1) shall not apply to any period of interruption of a person's full-time education which is likely to be followed immediately or which is followed immediately by a period during which—

    (a)  provision is made for the training of that person, and for an allowance to be payable to that person, under work-based training for young people or, in Scotland, Skillseekers training; or

    (b)  he is receiving education by virtue of his employment or of any office held by him.

*Circumstances in which a person who has ceased to receive full-time education is to be treated as continuing to fall within section 55(1) of the Act*

**5**—(1) Subject to sub-paragraphs (2) and (5), a person who has ceased to receive full-time education (which is not advanced education) shall, if—

    (a)  he is under the age of 16 when he so ceases, from the date on which he attains that age; or

    (b)  he is 16 or over when he so ceases, from the date on which he so ceases,

be treated as continuing to fall within section 55(1) of the Act up to and including the week including the terminal date, or if he attains the age of 19 on or before that date, up to and including the week including the last Monday before he attains that age.

(2) In the case of a person specified in sub-paragraph (1)(a) or (b) who had not attained the upper limit of compulsory school age when he ceased to receive full-time education, the terminal date shall be that specified in head (a), (b) or (c) of sub-paragraph (3), whichever next follows the date on which he would have attained that age.

(3) In this paragraph the 'terminal date' means—

    (a)  the first Monday in January; or

    (b)  the Monday following Easter Monday; or

    (c)  the first Monday in September,

whichever first occurs after the date on which the person's said education ceased.

(4) In this paragraph 'compulsory school age' means—

    (a)  in England and Wales, compulsory school age as determined in accordance with section 9 of the Education Act 1962;

    (b)  in Scotland, school age as determined in accordance with sections 31 and 33 of the Education (Scotland) Act 1980.

(5) A person shall not be treated as continuing to fall within section 55(1) of the Act under this paragraph if he is engaged in remunerative work, other than work of a temporary nature that is due to cease before the terminal date.

(6) Subject to sub-paragraphs (5) and (8), a person whose name was entered as

a candidate for any external examination in connection with full-time education (which is not advanced education), which he was receiving at the time, shall so long as his name continued to be so entered before ceasing to receive such education be treated as continuing to fall within section 55(1) of the Act for any week in the period specified in sub-paragraph (7).

(7) Subject to sub-paragraph (8), the period specified for the purposes of sub-paragraph (6) is the period beginning with the date when that person ceased to receive such education ending with—

(a) whichever of the dates in sub-paragraph (3) first occurs after the conclusion of the examination (or the last of them, if there is more than one); or

(b) the expiry of the week which includes the last Monday before his 19th birthday,

whichever is the earlier.

(8) The period specified in sub-paragraph (7) shall, in the case of a person who had not attained the age of 16 when he so ceased, begin with the date on which he did attain that age.

*Interpretation*

**6** In this Schedule—

'Education Acts 1944 to 1992' has the meaning prescribed in section 94(2) of the Further and Higher Education Act 1992;

'remunerative work' means work of not less than 24 hours a week—

(a) in respect of which payment is made; or

(b) which is done in expectation of payment;

'week' means a period of 7 days beginning with a Monday;

'work-based training for young people or, in Scotland, Skillseekers training' means—

(a) arrangements made under section 2 of the Employment and Training Act 1973 (functions of the Secretary of State) or section 2 of the Enterprise and New Towns (Scotland) Act 1990;

(b) arrangements made by the Secretary of State for the persons enlisted in Her Majesty's forces for any special term of service specified in regulations made under section 2 of the Armed Forces Act 1966 (power of Defence Council to make regulations as to engagement of persons in regular forces); or

(c) for the purposes of the application of Council Regulation (EEC) No 1408/71, any corresponding provisions operated in another member State,

for purposes which include the training of persons who, at the beginning of their training, are under the age of 18.

SCHEDULE 2                                                                Regulation 4(1)

MULTIPLE APPLICATIONS

*No maintenance calculation in force: more than one application for a maintenance calculation by the same person under section 4 or 6 or under sections 4 and 6 of the Act*

**1**—(1) Where an effective application is made or treated as made, as the case may be, for a maintenance calculation under section 4 or 6 of the Act and, before that calculation is made, the applicant makes a subsequent effective application under that section with respect to the same non-resident parent or person with care, as the case may be, those applications shall be treated as a single application.

(2) Where an effective application for a maintenance calculation is made, or treated as made, as the case may be, by a person with care—

(a)  under section 4 of the Act; or

(b)  under section 6 of the Act,

and, before that maintenance calculation is made, the person with care—

    (i)  in a case falling within head (a), is treated as making an application under section 6 of the Act; or

    (ii)  in a case falling within head (b), makes a subsequent effective application under section 4 of the Act,

with respect to the same non-resident parent, those applications shall, if the person with care does not cease to fall within section 6(1) of the Act, be treated as a single application under section 6 of the Act, and shall otherwise be treated as a single application under section 4 of the Act.

*No maintenance calculation in force: more than one application by a child under section 7 of the Act*

**2** Where a child makes an effective application for a maintenance calculation under section 7 of the Act and, before that calculation is made, makes a subsequent effective application under that section with respect to the same person with care and non-resident parent, both applications shall be treated as a single application for a maintenance calculation.

*No maintenance calculation in force: applications by different persons for a maintenance calculation*

**3**—(1)  Where the Secretary of State receives more than one effective application for a maintenance calculation with respect to the same person with care and non-resident parent, he shall, if no maintenance calculation has been made in relation to any of the applications, determine which application he shall proceed with in accordance with sub-paragraphs (2) to (11).

(2)  Where an application by a person with care is made under section 4 of the Act or is treated as made under section 6 of the Act, and an application is made by a non-resident parent under section 4 of the Act, the Secretary of State shall proceed with the application of the person with care.

(3)  Where there is an application for a maintenance calculation by a qualifying child under section 7 of the Act and a subsequent application is made with respect to that child by a person who is, with respect to that child, a person with care or a non-resident parent, the Secretary of State shall proceed with the application of that person with care or non-resident parent, as the case may be.

(4)  Where, in a case falling within sub-paragraph (3), there is made more than one subsequent application, the Secretary of State shall apply the provisions of sub-paragraphs (2), (7), (8), or (10), as is appropriate in the circumstances of the case, to determine which application he shall proceed with.

(5)  Where there is an application for a maintenance calculation by more than one qualifying child under section 7 of the Act in relation to the same person with care and non-resident parent, the Secretary of State shall proceed with the application of the elder or, as the case may be, eldest of the qualifying children.

(6)  Where there are two non-resident parents in respect of the same qualifying child and an effective application is received from each such person, the Secretary of State shall proceed with both applications, treating them as a single application for a maintenance calculation.

(7)  Where an application is treated as having been made by a parent with care under section 6 of the Act and there is an application under section 4 of the Act by another person with care who has parental responsibility for (or, in Scotland, parental rights over) the qualifying child or qualifying children with respect to whom the application under section 6 of the Act was treated as made, the Secretary of State shall proceed with the application under section 6 of the Act by the parent with care.

(8) Where—

(a) more than one person with care makes an application for a maintenance calculation under section 4 of the Act in respect of the same qualifying child or qualifying children (whether or not any of those applications is also in respect of other qualifying children);

(b) each such person has parental responsibility for (or, in Scotland, parental rights over) that child or children; and

(c) under the provisions of regulation 8 of the Maintenance Calculations and Special Cases Regulations one of those persons is to be treated as a non-resident parent,

the Secretary of State shall proceed with the application of the person who does not fall to be treated as a non-resident parent under the provisions of regulation 8 of those Regulations.

(9) Where, in a case falling within sub-paragraph (8), there is more than one person who does not fall to be treated as a non-resident parent under the provisions of regulation 8 of those Regulations, the Secretary of State shall apply the provisions of paragraph (10) to determine which application he shall proceed with.

(10) Where—

(a) more than one person with care makes an application for a maintenance calculation under section 4 of the Act in respect of the same qualifying child or qualifying children (whether or not any of those applications is also in respect of other qualifying children); and

(b) either—

    (i) none of those persons has parental responsibility for (or, in Scotland, parental rights over) that child or children; or

    (ii) the case falls within sub-paragraph (8)(b) but the Secretary of State has not been able to determine which application he is to proceed with under the provisions of sub-paragraph (8),

the Secretary of State shall proceed with the application of the principal provider of day to day care, as determined in accordance with sub-paragraph (11).

(11) Where—

(a) the applications are in respect of one qualifying child, the application of that person with care to whom child benefit is paid in respect of that child;

(b) the applications are in respect of more than one qualifying child, the application of that person with care to whom child benefit is paid in respect of those children;

(c) the Secretary of State cannot determine which application he is to proceed with under head (a) or (b) the application of that applicant who in the opinion of the Secretary of State is the principal provider of day to day care for the child or children in question.

(12) Subject to sub-paragraph (13), where, in any case falling within sub-paragraphs (2) to (10), the applications are not in respect of identical qualifying children, the application that the Secretary of State is to proceed with as determined by those sub-paragraphs shall be treated as an application with respect to all of the qualifying children with respect to whom the applications were made.

(13) Where the Secretary of State is satisfied that the same person with care does not provide the principal day to day care for all of the qualifying children with respect to whom an application would but for the provisions of this paragraph be made under sub-paragraph (12), he shall make separate maintenance calculations in relation to each person with care providing such principal day to day care.

(14) For the purposes of this paragraph 'day to day care' has the same meaning as in the Maintenance Calculations and Special Cases Regulations.

*Maintenance calculation in force: subsequent application with respect to the same persons*

**4** Where a maintenance calculation is in force and a subsequent application is made or treated as made, as the case may be, under the same section of the Act for a maintenance calculation with respect to the same person with care, non-resident parent, and qualifying child or qualifying children as those with respect to whom the maintenance calculation in force has been made, that application shall not be proceeded with.

[SCHEDULE 3]                                                         Regulation 31(1B)

MULTIPLE APPLICATIONS—TRANSITIONAL PROVISIONS

*No maintenance assessment or calculation in force: more than one application for*
*maintenance by the same person under section 4 or 6, or under sections 4 and 6, of the*
*former Act and of the Act.*

**1**—(1) Where an assessment application is made and, before a maintenance assessment under the former Act is made, the applicant makes or is treated as making, as the case may be, a calculation application under section 4 or 6 of the Act, with respect to the same person with care or with respect to a non-resident parent who is the absent parent with respect to the assessment application, as the case may be, those applications shall be treated as a single application.

   (2) Where an assessment application is made by a person with care—
   (a)   under section 4 of the former Act; or
   (b)   under section 6(1) of the former Act,
and, before a maintenance assessment under the former Act is made, the person with care—
      (i)    in a case falling within head (a), is treated as making a calculation application under section 6(1) of the Act; or
      (ii)   in a case falling within head (b), makes a calculation application under section 4 of the Act,
with respect to a non-resident parent who is the absent parent with respect to the assessment application, those applications shall, if the person with care does not cease to fall within section 6(1) of the Act, be treated as a single application under section 6(1) of the former Act or of the Act, as the case may be, and shall otherwise be treated as a single application under section 4 of the former Act or of the Act, as the case may be.

*No maintenance assessment or calculation in force: more than one application for*
*maintenance by a child under section 7 of the former Act and of the Act*

**2** Where a child makes an assessment application under section 7 of the former Act and, before a maintenance assessment under the former Act is made, makes a calculation application under section 7 of the Act with respect to the same person with care and a non-resident parent who is the absent parent with respect to the assessment application, both applications shall be treated as a single application.

*No maintenance assessment or calculation in force: applications by different persons for*
*maintenance*

**3**—(1) Where the Secretary of State receives more than one application for maintenance with respect to the same person with care and absent parent or non-resident parent, as the case may be, he shall, if no maintenance assessment under the former Act or maintenance calculation under the Act, as the case may be, has been made in relation to any of the applications, determine which application he shall proceed with in accordance with sub-paragraphs (2) to (11).

(2) Where an application by a person with care is made under section 4 of the former Act or of the Act, or is made under section 6 of the former Act, or is treated as made under section 6 of the Act, and an application is made by an absent parent or non-resident parent under section 4 of the former Act or of the Act, as the case may be, the Secretary of State shall proceed with the application of the person with care.

(3) Where there is an assessment application by a qualifying child under section 7 of the former Act and a calculation application is made with respect to that child by a person who is, with respect to that child, a person with care or a non-resident parent, the Secretary of State shall proceed with the application of that person with care or non-resident parent, as the case may be.

(4) Where, in a case falling within sub-paragraph (3), there is made more than one subsequent application, the Secretary of State shall apply the provisions of sub-paragraphs (2), (7), (8) or (10), as appropriate in the circumstances of the case, to determine which application he shall proceed with.

(5) Where there is an assessment application and a calculation application by more than one qualifying child under section 7 of the former Act or of the Act, in relation to the same person with care and absent parent or non-resident parent, as the case may be, the Secretary of State shall proceed with the application of the elder or, as the case may be, eldest of the qualifying children.

(6) Where there is one absent parent and one non-resident parent in respect of the same qualifying child and an assessment application and a calculation application is received from each such person respectively, the Secretary of State shall proceed with both applications, treating them as a single application.

(7) Where a parent with care is required to authorise the Secretary of State to recover child support maintenance under section 6 of the former Act and there is a calculation application under section 4 of the Act by another person with care who has parental responsibility for (or, in Scotland, parental rights over) the qualifying child or qualifying children with respect to whom the application was made under section 6 of the former Act, the Secretary of State shall proceed with the assessment application under section 6 of the former Act by the parent with care.

(8) Where—

(a) a person with care makes an assessment application under section 4 of the former Act and a different person with care makes a calculation application under section 4 of the Act and those applications are in respect of the same qualifying child or qualifying children (whether or not any of those applications is also in respect of other qualifying children);

(b) each such person has parental responsibility for (or, in Scotland, parental rights over) that child or children; and

(c) under regulation 20 of the Child Support (Maintenance Assessments and Special Cases) Regulations 1992 ('the Maintenance Assessments and Special Cases Regulations') one of those persons is to be treated as an absent parent or under the provisions of regulation 8 of the Maintenance Calculations and Special Cases Regulations one of those persons is to be treated as a non-resident parent, as the case may be,

the Secretary of State shall proceed with the application of the person who does not fall to be treated as an absent parent under regulation 20 of the Maintenance Assessments and Special Cases Regulations, or as a non-resident parent under regulation 8 of the Maintenance Calculations and Special Cases Regulations, as the case may be.

(9) Where, in a case falling within sub-paragraph (8), there is more than one person who does not fall to be treated as an absent parent under regulation 20 of

the Maintenance Assessments and Special Cases Regulations or as a non-resident parent under regulation 8 of the Maintenance Calculations and Special Cases Regulations, as the case may be, the Secretary of State shall apply the provisions of paragraph (10) to determine which application he shall proceed with.

(10) Where—

(a) a person with care makes an assessment application under section 4 of the former Act and a different person with care makes a calculation application under section 4 of the Act and those applications are in respect of the same qualifying child or qualifying children (whether or not any of those applications is also in respect of other qualifying children); and

(b) either—

    (i) none of those persons has parental responsibility for (or, in Scotland, parental rights over) that child or children; or

    (ii) the case falls within sub-paragraph (8)(b) but the Secretary of State has not been able to determine which application he is to proceed with under the provisions of sub-paragraph (8),

the Secretary of State shall proceed with the application of the principal provider of day to day care, as determined in accordance with sub-paragraph (11).

(11) For the purposes of sub-paragraph (10), the application of the principal provider is, where—

(a) the applications are in respect of one qualifying child, the application of that person with care to whom child benefit is paid in respect of that child;

(b) the applications are in respect of more than one qualifying child, the application of that person with care to whom child benefit is paid in respect of those children;

(c) the Secretary of State cannot determine which application he is to proceed with under head (a) or (b), the application of that applicant who in the opinion of the Secretary of State is the principal provider of day to day care for the child or children in question.

(12) Subject to sub-paragraph (13), where, in any case falling within sub-paragraphs (2) to (10), the applications are not in respect of identical qualifying children, the application that the Secretary of State is to proceed with as determined by those sub-paragraphs shall be treated as an application with respect to all of the qualifying children with respect to whom the applications were made.

(13) Where the Secretary of State is satisfied that the same person with care does not provide the principal day to day care for all of the qualifying children with respect to whom an application would but for the provisions of this paragraph be made under sub-paragraph (12), he shall make separate maintenance assessments under the former Act or maintenance calculations under the Act, as the case may be, in relation to each person with care providing such principal day to day care.

(14) For the purposes of this paragraph 'day to day care' has the same meaning as in the Maintenance Assessments and Special Cases Regulations or the Maintenance Calculations and Special Cases Regulations, as the case may be.

*Maintenance assessment in force: subsequent application with respect to the same persons*

**4** Where—

(a) a maintenance assessment is in force under the former Act;

(b) a calculation application is made or treated as made under the section of the Act which is the same section as the section of the former Act under which the assessment application was made; and

(c) the calculation application relates to—

    (i) the same person with care and qualifying child or qualifying children as the maintenance assessment; and

   (ii) a non-resident parent who is the absent parent with respect to the
     maintenance assessment,
the calculation application shall not be proceeded with.

*Interpretation*

**5** In this Schedule, 'absent parent', 'former Act' and 'maintenance assessment'
have the meanings given in regulation 31(8)(a).]
**Note.** Schedule 3 inserted by SI 2003 No 328 as from 21 February 2003.

## EUROPEAN COMMUNITIES (MATRIMONIAL JURISDICTION) REGULATIONS 2001

**Dated** February 2001

## SI 2001 No 310

These regulations amend s 5 and para 91) of Sch 1 to the Domicile and
Matrimonial Proceedings Act 1973, s 12 of the Child Abduction and Custody Act
1985 and ss 2(1), 5(2), 42(1), 45 and 54(1) of the Family Law Act 1986 with effect
from 1 March 2001.

## COMMUNITY LEGAL SERVICE (FUNDING) (COUNSEL IN FAMILY PROCEEDINGS) ORDER 2001

**Dated** 15 March 2001

## SI 2001 No 1077

PART I

GENERAL

**1 Citation and commencement** This Order may be cited as the Community
Legal Service (Funding) (Counsel in Family Proceedings) Order 2001 and shall
come into force on 1st May 2001.

**2 Interpretation** In this Order:
 'the Act' means the Access to Justice Act 1999;
 ['Advocates Meeting' means an Advocates Meeting held in accordance with
  paragraph 4.5 or 5.2 of the Children Act Protocol and the expression
  'Advocates Meeting' does not include communications between the
  advocates under paragraph 5.2 other than a meeting;]
 'assessment of costs' means the determination of all costs and disbursements
  due under the relevant certificate in relation to proceedings in which
  counsel has submitted a claim for payment under this Order;
 ['care proceedings' means proceedings under Part IV of the Children Act 1989;
 ['Case Management Conference' means a Case Management Conference held
  in accordance with step 4 of the Children Act Protocol;]
 'certificate' means a certificate issued under the Funding Code certifying a
  decision to fund services for the client;
 ['Children Act Protocol' means the Protocol annexed to the Practice Direction
  *(Care Cases: Judicial Continuity and Judicial Case Management)* made by the
  President of the Family Division;]

'client' means an individual who receives funded services from the Commission as part of the Community Legal Service under sections 4 to 11 of the Act;

'the Commission' means the Legal Services Commission established under section 1 of the Act;

'Cost Appeals Committee' means a committee appointed by the Commission for the purpose of considering appeals from the Costs Committee;

'Costs Committee' means a committee appointed by the Commission for the purpose of considering appeals in relation to costs, whether under this Order or generally;

'counsel' means a barrister in independent practice;

'family proceedings' means proceedings, other than proceedings for judicial review, which arise out of family relationships, including proceedings in which the welfare of children is determined, and including all proceedings under one or more of the following:

(a) the Matrimonial Causes Act 1973;

(b) *the Inheritance (Provision for Family and Dependants) Act 1975*;

(c) the Adoption Act 1976;

(d) the Domestic Proceedings and Magistrates' Courts Act 1978;

(e) Part III of the Matrimonial and Family Proceedings Act 1984;

(f) Parts I to V of the Children Act 1989;

(g) Part IV of the Family Law Act 1996; and

(h) the inherent jurisdiction of the High Court in relation to children;

[but excluding proceedings under either the Inheritance (Provision for Family and Dependants) Act 1975 or the Trusts of Land and Appointment of Trustees Act 1996;]

'function F1' means all work, other than conferences:

(a) which is carried out prior to the issue of proceedings; or

(b) which does not fall within functions F2 to F5;

'function F2' means all work carried out in connection with a hearing relating to injunctive relief or enforcement procedures, other than work which falls within function F5, including but not limited to preparation, advocacy, advising and drafting;

'function F3' means all work carried out in connection with a hearing [or, in care proceedings, an Advocates Meeting, Case Management Conference or Pre-Hearing Review], other than work which falls within function F2 or F5, including but not limited to preparation, advocacy, advising and drafting;

'function F4' means all work carried out in connection with a conference (including a telephone or video conference), other than any conference which takes place on the same day as a hearing for which payment is claimed under function F5, including but not limited to preparation and advice;

'function F5' means all work carried out in connection with the main hearing [and, in care proceedings, where the same counsel attends both the Pre-Hearing Review and the main hearing on behalf of a client, the Pre-Hearing Review] , including but not limited to preparation, advocacy, advising and drafting;

'Funding Code' means the code approved under section 9 of the Act;

'Funding Review Committee' means a committee appointed by the Commission for the purpose of considering appeals in relation to the discharge or revocation of a certificate, whether under this Order or generally;

'the main hearing' means the hearing at which the substantive issues are listed to be determined and are considered by the court;

['Pre-Hearing Review' means a Pre-Hearing Review held in accordance with step 5 of the Children Act Protocol;]

'the primary hearing unit' means the first day of the main hearing;

'Regional Director' means any Regional Director appointed by the Commission under the Funding Code and includes any person authorised to act on his behalf, other than a solicitor authorised by contract to determine applications on behalf of the Commission; and

'the secondary hearing unit' means any day of the main hearing other than the first.

**Note.** Words in italics and words in square brackets inserted by SI 2003 No 2590, art 3(a)-(f) as from 1 November 2003.

**3 Transitional provisions** This Order applies to all fees mentioned in article 4(2) payable to counsel under a certificate granted on or after 1st May 2001, and such fees payable under a certificate granted before that date shall be treated as if this Order had not been made.

**4 Scope—**(1) In respect of proceedings to which this Order applies, the Commission shall fund services as part of the Community Legal Service in accordance with the provisions of the following articles.

(2) Subject to article 3 and paragraphs (3) to (6), and to any limitations on the relevant certificate, this Order applies to counsel's fees in respect of all family proceedings in the High Court, county courts and magistrates' courts.

(3) This Order does not apply to proceedings where the length of the main hearing exceeds 10 days.

(4) This Order does not apply to appeals to:
   (a) the Divisional Court of the High Court;
   (b) the Court of Appeal; or
   (c) the House of Lords.

(5) Where the Commission issues a High Cost Case Contract under the Funding Code, this Order applies except to the extent that the terms of such contract provide otherwise.

(6) Nothing in this Order shall affect any determination of the amount of costs payable under an order or agreement which provides that another party to proceedings or prospective proceedings shall pay all or part of the costs of a client.

**5 Graduated fees—**(1) The amount of the graduated fee for counsel shall be the base fee or the hearing unit fee, as appropriate, in respect of the function for which the fee is claimed, which is specified in the Schedules to this Order as applicable to the category of proceedings and the counsel instructed, increased by any:
   (a) settlement supplement ('SS') or additional payment;
   (b) special issue payment ('SIP'); and
   (c) court bundle payment;
so specified.

(2) The total graduated fee, as set out in paragraph (1), shall be increased by 33% in respect of all work carried out while the proceedings are in the High Court.

**6 Mixed and multiple claims—**(1) Only one base fee may be claimed in respect of each of functions F1 and F4 in relation to any single set of proceedings.

(2) Where counsel carries out work relating to more than one category of proceedings within the same function in a single set of proceedings, he may claim the fee for one category only.

(3) Counsel shall specify the category of proceedings upon which the fee payable under this Order is to be based when he submits his claim for payment.

(4) For the purposes of this Order, applications to the court constitute a single set of proceedings irrespective of whether they are made separately or together, where they are:

(a) heard together or consecutively; and

(b) treated by the court as a single set of proceedings.

**7 Representation of more than one party** Subject to article 9(1)(c), where counsel represents more than one party in the same set of proceedings, payment shall be made as if counsel represented a single party.

PART II

RULES REGARDING FEES

**8 Hearing units—**(1) Where:

(a) preparatory work for a hearing is carried out but that hearing does not take place; or

[(aa)  in care proceedings, the advocates concerned are able to discuss all relevant matters without the need for an Advocates Meeting under paragraph 5.2 of the Children Act Protocol; or]

(b) preparatory work for the main hearing is carried out but counsel is prevented from representing his client because:

(i)  he has withdrawn from the proceedings with the permission of the court because of his professional code of conduct or to avoid embarrassment in the exercise of his profession; or

(ii)  he has been dismissed by his client

one half of the relevant hearing unit fee, without special issue payments or court bundle payments, shall be paid [and for the purposes of this paragraph 'hearing' shall, in care proceedings, include a Case Management Conference or a Pre-Hearing Review].

(2) For the purpose of functions F2 and F3:

(a) one hearing unit fee shall be paid for each period of two and a half hours or less for which the hearing continues;

(b) the hearing shall:

(i)  [subject to paragraph (2A),] commence at the time at which it is listed to begin or at the time at which counsel is specifically directed by the court to attend for that particular hearing, whichever is earlier;

(ii)  end when it concludes or at 5pm, whichever is earlier; and

(iii)  take no account of any luncheon adjournment; and

(c) where a hearing continues after 5pm and concludes on that same day, an additional one half of the hearing unit fee shall be paid in respect of the time on that day after 5pm.

[(2A) For the purpose of function F3, where, in care proceedings, an Advocates Meeting is held on the same day as a Case Management Conference or Pre-Hearing Review, a hearing unit fee shall be paid as if the Advocates Meeting and the Case Management Conference or (as the case may be) Pre-Hearing Review together formed a single hearing, beginning at the time when the Advocates Meeting began and ending when the Case Management Conference or (as the case may be) Pre-Hearing Review ended.]

(3) For the purpose of function F5:

(a) where the hearing takes place on one day, the primary hearing unit fee shall be paid for the period from the time at which the hearing begins until 5pm on that day;

(b) where the hearing takes place over more than one day, whether by reason of being adjourned, split or otherwise:

(i)  the hearing on the first day shall be paid at the primary hearing unit rate; and

(ii)  the hearing on any subsequent date shall be paid at the secondary hearing unit rate; and

(c) where a hearing continues after 5pm and ends on that same day, an additional one half of the appropriate hearing unit fee (whether primary or secondary) shall be paid in respect of the time on that day after 5pm;

[(d) where, in care proceedings, the same counsel attends both the Pre-Hearing Review and the main hearing on behalf of a client, a function F5 primary hearing unit fee shall be paid in respect of the Pre-Hearing Review and the main hearing shall be paid at the secondary hearing unit rate;

(e) where, in care proceedings, counsel makes written submissions as to orders consequential to the main hearing an additional secondary hearing unit fee shall be paid.]

**Note.** Words in square brackets inserted by SI 2003 No 2590, art 4(1)-(5) as from 1 November 2003.

**9 Special issue payments—**(1) A special issue may arise where the proceedings involve, or, with regard to sub-paragraphs (e) to (g), are alleged to involve:
(a) a litigant in person;
(b) more than two parties;
(c) representation of more than one child by counsel submitting a claim for payment under this Order;
(d) more than one expert;
(e) a relevant foreign element;
(f) relevant assets which are not or may not be under the exclusive control of any of the parties; or
(g) a party who has or may have been involved in the following:
　(i) conduct by virtue of which a child who is the subject of the proceedings has, may have or might suffer very significant harm; or
　(ii) intentional conduct which has, could have or might significantly reduce the assets available for distribution by the court.

(2) The judge hearing the case shall, at the conclusion of the relevant hearing, certify on a form provided for that purpose any special issues mentioned in paragraph (1)(a) to (c), and any mentioned in paragraph (1)(d) to (g) which were of substance and relevant to any of the issues before the court.

(3) The decision of the judge under paragraph (2) shall be final save on a point of law.

(4) Subject to paragraph (7):
(a) a special issue payment shall be made for each special issue certified in relation to functions F2, F3 and F5;
(b) such payment shall equate to the percentage of the single hearing unit fee applicable to the function in which the issue arises which is specified in Schedule 1 for that special issue.

(5) Subject to paragraph (8):
(a) counsel may, when he submits his claim for payment, claim a special issue payment in respect of any special issue which arises in relation to functions F1 and F4;
(b) such payment shall equate to the percentage of the single base fee applicable to the function in which the issue arises which is specified in Schedule 1 for that special issue.

(6) The Regional Director shall, in considering any claim made under paragraph (5), consider whether the work in question was reasonably carried out and, in respect of any special issues mentioned in paragraph (1)(d) to (g), whether the issue was of substance and relevant to any of the issues before the court.

(7) With regard to functions F2 and F3, where more than one hearing has taken place in a single set of proceedings, a special issue payment shall be made only in respect of one such hearing in relation to any special issue certified in

respect of that hearing, and counsel shall specify in respect of which hearing in each function it shall be made.

(8) With regard to function F4, where more than one conference has taken place counsel shall specify in respect of which single conference the special issue payment shall be made.

**10 Financial Dispute Resolution hearing payments** In respect of a set of proceedings which include proceedings for ancillary relief, an additional payment shall be paid at a rate of £150 in respect of Queen's Counsel, and £60 in respect of counsel other than Queen's Counsel, in respect of the Financial Dispute Resolution hearing in function F3.

**[10A** In respect of care proceedings, an additional payment shall be paid at a rate of £206.25 in respect of Queen's Counsel, and £82.50 in respect of counsel other than Queen's Counsel, in respect of the Case Management Conference in function F3.]

**Note.** Inserted by SI 2003 No 2590, art 5 as from 1 November 2003; for transitional provisions see art 2 thereof.

**11 Court bundle payments—**(1) A court bundle payment shall be made:
  (a) where the court bundle comprises between 176 and 350 pages;
  (b) where the court bundle comprises *between 351 and 700 pages* [comprises more than 350 pages]; and
  (c) [in addition to the payment under sub-paragraph (b)] as a special preparation fee in accordance with article 16 where the court bundle comprises more than 700 pages.

(2) Where there is no court bundle, equivalent provisions to those in paragraph (1) shall apply to counsel's brief.

**Note.** Para (1)(b)(c): words in italics and words in square brackets inserted by SI 2003 No 2590, art 6(1), (2) as from 1 November 2003; for transitional provisions see art 2 thereof.

**12 Early settlement payments—**(1) Subject to paragraphs (2) and (3), one settlement supplement shall be paid, as a percentage of the base fee or the hearing unit fee, as appropriate, applicable to the function in which the settlement takes place, where a settlement takes place which leads to the resolution of the set of proceedings.

(2) Subject to paragraph (3), no settlement supplement shall be paid in respect of a settlement which takes place in:
  (a) function F1;
  (b) function F4;
  (c) the primary hearing unit of function F5 where the proceedings have been listed for less than 2 days; or
  (d) the secondary hearing unit of function F5.

(3) In respect of a set of proceedings which include proceedings for ancillary relief, an additional payment shall be paid at a rate of £171.88 in respect of Queen's Counsel, and £68.75 in respect of counsel other than Queen's Counsel, where a settlement takes place in function F1 which leads to the resolution of the set of proceedings.

**13 Incidental items** An incidental item payment may be claimed, where it was reasonably and necessarily incurred, in respect of the following:
  (a) listening to or viewing evidence recorded on tape, disc or video cassette, once in respect of each item, at a rate of £10.90 per 10 minutes running time; and
  (b) *except where the court is within 40 kilometres from Charing Cross or where there is a*

*local Bar which the Commission considers to be sufficiently specialist in, or within 40 kilometres of, the court town:*
- (i)   time spent travelling, at an hourly rate of £13.60;
- (ii)  incurring travel expenses at a mileage rate of 45p per mile or at the rate of the cheapest second class fare reasonably available, as appropriate; and
- (iii) incurring hotel expenses at an overnight subsistence rate of £85.25 in respect of hotels situated within the London Region of the Commission and £55.25 elsewhere.

**Note.** Words in italics omitted by SI 2003 No 2590, art 7 as from 1 November 2003; for transitional provisions see art 2 thereof.

**14 Replacement counsel** Where one counsel replaces another during the course of a function, payment shall be made to the replacement counsel and shall be divided by agreement between them.

**15 Applications after the main hearing—**(1) Claims for payment in respect of work carried out after the main hearing shall be paid at the appropriate function rate.

(2) For the purposes of this Order, an appeal from a District Judge to a Circuit Judge or a High Court Judge, and all work relating thereto including but not limited to an advice on appeal, shall be treated as the commencement of a new set of proceedings.

**16 Special preparation fee—**(1) Where this article applies, counsel may claim a special preparation fee in addition to the graduated fee payable under this Order.

(2) This article applies where:
- (a) the proceedings to which the relevant certificate relates involve exceptionally complex issues of law or fact [, or was otherwise an exceptional case of its nature]; or
- (b) in public law children proceedings, in relation to work carried out within the secondary hearing unit of function F5, where the main hearing is split so that a period of at least four months elapses between its commencement and the time at which it resumes

such that it has been necessary for counsel to carry out work by way of preparation substantially in excess of the amount normally carried out for proceedings of the same type; or
- (c) the court bundle comprises more than 700 pages.

(3) The amount of the special preparation fee shall be calculated by multiplying the number of hours of preparation in excess of the amount normally carried out for proceedings of the same type, by an hourly rate of £100.50 in respect of Queen's Counsel, and £40.20 in respect of counsel other than Queen's Counsel.

(4) Where counsel claims a special preparation fee for work carried out within functions F1 and F4, or within functions F2, F3 and F5 where no hearing takes place, he shall, when submitting his claim for payment, supply such information and documents as may be required by the Regional Director as proof of the complexity of the relevant issues of law or fact and of the number of hours of preparation, and the Regional Director shall decide what special preparation fee, if any, shall be paid.

(5) Where counsel claims a special preparation fee for work carried out within functions F2, F3 and F5 he shall apply accordingly to the judge hearing the case at the relevant hearing, who shall decide what additional fee, if any, shall be paid, and whose decision shall be final save on a point of law.

**Note.** Para (2): words in square brackets inserted by SI 2003 No 2590, art 8 as from 1 November 2003; for transitional provisions see art 2.

**17 Claims for payment—**(1) Claims for payment in respect of work to which this Order applies shall be submitted to the Regional Director and shall contain full details of the claim and copies of all relevant documents.

(2) Counsel may submit a claim for payment:

(a) when the proceedings to which the certificate relates are concluded;

(b) when the certificate under which the work has been carried out is discharged or revoked and any review by the Commission or the Funding Review Committee has been completed;

(c) when he has completed all work in respect of which he has been instructed up to and including function F2 or F3, as appropriate;

(d) when he has completed all work in respect of which he has been instructed in function F5; and

(e) where he has received no instructions from the instructing solicitor for a period of 3 months.

(3) Only one claim for payment may be submitted under paragraph (2)(c) in respect of any one set of proceedings.

(4) Only one claim for payment may be submitted in respect of function F4 in respect of any one set of proceedings.

(5) Any claim for payment may include a claim in respect of all work carried out in the proceedings for which counsel has not previously submitted a claim.

(6) Counsel shall submit his claim for payment within 3 months of the discharge or revocation of the certificate to which it relates and, if he fails to do so, the Regional Director may reduce the amount payable under this Order; provided that the amount payable shall not be reduced unless counsel has been allowed a reasonable opportunity to show cause in writing why the amount should not be reduced.

(7) Any claim for payment shall include a claim in respect of all special issue payments, court bundle payments, settlement supplements and additional payments in respect of any functions for which the base fee or hearing unit fee, as appropriate, has been claimed and no later claim may be made in this respect.

(8) The Regional Director shall consider claims for payment under this Order and all relevant information and shall pay counsel such sums as are properly and reasonably due under this Order for work carried out within the scope of any relevant certificate or contract.

(9) No claims for payment on account of sums payable under this Order may be made.

**18 Appeals—**(1) If counsel is dissatisfied with any decision of the Regional Director with regard to the assessment of his fees under this Order, he may, within 21 days of the date of the assessment, (or such longer period as the Regional Director may allow) make written representations to the Costs Committee by way of an appeal.

(2) In any appeal under paragraph (1) the Costs Committee shall review the assessment and shall confirm, increase or decrease the amount assessed.

(3) If counsel is dissatisfied with the decision of the Costs Committee he may, within 21 days of the date of the reviewed assessment, apply to that Committee to certify a point of principle of general importance.

(4) Where the Costs Committee certifies a point of principle of general importance, counsel may, within 21 days of the date of the certification, appeal in writing to the Cost Appeals Committee against the reviewed assessment.

(5) If the Regional Director is dissatisfied with any reviewed assessment under paragraph (2), he may, within 21 days of the date of such reviewed assessment, certify a point of principle of general importance and appeal in writing to the Cost Appeals Committee.

(6) In any appeal under paragraph (5) the Regional Director shall serve notice

of the appeal on counsel who may, within 21 days of the date of such notice, make written representations to the Cost Appeals Committee.

(7) In any appeal under paragraph (4) or (5) the Cost Appeals Committee shall review the decision of the Costs Committee and shall confirm, increase or decrease the reviewed assessment.

**19 Review of payments—**(1) Subject to the provisions of this article and article 4, payments under this Order shall be final payments.

(2) Nothing in this Order shall affect any right of a client with a financial interest in an assessment of costs to make representations after the conclusion of the set of proceedings with regard to such payments.

(3) Representations under paragraph (2) above may include representations as to the use of counsel in proceedings and as to the sums payable to counsel under this Order.

(4) Where a contract entered into by the Commission in accordance with section 6(3)(a) of the Act includes rules for the assessment of costs in proceedings in which fees have been paid or are payable to counsel under this Order, and such costs are to be assessed by the court, the court shall carry out such assessment in accordance with those rules.

(5) Where in any assessment of costs it appears that payments made to counsel are in excess of the amount properly and reasonably due to counsel under this Order or any relevant certificate, counsel's fees shall be reduced accordingly.

(6) Where in any assessment of costs payment to counsel under this Order alone would exceed any limit set by the Commission on the total costs payable under the relevant certificate or contract, counsel's fees shall be reduced accordingly.

(7) Counsel shall be informed of any reduction in his fees under this article and shall have the same rights to make representations with regard to any such reduction as would a solicitor, in accordance with the relevant rules of court, contract and regulations, as applicable.

(8) Where payment has been made under this Order which is in excess of the amount properly and reasonably due to counsel, the Commission may recover the excess payment either by way of repayment by counsel or by way of deduction from any other sum which may be due to him.

SCHEDULE 1

TABLES OF FEES

**1** In respect of the proceedings mentioned in paragraph 1 of Schedule 2, the amount of the graduated fee shall be as follows:

(a)  in respect of Queen's Counsel:

| | Base fee | Hearing unit fee | SS | $CBP_1$ | $CBP_2$ |
|---|---|---|---|---|---|
| F1 | £150 | — | — | £40 | £79 |
| F2 | — | £287.50 | 100% | £47 | £94 |
| F4 | £125 | — | — | £33 | £67 |
| F5 primary | — | £800 | 10% | £221 | £442 |
| F5 secondary | — | £550 | — | £135 | £271 |
| Special Issue Payments | | | | | |
| Litigant in person | 5% | | | | |
| More than two parties | 5% | | | | |
| More than one child | 5% | | | | |

| | Base fee | Hearing unit fee | SS | $CBP_1$ | $CBP_2$ |
|---|---|---|---|---|---|
| More than one expert | 10% | | | | |
| Foreign | 0% | | | | |
| Assets | 0% | | | | |
| Conduct | 0% | | | | |

[1] where the court bundle comprises between 176 and 350 pages
[2] *where the court bundle comprises between 351 and 700 pages* [where the court bundle comprises more than 350 pages]

(b)  in respect of counsel other than Queen's Counsel:

| | Base fee | Hearing unit fee | SS | $CBP_1$ | $CBP_2$ |
|---|---|---|---|---|---|
| F1 | £60 | — | — | £16 | £32 |
| F2 | — | £115 | 100% | £19 | £37.50 |
| F4 | £50 | — | — | £13 | £27 |
| F5 primary | — | £320 | 10% | £88 | £177 |
| F5 secondary | — | £220 | — | £54 | £108 |
| Special Issue Payments | | | | | |
| Litigant in person | 5% | | | | |
| More than two parties | 5% | | | | |
| More than one child | 5% | | | | |
| More than one expert | 10% | | | | |
| Foreign | 0% | | | | |
| Assets | 0% | | | | |
| Conduct | 0% | | | | |

[1] where the court bundle comprises between 176 and 350 pages
[2] *where the court bundle comprises between 351 and 700 pages* [where the court bundle comprises more than 350 pages]

**2**  In respect of proceedings mentioned in paragraph 2 of Schedule 2, the amount of the graduated fee shall be as follows:
(a)  in respect of Queen's Counsel:

| | Base fee | Hearing unit fee | SS | $CBP_1$ | $CBP_2$ |
|---|---|---|---|---|---|
| F1 | £175 | — | — | £40 | £79 |
| F2 | — | £212.50 | 100% | £47 | £94 |
| F3 | — | £412.50 | 100% | £82 | £165 |
| F4 | £150 | — | — | £33 | £67 |
| F5 primary | — | £1,075 | 20% | £221 | £442 |
| F5 secondary | — | £575 | — | £135 | £271 |
| Special Issue Payments | | | | | |
| Litigant in person | 40% | | | | |
| More than two parties | 40% | | | | |
| More than one child | 5% | | | | |
| More than one expert | 20% | | | | |
| Foreign | 30% | | | | |
| Assets | 0% | | | | |
| Conduct | 50% | | | | |

[1] where the court bundle comprises between 176 and 350 pages
[2] *where the court bundle comprises between 351 and 700 pages* [where the court bundle comprises more than 350 pages]

(b)  in respect of counsel other than Queen's Counsel:

|  | Base fee | Hearing unit fee | SS | CBP$_1$ | CBP$_2$ |
|---|---|---|---|---|---|
| F1 | £70 | — | — | £16 | £32 |
| F2 | — | £85 | 100% | £19 | £37.50 |
| F3 | — | £165 | 100% | £33 | £66 |
| F4 | £60 | — | — | £13 | £27 |
| F5 primary | — | £430 | 20% | £88 | £177 |
| F5 secondary | — | £230 | — | £54 | £108 |
| Special Issue Payments |  |  |  |  |  |
| Litigant in person |  | 40% |  |  |  |
| More than two parties |  | 40% |  |  |  |
| More than one child |  | 5% |  |  |  |
| More than one expert |  | 20% |  |  |  |
| Foreign |  | 30% |  |  |  |
| Assets |  | 0% |  |  |  |
| Conduct |  | 50% |  |  |  |

[1] where the court bundle comprises between 176 and 350 pages
[2] *where the court bundle comprises between 351 and 700 pages* [where the court bundle comprises more than 350 pages]

**3** In respect of proceedings mentioned in paragraph 3 of Schedule 2, the amount of the graduated fee shall be as follows:
  (a)  in respect of Queen's Counsel:

|  | Base fee | Hearing unit fee | SS | CBP$_1$ | CBP$_2$ |
|---|---|---|---|---|---|
| F1 | £150 | — | — | £40 | £79 |
| F2 | — | £187.50 | 100% | £47 | £94 |
| F3 | — | £300 | 100% | £82 | £165 |
| F4 | £125 | — | — | £33 | £67 |
| F5 primary | — | £812.50 | 10% | £221 | £442 |
| F5 secondary | — | £550 | — | £135 | £271 |
| Special Issue Payments |  |  |  |  |  |
| Litigant in person |  | 30% |  |  |  |
| More than two parties |  | 30% |  |  |  |
| More than one child |  | 5% |  |  |  |
| More than one expert |  | 50% |  |  |  |
| Foreign |  | 30% |  |  |  |
| Assets |  | 0% |  |  |  |
| Conduct |  | 50% |  |  |  |

[1] where the court bundle comprises between 176 and 350 pages
[2] *where the court bundle comprises between 351 and 700 pages* [where the court bundle comprises more than 350 pages]

(b)  in respect of counsel other than Queen's Counsel:

| | Base fee | Hearing unit fee | SS | CBP$_1$ | CBP$_2$ |
|---|---|---|---|---|---|
| F1 | £60 | — | — | £16 | £32 |
| F2 | — | £75 | 100% | £19 | £37.50 |
| F3 | — | £120 | 100% | £33 | £66 |
| F4 | £50 | — | — | £13 | £27 |
| F5 primary | — | £325 | 10% | £88 | £177 |
| F5 secondary | — | £220 | — | £54 | £108 |
| Special Issue Payments | | | | | |
| Litigant in person | | 30% | | | |
| More than two parties | | 30% | | | |
| More than one child | | 5% | | | |
| More than one expert | | 50% | | | |
| Foreign | | 30% | | | |
| Assets | | 0% | | | |
| Conduct | | 50% | | | |

[1] where the court bundle comprises between 176 and 350 pages
[2] *where the court bundle comprises between 351 and 700 pages* [where the court bundle comprises more than 350 pages]

**4** In respect of proceedings mentioned in paragraph 4 of Schedule 2, the amount of the graduated fee shall be as follows:
  (a)  in respect of Queen's Counsel:

| | Base fee | Hearing unit fee | SS | CBP$_1$ | CBP$_2$ |
|---|---|---|---|---|---|
| F1 | £150 | — | —* | £40 | £79 |
| F2 | — | £162.50 | 50% | £47 | £94 |
| F3 | — | £300 | 50% | £82 | £165 |
| F4 | £125 | — | — | £33 | £67 |
| F5 primary | — | £812.50 | 10% | £221 | £442 |
| F5 secondary | — | £550 | — | £135 | £271 |
| Special Issue Payments | | | | | |
| Litigant in person | | 10% | | | |
| More than two parties | | 10% | | | |
| More than one child | | 5% | | | |
| More than one expert | | 10% | | | |
| Foreign | | 25% | | | |
| Assets | | 50% | | | |
| Conduct | | 50% | | | |

* see article 12(3)
[1] where the court bundle comprises between 176 and 350 pages
[2] *where the court bundle comprises between 351 and 700 pages* [where the court bundle comprises more than 350 pages]

(b)  in respect of counsel other than Queen's Counsel:

|  | Base fee | Hearing unit fee | SS | CBP$_1$ | CBP$_2$ |
|---|---|---|---|---|---|
| F1 | £60 | — | —* | £16 | £32 |
| F2 | — | £65 | 50% | £19 | £37.50 |
| F3 | — | £120 | 50% | £33 | £66 |
| F4 | £50 | — | — | £13 | £27 |
| F5 primary | — | £325 | 10% | £88 | £177 |
| F5 secondary | — | £220 | — | £54 | £108 |
| Special Issue Payments |  |  |  |  |  |
| Litigant in person | 10% |  |  |  |  |
| More than two parties | 10% |  |  |  |  |
| More than one child | 5% |  |  |  |  |
| More than one expert | 10% |  |  |  |  |
| Foreign | 25% |  |  |  |  |
| Assets | 50% |  |  |  |  |
| Conduct | 50% |  |  |  |  |

* see article 12(3)

[1] where the court bundle comprises between 176 and 350 pages

[2] *where the court bundle comprises between 351 and 700 pages* [where the court bundle comprises more than 350 pages]

**Note.** Words in italics omitted and words in square brackets inserted by SI 2003 No 2590, art 9 as from 1 November 2003; for transitional provisions see art 2.

## SCHEDULE 2

## CATEGORIES OF PROCEEDINGS

**1** Category of proceedings: family injunctions.

Family proceedings (other than those for ancillary relief) for an injunction, committal order, or other order for the protection of a person (other than proceedings for the protection of children within paragraph 2).

**2** Category of proceedings: public law children.

Family proceedings under Parts III, IV or V of the Children Act 1989, adoption proceedings (including applications to free for adoption) [, proceedings under the Child Abduction and Custody Act 1985], and other family proceedings within the inherent jurisdiction of the High Court concerning the welfare of children (other than proceedings for ancillary relief).

**3** Category of proceedings: private law children.

Family proceedings between individuals concerning the welfare of children (other than those for ancillary relief or within paragraph 2).

**4** Category of proceedings: ancillary relief and all other family proceedings.

All other family proceedings not within paragraphs 1 to 3.

**Note.** Para (2): words in square brackets inserted by SI 2003 No 2590, art 10 with effect from 1 November 2003; for transitional provisions see art 2.

## LITIGANTS IN PERSON (COSTS AND EXPENSES) (MAGISTRATES' COURTS) ORDER 2001

**Dated**  15 October 2001

**SI 2001 No 3438**

**1 Citation, commencement and interpretation—**(1) This Order may be cited as the Litigants in Person (Costs and Expenses) (Magistrates' Courts) Order 2001 and shall come into force on 15th November 2001.

(2) In this Order any reference to a section by number alone refers to the section so numbered in the Litigants in Person (Costs and Expenses) Act 1975.

**2 Specification of magistrates' courts**  For the purposes of section 1(1) there are specified all magistrates' courts in England and Wales, and accordingly that subsection applies to civil proceedings in or before those courts.

**3 Rules of court**  In section 1 'rules of court', in relation to magistrates' courts in England and Wales, shall mean rules made under section 144 of the Magistrates' Courts Act 1980.

## RECIPROCAL ENFORCEMENT OF MAINTENANCE ORDERS (DESIGNATION OF RECIPROCATING COUNTRIES) ORDER 2001

**Dated**  31 October 2001

**SI 2001 No 3501**

**1** This Order may be cited as the Reciprocal Enforcement of Maintenance Orders (Designation of Reciprocating Countries) Order 2001 and shall come into force on 10th December 2001.

**2** The territory specified in column (1) of the Schedule to this Order is hereby designated as a reciprocating country for the purposes of Part I of the Act as regards maintenance orders of the description specified in respect of that territory on column (2) of the Schedule to this Order.

SCHEDULE

TERRITORY DESIGNATED AS A RECIPROCATING COUNTRY AND EXTENT OF DESIGNATION

| (1) Territory | (2) Description of maintenance orders to which designation extends |
| --- | --- |
| Nunavut | Maintenance orders other than— <br> (a) affiliation orders; <br> (b) maintenance orders of the description contained in paragraph (b) of the definition of 'maintenance order' in section 21(1) of the Act; and <br> (c) orders obtained by or in favour of a public authority. |

**CIVIL JURISDICTION AND JUDGMENTS (AUTHENTIC INSTRUMENTS AND COURT SETTLEMENTS) ORDER 2001**

**SI 2001 No 3928**

**Dated** 11 December 2001

**1**—(1) This Order may be cited as the Civil Jurisdiction and Judgments (Authentic Instruments and Court Settlements) Order 2001 and shall come into force on 1st March 2002.

(2) In this Order—

'the Act' means the Civil Jurisdiction and Judgments Act 1982;

'the Regulation' means Council Regulation (EC) No 44/2001 of 22nd December 2000 on jurisdiction and the recognition and enforcement of judgments in civil and commercial matters;

'Regulation State' in any provision, in the application of that provision in relation to the Regulation, has the same meaning as 'Member State' in the Regulation, that is all Member States except Denmark;

'the 2001 Order' means the Civil Jurisdiction and Judgments Order 2001.

(3) In this Order—

(a) references to authentic instruments and court settlements are references to those instruments and settlements referred to in Chapter IV of the Regulation; and

(b) references to judgments and maintenance orders are references to judgments and maintenance orders to which the Regulation applies.

**2**—(1) Subject to the modifications specified in paragraphs (2) and (3), paragraphs 1 to 6 of Schedule 1 to the 2001 Order shall apply, as appropriate, to authentic instruments and court settlements which—

(a) do not concern maintenance as if they were judgments,

(b) concern maintenance as if they were maintenance orders.

(2) In the application of paragraph 2(2) of Schedule 1 to the 2001 Order to authentic instruments and court settlements, for the words 'as if the judgment had been originally given' there shall be substituted 'as if it was a judgment which had been originally given'.

(3) In the application of paragraph 3(3) of Schedule 1 to the 2001 Order to authentic instruments and court settlements, for the words 'as if the order had been originally made' there shall be substituted the words 'as if it was an order which had been originally made'.

(4) Paragraph 8 of Schedule 1 to the 2001 Order shall apply to authentic instruments as if they were judgments and in its application—

(a) for sub-paragraph (1)(b) there shall be substituted the following—

'(b) a certificate obtained in accordance with Article 57 and Annex VI shall be evidence, and in Scotland sufficient evidence, that the authentic instrument is enforceable in the Regulation State of origin.'; and

(b) for sub-paragraph (2) there shall be substituted the following—

'(2) A document purporting to be a copy of an authentic instrument drawn up or registered, and enforceable, in a Regulation State other than the United Kingdom is duly authenticated for the purposes of this paragraph if it purports to be certified to be a true copy of such an instrument by a person duly authorised in that Regulation State to do so.'.

(5) Paragraph 8 of Schedule 1 to the 2001 Order shall apply to court settlements as if they were judgments and in its application for 'Article 54' there shall be substituted 'Article 58'.

**3** The disapplication of section 18 of the Act (enforcement of United Kingdom judgments in other parts of the United Kingdom) by section 18(7) will extend to authentic instruments and court settlements enforceable in a Regulation State outside the United Kingdom which will fall to be treated for the purposes of their enforcement as judgments of a court of law in the United Kingdom by virtue of registration under the Regulation.

**4** Section 48 of the Act (matters for which rules of court may provide) will apply to authentic instruments and court settlements as if they were judgments or maintenance orders, as appropriate, to which the Regulation applies.

## CIVIL JURISDICTION AND JUDGMENTS ORDER 2001

### SI 2001 No 3929

**Dated** 11 December 2001

**1 Citation and commencement** This Order may be cited as the Civil Jurisdiction and Judgments Order 2001 and shall come into force—
(a) as to articles 1 and 2, paragraphs 1(a), 1(b)(ii) and 17 of Schedule 2 and, so far as it relates to those paragraphs, article 4, on 25th January 2002; and
(b) as to the remainder of this Order, on 1st March 2002.

**2 Interpretation**—(1) In this Order—
'the Act' means the Civil Jurisdiction and Judgments Act 1982;
'the Regulation' means Council Regulation (EC) No 44/2001 of 22nd December 2000 on jurisdiction and the recognition and enforcement of judgments in civil and commercial matters;
'Regulation State' in any provision, in the application of that provision in relation to the Regulation, has the same meaning as 'Member State' in the Regulation, that is all Member States except Denmark.
(2) In Schedule 2 to this Order, a section, Part, Schedule or paragraph referred to by number alone is a reference to the section, Part, Schedule or paragraph so numbered in the Act.

**3 The Regulation** Schedule 1 to this Order (which applies certain provisions of the Act with modifications for the purposes of the Regulation) shall have effect.

**4 Amendments to the Civil Jurisdiction and Judgments Act 1982** Schedule 2 to this Order (which makes amendments to the Act) shall have effect.

**5 Consequential amendments** Schedule 3 to this Order (which makes consequential amendments) shall have effect.

**6 Transitional provisions**—(1) Where proceedings are begun before 1st March 2002 in any part of the United Kingdom on the basis of jurisdiction determined in accordance with section 16 of, and Schedule 4 to, the Act, the proceedings may be continued as if the amendments made by paragraphs 3 and 4 of Schedule 2 to this Order had not been made and those amendments shall not apply in respect of any proceedings begun before that date.
(2) Where proceedings are begun before 1st March 2002 in any court in Scotland on the basis of jurisdiction determined in accordance with section 20 of, and Schedule 8 to, the Act, the proceedings may be continued as if the

amendments made by paragraphs 6 and 7 of Schedule 2 to this Order had not been made and those amendments shall not apply in respect of any proceedings begun before that date.

SCHEDULE 1                                                             Article 3

THE REGULATION

*Interpretation*

**1**—(1) In this Schedule—
    'court', without more, includes a tribunal;
    'judgment' has the meaning given by Article 32 of the Regulation;
    'magistrates' court', in relation to Northern Ireland, means a court of summary
        jurisdiction;
    'maintenance order' means a maintenance judgment within the meaning of the
        Regulation;
    'part of the United Kingdom' means England and Wales, Scotland or Northern
        Ireland;
    'payer', in relation to a maintenance order, means the person liable to make the
        payments for which the order provides;
    'prescribed' means prescribed by rules of court.
    (2) In this Schedule, any reference to a numbered Article or Annex is a reference to the Article or Annex so numbered in the Regulation, and any reference to a sub-division of a numbered Article shall be construed accordingly.
    (3) References in paragraphs 2 to 8 to a judgment registered under the Regulation include, to the extent of its registration, references to a judgment so registered to a limited extent only.
    (4) Anything authorised or required by the Regulation or paragraphs 2 to 8 to be done by, to or before a particular magistrates' court may be done by, to or before any magistrates' court acting for the same petty sessions area (or, in Northern Ireland, petty sessions district) as that court.

*Enforcement of judgments other than maintenance orders (section 4)*

**2**—(1) Where a judgment is registered under the Regulation, the reasonable costs or expenses of and incidental to its registration shall be recoverable as if they were sums recoverable under the judgment.
    (2) A judgment registered under the Regulation shall, for the purposes of its enforcement, be of the same force and effect, the registering court shall have in relation to its enforcement the same powers, and proceedings for or with respect to its enforcement may be taken, as if the judgment had been originally given by the registering court and had (where relevant) been entered.
    (3) Sub-paragraph (2) is subject to Article 47 (restriction on enforcement where appeal pending or time for appeal unexpired), to paragraph 5 and to any provision made by rules of court as to the manner in which and conditions subject to which a judgment registered under the Regulation may be enforced.

*Recognition and enforcement of maintenance orders (section 5)*

**3**—(1) The Secretary of State's function (under Article 39 and Annex II) of transmitting an application for the recognition or enforcement in the United Kingdom of a maintenance order (made under Article 38) to a magistrates' court shall be discharged—
    (a) as respects England and Wales and Northern Ireland, by the Lord
        Chancellor;

(b) as respects Scotland, by the Scottish Ministers.

(2) Such an application shall be determined in the first instance by the prescribed officer of the court having jurisdiction in the matter.

(3) A maintenance order registered under the Regulation shall, for the purposes of its enforcement, be of the same force and effect, the registering court shall have in relation to its enforcement the same powers, and proceedings for or with respect to its enforcement may be taken, as if the order had been originally made by the registering court.

(4) Sub-paragraph (3) is subject to Article 47 (restriction on enforcement where appeal pending or time for appeal unexpired), to paragraph 5 and to any provision made by rules of court as to the manner in which and conditions subject to which an order registered under the Regulation may be enforced.

(5) A maintenance order which by virtue of the Regulation is enforceable by a magistrates' court in England and Wales shall, subject to the modifications of sections 76 and 93 of the Magistrates' Courts Act 1980 specified in sections 5(5B) and 5(5C) of the Act, be enforceable in the same manner as a magistrates' court maintenance order made by that court.

In this sub-paragraph 'magistrates' court maintenance order' has the same meaning as in section 150(1) of the Magistrates' Courts Act 1980.

(6) A maintenance order which by virtue of the Regulation is enforceable by a magistrates' court in Northern Ireland shall, subject to the modifications of Article 98 of the Magistrates' Courts (Northern Ireland) Order 1981 specified in section 5(6A) of the Act, be enforceable as an order made by that court to which that Article applies.

(7) The payer under a maintenance order registered under the Regulation in a magistrates' court in England and Wales or Northern Ireland shall give notice of any changes of address to the proper officer of that court.

A person who without reasonable excuse fails to comply with this sub-paragraph shall be guilty of an offence and liable on summary conviction to a fine not exceeding level 2 on the standard scale.

(8) In sub-paragraph (7) 'proper officer' means—

(a) in relation to a magistrates' court in England and Wales, the justices' chief executive for the court; and

(b) in relation to a magistrates' court in Northern Ireland, the clerk of the court.

*Appeals under Article 44 and Annex IV (section 6)*

**4**—(1) The single further appeal on a point of law referred to under Article 44 and Annex IV in relation to the recognition or enforcement of a judgment other than a maintenance order lies—

(a) in England and Wales or Northern Ireland, to the Court of Appeal or to the House of Lords in accordance with Part II of the Administration of Justice Act 1969 (appeals direct from the High Court to the House of Lords);

(b) in Scotland, to the Inner House of the Court of Session.

(2) Paragraph (a) of sub-paragraph (1) has effect notwithstanding section 15(2) of the Administration of Justice Act 1969 (exclusion of direct appeal to the House of Lords in cases where no appeal to that House lies from a decision of the Court of Appeal).

(3) The single further appeal on a point of law referred to in Article 44 and Annex IV in relation to the recognition or enforcement of a maintenance order lies—

(a) in England and Wales, to the High Court by way of case stated in accordance with section 111 of the Magistrates' Courts Act 1980;

(b) in Scotland, to the Inner House of the Court of Session;

(c) in Northern Ireland, to the Court of Appeal.

*Interest on registered judgments (section 7)*

**5**—(1) Subject to sub-paragraph (3), where in connection with an application for registration of a judgment under the Regulation the applicant shows—

(a) that the judgment provides for the payment of a sum of money; and

(b) that in accordance with the law of the Regulation State in which the judgment was given interest on that sum is recoverable under the judgment from a particular date or time,

the rate of interest and the date or time from which it is so recoverable shall be registered with the judgment and, subject to rules of court, the debt resulting, apart from paragraph 2(1), from the registration of the judgment shall carry interest in accordance with the registered particulars.

(2) Costs or expenses recoverable by virtue of paragraph 2(1) shall carry interest as if they were the subject of an order for the payment of costs or expenses made by the registering court on the date of registration.

(3) Interest on arrears of sums payable under a maintenance order registered under the Regulation in a magistrates' court in England and Wales or Northern Ireland shall not be recoverable in that court, but without prejudice to the operation in relation to any such order of section 2A of the Maintenance Orders Act 1958 or section 11A of the Maintenance and Affiliation Orders Act (Northern Ireland) 1966 (which enable interest to be recovered if the order is re-registered for enforcement in the High Court).

(4) Except as mentioned in sub-paragraph (3), debts under judgments registered under the Regulation shall carry interest only as provided by this paragraph.

*Currency of payment under registered maintenance orders (section 8)*

**6**—(1) Sums payable in the United Kingdom under a maintenance order by virtue of its registration under the Regulation, including any arrears so payable, shall be paid in the currency of the United Kingdom.

(2) Where the order is expressed in any other currency, the amounts shall be converted on the basis of the exchange rate prevailing on the date of registration of the order.

(3) For the purposes of this paragraph, a written certificate purporting to be signed by an officer of any bank in the United Kingdom and stating the exchange rate prevailing on a specified date shall be evidence, and in Scotland sufficient evidence, of the facts stated.

**7 [*Not reproduced*]**

*Proof and admissibility of certain judgments and related documents (section 11)*

**8**—(1) For the purposes of the Regulation—

(a) a document, duly authenticated, which purports to be a copy of a judgment given by a court of a Regulation State other than the United Kingdom shall without further proof be deemed to be a true copy, unless the contrary is shown; and

(b) a certificate obtained in accordance with Article 54 and Annex V shall be evidence, and in Scotland sufficient evidence, that the judgment is enforceable in the Regulation State of origin.

(2) A document purporting to be a copy of a judgment given by any such court as is mentioned in sub-paragraph (1)(a) is duly authenticated for the purposes of this paragraph if it purports—

(a) to bear the seal of that court; or

(b) to be certified by any person in his capacity as a judge or officer of that court to be a true copy of a judgment given by that court.

(3) Nothing in this paragraph shall prejudice the admission in evidence of any document which is admissible apart from this paragraph.

*Domicile of individuals (section 41)*

**9**—(1) Subject to Article 59 (which contains provisions for determining whether a party is domiciled in a Regulation State), the following provisions of this paragraph determine, for the purposes of the Regulation, whether an individual is domiciled in the United Kingdom or in a particular part of, or place in, the United Kingdom or in a state other than a Regulation State.

(2) An individual is domiciled in the United Kingdom if and only if—

(a) he is resident in the United Kingdom; and

(b) the nature and circumstances of his residence indicate that he has a substantial connection with the United Kingdom.

(3) Subject to sub-paragraph (5), an individual is domiciled in a particular part of the United Kingdom if and only if—

(a) he is resident in that part; and

(b) the nature and circumstances of his residence indicate that he has a substantial connection with that part.

(4) An individual is domiciled in a particular place in the United Kingdom if and only if he—

(a) is domiciled in the part of the United Kingdom in which that place is situated; and

(b) is resident in that place.

(5) An individual who is domiciled in the United Kingdom but in whose case the requirements of sub-paragraph (3)(b) are not satisfied in relation to any particular part of the United Kingdom shall be treated as domiciled in the part of the United Kingdom in which he is resident.

(6) In the case of an individual who—

(a) is resident in the United Kingdom, or in a particular part of the United Kingdom; and

(b) has been so resident for the last three months or more,

the requirements of sub-paragraph (2)(b) or, as the case may be, sub-paragraph (3)(b) shall be presumed to be fulfilled unless the contrary is proved.

(7) An individual is domiciled in a state other than a Regulation State if and only if—

(a) he is resident in that state; and

(b) the nature and circumstances of his residence indicate that he has a substantial connection with that state.

**10 and 11 [not reproduced]**

*Domicile of trusts (section 45)*

**12**—(1) The following provisions of this paragraph determine for the purposes of the Regulation where a trust is domiciled.

(2) A trust is domiciled in the United Kingdom if and only if it is by virtue of sub-paragraph (3) domiciled in a part of the United Kingdom.

(3) A trust is domiciled in a part of the United Kingdom if and only if the system of law of that part is the system of law with which the trust has its closest and most real connection.

SCHEDULE 2                                                           Article 4

AMENDMENTS TO THE CIVIL JURISDICTION AND JUDGMENTS ACT 1982

PART I—
IMPLEMENTATION OF THE CONVENTIONS

\*     \*     \*     \*     \*

**FOSTERING SERVICES REGULATIONS 2002**

**Dated** 14 January 2002

**SI 2002 No 57**

PART I

GENERAL

**1 Citation, commencement and extent—**(1) These Regulations may be cited as
the Fostering Services Regulations 2002 and shall come into force on 1st April
2002.

(2) These Regulations extend to England only.

**Note.** The Fostering Services (Wales) Regulations 2003 (SI 2003 No 237) came into force on
1 April 2003. Generally the regulations are the same as the 'English' regulations printed
below with minor variations particular to Wales.

**2 Interpretation—**(1) In these Regulations, unless the context otherwise
requires—

'the 1989 Act' means the Children Act 1989;

'the 2000 Act' means the Care Standards Act 2000;

'approval' means approval as a foster parent in accordance with regulation 28
    and references to a person being approved shall be construed accordingly;

'area authority' means the local authority in whose area a child is placed, in any
    case where that local authority is not the child's responsible authority;

'assessment' shall be construed in accordance with regulation 27(1);

'child protection enquiries' has the meaning given to it by regulation 12(4);

'children's guide' means the written guide produced in accordance with
    regulation 3(3);

['Commission' means the Commission for Social Care Inspection;]

'foster care agreement' has the meaning given to it by regulation 28(5)(b);

'foster placement agreement' has the meaning given to it by regulation 34(3);

['foster parent' means a person with whom a child is placed, or may be placed
    under these Regulations, except that, in Parts IV and V of these Regulations
    it does not include a person with whom a child is placed under regulation
    38(2);]

'fostering panel' means a panel established in accordance with regulation 24;

'fostering service' means—

    (a) a fostering agency within the meaning of section 4(4) of the 2000 Act;
        or

    (b) a local authority fostering service;

'fostering service provider' means—

    (a) in relation to a fostering agency, a registered person; or

    (b) in relation to a local authority fostering service, a local authority;

*'general practitioner' means a registered medical practitioner who—*

    *(a) provides general medical services under Part II of the National Health Service
        Act 1977;*

(b) performs personal medical services in connection with a pilot scheme under the National Health Service (Primary Care) Act 1997; or

(c) provides services which correspond to services provided under Part II of the National Health Service Act 1977 otherwise than in pursuance of that Act;

['general practitioner' means a person who—

(a) provides primary medical services pursuant to Part I of the National Health Service Act 1977; or

(b) provides services which correspond to primary medical services provided under Part I of that Act, otherwise than in pursuance of that Act;]

'independent fostering agency' means a fostering agency falling within section 4(4)(a) of the 2000 Act (discharging functions of local authorities in connection with the placing of children with foster parents);

'local authority fostering service' means the discharge by a local authority of relevant fostering functions within the meaning of section 43(3)(b) of the 2000 Act;

'organisation' means a body corporate or any unincorporated association other than a partnership;

'parent' in relation to a child, includes any person who has parental responsibility for him;

'placement' means any placement of a child made by—

(a) a local authority under section 23(2)(a) of the 1989 Act or a voluntary organisation under section 59(1)(a) of the 1989 Act which is not—

(i) a placement with a person who falls within section 23(4) of that Act; or

(ii) a placement for adoption; and

(b) except in Part V of these Regulations includes a placement arranged by an independent fostering agency acting on behalf of a local authority,

and references to a child who is placed shall be construed accordingly;

['Primary Care Trust' means a Primary Care Trust established under section 16A of the National Health Service Act 1977;]

'registered manager' in relation to a fostering agency means a person who is registered under Part II of the 2000 Act as the manager of the fostering agency;

'registered person' in relation to a fostering agency means any person who is the registered provider or the registered manager of the fostering agency;

'registered provider' in relation to a fostering agency means a person who is registered under Part II of the 2000 Act as the person carrying on the fostering agency;

'responsible authority' means, in relation to a child, the local authority or voluntary organisation as the case may be, responsible for the child's placement;

'responsible individual' shall be construed in accordance with regulation 5(2)(c)(i);

'statement of purpose' means the written statement compiled in accordance with regulation 3(1).

(2) In these Regulations, a reference—

(a) to a numbered regulation or Schedule is to the regulation in, or Schedule to, these Regulations bearing that number;

(b) in a regulation or Schedule to a numbered paragraph, is to the paragraph in that regulation or Schedule bearing that number;

(c) in a paragraph to a lettered or numbered sub-paragraph is to the sub-paragraph in that paragraph bearing that letter or number.

(3) In these Regulations, references to employing a person include employing a person whether or not for payment, and whether under a contract of service or a

contract for services, and allowing a person to work as a volunteer, but do not include allowing a person to act as a foster parent, and references to an employee or to a person being employed shall be construed accordingly.

**Note.** Para (1): definition 'Commission' inserted by SI 2004 No 664, art 3, Sch 2 as from 1 April 2004. definition 'foster parent' substituted by SI 2002 No 865, reg 7(1), (2) as from 18 April 2002; definition 'general practitioner' substituted by SI 2004 No 865, art 119, Sch 1, para 31 as from 1 April 2004; definition of 'Primary Care Trust' inserted by SI 2002 No 2469, reg 11, Sch 8 as from 1 October 2002.

**3 Statement of purpose and children's guide**—(1) The fostering service provider shall compile, in relation to the fostering service, a written statement (in these Regulations referred to as 'the statement of purpose') which shall consist of—

(a) a statement of the aims and objectives of the fostering service; and

(b) a statement as to the services and facilities to be provided by the fostering service.

(2) The fostering service provider shall provide a copy of the statement of purpose to the Commission and shall make it available, upon request, for inspection by—

(a) any person working for the purposes of the fostering service;

(b) any foster parent or prospective foster parent of the fostering service;

(c) any child placed with a foster parent by the fostering service; and

(d) the parent of any such child.

(3) The fostering service provider shall produce a written guide to the fostering service (in these Regulations referred to as 'the children's guide') which shall include—

(a) a summary of the statement of purpose;

(b) a summary of the procedure established—

(i) in the case of an independent fostering agency, under regulation 18(1);

(ii) in the case of a local authority fostering service, under section 26(3) of the 1989 Act; and

(iii) in the case of a fostering agency falling within section 4(4)(b) of the 2000 Act, under section 59(4)(b) of the 1989 Act; and

(c) the address and telephone number of the Commission.

(4) The fostering service provider shall provide a copy of the children's guide to the Commission, to each foster parent approved by the fostering service provider and (subject to his age and understanding), to each child placed by it.

(5) Subject to paragraph (6) of this regulation the fostering service provider shall ensure that the fostering service is at all times conducted in a manner which is consistent with its statement of purpose.

(6) Nothing in paragraph (5) shall require or authorise the fostering service provider to contravene or not comply with—

(a) any other provision of these Regulations; or

(b) in the case of a fostering agency, any conditions for the time being in force in relation to the registration of the registered person under Part II of the 2000 Act.

**4 Review of statement of purpose and children's guide** The fostering service provider shall—

(a) keep under review and where appropriate revise the statement of purpose and children's guide;

(b) notify the Commission of any such revision within 28 days; and

(c) if the children's guide is revised, supply a copy to each foster parent approved by the fostering service provider and (subject to his age and understanding), to each child placed by it.

PART II

REGISTERED PERSONS AND MANAGEMENT OF LOCAL AUTHORITY FOSTERING SERVICE

**5 Fostering agency—fitness of provider—**(1) A person shall not carry on a fostering agency unless he is fit to do so.

(2) A person is not fit to carry on a fostering agency unless the person—

(a) in the case of an independent fostering agency, is an individual who carries on the fostering agency—

(i) otherwise than in partnership with others and he satisfies the requirements set out in paragraph (3);

(ii) in partnership with others, and he and each of his partners satisfies the requirements set out in paragraph (3);

(b) is a partnership, and each of the partners satisfies the requirements set out in paragraph (3);

(c) is an organisation and—

(i) the organisation has given notice to the Commission of the name, address and position in the organisation of an individual (in these Regulations referred to as 'the responsible individual') who is a director, manager, secretary or other officer of the organisation and is responsible for supervising the management of the fostering agency; and

(ii) that individual satisfies the requirements set out in paragraph (3).

(3) The requirements are that—

(a) he is of integrity and good character;

(b) he is physically and mentally fit to carry on the fostering agency; and

(c) full and satisfactory information is available [in relation to him in respect of each of the matters specified in Schedule 1].

*(4) This paragraph applies where any certificate or information on any matters referred to in paragraph 2 of Schedule 1 is not available to an individual because any provision of the Police Act 197 has not been brought into force.*

(5) A person shall not carry on a fostering agency if—

(a) he has been adjudged bankrupt or sequestration of his estate has been awarded and (in either case) he has not been discharged and the bankruptcy order has not been annulled or rescinded; or

(b) he has made a composition or arrangement with his creditors and has not been discharged in respect of it.

**Note.** Para (3): in sub-para (c) words from 'in relation to him' to 'in Schedule 1' in square brackets substituted by SI 2002 No 865, reg 6(1), (2)(a) as from 18 April 2002. Para (4): revoked by SI 2002 No 865, reg 6(1), (2)(b) as from 18 April 2002.

**6 Fostering agency—appointment of manager—**(1) The registered provider shall appoint an individual to manage the fostering agency.

(2) Where the registered provider is—

(a) an organisation, it shall not appoint the person who is the responsible individual as the manager;

(b) a partnership, it shall not appoint any of the partners as the manager.

(3) The registered provider shall forthwith notify the Commission of—

(a) the name of any person appointed in accordance with this regulation; and

(b) the date on which the appointment is to take effect.

**7 Fostering agency—fitness of manager—**(1) A person shall not manage a fostering agency unless he is fit to do so.

(2) A person is not fit to manage a fostering agency unless—

(a) he is of integrity and good character;

(b) having regard to the size of the fostering agency, its statement of purpose, and the numbers and needs of the children placed by it—

      (i)  he has the qualifications, skills and experience necessary for managing the fostering agency; and

      (ii)  he is physically and mentally fit to manage a fostering agency;

  (c)  full and satisfactory information is available [in relation to him in respect of each of the matters specified in Schedule 1].

    *(3) This paragraph applies where any certificate or information on any matters referred to in paragraph 2 of Schedule 1 is not available to an individual because any provision of the Police Act 1997 has not been brought into force.*

**Note.** Para (2): in sub-para (c) words from 'in relation to him' to 'in Schedule 1' in square brackets substituted by SI 2002 No 865, reg 6(1), (3)(a) as from 18 April 2002: Para (3): revoked by SI 2002 No 865, reg 6(1), (3)(b) as from 18 April 2002.

**8 Registered person—general requirements—**(1) The registered provider and the registered manager shall, having regard to—

  (a)  the size of the fostering agency, its statement of purpose, and the numbers and needs of the children placed by it; and

  (b)  the need to safeguard and promote the welfare of the children placed by the fostering agency,

carry on or manage the fostering agency (as the case may be) with sufficient care, competence and skill.

    (2) If the registered provider is—

  (a)  an individual, he shall undertake;

  (b)  an organisation, it shall ensure that the responsible individual undertakes;

  (c)  a partnership, it shall ensure that one of the partners undertakes,

from time to time such training as is appropriate to ensure that he has the experience and skills necessary for carrying on the fostering agency.

    (3) The registered manager shall undertake from time to time such training as is appropriate to ensure that he has the experience and skills necessary for managing the fostering agency.

**9 Notification of offences** Where the registered person or the responsible individual is convicted of any criminal offence, whether in England and Wales or elsewhere, he shall forthwith give notice in writing to the Commission of—

  (a)  the date and place of the conviction;

  (b)  the offence of which he was convicted; and

  (c)  the penalty imposed on him in respect of the offence.

**10 Local authority fostering service—manager—**(1) Each local authority shall appoint one of its officers to manage the local authority fostering service, and shall forthwith notify the Commission of—

  (a)  the name of the person appointed; and

  (b)  the date on which the appointment is to take effect.

    (2) Regulations 7, 8 and 9 shall apply to the manager of a local authority fostering service, in relation to that service, as they apply to the manager of a fostering agency in relation to the fostering agency.

    (3) The local authority shall forthwith notify the Commission if the person appointed under paragraph (1) ceases to manage the local authority fostering service.

PART III

CONDUCT OF FOSTERING SERVICES

**11 Independent fostering agencies—duty to secure welfare** The registered person in respect of an independent fostering agency shall ensure that—

  (a)  the welfare of children placed or to be placed with foster parents is safeguarded and promoted at all times; and

   (b)  before making any decision affecting a child placed or to be placed with foster parents due consideration is given to—
>    (i)  the child's wishes and feelings in the light of his age and understanding; and
>    (ii)  his religious persuasion, racial origin and cultural and linguistic background.

**12 Arrangements for the protection of children**—(1) The fostering service provider shall prepare and implement a written policy which—
   (a)  is intended to safeguard children placed with foster parents from abuse or neglect; and
   (b)  sets out the procedure to be followed in the event of any allegation of abuse or neglect.

(2) The procedure under paragraph (1)(b) shall, subject to paragraph (3), provide in particular for—
   (a)  liaison and co-operation with any local authority which is, or may be, making child protection enquiries in relation to any child placed by the fostering service provider;
   (b)  the prompt referral to the area authority of any allegation of abuse or neglect affecting any child placed by the fostering service provider;
   (c)  notification of the instigation and outcome of any child protection enquiries involving a child placed by the fostering service provider, to the Commission;
   (d)  written records to be kept of any allegation of abuse or neglect, and of the action taken in response;
   (e)  consideration to be given to the measures which may be necessary to protect children placed with foster parents following an allegation of abuse or neglect; and
   (f)  arrangements to be made for persons working for the purposes of a fostering service, foster parents and children placed by the fostering service, to have access to information which would enable them to contact—
>    (i)  the area authority; and
>    (ii)  the Commission,

regarding any concern about child welfare or safety.

(3) Sub-paragraphs (a), (c) and (f)(i) of paragraph (2) do not apply to a local authority fostering service.

(4) In this regulation 'child protection enquiries' means any enquiries carried out by a local authority in the exercise of any of its functions conferred by or under the 1989 Act relating to the protection of children.

**13 Behaviour management and absence from foster parent's home**—(1) The fostering service provider shall prepare and implement a written policy on acceptable measures of control, restraint and discipline of children placed with foster parents.

(2) The fostering service provider shall take all reasonable steps to ensure that—
   (a)  no form of corporal punishment is used on any child placed with a foster parent;
   (b)  no child placed with foster parents is subject to any measure of control, restraint or discipline which is excessive or unreasonable; and
   (c)  physical restraint is used on a child only where it is necessary to prevent likely injury to the child or other persons or likely serious damage to property.

(3) The fostering service provider shall prepare and implement a written procedure to be followed if a child is absent from a foster parent's home without permission.

**14 Duty to promote contact** The fostering service provider shall, subject to the provisions of the foster placement agreement and any court order relating to contact, promote contact between a child placed with a foster parent and his parents, relatives and friends unless such contact is not reasonably practicable or consistent with the child's welfare.

**15 Health of children placed with foster parents—**(1) The fostering service provider shall promote the health and development of children placed with foster parents.

(2) In particular the fostering service provider shall ensure that—

(a) each child is registered with a general practitioner;

(b) each child has access to such medical, dental, nursing, psychological and psychiatric advice, treatment and other services as he may require;

(c) each child is provided with such individual support, aids and equipment which he may require as a result of any particular health needs or disability he may have; and

(d) each child is provided with guidance, support and advice on health, personal care and health promotion issues appropriate to his needs and wishes.

**16 Education, employment and leisure activities—**(1) The fostering service provider shall promote the educational attainment of children placed with foster parents.

(2) In particular the fostering service provider shall—

(a) establish a procedure for monitoring the educational attainment, progress and school attendance of children placed with foster parents;

(b) promote the regular school attendance and participation in school activities of school aged children placed with foster parents; and

(c) provide foster parents with such information and assistance, including equipment, as may be necessary to meet the educational needs of children placed with them.

(3) The fostering service provider shall ensure that any education it provides for any child placed with foster parents who is of compulsory school age but not attending school is efficient and suitable to the child's age, ability, aptitude, and any special educational needs he may have.

(4) The fostering service provider shall ensure that foster parents promote the leisure interests of children placed with them.

(5) Where any child placed with foster parents has attained the age where he is no longer required to receive compulsory full-time education, the fostering service provider shall assist with the making of, and give effect to, the arrangements made for his education, training and employment.

**17 Support, training and information for foster parents—**(1) The fostering service provider shall provide foster parents with such training, advice, information and support, including support outside office hours, as appears necessary in the interests of children placed with them.

(2) The fostering service provider shall take all reasonable steps to ensure that foster parents are familiar with, and act in accordance with the policies established in accordance with regulations 12(1) and 13(1) and (3).

(3) The fostering service provider shall ensure that, in relation to any child placed or to be placed with him, a foster parent is given such information, which is kept up to date, as to enable him to provide appropriate care for the child, and in particular that each foster parent is provided with appropriate information regarding—

(a) the state of health and health needs of any child placed or to be placed with him; and

(b) the arrangements for giving consent to the child's medical or dental examination or treatment.

**18 Independent fostering agencies—complaints and representations—**(1) Subject to paragraph (7), the registered person in respect of an independent fostering agency shall establish a written procedure for considering complaints made by or on behalf of children placed by the agency and foster parents approved by it.

(2) The procedure shall, in particular, provide—

(a) for an opportunity for informal resolution of the complaint at an early stage;

(b) that no person who is the subject of a compliant takes part in its consideration other than, if the registered person considers it appropriate, at the informal resolution stage only;

(c) for dealing with complaints about the registered person;

(d) for complaints to be made by a person acting on behalf of a child;

(e) for arrangements for the procedure to be made known to—

    (i) children placed by the agency;

    (ii) their parents;

    (iii) persons working for the purposes of the independent fostering agency.

(3) A copy of the procedure shall be supplied on request to any of the persons mentioned in paragraph (2)(e).

(4) The copy of the procedure supplied under paragraph (3) shall include—

(a) the name, address and telephone number of the Commission; and

(b) details of the procedure (if any) which has been notified to the registered person by the Commission for the making of complaints to it relating to independent fostering agencies.

(5) The registered person shall ensure that a written record is made of any complaint or representation, the action taken in response to it, and the outcome of the investigation.

(6) The registered person shall ensure that—

(a) children are enabled to make a complaint or representation; and

(b) no child is subject to any reprisal for making a complaint or representation.

(7) The registered person shall supply to the Commission at its request a statement containing a summary of any complaints made during the preceding twelve months and the action taken in response.

(8) This regulation (apart from paragraph (5)) does not apply in relation to any matter to which the Representations Procedure (Children) Regulations 1991 applies.

**19 Staffing of fostering service**   The fostering service provider shall ensure that there is, having regard to—

(a) the size of the fostering service, its statement of purpose, and the numbers and needs of the children placed by it; and

(b) the need to safeguard and promote the health and welfare of children placed with foster parents,

a sufficient number of suitably qualified, competent and experienced persons working for purposes of the fostering service.

**20 Fitness of workers—**(1) The fostering service provider shall not—

(a) employ a person to work for the purposes of the fostering service unless that person is fit to work for the purposes of a fostering service; or

(b) allow a person to whom paragraph (2) applies, to work for the purposes of the fostering service unless that person is fit to work for the purposes of a fostering service.

(2) This paragraph applies to any person who is employed by a person other than the fostering service provider in a position in which he may in the course of his duties have regular contact with children placed by the fostering service.

(3) For the purposes of paragraph (1), a person is not fit to work for the purposes of a fostering service unless—

(a) he is of integrity and good character;

(b) he has the qualifications, skills and experience necessary for the work he is to perform;

(c) he is physically and mentally fit for the work he is to perform; and

(d) full and satisfactory information is available [in relation to him in respect of each of the matters specified in Schedule 1].

*(4) This paragraph applies where any certificate or information on any matters referred to in paragraph 2 of Schedule 1 is not available to an individual because any provision of the Police Act 1997 has not been brought into force.*

(5) The fostering service provider shall take reasonable steps to ensure that any person working for a fostering service who is not employed by him and to whom paragraph (2) does not apply, is appropriately supervised while carrying out his duties.

(6) Subject to regulation 50(7), the fostering service provider shall not employ to work for the purposes of the fostering service in a position to which paragraph (7) applies, a person who is—

(a) a foster parent approved by the fostering service; or

(b) a member of the household of such a foster parent.

(7) This paragraph applies to any management, social work or other professional position, unless in the case of a position which is not a management or a social work position, the work is undertaken on an occasional basis, as a volunteer, or for no more than 5 hours in any week.

**Note.** Para (3): in sub-para (d) words from 'in relation to him' to 'in Schedule 1' in square brackets substituted by SI 2002 No 865, reg 6(1), (4)(a) as from 18 April 2002. Para (4): revoked by SI 2002 No 865, reg 6(1), (4)(b) as from 18 April 2002.

**21 Employment of staff—**(1) The fostering service provider shall—

(a) ensure that all permanent appointments are subject to the satisfactory completion of a period of probation; and

(b) provide all employees with a job description outlining their responsibilities.

(2) The fostering service provider shall operate a disciplinary procedure which, in particular—

(a) provides for the suspension of an employee where necessary in the interests of the safety or welfare of children placed with foster parents;

(b) provides that the failure on the part of an employee to report an incident of abuse, or suspected abuse of a child placed with foster parents to an appropriate person is a ground on which disciplinary proceedings may be instituted.

(3) For the purposes of paragraph (2)(b), an appropriate person is—

(a) in any case—

(i) the registered person, or the manager of the local authority fostering service as the case may be;

(ii) an officer of the Commission;

(iii) an officer of the area authority if applicable;

(iv) a police officer;

(v) an officer of the National Society for the Prevention of Cruelty to Children;

(b) in the case of an employee of an independent fostering agency, an officer of the responsible authority;

(c) in the case of an employee of a fostering agency, an officer of the local authority in whose area the agency is situated.

(4) The fostering service provider shall ensure that all persons employed by him—

(a) receive appropriate training, supervision and appraisal; and

(b) are enabled from to time to time to obtain further qualifications appropriate to the work they perform.

**22 Records with respect to fostering services—**(1) The fostering service provider shall maintain and keep up to date the records specified in Schedule 2.

(2) The records referred to in paragraph (1) shall be retained for at least 15 years from the date of the last entry.

**23 Fitness of premises—**(1) The fostering service provider shall not use premises for the purposes of a fostering service unless the premises are suitable for the purpose of achieving the aims and objectives set out in the statement of purpose.

(2) A fostering service provider shall ensure—

(a) that there are adequate security arrangements at the premises, in particular that there are secure facilities for the storage of records; and

(b) that any records which are stored away from the premises are kept in conditions of appropriate security.

PART IV

APPROVAL OF FOSTER PARENTS

**24 Establishment of fostering panel—**(1) Subject to paragraph (5), the fostering service provider shall establish at least one panel, to be known as a fostering panel, in accordance with this regulation.

(2) The fostering service provider shall appoint to chair the panel either—

(a) a senior member of staff of the fostering service provider who is not responsible for the day to day management of any person carrying out assessments of prospective foster parents; or

(b) such other person not being an employee, member, partner or director of the fostering service provider, who has the skills and experience necessary for chairing a fostering panel.

(3) Subject to paragraph (5), the fostering panel shall consist of no more than 10 members including the person appointed under paragraph (2) and shall include—

(a) two social workers employed by the fostering service provider, one of whom has child care expertise and the other of whom has expertise in the provision of a fostering service;

(b) in the case of a fostering agency—

(i) if the registered provider is an individual, that individual;

(ii) if the registered provider is an organisation, at least one of its directors or the responsible individual;

(iii) if the registered provider is a partnership, at least one of the partners;

(c) in the case of a local authority fostering service, at least one elected member of the local authority; and

(d) at least four other persons (in this regulation referred to as 'independent members'), including at least one person who is, or within the previous two years has been, a foster parent for a fostering service provider other than the one whose fostering panel is being established.

(4) The fostering service provider shall appoint a member of the fostering panel who will act as chair if the person appointed to chair the panel is absent or his office is vacant ('the vice chair').

(5) A fostering panel may be established jointly by any two but not more than three fostering service providers, and if such a fostering panel is established—

(a) the maximum number of members who may be appointed to that panel is eleven;

(b) each fostering service provider shall appoint two persons to the panel, one of whom falls within paragraph (3)(a), and the other of whom falls within paragraph (3)(b) or (c), as the case may be;

(c) by agreement between the fostering service providers there shall be appointed—

(i) a person to chair the panel;

(ii) at least four independent members including at least one person who is, or within the previous two years has been, a foster parent for a fostering service provider other than any of those whose fostering panel is being established; and

(iii) a member of the panel who will act as chair if the person appointed to chair the panel is absent or his office is vacant ('the vice chair').

(6) A fostering panel member shall hold office for a term not exceeding three years, and may not hold office for the panel of the same fostering service provider for more than two consecutive terms.

(7) Any panel member may resign his office at any time by giving one month's notice in writing to the fostering service provider.

(8) Where a fostering service provider is of the opinion that any member of the fostering panel is unsuitable or unable to remain in office, it may terminate his office at any time by giving him notice in writing.

(9) A person shall not be appointed as an independent member of a fostering panel if—

(a) he is a foster parent approved by the fostering service provider;

(b) he is employed by the fostering service provider;

(c) he is concerned in the management of the fostering service provider;

(d) in the case of a local authority fostering service, he is an elected member of the local authority; or

(e) in the case of a fostering agency, he is related to an employee of the registered provider, or to any person concerned in the management of the fostering agency.

(10) For the purposes of paragraph (9)(e), a person ('person A') is related to another person ('person B') if he is—

(a) a member of the household of, or married to person B;

(b) the son, daughter, mother, father, sister or brother of person B; or

(c) the son, daughter, mother, father, sister or brother of the person to whom person B is married.

**25 Meetings of fostering panel**—(1) Subject to paragraph (3), no business shall be conducted by a fostering panel unless at least five of its members, including the person appointed to chair the panel, or the vice chair, at least one of the social workers employed by the fostering service and at least two of the independent members, meet as a panel.

(2) A fostering panel shall make a written record of its proceedings and the reasons for its recommendations.

(3) In the case of a joint fostering panel, no business shall be conducted unless at least six of its members, including the person appointed to chair the panel, or the vice chair, and one social worker from each fostering service, meet as a panel.

**26 Functions of fostering panel**—(1) The functions of the fostering panel in respect of cases referred to it by the fostering service provider are—

(a)  to consider each application for approval and to recommend whether or not a person is suitable to act as a foster parent;

(b)  where it recommends approval of an application, to recommend the terms on which the approval is to be given;

(c)  to recommend whether or not a person remains suitable to act as a foster parent, and whether or not the terms of his approval remain appropriate—

    (i)   on the first review carried out in accordance with regulation 29(1); and

    (ii)   on the occasion of any other review when requested to do so by the fostering service provider in accordance with regulation 29(5); and

(d)  to consider any case referred to it under regulation 28(8) or 29(9).

(2)  The fostering panel shall also—

(a)  advise on the procedures under which reviews in accordance with regulation 29 are carried out by the fostering service provider and periodically monitor their effectiveness;

(b)  oversee the conduct of assessments carried out by the fostering service provider; and

(c)  give advice and make recommendations on such other matters or cases as the fostering service provider may refer to it.

(3)  In this regulation 'recommend' means recommend to the fostering service provider.

**27 Assessment of prospective foster parents**—(1) The fostering service provider shall carry out an assessment of any person whom it considers may be suitable to become a foster parent, in accordance with this regulation.

(2)  If the fostering service provider considers that a person may be suitable to act as a foster parent it shall—

(a)  obtain the information specified in Schedule 3 relating to the prospective foster parent and other members of his household and family, and any other information it considers relevant;

(b)  interview at least two persons nominated by the prospective foster parent to provide personal references for him, and prepare written reports of the interviews;

(c)  subject to paragraph (3), consult with, and take into account the views of, the local authority in whose area the prospective foster parent lives;

(d)  having regard to these matters consider whether the prospective foster parent is suitable to act as a foster parent and whether his household is suitable for any child in respect of whom approval may be given;

(e)  prepare a written report on him which includes the matters set out in paragraph (4); and

(f)  refer the report to the fostering panel and notify the prospective foster parent accordingly.

(3)  Paragraph (2)(c) does not apply where the fostering service provider is a local authority and the applicant lives in the area of that authority.

(4)  The report referred to in paragraph (2)(e) shall include the following matters in relation to the prospective foster parent—

(a)  the information required by Schedule 3 and any other information the fostering service provider considers relevant;

(b)  the fostering service provider's assessment of his suitability to act as a foster parent; and

(c)  the fostering service provider's proposals about the terms and conditions of any approval.

(5)  Subject to paragraph (6), a person shall not be regarded as suitable to act as a foster parent if he or any member of his household aged 18 or over—

(a)  has been convicted of a specified offence committed at the age of 18 or over; or

(b) has been cautioned by a constable in respect of any such offence which, at the time the caution was given, he admitted.

(6) The fostering service provider may regard a person to whom paragraph (5) would, apart from this paragraph apply, as suitable to act or to continue to act, as the case may be, as a foster parent in relation to a particular named child or children if the fostering service provider is satisfied that the welfare of that child or those children requires it, and either—

(a) the person, or a member of his household, is a relative of the child; or

(b) the person is already acting as a foster parent for the child.

(7) In this regulation 'specified offence' means—

(a) an offence against a child;

(b) an offence specified in Schedule 4;

(c) an offence contrary to section 170 of the Customs and Excise Management Act 1979 in relation to goods prohibited to be imported under section 42 of the Customs Consolidation Act 1876 (prohibitions and restrictions relating to pornography) where the prohibited goods included indecent photographs of children under the age of 16;

(d) any other offence involving bodily injury to a child *or young person*, other than an offence of common assault or battery, and

the expression 'offence against a child' has the meaning given to it by section 26(1) of the Criminal Justice and Court Services Act 2000 except that it does not include an offence contrary to sections 6, 12 or 13 of the Sexual Offences Act 1956 (sexual intercourse with a girl aged 13 to 16, buggery, or indecency between men) in a case where the offender was under the age of 20 at the time the offence was committed.

**Note.** Para (7): in sub-para (d) words omitted revoked by SI 2002 No 865, reg 7(1), (3) as from 18 April 2002.

**28 Approval of foster parents**—(1) A fostering service provider shall not approve a person who has been approved as a foster parent by another fostering service provider, and whose approval has not been terminated.

(2) A fostering service provider shall not approve a person as a foster parent unless—

(a) it has completed its assessment of his suitability; and

(b) its fostering panel has considered the application.

(3) A fostering service provider shall in deciding whether to approve a person as a foster parent and as to the terms of any approval, take into account the recommendation of its fostering panel.

(4) No member of its fostering panel shall take part in any decision made by a fostering service provider under paragraph (3).

(5) If a fostering service provider decides to approve a person as a foster parent it shall—

(a) give him notice in writing specifying the terms of the approval, for example, whether it is in respect of a particular named child or children, or number and age range of children, or of placements of any particular kind, or in any particular circumstances; and

(b) enter into a written agreement with him covering the matters specified in Schedule 5 (in these Regulations referred to as the 'foster care agreement').

(6) If a fostering service provider considers that a person is not suitable to act as a foster parent it shall—

(a) given him written notice that it proposes not to approve him, together with its reasons and a copy of the fostering panel's recommendation; and

(b) invite him to submit any written representations within 28 days of the date of the notice.

(7) If the fostering service provider does not receive any representations within the period referred to in paragraph (6)(b), it may proceed to make its decision.

(8) If the fostering service provider receives any written representations within the period referred to in paragraph (6)(b), it shall—

(a) refer the case to the fostering panel for further consideration; and

(b) make its decision, taking into account any fresh recommendation made by the fostering panel.

(9) As soon as practicable after making the decision referred to in paragraph (7) or (8)(b) as the case may be, the fostering service provider shall notify the prospective foster parent in writing and—

(a) if the decision is to approve the person as a foster parent, comply with paragraph (5) in relation to him; or

(b) if the decision is not to approve the person, provide written reasons for its decision.

**29 Reviews and terminations of approval—**(1) The fostering service provider shall review the approval of each foster parent in accordance with this regulation.

(2) A review shall take place not more that a year after approval, and thereafter whenever the fostering service provider considers it necessary, but at intervals of not more than a year.

(3) When undertaking a review, the fostering service provider shall—

(a) make such enquiries and obtain such information as it considers necessary in order to review whether the person continues to be suitable as to act as a foster parent and his household continues to be suitable; and

(b) seek and take into account the views of—

(i) the foster parent;

(ii) (subject to the child's age and understanding) any child placed with the foster parent; and

(iii) any responsible authority which has within the preceding year placed a child with the foster parent.

(4) At the conclusion of the review the fostering service provider shall prepare a written report, setting out whether—

(a) the person continues to be suitable to act as a foster parent and his household continues to be suitable; and

(b) the terms of his approval continue to be appropriate.

(5) The fostering service provider shall on the occasion of the first review under this regulation, and may on any subsequent review, refer its report to the fostering panel for consideration.

(6) If the fostering service provider decides, taking into account any recommendation made by the fostering panel, that the foster parent and his household continue to be suitable and that the terms of his approval continue to be appropriate, it shall give written notice to the foster parent of its decision.

(7) If, taking into account any recommendation made by the fostering panel, the fostering service provider is no longer satisfied that the foster parent and his household continue to be suitable, or that the terms of the approval are appropriate, it shall—

(a) give written notice to the foster parent that it proposes to terminate, or revise the terms of, his approval as the case may be, together with its reasons, and

(b) invite him to submit any written representations within 28 days of the date of the notice.

(8) If the fostering service provider does not receive any representations within the period referred to in paragraph (7)(b), it may proceed to make its decision.

(9) If the fostering service provider receives any written representations within the period referred to in paragraph (7)(b), it shall—

(a)  refer the case to the fostering panel for its consideration; and

(b)  make its decision, taking into account any recommendation made by the fostering panel.

(10)  As soon as practicable after making the decision referred to in paragraph (8) or (9)(b), the fostering service provider shall give written notice to the foster parent stating, as the case may be—

(a)  that the foster parent and his household continue to be suitable, and that the terms of the approval continue to be appropriate;

(b)  that his approval is terminated from a specified date, and the reasons for the termination; or

(c)  the revised terms of the approval and the reasons for the revision.

(11)  A foster parent may give notice in writing to the fostering service provider at any time that he no longer wishes to act as a foster parent, whereupon his approval is terminated with effect from 28 days from the date on which the notice is received by the fostering service provider.

(12)  A copy of any notice given under this regulation shall be sent to the responsible authority for any child placed with the foster parent (unless the responsible authority is also the fostering service provider), and the area authority.

**30  Case records relating to foster parents and others**—(1)  A fostering service provider shall maintain a case record for each foster parent approved by it which shall include copies of the documents specified in paragraph (2) and the information specified in paragraph (3).

(2)  The documents referred to in paragraph (1) are, as the case may be—

(a)  the notice of approval given under regulation 28(5)(a);

(b)  the foster care agreement;

(c)  any report of a review of approval prepared under regulation 29(4);

(d)  any notice given under regulation 29(10);

(e)  any agreement entered into in accordance with regulation 38(1)(a);

(f)  the report prepared under regulation 27(2)(e) and any other reports submitted to the fostering panel; and

(g)  any recommendations made by the fostering panel.

(3)  The information referred to in paragraph (1) is, as the case may be—

(a)  a record of each placement with the foster parent, including the name, age and sex of each child placed, the dates on which each placement began and terminated and the circumstances of the termination;

(b)  the information obtained by the fostering service provider in relation to the assessment and approval of the foster parent and in relation to any review or termination of the approval.

(4)  A local authority shall maintain a case record for each person with whom a child is placed under regulation 38(2) which shall include in relation to that person—

(a)  the agreement entered into in accordance with regulation 38(2)(b);

(b)  a record in relation to the placement, including the name, age and sex of each child placed, the dates on which the placement began and terminated, and the circumstances of the termination; and

(c)  the information obtained in relation to the enquiries carried out under regulation 38(2).

(5)  The fostering service provider shall compile a record for each person whom it does not approve as a foster parent, or who withdraws his application prior to approval, which shall included in relation to him—

(a)  the information obtained in connection with the assessment;

(b)  any report submitted to the fostering panel and any recommendation made by the fostering panel; and

(c)  any notification given under regulation 28.

**31 Register of foster parents—**(1) The fostering service provider shall enter, in a register kept for the purpose, the particulars specified in paragraph (2) and in the case of a local authority fostering service, it shall also enter the particulars specified in paragraph (3).

(2) The particulars are—

(a) the name, address, date of birth and sex of each foster parent;

(b) the date of his approval and of each review of his approval; and

(c) the current terms of his approval.

(3) Each local authority shall enter in its register—

(a) the name and address of each person with whom it has placed a child under regulation 38(2);

(b) the date of each agreement entered into in accordance with regulation 38(2)(b); and

(c) the terms of any such agreement for the time being in force.

**32 Retention and confidentiality of records—**(1) The records compiled in relation to a foster parent under regulation 30(1), and any entry relating to him in the register maintained under regulation 31(1) shall be retained for at least 10 years from the date on which his approval is terminated.

(2) The records compiled by a local authority under regulation 30(4) in relation to a person with whom a child is placed under regulation 38(2), and any entry relating to such a person in the register maintained under regulation 31(1), shall be retained for at least 10 years from the date on which the placement is terminated.

(3) The records compiled under regulation 30(5) shall be retained for at least 3 years from the refusal or withdrawal, as the case may be, of the application to become a foster parent.

(4) The requirement in paragraphs (1) to (3) may be complied with by retaining the original written records or copies of them, or by keeping all or part of the information contained in them in some other accessible form such as a computer record.

(5) Any records or register maintained in accordance with regulation 30 or 31 shall be kept securely and may not be disclosed to any person except in accordance with—

(a) any provision of, or made under, or by virtue of, a statute under which access to such records is authorised;

(b) any court order authorising access to such records.

PART V

PLACEMENTS

**33 General duty of responsible authority** A responsible authority shall not place a child with a foster parent unless it is satisfied that—

(a) it is the most suitable way of performing its duty under (as the case may be) section 22(3) or 61(1)(a) and (b) of the 1989 Act; and

(b) a placement with the particular foster parent is the most suitable placement having regard to all the circumstances.

**34 Making of placements—**(1) Except in the case of an emergency or immediate placement under regulation 38, a responsible authority may only place a child with a foster parent if—

(a) the foster parent is approved—

(i) by the responsible authority proposing to make the placement; or

(ii) provided the conditions specified in paragraph (2) are satisfied, by another fostering service provider;

(b) the terms of his approval are consistent with the proposed placement; and

(c) he has entered into a foster care agreement.

(2) The conditions referred to in paragraph (1)(a)(ii) are—

(a) that the fostering service provider by whom the foster parent is approved, consents to the placement;

(b) that any other responsible authority which already has a child placed with the foster parent, consents to the placement;

(c) where applicable, that the area authority is consulted, its views are taken into account, and it is given notice if the placement is made; and

(d) where the foster parent is approved by an independent fostering agency, the requirements of regulation 40 are complied with.

(3) Before making a placement, the responsible authority shall enter into a written agreement (in these regulations referred to as the 'foster placement agreement') with the foster parent relating to the child, which covers the matters specified in Schedule 6.

**35 Supervision of placements**—(1) A responsible authority shall satisfy itself that the welfare of each child placed by it continues to be suitably provided for by the placement, and for that purpose the authority shall make arrangements for a person authorised by the authority to visit the child, in the home in which he is placed—

(a) from time to time as circumstances may require;

(b) when reasonably requested by the child or the foster parent; and

(c) in any event (subject to regulation 37)—

(i) in the first year of the placement, within one week from its beginning and then at intervals of not more than six weeks;

(ii) subsequently, at intervals of not more than 3 months.

(2) In the case of an immediate placement under regulation 38, the local authority shall arrange for the child to be visited at least once in each week during the placement.

(3) On each occasion on which the child is visited under this regulation the responsible authority shall ensure that the person it has authorised to carry out the visit—

(a) sees the child alone unless the child, being of sufficient age and understanding to do so, refuses; and

(b) prepares a written report of the visit.

**36 Termination of placements**—(1) A responsible authority shall not allow the placement of a child with a particular person to continue if it appears to them that the placement is no longer the most suitable way of performing their duty under (as the case may be) section 22(3) or 61(1)(a) and (b) of the Act.

(2) Where it appears to an area authority that the continuation of a placement would be detrimental to the welfare of the child concerned, the area authority shall remove the child forthwith.

(3) An area authority which removes a child under paragraph (2) shall forthwith notify the responsible authority.

**37 Short-term placements**—(1) This regulation applies where a responsible authority has arranged to place a child in a series of short-term placements with the same foster parent and the arrangement is such that—

(a) no single placement is to last for more than four weeks; and

(b) the total duration of the placements is not to exceed 120 days in any period of 12 months.

(2) A series of short-term placements to which this regulation applies may be treated as a single placement for the purposes of these Regulations, but with the modifications set out in paragraphs (3) and (4).

(3) Regulation 35(1)(c)(i) and (ii) shall apply as if they required arrangements to be made for visits to the child on a day when he is in fact placed ('a placement day')—

(a) within the first seven placement days of a series of short-term placements; and

(b) thereafter, if the series of placements continues, at intervals of not more than six months or, if the interval between placements exceeds six months, during the next placement.

(4) Regulation 41 shall apply as if it required arrangements to be made for visits to the child on a placement day within the first seven placement days of a series of short-term placements.

**38 Emergency and immediate placements by local authorities**—(1) Where a child is to be placed in an emergency, a local authority may for a period not exceeding 24 hours place the child with any foster parent approved by the local authority or any other fostering service provider provided that—

(a) the foster parent has made a written agreement with the local authority to carry out the duties specified in paragraph (3); and

(b) the local authority are satisfied as to the provisions of regulation 33(a).

(2) Where a local authority are satisfied that the immediate placement of a child is necessary, they may place the child with a person who is not a foster parent after interviewing him, inspecting the accommodation and obtaining information about other persons living in his household, for a period not exceeding six weeks, provided that—

(a) the person is a relative or friend of the child;

(b) the person has made a written agreement with the local authority to carry out the duties specified in paragraph (3); and

(c) the local authority are satisfied as to the provisions of regulation 33(a).

(3) The duties referred to in paragraphs (1)(a) and (2)(b) are—

(a) to care for the child as if he were a member of that person's family;

(b) to permit any person authorised by the local authority or (if applicable) the area authority, to visit the child at any time;

(c) where regulation 36 applies, to allow the child to be removed at any time by the local authority or (if applicable) the area authority;

(d) to ensure that any information which that person may acquire relating to the child, his family or any other person, which has been given to him in confidence in connection with the placement is kept confidential and is not disclosed except to, or with the agreement of, the local authority; and

(e) to allow contact with the child in accordance with the terms of any court order relating to contact or any arrangements made or agreed by the local authority.

(4) Where a local authority make a placement under this regulation outside their area they shall notify the area authority.

**39 Placements outside England**—(1) A voluntary organisation shall not place a child outside the British Islands.

(2) Where a responsible authority makes arrangements to place a child outside England it shall ensure, so far as reasonably practicable, that the requirements which would have applied under these Regulations had the child been placed in England, are complied with.

*(3) In the case of a placement by a local authority outside England or Wales, paragraph (2) is subject to the provisions of paragraph 19 of Schedule 2 to the 1989 Act (arrangements to assist children to live abroad).*

**Note.** Para (3): revoked by SI 2002 No 865, reg 7(1), (4) as from 18 April 2002.

**40 Independent fostering agencies—discharge of local authority functions—**
(1) A local authority may make arrangements in accordance with this regulation for the duties imposed on it as a responsible authority by regulations 34, 35, 36(1) and 37 and where paragraph (3) applies, 33(b) to be discharged on its behalf by a registered person.

(2) Subject to paragraph (3), no arrangements may be made under this regulation in respect of a particular child, unless a local authority has performed its duties under regulation 33 in relation to that child.

(3) Where a local authority makes arrangements with a registered person for the registered person to provide foster parents for the purposes of a short-term placement within the meaning of regulation 37(1), the local authority may also make arrangements for the registered person to perform the local authority's duty under regulation 33(b) in relation to that placement on its behalf.

(4) No arrangements may be made under this regulation unless a local authority has entered into a written agreement with the registered person which sets out—

(a) which of its duties the local authority proposes to delegate in accordance with this regulation;

(b) the services to be provided to the local authority by the registered person;

(c) the arrangements for the selection by the local authority of particular foster parents from those approved by the registered person;

(d) a requirement for the registered person to submit reports to the local authority on any placement as may be required by the authority, and in particular following any visit carried out under regulation 35; and

(e) the arrangements for the termination of the agreement.

(5) Where a local authority proposes to make an arrangement under this regulation in respect of a particular child the local authority shall enter into an agreement with the registered person in respect of that child which sets out—

(a) details of the particular foster parent with whom the child is to be placed;

(b) details of any services the child is to receive;

(c) the terms (including as to payment) of the proposed foster placement agreement;

(d) the arrangements for record keeping about the child, and for the return of records at the end of the placement;

(e) a requirement for the registered person to notify the local authority immediately in the event of any concerns about the placement; and

(f) whether and on what basis other children may be placed with the foster parent.

(6) A foster parent with whom a child is placed in accordance with arrangements made under this regulation is, in relation to that placement, to be treated for the purposes of paragraph 12(d) of Schedule 2 to the 1989 Act as a local authority foster parent.

(7) A local authority shall report to the Commission any concerns it may have about the services provided by a registered person.

(8) In this regulation 'registered person' means a person who is the registered person in respect of an independent fostering agency.

LOCAL AUTHORITY VISITS

**41 Local authority visits to children placed by voluntary organisations—**(1) Every local authority shall arrange for a person authorised by the local authority to visit every child who is placed with a foster parent within their area by a voluntary organisation as follows—

(a) subject to regulation 37(4), within 28 days of the placement;

(b) within 14 days of receipt of a request from the voluntary organisation which made the placement to visit a child;

(c)  as soon as reasonably practicable if it is informed that the welfare of the child may not be being safeguarded or promoted; and

(d)  at intervals of not more than six months where the local authority are satisfied, following a visit to a child under this regulation that the child's welfare is being safeguarded and promoted.

(2)  Every local authority shall ensure that a person carrying out a visit in accordance with paragraph (1)—

(a)  sees the child during the course of the visit, or if the child is not there, makes arrangements to see the child as soon as reasonably practicable; and

(b)  takes steps to discover whether the voluntary organisation which placed the child have made suitable arrangements to perform their duties under these Regulations, and those under section 61 of the 1989 Act.

(3)  A local authority shall report to the Commission any concerns it may have about the voluntary organisation.

PART VII

FOSTERING AGENCIES—MISCELLANEOUS

**42 Review of quality of care—**(1) The registered person shall establish and maintain a system for—

(a)  monitoring the matters set out in Schedule 7 at appropriate intervals; and

(b)  improving the quality of foster care provided by the fostering agency.

(2)  The registered person shall supply to the Commission a report in respect of any review conducted by him for the purposes of paragraph (1) and make a copy of the report available upon request to the persons mentioned in regulation 3(2).

(3)  The system referred to in paragraph (1) shall provide for consultation with foster parents, children placed with foster parents, and their responsible authority (unless, in the case of a fostering agency which is a voluntary organisation, it is also the responsible authority).

**43 Notifiable events—**(1) If, in relation to a fostering agency, any of the events listed in column 1 of the table in Schedule 8 takes place, the registered person shall without delay notify the persons indicated in respect of the event in column 2 of the table.

(2)  Any notification made in accordance with this regulation which is given orally shall be confirmed in writing.

**44 Financial position—**(1) The registered provider shall carry on the fostering agency in such manner as is likely to ensure that it will be financially viable for the purpose of achieving the aims and objectives set out in its statement of purpose.

(2)  The registered provider shall—

(a)  ensure that adequate accounts are maintained and kept up to date in respect of the fostering agency; and

(b)  supply a copy of the accounts, *certified by an accountant* [if requested to do so,] to the Commission.

(3)  The registered provider shall, if the Commission so requests, provide the Commission with such information as it may require for the purpose of considering the financial viability of the fostering agency, including—

(a)  the annual accounts of the fostering agency, certified by an accountant;

(b)  a reference from a bank expressing an opinion as to the registered provider's financial standing;

(c)  information as to the financing and financial resources of the fostering agency;

(d)  where the registered provider is a company, information as to any of its associated companies; and

(e) a certificate of insurance for the registered provider in respect of liability which may be incurred by him in relation to the fostering agency in respect of death, injury, public liability, damage or other loss.

(4) In this regulation one company is associated with another if one of them has control of the other, or both are under the control of the same person.

**Note.** Para (2): in sub-para (b) words 'if requested to do so,' in square brackets substituted by SI 2002 No 865, reg 7(1), (5) as from 18 April 2002.

**45 Notice of absence—**(1) Where the registered manager proposes to be absent from the fostering agency for a continuous period of 28 days or more, the registered person shall give notice in writing to the Commission of the proposed absence.

(2) Except in the case of an emergency, the notice referred to in paragraph (1) shall be given no later than one month before the proposed absence is to start, or within such shorter period as may be agreed with the Commission, and the notice shall specify—

(a) the length or expected length of the proposed absence;

(b) the reason for the proposed absence;

(c) the arrangements which have been made for the running of the fostering agency during that absence;

(d) the name, address and qualifications of the person who will be responsible for the fostering agency during the absence; and

(e) the arrangements that have been made or are proposed to be made for appointing another person to manage the fostering agency during the absence, including the proposed date by which the appointment is to start.

(3) Where the absence arises as a result of an emergency, the registered person shall give notice of the absence within one week of its occurrence, specifying the matters mentioned in sub-paragraphs (a) to (e) of paragraph (2).

(4) Where the registered manager has been absent from the fostering agency for a continuous period of 28 days or more, and the Commission has not been given notice of the absence, the registered person shall without delay give notice in writing to the Commission specifying the matters mentioned in paragraph (2).

(5) The registered person shall notify the Commission of the return to duty of the registered manager not later than 7 days after the date of his return.

**46 Notice of changes—**(1) The registered person shall give notice in writing to the Commission as soon as it is practicable to do so if any of the following events takes place or is proposed to take place—

(a) a person other than the registered person carries on or manages the fostering agency;

(b) a person ceases to carry on or manage the fostering agency;

(c) where the registered provider is an individual, he changes his name;

(d) where the registered provider is a partnership, there is any change in the membership of the partnership;

(e) where the registered provider is an organisation—

(i) the name or address of the organisation is changed;

(ii) there is any change of director, manager, secretary or other similar officer of the organisation;

(iii) there is to be any change in the identity of the responsible individual;

(f) where the registered provider is an individual, a trustee in bankruptcy is appointed or he makes any composition or arrangement with his creditors; or

(g) where the registered provider is a company, or a partnership, a receiver, manager, liquidator or provisional liquidator is appointed in respect of the registered provider.

(2) The registered provider shall notify the Commission in writing and without delay of the death of the registered manager.

**47 Appointment of liquidators etc—**(1) Any person to whom paragraph (2) applies shall—

(a) forthwith notify the Commission of his appointment indicating the reasons for it;

(b) appoint a manager to take full-time day to day charge of the fostering agency in any case where there is no registered manager; and

(c) not more than 28 days after his appointment notify the Commission of his intentions regarding the future operation of the fostering agency.

(2) This paragraph applies to any person appointed as—

(a) the receiver or manager of the property of a company or partnership which is a registered provider of a fostering agency;

(b) a liquidator or provisional liquidator of a company which is the registered provider of a fostering agency; or

(c) the trustee in bankruptcy of a registered provider of a fostering agency.

**48 Offences—**(1) A contravention or failure to comply with any of the provisions of regulations 3 to 23 and 42 to 46 shall be an offence.

(2) The Commission shall not bring proceedings against a person in respect of any contravention or failure to comply with those regulations unless—

(a) subject to paragraph 4, he is a registered person;

(b) notice has been given to him in accordance with paragraph (3);

[(c) the period specified in the notice, within which the registered person may make representations to the Commission, has expired; and

(d) in a case where, in accordance with paragraph (3)(b), the notice specifies any action that is to be taken within a specified period, the period has expired and the action has not been taken within that period].

(3) Where the Commission considers that the registered person has contravened or failed to comply with any of the provisions of the regulations mentioned in paragraph (1), it may serve a notice on the registered person specifying—

(a) in what respect in its opinion the registered person has contravened or is contravening any of the regulations, or has failed or is failing to comply with the requirements of any of the regulations;

[(b) where it is practicable for the registered person to take action for the purpose of complying with any of those regulations, the action which, in the opinion of the Commission, the registered person should take for that purpose;

(c) the period, not exceeding three months, within which the registered person should take any action specified in accordance with sub-paragraph (b);

(d) the period, not exceeding one month, within which the registered person may make representations to the Commission about the notice].

(4) The Commission may bring proceedings against a person who was once, but no longer is, a registered person, in respect of a failure to comply with regulation 22 *or 32* and for this purpose, references in paragraphs (2) and (3) to a registered person shall be taken to include such a person.

**Note.** Para (2): sub-paras (c), (d) substituted by SI 2002 No 865, reg 7(1), (6)(a) as from 18 April 2002. Para (3): sub-paras (b)–(d) substituted, for sub-paras (b), (c) as originally enacted, by SI 2002 No 865, reg 7(1), (6)(b) as from 18 April 2002. Para (4): words omitted revoked by SI 2002 No 865, reg 7(1), (6)(c) as from 18 April 2002.

**49 Compliance with regulations** Where there is more than one registered person in respect of a fostering agency, anything which is required under these

Regulations to be done by the registered person shall, if done by one of the registered persons, not be required to be done by any of the other registered persons.

PART VIII

MISCELLANEOUS

**50 Transitional provisions—**(1) This paragraph applies to a fostering agency falling within section 4(4)(b) of the 2000 Act (a voluntary organisation which places children with foster parents under section 59(1) of the 1989 Act) which has, before the coming into force of these Regulations duly made an application for registration under Part II of the 2000 Act.

(2) These Regulations shall apply to a fostering agency to which paragraph (1) applies, as if any reference in them to a registered person is a reference to the person who carries on the agency—
  (a) until such time as the application for registration is granted, either unconditionally or subject only to conditions which have been agreed in writing between that person and the Commission; or
  (b) if the application is granted subject to conditions which have not been so agreed, or it is refused—
      (i) if no appeal is brought, until the expiration of the period of 28 days after service on that person of notice of the Commission's decision; or
      (ii) if an appeal is brought, until it is determined or abandoned.

(3) This paragraph applies to an independent fostering agency which is carried on by a voluntary organisation, which has, before the coming into force of these Regulations, duly made an application for registration under Part II of the 2000 Act.

(4) Where a local authority looking after a child is satisfied that the child should be placed with foster parents, they may make arrangements, subject to paragraph (5), for the duties imposed on them by regulations 34, 35, 36(1) and 37 to be discharged on their behalf by the voluntary organisation to which paragraph (3) applies ('an unregistered independent voluntary provider')—
  (a) until such time as the application for registration is granted, either unconditionally or subject only to conditions which have been agreed in writing between that provider and the Commission; or
  (b) if the application is granted subject to conditions which have not been so agreed, or it is refused—
      (i) if no appeal is brought, until the expiration of the period of 28 days after service on that provider of notice of the Commission's decision; or
      (ii) if an appeal is brought, until it is determined or abandoned.

(5) A local authority may not make arrangements under paragraph (4) unless they—
  (a) are satisfied—
      (i) as to the capacity of the unregistered independent voluntary provider to discharge duties on their behalf; and
      (ii) that those arrangements are the most suitable way for those duties to be discharged; and
  (b) enter into a written agreement with the unregistered independent voluntary provider about the arrangements, providing for consultation and exchange of information and reports between the local authority and the unregistered independent voluntary *agency* [provider].

(6) Paragraphs (2) and (4) are subject to the provisions of Article 2 of, and sub-paragraphs (5) and (6) of paragraph 15 of Schedule 1 to, the Care Standards Act

2000 (Commencement No 9 (England) and Transitional Provisions) Order 2001 (application by the Commission to a justice of the peace).

(7) Regulation 20(6) shall not apply to any person to whom it would, apart from this regulation apply, if he is on 1st April 2002 already employed by a fostering service provider in a position to which paragraph (7) of that regulation applies.

**Note.** Para (5): in sub-para (b) word 'provider' in square brackets substituted by SI 2002 No 865, reg 7(1), (7) as from 18 April 2002.

**51 Revocation** The following Regulations are revoked—
  (a)  the Foster Placement (Children) Regulations 1991;
  (b)  regulation 2 of the Children (Short-term Placements) (Miscellaneous Amendments) Regulations 1995;
  (c)  regulation 3 of the Children (Protection from Offenders) (Miscellaneous Amendments) Regulations 1997;
  (d)  regulation 2 of the Children (Protection from Offenders) (Amendment) Regulations 1999 so far as it amends the Foster Placement (Children) Regulations 1991; and
  (e)  regulation 2 of the Foster Placement (Children) and Adoption Agencies Amendment (England) Regulations 2001.

SCHEDULE 1                                                        Regulations 5, 7, 20

INFORMATION REQUIRED IN RESPECT OF PERSONS SEEKING TO CARRY ON, MANAGE OR WORK FOR THE PURPOSES OF A FOSTERING SERVICE

**1** Positive proof of identity including a recent photograph.

**2** Either—
  (a)  where the certificate is required for a purpose relating to section 115(5)(ea) of the Police Act 1997 (registration under Part II of the 2000 Act), or the position falls within section 115(3) of that Act, an enhanced criminal record certificate issued under section 115 of that Act; or
  (b)  in any other case, a criminal record certificate issued under sections 113 of that Act,
including, where applicable, the matters specified in sections 113(3A) or 115(6A) of that Act.

**3** Two written references, including a reference from the person's most recent employer, if any.

**4** Where a person has previously worked in a position whose duties involved work with children or vulnerable adults, so far as reasonably practicable verification of the reason why the employment or position ended.

**5** Documentary evidence of any relevant qualification.

**6** A full employment history, together with a satisfactory written explanation of any gaps in employment.

**7** Details of any criminal offences—
  (a)  *of which the person has been convicted, including details of any convictions which are spent within the meaning of section 1 of the Rehabilitation of Offenders Act 2974 and which may be disclosed by virtue of the Rehabilitation of Offenders Act 1974 (Exceptions) Order 1975; or*

(b)   in respect of whci he has been cautioned by a constable and which, at the time the caution was given, he admitted.

**Amendment**   Para 7: revoked by SI 2002 No 865, reg 6(1), (5) with effect from 18 April 2002.

SCHEDULE 2                                                                                   Regulation 22

RECORDS TO BE KEPT BY FOSTERING SERVICE PROVIDERS

**1** A record in the form of a register showing in respect of each child placed with foster parents—

(a)   the date of his placement;
(b)   the name and address of the foster parent;
(c)   the date on which he ceased to be placed there;
(d)   his address prior to the placement;
(e)   his address on leaving the placement;
(f)   his responsible authority (if it is not the fostering service provider);
(g)   the statutory provision under which he is placed with foster parents.

**2** A record showing in respect of each person working for the fostering service provider—

(a)   his full name;
(b)   his sex;
(c)   his date of birth;
(d)   his home address;
(e)   his qualifications relevant to, and experience of, work involving children;
(f)   whether he is employed by the fostering service provider under a contract of service or a contract for services, or is employed by someone other than the fostering service provider;
(g)   whether he works full-time or part-time and, if part-time, the average number of hours worked per week.

**3** A record of all accidents occurring to children whilst placed with foster parents.

SCHEDULE 3                                                                                   Regulation 27

INFORMATION AS TO PROSPECTIVE FOSTER PARENT AND OTHER
MEMBERS OF HIS HOUSEHOLD AND FAMILY

**1** His full name, address and date of birth.

**2** Details of his health (supported by a medical report), personality, marital status and details of his current and any previous marriage or similar relationship.

**3** Particulars of any other adult members of his household.

**4** Particulars of the children in his family, whether or not members of his household, and any other children in his household.

**5** Particulars of his accommodation.

**6** His religious persuasion, and his capacity to care for a child from any particular religious persuasion.

**7** His racial origin, his cultural and linguistic background and his capacity to care for a child from any particular origin or cultural or linguistic background.

**8** His past and present employment or occupation, his standard of living and leisure activities and interests.

**9** His previous experience (if any) of caring for his own and other children.

**10** His skills, competence and potential relevant to his capacity to care effectively for a child placed with him.

**11** The outcome of any request or application made by him or any other member of his household to foster or adopt children, or for registration for child minding or day care, including particulars of any previous approval or refusal of approval relating to him or to any other member of his household.

**12** The names and addresses of two persons who will provide personal references for the prospective foster parent.

**13** In relation to the prospective foster parent, either—
  (a) an enhanced criminal record certificate issued under section 115 of the Police Act 1997 including the matters specified in section 115(6A) of that Act; or
  (b) where any certificate of information on any matters referred to in sub-paragraph (a) is not available to an individual because any provision of the Police Act 1997 has not been brought into force, details of any criminal offences—
      (i) of which the person has been convicted, including details of any convictions which are spent within the meaning of section 1 of the Rehabilitation of Offenders Act 1974 and which may be disclosed by virtue of the Rehabilitation of Offenders Act 1974 (Exceptions) Order 1975; or
      (ii) in respect of which he has been cautioned by a constable and which, at the time the caution was given, he admitted; and

in relation to each member of the household aged 18 or over, details of any criminal offences such as are mentioned in sub-paragraphs (i) and (ii) of paragraph 13(b).

SCHEDULE 4                                              Regulation 27(7)(b)

**OFFENCES SPECIFIED FOR THE PURPOSES OF REGULATION 27(7)(B)**

*Offences in Scotland*

**1** An offence of rape.

**2** An offence specified in Schedule 1 to the Criminal Procedure (Scotland) Act 1995 except, in a case where the offender was under the age of 20 at the time the offence was committed, an offence contrary to section 5 of the Criminal Law (Consolidation) (Scotland) Act 1995 (intercourse with a girl under 16), an offence of shameless indecency between men or an offence of sodomy.

**3** An offence of plagium (theft of a child below the age of puberty).

**4** Section 52 or 52A of the Civic Government (Scotland) Act 1982 (indecent photographs of children).

**5** An offence under section 3 of the Sexual Offences (Amendment) Act 2000 (abuse of trust).

*Offences in Northern Ireland*

**6** An offence of rape.

**7** An offence specified in Schedule 1 to the Children and Young Persons Act (Northern Ireland) 1968, except in the case where the offender was under the age of 20 at the time the offence was committed, an offence contrary to sections 5 or 11 of the Criminal Law Amendment Act 1885 (unlawful carnal knowledge of a girl under 17 and gross indecency between males), or an offence contrary to section 61 of the Offences against the Person Act 1861 (buggery).

**8** An offence under Article 3 of the Protection of Children (Northern Ireland) Order 1978 (indecent photographs).

**9** An offence contrary to Article 9 of the Criminal Justice (Northern Ireland) Order 1980 (inciting girl under 16 to have incestuous sexual intercourse).

**10** An offence contrary to Article 15 of the Criminal Justice (Evidence, etc) (Northern Ireland) Order 1988 (possession of indecent photographs of children).

**11** An offence under section 3 of the Sexual Offences (Amendment) Act 2000 (abuse of trust).


SCHEDULE 5                                               Regulation 28(5)(b)

MATTERS AND OBLIGATIONS IN FOSTER CARE AGREEMENTS

**1** The terms of the foster parent's approval.

**2** The amount of support and training to be given to the foster parent.

**3** The procedure for the review of approval of a foster parent.

**4** The procedure in connection with the placement of children and the matters to be included in any foster placement agreement.

**5** The arrangements for meeting any legal liabilities of the foster parent arising by reason of a placement.

**6** The procedure available to foster parents for making representations.

**7** To give written notice to the fostering service provider forthwith, with full particulars, of—
    (a) any intended change of the foster parent's address;
    (b) any change in the composition of his household;
    (c) any other change in his personal circumstances and any other event affecting either his capacity to care for any child placed or the suitability of his household; and
    (d) any request or application to adopt children, or for registration for child minding or day care.

**8** Not to administer corporal punishment to any child placed with him.

**9** To ensure that any information relating to a child placed with him, to the child's family or to any other person, which has been given to him in confidence in connection with a placement is kept confidential and is not disclosed to any person without the consent of the fostering service provider.

**10** To comply with the terms of any foster placement agreement.

**11** To care for any child placed with him as if the child were a member of the foster parent's family and to promote his welfare having regard to the long and short-term plans for the child.

**12** To comply with the policies and procedures of the fostering service provider issued under regulations 12 and 13.

**13** To co-operate as reasonably required with the Commission and in particular to allow a person authorised by the Commission to interview him and visit his home at any reasonable time.

**14** To keep the fostering service provider informed about the child's progress and to notify it immediately of any significant events affecting the child.

**15** To allow any child placed with him to be removed from his home if regulation 36 applies.

SCHEDULE 6                                                            Regulation 34(3)

MATTERS AND OBLIGATIONS IN FOSTER PLACEMENT AGREEMENTS

**1** A statement by the responsible authority containing all the information which the authority considers necessary to enable the foster parent to care for the child and, in particular, information as to—
  (a) the authority's arrangements for the child and the objectives of the placement in the context of its plan for the care of the child;
  (b) the child's personal history, religious persuasion and cultural and linguistic background and racial origin;
  (c) the child's state of health and identified health needs;
  (d) the safety needs of the child, including any need for any special equipment or adaptation;
  (e) the child's educational needs; and
  (f) any needs arising from any disability the child may have.

**2** The responsible authority's arrangements for the financial support of the child during the placement.

**3** The arrangements for giving consent to the medical or dental examination or treatment of the child.

**4** The circumstances in which it is necessary to obtain in advance the approval of the responsible authority for the child to take part in school trips, or to stay overnight away from the foster parent's home.

**5** The arrangements for visits to the child by the person authorised by or on behalf of the responsible authority, and the frequency of visits and reviews under the Review of Children's Cases Regulations 1991.

**6** The arrangements for the child to have contact with his parents and any other specified persons, and details of any court order relating to contact.

**7** Compliance by the foster parent with the terms of the foster care agreement.

**8** Co-operation by the foster parent with the responsible authority regarding any arrangements it makes for the child.

SCHEDULE 7                                Regulation 42(1)

MATTERS TO BE MONITORED BY THE REGISTERED PERSON

**1** Compliance in relation to each child placed with foster parents, with the foster placement agreement and the responsible authority's plan for the care of the child.

**2** All accidents, injuries and illnesses of children placed with foster parents.

**3** Complaints in relation to children placed with foster parents and their outcomes.

**4** Any allegations or suspicions of abuse in respect of children placed with foster parents and the outcome of any investigation.

**5** Recruitment records and conduct of required checks of new workers.

**6** Notifications of events listed in Schedule 8.

**7** Any unauthorised absence from the foster home of a child accommodated there.

**8** Use of any measures of control, restraint or discipline in respect of children accommodated in a foster home.

**9** Medication, medical treatment and first aid administered to any child placed with foster parents.

**10** Where applicable, the standard of any education provided by the fostering service.

**11** Records of assessments.

**12** Records of fostering panel meetings.

**13** Duty rosters of persons working for the fostering agency, as arranged and as actually worked.

**14** Records of appraisals of employees.

**15** Minutes of staff meetings.

SCHEDULE 8                                              Regulation 43(1)

EVENTS AND NOTIFICATIONS

| Column 1<br>*Event:* | Column 2<br>*To be notified to:*<br>Commission | Responsible authority | Secretary of State | Area authority | Police | *Health Authority* [Primary Care Trust] |
|---|---|---|---|---|---|---|
| Death of a child placed with foster parents | yes | yes | yes | yes | | yes |
| Referral to the Secretary of State pursuant to section 2(1)(a) of the Protection of Children Act 1999 of an individual working for a fostering service | yes | yes | | | | |
| Serious illness or serious accident of a child placed with foster parents | yes | yes | | | | |
| Outbreak at the home of a foster parent of any infectious disease which in the opinion of a registered medical practitioner attending the home is sufficiently serious to be so notified | yes | yes | | | | yes |
| Allegation that a child placed with foster parents has committed a serious offence | | yes | | | yes | |

| Column 1 Event: | Column 2 To be notified to: Commission | Responsible authority | Secretary of State | Area authority | Police | Health Authority [Primary Care Trust] |
|---|---|---|---|---|---|---|
| Involvement or suspected involvement of a child placed with foster parents in prostitution | yes | yes | | yes | yes | |
| Serious incident relating to a child placed with foster parents necessitating calling the police to the foster parent's home | yes | yes | | | | |
| Absconding by a child placed with foster parents | | yes | | | | |
| Any serious complaint about any foster parent approved by the fostering agency | yes | yes | | | | |
| Instigation and outcome of any child protection enquiry involving a child placed with foster parents | yes | yes | | | | |

**Note.** Column 2 heading 'Primary Care Trust' substituted by SI 2002 No 2469, reg 10(a), Sch 7 as from 1 October 2002.

## RECIPROCAL ENFORCEMENT OF MAINTENANCE ORDERS (DESIGNATION OF RECIPROCATING COUNTRIES) ORDER 2002

**Dated** 26 March 2002

## SI 2002 No 788

**1** This Order may be cited as the Reciprocal Enforcement of Maintenance Orders (Designation of Reciprocating Countries) Order 2002 and shall come into force on 28th May 2002.

**2** In this Order—

   (a) 'the 1920 Act' means the Maintenance Orders (Facilities for Enforcement) Act 1920;

   (b) 'the 1972 Act' means the Maintenance Orders (Reciprocal Enforcement) Act 1972;

   (c) 'column (1)' and 'column (2)' mean respectively columns (1) and (2) of the Schedule to this Order.

**3** The Country and the territory specified in column (1) is hereby designated as a reciprocating country for the purposes of Part I of the 1972 Act as regards maintenance orders of the description specified in respect of that Country or that territory in column (2).

**4**—(1) In this Article—

   (a) 'commencement date' means the date on which this Order comes into force;

   (b) 'registered' means registered in the High Court or the High Court of Justice in Northern Ireland under section 1 of the 1920 Act;

   (c) 'relevant maintenance order' means an order, other than an order of affiliation, for the periodic payments of sums of money.

   (2) Paragraph (3) shall apply if—

   (a) a relevant maintenance order is transmitted under section 2 or 3 of the 1920 Act to the Country or the territory specified in column (1); and

   (b) immediately before the commencement date the 1920 Act applied to that order.

   (3) Where this paragraph applies, sections 5, 12 to 15, 17, 18 and 21 of the 1972 Act shall apply in relation to a relevant maintenance order referred to in paragraph (1), as they apply in relation to a maintenance order of the same description—

   (a) sent to the Country or territory specified in column (1) pursuant to section 2 of the 1972 Act;

   (b) made under section 3 or 4 of the 1972 Act; and

   (c) confirmed by a competent court in that Country or territory.

   (4) Paragraph (5) shall apply if—

   (a) a relevant maintenance order is transmitted under section 2 or 3 of the 1920 Act to the Country or territory specified in column (1); and

   (b) immediately before the commencement date—

     (i) the 1920 Act applied to that order; and

     (ii) the order was not registered.

   (5) Where this paragraph applies, sections 8 to 21 of the 1972 Act shall apply in relation to a relevant maintenance order referred to under paragraph (1), as they apply in relation to a maintenance order of the same description made under the 1972 Act which is so registered.

   (6) Paragraph (7) shall apply if—

   (a) a relevant maintenance order has been confirmed by a court in England, Wales or Northern Ireland under section 4 of the 1920 Act; and

   (b) is in force immediately before the commencement date.

   (7) Where this paragraph applies, a relevant maintenance order as referred to under paragraph (1) shall be registered under section 7(5) of the 1972 Act in the same manner as if it had been confirmed by that court in England, Wales or Northern Ireland under subsection (2) of that section.

   (8) Any proceedings brought under or by virtue of any provision of the 1920 Act in a court in England, Wales or Northern Ireland which are pending immediately before the commencement date, being proceedings affecting a person resident in the Country or territory specified in column (1), shall be continued as if they had been brought under or by virtue of the corresponding provision of the 1972 Act.

SCHEDULE
COUNTRY AND TERRITORY DESIGNATED AS A RECIPROCATING COUNTRY
AND EXTENT OF DESIGNATION

| (1) Country or territory | (2) Description of maintenance orders to which designation extends |
| --- | --- |
| Brunei Darussalam | Maintenance orders other than lump sum orders |
| Newfoundland and Labrador (formerly known as Newfoundland) | Maintenance orders generally |

## PROTECTION OF CHILDREN AND VULNERABLE ADULTS AND CARE STANDARDS TRIBUNAL REGULATIONS 2002

**Dated** 25 March 2002

**SI 2002 No 816**

PART I

INTRODUCTORY

**1 Citation, commencement and interpretation**—(1) These Regulations may be cited as the Protection of Children and Vulnerable Adults and Care Standards Tribunal Regulations 2002 and shall come into force—
  (a)  for the purposes of—
      (i)   an appeal under section 86(1)(a) or (b) of the 2000 Act;
      (ii)  an application for leave to appeal under section 86(1)(b) of the 2000 Act;
      (iii) a determination, or an application for leave for a determination, under section 86(2) of the 2000 Act,
    on the first day on which sections 80 to 93 of the 2000 Act are in force;
  (b)  for all other purposes, on 1st April 2002.
  (2)  In these Regulations—
'the 1989 Act' means the Children Act 1989;
['the 1998 Act' means the School Standards and Framework Act 1998;]
'the 1999 Act' means the Protection of Children Act 1999;
'the 2000 Act' means the Care Standards Act 2000;
['the 2002 Act' means the Education Act 2002;]
'case' in Parts IV and VI means—
    (a)  an appeal under section 21 of the 2000 Act;
    (b)  an appeal under section 79M of the 1989 Act;
    (c)  an appeal under section 65A of the 1989 Act;
    (d)  an appeal under section 4(1)(a) or (b) of the 1999 Act;
    (e)  a determination under section 4(2) of the 1999 Act;
    (f)  an appeal under the Education Regulations;
    (g)  an appeal under section 86(1)(a) or (b) of the 2000 Act; *or*
    (h)  a determination under section 86(2) of the 2000 Act;
    [(i)  an appeal under section 68 of the 2000 Act; *or*
    (j)  an appeal under the Suspension Regulations;] [*or*
    (k)  an appeal under paragraph 10(1A) of Schedule 26 to the 1998 Act;]
        [or

(1)   an appeal under section 166 of the 2002 Act including an application for, or consideration by the Tribunal of the making of, an order under section 166(5);]

'application for leave' means an application to the Tribunal—

(a)  for leave to appeal under section 4(1)(b) of the 1999 Act or section 86(1)(b) of the 2000 Act;

(b)  for leave for a determination by the Tribunal under section 4(2) of the 1999 Act or section 86(2) of the 2000 Act;

'appropriate authority' means in relation to an appeal under section 65A of the 1989 Act the *Commission* [Commission for Social Care Inspection] or the Assembly;

'the Assembly' means the National Assembly for Wales;

'the Chief Inspector' means Her Majesty's Chief Inspector of Schools in England;

'the clerk' means, in relation to a hearing before the Tribunal, the person appointed by the Secretary to act as clerk to the Tribunal;

'the Commission' means the *National Care Standards Commission* [Commission for Social Care Inspection or the Commission for Healthcare Audit and Inspection];

'costs order' shall be construed in accordance with regulation 24;

['Council' means in relation to England, the General Social Care Council or in relation to Wales, the Care Council for Wales;]

'county court' has the same meaning as in the County Courts Act 1984;

'document' means information recorded in writing or in any other form;

'the Education Regulations' means the Education (Restriction of Employment) Regulations 2000;

'an institution within the further education sector' shall be construed in accordance with section 4(3) of the Education Act 1996;

'local authority' has the same meaning as in section 105 of the 1989 Act;

'local education authority' shall be construed in accordance with section 12 of the Education Act 1996;

'nominated chairman' means the chairman appointed by the President in accordance with regulation 5 to determine a case or an application for leave;

'a party' means either the applicant or the respondent;

'parties' means the applicant and the respondent;

'the POCA list' means the list kept under section 1 of the 1999 Act;

'the POVA list' means the list kept under section 81 of the 2000 Act;

'records' means the records of the Tribunal;

'registration authority' means—

(a) in relation to an appeal under section 21 of the 2000 Act, *the Commission* [Commission for Healthcare Audit and Inspection or the Commission for Social Care Inspection] or the Assembly; *and*

(b) in relation to an appeal under section 79M of the 1989 Act, the Chief Inspector or the Assembly;

[(c) in relation to an appeal under section 166 of the 2002 Act, the Secretary of State for Education and Skills or the Assembly;]

'relevant programme' means a programme included in a programme service within the meaning of the Broadcasting Act 1990;

'relevant social work' has the same meaning as in section 55(4) of the 2000 Act;

'the respondent' means—

(a)  in relation to an appeal under section 21 of the 2000 Act, the registration authority;

(b)  in relation to an appeal under section 79M of the 1989 Act, the registration authority;

(c) in relation to an appeal under section 65A of the 1989 Act, the appropriate authority;

(e) in relation to an appeal, an application for leave or a determination under section 4 of the 1999 Act, *the Secretary of State for Health* [the Secretary of State for Education and Skills];

(f) in relation to an appeal under the Education Regulations, the Secretary of State for Education and Skills or the National Assembly for Wales;

(g) in relation to an appeal, an application for leave or a determination under section 86 of the 2000 Act, the Secretary of State for Health;

[(h) in relation to an appeal under section 68 of the 2000 Act, the Council;

(i) in relation to an appeal under the Suspension Regulations, the Chief Inspector;]

[(j) in relation to an appeal under paragraph 10(1A) of Schedule 26 to the 1998 Act, the Chief Inspector;]

[(k) in relation to an appeal under section 166 of the 2002 Act, the registration authority.]

'residential family centre' has the same meaning as in section 4(2) of the 2000 Act;

'school' has the same meaning as in section 4 of the Education Act 1996;

'the Secretary' means the person for the time being acting as the Secretary to the Tribunal;

['the Suspension Regulations' means the Child Minding and Day Care (Suspension of Registration) (England) Regulations 2003;]

'vulnerable adult' means a person who is not a child and who—

(a) suffers from mental disorder within the meaning of the Mental Health Act 1983, or otherwise has a significant impairment of intelligence and social functioning; or

(b) has a physical disability or is suffering from a physical disorder;

'working day' means any day other than a Saturday, a Sunday, Christmas Day, Good Friday or a day which is a bank holiday within the meaning of the Banking and Financial Dealings Act 1971.

(3) In these Regulations, a reference—

(a) to a numbered regulation is to the regulation in these Regulations bearing that number;

(b) in a regulation to a numbered paragraph is to the paragraph of that regulation bearing that number;

(c) to a numbered Schedule, is to a Schedule in these Regulations bearing that number;

(d) in a paragraph to a numbered or lettered sub-paragraph is to the sub-paragraph of that paragraph bearing that number or letter.

**Note.** Words in square brackets and definitions added by SI 2003 No 626 as from 1 April 2003, SI 2003 No 1060 as from 30 April 2003 and SI 2003 No 2043 with effect from 1 September 2003; further amended in paras (1), (2) by SI 2004 No 664, art 2, Sch 1, para 7(1), (2)(a)(c) as from 1 April 2004 and SI 2004 No 2073, reg 2 as from 31 August 2004.

PART II

CONSTITUTION

**2 Powers and functions exercisable by the President and Secretary**—(1) Anything which must or may be done by the President (except under regulation 5(1), (2), (4) or (5) or 25(4)), may be done by a member of the chairmen's panel authorised by the President.

(2) Anything which must or may be done by the Secretary may be done by a member of the Tribunal's staff authorised by the Secretary.

**3 Requirements for membership of lay panel**—(1) A person may be appointed a member of the lay panel if he satisfies the requirements of—
  (a) paragraph (2);
  (b) paragraphs (3) and (4); or
  (c) paragraph (5).
  (2) The requirements of this paragraph are—
  (a) experience in the provision of services—
      (i) which must or may be provided by local authorities under the 1989 Act [or the Adoption Act 1976] or which are similar to such services;
      (ii) for vulnerable adults; or
      (iii) in a residential family centre; and
  (b) experience in relevant social work.
  (3) The requirements of this paragraph are—
  (a) experience in the provision of services by a Health Authority, a Special Health Authority, a National Health Service trust [, an NHS foundation trust] or a Primary Care Trust;
  (b) experience in the provision of education in a school or in an institution within the further education sector; or
  (c) experience of being employed by a local education authority in connection with the exercise of its functions under Part I of the Education Act 1996.
  (4) The requirements of this paragraph are—
  (a) experience in the conduct of disciplinary investigations;
  (b) experience as a member of an Area Child Protection Committee, or similar experience;
  (c) experience of taking part in child protection conferences or in child protection review conferences, or similar experience; or
  (d) experience in negotiating the conditions of service of employees.
  (5) The requirements of this paragraph are—
  (a) experience in carrying out inspections under Part II of the 2000 Act;
  (b) experience in carrying out inspections under the Registered Homes Act 1984;
  (c) experience in carrying out inspections under the 1989 Act [or the Adoption Act 1976];
  (d) experience in managing an establishment or agency under Part II of the 2000 Act;
  (e) experience in managing a children's home under the 1989 Act;
  [(ee) experience in managing an adoption society approved under the Adoption Act 1976;]
  (f) experience in managing a nursing home, mental nursing home or residential care home under the Registered Homes Act 1984;
  (g) experience in managing the provision of local authority social services;
  (h) that the person is a registered nurse or registered medical practitioner who has experience of the provision of health care services;
  (i) experience in managing or inspecting child minding and day care provision for children under 8 years of age; or
  (j) experience in a professional, managerial or supervisory position in the provision of early childhood education [, child minding or day care] or child development.

**Note.** Paras (2), (3), (5): words in square brackets added by SI 2003 No 1060, reg 3(a)-(d) as from 30 April 2003. Para (3): in sub-para (a) words ', an NHS foundation trust' in square brackets inserted by SI 2004 No 696, art 3(4), Sch 4 as from 1 April 2004.

PART III

APPEALS, DETERMINATIONS AND APPLICATIONS FOR LEAVE

**4 Procedure for appeals, determinations and applications for leave**—(1) In the case of an appeal under section 21 of the 2000 Act, the procedure set out in Schedule 1 shall apply.

(2) In the case of an appeal under section 79M of the 1989 Act, the procedure set out in Schedule 2 shall apply.

(3) In the case of an appeal under section 65A of the 1989 Act, the procedure set out in Schedule 3 shall apply.

(4) In the case of—

(a) an application for leave under section 4(1)(b) or (2) of the 1999 Act;

(b) an appeal under section 4(1)(a) of the 1999 Act against a decision to include an individual in the POCA list;

(c) an appeal under section 4(1)(b) of the 1999 Act against a decision not to remove an individual from the POCA list under section 1(3) of that Act;

(d) a determination under section 4(2) of the 1999 Act as to whether an individual should be included in the POCA list;

(e) an appeal under regulation 13 of the Education Regulations against a decision to give a direction under regulation 5 of those Regulations; or

(f) an appeal under regulation 13 of the Education Regulations against a decision not to revoke or vary such a direction,

the procedure set out in Schedule 4 shall apply.

(5) In the case of—

(a) an application for leave to the Tribunal under section 86(1)(b) or (2) of the 2000 Act;

(b) an appeal under section 86(1)(a) of the 2000 Act against a decision to include an individual in the POVA list;

(c) an appeal under section 86(1)(b) of the 2000 Act against a decision not to remove an individual from the POVA list; or

(d) a determination under section 86(2) of the 2000 Act as to whether an individual should be included in the POVA list,

the procedure set out in Schedule 5 shall apply.

[(6) In the case of an appeal under section 68 of the 2000 Act against a decision of the Council under Part IV of the 2000 Act, the procedure set out in Schedule 6 shall apply.

(7) In the case of—

(a) an appeal under regulation 8(1)(a) of the Suspension Regulations against a decision to suspend the registration of a person acting as a child minder or providing day care; or

(b) an appeal under regulation 8(1)(b) of the Suspension Regulations against a refusal to lift the suspension of such registration,

the procedure set out in Schedule 7 shall apply.]

[(8) In the case of an appeal under paragraph 10(1A) of Schedule 26 to the 1998 Act against a decision of the Chief Inspector, the procedure set out in Schedule 8 shall apply.]

[(9) In the case of an appeal under section 166 of the 2002 Act (including in relation to the making of an order under section 166(5)), the procedure set out in Schedule 9 shall apply.]

**Note.** Paras (6) and (7) inserted by SI 2003 No 626, reg 3, 4 as from 1 April 2003. Para (8) added by SI 2003 No 1060 as from 30 April 2003. Para (9) inserted by SI 2003 No 2043, reg 3 as from 1 September 2003.

**[4A Misconceived appeals or applications etc]**—[(1) The President or the nominated chairman may at any time strike out an appeal or application for leave mentioned in regulation 4 on the grounds that—

- (a)  it is made otherwise than in accordance with the provision in these Regulations for—
    - (i)   initiating that appeal; or
    - (ii)  applying for leave;
- (b)  it is outside the jurisdiction of the Tribunal or is otherwise misconceived; or
- (c)  it is frivolous or vexatious.

(2)  Before striking out an appeal or application for leave under this paragraph, the President or the nominated chairman must—

- (a)  invite the parties to make representations on the matter within such period as he may direct;
- (b)  if, within the period specified in the direction, the applicant so requests in writing, afford the parties an opportunity to make oral representations; and
- (c)  consider any representations the parties may make.

(3)  Where the President or the nominated chairman strikes out an appeal or an application for leave under paragraph (1), regulation 24 (costs) shall apply as if the references to 'the Tribunal' were instead references to 'the President or the nominated chairman'.

(4)  Where, under paragraph (1), the President or the nominated chairman has made a determination to strike out an appeal or application for leave ('the determination'), the applicant may apply to the President, or to that nominated chairman, for the determination to be set aside.

(5)  An application under paragraph (4) must—

- (a)  be made not later than 10 working days after the date on which notice of the determination was sent to the applicant; and
- (b)  must be in writing stating the grounds in full.

(6)  In the case of an application under paragraph (4), the President, or the nominated chairman, may, if he considers that it is appropriate to do so, set aside the determination (including, where applicable, a costs order made pursuant to paragraph (3)), and may give such directions in exercise of his powers under Part IV of these Regulations as he considers appropriate.

(7)  Before setting aside the determination, the President or the nominated chairman may invite the parties to make representations on the matter within such period as he may direct.

(8)  Where the determination is set aside, the Secretary shall alter the relevant entry in the records.]

**Note.** Inserted by SI 2004 No 2073, reg 3 as from 31 August 2004.

PART IV

CASE MANAGEMENT

**5 Appointment of Tribunal—**(1) The President shall, at such time as he considers it appropriate to do so, nominate a chairman (who may be himself) and two members of the lay panel to determine the case.

(2)  The President shall, at such time as he considers it appropriate to do so, nominate a chairman (who may be himself) to determine an application for leave.

(3)  The President or the nominated chairman may determine any application made in relation to the case or any application for leave.

(4)  The President may at any time before the hearing (or, if the case is to be determined without an oral hearing, before the case is determined) nominate from the appropriate panel another person in substitution for the chairman or other member previously nominated.

(5)  The President shall nominate members of the lay panel who appear to him to have experience and qualifications relevant to the subject matter of the case.

**6 Directions—**[(Z1) This regulation shall not apply in the case of an appeal under the Suspension Regulations] [or in relation to an application for an order under section 166(5) of the 2002 Act pursuant to paragraph 7(1) of Schedule 9].

(1) If either party has requested that there shall be a preliminary hearing, or if the President or the nominated chairman considers that a preliminary hearing is necessary, the President or the nominated chairman, as the case may be, shall fix a date for the preliminary hearing, as soon as possible after the expiry of the 5 working days referred to *in paragraph 6 of Schedule 1, 2 or 3* [*in paragraph 6 of Schedule 1, 2, 3 or 6*] [*in paragraph 6 of Schedule 1, 2, 3, 6 or 8*] [in paragraph 6 of Schedule 1, 2, 3, 6, 8 or 9] or paragraph 9 of Schedule 4 or 5, as the case may be.

(2) At the preliminary hearing, or if a preliminary hearing is not to be held, as soon as possible after, and in any event not later than 10 working days after, the expiry of the 5 working days referred to in paragraph (1) the President or the nominated chairman—

(a) shall give directions as to the dates by which any document, witness statement or other material upon which any party is intending to rely shall be sent to the Tribunal, and, if the President or the nominated chairman considers it appropriate, to the other party;

(b) may give any other direction in exercise of his powers under this Part which he considers appropriate; and

(c) shall, where the applicant has requested that the case be determined without an oral hearing, give a direction as to the date, which shall be not less than 10 working days after the last date on which he has directed that any document, witness statement or other evidence be sent to the Tribunal, by which the parties shall send any written representations regarding their appeal to the Tribunal.

(3) The President or the nominated chairman may direct that exchange of witness statements or other material shall be simultaneous or sequential, as he considers appropriate.

(3A) If, at any time, it appears to the President or the nominated chairman that the appeal is of such a nature that it should be determined at an oral hearing, he may (after considering any representations from the parties) direct that such a hearing shall be held, but otherwise the case shall be determined without an oral hearing if the applicant has so requested.]

(4) The Secretary shall notify the parties as soon as possible in writing of any directions the President or the nominated chairman gives in writing under paragraphs (2) and (3) above.

(5) The Secretary shall notify the parties as soon as possible, and in any event not less than 5 working days before the hearing of the date, time and place of any preliminary hearing.

(6) The parties may be represented or assisted at any preliminary hearing by any person.

**Note.** Sub-para (Z1) inserted, words in italics in para (1) omitted and words in square brackets inserted by SI 2003 No 626, reg 4(a) as from 1 April 2003. Words at the end of this sub-para and reference to schedules in sub-para (1) substituted by SI 2003 No 2043 as from 1 September 2003. Words in italics omitted and words in square brackets substituted by SI 2003 No 1060 as from 30 April 2003. Para (3A) inserted by SI 2004 No 2073, reg 4(b) as from 31 August 2004.

*[Directions: appeals under the Suspension Regulations*

**6A—**(1) This regulation shall apply in the case of an appeal under the Suspension Regulations [and in the case of an application for an order under section 166(5) of the 2002 Act].

(2) The President or the nominated chairman may, if he considers it necessary or expedient (and whether at the request of either party or otherwise)—

    (a)  give directions as to the dates by which any document, witness statement or other material upon which any party is intending to rely shall be sent to the Tribunal, and, if the President or the nominated chairman considers it appropriate, to the other party;

    (b)  give any other direction in exercise of his powers under this Part;

    (c)  where the applicant has requested that the case be determined without an oral hearing, give a direction as to the date by which the parties shall send any written representations, regarding the appeal, to the Tribunal.

(3) The President or the nominated chairman may direct that exchange of witness statements or other material shall be simultaneous or sequential, as he considers appropriate.

(4) The Secretary shall notify the parties as soon as possible in writing of any directions the President or the nominated chairman gives in writing under paragraphs (2) and (3).]

**Note.** Regulation 6A added by SI 2003 No 626, reg 5 as from 1 April 2003. Words in square brackets in para (1) inserted by SI 2003 No 2043, reg 5 as from 1 September 2003.

**7 Fixing and notification of hearing—**[(Z1) This regulation shall not apply in relation to an application for an order under section 166(5) of the 2002 Act.]

(1) The Secretary must, in consultation with the President or the nominated chairman, fix a date for the hearing of the case unless the applicant has requested in writing that the case be determined without a hearing [, and the President or nominated chairman has not directed that there be a hearing pursuant to regulation 6(3A)].

(2) *The date* [Except in the case of an appeal under the Suspension Regulations, the date] fixed for the hearing shall be the earliest practicable date having regard to any directions which have been made by the President or the nominated chairman with regard to the preparation of evidence but shall be no sooner than 15 working days after the latest date on which the President or the nominated chairman has directed that the evidence of the parties (including the statements of any witnesses or experts) shall be filed or exchanged.

[(2A) In the case of an appeal under the Suspension Regulations, the date fixed for the hearing shall be the earliest practicable date having regard to any directions which have been made by the President or the nominated chairman with regard to the preparation of evidence but shall be not later than 10 working days after the date on which the Secretary receives the written response from the respondent under paragraph 3 of Schedule 7.]

(3) *The Secretary* [Except in the case of an appeal under the Suspension Regulations, the Secretary] must inform the parties in writing of the date, time and place of the hearing no less than 20 working days before the date fixed for the hearing.

[(3A) In the case of an appeal under the Suspension Regulations, the Secretary must inform the parties in writing of the date, time and place of the hearing—

    (a)  subject to sub-paragraph (b), by no later than 5 working days before the date fixed for the hearing, or by such later date as the parties may agree;

    (b)  where it appears to the President or the nominated chairman that it is necessary or expedient for the parties to be informed of the hearing at a date later than 5 working days before the date fixed for the hearing, by such date as the President or the nominated chairman may direct.]

(4) The Secretary may, in consultation with the President or the nominated chairman, alter the place of the hearing and, if he does, he must without delay inform the parties in writing of the alteration.

(5) Subject to paragraph (6), the President or the nominated chairman may adjourn the hearing, either on the application of either party or on his own initiative.

(6) The President or the nominated chairman shall not adjourn the hearing unless satisfied that refusing the adjournment would prevent the just disposal of the case.

(7) If the President or the nominated chairman adjourns the hearing, then the Secretary must, without delay, inform the parties in writing of the date, time and place at which the hearing will be resumed.

**Note.** Words in italics in paras (2) and (3) omitted and words in square brackets substituted and paras (2A) and (3A) added by SI 2003 No 626, reg 6(a)-(d) as from 1 April 2003. Para (Z1) inserted by SI 2003 No 2043, reg 6 as from 1 September 2003. Para (1): words from ', and the President' to 'to regulation 6(3A)' in square brackets inserted by SI 2004 No 2073, reg 5 as from 31 August 2004.

**8 Multiple appeals—**(1) Subject to paragraphs (2) and (3), where two or more cases relate to the same person, establishment or agency, the President or the nominated chairman may, on the application of either party or on his own initiative, direct that such cases shall be heard together if he considers it appropriate to do so.

(2) Where a person ('the applicant') has by virtue of section 92(1) and (2) of the 2000 Act been included in the POVA list pursuant to a reference under section 2, 2A, or 2D of the 1999 Act or as a result of being named in a relevant inquiry within the meaning of section 2B of that Act, then subject to paragraph (4) any appeal against inclusion in the POVA list shall be joined with any appeal against inclusion in the POCA list and in that event the appeal against inclusion in the POCA list shall be heard first.

(3) Where a person ('the applicant') has by virtue of section 2C of the 1999 Act been included in the POCA list pursuant to a reference made under section 82, 83 or 84 of the 2000 Act or as a result of being named in a relevant inquiry within the meaning of section 85 of that Act, then subject to paragraph (4) any appeal against inclusion in the POCA list shall be joined with any appeal against inclusion in the POVA list and in that event the appeal against inclusion in the POVA list shall be heard first.

(4) The applicant may request the President or the nominated chairman in writing to give a direction that the appeals referred to in paragraph (2) or (3) shall be heard separately.

(5) Before making any direction under paragraph (1) the President or the nominated chairman shall—

(a) where the direction which he proposes to give is at the request of either party, give the other party the opportunity *to make written representations* [to make—
    (i) in the case of an appeal under the Suspension Regulations, oral representations at the commencement of the hearing; or
    (ii) in any other case, written representations.]

(b) where the direction which he proposes to give is on his own initiative, give both parties the opportunity *to make written representations* [to make—
    (i) in the case of an appeal under the Suspension Regulations, oral representations at the commencement of the hearing; or
    (ii) in any other case, written representations.]

(6) In considering whether to give a direction under paragraph (1), the President or the nominated chairman shall take into account the following matters—

(a) *any written representations made by either party;*
[(a) any representations made by either party under paragraph (5);]
(b) the increased cost of hearing the cases together or separately; and
(c) any unreasonable delay in hearing any case which would be caused by hearing the appeals together or separately.

(7) In considering whether to give a direction under paragraph (4) the President or the nominated chairman shall take into account the following matters—
  (a) any representations from the applicant which show he would be significantly disadvantaged if the appeals were to be heard together;
  (b) the increased cost of hearing the appeals together or separately; and
  (c) any unreasonable delay in hearing either appeal which would be caused by hearing the appeals together or separately,
and shall give a direction that the appeals be heard separately where he is satisfied that it would be unfair in all the circumstances to hear the appeals together.

**Note.** Words in italics in paras (5) and (6) omitted and words in square brackets substituted by SI 2003 No 626 as from 1 April 2003.

**9 Further directions—**(1) The President or the nominated chairman may at any time on the application of either party or on his own initiative, vary any direction which he has given or give any further direction in exercise of any of his powers under this Part as he considers appropriate.

(2) Before making any further direction, or varying any direction under paragraph (1)—
  (a) the President or the nominated chairman shall, where the variation or further direction which he proposes to give—
    (i) is at the request of either party, give the other party the opportunity to make written representations; or
    (ii) is on his own initiative, give both parties the opportunity to make written representations;
  (b) [except in relation to an application for an order under section 166(5) of the 2002 Act,] the President or the nominated chairman may direct that there shall be a preliminary hearing in relation to any proposed variation or further direction if he considers it appropriate or if a preliminary hearing has been requested by either party.

**Note.** Words in square brackets in para (2)(b) inserted by SI 2003 No 2043, reg 7 as from 1 September 2003.

**10 Unless orders—**(1) The President or the nominated chairman may at any time make an order to the effect that, unless the party to whom the order is addressed takes a step specified in the order within the period specified in the order, the case may be determined in favour of the other party.

(2) The Secretary shall give written notification of the order to the party to whom it is addressed and to the other party and shall inform him of the effect of paragraph (3).

(3) If a party fails to comply with an order addressed to him under this regulation, the President or the nominated chairman may determine the case in favour of the other party.

[(4) If, in the opinion of the President or the nominated chairman, the party to whom an order referred to in paragraph (1) is addressed has acted unreasonably in failing to comply with an order addressed to him under this regulation, the President or the nominated chairman may make an order for costs ('a costs order') pursuant to regulation 24 requiring that party ('the paying party') to make a payment to the other party ('the receiving party') to cover costs incurred by the receiving party and, in such a case, the references in regulation 24 to 'the Tribunal' shall have effect as if they were references to 'the President or the nominated chairman'.

(5) Where, in accordance with paragraph (3), the President or the nominated chairman has determined the case in favour of the other party, the party to whom the order was addressed may apply to the President, or that nominated chairman (as the case may be), for that determination to be set aside.

(6) An application under paragraph (5) must—
(a) be made not later than 10 working days after the date upon which the notice of the determination was sent to the party to whom the order was addressed; and
(b) must be in writing stating the grounds in full.

(7) In the case of an application under paragraph (5), the President, or the nominated chairman, may, if he considers that it is appropriate to do so, direct that the determination, and any costs order made pursuant to paragraph (4), be set aside and may give such directions in exercise of his powers under this Part as he considers appropriate.

(8) Before making a direction setting aside the determination, or any costs order, the President or the nominated chairman may invite the parties to make representations on the matter within such period as he may direct.

(9) Where the determination, or any costs order, is set aside, the Secretary shall alter the relevant entry in the records.]

**Note.** Paras (4)-(9) inserted by SI 2004 No 2073, reg 6 as from 31 August 2004.

**11 Copies of documents—**(1) The President or the nominated chairman may give a direction as to the number of copies of relevant material, which each party must send to the Tribunal and relevant material means, all documents, witness statements and other material on which the parties intend to rely or which they have been ordered by the President or the nominated chairman to send to the Secretary under this Part.

(2) The President or the nominated chairman may, if he considers it appropriate to do so, direct the form and order in which relevant material shall be supplied to the Tribunal.

**12 Disclosure of information and documents—**(1) Subject to paragraphs (3) to (5), the President or the nominated chairman may give directions—
(a) requiring a party to send to the Secretary any document or other material which he considers may assist the Tribunal in determining the case and which that party is able to send, and the Secretary shall take such steps as the President or the nominated chairman may direct, to supply copies of any information or document obtained under this paragraph to the other party;
(b) granting to a party the right to inspect and take copies of any document or other material which it is in the power of the other party to disclose, and appointing the date, time and place at which any such inspection and copying is to be done.

(2) Subject to paragraphs (3) to (5), the President or the nominated chairman may give a direction on the application of either party, requiring a person who is not a party to the proceedings to disclose any document or other material to the party making the application, if he is satisfied that—
(a) the documents or other material sought are likely to support the applicant's case or adversely affect the case of the other party;
(b) it is within the power of the person subject to the direction to disclose any document or other material; and
(c) disclosure is necessary for the fair determination of the case.

(3) It shall be a condition of the supply of any document or material under paragraph (1) or (2) that a party shall use it only for the purpose of the proceedings.

(4) Paragraphs (1) and (2) do not apply in relation to any document or material which the party could not be compelled to produce in legal proceedings in a county court.

(5) Before making a direction under paragraph (1) or (2), the President or the nominated chairman shall take into account the need to protect any matter which

relates to intimate personal or financial circumstances, is commercially sensitive, or was communicated or obtained in confidence.

**13 Expert evidence—**(1) The President or the nominated chairman may, if he thinks that any question arises in relation to the case on which it would be desirable for the Tribunal to have the assistance of an expert, appoint a person having appropriate qualifications to enquire into and report on the matter.

(2) The Secretary must supply the parties with a copy of any written report received under paragraph (1) in advance of the hearing (or, if the case is to be determined without an oral hearing, before the case is determined).

(3) If the President or the nominated chairman sees fit, he may direct that the expert shall attend the hearing, and give evidence.

(4) The Tribunal shall pay such reasonable fees as the President or the nominated chairman may determine to any person appointed under this regulation.

**14 Evidence of witnesses—**(1) The President or the nominated chairman may direct that the parties send to each other by the date specified in the direction a copy of a witness statement in respect of each witness on whose evidence he wishes to rely.

(2) A witness statement must contain the words 'I believe that the facts stated in this witness statement are true', and be signed by the person who makes it.

(3) The President or the nominated chairman (before the hearing or, if the case is to be determined without an oral hearing, before the case is determined) or the Tribunal may direct that a document or the evidence of any witness other than the applicant shall be excluded from consideration because—

(a)   it would be unfair in all the circumstances to consider it;

(b)   the party wishing to rely on the document or evidence has failed to submit the document, or witness statement containing it, in compliance with any direction; or

(c)   it would not assist the Tribunal in determining the case.

(4) Instead of excluding evidence under this regulation the President or the nominated chairman or the Tribunal may permit it to be considered on such terms as he or it thinks fit, including, subject to regulation 24, the making of a costs order.

(5) The President or the nominated chairman may direct that a witness (other than the applicant) shall not give oral evidence.

**15 Withholding medical report from disclosure in exceptional circumstances—**(1) This regulation applies where the respondent wishes the Tribunal, in determining the case, to consider a medical report and the President or the nominated chairman is satisfied—

(a)   that disclosure to the applicant of all or any part of the contents of the report would be so harmful to his health or welfare that it would be wrong to disclose it to him; and

(b)   that in all the circumstances it would not be unfair if the report or that part of it is considered by the Tribunal.

(2) The President or the nominated chairman may appoint a person having appropriate skills or experience to—

(a)   assess whether disclosure of the report to the applicant would be harmful to the applicant's health or welfare; and

(b)   report on the matter to the President or the nominated chairman.

(3) The President or the nominated chairman may direct that—

(a)   the report may be considered by the Tribunal; and

(b)   all or any part of its contents must not be disclosed to the applicant.

**16 Summoning of witnesses—**(1) The President or the nominated chairman may, on the application of either party or on his own initiative, issue a summons requiring any person—

(a) to attend as a witness at the hearing, at the date, time and place set out in the summons; and

(b) to answer any questions or produce any documents or other material in his possession or under his control which relate to any matter in question in the case.

(2) The summons must—

(a) explain that it is an offence under section 9(5)(c) of the 1999 Act to fail, without reasonable excuse, to comply with it; and

(b) explain the right to apply under this regulation to have it varied or set aside.

(3) A person summoned under this regulation may apply in writing to the Secretary for the summons to be varied or set aside by the President or the nominated chairman, and—

(a) the President or the nominated chairman may do so if he sees fit; and

(b) the Secretary must notify him and the parties in writing of the decision.

(4) No person shall be required to attend, answer questions or produce any document in obedience to a summons issued under this regulation unless—

(a) he has been given at least 5 working days' notice of the *hearing* [or has consented to a shorter period of notice]; and

(b) the necessary expenses of his attendance are paid or tendered to him by the party who requested his attendance or by the Tribunal, as the President or the nominated chairman shall direct.

(5) No person shall be required under this regulation to give any evidence or produce any document or other material that he could not be required to produce in legal proceedings in a county court.

**Note.** Words in italics in para (4)(a) omitted and words in square brackets substituted by SI 2003 No 626 as from 1 April 2003.

**17 Child and vulnerable adult witnesses—**(1) A child shall only give evidence in person where—

(a) the President or the nominated chairman has given the parties an opportunity to make written representations before the hearing or representations at the hearing; and

(b) having regard to all the available evidence, and the representations of the parties, the President or the nominated chairman considers that the welfare of the child will not be prejudiced by so doing.

(2) If he directs that a child shall give evidence in person, the President or the nominated chairman shall—

(a) secure that any arrangements he considers appropriate (such as the use of a video link) are made to safeguard the welfare of the child; and

(b) appoint for the purpose of the hearing a person with appropriate skills or experience in facilitating the giving of evidence by children.

(3) Where the President or the nominated chairman believes that it might not be in the best interests of a vulnerable adult for the vulnerable adult to give oral evidence to the Tribunal, the President or the nominated chairman shall—

(a) give the parties the opportunity to make written representations before the hearing or representations at the hearing; and

(b) having regard to all the available evidence, including any written representations made by the parties consider whether it would prejudice the vulnerable adult's welfare to give oral evidence to the Tribunal—

(i) in any circumstances; or

(ii) otherwise than in accordance with paragraph (5).

(4) If the President or the nominated chairman considers that—

(a) it would prejudice the vulnerable adult's welfare to give oral evidence to the Tribunal in any circumstances, he shall direct that the vulnerable adult shall not do so; or

(b) it would prejudice the vulnerable adult's welfare to give oral evidence to the Tribunal otherwise than in accordance with paragraph (5) he shall direct that paragraph (5) shall apply in relation to the vulnerable adult.

(5) If he directs that this paragraph shall apply in relation to the vulnerable adult, the President or the nominated chairman shall—

(a) secure that any arrangements he considers appropriate (such as the use of a video link) are made to safeguard the welfare of the vulnerable adult; and

(b) appoint for the purpose of the hearing a person with appropriate skills or experience in facilitating the giving of evidence by vulnerable adults.

(6) The President or the nominated chairman shall pay such fees as he may determine to any person appointed under this regulation.

**18 Restricted reporting orders** (1) If it appears appropriate to do so, the President or the nominated chairman (or, at the hearing, the Tribunal) may make a restricted reporting order.

(2) A restricted reporting order is an order prohibiting the publication (including by electronic means) in a written publication available to the public, or the inclusion in a relevant programme for reception in England and Wales, of any matter likely to lead members of the public to identify the applicant, any child, any vulnerable adult or any other person who the President or the nominated chairman or the Tribunal considers should not be identified.

(3) An order that may be made under this regulation may be made in respect of a limited period and may be varied or revoked by the President or the nominated chairman before the hearing (or by the Tribunal at the hearing).

**19 Exclusion of press and public—**(1) Where paragraph (2) applies, the President or the nominated chairman (or, at the hearing, the Tribunal) may on his (or its) own initiative, or on a written request by either party that the hearing or any part of it should be conducted in private, direct that—

(a) any member of the public specified in the direction;

(b) members of the public generally; or

(c) members of the press and members of the public,

be excluded from all or part of the hearing.

(2) This paragraph applies where the President or the nominated chairman (or, at the hearing, the Tribunal) is satisfied that a direction under paragraph (1) is necessary in order to—

(a) safeguard the welfare of any child or vulnerable adult;

(b) protect a person's private life; or

(c) avoid the risk of injustice in any legal proceedings.

PART V

HEARING

**20 Procedure at the hearing—**(1) The Tribunal may regulate its own procedure.

(2) At the beginning of the hearing the chairman must explain the order of proceedings which the Tribunal proposes to adopt.

(3) The parties may be represented or assisted at the hearing by any person.

(4) If either party fails to attend or be represented at the hearing, the Tribunal may hear and determine the case in that party's absence.

**21 Hearing to be in public—**(1) The hearing must be in public except in so far as any person is excluded under regulation 19.

(2) Whether or not the hearing is held in public—

(a) a member of the Council on Tribunals;

(b) the President;

(c) the clerk; and

(d) any person whom the President or the nominated chairman permits to be present in order to assist the Tribunal,

are entitled to attend the hearing.

(3) Whether or not the hearing is held in public—

(a) a member of the Council on Tribunals; and

(b) the President,

may remain present during the Tribunal's deliberations, but must not take part in the deliberations.

**22 Evidence—**(1) The Tribunal may consider any evidence, whether or not such evidence would be admissible in a court of law.

(2) The applicant has the right to give evidence at the hearing in person, and any other witness may do so unless the President or the nominated chairman has directed otherwise.

(3) No child may be asked any question except by the Tribunal or a person appointed under regulation 17(2).

(4) Where a direction has been made under regulation 17 that paragraph (5) of that regulation shall apply to any vulnerable adult, the vulnerable adult may not be asked any question except by the Tribunal or a person appointed under regulation 17(5).

(5) The Tribunal may require any witness to give evidence on oath or affirmation which may be administered for the purpose by the chairman or the clerk.

PART VI

DECISION

**23 The decision—**(1) The Tribunal's decision may be taken by a majority and the decision shall record whether it was unanimous or taken by a majority.

(2) The decision may be made and announced at the end of the hearing or reserved, and in any event, whether there has been a hearing or not, the decision must be recorded without delay in a document signed and dated by the chairman (or if as a result of his death or incapacity he is unable to sign, or if he ceases to be a member of the chairman's panel, by another member of the Tribunal).

(3) The document mentioned in paragraph (2) must also state—

(a) the reasons for the decision; and

(b) what, if any, order the Tribunal has made as a result of its decision.

(4) The Secretary must, as soon as reasonably possible, send to each party a copy of the document mentioned in paragraph (2) and [(except where the decision relates to the making of an order under section 166(5) of the 2002 Act)] a notice explaining to the parties any right of appeal which they may have against the Tribunal's decision and the right to apply for a review of the Tribunal's decision.

(5) Where the appeal was against an order made by a justice of the peace under section 20 of the 2000 Act or section 79K of the 1989 Act, the Secretary must, as soon as reasonably practicable, send a copy of the document mentioned in paragraph (2) to the justice of the peace who made the order.

(6) Except where a decision is announced at the end of the hearing, the decision shall be treated as having been made on the day on which a copy of the document mentioned in paragraph (2) is sent to the applicant.

(7)  The decision shall be entered in the records.

**Note.** Words in square brackets in para (4) added by SI 2003 No 2043, reg 8 as from 1 September 2003.

**24  Costs**—(1) Subject to regulation 31 and to paragraph (2) below, if in the opinion of the Tribunal a party has acted unreasonably in bringing or conducting the proceedings, it may make an order (a 'costs order') requiring that party ('the paying party') to make a payment to the other party ('the receiving party') to cover costs incurred by the receiving party.

(2)  Before making a costs order against a party, the Tribunal must—

(a)  invite the receiving party to provide to the Tribunal a schedule of costs incurred by him in respect of the proceedings; and

(b)  invite representations from the paying party and consider any representations he makes, consider whether he is able to comply with such an order and consider any relevant written information which he has provided.

(3)  When making a costs order, the Tribunal must—

(a)  order the payment of any sum which the parties have agreed should be paid;

(b)  order the payment of any sum which it considers appropriate having considered any representations the parties may make; or

(c)  order the payment of the whole or part of the costs incurred by the receiving party in connection with the proceedings as assessed.

(4)  Any costs required by an order under this regulation to be assessed may be assessed in a county court according to such rules applicable to proceedings in a county court as shall be directed in the order.

(5)  A costs order may, by leave of a county court, be enforced in the same manner as a judgment or order of that court to the same effect.

**25  Review of the Tribunal's decision**—[(Z1) This regulation shall not apply in relation to an application for an order under section 166(5) of the 2002 Act.]

(1)  A party may apply to the President for the Tribunal's decision to be reviewed on the grounds that—

(a)  it was wrongly made as a result of an error on the part of the Tribunal staff;

(b)  a party, who was entitled to be heard at a hearing but failed to appear or to be represented, had good and sufficient reason for failing to appear; or

(c)  there was an obvious error in the decision.

(2)  An application under this regulation must—

(a)  be made not later than ten working days after the date on which the decision was sent to the party applying for the Tribunal's decision to be reviewed; and

(b)  must be in writing stating the grounds in full.

(3)  An application under this regulation may be refused by the President, or by the chairman of the Tribunal which decided the case, if in his opinion it has no reasonable prospect of success.

(4)  Unless an application under this regulation is refused under paragraph (3), it shall be determined, after the parties have had an opportunity to be heard, by the Tribunal which decided the case or, where that is not practicable, by another Tribunal appointed by the President.

(5)  The Tribunal may on its own initiative propose to review its decision on any of the grounds referred to in paragraph (1) above, in which case—

(a)  the Secretary shall serve notice on the parties not later than ten working days after the date on which the decision was sent to them; and

(b)  the parties shall have an opportunity to be heard.

(6)  If, on the application of a party or on its own initiative the Tribunal is satisfied as to any of the grounds referred to in paragraph (1)—

(a) it shall order that the whole or a specified part of the decision be reviewed; and

(b) it may give directions to be complied with before or after the hearing of the review.

(7) The power to give directions under paragraph (6) includes a power to give a direction requiring a party to provide such particulars, evidence or statements as may reasonably be required for the determination of the review.

**Note.** Para (Z1) added by SI 2003 No 2043, reg 9 as from 1 September 2003.

**26 Powers of Tribunal on review—**[(Z1) This regulation shall not apply in relation to an application for an order under section 166(5) of the 2002 Act.]

(1) The Tribunal may, having reviewed all or part of a decision—

(a) set aside or vary the decision by certificate signed by the chairman (or if as a result of his death or incapacity he is unable to sign, or if he ceases to be a member of the chairmen's panel, by another member of the Tribunal); and

(b) substitute such other decision as it thinks fit or order a rehearing before the same or a differently constituted Tribunal.

(2) If any decision is set aside or varied (whether as a result of a review or by order of the High Court), the Secretary shall alter the relevant entry in the records to conform to the chairman's certificate or the order of the High Court and shall notify the parties accordingly.

(3) Any decision of the Tribunal under this regulation may be taken by a majority and the decision shall record whether it was unanimous or taken by a majority.

**Note.** Para (Z1) added by SI 2003 No 2043, reg 10 as from 1 September 2003.

**27 Publication—**(1) The President must make such arrangements as he considers appropriate for the publication of Tribunal decisions.

(2) Decisions may be published electronically.

(3) The decision may be published in an edited form, or subject to any deletions, if the President or the nominated chairman considers it appears appropriate bearing in mind—

(a) the need to safeguard the welfare of any child or vulnerable adult;

(b) the need to protect the private life of any person;

(c) any representations on the matter which either party has provided in writing;

(d) the effect of any subsisting restricted reporting order; and

(e) the effect of any direction under regulation 15.

PART VII

SUPPLEMENTARY

**28 Method of sending documents—**(1) Any document may be sent to the Secretary by post, by fax, electronically or through a document exchange, unless the President or the nominated chairman directs otherwise.

(2) Any notice or document which these Regulations authorise or require the Secretary to send to a party shall be sent—

(a) by first-class post to the address given for the purpose by that party in accordance with these Regulations;

(b) by fax or electronically to a number or address given by that party for the purpose; or

(c) where the party has given for the purpose an address which includes a numbered box number at a document exchange, by leaving the notice or document addressed to that numbered box at that document exchange or at a document exchange which transmits documents on every working day to that exchange.

(3) If a notice or document cannot be sent to a party in accordance with paragraph (2), the President or the nominated chairman may dispense with service of it or direct that it be served on that party in such manner as he thinks appropriate.

(4) Any notice or document sent by the Secretary to a party in accordance with these Regulations shall be taken to have been received—

(a) if sent by post and not returned, on the second working day after it was posted;

(b) if sent by fax or electronically, unless the Secretary has been notified that the transmission has been unsuccessful, on the next working day after it was sent;

(c) if left at a document exchange in accordance with paragraph (2), on the second working day after it was left; and

(d) if served in accordance with a direction under paragraph (3), on the next working day after it was so served.

**29 Irregularities—**(1) An irregularity resulting from failure to comply with any provision of these Regulations or any direction given in accordance with them before the Tribunal has reached its decision shall not of itself render the proceedings void.

(2) Where any irregularity comes to the attention of the President or the nominated chairman (before the hearing) or the Tribunal he or it may and, if it appears that any person may have been prejudiced by the irregularity, shall, before reaching a decision, give such directions as he or it thinks just to cure or waive the irregularity.

(3) Clerical mistakes in any document recording the decision of the Tribunal or a direction or decision of the President or the nominated chairman, or errors arising in such documents from accidental slips or omissions, may at any time be corrected by the chairman or, as the case may be, the President, or nominated chairman by means of a certificate signed by him.

(4) The Secretary shall as soon as practicable where a document is corrected in accordance with paragraph (3) send the parties a copy of any corrected document together with reasons for the decision to correct the document.

**30 Application on behalf of person under a disability—**(1) A person may, by writing to the Secretary, request authorisation by the President or the nominated chairman to make any application to the Tribunal on behalf of any person who is prevented by mental or physical infirmity from acting on his own behalf.

(2) A person acting in accordance with an authorisation under this regulation may on behalf of the other person take any step or do anything which that person is required or permitted to do under these Regulations, subject to any conditions which the President or the nominated chairman may impose.

**31 Death of applicant** If the applicant dies, before the case or application for leave is determined, the President or the nominated chairman may—

(a) strike out the case or application for leave in so far as it relates to that individual without making a costs order;

(b) appoint such person as he thinks fit to proceed with the appeal in the place of the deceased applicant.

**32 Amendment of appeal, application for leave or response—**(1) The applicant may amend the reasons he gives in support of the case or application for leave as the case may be, but only with the leave of the President or the nominated chairman (or at the hearing, with the leave of the Tribunal).

(2) The respondent may amend the reasons he gives for opposing the applicant's case or application for leave, as the case may be, but only with the leave of the President or the nominated chairman (or at the hearing, with the leave of the Tribunal).

(3) Where the President, the nominated chairman or Tribunal gives leave to either party to amend the reasons given in support of his case, he may do so on such terms as he thinks fit (including, subject to regulation 24, the making of a costs order).

**33 Withdrawal of proceedings or opposition to proceedings**—(1) If the applicant at any time notifies the Secretary in writing, or states at a hearing, that he no longer wishes to pursue the proceedings, the President or the nominated chairman (or at the hearing, the Tribunal) must dismiss the proceedings, and may, subject to regulation *24(2)* [24] and (3) make a costs order.

(2) If the respondent notifies the Secretary in writing, or states at a hearing, that he does not oppose or no longer opposes the proceedings, the President (or at the hearing, the Tribunal)—

(a) must without delay determine the case or, as the case may be, the application for leave in the applicant's favour;

(b) subject to regulation *24(2) and (3)* [24] may make a costs order; and

(c) must consider making one.

[(3) Where the President or the nominated chairman dismisses the proceedings under paragraph (1) or determines the case, or the application for leave in the applicant's favour under paragraph (2), the references to 'the Tribunal' in regulation 24 shall be read as if they were references to 'the President or the nominated chairman'.]

**Note.** Para (1), (2)(b) reference to '24' substituted by SI 2004 No 2073, reg 7(a) as from 31 August 2004. Para (3) inserted by SI 2004 No 2073, reg 7(b) as from 31 August 2004.

**34 Proof of documents and certification of decisions**—(1) A document purporting to be issued by the Secretary shall be taken to have been so issued, unless the contrary is proved.

(2) A document purporting to be certified by the Secretary to be a true copy of a document containing—

(a) a decision of the Tribunal; or

(b) an order of the President or the nominated chairman or of the Tribunal,

shall be sufficient evidence of the matters contained in it, unless the contrary is proved.

**35 Time**—(1) The President or the nominated chairman may [, having consulted the parties in the case,] extend any time limit mentioned in these Regulations if in the circumstances—

(a) it would be unreasonable to expect it to be, or to have been, complied with; and

(b) it would be unfair not to extend it.

[(1A) The President or the nominated chairman may reduce any time limit mentioned in these Regulations if he considers it reasonable to do so and the parties in the case agree to the reduction.]

(2) Where the time prescribed by these Regulations, or specified in any direction given by the President or the nominated chairman, for taking any step expires on a day which is not a working day, the step must be treated as having been done in time if it is done on the next working day.

*(3) This regulation does not apply to the time limits provided for initiating an appeal in paragraph (1) of Schedule 1 and paragraph 1 of Schedule 2.*

[(3) This regulation does not apply to the time limits provided for initiating an appeal mentioned in paragraph (1) of *Schedule 2, 6 or 7* [*Schedule 2, 6, 7 or 8*] [Schedule 2, 6, 7, 8 or 9.].]

**Note.** Para (3) in italics omitted and para (3) in square brackets substituted by SI 2003 No 626, reg 9 as from 1 April 2003. Words in italics in para (3) as so substituted, further substituted by the words in square brackets by SI 2003 No 1060 as from 30 April 2003 and further substituted by SI 2003 No 2043, reg 11 as from 1 September 2003. Para (1): words ', having consulted the parties in the case,' in square brackets inserted by SI 2004 No 2073, reg 8(a) as from 31 August 2004. Para (1A): inserted by SI 2004 No 2073, reg 8(b) as from 31 August 2004.

## PART VIII

### MISCELLANEOUS

**36 Revocation—**(1) The Protection of Children Act Tribunal Regulations 2000 ('the 2000 Regulations') are hereby revoked.

(2) Any application or appeal which—

(a) was made to the Tribunal under the 2000 Regulations before 1st April 2002; and

(b) the Tribunal has not determined before that date,

shall for the purposes of these Regulations be treated as having been made to the Tribunal under these Regulations.

(3) Any direction or notice given, or thing done, by the Tribunal before 1st April 2002 shall for the purposes of these Regulations be treated as having been given or done by the Tribunal under these Regulations.

SCHEDULE 1                                                                              Regulation 4(1)

APPEAL UNDER SECTION 21 OF THE 2000 ACT AGAINST A DECISION OF THE REGISTRATION AUTHORITY OR AN ORDER OF A JUSTICE OF THE PEACE

*Initiating an appeal*

**1—**(1) A person who wishes to appeal to the Tribunal under section 21 of the 2000 Act against a decision of the registration authority under Part II of the 2000 Act, or an order made by a justice of the peace under section 20 of that Act, must do so by application in writing to the Secretary.

(2) An application under this paragraph may be made on the application form available from the Secretary.

(3) An application under this paragraph must—

(a) give the applicant's name and full postal address, if the applicant is an individual his date of birth and, if the applicant is a company, the address of its registered office;

(b) give the name, address and profession of the person (if any) representing the applicant;

(c) give the address within the United Kingdom to which the Secretary should send documents concerning the appeal;

(d) give, where these are available, the applicant's telephone number, fax number and e-mail address and those of the applicant's representative;

(e) identify the decision or order against which the appeal is brought and give particulars of—

(i) whether the appeal is against a refusal of registration, an imposition or variation of conditions of registration, a refusal to remove or vary any condition, *or a cancellation of registration* [a cancellation of registration pursuant to sections 14 or 20 of the 2000 Act, or a refusal to grant an application for cancellation of registration pursuant to section 15(1)(b) of that Act];

     (ii)   whether the appeal is against a decision of the registration authority or an order made by a justice of the peace;

    (iii)   where the appeal is in respect of a cancellation of registration, whether the establishment or agency in respect of which the appeal is made remains open and, in the case of an establishment, the number of residents in that establishment;

(f)  give a short statement of the grounds of appeal; and

(g)  be signed and dated by the applicant.

*Acknowledgement and notification of application*

**2**—(1) On receiving an application, made within the period for bringing an appeal specified in section 21 of the 2000 Act, the Secretary must—

(a)  immediately send an acknowledgement of its receipt to the applicant; and

(b)  enter particulars of the appeal, and the date of its receipt in the records and send a copy of it, together with any documents supplied by the applicant in support of it, to the respondent.

(2)  If in the Secretary's opinion there is an obvious error in the application—

(a)  he may correct it;

(b)  he must notify the applicant in writing that he has done so; and

(c)  unless, within five working days of receipt of notification under head (b) of this sub-paragraph the applicant notifies the Secretary in writing that he objects to the correction, the application shall be amended accordingly.

*Response to application*

**3**—(1) The Secretary must send the information provided by the applicant under paragraph 1 to the respondent together with a request that it respond to the application within 20 working days of receiving it.

(2) If the respondent fails to respond as requested, it shall not be entitled to take any further part in the proceedings.

(3) The response must—

(a)  acknowledge that the respondent has received a copy of the application;

(b)  indicate whether or not the respondent opposes it, and if it does, give the reasons why it opposes the application;

(c)  provide the following information and documents—

     (i)   the name, address and profession of the person (if any) representing the respondent and whether the Secretary should send documents concerning the appeal to the representative rather than to the respondent; and

    (ii)   in the case of an appeal under section 21(1)(a) of the 2000 Act, a copy of the written notice of the decision (which is the subject of the appeal) served under section 19(3) of that Act, and the reasons for the decision; or

    (iii)   in the case of an appeal under section 21(1)(b) of the 2000 Act, a copy of the order made by the justice of the peace.

(4) The Secretary must without delay send to the applicant a copy of the response and the information and documents provided with it.

   ...

*Misconceived appeals etc*

**4**—*(1) The President or the nominated chairman may at any time strike out the appeal on the grounds that—*

*(a)  it is made otherwise than in accordance with paragraph 1;*

*(b)  it is outside the jurisdiction of the Tribunal or is otherwise misconceived; or*

*(c)  it is frivolous or vexatious.*

(2)  *Before striking out an appeal under this paragraph, the President or the nominated chairman must—*

    (a)  *invite the parties to make representations on the matter within such period as he may direct;*

    (b)  *if within the period specified in the direction the applicant so requests in writing, afford the parties an opportunity to make oral representations;*

    (c)  *consider any representations the parties may make.*

*Further information to be sent by the applicant and respondent*

**5**—(1)  As soon as the respondent has provided the information set out in paragraph 3, the Secretary must write to each party requesting that he send to the Secretary within 15 working days after the date on which he receives the Secretary's letter the following information—

    (a)  the name of any witness whose evidence the party wishes the Tribunal to consider (and whether the party may wish the Tribunal to consider additional witness evidence from a witness whose name is not yet known) and the nature of that evidence;

    (b)  whether the party wishes the President or the nominated chairman to give any directions or exercise any of his powers under Part IV of these Regulations;

    (c)  whether the party wishes there to be a preliminary hearing with regard to directions;

    (d)  a provisional estimate of the time the party considers will be required to present his case;

    (e)  the earliest date by which the party considers he would be able to prepare his case for hearing; and

    (f)  in the case of the applicant, whether he wishes his appeal to be determined without a hearing.

(2)  Once the Secretary has received the information referred to in sub-paragraph (1) from both parties, he must without delay send a copy of the information supplied by the applicant to the respondent and that supplied by the respondent to the applicant.

*Changes to further information supplied to the Tribunal*

**6**—(1)  Either party, within 5 working days of receiving the further information in respect of the other party from the Secretary, may ask the Secretary in writing to amend or add to any of the information given under paragraph 5(1).

(2)  If the Secretary receives any further information under sub-paragraph (1) from either party he must, without delay, send a copy of it to the other party.

**Note.**  Para 1: in sub-para (3)(e)(i) words from 'a cancellation of registration' to 'of that Act' in square brackets substituted by SI 2004 No 2073, reg 9(a) as from 31 August 2004. Para 4: revoked by SI 2004 No 2073, reg 9(b) as from 31 August 2004.

SCHEDULE 2                                    Regulation 4(2)

APPEAL UNDER SECTION 79M OF THE 1989 ACT AGAINST A DECISION OF THE REGISTRATION AUTHORITY OR AN ORDER OF A JUSTICE OF THE PEACE

*Initiating an appeal*

**1**—(1)  *A person who wishes to appeal to the Tribunal under section 79M of the 1989 Act, against the taking of any step mentioned in section 79L(1), or an order under section 79K, of that Act, must do so by application in writing to the Secretary.*

[(1) A person who wishes to appeal to the Tribunal under section 79M of the 1989 Act against—
(a) the taking of any step mentioned in section 79L(1) of that Act;
(b) an order under section 79K of that Act; or
(c) a determination in relation to the disqualification of a person for registration for child minding or providing day care under paragraph 4 of Schedule 9A to that Act,
must do so by application in writing to the Secretary.]

(2) An application under this paragraph must be received by the Secretary no later than 28 days after service on the applicant of notice of the decision to take the step in question or the order.

(3) An application under this paragraph may be made on the application form available from the Secretary.

(4) An application under this paragraph must—
(a) give the applicant's name and full postal address, if the applicant is an individual his date of birth and, if the applicant is a company, the address of its registered office;
(b) give the name, address and profession of the person (if any) representing the applicant;
(c) give the address within the United Kingdom to which the Secretary should send documents concerning the appeal;
(d) give, where these are available, the applicant's telephone number, fax number and e-mail address and those of the applicant's representative;
(e) identify the decision against which the appeal is brought and give particulars of—
> (i) *whether the appeal is against the refusal or cancellation of registration, or the imposition, removal or variation of any condition of registration, or a refusal to remove or vary any condition;*
> (ii) *whether the appeal is against a decision of the registration authority or a justice of the peace;*
>
> [(i) whether the appeal is against—
>> (aa) the refusal or cancellation of registration;
>> (bb) the imposition, removal or variation of any condition of registration;
>> (cc) the refusal to remove or vary any such condition; or
>> (dd) a determination in relation to disqualification from registration;]
(f) give a short statement of the grounds of appeal; and
(g) be signed and dated by the applicant.

*Acknowledgement and notification of application*

**2**—(1) On receiving an application, the Secretary must—
(a) immediately send an acknowledgement of its receipt to the applicant;
(b) enter particulars of the appeal, and the date of its receipt in the records and send a copy of it, together with any documents supplied by the applicant in support of it, to the respondent.

(2) If in the Secretary's opinion there is an obvious error in the application—
(a) he may correct it;
(b) he must notify the applicant in writing that he has done so; and
(c) unless within five working days of receipt of notification under head (b) of this sub-paragraph the applicant notifies him in writing that he objects to the correction, the application shall be amended accordingly.

*Response to application*

**3**—(1) The Secretary must send the information provided by the applicant under paragraph 1 to the respondent together with a request that he respond to the application within 20 working days of receiving it.

(2) If the respondent fails to respond as directed, he shall not be entitled to take any further part in the proceedings.

(3) The response must—

(a)   acknowledge that the respondent has received a copy of the application;

(b)   indicate whether or not the respondent opposes it, and if he does, give the reasons why he opposes the application;

(c)   provide the following information and documents—

    (i)   the name, address and profession of the person (if any) representing the respondent and whether the Secretary should send documents concerning the appeal to the representative rather than to the respondent; and

    (ii)   a copy of the written notice of the decision to take the step in question (which is the subject of the appeal) served under section 79L of the 1989 Act, and the reasons for the decision; *or*

    (iii)   where the appeal is against an order of a justice of the peace under section 79K of the 1989 Act, a copy of the order and a copy of the statement referred to in subsection (5)(b) of that section [or

    (iv)   where an appeal is against a determination in relation to disqualification from registration, a copy of the written notice of the determination and the reasons for it].

(4) The Secretary must without delay send to the applicant a copy of the response and the information and documents provided with it.

...

*Misconceived appeals etc*

**4**—*(1) The President or the nominated chairman may at any time strike out the appeal on the grounds that—*

(a)   *it is made otherwise than in accordance with paragraph 1;*

(b)   *it is outside the jurisdiction of the Tribunal or is otherwise misconceived; or*

(c)   *it is frivolous or vexatious.*

*(2) Before striking out an appeal under this paragraph, the President or the nominated chairman must—*

(a)   *invite the parties to make representations on the matter within such period as he may direct;*

(b)   *if within the period specified in the direction the applicant so requests in writing, afford the parties an opportunity to make oral representations;*

(c)   *consider any representations the parties may make.*

*Further information to be sent by the applicant and respondent*

**5**—(1) As soon as the respondent has provided the information set out in paragraph 3, the Secretary must write to each party requesting that he send to the Secretary, within 15 working days after the date on which he receives the Secretary's letter, the following information—

(a)   the name of any witness whose evidence the party wishes the Tribunal to consider (and whether the party may wish the Tribunal to consider additional witness evidence where the name of the party is not yet known) and the nature of that evidence;

(b)   whether the party wishes the President [or nominated chairman] to give any directions or exercise any of his powers under Part IV of these Regulations;

(c) whether the party wishes there to be a preliminary hearing with regard to directions;

(d) a provisional estimate of the time the party considers will be required to present his case;

(e) the earliest date by which the party considers he would be able to prepare his case for hearing; and

(f) in the case of the applicant, whether he wishes his appeal to be determined without a hearing.

(2) Once the Secretary has received the information referred to in sub-paragraph (1) from both parties, he must without delay send a copy of the information supplied by the applicant to the respondent and that supplied by the respondent to the applicant.

*Changes to further information supplied to the Tribunal*

**6**—(1) Either party, within 5 working days of receiving the further information in respect of the other party from the Secretary, may ask the Secretary in writing to amend or add to any of the information given under paragraph 5(1).

(2) If the Secretary receives any further information under sub-paragraph (1) from either party he must, without delay, send a copy of it to the other party.

**Note.** Para 1: words in square brackets substituted and words inserted by SI 2004 No 2073, reg 10(1), (2)(a)(b), (3)(a)(b), (4) as from 31 August 2004. Words in square brackets in para (5)(1)(b) added by SI 2003 No 1060, reg 7 as from 30 April 2003.

SCHEDULE 3                                                      Regulation 4(3)

APPEAL UNDER SECTION 65A OF THE 1989 ACT AGAINST A DECISION OF THE APPROPRIATE AUTHORITY REFUSING TO GIVE CONSENT UNDER SECTION 65 OF THAT ACT

*Initiating an appeal*

**1**—(1) A person who wishes to appeal to the Tribunal under section 65A of the 1989 Act against a decision of the appropriate authority must do so by application in writing to the Secretary.

(2) An application under this paragraph must be received by the Secretary no later than the first working day after the expiry of three months from the date of the letter informing the applicant of the decision.

(3) An application under this paragraph may be made on the application form available from the Secretary.

(4) An application under this paragraph must—

(a) give the applicant's name and full postal address, if the applicant is an individual his date of birth and, if the applicant is a company, the address of its registered office;

(b) give the name, address and profession of the person (if any) representing the applicant;

(c) give the address within the United Kingdom to which the Secretary should send documents concerning the appeal;

(d) give, where these are available, the applicant's telephone number, fax number and e-mail address and those of the applicant's representative;

(e) give sufficient information concerning the decision appealed against to make it clear whether it falls within section 65(1) or (2) of the 1989 Act;

(f) give a short statement of the grounds of appeal; and

(g) be signed and dated by the applicant.

*Acknowledgement and notification of application*

**2**—(1) On receiving an application, the Secretary must—
    (a) immediately send an acknowledgement of its receipt to the applicant; and
    (b) subject to the following provisions of this paragraph, enter particulars of the appeal and the date of its receipt in the records and send a copy of it, together with any documents supplied by the applicant in support of it, to the respondent.

(2) If the President is of the opinion that the applicant is asking the Tribunal to do something which it cannot do, he may notify the applicant in writing—
    (a) of the reasons for his opinion; and
    (b) that the appeal will not be entered in the records unless within five working days the applicant notifies the President in writing that he wishes to proceed with it.

(3) If in the Secretary's opinion there is an obvious error in the application—
    (a) he may correct it;
    (b) he must notify the applicant accordingly; and
    (c) unless within five working days of receipt of notification under heading (b) of this sub-paragraph the applicant notifies the Secretary in writing that he objects to the correction, the application shall be amended accordingly.

*Response to application*

**3**—(1) The Secretary must send the information provided by the applicant under paragraph 1 to the respondent together with a request that it respond to the application within 20 working days of receiving it.

(2) If the respondent fails to respond as requested it shall not be entitled to take any further part in the proceedings.

(3) The response must—
    (a) acknowledge that the respondent has received a copy of the application;
    (b) indicate whether or not it opposes it, and if it does, why; and
    (c) provide the following information and documents—
        (i) the name, address and profession of the person (if any) representing the respondent and whether the Secretary should send documents concerning the appeal to the representative rather than to the respondent; and
        (ii) a copy of the written notice of the decision which is the subject of the appeal and the reasons for the decision.

(4) The Secretary must without delay send to the applicant a copy of the response and the information and documents provided with it.
    ....

*Misconceived appeals etc*

**4**—*(1) The President or the nominated chairman may at any time strike out the appeal on the grounds that—*
    *(a) it is made otherwise than in accordance with paragraph 1;*
    *(b) it is outside the jurisdiction of the Tribunal or is otherwise misconceived; or*
    *(c) it is frivolous or vexatious.*

*(2) Before striking out an appeal under this paragraph, the President or the nominated chairman must—*
    *(a) invite the parties to make representations on the matter within such period as he may direct;*
    *(b) if within the period specified in the direction the applicant so requests in writing, afford the parties an opportunity to make oral representations; and*
    *(c) consider any representations the parties may make.*

*Further information to be sent by the applicant and respondent*

**5**—(1) As soon as the respondent has provided the information set out in paragraph 3 the Secretary must write to each party requesting that he send to the Secretary within 15 working days after the date on which he receives the Secretary's letter the following information—

(a) the name of any witness whose evidence the party wishes the Tribunal to consider (and whether the party may wish the Tribunal to consider additional witness evidence from a witness whose name is not yet known) and the nature of that evidence;

(b) whether the party wishes the President or the nominated chairman to give any directions or exercise any of his powers under Part IV of these Regulations;

(c) whether the party wishes there to be a preliminary hearing with regard to directions;

(d) a provisional estimate of the time the party considers will be required to present his case;

(e) the earliest date by which the party considers he would be able to prepare his case for hearing; and

(f) in the case of the applicant, whether he wishes his appeal to be determined without a hearing.

(2) Once the Secretary has received the information referred to in sub-paragraph (1) from both parties, he must without delay send a copy of the information supplied by the applicant to the respondent and that supplied by the respondent to the applicant.

*Changes to further information supplied to the Tribunal*

**6**—(1) Either party, within 5 working days of receiving the further information in respect of the other party from the Secretary, may ask the Secretary in writing to amend or add to any of the information given under paragraph 5(1).

(2) If the Secretary receives any further information under sub-paragraph (1) from either party he must, without delay, send a copy of it to the other party.

**Note.** Para (4) revoked by SI 2004 No 2073, reg 11 as from 31 August 2004.

SCHEDULE 4                                                    Regulation 4(4)

APPEALS AND APPLICATIONS FOR LEAVE TO APPEAL UNDER SECTION 4 OF THE 1999 ACT AND APPEALS UNDER REGULATION 13 OF THE EDUCATION REGULATIONS

*Initiating an appeal*

**1**—(1) A person who wishes to appeal to the Tribunal—

(a) under section 4(1)(a) of the 1999 Act, against a decision to include him in the POCA list;

(b) under regulation 13 of the Education Regulations, against a decision to give a direction under regulation 5 of those Regulations; or

(c) under regulation 13 of the Education Regulations, against a decision not to revoke or vary such a direction,

must do so by application in writing to the Secretary.

(2) An application under this paragraph must be received by the Secretary no later than the first working day after the expiry of three months from the date of the letter informing the applicant of the decision.

(3) An application under this paragraph may be made on the application form available from the Secretary.

(4) An application under this paragraph must—

(a) give the applicant's name, date of birth and full postal address;

(b) give sufficient information concerning the decision appealed against to make it clear whether it falls within sub-paragraph (1)(a), (1)(b) or (1)(c);

(c) give the reasons why the applicant believes he should not be included in the POCA list, or why he believes the direction should not have been given, or why that direction should be revoked or varied, as the case may be;

(d) give the name, address and profession of the person (if any) representing the applicant;

(e) give the address within the United Kingdom to which the Secretary should send documents concerning the appeal;

(f) give, where these are available, the applicant's telephone number, fax number and e-mail address and those of the applicant's representative; and

(g) be signed and dated by the applicant.

*Applying for leave*

**2**—(1) An application for leave—

(a) to appeal to the Tribunal under section 4(1)(b) of the 1999 Act against a decision not to remove the applicant from the POCA list; or

(b) to have the issue of the applicant's inclusion in the POCA list determined under section 4(2) of the 1999 Act by the Tribunal,

must be made in writing to the Secretary.

(2) An application under sub-paragraph (1)(a) must be received by the Secretary no later than the first working day after the expiry of three months from the date of the letter informing the applicant of the decision.

(3) An application under this paragraph may be made on the application form available from the Secretary.

(4) An application under this paragraph must—

(a) give the applicant's name, date of birth and full postal address;

(b) give sufficient information to make it clear whether the application falls within sub-paragraph (1)(a) or (b);

(c) give the reasons why the applicant believes the decision was wrong or, as the case may be, why he believes he should not be included in the POCA list;

(d) give the dates of any previous appeal under the 1999 Act and (where applicable) application for leave the applicant has made to the Tribunal;

(e) give details of any new evidence or material change of circumstances since that appeal and (where applicable) application for leave was determined which might lead the Tribunal to a different decision;

(f) in the case of an application to have the issue of his inclusion in the POCA list determined by the Tribunal, give details of any civil or criminal proceedings relating to the misconduct of which the applicant is alleged to have been guilty;

(g) give the name, address and profession of the person (if any) representing the applicant;

(h) give an address within the United Kingdom to which the Secretary should send documents concerning the appeal and application for leave;

(i) give, where these are available, the applicant's telephone number, fax number and e-mail address and those of the applicant's representative; and

(j) be signed and dated by the applicant.

*Acknowledgement and notification of application*

**3**—(1) On receiving an application, the Secretary shall—

(a) immediately send an acknowledgement of its receipt to the applicant;

(b) subject to the following provisions of this paragraph, enter particulars of the application and the date of its receipt in the records and send a copy of it, together with any documents supplied by the applicant in support of it, to the respondent.

(2) If the President is of the opinion that the applicant is asking the Tribunal to do something which it cannot do, he may notify the applicant in writing—
  (a) of the reasons for his opinion; and
  (b) that the application will not be entered in the records unless within five working days the applicant notifies the President in writing that he wishes to proceed with it.

(3) If in the Secretary's opinion there is an obvious error in the application—
  (a) he may correct it;
  (b) he shall notify the applicant accordingly; and
  (c) unless within five working days of receipt of notification under head (b) of this sub-paragraph the applicant notifies the Secretary in writing that he objects to the correction, the application shall be amended accordingly.

*Response to application*

**4**—(1) The Secretary must send information provided by the applicant under paragraph 1 or 2, as the case may be, to the respondent together with a request that he respond to the application within 20 working days of receiving it.

(2) If the respondent fails to respond as requested, he shall not be entitled to take any further part in the proceedings.

(3) The response must—
  (a) acknowledge that the respondent has received a copy of the application;
  (b) indicate whether or not he opposes it, and if he does, why; and
  (c) provide the following information and documents—
    (i) the name, address and profession of the person (if any) representing the respondent and whether the Secretary should send documents concerning the application to the representative rather than to the respondent;
    (ii) copies of any letters informing the applicant of the decision which is the subject of the appeal or application for leave, as the case may be;
    (iii) copies of any information submitted with a reference under section 2, 2A, 2B or 2D of the 1999 Act and of any observations submitted on it by the applicant;
    (iv) copies of any evidence and expert evidence relied on by the respondent in making a decision under the Education Regulations.

(4) The Secretary must without delay send to the applicant a copy of the response and the information and documents provided with it (subject, in the case of any material provided in accordance with sub-paragraph (3)(c)(iv), to any direction of the President or the nominated chairman under regulation 15).

...

*Misconceived applications etc*

**5**—*(1) The President or the nominated chairman may at any time strike out the appeal or, as the case may be application for leave, on the grounds that—*
  *(a) it is made otherwise than in accordance with paragraph 1 or 2 (as the case may be);*
  *(b) it is outside the jurisdiction of the Tribunal or is otherwise misconceived; or*
  *(c) it is frivolous or vexatious.*

*(2) Before striking out an appeal or, as the case may be, application for leave, under this paragraph, the President or the nominated chairman must—*
  *(a) invite the parties to make representations on the matter within such period as he may direct;*

   (b)   *if within the period specified in the direction the applicant so requests in writing, afford the parties an opportunity to make oral representations; and*

   (c)   *consider any representations the parties may make.*

*Grant or refusal of leave*

**6**—(1) The President or the nominated chairman shall grant or refuse leave in relation to an application under paragraph 2 without a hearing, as he sees fit.

(2) Subject to paragraph 7, if the President or the nominated chairman refuses leave the application shall be dismissed.

(3) The Secretary must without delay notify the parties in writing of the President or the nominated chairman's decision, and if he has refused leave—

   (a)   must notify them of his reasons for doing so; and

   (b)   must inform the applicant of his right to request a reconsideration of the decision under paragraph 7.

*Reconsideration of leave*

**7**—(1) The President or the nominated chairman must reconsider a decision to refuse leave if within ten working days after receipt of a notice under paragraph 6(3) the Secretary receives a written request to do so from the applicant.

(2) If in his request under sub-paragraph (1) the applicant has asked to make representations about leave at a hearing, the Secretary must fix a hearing for those representations to be heard.

(3) The Secretary must notify the respondent of any hearing fixed for the purpose of considering whether to grant leave, and the applicant and the respondent may appear or be represented by any person at that hearing.

(4) If the President or the nominated chairman again refuses leave after reconsideration—

   (a)   he must give his reasons for doing so in writing; and

   (b)   the Secretary must without delay send to the parties a copy of the President or the nominated chairman's decision and if he has refused leave, of his reasons for doing so.

*Further information to be sent by the applicant and respondent*

**8**—(1) As soon as the respondent has provided the information set out in paragraph 4, or as soon as leave has been granted under paragraph 6 or 7, the Secretary must write to each party requesting that he send to the Secretary, within 20 working days after the date on which he receives the Secretary's letter, the following information—

   (a)   the name of any witness whose evidence the party wishes the Tribunal to consider (and whether the party may wish the Tribunal to consider additional witness evidence from a witness whose name is not yet known) and the nature of that evidence;

   (b)   whether the party wishes the President [or nominated chairman] to give any directions or exercise any of his powers under Part IV of these Regulations;

   (c)   whether the party wishes there to be a preliminary hearing with regard to directions;

   (d)   a provisional estimate of the time the party considers will be required to present his case;

   (e)   the earliest date by which the party considers he would be able to prepare his case for hearing; and

   (f)   in the case of the applicant, whether he wishes his case to be determined without a hearing.

(2) Once the Secretary has received the information referred to in sub-paragraph (1) from both parties, he must without delay send a copy of the information supplied by the applicant to the respondent and that supplied by the respondent to the applicant.

*Changes to further information supplied to the Tribunal*

**9—**(1) Either party, within 5 working days of receiving the further information in respect of the other party from the Secretary, may ask the Secretary in writing to amend or add to any of the information given under paragraph 8(1).

(2) If the Secretary receives any further information under sub-paragraph (1) from either party he must, without delay, send a copy of it to the other party.

**Note.** Para (5) revoked by SI 2004 No 2073, reg 12 as from 31 August 2004. Words in square brackets in para (8)(1)(b) added by SI 2003 No 1060, reg 7 as from 30 April 2003.

SCHEDULE 5                                                                 Regulation 4(5)

APPEALS AND APPLICATIONS FOR LEAVE UNDER SECTION 86 OF THE 2000 ACT

*Initiating an appeal*

**1—**(1) A person who wishes to appeal to the Tribunal under section 86(1)(a) of the 2000 Act, against a decision to include him in the POVA list must do so by application in writing to the Secretary.

(2) An application under this paragraph must be received by the Secretary no later than the first working day after the expiry of three months from the date of the letter informing the applicant of the decision.

(3) An application under this paragraph may be made on the application form available from the Secretary.

(4) An application under this paragraph must—

(a)  give the applicant's name, date of birth and full postal address;

(b)  give the reasons why the applicant believes he should not be included in the POVA list;

(c)  give the name, address and profession of the person (if any) representing the applicant;

(d)  give the address within the United Kingdom to which the Secretary should send documents concerning the appeal;

(e)  give, where these are available, the applicant's telephone number, fax number and e-mail address and those of the applicant's representative; and

(f)  be signed and dated by the applicant.

*Applying for leave*

**2—**(1) An application for leave—

(a)  to appeal to the Tribunal under section 86(1)(b) of the 2000 Act against a decision not to remove the applicant from the POVA list; or

(b)  to have the issue of the applicant's inclusion in the POVA list determined under section 86(2) of the 2000 Act by the Tribunal,

must be made in writing to the Secretary.

(2) An application under sub-paragraph (1)(a) must be received by the Secretary no later than the first working day after the expiry of three months from the date of the letter informing the applicant of the decision.

(3) An application under this paragraph may be made on the application form available from the Secretary.

(4) An application under this paragraph must—

(a)  give the applicant's name, date of birth and full postal address;
(b)  give sufficient information to make it clear whether the appeal falls within sub-paragraph (1)(a) or (b);
(c)  give the reasons why the applicant believes the decision was wrong or, as the case may be, why he believes he should not be included in the POVA list;
(d)  give the dates of any previous appeal under section 86 of the 2000 Act and (where applicable) application for leave, he has made to the Tribunal;
(e)  give details of any new evidence or material change of circumstances since that appeal and (where applicable) application for leave was determined which might lead the Tribunal to a different decision;
(f)  in the case of an application to have the issue of his inclusion in the POVA list determined by the Tribunal, give details of any civil or criminal proceedings relating to the misconduct of which the applicant is alleged to have been guilty;
(g)  give the name, address and profession of the person (if any) representing the applicant;
(h)  give the address within the United Kingdom to which the Secretary should send documents concerning the appeal and the application for leave;
(i)  give, where these are available, the applicant's telephone number, fax number and e-mail address and those of the applicant's representative; and
(j)  be signed and dated by the applicant.

*Acknowledgement and notification of application*

**3**—(1)  On receiving an application, the Secretary must—
(a)  immediately send an acknowledgement of its receipt to the applicant; and
(b)  subject to the following provisions of this paragraph, enter particulars of the application and the date of its receipt in the records and send a copy of it, together with any documents supplied by the applicant in support of it, to the respondent.

(2)  If the President is of the opinion that the applicant is asking the Tribunal to do something which it cannot do, he may notify the applicant in writing—
(a)  of the reasons for his opinion; and
(b)  that the application will not be entered in the records unless within five working days the applicant notifies the President in writing that he wishes to proceed with it.

(3)  If in the Secretary's opinion there is an obvious error in the application—
(a)  he may correct it;
(b)  he shall notify the applicant accordingly; and
(c)  unless within five working days of receipt of notification under head (b) of this sub-paragraph the applicant notifies the Secretary in writing that he objects to the correction, the application shall be amended accordingly.

*Response to application*

**4**—(1)  The Secretary must send the information provided by the applicant under paragraph 1 or 2, as the case may be, to the respondent together with a request that he respond to the application within 20 working days of receiving it.

(2)  If the respondent fails to respond as directed, he shall not be entitled to take any further part in the proceedings.

(3)  The response must—
(a)  acknowledge that the respondent has received a copy of the application;
(b)  indicate whether or not he opposes it, and if he does, why;
(c)  provide the following information and documents—
    (i)  the name, address and profession of the person (if any) representing the respondent and whether the Secretary should send documents

concerning the appeal or, as the case may be, application for leave, to the representative rather than to the respondent;

(ii) copies of any letters informing the applicant of the decision which is the subject of the appeal or, as the case may be, application for leave;

(iii) copies of any information submitted with a reference under section 82(1), 83(1), 84(1) or 85 of the 2000 Act and of any observations submitted on it by the applicant.

(4) The Secretary must without delay send to the applicant a copy of the response and the information and documents provided with it.

...

*Misconceived applications etc*

**5**—*(1) The President or the nominated chairman may at any time strike out the appeal or, as the case may be, application for leave, on the grounds that—*

(a) *it is made otherwise than in accordance with paragraph 1 or 2 (as the case may be);*

(b) *it is outside the jurisdiction of the Tribunal or is otherwise misconceived; or*

(c) *it is frivolous or vexatious.*

*(2) Before striking out an appeal or application for leave, as the case may be, under this paragraph, the President or the nominated chairman must—*

(a) *invite the parties to make representations on the matter within such period as he may direct;*

(b) *if within the period specified in the direction the applicant so requests in writing, afford the parties an opportunity to make oral representations; and*

(c) *consider any representations the parties may make.*

*Grant or refusal of leave*

**6**—(1) The President or the nominated chairman shall grant or refuse leave in relation to an application under paragraph 2 without a hearing, as he sees fit.

(2) Subject to paragraph 7, if the President or the nominated chairman refuses leave the application shall be dismissed.

(3) The Secretary must without delay notify the parties in writing of the President or the nominated chairman's decision, and if he has refused leave—

(a) must notify them of his reasons for doing so; and

(b) must inform the applicant of his right to request a reconsideration of the decision under paragraph 7.

*Reconsideration of leave*

**7**—(1) The President or the nominated chairman must reconsider a decision to refuse leave if within ten working days after receipt of a notice under paragraph 6(3) the Secretary receives a written request to do so from the applicant.

(2) If in his request under sub-paragraph (1) the applicant has asked to make representations about leave at a hearing, the Secretary must fix a hearing for those representations to be heard.

(3) The Secretary must notify the respondent of any hearing fixed for the purpose of considering whether to grant leave, and the applicant and the respondent may appear or be represented by any person at that hearing.

(4) If the President or the nominated chairman again refuses leave after reconsideration—

(a) he must give his reasons for doing so in writing; and

(b) the Secretary must without delay send to the parties a copy of the President or the nominated chairman's decision and if he has refused leave his reasons for doing so.

*Further information to be sent by the applicant and the respondent*

**8**—(1) As soon as the respondent has provided the information set out in paragraph 4, or as soon as leave has been granted under paragraph 6 or 7, the Secretary must write to each party requesting that he send to the Secretary, within 20 working days after the date on which he receives the Secretary's letter, the following information—

(a) the name of any witness whose evidence the party wishes the Tribunal to consider (and whether the party may wish the Tribunal to consider additional witness evidence from a witness whose name is not yet known) and the nature of that evidence;

(b) whether the party wishes the President [or nominated chairman] to give any directions or exercise any of his powers under Part IV of these Regulations;

(c) whether the party wishes there to be a preliminary hearing with regard to directions;

(d) a provisional estimate of the time the party considers will be required to present his case;

(e) the earliest date by which the party considers he would be able to prepare his case for hearing; and

(f) in the case of the applicant, whether he wishes his case to be determined without a hearing.

(2) Once the Secretary has received the information referred to in sub-paragraph (1) from both parties, he must without delay send a copy of the information supplied by the applicant to the respondent and that supplied by the respondent to the applicant.

*Changes to further information supplied to the Tribunal*

**9**—(1) Either party, within 5 working days of receiving the further information in respect of the other party from the Secretary, may ask the Secretary in writing to amend or add to any of the information given under paragraph 8(1).

(2) If the Secretary receives any further information under sub-paragraph (1) from either party he must, without delay, send a copy of it to the other party.

**Note.** Para (5) revoked by SI 2004 No 2073, reg 13 as from 31 August 2004. Words in square brackets in para (8)(1)(b) added by SI 2003 No 1060, reg 7 as from 30 April 2003.

[SCHEDULE 6                                Regulation 4(6)

APPEAL UNDER SECTION 68 OF THE 2000 ACT AGAINST A DECISION OF A COUNCIL IN RESPECT OF REGISTRATION UNDER PART IV OF THAT ACT

*Initiating an appeal*

**1**—(1) A person who wishes to appeal to the Tribunal under section 68 of the 2000 Act against a decision of the Council under Part IV of the 2000 Act in respect of registration must do so by application in writing to the Secretary.

(2) An application under this paragraph may be made on the application form available from the Secretary.

(3) An application under this paragraph must be received by the Secretary no later than 28 days after the date of service on the applicant of notice of the decision.

(4) An application under this paragraph must—

(a) give the applicant's name, date of birth and full postal address;

(b) give the name, address and profession of the person (if any) representing the applicant;

    (c)  give the address within the United Kingdom to which the Secretary should send documents concerning the appeal;

    (d)  give the applicant's telephone number, fax number and e-mail address and those of the applicant's representative where these are available;

    (e)  identify the decision against which the appeal is brought and give particulars of whether the appeal is against—

        (i)  the refusal of registration of the applicant as a social worker or, as the case may be, a social care worker in the relevant part of the register;

       (ii)  the removal of the applicant from a part of the register;

      (iii)  the suspension, or the refusal to terminate the suspension, of the applicant from a part of the register;

      (iv)  the grant of an application for registration subject to conditions; or

       (v)  the removal, alteration or restoration of an entry relating to the applicant in a part of the register;

    (f)  give a short statement of grounds for the appeal; and

    (g)  be signed and dated by the applicant.

    (5) In this Schedule, 'register' means the register maintained by the Council under section 56(1) of the Act and 'relevant part' of the register means—

    (a)  in relation to a social worker, the part of the register for social workers; and

    (b)  in relation to a social care worker of a specified description, the part of the register for a social care worker of that description.

*Acknowledgement and notification of application*

**2**—(1)  On receiving an application, the Secretary must—

    (a)  immediately send an acknowledgement of its receipt to the applicant; and

    (b)  enter particulars of the appeal and the date of its receipt in the records and send a copy of it, together with any documents supplied by the applicant in support of it, to the respondent.

    (2)  If, in the Secretary's opinion, there is an obvious error in the application—

    (a)  he may correct it;

    (b)  he shall notify the applicant in writing accordingly; and

    (c)  unless within five working days of receipt of notification under head (b) the applicant notifies him in writing that he objects to the correction, the application shall be amended accordingly.

*Response to application*

**3**—(1) The Secretary must send the information provided by the applicant under paragraph 1 to the respondent together with a request that he respond to the application within 20 working days of receiving it.

    (2) If the respondent fails to respond as requested, he shall not be entitled to take any further part in the proceedings.

    (3) The response must—

    (a)  acknowledge that the respondent has received a copy of the application;

    (b)  indicate whether or not he opposes it, and if he does, why; and

    (c)  provide the following information and documents—

        (i)  the name, address and profession of the person (if any) representing the respondent and whether the Secretary should send documents concerning the appeal to the representative rather than to the respondent;

       (ii)  a copy of the decision which is the subject of the appeal and the reasons for the decision; and

      (iii)  a copy of the relevant entry in the register.

    (4) The Secretary must without delay send to the applicant a copy of the response and the information and documents provided with it.

    ...

*Misconceived appeals etc*

**4**—(1)   The President or the nominated chairman may at any time strike out the appeal on the grounds that—
  (a)   it is made otherwise than in accordance with paragraph 1;
  (b)   it is outside the jurisdiction of the Tribunal or is otherwise misconceived; or
  (c)   it is frivolous or vexatious.
  (2)   Before striking out an appeal under this paragraph, the President or the nominated chairman must—
  (a)   invite the parties to make representations on the matter within such period as he may direct;
  (b)   if within the period specified in the direction the applicant so requests in writing, afford the parties an opportunity to make oral representations; and
  (c)   consider any representations the parties may make.

*Further information to be sent by the applicant and the respondent*

**5**—(1)   As soon as the respondent has provided the information set out in paragraph 3, the Secretary must write to each party requesting that he send to the Secretary, within 15 working days after the date on which he receives the Secretary's letter, the following information—
  (a)   the name of any witness whose evidence the party wishes the Tribunal to consider (and whether the party may wish the Tribunal to consider additional witness evidence from a witness whose name is not yet known) and the nature of that evidence;
  (b)   whether the party wishes the President or the nominated chairman to give any directions or exercise any of his powers under Part IV of these Regulations;
  (c)   whether the party wishes there to be a preliminary hearing with regard to directions;
  (d)   a provisional estimate of the time the party considers will be required to present his case;
  (e)   the earliest date by which the party considers he would be able to prepare his case for hearing; and
  (f)   in the case of the applicant, whether he wishes his appeal to be determined without a hearing.
  (2)   Once the Secretary has received the information referred to in sub-paragraph (1) from both parties, he must without delay send a copy of the information supplied by the applicant to the respondent and that supplied by the respondent to the applicant.

*Changes to further information supplied to the Tribunal*

**6**—(1)   Either party, within 5 working days of receiving the further information in respect of the other party from the Secretary, may ask the Secretary in writing to amend or add to any of the information given under paragraph 5(1).
  (2)   If the Secretary receives any further information under sub-paragraph (1) from either party he must, without delay, send a copy of it to the other party.]

**Note.**   Schedule 6 inserted by SI 2003 No 626, reg 10, Schedule as from 1 April 2003. Para 4 revoked by SI 2004 No 2073, reg 14 as from 31 August 2004.

[SCHEDULE 7                                              Regulation 4(7)

APPEALS UNDER THE SUSPENSION REGULATIONS

*Initiating an appeal*

**1**—(1)  A person who wishes to appeal to the Tribunal—
  (a)  under regulation 8(1)(a) of the Suspension Regulations against a decision to suspend the registration of a person acting as a child minder or providing day care; or
  (b)  under regulation 8(1)(b) of the Suspension Regulations against a refusal to lift the suspension of such registration,
must do so by application in writing to the Secretary.

(2)  An application under sub-paragraph (1)(a) must be received by the Secretary no later than 10 working days after service on the applicant of a notice suspending his registration.

(3)  An application under sub-paragraph (1)(b) must be received by the Secretary no later than 10 working days after service on the applicant of a notice informing him of the decision not to lift his suspension.

(4)  An application under this paragraph may be made on the application form available from the Secretary.

(5)  An application under this paragraph must—
  (a)  give the applicant's name, full postal address and, if the applicant is an individual, his date of birth or, where the applicant is a company, the address of its registered office;
  (b)  give the name, address and profession of the person (if any) representing the applicant;
  (c)  give the address within the United Kingdom to which the Secretary should send documents concerning the appeal;
  (d)  give, where these are available, the applicant's telephone number, fax number and e-mail address and those of the applicant's representative;
  (e)  identify the decision against which the appeal is brought and give particulars of whether the appeal is made under sub-paragraph (1)(a) or (1)(b) or both;
  (f)  set out the reasons for and grounds upon which the applicant is appealing;
  (g)  state whether or not the applicant wishes the Tribunal to determine the appeal by way of an oral hearing;
  (h)  where the applicant wishes the Tribunal to determine the appeal by way of an oral hearing—
    (i)  insofar as the applicant is able to identify them at that stage, give the names of any witnesses that the applicant will be calling or is likely to call to support his case and provide a statement as to the nature of the evidence to be given by those witnesses; and
    (ii)  specify any working days within the 20 working days following the date of the application when the applicant or any such witnesses will not be available to attend a hearing before the Tribunal, and the reasons for which he or they (as the case may be) will not be so available; and
  (i)  be signed and dated by the applicant and must contain a statement as follows: 'To the best of my knowledge, information and belief, the facts contained in this application are true'.

(6)  The applicant must, so far as it is practicable to do so, ensure that the application includes a copy of any documentary evidence (including any statements from witnesses) that the applicant intends to rely upon in presenting his case.

(7)  At the same time as he sends the application to the Secretary, the applicant must send a copy of his application to the respondent.

*Acknowledgement and notification of application*

**2**—(1) On receiving an application, the Secretary must—

(a) immediately send to the applicant an acknowledgement of its receipt;

(b) enter particulars of the appeal and the date of its receipt in the records and send a copy of it, together with any documents supplied by the applicant in support of the appeal, to the respondent.

(2) If in the Secretary's opinion there is an obvious error in the application—

(a) he may correct it;

(b) he must as soon as reasonably practicable and wherever possible, in advance of any determination of the appeal notify the applicant that he has done so; and

(c) amend the application accordingly unless, at any stage prior to the determination of the appeal by the Tribunal, the applicant notifies the Secretary that he objects to the correction.

*Response to application*

**3**—(1) The respondent must, within 3 working days of the date of receipt of the application from the applicant or the Secretary (whichever is the earliest) send to the Secretary and to the applicant a written response to the application.

(2) Where the respondent fails to respond as directed under sub-paragraph (1), he shall not be entitled to take any further part in the proceedings.

(3) The response must—

(a) acknowledge that the respondent has received a copy of the application and any documentary evidence enclosed with it;

(b) indicate whether or not the respondent opposes the appeal;

(c) provide a copy of the notice referred to in paragraph 1(2) or (3) that was served on the applicant;

(d) provide a provisional estimate of the time the respondent considers he will require to present his case;

(e) state whether the respondent wishes the President or the nominated chairman to give any directions or exercise any of his powers under Part IV of these Regulations;

(f) provide the name, address and profession of the person (if any) representing the respondent and whether the Secretary should send any further documents relating to the appeal to the representative rather than the respondent;

(g) where the applicant has requested an oral hearing—

(i) insofar as the respondent is able to identify them at that stage, give the names of any witnesses that the respondent will be calling or is likely to call to support his case and provide a statement as to the nature of the evidence to be given by those witnesses;

(ii) specify any forthcoming working days within the period of 20 working days after the date of the application when the respondent or any such witnesses will not be available to attend a hearing before the Tribunal, and the reasons for which he or they (as the case may be) will not be so available.

(4) The respondent must, so far as it is practicable to do so, ensure that the response includes a copy of any documentary evidence (including any statements from witnesses) that the respondent intends to rely upon in presenting his case.

*Further evidence*

**4**—(1) Subject to sub-paragraph (2), either party shall, at the earliest practicable date after he sent his application or response (as the case may be) to the Secretary, send to the Secretary and to the other party—

(a) any further documentary evidence which he intends to rely upon at the hearing (or wishes the Tribunal to take into consideration in otherwise determining the appeal); and

(b) the names of any witnesses or any further witnesses that he will be calling or is likely to call to support his case and a statement as to the nature of the evidence to be given by those witnesses.

(2) The evidence or information referred to in sub-paragraph (1)(a) or (b) must be received by the Secretary and the other party no later than 5 working days before the hearing or the determination of the appeal or, where it appears to the President or the nominated chairman that it is necessary or expedient for a later date to be substituted, by such date as the President or the nominated chairman may direct.

...

*Misconceived appeals etc*

**5**—*(1) Subject to sub-paragraph (2), the President or the nominated chairman may at any time strike out the appeal on the grounds that—*

*(a) it is made otherwise than in accordance with paragraph 1;*

*(b) it is outside the Tribunal's jurisdiction or is otherwise misconceived; or*

*(c) it is frivolous or vexatious.*

*(2) Before striking out an appeal under this paragraph, the President or the nominated chairman must—*

*(a) invite the parties to make representations on the matter within such period as he may direct;*

*(b) if within the period specified in the direction, the applicant so requests in writing, afford the parties an opportunity to make oral representations; and*

*(c) consider any representations the parties may make.]*

**Note.** Schedule 7 added by SI 2003 No 626, reg 10, Schedule as from 1 April 2003. Para (5) revoked by SI 2004 No 2073, reg 15 as from 31 August 2004.


[SCHEDULE 8]                                                        Regulation 4(8)

APPEAL UNDER PARAGRAPH 10(1A) OF SCHEDULE 26 TO THE 1998 ACT AGAINST A DECISION OF THE CHIEF INSPECTOR

*Initiating an appeal*

**1**—(1) A person who wishes to appeal to the Tribunal under paragraph 10(1A) of Schedule 26 to the 1998 Act against a decision of the Chief Inspector must do so by application in writing to the Secretary.

(2) An application under this paragraph may be made on the application form available from the Secretary.

(3) An application under this paragraph must be received by the Secretary no later than 28 days after the date of service on the applicant of notice of the decision of the Chief Inspector.

(4) An application under this paragraph must—

(a) give the applicant's name, date of birth and full postal address;

(b) give the name, address and profession of the person (if any) representing the applicant;

(c) give the address within the United Kingdom to which the Secretary should send documents concerning the appeal;

(d) give the applicant's telephone number, fax number and e-mail address and those of the applicant's representative where these are available;

(e) identify the decision against which the appeal is brought and give particulars of whether the appeal is against—

> > > (i)   the refusal of the Chief Inspector to renew the registration of the applicant as a nursery education inspector or an early years child care inspector;
> > > (ii)   the imposition or variation of any condition subject to which the applicant is registered; or
> > > (iii)   the removal of the name of the applicant from the register;
> > (f)   give a short statement of grounds for the appeal; and
> > (g)   be signed and dated by the applicant.

(5)   In this Schedule, 'register' means the register maintained by the Chief Inspector under paragraph 8(1) of Schedule 26 to the 1998 Act or section 79P(1) of the 1989 Act, and 'registration' and 'registered' shall be construed accordingly.

*Acknowledgement and notification of application*

**2**—(1)   On receiving an application, the Secretary must—
> (a)   immediately send an acknowledgement of its receipt to the applicant; and
> (b)   enter particulars of the appeal and the date of its receipt in the records and send a copy of it, together with any documents supplied by the applicant in support of it, to the respondent.

(2)   If, in the Secretary's opinion, there is an obvious error in the application—
> (a)   he may correct it;
> (b)   he shall notify the applicant in writing accordingly; and
> (c)   unless within five working days of receipt of notification under head (b) the applicant notifies him in writing that he objects to the correction, the application shall be amended accordingly.

*Response to application*

**3**—(1)   The Secretary must send the information provided by the applicant under paragraph 1 to the respondent together with a request that he respond to the application within 20 working days of receiving it.

(2)   If the respondent fails to respond as requested, he shall not be entitled to take any further part in the proceedings.

(3)
The response must—
> (a)   acknowledge that the respondent has received a copy of the application;
> (b)   indicate whether or not he opposes it, and if he does, why; and
> (c)   provide the following information and documents—
> > (i)   the name, address and profession of the person (if any) representing the respondent and whether the Secretary should send documents concerning the appeal to the representative rather than to the respondent;
> > (ii)   a copy of the decision which is the subject of the appeal and the reasons for the decision; and
> > (iii)   a copy of the relevant entry in the register.

(4)   The Secretary must without delay send to the applicant a copy of the response and the information and documents provided with it.

...

*Misconceived appeals etc*

**4**—*(1)   The President or the nominated chairman may at any time strike out the appeal on the grounds that*—
> *(a)   it is made otherwise than in accordance with paragraph 1;*
> *(b)   it is outside the jurisdiction of the Tribunal or is otherwise misconceived; or*
> *(c)   it is frivolous or vexatious.*

(2) Before striking out an appeal under this paragraph, the President or the nominated chairman must—

(a) invite the parties to make representations on the matter within such period as he may direct;

(b) if within the period specified in the direction the applicant so requests in writing, afford the parties an opportunity to make oral representations; and

(c) consider any representations the parties may make.

*Further information to be sent by the applicant and the respondent*

**5**—(1) As soon as the respondent has provided the information set out in paragraph 3, the Secretary must write to each party requesting that he send to the Secretary, within 15 working days after the date on which he receives the Secretary's letter, the following information—

(a) the name of any witness whose evidence the party wishes the Tribunal to consider (and whether the party may wish the Tribunal to consider additional witness evidence from a witness whose name is not yet known) and the nature of that evidence;

(b) whether the party wishes the President or the nominated chairman to give any directions or exercise any of his powers under Part IV of these Regulations;

(c) whether the party wishes there to be a preliminary hearing with regard to directions;

(d) a provisional estimate of the time the party considers will be required to present his case;

(e) the earliest date by which the party considers he would be able to prepare his case for hearing; and

(f) in the case of the applicant, whether he wishes his appeal to be determined without a hearing.

(2) Once the Secretary has received the information referred to in sub-paragraph (1) from both parties, he must without delay send a copy of the information supplied by the applicant to the respondent and that supplied by the respondent to the applicant.

*Changes to further information supplied to the Tribunal*

**6**—(1) Either party, within 5 working days of receiving the further information in respect of the other party from the Secretary, may ask the Secretary in writing to amend or add to any of the information given under paragraph 5(1).

(2) If the Secretary receives any further information under sub-paragraph (1) from either party he must, without delay, send a copy of it to the other party.]

**Note.** Schedule 8 added by SI 2003 No 1060, reg 8, Schedule as from 30 April 2003. Para (4) revoked by SI 2004 No 2073, reg 16 as from 31 August 2004.

[SCHEDULE 9                                                      Regulation 4(9)

### APPEALS AGAINST REFUSALS, DETERMINATIONS OR ORDERS OF THE REGISTRATION AUTHORITY UNDER THE 2002 ACT

*Initiating an appeal*

**1**—(1) A person who wishes to appeal to the Tribunal under section 166 of the 2002 Act against a refusal, determination or order made by the registration authority must do so by application in writing to the Secretary.

(2) An application under this paragraph may be made on the application form available from the Secretary.

(3) An application under this paragraph must—

(a) give the applicant's name and full postal address, if the applicant is an individual his date of birth and, if the applicant is a company, the address of its registered office;

(b) give the name, address and profession of the person (if any) representing the applicant;

(c) give the address within the United Kingdom to which the Secretary should send documents concerning the appeal;

(d) give, where these are available, the applicant's telephone number, fax number and e-mail address and those of the applicant's representative;

(e) give particulars of whether the appeal is against—

    (i) a refusal under section 162 of the 2002 Act to approve a material change;

    (ii) a determination under section 165 of the 2002 Act to remove the school from the register;

    (iii) an order under section 165(8) of the 2002 Act requiring the taking of specified action; or

    (iv) a refusal under section 165(10) of the 2002 Act to vary or revoke such an order;

(f) give a short statement of the grounds of the appeal; and

(g) be signed and dated by the applicant.

*Acknowledgement and notification of application*

**2**—(1) On receiving an application made within the period for bringing an appeal specified in section 166(2) of the 2002 Act, the Secretary must—

(a) immediately send an acknowledgement of its receipt to the applicant; and

(b) enter particulars of the appeal and the date of its receipt in the records and send a copy of it, together with any documents supplied by the applicant in support of it, to the respondent.

(2) If, in the Secretary's opinion, there is an obvious error in the application—

(a) he may correct it;

(b) he must notify the applicant in writing that he has done so; and

(c) unless within five working days of receipt of notification under head (b) of this sub-paragraph the applicant notifies him in writing that he objects to the correction, the application shall be amended accordingly.

*Response to application*

**3**—(1) The Secretary must send the information provided by the applicant under paragraph 1 to the respondent together with a request that he respond to the application within 20 working days of receiving it.

(2) If the respondent fails to respond as directed, he shall not be entitled to take any further part in the proceedings.

(3) The response must—

(a) acknowledge that the respondent has received a copy of the application;

(b) indicate whether or not the respondent opposes it, and if he does, give the reasons why he opposes the application;

(c) provide the following information and documents—

    (i) the name, address and profession of the person (if any) representing the respondent and whether the Secretary should send documents concerning the appeal to the representative rather than to the respondent; and

    (ii) a copy of the notice of the refusal, determination or order which is the subject of the appeal and the reasons for it.

(4) The Secretary must without delay send the applicant a copy of the response and the information and documents provided with it.

...

*Misconceived appeals etc*

**4**—(*1*) *The President or the nominated chairman may at any time strike out the appeal on the grounds that—*
 (*a*) *it is made otherwise than in accordance with paragraph 1;*
 (*b*) *it is outside the jurisdiction of the Tribunal or is otherwise misconceived; or*
 (*c*) *it is frivolous or vexatious.*
 (*2*) *Before striking out an appeal under this paragraph, the President or the nominated chairman must—*
 (*a*) *invite the parties to make representations on the matter within such period as he may direct;*
 (*b*) *if within the period specified in the direction the applicant so requests in writing, afford the parties an opportunity to make oral representations; and*
 (*c*) *consider any representations the parties may make.*

*Further information to be sent by the applicant and respondent*

**5**—(1) As soon as the respondent has provided the information set out in paragraph 3, the Secretary must write to each party requesting that he sends the Secretary, within 15 working days after the date on which he receives the Secretary's letter, the following information—
 (a) name of any witness whose evidence the party wishes the Tribunal to consider (and whether the party may wish the Tribunal to consider additional witness evidence from a witness whose name is not yet known) and the nature of that evidence;
 (b) whether the party wishes the President or the nominated chairman to give any directions or exercise any of his powers under Part IV of these Regulations;
 (c) whether the party wishes there to be a preliminary hearing with regard to directions;
 (d) a provisional estimate of the time the party considers will be required to present his case;
 (e) the earliest date by which the party considers he would be able to prepare his case for the hearing; and
 (f) in the case of the applicant, whether he wishes his appeal to be determined without a hearing.
 (2) Once the Secretary has received the information referred to in sub-paragraph (1) from both parties, he must without delay send a copy of the information supplied by the applicant to the respondent and that supplied by the respondent to the applicant.

*Changes to further information supplied to the Tribunal*

**6**—(1) Either party, within 5 working days of receiving the further information in respect of the other party from the Secretary, may ask the Secretary in writing to amend or add to any of the information given under paragraph 5(1).
 (2) If the Secretary receives any further information under sub-paragraph (1) from either party he must, without delay, send a copy of it to the other party.

*Orders under section 166(5) of the 2002 Act*

**7**—(1) Where the respondent in relation to an appeal under section 166 of the 2002 Act wishes the Tribunal to make an order under section 166(5) of that Act, he must make an application in writing to the Secretary and, at the same time, send a copy of that application to the applicant in the appeal.
 (2) The respondent may make an application under this paragraph at any time from the date he receives the copy of the application under paragraph 3(1) until 20 working days following that date.

(3) An application under this paragraph must—

(a) set out the grounds for the application;

(b) give the names of any witnesses that the respondent will be calling to support his application and provide a statement as to the nature of the evidence to be given by those witnesses;

(c) specify any working days within the 28 working days following the making of the application when the respondent or any such witnesses will not be available to attend a hearing before the Tribunal, and the reasons why the respondent or they (as the case may be), will not be so available; and

(d) be signed and dated by or on behalf of the respondent.

(4) The respondent must, so far as it is practicable to do so, ensure that the application includes a copy of any documentary evidence (including any statements from witnesses) that the respondent intends to rely upon in relation to the application.

(5) On receiving an application under this paragraph, the Secretary must immediately send a copy of it together with any documents supplied by the respondent in support of the application, to the applicant.

(6) The applicant must within 10 working days of receipt of the application from the Secretary, send to the Secretary and the respondent a written response to the application which must—

(a) acknowledge that he has received a copy of the application and any documentary evidence enclosed with it;

(b) state whether he wishes the Tribunal to determine the application without an oral hearing, and if that is not the case, give the names of any witnesses that he will be calling or is likely to call to support his case and provide a statement as to the nature of the evidence to be given by those witnesses;

(c) unless he wishes the Tribunal to determine the application without an oral hearing, specify any working days within the 28 working days following the date of the application when he or any such witnesses will not be available to attend a hearing in respect of the application and the reasons why he or they (as the case may be) will not be so available.

(7) The applicant must, so far as it is practicable to do so, ensure that the response includes a copy of any documentary evidence (including any statements from witnesses) that he intends to rely upon in opposing the application.

(8) If the applicant fails to respond as required by sub-paragraph (6), he shall not be entitled to take any further part in the proceedings under this paragraph.

(9) An application shall be determined by way of oral hearing unless the applicant in the appeal requests that it be determined without an oral hearing.

(10) The date fixed for a hearing shall be the earliest practicable date having regard to any directions which have been made by the President or the nominated chairman with regard to the preparation of evidence but shall not be later than 10 working days after—

(a) the date on which the Secretary receives the written response from the applicant; or

(b) if the applicant fails to respond within the time limit set out in sub-paragraph (6), the date of the expiry of that time limit,

and the Secretary must then inform the parties of the date of the hearing by no later than 5 working days before the date fixed for the hearing, or (where the President or the nominated chairman considers it necessary or expedient) by such later date as the President or the nominated chairman may direct.

(11) This sub-paragraph applies where the respondent has not made an application under sub-paragraph (1) but the Tribunal is considering whether to make an order under section 166(5) of the 2002 Act.

(12) Subject to sub-paragraph (13), where sub-paragraph (11) applies, the President or the nominated chairman may—

    (a)  give directions as to the dates by which any document, witness statement or any other material which the parties wish the Tribunal to take into account, shall be sent to the Secretary; and

    (b)  give any other direction in exercise of his powers under Part IV of these Regulations.

(13) Where sub-paragraph (11) applies, the President or the nominated chairman may not make an order under section 166(5) of the 2002 Act unless the applicant has been given an opportunity of appearing before the Tribunal and being heard on the question of whether such an order should be made, in which case the date for the hearing shall be the earliest practicable date having regard to any direction made.]

**Note.** Schedule 9 added by SI 2003 No 2043, reg 12, Schedule as from 1 September 2003. Para (4) revoked by SI 2004 No 2073, reg 17 as from 31 August 2004.

## CHILD SUPPORT APPEALS (JURISDICTION OF COURTS) ORDER 2002

**Dated** 20 July 2002

**SI 2002 No 1915**

*Citation, commencement, interpretation and extent*

**1**—(1) This Order may be cited as the Child Support Appeals (Jurisdiction of Courts) Order 2002.

    (2) Subject to paragraph (3) this Order shall come into force on the day after the date on which it is made.

    (3) This Order shall not have effect in relation to a particular type of case until the day on which section 10 of the Child Support, Pensions and Social Security Act 2000 comes into force for the purposes of that type of case.

    (4) In this Order—

    (a)  'the Act' means the Child Support Act 1991; and

    (b)  'the Regulations' means the Social Security and Child Support (Decisions and Appeals) Regulations 1999.

    (5) This Order extends to England and Wales only.

*Revocation*

**2** The Child Support Appeals (Jurisdiction of Courts) Order 1993, to the extent to which it applies in England and Wales, is revoked.

*Parentage appeals to be made to courts*

**3** An appeal under section 20 of the Act shall be made to a court instead of to an appeal tribunal in the circumstances mentioned in article 4.

**4** The circumstances are that—

    (a)  the appeal will be an appeal under section 20(1)(a) or (b) of the Act;

    (b)  the determination made by the Secretary of State in making the decision to be appealed against included a determination that a particular person (whether the applicant or some other person) either was, or was not, a parent of the qualifying child in question ('a parentage determination'); and

    (c)  the ground of the appeal will be that the decision to be appealed against should not have included that parentage determination.

**5** Regulations 31 and 32 of the Regulations shall apply to appeals brought under this Order with the following modifications—

(a) for the words 'an appeal tribunal' shall be substituted 'a court';

(b) for the words 'legally qualified panel member' and 'panel member' shall be substituted 'justices' clerk or the court'; and

(c) in regulation 32(10) for the words 'such written form as has been approved by the President' shall be substituted 'written form'.

## RECOVERY ABROAD OF MAINTENANCE (CONVENTION COUNTRIES) ORDER 2002

**Dated** 20 November 2002

**SI 2002 No 2839**

This order varies the Recovery Abroad of Maintenance (Convention Countries) Order 1975 by adding Ireland to the schedule with effect from 15 January 2003.

## INTERCOUNTRY ADOPTION (HAGUE CONVENTION) REGULATIONS 2003

**Dated** 26 January 2003

**SI 2003 No 118**

PART 1

GENERAL

**1 Citation, commencement and application** (1) These Regulations may be cited as the Intercountry Adoption (Hague Convention) Regulations 2003 and shall come into force on 1st June 2003.

(2) These Regulations apply to England and Wales only.

**2 Interpretation** In these Regulations—

'the 1976 Act' means the Adoption Act 1976;

'the 1999 Act' means the Adoption (Intercountry Aspects) Act 1999;

'the Adoption Agencies Regulations' means the Adoption Agencies Regulations 1983 subject to the modifications set out in Schedule 4;

'adoption agency' means a local authority or an appropriate voluntary organisation which is an accredited body for the purposes of the Convention;

'adoption panel' has the same meaning as in the Adoption Agencies Regulations;

'CA of the receiving State' means, in relation to a Convention country other than the United Kingdom, the Central Authority of the receiving State;

'CA of the State of origin' means, in relation to a Convention country other than the United Kingdom, the Central Authority of the State of origin;

'contact order' has the meaning given in section 8(1) of the Children Act 1989;

'eligible to adopt', except in regulation 8(4)(a), has the meaning given in regulation 4;

['independent review panel' means a panel constituted under section 9A of the 1976 Act;]

'prospective adopter' means a married couple or a person who makes an application under regulation 3;
'receiving State' has the same meaning as in Article 2 of the Convention;
'relevant Central Authority' means—
  (a) in Part 2—
      (i) in relation to a prospective adopter who is habitually resident in England, the Secretary of State; and
      (ii) in relation to a prospective adopter who is habitually resident in Wales, the National Assembly for Wales; and
  (b) in Part 3—
      (i) in relation to a local authority in England, the Secretary of State; and
      (ii) in relation to a local authority in Wales, the National Assembly for Wales;
'relevant local authority' in Part 2 has the meaning given in regulation 15;
'State of origin' has the same meaning as in article 2 of the Convention.

**Note.** Definition 'Independent review panel' inserted, in relation to England, by SI 2004 No 1868, reg 2(1), (2) as from 20 August 2004.

PART 2
REQUIREMENTS, PROCEDURE, RECOGNITION AND EFFECT OF ADOPTION IN ENGLAND AND WALES WHERE THE UNITED KINGDOM IS THE RECEIVING STATE

**3 Application for determination of eligibility, and assessment of suitability, to adopt**—(1) A married couple or a person habitually resident in the British Islands who wishes to adopt a child habitually resident in a Convention country outside the British Islands shall apply to an adoption agency for a determination of eligibility, and an assessment of his suitability, to adopt.

(2) An application under this regulation shall be made in writing and include such information as the agency may require.

**4 Eligibility requirements** An adoption agency may not consider any person eligible to adopt unless the application under regulation 3 is made by a married couple or one person and—
  (a) in the case of an application by a married couple they have both—
      (i) attained the age of 21 years; and
      (ii) been habitually resident in any part of the British Islands for a period of not less than 1 year ending with the date of the application; or
  (b) in the case of an application by one person, he—
      (i) has attained the age of 21 years; and
      (ii) has been habitually resident in any part of the British Islands for a period of not less than 1 year ending with the date of the application.

**5 Requirement to provide counselling and information**—(1) Where an application is made in accordance with regulation 3, the adoption agency must—
  (a) provide a counselling service for the prospective adopter;
  (b) explain to him the legal implications of adoption and the procedure in relation to adopting a child under the Convention; and
  (c) provide him with written information about the matters referred to in sub-paragraph (b).

(2) Paragraph (1) does not apply if the adoption agency is satisfied that the requirements set out in that paragraph have been carried out in respect of the prospective adopter by another adoption agency.

**6 Requirement to carry out police checks—**(1) An adoption agency must take steps to obtain—

(a) in respect of the prospective adopter, an enhanced criminal record certificate within the meaning of section 115 of the Police Act 1997 including the matters specified in subsection (6A) of that section; and

(b) in respect of any other member of his household aged 18 or over, an enhanced criminal record certificate under section 115 of that Act.

(2) An adoption agency may not consider a person to be suitable to be an adoptive parent if he or any member of his household aged 18 or over—

(a) has been convicted of an offence specified in Schedule 2 to the Adoption Agencies Regulations committed at the age of 18 or over; or

(b) has been cautioned by a constable in respect of such an offence which, at the time the caution was given, he admitted.

**7 Requirement to notify—**(1) The adoption agency must notify a prospective adopter in writing as soon as possible after becoming aware that—

(a) he is not eligible to adopt because he does not meet the requirements of regulation 4; or

(b) he is not suitable to be an adoptive parent by virtue of regulation 6.

(2) In a case to which paragraph (1)(b) applies the notification must specify the conviction, or as the case may be, the caution in question.

**8 Procedure in respect of carrying out an assessment—**(1) Where the adoption agency—

(a) is satisfied that the prospective adopter is eligible to adopt in accordance with the provisions in regulation 4; and

(b) considers he may be suitable to be an adoptive parent following any information provided or made available as a consequence of the carrying out of the requirements imposed by regulation 5 or otherwise,

it must set up a case record in respect of him and place on it any information obtained under that regulation or otherwise.

(2) The adoption agency must obtain such particulars as are referred to in Part VI of Schedule 1 to the Adoption Agencies Regulations together with, so far as is reasonably practicable, any other relevant information which may be required by the adoption panel.

(3) The adoption agency must obtain a written report—

(a) from a registered medical practitioner about the health of the prospective adopter which must deal with matters specified in Part VII of Schedule 1 to the Adoption Agencies Regulations;

(b) about the premises where the prospective adopter intends to live with any child who might be adopted by him; and

(c) of each of the interviews with the persons nominated by the prospective adopter to provide personal references for him,

and in a case where the agency is not the local authority in whose area the prospective adopter has his home, it must also obtain a written report about him from that authority.

(4) The adoption agency must prepare a written report which must—

(a) state the Convention country from which the prospective adopter wishes to adopt a child, confirm that he is eligible to adopt a child under the law of that Convention country and provide any other information which that Convention country usually requires;

(b) include the agency's assessment of the prospective adopter's suitability to be an adoptive parent;

(c) include any other observations of the agency on the matters referred to in regulations 3 to 6 and this regulation; and

(d) include information and observations regarding the prospective adopter's identity, background, family and medical history, social environment, reasons for adoption, ability to undertake an intercountry adoption as well as the characteristics of the children for whom he would be qualified to care for and any other information which may be relevant.

(5) The adoption agency must notify the prospective adopter that his application is to be referred to the adoption panel and at the same time send him a copy of the agency's report referred to in paragraph (4), inviting him to send any observations in writing to the agency on the report within 28 days, beginning with the date on which the notification was sent.

(6) At the end of the period of 28 days referred to in paragraph (5) (or earlier if any observations made by the prospective adopter are received before the 28 days has expired) the adoption agency must pass the report referred to in paragraph (4) together with all relevant information obtained by it under this regulation (including the prospective adopter's observations on the report), to the adoption panel.

**9 Function of adoption panel—**(1) Subject to paragraph (2), the function of an adoption panel is to consider the case of the prospective adopter referred to it by the adoption agency and make a recommendation to that agency as to whether the prospective adopter is suitable to be an adoptive parent.

(2) In considering what recommendation to make, the adoption panel—

(a) must consider and take into account all information and reports passed to it in accordance with regulation 8(6);

(b) may request the adoption agency to obtain any other relevant information which the panel considers necessary; and

(c) may obtain legal advice as it considers necessary in relation to the case.

**10 Adoption agency decision and notification—**(1) The adoption agency must take into account the recommendation of the adoption panel in coming to a decision about whether the prospective adopter is suitable to be an adoptive parent.

(2) No member of an adoption panel [ or an independent review panel] shall take part in any decision made by the adoption agency under paragraph (1).

(3) If the adoption agency decide to approve the prospective adopter as suitable to be an adoptive parent, it must notify him in writing of its decision.

(4) If the adoption agency consider that the prospective adopter is not suitable to be an adoptive parent, it must—

(a) notify the prospective adopter in writing that it proposes not to approve him as suitable to be an adoptive parent;

(b) send with that notification its reasons together with a copy of the recommendations of the adoption panel, if different; and

(c) *invite the prospective adopter to submit any representations he wishes to make within 28 days.*

[(c) notify the prospective adopter in writing that within 28 days he may—

(i) submit any representations he wishes to make in writing to the adoption agency; or

(ii) apply to the Secretary of State for a review by an independent review panel of the adoption agency's proposal not to approve him as suitable to be an adoptive parent (referred to in this regulation as a 'qualifying determination')]

(5) If within the period of 28 days referred to in paragraph (4), *the prospective adopter has not made any representations* [the prospective adopter has not applied to the Secretary of State for a review by an independent review panel of the qualifying determination or made any representations to the adoption agency], the adoption

agency may proceed to make its decision and shall notify the prospective adopter in writing of its decision together with the reasons for that decision.

[(5A) If the adoption agency receives notification from the Secretary of State that a prospective adopter has applied to the Secretary of State for a review by an independent review panel of the qualifying determination, it shall within 7 days after the date of that notification submit to the Secretary of State—

  (a)  all of the documents and information which were passed to the adoption panel in accordance with regulation 8(6);

  (b)  any relevant information in relation to the prospective adopter which was obtained by the adoption agency after the date on which the documents and information referred to in sub-paragraph (a) were passed to the adoption panel; and

  (c)  the documents referred to in paragraph (4)(a) and (b).]

(6) If within the period of 28 days referred to in paragraph (4), the adoption agency receive further representations from the prospective adopter, it may refer the case together with all the relevant information to the adoption panel for further consideration.

(7) The adoption panel must reconsider any case referred to it under paragraph (6) and make a fresh recommendation to the adoption agency as to whether the prospective adopter is suitable to be an adoptive parent.

*(8)   The adoption agency must make a decision on the case but if the case has been referred to the adoption panel under paragraph (6) it must make the decision only after taking into account any recommendation of the adoption panel made under paragraph (7).*

[(8) The adoption agency shall make a decision on the case and, in addition to the requirements of paragraph (1),—

  (a)  if the prospective adopter has applied to the Secretary of State for a review by an independent review panel of the qualifying determination, it shall make the decision only after taking into account any recommendation of that panel made in accordance with the Independent Review of Determinations (Adoption) Regulations 2004; or

  (b)  if the case has been referred to an adoption panel under paragraph (6), it shall make the decision only after taking into account any recommendation of the adoption panel made by virtue of paragraph (7).]

(9) As soon as possible after making the decision under paragraph (8), the adoption agency must notify the prospective adopter in writing of its decision, stating its reasons for that decision if they do not consider the prospective adopter to be suitable to be an adoptive parent, and *of the adoption panel's recommendations, if this is different from the adoption agency's decision* [, if the case has been referred to an adoption panel under paragraph (6), of the adoption panel's recommendation, if this is different from the adoption agency's decision].

[(10) In a case where an independent review panel has made a recommendation, the adoption agency shall send to the independent review panel a copy of the notification referred to in paragraph (9).]

**Note.** Para (2): words 'or an independent review panel' in square brackets inserted, in relation to England, by SI 2004 No 1868, reg 2(1), (3)(a) as from 20 August 2004. Para (4): sub-para (c) substituted, in relation to England, by SI 2004 No 1868, reg 2(1), (3)(b) as from 20 August 2004. Para (5): words 'the prospective adopter has not made any representations' in italics revoked and subsequent words in square brackets substituted, in relation to England, by SI 2004 No 1868, reg 2(1), (3)(c) as from 20 August 2004. Para (5A): inserted, in relation to England, by SI 2004 No 1868, reg 2(1), (3)(d) as from 20 August 2004. Para (8): substituted, in relation to England, by SI 2004 No 1868, reg 2(1), (3)(e) as from 20 August 2004. Para (9): words 'of the adoption panel's recommendations, if this is different from the adoption agency's decision' in italics revoked and subsequent words in square brackets substituted, in relation to England, by SI 2004 No 1868, reg 2(1), (3)(f) as from 20 August 2004. Para (10): inserted, in relation to England, by SI 2004 No 1868, reg 2(1), (3)(g) as from 20 August 2004.

**11 Procedure following approval by adoption agency**—(1) Where the adoption agency is satisfied that the prospective adopter is eligible to adopt and has approved him as suitable to be an adoptive parent ('the decision') it must send to the relevant Central Authority—

(a)  written confirmation of the decision; and

(b)  the report prepared for the purpose of regulation 8(4).

(2) The relevant Central Authority may seek further information from the adoption agency, if that Authority considers it is appropriate to do so.

(3) If the relevant Central Authority is satisfied that the adoption agency has complied with these Regulations and that all the relevant information has been supplied by that agency, the Authority must send to the CA of the State of origin—

(a)  a certificate in the form set out in Schedule 1 confirming that the—

    (i)  prospective adopter is eligible to adopt;

    (ii)  prospective adopter has been assessed in accordance with these Regulations;

    (iii)  prospective adopter has been approved as suitable to be an adoptive parent;

    (iv)  child will be authorised to enter and reside permanently in the United Kingdom if entry clearance, and leave to enter or remain as may be necessary, is granted and not revoked or curtailed and a Convention adoption order or Convention adoption is made;

(b)  a copy of the decision; and

(c)  a copy of the report prepared for the purpose of regulation 8(4).

(4) The relevant Central Authority must notify the adoption agency and the prospective adopter in writing that the certificate and the documents referred to in paragraph (3) have been sent to the CA of the State of origin.

**12 Procedure following receipt of the Article 16 Information from the CA of the State of origin**—(1) Where the relevant Central Authority receive from the CA of the State of origin, the Article 16 Information relating to the child whom the CA of the State of origin considers should be placed for adoption with the prospective adopter, the relevant Central Authority must send that Information to the adoption agency.

(2) The adoption agency must consider the Article 16 Information and—

(a)  send that Information to the prospective adopter;

(b)  meet with him to discuss the Article 16 Information and the proposed placement; and

(c)  if appropriate, offer a counselling service and further information as required.

(3) Where—

(a)  the procedure in paragraph (2) has been followed;

(b)  the prospective adopter (and where the prospective adopters are a married couple each of them) has visited the child in the State of origin; and

(c)  after that visit to the child, the prospective adopter confirmed in writing that he—

    (i)   has visited that child; and

    (ii)   wishes to proceed to adopt the child,

the adoption agency must notify the relevant Central Authority that the requirements specified in sub-paragraph (a), (b) and (c) have been satisfied and at the same time it must confirm that it is content that the adoption should proceed.

(4) Where the relevant Central Authority has received notification from the adoption agency under paragraph (3), the relevant Central Authority shall—

(a)  notify the CA of the State of origin that—

    (i)  the prospective adopter wishes to proceed to adopt the child;

    (ii)  it is prepared to agree with the CA of the State of origin that the adoption may proceed; and

(b) confirm to the CA of the State of origin that—
    (i) in the case where the requirements specified in section 1(5A) of the British Nationality Act 1981 are met that, the child will be authorised to enter and reside permanently in the United Kingdom; and
    (ii) in any other case, if entry clearance and leave to enter and remain, as may be necessary, is granted and not revoked or curtailed and a Convention adoption order or a Convention adoption is made, the child will be authorised to enter and reside permanently in the United Kingdom.

(5) The relevant Central Authority must inform the adoption agency and the prospective adopter when the agreement under Article 17(c) of the Convention has been made.

(6) If, at any stage before the agreement under Article 17(c) of the Convention is made, the CA of the State of origin notifies the relevant Central Authority that it has decided the proposed placement should not proceed, the relevant Central Authority must inform the adoption agency of the CA of the State of origin's decision and the agency must then inform the prospective adopter and return the documents referred to in paragraph (2) to that Authority who must then return them to the CA of the State of origin.

(7) If, at any stage before the child is placed with him, the prospective adopter notifies the adoption agency that he does not wish to proceed with the adoption of the child, that agency must inform the relevant Central Authority and return the documents to that Authority who must in turn notify the CA of the State of origin of the prospective adopter's decision and return the documents to the CA of the State of origin.

(8) Following any agreement under Article 17(c) of the Convention and the placement of the child by the adoption agency with the prospective adopter, the prospective adopter must accompany the child on entering the United Kingdom unless, in the case of a married couple, the agency and the CA of the State of origin have agreed that it is necessary for only one of them to do so.

(9) For the purposes of this regulation 'the Article 16 Information' means—
(a) the report referred to in Article 16(1) of the Convention including information about the child's identity, adoptability, background, social environment, family history, medical history including that of the child's family, and any special needs of the child;
(b) proof of confirmation that the consents of the persons, institutions and authorities whose consents are necessary for adoption have been obtained in accordance with Article 4 of the Convention; and
(c) the reasons for the CA of the State of origin's determination on the placement.

**13 Duty of adoption agency before the arrival of the child in England or Wales** Where the adoption agency is informed by the relevant Central Authority that the agreement under Article 17(c) of the Convention has been made and the adoption may proceed, that agency must—
(a) send a written report of the child's health history and current state of health, so far as it is known, to the prospective adopter's registered medical practitioner, if any, together with particulars of the placement;
(b) in a case where the adoption agency is not the local authority within whose area the prospective adopter has his home, notify that authority of the particulars of the placement; and
(c) notify the local education authority within whose area the prospective adopter has his home in writing of the particulars of the placement if the child is of compulsory school age within the meaning of section 8 of the Education Act 1996 or the adoption agency's medical adviser considers the child to have special needs or to be disabled.

**14 Requirements following arrival of the child in the United Kingdom but no Convention adoption is made in the State of origin** Regulations 15 to 19 apply where, following agreement between the relevant Central Authority and the CA of the State of origin under Article 17(c) of the Convention that the adoption may proceed, no Convention adoption is made, or applied for, in the State of origin but the child is placed with the prospective adopter in the State of origin and he then returns to England or Wales with the child.

**15 Duty of prospective adopter to notify local authority** A prospective adopter with whom the child is placed must within the period of fourteen days beginning with the date on which he brings the child into the United Kingdom give notice to the local authority within whose area he has his home ('the relevant local authority') of—

   (a)  his intention to apply for an adoption order to be made as a Convention adoption order in accordance with section 22 of the 1976 Act (notification to local authority of adoption application); or

   (b)  his intention not to give the child a home.

**16 Duty of prospective adopter where the child is placed with them**—(1) The prospective adopter with whom the child is placed is not required to allow the child to visit or stay with any person, or otherwise to allow contact between the child and any person, except under a contact order.

(2) Subject to paragraphs (3) and (4), the prospective adopter may not cause or permit—

   (a)  the child to be known by a new surname; or

   (b)  the child to be removed from the United Kingdom,

unless the court gives leave or the relevant local authority agree.

(3) Paragraph (2)(a) does not apply if the competent authority of the State of origin has agreed the child may be known by a new surname.

(4) Paragraph (2)(b) does not apply if the removal of the child is for a period of less than one month by the prospective adopter.

**17 Prospective adopter unable to proceed with application to adopt** Where the child is placed with the prospective adopter or regulation 20 applies and the prospective adopter gives notice to the relevant local authority that he does not wish to proceed with the adoption and no longer wishes to give the child a home, that authority must—

   (a)  receive the child from him before the end of the period of 7 days beginning with the giving notice; and

   (b)  notify the relevant Central Authority of his decision not to proceed with the adoption.

**18 Removal of the child by the relevant authority**—(1) Subject to paragraph (4), where the child is placed with the prospective adopter or regulation 20 applies and the relevant local authority are of the opinion that—

   (a)  the continued placement of the child with the prospective adopter is not in the child's best interests; and

   (b)  the child should not remain with the prospective adopter,

that authority must give notice to the prospective adopter of their opinion.

(2) The prospective adopter must, not later than the end of the period of 7 days beginning with the giving of notice, return the child to the authority.

(3) Where the relevant local authority give notice under paragraph (1), they must also give notice to the relevant Central Authority that they have requested the return of the child.

(4) Where a notice under paragraph (1) is given, but—

(a) before the notice was given an application for a Convention adoption order was made; and

(b) the application has not been disposed of,

the prospective adopter is not required by virtue of the notice to return the child to the authority unless the court so orders.

(5) This regulation does not affect the exercise by any local authority or other person of any power conferred by any enactment or the exercise of any power of arrest.

**19 Breakdown of placement—**(1) This regulation applies where—

(a) the prospective adopter notifies the relevant local authority under regulation 17 that he does not wish to proceed with the adoption;

(b) the relevant local authority have removed the child from the home of the prospective adopter in accordance with regulation 18; or

(c) an application for a Convention adoption order is refused, or a Convention adoption or a Convention adoption order is annulled pursuant to section 53(1) of the 1976 Act.

(2) Where the relevant local authority are satisfied that it would be in the child's best interests to be placed for adoption with another prospective adopter habitually resident in the United Kingdom they must seek to identify a suitable adoptive parent for the child.

(3) Where the relevant local authority have identified another prospective adopter who is eligible to adopt and has been assessed in accordance with these Regulations and approved as suitable to be an adoptive parent in accordance with regulations 3 to 10—

(a) that authority must notify the relevant Central Authority in writing that—

(i) another prospective adopter has been identified; and

(ii) the requirements, procedures and notifications as provided for in regulations 3 and 10 have been complied with; and

(b) the requirements specified in regulation 11(1) shall apply in respect of that prospective adopter.

(4) Where the relevant Central Authority has been notified in accordance with paragraph (3)—

(a) regulation 11(2) to (4) shall apply in respect of that other prospective adopter;

(b) it shall inform the CA of the State of origin of the proposed placement; and

(c) it shall agree that placement with the CA of the State of origin in accordance with the provisions in this Part of these Regulations.

(5) Where the relevant local authority are not satisfied it would be in the child's best interests to be placed for adoption with another prospective adopter in England or Wales, it must liaise with the relevant Central Authority to arrange for the return of the child to his State of origin.

(6) Before coming to any decision under this regulation, the relevant local authority must have regard to the wishes and feelings of the child, having regard to his age and understanding, and, where appropriate, obtain his consent in relation to measures to be taken under this regulation.

**20 Convention adoptions subject to a probationary period—**(1) This regulation applies where—

(a) the child has been placed with the prospective adopters by the competent authority of the State of origin and a Convention adoption has been applied for by the prospective adopter in the State of origin but the child's placement with the prospective adopter is subject to a probationary period before the Convention adoption is made; and

(b) the prospective adopter returns to England or Wales with the child before that probationary period is completed and the Convention adoption is made in the State of origin.

(2) The relevant local authority must, if requested by the competent authority of the State of origin, submit a report about the placement to that authority and such a report must be prepared within such timescale and contain such information as the competent authority may reasonably require.

**21 Prescribed requirements for the purposes of making a Convention adoption order**—(1) For the purposes of section 17 of the 1976 Act (requirements in respect of adoption order made as a Convention adoption order), where the United Kingdom is the receiving State the prescribed requirements are—

(a) both spouses (in the case of an application by a married couple) or the applicant (in the case of an application by one person) have been habitually resident in any part of the British Islands for a period of not less than 1 year ending with the date of the application;

(b) the child to be adopted has not attained the age of 18 years on the date of the application;

(c) the child to be adopted was, on the date on which the agreement under Article 17(c) was made, habitually resident in a Convention country outside the British Islands; and

(d) in a case where the applicant (in the case of an application by one person) or one of the spouses (in the case of an application by a married couple) is not a British citizen by virtue of the British Nationality Act 1981, the Home Office has confirmed that the child is authorised to enter and reside permanently in the United Kingdom.

**22 Procedural requirements following a Convention adoption order or Convention adoption**—(1) Where a Convention adoption order is made by a court in England or Wales, the court must send a copy of that order to the relevant Central Authority.

(2) On receipt of an order under paragraph (1), the relevant Central Authority must issue a certificate in the form set out in Schedule 2 certifying that the adoption has been made in accordance with the Convention.

(3) A copy of the certificate issued under paragraph (2) must be sent to—

(a) the CA of the State of origin;

(b) the adoptive parents; and

(c) the adoption agency and, if different, the relevant local authority.

(4) Where the relevant Central Authority receive a certificate under Article 23 of the Convention in respect of a Convention adoption made in that Convention country, the relevant Central Authority must send a copy of that certificate to—

(a) the adoptive parents; and

(b) the adoption agency.

**23 Refusal of a court in England or Wales to make a Convention adoption order** Where an application for a Convention adoption order is refused by the court or is withdrawn, the prospective adopter must return the child to the relevant local authority within the period determined by the court.

**24 Annulment of a Convention adoption order or a Convention adoption** Where a Convention adoption order or a Convention adoption is annulled under section 53(1) of the 1976 Act the court must send a copy of the order to—

(a) the relevant Central Authority for onward transmission to the CA of the State of origin;

(b)  the adoptive parents; and
(c)  the adoption agency and, if different, the relevant local authority.

PART 3

REQUIREMENTS AND PROCEDURE IN ENGLAND AND WALES WHERE THE UNITED KINGDOM IS THE STATE OF ORIGIN

**25 Duty of adoption agency in respect of assessment of a child—**(1) This regulation applies where—
(a)  a local authority (referred to in this Part as 'the LA')—
    (i)  has decided that adoption is in the best interests of a child under regulation 11(1) of the Adoption Agencies Regulations ('the first decision');
   (ii)  has considered the possibilities for placement of that child within the British Islands; and
  (iii)  considers that adoption by a person habitually resident in a Convention country outside the British Islands may be in the child's best interests; and
(b)  the child is free for adoption by virtue of an order made under section 18 of the 1976 Act, section 18 of the Adoption (Scotland) Act 1978 or Article 17(1) or 18(1) of the Adoption (Northern Ireland) Order 1987.
(2)  The LA must refer the case of the child to the adoption panel together with—
(a)  the documents referred to in regulation 7(2)(e) of the Adoption Agencies Regulations originally sent to the adoption panel; and
(b)  a report from the child's social worker—
    (i)  as to why he considers that adoption by a person habitually resident in a Convention country outside the British Islands may be in the child's best interests, and
   (ii)  if appropriate, having regard to the child's age and understanding, on the child's views and wishes in relation to adoption.

**26 Function of adoption panel—**(1) The adoption panel must consider the case of the child and make a recommendation to the LA as to whether adoption by a person habitually resident in a Convention country outside the British Islands is in the best interests of the child.
(2)  In considering what recommendation to make, the adoption panel must have regard to the duties imposed upon the LA by sections 6 and 7 of the 1976 Act (duty to promote the welfare of the child and religious upbringing of adopted child) and must—
(a)  consider and take into account all the information and reports passed to it under regulation 25(2);
(b)  request the LA to obtain any other relevant information which the adoption panel considers necessary; and
(c)  obtain legal advice in relation to the case as may be necessary.

**27 Decision and notification—**(1) The LA must make a decision on the case referred to the adoption panel only after taking into account the recommendation of the adoption panel.
(2)  No member of an adoption panel shall take part in any decision made by the LA under paragraph (1).
(3)  The LA must notify the relevant Central Authority—
(a)  of the name and age of the child;
(b)  of the reasons why they consider that the child may be suitable for adoption by a person habitually resident in a Convention country outside the British Islands;

   (c)  of the date the freeing order under section 18 of the 1976 Act, section 18 of the Adoption (Scotland) Act 1978 or Article 17(1) or 18(1) of the Adoption (Northern Ireland) Order 1987 was made; and

   (d)  of any other information that Authority may require.

   (4) The relevant Central Authority is to maintain a list of children who are notified to that Authority under paragraph (3) and shall make the contents of that list available for consultation by other Central Authorities within the British Islands.

   (5) Where a LA—

   (a)  places for adoption a child whose details have been notified to the relevant Central Authority under paragraph (3); or

   (b)  determines that adoption by a person habitually resident in a Convention country outside the British Islands is no longer in the best interests of such a child,

they must notify the relevant Central Authority accordingly and that Authority must remove the details relating to that child from the Convention list.

   (6) In this regulation and regulation 28 'Convention list' means—

   (a)  in relation to a relevant Central Authority, a list of children notified to that Authority in accordance with paragraph (3); or

   (b)  in relation to any other Central Authority within the British Islands, a list of children notified to that Authority in accordance with provisions which correspond to paragraph (3).

**28 Receipt of the Article 15 Report from the CA of the receiving State—**(1) This regulation applies where—

   (a)  the relevant Central Authority receives a report from the CA of the receiving State which has been prepared for the purposes of Article 15 of the Convention ('the Article 15 Report');

   (b)  the Article 15 Report relates to a prospective adopter who is habitually resident in that receiving State ('a Convention prospective adopter'); and

   (c)  the Convention prospective adopter wishes to adopt a child who is habitually resident in England or Wales.

   (2) If the relevant Central Authority is satisfied the Convention prospective adopter meets the following requirements—

   (a)  in respect of age and marital status as provided for in sections 14 and 15 of the 1976 Act; and

   (b)  in the case of a married couple, both Convention prospective adopters are, or in the case of a single Convention prospective adopter, that prospective adopter is habitually resident in a Convention country outside the British Islands,

the Authority must consult the Convention list and may, if the Authority considers it appropriate, consult any Convention list maintained by another Central Authority within the British Islands.

   (3) The relevant Central Authority may pass a copy of the Article 15 Report to any other Central Authority within the British Islands for the purpose of enabling that Authority to consult its Convention list.

   (4) Where the relevant Central Authority identifies a child on the Convention list who may be suitable to be adopted by the Convention prospective adopter, that Authority must send the Article 15 Report to the LA which referred the child's details to the Authority.

   (5) The LA must consider the Article 15 Report and where it considers that it may be appropriate to place the child for adoption with the Convention prospective adopter it must refer the proposed placement for adoption to the adoption panel together with—

   (a)  the Article 15 Report;

    (b)  the documents and report referred to in regulation 25(2);

    (c)  its observations on the proposed placement; and

    (d)  any other relevant information about the child.

**29 Duty of adoption panel in respect of proposed placement—**(1) The adoption panel must consider the proposed placement referred to it by the LA under regulation 25 and make a recommendation to the LA, as to whether—

    (a)  the Convention prospective adopter is a suitable adoptive parent for the child; and

    (b)  the proposed placement is in the best interests of the child.

    (2) In considering what recommendation to make under paragraph (1), the adoption panel—

    (a)  must have regard to the child's upbringing and his ethnic, religious and cultural background;

    (b)  must have regard to the duties imposed upon the LA by sections 6 and 7 of the 1976 Act (duty to promote welfare of child and religious upbringing of adopted child);

    (c)  must have regard to the documents and the Article 15 Report referred to it under regulation 28(4);

    (d)  may request the LA to obtain any other relevant information which the adoption panel considers necessary; and

    (e)  may obtain legal advice as it considers necessary in relation to the case.

**30 LA decision in respect of placement—**(1) The LA must make a decision about the proposed placement only after having taken into account the recommendations of the adoption panel.

    (2) No member of an adoption panel shall take part in any decision made by the LA under paragraph (1).

**31 Preparation of the Article 16 information for the CA of the receiving State—**(1) Where the LA decides under regulation 30 that the proposed placement is in the best interests of the child and the adoption may proceed, it must prepare a report for the purposes of Article 16(1) of the Convention which must include—

    (a)  information about the child's identity, suitability for adoption, background, social environment, family history, medical history including that of the child's family, and any special needs of the child; and

    (b)  the reasons for their decision.

    (2) The LA must send the report referred to in paragraph (1) to the relevant Central Authority together with—

    (a)  evidence that a freeing order has been made in respect of the child;

    (b)  written observations relating to the child's upbringing and to his or her ethnic, religious and cultural background; and

    (c)  the report, if any, referred to in regulation 25(2)(b)(ii).

    (3) The relevant Central Authority must send the report and information referred to it under paragraph (2) to the CA of the receiving State.

    (4) The relevant Central Authority may notify the CA of the receiving State that it is prepared to agree that the adoption may proceed provided that CA has confirmed that—

    (a)  the Convention prospective adopter has agreed to adopt the child and has received such counselling as may be necessary;

    (b)  the Convention prospective adopter has confirmed that he will accompany the child to the receiving State, unless where the Convention prospective adopter is a married couple, the LA and the CA of the receiving State have agreed that it is necessary for only one of them to do so;

  (c)  it is content for the adoption to proceed; and
  (d)  the child is or will be authorised to enter and reside permanently in the Convention country if a Convention adoption is made in that Convention country or a Convention adoption order is made in the United Kingdom.
  (5)  Subject to paragraph (7), the relevant Central Authority may not make an agreement under Article 17(c) of the Convention with the CA of the receiving State unless the LA have confirmed to that Authority that—
  (a)  it has met the Convention prospective adopter;
  (b)  the Convention prospective adopter has visited the child; and
  (c)  the Convention prospective adopter is content for the adoption to proceed.
  (6)  A LA may not place a child for adoption with a Convention prospective adopter unless the agreement under Article 17(c) of the Convention has been made and the relevant Central Authority must advise the LA when that agreement has been made.
  (7)  In paragraph (5), the reference to 'Convention prospective adopter' means in the case where the Convention prospective adopters are a married couple, both of them.

**32 Prescribed requirements for the purposes of making a Convention adoption order**  For the purposes of section 17 of the 1976 Act (requirements in respect of an adoption order made as a Convention adoption order) the prescribed requirements are in the case where the United Kingdom is the State of origin—
  (a)  both spouses (in the case of an application by a married couple) are, or the applicant (in the case of an application by one person) is, habitually resident in a Convention country outside the British Islands on the date of the application;
  (b)  the child to be adopted is free for adoption by virtue of an order made under section 18 of the 1976 Act, section 18 of the Adoption (Scotland) Act 1978, or Article 17(1) or 18(1) of the Adoption (Northern Ireland) Order 1987;
  (c)  the child to be adopted is habitually resident in any part of the British Islands on the date of the application; and
  (d)  the child to be adopted has not attained the age of 18 years on the date of the application.

**33 Procedural requirements following a Convention adoption order or Convention adoption—**(1) Where a Convention adoption order is made by a court in England or Wales, the court must send a copy of that order to the relevant Central Authority.
  (2)  On receipt of an order under paragraph (1), the relevant Central Authority must issue a certificate in the form set out in Schedule 2 certifying that the Convention adoption order has been made in accordance with the Convention.
  (3)  A copy of the certificate must be sent to the—
  (a)  CA of the receiving State; and
  (b)  LA.
  (4)  Where the relevant Central Authority receives a certification of the adoption having been made in accordance with the Convention from the competent authority of the receiving State, the relevant Central Authority must send a copy of that certification to the LA.

PART 4

MISCELLANEOUS

**34 Application, with or without modifications, of provisions of the 1976 Act—**(1)  The provisions of the 1976 Act set out in column 1 of Schedule 3 to these Regulations shall apply with the modifications set out in column 2 of that Schedule in relation to adoptions under the Convention.

(2)  Paragraph (1) does not preclude the application of provisions of the 1976 Act, which do not require modifications, to adoptions under the Convention.

**35 Application, with modifications, of provisions of the Adoption Agencies Regulations**  The Adoption Agencies Regulations shall apply together with the modifications set out in Schedule 4 to these Regulations in relation to adoptions under the Convention.

**36 Offences**  Any person who contravenes or fails to comply with—
  (a)  regulation 15 (notification to local authority);
  (b)  regulation 18(2) (return of child to relevant local authority);
  (c)  regulation 18(4) (return of child to relevant authority as ordered by the court); or
  (d)  regulation 23 (return of child to relevant authority within period prescribed by court),
without reasonable excuse is guilty of an offence and liable on summary conviction to imprisonment for a term not exceeding three months, or a fine not exceeding level 5 on the standard scale, or both.

**37 Transitional and consequential provisions—**(1) These Regulations shall not apply in relation to the case of any prospective adopter who wishes to adopt a child from a Convention country outside the British Islands which has been referred by the adoption agency (dealing with the case) to the adoption panel before the date on which these Regulations come into force.

(2)  No application may be made for a Convention adoption order under section 17 of the 1976 Act unless the arrangements for the adoption of the child have been made in accordance with these Regulations.

SCHEDULE 1                                                                 Regulation 11

CERTIFICATE OF ELIGIBILITY AND APPROVAL

To the Central Authority of the State of origin
Re . . . [name of applicant]
  In accordance with Article 5 of the Convention, I hereby certify on behalf of the Central Authority for [England] [Wales] that . . . [name of applicant] has been counselled, is eligible to adopt and has been assessed and approved as suitable to adopt a child from . . . [State of origin] by . . . [a local authority in England or Wales or an accredited body for the purpose of the Convention].
  The attached report has been prepared in accordance with Article 15 of the Convention for presentation to the competent authority in . . . [State of origin].
  This certificate of eligibility and approval and the report under Article 15 of the Convention are provided on the condition that a Convention adoption or Convention adoption order will not be made until the agreement under Article 17(c) of the Convention has been made.
  I confirm on behalf of the Central Authority that if, following the agreement under Article 17(c) of the Convention that—

[(i) in the case, where the requirements specified in section 1(5A) of the British Nationality Act 1981 are met that the child . . . [name] will be authorised to enter and reside permanently in the United Kingdom]

OR

[(ii) in any other case, if entry clearance and leave to enter and remain, as may be necessary, is granted and not revoked or curtailed and a Convention adoption order or Convention adoption is made, the child . . . [name] will be authorised to enter and reside permanently in the United Kingdom.]

Signed

On behalf of [the Secretary of State Central Authority for England]
[the National Assembly for Wales Central Authority for Wales]

SCHEDULE 2                                                           Regulations 22 and 33

CERTIFICATE THAT THE CONVENTION ADOPTION ORDER HAS BEEN MADE IN ACCORDANCE WITH THE CONVENTION

1   The Central Authority as the competent authority for [England] [Wales] being the country in which the Convention adoption order was made hereby certifies, in accordance with Article 23(1) of the Convention, that the child:

(a) name: ................................................. [name on birth certificate, also known as/now known as]

sex: ..........................
date and place of birth: .........................................
habitual residence at the time of adoption: .........................................
State of origin: .........................................

(b) was adopted on: .........................................
by order made by: ......................................... court in [England] [Wales]

(c) by the following person(s):

(i) —   family name and first name(s): .........................................
—   sex: .........................................
—   date and place of birth: .........................................
—   habitual residence at the time of the adoption: .........................................
.........................................

(ii) —   family name and first name(s): .........................................
—   sex: .........................................
—   date and place of birth: .........................................
—   habitual residence at the time of the adoption: .........................................
.........................................

2   The competent authority for [England] [Wales] in pursuance of Article 23(1) of the Convention hereby certifies that the adoption was made in accordance with the Convention and that the agreement under Article 17(c) was given by:

(a) —   Name and address of the Central Authority in the State of origin: ........
.........................................
.........................................

Date of the agreement: .........................................

(b) —   Name and address of the Central Authority in the receiving State:
.........................................
.........................................

—   Date of the agreement: .........................................

Signed .........................................       Dated .........................................

SCHEDULE 3                                                    Regulation 34(1)

APPLICATION, WITH MODIFICATIONS, OF THE PROVISIONS OF THE 1976 ACT

| Column 1<br>Provisions of the 1976 Act<br>Modifications | Column 2 |
| --- | --- |
| Section 12<br><br>(adoption orders) | As if at the beginning of subsections (5) and (7) there were inserted the words 'Subject to paragraph (8),'. As if there were inserted at the end '(8) A Convention adoption order may not be made in relation to a person who has attained the age of 19 years.'. |
| Section 16 (parental agreement) | As if for subsection (1) there were substituted 'A Convention adoption order shall not be made unless an agreement under Article 17(c) of the Convention has been made in respect of the child' and subsections (2) to (5) were omitted. |
| Section 22 (notification to local authority of adoption application) | As if the words in subsection (1) 'not placed with the applicant by an adoption agency' there were substituted 'entrusted to the applicants by a competent authority in accordance with Article 17 of the Convention'. |
| Section 27 (restrictions on removal where adoption agreed) | As if for subsection (1) there were substituted 'Where an application for a Convention adoption order is pending the parent or guardian is not entitled to remove the child from the home of the applicant except with the leave of the court.', subsections (2) and (2A) were omitted, and in subsection (3) 'or (2)' were omitted. |
| Sections 30 and 31 (application of section 30 where child not placed for adoption) | As if sections 30 and 31 were omitted. |

SCHEDULE 4                                               Regulation 35

APPLICATION, WITH MODIFICATIONS, OF THE PROVISIONS OF THE
ADOPTION AGENCIES REGULATIONS

| Column 1<br>Provision of the Adoption Agencies<br>Regulations | Column 2<br>Modifications |
| --- | --- |
| Regulation 7 | In relation to a case where the UK is the receiving State as if regulation 7 were omitted. |
| Regulations 8 to 12 | As if regulations 8 to 12 were omitted. |
| Regulation 14 | As if in paragraph (2) the words—<br>(i) 'regulations 7(2)(a), 8(2)(a) or 9(3)' were substituted by the words 'regulation 7(2)(a) or under the Intercountry Adoption (Hague Convention) Regulations 2003' and;<br>(ii) 'these regulations' were substituted by the words 'those regulations'. |

## VOLUNTARY ADOPTION AGENCIES AND ADOPTION AGENCIES (MISCELLANEOUS AMENDMENTS) REGULATIONS 2003

**Dated** 25 February 2003

**SI 2003 No 367**

PART I

GENERAL

**1 Citation, commencement and interpretation**—(1) These Regulations may be cited as the Voluntary Adoption Agencies and the Adoption Agencies (Miscellaneous Amendments) Regulations 2003 and shall come into force on 30th April 2003.

(2) In these Regulations—
'the Act' means the Care Standards Act 2000;
'agency' means an appropriate voluntary organisation;
'branch manager' shall be construed in accordance with regulation 6(1)(b);
['Commission' means the Commission for Social Care Inspection;]
'complaints procedure' shall be construed in accordance with regulation 11(1);
'guardian' has the meaning given to it in section 5 of the Children Act 1989;
'manager' shall be construed in accordance with regulation 6(1)(a);
'organisation' means a body corporate other than a public or local authority the activities of which are not carried on for profit;
'registered provider' means, in relation to an agency, a person who is registered under Part II of the Act as the person carrying on the agency;
'registration authority' means, in relation to an agency, the registration authority which may exercise, in relation to that agency, functions to which section 36A of the Act applies;
'responsible individual' shall be construed in accordance with regulation 5(2);
'statement of purpose' means the written statement compiled in accordance with regulation 3(1).

(3) In these Regulations, references to employing a person include employing a person whether or not for payment, and whether under a contract of service or a contract for services, and allowing a person to work as a volunteer, and references to an employee or to a person being employed shall be construed accordingly.

**Note.** Para (2): definition 'Commission' inserted by SI 2004 No 664, art 3, Sch 2 s from 1 April 2004.

**2 Application for registration under Part II of the Act** No application for registration under Part II of the Act shall be made in respect of a voluntary adoption agency which is an unincorporated body.

**3 Statement of purpose—**(1) The registered provider and the manager shall compile in relation to the agency a written statement (in these Regulations referred to as 'the statement of purpose') which shall consist of a statement as to the matters listed in Schedule 1.

(2) The registered provider and the manager shall provide a copy of the statement of purpose to the registration authority and—

(a) if the registration authority is the Commission and the agency has a branch in Wales, to the Assembly;

(b) if the registration authority is the Assembly and the agency has a branch in England, to the Commission.

(3) The registered provider and the manager shall make a copy of the statement of purpose available, upon request, for inspection by—

(a) any person working for the purposes of the agency;

(b) children who may be adopted, their parents and guardians;

(c) persons wishing to adopt a child;

(d) adopted persons, their parents, natural parents and former guardians;

(e) any local authority.

(4) Subject to paragraph (5), the registered provider and the manager shall ensure that the agency is at all times conducted in a manner which is consistent with its statement of purpose.

(5) Nothing in paragraph (4) shall require or authorise the registered provider, the manager or the branch manager (if any), to contravene, or not comply with—

(a) any other provision of these Regulations;

(b) any conditions for the time being in force in relation to the registration of the registered provider under Part II of the Act.

**4 Review of statement of purpose** The registered provider and the manager shall—

(a) keep under review and, where appropriate, revise the statement of purpose; and

(b) notify the registration authority and—

(i) if the registration authority is the Commission and the agency has a branch in Wales, the Assembly;

(ii) if the registration authority is the Assembly and the agency has a branch in England, the Commission,

of any such revision within 28 days.

PART II

REGISTERED PROVIDERS, RESPONSIBLE INDIVIDUALS AND MANAGERS

**5 Fitness of registered provider—**(1) An organisation shall not carry on an agency unless it is fit to do so.

(2) An organisation is not fit to carry on an agency unless—

(a) it has given notice to the registration authority of the name, address and position in the organisation of an individual (in these Regulations referred to as 'the responsible individual') who is a director, manager, secretary or other officer of the organisation and is responsible for supervising the management of the agency; and

(b) that individual satisfies the requirements set out in paragraph (3).

(3) The requirements are that—

(a) he is of integrity and good character;

(b) he is physically and mentally fit to carry on the agency; and

(c) full and satisfactory information is available in relation to him in respect of each of the matters specified in Schedule 2.

**6 Appointment of manager and branch manager—**(1) The registered provider shall appoint—

(a) an individual to manage the agency (in these Regulations referred to as 'the manager'); and

(b) where the agency has a branch, an individual to manage that branch (in these Regulations referred to as 'the branch manager').

(2) The registered provider shall forthwith notify the registration authority of—

(a) the name of any person appointed in accordance with this regulation; and

(b) the date on which the appointment is to take effect.

**7 Fitness of manager and branch manager—**(1) The registered provider shall not allow a person to manage the agency or any branch of the agency unless he is fit to do so.

(2) A person is not fit to manage an agency or (as the case may be) branch unless—

(a) he is of integrity and good character;

(b) having regard to the size of the agency or branch and the agency's statement of purpose—

(i) he has the qualifications, skills and experience necessary for managing the agency or branch; and

(ii) he is physically and mentally fit to manage the agency or branch; and

(c) full and satisfactory information is available in relation to him in respect of each of the matters listed in Schedule 2.

**8 Registered provider, manager and branch manager—general requirements—**(1) The registered provider, the manager, and the branch manager (if any) shall, having regard to—

(a) the size of the agency or (as the case may be) branch and the agency's statement of purpose; and

(b) the need to safeguard and promote the welfare of children who may be, or have been, placed for adoption by the agency,

carry on or manage the agency or (as the case may be) branch, with sufficient care, competence and skill.

(2) The registered provider shall ensure that the responsible individual undertakes from time to time such training as is appropriate to ensure that he has the experience and skills necessary for carrying on the agency.

(3) The registered provider shall ensure that the manager and branch manager (if any), undertake from time to time such training as is appropriate to ensure that he has the experience and skills necessary for managing the agency or (as the case may be) branch.

**9 Notification of offences** Where the registered provider, responsible individual, manager or branch manager (if any) is convicted of any criminal offence, whether in England and Wales or elsewhere, he shall forthwith give notice in writing to the registration authority of—

(a)   the date and place of the conviction;

(b)   the offence of which he was convicted; and

(c)   the penalty imposed on him in respect of the offence.

PART III

CONDUCT OF AGENCIES

**10  Arrangements for the protection of children—**(1)  The registered provider and the manager shall prepare and implement a written policy which—

(a)   is intended to safeguard from abuse or neglect children placed for adoption—

   (i)   by the agency; or

   (ii)   by another adoption agency but with prospective adopters approved by the agency as suitable to be adoptive parents in accordance with the Adoption Agencies Regulations 1983; and

(b)   sets out the procedure to be followed in the event of any allegation of abuse or neglect.

(2)  The procedure under paragraph (1)(b) shall provide in particular for—

(a)   liaison and co-operation with any local authority which is, or may be, making child protection enquiries in respect of the child;

(b)   where the child is placed with prospective adopters, the prompt referral to the local authority in whose area the child is placed of any allegation of abuse or neglect;

(c)   where the child is not placed with prospective adopters, the prompt referral to the local authority in whose area the principal office of the agency is located of any allegation of abuse or neglect;

(d)   notification to the registration authority of the instigation and outcome of any child protection enquiries;

(e)   written records to be kept of any allegation of abuse or neglect and the action taken in response;

(f)   consideration to be given to the measures that may be necessary to protect children placed with prospective adopters following an allegation of abuse or neglect;

(g)   arrangements to be made for persons working for the purposes of the agency, prospective adopters and children who have been placed for adoption by the agency, to have access to information that would enable them to contact—

   (i)   the local authority referred to in sub-paragraph (b) or (c) (as the case may be); and

   (ii)   the registration authority,

regarding any concern about child welfare or safety.

(3)  In this regulation 'child protection enquiries' means any enquiries carried out by a local authority in the exercise of any of its functions conferred by or under the Children Act 1989 relating to the protection of children.

**11  Complaints—**(1)  The registered provider and the manager shall establish a written procedure for considering complaints (referred to in these Regulations as 'the complaints procedure') made by or on behalf of—

(a)   children who may be adopted, their parents and guardians;

(b)   persons wishing to adopt a child;

(c)   adopted persons, their parents, natural parents and former guardians.

(2)  The complaints procedure shall, in particular, provide—

(a)   for an opportunity for informal resolution of a complaint at an early stage;

  (b) that no person who is the subject of a complaint takes part in its consideration other than, if the registered provider or the manager considers it appropriate, at the informal resolution stage only;

  (c) for dealing with complaints about the registered provider, the responsible individual, the manager and branch manager (if any); and

  (d) for complaints to be made by a person acting on behalf of a child.

  (3) The registered provider and the manager shall provide a copy of the complaints procedure to every person working for the purposes of the agency and shall provide, upon request, a copy of the procedure to any person mentioned in paragraph (1)(a) to (c).

  (4) The copy of the complaints procedure supplied under paragraph (3) shall include—

  (a) the name, address and telephone number of the registration authority; and

  (b) details of the procedure (if any) which has been notified to the registered provider by the registration authority for the making of complaints to the registration authority that relate to the agency.

**12 Complaints—further requirements—**(1) The registered provider and the manager shall ensure that any complaint made under the complaints procedure is fully investigated.

  (2) The registered provider and the manager shall, so far as is reasonably practicable, within a period of 28 days beginning on the date on which the complaint is received by the agency, inform the complainant of the outcome of the investigation and the action (if any) that is to be taken in consequence.

  (3) The registered provider and the manager shall ensure that a written record is made of any complaint, including details of the investigation made, the outcome and any action taken in consequence, and for that record to be retained for at least 3 years from the date that it is made.

  (4) The registered provider and the manager shall take all reasonable steps to ensure that—

  (a) children are enabled to make a complaint; and

  (b) no person is subject to any reprisal by the agency for making a complaint.

  (5) The registered provider shall supply to the registration authority at its request a statement containing a summary of any complaints made in accordance with the complaints procedure during the preceding 12 months and any action taken in consequence.

**13 Staffing of agency** The registered provider, the manager and, in relation to any branch, the branch manager, shall ensure that there is, having regard to—

  (a) the size of the agency or (as the case may be) branch and the agency's statement of purpose; and

  (b) the need to safeguard and promote the health and welfare of children placed for adoption—

    (i) by the agency; or

    (ii) by another adoption agency but with prospective adopters approved by the agency as suitable to be adoptive parents in accordance with the Adoption Agencies Regulations 1983,

a sufficient number of suitably qualified, competent, and experienced persons working for the purposes of the agency or (as the case may be) branch.

**14 Fitness of workers—**(1) The registered provider, the manager and, in relation to any branch, the branch manager, shall not—

  (a) employ a person to work for the purposes of the agency unless that person is fit to work for the purposes of an agency; or

  (b) allow a person to whom paragraph (2) applies, to work for the purposes of the agency unless that person is fit to work for the purposes of an agency.

(2) This paragraph applies to any person who is employed by a person other than the registered provider, in a position in which he may in the course of his duties have regular contact with children who may be, or have been, placed for adoption by the agency.

(3) For the purposes of paragraph (1), a person is not fit to work for the purposes of an agency unless—

(a) he is of integrity and good character;

(b) he has the qualifications, skills and experience necessary for the work he is to perform;

(c) he is physically and mentally fit for the work he is to perform; and

(d) full and satisfactory information is available in relation to him in respect of each of the matters specified in Schedule 2.

(4) The registered provider, the manager and, in relation to any branch, the branch manager, shall take reasonable steps to ensure that any person working for the agency who is not employed by the agency and to whom paragraph (2) does not apply is appropriately supervised while carrying out his duties.

**15 Employment of staff**—(1) The registered provider, the manager and, in relation to any branch, the branch manager, shall—

(a) ensure that all permanent appointments of staff are subject to the satisfactory completion of a period of probation; and

(b) provide all employees with a job description outlining their responsibilities.

(2) The registered provider, the manager and, in relation to any branch, the branch manager, shall ensure that all persons employed by the agency—

(a) receive appropriate training, supervision and appraisal; and

(b) are enabled from time to time to obtain further qualifications appropriate to the work they perform.

**16 Staff disciplinary procedure**—(1) The registered provider and the manager shall operate a disciplinary procedure which, in particular—

(a) provides for the suspension of an employee where necessary in the interests of the safety or welfare of children placed for adoption by the agency;

(b) provides that the failure on the part of an employee to report, to an appropriate person, an incident of abuse, or suspected abuse of a child placed for adoption by the agency is a ground on which disciplinary proceedings may be instituted.

(2) For the purposes of paragraph (1)(b), an appropriate person is—

(a) the registered provider, the manager, or in relation to any person working at any branch of the agency, the branch manager;

(b) an officer of the registration authority;

(c) a police officer;

(d) an officer of the National Society for the Prevention of Cruelty to Children;

(e) an officer of a local authority in whose area the agency or (as the case may be) branch is situated; or

(f) an officer of a local authority in whose area the child is placed for adoption.

**17 Records with respect to staff**—(1) The registered provider, the manager and, in relation to any person working at any branch of the agency, the branch manager, shall maintain and keep up to date the records specified in Schedule 3.

(2) The records referred to in paragraph (1) shall be retained for at least 15 years from the date of the last entry.

**18 Fitness of premises**—(1) The registered provider shall not use premises for the purposes of the agency unless the premises are suitable for the purpose of achieving the aims and objectives set out in the statement of purpose.

(2) The registered provider, the manager and, in relation to any branch, the branch manager, shall ensure—

    (a) that there are adequate security arrangements at the premises, in particular that there are secure facilities for the storage of records; and

    (b) that any records which are, for any reason, not on the premises are nevertheless kept in conditions of appropriate security.

## PART IV

### MISCELLANEOUS—AGENCIES

**19 Notifiable events—**(1) If, in relation to an agency, any of the events listed in column 1 of the table in Schedule 4 takes place, the registered provider and the manager shall without delay notify the person indicated in respect of the event in column 2 of that table.

(2) Any notification made in accordance with this regulation which is given orally shall be confirmed in writing within 14 days.

(3) In the table—

'approved by the agency' means approved by the agency as suitable to be an adoptive parent in accordance with the Adoption Agencies Regulations 1983;

'area authority' means the local authority in whose area the child is placed for adoption;

'placing agency' means the adoption agency that placed the child for adoption with the prospective adopter;

'Primary Care Trust' means the Primary Care Trust in whose area the child is placed for adoption by the agency; and

'Local Health Board' means the Local Health Board in whose area the child is placed for adoption by the agency.

**20 Financial position—**(1) The registered provider shall carry on the agency in such a manner as is likely to ensure that it will be financially viable for the purpose of achieving the aims and objectives set out in its statement of purpose.

(2) The registered provider shall, if the registration authority so requests, provide the authority with such information and documents as it may require for the purpose of considering the financial viability of the agency, including—

    (a) the annual accounts of the agency certified by an accountant; and

    (b) a certificate of insurance for the registered provider in respect of liability which may be incurred by him in relation to the agency in respect of death, injury, public liability, damage or other loss.

**21 Notice of absence—**(1) Where—

    (a) the manager proposes to be absent from the agency; or

    (b) the branch manager proposes to be absent from the branch of the agency,

for a continuous period of 28 days or more, the registered provider and the manager shall give notice in writing to the registration authority of the proposed absence.

(2) Except in the case of an emergency, the notice referred to in paragraph (1) shall be given no later than one month before the proposed absence is to start, or within such shorter period as may be agreed with the registration authority, and the notice shall specify—

    (a) the length or expected length of the proposed absence;

    (b) the reason for the proposed absence;

    (c) the arrangements which have been made for the running of the agency or (as the case may be) branch during that absence;

(d) the name, address and qualifications of the person who will be responsible for the management of the agency or (as the case may be) branch during the absence; and

(e) the arrangements that have been made or are proposed to be made for appointing another person to manage the agency or (as the case may be) branch during the absence, including the proposed date by which the appointment is to start.

(3) Where the absence arises as a result of an emergency, the registered provider and the manager shall give notice of the absence within one week of its occurrence, specifying the matters mentioned in paragraph (2)(a) to (e).

(4) Where the manager or branch manager has been absent from the agency or (as the case may be) branch for a continuous period of 28 days or more, and the registration authority has not been given notice of the absence, the registered provider and the manager shall without delay give notice in writing to the authority specifying the matters mentioned in paragraph (2)(a) to (e).

(5) The registered provider and the manager shall notify the registration authority of the return to duty of the manager or branch manager not later than 7 days after the date of his return.

**22 Notice of changes—**(1) The registered provider and the manager shall give notice in writing to the registration authority as soon as it is practicable to do so if any of the following events takes place or is proposed to take place—

(a) a person other than the registered provider carries on the agency;

(b) a person ceases to manage the agency;

(c) the name or address of the registered provider is changed;

(d) there is any change of trustee, or director, manager, secretary, or other similar officer, of the registered provider;

(e) there is to be any change in the identity of the responsible individual;

(f) a receiver, manager, liquidator or provisional liquidator is appointed in respect of the registered provider; or

(g) the agency intends to cease to act or exist as such.

(2) The registered provider shall notify the registration authority in writing and without delay of the death of the responsible individual, the manager or branch manager (if any).

**23 Appointment of liquidators etc—**(1) Any person to whom paragraph (2) applies shall—

(a) forthwith notify the registration authority of his appointment indicating the reasons for it;

(b) appoint a manager to take full-time day to day control of the agency in any case where there is no manager; and

(c) not more than 28 days after his appointment notify the registration authority of his intentions regarding the future operation of the agency.

(2) This paragraph applies to any person appointed as—

(a) the receiver or manager of the property of a registered provider;

(b) the liquidator or provisional liquidator of a registered provider.

**24 Compliance with regulations** Where anything is required under these Regulations to be done by more than one person, it shall, if done by one of those persons, not be required to be done by the other person or, as the case may be, persons.

**ADOPTION (BRINGING CHILDREN INTO THE UNITED KINGDOM) REGULATIONS 2003**

**SI 2003 No 1173**

**Dated** 28 April 2003

**1 Citation, commencement and application—**(1) These Regulations may be cited as the Adoption (Bringing Children into the United Kingdom) Regulations 2003 and shall come into force on 1st June 2003.

(2) This regulation and regulations 2, 3, 5 and 6 apply to England and Wales.

(3) Regulation 4 applies to England only.

**2 Interpretation** In these Regulations—
'the 1976 Act' means the Adoption Act 1976;
'relevant foreign authority' means a person, outside the British Islands performing functions in the country in which the child is habitually resident which correspond to the functions of an adoption agency or to the functions of the Secretary of State in respect of adoptions with a foreign element.

**3 Requirements applicable in respect of bringing or causing a child to be brought into the United Kingdom** A person intending to bring, or to cause another to bring, a child into the United Kingdom in circumstances where section 56A of the 1976 Act applies must—
(a) apply in writing to an adoption agency for an assessment of his suitability to adopt; and
(b) give the adoption agency any information it may require for the purposes of the assessment.

**4 Duties of an adoption agency** In a case where the adoption agency has determined and approved a person who has applied for an assessment under regulation 3 as eligible and suitable to adopt in accordance with the Adoption Agencies Regulations 1983, that agency must notify the Secretary of State in writing of that decision and provide to him—
(a) all the information considered by the adoption panel before making a recommendation to the agency as to whether the prospective adopter is suitable to be an adoptive parent; and
(b) such other information relating to the case as he and the relevant foreign authority may require.

**5 Conditions applicable in respect of a child brought into the United Kingdom** The prescribed conditions for the purposes of section 56A(5) of the 1976 Act (conditions to be met in respect of a child brought into the United Kingdom in circumstances where that section applies) are—
(a) prior to the child's entry into the United Kingdom, a person must receive in writing, notification from the Secretary of State that he has issued a certificate confirming to the relevant foreign authority—
(i) that the person has been assessed and approved as eligible and suitable to be an adoptive parent; and
(ii) if entry clearance and leave to enter and remain, as may be necessary, is granted and not revoked or curtailed, and an adoption order is made or an overseas adoption is effected, the child will be authorised to enter and reside permanently in the United Kingdom;
(b) except where an overseas adoption is effected, within the period of 14 days beginning with the date on which the child is brought into the United

Kingdom, the person must give notice to the local authority within whose area he has his home of his intention—
  (i)   to apply for an adoption order, in accordance with section 22 of the 1976 Act; or
  (ii)  not to give the child a home.

**6 Application of section 13 of the 1976 Act**—(1) Where a child is brought into the United Kingdom for adoption in circumstances where section 56A of the 1976 Act applies, section 13(1) of that Act shall not apply and the remaining provisions in section 13 shall apply with the modification as set out in paragraph (2).

(2) Subsection (1A) (child to live with adopters before order made) shall apply as if the words from 'Where' to 'the order' there were substituted 'Where a child is brought into the United Kingdom for adoption in circumstances where section 56A of the 1976 Act applies and in accordance with regulations made by virtue of that section, an adoption order'.

**7 Revocation** The Adoption of Children from Overseas Regulations 2001 are hereby revoked.

## REGISTRATION OF FOREIGN ADOPTIONS REGULATIONS 2003

**Dated** 7 May 2003

**SI 2003 No 1255**

**1 Citation, commencement and interpretation**—(1) These Regulations may be cited as the Registration of Foreign Adoptions Regulations 2003 and shall come into force on 1st June 2003.

(2) In these Regulations 'the 1976 Act' means the Adoption Act 1976.

**2 Registrable foreign adoption** For the purposes of paragraph 3(4) of Schedule 1 to the 1976 Act (meaning of registrable foreign adoption), the specified requirement is that at the time the Convention or overseas adoption is effected, the adoptive parent, or in the case of a married couple, both adoptive parents, are habitually resident in England or Wales.

**3 Form of an entry in the Adopted Children Register** For the purposes of paragraph 3(2) of Schedule 1 to the 1976 Act (form of entry in the Adopted Children Register) the specified form—
  (a) in the case of an adopted child habitually resident in England, is the form set out in Schedule 1;
  (b) in the case of an adopted child habitually resident in Wales, is the form set out in Schedule 2.

**4 Person who may make an application** For the purposes of paragraph 3(3) of Schedule 1 to the 1976 Act (persons who may make an application), the specified persons are—
  (a) in the case of—
    (i)   an adoption by a married couple, one of the adoptive parents of the adopted child;
    (ii)  an adoption by one person, the adoptive parent of the adopted child;
  (b) any other person who has parental responsibility within the meaning of section 3 of the Children Act 1989 for the adopted child;
  (c) the adopted child who has attained the age of 18 years.

**5 Application—**(1) An application under paragraph 3 of Schedule 1 to the 1976 Act (entry of registrable foreign adoptions in Adopted Children Register) shall be made in the manner specified in this regulation.

(2) An application must be—

(a) made in writing; and

(b) signed by the person making the application.

(3) An application made in accordance with paragraph (2) shall be sent to the Registrar General together with—

(a) in the case where the application is not in English or Welsh, a translation into English of that application;

(b) in the case of a Convention adoption, the copy of the certificate sent to the adoptive parents by the relevant Central Authority in accordance with regulation 22 of the Intercountry Adoption (Hague Convention) Regulations 2003; and

(c) in the case of an overseas adoption, the evidence in accordance with article 4 of the Adoption (Designation of Overseas Adoptions) Order 1973, that the adoption has been effected.

**6 Particulars to be given in the application—**(1) An application made under paragraph 3 of Schedule 1 to the 1976 Act shall contain the particulars specified in this regulation.

(2) Subject to paragraphs (3) and (4), the specified particulars are—

(a) date of birth of the adopted child;

(b) place and country of birth of adopted child;

(c) gender of the adopted child;

(d) full name and any previous names of the adopted child;

(e) full name and any previous names of the natural father and natural mother;

(f) in the case of an adoption by a married couple, the full name, any previous names, address and occupation of the adoptive mother and adoptive father;

(g) in the case of an adoption by one person, the full name, any previous names, address and occupation of the adoptive parent;

(h) the date on which the Convention adoption or overseas adoption was effected; and

(i) the capacity in which the person is making the application.

(3) In a case where the person making the application does not know the full particulars specified in paragraph (2), that person shall state in the appropriate place in the application the extent to which such particulars are not known.

(4) In a case where an application is translated into English, the translated version of that application shall be duly signed and endorsed by the translator with the following particulars—

(a) the name, address and occupation of translator; and

(b) a statement to the effect that the translation is true and accurate.

SCHEDULE 1             Regulation 3(a)

FORM OF ENTRY TO BE MADE IN THE ADOPTED CHILDREN REGISTER IN RESPECT OF A REGISTRABLE FOREIGN ADOPTION (ENGLAND)

---

1    No of entry

---

2    Date                    and place and country of birth of child

---

3    Name and surname of child

---

4    Sex of child

---

5    Name and surname

 

address

 

and occupation of adopter or adopters

---

6    Date of adoption order or date the adoption was effected

 

and description of court or by whom effected

---

7    Date of entry

---

8    Signature of officer deputed by Registrar General to attest the entry

---

(*Sch 2 relating to Wales not printed.*)

**ADOPTION SUPPORT SERVICES (LOCAL AUTHORITIES) (ENGLAND) REGULATIONS 2003**

**Dated** 21 May 2003

**SI 2003 No 1348**

**1 Citation, commencement, application and interpretation—**(1) These Regulations may be cited as the Adoption Support Services (Local Authorities) (England) Regulations 2003 and shall come into force on 31st October 2003.

(2) These Regulations apply to England only.

(3) In these Regulations—

'the 2002 Act' means the Adoption and Children Act 2002;

'the 1983 Regulations' means the Adoption Agencies Regulations 1983;

'adoption agency' has the same meaning as in the Adoption Act 1976;

'adoption support services' shall be construed in accordance with regulation 2(1);

'adoptive child' means, subject to paragraph (5), a child who is an agency adoptive child or a non-agency adoptive child;

'adoptive family' means an adoptive child, the adoptive parent of the adoptive child, and any child of the adoptive parent, and references to the adoptive family of a person, or to an adoptive family in relation to a person, shall be construed as the adoptive family of which that person is a member;

'adoptive parent' means a person—

    (a) who an adoption agency has decided in accordance with regulation 11(1) of the 1983 Regulations would be a suitable adoptive parent for a particular child;

    (b) with whom an adoption agency has placed a child for adoption;

    (c) who has given notice under section 22(1) of the Adoption Act 1976 of his intention to apply for an adoption order for a child; or

    (d) who has adopted a child,

but does not include a person where the child is no longer a child, or where the person is the step-parent or natural parent of the child, or was the step-parent of the child before he adopted the child;

'agency adoptive child' means a child—

    (a) in respect of whom an adoption agency has decided in accordance with regulation 11(1) of the 1983 Regulations that a person would be a suitable adoptive parent for the child;

    (b) whom an adoption agency has placed for adoption; or

    (c) who has been adopted after having been placed for adoption by an adoption agency;

'child' means, subject to paragraph (5), a person who has not attained the age of 18 years;

'child of an adoptive parent', in any case where the provision of adoption support services, or any assessment in respect of adoption support services, is in relation to the adoption or prospective adoption of an adoptive child by an adoptive parent, means a child, other than that adoptive child, of the adoptive parent;

'child tax credit' has the same meaning as in the Tax Credits Act 2002;

'foster parent' has the same meaning as in the Fostering Services Regulations 2002;

'income support' means income support under Part VII of the Social Security Contributions and Benefits Act 1992;

'jobseeker's allowance' has the same meaning as in the Jobseekers Act 1995;

'local education authority' has the same meaning as in the Education Act 1996;

'non-agency adoptive child' means a child—

    (a) in respect of whom a person—

        (i) has given notice under section 22(1) of the Adoption Act 1976 of his intention to apply for an adoption order; and

        (ii) is not the natural parent or step-parent of the child; or

    (b) who has been adopted by a person who—

        (i) is not the natural parent of the child; and

        (ii) was not the step-parent of the child before he adopted the child,

but does not include an agency adoptive child;

'notify' means notify in writing;

'person entitled to be assessed' means—

    (a) an adoptive parent;

    (b) an adoptive child;

    (c) a child of an adoptive parent; or

    (d) a related person;

'plan' shall be construed in accordance with regulation 11;

'related person' means a person, other than an adoptive child, referred to in regulation 2(1)(c)(i) or (ii).

(4) In these Regulations—

(a) any reference to a child who is looked after by a local authority has the same meaning as it has in the Children Act 1989;

(b) any reference to a person's adoptive child is to a child who is an adoptive child in relation to that person;

(c) any reference to a child's adoptive parent is to a person who is an adoptive parent in relation to that child;

(d) references (other than references in this sub-paragraph) to a child being placed, or being placed for adoption—

    (i) are to the child being placed for adoption with a prospective adopter by an adoption agency;

    (ii) include, where the child has been placed with a person by an adoption agency, leaving the child with him as a prospective adopter.

(5) In any case where—

(a) a person has attained the age of 18 years and is in full-time education or training; and

(b) immediately before he attained the age of 18 years—

    (i) he was an adoptive child; and

    (ii) financial support was payable in relation to him,

the definitions of 'adoptive child' and 'child' shall, for the purposes of the continued provision of financial support and any review of financial support, have effect in relation to him as if he had not attained the age of 18 years.

**2 Provision of adoption support services—**(1) For the purposes of section 2(6) of the 2002 Act (definition of 'adoption support services'), the following services are prescribed—

(a) financial support payable under regulation 3;

(b) services to enable groups of adoptive parents and adoptive children to discuss matters relating to adoption;

(c) assistance in relation to arrangements for contact between an adoptive child and—

    (i) a natural parent or relative of the adoptive child; or

    (ii) any person with whom the adoptive child has a relationship which appears to the local authority to be beneficial to the welfare of the child having regard to the matters referred to in sub-paragraphs (i) to (iii) of section 1(4)(f) of the 2002 Act;

(d) services that may be provided in relation to the therapeutic needs of an adoptive child;

(e) assistance for the purpose of ensuring the continuance of the relationship between the child and his adoptive parent, including—

    (i) training for adoptive parents for the purpose of meeting any special needs of the child;

    (ii) respite care.

(2) Subject to paragraph (3), local authorities shall make arrangements for the purpose of providing any service specified in column (1) of the table in the Schedule for persons who are of a description specified in the corresponding entry in column (2) of the table.

(3) The arrangements referred to in paragraph (2) in respect of any service are required to be made whether or not the local authority have decided to provide the service to any person.

(4) The services prescribed in paragraph (1)(b) to (e) may include—

(a) giving assistance in cash;

(b) making arrangements with other persons for the purpose of providing those services.

(5) These Regulations shall apply to a local authority in respect of a person who lives in the area of the local authority or, in the circumstances specified in paragraph (6), a person ('the individual') who lives outside that area.

(6) The circumstances specified are where—

(a) a person entitled to be assessed lives in that area;

(b) the individual, or a person entitled to be assessed—

    (i) has at any time in the preceding six months lived in that area; or

    (ii) intends to live in that area; or

(c) the individual (if he is the adoptive child), or the adoptive child—

    (i) is looked after by the local authority;

    (ii) has not been adopted but has been placed by the local authority for adoption; or

    (iii) has been adopted and, before the adoption order was made, was placed for adoption with the adoptive parents by the local authority;

(d) the individual is not the adoptive child and the local authority have assessed the individual's needs for adoption support services in relation to the adoption or prospective adoption of the adoptive child.

**3 Circumstances in which financial support may be paid**—(1) Financial support may be paid only to an adoptive parent, and only where one or more of the circumstances specified in paragraph (2) exists.

(2) The circumstances referred to in paragraph (1) are—

(a) where the child has not been placed with the adoptive parents for adoption, and financial support is necessary to ensure that the adoptive parents can look after the child if placed with them;

(b) where the child has been placed with the adoptive parents for adoption, and financial support is necessary to ensure that the adoptive parents can continue to look after the child;

(c) where the child has been adopted, and financial support is necessary to ensure that the adoptive parents can continue to look after the child;

(d) where the local authority are satisfied that the child has established a strong and important relationship with the adoptive parent before the adoption order is made;

(e) where it is desirable that the child be placed with the same adoptive parent as his brother or sister (whether of the full blood or half blood), or with a child with whom he has previously shared a home;

(f) where the child needs special care which requires a greater expenditure of resources by reason of illness, disability, emotional or behavioural difficulties or the continuing consequences of past abuse or neglect;

(g) where on account of the age, sex or ethnic origin of the child it is necessary for the local authority to make special arrangements to facilitate the placement of the child for adoption.

(3) Before financial support is payable the local authority shall require the adoptive parents to have agreed to—

(a) inform the local authority immediately if—

    (i) they change their address;

    (ii) the child no longer has his home with them (or either of them), or dies; or

    (iii) there is any change in their financial circumstances or the financial needs or resources of the child,

and, where the information is given orally, to confirm it in writing within seven days;

(b) complete and supply the local authority with an annual statement as to the matters referred to in regulation 13(2)(a)(i) to (iii).

**4 Adoption support services adviser**—(1) The local authority shall appoint a person (an 'adoption support services adviser') to carry out the function specified in paragraph (2).

(2) The function of the adoption support services adviser shall be to give advice and information, to persons who may be affected by the adoption or proposed adoption of a child, as to—

(i) services that may be appropriate to those persons; and

(ii) how those services may be made available to them.

(3) The local authority shall not appoint a person as an adoption support services adviser unless satisfied that his knowledge and experience of—

(a) the process of adoption; and

(b) the effect of the adoption of a child on persons likely to be affected by the adoption,

is sufficient for the purposes of the work that he is to perform.

**5 Requirement for assessment**—(1) Subject to paragraph (10), a local authority shall, at the request of—

(a) an adoptive parent;

(b) an adoptive child; or

(c) a child of an adoptive parent,

carry out an assessment of his needs for adoption support services.

(2) Subject to paragraph (11), where—

(a) a related person requests a local authority to carry out an assessment of his need for assistance in relation to arrangements for contact between him and an adoptive child; and

(b) arrangements for such contact have been made before the request for an assessment,

the local authority shall carry out the assessment.

(3) Where a local authority are considering adoption for a child, they shall, before completing the written report required under regulation 7(2)(e) of the 1983 Regulations, carry out an assessment of the child's needs for adoption support services.

(4) Where a local authority propose to place a particular child for adoption with a prospective adopter, they shall, before completing the written report required under regulation 9(1) of the 1983 Regulations, carry out an assessment of the needs of each member of the adoptive family for adoption support services.

(5) Where—

(a) a local authority are reviewing the placement for adoption of a child under regulation 12(2)(k) of the 1983 Regulations; and

(b) they have not carried out an assessment in accordance with paragraph (4) in respect of each member of the adoptive family,

they shall, before completing the review, carry out an assessment of the needs of each member of the adoptive family for adoption support services.

(6) Where a person's request for an assessment under paragraph (1) relates to a particular adoption support service, or it appears to the local authority that the person's needs for adoption support services may be adequately assessed by reference to a particular adoption support service, the local authority may carry out the assessment by reference only to that service.

(7) In this regulation a reference to a particular adoption support service is to any of the following services—

(a) counselling, advice and information in relation to adoption; or

(b) a service specified in regulation 2(1).

(8) This paragraph applies where an adoptive child—

(a) is looked after by the local authority; or

(b) has not been adopted but has been placed by the local authority for adoption.

(9) This paragraph applies where an adoptive child—

(a) has been adopted by his adoptive parents; and

(b) before the adoption order was made, was placed for adoption with the adoptive parents by the local authority.

(10) The local authority shall not be required under paragraph (1) to carry out an assessment of a person's needs unless—

(a) paragraph (8) applies;

(b) paragraph (9) applies and the person requests the assessment—

    (i) not more than one year after the date of the adoption order; or

    (ii) not more than three years after the date on which the adoptive child was placed with the adoptive parents; or

(c) sub-paragraphs (a) and (b) do not apply and the person lives in the area of the local authority.

(11) The local authority shall not be required under paragraph (2) to carry out an assessment of a related person's needs unless—

(a) paragraph (8) or (9) applies; or

(b) paragraphs (8) and (9) do not apply and the related person lives in the area of the local authority.

**6 Procedure for assessment**—(1) Where the local authority carry out an assessment of a person's needs for adoption support services they shall, in carrying out the assessment, have regard to the following considerations—

(a) subject to paragraph (4), the needs of the person being assessed;

(b) the needs of the adoptive child and his adoptive family;

(c) in the case of a child who has been placed for adoption, the circumstances that led to the child being placed for adoption.

(2) In carrying out an assessment in respect of a person—

(a) where it appears to the local authority that—

    (i) there may be a need for the provision of services to that person by a Primary Care Trust; or

    (ii) there may be a need for the provision to him of any services which fall within the functions of a local education authority,

the local authority shall notify that Primary Care Trust or local education authority;

(b) where the assessment is for the purposes of regulation 5(4) and the prospective adopter lives in the area of another local authority, they shall consult that other local authority.

(3) The local authority shall, where it considers it appropriate to do so—

(a) interview the person and, where the person is an adoptive child, his adoptive parents;

(b) prepare a written report of the assessment.

(4) Where the assessment is being carried out at the request of a related person, the local authority shall have regard to his needs only so far as they relate to his need for assistance so as to enable him to take part in arrangements for contact with the adoptive child that were made before the request for an assessment.

**7 Amount of financial support**—(1) This regulation applies where the local authority carry out an assessment of a person's need for financial support.

(2) In determining the amount of financial support the local authority shall take into account—

(a) any recommendations, in relation to the adoptive parent or the adoptive child, made by the adoption panel to the local authority on a matter referred to in regulation 10(1)(a) or (c) of the 1983 Regulations;

(b) the financial resources available to the adoptive parents including child tax credit and any other financial benefit which would be available in respect of the child if the child lived with them;

(c) the amount required by the adoptive parents in respect of their reasonable outgoings and commitments (excluding outgoings in respect of the child);

(d) the financial needs and resources of the child;

(e) expenditure for the purposes of facilitating the placement of the child with the adoptive parents for adoption, including—

    (i) expenditure for the purpose of introducing the child to his adoptive parents;

    (ii) initial expenditure necessary for the purpose of accommodating the child, including the provision of furniture and domestic equipment, alterations to and adaptations of the home, provision of means of transport and provision of clothing, toys and other items necessary for the purpose of looking after the child;

    (iii) legal costs, including fees payable to a court, in relation to the adoption of the child;

    (iv) cost of equipment for the purpose of meeting any special needs of the child;

    (v) cost of damage in the home where the child is accommodated where such cost arises out of special behavioural difficulties of the child;

    (vi) the cost of placing a child in a boarding school where the placement is necessary to meet the special needs of the child;

    (vii) the cost of meeting the special needs of the child, including needs arising out of a serious disability or illness;

    (viii) expenditure on travel for the purpose of visits between the child and a related person.

(3) Financial support may not be paid to meet any needs in so far as any benefit or allowance applicable to the adoptive parents as a result of their adoption of the child, is payable or available to them in respect of those needs.

(4) Except where paragraphs (5) and (6) apply, the financial support payable by the local authority shall not include any element of remuneration for the care of the child by the adoptive parents.

(5) This paragraph applies where—

(a) the adoptive parent is or has been a foster parent in respect of the child;

(b) it appears to the local authority that any financial assistance or allowances given to the adoptive parents in respect of their fostering of the child has ceased, or will cease;

(c) the local authority have decided in accordance with regulation 11(1) of the 1983 Regulations that the adoptive parent would be a suitable adoptive parent for the child;

(d) before the adoption order is made the local authority decide to pay financial support and determine that the financial support is to be paid periodically.

(6) This paragraph applies—

(a) at any time until the day ('the second anniversary') occurring two years after the date of the adoption order in respect of the child; and

(b) at any time after the second anniversary, in a case where any of the circumstances specified in regulation 3(2)(a), (b), (e), (f) or (g) exists on the date on which the local authority decide, in accordance with paragraph (5)(d), to pay financial support.

**8 Proposal to provide adoption support services**—(1) The local authority shall, after carrying out an assessment under regulation 5—

    (a)   supply in accordance with regulation 10 the information specified in paragraph (2);

    (b)   give notice in accordance with paragraph (3) and regulation 10.

    (2)  The matters specified are—

    (a)   a statement of the person's needs for adoption support services;

    (b)   where the assessment relates to the person's need for financial support, the basis upon which financial support is determined;

    (c)   whether the local authority propose to provide adoption support services to the person;

    (d)   the services (if any) that are proposed to be provided to him;

    (e)   if financial support is to be paid to him—

        (i)   the proposed amount which would be payable; and

        (ii)  whether the financial support should be paid subject to any conditions that may be imposed in accordance with regulation 9(4).

    (3)  A notice to be given to a person under paragraph (1)(b) shall state the period of time within which he may make representations to the local authority concerning the proposed decision; and the local authority shall not make a decision under regulation 9 until either—

    (a)   the person has—

        (i)   made representations to the local authority; or

        (ii)  notified the local authority that he is satisfied with the proposed decision; or

    (b)   the period of time for making representations has expired.

    (4)  Where the assessment relates only to the provision of information, the requirement in paragraph (1)(b) to give notice shall not apply where the local authority do not consider it appropriate to give such notice.

**9 Decision as to adoption support services—**(1) The local authority shall, having regard to the assessment, and after considering any representations received within the period specified in the notice to be given under regulation 8(1)(b), decide—

    (a)   whether the person has needs for adoption support services;

    (b)   if so, whether any such services are to be provided to him,

and shall give notice of that decision in accordance with regulation 10, which shall include the reasons for the decision.

    (2)  Where the assessment relates only to the provision of information, the requirement in paragraph (1) to give notice shall not apply where the local authority do not consider it appropriate to give such notice.

    (3)  If the local authority decide that financial support is to be paid—

    (a)   they shall determine, in accordance with regulation 7, the amount that is to be payable;

    (b)   they shall decide the conditions, if any, which are to be imposed in accordance with paragraph (4); and

    (c)   the notice required to be given under paragraph (1) shall include the matters specified in paragraph (6).

    (4)  Where the local authority decide that financial support is to be paid for a particular purpose, they may pay the financial support subject to a condition as to how the payment is to be used and may specify the date by which the condition is to be met.

    (5)  Where the local authority decide that financial support is to be paid, it shall be paid as a single payment except that—

    (a)   the local authority and the person to whom financial support is to be paid may agree that it shall be paid—

        (i)   in instalments on such dates as the local authority may specify; or

        (ii)  periodically until such date (if any) as the local authority may specify;

(b) where the local authority decide that financial support is to be paid to meet any needs which are likely to give rise to expenditure which is likely to be recurring, they may determine that financial support shall be paid—
 (i) in instalments on such dates as the local authority may specify; or
 (ii) periodically until such date (if any) as the local authority may specify.
(6) The following matters are specified—
(a) the method of the determination of the amount of financial support;
(b) where financial support is to be paid in instalments or periodically—
 (i) the amount of financial support;
 (ii) the frequency with which the payment will be made;
 (iii) the date (if any) until which financial support is to be paid;
 (iv) the date of the first payment of financial support;
(c) where financial support is to be paid as a single payment, the date on which the payment is to be made;
(d) where financial support is to be paid subject to any conditions, those conditions, the date (if any) by which the conditions are to be met and the consequences of failing to meet the conditions;
(e) the arrangements and procedure for review, variation and termination of financial support;
(f) the responsibilities of—
 (i) the local authority under regulation 13 (review of financial support); and
 (ii) the adoptive parents pursuant to their agreement under regulation 3(3).
(7) Where the local authority are satisfied that a condition notified under paragraph (3) has not been met by the date, if any, specified in the notice, they may require that the payment or an appropriate part of the payment be repaid.

**10 Notices—**(1) Any information required to be supplied, or notice required to be given, under regulation 8, 9, 11, 12 or 13 shall be given in writing—
(a) where the person is an adult, to that person;
(b) where the person is a child and paragraph (2) applies—
 (i) to the child; and
 (ii) except where it appears inappropriate to do so, to the adoptive parents;
(c) where the person is a child and paragraph (2) does not apply, to the adoptive parents.
(2) This paragraph applies where—
(a) it appears to the local authority that the child is of sufficient age and understanding for it to be appropriate to give him such notice; and
(b) in all the circumstances it does not appear inappropriate to give him such notice.

**11 Plan—**(1) If the local authority decide under regulation 9 to provide any adoption support services to a person, they shall—
(a) prepare a plan ('the plan') in accordance with which the services are to be provided; and
(b) give notice of the plan in accordance with regulation 10,
except where the services to be provided are to consist of services to be provided on a single occasion.
(2) The local authority shall for the purpose of preparing the plan consult—
(a) any person who is to be given notice of the plan under paragraph (1);
(b) where it appears to the local authority that—
 (i) there may be a need for the provision of services to that person by a Primary Care Trust; or

>>> (ii) there may be a need for the provision to him of any services which fall within the functions of a local education authority,

that Primary Care Trust or local education authority.

(3) If the local authority decide under regulation 9 to provide any adoption support services to a person, and are required under that regulation to give notice of that decision, they shall—

>> (a) nominate an individual who shall monitor the provision of the services that are to be provided; and

>> (b) notify the person of the nomination when they notify him of their decision under regulation 9(1).

**12 Review of the provision of adoption support services—**(1) Where the local authority provide adoption support services for a person, they shall review the provision of such services if any change in the person's circumstances comes to their notice.

(2) This regulation shall not apply to a review of the provision of financial support where the financial support is payable in instalments or periodically.

(3) Regulations 6 to 8 shall apply in relation to a review under this regulation as they apply in relation to an assessment under regulation 5.

(4) The local authority shall, having regard to the review and after considering any representations received within the period specified in the notice to be given in accordance with regulation 8(1)(b)—

>> (a) decide whether to vary or terminate the provision of adoption support services for the person; and

>> (b) review and, where appropriate, revise the plan.

(5) If the local authority decide to vary or terminate the provision of adoption support services for the person, or revise the plan, they shall give notice of their decision in accordance with regulation 10, which shall include the reasons for the decision; and paragraphs (2) to (7) of regulation 9 shall apply to a decision under paragraph (4) as they apply to a decision under paragraph (1) of that regulation.

**13 Review of financial support—**(1) This regulation shall apply where financial support is payable in instalments or periodically.

(2) The local authority shall review the financial support—

>> (a) annually, on receipt of a statement from the adoptive parents as to—

>>> (i) their financial circumstances;

>>> (ii) the financial needs and resources of the child;

>>> (iii) their address and whether the child still has a home with them (or either of them); and

>> (b) if any change in the circumstances of the adoptive parents or the child, including any change of address, comes to their notice.

(3) The local authority shall, having regard to the review, and in particular whether the adoptive parents' need for financial support has changed or ceased since the amount of financial support was last determined, and after considering any representations received within the period specified in the notice to be given in accordance with regulation 8(1)(b)—

>> (a) decide whether to vary, suspend or terminate payment of the financial support;

>> (b) review and, where appropriate, revise the plan.

(4) Where the adoptive parents fail to supply the local authority with an annual statement in accordance with their agreement under regulation 3(3)(b), the local authority may suspend payment of the financial support until such time as a statement is supplied.

(5) The local authority shall terminate payment of financial support when—

>> (a) the child ceases to have a home with the adoptive parents (or either of them);

(b) the child ceases full-time education or training and commences employment;

(c) the child qualifies for income support or jobseeker's allowance in his own right; or

(d) the child attains the age of 18, unless he continues in full-time education or training, when it may continue until the end of the course of education or training he is then undertaking.

(6) Regulations 6 to 8 shall apply in relation to a review under this regulation as they apply in relation to an assessment under regulation 5.

(7) If the local authority decide to vary, suspend or terminate payment of the financial support, or revise the plan, they shall give notice of their decision in accordance with regulation 10, which shall include the reasons for the decision.

(8) Paragraphs (3) to (7) of regulation 9 shall apply to a decision under paragraph (3) as they apply to a decision under paragraph (1) of that regulation.

**14 Recovery of expenses between local authorities—**(1) Where—

(a) a local authority ('the placing authority')—

    (i) are considering adoption for the child but the child has not been placed; or

    (ii) have placed a child for adoption; and

(b) another local authority ('the recovering authority') provide any adoption support services in relation to the child,

the recovering authority may, subject to paragraphs (2) and (3), recover from the placing authority the expenses of providing the adoption support services.

(2) Paragraph (1) shall not apply in respect of the expenses of providing adoption support services to the extent that those services consist of the provision of advice or information.

(3) Paragraph (1) shall apply in respect of the expenses of providing adoption support services in relation to a child only to the extent that—

(a) the placing authority have decided to provide such services; and

(b) the services are provided in accordance with the plan prepared by the placing authority.

(4) References in paragraph (3) to adoption support services include any allowance that by virtue of regulation 15(2) is treated as financial support payable under these Regulations.

**15 Amendment of the Adoption Allowance Regulations 1991 and transitional provision—**(1) In regulation 1(2) of the Adoption Allowance Regulations 1991, in the definition of 'adoption agency', the words 'or a local authority' shall be omitted.

(2) Any allowance which is payable by a local authority under the Adoption Allowance Regulations 1991 immediately before 31st October 2003 ('the allowance') shall be treated with effect from that date as financial support payable under these Regulations, and the financial support shall be of the same amount, method and frequency of payment, and payable for the same period, as the allowance.

SCHEDULE                                          Regulation 2(2)

| *(1) Service* | *(2) Description of person* |
|---|---|
| The service specified in regulation 2(1)(a) (financial support) | Adoptive parent of an agency adoptive child |
| The service specified in regulation 2(1)(b) (support group) | Adoptive parent who has adopted an agency adoptive child, or with whom an agency adoptive child has been placed for adoption |
| | Agency adoptive child who has been placed for adoption or has been adopted |
| The service specified in regulation 2(1)(c) (contact) | Agency adoptive child who has been placed for adoption or has been adopted |
| | A related person |
| The service specified in regulation 2(1)(d) (therapeutic services) | Adoptive parent who has adopted an agency adoptive child, or with whom an agency adoptive child has been placed for adoption |
| | Agency adoptive child who has been placed for adoption or has been adopted |
| | Any child of an adoptive parent who has adopted an agency adoptive child, or with whom an agency adoptive child has been placed for adoption |
| The service specified in regulation 2(1)(e) (services to ensure continuance of relationship) | Adoptive parent who has adopted an agency adoptive child, or with whom an agency adoptive child has been placed for adoption |
| | Agency adoptive child who has been placed for adoption or has been adopted |
| | Any child of an adoptive parent who has adopted an agency adoptive child, or with whom an agency adoptive child has been placed for adoption |
| Counselling, advice and information | Adoptive parent |
| | Adoptive child |
| | Any child of an adoptive parent |

## CHILDREN ACT 1989, SECTION 17(12) REGULATIONS 2003

**Dated** 11 August 2003

**SI 2003 No 2077**

**1 Citation and commencement** These Regulations may be cited as the Children Act 1989, Section 17(12) Regulations 2003 and shall come into force on 1st September 2003.

**2 Interpretation** In these Regulations—

'child care' has the meaning in the Working Tax Credit (Entitlement and Maximum Rate) Regulations 2002;

'relevant child care charges' has the meaning given in regulation 14(1) of those Regulations.

**3 Treating a person as in receipt of working tax credit or of any element of child tax credit other than the family element** A person shall be treated, for the purposes of Part 3 of the Children Act 1989, as in receipt of working tax credit, or of any element of child tax credit other than the family element, where—

(a) the person is in receipt of assistance under section 17 of that Act, or of a direct payment or voucher under section 17A or 17B of that Act; and

(b) that assistance consists in the provision (or a direct payment or voucher to secure the provision) of child care, the cost of which (if paid for by the person out of his own resources) would—

(i) be relevant child care charges in relation to that person, and

(ii) cause that person (in circumstances where, but for that cost, he would otherwise not be) to be entitled to working tax credit, or to any element of child tax credit other than the family element.

## TRANSFER OF FUNCTIONS (CHILDREN, YOUNG PEOPLE AND FAMILIES) ORDER 2003

**2003 No 3191**

### MINISTERS OF THE CROWN

*Made*................................................*10th December 2003*
*Laid before Parliament*............*22nd December 2003*
*Coming into force* ...................*12th January 2004*

At the Court at Buckingham Palace, the 10th day of December 2003

Present,

The Queen's Most Excellent Majesty in Council

Her Majesty, in pursuance of section 1 of the Ministers of the Crown Act 1975, is pleased, by and with the advice of Her Privy Council, to order, and it is hereby ordered, as follows:

**1 Citation and commencement—**(1) This Order may be cited as the Transfer of Functions (Children, Young People and Families) Order 2003.

(2) This Order comes into force on 12th January 2004.

**2 Interpretation—**(1) In this Order 'instrument', without prejudice to the generality of that expression, includes in particular judgements, decrees, orders, rules, regulations, schemes, bye-laws, awards, contracts and other agreements, memoranda and articles of association, warrants, certificates and other documents.

(2) Any reference in this Order to the functions of a Minister under an enactment includes a reference to the functions of that Minister under an instrument having effect under that enactment.

**3 Transfer of functions from the Lord Chancellor** The functions of the Lord Chancellor under—

  (a) section 4(1B) of the Children Act 1989,
  (b) section 22 of the Family Law Act 1996,
  (c) section 62(3A) of the Justices of the Peace Act 1997, and
  (d) sections 12, 19, 20 and 23 of, and Schedules 2 and 3 to, the Criminal Justice and Court Services Act 2000,

are transferred to the Secretary of State.

**4 Property, rights and liabilities** All property, rights and liabilities to which the Lord Chancellor is entitled or subject at the coming into force of this Order in connection with the functions transferred by article 3 are transferred to the Secretary of State for Education and Skills.

**5 Supplementary—**(1) This Order does not affect the validity of anything done (or having effect as if done) by or in relation to the Lord Chancellor before the coming into force of this Order.

(2) Anything (including legal proceedings) which, at the coming into force of this Order, is in the process of being done by or in relation to the Lord Chancellor may, so far as it relates to anything transferred by article 3 or 4, be continued by or in relation to the Secretary of State for Education and Skills.

(3) Anything done (or having effect as if done) by or in relation to the Lord Chancellor in connection with anything transferred by article 3 or 4 has effect, so far as necessary for continuing its effect after the coming into force of this Order, as if done by or in relation to the Secretary of State for Education and Skills.

(4) Documents or forms printed for use in connection with the functions transferred by article 3 may be used in connection with those functions even though they contain, or are to be read as containing, references to the Lord Chancellor, the Lord Chancellor's Department or an officer of the Lord Chancellor; and for the purposes of the use of any such documents or forms after the coming into force of this Order, those references are to be read as references to the Secretary of State for Education and Skills, the Department for Education and Skills or an officer of the Secretary of State for Education and Skills (as appropriate).

(5) Any enactment or instrument passed or made before the coming into force of this Order has effect—

  (a) so far as is necessary for the purposes of or in consequence of article 3, as if references to (and references which are to be read as references to) the Lord Chancellor, the Lord Chancellor's Department or an officer of the Lord Chancellor were references to the Secretary of State, his department or an officer of his (as appropriate), and

  (b) so far as is necessary for the purposes of or in consequence of article 4, as if references to (and references which are to be read as references to) the Lord Chancellor, the Lord Chancellor's Department or an officer of the Lord Chancellor were references to the Secretary of State for Education and Skills, the Department for Education and Skills or an officer of the Secretary of State for Education and Skills (as appropriate).

**6 Consequential amendments** The Schedule (consequential amendments) has effect.

*A K Galloway*

Clerk of the Privy Council

SCHEDULE                                                              Article 6

CONSEQUENTIAL AMENDMENTS

*Children Act 1989 (c 41)*

**1** In the Children Act 1989, in section 4(1B) (registration as father), for 'Lord Chancellor' substitute 'Secretary of State'.

*Family Law Act 1996 (c 27)*

**2** In the Family Law Act 1996, in section 22 (funding for marriage support services) for 'Lord Chancellor' in each place substitute 'Secretary of State'.

*Justices of the Peace Act 1997 (c 25)*

**3** In the Justices of the Peace Act 1997, in section 62(3A) (inspection of CAFCASS) for 'Lord Chancellor' in each place substitute 'Secretary of State'.

*Criminal Justice and Court Services Act 2000 (c 43)*

**4**—(1)  The Criminal Justice and Court Services Act 2000 is amended as follows.

(2)  In sections 19, 20 and 23 and in paragraph 5 of Schedule 3 (Probation Service and CAFCASS property and staff), for 'Minister' or 'appropriate Minister' in each place substitute 'Secretary of State'.

(3)  In section 25 (interpretation)—

(a)  omit the definition of 'appropriate Minister', and

(b)  in the definition of 'regulations', for paragraphs (a) and (b) substitute—

'(a)  in the case of regulations under section 15, regulations made by the Lord Chancellor, and

(b)  in any other case, regulations made by the Secretary of State.'

(4)  In Schedule 2 to that Act (CAFCASS), for 'Lord Chancellor' in each place, substitute 'Secretary of State'.

EXPLANATORY NOTE

*(This note is not part of the Order)*

This Order in Council is made under section 1 of the Ministers of the Crown Act 1975.

Article 3 transfers to the Secretary of State the functions of the Lord Chancellor under the enactments listed there. This is with a view to the functions being exercised by the Secretary of State for Education and Skills, and accordingly article 4 transfers to that Secretary of State any property, rights and liabilities to which the Lord Chancellor is entitled or subject in connection with the functions transferred.

Article 5 contains supplementary provision in connection with the transfers. Article 6 and the Schedule make consequential amendments to legislation.

Nothing in this Order alters the functions of the National Assembly for Wales, the Scottish Ministers or the devolved authorities in Northern Ireland.

# INDEPENDENT REVIEW OF DETERMINATIONS (ADOPTION) REGULATIONS 2004

## 2004 No 190

SOCIAL CARE, ENGLAND

CHILDREN AND YOUNG PERSONS, ENGLAND

*Made* ...................................... *2nd February 2004*
*Laid before Parliament* ........... *5th February 2004*
*Coming into force* .................. *30th April 2004*

The Secretary of State, in exercise of the powers conferred upon him by sections 9(2) and (3), 9A(1) to (3) and 67(5) of the Adoption Act 1976 hereby makes the following Regulations—

PART 1
GENERAL

**1 Citation, commencement, application and interpretation**—(1) These Regulations may be cited as the Independent Review of Determinations (Adoption) Regulations 2004 and shall come into force on 30th April 2004.

(2) These Regulations apply to England only.

(3) These Regulations shall apply to cases where the most recent consideration by an adoption panel of a prospective adopter's suitability to be an adoptive parent—

(a) *is under regulation 10(1)(b) of the 1983 Regulations; and*

(b) *takes place on or after 30 April 2004*

[(a) is under regulation 10(1)(b) of the 1983 Regulations and takes place on or after 30th April 2004; or

(b) is under regulation 9(1) of the 2003 Regulations and takes place on or after 20th August 2004].

(4) In these Regulations—

'the Act' means the Adoption Act 1976;

'the 1983 Regulations' means the Adoption Agencies Regulations 1983;

['the 2003 Regulations' means the Intercountry Adoption (Hague Convention) Regulations 2003;]

'adoption panel' means a panel established in accordance with regulation 5 of the 1983 Regulations;

'the central list' shall be construed in accordance with regulation 3(2);

'panel' means a panel constituted in accordance with regulation 3(1);

. . .

'review meeting' means a meeting convened in accordance with regulation 10 for the purposes of reviewing a qualifying determination; and

'social worker' means a social worker within the meaning of Part IV of the Care Standards Act 2000.

**Note.** Para (3)(a), (b) substituted by SI 2004/1868, reg 3(1), (2)(a), as from 20 August 2004.

In para (4) definition 'the 2003 Regulations' inserted by SI 2004/1868, reg 3(1), (2)(b)(i), as from 20 August 2004. In para (4) definition 'prospective adopter' (omitted) revoked by SI 2004/1868, reg 3(1), (2)(b)(ii), as from 20 August 2004.

**2 Qualifying determination** For the purposes of section 9A(1) of the Act, a qualifying determination is a determination that has been made by an adoption agency in accordance *with regulation 11A of the 1983 Regulations, that* [with—

(a)  regulation 11A of the 1983 Regulations; or

(b)  regulation 10 of the 2003 Regulations,

that] the adoption agency considers that a prospective adopter is not suitable to be an adoptive parent and does not propose to approve him as suitable to be an adoptive parent.

**Note.** Paras (a), (b) and word 'with—' immediately preceding them and word 'that' immediately following them substituted for words in italics by SI 2004/1868, reg 3(1), (3), as from 20 August 2004.

PART 2

PANELS

**3 Constitution and functions of panels—**(1) The Secretary of State shall, on receipt of the application by a prospective adopter made in accordance with regulation 9, constitute a panel for the purpose of reviewing a qualifying determination.

(2)  The members of the panel shall be appointed by the Secretary of State from a list of persons (in these Regulations referred to as 'the central list') kept by the Secretary of State.

(3)  The members of the central list shall include—

(a)  social workers;

(b)  registered medical practitioners; and

(c)  other persons who are considered by the Secretary of State to be suitable as members, to include, where reasonably practicable—

(i)   adopted persons who have reached the age of 18 years; and

(ii)  adoptive parents.

(4)  A panel established under paragraph (1) shall—

(a)  review the qualifying determination; and

(b)  make to the adoption agency which made the qualifying determination a recommendation as to whether or not a prospective adopter is suitable to be an adoptive parent.

(5)  In considering what recommendation to make, the panel—

(a)  must consider and take into account all of the information passed to it in accordance *with regulation 11A of the 1983 Regulations* [with, as the case may be—

(i)   regulation 11A of the 1983 Regulations; or

(ii)  regulation 10 of the 2003 Regulations];

(b)  may request the adoption agency to obtain any other relevant information which the panel considers necessary or to provide such other assistance as the panel may request; and

(c)  may obtain such legal advice as it considers necessary in relation to the case.

**Note.** In para (5)(a) words from 'with, as the case may be' to 'the 2003 Regulations' in square brackets substituted for words in italics by SI 2004/1868, reg 3(1), (4), as from 20 August 2004.

**4 Membership of panels—**(1) The maximum number of people who may be appointed to a panel is 10.

(2)  The panel shall include at least—

(a)  two persons falling within regulation 3(3)(a);

(b)  one person falling within regulation 3(3)(b); and

(c)  in addition at least four other persons falling within regulation 3(3)(c).

(3)  A person shall not be appointed to a panel if—

(a)  he or a member of his family was involved in the making of the qualifying determination in question;

(b)  he is employed by the adoption agency which made the qualifying determination in question or was employed by that agency within the period of two years prior to the date on which the qualifying determination was made;

(c) where the adoption agency which made the qualifying determination is a local authority, he is an elected member of that local authority or was such a member within the period of two years prior to the date on which the qualifying determination was made;

(d) where the adoption agency which made the qualifying determination is an appropriate voluntary organisation, he is concerned with the management of that agency or was so concerned within the period of two years prior to the date on which the qualifying determination was made;

(e) he was approved as a prospective adopter by the adoption agency which made the qualifying determination in question;

(f) in the case of an adopted person, the adoption agency which made the qualifying determination in question was the adoption agency which arranged his adoption; or

(g) he knows, in a personal or professional capacity, the person making the application under regulation 9.

(4) In this regulation—

(a) 'employed' includes employed whether or not for payment and whether under a contract of service or a contract for services or as a volunteer; and

(b) 'a member of his family' means—

(i) his spouse;

(ii) a member of his household; or

(iii) a son, daughter, mother, father, sister or brother of his or of his spouse.

**5 Chair and vice chair—**(1) The Secretary of State shall appoint to chair the panel a person who has expertise in adoption work and the skills and experience necessary for chairing a panel.

(2) The Secretary of State shall appoint one of the members of the panel as vice chair to act as chair if the person appointed to chair the panel is absent.

**6 Expenses of panel members** The Secretary of State may pay to any member of a panel such sum in respect of expenses as the Secretary of State considers to be reasonable.

**7 Meetings of panels** The proceedings of the panel will not be invalidated provided at least six of its members including the chair or vice chair and a social worker are present.

**8 Records** The Secretary of State shall ensure that a written record of a panel's review of a qualifying determination, including the reasons for its recommendation and whether the recommendation was unanimous or that of a majority, is retained—

(a) for a period of 12 months from the date on which the recommendation is made; and

(b) in conditions of appropriate security.

PART 3

PROCEDURE

**9 Application by prospective adopter for review of qualifying determination** An application by a prospective adopter to the Secretary of State for a review of a qualifying determination made in his case must be in writing and include the grounds of the application.

**10 Appointment of panel and conduct of review** Upon receipt of an application which has been made in accordance with regulation 9, the Secretary of State shall—

(a) notify the adoption agency which made the qualifying determination that the application has been made by sending to the agency a copy of the application;

(b) send a written acknowledgment of the application to the prospective adopter and notify him of the steps taken under sub-paragraph (a);

(c) appoint a panel in accordance with regulations 3 and 4;

(d) fix a date, time and venue for the panel to meet for the purposes of a review meeting;

(e) after taking the steps prescribed in sub-paragraph (d), inform in writing the prospective adopter who made the application and the adoption agency which made the qualifying determination of—

    (i) the appointment of the panel; and

    (ii) the date, time and venue of the review meeting; and

(f) inform the prospective adopter in writing that he may, if he wishes, provide to the panel further details of the grounds of his application in writing in the period up to two weeks before the review meeting and orally at the review meeting.

**11 Recommendation of panel—**(1) The panel's recommendation may be that of the majority.

(2) The recommendation and the reasons for it and whether it was unanimous or that of a majority must be recorded without delay in a document signed and dated by the chair.

(3) The panel must without delay send a copy of the recommendation and the reasons for it to the prospective adopter and to the adoption agency which made the qualifying determination.

**12 Order for payment of costs** The panel may make an order for the payment by the adoption agency by which the qualifying determination reviewed was made of such costs as [the panel] considers reasonable.

**Note.** Words 'the panel' in square brackets substituted by SI 2004/1081, reg 3, as form 30 April 2004.

**13 Amendment of the 1983 Regulations—**(1) The 1983 Regulations shall be amended in accordance with the following paragraphs.

(2) In regulation 1(3) (interpretation)—

(a) at the appropriate place insert—

'"independent review panel" means a panel constituted under section 9A of the Act;'; and

(b) in the definition of 'registration authority', after the second 'the' insert '2000'.

(3) In regulation 11A (adoption agency decisions and notifications- prospective adopters)—

(a) in paragraph (2), after 'panel' insert 'or an independent review panel';

(b) for paragraph (4)(c) substitute—

'(c) notify the prospective adopter in writing that within 28 days—

    (i) he may submit any representations he wishes to make in writing to the agency; or

    (ii) he may apply to the Secretary of State for a review by an independent review panel of the agency's proposal not to approve him as suitable to be a prospective adopter (referred to in this regulation as a 'qualifying determination').';

(c)  in paragraph (5) for 'the prospective adopter has not made any representations' substitute 'the prospective adopter has not applied to the Secretary of State for a review by an independent review panel of the qualifying determination or made any representations to the agency';

(d)  after paragraph (5) insert—

'(5A) If the agency receives notification from the Secretary of State that a prospective adopter has applied to the Secretary of State for a review by an independent review panel of the qualifying determination, it shall within 7 days after the date of that notification submit to the Secretary of State—

(a)  the written report in respect of the prospective adopter referred to in regulation 8(2)(g);

(b)  any written representations made by the prospective adopter in accordance with regulation 8(2)(h);

(c)  all of the information obtained by the agency in respect of the prospective adopter under regulation 8 or otherwise;

(d)  the documents referred to in paragraph (4)(a) and (b).';

(e)  for paragraph (8) substitute—

'(8) The agency shall make a decision on the case and, in addition to the requirements of paragraph (1),—

(a)  if the prospective adopter has applied to the Secretary of State for a review by an independent review panel of the qualifying determination, it shall make the decision only after taking into account any recommendation of that panel made in accordance with the Independent Review of Determinations (Adoption) Regulations 2004; or

(b)  if the case has been referred to an adoption panel under paragraph (6), it shall make the decision only after taking into account any recommendation of the adoption panel made by virtue of paragraph (7).';

(f)  in paragraph (9) after 'and' insert ', if the case has been referred to an adoption panel under paragraph (6),'; and

(g)  after paragraph (9) insert—

'(9A) In a case where an independent review panel has made a recommendation, the agency shall send to the independent review panel a copy of the notification referred to in paragraph (9).'.

*Margaret Hodge*

Minister of State,
Department for Education and Skills
2nd February 2004

## EXPLANATORY NOTE

*(This note is not part of the Regulations)*

These Regulations are made under the Adoption Act 1976. They apply in respect of England only and in relation to specified cases only. They make provision for the review by an independent panel of a determination made by an adoption agency that it does not propose to approve a prospective adopter as suitable to be an adoptive parent.

Regulation 2 defines a 'qualifying determination'. Part 2 makes provision for the constitution, functions, membership, payment of expenses, meetings and record keeping of the panels which are appointed by the Secretary of State to review qualifying determinations.

Part 3 makes provision for the procedure to be followed when a review of a qualifying determination by a panel constituted under Part 2 is sought by a prospective adopter and for the amendment of the Adoption Agencies Regulations 1983 to take account of this review procedure.

A regulatory impact assessment has been prepared for these Regulations and a copy has been placed in the library of each House of Parliament. Copies of the regulatory impact assessment can be obtained from the Adoption Team, Looked After Children Division, Area 104, Wellington House, 133–155 Waterloo Road, London, SE1 8UG. Alternatively it may be viewed on www.doh.gov.uk/adoption/law.htm#ria or the Department for Education and Skills's website http://www.dfes.gov.uk/ria/current.shtml.

## CHILDREN AND FAMILY COURT ADVISORY AND SUPPORT SERVICE (REVIEWED CASE REFERRAL) REGULATIONS 2004

### 2004 No 2187

CHILDREN AND YOUNG PERSONS, ENGLAND AND WALES

*Made*.....................................*16th August 2004*
*Laid before Parliament*...........*26th August 2004*
*Coming into force* ...................*27th September 2004*

The Lord Chancellor, in exercise of the powers conferred upon him by sections 26(2C) and 104(4) of the Children Act 1989, makes the following Regulations:

**1 Commencement and citation** These Regulations may be cited as the Children and Family Court Advisory and Support Service (Reviewed Case Referral) Regulations 2004 and shall come into force on 27th September 2004.

**2 Interpretation** In these Regulations—
a 'claim for judicial review' means a claim to review the lawfulness of—
    (a) an enactment; or
    (b) a decision, action or failure to act in relation to the exercise of a public function;
'court' means the House of Lords, the Court of Appeal, the High Court, a county court or a magistrates court;
'independent reviewing officer' means an independent reviewing officer referred to in regulation 2A of the Review of Children's Cases Regulations 1991;
'proceedings' means court proceedings;
'the Service' means the Children and Family Court Advisory and Support Service;
'referral' means a referral under section 26(2A)(c) of the Children Act 1989.

**3 Extension of the functions of officers of the Service** The functions of the Service in respect of family proceedings (within the meaning of section 12 of the Criminal Justice and Court Services Act 2000) are extended so that they can be exercised in respect of any —
    (a) proceedings under section 7(1) of the Human Rights Act 1998;
    (b) claim for judicial review; and
    (c) other proceedings,
in connection with a referral by an independent reviewing officer.

**4 Manner in which the functions of the officers of the Service are to be performed** On referral of a case by an independent reviewing officer, the functions of an officer of the Service shall be performed in the manner prescribed by regulations 5 to 9 below.

**5 Appointment of an officer of the Service—**(1) Following receipt of a referral by an independent reviewing officer, the Service shall appoint an officer to assess the case.

(2) The officer of the Service shall decide on a course of action and submit a written report of the decision to—

(a) the independent reviewing officer;

(b) the Chief Executive of the local authority which appointed the independent reviewing officer;

(c) any person specified by the independent reviewing officer in the referral; and

(d) any other person the officer of the Service considers should be informed, stating the reasons for the decision and the information taken into account, including where appropriate the ascertainable wishes and feelings of the child.

(3) The officer of the Service must seek to submit the report referred to in paragraph (2) to the persons referred to in that paragraph within two weeks of the referral.

(4) If the officer of the Service does not submit a written report within two weeks of the referral, he shall—

(a) send written notice within two weeks of the referral to the persons referred to in paragraph (2) (a) to (d) explaining that it has not been possible to send the report within that period; and

(b) submit the report as soon as is reasonably practicable thereafter and shall include in the report an explanation for the delay.

**6 Inappropriate referral of a case** If the officer of the Service appointed under regulation 5(1) considers that the case has been inappropriately referred to him by the independent reviewing officer, that officer may—

(a) require further written information as to the steps taken before the referral; or

(b) proceed with the referral irrespective of whether he considers that the referral was appropriate.

**7 Issue of proceedings—**(1) Where the decision made under regulation 5(2) is to bring proceedings, the officer of the Service must seek to bring them within six weeks of receipt by the Service of the referral by the independent reviewing officer.

(2) If the proceedings cannot be brought within six weeks, the proceedings shall be brought as soon as is reasonably practicable thereafter.

**8 Settlement of the case without a court hearing** Notwithstanding whether proceedings have been issued or not, the officer of the Service may seek to settle the case by alternative dispute resolution or other means—

(a) following the issue of proceedings, at any time before the date set for the final hearing of the proceedings; or

(b) in a case where proceedings have not been issued, at any time.

**9 Report following the conclusion of the case—**(1) On the conclusion of every case, whether following judgment of the court or settlement before or after proceedings were brought, the officer of the Service shall provide a written report to the persons referred to in regulation 5(2)(a) to (d) within six weeks of the judgment or settlement.

(2) The report under regulation 9(1) shall contain—

(a) the reasons for the decision to bring proceedings or the decision to settle;

(b) where applicable, the reasons for any delay where the time limits in regulations 5(3) or 7(1) have not been complied with;

(c)  full details of the court order or other settlement; and

(d)  any comments or recommendations the officer of the Service may have in respect of the case.

Signed by authority of the Lord Chancellor

*Filkin*

Parliamentary Under Secretary of State,

Department for Constitutional Affairs

Dated 16th August 2004

## EXPLANATORY NOTE

*(This note is not part of the Regulations)*

These Regulations provide for an extension of the functions of the Children and Family Court Advisory and Support Service, enabling court proceedings to be brought as necessary following a referral from an independent reviewing officer under section 26(2A)(c) of the Children Act 1989 (inserted by section 118 of the Adoption and Children Act 2002).

The Regulations further provide for the manner in which any functions of the officers of the Service are to be exercised following such a referral. For example, the officer of the service will assess the case, decide on a course of action, issue court proceedings if appropriate and report back to the independent reviewing officer on the outcome of any action taken.

# European Material

**COUNCIL REGULATION (EC) NO 1347/2000**

**of 29 May 2000**

on the jurisdiction and the recognition and enforcement of judgments in matrimonial matters and in matters of parental responsibility for children of both spouses

(repealed by Council Regulation (EC) NO 2201/2003 as from 1 March 2005.)

*THE COUNCIL OF THE EUROPEAN UNION*

*Having regard to the Treaty establishing the European Community, and in particular Article 61(c) and Article 67(1) thereof,*

*Having regard to the proposal from the Commission,*

*Having regard to the opinion of the European Parliament,*

*Having regard to the opinion of the Economic and Social Committee,*

*Whereas:*

*(1) The Member States have set themselves the objective of maintaining and developing the Union as an area of freedom, security and justice, in which the free movement of persons is assured. To establish such an area, the Community is to adopt, among others, the measures in the field of judicial cooperation in civil matters needed for the proper functioning of the internal market.*

*(2) The proper functioning of the internal market entails the need to improve and simplify the free movement of judgments in civil matters.*

*(3) This is a subject now falling within the ambit of Article 65 of the Treaty.*

*(4) Differences between certain national rules governing jurisdiction and enforcement hamper the free movement of persons and the sound operation of the internal market. There are accordingly grounds for enacting provisions to unify the rules of conflict of jurisdiction in matrimonial matters and in matters of parental responsibility so as to simplify the formalities for rapid and automatic recognition and enforcement of judgments.*

*(5) In accordance with the principles of subsidiarity and proportionality as set out in Article 5 of the Treaty, the objectives of this Regulation cannot be sufficiently achieved by the Member States and can therefore be better achieved by the Community. This Regulation does not go beyond what is necessary to achieve those objectives.*

*(6) The Council, by an Act dated 28 May 1998, drew up a Convention on jurisdiction and the recognition and enforcement of judgments in matrimonial matters and recommended it for adoption by the Member States in accordance with their respective constitutional rules. Continuity in the results of the negotiations for conclusion of the Convention should be ensured. The content of this Regulation is substantially taken over from the Convention, but this Regulation contains a number of new provisions not in the Convention in order to secure consistency with certain provisions of the proposed regulation on jurisdiction and the recognition and enforcement of judgments in civil and commercial matters.*

*(7) In order to attain the objective of free movement of judgments in matrimonial matters and in matters of parental responsibility within the Community, it is necessary and appropriate that the cross-border recognition of jurisdiction and judgments in relation to the dissolution of matrimonial ties and to parental responsibility for the children of both spouses be governed by a mandatory, and directly applicable, Community legal instrument.*

*(8) The measures laid down in this Regulation should be consistent and uniform, to enable people to move as widely as possible. Accordingly, it should also apply to nationals of non-member States whose links with the territory of a Member State are sufficiently close, in keeping with the grounds of jurisdiction laid down in the Regulation.*

*(9) The scope of this Regulation should cover civil proceedings and non-judicial proceedings in matrimonial matters in certain States, and exclude purely religious procedures. It should therefore be provided that the reference to 'courts' includes all the authorities, judicial or otherwise, with jurisdiction in matrimonial matters.*

*(10) This Regulation should be confined to proceedings relating to divorce, legal separation or marriage annulment. The recognition of divorce and annulment rulings affects only the dissolution of matrimonial ties; despite the fact that they may be interrelated, the Regulation does not affect issues such as the fault of the spouses, property consequences of the marriage, the maintenance obligation or any other ancillary measures.*

*(11) This Regulation covers parental responsibility for children of both spouses on issues that are closely linked to proceedings for divorce, legal separation or marriage annulment.*

*(12) The grounds of jurisdiction accepted in this Regulation are based on the rule that there must be a real link between the party concerned and the Member State exercising jurisdiction; the decision to include certain grounds corresponds to the fact that they exist in different national legal systems and are accepted by the other Member States.*

*(13) One of the risks to be considered in relation to the protection of the children of both spouses in a marital crisis is that one of the parents will take the child to another country. The fundamental interests of the children must therefore be protected, in accordance with, in particular, the Hague Convention of 25 October 1980 on the Civil Aspects of the International Abduction of Children. The lawful habitual residence is accordingly maintained as the grounds of jurisdiction in cases where, because the child has been moved or has not been returned without lawful reason, there has been a de facto change in the habitual residence.*

*(14) This Regulation does not prevent the courts of a Member State from taking provisional, including protective, measures, in urgent cases, with regard to persons or property situated in that State.*

*(15) The word 'judgment' refers only to decisions that lead to divorce, legal separation or marriage annulment. Those documents which have been formally drawn up or registered as authentic instruments and are enforceable in one Member State are treated as equivalent to such 'judgments'.*

*(16) The recognition and enforcement of judgments given in a Member State are based on the principle of mutual trust. The grounds for non-recognition are kept to the minimum required. Those proceedings should incorporate provisions to ensure observance of public policy in the State addressed and to safeguard the rights of the defence and those of the parties, including the individual rights of any child involved, and so as to withhold recognition of irreconcilable judgments.*

*(17) The State addressed should review neither the jurisdiction of the State of origin nor the findings of fact.*

*(18) No procedures may be required for the updating of civil-status documents in one Member State on the basis of a final judgment given in another Member State.*

*(19) The Convention concluded by the Nordic States in 1931 should be capable of application within the limits set by this Regulation.*

*(20) Spain, Italy and Portugal had concluded Concordats before the matters covered by this Regulation were brought within the ambit of the Treaty: It is necessary to ensure that these States do not breach their international commitments in relation to the Holy See.*

*(21) The Member States should remain free to agree among themselves on practical measures for the application of the Regulation as long as no Community measures have been taken to that end.*

*(22) Annexes I to III relating to the courts and redress procedures should be amended by the Commission on the basis of amendments transmitted by the Member State concerned. Amendments to Annexes IV and V should be adopted in accordance with Council Decision 1999/468/EC of 28 June 1999 laying down the procedures for the exercise of implementing powers conferred on the Commission.*

*(23) No later than five years after the date of the entry into force of this Regulation, the Commission is to review its application and propose such amendments as may appear necessary.*

*(24) The United Kingdom and Ireland, in accordance with Article 3 of the Protocol on the position of the United Kingdom and Ireland annexed to the Treaty on European Union and the Treaty establishing the European Community, have given notice of their wish to take part in the adoption and application of this Regulation.*

*(25) Denmark, in accordance with Articles 1 and 2 of the Protocol on the position of Denmark annexed to the Treaty on European Union and the Treaty establishing the European Community, is not participating in the adoption of this Regulation, and is therefore not bound by it nor subject to its application,*

HAS ADOPTED THIS REGULATION:

## CHAPTER I

SCOPE

*Article 1*

1.   This Regulation shall apply to:

(a)   civil proceedings relating to divorce, legal separation or marriage annulment;

(b)   civil proceedings relating to parental responsibility for the children of both spouses on the occasion of the matrimonial proceedings referred to in (a).

2.   Other proceedings officially recognised in a Member State shall be regarded as equivalent to judicial proceedings. The term 'court' shall cover all the authorities with jurisdiction in these matters in the Member States.

3.   In this Regulation, the term 'Member State' shall mean all Member States with the exception of Denmark.

## CHAPTER II

JURISDICTION

SECTION 1
GENERAL PROVISIONS

*Article 2*

**Divorce, legal separation and marriage annulment**

1.   In matters relating to divorce, legal separation or marriage annulment, jurisdiction shall lie with the courts of the Member State:

(a)   in whose territory:
–   the spouses are habitually resident, or
–   the spouses were last habitually resident, in so far as one of them still resides there, or
–   the respondent is habitually resident, or
–   in the event of a joint application, either of the spouses is habitually resident, or
–   the applicant is habitually resident if he or she resided there for at least a year immediately before the application was made, or
–   the applicant is habitually resident if he or she resided there for at least six months immediately before the application was made and is either a national of the Member State in question or, in the case of the United Kingdom and Ireland, has his 'domicile' there;

(b)   of the nationality of both spouses or, in the case of the United Kingdom and Ireland, of the 'domicile' of both spouses.

2.   For the purpose of this Regulation, 'domicile' shall have the same meaning as it has under the legal systems of the United Kingdom and Ireland.

*Article 3*

**Parental responsibility**

1. The Courts of a Member State exercising jurisdiction by virtue of Article 2 on an application for divorce, legal separation or marriage annulment shall have jurisdiction in a matter relating to parental responsibility over a child of both spouses where the child is habitually resident in that Member State.

2. Where the child is not habitually resident in the Member State referred to in paragraph 1, the courts of that State shall have jurisdiction in such a matter if the child is habitually resident in one of the Member States and:

(a)   at least one of the spouses has parental responsibility in relation to the child;
and

(b)   the jurisdiction of the courts has been accepted by the spouses and is in the best interests of the child.

3.   The jurisdiction conferred by paragraphs 1 and 2 shall cease as soon as:

(a)   the judgment allowing or refusing the application for divorce, legal separation or marriage annulment has become final;

or

(b)   in those cases where proceedings in relation to parental responsibility are still pending on the date referred to in (a), a judgment in these proceedings has become final;

or

(c)   the proceedings referred to in (a) and (b) have come to an end for another reason.

## Article 4

### Child abduction

The courts with jurisdiction within the meaning of Article 3 shall exercise their jurisdiction in conformity with the Hague Convention of 25 October 1980 on the Civil Aspects of International Child Abduction, and in particular Articles 3 and 16 thereof.

## Article 5

### Counterclaim

The court in which proceedings are pending on the basis of Articles 2 to 4 shall also have jurisdiction to examine a counterclaim, in so far as the latter comes within the scope of this Regulation.

## Article 6

### Conversion of legal separation into divorce

Without prejudice to Article 2, a court of a Member State which has given a judgment on a legal separation shall also have jurisdiction for converting that judgment into a divorce, if the law of that Member State so provides.

## Article 7

### Exclusive nature of jurisdiction under Articles 2 to 6

A spouse who:

(a)   is habitually resident in the territory of a Member State;

or

(b)   is a national of a Member State, or, in the case of the United Kingdom and Ireland, has his or her 'domicile' in the territory of one of the latter Member States,

may be sued in another Member State only in accordance with Articles 2 to 6.

## Article 8

### Residual jurisdiction

1.   Where no court of a Member State has jurisdiction pursuant to Articles 2 to 6, jurisdiction shall be determined, in each Member State, by the laws of that State.

2.   As against a respondent who is not habitually resident and is not either a national of a Member State or, in the case of the United Kingdom and Ireland, does not have his 'domicile' within the territory of one of the latter Member States, any national of a Member State who is habitually resident within the territory of another Member State may, like the nationals of that State, avail himself of the rules of jurisdiction applicable in that State.

EXAMINATION AS TO JURISDICTION AND ADMISSIBILITY

### Article 9

**Examination as to jurisdiction**

*Where a court of a Member State is seised of a case over which it has no jurisdiction under this Regulation and over which a court of another Member State has jurisdiction by virtue of this Regulation, it shall declare of its own motion that it has no jurisdiction.*

### Article 10

**Examination as to admissibility**

*1. Where a respondent habitually resident in a State other than the Member State where the action was brought does not enter an appearance, the court with jurisdiction shall stay the proceedings so long as it is not shown that the respondent has been able to receive the document instituting the proceedings or an equivalent document in sufficient time to enable him to arrange for his defence, or that all necessary steps have been taken to this end.*

*2. Article 19 of Council Regulation (EC) No 1348/2000 of 29 May 2000 on the service in the Member States of judicial and extrajudicial documents in civil or commercial matters, shall apply instead of the provisions of paragraph 1 of this Article if the document instituting the proceedings or an equivalent document had to be transmitted from one Member State to another pursuant to that Regulation.*

*3. Where the provisions of Council Regulation (EC) No 1348/2000 are not applicable, Article 15 of the Hague Convention of 15 November 1965 on the service abroad of judicial and extrajudicial documents in civil or commercial matters shall apply if the document instituting the proceedings or an equivalent document had to be transmitted abroad pursuant to that Convention.*

SECTION 3

LIS PENDENS AND DEPENDENT ACTIONS

### Article 11

*1. Where proceedings involving the same cause of action and between the same parties are brought before courts of different Member States, the court second seised shall of its own motion stay its proceedings until such time as the jurisdiction of the court first seised is established.*

*2. Where proceedings for divorce, legal separation or marriage annulment not involving the same cause of action and between the same parties are brought before courts of different Member States, the court second seised shall of its own motion stay its proceedings until such time as the jurisdiction of the court first seised is established.*

*3. Where the jurisdiction of the court first seised is established, the court second seised shall decline jurisdiction in favour of that court.*

*In that case, the party who brought the relevant action before the court second seised may bring that action before the court first seised.*

*4. For the purposes of this Article, a court shall be deemed to be seised:*

*(a) at the time when the document instituting the proceedings or an equivalent document is lodged with the court, provided that the applicant has not subsequently failed to take the steps he was required to take to have service effected on the respondent;*

*or*

*(b) if the document has to be served before being lodged with the court, at the time when it is received by the authority responsible for service, provided that the applicant has not subsequently failed to take the steps he was required to take to have the document lodged with the court.*

SECTION 4

PROVISIONAL, INCLUDING PROTECTIVE, MEASURES

*Article 12*

*In urgent cases, the provisions of this Regulation shall not prevent the courts of a Member State from taking such provisional, including protective, measures in respect of persons or assets in that State as may be available under the law of that Member State, even if, under this Regulation, the court of another Member State has jurisdiction as to the substance of the matter.*

CHAPTER III

RECOGNITION AND ENFORCEMENT

*Article 13*

**Meaning of 'judgment'**

*1. For the purposes of this Regulation, 'judgment' means a divorce, legal separation or marriage annulment pronounced by a court of a Member State, as well as a judgment relating to the parental responsibility of the spouses given on the occasion of such matrimonial proceedings, whatever the judgment may be called, including a decree, order or decision.*

*2. The provisions of this chapter shall also apply to the determination of the amount of costs and expenses of proceedings under this Regulation and to the enforcement of any order concerning such costs and expenses.*

*3. For the purposes of implementing this Regulation, documents which have been formally drawn up or registered as authentic instruments and are enforceable in one Member State and also settlements which have been approved by a court in the course of proceedings and are enforceable in the Member State in which they were concluded shall be recognised and declared enforceable under the same conditions as the judgments referred to in paragraph 1.*

SECTION 1

RECOGNITION

*Article 14*

**Recognition of a judgment**

*1. A judgment given in a Member State shall be recognised in the other Member States without any special procedure being required.*

*2. In particular, and without prejudice to paragraph 3, no special procedure shall be required for up-dating the civil-status records of a Member State on the basis of a judgment relating to divorce, legal separation or marriage annulment given in another member State, and against which no further appeal lies under the law of that Member State.*

*3. Any interested party may, in accordance with the procedures provided for in Sections 2 and 3 of this Chapter, apply for a decision that the judgment be or not be recognised.*

*4. Where the recognition of a judgment is raised as an incidental question in a court of a Member State, that court may determine that issue.*

*Article 15*

**Grounds of non-recognition**

*1. A judgment relating to a divorce, legal separation or marriage annulment shall not be recognised:*

    *(a)   if such recognition is manifestly contrary to the public policy of the Member State in which recognition is sought;*

    *(b)   where it was given in default of appearance, if the respondent was not served with the*

document which instituted the proceedings or with an equivalent document in sufficient time and in such a way as to enable the respondent to arrange for his or her defence unless it is determined that the respondent has accepted the judgment unequivocally;

(c)   if it is irreconcilable with a judgment given in proceedings between the same parties in the Member State in which recognition is sought;

*or*

(d)   if it is irreconcilable with an earlier judgment given in another Member State or in a non-member State between the same parties, provided that the earlier judgment fulfils the conditions necessary for its recognition in the Member State in which recognition is sought.

2.   A judgment relating to the parental responsibility of the spouses given on the occasion of matrimonial proceedings as referred to in Article 13 shall not be recognised:

(a)   if such recognition is manifestly contrary to the public policy of the Member State in which recognition is sought taking into account the best interests of the child;

(b)   if it was given, except in case of urgency, without the child having been given an opportunity to be heard, in violation of fundamental principles of procedure of the Member State in which recognition is sought;

(c)   where it was given in default of appearance if the person in default was not served with the document which instituted the proceedings or with an equivalent document in sufficient time and in such a way as to enable that person to arrange for his or her defence unless it is determined that such person has accepted the judgment unequivocally;

(d)   on the request of any person claiming that the judgment infringes his or her parental responsibility, if it was given without such person having been given an opportunity to be heard;

(e)   if it is irreconcilable with a later judgment relating to parental responsibility given in the Member State in which recognition is sought;

*or*

(f)   if it is irreconcilable with a later judgment relating to parental responsibility given in another Member State or in the non-member State of the habitual residence of the child provided that the later judgment fulfils the conditions necessary for its recognition in the Member State in which recognition is sought.

## Article 16

### Agreement with third States

A court of a Member State may, on the basis of an agreement on the recognition and enforcement of judgments, not recognise a judgment given in another Member State where, in cases provided for in Article 8, the judgment could only be founded on grounds of jurisdiction other than those specified in Articles 2 to 7.

## Article 17

### Prohibition of review of jurisdiction of court of origin

The jurisdiction of the court of the Member State of origin may not be reviewed. The test of public policy referred to in Article 15(1)(a) and (2)(a) may not be applied to the rules relating to jurisdiction set out in Articles 2 to 8.

## Article 18

### Differences in applicable law

The recognition of a judgment relating to a divorce, legal separation or a marriage annulment may not be refused because the law of the Member State in which such recognition is sought would not allow divorce, legal separation or marriage annulment on the same facts.

## Article 19

### Non-review as to substance

*Under no circumstances may a judgment be reviewed as to its substance.*

## Article 20

### Stay of proceedings

*1. A court of a Member State in which recognition is sought of a judgment given in another Member State may stay the proceedings if an ordinary appeal against the judgment has been lodged.*

*2. A court of a Member State in which recognition is sought of a judgment given in Ireland or the United Kingdom may stay the proceedings if enforcement is suspended in the Member State of origin by reason of an appeal.*

## SECTION 2

### ENFORCEMENT

## Article 21

### Enforceable judgments

*1. A judgment on the exercise of parental responsibility in respect of a child of both parties given in a Member State which is enforceable in that Member State and has been served shall be enforced in another Member State when, on the application of any interested party, it has been declared enforceable there.*

*2. However, in the United Kingdom, such a judgment shall be enforced in England and Wales, in Scotland or in Northern Ireland when, on the application of any interested party, it has been registered for enforcement in that part of the United Kingdom.*

## Article 22

### Jurisdiction of local courts

*1. An application for a declaration of enforceability shall be submitted to the court appearing in the list in Annex I.*

*2. The local jurisdiction shall be determined by reference to the place of the habitual residence of the person against whom enforcement is sought or by reference to the habitual residence of any child to whom the application relates.*

*Where neither of the places referred to in the first subparagraph can be found in the Member State where enforcement is sought, the local jurisdiction shall be determined by reference to the place of enforcement.*

*3. In relation to procedures referred to in Article 14(3), the local jurisdiction shall be determined by the internal law of the Member State in which proceedings for recognition or non-recognition are brought.*

## Article 23

### Procedure for enforcement

*1. The procedure for making the application shall be governed by the law of the Member State in which enforcement is sought.*

*2. The applicant must give an address for service within the area of jurisdiction of the court applied to. However, if the law of the Member State in which enforcement is sought does not provide for the furnishing of such an address, the applicant shall appoint a representative ad litem.*

*3. The documents referred to in Articles 32 and 33 shall be attached to the application.*

*Article 24*

**Decision of the court**

1. The court applied to shall give its decision without delay. The person against whom enforcement is sought shall not at this stage of the proceedings be entitled to make any submissions on the application.

2. The application may be refused only for one of the reasons specified in Articles 15, 16 and 17.

3. Under no circumstances may a judgment be reviewed as to its substance.

*Article 25*

**Notice of the decision**

The appropriate officer of the court shall without delay bring to the notice of the applicant the decision given on the application in accordance with the procedure laid down by the law of the Member State in which enforcement is sought.

*Article 26*

**Appeal against the enforcement decision**

1. The decision on the application for a declaration of enforceability may be appealed against by either party.

2. The appeal shall be lodged with the court appearing in the list in Annex II.

3. The appeal shall be dealt with in accordance with the rules governing procedure in contradictory matters.

4. If the appeal is brought by the applicant for a declaration of enforceability, the party against whom enforcement is sought shall be summoned to appear before the appellate court. If such person fails to appear, the provisions of Article 10 shall apply.

5. An appeal against a declaration of enforceability must be lodged within one month of service thereof. If the party against whom enforcement is sought is habitually resident in a Member State other than that in which the declaration of enforceability was given, the time for appealing shall be two months and shall run from the date of service, either on him or at his residence. No extension of time may be granted on account of distance.

*Article 27*

**Courts of appeal and means of contest**

The judgment given on appeal may be contested only by the proceedings referred to in Annex III.

*Article 28*

**Stay of proceedings**

1. The court with which the appeal is lodged under Articles 26 or 27 may, on the application of the party against whom enforcement is sought, stay the proceedings if an ordinary appeal has been lodged in the Member State of origin or if the time for such appeal has not yet expired. In the latter case, the court may specify the time within which an appeal is to be lodged.

2. Where the judgment was given in Ireland or the United Kingdom, any form of appeal available in the Member State of origin shall be treated as an ordinary appeal for the purposes of paragraph 1.

*Article 29*

**Partial enforcement**

1. Where a judgment has been given in respect of several matters and enforcement cannot be authorised for all of them, the court shall authorise enforcement for one or more of them.
  2. An applicant may request partial enforcement of a judgment.

*Article 30*

**Legal aid**

An applicant who, in the Member State of origin, has benefited from complete or partial legal aid or exemption from costs or expenses shall be entitled, in the procedures provided for in Articles 22 to 25, to benefit from the most favourable legal aid or the most extensive exemption from costs and expenses provided for by the law of the Member State addressed.

*Article 31*

**Security, bond or deposit**

No security, bond or deposit, however described, shall be required of a party who in one Member State applies for enforcement of a judgment given in another Member State on the following grounds:
  (a)  that he or she is not habitually resident in the Member State in which enforcement is sought;
  or
  (b)  that he or she is either a foreign national or, where enforcement is sought in either the United Kingdom or Ireland, does not have his or her "domicile" in either of those Member States.

SECTION 3

COMMON PROVISIONS

*Article 32*

**Documents**

1. A party seeking or contesting recognition or applying for a declaration of enforceability shall produce:
  (a)  a copy of the judgment which satisfies the conditions necessary to establish its authenticity;
  and
  (b)  a certificate referred to in Article 33.
  2.  In addition, in the case of a judgment given in default, the party seeking recognition or applying for a declaration of enforceability shall produce:
  (a)  the original or certified true copy of the document which establishes that the defaulting party was served with the document instituting the proceedings or with an equivalent document;
  or
  (b)  any document indicating that the defendant has accepted the judgment unequivocally.

*Article 33*

**Other documents**

The competent court or authority of a Member State where a judgment was given shall issue, at the request of any interested party, a certificate using the standard form in Annex IV (judgments in matrimonial matters) or Annex V (judgments on parental responsibility).

## Article 34

**Absence of documents**

1. If the documents specified in Article 32(1)(b) or (2) are not produced, the court may specify a time for their production, accept equivalent documents or, if it considers that it has sufficient information before it, dispense with their production.

2. If the Court so requires, a translation of such documents shall be furnished. The translation shall be certified by a person qualified to do so in one of the Member States.

## Article 35

**Legalisation or other similar formality**

No legalisation or other similar formality shall be required in respect of the documents referred to in Articles 32, 33 and 34(2) or in respect of a document appointing a representative ad litem.

## CHAPTER IV
## GENERAL PROVISIONS

## Article 36

**Relation with other instruments**

1. Subject to the provisions of Articles 38, 42 and paragraph 2 of this Article, this Regulation shall, for the Member States, supersede conventions existing at the time of entry into force of this Regulation which have been concluded between two or more Member States and relate to matters governed by this Regulation.

(2)

(a) Finland and Sweden shall have the option of declaring that the Convention of 6 February 1931 between Denmark, Finland, Iceland, Norway and Sweden comprising international private law provisions on marriage, adoption and guardianship, together with the Final Protocol thereto, will apply, in whole or in part, in their mutual relations, in place of the rules of this Regulation. Such declarations shall be annexed to this Regulation and published in the Official Journal of the European Communities. They may be withdrawn, in whole or in part, at any moment by the said Member States.

(b) The principle of non-discrimination on the grounds of nationality between citizens of the Union shall be respected.

(c) The rules of jurisdiction in any future agreement to be concluded between the Member States referred to in subparagraph (a) which relate to matters governed by this Regulation shall be in line with those laid down in this Regulation.

(d) Judgments handed down in any of the Nordic States which have made the declaration provided for in subparagraph (a) under a forum of jurisdiction corresponding to one of those laid down in Chapter II, shall be recognised and enforced in the other Member States under the rules laid down in Chapter III.

3. Member States shall send to the Commission:

(a) a copy of the agreements and uniform laws implementing these agreements referred to in paragraphs 2(a) and (c);

(b) any denunciations of, or amendments to, those agreements or uniform laws.

## Article 37

**Relations with certain multilateral conventions**

In relations between Member States, this Regulation shall take precedence over the following Conventions in so far as they concern matters governed by this Regulation:

–   the Hague Convention of 5 October 1961 concerning the Powers of Authorities and the Law Applicable in respect of the Protection of Minors,

- the Luxembourg Convention of 8 September 1967 on the Recognition of Decisions Relating to the Validity of Marriages,
- the Hague Convention of 1 June 1970 on the Recognition of Divorces and Legal Separations,
- the European Convention of 20 May 1980 on Recognition and Enforcement of Decisions concerning Custody of Children and on Restoration of Custody of Children,
- the Hague Convention of 19 October 1996 on Jurisdiction, Applicable law, Recognition, Enforcement and Cooperation in Respect of Parental Responsibility and Measures for the Protection of Children, provided that the child concerned is habitually resident in a Member State.

*Article 38*

**Extent of effects**

1. The agreements and conventions referred to in Articles 36(1) and 37 shall continue to have effect in relation to matters to which this Regulation does not apply.

2. They shall continue to have effect in respect of judgments given and documents formally drawn up or registered as authentic before the entry into force of this Regulation.

*Article 39*

**Agreements between Member States**

1. Two or more Member States may conclude agreements or arrangements to amplify this Regulation or to facilitate its application.

Member States shall send to the Commission:

(a) a copy of the draft agreements;

and

(b) any denunciations of, or amendments to, these agreements.

2. In no circumstances may the agreements or arrangements derogate from Chapters II or III.

*Article 40*

**Treaties with the Holy See**

1. This Regulation shall apply without prejudice to the International Treaty (Concordat) between the Holy See and Portugal, signed at the Vatican City on 7 May 1940.

2. Any decision as to the invalidity of a marriage taken under the Treaty referred to in paragraph 1 shall be recognised in the Member States on the conditions laid down in Chapter III.

3. The provisions laid down in paragraphs 1 and 2 shall also apply to the following international treaties (Concordats) with the Holy See:

(a) Concordato lateranense of 11 February 1929 between Italy and the Holy See, modified by the agreement, with additional Protocol signed in Rome on 18 February 1984;

(b) Agreement between the Holy See and Spain on legal affairs of 3 January 1979.

4. Recognition of the decisions provided for in paragraph 2 may, in Italy or in Spain, be subject to the same procedures and the same checks as are applicable to decisions of the ecclesiastical courts handed down in accordance with the international treaties concluded with the Holy See referred to in paragraph 3.

5. Member States shall send to the Commission:

(a) a copy of the Treaties referred to in paragraphs 1 and 3;

(b) any denunciations of or amendments to those Treaties.

*Article 41*

**Member States with two or more legal systems**

With regard to a Member State in which two or more systems of law or sets of rules concerning matters governed by this Regulation apply in different territorial units:

(a)   any reference to habitual residence in that Member State shall refer to habitual residence in a territorial unit;

(b)   any reference to nationality, or in the case of the United Kingdom 'domicile', shall refer to the territorial unit designated by the law of that State;

(c)   any reference to the authority of a Member State having received an application for divorce or legal separation or for marriage annulment shall refer to the authority of a territorial unit which has received such an application;

(d)   any reference to the rules of the requested Member State shall refer to the rules of the territorial unit in which jurisdiction, recognition or enforcement is invoked.

## CHAPTER V

## TRANSITIONAL PROVISIONS

### Article 42

1. The provisions of this Regulation shall apply only to legal proceedings instituted, to documents formally drawn up or registered as authentic instruments and to settlements which have been approved by a court in the course of proceedings after its entry into force.

2. Judgments given after the date of entry into force of this Regulation in proceedings instituted before that date shall be recognised and enforced in accordance with the provisions of Chapter III if jurisdiction was founded on rules which accorded with those provided for either in Chapter II of this Regulation or in a convention concluded between the Member State of origin and the Member State addressed which was in force when the proceedings were instituted.

## CHAPTER VI

## FINAL PROVISIONS

### Article 43

**Review**

No later than 1 March 2006, and every five years thereafter, the Commission shall present to the European Parliament, the Council and the Economic and Social Committee a report on the application of this Regulation, and in particular Articles 36, 39 and 40(2) thereof. The report shall be accompanied if need be by proposals for adaptations.

### Article 44

**Amendment to lists of courts and redress procedures**

1. Member States shall notify the Commission of the texts amending the lists of courts and redress procedures set out in Annexes I to III. The Commission shall adapt the Annexes concerned accordingly.

2. The updating or making of technical amendments to the standard forms set out in Annexes IV and V shall be adopted in accordance with the advisory procedure set out in Article 45(2).

### Article 45

1. The Commission shall be assisted by a committee.

2. Where reference is made to this paragraph, Articles 3 and 7 of Decision 1999/468 EC shall apply.

3. The committee shall adopt its rules of procedure.

*Article 46*

**Entry into force**

*This Regulation shall enter into force on 1 March 2001*

*This Regulation shall be binding in its entirety and directly applicable in the Member States in accordance with the Treaty establishing the European Community.*

*Done at Brussels, 29 May 2000.*

## ANNEX I

*The applications provided for by Article 22 shall be submitted to the following courts:*
- in Belgium, the 'tribunal de première instance'/'rechtbank van eerste aanleg'/'erstinstanzliches Gericht',
- in Germany:
  - in the district of the 'Kammergericht' (Berlin), the 'Familiengericht' Pankow/Weissensee',
  - in the districts of the remaining 'Oberlandesgerichte' to the 'Familiengericht' located at the seat of the respective 'Oberlandesgericht'
- in Greece, the [not reproduced, see original],
- in Spain, the 'Juzgado de Primera Instancia',
- in France, the presiding Judge of the 'tribunal de grande instance',
- in Ireland, the High Court,
- in Italy, the 'Corte d'apello',
- in Luxembourg, the presiding Judge of the 'Tribunal d'arrondissement',
- in the Netherlands, the presiding Judge of the 'arrondissementsrechtbank',
- in Austria, the 'Bezirksgericht',
- in Portugal, the 'Tribunal de Comarca' or 'Tribunal de Familia',
- in Finland, the 'käräjäoikeus'/'tingsrätt',
- in Sweden, the 'Svea hovrätt',
- in the United Kingdom:
  - (a) in England and Wales, the High Court of Justice;
  - (b) in Scotland, the Court of Session;
  - (c) in Northern Ireland, the High Court of Justice;
  - (d) in Gibraltar, the Supreme Court.

## ANNEX II

*The appeal provided for by Article 26 shall be lodged with the courts listed below:*
- in Belgium:
  - (a) a person applying for a declaration of enforceability may lodge an appeal with the 'cour d'appel' or the 'hof van beroep';
  - (b) the person against whom enforcement is sought may lodge opposition with the 'tribunal de première instance'/'rechtbank van eerste aanleg'/'erstinstanzliches Gericht',
- in Germany, the 'Oberlandesgericht',
- in Greece, the [not reproduced, see original],
- in Spain, the 'Audiencia Provincial',
- in France, the 'Cour d'appel',
- in Ireland, the High Court,
- in Italy, the 'Corte d'apello',
- Luxembourg, the 'Cour d'appel',
- in the Netherlands:
  - (a) if the applicant or the respondent who has appeared lodges the appeal: with the 'gerechtshof';
  - (b) if the respondent who has been granted leave not to appear lodges the appeal: with the 'arrondissementsrechtbank',

- in Austria, the 'Bezirksgericht',
- in Portugal, the 'Tribunal da Relação',
- in Finland, the 'hovioikeus'/'hovrätt',
- in Sweden, the 'Svea hovrätt',
- in the United Kingdom:
  - (a) in England and Wales, the High Court of Justice;
  - (b) in Scotland, the Court of Session;
  - (c) in Northern Ireland, the High Court of Justice;
  - (d) in Gibraltar, the Court of Appeal.

## ANNEX III

The appeals provided for by Article 27 may be brought only:
- in Belgium, Greece, Spain, France, Italy, Luxembourg and in the Netherlands, by an appeal in cassation,
- in Germany, by a 'Rechtsbeschwerde',
- in Ireland, by an appeal on a point of law to the Supreme Court,
- in Austria, by a 'Revisionsrekurs',
- in Portugal, by a 'recurso restrito à matéria de direito',
- in Finland, by an appeal to 'korkein oikeus'/'högsta domstolen',
- in Sweden, by an appeal to the 'Högsta domstolen',
- in the United Kingdom, by a single further appeal on a point of law.

## ANNEX IV

Certificate referred to in Article 33 concerning judgments in matrimonial matters
1. Country of origin:_____
2. Court or authority issuing the certificate:_____
   - 2.1. Name:_____
   - 2.2. Address:_____
   - 2.3. Tel/fax/E-mail:_____
3. Marriage
   - 3.1. Wife
     - 3.1.1. Full name:_____
     - 3.1.2. Country and place of birth:_____
     - 3.1.3. Date of birth:_____
   - 3.2. Husband
     - 3.2.1. Full name:_____
     - 3.2.2. Country and place of birth:_____
     - 3.2.3. Date of birth:_____
   - 3.3. Country, place (where available) and date of marriage
     - 3.3.1. Country of marriage:_____
     - 3.3.2. Place of marriage (where available):_____
     - 3.3.3. Date of marriage_____
4. Court which delivered the judgment
   - 4.1. Name of Court:_____
   - 4.2. Place of Court:_____
5. Judgment _____
   - 5.1. Date:_____
   - 5.2. Reference number:_____
   - 5.3. Type of judgment
     - 5.3.1. Divorce                                        ☐
     - 5.3.2. Marriage annulment                            ☐
     - 5.3.3. Legal separation                              ☐
   - 5.4. Was the judgment given in default of appearance?
     - 5.4.1. No                                            ☐
     - 5.4.2. Yes[1]                                        ☐

6. Names of parties to whom legal aid has been granted:_____
7. Is the judgment subject to further appeal under the law of the Member State of origin?
    7.1. ☐
    7.2. ☐
8. Date of legal effect in the Member State where the judgment was given
    8.1. Divorce:_____
    8.2. Legal separation:_____

Done at:_____ Date:_____

*Signature and/or stamp*
[1] Documents referred to in Article 32(2) must be attached.

## ANNEX V
*Certificate referred to in Article 33 concerning judgments on parental responsibility*

1. Country of origin:_____
2. Court or authority issuing the certificate
    2.1. Name:_____
    2.2. Address:_____
    2.3. Tel/Fax/E-mail:_____
3. Parents
    3.1. Mother
        3.1.1. Full name:_____
        3.1.2. Date and place of birth:_____
    3.2. Father
        3.2.1. Full name:_____
        3.2.2. Date and place of birth:_____
4. Court which delivered the judgment
    4.1. Name of Court:_____
    4.2. Place of Court:_____
5. Judgment
    5.1. Date:_____
    5.2. Reference number:_____
    5.3. Was the judgment given in default of appearance?
        5.3.1. No ☐
        5.3.2. Yes[1] ☐
6. Children who are covered by the judgment[2]
    6.1. Full name and date of birth:_____
    6.2. Full name and date of birth:_____
    6.3. Full name and date of birth:_____
    6.4. Full name and date of birth:_____
7. Names of parties to whom legal aid has been granted:_____
8. Attestation of enforceability and service
    8.1. Is the judgment enforceable according to the law of the Member State of origin?
        8.1.1. Yes ☐
        8.1.2. No ☐
    8.2. Has the judgment been served on the party against whom enforcement is sought?
        8.2.1. Yes ☐
        8.2.1.1. Full name of the party:_____
        8.2.1.2. Date of service:_____
        8.2.2. No ☐

Done at:_____ Date:_____
*Signature and/or stamp*
[1] Documents referred to in Article 32(2) must be attached.
[2] If more than four children are covered, use a second form.

## COUNCIL REGULATION (EC) NO 1348/2000

**of 29 May 2000**

on the service in the Member States of judicial and extrajudicial documents in civil or commercial matters

*       *       *       *       *

## CHAPTER III

JUDICIAL DOCUMENTS

SECTION 2

*Article 19*

*Defendant not entering an appearance*

1. Where a writ of summons or an equivalent document has had to be transmitted to another Member State for the purpose of service, under the provisions of this Regulation, and the defendant has not appeared, judgment shall not be given until it is established that:

    (a)  the document was served by a method prescribed by the internal law of the Member State addressed for the service of documents in domestic actions upon persons who are within its territory; or

    (b)  the document was actually delivered to the defendant or to his residence by another method provided for by this Regulation;

and that in either of these cases the service or the delivery was effected in sufficient time to enable the defendant to defend.

2. Each Member State shall be free to make it known, in accordance with Article 23(1), that the judge, notwithstanding the provisions of paragraph 1, may give judgment even if no certificate of service or delivery has been received, if all the following conditions are fulfilled:

    (a)  the document was transmitted by one of the methods provided for in this Regulation;

    (b)  a period of time of not less than six months, considered adequate by the judge in the particular case, has elapsed since the date of the transmission of the document;

    (c)  no certificate of any kind has been received, even though every reasonable effort has been made to obtain it through the competent authorities or bodies of the Member State addressed.

3. Notwithstanding paragraphs 1 and 2, the judge may order, in case of urgency, any provisional or protective measures.

4. When a writ of summons or an equivalent document has had to be transmitted to another Member State for the purpose of service, under the provisions of this Regulation, and a judgment has been entered against a defendant who has not appeared, the judge shall have the power to relieve the defendant from the effects of the expiration of the time for appeal from the judgment if the following conditions are fulfilled:

    (a)  the defendant, without any fault on his part, did not have knowledge of the document in sufficient time to defend, or knowledge of the judgment in sufficient time to appeal; and

    (b)  the defendant has disclosed a prima facie defence to the action on the merits.

An application for relief may be filed only within a reasonable time after the defendant has knowledge of the judgment.

Each Member State may make it known, in accordance with Article 23(1), that such application will not be entertained if it is filed after the expiration of a time to be stated by it in that communication, but which shall in no case be less than one year following the date of the judgment.

5. Paragraph 4 shall not apply to judgments concerning status or capacity of persons.

## COUNCIL REGULATION (EC) NO 44/2001

### of 22 December 2000

On jurisdiction and the recognition and enforcement of judgments in civil and commercial matters

THE COUNCIL OF THE EUROPEAN UNION,

Having regard to the Treaty establishing the European Community, and in particular Article 61(c) and Article 67(1) thereof,

Having regard to the proposal from the Commission[1],

Having regard to the opinion of the European Parliament[2],

Having regard to the opinion of the Economic and Social Committee[3],

Whereas:

(1) The Community has set itself the objective of maintaining and developing an area of freedom, security and justice, in which the free movement of persons is ensured. In order to establish progressively such an area, the Community should adopt, amongst other things, the measures relating to judicial cooperation in civil matters which are necessary for the sound operation of the internal market.

(2) Certain differences between national rules governing jurisdiction and recognition of judgments hamper the sound operation of the internal market. Provisions to unify the rules of conflict of jurisdiction in civil and commercial matters and to simplify the formalities with a view to rapid and simple recognition and enforcement of judgments from Member States bound by this Regulation are essential.

(3) This area is within the field of judicial cooperation in civil matters within the meaning of Article 65 of the Treaty.

(4) In accordance with the principles of subsidiarity and proportionality as set out in Article 5 of the Treaty, the objectives of this Regulation cannot be sufficiently achieved by the Member States and can therefore be better achieved by the Community. This Regulation confines itself to the minimum required in order to achieve those objectives and does not go beyond what is necessary for that purpose.

(5) On 27 September 1968 the Member States, acting under Article 293, fourth indent, of the Treaty, concluded the Brussels Convention on Jurisdiction and the Enforcement of Judgments in Civil and Commercial Matters, as amended by Conventions on the Accession of the New Member States to that Convention (hereinafter referred to as the 'Brussels Convention')[4]. On 16 September 1988 Member States and EFTA States concluded the Lugano Convention on Jurisdiction and the Enforcement of Judgments in Civil and Commercial Matters, which is a parallel Convention to the 1968 Brussels Convention. Work has been undertaken for the revision of those Conventions, and the Council has approved the content of the revised texts. Continuity in the results achieved in that revision should be ensured.

(6) In order to attain the objective of free movement of judgments in civil and commercial matters, it is necessary and appropriate that the rules governing jurisdiction and the recognition and enforcement of judgments be governed by a

Community legal instrument which is binding and directly applicable.

(7) The scope of this Regulation must cover all the main civil and commercial matters apart from certain well-defined matters.

(8) There must be a link between proceedings to which this Regulation applies and the territory of the Member States bound by this Regulation. Accordingly common rules on jurisdiction should, in principle, apply when the defendant is domiciled in one of those Member States.

(9) A defendant not domiciled in a Member State is in general subject to national rules of jurisdiction applicable in the territory of the Member State of the court seised, and a defendant domiciled in a Member State not bound by this Regulation must remain subject to the Brussels Convention.

(10) For the purposes of the free movement of judgments, judgments given in a Member State bound by this Regulation should be recognised and enforced in another Member State bound by this Regulation, even if the judgment debtor is domiciled in a third State.

(11) The rules of jurisdiction must be highly predictable and founded on the principle that jurisdiction is generally based on the defendant's domicile and jurisdiction must always be available on this ground save in a few well-defined situations in which the subject-matter of the litigation or the autonomy of the parties warrants a different linking factor. The domicile of a legal person must be defined autonomously so as to make the common rules more transparent and avoid conflicts of jurisdiction.

(12) In addition to the defendant's domicile, there should be alternative grounds of jurisdiction based on a close link between the court and the action or in order to facilitate the sound administration of justice.

(13) In relation to insurance, consumer contracts and employment, the weaker party should be protected by rules of jurisdiction more favourable to his interests than the general rules provide for.

(14) The autonomy of the parties to a contract, other than an insurance, consumer or employment contract, where only limited autonomy to determine the courts having jurisdiction is allowed, must be respected subject to the exclusive grounds of jurisdiction laid down in this Regulation.

(15) In the interests of the harmonious administration of justice it is necessary to minimise the possibility of concurrent proceedings and to ensure that irreconcilable judgments will not be given in two Member States. There must be a clear and effective mechanism for resolving cases of lis pendens and related actions and for obviating problems flowing from national differences as to the determination of the time when a case is regarded as pending. For the purposes of this Regulation that time should be defined autonomously.

(16) Mutual trust in the administration of justice in the Community justifies judgments given in a Member State being recognised automatically without the need for any procedure except in cases of dispute.

(17) By virtue of the same principle of mutual trust, the procedure for making enforceable in one Member State a judgment given in another must be efficient and rapid. To that end, the declaration that a judgment is enforceable should be issued virtually automatically after purely formal checks of the documents supplied, without there being any possibility for the court to raise of its own motion any of the grounds for non-enforcement provided for by this Regulation.

(18) However, respect for the rights of the defence means that the defendant should be able to appeal in an adversarial procedure, against the declaration of enforceability, if he considers one of the grounds for non-enforcement to be present. Redress procedures should also be available to the claimant where his application for a declaration of enforceability has been rejected.

(19) Continuity between the Brussels Convention and this Regulation should be ensured, and transitional provisions should be laid down to that end. The same

need for continuity applies as regards the interpretation of the Brussels Convention by the Court of Justice of the European Communities and the 1971 Protocol[5] should remain applicable also to cases already pending when this Regulation enters into force.

(20) The United Kingdom and Ireland, in accordance with Article 3 of the Protocol on the position of the United Kingdom and Ireland annexed to the Treaty on European Union and to the Treaty establishing the European Community, have given notice of their wish to take part in the adoption and application of this Regulation.

(21) Denmark, in accordance with Articles 1 and 2 of the Protocol on the position of Denmark annexed to the Treaty on European Union and to the Treaty establishing the European Community, is not participating in the adoption of this Regulation, and is therefore not bound by it nor subject to its application.

(22) Since the Brussels Convention remains in force in relations between Denmark and the Member States that are bound by this Regulation, both the Convention and the 1971 Protocol continue to apply between Denmark and the Member States bound by this Regulation.

(23) The Brussels Convention also continues to apply to the territories of the Member States which fall within the territorial scope of that Convention and which are excluded from this Regulation pursuant to Article 299 of the Treaty.

(24) Likewise for the sake of consistency, this Regulation should not affect rules governing jurisdiction and the recognition of judgments contained in specific Community instruments.

(25) Respect for international commitments entered into by the Member States means that this Regulation should not affect conventions relating to specific matters to which the Member States are parties.

(26) The necessary flexibility should be provided for in the basic rules of this Regulation in order to take account of the specific procedural rules of certain Member States. Certain provisions of the Protocol annexed to the Brussels Convention should accordingly be incorporated in this Regulation.

(27) In order to allow a harmonious transition in certain areas which were the subject of special provisions in the Protocol annexed to the Brussels Convention, this Regulation lays down, for a transitional period, provisions taking into consideration the specific situation in certain Member States.

(28) No later than five years after entry into force of this Regulation the Commission will present a report on its application and, if need be, submit proposals for adaptations.

(29) The Commission will have to adjust Annexes I to IV on the rules of national jurisdiction, the courts or competent authorities and redress procedures available on the basis of the amendments forwarded by the Member State concerned; amendments made to Annexes V and VI should be adopted in accordance with Council Decision 1999/468/EC of 28 June 1999 laying down the procedures for the exercise of implementing powers conferred on the Commission[6],

HAS ADOPTED THIS REGULATION:

[1] OJ C 376, 28.12.1999, p 1.
[2] Opinion delivered on 21 September 2000 (not yet published in the Official Journal).
[3] OJ C 117, 26.4.2000, p 6.
[4] OJ L 299, 31.12.1972, p 32. OJ L 304, 30.10.1978, p 1. OJ L 388, 31.12.1982, p 1. OJ L 285, 3.10.1989, p 1. OJ C 15, 15.1.1997, p 1. For a consolidated text, see OJ C 27, 26.1.1998, p 1.
[5] OJ L 204, 2.8.1975, p 28. OJ L 304, 30.10.1978, p 1. OJ L 388, 31.12.1982, p 1. OJ L 285, 3.10.1989, p. 1. OJ C 15, 15.1.1997, p 1. For a consolidated text see OJ C 27, 26.1.1998, p 28.
[6] OJ L 184, 17.7.1999, p 23.

## CHAPTER I

## SCOPE

*Article 1*

1. This Regulation shall apply in civil and commercial matters whatever the nature of the court or tribunal. It shall not extend, in particular, to revenue, customs or administrative matters.

2. The Regulation shall not apply to:
(a) the status or legal capacity of natural persons, rights in property arising out of a matrimonial relationship, wills and succession;
(b) bankruptcy, proceedings relating to the winding-up of insolvent companies or other legal persons, judicial arrangements, compositions and analogous proceedings;
(c) social security;
(d) arbitration.

3. In this Regulation, the term 'Member State' shall mean Member States with the exception of Denmark.

## CHAPTER II

## JURISDICTION

### Section 1

#### General provisions

*Article 2*

1. Subject to this Regulation, persons domiciled in a Member State shall, whatever their nationality, be sued in the courts of that Member State.

2. Persons who are not nationals of the Member State in which they are domiciled shall be governed by the rules of jurisdiction applicable to nationals of that State.

*Article 3*

1. Persons domiciled in a Member State may be sued in the courts of another Member State only by virtue of the rules set out in Sections 2 to 7 of this Chapter.

2. In particular the rules of national jurisdiction set out in Annex I shall not be applicable as against them.

*Article 4*

1. If the defendant is not domiciled in a Member State, the jurisdiction of the courts of each Member State shall, subject to Articles 22 and 23, be determined by the law of that Member State.

2. As against such a defendant, any person domiciled in a Member State may, whatever his nationality, avail himself in that State of the rules of jurisdiction there in force, and in particular those specified in Annex I, in the same way as the nationals of that State.

### Section 2

#### Special jurisdiction

*Article 5*

A person domiciled in a Member State may, in another Member State, be sued:
1.
(a) in matters relating to a contract, in the courts for the place of performance of the obligation in question;

   (b)  for the purpose of this provision and unless otherwise agreed, the place of performance of the obligation in question shall be:
- in the case of the sale of goods, the place in a Member State where, under the contract, the goods were delivered or should have been delivered,
- in the case of the provision of services, the place in a Member State where, under the contract, the services were provided or should have been provided,

   (c)  if subparagraph (b) does not apply then subparagraph (a) applies;

2.  in matters relating to maintenance, in the courts for the place where the maintenance creditor is domiciled or habitually resident or, if the matter is ancillary to proceedings concerning the status of a person, in the court which, according to its own law, has jurisdiction to entertain those proceedings, unless that jurisdiction is based solely on the nationality of one of the parties;

3.  in matters relating to tort, delict or quasi-delict, in the courts for the place where the harmful event occurred or may occur;

4.  as regards a civil claim for damages or restitution which is based on an act giving rise to criminal proceedings, in the court seised of those proceedings, to the extent that that court has jurisdiction under its own law to entertain civil proceedings;

5.  as regards a dispute arising out of the operations of a branch, agency or other establishment, in the courts for the place in which the branch, agency or other establishment is situated;

6.  as settlor, trustee or beneficiary of a trust created by the operation of a statute, or by a written instrument, or created orally and evidenced in writing, in the courts of the Member State in which the trust is domiciled;

7.  as regards a dispute concerning the payment of remuneration claimed in respect of the salvage of a cargo or freight, in the court under the authority of which the cargo or freight in question:

   (a)  has been arrested to secure such payment, or

   (b)  could have been so arrested, but bail or other security has been given; provided that this provision shall apply only if it is claimed that the defendant has an interest in the cargo or freight or had such an interest at the time of salvage.

## Article 6

A person domiciled in a Member State may also be sued:

1.  where he is one of a number of defendants, in the courts for the place where any one of them is domiciled, provided the claims are so closely connected that it is expedient to hear and determine them together to avoid the risk of irreconcilable judgments resulting from separate proceedings;

2.  as a third party in an action on a warranty or guarantee or in any other third party proceedings, in the court seised of the original proceedings, unless these were instituted solely with the object of removing him from the jurisdiction of the court which would be competent in his case;

3.  on a counter-claim arising from the same contract or facts on which the original claim was based, in the court in which the original claim is pending;

4.  in matters relating to a contract, if the action may be combined with an action against the same defendant in matters relating to rights in rem in immovable property, in the court of the Member State in which the property is situated.

## Article 7

Where by virtue of this Regulation a court of a Member State has jurisdiction in actions relating to liability from the use or operation of a ship, that court, or any other court substituted for this purpose by the internal law of that Member State, shall also have jurisdiction over claims for limitation of such liability.

## SECTION 3

### JURISDICTION IN MATTERS RELATING TO INSURANCE

*Article 8*

In matters relating to insurance, jurisdiction shall be determined by this Section, without prejudice to Article 4 and point 5 of Article 5.

*Article 9*

1. An insurer domiciled in a Member State may be sued:
   (a) in the courts of the Member State where he is domiciled, or
   (b) in another Member State, in the case of actions brought by the policyholder, the insured or a beneficiary, in the courts for the place where the plaintiff is domiciled,
   (c) if he is a co-insurer, in the courts of a Member State in which proceedings are brought against the leading insurer.
   2. An insurer who is not domiciled in a Member State but has a branch, agency or other establishment in one of the Member tates shall, in disputes arising out of the operations of the branch, agency or establishment, be deemed to be domiciled in that Member State.

*Article 10*

In respect of liability insurance or insurance of immovable property, the insurer may in addition be sued in the courts for the place where the harmful event occurred. The same applies if movable and immovable property are covered by the same insurance policy and both are adversely affected by the same contingency.

*Article 11*

1. In respect of liability insurance, the insurer may also, if the law of the court permits it, be joined in proceedings which the injured party has brought against the insured.
   2. Articles 8, 9 and 10 shall apply to actions brought by the injured party directly against the insurer, where such direct actions are permitted.
   3. If the law governing such direct actions provides that the policyholder or the insured may be joined as a party to the action, the same court shall have jurisdiction over them.

*Article 12*

1. Without prejudice to Article 11(3), an insurer may bring proceedings only in the courts of the Member State in which the defendant is domiciled, irrespective of whether he is the policyholder, the insured or a beneficiary.
   2. The provisions of this Section shall not affect the right to bring a counter-claim in the court in which, in accordance with this Section, the original claim is pending.

*Article 13*

The provisions of this Section may be departed from only by an agreement:
   1. which is entered into after the dispute has arisen, or
   2. which allows the policyholder, the insured or a beneficiary to bring proceedings in courts other than those indicated in this Section, or

3. which is concluded between a policyholder and an insurer, both of whom are at the time of conclusion of the contract domiciled or habitually resident in the same Member State, and which has the effect of conferring jurisdiction on the courts of that State even if the harmful event were to occur abroad, provided that such an agreement is not contrary to the law of that State, or

4. which is concluded with a policyholder who is not domiciled in a Member State, except in so far as the insurance is compulsory or relates to immovable property in a Member State, or

5. which relates to a contract of insurance in so far as it covers one or more of the risks set out in Article 14.

*Article 14*

The following are the risks referred to in Article 13(5):
1. any loss of or damage to:
(a) seagoing ships, installations situated offshore or on the high seas, or aircraft, arising from perils which relate to their use for commercial purposes;
(b) goods in transit other than passengers' baggage where the transit consists of or includes carriage by such ships or aircraft;
2. any liability, other than for bodily injury to passengers or loss of or damage to their baggage:
(a) arising out of the use or operation of ships, installations or aircraft as referred to in point 1(a) in so far as, in respect of the latter, the law of the Member State in which such aircraft are registered does not prohibit agreements on jurisdiction regarding insurance of such risks;
(b) for loss or damage caused by goods in transit as described in point 1(b);
3. any financial loss connected with the use or operation of ships, installations or aircraft as referred to in point 1(a), in particular loss of freight or charter-hire;
4. any risk or interest connected with any of those referred to in points 1 to 3;
5. notwithstanding points 1 to 4, all 'large risks' as defined in Council Directive 73/239/EEC[1], as amended by Council Directives 88/357/EEC[2] and 90/618/EEC[3], as they may be amended.

[1] OJ L 228, 16.8.1973, p 3. Directive as last amended by Directive 2000/26/EC of the European Parliament and of the Council (OJ L 181, 20.7.2000, p 65).
[2] OJ L 172, 4.7.1988, p 1. Directive as last amended by Directive 2000/26/EC.
[3] OJ L 330, 29.11.1990, p 44.

SECTION 4

JURISDICTION OVER CONSUMER CONTRACTS

*Article 15*

1. In matters relating to a contract concluded by a person, the consumer, for a purpose which can be regarded as being outside his trade or profession, jurisdiction shall be determined by this Section, without prejudice to Article 4 and point 5 of Article 5, if:
(a) it is a contract for the sale of goods on instalment credit terms; or
(b) it is a contract for a loan repayable by instalments, or for any other form of credit, made to finance the sale of goods; or
(c) in all other cases, the contract has been concluded with a person who pursues commercial or professional activities in the Member State of the consumer's domicile or, by any means, directs such activities to that Member State or to several States including that Member State, and the contract falls within the scope of such activities.
2. Where a consumer enters into a contract with a party who is not domiciled in the Member State but has a branch, agency or other establishment in one of the

Member States, that party shall, in disputes arising out of the operations of the branch, agency or establishment, be deemed to be domiciled in that State.

3. This Section shall not apply to a contract of transport other than a contract which, for an inclusive price, provides for a combination of travel and accommodation.

*Article 16*

1. A consumer may bring proceedings against the other party to a contract either in the courts of the Member State in which that party is domiciled or in the courts for the place where the consumer is domiciled.

2. Proceedings may be brought against a consumer by the other party to the contract only in the courts of the Member State in which the consumer is domiciled.

3. This Article shall not affect the right to bring a counter-claim in the court in which, in accordance with this Section, the original claim is pending.

*Article 17*

The provisions of this Section may be departed from only by an agreement:
  1. which is entered into after the dispute has arisen; or
  2. which allows the consumer to bring proceedings in courts other than those indicated in this Section; or
  3. which is entered into by the consumer and the other party to the contract, both of whom are at the time of conclusion of the contract domiciled or habitually resident in the same Member State, and which confers jurisdiction on the courts of that Member State, provided that such an agreement is not contrary to the law of that Member State.

SECTION 5

JURISDICTION OVER INDIVIDUAL CONTRACTS OF EMPLOYMENT

*Article 18*

1. In matters relating to individual contracts of employment, jurisdiction shall be determined by this Section, without prejudice to Article 4 and point 5 of Article 5.

2. Where an employee enters into an individual contract of employment with an employer who is not domiciled in a Member State but has a branch, agency or other establishment in one of the Member States, the employer shall, in disputes arising out of the operations of the branch, agency or establishment, be deemed to be domiciled in that Member State.

*Article 19*

An employer domiciled in a Member State may be sued:
  1. in the courts of the Member State where he is domiciled; or
  2. in another Member State:
  (a) in the courts for the place where the employee habitually carries out his work or in the courts for the last place where he did so, or
  (b) if the employee does not or did not habitually carry out his work in any one country, in the courts for the place where the business which engaged the employee is or was situated.

*Article 20*

1. An employer may bring proceedings only in the courts of the Member State in which the employee is domiciled.

2. The provisions of this Section shall not affect the right to bring a counter-claim in the court in which, in accordance with this Section, the original claim is pending.

### Article 21

The provisions of this Section may be departed from only by an agreement on jurisdiction:

    1. which is entered into after the dispute has arisen; or

    2. which allows the employee to bring proceedings in courts other than those indicated in this Section.

### SECTION 6

#### EXCLUSIVE JURISDICTION

### Article 22

The following courts shall have exclusive jurisdiction, regardless of domicile:

    1. in proceedings which have as their object rights in rem in immovable property or tenancies of immovable property, the courts of the Member State in which the property is situated.However, in proceedings which have as their object tenancies of immovable property concluded for temporary private use for a maximum period of six consecutive months, the courts of the Member State in which the defendant is domiciled shall also have jurisdiction, provided that the tenant is a natural person and that the landlord and the tenant are domiciled in the same Member State;

    2. in proceedings which have as their object the validity of the constitution, the nullity or the dissolution of companies or other legal persons or associations of natural or legal persons, or of the validity of the decisions of their organs, the courts of the Member State in which the company, legal person or association has its seat. In order to determine that seat, the court shall apply its rules of private international law;

    3. in proceedings which have as their object the validity of entries in public registers, the courts of the Member State in which the register is kept;

    4. in proceedings concerned with the registration or validity of patents, trade marks, designs, or other similar rights required to be deposited or registered, the courts of the Member State in which the deposit or registration has been applied for, has taken place or is under the terms of a Community instrument or an international convention deemed to have taken place.

Without prejudice to the jurisdiction of the European Patent Office under the Convention on the Grant of European Patents, signed at Munich on 5 October 1973, the courts of each Member State shall have exclusive jurisdiction, regardless of domicile, in proceedings concerned with the registration or validity of any European patent granted for that State;

    5. in proceedings concerned with the enforcement of judgments, the courts of the Member State in which the judgment has been or is to be enforced.

### SECTION 7

#### PROROGATION OF JURISDICTION

### Article 23

1. If the parties, one or more of whom is domiciled in a Member State, have agreed that a court or the courts of a Member State are to have jurisdiction to settle any disputes which have arisen or which may arise in connection with a particular legal relationship, that court or those courts shall have jurisdiction. Such

jurisdiction shall be exclusive unless the parties have agreed otherwise. Such an agreement conferring jurisdiction shall be either:

(a) in writing or evidenced in writing; or

(b) in a form which accords with practices which the parties have established between themselves; or

(c) in international trade or commerce, in a form which accords with a usage of which the parties are or ought to have been aware and which in such trade or commerce is widely known to, and regularly observed by, parties to contracts of the type involved in the particular trade or commerce concerned.

2. Any communication by electronic means which provides a durable record of the agreement shall be equivalent to 'writing'.

3. Where such an agreement is concluded by parties, none of whom is domiciled in a Member State, the courts of other Member States shall have no jurisdiction over their disputes unless the court or courts chosen have declined jurisdiction.

4. The court or courts of a Member State on which a trust instrument has conferred jurisdiction shall have exclusive jurisdiction in any proceedings brought against a settlor, trustee or beneficiary, if relations between these persons or their rights or obligations under the trust are involved.

5. Agreements or provisions of a trust instrument conferring jurisdiction shall have no legal force if they are contrary to Articles 13, 17 or 21, or if the courts whose jurisdiction they purport to exclude have exclusive jurisdiction by virtue of Article 22.

*Article 24*

Apart from jurisdiction derived from other provisions of this egulation, a court of a Member State before which a defendant enters an appearance shall have jurisdiction. This rule shall not apply where appearance was entered to contest the jurisdiction, or where another court has exclusive jurisdiction by virtue of Article 22.

SECTION 8

EXAMINATION AS TO JURISDICTION AND ADMISSIBILITY

*Article 25*

Where a court of a Member State is seised of a claim which is principally concerned with a matter over which the courts of another Member State have exclusive jurisdiction by virtue of Article 22, it shall declare of its own motion that it has no jurisdiction.

*Article 26*

1. Where a defendant domiciled in one Member State is sued in a court of another Member State and does not enter an appearance, the court shall declare of its own motion that it has no jurisdiction unless its jurisdiction is derived from the provisions of this Regulation.

2. The court shall stay the proceedings so long as it is not shown that the defendant has been able to receive the document instituting the proceedings or an equivalent document in sufficient time to enable him to arrange for his defence, or that all necessary steps have been taken to this end.

3. Article 19 of Council Regulation (EC) No 1348/2000 of 29 May 2000 on the service in the Member States of judicial and extrajudicial documents in civil or commercial matters[1] shall apply instead of the provisions of paragraph 2 if the

document instituting the proceedings or an equivalent document had to be transmitted from one Member State to another pursuant to this Regulation.

4. Where the provisions of Regulation (EC) No 1348/2000 are not applicable, Article 15 of the Hague Convention of 15 November 1965 on the Service Abroad of Judicial and Extrajudicial Documents in Civil or Commercial Matters shall apply if the document instituting the proceedings or an equivalent document had to be transmitted pursuant to that Convention.

[1] OJ L 160, 30.6.2000, p 37.

## SECTION 9

### LIS PENDENS — RELATED ACTIONS

*Article 27*

1. Where proceedings involving the same cause of action and between the same parties are brought in the courts of different Member States, any court other than the court first seised shall of its own motion stay its proceedings until such time as the jurisdiction of the court first seised is established.

2. Where the jurisdiction of the court first seised is established, any court other than the court first seised shall decline jurisdiction in favour of that court.

*Article 28*

1. Where related actions are pending in the courts of different Member States, any court other than the court first seised may stay its proceedings.

2. Where these actions are pending at first instance, any court other than the court first seised may also, on the application of one of the parties, decline jurisdiction if the court first seised has jurisdiction over the actions in question and its law permits the consolidation thereof.

3. For the purposes of this Article, actions are deemed to be related where they are so closely connected that it is expedient to hear and determine them together to avoid the risk of irreconcilable judgments resulting from separate proceedings.

*Article 29*

Where actions come within the exclusive jurisdiction of several courts, any court other than the court first seised shall decline jurisdiction in favour of that court.

*Article 30*

For the purposes of this Section, a court shall be deemed to be seised:

1. at the time when the document instituting the proceedings or an equivalent document is lodged with the court, provided that the plaintiff has not subsequently failed to take the steps he was required to take to have service effected on the defendant, or

2. if the document has to be served before being lodged with the court, at the time when it is received by the authority responsible for service, provided that the plaintiff has not subsequently failed to take the steps he was required to take to have the document lodged with the court.

## SECTION 10

### PROVISIONAL, INCLUDING PROTECTIVE, MEASURES

*Article 31*

Application may be made to the courts of a Member State for such provisional, including protective, measures as may be available under the law of that State, even if, under this Regulation, the courts of another Member State have jurisdiction as to the substance of the matter.

## CHAPTER III

## RECOGNITION AND ENFORCEMENT

*Article 32*

For the purposes of this Regulation, 'judgment' means any judgment given by a court or tribunal of a Member State, whatever the judgment may be called, including a decree, order, decision or writ of execution, as well as the determination of costs or expenses by an officer of the court.

SECTION 1

RECOGNITION

*Article 33*

1. A judgment given in a Member State shall be recognised in the other Member States without any special procedure being required.

2. Any interested party who raises the recognition of a judgment as the principal issue in a dispute may, in accordance with the procedures provided for in Sections 2 and 3 of this Chapter, apply for a decision that the judgment be recognised.

3. If the outcome of proceedings in a court of a Member State depends on the determination of an incidental question of recognition that court shall have jurisdiction over that question.

*Article 34*

A judgment shall not be recognised:

1. if such recognition is manifestly contrary to public policy in the Member State in which recognition is sought;

2. where it was given in default of appearance, if the defendant was not served with the document which instituted the proceedings or with an equivalent document in sufficient time and in such a way as to enable him to arrange for his defence, unless the defendant failed to commence proceedings to challenge the judgment when it was possible for him to do so;

3. if it is irreconcilable with a judgment given in a dispute between the same parties in the Member State in which recognition is sought;

4. if it is irreconcilable with an earlier judgment given in another Member State or in a third State involving the same cause of action and between the same parties, provided that the earlier judgment fulfils the conditions necessary for its recognition in the Member State addressed.

*Article 35*

1. Moreover, a judgment shall not be recognised if it conflicts with Sections 3, 4 or 6 of Chapter II, or in a case provided for in Article 72.

2. In its examination of the grounds of jurisdiction referred to in the foregoing paragraph, the court or authority applied to shall be bound by the findings of fact on which the court of the Member State of origin based its jurisdiction.

3. Subject to the paragraph 1, the jurisdiction of the court of the Member State of origin may not be reviewed. The test of public policy referred to in point 1 of Article 34 may not be applied to the rules relating to jurisdiction.

*Article 36*

Under no circumstances may a foreign judgment be reviewed as to its substance.

*Article 37*

1. A court of a Member State in which recognition is sought of a judgment given in another Member State may stay the proceedings if an ordinary appeal against the judgment has been lodged.

2. A court of a Member State in which recognition is sought of a judgment given in Ireland or the United Kingdom may stay the proceedings if enforcement is suspended in the State of origin, by reason of an appeal.

SECTION 2

ENFORCEMENT

*Article 38*

1. A judgment given in a Member State and enforceable in that State shall be enforced in another Member State when, on the application of any interested party, it has been declared enforceable there.

2. However, in the United Kingdom, such a judgment shall be enforced in England and Wales, in Scotland, or in Northern Ireland when, on the application of any interested party, it has been registered for enforcement in that part of the United Kingdom.

*Article 39*

1. The application shall be submitted to the court or competent authority indicated in the list in Annex II.

2. The local jurisdiction shall be determined by reference to the place of domicile of the party against whom enforcement is sought, or to the place of enforcement.

*Article 40*

1. The procedure for making the application shall be governed by the law of the Member State in which enforcement is sought.

2. The applicant must give an address for service of process within the area of jurisdiction of the court applied to. However, if the law of the Member State in which enforcement is sought does not provide for the furnishing of such an address, the applicant shall appoint a representative ad item.

3. The documents referred to in Article 53 shall be attached to the application.

*Article 41*

The judgment shall be declared enforceable immediately on completion of the formalities in Article 53 without any review under Articles 34 and 35. The party against whom enforcement is sought shall not at this stage of the proceedings be entitled to make any submissions on the application.

*Article 42*

1. The decision on the application for a declaration of enforceability shall forthwith be brought to the notice of the applicant in accordance with the procedure laid down by the law of the Member State in which enforcement is sought.

2. The declaration of enforceability shall be served on the party against whom enforcement is sought, accompanied by the judgment, if not already served on that party.

*Article 43*

1. The decision on the application for a declaration of enforceability may be appealed against by either party.

2. The appeal is to be lodged with the court indicated in the list in Annex III.

3. The appeal shall be dealt with in accordance with the rules governing procedure in contradictory matters.

4. If the party against whom enforcement is sought fails to appear before the appellate court in proceedings concerning an appeal brought by the applicant, Article 26(2) to (4) shall apply even where the party against whom enforcement is sought is not domiciled in any of the Member States.

5. An appeal against the declaration of enforceability is to be lodged within one month of service thereof. If the party against whom enforcement is sought is domiciled in a Member State other than that in which the declaration of enforceability was given, the time for appealing shall be two months and shall run from the date of service, either on him in person or at his residence. No extension of time may be granted on account of distance.

*Article 44*

The judgment given on the appeal may be contested only by the appeal referred to in Annex IV.

*Article 45*

1. The court with which an appeal is lodged under Article 43 or Article 44 shall refuse or revoke a declaration of enforceability only on one of the grounds specified in Articles 34 and 35. It shall give its decision without delay.

2. Under no circumstances may the foreign judgment be reviewed as to its substance.

*Article 46*

1. The court with which an appeal is lodged under Article 43 or Article 44 may, on the application of the party against whom enforcement is sought, stay the proceedings if an ordinary appeal has been lodged against the judgment in the Member State of origin or if the time for such an appeal has not yet expired; in the latter case, the court may specify the time within which such an appeal is to be lodged.

2. Where the judgment was given in Ireland or the United Kingdom, any form of appeal available in the Member State of origin shall be treated as an ordinary appeal for the purposes of paragraph 1.

3. The court may also make enforcement conditional on the provision of such security as it shall determine.

*Article 47*

1. When a judgment must be recognised in accordance with this regulation, nothing shall prevent the applicant from availing himself of provisional, including protective, measures in accordance with the law of the Member State requested without a declaration of enforceability under Article 41 being required.

2. The declaration of enforceability shall carry with it the power to proceed to any protective measures.

3. During the time specified for an appeal pursuant to Article 43(5) against the declaration of enforceability and until any such appeal has been determined, no measures of enforcement may be taken other than protective measures against the property of the party against whom enforcement is sought.

*Article 48*

1. Where a foreign judgment has been given in respect of several matters and the declaration of enforceability cannot be given for all of them, the court or competent authority shall give it for one or more of them.

2. An applicant may request a declaration of enforceability limited to parts of a judgment.

*Article 49*

A foreign judgment which orders a periodic payment by way of a penalty shall be enforceable in the Member State in which enforcement is sought only if the amount of the payment has been finally determined by the courts of the Member State of origin.

*Article 50*

An applicant who, in the Member State of origin has benefited from complete or partial legal aid or exemption from costs or expenses, shall be entitled, in the procedure provided for in this Section, to benefit from the most favourable legal aid or the most extensive exemption from costs or expenses provided for by the law of the Member State addressed.

*Article 51*

No security, bond or deposit, however described, shall be required of a party who in one Member State applies for enforcement of a judgment given in another Member State on the ground that he is a foreign national or that he is not domiciled or resident in the State in which enforcement is sought.

*Article 52*

In proceedings for the issue of a declaration of enforceability, no charge, duty or fee calculated by reference to the value of the matter at issue may be levied in the Member State in which enforcement is sought.

SECTION 3

COMMON PROVISIONS

*Article 53*

1. A party seeking recognition or applying for a declaration of enforceability shall produce a copy of the judgment which satisfies the conditions necessary to establish its authenticity.

2. A party applying for a declaration of enforceability shall also produce the certificate referred to in Article 54, without prejudice to Article 55.

*Article 54*

The court or competent authority of a Member State where a judgment was given shall issue, at the request of any interested party, a certificate using the standard form in Annex V to this Regulation.

*Article 55*

1. If the certificate referred to in Article 54 is not produced, the court or competent authority may specify a time for its production or accept an equivalent document or, if it considers that it has sufficient information before it, dispense with its production.

2. If the court or competent authority so requires, a ranslation of the documents shall be produced. The translation shall be certified by a person qualified to do so in one of the Member States.

### Article 56

No legalisation or other similar formality shall be required in respect of the documents referred to in Article 53 or Article 55(2), or in respect of a document appointing a representative ad litem.

## CHAPTER IV

### AUTHENTIC INSTRUMENTS AND COURT SETTLEMENTS

### Article 57

1. A document which has been formally drawn up or registered as an authentic instrument and is enforceable in one Member State shall, in another Member State, be declared enforceable there, on application made in accordance with the procedures provided for in Articles 38, et seq. The court with which an appeal is lodged under Article 43 or Article 44 shall refuse or revoke a declaration of enforceability only if enforcement of the instrument is manifestly contrary to public policy in the Member State addressed.

2. Arrangements relating to maintenance obligations concluded with administrative authorities or authenticated by them shall also be regarded as authentic instruments within the meaning of paragraph 1.

3. The instrument produced must satisfy the conditions necessary to establish its authenticity in the Member State of origin.

4. Section 3 of Chapter III shall apply as appropriate. The competent authority of a Member State where an authentic instrument was drawn up or registered shall issue, at the request of any interested party, a certificate using the standard form in Annex VI to this Regulation.

### Article 58

A settlement which has been approved by a court in the course of proceedings and is enforceable in the Member State in which it was concluded shall be enforceable in the State addressed under the same conditions as authentic instruments. The court or competent authority of a Member State where a court settlement was approved shall issue, at the request of any interested party, a certificate using the standard form in Annex V to this Regulation.

## CHAPTER V

### GENERAL PROVISIONS

### Article 59

1. In order to determine whether a party is domiciled in the Member State whose courts are seised of a matter, the court shall apply its internal law.

2. If a party is not domiciled in the Member State whose courts are seised of the matter, then, in order to determine whether the party is domiciled in another Member State, the court shall apply the law of that Member State.

### Article 60

1. For the purposes of this Regulation, a company or other legal person or association of natural or legal persons is domiciled at the place where it has its:

(a) statutory seat, or
(b) central administration, or
(c) principal place of business.

2. For the purposes of the United Kingdom and Ireland 'statutory seat' means the registered office or, where there is no such office anywhere, the place of incorporation or, where there is no such place anywhere, the place under the law of which the formation took place.

3. In order to determine whether a trust is domiciled in the Member State whose courts are seised of the matter, the court shall apply its rules of private international law.

### Article 61

Without prejudice to any more favourable provisions of national laws, persons domiciled in a Member State who are being prosecuted in the criminal courts of another Member State of which they are not nationals for an offence which was not intentionally committed may be defended by persons qualified to do so, even if they do not appear in person. However, the court seised of the matter may order appearance in person; in the case of failure to appear, a judgment given in the civil action without the person concerned having had the opportunity to arrange for his defence need not be recognised or enforced in the other Member States.

### Article 62

In Sweden, in summary proceedings concerning orders to pay (betalningsföreläggande) and assistance (handräckning), the expression 'court' includes the 'Swedish enforcement service' (kronofogdemyndighet).

### Article 63

1. A person domiciled in the territory of the Grand Duchy of Luxembourg and sued in the court of another Member State pursuant to Article 5(1) may refuse to submit to the jurisdiction of that court if the final place of delivery of the goods or provision of the services is in Luxembourg.

2. Where, under paragraph 1, the final place of delivery of the goods or provision of the services is in Luxembourg, any agreement conferring jurisdiction must, in order to be valid, be accepted in writing or evidenced in writing within the meaning of Article 23(1)(a).

3. The provisions of this Article shall not apply to contracts for the provision of financial services.

4. The provisions of this Article shall apply for a period of six years from entry into force of this Regulation.

### Article 64

1. In proceedings involving a dispute between the master and a member of the crew of a seagoing ship registered in Greece or in Portugal, concerning remuneration or other conditions of service, a court in a Member State shall establish whether the diplomatic or consular officer responsible for the ship has been notified of the dispute. It may act as soon as that officer has been notified.

2. The provisions of this Article shall apply for a period of six years from entry into force of this Regulation.

### Article 65

1. The jurisdiction specified in Article 6(2), and Article 11 in actions on a warranty of guarantee or in any other third party proceedings may not be resorted

to in Germany and Austria. Any person domiciled in another Member State may be sued in the courts:

(a) of Germany, pursuant to Articles 68 and 72 to 74 of the Code of Civil Procedure (Zivilprozessordnung) concerning third-party notices,

(b) of Austria, pursuant to Article 21 of the Code of Civil Procedure (Zivilprozessordnung) concerning third-party notices.

2. Judgments given in other Member States by virtue of Article 6(2), or Article 11 shall be recognised and enforced in Germany and Austria in accordance with Chapter III. Any effects which judgments given in these States may have on third parties by application of the provisions in paragraph 1 shall also be recognised in the other Member States.

## CHAPTER VI

## TRANSITIONAL PROVISIONS

### Article 66

1. This Regulation shall apply only to legal proceedings instituted and to documents formally drawn up or registered as authentic instruments after the entry into force thereof.

2. However, if the proceedings in the Member State of origin were instituted before the entry into force of this Regulation, judgments given after that date shall be recognised and enforced in accordance with Chapter III,

(a) if the proceedings in the Member State of origin were instituted after the entry into force of the Brussels or the Lugano Convention both in the Member State or origin and in the Member State addressed;

(b) in all other cases, if jurisdiction was founded upon rules which accorded with those provided for either in Chapter II or in a convention concluded between the Member State of origin and the Member State addressed which was in force when the proceedings were instituted.

## CHAPTER VII

## RELATIONS WITH OTHER INSTRUMENTS

### Article 67

This Regulation shall not prejudice the application of provisions governing jurisdiction and the recognition and enforcement of judgments in specific matters which are contained in Community instruments or in national legislation harmonised pursuant to such instruments.

### Article 68

1. This Regulation shall, as between the Member States, supersede the Brussels Convention, except as regards the territories of the Member States which fall within the territorial scope of that Convention and which are excluded from this Regulation pursuant to Article 299 of the Treaty.

2. In so far as this Regulation replaces the provisions of the Brussels Convention between Member States, any reference to the Convention shall be understood as a reference to this Regulation.

### Article 69

Subject to Article 66(2) and Article 70, this Regulation shall, as between Member States, supersede the following conventions and treaty concluded between two or more of them:

– the Convention between Belgium and France on Jurisdiction and the

Validity and Enforcement of Judgments, Arbitration Awards and Authentic Instruments, signed at Paris on 8 July 1899,

- the Convention between Belgium and the Netherlands on Jurisdiction, Bankruptcy, and the Validity and Enforcement of Judgments, Arbitration Awards and Authentic Instruments, signed at Brussels on 28 March 1925,
- the Convention between France and Italy on the Enforcement of Judgments in Civil and Commercial Matters, signed at Rome on 3 June 1930,

[- the Convention between the United Kingdom and the French Republic providing for the reciprocal enforcement of judgments in civil and commercial matters, with Protocol, signed at Paris on 18 January 1934,
- the Convention between the United Kingdom and the Kingdom of Belgium providing for the reciprocal enforcement of judgments in civil and commercial matters, with Protocol, signed at Brussels on 2 May 1934,]
- the Convention between Germany and Italy on the Recognition and Enforcement of Judgments in Civil and Commercial Matters, signed at Rome on 9 March 1936,
- the Convention between Belgium and Austria on the Reciprocal Recognition and Enforcement of Judgments and Authentic Instruments relating to Maintenance Obligations, signed at Vienna on 25 October 1957,
- the Convention between Germany and Belgium on the Mutual Recognition and Enforcement of Judgments, Arbitration Awards and Authentic Instruments in Civil and Commercial Matters, signed at Bonn on 30 June 1958,
- the Convention between the Netherlands and Italy on the Recognition and Enforcement of Judgments in Civil and Commercial Matters, signed at Rome on 17 April 1959,
- the Convention between Germany and Austria on the Reciprocal Recognition and Enforcement of Judgments, Settlements and Authentic Instruments in Civil and Commercial Matters, signed at Vienna on 6 June 1959,
- the Convention between Belgium and Austria on the Reciprocal Recognition and Enforcement of Judgments, Arbitral Awards and Authentic Instruments in Civil and Commercial Matters, signed at Vienna on 16 June 1959,

[- the Convention between the United Kingdom and the Federal Republic of Germany for the reciprocal recognition and enforcement of judgments in civil and commercial matters, signed at Bonn on 14 July 1960,
- the Convention between the United Kingdom and Austria providing for the reciprocal recognition and enforcement of judgments in civil and commercial matters, signed at Vienna on 14 July 1961, with amending Protocol signed at London on 6 March 1970,]
- the Convention between Greece and Germany for the Reciprocal Recognition and Enforcement of Judgments, Settlements and Authentic Instruments in Civil and Commercial Matters, signed in Athens on 4 November 1961,
- the Convention between Belgium and Italy on the Recognition and Enforcement of Judgments and other Enforceable Instruments in Civil and Commercial Matters, signed at Rome on 6 April 1962,
- the Convention between the Netherlands and Germany on the Mutual Recognition and Enforcement of Judgments and Other Enforceable Instruments in Civil and Commercial Matters, signed at The Hague on 30 August 1962,
- the Convention between the Netherlands and Austria on the Reciprocal Recognition and Enforcement of Judgments and Authentic Instruments in Civil and Commercial Matters, signed at The Hague on 6 February 1963,

[– the Convention between the United Kingdom and the Republic of Italy for the reciprocal recognition and enforcement of judgments in civil and commercial matters, signed at Rome on 7 February 1964, with amending Protocol signed at Rome on 14 July 1970,]

– the Convention between France and Austria on the Recognition and Enforcement of Judgments and Authentic Instruments in Civil and Commercial Matters, signed at Vienna on 15 July 1966,

[– the Convention between the United Kingdom and the Kingdom of the Netherlands providing for reciprocal recognition and enforcement of judgments in civil matters, signed at The Hague on 17 November 1967,]

– the Convention between Spain and France on the Recognition and Enforcement of Judgment Arbitration Awards in Civil and Commercial Matters, signed at Paris on 28 May 1969,

– the Convention between Luxembourg and Austria on the Recognition and Enforcement of Judgments and Authentic Instruments in Civil and Commercial Matters, signed at Luxembourg on 29 July 1971,

– the Convention between Italy and Austria on the Recognition and Enforcement of Judgments in Civil and Commercial Matters, of Judicial Settlements and of Authentic Instruments, signed at Rome on 16 November 1971,

– the Convention between Spain and Italy regarding Legal Aid and the Recognition and Enforcement of Judgments in Civil and Commercial Matters, signed at Madrid on 22 May 1973,

– the Convention between Finland, Iceland, Norway, Sweden and Denmark on the Recognition and Enforcement of Judgments in Civil Matters, signed at Copenhagen on 11 October 1977,

– the Convention between Austria and Sweden on the Recognition and Enforcement of Judgments in Civil Matters, signed at Stockholm on 16 September 1982,

– the Convention between Spain and the Federal Republic of Germany on the Recognition and Enforcement of Judgments, Settlements and Enforceable Authentic Instruments in Civil and Commercial Matters, signed at Bonn on 14 November 1983,

– the Convention between Austria and Spain on the Recognition and Enforcement of Judgments, Settlements and Enforceable Authentic Instruments in Civil and Commercial Matters, signed at Vienna on 17 February 1984,

– the Convention between Finland and Austria on the Recognition and Enforcement of Judgments in Civil Matters, signed at Vienna on 17 November 1986, and

– the Treaty between Belgium, the Netherlands and Luxembourg in Jurisdiction, Bankruptcy, and the Validity and Enforcement of Judgments, Arbitration Awards and Authentic Instruments, signed at Brussels on 24 November 1961, in so far as it is in force.

Amended by the Corrigenda to Council Regulation (EC) No 44/2001 of 22 December 2000.

*Article 70*

1. The Treaty and the Conventions referred to in Article 69 shall continue to have effect in relation to matters to which this Regulation does not apply.

2. They shall continue to have effect in respect of judgments given and documents formally drawn up or registered as authentic instruments before the entry into force of this Regulation.

*Article 71*

1. This Regulation shall not affect any conventions to which the Member States are parties and which in relation to particular matters, govern jurisdiction or the recognition or enforcement of judgments.

2. With a view to its uniform interpretation, paragraph 1 shall be applied in the following manner:

   (a) this Regulation shall not prevent a court of a Member State, which is a party to a convention on a particular matter, from assuming jurisdiction in accordance with that convention, even where the defendant is domiciled in another Member State which is not a party to that convention. The court hearing the action shall, in any event, apply Article 26 of this Regulation;

   (b) judgments given in a Member State by a court in the exercise of jurisdiction provided for in a convention on a particular matter shall be recognised and enforced in the other Member States in accordance with this Regulation. Where a convention on a particular matter to which both the Member State of origin and the Member State addressed are parties lays down conditions for the recognition or enforcement of judgments, those conditions shall apply. In any event, the provisions of this Regulation which concern the procedure for recognition and enforcement of judgments may be applied.

*Article 72*

This Regulation shall not affect agreements by which Member States undertook, prior to the entry into force of this Regulation pursuant to Article 59 of the Brussels Convention, not to recognise judgments given, in particular in other Contracting States to that Convention, against defendants domiciled or habitually resident in a third country where, in cases provided for in Article 4 of that Convention, the judgment could only be founded on a ground of jurisdiction specified in the second paragraph of Article 3 of that Convention.

## CHAPTER VIII
## FINAL PROVISIONS

*Article 73*

No later than five years after the entry into force of this Regulation, the Commission shall present to the European Parliament, the Council and the Economic and Social Committee a report on the application of this Regulation. The report shall be accompanied, if need be, by proposals for adaptations to this Regulation.

*Article 74*

1. The Member States shall notify the Commission of the texts amending the lists set out in Annexes I to IV. The Commission shall adapt the Annexes concerned accordingly.

2. The updating or technical adjustment of the forms, specimens of which appear in Annexes V and VI, shall be adopted in accordance with the advisory procedure referred to in Article 75(2).

*Article 75*

1. The Commission shall be assisted by a committee.

2. Where reference is made to this paragraph, Articles 3 and 7 of Decision 1999/468/EC shall apply.

3. The Committee shall adopt its rules of procedure.

*Article 76*

This Regulation shall enter into force on 1 March 2002.

This Regulation is binding in its entirety and directly applicable in the Member States in accordance with the Treaty establishing the European Community.

Done at Brussels, 22 December 2000.

## ANNEX I

Rules of jurisdiction referred to in Article 3(2) and Article 4(2) The rules of jurisdiction referred to in Article 3(2) and Article 4(2) are the following:

- in Belgium: Article 15 of the Civil Code (*Code civil/Burgerlijk Wetboek*) and Article 638 of the Judicial Code (*Code judiciaire/Gerechtelijk Wetboek*);
- in Germany: Article 23 of the Code of Civil Procedure (*Zivilprozessordnung*),
- in Greece, Article 40 of the Code of Civil Procedure '[*Not reproduced, see original*]',
- in France: Articles 14 and 15 of the Civil Code (*Code civil*),
- in Ireland: the rules which enable jurisdiction to be founded on the document instituting the proceedings having been served on the defendant during his temporary presence in Ireland,
- in Italy: Articles 3 and 4 of Act 218 of 31 May 1995,
- in Luxembourg: Articles 14 and 15 of the Civil Code (*Code civil*),
- in the Netherlands: Articles 126(3) and 127 of the Code of Civil Procedure (*Wetboek van Burgerlijke Rechtsvordering*),
- in Austria: Article 99 of the Court Jurisdiction Act (*Jurisdiktionsnorm*),
- in Portugal: Articles 65 and 65A of the Code of Civil procedure (*Código de Processo Civil*) and Article 11 of the Code of Labour Procedure (*Código de Processo de Trabalho*),
- in Finland: the second, third and fourth sentences of the first paragraph of Section 1 of Chapter 10 of the Code of Judicial Procedure (*oikeudenkäymiskaari/rättegångsbalken*),
- in Sweden: the first sentence of the first paragraph of Section 3 of Chapter 10 of the Code of Judicial Procedure (*rättegångsbalken*),
- in the United Kingdom: rules which enable jurisdiction to be founded on:
  - (a) the document instituting the proceedings having been served on the defendant during his temporary presence in the United Kingdom; or
  - (b) the presence within the United Kingdom of property belonging to the defendant; or
  - (c) the seizure by the plaintiff of property situated in the United Kingdom.

## ANNEX II

The courts or competent authorities to which the application referred to in Article 39 may be submitted are the following:

- in Belgium, the '*tribunal de première instance*' or '*rechtbank van eerste aanleg*' or '*erstinstanzliches Gericht*',
- in Germany, the presiding judge of a chamber of the '*Landgericht*',
- in Greece, the '[*Not reproduced, see original*]'
- in Spain, the '*Juzgado de Primera Instancia*',
- in France, the presiding judge of the '*tribunal de grande instance*',
- in Ireland, the High Court,
- in Italy, the '*Corte d'appello*',
- in Luxembourg, the presiding judge of the '*tribunal d'arrondissement*',
- in the Netherlands, the presiding judge of the '*arrondissementsrechtbank*';
- in Austria, the '*Bezirksgericht*',
- in Portugal, the '*Tribunal de Comarca*',
- in Finland, the '*käräjäoikeus/tingsrätt*',

- in Sweden, the '*Svea hovrätt*',
- in the United Kingdom:
  - (a) in England and Wales, the High Court of Justice, or in the case of a maintenance judgment, the Magistrate's Court on transmission by the Secretary of State;
  - (b) in Scotland, the Court of Session, or in the case of a maintenance judgment, the Sheriff Court on transmission by the Secretary of State;
  - (c) in Northern Ireland, the High Court of Justice, or in the case of a maintenance judgment, the Magistrate's Court on transmission by the Secretary of State;
  - (d) in Gibraltar, the Supreme Court of Gibraltar, or in the case of a maintenance judgment, the Magistrates' Court on transmission by the Attorney General of Gibraltar.

## ANNEX III

The courts with which appeals referred to in Article 43(2) may be lodged are the following:
- in Belgium,
  - (a) as regards appeal by the defendant: the '*tribunal de première instance*' or '*rechtbank van eerste aanleg*' or '*erstinstanzliches Gericht*',
  - (b) as regards appeal by the applicant: the '*Cour d'appel*' or '*hof van beroep*',
- in the Federal Republic of Germany, the '*Oberlandesgericht*',
- in Greece, the '[*Not reproduced, see original*]'
- in Spain, the '*Audiencia Provincial*',
- in France, the '*cour d'appel*',
- in Ireland, the High Court,
- in Italy, the '*corte d'appello*',
- in Luxembourg, the '*Cour supérieure de Justice*' sitting as a ourt of civil appeal,
- in the Netherlands:
  - (a) for the defendant: the '*arrondissementsrechtbank*',
  - (b) for the applicant: the '*gerechtshof*',
- in Austria, the '*Bezirksgericht*',
- in Portugal, the '*Tribunal de Relação*',
- in Finland, the '*hovioikeus/hovrätt*',
- in Sweden, the '*Svea hovrätt*',
- in the United Kingdom:
  - (a) in England and Wales, the High Court of Justice, or in the case of a maintenance judgment, the Magistrate's Court;
  - (b) in Scotland, the Court of Session, or in the case of a maintenance judgment, the Sheriff Court;
  - (c) in Northern Ireland, the High Court of Justice, or in the case of a maintenance judgment, the Magistrate's Court;
  - (d) in Gibraltar, the Supreme Court of Gibraltar, or in the case of a maintenance judgment, the Magistrates' Court.

## ANNEX IV

The appeals which may be lodged pursuant to Article 44 are the following
- in Belgium, Greece, Spain, France, Italy, Luxembourg and the Netherlands, an appeal in cassation,
- in Germany, a '*Rechtsbeschwerde*',
- in Ireland, an appeal on a point of law to the Supreme Court,
- in Austria, a '*Revisionsrekurs*',
- in Portugal, an appeal on a point of law,
- in Finland, an appeal to the '*korkein oikeus/högsta domstolen*',
- in Sweden, an appeal to the '*Högsta domstolen*',
- in the United Kingdom, a single further appeal on a point of law.

## ANNEX V

*Certificate referred to in Articles 54 and 58 of the Regulation on judgments and court settlements*

*(English, inglés, anglais, inglese)*

1. Member State of origin
2. Court or competent authority issuing the certificate
    2.1. Name
    2.2. Address
    2.3. Tel/fax/e-mail
3. Court which delivered the judgment/approved the court settlement*
    3.1. Type of court
    3.2. Place of court
4. Judgment/court settlement*
    4.1. Date
    4.2. Reference number
    4.3. The parties to the judgment/court settlement*
        4.3.1. Name(s) of plaintiff(s)
        4.3.2. Name(s) of defendant(s)
        4.3.3. Name(s) of other party(ies), if any
    4.4. Date of service of the document instituting the proceedings where judgment was given in default of appearance
    4.5. Text of the judgment/court settlement* as annexed to this certificate
5. Names of parties to whom legal aid has been granted

The judgment/court settlement* is enforceable in the Member State of origin (Articles 38 and 58 of the Regulation) against:

Name:

Done at ................................. date ...........................

Signature and/or stamp ...........................................
    * Delete as appropriate.

## ANNEX VI

*Certificate referred to in Article 57(4) of the Regulation on authentic instruments*

*(English, inglés, anglais, inglese)*

1. Member State of origin
2. Competent authority issuing the certificate
    2.1. Name
    2.2. Address
    2.3. Tel/fax/e-mail
3. Authority which has given authenticity to the instrument
    3.1. Authority involved in the drawing up of the authentic instrument (if applicable)
        3.1.1. Name and designation of authority
        3.1.2. Place of authority
    3.2. Authority which has registered the authentic instrument (if applicable)
        3.2.1. Type of authority
        3.2.2. Place of authority

4.    Authentic instrument
     4.1.    Description of the instrument
     4.2.    Date
          4.2.1.    on which the instrument was drawn up
          4.2.2.    if different: on which the instrument was registered
     4.3.    Reference number
     4.4.    Parties to the instrument
          4.4.1.    Name of the creditor
          4.4.2.    Name of the debtor
5.    Text of the enforceable obligation as annexed to this certificate

The authentic instrument is enforceable against the debtor in the Member State of origin (Article 57(1) of the Regulation)

Done at ................................. date ...........................

Signature and/or stamp ...........................................

# COUNCIL REGULATION (EC) NO 1206/2001

## of 28 May 2001

on cooperation between the courts of the Member States in the taking of evidence in civil or commercial matters

THE COUNCIL OF THE EUROPEAN UNION,

Having regard to the Treaty establishing the European Community, and in particular Article 61(c) and Article 67(1) thereof,
    Having regard to the initiative of the Federal Republic of Germany(1),
    Having regard to the opinion of the European Parliament(2),
    Having regard to the opinion of the Economic and Social Committee(3),
    Whereas:
    (1) The European Union has set itself the objective of maintaining and developing the European Union as an area of freedom, security and justice in which the free movement of persons is ensured. For the gradual establishment of such an area, the Community is to adopt, among others, the measures relating to judicial cooperation in civil matters needed for the proper functioning of the internal market.
    (2) For the purpose of the proper functioning of the internal market, cooperation between courts in the taking of evidence should be improved, and in particular simplified and accelerated.
    (3) At its meeting in Tampere on 15 and 16 October 1999, the European Council recalled that new procedural legislation in cross-border cases, in particular on the taking of evidence, should be prepared.
    (4) This area falls within the scope of Article 65 of the Treaty.
    (5) The objectives of the proposed action, namely the improvement of cooperation between the courts on the taking of evidence in civil or commercial matters, cannot be sufficiently achieved by the Member States and can therefore be better achieved at Community level. The Community may adopt measures in accordance with the principle of subsidiarity as set out in Article 5 of the Treaty. In accordance with the principle of proportionality, as set out in that Article, this Regulation does not go beyond what is necessary to achieve those objectives.
    (6) To date, there is no binding instrument between all the Member States concerning the taking of evidence. The Hague Convention of 18 March 1970 on the taking of evidence abroad in civil or commercial matters applies between only 11 Member States of the European Union.

(7) As it is often essential for a decision in a civil or commercial matter pending before a court in a Member State to take evidence in another Member State, the Community's activity cannot be limited to the field of transmission of judicial and extrajudicial documents in civil or commercial matters which falls within the scope of Council Regulation (EC) No 1348/2000 of 29 May 2000 on the serving in the Member States of judicial and extrajudicial documents in civil or commercial matters(4). It is therefore necessary to continue the improvement of cooperation between courts of Member States in the field of taking of evidence.

(8) The efficiency of judicial procedures in civil or commercial matters requires that the transmission and execution of requests for the performance of taking of evidence is to be made directly and by the most rapid means possible between Member States' courts.

(9) Speed in transmission of requests for the performance of taking of evidence warrants the use of all appropriate means, provided that certain conditions as to the legibility and reliability of the document received are observed. So as to ensure the utmost clarity and legal certainty the request for the performance of taking of evidence must be transmitted on a form to be completed in the language of the Member State of the requested court or in another language accepted by that State. For the same reasons, forms should also be used as far as possible for further communication between the relevant courts.

(10) A request for the performance of the taking of evidence should be executed expeditiously. If it is not possible for the request to be executed within 90 days of receipt by the requested court, the latter should inform the requesting court accordingly, stating the reasons which prevent the request from being executed swiftly.

(11) To secure the effectiveness of this Regulation, the possibility of refusing to execute the request for the performance of taking of evidence should be confined to strictly limited exceptional situations.

(12) The requested court should execute the request in accordance with the law of its Member State.

(13) The parties and, if any, their representatives, should be able to be present at the performance of the taking of evidence, if that is provided for by the law of the Member State of the requesting court, in order to be able to follow the proceedings in a comparable way as if evidence were taken in the Member State of the requesting court. They should also have the right to request to participate in order to have a more active role in the performance of the taking of evidence. However, the conditions under which they may participate should be determined by the requested court in accordance with the law of its Member State.

(14) The representatives of the requesting court should be able to be present at the performance of the taking of evidence, if that is compatible with the law of the Member State of the requesting court, in order to have an improved possibility of evaluation of evidence. They should also have the right to request to participate, under the conditions laid down by the requested court in accordance with the law of its Member State, in order to have a more active role in the performance of the taking of evidence.

(15) In order to facilitate the taking of evidence it should be possible for a court in a Member State, in accordance with the law of its Member State, to take evidence directly in another Member State, if accepted by the latter, and under the conditions determined by the central body or competent authority of the requested Member State.

(16) The execution of the request, according to Article 10, should not give rise to a claim for any reimbursement of taxes or costs. Nevertheless, if the requested court requires reimbursement, the fees paid to experts and interpreters, as well as the costs occasioned by the application of Article 10(3) and (4), should not be borne by that court. In such a case, the requesting court is to take the necessary

measures to ensure reimbursement without delay. Where the opinion of an expert is required, the requested court may, before executing the request, ask the requesting court for an adequate deposit or advance towards the costs.

(17) This Regulation should prevail over the provisions applying to its field of application, contained in international conventions concluded by the Member States. Member States should be free to adopt agreements or arrangements to further facilitate cooperation in the taking of evidence.

(18) The information transmitted pursuant to this Regulation should enjoy protection. Since Directive 95/46/EC of the European Parliament and of the Council of 24 October 1995 on the protection of individuals with regard to the processing of personal data and on the free movement of such data(5), and Directive 97/66/EC of the European Parliament and of the Council of 15 December 1997 concerning the processing of personal data and the protection of privacy in the telecommunications sector(6), are applicable, there is no need for specific provisions on data protection in this Regulation.

(19) The measures necessary for the implementation of this Regulation should be adopted in accordance with Council Decision 1999/468/EC of 28 June 1999(7) laying down the procedures for the exercise of implementing powers conferred on the Commission.

(20) For the proper functioning of this Regulation, the Commission should review its application and propose such amendments as may appear necessary.

(21) The United Kingdom and Ireland, in accordance with Article 3 of the Protocol on the position of the United Kingdom and Ireland annexed to the Treaty on the European Union and to the Treaty establishing the European Community, have given notice of their wish to take part in the adoption and application of this Regulation.

(22) Denmark, in accordance with Articles 1 and 2 of the Protocol on the position of Denmark annexed to the Treaty on European Union and to the Treaty establishing the European Community, is not participating in the adoption of this Regulation, and is therefore not bound by it nor subject to its application,

HAS ADOPTED THIS REGULATION:

## CHAPTER I

## GENERAL PROVISIONS

*Article 1*

*Scope*

1. This Regulation shall apply in civil or commercial matters where the court of a Member State, in accordance with the provisions of the law of that State, requests:

  (a) the competent court of another Member State to take evidence; or

  (b) to take evidence directly in another Member State.

2. A request shall not be made to obtain evidence which is not intended for use in judicial proceedings, commenced or contemplated.

3. In this Regulation, the term 'Member State' shall mean Member States with the exception of Denmark.

*Article 2*

*Direct transmission between the courts*

1. Requests pursuant to Article 1(1)(a), hereinafter referred to as 'requests', shall be transmitted by the court before which the proceedings are commenced or contemplated, hereinafter referred to as the 'requesting court', directly to the competent court of another Member State, hereinafter referred to as the 'requested court', for the performance of the taking of evidence.

2. Each Member State shall draw up a list of the courts competent for the performance of taking of evidence according to this Regulation. The list shall also indicate the territorial and, where appropriate, the special jurisdiction of those courts.

*Article 3*

*Central body*

1. Each Member State shall designate a central body responsible for:
   (a) supplying information to the courts;
   (b) seeking solutions to any difficulties which may arise in respect of a request;
   (c) forwarding, in exceptional cases, at the request of a requesting court, a request to the competent court.

   2. A federal State, a State in which several legal systems apply or a State with autonomous territorial entities shall be free to designate more than one central body.

   3. Each Member State shall also designate the central body referred to in paragraph 1 or one or several competent authority(ies) to be responsible for taking decisions on requests pursuant to Article 17.

## CHAPTER II

## TRANSMISSION AND EXECUTION OF REQUESTS

### SECTION 1

#### TRANSMISSION OF THE REQUEST

*Article 4*

*Form and content of the request*

1. The request shall be made using form A or, where appropriate, form I in the Annex. It shall contain the following details:
   (a) the requesting and, where appropriate, the requested court;
   (b) the names and addresses of the parties to the proceedings and their representatives, if any;
   (c) the nature and subject matter of the case and a brief statement of the facts;
   (d) a description of the taking of evidence to be performed;
   (e) where the request is for the examination of a person:
     - the name(s) and address(es) of the person(s) to be examined,
     - the questions to be put to the person(s) to be examined or a statement of the facts about which he is (they are) to be examined,
     - where appropriate, a reference to a right to refuse to testify under the law of the Member State of the requesting court,
     - any requirement that the examination is to be carried out under oath or affirmation in lieu thereof, and any special form to be used,
     - where appropriate, any other information that the requesting court deems necessary;
   (f) where the request is for any other form of taking of evidence, the documents or other objects to be inspected;
   (g) where appropriate, any request pursuant to Article 10(3) and (4), and Articles 11 and 12 and any information necessary for the application thereof.

   2. The request and all documents accompanying the request shall be exempted from authentication or any equivalent formality.

   3. Documents which the requesting court deems it necessary to enclose for the execution of the request shall be accompanied by a translation into the language in which the request was written.

*Article 5*

*Language*

The request and communications pursuant to this Regulation shall be drawn up in the official language of the requested Member State or, if there are several official languages in that Member State, in the official language or one of the official languages of the place where the requested taking of evidence is to be performed, or in another language which the requested Member State has indicated it can accept. Each Member State shall indicate the official language or languages of the institutions of the European Community other than its own which is or are acceptable to it for completion of the forms.

*Article 6*

*Transmission of requests and other communications*

Requests and communications pursuant to this Regulation shall be transmitted by the swiftest possible means, which the requested Member State has indicated it can accept. The transmission may be carried out by any appropriate means, provided that the document received accurately reflects the content of the document forwarded and that all information in it is legible.

SECTION 2

RECEIPT OF REQUEST

*Article 7*

*Receipt of request*

1. Within seven days of receipt of the request, the requested competent court shall send an acknowledgement of receipt to the requesting court using form B in the Annex. Where the request does not comply with the conditions laid down in Articles 5 and 6, the requested court shall enter a note to that effect in the acknowledgement of receipt.

2. Where the execution of a request made using form A in the Annex, which complies with the conditions laid down in Article 5, does not fall within the jurisdiction of the court to which it was transmitted, the latter shall forward the request to the competent court of its Member State and shall inform the requesting court thereof using form A in the Annex.

*Article 8*

*Incomplete request*

1. If a request cannot be executed because it does not contain all of the necessary information pursuant to Article 4, the requested court shall inform the requesting court thereof without delay and, at the latest, within 30 days of receipt of the request using form C in the Annex, and shall request it to send the missing information, which should be indicated as precisely as possible.

2. If a request cannot be executed because a deposit or advance is necessary in accordance with Article 18(3), the requested court shall inform the requesting court thereof without delay and, at the latest, within 30 days of receipt of the request using form C in the Annex and inform the requesting court how the deposit or advance should be made. The requested Court shall acknowledge receipt of the deposit or advance without delay, at the latest within 10 days of receipt of the deposit or the advance using form D.

*Article 9*

*Completion of the request*

1. If the requested court has noted on the acknowledgement of receipt pursuant to Article 7(1) that the request does not comply with the conditions laid down in Articles 5 and 6 or has informed the requesting court pursuant to Article 8 that the request cannot be executed because it does not contain all of the necessary information pursuant to Article 4, the time limit pursuant to Article 10 shall begin to run when the requested court received the request duly completed.

2. Where the requested court has asked for a deposit or advance in accordance with Article 18(3), this time limit shall begin to run when the deposit or the advance is made.

SECTION 3

TAKING OF EVIDENCE BY THE REQUESTED COURT

*Article 10*

*General provisions on the execution of the request*

1. The requested court shall execute the request without delay and, at the latest, within 90 days of receipt of the request.

2. The requested court shall execute the request in accordance with the law of its Member State.

3. The requesting court may call for the request to be executed in accordance with a special procedure provided for by the law of its Member State, using form A in the Annex. The requested court shall comply with such a requirement unless this procedure is incompatible with the law of the Member State of the requested court or by reason of major practical difficulties. If the requested court does not comply with the requirement for one of these reasons it shall inform the requesting court using form E in the Annex.

4. The requesting court may ask the requested court to use communications technology at the performance of the taking of evidence, in particular by using videoconference and teleconference.

The requested court shall comply with such a requirement unless this is incompatible with the law of the Member State of the requested court or by reason of major practical difficulties.

If the requested court does not comply with the requirement for one of these reasons, it shall inform the requesting court, using form E in the Annex.

If there is no access to the technical means referred to above in the requesting or in the requested court, such means may be made available by the courts by mutual agreement.

*Article 11*

*Performance with the presence and participation of the parties*

1. If it is provided for by the law of the Member State of the requesting court, the parties and, if any, their representatives, have the right to be present at the performance of the taking of evidence by the requested court.

2. The requesting court shall, in its request, inform the requested court that the parties and, if any, their representatives, will be present and, where appropriate, that their participation is requested, using form A in the Annex. This information may also be given at any other appropriate time.

3. If the participation of the parties and, if any, their representatives, is requested at the performance of the taking of evidence, the requested court shall determine, in accordance with Article 10, the conditions under which they may participate.

4. The requested court shall notify the parties and, if any, their representatives, of the time when, the place where, the proceedings will take place, and, where appropriate, the conditions under which they may participate, using form F in the Annex.

5. Paragraphs 1 to 4 shall not affect the possibility for the requested court of asking the parties and, if any their representatives, to be present at or to participate in the performance of the taking of evidence if that possibility is provided for by the law of its Member State.

### Article 12

*Performance with the presence and participation of representatives of the requesting court*

1. If it is compatible with the law of the Member State of the requesting court, representatives of the requesting court have the right to be present in the performance of the taking of evidence by the requested court.

2. For the purpose of this Article, the term 'representative' shall include members of the judicial personnel designated by the requesting court, in accordance with the law of its Member State. The requesting court may also designate, in accordance with the law of its Member State, any other person, such as an expert.

3. The requesting court shall, in its request, inform the requested court that its representatives will be present and, where appropriate, that their participation is requested, using form A in the Annex. This information may also be given at any other appropriate time.

4. If the participation of the representatives of the requesting court is requested in the performance of the taking of evidence, the requested court shall determine, in accordance with Article 10, the conditions under which they may participate.

5. The requested court shall notify the requesting court, of the time when, and the place where, the proceedings will take place, and, where appropriate, the conditions under which the representatives may participate, using form F in the Annex.

### Article 13

*Coercive measures*

Where necessary, in executing a request the requested court shall apply the appropriate coercive measures in the instances and to the extent as are provided for by the law of the Member State of the requested court for the execution of a request made for the same purpose by its national authorities or one of the parties concerned.

### Article 14

*Refusal to execute*

1. A request for the hearing of a person shall not be executed when the person concerned claims the right to refuse to give evidence or to be prohibited from giving evidence,

   (a) under the law of the Member State of the requested court; or

   (b) under the law of the Member State of the requesting court, and such right has been specified in the request, or, if need be, at the instance of the requested court, has been confirmed by the requesting court.

2. In addition to the grounds referred to in paragraph 1, the execution of a request may be refused only if:

   (a) the request does not fall within the scope of this Regulation as set out in Article 1; or

(b) the execution of the request under the law of the Member State of the requested court does not fall within the functions of the judiciary; or

(c) the requesting court does not comply with the request of the requested court to complete the request pursuant to Article 8 within 30 days after the requested court asked it to do so; or

(d) a deposit or advance asked for in accordance with Article 18(3) is not made within 60 days after the requested court asked for such a deposit or advance.

3. Execution may not be refused by the requested court solely on the ground that under the law of its Member State a court of that Member State has exclusive jurisdiction over the subject matter of the action or that the law of that Member State would not admit the right of action on it.

4. If execution of the request is refused on one of the grounds referred to in paragraph 2, the requested court shall notify the requesting court thereof within 60 days of receipt of the request by the requested court using form H in the Annex.

## Article 15

### Notification of delay

If the requested court is not in a position to execute the request within 90 days of receipt, it shall inform the requesting court thereof, using form G in the Annex. When it does so, the grounds for the delay shall be given as well as the estimated time that the requested court expects it will need to execute the request.

## Article 16

### Procedure after execution of the request

The requested court shall send without delay to the requesting court the documents establishing the execution of the request and, where appropriate, return the documents received from the requesting court. The documents shall be accompanied by a confirmation of execution using form H in the Annex.

## SECTION 4

### DIRECT TAKING OF EVIDENCE BY THE REQUESTING COURT

## Article 17

1. Where a court requests to take evidence directly in another Member State, it shall submit a request to the central body or the competent authority referred to in Article 3(3) in that State, using form I in the Annex.

2. Direct taking of evidence may only take place if it can be performed on a voluntary basis without the need for coercive measures.

Where the direct taking of evidence implies that a person shall be heard, the requesting court shall inform that person that the performance shall take place on a voluntary basis.

3. The taking of evidence shall be performed by a member of the judicial personnel or by any other person such as an expert, who will be designated, in accordance with the law of the Member State of the requesting court.

4. Within 30 days of receiving the request, the central body or the competent authority of the requested Member State shall inform the requesting court if the request is accepted and, if necessary, under what conditions according to the law of its Member State such performance is to be carried out, using form J.

In particular, the central body or the competent authority may assign a court of its Member State to take part in the performance of the taking of evidence in order to ensure the proper application of this Article and the conditions that have been set out.

The central body or the competent authority shall encourage the use of communications technology, such as videoconferences and teleconferences.

5. The central body or the competent authority may refuse direct taking of evidence only if:

(a) the request does not fall within the scope of this Regulation as set out in Article 1;

(b) the request does not contain all of the necessary information pursuant to Article 4; or

(c) the direct taking of evidence requested is contrary to fundamental principles of law in its Member State.

6. Without prejudice to the conditions laid down in accordance with paragraph 4, the requesting court shall execute the request in accordance with the law of its Member State.

## SECTION 5

### COSTS

*Article 18*

1. The execution of the request, in accordance with Article 10, shall not give rise to a claim for any reimbursement of taxes or costs.

2. Nevertheless, if the requested court so requires, the requesting court shall ensure the reimbursement, without delay, of:

— the fees paid to experts and interpreters, and

— the costs occasioned by the application of Article 10(3) and(4).

The duty for the parties to bear these fees or costs shall be governed by the law of the Member State of the requesting court.

3. Where the opinion of an expert is required, the requested court may, before executing the request, ask the requesting court for an adequate deposit or advance towards the requested costs. In all other cases, a deposit or advance shall not be a condition for the execution of a request.

The deposit or advance shall be made by the parties if that is provided for by the law of the Member State of the requesting court.

## CHAPTER III

### FINAL PROVISIONS

*Article 19*

*Implementing rules*

1. The Commission shall draw up and regularly update a manual, which shall also be available electronically, containing the information provided by the Member States in accordance with Article 22 and the agreements or arrangements in force, according to Article 21.

2. The updating or making of technical amendments to the standard forms set out in the Annex shall be carried out in accordance with the advisory procedure set out in Article 20(2).

*Article 20*

*Committee*

1. The Commission shall be assisted by a Committee.

2. Where reference is made to this paragraph, Articles 3 and 7 of Decision 1999/468/EC shall apply.

3. The Committee shall adopt its Rules of Procedure.

*Article 21*

*Relationship with existing or future agreements or arrangements between Member States*

1. This Regulation shall, in relation to matters to which it applies, prevail over other provisions contained in bilateral or multilateral agreements or arrangements concluded by the Member States and in particular the Hague Convention of 1 March 1954 on Civil Procedure and the Hague Convention of 18 March 1970 on the Taking of Evidence Abroad in Civil or Commercial Matters, in relations between the Member States party thereto.

2. This Regulation shall not preclude Member States from maintaining or concluding agreements or arrangements between two or more of them to further facilitate the taking of evidence, provided that they are compatible with this Regulation.

3. Member States shall send to the Commission:
(a) by 1 July 2003, a copy of the agreements or arrangements maintained between the Member States referred to in paragraph 2;
(b) a copy of the agreements or arrangements concluded between the Member States referred to in paragraph 2 as well as drafts of such agreements or arrangements which they intend to adopt; and
(c) any denunciation of, or amendments to, these agreements or arrangements.

*Article 22*

*Communication*

By 1 July 2003 each Member State shall communicate to the Commission the following:
(a) the list pursuant to Article 2(2) indicating the territorial and, where appropriate, the special jurisdiction of the courts;
(b) the names and addresses of the central bodies and competent authorities pursuant to Article 3, indicating their territorial jurisdiction;
(c) the technical means for the receipt of requests available to the courts on the list pursuant to Article 2(2);
(d) the languages accepted for the requests as referred to in Article 5.

Member States shall inform the Commission of any subsequent changes to this information.

*Article 23*

*Review*

No later than 1 January 2007, and every five years thereafter, the Commission shall present to the European Parliament, the Council and the Economic and Social Committee a report on the application of this Regulation, paying special attention to the practical application of Article 3(1)(c) and 3, and Articles 17 and 18.

*Article 24*

*Entry into force*

1. This Regulation shall enter into force on 1 July 2001.

2. This Regulation shall apply from 1 January 2004, except for Articles 19, 21 and 22, which shall apply from 1 July 2001.

This Regulation shall be binding in its entirety and directly applicable in the Member States in accordance with the Treaty establishing the European Community.

Done at Brussels, 28 May 2001.

For the Council

The President

T. Bodström

[1] OJ C 314, 3.11.2000, p. 2.
[2] Opinion delivered on 14 March 2001 (not yet published in the Official Journal).
[3] Opinion delivered on 28 February 2001 (not yet published in the Official Journal).
[4] OJ L 160, 30.6.2000, p. 37.
[5] OJ L 281, 23.11.1995, p. 31.
[6] OJ L 24, 30.1.1998, p. 1.
[7] OJ L 184, 17.7.1999, p. 23.

## ANNEX

## COUNCIL REGULATION (EC) NO 2201/2003

### of 27 November 2003

concerning jurisdiction and the recognition and enforcement of judgments in matrimonial matters and the matters of parental responsibility, repealing Regulation (EC) No 1347/2000

THE COUNCIL OF THE EUROPEAN UNION

Having regard to the Treaty establishing the European Community, and in particular Article 61(c) and Article 67(1) thereof,

Having regard to the proposal from the Commission,

Having regard to the opinion of the European Parliament,

Having regard to the opinion of the Economic and Social Committee,

Whereas:

(1) The European Community has set the objective of creating an area of freedom, security and justice, in which the free movement of persons is ensured. To this end, the Community is to adopt, among others, measures in the field of judicial cooperation in civil matters that are necessary for the proper functioning of the internal market.

(2) The Tampere European Council endorsed the principle of mutual recognition of judicial decisions as the cornerstone for the creation of a genuine judicial area, and identified visiting rights as a priority.

(3) Council Regulation (EC) No 1347/2000 sets out rules on jurisdiction, recognition and enforcement of judgments in matrimonial matters and matters of parental responsibility for the children of both spouses rendered on the occasion of the matrimonial proceedings. The content of this Regulation was substantially taken over from the Convention of 28 May 1998 on the same subject matter.

(4) On 3 July 2000 France presented an initiative for a Council Regulation on the mutual enforcement of judgments on rights of access to children.

(5) In order to ensure equality for all children, this Regulation covers all decisions on parental responsibility, including measures for the protection of the child, independently of any link with a matrimonial proceeding.

(6) Since the application of the rules on parental responsibility often arises in the context of matrimonial proceedings, it is more appropriate to have a single instrument for matters of divorce and parental responsibility.

(7) The scope of this Regulation covers civil matters, whatever the nature of the court or tribunal.

(8) As regards judgments on divorce, legal separation or marriage annulment, this Regulation should apply only to the dissolution of matrimonial ties and should not deal with issues such as the grounds for divorce, property consequences of the marriage or any other ancillary measures.

(9) As regards the property of the child, this Regulation should apply only to measures for the protection of the child, ie (i) the designation and functions of a person or body having charge of the child's property, representing or assisting the child, and (ii) the administration, conservation or disposal of the child's property. In this context, this Regulation should, for instance, apply in cases where the parents are in dispute as regards the administration of the child's property. Measures relating to the child's property which do not concern the protection of the child should continue to be governed by Council Regulation (EC) No 44/2001 of 22 December 2000 on jurisdiction and the recognition and enforcement of judgments in civil and commercial matters.

(10) This Regulation is not intended to apply to matters relating to social security, public measures of a general nature in matters of education or health or to decisions on the right of asylum and on immigration. In addition it does not apply to the establishment of parenthood, since this is a different matter from the attribution of parental responsibility, nor to other questions linked to the status of persons. Moreover, it does not apply to measures taken as a result of criminal offences committed by children.

(11) Maintenance obligations are excluded from the scope of this Regulation as these are already covered by Council Regulation No 44/2001. The courts having jurisdiction under this Regulation will generally have jurisdiction to rule on maintenance obligations by application of Article 5(2) of Council Regulation No 44/2001.

(12) The grounds of jurisdiction in matters of parental responsibility established in the present Regulation are shaped in the light of the best interests of the child, in particular on the criterion of proximity. This means that jurisdiction should lie in the first place with the Member State of the child's habitual residence, except for certain cases of a change in the child's residence or pursuant to an agreement between the holders of parental responsibility.

(13) In the interest of the child, this Regulation allows, by way of exception and under certain conditions, that the court having jurisdiction may transfer a case to a court of another Member State if this court is better placed to hear the case. However, in this case the second court should not be allowed to transfer the case to a third court.

(14) This Regulation should have effect without prejudice to the application of public international law concerning diplomatic immunities. Where jurisdiction under this Regulation cannot be exercised by reason of the existence of diplomatic immunity in accordance with international law, jurisdiction should be exercised in accordance with national law in a Member State in which the person concerned does not enjoy such immunity.

(15) Council Regulation (EC) No 1348/2000 of 29 May 2000 on the service in the Member States of judicial and extrajudicial documents in civil or commercial matters should apply to the service of documents in proceedings instituted pursuant to this Regulation.

(16) This Regulation should not prevent the courts of a Member State from taking provisional, including protective measures, in urgent cases, with regard to persons or property situated in that State.

(17) In cases of wrongful removal or retention of a child, the return of the child should be obtained without delay, and to this end the Hague Convention of 25 October 1980 would continue to apply as complemented by the provisions of this Regulation, in particular Article 11. The courts of the Member State to or in which the child has been wrongfully removed or retained should be able to oppose his or her return in specific, duly justified cases. However, such a decision could be replaced by a subsequent decision by the court of the Member State of habitual residence of the child prior to the wrongful removal or retention. Should that judgment entail the return of the child, the return should take place without any

special procedure being required for recognition and enforcement of that judgment in the Member State to or in which the child has been removed or retained.

(18) Where a court has decided not to return a child on the basis of Article 13 of the 1980 Hague Convention, it should inform the court having jurisdiction or central authority in the Member State where the child was habitually resident prior to the wrongful removal or retention. Unless the court in the latter Member State has been seised, this court or the central authority should notify the parties. This obligation should not prevent the central authority from also notifying the relevant public authorities in accordance with national law.

(19) The hearing of the child plays an important role in the application of this Regulation, although this instrument is not intended to modify national procedures applicable.

(20) The hearing of a child in another Member State may take place under the arrangements laid down in Council Regulation (EC) No 1206/2001 of 28 May 2001 on cooperation between the courts of the Member States in the taking of evidence in civil or commercial matters.

(21) The recognition and enforcement of judgments given in a Member State should be based on the principle of mutual trust and the grounds for non-recognition should be kept to the minimum required.

(22) Authentic instruments and agreements between parties that are enforceable in one Member State should be treated as equivalent to 'judgments' for the purpose of the application of the rules on recognition and enforcement.

(23) The Tampere European Council considered in its conclusions (point 34) that judgments in the field of family litigation should be 'automatically recognised throughout the Union without any intermediate proceedings or grounds for refusal of enforcement'. This is why judgments on rights of access and judgments on return that have been certified in the Member State of origin in accordance with the provisions of this Regulation should be recognised and enforceable in all other Member States without any further procedure being required. Arrangements for the enforcement of such judgments continue to be governed by national law.

(24) The certificate issued to facilitate enforcement of the judgment should not be subject to appeal. It should be rectified only where there is a material error, ie where it does not correctly reflect the judgment.

(25) Central authorities should cooperate both in general matter and in specific cases, including for purposes of promoting the amicable resolution of family disputes, in matters of parental responsibility. To this end central authorities shall participate in the European Judicial Network in civil and commercial matters created by Council Decision 2001/470/EC of 28 May 2001 establishing a European Judicial Network in civil and commercial matters.

(26) The Commission should make publicly available and update the lists of courts and redress procedures communicated by the Member States.

(27) The measures necessary for the implementation of this Regulation should be adopted in accordance with Council Decision 1999/468/EC of 28 June 1999 laying down the procedures for the exercise of implementing powers conferred on the Commission.

(28) This Regulation replaces Regulation (EC) No 1347/2000 which is consequently repealed.

(29) For the proper functioning of this Regulation, the Commission should review its application and propose such amendments as may appear necessary.

(30) The United Kingdom and Ireland, in accordance with Article 3 of the Protocol on the position of the United Kingdom and Ireland annexed to the Treaty on European Union and the Treaty establishing the European Community, have given notice of their wish to take part in the adoption and application of this Regulation.

(31) Denmark, in accordance with Articles 1 and 2 of the Protocol on the position of Denmark annexed to the Treaty on European Union and the Treaty establishing the European Community, is not participating in the adoption of this Regulation and is therefore not bound by it nor subject to its application.

(32) Since the objectives of this Regulation cannot be sufficiently achieved by the Member States and can therefore be better achieved at Community level, the Community may adopt measures, in accordance with the principle of subsidiarity as set out in Article 5 of the Treaty. In accordance with the principle of proportionality, as set out in that Article, this Regulation does not go beyond what is necessary in order to achieve those objectives.

(33) This Regulation recognises the fundamental rights and observes the principles of the Charter of Fundamental Rights of the European Union. In particular, it seeks to ensure respect for the fundamental rights of the child as set out in Article 24 of the Charter of Fundamental Rights of the European Union,

HAS ADOPTED THE PRESENT REGULATION:

CHAPTER I

SCOPE AND DEFINITIONS

*Article 1*

*Scope*
1.   This Regulation shall apply, whatever the nature of the court or tribunal, in civil matters relating to:
   (*a*)   divorce, legal separation or marriage annulment;
   (*b*)   the attribution, exercise, delegation, restriction or termination of parental responsibility.
2.   The matters referred to in paragraph 1(*b*) may, in particular, deal with:
   (*a*)   rights of custody and rights of access;
   (*b*)   guardianship, curatorship and similar institutions;
   (*c*)   the designation and functions of any person or body having charge of the child's person or property, representing or assisting the child;
   (*d*)   the placement of the child in a foster family or in institutional care;
   (*e*)   measures for the protection of the child relating to the administration, conservation or disposal of the child's property.
3.   This Regulation shall not apply to:
   (*a*)   the establishment or contesting of a parent-child relationship;
   (*b*)   decisions on adoption, measures preparatory to adoption, or the annulment or revocation of adoption;
   (*c*)   the name and forenames of the child;
   (*d*)   emancipation;
   (*e*)   maintenance obligations;
   (*f*)   trusts or succession;
   (*g*)   measures taken as a result of criminal offences committed by children.

*Article 2*

*Definitions*
For the purposes of this Regulation:
1.   the term 'court' shall cover all the authorities in the Member States with jurisdiction in the matters falling within the scope of this Regulation pursuant to Article 1;
2.   the term 'judge' shall mean the judge or an official having powers equivalent to those of a judge in the matters falling within the scope of the Regulation;

3. the term 'Member State' shall mean all Member States with the exception of Denmark;

4. the term 'judgment' shall mean a divorce, legal separation or marriage annulment, as well as a judgment relating to parental responsibility, pronounced by a court of a Member State, whatever the judgment may be called, including a decree, order or decision;

5. the term 'Member State of origin' shall mean the Member State where the judgment to be enforced was issued;

6. the term 'Member State of enforcement' shall mean the Member State where enforcement of the judgment is sought;

7. the term 'parental responsibility' shall mean all rights and duties relating to the person or the property of a child which are given to a natural or legal person by judgment, by operation of law or by an agreement having legal effect. The term shall include rights of custody and rights of access;

8. the term 'holder of parental responsibility' shall mean any person having parental responsibility over a child;

9. the term 'rights of custody' shall include rights and duties relating to the care of the person of a child, and in particular the right to determine the child's place of residence;

10. the term 'rights of access' shall include in particular the right to take a child to a place other than his or her habitual residence for a limited period of time;

11. the term 'wrongful removal or retention' shall mean a child's removal or retention where:

(a) it is in breach of rights of custody acquired by judgment or by operation of law or by an agreement having legal effect under the law of the Member State where the child was habitually resident immediately before the removal or retention;

and

(b) provided that, at the time of removal or retention, the rights of custody were actually exercised, either jointly or alone, or would have been so exercised but for the removal or retention. Custody shall be considered to be exercised jointly when, pursuant to a judgment or by operation of law, one holder of parental responsibility cannot decide on the child's place of residence without the consent of another holder of parental responsibility.

## CHAPTER II

## JURISDICTION

### SECTION 1

### DIVORCE, LEGAL SEPARATION AND MARRIAGE ANNULMENT

*Article 3*

*General jurisdiction*

1. In matters relating to divorce, legal separation or marriage annulment, jurisdiction shall lie with the courts of the Member State

(a) in whose territory:

– the spouses are habitually resident, or

– the spouses were last habitually resident, insofar as one of them still resides there, or

– the respondent is habitually resident, or

– in the event of a joint application, either of the spouses is habitually resident, or

- the applicant is habitually resident if he or she resided there for at least a year immediately before the application was made, or
- the applicant is habitually resident if he or she resided there for at least six months immediately before the application was made and is either a national of the Member State in question or, in the case of the United Kingdom and Ireland, has his or her 'domicile' there;

(*b*) of the nationality of both spouses or, in the case of the United Kingdom and Ireland, of the 'domicile' of both spouses.

2. For the purpose of this Regulation, 'domicile' shall have the same meaning as it has under the legal systems of the United Kingdom and Ireland.

## Article 4

### Counterclaim

The court in which proceedings are pending on the basis of Article 3 shall also have jurisdiction to examine a counterclaim, insofar as the latter comes within the scope of this Regulation.

## Article 5

### Conversion of legal separation into divorce

Without prejudice to Article 3, a court of a Member State that has given a judgment on a legal separation shall also have jurisdiction for converting that judgment into a divorce, if the law of that Member State so provides.

## Article 6

### Exclusive nature of jurisdiction under Articles 3, 4 and 5

A spouse who:

(*a*) is habitually resident in the territory of a Member State; or

(*b*) is a national of a Member State, or, in the case of the United Kingdom and Ireland, has his or her 'domicile' in the territory of one of the latter Member States,

may be sued in another Member State only in accordance with Articles 3, 4 and 5.

## Article 7

### Residual jurisdiction

1. Where no court of a Member State has jurisdiction pursuant to Articles 3, 4 and 5, jurisdiction shall be determined, in each Member State, by the laws of that State.

2. As against a respondent who is not habitually resident and is not either a national of a Member State or, in the case of the United Kingdom and Ireland, does not have his 'domicile' within the territory of one of the latter Member States, any national of a Member State who is habitually resident within the territory of another Member State may, like the nationals of that State, avail himself of the rules of jurisdiction applicable in that State.

## SECTION 2

### PARENTAL RESPONSIBILITY

## Article 8

### General jurisdiction

1. The courts of a Member State shall have jurisdiction in matters of parental responsibility over a child who is habitually resident in that Member State at the time the court is seised.

2. Paragraph 1 shall be subject to the provisions of Articles 9, 10 and 12.

*Article 9*

*Continuing jurisdiction of the child's former habitual residence*

1.   Where a child moves lawfully from one Member State to another and acquires a new habitual residence there, the courts of the Member State of the child's former habitual residence shall, by way of exception to Article 8, retain jurisdiction during a three-month period following the move for the purpose of modifying a judgment on access rights issued in that Member State before the child moved, where the holder of access rights pursuant to the judgment on access rights continues to have his or her habitual residence in the Member State of the child's former habitual residence.

2.   Paragraph 1 shall not apply if the holder of access rights referred to in paragraph 1 has accepted the jurisdiction of the courts of the Member State of the child's new habitual residence by participating in proceedings before those courts without contesting their jurisdiction.

*Article 10*

*Jurisdiction in cases of child abduction*

In case of wrongful removal or retention of the child, the courts of the Member State where the child was habitually resident immediately before the wrongful removal or retention shall retain their jurisdiction until the child has acquired a habitual residence in another Member State and:

(*a*)   each person, institution or other body having rights of custody has acquiesced in the removal or retention;

or

(*b*)   the child has resided in that other Member State for a period of at least one year after the person, institution or other body having rights of custody has had or should have had knowledge of the whereabouts of the child and the child is settled in his or her new environment and at least one of the following conditions is met:

   (i)   within one year after the holder of rights of custody has had or should have had knowledge of the whereabouts of the child, no request for return has been lodged before the competent authorities of the Member State where the child has been removed or is being retained;

   (ii)   a request for return lodged by the holder of rights of custody has been withdrawn and no new request has been lodged within the time limit set in paragraph (i);

   (iii)   a case before the court in the Member State where the child was habitually resident immediately before the wrongful removal or retention has been closed pursuant to Article 11(7);

   (iv)   a judgment on custody that does not entail the return of the child has been issued by the courts of the Member State where the child was habitually resident immediately before the wrongful removal or retention.

*Article 11*

*Return of the child*

1.   Where a person, institution or other body having rights of custody applies to the competent authorities in a Member State to deliver a judgment on the basis of the Hague Convention of 25 October 1980 on the Civil Aspects of International Child Abduction (hereinafter 'the 1980 Hague Convention'), in order to obtain the return of a child that has been wrongfully removed or retained in a Member State other than the Member State where the child was habitually resident immediately before the wrongful removal or retention, paragraphs 2 to 8 shall apply.

2.  When applying Articles 12 and 13 of the 1980 Hague Convention, it shall be ensured that the child is given the opportunity to be heard during the proceedings unless this appears inappropriate having regard to his or her age or degree of maturity.

3.  A court to which an application for return of a child is made as mentioned in paragraph 1 shall act expeditiously in proceedings on the application, using the most expeditious procedures available in national law.

Without prejudice to the first subparagraph, the court shall, except where exceptional circumstances make this impossible, issue its judgment no later than six weeks after the application is lodged.

4.  A court cannot refuse to return a child on the basis of Article 13b of the 1980 Hague Convention if it is established that adequate arrangements have been made to secure the protection of the child after his or her return.

5.  A court cannot refuse to return a child unless the person who requested the return of the child has been given an opportunity to be heard.

6.  If a court has issued an order on non-return pursuant to Article 13 of the 1980 Hague Convention, the court must immediately either directly or through its central authority, transmit a copy of the court order on non-return and of the relevant documents, in particular a transcript of the hearings before the court, to the court with jurisdiction or central authority in the Member State where the child was habitually resident immediately before the wrongful removal or retention, as determined by national law. The court shall receive all the mentioned documents within one month of the date of the non-return order.

7.  Unless the courts in the Member State where the child was habitually resident immediately before the wrongful removal or retention have already been seised by one of the parties, the court or central authority that receives the information mentioned in paragraph 6 must notify it to the parties and invite them to make submissions to the court, in accordance with national law, within three months of the date of notification so that the court can examine the question of custody of the child. Without prejudice to the rules on jurisdiction contained in this Regulation, the court shall close the case if no submissions have been received by the court within the time limit.

8.  Notwithstanding a judgment of non-return pursuant to Article 13 of the 1980 Hague Convention, any subsequent judgment which requires the return of the child issued by a court having jurisdiction under this Regulation shall be enforceable in accordance with Section 4 of Chapter III below in order to secure the return of the child.

*Article 12*

*Prorogation of jurisdiction*

1. The courts of a Member State exercising jurisdiction by virtue of Article 3 on an application for divorce, legal separation or marriage annulment shall have jurisdiction in any matter relating to parental responsibility connected with that application where:

(*a*)  at least one of the spouses has parental responsibility in relation to the child;

and

(*b*)  the jurisdiction of the courts has been accepted expressly or otherwise in an unequivocal manner by the spouses and by the holders of parental responsibility, at the time the court is seised, and is in the superior interests of the child.

2.  The jurisdiction conferred in paragraph 1 shall cease as soon as:

(*a*)  the judgment allowing or refusing the application for divorce, legal separation or marriage annulment has become final;

(*b*)   in those cases where proceedings in relation to parental responsibility are still pending on the date referred to in (*a*), a judgment in these proceedings has become final;

(*c*)   the proceedings referred to in (*a*) and (*b*) have come to an end for another reason.

3.   The courts of a Member State shall also have jurisdiction in relation to parental responsibility in proceedings other than those referred to in paragraph 1 where:

(*a*)   the child has a substantial connection with that Member State, in particular by virtue of the fact that one of the holders of parental responsibility is habitually resident in that Member State or that the child is a national of that Member State;

and

(*b*)   the jurisdiction of the courts has been accepted expressly or otherwise in an unequivocal manner by all the parties to the proceedings at the time the court is seised and is in the best interests of the child.

4.   Where the child has his or her habitual residence in the territory of a third State which is not a contracting party to the Hague Convention of 19 October 1996 on jurisdiction, applicable law, recognition, enforcement and cooperation in respect of parental responsibility and measures for the protection of children, jurisdiction under this Article shall be deemed to be in the child's interest, in particular if it is found impossible to hold proceedings in the third State in question.

### Article 13

*Jurisdiction based on the child's presence*

1.   Where a child's habitual residence cannot be established and jurisdiction cannot be determined on the basis of Article 12, the courts of the Member State where the child is present shall have jurisdiction.

2.   Paragraph 1 shall also apply to refugee children or children internationally displaced because of disturbances occurring in their country.

### Article 14

*Residual jurisdiction*

Where no court of a Member State has jurisdiction pursuant to Articles 8 to 13, jurisdiction shall be determined, in each Member State, by the laws of that State.

### Article 15

*Transfer to a court better placed to hear the case*

1.   By way of exception, the courts of a Member State having jurisdiction as to the substance of the matter may, if they consider that a court of another Member State, with which the child has a particular connection, would be better placed to hear the case, or a specific part thereof, and where this is in the best interests of the child:

(*a*)   stay the case or the part thereof in question and invite the parties to introduce a request before the court of that other Member State in accordance with paragraph 4; or

(*b*)   request a court of another Member State to assume jurisdiction in accordance with paragraph 5.

2.   Paragraph 1 shall apply:

(*a*)   upon application from a party; or

(*b*)   of the court's own motion; or

  (*c*)  upon application from a court of another Member State with which the child has a particular connection, in accordance with paragraph 3.

A transfer made of the court's own motion or by application of a court of another Member State must be accepted by at least one of the parties.

    3. The child shall be considered to have a particular connection to a Member State as mentioned in paragraph 1, if that Member State:

  (*a*)  has become the habitual residence of the child after the court referred to in paragraph 1 was seised; or

  (*b*)  is the former habitual residence of the child; or

  (*c*)  is the place of the child's nationality; or

  (*d*)  is the habitual residence of a holder of parental responsibility; or

  (*e*)  is the place where property of the child is located and the case concerns measures for the protection of the child relating to the administration, conservation or disposal of this property.

    4. The court of the Member State having jurisdiction as to the substance of the matter shall set a time limit by which the courts of that other Member State shall be seised in accordance with paragraph 1.

If the courts are not seised by that time, the court which has been seised shall continue to exercise jurisdiction in accordance with Articles 8 to 14.

    5. The courts of that other Member State may, where due to the specific circumstances of the case, this is in the best interests of the child, accept jurisdiction within six weeks of their seisure in accordance with paragraph 1(*a*) or 1(*b*). In this case, the court first seised shall decline jurisdiction. Otherwise, the court first seised shall continue to exercise jurisdiction in accordance with Articles 8 to 14.

    6. The courts shall cooperate for the purposes of this Article, either directly or through the central authorities designated pursuant to Article 53.

SECTION 3

COMMON PROVISIONS

*Article 16*

*Seising of a Court*

1. A court shall be deemed to be seised:

  (*a*)  at the time when the document instituting the proceedings or an equivalent document is lodged with the court, provided that the applicant has not subsequently failed to take the steps he was required to take to have service effected on the respondent;

or

  (*b*)  if the document has to be served before being lodged with the court, at the time when it is received by the authority responsible for service, provided that the applicant has not subsequently failed to take the steps he was required to take to have the document lodged with the court.

*Article 17*

*Examination as to jurisdiction*

Where a court of a Member State is seised of a case over which it has no jurisdiction under this Regulation and over which a court of another Member State has jurisdiction by virtue of this Regulation, it shall declare of its own motion that it has no jurisdiction.

*Article 18*

*Examination as to admissibility*

1. Where a respondent habitually resident in a State other than the Member State where the action was brought does not enter an appearance, the court with jurisdiction shall stay the proceedings so long as it is not shown that the respondent has been able to receive the document instituting the proceedings or an equivalent document in sufficient time to enable him to arrange for his defence, or that all necessary steps have been taken to this end.

2. Article 19 of Regulation (EC) No 1348/2000 shall apply instead of the provisions of paragraph 1 of this Article if the document instituting the proceedings or an equivalent document had to be transmitted from one Member State to another pursuant to that Regulation.

3. Where the provisions of Regulation (EC) No 1348/2000 are not applicable, Article 15 of the Hague Convention of 15 November 1965 on the service abroad of judicial and extrajudicial documents in civil or commercial matters shall apply if the document instituting the proceedings or an equivalent document had to be transmitted abroad pursuant to that Convention.

*Article 19*

*Lis pendens and dependent actions*

1. Where proceedings relating to divorce, legal separation or marriage annulment between the same parties are brought before courts of different Member States, the court second seised shall of its own motion stay its proceedings until such time as the jurisdiction of the court first seised is established.

2. Where proceedings relating to parental responsibility relating to the same child and involving the same cause of action are brought before courts of different Member States, the court second seised shall of its own motion stay its proceedings until such time as the jurisdiction of the court first seised is established.

3. Where the jurisdiction of the court first seised is established, the court second seised shall decline jurisdiction in favour of that court.

In that case, the party who brought the relevant action before the court second seised may bring that action before the court first seised.

*Article 20*

*Provisional, including protective, measures*

1. In urgent cases, the provisions of this Regulation shall not prevent the courts of a Member State from taking such provisional, including protective, measures in respect of persons or assets in that State as may be available under the law of that Member State, even if, under this Regulation, the court of another Member State has jurisdiction as to the substance of the matter.

2. The measures referred to in paragraph 1 shall cease to apply when the court of the Member State having jurisdiction under this Regulation as to the substance of the matter has taken the measures it considers appropriate.

## CHAPTER III
## RECOGNITION AND ENFORCEMENT

### SECTION 1

#### RECOGNITION

*Article 21*

*Recognition of a judgment*

1. A judgment given in a Member State shall be recognised in the other Member States without any special procedure being required.

2. In particular, and without prejudice to paragraph 3, no special procedure shall be required for updating the civil-status records of a Member State on the basis of a judgment relating to divorce, legal separation or marriage annulment given in another Member State, and against which no further appeal lies under the law of that Member State.

3. Without prejudice to Section 4 of this Chapter, any interested party may, in accordance with the procedures provided for in Section 2 of this Chapter, apply for a decision that the judgment be or not be recognised.

The local jurisdiction of the court appearing in the list notified by each Member State to the Commission pursuant to Article 68 shall be determined by the internal law of the Member State in which proceedings for recognition or non-recognition are brought.

4. Where the recognition of a judgment is raised as an incidental question in a court of a Member State, that court may determine that issue.

*Article 22*

*Grounds of non-recognition for judgments relating to divorce, legal separation or marriage annulment*

A judgment relating to a divorce, legal separation or marriage annulment shall not be recognised:

(a) if such recognition is manifestly contrary to the public policy of the Member State in which recognition is sought;

(b) where it was given in default of appearance, if the respondent was not served with the document which instituted the proceedings or with an equivalent document in sufficient time and in such a way as to enable the respondent to arrange for his or her defence unless it is determined that the respondent has accepted the judgment unequivocally;

(c) if it is irreconcilable with a judgment given in proceedings between the same parties in the Member State in which recognition is sought; or

(d) if it is irreconcilable with an earlier judgment given in another Member State or in a non-Member State between the same parties, provided that the earlier judgment fulfils the conditions necessary for its recognition in the Member State in which recognition is sought.

*Article 23*

*Grounds of non-recognition for judgments relating to parental responsibility*

A judgment relating to parental responsibility shall not be recognised:

(a) if such recognition is manifestly contrary to the public policy of the Member State in which recognition is sought taking into account the best interests of the child;

(b) if it was given, except in case of urgency, without the child having been given an opportunity to be heard, in violation of fundamental principles of procedure of the Member State in which recognition is sought;

(c) where it was given in default of appearance if the person in default was not served with the document which instituted the proceedings or with an equivalent document in sufficient time and in such a way as to enable that person to arrange for his or her defence unless it is determined that such person has accepted the judgment unequivocally;

(d) on the request of any person claiming that the judgment infringes his or her parental responsibility, if it was given without such person having been given an opportunity to be heard;

(e) if it is irreconcilable with a later judgment relating to parental responsibility given in the Member State in which recognition is sought;

(f) if it is irreconcilable with a later judgment relating to parental responsibility given in another Member State or in the non-Member State of the habitual residence of the child provided that the later judgment fulfils the conditions necessary for its recognition in the Member State in which recognition is sought.

or

(g) if the procedure laid down in Article 56 has not been complied with.

### Article 24

*Prohibition of review of jurisdiction of the court of origin*

The jurisdiction of the court of the Member State of origin may not be reviewed. The test of public policy referred to in Articles 22(a) and 23(a) may not be applied to the rules relating to jurisdiction set out in Articles 3 to 14.

### Article 25

*Differences in applicable law*

The recognition of a judgment may not be refused because the law of the Member State in which such recognition is sought would not allow divorce, legal separation or marriage annulment on the same facts.

### Article 26

*Non-review as to substance*

Under no circumstances may a judgment be reviewed as to its substance.

### Article 27

*Stay of proceedings*

1. A court of a Member State in which recognition is sought of a judgment given in another Member State may stay the proceedings if an ordinary appeal against the judgment has been lodged.

2. A court of a Member State in which recognition is sought of a judgment given in Ireland or the United Kingdom may stay the proceedings if enforcement is suspended in the Member State of origin by reason of an appeal.

SECTION 2
APPLICATION FOR A DECLARATION OF ENFORCEABILITY

### Article 28

*Enforceable judgments*

1. A judgment on the exercise of parental responsibility in respect of a child given in a Member State which is enforceable in that Member State and has been served

shall be enforced in another Member State when, on the application of any interested party, it has been declared enforceable there.

2. However, in the United Kingdom, such a judgment shall be enforced in England and Wales, in Scotland or in Northern Ireland only when, on the application of any interested party, it has been registered for enforcement in that part of the United Kingdom.

*Article 29*

*Jurisdiction of local courts*

1. An application for a declaration of enforceability shall be submitted to the court appearing in the list notified by each Member State to the Commission pursuant to Article 68.

2. The local jurisdiction shall be determined by reference to the place of habitual residence of the person against whom enforcement is sought or by reference to the habitual residence of any child to whom the application relates. Where neither of the places referred to in the first subparagraph can be found in the Member State of enforcement, the local jurisdiction shall be determined by reference to the place of enforcement.

*Article 30*

*Procedure*

1. The procedure for making the application shall be governed by the law of the Member State of enforcement.

2. The applicant must give an address for service within the area of jurisdiction of the court applied to. However, if the law of the Member State of enforcement does not provide for the furnishing of such an address, the applicant shall appoint a representative ad litem.

3. The documents referred to in Articles 37 and 39 shall be attached to the application.

*Article 31*

*Decision of the court*

1. The court applied to shall give its decision without delay. Neither the person against whom enforcement is sought, nor the child shall, at this stage of the proceedings, be entitled to make any submissions on the application.

2. The application may be refused only for one of the reasons specified in Articles 22, 23 and 24.

3. Under no circumstances may a judgment be reviewed as to its substance.

*Article 32*

*Notice of the decision*

The appropriate officer of the court shall without delay bring to the notice of the applicant the decision given on the application in accordance with the procedure laid down by the law of the Member State of enforcement.

*Article 33*

*Appeal against the decision*

1. The decision on the application for a declaration of enforceability may be appealed against by either party.

2. The appeal shall be lodged with the court appearing in the list notified by each Member State to the Commission pursuant to Article 68.

3. The appeal shall be dealt with in accordance with the rules governing procedure in contradictory matters.

4. If the appeal is brought by the applicant for a declaration of enforceability, the party against whom enforcement is sought shall be summoned to appear before the appellate court. If such person fails to appear, the provisions of Article 18 shall apply.

5. An appeal against a declaration of enforceability must be lodged within one month of service thereof. If the party against whom enforcement is sought is habitually resident in a Member State other than that in which the declaration of enforceability was given, the time for appealing shall be two months and shall run from the date of service, either on him or at his residence. No extension of time may be granted on account of distance.

### Article 34

*Courts of appeal and means of contest*

The judgment given on appeal may be contested only by the proceedings referred to in the list notified by each Member State to the Commission pursuant to Article 68.

### Article 35

*Stay of proceedings*

1. The court with which the appeal is lodged under Articles 33 or 34 may, on the application of the party against whom enforcement is sought, stay the proceedings if an ordinary appeal has been lodged in the Member State of origin, or if the time for such appeal has not yet expired. In the latter case, the court may specify the time within which an appeal is to be lodged.

2. Where the judgment was given in Ireland or the United Kingdom, any form of appeal available in the Member State of origin shall be treated as an ordinary appeal for the purposes of paragraph 1.

### Article 36

*Partial enforcement*

1. Where a judgment has been given in respect of several matters and enforcement cannot be authorised for all of them, the court shall authorise enforcement for one or more of them.

2. An applicant may request partial enforcement of a judgment.

### SECTION 3

PROVISIONS COMMON TO SECTIONS 1 AND 2

### Article 37

*Documents*

1. A party seeking or contesting recognition or applying for a declaration of enforceability shall produce:
   (*a*) a copy of the judgment which satisfies the conditions necessary to establish its authenticity;
   and
   (*b*) the certificate referred to in Article 39.

2. In addition, in the case of a judgment given in default, the party seeking recognition or applying for a declaration of enforceability shall produce:
   (*a*) the original or certified true copy of the document which establishes that the defaulting party was served with the document instituting the proceedings or with an equivalent document;

or
(*b*) any document indicating that the defendant has accepted the judgment unequivocally.

### Article 38

*Absence of documents*

1. If the documents specified in Article 37(1)(*b*) or (2) are not produced, the court may specify a time for their production, accept equivalent documents or, if it considers that it has sufficient information before it, dispense with their production.
    2. If the court so requires, a translation of such documents shall be furnished. The translation shall be certified by a person qualified to do so in one of the Member States.

### Article 39

*Certificate concerning judgments in matrimonial matters and certificate concerning judgments on parental responsibility*

The competent court or authority of a Member State of origin shall, at the request of any interested party, issue a certificate using the standard form set out in Annex I (judgments in matrimonial matters) or in Annex II (judgments on parental responsibility).

### SECTION 4
ENFORCEABILITY OF CERTAIN JUDGMENTS CONCERNING RIGHTS OF ACCESS AND OF CERTAIN JUDGMENTS WHICH REQUIRE THE RETURN OF THE CHILD

### Article 40

*Scope*

1. This Section shall apply to:
    (*a*) rights of access;
    and
    (*b*) the return of a child entailed by a judgment given pursuant to Article 11(8).
    2. The provisions of this Section shall not prevent a holder of parental responsibility from seeking recognition and enforcement of a judgment in accordance with the provisions in Sections 1 and 2 of this Chapter.

### Article 41

*Rights of access*

1. The rights of access referred to in Article 40(1)(*a*) granted in an enforceable judgment given in a Member State shall be recognised and enforceable in another Member State without the need for a declaration of enforceability and without any possibility of opposing its recognition if the judgment has been certified in the Member State of origin in accordance with paragraph 2.
Even if national law does not provide for enforceability by operation of law of a judgment granting access rights, the court of origin may declare that the judgment shall be enforceable, notwithstanding any appeal.
    2. The judge of origin shall issue the certificate referred to in paragraph 1 using the standard form in Annex III (certificate concerning rights of access) only if:
    (*a*) where the judgment was given in default, the person defaulting was served with the document which instituted the proceedings or with an equivalent document in sufficient time and in such a way as to enable that person to

arrange for his or her defense, or, the person has been served with the document but not in compliance with these conditions, it is nevertheless established that he or she accepted the decision unequivocally;

(*b*) all parties concerned were given an opportunity to be heard; and

(*c*) the child was given an opportunity to be heard, unless a hearing was considered inappropriate having regard to his or her age or degree of maturity.

The certificate shall be completed in the language of the judgment.

3. Where the rights of access involve a cross-border situation at the time of the delivery of the judgment, the certificate shall be issued ex officio when the judgment becomes enforceable, even if only provisionally. If the situation subsequently acquires a cross-border character, the certificate shall be issued at the request of one of the parties.

### Article 42

#### Return of the child

1. The return of a child referred to in Article 40(1)(*b*) entailed by an enforceable judgment given in a Member State shall be recognised and enforceable in another Member State without the need for a declaration of enforceability and without any possibility of opposing its recognition if the judgment has been certified in the Member State of origin in accordance with paragraph 2.

Even if national law does not provide for enforceability by operation of law, notwithstanding any appeal, of a judgment requiring the return of the child mentioned in Article 11(*b*)(8), the court of origin may declare the judgment enforceable.

2. The judge of origin who delivered the judgment referred to in Article 40(1)(*b*) shall issue the certificate referred to in paragraph 1 only if:

(*a*) the child was given an opportunity to be heard, unless a hearing was considered inappropriate having regard to his or her age or degree of maturity;

(*b*) the parties were given an opportunity to be heard; and

(*c*) the court has taken into account in issuing its judgment the reasons for and evidence underlying the order issued pursuant to Article 13 of the 1980 Hague Convention.

In the event that the court or any other authority takes measures to ensure the protection of the child after its return to the State of habitual residence, the certificate shall contain details of such measures.

The judge of origin shall of his or her own motion issue that certificate using the standard form in Annex IV (certificate concerning return of the child(ren)).

The certificate shall be completed in the language of the judgment.

### Article 43

#### Rectification of the certificate

1. The law of the Member State of origin shall be applicable to any rectification of the certificate.

2. No appeal shall lie against the issuing of a certificate pursuant to Articles 41(1) or 42(1).

### Article 44

#### Effects of the certificate

The certificate shall take effect only within the limits of the enforceability of the judgment.

*Article 45*

*Documents*

1. A party seeking enforcement of a judgment shall produce:
   (*a*) a copy of the judgment which satisfies the conditions necessary to establish its authenticity;
   and
   (*b*) the certificate referred to in Article 41(1) or Article 42(1).
2. For the purposes of this Article,
   – the certificate referred to in Article 41(1) shall be accompanied by a translation of point 12 relating to the arrangements for exercising right of access,
   – the certificate referred to in Article 42(1) shall be accompanied by a translation of its point 14 relating to the arrangements for implementing the measures taken to ensure the child's return.

The translation shall be into the official language or one of the official languages of the Member State of enforcement or any other language that the Member State of enforcement expressly accepts. The translation shall be certified by a person qualified to do so in one of the Member States.

SECTION 5

AUTHENTIC INSTRUMENTS AND AGREEMENTS

*Article 46*

Documents which have been formally drawn up or registered as authentic instruments and are enforceable in one Member State and also agreements between the parties that are enforceable in the Member State in which they were concluded shall be recognised and declared enforceable under the same conditions as judgments.

SECTION 6

OTHER PROVISIONS

*Article 47*

*Enforcement procedure*

1. The enforcement procedure is governed by the law of the Member State of enforcement.
   2. Any judgment delivered by a court of another Member State and declared to be enforceable in accordance with Section 2 or certified in accordance with Article 41(1) or Article 42(1) shall be enforced in the Member State of enforcement in the same conditions as if it had been delivered in that Member State.

In particular, a judgment which has been certified according to Article 41(1) or Article 42(1) cannot be enforced if it is irreconcilable with a subsequent enforceable judgment.

*Article 48*

*Practical arrangements for the exercise of rights of access*

1. The courts of the Member State of enforcement may make practical arrangements for organising the exercise of rights of access, if the necessary arrangements have not or have not sufficiently been made in the judgment delivered by the courts of the Member State having jurisdiction as to the substance of the matter and provided the essential elements of this judgment are respected.

2.   The practical arrangements made pursuant to paragraph 1 shall cease to apply pursuant to a later judgment by the courts of the Member State having jurisdiction as to the substance of the matter.

*Article 49*

*Costs*

The provisions of this Chapter, with the exception of Section 4, shall also apply to the determination of the amount of costs and expenses of proceedings under this Regulation and to the enforcement of any order concerning such costs and expenses.

*Article 50*

*Legal aid*

An applicant who, in the Member State of origin, has benefited from complete or partial legal aid or exemption from costs or expenses shall be entitled, in the procedures provided for in Articles 21, 28, 41, 42 and 48 to benefit from the most favourable legal aid or the most extensive exemption from costs and expenses provided for by the law of the Member State of enforcement.

*Article 51*

*Security, bond or deposit*

No security, bond or deposit, however described, shall be required of a party who in one Member State applies for enforcement of a judgment given in another Member State on the following grounds:

(*a*)  that he or she is not habitually resident in the Member State in which enforcement is sought; or

(*b*)  that he or she is either a foreign national or, where enforcement is sought in either the United Kingdom or Ireland, does not have his or her 'domicile' in either of those Member States.

*Article 52*

*Legalisation or other similar formality*

No legalisation or other similar formality shall be required in respect of the documents referred to in Articles 37, 38 and 45 or in respect of a document appointing a representative ad litem.

## CHAPTER IV

## COOPERATION BETWEEN CENTRAL AUTHORITIES IN MATTERS OF PARENTAL RESPONSIBILITY

*Article 53*

*Designation*

Each Member State shall designate one or more central authorities to assist with the application of this Regulation and shall specify the geographical or functional jurisdiction of each. Where a Member State has designated more than one central authority, communications shall normally be sent direct to the relevant central authority with jurisdiction. Where a communication is sent to a central authority without jurisdiction, the latter shall be responsible for forwarding it to the central authority with jurisdiction and informing the sender accordingly.

## Article 54

*General functions*

The central authorities shall communicate information on national laws and procedures and take measures to improve the application of this Regulation and strengthening their cooperation. For this purpose the European Judicial Network in civil and commercial matters created by Decision No 2001/470/EC shall be used.

## Article 55

*Cooperation on cases specific to parental responsibility*

The central authorities shall, upon request from a central authority of another Member State or from a holder of parental responsibility, cooperate on specific cases to achieve the purposes of this Regulation. To this end, they shall, acting directly or through public authorities or other bodies, take all appropriate steps in accordance with the law of that Member State in matters of personal data protection to:

    (a) collect and exchange information:
        (i)   on the situation of the child;
        (ii)  on any procedures under way; or
        (iii) on decisions taken concerning the child;
    (b) provide information and assistance to holders of parental responsibility seeking the recognition and enforcement of decisions on their territory, in particular concerning rights of access and the return of the child;
    (c) facilitate communications between courts, in particular for the application of Article 11(6) and (7) and Article 15;
    (d) provide such information and assistance as is needed by courts to apply Article 56; and
    (e) facilitate agreement between holders of parental responsibility through mediation or other means, and facilitate cross-border cooperation to this end.

## Article 56

*Placement of a child in another Member State*

1. Where a court having jurisdiction under Articles 8 to 15 contemplates the placement of a child in institutional care or with a foster family and where such placement is to take place in another Member State, it shall first consult the central authority or other authority having jurisdiction in the latter State where public authority intervention in that Member State is required for domestic cases of child placement.

2. The judgment on placement referred to in paragraph 1 may be made in the requesting State only if the competent authority of the requested State has consented to the placement.

3. The procedures for consultation or consent referred to in paragraphs 1 and 2 shall be governed by the national law of the requested State.

4. Where the authority having jurisdiction under Articles 8 to 15 decides to place the child in a foster family, and where such placement is to take place in another Member State and where no public authority intervention is required in the latter Member State for domestic cases of child placement, it shall so inform the central authority or other authority having jurisdiction in the latter State.

*Article 57*

*Working method*

1. Any holder of parental responsibility may submit, to the central authority of the Member State of his or her habitual residence or to the central authority of the Member State where the child is habitually resident or present, a request for assistance as mentioned in Article 55. In general, the request shall include all available information of relevance to its enforcement. Where the request for assistance concerns the recognition or enforcement of a judgment on parental responsibility that falls within the scope of this Regulation, the holder of parental responsibility shall attach the relevant certificates provided for in Articles 39, 41(1) or 42(1).

2. Member States shall communicate to the Commission the official language or languages of the Community institutions other than their own in which communications to the central authorities can be accepted.

3. The assistance provided by the central authorities pursuant to Article 55 shall be free of charge.

4. Each central authority shall bear its own costs.

*Article 58*

*Meetings*

1. In order to facilitate the application of this Regulation, central authorities shall meet regularly.

2. These meetings shall be convened in compliance with Decision No 2001/470/EC establishing a European Judicial Network in civil and commercial matters.

## CHAPTER V

## RELATIONS WITH OTHER INSTRUMENTS

*Article 59*

*Relation with other instruments*

1. Subject to the provisions of Articles 60, 63, 64 and paragraph 2 of this Article, this Regulation shall, for the Member States, supersede conventions existing at the time of entry into force of this Regulation which have been concluded between two or more Member States and relate to matters governed by this Regulation.

2.

 (*a*) Finland and Sweden shall have the option of declaring that the Convention of 6 February 1931 between Denmark, Finland, Iceland, Norway and Sweden comprising international private law provisions on marriage, adoption and guardianship, together with the Final Protocol thereto, will apply, in whole or in part, in their mutual relations, in place of the rules of this Regulation. Such declarations shall be annexed to this Regulation and published in the Official Journal of the European Union. They may be withdrawn, in whole or in part, at any moment by the said Member States.

 (*b*) The principle of non-discrimination on the grounds of nationality between citizens of the Union shall be respected.

 (*c*) The rules of jurisdiction in any future agreement to be concluded between the Member States referred to in subparagraph (*a*) which relate to matters governed by this Regulation shall be in line with those laid down in this Regulation.

 (*d*) Judgments handed down in any of the Nordic States which have made the declaration provided for in subparagraph (*a*) under a forum of jurisdiction corresponding to one of those laid down in Chapter II of this Regulation, shall be recognised and enforced in the other Member States under the rules laid down in Chapter III of this Regulation.

3. Member States shall send to the Commission:

   (*a*) a copy of the agreements and uniform laws implementing these agreements referred to in paragraph 2(*a*) and (*c*);

   (*b*) any denunciations of, or amendments to, those agreements or uniform laws.

### Article 60

*Relations with certain multilateral conventions*

In relations between Member States, this Regulation shall take precedence over the following Conventions in so far as they concern matters governed by this Regulation:

   (*a*) the Hague Convention of 5 October 1961 concerning the Powers of Authorities and the Law Applicable in respect of the Protection of Minors;

   (*b*) the Luxembourg Convention of 8 September 1967 on the Recognition of Decisions Relating to the Validity of Marriages;

   (*c*) the Hague Convention of 1 June 1970 on the Recognition of Divorces and Legal Separations;

   (*d*) the European Convention of 20 May 1980 on Recognition and Enforcement of Decisions concerning Custody of Children and on Restoration of Custody of Children;

and

   (*e*) the Hague Convention of 25 October 1980 on the Civil Aspects of International Child Abduction.

### Article 61

*Relation with the Hague Convention of 19 October 1996 on Jurisdiction, Applicable law, Recognition, Enforcement and Cooperation in Respect of Parental Responsibility and Measures for the Protection of Children*

As concerns the relation with the Hague Convention of 19 October 1996 on Jurisdiction, Applicable law, Recognition, Enforcement and Cooperation in Respect of Parental Responsibility and Measures for the Protection of Children, this Regulation shall apply:

   (*a*) where the child concerned has his or her habitual residence on the territory of a Member State;

   (*b*) as concerns the recognition and enforcement of a judgment given in a court of a Member State on the territory of another Member State, even if the child concerned has his or her habitual residence on the territory of a third State which is a contracting Party to the said Convention.

### Article 62

*Scope of effects*

1. The agreements and conventions referred to in Articles 59(1), 60 and 61 shall continue to have effect in relation to matters not governed by this Regulation.

   2. The conventions mentioned in Article 60, in particular the 1980 Hague Convention, continue to produce effects between the Member States which are party thereto, in compliance with Article 60.

*Article 63*

*Treaties with the Holy See*

1. This Regulation shall apply without prejudice to the International Treaty (Concordat) between the Holy See and Portugal, signed at the Vatican City on 7 May 1940.

2. Any decision as to the invalidity of a marriage taken under the Treaty referred to in paragraph 1 shall be recognised in the Member States on the conditions laid down in Chapter III, Section 1.

3. The provisions laid down in paragraphs 1 and 2 shall also apply to the following international treaties (Concordats) with the Holy See:

　(*a*) 'Concordato lateranense' of 11 February 1929 between Italy and the Holy See, modified by the agreement, with additional Protocol signed in Rome on 18 February 1984;

　(*b*) Agreement between the Holy See and Spain on legal affairs of 3 January 1979.

4. Recognition of the decisions provided for in paragraph 2 may, in Italy or in Spain, be subject to the same procedures and the same checks as are applicable to decisions of the ecclesiastical courts handed down in accordance with the international treaties concluded with the Holy See referred to in paragraph 3.

5. Member States shall send to the Commission:

　(*a*) a copy of the Treaties referred to in paragraphs 1 and 3;

　(*b*) any denunciations of or amendments to those Treaties.

## CHAPTER VI

## TRANSITIONAL PROVISIONS

*Article 64*

1. The provisions of this Regulation shall apply only to legal proceedings instituted, to documents formally drawn up or registered as authentic instruments and to agreements concluded between the parties after its date of application in accordance with Article 72.

2. Judgments given after the date of application of this Regulation in proceedings instituted before that date but after the date of entry into force of Regulation (EC) No 1347/2000 shall be recognised and enforced in accordance with the provisions of Chapter III of this Regulation if jurisdiction was founded on rules which accorded with those provided for either in Chapter II or in Regulation (EC) No 1347/2000 or in a convention concluded between the Member State of origin and the Member State addressed which was in force when the proceedings were instituted.

3. Judgments given before the date of application of this Regulation in proceedings instituted after the entry into force of Regulation (EC) No 1347/2000 shall be recognised and enforced in accordance with the provisions of Chapter III of this Regulation provided they relate to divorce, legal separation or marriage annulment or parental responsibility for the children of both spouses on the occasion of these matrimonial proceedings.

4. Judgments given before the date of application of this Regulation but after the date of entry into force of Regulation (EC) No 1347/2000 in proceedings instituted before the date of entry into force of Regulation (EC) No 1347/2000 shall be recognised and enforced in accordance with the provisions of Chapter III of this Regulation provided they relate to divorce, legal separation or marriage annulment or parental responsibility for the children of both spouses on the occasion of these matrimonial proceedings and that jurisdiction was founded on rules which accorded with those provided for either in Chapter II of this

Regulation or in Regulation (EC) No 1347/2000 or in a convention concluded between the Member State of origin and the Member State addressed which was in force when the proceedings were instituted.

## CHAPTER VII

## FINAL PROVISIONS

*Article 65*

*Review*

No later than 1 January 2012, and every five years thereafter, the Commission shall present to the European Parliament, to the Council and to the European Economic and Social Committee a report on the application of this Regulation on the basis of information supplied by the Member States. The report shall be accompanied if need be by proposals for adaptations.

*Article 66*

*Member States with two or more legal systems*

With regard to a Member State in which two or more systems of law or sets of rules concerning matters governed by this Regulation apply in different territorial units:
  (*a*)  any reference to habitual residence in that Member State shall refer to habitual residence in a territorial unit;
  (*b*)  any reference to nationality, or in the case of the United Kingdom 'domicile', shall refer to the territorial unit designated by the law of that State;
  (*c*)  any reference to the authority of a Member State shall refer to the authority of a territorial unit within that State which is concerned;
  (*d*)  any reference to the rules of the requested Member State shall refer to the rules of the territorial unit in which jurisdiction, recognition or enforcement is invoked.

*Article 67*

*Information on central authorities and languages accepted*

The Member States shall communicate to the Commission within three months following the entry into force of this Regulation:
  (*a*)  the names, addresses and means of communication for the central authorities designated pursuant to Article 53;
  (*b*)  the languages accepted for communications to central authorities pursuant to Article 57(2);
and
  (*c*)  the languages accepted for the certificate concerning rights of access pursuant to Article 45(2).
The Member States shall communicate to the Commission any changes to this information.
The Commission shall make this information publicly available.

*Article 68*

*Information relating to courts and redress procedures*

The Member States shall notify to the Commission the lists of courts and redress procedures referred to in Articles 21, 29, 33 and 34 and any amendments thereto.
  The Commission shall update this information and make it publicly available through the publication in the Official Journal of the European Union and any other appropriate means.

*Article 69*

*Amendments to the Annexes*

Any amendments to the standard forms in Annexes I to IV shall be adopted in accordance with the consultative procedure set out in Article 70(2).

*Article 70*

*Committee*

1. The Commission shall be assisted by a committee (committee).
   2. Where reference is made to this paragraph, Articles 3 and 7 of Decision 1999/468/EC shall apply.
   3. The committee shall adopt its rules of procedure.

*Article 71*

*Repeal of Regulation (EC) No 1347/2000*

1. Regulation (EC) No 1347/2000 shall be repealed as from the date of application of this Regulation.
   2. Any reference to Regulation (EC) No 1347/2000 shall be construed as a reference to this Regulation according to the comparative table in Annex V.

*Article 72*

*Entry into force*

This Regulation shall enter into force on 1 August 2004.

The Regulation shall apply from 1 March 2005, with the exception of Articles 67, 68, 69 and 70, which shall apply from 1 August 2004.

This Regulation shall be binding in its entirety and directly applicable in the Member States in accordance with the Treaty establishing the European Community.

Done at Brussels, 27 November 2003.

## ANNEX I

CERTIFICATE REFERRED TO IN ARTICLE 39 CONCERNING JUDGMENTS IN MATRIMONIAL MATTERS

1. Member State of origin
2. Court or authority issuing the certificate
   2.1. Name
   2.2. Address
   2.3. Tel./fax/e-mail
3. Marriage
   3.1. Wife
   3.1.1. Full name
   3.1.2. Address
   3.1.3. Country and place of birth
   3.1.4. Date of birth
   3.2. Husband
   3.2.1. Full name
   3.2.2. Address
   3.2.3. Country and place of birth
   3.2.4. Date of birth
   3.3. Country, place (where available) and date of marriage
   3.3.1. Country of marriage
   3.3.2. Place of marriage (where available)
   3.3.3. Date of marriage

4. Court which delivered the judgment
    4.1. Name of Court
    4.2. Place of Court
5. Judgment
    5.1. Date
    5.2. Reference number
    5.3. Type of judgment
        5.3.1. Divorce
        5.3.2. Marriage annulment
        5.3.3. Legal separation
    5.4. Was the judgment given in default of appearance?
        5.4.1. No
        5.4.2. Yes
6. Names of parties to whom legal aid has been granted
7. Is the judgment subject to further appeal under the law of the Member State of origin?
    7.1. No
    7.2. Yes
8. Date of legal effect in the Member State where the judgment was given
    8.1. Divorce
    8.2. Legal separation

Done at ............................., date ...........................

Signature and/or stamp.......................................

## ANNEX II

### CERTIFICATE REFERRED TO IN ARTICLE 39 CONCERNING JUDGMENTS ON PARENTAL RESPONSIBILITY

1. Member State of origin
2. Court or authority issuing the certificate
    2.1. Name
    2.2. Address
    2.3. Tel./Fax/e-mail
3. Person(s) with rights of access
    3.1. Full name
    3.2. Address
    3.3. Date and place of birth (where available)
4. Holders of parental responsibility other than those mentioned under 3(2)
    4.1.
        4.1.1. Full name
        4.1.2. Address
        4.1.3. Date and place of birth (where available)
    4.2.
        4.2.1. Full Name
        4.2.2. Address
        4.2.3. Date and place of birth (where available)
    4.3.
        4.3.1. Full name
        4.3.2. Address
        4.3.3. Date and place of birth (where available)
5. Court which delivered the judgment
    5.1. Name of Court
    5.2. Place of Court

6.  Judgment
    6.1.  Date
    6.2.  Reference number
    6.3.  Was the judgment given in default of appearance?
        6.3.1.  No
        6.3.2.  Yes
7.  Children who are covered by the judgment
    7.1.  Full name and date of birth
    7.2.  Full name and date of birth
    7.3.  Full name and date of birth
    7.4.  Full name and date of birth
8.  Names of parties to whom legal aid has been granted
9.  Attestation of enforceability and service
    9.1.  Is the judgment enforceable according to the law of the Member State of origin?
        9.1.1.  Yes
        9.1.2.  No
    9.2.  Has the judgment been served on the party against whom enforcement is sought?
        9.2.1.  Yes
            9.2.1.1.  Full name of the party
            9.2.1.2.  Address
            9.2.1.3.  Date of service
        9.2.2.  No
10.  Specific information on judgments on rights of access where 'exequatur' is requested under Article 28. This possibility is foreseen in Article 40(2).
    10.1.  Practical arrangements for exercise of rights of access (to the extent stated in the judgment)
        10.1.1.  Date and time
            10.1.1.1.  Start
            10.1.1.2.  End
        10.1.2.  Place
        10.1.3.  Specific obligations on holders of parental responsibility
        10.1.4.  Specific obligations on the person with right of access
        10.1.5.  Any restrictions attached to the exercise of rights of access
11.  Specific information for judgments on the return of the child in cases where the 'exequatur' procedure is requested under Article 28. This possibility is foreseen under Article 40(2).
    11.1.  The judgment entails the return of the child
    11.2.  Person to whom the child is to be returned (to the extent stated in the judgment)
        11.2.1.  Full name
        11.2.2.  Address

Done at ..........................., date ..........................

Signature and/or stamp........................................

ANNEX III

CERTIFICATE REFERRED TO IN ARTICLE 41(1) CONCERNING JUDGMENTS ON RIGHTS OF ACCESS

1.  Member State of origin
2.  Court or authority issuing the certificate
    2.1.  Name
    2.2.  Address
    2.3.  Tel./fax/e-mail

3.  Person(s) with rights of access
    3.1.  Full name
    3.2.  Address
    3.3.  Date and place of birth (where available)
4.  Holders of parental responsibility other than those mentioned under 3
    4.1.
        4.1.1.  Full name
        4.1.2.  Address
        4.1.3.  Date and place of birth (where available)
    4.2.
        4.2.1.  Full name
        4.2.2.  Address
        4.2.3.  Date and place of birth (where available)
    4.3.  Other
        4.3.1.  Full name
        4.3.2.  Address
        4.3.3.  Date and place of birth (where available)
5.  Court which delivered the judgment
    5.1.  Name of Court
    5.2.  Place of Court
6.  Judgment
    6.1.  Date
    6.2.  Reference number
7.  Children who are covered by the judgment
    7.1.  Full name and date of birth
    7.2.  Full name and date of birth
    7.3.  Full name and date of birth
    7.4.  Full name and date of birth
8.  Is the judgment enforceable in the Member State of origin?
    8.1.  Yes
    8.2.  No
9.  Where the judgment was given in default of appearance, the person defaulting was served with the document which instituted the proceedings or with an equivalent document in sufficient time and in such a way as to enable that person to arrange for his or her defence, or the person has been served with the document but not in compliance with these conditions, it is nevertheless established that he or she accepted the decision unequivocally
10. All parties concerned were given an opportunity to be heard
11. The children were given an opportunity to be heard, unless a hearing was considered inappropriate having regard to their age or degree of maturity
12. Practical arrangements for exercise of rights of access (to the extent stated in the judgment)
    12.1.  Date and time
        12.1.1. Start
        12.1.2. End
    12.2.  Place
    12.3.  Specific obligations on holders of parental responsibility
    12.4.  Specific obligations on the person with right of access
    12.5.  Any restrictions attached to the exercise of rights of access
13. Names of parties to whom legal aid has been granted

Done at ..........................., date ...........................

Signature and/or stamp...........................................

ANNEX IV

## CERTIFICATE REFERRED TO IN ARTICLE 42(1) CONCERNING THE RETURN OF THE CHILD

1. Member State of origin
2. Court or authority issuing the certificate
   2.1. Name
   2.2. Address
   2.3. Tel./fax/e-mail
3. Person to whom the child has to be returned (to the extent stated in the judgment)
   3.1. Full name
   3.2. Address
   3.3. Date and place of birth (where available)
4. Holders of parental responsibility
   4.1. Mother
      4.1.1. Full name
      4.1.2. Address (where available)
      4.1.3. Date and place of birth (where available)
   4.2. Father
      4.2.1. Full name
      4.2.2. Address (where available)
      4.2.3. Date and place of birth (where available)
   4.3. Other
      4.3.1. Full name
      4.3.2. Address (where available)
      4.3.3. Date and place of birth (where available)
5. Respondent (where available)
   5.1. Full name
   5.2. Address (where available)
6. Court which delivered the judgment
   6.1. Name of Court
   6.2. Place of Court
7. Judgment
   7.1. Date
   7.2. Reference number
8. Children who are covered by the judgment
   8.1. Full name and date of birth
   8.2. Full name and date of birth
   8.3. Full name and date of birth
   8.4. Full name and date of birth
9. The judgment entails the return of the child
10. Is the judgment enforceable in the Member State of origin?
    10.1. Yes
    10.2. No
11. The children were given an opportunity to be heard, unless a hearing was considered inappropriate having regard to their age or degree of maturity
12. The parties were given an opportunity to be heard
13. The judgment entails the return of the children and the court has taken into account in issuing its judgment the reasons for and evidence underlying the decision issued pursuant to Article 13 of the Hague Convention of 25 October 1980 on the Civil Aspects of International Child Abduction
14. Where applicable, details of measures taken by courts or authorities to ensure the protection of the child after its return to the Member State of habitual residence
15. Names of parties to whom legal aid has been granted

Done at ............................, date ..........................

Signature and/or stamp.........................................

## ANNEX V

COMPARATIVE TABLE WITH REGULATION (EC) No 1347/2000

[ ]

| Articles repealed | Corresponding Articles of new text | Articles repealed Articles of new text | Corresponding |
|---|---|---|---|
| 1 | 1, 2 | 27 | 34 |
| 2 | 3 | 28 | 35 |
| 3 | 12 | 29 | 36 |
| 4 | | 30 | 50 |
| 5 | 4 | 31 | 51 |
| 6 | 5 | 32 | 37 |
| 7 | 6 | 33 | 39 |
| 8 | 7 | 34 | 38 |
| 9 | 17 | 35 | 52 |
| 10 | 18 | 36 | 59 |
| 11 | 16, 19 | 37 60, | 61 |
| 12 | 20 | 38 | 62 |
| 13 | 2, 49, 46 | 39 | |
| 14 | 21 | 40 | 63 |
| 15 | 22, 23 | 41 | 66 |
| 16 | | 42 | 64 |
| 17 | 24 | 43 | 65 |
| 18 | 25 | 44 | 68, 69 |
| 19 | 26 | 45 | 70 |
| 20 | 27 | 46 | 72 |
| 21 | 28 | Annex I | 68 |
| 22 | 21, 29 | Annex II | 68 |
| 23 | 30 | Annex III | 68 |
| 24 | 31 | Annex IV | Annex I |
| 25 | 32 | Annex V | Annex II |
| 26 | 33 | | |

## ANNEX VI

Declarations by Sweden and Finland pursuant to Article 59(2)(a) of the Council Regulation concerning jurisdiction and the recognition and enforcement of judgments in matrimonial matters and matters of parental responsibility, repealing Regulation (EC) No 1347/2000.

Declaration by Sweden:

Pursuant to Article 59(2)(*a*) of the Council Regulation concerning jurisdiction and the recognition and enforcement of judgments in matrimonial matters and matters of parental responsibility, repealing Regulation (EC) No 1347/2000, Sweden hereby declares that the Convention of 6 February 1931 between Denmark, Finland, Iceland, Norway and Sweden comprising international private law provisions on marriage, adoption and guardianship, together with the Final Protocol thereto, will apply in full in relations between Sweden and Finland, in place of the rules of the Regulation.

Declaration by Finland:

Pursuant to Article 59(2)(*a*) of the Council Regulation concerning jurisdiction and the recognition and enforcement of judgments in matrimonial matters and matters of parental responsibility, repealing Regulation (EC) No 1347/2000, Finland hereby declares that the Convention of 6 February 1931 between Finland, Denmark, Iceland, Norway and Sweden comprising international private law provisions on marriage, adoption and guardianship, together with the Final Protocol thereto, will apply in full in relations between Finland and Sweden, in place of the rules of the Regulation.

# Court Fees

# Court Fees

In the Principal Registry, the divorce county courts and district registries fees are taken in cash. The court fees payable under the Family Proceedings Fees Order 1999 (as amended) are set out in the following table. As to remission of and exemption from fees, see clauses 4, 5 and 5A of the Order. Relevant fees derived from the Supreme Court Fees Order 1999 (as amended) and the County Court Fees Order 1999 (as amended) are also set out.

| | NO OF FEE | | | AMOUNT |
|---|---|---|---|---|
| | S.C. FEES ORDER | F.P. FEES ORDER | C.C. FEES ORDER | £ |
| ADOPTION: | | | | |
| On commencing proceedings under the Adoption Act 1976 other than s 21 thereof . . . | | 3.1 | | 120.00 |
| On commencing proceedings under s 21 of the Act . . . | | 3.2 | | 120.00 |
| (*Note. County Court fee 1(iii) has been revoked: these fees are payable on an application for an adoption in the county court.*) | | | | |
| AFFIDAVITS:— | | | | |
| filing each . . . . . | | | | (No fee) |
| swearing each . . . . . | 8.1 | 15.1* | | 5.00 |
| ALLOCATUR . . . . . | | | | (No fee) |
| AMENDED PETITION . . . | | | | 50.00 |
| ANCILLARY RELIEF:— | | | | |
| filing notice in Form A or B: | | | | |
| (a) by consent . . . . | | 4.1 | | 30.00 |
| (b) otherwise . . . . | | 4.4 | | 120.00 |
| ANSWER TO PETITION/CROSS PETITION:— | | | | |
| filing . . . . . | | | | 100.00 |
| APPEAL TO COURT OF APPEAL:— | | | | |
| On filing notice of appeal . | 9.1 | | | 200.00 |
| On filing a notice of cross appeal or a respondent's notice under CPR Part 52 . . . . | 9.2 | | | 100.00 |

* Fee 15.1 applies only to proceedings pending in the High Court.

| | No of Fee | | | Amount |
|---|---|---|---|---|
| | S.C. Fees Order | F.P. Fees Order | C.C. Fees Order | £ |
| On any application notice . . | 9.3 | | | 100.00 |
| APPEAL TO DIVISIONAL COURT:— | | | | |
| On filing— | 2.3 | | | |
|   (a) an appellant's notice | | | | 100.00 |
|   (b) on filing a respondent's notice where the respondent is appealing or wishes to ask the appeal court to uphold the order of the lower court for reasons different from or in addition to those given by the lower court | | | | |
| APPEAL FROM A DISTRICT JUDGE:— | | | | |
| On filing a notice of appeal from a district judge . . . . | | 5.1 | | 60.00 |
| APPLICATION | | | | |
|   (i) on an application for an order without notice or by consent except where otherwise provided . . | | 4.1 | | 30.00 |
|   (ii) on any application on notice except where otherwise provided . . | | 4.3 | | 60.00 |
| APPOINTMENT:— | | | | |
| for examination in aid of execution . . . . . | 12.3 | 14.2 | | 40.00 |
| ATTACHMENT OF EARNINGS:— | | | | |
| To enforce an order for maintenance . . . . | | 12.7 | | 60.00 |
| THIRD PARTY DEBT ORDERS:— | | | | |
| Proceedings in the High Court other than prescribed proceedings . . . . . . | 3.3 | | | 60.00 |
| Family proceedings in the High Court . . . . . . | | 12.4 | | 60.00 |
| Proceedings in a divorce county court . . . . . . | | 14.3 | | 60.00 |
| CHILDREN | | | | |
| *Proceedings under the Children Act 1989* | | | | |
| On filing an application or requesting leave under the following provisions of the Children Act 1989— | | | | |
| *Parental responsibility, guardians, section 8 orders etc* | | | | |
|   section 4(1)(a), or (3), 5(1), 10(1) or (2) . . . . | | 2(1) | | 90.00 |
|   section 6(7), or 13(1) . . . | | 2(1) | | 90.00 |

| | No of fee | | | Amount |
|---|---|---|---|---|
| | S.C. Fees Order | F.P. Fees Order | C.C. Fees Order | £ |
| *Financial provision for children* | | | | |
| paragraph 1(1), 2(1), 6(5) or 14(1) of Schedule 1 . . . | | 2(2) | | 90.00 |
| paragraph 1(4), 2(5), 5(6), 6(7), 6(8), 8(2), 10(2), or 11 of Schedule 1 . . . . | | 2(1) | | 90.00 |
| *Secure accommodation* | | | | |
| section 25. . . . . | | 2(3) | | 90.00 |
| *Care, supervision, etc* | | | | |
| section 31. . . . . | | 2(4) | | 90.00 |
| section 33(7), 38(8)(b), 39(1), (2), (3) or (4), paragraph 6 of Schedule 3 or paragraph 11(3) of Schedule 14. . . . | | 2(5) | | 90.00 |
| *Contact with child in care* | | | | |
| section 34(2), (3), (4) or (9). . | | 2(6) | | 90.00 |
| *Placement abroad* | | | | |
| paragraph 19(1) of Schedule 2 . | | 2(7) | | 90.00 |
| *Education supervision* | | | | |
| section 36(1) . . . . | | 2(8) | | 90.00 |
| paragraph 15(2) or 17(1) of Schedule 3 . . . . | | 2(9) | | 90.00 |
| *Child assessment order* | | | | |
| section 43(1) . . . . | | 2(10) | | 90.00 |
| *Emergency protection* | | | | |
| section 43(12) . . . . | | 2(11) | | 90.00 |
| section 44, 45, 46 or 48 . . . | | 2(11) | | 90.00 |
| *Recovery of children* | | | | |
| section 50. . . . . | | 2(12) | | 90.00 |
| *Miscellaneous* | | | | |
| section 102 . . . . | | 2(13) | | 90.00 |
| On commencing an appeal under section 94 of, or paragraph 23(11) of Schedule 2 to, the Children Act 1989 . . . | | 2(2) | | 90.00 |
| On an application to register a custody order in another part of the United Kingdom . . . | 13.5 | | | 30.00 |
| (*The fee payable to the county court has been revoked.*) | | | | |
| Copies:— | | | | |
| For a copy of any document, held by the court except where Fee 7.2 applies | | | | |
| (a) for the first page of a document . . . . | 7(1)(b) | 7(1)(a) | 6(1)(a) | 1.00 |
| (b) per page for subsequent pages . . . . | 7(1)(b) | 7(1)(b) | 6(1)(b) | 0.20 |
| On a request for a copy of a document required in connection with proceedings and supplied by the party making the request at the time of copying . . . . | 7.2 | | | 0.20 |

| | No of Fee | | | Amount |
|---|---|---|---|---|
| | S.C. Fees Order | F.P. Fees Order | C.C. Fees Order | £ |
| On a request for a copy of a document on a computer disk or in other electronic form, for each copy | 7.3 | | | 3.00 |
| COSTS:— | | | | |
| Filing bill of costs/request for detailed assessment/detailed assessment hearing/request for hearing date for assessment under Part III Solicitors Act 1974 in respect of a family LSC (legal aid) detailed assessment | | 8.1 | | 100.00 |
| Where there is an inter partes element to the detailed assessment | | | | 160.00 |
| Request for detailed assessment of costs | | 8.2 | | 160.00 |
| Request for review of taxation or an appeal against taxation/detailed assessment. | | 8.4 | | 100.00 |
| Application for court's approval of a Legal Aid Taxation/Assessment Certificate | | 8.3 | | 30.00 |
| On application for a default costs certificate | | | | 40.00 |
| On an appeal against a decision made in detailed assessment proceedings | | 8.5 | | 30.00 |
| On an application to set aside a default costs certificate | | 8.6 | | 60.00 |
| DECREE ABSOLUTE, application for | | 4.1 | | 30.00 |
| DIRECTIONS FOR TRIAL:— | | | | |
| On a request for directions for trial (other than uncontested divorce proceedings) | | 4.2 | | 30.00 |
| EXHIBITS, marking each | 8.2 | 15.1* | | 2.00 |
| FAMILY LAW ACT 1996:— | | | | |
| On making an application for an order under Part IV of the Act | | 1(c) | | 30.00 |
| THIRD PARTY DEBT ORDER:— | | | | |
| On the issue of a third party debt order to enforce an order of the divorce county court or the High Court | 3.3 | 14.3 | 4.4 | 50.00 |
| INJUNCTION:— | | | | |
| On applying for an injunction under Part IV of the Family Law Act 1996 | | | 1.3 | 130.00 |

\* Fee 15.1 applies only to proceedings pending in the High Court.

| | No of fee | | Amount |
|---|---|---|---|
| | S.C. Fees Order | F.P. Fees Order | C.C. Fees Order | £ |

| | S.C. Fees Order | F.P. Fees Order | C.C. Fees Order | £ |
|---|---|---|---|---|
| INHERITANCE (PROVISION FOR FAMILY AND DEPENDANTS) ACT 1975:— On filing originating proceedings | | | 1.1 | 130.00 |
| INTERLOCUTORY APPLICATIONS:— On any application in family proceedings . . . . | | 4.3 | | 60.00 |
| (*See also item headed* 'CHILDREN') INTERROGATORIES, filing each set . | | | | (No fee) |
| JUDGMENT SUMMONS (payable in *all* proceedings, whether High Court or divorce county court) . . | 3.4 | 14.4 | 4.5 | 90.00 |
| MEDICAL INSPECTION:— filing report . . . . | | | | (No fee) |
| NOTATION OF GRANT OF REPRESENTATION . . . | | | | (No fee) |
| OATH, administering to each deponent . . . . . | 3.1 | 15.1* | | 5.00 |
| ORIGINATING APPLICATION, filing . . | | 1.1 | | 130.00 |
| ORIGINATING SUMMONS . . . | | 1.1 | | 130.00 |
| PARTICULARS, filing . . . | | | | (No fee) |
| Petition, filing, save under FPR, r 2.6(4) . . . . . | | 1.2 | | 180.00 |
| filing a second or subsequent petition with leave under FPR, r 2.6(4) . . . . . | | 1.4 | | 50.00 |
| REGISTRATION OF MAINTENANCE ORDERS (payable in all proceedings whether High Court or county court) on an application for a maintenance order to be— (a) registered under the Maintenance Orders Act 1950 or the Maintenance Orders Act 1958 . . . | | 9.1 | | 30.00 |
| (b) sent abroad for enforcement under the Maintenance Orders (Reciprocal Enforcement) Act 1972 . . . . | | 9.2 | | 30.00 |
| and (c) on an application to transmit a maintenance order abroad under the Maintenance Orders (Facilities for Enforcement) Act 1920 . . | | 9.2 | | 30.00 |
| REGISTRATION OF CUSTODY ORDERS:— On an application to register a custody order in another part of the United Kingdom . . . (*The fee payable in the county court has been revoked.*) | 3.5 | | | 30.00 |

\* Fee 15.1 applies only to proceedings pending in the High Court.

| | NO OF FEE | | AMOUNT |
| --- | --- | --- | --- |
| | S.C. FEES ORDER | F.P. FEES ORDER | C.C. FEES ORDER | £ |

| | S.C. FEES ORDER | F.P. FEES ORDER | C.C. FEES ORDER | £ |
| --- | --- | --- | --- | --- |
| REPORT, of medical inspector of court welfare officer | | | | (No fee) |
| (i) filing | | | | (No fee) |
| (ii) for supplying a copy of a report | | | | (No fee) |
| SEARCHES:— | | | | |
| (1) for making a search of the index of decrees absolute for any specified period of ten calendar years or, if no such period is specified, for the ten most recent years and, where appropriate, providing a certificate of decree absolute | | 6.1 | | 20.00 |
| (2) or making a search in the central index of parental responsibility agreements kept at the Principal Registry | | 6.2 | | 20.00 |
| (3) on making a search in an index of decrees absolute kept at any divorce county court or district registry for any specified period of ten calendar years or, if no such period is specified, for the ten most recent years and, if appropriate, providing a certificate of decree absolute | | 6.3 | | 5.00 |
| SERVICE, ex parte application for substituted service to deem service or to dispense with service | | 4.1 | | 30.00 |
| by bailiff | | | 2 | 10.00 |
| by bailiff in family proceedings | | 11.1 | | 10.00 |
| SUBPOENA | | | | (No fee) |
| VARIATION OF SETTLEMENTS, on filing notice in Form A or B: | | | | |
| (a) by consent | | 4.1 | | 30.00 |
| (b) other than by consent | | 4.2 | | 50.00 |
| WARRANT OF EXECUTION AGAINST GOODS, issuing | | 12(a) | | 30 |
| WARDSHIP:— | | | | |
| on sealing an originating summons | | 3.2 | | 130.00 |
| WRITS, *fi. fa.*; sequestration | 3.1 | 14.1 | | |
| sealing | | | | 30.00 |

## FEES PAYABLE IN MAGISTRATES' COURTS

The fees set out in this table are prescribed by Part I of Schedule 6 to the Magistrates' Courts Act 1980 as amended by the Magistrates' Courts Fees (Amendment) Order 1993 with effect from 1 August 1993.

FAMILY PROCEEDINGS

### 1. Case for the opinion of the High Court
- Drawing the case, copies, taking recognizance and enlargements and renewals thereof,
- where the application to state a case is made on or after 1 April 1992 . . . . . . . . . . . **£382.00**
  Certificate of refusal of case, where the application is so made **£8.00**

### 2. Child Support Act 1991
- Application for a liability order (each child) (payable on making the application) . . . . . . . . **£0.70**
- Paternity application (each child) . . . . . . **.£30.00**
- Appeal against a deduction from earnings order . . . . **£10.00**
- Complaint or application and summons . . . . **£10.00**
- Warrant of arrest . . . . . . . . . **£10.00**
- Commitment order (payable on the making of the order) . **£40.00**

### 3. Copies
- First photocopy or 90-word folio of any document . . **£1.10**
- Each folio of succeeding 90 words . . . . . . **55p**
- Each additional photocopy . . . . . . **10p**

But no fee is payable under this provision for a copy of a summons, an order or warrant where a fee is specifically provided in the Order.

### 4. Duplicate
For a duplicate document . . . . . . . . . **£5.00**

### 5. Family Proceedings
- Applications under: Part I or II of the Children Act 1989; s.30, Human Fertilisation & Embryology Act 1990; Part I of the Domestic Proceedings and Magistrates' Courts Act 1978 (except s.16 – protection of a spouse or child from violence); Adoption Act 1976 (except s.21 – variation of s. 18 order so as to transfer parental responsibility from one adoption agency to another); all applications for financial orders (other than applications to vary or discharge such orders or in respect of claims for maintenance or maintenance orders made to the benefit of or against a person residing outside the UK) . . **£30.00**
- Applications under Children Act 1989, s.31 (care or supervision order), s.36 (education supervision order), or s.43 (child assessment order) . . . . . . . . . **£50.00**
- Applications to vary, extend or discharge an order; for contact or refusal of contact with a child in care, to change a child's surname or remove the child from the jurisdiction; and under s.21 Adoption Act 1976 . . . . . . . **£20.00**
- Applications under Part X Children Act 1989 (affecting the registration of a child minder or day carer, including appeals against cancellation or varying the conditions of the registration) and Sched. 8, para 8(1) Children Act 1989 (appeals concerning foster parenting) . . . . . . **£50.00**

When an application requires the leave of the court, the relevant fee applies where leave is sought, but no further fee is charged if leave is granted and the application is made.